Blue Book of Electric Guitars™

7th Edition

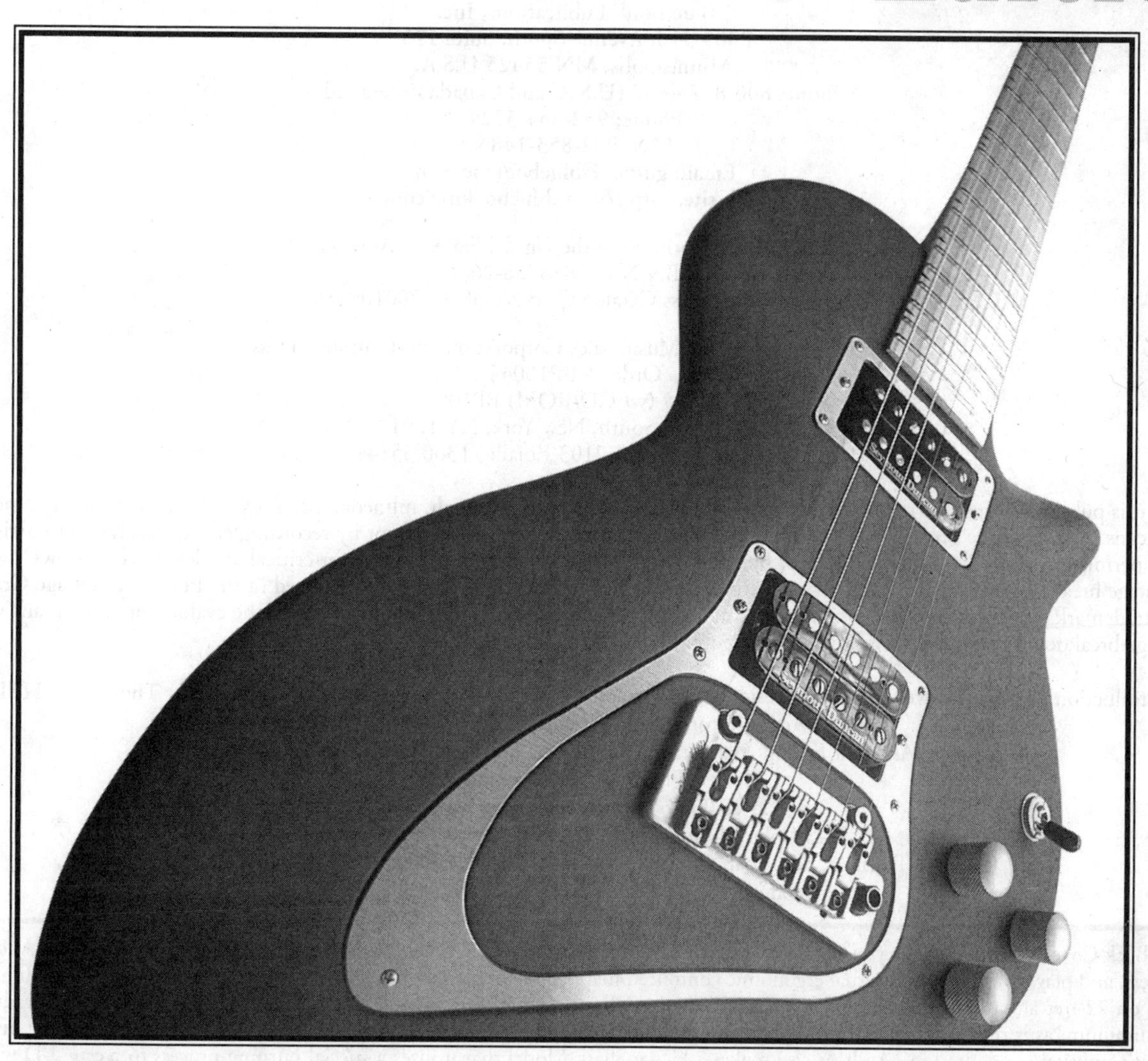

Edited by S.P. Fjestad
Text by Gurney Brown

$29.95
Publisher's Softcover Suggested List Price

Publisher's Limited Edition Hardcover Suggested List Price - $49.95

Access Code: E0107O9

7th EDITION BLUE BOOK OF ELECTRIC GUITARS™

Publisher's Note: This book is the result of nonstop and continual guitar research obtained by attending guitar shows, communicating with guitar dealers and collectors throughout the country each year, and staying on top of trends as they occur. This book represents an analysis of prices for which both recently manufactured and collectible guitars have actually been selling for during that period at an average retail level.

Although every reasonable effort has been made to compile an accurate and reliable guide, guitar prices may vary significantly depending on such factors as the locality of the sale, the number of sales we were able to consider, famous musician endorsement of certain models, regional economic conditions, and other critical factors.

Accordingly, no representation can be made that the guitars listed may be bought or sold at prices indicated, nor shall the editor or publisher be responsible for any error made in compiling and recording such prices.

Blue Book Publications, Inc.
8009 34th Avenue South, Suite 175
Minneapolis, MN 55425 U.S.A.
Phone: 800-877-4867 (U.S.A. and Canada orders only)
Phone: 952-854-5229
FAX: 952-853-1486
Email: guitars@bluebookinc.com
Web site: http://www.bluebookinc.com

Published and printed in the United States of America
ISBN No. 1-886768-26-9
Library of Congress Catalog Card Number: 2001093894

Distributed in part by Music Sales Corporation and Omnibus Press
Order # BP10044
Order # (w/ CD-ROM) BP10046
257 Park Avenue South, New York, NY 10010 USA
Phone: 212-254-2100 Fax: 212-254-2103 Email: 71360.3514@compuserve.com

Production Manager, Cover Layout & Design, Text Formatting & Layout, Compositing, and Lettering - **Thomas D. Heller**
Assistant Art Director, Photo Formatting & Layout - **Clint Schmidt**
Assistant Editor, Manuscript Madness & Mayhem - **Cassandra Faulkner**
Proofing: **Rob Niemala**
Cover Photography & Design - **S.P. Fjestad**
PGS Color Photography - **Dale Hanson, Beowulf Studios**
Taurus & Suburban Courier Services - **Beth Marthaler & Zach Fjestad**
Printer - **Von Hoffman Graphics, Owensville, MO**

Front & Back Cover Explanation: So you've already figured out its not a Strat or LP. Killer thinking Bubba! Made in Austria, this Andreas Blue Shark reeks of coolness, and plays even better! Unusual ergonomic contoured maple body gets a unique, difficult to apply, smooth (soft) satin finish. Maple neck features glued on 22-fret aluminum fretboard with machined, hollowed out aluminum headstock that's pressure fitted into the neck radius. Back cover plate is also aluminum, as is the hardware and pickup trim rings. Seymour Duncan pickups, a Schaller bridge with vibrato, and a graphite nut complete this instrument's unusual configuration. Andreas also makes a Fierce Shark Model that utilizes a special burning process to create 3-D wood layering on the body. Instrument courtesy Andreas Guitars.

Inside Front Cover Explanation: Anybody recognize this distinctive new body shape, sprayed in the subtle colors of Orange, Purple, and Yellow? Again, don't worry if you haven't. Not many people have seen Lace Music Products' new Lace Helix guitar, using Lace's unique neck design and famous pickups. Innovations include a patented Lace Helix twisted neck with a 20 degree neck twist at the nut that follows the natural twist of your hand as it moves up and down the fingerboard. Radical body style and neck joint appear to have spent time in a wind tunnel finalizing this sleek design. What else would you expect from a couple of brothers from California who restore older Airstreams and feature chicken wing recipes on their company web site? Vintage Gibson perverts will immediately pick up on the 1967 Pelham Blue ES-335 TD with Bigsby. Current owner is from LaCrosse, WI, but this instrument may make a permanent trip across the Mississippi shortly to a better state! Instruments courtesy of Lace Music Products and Dave's Guitar Shop.

Inside Back Cover Explanation: Samick makes over 50% of the world's guitars, and here's a good reason why. In addition to being an OEM (original equipment manufacturer) for many of the world's most recognizable trademarks, Samick also manufactures a complete lineup of electric and acoustic guitars and basses, including this limited edition Signature "Hoo Doo Man" solid body, made for blues artist C.D. Morris. Samick is well known for their high quality manufacturing and aggressive consumer pricing. Instrument courtesy of Samick Music USA.

This publication was published and printed in the United States of America.

CONTENTS

GENERAL INFORMATION

While many of you have probably dealt with our company for a while, it may be helpful for you to know a little bit more about our operation and what we are currently publishing. We are also the leaders in online informational services on collectibles. As this edition goes to press, the following titles/products/services are currently available.

Online Guitar & Gun Services: www.bluebookinc.com

7th Edition *Blue Book of Electric Guitars*, edited by S.P. Fjestad, text by Gurney Brown
7th Edition *Blue Book of Acoustic Guitars*, edited by S.P. Fjestad, text by Gurney Brown
7th Editions *Blue Book of Guitars* CD-ROM (includes both books) with inventory program

The Nethercutt Collection - The Cars of San Sylmar, Deluxe Edition, by Dennis Adler (also available on CD-ROM)

2nd Edition *Blue Book of Pool Cues*, by Brad Simpson, edited by Victor Stein and Paul Rubino
2nd Edition *The Billiard Encyclopedia*, by Victor Stein and Paul Rubino

22nd Edition *Blue Book of Gun Values* by S.P. Fjestad
GunTracker, CD-ROM firearms inventory software program
Colt Black Powder Reproductions & Replicas by Dennis Adler
1st Edition *Blue Book of Airguns* by Dennis Adler, edited by S.P. Fjestad & Dr. Robert Beeman
1st Edition *Blue Book of Modern Black Powder Values* by Dennis Adler

If you would like to order or get more information about any of the above publications/products, simply contact us at:

Blue Book Publications, Inc.
8009 34th Avenue South, Suite 175
Minneapolis, MN 55425 U.S.A.
www.bluebookinc.com
800-877-4867 (toll free domestic)
952-854-5229 (non-domestic) • Fax: 952-853-1486

Since our phone system is equipped with voicemail, you may also wish to know extension numbers and email addresses which have been provided below:

Gurney Brown	guitars@bluebookinc.com
Ext. No.: 11 - Tom Stock	toms@bluebookinc.com
Ext. No.: 18 - Katie Sandin	katies@bluebookinc.com
Ext. No.: 12 - Production Room	
Ext. No.: 19 - Cassandra Faulkner	cassandraf@bluebookinc.com
Ext. No.: 13 - S.P. Fjestad	stevef@bluebookinc.com
Ext. No.: 20 - Clint Schmidt	clints@bluebookinc.com
Ext. No.: 22 - Zach Fjestad	zachf@bluebookinc.com
Ext. No.: 15 - Thomas D. Heller	tomh@bluebookinc.com
Ext. No.: 25 - Beth Marthaler	bethm@bluebookinc.com
Ext. No.: 16 - John Allen	johna@bluebookinc.com
Ext. No.: 27 - Shipping	

Office hours are: 8:30 a.m. - 5:00 p.m. CST, Monday - Friday.
Orders Only: 800-877-4867 Phone No.: 952-854-5229
Additionally, an after hours answering service is available for both ordering and leaving messages.
Fax No.: 952-853-1486 (available 24 hours a day)
E-Mail: guitars@bluebookinc.com (checked several times daily)
Website: http://www.bluebookinc.com

We would like to thank all of you for your business in the past - you are the reason(s) we are successful. Our goal remains the same to give you the best products, the most accurate and up-to-date information for the money, and the highest level of customer service available in today's marketplace. If something's right, tell the world over time. If something's wrong, please tell us immediately.

ACKNOWLEDGMENTS

Whenever possible, the *Blue Book of Electric Guitars* has pointed out proper reference sources within a section (see Guitar Reference & Periodicals pages for complete listings). These books are invaluable resources for gaining additional knowledge within the wide variety of the guitar marketplace.

CONTRIBUTING EDITORS

The publisher extends a special thanks to those Contributing Editors listed below who took their valuable time to make important revisions, corrections, and additions - all making this a better publication. We couldn't have done it without them.

Dave Rogers and **Eddy Thurston** - Dave's Guitar Shop
Mark Pollock, Danny Collier, Jeannie, & The Bidet - Charley's Guitar Shop
Fred Oster
Dave Hull
Jay Pilzer - *20th Century Guitar* magazine
Larry Meiners
Rick Wilkowicz
Jack in the Box! - Ft. Worth, TX
Anthony Huvard - Luthiers Around the World
Jay Wolfe - Wolfe Guitars
Doug Tulloch
Scott Sanders
Kwinn Kastrosky
David Newell
John Beeson - The Music Shop
Rick Powell - Mars Music
Keith Smart - Zematis Guitar Owners Club
Walter Murray - Frankenstein Fretworks
R. Steven Graves
Stan Jay - Mandolin Bros.
Hal Hammer, Jr.
Dan Lenard - Luthier Access Group

FACTORY SUPPORT & ASSISTANCE

The following factory people really went out of their way (as if they're not busy enough already) to either give us or track down the information we requested. A special thanks to all of you for your unselfishness - there's no greater gift than someone's time.

Lon Werner - Martin Guitar Company
Robert & Cindy Benedetto
Paul Jernigan - Fender
Thom Fowle, David Rohrer, Gypsy Carns & Rick Gembar - Gibson Nashville
Sam Catalona - Gibson Montana
Will Jones - Epiphone
Dino Fererri - Andreas Guitars
Tom Wayne & David Brown - Yamaha
Steve Helgeson - Moonstone
Andy Robinson - Taylor
Larry Urie - PRS Guitars
Jim Donahue - Ibanez
Tommy Thomasson - Rickenbacker International Corp.
Frank Rindone - Hamer
Tom Anderson & Laurie Berg - Tom Anderson Guitarworks
Tom Nguyen - Yamaha

ADVISORY BOARD

The Advisory Board members listed below are generally people who let us pick their already ravaged, sometimes tortured and demented brains, and we highly value their range of attitudes and opinions (no shortage there). Very little 9-5 mentality here! These elite, card-carrying members pretty much span the humanitarian gamut in guitar intelligence (guitarded?). Occasionally, you might even see some cocktails exchanged among various members of this group, sometimes disguised as rogues lurking in the dark shadows, boisterously discussing their next move on the ever-changing guitar chessboard. And unlike Richard Nixon, there are no tapes of these rocket science summits! These people carry their cards proudly!

Don & Jeff Lace - Lace Music Products
Dave Rogers and Eddy Thurston - Dave's Guitar Shop
Mr. Hartley Peavey - Peavey Electronics Corporation
Robert and Cindy (they work weekends!) Benedetto - Benedetto Archtop Guitars
Charles H. Chapman
Rick Turner
Dino Fererri
Chris F. Martin IV - C.F. Martin & Co.
John and Rhonda Kinnemire - JK Lutherie
John Page - Fender Museum of Music & Arts Director
The hard working dicks at the Fender Custom Shop
David Maddux -Fender U.S. Production
Henry Lowenstein
Art Wiggs - Wings Guitar Products
Texas Amigos - John Brinkmann, Dave Crocker, & Eugene Robertson
Chad Speck - Encore Music
Larry Linkin & Joe Lamond - NAMM
Willie G. Moseley
Jim Fisch & L.B. Fred
Paul Day
Walter Carter
George Gruhn
Charles "Duke" Kramer
Jimmy Triggs
Dr. Thomas Van Hoose
Jim Rosenberg - Epiphone
Larry Briggs - Strings West
Greg Rich
Motoyosi "Morry" Takashima - First Guitar
Trent Salter - Music Hotbid.com
Chris Trider
Zebuelon Cash-Lane (and Dumpmaster)
Barry Clark
Dale B. Hanson - Beowulf Studios
Lawrence & James Acunto - *20th Century Guitar*
Gregg Hopkins - Vintage Amp Restoration
Steve Helgeson - Moonstone Guitars
Larry Jenssen - Slow Hand Guitars
Norm Harris & David Swartz - Norman's Rare Guitars
Paul Reed Smith - PRS Guitars
Tom "Murphdog" Murphy - Guitar Preservation
Dave Amato - lead guitarist, REO Speedwagon
Joe Naylor - Reverend Guitars
Mike and Margaret Overly - The Guitar Encyclomedia
Seymour Duncan - Seymour Duncan Pickups
Dave Prescott - Arista Records
Mark Pollock & bidet - Charley's Guitar Shop & Dallas Guitar Show
Lisa Sharken - *Guitar Shop* magazine
Kent Armstrong - Kent Armstrong Pickups
Mike & John Justin - Eclipse Music
Rick Nielsen - Cheap Trick
Jeff "Skunk" Baxter - Steely Dan
Steve Cropper - Booker T & the MGs
Ray Kennedy
Jimmy Gravity - Gravity Strings
Pete Wagener - LaVonne Wagener Music
Nate Westgor - Willie's American Guitars
Robbie Bakes - Bakes Guitars (& Moonlight Madness)
Gerald Weber -Kendrick Amplifiers
Jimmy Wallace - Sound Southwest
The Podium - Minneapolis, MN
Ari Latella - Toys From the Attic
Rock and Roll Hall of Fame Museum, Cleveland, OH
Dick Messer - Petersen Automotive Museum, Los Angeles, CA
Dave Hinson - Killer Vintage
Steven A. Wilson - Music Sales Corp.
Rob Griffin & crew - The Adolphus Hotel, Dallas, TX (*****+)
The Angry Dog Restaurant & Blue Cat Blues, Deep Ellum, TX
Mike's Butcher Shop - St. Paul, MN

PHOTO ACKNOWLEDGEMENTS

The people/companies listed below have either given us instruments to photograph and/or have performed photographic services in the past. Thanks again!

Dale Hanson - Beowulf Studios
Dave Hull
Dave's Guitar Shop
Willie's American Guitars
LaVonne Wagener Music
S.P. Fjestad
Leonard Shapiro
Paul Goodwin
Sandy Njoes
Glenn Wetterlund
Kari Larson
Dr. Steven Aaker, D.D.S.
Clint Schmidt
Hoffman Guitars
Hal Hammer, Jr.

Also note cover Acknowledgements (page 2).

And thanks to all the dealers, collectors, and individuals who have been nice enough to let the digital "drive by catch & release" photo crew (mostly seen in Texas) from Blue Book Publications, Inc. photograph their guitar(s). We haven't lost an instrument yet!

Foreword & Electric Guitar Marketplace Overview

S.P. Fjestad, Paul Reed Smith, and 6th Ed. cover PRS at Dave's Guitar Shop.

FOREWORD

The 7th Edition *Blue Book of Electric Guitars* continues to set new standards for the amount of electric guitar information and pricing in a single publication. Our digital color Photo Grading System (PGS) remains the standard for determining the proper grading of instruments. Many new B&W photos have also been added within the text, while the important Trademark Index has been thoroughly updated. Now with over 925 pages, the 7th Edition *Blue Book of Electric Guitars* continues to give you more volume using the same power.

So what else is new? The guitar book databases are now available online (www.bluebookinc.com). We suggest that you visit our web site for more information. After all, good information never sleeps.

While attending a St. Paul guitar show recently, one of the local dealers stopped by the booth for a chat. He mentioned that many guitar buyers prefer to go to his shop and play the instruments they are interested in. While Ebay might offer an alternative method of purchasing, it gives the consumer no chance to "road test" the guitar they're buying. While I used to think there was more variance within acoustic instruments for sound quality, electric instruments also have individual characteristics that can vary significantly from one guitar to the next. After all, isn't selecting the right instrument(s) for you supposed to be a personal decision, based on doing the homework for the choices you've selected? To think that every guitar is created approximately equal at particular price point is a big mistake.

CD-ROM! The new version 2.0 will be available shortly, and has an updated inventory program suitable for both consumers and dealers. Also, the price has been reduced to only $19.95. For more information, please look at the inside back cover, or use convenient tear out card for ordering.

On this 7th Edition, Gurney "The Gurnmeister" Brown was once again responsible for most of the new model information and pricing. To say that it's a big job is a gross understatement, and getting both books through the production cycles requires a maximum of both human resources and equipment.

Make sure you look at page 64 for a listing of recent electric book titles from Music Sales Corp. Also, JK Lutherie carries many of the reference titles used in this text – please visit him at www.jklutherie.com. We are also selling Larry Meiners' new Gibson books, *Gibson Shipment Totals 1937-1979* (a must for any Gibson fan) and *The Flying V – The Illustrated History of this Modernistic Guitar* – tear out order cards are provided in the G section. The guitar industry is fortunate to have had so many good books published on the subject within the past 3 decades. And owning them is an investment unto itself – it's like getting paid to be educated!

ELECTRIC GUITAR MARKETPLACE OVERVIEW

It's really not that hard. You just have to thoroughly examine the current state of today's electric guitar marketplace, and then think about it for awhile. The current electric guitar sales arena, with the anything goes, free for all, turbulent marketplace, while offering the consumer an unprecedented variety of good quality instruments at unequalled low prices, is a constant struggle and challenge for many high volume manufacturers. Most major trademarks, including Gibson, Fender, Gretsch, Yamaha, Guild, Ibanez, and others sell directly to dealers. These dealers usually include independent music stores, guitar shops, small retail chains, super centers (i.e., Mars Music, Guitar Center, etc.), plus the catalog merchandisers (i.e., Musician's Friend, Musician's Hotline, etc). What do all these very diversified retailers have in common? They (and their customers) are very price conscious, and there is a constant marketing/advertising battle going on within the typical 25%-35% "discount zone" on most MSRs (manufacturer's suggested retails) for mass produced instruments.

Since discounting has become an accepted method to entice more sales from consumers, some manufacturers are publishing MAPs (minimum advertised prices) for all their models. Under this arrangement, dealers may not advertise an instrument below a manufacturer's MAP.

OK, so here's the math. Let's take a new, commonly sold electric guitar, like an American Fender Strat. Say this model has a current MSR of $1,000. If Fender has a MAP price of $700 (30% off), it means the price range that a consumer can expect to pay is probably going to be in the $700-$850 range, depending on how or where the instrument was purchased.

It's no huge trade secret that many large guitar manufacturers sell their instruments directly to dealers at 50% off the MSR. Maybe larger orders, seasonal sales, and/or special model discounting could knock off another 3%-10%. So, if some web site merchant or superstore is selling Fenders at 35% off, his profit margin is approximately 15%. On the $1,000 American Strat that got blown out on Ebay for $650, the person/company made at least $150. Maybe that same model would sell in the $850 range if offered in a professional sales environment, specializing in a high level of product knowledge and a personalized approach to customer sales. These additional services, seen by many as an unnecessary expense, may well be worth every penny to make sure you are getting the instrument that's really right for you. It's just like automobiles really. Some people want/need a Viper, and others can get by with a Yugo.

Foreword & Electric Guitar Marketplace Overview

So, if a new guitar retails for $1,000, but can be bought for as low as $650, what's a used model worth? The math gets a little brutal here, but it's still correct. Let's say Johnny walks into Jimbo's Guitar Shop, and wants to buy that Fender American Strat with an MSR of $1,000. The price has been reduced to $625, and includes a hardshell case, and 10 guitar lessons. So Johnny buys his $625 Strat, and after 2 lessons, discovers he really wants to play bass guitar, and he brings the 2-week-old Fender back to Jimbo's to either trade or sell. He could really use the money more than anything else right now. Jimbo tells him that if he wants to trade for a bass guitar of equal or more money, he'd give him $500 towards the trade. "If you want the cash, I'll give you $450." "$450?" says Johnny, "You're kidding, I've only played it 3 times – it's like new." Jimbo calmly replies, "If I can buy a new one for $500 with full factory warranty that hasn't been previously sold, why would I want to pay you my cost on your now used instrument?". Johnny takes the $450 (must be cash), but still can't help feeling that he got ripped off. After all, he bought a new guitar 2 weeks ago, played it 3 times, and lost $175.

So who's the bad guy in this story? Not Jimbo, not the guitar, and certainly not Johnny. It's today's mass guitar marketplace antics, and its runaway marketing directed at these strategic discount levels, now reinforced by MAPs. The real problem here is the major level of discounting. It's pretty hard to go out and expect to buy a new automobile, boat, or house at 35% off. Yet, the mass guitar marketplace and its consumers now almost demand these types of large discounts, and it may be too late to reform this discounted pricing formula. Some manufacturers are no longer publishing MSRs, but do have dealer agreements on MAPs (non-published).

As a general guideline, an expensive new guitar from a major trademark/manufacturer will hold its value considerably better than an equally priced product from a little known company. Because of the overall large demand factor, Fenders, Gretschs, Gibsons, and PRSs will always have secondary marketplace appeal due to both trademark notoriety and a high level of quality. Lower priced, non-major trademarks from Asia will have their competitive price tags determine by the playability alone. You can't charge extra for something that you don't have yet – a reputation!

Now let's look at another area of newly manufactured electric guitars. These companies/individuals manufacture a much lower quantity of instruments annually – perhaps as few as 10, but usually not more than 250-300. Who are these guitars sold to? Not to dealers – except maybe occasionally at a smaller 10%-15% discount. They're mostly sold to individuals, who typically custom order them at little or no discount. There are no MAPs. So what's the gig here? Obviously, this is a much different economic scenario than the big dogs. These smaller manufacturers/companies are selling directly to consumers – most do not have a dealer base, and the majority of their sales are custom orders.

So what's a custom instrument made by a small manufacturer really worth? The answer is, it depends on how famous is the builder, instrument configuration desirability, and how much of a back order situation is the builder currently experiencing? If people are waiting a year to get an instrument, a used specimen will be worth anywhere from current MSR for that model variation, to 20%-25% off, depending on the overall configuration and desirability. Because of this, pricing low volume custom instruments can be very tricky, and depends on the tenure, collectibility/notoriety, playability, and the overall desirability of the luthier/trademark.

So how's the vintage marketplace doing overall? Actually, pretty well, if you have the right instruments. Since the dollar is so strong, it has slowed down a lot of foreign purchasing, yet the domestic marketplace remains relatively stable at a time when everyone else is talking about the downturn in our economy. Good condition, original Fender, Gibson, Gretsch, PRS, and other major trademarks have always led the pack in terms of overall desirability (and top prices). I see no need for that to change. Maybe the best advice I ever got was from a grizzled, traveled guitar show veteran who said, "Don't try to figure it out Steve, just have another box of price tags ready". On the other hand, a major dealer recently confessed that if he could of bought anything (guitars, cars, stocks, real estate, guns, etc.) back in the late 80s and early 90s, his choice now would have been high end PRSs, maybe even a Dragon or two.

In closing, we hope that you will appreciate and use the information contained within these pages. The sister publication, the 7th Edition *Blue Book of Acoustic Guitars*, contains similar information on acoustic and acoustic electric instruments. Together, they are over 1,500 pages and weigh over 7 lbs.! No other 2 books provide with as much guitar information and up-to-date pricing. As in the past, thanks for supporting this project, and we will continue to earn your patronage in future editions.

Sincerely,

S.P. Fjestad
Editor & Publisher
Blue Book of Electric Guitars

DEDICATION

Since ushering in the new millenium, we have lost some great guitar players and industry leaders: Joey Ramone, Ted McCarty, John Lee Hooker, Scott Chinery, and most recently, Chet Atkins. Over 150 albums were recorded between Hooker, Ramone, & Atkins! Ted McCarty, Gibson's youngest president, is credited with the Les Paul, Flying V, ES-175, ES-335, Explorer, Firebird, and others. Scott Chinery created one of the world's finest guitar collections. All these people had one thing in common – they took the guitar very seriously, and used it to speak to us in the world's only true universal language – music. We will miss their licks, their presence, and their contributions – they gave us all so much. Hopefully, a new crop of guitarists will grow up appreciating their achievements, and take their musical ability to a higher level. Hope the big guy likes the new members in the band – must be a killer guitar section by now.

INTRODUCTION

by Gurney Brown

Gurney "The Gurnmeister" Brown

Congratulations - you are reading the most up-to-date book on electric guitars published so far in our new millennium! This 7th Edition of the *Blue Book of Electric Guitars* represents countless hours of reading, research, discussion, and cataloging - after which it needs formatting and correct entry into a database. Big job. As with previous editions, we have made every effort to keep you up to date with current pricing on vintage guitars and basses as well as currently produced models. We have also worked to expand sections of the book where only a few well-known models were previously listed. For example, many sections have been greatly expanded, including Danelectro, Hagstrom, and Silvertone. Additionally, Epiphone, Fender, Gibson, Gretsch, Peavey, and others have been completely updated - including vintage pricing updates. This edition's Trademark Index might be the most up-to-date electric guitar reference listing ever compiled. Many new photographs have also been added. Page count is up over 10% from the 6th Edition!

As part of our effort to stay informed, we attend a large number of shows, both trade (summer & winter NAMM) and guitar shows. During these events, we are able to monitor pricing and try to dissimulate the chicken salad from the chicken poop. We spend time talking with manufacturers, exhibitors, consumers, and assorted vendors. These are places where lots of information can be gathered under one roof over a 2-3 day period. We strongly urge you to attend a show of this caliber such as The Dallas Guitar Show or The Arlington Texas Guitar Show. We guarantee a memorable experience.

This year we have already lost too many guitar giants. The deaths of John Lee Hooker and Chet Atkins saddened us greatly. Both masters of their own techniques will continue to play… in our hearts. Another giant, Ted McCarty, former President of Gibson and designer of many historic Gibson models, passed away in January. I had the privilege of talking with him for about 5 minutes in the Paul Reed Smith booth at last year's Summer NAMM. For me, those 5 minutes were the highlight of the show!

We continue to see an endless stream of good quality, lower priced models flowing out of Korea by many of the major manufacturers. This is great news for the beginning player, since $200.00 will now buy you a good quality guitar that will go a long way before needing to be upgraded. $300.00 will buy you a very nice guitar! For those of you with larger pockets, Fender, Gibson and the other major manufacturers continue to produce an ever expanding range of fine, high end instruments. Check out Gibson's new Les Paul Acoustic model or Fender's baritone Stratocaster. Innovation flows in the veins of these designers, and we the consumers, reap the benefits!

I would like to sincerely thank the production staff at Blue Book Publications, Inc. Special thanks to Assistant Editor Cassandra Faulkner, who reformatted the entire book and helped compile the endless informational updates from contributing editors and manufacturers. Art Director Tom Heller deserves the podium for his untiring efforts while grinding through over 925 pages of text. Clint Schmidt, Assistant Art Director, photographer, and TX Guitar Show pervert in March & Oct., also gets high marks for rapid picture positioning. And finally, thanks to Editor & Publisher S.P. Fjestad, for allowing me the opportunity to work on this project. It is most rewarding work!

Finally, I would like to thank my wife Kathy for allowing me the time and space to work on these two editions when I probably should have been doing "family" things. She has seldom seen me after 6:00 p.m. for the past four months, except when bringing me coffee or a Coke so that I did not have to leave the computer. Every day I thank God that I met her!

Gurney Brown - "The Gurnmeister"
Blue Book Publications, Inc.

How to Use This Book

This most recent Seventh Edition of the ***Blue Book of Electric Guitars™***, when used properly, will provide you with more up-to-date electric guitar information and pricing than any other single source. This revised Seventh Edition, now with over 925 pages of specific guitar models and pricing, continues to be more of a complete informational source than a simple "hold-your-hand" pricing guide. In theory, you should be able to identify the trademark/name off the guitar's headstock (whenever applicable), and be able to find out the country of origin, date(s) produced, and other company/model-related facts for that guitar. **Many smaller, out-of-production trademarks and/or companies which are only infrequently encountered in the secondary marketplace are intentionally not priced in this text, as it is pretty hard to pin a tail on a donkey that is nowhere to be seen.** Unfortunately, the less information known about a trademark is typically another way of asking the seller, "Would you take any less? After all, nobody seems to know anything about it." In other words, don't confuse rarity with desirability when it comes to these informational "black-holes." As in the past, if you own a current Seventh Edition of the ***Blue Book of Electric Guitars™*** and still have questions, we will try to assist you in identifying/pricing your guitar(s). Please refer to page 29 for this service.

The prices listed in the Seventh Edition *Blue Book of Electric Guitars™* are based on average national retail prices for both vintage and currently manufactured guitars. This is NOT a wholesale pricing guide - prices reflect the numbers you typically see on a guitar's price tag. More importantly, do not expect to walk into a music store, guitar, or pawn shop and think that the proprietor should pay you the retail price listed within this text for your instrument(s). Dealer offers on most models could be 20%-50% less than values listed, depending upon desirability, locality, and profitability.

In other words, if you want to receive 100% of the price (retail value), then you have to do 100% of the work (become the retailer, which also includes assuming 100% of the risk). Suceeding in business usually means making a profit, and is essential in today's tough retail environment.

Currently manufactured guitars are typically listed with 60%-100% condition factors, since condition below 60% is seldom encountered and obviously, less desirable. A few older vintage instruments may only have the 20%-90% condition factors listed, since 95%+ condition factors are seldom encountered and are difficult to price accurately. Please consult the revised, 31 page, digital color **Photo Grading System™** (pages 33-63) to learn more about the condition of your electric guitar(s). The ***Blue Book of Electric Guitars™*** will continue using selected photos to illustrate real world condition factors, and/or problems. Guitar porno, it isn't. Since condition is the overriding factor in price evaluation, study these photos carefully to learn more about the condition of your instrument(s). **Remember, the price will be wrong if the condition factor isn't right.**

For your convenience, an explanation of guitar grading systems, how to convert them, and descriptions of individual conditions appears on page 32 (Explanation & Converting Guitar Grading Systems) to assist you in learning more about guitar grading systems and individual condition factors. Please read this page carefully, as the values in this publication are based on the grading/condition factors listed. This will be especially helpful when evaluating older vintage instruments.

All values within this text assume original condition. From the vintage marketplace or (especially) a collector's point of view, any repairs, alterations, modifications, "enhancements", "improvements", "professionally modified to a more desirable configuration", or any other non-factory changes usually detract from an instrument's value. Please refer to page 31 regarding an explanation on finishes, repairs, alterations/modifications, and other elements which have to be factored in before determining the correct condition. Depending on the seriousness of the modification/alteration, you may have to go down 1-3 condition factors when re-computing price for these alterations. Determining values for damaged and/or previously repaired instruments will usually depend on the parts and labor costs necessary to return them to playable and/or original specifications. The grading lines within the Seventh Edition continue to incorporate other grading nomenclature and are listed under the respective percentages of original condition.

You may note that this new Seventh Edition contains many new black-and-white photos of individual electric models/variations to assist you with more visual identification. **Remember, the photos may not necessarily be on the same page as the model listing/descriptions.**

The Seventh Edition ***Blue Book of Electric Guitars™*** provides many company histories, notes on influential luthiers and designers, and other bits of knowledge as a supplement to the straight pricing text. Hopefully, this information will be shared to alleviate those "grey areas" of the unknown, and shed light on the efforts of those new luthiers/companies who keep pushing the envelope.

We have designed an easy-to-use (and consistent) text format throughout this publication to assist you in finding specific information within the shortest amount of time, and there is a lot of information!

How to Use This Book

1. Trademark, manufacturer, company names (if luthier or individual, last name will appear first), brand name, or importer is listed in bold face type and will appear alphabetically as follows:

B.C. RICH
FERNANDES
GUILD
RENO, G.H.

2. Manufacturer information and production dates (if possible) are listed directly beneath the trademark heading:

Instruments previously produced in Japan circa 1970s. Distributed by Sam Ash of New York, NY. Later distribution by Guitar Centers.

3. A company overview, brief history, additional model information, and/or other useful pieces of related information may follow within a smaller block of text. They appear as:

Luthier/designer Tom Anderson founded Tom Anderson Guitarworks in 1984, following a stint at Schecter as vice president from 1977 to 1984. Anderson's interest and exploration of tonewoods and the overall interaction of the guitar's parts have led to a refined and defined tone in his instruments.

4. When a proper model-by-model listing is not available, a small paragraph may follow with condensed information on current models and pricing. An example will appear as follows:

The current Mayan Gold Series basses feature an offset cocobolo body design with lengthened bass horn. Designed by Bishop Cochran, these handcrafted instruments feature a deep cutaway on the upper bout to provide full access to all 24-frets. The BC-1 bass has a list price of $1,995, the BC-20 bass retails at $1,695, and the BC Standard bass retails at $1,795.

5. The next major classification under a heading name may include a category name which appears in upper-case, is flush left, and inside a darkly shaded box. A category name refers mostly to a guitar's primary configuration:

ELECTRIC

ELECTRIC BASS

6. A sub-classification of the category name (upper and lower-case description inside a lighter shaded box) usually indicates a grouping or series within the classification of the category name:

Chet Atkins Series

RD Bass Series

7. A category note may follow either a category or subcategory heading, and contains information specific to that category or subcategory. A good example would be:

Early Guild basses have a specially designed Guild single coil pickup made by Hagstrom in Sweden that is often mistaken for a humbucker. Some of these basses have an extra switch that activated a passive circuit and eliminated the hum associated with single coil pickups. This feature makes the basses more desirable and collectible.

These category notes may also list general pricing for models covered within that category (typically bold face).

8. Model names appear flush left, are bolded in upper case, and appear in alpha-numerical (normally) sequence which are grouped under various category/subcategory listings:

PIZZA FACE, ELIMINATOR, TAL FARLOW (HSTF prefix), SG, SUPERSWEDE, T-60

Parentheses after a model or submodel name refers to either a previous model name or the factory family code/number to assist in proper identification. In some cases, it may include both.

9. Variations within a model appear as sub-models, are indented, and appear in both upper and lower case type:

M-4 Deluxe, California Fat Tele (U.S. Mfg.), ES-225 TD, Parson Street III, Falcon Standard

Model sub-variations follow in the text under the description/pricing of the main model(s).

How to Use This Book

10. Model/sub-model descriptions appear directly under model/sub-model names and appear as follows:

- hollow bound maple body, arched spruce top, f-holes, raised tortoise pickguard, maple neck, 14/20 fret rosewood fingerboard with white dot inlay, adjustable rosewood bridge/trapeze tailpiece, blackface peghead with engraved logo, Electromatic vertically engraved onto peghead, 3 per side tuners with plastic buttons, chrome hardware, exposed DeArmond pickup, volume/tone control, available in Natural (Model 6185N) and Sunburst (Model 6185) finishes. Mfg. 1940 to 1959.

Model/submodel descriptions are where most of the critical information regarding that model will be located. Typically, they list configuration first, type of wood(s) second, fretboard description, bridge/tuner specifications, pickup(s)/electronics, and factory finish descriptions. If possible, years of production are listed last. In many cases, this allows the last MSR and date of a discontinued model to be known. Whenever possible, black & white photos have been provided on the right hand pages, even though they may not appear on the same page as the model name/description.

11. Pricing. Typically, pricing is located directly underneath the model description. The primary pricing line example in this book is listed below. **When this price line is encountered,**

GRADING		100% MINT	98% NEAR MINT	95% EXC+	90% EXC	80% VG+	70% VG	60% G
MSR	$995	$695	$575	$500	$450	$400	$350	$300

it automatically indicates the guitar is currently manufactured and the manufacturer's suggested retail price (MSR) is shown left of the 100% column. The 100% price on a currently manufactured instrument is what you can typically expect to pay for that model, and may reflect a discount off the MSR. Musical instruments, like other consumer goods, may be discounted to promote consumer spending. Discounting is generally used as a sales tool within the music industry and includes many music/guitar establishments, chain stores, mail-order companies, Ebay, and other retailers to help move merchandise. Discounted prices depend on the local market (some markets may not discount at all, but offer quality service and support/advice after your purchase). With the advent of manufacturer MAPs (minimum advertised prices), discounting seems to become more manageable than it was in the 90s. 25%-35% off MSR seems to be the rule for most manufacturer's MAPs.

The 100% condition factor, when encountered in a currently manufactured guitar, assumes the guitar has not been previously sold at retail and includes a factory warranty. A currently manufactured new instrument must include EVERYTHING the factory originally provided with the instrument - including the case (if originally included), warranty card, instruction manual (if any), hang tags (if any), etc. Because of this, a slightly used instrument that appears new, but has had its warranty card sent in, may be worth only approx. 50% of its current MSR. The values for the remaining 98%-60% condition factors represent actual selling prices for instruments in various conditions. Simply refer to the correct condition column of the instrument in question and refer to the price listed directly underneath.

Please consult the Photo Grading System™ on pages 33-63 to learn more about how to visually determine electric guitar condition factors accurately. It is also recommended to read pages 31-32 thoroughly to understand and convert the various guitar grading systems - individual grades are also explained in detail. An "N/A" instead of a price means that either that model hasn't been produced long enough for wear to occur, or the rarity factor precludes this price.

A price line with 7 values listed (as the example below demonstrates) indicates a

GRADING	100%	98%	95%	90%	80%	70%	60%
	$895	$775	$650	$525	$450	$400	$350

discontinued, out of production model with values shown for 100%-60% conditions. Obviously, "MSR" will not appear in the left margin, but a model note may appear below the price line indicating the last MSR. In the 7th Edition, 1994 has typically been used for the cutoff on some 100% values (i.e., Gibson, Gretsch, Guild). An N/A (Not Available) may appear in place of values for instruments that are not commonly encountered in lower condition factor(s). The longer an instrument has been discontinued, the less likely you will find it in 100% condition. Some instruments that are only 10 years old and have never been taken out-of-the-case (unplayed), may not be 100% (new), as the finish may have slightly cracked, tarnished, faded, or deteriorated. **100% is new - no excuses, period.**

How to Use This Book

The following price line indicates that either

MSR $3,995

this model is produced in small enough quantities and is not discounted (perhaps consumer direct sales only), or has only been in production for a short time, and used guitars simply do not exist yet. As time goes on, these slots will need to be filled in.

12. While the MSR price is included in the regular pricing line of currently manufactured instruments, the Last MSR for discontinued, out of production models may appear in smaller typeface to the right:

Last MSR was $489.

13. Manufacturer's notes, model information, and available options appear in smaller type, typically following price lines, and are significant since they contain both important model changes and other related information:

The Wildwood finish was the result of a seven year process in Germany where dye was injected into growing beech trees. After the trees were harvested, veneers were cut and laminated to the guitar tops. Pickguard numbers (I-VI) refer to the dye color (primary color of green, blue, and gold) and the applied finish.

14. Extra cost features/special orders and other value added/subtracted items (add-ons for currently manufactured guitars reflect an option's retail price), are placed directly under individual price lines, and appear bolder than other descriptive typeface:

Add 50% for rare factory Dupont colors.

Subtract approx. 50% if professionally refinished.

15. Grading lines will appear at the top of each page where applicable or wherever pricing lines change. The most commonly encountered grading line (with corresponding price line for currently manufactured instruments) in this text is 100%-60%:

GRADING		100% MINT	98% NEAR MINT	95% EXC+	90% EXC	80% VG+	70% VG	60% G
MSR	$1,995	$1,395	$1,175	$995	$875	$750	$625	$550

A few electric vintage instruments (mainly pre-WWII) may require the grading line listed below.

GRADING	90%	80%	70%	60%	50%	40%	20%

Values are listed for 90%-20% condition factors only since condition over 90% is seldom encountered and almost impossible to accurately value.

To find a particular electric guitar in this book, first try to identify the name/trademark on the headstock. This will usually identify the manufacturer, trademark, importer, or possible brand/trade name. Then refer to this listing within the correct alphabetical section. Next, locate the correct category name, Electric, Electric Basses, etc. Models will be listed first alphanumerically, example: DM-1, DM-2, etc., then by model name example: Ripper, Thunderbird, etc.

Once you find the correct model or sub-model under its respective subheading, determine that particular electric guitar's percentage of original condition (see the Photo Grading System™ on pages 33-63), and simply find the corresponding grading column to ascertain price. Special/limited editions usually appear last under a manufacturer's heading. When using serialization charts, make sure your model is listed, and find the serial number within the yearly range listings. However, do not date your instrument on serial number information alone! Double check parts/finish variations in the text accompanying the model, or reference the coding on your instrument's potentiometers (tone and volume controls), if applicable.

In order to save time when looking up a particular model(s), you may want to look first at our expanded Index on pages 915-927. Also, the Trademark Index located on pages 893-914, is the only up-to-date and comprehensive listing of current electric manufacturers and luthiers in print - use both of them, they can be very helpful! Another Trademark Index on Amps/Effects/Strings/Pickups is also provided on pages 886-892. Once again, the Glossary and Anatomy of a Guitar sections have been updated - there's a lot of information in both.

ANATOMY OF AN ELECTRIC GUITAR

Trademark & Model (Fender Stratocaster)
Tuner
6-on-one-side Headstock
Truss Rod "Bullet"
Nut
Maple Finger Board
Fret
Black Dot Inlay (Fret Marker)
Bolt-on Neck
Strap Pin
Pickguard
Pickup Pole Pieces
Single Coil Neck Pickup
Bridge Cover
Five-Way Pickup Selector Switch
2-Tone Sunburst Finish
1 Volume Control
2 Tone Controls
Contoured Lower Bout
Tremolo Arm (Whammy Bar or Wang Bar)
Body (one-piece)
Output Jack
Trademark & Model (Gibson Les Paul Deluxe)
3-per-side Headstock
Tuner
Bell
Nut
Fret
Rosewood Finger Board
Set Neck (glued in)
Pearl Trapezoid Inlay
Bill Lawrence "Blade" Humbucker Pickup (non-factory)
Bass Bout
Three Position Pickup Switch
Cutaway
Treble Bout
Raised Pickguard
Bridge Pickup
Tune-o-matic Bridge
2 Volume Controls
Lower Bout
Output Jack
2 Tone Controls
Stop Tailpiece (non-original)
Strap Pin
Painted Gold Top Finish

GLOSSARY

This glossary is divided into 4 sections: General Glossary, Hardware: Bridges, Pegs, Tailpieces, and Tuners, Pickups/Electronics, and Book Terminology. If you are looking for something and can't find it in one section, please check the others. You may also want to refer to Anatomy of An Electric Guitar (page 13) for visual identification on many of the terms listed below.For wood terminology, please see "Know Your Woods" section.

GENERAL GLOSSARY

Abalone -Shellfish material used in instrument ornamentation.
Action - Action is the height the strings are off of the fingerboard, stretched between the nut and bridge.
Arch/Arched Top -The top of an instrument that has been carved or pressed to have a "rounded" top.
Avoidire – blonde mahogany.
Back Plate – Refers to the cover plate on the back of an instrument allowing access into the body cavity for repair/alterations.
Bass Bout – Upper left hand part of body (left side of lower fingerboard on right hand guitars).
Bell – Truss Rod cover located directly above nut. Most are bell shaped, and may have model/make information on the outside.
Binding (bound) -Trim that goes along the outer edge of the body, neck or headstock. It is made out of many different materials, natural and synthetic.
"Black Beauty" - This term is generally used in reference to early (1955-1960) Gibson Les Paul Customs, due to their glossy black finish.
Body - The main bulk of the instrument, usually. It is where the bridge, tailpiece and pickguard are located. On electrics it is where the pickups are routed into and the electronics housing is stored. It is what the player cradles.
Bolt On/Bolt On Neck - Construction technique that involves attaching the neck to the body by means of bolts or screws. Bolt-on necks are generally built and finished separately from the guitar body, and parts are assembled together later.
Bookmatched – Refers to the process where a single wood block is cut in half, and both pieces are carefully aligned and glued in the middle, matching the grain from left to right. Very popular on instruments with maple backs and a lot of flame.
Bound - See BINDING.
Bout/Bouts – Also see Bass Bout, Lower Bout, and Treble Bout. The rounded, generally, side/sides on the top and bottom of an instrument's body.
Bridge - Component that rests on the top of the instrument and transfers vibrations from string to body. It is usually attached by glue or screws but is also found to be held in place by string tension, the same as a violin.
Carved Top - See ARCH TOP.
Cello Tail Adjuster - The Cello tail adjuster is a 1/8" diameter black nylon-type material that attaches to the tailpiece and loops around an endpin jack (or ebony endpin). Nylon, of course, replaced the real (if unstable) gut material several years ago. This tail adjuster is used on virtually every cello tailpiece in the world, and figures prominently in a number of archtop guitar designs.
Cutaway - An area that has been cut away on the treble bout, or both bouts, to allow access to the higher frets. See FLORENTINE and VENETIAN.
Ding - small mark or dent on a guitar. Also the noise you swear you hear when your guitar hits another object, thus causing the mark.
Ebonized - A process by which the wood has been stained dark to appear to be ebony; alternatively, also referring to something black in color (such as bridge adjuster wheels) made to blend in with ebony fittings on an archtop guitar.
Ebonol - A synthetic material that is used as replacement for wood (generally as a fingerboard).
F-Hole - Stylized "f" shaped soundhole that is carved into the top of various instruments, most commonly acoustic. It usually comes in pairs.
Fingerboard - An area on top of the neck that the string is pressed against to create the desired note (frequency).
Finish - The outer coat of an instrument. The sealant of the wood. The protector of the instrument. Finishes include Gloss, Satin, Nitrocellulose, Matte, Spar, Polyurethane, Tongue Oil, etc.
Florentine - sharp point on the treble forward horn of a body cutaway. See also VENETIAN.
Fret - A strip of metal that is embedded at specific intervals into the fingerboard.
Fretboard - Another way of saying fingerboard and specifying that it has frets embedded into it.
Fretless Fingerboard -Commonly found on bass instruments, this fingerboard is smooth, with no frets.
Graphite - Used in various forms of instrument construction because of its rigidity and weight, this type of synthetic material may be used in the body, neck, nut, saddle, etc.
Hardware -Generic term typically used for the bridge, tailpiece, tuners, and/or vibrato system.
Headless - This means the instrument has no headstock.
Headstock – Top portion of the neck assembly where the tuning machines are located. Headstock design is a field unto itself, and many makes/models can be instantly identified by simply looking at an instrument's headstock design/configuration. Additional information about the instrument, such as serialization (typically on back side or top), model number, and/or distinctive logo/trademark may also be part of the headstock.
Heel - On the backside of an instrument, the heel is located at the base of the lower neck where the neck meets the body. May be bound, inlaid, or carved as well.
Inlay - Decoration or identifying marks on an instrument that are inlaid into one of the surface areas. They are made of a number of materials, though abalone, pearl and wood are the most common.
Locking Tuners - These tuners are manufactured with a locking mechanism built right into them, thus preventing string slippage.
Logo - An identifying feature on an instrument: it could be a symbol or a name; and it could appear as a decal, an inlay, or painted on (and it could be missing).
Lower Bout(s) – Refers to the lower part of an instrument's contour(s). A lower bout measurement is the maximum distance between an instrument's 2 lower bouts.
Mortise – Wood construction procedure where one piece of wood is carefully fitted to join another.

GLOSSARY

Mother-of-Pearl - A shellfish (oyster/clam) material used for inlay.
Nato - A lower grade or quality of mahogany, sometimes referred to as "lumberyard" mahogany.
Neck - The area that the strings of the instrument are stretched along, the headstock sits at the top, and the body lies below the last fret.
Neck Angle – The angle at which the neck joins the body (more common on set neck instruments). Different neck angles can affect both tone & volume, especially on acoustic guitars.
Octave - In Western Notation, every 12 frets on a stringed instrument is an octave in the musical scale.
Pearl - Short for mother-of-pearl, the inside shell from a shellfish. See MOTHER-OF-PEARL.
Pearloid - A synthetic material made of plastic and pearl dust.
Peghead – See HEADSTOCK. Originally used to describe the pegs/tuners extruding from the guitar head.
Phenolic -A synthetic material that is used as fingerboard wood replacement.
Pickguard - A piece of material used to protect the instrument's top or finish from gouges that are caused by the pick or your fingers.
Pickup - An electronic device utilizing magnetic induction to transform string vibrations into electronic signals needed for sound amplification. Pickups can either be high (most popular) or low (less output) impedance.
Position Marker – Usually, some form of decorative inlay which is inlaid into the neck to help the player identify fret position.
"Pre-CBS" - Collector's terminology that refers to the CBS purchase of Fender Instruments in 1965. A "Pre-CBS" instrument is one built by Leo Fender's original company.
Purfling - Decorative trim that is found running along the inside of the binding.
Relief - The upward slope of the fingerboard that keeps the strings off the frets.
Reverse Headstock - On this instrument the headstock has been flipped over from the normal configuration and the tuners are all on the highest note side of the instrument (tuners are all located on one side).
Rims – also referred to as Sides – refers to the sides of an instrument, typically between 1½ -5 inches deep.
Saddle - A natural or synthetic component generally attached to the bridge on which the strings rest, enabling the strings to resonate properly through the bridge and instrument top, and to assist in intonation.
Scale Length - The length measured in inches between the nut and the bridge/saddle/tailpiece.
Scalloped - This is what the area on the fingerboard between the frets is called when it has been scooped out, creating a dip between the frets.
Scratch Plate - Slang for Pickguard. - See PICKGUARD.
Semi-Acoustic - term used to describe a shallow bodied instrument that is constructed with a solid piece of wood running the length of the center of the body.
Sides – also referred to as Rims – refers to the sides of an instrument, typically between 1½ -5 inches deep.
Slotted Headstock – A headstock design usually associated with acoustic guitars, featuring 2 internal "slotted" areas where the strings are guided and the tuning machines spindles are placed horizontally.
Strings – Typically made from gut (older), nylon, steel, or bronze. Metal strings may or may not be coated also. They range in a variety of sizes, both in diameter and length. The weight of the string is what determines the range of frequencies it will cover.
Sunburst (Sunburst Finish) – Typically, either a 2 or 3 color finish that is applied around the outside of the body (may include rims, back, and neck also), leaving the inside a lighter, unstained natural color.
Thinline - Original Gibson terminology referring to a hollow bodied instrument that has a shallow depth of body.
Through Body (Thru Body; Neck Through) - Type of construction that consists of the neck wood extending through the entire length of the instrument and the pieces of wood that make up the body being attached to the sides of the neck wood (called "wings").
Treble Bout – Upper right hand part of body (right side of lower fingerboard on right hand guitars).
Tremolo - An increase of decrease in the frequency of a tone. Tremolo in relation to guitars usually refers to a tremolo unit, or tremolo effects. Please refer to individual listings.
Truss Rod - Typically, an adjustable rod (usually metal) placed in an instrument's neck, adding stability, and allowing for a neck adjustment in the case of a warped/curved neck.
Venetian - rounded point on the treble forward horn of a body cutaway. See also FLORENTINE.
Vibrato - The act of physically lengthening or shortening the medium (in this case, it will be strings) to produce a fluctuation in frequency. The pitch altering mechanism on your guitar is a vibrato, not a tremolo!
Volute (also Neck Volute) - Additional protruding wood used as a strengthening support where an angled back of the headstock is spliced to the end of the neck. This carved (or shaped) piece of the neck is also referred to as a "handstop".
Warpage – Generally refers to a neck that becomes bowed or warped, making playability difficult/impossible. On necks with truss rods, the neck may be adjusted to become straight again. On instruments with set necks, often times the neck must be taken off and repaired, or needs to be replaced.
Wings - The body pieces attached to the sides of a through body neck blank, thus forming a complete body.
Zero Fret - The zero fret is a length of fret wire fitted into a fret slot which is cut at the exact location as that of a conventional nut. The fingerboard is generally cut off 1/8" longer than usual, at which point the nut is fitted. When used in conjunction with the zero fret, the nut serves as a string guide. The fret wire used on the zero fret is usually slightly larger than that used on the fingerboard itself - the slightly higher zero fret establishes the open string's height above the fingerboard.

HARDWARE: BRIDGES, PEGS, TAILPIECES AND TUNERS

Banjo Tuners - tuners that are perpendicular to the headstock and pass through it, as opposed to being mounted on the side of the headstock, (like classic style headstock tuners).
Bigsby Vibrato - A vibrato system that involves a roller bar with lit-

GLOSSARY

tle pegs that run in a perpendicular line, around which you hook the string balls. One end of the bar has an arm coming off of it, a spring is located under the arm, and the entire apparatus is connected to a trapeze tailpiece. The bridge is separate from the vibrato system. This vibrato was designed by Paul Bigsby.

Bridge - Component that connects the strings to the body of the instrument. Bridge materials may be wood, metal, alloy, synthetic, or even a combination. It is usually attached to the top of an instrument's body by glue or screws but can also be held in place by string tension, the same as a violin. Bridge placement is determined by the instrument's scale length.

Bridge Pins – Pins or dowels used to secure string to bridge. These pins usually utilize friction to seat properly, and are typically made from hard wood, synthetic materials (ivoroid is popular), or ivory. Also referred to as Pegs.

Double Locking Vibrato - A vibrato system that locks the strings into place by tightening down screws on each string, thus stopping the string's ability to slip. There is also a clamp at the top of the fingerboard that holds the strings from the tuners. These more modern designs were formulated separately by Floyd Rose and the Kahler Company. As guitarist Billy Gibbons (ZZ Top) is fond of saying, the locking vibratos give you the ability to "turn Steel into Rubber, and have 'er bounce back on a dime". - See VIBRATO SYSTEM.

Fixed Bridge - Body hardware component that typically contains the saddles, bridge, and tailpiece in one integrated unit, and is usually mounted utilizing screws/studs.

Headless - Term meaning that the instrument's headstock is missing (example: Steinberger). The top of the neck is capped with a piece of hardware that acts like a regular tailpiece on the instrument body.

Locking Tuners - These tuners are manufactured with a locking mechanism built into them, thus preventing string slippage.

Nut - Device located at the top of the fingerboard (opposite from the bridge) that determines the action and spacing of the strings.

Pegs – Can refer to either the small pegs used to secure the strings in the bridge or older tuners used on some vintage instruments (hence the term peghead).

Pins - Pegs that are used to anchor the strings in place on the bridge.

Roller Bridge - This is a Gretsch trademark feature. It is an adjustable metal bridge that sits on a wooden base, the saddles of this unit sit on a threaded bar and are easily moved back and forth to allow personal string spacing.

Saddle/Saddles - A part of the bridge that holds the string/strings in place, helps transfer vibrations to the instrument body and helps in setting the action.

Set- In Neck - Guitar construction that involves attaching the neck to the body by gluing a joint (such as a dovetail). Set necks cannot be adjusted by shims as their angle of attachment to the body is preset in the design.

Sideways Vibrato - Built off the trapeze tailpiece concept, this unit has a lever that pulls the string attachment bar back along a pair of poles that have springs attached them to push the bar back into place. This is all covered by a plate with a design on it.

Single Locking Vibrato - A vibrato system that locks the strings on the unit to keep them from going out of tune during heavy arm use. This style of vibrato does not employ a clamping system at the top of the fingerboard.

Standard Vibrato - Usually associated with the Fender Stratocaster, this unit has the saddles on top and an arm off to one side. The arm allows you to bend the strings, making the frequencies (notes) rise or drop. All of this sits on a metal plate that rocks back and forth. Strings may have an area to attach to on top or they may pass through the body and have holding cups on the back side. A block of metal, usually called the Inertia Block, is generally located under the saddles to allow for increased sustain. The block travels through the instrument's body and has springs attached to it to create the tension necessary to keep the strings in tune. - See VIBRATO SYSTEM.

Steinberger Bridge - A bridge designed by Ned Steinberger, it combines the instrument bridge and tuners all in one unit. It is used with headless instruments.

Steinberger Vibrato - A vibrato system that has the instrument's bridge, vibrato and tuners all in one unit. Like the Steinberger Bridge, this was also designed by Ned Steinberger. It is also used with headless instruments.

Stop Tailpiece - Machined metal part attached to lower body by screws, which is usually slotted to hold the string balls. Generally used with a tune-o-matic bridge.

Strap button – Typically refers to oversized metal buttons on the outside of an instrument allowing the player to attach a strap to the instrument.

String Through Anchor Block – Refers to a steel block located in a tremolo unit to help sustain and anchor strings.

Strings Through Body (Anchoring) - A tailpiece that involves the strings passing through an instrument's body and the string balls are held in place by recessed cups on the back side.

Stud Tailpiece - See STOP TAILPIECE.

Tailpiece - The device that holds and typically positions (along with a possible bridge) the strings at the lower body. It may be all in one unit that contains the saddle/saddles also, or stands alone. Electric tailpieces are mostly metal construction, although metal, wood, alloy, synthetic or other materials have also been used.

Trapeze Tailpiece - A type of tailpiece that is hinged, has one end attached to either the lower bout or bottom rim of the instrument, and the top portion has internal grooves to hold the string balls.

Tremolo Unit – Refers to a mechanical device typically incorporated into the bridge of an instrument utilizing a tremolo (whammy) bar to produce changes in frequencies.

Truss Rod - Refers to a metal truss rod fitted into the back of an instrument's neck, adding stability, and allowing for a neck adjustment in the case of a warped/curved neck. Gibson invented this solution for neck adjusting in the mid 1920s.

Tuner(s)/Tuning Machine(s) - Mechanical device that is used to stretch the strings to the right tension for adjustable tuning. These are typically located on the headstock.

Tunable Stop Tailpiece - A tailpiece that rests on a pair of posts and has small fine-tuning machines mounted on top of it.

Tune-o-matic Bridge - A bridge that is attached to the instrument's top by two metal posts and has adjustable small moving saddles allowing for the intonation of individual strings. Tune-o-matic was originally a proprietary Gibson trademark that was designed by the late Ted McCarty in 1952, and introduced in 1954 on the Gibson Les Paul Custom.

Vibrato - Generic term used to describe Vibrato System.

Vibrato System - A device that increases or decreases the string tension by using a lever (whammy bar) and a fulcrum (typically pivot pins or blades).

Wang Bar - Slang term used for Vibrato System.

Whammy (Whammy Bar) - Slang term used for Vibrato System.

Wraparound Tailpiece – Design allowing strings to be wrapped around the tailpiece, then secured.

Wrapover Bridge - A self contained bridge/tailpiece bar device that is attached to the body, with the strings wrapping over the bar.

Wrapunder Bridge - The same as above except the strings wrap under the bar.

PICKUPS/ELECTRONICS

The Pickup Principle follows this idea: your instrument's pickup is composed of a magnetic core that has wire wrapped about it. This creates a magnetic field that the strings pass through. As the string is plucked it vibrates in this field and creates fluctuations. These fluctuations are then translated into electronic pulses by induction; the magic of having electrons excited into activity by being wrapped next to each other via the wire coils. Once the fluctuations are in electron form they move along the wires in groups called waveforms, which move to an amplifier and get enlarged. The rest is up to you.

Active Electronics - A form of electronic circuitry that involves some power source, usually a 9-volt battery. Most of the time the circuit is an amplification circuit, though it may also be onboard effects circuitry.

Alnico Pickup – A pickup utilizing an alloy magnet consisting of Aluminum, Nickel and Cobalt.

Amplify/Amplification - To increase, in this case to increase the volume of the instrument.

Blade - A pickup that uses a blade or rail instead of polepieces.

Bobbin - The structure, usually plastic, that the coil wires are wound around. See COILS.

Ceramic - A substance used in pickup magnets that consists of magnetic particles mixed with a clay- like base.

Coils - Insulated wire wrapped around a nonconductive material.

Coil Split - A switch and a term that means you are splitting the coils in a humbucker and turning it into two single coil pickups. - See SPLIT PICKUP.

Coil Tap - A term and a switch that refers to accessing a coil tap in a pickup. - See TAPPED.

Control/Controls - See POT and POTENTIOMETERS

Decade Switch – Typically, a switch or potentiometer involved in the tone circuitry that changes an instrument's sound by altering resistance levels.

Dirty Fingers - Coverless humbucker pickups that have black and white bobbins.

Equalizer - An effect that allows you to boost or cut certain frequencies.

'Floating' pickup - A magnetic pickup that is suspended over (versus being built into) the top of the guitar, just below the fingerboard. This enables the guitar to be used acoustically or electrically. Examples include the Benedetto pickup, the DeArmond #1100G, or the Gibson Johnny Smith pickup.

Hex Pickup - A device that has six individual pickups, one for each string, housed in a single unit. This unit is used to provide the signals for synth (synthesizer) instruments.

'Horseshoe' Pickup - Generally refers to Rickenbacker's original "frying pan" design pickups that resemble a horseshoe. The pickup "wings" extend up and back over the strings, but do not meet in the middle (split).

Humbucker - Consists of two single coil pickups being placed side by side and wired together in such a fashion that the hum is canceled out of the single coils.

J- Style - A single coil pickup, though some are humbucker pickups, designed for electric bass and usually placed near the bridge. It is largely associated with the Fender Jazz Bass.

"Jazz" Pickup - A pickup, suspended ('floating') or built- in on an archtop guitar that gives the instrument a traditional, mainstream jazz sound.

Lace Sensor - A pickup developed by Don Lace that takes a single bobbin and windings and places it inside a magnetic housing with an open top. This creates an electromagnetic shielding effect and allows only the area directly over the pickup to sense string vibration. As a result, the magnetic force ("string pull") on the string is lessened.

Lipstick (or Lipstick Tube) Pickup - Term coined in the vintage guitar market to describe the chrome single coil pickups found in Danelectro guitar models. The wound single coil pickups were actually placed in two chromed halves of lipstick casings (Danelectro bought the casings from a manufacturer who serviced the cosmetic industry). Since then, the 'Lipstick Tube' term has been applied to any similar single coil pickup in a chromed tube cover.

Mini-humbucker – similar to humbucker, except is smaller in size.

Onboard - Usually referencing effects, it means built into the instrument.

Out Of Phase - When a signal from two pickups are run through a switch that puts their respective signals 180 degrees out of phase with each other.

P-90 – original Gibson terminology for single coil pickup (also referred to as Soapbar).

P- Style - An offset pickup with two magnets per half. They are usually located near the neck and are associated with the Fender Precision Bass.

P.A.F. (Patent Applied For) - Common term used to mean the pickup that Seth Lover designed for Gibson in 1955. The patent was not awarded till 1959, so pickups used in the meantime had the P.A.F. stickers underneath the housing.

Parametric Equalizer - An equalizer that allows you to specifically choose which range of frequencies you wish to affect.

Passive Electronics - Electronic circuitry that has no power supply. Usually it consists of filter circuitry.

Phase Switch - A switch used to accomplish the feat of putting the signal out of phase. - See OUT OF PHASE.

Pickup - An electronic device utilizing magnetic induction to transform string vibrations into electronic signals needed for sound amplification. Pickups can either be high (most popular) or low (less output) impedance.

Pickup Trim Ring – A trim ring that goes around the outside of the

pickup. Typically used w/o pickguard, and may be recessed into body.
Piezo (piezoelectric) - A crystalline substance that induces an electrical current caused by pressure or vibrations.
Polepiece/Polepieces - Small magnetic rods that are found inside the pickup coils and, usually, situated under the instrument's strings. Some of these polepieces are adjustable.
Pot - Short for "potentiometer".
Potentiometer - A variable resistor that is typically used to make tone and volume adjustments on an instrument.
Preamp - An electronic circuit that amplifies the signal from the pickup/s and preps it for the amplifier.
Rail Pickup- See BLADE.
Shielding - Term used to describe materials (usually copper) used to protect the signal in electronic instruments from outside electrical interference.
Single Coil - See opening paragraph for this section, it applies to this term.
Soap Bar - Term used to describe a specific Gibson single coil pickup, model number: P- 90.
Split Pickup - A humbucker that has been wired so it has the capability of being split into two single coil pickups.
Stacked Coil - A form of humbucker pickup that is in a stacked configuration so it can be installed as a replacement for a single coil.
Tapped - The process of taking a wire out of the midst of the windings in a pickup and leaving it open for hookup to a switch. This can be done a number of times in one pickup. "Tapping" the pickup allows access to a different amount of winding (a percentage of the full winding) and thus different sounds from the same pickup.
Transducer/Transducer Pickup - A device that converts energy from one form to another, in this instance it is the vibrations caused by the strings, moving along the wood and being converted into electrical energy for amplification.

BOOK TERMINOLOGY

This glossary section should help you understand the jargon used in the model descriptions of the instruments in this text.
3-per-side - Three tuners on each side of the headstock on a six string instrument.
3/2-per-side - This is in reference to a 5-string instrument with three tuners on one side of the headstock and two tuners on the other.
335 Style - refers to an instrument that has a semi- hollowbody cutaway body style similar to that of the Gibson 335.
4-on-one-side - Four tuners on one side of the headstock on a 4-string instrument.
4-per-side - Four tuners on each side of the headstock an eight-string instrument.
4/1-per-side - On an instrument with five strings this would mean four tuners are on one side of the headstock, and one is on the other.
4/2-per-side - Four tuners on one side and two on the other side of a headstock.
4/3-per-side - This instrument has seven strings with four of the tuners located on one side of the headstock and three on the other side.
5-on-one-side - All the tuners on one side of the headstock on a 5-string instrument.
6-on-one-side - All six tuners on one side of the headstock on a 6-string instrument.
6-per-side - Six tuners on each side of the headstock on an twelve string instrument.
6/1-per-side - A seven string instrument with six tuners on one side and one on the other.
7-on-one-side - A term referring to a seven-string instrument with al the tuners on the headstock are on one side.
14/20-Fret - Term in which the first number describes the fret at which the neck joins the body, and the second number is the total number of frets on the fingerboard.
Contoured Body - A body design that features some carved sections that fit easier to the player's body (a good example is the Fender Stratocaster).
Dual Cutaway - Guitar design with two forward horns, both extending forward an equal amount (See OFFSET DOUBLE CUTAWAY, SINGLE CUTAWAY).
Explorer style - The instrument's body shape, a unique 'hourglass' shape, is similar to the original Gibson Explorer model.
Jazz Style - A body shape similar to the traditional jazz archtop or semi-hollowbody design, or some parts/designs of a traditional jazz archtop.
Les Paul (LP) Body Style – Typically refers to original Gibson Les Paul style body.
Offset Double Cutaway - Guitar design with two forward horns, the top (bass side) horn more prominent of the two (See DUAL CUTAWAY, SINGLE CUTAWAY).
Point Fingerboard - A fingerboard that has a "V-ed" section on it at the body end of the fingerboard.
Point(y) Headstock - Tip of the headstock narrows (i.e. Charvel/Jackson or Kramer models).
Precision Style (P- Style) - A bass guitar body shape similar to the original Fender Precision Bass; also refers to the split single coil design of the pickup.
Single Cutaway - Guitar design with a single curve into the body, allowing the player access to the upper frets of the fretboard (See DUAL CUTAWAY, OFFSET DOUBLE CUTAWAY).
Sleek - A more modern body style, perhaps having longer forward horns, more contoured body, or a certain aerodynamic flair (!).
Strat Style – Typically refers to a Fender Stratocaster body style.
Tele Style - A single cutaway 'plank' body similar to the original Fender Telecaster; also refers to the style of fixed bridge.
Through Body (Neck-Through Construction) - Type of construction that consists of the neck wood extending through the entire length of the instrument and the pieces of wood that make up the body being attached to the sides of the neck wood.
Tune-o-matic Stop Tailpiece - This unit is a combination bridge/tailpiece that has adjustable (tune-o-matic) saddles mounted on a wrap around tailpiece.
V Style - The instrument's body shape, a unique 'V' shape, is similar to the original Gibson Flying V model.
Volume/Tone Control - When encountered, refers to an instrument which has a volume and/or tone control. A numerical prefix (2 or 3 preceding the term indicates the amount of volume/tone controls.

Rudolf Schenker of The Scorpions 8/11/99

Merle Haggard 10/2/99

Wynonna 10/14/99

Brian Setzer 10/29/99

Sammy Hagar 1/26/01

Brad Whitford of Aerosmith 5/3/99

Ted Nugent 9/5/99
Gene Simmons of KISS 3/17/00
Ace Frehley of KISS 3/17/00
Paul Stanley of KISS 3/17/00
Paul Stanley and Jerry Adler 2/15/98
For my fourth appearance in the "Blue Book of Electric Guitars" I am featuring my favorite rock band - KISS.
The group is hanging up their platform shoes after 27 years!
These photos were taken last year on their Farewell Tour. Also several of my other favorite country and rock musicians.
The photo of Paul Stanley and myself was taken in Feb. 1998 as we were in line to go see The Rolling Stones concert at The Hard Rock Hotel in Las Vegas.

Backstage With Deep Purple

By Judi Glover

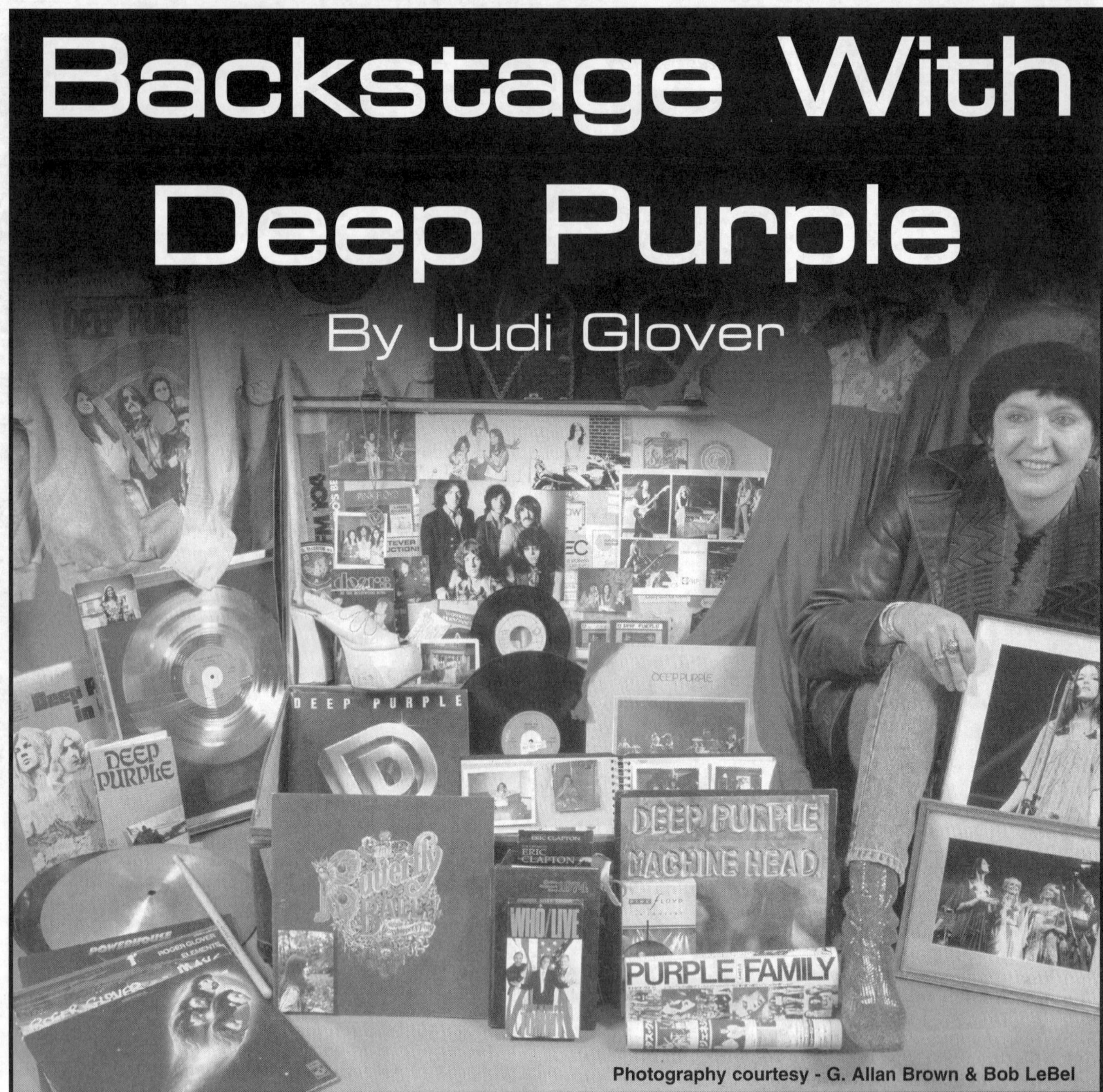

Photography courtesy - G. Allan Brown & Bob LeBel

The year was 1970. At the time I was in college at Georgia State University. I sat in the coliseum in Atlanta, to see a rock concert - in company with my cousin. We were both obsessed with music. I didn't realize until later that she had other objectives. In those days, there were two support bands before the main act. By the time the British band, Deep Purple, came on, we were quite stoned. Marijuana was used fairly openly and whether you were "using" or not, the air was pungent and intoxicating.

Deep Purple took the stage and gave us all a thunderous wake-up call. Their album "In Rock" was on top of the charts. They were, at that time, the top selling band in the world. It was the best gig I'd seen to that point.

A year or so later, I was working in a club called "The Headrest." It was a place where such bands as Lynyrd Skynyrd were discovered. I was modeling and working nights to supplement expenses of going to college.

Deep Purple was back in town, but I had to work. That night, some of the band came to the club. I recognized two of them. The third, Roger Glover, told me that he was Ritchie Blackmore's "roadie." At the end of the night, he invited me to their concert in Birmingham, Alabama, the following weekend.

I asked my cousin to come along – not knowing she had already planned to go. She'd been seeing one of the members on their Atlanta visits for a time. This trip would change my life forever!

We went to Birmingham, and stayed out of the way. We knew the promoter, which always proved helpful. Fleetwood Mac was the support band. After they finished, I began a conversation with Mick Fleetwood. There was the usual equipment change, and then Purple took the stage. As Roger went by, he winked at me. I fully expected him to get Ritchie's guitar and hand it to him – as roadies do. That didn't happen. I asked Mick who Roger was. He told me he was the bass player! We spent the rest of the concert spraying water pistols at Deep Purple!

That was the beginning of the long lists of non-truths I would hear from Roger – one of the hazards of falling for a rock star! Shortly afterwards, I flew to Miami for another gig. The "Small Faces" were the support band. We celebrated after the show - Rod Stewart among us - by setting the straw roofs of the beach cabanas on fire. Once inside, there was a round of exploding televisions out the windows. My baptism to backstage rock 'n roll! The touring began.

Rock stars are almost always looking for willing "talent" – and that's another way roadies come in...

At first, touring was great. Different cities, states, countries, different cultures, characters, cuisines, hotels, etc. But it soon became very repetitive, and boring. You don't *see* the countries, you see airports, hotels, restaurants, the concert halls and maybe a local nightclub. More time is spent in travel, sound checks, interviews, with press and preparation. You rearrange furniture, smash things, play pranks, and so forth, out of boredom.

For a long time, I was the only band member's "woman" on the road. Ritchie had the final say in most things. He decided I could be along for the ride. I never told the other wives or girl friends about the indiscretions of certain members. That was partly due to the fact that I didn't know them well enough for a long time. I wasn't always around during the performances. In six tours of Japan, I was off enjoying the culture, not sitting backstage watching, listening, absorbing.

Being backstage can be like watching a pre-show performance. Primping, posing, positioning and pick-ups. The band had different dressing rooms: one for Ritchie, the other for the remaining members. The dressing room was a mixture of other musicians, show business luminaries, "liggers" (how did *they* get in here?), sometimes relatives, but *always* groupies.

Jon Lord and "friends" backstage.

Rock stars are almost always looking for willing "talent" – and that's another way roadies come in. Part of their job is to seek out attractive females, give them backstage passes and hope the bosses will be well entertained. This, along with his interest in black magic, were two of the reasons why Ritchie had his own dressing room. The rest of the band wanted no part of his amusement. His roadies were always very busy. He insisted on "action" before and after the gig.

"Which one do you want to sleep with?" This was a common question asked of me as I sat outside of the Purple dressing rooms. Early on in my time with them, it became somewhat of a habit for the guys to hand me rings, wallets, photos or whatever else they didn't feel comfortable leaving in the dressing room. Before concerts, the band would usually socialize with each other, and guests. They didn't always communicate enroute. After the gig, they would file into the room, close the door, and review, discuss and tear-

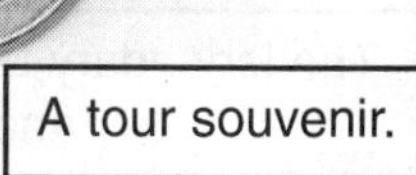

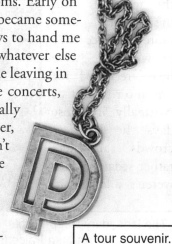

A tour souvenir.

apart the gig.

So, I sat outside. Quite a change from being on-stage all along. I was never allowed to walk to the stage with Roger. Management felt it ruined the illusion of "bad boys" and availability. It wasn't Roger's decision. After the show began, I was carefully seated behind the stacks of amps – usually to drummer Ian Paice's right. There, no other females made contact with me.

I would hardly reply when these girls asked whom I wanted. I would wait until the band filed out, and took their belongings from me. Then Roger would come out, kiss me, take my hand and we'd walk away. I was so proud!

There were a lot of things I liked about being on the road. The pampering, private jets, the best hotels (until they experience your antics), the attention. Almost everything is done for you besides eating, sex and going to the bathroom! Leave your bags one place, and they magically show up in your room at the next destination!

But, there were things I didn't like. I guess that's what ultimately ruined my marriage. I hated the sleaze and the often cheap way women were treated . . . the debauchery and "anything goes" mentality. There were no drugs (honestly), but Jack Daniels, groupies and rock 'n roll go together. Alcohol helped dull boredom, repetitiveness and loneliness.

In 1972, I was part of the ultimate behind the scenes backstage experience. It was at the time Deep Purple recorded their Japanese tour for "Made in Japan." It was thrilling to see the reaction from the crowds – even more so since they knew they were being recorded for immortality! Normally in those days the Japanese crowds sat there rather sedately; they weren't allowed to jump around, and express their feelings. But, this time, they broke loose, and went crazy. It was something to watch!

In 1973, Roger left the band. All of the guys were burnt out. Six tours of America a year, plus the rest of the world - and at least one album per year - left little time for anything else. Tempers flared constantly. After an emotional close in Osaka, Japan, it was over. It took Roger about two years to regroup.

Roger went on to join Rainbow, pursued solo deals and produced many other successful groups, among them Judas Priest, Nazareth, Rory Gallagher and Rainbow. I rarely went backstage again.

The last time I went backstage, I was one of the performers. Roger wrote an album called "The Butterfly Ball." It was a compilation of songs written to poems from the 1800s, and illustrated by Alan Aldridge. He was responsible for the "Yellow Submarine" animations and designing the "Brown Dirt Cowboy" album cover for Elton John – among other accomplishments. Vincent Price, the actor, narrated and Twiggy (famous model of the 1960s) performed the final song. Twiggy and I did the encore together. Among other rock performers starring in this concert were Jon Lord, Glenn Hughes (who had replaced Roger in Deep Purple),

The legendary Deep Purple, circa 1969. Left to right: Ritchie Blackmore, Ian Gillan (sitting), Roger Glover, John Lord, and Ian Paice (sitting). DP's six Tokyo concerts changed Japan's rock adolescents forever.

David Coverdale (who replaced Ian Gillian), and Ronnie James Dio (who went from Rainbow to Black Sabbath!). It was a very different kind of backstage, much more theatrical. It was also a sort of disjointed, expanded, but satisfactory Deep Purple reunion. The project was a great success. In 2000 the long playing album was re-released as a 25th anniversary CD. The pictures inside the jacket cover showed, Roger, and Twiggy and me singing. In the audience, a packed house, were the likes of Robert Plant and Ian Gillian.

I don't regret anything. It was a fabulous life experience. I still go behind the scenes to see other friends, from the old days, perform.

Our daughter, Gillian, now 24, has seen the band around the world, and has embarked on her own singing career. Roger is still performing with four of the original members of Deep Purple. Ritchie is gone. To this day, Gillian sees her father – who rejoined Purple in the mid-1980s – and his bandmates perform all over the world. She has a lot to tell, from *her* point of view, but, that's another story . . . .

You are invited to a Pre-View Showing
of
"THE BUTTERFLY BALL"
on Wednesday 7th July 1976
at
THE PRINCESS ANNE THEATRE,
BRITISH ACADEMY OF FILM AND TELEVISION ARTS,
195 PICADILLY,
LONDON, W1V 9LG.
The bar will be open from 7.00 p.m. and the film will commence promptly at **7.30 p.m.**

Deep Purple onstage, 1970.

Thanks for the Memories

Kids always love the blow-up Fender Tele.

Seymour Duncan rips on the giant Gibson.

Triggs and the heat.

Yasuhiko Iwanade (author of Beauty of the Burst & Galaxy of Strats) and wife.

Dr. Tom Van Hoose, lost in his music, on a 335.

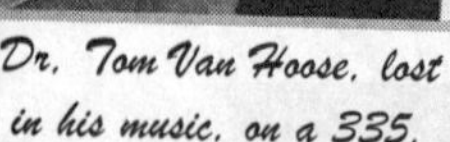

Bassist Billy Sheehan checking out intonation on a Turner.

Jimmy Wallace (co-owner of Dallas Guitar Show & axe grinder extraordinare) and son.

Andreas Pichler of Andreas Guitars with Blue Shark

ESP's Cuctom shop can do any-thing- train kept a rollin'.

Guitarist Robben Ford takes an sutograph break

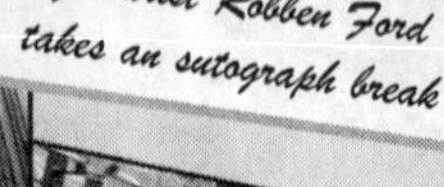

Mark Pollock of Charley's Guitar Shop, struttin' his stuff.

Music Sales' Steve Wilson (l), Joey Lyons, and Dave McCumsky (r).

Fender alwayts has an impressive NAMM display.

1950 Fender Broadcaster, originally approx. $189, now $50k. Do the math.

Bob & Cindy Benedetto

Dave Rogers from Dave's Guitar Shop.

1959 Les Paul Standard from Dave's Guitar Shop.

Don Lace with from Lace Music Products with his new Lace Helix guitar.

I Dream of Jeannie "rubbing" her custom Strat.

John Brinkmann, one of the Texas Amigos, and guitar show pioneer.

Where else but the Ernie Ball booth?

Add a soft touch to your Vox amp.

Where else but in CA? She said she felt really high!

George Gruhn with a pair of Tacoma Papooses!

BBP's secret NAMM weapon - Zachary Fjestad, doing solo time in booth

Inside Gibson trailer with Gibson Personel and Dave Amato (REO Speedwagon's Guitarist).

Blue Book road crew - Clint Schmidt, Jack in the Box, the Gurnmesiter, and S.P. Fjestad.

Master Pickup builder and recent U.S. citizen Kent Armstrong (r), with friend

KNOW YOUR WOODS!

Throughout the text of this book, readers may notice the different woods used in the construction of guitars and basses. In addition to wood types, we have also listed wood trade names as well (i.e., Smartwood, Certified Wood, Plywood, Wildwood, etc.). The following table is presented to help understand the names, family references, and many other common names that describe the woods used in guitar building. Without these woods, guitar building would be on a much lower plateau.

WOOD VARIETIES (SOFT & HARDWOOD) TRADENAMES, & RELATED INFORMATION

Common Name	Latin Name	Family	Other Names/Information
American Woods			
Alder	—	—	—
Ash	—	—	—
Cedar, Western Red	—	—	Typically harvested in California & Washington
Certified Wood	—	—	Term used by Smartwood Certified Forestry designating that the wood comes only from a certified forest.
Cherry	—	—	—
Deadwood	—	—	Stage following old wood, indigenous to a small area in South Dakota north of Rapid City.
Madrone	Arbutus Menziessi	Ericaceae	—
Maple (generic)	Acer Macrophyllum	Aceraceae	—
Big Leaf Maple	—	—	—
Bird's Eye Maple	—	—	Bird's Eye, "dot-top", denoted by dark, small circular patterns, somewhat resembling bird's eyes.
Flame Maple	—	—	Flametop, denoted by discernible lines showing the dark and light contrast of the grain. Can be either wide or narrow.
Quilt Maple	—	—	Quilted, denoted by swirly, puffy, cloud-like patterns.
Rock Maple	Acer Saccharum	Aceraceae	Hard Maple, White Maple
Good quality rock maple is straight grained, and almost white.			
Oak	—	—	Red or White Oak (mostly acoustic production)
Plywood	Cheapus Waytoomuchus	American Big Business	—
Utilized in more recently mfg. instruments, allowing good overall tonal wood characteristics at a price point.			
Smartwood	Politicus Correctus	Treehuggers	Certified Wood
The term Smartwood represents an organization called Smartwood Certified Forestry, run by the Rainforest Alliance, and governed by the Forest Stewardship Council. The Smartwood Certified Forestry program ensures that Smartwood is harvested only from certified managed forests that have been independently evaluated, ensuring that they meet internationally recognized environmental and socioeconomic standards.			
Spruce	—	—	Many variations
The 3 main variations of American Spruce are Sitka Spruce, grown in the coastal region between Northern California & Alaska, Engelmann Spruce is indigenous to the Rocky Mountain Range, including New Mexico, Idaho, and Montana, and Adirondack Spruce, which comes from the Adirondack region in the eastern U.S. Other variations do exist.			
Sycamore	Acer Pseudoplatanus	Aceraceae	—
Tonewood (universal term)	—	—	—
Generic term referring to any wood selected in the manufacturing process for tonal quality and performance. Tonewoods usually include maple, mahogany, rosewood, ebony, spruce, koa, cedar, walnut, etc.			
Walnut	Juglans Hindsii	Juglancaceae	California Walnut, Claro Walnut
Wildwood	—	—	—
Refers to Fender trademark for process utilizing German beech trees injected with dyes that have been cut into veneers and laminated to the top of the instrument, circa 1967-1970.			
South and Central American Woods			
Bocate	Cordia spp.	—	Mexican Rosewood
Brazilian Rosewood	Harvest Interuptus	Mucho Centavos	—
Brazilian Rosewood was mostly discontinued after 1968, the last legal year of importation. Current legal mfg. requires C.I.T.E.S. certification beginning 1992. Since this now very controlled hardwood has achieved almost cult-like status, prices for instruments utilizing Brazilian Rosewood (mostly back & sides) have skyrocketed - both on new and vintage instruments.			
Cocobola	Dalbergia Retusa	Leguminosae	Granadillo
Imbuia	—	—	—
Indigenous in southern Brazil			
Mahogany	Swietinia Macrophylla	Meliaceae	—
Nato	—	—	—
Utility Grade Mahogany, not as high grade as African or Indian mahogany.			
Purpleheart	Peltogne spp.	Leguminosae	Amaranth, Violetwood, Morado, Saka, Koroboreli, Tananeo, Pau Roxo
Tulipwood	Dalbergia Fructescens	Leguminosae	Jacaranda Rosa, Pinkwood, Pau Rosa
African Woods			
Bubinga	Guibouria Demusi	Leguminosae	African Rosewood
Cocobola	Microberlinia	Leguminosae	Zebrano, Zingana, Brazzavillensis, Allene, Ele, Amouk
Ebony	Diospryus Crassiflora	Ebenaceae	Gabon Ebony
(African ebony is generally categorized by the country of orgin, i.e., Madagascar, etc.)			
Mahogany	—	—	—
South America			
Ovangkol	—	—	—
Pink Ivory	—	—	—
Sapele	—	—	—
Wenge	Millettia Laurentii	Leguminosae	Panga Panga
Zebrawood	—	—	—
European Woods			
Spruce	—	—	typically German Spruce
Indian Woods			
Ebony	Diospryus Ebenaceae	Ebenaceae	—
Macassar Ebony	Diospryus Celebica	Ebenaceae	Striped Ebony
Indian Rosewood	Dalbergia Latifoloa	Leguminosae	Bombay Rosewood, Sissoo, Biti, Ervadi, Kalaruk
(most currently manufactured guitars using rosewood are made from Indian rosewood - C.I.T.E.S. approval not needed)			
Vermillion	Pterocarpu Dalbergoides	Leguminosae	Paduak, Andaman Rosewood
Pacific Region Woods			
Koa	Acacia Koa	—	—
Lacewood	Carwellia Sublimis	Protaceae	Australian Silky Oak
Mahogany	—	—	Phillipine Mahogany, widely acclaimed for its tonal characteristics.

(Wood information courtesy Mica Wickersham, Alembic, & S.P. Fjestad)

INTERESTED IN CONTRIBUTINNG

The good thing about publishing a book on an annual basis is that you will find out what you don't know yearly. Each new edition should be an improvement on the last. Even though you can't do it all in one, 10, or even 20 editions, accumulating the new research is an ongoing process, with the results being published in each new edition.

The *Blue Book of Electric Guitars*™ has been the result of non-stop and continual guitar research obtained by getting the information needed from both manufacturers and luthiers (including visiting their production facilities whenever we get the opportunity). Also of major importance is speaking directly with acknowledged experts (both published and unpublished), reading books, catalogues, and company promo materials, gathering critical and up-to-date manufacturer/luthier information obtained from the NAMM Shows and the makers themselves, and observing and analyzing market trends by following major vintage dealer and collector pricing and trends.

We also have a great batch of contributing editors and advisory board members that pump out a lot of good information annually - including vintage pricing updates. Going to a lot of guitar/trade shows, in addition to visiting a variety of music stores, guitar shops, pawn shops, second-hand stores also hone our chops.

If you feel that you can contribute in any way to the materials published herein, you are encouraged to submit hard copy regarding your potential additions, revisions, corrections, or any other pertinent information that you feel would enhance the benefits this book provides to its readers. Unfortunately, we are unable to take your information over the phone (this protects both of us)! Earn your way into the ranks of the truly twisted, join the motley crew of contributing editors, and see that your information can make a difference! We thank you in advance for taking the time to make this a better publication.

All materials sent in for possible inclusion into upcoming editions of the Blue Book of Electric Guitars™ should be either mailed, faxed, or emailed to us at the address listed below:

Blue Book Publications, Inc.
Attn: Guitar Contributions
8009 34th Avenue South, Ste. 175
Minneapolis, MN 55425 USA
Fax: 952-853-1486
Email: guitars@bluebookinc.com
Web: http://www.bluebookinc.com

If you're emailing us an image, please make sure it is in TIF or JPEG format. Poor quality images cannot be used for publication.

CORRESPONDENCE INQUIRIES

Can't find your guitar in the book? No one's ever seen/heard of this make/model? Color/feature not listed? What's this thing worth? When was it manufactured? These are the most common type of questions we get when conducting research. This type of researching is a big job, and to do it properly, you must have a good working knowledge of instruments and their values, an up-to-date reference library, the right contacts (huge), keep going to guitar/trade shows, and actually read the guitar mags. We have helped out hundreds of people in the past, and hope to maintain this service in the future as well.

As with any ongoing publication, certain makes and models will not be included within the scope of the text. As expanded research uncovers model variations and new companies, the book's body of text will always have some unlisted instruments. Not believing in ivory towers and one-way traffic, this editor/publisher offers a mechanism for the consumer to get further information about makes/models not listed in these pages. For those reasons, we are offering correspondence inquiries to help you obtain additional information on items not listed, or even questions you may have regarding values and other related information.

Answering your correspondence (including letters, faxes, and email) under normal circumstances takes us between 10-14 working days. On hard to research items, more time is necessary. To make sure we can assist you with any correspondence, please include good quality photos of the specimen in question, any information available about that particular specimen - including manufacturer/trademark, model, body style, color/finish, unusual or other discernible features (if any) that will assist us with identifying your guitar(s). If you're emailing us an image, please make sure it is in TIF or JPEG format. Poor quality images cannot be properly used for determining value. The charge for this comprehensive research program is $20.00 per instrument. In addition to payment, be sure to include both your address and phone number, giving us an option of how to contact you for best service. To keep up with this constant onslaught of correspondence, we have a large network of both dealers and collectors who can assist us (if necessary) to answer most of your questions within this time frame.

Remember, the charge for this research service is $20.00 per guitar and payment must accompany your correspondence, and will be answered in a FIFO system (first in first out). Thank you for your patience. Sometimes proper research can't be hurried.

You may also want to check our web site for additional guitar information, including the Photo Grading System™ for ascertaining guitar condition factors. Good information never sleeps!

All correspondence regarding information and appraisals (not potential contributions or buying/selling guitars) should be directed to:

Blue Book Publications, Inc.
Attn: Guitar Contributions
8009 34th Avenue South, Ste. 175
Minneapolis, MN 55425 USA
Toll-free (U.S. & Canada): 800-877-4867 (voicemail only)
Fax: 952-853-1486
Email: guitars@bluebookinc.com
Web: http://www.bluebookinc.com

SORRY - No order or request for research paid by credit card will be processed without a credit card expiration date.

BUYING, SELLING, or TRADING

Interested in buying or selling a particular guitar(s)? Not sure about Ebay, or perhaps another risky alternative? Does consigning scare you? Or maybe you're just hesitating because you're not sure what a fair market price is? To be sure that you are getting a fair price/getting what you paid for, a buy/sell referral contact will be made, typically based on your interest(s) and geographical location. This referral service is designed to help all those people who are worried or scared about purchasing a potentially "bad guitar" or getting "ripped off" when selling. There is no charge for this referral service - we are simply connecting you with the best person(s) possible within your interest(s), making sure that you get a fair deal. This sort of matchmaking (no easy task) can make a world of difference on potentially buying or selling a guitar. Please contact the ***Blue Book of Electric Guitars*™** with your request(s) (email or fax preferred). If selling or trading, please mail or email (TIF or JPEG format) us a good quality image(s). On buy request, please as specific as possible. All replies are treated strictly confidentially, and should be directed to:

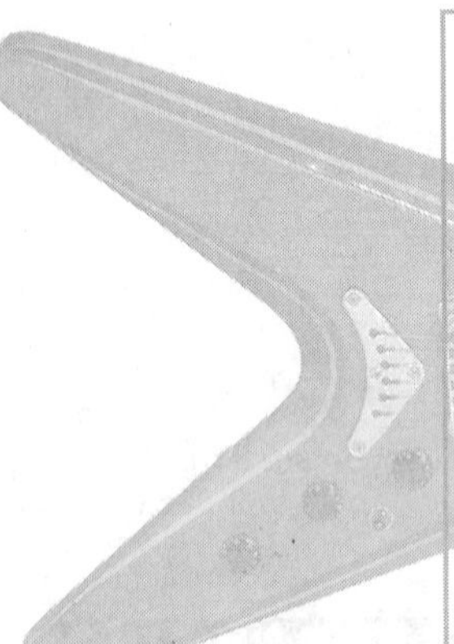

Blue Book Publications, Inc.
Attn: Guitars B/S/T
8009 34th Ave. S., Ste. 175
Minneapolis, MN 55425 USA
Email: guitars@bluebookinc.com
Web: http://www.bluebookinc.com
Fax: 952-853-1486
Toll-free (U.S. & Canada): 800-877-4867
Non-domestic: 952-854-5229

COMMON GUITAR ABBREVIATIONS

These abbreviations listed below may be found as prefixes and suffixes with a company's model names, and may indicate a special quality about that particular designation. This list should be viewed as being a guide only; abbreviations specifically relating to individual trademarks (i.e., Fender, Gibson, Martin) are listed separately within their sections.

A	-Ash
AE	-Acoustic Electric
B	-Bass, Brazilian Rosewood, or Blue (finish)
BLK, BK, BL	- Black (finish)
B & S	-Back & Sides (not BS, that's the sales pitch!)
C	-Cutaway
CH	-Channel
C.I.T.E.S.	-Convention for International Trade of Endangered Species (July 1,1975)
D	-Dreadnought or Double
DC	-Double Cutaway
E	-Electric
EQ	-Equalizer
ES	-Electric (Electro) Spanish
F	-Fretless or Florentine
FB	-Fingerboard
H	-Herringbone
HB	-Humbucker
HC	-Hard Case
HDWR	-Hardware
HS	-Headstock
J	-Jumbo
K	-Koa
L, LH	-Left Handed
LE	-Limited Edition
M	-Mahogany or Maple
MFG.	-Manufactured
MPL	-Maple
MSR	-Manufacturer's Suggested Retail
N, NAT	-Natural
N/A	-(Also $N/A) Not Available.
NOS	-New Old Stock
OEM	-Original Equipment Manufacture
OH	-Original Hardshell
OHSC	-Original Hardshell Case
OM	-Orchestra Model
OSC	-Original Soft Case
PG	-Pickguard
PU (P.U.)	-Pickup
R	-Reverse (headstock) Red (finish), or Rosewood
REFIN	-Refinished
REFRET	-Refretted
REPRO	-Reproduction
RSH	-Round Soundhole
S	-Spanish, Solid Body, Special or Super
SB, S/B	-Sunburst
Ser. No.	-Serial Number
SG	-Solid Guitar
SGL	-Single
SJ	-Super Jumbo
SN	-Serial Number
STD	-Standard
SWD	-Smartwood
T	-Tremolo or Thinline
TOB	-Tobacco
TREM	-Tremolo
TV	-TV Color Finish
V	-V shaped Neck, Venetian, Vibrato or Vintage Series
VIB	-Vibrato
W/	-With
W/O	-Without
WOB	-Wood Out Binding

CONDITION FACTORS

Rating the condition factor of a guitar is, at best, still subjective, while at worst, totally misrepresentative. We've attempted to give a few examples of things that may affect the pricing and desirability of vintage electric guitars, but it's almost impossible to accurately ascertain the correct condition factor (especially true on older instruments) without knowing what to look for - which means having the instrument in your hands (or someone else's whose checked out). Even then, three different experienced sources will probably come up with slightly different grades, not to mention different values based on different reasons. Listed below are major factors to consider when determining both the condition and value of any used electric instrument. Also, please study the PGS digital color photographs carefully on pages 33-63 to learn more about the factors described below.

Finish (read that original finish) - Original finish in good shape is, of course, the most desirable, and is the Holy Grail for collectors when hooked up with a major trademark and desirable model. A light professional overspray will negatively affect the value of a guitar somewhat. Professionally refinished instruments are typically worth 50% of the value of an original, and a poor refin is below that. An exception might be a case where there's only one or two examples of a highly desirable item, and condition may take a back seat to rarity.

Major repairs - Many older guitars have had repairs, of course. A well-done neck reset won't affect the overall value that much. Replaced bridges will have an affect, but the better the work, the better the resale value. A replaced neck, fingerboard, part of a side, top or back will cause the price to drop noticeably. Again, if it's an especially rare item, the rarity factor might negate the major repair(s).

Modifications - Any non-factory modification on an original guitar is going to hurt the value. Deciding to refinish the top of your 1959 LP Standard for example, will cost you the price of refinishing, plus another $15,000-$40,000 for non-originality! Modifications on pickups, tailpieces, and even installing a tremelo unit will also subtract from a guitars value. Think really really hard before you do any of these things to your vintage guitar. You won't get a second chance to make it original.

Replacement Tuners and other non-original parts - Many older guitars have been fitted with new tuners at some point. These days, there are good replacement tuners available that fit the original holes, etc. There are also sleeves that will make an oversized hole into the correct size for original style tuners. Even a good, appropriate replacement set will have a negative affect on value, even though it constitutes a playing improvement over what was available when the instrument was manufactured.

Cracks - Electric guitars are made of wood and cracks do happen. Unfortunately, unattended cracks tend to get bigger and usually do not go back together perfectly. Any crack will affect value, but a small, professionally well repaired crack will take much less of a bite out of the price than a large gaping crack that wouldn't go together properly.

Frets - A good analogy for frets would be found in the vintage car market: you rarely find a vintage car with original tires. Guitars were made to be played and frets do wear out. A good professional fret job using factory spec parts should not affect the value of your instrument. Again, this question won't come up with a mint, unplayed guitar.

Cosmetics - The cleaner an instrument, the more it's worth. Don't ever underestimate the value of eye appeal. A mint, unplayed, original condition guitar with tags will always bring more than the prices for "excellent" condition. On the other hand, an instrument with most of the finish worn off from years of use might bring less than the average shown here.

General Guitar Maintenance & Tips - Airplanes are meant to be flown, cars are meant to be driven, and guitars are meant to be played. Since instrument construction is typically wood, and wood expands/contracts like many other natural materials, don't allow instruments to go from one extreme temp./humidity factor to another (i.e., don't ship your Gibson Super 400 CES from Ft. Meyers, FL to Thief River Falls, MN in Jan.). Try to maintain a stable temp. and humidity level. Also, use good quality, professional products to clean, polish, and maintain (Virtuoso is recommended, www.virtuosopolish.com) your instruments (investments). Remember, maintaining a fine guitar requires some common sense and TLC.

Guitars, even vintage ones, are meant to be played. Enjoy yours, take proper care of it, play it once in awhile, and don't let temperature and/or humidity factors get to extremes.

Explanation & Converting Guitar Grading Systems

Since the 7th Edition *Blue Book of Electric Guitars*™ continues to use the **Photo Grading System**™ (PPGS) to describe condition, please study the color electric guitar condition photos on the following pages carefully to help understand and identify each electric guitar's unique condition factor. These photos, with condition factors, serve as a guideline, not an absolute. Remember, if the condition factor isn't right, the price is wrong!

The conversion chart listed below has been provided to help you convert the Photo Grading System™ to several other grading systems. All percentage descriptions and/or possible conversions made thereof, are based on original condition - alterations, repairs, refinishing work, and any other non-original alterations that have changed the condition of an instrument must be listed additionally, and typically subtracted from the values based on condition throughout this text (please refer to page 31 for an explanation of these critical factors affecting both condition and price).

Electric Guitar PGS Condition Factors with Explanations & Conversions

100% - New - Factory new with all factory materials, including warranty card, owner's manual, case, and other items that were originally included by the manufacturer. On currently manufactured instruments, the 100% price refers to an instrument not previously sold at retail. Even if a new instrument was played only twice, and traded in a week later, it no longer qualifies at 100%. On out-of-production instruments (including dealer "new, old stock," or NOS), the longer a guitar has been discontinued, the less likely you will find it in 100% condition. Some instruments that are less than 20 years old and have never been taken out-of-the-case (unplayed) may not be 100% (new), as the finish may have slightly cracked, tarnished, faded, or deteriorated. **Remember, there are no excuses in 100% condition.** See Photo 32 (refinished).

98% - Near Mint, Excellent++, 9.8 - Only very slightly used and/or played very little - may have minor "case" wear or light dings on exterior finish only, without finish cracking, very close to new condition, also refers to a currently manufactured instrument that has previously sold at retail, even though it may not have been played. May have a slight scratch - otherwise as new. Also, should have original case.

95% - Excellent+ (Exc.+), 9.5 - Very light observable wear, perhaps some very light plating deterioration on metal parts, extremely light finish scratching, may have slight neck wear.

90% - Excellent (Exc.), 9.0 - Light exterior finish wear with a few minor dings, no paint chips down to the wood, normal nicks and scratches, light observable neck wear in most cases, 9 quesadillas with homemade guacamole and salsa.

80% - Very Good+ (VG+), Above Average, approx. 8.0 - More exterior finish wear (20% of the original finish is gone) that may include minor chips that extend down to the wood, body wear, but nothing real serious, nice shape overall, with mostly honest player wear.

70% - Very Good (VG), Average, approx. 7.0 - More serious exterior finish wear that could include some major gauges and nicks, player arm wear, and/or fret deterioration.

60% - Good (G), Sub-average, approx. 6.0 - Noticeable wear on most areas - normally this consists of some major belt buckle wear and finish deterioration, may include cracking, possible repairs or alterations. When this condition factor is encountered, normally an instrument should have all logos intact, original pickups, minor headstock damage, and perhaps a few non-serious alterations, with or without original case.

40% - Fair (F), Below Average, approx. 3.0 to 5.0 - Major features are still discernible, major parts missing, probably either refinished or repaired, structurally sound, though many times encountered with non-factory alterations.

20% - Poor (P), approx. 2.0 - Ending a life sentence of hard labor, must still be playable, most of the licks have left, family members should be notified immediately, normally not worthy unless the ad also mentions first year Tele. May have to double as kindling if in a tight spot on a cold night.

1994 Fender Telecaster '52 Reissue - Ser. #17616. Blonde Natural finish, new condition (mint, 10, 100%). Light ash body with maple neck and black pickguard. Most reissues like this always like it when the case gets opened - it's the only time they ever see daylight! This Tele lives quietly in its vintage tweed case, complete with all the original hang tags, paperwork, and other "case candy". Since most recent reissues remain in new condition, the real question is, "How many years do I have to leave this thing in the closet before it can make me some money?" Got time? Courtesy Dale Hanson.

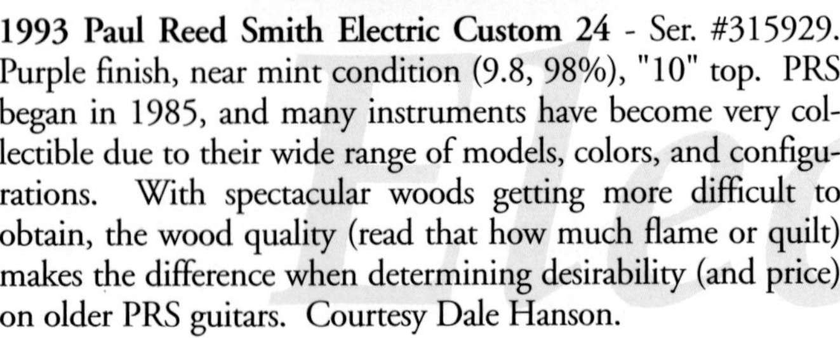

1993 Paul Reed Smith Electric Custom 24 - Ser. #315929. Purple finish, near mint condition (9.8, 98%), "10" top. PRS began in 1985, and many instruments have become very collectible due to their wide range of models, colors, and configurations. With spectacular woods getting more difficult to obtain, the wood quality (read that how much flame or quilt) makes the difference when determining desirability (and price) on older PRS guitars. Courtesy Dale Hanson.

1981 G&L F-100 Series II - Ser. #G005289. Gold metallic finish, near mint condition (9.8, 98%). Note ebony fingerboard - this model was also available with a maple fingerboard, as well as an ash, maple, or mahogany body. A great early G&L guitar from George Fullerton & Leo Fender. Early models and variations with rare/special order features from a new company are usually worth more than later production, unless playing is negatively affected. Courtesy Dale Hanson.

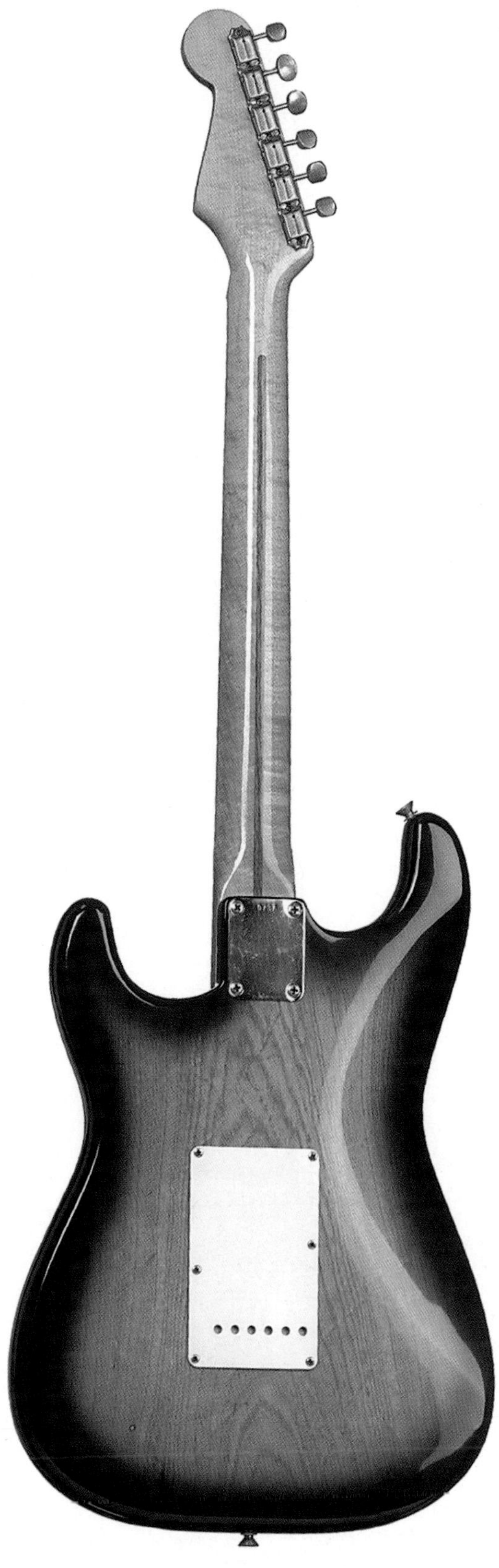

1954 Fender Stratocaster - Ser. #0737. 2-Tone Sunburst finish, mint refinished condition, (10 refin, 100% refinished). Well-trained, advanced "Stratmasters" can usually smell this type of refinish before they actually see it. Problem - the color's wrong. Retaining all the original parts except for the knobs, the pickups were rewound by Seymour Duncan, and the guitar was recently refinished to new condition. Most good-quality refins are worth at least 50% less than their original, excellent condition counterparts. On poor or average refins, the price is reduced to player value only, since collector interest has been killed. Bottom line - $15,000 for an original mint '54 Strat - $4,000 for this guitar. Courtesy Dale Hanson.

1990s Heritage Super Eagle Custom - Ser. #K03401. Vintage Sunburst Translucent finish, near mint condition (9.8 or 98%). This guitar is one of two Heritage Super Eagles to feature special order Gibson P-90 pickups, installed at the time of manufacture. Note the 18 inch body (bound front and back), perfect book matched backside with super flame, and unique headstock inlays. This model is next to the top-of-the-line in their electric archtop series. Heritage was started in Kalamazoo, MI, during April of 1985 (after Gibson moved to Nashville) by 3 ex-Gibson employees, using Gibson's original 1917 building. Courtesy Jeff Radtke.

1997 ToneSmith 316 Custom - Ser. #003097. Vintage Tobacco Sunburst finish, near mint condition (9.8, 98%). A nice example of a new bunch of luthiers who are building quality instruments their own way. Notice the unusually shaped F-hole, pickups consisting of two mini-humbuckers and a lipstick, and the Bigsby vibrato tailpiece. This type of quality made instrument is giving the larger trademark custom shops a run for their money. Currently priced in the $2,000 range, depending on options, this type of new custom guitar has yet to establish itself in the secondary marketplace. Stay away from sharp objects once your local dealer insults you on what he/she will pay you when you're hard up. Courtesy Dale Hanson.

Early 1966 Fender Jazz Bass - Ser. #139026. 3-Tone Sunburst finish, Excellent condition, (9, 90%). A prominent Lakeville, MN dentist bought this Fender Jazz Bass new for $250, after his P-Bass was stolen the year before the Chevelle SS396 was introduced. Having seen little use, this creampuff is only on its 2nd set of strings! OHSC is near mint. Current value? The right person might count out 35-40 C-notes before claiming title, depending on the level of interest (usually high, with this amount of original condition). $250 after "marinating" in a bank for approx. 35 years at 6% would cash out today at a measly $1,921.52! Like money? Got Wood? Courtesy Dr. Steven Aaker, D.D.S.

1962 Fender Jazzmaster - Ser. #77839. Fiesta Red finish, Excellent refinished condition (9 refin, 90% refinished). This instrument was probably professionally refurbished sometime during the 1980s, and hasn't seen much barroom smoke after that. Careful inspection will reveal a few touched up belt buckle marks, a few nicks on the lower back, and for whatever reason, tape around the outside of the peghead. Current book value on this instrument, assuming original condition, is in the $2,300 range ($1,900 + 20% for this factory custom color). As a correct refinish (all original parts and factory paint color, headstock decal not removed), today's realistic price is $1,000-$1,200 range. Courtesy S. P. Fjestad.

1973 Guild JS (Jet Star) Bass II - Ser. #79759. Natural finish, Very Good + condition (VG+, 8, 80%). This guitar is like Rodney Dangerfield - it gets no respect. Depicted with normal nicks, scratches and dings. Probably started its R&R career playing the bottom line on "Frankenstein" or "We're An American Band". Courtesy Dale Hanson.

1979 Music Man Sabre Bass - Ser. #C002026. Natural finish, Very Good + condition (VG+, 8, 80%). An above average example of a pre-Ernie Ball Sabre Bass designed by Leo Fender before the break up with Music Man. Players set the values today, regardless of condition. Last retail in 1991 was $1,095 - a super clean one will bring that today. Courtesy Dave's Guitar Shop.

1958 Gretsch Anniversary (Model 6125) - Ser. #28914. Two-tone Smoke Green finish, Very Good + condition (VG+, 8, 80%). Cool vintage guitar color. Examine the color difference between the top and bottom body binding - a tell-tale indication that the top binding had been poorly repaired at an earlier date, probably due to shrinkage. This is quite common on Gretsch instruments. Trapeze tailpiece and pickup show little oxidation, considering this instrument has already had its 40th birthday. If you had been a recent college grad with an engineering degree, you could have started work with the newly created NASA, established after Russia put a Sputnik into orbit the year before. Courtesy Willie's American Guitars.

1980 Gibson Flying V II - Ser. #80700032. Natural finish, Very Good + condition (VG+, 8, 80%). Initially designed to counteract the success of Fender's electric models, the original Flying V (Korina) was released in 1958 with a retail price of $247.50 - for $2 more you could have had a Stratocaster without tremolo! Most people bought the Strat. Having been reissued more than once, there are quite a few Gibson Flying V variations. It's not surprising that someone administered a lethal dosage of new body routing (observe partial hole below bridge pickup) to accept a standard humbucker, since the original V-shaped humbuckers were definitely B-class cheerleaders. Courtesy Dale Hanson.

Circa Mid-60s Kay. Red finish, Very Good + condition (VG+, 8, 80%). Once a large company, Kay Musical Instrument Company produced many of the Silvertones for Sears. This unidentified model was built around the time Kay moved into their new million dollar production facility next to Chicago's O'Hare airport. Due to an oversaturated marketplace, Kay production had ceased by 1970. Typically built to a price point, many student grade and entry level Kays worked out better as kindling than as musicmakers. Close to being cool, it's surprising this little axe never got butchered. Potentiometer dating can be a reliable method in figuring out years of manufacture on many secondary trademark electrics. Courtesy Dale Hanson.

1960 Gibson ES-125T - Ser. #R67953. Sunburst finish, Very Good condition (VG, 7.5, 75%). One of the original thinline electric designs (Gibson's terminology was "wonder-thin silhouette"), this ES-125T ("T" suffix designates thinline) retailed for approx. $175 when new. Everything is original, with the exception of the strap/tuner buttons and volume/tone knobs - not serious, even for original condition freaks. Note normal finish cracking, verifying its originality and age, and ser. no. in body, not on neck back. This model came standard with maple front and back, mahogany neck and rims, and a single P-90 pickup. The two pickup model was the ES-125TD ("D" suffix denotes double pickups). Courtesy Dale Hanson.

1960 Gretsch Country Club (Model 6196) - Ser. #35384. Cadillac Green finish, Very Good condition (VG, 7-7.5, 70%-75%). How can you not like this instrument? Compare neck and headstock bindings on this Gretsch to the body only bindings on Models 6125 (pg. 41) and 6120 (pg. 360). Broken pickup rings (not unusual) and a little honest wear are the only things that can be faulted - no major problems here. Rare colors, finishes, and special features/orders on most major trademark instruments can make major price differences, especially when original condition is high. Knowing this "desirability mix" is crucial in figuring out the correct value. Courtesy Glenn Wetterlund.

1963 Fender Jaguar - Ser. #87775. Three-tone Sunburst finish, Very Good condition (VG, 7, 70%). Overall, a nice original Jaguar, with some unusual, non-standard features. Notice the unexplainable pearl dot fingerboard (new 1964), one-piece pickguard, white roller pots retained by 2 slotted screws, tooth shaped switches on upper controls, and a Strat-style jackplate. Who said Fender didn't have a custom shop back in the early '60s? Wear is where it should be - outside edges (note chipping, scratches, and other scrapes on front and back), normal neck wear on back. The overall condition factor of this guitar correctly "adds up" - no one area, part, or finish is "overworn". Courtesy Glenn Wetterlund.

1973 Gibson Les Paul Deluxe Gold Top - Ser. #204029. Gold Top finish, Very Good condition (VG, 7, 70%). If you had 100 words, could you describe everything that's wrong with this guitar? Careful inspection of the headstock (below volute, above neck binding) indicates an earlier break, original humbucking pickups have been replaced with Bill Lawrence "blades", bridge is non-original, tuning machines have been changed to Schallers (note extra holes), back of body has been oversprayed, and it's a factory second - observe "2" over the ser. no. Were these factory deuces really flawed, or did Gibson use them as a discounted sales tool when inventories became too high? Courtesy S. P. Fjestad.

Circa 1960 Gibson L-5 CES - Ser. #S13576. Sunburst finish, Very Good condition (VG, 7, 70%). For whatever reason(s), the back of this instrument has fared much better than the front. Typical plating wear on the pickup covers and trapeze tailpiece. Close scrutiny reveals non-original tuners and bridge saddle. The eye appeal of this guitar has been negatively affected by the extensive crystallization of the pickguard, which suffered from an earlier repair attempt using epoxy. Replacing this damaged pickguard with an original (they don't grow on trees) would make a big difference on the initial condition reaction. Current retail on a new L-5 CES in Natural Finish? $14,444 - any questions? Courtesy Leonard Shapiro.

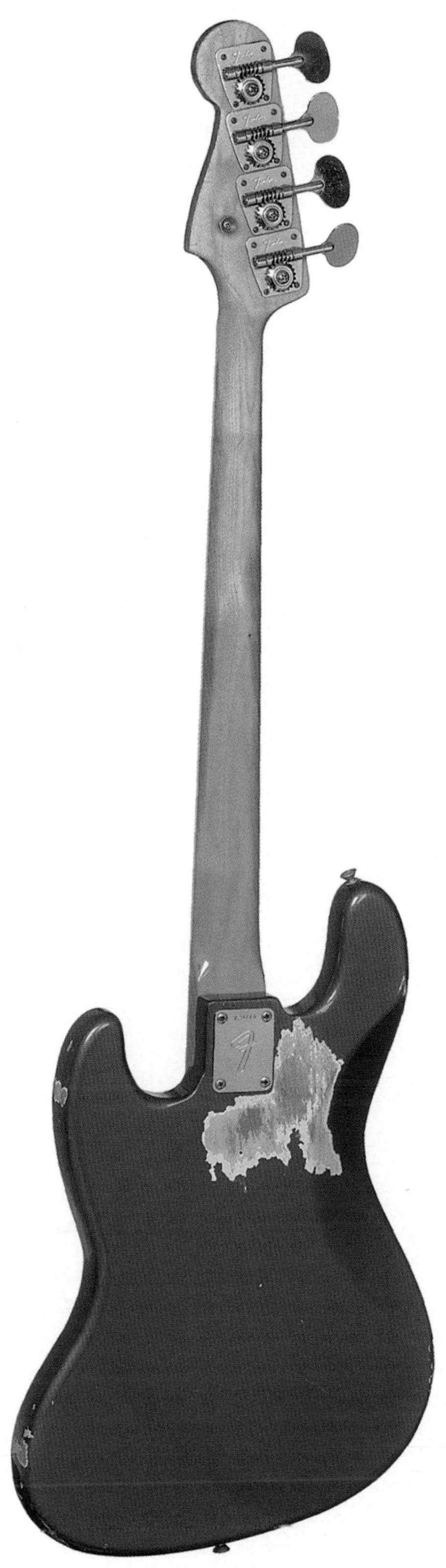

1966 Fender Jazz Bass - Ser. #129119. Sherwood Green Metallic finish, Very Good condition (VG, 7, 70%). Another good example of one side being in a lot better condition than the other. The back is probably a 6-7 (due to excessive belt buckle wear), but the front is a good 7-8. In some cases, it is better off to describe both sides individually, rather than try to average a condition factor. Many collectors are more concerned about how bad the instrument is on the down side, rather than concentrating on how good it is on the "flip" side. Missing bridge cover doesn't affect this instrument's value that much - still around $4,000. Courtesy Glenn Wetterlund.

1967 Gibson ES 335TD - Ser. #871604. Cool Pelham Blue finish, Very Good condition (VG, 7, 70%). If you're a major trademark, rare color collector, you'd better leave home without your American Express card, because this instrument might put you over your limit! All original parts and finish, including a special order, original factory installed Bigsby vibrato. Observe block inlays on neck - Gibson changed from the dot neck construction to block pearl inlays during 1962. Note the extensive neck wear - it's about the only thing you can fault (and try to get the price reduced) on this amazing instrument. Courtesy Dave's Guitar Shop.

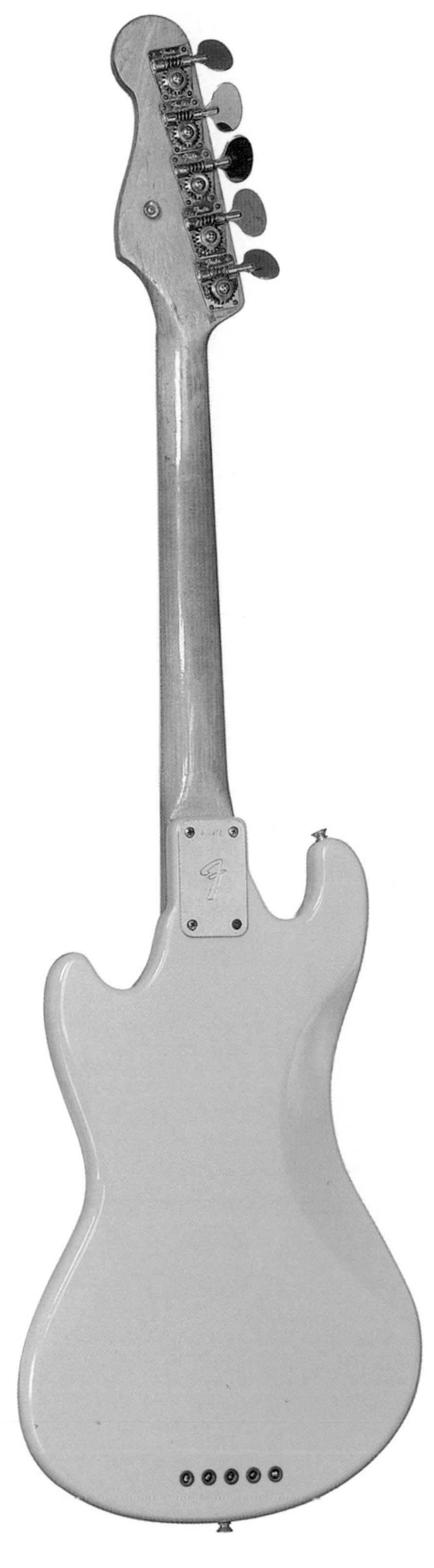

1967 Fender Bass V - Ser. #600972. Sea Foam Green finish, Very Good condition (VG, 7, 70%). Leo was definitely not afraid of trying out different body designs and colors, as evidenced here. Fender aficionados will immediately spot the refinished body and missing bridge cover. Note how the back neck wear does not match the "fresh paint" of the body. Many people think that 5+ string bass guitars are a recent development in the guitar world - both Fender & Gibson offered 5 & 6 string basses in the early '60s. Value? Because of the body refin, the price get lowered from $1,750-$2,000 (if original) to approx. $1,000 the way it is. Courtesy Dave's Guitar Shop.

1966 Fender Jazzmaster - Ser. #156616 (F-plate). Charcoal frost metallic finish, Very Good condition (VG, 7-7.5, 70%-75%). No surprises here - with the exception of the Mustang bridge, this Fender is all original, including the black tremolo tip, switches and knobs - correct for this rare color Jazzmaster. Light body perimeter nicks/chips and minor mid-neck wear. Add up all these rare production goodies and the amount of original finish on this color, and the price tag escalates considerably. In this case, a Sunburst model of the same year and in similar condition would top out at approx. $1,500 - this instrument is currently priced in the $2,500-$3,000 range. Courtesy Glenn Wetterlund.

Late 1965 Fender Jaguar - Ser. #123729. Blonde finish, Very Good condition (VG, 7, 70%). Observe wear on this Jaguar, compared to the Jazzmaster on the preceding page - both instruments are pretty similar (including dot inlays with bound fingerboard), except this specimen has a little bit more wear to the front of the body. Nothing exceptional here, but no problems either - just good, clean licks! If the purchase price is within reason, it's pretty hard to lose money on this type and condition guitar. 35 years after manufacture, this Jaguar has to feel pretty good about retaining this amount of original condition. Courtesy Dave's Guitar Shop.

Circa 1967 Mosrite Joe Maphis Model - Ser. #2J215. Metallic Blue finish, Very Good condition (VG, 7, 70%). No electric photo section would be complete without a doubleneck. Mosrite guitars were endorsed by The Ventures, whose organization doubled as the main distributor. Semie Mosley (the Mos of Mosrite) originally worked for Rickenbacker, and later teamed up with Rev. Ray Boatright (the rite) to produce Mosrite Guitars for nearly a decade. Between 1963-1969, Mosrite employed up to 105 employees, and produced as many as 300 guitars a month. The most obvious condition problem is belt buckle wear on back - see the "fanned" tuning machines on the 12-string neck? Anybody catch the non-original knobs? Courtesy Willie's American Guitars.

1963 Fender Telecaster - Ser. #L20086, mahogany body. Natural finish, Very Good condition (VG, 7, 70%). The differences between the neck and body wear are a giveaway to the refinished body. Having all original parts, this mahogany body Tele is certainly an ultra rarity, since virtually all were made from ash or alder. This is the type of instrument that could find its way into a pawn shop, and unless the store personnel knew the rarity factor associated with the mahogany body, it might get pawned for $350-$400. Even with the refinish, this Tele checks out today in the $3,000 range. Courtesy Dave's Guitar Shop.

1963 Gibson Firebird V - Ser. #142054. Tobacco Sunburst finish, Very Good Minus condition (VG-, 6.5, 65%). Look carefully next to the maestro tremelo bar on the left side. There's a tell-tale round circle where the body was plugged after the non-original stop tailpiece was probably changed back to the original trapeze style. Also, the pickguard is too clean to match the rest of this instrument's condition, indicating replacement. How serious are these repairs? Pretty serious - the price goes from $7,500 for original condition, to $4,500 for this Firebird. On major trademarks, originality and superior condition remain Polar North for today's collectors and investors. Courtesy Dave's Guitar Shop.

1938 Gibson ES-150 - Ser. #D6E 5437. Sunburst finish, Very Good Minus condition (VG-, 6.5, 65%). Also referred to as the Charlie Christian model. Remember, when this guitar was built, the Hoover dam was 2 years old, and rock and roll was only a dream a couple of generations away. The earlier an electric instrument, the more chances of finding alterations and/or modifications, as pickup technology and performance have vastly improved during the last 40 years. Having all original parts, this senior citizen can still pump serious iron. No, that's not a battery/pre-amp box built into the upper left rim (it just looks like it). Courtesy Dave Hull.

1961 Gretsch Silver Jet (Model 6129) - Ser. #39933. Silver Sparkle finish, Very Good Minus condition (VG-, 6.5, 65%). Note how the top is showing some shrinking around the body binding. This is very typical on this Gretsch model, as the silver sparkle plastic laminate was mostly used on their drums, not guitars. While a lot of people confuse this with a finish problem, it's actually a laminate shrinkage problem. Close inspection reveals that the finish, tuners, pickguard, bridge and pickups are original to this guitar, but the pickup rings are cracked, and the peghead has been broken and professionally repaired by the volute (darkened wood covers up break). Courtesy Willie's American Guitars.

1957 Gibson Byrdland - Ser. #A25594. Sunburst finish, Good condition (G, 6, 60%). Imagine - walking into your Chevrolet dealership in 1957 and finally buying the new Venetian Red Corvette ($3,176 base price) you've had your eyes on, then stopping by the music store on the way home to make the final payment on this instrument that you've had on layaway for the past 6 months ($625 w/case). Strats were $275. Life is good. If you were lucky, "Jailhouse Rock" was blaring so loud from the Wonderbar AM radio, that your new Byrdland in the trunk was already getting excited. Honest and normal wear - note finish cracking on back and non-original tuners (see extra holes) and pickguard. Courtesy Dave's Guitar Shop.

1962 Fender Jazzmaster - Ser. #78457. Black finish, Good condition (G, 6, 60%). Observe the paint wear carefully - originally factory finished in Sunburst, this instrument was resprayed in black by the factory before it was shipped. Chances are Fender had some stock, unfinished Sunburst instruments on hand, and decided to use this one to fill a black custom color special order. This condition factor is pretty well represented with the fair amount of wear on back of the neck, serious chipping along both the upper and lower body bouts, and some belt buckle grinding. Why can't today's relics look this cool? Got paint? Courtesy Dave's Guitar Shop.

1981 Gibson Les Paul Heritage Series Standard 80 - Ser. #82431520. Cherry Sunburst finish, Good condition (G, 6, 60%). Good example of the front of an instrument being in better condition than the back. The previous owners must have been wearing their rodeo champion belt buckles to produce this much belt buckle wear. While the finish, tuners, pickguard and pickups are all original on this guitar, observe the replaced bridge. A good, playable used instrument for someone who won't compromise on the weight of genuine LP mahogany hanging around his/her neck, and doesn't mind some previous wear. Courtesy Dale Hanson.

1960s Danelectro DC Bass - No Ser. #. Copper finish, Good Minus condition (G-, 5, 50%). If this instrument could talk, it would probably have enough eyewitness accounts to indict several people! A true road warrior, this Danelectro has pumped out serious bass lines for decades, based on the amount of finish deterioration. Note the extreme wear (top to bottom) on the back of the neck, relocated strap button, missing pickguard (silhouette still visible), and poorly made replacement rear cavity cover. Instruments like this never seem to die, they just keep reshuffling in and out of pawn shops. Courtesy Dave's Guitar Shop.

1960s Silvertone Electric - No Ser. #. Black finish, Good Minus condition (G-, 5, 50%). Probably made by Harmony, this was a pretty cool piece of cheesecake at one time! Unfortunately, time has not been on the side of this instrument. Observe the playing wear both front and back, missing pickguard, and nasty rim crack that warranted adding a jackplate. Remember, Silvertone was a Sears trademark, not a company or a factory. Anybody pick up (no pun intended) on the Gibson pickups? That's another way of saying this $250 instrument, after the Gibson pickups are sold for $200, could now be a $50 organ donor with hippy artwork. Got parts? Courtesy Dale Hanson.

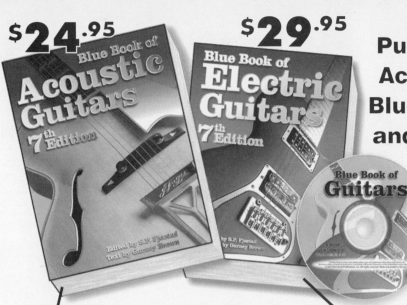

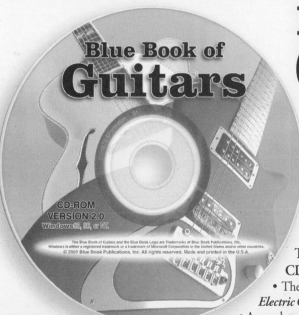

Section A

A

See chapter on House Brands.

This trademark has been identified as a House Brand of the Alden department store chain. One of the models shares similarities with the Harmony-built Stratotone of the 1960s, while a previously identified model dates back to the 1950s.

(Source: Willie G. Moseley, Stellas & Stratocasters)

A BASSES

Instruments currently built in Waltham-Boston, Massachusetts.

A Basses, working with high profile bassist Darryl Jones (sideman to the Rolling Stones), currently offers three editions of the Darryl Jones Signature bass and the **World Bass** model. These high quality instruments base their design on Fender's Jazz model, with numerous upgrade touches that one does not encounter on production models.

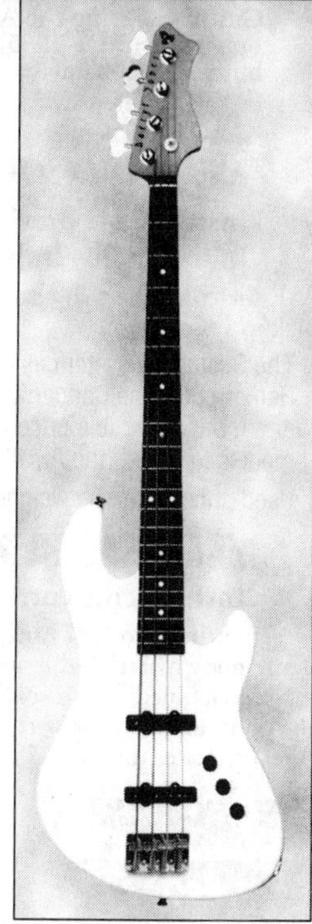

A Basses Darryl Jones
courtesy A Basses

ELECTRIC BASS

Darryl Jones Signature

All three models are offered in active or passive versions.

DARRYL JONES STANDARD EDITION - offset double cutaway alder body, bolt-on maple neck, 21-fret rosewood fingerboard with dot inlay, bridge, 4-on-a-side tuners, 2 Seymour Duncan pickups (see specs below), 2 volume/tone controls. Disc.

Passive electronics: Basslines Hot Jazz pickups.

Last MSR was $1,595.

Active Electronics: Basslines Lightning Rod pickups/slap contour/3-band EQ.

Last MSR was $1,795.

Darryl Jones Signature Model similar to Darryl Jones Standard Edition, except has Aero pickups. Optional Aguilar pre-amp. Current mfg.

MSR $1,995

Darryl Jones Deluxe Edition - similar to the Darryl Jones Standard, except features a Quilted maple laminate top, available in 3-Color Sunburst finish. Disc.

Passive electronics: Basslines Hot Jazz pickups.

Last MSR was $1,795.

Active Electronics: Basslines Lightning Rod pickups/slap contour/3-band EQ.

Last MSR was $1,995.

Darryl Jones 5-String - similar to the Darryl Jones Standard, except features a 5-string configuration. Disc.

Passive electronics: Basslines Hot Jazz pickups.

Last MSR was $1,795.

Active Electronics: Basslines Lightning Rod pickups/slap contour/3-band EQ.

Last MSR was $1,995.

Jade Bass Series - alder or Swamp ash body, maple neck, choice of fingerboards, fretted or fretless, optional figured maple top and/or Aguilar pre-amp. Current mfg.

MSR $1,995

World Bass Series

The World Bass has an alder or Swamp ash body with figured top, extra long ebony fingerboard, Aero pickups, optional Aguilar pre-amp. Current mfg. List price is $3,195.

A Basses Jade Bass
courtesy A Basses

APP

Instruments previously built in the early 1940s in Burlington, Iowa; later models were built in the early 1960s.

Guitar instructor/inventor O.W. Appleton was another forerunner of the electric solid body guitar concept. In the early 1940s, Appleton built a carved top solid body guitar that featured a single cutaway design, raised bridge/trapeze tailpiece, and single coil pickup. APP even went so far as to put a Gibson neck on his design, but received no interest from the Gibson company. Comparing an APP to the later 1952 Gibson Les Paul is somewhat akin to comparing a Bigsby guitar to Fender's Telecaster model (it's deja vu all over again!).

Of course, Rickenbacker in Los Angeles had marketed the solid body lap steel since the 1930s; Lloyd Loar's Vivi-Tone company had attempted to market an electric Spanish guitar. In 1941, guitar marvel Les Paul had begun work on *The Log*, a solid 4" x 4" neck-through design with pickups. Les Paul attached body *wings* from an Epiphone archtop guitar to the sides of the neck (the Log was constructed after hours at the original Epiphone facilities in New York). It is interesting now to look back and view how many people were working towards the invention of the solid body electric guitar.

(Source: Tom Wheeler, American Guitars)

Guitars bearing the APP trademark appeared in the early 1960s. One such model appeared in Teisco Del Rey's column in Guitar Player magazine (June 1985), and featured an offset double cutaway body that was shaped like an inverted *V*. Appleton later retired to Arizona, but the 1960s models are still a mystery.

ASI

Also AUDIO SOUND INTERNATIONAL.

Instruments previously built in Korea. Previously distributed in the U.S. market by Audio Sound International, Inc. of Indianapolis, Indiana.

ASI, the company that also supplied Quantum amplifiers and Rackmaster gear, developed a number of solid body guitars to market the *Sustainiac* pickup system.

The Sustainiac system as developed by Maniac Music features on-board magnetic circuitry to create real string sustain. Similar to the system that Kaman/Hamer put in the Chaparral Elite, ASI used both the GA2 and GA4 in a number of Taiwan-, Korean-, and Japanese-built guitars in an effort to bring the system at a more affordable price in the guitar market. The AE 7S was an earlier model from 1990, and was followed by the AS-121 in 1991. Two more maple-bodied models followed (the AS 100 and AS 85).

Used prices must be weighed from the pickup system against the quality of the guitar it is installed in. Average prices run from $150 up to $250.

ABEL AXE

Instruments currently built in Evanston, Wyoming since 1992. Distributed by Abel Axe of Evanston, Wyoming.

Designer/inventor Jeff Abel spent two years in research and development refining his aluminum body/wood neck concept. Due to the nature of the dense body material, the sustain and harmonics produced are markedly different compared to traditional wood technologies. The **Abel Axe** body is CNC machined from a solid slab of aircraft grade aluminum and the finished guitar weighs in at only 8 pounds. The colors offered are then anodized to the body, and become part of the aluminum during the process. Assisted by his brother, Jim Abel, Jeff Abel currently produces limited to custom orders. Abel estimates that over 250 guitars have been produced to date.

ELECTRIC

Pro Series

Pro Series guitars are offered factory direct from Abel Axe. Abel Axe also offers the aluminum body separately (with strap buttons and back plate) directly from the factory for those players interested in creating their own custom instrument. The tuning machines can be anodized to match body color.

ABEL AXE - offset double cutaway aluminum body, circular body hollows, bolt-on maple neck, 22-fret rosewood (or maple) fingerboard with dot inlay, strings through bridge, 6-on-a-side Sperzel tuners, black hardware, 2 Kent Armstrong humbucker pickups, volume control, 3-position switch, available in Red, Black, Blue, Teal, Violet, and Aluminum (Silver) anodized finishes. New 1994.

MSR $1,000

This model is available with optional locking tremolo (Abel Axe T).

ABEL AXE 211 - offset double cutaway aluminum body, slot-style body hollows, bolt-on maple neck, 22-fret rosewood fingerboard with dot inlay, string through tailpiece, 6-on-a-side Sperzel tuners, black hardware, Kent Armstrong humbucker pickup(s), volume control, available in Red, Black, Blue, Teal, Violet, and Aluminum (Silver) anodized finishes. New 1996.

MSR $490

ELECTRIC BASS

ABEL AXE BASS - offset double cutaway body, bolt-on maple neck, 22-fret rosewood (or maple) fingerboard with dot inlay, 34" scale, fixed brass bridge, 4-on-a-side Gotoh tuners, black hardware, Kent Armstrong pickup, volume control, available in Red, Black, Blue, Teal, Violet, and Aluminum (Silver) anodized finishes. New 1995.

MSR $1,100

ABILENE

Instruments currently produced in Korea by Samick. Distributed in the U.S. by Advantage Worldwide.

The Abilene trademark is distributed in the U.S. by Advantage Worldwide. The Abilene trademark is offered on a range of acoustic, acoustic/electric, and solid body electric guitars and practice amplifiers. The guitars are built by Samick of Korea, and the electric guitar models feature designs based on popular American models.

ELECTRIC

Abilene has two "LP" models, the **ASL 21 GS** (slab body, 2 humbuckers) and the **ALSE 450 HS** (arched top, raised pickguard). All other models are straight out of Fenderville: The **AS 10** (rosewood fingerboard) and **AS 100** (maple fingerboard) are double cutaway/3 single coil traditional Strat styles, while the **ALM 80T** has a single/humbucker pickup combination. The **AP 757 BK** is a single cutaway/2 single coil Tele with a maple neck, and the **AB 11** is a traditional shaped Precision-type bass.

ABYSS

Instruments currently built in Forest City, Iowa.

Al Stokka's Abyss Guitar Company specializes in custom-made 7-string (and some 6-string) electric guitars. Stokka offers a number of options on these custom-built models, and all are currently made to order by commission.

Abyss guitars feature handpicked tops and neck woods, alder bodies, and quartersawn hard maple necks. "Although prices and woods may vary," says Stokka, "Meticulous construction techniques do not - which ensures a great sounding, stable guitar." Contact the Abyss Guitar Company for a current price quote and specifications.

ACACIA

Instruments currently built in Southampton, Pennsylvania since 1986.

Luthier Matt Friedman has been designing and building high quality custom instruments actively for the past seven years. Friedman began carving bodies back in 1980, and spent a number of years doing repair work for local music stores. In 1989 he began full-time production of instruments.

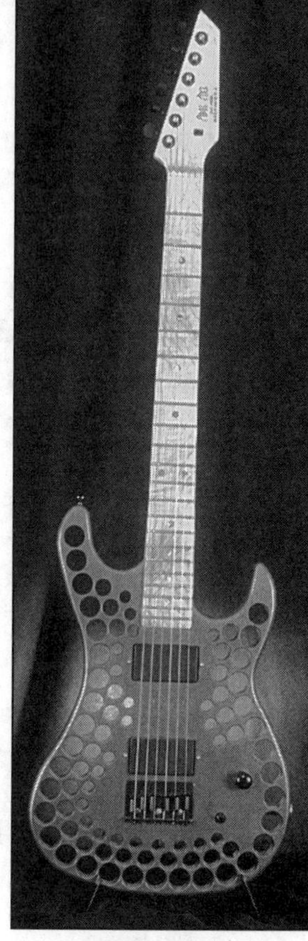

Abel Axe Pro
courtesy Abel Axe

ELECTRIC BASS

All Acacia bass body contours are hand carved. The 24-fret neck is available in any scale lengths at no additional charge. Hardware is available in gold or black. Basses can be ordered with electronics by Lane Poor, Bartolini, Aero, and John East. Friedman also offers choices of bookmatched tops such as striped ebony, tulipwood, leopardwood, kingwood, or pink ivory (call for pricing).

Add $500 for Novax *Fanned Fret* fretboard (licensed by Ralph Novak).

Add $225 for Bartolini pickups/preamp/3-band EQ.

Add $270 for John East preamp/3-band EQ with mid-sweep.

Add $300 for left-handed configuration.

Add Lightwave Optical Bridge System – Call for price.

CUSTOM - sleek offset double cutaway mahogany body, bookmatched exotic wood top/back, through-body multilaminated neck (4- and 5-string basses feature a 9-piece design while the 6- and 7-string models feature a 13-piece neck) of Wenge, Mahogany, and other exotic woods with graphite epoxy reinforcement, 24-fret ebony or snakewood fingerboard, customer's choice of electronics/preamp/EQ, available in Natural Oil finish. New 1986.

Custom 4-string
MSR $3,800

Custom 5-string
MSR $4,000

Custom 6-string
MSR $4,200

Custom 7-string
MSR $4,400

EMOTION - sleek offset double cutaway body, bookmatched exotic wood top/back, through-body multilaminated Wenge or zebrawood neck, ebony fretless fingerboard, ebony bridge, Aero twin coil pickup, RMC bridge-mounted piezo pickup, volume/blend/EQ controls, John East preamp, available in Natural Oil finish. New 1995.

Emotion 4-string
MSR $4,200

Emotion 5-string
MSR $4,400

Emotion 6-string
MSR $4,600

Emotion 7-string
MSR $4,800

THE GRUV (GLB) - sleek offset double cutaway swamp ash body, bolt-on 5-piece neck, 24-fret ebony fingerboard with sterling silver side dot inlay, Ebony bridge, Hipshot Ultralite tuners, 2 Custom Aero pickups, volume/blend/tone controls, available in Natural finish. New 1996.

Gruv 4-string
MSR $3,600

Gruv 5-string
MSR $3,800

This model has an optional bookmatched figured maple top, a set-in neck, and numerous different transparent finishes.

ACOUSTIC

Instruments previously produced in Japan during the early 1970s. Distributed by the Acoustic amplifier company of California.

While the Acoustic company was going strong in the amplifier business with models like the 360, they decided to add a guitar and bass model to the product line. The first Black Widows were produced in Japan, and distributed through the Acoustic company. Towards the end of the model, production actually switched to Semie Moseley of Mosrite (model neck dimensions correspond to the Mosrite feel). There has been some indication that Paul Barth's Bartell company may have built some as well.

The most striking feature of the Acoustic Black Widow is the finish. The darkened rosewood fingerboard and deep black maple body, combined with the red pad in the back supposedly resembles the markings of a black widow spider.

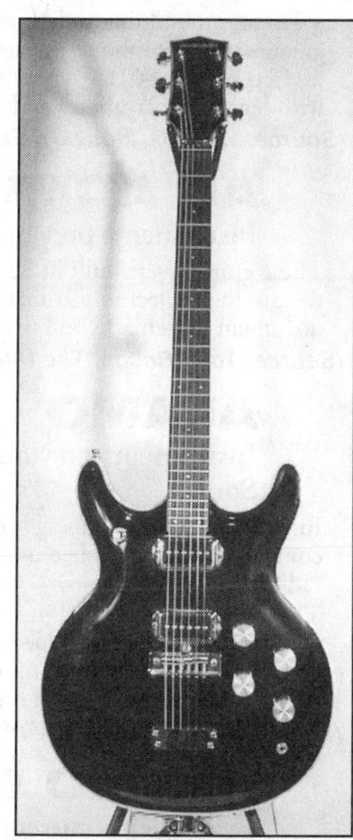

Acoustic 335
courtesy The Music Shoppe

GRADING	100% MINT	98% NEAR MINT	95% EXC+	90% EXC	80% VG+	70% VG	60% G

ELECTRIC

BLACK WIDOW - double cutaway semi-hollow maple body, maple neck, 24-fret rosewood fingerboard, bridge/stop tailpiece, 3-per-side Grover Rotomatic tuners, chrome hardware, 2 humbucker pickups, volume/tone controls, 3-position selector, available in Black lacquer finish. Mfg. circa 1972-74.

$375	$325	$275	$250	$200	$150	$100

Last MSR was $415.

This model has a red pad attached to the back of the instrument.

ELECTRIC BASS

BLACK WIDOW BASS - double cutaway semi-hollow maple body, maple neck, 20-fret rosewood fingerboard, bridge/stop tailpiece, 2-per-side Grover Rotomatic tuners, chrome hardware, humbucker pickups volume/tone controls, available in Black lacquer finish. Mfg. circa 1972-74.

$350	$300	$275	$250	$200	$150	$100

Last MSR was $415.

This model has a red pad attached to the back of the instrument.

AELITA

Instruments previously built in Russia during the 1970s.

(Headstock lettering in Cyrillic may appear as a capital A, backwards e, r, u, m, or a. We have anglicized the brand name.)

These solid bodied guitars were produced by the Rostov-on-Don accordion factory, and the design may strike the casual observer as favoring classic Italian designs of the 1960s.

(Source: Tony Bacon, The Ultimate Guitar Book)

AIRCRAFT

Instruments currently built in Japan.

Guitars carrying the Aircraft logo are actually manufactured by the Morris company, which also builds instruments for such brand names as their own Morris trademark, and the Hurricane logo.

AIRLINE

See SUPRO.

Instruments previously manufactured by Valco in Chicago, Illinois during the 1960s. See chapter on House Brands.

This trademark has been identified as a *House Brand* of the Montgomery Wards department store chain. Author/researcher Willie G. Moseley indicates that the unique body design is proprietary to the Airline brand. Models can be found constructed of both *Res-O-Glas* (a hollow fiberglass body) and wood.

Valco began building solid body wood instruments in 1952, and built fiberglass body electric guitars from 1962 to 1966. The basic Airline wood body guitar came in sunburst finishes; and the deluxe *Res-O-Glas* two piece modeled bodies came with either one or two pickups, a wood bolt-on neck, and 20 frets on the 24 1/2" scale neck. The top of Airline headstocks, just like the Nationals, ran low-to-high from the left to the right. Not that it matters with regard to playability and tone, but Supros dipped the headstock in the opposite way.

(Source: Willie G. Moseley, Stellas & Stratocasters)

AK ADMIRAL

Instruments previously produced in Russia in the early 1980s.

These guitars were built in Leningrad as part of a project to mass produce good quality electrics. While the styling and hardware seem more modern in design, the project unfortunately failed. The *Blue Book of Electric Guitars* welcomes any information on Russian-built guitars in our attempt to document trademarks and brands of the world.

(Source: Tony Bacon, The Ultimate Guitar Book)

ALAMO

Instruments previously manufactured in San Antonio, Texas from 1960 to 1970. Distributed in part by C. Bruno & Sons.

In 1947, Charles Eilenberg was recruited by Milton Fink to manufacture electronic gear in San Antonio, Texas. Fink, the owner of Southern Music company, was a publisher and music wholesaler. By 1950, the company was producing instrument cases, tube amplifiers, and lap steel guitars (as well as radios and phonographs).

The company continued to expand, and in 1960 introduced its first electric Spanish guitar. Alamo offered both solid body and semi-hollow electrics that were generally entry level quality, and designed with the student or beginner player in mind. Outside of a few Valco-produced models, all Alamo guitars were built in San Antonio during the ten year period. The company also continued to produce tube amplifiers until 1970, then solid state models. Alamo went out of business in 1982.

(Source: Michael Wright, Vintage Guitar Magazine)

ALAMO GUITARS

Instruments currently made in Houston, Texas. Distributed by Alamo Music Products.

Alamo Guitars manufactures several models, including the Tonemonger (MSR - $1,760),Tonemonger Custom (MSR - $1,970), Tonemonger Custom with exotic top (MSR - $$2,195), and the Tonemonger Custom 5 (MSR - $$2,070). Features include a Strat style body from Swamp ash or African Fakimba, nitrocellulose lacquer finish, maple neck, with choice of maple or rosewood fingerboard, custom center point tremelo system, master volume and tone control, with 5-way selector switch, includes hardshell case. Please contact the company directly for more information (see Trademark Index).

ALEMBIC

Instruments currently built in Santa Rosa, California. Previous production was centered in San Francisco, California. Distribution is handled by Alembic, Inc. of Santa Rosa, California.

The Alembic company was founded in San Francisco in 1969, primarily to incorporate new ways to clarify and amplify the sound of the rock group *The Grateful Dead.* The Alembic workshop covered three main areas: a recording studio, PA/sound reinforcement, and guitar electronics. Wickersham was developing a low impedance pickup coupled with active electronics. Up until this point all electronics in production guitars and basses were passive systems. Artists using these "Alembicized" instruments early on include David Crosby (a Guild 12-string), Jack Casady (Guild bass), and Phil Lesh (SG and Guild basses). Both Bob Weir's and Jerry Garcia's guitars were converted as well. Wickersham found that mounting the active circuitry in the instrument itself gave the player a greater degree of control over his tone than ever before.

The new company turned from customizing existing instruments in 1970 to building new ones in 1971. Founder Ron Wickersham, an electronics expert, was joined by luthier/designer Rick Turner, Bob Matthews (a recording engineer), and Jim Furman (later to start his own Furman Sound Company) among others. When Alembic incorporated in 1970, Wickersham, Turner, and Matthews were the principal shareholders. In addition to running a state-of-the-art 16-track recording studio on Brady Street, Alembic opened a music store in 1971 that sold their own guitars and basses, as well as cabinets (with tie-dyed speaker cloth) and PA gear. Alembic continued to work with the Grateful Dead for taping and PA requirements, and in 1972 also produced a monthly critique column for Guitar Player magazine (The Alembic Report).

In 1973, Alembic received a distribution offer from the L D Heater company, a subsidiary of Norlin. Wickersham and Turner then began tooling up for production in earnest. Turner's choices in exotic woods and laminated bodies gained attention for the craftsmanship involved. The right combination of a new distributor and a new jazz talent named Stanley Clarke actively playing an Alembic bass propelled the company into the spotlight in the mid 1970s.

In 1974, Alembic began to focus on the manufacturing side of their high-end instruments. The company sold off the assets of the recording studio, and sold the music store to Stars Guitars (Stars Guitars' Ron Armstrong later wrote the Product Profile column for Guitar Player magazine after the Alembic Report was discontinued). Bob Matthews' shares were bought out by Alembic. A new distribution deal was started with Rothchild Musical Instruments (San Francisco) in 1976, after the original L D Heater/Norlin distribution deal.

Geoff Gould, an aerospace engineer and bass player, was intrigued by an Alembic-customized bass he saw at a Grateful Dead concert. Assuming that the all-wood construction was a heavy proposition, he fashioned some samples of carbon graphite and presented them to Alembic. An experimental model with a graphite neck was displayed in 1977, and a patent issued in 1978. Gould formed the Modulus Graphite company with other ex-aerospace partners to provide necks for Alembic, and also build necks for Music Man's Cutlass bass model as well as their own Modulus Graphite guitars.

Rick Turner left Alembic in 1978 to form Turner Guitars, the same year that Alembic decided to forego future distribution deals and fulfill distribution themselves. As the company expanded, the workshop continued to move from San Francisco to Cotati to Santa Rosa. In addition to guitar and bass production, the 1980s saw expansion in F2B preamp demand as well as the production of modular-based (no soldering) *Activator* pickups and active electronics. In 1989 Alembic settled into a larger facility in Santa Rosa, and currently has a twenty-five person staff.

(Company history courtesy Mica and Susan Wickersham, Alembic)

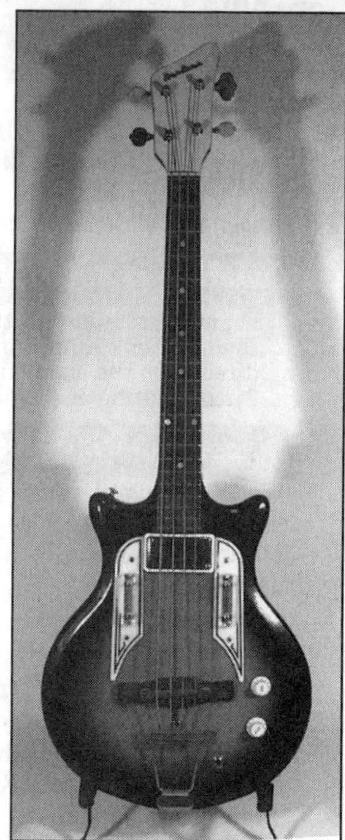

Airline Bass
courtesy The Bass Place

The tops of Alembic instruments are bookmatched and the wood types vary widely, though the most consistently used woods are as follows: bocate, bubinga, cocobola, figured (bird's eye, burl, flame, quilted) maple, figured (burl and flame) walnut, flame koa, lacewood, rosewood (and burl rosewood), tulipwood, vermillion and zebrawood.

MODEL IDENTIFICATION

Model Identification Via Serial Number

Alembic models can be identified in the serial number: The first two digits indicate the year built, and the letter codes directly after the first two digits indicate the model. As the body style, peghead style, and electronic/hardware configurations and combinations may vary from instrument to instrument due to Alembic's numerous options, identification can be made from this letter coding.

Model	Letter Code
20th Anniversary	AM
Custom	C
Distillate	D
Elan	H
Electrum	E
Epic	W
Essence	K
Europa	U
Mark King Deluxe	MK
Mark King Standard	MJ
Orion (Bass)	OW
Orion (Guitar)	O
Persuader	P (or V or F)
Rogue	Q
Series I	(Blank)
Series II	(Blank)
Spectrum	BG (or M)

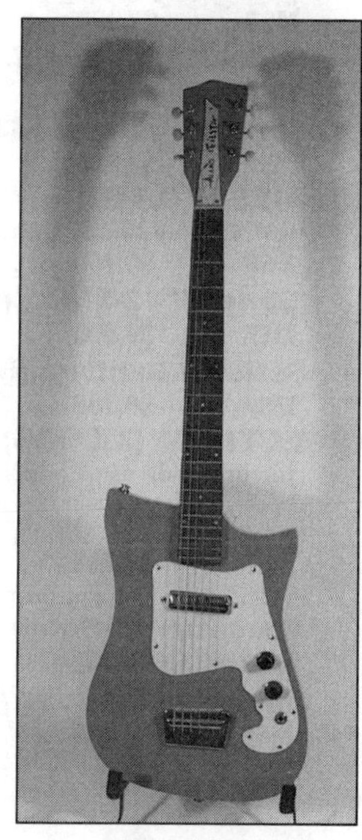

Alamo Fiesta
courtesy Austin Thomerson

GRADING	100% MINT	98% NEAR MINT	95% EXC+	90% EXC	80% VG+	70% VG	60% G

Spoiler	S
Spoiler (3/4 size)	R
Stanley Clarke Deluxe	SC
Standard	SJ

Furthermore, all series between 1972 to 1976 carry either an AE (Alembic Export General) or AC (Alembic Export Canada) stamp.

Location of Serial Number

On new instruments, the serial number is stamped on the truss rod cover and also in the electronics cavity (Epic and Orion models have the number stamped in the back of the peghead and in the electronics cavity). On older instruments, the serial number is stamped directly on the ebony fingerboard below the 24th fret. Earliest Alembic models have serial numbers stamped on top of the headstock (for further dating of Alembic instruments, see the Serialization section in the back of this edition).

Discontinuation Notice

If an Alembic model is noted as "Disc." (as in disc), it does not mean that the company will not build any more instruments to those specifications. It may mean that the model is not carried on the current price sheet: 7-, 8-, 10-, 12-string, and doubleneck configurations are currently available on some models as a "Call for Price Quote" listing. Even though certain models or configurations may not be currently offered by Alembic, the design templates are on storage for a customer's special order.

ELECTRIC

CALIFORNIA SPECIAL (CSLG6) - offset double cutaway maple body, through-body maple neck, brass truss rod cover plate, 24-fret ebony fingerboard with pearl oval inlay, double locking vibrato, brass nut, body matching peghead with bronze logo, 6-on-a-side tuners, chrome hardware, 2 single coil/1 humbucker Alembic pickups, volume/tone control, 3 mini switches, available in Natural, Metal Ruby Red, Metal Sapphire Blue, Transparent Ruby Red, and Transparent Sapphire Blue finishes. Current mfg.

MSR $3,900 **$3,125 $2,750 $2,350 $N/A $N/A $N/A $N/A**

California Special 12-String (CSLSG12) - similar to the California Special, except in a 12-string configuration. New 1997.

MSR $4,400

California Special Baritone (CSBSG6) - similar to the California Special, except in a longer 28" scale. New 1997.

MSR $3,900

ORION (OLSB6) - offset sweeping double cutaway mahogany body, flame maple (or Flame California Walnut, Birds eye Maple, Wenge, Zebrawood, Bocate, Bubinga, or Vermillion) top, walnut accent veneer, 3-piece maple set neck, 25 3/4" scale, 24-fret ebony fingerboard with pearl oval inlay, six on a side Alembic-Gotoh tuners, brass nut, gold hardware, 2 Alembic HG humbucking pickups, volume/treble/bass controls, pickup selector switch, available in a satin polyurethane finish. New 1996.

MSR $2,250

Orion Baritone (OBSG6) - similar to the Orion, except has a 28" scale. New 1996.

MSR $2,250

SERIES I (LSGI-6) - similar to California Special, except has treble/bass volume/tone control, treble Q/bass Q/pickup switch, 5-pin stereo output jack. Current mfg.

MSR $7,000 **$5,600 $5,000 $4,550 $N/A $N/A $N/A $N/A**

Series I 12-String (LSGI-12) - similar to the Series I model, except in a 12-string configuration. Current mfg.

MSR $7,300 **$5,800 $5,200 $4,700 $N/A $N/A $N/A $N/A**

Series I Baritone (BSGI-6) - similar to the Series I model, except in a longer 28" scale. Current mfg.

MSR $7,000 **$5,600 $5,000 $4,550 $N/A $N/A $N/A $N/A**

SERIES II (LSGII-6) - similar to California Special, except has master/treble/bass volume control, treble/bass tone control, treble CVQ/bass CVQ/pickup switch, 5-pin stereo output jack. Current mfg.

MSR $8,700 **$7,000 $6,100 $5,600 $N/A $N/A $N/A $N/A**

Series II 12-String (LSG12-II) - similar to the Series II model, except in a 12-string configuration. Current mfg.

MSR $9,000 **$7,200 $6,300 $5,900 $N/A $N/A $N/A $N/A**

Series II Baritone (BSG6-II) - similar to the Series II model, except in a longer 28" scale. Current mfg.

MSR $8,700 **$7,000 $6,100 $5,600 $N/A $N/A $N/A $N/A**

SPECTRUM (MLSG6) - offset double cutaway mahogany body, figured maple (or Bocate, Bubinga, Walnut, or Zebrawood) top, 25 ¾" scale, through-body maple/purpleheart laminate neck, 24-fret ebony fingerboard with pearl oval inlay, fixed solid brass bridge/string retainer, brass nut, body matching peghead with bronze logo, 6-on-a-side Alembic-Gotoh tuners, gold hardware, 2 single coil/1 humbucker Alembic pickups, volume/pan/low pass filter (with q switch) controls, 5-way selector, available in natural gloss polyester finish. Current mfg.

MSR $4,200

The Spectrum guitar model is the complement to the Europa bass.

Spectrum 12-String (MLSG12) - similar to the Spectrum, except in a 12-string configuration. New 1997.

MSR $4,700

Spectrum Baritone (MBSG6) - similar to the Spectrum, except in a longer 28" scale. New 1997.

MSR $4,200

GRADING	100% MINT	98% NEAR MINT	95% EXC+	90% EXC	80% VG+	70% VG	60% G

ELECTRIC BASS

All models have through-body maple, or maple/mahogany laminate neck construction, dual truss rods, 24-fret ebony fingerboard with pearl oval inlay (unless otherwise listed), adjustable brass saddles/bridge/tailpiece/nut (these items may be chrome or gold plated), active electronics, ebony fingerboard and clear gloss finish.

A number of the earlier instruments were custom ordered so there are variations that may be found that are not standard items. The Omega Cut refers to the stylish rounded cut in the lower bout sometimes found on Series I and II models - it's a custom option.

20TH ANNIVERSARY - slightly offset double cutaway body with Omega Cut on lower bout, maple core Quilted maple top and back with Purpleheart accents or walnut core/Burl walnut top and back with vermilion accents, through-body maple/purpleheart laminated neck, 24-fret ebony fingerboard with oval inlays, 4-on-a-side tuners, brass hardware, 2 Alembic AXY pickups, 2 volume/2 filter (with q switch) controls, 4-position selector switch, mono/stereo switch, active electronics, available in Natural finish. Mfg. 1989 only.

		100%	98%	95%	90%	80%	70%	60%
		$2,400	$2,250	$2,000	$1,600	$N/A	$N/A	$N/A

Last MSR was $3,630.

Only 200 instruments were built.

The current 25th Anniversary Edition is limited to only 25 pieces. Contact Alembic for specifications and pricing.

CLASSICO UPRIGHT - updated upright bass-shaped semi-hollow mahogany body, figured maple top, 41 ½" scale, 3-piece maple neck, rosewood fingerboard, ebony nut, 2+2 open headstock, maple bridge, rosewood tailpiece, Alembic Magnetic CS-2 pickups, volume/bass/treble controls, available in hand rubbed satin polyester finish.

		100%	98%	95%	90%	80%	70%	60%
4-string - 4-on-a-side tuners. New 1994.								
MSR	$5,795	$4,650	$4,100	$N/A	$N/A	$N/A	$N/A	$N/A
5-string - 4/1 per side tuners. New 1994.								
MSR	$6,495	$5,200	$4,600	$N/A	$N/A	$N/A	$N/A	$N/A
6-string - 3-per-side tuners. New 1994.								
MSR	$7,095	$5,700	$5,000	$N/A	$N/A	$N/A	$N/A	$N/A

ELAN - offset double cutaway asymmetrical body, Honduras mahogany back, brass truss rod plate, body matching peghead with bronze logo, gold Alembic-Gotoh tuners, 2 P-style Alembic pickups, volume/tone/balance control, active electronics switch. Mfg. 1985-1997.

	100%	98%	95%	90%	80%	70%	60%
4-string - 4-on-a-side tuners.	$2,200	$1,650	$1,375	$1,100	$N/A	$N/A	$N/A
	Last MSR was $2,770.						
5-string - 4/1 per side tuners.	$2,475	$1,850	$1,550	$1,225	$N/A	$N/A	$N/A
	Last MSR was $3,090.						
6-string - 3-per-side tuners.	$2,725	$2,100	$1,700	$1,425	$N/A	$N/A	$N/A
	Last MSR was $3,415.						
7-string - 4/3-per-side tuners.	$4,175	$3,125	$2,600	$2,100	$N/A	$N/A	$N/A
	Last MSR was $5,220.						
8-string - 4-per-side tuners.	$2,850	$2,150	$1,775	$1,425	$N/A	$N/A	$N/A
	Last MSR was $3,570.						
10-string - 5-per-side tuners.	$3,450	$2,595	$2,275	$1,825	$N/A	$N/A	$N/A
	Last MSR was $4,325.						

EPIC - offset double cutaway mahogany body, standard woods top, 34" scale, 3-piece maple set neck, 24-fret ebony fingerboard, brass truss rod plate, body matching peghead with brass logo, chrome Alembic-Gotoh tuners, 2 Alembic MXY pickups, volume/pan/treble/bass controls, active electronics, satin polyurethane finish.

		100%	98%	95%	90%	80%	70%	60%
4-string (WLB4) - 2-per-side tuners. New 1994.								
MSR	$1,950	$1,550	$1,375	$1,250	$1,075	$N/A	$N/A	$N/A
5-string (WLB5) - 3/2-per-side tuners. New 1994.								
MSR	$2,250	$1,800	$1,575	$1,450	$1,225	$N/A	$N/A	$N/A
6-string (WLB6) - 5-piece maple set neck, 3-per-side tuners. New 1995.								
MSR	$2,550	$2,050	$1,775	$1,650	$1,400	$N/A	$N/A	$N/A

ESSENCE - offset double cutaway body, flame maple top, rock maple back, brass truss rod plate, body matching peghead with bronze logo, chrome Alembic-Gotoh tuners, 2 Alembic MXY pickups, volume/tone/balance control.

		100%	98%	95%	90%	80%	70%	60%
4-string (KLB4) - 2-per-side tuners. New 1991.								
MSR	$2,700	$2,200	$1,900	$1,750	$1,475	$N/A	$N/A	$N/A

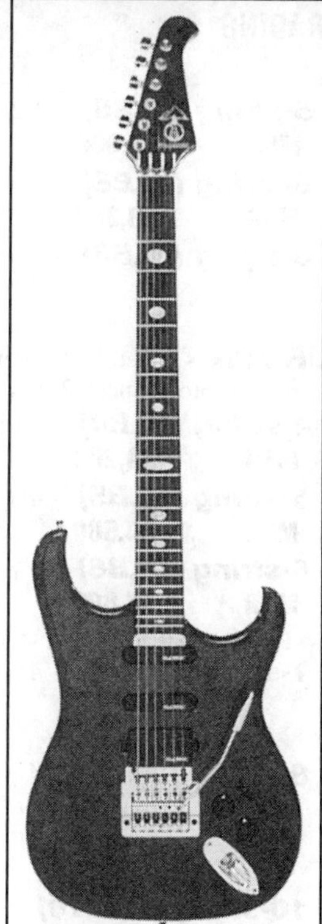

Alembic California Special
courtesy Alembic

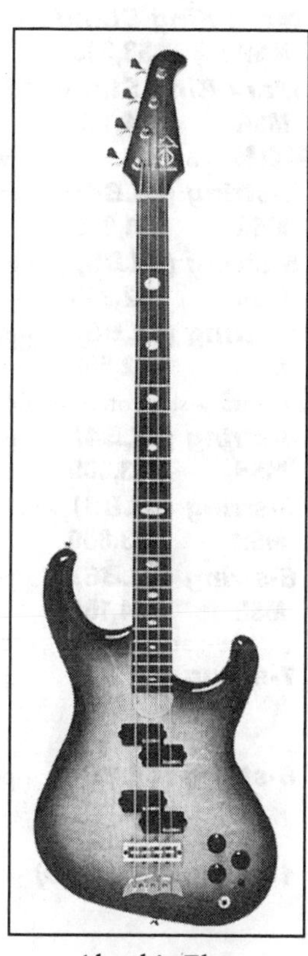

Alembic Elan
courtesy Alembic

GRADING		100% MINT	98% NEAR MINT	95% EXC+	90% EXC	80% VG+	70% VG	60% G

5-string (KLB5) - 3/2-per-side tuners. New 1991.

MSR	$3,000	$2,400	$2,100	$1,950	$1,650	$N/A	$N/A	$N/A

6-string (KLB6) - 3-per-side tuners. New 1993.

MSR	$3,300	$2,650	$2,300	$2,150	$1,825	$N/A	$N/A	$N/A

8-string (KLB8) - 3-per-side tuners. Mfg. 1996-98.

		$3,100	$2,400	$2,000	$1,700	$N/A	$N/A	$N/A

Last MSR was $3,950.

EUROPA - offset double cutaway asymmetrical Honduras mahogany body, brass truss rod plate, body matching peghead with bronze logo, gold Alembic-Gotoh tuners, 2 Alembic MXY pickups, volume/tone/balance control, bass/treble/Q switches.

4-string (ULB4) - 4-on-a-side tuners. New 1986.

MSR	$4,200	$3,350	$2,950	$2,650	$2,300	$N/A	$N/A	$N/A

5-string (ULB5) - 4/1 per side tuners. New 1986.

MSR	$4,500	$3,600	$3,250	$2,925	$2,475	$N/A	$N/A	$N/A

6-string (ULB6) - 3-per-side tuners. New 1986.

MSR	$4,800	$3,850	$3,350	$3,200	$2,650	$N/A	$N/A	$N/A

7-, 8-, and 10-string configurations currently available by special order only.

7-string (ULB7) - 4/3-per-side tuners. Mfg. 1986-1998.

		$4,600	$3,700	$3,000	$N/A	$N/A	$N/A	$N/A

Last MSR was $5,850.

8-string (ULB8) - 4-per-side tuners. New 1986.

		$3,900	$2,700	$2,100	$1,750	$N/A	$N/A	$N/A

Last MSR was $5,150.

10-string (ULB10) - 5-per-side tuners. New 1993.

		$4,800	$3,600	$3,000	$2,400	$N/A	$N/A	$N/A

Last MSR was $6,050.

MARK KING SERIES - offset double cutaway body with bottom bout point, long scale length, Mark King signature on peghead with gold plated sterling silver logo, 2-per-side gold Alembic-Gotoh tuners.

Mark King Deluxe 4 (MKLB4) - 5-piece body with mahogany core/exotic woods top, 2-per-side tuners. New 1989.

MSR	$4,800	$3,850	$3,350	$3,200	$2,650	$N/A	$N/A	$N/A

Mark King Deluxe 5 (MKLB5) - 5-piece body with mahogany core/exotic woods top, 2/3-per-side tuners. New 1989.

MSR	$5,100	$4,100	$3,575	$3,300	$2,800	$N/A	$N/A	$N/A

Mark King Standard 4 (MJLB4) - 3-piece mahogany body, 2-per-side tuners. New 1990.

MSR	$3,800	$3,100	$2,650	$2,500	$2,100	$N/A	$N/A	$N/A

Mark King Standard 5 (MJLB5) - 3-piece mahogany body, 2/3-per-side tuners. New 1990.

MSR	$4,100	$3,300	$2,875	$2,650	$2,250	$N/A	$N/A	$N/A

ORION - offset double cutaway mahogany body, walnut top with maple veneer, maple/walnut laminated neck, active electronics.

4-string (OLB4) - 4-in-line tuners. New 1996.

MSR	$1,950	$1,450	$1,325	$1,175	$995	$N/A	$N/A	$N/A

5-string (OLB5) - 5-in-line tuners. New 1996.

MSR	$2,250	$1,700	$1,625	$1,350	$1,200	$N/A	$N/A	$N/A

6-string (OLB6) - 5-piece maple set neck, 6-in-line tuners. New 1996.

MSR	$2,550	$1,950	$1,775	$1,525	$1,450	$N/A	$N/A	$N/A

ROGUE - sleek offset double cutaway mahogany body, vermillion top with maple accents, maple/walnut laminated neck, active electronics.

4-string (QLB4) - 2-per-side tuners. New 1996.

MSR	$3,500	$2,800	$2,450	$2,275	$1,900	$N/A	$N/A	$N/A

5-string (QLB5) - 3/2-per-side tuners. New 1996.

MSR	$3,800	$3,100	$2,650	$2,400	$2,100	$N/A	$N/A	$N/A

6-string (QLB6) - 3-per-side tuners. New 1996.

MSR	$4,100	$3,275	$2,850	$2,650	$2,250	$N/A	$N/A	$N/A

7-, 8-, and 10-string configurations currently available by special order only.

7-string (QLB7) - 4/3-per-side tuners. Mfg. 1996-98.

		$3,875	$3,200	$3,775	$2,450	$N/A	$N/A	$N/A

Last MSR was $4,700.

8-string (QLB8) - 4-per-side tuners. Mfg. 1996-98.

		$3,100	$2,500	$2,250	$2,000	$N/A	$N/A	$N/A

Last MSR was $4,000.

10-string (QLB10) - 5-per-side tuners. Mfg. 1996-98.

		$4,000	$3,400	$3,000	$2,650	$N/A	$N/A	$N/A

Last MSR was $4,900.

GRADING		100% MINT	98% NEAR MINT	95% EXC+	90% EXC	80% VG+	70% VG	60% G

SERIES I - offset double cutaway mahogany core body with bottom bout point, figured wood top/back, brass truss rod plate, body matching peghead with sterling silver logo, chrome Schaller tuners, chrome plated hardware, single coil/dummy humbucker/single coil pickups, treble/bass volume/tone control, treble Q/bass Q/pickup switch, 5-pin stereo output jack.

4-string (LBI4) - 2-per-side tuners. New 1971.

MSR	$7,000	$5,600	$4,900	$4,550	$3,850	$N/A	$N/A	$N/A

5-string (LBI5) - 3/2-per-side tuners. New 1971.

MSR	$7,300	$5,900	$5,000	$4,750	$4,000	$N/A	$N/A	$N/A

6-string (LBI6) - 3-per-side tuners. New 1971.

MSR	$7,600	$6,200	$5,325	$5,000	$4,200	$N/A	$N/A	$N/A

7-, 8-, and 10-string configurations currently available by special order only.

7-string (LBI7) - 4/3-per-side tuners. Disc. 1998.

		$7,400	$6,000	$5,300	$4,500	$N/A	$N/A	$N/A

Last MSR was $8,800.

8-string (LBI8) - 4-per-side tuners. Disc. 1998.

		$6,700	$5,250	$4,600	$3,775	$N/A	$N/A	$N/A

Last MSR was $8,100.

10-string (LBI10) - 5-per-side tuners. Mfg. 1993-98.

		$7,600	$6,200	$5,500	$4,700	$N/A	$N/A	$N/A

Last MSR was $9,000.

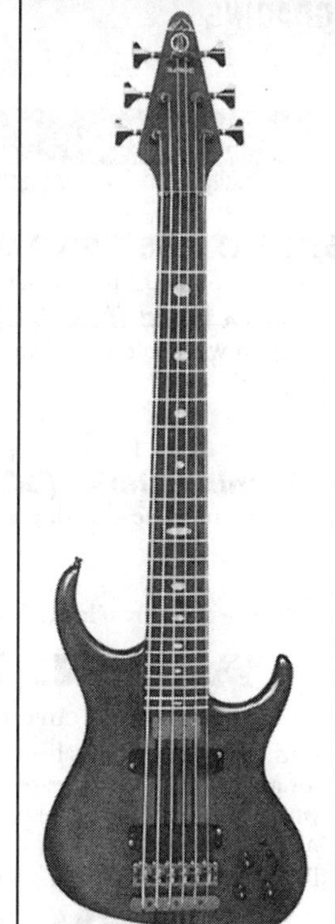

Alembic Europe
courtesy Alembic

SERIES II - offset double cutaway mahogany core body, figured wood top/back, 34" scale, 7-piece neck, brass truss rod plate, body matching peghead with gold plated sterling silver logo, gold Schaller tuners, gold plated hardware, single coil/dummy humbucker/single coil pickups, master/treble/bass volume control, treble/bass tone control, treble CVQ/bass CVQ/pickup switch, 5-pin stereo output jack, side position LED fret markers.

4-string (LBII4) - 2-per-side tuners. New 1971.

MSR	$8,700	$7,000	$6,100	$5,650	$4,800	$N/A	$N/A	$N/A

5-string (LBII5) - 3/2-per-side tuners. New 1971.

MSR	$9,000	$7,200	$5,600	$5,850	$5,000	$N/A	$N/A	$N/A

6-string (LBII6) - 3-per-side tuners. New 1971.

MSR	$9,300	$7,500	$6,500	$6,000	$5,200	$N/A	$N/A	$N/A

7-, 8-, and 10-string configurations currently available by special order only.

7-string (LBII7) - 4/3-per-side tuners. Disc. 1998.

		$9,200	$7,700	$6,800	$6,200	$N/A	$N/A	$N/A

Last MSR was $10,500.

8-string (LBII8) - 4-per-side tuners. Disc. 1998.

		$8,400	$7,000	$6,100	$5,500	$N/A	$N/A	$N/A

Last MSR was $9,800.

10-string (LBII10) - 5-per-side tuners. Mfg. 1993-98.

		$9,400	$7,900	$7,000	$6,400	$N/A	$N/A	$N/A

Last MSR was $10,700.

SPOILER - offset double cutaway Honduras mahogany body, brass truss rod plate, body matching peghead with bronze logo, chrome Alembic-Gotoh tuners, 2 humbucker pickups, volume/tone control, pickup/Q switch. New 1980.

4-string - 2-per-side tuners.

MSR	$3,200	$2,550	$2,250	$2,100	$1,750	$N/A	$N/A	$N/A

The Spoiler was also offered in a 3/4 size model between 1986 to 1996.

5-string - 3/2-per-side tuners.

MSR	$3,500	$2,800	$2,450	$2,275	$1,925	$N/A	$N/A	$N/A

6-string - 3-per-side tuners.

MSR	$3,800	$3,100	$2,650	$2,475	$2,100	$N/A	$N/A	$N/A

STANLEY CLARKE SERIES - offset double cutaway body with rounded bottom bout, short scale length, Stanley Clarke signature on peghead with gold plated sterling silver logo, 2-per-side gold Alembic-Gotoh tuners.

Stanley Clarke Deluxe 4 (SCSB4) - 5-piece body with mahogany core/exotic woods top, 2-per-side tuners. New 1986.

MSR	$4,800	$3,850	$3,350	$3,100	$2,650	$N/A	$N/A	$N/A

Stanley Clarke Deluxe 5 (SCSB5) - 5-piece body with mahogany core/exotic woods top, 2/3-per-side tuners. New 1986.

MSR	$5,100	$4,100	$3,575	$3,300	$2,800	$N/A	$N/A	$N/A

Stanley Clarke Standard 4 (SJSB4) - 3-piece mahogany body, 2-per-side tuners. New 1990.

MSR	$3,800	$3,100	$2,650	$2,500	$2,100	$N/A	$N/A	$N/A

Stanley Clarke Standard 5 (SJSC5) - 3-piece mahogany body, 2/3-per-side tuners. New 1990.

MSR	$4,100	$3,300	$2,900	$2,700	$2,250	$N/A	$N/A	$N/A

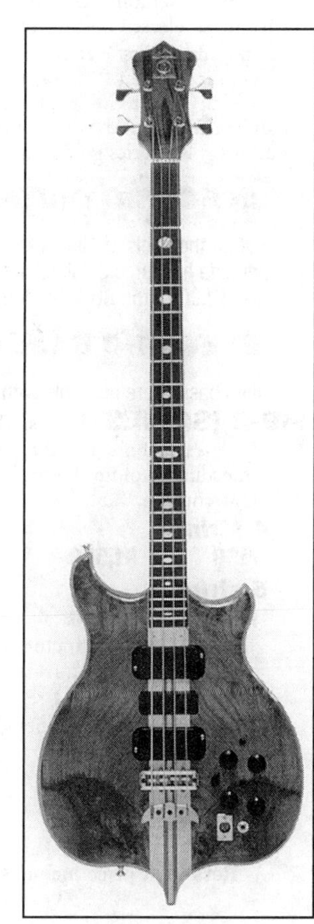

Alembic Series I
courtesy Alembic

GRADING	100% MINT	98% NEAR MINT	95% EXC+	90% EXC	80% VG+	70% VG	60% G

Artist Signature Series

Originally, both Stanley Clarke and Mark King had specific signature models. These models lead to the individual Stanley Clarke Series and Mark King Series models.

SIGNATURE SERIES - brass truss rod plate, body matching peghead with gold plated sterling silver logo, brass hardware, 2 humbucker pickups, volume/2 tone/balance controls, 2 Q switches, 5-pin stereo output jack.

Mark King (MKLSB) - offset double cutaway mahogany core body with bottom bout point, long scale length, Mark King signature on peghead with gold plated sterling silver logo, 2-per-side gold Alembic-Gotoh tuners. Disc. 1993.

$1,975 $1,700 $1,400 $1,125 $N/A $N/A $N/A
Last MSR was $2,815.

See Mark King Series for current models.

Stanley Clarke (SCSSB) - offset double cutaway mahogany core body with rounded bottom bout, short scale length, Stanley Clarke signature on peghead with gold plated sterling silver logo, 2-per-side gold Alembic-Gotoh tuners. Disc. 1993.

$2,000 $1,750 $1,500 $1,200 $N/A $N/A $N/A
Last MSR was $2,815.

See Stanley Clarke Series for current models.

ALLEN, RICHARD C.

Instruments currently built in Almonte, California.

Luthier R.C. Allen has been playing guitar since his high school days in the late 1940s. Allen has been playing, collecting, repairing, and building guitars for a great number of years. After working sixteen years as a warehouseman for a paper company, Allen began doing repair work for West Coast guitar wholesaler/distributors like C. Bruno and Pacific Music. In 1972, Allen began building guitars full time.

Allen's designs focus on hollowbody and semi-hollowbody guitars. While he has built some electrics, the design was semi-hollow (similar to the Rickenbacker idea) with a flat top/back and f-holes. Currently, Allen focuses on *jazz*-style archtops.

ALLEN, ROB

Instruments currently built in Santa Monica, California since 1996. Distributed by Rob Allen Guitars (Santa Monica), LA Bass Exchange (San Fernando Valley), and Rudy's Music (New York).

Luthier Rob Allen has a background as both a musical artist and a fine craftsman. It is a culmination of his experiences that make his instruments distinctly musical, organic in concept, and naturally appealing to the player. As a musician, Allen has played guitar with Melissa Etheridge (World Tour '92-'93), Ceremony (Geffen Records), and Kindred Spirit (I.R.S.). Allen has taught guitar at UCLA, and has recorded his own solo album (Mysterious Measures, released on the Suppletone label).

Allen built his first electric guitar from raw materials at the age of seventeen, and shortly thereafter served as an apprentice to Seymour Duncan (Seymour Duncan Pickups) for three years. Allen has also had an apprenticeship with luthier Rick Turner, the well known co-founder of Alembic and now Rick Turner Guitars. In addition to working on his own designs, Allen has drawn from both of these modern pioneers. Since 1996, Allen has been handcrafting 4- and 5-string basses that feature internal hollow tone chambers, and Fishman piezo electronics (no magnetic pickups). Allen also custom builds his RA series guitars and BB series Baritone guitars.

ELECTRIC GUITAR

Hot on the heels of Allen's **MB** series basses are the **BB** series Baritone guitars. The **BB** model Baritone has a semi-hollow offset double cutaway body, 4/2-per-side headstock, 2 lipstick tube pickups, and a fixed bridge. The **BB-1** Baritone has ultra-premium grade woods, bound headstock, and gloss lacquer finish (list $2,000); the **BB-2** Baritone has premium grade woods and an oil finish (list $1,500).

ELECTRIC BASS

Allen basses are available with either fretted or fretless fingerboards at no extra charge.

MB-2 (SERIES 2) - sleek offset double cutaway swamp ash body with internal tone chambers, quilted maple top, bolt-on birds eye maple neck, fretless cocobola fingerboard, through-body stringing, carved cocobola bridge, 2-per-side Hipshot Ultralite tuners, Fishman Acoustic Matrix Natural transducer, volume control (mounted on bridge), trim pot (in controls area in back), Fishman electronics, available in Tung Oil/Carnuba Wax finish. Current mfg.

4-string
MSR $1,500

5-string
MSR $1,700

Retail list price includes a padded gig bag.
Options include a fretted fingerboard, alder body, inlaid fret markers, or a wood thumbrest.

MB-1 (SERIES 1) - similar to the MB-2, except features ultra premium wood selection, bound headstock, available in Natural, Plum, Red, Sunburst, and Vintage Amber gloss finishes. Current mfg.

4-string
MSR $2,000

5-string
MSR $2,200

Retail list price includes a deluxe padded gig bag.

GRADING	100% MINT	98% NEAR MINT	95% EXC+	90% EXC	80% VG+	70% VG	60% G

ALLIGATOR

Instruments previously built in England in 1983.

In celebration of Alligator Amplifications' first anniversary, Reeve Guitars (UK) built a number of instruments designed by Pete Tulett.

(Source: Tony Bacon and Paul Day, The Guru's Guitar Guide)

ALOHA

Instruments previously built in San Antonio, Texas, and Chicago, Illinois. Distributed by the Aloha Publishing and Musical Instrument Company of Chicago, Illinois.

The Aloha company was founded in 1935 by J. M. Raleigh. True to the nature of a "House Brand" distributor, Raleigh's company distributed both Aloha instruments and amplifiers and Raleigh brand instruments through his Chicago office. Acoustic guitars were supplied by Harmony, and initial amplifiers and guitars were supplied by the Alamo company of San Antonio. By the mid 1950s, Aloha was producing its own amps, but continued using Alamo products.

(Source: Michael Wright, Vintage Guitar Magazine)

ALRAY

Instruments previously built in Neodesha, Kansas circa 1967. Distributed by Holman-Woodell, Inc. of Neodesha, Kansas.

The Holman-Woodell company built guitars during the late 1960s in Neodesha, Kansas (around 60 miles due south from Topeka). After they had produced guitars for Wurlitzer, they also built guitars under the trademark names of Holman, Alray, and 21st Century. The Holman-Woodell company is also famous for building the La Baye 2 x 4 guitars for Wisconsin-based designer Dan Helland.

(Source: Michael Wright, Guitar Stories Volume One)

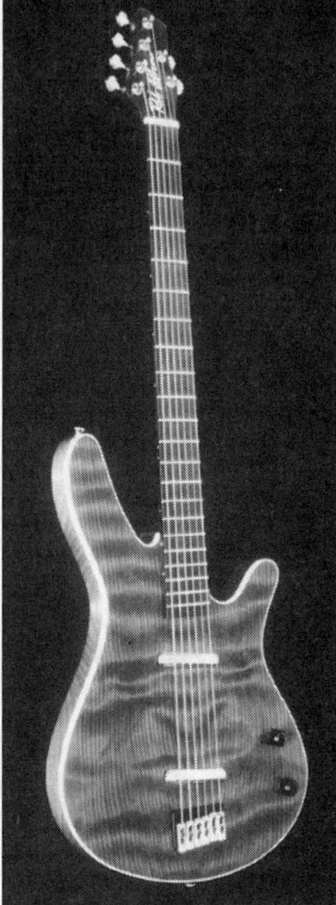

Rob Allen BB-1
courtesy Rob Allen

ALVAREZ

Instruments currently manufactured in either Japan or Korea. Distributed by St. Louis Music of St. Louis, Missouri.

The St. Louis Music Supply Company was originally founded in 1922 by Bernard Kornblum as a violin shop. In 1957, Gene Kornblum (Bernard's son) joined the family business.

The Alvarez trademark was established in 1965, and the company was the earliest of Asian producers to feature laminate-body guitars with solid wood tops. Initially, Alvarez guitars were built in Japan during the late 1960s, and distributed through St. Louis Music.

St. Louis Music also distributed the Electra and Westone brands of solid body electrics. St. Louis Music currently manufactures Crate and Ampeg amplifiers in the U.S., while Alvarez instruments are designed in St. Louis and produced overseas.

ELECTRIC

Classic Series

AE 10 BK CLASSIC I - single cutaway solid alder body, bolt-on maple neck, 21-fret maple fingerboard with black dot inlay, fixed bridge, 6-on-a-side die cast tuners, chrome hardware, white pickguard, 2 single coil pickups, volume/tone controls on metal plate, 3-way selector, available in Gloss Black finish. Mfg. 1994-99.

$285 $250 $225 $195 $160 $125 $100

Last MSR was $379.

AE 15 BK CLASSIC II (AE 15 SB) - offset double cutaway solid alder body, bolt-on maple neck, 21-fret rosewood fingerboard with white dot inlay, vintage tremolo, 6-on-a-side Alvarez tuners, chrome hardware, white pickguard, 2 single coil/1 humbucker pickups, volume/2 tone controls, 5-position switch, available in Gloss Black (Model AE 15 BK) and Sunburst (Model AE 15 SB) finishes. Disc. 1999.

$285 $250 $225 $195 $160 $125 $100

Last MSR was $379.

AE 20 CLASSIC II - offset double cutaway alder body, bolt-on maple neck, 21-fret maple fingerboard with black dot inlay, standard vibrato, 3-per-side tuners, chrome hardware, pearloid pickguard, 2 single coil/1 humbucker pickups, volume/2 tone controls, 5-position switch, available in Black and Sunburst finishes. Mfg. 1994-97.

$250 $200 $175 $150 $125 $100 $85

Last MSR was $350.

In 1995, Black finish was introduced.

AE 25 BK CLASSIC STANDARD (AE 25 NA) - offset double cutaway solid alder body, bolt-on maple neck, 22-fret rosewood fingerboard with white dot inlay, vintage-style tremolo, 6-on-a-side Alvarez tuners, chrome hardware, black pickguard, 2 single coil/1 humbucker pickups, volume/tone controls, 5-position switch, available in Gloss Black (Model AE 25 BK) and Natural Satin (Model AE 25 NA) finishes. Disc. 1999.

$325 $285 $250 $215 $180 $145 $110

Last MSR was $439.

Subtract $10 for Satin Natural finish (Model AE 25 NA), retail list is $429.

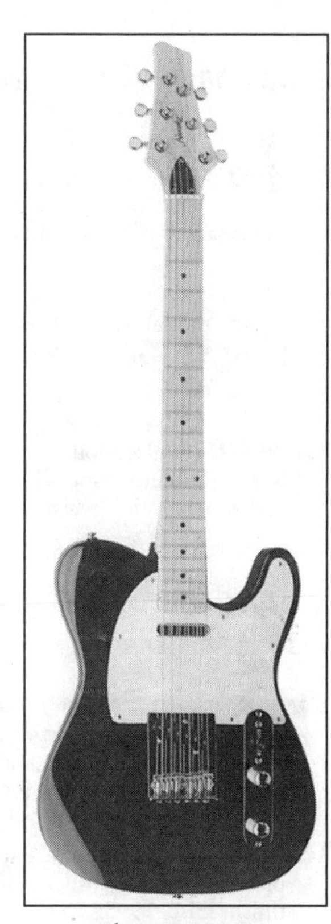

Alvarez AE 10
BK Classic 1
courtesy Alvarez

GRADING	100% MINT	98% NEAR MINT	95% EXC+	90% EXC	80% VG+	70% VG	60% G

AE 30 BK CLASSIC III (AE 30 SB, AE 30 TB, AE 30 TR) - offset double cutaway solid alder body, bolt-on maple neck, 22-fret rosewood fingerboard with white dot inlay, Accutune II tremolo, 6-on-a-side Alvarez die cast tuners, chrome hardware, white pickguard, 2 single coil/1 humbucker pickups, volume/2 tone controls, 5-position switch, available in Gloss Black (**Model AE 30 BK**), Sunburst (**Model AE 30 TB**), Transparent Blue (**Model AE 30 TB**), and Transparent Red (**Model AE 30 TR**) finishes. Disc. 1999.

$350 $300 $265 $225 $195 $160 $120
Last MSR was $469.

AE 40 FB CLASSIC DELUXE (AE 40 SB) - offset double cutaway alder body, bolt-on maple neck, 22-fret rosewood fingerboard with pearl dot inlay, fixed bridge, 6-on-a-side Alvarez die cast tuners, chrome hardware, white pearloid pickguard, 2 single coil/1 humbucker pickups, volume/tone controls, 5-position switch, available in Tobacco Sunburst and Walnut finishes. Mfg. 1994-99.

$450 $395 $350 $295 $250 $195 $150
Last MSR was $599.

In 1996, Faded Blue (**Model AE 40 FB**) and Sunburst (**Model AE 40 SB**) finishes replaced Tobacco Sunburst and Walnut finishes, and vintage-style tremolo and gold hardware replaced original parts/design.

AE 50 Classic V - similar to AE 40 Classic Deluxe, except has standard tremolo, roller nut, gold hardware, available in Ivory and Vintage Sunburst finishes. Mfg. 1994-96.

$400 $350 $300 $275 $225 $185 $150
Last MSR was $575.

In 1995, Ivory finish was introduced.

AE 60 FB Classic (AE 60 SB) - similar to AE 40 Classic Deluxe, except has Wilkinson tremolo, Sperzel locking tuners, pearloid pickguard, volume/tone controls, available in Faded Blue (**Model AE 60 FB**) and Sunburst (**Model AE 60 SB**) finishes. Disc. 1999.

$715 $625 $550 $465 $385 $300 $225
Last MSR was $949.

Dana Scoop Series

The Scoop guitar model was designed by luthier Dana Sutcliffe in 1988, and won the Music and Sound Retailer magazine's "Most Innovative Guitar of the Year Award" in 1992. Produced between 1992 and 1995, the scoop-shaped slot in the guitar body's design reinforces and channels neck vibrations into a single point where the neck and body meet.

AE 600 - offset double cutaway maple body with a "scoop" cutaway, bolt-on maple neck, 22-fret rosewood fingerboard with pearl block inlay, double locking vibrato, 6-on-a-side tuners, black hardware, single coil/humbucker pickups, volume/tone control, 3-position switch, available in Dark Metallic Blue and Fire Red finishes. Disc. 1995.

$550 $500 $425 $350 $300 $250 $225
Last MSR was $850.

In 1994, active electronics, Blue Pearl and Red Glow finishes were added.

AE 600 MA - similar to AE 600, except has figured maple top, maple fingerboard, available in Honey Burst finish. Mfg. 1994 only.

$725 $650 $550 $425 $395 $350 $325
Last MSR was $1,090.

AE 6001 - similar to AE 600, except has Modulus Graphite neck/fingerboard, available in Black finish. Disc. 1993.

$600 $550 $450 $350 $300 $250 $200
Last MSR was $900.

AE 650 - offset double cutaway maple body with a "scoop" cutaway, bolt-on maple neck, 22-fret rosewood fingerboard with pearl dot inlay, double locking vibrato, 6-on-a-side tuners, black hardware, single coil/triple *Dana* pickups, volume/tone control, 5-position switch, available in Black and Transparent White finishes. Mfg. 1994 only.

$525 $475 $400 $325 $295 $250 $225
Last MSR was $800.

This model was also available with a maple fingerboard with black dot inlay.

AE 655 - similar to AE 650, except has maple fingerboard with black dot inlay, gold hardware.

$600 $550 $450 $350 $315 $275 $250
Last MSR was $900.

AE 3000 - offset double cutaway alder body with a "scoop" cutaway, bolt-on maple neck, 22-fret rosewood fingerboard with pearl dot inlay, double locking vibrato, 3-per-side tuners, smoked chrome hardware, 2 single coil/1 humbucker *Dana* pickups, volume/tone control, 5-position switch, active electronics, available in Ivory finish. Mfg. 1994 only.

$525 $475 $400 $325 $275 $250 $225
Last MSR was $800.

AE 5000 - similar to AE 3000, except has fixed bridge.

$450 $400 $350 $280 $250 $225 $200
Last MSR was $700.

Dana Signature Series

Designer/luthier Dana Sutcliffe has over twenty years' experience in the music industry. Combining his experiences as a practicing musician, Sutcliffe has been designing quality forward-thinking guitars and amplifiers. In 1990, Sutcliffe co-designed the Alvarez Electric Guitar line for St. Louis Music. Innovative designs include the "Tri-Force" pickups, the Dana "Scoop" slotted body design, and the Dana "Off Set" bass design.

AED 100 - offset double cutaway alder body, bolt-on maple neck, 22-fret rosewood fingerboard with pearl block inlay, tune-o-matic bridge/stop tailpiece, 6-on-a-side tuners, chrome hardware, 2 DSR humbucker pickups, volume/2 tone controls, 3-position and coil tap switches, available in Black finish. Disc. 1995.

$350 $300 $250 $200 $180 $165 $150
Last MSR was $500.

GRADING	100% MINT	98% NEAR MINT	95% EXC+	90% EXC	80% VG+	70% VG	60% G

AED 200 - offset double cutaway hardwood body, bolt-on maple neck, 22-fret maple fingerboard with black dot inlay, standard vibrato, 6-on-a-side tuners, chrome hardware, 2 single coil/1 humbucker Alvarez pickups, volume/tone control, 5-position switch, available in Black and White finishes. Mfg. 1994 only.

$250 $225 $195 $150 $135 $100 $95
Last MSR was $375.

AED 250 - similar to the AED 200, except features 22-fret rosewood fingerboard with pearl dot inlay, fixed bridge, 3-per-side tuners, single coil/triple Dana pickup, available in Red finish. Mfg. 1994 only.

$265 $235 $200 $160 $140 $115 $100
Last MSR was $390.

AED 260 - similar to AED 250, except has alder body, figured maple top, transparent pickguard, maple fingerboard with black dot inlay, gold hardware, available in Transparent Red finish. Mfg. 1994-96.

$400 $325 $275 $225 $185 $140 $100
Last MSR was $550.

AED 275 - offset double cutaway alder body, transparent pickguard, bolt-on maple neck, 22-fret rosewood fingerboard with pearl dot inlay, double locking vibrato, 3-per-side tuners, chrome hardware, single coil/triple Dana pickup, 1 volume/2 tone controls, 5-position switch, available in Red and White finishes. Mfg. 1994-96.

$425 $350 $300 $250 $200 $150 $115
Last MSR was $575.

Add $50 for Blue Pearl/Transparent Red finish (AED 275 VR).

AED 280 - similar to AED 275, except has humbucker/single coil/humbucker pickups, available in Blue Pearl finish. Mfg. 1994-96.

$450 $365 $325 $275 $225 $165 $125
Last MSR was $635.

AED 300 - offset double cutaway alder body, bolt-on maple neck, 22-fret rosewood fingerboard with pearl dot inlay, double locking vibrato, 6-on-a-side tuners, black hardware, 2 single coil/1 humbucker DSR pickups, volume/2 tone controls, 5-position switch, available in Fire Red and White finishes. Disc. 1995.

$325 $300 $250 $200 $175 $145 $125
Last MSR was $500.

In 1994, White finish became available.

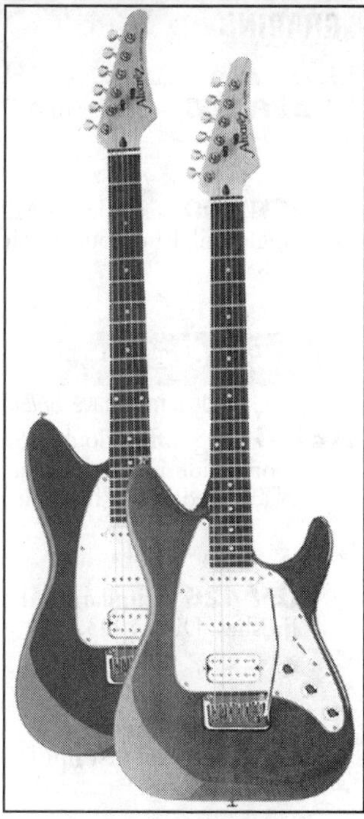
Alvarez AE 30 Classic 3
courtesy Alvarez

Regulator Series

AE 100 - offset double cutaway alder body, black pickguard, bolt-on maple neck, 22-fret maple fingerboard with black dot inlay, standard vibrato, 6-on-a-side tuners, chrome hardware, 2 single coil/1 humbucker EMG pickups, volume/2 tone controls, 5-position switch, available in Transparent Blue and Transparent Red finishes. Disc. 1993.

$325 $275 $225 $200 $180 $150 $115
Last MSR was $450.

AE 200 - similar to AE 100, except has maple body, rosewood fingerboard with pearl dot inlay, gold hardware and humbucker/single coil/humbucker EMG pickups, available in Cherry Sunburst finish. Disc. 1995.

$450 $395 $325 $260 $200 $175 $135
Last MSR was $650.

AE 300 - similar to AE 100, except has maple body, Modulus Graphite neck/fingerboard, gold hardware and humbucker/single coil/humbucker EMG pickups, available in Black finish. Disc. 1993.

$350 $300 $250 $200 $180 $165 $135
Last MSR was $500.

AE 400 - offset double cutaway alder body, black pickguard, bolt-on maple neck, 22-fret maple fingerboard with black dot inlay, double locking vibrato, 3-per-side tuners, chrome hardware, 1 single coil/1 triple Alvarez pickups, volume/tone control, 5-position switch, available in Black finish. Mfg. 1994 only.

$425 $375 $300 $250 $225 $185 $145
Last MSR was $600.

AE 500 - similar to the AE 400, except has black hardware and single coil/humbucker Dan Armstrong pickups. Mfg. 1994 only.

$400 $360 $300 $240 $200 $165 $125
Last MSR was $600.

Trevor Rabin Signature Series

This series was designed in conjunction with guitarist Trevor Rabin of the band Yes.

AER 100 - offset double cutaway alder body, arched maple top, maple neck, 24-fret ebony fingerboard with slanted abalone inlay, double locking Kahler vibrato, 6-on-a-side tuners, black hardware, 2 Alnico humbucker pickups, volume/2 tone controls, 3-position switch, available in Black and White finishes. Disc. 1995.

$600 $550 $475 $395 $325 $275 $240
Last MSR was $925.

In 1993, Black finish was disc.

GRADING	100% MINT	98% NEAR MINT	95% EXC+	90% EXC	80% VG+	70% VG	60% G

AER 200 - similar to AER 100, except has fixed bridge, gold hardware and 1 tone control, available in White finish. Disc. 1993.

		$825	$750	$650	$525	$475	$400	$350

Last MSR was $1,300.

AER 300 - similar to AER 100, except has bolt-on maple neck, rosewood fingerboard with pearl dot inlay, standard vibrato, chrome hardware, 2 single coil/1 humbucker pickups and 5-position switch, available in Red finish. Disc. 1993.

		$650	$575	$500	$400	$350	$300	$250

Last MSR was $1,000.

Villain Series

Some models may have *Select by EMG* pickups.

AEV 410 - offset double cutaway alder body, bolt-on maple neck, 22-fret rosewood fingerboard with pearl dot inlay, double locking Kahler vibrato, 6-on-a-side tuners, chrome hardware, 2 single coil/1 humbucker Dan Armstrong pickups, volume/tone controls, 5-position switch, available in Black, Red and White finishes. Disc. 1993.

		$425	$375	$325	$250	$225	$200	$185

Last MSR was $650.

AEV 425 - similar to AEV 410, except has Modulus Graphite neck/fingerboard and black hardware, available in Dark Grey Metallic and Red Pearl finishes. Disc. 1993.

		$525	$450	$375	$325	$275	$225	$195

Last MSR was $800.

AEV 520 - similar to AEV 410, except has maple body, black hardware and humbucker/single coil/humbucker Dan Armstrong pickups, available in Cherry Sunburst finish. Disc. 1993.

		$550	$500	$425	$325	$275	$225	$185

Last MSR was $900.

ASG SERIES

ASG2 - contoured double cutaway solid alder body, quilted maple top with transparent colors, bolt-on maple neck, 6-on-a-side tuners, rosewood fingerboard with dot position markers, 25 ½" scale, 2 Alnico SC single coil pickups and 1 Alnico HB Humbucker pickup, 1 volume/2 tone switches, 5-position switch, Wilkinson vibrato, Kluson-style locking tuners, nickel hardware, available in Surf Green and Purple Hayes and Black Cherry and Amber Burst on quilted maple tops. New 2000.

MSR	$459	$350	$300	$250	$200	$175	$150	$120

Add $30 for Black Cherry and Amber Burst finishes.

ASG3 contoured double cutaway solid alder body, bolt-on one piece maple neck and fingerboard, 6-on-one-side tuners, black dot position markers, 25 ½" scale, 3 Alnico SC single coil pickups, 1 volume/2 tone controls, 5-position switch, vintage vibrato, Kluson-style tuners, nickel hardware, available in 3-Tone Sunburst, Vintage White and Burgundy Metallic finishes. New 2000.

MSR	$379	$285	$245	$210	$180	$150	$125	$100

ASG4 contoured single cutaway solid alder body, bolt-on one piece maple neck and fingerboard, 6-on-one-side tuners, black dot position markers, 25 ½" scale, 3 Alnico SC sincle coil pickups, 1 volume/2 tone switches, 5-position switch, vintage fixed bridge, Kluson-style tuners, nickel hardware, available in Gold Metallic, Red Pearl, and black finishes. New 2000.

MSR	$379	$285	$245	$210	$180	$150	$125	$100

ELECTRIC BASS

Dana Signature Series

The Alvarez Dana "Off Set" Bass design, designed by Dana Sutcliffe, was nominated for the 1992 "Most Innovative Bass of the Year" award during its first year of production.

AE 700 - offset double cutaway asymmetrical alder body, bolt-on maple neck, 24-fret rosewood fingerboard with pearl block inlay, fixed bridge, 4-on-a-side tuners, black hardware, P/J-style pickups, volume/2 tone controls, 3-position switch, available in Black and Dark Blue Metallic finishes. Disc. 1993.

		$450	$400	$325	$250	$225	$200	$175

Last MSR was $700.

Pantera Series

AEB P 1 - offset double cutaway alder body, bolt-on maple neck, 24-fret ebony fingerboard with abalone slant inlay, fixed bridge, 2 on one side tuners, gold hardware, 2 pickups, volume/2 tone controls, 3-position switch, available in Black and White finishes. Disc. 1995.

		$495	$450	$375	$300	$275	$225	$200

Last MSR was $750.

In 1993, Black finish was disc.

AEB P 2 - similar to AEB P 1, except has rosewood fingerboard with pearl dot inlay and chrome hardware, available in Black finish. Disc. 1993.

		$575	$500	$450	$350	$325	$300	$275

Last MSR was $900.

GRADING	100% MINT	98% NEAR MINT	95% EXC+	90% EXC	80% VG+	70% VG	60% G

Villain Series

AE 800 - offset double cutaway alder body, bolt-on maple neck, 24-fret rosewood fingerboard with pearl dot inlay, fixed bridge, 2-per-side tuners, black hardware, P/J-style EMG pickups, 2 volume/1 tone controls, available in Black, Red Pearl, Transparent Black and Transparent Red finishes. Disc. 1995.

$425	$375	$325	$250	$225	$175	$150

Last MSR was $685.

AE 800 CS - similar to AE 800, except has maple body. Disc. 1993.

$525	$450	$375	$300	$275	$245	$225

Last MSR was $750.

AE 800 WA - similar to AE 800, except has Natural finish. Mfg. 1994 only.

$475	$425	$350	$295	$250	$225	$200

Last MSR was $725.

AE 900 5-string - similar to AE 800, except has 5 strings, 3/2-per-side tuners. Disc. 1993.

$450	$395	$325	$275	$225	$195	$175

Last MSR was $650.

AE 7000 - offset double cutaway asymmetrical alder body, bolt-on maple neck, 24-fret rosewood fingerboard with pearl dot inlay, brass fixed bridge, 2-per-side tuners, chrome hardware, J/P/J-style Dana pickups, volume/treble/mid/bass controls, 3-position switch, available in Transparent Black and Transparent Red finishes. Mfg. 1994 only.

$525	$450	$375	$300	$275	$245	$225

Last MSR was $750.

AE 7050 - similar to AE 7000, except has fretless ceramic fingerboard, available in Transparent White finish. Mfg. 1994 only.

$475	$425	$350	$275	$250	$225	$200

Last MSR was $775.

AEB 200 NA VILLAIN BASS (AEB 200 TBK, AEB 200 TRD) - offset double cutaway solid alder body, bolt-on maple neck, 22-fret rosewood fingerboard with offset pearl dot inlay, die cast fixed bridge, 2-per-side Alvarez die cast tuners, chrome hardware, P/J-style pickups, 2 volume/1 tone controls, available in Natural (Model AEB 200 NA), Transparent Black (Model AEB 200 TBK), and Transparent Red (Model AEB 200 TRD) finishes. Mfg. 1994-99.

$400	$350	$300	$265	$225	$175	$135

Last MSR was $539.

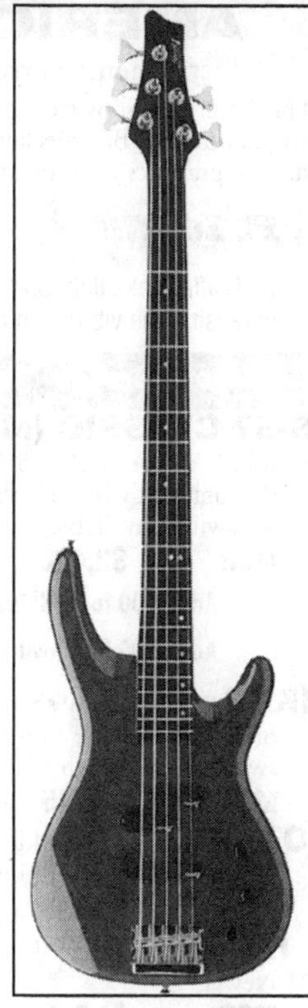
Alvarez AEB 250 TRD courtesy Alvarez

AEB 250 NA VILLAIN 5-STRING (AEB 250 TRD) - similar to AEB 200, except has 5-string configuration, 3/2-per-side tuners, active electronics, available in Natural (Model AEB 250 NA) and Transparent Red (Model AEB 250 TRD) finishes. Mfg. 1995-99.

$475	$425	$375	$325	$265	$215	$160

Last MSR was $639.

AEB 260 WA VILLAIN 6-STRING - similar to AEB 200, except has 6-string configuration, 3-per-side tuners, 2 Alvarez custom J-style pickups, active electronics, available in Natural Walnut finish. Mfg. 1995-99.

$675	$585	$525	$450	$375	$295	$225

Last MSR was $899.

AEB4 contoured double cutaway solid alder body with quilted maple top, bolt-on maple neck, rosewood fingerboard with dot position markers, 25 ½" scale, 2 custom Alvarez HB Humbucker pickups, 2 volume/1 tone control, high mass die cast bridge, Alvarez custon die cast tuners, 2-per-side tuners, chrome hardware, available in Amber Burst, Black Cherry and Purple Burst on Quilted Maple.

MSR	$539							
		$400	$375	$350	$300	$275	$250	$200

Also available in 5-string (AEB5, Sug. Retail $639) and 6-string (AEB6, Sug. Retail $899) models.

AMBUSH CUSTOM BASSES

Instruments currently built in Frederick, Maryland.

Luthier/bassist Scott Ambush has been playing bass for 26 years, and professionally with the jazz group Spiro Gyra for the past 6 years. Ambush has been building basses as a hobby for the past 10 years, and decided to offer them to players in 1998.

ELECTRIC BASS

The **Ambush Custom 5-String** bass (retail list $3,975) features an asymmetrical deep double cutaway ash or alder body, choice of (1/4" thick) exotic wood top, 34" or 35" scale, graphite reinforced composite constructed neck, 22-fret resin impregnated wood fingerboard, Hipshot tuners/'B' bridge, Bartolini J-style or double humbucker pickups, volume/blend controls, and treble/mid/mid position/bass cut and boost controls. Ambush basses are optionally available with 24-fret birds eye maple, rosewood, or ebony fingerboards; and black, gold, and silver hardware.

AMERICAN ACOUSTECH

Instruments currently produced in Rochester, New York.

American Acoustech is currently producing guitar models. For further information, please contact American Acoustech via the Index of Current Manufacturers located in the back of this edition.

AMERICAN SHOWSTER

Instruments currently built in Bayville, New Jersey since 1995.

The American Showster company first debuted the tailfin-bodied AS-57 solid body guitar at the NAMM show in the late 1980s. In addition to the original model, Bill Meeker and David Haines are continuing to debut new exciting guitar designs. American Showster guitars are also available with custom graphics (call for price quote).

ELECTRIC

The tailfin brake light on the AS-57 model is fully functional. The brake light is activated by either the push-pull tone pot on the fixed-bridge model or by depressing the vibrola on the Floyd Rose-equipped model.

Custom Series

AS-57 CLASSIC (Model AS-57-FX) - alder body shaped like the tailfin of a '57 Chevy, operational chromed tailfin brake-light assembly, 6-bolt maple neck, 25 1/2" scale, 22-fret rosewood or maple fingerboard with dot inlay, 6-on-a-side Schaller tuners, tune-o-matic bridge/custom through-body bolt chevron *V* stop tailpiece, chrome hardware, 3 *ER* single coil pickups, master volume/master treble-cut tone controls, 5-way selector switch, available in Black, Red, Turquoise, and Yellow finishes. New 1987.

MSR $2,400

Add $100 for Wilkinson VSV tremolo (Model AS-57-VT).

Add $200 for Floyd Rose tremolo (Model AS-57-FR).

BIKER - alder body shaped like gas tank on a motorcycle, 6-bolt maple neck, 25 1/2" scale, 22-fret rosewood or maple fingerboard with dot inlay, 6-on-a-side Schaller tuners, Wilkinson VSV tremolo, 3 Lace Sensor single coil pickups, master volume/master treble-cut tone controls, 5-way selector switch, available in Black Flame, Red Flame, and Yellow Flame finishes. New 1997.

MSR $1,795

HOT ROD 327 - alder body, bolt-on maple neck, rosewood fingerboard, chrome hardware, volume/tone controls, 5-way selector, 3 DiMarzio single coil pickups, Wilkinson VSV tremolo, available in Flame Fade finish. New 1997.

MSR $1,795

Hot Rod 409 - similar to the Hot Rod 327, except features korina body, tune-o-matic bridge/stop tailpiece, 2 DiMarzio humbucking pickups. New 1997.

MSR $1,650

Standard Series

The Standard Series is produced in Czechoslovakia.

AS-57 - alder body shaped like the tailfin of a '57 Chevy, operational chromed tailfin brake-light assembly, 6-bolt maple neck, 25 1/2" scale, 22-fret rosewood fingerboard with dot inlay, 6-on-a-side Schaller tuners, Schaller tune-o-matic bridge/V-shaped stop tailpiece, chrome hardware, 3 Showster single coil pickups, volume/tone controls, 5-way selector switch, available in Black, Red, and Turquoise finishes. New 1997.

MSR $1,399

BIKER-FM - alder body shaped like a gas tank on a motorcycle, 6-bolt maple neck, 25 1/2" scale, 22-fret rosewood fingerboard with dot inlay, 6-on-a-side Schaller tuners, chrome hardware, Schaller tune-o-matic bridge/V-shaped stop tailpiece, 3 Showster single coil pickups, volume/tone controls, 5-way selector switch, available in Black with Hot 3-Tone Flame finish. New 1997.

MSR $1,199

This model is also available with 2 Showster Humbucking pickups (with individual splitters).

Biker-TD - similar to the Biker-FM, available in Black, Red, and Turquoise Two-Tone Tear Drop finishes. New 1997.

MSR $999

This model is also available with 2 Showster Humbucking pickups (with individual splitters).

ICE PICK - offset double cutaway alder body, bolt-on neck, 25 1/2" scale, 22-fret fingerboard with dot inlay, Schaller tune-o-matic bridge/V-shaped stop tailpiece, 6-on-a-side Schaller tuners, 3 Showster single coil pickups, chrome hardware, volume/tone controls, 5-way selector, available in Black, Sea Foam (Green), Transparent Green, and Transparent Red finishes. New 1997.

MSR $799

This model is also available with 2 single coil/humbucker (with splitter) pickups.

ELECTRIC BASS

AS-57 BASS (Model AS-57-B) - alder body shaped like the tailfin of a '57 Chevy, operational chromed tailfin brake-light assembly, 6-bolt maple neck, 22-fret rosewood or maple fingerboard with dot inlay, 4-on-a-side Schaller tuners, BadAss II bridge, chrome hardware, P/J-style EMG pickups, volume/tone controls, pickup selector switch, available in Black, Red, Turquoise, and Yellow finishes. New 1996.

MSR $2,600

AMKA

Instruments previously built in Holland.

Amka instruments were produced by the Veneman family. Later, Kope Veneman moved to the U.S. and opened a music store in Maryland. In the 1960s, Kope Veneman introduced the Kapa instrument line, and his crown shield logo was similar to his father's Amka logo.

(Source: Michael Wright, Guitar Stories Volume One)

AMPEG/DAN ARMSTRONG AMPEG

See also ARMSTRONG, DAN.

Instruments previously built in the U.S. from the early 1960s through the early 1970s.

Burns by Ampeg instruments were imported from Britain between 1963 to 1964.

GRADING	100% MINT	98% NEAR MINT	95% EXC+	90% EXC	80% VG+	70% VG	60% G

Some Ampeg AEB-1 style models with magnetic pickups were built in Japan, and distributed by both Ampeg and Selmer (circa 1970s).

Current models are built in the U.S., and distributed by St. Louis Music, Inc. of St. Louis, Missouri.

The Ampeg company was founded in late 1940s by Everett Hull and Jess Oliver. While this company is perhaps better known for its **B-15 "flip top" Portaflex** or **SVT** bass amplifiers, the company did build various electric guitar and bass designs during the 1960s. As both Hull and Oliver came from jazz music traditions (and were musicians), the first Ampeg bass offered was an electric upright-styled **Baby Bass**. Constructed of fiberglass bodies and wood necks, a forerunner to the Baby Bass was produced by the Dopyera Brothers (See DOBRO and VALCO) as an electric pickup-equipped upright *mini-bass* under the **Zorko** trademark. In 1962, Everett Hull from Ampeg acquired the rights to the design. Hull and others improved the design, and Jess Oliver devised a new 'diaphragm-style' pickup.

During the early 1960s, Ampeg imported Burns-built electric guitars and basses from England. Burns instruments had been available in the U.S. market under their own trademark prior to the distribution deal. Five models were briefly distributed by Ampeg, and bear the *Ampeg by Burns of London* designation on the pickguard.

With the relative success of the Ampeg electric upright and their tube bass amps among jazz and studio musicians, Ampeg launched their first production solid body electric bass in 1966. Named the **AEB-1** (Ampeg Electric Bass), this model was designed by Dennis Kager. Ampeg also offered the **AUB-1** (Ampeg Unfretted Bass) in late 1966. Conversely, the Fender Instrument company did not release a fretless model until 1970, and even then Fender's first model was a fretless *Precision* (which is ironic considering the name, and Leo Fender's design intention back in 1951). Both instruments featured the Ampeg *scroll* headstock, and a pair of f-holes that were designed through the body. A third model, the ASB-1/AUSB-1, was designed by Mike Roman.

Both the fretted and fretless models feature exaggerated body horns, which have been nicknamed "devil horns" by vintage guitar collectors.

Everett Hull sold the Ampeg company to a group of investors in 1967. Unimusic, lead by Al Dauray, John Forbes, and Ray Mucci, continued to offer the inventively shaped Ampeg basses through 1970. Ampeg introduced the SVT bass amplifier and V-4 guitar amp stack in 1968, again making their mark in the music business.

In 1969, luthier/designer Dan Armstrong devised a guitar that had a wood neck and a plastic lucite body. The use of the lucite was to increase sustain, and was not intended as a gimmick. Never the less, the guitars and basses gained the nickname *see-through*, and were produced from 1969 to 1971. The instruments featured formica pickguards that read *Dan Armstrong Ampeg* and clear acrylic bodies (although a small number were cast in black acrylic as well).

Ampeg continued to offer guitars and basses during the mid-1970s. The Stud series of guitar and bass models were produced in Asia. In the late 1970s, Ampeg teamed up with the Swedish Hagstrom company to design an early guitar synthesizer. Dubbed the *Patch 2000*, the system consisted of a guitar and a footpedal-controlled box which generated the synthesizer sounds. While advertising included both guitar and bass models, it is unlikely that any of the bass systems ever got beyond the prototype stage.

In 1997, Ampeg released a number of updated designs and re-issue models. Both the AEB-2 and AUB-2 combine modern pickup design and construction with the looks of their 1960s counterparts; the Baby Bass was re-introduced; and even the Dan Armstrong-approved Lucite guitars were reproduced.

(Source: Tony Bacon and Barry Moorhouse, The Bass Book; and Paul Day, The Burns Book)

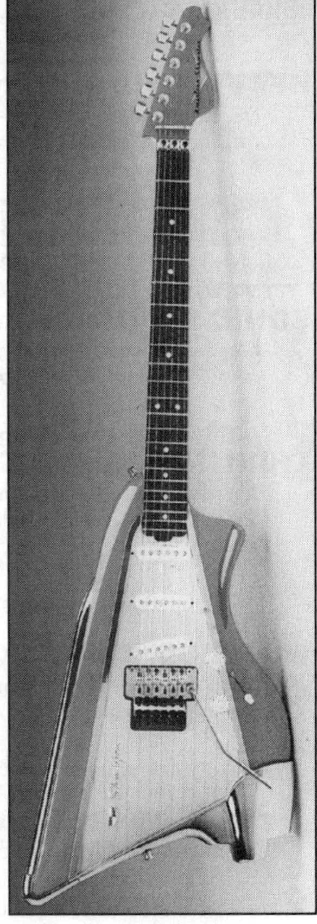

American Showster AS-57
courtesy American Showster

In 1966, Jess Oliver left Ampeg to form Oliver Sound, and released a number of his own musical products. Oliver is still offering electronic services of repairs and modifications through the Oliver Sound company:
225 Avoca Avenue
Massapequa Park, NY 11762
(Phone) 516.799.5267

MODEL DATING IDENTIFICATION

Due to various corporate purchases of Ampeg, production records have been lost or accidentally destroyed. Model productions are estimates based on incomplete records.

1962: Ampeg debuts the Baby Bass.

1963-1964: Importation of electric guitars and basses built by Burns; the five models are identical to the Burns models, except feature a pickguard inscribed *Ampeg by Burns of London*.

1966-1970: Production of Ampeg's *Horizontal* bass models (AEB-1/AUB-1, ASB-1/AUSB-1, SSB-1/SSUB-1).

1969-1971: Dan Armstrong invents the Lucite-bodied guitar, nicknamed the *See-Through*.

Mid 1970s: The Stud series is imported in from Asian production.

Late 1970s: Introduction of the Hagstrom-built *Patch 2000* guitar synthesizer system.

ELECTRIC

ARMG-2 DAN ARMSTRONG - clear lucite body, bolt-on maple neck, 24 1/2" scale, 24-fret rosewood fingerboard, Schaller (or Grover) tuners, adjustable straight bar bridge, 1 (interchangeable) pickup, volume/tone controls. Mfg. 1970-71.

$1,200	$1,000	$950	$840	$725	$620	$400

Last MSR was $340.

Add 20% for Black lucite bodies (end of production)

This model is nicknamed the "See-Through" guitar; Ampeg later had this title copy written for the model.

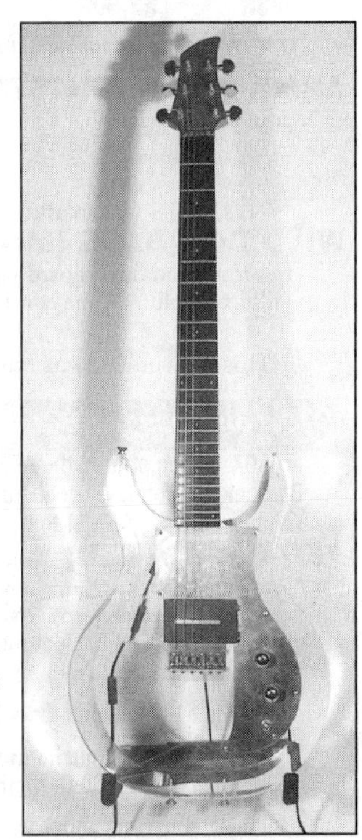

Ampeg Dan Armstrong
courtesy Fly by Night

GRADING	100% MINT	98% NEAR MINT	95% EXC+	90% EXC	80% VG+	70% VG	60% G

HEAVY STUD (Japan Mfg.) - single cutaway body, bolt-on maple neck, 21-fret maple fingerboard with white block inlay, 3-per-side tuners, chrome hardware, tele-style bridge, white pickguard, covered humbucker/single coil pickups, volume/tone controls, 3-way pickup selector, controls mounted on metal plate.

$325 $275 $245 $225 $175 $150 $120

Ampeg by Burns of London Series

Between 1963 to 1964, Ampeg made an agreement with Burns of London to import in 5 models built in England. All 5 are directly identical to the Burns version, with the exception that the pickguard's logo read "Ampeg by Burns of London". All 5 models were renamed for the U.S. market.

SONIC SIX (Model EGSS) - offset double cutaway hardwood body with short horns, 23 3/8" scale, bolt-on neck, 22-fret rosewood fingerboard with white dot inlay, 6-on-a-side tuners, chrome hardware, black inscribed pickguard, 2 Burns 'Nu-Sonic' single coil pickups, bridge/tremolo tailpiece, volume/2 tone controls, 3-way selector switch, available in Cherry finish. Mfg. 1963-64.

$400 $350 $300 $265 $225 $190 $150

This model was built by the Burns Guitar company, and basically is a renamed Nu-Sonic.

THINLINE (Model EGT-1) - offset double cutaway semi-solid body (solid center section), 2 f-holes, white body binding, bolt-on neck, 24 3/4" scale, 22-fret bound rosewood fingerboard with white dot inlay, 3-per-side tuners, bound headstock, bridge/tremolo tailpiece, 2 Burns 'Ultra-Sonic' pickups, raised black inscribed pick guard with volume/bass/treble roller controls mounted underneath, 3-way selector switch, available in Red Sunburst finish. Mfg. 1963-64.

$400 $350 $300 $265 $225 $190 $150

This instrument was built by the Burns Guitar company, and basically is a renamed TR 2 (originally "TRansistorized 2 Pickup" designation).

WILD DOG (Model EG1-S) - offset double cutaway hardwood body with inward curving horns, 23 3/8" scale, bolt-on neck, 22-fret rosewood fingerboard with white dot inlay, 6-on-a-side tuners, chrome hardware, black inscribed pickguard, 3 Burns 'Split-Sonic' pickups, bridge/tremolo tailpiece, volume/tone controls, 4-way selector switch, available in Red Sunburst finish. Mfg. 1963-64.

$425 $365 $315 $280 $240 $200 $175

This instrument was built by the Burns Guitar company, and basically is a renamed Jazz Split Sound. The 4 notable tone settings on this model include *Treble*, *Bass*, *Split-Sound*, and mondo-popular *Wild Dog*.

Deluxe Wild Dog (Model EG-3) - similar to the Wild Dog, except has a shorter horn double cutaway body, 24 3/4" scale, available in Red Sunburst finish. Mfg. 1963-64.

$425 $375 $325 $295 $250 $215 $180

This instrument was built by the Burns Guitar company, and basically is a renamed Split Sonic.

ELECTRIC BASS

ABB-1 BABY BASS (Current Mfg.) - upright sloped shoulder urethane foam/fiberglass body with internal aluminum structure, bolt-on tilt-adjustable hard rock maple neck, 41 1/2" scale, fretless Macassar ebony fingerboard, open slot scroll headstock, 2-per-side chrome tuners, rock maple bridge, black finished aluminum tailpiece, dual coil Alnico magnetic diaphragm pickup, dual piezo-electric element pickups, Master volume/active blend/tone controls, available in Solid Black (Model ABB-1 BK), Solid Red (Model ABB-1 RD), Solid White (Model ABB-1 WH), and Sunburst (Model ABB-1 SB) finishes. New 1997.

MSR $3,600

Add $100 for Sunburst (Model ABB-1 SB) finish.

ARMB-2 DAN ARMSTRONG BASS - clear lucite body, bolt-on maple neck, 30 1/2" scale, 24-fret rosewood fingerboard, Schaller tuners, adjustable straight bar bridge, 2 (stacked) pickups, volume/tone controls, pickup selector switch. Mfg. 1970-71.

$1,200 $1,000 $950 $840 $725 $620 $400

Last MSR was $340.

This model was available with a fretless fingerboard.

WILD DOG BASS (Model EB-3) - offset double (almost dual) cutaway hardwood body with short horns, 31 1/2" scale, bolt-on neck, 20 fret rosewood fingerboard with white dot inlay, 4-on-a-side tuners, chrome hardware, black inscribed pickguard, 3 Burns 'Tri-Sonic' pickups, bridge/tailpiece, volume/tone controls, 4-way selector switch, available in Red Sunburst finish. Mfg. 1963-64.

$425 $375 $325 $295 $250 $215 $180

This instrument was built by the Burns Guitar company, and basically is a renamed Vista Sonic.

Scroll Bass (AEB-2 and AUB-2) Series

In 1997, Ampeg offered the **AEB-2** and the **AUB-2**. Designed and developed by Bruce Johnson (Johnson's Extremely Strange Musical Instrument Company of Burbank, California) in cooperation with Ampeg beginning in 1995, the first prototypes were completed in November, 1996. Rather than just release a *historic reissue*, Johnson sought to marry the eye-catching original body design to state-of-the-art electronics and neck construction.

AEB-2 (FRETTED) - offset double cutaway western ash body, bolt-on rock maple neck, 35" scale, 20-fret ebony fingerboard with white dot inlay, scroll headstock, aluminum bridge, brass tailpiece and nut, 2-per-side Schaller tuners, chrome hardware, humbucking magnetic pickup, bridge-mounted piezo pickups, 2 volume/tone controls, 3-position tone select switch, available in Solid Black (**Model AEB-2 BL**), Black with Natural Neck (**Model AEB-2 BT**), Natural (**Model AEB-2 NT**), and Sunburst (**Model AEB-2 SB**) finishes. New 1997.

MSR $2,000

Add $100 for Solid Black (Model AEB-2 BL) and Sunburst (Model AEB-2 SB) finishes.

Add $100 for Gold hardware: Solid Black (Model AEB-2 BL G), Black with Natural Neck (Model AEB-2 BT G), Natural (Model AEB-2 NT G), and Sunburst (Model AEB-2 SB G) finishes.

The pickup/on-board 18-volt preamp system was developed by Rick Turner.

GRADING	100% MINT	98% NEAR MINT	95% EXC+	90% EXC	80% VG+	70% VG	60% G

AUB-2 (Fretless) - similar to the AEB-2, except has fretless fingerboard, available in Solid Black (Model AUB-2 BL), Black with Natural Neck (Model AUB-2 BT), Natural (Model AUB-2 NT), and Sunburst (Model AUB-2 SB) finishes. New 1997.

MSR $2,000

Add $100 for Left-Handed configuration ("L" code designation).

Add $100 for Solid Black (Model AUB-2 BL) and Sunburst (Model AUB-2 SB) finishes.

Add $100 for Gold hardware: Solid Black (Model AUB-2 BL G), Black with Natural Neck (Model AUB-2 BT G), Natural (Model AUB-2 NT G), and Sunburst (Model AUB-2 SB G) finishes.

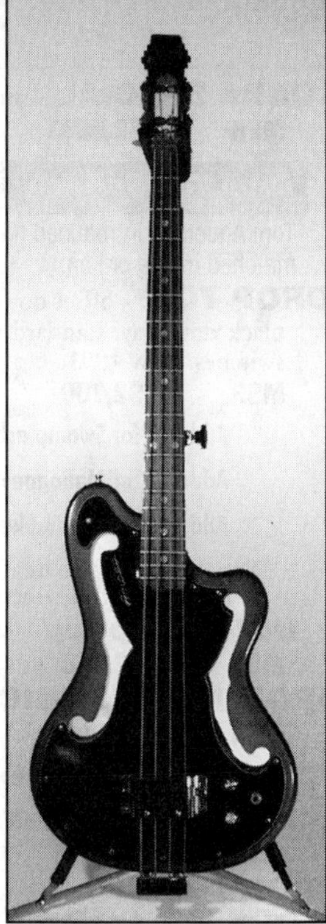

Ampeg Scroll Bass
courtesy Bass Palace

ANDERBILT

Instruments previously built in Corpus Christi or Brownsville, Texas during the mid to late 1960s.

With the help of repairman Gene Warner of Meteor Music (San Antonio), Teisco Del Rey attempted to track down the origins of the Anderbilt (also possibly ANDERTONE) guitars. The builder was rumored to be a Baptist minster; and the educated guess was made that his last name was Anderson.

The most striking feature of Anderbilt guitars is the vibrato: rather than being located on the bridge or tailpiece, the neck is the mechanism! Built in the style of a pump shotgun, the entire neck has to be pushed in toward the body and pulled away to raise or lower the pitch. Features on the guitar include a six on a side headstock, 2 pickups, a "coat-of-arms" body design, and separate volume and tone knobs for each pickup. Anyone with further information to share on the Anderbilt guitars is invited to write to the *Blue Book of Electric Guitars.*

(Source: Teisco Del Rey, Guitar Player magazine, October 1988)

TOM ANDERSON GUITARWORKS

Instruments currently produced in Newbury Park, California since 1984.

Luthier/designer Tom Anderson founded Tom Anderson Guitarworks in 1984, following a stint at Schecter as vice president from 1977 to 1984. Anderson's interest and exploration of tonewoods and the overall interaction of the guitar's parts have led to a refined and defined tone in his instruments.

All specs and orders are maintained on the company database. For anyone interested in recreating his or her favorite Anderson instrument, each guitar has a file in the database. Furthermore, there's a good chance the original builder is still on staff - and that someone will probably remember building the first instrument!

According to Roy Fought, nearly 6,000 instruments have been produced in the company's eight year history. According to Fought, the company is structured towards building guitars for the individual player's style, and that the tonewood and pickup combinations are combined to enhance what the player wants to get out of his instrument.

ELECTRIC

All models in this series are available in these finishes: 6120 Orange, Baby Blue, Black, Blonde, Bora Bora Blue, Cherry Burst, Honey Burst, Metallic Purple, Natural, Seafoam Green, Three-Color Burst, Tobacco Burst, Transparent Amber, Transparent Blonde, Transparent Blue, Transparent Green, Transparent Magenta, Transparent Purple, Transparent Red, Transparent White, Transparent Yellow, White and White Pearl. A special Cajun Red or Cajun Magenta is an option at an additional $90.

Metallic colors are offered as an additional $100 option. These finishes include Anthracite (Grey), Black Cherry, Burgundy Mist, Candy Apple Red, Electric Blue, Lake Placid Blue, Ruby, Sapphire, Sparkle Gold, Sparkle Plum, Sparkle Purple, and Shoreline Gold.

Anderson guitars are available with variations of the 5-way switching, or Anderson's own *Switcheroo* system. The *Switcheroo* consists of a four switch passive system - the three mini-switches are used for selecting any combination of neck/middle/bridge pickups, while the fourth *Blower* mini-switch goes from any pickup selection directly to the bridge pickup at full output.

Chrome hardware is stock on the guitar models. In 1996, Anderson adopted the Buzz Feiten Tuning system as standard for all guitars produced. This system helps compensate for inaccuracies inherent in guitar design (other builders such as Washburn have also begun using this system). For other model options and wood choices, please contact the company.

Add $80 for the black hardware option.

Add $150 for the gold hardware option.

Add $450 for L.R. Baggs *X-Bridge* (an acoustic bridge transducer and preamp circuit).

COBRA - single cutaway mahogany body, bound figured maple top, 24 3/4" scale, bolt-on mahogany neck, 22-fret rosewood fingerboard with pearl dot inlay, fixed bridge, 6-on-a-side locking tuners, chrome hardware, 2 humbucker pickups, volume/tone control, 5-position switch. New 1993.

MSR	$2,700	$2,100	$1,650	$1,475	$1,200	$N/A	$N/A	$N/A

This model is available with a vintage tremolo bridge.

Hollow Cobra - similar to Cobra, except has two hollow internal sound chambers. New 1994.

MSR	$2,760	$2,100	$1,800	$1,525	$1,250	$N/A	$N/A	$N/A

COBRA S - similar to the Cobra, except features a double cutaway body. New 1997.

MSR	$2,700	$2,100	$1,650	$1,475	$1,200	$N/A	$N/A	$N/A

Hollow Cobra S - similar to Cobra S, except has two hollow internal sound chambers. New 1994.

MSR	$2,760	$2,100	$1,800	$1,525	$1,250	$N/A	$N/A	$N/A

Anderson Hollow Cobra
courtesy Tom Anderson

GRADING		100% MINT	98% NEAR MINT	95% EXC+	90% EXC	80% VG+	70% VG	60% G

COBRA SPECIAL - similar to the Cobra, except features all mahogany body, 2 P-90 style (Anderson P1 and P3) pickups. New 1998.

MSR	$2,500	$1,875	$1,675	$1,475	$1,150	$N/A	$N/A	$N/A

Drop Top Series

Tom Anderson introduced the Drop Top model in 1992. The *Dropped* or *bent* top feel is the contouring similar to other models, but features a thick top of book-matched maple or koa.

DROP TOP - offset double cutaway basswood body, 25 1/2" scale, bound figured maple top, bolt-on maple neck, 22-fret maple fingerboard with black dot inlay, standard vibrato, 6-on-a-side locking tuners, chrome hardware, 2 single coil/1 humbucker pickups, volume/tone control, 4 mini switches. New 1991.

MSR	$2,700	$2,100	$1,650	$1,475	$1,200	$N/A	$N/A	$N/A

Add $70 for Swamp ash body.

Add $70 for Mahogany back.

Add $100 for bound koa top.

This model is also available with the following options: alder or lacewood body; pau ferro, palisander or rosewood fingerboard; fixed bridge or double locking vibrato; and left-handed configuration.

Hollow Drop Top - similar to the Drop Top, except has hollowed internal tone chambers. New 1996.

MSR	$2,760	$2,100	$1,800	$1,525	$1,250	$N/A	$N/A	$N/A

DROP TOP CLASSIC - similar to Drop Top, except has pearloid or black satin pickguard. New 1993.

MSR	$2,700	$2,100	$1,650	$1,475	$1,200	$N/A	$N/A	$N/A

Add $100 for bound koa top.

Hollow Drop Top Classic - similar to the Drop Top, except has hollowed internal tone chambers. New 1996.

MSR	$2,760	$2,100	$1,800	$1,525	$1,250	$N/A	$N/A	$N/A

DROP TOP T - similar to Drop Top, except has single cutaway body. New 1993.

MSR	$2,700	$2,100	$1,650	$1,475	$1,200	$N/A	$N/A	$N/A

Add $70 for Swamp ash body.

Add $70 for Mahogany back.

Add $100 for bound koa top.

This model is also available with the following options: alder or lacewood body; pau ferro, palisander or rosewood fingerboard; fixed bridge or double locking vibrato; and left-handed configuration.

GRAND AM - offset double cutaway lacewood body, 25 1/2" scale, bolt-on maple neck, 22-fret maple fingerboard with black dot inlay, double locking vibrato, 6-on-a-side tuners, chrome hardware, 2 single coil/1 humbucker pickups, volume/tone control, 4 mini switches. Disc. 1994.

		$1,700	$1,475	$1,250	$1,000	$N/A	$N/A	$N/A

Last MSR was $2,400.

This model was available with all the Anderson options when it was offered. The *exotic*, upscale cousin to the Pro Am model.

Hollow T Series

The Hollow T series features a swamp ash or basswood body with hollowed out sides and a solid central section (slightly wider than the pickup's width). These hollow internal tone chambers help produce a light weight guitar that still has the tonal characteristics of solid body models. This idea has been offered on other models in the Anderson line as well.

HOLLOW T - single cutaway swamp ash body with two internal hollow sound chambers, 25 1/2" scale, bolt-on maple neck, 22-fret maple fingerboard with black dot inlay, fixed bridge, 6-on-a-side locking tuners, chrome hardware, 2 hum-cancelling pickups, volume/tone control, 4 mini switches. Current mfg.

MSR	$2,500	$1,875	$1,625	$1,400	$1,125	$N/A	$N/A	$N/A

Add $200 for maple top.

This model is available with these options: pau ferro, palisander or rosewood fingerboard with pearl dot inlay; standard or double locking vibrato, choice of pickups; and left-handed configuration.

Hollow T Contoured - similar to Hollow T, except has contoured top/back, redesigned sound chambers. New 1995.

MSR	$2,560	$1,925	$1,650	$1,475	$1,150	$N/A	$N/A	$N/A

HOLLOW T CLASSIC - similar to Hollow T, except has white pickguard and metal plate containing volume/tone controls and 5-way selector switch. Current mfg.

MSR	$2,500	$1,875	$1,625	$1,400	$1,125	$N/A	$N/A	$N/A

Add $200 for maple top.

Hollow T Classic Contoured - similar to Hollow T, except has contoured top/back, redesigned sound chambers, pearloid pickguard, 2 single coil pickups, 5-position switch. New 1995.

MSR	$2,560	$1,925	$1,650	$1,475	$1,150	$N/A	$N/A	$N/A

GRADING		100% MINT	98% NEAR MINT	95% EXC+	90% EXC	80% VG+	70% VG	60% G

PRO AM - offset double cutaway swamp ash body, 25 1/2" scale, bolt-on maple neck, 22-fret pau ferro fingerboard with pearl dot inlay, double locking vibrato, 6-on-a-side tuners, chrome hardware, volume/tone control, 4 mini switches. New circa mid 1980s.

MSR	$2,280	$1,700	$1,475	$1,250	$1,050	$N/A	$N/A	$N/A

Add $70 for mahogany body.

This model is also available with the following options: alder or basswood body; maple, palisander or rosewood fingerboard; fixed bridge or standard vibrato; locking tuners; left-handed configuration.

THE CLASSIC - offset double cutaway swamp ash body, 25 1/2" scale, white pickguard, bolt-on maple neck, 22-fret maple fingerboard with black dot inlay, standard vibrato, 6-on-a-side locking tuners, chrome hardware, 3 single coil pickups, volume/tone control, 4 mini switches. Current mfg.

MSR	$2,280	$1,700	$1,475	$1,250	$1,050	$N/A	$N/A	$N/A

This model is also available with the following options: alder or basswood body; black satin pickguard; palisander, pau ferro or rosewood fingerboard with pearl dot inlay; fixed bridge or double locking vibrato; and left-handed configuration.

Baritom Classic

MSR	$2,480	$1,875	$1,625	$1,425	1,125	$N/A	$N/A	$N/A

Hollow Classic - similar to The Classic model, except has hollowed internal tone chambers. Mfg. 1996 to date.

MSR	$2,560	$1,925	$1,650	$1,475	$1,150	$N/A	$N/A	$N/A

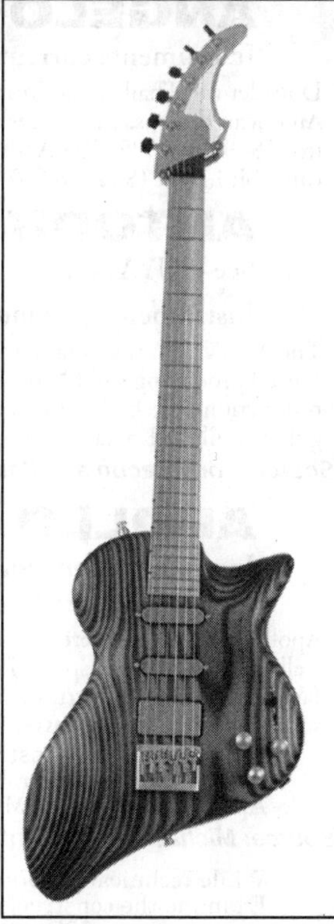

Andreas Fierce Shark
courtesy Andreas

ANDREAS

Instruments currently manufactured in Dollach, Austria since 1995. Distributed in North America by Connolly & Co, located in East Northport, NY.

All models feature brushed galvanized aluminum fingerboards glued to maple necks, 24 frets, graphite nut, 4-bolt necks, ergonomically contoured bodies, Gotoh Side Adjuster truss rod, matte chrome finish Schaller hardware and matte-finished bodies.

ELECTRIC

BLUE SHARK/GRAY SHARK single cutaway ergonomically contoured body, maple body, aluminum fingerboard and headstock, 22 jumbo frets, 6-on-a-side tuners, available with 2 EMG SA single coil pickups and 1 EMG 85 humbucker pickup, or with 1 Seymour Duncan Pearly Gates 1 pickup and 1 Seymour Duncan SH5 pickup, Schaller locking tuners, Schaller 2000 tremelo or Schaller 3D-6 stop tailpiece, available in a soft finish stained Matte Blue (Blue Shark) or Nature Sunburst White (Gray Shark) finishes.

MSR $1,879 - $2,615 depending on options

FIERCE SHARK similar to Blue and Gray Sharks, except body is constructed of Western Larch, then sandblasted, stained, and literally burned to give it its 3-D layered appearance, available in Sandblasted, Stained, Burnt finish. Current Mfg.

MSR $2,005 - $2,615 depending on options

SILVERTIP SHARK similar to other Shark models except has two single coil pickups and 1 humbucker pickup, available in Nature White Sunburst, Nature Black Sunburst, and stained Black Matte finishes. Current Mfg.

MSR $1,425

BLACK SHARK similar to other Shark models, available with Andreas Custom made pickups, EMG or Seymour Duncan pickups, available in soft stained Black Matte finish. Current Mfg.

MSR $1,879 - $2,530 depending on options

Bass Guitars

BASKING SHARK choice of maple or ash body, 5-strings, balanced ergonomically designed body, aluminum fingerboard, Schaller BM Light tuners, Schaller 2000 Series 3 dimensionally adjustable bridge, 2 Alembic AE-3 Soapbar pickups with active circuitry, Volume, Balance, Bass and High controls, handmade Thomastik-Infeld strings, also available in 4-string and fretless configurations, available in Stained Sunburst, Sunburst Orange, Sunburst Blue, and nature Sunburst matte finishes. Current Mfg.

MSR $2,905 - $3,055 depending on options.

BULL SHARK similar to Basking Shark except has Tobacco Sunburst Matte finish, also available in a 4-string and fretless configurations. Current Mfg.

MSR $2,940 - $2,800 depending on options.

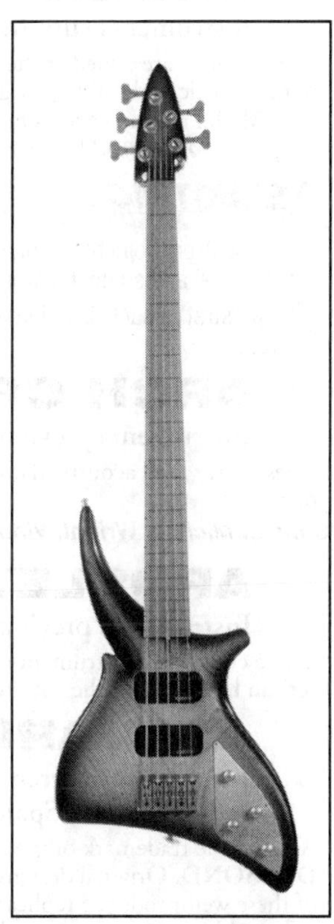

Andreas Basking Shark
courtesy Andreas

ANGELICA

Instruments previously built in Japan from circa 1967 to 1975.

The Angelica trademark is a brand name used by UK importers Boosey & Hawkes on these entry level guitars and basses based on classic American designs. Some of the original designs produced for Angelica are actually better in quality.

(Source: Tony Bacon and Paul Day, The Guru's Guitar Guide)

Angelica instruments were not distributed to the U.S. market. Some models may be encountered on the Eastern Seaboard, but the average price for these guitars ranges around $100 to $150.

ANGELO

Instruments currently produced in Thailand. Distributed by T. Angelo Industrial Co., Ltd., of Bangkok, Thailand.

Don't let the Thailand address fool you - the T. Angelo Industrial company is building credible acoustic and electric guitar models based on classic American designs. The prices are in the entry to intermediate players range, with acoustic retailing between $185 to $260, acoustic/electrics ranging from $499 to $595. The **A'50** and **A'60 Vintage** Strat-ish models fall between $450 to $545. Hot-rodded modern designs with locking tremolo systems run a bit higher ($540 to $675).

ANTORIA

See GUYATONE.

Instruments previously built in Japan in the 1950s, later switching to Korean-built models.

The ANTORIA trademark was a brand name used by a UK importer for guitars produced by Guyatone. Guyatone began building guitars in 1933, and started producing solid body electrics in the late 1950s. While the original Antorias were cheap entry level models, the quality level rose when production switched to the same factory that was producing Ibanez guitars. Currently, the trademark has been applied to solid and semi-hollowbody guitars built in Korea.

(Source: Tony Bacon and Paul Day, The Guru's Guitar Guide)

APOLLO

Instruments previously produced in Japan from early to mid 1970s. Distributed in the U.S. by St. Louis Music of St. Louis, Missouri.

Apollo instruments were generally entry level to student quality guitars that featured original designs which incorporated some American design ideas as well as some Burns-inspired *pointy* body shapes. St. Louis Music, the American distributors, switched from Valco-built Custom Craft models to the Japanese-produced instruments in 1970s when domestic sources dried up. This product line included thinline hollow body electric archtops as well as solid body guitars and basses.

Most of the Apollo instruments were built by Kawai, who also produced Teisco guitars during this time period. St. Louis Music also introduced their Electra trademark in 1971 (classic American-based designs), and phased out Apollo instruments sometime in the mid 1970s. Apollo was St. Louis Music's budget line brand.

(Source: Michael Wright, Vintage Guitar Magazine)

While technically a *vintage* instrument (based on date of production), market desirability dictates the prices found for Apollo guitars. Examine the construction quality of the hollowbody models (especially the neck pocket) before spending the big bucks! Prices should range between $75 to $125, depending on condition and playability.

ARBITER

Instruments previously built in Japan during the mid 1960s to late 1970s.

The ARBITER trademark is the brand of a UK importer. Original models are of entry level quality, later models are good quality copy designs and some original designs.

(Source: Tony Bacon and Paul Day, The Guru's Guitar Guide)

ARBOR

Instruments currently manufactured in Asia. Distributed in the U.S. by Midco International of Effingham, Illinois.

Arbor guitars are aimed at the entry level student to the intermediate player. The Midco International company has been importing and distributing both acoustic and solid body guitars to the U.S. market for a good number of years, and now offers a five-year warranty on their acoustic guitar line.

Model coding carries an *A* for an acoustic model. The double digits after the prefix (such as A30) indicates a regular acoustic, and triple digits following the prefix (like A700) for acoustic/electric models.

ELECTRIC

Electric Arbor solid body guitars feature a range of designs based on classic American designs. Again, hardware and pickup options are geared towards the entry level and student players. Most models feature bolt-on neck designs, laminate bodies and solid finishes, and adjustable truss rods.

'Superstrat' models built in the early 1990s had new retail list prices ranging from $319 to $399. 4-string bass models with P/J pickups ranged from $369 to $429.

ARCH CRAFT

Instruments previously built by the Kay Musical Instrument Company of Chicago, Illinois during the early 1930s.

These entry level acoustic flattop and archtop guitars were built by Kay (one of the three U.S. *jobber* guitar companies), and distributed through various outlets.

(Source: Michael Wright, Vintage Guitar Magazine)

ARDSLEYS

Instruments previously built in Japan during the mid 1960s.

These entry level instruments can also be found with **Elite** or **Canora** on the headstock, depending on the U.S. importer. A fine example of a matching set can be found on the cover of The Shaggs "Philosophy of the World" LP (reissued by Rounder Records).

ARIA/ARIA PRO II

Instruments currently produced in Japan since 1957. Current models are produced in the U.S., Japan, Korea, China, Indonesia, and Spain. Distributed in the U.S. market by Aria USA/NHF of Pennsauken, New Jersey.

ARIA is the trademark of the Aria Company of Japan, which began producing guitars in 1957. Prior to 1975, the trademark was either **ARIA**, or **ARIA DIAMOND**. Original designs in the 1960s gave way to a greater emphasis on replicas of American designs in the late 1970s. Ironically, the recognition of these well-produced replicas led to success in later years as the company returned to producing original designs. The Aria trademark has always reflected high production quality, and currently there has been more emphasis on stylish designs (such as the Fullerton guitar series, or in bass designs such as the AVB-SB).

The Aria company has produced instruments under their Aria/Aria Diamond/Aria Pro II trademark for a number of years. They have also built instruments distributed under the Univox and Cameo labels as well. Aria also offers the Ariana line of acoustic steel-string and nylon-string models.

ELECTRIC

615 Series

This series has bolt-on maple necks (with 5 bolts), pearloid pickguard with 3-Tone Sunburst and Red finishes, red pickguard with White finish.

5 615 CST (U.S. Mfg.) - single sharp cutaway alder body, pickguard, metal controls plate, 22-fret rosewood fingerboard with pearl dot inlay, strings through Wilkinson bridge, screened peghead logo, 6-on-a-side tuners with pearloid buttons, chrome hardware, 3 single coil Seymour Duncan pickups, volume/tone controls, one 5-position/1 mini-rhythm switches, available in 3-Tone Sunburst, See-Through Red and Off White finishes. Mfg. 1995-98.

$795 $595 $500 $400 $350 $325 $275
Last MSR was $999.

5 615 DLX (U.S. Mfg.) - similar to 5 615 CST, except has 3 Don Lace single coil pickups. Mfg. 1995-98.

$675 $500 $425 $350 $300 $275 $250
Last MSR was $850.

5 615 SPL - similar to 5 615 CST, except has 2 single coil Aria pickups, available in 3-Tone Sunburst, Red and White finishes. Mfg. 1995-98.

$350 $315 $295 $240 $215 $185 $145
Last MSR was $399.

5 615 STD - similar to 5 615 CST, except has 3 Aria single coil pickups, available in 3-Tone Sunburst, See-Through Red and Off White finishes. Mfg. 1995-98.

$525 $450 $395 $335 $295 $250 $185
Last MSR was $679.

Aria Pro II 615 CST
courtesy Aria Pro II

Aquanote Series

CR 60 - offset double cutaway alder body, bolt-on maple neck, 24-fret rosewood fingerboard with pearl dot inlay, standard vibrato, 6-on-a-side locking tuners, chrome hardware, 2 single coil/1 humbucker pickups, volume/tone control, 5-position switch, coil split on tone control, available in Black, Midnight Cherry, Navy Blue and Pearl White finishes. Disc. 1993.

$595 $500 $425 $340 $305 $280 $255
Last MSR was $850.

CR 65 - similar to CR 60, except has black hardware, single coil/humbucker pickups, 3-position and separate coil split switches, available in Amber Natural, Dark Red Shade and Purple Shade finishes. Disc. 1993.

$665 $575 $475 $380 $345 $315 $285
Last MSR was $950.

CR 65/12 - similar to CR 60, except has 12 strings, fixed bridge. Disc. 1993.

$595 $500 $425 $340 $305 $280 $255
Last MSR was $850.

CR 80 - offset double cutaway carved top alder body, set in maple neck, 24-fret rosewood fingerboard with pearl dot inlay, non-locking vibrato, 6-on-a-side locking tuners, black hardware, CS-2AL single coil/humbucker pickups, volume/tone control, 3-position switch, coil split in tone control, available in Black, Midnight Cherry, and Pearl White finishes. Disc. 1993.

$650 $600 $550 $500 $440 $395 $350
Last MSR was $1,000.

CR 100 - offset double cutaway carved top ash body, set in maple neck, 24-fret rosewood fingerboard with pearl oval inlay, non-locking vibrato, 6-on-a-side locking tuners, silver black hardware, Seymour Duncan single coil/humbucker pickups, volume/tone control, 3-position switch, coil split in tone control, available in Blue Shade, Dark Red Shade, Purple Shade and Vintage Sunburst finishes. Disc. 1993.

$1,050 $900 $750 $600 $540 $495 $450
Last MSR was $1,500.

Black 'N Gold Limited Edition

In 1983, Aria released a number of guitar and bass models under the **Black 'N Gold Limited Editions**, which featured a Gloss Black finish and gold hardware. Guitar models included the **CS-400, PE-60, PE-R 80, TA-60,** and **TS-500**; Bass models included the **CSB-450** and **SB-R 80.**

Excel Series

XL STD 3 - offset double cutaway hardwood body, bolt-on maple neck, 22-fret bound rosewood fingerboard with pearl wedge inlay, standard vibrato, 6-on-a-side tuners, black hardware, 2 single coil/1 humbucker pickups, volume/tone control, 5-position switch, coil split in tone control, available in Black, Candy Apple, Midnight Blue and White finishes. Disc. 1995.

$280 $240 $200 $160 $145 $130 $120
Last MSR was $400.

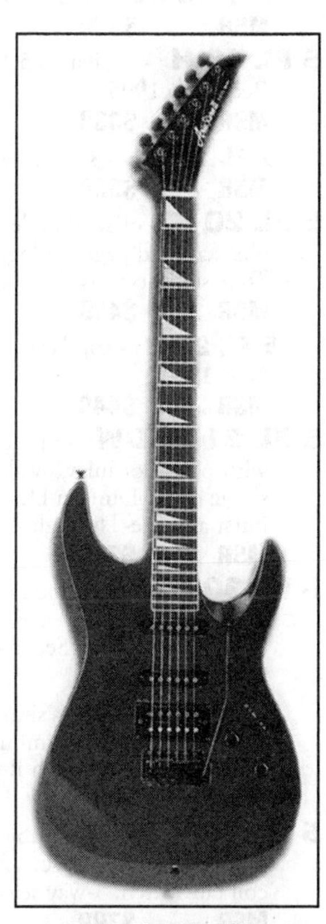

Aria Pro II XL STD 3
courtesy Aria Pro II

GRADING	100% MINT	98% NEAR MINT	95% EXC+	90% EXC	80% VG+	70% VG	60% G

XL SPT 3 - similar to XL STD 3, except has KKT-2 double locking vibrato. Disc. 1991.

	$350	$300	$250	$200	$185	$165	$150

Last MSR was $500.

XL DLX 3 - similar to XL STD 3, except has ART-10 double locking vibrato. Disc. 1995.

	$360	$275	$260	$220	$200	$180	$165

Last MSR was $500.

XL CST 3 - similar to XL STD 3, except has curly maple top/back, ART-10 double locking vibrato, gold hardware, available in Transparent Black, Transparent Blue and Transparent Red finishes. Disc. 1994.

	$420	$360	$300	$240	$215	$195	$180

Last MSR was $600.

Full Acoustic (FA) Series

5 FA 50 EBS - all mahogany non-cutaway arched top with single floating mini-humbucker, vintage tuners, volume and tone controls mounted on pickguard, available in Brown Sunburst finish. New 1999.

MSR $629	$475	$395	$350	$325	$295	$250	$200

5 FA 70 VS - single round cutaway hollow style, arched maple top/back/sides, bound body/f-holes, raised black pickguard, maple neck, 20-fret bound rosewood fingerboard with pearl split block inlay, rosewood bridge, trapeze tailpiece, bound peghead with pearl Aria Pro II logo and dove inlay, 3-per-side tuners, gold hardware, 2 humbucker pickups, 2 volume/tone controls, 3-position switch, available in Brown Sunburst and Vintage Sunburst finishes. New 1991.

MSR $999	$750	$650	$570	$490	$415	$330	$250

In 1993, Brown Sunburst finish was disc. A similar model, the FA 70 TR was offered until 1992. This model had a tremolo tailpiece and the same construction. Later superseded by the FA 75 TR model.

FA 75 TR - similar to 5 FA 70 VS, except has rosewood/metal bridge, vibrato tailpiece. Disc. 1993.

	$560	$480	$400	$320	$290	$265	$240

Last MSR was $800.

Fullerton Series

5 FL 05 - offset double cutaway alder body, white pickguard, bolt-on maple neck, 22-fret maple fingerboard with black dot inlay, stop tailpiece, screened peghead logo, 6-on-a-side tuners, chrome hardware, 3 single coil pickups, 1 volume/2 tone controls, 5-position switch, available in 3-Tone Sunburst, Black, Blue and Red finishes. New 1995.

MSR $299	$225	$195	$170	$150	$125	$100	$75

5 FL 10 S - similar to 5 FL 05, except has vintage tremolo, available in 3-Tone Sunburst, Black, Blue and Red finishes. New 1995.

MSR $329	$250	$215	$190	$165	$140	$115	$85

5 FL 10 SL - similar to 5 FL 10 S, except in left-handed configuration, available in 3-Tone Sunburst and Black finishes. New 1995.

MSR $359	$270	$240	$215	$180	$150	$120	$90

5 FL 10 H - similar to 5 FL 05, except has standard vibrato, 2 single coil/1 humbucker pickups, coil tap, available in 3-Tone Sunburst, Black, and Red. New 1995.

MSR $339	$255	$220	$195	$170	$140	$115	$85

5 FL 10 HL - similar to 5 FL 10 H, except in left-handed configuration, available in 3-Tone Sunburst and Black finishes. New 1995.

MSR $369	$275	$240	$215	$185	$150	$125	$95

5 FL 20 S - offset double cutaway alder body, white pickguard, bolt-on maple neck, 22-fret rosewood fingerboard with pearl dot inlay, vintage tremolo, screened peghead logo, 6-on-a-side tuners, chrome hardware, 3 single coil pickups, 1 volume/2 tone controls, 5-position switch, available in 3-Tone sunburst, See-Through Blue and See-Through Red finishes. New 1995.

MSR $429	$325	$280	$250	$215	$180	$145	$110

5 FL 20 H - similar to 5 FL 20 S, except has 2 single coil/1 humbucker pickups, 1 volume/1 tone controls, 5-position switch, 1 coil tap switch. New 1995.

MSR $449	$340	$290	$255	$220	$185	$150	$115

5 FL 21 HSDW - offset double cutaway alder body, flamed tiger maple top, pearl pickguard, bolt-on maple neck, 22-fret rosewood fingerboard with pearl dot inlay, Wilkinson VS-50 tremolo, screened peghead logo, 6-on-a-side Gotoh tuners, chrome hardware, 2 Duncan Designed SC-101 single coil/1 Duncan Designed HB-103 humbucking pickups, 1 volume/1 tone controls, 5-position switch, coil tap switch, available in 3-Tone sunburst and See-Through Blue finishes. New 1996.

MSR $799	$595	$520	$460	$395	$330	$265	$200

5 FL 30 H - offset double cutaway ash body, pearloid pickguard, bolt-on maple neck, 22-fret rosewood fingerboard with pearl dot inlay, knife edge tremolo system, screened peghead logo, 6-on-a-side Gotoh tuners, black hardware, 2 single coil/1 humbucker pickups, coil tap switch, 5-way selector switch, available in See-Through Black, See-Through Blue, and See-Through Red finishes. New 1995.

MSR $579	$435	$375	$330	$285	$235	$190	$145

5 FL 30 HSDW - similar to the 5 FL 30 H, except features a Wilkinson VS-50 tremolo and 2 Duncan Designed SC-101 single coil/1 Duncan Designed HB-103 humbucking pickups, 1 volume/1 tone controls, 5-position switch, coil tap switch, available in See-Through Black, See-Through Blue, and See-Through Red finishes. New 1995.

MSR $839	$625	$545	$480	$415	$350	$280	$215

5 FL 40 W - offset double cutaway ash body, black pearl pickguard, bolt-on maple neck, 22-fret rosewood fingerboard with pearl dot inlay, Wilkinson VS-50 tremolo, screened peghead logo, 6-on-a-side Gotoh tuners, chrome hardware, humbucker/single coil/humbucker pickups, bridge pickup coil tap switch, 5-way selector switch, available in Natural and See-Through Red finishes. New 1995.

MSR $799	$595	$520	$460	$395	$330	$265	$200

GRADING	100% MINT	98% NEAR MINT	95% EXC+	90% EXC	80% VG+	70% VG	60% G

5 FL 50 S (5 FL 50 SSDW, U.S. Mfg.) - offset double cutaway alder body, white pickguard, bolt-on (5-bolt neck joint) maple neck, 22-fret rosewood fingerboard with pearl dot inlay, Wilkinson VS-50 vibrato, screened peghead logo, 6-on-a-side Sperzel locking tuners, chrome hardware, 3 single coil Don Lace pickups, volume/tone controls, available in 3-Tone Sunburst, Blue, Candy Apple Red and White finishes. Mfg. 1995-99.

$799 $599 $500 $400 $360 $330 $300
Last MSR was $999

In 1996, Blue, Candy Apple Red, and White finishes were disc.; See-Through Red finish was introduced.

5 FL 60 H (5 FL 60 HSDW, U.S. Mfg.) - similar to 5 FL 50, except has a pearloid pickguard, Wilkinson VS-100 tremolo, 2 single coil/1 mini humbucker Seymour Duncan pickups, available in See-Through Red and White finishes. Mfg. 1995-99.

$1,039 $779 $650 $520 $470 $430 $390
LastMSRwas$1,299

This instrument has white pearloid pickguard with Red finish, red pearloid pickguard with White finish. In 1996, 3-Tone Sunburst finish was introduced. In 1998, White finish was disc.; See-Through Black finish was introduced.

FL MID - offset double cutaway alder body, flamed maple or ash top, bolt-on maple neck, 22-fret rosewood fingerboard with pearl dot inlay, bridge/stop tailpiece, screened peghead logo, 6-on-a-side tuners, gold hardware, 2 single coil/1 humbucking Duncan Designed pickups, piezo bridge pickups, magnetic pickup volume/tone controls, synth volume/piezo volume controls, magnetic pickup selector switch, magnetic/piezo selector switch, S1/S2 controller switches. 1/4" phono output and 13-pin DIN connector jack mounted on side, available in See-Through Black, See-Through Red, and Tobacco Sunburst finishes. Disc. 1994.

$560 $480 $400 $320 $290 $265 $240

Headstock may read *Aria Custom Shop/Fullerton (model series)*. This model was designed to interface with a Roland GR-09 MIDI device.

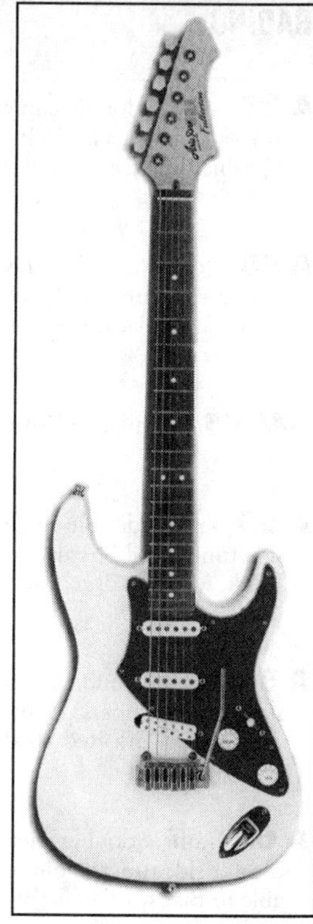
Aria Pro II FL 60
courtesy Aria Pro II

Magna Series

Instruments in this series had "crystal shape" carved tops.

MA 09 - offset double cutaway hardwood body, bolt-on maple neck, 24-fret maple fingerboard with black dot inlay, standard vibrato, 6-on-a-side tuners, chrome hardware, 2 single coil/1 humbucker pickups, volume/tone controls, 5-position switch, available in Black, Blue and Red finishes. Mfg. 1994 only.

$250 $225 $175 $150 $135 $125 $100
Last MSR was $370.

MA 10 - offset double cutaway alder body, bolt-on maple neck, 22-fret rosewood fingerboard with pearl dot inlay, standard vibrato, roller nut, 6-on-a-side tuners, black hardware, 2 single coil/1 humbucker pickups, volume control, push/pull tone control with humbucker coil tap, 5-position switch, available in Black, Fiero Red, Metallic Red Shade, Metallic Blue Shade and White finishes. Disc. 1996.

$325 $250 $200 $175 $150 $135 $125
Last MSR was $400.

In 1993, Fiero Red finish was disc.

MA 15 - similar to MA 10, except has sen body, available in Transparent Black, Transparent Blue and Transparent Red finishes. Mfg. 1994-96.

$400 $300 $250 $200 $175 $150 $125
Last MSR was $500.

MA 15 ST - similar to MA 10, except has sen body, fixed strings through bridge, available in Transparent Blue and Transparent Red finishes. Mfg. 1994-96.

$350 $250 $225 $175 $150 $135 $125
Last MSR was $430.

MA 22 (MA 20) - similar to MA 10, except has double locking vibrato, chrome hardware, available in Metallic Red Shade, Purple Pearl Burst and Silver Metallic finishes. Disc. 1996.

$375 $295 $250 $200 $175 $150 $135
Last MSR was $550.

MA 28 - similar to MA 10, except has flamed maple top/alder body, double locking vibrato, available in Transparent finishes. Disc. 1996.

$375 $300 $275 $225 $200 $175 $150
Last MSR was $600.

MA 28 G - similar to MA 28, except has gold hardware, available in Brown sunburst, Dark Blue shade, and Dark Red shade finishes. Disc. 1994.

$425 $300 $275 $225 $200 $175 $150

MA 29 - similar to MA 10, except has ash carved top body, single coil/humbucker pickups, available in Natural and Paduak Red semi-gloss finishes. Disc. 1994.

$425 $300 $275 $225 $200 $175 $150

MA 30 - similar to MA 10, except has 24-fret fingerboard, double locking vibrato, available in Black, Navy Blue, Purple Cherry and Pearl White finishes. Disc. 1996.

$525 $450 $400 $300 $275 $250 $225
Last MSR was $900.

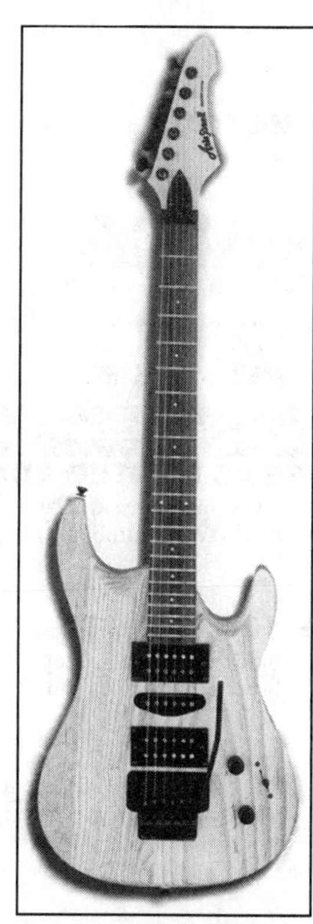
Aria Pro II MA 29
courtesy Aria Pro II

GRADING	100% MINT	98% NEAR MINT	95% EXC+	90% EXC	80% VG+	70% VG	60% G

MA 35 - offset double cutaway alder body, bolt-on maple neck, 24-fret rosewood fingerboard with pearl dot inlay, double locking vibrato, roller nut, 6-on-a-side tuners, black hardware, single coil/humbucker pickups, volume/tone control, 3-position switch, coil split in tone control, available in Metallic Blue, Metallic Burgundy and Metallic Violet finishes. Mfg. 1991 only.

$625	$550	$450	$375	$325	$300	$275

Last MSR was $900.

MA 40 - offset double cutaway alder body, bolt-on maple neck, 24-fret rosewood fingerboard with pearl dot inlay, double locking vibrato, roller nut, 6-on-a-side tuners, black hardware, 2 single coil/1 humbucker pickups, volume/2 EQ controls, 3-position and 2 EQ switches, active electronics, available in Black, Metallic Blue, Metallic Burgundy, Metallic Violet, Navy Blue, Pearl White and Purple Cherry finishes. Mfg. 1991 only.

$625	$575	$475	$395	$350	$325	$295

Last MSR was $960.

MA 45 - similar to MA 40, except has bound fingerboard with pearl oval inlay, tune-o-matic bridge/stop tailpiece, gold hardware. Disc. 1992.

$650	$600	$550	$450	$375	$350	$300

Last MSR was $1,025.

MA 50 - offset double cutaway alder body, bolt-on maple neck, 24-fret rosewood fingerboard with pearl dot inlay, standard vibrato, roller nut, 6-on-a-side tuners, gold hardware, 2 single coil/1 humbucker pickups, volume/tone control, three 3-position switches, coil split in tone control, available in Black, Metallic Blue, Metallic Burgundy, Metallic Violet, Navy Blue, Pearl White and Purple Cherry finishes. Disc. 1993.

$700	$600	$500	$400	$350	$325	$300

Last MSR was $1,000.

MA 55 - offset double cutaway sen body, bolt-on maple neck, 24-fret rosewood fingerboard with pearl dot inlay, standard vibrato, roller nut, 6-on-a-side locking tuners, 2 single coil/1 humbucker pickups, volume/tone control, 5-position and coil split switches, available in Amber Natural, Blue Shade and Dark Red Shade finishes. Mfg. 1992 only.

$725	$650	$525	$425	$375	$350	$325

Last MSR was $1,050.

MA 60 - offset double cutaway alder body, maple neck, 24-fret bound rosewood fingerboard with pearl oval inlay, double locking vibrato, roller nut, 6-on-a-side tuners, gold hardware, 2 single coil/1 humbucker pickups, volume/2 EQ controls, 3-position and 2 EQ switches, active electronics, available in Black, Metallic Blue, Metallic Burgundy, Metallic Violet, Navy Blue, Pearl White and Purple Cherry finishes. Mfg. 1991-92.

$750	$675	$550	$450	$395	$350	$325

Last MSR was $1,100.

MA 75 - offset double cutaway sen body, bolt-on maple neck, 22-fret rosewood fingerboard with pearl oval inlay, double locking vibrato, 6-on-a-side tuners, gold hardware, humbucker/single coil/humbucker pickups, volume/tone control, 5-position and coil split switches, available in Amber Natural, Cherry Sunburst, Purple Shade and Vintage Sunburst finishes. Mfg. 1992 only.

$750	$695	$575	$450	$425	$375	$350

Last MSR was $1,150.

MA 90 - offset double cutaway alder body, bolt-on maple neck, 24-fret bound rosewood neck with pearl oval inlay, double locking vibrato, 6-on-a-side tuners, silver black hardware, 2 single coil/Seymour Duncan humbucker pickups, volume/tone control, 5-position switch, coil split in tone control, available in Emerald Green Sunburst, Gun metal Grey, Navy Blue Sunburst and Rose Red Sunburst finishes. Mfg. 1991-92.

$800	$750	$675	$525	$475	$425	$375

Last MSR was $1,295.

MA 100 - similar to MA-90, except has set neck, available in Gun Metal Grey finish. Mfg. 1991-92.

$825	$775	$725	$575	$500	$450	$400

Last MSR was $1,400.

Neo Series

5 NEO X 10 - small, lightweight alder body with bolt-on neck, two single coil and one humbucker pickup, 24-frets, VFT-1C tremolo, 5-position selector switch, chrome hardware, available in Antique Violin Color, See-Through Blue Shade, Cherry Sunburst and Vintage Sunburst finishes. New 1999.

MSR	$359	$269	$225	$200	$175	$150	$100	$75

Pro Electric Series

5 PE 40 LIMITED EDITION 40TH ANNIVERSARY MODEL - single sharp cutaway mahogany body, bound quilted maple top, set-in maple neck, 22-fret bound ebony fingerboard with fancy abalone inlays, tune-o-matic bridge/stop tailpiece, 3-per-side locking tuners, gold hardware, 2 humbucker pickups, 2 volume/2 tone controls, 1 selector switch, available in Antique Violin Shade finish only. Mfg. 1996-99.

$899	$780	$685	$590	$495	$395	$300

Last MSR was $1,199.

PE 1000 - single sharp cutaway mahogany body, bound curly maple top, set-in maple neck, 22-fret bound rosewood fingerboard with abalone/pearl block inlay, bridge/stop tail piece, 3-per-side tuners, gold hardware, 2 humbucker pickups, 2 volume/2 tone controls, available in See-Through Blue, See-Through Red, and Vintage Sunburst. Mfg. 1991-92.

$860	$730	$600	$470	$420	$380	$330

Last MSR was $1,200.

PE 1000 TR - similar to the PE 1000, except has abalone/pearl split block inlay, non-locking tremolo system, 3-per-side locking tuners, volume/tone controls, 3-way pickup selector switch, available in Blondy Natural, Transparent Scarlet and Twilight Black finishes. Mfg. 1991-92.

$910	$780	$650	$520	$470	$430	$390

Last MSR was $1,300.

GRADING		100% MINT	98% NEAR MINT	95% EXC+	90% EXC	80% VG+	70% VG	60% G

PE 1500 - similar to the PE 1000, except has mahogany body, carved maple top and back, 2 Seymour Duncan humbuckers, abalone/pearl snowflake inlay, available in Antique Violin finish. Mfg. 1991-92.

		$970	$820	$750	$620	$550	$450	$395

Last MSR was $1,400.

PE JR 600 - single sharp cutaway maple body, bolt-on maple neck, 22-fret rosewood fingerboard with pearl dot inlay, tune-o-matic bridge/stop tailpiece, 3-per-side tuners, chrome hardware, 2 single coil pickups, 2 volume/tone controls, 3-position switch, available in Black, Metallic Blue Shade and Metallic Violet Shade finishes. Disc. 1992.

		$540	$460	$385	$310	$280	$255	$230

Last MSR was $775.

PE JR 750 - similar to PE JR 600, except has bound body, vibrato tailpiece, gold hardware, volume/tone control, available in Cherry Sunburst, Pearl White and Vintage Sunburst finishes. Disc. 1992.

		$700	$600	$500	$400	$360	$330	$300

Last MSR was $1,000.

5 PE CLS - single sharp cutaway semi-hollow alder body, bound flame maple top, set in maple neck, 25 1/2" scale, four *wave*-shaped soundholes, 24-fret bound rosewood fingerboard with abalone/pearl block inlay, string through rosewood tailpiece, 3-per-side tuners with pearl button pegs, slotted headstock, gold hardware, Fishman AG-125 piezo system, volume/active treble/middle/bass controls, available in Rose Natural finish. Mfg. 1994-99.

		$1,000	$895	$775	$665	$550	$445	$325

Last MSR was $1,299.

5 PE DLX - single sharp cutaway alder body, bound flamed maple top, bolt-on maple neck, 22-fret bound rosewood fingerboard with pearl block inlay, tune-o-matic bridge/stop tailpiece, 3-per-side locking tuners, gold hardware, 2 humbucker pickups, 2 volume/2 tone controls, 1 selector switch, available in See-Through Black, See-Through Blue, See-Through Green, See-Through Purple, Violin Shade, and See-Through Wine Red finishes. Current mfg.

MSR	$699	$525	$455	$400	$345	$290	$230	$175

5 PE DLX L SBL - similar to the 5 PE DLX, except has left-handed configuration, available in See-Through Blue finish only. New 1998.

MSR	$769	$575	$500	$440	$375	$315	$250	$195

5 PE STD - similar to the 5 PE DLX, except has a maple top, chrome hardware, bolt-on neck, available in Violin Shade finish only. New 1997.

MSR	$599	$450	$390	$350	$295	$250	$200	$150

5 PE PRO - similar to 5 PE DLX except has gold hardware, available in black, Vintage Sunburst, and Wine Red finishes. New 1999.

MSR	$649	$485	$410	$375	$325	$275	$225	$200

5 PE SPL - similar to 5 PE DLX, except features a set-in neck, available in Natural Violin Shade finish only. New 1994.

MSR	$899	$675	$585	$515	$440	$370	$300	$225

PE DLX MID - single sharp cutaway mahogany body, flamed maple carved top, set-in maple neck, 22-fret rosewood fingerboard with pearl block inlay, bridge/stop tailpiece, screened peghead logo, 3+3 tuners, gold hardware, 2 humbucker Duncan Designed pickups, piezo bridge pickups, magnetic pickup volume/tone controls, synth volume/piezo volume controls, magnetic pickup selector switch, magnetic/piezo selector switch, S1/S2 controller switches. 1/4" phono output and 13-pin DIN connector jack mounted on side, available in Vintage Sunburst finish only. Disc. 1994.

		$575	$475	$400	$325	$295	$265	$235

Headstock may read Aria Custom Shop. This model was designed to interface with a Roland GR-09 MIDI device. Aria also offered a PE CLS MID model (a MIDI version of the PE CLS).

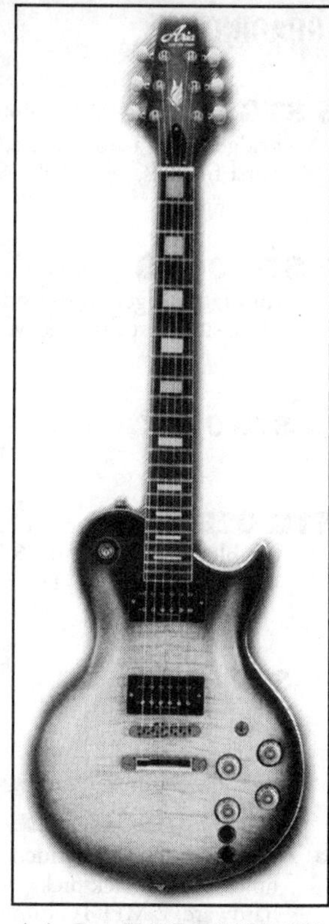

Aria Pro II PE DLX MID
courtesy Aria Pro II

STG Series

5 STG 003 - offset double cutaway hardwood body, white pickguard, bolt-on maple neck, 25 1/2" scale, 22-fret rosewood fingerboard with white dot inlay, vintage style tremolo, 6-on-a-side tuners, chrome hardware, 3 single coil pickups, volume/2 tone controls, 5-position switch, available in 3-Tone Sunburst, Black, Red, and White finishes. New 1996.

MSR	$279	$210	$180	$160	$135	$110	$90	$65

In 1997, 3-Tone Sunburst finish was disc.; Blue and Green finishes were introduced.

5 STG 003 L - similar to 5 STG 003, except in left-handed configuration, available in Black finish only. New 1996.

MSR	$299	$225	$195	$170	$145	$120	$95	$70

5 STG 002 - similar to 5 STG 003, except has maple fingerboard, available in Black, Blue, Red, and White finishes. New 1998.

MSR	$279	$210	$180	$160	$135	$110	$90	$65

5 STG 004 - similar to 5 STG 003, except features 2 single coil/humbucker pickups, vintage-style VFT-1M tremolo, available in 3-Tone Sunburst, Natural, See-Through Blue, See-Through Green, and See-Through Wine Red finishes. New 1998.

MSR	$299	$225	$195	$170	$145	$120	$95	$70

In 1998, Midnight Blue, Metallic Black, Metallic Green, Metallic Lavender, and Metallic Silver finishes were introduced.

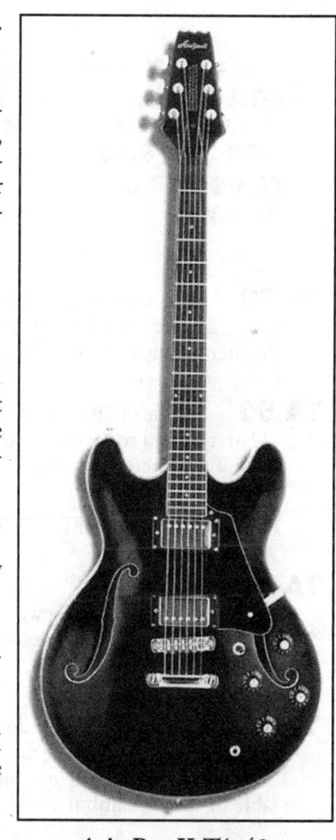

Aria Pro II TA 40
courtesy Aria Pro II

GRADING	100% MINT	98% NEAR MINT	95% EXC+	90% EXC	80% VG+	70% VG	60% G

5 STG 012 S - offset double cutaway hardwood body, white pickguard, bolt-on maple neck, 22-fret maple fingerboard with black dot inlay, fixed bridge, 6-on-a-side tuners, chrome hardware, 2 single coil pickups, volume/tone control, 3-position switch, available in Black, Blue and 3-Tone Sunburst finishes. Mfg. 1994-97.

	$200	$150	$125	$95	$85	$80	$75

Last MSR was $279.

5 STG 013 S - offset double cutaway hardwood body, white pickguard, bolt-on maple neck, 22-fret maple fingerboard with black dot inlay, strings through bridge, 6-on-a-side tuners, chrome hardware, 3 single coil pickups, volume/tone controls, 5-position switch, available in Black, Blue and 3-Tone sunburst finishes. Mfg. 1994-97.

	$275	$195	$150	$120	$110	$100	$90

Last MSR was $349.

STG 013 X - similar to STG 013 S, except has standard vibrato, 2 single coil/1 humbucker pickups. Mfg. 1994-97.

	$295	$225	$175	$150	$135	$125	$110

Last MSR was $360.

STG 023 C - offset double cutaway figured maple body, black pickguard, bolt-on maple neck, 22-fret rosewood fingerboard with pearl dot inlay, double locking vibrato, 6-on-a-side tuners, chrome hardware, 2 single coil/1 humbucker pickups, volume/tone control, 5-position switch, available in Dark Blue Shade, Dark Red Shade and Tobacco Sunburst finishes. Mfg. 1994-96.

	$350	$275	$225	$175	$150	$135	$125

Last MSR was $440.

STG 023 X - similar to STG 023 C, except had gold hardware. Mfg. 1994-96.

	$450	$325	$275	$225	$200	$175	$150

Last MSR was $550.

Thin Acoustic (TA) Series

5 TA 40 - double rounded cutaway semi-hollow style, mahogany arched top/back/sides, bolt-on mahogany neck, 24 3/4" scale, bound body, bound f-holes, raised black pickguard, 22-fret bound rosewood fingerboard with pearl dot inlay, tune-o-matic bridge/stop tailpiece, 3-per-side tuners, chrome hardware, 2 MH-1C humbucker pickups, 2 volume/tone controls, 3-position switch, available in Walnut and Wine Red finishes. Current mfg.

MSR $569	$425	$370	$325	$280	$235	$190	$145

In 1999, black finish was added.

5 TA 60 - similar to 5 TA 40, except features block inlay on fingerboard, gold hardware, 2 MH-1G humbucker pickups, available in Pearl Black, Walnut, and Wine Red finishes. Current mfg.

MSR $659	$595	$425	$370	$320	$270	$215	$160

In 1993, Walnut finish was disc.

5 TA 61 - similar to TA 60, except has maple arched top/back/sides, transparent pickguard, bound peghead, tone selector switch, available in Amber Natural, Cherry, and Vintage Sunburst finishes. Disc. 1997.

	$575	$500	$450	$395	$325	$250	$200

Last MSR was $799.

In 1993, Cherry finish was disc. In 1996, Wine Red finish was introduced.

5 TA 62 - similar to the 5 TA 60, except has maple arched top/back/sides, set-in maple neck, available in Amber Natural, Wine Red, and Vintage Sunburst finishes. New 1998.

MSR $799	$599	$520	$455	$395	$325	$265	$200

TA 65 TR - similar to TA 60, except has vibrato tailpiece, available in Amber Natural, Cherry, Vintage Sunburst, Walnut and Wine Red finishes. Disc. 1991.

	$490	$425	$350	$280	$250	$225	$200

Last MSR was $700.

TA 70 - double cutaway semi-hollow body, spruce arched top, mahogany arched back/sides, f-holes, bound body, raised black pickguard, maple set-neck, 22-fret bound rosewood fingerboard with pearl dot inlay, bridge/stop tailpiece, unbound peghead, 3-per-side tuners, chrome hardware, 2 humbucker pickups, 2 volume/tone controls, 3-position switch, available in Vintage Sunburst and Wine Red finishes. Disc. 1995.

	$495	$425	$350	$295	$250	$225	$180

TA 80 - double cutaway semi-hollow body, flamed maple arched top/back/sides, f-holes, bound body, raised tortoiseshell pickguard, maple set neck, 22-fret bound rosewood fingerboard with pearl dot inlay, bridge/stop tailpiece, bound peghead, 3-per-side tuners, gold hardware, 2 humbucker pickups, 2 volume/tone controls, 3-position switch, available in Antique Sunburst and Antique Violin color finishes. Disc. 1995.

	$500	$450	$375	$315	$275	$240	$195

TA 80 TR - similar to TA 80, except has vibrato tailpiece, available in Antique Sunburst and Antique Violin color finishes. Disc. 1995.

	$500	$450	$375	$300	$265	$230	$195

TA 900 (TA STD) - double cutaway semi hollow body, maple arched top/back/sides, f-holes, bound body, raised black pickguard, mahogany neck, 22-fret bound rosewood fingerboard with pearl dot inlay, bridge/stop tailpiece, unbound peghead, 3-per-side tuners, chrome hardware, 2 humbucker pickups, 2 volume/tone controls, 3-position switch, available in Black, Brown Sunburst and Transparent Red finishes. Mfg. 1991-92.

	$875	$750	$625	$500	$450	$415	$375

Last MSR was $1,250.

TA 1300 (TA DLX) - double rounded cutaway semi hollow style, sycamore top/back/sides, bound body, bound f-holes, raised bound tortoise pickguard, mahogany neck, 22-fret bound ebony fingerboard with abalone/pearl split block inlay, tune-o-matic bridge/stop tailpiece, bound peghead with pearl Aria Pro II logo and dove inlay, 3-per-side tuners, gold hardware, 2 humbucker pickups, 2 volume/tone controls, 3-position switch, available in Brown Sunburst and Vintage Sunburst finishes. Mfg. 1991-92.

	$1,225	$1,050	$875	$700	$630	$575	$525

Last MSR was $1,750.

GRADING	100% MINT	98% NEAR MINT	95% EXC+	90% EXC	80% VG+	70% VG	60% G

Viper Series

VP-30 - offset double cutaway maple body, bolt-on maple neck, 22-fret rosewood fingerboard with pearl dot inlay, standard vibrato, roller nut, 6-on-a-side tuners, chrome hardware, 2 single coil/1 humbucker pickups, volume/tone control, 5-position switch, available in Black, Fiero Red and White finishes. Mfg. 1991 only.

		$275	$235	$195	$155	$140	$125	$115

Last MSR was $390.

VP-40 - offset double cutaway alder body, pearloid pickguard, bolt-on maple neck, 22-fret rosewood fingerboard with pearl wedge inlay, locking vibrato, 6-on-a-side tuners, black hardware, 2 single coil/1 humbucker pickups, volume/tone control, 5-position switch, available in Black, Fiero Red, Navy Blue, Pearl White and White finishes. Mfg. 1991 only.

		$350	$300	$250	$200	$180	$165	$150

Last MSR was $500.

VP-50 - similar to VP-40, except has coil split switch, available in Black, Candy Apple, Navy Blue, Midnight Cherry and Pearl White finishes. Disc. 1995.

		$650	$540	$420	$300	$270	$245	$225

Last MSR was $1,000.

VP-65 - similar to VP-40, except has pearloid pickguard, humbucker/single coil/humbucker pickups, coil split switch, available in Black, Metallic Lavender Shade and Pearl Blue finishes. Disc. 1993.

		$695	$595	$500	$400	$360	$330	$300

Last MSR was $995.

VP-90 - semi-solid offset double cutaway maple body, figured maple top, wedge soundhole, bound body and soundhole, maple neck, 22-fret bound rosewood fingerboard with pearl dot inlay, standard vibrato, 6-on-a-side locking tuners, chrome hardware, volume/tone control, 3-position and coil split switch, available in Cherry Sunburst and Natural finishes. Disc. 1993.

		$170	$145	$120	$95	$85	$80	$75

Last MSR was $240.

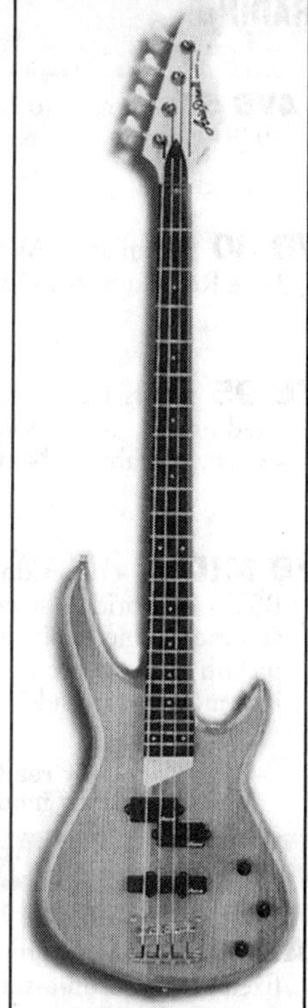

Aria Pro II AVB 40
courtesy Aria Pro II

ELECTRIC BASS

Avante Bass Series

6 AVB 20 - offset double cutaway alder body, bolt-on maple neck, 24-fret rosewood fingerboard with dot inlay, fixed bridge, 4-on-a-side tuners, chrome hardware, P/J-style pickups, 2 volume/1 tone controls, available in Black finish only. New 1995.

MSR	$549	$415	$355	$315	$270	$225	$185	$140

AVB 30 - offset double cutaway hardwood body, bolt-on maple neck, 24-fret rosewood fingerboard with dot inlay, fixed bridge, 4-on-a-side tuners, chrome hardware, P/J-style pickups, 2 volume/1 tone controls, available in Black, Blue, Red, and White finishes. Disc. 1996.

		$300	$245	$220	$195	$165	$120	$95

Last MSR was $400.

6 AVB 40 - offset double cutaway alder body, bolt-on maple neck, 24-fret rosewood fingerboard with dot inlay, fixed bridge, 4-on-a-side tuners, chrome hardware, P/J-style pickups, 2 volume/1 tone controls, available in Natural, See-Through Blue, See-Through Green, See-Through Purple, and See-Through Red finishes. New 1994.

MSR	$599	$450	$390	$340	$295	$250	$200	$150

6 AVB 40 FL - similar to 6 AVB 40, except in fretless configuration, available in Natural finish only. New 1996.

MSR	$599	$450	$390	$340	$295	$250	$200	$150

6 AVB 40 LN - similar to 6 AVB 40, except in left-handed configuration, available in Natural finish only. New 1996.

MSR	$649	$485	$420	$370	$315	$265	$215	$160

6 AVB 45 - offset double cutaway alder body, bolt-on maple neck, 24-fret rosewood fingerboard with pearl oval inlay, fixed bridge, 4-on-a-side tuners, black hardware, P/J-style pickups, volume/treble/bass/balance controls, active electronics, available in Natural, See-Through Blue and See-Through Red finishes. New 1994.

MSR	$849	$640	$550	$485	$415	$350	$285	$215

6 AVB 45/5 5-String - similar to AVB 45, except has 5-string configuration, 4/1 per side tuners, 2 J-style pickups. New 1994.

MSR	$899	$675	$585	$515	$435	$360	$285	$225

AVB 50 - offset double cutaway alder body, bolt-on maple neck, 24-fret rosewood fingerboard with pearl dot inlay, fixed bridge, 4-on-a-side tuners, chrome hardware, P-style/J-style pickups, 2 volume/1 tone controls, available in Black, Fiero Red and White finishes. New 1991.

		$345	$295	$245	$195	$175	$160	$150

Last MSR was $490.

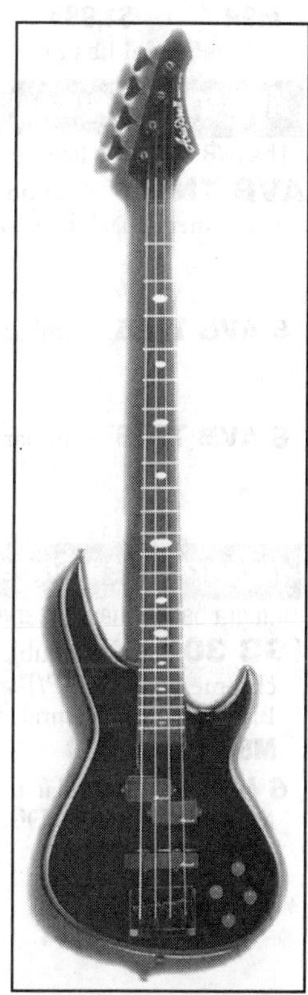

Aria Pro II AVB 45
courtesy Aria Pro II

GRADING	100% MINT	98% NEAR MINT	95% EXC+	90% EXC	80% VG+	70% VG	60% G

AVB 55 - similar to AVB 50, except has carved top and black hardware, available in Alsace Red, Black, Navy Blue and Pearl White finishes. Disc. 1993.

	$595	$500	$425	$340	$305	$280	$255

Last MSR was $850.

AVB 80 - similar to AVB 50, except has carved top, gold hardware and active electronics, available in Black, Navy Blue Sunburst, Pearl White and Rose Red Sunburst. Disc. 1993.

	$775	$650	$550	$440	$395	$350	$325

Last MSR was $1,100.

AVB 95 - offset double cutaway mahogany body, walnut carved top/back, bolt-on maple neck, 24-fret rosewood fingerboard with pearl dot inlay, fixed bridge, 4-on-a-side tuners, gun metal hardware, 2 Seymour Duncan humbucking pickups, volume/balance/bass/treble active controls, bypass switch, available in Natural Walnut finish. Disc. 1996.

	$1,200	$800	$750	$595	$500	$450	$400

Last MSR was $1,600.

AVB MID 4 - offset double cutaway alder body, flamed maple carved top, bolt-on maple neck, 24-fret rosewood fingerboard with pearl dot inlay, BST-4 bass bridge, screened peghead logo, 4-on-a-side tuners, black hardware, 2 single coil SJS-04 pickups, piezo bridge pickups, magnetic pickup volume/magnetic pickup balance stacked controls, synth volume/magnetic pickup active bass EQ stacked controls, piezo pickup volume/magnetic pickup active treble EQ stacked controls, magnetic/piezo selector switch, S1/S2 controller switches. 1/4" phono output and 13-pin DIN connector jack mounted on side, available in Tobacco Sunburst finish only. Disc. 1994.

	$575	$495	$400	$350	$295	$250	$225

Headstock may read *Aria Custom Shop*. This model was designed to interface with a Roland GI-10 MIDI device. Aria also offered AVB MID 5 (5-string model), and the AVB MID 6 (6-string model).

AVB Steve Bailey Series

These AVB models were designed in collaboration with bassist Steve Bailey and Trev Wilkinson. Steve Bailey AVB bass models debuted in 1994.

6 AVB SB 4 D - offset double cutaway ash body, tortoiseshell pickguard, bolt-on maple neck, 24-fret rosewood fingerboard with pearl dot inlay, fixed bridge, 4-on-a-side tuners, pearl black hardware, 2 J-style Basslines by Seymour Duncan pickups, volume/concentric treble/bass controls, USA Seymour Duncan active electronics, available in 3-Tone Sunburst finish. New 1994.

MSR	$1,499	$1,125	$975	$855	$735	$615	$495	$375

See-Through Black finish added in 1999. This model has an optional fretless ebony fingerboard (AVB SB 4 FL).

6 AVB SB 5 D - similar to 6 AVB SB 4 D, except has 5-string configuration, 4/1 per side tuners, available in Three Tone Sunburst finish. New 1994.

MSR	$1,699	$1,275	$1,100	$965	$830	$695	$560	$425

This model has an optional fretless ebony fingerboard (AVB SB 5 FL).

6 AVB SB 6 D - similar to 6 AVB SB 4 D, except has 6-string configuration, 4/2-per-side tuners, black hardware, 2 humbucker pickups, available in Three Tone Sunburst finish. New 1994.

MSR	$1,999	$1,499	$1,299	$1,140	$980	$825	$665	$500

This model has an optional fretless ebony fingerboard (AVB SB 6 FL).

AVB TN Series

The AVB TN series features a maple neck-through design and alder body.

6 AVB TN 4 - offset double cutaway alder body, through-body maple neck, 24-fret rosewood fingerboard with pearl oval inlay, fixed bridge, 4-on-a-side tuners, black hardware, 2 J-style pickups, 2 volume/1 tone controls, active electronics, available in Natural and Walnut finishes. Mfg. 1994-99.

	$860	$750	$660	$565	$475	$380	$290

Last MSR was $1,149.

6 AVB TN 5 - similar to AVB TN 4, except has 5-string configuration, 4/1 per side tuners. Mfg. 1994-99.

	$899	$780	$685	$590	$495	$400	$300

Last MSR was $1,199.

6 AVB TN 6 - similar to AVB TN 4, except has 6-string configuration, 4/2-per-side tuners. Mfg. 1994-99.

	$975	$845	$745	$640	$540	$435	$325

Last MSR was $1,299.

Integra Bass Series

Integra basses have a carved top and slightly elongated top horn.

6 IGB 30 - offset double cutaway alder body, bolt-on maple neck, 24-fret rosewood fingerboard with pearl dot inlay, fixed bridge, 2-per-side tuners, chrome hardware, P/J-style pickups, 2 volume/1 tone controls, vailable in Black and Brown Sunburst finishes. Disc. 1994. Reintroduced 1999 in Black, Stained Natural, and Stained Walnut finishes.

MSR	$599	$450	$375	$315	$250	$225	$205	$190

6 IGB 40 - similar to IGB 30, except has maple neck through-body, double coil pickups, black hardware, available in Dark Oak and Natural Mahogany finishes. Disc. 1994. Reintroduced 1999.

MSR	$849	$650	$450	$375	$325	$275	$250	$200

GRADING		100% MINT	98% NEAR MINT	95% EXC+	90% EXC	80% VG+	70% VG	60% G

6 *IGB 50* - similar to IGB 30, except has mahogany body, Infinity double coil and single pickups, matte chrome hardware, volume/balance/active treble/active bass controls, available in Dark Oak and Natural Mahogany finishes. Disc. 1994. Reintroduced 1999.

MSR	$849	$650	$450	$400	$350	$300	$275	$225

6 IGB 58 - Ash carved top with rosewood fingerboard, 24-frets, one MBH-4 bass humbucker pickup, active treble, middle and bass controls, coil tap switch, bypass switch, matte chrome hardware, available in See-Through Blue and Stained Natural finishes. New 1999.

MSR	$859	$650	$450	$400	$325	$275	$225	$200

IGB 60 - similar to IGB 30, except has mahogany body, maple neck-through-body design, black hardware, volume/balance/active treble/active bass controls, available in Dark Oak and Natural Mahogany finishes. Disc. 1994.

$675 $450 $410 $320 $290 $265 $240

IGB SPT - jazz style maple body, bolt-on maple neck, 24-fret rosewood fingerboard with pearl dot inlay, fixed bridge, 2-per-side tuners, black hardware, P-style/J-style pickups, 2 volume/1 tone controls, available in Alsace Red, Black, Navy Blue and White finishes. Disc. 1992.

$450 $375 $315 $250 $225 $205 $190
Last MSR was $630.

IGB STD - similar to IGB-SPT, except has chrome hardware. Disc. 1996.

$675 $450 $410 $320 $290 $265 $240
Last MSR was $900.

IGB CST - similar to IGB SPT, except has sen body, gold hardware and volume/bass/treble/mix controls, available in Blue Shade, Dark Red Shade, Transparent Black and Transparent White finishes. Disc. 1993.

$700 $600 $500 $400 $360 $330 $300
Last MSR was $1,000.

IGB DLX - similar to IGB SPT, except has black hardware, volume/bass/treble/mix controls. Disc. 1996.

$750 $500 $470 $360 $325 $300 $275
Last MSR was $1,000.

IGB DLX/5 - similar to IGB DLX, except has 5-strings, 4/1 per side tuners, black hardware, volume/bass/treble/mix controls. Disc. 1996.

$825 $550 $520 $400 $360 $330 $300
Last MSR was $1,100.

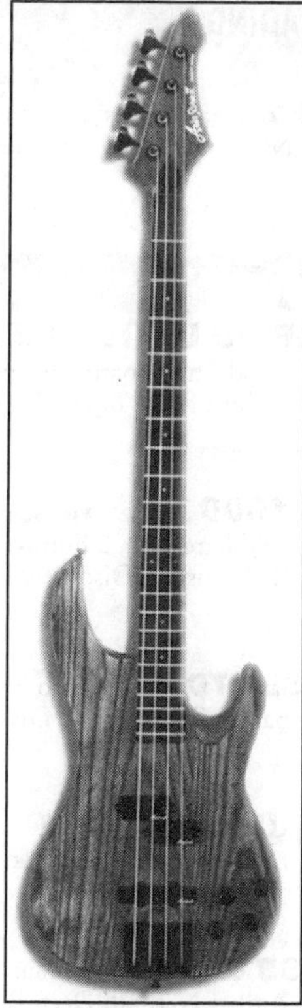
Aria Pro II MAB 50
courtesy Aria Pro II

Magna Bass Series

MAB 09 - offset double cutaway hardwood body, bolt-on maple neck, 22-fret maple fingerboard with black dot inlay, fixed bridge, 4-on-a-side tuners, chrome hardware, P/J-style pickups, 1 volume/2 tone controls, available in Black, Blue and Red finishes. Mfg. 1994 -96.

$325 $250 $200 $160 $145 $130 $120
Last MSR was $400.

MAB 20 - offset double cutaway alder body, bolt-on maple neck, 22-fret rosewood fingerboard with pearl dot inlay, fixed bridge, 4-on-a-side tuners, black hardware, P/J-style pickups, 2 volume/1 tone controls, available in Apple Red, Black, Midnight Blue and White finishes. Disc. 1996.

$400 $300 $250 $200 $180 $165 $150
Last MSR was $500.

MAB 20/5 - similar to MAB 20, except has 5-strings, 24-frets and 2 J-style pickups, available in Apple Red, Black and White finishes. Disc. 1996.

$395 $265 $250 $200 $180 $165 $150
Last MSR was $540.

MAB 25 - similar to MAB 20, except has P/J-style pickups, chrome hardware, available in Dark Oak, Natural, and See-Through Red semi-gloss finishes. Disc. 1994.

$525 $350 $320 $240 $215 $195 $180

MAB 40 - similar to MAB 20, except has active EQ in tone control, 3-position and bypass switch, available in Black, Midnight Cherry, Navy Blue, Pearl Black, Pearl White and White finishes. Disc. 1996.

$525 $350 $320 $240 $215 $195 $180
Last MSR was $700.

MAB 50 - similar to MAB 20, except has 24-frets, gold hardware, volume/bass/treble/mix controls, active electronics, available in Midnight Cherry, Pearl Black and Pearl White finishes. Disc. 1996.

$695 $595 $500 $400 $360 $330 $300
Last MSR was $995.

MAB 60 - offset double cutaway sen body, bolt-on maple neck, 24-fret rosewood fingerboard with pearl dot inlay, fixed bridge, 4-on-a-side tuners, gold hardware, 2 J-style pickups, volume/bass/treble/mix controls, available in Blue Shade, Dark Red Shade, Purple Shade and Vintage Sunburst finishes. Disc. 1992.

$835 $715 $600 $480 $430 $395 $360
Last MSR was $1,195.

GRADING	100% MINT	98% NEAR MINT	95% EXC+	90% EXC	80% VG+	70% VG	60% G

MAB 60/5 - similar to MAB-60, except has 5 strings, ebony fingerboard, black hardware and 2 double coil pickups, available in Midnight Cherry, Navy Blue, Pearl Black and Pearl White finishes. Disc. 1992.

	$835	$715	$600	$480	$430	$395	$360

Last MSR was $1,195.

Super Bass Series

6 SB 40 LIMITED EDITION 40TH ANNIVERSARY SUPER BASS - jazz style, alder body, bolt-on maple neck, 24-fret rosewood fingerboard with pearl dot inlay, fixed bridge, 2-per-side tuners, gold hardware, P/J-style active pickups, 2 volume/1 tone controls, available in Walnut finish only. Mfg. 1997-99.

	$675	$585	$525	$450	$375	$300	$225

Last MSR was $899.

SB 1000 - jazz style, sen body, maple/walnut through-body neck, 24-fret rosewood fingerboard with pearl dot inlay, fixed bridge, 2-per-side tuners, gold hardware, 2 humbucker pickups, 2 volume/1 tone controls, active electronics, available in Black, Light Oak, Transparent Black and Transparent Red finishes. Disc. 1993.

	$995	$850	$700	$550	$500	$450	$400

Last MSR was $1,400.

SB LTD - similar to SB 1000, except has ebony fingerboard with pearl oval inlay and Alembic pickups, available in Transparent Black and Transparent Red finishes. Disc. 1994.

	$1,250	$1,100	$900	$795	$675	$595	$525

Last MSR was $1,800.

SB JR 600 - jazz style, alder body, bolt-on maple neck, 24-fret rosewood fingerboard with pearl dot inlay, fixed bridge, 2-per-side tuners, black hardware, P/J-style pickup, 2 volume/1 tone controls, available in Midnight Cherry, Navy Blue, Pearl Black and Pearl White finishes. Disc. 1992.

	$595	$510	$425	$340	$305	$280	$255

Last MSR was $850.

SB JR 750 - similar to SB JR600, except has maple/walnut/sen body, gold hardware and volume/bass/treble and mixed controls, available in Amber Natural, Deep Blue and Dark Cherry Shade finishes. Disc. 1992.

	$770	$660	$550	$440	$395	$365	$330

Last MSR was $1,100.

STB Series

6 STB PB 01 - offset double cutaway hardwood body, black pickguard, bolt-on maple neck, 20-fret maple fingerboard with black dot inlay, fixed bridge, 4-on-a-side tuners, chrome hardware, P/J-style pickups, volume/tone controls, 3-position switch, available in Black, Blue, and 3-Tone Sunburst finishes. New 1994.

MSR $449	$340	$290	$255	$220	$185	$150	$115

6 STB PB 02 X - offset double cutaway hardwood body, flamed maple top and back, black pickguard, bolt-on maple neck, 20-fret rosewood fingerboard with white dot inlay, fixed bridge, 4-on-a-side tuners, gold hardware, P/J-style pickups, 2 volume/1 tone controls, 3-position switch, available in Dark Blue shade and Dark Red shade finishes. Disc. 1995.

	$325	$275	$225	$200	$180	$140	$100

Last MSR was $450.

6 STB PJ - offset double cutaway hardwood body, bolt-on maple neck, 20-fret rosewood fingerboard with pearl dot inlay, fixed bridge, 4-on-a-side tuners, chrome hardware, P/J-style pickups, volume/tone controls, 3-position switch, available in Black, Red, White, and 3-Tone Sunburst finishes. New 1995.

MSR $349	$260	$225	$200	$170	$145	$115	$90

6 STB PB - similar to above but with maple neck and fingerboard, one split pickup, volume and tone controls, available in Black, Blue, Red, and White finishes.

MSR $329	$250	$175	$150	$125	$100	$75	$50

6 STB PJ L - similar to the 6 STB PJ, except in left-handed configuration, available in Black finish only. New 1995.

MSR $379	$285	$250	$220	$190	$160	$125	$95

SWB Series

SWB basses were compact electric upright instruments equipped with Fishman pickups and Aria electronics. Original production was handled by the Aria Pro Custom Shop.

SWB 01 - sleek upright alder body, bolt-on neck, 41 1/3" scale, darkened maple fingerboard, 2-per-side slotted rounded headstock, maple bridge, Aria piezo pickup, chrome hardware, available in Black finish. Disc. 1994.

	$1,650	$1,275	$925	$850	$725	$625	$575

Last MSR was $2,899.

SWB 02 - sleek upright alder body, bolt-on neck, 41 1/3" scale, darkened maple fingerboard, 2-per-side slotted scroll headstock, maple bridge, Fishman BP-100 pickup, chrome hardware, available in Antique Violin color finish. Disc. 1994.

	$1,650	$1,275	$925	$850	$750	$650	$595

Last MSR was $2,999.

SWB 02/5 - similar to SWB 02, except has 5-string configuration, 2/3-per-side slotted scroll headstock, both Fishman BP-100 and BIR individual pickups, volume/active treble/active bass controls, pickup selector switch. Disc. 1994.

	$1,675	$1,300	$950	$875	$795	$675	$625

GRADING		100% MINT	98% NEAR MINT	95% EXC+	90% EXC	80% VG+	70% VG	60% G

SWB 04 - similar to SWB 02, except has alder back, maple carved top, ebony fingerboard, both Fishman BP-100 and BIS individual pickups, 2 f-holes, volume/attack/active treble/active bass controls, BIS and piezo on/off switches, BIS and piezo sensing controls, available in Brown Sunburst and Vintage Sunburst finishes. Current mfg.

MSR	$3,799	$2,850	$2,485	$2,250	$1,975	$1,700	$1,450	$1,100

ARIRANG

Instruments previously built in Korea during the early 1980s.

This trademark consists of entry level copies of American designs, and some original designs.

(Source: Tony Bacon and Paul Day, The Guru's Guitar Guide)

ARISTONE

See FRAMUS & BESSON.

Instruments previously built West Germany during the late 1950s through the early 1960s.

While ARISTONE was the brandname for a UK importer, these guitars were made by and identical to certain FRAMUS models. Research also indicates that the trademark BESSON was utilized as well.

(Source: Tony Bacon and Paul Day, The Guru's Guitar Guide)

ARITA

Instruments previously manufactured in Japan.

Arita instruments were distributed in the U.S. market by the Newark Musical Merchandise Company of Newark, New Jersey.

(Source: Michael Wright, Guitar Stories Volume One)

ARMSTRONG, DAN

See AMPEG.

Instruments previously produced in England between 1973 and 1975.

Luthier/designer Dan Armstrong has been involved in the music industry for over thirty years. Armstrong originally was a musician involved with studio recording in New York, and used to rent equipment from a music shop called Caroll's. The owner noticed that his rental instruments were coming back in better shape than when they went out, and began using Armstrong to repair guitars. In 1965, Armstrong opened his own luthier/repair shop on 48th Street across from Manny's Music, and one of his first customers was John Sebastian (Loving Spoonful). As his new business grew, his studio calls for standby work also had him working with numerous artists. Armstrong's shop was open from 1966 to 1968 (which was then demolished to make room for the Rockefeller building), and then he switched locations to a shop in Laguardia Place in the Village.

Armstrong's shop used to sell new instruments as well. Armstrong used to stabilize Danelectros by changing the factory tuners for after-market Klusons, and by replacing the factory bridges. Nat Daniels (Danelectro) once visited his shop, and upon discovering Armstrong's *stabilizing* techniques, got mad and left.

A year after MCA folded the Danelectro company in 1968, Armstrong met William C. Herring at a swap meet in New Jersey. Herring had bought the company from MCA in late 1968/early 1969, and Armstrong acquired some interest in the trademark. The facilities produced some 650 to 700 single cutaway models that had one humbucker, no peghead logo, and **Dan Armstrong Modified Danelectro** on the pickguard.

During the same time period, Armstrong was contracted by Ampeg to produce solid body guitars and basses. Prototypes of the lucite bodied-instruments were produced in 1969, and production ran from 1970 to 1971. Lucite was chosen for its sustaining properties but the novelty of a transparent body led to the nickname *See-Throughs* (which Ampeg later had copy written). The clear bodied guitars featured interchangeable pickups designed by Bill Lawrence; however, the plastic was prone to expanding when the body warmed up. While most of the production was clear lucite, a number of instruments were also cast in black lucite.

In 1973, Armstrong moved to England and produced wood body guitars based on the lucite designs. These guitars had the same sliding pickup design, and an anodized aluminum pickguard. The English wood body instruments were produced between 1973 and 1975.

Armstrong produced a number of non-guitar designs as well. Armstrong assisted in some designs for Ampeg's SVT bass amp and the V-4 guitar amplifiers. Musictronics produced the Dan Armstrong Boxes in the mid 1970s, while Armstrong was still living in England. These six small boxes of circuitry plugged into the guitar directly, and then a cable was attached to the amplifier. Modules included the Red Ranger (EQ), Blue Clipper (distortion), Purple Peaker (EQ), Green Ringer (ring modulator), Yellow Humper (EQ) and the acclaimed Orange Squeezer (compression). Armstrong also had a hand in devising the Mutron Octave divider, Volume Wah, and *Gizmo.*

Dan Armstrong stayed busy in the early to mid 1980s inventing circuit designs and building prototypes of amplifiers in a consulting fashion. Armstrong was featured in numerous ***Guitar Player*** magazine articles on aftermarket rewiring schematics that expanded the potential voicings of Fender and Gibson production guitar models. Armstrong built some guitar prototypes for the Westone product line in the late 1980s, and his most recent project was the *Hot Cabs* instrument speaker line for Cerwin Vega, and overseeing St. Louis Music/Ampeg's Reissue guitar models.

(Biographical information courtesy Dan Armstrong)

May/June 1996.

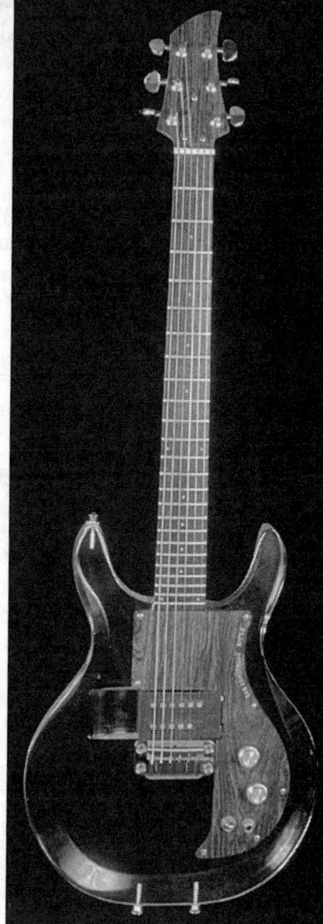

Dan Armstrong/Ampeg ARMG 2
courtesy Elliot Rubinson

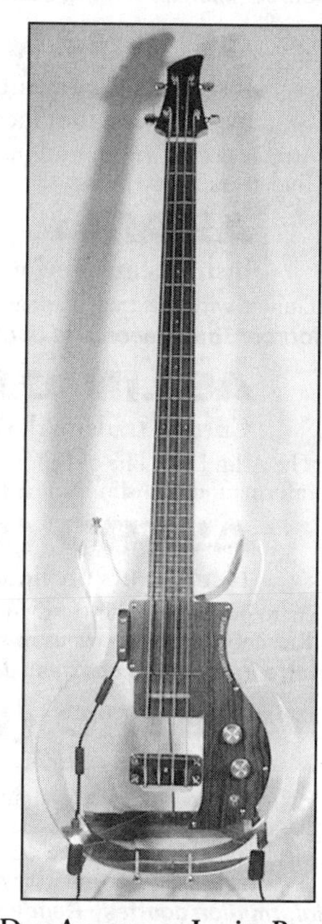

Dan Armstrong Lucite Bass
courtesy Jack Wadsworth

ARMSTRONG, ROB

Instruments previously built in England during the late 1970s, possibly also the early to mid 1980s as well.

Luthier Rob Armstrong is known for his custom guitar building. One of his more famous jobs appears to be a Kellogg's Corn Flakes box-turned-guitar for Simon Nicol (Fairport Convention).

(Source: Tony Bacon, The Ultimate Guitar Book)

ARPEGGIO KORINA

Instruments currently built in Pennsylvania since 1995. Distributed by the Arpeggio Korina Guitar Company, a division of Arpeggio Music, Inc.

Ron and Marsha Kayfield have been running Arpeggio Music, Inc. since 1992. Their music shop deals in new, used, and vintage guitars and amplifiers. Arpeggio Music also offers new and vintage refinishing, as well as restoration and repairs.

In 1995, Ron introduced the Korina model, which combines the best features of earlier guitar models in one new versatile package. Guitar players may note the *stingray*-shaped 3+3 headstock design and arrow-shaped truss rod cover. The access to the truss rod has been moved back away from the nut to avoid the potential *weak neck* syndrome inherent in other designs. Headstocks are tilted back 17 degrees, and the neck has custom-shaped '50s or '60s neck profiles. The Arpeggio Korina Guitar company also offers custom inlay in both abalone and mother-of-pearl (call for price quote) on their handmade guitars.

Arpeggio Korina Series

All Korina electronics feature Seymour Duncan pickups and custom wiring by Rusty Gray of Musician's Electronic Service. Both the volume and tone controls feature push/push potentiometers: The volume pot controls both the overall volume of the instrument, as well as controlling the pickups phase/out of phase while the selector is in the middle position; the tone pot controls both the overall tone of the instrument as well as coil tapping mode.

ARPEGGIO KORINA CUSTOM - single cutaway korina body, wood binding, hand-carved premium tiger maple book-matched top, korina set neck, Brazilian rosewood fingerboard with abalone diamond snowflake inlay, brass string-through *V*-shaped tailpiece/trapeze bridge, 3+3 *stingray*-shaped headstock, gold hardware, 2 Seymour Duncan '59 humbucking pickups, volume/tone push/push controls, 3-way selector switch, available in Chestnut Burst, Ice Tea Burst, Natural, Tequila Sunrise, Vintage Amber Burst, Vintage Natural, and other transparent nitrocellulose finishes. Current mfg.

MSR $3,600

Retail price includes a fitted hardshell case. Flamed tiger maple or tiger Koa fingerboards are options.

ARPEGGIO KORINA PLAYER - similar to the Korina Custom, except has an ebony or rosewood fingerboard, abalone or mother-of-pearl dot inlays, nickel hardware and custom brass *V*-shaped tailpiece, and no maple top.

MSR $2,800

Retail price includes a fitted hardshell case.

ARTISAN

Instruments previously produced in Japan.

Artisan instruments were distributed in the U.S. market by the Barth-Feinberg company of New York.

(Source: Michael Wright, Guitar Stories Volume One)

ARTISAN (CURRENT MFG.)

Instruments currently manufactured by Eikosha Musical Instrument Co., Inc. of Nagoya, Japan. Distributed in the U.S. by V.J. Rendano, located in Boardman, OH.

Artisan electric instruments include good quality archtop models. Please contact the distributor directly for more information and current pricing (See Trademark Index).

ASAMA

Instruments previously built in Japan during the early 1980s.

Guitars with this trademark are generally medium to good quality copies of American design as well as some original designs.

(Source: Tony Bacon and Paul Day, The Guru's Guitar Guide)

ASLIN DANE

Current trademark distributed by David Burns Musical Instruments Inc., located in West Islip, NY.

The Aslin Dane line of Fender styled electric guitars and basses are available in 4 various configurations. Please contact the distributor directly for more information on Aslin Dane instruments (see Trademark Index).

ASTRO (U.S. MFG.)

Instruments previously produced in California circa 1963.

Astro guitars were kit (ready to assemble) guitars produced in the Rickenbacker factory around 1963. There was no reference whatsoever to Rickenbacker (for obvious reasons). Research continues on Astro Guitars for upcoming editions of the *Blue Book of Electric Guitars*.

(Astro information courtesy John Hall, Rickenbacker International Corporation)

ASTRO (ITALY MFG.)

Instruments previously built in Italy during the mid to late 1960s. The U.S. distributor is currently unknown.

Astro guitars are entry level instruments, similar to other late 1960s *strat-y* import/exports. According to owner Randy Varrone, his two pickup model has a bolt-on neck (four bolts and a plate), a ply body, six-on-a-side headstock, and a white pickguard with 2 pickups and controls mounted on it. The electronic controls feature a pickup selector marked "B/ALL/T", a volume knob, and two tone knobs marked "B" and "G".

As these instruments were entry level to begin with, used models are generally priced between $79 and $119.

(Information courtesy Randy Varrone, Pulse Music of Logansport, Indiana)

ATELIER Z

Instruments currently produced in Japan. Previously distributed by the Day's Corporation of Tokyo, Japan.

Atelier Z instruments are high quality guitars and basses new to the U.S. market.

ELECTRIC

Progressive series guitars featured a Strat-ish sort of design, with a shorter rounded bass horn, alder body, Gotoh (or Schaller tuners) and 635 mm scale (25"). The **AG-STD** Standard (last retail was $1,320 in 1998) has 3 Atelier Z single coil pickups, while the **AG-DLX** Deluxe (last retail was $1,633 in 1998) has 2 single coils and a humbucker in the bridge position.

ELECTRIC BASS

M Standard model basses are similar to Jazz basses, except feature 2 volume/treble/bass controls and matching headstock finishes. The **MZ-188** Basic 4-string (list $1,400) has a 2-piece ash body and BadAss II bridge; the **M-245** 4-string ($1,750) and **M-265** ($1,900) Standard basses have a Bartolini XTCT preamp.

The more modern and sleek design of the **US** series feature a 2-piece ash body and maple neck/maple fingerboard. The **ZX-500** 5-string ($2,000) has Bartolini FN5W pickups, Bartolini NTMB preamp and volume/balancer/3-band EQ controls; the **ZAP-600** 6-string (list $2,500) has Bartolini FN6W pickups and a Demeter BEQP-1 preamp.

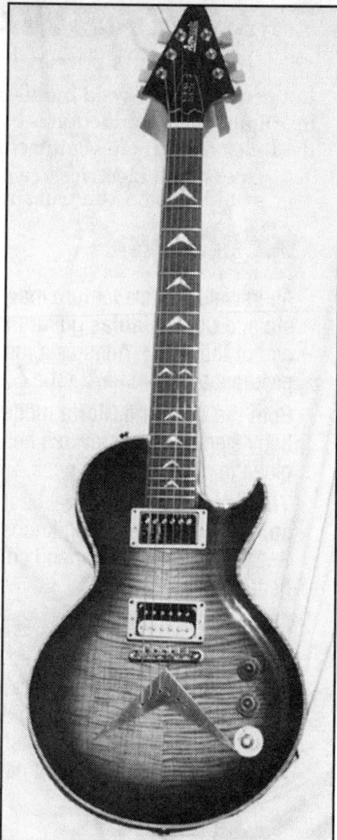

Arpeggio Korina Custom
courtesy Ron and
Marsha Kayfield

ATHELETE

Instruments previously built in New York, New York.

Luthier Fumi Nozawa created these high quality 4, 5, or 6-string acoustic basses, as well as acoustic guitars for several years.

ATLANSIA

Instruments currently built in Matsumoto (Nagano), Japan. Distributed by Atlansia Instrumental Technology, Ltd. of Matsumoto, Japan.

The best way to describe instruments designed and built by luthier N. Hayashi is *sleek*. Every curve on any model seems aerodynamic, and the instruments have a nice balance to them. During the early 1980s, models like the Concorde, Stealth, and Galaxie were offered in the U.S. market (the U.S. distributor was based in Texas). These models, and many more, are still available through the manufacturer in Japan.

Atlansia guitars and basses are readily identifiable by the Atlansia logo on the headstock (or body). Models will feature either covered single coil or humbucker pickups; Atlansia also produces the ARS individual round pickups (generally one per string) which are the size of dimes. These pickups are similar to the individual round Bunker designs in that each one contains its own pole piece and winding.

ELECTRIC

While bass models seem to "rule the roost" at Atlansia, there are at least 5 guitar models regularly produced. The **Century** is a semi-hollow design with a single cutaway body and 2 f-holes. The **Stroke** is offset double cutaway solid body, with either a single or two single coil pickups. The **Pentagon, Victoria**, and **Stealth** guitar models have matching bass model conterparts.

ELECTRIC BASS

The **Pentagon** bass model has a sleek, single cutaway body. The **Garland** model has a slightly offset double cutaway shape, with extra shaping in the lower bout. **Concord** models have an extended bass horn, and mild cutaway on the treble side. The **Stealth** model has a similar body shape, but features a slim 4-in-line tuning machine profile (as opposed to the Concord's 3/1 per side headstock). **Victoria** basses have a scrolled bass horn; **Galaxy** and **Pegasus** models have a very extended bass horn and sloped treble bout (no treble side horn). The **Solitaire** featured a body shaped like a pool cue with a single string, bridge unit, and one pickup (you would think that a single string bass model would appeal to 'heavy metal' bass players in the mid 1980s!). The other models are not that extreme; any of the 4-, 5-, or 6-string models are well-balanced and eminently playable.

ATLAS

See chapter on House Brands.

This trademark has been identified as a "House Brand" of the RCA Victor Records Stores.

(Source: Willie G. Moseley, Stellas & Stratocasters)

AUDITION

See chapter on House Brands.

This trademark has been identified by researcher Willie G. Moseley as a "House Brand" of the F. W. Woolworth (Woolco) department stores.

Further information from authors Tony Bacon and Paul Day indicate that guitars with this trademark originated in Japan (later Korea) during the 1960s and 1970s.

(Source: Tony Bacon and Paul Day, The Guru's Guitar Guide)

AUERSWALD

Instruments currently built in Konstanz, Germany since the early 1990s.

Luthier Jerry Auerswald builds high quality original design solid body guitars and basses that are visually exciting as well. Auerswald hand crafts all his instruments, so production is based on his output alone. For further information regarding specifications and pricing, please contact Auerswald through the Index of Current Manufacturers located in the back of this book.

Auerswald electrics are easily identified by the unique body/neck design, the additional *sustain bow* on three of the models, and the Auerswald logo on the truss rod cover and bridge hardware. All models feature Auerswald hardware (bridge, string rider, tremolo).

ELECTRIC

Auerswald models feature maple bodies, cherry/wenge necks, EMG pickups, Sperzel hardware, and Auerswald custom tremolo and EQ systems. The **Anastasia** and **Chico Hablas** guitar models both feature a *sustain bow* (a body arm that attaches to the headstock and provides extra stiffening support to the upper end of the neck). Anastasia models feature wenge bodies, cherry necks, 33-fret ebony fingerboards (66 cm scale), 2 EMG single coil/humbucker (model 81) pickups, and volume/2 tone controls.

Both the **Diva** and **Gloria** models feature angular semi-hollow bodies and reverse headstock designs as well as *V*-shaped f-holes. The **Naomi** and **Viva** solid body electrics have reverse headstocks, and exaggerated top horns to accentuate the sleek body contours. The Naomi *Power Slam* model has a maple body, glued-in cherry/wenge neck, 27-fret ebony fingerboard (66 cm scale), 2 EMG 89 humbuckers, and Sperzel tuners.

The **Venus** 8-string model has a pair of sustain bows on either side of the neck, culminating in an open triangular headpiece. This model features reverse stringing, and the tuning knobs are cleverly concealed on the back of the lower bout. The **Aliki** acoustic/electric model has three *cat's eye*-shaped f-holes, a 3+3 slotted headstock, and controls mounted on the side of the upper bout. This model is also offered in a 4-string acoustic/electric bass, with a 2+2 solid headstock.

ELECTRIC BASS

The **Hammer** bass model has a cherry wood body with extended bass and treble horns, glued-in neck, 25-fret ebony fingerboard (86.4 cm scale), and reverse stringing (tuners near bridge). Electronics consist of a set of EMG P/J pickups, 2 volume/one tone controls. Auerswald also offers the **Cleo** bass model, which features a **sustain bow**: a body arm that attaches to the headstock and provides extra stiffening support to the upper end of the neck. Cleo basses feature wenge bodies, cherry wood necks, 24-fret ebony fingerboards (86.4 cm scale), 2 Auerswald (or EMG) humbuckers, and 2 volume/one tone controls.

AUROC

Instruments currently built in England since 1988.

Luthier Pat Luckett builds guitars with a 'strat'-styled synthetic marble body coupled with a graphite neck. A promising design that may eliminate the "tweakage" phenomenon of wood necks. The *Blue Book of Electric Guitars* encourages anyone with further information to contact us for future edition updates.

AUSTIN

Instruments currently built in Korea and China. Distributed by St. Louis Music of St. Louis, Missouri.

Asian-produced Austin instruments are good quality entry or student level acoustic and electric guitars.

ELECTRIC

The **Austin Era Standard** (retail $199) has a 'Strat'-style ply body, with three single coil pickups; the **Era Deluxe** (retail $249) has a rosewood fingerboard and 2 single coil/humbucker pickups. The **Era Deluxe** is also available in a left-handed configuration.

The **Austin Mini Era** (retail list $149) is a scaled-down electric with one single coil pickup, volume control, and adjustable bridge; the **Mini Era Deluxe** (list $179) has 3 single coils, volume and tone controls, and a traditional tremolo.

The **Vintage Rock** (list $329) is an archtop model with multi-layer celluloid body binding, 2 humbuckers, and a tune-o-matic bridge.

ELECTRIC BASS

Austin bass models feature hardwood bodies, bolt-on maple necks, and fixed bridges. The **AU 759** P-style bass (list $269) has a split P-style pickup; this model has an optional left-handed configuration (**Model AU 770**), or in Black, Red, Sunburst, or Transparent Blue finishes. The **AU 769** PJ-style bass has P/J-style pickups and a rosewood fingerboard (list $299). The **AU 779 Intruder Bass** has 2 J-style pickups, rosewood fingerboard, and chrome hardware.

AUSTIN HATCHET

Trademark of instruments previously distributed by Targ and Dinner of Chicago, Illinois circa mid 1970s to early 1980s. Instrument production location unknown.

The Austin Hatchet was one of the first *travel guitars* (along with Erlewine's Chiquita model) available for the "musician on the move".

ELECTRIC

The **Austin Hatchet** is a scaled down electric with a wedge-shaped body, 22-fret fingerboard, 3-per-side *arrowhead* headstock, 2 humbuckers, fixed bridge, 2 volume/1 tone knobs, pickup selector switch, and phase switch.

The company also offered a **Flying V**-style model, with gold hardware, brass nut, 2 humbuckers, and a "lead" switch. The **Flying V** model was 43" long, and 17" across the bottom "V" wings.

Austin Hatchet models in good condition may range between $150 and $200.

AVALON

See WANDRE'.

Instruments such as Avalon's Rock Oval model were produced in Italy during the 1960s.

AVANTI

Instruments previously produced in Europe during the 1960s.

Research continues into this trademark. Most models that are encountered seem to have a resounding feel of 1960s entry level Italian production. Further information will be updated in future editions of the *Blue Book of Electric Guitars*.

(Source: Rittor Books, 60s Bizarre Guitars)

AVON

Instruments previously built in Japan during the early to late 1970s.

The AVON trademark is the brandname of a UK importer. Avons are generally low to medium quality copies of American designs.

(Source: Tony Bacon and Paul Day, The Guru's Guitar Guide)

AW SHADOWS GUITARS

Instruments currently built in Princeton, Minnesota.

In 1998, AW Shadows introduced a new take on guitar body shapes: Curved! The **CRS Curve** guitar incorporates a traditional single cutaway body design with an ergonomic vertical curve in the lower bout, beginning after the bridge/stop tailpiece. This patent-pending design lets players keep their arms in a natural position close to the body, eliminating "playing-related maladies such as tendinitis, carpal tunnel syndrome, muscle strain, and back pain," as the company claims.

The CRS Curve model features a cherry wood body with walnut accents, maple neck-through design, 24 1/2" scale, rosewood or ebony fingerboards, custom made ebony saddle, 3-per-side tuners, 2 humbuckers, 2 volume/2 tone controls, and 3-way toggle switch. Currently available in a Natural finish (price $TBA).

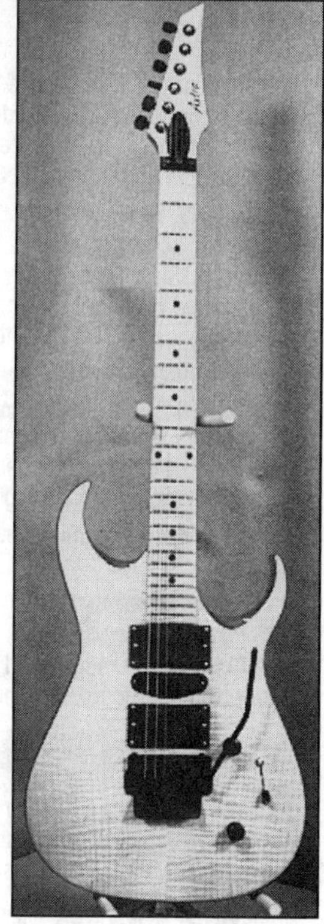

Axtra Custom
courtesy Bill Michaelis

AXE

Instruments previously built in Korea from 1988 to 1989.

Entry level two pickup guitar that came in a "starter pack". Although we're not familiar with the guitar, the idea of a package containing all sorts of guitar paraphernalia (how-to booklet, strings, tuner of some sort, strap, etc.) actually sounds like a novel idea if coupled with lessons.

(Source: Tony Bacon and Paul Day, The Guru's Guitar Guide)

AXELSON

Instruments currently built in Duluth, Minnesota.

Luthier Randy Axelson has been providing top-notch guitar repair, restoration, and custom guitar building on a regular basis. For information, pricing, and availability contact luthier Axelson through the Index of Current Manufacturers located in the back of this book.

AXEMAN

Instruments previously built in Japan during the late 1970s.

The AXEMAN trademark is the brand name of a UK importer. The guitars are generally medium quality copies of American designs.

(Source: Tony Bacon and Paul Day, The Guru's Guitar Guide)

AXIS

Instruments previously built in Korea circa 1989.

The AXIS trademark is the brand name of a UK importer. Axis guitars are entry level to medium quality solid body copies of American designs.

(Source: Tony Bacon and Paul Day, The Guru's Guitar Guide)

AXTECH

Instruments currently built in Korea.

Axtech instruments are generally entry level to medium quality solid body and acoustic guitars based on Classic American designs.

AXTRA

Instruments currently built in Kenosha, Wisconsin since 1985. Distributed by Axtra Guitars, Inc. of Kenosha, Wisconsin.

Axtra Guitars, Inc. was founded in 1985 by Bill Michaelis, who heads the organization. His tremendous creativity, experience, innovativeness, and commitment to the highest standards of manufacturing excellence has been the key to the great satisfaction of guitar players who own Axtra instruments.

This company is not a huge impersonal organization, but a custom specialty shop that also manufactures a standard line of guitars and basses. Personally run by Bill, where dedication to the finest quality products, service, and customer satisfaction is the basic aim. The result is a modern, progressive company dedicated to meeting the needs of every musician: Great Sound - Versatility - Reliability - Durability - Individual Custom Features. Everyone at Axtra takes great pride in producing the highest quality guitars and basses.

(Source: Bill Michaelis, Axtra Guitars)

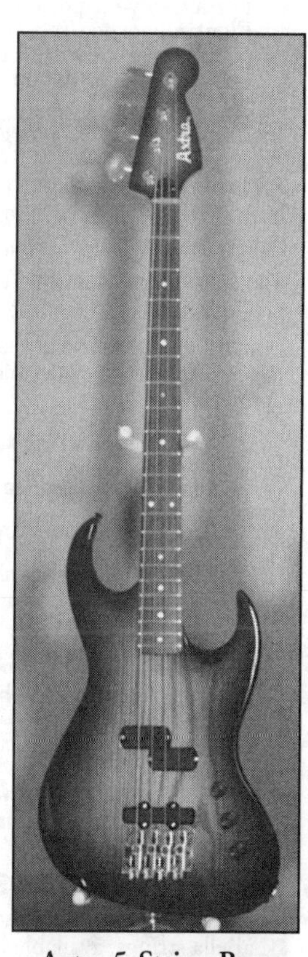

Axtra 5-String Bass
courtesy Bill Michaelis

ELECTRIC

Michaelis offers a number of body designs, as well as the flexibility of a custom design (hardware, pickups, and other options are at the customer's choice). Some of the Axtra standard designs include bolt-on or set-neck designs; quartersawn maple or mahogany necks; maple, rosewood, ebony, pau ferro, bubinga, or wenge fingerboards; figured maple or curly birch tops; ash, mahogany, basswood, and maple bodies; locking or non-locking tremolos, or tune-o-matic bridges; Sperzel tuners; and Seymour Duncan pickups. Instruments are finished in transparent or solid colors, or custom graphics.

Bolt-On Neck Models

The Axtra "Strat"-style guitar model (suggested list price starts at $1,200, and up) features a choice of basswood or maple or mahogany body, maple bolt-on neck, maple fretboard, Seymour Duncan pickups, and Wilkinson hardware. A "Tele"-style guitar model had a single cutaway body design, but similar construction details as the 'Strat'. The list price starts at $1,600 and up, depending on options.

Designer Models

Axtra offers a number of specialty models based on the "strat" or "super strat" configuration. The 7/8 Strat has a flame maple top/basswood body, maple neck, 22-fret rosewood fingerboard, 25 1/2" scale, Wilkinson bridge, and many options to explore at a list price of $1,800. A full sized mahogany body with curly birch top is offered beginning at $2,000; the same mahogany body can be matched with a carved curly birch top for $2,400.

A custom 7-string semi-hollow "Tele" is available with a flamed maple body, special Seymour Duncan pickups, custom bridge, and ebony fingerboard at $2,400.

Stylist Series

The Axtra Stylist (suggested list price starts at $1,800 and up) features a flame maple top, basswood body, maple set-in neck, 25 1/2" scale, 24-fret bound pau ferro fingerboard with musical note inlay, and Gotoh bridge. Also offered in a 24-fret bolt-on neck design for $2,000.

ELECTRIC BASS

Axtra offers both a P-style and a P/J-styled model bass in 4-, 5-, and 6-string configurations. The suggested list price begins at $1,500 (and up). Many options (like a Northern Ash body, bubinga fingerboard, and quartersawn maple neck) are available on the bass models. Axtra also has their own sleek bass design in a maple body and Bartolini soapbar pickups that starts at $2,400.

AZOLA BASSES

Instruments currently built in Ramona, CA. Previously built in San Marcos, CA.

Since bringing the Baby Bass back to life and giving it their own twist and modern versatility, Azola's line of electric uprights has grown dramatically. In 1997, the evolution of the Baby Bass came full circle when Ampeg contracted Azola to manufacture the official re-issue Ampeg Baby Bass with its fiberglass body and magnetic diaphragm pickup system plus piezo bridge pickups (fiberglass-bodied Ampeg Baby Basses are available through Ampeg dealers only).

Azola offers Baby Basses under their own name in a hardwood hollow body version available with any of their various pickup options (and they still offer replacement parts and accessories for vintage Ampeg and Zorko Baby Basses). Bassbegruven!

For a two year period, Azola offered an upright, violin-shaped Mahogany body StradiBass model, which featured a Clevinger-designed Floating spruce Top, figured maple laminated neck, ebony fingerboard, 41.5" scale, maple bridge, gold hardware, and a multi-piezo bridge pickup system with 3-band active EQ at a retail price of $4,995. Many aspects of this design have either been incorporated into the current models, or have become options available to all models.

ELECTRIC UPRIGHT BASS

Azola offers three different models in either **Standard** or **Floating Top** configuration, and a large number of options to choose from. The **Standard Series** bass configuration shares these features: ash bodies, 2-piece maple tilt-adjust neck, bubinga fingerboard, 41.5" scale, piezo bridge pickups with passive volume control, adjustable endpin and bout, black hardware, LaBella strings, and are finished in a natural semi-gloss finish.

The semi-hollow **Floating Top** configuration features an arched spruce top on an ash body (a design concept from Martin Clevinger), a bass bar and sound post, passive bass boost/arco sensitive control, Thomastik strings, and an ebony fingerboard.

Options, upgrades and accessories available for all the listed models include six different types of pickup systems, such as the Clevinger-design bridge/dual piezo system, multi-piezo bridge pickup system, and the *Latin* (and Latin+) pickup system. Custom color high gloss finishes are also available on all three models.

Add $75 for position markers.

Add $100 for "Iced Tea" sunburst semi-gloss finish.

Add $150 for ebony fingerboard.

Add $300 for on-board preamp with active EQ.

Add $500 for 5-string configuration.

STANDARD BABY BASS - classical shape, ash body, 2-piece maple tilt-adjust neck, bubinga fingerboard, 41.5" scale, 2-per-side tuners on slotted headstock, scroll headpiece, piezo bridge pickups with passive volume control, adjustable endpin and bout, black hardware, LaBella strings, available in Natural semi-gloss finish. Current mfg.

MSR $3,495

Floating Top Baby Bass - similar to the Standard Baby Bass, except features semi-hollow body construction, arched spruce top, ebony fingerboard, bass bar, soundpost. New 1998.

MSR $4,495

STANDARD BUGBASS - ultra compact upright body style, ash body, 2-piece maple tilt-adjust neck, bubinga fingerboard, 41.5" scale, 2-per-side tuners on slotted headstock, rounded headpiece, piezo bridge pickups with passive volume control, adjustable endpin and bout, black hardware, LaBella strings, available in Natural semi-gloss finish. Current mfg.

MSR $1,495

Floating Top BugBass - similar to the Standard BugBass, except features semi-hollow body construction, arched spruce top, ebony fingerboard, bass bar, sound post. New 1998.

MSR $2,495

STANDARD MINIBASS - sleek contoured violin-shaped upright body, ash body, 2-piece maple tilt-adjust neck, bubinga fingerboard, 41.5" scale, 2-per-side tuners on slotted headstock, scroll headpiece, piezo bridge pickups with passive volume control, adjustable endpin and bout, black hardware, LaBella strings, available in Natural semi-gloss finish. Current mfg.

MSR $2,295

Floating Top MiniBass - similar to the Standard MiniBass, except features semi-hollow body construction, arched spruce top, ebony fingerboard, bass bar, sound post. New 1998.

MSR $3,495

Azola Custom Shop

The Azola Custom Shop's special Deco Bass model (call for list price) features an arched spruce top over a hollow body, maple neck, upright-style fingerboard, 34" scale, and multi-piezo bridge pickup system. Contact Azola for further specifications.

The Limited Edition Package of the Bugbass, Minibass, and Baby Bass instruments are handcrafted in a variety of fine hardwoods in a sculpted body style, figured tops and necks, and gloss finishes (call for prices).

Jazzman Series

Azola's Jazzman Series is part of their Custom Shop operations. The **Jazzman I** features an offset double cutaway body, J-style neck and fingerboard/4-on-a-side tuners, one Basslines humbuckering pickup, 3-band active EQ, and a semi-gloss finish. Prices begin at $1,295. The **Jazzman II** (prices start at $1,295) is similar in design, but features 2 Bassline humbuckers (with coil switching), and passive volume and tone controls. The semi-hollow **Jazzman III** has a spruce top, upright style fingerboard, magnetic or piezo pickup, and passive volume and tone controls. The **Jazzman III's** list price begins at $1,995.

Jazzman model Upgrades include exotic woods (call for prices), a figured top (add $250), custom color or sunburst gloss finish (add $250), the "Vintage Package" of pickguard and control plate (add $100), and an active EQ (add $250).

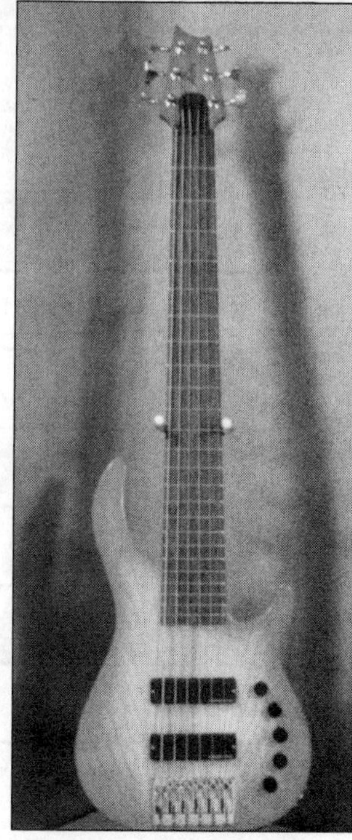

Axtra 6-String Bass
courtesy Axtra Guitars

AZUMI

See LEW CHASE.

Instruments previously built in Japan during the early 1980s.

Azumi guitars were generally medium quality solidbodys of original design. Research continues to document these body designs.

(Source: Tony Bacon and Paul Day, The Guru's Guitar Guide)

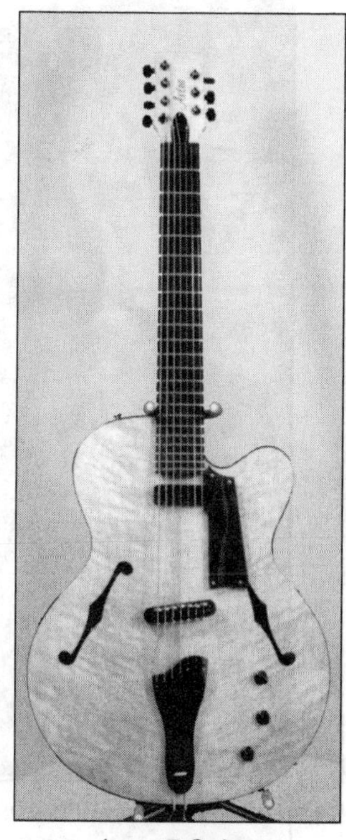

Axtra 7-String
Semi Acoustic
courtesy Bill Michaelis

NOTES

The Legendary Bill Carson outside the Fender booth with a maple neck. Bill has to be the second hardest working man in the music business.

Section B

B & G

See chapter on House Brands.

B & G instruments were built by Danelectro in Neptune City, New Jersey in the late 1950s/early 1960s.

(Source: Willie G. Moseley, Stellas & Stratocasters)

B & J

See chapter on House Brands.

This trademark has been identified as a House Brand of the B & J company.

(Source: Willie G. Moseley, Stellas & Stratocasters)

B.C. RICH

Instruments currently built in Hesperia, California (American Handmade series) and Asia (N.J., Platinum and Bronze series). Distributed by B.C. Rich Guitars International, Inc. of San Bernadino, California and B.C. Rich Guitars USA. Import models (N.J., Platinum, and Bronze Series) distributed by Davitt & Hanser Music of Cincinnati, Ohio.

Luthier Bernardo Chavez Rico used to build classical and flamenco guitars at Bernardo's Valencian Guitar Shop, the family's business in Los Angeles. During the mid 1960s folk music boom (and boom in guitar sales), a distributor suggested a name change - and B.C. Rich guitars was born. Between 1966 and 1968, Rico continued to build acoustic guitars, then changed to solid body electrics. The company began producing custom guitars based on Fender and Gibson designs, but Rico wanted to produce designs that represented his tastes and ideals. The Seagull solid body (first produced in 1971) was sleek, curvy, and made for rock & roll. Possessing a fast neck, hot-rodded circuitry and pickups, and a unique body profile was (and still is) an eye-catching design.

In 1974, Neal Mosher joined the company. Mosher also had a hand in some of the guitars designed, and further explored other designs with models like the Mockingbird, Eagle, Ironbird, and the provocatively-named Bich. The first 6-tuners-on-a-side headstocks began to appear in 1981. In the mid 1980s, B.C. Rich moved from Los Angeles to El Monte, California.

The company began to import models in the **U.S. Production Series**, Korean-produced kits that were assembled in the U.S. between 1984 to 1986. In 1984, the Japanese-built **N.J. Series** line of B.C. Rich designs were introduced, and were built by the Terada company for two years. Production of the N.J. series was moved to Korea in 1986 (models were built in the Cort factory).

In 1988, Rico licensed the Korean-built lower priced **Platinum** and entry level **Rave Series** to the Class Axe company, and later licensed the B.C. Rich name and designs in 1989. Class Axe moved production of the U.S.-built guitars to a facility in Warren, New Jersey, and stepped up importation of the N.J. (named after Nagoya, Japan - not New Jersey), Platinum, and Rave Series models.

Unfortunately, the lower priced series soon began to show a marked drop in quality. In 1994, Rico came back out of semi-retirement, retook control over his trademark, and began to rebuild the company. Rico became partners with Bill Shapiro, and the two divided up areas of responsibility. Rico once more began building acoustic and high end electrics at his Hesperia facilities; and Shapiro began maintaining quality control over the imported N.J., Platinum, and U.S. series in San Bernadino. In 1998, Davitt & Hanser Music of Cincinnati, Ohio began distributing the import models (N.J., Platinum, and Bronze Series).

(Additional model commentary courtesy Bernie Rich, President/Founder of B.C. Rich International, May 1997)

Model Series Identification

B.C. Rich models all have different body profiles. However, this distinct model profile may be offered in one of five different series, and those different series have different price levels based on construction and distinctions.

American Production: Any American-built **neck-through** guitar or bass with **B.C. Rich, Rico**, or **R** logos has a new retail price between $1,499 to $1,999 (Robert Conti models and double neck 6/12 models run higher).

The American-built guitars and basses with **bolt-on neck** construction are priced in a lower range between $1,199 to $1,299.

Import Production: Overall, the **Elite Series** import instruments feature a bolt-on neck and entry level hardware and pickups. There are three current branches to the Elite Series Electric guitars: Bronze (formerly U.S.), Platinum, and N.J.

Bronze series (formerly the **U.S.** series): These 2 models are priced slightly above where the discontinued **Rave/U.S.** series were: between $349 and $369.

Platinum series: This is the more moderate series, and the 6 models are priced between $499 and $599.

N.J. series: These 3 models are priced at $699. With each step up in pricing, there is an equivalent step up in quality (construction and hardware).

B.C. Rich Active Electronics

B.C. Rich has a long history of offering on-board active electronic packages. Here's a short guide to all those extra switches and knobs:

GRADING	100% MINT	98% NEAR MINT	95% EXC+	90% EXC	80% VG+	70% VG	60% G

The **Active Electronic** package available on Mockingbird Supreme and Eagle Supreme (guitar and bass models) consists of (listed top to bottom, as if the guitar was held by the neck): Master Volume knob, Pickup Selector Switch, Pre-Amp Volume Knob, Pre-Amp On/Off switch, a 6-position Vari-Tone 'chicken head' knob, phase mini-switch, Rhythm pickup coil tap switch, Lead pickup coil tap switch, Master Tone knob.

Due to space constraints, the **Full Active Electronic** package is only available on the Bich models. This package consists of (listed top to bottom): Master Volume knob, Pickup Selector Switch, Pre-Amp #1 On/Off mini-switch, Pre-Amp #2 On/Off mini-switch, phase mini-switch, Pre-Amp #1 Volume Knob, Pre-Amp #2 Volume Knob, Rhythm pickup Volume, a 6-position Vari-Tone 'chicken head' knob, Master Tone knob, Rhythm pickup coil tap switch, Lead pickup coil tap switch. Now that's tonal variety!

(For further information and controls diagram, visit the B.C. Rich website at www.bcrichguitars.com)

ELECTRIC

B.C. Rich offers numerous options for the current instrument line through their Custom Shop. There is no additional charge for left-handed configuration. For information and pricing on custom inlays, graphic paint jobs, and exotic woods, please contact the B.C. Rich Custom Shop.

Listings within this section are alphabetized by series.

Add $40 for black hardware.

Add $40 for coil tap switch.

Add $40 for phase switch.

Add $40 for rosewood fingerboard.

Add $50 for paint matching headstock.

Add $75 for headstock binding.

Add $75 for fingerboard binding.

Add $75 for ebony fingerboard.

Add $100 for gold hardware.

Add $125 for Sunburst finish.

Add $125 for Pearl or Candy finishes.

Add $150 for Marble finish (this option was discontinued in 1998).

Add $150 for active electronics (Mockingbird Supreme and Eagle Supreme, Guitars and Basses).

Add $250 for full active electronics (due to space constraints, Bich models only).

Add $200 for Floyd Rose tremolo.

Add $200 for full active electronics.

Add $225 for urethane Transparent finish.

Add $250 for nitrocellulose lacquer finish.

Assassin Series

The Assassin model was introduced in 1986.

ASM 1 [U.S.: Neck-through-body] - offset double cutaway body, mahogany body wings, figured maple top, maple neck-through design, 25 ½" scale, 24-fret bound ebony fingerboard with diamond 'insert' inlays, locking Floyd Rose vibrato, 6-on-a-side tuners, chrome hardware, 2 Seymour Duncan humbucker pickups, volume/tone controls, 3-way selector switch, available in Amber Burst, Cherry Sunburst, Transparent Black, Transparent Blue, and Transparent Red finishes. Mfg. 1998 to date.

MSR $1,899 $1,525 $1,325 $1,125 $925 $825 $725 $595

ASM 2 [U.S.: Neck-through-body] - similar to the ASM 1, except features pearl diamond fingerboard inlay, black hardware, unbound fingerboard/headstock, pickup selector mini-switches. Mfg. 1998 to date.

MSR $1,699 $1,275 $1,075 $875 $775 $675 $575 $475

ASM 3 [U.S.: Bolt-On Neck] - similar to the ASM 1, except features basswood body, bolt-on maple neck, pearl 'teardrop' fingerboard inlay, unbound fingerboard/headstock. Mfg. 1998 to date.

MSR $1,549 $1,165 $1,050 $850 $750 $650 $550 $450

ASM B [U.S.: Bolt-On Neck] - similar to the ASM 1, except features basswood body, figured maple top, bolt-on maple neck, available in Amber Burst, Cherry Sunburst, Transparent Blue, and Transparent Magenta finishes. Mfg. 1998 to date.

MSR $1,549 $1,165 $1,050 $850 $750 $650 $550 $450

ASSASSIN [U.S.: Neck-through-body] - offset double cutaway body, alder body wings/maple neck-through design, 24 5/8" scale, 24-fret ebony fingerboard with diamond-shaped inlays, double locking Floyd Rose vibrato, blackface peghead with screened logo, 6-on-a-side Sperzel tuners, black hardware, 2 Seymour Duncan humbucker pickups, 2 volume/1 tone controls, 3-way selector, available in Black, Blue, Emerald Green, Golden Yellow, Magenta, Red and Tangerine translucent finishes. Mfg. 1986 to 1998.

$1,000 $900 $800 $675 $575 $450 $325

Last MSR was $1,399.

In 1994, Black, Purple, Red, and White finishes replaced previous item.
In 1995, rosewood fingerboard, fixed bridge replaced previous item.
This model was previously available with other pickup configurations: 3 single coil pickups (with 3 mini switches), single coil/humbucker pickups (with mini switches).

GRADING	100% MINT	98% NEAR MINT	95% EXC+	90% EXC	80% VG+	70% VG	60% G

Assassin MMT (Maple Molded Top) [U.S.: Neck-through-body] - similar to the Assassin model, except has offset double cutaway mahogany body, figured maple top, 2 DiMarzio humbucker pickups, 2 volume/1 tone controls, 3-position switch, available in Emerald Green, Red Tangerine, Transparent Blue, Transparent Gold and Transparent Purple finishes. Disc. 1995.

$1,050 $900 $795 $695 $575 $475 $375

Last MSR was $1,499.

This model had an optional B.C. Rich stop bridge/tailpiece or standard Wilkinson vibrato.

In 1995, pearl blade fingerboard inlay, Translucent Blue, Translucent Cherry Red, Translucent Emerald Green and Translucent Pagon Gold finishes were introduced. Emerald Green, Red Tangerine, Transparent Blue, Transparent Gold and Transparent Purple finishes were discontinued.

Assassin Hollow [U.S.: Neck-through-body] - offset double cutaway semi hollow mahogany body, figured maple top, f-holes, set maple neck, 24-fret ebony fingerboard, B.C. Rich stop bridge/tailpiece, blackface peghead with screened logo, 6-on-a-side tuners, black hardware, 2 humbucker DiMarzio pickups, 2 volume/1 tone controls, 3-position switch, available in Emerald Green, Translucent Blue, Translucent Pagan Gold and Translucent Cherry Red finishes. Disc. 1995.

$1,100 $950 $825 $725 $625 $525 $425

Last MSR was $1,499.

ASSASSIN STANDARD [U.S.: Bolt-On Neck] - offset double cutaway alder body, bolt-on maple neck, 24-fret ebony fingerboard with abalone blade inlay at 12th fret, double locking Floyd Rose vibrato, blackface peghead with screened logo, 6-on-a-side Sperzel tuners, black hardware, Seymour Duncan single coil/humbucker pickups, 2 volume/1 tone controls, 3-position switch, available in Black, Candy Blue, Candy Red, Deep Metallic Purple, Pearl Emerald, Red, and various Transparent Colors finishes. Disc. 1998.

$800 $725 $650 $550 $475 $375 $300

Last MSR was $1,199.

In 1995, Blue, Purple, Turquoise and White finishes were introduced, Candy Color finishes became options, Deep Metallic Purple, Pear Emerald and Transparent Color finishes were discontinued.

In 1996, Cobalt Blue finish was introduced, and Turquoise finish was discontinued.

Assassin MMT (Maple Molded Top) [U.S.: Bolt-On Neck] - similar to Assassin Standard, except has mahogany body, quilted maple top, chrome hardware, no Blade inlay at 12th fret, available in Translucent Black, Translucent Blue, Translucent Emerald Green, Translucent Golden Yellow, Translucent Magenta, Translucent Red and Translucent Tangerine. Disc. 1998.

$1,050 $900 $800 $675 $575 $450 $350

Last MSR was $1,399.

In 1995, Translucent Pagan Gold and Translucent Purple finishes were introduced; Translucent Black, Translucent Golden Yellow, Translucent Magenta, and Translucent Tangerine finishes were discontinued.

MB 1 (MASON BERNARD) [U.S.: Bolt-On Neck] - offset double cutaway alder (or poplar) body, bolt-on maple neck, 25 1/2 " scale, 24-fret ebony fingerboard, locking Floyd Rose vibrato, blackface peghead with screened logo, 6-on-a-side tuners, chrome hardware, Seymour Duncan single coil/humbucker pickups, volume/tone controls, 3-position switch, available in Black, Gunmetal Grey, Metallic Red, Wine Purple, and White finishes. Disc. 1998.

MSR $1,199 $895 $795 $695 $595 $495 $395 $250

MB 2 (Mason Bernard) [U.S.: Bolt-On Neck] - similar to the MB 1, except features 2 Seymour Duncan humbucking pickups. Mfg. 1998 to date.

MSR $1,249 $935 $825 $725 $625 $525 $425 $295

Bich Series

The Bich model was introduced in 1976. The first bolt-on neck versions were offered in 1977.

BICH STANDARD [U.S.: Neck-through-body] - offset double cutaway body with bottom bout cutaways, through-body mahogany neck, alder (or poplar) wings, 24 5/8" scale, 24-fret rosewood fingerboard with pearl diamond inlay, Quadmatic stop bridge/tailpiece, blackface peghead with screened logo, 3-per-side tuners, chrome hardware, 2 DiMarzio humbucker pickups, 2 volume/1 tone controls, 3-position switch, available in Black, Blue, Red, White and Yellow finishes. Current Mfg.

MSR $1,499 $1,195 $1,050 $925 $775 $650 $500 $375

In 1995, maple neck, black hardware, Seymour Duncan humbuckers replaced previous items. Purple finish was introduced; Blue and Yellow finishes were discontinued.

In 1998, maple neck replaced the mahogany neck; DiMarzio pickups and Blue finish re-introduced.

Bich Doubleneck [U.S.: Neck-through-body] - similar to the Bich Standard, except has mahogany body wings, maple through-body necks in 6- and 12-string configurations, abalone cloud inlays, Imperial-style tuning machines, full active electronics on 6-string neck, 2 volume/1 tone controls on 12-string neck, available in Transparent Blue, Transparent Emerald Green, Transparent Oriental Blue, Transparent Pagan Gold, and Transparent Red finishes. Mfg. circa 1978 to date.

1978-1998 $3,600 $3,200 $2,850 $2,350 $1,975 $1,550 $1,195

MSR $POR

P.O.R. is B.C. Rich's term for Price On Request (in other words, call for details on pricing and availability).

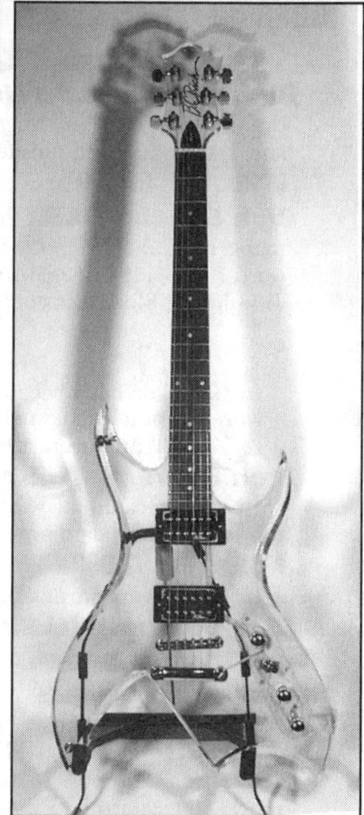

B.C. Rich Bich
courtesy Dave Anderson

B.C. Rich Seagull
courtesy Jeff Mikols

GRADING			100% MINT	98% NEAR MINT	95% EXC+	90% EXC	80% VG+	70% VG	60% G

Bich Deluxe [U.S.: Neck-through-body] - similar to the Bich Standard, except features mahogany/maple body, mahogany neck-through design, ebony fingerboard, Imperial-style tuning machines, available in Natural, Transparent Black, Transparent Blue, Transparent Green, and Transparent Red finishes. Mfg. 1998 to date.

MSR	$1,699	$1,275	$1,150	$1,050	$950	$850	$750	$650

Bich Special [U.S.: Neck-through-body] - offset double cutaway maple (or koa) body with bottom bout cutaways, through-body maple neck, 24-fret ebony fingerboard with abalone diamond inlay, Quadmatic fixed bridge, blackface peghead with pearl logo inlay, chrome hardware, 3-per-side Imperial-style tuning machines, 2 DiMarzio humbucker pickups, 2 volume/1 tone controls, 3-position switch, available in Natural, Translucent Blue, Translucent Emerald Green, Translucent Purple, Translucent Tangerine, and Translucent Red finishes. Disc. 1998.

$1,100	$950	$850	$750	$625	$525	$400

Last MSR was $1,599.

In 1995, koa body became an option, Translucent Black, Translucent Cherry Red, Translucent Emerald, and Translucent Orange finishes were introduced; Translucent Tangerine finish was discontinued.

In 1996, Translucent Cherry Red, Translucent Emerald, and Translucent Orange finishes were discontinued.

Bich Supreme [U.S.: Neck-through-body] - similar to the Bich Deluxe, except has quilted maple or koa body, bound fingerboard with abalone cloud inlay, bound peghead, Imperial-style tuning machines, active electronics (2 coil tap/1 phase mini switches, 6-position rotary Vari-tone switch, on-board pre-amp switch, volume control), available in Natural finish. Current Mfg.

MSR	$2,099	$1,675	$1,450	$1,250	$1,100	$895	$700	$525

In 1998, Transparent Black, Transparent Blue, and Transparent Red finishes were introduced.

Bich 10 String [U.S.: Neck-through-body] - similar to the Bich Standard, except features 10-String configuration, mahogany/maple body, ebony fingerboard, 3-per-side headstock/4 tuners on bass bout, Imperial-style tuning machines, available in Natural, Transparent Black, Transparent Blue, Transparent Green, and Transparent Red finishes. Mfg. 1998 to date.

MSR	$2,299	$1,725	$1,525	$1,425	$1,325	$1,225	$1,125	$950

BICH BOLT-ON [U.S.: Bolt-On Neck] - offset double cutaway alder (or poplar) body, bottom bout cutaways, maple bolt-on neck, 25 1/2" scale, 24-fret rosewood fingerboard with pearl dot inlay, Floyd Rose tremolo, 6-on-a-side tuners, black hardware, 2 humbucker pickups, 2 volume/1 tone controls, 3-position switch, available in Black, Purple, Red, White and Yellow finishes. Current Mfg.

MSR	$1,199	$950	$850	$750	$625	$525	$400	$295

In 1998, Blue finish was introduced; Purple and Yellow finishes were discontinued.

This model is available with a Quadmatic stop tailpiece/bridge.

Bich (N.J. Series) - similar to the Bich U.S.: Bolt-on, except has 24 3/4" scale, B.C. Rich angled headstock with N.J. logo, die cast tuners, additional toggle switch, available in Black, Metallic Red, or White finishes. Current Mfg.

MSR	$669	$465	$415	$365	$315	$265	$215	$165

Add $25 for Transparent Blue, Transparent Purple, or Transparent Red finishes (Transparent Blue and Transparent Purple finishes were discontinued in 1998).

Add $20 for Blue Burst finish.

In 1998, Blood Red finish was introduced; Metallic Red finish was discontinued.

In 2000, Transparent Red finish was discontinued; Blue Burst finish was introduced.

Bich (Platinum Series) - similar to the Bich U.S.: Bolt-on, except has 24 3/4" scale, B.C. Rich 3-per-side headstock with Platinum logo, die cast tuners, additional toggle switch, available in Black, Metallic Red, or White finishes. Current Mfg.

MSR	$499	$360	$300	$275	$260	$200	$165	$100

Add $25 for Transparent Purple or Transparent Red finishes (Transparent Purple finish was discontinued in 1998).

Add $20 for Blue Burst finish.

Add $200 for Acrylic Green and Acrylic Red finishes.

In 1998, Blood Red finish was introduced; Metallic Red finish was discontinued.

In 1999, Transparent Red and white finishes were discontinued.

In 2000, Blue Burst, Acrylic Green and Acrylic Red finishes were introduced.

Blaster Series

BLASTER (U.S. Series) - single cutaway alder laminated body, bolt-on hard maple neck, 25 1/2" scale, 21-fret maple fingerboard with black dot inlay, 6-saddle tele-style bridge, B.C. Rich *vintage* headstock, 6-on-a-side tuners, white pickguard, chrome hardware, 2 humbucker pickups, volume/tone controls, 3-position switch, control plate, available in Black, Bright Green, Creme, Red, and White finishes. Disc. 1998.

$225	$200	$175	$150	$125	$100	$75

Last MSR was $329.

Outlaw Blaster (U.S. Series) - similar to the Blaster, except has 6-on-a-side B.C. Rich angled headstock. Disc. 1998.

$250	$225	$195	$175	$135	$100	$90

Last MSR was $359.

OUTLAW (U.S. Series) - offset double cutaway alder laminated body, bolt-on maple neck, 25 1/2" scale, 21-fret maple fingerboard with black position dots, ST-style tremolo, B.C. Rich angled headstock, 6-on-a-side tuners, chrome hardware, 2 humbucker pickups, volume/tone controls, 3-position switch, available in Black, Blue, Purple, Red, and White finishes. Mfg. 1987 to 1998.

$250	$225	$195	$165	$125	$100	$85

Last MSR was $349.

GRADING	100% MINT	98% NEAR MINT	95% EXC+	90% EXC	80% VG+	70% VG	60% G

B.C. Rich Outlaw Blaster
courtesy B.C. Rich

Condor Series

"The first **Condor** was designed and made in 1983. The Condor was of archtop design with a 24 5/8" scale. As with all B.C. Rich guitars of that period, it was of neck-through construction with a mahogany neck and body, with a maple contoured top. Basically, the present **Eagle Arch Top Supreme** is the predecessor to the **Condor**."

Robert Conti Series

In the mid 1980s, guitarist Robert Conti also inspired B.C. Rich to build archtop jazz guitar models such as the **RTJG** and **RTSG**.

ROBERT CONTI 8 STRING JAZZ (CONTOURED TOP) [U.S.: Neck-through-body] - single rounded cutaway mahogany body, bound carved maple top, through-body multi-laminated maple neck, 25 1/2" scale, 24-fret bound ebony fingerboard with abalone block inlay, trapeze bridge/stop tailpiece, gold hardware, bound peghead with rosewood veneer and pearl logo inlay, 4-per-side tuners, Bartolini custom wound humbucker pickup, volume/tone controls, available in Burgundy Pearl, Cream, Emerald Green, Gold, Metallic Blue, Pearl White, Porsche Red, Solid Black, Solid White, Tropical Blue, Translucent Red and Violet finishes. Current Mfg.

MSR $3,000 — $2,400 $2,100 $1,825 $1,595 $N/A $N/A $N/A

This model is also available in a 7-string configuration.

Conti 6 String [U.S.: Neck-through-body] - similar to the Robert Conti 8 String Jazz (Contoured Top), except has extra select figured maple top, 3-per-side headstock, 2 Seymour Duncan Jazz pickups, 2 volume/2-Tone controls, 3-way selector, available in Transparent Black, Transparent Blue, Transparent Root Beer, and Solid Black. Current Mfg.

MSR $2,499 — $2,000 $1,750 $1,525 $1,300 $N/A $N/A $N/A

This model is available with chrome hardware.

Eagle Series

The Eagle model was introduced in 1994.

EAGLE STANDARD [U.S.: Neck-through-body] - offset double cutaway poplar body, through-body maple neck, 24 5/8" scale, 24-fret rosewood fingerboard with abalone diamond inlay, tune-o-matic bridge/stop tailpiece, chrome hardware, 3-per-side tuners, 2 DiMarzio humbucker pickups, 2 volume/1 tone controls, 3-position switch, available in Black, Blue, Red, and White finishes. Mfg. 1998 to date.

MSR $1,499 — $1,150 $1,000 $875 $750 $625 $500 $375

Eagle Deluxe [U.S.: Neck-through-body] - similar to the Eagle Standard, except has mahogany body, mahogany through-body neck, bound ebony fingerboard with pearl triangle inlay, bound headstock, available in Natural, Transparent Black, Translucent Blue, Translucent Green, and Translucent Red finishes.

MSR $1,699 — $1,275 $1,075 $950 $850 $750 $650 $525

Eagle Special [U.S.: Neck-through-body] - similar to the Eagle Standard, except has maple or koa body, ebony fingerboard with abalone diamond inlay, Quadmatic bridge/stop tailpiece, blackface peghead with pearl logo inlay, available in Natural, Translucent Blue, Translucent Emerald Green, Translucent Purple, Translucent Tangerine and Translucent Red finishes. Disc. 1998.

$1,100 $950 $850 $750 $625 $525 $400

Last MSR was $1,599.

In 1995, koa body became an option, Translucent Black, Translucent Cherry Red, Translucent Emerald, and Translucent Orange finishes were introduced; Translucent Tangerine finish was discontinued.

In 1996, Translucent Cherry Red, Translucent Emerald, and Translucent Orange finishes were discontinued.

Eagle Supreme [U.S.: Neck-through-body] - similar to the Eagle Special, except has maple/mahogany body, mahogany through-body neck, bound ebony fingerboard with abalone cloud inlay, bound peghead, active electronics (2 coil tap/1 phase mini switches, 6-position rotary Vari-tone switch, on-board pre-amp switch, volume control), available in Natural finish. Current Mfg.

MSR $2,099 — $1,675 $1,450 $1,275 $1,100 $925 $725 $550

In 1998, Transparent Black, Transparent Blue, Transparent Green, and Transparent Red finishes were introduced.

Eagle Arch Top Supreme [U.S.: Neck-through-body] - similar to the Eagle Special, except has mahogany body, carved quilted or flame maple top, through-body mahogany neck, 24 5/8" scale, white body binding, bound fingerboard with green abalone cloud inlay, bound peghead, 2 Seymour Duncan custom (or DiMarzio) humbuckers, available in Gold Top, Transparent Blue, Transparent (Emerald) Green, Transparent Purple, Transparent Tangerine, and Transparent Red finishes. Mfg. 1994 to date.

MSR $2,099 — $1,675 $1,450 $1,275 $1,100 $925 $725 $550

In 1995, Gold Top and Transparent Tangerine finishes were discontinued.

In 1998, Butterscotch Sun, Cherry Sunburst, Magenta Burst, and Transparent Black finishes were introduced; Transparent Blue and Transparent Purple finishes were discontinued.

Eagle (Platinum Series) - offset double cutaway solid alder body, bolt-on hard maple neck, 24 3/4" scale, 22-fret rosewood fingerboard with white dot inlay, tune-o-matic bridge, 6-on-a-side headstock, die cast tuners, chrome hardware, 2 humbucker pickups, 2 volume/1 tone controls, 1 toggle switch, 3-position selector, available in Black, Metallic Red, and White finishes. Disc. 1997.

$350 $295 $250 $225 $195 $175 $125

Last MSR was $489.

Add $25 for Transparent Purple and Transparent Red finishes.

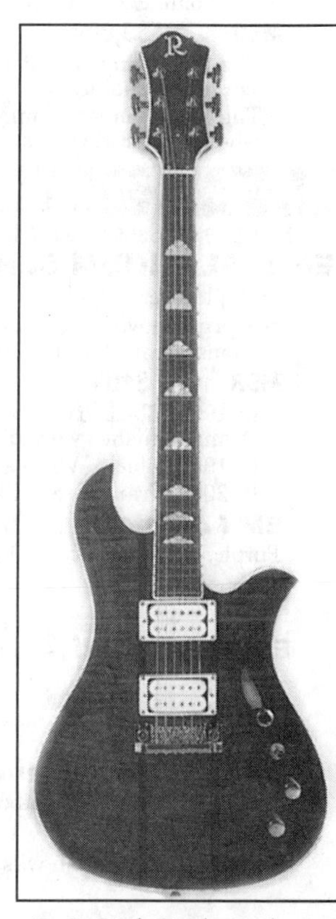

B.C. Rich Eagle Archtop Supreme
courtesy B.C. Rich

GRADING		100% MINT	98% NEAR MINT	95% EXC+	90% EXC	80% VG+	70% VG	60% G

Exclusive Series

Exclusive Series models feature neck-through construction, and are hand crafted in the U.S.

EXCLUSIVE MODEL ACT (ABALONE ARCH TOP) - slightly offset double cutaway mahogany body, bound highly figured carved maple top, abalone body binding, through-body mahogany neck, 24 5/8" scale, 24-fret bound ebony fingerboard with abalone oval inlay, tune-o-matic bridge/stop tailpiece, chrome hardware, bound blackface peghead with pearl logo inlay, 3-per-side tuners, 2 Seymour Duncan Alnico Pro humbucker pickups, 2 volume/1 tone controls, 3-position switch, available in Butterscotch Sun, Cherry Sunburst, Transparent Black, Transparent Magenta, and Translucent Red finishes. Current Mfg.

MSR $3,000 $2,500 $2,150 $1,875 $1,595 $1,300 $1,050 $750

This model was originally available in Burgundy Pearl, Cream, Emerald Green, Gold, Metallic Blue, Pearl White, Porsche Red, Solid Black, Solid White, Tropical Blue, and Violet finishes (current colors were introduced in 1998).

This model was briefly available with an unbound fingerboard and headstock (This option, discontinued in 1998, originally had a retail list price of $2,150).

Exclusive Model CT (Arch Top) - similar to the Exclusive Model ACT, except does not feature the abalone inlay on the top, available in Black, Butterscotch Sun, Cherry Sunburst, Gold Top Pearl, Transparent Magenta, and White finishes. Current Mfg.

MSR $2,100 $1,675 $1,475 $1,275 $1,100 $925 $750 $525

Exclusive Model FT 1 (Flat Top) - similar to the Exclusive Model ACT, except does not feature the carved arched top, available in Cherry Sunburst, Transparent Green, Transparent Magenta, and Transparent Pagan Gold finishes. Current Mfg.

MSR $1,599 $1,275 $1,100 $950 $825 $675 $550 $400

This model was briefly available without the abalone inlay on top (This option was discontinued in 1998).

Exclusive Model FT 2 (Flat Top) - similar to the Exclusive Model FT 1, except features an alder or poplar body, rosewood fingerboard, available in Black, Blue, Gunmetal Grey, and White finishes. Current Mfg.

MSR $1,299 $1,000 $900 $775 $675 $550 $450 $325

EXCLUSIVE DOUBLENECK 6/12 - offset double cutaway mahogany body, white bound figured carved maple top, through-body mahogany necks, 24-fret rosewood fingerboards with abalone block inlay, trapeze bridge/stop tailpiece, chrome hardware, blackface peghead with pearl logo inlay, 3-per-side tuners (6 string), 6-per-side tuners (12 string). Both necks each feature 2 humbucker pickups, 2 volume/1 tone controls, 3-position switch, plus master neck selector switch, available in Acapulco Blue, Black, White, and Wine Purple finishes. Disc. 1998.

$2,800 $2,450 $2,150 $1,825 $N/A $N/A $N/A

Last MSR was $3,499.

Add $225 for Transparent Emerald Green, Transparent Oriental Blue, Transparent Pagan Gold, Transparent Purple, and Transparent Red finishes.

VICTOR SMITH COMMEMORATIVE EXCLUSIVE - slightly offset double cutaway mahogany body, bound highly figured carved maple top, through-body mahogany neck, 24 5/8" scale, 24-fret bound ebony fingerboard with abalone block inlay, tune-o-matic bridge/stop tailpiece, gold hardware, bound blackface peghead with pearl 'B.C. Rich' logo inlay, 3-per-side tuners, 2 Seymour Duncan *Seth Lover* humbucker pickups, 2 volume/2-Tone controls, 3-position switch, available in Butterscotch Sun, Cherry Sunburst, and Magenta Burst finishes. Mfg. 1998 to date.

MSR $3,000 $2,250 $2,050 $1,850 $1,650 $1,450 $1,250 $1,050

The Victor Smith model is available in two different body weights: SL (Slim Line) and HV (Heavier Weight, for those players who want a 'chunkier' sound).

The Victor Smith Commemorative is named after the early guitar pickup designer. In 1929, Smith introduced the first commercial Spanish-style electric guitar while working at the Dobro Guitar company.

Exclusive EM Series

Exclusive EM Series models feature bolt-on neck construction, and are imported to the U.S. market.

EM I (PLATINUM SERIES) (EXCLUSIVE EM I) - slightly offset double cutaway solid alder body, bolt-on maple neck, 24 3/4" scale, multiple layer bound body, 24-fret rosewood fingerboard with pearloid rectangular position markers, tune-o-matic bridge, chrome hardware, blackface peghead with logo inlay, 3-per-side tuners, Exclusive-style headstock, 2 humbucker pickups, 2 volume/1 tone controls, 3-way selector, available in Transparent Blue, Transparent Natural, Transparent Purple, and Translucent Orange finishes. Mfg. 1996 to date.

MSR $499 $350 $295 $250 $195 $150 $125 $95

In 1998, Black, Transparent Red, and White finishes were introduced; Transparent Natural, Transparent Purple, and Transparent Orange finishes were discontinued.

In 1999, Black, White and Transparent Red finishes were discontinued.

In 2000, Transparent Black was introduced.

EM I Archtop - similar to the Exclusive EM I, except has carved arched top, available in Transparent Blue, Transparent Natural, Transparent Purple, and Translucent Orange finishes. Mfg. 1996 to 1998.

$550 $495 $450 $375 $300 $250 $175

Last MSR was $699.

Exclusive EM II - similar to the Exclusive EM I, except has single layer body binding, available in Black, Purple, Red, and White finishes. Mfg. 1996 to 1998.

$450 $375 $350 $295 $250 $195 $150

Last MSR was $549.

EM 3 (Platinum Series) (Exclusive EM III) - similar to the Exclusive EM I, exept has single coil/humbucker pickups, tele-style bridge, dot position markers, and 6-on-a-side Exclusive-style headstock, available in Black, Gun Metal Gray, Red, and White finishes. Mfg. 1996 to date.

MSR $499 $375 $325 $295 $250 $200 $165 $125

In 1998, Red finish was discontinued.

GRADING	100% MINT	98% NEAR MINT	95% EXC+	90% EXC	80% VG+	70% VG	60% G

Exclusive Series Bolt-On

Exclusive Bolt-On Series models have the similar body design as the Exclusive series models, but feature bolt-on necks. Constructed in the U.S.

EXCLUSIVE MODEL TBH - slightly offset double cutaway mahogany body, highly figured carved maple top, bolt-on maple neck, 24 5/8" scale 24-fret ebony fingerboard with abalone dot inlay, tele-ish bridge, chrome hardware, blackface peghead with pearl logo inlay, 3-per-side tuners, single coil/humbucker pickups, volume/tone controls, 5-way selector, control plate, available in Burgundy Pearl, Cream, Emerald Green, Gold, Metallic Blue, Pearl White, Porsche Red, Solid Black, Solid White, Tropical Blue, Translucent Red and Violet finishes. Disc. 1998.

$1,000 $900 $800 $675 $575 $450 $350
Last MSR was $1,399.

Later production models may feature an alder or poplar body and rosewood fingerboard.
This model was also available with 2 humbucker pickups, volume/tone controls, and 3-way selector switch as the Model EXB O.

Exclusive Model TBS - similar to the Exclusive Model TBH, except has single coil pickup in bridge position.

$1,000 $900 $800 $675 $575 $450 $350
Last MSR was $1,399.

Fat Bob Series

FAT BOB - *motorcycle gas tank* style alder body, bolt-on maple neck, 25 1/2" scale, 22-fret rosewood fingerboard with pearl flames inlay, tremolo, 6-on-a-side tuners, chrome hardware, humbucker pickup, volume control, available in Black with Red/White/Yellow flames finish. Mfg. 1984 to 1986.

$900 $800 $750 $675 $625 $550 $460

G STRING - Mfg. mid 1980s.
Research continues on this model.

Gunslinger Series

The Gunslinger model was introduced in 1987.

GUNSLINGER [U.S.: Bolt-On Neck] - offset double cutaway alder body, bolt-on maple neck, 25 1/2" scale, 22-fret maple fingerboard with black dot inlay, standard Wilkinson vibrato, reverse blackface peghead with screened logo, 6-on-a-side tuners, black hardware, humbucker pickup, volume control, dual sound switch, available in Black, Cobalt Blue, Emerald Green, Purple, Red, White and Yellow finishes. Mfg. 1994 to 1998.

$700 $600 $525 $450 $395 $325 $250
Last MSR was $999.

Add $125 for optional Candy Color finishes.

In 1995, double locking Floyd Rose vibrato replaced original part/design; Candy Color finishes became optional, Powder Blue finish was briefly introduced (1 year), Emerald Green and Yellow finishes were discontinued.

Gunslinger 2 [U.S.: Bolt-On Neck] - similar to Gunslinger, except has alder or poplar body, 24-fret rosewood fingerboard, 2 Seymour Duncan humbuckers, 2 volume/1 tone controls, 3-way selector, available in Black, Gunmetal Grey, Red, and White finishes. Mfg. 1994 to date.

MSR $1,199 $950 $825 $725 $600 $500 $400 $295

Jeff Cook Alabama Signature Series

These models were designed in conjunction with guitarist Jeff Cook (Alabama).

JEFF COOK MODEL 1 [U.S.: Bolt-On Neck] - offset double cutaway alder body, bolt-on maple neck, maple fingerboard with abalone dot inlay, tele-style bridge, chrome hardware, 6-on-a-side tuners, 2 single coil pickups, volume/tone controls, 3-way selector, available in Black, Blue Metallic, Emerald Green, Glitter Rock White, Purple, Red, and White finishes. Disc. 1998.

$1,000 $900 $800 $675 $575 $450 $350
Last MSR was $1,399.

Add $225 for optional transparent finish.

Jeff Cook Model 2 [U.S.: Bolt-On Neck] - similar to the Jeff Cook Model 1, except has humbucker in the bridge position. Disc. 1998.

$1,000 $900 $800 $695 $595 $475 $375
Last MSR was $1,399.

B.C. Rich Fat Bob Model
courtesy Dan Choles

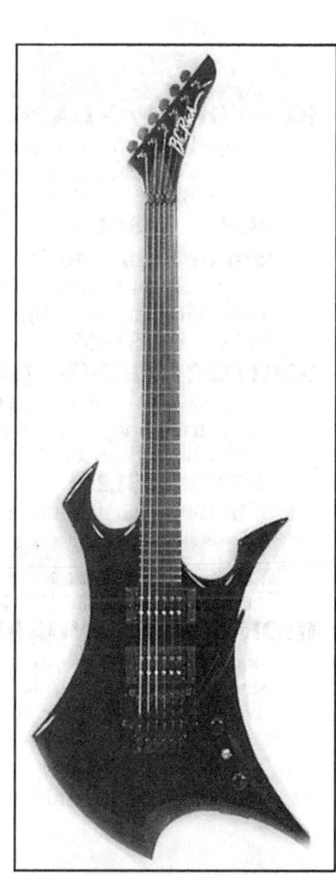

B.C. Rich Ignitor Standard
courtesy B.C. Rich

GRADING	100% MINT	98% NEAR MINT	95% EXC+	90% EXC	80% VG+	70% VG	60% G

B

Junior V Series

JUNIOR V STANDARD [U.S.: Neck-through-body] - flying V-shaped body, alder body wings, through-body maple neck, 24 5/8" scale, 24-fret rosewood fingerboard with diamond inlays at 12th fret, tune-o-matic fixed bridge, 6-on-the-other-side tuners, reverse blackface headstock with logo, black (or chrome) hardware, 2 Seymour Duncan custom humbuckers, volume/tone controls, 3-way selector, available in Black, Purple, Red, and White finishes. Current Mfg.

MSR	$1,499	$1,200	$1,000	$875	$750	$625	$500	$375

In 1998, poplar body wings replaced the alder body wings; DiMarzio humbuckers replaced the Seymour Duncan humbuckers; Blue finish was introduced; Purple finish was discontinued.

Junior V Supreme [U.S.: Neck-through-body] - similar to the Junior V Standard, except has mahogany body wings, mahogany neck, bound figured maple top, bound ebony fingerboard with abalone 'V' inlays, bound unreversed headstock, locking Floyd Rose tremolo or fixed bridge, available in Transparent Sunburst Emerald Green, Transparent Sunburst Gold, Transparent Sunburst Pagan Blue, and Transparent Sunburst Red finishes. Current Mfg.

MSR	$2,499	$1,995	$1,750	$1,525	$1,300	$1,075	$850	$625

In 1998, the figured maple top was discontinued (all mahogany body).

In 1998, Transparent Black, Transparent Blue, Transparent Magenta, and Transparent Red finishes were introduced; Transparent Sunburst Emerald Green, Transparent Sunburst Gold, Transparent Sunburst Pagan Blue, and Transparent Sunburst Red finishes were discontinued.

KKV KERRY KING SIGNATURE JUNIOR V [U.S.: Neck-through-body] - similar to the Junior V Standard, except has mahogany body wings, mahogany neck, figured maple top, ebony fingerboard with abalone diamond inlays, blackface reverse headstock with Kerry King/B.C. Rich logos, locking Floyd Rose or Kahler tremolo, available in Transparent Black Sunburst, Transparent Blue, and Transparent Magenta finishes. Mfg. 1998 to date.

MSR	$2,499	$1,875	$1,675	$1,475	$1,275	$1,075	$875	$650

JUNIOR V BOLT-ON [U.S.: Bolt-On Neck] - flying V-shaped alder body, bolt-on maple neck, 25 1/2" scale, 24-fret rosewood fingerboard with dot inlays, fixed bridge, chrome hardware, 6-on-a-side tuners, 2 humbuckers, 2 volume/1 tone controls, 3-way selector, available in Black, (Cobalt) Blue, Red, and White finishes. Current Mfg.

MSR	$1,199	$950	$850	$750	$625	$525	$400	$295

In 1998, poplar body replaced the alder body.

Jr. V (Platinum Series) - flying V-shaped solid alder body, bolt-on hard maple neck, 24 3/4" scale, 22-fret rosewood fingerboard with white dot inlay, tune-o-matic bridge, 6-on-a-side headstock, die cast tuners, chrome hardware, 2 humbucker pickups, 2 volume/1 tone controls, 1 toggle switch, 3-position selector, available in Black, Metallic Red, and White finishes. Current Mfg.

MSR	$599	$475	$425	$375	$325	$250	$200	$150

Add $25 for Transparent Purple and Transparent Red finishes (Transparent finishes were discontinued in 1998).

In 1999, Metallic Red and white finishes were discontinued.

In 1998, Gunmetal Grey finish was introduced; Metallic Red finish was discontinued.

Ignitor Series

IGNITOR STANDARD [U.S.: Neck-through-body] - offset double cutaway alder (or poplar) body, pointed forward horns, scooped lower bout cutaway, bolt-on maple neck, 24 5/8" scale, 24-fret rosewood fingerboard with inlay at 12th fret, blackface headstock with silk-screened logo, Quadmatic fixed bridge, chrome hardware, 6-on-a-side tuners, 2 DiMarzio humbuckers, volume/tone controls, 3-way selector, available in Black, Blood Red, Gunmetal Grey, and White finishes. Mfg. 1998 to date.

MSR	$1,499	$1,200	$1,050	$925	$775	$650	$500	$375

Ignitor Supreme [U.S.: Neck-through-body] - similar to Ignitor Standard, except has a maple/mahogany body, mahogany through-body neck, 24-fret ebony fingerboard, locking Floyd Rose or Quadmatic fixed bridge, available in Blue Sunburst, Transparent Black, and Transparent Pagan Gold finishes. Mfg. 1998 to date.

MSR	$1,899	$1,500	$1,325	$1,150	$975	$825	$650	$475

IGNITOR BOLT-ON [U.S.: Bolt-On Neck] - offset double cutaway alder (or poplar) body, pointed forward horns, scooped lower bout cutaway, bolt-on maple neck, 25 1/2" scale, 24-fret rosewood fingerboard with inlay at 12th fret, blackface headstock with silk-screened logo, Quadmatic fixed bridge, chrome hardware, 6-on-a-side tuners, 2 DiMarzio humbuckers, volume/tone controls, 3-way selector, available in Black, Blood Red, Cobalt Blue, and White finishes. Current Mfg.

MSR	$1,299	$1,000	$900	$795	$650	$525	$425	$325

In 1998, Cobalt Blue finish was discontinued.

Ironbird Series

The Ironbird model was introduced in 1983.

IRONBIRD STANDARD [U.S.: Neck-through-body] - angular offset cutaway body, pointed treble bout/rear body bouts, alder body wings, 24 5/8" scale, through-body maple neck, 24-fret rosewood fingerboard with pearl diamond inlay, fixed bridge, blackface peghead with screened logo, 3-per-side tuners, black hardware, 2 Seymour Duncan custom humbucker pickups, 2 volume/1 tone controls, 3-position switch, available in Black, Blue, Red, White and Yellow finishes. Disc. 1998.

		$1,000	$900	$800	$675	$575	$450	$350

Last MSR was $1,399.

In 1995, Purple finish was introduced, Blue and Yellow finishes were discontinued.

GRADING		100% MINT	98% NEAR MINT	95% EXC+	90% EXC	80% VG+	70% VG	60% G

Ironbird [U.S.: Bolt-On Neck] - angular offset double cutaway alder body with pointed treble bout/rear body bouts, bolt-on maple neck, 25 1/2" scale, 22-fret rosewood fingerboard with white dot inlay, double locking Floyd Rose vibrato, 6-on-a-side tuners, black hardware, 2 humbucker pickups, 2 volume/1 tone controls, 3-position switch, available in Black, Blue, Emerald Green, Red, White, and Yellow finishes. Disc. 1998.

$775 $650 $575 $500 $425 $350 $275

Last MSR was $1,099.

Add $125 for optional Candy Color finish.

In 1995, Candy Color finishes became optional, Purple finish was introduced, Blue and Emerald Green finishes were discontinued.

Ironbird (N.J. Series) - similar to the Ironbird [U.S.: Bolt-On Neck], except has 24 3/4" scale, diamond inlays, N.J. logo on headstock, die cast tuners, additional toggle switch, available in Black, Metallic Red, and White finishes. Disc. 1998, 2000 to date.

MSR $689 $475 $425 $375 $325 $275 $225

Add $25 for Transparent Blue or Transparent Red finishes. (Disc. 1998)

In 1998, Metallic Red and white finishes were discontinued.

Mockingbird Series

The Mockingbird model was introduced in 1976.

MOCKINGBIRD ARCH TOP [U.S.: Neck-through-body] - offset double cutaway mahogany body, extended pointed treble bout/rounded lower bout, carved highly figured quilted maple top, white body binding, through-body mahogany neck, 24 5/8" scale, 24-fret bound ebony fingerboard with green abalone cloud inlay, Quadmatic fixed bridge, 3-per-side tuners, chrome hardware, 2 DiMarzio (or Seymour Duncan Alnico Pro) humbucker pickups, 2 volume/1 tone controls, 3-way selector, available in Transparent Black, Transparent Blue, Transparent (Emerald) Green, Transparent Purple, and Transparent Red finishes. Mfg. 1995 to date.

MSR $2,099 $1,675 $1,450 $1,250 $1,100 $895 $700 $525

This model was designed for Slash (Guns 'n Roses).

In 1998, Butterscotch Sun, Cherry Sunburst, Magenta Burst finishes were introduced; Transparent Blue and Transparent Purple finishes were discontinued.

MOCKINGBIRD STANDARD [U.S.: Neck-through-body] - offset double cutaway body, extended pointed treble bout/rounded lower bout, alder (or poplar) body wings, through-body maple neck, 24 5/8" scale, 24-fret rosewood fingerboard with pearl diamond inlay, Quadmatic fixed bridge, blackface peghead with logo, 3-per-side tuners, black hardware, 2 Seymour Duncan custom humbucker pickups, 2 volume/1 tone controls, 3-position switch, available in Black, Blue, Red, White, and Yellow finishes. Current Mfg.

MSR $1,499 $1,200 $1,000 $875 $750 $625 $500 $375

In 1995, Purple finish was introduced, Blue and Yellow finishes were discontinued.

In 1998, DiMarzio humbuckers replaced Seymour Duncan humbuckers; Blue finish reintroduced; Purple finish was discontinued.

Mockingbird Deluxe [U.S.: Neck-through-body] - similar to the Mockingbird Standard, except features mahogany body wings, figured maple top, mahogany through-body neck, ebony fingerboard, 2 DiMarzio humbuckers, available in Natural, Translucent Black, Translucent Blue, Translucent Green, and Translucent Red finishes. Mfg. 1998 to date.

MSR $1,699 $1,350 $1,195 $1,050 $875 $725 $575 $425

Mockingbird Special [U.S.: Neck-through-body] - offset double cutaway body, extended pointed treble bout/rounded lower bout, maple or koa body wings, through-body maple neck, 24 5/8" scale, 24-fret ebony fingerboard with abalone diamond inlay, Quadmatic bridge/stop tailpiece, blackface peghead with pearl logo inlay, 3-per-side tuners, 2 DiMarzio humbucker pickups, 2 volume/1 tone controls, 3-position switch, available in Natural, Translucent Blue, Translucent Emerald Green, Translucent Purple, Translucent Tangerine and Translucent Red finishes. Disc. 1998.

$1,100 $995 $850 $750 $625 $525 $400

Last MSR was $1,599.

In 1995, koa body became optional, Translucent Black, Translucent Cherry Red, Translucent Emerald, and Translucent Orange finishes were introduced; Translucent Tangerine finish was discontinued.

In 1996, Translucent Cherry Red, Translucent Emerald, and Translucent Orange finishes were discontinued.

Mockingbird Supreme [U.S.: Neck-through-body] - similar to the Mockingbird Special, except has quilted maple or koa body, bound fingerboard with abalone cloud inlay, bound peghead, active electronics (2 coil tap/1 phase mini switches, 6-position rotary Vari-tone switch, on-board pre-amp switch, volume control), available in Natural finish. Current Mfg.

MSR $2,099 $1,675 $1,450 $1,250 $1,100 $895 $700 $525

In 1998, the koa body was discontinued; Translucent Black, Translucent Blue, Translucent Green, and Translucent Red finishes were introduced.

Mockingbird SL (Slash Limited Edition) [U.S.: Neck-through-body] - similar to the Mockingbird Special, except features a mahogany body/neck, quilted maple top, locking Floyd Rose 2 Tremolo, 2 DiMarzio (or Seymour Duncan Alnico Pro) humbuckers, black hardware, available in Transparent Red finish. Current Mfg.

MSR $1,799 $1,450 $1,250 $1,100 $950 $775 $600 $450

In 1998, Transparent Black, Transparent Blue, and Transparent Green finishes were introduced.

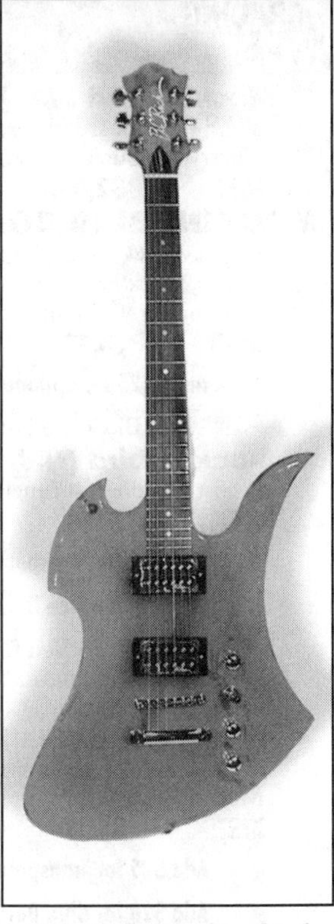

B.C. Rich Mockingbird
courtesy Dave Anderson

B.C. Rich Mockingbird Supreme
courtesy B.C. Rich

GRADING	100% MINT	98% NEAR MINT	95% EXC+	90% EXC	80% VG+	70% VG	60% G

B

Mockingbird SLP [U.S.: Neck-through-body] - similar to the Mockingbird SL, except features bound body/neck/peghead, abalone cloud fingerboard inlays, tune-o-matic bridge, 2 DiMarzio humbuckers, chrome hardware, 2 volume/2-Tone controls, available in Butterscotch Sun, Cherry Sunburst, Magenta Burst, Transparent Black, Transparent Green, and Transparent Red finishes. Mfg. 1998 to date.

MSR $2,099 — $1,675 $1,450 $1,250 $1,100 $895 $700 $525

MOCKINGBIRD BOLT-ON [U.S.: Bolt-On Neck] - offset double cutaway alder (or poplar) body, extended pointed treble bout/ rounded lower bout, bolt-on maple neck, 25 1/2" scale, 24-fret rosewood fingerboard with pearl dot inlay, locking Floyd Rose 2 tremolo, 6-on-a-side tuners, black hardware, 2 DiMarzio humbucker pickups, 2 volume/1 tone controls, 3-way selector, available in Black, Purple, Red, White, and Yellow finishes. Current Mfg.

MSR $1,199 — $950 $850 $750 $625 $525 $400 $300

Add $125 for optional Candy Color finish.

In 1998, Blood Red and Blue finishes were introduced; Purple, Red, and Yellow finishes were discontinued.

Mockingbird (N.J. Series) - similar to the Mockingbird [U.S.: Bolt-On Neck], except has 24 3/4" scale, diamond inlays, N.J. logo on headstock, die cast tuners, additional toggle switch, available in Black, Metallic Red, and White finishes. Current Mfg.

MSR $669 — $465 $425 $350 $295 $225 $175 $150

Add $25 for Transparent Blue or Transparent Red finishes (Transparent Blue finish was discontinued in 1998).

Add $20 for Blue Burst finish.

In 1998, Blood Red finish was introduced; Metallic Red finish was discontinued.
In 1999, Transparent Red and white finishes were discontinued.
In 2000, Blue Burst finish was introduced.

Mockingbird (Platinum Series) - similar to the Mockingbird [U.S.: Bolt-On Neck], except has 24 3/4" scale, white inlay dots, B.C. Rich 3-per-side headstock with Platinum logo, fixed bridge, die cast tuners, chrome hardware, additional toggle switch, available in Black, Blood Red, Metallic Red, and White finishes. Current Mfg.

MSR $499 — $350 $295 $250 $225 $175 $150 $125

Add $25 for Transparent Blue and Transparent Red finishes (Transparent Blue finish was discontinued in 1998).

Add $20 for Blue Burst finish.

Add $200 for Acrylic Red and Acrylic Green finishes.

In 1998, Metallic Red finish was discontinued.
In 1999, white finish was discontinued.
In 2000, Blue Burst, Acrylic Green and Acrylic Red finishes were introduced.

Mockingbird (Bronze Series) - similar to the Mockingbird [U.S.: Bolt-On Neck], except has laminated alder body, headstock with B.C. Rich/Bronze logos, covered machine heads, chrome hardware, available in Black, Red, and White finishes. Mfg. 1998 to date.

MSR $369 — $275 $250 $225 $175 $150 $125 $95

Nighthawk/Phoenix Series

"The **NightHawk** was the first attempt for a bolt on neck guitar for B.C. Rich. It was introduced around 1979. This model, along with the **Phoenix**, were made as an affordable B.C. Rich guitar for those times. The **NightHawk** was in the *Eagle* shape and the **Phoenix** was in the *Mockingbird* shape."

"Both the NightHawk and the Phoenix were made with mahogany body and maple neck, 25 1/2" scale, rosewood fingerboard with round position markers, and 2 DiMarzio Super Distortion pickups."

Seagull Series

The Seagull model was first introduced in 1971. "These models were the first production B.C. Rich electric guitars. To my knowledge [writes Bernie Rico], the Seagull Guitar and Bass were the first guitars to offer the neck-through design featuring total access with the heel-less neck-through concept."

Earlier Seagull models from the 1970s are generally priced between $1,000-$1,500.

SEAGULL WOODIE JR [U.S.: Neck-through-body] - sculpted single cutaway mahogany body, maple set neck, 22-fret rosewood fingerboard with pearl dot inlay, B.C. Rich bridge/stop tailpiece, blackface peghead with pearl logo inlay, 3-per-side Grover Imperial tuners, chrome hardware, 2 DiMarzio humbucker pickups, 2 volume/1 tone controls, 3-position switch, available in Black, Blue, DiMarzio Creme, Porsche Red, Translucent Blue and White finishes. Mfg. 1995 to 1996.

$800 $600 $525 $450 $395 $325 $250

Last MSR was $1,000.

ST Series

The ST (*Strat*) model was introduced in 1987.

ST MSS (Maple Molded Top) [U.S.: Neck-through-body] - offset double cutaway mahogany body, contoured quilted maple top, through-body maple neck, 24-fret ebony fingerboard with tear drop inlay, double locking Floyd Rose tremolo, 6-on-a-side tuners, chrome hardware, 2 Seymour Duncan custom humbucker pickups, 2 volume/1 tone controls, 3-way selector, available in Translucent Blue, Translucent Pagan Gold, Translucent Purple, and Translucent Red finishes. Mfg. 1995 to 1998.

$1,125 $950 $850 $750 $625 $525 $400

Last MSR was $1,599.

This model was part of the Tony MacAlpine Signature series.

GRADING	100% MINT	98% NEAR MINT	95% EXC+	90% EXC	80% VG+	70% VG	60% G

ST MSS [U.S.: Bolt-On Neck] - offset double cutaway alder body, contoured quilted maple top, bolt-on maple neck, 25 1/2" scale, 24-fret ebony fingerboard with tear drop inlay, locking Floyd Rose tremolo, 6-on-a-side tuners, chrome hardware, 2 Seymour Duncan custom humbucking pickups, 2 volume/1 tone controls, 3-way selector, available in Translucent Black, Translucent (Oriental) Blue, Translucent Magenta, Translucent Purple, and Translucent Red finishes. Current Mfg.

MSR $1,599	$1,275	$1,100	$950	$825	$675	$550	$400

In 1998, basswood body replaced the alder body; Transparent Root Beer finish was introduced; Translucent Purple finish was discontinued.

This model was previously available with 2 single coil/1 humbucker pickup configuration.

ST 2001 [U.S.: Bolt-On Neck] - similar to the ST MSS [U.S.: Bolt-On Neck], except has mahogany body, non-contoured quilted maple top, 22-fret maple fingerboard with black dot inlay, double locking Floyd Rose or Wilkinson fixed bridge, reverse headstock, available in Translucent Blue, Translucent Emerald Green, Translucent Pagan Gold, and Translucent Red finishes. Mfg. 1994 to 1998.

$900	$775	$695	$600	$500	$425	$325

Last MSR was $1,299.

ST (Platinum Series) - offset double cutaway solid alder body, bolt-on hard maple neck, 24 3/4" scale, 22-fret rosewood fingerboard with white inlay dots, B.C. Rich vintage-style 6-on-a-side headstock with Platinum logo, accu-tune tremolo, die cast tuners, chrome hardware, 2 single coil/1 humbucker pickups, volume/tone controls, additional mini toggle switch, 5-way selector, available in Black, Metallic Red, and White finishes. Disc. 1998.

$350	$295	$250	$225	$195	$150	$125

Last MSR was $489.

Add $25 for Transparent Blue and Transparent Red finishes.

ST (Bronze Series) (U.S. Series) - offset double cutaway laminated alder body, bolt-on hard maple neck, 25 1/2" scale, 21-fret maple fingerboard with black inlay dots, B.C. Rich vintage-style 6-on-a-side headstock, ST-style tremolo, covered machine heads, chrome hardware, 2 humbucker pickups, 2 volume/1 tone controls, 3-way selector, available in Black, Red, and White finishes. Current Mfg.

MSR $349	$275	$250	$225	$175	$150	$125	$95

ST (U.S. Series) models were available in Black, Blue, Purple, Red, and White finishes (until model transition in 1998).

ST III (U.S. Series) - similar to the ST (U.S. Series), except features 3 single coil pickups, 5-way selector switch. Disc. 1998.

$225	$195	$175	$150	$125	$95	$75

Last MSR was $299.

ST B1 (U.S. Series) - similar to the ST (U.S. Series), except has a bound laminated alder body, single coil/humbucker pickups. Disc. 1998.

$225	$200	$175	$150	$125	$100	$80

Last MSR was $329.

ST-1 (Rave Series) - similar to the ST III (U.S. Series), except has only 1 pickup. Disc. 1993.

$195	$170	$150	$130	$110	$90	$65

Last MSR was $279.

ST-3 (Rave Series) - similar to the ST III (U.S. Series), and features 3 single coil pickups. Disc. 1993.

$225	$200	$175	$150	$125	$100	$85

Last MSR was $339.

Stealth Series

The Stealth model was introduced in 1983. "The Stealth was designed in collaboration with Rick Derringer and Bernie Rich. Due to trend changes and slow sales, production was discontinued in 1989 and was only made through the Custom Shop." The Stealth model was briefly offered again as a production model in the late 1990s, then returned to its Custom Shop niche in 1998.

STEALTH STANDARD [U.S.: Neck-through-body] - offset double cutaway body, alder body wings, through-body maple neck, 24 5/8" scale, 24-fret rosewood fingerboard with pearl diamond inlay, fixed bridge, blackface peghead with logo, 3-per-side tuners, black hardware, 2 Seymour Duncan custom humbucker pickups, 2 volume/1 tone controls, 3-position switch, available in Black, Purple Red, White finishes. Disc. 1998.

$1,000	$900	$800	$675	$575	$450	$350

Last MSR was $1,399.

Stealth [U.S.: Bolt-On Neck] - similar to the Stealth Standard, except has alder body, bolt-on maple neck, 25 1/2" scale, 22-fret fingerboard with dot inlay, 2 DiMarzio custom humbuckers, available in Black, Cobalt Blue, Red, and White finishes. Disc. 1998.

$800	$725	$650	$550	$475	$375	$295

Last MSR was $1,199.

TS Series

TS series models were produced in the U.S. during the mid 1980s. The two models (**TS-100** and **TS-200**) both featured a tele-style design, and a bolt-on maple neck.

B.C. Rich Conti 8-string Jazz
courtesy B.C. Rich

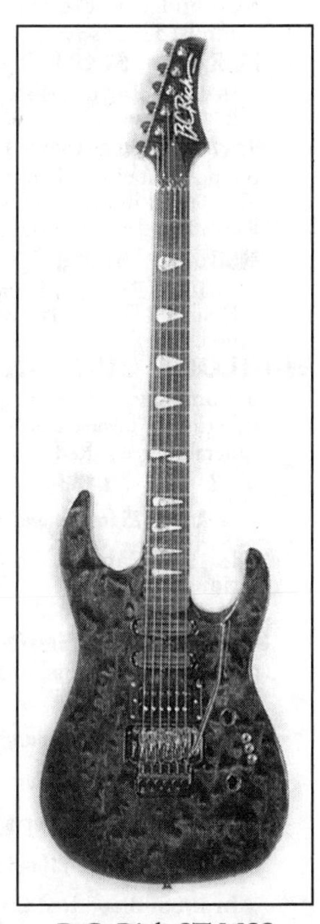

B.C. Rich ST MSS
courtesy B.C. Rich

GRADING	100% MINT	98% NEAR MINT	95% EXC+	90% EXC	80% VG+	70% VG	60% G

Virgin Series

The Virgin model was introduced in 1987.

VIRGIN [U.S.: Neck-through-body] - offset double cutaway body, pointed forward horns, rounded bottom bout, Honduran mahogany body wings, through-body maple neck, 22-fret rosewood fingerboard with pearl diamond inlay, Kahler Steeler tremolo, blackface peghead with logo, 3-per-side Sperzel tuners, black hardware, 2 Seymour Duncan humbucker pickups, volume/tone controls, 3-way selector, available in Black, Gun Metal Gray, Natural, Pearl Blue, Pearl Purple, Pearl White, Pearl Violet, Red, and Yellow finishes. Disc. 1993.

$1,300 $1,100 $1,000 $900 $775 $650 $525
Last MSR was $2,099.

Add $100 for optional Candy Color finishes.

Add $150 for optional translucent finishes.

Virgin [U.S.: Bolt-On Neck] - similar to the Virgin [U.S.: Neck-through-body], except has mahogany body, bolt-on maple neck. Disc. 1993.

$850 $725 $650 $550 $475 $400 $325
Last MSR was $1,299.

Virgin (N.J. Series) - similar to the Virgin [U.S.: Bolt-On Neck], except has diamond position markers, double locking Floyd Rose tremolo, EMG Select pickups, available in Black and Red finishes. Disc. 1993, 2000 to

MSR $689 $485 $335 $300 $250 $225 $175 $150

Add $20 for reverse headstock.

Add $70 for optional translucent finishes.

Red finish discontinued in 1993.

Virgin (Platinum Series) - similar to the Virgin [U.S.: Bolt-On Neck], except has dot position markers, double locking Floyd Rose tremolo, available in Black and Red finishes. Disc. 1993.

$300 $250 $225 $200 $175 $150 $100
Last MSR was $469.

Warlock Series

The Warlock model was introduced in 1981.

WARLOCK STANDARD [U.S.: Neck-through-body] - offset double cutaway body, pointed forward horns, centered large *V* cutaway in bottom bout, alder (or poplar) body wings, through-body maple neck, 24 5/8" scale, 24-fret rosewood fingerboard with pearl diamond inlay, fixed bridge, blackface peghead with logo, 6-on-a-side tuners, black hardware, 2 Seymour Duncan custom humbucker pickups, 2 volume/1 tone controls, 3-way selector, available in Black, Purple, Red, and White finishes. Current Mfg.

MSR $1,499 $1,200 $1,000 $875 $750 $625 $500 $375

In 1998, Floyd Rose 2 tremolo replaced the fixed bridge; Blood Red and Blue finishes were introduced; Purple and Red finishes were discontinued.

Warlock Supreme [U.S.: Neck-through-body] - similar to the Warlock Standard, except has mahogany body wings, mahogany neck, bound figured maple top, bound ebony fingerboard with abalone blade inlays, 3-per-side tuners, bound headstock, Floyd Rose tremolo or Quadmatic fixed bridge, 2 DiMarzio humbuckers, available in Transparent Sunburst Emerald Green, Transparent Sunburst Gold, Transparent Sunburst Pagan Blue, and Transparent Sunburst Red finishes. Current Mfg.

MSR $1,999 $1,500 $1,300 $1,150 $975 $825 $650 $500

In 1998, Blue Sunburst, Transparent Black, Transparent Green, and Transparent Red finishes were introduced; Transparent Sunburst Emerald Green, Transparent Sunburst Gold, Transparent Sunburst Pagan Blue, and Transparent Sunburst Red finishes were discontinued.

WARLOCK BOLT-ON [U.S.: Bolt-On Neck] - offset double cutaway alder body, pointed forward horns, centered large *V* cutaway in bottom bout, bolt-on maple neck, 25 1/2" scale, 24-fret rosewood fingerboard with white dot inlay, locking Floyd Rose 2 tremolo, 6-on-the-other-side tuners, reverse headstock, black hardware, 2 DiMarzio humbucker pickups, 2 volume/1 tone controls, 3-way selector, available in Black, Blue, Emerald Green, Red, White and Yellow finishes. Current Mfg.

MSR $1,199 $950 $825 $725 $600 $500 $395 $295

Add $125 for optional Candy Color finish.

In 1995, Candy Color finishes became optional, Purple finish was introduced, and Blue, Emerald Green, and Yellow finishes were discontinued.
In 1998, poplar body replaced the alder body; Blue finish was re-introduced; Purple and White finishes were discontinued.

Warlock (N.J. Series) - similar to the Warlock [U.S.: Bolt-On Neck], except has 24 3/4" scale, diamond inlays, N.J. logo on headstock, die cast tuners, additional toggle switch, available in Black, Metallic Red, and White finishes. Current Mfg.

MSR $669 $465 $425 $350 $295 $225 $175 $125

Add $25 for Transparent Blue or Transparent Red finishes (Transparent Blue finish was discontinued in 1998).

Add $20 for Blue Burst finish.

Add $100 for Supreme Black finish.

Add $25 for Left Hand Model with black finish.

In 1998, Blood Red finish was introduced; Metallic Red finish was discontinued.
In 1999, Transparent Red finish was discontinued.
In 2000, Blue Burst and Supreme Black finishes were introduced.

B

GRADING		100% MINT	98% NEAR MINT	95% EXC+	90% EXC	80% VG+	70% VG	60% G

Warlock (Platinum Series) - similar to the Warlock [U.S.: Bolt-On Neck], except has 24 3/4" scale, white inlay dots, B.C. Rich angled headstock with Platinum logo, 6-on-a-side die cast tuners, chrome hardware, accu-tune tremolo, additional toggle switch, available in Black, Metallic Red, and White finishes. Current Mfg.

MSR	$499	$350	$295	$250	$225	$175	$150	$125

Add $25 for Transparent Blue, Transparent Purple, and Transparent Red finishes (Transparent Blue and Transparent Purple finishes were discontinued in 1998).

Add $20 for Blue Burst finish.

Add $100 for Supreme Black finish.

Add $200 for Acrylic Red and Acrylic Green finishes.

Add $25 for Left Hand Model with black finish.

In 1998, Blood Red finish was introduced; Metallic Red finish was discontinued.
In 1999, Transparent Red finish was discontinued.
In 2000, Blue Burst, Supreme Black, Acrylic Green and Acrylic red finishes were introduced.

Warlock (Bronze Series, Warlock WG-5T) - similar to the Warlock [U.S.: Bolt-On Neck], except has laminated body, 24 3/4" scale, dot position markers, B.C. Rich angled headstock, 6-on-a-side covered tuners, chrome hardware, tremolo, available in Black, Red, and White finishes. Current Mfg.

MSR	$369	$275	$250	$225	$175	$150	$125	$95

Warlock WG-1 (Rave Series) - similar to the Warlock WG-5T, except has only 1 pickup. Disc. 1993.

$225	$195	$175	$150	$125	$95	$75

Last MSR was $309.

Warlock WG-2 (Rave Series) - similar to the Warlock WG-5T, and features 2 pickups. Disc. 1993.

$235	$200	$175	$150	$125	$100	$85

Last MSR was $339.

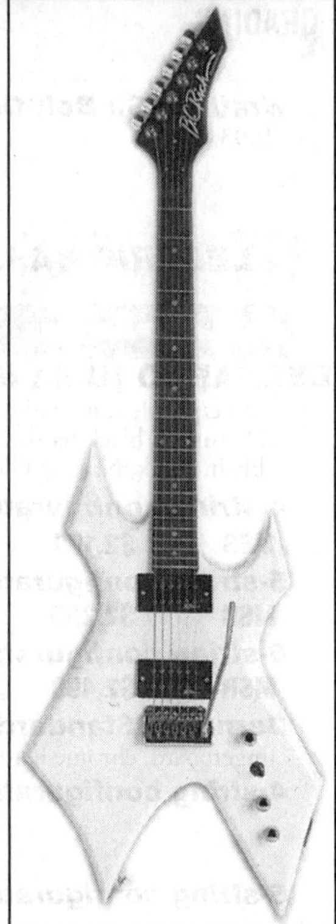
B.C. Rich Warlock (Platinum Series) courtesy B.C. Rich

Wave Series

The Wave model was introduced in 1983.

WAVE [U.S.: Neck-through-body] - offset double cutaway body with curled bottom bout cutaway, ash/mahogany body wings, through-body rock maple neck, 24 3/4" scale, 22-fret rosewood (or ebony) fingerboard with pearl diamond inlay, Kahler Steeler tremolo, blackface peghead with pearl logo inlay, 3-per-side tuners, chrome hardware, 2 DiMarzio humbucker pickups, 2 volume/1 tone controls, 3-position switch, available in Black, Gun Metal Gray, Natural, Pearl Blue, Pearl Purple, Pearl White, Pearl Violet, Red, and Yellow finishes. Disc. 1993.

$1,300	$1,150	$1,000	$900	$775	$650	$525

Last MSR was $2,099.

Add $100 for optional Candy Color finishes.

Add $150 for optional translucent finishes.

Wave Supreme [U.S.: Neck-through-body] - similar to the Wave, except has figured maple body, 24-fret bound ebony fingerboard with pearl cloud inlay, Leo Quan wraparound bridge, 2 volume/2-Tone controls, 4 mini switches, on-board preamp, available in Translucent Blue, Translucent Emerald Green, Natural, Translucent Pagan Gold, and Translucent Red finishes. Disc. 1989.

$1,600	$1,350	$1,200	$1,000	$900	$795	$650

Wave [U.S.: Bolt-On Neck] - similar to the Wave Bass [U.S.: Neck-through-body], except has Honduran mahogany body, bolt-on maple neck. Disc. 1993.

$900	$775	$650	$525	$475	$395	$325

Last MSR was $1,299.

Widow Series

The Widow model was introduced in 1983. "The Widow was designed in collaboration with Blackie Lawless (W.A.S.P.). The Widow was made in a guitar and bass configuration. This model was never part of our production lineup; however, we did make quite a few Widow guitars and basses in the Custom Shop."

Wrath Series

WRATH [U.S.: Neck-through-body] - offset double cutaway body, pointed forward horns, asymmetrical waist/rounded bottom bout, Honduran mahogany body wings, through-body maple neck, 22-fret rosewood fingerboard with pearl diamond inlay, Kahler Steeler tremolo, blackface peghead with logo, 3-per-side Sperzel tuners, black hardware, 2 Seymour Duncan humbucker pickups, volume/tone controls, 3-way selector, available in Black, Gun Metal Gray, Natural, Pearl Blue, Pearl Purple, Pearl White, Pearl Violet, Red, and Yellow finishes. Disc. 1993.

$1,300	$1,150	$1,000	$900	$775	$650	$525

Last MSR was $2,099.

Add $100 for optional Candy Color finishes.

Add $150 for optional translucent finishes.

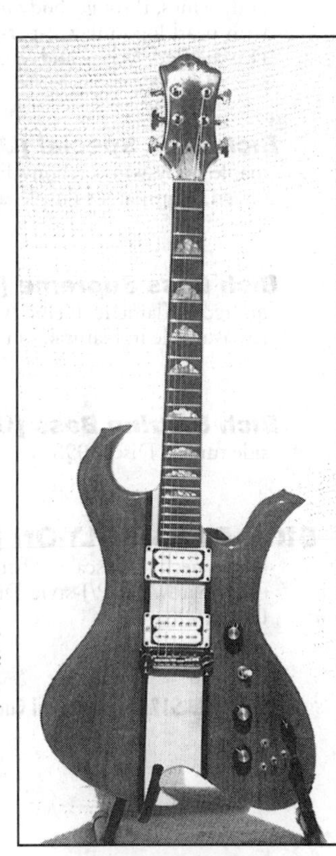
B.C. Rich Wave courtesy B.C. Rich

GRADING	100% MINT	98% NEAR MINT	95% EXC+	90% EXC	80% VG+	70% VG	60% G

Wrath [U.S.: Bolt-On Neck] - similar to the Wrath [U.S.: Neck-through-body], except has mahogany body, bolt-on maple neck. Disc. 1993.

$850	**$725**	**$650**	**$550**	**$475**	**$400**	**$325**

Last MSR was $1,299.

ELECTRIC BASS

Bernardo Series

BERNARDO [U.S.: Neck-through-body] (BERNARDO ARTIST/BERNARDO DELUXE) - offset double cutaway maple/purpleheart body, through-body maple neck, 34" scale, 24-fret ebony fingerboard with abalone oval inlays, black peghead with logo, 2-per-side tuners, black hardware, 2 Seymour Duncan Bassline soapbar pickups, volume/blend/stacked bass/mid/treble controls, active electronics, available in Black, Natural Gloss, Transparent Black, Transparent Red, White, and Natural hand-rubbed Oil finishes. Current Mfg.

4-string configuration.

MSR	$2,199	$1,750	$1,550	$1,350	$1,100	$950	$750	$550

5-string configuration (3/2-per-side tuners).

MSR	$2,299	$1,850	$1,600	$1,395	$1,195	$975	$775	$575

6-string configuration (3-per-side tuners).

MSR	$2,499	$2,000	$1,750	$1,525	$1,300	$1,075	$850	$625

Bernardo Standard [U.S.: Neck-through-body] - similar to the Bernardo Deluxe, except featured less figured woods, pau ferro fingerboard, chrome hardware, available in Acapulco Blue, Black, Cream, White, and Wine Purple solid finishes. Disc. 1998.

4-string configuration.

$1,300	**$1,175**	**$1,000**	**$875**	**$725**	**$595**	**$425**

Last MSR was $1,699.

5-string configuration.

$1,400	**$1,250**	**$1,100**	**$950**	**$775**	**$625**	**$450**

Last MSR was $1,799.

6-string configuration.

$1,500	**$1,325**	**$1,150**	**$995**	**$825**	**$650**	**$475**

Last MSR was $1,899.

Bich Bass Series

BICH BASS STANDARD [U.S.: Neck-through-body] - offset double cutaway body, asymmetrical bottom bout cutaways, maple body wings, through-body maple neck, 34" scale, 24-fret rosewood fingerboard with pearl diamond inlay, fixed Wilkinson bridge, blackface peghead with pearl logo inlay, 2-per-side tuners, black hardware, P/J-style DiMarzio pickups, 2 volume/1 tone controls, 3-way selector, available in Black, Porsche Red, White and Wine Purple finishes. Disc. 1998.

$1,000	**$900**	**$795**	**$695**	**$575**	**$475**	**$350**

Last MSR was $1,499.

Bich Bass Special [U.S.: Neck-through-body] - similar to the Bich Standard, except has hard rock maple neck, quilted or flame maple body wings, ebony fingerboard with abalone cloud inlays, active electronics, available in Natural, Transparent Blue, Transparent Emerald Green, Transparent Purple, and Transparent Red finishes. Disc. 1998.

$1,100	**$950**	**$850**	**$750**	**$625**	**$525**	**$400**

Last MSR was $1,599.

Bich Bass Supreme [U.S.: Neck-through-body] - similar to the Bich Standard, except has hard rock maple neck, AAA select quilted or flame maple body wings, bound ebony fingerboard and headstock, abalone cloud inlays, 2 DiMarzio P-style pickups, full active electronics, available in Natural, Transparent Blue, Transparent Emerald Green, Transparent Purple, and Transparent Red finishes. Disc. 1998.

$1,400	**$1,150**	**$1,000**	**$900**	**$825**	**$675**	**$500**

Last MSR was $1,999.

Bich 8 String Bass [U.S.: Neck-through-body] - similar to the Bich Supreme, except in an 8-string configuration, 30" scale, 4-per-side tuners. Disc. 1998.

$1,600	**$1,475**	**$1,200**	**$1,000**	**$N/A**	**$N/A**	**$N/A**

Last MSR was $2,100.

BICH BASS BOLT-ON [U.S.: Bolt-On Neck] - offset double cutaway maple body with asymmetrical bottom bout cutaways, bolt-on maple neck, 34" scale, 22-fret rosewood fingerboard with pearl diamond inlay, fixed bridge, blackface peghead with logo inlay, 2-per-side tuners, black hardware, P/J-style DiMarzio pickups, 2 volume/1 tone controls, 3-way selector, available in Black, Red, White and Wine Purple finishes. Disc. 1998.

$900	**$775**	**$695**	**$600**	**$500**	**$425**	**$325**

Last MSR was $1,299.

Add $125 for optional Candy Color finish.

GRADING	100% MINT	98% NEAR MINT	95% EXC+	90% EXC	80% VG+	70% VG	60% G

Eagle Bass Series

The Eagle Bass model was introduced in 1977.

EAGLE SUPREME [U.S.: Neck-through-body] - offset double cutaway figured maple body, through-body maple neck with koa stringers, 24-fret ebony fingerboard with pearl cloud inlay, fixed Wilkinson bridge, blackface peghead with pearl logo inlay, 2-per-side tuners, black hardware, P/J-style pickups, 2 volume/1 tone controls, available in Natural finish. Disc. 1996.

		100%	98%	95%	90%	80%	70%	60%
		$1,200	$1,050	$925	$825	$700	$595	$475

Last MSR was $1,899.

This model had an optional koa body/neck.

In 1995, active electronics, Translucent Blue, Translucent Emerald Green, Translucent Pagan Gold and Translucent Red finishes were introduced, bound fingerboard/peghead replace original part/designs.

Exxclusive Arch Top Bass Series

EXXCLUSIVE ARCH TOP BASS [U.S.: Neck-through-body] - offset double cutaway mahogany body, bound figured maple top, through-body maple neck, 34" scale, 24-fret bound ebony fingerboard with pearl block inlay, fixed bridge, blackface peghead with pearl 'R' inlay, 2-per-side tuners, chrome hardware, P/J-style Bassline pickups, 2 volume/1 tone controls, 3-way selector, available in Cherry Sunburst, Natural, Transparent Black, Transparent Magenta, and Transparent Red finishes. Mfg. 1998 to date.

		100%	98%	95%	90%	80%	70%	60%
MSR	$2,400	$1,800	$1,600	$1,400	$1,200	$1,000	$900	$750

Gunslinger Bass Series

GUNSLINGER BASS [U.S.: Bolt-On Neck] - offset double cutaway swamp ash body, bolt-on maple neck, 34" scale, 22-fret rosewood fingerboard with pearl dot inlay, fixed bridge, blackface peghead with logo, 4-on-a-side tuners, chrome hardware, DiMarzio High Output P-style pickup, volume/tone controls, available in Black, Creme, Porsche Red, and White finishes. Disc. 1998.

		100%	98%	95%	90%	80%	70%	60%
		$850	$725	$650	$550	$475	$395	$325

Last MSR was $1,199.

Add $40 for optional black hardware.

Ignitor Bass Series

IGNITOR BASS [U.S.: Bolt-On Neck] - offset double cutaway maple body, pointed forward horns, scooped lower bout cutaway, bolt-on maple neck, 34" scale, 22-fret rosewood fingerboard with dot inlays, fixed bridge, black hardware, 4-on-a-side tuners, P/J-style DiMarzio pickups, 2 volume/1 tone controls, 3-way selector, available in Black, Red, White, and Wine Purple finishes. Disc. 1998.

		100%	98%	95%	90%	80%	70%	60%
		$900	$775	$695	$600	$500	$425	$325

Last MSR was $1,299.

Innovator Bass Series

The Innovator Bass model was introduced in 1987.

INNOVATOR BASS 4 [U.S.: Neck-through-body] - offset double cutaway maple/purpleheart body, maple through-body neck, 34" scale, 24-fret ebony fingerboard with abalone block inlay, fixed bridge, 4-on-a-side tuners, chrome hardware, 2 Seymour Duncan Bassline soapbar pickups, 2 volume/blend/tone controls, active electronics, available in Natural hand-rubbed Oil finish. Mfg. 1987 to date.

		100%	98%	95%	90%	80%	70%	60%
MSR	$1,699	$1,300	$1,195	$1,050	$895	$725	$575	$425

Add $225 for optional transparent color Urethane finish.

Innovator Bass 5 [U.S.: Neck-through-body] - similar to Innovator Bass 4, except has 5-string configuration, 3/2-per-side tuners. Disc. 1998.

		100%	98%	95%	90%	80%	70%	60%
		$1,100	$950	$850	$750	$600	$500	$400

Last MSR was $1,599.

Innovator Bass 6 [U.S.: Neck-through-body] - similar to Innovator Bass 4, except has 6-string configuration, through-body maple neck with rosewood stringers, ebony fingerboard with pearl cloud inlay, 3-per-side tuners, 2 humbucker Bartolini pickups. Disc. 1997.

		100%	98%	95%	90%	80%	70%	60%
		$1,350	$1,150	$1,000	$925	$775	$650	$475

Last MSR was $2,000.

INNOVATOR [U.S.: Bolt-On Neck] - offset double cutaway swamp ash body, bolt-on maple neck, 34" scale, 22-fret pau ferro fingerboard with pearl dot inlay, fixed bridge, blackface peghead with logo, 4-on-a-side tuners, chrome hardware, Seymour Duncan Bassline soapbar pickup, volume/tone controls, active electronics, available in Black, Creme, Porsche Red, and White finishes. Disc. 1998.

		100%	98%	95%	90%	80%	70%	60%
		$900	$775	$695	$600	$500	$425	$325

Last MSR was $1,299.

Add $100 for optional gold hardware.

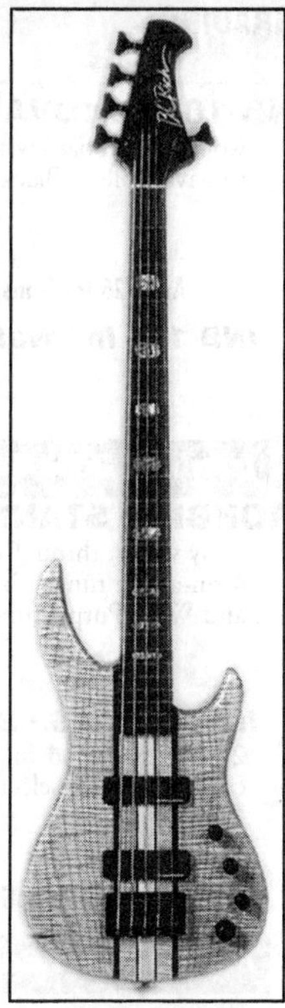

B.C. Rich Innovator Bass courtesy B.C. Rich

GRADING	100% MINT	98% NEAR MINT	95% EXC+	90% EXC	80% VG+	70% VG	60% G

B

INB-104 INNOVATOR BASS 4 STRING - offset double cutaway solid ash and maple body, bolt-on maple neck, 34" scale, 22-fret rosewood fingerboard with dot inlay, fixed bridge, 4-on-a-side tuners, chrome hardware, 2 active soapbar pickups, 2 volume/1 tone controls, 3-way selector, available in Black, Natural, Red, and White finishes. Disc. 1998.

	$475	$395	$350	$300	$250	$200	$150

Last MSR was $649.

Add $25 for Transparent Blue, Transparent Purple, or Transparent Red finishes.

INB-105 Innovator Bass 5 String - similar to the INB-104 Innovator Bass, except in a 5-string configuration. Disc. 1998.

	$495	$425	$375	$325	$275	$225	$175

Last MSR was $699.

Ironbird Bass Series

IRONBIRD STANDARD [U.S.: Neck-through-body] - angular offset cutaway body, pointed treble bout/rear body bouts, maple body wings, through-body maple neck, 34" scale, 24-fret rosewood fingerboard with pearl diamond inlay, fixed bridge, blackface peghead with logo, 4-on-a-side tuners, black hardware, P/J-style DiMarzio pickups, 2 volume/1 tone controls, 3-way selector, available in Black, Porsche Red, White, and Wine Purple finishes. Disc. 1998.

	$1,100	$900	$795	$695	$575	$475	$350

Last MSR was $1,499.

Ironbird [U.S.: Bolt-On Neck] - angular offset cutaway maple body, pointed treble bout/rear body bouts, bolt-on maple neck, 34" scale, 22-fret rosewood fingerboard with pearl dot inlay, fixed bridge, 4-on-a-side tuners, black hardware, P/J-style DiMarzio pickups, 2 volume/1 tone controls, 3-way selector, available in Black, Red, and White finishes. Disc. 1998.

	$900	$775	$695	$600	$500	$425	$325

Last MSR was $1,299.

Add $125 for optional Candy Color finishes.

Mockingbird Bass Series

MOCKINGBIRD BASS STANDARD [U.S.: Neck-through-body] - offset double cutaway asymmetrical body, maple body wings, through-body maple neck, 34" scale, 24-fret rosewood fingerboard with pearl diamond inlay, fixed bridge, blackface peghead with pearl logo inlay, 2-per-side tuners, black hardware, P/J-style DiMarzio pickups, 2 volume/1 tone controls, 3-position switch, available in Black, Porsche Red, White, and Wine Purple finishes. Current Mfg.

MSR $1,499	$1,150	$1,000	$875	$750	$625	$500	$375

In 1998, Porsche Red and Wine Purple finishes were discontinued; Blood Red and Metallic Red finishes were introduced.

Mockingbird Arch Top Bass [U.S.: Neck-through-body] - similar to the Mockingbird Standard, except has mahogany body wings, carved maple top, mahogany through-body neck, chrome hardware, available in Black, Oriental Blue, Purple, Red, and White finishes. Disc. 1998.

	$1,350	$1,195	$1,050	$895	$725	$575	$425

Last MSR was $1,699.

Mockingbird Bass Special [U.S.: Neck-through-body] - similar to the Mockingbird Standard, except has quilted or flame maple body wings, hard rock maple neck-through-body, ebony fingerboard with abalone cloud inlays, 2 P-style DiMarzio pickups, active electronics, available in Natural, Transparent Blue, Transparent Emerald Green, Transparent Purple, and Transparent Red finishes. Disc. 1998.

	$1,125	$995	$850	$750	$625	$525	$400

Last MSR was $1,599.

Mockingbird Bass Supreme [U.S.: Neck-through-body] - similar to the Mockingbird Standard, except has AAA select quilted or flame maple body wings, hard rock maple neck-through-body, bound ebony fingerboard with abalone cloud inlays, bound headstock, 2 P-style DiMarzio pickups, full active electronics, available in Natural, Transparent Blue, Transparent Emerald Green, Transparent Purple, and Transparent Red finishes. Disc. 1998.

	$1,550	$1,300	$1,100	$1,000	$895	$750	$550

Last MSR was $1,999.

MOCKINGBIRD BASS BOLT-ON [U.S.: Bolt-On Neck] - offset double cutaway asymmetrical maple body, bolt-on maple neck, 34" scale, 22-fret rosewood fingerboard with pearl dot inlay, fixed bridge, 2-per-side tuners, black hardware, P/J-style DiMarzio pickups, 2 volume/1 tone controls, 3-position switch, available in Black, Red, White, and Wine Purple finishes. Disc. 1998.

	$900	$775	$695	$600	$500	$425	$325

Last MSR was $1,299.

Add $125 for optional Candy Color finishes.

Mockingbird 4 String (Platinum Series) - similar to the Mockingbird [U.S.: Bolt-On Neck), except has solid maple body, dot position markers, 2-per-side headstock with Platinum logo, chrome hardware, 2 P-style pickups, available in Black, Red, and White finishes. Disc. 1998.

	$425	$350	$325	$275	$225	$195	$175

Last MSR was $599.

Add $25 for Transparent Blue, Transparent Green, or Transparent Purple finishes.

GRADING	100% MINT	98% NEAR MINT	95% EXC+	90% EXC	80% VG+	70% VG	60% G

Seagull Bass Series

The Seagull model was introduced in 1972. "The **Eagle Bass** was formerly called the **Bodine Bass**. It was named after a very good friend named Bill Bodine, who at the time was the bass player for Olivia Newton-John. After the Seagull went through a slight design change that it was renamed the Bodine Bass. The original Seagull featured a shorter upper horn and the Bodine/Eagle featured a longer upper horn. The upper horn was modified to give the bass better balance."

ST Series

ST BASS (U.S. Series) - offset double cutaway laminated alder body, bolt-on hard maple neck, 34" scale, 21-fret maple fingerboard with black dot inlay, vintage-style fixed bridge, 4-on-a-side vintage-style headstock, open gear tuners, chrome hardware, P-style pickup, volume/tone controls, available in Black, Bright Green, Creme, Red, and White finishes. Disc. 1998.

MSR $399 — $275 $250 $200 $175 $150 $125 $100

TBB Series

TBB BASS [U.S.: Neck-through-body] - offset double cutaway body, mahogany body wings, through-body maple neck, 34" scale, 22-fret rosewood fingerboard with pearl diamond inlay, fixed bridge, 2-per-side tuners, chrome hardware, P/J-style DiMarzio pickups, 2 volume/2-Tone controls, 3-way selector, available in Black, Creme, Red, and White finishes. Disc. 1998.

$1,000 $900 $795 $695 $575 $475 $350
Last MSR was $1,499.

Virgin Bass Series

VIRGIN BASS [U.S.: Neck-through-body] - offset double cutaway body, pointed forward horns, rounded bottom bout, Honduran mahogany body wings, through-body maple neck, 34" scale, 22-fret rosewood fingerboard with pearl diamond inlay, fixed bridge, blackface peghead with logo, 4-on-a-side tuners, black hardware, P/J-style Seymour Duncan pickups, volume/tone controls, 3-way selector, available in Black, Gun Metal Gray, Natural, Pearl Blue, Pearl Purple, Pearl White, Pearl Violet, Red, and Yellow finishes. Disc. 1993.

$1,395 $1,150 $1,000 $900 $795 $675 $525
Last MSR was $2,099.

Add $100 for optional Candy Color finishes.

Add $150 for optional translucent finishes.

Virgin Bass [U.S.: Bolt-On Neck] - similar to the Virgin Bass [U.S.: Neck-through-body], except has mahogany body, bolt-on maple neck. Disc. 1993.

$850 $725 $650 $550 $475 $400 $325
Last MSR was $1,299.

Virgin Bass 4 String (N.J. Series) - similar to the Virgin Bass [U.S.: Bolt-On Neck], except has diamond position markers, EMG Select pickups, available in Black and Red finishes. Disc. 1993.

$425 $350 $300 $275 $250 $195 $150
Last MSR was $629.

Add $20 for reverse headstock.

Add $70 for optional translucent finishes.

Virgin Bass 4 String (Platinum Series) - similar to the Virgin Bass [U.S.: Bolt-On Neck], except has dot position markers, available in Black and Red finishes. Disc. 1993.

$300 $250 $225 $200 $175 $150 $125
Last MSR was $469.

Warlock Bass Series

WARLOCK BASS STANDARD [U.S.: Neck-through-body] - offset double cutaway body, pointed forward horns, centered large *V* cutaway in bottom bout, maple body wings, through-body maple neck, 34" scale, 24-fret rosewood fingerboard with pearl diamond inlay, fixed bridge, blackface peghead with pearl logo inlay, 2-per-side tuners, black hardware, P/J-style DiMarzio pickups, 2 volume/1 tone controls, 3-position switch, available in Black, Porsche Red, White and Wine Purple finishes. Current Mfg.

MSR $1,499 — $1,150 $1,050 $925 $775 $650 $500 $375

In 1998, Porsche Red and Wine Purple finishes were discontinued; Blood Red and Metallic Red finishes were introduced.

WARLOCK [U.S.: Bolt-On Neck] - offset double cutaway maple body, pointed forward horns, centered large *V* cutaway in bottom bout, bolt-on maple neck, 34" scale, 22-fret rosewood fingerboard with pearl dot inlay, fixed bridge, 2-per-side tuners, black hardware, P/J-style DiMarzio pickups, 2 volume/1 tone controls, 3-position switch, available in Black, Red, White, and Wine Purple finishes. Current Mfg.

$900 $775 $695 $600 $500 $425 $325
Last MSR was $1,299.

This model had optional Candy Color finishes.

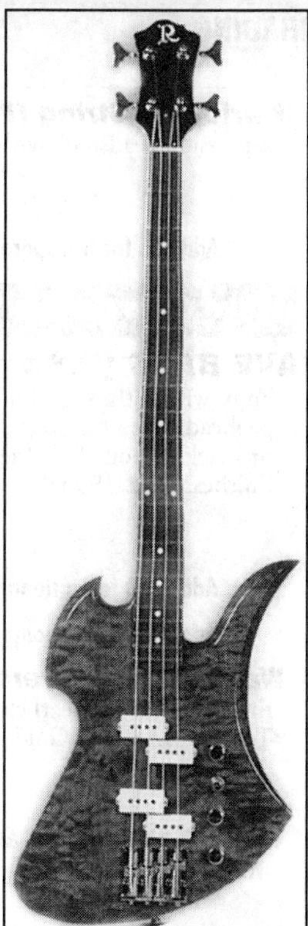

B.C. Rich Mockingbird Bass Bolt-On courtesy B.C. Rich

GRADING	100% MINT	98% NEAR MINT	95% EXC+	90% EXC	80% VG+	70% VG	60% G

Warlock 4 String (Platinum Series) - similar to the Warlock [U.S.: Bolt-On Neck], except has solid maple body, dot position markers, 2-per-side headstock with Platinum logo, P/J-style pickups, available in Black, Red, and White finishes. Current Mfg.

$425	$375	$325	$275	$225	$195	$150

Last MSR was $599.

Add $25 for Transparent Blue, Transparent Green, or Transparent Purple finishes.

Wave Bass Series

WAVE BASS [U.S.: Neck-through-body] - offset double cutaway body with curled bottom bout cutaway, maple (ash or mahogany) body wings, through-body rock maple neck, 34" scale, 22-fret rosewood (or ebony) fingerboard with pearl diamond inlay, fixed bridge, blackface peghead with pearl logo inlay, 2-per-side tuners, black hardware, P/J-style DiMarzio pickups, 2 volume/2-Tone controls, 3-position switch, available in Black, Blood Red, Metallic Red, Natural, Translucent Blue, Translucent Emerald Green, Translucent Pagan Gold, Translucent Red, and White finishes. Disc. 1995.

$1,350	$1,150	$1,000	$900	$775	$650	$525

Last MSR was $2,099.

Add $100 for optional Candy Color finishes.

Add $150 for optional translucent finishes.

Wave Bass Supreme [U.S.: Neck-through-body] - similar to the Wave Bass, except has figured maple body, 24-fret bound ebony fingerboard with pearl cloud inlay, 2 volume/2-Tone controls, on-board preamp, available in Translucent Blue, Translucent Emerald Green, Natural, Translucent Pagan Gold, and Translucent Red finishes. Disc. 1995.

$1,425	$1,250	$1,050	$925	$875	$750	$595

Last MSR was $1,899.

Wave Bass [U.S.: Bolt-On Neck] - similar to the Wave Bass [U.S.: Neck-through-body], except has ash body, bolt-on maple neck, rosewood fingerboard, 2 volume/1 tone controls, available in Black, Sunburst, Turquoise, and White finishes. Disc. 1995.

$900	$775	$650	$525	$475	$425	$375

Last MSR was $1,299.

Wrath Bass Series

WRATH BASS [U.S.: Neck-through-body] - offset double cutaway body, pointed forward horns, asymmetrical waist/rounded bottom bout, Honduran mahogany body wings, through-body maple neck, 34" scale, 22-fret rosewood fingerboard with pearl diamond inlay, fixed bridge, blackface peghead with logo, 4-on-a-side tuners, black hardware, P/J-style pickups, volume/tone controls, 3-way selector, available in Black, Gun Metal Gray, Natural, Pearl Blue, Pearl Purple, Pearl White, Pearl Violet, Red, and Yellow finishes. Disc. 1993.

$1,395	$1,150	$1,050	$900	$795	$675	$525

Last MSR was $2,099.

Add $100 for optional Candy Color finishes.

Add $150 for optional translucent finishes.

Wrath Bass [U.S.: Bolt-On Neck] - similar to the Wrath Bass [U.S.: Neck-through-body], except has mahogany body, bolt-on maple neck. Disc. 1993.

$895	$750	$650	$550	$475	$400	$325

Last MSR was $1,299.

BD DEY

Instruments previously built in the Czech Republic. Previously distributed by BD Dey Musical Instruments of the Czech Republic.

The Czech Republic is the popular place for companies looking for an alternative to Asian guitar production. Various areas in the Czech Republic have a reputation for excellent instrument craftsmanship, evolving from the earlier days of violin and viola production. B D Dey offered 5 different electric guitar models, and a 6- and 12-string jumbo acoustic guitar model.

ELECTRIC

All B D Dey electric guitar models feature Gotoh hardware, Kent Armstrong or Porizta pickups, and S I T strings. The **Dey 01** has a double cutaway mahogany body with sharp forward horns, mahogany neck, 24-fret ebony fingerboard, 6-per-side tuners, and 2 humbucking pickups. The **Dey 02** has a similar design, with slimmed down maple body, maple neck, and rosewood fingerboard; the **Dey 03** features a semi-hollow walnut body, mahogany neck, and 3 Kent Armstrong single coils. The **Dey 04** is more of a 'superstrat' style, with basswood body, maple neck, ebony fingerboard, 6-on-a-side tuners, and 2 humbuckers. The **Dey 05** is a throwback to the 1980s 'heavy metal' guitar years, and features a 'chopped' explorer-style alder body and maple neck.

BM

Instruments previously built in both Japan and Britain during the early 1960s through the mid 1980s.

The B M trademark was utilized by the UK importer Barnes & Mullins. While the company did import some entry level to medium quality guitars in from Japan, they also distributed some British-built SHERGOLD originals under their trademark.

(Source: Tony Bacon and Paul Day, The Guru's Guitar Guide)

B

BSX BASS, INC.

Instruments currently built in Aliquippa, Pennsylvania since 1989.

BSX has been producing a sleek electric upright bass for the past decade. BSX's current model line consists of 3 different upright models, and a conventional electric bass with through-neck construction. BSX basses fit the niche when you want that upright feel and sound, but can't put an upright acoustic bass in the back seat of your economy car!

In nine years of operation, BSX estimates that over 500 instruments have been produced. BSX briefly offered the BSX Traveler, which featured a detachable neck and a piezo bridge pickup. These innovations have been incorporated into the T Series model.

ELECTRIC BASS

Add $30 for position dots.

Add $50 for left-handed configuration.

Add $50 for inlaid fret lines.

Add $75 for Sapphire Blue, Vintage Yellow, Crimson Red, or Emerald Green Translucent colors.

Add $80 for Walnut, Maple, or Ash body woods.

Add $80 for Walnut, Maple, Cherry, or Purpleheart top woods.

Add $90 for graphite fingerboard.

BSX T 4 - slim upright poplar body, detachable tilting rock maple neck, 41 1/2" scale, fretless ebony fingerboard, 5" tall wood bridge, 2-per-side Hipshot tuners, open center peghead, rotating tummy rest, adjustable endpin, multi-sensor piezo bridge pickup, volume control per string, treble/mid/bass EQ controls, active Bartolini electronics, available in Burgundy or Tobacco gloss (or satin) finishes. Current Mfg.

Body Length - 55 inches, Body Width - 5 1/2 inches, Weight - 12 lbs.

MSR **$2,900**

Add $35 for Thigh rest addition.

BSX T 5 - similar to the T 4, except features 5-string configuration, 3/2-per-side tuners. Current Mfg.

MSR **$3,000**

BSX T 6 - similar to the T 4, except features 6-string configuration, 3-per-side tuners. Current Mfg.

MSR **$3,200**

BSX ST 4 - similar to the BSX T 4, except features non-removable neck, 3" tall wood bridge, 39" to 41 1/2" scale (specify when ordering), solid "paddle" headstock, available in Burgundy or Tobacco gloss (or satin) finishes. Current Mfg.

Body Length - 50 inches, Body Width - 5 inches, Weight - 9 lbs.

MSR **$1,600**

Add $35 for Thigh rest addition.

Add $105 for modified Tripod Stand.

BSX ST 5 - similar to the ST 4, except features 5-string configuration, 3/2-per-side tuners. Current Mfg.

MSR **$1,800**

BSX ST 6 - similar to the ST 4, except features 6-string configuration, 3-per-side tuners. Current Mfg.

MSR **$1,900**

BSX FLIP 4 - slim poplar body, set-in rock maple neck, 34" scale, fretless ebony fingerboard, wood bridge, 2-per-side Hipshot tuners, solid peghead, multi-sensor piezo bridge pickup, volume control per string, treble/mid/bass EQ controls, active Bartolini electronics, available in Burgundy or Tobacco gloss (or satin) finishes. Current Mfg.

Body Length - 43 inches, Body Width - 5 1/2 inches, Weight - 7 lbs.

MSR **$1,100**

Add $105 for modified Tripod Stand.

The BSX Flip model is not available with a Tummy rest, Thigh rest, or End Pin. The BSX Flip can be played upright or strapped on like a conventional electric bass.

BSX Flip 5 - similar to the Flip 4, except features 5-string configuration, 3/2-per-side tuners. Current Mfg.

MSR **$1,250**

BSX J 4 - offset double cutaway body with elongated bass horn, through-body maple neck, 34" scale, 24-fret ebony fingerboard with pearl dot inlay, Hipshot fixed bridge, 2-per-side Hipshot tuners, black chrome hardware, 2 J-style Bartolini pickups, volume/tone controls, Bartolini electronics, available in Natural satin or gloss finishes. Current Mfg.

MSR **$1,500**

Add $50 for Sapphire Blue, Vintage Yellow, Crimson Red, or Emerald Green Translucent colors.

BSX J 5 - similar to the J 4, except features 5-string configuration, 3/2-per-side tuners. Current Mfg.

MSR **$1,700**

GRADING			100% MINT	98% NEAR MINT	95% EXC+	90% EXC	80% VG+	70% VG	60% G

BACHMANN

Instruments currently built in Antholz-Mittertal, Germany.

This independent luthier is currently building a number of high quality guitars. For further information regarding specifications and pricing, please contact Bachmann Guitars directly (see Trademark Index).

BAKER

Instruments currently built in Riverside, California. Distributed in the U.S. by Baker Guitars U.S.A. and Intertune, Inc. in Japan.

Gene Baker began playing guitar at age eleven, and honed his woodworking skills in Junior High preparing for his guitar-building career. Baker attended the Guitar Institute of Technology (G.I.T.) to further his playing abilities. After graduation, Baker served as a teacher/repair man for various stores, and briefly worked at Ernie Ball/Music Man. Baker built a number of guitars in a limited partnership under the **Mean Gene** trademark between 1989 to 1991.

Baker then took a Masters apprentice job at the Gibson West Custom Shop, serving under Roger Griffin. His duties included warranty repairs, vintage restorations, and custom building guitars. After Gibson closed down the shop, Baker moved to the Fender Custom Shop in Corona. Baker's first production work at Fender included working on the Robben Ford Signature Series, as well as the Carved Top Strat. In 1995, Baker was promoted to Master Builder (at age 28), and continued to produce around 60 custom Fender guitars a year.

In his spare time, Baker produces a limited amount of Baker guitars in his own workshop. Baker guitars strive to meld Gibson and Fender designs while keeping as much individuality and vintage values in the instrument.

ELECTRIC

Baker offers a number of custom options on his models, such as a Bigsby tailpiece, Korina bodies, or gold hardware (call for pricing). Suggested list prices include hardshell case.

B1 - single white bound mahogany body, figured maple top, set-in mahogany neck, 25 1/2 " scale, 22-fret bound rosewood fingerboard with custom side block inlays, Grover tuners, nickel hardware, Tune-o-matic bridge/stop tailpiece, 2 Seymour Duncan humbuckers, 2 volume/2-Tone controls, pickup selector, available in 2-Tone Sunburst, Cherry Burst, Gold Top with Natural or Transparent Brown back, Honey Burst, Transparent Amber, Transparent Bing Cherry, Transparent Blue, Transparent Blue Burst, and Transparent Red finishes. Mfg. 1997 to date.

MSR $3,450 $2,595 $2,395 $2,195 $1,995 $1,795 $1,595 $1,395

This model is available with optional Bigsby tailpiece and gold hardware.

B1 Chambered (B1C) similar to the B1H , except does not have Talon f-hole, carved flamed maple top, available in Watermelon, Aged Cherry Burst, Cherry Sun Burst, Tequila Sunrise, Antique Burst, Two-tone Sun Burst, Binge Cherry and Ice Tea Burst finishes. Current Mfg.

MSR $3,615 $2,700 $2,400 $2,100 $1,800 $1,500 $1,200 $999

B1 Hollow (B1H) - similar to the B1, except has single white bound mahogany neck/headstock/body, 3/4 chambered body, carved undertop with bound f-hole. Mfg. 1997 to date.

MSR $3,950 $2,950 $2,650 $2,350 $2,050 $1,750 $1,450 $1,150

This model is available with optional Bigsby tailpiece and gold hardware.

B1 Seven String - similar to the B1, except in a 7-string configuration, top bound solid mahogany body, highly figured carved maple top, mahogany set neck, 22-fret rosewood fingerboard with custom side block position markers, medium jumbo frets, 2 DiMarzio Custom Humbucking pickups, Tone Pros/Baker Nashville Tune-O-Matic bridge, 1 volume/2-Tone controls, 5-way pickup selector, Schaller tuners, nickel hardware, available in watermelon, Aged Cherry Burst, Chery Sun Burst, Tequila Sunrise, Antique Burst, Two-tone Sunburst, Binge Cherry and Ice Tea Burst finishes. Current Mfg.

MSR $3,780 $2,850 $2,550 $2,250 $1,950 $1,650 $1,350 $999

BJ - mahogany body, set-in mahogany neck, 24 5/8" scale, 22-fret rosewood fingerboard with pearl dot inlays, Grover tuners, nickel hardware, Wilkinson wrap around/stop tailpiece, 2 P-90 pickups, volume/tone controls, pickup selector, available in 2-Tone Sunburst, Transparent Amber, Transparent Red, and TV Yellow finishes. Mfg. 1997 to date.

MSR $2,615 $1,965 $1,750 $1,550 $1,350 $1,150 $950 $750

This model is available with optional Korina neck and body.

BJ Hollow similar to the BJ, except has hollow mahogany body, highly figured maple top, medium jumbo frets, available with two P-90's or 2 humbucking pickups, Schaller Nashville Tune-O-Matic bridge, 2 volume/1 tone control, 3-way pickup selector, Schaller tuners, nickel hardware, available in Watermelon, Aged Cherry Burst, Cherry Sun Burst, Tequila Sunrise, Antique Burst, Two-tone Sunburst, Binge Cherry and Ice tea Burst finishes. Current Mfg.

MSR $3,030 $2,275 $2,075 $1,875 $1,675 $1,450 $1,250 $1,050

BNT - mahogany body, figured maple top, mahogany neck-through-body, 25 1/2 " scale, 22-fret bound rosewood fingerboard with custom side block inlays, Grover tuners, nickel hardware, Wilkinson tremolo, 2 Seymour Duncan humbuckers, volume/tone (push/pull) controls, pickup selector, available in 2-Tone Sunburst, Cherry Burst, Honey Burst, Transparent Amber, Transparent Bing Cherry, Transparent Blue, Transparent Blue Burst, and Transparent Red finishes. Mfg. 1997 to 2000.

$2,550 $2,350 $2,150 $1,950 $1,750 $1,550 $1,350

Last MSR was $3,400.

ELECTRIC BASS

B1 BASS - single white bound mahogany body, figured maple carved top, set-in mahogany neck, 34" scale, 21-fret bound rosewood fingerboard with custom side block inlays, Grover tuners, nickel hardware, Badass fixed bridge, 2 Seymour Duncan pickups, active controls, available in 2-Tone Sunburst, Cherry Burst, Gold Top with Natural or Transparent Brown back, Honey Burst, Transparent Bing Cherry, Transparent Blue, Transparent Blue Burst, and Transparent Red finishes. Mfg. 1997 to date.

MSR $4,400 $3,300 $2,995 $2,695 $2,395 $1,995 $1,695 $1,395

BAKER, JAMES R.

Instruments currently built in Shoreham, New York.

Luthier James R. Baker has been building conventional archtop guitars as well as experimental archtop designs that enhance the electric capabilities of the guitar. While his **Classic** features traditionally placed f-holes, Baker's innovative **Legend** and **Special** models have teardrop-shaped soundholes in the lower bout, and a patented structure which eliminates feedback and increases sustain. All models now feature Kent Armstrong pickups.

James R. Baker Legend
courtesy James R. Baker

ELECTRIC ARCHTOP

THE CLASSIC - single rounded cutaway body design, bookmatched spruce and bookmatched flame maple materials, 3" depth, 17" width across the lower bout, 25 1/2" scale, antiqued ivoroid body/f-hole binding, ebony fingerboard, matching maple pickguard/violin style bridge/wood fingerjointed hinge tailpiece, 3-per-side headstock with *note* design, Schaller or Grover tuning machines, Kent Armstrong or EMG floating pickup, pickguard-mounted volume control, available in Honey Blond lacquer finish. Current Mfg.

Mfg.'s Base Price **$4,500 + options**

Price includes a premium luggage case.

The Legend - similar to the Classic, except has Spanish cedar top, bookmatched African mahogany neck and sides, African Sapele with inlaid art work of rosewood/ebony/zebrawood, 2 lower bout teardrop soundholes, 2 upper bout smaller teardrop soundholes, EMG 91 active/passive floating pickup, available in clear Natural lacquer finish. Current Mfg.

Mfg.'s Base Price **$4,500 + options**

Price includes a premium luggage case.

The Special - similar to the Classic, except has 2 teardrop soundholes in lower bout instead of f-holes, ebony or maple pickguard, available in clear Natural or Black Burst lacquer finish. Current Mfg.

Mfg.'s Base Price **$4,500 + options**

Price includes a premium luggage case.

ONE-PIECE SOLID BODY MODEL carved from a single book matched billet of tonewood, single cutaway design, Kent Armstrong pickups, "Equal Space" TM neck profile, available in a large quantity of exotic tonewoods and finishes. Current Mfg.

Mfg.'s Base Price **$3,500 + options**

BAKES GUITARS

Instruments currently built in Elgin, Illinois since 1983. Distributed by Bakes Guitars of Elgin, Illinois.

Luthier Robert Bakes has been handcrafting fine guitars since 1983. Over the past twelve years, Bakes has been performing repairs and custom building instruments out of the Bakes Guitars shop in Elgin, Illinois. Ably assisted by his wife Beverly, Bakes also produces the classic vintage instrument show, "Guitar Madness". This show is held yearly in September. For information regarding either the guitars or the guitar show, please contact Bakes Guitars directly (see Trademark Index).

BALDWIN

Instruments previously produced between 1965 to 1970. Baldwin guitars and basses were initially built in England by Burns; later models were shipped by components and assembled in Booneville, Arkansas. Distributed by the Baldwin Piano Company of Cinncinnati, Ohio.

In 1962, as Leo Fender's health was faltering, he discussed the idea of selling Fender Electric Instruments company to Don Randall (head of Fender Sales). While Randall toyed with the idea even as late as the summer of 1963, they eventually concluded to sell to a third party who had money. Negotiations began with the Baldwin Piano Company in April of 1964, who offered $5 million (minus Fender's liabilities). When talks bogged down over acoustic guitar and electric piano operations, Randall met with representatives of the Columbia Broadcasting System (CBS). An agreement with CBS was signed in October, 1964, for $13 million that took effect in January of 1965.

Baldwin, outbid by CBS but still looking to diversify its product lines, then bought the Burns manufacturing facilities from Jim Burns (regarded as "the British Leo Fender") in September, 1965. U.S. distributed models bore the Baldwin trademark. During Baldwin's first year of ownership, only the logos were changed on the imported guitars. In 1966, the Burns-style scroll headstock was redesigned; and in 1967 the *700* series was debuted. The Baldwin company then began assembling the imported Burns parts in Booneville, Arkansas.

Baldwin acquired the Gretsch trademark when Fred Gretsch, Jr. sold the company in 1967. As part of a business consolidation, the New York Gretsch operation was moved to the Arkansas facility in 1970. Baldwin then concentrated its corporate interests in the Gretsch product line, discontinuing further Baldwin/Burns models. However, it is interesting to note that many Burns-style features (like the bridge vibrato) began to turn up on Gretsch models after 1967. For further Baldwin/Gretsch history, see GRETSCH.

(Source: Paul Day, The Burns Book; and Michael Wright, Vintage Guitar Magazine)

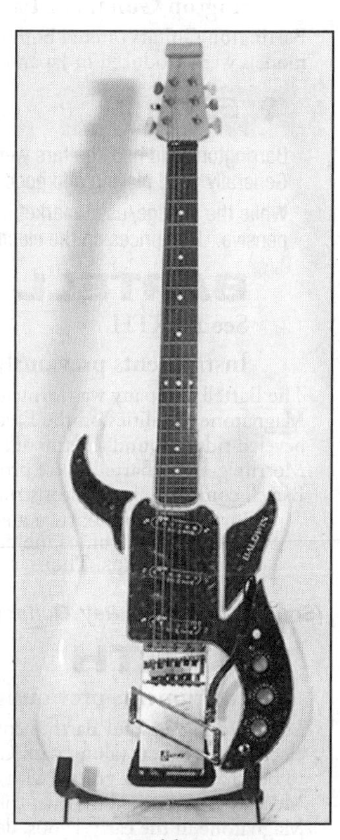

Baldwin
courtesy Encore Music

BALEANI

Instruments previously built in Italy during the mid 1960s.

These solid body guitars are generally entry level quality, but the sparkle/pearloid plastic finish says "Las Vegas" every time!

(Source: Tony Bacon and Paul Day, The Guru's Guitar Guide)

B

BAMBU

Instruments previously built in Japan in the late 1970s.

The model CB625 was a solid body built by the Maya company, and featured a laminated bamboo neck, two humbuckers and active circuitry.

(Source: Tony Bacoa and Paul Day, The Guru's Guitar Guide)

BARCLAY

Instruments previously produced in Japan during the 1960s.

Barclay instruments were generally entry level quality guitars with shorter scale necks that appealed to beginners. Built in Japan, the American distributor is unknown. The product line included thinline hollow body electric archtop as well as solid body guitars and basses. Some models appear to be built by Kawai/Teisco, although this has not yet been confirmed.

(Source: Michael Wright, Vintage Guitar Magazine)

BARKER GUITARS, LTD.

Instruments currently built in Rockford, Illinois.

Dwayne Barker is currently producing custom guitars in Rockford, Illinois. For further information, please contact Barker Guitars, Ltd. directly (see Trademark Index).

BARON (JAPAN MFG.)

See DOMINO.

Instruments previously manufactured in Japan circa mid to late 1960s. Distributed by Maurice Lipsky Music Company, Inc., of New York, New York.

Baron solid body guitars were advertised as "Perfect for the Beginner", and featured an offset double cutaway body, 6-on-a-side headstock, Jaguar-ish tremolo bridge, and one large pickguard with an individual on/off pickup switch (per pickup), volume/tone knobs, and a phase on/off switch. The **Model 401** was offered with one pickup (retail list $57.00), two pickups (retail list $69.00), three pickups (retail list $85.00), or four pickups (retail list $97.00). These guitars were all finished in solid colors, no doubt in order to cover the plywood nature of the body!

(Domino catalog courtesy John Kinnemeyer, JK Lutherie)

BARON (U.S. MFG.)

See chapter on House Brands.

This trademark has been identified as a *House Brand* of the RCA Victor Records Store; furthermore, KAY exported guitars bearing this trademark to the Thibouville-Lamy company of France.

(Source: Willie G. Moseley, Stellas & Stratocasters)

BARRINGTON

Instruments previously produced in Japan during the late 1980s. Distribution in the U.S. market was handled by Barrington Guitars of Barrington, Illinois.

Barrington Guitars offered both solid body electric guitars and basses during the late 1980s, as well as acoustic and acoustic/electric models. The guitar models were produced in Japan by Terada. The company now specializes in brass instruments as the L.A. Sax Company of Barrington, Illinois.

ELECTRIC

Barrington solid body guitars were styled after the 'superstrat' design prevalent in the late 1980s, and were built in Japan (possibly by the Terada company). Generally good playing and good looking guitars.

While the vintage/used market is currently focusing on vintage-style designs, models like these are generally overlooked - and as a result are generally inexpensive. Used prices on the electrics range between $295 to $450, $250 to $450 on the semi-hollow body models, and $225 to $500 on the acoustic models.

BARTELL

See BARTH.

Instruments previously built in Riverside, California between 1964 and 1969.

The Bartell company was formed by Paul Barth (engineer) and Ted Peckles (owner and company president) in the mid 1960s after Barth returned from Magnatone's facilities on the East Coast. One of Barth's co-workers at Rickenbacker was Roger Rossmeisel, who introduced the "German Carve" (a beveled ridge around the top of a guitar) to Rickenbacker, and later Fender designs. The same "German Carve" can be found on both Bartell and Mosrite guitars. Bartells were produced from 1964 to 1969, and former owner Peckles estimates that around 2,000 instruments were produced. The Bartell company also built instruments for rebranding for **Hohner, St. George**, and later edition Acoustic **Black Widow** models.

Bartell guitars feature a strat-style offset double cutaway body, a Mosrite-inspired headstock, "German Carve" ridge, and two single coil pickups. Electronics include a volume and tone knob, two on/off pickup selector switches, and a third switch for in/out of phase between the two pickups. There is also mention of a semi-hollowbody that features a design that is a cross between the above model and an ES-335.

(Source: Teisco Del Rey, Guitar Player magazine)

BARTH

Instruments previously built in Southern California during the mid to late 1950s.

Luthier/designer Paul Barth, nephew to National's John Dopyera, was one of the three men responsible for Rickenbacker's "Frying Pan" solid body electric steel guitar (along with George Beauchamp and Adolph Rickenbacker). Barth left Rickenbacker in 1956, and formed his own company briefly to build and market guitars with the Barth trademark. One of Paul Barth's employees at Rickenbacker was Semie Moseley in the early 1950s; and when Moseley later formed his own company, Barth briefly used Moseley's finishing skills to complete an order of guitars. Barth later went to work for Magnatone in the early 1960s, designing models at Magnatone's Torrance, California facilities.

For further biographical information, see BARTELL.

(Source: Teisco Del Rey, Guitar Player magazine)

BARTOLINI

Instruments previously built in Italy during the 1960s.

Author Tony Bacon in his book, *The Ultimate Guitar Book*, notes that Italy, like many other European countries, experienced the 1960's pop music popularity that led to a larger demand for electric guitars. However, many electric guitar builders were also manufacturers of accordions. As a result, many guitars ended up with accordion-style finishes. Wacky or not, Leo Fender was using this same sort of heat-molded acetate finish on some of his lap steel models in the early 1950s. What Leo wasn't using was the accordion-style push buttons, however.

BARTOLINI, BILL

Instruments previously built in 1960s.

Bartolini now produces a line of high quality guitar pickups in Livermore, California.

Luthier Bill Bartolini used to build classical guitars in California during the 1960s. Bartolini estimates that perhaps only a dozen guitars were built. Research on resonances produced during this time formed the basis for his pickup designs, and his clear, high quality pickups are standard features on numerous luthiers' creations.

(Information courtesy Bill Bartolini)

BASS COLLECTION

Instruments previously manufactured in Japan from 1985 to 1992. Distributed by Meisel Music, Inc. of Springfield, New Jersey.

Bass Collection (and Guitar Collection) instruments are medium grade instruments with good hardware, and a modern, rounded body design. Their current appeal may fall in the range of the novice to intermediate player looking for a solid-feeling instrument.

Bass Collection instruments were originally distributed by Meisel Music, Inc. for a number of years between 1985 to 1992. Their on-hand stock was purchased by the Sam Ash music store chain of New York in 1994 and sold through the Sam Ash stores.

ELECTRIC BASS

300 Series

SB301 - offset double cutaway alder body, bolt-on maple neck, 24-fret rosewood fingerboard, fixed bridge, 2-per-side Gotoh tuners, black hardware, P/J-style pickups, 2 volume/2-Tone controls, available in Black, Magenta, Metallic Grey and Sunburst finishes. Disc. 1994.

$450 $400 $325 $275 $250 $225 $200
Last MSR was $700.

This model had an optional ash body with Transparent Red finish.

SB302 - similar to SB301, except has fretless fingerboard, available in Black, Magenta and Metallic Grey finishes.

$450 $400 $325 $275 $250 $225 $200
Last MSR was $700.

This model had an optional ash body with Transparent Red finish.

SB305 - similar to SB301, except has 5 strings, 2 J-style pickups.

$495 $425 $350 $300 $275 $250 $225
Last MSR was $670.

This model had an optional ash body with Transparent Red finish.

SB305FL - similar to SB301, except has 5-string configuration, fretless fingerboard, 2 J-style pickups.

$550 $475 $400 $325 $295 $275 $225
Last MSR was $800.

This model had an optional ash body with Transparent Red finish.

400 Series

SB401 - offset double cutaway basswood body, bolt-on maple neck, 24-fret rosewood fingerboard, fixed bridge, 2-per-side Gotoh tuners, black hardware, P/J-style pickups, 2 volume/2-Tone controls, active electronics, 2-band EQ, available in Black, Metallic Red and Pearl White finishes. Disc. 1994.

$695 $595 $500 $400 $350 $325 $275
Last MSR was $995.

SB402 - similar to SB401, except has fretless fingerboard.

$695 $595 $500 $400 $375 $325 $275
Last MSR was $995.

SB405 - similar to SB401, except has 5-string configuration, 2 J-style pickups.

$725 $675 $600 $495 $450 $375 $325
Last MSR was $1,195.

GRADING	100% MINT	98% NEAR MINT	95% EXC+	90% EXC	80% VG+	70% VG	60% G

500 Series

SB501 - offset double cutaway alder body, bolt-on 3-piece maple neck, 24-fret ebony fingerboard, fixed bridge, 2-per-side tuners, black hardware, P/J-style pickups, 2 volume/2-Tone controls, active electronics with 2-band EQ, available in Black, Natural and Pearl White finishes. Disc. 1994.

$700 $650 $600 $475 $425 $350 $300
Last MSR was $1,195.

Add $100 for left-handed version.

SB502 - similar to SB501, except has fretless fingerboard.

$725 $675 $600 $475 $425 $350 $300
Last MSR was $1,195.

Add $200 for left-handed version.

SB505 - similar to SB501, except has 5-string configuration.

$750 $700 $650 $500 $450 $400 $325
Last MSR was $1,395.

This model had an optional ash body with Transparent Red finish.

600 Series

SB611 - offset double cutaway asymmetrical maple body with padauk or walnut top, bolt-on maple neck, 24-fret ebony fingerboard, fixed bridge, 2-per-side Gotoh tuners, gold hardware, P/J-style pickups, 2 volume/2-Tone controls, active electronics with 2-band EQ, available in Oil finishes. Disc. 1994

$850 $795 $700 $650 $575 $475 $395
Last MSR was $1,495.

This model had an optional fretless fingerboard (Model SB612).

SB615 - similar to SB611, except has 5-string configuration.

$875 $825 $750 $695 $595 $500 $450
Last MSR was $1,650.

DB Series

DB41R - asymmetrical double cutaway ash body, bolt-on maple neck, 24-fret rosewood fingerboard with abalone dot inlay, fixed bridge, 2-per-side tuners, chrome hardware, 2 J-style pickups, 2 volume/2-Tone controls, available in Transparent Black and Transparent Red finishes. Disc. 1994.

$725 $675 $600 $495 $425 $375 $325
Last MSR was $1,150.

DB43E - similar to DB41R, except has padauk/maple/mahogany laminated or walnut/maple/mahogany laminated body, ebony fingerboard, gold hardware, 2 humbucker pickups, available in Oil finishes. Disc. 1994.

$850 $800 $725 $650 $575 $475 $425
Last MSR was $1,630.

DB51R - similar to DB41R, except has 5-string configuration.

$825 $750 $675 $625 $550 $500 $450
Last MSR was $1,560.

DB53E - similar to DB41R, except has 5 strings, padauk/maple/mahogany laminated or walnut/maple/mahogany laminated body, ebony fingerboard, gold hardware, 2 humbucker pickups, available in Oil finishes. Mfg. 1991 to 1992.

$900 $850 $750 $700 $650 $595 $500
Last MSR was $2,000.

BASS O LIN

Instruments currently built in New York, New York since 1994. Distributed by Bass O Lin (Dan Agostino) of Lanoka Harbor, New Jersey.

Designer Danny Agostino is currently offering *the world's most versatile electric bass.* Inspired in the early 1970s by Jimmy Page's explorations of a Les Paul and a violin bow, Agostino developed a bass design in the early 1980s that could be played by tapping, plucking, or bowing. The Bass O Lin's bridge is constructed similar to an upright bass's bridge, with different string planes for bowing access.

The bass's unique design allows 10 different playing positions: 3 different strap configurations - standing, or on either leg in a sitting position; and five different positions seated or standing with the optional quick- release playing stand. This stand features non-dampening rubber mounts that allows the instrument to vibrate freely.

ELECTRIC BASS

While compact, the instrument has a 34" scale. Models are offered with 3-piece curly maple necks, African Mahogany or Quilted Maple bodies, fretted or fretless Rosewood or Ebony fingerboards, Sperzel locking tuners, High Resolution Micro U pickup, and gold-plated brass tailpiece and electronics rear cover. The custom designed Agostino radiused pickup combines with an RMC Pizz-Arco piezo bridge, and active preamp circuitry featuring a master volume and master pickup blend controls. The rear of the body has the locking strap/playing stand jacks and a knee pad for bowing leverage and comfort.

GRADING	100% MINT	98% NEAR MINT	95% EXC+	90% EXC	80% VG+	70% VG	60% G

BASSLINE

Instruments currently built in Krefeld, Germany. Distributed in the U.S. by Salwender International of Trabuco Canyon, California.

The Bassline Custom Shop currently offers both electric upright models as well as 4-, 5-, and 6-string electric bass guitars. Salwender International is currently offering the **Universal** model in the U.S. Market.

The Buster Art-Line models are set-neck, while the Buster Bolt-On is a bolt-neck design. Both versions feature Gotoh/ETS tuners, and EMG or Seymour Duncan pickups. Models are available in 4-, 5-, and 6-string versions; and currently available in Europe.

ELECTRIC BASS

After 10 years of research and development, Bassline introduced the **Universal** electric upright model. The Universal (retail list price $5,659) has an enlarged neck for stability and tone. Equipped with piezo and magnetic pickups, this 36" scale instrument is constructed of one-piece flamed maple body and curved ebony fingerboard, and flamed maple bridge/ ebony string holders. Models are available in 4- and 5-string configurations, and can be played both arco or pizz-style upright.

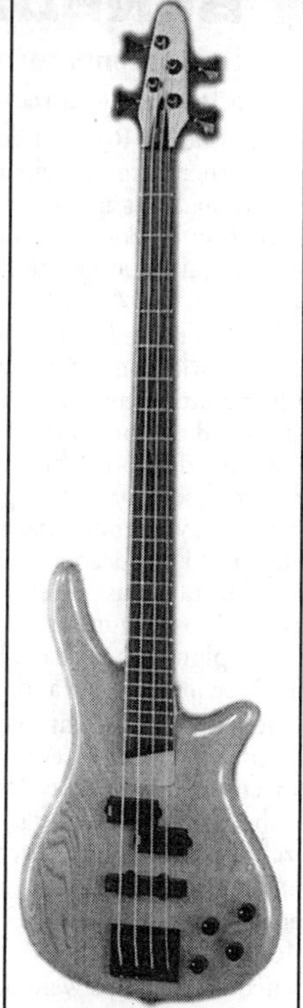

Bass Collection
SB 501 AN
courtesy
Bass Collection

BATMAN

See C & R GUITARS.

BELIGER GUITARS

Instruments currently built in Garden City, Michigan.

Luthier Lemon James is handcrafting a line of Foxey electric guitars, which share a unique and original "flowing", curved body shape. Two current eye- catching models include a Burl Maple body, and the Transparent (lucite material) body with clear headstock and 8 super bright red LEDs that illuminate the body in the dark. For further information regarding these handcrafted custom guitars, contact luthier James directly (see Trademark Index).

BELLA

Instruments currently built in Chalmette, Louisiana.

Bella Guitars offers the Bella Deluxe model ($2,400), which features a mahogany body, curly maple or quilted maple (or other exotic tops), rosewood fingerboard, Schaller tuners, Seymour Duncan or DiMarzio pickups, and a 25 1/2" scale.

BELLTONE

Instruments previously manufactured in Japan, or constructed of Japanese-produced parts during the late 1960s.

Belltone was the brand name of the Peter Sorkin Music Company. The Sorkin company distributed Premier guitars, which were built at the Multivox company of New York. Other guitars built or distributed (possibly as rebrands) were ROYCE, STRAD-O-LIN, BELLTONE, and MARVEL. Parts varied, as pickups were Japanese, while the roller bridges may have been Italian or Japanese.

(Source: Michael Wright, Guitar Stories Volume One)

BELTONE

See chapter on House Brands.

This trademark has been identified as a *House Brand* of the Monroe Catalog House. Various Beltone instruments appear to be rebranded Zen-On instruments. **Zen-On** guitars were produced in Japan during the 1960s.

(Source: Willie G. Moseley, Vintage Guitar Magazine)

BENAVENTE

Instruments currently built in Grants Pass, Oregon.

Luthier Chris Benavente is currently producing custom built guitars. Each instrument is completely hand crafted, and feature exotic woods and multiple piece laminated neck-through design. Custom instruments are also available on request.

ELECTRIC

Benavente currently offers a variety of models: The **100 Series** (list $1,899), the **200 Series** (list $2,100), the **2K Series** (list $2,500), **2KDC Series** (list $2,500), and the **2K Archtop Series** (list $3,900). All models feature customer's choice of body wood, 5-piece neck-through-body design, rosewood fingerboard, EMG active electronics, and chrome (or black or gold) hardware. A wide variety of endless options are available on all Benavente Guitars - limited only by the customer's imagination.

ELECTRIC BASS

Benavente's bass models follow the sleek offset lines of the the **219 Bass Series** (list $2,500), and the **Singlecut Bass Series** (list $3,300). Standard construction is similar to the guitar models, except feature a 21-fret fingerboard, 34" scale, and a Schaller roller bridge. Benavente also offers the **J 150** model, which is a classic J-styled bass with a maple neck, ebony fingerboard, and EMG pickups (list $2,100). Prices are suggested list retail. The factory recommends calling your local Benavente dealer for a price and delivery time.

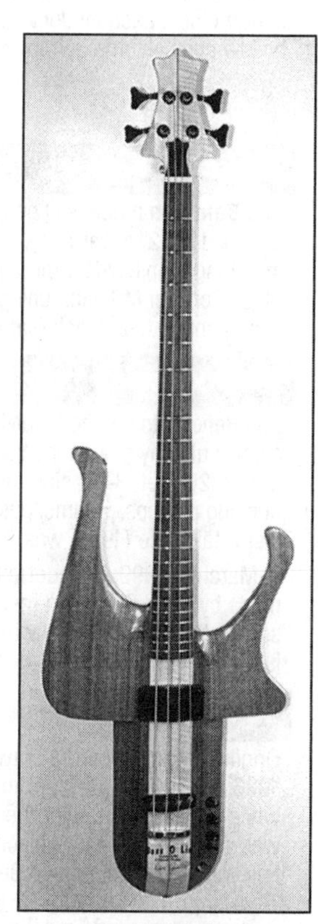

Bass O Lin
courtesy Danny Agostino

B

BENEDETTO, ROBERT

Instruments currently built in Nashville, TN by the Guild Custom Shop (select models only) beginning in 2000, through a licensing agreement with the Fender Musical Instrument Corporation (FMIC).

Master Luthier Robert Benedetto has been handcrafting fine archtop guitars since 1968. Benedetto was born in New York in 1946. Both his father and grandfather were master cabinetmakers, and Benedetto's uncles were musicians. While growing up in New Jersey, Benedetto began playing the guitar professionally at age thirteen. Being near the New York/New Jersey jazz music scene, Benedetto had numerous opportunities to perform repair and restoration work on other classic archtops. Benedetto built his first archtop in 1968, and his pre-eminence in the field is evidenced by his having made archtop guitars longer than any living builders and has a growing list of endorsers. Current endorsers range from Jimmy Bruno and Kenny Burrell to Earl Klugh and Andy Summers.

Benedetto moved to Homosassa, Florida in 1976. Three years later, he relocated to Clearwater, Florida. A veteran innovator, Benedetto began concentrating on the acoustic properties of the guitar designs, and started a movement to strip away unnecessary adornment (inlays, bindings) in 1982. While continuing his regular work on archtop building, Benedetto also built violins between 1983-1987. Violinist extraordinaire Stephane Grappelli purchased one of his violins in 1993. Benedetto even built a small number of electric solid body guitars and basses (which debuted at the 1987 NAMM show) in addition to his regular archtop production schedule. After 10 years in East Stroudsburg, PA, Benedetto relocated back to Florida during 2000. His endorsers span three generations of jazz guitarists. Not since John D'Angelico has anyone made as many archtop guitars nor had as many well known players endorsing and recording with his guitars. Closer scrutiny reveals nuances found only from a maker of his stature. His minimalist delicate inlay motif has become a trademark as have his novel use of black, rather than gold, tuning machines, black bridge height adjustment wheels, and an ebony nut (versus bone), all of which harmonize with the ebony fittings throughout the guitar. He is the originator of the solid ebony tailpiece, uniquely fastened to the guitar with cello tail adjustor. Likewise, he was the first to use exotic and natural wood veneers on the headstock and pioneered the use of violin- pigments to shade his guitars. His "honey blonde" finish is now widely used within the guitar industry. Benedetto is also well known for refining the 7- string archtop and is that unique model's most prolific maker.

Benedetto is the Archtop Guitar Construction Editor and "Guitar Maintenance" columnist for "Just Jazz Guitar" magazine, and is the author of *Making an Archtop Guitar* (Center stream Publishing, 1994). He released his 9 1/2 hour instructional video, "Archtop Guitar Design & Construction", in November 1996. He is currently at work on a second book tentatively entitled *Anecdotes, Insights, and Facts about Archtop Guitar Construction.* His forthcoming biography is being written by eminent jazz guitar historian Adrian Ingram. He also markets the Benedetto "floating" pickup, a standard size humbucking pickup, and solid ebony tailpiece for his (and other) archtop acoustic guitars.

In March 1999, through a licensing agreement with the Fender Musical Instrument Corporation (FMIC), Benedetto licensed the Benny & Bambino series to be made at the Guild custom shop in Nashville, TN, beginning in 2000. As of March 1, 1999, Robert Benedetto stopped making standard Models.

Benedetto pickups were licensed in late 1999 to be sold exclusively by Seymour Duncan.

As of spring 2001, Benedetto has built over 750 musical instruments. While the majority (466) are archtop guitars, he has produced 157 electric solid body guitars, 52 electric basses, 48 violins, 5 violas, 2 mandolins and 1 cello. Benedetto currently schedules his production to 6 archtop guitar instruments per year, as well as a few violins.

(Biographical information courtesy Cindy Benedetto)

SEMI-HOLLOW ELECTRIC

During his archtop building career, Benedetto built 8 semi-hollow body electric guitars (6 of which that were built between 1982 to 1983 have been dubbed Semi-dettos by author Adrian Ingram). These versatile guitars feature a carved top, dual cutaway body design with two separate tone chambers and a solid center block. Each model was crafted to the original owner's needs and specifications, resulting in slight differences between the models. The other two semi-hollow body electric guitars were prototypes built by Benedetto in 1997.

ELECTRIC

Bambino Series

The **Bambino** model will be introduced in 2000, and will be manufactured under license by the Guild Custom Shop, located in Nashville, TN. This model features a 14 1/2" lower body, 2 1/4" body depth, single florentine cutaway, carved two-piece Sitka spruce top, carved two-piece American Maple back with matching maple sides, three-piece American Maple neck, solid ebony fingerboard, nut, saddle, bridge, trussrod cover, and tailpiece and narrow finger rest. Black Schaller M6 mini tuning machines with ebony buttons, one Benedetto B-6 built-in pickup with volume/tone controls, and abalone "Benedetto" logo inlaid in serpentine headstock (same size and shape as Benny model). Retail price is $10,000.

Benny Series

Bob Benedetto stopped individually making his standard Benny model mid-1999. Some of the features of the Benedetto made **Benny** electric model include a single cutaway mahogany body with routed tone chambers, carved spruce top, set-in mahogany neck, 25" scale, ebony fingerboard with a single abalone inlay at the 12th fret, 3-per-side tuners, gold plated hardware, Leo Quan Badass bridge, 2 custom Kent Armstrong (1998 and earlier) or Benedetto (new 1999) humbucking pickups, volume/push-pull tone controls, 3-way selector switch, available in Honey Blonde or Sunburst top with Wine back/sides/neck finishes. His last retail price (1999) was $5,000.

In March of 1999, Benedetto licensed his name to the Fender Musical Instruments Corp. (FMIC) for his standard models (including the Benny Series) to be made by Guild Guitars in their custom shop located in Nashville, TN. Features include a mahogany body with routed tone chambers, mahogany neck, carved spruce top, 14 1/2" body with 2" body depth, 2 Seymour Duncan pickups, Leo Quan Badass bridge, gold Schaller tuners with ebony buttons. The retail price is $5,000, $6,000 for the Benny 7 (7-string).

1000 Series

Originally a joint venture between Robert Benedetto and John Buscarino, these solid body electric instruments were made in Clearwater, Florida between May, 1986 - April, 1987. All instruments were completely handmade on the premises, without using premade necks or bodies. Buscarino focused on the electronics, while Benedetto brought the feel of his jazz guitar necks to the models. Following the electric line's debut at the January 1987 NAMM show, the partnership was dissolved. Benedetto continued working alone through April, 1987. While the instruments were well received, he could not produce them fast enough. The line was discontinued and Benedetto resumed making archtop guitars full-time.

A separate serial number was maintained, starting at #1001. A decal, (in black or white) with the name "Benedetto" in all lower case letters, was used on all models. 157 electric guitars and 52 electric basses were produced.

1000S - offset double cutaway poplar body, bolt-on rock maple neck, 25 1/2" scale, 22-fret rosewood fingerboard, graphite/teflon nut, 6-on-a-side Grover mini tuners, chrome hardware, Gotoh GE-1055T fulcrum tremolo, 3 Select by EMG single coil pickups, volume/tone controls, 5-way selector switch, available in Black, Red, and White Durocoat finishes. Mfg. 1986 to 1987.

Model has not traded sufficiently to quote pricing.

For historical interest, the 1987 retail list price was $469.

1000T - similar to the 1000S, except features a single cutaway poplar body, Gotoh GTC-301C bridge, single coil/humbucker Select by EMG pickups, 3-way selector switch.

Model has not traded sufficiently to quote pricing.

For historical interest, the 1987 retail list price was $439.

Robert Benedetto courtesy Robert and Cindy Benedetto

3000 Series

3000S - offset double cutaway poplar body, bolt-on rock maple neck, 25 1/2" scale, 22-fret rosewood fingerboard, graphite/teflon nut, 6-on-a-side Grover mini tuners, black headstock, black chrome hardware, Gotoh GE-1055T fulcrum tremolo, 3 Select by EMG single coil pickups, volume/tone controls, 5-way selector switch, available in Black, Red, Taxi Yellow, and White Durocoat finishes. Mfg. 1986 to 1987.

Model has not traded sufficiently to quote pricing.

This model had an optional a 2-piece alder body with Prussian Blue Sunburst or Brown Maple Sunburst finishes (an additional $120), or Black neck finish (an additional $40).

For historical interest, the 1987 retail list price was $569.

3000T - similar to the 3000S, except features a single cutaway poplar body, Gotoh GTC-301B bridge, single coil/humbucker Select by EMG pickups, 3-way selector switch.

Model has not traded sufficiently to quote pricing. For historical interest, the 1987 retail list price was $539.

Wave Series

The Wave Series was the top of the Benedetto 1986-1987 electric solid body line, and featured one guitar model and one bass guitar model. The specifications are similar to the 3000 Series instruments, except featured a choice of exotic wood (quilted and highly figured curly maple, burl, etc.), ebony fingerboard, EMG active electronics, and upgraded hardware. A limited number of the very custom Wave instruments were produced. The base retail list price in 1987 was $999.

ELECTRIC BASS

1000B - offset double cutaway poplar body, bolt-on rock maple neck, 34" scale, 22-fret rosewood fingerboard, graphite/teflon nut, 4-on-a-side Grover mini tuners, chrome hardware, Gotoh GEB-204C bridge, P/J-style Select by EMG pickups, volume/tone controls, 3-way selector switch, available in Black, Red, or White Durocoat finishes. Mfg. 1986 to 1987.

Model has not traded sufficiently to quote pricing.

This model had an optional fretless fingerboard (an additional $60). For historical interest, the 1987 retail list price was $399.

3000B - similar to the 1000B, except features black headstock, black chrome hardware, available in Black, Red, Taxi Yellow, and White Durocoat finishes. Mfg. 1986 to 1987.

Model has not traded sufficiently to quote pricing.

This model had an optional 2-piece alder body with Prussian Blue Sunburst or Brown Maple Sunburst finishes (an additional $120), or Black neck finish (an additional $40). For historical interest, the 1987 retail list price was $499.

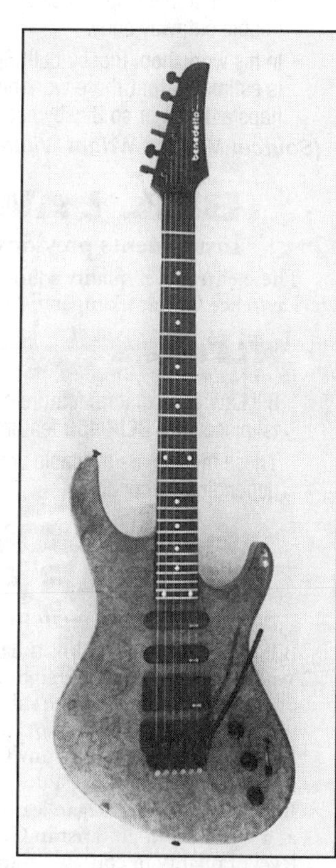

Benedetto Wave (circa 1987) courtesy Robert and Cindy Benedetto

BENEDICT GUITARS

Instruments currently built in Cedar, Minnesota since 1981. Distributed by the Benedict Guitar Company of Cedar, Minnesota.

Luthier Roger Benedict began building guitars back in 1974 out east in Elizabethtown, New York. Benedict moved to Minneapolis, Minnesota in 1981, and continued to build custom guitars. In 1988, he unveiled the Groovemaster model (as named by Jackson Browne, who owns two), a Strat-styled semi-hollowbody design. Unfortunately, Benedict passed away in 1994. He was remembered all over Minneapolis by musicians as a generous man who was easy-going and a great luthier.

In late 1995, Bill Hager purchased the rights to the trademark and designs from the estate, and continues to produce Benedict guitars. Hager, a printer and luthier, was apprenticed to Roger Benedict for five years. Hager continues to offer the Groovemaster, as well as a baritone guitar, an acoustic/electric, and continues to build custom models.

BENTLY

Instruments currently manufactured in Asia. Distributed by the St. Louis Music company of St. Louis, Missouri.

Bently instruments are entry level to medium quality solid body guitars and basses that feature designs based on classic American favorites.

BERT WEEDON

Please refer to the W section in this text.

B

BESSON

See FRAMUS & ARISTONE.

Instruments previously built in West Germany during the late 1950s through the early 1960s.

While BESSON was the brand name for a UK importer, these guitars were made by and identical to certain FRAMUS models. Research also indicates that the trademark ARISTONE was utilized as well.

(Source: Tony Bacon and Paul Day, The Guru's Guitar Guide)

BEVERLY

See chapter on House Brands.

This trademark has been identified as a "House Brand" of SELMER UK in England.

(Source: Willie G. Moseley, Stellas & Stratocasters)

BIAXE

Instruments previously built in Stamford, Connecticut from 1978 to 1985.

The original Biaxe Guitar company manufactured instruments for roughly eight years. When the company briefly reformed, they focused on retrofit devices that yielded the sound of a fretless bass on a fretted neck bass guitar. Dubbed **The Fretless Wizard**, the kits were produced for 4-, 5-, and 6-string basses, and included an instructional cassette (these retrofit devices are no longer offered).

BIGSBY, PAUL

Instruments previously built in Downey, California from 1947 to 1965.

Paul Arthur Bigsby was a pattern-maker who was fond of motorcycle repair and racing. During the 1940s, Bigsby was contacted by country music star Merle Travis to repair a worn-out Vibrola on his Gibson L-10. Rather than just repair it, Bigsby produced a better vibrato tailpiece. The Bigsby vibrato was marketed for a number of years after he finished the first prototype. In 1965, Ted McCarty (ex-Gibson president) bought Bigsby's vibrato company, and Bigsby vibrato models are still available today.

In 1947-1948 Travis and Bigsby collaborated on a solid body electric which featured a 6-on-a-side headstock, single cutaway, neck-through-body construction, and a string-through-body bridge and tailpiece. Bigsby produced solid body guitars like this in small numbers on a custom order basis. Bigsby also had success with his electric pedal steel guitar beginning in the late 1940s and after. In 1956, Bigsby designed **Magnatone's** Mark IV (one pickup/trapeze tailpiece), and Mark V (two pickups/Bigsby tremolo) model electric guitars. These guitars were produced in Magnatone's factory. Paul Bigsby passed away in 1968.

Bigsby serialization can be found on the guitars stamped down by the lower strap button, and on pedal steels near the leg attachment. Serialization corresponds with the date produced (month/day/year).

ELECTRIC

While Bigsby's instruments were built on a custom order basis, there is some overall uniformity to the differences in models. One model was based on Merle Travis' neck-through/semi-hollowbody/single Florentine cutaway original design. The **Electric Standard** was similar, except had different scroll appointments and adjustable pole pieces on the pickups. A model built for Jack Parsons again had a single pointed cutaway, but a 3" deep body. Bigsby's last design had a double cutaway body.

In his workshop, Bigsby built Spanish guitars, mandolins, electric guitars, pedal steel guitars, and neck replacements on other company's acoustic guitars. It is estimated that there were only 25 to 50 *electric Spanish* guitars built (and only 3 or 4 doublenecks), 6 mandolins, around 150 pedal steel guitars, and perhaps a dozen or so Bigsby neck replacements.

(Source: Michael Wright, Vintage Guitar Magazine; and Tom Wheeler, American Guitars)

BILL LAWRENCE

Instruments previously produced in Korea by the Moriadara Guitar company.

These entry level quality solid body guitars feature designs based on classic American favorites. While they do bear his name, Bill Lawrence (Bill Lawrence Guitar Company, Keystone Pickups) is not associated with these models.

ELECTRIC

Bill Lawrence guitars feature designs based on American designs. The **MB-120** features an offset cut body, 3+3 headstock, 2 humbucking pickups, and a stop tailpiece. The **BLIR-150** features more of a Strat-style design, and has two humbuckers, a volume knob, and a pickup selector switch.

These models are available primarily in Japan. Instruments may turn up in the western states in the U.S. market. Estimated prices may run from $250 to $450, depending on condition.

BILL LAWRENCE GUITAR COMPANY, LLC

Instruments currently built in Pennsylvania.

Bill Lawrence, a legend in the field of guitar and pickup design, also had a career as a well known jazz guitarist in Germany. Born Willi Lorenz Stich in Wahn-Heide, Germany (eight miles south east of Cologne) on March 24, 1931, Lawrence began violin lessons and the study of counterpoint at the age of eight. Five years later he suffered a childhood accident that fractured his left hand and ended his violin-playing career. At age 14, Lawrence became an interpreter for the American and British armies after World War II. After being exposed to recordings of the Les Paul Trio, King Cole Trio, Glenn Miller, Lionel Hampton, and Benny Goodman, Lawrence became interested in the guitar playing styles of such notables as Charlie Christian, Barney Kessel, Oscar Moore, and Les Paul.

In 1946, Lawrence began learning to play the guitar - and by 1947 was performing in Cologne at the Hot Club '47. By 1951, Lawrence was established as a well known guitarist in Germany. Two years later, he met Frederick Wilfer, president of the Framus Guitar Company. After complaining about the level of quality in contemporary guitar models, Wilfer created a prototype of a guitar based on Lawrence's ideas. When the decision was made to market this new guitar model, Lawrence (nee' Stich) changed his performing name to **Billy Lorento**. This performing name was applied to Framus' top of the line model, and Lawrence used the Lorento name over the next ten years while performing publicly.

During that time, Lawrence was working for Framus as a consultant. His main job was to improve the sound and playability of their guitars. In 1962, Lawrence left Framus and changed his name to Bill Lawrence to endorse Fender guitars in Germany (the 'Billy Lorento' name was owned by Framus). In 1965, he started his first pickup company and came to the United States to meet designer Dan Armstrong. The two spent a couple of years discussing guitar design aspects, and later collaborated on Armstrong's **Dan Armstrong** Lucite guitar (Lawrence built the prototypes for the pickups).

After working with Armstrong, Lawrence worked as a designer with the Gibson Guitar Company during the early 1970s. After a brief return to Framus, Lawrence came back to Gibson and helped design features for models like the S- 1, L6-S, and Howard Roberts model guitars as well as the G-3 and Ripper bass. While designing other products at Gibson, Lawrence came up with a prototype for a flat-top pickup. When people at Gibson suggested he market it on his own, Lawrence founded the *Lawrence Sound Research* in 1975. Lawrence currently produces **Keystone** pickups, and is debuting the new high quality Wilde USA guitar design that feature his own pickups.

Lawrence's Keystone series of pickups are available in single coil and humbucking models for guitars as well as 'P', 'J', and 'Soapbar' styles for basses. These models are designed for aftermarket installation and as OEM- based parts for guitar companies.

Wilde Guitars Series

Lawrence is currently offering his guitar design that feature Lawrence's special own Noise free pickups. Wilde guitar models have an offset, double cutaway alder body, flamed maple top, bolt-on rock maple neck with 22-fret rosewood fret-board (25 1/2" scale) or solid rock maple neck/no fingerboard, fixed bridge, pickguard, 2 single coil/humbucker pickup configuration, volume and tone controls, and a 2 position, Series to Parallel, Selector-switch to change the inductance of the lead pickup from 4.8 to 1.2 Henry (high to medium impedance). The guitar is also available with different pickup combinations. The pickup systems are interchangeable. The **Standard** model (suggested list $1,500) features popular classic colors, while the **Deluxe** (suggested retail $1,650) features a selected flame maple top and translucent finishes. All models are hand finished with thin coats of high impact varnish. Lawrence's Wilde guitars are available through direct dealers only.

BISCAYNE

See also PALMER.

Instruments currently produced in Asia. Distributed by Tropical Music Corporation of Miami, Florida.

Biscayne electric guitars and basses are entry level instruments based on traditional American designs. Biscayne models are distributed by Tropical Music Corporation, which has been servicing customers throughout Central and South America, Caribbean, and the West Indies since 1975. Biscayne instruments are also available in the U.S. market through various wholesale catalogs.

Biscayne electric guitars and basses are usually priced in used condition from $79 up to $299.

BLACK HILLS

See chapter on House Brands.

This trademark has been identified as a *House Brand* of the Wall Drug stores.

(Source: Willie G. Moseley, Stellas & Stratocasters)

BLACKHURST

Instruments currently built in Roseville, California.

Luthier Dave Blackhurst is presently building high quality custom designed guitars and basses that feature numerous options. Retail prices listed below are the base price; other customer-chosen options are priced extra.

ELECTRIC

In 1996, Blackhurst introduced a new custom model that was called **The Big One** (retail list $2,000 and up). **The Big One** is a playable hand-carved guitar or bass shaped like a fish - bluegill, halibut, bass (you name it). This fully functional instrument can also be mounted on your wall, like the trophy catch that it is!

Other models offered in the past include the more traditional **STX** and **TLX** that feature deeper body cutaways.

Tigershark Series

The **Tigershark** series has a sleek double cutaway body design. The **Tigershark I/II F** has an alder body with cutaway neck heel, maple neck, ebony fingerboard, fixed bridge, and Seymour Duncan pickups (retail list $1,295 and up).

The **Tigershark I/II NL** is the non-locking tremolo version (list $1,350 and up), while the **Tigershark I/II-12** is the 12-string version. The **Tigershark I/II-12** has 6 tuners on the lower bout, and 6 tuners on the headstock (list $1,350 and up). The limited production **Tigershark II C/F** features a highly flamed maple carved top and an alder body (list $2,250 and up). Prices range from $1,295 up to $2,250.

ELECTRIC BASS

Blackhurst's **Home Bass** is a headless model constructed of koa or light ash, and has a 24-fret ebony fingerboard (list price $1,495 and up). This model is available in a fretless fingerboard configuration.

The **Tigershark Bass** is styled after the Tigershark guitar model, and is available in 4-, 5-, and 6-string configurations in customer's choice of woods (list $1,150 and up). Both bass models are available in a variety of pickup configurations.

GRADING	100% MINT	98% NEAR MINT	95% EXC+	90% EXC	80% VG+	70% VG	60% G

BLACKJACK

Instruments previously produced in Japan circa 1960s.

The Blackjack brand name appears on these electric hollowbody guitars and basses. Both the Japanese manufacturer (some models may have been built by Aria) and the U.S. distributor have not been identified.
Violin-shaped Blackjack instruments are generally entry level to medium quality, and hold little fascination in the vintage market. Prices should range between $75 to $150 (in excellent or 90% condition).
(Source: Michael Wright, Vintage Guitar Magazine)

BLADE

Instruments currently produced in England and Japan. Distributed in the U.S. & Canada exclusively by Lasar Music Corporation, located in Brentwood, Tennessee. Previously distributed by Musician's Friend of Medford, Oregon through 1998. Distributed internationally by L-TEK International of Allschwil, Switzerland.

Designer Gary Levinson began building guitars in Illinois in 1964. Levinson approached his guitar building from an analytical standpoint based on his multiple university degrees in applied and natural sciences. As a result, Blade guitars combine traditional designs with quality craftsmanship and modern updated hardware, on-board electronics, and pickup combinations. The resulting instruments had more tonal options than previous vintage models, but still maintained the *feel* that players are familiar with.
Levinson's design headquarters and Custom Shop are located in Allschwil (near Basel), Switzerland. The Custom Shop is the driving force in product development, derived in part from the input received from working musicians.
The on-board *Variable Spectrum Control* electronics devised by Levinson give the Blade guitar player additional control over the guitar's tone. Trim pots on the VSC (accessed through the back of the guitar) preset tone controls, and were activated through the VSC mini-switch (or push/pull pot) mounted near the volume and tone controls.
It is estimated that Blade has sold over 27,000 instruments worldwide in the past 10 years.

ELECTRIC

Blade VSC (Variable Spectrum Control) Electronics

The Guitar VSC package offered a midrange boost (0 to 12 dB at 650 Hz) in the mini-switch's up (1) position, VSC bypass in middle (2) position, and treble and bass boost/cut in down (3) position. The treble control ranged from -4 dB to +12 db at 7500 Hz, and the bass control ranged from -4 dB to +12 db at 160 Hz.
The Bass VSC package offered two preset EQ curves and two separate *hum trimmer* controls. In the mini-switch's up (2) position, the VSC went to the user's preset EQ curve, and in the down (1) position defaulted to the factory setting. Both EQ presets offered a three band (treble, mid, bass) separate cut/boost switch.

R 3 (Model R3-MB) - offset double cutaway soft maple body, white pickguard, bolt-on maple neck, 22-fret maple fingerboard with black dot inlay, Falcon tremolo system, graphite nut, 6-on-a-side Sperzel Trimlock tuners, black hardware, 3 SS-1 single coil pickups, volume/tone control, 5-position pickup selector switch, VSC switch, Variable Spectrum Control electronics, available in Black, Ice Blue, Iridescent White and Purple Rain opaque finishes. Mfg. 1988 to 1992.

$1,000 $875 $775 $695 $600 $525 $425
Last MSR was $1,675.

Add $75 for ebony fingerboard with pearl dot inlay (R3-EB).

This model was available with chrome hardware.

RH 3 (Model RH3-MB) - similar to R 3 (R3-MB), except has 2 SS-1 single coil/1 LH-4 humbucker pickups. Mfg. 1988 to 1992.

$1,050 $900 $800 $725 $625 $525 $425
Last MSR was $1,700.

Add $100 for ebony fingerboard with pearl dot inlay (RH3-EB).

R 4 (Model R4-MB) - offset double cutaway light ash body, black pickguard, bolt-on maple neck, 22-fret maple fingerboard with black dot inlay, Falcon tremolo system, graphite nut, 6-per-side Sperzel Trimlock tuners, black hardware, 3 SS-1 single coil pickups, volume/tone control, 5-position pickup selector switch, VSC switch, Variable Spectrum Control active electronics, available in Ocean Blue and See-Through Red translucent finishes. Mfg. 1988 to 1992.

$1,100 $950 $850 $750 $650 $550 $450
Last MSR was $1,800.

Add $100 for ebony fingerboard with pearl dot inlay (R4-EB).

R4-MG - similar to R4-MB, except has gold hardware, available in Honey, Misty Violet, Nightwood and 2-Tone Sunburst translucent finishes. Mfg. 1988 to 1992.

$1,125 $975 $875 $775 $675 $575 $475
Last MSR was $1,870.

Add $90 for ebony fingerboard with pearl dot inlay (R4-EG).

ABILENE - offset double cutaway sen ash body, white pearloid pickguard, bolt-on maple neck, 22-fret maple fingerboard with black dot inlay, FT-3 Vint-Edge tremolo, graphite nut, 6-on-a-side Sperzel Trimlock tuners, chrome hardware, white knobs and pickup covers, 3 V-1 humcancelling single coil pickups, volume/tone control, 5-position pickup selector switch, VSC-Gain boost electronics, available in Harvest Gold and 2-Tone Sunburst translucent finish. Mfg. 1993 only.

$1,000 $875 $775 $695 $600 $525 $425

This model was also available with a rosewood fingerboard and pearl dot inlays.

GRADING	100% MINT	98% NEAR MINT	95% EXC+	90% EXC	80% VG+	70% VG	60% G

Austin - similar to the Abilene, except has rosewood fingerboard, black pearloid pickguard, black hardware, 2 V-1 single coil/1 LM humbucker pickups, black knobs and pickup covers, available in Harvest Gold, Nightwood, and Ocean Blue translucent finishes. Mfg. 1993 only.

		$1,100	$950	$850	$750	$650	$550	$450

California Series

CALIFORNIA STANDARD (Model CS) - offset double cutaway swamp ash body, bolt-on hard rock maple neck, 22-fret rosewood fingerboard with pearl dot inlay, Wilkinson VS-50K tremolo, graphite nut, 6-on-a-side die cast tuners, chrome hardware, white pearloid pickguard, 2 VS-1 single coil/HD-4 humbucker pickups, volume/tone (push-pull coil tap) control, 5-position selector switch, VSC mini-switch, Variable Spectrum Control electronics, available in Black, Sparkling Blue, and Sparkling Purple finishes. Mfg. 1994 to date.

MSR	$999	$599	$500	$450	$400	$350	$300	$250

Some early models may have an alder body instead of swamp ash.

In 1996, Black, Sparkling Blue, and Sparkling Purple finishes were discontinued; Aegean (Adriatic) Blue Burst, Cherry Sunburst, and Honey Burst finishes were introduced.

California Deluxe - similar to the California Standard, except featured a mahogany body, figured maple top, Levinson FT-4 tremolo, Sperzel Trimlock tuners, VSC-2 electronics, available in Natural Silk satin finish. Mfg. 1994 to 1995.

		$1,250	$1,000	$900	$825	$725	$595	$500

This model had 3 VS-3 single coils as a pickup configuration option.

California Hybrid - similar to the California Standard, except features a hexaphonic piezo bridge pickup system, EA (electric/acoustic) mix control, EA system switch, available in Aegean Blue Burst, Cherry Sunburst, and Honey Burst finishes. Mfg. 1998 to date.

MSR	$1,599	$1,125	$975	$850	$750	$625	$525	$400

CALIFORNIA CUSTOM (Model CC) - similar to the California Standard, except features a swamp ash body/figured maple top, ebony fingerboard, Levinson Falcon FT-4 tremolo, chrome Sperzel Trimlock tuners, translucent pickguard, 2 V-1 Humcanceller single coil/LH-55 humbucker pickups, available in Aegean Blue Burst, Cherry Sunburst, Honey Burst, and Violet Burst finishes. Mfg. 1994 to date.

MSR	$2,399	$1,925	$1,675	$1,450	$1,250	$1,000	$825	$600

This model is custom built in Switzerland.

Classic Series

DELTA T 2 (Model T2) (Model DET2) - single cutaway sen ash body, bolt-on hard rock maple neck, 22-fret rosewood fingerboard with pearl dot inlay, black pickguard, fixed bridge, graphite nut, 6-on-a-side Levinson SG-36 tuners, gold hardware, 2 single coil Levinson T 4/2 Calibrated pickups, volume/tone control, 3-position selector switch, VSC switch, chrome controls plate, Variable Spectrum Control electronics, available in Honey, Ocean Blue, and Sunset Purple See-through finishes. Current Mfg.

MSR	$1,699	$1,200	$1,000	$875	$775	$650	$550	$425

This model is also available with a one piece maple neck (limited quantities).

In 1998, 3-Tone Sunburst and Fire Red finishes were introduced.

Delta T 1 (Model T1) - similar to the Delta T 2, except features hardwood body, chrome hardware, available in Black and Vintage White finishes. Mfg. 1998 to date.

MSR	$599	$425	$375	$325	$275	$250	$195	$150

THINLINE (Model THS/DTHS) - similar to the Delta T 2, except features a semi-solid sen ash body, unbound f-hole, rounded white pearl pickguard, no chrome controls plate, available in Honey, Ocean Blue, and Sunset Purple translucent finishes. Mfg. 1994 to date.

MSR	$1,859	$1,300	$1,125	$995	$875	$725	$600	$475

This model is also available with a one piece maple neck (limited quantities).

In 1998, 3-Tone Sunburst and Fire Red finishes were introduced.

Thinline (Model THH/DTHH) - similar to the Thinline (Model THS), except features a LH-55 humbucker/T 4 Bridge single coil pickups, push/pull tone (humbucker coil tap) control, available in 3-Tone Sunburst, Fire Red, Honey Burst, Ocean Blue, and Sunset Purple finishes. Mfg. 1993 to date.

MSR	$1,859	$1,300	$1,125	$995	$875	$725	$600	$475

This model was originally listed as the Delta Queen (1993-1994), and was offered in Harvest Gold, Misty Violet, Ocean Blue, and 3-Tone Sunburst finishes.

T 2 (Model T2-MG) - single cutaway light ash body, bolt-on maple neck, 22-fret maple fingerboard with black dot inlay, fixed bridge, graphite nut, 6-on-a-side tuners, gold hardware, 2 single coil pickups, volume/tone control, 3-position switch, VSC switch, Variable Spectrum Control electronics, available in Harvest Gold, Misty Violet, Ocean Blue, and See-through Red translucent finishes. Mfg. 1991 to 1992.

		$775	$675	$600	$525	$475	$400	$325

Last MSR was $1,290.

Add $40 for rosewood fingerboard with pearl dot inlay (T2-RG).

GRADING		100% MINT	98% NEAR MINT	95% EXC+	90% EXC	80% VG+	70% VG	60% G

RH 4-MB - offset double cutaway light ash body, black pickguard, bolt-on maple neck, 22-fret maple fingerboard with black dot inlay, Falcon tremolo system, graphite nut, 6-per-side Sperzel Trimlock tuners, black hardware, 2 SS-1 single coil/1 LH-4 humbucking pickups, volume/tone control, 5-position pickup selector switch, VSC switch, Variable Spectrum Control active electronics, available in Nightwood, Ocean Blue and See-through Red translucent finishes. Mfg. 1988 to 1992.

$1,100 $925 $825 $750 $650 $575 $475
Last MSR was $1,850.

Add $100 for ebony fingerboard with pearl dot inlay (RH4-EB).

RH 4-MG - similar to RH4-MB, except has gold hardware, available in Honey and Misty Violet finishes. Mfg. 1988 to 1992.

$1,150 $950 $850 $775 $675 $575 $475
Last MSR was $1,900.

Add $100 for ebony fingerboard with pearl dot inlay (RH4-EG).

RH 4 STANDARD (Model RS4) - offset double cutaway sen ash body, bolt-on hard rock maple neck, 22-fret rosewood fingerboard with pearl dot inlay, Levinson Vint-Edge FT-3 tremolo, graphite nut, 6-per-side Gotoh MG7 Magnum Lock tuners, chrome hardware, sepia mirror pickguard, 2 V-3 stacked coil/1 LH-55 humbucker pickups, volume/push-pull tone (humbucker coil tap) controls, 5-position selector switch, VSC switch, Variable Spectrum Control active electronics, available in Honey, Misty Violet, Ocean Blue, and See-through Red finishes. Mfg. 1996 to date.

MSR $1,799 $1,000 $900 $825 $725 $625 $550 $450

This model is available with a one piece maple neck (limited quantities), or 3 single coil pickups.
Early versions of this model may have black pickguards.

RH 4 Classic (Model RH4) - similar to the RH 4 Standard, except features an ebony or flamed maple fingerboard, Levinson Falcon tremolo, Sperzel Trimlock tuners, and gold hardware. Mfg. 1996 to date.

MSR $2,199 $1,300 $1,100 $995 $875 $775 $650 $550

This model is available with a one piece flamed maple neck (limited quantities), or 3 single coil pickups.

TEXAS (Model TE) - offset double cutaway alder body, bolt-on maple neck, 22-fret rosewood fingerboard with pearl dot inlay, Levinson Vint-Edge FT-2 tremolo, graphite nut, 6-on-a-side Levinson Staggered tuners, chrome hardware, white pearloid pickguard, 3 single coil pickups, volume/tone control, 5-position pickup selector switch, bypass mini-switch, gain boost electronics, available in Black and 3-Tone Sunburst finishes. Mfg. 1994 to 1997.

$800 $695 $625 $550 $475 $400 $325
Last MSR was $1,299.

This model was available with a one piece maple neck, and/or a black pickguard with 2 single coil/humbucker pickups.

Texas Deluxe - similar to the Texas TE, except had sen ash body, 2 single coil/1 humbucker pickups, Levinson FT-4 tremolo, Sperzel Trimlock tuners, VSC-2 mini-switch, VSC-2 electronics, available in Fire Red, Ocean Blue, Purple, and 2-Tone Sunburst finishes. Mfg. 1994 to 1995.

$950 $850 $750 $650 $575 $475 $375

Texas JR - similar to the Texas TE, except had sen ash body, 2 single coil/1 humbucker pickups, Levinson FT- 3 tremolo, Sperzel Trimlock tuners, variable mid boost electronics (push/pull tone knob), available in Blue Oil, Purple Oil, and Red Oil finishes. Mfg. 1994 to 1995.

$975 $875 $795 $675 $695 $500 $400

TEXAS STANDARD (Model TE-2) - offset double cutaway North American alder body, bolt-on hard rock maple neck, 22-fret maple fingerboard with black dot inlay, Levinson FT-3 tremolo, graphite nut, 6-on-a-side Staggered SG-36 tuners, chrome hardware, white pickguard, 3 VS-1 single coil pickups, volume/tone controls, 5-position selector switch, gain boost mini-switch, gain boost electronics, available in 3-Tone Sunburst, Black, Candy Apple Red, Lake Placid Blue, and Olympic White finishes. Mfg. 1998 to date.

MSR $899 $650 $550 $475 $425 $350 $295 $225

This model has an optional rosewood fingerboard with pearl dot inlay.

Texas Special (Model TS) - similar to the Texas Standard (TE-2), except has sen ash body, and an LH-55 humbucker (bridge position), available in Fire Red, Honey, Ocean Blue, and Sunset Purple See-through finishes. Mfg. 1994 to date.

MSR $1,399 $850 $725 $650 $575 $500 $425 $350

This model has an optional rosewood fingerboard with pearl dot inlay, or one-piece maple neck (limited quantities).

Texas Vintage (Model TV) - similar to the Texas TE, except has sen ash body, available in 3-Tone Sunburst, Black, Candy Apple Red, Indian Turquoise, Sea Foam Green, Sonic Blue, and Tobacco Sunburst finishes. Mfg. 1998 to date.

MSR $1,599 $1,125 $975 $850 $750 $625 $525 $400

This model has an optional one-piece maple neck (Tobacco Sunburst finish only).

Durango Series

DURANGO (Model DU) - offset double cutaway alder body, bolt-on maple neck, 22-fret rosewood fingerboard with pearl dot inlay, Wilkinson HT100T tremolo, graphite nut, 6-on-a-side Sperzel non-locking tuners, chrome hardware, white pearloid pickguard, 1 single coil/1 humbucker pickups, volume/tone control, 3-position pickup selector switch, bypass mini-switch, gain boost electronics, available in Amber, Black, Candy Apple Red, Purple, and Turquoise finishes. Mfg. 1994 to 1997.

$900 $775 $695 $625 $525 $450 $375
Last MSR was $1,499.

DURANGO STANDARD (Model DS) - offset double cutaway mahogany body, bolt-on hard rock maple neck, 25 1/2" scale, 22-fret rosewood fingerboard with pearl dot inlay, Wilkinson VS-50K tremolo, graphite nut, 6-on-a-side die cast tuners, chrome hardware, white pearloid pickguard, 2 VS-1 single coil/LH-55 humbucker pickups, volume/tone controls, 5-position pickup selector switch, available in Blue Metallic, Cherry, and Natural Oil finishes. Mfg. 1996 to date.

MSR $799 $499 $399 $350 $325 $275 $225 $200

In 1997, Black and Matt Stained Mahogany finishes were introduced; Blue Metallic, Cherry, and Natural Oil finishes were discontinued.

GRADING		100% MINT	98% NEAR MINT	95% EXC+	90% EXC	80% VG+	70% VG	60% G

Durango Deluxe (Model DD) - similar to the Durango Standard, except features North American alder body, Levinson FT-4 tremolo, chrome Sperzel Trimlock tuners, and Seymour Duncan L'il 59 mini-humbucker/HD-4 humbucker pickups, volume/push-pull tone (humbucker coil tap) controls, gain boost electronics, available in Amber, Black, Candy Apple Red, Cherry, Purple, and Turquoise finishes. Mfg. 1994 to date.

MSR	$1,699	$1,175	$1,000	$875	$775	$650	$550	$425

Add $150 for 2 single coil/humbucker pickups with VSC electronics configuration.

This model is custom built in Switzerland.

In 1997, Ice Blue finish was introduced; Amber, Cherry, Purple, and Turquoise finishes were discontinued.

Durango Magnum (Model DM) - similar to the Durango Standard, available in Black, See-through Cherry, Blue Metallic, and See-through Matt Stained Mahogany finishes. Mfg. 1998 to date.

MSR	$899	$625	$550	$475	$425	$350	$295	$225

Durango T (Model DT) - similar to the Durango Standard, except features set-in mahogany neck, 24 3/4" scale, tune-o-matic bridge/stop tailpiece, 2 LP-90 oversized single coil pickups, volume/tone push-pull (gain boost on/off) controls, 3-way selector switch, available in See-through Cherry and Tobacco Sunburst finishes. Mfg. 1997 to date.

MSR	$959	$625	$550	$475	$425	$350	$295	$225

DURANGO T HYBRID (Model DTH) - offset single cutaway mahogany body, hard rock maple neck, 25 1/2" scale, 22-fret rosewood fingerboard with pearl dot inlay, hexaphonic piezo bridge/stop tailpiece, graphite nut, 6-on-a-side SG-36 tuners, chrome hardware, curved white pearloid pickguard, 2 single coil/humbucker magnetic pickups, master volume/tone/EA (electric/acoustic) mix controls, 5-position magnetic pickup selector switch, EA system switch, "hideaway" push-in piezo treble/bass boost controls (on bass bout), available in Sunburst finish only. Mfg. 1997 to date.

MSR	$1,299	$950	$795	$700	$600	$525	$425	$325

ELECTRIC BASS

Blade basses were offered with a fretted or fretless fingerboard.

B 3 - offset double cutaway contoured soft maple body, bolt-on maple neck, 21-fret ebony fingerboard with pearl dot inlay, fixed bridge, 4-on-a-side Gotoh tuners, 2 J-style pickups, black hardware, volume/pickup balance/tone controls, VSC switch, Variable Bass Spectrum Control II electronics, available in Black, Ice Blue, Purple Rain, and Snow White opaque finishes. Mfg. 1991 to 1992.

$1,100	$895	$800	$695	$625	$525	$425

Last MSR was $1,740.

B 4 - similar to B 3, except has light ash body, and gold hardware, available in Honey, Misty Violet, Ocean Blue, and See-through Red translucent finishes. Mfg. 1991 to 1992.

$1,195	$995	$895	$800	$700	$595	$495

Last MSR was $1,970.

B 4 Custom - similar to the B 4, except featured mahogany body. Mfg. 1991 to 1992.

$1,200	$1,000	$900	$800	$700	$600	$500

Last MSR was $1,970.

PENTA 5 - offset double cutaway contoured sen ash body, bolt-on maple neck, 5-string configuration, 21-fret rosewood fingerboard with pearl dot inlay, fixed bridge, 4/1 per side Gotoh tuners, 2 JHB-25 J-style pickups, gold hardware, master volume/pickup balance/Treble boost/Bass boost controls, Variable Bass Spectrum Control 2 (VSC 2) active electronics, available in Honey, Misty Violet, Nightwood, Ocean Blue, and See-through Red translucent finishes. Mfg. 1993 only.

$1,195	$995	$895	$800	$700	$595	$495

The Bass push/pull control activates the VSC 2 setting. Trim pots in the back of the Penta 5 pre-set a different EQ setting.

TETRA 4 - offset double cutaway contoured sen ash body, bolt-on maple neck, 4-string configuration, 21-fret rosewood fingerboard with pearl dot inlay, fixed bridge, 4-on-a-side Gotoh tuners, 2 JHB-2 J-style pickups, gold hardware, master volume/pickup balance/Treble boost/Bass boost controls, Variable Bass Spectrum Control 2 (VSC 2) active electronics, available in Honey, Misty Violet, Nightwood, Ocean Blue, and See-through Red translucent finishes. Mfg. 1993 only.

$1,100	$895	$800	$695	$625	$525	$425

The Bass push/pull control activates the VSC 2 setting. Trim pots in the back of the Tetra 4 pre-set a different EQ setting.

BLAIR GUITARS LTD.

Instruments currently built in Ellington, Connecticut.

Designer Douglas Blair has over twenty years experience in the music field, and has been building his own guitars since his teens. Blair has recorded 3 independent EP/LPs, and toured with acts like *Run 21* and *W.A.S.P.* Throughout his professional playing career, Blair found himself constantly switching between his electric guitar and an Ovation acoustic on a stand for live performances. In 1990, Blair conceived of the **Mutant Twin** guitar model as a way to solve the problem, which combined a solid body half with an "acoustic" half (with hollow tuned sound chamber and Fishman preamp). Prototypes were developed with the aid of Ovation R & D designer Don Johnson in 1990, and the guitar debuted in Boston in 1991. Blair Guitars Ltd. debuted at the 1994 NAMM winter show.

In 1997, Blair's design was licensed to Guild (FMIC) as the new Slash signature Crossroads custom design doubleneck guitar. This model is available in Black or Crimson Transparent finishes (Guild retail list $4,000).

ELECTRIC

Doug Blair's **Blair Guitars Ltd**. currently offers the **Mutant Twin Standard 6**, which carries a suggested retail price of $2,299 (these guitars originally were available as a custom order only). The double necked guitar had a solid mahogany "common" body, solid cedar or spruce braced soundboard (on the acoustic half) over a tuned acoustic sound chamber in the body. The two Warmouth necks had Graph Tech nuts and Schaller tuning machines. The acoustic side of the guitar had a custom 'pinless' rosewood bridge and Fishman piezo bridge pickup (and preamp); the electric side had Gibson humbuckers and either a Schaller or Wilkinson locking tremolo.

The **Mutant Twin Standard 12** (list price $2,799) is the 6-string electric/12-string acoustic doubleneck configuration. Other variations include the **Mutant Twin Memphis Belle 6** (list price $2,799), which has 6 string electric/6-string dobro resophonic 'Tele'-style downsized alder body, tricone resonator, biscuit bridge, Fishman pickup and preamp, maple necks with maple or rosewood fingerboards, DiMarzio pickups (electric half), and a nitrocellulose finish. The **Mutant Twin Madrid Eyes 6** (list price $2,799) is similar to the Standard 6 but pairs the electric side's two Gibson '57 humbuckers with a nylon string half, along with an ebony fingerboard and an X-braced cedar top. The **Mutant Twin Bristol Shores 6** (list price $2,299) is also similar to the Standard 6, but has 3 Dimarzio "Class of '55" single coil pickups, a 5-way selector, and a Wilkinson non-locking tremolo bridge. The Bristol Shores is also available in a 12-string/6-string configuration (list $2,799).

ELECTRIC BASS

Blair has also introduced the **Generation X 8** bass model which has a Les Paul Jr.-style body, "Dual Format 8-string configuration with P/J-style pickups and Fishman piezo bridge pickups (on octave strings only), active tone/EQ controls, discrete outputs, and a 3-way magnetic/piezo pickup selector (list price $1,999)."

BLUE SAGE

See MELODY.

The Italian-built Blue Sage series debuted in 1982, and was part of the overall Melody guitar line. The Blue Sage series of original designs was of higher quality than the traditional offerings of the company.

(Source: Tony Bacon, Ultimate Guitar Book)

BLUE STAR GUITAR COMPANY

Instruments currently built in Fennville, Michigan since 1981. Distributed by Elderly Instruments of Lansing, Michigan.

Luthier Bruce Herron has been building guitars since 1979. The first Blue Star electric guitar was built in 1984. Herron's initial production model, the Travelcaster (a travel-sized 6-string electric) was introduced in 1990. In his one-man shop, Herron now offers a range of electric stringed instruments distributed both in his home town near Holland, Michigan, as well as Elderly Instruments.

Other stringed instruments produced by Herron include the Mandoblaster (Model BSMB), a 4- or 5-string electric solid body mandolin. Mandoblasters have been the most popular since introduced; and feature one single coil pickup, double cutaway body, adjustable truss rod, volume/tone controls, and choice of maple or rosewood fingerboards. The retail list for the BSMB-4 (4-string) or the BSMB (5-string) is $600 factory direct (retail price at Elderly is $490). Herron's Lapmaster is a electric lap steel with one humbucker, volume and tone controls, and carpeted (like amplifier covering) back and sides (retail list is $300 factory direct - list price at Elderly is $210).

In 1997, Herron introduced the Banjocaster. A 5-string double cutaway electric banjo with 2-lipstick pickups, 4-on-a-side peghead and Schaller geared 5th peg, string through-body bridge, adjustable truss rod, volume/tone controls, 3-way pickup selector switch, and choice of maple or rosewood, and scalloped or radius options for the fingerboard. List price is $850, factory or Elderly price is $595.

New in 1998 will be the "Otis Taylor-Bluesman" model Banjocaster. A cool body shape with 3 mini-lipstick pickups and personally autographed by Otis Taylor. List price is $995 factory direct, or $696.50 at Elderly Instruments. The Otis Taylor Bluesman model is also available at Otis' favorite hometown music store, the Denver Folklore Center.

Herron's Konablaster Ukulele has a pineapple-shaped body, Pacific Blue top/non-slip Ozite carpeted back and sides, one single coil pickup, and a nickel plated "thirty-aught-six" shell casing tailpiece! The headstock on this model is personally signed by Allan Woody (Allman Brothers, Gov't Mule). Retail price on the BSKB is $210.

ELECTRIC

Blue Star instruments feature solid wood construction topped with an eye-catching, psychedelic Phenolic *burst* top. This durable reflective material is occasionally found on drum sets (Herron admits that his inspiration began with '50s Gretsch drum sets and guitars). All models have a chip-resistant finish on the sides and back, chrome hardware, and a limited lifetime warranty from Herron, available in Blueburst, Chromeburst, Goldburst, Redburst, and Silverburst.

The **Travelcaster (Model BS-1)** has a 22" scale, one humbucker, double cutaway body, 3-per-side headstock, rosewood fingerboard, adjustable truss rod, and a tune-o-matic type bridge. Retail list is $550 factory direct, (retail price at Elderly is $385). The left-handed Travelcaster (Model BS-1L) has a retail price of $420.

Herron's full scale guitar, the **Psychocaster (Model PC)**, is a Telecaster-style design that features two single coil pickups, string through-body bridge, adjustable truss rod, volume/tone controls, 3-way pickup selector switch, and choice of maple or rosewood fingerboards. The **PC** lists at $560 factory direct (retail price at Elderly is $462); the left-handed **PCL's** retail price is $504.

BLUE STAR MUSIC

Instruments currently built in Lovingston, Virginia since 1995.

Luthier Joe Madison began operating Blue Star Music in 1988. He thought he had "seen it all" until artist Willie Kirschbaum brought in a hand-sculpted guitar body that featured a beautifully carved face with long flowing hair. Originally the bodies were displayed at art shows and galleries, and sparked a lot of interest. Jack Roy, an electronics specialist and vintage Fender aficionado, was also impressed. The three combined their talents to create these uniquely beautiful guitars, with hand-carved headstocks that echo the body design.

Each guitar has a unique figure carved into the wood, be it a dragon, a face, a snake, or almost any design. Custom guitars can be standard shape or radical designs with many wood choices and unlimited electronic configurations. Prices range from $1,000 to $4,500, depending on the intricacy of the sculpting and design. All are outfitted with top quality hardware.

B

BLUESOUTH

Instruments currently built in Muscle Shoals, Alabama.

Ronnie Knight began Bluesouth Guitars in 1991 with the idea of building stringed musical instruments which celebrate the musical heritage of the American South. Blues, jazz, country, rock, and spiritual music were all created in the southern American states. This small area from Texas to the Carolinas, from Kentucky to Florida, has been the hotbed of the world's musical culture in the twentieth century. Several small towns within the southeast have had a huge impact on today's popular music: Muscle Shoals, Alabama; Macon, Georgia; and Clarksdale, Mississippi.

The results of this project have been unique, light-bodied guitars with large, comfortable necks. Bluesouth contends that "fierce individualism" is the key ingredient in their guitar making operation. Starting in a small shop over a record store in early 1992, Bluesouth moved to a much larger industrial facility in the spring of 1995. To date, the company offers 7 models, including 2 electric basses. Bluesouth also builds its own cases and pickups in-house.

(Company history courtesy Ronnie Knight, April 17, 1996)

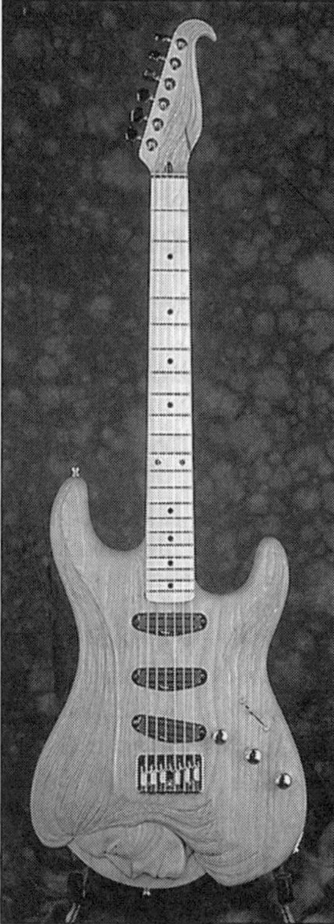

Blue Star Music Carved Face Custom courtesy Jack Roy

ELECTRIC

All Bluesouth instruments feature mahogany or swamp ash bodies in sleek ergonomic designs, a mahogany set-neck with 22-fret fingerboard, 24 3/4" scale, Sperzel tuners, Wilkinson or Gotoh hardware, and Bluesouth's own pickups.

Models run from the **Clarksdale** (list $1,295), which has a mahogany body, rosewood fingerboard, 2 Bluesouth 'soapbar' pickups, and a tune-o-matic bridge; to the **Macon** ($1,895), which has a carved top mahogany body, ebony fingerboard, Schaller humbuckers, and an ivoroid bound body. The **Jimmy Johnson "Original Swamper"** (list $1,895) has a single cut away 'Tele'-style swamp ash body, bolt on maple neck, and 2 single coil pickups. The **Muscle Shoals** ($1,495) model has a swamp ash body, rosewood fingerboard, 3 Bluesouth single coil pickups, and a Wilkinson HT-100C bridge; the **Muscle Shoals DLX** ($2,095) has a carved top ivoroid bound mahogany body, 2 Bluesouth "soapbar" pickups, and rosewood fingerboard.

ELECTRIC BASS

The **Clarksdale** 4-string bass (30" or 34" scale) retails at $1,895 (5-string is optional). The **Clarksdale** has a mahogany body, set-in mahogany neck, rosewood or ebony fingerboard (21, 22, or 24-fret), and 2 EMG J-style pickups. For further information, y'all call the boys from Bluesouth directly (see Trademark Index).

BLUNDELL

Instruments previously built in England during the early 1980s.

These British-built solid body guitars were patterned after the Explorer and Flying V designs.

(Source: Tony Bacon and Paul Day, The Guru's Guitar Guide)

BOGART

Instruments currently built in Germany since 1991. Distributed in the U.S. market by Salwender International of Orange, California.

Bogart has been producing high quality basses since 1991. Models feature a patented *Blackstone* material for the bodies and bolt-on graphite necks. Bogart basses have Bartolini pickups, solid brass bridge (with fine tuners) and Schaller tuning machines.

The *Blackstone* material consists of a wood core surrounded by epoxy foam. However, the neck, pickups, and hardware all bolt to the wood core.

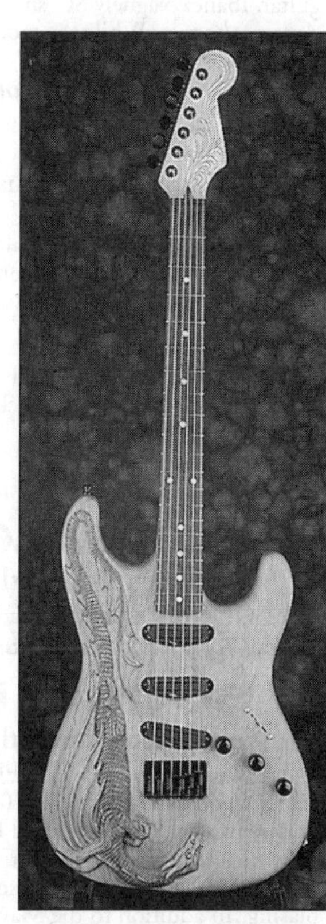

Blue Star Music Carved Dragon Custom courtesy Jack Roy

ELECTRIC BASS

Basic Series

Basic model options include black or blacknickel hardware, and Bartolini J-Bass pickups.

Add $84 for fretless Phenolic fingerboard.

BASIC CLASSIC 4 - offset double cutaway *Blackstone* body, bolt-on graphite neck, 86.4 cm scale, 24-fret graphite fingerboard, 3/1 per side Schaller tuners, chrome hardware, Bartolini humbucker, bridge/stop tailpiece with fine tuners, volume/tone control, passive electronics, available in Black, Pink, Red, Sky Blue, White, and Yellow Struktur finishes. Current Mfg.

MSR $2,795

Basic Classic 5 - similar to the Basic 4, except has 4/1 per side headstock and 5-string configuration. Current Mfg.

MSR $3,064

Basic Classic 6 - similar to the Basic 4, except has 4/2-per-side headstock and 6-string configuration. Current Mfg.

MSR $3,656

BASIC II/4 - similar to the Basic 4, except features a hardwood body, bridge/stop tailpiece. Current Mfg.

MSR $1,695

Basic II/5 - similar to the Basic II/4, except has 4/1 per side headstock and 5-string configuration. Current Mfg.

MSR $1,895

GRADING	100% MINT	98% NEAR MINT	95% EXC+	90% EXC	80% VG+	70% VG	60% G

B

Custom Basic Series

Custom Basic model options include gold hardware, and custom Multicolor painting.

Add $84 for fretless Phenolic fingerboard.

COLLIER BOGART 4 - offset double cutaway mahogany or European maple body, set-in graphite neck, 86.4 cm scale, 24-fret phenolic fingerboard, 3/1 per side Schaller tuners, black hardware, Bartolini soapbar humbucker, ETS bridge, volume control, 2 or 3-band EQ controls, available in Natural satin-like polyester finish. Mfg. 1997 to date.

MSR $2,881

Collier Bogart 5 - similar to the Collier Bogart 4, except has 4/1 per side headstock and 5-string configuration. Mfg. 1997 to date.

MSR $3,15

Collier Bogart 6 - similar to the Collier Bogart 4, except has 4/2-per-side headstock and 6-string configuration. Current Mfg.

MSR $3,504

CUSTOM BASIC 4 - offset double cutaway *Blackstone* body, bolt-on graphite neck, 86.4 cm scale, 24-fret graphite fingerboard, 3/1 per side Schaller tuners, black or blacknickel hardware, Bartolini soapbar humbucker, bridge/stop tailpiece with fine tuners, volume control, treble/mid/bass EQ controls, BBA3 active EQ, available in Black, Burgundy, Green, Light Red, Light Green, Midnight Blue, White, and Yellow Blackstone finishes. Current Mfg.

MSR $2,617

Custom Basic 5 - similar to the Custom Basic 4, except has 4/1 per side headstock and 5-string configuration. Current Mfg.

MSR $2,881

Custom Basic 6 - similar to the Custom Basic 4, except has 4/2-per-side headstock and 6-string configuration. Current Mfg.

MSR $3,504

BOGUE, REX

Previous trademark of instruments built in San Gabriel, California circa early 1970s. Previously distributed by Rex Bogue Guitars of San Gabriel, California.

Designer Rex Bogue was an independent luthier perhaps best known for his association with jazz guitarist Mahavishnu John McLaughlin, and the heavily inlaid doubleneck "Double Rainbow" guitar that Bogue created for him. Bogue credited the inlay work from S.S. Stewart banjo inlays and the French *art nouveau* painted Alphonse Mucha as inspiration for the "Tree of Life" fingerboard inlay design on McLaughlin's guitar.

Luthier Bogue was associated with the Ren Ferguson Guitar Company in Venice, California when the "Double Rainbow" was created; he later formed his own Rex Bogue Guitars in San Gabriel. Bogue created a number of other custom inlay commissioned works during the early 1970s, including a 4-string bass/6-string guitar doubleneck for bassist Miraslav Vitous (ex-Weather Report).

McLaughlin's doubleneck also attracted the attention of Jeff Hasselberger at Ibanez, who received Bogue's permission to duplicate the "look" of the guitar. Ibanez' vaguely SG-shaped doubleneck re-creation debuted in the 1975 Ibanez catalog as the model 2670, under the *Professional* or *Artist Autograph* series. While the model 2670 was available from 1975 through 1980, it is estimated that only a dozen were actually produced (1970s retail list was $1,500).

(Ibanez connection information courtesy Michael Wright, Guitar Stories Vol. 1)

BOND

Instruments previously built in England between 1984 and 1986.

Advanced design Bond guitars were designed by Scotland's Andrew Bond. The Electraglide model featured such innovations as a graphite body, *stepped ridges* instead of a conventional fretted neck, and a digital LED readout. Despite interest in the innovations and feel of the guitar, production lagged and the retail cost climbed. The company eventually closed in 1986, despite considerable financial investment and endorsements by The Edge (U2's guitarist). Production amounts are limited (understandably).

(Source: Greg Smith)

ELECTRAGLIDE - dual cutaway graphite body, synthetic *stepped ridges* fingerboard with dot inlay, 3+3 headstock, bridge/stop tailpiece, 'raised' pickguard, 3 single coil pickups, 5 pushbutton-type pickup selectors, 3 rocker switches, digital LED preset control, available in Black finish. Mfg. 1984 to 1986.

	100%	98%	95%	90%	80%	70%	60%
	$950	**$825**	**$755**	**$680**	**$600**	**$524**	**$450**

This model was available with an optional vibrato.

BOOGALOO

Instruments currently built in Britain since 1986.

The BOOGALOO trademark is used by luthier Frank Lemaux on his original designed high quality solid body guitars.

(Source: Tony Bacon and Paul Day, The Guru's Guitar Guide)

BOOGIE BODY

Instruments currently built in Gig Harbor, Washington.

Over twenty years ago, Lynn Ellsworth and Wayne Charvel founded Boogie Body guitars, a two-man company that produced electric guitar bodies of exotic woods. During the 1970s, Boogie Body had an impressive client roster of Eddie Van Halen (the red and white striped guitars), The Who, and Steppenwolf. Ellsworth closed Boogie Body in 1982, but reopened the company later in Gig Harbor, Washington.

Ellsworth recently developed the 2TEK bridge, an innovative through-body bridge system that improves the overall sound of guitars and basses. Boogie Body/VVT Technologies is also building Speedster hand-crafted amplifiers, an innovative design that features front panel control over the tube amp's biasing. In addition to the Mayan Gold series basses, Boogie Body also offers the BC-1 guitar model.

The current **Mayan Gold Series** basses feature an offset cocobolo body design with lengthened bass horn. Designed by Bishop Cochran, these handcrafted instruments feature a deep cutaway on the upper bout to provide full access to all 24-frets. Other features include a six bolt aluminum plate joining the neck to the body with machine screws and threaded brass inserts, EMG or Seymour Duncan pickups, and a 2TEK bridge. The **BC-1** bass has a list price of $1,995, the **BC-20** bass retails at $1,695, and the **BC Standard** bass retails at $1,495.

GRADING	100% MINT	98% NEAR MINT	95% EXC+	90% EXC	80% VG+	70% VG	60% G

BORJES, RALF

Instruments currently built in Bad Zwischenahn, Germany. Distributed by Dacapo Musik of Bad Zwischenahn, Germany, and Ralf Schulte of Palm Beach, Florida.

Designer Ralf Borjes offers 3 guitar and 3 bass models, as well as Dacapo Basstronic on-board preamp/EQs and other bass related electronics. All instruments are very good quality, and have transparent finishes.

ELECTRIC

Borjes' **Hunter** model has a 'superstrat' body, 2 Seymour Duncan humbuckers, special 5-way switch, 24-fret neck, double locking Floyd Rose bridge, and 6-on-a-side tuners. The **ST-Maniac** features a strat-styled body, 3 Seymour Duncan single coils or 2 singles/1 humbucker, vintage tremolo or locking Floyd Rose, and 22-fret neck. The third design, the T-Master, is a tele-shaped guitar with 2 Seymour Duncan or Joe Barden single coils, fixed bridge, and 22-fret neck. Retail prices start at $1,995.

ELECTRIC BASS

The JB-Custom bass has a Jazz-style alder (or alder with maple top) body, bolt-on maple neck, 21-fret rosewood or maple fingerboard, 2 Kent Armstrong single coil or humbucker pickups, and is available in 4- and 5-string configurations. Borjes' Groover model features an original body design with extended bass horn and narrow waist in cherry or flamed maple, bolt-on 3-piece maple neck, 24-fret ebony fingerboard, 2 Kent Armstrong *soapbar* pickups with single coil switch, and can be had in a 4-, 5-, or 6-string configuration. Basses in 4-string configuration have a 34" scale, while the 5- and 6-string models have a 36" scale. Retail prices start at $2,100.

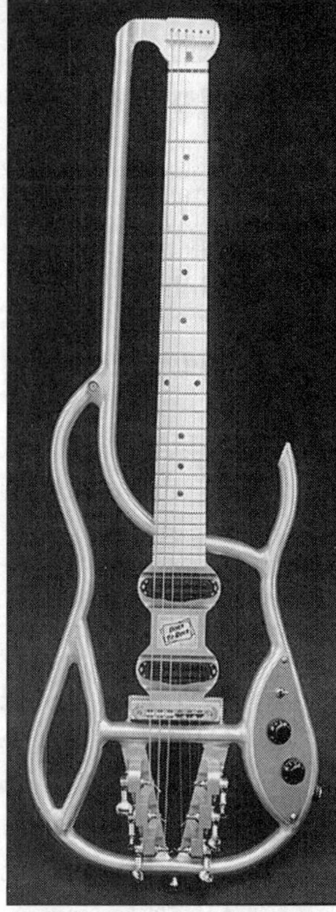

Born To Rock Model F4C
courtesy Robert Kunstadt

BORN TO ROCK

Instruments currently built in New York, New York.

Designer Robert Kunstadt came up with a new way to answer the age-old problem of neck warpage: by redesigning the nature of the neck/body/headstock interface, and by building the resulting innovative design out of aluminum tubing. The hollow aluminum tubing adds a new dimension to the instrument's sustain, and the neck joint assures that the neck will always line up straight with the strings.

ELECTRIC

Both the 6-string guitar (Model F4c) and 4-string bass (Model F4b) carry a new retail price of $3,380 each.

BORYS

Instruments currently built in Burlington, Vermont beginning in the mid 1970s.

Luthier Roger Borys began guitar repair work in the early 1970s, and completed building his first guitar in 1976. Borys has concentrated on building versatile, high quality instruments designed for the jazz guitarist. In 1980, Borys united with James D'Aquisto and musician Barry Galbraith to design the BG 100 Jazz electric. This instrument, later labeled the **Model B 120**, was co-built between Borys and Chip Wilson. Other instruments have included the **B 222 Jazz Solid**, which has a solid jazz *voice*, but can be used in playing other forms of music. For further information regarding model specifications, please contact Roger Borys directly (see Trademark Index).

BOSS AXE

Instruments currently produced in Japan.

Although the U.S. distributor is unknown, Boss Axe instruments are built in Japan by the Shimokura company.

BOSSA

Instruments currently built in Japan. Exclusively distributed by Soniq Trading, Inc. of North Hollywood, California.

Luthier Toshio Setozaki hand crafts exquisite looking and sounding basses and guitars.

ELECTRIC

OG Series

OG models are available in Natural Hand Rubbed Oil, Walnut Hand Rubbed Oil, Transparent Black, Transparent Blue, Transparent Red, Transparent Violet, Honey Sunburst, Turquoise Sunburst, 2-Tone Sunburst, and Snow White finishes.

Add $200 for Spalted maple top/Honduras mahogany back.

OG-1 JAY GRAYDON SIGNATURE - offset double cutaway asymmetrical Honduras mahogany body, quilted maple top, 24 3/4" scale, hardrock maple neck, 24-fret ebony (or maple) fingerboard with pearl dot inlays, 6-on-a-side Gotoh tuners, Floyd Rose locking tremolo, chrome hardware, 2 Bossa/Jay Graydon custom Dimarzio humbuckers, master volume/master tone controls, 3-way pickup selector switch, 2 coil tap switches. Mfg. 1996 to date.

MSR	$2,550	$2,100	$1,650	$1,425	$1,200	$N/A	$N/A	$N/A

This model was designed in conjunction with guitarist Jay Graydon.
This model comes standard with a hard shell case.

GRADING		100% MINT	98% NEAR MINT	95% EXC+	90% EXC	80% VG+	70% VG	60% G

B

OG-2 Jay Graydon Standard - similar to the OG-1 Jay Graydon, except features a light ash body. Mfg. 1996 to date.

MSR	$2,000	$1,650	$1,300	$1,125	$950	$N/A	$N/A	$N/A

OG-3 - offset double cutaway contoured body, 25 1/2" scale, hardrock maple neck, 22-fret ebony (or maple) fingerboards with pearl dot inlay, Wilkinson VS-100 tremolo by Gotoh, 6-on-a-side Gotoh tuners, logo peghead decal, chrome hardware, 2 Bossa custom Dimarzio humbucker pickups, 1 Bossa custom single coil, master volume/master tone controls, 3-position pickup selector switch, coil tap switches, center single coil on/off switch. Mfg. 1997 to date.

Light Ash body

MSR	$1,950	$1,600	$1,250	$1,075	$900	$N/A	$N/A	$N/A

Mahogany body and quilted maple top

MSR	$2,350	$1,900	$1,450	$1,225	$1,000	$N/A	$N/A	$N/A

OG-5 - similar to the OG-3, except features a quilted maple top, Honduras mahogany body, stop tailpiece. Mfg. 1998 to date.

MSR	$2,550	$2,100	$1,650	$1,425	$1,200	$N/A	$N/A	$N/A

This model comes standard with a hard shell case.

BASS

Bossa basses are available in Natural Hand Rubbed Oil, Walnut Hand Rubbed Oil, Transparent Black, Transparent Blue, Transparent Red, Transparent Violet, Honey Sunburst, Turquoise Sunburst, 2-Tone Sunburst, and Snow White finishes (Antique White was offered on the OB series until 1995).

Pau Ferro fingerboards were offered on both bass models until 1998.

OB and **OBJ** models have an optional on-board 18 volt active circuit, C.A.T. (Convertible Action Tremolo) system, and black or gold hardware.

Add $40 for a clear pickguard.

Add $80 for quilted maple wood *Pickup Fence* (string cover).

Add $100 for fretless fingerboard.

Add $400 for 4-string custom C.A.T. tremolo bridge.

Add $500 for 5-string custom C.A.T. tremolo bridge.

Add $600 for 6-string custom C.A.T. tremolo bridge.

Add 20% for left-handed configuration.

OB Series

Add $50 for Coil Tap Balancer Switch.

Add $200 for solid walnut body.

Add $500 for Quilted maple top/Light ash back body.

OB-4 - offset double cutaway asymmetrical solid Light ash body, 3-piece hardrock maple neck, 34" scale, 25-fret Maple (or ebony) fingerboards with pearl dot inlay, fixed bridge, 2-per-side Gotoh tuners, logo peghead decal, chrome hardware, 2 humbucker pickups, volume/pickup balance controls, treble/mid/bass EQ controls. Current Mfg.

MSR	$2,000	$1,600	$1,450	$1,250	$1,100	$N/A	$N/A	$N/A

OB-5 - similar to the OB-4, except features 5-string configuration, 3/2-per-side tuners. Current Mfg.

MSR	$2,300	$1,850	$1,600	$1,350	$1,200	$N/A	$N/A	$N/A

OB-6 - similar to the OB-4, except features 6-string configuration, 3-per-side tuners. Current Mfg.

MSR	$2,600	$2,100	$1,800	$1,500	$1,300	$N/A	$N/A	$N/A

OBJ Series

Add $200 for solid walnut body.

Add $500 for Quilted maple top/light ash back body.

OBJ-4 - offset double cutaway solid Light ash contoured body, 3-piece hardrock maple neck, 34" scale, 24-fret Maple (or ebony) fingerboards with pearl dot inlay, fixed bridge, 2-per-side Gotoh tuners, logo peghead decal, chrome hardware, 2 humbucker pickups, volume/pickup balance controls, coil tap balancer switch, treble/mid/bass EQ controls. Mfg. 1997 to date.

MSR	$2,100	$1,675	$1,475	$1,275	$1,100	$N/A	$N/A	$N/A

OBJ-5 - similar to the OBJ-4, except features 5-string configuration, 3/2-per-side tuners. Current Mfg.

MSR	$2,400	$1,925	$1,700	$1,450	$1,200	$N/A	$N/A	$N/A

OBJ-6 - similar to the OBJ-4, except features 6-string configuration, 3-per-side tuners. Current Mfg.

MSR	$2,700	$2,150	$1,900	$1,650	$1,350	$N/A	$N/A	$N/A

BOUVIER

Instruments currently built in Ocean Gate, New Jersey.

Dennis Bouvier Bourke, a professional guitarist and recording studio owner, debuted a new guitar design in 1997 that mates a mahogany body with a DuPont Corian top as a way to deliver a consistent, rich sound. The DuPont Corian is available in over sixty colors, and is guaranteed to never fade or discolor.

The **Bouvier Guitar - Revolution #1** is available in 2 models. The **Custom** (retail list $1,600 to $2,000) features a choice mahogany body, 1/4" Corian top, maple neck, maple or rosewood fingerboard, 1/2" Corian forearm rest, 2 humbucker pickups, and chrome (or black or gold) hardware. The Deluxe (retail list $1,900 to $2,500) is similar in design, but features 2 'soapbar' P-90 pickups, Bigsby tremolo, Schaller roller saddle, and vintage-style locking tuners. Both models retail price varies according to choices of Corian color, pickups, and hardware.

Bouvier also offers the **Coritone** electric bass, designed by Michael Tobias. Construction details are similar to the guitar models, and also feature passive P/J-style pickups. The retail list price runs from $1,600 to $2,000.

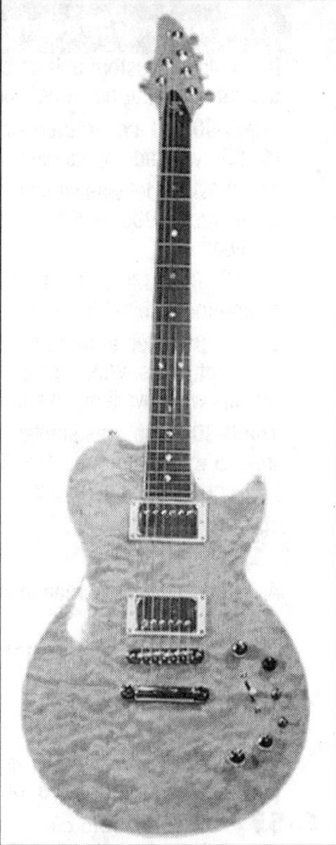

Brian Moore I2-13
courtesy Rich Gasciato

BOWN, RALPH S.

Instruments currently built in York, England.

This independent luthier is currently building high quality guitars. For further information, please contact Ralph Bown directly (see Trademark Index).

BOY LONDON

Current trademark established in 1976, and On You Co., Ltd., located in Osaka, Japan, is the exclusive agent.

Boy London guitars include both acoustic, acoustic electric, and electric guitars and basses. There are a wide variety of configurations, styles, colors, and features. Boy London also includes a line of amplifiers. For current model information and pricing, please contact the agent directly (see Trademark Index).

BRADFORD

See chapter on House Brands.

This trademark has been identified as a *House Brand* of the W. T. Grant company, one of the old style *Five and Dime* retail stores. W. T. Grant offered the Bradford trademarked guitars during the mid 1960s. Many of the instruments have been identified as produced by Guyatone in Japan. Bradford models ranged from flattop acoustics to thinline hollowbody and solidbody electric guitars and basses.

(Source: Michael Wright, Vintage Guitar Magazine)

BRADLEY

Instruments previously produced in Japan.

The American distributor for this trademark was Veneman Music of Bethesda, Maryland.

(Source: Michael Wright, Guitar Stories Vol. 1)

BRANDONI

Instruments currently produced in Wembley, England.

Roberto Brandoni was born and raised in Castelfidardo, Italy's premier musical instrument production area. By age six, he was already helping out in his father's accordion factory. In 1972, Brandoni resettled in England and has become part of the British music industry. After working for UK distributors Dallas-Arbiter, Brandoni started his own firm specializing in music related accessories like Quik-Lok stands and cases.

Brandoni became involved in guitar production after buying out leftover Vox and Hayman spare parts. Setting up workshops in Wembley, he produced and customized a number of instruments over the years (such as **Graffiti of London**). In 1987, Brandoni acquired the remaining inventory of **EKO** parts after the company closed down. Brandoni also purchased the contents of the **Welson** factory (another leading Italian guitar builder). At present, the Brandoni Custom Guitar catalog is 24 pages long!

Brandoni is currently offering guitars built of parts from decommissioned EKO, Vox, and Welson factories. Models include laminate-top archtops with no f-holes and pearloid-covered bodies, pearloid-covered Tele style guitars, as well as 9-string guitars. Other catalog listings include unmounted necks, bodies, pickups, parts, and hardware.

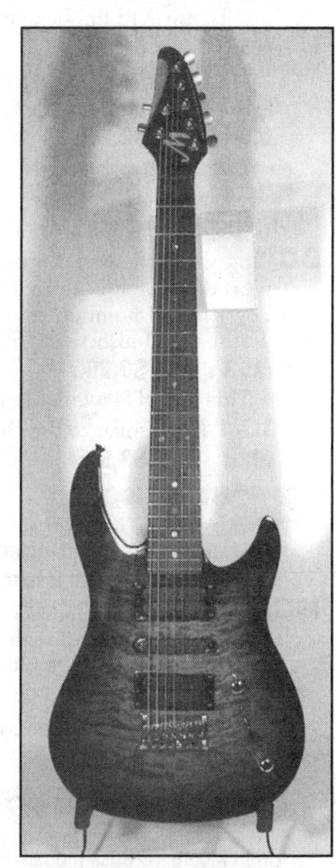

Brian Moore 7-String
courtesy Brook Mays

BRIAN EASTWOOD GUITARS

Instruments currently built in England.

Brian Eastwood has been making guitars since childhood. He builds, repairs and restores all types of electric and acoustic guitars. Custom instruments made to individual specifications are a specialty. Standard models include the Distortorcaster, Jellycaster, Burnt Marvel and Collision Bass. Brians "Blue Moon" is featured in Tony Bacon's book, **The *Ultimate Guitar Book*** and is possibly the most photographed guitar in the world.

BRIAN MOORE CUSTOM GUITARS

Instruments produced in Brewster, New York since 1994. Distributed by Brian Moore Custom Guitars of Brewster, New York.

Pat Cummings and Brian Moore teamed up with Kevin Kalagher in 1992 to begin prototype designs on the MC/1. Both Cummings and Moore had prior experience in producing guitars for another company, but elected to stay in New York when their division was moved south by headquarters. Moore designed the composite body shapes and incorporated the tonewood tops while Cummings arranged the electronics and pickup configurations. After testing seven prototypes, the MC (Moore/Cummings) 1 debuted in 1993.

After continued success both in the U.S. and Japan, the company expanded the product line with the **C Series**. Designed similar to the MC/1, the different models featured all wood bodies and bolt-on necks. The MC/1 was also offered with elaborate fretboard inlays (the Art Guitars), or with built-in MIDI equipment.

Brian Moore Art Guitars feature custom inlay work, and is available on any of the models (call for details). Brian Moore guitars are available with an installed MIDI system. The RMC MIDI Ready System is currently the featured product, and is compatible with all 13-pin guitar synthesizer inputs. The RMC system uses piezo saddles as the MIDI pickup, and all hardware and electronics is mounted internally. As a result, there are full blending capabilities between MIDI, piezo pickups, and magnetic pickups.

Transitional Models

Brian Moore Custom guitars briefly produced a number of models that lead to the expansion of the C Series guitars. These transition models are referred to in the catalogs, but not widely produced:

The **C-50** had a contoured alder body, bolt-on maple neck, Wilkinson tremolo, and 2 Seymour Duncan humbuckers. The suggested retail price was $1,695 ($1,850 with additional piezo bridge pickup).

The **C-70** model was similar in construction, but featured a swamp ash body and 2 single coil/1 humbucker Seymour Duncan pickups. Announced retail list price was $1,995, or $2,150 with the optional piezo bridge. Again, these were transition models only, and mention is listed to avoid any confusion with older catalogs.

In 1997, Brian Moore Custom Guitars offered a pair of models in the **C Series** that were the "entry level" models to the entire product line (these models were discontinued in 1998):

The **C-10** model featured the Brian Moore-style offset double cutaway contoured basswood body, a bolt-on maple neck, a 22-fret rosewood fingerboard with pearl dot inlays, Wilkinson standard vibrato, chrome hardware, 2 Duncan Design humbucker pickups, volume/tone controls, and a 3 way selector switch. C-10 models were available in solid color finishes. The listed retail price was $795, and the **C-10 P** model with the additional piezo bridge pickup was $1,045).

The **C-30** model was similar to the C-10, except featured an ash body, 2 Duncan Design single coils/1 Duncan Design humbucker pickups, volume/tone controls, 5 way selector switch. The C-30 was available in transparent finishes. The suggested retail list price was $995 (the **C-30 P** model had an additional piezo bridge pickup, and a retail price of $1,245).

ELECTRIC

All pegheads have screened logos with 2/4-per-side tuners. Models are also available in left-handed configuration (consult your Brian Moore Custom Guitar dealer).

Add $525 for RMC MIDI Ready System.

C Series

In 1996, the company offered variations in the C-series design, but with solid wood bodies and no synthetic backs. The C- series originally offered different pickup configurations and tonewood tops.

C-55 - offset double cutaway contoured mahogany body, figured maple top, bolt-on maple neck, 25 1/2" scale, 22 fret rosewood fingerboard with pearl dot inlays, 2/4-per-side sculpted headstock with Sperzel tuners, Wilkinson standard vibrato, chrome hardware, 2 Seymour Duncan humbucker pickups, volume/tone controls, 5-way selector switch. Available in Transparent colors and Sunburst finishes. Mfg. 1997 to date.

MSR $1,895

C-55 P - similar to the C-55, except features an additional piezo bridge pickup. Mfg. 1997 to date.

MSR $2,145

C-90 - offset double cutaway contoured mahogany body, figured maple top, bolt-on figured maple neck, 25 1/2" scale, 22 fret rosewood fingerboard with pearl dot inlays, 2/4-per-side sculpted headstock with Sperzel tuners, Wilkinson standard vibrato, gold hardware, Seymour Duncan humbucker/single coil/humbucker pickups, volume/tone controls, 5-way selector switch. Available in Blue, Gray, Green, Natural, Purple, Red, and Yellow Transparent finishes, and Sunburst-style finishes. Mfg. 1996 to date.

MSR $2,495

This model was briefly offered with a swamp ash body/figured maple top.

C-90 P - similar to the C-90, except features an additional piezo bridge pickup. Mfg. 1997 to date.

MSR $2,745

DC/1 Series

The DC/1 model was a joint design with luthier/sound engineer Tom Doyle and Patrick Cummings (DC = Doyle/Cummings).

DC/1 - single cutaway contoured mahogany body, figured maple top, set-in mahogany neck, 24 3/4" scale, 22-fret bound rosewood fingerboard with pearl dot inlays, 2/4-per-side sculpted headstock with Sperzel tuners, tune-o-matic bridge/stop tailpiece, gold hardware, 2 Seymour Duncan Seth Lover model humbucker pickups, volume/tone controls, 3-way selector switch. Available in Blue, Gray, Green, Natural, Purple, Red, and Yellow Transparent finishes, and Sunburst-style finishes. Mfg. 1997 to date.

MSR $3,295

This model is available with the T.W. Doyle pickup system.

DC/1 P - similar to the DC/1, except features an additional piezo bridge pickup. Mfg. 1998 to date.

MSR $3,545

MC/1 Series

MC/1 guitars feature an offset double cutaway body and neck of one solid piece of composite material, and a variety of figured wood tops with natural binding. Various pickup and electronic configurations are optionally offered along with choice of hardware.

MC/1 - offset double cutaway neck-through contoured composite body, arched figured maple top with wood binding, 25 1/2" scale, 24-fret ebony or rosewood fingerboard with pearl dot inlays, chrome or gold hardware, 2/4-per-side sculpted headstock, Wilkinson or Floyd Rose tremolo, 2 humbucking pickups, volume/tone controls, custom 5-way pickup selector switch. Mfg. 1993 to date.

MSR $3,795

MC/1 P - similar to the MC/1, except features an additional piezo bridge pickup. Mfg. 1998 to date.

MSR $3,795

ELECTRIC BASS

Brian Moore TC Bass models are a joint design with Michael Tobias (MTD/Michael Tobias Design) and Patrick Cummings.

All electric bass models are optionally available with a piezo bridge pickup system (contact your Brian Moore Custom Guitar dealer).

B

TC/4 - offset double cutaway contoured swamp ash body, bolt-on maple neck, 34" scale, 21-fret rosewood fingerboard with pearl dot inlays, 1/3 per side sculpted headstock with Sperzel tuners, Wilkinson bridge, gold or chrome hardware, Seymour Duncan Bassline passive pickups, volume/blend/tone controls. Available in Transparent colors and Sunburst-style finishes. Mfg. 1997 to date.

MSR $1,995

This model is available with Bartolini pickups.

TC/4+ - similar to the TC/4, except features highly figured wood top and Seymour Duncan Bassline active electronics. Mfg. 1997 to date.

MSR $2,495

TC/5 - offset double cutaway contoured swamp ash body, bolt-on maple neck, 34" scale, 21-fret rosewood fingerboard with pearl dot inlays, 2/3 per side sculpted headstock with Sperzel tuners, Wilkinson bridge, gold or chrome hardware, Seymour Duncan Bassline passive pickups, volume/blend/tone controls. Available in Transparent colors and Sunburst-style finishes. Mfg. 1997 to date.

MSR $2,195

This model is available with Bartolini pickups.

TC/5+ - similar to the TC/5, except features highly figured wood top and Seymour Duncan Bassline active electronics. Mfg. 1997 to date.

MSR $2,695

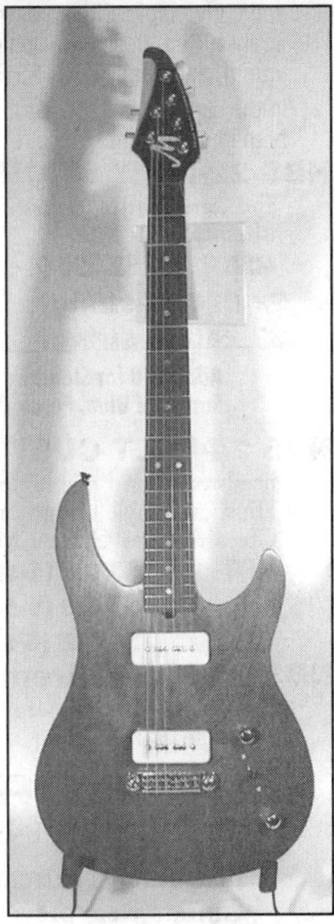

Brian Moore C-45
courtesy Brook Mays

BRIDWELL WORKSHOP

Instruments currently produced in Palatine, Illinois.

The Bridwell Workshop is currently building high quality guitars. For further information, please contact the Bridwell Workshop directly (see Trademark Index).

BROADWAY

Instruments previously built in Britain, Japan, and West Germany in the early to late 1960s.

The Broadway trademark is the brand name of a UK importer. The solid and semi-hollowbody guitars were of original design, but entry level quality.

(Source: Tony Bacon and Paul Day, The Guru's Guitar Guide)

BROCK, A. R.

Instruments previously built in Brooklyn, New York, circa unknown.

An example of an A.R. Brock Harp Guitar surfaced at a Texas Guitar show in 1996. The instrument's only company clue appears on the headstock, and read *Brooklyn, New York*. The guitar was decently built, and sounded okay when plugged into an amp. Research is still continuing into this trademark.

BRONSON

See chapter on House Brands.

While this trademark has been identified as a *House Brand*, the distributor is still unknown.

(Source: Willie G. Moseley, Stellas & Stratocasters)

BRUBAKER

Instruments currently built in Westminster, Maryland since 1993.

During the last year luthier/designer Kevin Brubaker has added Xtreme custom shop models to his handcrafted bases and guitars. While his instruments always featured carved flame or quilt maple tops and innovations such as his smooth sculpted heel, this new line offers colored, figured maple fingerboards, natural bindings and the best available hardware and electronics. Brubaker instruments have tonal qualities of both a set neck and a bolt-on, thanks to this unique neck-through-bolt-on joint. The neck goes 10 inches into the body, giving lateral stability and sustain.

ELECTRIC

B2 STANDARD - lightweight ash or mahogany body, maple neck and fingerboard, 2 Seymour Duncan humbucking pickups, 1-volume/1 tone, 3-way switch, Hipshot chrome hardtail bridge, chrome Grover tuners, available in Black, White, Seafoam green, Royal Blue and Viper Red finishes. Hardshell case included. Current Mfg.

MSR $2,000

Add $200 for Standard Upgrade Package consisting of chrome Schaller locking tuners, Coil tap switch, and rosewood fingerboard, available in Translucent Amber, Mahogany Red, Sapphire Blue, Purple/Violet and Natural finishes.

B2 Custom - similar to B2 Standard, except has AAAAA Flame Maple Top with matching headstock, maple or mahogany neck with mahogany body, Satin or Gloss finish, maple, Birdseye maple or rosewood fingerboard, chrome Point Technologies Tremelo Bridge, available in Translucent Amber, Cherry Red, Sapphire Blue, Purple/Violet, Black, Emerald Green and Natural finishes. Hardshell case included. Current Mfg.

MSR $2,800

B2 Xtreme - similar to B2 Custom, except choice of lightweight ash, mahogany, swamp ash or paulownia body material, hard maple neck, available in Custom colors. Hardshell case included. Current Mfg.

MSR Call for pricing.

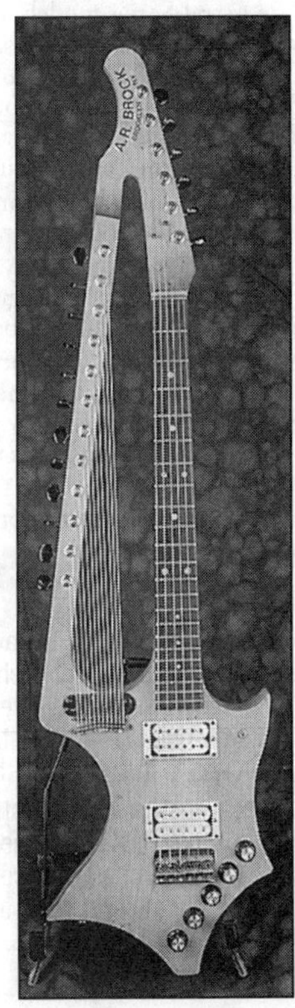

A.R. Brock
Harp Guitar
courtesy 19th
Annual Dallas Show

ELECTRIC BASS

The Lexa model is available in 4, 5, or 6-string configurations, and in either 34" or 35" scale lengths. The bolt-on one piece Hard maple neck has a 24-fret wenge fingerboard, and the soft maple body is topped with purpleheart or padauk and curly maple. Either passive or active Seymour Duncan pickups, Gotoh tuners, and a 2TEK bridge round out the package. Available in Natural, Cherry Red, Scarlett Red, Rose Red, Juniper Green, Forest Green, Sapphire Blue, and Indigo Waterborne lacquers. Retail list prices begin at $2,750 (4-string), to $3,100 (5-string), and finally up at $3,600 (6-string model). These models are disc.

In the summer of 1996, Brubaker introduced the Bo Axe, a slim bodied upright bass with 35" scale. The Bo Axe mounts to a support stand, and can be played both in an upright stance, or sideways by re-adjusting the stand. Disc.

NBS 22-FRET STANDARD - ash body, maple neck and fingerboard, single Bartolini Humbucker style pickup or Jazz pickups with a volume and tone control, chrome Hipshot B style bridge, chrome Hipshot tuners, available in Black, White, Seafoam green, Royal Blue and Viper Red finishes. Current Mfg.

MSR $2,390 (4-string)
$2,670 (5-string)
$3,240 (6-string)

Add $200 for Standard Upgrade Package consisting of rosewood fingerboard, AAA maple top, 3-band pre-amp, available in Translucent Amber, Cherry Red, Sapphire Blue, Purple/Violet, Black, Emerald Green or Natural finishes.

NBS 24-FRET CUSTOM - similar to NBS 22-fret Standard, except has 24-fret neck, AAAAA flame maple or quilted maple top with matching headstock, hard maple neck, Cocobolo or Birdseye Maple fingerboard, Bartolini P25 Soapbar pickups (quadcoil), with NTMB pre-amp, chrome Hipshot A Style bridge and chrome Hipshot tuners, available in Translucent Amber, Cherry Red, Sapphire Blue, Purple/Violet, Black and Emerald Green finishes. Current Mfg.

MSR $3,190 (4-string)
$3,470 (5-string)
$4,040 (6-string)

NBS 24-FRET Xtreme - similar to NBS 24-fret Custom, except has choice of lightweight ash, Swamp ash, alder or Paulownia body and custom colors. Current Mfg.

Please call the company directly for current pricing on this model.

BUNKER GUITARS

Also BUNKER INSTRUMENTS.

Instruments currently built in Mill Creek, Washington. Distributed by Bunker Guitars, LLC, of Mill Creek, Washington. Guitars were previously built in Tacoma, Washington between circa early 1960s to mid 1960s (Astral Series); 1976 to 1982 (Pro-Line).

Luthier/designer and musician David Bunker has been building guitars and basses for over the past 40 years. In 1955, Bunker built his first doubleneck Touch Guitar with his father, Joe Bunker. This model was named the Duo-Lectar. Bunker later received input from Irby Mandrell (Barbara Mandrell's father) regarding scale length. Bunker was granted his first patent in June of 1961. Bunker and his Touch Guitar was the foundation for **The Dave Bunker Show**, which was very popular in Las Vegas at the Golden Nugget between 1965 to 1974. Bunker also built other guitar models for his fellow performers in the band.

The **Astral Series** models, often described as "radically designed", debuted in the early 1960s. The advertising for Bunker guitars proclaimed them to be "The Guitars of Tomorrow!" Of course, the same advertising also had a favorite catchphrase: "It **Looks** Like No Other Guitar --- Because It **Is** Like No Other Guitar!" Rather than be different for different's sake, Bunker's Astral Series models were designed to solve certain inherent solid body design flaws. Bunker instruments are completely modular - you can change out any piece (neck or headstock or body or electronics, etc.) rather than repair the guitar, if you so chose. These detachable body and headstock pieces bolted to the center neck/minimalist body. Pickups and bridge hardware were also directly attached to the center "frame".

In 1976, Bunker built a small number of **Pro-Line** models (12, actually). These models are identifiable by their headless (reverse tuning) headstock, upswept lower bout with reverse tuners, and Bunker pickups. Even the cases were custom made, and built by Case's Inc. of Seattle, Washington.

After the Bunker company, David Bunker was later involved with **PBC Guitar Technology, Inc.** in Pennsylvania, which had noticeable success with the "Tension-Free" neck design and the *Wishbone* hollowbody series (see **PBC**). PBC was in business from 1989 to 1996, and produced a number of high quality bass and guitar models with innovative ideas.

After PBC closed their doors, Bunker relocated to Mill Creek, Washington. In 1998, Bunker was back to building the same quality PBC-style models, as well as the **Through-body Bridges**, a new Touch Guitar model, a new full body acoustic model, and **Tension Free** neck modifications. Bunker and a number of the key employees from PBC will be debuting the "new" Bunker models in the near future, but information and purchasing news is currently available at the company's website. So, for current information regarding the new Bunker instruments, contact Bunker Guitars directly (see Trademark Index).

(Bunker model information courtesy Ryland Fitchett of Rockohaulix)

MODEL CONSTRUCTION NOTES

Bunker instruments do have many similar innovative features. The Bunker "Split Bridge" bypassed the conventional single bridge piece for an individual bridge piece for each string. Each individual bridge was fully adjustable, and separated to prevent "electrical or acoustical cross-feed". Bunker's **Magnum** round pickups featured a 1/4" diameter Alnico V magnet with its own vertically wrapped wire coil. Instead of a common coil and magnets/pole pieces, the Magnum was an individual pickup per string. All Bunker models feature the "Floating Neck" design that was later utilized on various PBC and Treker models (as well as some high end Ibanez USA Prestige models).

Bunker instruments are strung in reverse, so tuning keys are on the end of the body similar to the Steinberger bridge. **Nova** and **Supernova** models featured "Peg Tuning", in which the string passed through the end of the body and was tuned by tightening a peg with a drum key (similar to autoharp stringing). After the primary tuning was completed, further tuning was accomplished by the "Fine Tuner", an additional piece between the bridge and tuning machines that used adjustment screws to deliver a "finer, more precise tuning of strings".

ELECTRIC

All Bunker models were available in "Fixed" (wings attached) or the optional "Snap-On"/Quick Change kit that allowed interchangeable wings to be attached to the body. As the catalog pointed out, "This invaluable device permits a performer to have many guitars in one - an advantage loved by the Pros". In addition to Eastern maple and Black Walnut, other Snap-On bodies include Satin Black, Silverflake vinyl, leather bound Blue Denim, Fire (Red and Black swirled) Naugahyde, Earth (Brown with Gold flecks) Naugahyde, and Charcoal (Black with Silver Flecks) Naugahyde.

GRADING	100% MINT	98% NEAR MINT	95% EXC+	90% EXC	80% VG+	70% VG	60% G

Optional Body Sets for the guitar models had a new retail price of $85 for **Fabric** (vinyl), $90 for **Wood**, and $110 for **Denim** (leather bound Denim).

Astral Series

HELLBENDER (Model HB-25-10) - minimalist neck-through eastern hard maple or black walnut body with 2 attached wings, 25" scale, bolt-on neck, 23-fret fingerboard with dot inlay, metal Bunker logo on headstock, 3-per-side tuners on end of body, 6 individual string brass bridge pieces, chrome hardware, 10 round Magnum pickups (in a dual bank), black 'roll' volume control, volume control/tone filter on/off switches, stainless steel controls plate, available in Natural finish. Mfg. circa 1960s.

$1,200 $1,100 $1,000 $825 $695 $550 $400
Last MSR was $830.

Hellbender (Model HB-25-10-FT) - similar to the Hellbender, except also features the Bunker Fine Tuner adjustable tuning system.

$1,200 $1,100 $1,000 $825 $695 $550 $400
Last MSR was $860.

Hellbender (Model HB-25-10-CK) - similar to the Hellbender, except features the Quick Change kit for interchangeable bodies.

$1,200 $1,100 $1,000 $825 $695 $550 $400
Last MSR was $860.

Hellbender (Model HB-25-10-FT-CK) - similar to the Hellbender, except features both the Bunker Fine Tuner and Quick Change kit.

$1,300 $1,100 $1,000 $895 $750 $675 $500
Last MSR was $810.

NOVA (Model N-25-6-FT) - minimalist neck-through eastern hard maple or black walnut body with 2 attached wings, 25" scale, bolt-on neck, 23-fret fingerboard with dot inlay, metal Bunker logo on headstock, 6-in-a-row brass Bunker Peg Tuner pegs/Delrin Brake Block/chrome string guard on end of body, 6 individual string brass bridge pieces, Bunker Fine Tuner, chrome hardware, 6 round Magnum pickups, black 'roll' volume control, volume control/tone filter on/off switches, stainless steel controls plate, available in Natural finish. Mfg. circa 1960s.

$1,200 $1,100 $1,000 $825 $695 $550 $400
Last MSR was $720.

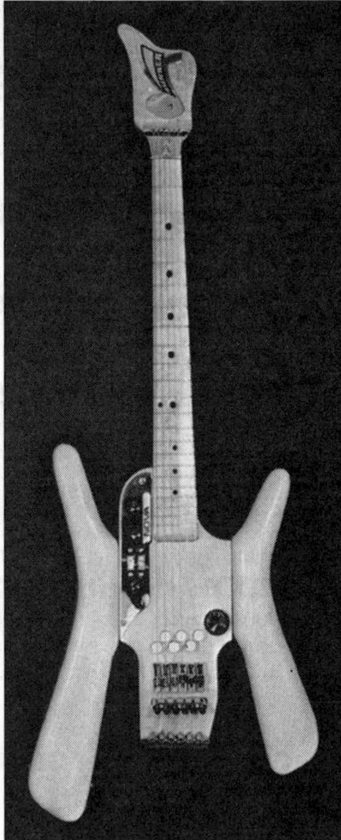

Bunker Nova
courtesy Ryland Fichett

Nova (Model N-25-6-FT-CK) - similar to the Nova, except features both the Bunker Fine Tuner and Quick Change kit.

$1,200 $1,100 $1,000 $895 $750 $675 $500
Last MSR was $750.

STARDUSTER (Model SD-25-6) - similar to the Nova, except features 3-per-side chromed solid brass tuners (in place of the Bunker Peg Tuner pegs, Fine Tuner adjustable tuning system), available in Natural finish. Mfg. circa 1960s.

$1,200 $1,100 $1,000 $825 $695 $550 $400
Last MSR was $740.

Starduster (Model SD-25-6-FT) - similar to the Starduster, except also features the Bunker Fine Tuner adjustable tuning system.

$1,200 $1,100 $1,000 $825 $695 $550 $400
Last MSR was $780.

Starduster (Model SD-25-6-CK) - similar to the Starduster, except features the Quick Change kit for interchangeable bodies.

$1,200 $1,100 $1,000 $825 $695 $550 $400
Last MSR was $770.

Starduster (Model SD-25-6-FT-CK) - similar to the Starduster, except features both the Bunker Fine Tuner and Quick Change kit.

$1,200 $1,100 $1,000 $825 $695 $550 $400
Last MSR was $810.

SUPERNOVA (Model SN-265-12-FT) - minimalist neck-through eastern hard maple or black walnut body with 2 attached wings, 26 1/2" scale, bolt-on neck, 24-fret fingerboard with dot inlay, metal Bunker logo on headstock, 6 in a row brass Bunker Peg Tuner pegs/Delrin Brake Block/chrome string guard on end of body, 6 individual string brass bridge pieces, Bunker Fine Tuner, chrome hardware, 12 round Magnum pickups (2 banks of 6), black 'roll' volume control, 2 volume control/2-Tone filter on/off/2 pickup on/off switches, hi-lo switch, stainless steel controls plate, available in Natural finish. Mfg. circa 1960s.

$1,200 $1,100 $1,000 $825 $695 $550 $400
Last MSR was $925.

Supernova (Model SN-265-12-FT-CK) - similar to the Supernova, except features both the Bunker Fine Tuner and Quick Change kit.

$1,300 $1,100 $1,000 $895 $750 $675 $500
Last MSR was $955.

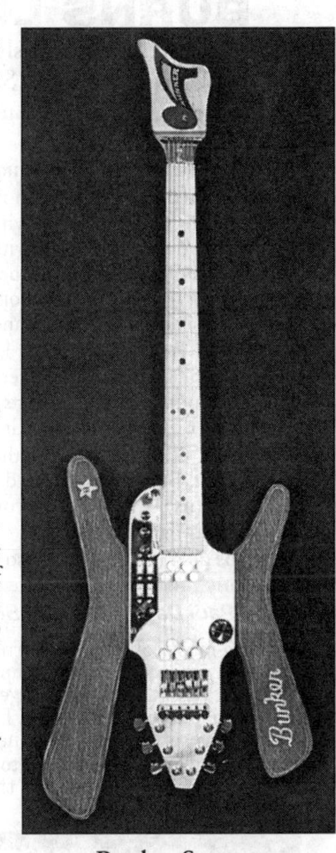

Bunker Sunstar
courtesy Ryland Fichett

GRADING	100% MINT	98% NEAR MINT	95% EXC+	90% EXC	80% VG+	70% VG	60% G

SUNSTAR (Model SS-265-12) - similar to the Supernova, except features 3-per-side tuners (in place of the Bunker Peg Tuner pegs, Fine Tuner adjustable tuning system), available in Natural finish. Mfg. circa 1960s.

$1,200	**$1,100**	**$1,000**	**$825**	**$695**	**$550**	**$400**

Last MSR was $945.

Sunstar (Model SS-265-12-FT) - similar to the Sunstar, except also features the Bunker Fine Tuner adjustable tuning system.

$1,200	**$1,100**	**$1,000**	**$825**	**$695**	**$550**	**$400**

Last MSR was $975.

Sunstar (Model SS-265-12-CK) - similar to the Sunstar, except features the Quick Change kit for interchangeable bodies.

$1,200	**$1,100**	**$1,000**	**$825**	**$695**	**$550**	**$400**

Last MSR was $965.

Sunstar (Model SS-265-12-FT-CK) - similar to the Sunstar, except features both the Bunker Fine Tuner and Quick Change kit.

$1,300	**$1,100**	**$1,000**	**$895**	**$750**	**$675**	**$500**

Last MSR was $995.

ELECTRIC BASS

Optional Body Sets for the bass models had a new retail price of $89 for **Fabric** (vinyl), $100 for **Wood**, and $114 for **Denim** (leather bound Denim).

GALAXY I (Model GL-305-4) - minimalist neck-through eastern hard maple or black walnut body with 2 attached wings, 30 1/2" scale, bolt-on neck, 23-fret fingerboard with dotted circle inlay, metal Bunker logo on headstock, 2-per-side tuners on end of body, 4 individual string brass bridge pieces, chrome hardware, 4 round Magnum pickups, volume control/tone filter on/off switches, stainless steel controls plate, available in Natural finish. Mfg. circa 1960s.

$1,200	**$1,100**	**$1,000**	**$825**	**$695**	**$550**	**$400**

Last MSR was $740.

Galaxy I (Model GL-305-4-CK) - similar to the Galaxy I, except features the Quick Change kit for interchangeable bodies.

$1,300	**$1,100**	**$1,000**	**$895**	**$750**	**$675**	**$500**

Last MSR was $820.

Galaxy II (Model GL-305-8) - similar to the Galaxy I, except features 8 round Magnum pickups (2 sets of 4), pickup bank selector switch. Mfg. circa 1960s.

$1,200	**$1,100**	**$1,000**	**$825**	**$695**	**$550**	**$400**

Last MSR was $860.

Galaxy II (Model GL-305-8-CK) - similar to the Galaxy II, except features the Quick Change kit for interchangable bodies.

$1,300	**$1,100**	**$1,000**	**$895**	**$750**	**$675**	**$500**

Last MSR was $890.

BURNS LONDON LTD./BURNS

Instruments previously built in Britain since the late 1950s. The exception being Baldwin-built Burns from 1965 to 1972, which were U.S. produced by assembling imported parts in Booneville, Arkansas. Current production is based in Surrey, England by Burns London Ltd. James O. Burns is acting as a consultant for Burns London Ltd.

Jim Burns has been hailed as *the British Leo Fender* due to his continual and on-going electric guitar designs and innovations. Widely accepted in England and Europe, Burns guitars never really caught on in the U.S. market.

James Ormsted Burns was born in 1925. Burns built his first lap steel while still serving in the Royal Air Force in 1944. By 1952 he completed his first solid body electric, and along with partner Alan Wooten, Burns built his first twenty guitars under the **Supersound** name in 1958. Burns' first production guitars were built with Henry Weill in 1959 under the Burns-Weill trademark, then later under the Burns logo. The **Burns, London** company (1960 to 1965) was the watermark of Jim Burns' career, as the company stayed very successful producing guitars, basses, amplifiers, and accessories. Even while many popular British artists used Burns instruments, Jim Burns then turned to exporting his instruments to the U.S. market briefly under both the Ampeg and Burns trademarks.

In 1965, the Baldwin company lost to CBS in its bid to acquire Fender. Searching for another proven winner, Baldwin bought Burns and began importing the instruments under the **Baldwin** or **Baldwin/Burns** trademarks. Jim Burns stayed on as managing director and "idea man" through 1966, then left to pursue other projects. Baldwin eventually began assembling imported parts in Booneville, Arkansas. By 1970, Baldwin decided to concentrate on production of Gretsch guitars and drums (acquired in 1967, the Gretsch operation was also moved down to Arkansas).

In 1969 Jim Burns returned to the musical instrument world as a design consultant to Dallas-Arbiter's Hayman trademark. Along with ex-Vox employee Bob Pearson, Burns was reunited with Jack Golder (ex-Burns mainstay) but only continued his affiliation until 1971. A new Burns organization arose in 1973 as **Burns, U.K.**, but this company met with less success than intended and folded in 1977. A later stab at affairs continued as the **Jim Burns Company** from 1979 to 1983.

Jim Burns died in 1998, and also served as an acting consultant at *Burns, London Ltd.* This Surrey, England-based company was established in 1992, and is currently producing authentic reproductions of the desirable 1960s-style Burns models.

(Source: Paul Day, The Burns Book)

The most collectable Burns instruments would be from the company's heyday between 1960 and 1965. The Burns-Weill models are relatively scarce, and the Ampeg by Burns of London models were only distributed from 1963 to 1964. Baldwin models, while not plentiful, do surface in the U.S. vintage market - and some examples pop up in Elvis Presley's 1960s movies! A Double-Six 12-string model is currently on display in Graceland. Later Burns' companies probably contributed smaller guitar productions, although the Burns U.K. Flite model has a pretty cool "jet plane"-shaped body design.

Jim Burns was the first to pioneer a number of distinct design ideas that are accepted worldwide in guitar production. Burns originated interesting features like the 24-fret fingerboard, the heel-less glued-in neck joint, knife-edge bearing vibrato unit, active electronics, and stacked-coil pickups.

Trademark Dating Identification

Jim Burn's career spanned from 1958 through 1984. Along the way, Burns founded a number of production companies and company trademarks. The following is an overview of his companies:

GRADING	100% MINT	98% NEAR MINT	95% EXC+	90% EXC	80% VG+	70% VG	60% G

1958: *Supersound*, with Alan Wooten.

1959: *Burns-Weill*, with Henry Weill. These models were Jim Burns' first production guitars.

1960-1965: *Burns London*.

1965-1970: *Baldwin, Baldwin/Burns*, importation by Baldwin to the U.S. market. Jim Burns stayed on with the company through 1966.

1973, 1974-1977: *Burns, U.K.*.

1979-1984: *Jim Burns* company.

1992-date: *Burns London, Ltd.* Jim Burns is an acting consultant to the current English company, which is specializing in authentic reproductions of the desirable 1960s-style models.

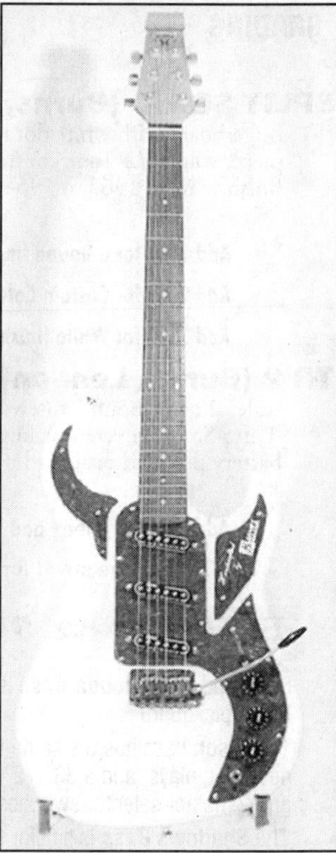

Burns Marquis
courtesy Mike Guther
at Top Gear LTD

ELECTRIC

The current Burns London Ltd. company is offering a number of new and reproduction Burns models. Model options include gold-plated hardware, Hiscox cases, and left-handed configuration. For current pricing specifications, please contact Burns London, Ltd. directly (see Trademark Index).

The **Bison** guitar has the familiar Burns double cutaway/inwards pointing horns design. Current models are constructed of a one-piece mahogany or tulipwood body, and feature a glued-in English beech or sycamore neck. The 22-fret rosewood fingerboard has pearl dot inlays, and a 24 3/4" scale. Bison guitars have 3 Rez-O-Matic pickups, Rez-O-Tube bridge/tailpiece, gold hardware, volume/rotary tone controls, and 2 master selector switches. Bison guitars are available in White (with grey pearl pickguard), and Black (with grey pearl or black pickguard) finishes.

The current 12-string **Double Six** model also features a Rez-O-Tube tremolo bridge! The offset double cutaway body features a glued-in maple neck, 6-per-side scrolled headstock, 21-fret ebony fingerboard, and a 25 1/2" scale. Electronics include 3 tri-sonic pickups, volume/rotary tone controls, and a 5-way selector switch. The Double Six is available in a Green Sunburst finish with 3-piece black pickguard.

The new **Flyte** guitar model has 2 split coil humbucker pickups and a Wilkinson tremolo unit, while the new **Burns Cobra** has vintage body styling, a scroll headstock, and Wilkinson tremolo unit.

Burns Limited Editions

The **30/50 Anniversary** limited edition model built in 1994 celebrates the 30th anniversary of the Shadows' changeover to Burns guitars, and the 50th anniversary of James Ormston Burns' first guitar built.

Legend Series

The **Legend Standard** has a double cutaway body, glued-in maple neck, 25 1/2" scale, 21-fret rosewood fingerboard with pearl dot inlay, 3-per-side tuners, scrolled headstock, 3-piece tortoiseshell pickguard, chrome hardware, 3 pickups, Rez-O-Tube tail piece, volume/rotary tone selector/push-pull tone controls, 5-way pickup selector. The **Deluxe (Shadows Model)** is similar, except features a slimline body and figured maple neck; the **Custom Deluxe (Shadows Model)** also features gold-plated hardware, a bound body, and unbound highly figured maple neck. Legend Series models are available in a white finish, but are also available in optional Green or Blue Sunburst finishes.

The **Legend 'S' Type** is a hollowed body version of the Standard. The guitar body is Brazilian mahogany with a Sycamore ripple top, and the glued-in beech neck has a rosewood fingerboard. The Legend 'S' Type is standard with a Green finish and white pearloid 3-piece pickguard.

Nu-Sonic Series

The **Nu Sonic model GB/98** features a single cutaway magnolia or mahogany body, glued-in maple neck, 25 1/2" scale, 22-fret rosewood fingerboard with pearl dot inlay, 3-per-side tuners, scrolled headstock, chrome hardware, black (or white) pickguard, 2 pickups, Rez-O-Tube tail piece, volume/rotary tone selector/push-pull tone controls, 3-way pickup selector. Model **GB/98 B** is similar in design, and features 3 pickups, a piezo transducer system, and a 5-way pickup selector; model **GB/98 B Custom** has a similar layout and gold-plated hardware. The **Steve Howe Signature** model has two pickups (which includes a split coil humbucker at the neck position). Nu-Sonic models are available in Black, White, or Fiesta Red; custom colors include Blue Sunburst and Green Sunburst. Body binding is optional

JAZZ SPLIT SOUND (Burns, London) - offset double cutaway hardwood body with inward curving horns, 23 3/8" scale, bolt-on neck, 22-fret rosewood fingerboard with white dot inlay, 6-on-a-side tuners, chrome hardware, black inscribed pickguard, 3 Burns 'Split-Sonic' pickups, bridge/tremolo tailpiece, volume/tone controls, 4-way tone selector switch (*Treble, Jazz, Split-Sound,* and *Wild Dog*), available in Red Sunburst finish. Mfg. 1962 to 1965.

$425	**$365**	**$315**	**$280**	**$240**	**$200**	**$175**

NU-SONIC (Burns, London) - offset double cutaway hardwood body with short horns, 23 3/8" scale, bolt-on neck, 22-fret rosewood fingerboard with white dot inlay, 6-on-a-side tuners, chrome hardware, black inscribed pickguard, 2 Burns 'Nu-Sonic' pickups, bridge/tremolo tailpiece, volume/2-Tone controls, 3-way selector switch, available in Black and Cherry finishes. Mfg. 1964 to 1965.

$400	**$350**	**$300**	**$265**	**$225**	**$190**	**$150**

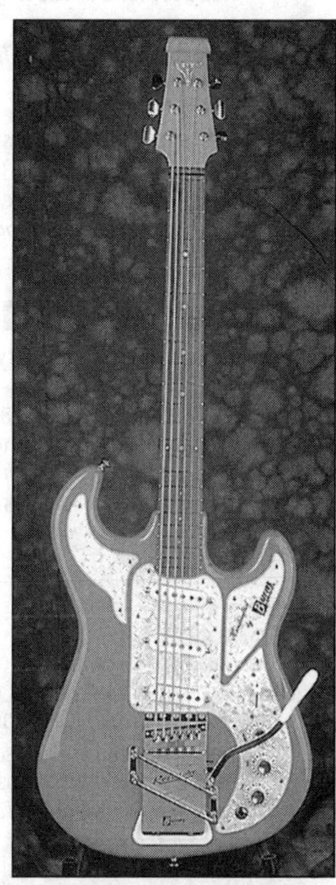

Burns London Ltd.
Baritone (Reissue)
courtesy Mark Sampson

GRADING	100% MINT	98% NEAR MINT	95% EXC+	90% EXC	80% VG+	70% VG	60% G

SPLIT SONIC (Burns, London) - offset double cutaway hardwood body with short horns, 24 3/4" scale, bolt-on neck, 22-fret rosewood fingerboard with white dot inlay, 6-on-a-side tuners, chrome hardware, black inscribed pickguard, 3 Burns 'Split-Sonic' pickups, bridge/tremolo tailpiece, volume/2-Tone controls, 4-way tone selector switch (Treble, Bass, Split-Sound, and Wild Dog), available in Red Sunburst and Custom Color finishes. Mfg. 1962 to 1964.

$425	$375	$325	$295	$250	$215	$180

Add 10% for a bound fingerboard.

Add 20% for Custom Color finishes.

Add 25% for White finish/inscribed White pickguard.

TR 2 (Burns, London) - offset double cutaway semi-solid body (solid center section), 2 f-holes, white body binding, bolt-on neck, 24 3/4" scale, 22-fret bound rosewood fingerboard with white dot inlay, 3-per-side tuners, bound headstock, bridge/'Mk. 9' tremolo tailpiece, 2 Burns 'Ultra-Sonic' covered pickups, raised black inscribed pickguard with volume/bass/treble roller controls mounted underneath, 3-way selector switch, battery powered on-board preamp, available in Cherry, Natural, and Red Sunburst finishes. Mfg. 1963 to 1964.

$400	$350	$300	$265	$225	$190	$150

Add 20% for Cherry and Natural finishes.

The TR 2 name stood for TR*ansistorized* 2 *Pickup* model.

ELECTRIC BASS

Burns' new **Barracuda Bass** is a 6-string bass/baritone guitar with a Rez-O-Tube tremolo bridge. Barracudas are offered in a Fiesta Red finish with an aged White pickguard.

The **Bison** bass has the same familiar Burns double cutaway/inwards pointing horns design as the Bison guitar model. The 22-fret rosewood fingerboard has pearl dot inlays, and a 33 1/2" scale. Bison basses have 3 Rez-O-Matic bass pickups, Rez-O-Tube tailpiece, chrome hardware, volume/rotary tone controls, and 2 master selector switches. Bison basses are available in White (with grey pearl pickguard), and Black (with grey pearl or black pickguard) finishes.

The **Shadows Bass** is similar to the Legend Deluxe (Shadows) guitar model. The offset double cutaway body is joined to a maple neck with a 22-fret rosewood fingerboard, and a 33 1/2" scale. Shadows Basses have 3 Rez-O-Matic bass pickups, Rez-O-Tube tailpiece, chrome hardware, volume/rotary tone controls, and a 5-way selector switch. Shadows Basses are available in White (with brown tortoise pickguard) or Green Sunburst (with black pickguard) finishes.

VISTA SONIC BASS (Burns, London) - offset double (almost dual) cutaway hardwood body with short horns, 31 1/2" scale, bolt-on neck, 20-fret rosewood fingerboard with white dot inlay, 4-on-a-side tuners, chrome hardware, black inscribed pickguard, 3 Burns 'Tri-Sonic' pickups, bridge/tailpiece, volume/tone controls, 4-way tone selector switch (*Treble, Bass, Contra-Bass, Wild Dog*), available in Red Sunburst finish. Mfg. 1962 to 1964.

$425	$375	$325	$295	$250	$215	$180

Add 20% for a bound fingerboard.

BURNSIDE

See GUILD.

Instruments previously built in Korea during the late 1980s.

Between 1987 and 1988, Guild introduced a line of imported entry level instruments to augment their sales line. The headstock trademark reads *Burnside by Guild* and consisted of 4 solid body guitar models and 2 bass models.

(Source: Michael Wright, Vintage Guitar Magazine)

Prices on these strat-styled instruments may range from $150 up to $225, depending on hardware/pickup packages.

BUSCARINO, JOHN

Instruments currently built in Largo, Florida. Distributed by the Buscarino Guitar Company of Largo, Florida.

Luthier John Buscarino apprenticed with Master acoustic guitar builder Augustino LoPrinzi for over a year in 1978, and with Bob Benedetto of archtop lutherie fame from 1979 to 1981. Later that year, Buscarino formed **Nova U.S.A.**, which built high quality solid body electrics, and acoustic/electric instruments. In 1990, **Buscarino** changed the company name to Buscarino Guitars to reflect the change to building acoustic instruments. Buscarino continues to produce limited production custom guitars, and is currently focusing on archtop guitar building.

For current information on John Buscarino's acoustic and acoustic archtop models, please refer to the 7th Edition ***Blue Book of Acoustic Guitars***.

ELECTRIC

Deluxe Series

Buscarino also built a number of solid body designs. Deluxe Series instruments featured bolt-on rock maple necks, rosewood fingerboards, chrome hardware, and Sperzel tuners. All models were available in Antique Cherry Sunburst, Black, Caribbean Blue Sunburst, Eggshell White, Tobacco Brown Sunburst, Transparent Blue, Transparent Red polyester finishes.

The **Classic** featured a Wilkinson tremolo, white pickguard, 3 EMG or Duncan SSL-2 single coil pickups, while the **Telstar** had a Gotoh Tele Tailpiece, no pickguard, and 2 single coil pickups. The **Nashville St.** featured a single cutaway body (with or without pickguard) and 3 Van Zant single coil pickups. The **Pro Bass** model had active EMJ P/J-style pickups, poplar or alder body, and 4 Sperzel Tuners. Retail prices ran from $1,245 up to $1,445.

Supreme Series

Instruments in the Supreme Series had highly figured exotic wood bodies with decorative binding/pinstriping, the Buscarino patented *Dead Bolt* releaseable bolt- on rock maple necks. The semi-acoustic **Hybrid** model allowed players to change from piezo to magnetic pickups. The upgraded TeleStar was available

GRADING	100% MINT	98% NEAR MINT	95% EXC+	90% EXC	80% VG+	70% VG	60% G

with numerous pickup and tone wood choices, while the **Mira** featured a flame or quilt maple top over alder or basswood body. Retail prices listed from $2,195 to $2,495.

Monarch Series

Monarch Series instruments are custom carved arched top electric guitars with bookmatched flame or quilt maple over mahogany or alder/basswood bodies. All models featured glued-in purpleheart/ebony/flame maple necks, contoured bodies, and gold hardware. List prices ranged from $2,995 to $3,995.

BYRD GUITAR CO.

Instruments currently built in Seattle, Washington.

The Byrd Guitar Co. makes a Super Avianti model with Balance Compensated Wing design, a modified Flying V configuration, with Orthocarve head/neck offsets. Please contact the company directly for more information and current pricing on this model (see Trademark Index)

NOTES

Section C

C & R GUITARS

Instruments previously built in Tulsa, Oklahoma circa 1989 to 1991.

Luthier/designer John Bolin and Bill Rich are the men behind those spectacular and rather rare **Batman** and **Joker** custom electric guitars. Bolin, who has created custom guitars for such players as Billy Gibbons, Rick Nielsen, and Albert King, teamed up with Rich and received full licensing rights from DC Comics to produce the guitars. The Batman model was introduced in 1989, the same year that director Tim Burton released the movie *Batman* (starring Jack Nicholson and Michael Keaton - more importantly, featuring music by Danny Elfman and Prince). Coincidence or savvy business practices?

The Batman model was produced in a limited run of 50 pieces. The Joker model was scheduled to be a limited run of 100 pieces, but only 42 were actually built. Rumors abound that there were models for the Penguin and Riddler to follow, but the licensing fee took an astronomical jump and put the ki-bosh on future plans. Ka-Blam! Quick, Robin, to the Batpole!

(Information courtesy Mitch Walters).

ELECTRIC

The **Batman** model has an SG-ish body shape with the Caped Crusader's face on the headstock, Batman chest logo in yellow, and an overall black finish. The 3-piece laminated mahogany neck runs through the body, and has mystery *Bat-wood* wings (the overall weight is pretty light - hmmm...) and a maple fingerboard with no inlay. All hardware is black, of course, and the guitar has a single humbucker pickup and one volume knob, 3-per-side tuners, and a bridge/stop tail-piece combination. The Batman guitar came in its own Bat Gigbag, with a Bat strap and certificate of authenticity. There were only 50 Batman guitars produced in this limited edition.

A year later, the team of Rich and Bolin struck again with the limited edition **Joker** guitar (and Joker gigbag). The Joker featured more of a explorer *winged* shape, with similar mahogany neck-through design and *mysterywood* wings. The guitar's body features a pinstriped purple finish, with a green neck and Joker face graphic on the headstock. C & R Guitars announced that there would be 100 instruments made in the limited edition - but only 42 were actually built. The first forty-one were numbered similar to their matching Batman counterpart, but the forty-second guitar was numbered #100.

No matter how you slice it, there are only 41 sets of Batman and Joker guitars. There is "#100" Joker, and 9 additional Batman models swinging loose in Gotham City right now. The last recorded asking price for the set of two was $5,000. Given the nature of the guitars themselves, it's a safe bet that it will be a seller's market when they are available for sale.

CMI

CLEARTONE MUSICAL INSTRUMENTS – see NED CALLAN.

Instruments previously produced in England, later imports were built in Japan during the 1970s and 1980s.

The CMI trademark was used by UK importer/distributor Cleartone Musical Instruments. Early instruments were built by NED CALLAN in England, but were later joined by Japanese-built copies.

(Source: Tony Bacon and Paul Day, The Guru's Guitar Guide)

CSL

Instruments previously built in Japan during the 1970s through the late 1980s.

The CSL trademark was used by UK importer C. Summerfield Ltd. The 1970s copies of American designs were built at the same source as IBANEZ (and Ibanez copies were good enough for a lawsuit from NORLIN!); later solid body designs in the 1980s look vaguely Fender-ish. C S L owners who want to testify about the quality of their instruments are invited to write to the *Blue Book of Electric Guitars*. Any photos used in future editions will probably be backlit and silhouetted, and placed in witness protection programs!

(Source: Tony Bacon and Paul Day, The Guru's Guitar Guide)

CAIRNES

Also see COLT.

Instruments previously built in Britain during the 1980s.

Company featured high quality and original designs on models named Solo, Stud, Starguard, and Colt Peacemaker. These solid body guitars also came equipped with luthier Jim Cairnes' own pickups and hardware.

(Source: Tony Bacon and Paul Day, The Guru's Guitar Guide)

CALLAHAM VINTAGE GUITARS

Instruments currently built in Winchester, Virginia.

Callaham Vintage Guitars creates vintage reproduction solid body electric guitars and amplifiers. Callaham feels that only a small number of guitars from the 1950s and 1960s are in proper playing condition - the majority are worn excessively, have replaced parts (or swapped parts), or rendered un-playable by incompetent repairmen through the years. With a large number of historical books on the market, it can be demonstrated that the large manufacturers' vintage reproductions are rough approximations. Rather than pay extreme prices on the vintage market, Callaham figures to offer reproductions of the vintage guitars that players are searching for, and to offer them at prices that players are prepared to pay.

Callaham manufactures all of their own bodies and necks, and is concentrating on their own line of guitars which have many custom features (they are not interested in making one-of-a-kind or replica guitars). While they do offer some of the parts (hardware and electronics) used on their guitars, they do not sell the necks and bodies separately.

Callaham also offers 3 different amplifiers. All three amps feature hand-wired point-to-point designs, Sprague electrolytic and orange drop caps, CTS and Clarostat pots, and solid core teflon insulated wire. Retail prices range from $1,175 to $1,300; contact the company for proper specifications and cabinet wood options.

ELECTRIC

Callaham Vintage Guitars' reproductions are based on Fender-style solid body electrics. Callaham's **S Model** features either a one-piece alder (solid color finishes) or one-piece Swamp ash (for Sunburst and Blonde finishes) offset double cutaway bodies, with bolt-on curly maple necks and rosewood fingerboards. Lindy Fralin single coil Vintage Pickups are used on all **S Models**, combined with a 5-way selector switch and volume/2 tone controls. **S Models** feature nickel vintage reproduction parts, and are available in 2-Tone or 3-Tone Sunbursts, Blonde, Black, Burgundy Purple Mist, Firemist Gold Metallic, Lake Placid Blue, Ocean Turquoise, and Shoreline Gold nitrocellulose lacquer finishes. Retail list price is $1,650.

The **S Model** has optional gold parts (add $80), Base Plate/Blender Pot combo (add $20), and matching painted headstock in solid colors (add $40). The Base Plate is located on the lead pickup, and helps boost the lows and mid range frequencies; the Blend Pot blends the neck and bridge pickups together.

The **T Model** (retail list $1,550) is a single cutaway body with similar construction to the **S Model**. However, 2 Seymour Duncan Alnico II single coil pickups are standard. There are three different bridge configurations: an original 3-saddle vintage-style bridge, a 6-saddle bridge, or an angled 3-saddle bridge. The angled 3-saddle bridge is an additional $25.

CAMP, MICHAEL

Instruments previously built in Plymouth, Michigan.

Luthier Michael Camp handcrafted high quality electric guitars. These instruments feature single piece mahogany necks, offset double cutaway mahogany bodies with flame maple tops, Wilkinson fixed bridges or tremolo systems, Schaller tuners, 3-per-side headstocks, Seymour Duncan humbucker pickups, and nitrocellulose lacquer finishes. The **Master Series** models feature ebony fingerboards, gold hardware, and matching headstock finishes; while the **Players Series** models have rosewood fingerboards, chrome hardware, and black headstocks. The **Bolt-On Series** features the 'zing' delivered by bolt-on necks, maple or rosewood fingerboards, 2 or 3 single coil pickups, and natural wood headstocks.

CARLO ROBELLI

Please refer to the R section of this text.

CARLSON GUITAR COMPANY

Instruments currently built in St. Joseph, Missouri.

In addition to handcrafting his own custom-built instruments, Jim Carlson is the owner and operator of a lutherie shop where he currently performs repair and refinishing work for some of the St. Joseph and Kansas City area music stores.

As Jim explains, "My earliest recollection of my love for stringed instruments (especially the guitar) was around the age of five or six." All of Carlson's family members play stringed instruments of some kind, "Even my Grandmother, who can play just about anything on anything - a very gifted woman. My father used to play his guitar around the house in his spare time, and I found myself glued to the floor right in front of his chair in total amazement of the sounds being produced by the movement of his fingers on the fretboard. So as far back as I can recall music and the instruments that create it have been my life."

"I began playing at the age of eight, and have thoroughly enjoyed it for the last twenty-seven years. But the intrigue didn't stop with just the sounds that musical instruments produce - I also found myself very fascinated with the instruments themselves: the beauty of the finish, the way they felt, and the various woods that were being used to make them. By the age of fifteen, I was tinkering with my guitars and adjusting the action to try and get it as low as possible - after all, at age fifteen I was bound to be the world's next David Gilmour or Eric Clapton! Well, at least that's how most of us young musicians felt when we were fifteen."

"My parents didn't take things nearly as serious as I had, so needless to say they wouldn't pay for my expensive refins or buy me the beautiful Les Paul Custom that I had my eye on. I began a self-taught quest to build guitars (my own guitars) with the help of a few good pointers from books to auto body shops - believe it or not, there is some good information that you can pick up from paint and body mechanics concerning finish work. My first guitar was a success, in fact I have used it on a CD that I was invited to do some guitar playing. Some twenty years have come and gone since I first started seriously tinkering with my old Univox and Stratocaster, and I have continued to build custom guitars. Oh, and by the way, I did finally get that 1978 Les Paul Custom that I had my eye on!"

(Biography courtesy Jim and Pam Carlson)

ELECTRIC

Carlson offers 4 distinct models, and the hardware and finish can be altered upon request at the time of commission. The **Elite** has a single cutaway body, maple neck-through design, flamed maple carved arched top, 22-fret ebony fingerboard with dot inlay, 3-per-side tuners, tune-o-matic/stop tailpiece bridge, 2 Gibson *'57 Classic* humbuckers, volume and tone controls, 3-way toggle, and top-mounted cord jack. The **Retro** model has similar construction features, but has a sloped shoulder/cutaway body, bookmatched zebrawood top, PRS-style tremolo, 3-per-side Sperzel locking tuners, and 2 DiMarzio *Super Distortion* humbuckers. The **Signature** model has a through-body mahogany neck/mahogany top, bound single cutaway body, bound ebony fingerboard, gold-plated hardware, Schaller bridge, 3-per-side Grover tuners, and 2 Gibson *'57 Classic* humbuckers.

For all the single coil pickup fans, Carlson offers an almost-dual cutaway model called the **Honeymoon**. The **Honeymoon** features a laminated maple/mahogany neck-through design, maple core/mahogany top body, 22-fret ebony fingerboard, PRS-style tremolo, 3-per-side Grover tuners, 3 active EMG SA single coil pickups (with SPC control), volume and 2 tone controls, and a 5-way selector switch.

In addition to his custom instruments, Carlson continues to offer repair work for the professional and semi-professional players in his area. For questions regarding specifications and pricing, contact Jim Carlson at Carlson Lutherie directly (see Trademark Index).

CARMINE STREET GUITARS

Instruments currently built in New York City, New York.

In addition to their guitar sales and repair work, Carmine Street Guitars offers good quality custom-built instruments.

ELECTRIC

The **Kellycaster** model is offered in a solid body or sound chambered version, with carved tops and one-piece necks. The suggested retail price is $1,500 and features different pickup and bridge options.

Kelly Kustoms begin at a retail price of $1,000 for custom-shaped one-of-a-kind designs that are customer specified, or one of the over 20 ideas from the shop. For further information regarding pricing and specifications, contact Carmine Street Guitars directly (see Trademark Index).

CARRIVEAU

Instruments currently built in Phoenix, Arizona.

Carriveau custom-built instruments have been described as high quality, well built guitars. Research concerning the Carriveau trademark is still on-going; further updates will appear in future editions of the *Blue Book of Electric Guitars.*

CARRUTHERS, JOHN

Instruments currently built in Venice, California.

Luthier/designer John Carruthers is currently offering a number of custom-built guitars and an SUB-1 Upright Bass. Carruthers has been a consultant and subcontractor for the Fender, Ibanez, and Yamaha guitar companies. In addition, he also wrote numerous articles and reviews for *Guitar Player* magazine for a ten year period.

ELECTRIC

Carruthers is currently offering a wide range of custom-built solidbody and acoustic electric semi-hollow steel string guitars. All models are built with high quality hardware and pickups, and range in price from $1,895 up to $2,995. Model descriptions and specifications are available from Carruthers Guitars.

ELECTRIC BASS

Carruthers bass models all feature an alder body and EMG pickups. The **CB 4C** (list $1,795) has a bolt-on maple neck, striped ebony fingerboard, and active electronics; the **CB 4B** (list $2,095) has similar construction but features a figured maple top. The **CB 4A** (list $2,595) has a set-in maple neck, figured maple top, and striped ebony fingerboard.

Carruthers 5-string models all have a 34 1/2" scale. The **CB 5C** (list $1,995) has a bolt-on maple neck, striped ebony fingerboard, and active electronics; the **CB 5B** (list $2,295) has similar construction but features a figured maple top. The **CB 4A** (list $2,795) has a set-in maple neck, figured maple top, and striped ebony fingerboard.

The Carruthers electric Stand-Up Bass (SUB-1) has a retail price of $2,795. This model is a high quality, portable electric upright 4-string bass guitar. It is constructed with an alder body, detachable maple neck, ebony fingerboard, and features piezo electric pickups. For further information, please contact Carruthers Guitars directly (see Trademark Index).

CARVIN

Instruments currently produced in Escondido, California since 1969. Previous production was located in Covina, California from 1949 to 1969. Carvin instruments are sold through direct catalog sales, as well as through their 5 factory stores in California: San Diego, Santa Ana, Sherman Oaks, Covina and Hollywood.

In 1946, Lowell Kiesel founded Kiesel Electronics in Los Angeles, California. Three years later, the Kiesel family settled in Covina, California, and began the original catalog business of manufacturing and distributing lap steel guitars, small tube amps and pickups. The Carvin trademark was derived from Kiesel's two oldest sons, Carson and Gavin. Guitars were originally offered in kit form, or by parts since 1949; Carvin began building complete guitars in 1956. By 1978, the glued set-neck design replaced the bolt-on necks. The majority of the current guitar and bass models currently feature a neck-through design.

Carvin has always been a mail-order only company, and offers the players a wide range of options on the individual models. Even though they can't be tried out before they're bought, Carvin offers a 10-day money back guarantee. Because Carvin sells factory direct, they are not stocked in music stores. It is suggested to request a current copy of their catalog (free of charge) to find out more about the company's current models and pricing.

Carvin offers a full range of guitar and bass replacement parts in their full line catalog. The Carvin company also offers mixing boards, power amplifiers, powered mixers, P.A. speakers, monitor speakers, guitar combo amps/heads/cabinets, and bass amps/cabinets as well.

ELECTRIC

All Carvin guitar models feature a 25" scale, except for the Bolt and Holdsworth models. There is no additional charge for models in a left-handed configuration. Carvin offers numerous additional custom options than those briefly listed below (they represent the more common custom options encountered). Contact Carvin for specifications and pricing on the other custom options.

In 1992, Carvin made a production change from double locking Carvin/Floyd Rose vibratos to locking Carvin/Floyd Rose vibratos with locking Sperzel tuners. In 1993, Carvin changed to a standard Carvin/Wilkinson vibrato and locking Sperzel tuners combination. In 1994, all tremolo versions were offered.

Carlson Elite
courtesy Carlson Luthier

GRADING	100% MINT	98% NEAR MINT	95% EXC+	90% EXC	80% VG+	70% VG	60% G

All neck-through-body guitar models (unless otherwise listed) are available in the following standard colors: Classic White, Ferrari Red, Jet Black, Pearl Blue, Pearl Red, and Pearl White. The Natural Tung Oil finish was discontinued in 1998.

Add $20 for black chrome plated hardware.

Add $40 for gold plated hardware.

Add $40 for translucent finish (Blueburst, Cherry Sunburst, Classic Sunburst, Clear finish, Crimson Red, Deep Purple, Emerald Green, Greenburst, Sapphire Blue, Tobacco Sunburst, or Vintage Yellow).

Add $200 for a translucent color over a 1/2" thick AAA flamed maple top.

Add $300 for a translucent color over a 1/2" thick AAA quilted maple top.

AE Series

AE150 - offset double cutaway poplar body, through-body maple neck, 24-fret ebony fingerboard with pearl dot inlay, fixed bridge, blackface peghead with screened logo, 6-on-a-side locking Sperzel tuners, 2 humbucker/1 acoustic bridge Carvin pickups, 1 volume/2 tone/1 mix controls, 3-position switch. Mfg. 1994 to 1996.

		$800	$600	$550	$500	$450	$400	$350

Last MSR was $1,600.

AE160 - single cutaway poplar body, through-body maple neck, 24-fret ebony fingerboard with pearl dot inlay, fixed bridge, blackface peghead with screened logo, 6-on-a-side locking Sperzel tuners, 2 humbucker/1 acoustic bridge Carvin pickups, 1 volume/2 tone/1 mix controls, 3-position switch. Mfg. 1994 to 1996.

		$800	$600	$550	$500	$450	$400	$350

Last MSR was $1,600.

AE185 - single cutaway mahogany body, internal acoustic chambers, AAA Englemann spruce top, through-body mahogany neck, 24-fret ebony fingerboard with pearl dot inlay, fixed bridge, blackface peghead with screened logo, 3-per-side tuners, 2 Carvin humbuckers (C22N and C22T), Carvin F60 acoustic bridge pickup, master volume control, tone (electric)/tone (acoustic)/blend controls, 3-position selector (electric) switch, dual output jacks. Mfg. 1996 to date.

MSR	$1,799	$799	$725	$675	$625	$550	$500	$450

AE185-12 - similar to the AE185, except in 12-string configuration, 6-per-side headstock. Mfg. 1997 to date.

MSR	$1,899	$849	$775	$725	$650	$595	$525	$475

Allan Holdsworth Signature Series

These models were developed in conjunction with guitarist Allan Holdsworth.

H1 - single rounded cutaway alder body, internal acoustic chambers, alder top, set-in alder neck, 25 1/2" scale, 24-fret ebony fingerboard with pearl dot inlays, graphite nut, 2/4 headstock design, locking Sperzel tuners, chrome hardware, tune-o-matic bridge and tailpiece, one Carvin H22 humbucker, volume/tone controls. Mfg. 1996 to date.

MSR	$1,699	$749	$675	$625	$575	$525	$475	$425

H1T - similar to the H1, except features a Carvin/Wilkinson tremolo. Mfg. 1996 to date.

MSR	$1,849	$799	$725	$675	$625	$575	$525	$475

H2 - similar to the H1, except features 2 Carvin H22 humbuckers. Mfg. 1996 to date.

MSR	$1,799	$799	$725	$675	$625	$550	$500	$450

H2T - similar to the H2, except features a Carvin/Wilkinson tremolo. Mfg. 1996 to date.

MSR	$1,949	$849	$775	$725	$675	$595	$550	$495

Bolt Series

Carvin's Bolt Series models feature a bolt-on maple neck.

THE BOLT - offset double cutaway alder body, bolt-on graphite reinforced maple neck, 25 1/2" scale, 22-fret ebony fingerboard with pearl dot inlay, maple headstock veneer, fixed bridge, graphite nut, 6-on-a-side Carvin tuners, chrome hardware, white multi-layer pickguard, 3 Carvin AP11 single coil pickups, volume/tone control, 5-way selector switch, available in Black, Natural (Tung Oil), Pearl Blue, Pearl Red, Pearl White, Red, White and Clear Gloss standard finishes. Mfg. 1997 to date.

MSR	$1,099	$489	$450	$425	$375	$350	$300	$275

Add $20 for Carvin C22T humbucker with coil tap in bridge position.

Add $20 for white pearloid or red tortoise style pickguard.

Add $30 for Sperzel locking tuners.

In late 1997, left-handed configuration was optional.

Bolt-T - similar to the Bolt, except features a Wilkinson tremolo system. Mfg. 1997 to date.

MSR	$1,199	$549	$495	$450	$425	$375	$325	$295

DC Series

DC120 - offset double cutaway poplar body, through-body maple neck, 24-fret ebony fingerboard with pearl block inlay, fixed bridge, graphite nut, 6-per-side locking Sperzel tuners, chrome hardware, 2 Carvin C22 humbucking pickups, volume/treble/bass and mix controls, bright boost, phase/coil split switches, active electronics. Current Mfg.

MSR	$1,679	$779	$700	$650	$595	$525	$475	$425

GRADING		100% MINT	98% NEAR MINT	95% EXC+	90% EXC	80% VG+	70% VG	60% G

DC125 - offset double cutaway poplar body, through-body maple neck, 24-fret ebony fingerboard with pearl dot inlay, fixed bridge, graphite nut, 6-on-a-side locking Sperzel tuners, chrome hardware, 1 Carvin humbucker pickup, volume control, one coil split switch. Mfg. 1991 to 1996.

		$525	$425	$375	$325	$275	$200	$150

Last MSR was $1,050.

DC125T - similar to DC125, except has standard Carvin vibrato. Mfg. 1991 to 1996.

		$600	$450	$395	$350	$275	$225	$175

Last MSR was $1,200.

DC127 - offset double cutaway alder body, through-body maple neck, 24-fret ebony fingerboard with pearl dot inlay, fixed bridge, graphite nut, 6-on-a-side locking Sperzel tuners, chrome hardware, 2 Carvin C22 humbucker pickups, volume/tone control, 3-position/2-coil split switches. Mfg. 1991 to date.

MSR	$1,149	$549	$495	$450	$400	$375	$325	$295

DC127C - similar to DC127, except has double locking Floyd Rose vibrato. Mfg. 1993 to date.

MSR	$1,369	$649	$575	$525	$475	$450	$395	$350

DC127T - similar to DC127, except has standard Carvin/Wilkinson vibrato. Current Mfg.

MSR	$1,299	$609	$550	$500	$450	$425	$375	$325

DC135 - offset double cutaway poplar body, through-body maple neck, 24-fret ebony fingerboard with pearl dot inlay, fixed bridge, graphite nut, 6-on-a-side locking Sperzel tuners, chrome hardware, 2 Carvin S60 single coil/1 Carvin C22 humbucker pickups, volume/tone control, 3 pickup mini switches. Mfg. 1991 to date.

MSR	$1,199	$569	$500	$450	$425	$375	$350	$300

DC135C - similar to DC135, except has double locking Floyd Rose vibrato. Current Mfg.

MSR	$1,429	$669	$600	$550	$525	$475	$425	$375

DC135T - similar to DC135, except has standard Carvin/Wilkinson vibrato. Current Mfg.

MSR	$1,349	$629	$575	$525	$475	$450	$395	$350

DC145 - offset double cutaway poplar body, through-body maple neck, 24-fret ebony fingerboard with pearl dot inlay, fixed bridge, graphite nut, reverse peghead, 6-on-a-side locking Sperzel tuners, chrome hardware, humbucker/single coil/humbucker Carvin pickups, volume/tone controls, 5-position/coil split switches. Mfg. 1991 to 1993.

		$600	$500	$450	$375	$325	$250	$195

Last MSR was $1,200.

DC145T - similar to DC145, except has standard Carvin/Wilkinson vibrato.

		$675	$600	$525	$450	$375	$295	$225

Last MSR was $1,370.

DC150 - double cutaway maple body, through-body maple neck, 24-fret maple fingerboard with black dot inlay, tune-o-matic bridge/stop tailpiece, 3-per-side tuners, black pickguard, chrome hardware, 2 Carvin M22 humbuckers, volume/tone controls, 3-position switch, 2-coil tap/1 phase mini switches, available in Classic White, Clear Maple, Ferrari Red, Jet Black, Pearl Blue, Pearl Red and Pearl White finishes. Mfg. 1977 to 1991.

		$500	$450	$400	$350	$300	$250	$200

Last MSR was $1,000.

This model was available with an ebony fingerboard with pearl dot inlays.

DC150C - similar to DC150, except has double locking Floyd Rose vibrato.

		$600	$550	$495	$425	$375	$300	$250

Last MSR was $1,200.

DC200 - offset double cutaway poplar body, through-body maple neck, 24-fret ebony fingerboard with pearl block inlay, fixed bridge, graphite nut, 3-per-side locking Sperzel tuners, chrome hardware, 2 Carvin humbucker pickups, volume/treble/bass and mix controls, bright boost, phase and coil split switches, active electronics. Current Mfg.

MSR	$1,449	$679	$600	$550	$525	$475	$425	$375

DC200C - similar to DC200, except has double locking Floyd Rose vibrato. Mfg. 1994 to date.

MSR	$1,679	$779	$700	$650	$595	$525	$475	$425

DC200T - similar to DC200, except has standard Carvin/Wilkinson vibrato. Current Mfg.

MSR	$1,599	$739	$675	$625	$575	$500	$450	$400

DC200 Koa - similar to DC200, except has Koa body/neck, brass nut/bridge/tailpiece, Schaller M6 mini tuners, available in Black or Natural finishes. Mfg. 1981 to 1986.

		$550	$495	$425	$375	$325	$275	$225

Last MSR was $560.

DC400 - offset double cutaway koa body, AAA bookmatched flamed maple top, koa through-body neck, 24-fret ebony fingerboard with abalone block inlay, fixed bridge, body matching headstock, graphite nut, 6-on-a-side locking Sperzel tuners, chrome hardware, 2 Carvin humbucker pickups, volume/treble/bass and mix controls, bright boost, phase and coil tap switches, available in Blueburst, Cherry Sunburst, Classic Sunburst, Clear finish, Crimson Red, Deep Purple, Emerald Green, Greenburst, Sapphire Blue, Tobacco Sunburst, and Vintage Yellow translucent finishes. Current Mfg.

MSR	$2,049	$899	$800	$750	$695	$625	$575	$525

In 1993, poplar body, through-body maple neck replaced original part/designs.
In 1996, alder body replaced poplar body.

Carvin AE 185
courtesy Carvin

C

GRADING		100% MINT	98% NEAR MINT	95% EXC+	90% EXC	80% VG+	70% VG	60% G

DC400C - similar to DC400, except has double locking Floyd Rose vibrato. Mfg. 1994 to date.

MSR	$2,279	$999	$895	$825	$775	$700	$625	$575

DC400T - similar to DC400, except has standard Carvin/Wilkinson vibrato. Current Mfg.

MSR	$2,199	$959	$875	$800	$750	$675	$625	$550

DC400 ANNIVERSARY - offset double cutaway koa body with rounded sides, highly figured flamed maple top, 5-piece koa/maple through-body neck, 24-fret ebony fingerboard with abalone block inlay, fixed bridge, flamed maple matching headstock, graphite nut, 6-on-a-side locking Sperzel tuners, chrome hardware, 2 Carvin humbucker pickups, volume/treble/bass and mix controls, bright boost, phase and coil split switches, available in Blueburst, Cherry Sunburst, Classic Sunburst, Clear finish, Crimson Red, Deep Purple, Emerald Green, Greenburst, Sapphire Blue, Tobacco Sunburst, and Vintage Yellow translucent finishes. Mfg. 1996 to date.

MSR	$2,249	$1,099	$995	$925	SN/A	SN/A	SN/A	SN/A

The Anniversary model celebrates Carvin's 50th year (1946-1996).

DN612 - offset sharp double cutaway poplar body, 2 maple through-body necks in a 12/6 configuration, 24-fret ebony fingerboards with pearl dot inlays, fixed bridges, graphite nut, 6-per-side on 12-string neck, 3-per-side on 6-string neck, locking Sperzel tuners, chrome hardware, 2 Carvin humbucker pickups, volume/tone control, two 3-way pickup selector/1 neck selector switches, 2 separate output jacks. Disc. 1996.

$1,600	$1,475	$1,325	$1,200	$1,000	$925	$800

Last MSR was $3,200.

This model was also available with 4-string bass neck instead of 12-string neck as the DN640, or with two bass necks (fretted and unfretted) as the DN440.

DN612 Koa - similar to the DN612, except has natural Koa body. Mfg. 1981 to 1986.

$1,800	$1,650	$1,500	$1,350	$1,195	$1,000	$850

DT650 - offset single cutaway hard rock maple body, 2 maple through-body necks in a 12/6 configuration, 22-fret ebony fingerboards with pearl block inlays, bridge/stop tailpieces, 6-per-side on 12-string neck, 3-per-side on 6-string neck, Schaller M6 tuners, chrome hardware, black pickguards, 2 Carvin APH-6S humbucker pickups, volume/tone control (per neck), 3-way pickup selector (per neck), 2-coil tap/1 phase mini switches (per neck), neck selector switch, 2 separate output jacks. Mfg. circa late 1970s.

$700	$600	$525	$450	$375	$325	$275

Last MSR was $599.

This model was also available with 4-string bass neck instead of 12-string neck as the DB630.

LS Series

LS175 - offset double cutaway poplar body, through-body maple neck, 22-fret ebony fingerboard with pearl dot inlay, tune-o-matic bridge/stop tailpiece, 6-on-a-side tuners, chrome hardware, 3 stacked humbucker Carvin pickups, volume/tone controls, 5-position switch, available in Classic White, Ferrari Red, Jet Blue, Natural, Pearl Blue, Pearl Red and Pearl White finishes. Disc. 1991.

$575	$525	$475	$425	$395	$325	$250

Last MSR was $1,140.

LS175C - similar to LS175, except has double locking Floyd Rose vibrato. Disc. 1991.

$675	$625	$550	$500	$450	$350	$295

Last MSR was $1,340.

SC Series

SC90 - single rounded cutaway alder body, through-body maple neck, 24-fret ebony fingerboard with pearl dot inlay, fixed bridge, graphite nut, 3-per-side locking Sperzel tuners, chrome hardware, 2 Carvin humbucker pickups, 2 volume/2 tone controls, 3-position switch. Disc. 1996.

$595	$550	$500	$450	$400	$350	$295

Last MSR was $1,199.

SC90C - similar to SC90, except has double locking Floyd Rose vibrato. Current Mfg.

MSR	$1,429	$669	$600	$550	$500	$450	$400	$350

SC90T - similar to SC90, except has standard Carvin/Wilkinson vibrato. Current Mfg.

MSR	$1,349	$629	$575	$525	$475	$450	$395	$350

SC90S - similar to the SC90, except features a tune-o-matic bridge/stop tailpiece. Current Mfg.

MSR	$1,199	$579	$525	$475	$425	$395	$350	$300

TL Series

TL60 - single cutaway poplar body, through-body maple neck, 24-fret ebony fingerboard with pearl dot inlay, fixed bridge, graphite nut, 6-per-side locking Sperzel tuners, chrome hardware, 2 Carvin S60 single coil pickups, volume/tone control, series/parallel mini switch, 3-position switch. Mfg. 1993 to date.

MSR	$1,149	$549	$495	$450	$425	$375	$325	$295

In 1996, alder body replaced poplar body.

TL60T - similar to TL60, except has standard Carvin/Wilkinson vibrato. Current Mfg.

MSR	$1,299	$609	$550	$500	$475	$425	$375	$325

Ultra V Series

ULTRA V - V-shape poplar body, maple through-body neck, 24-fret ebony fingerboard with pearl dot inlay, fixed bridge, graphite nut, 6-on-a-side locking Sperzel tuners, chrome hardware, 2 humbucker pickups, volume/tone control, 3-way switch. Mfg. 1991 to 1994.

$525	$495	$450	$400	$350	$300	$275

Last MSR was $1,060.

GRADING	100% MINT	98% NEAR MINT	95% EXC+	90% EXC	80% VG+	70% VG	60% G

Ultra VT - similar to Ultra V, except has standard Carvin/Wilkinson vibrato.

		$625	$575	$525	$475	$425	$375	$325

Last MSR was $1,220.

X Series

X220 - offset double cutaway V-shaped poplar body, maple through-body neck, 24-fret ebony fingerboard with pearl dot inlay, fixed bridge, graphite nut, 6-on-a-side locking Sperzel tuners, chrome hardware, 2 humbucker pickups, volume/tone control, 3-way/2-coil split switches. Mfg. 1991 to 1992.

		$575	$525	$475	$425	$375	$325	$275

Last MSR was $1,140.

X220C - similar to X220, except has standard Carvin/Wilkinson vibrato.

		$675	$625	$550	$500	$450	$395	$350

Last MSR was $1,340.

ELECTRIC BASS

In 1996, Carvin's combination bass bridge/tailpiece unit by Hipshot became standard on all Carvin bass models. This new design can be strung through the back of the bridge or through the body using string ferrules.

Carvin briefly offered (1996-1997) the 2-Tek bridge (add $150) as a custom option; the 2-Tek was not available on left-handed configurations.

The standard features on all neck-through-body bass models are: 34" scale, graphite-reinforced maple neck, 24-fret ebony fingerboard, graphite nut, and chrome hardware. Carvin bass models are available in these standard colors: Classic White, Ferrari Red, Jet Black, Pearl Blue, Pearl Red, and Pearl White. The Natural Tung Oil finish was discontinued in 1998.

Add $20 for fretless fingerboard with white inlaid lines.

Add $30 for fretless fingerboard with white inlaid lines and dot position markers.

Add $60 for factory installed Hipshot bass detuner.

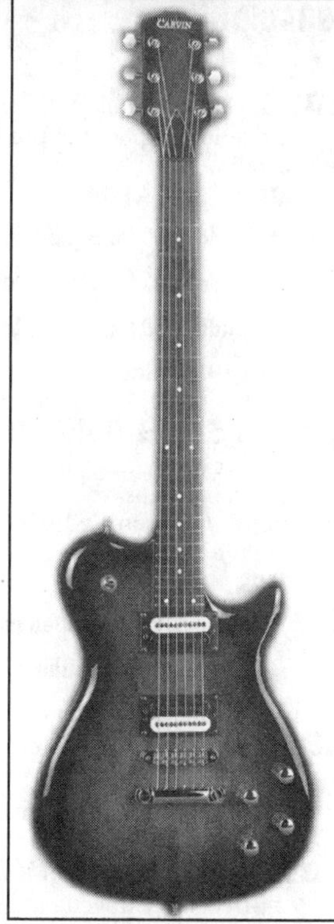

Carvin SC 90
courtesy Carvin

B (Bolt-On Neck) Series

B 4 - offset double cutaway alder body, bolt-on graphite-reinforced maple neck, 22-fret ebony fingerboard with offset pearl dot inlay, Hipshot fixed bridge, graphite nut, 4-on-a-side tuners, chrome hardware, 2 J-style H50N humbucking pickups, 2 volume/1 tone controls, available in Black, Pearl Blue, Pearl White, Red, White, and a Natural Tung Oil finish. Mfg. 1997 to date.

MSR	$999	$469	$425	$375	$300	$250	$175	$125

Add $70 for Passive/Active electronics package (master volume, pickup blend, active bass/mid /treble controls).

This model has an optional fretless fingerboard (B 4F).

B 5 - similar to the B 4, except features 5-string configuration, 3/2-per-side tuners. Mfg. 1997 to date.

MSR	$1,239	$599	$525	$450	$375	$300	$225	$150

Add $70 for Passive/Active electronics package (master volume, pickup blend, active bass/mid/treble controls).

This model has an optional fretless fingerboard (B 5F).

BB Series

BB Series basses were designed in conjunction with bassist Bunny Brunel. BB Series basses differ from the LB75 model with a slightly wider body, longer tapered bass horn, asymmetrical neck design, 1/4" wider at the 24th fret, and position dots are centered between the first four strings.

BB70 - offset double cutaway poplar body, through-body maple neck, 24-fret ebony fingerboard with offset pearl dot inlay, fixed bridge, graphite nut, 2-per-side tuners, chrome hardware, 2 J-style pickups, volume/treble/bass/mix controls, active electronics. Mfg. 1994 to date.

MSR	$1,649	$749	$675	$625	$575	$525	$475	$425

This model has an optional fretless fingerboard (BB70F).

BB75 (BUNNY BRUNEL LIMITED) - offset double cutaway poplar body, through-body maple neck, 24-fret ebony fingerboard with offset pearl dot inlay, fixed bridge, graphite nut, 3/2-per-side tuners, chrome hardware, 2 J-style pickups, volume/treble/bass and mix controls, active electronics. Current Mfg.

MSR	$1,799	$819	$725	$675	$625	$550	$500	$450

This model has an optional fretless fingerboard (BB75F).

LB Series

LB20 - offset double cutaway poplar body, through-body maple neck, 24-fret ebony fingerboard with pearl dot inlay, fixed bridge, graphite nut, 4-on-a-side locking Sperzel tuners, chrome hardware, 2 J-style H50N passive pickups, 2 volume/1 tone controls. Mfg. 1991 to date.

MSR	$1,199	$579	$525	$475	$425	$395	$350	$300

In 1996, alder body replaced poplar body.
This model has an optional fretless fingerboard (LB20F).

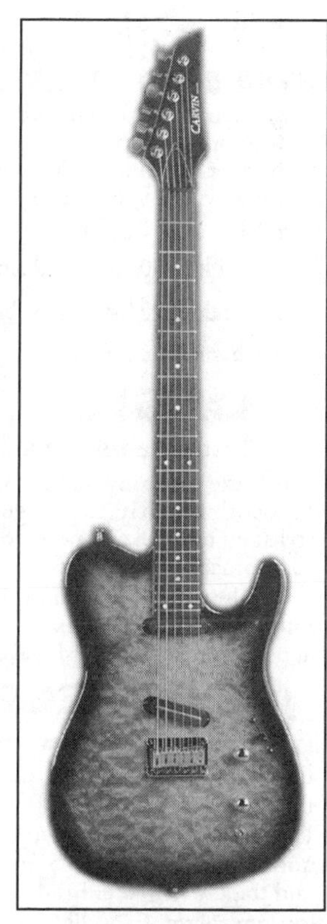

Carvin TL 60
courtesy Carvin

GRADING		100% MINT	98% NEAR MINT	95% EXC+	90% EXC	80% VG+	70% VG	60% G

LB70 - offset double cutaway poplar body, through-body maple neck, 24-fret ebony fingerboard with pearl dot inlay, fixed bridge, graphite nut, 4-on-a-side locking Sperzel tuners, chrome hardware, 2 J-style pickups, volume/blend/bass/mid/treble controls, passive/active electronics. Mfg. 1991 to date.

MSR	$1,299	$649	$575	$525	$475	$425	$375	$325

Add $100 for 5-piece laminated maple/koa stripes (5M) neck.

Add $100 for 5-piece laminated mahogany/maple stripes (5H) neck.

Add $150 for 5-piece laminated koa/maple stripes (5K) neck.

In 1996, alder body replaced poplar body.
This model has an optional fretless fingerboard (LB70F).

LB70A 50TH ANNIVERSARY - offset double cutaway laminated alder/koa body, flamed maple top, 5-piece koa/maple through-body neck, 24-fret ebony fingerboard with pearl dot inlay, Wilkinson fixed bridge, graphite nut, 4-on-a-side locking Sperzel tuners, chrome hardware, 2 Carvin J- style pickups, volume/bass/midrange/treble and blend controls, active electronics, available in Blueburst, Cherry Sunburst, Classic Sunburst, Clear finish, Crimson Red, Deep Purple, Emerald Green, Greenburst, Sapphire Blue, Tobacco Sunburst, and Vintage Yellow translucent finishes. Mfg. 1996 to date.

MSR	$3,250	$1,129	$1,000	$950	$N/A	$N/A	$N/A	$N/A

Add $100 for quilted maple top and matching headstock veneer.

Add $120 for abalone block inlays.

This model has an optional fretless fingerboard (LB70AF).

LB75 - similar to LB70, except has 5-string configuration, and 5-on-a-side tuners. Current Mfg.

MSR	$1,499	$719	$650	$595	$550	$475	$425	$375

This model has an optional fretless fingerboard (LB75F).
In 1992, 3/2-per-side tuners replaced original part/design.

LB75A 50TH ANNIVERSARY - offset double cutaway laminated alder/koa body, flamed maple top, 5-piece koa/maple through-body neck, 24-fret ebony fingerboard with pearl dot inlay, Wilkinson fixed bridge, graphite nut, 3/2-per-side locking Sperzel tuners, chrome hardware, 2 Carvin J-style pickups, volume/bass/midrange/treble and blend controls, active electronics, available in Blueburst, Cherry Sunburst, Classic Sunburst, Clear finish, Crimson Red, Deep Purple, Emerald Green, Greenburst, Sapphire Blue, Tobacco Sunburst, and Vintage Yellow translucent finishes. Mfg. 1996 to date.

MSR	$3,400	$1,199	$1,100	$1,050	$N/A	$N/A	$N/A	$N/A

Add $100 for quilted maple top and matching headstock veneer.

Add $120 for abalone block inlays.

This model has an optional fretless fingerboard (LB75AF).

LB76 - similar to LB70, except has 6-string configuration, 3-per-side headstock. Mfg. 1992 to date.

MSR	$1,799	$819	$750	$695	$625	$575	$500	$450

This model has an optional fretless fingerboard (LB76F).

LB76A 50TH ANNIVERSARY - offset double cutaway laminated alder/koa body, flamed maple top, 5-piece koa/maple through-body neck, 24-fret ebony fingerboard with pearl dot inlay, Wilkinson fixed bridge, graphite nut, 3-per-side per side locking Sperzel tuners, chrome hardware, 2 Carvin J-style pickups, volume/bass/midrange/treble and blend controls, active electronics, available in Blueburst, Cherry Sunburst, Classic Sunburst, Clear finish, Crimson Red, Deep Purple, Emerald Green, Greenburst, Sapphire Blue, Tobacco Sunburst, and Vintage Yellow translucent finishes. Mfg. 1996 to date.

MSR	$3,600	$1,299	$1,175	$1,100	$N/A	$N/A	$N/A	$N/A

Add $100 for quilted maple top and matching headstock veneer.

Add $120 for abalone block inlays.

This model has an optional fretless fingerboard (LB76AF).

CASIO

Instruments previously produced in Japan by Fuji Gen Gakki from 1987 to 1988.

The Casio company of Tokyo, Japan began producing keyboards in 1980. By the late 1980s, Casio unveiled the angular model MG-500 and vaguely Fenderish MG-510 electric guitars that could also be used as controllers by sending MIDI information. In 1988, Casio introduced the PG-380, a strat-styled guitar with an on-board synthesizer as well as a MIDI port. The PG-380 also has a companion module that takes up two rack spaces, and offers extra processing facilities.

Casio also produced a number of guitar shaped "Digital Guitars" in 1987. The DG10 is more self contained, while the DG20 can send processing information to an external synthesizer. Both models have plastic bodies, plastic "strings" and a number of buttons and built in features. These may appeal more to keyboard players, or entry level guitar synthesist enthusiasts.

CASTELFIDARDO

Instruments previously built in Italy, circa unknown.

Castelfidardo guitars are associated with Italian luthier Alfredo Bugari (see also **Stonehenge II**), but the distributor (if any) to the U.S. market is still unknown.

David Pavlick is the current owner of this "mystery guitar." The 3-per-side headstock features a decal which reads "Castelfidardo - Excelsior - New York", and features a 15 5/16" archtop body, two pickups, bound 22-fret neck, 2 volume/2 tone controls, 3-way pickup selector on the upper bass bout, and trapeze tailpiece. Inside both f-holes there is "1 52" stamped into the back wood. Research is still continuing on this trademark.

(Source: David J. Pavlick, Woodbury, Connecticut)

GRADING	100% MINT	98% NEAR MINT	95% EXC+	90% EXC	80% VG+	70% VG	60% G

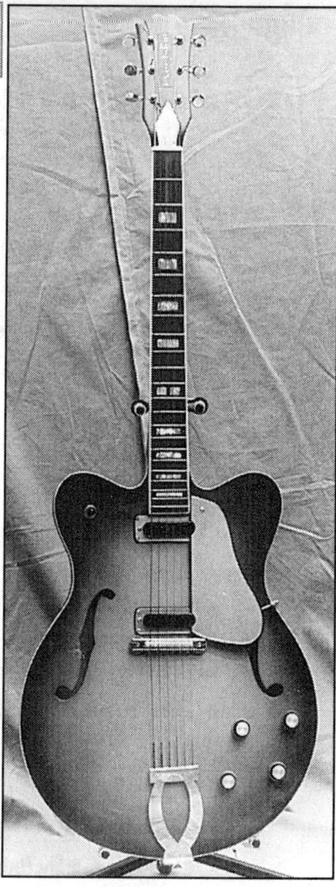
Castelfidardo Excelsior courtesy David J. Pavlick

CATALINA

See chapter on House Brands.

This trademark has been identified as a "House Brand" of the Abercrombie & Fitch company.

(Source: Willie G. Moseley, Stellas & Stratocasters)

CATALYST INSTRUMENTS USA

Instruments currently manufactured in West Islip, New York.

Catalyst Instruments currently manufactures a Panther (Strat style configuration), Tigress Bass (Jazz bass style), and the NXT (new design). For current information and prices regarding these models, please contact the company directly (see Trademark Index).

CHANDLER

Instruments previously built in Burlingame, California 1982-2000.

Chandler was located in Burlingame, California 1980-2000. The company originally focused on providing high quality replacement guitar parts, and then expanded to include guitar production beginning in 1985. Chandler's high quality models definitely feature some original design innovations!

In 1996, Chandler began offering a line of lap steels. The **RH-2** features a solid mahogany body, while the **RH-4** is a hollow body of mahogany or koa. The **RH-7** is a baritone model lap steel (30" scale length). Last retail list prices for the lap steel models was $399.

The company offered a line of guitar accessories such as the Super 60 hand wound pickups, Chandler vintage-style replacement pickups, the CC-90 soap bar pickup, replacement pickguards, as well as other related components. Chandler's electrical components featured the Stereo Digital Echo, an analog/digital rack unit that emulates a tape-driven echo effect; the Dynamo tube preamp, Tone-X active mid-boost circuit, and others.

ELECTRIC

555 Series

555 CLASSIC (Model 5552) - double sharp cutaway alder body, set-in maple neck, 25 1/2" scale, white pickguard, 22-fret rosewood fingerboard with pearl dot inlay, fixed bridge, slotted peghead, 3-per-side tuners, chrome hardware, pearl or tortoise shell pickguard, 3 mini humbucker Chandler pickups, volume/tone control, 5-position switch, available in Gloss Black (**Model 5552**), Crimson Red (**Model 5554**), Surf Green (**Model 5558**), Transparent Vintage Blonde, and Transparent Wine Red finishes. Mfg. 1992-2000.

$1,275 $1,100 $950 $825 $675 $550 $400
Last MSR was $1,598.

In 1993, Crimson Red finish was added, Transparent Wine Red finish was discontinued.

Add $100 for figured maple top (Model 5550).

555 Twin (Model 5560) - similar to the *555* Classic, except has two mini humbucker pickups, available in Vintage Blond finish. Mfg. 1993-98.

$1,295 $1,100 $975 $850 $725 $600 $475
Last MSR was $1,849.

AUSTIN SPECIAL - single offset sharp cutaway bound alder body, bolt-on maple neck, 25 1/2" scale, 22-fret rosewood fingerboard with pearl dot inlay, fixed bridge, 6-on-a-side tuners, chrome hardware, 1 single coil (neck)/ 2 dual single coils (bridge) lipstick tube pickups, volume and push/pull tone *chickenhead* control knobs, 3-position switch, available in Black finish. Mfg. 1992-96, 1998-2000.

$1,200 $1,050 $925 $775 $650 $500 $375
Last MSR was $1,499.

In 1993, White finish became available.

This model was developed by Ted Newman-Jones with input from Keith Richards (Rolling Stones).

Austin Special 5 - similar to Austin Special, except has 5-string configuration. Mfg. 1993 to 1995.

$1,350 $1,000 $850 $675 $550 $500 $425
Last MSR was $1,700.

Austin Special R - similar to Austin Special, except has traditional *tele-style* single coil in bridge position. Mfg. 1993 only.

$800 $675 $625 $575 $500 $450 $400
Last MSR was $998.

Austin Baritone - similar to Austin Special, except has 30" scale (longer neck), 2 single coil lipstick tube pickups, tremolo bridge, available in Gold Super sparkle, Red Super sparkle, and Surf Green finishes. Mfg. 1993 to 1995.

$1,500 $1,325 $1,000 $895 $725 $650 $575
Last MSR was $1,900.

GRADING	100% MINT	98% NEAR MINT	95% EXC+	90% EXC	80% VG+	70% VG	60% G

FUTURAMA (Model 1512) - offset double cutaway alder body, bolt-on maple neck, 25 1/2" scale, 22-fret rosewood fingerboard with dot inlay, custom tremolo, 6-on-a-side tuners, chrome hardware, 2-tone pickguard, 3 Chandler Super 60 pickups, volume/tone controls, 5-position switch, available in 3 Tone Sunburst, Black, Coral Pink, Fiesta Red, Olympic White, Surf Green. Mfg. 1996-2000.

$975 $850 $750 $625 $525 $400 $300

Last MSR was $1,199.

Add $40 for metallic finish (Model 1514).

Add $50 for Wilkinson tremolo.

Metro Series

METRO (Model 2010) - offset double cutaway alder body, bolt-on birds-eye maple neck, 25 1/2" scale, 22-fret rosewood or maple fingerboard with dot inlay, fixed bridge, 6-on-a-side tuners, chrome hardware, pearl or tortoise shell pickguard, P-90 style (neck)/humbucker (bridge) pickups, volume/tone control, 3-position switch, chrome controls plate, available in Fiesta Red. Mfg. 1995-2000.

$900 $795 $700 $600 $500 $395 $295

Last MSR was $1,139.

Add $50 for Wilkinson tremolo.

Metro Deluxe (Model 2100) - similar to Metro, except has sparkle finish and ivory (or shell or pearl) bound body. Mfg. 1995-98.

$1,100 $1,000 $895 $775 $595 $475 $375

Last MSR was $1,449.

Add $100 for figured maple top (Model 2140).

Metro Baritone (Model 8522) - similar to the Metro, except features a 30" scale, 24-fret rosewood fingerboard with pearl dot inlay, tremolo bridge, 2 single coil lipstick pickups, available in Black, Surf Green, and White finishes. Mfg. 1995-2000.

$1,200 $1,050 $925 $775 $650 $500 $375

Last MSR was $1,499.

Add $100 for ivory, shell, or pearl body binding (Model 8520).

Add $200 for sparkle finish and body binding (Model 8500).

SPITFIRE (Model 1210, Pathocaster) - offset double cutaway alder (or swamp ash or mahogany) body, bolt-on maple neck, 25 1/2" scale, 22-fret rosewood or maple fingerboard with dot inlay, fixed bridge, 6-on-a-side tuners, chrome hardware, pearl or tortoise shell pickguard, 3 Chandler single coil pickups, volume/2 tone controls, 5-position switch, available in Natural finish. Mfg. 1995-2000.

$725 $625 $550 $475 $375 $300 $225

Last MSR was $899.

Add $50 for Wilkinson tremolo.

Add $180 for vintage finish (Model 1214): 2 Tone Sunburst, 3 Tone Sunburst, Black, Olympic White, Surf Green.

Add $240 for vintage finish and 3 Chandler Super 60 pickups (Model 1220).

Add $340 for vintage finish and 3 Chandler Lipstick tube pickups (Model 1222).

Telepathic Series

TELEPATHIC BASIC (Model 1110) - single round cutaway alder body, pearloid pickguard, bolt-on maple neck, 25 1/2" scale, 22-fret maple or rosewood fingerboard with dot inlays, fixed bridge, 6-on-a-side Gotoh tuners, pearl or tortoise shell pickguard, chrome hardware, Chandler single coil pickup, volume/tone control, available in Natural finish. Mfg. 1994-2000.

$525 $475 $425 $375 $300 $250 $195

Last MSR was $649.

When the Telepathic model debuted in 1994, it was available in a wide range of finishes: 2 Tone Sunburst, 3 Tone Sunburst, Chandler Super sparkle, Cherry Sunburst, Gloss Black, Olympic White, Surf Green and Vintage Blonde. As the model's popularity grew, these finishes were designated to specific variations.

Telepathic Standard (Model 1114) - similar to Telepathic Basic, except has 2 Chandler single coil pickups, available in 2 Tone Sunburst finish. Mfg. 1994-98.

$900 $800 $675 $550 $450 $375 $295

Last MSR was $1,149.

Telepathic Deluxe (Model 1122) - similar to Telepathic Basic, except has ivory (or shell or pearl) body binding, 2 Chandler single coil pickups, available in 2 Tone Sunburst. Mfg. 1994-98.

$975 $875 $750 $695 $550 $450 $325

Last MSR was $1,249.

Add $100 for Chandler Super sparkle finish (Model 1130).

TELEPATHIC THINLINE TV (Model 1132) - similar to Telepathic, except has semi-hollow mahogany body, f-hole, and Seymour Duncan mini 59 pickup, available in TV Blond or SG Red finishes. Mfg. 1995-2000.

$1,050 $900 $775 $675 $550 $450 $325

Last MSR was $1,299.

GRADING	100% MINT	98% NEAR MINT	95% EXC+	90% EXC	80% VG+	70% VG	60% G

Telepathic Thinline (Model 1150) - similar to Telepathic Basic, except has semi-hollow mahogany body, figured maple top, f-hole, and 2 single coil pickups. Mfg. 1995 to 1998.

$1,200	$1,000	$875	$725	$600	$525	$395

Last MSR was $1,549.

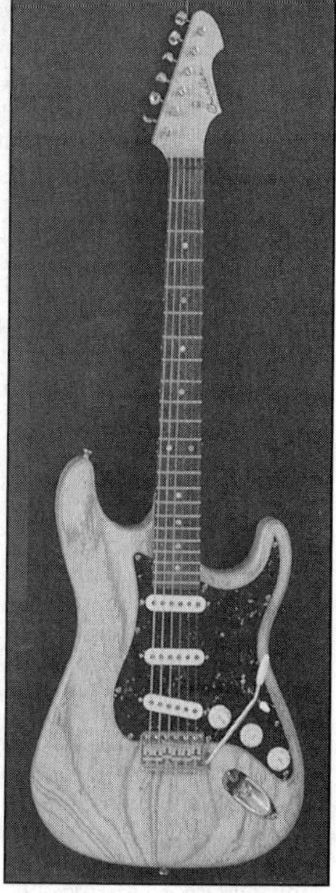
Chandler Spitfire
courtesy Chandler

ELECTRIC BASS

HI FIDELITY (Model 1610) - offset double cutaway *P-bass*-style alder body, bolt-on maple neck, 34" scale, 21-fret maple or rosewood fingerboard with dot inlay, chrome hardware, 4-on-a-side tuners, fixed bridge (with optional through-body stringing), tortoise shell pickguard, 2 Chandler Super 60 single coil pickups, 2 volume/1 tone controls, available in vintage finishes. Mfg. 1996-2000.

$1,150	$1,000	$825	$700	$575	$495	$350

Last MSR was $1,449.

Add $40 for metallic finish (Model 1612).

OFFSET CONTOUR BASS (Model 1622) - offset double cutaway *J-bass*-style alder body, bolt-on maple neck, 34" scale, 21-fret maple or rosewood fingerboard with dot inlay, chrome hardware, 4-on-a-side tuners, fixed bridge, tortoise shell pickguard, 2 Chandler single coil pickups, 2 volume/1 tone controls, available in Natural finish. Mfg. 1996-2000

$995	$875	$750	$695	$550	$450	$325

Last MSR was $1,249.

Add $200 for vintage finish (Model 1620).

ROYALE 12-STRING BASS (Model 1630) - single cutaway Honduran mahogany body, bolt-on graphite-reinforced maple neck, 21-fret rosewood fingerboard with pearl dot inlays, retro-designed layered plastic headstock, tortoise (or pearl or ivory) body binding with matching pickguard, 6-per-side tuners, chrome hardware, 1 split coil/2 soap bar Super 60 pickups, 3 volume controls, 3 on/off pickup selector switches. Mfg. 1996-2000.

Last MSR was $3,500.

This specialty model was designed in conjunction with Tom Petersson (Cheap Trick). Too few models exist for adequate secondary market information.

CHAPIN

Instruments currently built in San Jose, California.

Handcrafted Chapin guitars feature carefully thought out designs that provide ergonomic comfort and a wide palette of tones. All Chapin guitars are handcrafted by luthiers Bill Chapin and Fred Campbell; all guitars feature the Campbell/Chapin locking dovetail set-in neck joint.

The Chapin Insight guitar inspection camera features a small-bodied camera on a flexible mount that allows the luthier/repairman an inside view of the acoustic guitar to help solve internal problems. This low-light camera features 3.6 mm lens for ultra close crack inspection, and has an RCA output that feeds directly into a VCR or camcorder for video documentation. The Insight (list $349) operates on a 9-volt battery - so it is mobile as well. The importance to collectors? Now there is a tool for proper guitar authentication: the internal signatures and dates of an acoustic (or semi-hollow body) guitar can be read in seconds - and right at the guitar show, if necessary!

For current information on Chapin's acoustic electric models, please refer to the 7th Edition *Blue Book of Acoustic Guitars*.

ELECTRIC

The main Chapin electric design is based on the single cutaway body of a tele. The **Falcon** (list $1,750) has an alder or swamp ash body, maple neck with Campbell/Chapin locking dovetail joint, maple or rosewood fingerboard, 25 1/2" scale, 2 Van Zandt single coil pickups, volume/tone controls, 3-way selector, and a thin nitrocellulose lacquer finish. The **Falcon Special** (list $1,950) has Velvet Hammer pickups, custom wiring, and a 5-way switch; the **Falcon Deluxe** has a 24.9" scale, 2 Tom Holmes PAF or Filtertron style humbuckers, hardtail bridge, and gold hardware - with a Bigsby or tune-o-matic bridge/stop tailpiece as custom options (list $1,950).

The **Hawk** is a cross between the Tele and SG body designs. This model was originally designed for Billy Johnson (John Lee Hooker's band), and features a beveled mahogany or alder body, mahogany or maple neck, ebony or rosewood fingerboard, single coil/P-90-style or Tom Holmes humbucker pickups, 3-way switch, 25 1/2" scale, and a bolt-on or set neck (list $2,200). A Cherry nitrocellulose finish is standard.

The semi-hollow **Fatline** ($2,875) has a mahogany body with three different internal tuned chamber designs. The set-in figured maple neck is available in a 24.9" or 25 1/2" scale, with a bound 22-fret rosewood or African blackwood fingerboard. The 2 Velvet Hammer humbuckers are set into an AAAA grade figured maple or redwood top, and feature custom wiring. The all-out **Fatline TV** (list $3,875) was designed originally for guitarist Tim Volpicella, and features private stock aged tonewoods, quilted or flame maple top, koa pickguard/headstock plate/back plates, Brazilian rosewood fingerboard, vibrato bridge, gold hardware (call for more description of this model - these specs don't do it justice).

ELECTRIC BASS

The **Phoenix** (list $2,675) has a double cutaway one-piece alder body, quilted or flame maple top, set-in graphite-reinforced wenge neck, 34" scale, striped ebony fingerboard, Bartolini pickups (P/J, JJ, or soap bar), active TBT electronics, Mann Made bridge, Hipshot Ultralite tuners, and a nitrocellulose finish. The Phoenix has an optional 35" scale 5-string (list $2,975), 35" scale 6-string (list $3,195), with a fretless fingerboard, multi-laminated body, or in choice of woods.

GRADING	100% MINT	98% NEAR MINT	95% EXC+	90% EXC	80% VG+	70% VG	60% G

CHAPPELL

Instruments currently built in Richmond, California since 1969.

Luthier Sean Chappell has been building custom guitars and repairing musical instruments in the San Francisco Bay Area for the past 28 years. Chappell's partial list of clients includes John Lee Hooker, Tom Waits, Elvin Bishop, and David Newman. Recently, Chappell collaborated with guitarist Roy Rogers on a custom double neck dubbed Duo Chops, a blues guitar from hell.

CHARVEL

Trademark previously produced in Korea. The Charvel trademark established in 1978 by the Charvel Manufacturing Company. Distributed by Jackson/Charvel Guitar Company (Akai Musical Instruments) of Fort Worth, Texas. Charvel instruments were previously manufactured in the U.S between 1978 to 1985. Later (post-1985) production was in U.S., Japan, and Korea.

In the late 1970s, Wayne Charvel's Guitar Repair shop in Azusa, California acquired a reputation for making custom high quality bodies and necks. Grover Jackson began working at the shop in 1977, and a year later bought out Charvel and moved the company to San Dimas. Jackson debuted the Charvel custom guitars at the 1979 NAMM show, and the first catalog depicting the bolt-neck beauties and custom options arrived in 1981.

The standard models from *Charvel Manufacturing* carried a list price between $880 to $955, and the amount of custom options was staggering. In 1983, the Charvel company began offering neck-through models under the **Jackson** trademark.

Grover Jackson licensed the Charvel trademark to the International Music Corporation (IMC) in 1985; the company was sold to them a year later. In late 1986 production facilities were moved to Ontario, California. Distribution eventually switched from Charvel/Jackson to the Jackson/Charvel Guitar company, currently a branch of the Akai Musical Instruments company. As the years went by and the Charvel line expanded, its upper end models were phased out and moved into the Jackson line (which had been the Charvel/Jackson Company's line of custom made instruments) and were gaining more popularity. For example, the **Charvel Avenger** (Mfg. 1991 to 1992), became the **Jackson Rhoads EX Pro** (Mfg. 1992 to date). For further details, see the **Jackson** guitars section in this edition.

In 1988, Charvel sent a crew of luthiers to Japan for a year or so to crosstrain the Japanese builders on building methods for custom-built guitars. The resulting custom instruments had a retail list price between $1,000 to $1,300. U.S. custom-built guitars have a four digit serial number, the Japanese custom-built models have a six digit serial number. Numbers may be prefaced with a "C", which may stand for "Custom" made (this point has not been completely verified).

By the early 1990s, the only Charvel models left were entry level 'Strat'-style electrics and dreadnought and jumbo-style (full bodied and cut-a-ways) acoustic guitars. In the late 1990s, even the electrics were phased out in favor of the acoustic and acoustic/electric models. During 1999, instruments with the Charvel trademark had ceased production, and Wayne Charvel began building a new line of instruments utilizing the Wayne Guitars trademark.

(Early Charvel history courtesy Baker Rorick, Guitar Shop magazine; additional information courtesy Roland Lozier, Lozier Piano & Music)

Model Identification

As a general rule of thumb, you can identify the country of origin on earlier instruments that have the guitar-shaped **Charvel** logo by the color of the logo. The early model guitars with black or gold logos were manufactured in the U.S., and the ones with white logos were manufactured overseas. Early guitar-shaped logos have a '3-per-side headstock' in the graphic; current models have a 6-on-a-side headstock in the graphic.

Another way to determine the origin of manufacture is manufacturer's retail price point. In most cases, the lower the retail price (last retail price on discontinued models) the more likely the instrument was manufactured overseas.

Charvel **San Dimas** and **Charvel USA** guitars were built in California. Other production models are built in Japan; **CHS** series electrics were built in Korea.

The only production models under the Charvel trademark currently produced are the **550** and **625** series Acoustic models. These acoustics are built in Korea.

ELECTRIC

STANDARD 1 - offset double cutaway hardwood body, white pickguard, bolt-on maple neck, 22-fret maple fingerboard with black dot inlay, standard vibrato, 6-on-a-side tuners, chrome hardware, 1 DiMarzio humbucker pickup, volume control, available in Black, Blue, Red and White finish. Mfg. 1983 to 1985.

$675 $550 $450 $350 $325 $300 $275

Last MSR was $960.

Standard 2 - similar to Standard 1, except has 2 DiMarzio humbucker pickups, 3-position switch. Mfg. 1985 only.

$725 $575 $475 $375 $325 $300 $275

Last MSR was $1,030.

Standard 3 - similar to Standard 1, except has 3 DiMarzio single coil pickups, 3 mini switches. Mfg. 1983 to 1985.

$750 $600 $500 $375 $350 $300 $275

Last MSR was $1,040.

CHS Series

CHS 1 - offset double cutaway alder body, white pickguard, bolt-on maple neck, 22-fret rosewood fingerboard with pearl dot inlay, standard vibrato, screened peghead logo, 6-on-a-side tuners, black chrome hardware, 3 single coil exposed pickups, volume/tone controls, 5-position switch, available in Black, Bright Red, Metallic Blue, and Snow White finishes. Mfg. 1995 to 1997.

$225 $200 $175 $150 $125 $100 $85

Last MSR was $345.

CHS 2 - similar to CHS 1, except has 2 single coil/humbucker pickups, available in Black, Bright Red, Metallic Blue, and Snow White finishes. Mfg. 1995 to 1997.

$225 $200 $175 $150 $125 $100 $85

Last MSR was $345.

GRADING	100% MINT	98% NEAR MINT	95% EXC+	90% EXC	80% VG+	70% VG	60% G

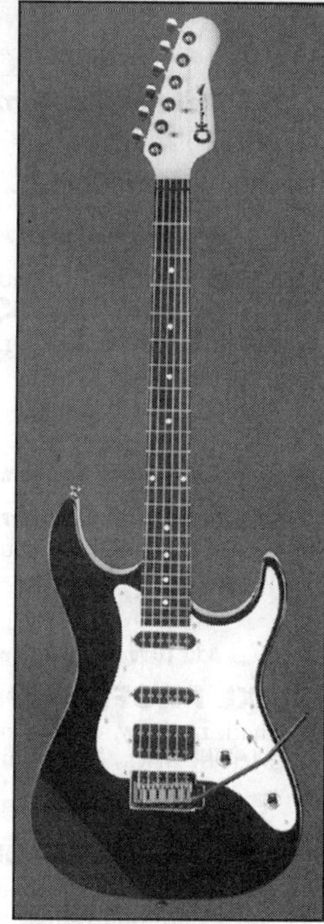
Charvel CHS 2
courtesy Charvel

CHS 3 - similar to CHS 1, except has no pickguard, 24-fret fingerboard, 2 exposed humbucker pickups, available in Black, Bright Red, Metallic Blue, and Snow White finishes. Mfg. 1995 to 1997.

$275	$225	$195	$150	$125	$100	$90

Last MSR was $395.

Classic Series

STX CUSTOM - offset double cutaway basswood body, pearloid pickguard, bolt-on maple neck, 22-fret rosewood fingerboard with pearl dot inlay, double locking vibrato, 6-on-a-side tuners, chrome hardware, 2 single coil/1 humbucker Jackson pickups, volume/tone control, 5-position switch, available in Black and Deep Metallic Blue finishes. Mfg. 1991 to 1994.

$625	$525	$450	$350	$325	$300	$275

Last MSR was $895.

STX Custom (Trans) - similar to STX Custom, except has ash body, available in Tobacco Sunburst, Transparent Blue and Transparent Red finishes. Mfg. 1991 to 1994.

$695	$595	$500	$400	$350	$325	$300

Last MSR was $995.

STX DELUXE - similar to STX Custom, except has standard vibrato, available in Black, Deep Metallic Blue, Dark Metallic Red, Pearl White and Turquoise finishes. Mfg. 1991 to 1994.

$475	$425	$350	$275	$250	$225	$200

Last MSR was $695.

TX CUSTOM (TE Custom) - single cutaway basswood body, pearloid pickguard, bolt-on maple neck, 22-fret maple fingerboard with black dot inlay, fixed bridge, 6-on-a-side tuners, chrome hardware, volume/tone control, 5-position switch, available in Black, Dark Metallic Red, Tobacco Sunburst, and Turquoise finishes. Mfg. 1992 to 1996.

$525	$400	$350	$275	$250	$200	$175

Last MSR was $795.

This model was also available with a rosewood fingerboard with pearl dot inlay.

TX Custom (Trans) - similar to TX Custom, except has ash body, available in Tobacco Sunburst finish. Disc. 1996.

$525	$400	$350	$295	$250	$225	$195

Last MSR was $795.

This model was also available with a rosewood fingerboard with pearl dot inlay.

TTX - single cutaway basswood body, pearloid pickguard, bolt-on maple neck, 24-fret maple fingerboard with black dot inlay, standard vibrato, 6-on-a-side locking tuners, chrome hardware, single coil/humbucker Jackson pickup, 3-position/mini switches, available in Black, Deep Metallic Blue, Deep Metallic Red, and Metallic Purple finishes. Mfg. 1993 only.

$400	$350	$300	$250	$225	$195	$150

Last MSR was $595.

TTX (Trans) - similar to TTX, except has ash body, available in Transparent Black, Transparent Blue and Transparent Red finishes. Mfg. 1993 only.

$425	$375	$325	$250	$225	$200	$175

Last MSR was $645.

Contemporary Series

275 DELUXE CLASSIC - offset double cutaway hardwood body, white pickguard, bolt-on maple neck, 22-fret maple fingerboard with black dot inlay, double locking vibrato, 6-on-a-side tuners, chrome hardware, single coil/humbucker pickups, volume control, 5-position switch, available in Candy Blue, Ferrari Red, Midnight Black and Snow White finishes. Mfg. 1991 to 1992.

$395	$350	$300	$250	$225	$175	$150

Last MSR was $600.

275 Deluxe Contemporary - similar to 275 Deluxe Classic, except has rosewood fingerboard with pearl dot inlay, black hardware, 3 stacked coil pickups (2 side by side at the bridge). Mfg. 1988 to 1991.

$450	$395	$350	$275	$250	$225	$200

Last MSR was $695.

375 DELUXE CLASSIC - offset double cutaway hardwood body, white pickguard, bolt-on maple neck, 22-fret maple fingerboard with black dot inlay, double locking vibrato, 6-on-a-side tuners, chrome hardware, 2 single coil/1 humbucker pickups, volume/tone controls, 5-position switch, available in Candy Red, Desert Crackle, Magenta, Metallic Black, Pearl Blue, Pearl White and Platinum finishes. Mfg. 1988 to 1991.

$495	$425	$350	$275	$250	$225	$200

Last MSR was $700.

Add 10% for figured wood body with Natural finish.

Charvel TX Custom
courtesy Charvel

GRADING	100% MINT	98% NEAR MINT	95% EXC+	90% EXC	80% VG+	70% VG	60% G

C

375 Deluxe Contemporary - similar to 375 Deluxe Classic, except has rosewood fingerboard with pearl dot inlay, available in Candy Red, Magenta, Metallic Black, Pearl Blue and Pearl White finishes. Mfg. 1991 to 1992.

$525 $475 $395 $325 $275 $250 $225
Last MSR was $795.

Add 10% for figured wood body with Natural finish.

This model has an optional maple fingerboard with black dot inlay.

475 SPECIAL CLASSIC - offset double cutaway hardwood body, white pickguard, bolt-on maple neck, 22-fret maple fingerboard with black dot inlay, double locking vibrato, 6-on-a-side tuners, chrome hardware, 2 stacked coil/1 Jackson humbucker pickups, volume/2 tone controls, 5-position switch, available in Candy Red, Desert Crackle, Magenta, Metallic Black, Pearl Blue and Pearl White finishes. Mfg. 1988 to 1991.

$495 $425 $350 $275 $250 $225 $200
Last MSR was $700.

Add 10% for figured wood body with Natural finish.

475 Special Contemporary - similar to 475 Special Classic, except has bound rosewood fingerboard with pearl shark fin inlay, bound peghead, black hardware, active electronics, available in Candy Red, Magenta, Metallic Black, Pearl Blue and Pearl White finishes. Mfg. 1991 to 1992.

$695 $595 $500 $400 $375 $325 $275
Last MSR was $995.

Add 10% for figured wood body with Natural finish.

550 XL PROFESSIONAL - offset double cutaway hardwood body, through-body maple neck, 22-fret bound rosewood fingerboard with pearl shark fin inlay, double locking vibrato, 6-on-a-side tuners, black hardware, Jackson humbucker pickup, volume control, available in Candy Red, Metallic Black, Pearl White, Platinum and Snow White finishes. Mfg. 1988 to 1991.

$675 $575 $475 $395 $350 $325 $275
Last MSR was $970.

650 XL CONTEMPORARY - offset double cutaway hardwood body, through-body maple neck, 22-fret bound rosewood fingerboard with pearl shark fin inlay, double locking vibrato, 6-on-a-side tuners, gold hardware, 2 stacked coil/1 Jackson humbucker pickups, volume/2 tone controls, 5-position switch, active electronics, available in Candy Red, Metallic Black, Pearl White and Snow White finishes. Mfg. 1991 to 1992.

$850 $775 $650 $525 $475 $425 $375
Last MSR was $1,295.

650 XL Professional - similar to 650 XL Contemporary, except has 2 single coil/1 humbucker pickups, available in Candy Red, Desert Crackle, Metallic Black, Pearl White, Platinum and Snow White finishes. Mfg. 1988 to 1991.

$775 $650 $550 $450 $395 $350 $300
Last MSR was $1,100.

750 XL PROFESSIONAL - offset double cutaway hardwood body, bolt-on maple neck, 22-fret bound rosewood fingerboard with pearl shark fin inlay, double locking vibrato, 6-on-a-side tuners, gold hardware, 2 Jackson humbucker pickups, volume/tone controls, 5-position switch, active electronics, available in Candy Red, Desert Crackle, Metallic Black, Pearl White, Platinum and Snow White finishes. Mfg. 1988 to 1991.

$795 $700 $575 $475 $425 $375 $325
Last MSR was $1,170.

Add 10% for figured maple top with Natural finish.

AVENGER - shark fin style hardwood body, bolt-on maple neck, 22-fret rosewood fingerboard with white dot inlay, double locking vibrato, 6-on-a-side Gotoh tuners, black hardware, 3 stacked coil Charvel pickups (2 side by side at the bridge), volume control, 5-position switch, available in Candy Blue, Ferrari Red, Midnight Black and Snow White finishes. Mfg. 1991 to 1992.

$475 $425 $350 $275 $250 $225 $200
Last MSR was $695.

PREDATOR - offset double cutaway hardwood body, bolt-on maple neck, 22-fret rosewood fingerboard with white dot inlay, double locking vibrato, reverse headstock, 6-on-a-side tuners, black hardware, blade stacked coil/humbucker Jackson pickups, volume control, 5-position switch, available in Candy Blue, Candy Red, Magenta, Midnight Black and Pearl White finishes. Mfg. 1991 only.

$550 $475 $395 $325 $275 $225 $200
Last MSR was $795.

SPECTRUM - similar to Predator, except has white pickguard, chrome hardware, 3 stacked coil Jackson pickups, active electronics with switch, available in Candy Red, Midnight Black, Sea Green and Tobacco Sunburst finishes. Mfg. 1991 only.

$625 $525 $450 $350 $325 $275 $250

Last MSR was $895.
This model was also available with maple fingerboard with black dot inlay.

CS Series

CS Series models were produced in Korea.

CS 10 - offset double cutaway alder body, bolt-on maple neck, 22-fret rosewood fingerboard with dot inlay, GR-6 steel fulcrum vibrato, 6-per-side tuners, chrome hardware, pickguard, 3 single coil pickups, volume/tone controls, 5-way switch, available in Black, Bright Red, Blue, and White finishes. Disc. 1998.

$225 $175 $150 $125 $115 $95 $75
Last MSR was $289.

C

GRADING	100% MINT	98% NEAR MINT	95% EXC+	90% EXC	80% VG+	70% VG	60% G

CS 20 - similar to the CS 10, except features 2 single coil/humbucker pickups. Disc. 1998.

$225	$175	$150	$125	$115	$95	$75

Last MSR was $289.

CX Series

This series was manufactured in Korea.

CX290 - strat-style basswood body, white pickguard, bolt-on maple neck, 22-fret rosewood fingerboard with pearl dot inlay, standard vibrato, 6-per-side tuners, chrome hardware, 3 single coil Jackson pickups, volume/tone control, 5-position switch, available in Black, Bright Red, Deep Metallic Blue, and Snow White finishes. Mfg. 1992 to 1996.

$250	$195	$175	$150	$125	$100	$95

Last MSR was $395.

This model also available with 2 single coil/humbucker pickup configuration (Model CX291).

CX390 - strat-style basswood body, black pickguard, bolt-on maple neck, 22-fret rosewood fingerboard with pearl dot inlay, double locking vibrato, 6-on-a-side tuners, chrome hardware, 2 single coil/1 Jackson humbucker pickups, volume/tone control, 5-position switch, available in Black, Bright Red, Deep Metallic Blue and Snow White finishes. Mfg. 1992 to 1996.

$275	$225	$200	$175	$150	$125	$100

Last MSR was $495.

This model also available with humbucker/single coil/humbucker pickup configuration (Model CX391).

Fusion Series

FUSION CUSTOM - offset double cutaway poplar body, bolt-on maple neck, 24-fret rosewood fingerboard with white dot inlay, double locking vibrato, 6-on-a-side tuners, black hardware, 2 rail stacked coil/1 Jackson humbucker pickups, volume/tone control, 5-position switch, available in Candy Blue, Candy Red, Metallic Black and Snow White finishes. Mfg. 1991 only.

$625	$525	$450	$350	$325	$295	$275

Last MSR was $895.

FUSION DELUXE - similar to Fusion Custom, except has chrome hardware, rail stacked coil/humbucker Jackson pickups, volume control. Mfg. 1991 only.

$550	$475	$395	$325	$275	$250	$225

Last MSR was $795.

This model was also available with maple fingerboard with black dot inlay.

FUSION PLUS - offset double cutaway ash body, bolt-on maple neck, 24-fret rosewood fingerboard with offset white dot inlay, double locking vibrato, 6-on-a-side tuners, black hardware, 2 humbucker Jackson pickups, volume/tone control, 5-position switch with coil split, available in Tobacco Sunburst, Transparent Amber, Transparent Red, Transparent Violet and Transparent White finishes. Disc. 1992.

$625	$525	$450	$350	$325	$300	$275

Last MSR was $895.

FUSION SPECIAL - offset double cutaway poplar body, through-body maple neck, 24-fret rosewood fingerboard with white dot inlay, double locking vibrato, 6-on-a-side tuners, black hardware, 3 stacked coil Charvel pickups (2 side by side at the bridge), volume control, 5-position switch, available in Candy Blue, Ferrari Red, Midnight Black and Snow White finishes. Mfg. 1991 only.

$485	$425	$350	$275	$250	$225	$200

Last MSR was $695.

LS Series

LS-1 - offset double cutaway asymmetrical bound carved mahogany body, mahogany neck, 22-fret bound rosewood fingerboard with pearl dot inlay, tune-o-matic bridge, string through-body tailpiece, bound blackface peghead with screened logo, 3-per-side tuners, chrome hardware, 2 humbucker Jackson pickups, volume/tone control, 3-position switch, available in Black, Deep Metallic Blue, and Gold finishes. Mfg. 1993 to 1996.

$650	$595	$500	$425	$350	$325	$250

Last MSR was $995.

LSX-I - offset double cutaway asymmetrical ash body, figured maple top, mahogany neck, 22-fret rosewood fingerboard with pearl dot inlay, Wilkinson vibrato, roller nut, blackface peghead with screened logo, 3-per-side tuners, black hardware, 2 humbucker Jackson pickups, volume/tone control, 3-position switch, available in Natural Green Sunburst, Natural Purple Sunburst, and Natural Red Sunburst finishes. Mfg. 1994 to 1996.

$575	$495	$450	$350	$325	$275	$225

Last MSR was $895.

LSX-II - offset double cutaway asymmetrical mahogany body, mahogany neck, 22-fret rosewood fingerboard with pearl dot inlay, double locking vibrato, blackface peghead with screened logo, 3-per-side tuners, black hardware, 2 humbucker Jackson pickups, volume/tone control, 3-position switch, available in Black and Transparent Red finishes. Mfg. 1994 to 1996.

$525	$450	$395	$325	$275	$250	$200

Last MSR was $795.

Charvel LSX 1
courtesy Charvel

GRADING	100% MINT	98% NEAR MINT	95% EXC+	90% EXC	80% VG+	70% VG	60% G

LSX-III - offset double cutaway asymmetrical ash body, mahogany neck, 22-fret rosewood fingerboard with pearl dot inlay, string through-body bridge, blackface peghead with screened logo, 3-per-side tuners, black hardware, 2 humbucker Jackson pickups, volume/tone control, 3-position switch, available in Tobacco Sunburst, Transparent Blue, and Transparent Red finishes. Mfg. 1994 to 1996.

$450 $425 $350 $275 $250 $225 $175
Last MSR was $695.

Model Series

MODEL 1 - offset double cutaway hardwood body, white pickguard, bolt-on maple neck, 22-fret maple fingerboard with black dot inlay, fixed bridge, 6-on-a-side tuners, chrome hardware, J90-C humbucker pickup, volume control, available in Ferrari Red, Midnight Black, Royal Blue and Snow White finishes. Mfg. 1987 to 1989.

$325 $275 $225 $195 $150 $125 $100
Last MSR was $400.

Model 1A - similar to Model 1, except has 3 single coil pickups, tone control, 5-position switch.

$350 $275 $225 $195 $150 $125 $100
Last MSR was $450.

MODEL 2 - similar to Model 1, except has standard vibrato. Mfg. 1986 to 1989.

$425 $325 $275 $225 $200 $175 $150
Last MSR was $550.

MODEL 3 - similar Model 1, except has 2 single coil/1 humbucker pickups, tone control, 5-position switch. Mfg. 1986 to 1989.

$450 $395 $325 $250 $225 $200 $175
Last MSR was $650.

Model 3A - similar to Model 3, except has 2 humbucker pickups, standard vibrato. Mfg. 1986 to 1988.

$425 $350 $300 $250 $225 $175 $150
Last MSR was $600.

MODEL 4 - similar to Model 1, except has standard vibrato, 2 humbucker pickups, tone control, 5-position switch, active electronics. Mfg. 1986 to 1989.

$595 $500 $425 $375 $325 $295 $275
Last MSR was $850.

MODEL 5 - similar to Model 1, except has through-body neck, standard vibrato, 2 humbucker pickups, tone control, 5-position switch. Mfg. 1986 to 1989.

$675 $575 $475 $375 $325 $300 $275
Last MSR was $950.

MODEL 6 - similar to Model 5, except has standard vibrato, 2 single coil/1 humbucker pickups, tone control, 5-position switch, active electronics. Mfg. 1986 to 1989.

$725 $625 $550 $450 $395 $350 $300
Last MSR was $1,050.

San Dimas Series

This series was entirely hand made at the Jackson Custom Shop located in Ontario, California.

SAN DIMAS I - offset double cutaway lacewood (or mahogany) body, bolt-on bird's-eye maple neck, 24-fret rosewood fingerboard with pearl dot inlay, double locking Floyd Rose vibrato, screened peghead logo, 6-on-a-side Gotoh tuners, gold hardware, 2 exposed humbucker DiMarzio pickups, volume control, 3-position switch, available in Natural Oil finish. Mfg. 1995 to 1997.

$925 $850 $725 $575 $525 $450 $350
Last MSR was $1,395.

Add $100 for koa body.

San Dimas II - similar to San Dimas I, except has standard Wilkinson vibrato, locking Sperzel tuners, black hardware, available in Natural Oil finish. Mfg. 1995 to 1997.

$850 $695 $650 $525 $475 $425 $325
Last MSR was $1,295.

Add $100 for koa body.

SAN DIMAS III - offset double cutaway mahogany body, quilted maple top, bolt-on bird's-eye maple neck, 24-fret pau ferro fingerboard with pearl dot inlay, double locking Floyd Rose vibrato, screened peghead logo, 6-on-a-side Gotoh tuners, black hardware, 2 single coil rail/1 exposed DiMarzio pickups, volume/tone controls, 5-position/coil tap switches, available in Transparent Green, Transparent Purple, Transparent Red and Vintage Sunburst finishes. Mfg. 1995 to 1997.

$975 $900 $750 $600 $550 $495 $375
Last MSR was $1,495.

San Dimas IV - similar to San Dimas III, except has koa body, bound quilted maple top, body matching peghead with screened logo, gold hardware, no coil tap, available in Transparent Green, Transparent Purple, Transparent Red, and Vintage Sunburst finishes. Mfg. 1995 to 1997.

$1,100 $950 $850 $675 $600 $550 $425
Last MSR was $1,695.

C

GRADING	100% MINT	98% NEAR MINT	95% EXC+	90% EXC	80% VG+	70% VG	60% G

SAN DIMAS STANDARD - offset double cutaway alder body, bolt-on maple neck, 24-fret rosewood fingerboard with pearl dot inlay, standard vibrato, screened peghead logo, 6-on-a-side locking Sperzel tuners, chrome hardware, 2 single coil/humbucker exposed DiMarzio pickups, volume/tone controls, 5-position switch, available in Black, Forest Green, Garnet Red, Sapphire Blue, and Snow White finishes. Mfg. 1995 to 1997.

$650 $595 $500 $400 $350 $300 $250
Last MSR was $995.

SAN DIMAS TRADITIONAL - offset double cutaway alder body, pearloid pickguard, bolt-on maple neck, 22-fret rosewood fingerboard with pearl dot inlay, standard Wilkinson vibrato, string tree, screened peghead logo, 6-on-a-side locking Sperzel tuners, black hardware, 3 single coil exposed DiMarzio pickups, volume/tone controls, 5-position switch, available in Black, Forest Green, Garnet Red, Sapphire Blue, and Snow White finishes. Mfg. 1995 to 1997.

$650 $595 $500 $400 $350 $300 $250
Last MSR was $995.

Surfcaster Series

SURFCASTER - offset double rounded cutaway asymmetrical semi hollow basswood body, offset wedge soundhole, bound body and soundhole, pearloid pickguard, bolt-on maple neck, 24-fret bound rosewood fingerboard with pearl shark fin inlay, standard vibrato, bound peghead, roller nut, 3-per-side tuners, chrome hardware, 2 single coil lipstick pickups, volume/tone control, 3-position switch, phase reversal in tone control, available in Black, Magenta and Turquoise finishes. Mfg. 1992 to 1994.

$695 $595 $500 $400 $350 $295 $275
Last MSR was $995.

Surfcaster (Trans) - similar to Surfcaster, except has figured maple top/mahogany body, available in Star Glo, Transparent Orange and Transparent Red finishes.

$775 $650 $550 $425 $395 $350 $300
Last MSR was $1,095.

SC1 (SURFCASTER HT) - offset double round cutaway asymmetrical semi hollow basswood body, bound wedge soundhole, bound body, pearloid pickguard, bolt-on maple neck, 24-fret bound rosewood fingerboard with pearl shark fin inlay, tune-o-matic bridge/trapeze tailpiece with stylized C, bound peghead with screened logo, 3-per-side tuners, chrome hardware, 2 single coil lipstick pickups, volume/tone control, 3-position switch, phase reversal in tone control, available in Black, Metallic Violet and Turquoise finishes. Mfg. 1992 to 1996.

$655 $575 $475 $400 $350 $300 $275
Last MSR was $895.

In early 1994, single coil/humbucker pickups configuration replaced original part/design. The phase reversal switch was discontinued in 1996.

Surfcaster HT (Trans) - similar to SC1 (Surfcaster HT), except has figured maple top/mahogany body, available in Natural Green Burst, Natural Red Burst, Star Glo, Tobacco Sunburst, Transparent Orange and Transparent Red finishes. Mfg. 1992 to 1994.

$725 $625 $525 $425 $375 $325 $275
Last MSR was $995.

In early 1994, Natural Green Burst, Natural Red Burst and Tobacco Sunburst finishes were introduced, single coil/humbuckers pickup configuration replaced original part/design, Star Glo, Transparent Orange and Transparent Red finishes were discontinued.

SURFCASTER 12 - offset double round cutaway asymmetrical semi hollow basswood body, bound wedge soundhole, bound body, pearloid pickguard, bolt-on maple neck, 24-fret bound ebony fingerboard with pearl shark fin inlay, fixed bridge, bound peghead with screened logo, roller nut, 6-per-side tuners, chrome hardware, 2 single coil lipstick pickups, volume/tone control, 3-position switch, phase reversal in tone control, available in Black, Magenta and Turquoise finishes. Mfg. 1992 to 1994.

$795 $675 $575 $475 $425 $375 $325
Last MSR was $1,050.

In early 1994, bound rosewood fingerboard replaced original part/design.

Surfcaster 12 (Trans) - similar to Surfcaster 12, except has figured maple top/mahogany body, available in Star Glo, Transparent Orange and Transparent Red finishes.

$850 $725 $615 $515 $465 $425 $385
Last MSR was $1,150.

ELECTRIC BASS

STANDARD 1 - offset double cutaway hardwood body, white pickguard, bolt-on maple neck, 21-fret maple fingerboard with black dot inlay, fixed bridge, 4-on-a-side tuners, chrome hardware, P-style Charvel pickups, volume/tone controls, available in Black, Red and White finishes. Mfg. 1985 only.

$675 $575 $475 $375 $325 $300 $275
Last MSR was $960.

STANDARD 2 - offset double cutaway asymmetrical hardwood body, bolt-on maple neck, 21-fret maple fingerboard with black dot inlay, fixed bridge, 4-on-a-side tuners, chrome hardware, 2 J-style Charvel pickups, 2 volume/1 tone controls, available in Black, Red and White finishes. Mfg. 1983 to 1985.

$725 $625 $500 $425 $375 $350 $300
Last MSR was $1,030.

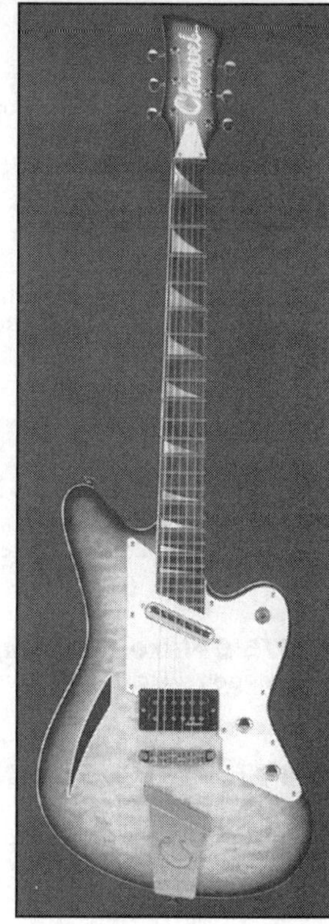

Charvel Surfcaster HT
courtesy Charvel

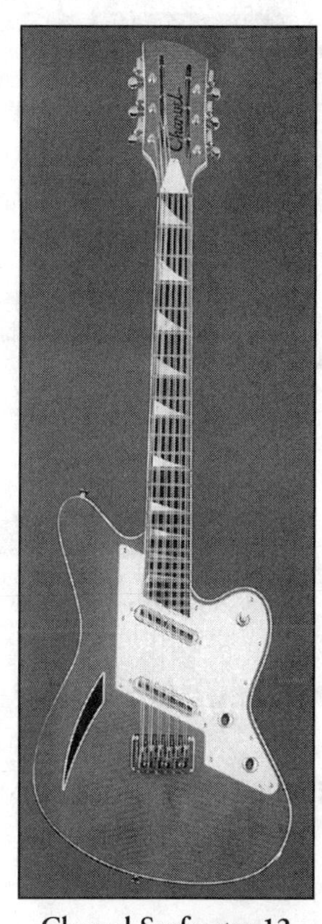

Charvel Surfcaster 12
courtesy Charvel

GRADING	100% MINT	98% NEAR MINT	95% EXC+	90% EXC	80% VG+	70% VG	60% G

ELIMINATOR - offset double cutaway hardwood body, bolt-on maple neck, 24-fret rosewood fingerboard with white dot inlay, fixed bridge, 4-on-a-side tuners, black hardware, P/J-style Charvel pickups, volume/treble/bass and mix controls, active electronics, available in Candy Blue, Ferrari Red, Midnight Black and Snow White finishes. Mfg. 1991 only.

$495 $425 $350 $295 $250 $225 $200
Last MSR was $695.

JX BASS - offset double cutaway asymmetrical poplar body, bolt-on maple neck, 22-fret rosewood fingerboard with pearl dot inlay, fixed bridge, 4-on-a-side tuners, chrome hardware, P/J-style Jackson pickups, volume/tone/mix controls, available in Black, Deep Metallic Blue, Dark Metallic Red, Snow White and Turquoise finishes. Mfg. 1992 to 1994.

$475 $425 $350 $295 $250 $225 $210
Last MSR was $695.

Contemporary Bass Series

575 DELUXE CLASSIC - offset double cutaway hardwood body, bolt-on maple neck, 21-fret rosewood fingerboard with white dot inlay, fixed bridge, 4-on-a-side tuners, chrome hardware, P/J-style pickups, 2 volume/2 tone controls, available in Candy Blue, Ferrari Red, Midnight Black, Platinum and Snow White finishes. Mfg. 1988 to 1991.

$425 $350 $300 $250 $225 $175 $150
Last MSR was $600.

575 Deluxe Contemporary - similar to 575 Deluxe Classic, except has rosewood fingerboard with pearl dot inlay, volume/tone control, 3-position switch, available in Candy Blue, Candy Red, Metallic Black and Snow White finishes. Mfg. 1991 to 1992.

$475 $425 $350 $275 $250 $225 $200
Last MSR was $695.

850 XL PROFESSIONAL - offset double cutaway hardwood body, bolt-on maple neck, 21-fret rosewood fingerboard with white dot inlay, fixed bridge, 4-on-a-side tuners, chrome hardware, P/J-style pickups, volume/treble/bass/mix controls, available in Candy Blue, Ferrari Red, Midnight Black, Platinum and Snow White finishes. Mfg. 1988 to 1991.

$700 $600 $500 $400 $350 $300 $250
Last MSR was $1,000.

CX Bass Series

CX490 - offset double cutaway poplar body, bolt-on maple neck, 22-fret rosewood fingerboard with pearl dot inlay, fixed bridge, 4-on-a-side tuners, chrome hardware, P/J-style Jackson pickups, volume/tone and mix controls, available in Black, Bright Red, Deep Metallic Blue, and Snow White finishes. Mfg. 1992 to 1995.

$325 $295 $250 $195 $175 $150 $125
Last MSR was $495.

Fusion Bass Series

FUSION IV - offset double cutaway hardwood body, bolt-on maple neck, 24-fret rosewood fingerboard with offset pearl dot inlay, pearl Charvel block inlay at 12th fret, fixed bridge, 4-on-a-side tuners, black hardware, P/J-style Charvel pickups, volume/treble/bass and mix controls, active electronics, available in Candy Blue, Ferrari Red, Magenta, Metallic Black and Pearl White finishes. Mfg. 1991 only.

$525 $475 $395 $325 $275 $250 $225
Last MSR was $795.

Fusion V - similar to Fusion IV, except has 5-string configuration, 3/2-per-side tuners.

$650 $595 $500 $400 $375 $325 $275
Last MSR was $995.

LS Bass Series

LS-1 BASS - offset double cutaway asymmetrical bound mahogany body, mahogany neck, 21-fret bound rosewood fingerboard with pearl dot inlay, tune-o-matic bridge, through-body ring and ball holder tailpiece, 2 Jackson pickups, volume/treble/bass/mix control, available in Black, Deep Metallic Blue, and Gold finishes. Mfg. 1993 to 1996.

$775 $650 $600 $525 $450 $395 $300
Last MSR was $1,195.

Model Bass Series

MODEL 1B - offset double cutaway hardwood body, bolt-on maple neck, 21-fret rosewood fingerboard with pearl dot inlay, fixed bridge, 4-on-a-side tuners, chrome hardware, P-style Charvel pickup, volume/tone controls, available in Black, Red and White finishes. Mfg. 1986 to 1989.

$325 $275 $225 $175 $150 $125 $100
Last MSR was $450.

MODEL 2B - similar to Model 1B, except has P/J-style pickups, 2 volume/2 tone controls. Mfg. 1986 to 1989.

$425 $350 $300 $250 $225 $175 $150
Last MSR was $600.

MODEL 3B - similar to Model 1B, except has through-body neck, 2 J-style pickups, 2 volume/2 tone controls. Mfg 1986 to 1989.

$595 $525 $425 $350 $300 $275 $225
Last MSR was $850.

GRADING	100% MINT	98% NEAR MINT	95% EXC+	90% EXC	80% VG+	70% VG	60% G

C

Surfcaster Bass Series

SURFCASTER BASS - sleek offset double rounded cutaway basswood body, pearloid pickguard, bolt-on maple neck, 21-fret bound rosewood fingerboard with offset pearl inlay, fixed bridge, bound peghead, 2-per-side tuners, chrome hardware, 2 single coil lipstick pickups, volume/tone control, 3-position switch, phase reversal in tone control, available in Black, Magenta and Turquoise finishes. Mfg. 1992 to 1994.

$695 $595 $500 $400 $360 $330 $300
Last MSR was $995.

Surfcaster Bass (Trans) - similar to Surfcaster Bass, except has figured maple top/mahogany body, available in Star Glo, Transparent Orange and Transparent Red finishes.

$765 $655 $545 $435 $395 $360 $330
Last MSR was $1,095.

CHARVETTE

Instruments previously produced in Korea from 1989 to 1994. Charvette, an entry level line to Charvel, was distributed by the International Music Corporation of Ft. Worth, Texas.

The Charvette trademark was distributed by the Charvel/Jackson company as a good quality entry level guitar based on their original Jackson USA "superstrat" designs. Where the Charvel and Jackson models may sport 'Jackson' pickups, Charvettes invariably had 'Charvel' pickups to support a company/product unity.

ELECTRIC

All models in this series were available in Ferrari Red, Midnight Black, Royal Blue, Snow White, and Splatter finishes, unless otherwise listed.

100 - offset double cutaway hardwood body, bolt-on maple neck, 22-fret rosewood fingerboard with white dot inlay, standard vibrato, reverse peghead, 6-on-a-side tuners, black hardware, stacked coil/humbucker Charvel pickup, volume/tone control, 3-position switch. Mfg. 1989 to 1992.

$250 $225 $175 $150 $125 $100 $75
Last MSR was $365.

150 - similar to 100, except has locking vibrato, standard peghead. Mfg. 1989 to 1992.

$275 $225 $195 $150 $125 $100 $75
Last MSR was $395.

170 - similar to 100, except has double locking vibrato, standard peghead, no tone control. Mfg. 1991 to 1992.

$325 $295 $250 $175 $150 $125 $100
Last MSR was $495.

175 - similar to 100, except has 24-fret fingerboard, standard peghead, no tone control. Mfg. 1989 to 1991.

$295 $250 $200 $175 $150 $125 $100
Last MSR was $420.

200 - similar to 100, except has 2 single coil/1 Charvel humbucker pickups. Mfg. 1989 to 1992.

$250 $200 $175 $150 $125 $100 $100
Last MSR was $375.

250 - similar to 100, except has locking vibrato, standard peghead, stacked coil/single coil/humbucker Charvel pickups. Mfg. 1989 to 1992.

$295 $250 $200 $175 $150 $125 $100
Last MSR was $425.

270 - similar to 100, except has double locking vibrato, standard peghead, stacked coil/single coil/humbucker Charvel pickups, no tone control. Mfg. 1991 to 1992.

$375 $325 $250 $200 $175 $150 $125
Last MSR was $525.

275 - similar to 100, except has 24-fret fingerboard, standard peghead, locking vibrato, stacked coil/single coil/humbucker pickups, no tone control. Mfg. 1989 to 1991.

$300 $250 $200 $175 $150 $125 $100
Last MSR was $430.

300 - similar to 100, except has 3 single coil Charvel pickups. Mfg. 1989 to 1992.

$325 $295 $250 $175 $150 $125 $100
Last MSR was $495.

ELECTRIC BASS

400 - offset double cutaway hardwood body, bolt-on maple neck, 21-fret rosewood fingerboard with pearl dot inlay, fixed bridge, 4-on-a-side tuners, chrome hardware, P-style Charvel pickup, volume/tone control. Mfg. 1989 to 1992.

$295 $250 $200 $175 $150 $125 $100
Last MSR was $425.

450 - similar to 400, except has P/J-style pickups, 2 volume/2 tone controls. Mfg. 1991 to 1992.

$350 $295 $250 $175 $150 $125 $100
Last MSR was $495.

CHATWORTH

Instruments currently built in England.

Luthier Andy Smith is currently building high quality guitars. For further information, please contact luthier Smith directly (see Trademark Index).

CHRIS

See chapter on House Brands.

This trademark has been identified as a separate budget line of guitars from the Jackson-Guldan company of Columbus, Ohio.

(Source: Willie G. Moseley, Stellas & Stratocasters)

CHRIS LARKIN CUSTOM GUITARS

Instruments currently built in Ireland since 1979.

Since 1977, Chris Larkin Custom Guitars have been based at Castlegregory, County Kerry, on the west coast of Ireland. Chris Larkin works alone hand building a range of original designs to custom order with a very high level of quality from the finest available materials. The range is wide ("it stops me from becoming bored!") including acoustic, electric, archtop, and semi-acoustic guitars; acoustic, electric, semi-acoustic, and upright 'stick' basses; and archtop mandolins. 'One-off' designs are also built and Chris admits to having made some very high spec copies when offered enough money!

(Company information courtesy Chris Larkin, Chris Larkin Custom Guitars)

As each instrument is hand made to order, the customer has a wide choice of woods, colors, fret type, fingerboard radius, neck profile, and dimensions within the design to enable the finished instrument to better suit the player. All Larkin instruments from 1980 on have a shamrock as the headstock inlay. Sales are worldwide through distributors in some areas, or direct from the maker.

Serialization

Since 1982, a simple six digit system has been used. The first two digits indicate the year, the next two the month, and the final two the sequence in that month. For example, 970103 was the third instrument in January 1997. Before 1982 the numbers are a bit chaotic! Chris Larkin has full documentation for almost every instrument that he has ever built, so he can supply a history from the serial number in most cases.

ELECTRIC

Larkin's **ASAD** model is a solid body electric guitar with set-in neck, mahogany body, and bookmatched exotic wood overlays. This model is available in **Standard** (flat topped with contours) at $2,280, and **Custom** (carved arched top) at $2,600.

ELECTRIC BASS

Reactor basses are similar in body style to the ASAD guitars, and feature laminated set-in necks, mahogany bodies, and bookmatched exotic wood tops. Reactor basses are available in 4- and 5-string configurations, and as a **Standard** (flat topped) and **Custom** (carved arched top). Prices range from $2,060 to $2,370 (4-string) and $2,240 to $2,550 (5-string). The Bassix 6-string price range is from $2,420 to $2,720; the **Basseven** 7-string (Larkin built one model as early as 1968) prices range from $2,590 to $2,890.

In addition to the high quality solid body basses, Larkin also builds minimalist body electric semi-hollow upright basses. The **Blen** Upright Electric Bass is available in 4-, 5-, and 6-string configurations. Prices range from $2,860 up to $3,300.

CIMAR

Instruments previously built in Japan during the 1970s and 1980s.

Cimar produced good-to-medium quality guitars that featured similar versions of classic American designs, as well as some original and thinline hollowbody designs.

(Source: Tony Bacon and Paul Day, The Guru's Guitar Guide)

CIPHER

Instruments previously produced in Japan circa 1960s.

Cipher guitars were distributed in the U.S. market by Inter-Mark, and featured oddly-shaped body designs.

(Source: Michael Wright, Guitar Stories Volume One)

CITATION

Instruments previously produced in Japan.

The U.S. distributor of Citation guitars was the Grossman company of Cleveland, Ohio.

(Source: Michael Wright, Guitar Stories Volume One)

CITRON, HARVEY

Instruments currently built in Woodstock, New York since 1983.

Luthier Harvey Citron has been building high quality, innovative, solid body guitars since the early 1970s. Citron, a noted guitarist and singer, co-founded the Veillette-Citron company in 1975. During the partnership's eight years, they were well known for the quality of their handcrafted electric guitars, basses, and baritone guitars. Citron also designed the **X-92 Breakaway** model for Guild and was a regular contributing writer for several guitar magazines.

Citron instruments are available direct from Harvey Citron, or through a limited number of dealers. Citron maintains a current price list and descriptions of his models at his web site. His **Basic Guitar Set-Up and Repair** instructional video is available from Homespun Tapes; and Citron's cleverly designed **Guitar Stand** has a list price of $499.

Citron Instrument Specifications

All Citron instruments are topped with figured/exotic woods such as Curly or Quilted Maple, Swamp ash, Korina, Purple Heart, Wenge, Macassar Ebony, and Rosewood. Bodies without the figured/exotic woods are available at a lower price (call for price quote). Necks are constructed from Hard Rock Maple and Mahogany, and fingerboards feature materials such as Ebony, Rosewood, Pau Ferro, Wenge, and Maple.

Citron welcomes custom orders, and offers choices in woods, colors, finish, electronics, hardware, and other specifications (call for price quote).

Citron instruments feature *custom blended* Citron pickups or pickups built by other custom pickup makers.

The standard finish on a Citron body is a hand rubbed oil finish. All retail prices include a hard shell case.

Add $250 for a gloss polyester finish (bolt-on style models).

ELECTRIC

All Electric guitar models feature a 25 1/2" scale.

CC1 - offset double cutaway body, internal hollowed chambers, bolt-on neck, 6-on-a-side headstock, tremolo, 3 pickups, volume/tone controls, 5-way selector switch. Current Mfg.

MSR **$3,699**

CC2 - similar to the CC1, except features 2 humbucker pickups, bridge/stop tailpiece. Mfg. 1998 to date.

MSR **$2,499**

CF1 - sleek, balanced reverse Firebird-style body, bolt-on neck, 6-on-a-side reverse headstock, fixed bridge, 2 pickups, volume/tone controls, 3-way selector switch. Current Mfg.

MSR **$2,899**

CS1 - offset double cutaway body, bolt-on neck, 6-on-a-side headstock, tremolo, 3 pickups, volume/tone controls, 5-way selector switch. Current Mfg.

MSR **$3,199**

CT1 - single cutaway body, bolt-on neck, 6-on-a-side headstock, fixed bridge, 3 pickups, volume/tone controls, 3-way selector switch. Current Mfg.

MSR **$2,799**

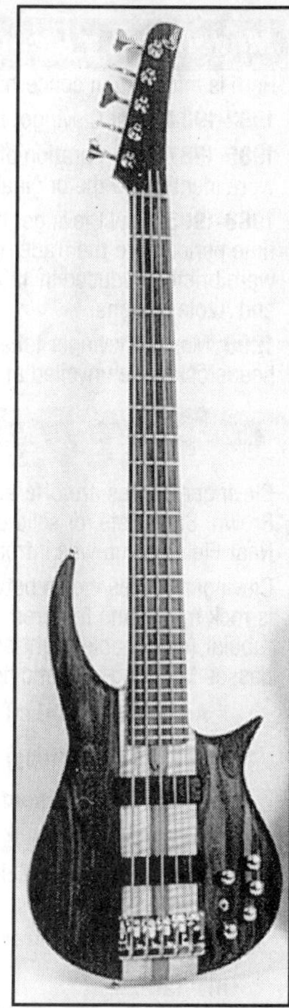

Citron NT 5 Bass
courtesy Harvey Citron

ELECTRIC BASS

All bass models feature active electronics.

Fingerboards available in fretless configuration at no additional cost.

BO4 - offset double cutaway body, 34" scale, bolt-on neck, four on a side headstock, 2 pickups, fixed bridge, active electronics, volume/blend/tone controls. Current Mfg.

MSR **$2,899**

BO5 - similar to the BO4, except has 35" scale, 5-string configuration. Current Mfg.

MSR **$3,099**

BO6 - similar to the BO4, except has 35" scale, 6-string configuration. Current Mfg.

MSR **$3,299**

NT4 - offset double cutaway body, 34" scale, neck-through-body construction, four on a side headstock, 2 pickups, fixed bridge, active electronics, volume/blend/tone controls. Current Mfg.

MSR **$3,599**

NT5 - similar to the NT4, except has 35" scale, 5-string configuration. Current Mfg.

MSR **$3,799**

NT6 - similar to the NT4, except has 35" scale, 6-string configuration. Current Mfg.

MSR **$3,999**

ED CLARK GUITARS, INC.

Please refer to the E section of this text.

CLEARSOUND

Instruments previously built in Japan during the 1970s.

Shades of Dan Armstrong! The Clearsound "Strat" model of the late 1970s was built of see-through plastic with a wood neck and three single coil pickups. If you begin the tally with the original Dan Armstrong/Ampeg lucite "See-Throughs", Renaissance company's original designs, the Univox and Ibanez "Dan Armstrong" copies, as well as the models currently built by George Fedden, this brings the total count of companies who produced these type of lucite guitars to six!

(Source for Clearsound: Tony Bacon, The Ultimate Guitar Book)

CLEVINGER

Instruments currently built in Oakland, California.

Martin Clevinger has been building solid body electric double basses since the early 1980s. As a working bassist on both the acoustic and bass guitar for many years, Clevinger knew that a more durable double bass could be built that would help lessen the wear and tear on a bassist's more expensive older upright, and at the same time be more adaptable in modern musical situations. Clevinger originally purchased and was dissatisfied with a Framus Triumph and a Zorko. He then set out to build prototypes that overcame their shortcomings. After building a few basses and playing them on his gigs, other bassists became interested and wanted Clevinger to build instruments for them.

(Company history and information courtesy Martin Clevinger)

Clevinger has reissued the original Clevinger Bass. These vintage models are faithful reproductions of the 1984 models. They retain the keyhole body shape, the cut scroll head with deep neck heel. The pickup system and controls have been updated (Clevinger Near Field pickup). Each is custom-built on demand, and carries a retail price of $3,595. This model has a choice of vintage gold transparent, vintage black with gold transparent neck, or custom colors.

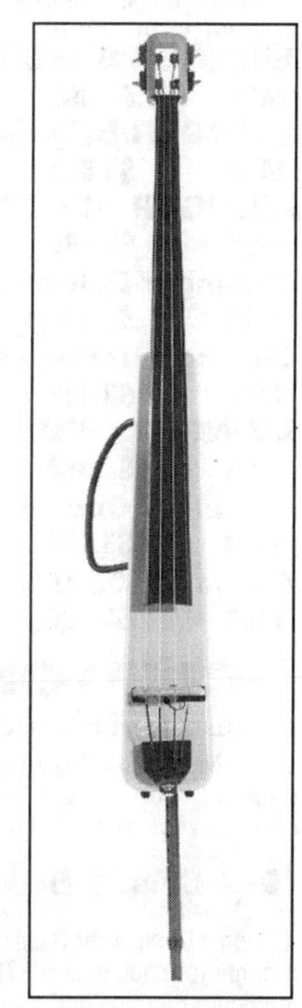

Clevinger Basic
courtesy
Martin Clevinger

C

Model Dating Identification

Here is information concerning production as well as the various brand names found on Clevinger upright basses:

1982-1984: First Clevinger basses produced by Ace Industries in San Francisco, California.

1985-1987: Incorporation of Ace Industries in 1985 resulted in the removal of the Clevinger name from basses produced by Able Tech, Inc. These instruments were identical to the original Clevinger basses but were labeled **Solid Acoustic**. Several hundred were produced. Able Tech, Inc. was dissolved by 1989.

1986-1995: New Clevinger bass models resulted from Martin Clevinger licensing all new Clevinger designs to Robert Lee Guitars. Instruments built during this time period bore the trademark **Clevinger by Robert Lee**. A joint design project between Clevinger, Azola Basses, and Robert Lee, dubbed the **C.A.L.** bass were briefly produced in 1995. Both companies currently offer a version or similar design options in their separate product lines, each incorporating Clevinger and Azola designs.

1996: Martin Clevinger takes sales in-house, producing instruments with the name *Clevinger.* The curvaceous Clevinger **Opus** models with elegant scrolled headstock were unveiled at the 1996 NAMM trade show.

ELECTRIC BASS

Clevinger Basses are offered in a Black highly polished polyurethane or Honey transparent urethane. Other custom colors, such as Golden Brown, Reddish Brown, Sunbursts, or solid colors are available. Clevinger also offers custom woods and different pickup options (call for price quotes). In 1997, the Clevinger Near Field pickup was introduced.

Clevinger basses weigh between 15 to 19 pounds, and range between 53" to 57" in length. These slim body basses are constructed of poplar, while the neck is rock maple and features an ebony fingerboard. The solid body instruments have a scale length of 41 1/2", have a telescoping endpin, and a black metal tubular (detachable) right bout (the left bout is an added accessory). Pickups technology is designed by Clevinger, and the tuners are by Hipshot. Clevinger basses featuring acoustic floating spruce tops are available for acoustic purists.

Add $100 (per string) for Clevinger Near Field pickup (standard equipment on Opus and Deluxe models).

Add $125 (per string) for RMC string saddle sensors.

Add $575 for Barbera pickup in Clevinger bridge (4-string only).

CLEVINGER/AZOLA VIRTUOSO - custom Azola violin body, floating spruce top, scrolled headstock, 2-per-side tuners, ebony fittings, Clevinger Near Field pickup, available in Tuscan Red Sunburst high gloss finish. Mfg. 1995 to date.

MSR $4,295

Clevinger also offered 5-string and 6-string configurations of this model: The Clevinger/Azola Virtuoso 5 had a 3/2-per-side headstock (MSR of $4,495), and the Clevinger/Azola Virtuoso 6 had a 3-per-side headstock (MSR of $4,695). These models may be custom options at this date.

CLEVINGER JR. BASS BOY X-FORMER - 36 1/2" scale, Clevinger Arco Virtuoso pickup, rounded headstock, 2-per-side tuners. Mfg. 1997 to date.

MSR $1,295

The Clevinger Jr., first introduced in 1987, was one of the first instruments to bridge the gap between the guitar-type basses and classical string bass. The 5-pound Bass Boy model is the current interpretation of the Clevinger Jr. This model may be played in an upright position, or may be strapped on for vertical playing.

CLEVINGER BASSIC - rounded headstock, 2-per-side tuners. Current Mfg.

MSR $2,395

CLEVINGER/BENNETT - acoustic hollowed body, floating spruce top, modified scroll headstock, 2-per-side tuners. Mfg. 1996 to date.

MSR $3,595

CLEVINGER DELUXE 4 - squared headstock, 2-per-side tuners. Mfg. 1996 to date.

MSR $2,795

Clevinger Deluxe 5 - similar to the Deluxe 4, except has 5 strings and a 3/2 headstock. Current Mfg.

MSR $2,995

Clevinger Deluxe 6 - similar to the Deluxe 4, except has 6 strings and a 3-per-side headstock. Current Mfg.

MSR $3,195

CLEVINGER OPUS 4 - contoured body, scrolled headstock. Mfg. 1996 to date.

MSR $2,995

Clevinger Opus 5 - similar to the Opus 4, except has 5 string configuration, 3/2-per-side headstock. Mfg. 1996 to date.

MSR $3,195

Clevinger Opus 6 - similar to the Opus 4, except has 6-string configuration, 3-per-side headstock. Mfg. 1996 to date.

MSR $3,395

CLIFTON

Instruments currently built in Blackheath, England since 1986.

Luthier Mo Clifton became involved in instrument design as a result of shoulder problems incurred from playing a bass guitar with a heavy headstock. As a result, Clifton basses have a balanced body design and no headstock (guitar and upright models do feature headstocks). Clifton also offers full luthier services, but asks that the visits are by appointment only.

ELECTRIC BASS

Clifton's **Downright** Bass derives its name from the New York jazz bassists who often refer to their electric bass guitar as the downright as opposed to their Upright (or double bass). The 5-string model has a solid mahogany body and select hardwood top, and a choice of 34" or 36" scale. The two octave ebony fingerboard has side dot position markers, and is available fretless (with or without lines). The headless neck is reverse strung to an ABM bridge, and the customer has a choice between Bartolini or EMG pickups (and one or two).

Clifton also offers a 5-string **Piccolo Bass** model. The original inspiration began from a repaired jumbo acoustic that was restrung with five strings tuned one octave above the strings on a bass. The resulting model has a single cutaway mahogany body that is partially hollowed to form an acoustic chamber, and either a spruce or cedar top. The neck is rock maple, and the fingerboard and bridge are ebony. The Piccolo bass has a 24" scale, and is available in 4-, 5-, and 6-string configurations. A 6-string guitar model also grew out of this project, and features a choice of Kent Armstrong single coil or humbucking pickups, and Schaller hardware.

Other Clifton stringed instruments include the **Clifton Upright**, a solid body electric upright bass with scroll headstock; the **Electric Cello**, a solid body cello outfitted with a Fishman transducer; an **Alibatta Cello**, Clifton's aluminum-bodied copy of the Stradivarius Batta cello; and the 6- or 7-string **Clifton Jazz Guitar**, a semi-acoustic jazz box with a custom designed humbucking pickup.

CLOVER

Instruments currently built in Recklinghausen, Germany. Distributed in the U.S. by Clover.

Clover hand-crafts custom basses in Germany, and the company prefers to build to order to fully satisfy all serious bassists. Clover basses are high quality instruments that feature non-endangered tone wood bodies, graphite necks, and Bartolini pickups.

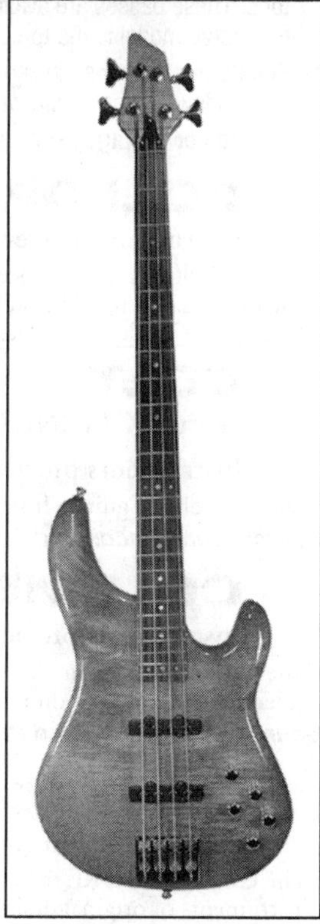

Clover Paragon Custom
courtesy Clover

ELECTRIC BASS

Avenger Series

Avenger Basses are available in both 4- and 5-string configurations. Current models have a maple body, bolt-on graphite neck, 21-fret ebonol fingerboard (86.4 cm scale), Clover tuning machines and *Quick Change* bridge, two Bartolini soapbar pickups, two-band active EQ circuit, and volume/balance/treble/bass controls. Avenger models (retail list $2,695) are finished in a durable urethane finish that feature custom colors such as simulated marble stone.

Bass-Tard Series

The **Bass-Tard 4** (list $3,195) is constructed with a solid Flame Maple body, bolt-on graphite neck (86.4 cm scale), 24-fret ebonol fingerboard, Gotoh tuning machines, Clover Special Design bridge, two Bartolini soapbar pickups, three band active EQ circuit, and volume/balance/treble/mid/bass controls. Bass-Tard models are wood-stained then finished in a high gloss.

The **Bass-Tard 5** (list $3,595) has a 5-string configuration, and is available with the 24-fret (86.4 cm scale) or the 25-fret (91.5 cm scale) neck. Either model can also be ordered in an Alder body with opaque finishes.

Slapper Series

Clover's Slapper Series features two models: The **Giant Five** 5-string (list $3,795) and the **Beelzebub** 6-string (list $3,995). Both models sport a reverse strung (no headstock) graphite neck-through-body design with select tops and backs, and the 25-fret *super long scale* 91.6 cm scale necks. Hardware is Schaller tuners and bridge, and Bartolini dual coil humbuckers. The on-board active/passive EQ is either a 2-band optimized or 3-band with parametric mid control. The **Giant 5 Bolt-On** model features a bolt-on neck, and a list price of $3,395.

Xpression Series

In 1998, Clover debuted the **Xpression** model (list $2,195). The Xpression has an offset double cutaway red alder or Swamp ash body, Canadian rock maple neck, 24-fret ebony or maple fingerboard (86.4 cm scale), 2-per-side tuners, fixed bridge, Bartolini humbucker pickup, volume/2-band EQ controls, and a white pickguard (the first Clover model to do so). The **Xpression** 5 five-string model has a retail list price of $2,495.

COBRA

See JOHN BIRCH.

Instruments previously built in England during the early 1980s.

Luthier John Birch, known for his custom guitar building, teamed up with Barry Kirby to create models under this trademark.

(Source: Tony Bacon and Paul Day, The Guru's Guitar Guide)

CODE

Instruments previously manufactured in New Jersey during the 1950s.

Luthier John D'Angelico supplied finished necks to the Code (pronounced ko-day) company for a series of plywood body guitars (Model G-7) that bear the D'Angelico trademark. The D'Angelico/Code guitars were similar in appearance to Gibson's ES-175.

(Source: Paul William Schmidt, Acquired of the Angels)

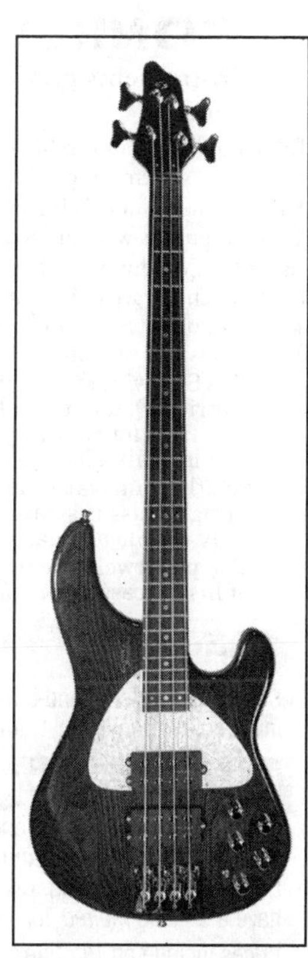

Clover Paragon Studio
courtesy Clover

COLLIER QUALITY BASSES

Instruments currently built in Belgium since 1988.

Ed Collier is currently offering a number of high quality, low quantity bass guitars. Prices range from $2,000 to $3,000.

ELECTRIC BASS

The **Collier Graphite** series feature a set-in Graphite neck, 24-fret phenol fingerboard (or Fretless) Basstec or Bartolini soapbar pickups, solid ETS hardware and a 2- or 3-band EQ. Wood choices include Olive Ash, figured Sycamore (Euopean Maple), different Mahoganies (also Pomele) or Red Alder together with a large choice of exotic or 5A selected wood for tops. These basses are available in 4-, 5-, and 6-string left/right versions. The **Standard** model features black hardware and a satin-like Polyester finish. The **Exclusive** model is the top of the line, and features rare and exotic woods, as well as the best bass components.

The **Collier Power** series are identical with the **Graphite** series, but with a wooden core and shell in and around the graphite neck (4EVER neck). This creates a wooden look and sound with the stability of graphite.

The **Collier Vintage** series are available in 4- or 5-string configurations and feels like a '62 Jazz Bass.

COLLOPY

Instruments currently built in San Francisco, California.

Luthier Rich Collopy has been building and performing repairs on guitars for the past 25 years. In the last year, Collopy opened a retail musical instrument shop in addition to his repairs and building. For further information concerning specifications and pricing, please contact luthier Collopy directly (see Trademark Index).

COLT

See also CAIRNES.

Instruments previously built in England in the late 1970s.

These solidbody guitars from the Guitarzan company were shaped like guns, and featured 2 pickups.

(Source: Tony Bacon and Paul Day, The Guru's Guitar Guide)

COLUMBUS

Instruments previously built in Japan, then manufacturing switched to Korea during the late 1960s.

The Columbus trademark was the brand name of a UK importer. Although the first models were cheap entry level guitars, subsequent Japanese-built guitars raised up to medium quality copies of American designs. The manufacturer then switched to Korean production.

(Source: Tony Bacon and Paul Day, The Guru's Guitar Guide)

COMMODORE

Instruments previously built in Japan during the late 1960s through the 1970s.

The COMMODORE trademark was the brand name of a UK importer. In an unusual switch, the Japanese-built guitars started out as cheap entry level instruments of original design and then progressed into copying American designs. To further this twist, one of the models copied was the Dan Armstrong "See-Through" lucite design!

(Source: Tony Bacon and Paul Day, The Guru's Guitar Guide)

CONCERTONE

See chapter on House Brands.

This trademark has been identified as a "House Brand" of Montgomery Wards. Instruments were built by either KAY or HARMONY.

(Source: Michael Wright, Guitar Stories Volume One)

CONKLIN

Instruments previously built in Springfield, Missouri since 1984. Distributed by Conklin Guitars of Springfield, Missouri.

Bill Conklin began producing one-of-a-kind custom instruments in 1984 after designing the **Quick Co-Necked** Double neck; a guitar and bass *component* system in which the individual instruments can be played separately or in their doubleneck configuration.

Early Conklin models incorporate traditional body styles as well as more outlandish signature models like the **Boomerang**, **Elec-trick**, or the **Shadow**. Conklin guitars were offered with many custom options, such as custom finishes and graphics, electronic packages, and fingerboard inlays.

In 1991, Conklin offered an entirely new guitar construction technique called **Melted Tops**. These 3-piece and 5-piece tops differ from the standard bookmatched variety in that they consist of different species of wood joined with virtually flawless joints. Each *Melted Top* is unique in its species selection, orientation, and grain patterns - which ensures a limitless combination of exotic tops. The *Melted Top* configuration is offered on all Session Model versions of Conklin instruments.

The Sidewinder 7-string bass was introduced in 1992, and offered such features as full stereo panning, pickup splitting, an on board parametric EQ, and the full range and versatility of up to a three octave fingerboard. Tuned from the low B to high F, the Sidewinder 7-string is perfect for chording, soloing, slap and funk styles. Currently, the Sidewinder body design is the basis for the New Century Bass series, and is available in 4- , 5-, 6-, and 7-string configurations.

Another innovative addition to the Conklin product line is the **M.E.U.** or Mobile Electric Upright bass. Introduced in 1995, this electric upright bass is strapped on like an electric bass but hangs on the body in an upright position. The *M.E.U.* can be plucked or bowed, and is fully mobile and easily transported. It's even small enough to fit the overhead compartment of most airplanes.

The past twelve years have shown tremendous growth from Bill Conklin and the staff from Conklin Guitars. Conklin credits a large part of his success to the practice of listening and catering to the wants and needs of each individual customer.

ELECTRIC

Conklin still offers hand-crafted instruments with numerous custom options. Custom instruments start at $3,600; prices vary by nature of the custom work involved. All Conklin instruments carry a limited lifetime warranty.

New Century Series Guitars

Currently, the Sidewinder and Crossover Guitar series are offered in three basic models. The **Club Model** has a solid Cherry body and no pickguard. At the next level, the **Tour Model** features a figured Maple top or a figured Maple pickguard over the Cherry body. Both Club and Tour models are available in Cellophane Blue, Cellophane Green, Cellophane Purple, Cellophane Red, and Natural in hand rubbed oil or Clearcoat finish. At the **Session Model** level, the instruments have a 3-piece *Melted Top* of Maple, Purpleheart, and Walnut over the cherry body, and are only available in a Natural finish.

Prices include an *Ultralite* case from Modern Case Company.

Add $500 for piezo bridge, gold hardware, Seymour Duncan pre-amp and 3-band EQ (Pro Package).

Add $500 for neck-through-body construction (Premium Package).

C

CROSSOVER 6-STRING - rounded single cutaway cherry body, bolt-on muti-laminated neck with tilt-back 3-per-side headstock, 25 1/2" scale, 24-fret rosewood or purpleheart fingerboard with *off-sides* dot inlays, Gotoh tuners, chrome or black hardware, straplock hardware, locking input jack. Current Mfg.

Model 101: tele-style bridge, 2 Seymour Duncan pickups, volume/tone controls, 3-way switch.

MSR (Club Model) **$1,997**
MSR (Tour Model) **$2,297**
MSR (Session Model) **$2,397**

Model 111: vintage-style fixed bridge, 3 Seymour Duncan single coil pickups, volume/tone controls, 5-way switch.

MSR (Club Model) **$1,997**
MSR (Tour Model) **$2,297**
MSR (Session Model) **$2,397**

Model 202: tune-o-matic bridge, arched top, 2 Seymour Duncan humbucking pickups, volume/tone controls, 3-way switch.

MSR (Club Model) **$2,197**
MSR (Tour Model) **$2,497**
MSR (Session Model) **$2,597**

Add $400 for Floyd Rose licensed tremolo and locking tuners (Plus Package).

Crossover 7-String - similar to the Crossover 6-string, except has a 7-string configuration, 4/3-per-side headstock, 5-piece Maple/Purpleheart laminated neck. Current Mfg.

Model 111: vintage-style fixed bridge, 3 Seymour Duncan single coil pickups, volume/tone controls, 5-way switch.

MSR (Club Model) **$2,197**
MSR (Tour Model) **$2,497**
MSR (Session Model) **$2,597**

Model 202: tune-o-matic bridge, arched top, 2 Seymour Duncan humbucking pickups, volume/tone controls, 3-way switch.

MSR (Club Model) **$2,397**
MSR (Tour Model) **$2,697**
MSR (Session Model) **$2,797**

Add $300 for 7-string non-locking tremolo and locking tuners.

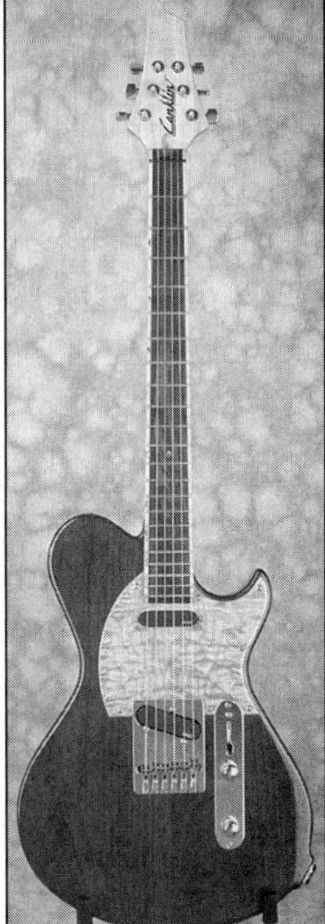

Conklin Guitar
courtesy Bill Conklin

Crossover 8-String - similar to the Crossover 6-string, except has an 8-string configuration, 4-per-side headstock, 5-piece Maple/Purpleheart laminated neck. Current Mfg.

Model 111: vintage-style fixed bridge, 3 Seymour Duncan single coil pickups, volume/tone controls, 5-way switch.

MSR (Club Model) **$2,797**
MSR (Tour Model) **$3,097**
MSR (Session Model) **$3,197**

Model 202: tune-o-matic bridge, arched top, 2 Seymour Duncan humbucking pickups, volume/tone controls, 3-way switch.

MSR (Club Model) **$2,997**
MSR (Tour Model) **$3,297**
MSR (Session Model) **$3,397**

SIDEWINDER 6-STRING - offset double cutaway asymmetrical cherry body, bolt-on muti-laminated neck with tilt-back 3-per-side headstock, 25 1/2" scale, 24-fret rosewood or purpleheart fingerboard with *off-sides* dot inlays, Gotoh tuners, chrome or black hardware, straplock hardware, locking input jack. Current Mfg.

Model 101: tele-style bridge, 2 Seymour Duncan pickups, volume/tone controls, 3-way switch.

MSR (Club Model) **$1,997**
MSR (Tour Model) **$2,297**
MSR (Session Model) **$2,397**

Model 111: vintage-style fixed bridge, 3 Seymour Duncan single coil pickups, volume/tone controls, 5-way switch.

MSR (Club Model) **$1,997**
MSR (Tour Model) **$2,297**
MSR (Session Model) **$2,397**

Model 202: tune-o-matic bridge, arched top, 2 Seymour Duncan humbucking pickups, volume/tone controls, 3-way switch.

MSR (Club Model) **$2,197**
MSR (Tour Model) **$2,497**
MSR (Session Model) **$2,597**

Add $400 for Floyd Rose licensed tremolo and locking tuners.

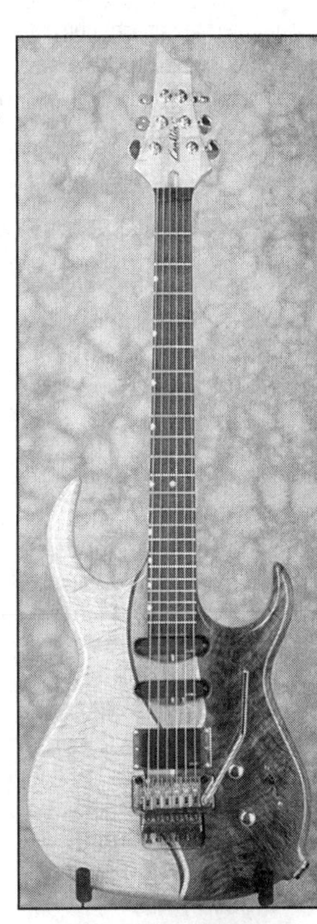

Conklin Guitar
courtesy Bill Conklin

C

Sidewinder 7 String - similar to the Sidewinder 6-string, except has a 7-string configuration, 4/3-per-side headstock, 5-piece Maple/Purpleheart laminated neck. Current Mfg.

Model 111: vintage-style fixed bridge, 3 Seymour Duncan single coil pickups, volume/tone controls, 5-way switch.

MSR (Club Model) **$2,197**
MSR (Tour Model) **$2,497**
MSR (Session Model) **$2,597**

Model 202: tune-o-matic bridge, arched top, 2 Seymour Duncan humbucking pickups, volume/tone controls, 3-way switch.

MSR (Club Model) **$2,397**
MSR (Tour Model) **$2,697**
MSR (Session Model) **$2,797**

Add $300 for 7-string non-locking tremolo and locking tuners.

Sidewinder 8 String - similar to the Sidewinder 6-string, except has an 8-string configuration, 4-per-side headstock, 5-piece Maple/Purpleheart laminated neck. Current Mfg.

Model 111: vintage-style fixed bridge, 3 Seymour Duncan single coil pickups, volume/tone controls, 5-way switch.

MSR (Club Model) **$2,797**
MSR (Tour Model) **$3,097**
MSR (Session Model) **$3,197**

Model 202: tune-o-matic bridge, arched top, 2 Seymour Duncan humbucking pickups, volume/tone controls, 3-way switch.

MSR (Club Model) **$2,997**
MSR (Tour Model) **$3,297**
MSR (Session Model) **$3,397**

Groove Tools

CGTG-7 - string, offset double cutaway solid cherry body, arched top and back, 5-piece maple/purpleheart laminated neck, 24-fret rosewood fingerboard, fixed bridge, string through-body, 2 custom humbucking pickups, 4/3 headstock configuration, 1 vol/1 push-pull tone control and coil tap switch, available in Cherry and Black finishes. Current Mfg.

MSR **$679**

CGTG -7T similar to CGTG-7, except has a non-locking tremelo and Sperzel locking tuners, available in Cherry and Black finishes. Current Mfg.

MSR **$779**

ELECTRIC BASS

New Century Series Basses

Currently, the Sidewinder Bass is offered in three different models. The **Club Model** has a solid cherry body. At the next configuration, the **Tour Model** features a figured maple top over the Cherry body. Both Club and Tour models are available in Cellophane Blue, Cellophane Green, Cellophane Purple, Cellophane Red, and Natural in hand rubbed oil or Clearcoat finish. At the **Session Model** level, the instruments have a 3-piece *Melted Top* of maple, purpleheart, and walnut over the cherry body, and are only available in a Natural finish.

Prices include an *Ultralite* case from Modern Case Company.

Add $200 for Seymour Duncan 3-band EQ (Plus Package).

Add $500 for gold hardware, piezo bridge, and Bartolini pre-amp and EQ (Pro Package).

Add $500 for neck-through-body construction (Premium Package).

SIDEWINDER BASS 4 - offset double cutaway asymmetrical cherry body, bolt-on muti-laminated neck with tilt-back 2-per-side headstock, 34" scale, 24-fret rosewood or purpleheart fingerboard with *off-sides* dot inlays, fixed bridge, Gotoh tuners, chrome or black hardware, 2 Seymour Duncan soapbar pickups, volume/blend/tone controls, straplock hardware, locking input jack. Current Mfg.

MSR (Club Model) **$2,197**
MSR (Tour Model) **$2,497**
MSR (Session Model) **$2,597**

Sidewinder Bass 5 - similar to the Sidewinder Bass 4, except has 5-string configuration, 3/2 headstock, 5-piece laminated Maple/Purpleheart necks. Current Mfg.

MSR (Club Model) **$2,397**
MSR (Tour Model) **$2,697**
MSR (Session Model) **$2,797**

Sidewinder Bass 6 - similar to the Sidewinder Bass 4, except has 6-string configuration, 3-per-side headstock, 7-piece laminated Maple/Purpleheart necks. Current Mfg.

MSR (Club Model) **$2,797**
MSR (Tour Model) **$2,997**
MSR (Session Model) **$3,197**

Sidewinder Bass 7 - similar to the Sidewinder Bass 4, except has 7-string configuration, 4/3 headstock, 7-piece laminated Maple/Purpleheart necks. Mfg. 1992 to date.

MSR (Club Model) **$2,797**
MSR (Tour Model) **$2,997**
MSR (Session Model) **$3,197**

Groove Tools

GT-4 - offset double cutaway Swamp ash body with figured maple top, 5-piece Wenge/Purpleheart laminated bolt-on neck, Purpleheart fingerboard, 2-per-side tuners, 24" scale, 24 medium/jumbo frets, Conklin active pickups, black hardware, available in Cellophane Wine or Clear Hard finishes. Current Mfg.

MSR $995

Add $100 for fretless fingerboard (Model GT-4FL).

GTRP-4 - co-designed with Rocco Prestia, 4-string special, 21-fret bolt-on neck, Sidewinder body style with Birdseye Maple pickguard, Bartolini P/J style pickups. New 2001.

MSR $1,395

GT-5 - similar to GT-4, except in a 5-string configuration, available in Cellophane Wine or Clear Hard finishes. Current Mfg.

MSR $1,095

Add $100 for fretless configuration (Model GT-5FL).

GT-7 b - similar to GT-4, except in a 7-string configuration, 7-piece Wenge/Purpleheart laminated neck, Bartolini active pickups. Available in Cellophane Wine and Clear Hard finishes. Current Mfg.

MSR $1,695

Add $100 for fretless configuration (Model GT-6FL).

GTBD-7 BILL DICKENS SIGNATURE MODEL - similar to GT-7, except has 7-piece maple/Purpleheart neck-through-body construction, gold hardware, custom bartolini pickups and electronics, available in Cellophane Purpleburst finish. Current Mfg.

MSR $2,395

M.E.U. (MOBILE ELECTRIC UPRIGHT) - cello-styled hollow swamp ash body, cherry top, bolt-on muti-laminated neck with tilt-back 2-per-side headstock, 34" scale, rosewood or ebony fingerboard, solid wood bridge and tailpiece, Gotoh tuners, removable *balance block*, chrome or black hardware, bridge mounted piezo pickups, volume/tone controls, straplock hardware. Includes custom case. Mfg. 1995 to date.

4-string

MSR $3,200

5-string

MSR $3,500

This electric upright bass is strapped on like an electric bass but hangs on the body in an upright position. Overall length is 52 inches.

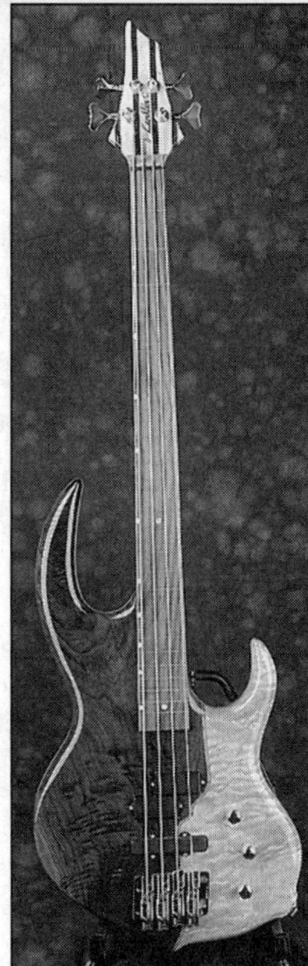

Conklin 4 String Bass
courtesy Bill Conklin

CONRAD

Instruments previously produced in Japan circa 1972 to 1978.

The Conrad trademark was a brand name used by U.S. importers David Wexler and Company of Chicago, Illinois. The Conrad product line consisted of 6- and 12-string acoustic guitars, thinline hollowbody electrics, solid body electric guitars and basses, mandolins, and banjos. Conrad instruments were produced by Kasuga International (Kasuga and Tokai USA, Inc.), and featured good quality designs specifically based on popular American designs.

(Source: Michael Wright, Guitar Stories Volume One)

CONTINENTAL

See also CONN.

Instruments previously produced in Japan.

As well as distributing the Conn guitars, the Continental Music Company of Chicago, Illinois also distributed their own brand name guitars under the Continental logo in the U.S.

(Source: Michael Wright, Guitar Stories Volume One)

COOG INSTRUMENTS

Instruments currently built in Santa Cruz, California.

Luthier Ronald Cook runs Coog Instruments as a hobby/semi-business. Cook's primary focus is on handcrafted folk instruments such as guitars and dulcimers, but has also constructed various electric guitars, hurdy-gurdies, and harpsichords through the years. Cook also performs repair work on antique or vintage stringed instruments.

Cook's building and repairs are conducted in his spare time; thus, the lead time on a custom guitar or dulcimer order is a bit longer than running down to your local "guitar club mega-gigantic store" and buying one off the wall. If patience and a custom-built folk instrument is what you're into, then please call luthier Cook directly (see Trademark Index).

CORAL

Instruments and amplifiers previously produced in Neptune City, New Jersey from 1967 to 1968 by the Danelectro Corporation. Distributed by MCA, after buying the Danelectro company and trademark.

In 1967, after MCA purchased the Danelectro Corporation, the Coral trademark was introduced. The Coral line was MCA's marketing strategy for direct wholesale selling to individual dealers, instead of Sears, Roebuck. Once the company went that route, however, they came up against competition from the larger guitar manufacturers at the dealer level. The Coral line of guitars and amplifiers was only produced for about one year.

CORT

Instruments currently produced in Inchon and Taejon, Korea; and Surabuya, Indonesia. Distributed in the U.S. by Cort Musical Instrument Company, Ltd. of Northbrook, Illinois.

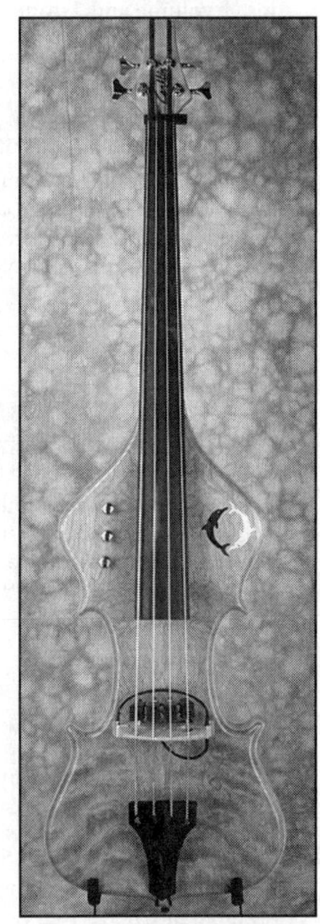

Conklin M.E.U.
courtesy Bill Conklin

GRADING	100% MINT	98% NEAR MINT	95% EXC+	90% EXC	80% VG+	70% VG	60% G

Since 1960, Cort has been providing students, beginners and mid-level guitar players quality acoustic, semi-hollow body, and solid body guitars and basses. All Cort instruments are produced in Asia in Cort company facilities, which were established in 1973. Cort is one of the few U.S. companies that owns their overseas production facilities. Cort also produces most of their own electronics (pickups, circuit boards, and other guitar parts); additional parts and custom pieces are available under the **Mightymite** trademark.

The Cort engineering and design center is located in Northbrook, Illinois. Wood is bought from the U.S. and Canada, and shipped to their production facilities in Korea. Cort instruments are then produced and assembled in the main Cort factories in Korea. After shipping the finished instruments back to the U.S., all instruments are checked in the Illinois facilities as part of quality control prior to shipping to the dealer.

In addition to their traditional designs, Cort also offers a large number of their own designs, as well as featured designs by other luthiers. Beginning in 1996, Cort began commissioning designs from noted luthier Jerry Auerswald; this lead to other designs from such noted U.S. luthiers as Jim Triggs, Bill Conklin, and Greg Curbow. Cort has also worked with guitarists Larry Coryell and Matt "Guitar" Murphy on their respective signature series models (the LCS-1 and the MGM-1).

In the mid 1980s, Cort licensed the Steinberger bridge/reverse tuner and double ball end string design for their minimalist body/headless instrument design. These Steinberger-derived models were available in both a guitar and bass model (either had a retail list price of $349). Both models featured neck-through construction, and were available in black or white finishes. The bass model had Powersound P/J-style pickups, and 2 volumes/1 tone control.

ELECTRIC

Cort's left-handed models are generally a special order, and produced in limited quantities. There is an additional $30 charge for left-handed configuration models in the current production line-up.

Hiram Bullock Series

The Cort HBS model was designed in conjunction with guitarist Hiram Bullock.

HBS - offset double cutaway light swamp ash body, birdseye hard maple neck, 25 ½" scale, 6-on-a-side tuners, rosewood fingerboard with dot position markers, 2 Mighty mite humbucking pickups and 1 Mighty mite single coil pickup, 1 Volume/1 Tone control, 5-way switch, Wilkinson VS50 II Tremelo bridge, chrome hardware, 3-Tone Sunburst finish, white pickguard. Current Mfg.

MSR $699 — $489 $385 $350 $295 $250 $195 $150

Joe Beck Signature Series

The Joe Beck Alto and Beck-6 were designed in conjunction with guitarist Joe Beck.

BECK-ALTO - single cutaway, semi-hollow body design with spruce top and flamed maple back and sides, maple neck with rosewood fingerboard and white dot inlays, 24 3/4" scale, custom made bass/treble split pickup, 2 volume and 1 tone control, toggle switch, dual jacks, special string gauge tuned A to A and incorporating a split signal allowing one to chord and play an accompanying bass line simultaneously, available in Natural Glossy and Vintage Sunburst finishes. 1999 to date.

MSR $1,195 — $825 $750 $650 $550 $450 $395 $350

BECK-6 - Joe Beck Signature Standard Model, single cutaway design, spruce top, maple back and sides, maple neck, Mightymite covered alnico pickups, 1 volume and 1-tone control, 2 uniquely shaped soundholes, available in Natural Glossy and Vintage Sunburst finishes. 1999 to date.

MSR $895 — $625 $525 $475 $425 $375 $325 $250

Larry Coryell Signature Series

The Cort **LCS-1** model was designed in conjunction with guitarist Larry Coryell.

LCS-1 - single cutaway semi-hollow bound body, spruce top, flamed maple back/sides, maple neck, 24 3/4" scale, 21-fret bound rosewood fingerboard with block inlays, bound headstock with Larry Coryell signature imprint inlay, raised pickguard, gold hardware, 3-per-side tuners, rosewood bridge/*C* trapeze tailpiece, 2 Duncan Designed humbucker pickups, 2 volume/2 tone controls, 3-way selector switch located on lower treble bout, available in Natural Glossy and Vintage Burst finishes. Natural Glossy finish disc. in 1999. Current Mfg.

MSR $1,595 — $1,125 $950 $825 $750 $595 $495 $395

LCS-II - similar to LCS-1 except has maple back and sides, Duncan designed pickups, available in Vintageburst, Natural and black finishes. New 2001

MSR $995 — $695 $595 $550 $495 $450 $395 $325

Matt "Guitar" Murphy Signature Series

The Cort **MGM-1** model was designed in conjunction with guitarist Matt "Guitar" Murphy (Blues Brothers).

MGM-1 - slightly offset double cutaway Agathis body, quilted maple top, set-in maple neck, 24 3/4" scale, 22-fret bound rosewood fingerboard with block inlays, bound headstock with abalone design inlay, gold hardware, 3-per-side tuners with white buttons, tun-o-matic bridge/stop tailpiece, 2 Mightymite humbucker pickups, volume/tone controls, 3-way selector switch, available in Amber Glossy and Transparent Purple finishes. 3-Tone Burst finish added in 1999. Current Mfg.

MSR $750 — $525 $475 $425 $376 $295 $245 $185

CL Series

CL 1500 - interesting new double cutaway body design, mahogany body with quilted maple top, chamber body with f-hole, mahogany neck with rosewood fingerboard with floral inlay pattern, set neck, 1 volume and 1 tone control, coil tap, Mightymite covered alnico humbuckers, toggle switch, Ivoroid binding, FK-1 combination bridge, gold hardware, available in Black, Cherry Sunburst and Vintage Burst finishes. 1999 to date.

MSR $995 — $695 $595 $550 $495 $450 $395 $350

CL 1400 - similar to CL1500, except has mahogany body with Flamed maple top, mahogany neck, rosewood fingerboard with split block position markers, 24 ¾" scale, 2 Mightymite covered vintage alnico humbucking pickups, 3-per-side tuners, FK-1 combination bridge, chrome hardware, available in Cherry Red Sunburst, Transparent Teal and Transparent Black finishes. New 2000.

MSR $895 — $625 $550 $495 $450 $395 $350 $295

GRADING			100% MINT	98% NEAR MINT	95% EXC+	90% EXC	80% VG+	70% VG	60% G

CL 1000 - similar to CL 1500, except does not have f-hole or chambered body, available in Transparent Blue, Transparent Red, and Cherry Sunburst finishes. 1999 to date.

MSR	$695	$485	$375	$350	$325	$275	$250	$175

CL 200 - similar to Cl 1000, except has mahogany body and mahogany bolt-on neck. Power Sound open pickups with Zebra bobbins, no binding, chrome hardware, available in Black, Transparent Blue and Transparent red finishes. 1999 to date.

MSR	$350	$250	$195	$175	$150	$125	$95	$65

G Series

G Series guitars have a offset double cutaway body, satin finished hard rock maple neck, various pickup combinations, 1-Volume/1-Tone control, 5-way switch.

G200 - agathis body, rosewood fingerboard, 3 single coil Powersound pickups, die-cast tuners, Full-Action II tremelo, available in Black, Blue, Red, Transparent Red, Transparent Blue and 2 Toneburst finishes. New 2001.

MSR	$225	$159	$125	$110	$95	$80	$65	$50

Add $10 for Transparent finishes and 2 Toneburst finish.
Add $35 for left-hand model (G200L).

G205 -similar to G200 except, has maple fingerboard, available in Red and Blue finishes. New 2001.

MSR

G210 - similar to G200 except, has 1 Powersound humbucking pickup and 2 Powersound single coil pickups, available in Black, Blue, Red, Transparent Blue, Transparent Red and 2 Toneburst finishes. New 2001

MSR	$259	$179	$150	$125	$95	$75	$55	$35

G250 - similar to G200 except, has basswood body, 1 Mighty mite humbucking pickup and 2 Mighty mite single coil pickups, Wilkinson VS50 II bridge, available in 2 Toneburst, Transparent Red and Transparent Blue finishes. New 2001.

MSR	$350	$245	$195	$150	$125	$95	$75	$50

G255 - similar to G250 exept, has Select by EMG pickups, available in Amber Stain, Walnut Stain, Bordeaux Red Metallic and Grey Nickel finishes. New 2001.

G260 - similar to G200 except has Light Swamp ash body, 3 Duncan Designed Hot Rail pickups, Wilkinson VS50 II bridge, available in Transparent Black, Natural and Honeyburst finishes. New 2001.

G270 - similar to G200 except, has light swamp ash body with flamed maple top, 1 Duncan Designed humbucking pickup and 2 Duncan Designed single coil pickups. Wilkinson VS50 II bridge, available in 3 Toneburst and Vintagevurst finishes. New 2001.

MSR	$595	$415	$375	$350	$295	$250	$225	$195

G290 - similar to G200 except, has light swamp ash body with quilted maple top, carved top, Seymour Duncan JB and Vintage staggered pickups, Sperzel Trim-Lok tuners, Wilkinson VS50 II bridge, available in Antique Violinburst and Cherry Red Sunburst finishes. New 2001.

MSR	$995	$695	$595	$550	$495	$450	$395	$350

JC Series

The three JC Series guitar models were introduced in 1998 and discontinued in 2001. Models include the **JC 2** (Last MSR was $269), **JC 3** (Last MSR was $259), and the **JC 4** (Last MSR was $279).

Luthite Series (Formerly EF Series)

Luthite series guitars feature Cort's patented *Environmentally Friendly* body material. The **JA 30** model is designed by Jerry Auerswald (Auerswald Guitars).

JA30 - offset double cutaway *EF (Luthite)* body, bolt-on hard maple neck, 25 1/2" scale, 22-fret rosewood fingerboard with offset dot inlays, chrome hardware, reverse headstock, 6-on-the-other-side side chrome tuners, Accutune II tremolo bridge, 2 single coil/1 humbucker Mightymite pickups, volume/tone controls, 5-way position switch, available in Atlantic Blue Metallic and Black finishes. Mfg. 1997-1999.

		$325	$275	$250	$225	$175	$150	$125

Last MSR was $450.

Mirage Series

MIRAGE 500 - offset double cutaway mahogany body, mahogany neck, 24 ¾" scale, rosewood fingerboard with dot position markers, 3-per-side tuners, 2 Mightymite covered vintage alnico humbucking pickups, 1 Volume/1-Tone control, 3-way switch, Tune-O-Matic bridge, chrome hardware, available in Bordeaux Red Metallic and Deep Blue Metallic finishes. New 2000.

MSR	$395	$275	$250	$225	$195	$175	$150	$125

Mirage 600 - similar to Mirage 500, except has bound top, available in Honeyburst and Antique Violin Dark finishes. New 2001.

MSR	$595	$425	$375	$325	$295	$250	$225	$175

GRADING	100% MINT	98% NEAR MINT	95% EXC+	90% EXC	80% VG+	70% VG	60% G

C

Mirage 700 - similar to Mirage 500 except, has Wilkinson VS50 II Tremelo bridge, gold hardware, available in Cherry Red Sunburst finish. Mfg. 2000 Only.

		$595	$495	$450	$425	$395	$350	$295

Last MSR was $850.

Performer Series

IMPALA - offset double cutaway Agathis body, bolt-on hard rock maple neck, 25 1/2" scale, 22-fret maple fingerboard with black dot inlay, vintage style tremolo, 6-on-a-side natural wood headstock, chrome hardware, white pickguard, 3 single coil Mightymite pickups, volume/2 tone controls, 5-way selector switch, available in 2-Tone Burst, Black, Gold Metallic, and Ivory finishes. Disc. 1999.

		$225	$195	$175	$150	$125	$100	$75

Last MSR was $299.

STATURE - similar to the Impala, except has rosewood fingerboard with white dot inlays, Accutune II tremolo, roller nut, black pickguard, 2 single coil/1 humbucker Mightymite pickups, available in Amber Burst, Black, See-Through Black, and See-Through Blue finishes. Disc. 1999.

		$325	$275	$250	$225	$175	$150	$125

Last MSR was $450.

Stature Gold - similar to the Stature, except has Wilkinson VS-50K tremolo, pearloid pickguard, and gold hardware, available in See-Through Black and Vintage Burst finishes. Disc. 1999.

		$350	$295	$275	$225	$195	$175	$125

Last MSR was $450.

In 1998, Amber Glossy and Black finishes were introduced; See-Through Black and Vintage Burst finishes were discontinued.

MEGA STANDARD - similar to the Stature, except features flamed maple top, white pickguard, gold hardware, 2 single coil/1 humbucker Select by EMG pickups, available in Amber Glossy, Blue Burst, Crimson Burst, and See-Through Black finishes. Disc. 1999

		$395	$325	$295	$250	$225	$175	$150.

Last MSR was $550

JC 65 - offset double cutaway slim-waisted Agathis body, bolt-on hard rock maple neck, 25 1/2" scale, 21-fret rosewood fingerboard with white dot inlay, bigsby-style JC tremolo, 6-on-a-side natural wood headstock, chrome hardware, white pickguard, 3 single coil Mightymite pickups, volume/2 tone controls, 5-way selector switch, available in Black, Foam Green, Shell Pink, and 2-Tone Burst finishes. Mfg. 1997 to 1998.

		$350	$300	$275	$225	$195	$150	$125

Last MSR was $500.

JC 67 - similar to the JC 65, available in Pink Sparkle and Silver Sparkle finishes. Mfg. 1998 to 1999.

		$275	$250	$225	$195	$150	$125	$100

Last MSR was $399.

VIVA GOLD - offset double cutaway contoured maple body, bolt-on hard rock maple neck, 25 1/2" scale, 24-fret rosewood fingerboard with offset white dot inlay, Lo-Pro Floyd Rose licensed tremolo, 6-on-a-side black headstock, chrome hardware, Mightymite humbucker/single coil/humbucker pickups, volume/tone controls, 5-way selector switch, available in Black, Natural Satin, Red Metallic, and Vintage Burst finishes. Disc. 1998.

		$525	$450	$395	$350	$275	$225	$195

Last MSR was $750.

Viva Gold II - similar to the Viva Gold, except features white silver hardware, available in Natural Stain and Walnut Stain finishes. Mfg. 1998 to date.

MSR	$650	$495	$425	$375	$325	$275	$225	$175

Solo Series

The Solo Series models feature a sleek *superstrat* style body, and slightly more exaggerated horns than the Performer Series models.

SOLO FA - offset double cutaway Agathis body, bolt-on hard rock maple neck, 25 1/2" scale, 24-fret rosewood fingerboard with offset white dot inlay, Full Action II tremolo, 6-on-a-side black headstock, chrome hardware, 2 single coil/1 humbucker Power Sound pickups, volume/tone controls, 5-way selector switch, available in Black, Blue Metallic, and Red Metallic finishes. Mfg. 1997 to 1999.

		$225	$175	$150	$125	$115	$95	$75

Last MSR was $289.

Solo WK - similar to the Solo FA, except has Wilkinson VS-50K tremolo, 2 Mightymite humbuckers, 3-way pickup selector, available in Black and Crimson Burst finishes. Mfg. 1997-1999

		$300	$275	$250	$200	$175	$150	$100

Last MSR was $429

Solo QM - similar to Solo FA, except has quilted mahogany top, Mightymite pickups, one volume switch, one tone switch with coil tap, 5-position switch, Floyd Rose licensed LO-PRO tremoloe, available in Transparent Red and Transparent Blue finishes. New 1999.

MSR	$599	$449	$375	$350	$325	$300	$275	$225

Solo SL - similar to the Solo FA, except has a maple fingerboard, FR III-S licensed Floyd Rose double locking tremolo, 2 Mightymite humbuckers, 3-way pickup selector, available in Black, Blue Metallic, and Red Metallic finishes. Disc. 2000.

		$335	$275	$250	$225	$195	$150	$125

Last MSR was $479.

Solo VS - similar to Solo FA, except has Wilkinson VS10 bridge, available in black, Blue Metallic and Red Metallic finishes. New 2001.

MSR	$289	$200	$165	$135	$95	$75	$50	$35

GRADING	100% MINT	98% NEAR MINT	95% EXC+	90% EXC	80% VG+	70% VG	60% G

Solo FR - similar to the Solo FA, except has Lo-Pro licensed Floyd Rose double locking tremolo, Mightymite humbucker/single coil/humbucker pickups, 5-way pickup selector, available in Black and Blue Metallic finishes. Disc. 1998.

	$450	$395	$350	$300	$250	$200	$150

Last MSR was $650.

S Series

Prior **S** Series models may be designated as **Sterling** or **Starlite** on the headstock.

S400 - sleek offset double cutaway Agathis body, bolt-on hard rock maple neck, 25 1/2" scale, 22-fret rosewood fingerboard with offset dot inlay, vintage style Full Action II tremolo, 3-per-side natural wood headstock, chrome hardware, white pickguard, 3 single coil Power Sound pickups, volume/2 tone controls, 5-way selector switch, available in Black, Foam Green, See-Through Red, and Shell Pink finishes. Mfg. 1997 to date.

MSR $269	$195	$175	$150	$125	$110	$95	$75

In 1998, See-through Blue finish was introduced.

S500 - similar to the S400, except has 2 single coil/humbucker Powersound pickups, volume/tone controls, available in Black, Foam Green, See-Through Blue, and See-Through Red finishes. Mfg. 1998 to 2000.

	$200	$175	$150	$125	$110	$95	$75

Last MSR was $279.

S2100 - similar to the S400, except has black headstock with silk screened logo, 2 single coil/1 humbucking Mightymite pickups, volume/tone controls, available in Black, Red Metallic, and White finishes. Mfg. 1997 to 1998.

	$275	$250	$200	$175	$150	$125	$100

Last MSR was $399.

S1000 - similar to the S400, except has mahogany body, black headstock with silk screened logo, fixed bridge, no pickguard, 2 Mightymite humbuckers, volume/tone controls, 3-way selector, available in Black and Cherry Red Sunburst finishes. Disc. 1999.

	$250	$225	$200	$175	$150	$125	$95

Last MSR was $359.

S2000 - similar to the S1000, except has maple fingerboard, natural wood headstock, Full Action II tremolo, 2 single coil/humbucking Mightymite pickups, 5-way selector switch, available in Black, Crimson Burst, and Walnut Satin finishes. Disc. 1998.

	$275	$250	$200	$175	$150	$125	$100

Last MSR was $399.

S2500 - similar to the S1000, except has maple body, Wilkinson VS-50K tremolo, 2 single coil/1 humbucking Mightymite pickups, 5-way selector switch, available in Amber Satin, Black, Cherry Red, and Oil Satin finishes. Mfg. 1996 to 1999.

	$325	$275	$250	$225	$195	$150	$125

Last MSR was $449.

S2500 M - similar to the S2500, except has mahogany body, available in Cherry Red and Oil Satin finishes. Mfg. 1996 to 1998.

	$350	$300	$275	$225	$200	$175	$125

Last MSR was $499.

S2550 - similar to S2500, except has soft maple body, hard maple neck, Mighty Mite pickups, one volume and one tone control, coil tap, 5-way switch, Wilkinson VS50K tremolo, available in Amber Satin, Walnut Satin and Vintage Burst finishes. Current Mfg.

MSR $429	$299	$250	$225	$200	$175	$150	$100

S2600 - similar to S2500, except has soft maple body, hard maple neck, Dincan designed hot rails, one volume and one tone switch, coil tap, 5-way switch, Wilkinson VS50K tremolo, available in Transparent Blue, Transparent Red and Vintage Burst finishes. Current Mfg.

MSR $499	$375	$325	$300	$250	$200	$175	$125

S2800 - similar to the S2500, except has maple body/quilted maple top, white pearloid pickguard, 2 single coil/humbucker Seymour Duncan pickups, satin gold hardware, available in Amber Satin, Walnut Stain, and Vintage Burst finishes. Mfg. 1998 to date.

MSR $795	$575	$495	$450	$375	$300	$250	$200

S2900 - similar to S2500, except has quilted maple top, arched body top, hard maple neck, has Seymour Duncan SSL-1 and TB-4 pickups, one volume control and one tone control with coil tap. Wilkinson VS50K tremolo and Sperzel Trimlok tuners, available in Cherry Red Sunburst and Blue Burst finishes. New 1999.

MSR $850	$595	$525	$465	$420	$375	$300	$250

S3000 - similar to the S2500, except has basswood body, Lo-Pro licensed Floyd Rose double locking tremolo system, Mightymite humbucker/single coil/humbucker pickups, available in Black, Blue Metallic, and See-Through Red finishes. Disc. 1998.

	$425	$350	$300	$275	$225	$175	$150

Last MSR was $590.

In 1997, See-Through Red finish was discontinued.

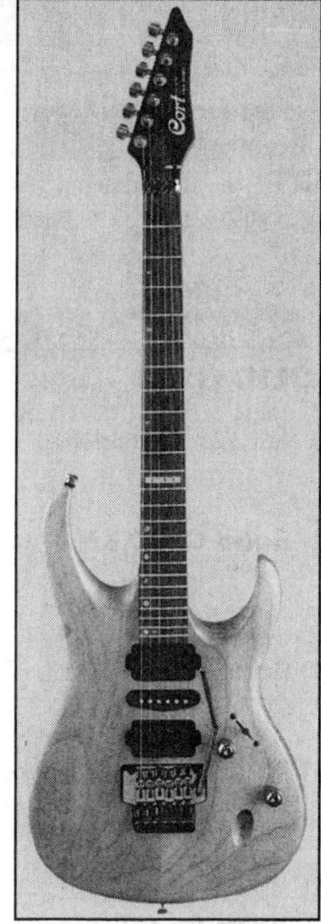

Cort Viva Gold
courtesy Cort

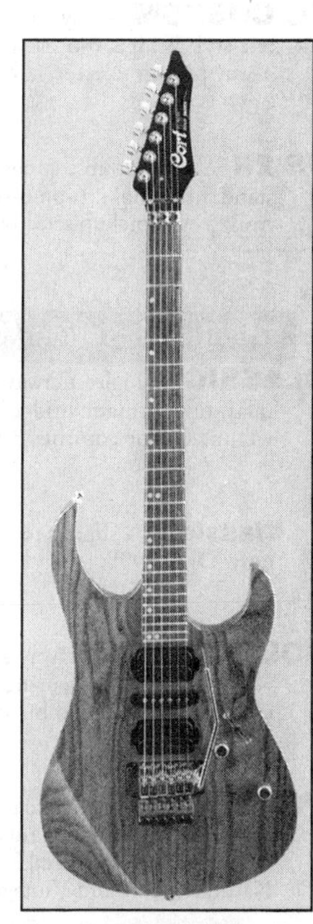

Cort Solo (Ash)
courtesy Cort

GRADING	100% MINT	98% NEAR MINT	95% EXC+	90% EXC	80% VG+	70% VG	60% G

C

Space Series

G3T - headless design licensed by Steinberger, maple body, hard maple neck, rosewood fingerboard, EMG Select pickups, one volume and one tone control, three mini toggles, available in black. Disc. 1999.

$425 $400 $350 $325 $300 $250 $200
Last MSR was $599.

Standard Series

SOLID G100 - single cutaway arched Agathis body, bolt-on hard rock maple neck, 24 3/4" scale, 22-fret rosewood fingerboard with white dot inlay, tune-o-matic bridge/stop tailpiece, 3-per-side black headstock, raised black pickguard, chrome hardware, 2 Power Sound humbucker pickups, 2 volume/2 tone controls, 3-way pickup selector, available in Black and Cherry Red finishes. Disc. 2000.

$250 $200 $175 $150 $125 $110 $95
Last MSR was $349.

Solid G100 LH - similar to the Solid G100, except in left-handed configuration, available in Black and Cherry Red Sunburst finishes. Disc. 1999.

$275 $225 $195 $175 $150 $125 $95
Last MSR was $379.

Solid G50 - Details of this model unknown by publishing date of this edition. Mfg. 1999 to 2000.

$175 $150 $125 $95 $75 $65 $50
Last MSR was $250.

STAT 2T - offset double cutaway Agathis body, bolt-on hard rock maple neck, 25 1/2" scale, 22-fret maple fingerboard with black dot inlay, vintage style Full Action II tremolo, 6-on-a-side natural wood headstock, chrome hardware, white pickguard, 3 Power Sound single coil pickups, volume/2 tone controls, 5-way selector switch, available in 2-Tone Burst, Black, Foam Green, Ivory, Red, and Shell Pink finishes. Disc. 1999.

$175 $150 $135 $115 $100 $85 $65
Last MSR was $239.

STAT 2T LH - similar to the Stat 2T, except in left-handed configuration, available in Black finish only. Disc. 1999.

$195 $175 $155 $135 $115 $95 $75
Last MSR was $269.

STAT 3T - similar to the Stat 2T, except has rosewood fingerboard with white dot inlay, 2 single coil/humbucker Power Sound pickups, available in 2-Tone Burst, Black, Ivory, and Red finishes. Disc. 1999.

$175 $150 $135 $115 $100 $85 $65
Last MSR was $259.

In 1998, See-Through Red finish was introduced; Ivory and Red finishes were discontinued.

TC CUSTOM - single cutaway Agathis body, bolt-on hard rock maple neck, 25 1/2" scale, 22-fret maple fingerboard with black dot inlay, 6-saddle tele-style bridge, 6-on-a-side natural wood headstock, chrome hardware, white pickguard, 2 Power Sound single coil pickups, volume/tone controls, 3-way pickup selector, chrome control plate, available in Black and Ivory finishes. Disc. 1998.

$195 $175 $150 $125 $115 $95 $75
Last MSR was $280.

VS 2R - offset double cutaway Agathis body, bolt-on hard rock maple neck, 25 1/2" scale, 22-fret rosewood fingerboard with black dot inlay, vintage standard tremolo, 6-on-a-side natural wood headstock, chrome hardware, white pickguard, 3 Power Sound single coil pickups, volume/2 tone controls, 5-way pickup selector, available in 2-Tone Burst, Black, and Ivory finishes. Mfg. 1998.

$195 $150 $135 $115 $100 $85 $65
Last MSR was $269.

Traditional Series

CLASSIC - single cutaway mahogany body, arched maple top, set-in mahogany neck, 24 3/4" scale, 22-fret rosewood fingerboard with white block inlay, tune-o-matic bridge/stop tailpiece, 3-per-side black headstock, gold hardware, raised pickguard, 2 covered Mightymite humbucker pickups, 2 volume/2 tone controls, 3-way pickup selector, available in Black and Cherry Red Sunburst finishes. Disc. 1999.

$495 $425 $375 $325 $275 $225 $175
Last MSR was $695.

Classic II - similar to the Classic, except has 2 exposed Mightymite humbuckers and chrome hardware, available in Cherry Red Sunburst finish only. Disc. 1998.

$495 $425 $375 $325 $275 $225 $175
Last MSR was $699.

SOURCE - dual cutaway semi-hollow bound body, maple top, maple back/sides, maple neck, 24 3/4" scale, 20-fret bound rosewood fingerboard with block inlays, fleur-de-lis/*Source* headstock inlay, raised pickguard, gold hardware, 3-per-side tuners, tune-o-matic bridge/stop tailpiece, 2 covered Mightymite humbucker pickups, 2 volume/2 tone controls, 3-way selector switch, available in Black and Vintage Burst finishes. Disc. 1998.

$595 $500 $450 $395 $325 $275 $225
Last MSR was $850.

YORKTOWN - single cutaway semi-hollow bound body, spruce top, flamed maple back/sides, maple neck, 24 3/4" scale, 20-fret bound rosewood fingerboard with block inlays, fleur-de-lis/*Yorktown* headstock inlay, raised black pickguard, gold hardware, 3-per-side tuners, rosewood bridge/*C* trapeze tailpiece, 2 covered Mightymite humbucker pickups, 2 volume/2 tone controls, 3-way selector switch located on lower treble bout, available in Natural Glossy and Vintage Burst finishes. Disc. 1998

$700 $595 $525 $450 $395 $325 $250
Last MSR was $995.

GRADING	100% MINT	98% NEAR MINT	95% EXC+	90% EXC	80% VG+	70% VG	60% G

Jim Triggs Signature Series

The Cort **TRG** model was designed in conjunction with luthier/designer Jim Triggs. Triggs has been building hand crafted instruments in his Nashville, Tennessee shop for the past 25 years.

TRG-1 - single sharp cutaway semi-hollow bound body, maple top, maple back/sides, 2 cat's-eye f-holes, set-in maple neck, 24 3/4" scale, 22-fret bound rosewood fingerboard, bound headstock with 'Triggs' signature imprint inlay, gold hardware, 3-per-side tuners with white buttons, rosewood bridge/trapeze tailpiece, Mightymite humbucker pickup, volume/tone controls, available in Robin's Egg Blue and See-Through Orange finishes. Mfg. 1998 to 2000.

		$500	$450	$395	$350	$275	$225	$175

Last MSR was $699.

TRG-2 - similar to TRG-1 except in a two pickup configuration, maple top, sides and back, 24 ¾" scale, maple neck, 2 Mightymite covered vintage alnico humbucking pickups, 2 cat's eye f-holes, "C" vibrato bridge, gold hardware, 3-per-side tuners, available in black and Transparent Orange finishes. New 2000.

MSR	$895	$625	$550	$475	$395	$325	$250	$195

TRG-CHAMBER - offset double cutaway, agathis top, back and sides, maple neck, rosewood fingerboard with dot position markers, 3-per-side tuners, 24 ¾" scale, 2 Powersound pickups, Tune-O-Matic bridge, chrome hardware, available in black and Robin's Egg Blue finishes. New 2000.

MSR	$350	$245	$195	$165	$135	$99	$75	$40

X Series

X GUITAR - dual cutaway Agathis body, bolt-on hard rock maple neck, 24 3/4" scale, 22-fret rosewood fingerboard with white dot inlay, wrap-around stop tailpiece, blackface headstock, 3-per-side tuners, chrome hardware, 2 Power Sound Humbucker pickups, 2 volume/2 tone controls, 3-way pickup selector, available in Black, Cherry Red Sunburst, and Ivory finishes. Mfg. 1998 to 1999.

		$195	$150	$135	$115	$100	$85	$65

Last MSR was $269.

X-2 - offset double cutaway basswood body, bolt-on hard rock maple neck, 2 Powersound humbucking pickups, 6-on-a-side die-cast tuners, Full-Action II tremelo bridge, available in Black, Red Metallic and Blue Metallic finishes. New 2001.

MSR	$259	$185	$150	$125	$95	$75	$50	$30

X-6 - similar to X-2 except, has 2 Mightymite humbucking pickups and 1 Mightymite single coil pickup, Floyd Rose Licensed SL tremelo bridge, available in Black, Iron Pruple Metallic and Blue Violet Metallic finishes. New 2001.

MSR	$380	$265	$225	$195	$175	$150	$125	$95

X-7 - similar to X-2 except, in a 7-string configuration, 3-piece hard maple neck, 2 Mightymite 7 humbucking pickups, Full-Action II-7 tremelo bridge, available in Black and Iron Purple Metallic finishes. New 2001.

MSR	$350	$245	$215	$175	$150	$125	$95	$65

X-9 - similar to X-2 except, has 2 Mightymite humbucking pickups and 1 Mightymite single coil pickup, Floyd Rose Licensed Lo-Pro tremelo bridge, available in Black, Iron Purple Metallic and Blue Violet Metallic finishes. New 2001.

MSR	$590	$415	$350	$295	$250	$225	$195	$165

X-CUSTOM - similar to X-2 except, has American Basswood body, custom-made neck, bolt-on hard rock maple neck, Seymour Duncan JB and Jazz pickups, Floyd Rose Liccensed Lo-Pro tremelo bridge, available in Black Metallic finish. New 2001.

MSR	$995	$695	$595	$550	$495	$450	$395	$295

ELECTRIC BASS

BILLY COX FREEDOM BASS - offset double cutaway ashwood body, maple neck, 34" scale, rosewood fingerboard with block position markers, 4-on-a-side tuners, 3 custom made single coil pickups, stacked volume and tone knobs, active to passive control, EB74 bridge, chrome hardware, available in 3-Tone Sunburst, white and black finishes. Current Mfg.

MSR	$750	$525	$450	$395	$350	$295	$250	$175

Artisan Bass Series

The **Artisan Bass** Series models are very similar to prior **C M Artist** Series models (the block inlay at 12th fret on those models read *C M Artist.*)

ARTISAN A4 - offset double cutaway select maple body, through-body wenge/maple laminated neck, 34" scale, 24-fret rosewood fingerboard with offset dot inlays, *Artisan* block inlay on 24th fret, black headstock, fixed bridge, gold hardware, squared headstock, 2-per-side tuners, 2 Mightymite soapbar pickups, 2 volume/2 tone controls, active electronics, available in Natural Satin, See-Through Red, and Walnut Stain finishes. Mfg. 1996 to 2000.

		$625	$550	$495	$425	$350	$295	$225

Last MSR was $895.

GRADING			100% MINT	98% NEAR MINT	95% EXC+	90% EXC	80% VG+	70% VG	60% G

C

Artisan A5 - similar to the Artisan A4, except in 5-string configuration and 2/3-per-side headstock, available in Amber Glossy, Natural Satin, and See-Through Red finishes. Mfg. 1996 to 2000.

$695 $595 $525 $475 $395 $325 $250

Last MSR was $995.

Artisan A6 - similar to the Artisan A4, except in 6-string configuration and 3-per-side headstock, available in Natural Satin and See-Through Blue finishes. Mfg. 1996 to 2000.

$775 $695 $625 $525 $450 $375 $275

Last MSR was $1,095.

In 1998, See-Through Red finish was introduced; See-Through Blue finish was discontinued.

ARTISAN B4 - similar to the Artisan A4, except features a bolt-on wenge neck, natural wenge headstock, and black hardware, available in Amber Glossy, Natural Satin, Vintage Burst and Walnut Satin finishes. Current Mfg.

MSR $695 $500 $425 $375 $325 $275 $225 $175

Artisan B4 FL - similar to the Artisan B4, except has fretless fingerboard, available in Amber Satin and Vintage Burst finishes. Mfg. 1997 to 2000.

$575 $475 $425 $375 $300 $250 $200

Last MSR was $795.

In 1998, Walnut Stain finish was introduced; Amber Satin and Vintage Burst finishes were discontinued.

Artisan B5 - similar to the Artisan B4, except in 5-string configuration, 2/3-per-side tuners, available in Natural Satin, Vintage Burst, and Walnut Satin finishes. Current Mfg.

MSR $850 $595 $500 $450 $395 $325 $275 $225

In 1998, Amber Satin and Vintage Burst finishes were introduced; Natural Satin, Vintage Burst, and Walnut Satin finishes were discontinued.

Artisan B5 FL - similar to the Artisan B5, except has fretless fingerboard, available in Amber Satin and Vintage Burst finishes. Mfg. 1997 to 2000.

$625 $550 $475 $425 $350 $295 $225

Last MSR was $895.

In 1998, Natural Satin and Walnut Satin were introduced; Amber Satin finish was discontinued.

Artisan B6 - similar to the Artisan B4, except in 6-string configuration, 3-per-side tuners, available in Oil Satin and Walnut Satin finishes. Disc.1999.

MSR $950 $695 $575 $500 $450 $375 $325 $250

Last MSR was $950.

In 1998, Vintage Burst finish was introduced; Walnut Satin finish was discontinued.

ARTISAN C4 - offset double cutaway Agathis body, bolt-on hard rock maple neck, 34" scale, 24-fret rosewood fingerboard with offset dot inlays, black squared headstock, fixed bridge, chrome hardware, 2-per-side tuners, 2 Mightymite soapbar pickups, volume/blend/tone controls, available in Amber Satin and Black finishes. Disc. 1999.

MSR $495 $375 $300 $275 $225 $195 $150 $125

Last MSR was $495.

In 1998, Blue Metallic and See-Through Red finishes were introduced; Amber Satin finish was discontinued.

Artisan C5 - similar to the Artisan C4, except in a 5-string configuration, 2/3-per-side tuners, available in Black finish only. Disc. 1999.

MSR $595 $425 $375 $325 $275 $250 $195 $150

Last MSR was $595.

Artisan NA4 - offset double cutaway body, neck-through-body, Wenge/Maple combinition neck, 34" scale, 2 Bartolini MK1 pickups, active EQ, Fortress bridge, platinum hardware, 2-per-side tuners, available in Natural, Transparent Red and Transparent Teal finishes. New 2000.

MSR $950 $665 $550 $495 $450 $395 $350 $295

Artisan NA5 - similar to Artisan NA4, except in a 5-string configuration, available in Natural, Transparent Red and Transparent Teal finishes. New 2000.

MSR $995 $695 $575 $525 $475 $425 $375 $325

Artisan NA6 - similar to Artisan NA4, except in a 6-string configuration, 3-per-side tuners, available in Natural and Transparent red finishes. New 2000.

MSR $1,095 $765 $675 $575 $49 $425 $375 $325

Artisan NB4 - offset double cutaway basswood body, Wenge neck, 34" scale, 2 Bartolini MK1 pickups, active EQ, Fortress Bridge, black hardware, available in Bordeaux Red Metallic, Deep Blue Metallic, Grey Nickel and Walnut Stain finishes. New 2000.

MSR $750 $525 $425 $375 $325 $275 $225 $175

Artisan NB5 - similar to Artisan NB4, except in a 5-string configuration, available in Bordeaux Red Metallic, Deep Blue Metallic and Walnut Stain finishes. New 2000.

MSR $850 $595 $495 $450 $395 $350 $295 $250

Luthite Series (EF Series)

Luthite series basses feature Cort's patented *Environmentally Friendly* body material. Luthite series basses are designed in conjunction with Jerry Auerswald (Auerswald Guitars) and Greg Curbow (Curbow Custom Basses).

C

GRADING		100% MINT	98% NEAR MINT	95% EXC+	90% EXC	80% VG+	70% VG	60% G

CURBOW 4 - slimmed down offset double cutaway luthite body, bolt-on hard rock maple neck, 34" scale, 24-fret ebanol fingerboard with white dot inlays, 2-per-side die cast tuners, fixed bridge, chrome hardware, Mightymite humbucker pickup, volume/treble/mid/bass controls, available in Lake Placid Blue and Red Metallic finishes. Mfg. 1998 to date.

MSR	$695	$485	$425	$375	$325	$275	$225	$150

Add $55 for Burled Walnut finish.

Add $100 for fretless configuration. (CURBOW 4FL).

This model was designed by Greg Curbow (Curbow Custom Basses).

Curbow 5 - similar to the Curbow 4, except features a 5-string configuration, 3/2-per-side tuners. Mfg. 1998 to date.

MSR	$795	$550	$475	$395	$350	$295	$245	$185

Add $55 for Burled Walnut finish.

Add $55 for fretless configuration (CURBOW 5FL).

This model was designed by Greg Curbow (Curbow Custom Basses).

EFVB1 - violin-shaped *EF (luthite)* body, bolt-on hard rock maple neck, 32" scale, 22-fret rosewood fingerboard with dot inlay, fixed bridge, chrome hardware, 2 on a side squared headstock, chrome tuners, 2 Mightymite pickups, volume/blend/tone controls on black control plate, available in Black finish only. Mfg. 1997-1998.

		$295	$250	$225	$195	$150	$125	$100

Last MSR was $399.

This model was designed by Jerry Auerswald (Auerswald Guitars).

JAB 70 - offset double cutaway *EF (luthite)* body, bolt-on hard rock maple neck, 34" scale, 24-fret rosewood fingerboard with offset dot inlays, fixed bridge, chrome hardware, reverse headstock, 4-on-the-other-side chrome tuners, P/J-style Select by EMG pickups, volume/blend/tone controls, available in Atlantic Blue Metallic and Black finishes. Mfg. 1997-1998.

		$350	$295	$250	$225	$195	$150	$125

Last MSR was $450.

This model was designed by Jerry Auerswald (Auerswald Guitars).

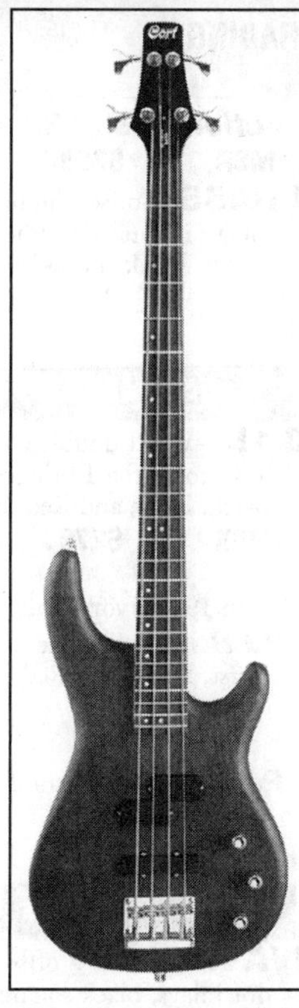

Cort Action Bass Ash
courtesy Cort

S Bass Series

SB10 - sleek offset double cutaway Agathis body, bolt-on hard rock maple neck, 34" scale, 22-fret rosewood fingerboard with white dot inlay, vintage style fixed bridge, natural wood headstock, 2-per-side tuners, chrome hardware, white pickguard, Mightymite humbucker pickup, volume/tone controls, available in Black, Foam Green, and See-Through Red finishes. Mfg. 1998 to date.

MSR	$299	$225	$195	$175	$150	$125	$100	$75

SB70 - similar to SB10 except, has soft maple body, alnico bass humbucker pickup, active EQ, black hardware, available in Amber Stain, Walnut Stain and Vintage Burst finishes. Current Mfg.

MSR	$550	$385	$350	$295	$250	$225	$195	$150

Space Series

B2A - headless bass design licensed by Steinberger, maple body, hard maple neck, rosewood fingerboard, 34" scale, EMG/Select pickups, two volume and one tone control with active EQ, one mini-toggle switch, available in Black finish. Disc. 1999.

		$450	$375	$325	$300	$275	$225	$195

Last MSR was $599.

B2AV - similar to B2A, only in a 5-string model with Mightymite bass humbucker pickups, Steinberger 5-String bridge, available in Black finish. Disc. 1999.

		$525	$475	$425	$400	$375	$325	$295

Last MSR was $695.

Standard Series Basses

ACTION BASS - offset double cutaway Agathis body, bolt-on hard rock maple neck, 34" scale, 24-fret rosewood fingerboard with offset dot inlays, black squared headstock, fixed bridge, chrome hardware, 2-per-side tuners, 2 Power Sound P/J-style pickups, volume/blend/tone controls, available in Black, See-Through Blue, and See-Through Red finishes. Current Mfg.

MSR	$299	$200	$185	$165	$145	$125	$95	$65

In 2000, Walnut Stain finish was introduced.

Action Bass V (Also Action Bass 5) - similar to the Action Bass, except in 5-string configuration, 2/3-per-side tuners, 2 Power Sound J- style pickups, available in Black and See-Through Red finishes. Current Mfg.

MSR	$389	$295	$250	$225	$195	$150	$125	$100

In 2000, Walnut Stain finish was introduced.

Action Bass Ash - similar to the Action Bass, except features a swamp ash body, gold hardware, available in Natural Satin and Padauk Satin finishes. Disc. 1998.

		$425	$375	$325	$275	$225	$195	$150

Last MSR was $600.

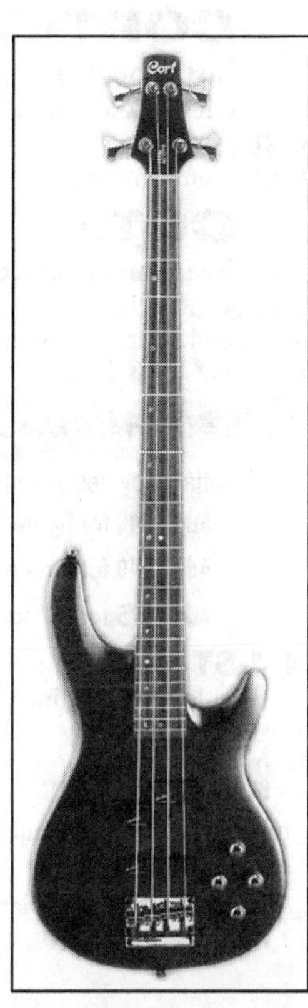

Cort Viva Active Bass
courtesy Cort

GRADING			100% MINT	98% NEAR MINT	95% EXC+	90% EXC	80% VG+	70% VG	60% G

C

Action Bass LH - similar to Action Bass, only in a left-handed version, available in Walnut Stain finish. Current Mfg.

MSR	$369	$295	$250	$200	$175	$150	$125	$100

JJ BASS - offset double cutaway slim-waisted Agathis body, bolt-on hard rock maple neck, 34" scale, 20 fret rosewood fingerboard with white dot inlays, natural wood headstock, fixed bridge, chrome hardware, 4-on-a-side tuners, 2 Power Sound J-style pickups, 2 volume/1 tone controls, available in Black and 2-Tone Burst finishes. Disc. 1998.

$225	$195	$175	$150	$125	$100	$75

Last MSR was $325.

Traditional Series

PB 1L - offset double cutaway Agathis body, bolt-on hard rock maple neck, 34" scale, 20 fret maple fingerboard with black dot inlays, natural wood headstock, fixed bridge, chrome hardware, 4-on-a-side tuners, Power Sound P bass-style pickup, volume/tone controls, available in 2-Tone Burst, Black, Ivory, and Red finishes. Disc. 1999.

MSR	$279	$200	$175	$150	$135	$115	$95	$75

Last MSR was $279.

In 1998, Ivory finish was discontinued.

PJ Bass - similar to the PB 1L, except has rosewood fingerboard with white dot inlays and Power Sound P/J-style pickups, available in 2-Tone Burst, Black, and Red finishes. Disc. 1999.

$200	$175	$150	$125	$100	$75	$50

Last MSR was $279.

PJ Bass LH - similar to the PJ Bass, except in left-handed configuration. Disc. 1999.

$215	$185	$165	$145	$125	$100	$75

Last MSR was $309.

Viva Bass Series

VIVA ACTIVE - offset double cutaway contoured maple body, bolt-on hard rock maple neck, 34" scale, 24-fret rosewood fingerboard with offset dot inlays, black squared headstock, fixed bridge, chrome hardware, 2-per-side tuners, P/J-style Select by EMG pickups, volume/blend/treble/bass controls, active EQ, available in Black, See-Through Black, See-Through Red, and Walnut Satin finishes. Disc. 1999

$375	$300	$275	$225	$195	$150	$125

Last MSR was $495.

Viva Active 5 - similar to the Viva Active, except has a 5-string configuration, 3/2-per-side tuners, and 2 J-style Select by EMG pickups, available in Black and Natural Satin finishes. Disc. 1999.

$425	$375	$325	$275	$250	$195	$150

Last MSR was $595.

CORTEZ

Instruments previously built in Japan circa 1969 to 1988. Distributed in the U.S. market by Westheimer Musical Industries of Chicago, Illinois.

Cortez acoustics were produced in Japan, and imported to the U.S. market as an affordable alternative in the acoustic guitar market. Westheimer's Cortez company and trademark could be viewed as a stepping stone towards his current Cort company (See CORT).

COTE'

Instruments currently built in Largo, Florida. Previously based in St. Petersburg, Florida.

Charles Cote' Basses is a family owned business that was founded in Atlanta, Georgia in 1992. Cote' began building guitars in 1987, and worked as a guitar builder from 1989 to 1991 at John Buscarino's Nova Guitar Company. A professional bassist for a number of years, Cote' brings his *player's experience* to his designs, and each instrument features a hand carved neck and body.

ELECTRIC BASS

The initial body design of the **R** series was inspired by a drawing by graphic artist Cris Rosario. List price includes a deluxe hardshell case.

Add $240 for figured maple top.

Add $240 for lacquer finish.

Add $275 for 35" scale length.

R4 4-STRING - offset double cutaway alder (or Southern ash or korina) body, bolt-on graphite reinforced rock maple neck, 34" scale, 24-fret morado or maple fingerboard, 2-per-side headstock, black hardware, BadAss II fixed bridge, 2 Kent Armstrong-wound Cote' humbucking pickups, volume/blend/tone controls, active electronics, available in Emerald Green, Amber, Natural, Ocean, and Scarlet hand rubbed oil finishes. Current Mfg.

MSR $1,820

R5 5 String - similar to the R4 4-string, except features a 5-string configuration, 2/3-per-side headstock, BadAss Bass V bridge. Current Mfg.

MSR $1,953

R6 6-string - similar to the R4 4-string, except features a 6-string configuration, 3-per-side headstock, custom Cote' bridge. Current Mfg.

MSR $2,310

Continuum Series

CONTINUUM BASIC 4 - similar to the R4 4-string, except has an ash body, bolt-on rock maple neck, 22-fret rosewood or maple fingerboard with pearl dot inlay, tortoiseshell pickguard, 2 Lindy Fralin single coil pickups, 2 volume/tone controls. Current Mfg.

MSR **$1,659**

This model is available with a fretless fingerboard and maple line marker inlays.

Continuum Standard 4 - similar to the Continuum Basic 4, except features alder or southern ash body, available in a variety of color lacquer finishes. Current Mfg.

MSR **$1,899**

Continuum Deluxe 4 - similar to the Continuum Basic 4, except features alder or southern ash body, figured maple top, available in a variety of color lacquer finishes. Current Mfg.

MSR **$1,999**

CRAFTSMAN

Instruments previously produced in Japan during the late 1970s through the mid 1980s.

Craftsman built entry level to medium quality copies of American designs.

(Source: Tony Bacon and Paul Day, The Guru's Guitar Guide)

CRATE

Also CRATE/ELECTRA.

Instruments currently produced in Korea. Distributed by St. Louis Music of St. Louis, Missouri.

St. Louis Music's Crate amplifier line featured a "Starter Pack" in 1997, which featured a Crate GX15 amp, cable, strap, and a **Crate** (or **Crate/Electra**) **Nashville Standard** model LP-style guitar. The **Nashville Standard** had a set-in neck, 2 humbuckers, 3-way selector, and a bound body/bound fingerboard. Retail on the **Nashville Standard** is $229.95; this model is available in Black, or an optional 2-Tone Tobacco Sunburst finish (**Model CRNSTB**).

The Crate/Electra International Series has an additional model: the **California Classic (CRCCB)** features a strat-style body and 2 single coil/humbucker pickup configuration. This model is available in Black, or optional Metallic Red (**Model CRCCR**) and 3-Tone Sunburst (**Model CRCCSB**) finishes.

Cripe SRC Lightning Bolt
courtesy S.R. Cripe estate

CRESTLINE

Instruments previously built in Japan circa mid to late 1970s. Distributed by the Grossman Music Corporation of Cleveland, Ohio.

These entry level to intermediate solid body guitars featured designs based on classic American favorites. Crestline offered a wide range of stringed instruments, including classical, folk, dreadnought, and 12-string acoustics; solid body electric guitars and basses; amplifiers; banjos, mandolins, and ukuleles. Considering the amount of instruments available, the Crestline trademark was probably used on guitars built by one of the bigger Japanese guitar producers and 'rebranded' for the U.S. market. One model reviewed at a vintage guitar show was based on Gibson's Les Paul design, and had Grover tuners, 2 Japanese covered humbuckers, and decent wood.

CRIPE, STEVE

Instruments previously built in Trilby, Florida from 1990 to 1996.

Although he is best known for building the *Lightning Bolt* and *Top Hat* guitars for Jerry Garcia, Stephen R. Cripe also built a number of guitars for other players across the country. A self-taught luthier, Cripe's guitar designs were based on photos and video footage of Jerry Garcia's performances, not actual guitar templates.

Steve Cripe was born and raised in southern Michigan, and spent his high school years in Elkhart, Indiana. In 1972 he moved with his parents to Marathon, Florida and purchased a boat for his living quarters. After developing his talents fixing up his boat, he turned to hand-building ornate wood interiors for sailboats.

In 1983, Cripe moved to North Carolina for a year, then later to Miami, Florida. While continuing to work on boats, he began to study guitars and their construction. Cripe started hand building guitars in 1990 mainly to learn to play, but found he enjoyed building them instead. Cripe selected and used exotic woods in his guitar building, and always finished them naturally (adding no stain or color).

A self-described Dead Head, Cripe studied photographs and videos of Jerry Garcia (*Grateful Dead*). Inspired by the Doug Irwin-built model that Garcia played, Cripe decided to create his own guitar for Garcia. "I figured that the building of the instrument would be easy, but getting it to him would be a challenge," Cripe said, "Once the guitar was finished, I contacted numerous music magazines requesting an address to which to send the guitar. No such luck."

Through a series of intermediaries, Cripe sent the guitar to Garcia. After five weeks of waiting, Cripe received a message on his answering machine that Garcia was 'fiddling around with the guitar' and 'was intrigued by it'. A relationship developed between Cripe and Garcia, and Cripe began building a few more guitars for him. After completing the *Top Hat*-named guitar, Cripe shipped it to Garcia. Garcia began playing it immediately, and continued using them up until his death.

Steve Cripe completed commissions for a number of anxious buyers, and found time to build a new workshop for guitar production. Unfortunately, Cripe died in a devastating explosion in his workshop on June 18, 1996.

(Source: Hal Hammer)

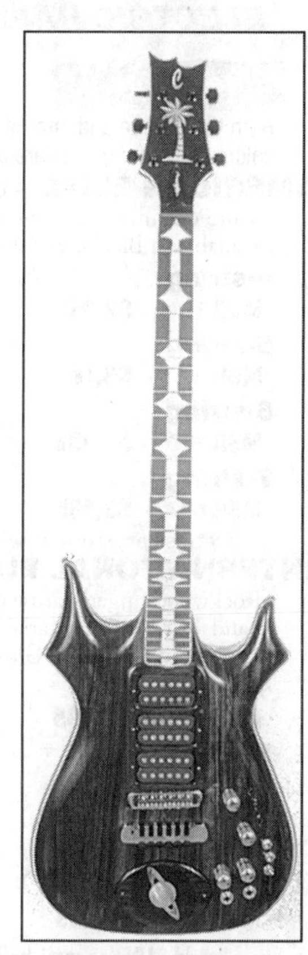

Cripe SRC Saturn
courtesy S.R. Cripe estate

CROWN

Instruments previously produced in Japan during the mid 1960s.

The U.S. distributor for the Crown trademark is still currently unknown, as well as the Japanese manufacturer. The Crown logo has been spotted on violin-shaped hollow body electric guitars and basses, as well as solid body electrics. The solid body guitars are reported as being generally cheap entry level instruments.

(Source: Tony Bacon and Paul Day, The Guru's Guitar Guide; and Michael Wright, Vintage Guitar Magazine)

CRUCIANELLI

See ELITE.

Instruments previously produced in Italy during the 1960s.

Author Tony Bacon notes in his book, *The Ultimate Guitar Book*, that Italy, like many other European countries, experienced the 1960's pop music popularity that led to a larger demand for electric guitars. However, many electric guitar builders were also manufacturers of accordions. As a result, many guitars ended up with accordion-style finishes. Wacky or not, Leo Fender was using this same sort of heat-molded acetate finish on some of his early lap steel models in the early 1950s.

CURBOW

Instruments currently built in Morgantown, Georgia.

Luthier Greg Curbow offers a line of high quality stringed instruments that feature **Rockwood** necks. The Rockwood material is a composite of birch and phenolic based resins formed under pressure and heat, which produces a neck unaffected by changes in temperature and humidity. Curbow basses and guitars are hand-crafted directly at the Curbow workshop in the North Georgia mountains.

For current information on Curbow acoustic electric basses, please refer to the 7th Edition *Blue Book of Acoustic Guitars*.

ELECTRIC

INTERNATIONAL EXOTIC PETITE CARVED TOP (SIX STRING) - offset double cutaway mahogany body, wenge (or zebra or bubinga or rock maple or figured maple or walnut or cherry) top, bolt-on Rockwood neck, 25 1/2" scale, 24-fret Rockwood fingerboard, 3-per-side headstock, chrome hardware, tune-o-matic bridge/stop tailpiece, 2 single coil/humbucker Bartolini or Seymour Duncan pickups, volume/2 band EQ controls, pickup selector switch. Mfg. 1994 to date.

MSR **$3,595**

Price includes a custom hardshell case.
This model is available with a tremolo bridge.
This model is available with a semi-hollow body (International Exotic Petite Carved Top Semi Hollow).

International Exotic Petite Carved Top (Seven String) - similar to the Petite Six, except features a 7-string configuration and 3/4-per-side headstock. Mfg. 1997 to date.

MSR **$3,896**

This model is available with a semi-hollow body (International Exotic Petite Carved Top Semi Hollow Seven String).

ELECTRIC BASS

Elite Series

Both the Grande and International Elite Series basses feature a hand-carved top of cherry, figured maple, rock maple, walnut, wenge, or zebra wood. Custom colors and other woods are available (please call for price quote).

AMERICAN ELITE - offset double cutaway maple or swamp ash body, bolt-on Rockwood neck, 34" scale, 24-fret Rockwood fingerboard with white dot inlays, 2-per-side headstock, brass bridge, Sperzel tuners, Bartolini Split Coil pickup, volume/3-band EQ controls, variable mid switch, available in Black Pearl, Ice Blue Pearl, Purple Pearl, Red Pearl, and White Pearl finishes. Mfg. 1997 to date.

4-string
MSR **$2,995**
5-string
MSR **$3,195**
6-string
MSR **$3,395**
7-string
MSR **$3,595**

Fretless or Fretless with lines fingerboards are available at no additional cost. Retail price includes a gig bag.

INTERNATIONAL ELITE - offset double cutaway mahogany body, hand carved exotic wood top, bolt-on Rockwood neck, 34" scale, 24-fret Rockwood fingerboard with white dot inlays, 2-per-side headstock, quick release bridge, Sperzel tuners, Bartolini Split-Coil pickup, volume/blend/3-band EQ controls, variable Midrange switch, slap contour switch, available in Amethyst Glow, Cocoa Burst, Grape Burst, Honey Burst, Scarlet Glow, and Turquoise Glow finishes. Also available in a Clear Coat or Oil & Wax finishes. Current Mfg.

4-string
MSR **$3,295**
5-string
MSR **$3,595**
6-string
MSR **$3,895**
7-string
MSR **$4,195**

Add $195 for semi-hollow body.

This model has optional choice of woods, gold hardware, and fretless or fretless with lines fingerboards are available at no additional cost. Retail price includes a lined hardshell case.

GRADING	100% MINT	98% NEAR MINT	95% EXC+	90% EXC	80% VG+	70% VG	60% G

Grande Elite - similar to the International Elite, except features an 18-volt 3-band EQ system, available in Amethyst Glow, Cocoa Burst, Grape Burst, Honey Burst, Scarlet Glow, Turquoise Glow and finishes. Also available in a Clear Coat or Oil & Wax finishes. Current Mfg.

4-string
MSR **$3,495**
5-string
MSR **$3,795**
6-string
MSR **$4,095**
7-string
MSR **$4,395**

Add $195 for semi-hollow body.

This model has optional choice of woods, gold hardware, and fretless or fretless with lines fingerboards are available at no additional cost. Retail price includes a lined hardshell case.

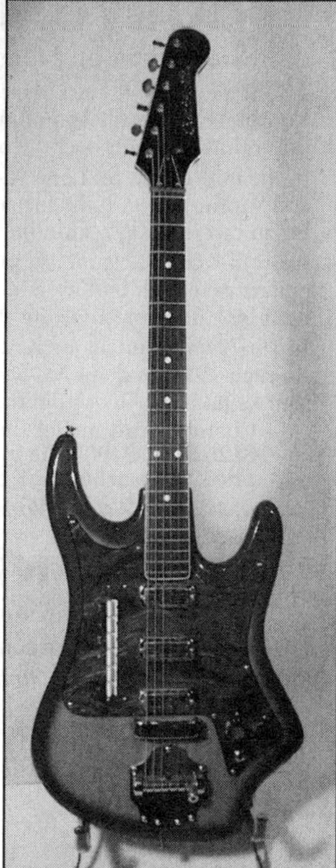

Crucianelli
courtesy TLC Amps & Guitars

Retro Series

RETRO - offset double cutaway maple or Swamp ash body, bolt-on Rockwood Lite neck, 34" scale, 24-fret Rockwood neck with white dot inlays, 2-per-side headstock, brass bridge, Sperzel tuners, Black Pearl or White Pearl pickguard, Bartolini Dual-Coil pickup, volume/treble/mid/bass controls, active 9-volt 3-band parametric EQ system, available in Black Pearl, Ice Blue Pearl, Red Pearl, and White Pearl finishes. Mfg. 1997 to date.

4-string
MSR **$1,995**
5-string
MSR **$2,195**
6-string
MSR **$2,395**

Fretless or Fretless with lines fingerboards are available at no additional cost. Retail price includes a gig bag.

Retro II - similar to the Retro, except features 2 Bartolini J-style pickups, 2 volume/tone controls. Current Mfg.

4-string
MSR **$2,095**
5-string
MSR **$2,295**
6-string
MSR **$2,495**

Add $200 for active 3-band EQ with variable mid switch.

Fretless or Fretless with lines fingerboards are available at no additional cost. Retail price includes a gig bag.

XT Series

XT-33 - offset double cutaway mahogany body, hand carved exotic wood top, bolt-on Rockwood neck, 34" scale, extended 33-fret Rockwood fingerboard with white dot inlays, 2-per-side headstock, brass bridge, Sperzel tuners, Bartolini Quad-Coil pickup, volume/blend controls, Bartolini 3-band EQ, 18-volt electronics, variable Midrange switch, slap contour switch, available in Amethyst Glow, Cocoa Burst, Grape Burst, Honey Burst, Scarlet Glow, and Turquoise Glow finishes. Also available in a Clear Coat or Oil & Wax finishes. Current Mfg.

4-string
MSR **$3,595**
5-string
MSR **$3,895**
6-string
MSR **$4,195**
7-string
MSR **$4,495**

Add $195 for semi-hollow body.

This model has optional choice of woods, gold hardware, and lined or unlined fretless fingerboard.

CUSTOM GUITAR COMPANY

Instruments currently built in Sunnyvale, CA, previously built in Santa Clara, CA.

These quality custom instruments are built in Southern California. For more information on the curernt model lineup, please contact the company directly (see Trademark Index).

CUSTOM KRAFT

See chapter on House Brands.

This trademark has been identified as a House Brand of St. Louis Music. The St. Louis Music Supply Company was founded in 1922 by Bernard Kornblum, originally as an importer of German violins. The St. Louis, Missouri-based company has been a distributor, importer, and manufacturer of musical instruments over the past seventy-five years.

In the mid 1950s, St. Louis Music distributed amplifiers and guitars from other producers such as Alamo, Harmony, Kay, Magnatone, Rickenbacker, and Supro. By 1960, the focus was on Harmony, Kay, and Supro: all built "upstream" in Chicago, Illinois. 1960 was also the year that St. Louis Music began carrying Kay's **Thinline** single cutaway electric guitar.

Custom Kraft was launched in 1961 as St. Louis Music's own house brand. The first series of semi-hollowbody Custom Kraft **Color Dynamic** Electric guitars were built by **Kay**, and appear to be Thinline models in Black, Red, and White finishes. In 1963, a line of solid body double cutaway electrics built by **Valco** were added to the catalog under the Custom Kraft moniker, as well as Kay-built archtop and flat-top acoustic.

In 1967, Valco purchased Kay, a deal that managed to sink both companies by 1968. St. Louis Music continued advertising both companies models through 1970, perhaps NOS supplies from their warehouse. St. Louis Music continued to offer Custom Kraft guitars into the early 1970s, but as their sources had dried up so did the trademark name. St. Louis Music's next trademark guitar line was **Electra** (then followed by **Westone**, and **Alvarez**).

Custom Kraft models are generally priced according to the weirdness/coolness factor, so don't be surprised to see the range of prices from $125 up to $400! The uncertainty indicates a buyer-directed market, so if you find one that you like, don't be afraid to haggle over the price. The earlier KAY and VALCO built guitars date from the 1960s, while later models were probably built in Japan.

(Source: Michael Wright, Vintage Guitar magazine)

CYCLONE

Instruments previously produced in Japan.

Cyclone guitars were distributed in the U.S. market by Leban Imports of Baltimore, Maryland.

(Source: Michael Wright, Guitar Stories Volume One)

Section D

D. C. HILDER BUILDER

Instruments currently built in Guelph (Ontario), Canada.

D.C. Hilder's Garcia's Guitar model features seven laminated layers of hard wood, which are then hand carved for the top and back contouring. The bound neck is inlaid with "museum grade" jewelry work. These models have optional three split coil pickups. Suggested retail list price is $1,323.

(Source: Guitar Player magazine)

D'AGOSTINO

Instruments previously produced in Italy by the EKO company between 1978 and 1982. Instrument production was contracted to the EKO Custom Shop in Milwaukee, Wisconsin, and distributed by PMS Music of New York, New York. After 1982, instruments were produced in Japan.

Pat D'Agostino (ex-Gibson/Maestro Effects) began his own instrument importing company in 1975. The D'Agostino Corporation of New Jersey began importing acoustic dreadnoughts, then introduced the Italian-built **Benchmark Series** of guitars in 1977. These models featured laminated neck-through designs, two humbuckers, and a 3+3 headstock. Production then moved to Korea in the early 1980's, although some better models were built in Japan in the 1990's. Pat, assisted by Steven D'Agostino and Mike Confortti, have always maintained a high quality control level and limited quantities.

D'ANGELICO

Instruments previously built in New York City, New York between 1932 and 1964.

Master Luthier John D'Angelico (1905-1964) was born and raised in New York City, New York. In 1914, he apprenticed to his Greatuncle, and learned the luthier trade of building and repairing stringed instruments. After 18 years of working on stringed instruments, he opened his own shop on Kenmare Street (D'Angelico was 27). D'Angelico guitars were entirely handcrafted by D'Angelico with assistance by shop employees such as Vincent DiSerio (assistant/apprentice from 1932 to 1959). In the early 1950s, D'Angelico's workshop had a bench and counter for guitar work, and a showcase with new United or Favilla guitars, used "trade-ins" and a few amplifiers from Nat Daniel's Danelectro or Everett Hull's Ampeg company. A very young James D'Aquisto became the second assistant to the shop in 1953.

In 1959, the building where D'Angelico worked and lived was condemned by the city due to an unsafe foundation. While scouting out new locations, D'Angelico and DiSerio had a serious argument over finances. DiSerio left and accepted work at the Favilla guitar plant. After a number of months went by, D'Angelico and D'Aquisto finally reopened the guitar shop at its new location. Unfortunately, D'Angelico's health began to take a turn for the worse. John D'Angelico passed away in his sleep in September of 1964.

John D'Angelico created 1,164 serialized acoustic guitars (electric models were not part of the serialization ledgers), as well as unnumbered mandolins, and novelty instruments.

(Source: Paul William Schmidt, Acquired of the Angels)

D'Angelico Electric Models

Although John D'Angelico prided himself on producing the finest acoustic archtop guitars, many of his customers ultimately outfitted them with DeArmond floating pickups as the guitar's role in modern music changed. Though he did make a few acoustic instruments with built-in pickups, D'Angelico electric guitars - sometimes referred to as the model "G-7" after the numbers stamped inside their bodies - were the luthier's concession to those clients wanting a non-carved, utilitarian guitar with built-in pickups.

The plywood, maple cutaway bodies were obtained from either the United or Code companies, both located in New Jersey. To these, he affixed his hand fashioned maple neck, replete with ebony fingerboard, block inlays, adjustable truss rod, and a distinctive 5-point, flared headstock. As was typical of most of his instruments, the pearl D'Angelico script inlay adorned the headstock.

Pickups vary from model to model, and they often reflected the requests of a particular customer. It is common to see non-original pickups in these electric guitars, as it reflected the working musician's desire to keep up with the latest electronic technology. Both single and double pickup, blonde, and sunburst models were produced.

Body size was typically 16-16 1/2" wide, and body depth varied from 2 1/4-2 3/4". One seldom sees two identical D'Angelico electric guitars. In addition to all of the above, pickguards, tailpieces, knobs, and decorative headstock inlays changed according to what the luthier seems to have had on hand. Electric guitars are not recorded as part of the serialization in the D'Angelico ledgers. These guitars bring significantly less on the vintage market than comparable acoustic models.

D'Angelico Electric Pricing: Prices for original instruments with no modifications/alterations are currently in the $9,000-$10,000 range, assuming Excellent condition. It is highly recommended that several professional appraisals be secured before buying/selling/trading any D'Angelico electric instrument.

(The publisher wishes to express his thanks to Mr. Jim Fisch for the above information.)

D'ANGELICO II

Instruments currently built in the U.S. Distributed by Archtop Enterprises, Inc. of Merrick, New York.

The D'Angelico II company is currently building a semi-hollow body electric archtop.

The Fusion ($3,750) is offered in an Antique Natural, New Yorker Sunburst, or Flaming Red nitro cellulose lacquer finish.

D'ANGELICO BY VESTAX

Instruments currently built in Japan. These models are not distributed in the U.S. market.

Vestax is currently offering a number of high quality D'Angelico archtop guitar models in other parts of the world's musical instrument market (i.e. not the U.S. market). These models remain true to the D'Angelico designs from which they are derived, and do have high quality workmanship.

Retail list pricing from specification sheets were in Japanese Yen - but as they do not apply to the U.S. market, they will not be quoted below. Various body widths and specifications are unknown to date.

ELECTRIC

There are 5 different D'Angelico models offered by Vestax; four are full acoustics which are augmented by floating pickups, and the fifth is a semi-hollow body model with 2 humbuckers. The **D'Angelico New Yorker (Model Big Body NYI-1)** has a single rounded cutaway bound body, set-in neck, 22-fret bound fingerboard with pearl block inlays, bound headstock, bound pickguard, adjustable rosewood bridge/'stairstep' rosewood solid tailpiece, gold hardware, pearl logo/ 'New Yorker' logo inlay, pearl truss rod cover, gold plated hardware, and 3-per-side 'butterbean' tuners. This model is offered in a smaller body width as the **New Yorker (Model Small Body NYS-1)** with similar construction details.

The **New Yorker (Model Big Body NYL-2)** is also similar to the **NYL-1**, but features an adjustable rosewood bridge/gold-plated metal 'stairstep' bridge, re-issue Grover Imperial tuners. This model is offered in a smaller body width as the **New Yorker (Model Small Body NYS-2)**. Both of the "-2" have retail list prices that are roughly 1/3 the list price of the "-1" series, leading to the question of laminated bodies versus hand carved bodies. This question has not yet been resolved.

The Semi-Acoustic (or semi-hollow body) **New Yorker Semi Acoustic Type (Model NY22-3)** has a single cutaway bound body, 2 bound f-holes, bound neck/ headstock/raised pickguard, 2 humbuckers, tune-o-matic bridge/stop tailpiece, gold hardware, 2 volume/2 tone controls, 3-way selector switch. The headstock detail is similar to the 4 full acoustic models.

D'AQUISTO

Instruments previously built in Huntington, New York (as well as Greenport, New York) between 1965 to 1995.

Master Luthier James L. D'Aquisto (1935-1995) met John D'Angelico around 1953. At the early age of 17, D'Aquisto became D'Angelico's apprentice, and by 1959 was handling the decorative procedures and other lutherie jobs. When D'Angelico had a falling out with another member of the shop during the move of the business, D'Aquisto began doing actual building and shaping work. This lutherie work continued until the time of D'Angelico's death in 1964. The loss of D'Angelico in 1964 not only affected D'Aquisto personally, but professionally. Although he took over the business and shop with the encouragement of D'Angelico's brother, business under his own trademark started slowly. D'Aquisto continued to work in D'Angelico's shop repairing instruments at the last address - 37 Kenmare Street, New York City, New York. Finally, one year after D'Angelico's death, D'Aquisto summoned the nerve to build a guitar with the **D'Aquisto** inlay on the headpiece.

In 1965, D'Aquisto moved his shop to Huntington, New York, and sold his first instrument, styled after a D'Angelico New Yorker. Most of D'Aquisto's traditional design instruments are styled after John D'Angelico's Excel and New Yorker, with D'Aquisto adding refinements and improvements. D'Aquisto set up a deal with the Swedish-based Hagstrom company to produce guitars based on his designs in 1968, and the Ampeg company was one of the U.S. distributors. In 1973, D'Aquisto relocated his business once again, this time setting up shop in Farmingdale, New York. He produced his first flat top guitar in 1975, and his first solid body electric one year later. The Fender Musical Instrument Corporation produced a number of D'Aquisto-designed guitars beginning in the 1980s, and two models in the Designer series (D'Aquisto Ultra and Deluxe) are still in production today at the Fender USA Custom shop.

In the late 1980s, D'Aquisto again moved his shop to Greenport, New York, and continued to produce instruments from that location. In 1987, D'Aquisto broke away from archtop design tradition when he debuted the **Avant Garde**. The Excel and New Yorker style models were disc in 1991, as D'Aquisto concentrated on creating more forward-looking and advanced archtops. In 1994, models such as the **Solo** with four soundholes (only nine built), and Centura models were introduced. James L. D'Aquisto passed away in April, 1995.

(Source: Paul William Schmidt, Acquired of the Angels)

James D'Aquisto built several hundred instruments, from archtops to flat tops to solid body electrics. Even thouough D'Aquisto is more famous for his acoustic archtops, his electric guitars are also very special. D'Aquisto electric instruments typically range between $7,500-$20,000, depending on the desirability of the configuration and embellishments/special orders. Like D'Angelico, most of D'Aquisto's instruments were made to order and varied in dimensions and details. When buying/selling/appraising a D'Aquisto, it is the recommendation of the ***Blue Book of Electric Guitars*** that two or three professional appraisals be obtained.

D'HAITRE

Instruments previously built in Maple Falls, Washington during the early 1990s.

Luthier Andy Beech offered several quality solid body guitar and bass models that featured a neck-through-body design. Beech, with 18 years experience playing and building guitars, offered handcrafted work and select hardwoods in his constructions. The ***Blue Book of Electric Guitars*** will continue to research luthier Beech and the D'Haitre trademark for future editions.

D'LECO

Instruments currently built in Oklahoma City, Oklahoma since 1992. Distributed by the D'Leco company of Oklahoma City, Oklahoma.

James Dale, Jr., like his father, had a background in cabinet making that the two shared since 1953. Recently, Dale decided to begin building guitars full time. It was the love of jazz guitars that sparked the desire to build archtops. In the summer of 1992, Dale met a young jazz guitarist and entrepreneur named Maurice Johnson. After seeing one of Dale's archtops, Maurice was impressed and proposed a collaboration to build and market D'Leco guitars. In 1994, D'Leco acquired the rights to produce the **Charlie Christian Tribute** model. In 1995, Samick/Valley Arts began backing the proposed tribute model, and signed an exclusive agreement to build three unique production models based on the original guitars that was designed by D'Leco.

(Source: Hal Hammer)

D'Leco offers the Charlie Christian Tribute model. The Solo Flight S-15 ($5,000) electric hollowbody has a hand carved top, 15" bout, 17th fret neck joint, 5-layer binding, gold plated humbuckers, ebony or cocobolo fretboard, bridge and pickguard. The Solo Flight S-16 has a hand carved spruce top, curly maple back and sides, 16" bout, 15th fret neck joint, bound fretboard, Charlie Christian Straight Bar 'floating' pickup, and hand rubbed lacquer. Portions of the sales proceeds go to the Christian family.

D'Leco also offers electric solid body bass guitars custom built by a young Oklahoma City luthier named David Stys. Stys was discovered by James Dale while he was building basses, and accepted the opportunity to join the D'Leco company and further his skills and development. D'Leco/Stys basses feature exotic wood tops, through-body neck, hand-contoured body shaping, and the player's choice of electronics package. D'Leco/Stys basses are built on a custom order basis, and have a retail price of $4,000.

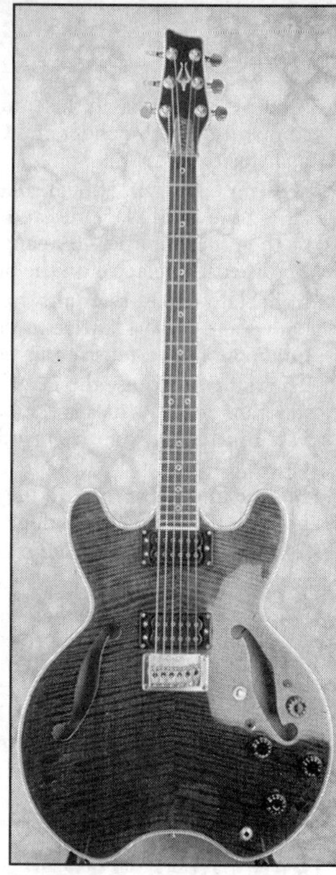

Daion HH
courtesy Darryl Alger

DAIMARU

Instruments previously produced in Japan.

Daimaru guitars were distributed in the U.S. by the Daimaru New York Corporation of New York, New York.

(Source: Michael Wright, Guitar Stories Volume One)

DAION

Instruments previously built in Japan circa late 1970s through the mid 1980s. Some guitars may also carry the trademark of JOODEE or YAMAKI. Distributed by MCI, Inc. of Waco, Texas.

Originally, these Japanese-produced high quality guitars were based on popular U.S. designs in the 1970s, but turned to original designs in the 1980s. The Daion logo was applied to a range of acoustic, semi-hollow body, and solid body guitars and basses. Some Daion headstocks also feature a stylized tuning fork logo.

ELECTRIC

Within the trends of the late 1970s, the electric guitar models had brass nuts and brass hardware, set-neck construction, and generally good finishes that seem to concentrate on light and dark brown, and translucent green. The **Headhunter** series semi-hollowbody models resemble an ES-335, except for the dip in the lower bout by the strap peg (not recommended, but a great party trick is to balance these guitars standing up). The Headhunter **Model HH-555** originally had a retail list price of $695. Models were offered between the late 1970s through the early 1980s.

Retail new prices ranged from $600 to $800 on the electric models. Current used prices range from $350 to $600, which is based on comparing these models with contemporary models.

ELECTRIC BASS

The Power Series solid body bass models had brass nuts/hardware, multi-laminated necks with through-body designs or set-neck construction.

New prices ranged from $675 to $895 on the electric bass models. Current used prices range from $375 to $600, based in part on comparisons between these models and similar construction (neck-through design) contemporary models.

DALLAS

Instruments previously made in England, West Germany, and Japan during the early to mid 1960s.

Some guitars may also carry the trademark of TUXEDO.

The DALLAS and TUXEDO trademarks are the brand names used by a UK importer/distributor. Early solid body guitars were supplied by either FENTON-WEILL or VOX in Britain, with entry level German and Japanese original design guitars imported in.

(Source: Tony Bacon and Paul Day, The Guru's Guitar Guide)

DANELECTRO (1954-1969 MFG.)

Instruments originally manufactured in Red Bank, New Jersey from 1953 to mid-1958, then production moved to Neptune, New Jersey through company's demise in 1969.

Between (roughly) 1956 to 1967, distribution was handled by the Danelectro Corporation of Neptune, New Jersey. However, the majority of instruments were sold or distributed through the Sears & Roebuck chain. At the end (1967-1969), distribution was handled by the MCA Corporation after they purchased Danelectro.

Nathan I. Daniels (1912-1994) was a New York electronics buff who began assembling amplifiers at home in 1934. In the mid 1930s, he was contracted by Epiphone (NYC) to build Electar amps, and successfully created a reputation and finances to start the Danelectro Corporation in 1948. Daniels' new company had offices and a factory in Red Bank, New Jersey.

By 1953, the first guitar was designed, and introduced in 1954. It has been indicated that Daniels had consulted his long time friend John D'Angelico for assistance in the fret spacing and bridge placement. While most people believe the body frame under the masonite is pine, Paul Bechtoldt confirmed that the body is poplar (and his source was Vinnie Bell!). In 1959 or 1960 the company moved to 207 West Sylvania Avenue in Neptune City, New Jersey, where it remained until its demise in 1968.

All models were assembled in the Neptune City factory, and the majority were sold to Sears, Roebuck under their Silvertone trademark. Many of the popular designs should be considered "semi-hollowbodies", for they have a masonite top and back mounted on a pine frame. The renowned "Lipstick Tube" pickups are exactly that: Danelectro bought the lipstick casings from a manufacturer who serviced the cosmetics industry, and then sent them to another contractor for plating before the pickup was installed inside.

The company grew during the 1960s guitar boom from under 100 employees to a peak of 503. George Wooster, Danelectro's production manager, estimated that the company produced 150 to 200 guitars a day during peak periods.

In late 1967 MCA (the entertainment conglomerate) bought Danelectro. In the same year, they introduced the Coral line. While 85% of Danelectro's output (guitars and amps) was for Sears, the Coral line was Danelectro's catalog line. The bodies for the Coral series were built in Japan, but the parts and assembly were done in the New Jersey plant.

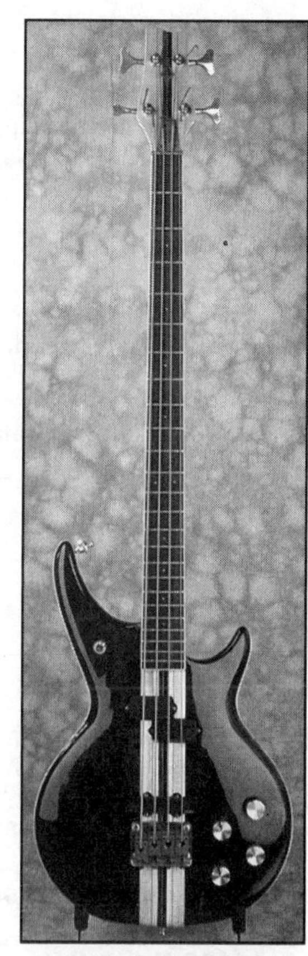

Daion Power XX-B Bass
courtesy
William Rutschman

GRADING	100% MINT	98% NEAR MINT	95% EXC+	90% EXC	80% VG+	70% VG	60% G

After MCA purchased the company, they began to do business with individual music shops instead of the big distributors - which brought them into competition with Fender and Gibson. Rather than point out the problem with that corporate thinking, let history do the talking: MCA folded Danelectro in 1968.

William C. Herring bought Danelectro's factory from MCA for $20,000 in late 1968 or 1969. Herring met Dan Armstrong (ex-Ampeg) and the pair visited the empty facilities and found numerous partially completed guitars and machinery. Armstrong contracted to build Danelectros for Ampeg, but by then the amplifier company was in financial straits and couldn't pay for them. These models have the single cutaway bodies, and **Dan Armstrong Modified Danelectro** on the pickguard.

D

In the late 1980s, the rights to the Danelectro name was acquired by Anthony Marks, who set about building "new" Danelectros with Asian-built bodies and NOS Danelectro necks. While the *Blue Book of Electric Guitars* has heard of this project, there have been no guitars witnessed to date. It is unknown how extensive this undertaking was.

The rights to license the Danelectro name was purchased by the Evets company in late 1995. By 1997, the "new" Danelectro company debuted three different effects pedals at the NAMM industry trade show in January, 1997. The new Danelectro effects pedals included the **Daddy O** overdrive ($79), **Fab Tone** distortion ($79), and the **Cool Cat** chorus ($99). In 1998, the company debuted the **Dan-O-Matic** on-stage tuner ($79), and the **Dan-Echo** tape echo-style pedal ($129).

But the important news to the guitar community is that the Danelectro company began offering guitars! The Danelectro re-issue **56-U2** is based on the popular U2 model that originated in 1956. Produced in Asia, the 56-U2 has a retail price of $299 - another nod to the original Danelectro concept!

(Source: Paul Bechtoldt and Doug Tulloch, Guitars From Neptune; and Mark Wollerman, Wollerman Guitars)

The vintage market is stronger now on Danelectros and Silvertones than in the past. With the arrival of a solid reference book to help differentiate between the models produced (Bechtoldt and Tulloch's *Guitars from Neptune*), and a time frame indicated for model production, dealers are more confident in displaying model nomenclature. Danelectros have a different tone, feel, and vibe from Fenders, Gibsons, and Rickenbackers - and perhaps the baby boomer players and dealers are beginning to respond.

Keep in mind, a Danelectro guitar was a modern production-built instrument, and the company made quite a few of them (and quite a few is an understatement). But as in any marketplace, when the demand/supply ratio changes, prices can go up.

(The publisher would like to thank Mr. Doug Tulloch for his significant contributions to this Danelectro section.)

ELECTRIC

1954 FIRST MODEL - single cutaway poplar wood body w/vinyl edging, neck reinforcement consisted of a ¾" square aluminum rod which ran from nut to bridge, "Bell" shaped headstock with large rear volute and angled stenciled logo with "curly-cue" design {soon changed to vertical stenciled logo}. Early versions had one or two pre-Lipstick tube pickups concealed under a thin single-ply white plastic pickguard, soon changed to Lipstick tube pickups w/clear pickguard with stenciled "D" logo and perimeter stripe. Available in a variety of finishes and textured coverings including Black, Red, Bronze, Blue, and Yellow, extremely rare model, introduced 1954, phased out 1955.

Model	100%	98%	95%	90%	80%	70%	60%
One pickup	$850	$800	$750	$650	$600	$550	$500
Two pickup	$1,200	$1,100	$1,000	$850	$815	$750	$700

"C" SERIES - single cutaway wood {smaller 11 ¼" "Peanut" size} body w/vinyl edging, one or two pickups, early versions have brown vinyl tape wrapped pickups then Lipstick covers, clear pickguard w/contrasting underlay, input jack on lower body edge, available in a ginger colored vinyl rare model, introduced 1955, phased out 1956.

Model	100%	98%	95%	90%	80%	70%	60%
One pickup	$500	$475	$450	$425	$400	$350	$275
Two pickup	$700	$675	$650	$625	$600	$575	$500

"U" SERIES - single cutaway Masonite body w/vinyl edging, one or two pickups {three pickups avail. in 1957}, stenciled "D" logo and perimeter stripe on clear pickguard, input jack on lower body edge, "Coke bottle" headstock, two and three pickup models have stacked concentric knobs, available in Gleaming Black, Antique Bronze, *Grained Ivory Leatherette, *Jade Green, *Bermuda Coral, and *Lagoon Aqua, introduced 1956, phased out 1958.

Add 50%-75% for custom color on the models listed below.

Model	100%	98%	95%	90%	80%	70%	60%
U-1	$300	$275	$250	$225	$200	$175	$150
U-2	$750	$650	$600	$500	$450	$400	$375
U-3 (rare)	$1,200	$1,100	$1,000	$900	$800	$700	$650
UB-2 6 string bass	$1,200	$1,100	$1,000	$900	$800	$700	$650

LONGHORN - "lyre" shaped Masonite body w/vinyl edging, two pickups, wooden pointer concentric knobs, clear pickguard, input jack on lower body edge, "Coke bottle" headstock, pickups on early versions are mounted close together in the neck position as with the Guitarlin, later versions had wide pickup spacing {neck & bridge}. Bronze and White Sunburst only, introduced 1958, available through 1969.

Model	100%	98%	95%	90%	80%	70%	60%
#4423 4 String Bass	$1,200	$1,000	$900	$850	$800	$750	$650
#4623 6 String Bass	$1,200	$1,000	$900	$850	$800	$750	$650
#4123 Guitarlin	$1,200	$1,000	$900	$850	$800	$750	$650

GRADING	100% MINT	98% NEAR MINT	95% EXC+	90% EXC	80% VG+	70% VG	60% G

Danelectro 6-String/Baritone courtesy Atomic Guitars

DOUBLENECK 4 string bass/6 string guitar, "Shorthorn" style Masonite body w/vinyl edging, two pickups, concentric knobs, clear pickguards, input jack on lower body edge, "Coke bottle" headstocks, Bronze and White Sunburst only, introduced 1958, phased out 1969.

Model	100%	98%	95%	90%	80%	70%	60%
#3923	$1,200	$1,100	$1000	$850	$750	$650	$600

SHORTHORN STANDARD - double cutaway Masonite body w/vinyl edging, one or two pickups, "Coke bottle" headstock, early versions had a clear "Kidney" shaped pickguard with a separate white vinyl underlay and the input jack mounted on the lower body edge. This was soon changed to the input jack mounted on a white painted "Seal" shaped pickguard. Available in Black, Bronze, and Blonde, introduced 1958, phased out 1966.

Model	100%	98%	95%	90%	80%	70%	60%
#3011 Black, one pickup	$275	$250	$225	$200	$175	$150	$125
#3012 Bronze, one pickup	$275	$250	$225	$200	$175	$150	$125
#3021 Black, two pickup	$1,000	$950	$900	$850	$700	$600	$500

Note: The above model #3021 is closely associated with Led Zeppelin guitarist Jimmy Page and has strong collector appeal. Specs. MUST be as follows: Black finish, two pickups, "Coke bottle" headstock, concentric knobs, "Seal" shaped pickguard, NO tremolo.

Model	100%	98%	95%	90%	80%	70%	60%
#3022 Bronze, two pickup	$750	$650	$600	$550	$500	$475	$450
#5025 Blonde, two pickup	$850	$750	$700	$650	$600	$550	$500

SHORTHORN DELUXE - double cutaway Masonite body w/vinyl edging, one, two, or three pickups, "Coke bottle" headstock, available in White w/brown body binding or Walnut w/white body binding, input jack on lower body edge, headstock and back of neck painted white, glued on pickguard, Kluson Deluxe tuners. Two and three pickup models have wooden pointer style concentric knobs, introduced 1958, phased out 1966.

Model	100%	98%	95%	90%	80%	70%	60%
#6016 White, one pickup	$350	$325	$300	$275	$250	$225	$200
#6017 Walnut, one pickup	$350	$325	$300	$275	$250	$225	$200
#6026 White, two pickup	$650	$600	$550	$500	$450	$375	$350
#6027 Walnut, two pickup	$650	$600	$550	$500	$450	$375	$350
#6036 White, three pickup	$750	$700	$675	$650	$600	$550	$500
#6037 Walnut, three pickup	$750	$700	$675	$650	$600	$550	$500

SHORTHORN BASS - double cutaway Masonite body w/vinyl edging, one pickup, white painted "Seal" shaped pickguard, "Coke bottle" headstock, pickguard mounted input jack, four and six string versions, available in Bronze finish only, introduced 1958, phased out 1966.

Model	100%	98%	95%	90%	80%	70%	60%
#3412 4 string	$375	$350	$325	$300	$275	$250	$225
#3612 6 string	$500	$475	$450	$425	$400	$350	$300

HAND VIBRATO GUITAR - double cutaway Masonite body w/vinyl edging, one or two pickups, Batwing headstock w/raised chrome script logo, all equipped with "Vibrato" bridge, large white painted pickguard which surrounds pickups, pickguard mounted input jack, Gleaming Black finish only, introduced 1965, phased out 1967.

Model	100%	98%	95%	90%	80%	70%	60%
#4011, one pickup	$375	$350	$325	$300	$275	$250	$225
#4021 two pickup	$500	$450	$425	$400	$375	$350	$325

CONVERTIBLE - double cutaway Masonite body w/vinyl edging and round soundhole, floating bridge, NO pickguard, body mounted input jack, "Coke bottle" headstock with decal logo through 1967, then 6-in-line headstock w/raised chrome script logo through 1969. Offered with or without electronics {hence the name Convertible}. If without electronics, chrome "decorative" inserts are fitted in the control holes. Early versions have a single screw mounting the tailpiece and only two allen screws on the rosewood bridge, later versions have two screws mounting the tailpiece with three allen screws on the rosewood bridge, available in Blonde, Red, or Blue finishes, introduced 1958 and available through 1969.

Add 25% for Red or Blue finish.

Model	100%	98%	95%	90%	80%	70%	60%
#5005 without electronics	$300	$275	$250	$225	$200	$175	$150

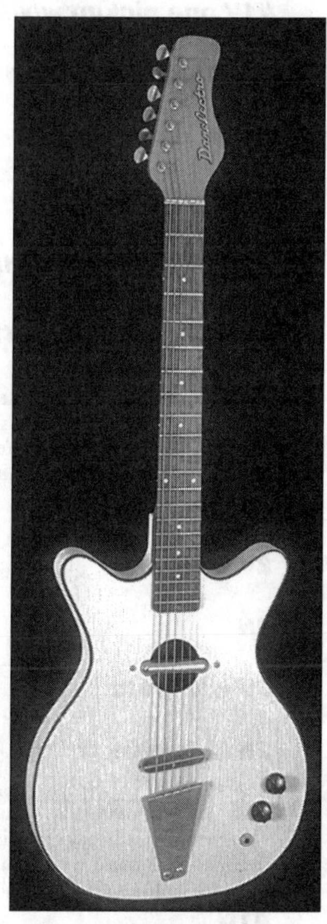

Danelectro Convertible courtesy Steve Burgess

D

GRADING	100% MINT	98% NEAR MINT	95% EXC+	90% EXC	80% VG+	70% VG	60% G

#5015 with electronics

$375	$350	$300	$275	$250	$225	$175

Companion - Similar to Convertible except has two pickups, concentric knobs, white painted pickguard, pickguard mounted input jack, NO soundhole, introduced 1958, phased out 1960.

#5025

$650	$600	$550	$500	$475	$400	$375

BELLZOUKI - three body variations centered around a Masonite teardrop shaped body, one or two pickups, body mounted input jack, tortoise shell pickguard and pickup surround, "Batwing" headstock, raised chrome script logo, Tobacco Brown Sunburst only, introduced 1961, phased out 1967.

Model	100%	98%	95%	90%	80%	70%	60%
#7010 one pickup	$475	$450	$425	$400	$375	$350	$300
#7020 two pickup	$675	$650	$600	$500	$450	$400	$375
#7021 two pickup - "Coral Sitar" style body w/treble horn, white "reflective stylized" pickguard {rare model}	$800	$750	$700	$675	$650	$550	$500

PRO 1 - square-ish offset Masonite body w/vinyl edging, one pickup, white baked melamine triangular pickguard, Brown w/sparkle accents only, introduced in 1963, phased out in 1964.

$500	$450	$425	$400	$375	$300	$275

SITAR - oval shaped wood body, keyhole shaped headstock, one pickup w/chrome surround, "Reflective Stylized" pickguard w/stenciled border design, chrome plated lap mount, "Sitarmatic" bridge, NO drone strings as on Coral version, very rare model, introduced 1968 through 1969.

$1,200	$1,100	$1,000	$950	$850	$750	$700

HAWAIIAN GUITAR - staggered three piece natural wood body w/brown felt backing, one pickup, 36-fret stenciled pattern on fingerboard, stenciled logo on Rosewood slab mounted to headstock, extremely rare model, introduced 1958 through 1959.

$500	$425	$350	$325	$300	$275	$250

HAWK - guitar, bass, and twelve string versions, offset solid wood body w textured finish, six-in-line matching headstock {twelve string resembles "Batwing" headstock}, one or two pickups {on two pickup models the lower half of the concentric knobs are painted to match body color}, raised chrome script logo, optional "Flexbridge" vibrato, white painted pickguard, available in Brilliant Red, Baby Blue, or Panther Black textured finishes, introduced 1967 through 1968.

Model	100%	98%	95%	90%	80%	70%	60%
#1N one pickup	$375	$350	$325	$300	$275	$250	$225
#1V one pickup w/vibrato Flexbridge	$375	$350	$325	$300	$275	$250	$225
#1N12 one pickup, 12-string	$375	$350	$325	$300	$275	$250	$225
#1B4 one pickup, 4-string bass	$400	$375	$350	$325	$300	$275	$250
#2N two pickup	$450	$425	$400	$375	$350	$325	$300
#2V two pickup, w/vibrato Flexbridge	$450	$425	$400	$375	$350	$325	$300
#2N12 two pickup, 12-string	$450	$425	$400	$375	$350	$325	$300

SLIMLINE six and twelve string guitar, offset Masonite semi-solid body w/vinyl edging, six-in-line matching headstock {twelve string resembles "Batwing" headstock} w/raised chrome script logo, two or three pickups {two for twelve string}, optional vibrato on six-string models, rear painted plastic pickguard w/perimeter stripe and pickguard mounted input jack, two volume/two tone with twin slider switches, available in White w/Black trim, Midnite Green w/White trim, Black and Yellow Sunburst w/White trim, introduced 1967 through 1969.

Model	100%	98%	95%	90%	80%	70%	60%
2N	$400	$375	$350	$325	$300	$275	$250
2V w/vibrato	$400	$375	$350	$325	$300	$275	$250
3N	$700	$675	$650	$625	$600	$575	$525
3V w/vibrato	$650	$600	$550	$500	$450	$375	$350
2N12 twelve string	$500	$475	$425	$400	$375	$350	$325

DANE "A" SERIES - guitar, bass, and twelve string versions. Offset solid wood body, six-in-line matching headstock {twelve string resembles "Batwing" headstock} w/raised chrome script logo, one or two pickups {one for bass}, optional "Flexbridge" vibrato on six string models, white painted pickguard w/pickguard mounted input jack, two pickup models have stacked concentric knobs, standard textured finish is Brown, textured custom colors were Red, Black, and Blue, introduced 1967 through 1969.

Model	100%	98%	95%	90%	80%	70%	60%
A1N	$275	$250	$225	$200	$175	$150	$125

GRADING	100% MINT	98% NEAR MINT	95% EXC+	90% EXC	80% VG+	70% VG	60% G
A2N							
	$375	$350	$325	$300	$275	$250	$225
A1V							
	$275	$250	$225	$200	$175	$150	$125
A2V							
	$375	$350	$325	$300	$275	$250	$225
A1N12							
	$275	$250	$225	$200	$175	$150	$125
A2N12							
	$375	$350	$325	$300	$275	$250	$225
A1B4							
	$275	$250	$225	$200	$175	$150	$125

"B" SERIES - guitar and twelve string versions, offset semi-solid "Durabody" w/vinyl edging, six-in-line matching headstock {twelve string resembles "Batwing" headstock} w/raised chrome script logo, two or three pickups w/ chrome surrounds, optional vibrato on six string models, black or white rear painted plastic pickguard w/contrasting perimeter stripe and pickguard mounted input jack, two volume/two tone with three slider switches {three pickup model has additional master volume control}, standard finish is White w/Black trim, custom finish is Green w/White trim.

B2N	$400	$375	$325	$300	$275	$250	$225
B3N	$650	$600	$550	$500	$450	$375	$350
B2V	$400	$375	$325	$300	$275	$250	$225
B3V	$650	$600	$550	$500	$450	$375	$350
B2N12	$400	$375	$325	$300	$275	$250	$225
B3N12	$650	$600	$550	$500	$450	$375	$350

"C" SERIES - guitar, bass {four and six1string}, twelve-string, offset semi-solid "Durabody" w/vinyl edging, six-in-line matching headstock {twelve string resembles "Batwing" headstock} w/raised chrome script logo, two or three pickups w/chrome surrounds, optional vibrato on six string models, black or white rear painted plastic pickguard w/contrasting perimeter stripe and pickguard mounted input jack, two volume/two tone with two slider switches {three pickup model has three slider switches and additional master volume control}, standard "Gator" textured finish is Gator Black w/Red trim, custom finishes are Gator Black w/Blue trim, and Gator Black w/Beige trim.

C2N	$400	$375	$325	$300	$275	$250	$225
C3N	$650	$600	$550	$500	$450	$375	$350
C2V	$400	$375	$325	$300	$275	$250	$225
C3V	$650	$600	$550	$500	$450	$375	$350
C2N12	$400	$375	$325	$300	$275	$250	$225
C3N12	$650	$600	$550	$500	$450	$375	$350
C2B4	$400	$375	$325	$300	$275	$250	$225
C2B6	$600	$550	$500	$450	$375	$350	$325

"D" SERIES - guitar, bass {four and six-string}, twelve-string, offset sculpted solid wood body, six-in-line matching headstock {twelve string resembles "Batwing" headstock} w/raised chrome script logo, two or three pickups w/chrome surrounds, optional vibrato on six string models, "Reflective Stylized" pickguard w/perimeter stripe, stainless control panel, two pickup model has individual volume for each pickup and master volume w/4 slider switches, three pickup model has individual volume for each pickup and master volume w/3 slider switches, available in Red, White, Black, Natural Black, Natural.

GRADING		100% MINT	98% NEAR MINT	95% EXC+	90% EXC	80% VG+	70% VG	60% G
D2N		$400	$375	$325	$300	$275	$250	$225
D3N		$650	$600	$550	$500	$450	$375	$350
D2V		$400	$375	$325	$300	$275	$250	$225
D3V		$650	$600	$550	$500	$450	$375	$350
D2N12		$400	$375	$325	$300	$275	$250	$225
D3N12		$650	$600	$550	$500	$450	$375	$350
D2B4		$400	$375	$325	$300	$275	$250	$225
D2B6		$600	$550	$500	$450	$375	$350	$325

DANELECTRO (CURRENT MFG.)

Instruments currently produced in Asia since 1998. Distributed by Danelectro Corporation of Laguna Hills, California.

ELECTRIC

56-U1 REISSUE - single cutaway semi-hollow body, masonite top and bottom, bolt on maple neck, adjustable truss rod, 21-fret rosewood fingerboard with white dot inlays, rosewood/metal stop tailpiece, "coke bottle" peghead with screened logo, 3-per-side sealed tuners, chrome hardware, 1 "Lipstick Tube" style single coil pickup, single stacked volume/tone control, available in Nifty Aqua, Limo Black, Daddy O.Yellow, Beatnik Burgundy, Commie Red, & Retro Purple. Mfg. 1998 to 1999.

		$160	$135	$110	$90	$75	$60	$50

Last MSR was $199.

56-U2 REISSUE - same as 56-U1 except has 2 "Lipstick Tube"-style single coil pickups, 2 sets stacked volume/tone controls, 3-way selector switch, available in Aqua Burst, Beatnik Burgundy, Blue Burst, Blue Suede, Commie Red, Cool Copper, Copper Burst, Daddy-O Yellow, Limo Black, Malt Shop Creme, and Nifty Aqua finishes. Mfg. 1998 to date.

MSR	$299	$240	$200	$175	$150	$125	$100	$75

In 1999, Beatnick Burgundy finish was disc.
In 2000, Black Burst finish was introduced.

56-U2 LEFTHANDED REISSUE - same as the 56-U2 only mirrored for the left-handed musician, available in Nifty Aqua, Limo Black, Daddy-O Yellow, Commie Red, Aqua Burst & Copper Burst, available 1998 to date.

MSR	$399	$319	$275	$250	$200	$150	$125	$100

56-U3 REISSUE - same as the 56-U2 but has three "Lipstick Tube" single coil pickups. Features Select-O-Matic switching allowing for seven different tone settings. Override switch allows for activation of all three pickups regardless of tone setting. Gotah tuners and individual string saddles, available in Limo Black, Commie Red, Burgundy Burst, Black Metal flake, Silver Metalflake, & Turquoise Metalflake. New 1999.

MSR	$399	$325	$275	$250	$200	$150	$125	$100

In 1999, Commie Red, Burgundy Burst and Black Metalflake finishes were disc.

59-DC REISSUE - similar to the 56-U2 only has double cutaway body style. Two "Lipstick Tube" style single coil pickups and two stacked volume/tone controls. 3-way selector switch, available in Daddy-O Yellow, Commie Red, Limo Black, Peachy Keen, Beatnik Burgundy, Cool Copper & Retro Purple. Mfg. 1998-1999.

		$240	$200	$175	$150	$125	$100	$75

Last MSR was $299.

'59 DC Pro - similar to 59 DC Reissue, except has adjustable bridge, Gotoh tuners, available in Silver Metalflake, Black/Gold Pearl and Deep Blue Pearl finishes. New 2000.

MSR	$349	$279	$250	$200	$150	$125	$100	$75

DC-3 REISSUE - same as the 56-U3 except has double cutaway body style, available in Blue Suede, Limo Black, Commie Red, Black Metalflake, Silver Metalflake, & Turquoise Metalflake. New 1999

MSR	$399	$325	$275	$250	$200	$150	$125	$100

In 1999, Blue Suede and Commie Red finishes were disc.

BARITONE REISSUE - 56 Body style with 24-fret rosewood fingerboard with white dot inlays. Dual "Lipstick Tube" single coil pickups & two stacked volume/tone controls. 3-way selector switch, available in Nifty Aqua, Limo Black, Daddy-O Yellow, Commie Red, Aqua Burst & Copper Burst. New 1999.

MSR	$399	$325	$275	$250	$200	$150	$125	$100

In 1999, Daddy-O Yellow, Aqua Burst and Copper Burst finishes were disc.

HEARSAY - offset double cutaway body, Hard Maple neck with rosewood fingerboard, dot position markers, 21-frets, 3 single coil "Dano Tuned" pickups with middle pickup reverse wound, volume, tone, built in distortion, distortion sweep, stereo jacks, (1 bypass and 1 effects), fulcrum style tremelo, available in Red Sparkle Burst, Black Sparkle and Blue Sparkle Burst finishes. New 2001.

MSR	$199	$159	$139	$125	$95	$75	$60	$45

GRADING		100% MINT	98% NEAR MINT	95% EXC+	90% EXC	80% VG+	70% VG	60% G

HODAD - double cutaway model with offset waist. Has 4 "Lipstick Tube" single coil pickups wired like two Humbuckers. Pull-on tone knobs for out of phase and coil-tap on each pickup set. Twelve tone variations, available with or without whammy bar. Dual tone and volume controls. Gotoh tuners, available in Black/Gold Pearl, Violet Pearl, Deep Blue Pearl, White/Violet Pearl, Red Pearl & Light Blue Metalflake. New 1999.

MSR	$399	$325	$275	$250	$200	$150	$125	$100
(w/Whammy)	$499	$400	$375	$350	$300	$250	$200	$150

HODAD BARITONE - similar to Hodad, except long scale, 3 "Lipstick" pickups, 7-tone Select-O-Matic switching, available in Black Metal Flake, Black/Gold Pearl and White/Violet Pearl finishes. New 2000.

MSR	$499	$399	$350	$295	$250	$195	$150	$95

HODAD 12-STRING - similar to Hodad, except in a 12-string configuration, 3 "Lipstick" pickups, 7-tone Select-O-Matic switching. 6-per-side tuners, available in Black/Gold Pearl, Deep Blue Pearl and White/Violet Pearl finishes. New 2000.

MSR	$499	$399	$350	$295	$250	$195	$150	$95

INNUENDO - offset double cutaway solid body, 3 single coil "Dano-Tuned" pickups with the middle pickup reverse wound, 4 built-in effects, push button Distortion, Chorus, Tremelo and Echo, volume, tone, distortion control and tremelo speed, pearloid pickguard, fulcrum style tremelo, 3-per-side tuners, graphite nut, stereo jacks (1 bypass, 1 effects), available in Limo Black, Gold Sparkle Burst and Blue/Silver Sparkle Burst finishes. New 2001.

MSR	$269	$215	$175	$150	$125	$95	$75	$50

Innuendo 12-String - similar to Innuendo, except in a 12-string configuration. 4 built-in effects, available in Black Sunburst, Red Sunburst and Blue Burst finishes. New 2001.

MSR	$299	$239	$195	$175	$150	$125	$95	$65

Innuendo Baritone - similar to Innuendo, exept has a long scale neck, 22-frets, 4 built-in effects, available in Red Sunburst, Black Sunburst and Blue Burst finishes. New 2001.

MSR	$299	$239	$195	$175	$150	$125	$95	$65

MOD - single cutaway body style, 2 single coil "Lipstick" pickups and 1 humbucker pickup, Select-O-Matic switching, coil tap, 11 tone variations, pearloid pickguard, available in 6 and 7-string sub-models, available in Black/Gold Pearl, White/Violet Pearl, Aqua Pearl and Violet Pearl finishes. New 2000.

MSR	$599	$479	$395	$350	$295	$250	$195	$150

GUITAR/MANDOLIN REISSUE - longhorn double cutaway styling with 31-fret neck. Lower frets used for normal guitar sounds. Upper frets are used for mandolin-like effect. Two "Lipstick Tube" single coil pickups and two stacked volume/tone controls. Selector switch, available in Commie Red, Black Metalflake, & Black Burst. New 1999.

MSR	$399	$325	$275	$250	$200	$150	$125	$100

12-string - 12-string variation of the 59-DC. Two single coil "Lipstick Tube" pickups and two stacked volume/tone controls. Has Gotoh tuners and adjustable bridge, available in Limo Black, White Pearl, Dark Blue Metalflake, Deep Purple Metalflake & Red Pearl. New 1999.

MSR	$399	$319	$275	$225	$195	$175	$150	$95

DOUBLENECK REISSUE - available as either a 6-string/12-string combo or a 6-string/baritone combo. Two "Lipstick Tube" single coil pickups per neck with separate stacked volume/tone controls for each. Selector switch. Gotoh tuners, available in Light Blue Pearl, White Pearl, & Black Burst. New 1999.

MSR	$599	$480	$425	$375	$325	$275	$250	$225

CONVERTIBLE REISSUE - acoustic/electric. Double cutaway design with a single "Lipstick Tube" style single coil pickup and stacked volume/tone control. Can be used as an acoustic or an electric guitar, available in Nifty Aqua, Limo Black, Beatnik Burgundy, Malt Shop Creme, Blue Burst, and Copper Burst. Mfg. 1999.

		$239	$200	$175	$150	$125	$100	$75

Last MSR was $299.

Convertible Pro - similar to Convertible Reissue, except has Gotoh tuners, available in Dark Blue Metalflake, Deep Purple Metalflake, Beep Blue Pearl and White Pearl finishes. New 2000.

MSR	$349	$279	$250	$195	$175	$150	$125	$95

ELECTRIC BASS

58-LONGHORN BASS REISSUE - double cutaway with extended "Horns". Two "Lipstick Tube" single coil pickups & two stacked volume/tone controls. 24-fret rosewood fingerboard with white dot inlays, available in Nifty Aqua, Blue Suede, Limo Black, Daddy-O Yellow, Beatnik Burgundy, Commie Red, Aqua Burst, Blue Burst, Copper Burst, Black Burst & Burgundy Burst. 1998 to 1999.

		$280	$250	$225	$200	$175	$150	$125

Last MSR was $349.

Longhorn Pro - similar to '58 Longhorn Bass Reissue, except has adjustable bridge and upgraded tuners, available in Deep Blue Pearl and Black/White Pearl Burst finishes. New 2000.

MSR	$399	$319	$250	$225	$195	$150	$125	$95

DC BASS - electronically similar to the 58-Longhorn except has normal double cutaway body style. Long scale rosewood neck with white dot inlays. Dual tone and volume controls, available in Cool Copper, Limo Black, Daddy-O Yellow, Commie Red, Black or Silver Metalflake. New 1999.

MSR	$349	$280	$250	$225	$200	$175	$150	$125

In 1999, Cool Copper and Daddy-O Yellow finishes were disc.

GRADING		100% MINT	98% NEAR MINT	95% EXC+	90% EXC	80% VG+	70% VG	60% G

DC LEFTHANDED BASS - as above except in left-handed configuration, available in Limo Black & Silver Metalflake. New 1999.

MSR	$449	$359	$299	$275	$250	$225	$175	$150

HODAD BASS - similar to Hodad in design, long scale, 3 single coil "Lipstick" pickups, 7-tone Select-O-Matic switching, available in Black/Gold Pearl, Deep Blue Pearl and White/Violet Pearl finishes. New 2000.

MSR	$499	$399	$350	$295	$250	$195	$150	$95

RUMOR BASS - offset double cutaway solid body, hard maple neck with rosewood fingerboard, 34" scale, 20-frets, "Dano-Tuned" bass pickups, Built in Chorus, adjustable bridge, 2-per-side tuners, available in Red Sparkle Burst, Blue Burst and Black Sparkle finishes. New 2001.

MSR	$199	$159	$139	$120	$95	$75	$55	$40

6-STRING BASS REISSUE - 56 Body style in a 6-string bass version. Two "Lipstick Tube" style single coil pickups and stacked volume/tone controls. Selector switch. Upgraded tuners, available in Limo Black & Turquoise Metalflake. New 1999.

MSR	$449	$359	$299	$275	$250	$225	$175	$150

DAVID ANDREW DESIGN RESEARCH

Instruments previously built in California during the mid 1980s.

David Andrew Design Research was founded in 1984 by David W. Newelll & Andrew Derosiers of Choes, NY. They received their first 2 U.S. patents 2 years later. Newell & Desoiers designed the first "Crusader" (later called Bladerunner by Guild guitars) prototype in the summer of 1984, and was featured in several guitar magazines later that year. The first guitars made their debut at Alex Music on 48th St. in NY during the fall of 1985. Newell & Desrosiers met J.J. French of Twisted Sister later that year, which bore their relationship with Mark Dronge of Guild Guitars. Guild adopted the Crusader guitar and bass design, and renamed it the Bladerunner in early 1986. The Bladerunner made its debut on the world market at the 1986 summer NAMM Show in New Orleans. The Bladerunner was in production through 1988, until Mark Dronge sold the company. The Bladerunner made its video debut in the Aerosmith/Run D.M.C. video, "Walk this Way". The Bladerunner was played by several top guitar players of the 1980s, including Joe Perry of Aerosmith, Howarde Leese of Heart, Eddie O'Jeda of Twisted Sister, and Ben Orr of The Cars.

The David Andrew Crusader/Bladerunner was an explorer-style solid body guitar with triangular cut-outs, a poplar body, dove tail glued in neck, 24-fret ebony fingerboard, Grover tuners, EMG pickups and electronics and lacquer finish and graphics, and came with a hard shell case. The last MSR was $1,500. Production continued through 1988.

(The publisher would like to thank Mr. David W. Newell for the above information.)

DAVID THOMAS MCNAUGHT GUITARS

Instruments currently built in Charlotte, North Carolina since 1989.

While he has been building guitars part time for the past eight years, David Thomas McNaught recently began building full time in 1997. McNaught's guitar playing background started in his childhood, performing to his favorite band's songs with a tennis racket! While learning to play an actual guitar, McNaught sometimes became dissatisfied with the construction. Many of his first guitars became *customized* (changing parts and pickups). This customizing combined his family's woodworking background and gave him the idea to begin building his own designs. Many of the ideas used in his guitar designs are based on a player's point of view. These handmade solid body arched top guitars are available in three different models (model configuration based on different bridges, body binding, and other specifications), and prices start at $2,500.

DAVIDSON STRINGED INSTRUMENTS

Instruments currently built in Lakewood, Colorado.

The Davidson Stringed Instrument company offers handcrafted electric guitars and basses with a wide selection of pickups and hardware options to choose from.

There are two models of guitars to choose from: The **Vintage Classic** (list price $2,395) which features a slightly offset double cutaway walnut body with a carved flame maple top, 5-piece maple/walnut neck which runs through the body, 24-fret rosewood fingerboard, stop tailpiece, and gold hardware (a Wilkinson tremolo is an additional $150). The Vintage Classic is available in Natural clear or Transparent finishes. The **Vintage Classic Sunburst** (list price $2,795) features similar construction, and has a 25-piece abalone/pearl inlay on the ebony fingerboard, flame maple binding, and choice of Sunburst finish.

Davidson **bass guitar** models are available in 4-, 5-, and 6-string configurations in a neck-through-body design. Prices start at $1,800 and up.

DAVIS, J. THOMAS

Instruments currently built in Columbus, Ohio.

Luthier Tom Davis estimates that while he builds a handful of custom guitars each year, his primary focus is on repair work. Davis has over twenty years experience in guitar building and repair. For further information about repair work or custom guitar pricing, please contact luthier Tom Davis directly (see Trademark Index).

K.D. DAVIS GUITARS

Instruments currently built in Sonoma, California.

Luthier Kevin D. Davis is currently building hand crafted custom guitars. For further information concerning model specifications and pricing, please contact luthier Kevin Davis directly (see Trademark Index).

DAVIS, WILLIAM

Instruments currently built in Boxford, Maine.

William Davis' hand built guitars are available through his Boxford, Maine lutherie. For up-to-date information concerning models and pricing, please contact luthier William Davis directly (see Trademark Index).

DAVOLI

See also WANDRE, GHERSON, and KRUNDAAL.

Instruments previously built in Italy from the early 1960s through the early 1970s.

The Davoli company built Wandre and Krundaal guitars in the 1960s, and progressed towards the Gherson trademark in the 1970s.

(Source: Tony Bacon and Paul Day, The Guru's Guitar Book)

GRADING	100% MINT	98% NEAR MINT	95% EXC+	90% EXC	80% VG+	70% VG	60% G

D

DE LACUGO

Instruments currently built in Atascadero, California.

De Lacugo Guitars offers 2 different models that feature mahogany bodies and 22-fret bolt-on maple necks. The **DC Guitar** (list $2,495) features a single cutaway Telecaster-ish body, 2 DiMarzio or Seymour Duncan humbucking pickups, fixed bridge, and a custom metal flake finish. The **Excelsior** guitar (list $2,595) has an extremely sculptured body, Floyd Rose or Wilkinson tremolo system, and candy-apple metal flake paint. An **Excelsior** bass guitar model is also available, with similar styled sculptured body and paint job (list $2,695). For more information, contact Tony De Lacugo directly (see Trademark Index).

DE WHALLEY

Instruments previously built in England during the mid 1980s.

This original design solid body was available in Standard, Deluxe, and Custom. Anyone with further information on the CV model is invited to write to the *Blue Book of Electric Guitars*. We will update future editions as the information becomes available.

(Source: Tony Bacon and Paul Day, The Guru's Guitar Guide)

DEAKON ROADS GUITARS

Instruments currently manufactured in Saskatoon, Saskatchewan, Canada beginning 1999.

Deakon Roads Guitars makes a Strat-like instrument that was designed for Deakon Roads by veteran Canadian guitar designer, Glen McDougall.

INTRUDER - offset double cutaway body constructed of soft maple, Eastern rock maple neck with walnut fingerboard (optional Eastern rock maple fingerboard), dot position markers, 25" scale, 22-frets, adjustable high-mass bridge, Grover Mini Roto-Matic tuners, chrome plated brass hardware, 3 single coil highly shielded pickups, black pickguard, 1 volume/1 tone control, 5-way switch, available in Electric Blue Metallic, Emerald Green Metallic, Teal Metallic, Pewter Metallic, Burgundy Metallic, Silver Metallic, Charcoal Metallic, Candy Apple Red, Midnight Black, Transparent Blue, Transparent Red, Transparent Green, Transparent Teal, Transparent Amber and Transparent Burgundy finishes. Current Mfg.

MSR $995 $895

DEAN

Current trademark owned by Dean Guitar Co., with headquarters located in Clearwater, Florida. Instruments currently produced in Plant City, Florida (Custom Shop and all the USA series) and Korea (the American Spirit series). Distributed by Armadillo Enterprises of Clearwater, Florida.

Dean guitars with the set-neck design were previously built in Evanston, Illinois from 1977 to 1986. In 1985, Dean began production of some models in Japan and Korea. Dean production from 1986 to 1993 was based in Asia.

The original Evanston, Illinois-based company was founded by Dean Zelinsky in 1977, after graduating from high school in 1976. Zelinsky, fond of classic Gibson designs, began building high quality electric solid body instruments and eventually started developing his own designs. Originally, there were three models: The V (similar to the Flying V), The Z (Explorer body shape), and the ML (sort of a cross between the V and an Explorer, and named after the initials of Matt Lynn, Zelinsky's best friend growing up). As the company's guitars gained popularity, production facilities were moved to Chicago in 1980.

Zelinsky originally got into the guitar building business to fill a void he felt the larger companies had: a high quality, set neck, eye-catching stage guitar. Though new designs continued to be developed, manufacturing of these instruments was shifted more and more to overseas builders. In 1986, Dean closed the USA Shop, leaving all construction to be completed overseas. The U.S. market had shifted towards the then-popular bolt neck *super-strat* design, and Zelinsky's personal taste leaned in the opposite direction.

Zelinsky sold Dean Guitars in 1990 to Oscar Medros, founder and owner of Tropical Music (based in Miami, Florida). The Dean Guitars facility in Plant City, Florida is currently run by Tracy Hoeft and Jon Hill, and new guitars are distributed to markets in the U.S., Japan, Korea, and Europe.

Zelinsky has estimated that between 6,000 and 7,000 (possibly 8,000) guitars were built in the U.S. between 1977 and 1986.

It has been estimated by various Dean collectors that the Japanese Dean models were built by the ESP Guitar company in Japan (circa 1986 to 1989).

In 1998, the Dean Guitar company introduced the Dean Stack in the Box (retail new $44.95), a stereo headphone amp that can be hooked up to home stereos; and the Dean Mean 16 (list $109.95), a 16-watt solid state amp with overdrive.

IDENTIFYING FEATURES

Headstock Variations

1977-1982: Guitars built between 1977 to 1982 had the large forked 'Dean' headstock.

1983-On: In 1983, the smaller headstock (nicknamed the "shrimp fork") was introduced for models with a tremolo; then all of U.S. made instruments were shifted over to the smaller forked peghead. Korean-built bolt neck 'superstrat' guitars have a pointy 6-on-a-side drooped design.

GRADING	100% MINT	98% NEAR MINT	95% EXC+	90% EXC	80% VG+	70% VG	60% G

Serialization

The serial numbers for U.S. produced Dean guitars were stamped into the back of the headstock, and have the year of production within the number. Imported Dean models do not carry the stamped and year-coded serial numbers.

Model Dating Identification

Author/researcher Michael Wright briefly discussed Dean guitar history in his book, *Guitar Stories Volume One* (Vintage Guitar Books, 1995). In the course of the Dean chapter, Wright provided some key developments in the company's history that helps date the various series offered.

1976-1978: Zelinsky opens his first factory in Evanston, Illinois; Introduction of the **ML, V**, and **Z** models.

1979-1980: Introduction of the **Cadillac** and **E'Lite** models; the company moves to a larger factory in Chicago.

1982: The downsized-body **Baby** models are presented. This series began production with the large V-shaped peghead, but shortly after switched to the small fork style peghead that is the most common found (the large V-shaped peghead was optionally offered). The **Baby** configuration has an unbound fingerboard and dot inlays, while the **Baby Deluxe** has a bound fingerboard and block inlays.

1983-1984: Bolt-neck **Bel Aire** 'superstrat' models.

1985: The Japanese-built **Hollywood** models were introduced.

1985-1987: Korean bolt-neck **Signature** 'superstrat' models.

1987-1990: More Korean bolt-neck designs arrive: the **Eighty-Eight** (perhaps a year early?), **Jammer**, and **Playmate** models.

1990: Zelinsky sells Dean Guitar Company to Tropical Music.

1991: The six screw bolt-neck 'superstrat' **90E, 91E**, and **92E** are introduced.

1993-1994: The U.S. built **Reissue Series** of the classic 1977 designs are briefly built in Northern California.

1994: **American Custom** ML, US Cadillac, and SL models first built in Cleveland, Ohio.

1995: New Dean facilities opened in Plant City, Florida. **American Custom** instruments are completely built in the U.S., while the **U.S. Series** instruments feature Dean USA necks, Korean bodies, and assembly in the U.S. The **D** Series is produced in Korea.

1997: U.S. built guitars are offered in the **Coupe, Deluxe, LTD**, and **Korina Series**; similar-styled imported Dean models fall under the various **American Spirit** series.

1998: The **American Spirit** terminology is disc, but the models retain their respective tiered pricing and quality levels. U.S. built guitars fall under the **USA Custom Shop: Coupe** and **LTD Series** are still maintained; **Flame, Ultima**, and **U.S. Phantom Series** are added; and the **Deluxe** (basically an Original Floyd Rose tremolo option) is disc. **European Custom** and **European Premium Series** are added; the **European Custom Series** takes over korina (**V** and **Z**) models from
the **U.S. Korina** models (a U.S. korina model would now be a USA Custom Shop model). Even more important, Dean acoustic guitars, acoustic/electric guitars, and even resonator models are introduced.

ELECTRIC

Listed below are standard configurations of instruments. Being a highly handcrafted product though, instruments can be found with numerous options. Several finishes were used throughout this trademark's early life, including *Cheetah, Tiger*, and *Zebra Graphic* finishes, and models are not necessarily limited to finishes listed.

90s Series

The series of 90E, 91E, and 92E models was manufactured 1991 to 1993 in Korea. All instruments in this series had a six bolt neck plate, and were available in Black, Blueburst, Grayburst, Red, and White finishes (unless otherwise listed).

90E - offset double cutaway alder body, bolt-on maple neck, 24-fret rosewood fingerboard with pearl wings inlay, standard vibrato, blackface peghead with screened logo, 6-on-one-side tuners, chrome hardware, 2 single coil/1 humbucker pickups, 1 volume/2 tone controls, 5-position switch. Mfg. 1991 to 1993.

$250 $225 $195 $175 $150 $125 $100

Last MSR was $400.

91E - similar to 90E, except has bound arched top, double locking Floyd Rose vibrato, humbucker/single coil/humbucker pickups, black hardware. Mfg. 1991 to 1993.

$400 $350 $300 $275 $225 $195 $150

Last MSR was $620.

92E - similar to 90E, except has carved maple top, double locking Floyd Rose vibrato, gold hardware, available in Sunburst finish. Mfg. 1991 to 1993.

$400 $350 $300 $275 $225 $195 $150

Last MSR was $620.

Bel Aire Series

The bodies for the Bel Aire models were produced and instruments were assembled in the USA by Dean (the serial numbers were stamped under the neck plate area), with the remaining parts being made in Japan by ESP. By 1985, total production had moved to Japan. Revived in 1987, the Bel Aire models were entirely produced in Korea through 1989.

GRADING	100% MINT	98% NEAR MINT	95% EXC+	90% EXC	80% VG+	70% VG	60% G

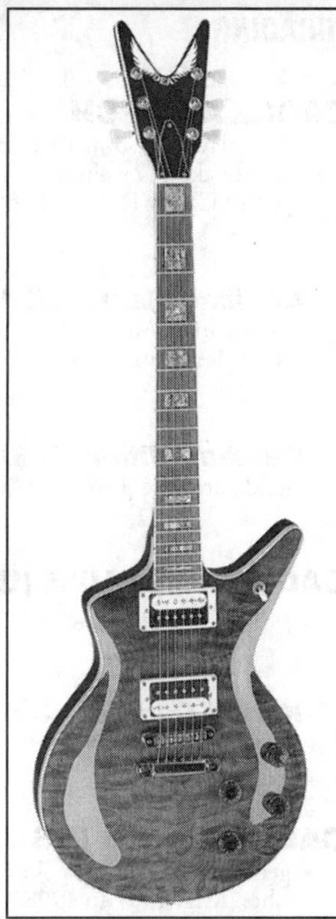
Dean Cadillac USA Custom
courtesy
Armadillo Enterprises

BEL AIRE - offset double cutaway maple body, bolt-on maple neck, 22-fret rosewood fingerboard with pearl dot inlay, standard vibrato, 3-per-side tuners, chrome hardware, 2 single coil/1 humbucker pickups, 2 volume/tone controls, 5-position switch, available in Black, Blueburst, Pearl, Pinkburst, and White finishes. Mfg. 1983 to 1984, 1987 to 1989.

$500 $425 $350 $295 $250 $225 $200
Last MSR was $1,050.

This model had an optional maple fingerboard.
In 1984, double locking Kahler vibrato became an option.
In 1985, 6-on-one-side tuners replaced original part/design.

HOLLYWOOD BEL AIRE - down-sized offset double cutaway hardwood body, bolt-on maple neck, 24-fret rosewood fingerboard with pearl dot inlay, tune-o-matic bridge/stop tailpiece, shrimp fork peghead with screened logo, 3-per-side tuners, chrome hardware, 2 humbucker pickups, volume/tone control, 3-position switch, available in Black, Blueburst, Bolt, Flames, Pearl Blue, Pearl Pink, Pearl Red, Pearl White, Red, Wedge, White, and Zebra Graphic finishes. Mfg. 1985 to 1987.

$200 $175 $150 $125 $100 $85 $65
Last MSR was $350.

Hollywood Bel Aire V - similar to Hollywood Bel Aire, except has double locking vibrato.

$225 $195 $150 $125 $100 $90 $75
Last MSR was $450.

Cadillac Series

The body design looks like a cross between a Les Paul and an Explorer with the rounded lower bout and Explorer-ish treble horn. The Cadillac version originally featured three pickups (versus the E'lite's two) but now the Cadillac name designates the body style.

CADILLAC - single horn cutaway round bottom bound mahogany body, mahogany neck, 22-fret bound ebony fingerboard with pearl block inlay, tune-o-matic bridge/stop tailpiece, blackface peghead with logo, 3-per-side tuners, gold hardware, 3 humbucker pickups, 2 volume/2 tone controls, 3-position switch, available in Braziliaburst, Caine White, Cherry, Cherryburst, Opaque Black and Walnut finishes. Mfg. 1979 to 1985.

$700 $600 $500 $400 $350 $325 $300
Last MSR was $1,600.

This model had optional 2 humbucker pickups.

U.S.A. SERIES CADILLAC-92 - single horn cutaway round bottom mahogany body, bound carved figured maple top, through-body mahogany neck, 22-fret bound ebony fingerboard with pearl dot inlay, Schaller tune-o-matic bridge/stop tailpiece, bound V-shape peghead with screened logo, 3-per-side tuners, chrome hardware, 3 exposed humbucker pickups, 2 volume/2 tone controls, 3-position switch, available in Cherry Sunburst, Natural, Transparent Blue and Transparent Red finishes. Mfg. 1992 to 1993.

$1,200 $1,050 $925 $775 $650 $525 $400
Last MSR was $1,600.

The U.S.A. series were produced in Northern California.

CADILLAC RESISSUE - single horn cutaway hardwood body, bound figured maple top, through-body mahogany neck, 24-fret bound rosewood fingerboard with pearl block inlay, tune-o-matic bridge/stop tailpiece, bound rosewood veneered peghead with screened logo, 3-per-side tuners, gold hardware, 2 covered humbucker pickups, 2 volume/2 tone controls, 3-position switch, available in Cherry Sunburst, Natural, Transparent Blue and Transparent Red finishes. Mfg. 1992 to 1994.

$650 $475 $395 $325 $275 $250 $225
Last MSR was $790.

The Reissue models were produced in Korea.

CADILLAC DELUXE - single horn cutaway round bottom mahogany body, bound arched mahogany top, set-in mahogany neck, 22-fret bound ebony fingerboard with pearl dot inlay, tune-o-matic bridge/stop tailpiece, bound V-shape peghead with screened logo, 3-per-side tuners, chrome hardware, 2 exposed Seymour Duncan humbuckers, 2 volume/2 tone controls, 3-position switch, available in Classic Black, Classic Red, Torrid Teal, and Wine Red finishes. Mfg. 1996 to 1997.

$1,200 $1,100 $950 $800 $675 $550 $425
Last MSR was $1,650.

Add $100 for flame maple top, mahogany body, available in Flame Black, Flame Blue, Flame Braziliaburst, Flame Cherry, Flame Cherry Sunburst, Flame Green, Flame Purple, Flame Teal, and Flame Vintage Sunburst finishes.

Add $125 for gold hardware and covered Seymour Duncan humbuckers (Model Cadillac DX GH).

Cadillac Standard - similar to the Cadillac Deluxe, except has a flat (non-arched) alder top, alder body, rosewood fingerboard. Mfg. 1996 to 1997.

$650 $575 $500 $425 $350 $295 $225
Last MSR was $875.

Add $20 for flame maple top, alder body, available in Flame Black, Flame Blue, Flame Braziliaburst, Flame Cherry, Flame Cherry Sunburst, Flame Green, Flame Purple, Flame Teal, and Flame Vintage Sunburst finishes.

Add $125 for gold hardware and covered Seymour Duncan humbuckers (Model Cadillac ST GH).

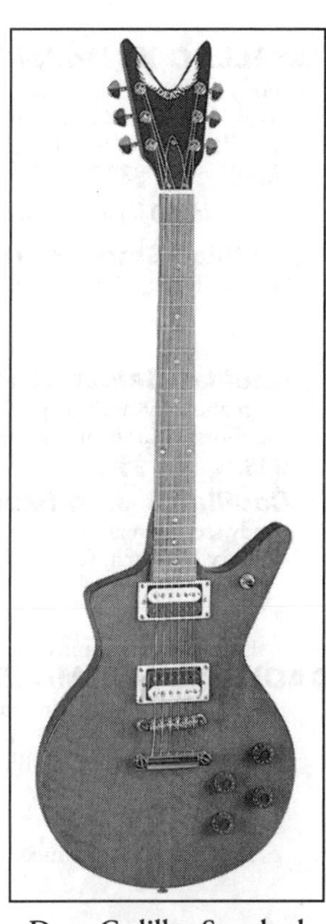
Dean Cadillac Standard
courtesy
Armadillo Enterprises

GRADING	100% MINT	98% NEAR MINT	95% EXC+	90% EXC	80% VG+	70% VG	60% G

D

CADILLAC ARCH - single horn cutaway round bottom mahogany body, arched top, set-in mahogany neck, 22-fret ebony fingerboard with pearl dot inlay, tune-o-matic bridge/stop tailpiece, V-shape peghead with screened logo, 3-per-side Grover tuners, chrome hardware, 2 Seymour Duncan humbuckers, 2 volume/2 tone controls, 3-position switch, available in Braziliaburst, Cherry Sunburst, Classic Black, Transparent Blue, and Transparent Candy Red finishes. Mfg. 1997 to 1998.

$1,000 $900 $850 $725 $600 $475 $350
Last MSR was $1,399.

Cadillac Flame (USA Custom Shop) - similar to the Cadillac Arch, except has arched flame maple top, wood body binding, available in Transparent Amber, Transparent Black, Transparent Blue, Transparent Candy Red, Transparent Green, Transparent Power Purple, and Transparent Root Beer finishes. Mfg. 1997 to 1998.

$1,350 $1,150 $1,000 $875 $750 $625 $475
Last MSR was $1,899.

Cadillac Ultima (USA Custom Shop) - similar to the Cadillac Flame, except has bound body/neck/peghead, block fingerboard inlays, gold hardware. Mfg. 1997 to 1999.

$1,850 $1,600 $1,425 $1,250 $1,000 $850 $695
Last MSR was $2,649.

CADILLAC COUPE (USA CUSTOM SHOP) - similar to the Cadillac Arch, except has flat (non-arched) mahogany body, available in Brite Blue, Canary Yellow, Cherry Sunburst, Classic Black, and Lipstick Red solid finishes. Mfg. 1997 to 1998.

$1,100 $975 $850 $750 $625 $500 $395
Last MSR was $1,599.

Korina Cadillac (U.S. Mfg.) - similar to the Cadillac Arch, except has flat (non-arched) korina body, available in Braziliaburst, Cherry Sunburst, Gloss Natural, Transparent Amber, and Transparent Red high gloss finishes. Mfg. 1997 to 1998.

$1,200 $1,000 $950 $850 $750 $650 $495
Last MSR was $1,899.

CADILLAC LTD (USA CUSTOM SHOP) - similar to the Cadillac Arch, except has flat (non-arched) mahogany body, bound body/fingerboard/headstock, gold hardware, available in Braziliaburst, Cherry Sunburst, Classic Black, Transparent Blue, and Transparent Candy Red finishes. Mfg. 1997 to 1998.

$1,350 $1,150 $1,000 $875 $750 $625 $475
Last MSR was $1,899.

Cadillac LTD 3 - similar to the Cadillac LTD, except has 3 Seymour Duncan humbuckers, custom fingerboard inlay. Mfg. 1997 to 1998.

$1,200 $1,000 $950 $850 $750 $650 $495
Last MSR was $1,899.

CADILLAC JUNIOR - similar to the Cadillac Arch, except has flat (non-arched) hardwood body, bolt-on maple neck, 22-fret rosewood fingerboard with dot inlays, fixed bridge, available in Classic Black, Classic Red, and Vintage Sunburst finishes. Mfg. 1997 to 1998.

$250 $225 $200 $175 $150 $125 $95
Last MSR was $349.

CADILLAC X (Model DGK-CADIX, AMERICAN SPIRIT CADILLAC X) - single horn cutaway round bottom basswood body, bolt-on maple neck, 22-fret rosewood fingerboard with dot inlays, tune-o-matic bridge/stop tailpiece, large V-shape peghead with screened logo, 3-per-side Grover tuners, chrome hardware, 2 "Zebra" humbuckers, 2 volume/2 tone controls, 3-position switch, available in (Transparent) Braziliaburst, Classic Black, Transparent Blue, and Transparent Red finishes. Mfg. 1997 to date.

MSR $3299 $245 $225 $195 $175 $150 $125 $95

Add $20 for left-handed configuration (Model DGK-CADIXL), available in Classic Black and Transparent Red finishes.

Cadillac Standard (Model DGK-CADIST) - similar to the Cadillac X, except has mahogany body, set-in mahogany neck, available in Classic Black, Transparent Blue, Transparent Braziliaburst, and Transparent Red finishes. Mfg. 1998 to 1999.

$425 $375 $325 $275 $250 $195 $150
Last MSR was $599.

Cadillac Select (Model DGK-CADISE) - similar to the Cadillac X, except has mahogany body, triple bound arched flame maple top, set-in mahogany neck, triple bound headstock, block fingerboard inlays, gold hardware, available in Flame Amberburst, Flame Black, Flame Cherry Sunburst, Flame Purple, and Flame Red finishes. Mfg. 1998 to date.

MSR $599 $425 $375 $325 $275 $225 $175 $150

Cadillac 3 Ultra (Model DGK-CADI3, American Spirit Cadillac Ultra) - similar to the Cadillac X, except has mahogany body, set-in mahogany neck, bound body/fingerboard/headstock, fingerboard block inlays, 3 covered humbuckers, gold hardware, available in Cherry Sunburst, Classic Black, and Transparent Red finishes. Mfg. 1997 to 1999.

$495 $425 $375 $325 $275 $225 $175
Last MSR was $699.

Earlier models may have 3 "Zebra" humbuckers, or a Metallic Red finish.

CADILLAC ULTIMA EUROPEAN CUSTOM (Model DGE-CAUL) - single horn cutaway round bottom mahogany body, arched flame top, set-in mahogany neck, 22-fret rosewood fingerboard with pearl block inlay, tune-o-matic bridge/stop tailpiece, large V-shape peghead with screened logo, 3-per-side Schaller tuners, chrome hardware, 2 "Zebra" humbuckers, 2 volume/2 tone controls, 3-position switch, available in Flame Amber, Flame Blue, Flame Green, Flame Red, 24K Gold Sparkle, Ruby Sparkle, and Silver Sparkle finishes. Mfg. 1998 to 1999.

$795 $675 $595 $525 $425 $350 $275
Last MSR was $1,099.

This model is produced in Europe.

GRADING	100% MINT	98% NEAR MINT	95% EXC+	90% EXC	80% VG+	70% VG	60% G

European Premium Cadillac Premium Ultima (DGE-PR-CU) - similar to the Cadillac Ultima European Custom, except features highly figured maple top, celluloid bound body/neck/headstock, gold hardware, 2 Seymour Duncan humbuckers, available in Flame Amber, Flame Amberburst, Flame Black, Flame Blue, Flame Cherry Sunburst, Flame Green, Flame Purple, and Flame Red finishes. Disc.

$950 $795 $700 $600 $525 $425 $325
Last MSR was $1,299.

This model was manufactured in Europe.

Chafin Series - named for Dean Custom Shop Senior Luthier Ben Chafin.

BOCA - double cutaway semi-hollow mahogany body, maple top, bolt-on maple neck, rosewood fingerboard with abalone dot position markers, 22 frets, 3-per-side chrome Grover tuners, 2 Dean humbucking pickups, Tune-O-Matic bridge, 1 volume/1 tone control, 3-way switch, chrome hardware, available in Classic Black, Metallic Charcoal and Metallic Red finishes. Current Mfg.

MSR $419 $315 $275 $250 $225 $195 $150 $95

Sarasota - similar to Boca, except has mahogany set neck, 2 Zebra humbucking pickups, Flame Maple top, single ply binding, available in Transparent Amber, Transparent Braziliaburst and Transparent red finishes. Current Mfg.

MSR $579 $435 $375 $325 $275 $250 $225 $175

Del Sol - similar to Sarasota Model, except has gold hardware, gold covered pickups, multi-ply binding, mother-of-pearl "Sun" position markers, available in Classic White, Transparent Amber, Transparent Blue and Transparent Red finishes. Current Mfg.

MSR $799 $599 $499 $450 $399 $350 $299 $250

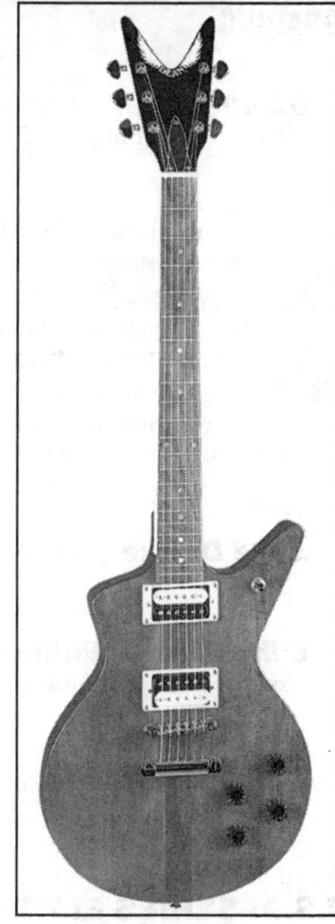

Dean Cadillac X courtesy Armadillo Enterprises

Custom Series

The Custom Series featured four special airbrushed color graphics.

BEAR METAL - offset double cutaway hardwood body, bolt-on maple neck, 22-fret rosewood fingerboard with pearl dot inlay, Floyd Rose tremolo, 6-on-a-side pointy headstock with screened logo, chrome hardware, EMG Select humbucker, volume/tone control, available in airbrushed claw/metal custom finish. Mfg. 1989 to 1991.

$350 $325 $300 $275 $250 $225 $200
Last MSR was $799.

Derri-Air - similar to the Bear Metal, except features airbrushed view of a butt in a bikini bottom custom finish. Mfg. 1989 to 1991.

$350 $325 $300 $275 $250 $225 $200
Last MSR was $799.

Pizza Face - similar to the Bear Metal, except features airbrushed likeness of Freddy Krueger ('Nightmare on Elm Street') custom finish. Mfg. 1989 to 1991.

$350 $325 $300 $275 $250 $225 $200
Last MSR was $799.

Space Angels - similar to the Bear Metal, except features airbrushed scene of two female 'angels' in space custom finish. Mfg. 1989 to 1991.

$350 $325 $300 $275 $250 $225 $200
Last MSR was $799.

D Series

The D Series/DS model guitars were produced in Korea from 1994 to 1996. Their body designs were similar to the 1990s Series models, except reverted to the 3-per-side 'shrimp fork' type headstock instead of 6-per-side tuners. D Series models have 4 bolt neckplates.

DS 90 - offset double cutaway hardwood body, bolt-on maple neck, 24-fret rosewood fingerboard with pearl wings inlay, standard vibrato, blackface peghead with screened logo, 3-per-side tuners, black hardware, 2 single coil/1 humbucker pickups, 1 volume/2 tone controls, 5-position switch, available in Black, Red, and White finishes. Mfg. 1994 to 1996.

$275 $250 $225 $175 $150 $125 $95
Last MSR was $375.

This model was offered in a left-handed configuration as the DS 90 L.

DS 87 - similar to the DS 90, except has 3 single coil pickups, 6-on-a-side headstock, chrome hardware, white pickguard, available in Classic Black, Classic Red, and Vintage Sunburst finishes. Mfg. 1996 to 1997.

$225 $175 $150 $125 $100 $90 $75
Last MSR was $285.

DS 91 - similar to DS 90, except has alder body, bound carved top, double locking Floyd Rose vibrato, humbucker/single coil/humbucker pickups, available in Black Flame Maple, Burgundy Flame Maple, Metallic Black, and Vintage Sunburst finishes. Mfg. 1994 to 1996.

$425 $350 $325 $275 $225 $175 $150
Last MSR was $555.

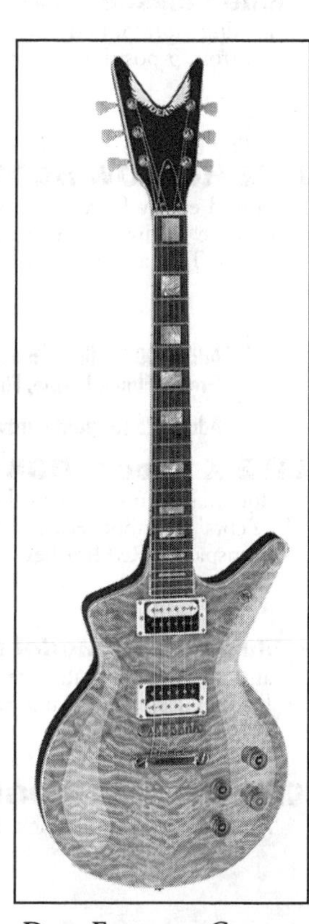

Dean European Custom Cadillac (Premium) courtesy Armadillo Enterprises

D

GRADING	100% MINT	98% NEAR MINT	95% EXC+	90% EXC	80% VG+	70% VG	60% G

DS 92 - similar to DS 90, except has carved maple top, double locking Floyd Rose vibrato, gold hardware, six on a side tuners, available in Black Flame Maple, Burgundy Flame Maple, Metallic Black, and Vintage Sunburst finishes. Mfg. 1994 to 1996.

$450 $395 $350 $295 $250 $200 $150
Last MSR was $595.

This model was offered in a left-handed configuration as the DS 92 L.

D

E'lite Series

The body design looks like a cross between a Les Paul and an Explorer with the rounded lower bout and Explorer-ish treble horn. The Cadillac version of the E'lite originally featured three pickups while the E'lite model had two, but now the Cadillac name is used to designate the body style on current models.

E'LITE - single horn cutaway round bottom mahogany body, mahogany neck, 22-fret bound rosewood fingerboard with pearl dot inlay, tune-o-matic bridge/stop tailpiece, blackface peghead with logo, 3-per-side tuners, chrome hardware, 2 DiMarzio exposed humbucker pickups, 2 volume/2 tone controls, 3-position switch, available in Braziliaburst, Caine White, Cherry, Cherryburst, Opaque Black and Walnut finishes. Mfg. 1978 to 1985.

$900 $825 $725 $650 $500 $475 $325
Last MSR was $1,030.

E'lite Deluxe - similar to E'lite, except has bound body, bound ebony fingerboard, available in Bursts and Natural finishes. Mfg. 1981 to 1985.

$925 $825 $750 $650 $525 $400 $350
Last MSR was $1,230.

E'lite Special Edition - similar to E'lite, except has bound curly maple top, bound ebony fingerboard with abalone dot inlay, gold hardware, covered pickups, available in Natural finish. Mfg. 1982 to 1984.

$825 $750 $625 $575 $495 $400 $325
Last MSR was $1,200.

Golden E'lite - similar to E'lite, except has bound body, bound ebony fingerboard with abalone dot inlay, gold hardware, covered pickups, available in Walnut finish. Mfg. 1979 to 1981.

$850 $750 $675 $595 $525 $425 $350
Last MSR was $1,200.

U.S.A. SERIES ELITE-92 - single horn cutaway mahogany body, bound carved figured maple top, through-body mahogany neck, 22 bound ebony fingerboard with pearl dot inlay, Schaller tune-o-matic bridge/stop tailpiece, bound V-shape peghead with screened logo, 3-per-side tuners, chrome hardware, 2 exposed humbucker pickups, 2 volume/2 tone controls, 3-position switch, available in Cherry Sunburst, Natural, Transparent Blue and Transparent Red finishes. Mfg. 1992 to 1993.

$1,200 $1,050 $925 $850 $750 $625 $495
Last MSR was $1,600.

The U.S.A. series were produced in Northern California.

Elite Reissue - single horn cutaway hardwood body, through-body mahogany neck, 22-fret rosewood fingerboard with pearl dot inlay, double locking vibrato, body matching peghead with screened logo, 3-per-side tuners, chrome hardware, 2 exposed humbucker pickups, 2 volume/2 tone controls, 3-position switch, available in Black, Blueburst, Grayburst, Red and White finishes. Mfg. 1992 to 1994.

$725 $650 $575 $500 $450 $350 $275
Last MSR was $790.

The Reissue models were produced in Korea.

ELITE HOLLOW BODY - semi-hollow single horn cutaway mahogany body, bound arched mahogany top, set-in mahogany neck, 22-fret bound ebony fingerboard with pearl dot inlay, tune-o-matic bridge/stop tailpiece, bound V-shape peghead with screened logo, 3-per-side tuners, chrome hardware, 2 exposed Seymour Duncan humbuckers, 2 volume/2 tone controls, 3-position switch, available in Classic Black, Classic Red, Torrid Teal, and Wine Red finishes. Mfg. 1996 to 1997.

$1,200 $1,100 $950 $800 $675 $550 $425
Last MSR was $1,650.

Add $100 for flame maple top, mahogany body, available in Flame Black, Flame Blue, Flame Braziliaburst, Flame Cherry, Flame Cherry Sunburst, Flame Green, Flame Purple, Flame Teal, and Flame Vintage Sunburst finishes.

Add $125 for gold hardware and covered Seymour Duncan humbuckers (Model Elite GH).

ELITE X (Model DGK-ELX) - single horn cutaway round bottom basswood body, bolt-on maple neck, 22-fret rosewood fingerboard with dot inlays, tune-o-matic bridge/stop tailpiece, small offset V-shape peghead with screened logo, 3-per-side Grover tuners, chrome hardware, 2 "Zebra" humbuckers, 2 volume/2 tone controls, 3-position switch, available in (Transparent) Braziliaburst, Classic Black, Transparent Blue, and Transparent Red finishes. Mfg. 1998 to 1999.

$275 $250 $225 $195 $175 $150 $125
Last MSR was $349.

Elite Select (Model DGK-ELSE) - similar to the Elite X, except has mahogany body, triple bound arched flame maple top, set-in mahogany neck, triple bound headstock, block fingerboard inlays, gold hardware, available in Flame Amberburst, Flame Black, Flame Cherry Sunburst, Flame Purple, and Flame Red finishes. Mfg. 1998.

$495 $425 $375 $325 $275 $225 $175
Last MSR was $699.

ELITE AX (Model DGK-ELAX) - similar to the Elite X, except features mahogany body, bound arched flame maple top, available in Flame Amberburst, Flame Black, Flame Blue, Flame Cherry Sunburst, and Flame Red finishes. Mfg. 1998.

$350 $300 $275 $225 $195 $150 $125
Last MSR was $499.

GRADING	100% MINT	98% NEAR MINT	95% EXC+	90% EXC	80% VG+	70% VG	60% G

Elite AXV (Model DGK-ELAXV) - similar to the Elite AX, except features a 2-point floating tremolo, available in Flame Amberburst, Flame Black, Flame Blue, Flame Cherry Sunburst, and Flame Red finishes. Mfg. 1998.

		$350	$300	$275	$225	$195	$150	$125

Last MSR was $499.

ELITE FLAME EUROPEAN CUSTOM (Model DGE-ELFL) - single horn cutaway round bottom mahogany body, arched flame top, set-in mahogany neck, 22-fret rosewood fingerboard with pearl dot inlay, tune-o-matic bridge/stop tailpiece, small offset V-shape peghead with screened logo, 3-per-side Schaller tuners, chrome hardware, 2 "Zebra" humbuckers, 2 volume/2 tone controls, 3-position switch, available in Flame Amber, Flame Amberburst, Flame Green, Flame Purple, and Flame Red finishes. Mfg. 1998.

		$695	$595	$525	$450	$375	$325	$250

Last MSR was $999.

This model is produced in Europe.

Eighty Eight Series

EIGHTY EIGHT - offset double cutaway maple body, bolt-on maple neck, 22-fret ebanol fingerboard with dot inlay, Floyd Rose tremolo, blackface peghead with screened logo, black pickguard, 6-on-a-side tuners, black hardware, 2 single coil/humbucker EMG Select pickups, volume/tone controls, 3 pickup selector mini-switches, available in Black, Blue Purpleburst, Gun Metal Grey, Pearl Purpleburst, Pearl Red, Pink, and White finishes. Mfg. 1987 to 1989.

		$275	$250	$225	$200	$175	$150	$125

Last MSR was $649.

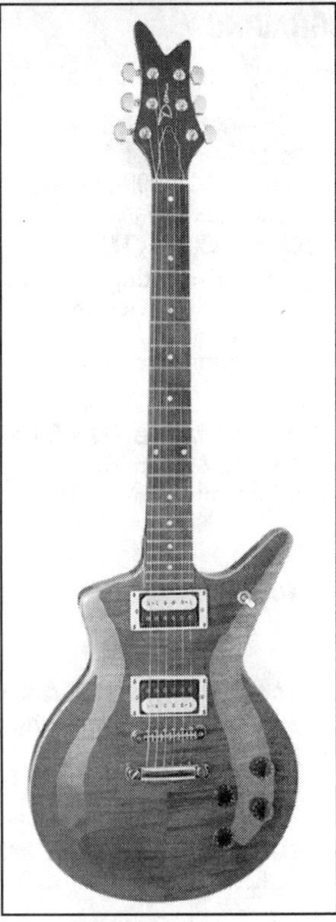

Dean European Custom Elite courtesy Armadillo Enterprises

EVO Series

EVO X - single cutaway basswood body, bolt-on maple neck, rosewood fingerboard with dot position markers, 24 ¾" scale, 22-frets, Tune-O-matic bridge, chrome hardware sealed tuners, 2 humbucking pickups, available in Classic White and Classic Black finishes. Current Mfg.

MSR	$299	$225	$195	$175	$150	$125	$95	$75

EVO FTX - similar to EVO X, except has exposed zebra-coil humbucking pickups and Grover tuners, available in Antique White, Transparent Amber, Transparent Black, Transparent Red and Transpaent Braziliaburst finishes. Current Mfg.

MSR	$369	$275	$250	$225	$195	$175	$150	$95

EVO FT - similar to EVO FTX, except has mahogany set neck, mahogany body, flame maple top, available in Antique White, Transparent Amber, Transparent Black, Transparent Green and Transparent Braziliaburst finishes. Current Mfg.

MSR	$449	$335	$275	$250	$225	$195	$175	$125

EVO 60 - similar to EVO FT, except has 2 Soapbar pickups, arched mahogany top, single ply binding, available in 24K Gold, Classic Black, Powder Blue and Silver Sparkle finish. Current Mfg.

MSR	$549	$410	$375	$350	$295	$250	$195	$150

Add $80 for left-hand configuration.

EVO Special - similar to EVO 60, except has 2 Dean humbucking pickups, arched Figured Maple top, fully bound, available in Classic Black and Quilt Amber finishes. Current Mfg.

MSR	$549	$410	$375	$350	$295	$250	$195	$150

EVO Special 7 - similar to EVO Special except in a 7-string configuration, mini Grover tuners, arched maple top. Available in Flame Blue, Flame Red, Quilt Amberburst and Quilt Black finishes. Current Mfg.

MSR	$599	$449	$399	$375	$325	$275	$225	$165

EVO Phantom - similar to EVO Special, except has triple black hardware, 2 Blade pickups, arched mahogany top, no binding, available in Classic Black finish. Current Mfg.

MSR	$599	$449	$399	$375	$325	$275	$225	$165

EVO Deluxe - similar to EVO Special, except has Schaller tuners, 2 Zebra humbucking pickups, ebony fingerboard, available in Flame Amberburst, Flame Amber, Flame Cherry Sunburst and Flame Red finishes. Current Mfg.

MSR	$999	$750	$650	$595	$550	$495	$450	$395

EVO DN76 - similar to EVO Special, except is not an archtop and is not bound, available in Metallic Charcoal finish. Current Mfg.

MSR	$789	$595	$495	$450	$395	$350	$295	$250

EVO Premium - similar to EVO Deluxe, except has gold hardware, 2 Seymour Duncan "Pearly Gates" humbucking pickups, block position markers, available in Flame Amber Burst, Flame Amber and Flame Cherry Sunburst finishes. Current Mfg.

MSR	$1,399	$1,050	$950	$850	$750	$650	$595	$550

EVO Millenium - similar to EVO Premium, except has V Schaller tuners, Honduras mahogany body, 5 Star Figured Maple top, Flame Maple neck, Wood binding, EVO Mother-of-Pearl inlay at the 12th fret, available in Flame Amber Burst finish. Current Mfg.

MSR	$3,299	$2,475	$2,175	$1,875	$1,575	$1,375	$1,175	$950

GRADING	100% MINT	98% NEAR MINT	95% EXC+	90% EXC	80% VG+	70% VG	60% G

D

Icon Series

Introduced in 1997, the Icon model is Dean's newest design. The Icon resembles a cross between a Les Paul and a PRS, and has a new 3-per-side offset 'V' headstock design.

ICON CONTOUR - offset double cutaway round bottom mahogany body, carved top, set-in mahogany neck, 22-fret ebony fingerboard with dot inlay, fixed bridge, chrome hardware, small offset V-shaped headstock, 3-per-side Grover tuners, 2 Seymour Duncan humbuckers, volume/tone controls, 3-way selector, available in Braziliaburst, Cherry Sunburst, Classic Black, Transparent Blue, and Transparent Candy Red finishes. Mfg. 1997 to 1998.

$1,000 $900 $825 $725 $600 $495 $350
Last MSR was $1,399.

Icon Flame (USA Custom Shop, Icon Exotic) - similar to the Icon Contour, except has carved flame maple top, available in Transparent Amber, Transparent Black, Transparent Blue, Transparent Candy Red, Transparent Green, Transparent Power Purple, and Transparent Root Beer finishes. Mfg. 1997 to 1999.

$1,350 $1,150 $1,000 $875 $750 $625 $475
Last MSR was $1,899.

Icon Exotic Plus - similar to the Icon Exotic, except has a piezo mounted tremolo bridge. Mfg. 1997 to 1998.

$1,200 $1,000 $950 $850 $750 $650 $495
Last MSR was $1,899.

Icon Ultima (USA Custom Shop) - similar to the Icon Exotic, except has carved quilted maple top, block fingerboard inlays, gold hardware. Mfg. 1997 to 1998.

$1,850 $1,600 $1,425 $1,250 $1,000 $850 $695
Last MSR was $2,649.

Early models may have a piezo mounted tremolo bridge.

Korina Icon (U.S. Mfg.) - similar to the Icon Contour, except has korina body, piezo mounted tremolo bridge, available in Braziliaburst, Cherry Sunburst, Gloss Natural, Transparent Amber, and Transparent Red high gloss finishes. Mfg. 1997 to 1998.

$1,350 $1,150 $1,000 $950 $800 $700 $525
Last MSR was $2,099.

ICON AX (Model DGK-ICAX) - offset double cutaway round bottom mahogany body, bound arched flame maple top, bolt-on maple neck, 22-fret rosewood fingerboard with dot inlay, tune-o-matic bridge/stop tailpiece, chrome hardware, offset V-shaped headstock, 3-per-side Grover tuners, 2 "Zebra" humbuckers, volume/tone controls, 3-way selector, available in Flame Black, Flame Blue, Flame Cherry Sunburst, and Flame Red finishes. Mfg. 1998.

$350 $300 $275 $225 $195 $150 $125
Last MSR was $499.

Icon AXV (Model DGK-ICAXV) - similar to the Icon AX, except features a 2-point floating tremolo, available in Flame Black, Flame Blue, Flame Cherry Sunburst, and Flame Red finishes. Mfg. 1998.

$350 $300 $275 $225 $195 $150 $125
Last MSR was $499.

ICON STANDARD (Model DGK-ICST) - offset double cutaway round bottom mahogany body, set-in mahogany neck, 22-fret rosewood fingerboard with dot inlay, tune-o-matic bridge/strings-through Icon wood bridge, chrome hardware, offset V-shaped headstock, 3-per-side Grover tuners, 2 "Zebra" humbuckers, volume/tone controls, 3-way selector, available in Cherry Sunburst, Classic Black, Transparent Blue, Transparent Braziliaburst, Transparent Purple, and Transparent Red finishes. Mfg. 1998 to date.

MSR $499 $350 $300 $275 $2250 $195 $150 $110

Icon Select (Model DGK-ICSE) - similar to the Icon Standard, except has triple bound arched flame maple top, triple bound headstock, block fingerboard inlays, gold hardware, available in Flame Amberburst, Flame Black, Flame Cherry Sunburst, Flame Purple, and Flame Red finishes. Mfg. 1998 to date.

MSR $599 $425 $350 $325 $275 $225 $175 $135

ICON PZ (Model DGK-ICPZ, AMERICAN SPIRIT ICON PZ) - offset double cutaway round bottom mahogany body, arched flame maple top, set-in mahogany neck, 22-fret rosewood fingerboard with dot inlay, 2-point floating tremolo, chrome hardware, offset V-shaped headstock, 3-per-side Grover tuners, 2 "Zebra" humbuckers, bridge-mounted piezo pickup, 2 volume/1 tone controls, 3-way magnetic pickup selector, 3-way magnetic/piezo pickups selector, available in Flame Cherry Sunburst, Flame Blue, Flame Purple, and Flame Red finishes. Mfg. 1997 to 1999.

$640 $560 $490 $420 $345 $275 $200
Last MSR was $799.

Earlier versions of this model were available in Transparent Cherry Sunburst, Transparent Blue, Transparent Purple, and Transparent Red high gloss finishes.

ICON FLAME EUROPEAN CUSTOM (Model DGE-ICFL) - offset double cutaway round bottom mahogany body, arched flame top, set-in mahogany neck, 22-fret rosewood fingerboard with pearl dot inlay, tune-o-matic bridge/stop tailpiece, small offset V-shape peghead with screened logo, 3-per-side Schaller tuners, chrome hardware, 2 "Zebra" humbuckers, volume/tone controls, 3-position switch, available in Flame Amber, Flame Amberburst, Flame Green, Flame Purple, and Flame Red finishes. Mfg. 1998 to 1999.

$695 $595 $525 $450 $375 $325 $250
Last MSR was $999.

This model is produced in Europe.

GRADING	100% MINT	98% NEAR MINT	95% EXC+	90% EXC	80% VG+	70% VG	60% G

European Premium Icon Premium Flame (DGE-PR-IC) - similar to the Icon Flame European Custom, except features highly figured maple top, wood bound body, pearl block fingerboard inlays, gold hardware, 2 Seymour Duncan humbuckers, available in Flame Amber, Flame Amberburst, Flame Black, Flame Blue, Flame Cherry Sunburst, Flame Green, Flame Purple, and Flame Red finishes. Mfg.1998-1999.

$950	$795	$700	$600	$525	$425	$325

Last MSR was $1,299.

This model is produced in Europe.

Jammer Series

JAMMER - offset double cutaway hardwood body, bolt-on maple neck, 22-fret rosewood fingerboard with dot inlay, locking tremolo, blackface peghead with screened logo, black pickguard, 6-on-a-side tuners, chrome hardware, 2 single coil/1 humbucker exposed pole piece pickups, volume/tone controls, 5-way pickup selector, available in Black, Blue Purpleburst, Gun Metal Grey, Pearl Purpleburst, Pearl Red, Pink, and White finishes. Mfg. 1987 to 1989.

$250	$225	$200	$175	$150	$150	$125

Last MSR was $549.

Mach Series

Both the Mach I and Mach V models were designed in 1985, and had a very limited production run in Korea. The Mach VII was designed the same year, but produced in the U.S. There are very few of the Mach Series instruments in circulation.

MACH V - single cutaway hardwood body, exaggerated treble horn/extended lower bout, bolt-on maple necks, 24-fret rosewood fingerboard with dot inlays, 3-per-side 'shrimp fork' headstock, traditional vibrato, chrome hardware, 2 humbuckers, volume/tone controls, available in Jet Black, Pearl Blueburst, Pearl Red, and Pearl White finishes. Mfg. 1985 to 1986.

Last MSR was $499.

Too few of these exist for accurate statistical representation.

MACH I - similar to the Mach V, except has a 6-on-a-side headstock, Mfg. 1985 to 1986.

Last MSR was $499.

Too few of these exist for accurate statistical representation.

Mach VII - similar to the Mach V construction (U.S. built), available in special Leopard, Tiger, and other exotic finishes. Mfg. 1985 to 1986.

Last MSR was $1,999.

Too few of these exist for accurate statistical representation. It is estimated that only a handful were built.

ML Series

The ML is a cross between the Flying V and the Explorer - designed like a Flying V with the treble horn of the Explorer up front.

ML FLAME - Flying V-style with treble horn mahogany body, 'V'-shaped strings plate, mahogany neck, 22-fret bound rosewood fingerboard with pearl dot inlay, tune-o-matic bridge/strings Through-body tailpiece, Dean 'wing' peghead with screened logo, 3-per-side Kluson tuners, chrome hardware, 2 DiMarzio humbucker pickups, 2 volume/1 tone controls, 3-position switch, available in Black, Braziliaburst, Cherry, Cherryburst, Metallic and White finishes. Mfg. 1978 to 1985.

$1,150	$1,000	$925	$795	$675	$525	$400

Last MSR was $1,100.

In 1981, Blueburst, Pearl and Pinkburst finishes were introduced.

ML Standard - similar to ML Flame, except has bound maple top, ebony fingerboard, Grover tuners, available in Black, Braziliaburst, Cherry, Cherryburst, Metallic and White finishes. Mfg. 1977 to 1986.

$1,200	$1,050	$950	$825	$695	$550	$425

Last MSR was $1,190.

This model had optional Black, Cream, Multiple, and White body binding.
In 1981, Blueburst, Pearl and Pinkburst finishes were introduced.

BABY ML - down-sized Flying V-style with treble horn poplar body, poplar neck, 22-fret rosewood fingerboard with pearl dot inlay, tunable wrap over tailpiece, body matching peghead with screened logo, 3-per-side tuners, chrome hardware, exposed Dimarzio humbucker pickups, volume/tone controls, available in Black, Blueburst, Pearl Blue, Pearl Pink, Pearl Red, Pearl White, Red, and White finishes. Mfg. 1982 to 1986.

$600	$550	$450	$375	$325	$250	$175

Last MSR was $660.

This model had an optional 24-fret fingerboard.

U.S.A. SERIES ML-92 - single horn cutaway V-shape mahogany body, carved figured maple top, V-shape strings plate, Through-body mahogany neck, 22-fret bound ebony fingerboard with pearl dot inlay, Schaller tune-o-matic bridge/strings through-body tailpiece, V-shape peghead with screened logo, 3-per-side tuners, chrome hardware, 2 exposed humbucker pickups, 2 volume/1 tone controls, 3-position switch, available in Cherry Sunburst, Natural, Transparent Blue and Transparent Red finishes. Mfg. 1992 to 1993.

$1,295	$1,100	$975	$850	$725	$625	$495

Last MSR was $1,600.

The U.S.A. series was manufactured in Northern California.

Dean ML Standard
courtesy
Armadillo Enterprises

D

GRADING	100% MINT	98% NEAR MINT	95% EXC+	90% EXC	80% VG+	70% VG	60% G

ML Reissue - single horn cutaway V-shape hardwood body, through-body mahogany neck, 22 bound rosewood fingerboard with pearl dot inlay, double locking vibrato, V-shape peghead with screened logo, 3-per-side tuners, chrome hardware, 2 exposed humbucker pickups, 2 volume/1 tone controls, 3-position switch, available in Black finish. Mfg. 1992 to 1994.

		$625	$525	$450	$375	$325	$275	$225

Last MSR was $800.

Add $60 for Lightning Graphic finish.

D

The Reissue series was manufactured in Korea.

ML NECK-THROUGH (Model ACML) - single horn cutaway V-shape alder body, V-shape strings plate, through-body maple neck, 22-fret bound rosewood fingerboard with pearl dot inlay, fixed bridge, V-shape peghead with screened logo, 3-per-side tuners, chrome hardware, 2 Seymour Duncan humbucker pickups, volume/2 tone controls, 3-position switch, available in Classic Black, Classic Red, Torrid Teal, and Wine Red finishes. Mfg. 1996 to 1997.

		$1,000	$875	$675	$600	$525	$425	$325

Last MSR was $1,345.

Add $30 for Floyd Rose tremolo.

ML Bolt-On (Model ACXML) - similar to the ML Neck-Through, except has a bolt-on maple neck, 2 Bill Lawrence humbuckers. Mfg. 1996 to 1997.

		$695	$600	$525	$450	$375	$300	$225

Last MSR was $925.

Add $30 for Floyd Rose tremolo.

USX ML - single horn cutaway V-shape alder body, bolt-on maple neck, 22-fret rosewood fingerboard with dot inlay, Floyd Rose licensed tremolo, blackface peghead with screened logo, 3-per-side tuners, chrome hardware, 2 Duncan Designed humbuckers, 1 volume/2 tone controls, 3-way switch, available in Cherry Sunburst, Classic Black, Metallic Red, and Vintage Sunburst finishes. Mfg. 1996 to 1997.

		$525	$450	$395	$350	$275	$225	$175

Last MSR was $689.

USX ML Pro - similar to the USX ML, except has ash body, Sperzel tuners, 2 Bill Lawrence L500 humbuckers, available in Transparent Black, Transparent Blue, Transparent Cherry, and Vintage Sunburst finishes. Mfg. 1996 to date.

		$595	$525	$450	$395	$325	$275	$200

Last MSR was $789.

ML COUPE (USA CUSTOM SHOP) - single horn cutaway V-shaped mahogany body, set-in mahogany neck, 22-fret ebony fingerboard with dot inlay, tune-o-matic bridge/V-shaped stop tailpiece, V-shaped peghead with screened logo, 3-per-side Grover tuners, chrome hardware, 2 Seymour Duncan humbucker pickups, volume/2 tone controls, 3-position switch, available in Brite Blue, Canary Yellow, Cherry Sunburst, Classic Black, and Lipstick Red solid finishes. Mfg. 1997 to 1998.

		$1,100	$975	$850	$750	$625	$500	$395

Last MSR was $1,599.

ML Deluxe - similar to the ML Coupe, except has Original Floyd Rose tremolo, available in Braziliaburst, Brite Blue, Canary Yellow, Classic Black, and Lipstick Red solid finishes. Mfg. 1997 to 1998.

		$1,000	$950	$875	$775	$650	$500	$375

Last MSR was $1,499.

ML LTD (USA Custom Shop) - similar to the ML Coupe, except has bound body/fingerboard/headstock, available in Braziliaburst, Cherry Sunburst, Classic Black, Transparent Blue, and Transparent Red finishes. Mfg. 1997 to 1998.

		$1,350	$1,150	$1,000	$875	$750	$625	$475

Last MSR was $1,899.

U.S. PHANTOM ML (USA CUSTOM SHOP) - single horn cutaway V-shaped mahogany body, set-in mahogany neck, 22-fret ebony fingerboard (no inlay), large V-shaped peghead with screened logo, 3-per-side Grover tuners, Original Floyd Rose tremolo, all black hardware, 2 Seymour Duncan humbucker pickups, 2 volume/1 tone controls, 3-position switch, available in Classic Black finish only. Mfg. 1996 to date.

MSR	$1,999	$1,400	$1,200	$1,000	$925	$775	$650	$500

ML Phantom X (Model DGK-MLPX) - similar to the U.S. Phantom ML, except has a basswood body, bolt-on maple neck, 22-fret rosewood fingerboard, tune-o-matic bridge/V-shaped stop tailpiece, 2 Dean Phantom Rail humbuckers, available in Classic Black finish only. Mfg. 1998 to date.

MSR	$429	$295	$270	$245	$215	$160	$135	$100

ML Phantom XT (Model DGK-MLPXT) - similar to the U.S. Phantom ML, except has a basswood body, bolt-on maple neck, 22-fret rosewood fingerboard, licensed Floyd Rose tremolo, 2 Dean Phantom Rail humbuckers, available in Classic Black finish only. Mfg. 1998 to date.

MSR	$529	$370	$320	$295	$245	$210	$160	$135

ML Phantom Standard (Model DGK-MLPST) - similar to the U.S. Phantom ML, except has 22-fret rosewood fingerboard, tune-o-matic bridge/V-shaped stop tailpiece, 2 Dean Phantom Rail humbuckers, available in Classic Black finish only. Mfg. 1998 to date.

MSR	$549	$395	$365	$335	$295	$250	$200	$125

ML (PHANTOM) STANDARD (Model DGK-MLST, AMERICAN SPIRIT ML STANDARD) - single horn cutaway V-shaped mahogany body, set-in mahogany neck, 22-fret rosewood fingerboard with dot inlay, tune-o-matic bridge/V-shaped stop tailpiece, chrome hardware, large V-shaped headstock, 3-per-side Grover tuners, 2 "Zebra" humbuckers, 2 volume/1 tone controls, 3-way selector, available in Classic Black, Transparent Blue, Transparent Braziliaburst, and Transparent Red finishes. Mfg. 1997 to date.

MSR	$549	$395	$345	$295	$250	$225	$175	$135

GRADING		100% MINT	98% NEAR MINT	95% EXC+	90% EXC	80% VG+	70% VG	60% G

ML Select (Model DGK-MLSE) - similar to the ML Standard, except has triple bound flame maple top, triple bound headstock, block fingerboard inlays, gold hardware, available in Flame Blue, Flame Braziliaburst, Flame Cherry Sunburst, Flame Red, Metallic Black, and Metallic Red finishes. Mfg. 1998 to date.

MSR	$599	$425	$375	$325	$275	$225	$175	$125

ML Ultra (Model DGK-MLUL, American Spirit ML Ultra) - similar to the ML Standard, except has licensed Floyd Rose tremolo, available in Classic Black, Transparent Blue, Transparent Braziliaburst, and Transparent Red finishes. Mfg. 1997 to 1999.

		$600	$525	$450	$395	$325	$250	$195

Last MSR was $749.

Add $20 for left-handed configuration (Model DGK-MLUL-L), available in Classic Black and Transparent Red finishes.

ML X (Model DGK-MLX, AMERICAN SPIRIT ML X) - single horn cutaway V-shaped basswood body, bolt-on maple neck, 22-fret rosewood fingerboard with dot inlays, tune-o-matic bridge/V-shaped stop tailpiece, large V-shape peghead with screened logo, 3-per-side Grover tuners, chrome hardware, 2 "Zebra" humbuckers, 2 volume/1 tone controls, 3-position switch, available in (Transparent) Braziliaburst, Classic Black, Transparent Blue, and Transparent Red finishes. Mfg. 1997 to date.

MSR	$299	$240	$225	$195	$175	$150	$125	$95

Add $20 for left-handed configuration (Model DGK-MLXL), available in Classic Black and Transparent Braziliaburst finishes.

ML XT (Model DGK-MLXT, American Spirit ML XT) - similar to the ML X, except has licensed Floyd Rose tremolo, available in (Transparent) Braziliaburst, Classic Black, Transparent Blue, and Transparent Red finishes. Mfg. 1997 to date.

MSR	$429	$315	$285	$265	$225	$195	$165	$125

Add $20 for left-handed configuration (Model DGK-MLXTL), available in Classic Black and Transparent Brazilliaburst finishes.

Playmate Series

PLAYMATE - offset double cutaway hardwood body, bolt-on maple neck, 22-fret rosewood fingerboard with dot inlay, traditional vibrato, blackface peghead with screened logo, black pickguard, 6-on-a-side tuners, chrome hardware, 3 single coil exposed pole piece pickups, volume/tone controls, 5-way pickup selector, available in Black, Red, and White finishes. Mfg. 1987 to 1989.

		$225	$195	$175	$150	$125	$100	$75

Last MSR was $349.

Signature Series

The Signature Series was Dean's first Korean production guitar series, and was introduced in 1985.

DEAN Z AUTOGRAPH - offset double cutaway hardwood body, bolt-on maple neck, 22-fret white painted fingerboard with dot inlay, double locking tremolo, blackface peghead with screened logo, mirror pickguard, 6-on-a-side tuners, chrome hardware, 2 single coil/1 humbucker exposed pole piece pickups, volume/tone controls, 5-way pickup selector, available in Electric Blue, Hot Flamingo, Ice White, Jet Black, Lemon-Lime, and Rock-It Red fluorescent finishes. Mfg. 1985 to 1987.

		$275	$225	$195	$175	$150	$125	$100

Last MSR was $349.

SS Series

The SS model was introduced in 1998, and features an offset double cutaway body similar to a 'superstrat' design.

Dean's Practice Pack (Model DGP-GPP1) is an all-in-one starter system that includes an SS-One electric guitar, a Stack in the Box headphone amp, a guitar strap, Dean picks, and a guitar tuner. This complete package retails for $349.

The Stagecoach (Model DGP-GSP2) is a similar all-in-one starter system that includes an SS-One electric guitar, a Dean Mean 16 guitar amp, a guitar strap, Dean picks, and a guitar tuner. This complete package retails for $449.

SS-ONE (Model DGK-SS1) - offset double cutaway basswood body, bolt-on maple neck, 22-fret rosewood fingerboard with dot inlays, 2-point floating tremolo, graphite nut, small offset V-shaped wood peghead with screened logo, 3-per-side Grover tuners, chrome hardware, white pearloid pickguard, 2 single coil/humbucker pickups, volume/2 tone controls, 5-position switch, available in Classic Black, Transparent Blue, and Transparent Red finishes. Mfg. 1998 to 1999.

		$225	$175	$150	$130	$110	$95	$75

Last MSR was $299.

Add $20 for left-handed configuration (Model DGK-SS1L), available in Classic Black and Transparent Red finishes.

SS Plus (Model DGK-SS+) - similar to the SS-One, except features flame maple top, available in Flame Black, Flame Blue, Flame Braziliaburst, Flame Cherry Sunburst, Flame Red, Metallic Black, Metallic Charcoal, and Metallic Red finishes with matching headstock. Mfg. 1998 to 1999.

		$275	$250	$225	$195	$150	$125	$100

Last MSR was $399.

Add $20 for left-handed configuration (Model DGK-SS+L), available in Flame Blue and Flame Braziliaburst finishes.

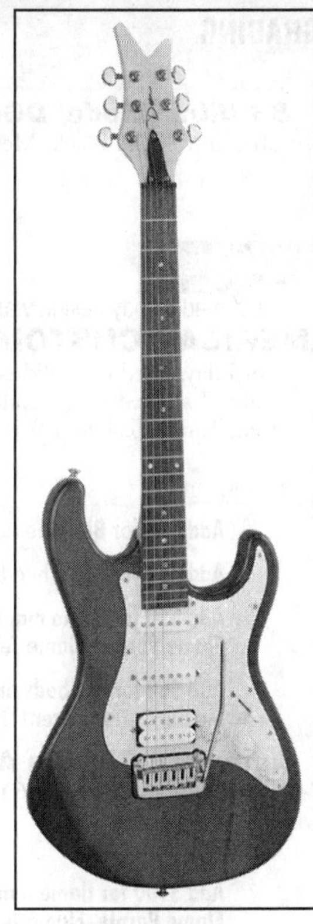

Dean SS One
courtesy
Armadillo Enterprises

D

GRADING	100% MINT	98% NEAR MINT	95% EXC+	90% EXC	80% VG+	70% VG	60% G

SS Ultra (Model DGK-SSUL) - similar to the SS-One, except features 24-fret fingerboard, no pickguard, licensed Floyd Rose tremolo, available in Metallic Black, Metallic Green, Metallic Purple, and Metallic Red finishes with matching headstock. Mfg. 1998 to 1999.

$425 $375 $325 $275 $250 $195 $150
Last MSR was $599.

X Series

The X model body design was a newer model to the 1990s, and had an offset double cutaway body that is reminiscent of a sleek 'superstrat' design.

AMERICAN CUSTOM ACX (Bolt-On) - offset double cutaway alder body, bolt-on maple neck, 24-fret rosewood fingerboard with pearl dot inlay, fixed or Wilkinson bridge (or Floyd Rose tremolo), 'shrimp fork' blackface peghead with screened logo, 3-per-side tuners, chrome hardware, 2 slanted single coil/humbucker Seymour Duncan pickups, 1 volume/2 tone controls, 5-position switch, available in Classic Black, Classic Red, Torrid Teal, and Wine Red finishes. Mfg. 1996 to 1997.

$595 $550 $500 $450 $350 $250 $200
Last MSR was $885.

Add $30 for Big V headstock (in Black).

Add $50 for Big V headstock (color matched).

Add $50 for flame maple top, alder body, available in Flame Black, Flame Blue, Flame Braziliaburst, Flame Cherry, Flame Cherry Sunburst, Flame Green, Flame Purple, Flame Teal, and Flame Vintage Sunburst finishes.

Add $60 for ash body and translucent finish, available in Translucent Black, Translucent Blue, Translucent Braziliaburst, Translucent Cherry, Translucent Cherry Sunburst, Translucent Green, Translucent Purple, Translucent Teal, and Translucent Vintage Sunburst finishes.

American Custom ACSL (Neck-Through) - similar to the American Custom ACX, except features a maple through-neck design, Floyd Rose tremolo. Mfg. 1996 to 1997.

$775 $675 $600 $550 $495 $400 $325
Last MSR was $1,299.

Add $100 for flame maple top, alder body, available in Flame Black, Flame Blue, Flame Braziliaburst, Flame Cherry, Flame Cherry Sunburst, Flame Green, Flame Purple, Flame Teal, and Flame Vintage Sunburst finishes.

Add $100 for ash body and translucent finish, available in Translucent Black, Translucent Blue, Translucent Braziliaburst, Translucent Cherry, Translucent Cherry Sunburst, Translucent Green, Translucent Purple, Translucent Teal, and Translucent Vintage Sunburst finishes.

USX - offset double cutaway alder body, bolt-on maple neck, 24-fret rosewood fingerboard with dot inlay, Wilkinson VS10 bridge, blackface peghead with screened logo, 6-on-a-side tuners, chrome hardware, 2 slanted single coil/1 humbucker Duncan Designed pickups, 1 volume/2 tone controls, 5-position switch, available in Cherry Sunburst, Classic Black, Metallic Red, and Vintage Sunburst finishes. Mfg. 1996 to 1997.

$350 $300 $275 $225 $195 $150 $125
Last MSR was $489.

USX Pro - similar to the USX, except has ash body, available in Transparent Black, Transparent Blue, Transparent Cherry, and Vintage Sunburst finishes. Mfg. 1996 to date.

$400 $350 $325 $295 $250 $195 $150
Last MSR was $589.

USXL - similar to the USX, except has Floyd Rose tremolo, available in Cherry Sunburst, Classic Black, Metallic Red, and Vintage Sunburst finishes. Mfg. 1996 to date.

$425 $375 $350 $325 $275 $225 $175
Last MSR was $589.

USXL Pro - similar to the USXL, except has ash body, available in Transparent Black, Transparent Blue, Transparent Cherry, and Vintage Sunburst finishes. Mfg. 1996 to date.

$450 $400 $375 $350 $300 $250 $200
Last MSR was $689.

V Series

The Dean V was Zelinsky's variation of a '58 Flying V.

V FLAME - Flying V-shaped mahogany body, V-shaped strings plate, mahogany neck, 22-fret bound rosewood fingerboard with pearl dot inlay, tune-o-matic bridge/strings Through-body tailpiece, V-shape peghead with screened logo, 3-per-side Kluson tuners, chrome hardware, 2 humbucker DiMarzio pickups, 2 volume/1 tone controls, 3-position switch, available in Black, Braziliaburst, Cherry, Cherryburst, Metallic and White finishes. Mfg. 1978 to 1985.

$1,100 $950 $875 $750 $650 $575 $425
Last MSR was $1,100.

In 1981, Blueburst, Pearl and Pinkburst finishes were introduced.

V Standard - similar to V Flame, except has bound maple top, ebony fingerboard, Grover tuners, available in Black, Braziliaburst, Cherry, Cherryburst, Metallic and White finishes. Mfg. 1977 to 1986.

$1,000 $900 $850 $700 $600 $525 $395
Last MSR was $1,190.

This model had an optional black, cream and white body binding.
In 1981, Blueburst, Pearl and Pinkburst finishes were introduced.

GRADING	100% MINT	98% NEAR MINT	95% EXC+	90% EXC	80% VG+	70% VG	60% G

BABY V - down-sized Flying V-shaped poplar body, poplar neck, 22-fret rosewood fingerboard with pearl dot inlay, tunable wrap over tailpiece, body matching peghead with screened logo, 3-per-side tuners, chrome hardware, exposed humbucker DiMarzio pickup, volume/tone controls, available in Black, Blueburst, Pearl Blue, Pearl Pink, Pearl Red, Pearl White, Red, and White finishes. Mfg. 1982 to 1986.

$700 $550 $495 $425 $375 $300 $250
Last MSR was $660.

This model had an optional 24-fret fingerboard.

HOLLYWOOD V - Flying V-shaped hardwood body, bolt-on maple neck, 24-fret rosewood fingerboard with pearl dot inlay, tune-o-matic bridge/stop tailpiece, body matching small fork peghead with screened logo, 3-per-side tuners, chrome hardware, 2 humbucker pickups, volume/tone controls, 3-position switch, available in Black, Blueburst, Bolt, Flames, Pearl Blue, Pearl Pink, Pearl Red, Pearl White, Red, Wedge, White, and Zebra Graphic finishes. Mfg. 1985 to 1987.

$300 $275 $225 $175 $150 $125 $95
Last MSR was $500.

Hollywood V V - similar to Hollywood V, except has double locking vibrato.

$350 $295 $250 $200 $175 $150 $125
Last MSR was $600.

V NECK-THROUGH (Model ACDV) - Flying V-shaped alder body, V-shaped strings plate, through-body maple neck, 22-fret bound rosewood fingerboard with pearl dot inlay, fixed bridge, V-shape peghead with screened logo, 3-per-side tuners, chrome hardware, 2 Seymour Duncan humbucker pickups, volume/2 tone controls, 3-position switch, available in Classic Black, Classic Red, Torrid Teal, and Wine Red finishes. Mfg. 1996 to 1997.

$900 $825 $750 $650 $575 $495 $395
Last MSR was $1,345.

Add $30 for Floyd Rose tremolo.

V Phantom (Model PHXDV) - similar to the V Neck-Through, except has no fingerboard inlays, black hardware, 2 Bill Lawrence humbuckers, available in Gloss Black finish only. Mfg. 1996 to 1997.

$695 $625 $575 $495 $425 $350 $275
Last MSR was $995.

Add $50 for Floyd Rose tremolo.

V Bolt-On (Model ACXDV) - similar to the V Neck-Through, except has a bolt-on maple neck, 2 Bill Lawrence humbuckers. Mfg. 1996 to 1997.

$595 $500 $425 $350 $300 $275 $225
Last MSR was $925.

Add $30 for Floyd Rose tremolo.

V COUPE (USA CUSTOM SHOP) - Flying V-shaped mahogany body, set-in mahogany neck, 22-fret ebony fingerboard with dot inlay, tune- o-matic bridge/V-shaped stop tailpiece, V-shaped peghead with screened logo, 3-per-side Grover tuners, chrome hardware, 2 Seymour Duncan humbucker pickups, volume/2 tone controls, 3-position switch, available in Brite Blue, Canary Yellow, Cherry Sunburst, Classic Black, and Lipstick Red solid finishes. Mfg. 1997 to 1998.

$1,100 $975 $850 $750 $625 $500 $395
Last MSR was $1,599.

V Deluxe - similar to the V Coupe, except has Original Floyd Rose tremolo, available in Braziliaburst, Brite Blue, Canary Yellow, Classic Black, and Lipstick Red solid finishes. Mfg. 1997 to 1998.

$1,100 $950 $850 $775 $650 $500 $375
Last MSR was $1,499.

V LTD (USA Custom Shop) - similar to the V Coupe, except has bound body/fingerboard/headstock, available in Braziliaburst, Cherry Sunburst, Classic Black, Transparent Blue, and Transparent Red finishes. Mfg. 1997 to 1998.

$1,350 $1,150 $1,000 $875 $750 $625 $475
Last MSR was $1,899.

Korina V (U.S. Mfg.) - similar to the V Coupe, except has korina body, available in Braziliaburst, Cherry Sunburst, Gloss Natural, Transparent Amber, and Transparent Red high gloss finishes. Mfg. 1997 to 1998.

$1,200 $1,050 $950 $850 $750 $650 $495
Last MSR was $1,899.

U.S. PHANTOM V (USA CUSTOM SHOP) - Flying V-shaped mahogany body, set in mahogany neck, 22-fret ebony fingerboard (no inlay), large V-shaped peghead with screened logo, 3-per-side Grover tuners, Original Floyd Rose tremolo, all black hardware, 2 Seymour Duncan humbucker pickups, 2 volume/1 tone controls, 3-position switch, available in Classic Black finish only. Mfg. 1998.

$1,400 $1,200 $1,000 $925 $775 $650 $500
Last MSR was $1,999.

GRADING	100% MINT	98% NEAR MINT	95% EXC+	90% EXC	80% VG+	70% VG	60% G

V STANDARD (Model DGK-VST) - Flying V-shaped mahogany body, set-in mahogany neck, 22-fret rosewood fingerboard with dot inlay, tune-o-matic bridge/V-shaped stop tailpiece, chrome hardware, large V-shaped headstock, 3-per-side Grover tuners, 2 "Zebra" humbuckers, 2 volume/1 tone controls, 3-way selector, available in Classic Black, Transparent Blue, Transparent Braziliaburst, and Transparent Red finishes. Mfg. 1998 to 1999.

$425 $375 $325 $275 $250 $195 $150
Last MSR was $599.

D

V Select (Model DGK-VSE) - similar to the V Standard, except has triple bound flame maple top, triple bound headstock, block fingerboard inlays, gold hardware, available in Flame Blue, Flame Braziliaburst, Flame Cherry Sunburst, Flame Red, Metallic Black, and Metallic Red finishes. Mfg. 1998 to date.

MSR $599 $425 $375 $325 $275 $225 $175 $125

V Ultra (Model DGK-VUL) - similar to the V Standard, except has licensed Floyd Rose tremolo, available in Classic Black, Transparent Blue, Transparent Braziliaburst, and Transparent Red finishes. Mfg. 1998.

$600 $525 $450 $395 $325 $250 $195
Last MSR was $749.

V X (Model DGK-VX, AMERICAN SPIRIT V X) - Flying V-shaped basswood body, bolt-on maple neck, 22-fret rosewood fingerboard with dot inlays, tune-o-matic bridge/V-shaped stop tailpiece, large V-shape peghead with screened logo, 3-per-side Grover tuners, chrome hardware, 2 "Zebra" humbuckers, 2 volume/1 tone controls, 3-position switch, available in (Transparent) Braziliaburst, Classic Black, Transparent Blue, and Transparent Red finishes. Mfg. 1997 to date.

MSR $299 $225 $195 $175 $150 $125 $100 $75

Add $20 for left-handed configuration (Model DGK-VXL), available in Classic Black finish only.

V XT (Model DGK-VXT) - similar to the V X, except has licensed Floyd Rose tremolo, available in (Transparent) Braziliaburst, Classic Black, Transparent Blue, and Transparent Red finishes. Mfg. 1998 to date.

MSR $419 $300 $275 $225 $195 $165 $125 $95

Add $20 for left-handed configuration (Model DGK-VXTL), available in Classic Black and Transparent Braziliaburst finishes.

KORINA V EUROPEAN CUSTOM (Model DGE-KV) - Flying V-shaped korina body, set-in korina neck, 22-fret rosewood fingerboard with pearl dot inlay, tune-o-matic bridge/V-shaped stop tailpiece, large V-shape peghead with screened logo, 3-per-side Schaller tuners, gold hardware, 2 "Zebra" humbuckers, 2 volume/1-tone controls, 3-position switch, available in Gloss Natural, Transparent Amber, Transparent Braziliaburst, and Transparent Red finishes. Mfg. 1998 to 1999.

$695 $595 $525 $450 $375 $325 $250
Last MSR was $999.

This model is produced in Europe.

Z Series

The Z was the first Dean model announced, and the body design resembles an Explorer.

Z FLAME - Explorer-style mahogany body, mahogany neck, 22-fret bound rosewood fingerboard with pearl dot inlay, tune-o-matic bridge/stop tailpiece, V-shape peghead with screened logo, 3-per-side Kluson tuners, chrome hardware, 2 humbucker DiMarzio pickups, 2 volume/1 tone controls, 3-position switch, available in Black, Braziliaburst, Cherry, Cherryburst, Metallic and White finishes. Mfg. 1978 to 1985.

$1,150 $1,000 $950 $825 $700 $595 $400
Last MSR was $1,100.

In 1981, Blueburst, Pearl and Pinkburst finishes were introduced.

Z Standard - similar to Z Flame, except has bound maple top, ebony fingerboard, Grover tuners, available in Black, Braziliaburst, Cherry, Cherryburst, Metallic and White finishes. Mfg. 1977 to 1986.

$1,000 $900 $800 $750 $600 $525 $375
Last MSR was $1,190.

This model had an optional black, cream and white body binding.
In 1981, Blueburst, Pearl and Pinkburst finishes were introduced.

HOLLYWOOD Z - Explorer-style hardwood body, bolt-on maple neck, 24-fret rosewood fingerboard with pearl dot inlay, tune-o-matic bridge/stop tailpiece, body matching small fork peghead with screened logo, 3-per-side tuners, chrome hardware, 2 humbucker pickups, volume/tone controls, 3-position switch, available in Black, Blueburst, Bolt, Flames, Pearl Blue, Pearl Pink, Pearl Red, Pearl White, Red, Wedge, White, and Zebra Graphic finishes. Mfg. 1985 to 1987.

$300 $250 $200 $175 $150 $125 $95
Last MSR was $350.

Hollywood Z V - similar to Hollywood Z, except has double locking vibrato.

$350 $295 $225 $195 $175 $150 $125
Last MSR was $450.

Z COUPE (USA CUSTOM SHOP) - Explorer-style mahogany body, set-in mahogany neck, 22-fret ebony fingerboard with dot inlay, tune-o- matic bridge/V-shaped stop tailpiece, V-shaped peghead with screened logo, 3-per-side Grover tuners, chrome hardware, 2 Seymour Duncan humbucker pickups, volume/2 tone controls, 3-position switch, available in Brite Blue, Canary Yellow, Cherry Sunburst, Classic Black, and Lipstick Red solid finishes. Mfg. 1997 to 1998.

$1,100 $975 $850 $750 $625 $500 $395
Last MSR was $1,599.

Z Deluxe - similar to the Z Coupe, except has Original Floyd Rose tremolo, available in Braziliaburst, Brite Blue, Canary Yellow, Classic Black, and Lipstick Red solid finishes. Mfg. 1997 to 1998.

$1,000 $950 $850 $750 $650 $500 $395
Last MSR was $1,499.

GRADING	100% MINT	98% NEAR MINT	95% EXC+	90% EXC	80% VG+	70% VG	60% G

Z LTD (USA Custom Shop) - similar to the Z Coupe, except has bound body/fingerboard/headstock, available in Braziliaburst, Cherry Sunburst, Classic Black, Transparent Blue, and Transparent Red finishes. Mfg. 1997 to 1998.

	$1,350	$1,150	$1,000	$875	$750	$625	$475

Last MSR was $1,899.

Korina Z (U.S. Mfg.) - similar to the Z Coupe, except has korina body, available in Braziliaburst, Cherry Sunburst, Gloss Natural, Transparent Amber, and Transparent Red high gloss finishes. Mfg. 1997 to 1998.

	$1,200	$1,050	$950	$850	$750	$650	$495

Last MSR was $1,899.

U.S. PHANTOM Z (USA CUSTOM SHOP) - Explorer-style mahogany body, set-in mahogany neck, 22-fret ebony fingerboard (no inlay), large V-shaped peghead with screened logo, 3-per-side Grover tuners, Original Floyd Rose tremolo, all black hardware, 2 Seymour Duncan humbucker pickups, 2 volume/1 tone controls, 3-position switch, available in Classic Black finish only. Mfg. 1998.

	$1,400	$1,200	$1,000	$925	$775	$650	$500

Last MSR was $1,999.

Z STANDARD (Model DGK-ZST, AMERICAN SPIRIT Z STANDARD) - Explorer-style mahogany body, set-in mahogany neck, 22-fret rosewood fingerboard with dot inlay, tune-o-matic bridge/V-shaped stop tailpiece, chrome hardware, large V-shaped headstock, 3-per-side Grover tuners, 2 "Zebra" humbuckers, 2 volume/1 tone controls, 3-way selector, available in Classic Black, Transparent Blue, Transparent Braziliaburst, and Transparent Red finishes. Mfg. 1998.

	$425	$375	$325	$275	$250	$195	$150

Last MSR was $599.

Z Select (Model DGK-ZSE) - similar to the Z Standard, except has triple bound flame maple top, triple bound headstock, block fingerboard inlays, gold hardware, available in Flame Blue, Flame Braziliaburst, Flame Cherry Sunburst, Flame Red, Metallic Black, and Metallic Red finishes. Mfg. 1998 to date.

MSR $599	$425	$375	$325	$275	$225	$175	$125

Z Ultra (Model DGK-ZUL, American Spirit Z Ultra) - similar to the Z Standard, except has licensed Floyd Rose tremolo, available in Classic Black, Transparent Blue, Transparent Braziliaburst, and Transparent Red finishes. Mfg. 1997 to 1998.

	$600	$525	$450	$395	$325	$250	$175

Last MSR was $749.

Z X (Model DGK-ZX, AMERICAN SPIRIT Z X) - Explorer-style basswood body, bolt-on maple neck, 22-fret rosewood fingerboard with dot inlays, tune-o-matic bridge/V-shaped stop tailpiece, large V-shape peghead with screened logo, 3-per-side Grover tuners, chrome hardware, 2 "Zebra" humbuckers, 2 volume/1 tone controls, 3-position switch, available in (Transparent) Braziliaburst, Classic Black, Transparent Blue, and Transparent Red finishes. Mfg. 1997 to date.

MSR $299	$225	$195	$175	$150	$125	$95	$65

Add $20 for left-handed configuration (Model DGK-ZXL), available in Transparent Red finish only.

Z XT (Model DGK-ZXT, American Spirit Z XT) - similar to the Z X, except has licensed Floyd Rose tremolo, available in (Transparent) Braziliaburst, Classic Black, Transparent Blue, and Transparent Red finishes. Mfg. 1997 to 1998.

	$325	$295	$275	$225	$195	$165	$125

Last MSR was $449.

KORINA Z EUROPEAN CUSTOM (Model DGE-KZ) - Explorer-style korina body, set-in korina neck, 22-fret rosewood fingerboard with pearl dot inlay, tune-o-matic bridge/V-shaped stop tailpiece, large V- shape peghead with screened logo, 3-per-side Schaller tuners, gold hardware, 2 "Zebra" humbuckers, 2 volume/1 tone controls, 3-position switch, available in Gloss Natural, Transparent Amber, Transparent Braziliaburst, and Transparent Red finishes. Mfg. 1998.

	$695	$595	$525	$450	$375	$325	$250

Last MSR was $999.

This model was produced in Europe.

Baby Z Series

The Baby Z model is basically the down-sized body version of the Z model.

BABY Z - down-sized Explorer-style poplar body, poplar neck, 22-fret rosewood fingerboard with pearl dot inlay, tunable wrap over tailpiece, 3-per-side tuners, chrome hardware, exposed humbucker DiMarzio pickup, volume/tone controls, available in Black, Blueburst, Pearl Blue, Pearl Pink, Pearl Red, Pearl White, Red and White finishes. Mfg. 1982 to 1986.

	$500	$425	$375	$325	$275	$200	$150

Last MSR was $660.

This model had an optional 24-fret fingerboard.

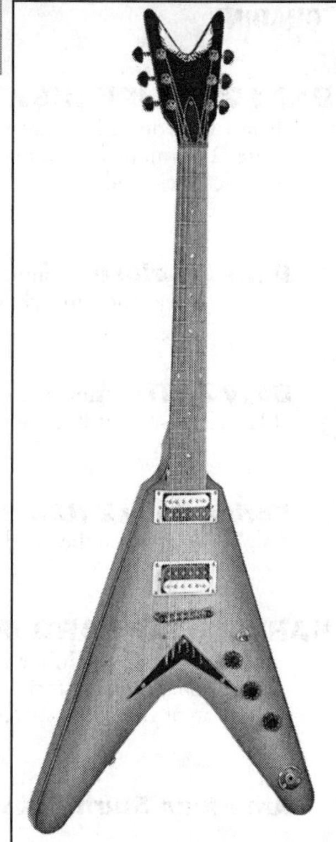

Dean V Standard
courtesy
Armadillo Enterprises

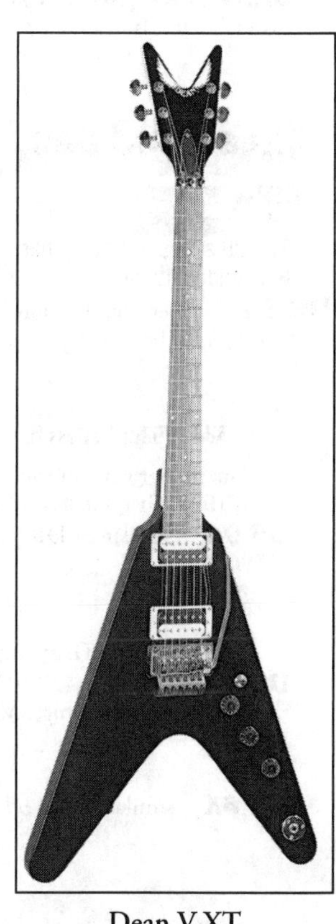

Dean V XT
courtesy
Armadillo Enterprises

GRADING	100% MINT	98% NEAR MINT	95% EXC+	90% EXC	80% VG+	70% VG	60% G

BABY Z COUPE (USA CUSTOM SHOP) - down-sized Explorer-style mahogany body, set-in mahogany neck, 22-fret ebony fingerboard with dot inlay, tune-o-matic bridge/V-shaped stop tailpiece, V-shaped peghead with screened logo, 3-per-side Grover tuners, chrome hardware, 2 Seymour Duncan humbucker pickups, volume/2 tone controls, 3-position switch, available in Brite Blue, Canary Yellow, Cherry Sunburst, Classic Black, and Lipstick Red solid finishes. Mfg. 1997 to 1998.

$1,100 $975 $850 $750 $625 $500 $395
Last MSR was $1,599.

Baby Z Deluxe - similar to the Baby Z Coupe, except has Original Floyd Rose tremolo, available in Braziliaburst, Brite Blue, Canary Yellow, Classic Black, and Lipstick Red solid finishes. Mfg. 1997 to 1998.

$1,000 $950 $850 $750 $650 $500 $395
Last MSR was $1,499.

Baby Z LTD - similar to the Baby Z Coupe, except has bound body/fingerboard/headstock, available in Braziliaburst, Cherry Sunburst, Classic Black, Transparent Blue, and Transparent Red finishes. Mfg. 1997 to 1998.

$1,350 $1,150 $1,000 $875 $750 $625 $475
Last MSR was $1,899.

Korina Baby Z (U.S. Mfg.) - similar to the Baby Z Coupe, except has korina body, available in Braziliaburst, Cherry Sunburst, Gloss Natural, Transparent Amber, and Transparent Red high gloss finishes. Mfg. 1997 to 1998.

$1,200 $1,000 $950 $850 $750 $650 $495
Last MSR was $1,899.

BABY Z STANDARD (Model DGK-BZST, AMERICAN SPIRIT BABY Z STANDARD) - down-sized Explorer-style mahogany body, set-in mahogany neck, 22-fret rosewood fingerboard with dot inlay, tune-o-matic bridge/strings-through-body, chrome hardware, large V-shaped headstock, 3-per-side Grover tuners, 2 "Zebra" humbuckers, volume/tone controls, 3-way selector, available in Classic Black, Transparent Blue, Transparent Braziliaburst, and Transparent Red finishes. Mfg. 1998.

$425 $375 $325 $275 $250 $195 $150
Last MSR was $599.

American Spirit Baby Z Ultra - similar to the American Spirit Baby Z Standard, except has Floyd Rose tremolo. Mfg. 1997 to 1998.

$500 $450 $400 $350 $300 $250 $195
Last MSR was $749.

BABY Z X (Model DGK-BZX, AMERICAN SPIRIT BABY Z X) - down-sized Explorer-style basswood body, bolt-on maple neck, 22-fret rosewood fingerboard with dot inlays, tune-o-matic bridge/strings-through-body, large V-shape peghead with screened logo, 3-per-side Grover tuners, chrome hardware, 2 "Zebra" humbuckers, volume/tone controls, 3-position switch, available in (Transparent) Braziliaburst, Classic Black, Transparent Blue, and Transparent Red finishes. Mfg. 1997 to 1999.

$275 $250 $225 $195 $175 $150 $125
Last MSR was $349.

BABY Z XT (Model DGK-BZXT, American Spirit Baby Z XT) - similar to the Baby Z X, except has licensed Floyd Rose tremolo, available in (Transparent) Braziliaburst, Classic Black, Transparent Blue, and Transparent Red finishes. Mfg. 1997 to 1998.

$325 $295 $275 $225 $195 $165 $125
Last MSR was $449.

ELECTRIC BASS

90s Series

The DB series of electric bass models were produced in Korea from 1991 to 1996. All instruments in this series were available in Black, Blueburst, Grayburst, Red, and White finishes (unless otherwise listed).

DB 91 - offset double cutaway alder body with slap contour area ('pop slot') on lower bout, bolt-on maple neck, 24-fret rosewood with pearl wings inlay, fixed bridge, 2-per-side tuners, chrome hardware, P/J-style pickups, 2 volume/1 tone controls, 3-position switch. Mfg. 1991 to 1996.

$325 $275 $250 $200 $175 $150 $100
Last MSR was $425.

Add $20 for fretless fingerboard (Model DB 91 F).

This model was offered in a left-handed configuration as the DB 91 L.
In 1995, Grayburst and Red finishes were disc; Flame Cherry Sunburst finish was introduced.

DB 94 - similar to DB 91, except has black hardware, volume/treble/bass/blend controls, no 3-position switch, active electronics. Mfg. 1991 to 1996.

$450 $395 $350 $295 $250 $200 $150
Last MSR was $595.

In 1995, Black, Grayburst, Red, and White finishes were disc; Black Flame Maple and Vintage Sunburst finishes were introduced.

DB 95 - similar to DB 91, except has 5-string configuration, 3/2-per-side tuners, gold hardware, volume/treble/bass/blend controls, no 3-position switch, active electronics. Mfg. 1991 to 1996.

$475 $400 $350 $300 $250 $200 $150
Last MSR was $630.

DB 6X - similar to DB 95, except has 6-string configuration, 3-per-side tuners. Mfg. 1995 to 1996.

$495 $425 $350 $300 $250 $200 $150
Last MSR was $640.

GRADING		100% MINT	98% NEAR MINT	95% EXC+	90% EXC	80% VG+	70% VG	60% G

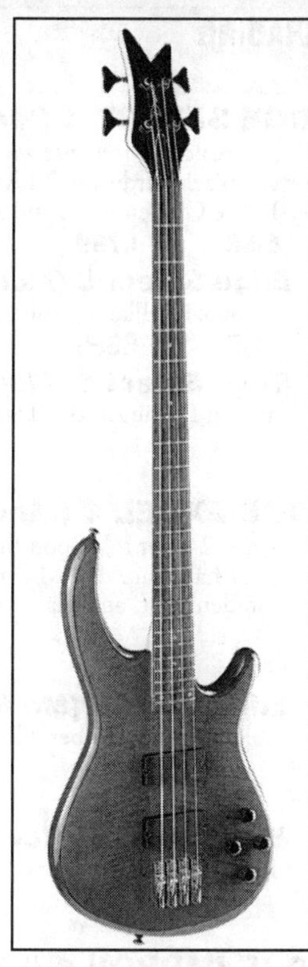
Dean Edge Custom PZ 4
courtesy
Armadillo Enterprises

Edge Series

The entire range of Edge bass models debuted in 1998.

The Bespeak (Model DGP-BP) is an all-in-one starter system that includes an Edge One electric bass, a Dean bass amp, a guitar strap, Dean picks, and a guitar tuner. This complete package retails for $469.

EDGE ONE (Model DGB-E1) - offset double cutaway basswood body, bolt-on maple neck, 24-fret rosewood fingerboard with white dot inlay, fixed bridge, small offset V-shaped peghead with screened logo, 2-per-side die cast tuners, chrome hardware, 2 'soapbar' pickups, 2 volume/1 tone controls, available in Classic Black and Classic White finishes. Mfg. 1998 to date.

MSR	$299	$225	$175	$150	$135	$115	$95	$75

EDGE 4 (Model DGB-EDGE4) - offset double cutaway basswood body, bolt-on laminated maple neck, 34" scale, 24-fret rosewood fingerboard with white dot inlay, fixed bridge, small offset V-shaped peghead with screened logo, 2-per-side die cast tuners, black hardware, 2 EMG-HZ 'soapbar' pickups, 2 volume/1 tone controls, available in Classic Black, Transparent Black, Transparent Blue, Transparent Goldenburst, Transparent Purple, and Transparent Red finishes. Mfg. 1998 to date.

MSR	$419	$290	$265	$240	$210	$165	$135	$100

Add $20 for left-handed configuration (Model DGB-EDGE4L), available in Transparent Black and Transparent Red finishes.

Edge 5 (Model DGB-EDGE5) - similar to the Edge 4, except features 5-string configuration, 35" scale, 3/2-per-side tuners, available in Classic Black, Transparent Black, Transparent Blue, Transparent Goldenburst, Transparent Purple, and Transparent Red finishes. Mfg. 1998 to date.

MSR	$499	$340	$305	$260	$235	$210	$175	$135

Add $20 for left-handed configuration (Model DGB-EDGE5L), available in Transparent Black and Transparent Red finishes.

Edge 6 (Model DGB-EDGE6) - similar to the Edge 4, except features 6-string configuration, 35" scale, 3-per-side tuners, available in Classic Black, Transparent Black, Transparent Blue, Transparent Goldenburst, Transparent Purple, and Transparent Red finishes. Mfg. 1998 to date.

MSR	$599	$425	$355	$325	$270	$250	$195	$160

Add $20 for left-handed configuration (Model DGB-EDGE6L), available in Transparent Black finish only.

EDGE 4 FRETLESS (Model DGB-E4FRLS) - similar to the Edge 4, except has a fretless fingerboard, available in Transparent Black, Transparent Goldenburst, and Transparent Red finishes. Mfg. 1998 to date.

MSR	$449	$300	$275	$250	$225	$175	$150	$125

Edge 5 Fretless (Model DGB-E5FRLS) - similar to the Edge 4 Fretless, except features 5-string configuration, 35" scale, 3/2-per-side tuners, available in Transparent Black, Transparent Goldenburst, and Transparent Red finishes. Mfg. 1998 to date.

MSR	$529	$360	$325	$275	$250	$225	$185	$145

EDGE 4 CUSTOM (Model DGB-EC4) - offset double cutaway mahogany body, flame maple top, bolt-on laminated maple neck, 34" scale, 24-fret rosewood fingerboard with white dot inlay, fixed bridge, small offset V-shaped peghead with screened logo, 2-per-side die cast tuners, black hardware, 2 EMG-HZ 'soapbar' pickups, 2 volume/1 tone controls, active electronics, available in Flame Amber, Flame Black, Flame Blue, Flame Goldenburst, and Flame Red finishes. Mfg. 1998 to date.

MSR	$619	$440	$385	$335	$295	$260	$195	$150

Add $20 for left-handed configuration (Model DGB-EC4L), available in Flame Amber finish only.

Edge 5 Custom (Model DGB-EC5) - similar to the Edge 4 Custom, except features 5-string configuration, 35" scale, 3/2-per-side tuners, available in Flame Amber, Flame Black, Flame Blue, Flame Goldenburst, and Flame Red finishes. Mfg. 1998 to date.

MSR	$699	$530	$425	$375	$325	$295	$250	$195

Add $20 for left-handed configuration (Model DGB-EC5L), available in Flame Amber finish only.

Edge 6 Custom (Model DGB-EC6) - similar to the Edge 4 Custom, except features 6-string configuration, 35" scale, 3-per-side tuners, available in Flame Amber, Flame Black, Flame Blue, Flame Goldenburst, and Flame Red finishes. Mfg. 1998.

		$525	$425	$375	$325	$295	$250	$195

Last MSR was $699.

EDGE 4 CUSTOM PZ (Model DGB-EC4PZ) - similar to the Edge 4 Custom, except has 2 EMG-HZ 'soapbar' pickups/Shadow piezo bridge pickup, 2 volume/2 tone controls, active electronics, available in Flame Black, Flame Blue, Flame Goldenburst, Flame Purple, and Flame Red finishes. Mfg. 1998 to 1999.

		$275	$250	$225	$195	$150	$125	$100

Last MSR was $399.

Edge 5 Custom PZ (Model DGB-EC5PZ) - similar to the Edge 4 Custom PZ, except features 5-string configuration, 35" scale, 3/2-per-side tuners, available in Flame Black, Flame Blue, Flame Goldenburst, Flame Purple, and Flame Red finishes. Mfg. 1998 to 1999.

		$325	$295	$250	$225	$195	$165	$125

Last MSR was $479.

GRADING		100% MINT	98% NEAR MINT	95% EXC+	90% EXC	80% VG+	70% VG	60% G

EDGE SELECT 4 (Model DGB-ES4) - offset double cutaway mahogany body, flame maple top, through-body laminated maple neck, 34" scale, 24-fret rosewood fingerboard with white dot inlay, fixed bridge, small offset V-shaped peghead with screened logo, 2-per-side die cast tuners, black hardware, 2 EMG-HZ 'soapbar' pickups, 2 volume/2 tone controls, active electronics, available in Flame Amber, Flame Black, Flame Blue, Flame Goldenburst, and Flame Red finishes. Mfg. 1998 to date.

MSR	$799	$575	$475	$425	$375	$325	$250	$195

Edge Select 5 (Model DGB-ES5) - similar to the Edge Select 4, except features 5-string configuration, 35" scale, 3/2-per-side tuners, available in Flame Amber, Flame Black, Flame Blue, Flame Goldenburst, and Flame Red finishes. Mfg. 1998 to date.

MSR	$869	$625	$550	$475	$425	$350	$295	$225

Edge Select 6 (Model DGB-ES6) - similar to the Edge Select 4, except features 6-string configuration, 35" scale, 3-per-side tuners, available in Flame Amber, Flame Black, Flame Blue, Flame Goldenburst, and Flame Red finishes. Mfg. 1998.

$550	$475	$425	$375	$325	$275	$225

Last MSR was $799.

EDGE EXCEL 4 (Model DGB-EE4) - offset double cutaway mahogany body, flame maple top, through-body laminated maple neck, 34" scale, 24-fret rosewood fingerboard with white block inlay, fixed bridge, small offset V-shaped peghead with screened logo, 2-per-side Grover tuners, gold hardware, 2 EMG pickups, 2 volume/2 tone controls, EMG active electronics, available in Flame Amber, Flame Black, Flame Blue, Flame Goldenburst, and Flame Red finishes. Mfg. 1998.

$695	$595	$525	$450	$375	$325	$250

Last MSR was $999.

Edge Excel 5 (Model DGB-EE5) - similar to the Edge Excel 4, except features 5-string configuration, 35" scale, 3/2-per-side tuners, available in Flame Amber, Flame Black, Flame Blue, Flame Goldenburst, and Flame Red finishes. Mfg. 1998.

$750	$650	$575	$500	$425	$350	$275

Last MSR was $1,049.

Edge Excel 6 (Model DGB-EE6) - similar to the Edge Excel 4, except features 6-string configuration, 35" scale, 3-per-side tuners, available in Flame Amber, Flame Black, Flame Blue, Flame Goldenburst, and Flame Red finishes. Mfg. 1998.

$795	$675	$595	$525	$450	$375	$295

Last MSR was $1,099.

EDGE IMPROV 4 (Model DGB-EI4) - offset double cutaway alder body, flame maple top, through-body laminated maple neck, 34" scale, 24-fret rosewood fingerboard with white block inlay, fixed bridge, small offset V- shaped peghead with screened logo, 2-per-side Schaller tuners, gold hardware, 2 EMG pickups, 2 volume/2 tone controls, active electronics, available in Flame Amber, Flame Blue, Flame Honeyburst, Flame Purple, Flame Red, and Satin Natural finishes. Mfg. 1998 to date.

MSR	$1,299	$775	$675	$575	$495	$395	$350	$275

Edge Improv 5 (Model DGB-EI5) - similar to the Edge Improv 4, except features 5-string configuration, 35" scale, 3/2-per-side tuners, available in Flame Amber, Flame Black, Flame Blue, Flame Goldenburst, and Flame Red finishes. Mfg. 1998 to date.

MSR	$1,450	$865	$750	$675	$575	$495	$395	$315

Eighty Eight Bass Series

EIGHTY EIGHT BASS - offset double cutaway maple body, bolt-on maple neck, 20-fret ebanol fingerboard with dot inlay, fixed bridge, blackface peghead with screened logo, black pickguard, 4-on-a-side tuners, chrome hardware, P-style EMG Select pickup, volume/tone controls, available in Black, Blue Purpleburst, Gun Metal Grey, Pearl Purpleburst, Pearl Red, Pink, and White finishes. Mfg. 1987 to 1989.

$275	$250	$225	$200	$175	$150	$125

Jeff Berlin Signature Series

JEFF BERLIN STANDARD - offset double cutaway alder body, bolt-on 3-piece maple neck with ebony fingerboard, 21 frets, dot position markers, 34" scale, Schaller tuners, gold hardware, Custom Bartolini pickups, available in Transparent Amberburst, Transparent Amber and Transparent Red finishes. Current Mfg.

MSR	$1,099	$825	$750	$695	$650	$595	$550	$475

Jeff Berlin Exotic - similar to Jeff Berlin Standard, except has choice of redwood burl, zebrawood or quilted maple top, available in Natural finish. Current Mfg.

MSR	$1,499	$1,125	$1,025	$925	$825	$725	$625	$525

Last MSR was $649.

Mach Series

These models were designed in 1985, and had very limited production runs. There are very few of either Mach bass guitar models in circulation.

MACH V BASS - single cutaway hardwood body, exaggerated treble horn/extended lower bout, bolt-on maple necks, 24-fret rosewood fingerboard with dot inlays, 2-per-side 'shrimp fork' headstock, fixed bridge, chrome hardware, P/J-style pickups, volume/tone controls, available in Jet Black, Pearl Blueburst, Pearl Red, and Pearl White finishes. Mfg. 1985 to 1986.

Last MSR was $499.

Too few of these exist for accurate statistical representation.

Mach VII Bass - similar to the Mach V construction (U.S. built), available in special Leopard, Tiger, and other exotic finishes. Mfg. 1985 to 1986.

Last MSR was $1,999.

Too few of these exist for accurate statistical representation.

GRADING	100% MINT	98% NEAR MINT	95% EXC+	90% EXC	80% VG+	70% VG	60% G

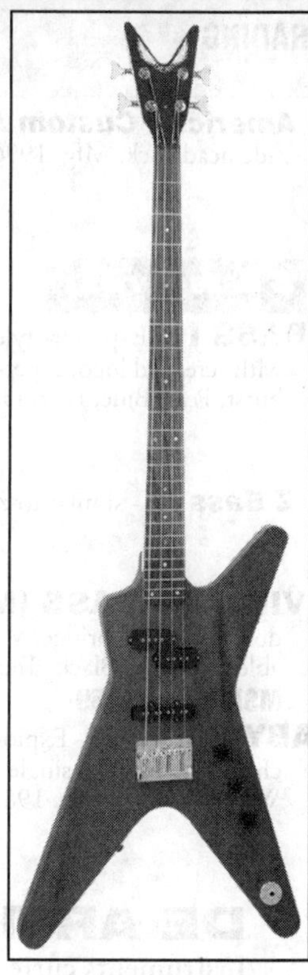
Dean ML Bass (Vintage Reissue) courtesy Armadillo Enterprises

ML Bass Series

ML BASS I - Flying V-style with treble horn mahogany body, maple neck, 22-fret bound rosewood fingerboard with pearl dot inlay, fixed bridge, wing shaped peghead with screened logo, 2-per-side Kluson tuners, chrome hardware, humbucker coil pickup, volume/tone controls, active electronics, available in Black, Blueburst, Pearl Blue, Pearl Pink, Pearl Red, Pearl White, Red, and White finishes. Mfg. 1980 to 1985.

$500 $425 $350 $295 $250 $225 $200
Last MSR was $1,050.

ML Bass II - similar to ML I, except has bound figured maple top, 2 humbucker pickups, 2 volume/1 tone controls.

$550 $475 $395 $325 $275 $250 $225
Last MSR was $1,200.

ML VINTAGE BASS (Model DGB-MLBX) - Flying V-style with treble horn basswood body, bolt-on maple neck, 24-fret rosewood fingerboard with white dot inlay, fixed bridge, V-shaped peghead with screened logo, 2-per-side tuners, chrome hardware, P/J-style pickups, 2 volume/1 tone controls, available in Classic Black, Transparent Blue, Transparent Braziliaburst, and Transparent Red finishes. Mfg. 1998 to date.

MSR $369 $250 $2225 $195 $150 $125 $95 $65

BABY ML BASS - down-sized Flying V-style with treble horn poplar body, poplar neck, 22-fret rosewood fingerboard with pearl dot inlay, fixed bridge, body matching peghead with screened logo, 2-per-side tuners, chrome hardware, single coil pickup, volume/tone controls, available in Black, Blueburst, Pearl Blue, Pearl Pink, Pearl Red, Pearl White, Red and White finishes. Mfg. 1983 to 1985.

$300 $250 $200 $175 $150 $125 $100
Last MSR was $800.

PLAYMATE BASS - offset double cutaway hardwood body, bolt-on maple neck, 20-fret rosewood fingerboard with dot inlay, fixed bridge, blackface peghead with screened logo, black pickguard, 4-on-a-side tuners, chrome hardware, P-style pickups, volume/tone controls, available in Black, Red, and White finishes. Mfg. 1987 to 1989.

$225 $195 $175 $150 $125 $100 $75
Last MSR was $359.

SB BASS - offset double cutaway alder or mahogany body, maple neck-through design, 34" scale, 24-fret rosewood with pearl dot inlay (wings inlay at 12th fret), fixed bridge, 2-per-side tuners, black hardware, 2 J-style pickups, volume/treble/bass/blend controls, active electronics. Mfg. 1995 to 1996.

$1,000 $925 $825 $725 $625 $525 $400
Last MSR was $1,695.

This model had an optional curly maple top.

X Bass Series

The X Bass model body design had a sleek, offset double cutaway body.

AMERICAN CUSTOM ACX B4 (Bolt-On) - offset double cutaway alder body, bolt-on maple neck, 34" scale, 24-fret rosewood fingerboard with pearl dot inlay, Dean fixed bridge, 'shrimp fork' peghead with screened logo, 2-per-side tuners, chrome hardware, 2 Seymour Duncan pickups, 2 volume/tone controls, available in Classic Black, Classic Red, Torrid Teal, and Wine Red finishes. Mfg. 1996 to 1997.

$675 $625 $550 $475 $395 $325 $250
Last MSR was $965.

Add $30 for flame maple top, alder body, available in Flame Black, Flame Blue, Flame Braziliaburst, Flame Cherry, Flame Cherry Sunburst, Flame Green, Flame Purple, Flame Teal, and Flame Vintage Sunburst finishes.

Add $100 for ash body and translucent finish, available in Translucent Black, Translucent Blue, Translucent Braziliaburst, Translucent Cherry, Translucent Cherry Sunburst, Translucent Green, Translucent Purple, Translucent Teal, and Translucent Vintage Sunburst finishes.

American Custom ACX B5 (Bolt-On) - similar to the American Custom ACX B4, except in a 5-string configuration, 3/2-per-side headstock. Mfg. 1996 to 1997.

$700 $650 $595 $525 $425 $350 $250
Last MSR was $1,050.

American Custom ACS B4 (Neck-Through) - similar to the American Custom ACX B4, except features a maple through-neck design, 2 Seymour Duncan 'soapbar' pickups. Mfg. 1996 to 1997.

$1,000 $900 $825 $750 $650 $575 $450
Last MSR was $1,550.

Add $100 for flame maple top, alder body, available in Flame Black, Flame Blue, Flame Braziliaburst, Flame Cherry, Flame Cherry Sunburst, Flame Green, Flame Purple, Flame Teal, and Flame Vintage Sunburst finishes.

Add $100 for ash body and translucent finish, available in Translucent Black, Translucent Blue, Translucent Braziliaburst, Translucent Cherry, Translucent Cherry Sunburst, Translucent Green, Translucent Purple, Translucent Teal, and Translucent Vintage Sunburst finishes.

GRADING	100% MINT	98% NEAR MINT	95% EXC+	90% EXC	80% VG+	70% VG	60% G

American Custom ACS B5 (Neck-Through) - similar to the American Custom ACS B4, except in a 5-string configuration, 3/2-per-side headstock. Mfg. 1996 to 1997.

	$1,100	$950	$875	$800	$695	$600	$475

Last MSR was $1,650.

Z Bass Series

Z BASS I - Explorer-style mahogany body, maple neck, 22-fret bound rosewood fingerboard with pearl dot inlay, fixed bridge, V-shaped peghead with screened logo, 2-per-side Kluson tuners, chrome hardware, humbucker pickup, volume/tone control, active electronics, available in Black, Blueburst, Pearl Blue, Pearl Pink, Pearl Red, Pearl White, Red and White finishes. Mfg. 1982 to 1985.

	$500	$425	$350	$275	$250	$225	$200

Last MSR was $1,050.

Z Bass II - similar to Z I, except has bound figured maple top, 2 humbucker pickups, 2 volume/1 tone controls.

	$550	$475	$395	$325	$275	$250	$235

Last MSR was $1,200.

Z VINTAGE BASS (Model DGB-ZBX) - Explorer-style basswood body, bolt-on maple neck, 24-fret rosewood fingerboard with white dot inlay, fixed bridge, V-shaped peghead with screened logo, 2-per-side tuners, chrome hardware, P/J-style pickups, 2 volume/1 tone controls, available in Classic Black, Transparent Blue, Transparent Braziliaburst, and Transparent Red finishes. Mfg. 1998 to date.

MSR $369	$250	$225	$195	$150	$125	$95	$65

BABY Z BASS - Explorer-style poplar body, poplar neck, 22-fret bound rosewood fingerboard with pearl dot inlay, fixed bridge, 2-per-side tuners, chrome hardware, single coil pickup, volume/tone controls, available in Black, Blueburst, Pearl Blue, Pearl Pink, Pearl Red, Pearl White, Red and White finishes. Mfg. 1983 to 1985.

	$300	$250	$225	$175	$150	$125	$100

Last MSR was $800.

DE ARMOND BY GUILD

Instruments currently produced in Korea. DeArmond by Guild instruments are not available in the U.S. market. Distributed in Europe by Fender Musical Instruments GmbH of Dusseldorf, Germany.

Another European conundrum! The DeArmond (DeArmond by Guild) trademark is applied to a series of Guild style instruments on a product line not available in the U.S. These instruments have the *DeArmond* logo across the headstock.

Fender Musical Instruments Corporation products are identified by a part number that consists of a three digit location/facility code, a four digit model code, and a hyphen that separates the two parts (there are additional digits that continue to identify the model). In the overall scheme, a 0 designates a Fender product without a Floyd Rose tremolo, a 1 indicates a Fender product with a Floyd Rose tremolo, and a 3 indicates a Guild product (see FENDER Production Model Codes).

A Rhode Island Guild product would thus be designated 3 50 - XXXX (X indicates the four digit model code). However, the DeArmond by Guild models carry a 0 35 - XXXX production code. Internal coding would thus indicate a Fender (non Guild) product from the Korean (33 versus 35) facility code; a 33 facility code is used for Korean-built Fender and Squire instruments. By the Fender production codes, the ***Blue Book of Electric Guitars*** has deduced that the following instruments are Korean products. All models listed below do not have a U.S. retail list price.

ELECTRIC

DE ARMOND JET-STAR (Model 035-0200) - offset double slightly cutaway mahogany body, set-in mahogany neck, 24 5/8" scale, 22-fret bound palisander fingerboard with white block inlay, adjustable metal bridge/stop tailpiece, 3-per-side tuners, chrome hardware, black pickguard, 2 DeArmond humbucking pickups, 2 volume/2 tone controls, 3-way switch, available in Black (-506), Crimson Red Transparent (-538), Moon Blue (-596), and Tyrian Purple (-582). Current Mfg.

This model is not sold in the U.S., and has no current domestic MSR.

DE ARMOND M 75 (Model 035-7500) - single round cutaway bound Agathis solid body, maple top, raised black pickguard, set-in maple neck, 24 5/8" scale, 22-fret bound palisander fingerboard with white block inlay, tune-o-matic bridge/metal 'Harp' tailpiece, 3-per-side tuners, chrome hardware, 2 DeArmond humbucker pickups, 2 volume/2 tone controls, 3-position switch, available in Antique Burst (-537), Black (-506), Moon Blue (-596), and Tyrian Purple (-582). Current Mfg.

This model is not sold in the U.S., and has no current domestic MSR.

De Armond M 75 T (Model 035-7600) - similar to the M 75, except features 2 DeArmond 2K single coil pickups, tune-o-matic bridge/Bigsby-style DeArmond tremolo, available in Antique Burst (-537), Black (-506), Blue Sparkle (-513), and Champagne Sparkle (-517). Current Mfg.

This model is not sold in the U.S., and has no current domestic MSR.

DE ARMOND STARFIRE II SPECIAL (Model 035-3000) - single Florentine cutaway laminated maple body, 2 f-holes, set-in maple neck, 24 5/8" scale, 22-fret bound palisander fingerboard with white dot inlay, tune-o-matic bridge/Bigsby-styled DeArmond tremolo, 3-per-side tuners, chrome hardware, raised black pickguard, 2 DeArmond 2K single coil pickups, 2 volume/2 tone controls, 3-position switch, available in Antique Burst (-537), Black (-506), and Crimson Red Transparent (-538). Current Mfg.

This model is not sold in the U.S., and has no current domestic MSR.

De Armond Starfire IV (Model 035-4000) - similar to the Starfire II Special, except features dual rounded cutaway semi-hollow bound laminated maple body, tune-o-matic bridge/metal 'Harp' tailpiece, 2 DeArmond humbucker pickups, available in Antique Burst (-537), Black (-506), Crimson Red Transparent (-538), and Natural (-521). Current Mfg.

This model is not sold in the U.S., and has no current domestic MSR.

DE ARMOND X-155 (Model 035-1700) - single round cutaway semi-hollow body, bound laminated maple top, 2 bound f-holes, raised black pickguard, laminated maple back/sides, set-in neck, 24 5/8" scale, 20-fret palisander fingerboard with white block inlay, adjustable rosewood bridge/metal 'Harp' tailpiece, 3-per-side tuners, chrome hardware, 2 DeArmond humbucker pickups, 2 volume/2 tone controls, 3-position switch, available in Antique Burst (-537), and Natural (-521). Current Mfg.

This model is not sold in the U.S., and has no current domestic MSR.

GRADING	100% MINT	98% NEAR MINT	95% EXC+	90% EXC	80% VG+	70% VG	60% G

ELECTRIC BASS

DE ARMOND JET-STAR BASS (Model 035-0500) - offset double slightly cutaway mahogany body, set-in maple neck, 30 ¾" scale, 21-fret palisander fingerboard with white dot inlay, fixed bridge, 2-per-side tuners, chrome hardware, 2 DeArmond 1B single coil pickups, volume/tone controls, 3-way switch, available in Black (-506), Crimson Red Transparent (-538), Moon Blue (-596), and Tyrian Purple (-582). Current Mfg.

This model is not sold in the U.S., and has no current domestic MSR.

DE ARMOND STARFIRE II BASS (Model 035-6000) - dual rounded cutaway semi-hollow bound laminated maple body, 2 f-holes, set-in maple neck, 30 ¾" scale, 21-fret bound palisander fingerboard with white dot inlay, fixed bridge, 2-per-side tuners, chrome hardware, 2 DeArmond 2B dual-coil pickups, 2 volume/2 tone controls, 3-position switch, available in Antique Burst (-537), Black (-506), and Crimson Red Transparent (-538). Current Mfg.

This model is not sold in the U.S., and has no current domestic MSR.

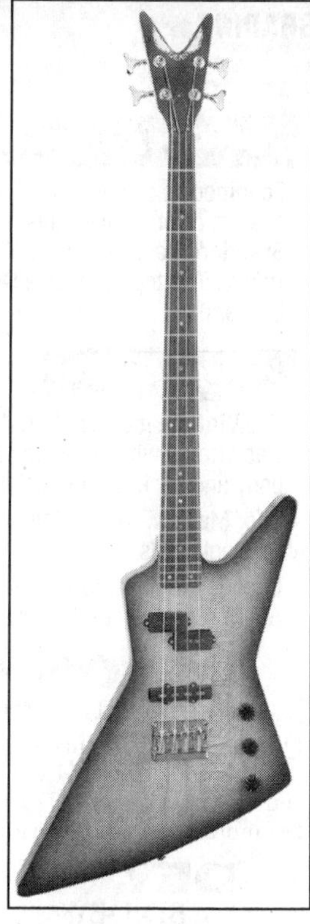

Dean Z Bass (Vintage Reissue) courtesy Armadillo Enterprises

DECCA

Instruments previously produced in Japan.

The Decca trademark was a brand name used by U.S. importers Decca Records.

(Source: Michael Wright, Guitar Stories Volume One)

DEERING

Instruments (guitar models) previously built in Lemon Grove, California from 1989 to 1991. Deering has produced high quality banjos in Lemon Grove since 1975.

In 1975, Greg and Janet Deering began producing the quality banjos for which the company is known. While continuing to offer innovative banjo designs, the Deerings also offer several models from entry level to professional play.

Deering offers a banjo model that is tuned and played like a guitar. The **MB-6** is designed for the guitar player who doesn't have to *learn banjo to play banjo.* The MB-6 is also available in a 12-string configuration.

In the late 1980s, Deering offered 4 different solid body guitar models in 2 variations that carried a retail price between $1,498-$2,850. The guitar models were also offered with some custom options, but were only produced for little over one year.

DEFIL

Instruments currently built in Poland.

The long-established Defil company is the only mass producer of guitars in Poland. Defil has a wide range of solid body and semi-hollow body designs.

(Source: Tony Bacon, The Ultimate Guitar Book)

DELACUGO, TONY

See TDL GUITAR WORKS.

DEMARINO

Instruments previously built in Copiague, New York 1973-2000.

Deeply rooted in music, Ronald J. DeMarino's career spanned four decades. DeMarino was playing New York clubs in 1956, when he had his first meeting with John D'Angelico (DeMarino was having his 1948 Gibson L-5 repaired!). D'Angelico took a liking to him, and after spending a great deal of time in his shop, DeMarino was fascinated with the idea of guitar building. DeMarino experimented for years, and finally launched his own shop.

DeMarino Guitars was established in 1967, and was in continuous operation since the inception of the business. DeMarino was a second generation family owned business, and for 27 years specialized in the restoration of fine instruments, as well as custom building special order guitars and basses.

(Source: Hal Hammer)

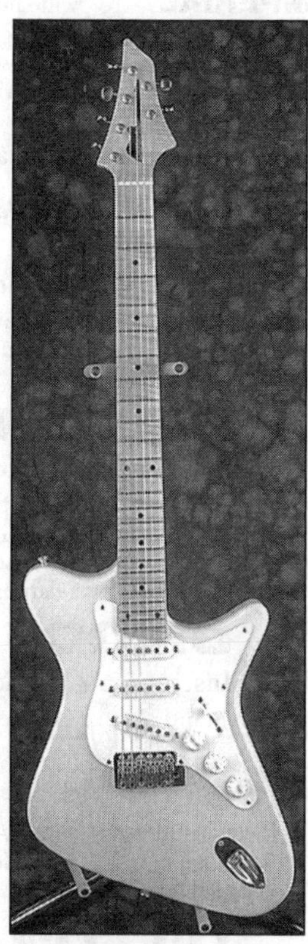

DeMarino "Mary K" courtesy Ronald J. Demarino

ELECTRIC

In addition to the quality standard model configurations, DeMarino also offered custom options such as flame maple or big leaf quilt maple tops, ebony fingerboards, abalone or mother-of-pearl inlays, and other exotic woods (spalted or burled maple, burled walnut, or lacewood).

Contour Series

The **Contour Standard** (last retail was $2,715) offerd a cutaway alder or ash body, a maple set-in neck, rosewood fingerboard, Sperzel tuners, EMG pickups, and either a DeMarino custom bridge or Wilkinson tremolo system.

The **Contour Custom** (last retail was $3,240) upgraded the body woods to a Honduran mahogany body and set-in neck, as well as a figured maple top and an ebony fingerboard. A DeMarino fixed bridge and a hand rubbed nitrocellulose finish completed the package.

On a slightly different note, the **Contour Pro** (last retail was $2,400) consisted of an alder body, a maple bolt-on neck with rosewood fingerboard, and a Wilkinson tremolo combined with locking Sperzel tuners (a Floyd Rose locking tremolo system is optional).

GRADING	100% MINT	98% NEAR MINT	95% EXC+	90% EXC	80% VG+	70% VG	60% G

Thin-Line Series

Four models comprised the Thin-Line Series. The primary models **Pro-1** (last retail was $1,900) and **Pro-2** (last retail was $1,900) both featured an alder body, custom color lacquer finishes, and a flat-mount Wilkinson bridge. The **Pro-1** had 2 single coil pickups, and the **Pro-2** had 2 EMG humbuckers. The **Thin-Line Standard** (last retail was $2,300) offered a swamp ash body topped with a figured maple top, rosewood fingerboard, EMG-T pickups, and a Wilkinson *Tele-bridge*. The top of the line **Custom** (last retail was $2,500) had a Honduran mahogany body under the Maple top, an ebony fingerboard, and two EMG humbuckers.

Vintage Series

The **Vintage** models offered a sleek single cutaway body design with finishes and parts that seem right at home in the vintage guitar market. The **TV Contour** was offered with either one single coil pickup (**Single**, last retail was $2,250) or two (**Double**, last retail was $2,350). Both models had a Honduran mahogany body and neck, a 'Vintage' limed mahogany finish, rosewood fingerboard, and a 'wrap-around' stud tailpiece.

The "**Mary K.**" (last retail was $2,250) combined a swamp ash body with a maple bolt-on neck, gold hardware, a 'see-through' blonde finish, and three EMG-SV single coils.

Change the finish to a *butter-scotch* lacquer, substitute a pair of EMG-T pickups and a black vintage-styled pickguard, and the results would be the *Black Guard* model (last retail was $2,150).

DEVON GUITARS

Instruments currently built in Pewaukee, Wisconsin.

Devon Guitars manufactures custom hand crafted bass instruments featuring unidirectional-fiber graphite necks. Models include the Diamond D ($1,150 for 4-string, $1,250 for 5-string), Diamond J ($1,050 for 4-string, $1,225 for 5-string), Diamond P ($1,050 for 4-string, $1,150 for 5-string), and the Grace Series ($975 for 4-string, $1,050 for 5-string, $1,350 for 6-string, $1,450 for 7-string, add approx. $200 for neck-through construction). For more information regarding these instruments, please contact the company directly (see Trademark Index).

DEY

See BD DEY.

DEYOE

Instruments currently built in Denver, Colorado.

Luthier Eric Deyoe has 13 years experience and is currently working at Colfax Guitar Shop in Denver, Colorado.

ELECTRIC

IMPERIAL - 18" wide hollow maple body with a single cutaway, f-holes, arched top and back, 4" body depth, 3-piece set maple neck, 24 3/4" scale, 22-fret bound ebony fingerboard, single layer cream body binding, Bigsby tremolo, gold or chrome hardware, 2 'soapbar' pickups, volume and tone controls, 3-way toggle switch, available in Apricot, Blue, Cherry, Green, Gold, Plum, Silver, and Teal sparkle finishes; and Black and Tobacco Sunburst finishes. Current Mfg.

MSR **$5,000**

This model is also available in a Thin Line model with 2" body depth.

DIAMOND

See ARIA.

Instruments previously built in Korea during the 1980s.

These entry level instruments were originally distributed by the Pennino Musical Corporation, and later by Aria USA. Designs mostly fell in the 'strat' or 'superstrat' guitar configuration, and a pointy headstock/sleek curves 'P-Bass' bass guitar. The trademark on the headstock generally read "DIAMOND by Aria".

DIAMOND-S

Instruments previously built in Independence, Virginia during the 1970s.

When Micro-Frets closed operations in Maryland in either 1974 or 1975, the company assets were purchased by David Sturgill. Sturgill, who served as the company president of Grammer Guitars for three years, let his sons John and Danny gain access to leftover Micro-Frets parts. In addition to those parts, they had also purchased the remains of New Jersey's Harptone guitar company. The two assembled a number of solid body guitars which were then sold under the 'Diamond-S' trademark. Unfortunately, that business venture did not catch on, and dissipated sometime in 1976.

DIEGO

Instruments previously built in Hannover, Germany. Distributed by Goldo Music of Hannover, Germany.

Diego brand Deluxe Guitars were offered by Dieter Golsdorf of Goldo Music. Diego instruments are vintage reproductions of late '50s Strats.

ELECTRIC

Diego instruments feature American alder bodies (shaped similar to a '59 strat), 22 jumbo fret slab-cut rosewood fingerboard, bolt-on maple necks, 3 '59 Grand Vintage single coil pickups, vintage-style tremolo, Gotoh Kluson Replica tuners, and aged-color pickguard/knobs/pickup covers, available in vintage-style finishes.

DILLON

Instruments currently built in Bloomsburg, Pennsylvania.

Dillon Guitars offers quality custom built instruments. For further information, contact Dillon Guitars directly (see Trademark Index).

DINGWALL DESIGNER GUITARS

Instruments currently built in Saskatoon, Canada.

Luthier Sheldon Dingwall founded Dingwall Designer Guitars in the mid 1980s, after years of actively playing music and doing guitar repair work. Dingwall moved from designing guitar models to bass models, specifically concentrating on fanned fretboard designs pioneered by Ralph Novak. Bass notables such as Lee Sklar, Michael Rhodes, Mike Brignardello, Mark Fain, and Hank Insell are all currently playing and recording with Dingwall basses. Disaster struck on October 8, 1996, when the warehouse where the Dingwall factory was located caught on fire. The fire eventually consumed the entire building, including the tooling and construction tools. When Dingwall began rebuilding the company, he received help from other Canadian luthiers such as Glenn MacDougall of Fury Guitars (see FURY) and Byron Olsen of Olsen Audio (a contract manufacturer of musical and audio equipment). As a result, the combined manufacturing experience totalled over 50 years! Local musicians and businesses held a benefit to raise funds for the re-tooling of the bass line. Dingwall basses were back to production 12 months later.

While Dingwall is concentrating on bass guitars, he used to offer several high quality electric guitar models. All models featured bolt-on necks, 3-per-side headstock with Sperzel or Gotoh tuners, and passive pickups. The Roadster featured a single cutaway body, stop tailpiece, mini-humbucker (neck position) and single coil (bridge). The ATV had an offset double cutaway body, tremolo bridge, and three single coils wired to a custom switching harness that delivered 10 distinct tones! The LVQ (Low Volume Resonance) model offered similar stylings to the ATV, except the design featured tone chambers (semi-hollowbody) and a stop tailpiece. Contact Dingwall Designer Guitars for availability.

Deyoe Imperial
courtesy Eric Deyoe

ELECTRIC BASS

All VooDoo series custom basses feature the Novax fanned fret system on the fingerboards. This system is licensed from famed inventor/luthier Ralph Novak, and contributes a more accurate intonation and harmonic system to the staggered bridge design developed by Dingwall.

Dingwall basses all have an innovative bridge design that allows each string the proper scale length to achieve optimum tone. Thus, the scale length is staggered from the low B string (37") up to the G string (34") on a five string bass.

Basses built prior to the fire featured 9-ply laminated necks and Kahler/Dingwall custom bridges. Since the fire and re-tooling, basses now feature a 5-ply laminated maple neck, a new 3 band switchable EQ, and Dingwall bridge.

Add $100 for lined fretless fingerboard.

Add $100 for 3 active/passive band EQ with switchable midrange.

Add $100 for Basslines pickups and electronics.

Add $100 for 2-Tone Sunburst finish.

Add $150 for 3-Tone Sunburst finish.

Add $200 for Hipshot Xtender key.

VooDoo Series

PRIMA 4-STRING - offset double cutaway American Black walnut body core, padauk bookmatched top/back, carbon fiber reinforced 5-ply laminated rock maple bolt-on neck, 24-fret pau ferro fingerboard, 2-per-side Gotoh tuners, 2 Bartolini custom soapbar pickups, black hardware, Dingwall custom aircraft aluminum bridge, volume/blend/2-band EQ controls, available in Oil finishes. Current Mfg.

MSR $2,695

Add $50 for Zebra model-style fretboard markers.

Add $75 for flame maple top and back.

Add $150 for quilted maple top.

Add $250 for Translucent polyurethane finish.

Prima 5-String - similar to the Prima 4-string, except has 5-string configuration, 2/3-per-side tuners. Current Mfg.

MSR $2,795

Prima 6-String - similar to the Prima 4-string, except has 6-string configuration, 3-per-side tuners. Current Mfg.

MSR $2,895

ZEBRA 4-STRING - similar to Prima, except features a solid Northern Ash body, available in Black Cherry Burst (BB), Colaburst (CB), Marylin's Lipstick Red (ML), Sticky Fingers Warm Caramel (SF), Stormy Monday Blue (SM), Sunlight through a Cola Deep Red/Brown (SC), and Whalepool Blue (WP) Transparent color finishes. Current Mfg.

MSR $2,695

The Zebra name is derived from the Transparent color finishes which highlight the wood's grain pattern.

Zebra 5-string - similar to the Zebra 4-string, except has 5-string configuration, 2/3-per-side tuners. Current Mfg.

MSR $2,795

Zebra 6-string - similar to the Zebra 4-string, except has 6-string configuration, 3-per-side tuners. Current Mfg.

MSR $2,895

DIPINTO

Instruments currently built in Korea.

Luthier Chris DiPinto handcrafts solid body electric guitars that recall the wackier side of the 1960s while still being solid, playable instruments (which sometimes can't be said for those 1960s inspirations!). Currently DiPinto guitars are manufactured in Korea then shipped to Philadelphia for final set-up and assembly.

DiPinto maintains a stock of colored sparkle and pearl materials for customized pickguards, as well as the more traditional tortoiseshell material. All models are available in a left-handed configuration at no additional charge.

Earlier versions of the Custom Series models featured 3-piece maple body, adjustable rosewood bridge/sparkle finish stop tailpiece, and 2 EMG single coil pickups.

D

ELECTRIC

All DiPinto **Custom Series** models feature neck-through construction, 24 3/4" scale, volume and tone controls, 2 on/off rocker pickup selectors, and a pre-set volume control *stomp switch.*

Custom Series

BELVEDERE - single cutaway poplar body, textured lizard skin top/sparkle plastic back overlays, through-body maple neck, 24 3/4" scale, 22-fret rosewood fingerboard with thumbnail sparkle inlay, 3-per-side tuners, 2 Wilde mini-humbucker pickups, chrome hardware, silver sparkle fixtures, adjustable tune-o-matic bridge/metal tailpiece, volume/tone controls, 2 pickup on/off rocker switches, preset volume control stomp switch, available in Black, Blue, and Red finishes. Disc.

Last MSR was $2,150.

Add $250 for gold hardware/gold sparkle fixtures/Beige finish.

Belvedere (Korean Mfg.) -similar to Belvedere, except has bolt-on neck, 2 Vintage Twang Humbucker pickups, available in Black & White, and Blue Sparkle finishes. Current Mfg.

MSR $649

Also available in Left-hand configuration at no extra charge.

MACH IV - offset double cutaway (Mosrite-ish) poplar body, through-body maple neck, 24 3/4" scale, 22-fret bound rosewood fingerboard with star inlay, 3-per-side tuners, 2 Wilde Noiseless single coil pickups, chrome hardware, white pickguard, Schaller roller bridge/sparkle covered stop tailpiece, volume/tone controls, 2 pickup on/off rocker switches, preset volume control stomp switch, available in Candy Apple Red and Hard Candy Blue finishes with a sporty White racing stripe. Disc.

Last MSR was $1,600.

Add $250 for Vibro*Star tremolo.

Mach IV (Korean Mfg.) - similar to Mack IV, except has bolt-on neck, 1 DiPinto single coil pickup, 1 DiPinto "Dual Single" humbucker pickup, Tune-O-Matic bridge with stop tailpiece, available in Candy Aplle Red, Hard Candy Blue and Sedated White finishes. Current Mfg.

MSR $599

Left-hand configuration available at no extra charge.

GALAXIE - offset double cutaway (pointy horns) poplar body, through-body maple neck, 24" scale, 22-fret rosewood fingerboard with V-wedge inlay, 6-on-a-side vintage style chrome button tuners, 2 Wilde Noiseless single coil pickups, chrome hardware, pearloid pickguard/chrome metal controls plate, Schaller roller bridge/pearloid finish Vibro*Star tremolo, volume/tone controls, 2 pickup on/off rocker switches, preset volume control stomp switch, available in Black (with Purple pickguard); Black, Navy, or Red (with White pickguard); and Dark Green and Light Blue (with Gold pickguard) finishes. Disc.

Last MSR was $1,600.

Add $50 for locking tuners.

GALAXIE (Korean Mfg.) - offset double cutaway, poplar body with bolt-on maple neck, 25 1/2" scale, rosewood fingerboard with dot or star inlays, six on a side pearl button tuners, four single coil pickups, five position selector switch, or two humbuckers with a three position switch, available in Red, Sunburst, Black, Silver Sparkle, Green Sunburst, or Pink Sparkle. Mfg. in Korea. 1999 to date.

MSR $549

Add $50 for tremelo.

Add $15 for Sparkle finish.

ELECTRIC BASS

In 1998, DiPinto teamed up with jazz bassist Jamaladeen Tacuma to design the 4-string Belvedere Bass.

BELVEDERE BASS STANDARD - single cutaway poplar body, through-body maple neck, 34" scale, 24-fret rosewood fingerboard with dot inlay, 2-per-side tuners, 2 Wilde pickups, chrome hardware, white pickguard, fixed bridge, volume/tone controls, 3-way toggle switch, available in a variety of color combinations. Disc.

Last MSR was $1,200.

Belvedere Bass (Korean Mfg.) similar to Belvedere Bass Standard, except has bolt-on neck, 2 mini-humbucker pickups, available in Black & White and Green Sparkle finishes. Current Mfg.

MSR $649

Custom - similar to the Belvedere Bass Standard, except features a white textured *lizard skin* top/laminated sparkle plastic back, 24-fret bound ebony fingerboard with thumbnail sparkle inlay, chrome hardware, 2 chrome covered mini-humbucker pickups, rosewood bridge/sparkle covered stop tailpiece, silver sparkle fixtures, volume/tone controls, 2 on/off pickup rocker switches, available in Black, Blue, and Red finishes. Disc.

Last MSR was $2,150.

Add $250 for gold hardware/gold sparkle fixtures/Beige finish.

GRADING	100% MINT	98% NEAR MINT	95% EXC+	90% EXC	80% VG+	70% VG	60% G

DOBRO

Current trademark of instruments currently built by Original Acoustic Instruments (OAI), located in Nashville, TN. Original Acoustic Instruments is a division of the Gibson Guitar Corporation. Previously manufactured by Original Musical Instruments Company, located in Huntington Beach, California. In 1997, production was moved to Nashville, Tennessee. Distributed by the Gibson Guitar Corporation of Nashville, Tennessee.

The original Dobro company was formed in 1928 in Los Angeles, California.

The Dopyera family emigrated from the Austro-Hungary area to Southern California in 1908. In the early 1920s, John and Rudy Dopyera began producing banjos in Southern California. They were approached by guitarist George Beauchamp to help solve his 'volume' (or lack thereof) problem with other instruments in the vaudeville orchestra. In the course of their conversation, the idea of placing aluminum resonators in a guitar body for amplification purposes was developed. John Dopyera and his four brothers (plus some associates, like George Beauchamp) formed National in 1925. The initial partnership between Dopyera and Beauchamp lasted for about two years, and then John Dopyera left National to form the Dobro company. The Dobro name was chosen as a contraction of the **Do**pyera **Bro**thers (and it also means *good* in Slavic languages).

The Dobro and National companies were later remerged by Louis Dopyera in 1931 or 1932. The company moved to Chicago, Illinois in 1936, and a year later granted Regal the rights to manufacture Dobros. The *revised* company changed its name to VALCO in 1943, and worked on war materials during World War II. In 1959, VALCO transferred the Dobro name and tools to Emil Dopyera. Between 1966 and 1967, the Dobro trademark was sold to Semie Moseley, of Mosrite fame. Moseley constructed the first Dobros out of parts from Emil's California plant, and later built his own necks and bodies. Moseley also built *Mobros*, a Mosrite-inspired Dobro design. After Mosrite collapsed, the name was still held by Moseley; so in the late 1960s, Emil's company produced resonator guitars under the trade name of **Hound Dog** and **Dopera** (note the missing 'y') Originals. When the Dobro name finally became available again, Emil and new associates founded the Original Musical Instruments Company, Inc. (OMI) in 1970. OMI has been producing Dobros ever since.

In 1985, Chester and Mary Lizak purchased OMI from Gabriela and Ron Lazar; and eight years later in 1993, OMI was purchased by the Gibson Guitar Corporation, and production continued to be centered in California. The production of Dobro instruments was moved to Nashville, Tennessee in the Spring of 1997.

(Early company history courtesy Bob Brozman, The History and Artistry of National Resonator Instruments)

DiPinto Belvedere
courtesy DiPinto Guitars

For further information regarding Dobro acoustic guitars, please refer to the 7th Edition *Blue Book of Acoustic Guitars*.

ELECTRIC

BLUESMAKER (Model DEBLU) - Available in BlackBurst, BlueBurst, CherryBurst, GreenBurst, PurpleBurst, VintageBurst, and WineBurst finishes. Mfg. 1996-2000.

	$1,120	$980	$855	$730	$600	$475	$350

Last MSR was $1,399.

BluesMaker Deluxe (Model DEBLU DLX) - similar to the Bluesmaker, except has fancier appointments. Mfg. 1996-2000.

	$1,280	$1,100	$960	$820	$680	$540	$400

Last MSR was $1,599.

DOBROLEKTRIC (Model DELEK/DELEKKB) - cutaway body with figured maple top, classic P90 and bridge Piezo pickups with blending, nickel hardware, single tone/volume controls, available in Ebony, BlackBurst (disc.), BlueBurst (disc.), CherryBurst (disc.), GreenBurst (disc.), PurpleBurst (disc.), VintageBurst, and WineBurst (disc.) finishes. Mfg. 1996 to date.

MSR $2,080	$1,500	$1,200	$1,050	$915	$780	$645	$510

VALPRO (Model DEVAL) - Available in Black, Coral Pink, Cream, Light Sky Blue, and Seafoam Green finishes. Mfg. 1996-2000.

	$1,200	$1,050	$915	$780	$645	$510	$375

Last MSR was $1,499.

ValPro Jr. (Model DEVJR) - Mfg. 1996-2000.

	$1,200	$1,050	$915	$780	$645	$510	$375

Last MSR was $1,499.

DODGE

Instruments currently built in Tallahassee, Florida since 1996. Distributed by Dodge Guitars of Pompano Beach, Florida.

Rick Dodge apprenticed to master stringed instrument maker Paris Bancetti in the mid 1970s, and has been a luthier for over 20 years, making both acoustic and electric guitars for personal use and for friends and family. Each guitar was carefully crafted from fine woods, and guitars made by Dodge achieved high quality aesthetics and sound. After building many electric guitars and experimenting with different electronic configurations, Dodge was struck with the idea of making a modular guitar that could completely exchange the electronics without sacrificing the high quality sound or beauty of a fine instrument. Dodge then developed the idea of a rear-mounted modular system: the pickups and electronics would be mounted on a section that could be inserted into the body area. Rick Dodge formed the **Dodge Guitar Company** in the spring of 1996. Production of the modular guitars began in September, 1996.

(Company information courtesy Janice Dodge, July, 1996)

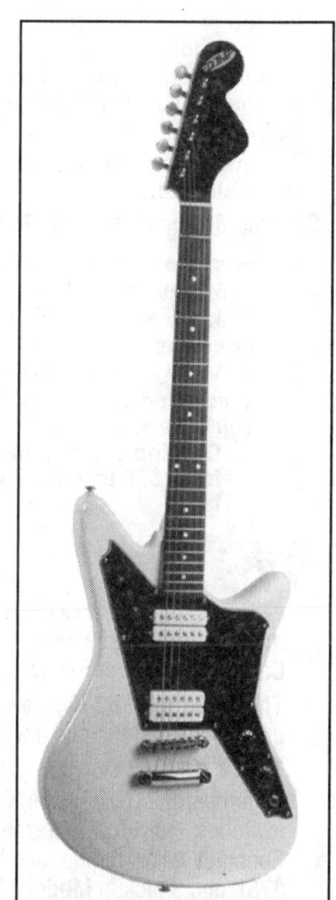

DiPinto Galaxie 2
courtesy DiPinto Guitars

ELECTRIC

Dodge guitar models with interchangeable pickup modules are available in two body styles, the DC-Classic and the **SC- Classic**. The **DC-Classic** has an off-set, short horned double cutaway body while the **SC-Classic** has a rounded single cutaway body. Standard features on both models include an Eastern hard rock maple body, figured birds-eye maple neck, 22-fret Brazilian rosewood fingerboard with dot inlay, 25 1/2" scale, MannMade hardtail brass bridge, locking Sperzel tuners, and a high gloss polyester finish. Dodge guitars have optional tremolo system, and Sunbust and Translucent finishes.

The standard package includes one electric guitar with three differently configured electronics-containing modules (pickup configurations similar to a Strat, Tele, and Les Paul). Other modules are available for the customer's own choice of pickups and configurations. Retail prices for both models is estimated at about $2,200 (each), but prices will vary considerably depending on what features are included and which brands and designs of electronics are installed.

D

ELECTRIC BASS

The **DC Classic Bass** (list $2,999) has a double cutaway maple body, birds-eye maple neck, rosewood fingerboard, Sperzel Trim Lok tuners, and a brass fixed bridge. The three bass modules feature Bassline pickups. Contact luthier Dodge directly for prices and customizing options (see Trademark Index).

DOLAN, MICHAEL

Instruments currently built in Sonoma County, California since 1977.

Luthier Michael Dolan has been handcrafting quality guitars for over twenty years. After Dolan graduated from Sonoma State University with a Bachelor of Arts degree in Fine Arts, he went to work for a prestigious bass and guitar manufacturer.

Dolan's full service shop offers custom built guitars and basses (solid body, arch-top, acoustic, neck-through, bolt-on, set-neck, and headless) as well as repairs and custom painting. He and his staff work in domestic and exotic woods, and use hardware and electronics from all well-known manufacturers. Finishes include their standard acrylic top coat/polyester base, nitrocellulose, and hand rubbed oil.

As luthier Dolan likes to point out, a "Custom Guitar is a unique expression of the vision of a particular individual. Because there are so many options and variables, offering a price list has proven to be impractical." However, Dolan's prices generally start at $1,200 - and the average cost may run between $1,500 to $2,000. Prices are determined by the nature of the project, and the costs of components and building materials.

Working with their custom guitar order form, Michael Dolan can provide a firm up-front price quote. All custom guitars are guaranteed for tone, playability, and overall quality.

DOLCE

See chapter on House Brands.

This trademark has been identified as the House Brand used by such stores as Marshall Fields, Macy's, and Gimbles.

(Source: Willie G. Moseley, Stellas & Stratocasters)

DOMINO

Instruments previously manufactured in Japan circa mid to late 1960s. Distributed by Maurice Lipsky Music Company, Inc., of New York, New York.

These Japanese-produced guitars and basses were imported to the U.S. market by the Maurice Lipsky company of New York, New York (Domino was a division of The Orpheum Manufacturing Company). Domino offered a wide range of Vox- and Fender-derived solid body models, and Gibson-esque 335 semi-hollow (or perhaps completely hollow) models. In 1967, the Domino design focus spotlighted copies of Fender's Jazzmaster/Jaguar and Mustang models renamed the **Spartan** and the **Olympic**. You just know that these guitars are the product of the 1960s, as the Domino catalog claimed that their guitars had "Lightning Fast Action - Psychedelic Sounds - Elegant Mod Styling". As they say on late night commercials, "Now how much will you pay?" But Wait!

The entire Domino product line featured Japanese hardware and pickups. Domino's **Thunder-Matic** line of drums featured 6 ply shells, and internal adjustable mufflers.

(Source: Michael Wright, Guitar Stories Volume One; Domino catalog courtesy John Kinnemeyer, JK Lutherie)

Sometimes you just can't stop. Here's some more "Features built into Every Domino:"
1) Mallory 'Full Range' adjustable pickups.
2) Mark Steel "Lightning Fast" Speed Scale Jazz Neck - the shorter distances between frets permits easier fingering and, naturally faster handling.
3) Mark Steel 3 ounce tremolo/micrometric roller bridge, 6 coats of gloss lacquer.
4) extra value(!) $400 worth of dramatic sound, features, superb styling, handling - yet Domino prices start as low as $22.50 - Compare and You'll Agree!

Domino guitars may look cool from a distance, but up close they're a tough tone nut to crack. Prices in the vintage market range from $75 to $175 (in excellent condition) as many players bypass the wacky 1960s models to look for a newer model entry level guitar.

ELECTRIC

All Domino electric models were offered with 1, 2, or 3 pickups, with a corresponding change in the model's designation number. For example, the Californian model was offered with 1 pickup (**Model 501**), 2 pickups (**Model 502**), or 3 pickups (**Model 503**). Models were also offered in a 12-string configuration: **A Californian Model 513** was a 12-string with 3 pickups. However, not all models follow this fairly simple system!

The model # **BB62 Beatle Guitar** was basically a Hofner design ripoff, with a single f-hole, raised pickguard, adjustable bridge/metal tailpiece, 2 pickups, volume/tone controls, and a 3-way toggle. Retail list price was $110.

The **(# 502) Californian** is frequently encountered at guitar shows. This model is based on the Vox Phantom, and features a 5-sided hardwood body, 21-fret fingerboard, 24 3/4" scale, 6-per-side tuners, a (big) richly grained rosewood pickguard, covered bridge/tremolo tailpiece, mallory pickups, pickup on/off switches, individual mute/solo/rhythm switches per pickup, and volume and tone controls. **Californian** models were available in Metallic Blue, Sunburst Red, Sunburst Yellow, White, and Yellow Mist finishes. The **Californian** model was offered as the 1 pickup **Model 501** (retail list $60), 2 pickup **Model 502** (list $75), and 3 pickup **Model 503** (list $90). The **Californian Model 513** (list $125) has a 12-string configuration and 3 pickups.

The **(# 80E2) Californian Rebel** looks like an expanded, floppy Californian model, and has single f-hole, pickup on/off switches, and volume and tone controls. The **Californian Rebel** model was offered as the 2 pickup **Model 80E2** (list $90), and 3 pickup **Model 80E3** (list $105). The **Californian Rebel** 12-string model had a retail list price of $140.

The Vox "teardrop" copy **(# 15E2) Fireball** model had a rounded hardwood body, single f-hole, 6-per-side headstock, volume and tone controls, and a 3-way switch. The **Fireball** model was offered with 2 pickups (list $90), and 3 pickups (list $105). The **Californian Rebel** 12-string model had a retail list price of $140.

The **(# 302) Spartan** model was a Fender Jaguar copy, with an unbound fingerboard with dot inlay, tremolo bridge, 6-on-a-side tuners, tortoise pickguard, metal controls plate, volume and 2 tone controls. The **Spartan** was offered as the 2 pickup **Model 302** (list $99.50), and the 3 pickup **Model 303** (list $110). The **Spartan** 12-string model had a retail list price of $125. An upscale version, the **(# D302) Spartan Deluxe** was the same as the Spartan, except featured block inlays, a bound fingerboard, and Mallory alnico pickups. The **Spartan Deluxe** was offered as the 2 pickup **Model D302** (list $149.95), and the 3 pickup **Model D303** (list $147.95). The **Model D313 Spartan Deluxe** 12-string model had a retail list price of $174.95. At the top of the list, the **(# DC302) Spartan Custom** was similar to the Spartan Deluxe, except had custom colors! These colors include (A) Sunset Red, (B) Sunburst Yellow, (C) Metallic Blue, (D) Palamino White, (E) Desert Sand, and (F) Diamond Blue. There was a $50 up charge for exotic *Starfire* wood grain finish. The **Spartan Custom** was offered as the 2 pickup **Model DC302** (list $174.95), and the 3 pickup **Model DC303** (list $199.95). The **Model DC313 Spartan Custom** 12-string model had a retail list price of $189.95.

From the Jaguar copy to the Music master copy! The **(# 202) Olympic** model had an offset double cutaway hardwood body, 24 3/4" scale, 21-fret unbound fingerboard with dot inlay, tremolo bridge, 6-on-a-side tuners, volume/2 tone controls (all controls were mounted on the pickguard). The **Olympic** model was offered as the 2 pickup **Model 202** (list $99.95), and as the 3 pickup **Model 203** (list $110). The **Olympic** 12-string model had a retail list price of $125. The **Olympic Deluxe** model is the same as the Olympic, except features block inlays, bound fingerboard, and Mallory alnico pickups. The **Olympic Deluxe** model was offered as the 2 pickup **Model D202** (list $124.95), and as the 3 pickup **Model D203** (list $149.95). The **Model D212 Olympic Deluxe** 12-string model had a retail list price of $174.95. The **Olympic Custom** model was similar to the Olympic Deluxe, except featured such custom colors as (A) Sunset Red, (B) Sunburst Yellow, (C) Metallic Blue, (D) Palamino White, (E) Desert Sand, and (F) Diamond Blue. The Olympic Custom model was offered as the 2 pickup **Model DC202** (list $149.95), and as the 3 pickup **Model DC203** (list $174.95). The **Model DC212 Olympic Custom** 12-string model had a retail list price of $199.95. There was a $50 up charge for the exotic "Starfire" wood grain finish.

The Domino **(# 40E2) Dawson** was a 335-style guitar, but fully hollow. This model had 2 f-holes, 24 3/4" scale, 21-fret bound fingerboard with white block inlay, raised black pickguard, bridge/attached tailpiece tremolo, chrome hardware, six per side headstock, volume/tone controls, 3-way pickup selector toggle switch. The **Dawson** model was available in Gunmetal Red, Yellow Sunburst, Sunburst Walnut, Silver-Red, and Golden-mist finishes. The **Dawson** model was offered as the 1 pickup **Model 40E1** (retail list $90), 2 pickup **Model 40E2** (list $110), and 3 pickup **Model 40E3** (list $120). The Dawson **Model 40E12** (list $150) has a 12-string configuration and 3 pickups.

Domino's **(# 22E2) Silverhawk** was similar to the **Dawson**, except featured unbound fingerboard with dot inlay, metal bridge with wood feet/tremolo tailpiece, 3-per-side tuners, chrome hardware, 2 pickups, volume and tone controls, and 2 toggle switches (one on bass bout, one on treble bout, both have an individual pickguard). **Silverhawk** models were available in White, Sunburst Red, Metallic Blue, Black, and Deep Red finishes. The **Silverhawk** model was offered as the 1 pickup **Model 22E1** (retail list $85) with tremolo, 2 pickup **Model 22E2** (list $110) with tremolo, and 3 pickup Model 22E3 (list $130) with tremolo. The Dawson **Model 22E12** (list $150) has a 12-string configuration and 2 pickups.

The **(# 7E1) Hawk** model has a single cutaway hollow body, 2 f-holes, same bridge/tremolo as the **Silverhawk**, raised black pickguard, 3-per-side tuners, one pickup, volume and tone controls, and a jack mounted on a metal controls plate, available in White finish only (retail list $75).

Dodge Guitar
courtesy Rick and Janice Dodge

ELECTRIC BASS

The model # **BB62 Beatle Bass** was basically a Hofner design ripoff, with a single f-hole, raised pickguard, adjustable bridge/metal tailpiece, 2 pickups, volume/tone controls, and a 3-way toggle. Retail list price was $129.95.

The **Californian Bass** model has a 5-sided hardwood body, 4-per-side tuners, a (big) richly grained rosewood pickguard, Mallory pickups, pickup on/off switches, and volume and tone controls. **Californian** models were available in Metallic Blue, Sunburst Red, Sunburst Yellow, White, and Yellow Mist finishes.The **Californian Bass** model was offered as the 1 pickup **Model 551** (retail list $100), and 2 pickup **Model 552** (list $115). The **Californian Rebel Bass** model had a retail list price of $105.

The Vox "teardrop" copy Fireball Bass model had a rounded hardwood body, single f-hole, 4-per-side headstock, 2 pickups, volume and tone controls, 3-way selector. (list $105).

The **Spartan Bass** model had an unbound fingerboard with dot inlay, 4-on-a-side tuners, tortoise pickguard, metal controls plate, volume and tone controls (list $115). The slightly upscale version **Spartan Deluxe Bass** was the same as the Spartan, except featured block inlays, a bound fingerboard, and Mallory alnico pickups. The **Spartan Deluxe Bass** was offered as the 2 pickup **Model D362** (list $154.95), and the 3 pickup **Model D363** (list $169.95). At the top of the list, the **Spartan Custom Bass** was similar to the Spartan Deluxe, except had custom colors like (A) Sunset Red, (B) Sunburst Yellow, (C) Metallic Blue, (D) Palamino White, (E) Desert Sand, and (F) Diamond Blue. The **Spartan Custom Bass** was offered as the 2 pickup **Model DC362** (list $179.95), and the 3 pickup **Model DC363** (list $189.95). There was a $50 up charge for exotic *Starfire* wood grain finish.

The **Olympic Bass** Music master copy had an offset double cutaway hardwood body, unbound fingerboard with dot inlay, 4-on-a-side tuners, volume/tone controls (all controls were mounted on the pickguard). The **Olympic Bass** model had a retail list price of $115. The **Olympic Deluxe Bass** model is the same as the Olympic, except features block inlays, bound fingerboard, and 2 Mallory alnico pickups. The **Model D262 Olympic Deluxe Bass** model had a retail list price of $129.95. The **Olympic Custom Bass** model was similar to the Olympic Deluxe, except featured such custom colors as (A) Sunset Red, (B) Sunburst Yellow, (C) Metallic Blue, (D) Palamino White, (E) Desert Sand, and (F) Diamond Blue. The **Model DC262 Olympic Custom Bass** model had a retail list price of $154.95. There was a $50 up charge for the exotic "Starfire" wood grain finish.

The **Dawson Bass (Model 40E62)** was a hollow, 335-style model (retail list $130). This model had 2 f-holes, bound fingerboard with white block inlay, fixed bridge, chrome hardware, 4-on-a-side headstock, 2 pickups, volume/tone controls, 3-way pickup selector toggle switch. The **Dawson Bass** was available in Gunmetal Red, Yellow Sunburst, Sunburst Walnut, Silver- Red, and Golden-mist finishes.

Domino's **Silverhawk Bass** was similar to the **Dawson Bass**, except featured unbound fingerboard with dot inlay, metal bridge with wood feet/metal tailpiece, 2-per-side tuners, chrome hardware, volume and tone controls, and 2 toggle switches (one on bass bout, one on treble bout, both have an individual pickguard). **Silverhawk** models were available in White, Sunburst Red, Metallic Blue, Black, and Deep Red finishes. The Silverhawk Bass model was offered as the 1 pickup **Model 22E61** (retail list $110) and the 2 pickup **Model 22E62** (list $130).

DORADO

Instruments previously produced in Japan circa early 1970s. Distributed in the U.S. by the Baldwin Piano and Organ Company of Cincinnati, Ohio.

The Dorado trademark was briefly used by Baldwin (during its Gretsch ownership) on a product line of Japanese-built acoustics and electric guitars and basses.

Dorado instruments are of decent quality, but are often found at slightly inflated asking prices due to the attachment of the Gretsch name. Remember, these are 1970s Japanese guitars imported in by Gretsch during their phase of Baldwin ownership! Dorados are sometimes rightly priced between $125 to $175; but many times they are tagged at prices double that. Of course, what a guitar is tagged at and what it sells at (cash talks, baby!) are always two different animals.

(Source: Walter Murray, Frankenstein Fretworks; and Michael Wright, Vintage Guitar Magazine)

DOUBLE EAGLE

Guitar parts previously produced in Japan.

As companies like Mighty Mite, Schecter, and DiMarzio pioneered the availability of high quality guitar components for the do-it-yourself builders, other companies joined in. Japan's Double Eagle company provided a wide range of quality parts.

DRAJAS

Instruments currently built in Hamburg, Germany.

Drajas is currently offering three different high quality guitar models.

Options for the Drajas guitar models include a mahogany body, bird's-eye or curly maple neck, ebony or pau ferro fingerboard, a bone nut, 25 1/2" or 24 3/4" scale length, Floyd Rose tremolo, and nitrocellulose or oil/wax finishes. There are additional charges for these options (call for pricing and availability).

ELECTRIC

All Drajas solid body guitars feature offset double cutaway alder bodies, bolt-on maple necks, 24-fret rosewood fingerboards with dot inlays, a 25 1/5" scale, graphite nut, 3-per-side Gotoh Magnum Lock tuners, Gotoh G510 tremolo, Drajas pickups, volume and tone controls, and a polyurethane finish.

The three Drajas models are offered in three different top styles: a *Flat* top, *Round* top (arched), and *Violin* shape. The Hornet has a locking tremolo system and humbucker/single coil/humbucker pickups; the **Hornet S** is similar save for a Floyd Rose tremolo system. The **Hornet V** has a fixed bridge and 2 humbucking pickups.

DRISKILL

Instruments currently built in Fort Worth, Texas. Distributed by Driskill Guitars of Fort Worth, Texas.

The Driskill Diablo and Diablo Blues are hand-crafted in Fort Worth, Texas by Joe Driskill. These are high quality electric guitars with exceptional tonewoods.

ELECTRIC

The Driskill **Diablo** features a sleek offset double cutaway and has a carved mahogany body with highly figured flame or quilted maple top. The neck is laminated mahogany with carbon fibre and double action truss rods,rosewood or ebony 24-fret rosewood fingerboard, fat or thin 25" scale, Schaller locking tuners, Schaller fixed bridge, custom wound Van Zandt pickups, volume and tone controls, 5-position selector switch, gold or chrome hardware. The **Diablo** model is available in custom finishes and colors. Form fitted hardshell case included. Retail price $2,800 - $4,000 depending on options.

The **Diablo Blues** features a carved solid ash highly figured body, set laminated hard maple neck, 22-fret fingerboard with paua abalone or Mother-of-Pearl dot inlay, fat or thin 25" scale, Schaller locking tuners, Schaller fixed bridge, single coil/humbucker (or 2 single coil/humbucker or 3 single coil) pickups, volume and tone controls, 5-position selector switch, custom inlays available, no-heel neck joint, chrome hardware, gold hardware option, optional piezo bridge. Form fitted hardshell case included. Retail price $2,200 - $2,800 depending on options.

MIDI control is available. For further information regarding specifications and pricing, please contact luthier Driskill directly (see Trademark Index).

DUBREUILLE, PHILIPPE

Instruments currently built in London, England. Previously built and distributed in Europe by Philippe Dubreuille of Bonnatrait, France.

Luthier/Designer Philippe Dubreuille custom crafted guitars that are playable works of art. Dubreuille's creations are played by a number of top guitarists, such as Iggy Pop, Joe Perry and Brad Whitford (Aerosmith), Robert Smith and Porl Thomson (The Cure), Dave Stewart, and Vernon Reid. As most of his creations were custom commissioned, specifications and pricing will vary by nature of the finished guitar.

DUESENBERG

Instruments previously built in Hannover, Germany. Distributed in the U.S. by Salwender International of Orange, California.

STARPLAYER I - single cutaway semi-hollow mahogany body, laminated maple/spruce top, hard rock maple neck, 25 ½" scale, 22-fret rosewood neck with dot inlays, 3-per-side Grover tuners, wrap-around fixed bridge, chrome hardware, tortoise shell or black pickguard, 2 Alnico humbuckers (or 2 P-99 single coil pickups), volume/tone controls, 5-way selector switch, available in Surf Green (Model DSP-SG), Silver Sparkle, and Transparent Orange (Model DSP-TO) finishes. Mfg. 1996 to date.

MSR $2,229

This model has an optional Silver Sparkle finish (Model DSP-SP).

Starplayer II - similar to the Starplayer I, except features a tune-o-matic bridge/Bigsby tremolo tailpiece.

MSR $2,229

This model has an optional Silver Sparkle finish (Model DDC-SP).

DOUBLE CAT - double cutaway semi-hollow alder body, hard rock maple neck, 22-fret rosewood neck with dot inlays, wrap-around fixed bridge, chrome hardware, 3-per-side Grover tuners, black or white pickguard, P-99 single coil/humbucker pickups, volume/tone controls, 5-way selector switch, available in Surf Green (Model DDC-SG), Silver Sparkle, and Transparent Orange (Model DDC-TO) finishes. Mfg. 1997 to date.

MSR $2,229

Add $150 for Silver Sparkle finish (Model DDC-SP).

Driskill Diablo
courtesy Driskill Guitars

D

DWIGHT

See chapter on House Brands.

Instruments previously produced by Valco of Chicago, Illinois (circa 1950s), and Epiphone of Kalamazoo, Michigan (circa 1963 to 1968). Distributed by the Sunny Shields Music Shop of East St. Louis, Illinois.

This trademark has been identified as a House Brand of the Sunny Shields Music Shop of East St. Louis, Illinois. The "Dwight" name was for the owner of Sunny Shields, Mr. Charles "Dwight" Shields.

The Sunny Shields Music Shop marketed some Supro (Valco-built) guitars. In addition, Shields also marketed a 'rebranded' Epiphone Coronet model between 1963 to 1968. According to Bob Vail, a retired employee from the Sunny Shields Music Shop, the Chicago Musical Instrument (C.M.I.) company always sold the 'rebranded' Epiphones on a *per dozen* basis to the store (which, of course, reinforces the notion of a House Brand instrument). Vail feels that before Gibson "bastardized" the Epiphone name, they made some pretty good guitars - the Dwight models are counted among the good ones.

In addition to the Supro and Epiphone "Dwight" model guitars, Shields also offered "Dwight" steel guitars and accordions. Vail estimates that there are probably plenty of "Dwight" instruments in basements and attics throughout Southwestern Illinois.

The Epiphone-built Dwight Coronet model has "Dwight" on the headstock and a "D" in the center of the pickguard. Epiphone guitars were built during this time period at the Gibson facilities in Kalamazoo, Michigan (American Epiphone production ran from 1961 to 1969), and were distributed by the Chicago Musical Instrument (C.M.I.) company.

(Source: Bob Vail, Sunny Shields Music Shop employee from 1949 to 1951, and 1955 to 1958; and Michael Wright, Vintage Guitar Magazine)

DYNELECTRON

Instruments previously built in Italy between 1974 and 1976.

This company specialized in reproducing the DANELECTRO 'Guitarlin' model. Like Jerry Jones, they took an existing model - and built it better! However, vintage Danelectro models are still more valuable to collectors.

(Source: Tony Bacon and Paul Day, The Guru's Guitar Guide)

Driskill Diablo
courtesy Driskill Guitars

NOTES

Section E

GRADING	100% MINT	98% NEAR MINT	95% EXC+	90% EXC	80% VG+	70% VG	60% G

ESH

Instruments currently produced in Trier, Germany. U.S. Distribution is by Esh USA/MTC of New York, NY. European distribution by Esh Gitarrenkonzeption GmbH of Trier, Germany.

Esh currently offers a range of neck-through and bolt-on model basses with original design double cutaway bodies (like a redesigned Jazz Bass).

Other custom Esh features include Esh electronics, Bartolini pickups, 24-fret rosewood fingerboards, rock maple or 5-piece rock maple/mahogany necks, Teflon wiring harnesses.

ELECTRIC

Models like the **Genuine, J-Bass, Sovereign**, and **Sovereign V** have select Hungarian ash bodies. Alder is featured on the sleek double cutaway **Stinger** and rounded bottom bout/narrow horn **Hero** models. All basses are finished in wax/oil natural, lacquer, transparent (See-Through) colors, or custom colors.

The **Notorious I** bass has a Music Man-style offset double cutaway body, while the **Notorious II** model is a Jazz bass-style body. Both models feature a selected Hungarian ash body, maple neck, maple or rosewood fingerboard with 21-frets and dot inlay, 'soapbar' (or 2 J-style or J/'soapbar') pickups, volume and tone controls, and an oil/wax finish. Notorious models have optional figured maple tops, high gloss lacquer finishes, bubinga body, wenge neck, and block inlays.

Esh's **Various** custom bass has an offset double cutaway alder body, bolt-on 3-piece maple neck, 24-fret rosewood fingerboard with dot inlay, 'soapbar' humbucker pickup. The **Various** model is available in Honey, Transparent Dark Blue, Transparent Dark Green, Transparent Dark Red, Satin lacquered, and oil/wax finishes.

ESP

Instruments currently produced in Tokyo, Japan since the early 1980s. Distributed in the U.S. by the ESP Guitar Company of Hollywood, California.

E S P was originally known as a source for high quality guitar components and replacement parts. In the early 1980s the company then focused on building Fender- and Gibson-derived designs, evolving to high quality *superstrat* models. Currently, ESP is offering newer designs that combine vintage tastes with modern designs.

In 1998, ESP introduced 4 new limited edition USA Custom Shop models, built at ESP's Custom Shop in California. These four models all feature one-piece mahogany bodies, figured maple tops with matching headstock overlay, bolt-on quartersawn maple necks, and ebony fingerboards with mother-of-pearl dot inlay.

ELECTRIC

The **ESP Guitar Company** was formed in 1985 as the USA distribution point (and custom work shop) for ESP guitars. These U.S. custom instruments are offered as custom option-outfitted equipment, and carry a higher premium than the standard production models.

In 1992, standard features were as follows: Transparent finishes had gold hardware, all other finishes had black hardware. Current models now feature chrome hardware. Pickup Upgrades (Seymour Duncan or ESP) are available in any model for an additional charge:

Add $100 for Seymour Duncan or ESP single coil.

Add $125 for Seymour Duncan or ESP humbucker.

Eclipse Series

ECLIPSE CUSTOM (First Version) - single cutaway bound mahogany body, bolt-on maple neck, 22-fret ebony fingerboard with pearl dot inlay, strings though bridge, blackface peghead with screened logo, 6-on-a-side tuners, black hardware, 2 exposed humbucker pickups, volume/tone controls, 3-position switch, available in Baby Blue, Black, Bubble Gum Pink, Candy Apple Blue, Fiesta Red, Metallic Blue, Metallic Red, Midnight Black, Mint Green, Snow White, Transparent Cherry Red, and Transparent Blue finishes. Mfg. 1986 to 1987.

$700	$625	$575	$500	$425	$350	$275

Last MSR was $1,150.

Eclipse Custom (Second Version) - similar to the Eclipse Custom (First Version), except has through-body maple neck, bound fingerboard, offset pearl block fingerboard inlay, redesigned bound peghead, chrome hardware, available in Cherry Sunburst, Pearl Gold, Pearl Pink, Pearl White, and Turquoise finishes. Mfg. 1987 to 1988.

$725	$650	$595	$525	$450	$375	$325

Last MSR was $1,150.

GRADING	100% MINT	98% NEAR MINT	95% EXC+	90% EXC	80% VG+	70% VG	60% G

Eclipse Custom T - similar to Eclipse Custom (Second Edition), except has double locking tremolo, available in Black, Cherry Sunburst, Pearl Gold, Pearl Pink, Pearl White, and Turquoise finishes. Mfg. 1987 to 1988.

$795 $700 $625 $550 $475 $425 $350
Last MSR was $1,750.

In 1988, Black, Cherry Sunburst, Pearl Gold and Pearl Pink finishes were disc; Burgundy Mist, Brite Red, Midnight Black and Pearl Silver finishes were introduced.

Eclipse Deluxe - similar to Eclipse Custom, except has standard vibrato. Mfg. 1986 to 1988.

$700 $600 $525 $425 $375 $325 $275
Last MSR was $1,450.

In 1988, Black, Cherry Sunburst, Pearl Gold and Pearl Pink finishes were disc, double locking vibrato replaced original part/design, Burgundy Mist, Brite Red, Midnight Black and Pearl Silver finishes were introduced.

E

ECLIPSE (SOLID BODY) - single cutaway mahogany body, bolt-on maple neck, 24-fret bound rosewood fingerboard with pearl dot inlay (logo block inlay at 12th fret), tune-o-matic bridge/stop tailpiece, 3-per-side tuners, bound headstock, chrome hardware, 2 ESP LH-200 humbucker pickups with nickel covers, volume/2-Tone controls, 3-position switch, available in Black, Gun metal Blue, Metallic Gold, and Pearl White finishes. Disc. 2000.

$950 $850 $750 $625 $525 $400 $300
Last MSR was $1,199.

In 1998, See-Through Blue, See-Through Green, See-Through Purple, and See-Through Red finishes were introduced as regular production finishes (these finishes were previously a $100 optional upgrade); Gunmetal Blue and Pearl White finishes were disc.

Add $300 for Original Floyd Rose locking tremolo (Model Eclipse with Floyd Rose).

Eclipse Arch Top - similar to the Eclipse Solid Body, except features a bound arched top semi-hollow mahogany body, cat's eye f-hole, 22-fret bound fingerboard, tune-o-matic bridge/trapeze tailpiece, available in Black, Metallic Gold, Pearl White, and Turquoise finishes. Mfg. 1996 to 2000.

$1,150 $1,000 $875 $750 $625 $500 $375
Last MSR was $1,429.

In 1998, See-Through Blue, See-Through Green, See-Through Purple, and See-Through Red finishes were introduced as regular production finishes (these finishes were previously a $100 optional upgrade); Pearl White and Turquoise finishes were disc.

Eclipse Semi-Acoustic - similar to the Eclipse Arch Top, except has rosewood bridge, piezo pickup, volume/tone controls, on-board active EQ system, available in Honey Sunburst, See-Through Black, See-Through Blue, See-Through Green, See-Through Purple, or See-Through Red finishes. Mfg. 1996 to 2000.

Steel string configuration, bound flame maple top.

$1,100 $950 $825 $695 $550 $425 $350
Last MSR was $1,349.

Nylon string configuration, spruce top, slotted headstock, available in Natural finish. Disc. 1999.

$1,100 $950 $825 $695 $550 $425 $350
Last MSR was $1,349.

ECLIPSE CUSTOM (USA CUSTOM SERIES) - single cutaway one-piece mahogany body, bound figured maple top, bolt-on maple neck, 24-fret bound rosewood fingerboard with mother-of-pearl dot inlay (logo block inlay at 12th fret), tune-o-matic bridge/stop tailpiece, 3-per-side Sperzel locking tuners, bound headstock, black hardware, 2 EMG-81 humbucker pickups with nickel covers, 2 volume/tone controls, 3-position switch, available in Amber, Natural Satin, See-Through Blue, See-Through Green, See-Through Purple, and See-Through Red finishes. Mfg. 1998 to 2000.

$1,550 $1,350 $1,150 $975 $800 $600 $500
Last MSR was $1,999.

E X P Series

E.X. (EXPLORER) - radical offset hourglass mahogany body, bolt-on maple neck, 22-fret rosewood fingerboard with pearl dot inlay, tune-o-matic bridge/stop tailpiece, black 'drooping' peghead with screened logo, 6-on-a-side tuners, black hardware, 2 EMG-81 humbucking pickups, volume/tone controls, 3-position switch, available in Black and Olympic White finishes. Mfg. 1996 to 2000.

$1,600 $1,350 $1,200 $1,000 $850 $675 $500
Last MSR was $1,999.

The price of the E.X.P. includes case.

ULTRATONE - offset double cutaway alder body, bolt-on maple neck, rosewood fingerboard with dot inlays, 22 XJ frets, white neck binding, Tune-O-Matic bridge, stop tailpiece, 3 Duncan Mini-Hum with Coil Split, 3-per-side tuners, pearloid pickguard, chrome hardware, available in 3-Tone Sunburst, black and Pearl White finishes. Mfg. 2000 Only.

$1,200 $1,100 $1,000 $900 $800 $700 $600
Last MSR was $1,499.

Horizon Series

HORIZON (First Version) - offset double cutaway bound ash body, bolt-on maple neck, 22-fret maple fingerboard with black dot inlay, standard vibrato, maple peghead with screened logo, 6-on-a-side tuners, chrome hardware, 3 single coil pickups, 1 volume/2-Tone controls, 5-position switch, available in Baby Blue, Black, Bubblegum Pink, Candy Apple Blue, Fiesta Red, Metallic Blue, Metallic Red, Midnight Black, Mint Green, Snow White, Transparent Cherry Red and Transparent Blue finishes. Disc. 1986.

$400 $350 $275 $225 $200 $175 $150

GRADING	100% MINT	98% NEAR MINT	95% EXC+	90% EXC	80% VG+	70% VG	60% G

Horizon (Second Version) - offset double cutaway arched top alder or ash body, "natural binding", bolt-on maple neck, 24-fret rosewood fingerboard, tune-o-matic bridge/stop tailpiece, 'curved point' peghead, 3-per-side tuners, chrome hardware, 2 ESP LH-200 humbuckers, volume/tone controls (with coil tap switching capability), pickup selector switch, available in Black, Gunmetal Blue, Metallic Gold, and Pearl White finishes. Mfg. 1996 to 2000.

$1,150	**$1,000**	**$875**	**$750**	**$625**	**$500**	**$375**

Last MSR was $1,429.

Add $300 for Original Floyd Rose tremolo (this option disc in 1998).

In 1998, Honey Sunburst, See-Through Blue, See-Through Green, See-Through Purple, and See-Through Red finishes were introduced as regular production finishes (these finishes were previously a $100 optional upgrade); Gunmetal Blue, Metallic Gold, and Pearl White finishes were disc.

HORIZON CUSTOM (USA CUSTOM SERIES) - offset double cutaway one-piece mahogany body, figured maple top, bolt-on maple neck, 24-fret bound rosewood fingerboard with mother-of-pearl dot inlay (logo block inlay at 12th fret), tune-o-matic bridge/stop tailpiece, 3-per-side Sperzel locking tuners, headstock, black hardware, 2 Seymour Duncan humbucker pickups (JB and '59 models), volume/tone controls, 3-position switch, available in Amber, Natural Satin, See-Through Blue, See-Through Green, See-Through Purple, and See-Through Red finishes. Mfg. 1998 to date.

MSR	$1,999	$1,600	$1,350	$1,200	$1,000	$850	$675	$500

HORIZON CUSTOM (JAPAN MFG.) - offset double cutaway arched top ash body, through-body maple neck, 24-fret bound ebony fingerboard, double locking vibrato, bound peghead, 6-on-a-side tuners, chrome hardware, single coil/humbucker EMG pickups, 1 volume/2-Tone controls, 3-position switch, available in Black, Fiesta Red, Magenta, Pearl Rose and Pearl White finishes. Mfg. 1987 to 1993.

$1,100	**$950**	**$795**	**$625**	**$575**	**$525**	**$450**

Last MSR was $2,195.

In 1988, Brite Red, Burgundy Mist, Gunmetal Blue, and Midnight Black finishes were introduced; Fiesta Red and Pearl Rose finishes were disc. In 1990, Candy Apple Red and Dark Metallic Blue finishes were introduced; black hardware replaced original part/design; Brite Red, Burgundy Mist, Magenta and Midnight Blue finishes were disc. In 1991, Dark Metallic Purple finish was introduced; bound fingerboard with 12th fret pearl logo block inlay, redesigned peghead, 3-per-side tuners replaced original part/designs.

In 1992, Metallic Green finish was introduced; Dark Metallic Blue finish was disc.

Horizon Deluxe - similar to Horizon Custom, except has bolt-on neck, 22-fret rosewood fingerboard with pearl dot inlay, gold hardware, available in Black, Brite Red, Burgundy Mist, Gunmetal Blue, Magenta and Pearl White finishes. Mfg. 1989 to 1992.

$850	**$725**	**$600**	**$495**	**$425**	**$400**	**$325**

Last MSR was $1,695.

In 1990, Candy Apple Red and Dark Metallic Blue finishes were introduced; black hardware replaced original part/design; Brite Red, Burgundy Mist and Magenta finishes were disc. In 1991, Transparent Blue, Transparent Purple and Transparent Red finishes were introduced; bound fingerboard with 12th fret pearl logo block inlay, tune-o-matic bridge/stop tailpiece, redesigned peghead, 3-per-side tuners replaced original part/designs; Candy Apple Red, Dark Metallic Blue and Gunmetal Blue finishes were disc. In 1992, Transparent Green finish was introduced; 24-fret fingerboard replaced original part/design; Cherry Sunburst finish was disc.

Horizon Deluxe T - similar to Horizon Custom, except has bolt-on neck, 24-fret bound rosewood fingerboard with offset pearl dot inlay/12th fret block logo inlay, black hardware, available in Black, Pearl White, Transparent Blue, Transparent Green, Transparent Purple and Transparent Red finishes. Mfg. 1992 to 1993.

$950	**$825**	**$675**	**$550**	**$495**	**$450**	**$400**

Last MSR was $1,895.

Horizon Classic (U.S. Mfg.) - similar to the Horizon Custom, except had offset double cutaway carved mahogany body, set-in mahogany neck, pearl dot fingerboard inlay/12th fret logo block inlay, available in Cherry Sunburst, Honey Sunburst, See-Through Black, See-Through Blue, See-Through Green, See-Through Purple, and See-Through Red finishes. Mfg. 1993 to 1995.

$1,900	**$1,675**	**$1,395**	**$1,100**	**$1,000**	**$895**	**$750**

Last MSR was $2,795.

Add $700 for mahogany body with figured maple top/matching headstock.

Horizon Classic instruments were all handcrafted in the USA to customer specifications. Price included hardshell case.

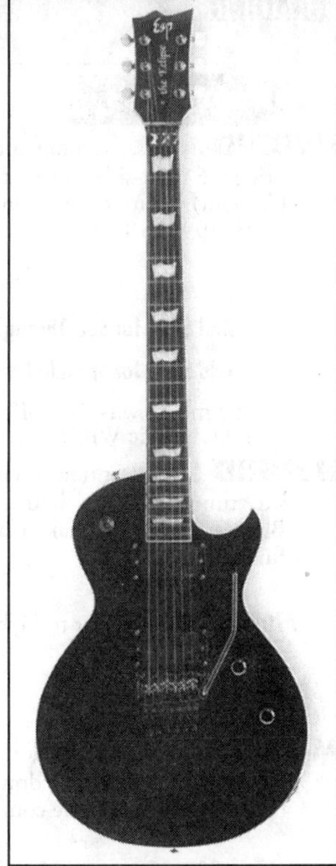

E.S.P. Eclipse
courtesy The ESP Guitar Co.

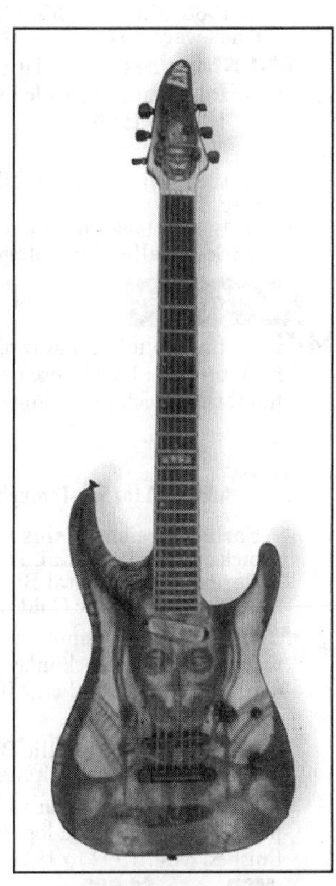

E.S.P. Horizon Custom
courtesy The ESP Guitar Co.

GRADING	100% MINT	98% NEAR MINT	95% EXC+	90% EXC	80% VG+	70% VG	60% G

Hybrid Series

HYBRID - offset double cutaway alder or mahogany body, maple neck, 22-fret rosewood fingerboard with pearl dot inlay, strings-through fixed bridge, 6-on-a-side tuners, chrome hardware, shell (or black) pickguard, TS-120 single coil/LH-200 humbucker ESP pickups, 3-way switch (on treble bout), volume/tone controls mounted on chrome control plate, available in Black, Metallic Gold, Pearl White, and Turquoise finishes. Mfg. 1993, 1996 to 1998.

$950 $800 $700 $590 $500 $425 $350

Last MSR was $1,395.

Add $100 for See-Through Blue, See-Through Green, See-Through Purple, or See-Through Red finishes.

Add $200 for Sparkle finishes, available in Blue Sparkle, Gold Sparkle, Purple Sparkle, Red Sparkle, and Silver Sparkle.

This model was first offered with a single ESP humbucker pickup, and additional finishes: Burgundy Mist, Fiesta Red, Lake Placid Blue, and Olympic White.

HYBRID I - offset double cutaway hardwood body, bolt-on maple neck, 22-fret rosewood fingerboard with pearl dot inlay, standard vibrato, 6-on-a-side tuners, chrome hardware, 2 single coil pickups, volume/tone control, 3-position switch, metal control plate, available in Baby Blue, Black, Blonde, Fiesta Red, Lake Placid Blue, Metallic Blue, Metallic Red, Natural, Olympic White, Salmon Pink, Two Tone Sunburst and 3-Tone Sunburst finishes. Disc. 1986.

$375 $325 $275 $225 $195 $175 $150

Hybrid II - similar to Hybrid I, except has 3 single coil pickups. Disc. 1986.

$375 $325 $275 $225 $195 $175 $150

M-I Series

M-I CUSTOM - offset double cutaway alder body, through-body maple neck, 24-fret bound rosewood fingerboard with pearl offset block inlay/logo block inlay at 12th fret, double locking vibrato, body matching bound peghead with screened logo, 6-on-a-side tuners, chrome hardware, ESP humbucker pickup, volume control, coil tap switch, available in Black, Fiesta Red, Snow White and Turquoise finishes. Mfg. 1987 to 1994.

$395 $350 $275 $225 $200 $175 $150

In 1988, Magenta, Metallic Black, Midnight Black, and Pearl Yellow were introduced; Bright Yellow and Cherry Sunburst finishes were disc.

In 1989, Dark Metallic Blue, Candy Apple Red, and Pearl White finishes were introduced; Fiesta Red, Metallic Black, Midnight Black, Snow White, and Turquoise finishes were disc.

M-I Deluxe - similar to the M-I Custom, except has bolt-on maple neck, 22-fret maple fingerboard with black dot inlay (or rosewood fingerboard with pearl dot inlay), black pickguard, 2 single coil/1 humbucker ESP pickups, 1 volume/2-Tone controls, 5-position switch, available in Bright Yellow, Candy Apple Red, Cherry Sunburst, Dark Metallic Blue, Pearl Pink Sunburst, and Pearl White finishes. Mfg. 1987 to 1989.

$350 $300 $250 $200 $175 $150 $125

In 1988, Magenta, Metallic Black, Midnight Black, and Pearl Yellow finishes were introduced; Bright Yellow and Cherry Sunburst finishes were disc.

M-I Standard - similar to the M-I Custom, except has hardwood body, bolt-on maple neck, 22-fret rosewood fingerboard with pearl dot inlay, standard vibrato, available in Bright Yellow, Candy Apple Red, Cherry Sunburst, Dark Metallic Blue, Pearl Pink Sunburst and Pearl White finishes. Mfg. 1987 to 1990.

$325 $275 $225 $195 $175 $150 $125

In 1988, Magenta, Metallic Black, Midnight Black, and Pearl Yellow were introduced; Bright Yellow and Cherry Sunburst finishes were disc.

In 1990, Black and Snow White finishes were introduced; black hardware, single coil/humbucker pickups replaced original part/designs; Dark Metallic Blue, Magenta, Metallic Black, Midnight Black, Pearl Pink Sunburst, Pearl White, and Pearl Yellow finishes were disc.

M-II Series

M-II - offset double cutaway alder or ash body, bolt-on maple neck, 24-fret maple or rosewood fingerboard with dot inlay (logo block inlay at 12th fret), Original Floyd Rose tremolo, reverse 'pointy' blackface peghead with screened logo, 6-on-the-other-side tuners, black hardware, 2 ESP LH-200 humbucker pickups, volume control, 3-position switch, available in Black, Brite Red and Snow White finishes. Mfg. 1989 to 1994, 1996 to 2000.

$1,000 $900 $795 $675 $550 $450 $325

Last MSR was $1,299.

Add $100 for See-Through Blue, See-Through Green, See-Through Purple, or See-Through Red finishes (this option was disc in 1998).

Earlier versions of this model may have 22-fret maple or rosewood fingerboards with offset dot inlays; and ESP single coil/humbucker pickups. In 1990, Candy Apple Red finish was introduced; Brite Red finish was disc. In 1996, Candy Apple Red and Snow White finishes were disc; Gunmetal Blue, Honey Sunburst, Metallic Purple, and Pearl White finishes were introduced. In 1997, Metallic Purple finish was disc; Metallic Gold finish was introduced. In 1998, ash body was disc; Metallic Purple finish was re-introduced.

M-II Custom - similar to the M-II, except has offset double cutaway alder body, through-body maple neck, 24-fret bound rosewood fingerboard with pearl offset block inlay (logo block inlay at 12th fret), reverse bound peghead, available in Black, Candy Apple Red, Gunmetal Blue, Magenta, and Pearl White finishes. Mfg. 1990 to 1994 and 2001.

MSR $2,195 $1,750 $1,500 $1,100 $1,000 $850 $700 $600

In 1991, Dark Metallic Blue and Dark Metallic Purple finishes were introduced; Magenta finish was disc. In 1992, Metallic Green finish was introduced; Dark Metallic Blue was disc. In 1993, pearl dot fingerboard inlay replaced original part/design.

M-II Deluxe - similar to M-II Custom, except has bolt-on neck, unbound fingerboard with pearl dot inlay/12th fret logo block inlay, unbound peghead with screened logo/model, available in Black, Pearl White, Transparent Blue, Transparent Green, Transparent Purple, and Transparent Red finishes. Mfg. 1992 to 1996 and 2000.

MSR $1,699 $1,350 $1,250 $1,150 $900 $700 $600 $450

Add $300 for Seymour Duncan Cool Rail/JB humbucker pickups.

This model has an optional maple fingerboard. From 1995 to 1996, a Koa wood body/oil finish replaced original part/design.

GRADING	100% MINT	98% NEAR MINT	95% EXC+	90% EXC	80% VG+	70% VG	60% G

M-III Series

M-III - offset double cutaway alder body, bolt-on maple neck, 22-fret rosewood (or maple) fingerboard with pearl dot inlay (logo block inlay at 12th fret), Original Floyd Rose tremolo, reverse blackface peghead with screened logo, 6-on-the-other-side tuners, black hardware, 2 ESP SH-100 single coil/LH-200 humbucker pickups, volume/tone controls, 5-position switch, available in Black, Metallic Purple, and Pearl White finishes. Mfg. 1989 to 1994, 1998 to 2000.

$1,100 $950 $825 $695 $550 $425 $350
Last MSR was $1,349.

Early models (1989-1994) had pearl offset block inlay (or maple fingerboard with black offset dot inlay) and Black, Brite Red, and Snow White finishes.

M-III CUSTOM W/WILKINSON BRIDGE (USA CUSTOM SERIES) - offset double cutaway one-piece mahogany body, walnut veneer top, bolt-on maple neck, 22-fret ebony fingerboard with pearl dot inlay (logo block inlay at 12th fret), Wilkinson VS-100 tremolo, matching peghead veneer, 6-on-a-side tuners, black hardware, white pickguard, EMG-81 humbucker/EMG-SA single coil/EMG-89R humbucker pickups, volume/tone controls, 5-position switch, available in Amber, Natural Satin, See-Through Blue, See-Through Green, See-Through Purple, and See-Through Red finishes. Mfg. 1998 to 1999.

$1,600 $1,350 $1,200 $1,000 $800 $700 $600
Last MSR was $1,999.

M-III Custom Reverse (USA CUSTOM SERIES) -similar to M-III Custom except has reverse headstock and EMG 81/SA/81 pickup combination. Mfg. 2000 only.

$1,750 $1,650 $1,550 $1,350 $1,250 $1,150 $950
Last MSR was $2,199.

M-III Custom W/Original Floyd Rose Bridge (USA Custom Series) - similar to the M-III Custom w/Wilkinson Bridge, except features an Original Floyd Rose tremolo. Mfg. 1998 to 1999.

$1,600 $1,350 $1,200 $1,000 $850 $675 $500
Last MSR was $1,999.

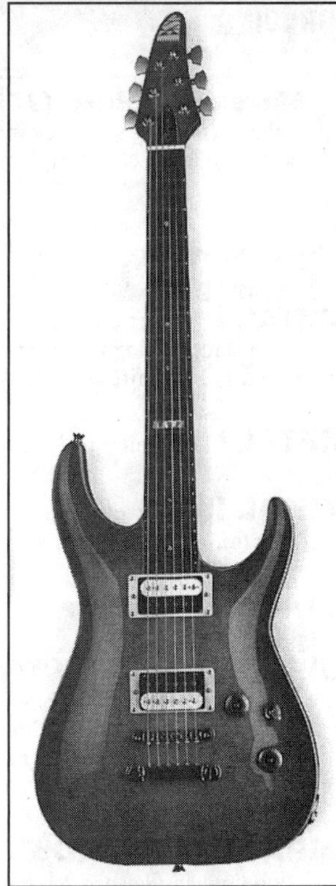

E.S.P. Horizon Classic
courtesy The ESP Guitar Co.

MH CUSTOM (USA CUSTOM SERIES) offset double cutaway mahogany body with figured maple top, bolt-on maple neck with ebony fingerboard, dot inlays, 6-on-a-side tuners, black hardware and black Sperzel tuners, Original Floyd Rose bridge, 24 XJ frets, two EMG-81 pickups, available in Amber Sunburst, See-Through Black Cherry, See-Through Aqua, Amber, natural Stain, See-Through Blue, See-Through Green, See-Through Purple and See-Through Red finishes. New 2000.

MSR $2,199 $1,750 $1,650 $1,550 $1,350 $1,250 $1,150 $950

MH DELUXE (USA DELUXE SERIES) similar to MH Custom except has alder body with maple neck, rosewood fingerboard with dot position markers with "Deluxe" at the 12th fret, Seymour Duncan TB-4 and SH-1 pickups. New 2001.

MSR $1,699 $1,350 $1,250 $1,150 $1,000 $900 $800 $700

MV CUSTOM (USA CUSTOM SERIES) -offset double cutaway design, mahogany body with flamed maple top, bolt-on maple neck with ebony fingerboard, abalone purfling, dot position markers with "Custom" at the 12th fret, black hardware and Sperzel locking tuners, Tune-O-Matic bridge with string-through-body, white top and neck binding, 24 XJ frets, Seymour Duncan SH-4 and SSL-1 pickups, 1 volume/1 tone control, 3-way toggle, available in See-Through Aqua and See-Through Orange finishes. New 2001.

MSR $1,999 $1,600 $1,500 $1,400 $1,300 $1,200 $1,100 $1,000

MV DELUXE (USA DELUXE SERIES) -similar to MV Custom except has alder body, maple neck with rosewood fingerboard, dot inlays with "Deluxe" at the 12th fret, available in Black Gold, Metallic Gold and Ice Blue finishes. New 2001.

MSR $1,499 $1,200 $1,100 $1,000 $900 $800 $700 $600

Maverick Series

MAVERICK - offset double cutaway hardwood body, bolt-on maple neck, 24-fret maple fingerboard with black offset dot inlay (or rosewood fingerboard with pearl dot inlay), double locking vibrato, blackface peghead with screened logo, 6-on-a-side tuners, black hardware, single coil/humbucker ESP pickups, volume control, 3-position switch, available in Black, Brite Yellow, Candy Apple Red, Dark Metallic Blue, Fluorescent Pink, and Snow White finishes. Mfg. 1989 to 1991.

$375 $325 $275 $225 $200 $175 $150

In 1990, Pearl White and Turquoise finishes were introduced; Brite Yellow, Fluorescent Pink, and Snow White finishes were disc. In 1991, Dark Metallic Purple and Gunmetal Blue finishes were introduced; Turquoise finish was disc.

Maverick Deluxe (1988) - similar to the Maverick, except has ash body, 24-fret rosewood fingerboard with pearl dot inlay, 2 ESP humbucker pickups, available in Brite Red, Brite Yellow, Fluorescent Pink, Fluorescent White, Gunmetal Blue, and Midnight Black finishes. Mfg. 1988 only.

$400 $350 $275 $225 $200 $175 $150

The neck position pickup was a stacked humbucker.

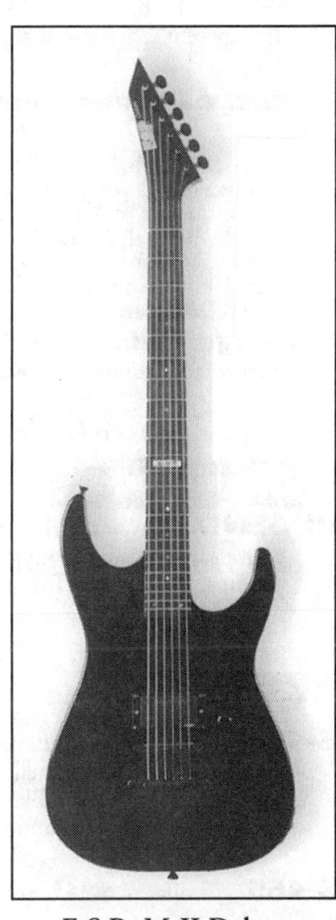

E.S.P. M-II Deluxe
courtesy The ESP Guitar Co.

GRADING	100% MINT	98% NEAR MINT	95% EXC+	90% EXC	80% VG+	70% VG	60% G

Maverick Deluxe (1992) - similar to the Maverick, except has ash body, pearloid pickguard, 24-fret rosewood fingerboard with pearl dot inlay/12th fret logo block inlay, maple peghead with screened logo, 2 single coil/1 humbucker ESP pickups, volume/tone controls, 5-position switch, available in Black, Pearl White, Transparent Blue, Transparent Green, Transparent Purple, and Transparent Red finishes. Mfg. 1992 only.

$750 $650 $525 $425 $395 $350 $325

Last MSR was $1,495.

Metal Series

METAL I - offset double cutaway alder body, bolt-on maple neck, 22-fret rosewood fingerboard with pearl dot inlay, standard vibrato, maple peghead with screened logo, 6-on-a-side tuners, gold hardware, exposed humbucker pickup, volume/tone control, available in Pearl Blue, Pearl Green, Pearl Pink, Pearl White and Metallic Purple. Mfg. 1986 only.

$350 $300 $250 $200 $175 $150 $125

METAL II - similar to Metal I, except has single horn cutaway V-shape body. Mfg. 1986 only.

$300 $250 $225 $175 $150 $125 $100

METAL III - reverse offset double cutaway asymmetrical alder body, bolt-on maple neck, 22-fret maple fingerboard with black dot inlay, standard vibrato, maple peghead with screened logo, 6-on-a-side tuners, gold hardware, exposed humbucker pickup, volume control. Mfg. 1986 only.

$325 $275 $225 $195 $175 $150 $125

Mirage Series

MIRAGE (FIRST EDITION) - offset double cutaway hardwood body, bolt-on maple neck, 22-fret bound rosewood fingerboard with pearl offset block inlay/logo block inlay at 12th fret, double locking vibrato, bound blackface peghead with screened logo, 6-on-a-side tuners, black hardware, 2 single coil/1 humbucker ESP pickups, volume/tone control, 5-position switch, available in Black, Candy Apple Red, Dark Metallic Blue, Dark Metallic Purple, Gunmetal Blue, and Pearl White finishes. Mfg. 1991 only.

$900 $825 $775 $700 $625 $525 $400

Last MSR was $1,695.

MIRAGE (SECOND EDITION) - offset double cutaway alder or ash body, maple neck, 22-fret rosewood fingerboard with pearl dot inlay (logo block inlay at 12th fret), Wilkinson VS-100 tremolo, reverse peghead, 6-on-a-side Sperzel locking tuners, black hardware, 2 SS-100 single coil/ 1 LH-200 humbucker ESP pickups, volume/tone control, 5-position switch, available in Black, Gunmetal Blue, Metallic Gold, and Pearl White finishes. Mfg. 1994 to 1998.

$950 $895 $800 $725 $625 $495 $375

Last MSR was $1,495.

Add $100 for See-Through Blue, See-Through Green, See-Through Purple, or See-Through Red finishes.

MIRAGE STANDARD - offset double cutaway mahogany body, bolt-on maple neck, 22-fret rosewood fingerboard with pearl dot inlay, strings through bridge, blackface peghead with screened logo, 6-on-a-side tuners, black hardware, exposed humbucker pickup, volume/tone controls, available in Baby Blue, Black, Bubblegum Pink, Candy Apple Blue, Fiesta Red, Metallic Blue, Metallic Red, Midnight Black, Mint Green, Snow White, Transparent Cherry Red and Transparent Blue finishes. Mfg. 1986 only.

$375 $325 $275 $225 $195 $175 $150

Mirage Custom - similar to Mirage Standard, except has 2 exposed humbucker pickups, 3-position switch. Mfg. 1986 to 1990.

$450 $395 $325 $250 $225 $200 $175

In 1987, Pearl Gold, Pearl Pink, Pearl White, and Turquoise finishes were introduced, through-body maple neck, 24-fret bound ebony fingerboard with offset pearl block inlay/logo block inlay at 12th fret, double locking vibrato, redesigned bound peghead, 2 single coil/1 humbucker pickups, 5-position switch replaced original part/designs, Baby Blue, Bubblegum Pink, Candy Apple Blue, Metallic Blue, Metallic Red, Mint Green, Snow White, Transparent Cherry Red, and Transparent Blue finishes were disc. In 1988, Brite Red, Gunmetal Blue, Magenta, Mediterranean Blue, and Pearl Silver finishes were introduced; Fiesta Red, Pearl Gold, and Pearl Pink finishes were disc. In 1989, Candy Apple Red and Lake Placid Blue finishes were introduced, 2 stacked coil/1 humbuckers replaced respective item, Brite Red, Mediterranean Blue, and Pearl Silver finishes were disc. In 1990, Magenta and Turquoise finishes were disc.

Mirage Deluxe - similar to Mirage Custom, except has bound rosewood fingerboard with pearl offset block inlay, double locking vibrato, stacked coil/humbucker pickups, available in Black, Fiesta Red, Pearl Gold, Pearl Pink, Pearl White and Turquoise finishes. Mfg. 1987 to 1990.

$425 $375 $300 $250 $225 $200 $175

Finish colors from 1988 to 1990 follow the same changes as the Mirage Custom.

Phoenix Series

PHOENIX - asymmetrical hourglass style mahogany body, white pickguard, through-body mahogany neck, 22-fret bound rosewood fingerboard with pearl dot inlay, double locking vibrato, bound blackface peghead with screened logo, 6-on-a-side tuners, black hardware, 2 covered humbucker pickups, 2 volume/2-Tone controls, 3-position switch, available in Black, Fiesta Red, Snow White and Turquoise finishes. Mfg. 1987 only.

$550 $475 $395 $325 $275 $225 $195

Last MSR was $1,550.

S Series

S-454 - offset double cutaway alder body, white pickguard, bolt-on maple neck, 22-fret maple fingerboard with black dot inlay, standard vibrato, maple peghead with screened logo, 6-on-a-side tuners, chrome hardware, 3 single coil exposed pickups, 1 volume/2-Tone controls, 5-position switch, available in Baby Blue, Black, Blonde, Fiesta Red, Lake Placid Blue, Metallic Blue, Metallic Red, Natural, Olympic White, Salmon Pink, Two Tone Sunburst and 3-Tone Sunburst finishes. Mfg. 1986 to 1987.

$350 $300 $250 $200 $175 $150 $125

S-465 - similar to S-454, except has rosewood fingerboard with pearl dot inlay. Mfg. 1986 to 1987.

$350 $300 $250 $200 $175 $150 $125

GRADING	100% MINT	98% NEAR MINT	95% EXC+	90% EXC	80% VG+	70% VG	60% G

S-487 DELUXE - offset double cutaway hardwood body, black lam pickguard, bolt-on maple neck, 22-fret rosewood fingerboard with pearl dot inlay, double locking vibrato, maple peghead with screened logo, 6-on-a-side tuners, chrome hardware, 3 single coil exposed pickups, 1 volume/2-Tone controls, 5-position switch, available in Black, Brite Red, Burgundy Mist, Cherry Sunburst, Mediterranean Blue and Snow White finishes. Mfg. 1987 to 1988.

$450 $375 $325 $250 $225 $200 $175

S-487 Standard - similar to S-487 Deluxe, except has black pickguard, standard vibrato, black hardware. Mfg. 1987 to 1988.

$375 $325 $275 $225 $200 $175 $125

This model had an optional maple fingerboard with black dot inlay.

S-500 - offset double cutaway ash body, bolt-on maple neck, 22-fret rosewood fingerboard with pearl dot inlay, vintage vibrato, graphite nut, 6-on-a-side locking Sperzel tuners, gold hardware, 2 single coil/1 humbucker ESP pickups, volume/tone control, 5-position switch, available in Black, Pearl White, Transparent Blue, Transparent Green, Transparent Purple and Transparent Red finishes. Mfg. 1991 to 1993.

$950 $875 $750 $600 $550 $495 $425
Last MSR was $1,495.

S-500 T - similar to S-500, except has double locking vibrato. Mfg. 1992 only.

$850 $725 $600 $475 $425 $400 $350
Last MSR was $1,695.

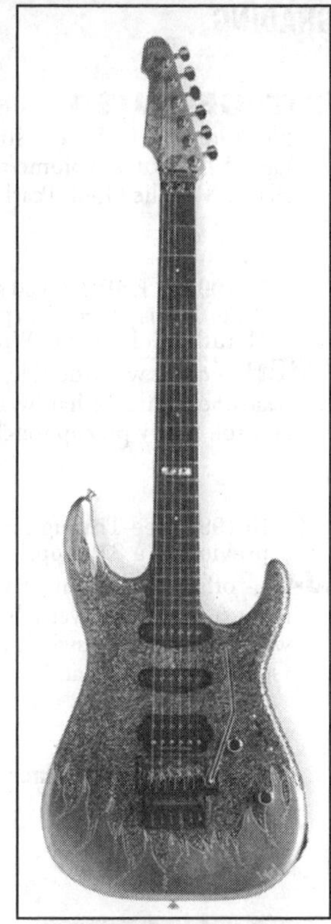

E.S.P. Mirage Custom
courtesy The ESP Guitar Co.

T Series

T-454 - single cutaway alder body, white pickguard, metal control plate, bolt-on maple neck, 22-fret maple fingerboard with black dot inlay, strings through bridge, maple peghead with screened logo, 6-on-a-side tuners, chrome hardware, 2 single coil pickups, volume/tone controls, 3-position switch, available in Baby Blue, Black, Blonde, Fiesta Red, Lake Placid Blue, Metallic Blue, Metallic Red, Natural, Olympic White, Salmon Pink, Two Tone Sunburst and 3-Tone Sunburst finishes. Mfg. 1986 to 1987.

$325 $275 $225 $195 $175 $150 $125

T-465 (T-463) - similar to T-454, except has bound body, rosewood fingerboard with pearl dot inlay. Mfg. 1986 to 1987.

$325 $275 $225 $195 $175 $150 $125

TRADITIONAL - offset double cutaway alder body, bolt-on maple neck, 21-fret rosewood fingerboard with pearl dot inlay, standard vibrato, maple peghead with screened logo, 6-on-a-side tuners, chrome hardware, 3 single coil ESP pickups, 1 volume/2-Tone controls, 5-position switch, available in Black, Candy Apple Red, Lake Placid Blue, Olympic White, Two Tone Sunburst and 3-Tone Sunburst finishes. Mfg. 1989 to 1990.

$895 $775 $650 $525 $450 $425 $375
Last MSR was $1,295.

This model had an optional maple fingerboard with black dot inlay.

Traditional Reissue - similar to Traditional, except has pearloid pickguard, 22-fret fingerboard with pearl dot inlay, locking tuners, available in Black, Burgundy, Candy Apple Red, Gunmetal Blue, Metallic Blue, Metallic Purple, Pearl Yellow and Pearl White finishes. Mfg. 1993 only.

$895 $775 $650 $525 $450 $425 $375
Last MSR was $1,295.

Vintage Plus Series

VINTAGE - offset double cutaway alder body, white lam pickguard, bolt-on maple neck, 22-fret maple or rosewood fingerboard with dot inlay, standard vibrato, 6-on-a-side tuners, chrome hardware, 3 single coil ESP pickups, 1 volume/2-Tone controls, 5-position switch, available in Black, Burgundy Mist, Candy Apple Red, Olympic White, 2-Tone Sunburst, 3-Tone Sunburst, and Turquoise finishes. Mfg. 1994 to 1995.

$795 $575 $475 $425 $395 $350 $300
Last MSR was $1,095.

VINTAGE PLUS S - offset double cutaway alder or ash body, bolt-on maple neck, 22-fret maple or rosewood fingerboard with dot inlay (logo block inlay at 12th fret), 2-point tremolo, 6-on-a-side Sperzel locking tuners, chrome hardware, pearloid pickguard, 3 Vintage Rail Seymour Duncan single coil pickups, 1 volume/2-Tone controls, 5-position switch, available in 2-Tone Sunburst, 3-Tone Sunburst, Black, Metallic Gold, Pearl White, and Turquoise finishes. Mfg. 1995 to 2000.

$1,000 $875 $775 $650 $550 $425 $325
Last MSR was $1,249.

In 1998, 3 ESP SS-120 single coil pickups replaced the 3 Vintage Rail Seymour Duncan pickups; Honey Sunburst, Transparent Blue, Transparent Green, Transparent Purple, and Transparent Red finishes were introduced (these finishes were previously a $100 optional upgrade); Metallic Gold, Pearl White, and Turquoise finishes were disc.

Vintage Plus S with Floyd Rose - similar to Vintage Plus S, except has double locking Floyd Rose vibrato, 2 single coil/1 humbucker ESP pickups, volume/tone control. Mfg. 1995 to 1998.

$1,200 $1,000 $925 $795 $650 $525 $400
Last MSR was $1,595.

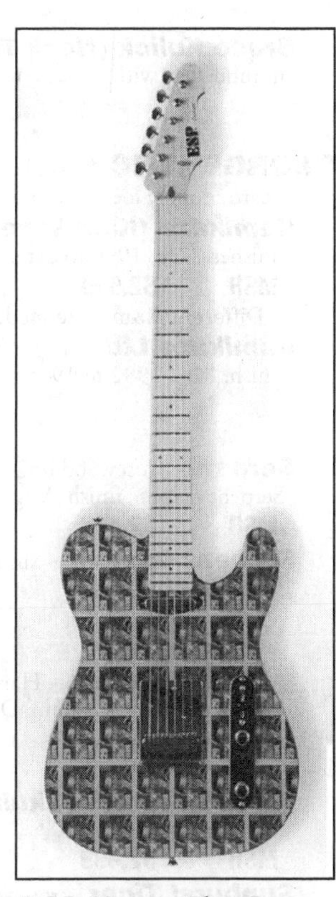

E.S.P. Vintage Plus Custom
courtesy The ESP Guitar Co.

GRADING	100% MINT	98% NEAR MINT	95% EXC+	90% EXC	80% VG+	70% VG	60% G

VINTAGE PLUS T - single cutaway bound alder or ash body, bolt on maple neck, 22-fret maple or rosewood fingerboard with dot inlay (logo block inlay at 12th fret), strings-through fixed bridge, 6-on-a-side tuners, chrome hardware, pearloid pickguard, 2 single coil Seymour Duncan Vintage '54 pickups, volume/tone control, 3-position switch, controls mounted on a chrome plate, available in 2-Tone Sunburst, 3-Tone Sunburst, Black, Metallic Gold, Pearl White, and Turquoise finishes. Mfg. 1994 to 2000.

$1,150 $1,000 $875 $750 $625 $500 $375
Last MSR was $1,449.

In 1998, 2 ESP TS-120 single coil pickups replaced the 2 Seymour Duncan Vintage '54 single coil pickups; Honey Sunburst, Transparent Blue, Transparent Purple, and Transparent Red finishes were introduced (these finishes were previously a $100 optional upgrade); Metallic Gold, Pearl White, Transparent Green, and Turquoise finishes were disc.

VIPER - offset waist/double cutaway mahogany body with pointed horns, bolt-on maple neck, 24-fret bound rosewood fingerboard, 3-per-side bound headstock, chrome hardware, tune-o-matic bridge/stop tailpiece, 2 ESP LH-200 humbuckers with nickel covers/black retaining rings, volume/tone control, 3-way pickup toggle switch, available in Black, Metallic Gold, Pearl White, and Turquoise finishes. Mfg. 1997 to 1999.

$975 $850 $750 $625 $525 $400 $300
Last MSR was $1,199.

In 1998, See-Through Blue, See-Through Green, See-Through Purple, and See-Through Red finishes were introduced (these finishes were previously a $100 optional upgrade); Metallic Gold and Turquoise finishes were disc.

XJ-6 - offset double cutaway alder or ash body with pointed bass bout/rounded treble bout, maple neck, 22-fret maple or rosewood neck with dot inlay, 6-on-a-side reverse headstock, shell pickguard, chrome hardware, fixed bridge, 2 Seymour Duncan mini-humbuckers, volume/tone control, 3-way pickup toggle switch (on treble bout), 3-way split/series/parallel mini-switch, available in 2-Tone Sunburst, 3-Tone Sunburst, Black, Metallic Gold, Pearl White, and Turquoise finishes. Mfg. 1996 to 1998.

$950 $895 $800 $725 $625 $495 $395
Last MSR was $1,495.

Add $100 for See-Through Blue, See-Through Green, See-Through Purple, or See-Through Red finishes.

XJ-12 - similar to the XJ-6, except has 12-string configuration, 4/8 reverse headstock, 2 ESP LH-200 humbuckers. Mfg. 1996 to 1998.

$1,100 $975 $900 $825 $675 $550 $425
Last MSR was $1,595.

Signature Series

All models in this series are built to their namesakes' specifications. The retail list price for Signature Series models include a hardshell case.

BRUCE KULICK (Bolt-On) - offset waist/double cutaway mahogany body with pointed horns, mahogany neck, 22-fret bound rosewood fingerboard with pearl parallelogram inlays, 3-per-side headstock with screened signature/logo, chrome hardware, shell pickguard, tune-o-matic bridge/stop tailpiece, 2 ESP LH-200 humbuckers with nickel covers/black retaining rings, volume/tone control, 3-way pickup toggle switch, available in Black finish. Mfg. 1996 to 1999.

$1,350 $1,175 $1,000 $900 $775 $650 $425
Last MSR was $1,699.

Bruce Kulick (Neck-Through) - similar to the Bruce Kulick (Bolt-On), except features neck-through-body design, 2 Seymour Duncan humbuckers with nickel covers. Mfg. 1996 to 1999.

$1,600 $1,400 $1,200 $1,050 $850 $675 $500
Last MSR was $1,999.

GEORGE LYNCH - All instruments in this group have the following items; offset double cutaway alder body, bolt-on maple neck, 22-fret fingerboard, double locking vibrato, reverse headstock, 6-on-a-side tuners, black hardware, single coil/humbucker pickups, pan control.

Kamikaze (Kamikaze I, II, III) - rosewood fingerboard with pearl dot inlay, available in black/brown/red camouflage Kamikaze graphic finishes. Mfg. 1990 to date.

MSR $2,599 $2,100 $1,875 $1,650 $1,450 $1,200 $1,000 $800

Different Kamikaze models have different color 'camouflage' graphic.

Kamikaze Ltd - maple fingerboard with black 'dropping bomb' inlay, reverse 'sawtooth' peghead, available in green/yellow/red Kamikaze graphic finish. Mfg. 1992 to 1995.

$1,800 $1,500 $1,350 $1,200 $1,000 $825 $650
Last MSR was $2,595.

Serpent - rosewood fingerboard with pearl dot inlay/ESP logo block inlay at 12th fret, peghead has screened logo/initial, available in Black/White Serpent graphic finish. Mfg. 1993 to date.

MSR $2,499 $2,050 $1,800 $1,595 $1,400 $1,095 $895 $675

Serpent Custom - similar to the Serpent configuration, available in Black/Brown Serpent graphic finish with Turquoise and white highlights. Mfg. 1994 to 1998.

$1,700 $1,500 $1,300 $1,100 $975 $795 $575
Last MSR was $2,295.

Skull & Bones - Hand Carved Maple body, maple bolt-on neck with ebony fingerboard, white dot inlays, 22 XJ frets, Original Floyd Rose bridge, Duncan Screamin' Demon pickup, vibrato bar, limited production, available in Bone finish. Mfg. 1999 Only.

$3,200 $2,700 $2,300 $2,000 $1,700 $1,400 $1,200
Last MSR was $3,999.

Skull & Snakes (Skull and Snakes Ltd) - rosewood fingerboard with pearl skull/swords inlay, available in Skulls & Snake graphic finish. Mfg. 1990 to date.

MSR $2,499 $2,050 $1,800 $1,595 $1,400 $1,095 $895 $675

Sunburst Tiger - rosewood fingerboard with pearl dot inlay, 6-on-a-side 'droopy' headstock, available in Purple/Red/Yellow Tiger Sunburst finish. Mfg. 1990 to date.

MSR $2,499 $2,050 $1,800 $1,595 $1,400 $1,095 $895 $675

GRADING	100% MINT	98% NEAR MINT	95% EXC+	90% EXC	80% VG+	70% VG	60% G

M-1 Tiger - similar to the Sunburst Tiger, except has M-I body design, 22-fret maple fingerboard with black dot inlay, exposed ESP humbucker, volume knob, available in Yellow/Black tiger stripe graphic finish with matching headstock. Mfg. 1996 to date.

MSR $2,199 — $1,800 $1,600 $1,400 $1,200 $950 $775 $600

GL-56 - Pre-aged offset double cutaway basswood body, bolt-on maple neck, 22-fret maple fingerboard with dot inlay, 6-on-a-side Sperzel locking tuners, 2-point tremolo bridge, chrome hardware, white pickguard, 3 Seymour Duncan Classic Stack pickups, 2 volume/tone controls, available in distressed Natural finish. Mfg. 1998 to date.

MSR $1,999 — $1,600 $1,400 $1,200 $1,000 $850 $675 $500

Ultra Tone - bound rosewood fingerboard with pearl dot inlay, 3-per-side 'vintage-style' tuners, screened logo/'Ultra Tone'/graphic on headstock, 3 Seymour Duncan covered mini-humbuckers, tune-o-matic bridge/stop tailpiece, chrome hardware, black/white 'marblized' pickguard, 3 control knobs, available in 3-Tone Sunburst, Black, and Pearl White finishes. Mfg. 1995 to 2000.

$1,200 $1,050 $900 $775 $650 $500 $375
Last MSR was $1,499.

JAKE E. LEE - offset double cutaway alder body, bolt-on maple neck, 24 3/4" scale, 22-fret maple or rosewood fingerboard with dot inlay, strings-through fixed bridge, screened peghead signature/logo, 6-on-a-side tuners, chrome hardware, white pickguard, 2 slanted single coil/1 humbucker ESP pickups, volume/tone controls, 5-position switch, available in Black, Metallic Purple, and Snow White finishes. Mfg. 1994 to 1996.

$895 $825 $725 $600 $500 $400 $295
Last MSR was $1,395.

This model has an optional rosewood fingerboard with pearl dot inlay.

JAMES HETFIELD JH-1 - Flying V-style mahogany body, 22-fret rosewood fingerboard with abalone custom inlay, 3-per-side headstock, fixed bridge, black hardware, 2 EMG humbuckers, volume/tone controls, 3-way selector, available in 'Hot Rod' flame graphic finish (Body and matching headstock) only. Mfg. 1997 only.

$2,150 $2,000 $1,750 $1,450 $1,200 $950 $725
Last MSR was $2,695.

Production of this model is limited to 200 pieces. List price includes hardshell case.

JAMES HETFIELD JH-2 - Explorer-style mahogany body, black Diamond-plate metal top, bolt-on maple neck, 22-fret rosewood fingerboard with pearl diamond custom inlay, 6-on-a-side headstock, tune-o-matic bridge/stop tailpiece, black hardware, 2 EMG (models 81/60) humbuckers, volume/tone controls, 3-way selector, available in Black finish with matching headstock. Mfg. 1998 only.

$2,200 $2,000 $1,750 $1,450 $1,200 $950 $725
Last MSR was $2,699.

This is a limited production model. List price includes hardshell case.

JAMES HETFIELD JH-3 - single cutaway mahogany body, maple-set neck with rosewood fingerboard, 22 XJ frets with custom flag inlays, Creme body and neck binding, tune-o-matic bridge, two EMG (models 81/60) humbucker pickups, gold hardware, two volume and two tone controls, limited production, available in Black finish with Pinstripes. New 1999.

MSR $2,699 — $2,200 $2,000 $1,750 $1,450 $1,200 $950 $725

JEFF HANNEMAN SIGNATURE - double cutaway maple neck-through-body with Alder sides, maple neck with rosewood fingerboard, white dot inlays with "Slayer" logo at 12th fret, 24 XJ frets, two EMG-81 humbucker pickups with SPC control, white neck binding, black hardware, Kahler Pro bridge, available in Black finish. New 1999.

MSR $2,999 — $2,460 $2,250 $1,900 $1,700 $1,500 $1,200 $1,000

KERRY KING KK STANDARD - Flying V-style mahogany body, set-in mahogany neck, 24-fret rosewood fingerboard with pearl diamond inlay, reverse curved headstock with screened signature/logo, 6-on-a-side tuners, Kahler Pro tremolo, black hardware, 2 EMG-81 humbuckers, volume/tone controls, 3-way selector, EMG PA-2 pre-amp, available in Black finish only. Disc. 1998.

$1,800 $1,600 $1,400 $1,200 $1,000 $800 $650
Last MSR was $2,395.

List price included a hardshell case.

Kerry King KK Custom - similar to the Kerry King KK Standard, except features neck-through-body construction, pearl eagle fingerboard inlays, available in red/black crackle finish. Disc. 1998.

$3,000 $2,800 $2,400 $N/A $N/A $N/A $N/A
Last MSR was $3,995.

List price included a hardshell case.

KIRK HAMMETT KH-1 - Flying V-style mahogany body, 22-fret rosewood fingerboard with pearl custom 'devil' inlay, 3-per-side headstock, Floyd Rose tremolo, black hardware, white pickguard, EMG-81 humbucker, volume controls, available in Black finish only. Disc. 1998.

$2,000 $1,800 $1,650 $1,400 $1,150 $950 $695
Last MSR was $2,695.

List price included a hardshell case.

KIRK HAMMETT KH-2 (CUSTOM M-II) - offset double cutaway alder body, bolt-on maple neck, 24-fret rosewood fingerboard with pearl skull & crossbones inlay, Floyd Rose tremolo, reverse pointed peghead with screened logo/initials, 6-on-a-side tuners, black hardware, 2 EMG-81 humbuckers, 1 volume/2-Tone controls, 5-position switch, available in Black finish only. Current Mfg.

MSR $2,399 — $1,700 $1,400 $1,200 $1,050 $900 $775 $600

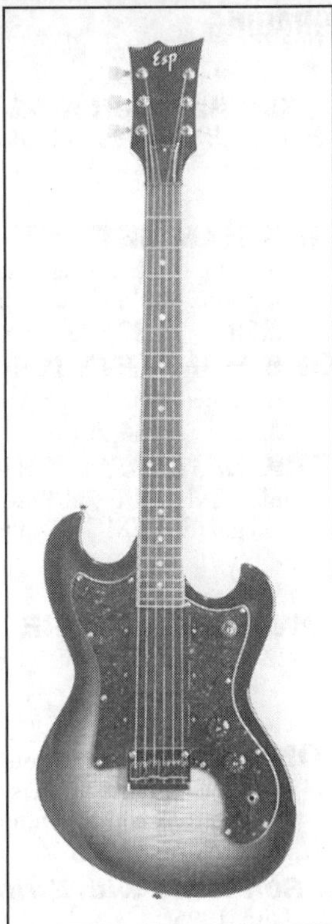

E.S.P. Ultratone (Prototype) courtesy The ESP Guitar Co.

E

GRADING		100% MINT	98% NEAR MINT	95% EXC+	90% EXC	80% VG+	70% VG	60% G

Kirk Hammett KH-2 (Custom M-II with Ouija Graphic) - similar to the Kirk Hammett KH-2, except has a custom *Ouija* graphic finish. Mfg. 1996 to 1999.

$2,000 $1,750 $1,525 $1,300 $1,075 $850 $625
Last MSR was $2,499.

KIRK HAMMETT KH-3 - single cutaway alder body, mahogany neck, 24-fret rosewood fingerboard with pearl skull & spider inlay, Floyd Rose tremolo, blackface peghead with screened signature/logo, 3-per-side tuners, black hardware, 2 EMG-81 humbuckers, 1 volume/2-Tone controls, 3-position switch, available in Black with Spider/Web graphic finish. Mfg. 1994 to date.

MSR $2,699 $2,200 $1,950 $1,725 $1,500 $1,200 $950 $725

KIRK HAMMETT KH-3 RELIC -exact reproduction of Kirk's main stage guitar showing wear and tear from use. Production limited to 100 instruments in 2001. Each guitar will include a certificate of authenticity signed by Kirk Hammett.

MSR $4,299

KIRK HAMMETT KH-4 - offset double cutaway body, alder wings, through-body maple neck, 24-fret rosewood fingerboard with pearl dot inlay, Original Floyd Rose tremolo, reverse pointed peghead with screened logo/initials, 6-on-the-other-side tuners, black hardware, white pearloid pickguard, 2 EMG-81 humbuckers, 2 volume/tone controls, 5-position switch, available in Black finish only. Disc. 1999.

$2,150 $1,850 $1,600 $1,375 $1,150 $900 $675
Last MSR was $2,699.

LOW G SIGNATURE - offset double cutaway Alder body, bolt-on maple neck with rosewood fingerboard, white dot inlays, white neck binding, 22 XJ frets, one EMG-81 pickup, tune-o-matic bridge, stop tailpiece, chrome hardware, available in Black & White Pearloid. Mfg. 1999 Only.

$2,800 $2,400 $2,025 $1,725 $1,475 $1,250 $995
Last MSR was $3,499.

RON WOOD - single round cutaway bound alder body, bolt-on maple neck, 22-fret maple fingerboard with black dot inlay, strings-through fixed bridge, 6-on-a-side tuners, natural headstock with screened signature/logo, chrome hardware, white pickguard, humbucker/single coil ESP pickups, volume/tone control on metal plate, 3-position switch, available in Black, Fiesta Red, and Metallic Blue finishes. Current Mfg.

MSR $1,399 $1,100 $995 $850 $725 $600 $475 $350

Ron Wood with Stringbender - similar to Ron Wood, except has pearloid pickguard, 2 humbucker pickups, Parsons-White Stringbender. Disc. 1995.

$1,200 $1,100 $995 $900 $850 $695 $575
Last MSR was $2,095.

STEPHEN CARPENTER SIGNATURE - double cutaway maple neck-through-body with alder sides, maple neck with ebony fingerboard, no inlays, white neck binding, 24 XJ frets, one Duncan TB-4 pickup, one ESP LH-200 and one ESP SS-120 pickup, tune-o-matic bridge, chrome hardware, available in See-Through Green, Snow White and Sonic Blue finishes. New 1999.

MSR $2,499 $1,999 $1,750 $1,425 $1,250 $1,000 $800 $700

STEPHEN CARPENTER 7 -similar to Stephen Carpenter Signature Model except in a 7-string configuration. Tune-O-Matic 7 bridge, Duncan JB-7, '59-7, and SSL-7 pickups, available in Black finish with pearl binding. Mfg. 2000 Only.

$2,150 $1,950 $1,750 $1,550 $1.350 $1,150 $950
Last MSR was $2,699.

MAX CAVALERA -offset double cutaway design similar to a SG, alder body maple neck, ebony fingerboard, soulfly logo position markers, XXX at 12-fet, Tune-O-Matic bridge, string-through-body, white neck binding, 24 XJ frets, one Seymour Duncan SH-6 pickup, 1 volume control, available in Brazil Green with graphic. New 2001.

MSR $2,799 $2,250 $2,150 $1,950 $1,750 $1,550 $1,350 $1,150

ELECTRIC BASS

Add $250 for Seymour Duncan bass pickup set.

B-1 - slightly offset double cutaway alder body, maple neck, 21-fret maple or rosewood fingerboard with dot inlay, 2-per-side headstock, fixed tailpiece, black hardware, Seymour Duncan MusicMan Basslines humbucker, volume/treble/bass controls, active EQ, available in Black, Candy Apple Red, Metallic Gold, and Pearl White. Mfg. 1997 to 2000.

$1,100 $950 $825 $700 $575 $450 $350
Last MSR was $1,349.

B Series

B-FIVE - sleek offset double cutaway ash body, maple neck, 24-fret rosewood fingerboard with pearl dot inlay, 3/2-per-side headstock, fixed bridge, black hardware, 2 ESP single coil pickups, 2 volume/blend/tone controls, 2 pickup selector switches, active CIR-1 EQ circuit, available in Black, Natural, See-Through Blue, See-Through Green, See-Through Purple, and See-Through Red finishes. Mfg. 1995 to 1997.

$1,150 $1,000 $925 $825 $700 $595 $475
Last MSR was $1,895.

Add $300 for 2-Tek bridge.

B-Four - similar to the B-5, except in a 4-string configuration, 2-per-side headstock. Mfg. 1996 to 1997.

$1,000 $900 $825 $725 $625 $525 $425
Last MSR was $1,695.

Add $300 for 2-Tek bridge.

GRADING	100% MINT	98% NEAR MINT	95% EXC+	90% EXC	80% VG+	70% VG	60% G

ECLIPSE BASS - single cutaway alder body, maple neck, 21-fret bound rosewood fingerboard with pearl dot inlay/logo block inlay at 12th fret, 2-per-side bound headstock, fixed bridge, chrome hardware, 2 ESP exposed humbucker pickups, volume/blend/tone controls, available in Black, Gunmetal Blue, Honey Sunburst, Metallic Gold, and Pearl White finishes. Mfg. 1996 to 1997.

$1,000 $895 $775 $695 $595 $500 $400
Last MSR was $1,595.

Add $300 for Transparent finish and EMG pickups (Available in See-Through Black, See-Through Blue, See-Through Green, See-Through Purple, and See-Through Red finishes).

This model had an optional mahogany body.

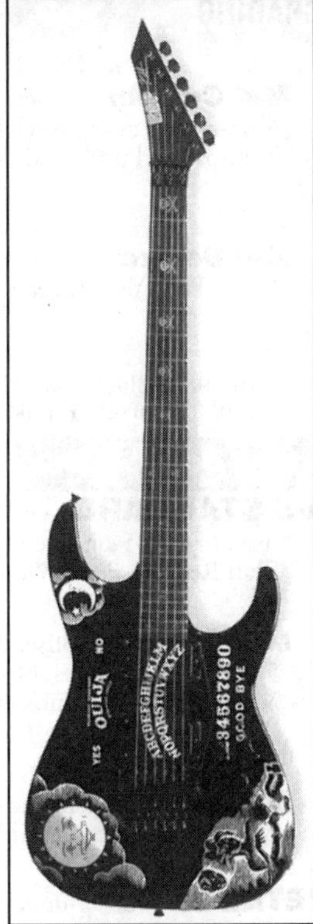

E.S.P. KH-2
courtesy
The ESP Guitar Co.

J Series

J-FOUR - offset double cutaway asymmetrical alder or ash body, bolt-on maple neck, 21-fret rosewood fingerboard with pearl dot inlay (logo block inlay at 12th fret), fixed bridge, 4-on-a-side tuners, chrome hardware, pearloid pickguard, 2 J-style ESP pickups, 2 volume/1 tone controls mounted on metal plate, available in 2-Tone Sunburst, 3-Tone Sunburst, Black, Candy Apple Red, Gunmetal Blue, and Pearl White finishes. Mfg. 1994 to 2000.

$875 $750 $650 $550 $450 $375 $275
Last MSR was $1,079.

In 1997, Candy Apple Red, Gunmetal Blue, 2-Tone Sunburst finishes were disc; Metallic Gold and Turquoise finishes were introduced. In 1998, See-Through Blue, See-Through Green, See-Through Purple, and See-Through Red finishes were introduced; Metallic Gold and Turquoise finishes were disc.

J-Five - similar to J-Four, except has 5-string configuration, 5-on-one -side tuners. Mfg.1994 to 2000

$950 $825 $725 $625 $500 $400 $295
Last MSR was $1,179.

J-464 - offset double cutaway asymmetrical hardwood body, bolt-on maple neck, 21-fret rosewood fingerboard with pearl dot inlay, fixed bridge, 4-on-a-side tuners, chrome hardware, white pickguard, 2 J-style pickups, 2 volume/1 tone controls, available in 2-Tone Sunburst, 3-Tone Sunburst, Baby Blue, Black, Blonde, Fiesta Red, Lake Placid Blue, Metallic Blue, Metallic Red, Natural, Olympic White, and Salmon Pink finishes. Mfg. 1986 only.

$275 $225 $195 $150 $125 $115 $95

This model had an optional tortoise pickguard.

Horizon Bass Series

HORIZON - offset double cutaway mahogany body, bolt-on maple neck, 21-fret maple fingerboard with black dot inlay, fixed bridge, 4-on-a-side tuners, black hardware, P-style pickup, volume/tone control, available in Baby Blue, Black, Bubblegum Pink, Candy Apple Blue, Fiesta Red, Metallic Blue, Metallic Red, Midnight Black, Mint Green, Snow White, Transparent Cherry Red and Transparent Blue finishes. Mfg. 1986 only.

$300 $250 $225 $175 $150 $125 $100

Horizon PJ - similar to Horizon, except has rosewood fingerboard with pearl dot inlay, P/J-style pickups, 2 volume/1 tone controls. Mfg. 1986 only.

$325 $275 $225 $195 $175 $150 $125

Horizon-4 - offset double cutaway maple body, bolt-on maple neck, 24-fret ebony fingerboard, fixed bridge, blackface peghead with screened logo, 2-per-side tuners, chrome hardware, P/J-style EMG pickups, volume/bass/treble/mix controls, active electronics, available in Black, Bright Red, Snow White and Turquoise finishes. Mfg. 1987 to 1993.

$1,400 $1,200 $1,000 $895 $795 $650 $550
Last MSR was $2,195.

In 1988, Gunmetal Blue, Mediterranean Blue, Midnight Black, Pearl Pink and Pearl Yellow finishes were introduced. In 1989, Burgundy Mist, Cherry Sunburst were introduced, through-body maple neck, bound fingerboard with offset pearl dot inlay, bound peghead, black hardware, replaced original part/designs, Mediterranean Blue, Midnight Black, Pearl Pink and Pearl Yellow finishes were disc. In 1990, Candy Apple Red, Dark Metallic Blue and Pearl White finishes were introduced, offset pearl dot fingerboard inlay/12th logo block inlay replaced respective items, Bright Red, Burgundy Mist, Cherry Sunburst, Snow White and Turquoise finishes were disc. In 1991, Dark Metallic Purple finish was introduced. In 1992, Metallic Green finish was introduced, Dark Metallic Blue finish was disc.

Horizon-5 - similar to Horizon-4, except has 5-string configuration, 3/2-per-side tuners. Mfg. 1987 to 1993.

$1,500 $1,300 $1,100 $950 $850 $750 $675
Last MSR was $2,395.

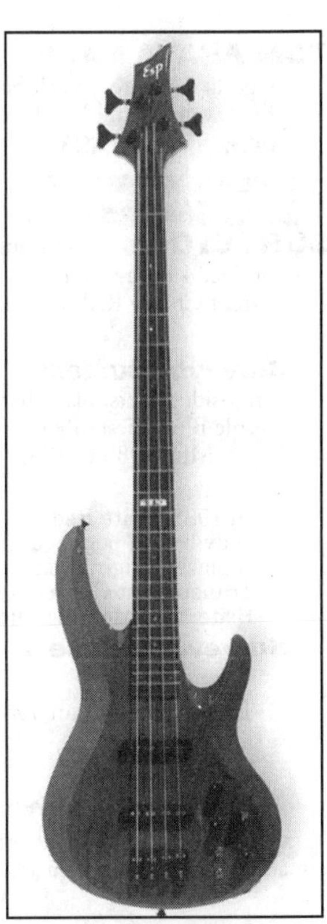

E.S.P. B-Four
courtesy
The ESP Guitar Co.

M-4 Bass Series

M-4 STANDARD - offset double cutaway alder body, bolt-on maple neck, 21-fret maple fingerboard with black dot inlay, fixed bridge, 4-on-a-side tuners, black hardware, P/J-style pickups, volume/tone controls, 3-position switch, available in Fiesta Red, Flip Flop Pearl Blue, Flip Flop Pearl Red, Pearl White and Turquoise finishes. Mfg. 1987 to 1993.

$695 $595 $500 $400 $350 $325 $300
Last MSR was $1,295.

In 1989, Black, Brite Red and Snow White finishes were introduced, rosewood fingerboard replaced original part/design, Fiesta Red, Flip Flop Pearl Blue, Flip Flop Pearl Red, Pearl White and Turquoise finishes were disc. In 1990, Candy Apple Red finish was introduced, Brite Red was disc. From 1990 to 1992, model was disc. In 1992, model was reintroduced, available in Black, Candy Apple Red, Gunmetal Blue, Metallic Green, Metallic Purple and Pearl White finishes.

GRADING	100% MINT	98% NEAR MINT	95% EXC+	90% EXC	80% VG+	70% VG	60% G

M-4 Custom - offset double cutaway asymmetrical ash body, bolt-on maple neck, 21-fret rosewood fingerboard with pearl dot inlay, fixed bridge, 4-on-a-side tuners, black hardware, P/J-style pickups, 2 volume/1 tone controls, available in Black, Cherry Sunburst, Pearl White, Transparent Blue, Transparent Purple and Transparent Red finishes. Mfg. 1991 only.

$800	$675	$575	$450	$400	$375	$325

Last MSR was $1,595.

M-4 Deluxe - similar to M-4 Standard, except has rosewood fingerboard with pearl dot inlay, available in Brite Red, Gunmetal Blue, Midnight Black, Pearl Yellow, Pearl White and Turquoise finishes. Mfg. 1988 to 1990.

$825	$725	$600	$475	$425	$395	$350

Last MSR was $1,195.

In 1989, Black, Candy Apple Red and Magenta finishes were introduced, redesigned bound peghead, P/J-style stacked coil pickups replaced original part/designs, Brite Red, Midnight Black and Turquoise finishes were disc. In 1990, Pearl Yellow finish was disc.

M-5 Bass Series

M-5 STANDARD - offset double cutaway asymmetrical hardwood body, bolt-on maple neck, 21-fret rosewood fingerboard with pearl dot inlay, fixed bridge, 5-on-one-side tuners, chrome hardware, 2 J-style pickups, 2 volume/1 tone controls, available in Black, Dark Metallic Blue, Flip Flop Pearl Red and Pearl White finishes. Mfg. 1987 only.

$300	$250	$225	$175	$150	$125	$100

M-5 Custom - offset double cutaway asymmetrical ash body, bolt-on maple neck, 21-fret rosewood fingerboard with pearl dot inlay, fixed bridge, 5-on-one-side tuners, black hardware, P/J-style pickups, 2 volume/1 tone controls, available in Black, Candy Apple Red, Dark Metallic Blue, Dark Metallic Purple, Gunmetal Blue and Pearl White finishes. Mfg. 1991 only.

$850	$725	$600	$495	$425	$375	$325

Last MSR was $1,695.

M-5 Deluxe - similar to M-5 Standard, except has rosewood fingerboard with pearl dot inlay, available in Brite Red, Gunmetal Blue, Midnight Black, Pearl Yellow, Pearl White and Turquoise finishes. Mfg. 1988 only.

$325	$275	$225	$195	$175	$150	$125

METAL IV - offset double cutaway hardwood body, bolt-on maple neck, 21-fret maple fingerboard with black dot inlay, fixed bridge, 4-on-a-side tuners, gold hardware, P/J-style pickups, 2 volume/1 tone controls, available in Pearl Blue, Pearl Green, Pearl Pink, Pearl White and Metallic Purple. Mfg. 1986 only.

$275	$225	$195	$150	$135	$125	$115

P-457 - offset double cutaway hardwood body, white pickguard, bolt-on maple neck, 21-fret maple fingerboard with black dot inlay, fixed bridge, 4-on-a-side tuners, chrome hardware, P-style pickup, 2 volume/1 tone controls, available in Baby Blue, Black, Blonde, Fiesta Red, Lake Placid Blue, Metallic Blue, Metallic Red, Natural, Olympic White, Salmon Pink, Two Tone Sunburst and 3-Tone Sunburst finishes. Mfg. 1986 only.

$300	$250	$225	$175	$150	$125	$100

P-464 - similar to P-457, except has tortoise pickguard, rosewood fingerboard with pearl dot inlay.

$300	$250	$225	$175	$150	$125	$100

TOM ARAYA BASS -offset double cutaway gothic look, alder body and maple neck, ebony gingerboard with pentagram position markers, Slayer logo at 12th fret, black hardware, 2-per-side tuners, Gotoh 206 bridge, 24 XJ frets, two EMG-35-DC pickups, volume, pan, EMG-BQS, Active EQ, available in black finish. New 2001.

MSR	$3,499							
		$2,800	$2,600	$2,400	$2,200	$2,000	$1,800	$1,600

Surveyor Series

SURVEYOR - offset double cutaway mahogany body, black pickguard, bolt-on maple neck, 21-fret ebony fingerboard with pearl dot inlay, fixed bridge, 4-on-a-side tuners, black hardware, P/J-style pickups, 2 volume/1 tone controls, available in Black, Bright Yellow, Snow White and Transparent Cherry Red finishes. Mfg. 1987 only.

$350	$275	$250	$195	$175	$150	$125

Surveyor Custom - offset double cutaway mahogany body, black pickguard, bolt-on maple neck, 21-fret ebony fingerboard, fixed bridge, 4-on-a-side tuners, black hardware, P/J-style pickups, volume/tone control, 3-position switch, available in Baby Blue, Black, Bubblegum Pink, Candy Apple Blue, Fiesta Red, Metallic Blue, Metallic Red, Midnight Black, Mint Green, Snow White, Transparent Cherry Red and Transparent Blue finishes. Mfg. 1986 to 1989.

$375	$325	$250	$200	$175	$150	$125

In 1988, Brite Red, Gunmetal Blue, Mediterranean Blue, Pearl Yellow, Pearl White and Turquoise finishes were introduced, redesigned body/bound peghead, through-body maple neck, 24-fret bound fingerboard with offset pearl block inlay/logo block inlay at 12th fret replaced original part/designs, Baby Blue, Bubblegum Pink, Candy Apple Blue, Fiesta Red, Metallic Blue, Metallic Red, Mint Green, Transparent Cherry Red and Transparent Blue finishes were disc. In 1989, Candy Apple Red and Magenta finishes were introduced, Brite Red, Mediterranean Blue, Snow White and Turquoise finishes were disc.

Surveyor Deluxe - similar to Surveyor Custom, except has pearl dot fingerboard inlay. Mfg. 1986 only.

$375	$325	$250	$200	$175	$150	$125

This model had an optional rosewood fingerboard with black dot inlay.

EAGLE

Instruments currently built in Murr, Germany.

Eagle Country Instruments produces the smallest full-size electric bass guitar (34" scale, 36" overall length). This innovative design features a padauk/maple/mahogany construction, reverse stringing/no headstock. Retail prices run from $1,480 (4-string) to $1,620 (5-string).

ECCLESHALL

Instruments currently built in England since the early 1970s.

Luthier Christopher J. Eccleshall is known for the high quality guitars that he produces. Eccleshall also builds violins, mandolins, and banjos. Some of his original designs carry such model designations like **Excalibur, EQ**, and **Craftsman**. Luthier Eccleshall was also the first UK maker to have Japanese-built solid body guitars.

(Source: Tony Bacon and Paul Day, The Guru's Guitar Guide)

ECHEVERRIA GUITARS

Instruments previously built in Morrow, Georgia.

Luthier Richard Echeverria designed, built, restored and sold guitars for over twenty years. He has been a member of both G.A.L. (since 1980) and A.S.I.A. (since 1989) lutherie groups, and introduced his formalized line of guitars after years of building custom one-of-a-kind instruments.

Mahogany was one of Echeverria's favorite woods that he extensively used to create his original design electrics. All models had a tongue-and-groove set-in neck design, and were finished in a nitrocellulose lacquer finish. Echeverria uses a wide range of quality (and some custom) pickups from Tom Holmes, Joe Barden, Van Zandt, Seymour Duncan, and Dimarzio.

ELECTRIC

The **Aztore** model is a hybrid of design ideas from Gibson's Firebird and Explorer models, combined with an original modernistic body design. Echeverria favors Korina and mahogany in the construction, a 24 5/8" scale, 6-on-a-side reverse banjo style tuners with pearloid buttons, a tune-o-matic stop tailpiece, and 2 humbuckers. Last MSR - $1,495.

The **Magnolia** (list $3,200) shares a similar 24 5/8" scale and Gibson-esque vibe, but this model has a single rounded/Florentine cutaway mahogany body and an arched flame maple top. Body, fingerboard, and headstock are all bound, and the fingerboard has block inlays. 2 humbuckers and a tune-o-matic bridge/stop tailpiece wrap up this classicly designed model, thus proving that "Les" is more!

The **Echo** has a Fender-y Jazzmaster feel to the offset double cutaway mahogany (or alder or swamp ash) body. The 25 ½" scale is combined with a 3-per-side headstock, 2 humbuckers, and a tune-o-matic bridge/stop tailpiece - offering a different tonal feel to a Fender-scale guitar. This model is also available with a flame maple top (Last MSR -$1,995).

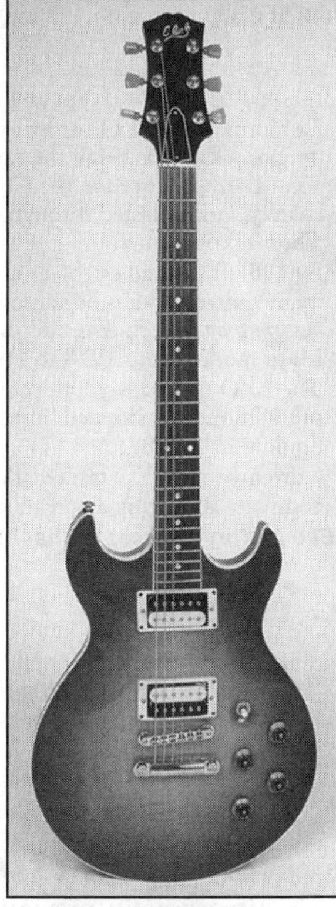

Ed Clark Nouveav Classique
courtesy
Ed Clark Guitars, Inc..

ECLECTIC

Instruments currently built in Duncan, South Carolina.

Luthier Brad Armstrong offers custom-crafted, custom-designed electric guitars. Armstrong offers a wide range of exotic woods such as Lacewood, Purpleheart, and Zebrawood in his creations. For further information concerning specicifications and pricing, please contact luthier Armstrong directly (see Trademark Index).

ED CLARK GUITARS, INC.

Instruments currently built in Ronkonkoma, New York.

Luthier and repairman Ed Clark specializes in all phases of guitar repair work, fretwork, bridge installations, as well as custom building guitars and basses. Clark is also the author of the monthly column Shop Talk in *20th Century Guitar* magazine.

EGMOND

See ROSETTI and LION.

Instruments previously built in Holland between 1960 and 1972.

In response to the pop music boom of the 1960s, guitar companies kept turning out instruments to try to meet the generated demand. These entry level guitars were aimed at the novice guitar player, and featured a line of Dutch-built solid and semi-hollow body designs.

(Source: Tony Bacon and Paul Day, The Guru's Guitar Guide)

EGYPT

Instruments previously produced in England between 1985 and 1987.

The EGYPT trademark was utilized by Scottish builders Maurice Bellando and James Cannell in the mid to late 1980s. These high quality, strikingly original solid body designs also featured Egyptian names. The luthiers also produced a range of Fender/Gibson-style models as well.

(Source: Tony Bacon and Paul Day, The Guru's Guitar Guide)

EKO

Trademark of instruments currently built the Czech Republic, Asia, Spain (classical), and Italy. EKO is now part of the E Group, which is split into EKO (Italian distributor of musical instruments), Esound (Italian distributor of musical instruments), Etek (professional audio producer and world wide musical instruments distributor), and Res (service society).

Instruments were formerly built in Italy from the early 1960s through 1987. Distribution in the U.S. market by the LoDuca Bros. of Milwaukee, Wisconsin.

The LoDuca Bros. musical distribution company was formed in 1941 by brothers Tom and Guy LoDuca. Capitalizing on money made through their accordion-based vaudevillian act, lessons, and accordion repair, the LoDucas began importing and selling Italian accordions. Throughout the 1940s and 1950s, the LoDucas built up a musical distributorship with accordions and sheet music. By the late 1950s, they were handling Magnatone amplifiers and guitars.

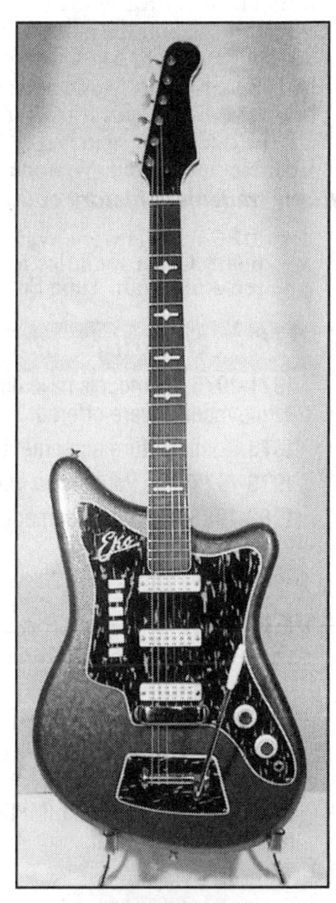

EKO 500-3V
courtesy J.R. Guitars

GRADING	100% MINT	98% NEAR MINT	95% EXC+	90% EXC	80% VG+	70% VG	60% G

In 1961, the LoDucas teamed up with Italy-based Oliviero Pigini & Company to import guitars. Pigini, one of the LoDuca's accordion manufacturers, had formed the EKO company in anticipation of the boom in the guitar market. The LoDucas acted as technical designers and gave input on EKO designs (as well as being the exclusive U.S. dealers), and EKO built guitars for their dealers. Some of the sparkle finishes were no doubt inspired by the accordions produced in the past. In fact, the various on/off switches and tone settings are down right reminiscent of accordion voice settings! The plastic covered-guitars lasted through to the mid 1960s, when more conventional finishes were offered. EKO also built a number of guitars for Vox, Goya, and Thomas companies.

By 1967 EKO had established dealers in 57 countries around the world. During the late 1960s and early 1970s the guitar market began to get soft, and many guitar builders began to go out of business. EKO continued on, but cut back the number of models offered. In the late 1970s, EKO introduced a *custom shop* branch that built neck-through designed guitars for other trademarks. Once such company was D'Agostino, and EKO produced the **Bench Mark** models from 1978 to 1982.

The EKO company kept producing models until 1985. By the mid-1980s, the LoDuca Bros. company had begun concentrating on guitar case production, and stopped importing the final *Alembic-styled* set-neck guitars that were being produced. The original EKO company's holdings were liquidated in 1987.

Currently, the EKO trademark has again been revived in Italy, and appears on entry level solid body guitars built in various countries. The revived company is offering a wide range of acoustic, classical, and solid body electric guitars and amplifiers - all with contemporary market designs.

(Eko history source: Michael Wright, Guitar Stories Volume One)

ELECTRIC

EKO produced a number of different models, like the semi-hollowbody 335-ish **Barracuda** series; or electric/acoustic cutaway models like the **Escort, Commander**, and **Mascot**. EKO offered violin-shaped guitars and basses; and solid body guitars like the double offset cutaway **Lancer** series, or the rocket ship-shaped **Roke** guitars and basses. More traditional were the **Kadett** and **Cobra** lines. A number of EKO designs were based on Fender's Jazzmaster model. Current models are Gibson- and Fender-based electric guitar designs, and dreadnought style acoustics.

Prices on vintage EKO models typically range $175-$350 – some models may be priced as high as $550-$600, depdning on condition, appeal, and relative coolness of the piece.

ELECTRA

Instruments previously built in Japan circa 1971 to 1983/1984. Distributed by the St. Louis Music Supply Company of St. Louis, Missouri.

Electra guitars, like Alvarez, was a brand name used by the St. Louis Music Supply company. The Electra and Apollo brands were introduced in 1971 as a replacement for the U.S.-built Custom Kraft instruments (Apollo was the budget brand line). Many models were bolt-neck versions of popular American instruments.

Tom Presley was hired by St. Louis Music in 1975 to work on the Modular Powered Circuits (MPC) program. The MPC line of guitars (mostly a Les Paul-ish style) featured cavities in the back of the instrument where 2 battery-powered effects modules could be plugged in. Thus, the guitarists' effects would be mounted in the instrument instead of located on the floor like *stomp box* effects. The effect modules had controls that could be preset after being plugged in; the guitar face had on/off toggle switches. The MPC idea is actually pretty clever! The distortion MPC modules also led to the development of SLM's Crate guitar amplifiers.

In 1983, St. Louis Music noticed that a west coast dealer had begun selling low end imported guitars using the *Electra* trademark. Although prior use belonged to St. Louis Music, it was felt that there would be some confusion with dealers and the public sorting out the differing levels of quality. Right off, the trademark switched to Electra/Phoenix. Then, in 1984, St. Louis Music announced that the Electra trademark would be merged with another Japanese-built brand, Westone. Models were sold under the Electra/Westone imprint for a year, then finally Westone only as the Electra aspect was disc.

(Early trademark history courtesy Michael Wright, Vintage Guitar Magazine)

MPC models were available in 11 different types of effects: The Phase Shifter and Booster modules were included with the MPC instrument. Other modules available were the Power Overdrive, Treble/Bass Expander, Electronic Fuzz, Tank Tone, Frog Nose, Triggered Filter, Auto Wah, Tube Sound, Octave Splitter, and Flanger.

Model Identification

1971-1975: All models have bolt-on necks, and resemble models offered by Univox during the same time period. By 1975 a wide range of Fender-ish/Gibson-esque models were offered.

1975: Joint venture agreement signed with a guitar company in Matsumoku, Japan; Tom Presley hired to oversee guitar design.

1976-1977: Les Paul-styled guitars switch to glued (set-in) necks. MPC guitar models introduced.

1983-1985: Electra trademark phased out in favor of Westone name.

ELECTRIC

AVENGER - offset double cutaway hardwood body, bolt-on maple neck, 22-fret maple fingerboard with black dot inlays, tremolo bridge, chrome hardware, 6-on-a-side tuners, white pickguard, 3 single coil pickups, volume/tone controls, available in Cream, Jet Black, and Sunburst finishes. Mfg. 1972 to 1979.

$250	$200	$175	$165	$145	$125	$95

MPC Series

Modular Powered Circuit (MPC) model guitars were introduced in 1976. The purpose of the design was to place effects typically found in pedals directly onboard the guitar itself.

GRADING	100% MINT	98% NEAR MINT	95% EXC+	90% EXC	80% VG+	70% VG	60% G

MPC - single cutaway mahogany body, maple top, set-in maple neck, 22-fret rosewood fingerboard with abalone block inlays, chrome hardware, 3-per-side headstock, bridge/stop tailpiece, white raised pickguard, 2 covered Magnaflux humbucker pickups, volume/tone controls, 2 effects control knobs, 2 effects on/off switches, 5-way pickup selector switch on upper bass bout, available in Natural and Sunburst finishes. Mfg. 1976 to 1977.

$350 $325 $295 $275 $250 $225 $195
Last MSR was $599.

This model has a hinged cover on the back of the instruments that allows access to MPC modules. This cavity holds two MPC modules, and is powered by a 9-volt battery.

MPC Standard - similar to the MPC, except has redesigned headstock, available in Antique Sunburst, Jet Black, Transparent Apple Red, Satin Jacaranda, and Sunburst Curly Maple finishes. Mfg. 1978 to 1984.

$350 $325 $295 $275 $250 $225 $195
Last MSR was $695.

After 1978, fancier versions such as the MPC Custom, Ultima MPC (special back/heel contour), and double cutaway Leslie West MPC were also offered.

MPC Outlaw - similar to the MPC Standard, except had a dual cutaway body, mahogany neck-through design, black pickguard, available in Charcoal Grey Sunburst, Natural Mahogany, and Tobacco Sunburst finishes. Mfg. 1978 to 1984.

$375 $350 $325 $295 $275 $250 $225
Last MSR was $775.

ELECTRA ROCK - single cutaway bound mahogany body, birds-eye maple (or jacaranda) top, bolt-on maple neck, 22-fret maple fingerboard with black trapezoidal inlays, chrome or gold hardware, 3-per-side headstock, bridge/stop tailpiece, white raised pickguard, 2 humbucker pickups, 2 volume/2-Tone controls, 3-way selector, available in Apple Red, Black, Goldtop, and Sunburst finishes. Mfg. 1972 to 1975.

$275 $225 $195 $175 $150 $125 $95

SUPER ROCK (Model 2245) - single cutaway bound mahogany body, maple top, bolt-on maple neck, 22-fret rosewood fingerboard with pearl crown inlays, chrome or gold hardware, 3-per-side headstock, bridge/stop tailpiece, white raised pickguard, 2 humbucker pickups, 2 volume/2-Tone controls, 3-way selector, available in Apple Red, Black, Goldtop, and Sunburst finishes. Mfg. 1972 to 1977.

$325 $250 $200 $175 $150 $125 $100

Magnum II - similar to the Super Rock, except has black body binding, black bound maple fingerboard with black crown inlay, clear pickguard, available in Natural finish only. Mfg. 1974 to 1977.

$285 $250 $205 $185 $160 $140 $110

Omega - similar to the Super Rock, except has *Tone Spectrum Circuit*: 5-way rotary pickup selector switch on upper bass bout. Mfg. 1976 to 1978.

$285 $250 $205 $185 $160 $140 $110

TREE OF LIFE - single cutaway bound mahogany body, leaf-design carved maple top, bolt-on maple neck, 22-fret maple fingerboard with vine design inlay, chrome hardware, 3-per-side headstock, tune-o-matic bridge/stop tailpiece, raised transparent pickguard, 2 humbucker pickups (1 covered, 1 exposed coils), 2 volume/2-Tone controls, 3-way selector, available in Natural finish. Mfg. circa 1973 to 1975.

$275 $225 $195 $175 $150 $125 $95

ELECTRIC BASS

MPC Series

MPC OUTLAW BASS - dual cutaway body, neck-through-body construction, 20-fret rosewood fingerboard with *bowtie* abalone inlays, brass nut, chrome hardware, 2 on a side headstock, fixed bridge, black pickguard, covered Magnaflux humbucker (neck position)/P-style pickup, volume/tone controls, 2 effects control knobs, 2 effects on/off switches, 5-way pickup selector switch on upper bass bout, available in Antique Sunburst and Charcoal Sunburst finishes. Mfg. 1978 to 1984.

$350 $300 $275 $250 $225 $200 $175
Last MSR was $695.

This model has a hinged cover on the back of the instrument that allows access to MPC modules. This cavity holds two MPC modules, and is powered by a 9-volt battery.

EL MAYA

See MAYA.

Instruments previously built in Japan from the mid 1970s to the mid 1980s.

The El Maya instruments were generally good quality solid body guitars featuring original designs and some based on Fender styles. The El Maya trademark was part of range offered by the Maya guitar producer.

(Source: Tony Bacon and Paul Day, The Guru's Guitar Guide)

ELECTRA/PHOENIX

See ELECTRA.

In 1983, St. Louis Music's Electra trademark was switched to Electra/Phoenix. These instruments were built in Japan from 1983 to 1984, and featured brass or black chrome hardware, active EQ, and custom paint jobs.

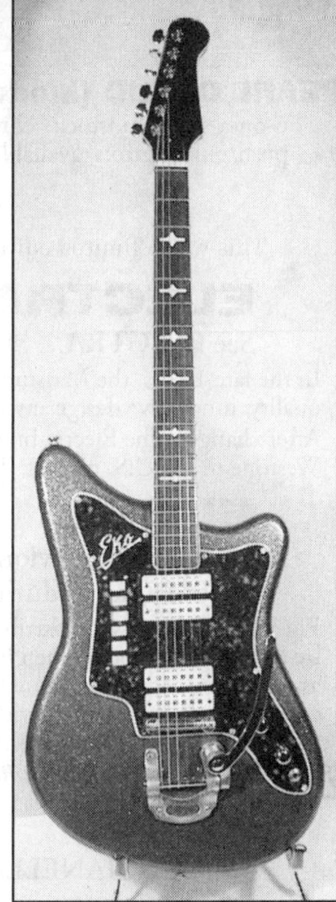
EKO 500-4V
courtesy J.R. Guitars

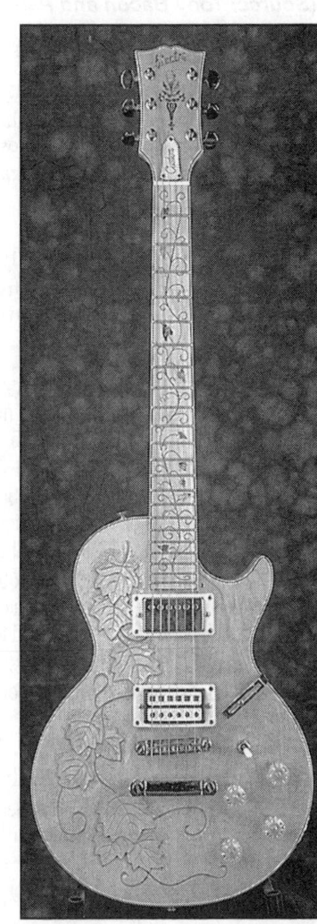
Electra "Tree of Life"
courtesy John Boyer

GRADING	100% MINT	98% NEAR MINT	95% EXC+	90% EXC	80% VG+	70% VG	60% G

PEARL CLOUD (Model X155) - offset double cutaway body, bolt-on rock maple neck, 21-fret rosewood fingerboard with white dot inlay, 6-on-a-side headstock, chrome hardware, fixed bridge/through-body stringing, blackface peghead, 2 Magnaflux humbuckers, 2 volume/2-Tone push/pull controls, available in Pearl Cloud White finish. Mfg 1982 to 1983.

$250	**$200**	**$175**	**$150**	**$125**	**$115**	**$100**

Last MSR was $379.

This was a limited edition production instrument. The push/pull controls allowed access to pickup coil tapping and phase reversal.

ELECTRA BY WESTONE

See ELECTRA.

In the late 1970s, the Matsumoku factory in Japan was beginning to build and market Westone guitars. The majority of these instruments were high quality, innovative design instruments with limited (not mass) production. Westone guitars were first introduced to the U.K. market by 1981.

After changing the Electra brandname to Electra/Phoenix in 1984, St. Louis Music announced that the Electra trademark would be merged with Westone in the U.S. market. Through 1984 to 1985, models were sold under the Electra by Westone, or Electra/Westone imprint.

ELGER

Instruments previously produced in Ardmore, Pennsylvania from 1959 to 1965. Elger began importing instruments produced in Japan during the early 1960s.

Elger instruments were distributed in the U.S. by the Elger Company of Ardmore, Pennsylvania. The roots of the Elger company were founded in 1954 by Harry Rosenbloom when he opened Medley Music in Bryn Mawr, Pennsylvania. In 1959, Rosenbloom decided to produce his own acoustic guitars as the Elger Company (named after his children, Ellen and Gerson). Rosenbloom soon turned from U.S. production to Japanese when the Elger company became partners with Hoshino Gakki Gen, and introduced the **Ibanez** trademark to the U.S. market. Elger did maintain the Pennsylvania facilities to check incoming shipments and correct any flaws prior to shipping merchandise out to their dealers. For further company history, see **Ibanez**.

(Source: Michael Wright, Guitar Stories Volume One)

ELITE

See CRUCIANELLI.

Instruments previously built in Italy during the mid 1960s.

Entry level solid body guitars that featured similar accordion-style finishes. Many Italian instrument producers were building accordions before the worldwide explosion of guitar popularity in the 1960s, and pearloid finishes are the direct result. Elite's semi-hollowbody guitars were more normal in appearance.

(Source: Tony Bacon and Paul Day, The Guru's Guitar Guide)

ELK

Instruments previously produced in Japan during the 1960s.

Elk instruments were mid-quality solid body guitars that featured some designs based on classic American favorites. Elk also produced a line of amplifiers with circuitry and cosmetics similar to Fender amps.

(Source: Rittor Books, 60s Bizarre Guitars)

ELRICK

Instruments currently built in Chicago, Illinois.

Luthier Robert Elrick handcrafts custom bass guitars. All instruments are constructed with bodies of koa or swamp ash, and feature bookmatched exotic wood tops and backs. Elrick favors Bartolini pickups and 3-band active/passive EQ pre-amps.

ELECTRIC BASS

The **Elrick Bass Guitar** has a neck-through design that features either hard maple or wenge necks reinforced with graphite stiffening rods. A 24-fret phenolic fingerboard is standard at a 35" scale, however, both 34" and 36" scale lengths are offered. The **Elrick Bass 4-String** retail lists at $3,200, the **Elrick Bass 5-string** at $3,400, **Elrick Bass 6-string** at $3,600, and the **Elrick Bass 7-String** at $3,800.

Elrick's **Empire** Bolt-On Neck bass guitar has similar construction to the neck-through model, except has a *heel-less* design and 5 bolts attaching the neck to the swamp ash or white ash body. The **Empire** is available in 4 different string configurations as the **Empire 4-String** ($2,700), **Empire 5-string** ($2,900), **Empire 6-string** ($3,100), and the **Empire 7-String** ($3,300).

The **Foundation** Bolt-On Neck bass guitar model has a solid swamp ash body, bolt-on quarter sawn wenge neck, wenge (or bubinga) fingerboard, Bartolini pickups, and 3-band active/passive preamp. The **Foundation** bass is available in 3 different string configurations as the **Foundation 4-tring** ($1,995), **Foundation 5-string** ($2,295), and the **Foundation 6-string** ($2,595).

A **Piccolo Bass Guitar** with a 28 5/8" scale (tuned one octave higher than regular bass) is offered as a custom instrument in 4-, 5-, 6-, 7-, and 8-string configurations. For further information regarding prices and specifications, contact Robert Elrick directly (see Trademark Index).

EMERY

Instruments currently built in Britt, Minnesota. Distributed by Resound Vintage Guitars of Britt, Minnesota.

Luthier Jean-Paul Emery has been customizing and building guitars as well as performing restoration work on vintage instruments for several years. For further information, contact luthier Emery directly (see Trademark Index).

GRADING	100% MINT	98% NEAR MINT	95% EXC+	90% EXC	80% VG+	70% VG	60% G

EMINENCE

Instruments currently built in Minneapolis, Minnesota.

G. Edward Lutherie, Inc. is currently offering a portable upright bass that has a fully acoustic body (that's right, it's hollow). The laminated arched spruce top is mated to laminated arched curly maple back, and combined with piezo pickups and an *L.R. Baggs Para Acoustic D.I.* This bass has an overall length of 63", and total weight of 11 pounds. Retail list price is $3,290. For further information, please contact G. Edward Lutherie, Inc. directly (see Trademark Index).

EMMONS

Instruments previously built in Burlington, North Carolina circa early 1970s. Distributed by the Emmons Guitar Company, Inc. of Burlington, North Carolina.

The Emmons Guitar Company, Inc., perhaps more well known for their steel guitars produced between the early 1970s to the early 1980s, constructed 4 different bass models in the early 1970s.

ELECTRIC BASSES

It has been estimated that the initials of the bass models correspond with the description of the bass models: For example, does the **LSB-U** model stand for "**Long Scale Bass - Unfretted**"? Because that's exactly what the model is.

LS-B - offset double cutaway (solid) body, 34" scale, 21-fret rosewood fingerboard, 2-per-side Kluson tuners, adjustable bridge, chrome hardware, black pickguard, one Emmons pickup, volume/tone controls. Mfg. circa early 1970s.

Length 46", Body Width 13".

$475	$425	$375	$325	$275	$225	$200

Last MSR was $325.

LSB-U - similar to the LS-B, except has a fretless rosewood fingerboard. Mfg. circa early 1970s.

Length 46", Body Width 13".

$475	$425	$375	$325	$275	$225	$200

Last MSR was $315.

SS-B - offset double cutaway (solid) body, 30" scale, 22-fret rosewood fingerboard, 2-per-side Kluson tuners, adjustable bridge, chrome hardware, black pickguard, one Emmons pickup, volume/tone controls. Mfg. circa early 1970s.

Length 43 1/2", Body Width 13".

$475	$425	$375	$325	$275	$225	$200

Last MSR was $325.

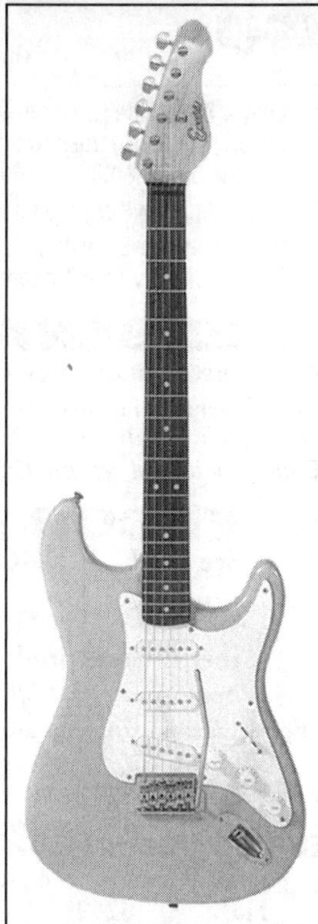

Encore E 76 IB courtesy John Hornby Skewes & Co.

EMPERADOR

Instruments previously built in Japan by the Kasuga company circa 1966 to 1992. Distributed by Westheimer Musical Instruments of Chicago, Illinois.

The Emperador trademark was a brand name used in the U.S. market by the Westheimer Musical Instruments of Chicago, Illinois. The Emperador trademark was the Westheimer company's entry level line to their Cort products line through the years. Emperador models are usually shorter-scaled entry level instruments, and the trademark can be found on both jazz-style thinline acoustic/electric archtops and solid body electric guitars and basses.

ENCORE

Instruments currently produced in Asia. Distributed by John Hornby Skewes & Co., Ltd. of Garforth (Leeds), England.

The Encore trademark is the brand name of UK importer John Hornby Skewes & Co., Ltd. The company was founded in 1965 by the namesake, Mr. John Hornby Skewes. The Encore line consists of solidly built guitars and basses that feature designs based on popular American favorites. Encore instruments are of medium to good quality, and their model E83 bass was named *Most Popular U.K. Bass Guitar* in 1992, 1993, 1994, and 1995.

In addition to the Encore line, the John Hornby Skewes company distributes the Vintage instruments line (see VINTAGE).

ELECTRIC

Though not available in the U.S. market, Encore's **RK** series is based on popular Rickenbacher stylings. For a listing of current Encore models and pricing (in English pounds), please visit John Hornby's web site: wwww.jhs.co.uk.

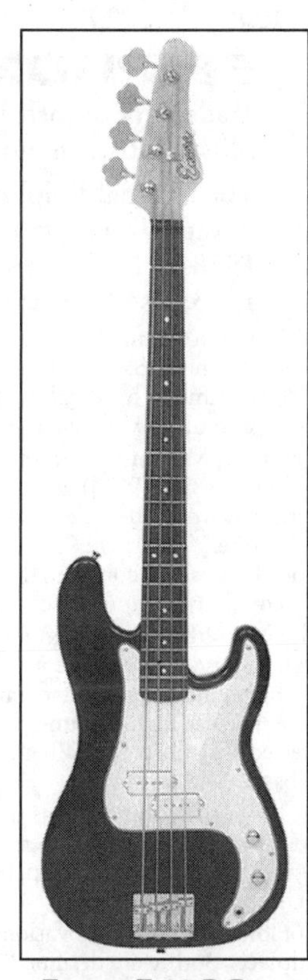

Encore E 83 B Bass courtesy John Hornby Skewes & Co.

ENGLISH GUITARS

Instruments currently built in Jamul, California since 1993.

English Guitars was founded in 1993 by Jim English. English, disappointed at the quality, price, and playability of current new guitars, decided to offer an alternative with his hand crafted Gretsch-ish guitar models. These models definitely catch the vibe of the 1950s and 1960s, and offer the guitarist the "smooth warm Nashville sound, similar to those that Chuck Berry, Duane Eddy, and Brian Setzer have, according to the catalog.

ELECTRIC

The English guitar model has a single cutaway laminated maple (plain, flame, or quilted) body, 2 bound f-holes, set-in rock maple neck, multiple-ply binding on body/neck/headstock, ebony fingerboard with gold or white mother-of-pearl

GRADING	100% MINT	98% NEAR MINT	95% EXC+	90% EXC	80% VG+	70% VG	60% G

inlays, 3-per-side Grover Imperial tuners, 2 Filtertron pickups, gold or chrome hardware, Bigsby vibrato tailpiece, 23 karat white or yellow gold leaf under raised pickguard/truss rod cover/pickup rings, master volume/individual pickup volumes/tone controls, and a pickup selector switch. The body width is 17", and the body depth is 3". English guitars are available in Black, Blue, Country Orange, Fire Orange, Honey Blonde, Sunburst, Walnut, and White finishes.

English's **Jazz King** model is similar in construction, except features a 3 1/4" body depth and a solid tailpiece.

Price range for English guitars is $3,440 - $4,600, depending on accessories. For further information regarding prices and specifications, please contact Jim English directly (see Trademark Index).

ENSENADA

Instruments previously produced in Japan, circa 1970s. Distributed by Strum & Drum of Chicago, Illinois.

The Ensenada trademark was a brandname of U.S. importers Strum & Drum of Chicago, Illinois. Strum and Drum were later owners of the National trademark, acquired when Valco's holdings were auctioned off. Ensenada instruments were distributed between roughly 1973 to 1974.

(Source: Michael Wright, Guitar Stories Volume One)

EPCORE

See BILL GRUGGETT.

EPI

Instruments produced in China or Indonesia. Distributed by Epiphone (Gibson Musical Instruments) of Nashville, Tennessee.

Epi stringed instruments are the entry level line to the current Epiphone range of guitars and basses.

ELECTRIC

ES-200 (Model ES20) - offset double cutaway plywood body, bolt-on maple neck, maple fingerboard, 6-on-a-side tuners, chrome hardware, standard tremolo, two pickups, volume/tone controls, 3-way switch, available in Ebony, Red, Vintage Sunburst, and White finishes. Current Mfg.

MSR	$249	$145	$125	$110	$100	$85	$70	$55

ES-300 (Model ES30) - similar to ES-200, except has three pickups, available in Ebony, Red, Vintage Sunburst, and White finishes. Current Mfg.

MSR	$259	$145	$125	$110	$100	$85	$70	$55

ELECTRIC BASS

EB-100 (Model EB10) - offset double cutaway plywood body, bolt-on maple neck, maple fingerboard, 4-on-a-side tuners, chrome hardware, P- style pickup, volume/tone controls, available in Ebony, Red, Vintage Sunburst, and White finishes. Current Mfg.

MSR	$289	$145	$125	$110	$100	$85	$70	$55

EPIPHONE

Trademark of instruments currently produced in Korea since 1983. Epiphone is a division of and distributed by Gibson Musical Instruments of Nashville, Tennessee.

The original Epiphone company was based in New York, New York from 1930 to 1953, and later in Philadelphia, Pennsylvania from 1954 to 1957. When Epiphone was purchased by Gibson, production moved to Kalamazoo, Michigan from 1958 to 1969; then to Japan from 1970 to 1983. Some specialty models were built in Nashville, Tenesee in 1982 to 1983, also from 1989 to 1994.

According to family history, Anastasios Stathopoulo (b. 1863) began constructing musical instruments in his home town of Sparta, Greece in 1873. He moved to the U.S. with his family is 1903, settling in New York City, where he produced a full range of stringed instruments bearing his own name up until the time of his death in 1915. The company, which soon became known as "The House of Stathopoulo", continued under the direction and ownership of his wife, Marianthe (b. 1875) and eldest son, Epaminondas (Epi [b. 1893]).

Following Marianthe's death in 1923, The House of Stathopoulo was incorporated with Epi as president and majority shareholder, his sister Alkminie (Minnie [1897-1984]) as treasurer, and brother Orpheus (Orphie [1899-1973]) as secretary. They immediately announced "The new policy of business" would be "the production of banjos, tenor banjos, banjo mandolins, banjo guitars, and banjo ukuleles under the registered trademark of **Epiphone.**" The name "Epiphone" was a combination of Epi's nickname with "phone", the Greek word for sound. Their elegant "Recording" line of tenor banjos was considered to be amongst the finest ever made. These were joined in the late 1920s by a full line of Recording model guitars. In 1928, the company's name was changed to "The Epiphone Banjo Co."

The **Masterbilt** series of guitars was introduced in 1931 and marked Epiphone's entrance into the production of modern, carved, "f"-hole archtop guitars, based on violin construction principles. Indeed, at the time of their introduction, the Masterbilt guitar line was the most complete selection of "f"-hole guitars available from any instrument maker in the world. Complementary Spanish and Hawaiian flattop models and carved-top mandolins were likewise included under the Masterbilt aigis. Soon, Epiphone advertisements would claim that it was "The World's Largest Producer of First Grade Fretted Instruments." Whether this was an accurate boast or not, it set the stage for a two decade rivalry between Epiphone and its largest competitor, Gibson.

By 1935, the company was now known simply as "Epiphone, Inc.", and was producing its "Electar" brand of electric Hawaiian and Spanish guitars, as well as amplifiers which were designed by electronics pioneer and Danelectro founder, Nat Daniels (1912-1994). That same year marked the introduction of the flagship 18 3/8" **Emperor** model archtop guitar and signaled the re-design and enlargement of the company's entire Masterbilt archtop line.

Notable Epiphone innovations in this era included the first patented electronic pickup with individual pole pieces and the distinctive "Frequensator" tailpiece. Both were designed by salesman and acknowledged jack-of-all-trades, Herb Sunshine (1906-1988), and in production by 1937. In 1940, the company also introduced a full line of well respected bass violins produced under the watchful eye of the youngest of the Stathopoulo brothers, Frixo (b. 1905) who had joined the firm in the early 1930s.

During this period, Epiphone's growing product line was considered second to none, and could boast such endorsers as George Van Eps (with the Ray Noble Orchestra), Carmen Mastren (with Tommy Dorsey), Allan Reuss (with Benny Goodman's band), and many, many more.

Epi Stathopoulo died from leukemia in 1943 at the age of 49, and this, combined with the many hardships incurred during World War II, set the company on a downward spiral. Orphie Stathopoulo, who took over as president, was unable to recapture the momentum of the prewar years, and constant friction between he and his brother Frixo (now vice-president) began to pull the company apart at the seams.

In 1951, simmering labor problems resulted in a strike which shut down the New York plant for several months. During this time, Orphie sold a stake in the business to the large distribution company, Continental Music. Continental moved production to Philadelphia, and most instruments manufactured from 1952 to 1957 were made there. It is doubtful, however, if much was produced in the final two years, as Epiphone was rapidly being overtaken by new entrants into the guitar market, notably Fender and Guild, the later of which had ironically been started by many former Epiphone employees under the leadership of Alfred Dronge and former Epiphone executive, George Mann.

It had become increasingly apparent that Epiphone was no longer capable of developing the new products necessary to capture the imagination of the guitar-buying public and its financial viability had come to an end. Following Frixo's sudden death in 1957, Orphie, by now the company's sole owner, approached Gibson president Ted McCarty, who had previously expressed interest in buying Epiphone's bass violin production. A deal was signed and trucks were dispatched from Kalamazoo to New York and Philadelphia to make the move. Records during this time period indicate that the out-of-work ex-Epiphone workers in New Berlin, New York "celebrated" by hosting a bonfire behind the plant with any available lumber (both finished and unfinished!). When the vans returned to the Gibson warehouse in Michigan, McCarty realized (much to his surprise) that not only had he received the bass-making operation, but all the jigs, fixtures, and machinery necessary for making guitars, plus much of the work in progress. For the sum of $20,000, Gibson had acquired it's once mighty rival (including what would become the most profitable trademark) lock, stock, and barrel.

It was decided that Epiphone would be re-established as a first rate guitar manufacturer, so that Gibson's parent company CMI (Chicago Musical Instruments) could offer a product comparable in every way to Gibson. This was done primarily as a way of offering music stores which, due to existing contractual obligations in a particular sales area, were not allowed to carry the exclusive Gibson line. The Epiphone brand could now be offered to competing retailers who were also carrying many of the other well-known brands which were distributed by the giant CMI. Though Epiphone was set up as an autonomous company, in a separate part of the Gibson complex, parallel product lines were soon established, and Gibson was (in effect) competing with itself.

After Epiphone was moved to Kalamazoo, instruments were built in the U.S through 1969. In 1970, production was moved overseas. Instruments were originally built in Japan (1970-1983), but during the early 1980s, Japanese production costs became pricey due to the changing ratio of the dollar/yen.

Since 1984, the majority of guitars have been produced in Korea. However, there have been a number of models like the Spirit, Special, USA Pro, and USA Coronet that were produced in Nashville, Tennessee. These models are the exception to the rule. Epiphone currently offers a very wide range of acoustic, semi-hollow, and solid body electric guitars.

In 1998, Epiphone offered the new **EZ-Bender**, a detachable "B" string bender that can be installed on any guitar equipped with a stop bar tailpiece. The EZ-Bender can be installed with no modifications whatsoever to the guitar.

(Source: N.Y. Epiphone information by L.B. Fred and Jim Fisch, Epiphone: The House of Stathopoulo)

(Additional Epiphone history courtesy Walter Carter, Epiphone: The Complete History)

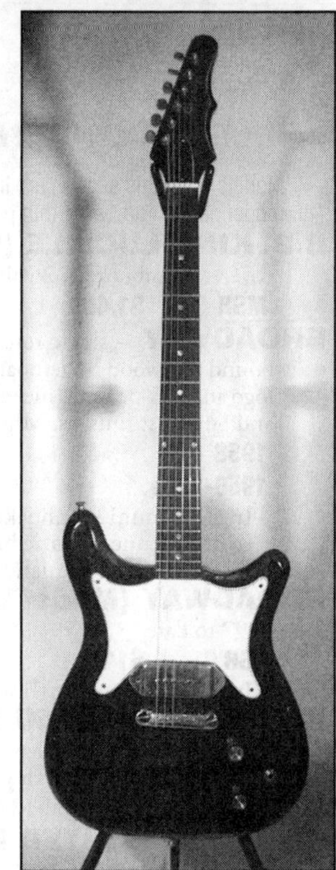

Epiphone courtesy Willies American Guitars

PRODUCTION LOCATION:

Epiphone guitars have been produced in a wide range of places. The following list gives a rough approximation to production facilities by year.

Epiphone-owned production:

Guitars produced from the late 1920s up to the time of Gibson's purchase of the company are known by collectors as "New York Epiphones".

New York, NY	**Late 1920s to 1952**
Philadelphia, PA	**1952 to 1957**

Gibson-owned production:

Kalamazoo, MI	**1958 to 1969**
Japan	**1970 to 1983**
Taiwan	**1979 to 1981**
Nashville, TN	**1982 to 1983 (Spirit, Special, U.S. Map)**
Korea	**1983 to date**
Japan	**1988 to 1989 (Spotlights, Thinlines)**
Nashville, TN	**1989 to 1994 (USA Pro)**
Nashville, TN	**1991 to 1994 (USA Coronet)**
China	**1997 to date**
Indonesia	**1997 to date**

For further information on Epiphone acoustic models, please refer to the 7th Edition ***Blue Book of Acoustic Guitars***. The Epiphone Chet Atkins Series models will be found in the Acoustic edition.

GRADING		100% MINT	98% NEAR MINT	95% EXC+	90% EXC	80% VG+	70% VG	60% G

ELECTRIC ARCHTOP

Models witin this section are listed alphbetically first, then by series in alphabetical order. On many models, the Epiphone family model name is listed after the model name/number within parentheses. Also, any older nomenclature may appear with the parentheses.

B.B. KING LUCILLE (Model ETBB) - dual cutaway semi-hollow body, 22-fret rosewood fingerboard with block inlay, gold hardware, 2 covered humbuckers, 2 volume/2-Tone controls, 3-way toggle switch, 6-position Vari-Phase switch, available in Ebony finish. Current Mfg.

		100%	98%	95%	90%	80%	70%	60%
MSR	$1,499	$1,100	$950	$850	$750	$625	$525	$375

BROADWAY - single round cutaway hollow style, spruce top, f-holes, raised bound black pickguard, bound body, maple back/sides/neck, 20-fret bound rosewood fingerboard with pearl block inlay, adjustable rosewood bridge/Frequensator tailpiece, bound blackface peghead with pearl column/logo inlay, 3-per-side nickel tuners with plastic buttons, 2 single coil pickups, volume/tone control, 3-position switch, available in Blonde, Cherry and Sunburst finishes. Mfg. 1958 to 1970.

	100%	98%	95%	90%	80%	70%	60%
1958	$2,750	$2,500	$2,200	$2,000	$1,750	$1,575	$1,300
1959-1970	$1,600	$1,300	$1,050	$900	$740	$675	$550

In 1961, mini humbucker pickups replaced original part/designs.
In 1963, tune-o-matic bridge replaced original part/design.
In 1967, Cherry finish became an option.

BROADWAY (Model ETBW) - contemprary re-issue, available in Antique Sunburst, Ebony, Natural, and Vintage Cherry Sunburst. Mfg. 1997 to date.

		100%	98%	95%	90%	80%	70%	60%
MSR	$1499	$1,050	$925	$825	$725	$600	$500	$375

In 2000, Ebony finish was disc.

FLAMEKAT LIMITED EDITION (HELLKAT, Model ETA1) - single cutaway design, laminated maple top, mahogany body, maple set neck with rosewood fingeboard, dice inlays, f-holes, chrome hardware, 2 "New York" Mini-Humbucker pickups, Vibratone tailpiece, dice knobs. Ebony finish with yellow and red flames. New 1999.

		100%	98%	95%	90%	80%	70%	60%
MSR	$1,159	$815	$715	$600	$550	$500	$450	$400

ALLEYKAT LIMITED EDITION (Model ETAK) -single cutaway semi-hollow body design, mahogany body, flame maple top, maple set neck, rosewood fingerboard with pearl block inlays, 3-per-side tuners, f-holes, chrome hardware, 1 New York mini humbucker in the neck position and 1 '57 classic humbucker in the bridge position, Tune-O-Matic bridge, stop tailpiece, master volume, available in Heritage Cherry Sunburst, Transparent Black, and Vintage Sunburst finishes. New 2000.

		100%	98%	95%
MSR	$799	$525	$400	$300

WILDKAT LIMITED EDITION (Model ETBK) -single cutaway semi-hollow body design, mahogany body, flame maple top, maple set neck, rosewood fingerboard with dot inlays, 3-per-side tuners, f-holes, chrome hardware, 2 Alnico-V P-90 pickups, Vibrotone tailpiece, master volume, available in Transparent Black, Turquoise, and Antique Natural finishes. New 2000.

		100%	98%	95%
MSR	$799	$525	$400	$300

Caiola Series

CAIOLA CUSTOM - 16" body width, thin double cutaway body, laminated top, multiple body binding, 25 1/2" scale, bound rosewood fingerboard with block inlay and "Custom" on end of neck, zero fret, ebony adjustable bridge/trapeze tailpiece with Caiola Model inlaid in trapeze insert, bound peghead, peghead inlay, 2 mini-humbucker pickups, 2 volume controls, 5 switches, pickup selector switch, available in Black, Walnut, and Yellow Sunburst finishes. Mfg. 1963 to 1970.

100%	98%	95%	90%	80%	70%	60%
$1,350	$1,200	$1,075	$950	$900	$850	$700

Caiola Standard - similar to Caiola Custom, except features single body binding, dot fingerboard inlay, unbound peghead, no peghead inlay, 2 P-90 pickups. Mfg. 1966 to 1970.

100%	98%	95%	90%	80%	70%	60%
$1,150	$1,050	$950	$900	$850	$800	$650

Casino Series

CASINO - 16" body width, thin double rounded cutaway hollow body, bound laminate body, 24 3/4" scale, bound fingerboard with dot inlay, tune-o-matic bridge/trapeze tailpiece, white 3-ply pickguard, 2 P-90 pickups (early models had 1 pickup), volume/tone controls, pickup selector switch, available in Royal Tan or Sunburst finishes. Mfg. 1962 to 1969.

	100%	98%	95%	90%	80%	70%	60%
1961-1965	$2,300	$2,100	$1,900	$1,500	$1,200	$1,000	$900
1966-1969	$1,600	$1,200	$950	$900	$850	$750	$650

Some models may feature a single humbucker pickup.

CASINO (Model ETCA) - contemporary re-issue, available in Cherry, Ebony, Natural, and Vintage Cherry Sunburst finishes. Current Mfg.

		100%	98%	95%	90%	80%	70%	60%
MSR	$999	$700	$595	$425	$375	$325	$295	$250

Add $150 for metallic finishes: Black Metallic, Metallic Light Blue, Metallic Burgundy Mist, and Turquoise finishes.

Add $250 for metal flake finishes: Gold Flake and Silver Flake finishes.

Vintage Cherry Sunburst finish disc.

All metallic finishes disc except turquoise which is now included without the premium.

All metal flake finishes disc.

Casino Reissue with Vibrotone (Model ETCA) - Available in Ebony, Gold Flake, Natural, Silver Flake, Turquoise, and Vintage Cherry Sunburst. Mfg. 1997 to date.

		100%	98%	95%	90%	80%	70%	60%
MSR	$1,249	$950	$875	$775	$650	$550	$425	$325

GRADING		100% MINT	98% NEAR MINT	95% EXC+	90% EXC	80% VG+	70% VG	60% G

Casino Left-Handed (Model ETCAL) - Available in Vintage Cherry Sunburst finish. Mfg. 1997 to 1999.

		$875	$750	$650	$575	$495	$400	$275

Last MSR was $1,099.

JOHN LENNON "1965" CASINO (Model USC 5) - assembled in the USA, original body shape, mid-60's Kalamazoo tooling specs, five-layer body of maple and birch, top contour bracing, one piece mahogany neck with 14 degree grain orientation, rosewood fingerboard with Pearloid parallelogram fret markers, neck joint at 17th fret, neck binding covers fret ends, Corian nut, mother-of-pearl headstock logo, Gibson-factory electronics, nickel plated P-90 pickup covers, Switchcraft 3-way toggle switch with old style black washer, nickel ABR bridge with nylon saddles, 3-ply pickguard, nickel Gibson-factory hardware with nickel Gotoh Kluson style machine heads, available in Vintage Sunburst nitrocellulose finish. Vintage style case with shroud included. Mfg. 1999 to date.

MSR	$2,995	$2,100	$1,500	$1,200	$1,000	$875	$800	$725

JOHN LENNON "REVOLUTION" CASINO (Model USCR) - similar to John Lennon "1965" Casino, except has "Stripped" Vintage Natural nitrocellulose finish as John's original guitar appeared after being refinished. Also features gold Grover tuners and dents, holes from original Kluson tuners for authenticity. Vintage style case with shroud included. 1999 to date.

MSR	$2,995	$2,100	$1,500	$1,200	$1,000	$875	$800	$725

CENTURY (1939-1957 Mfg.) - single bound laminated mahogany body, 14/20-fret bound rosewood fingerboard with dot inlays, single (non-adjustable) pickup with handrest, bakelite pickguard, trapeze tailpiece, individual tuners with plastic buttons, metal peghead logo plate, volume/tone controls (octagon knobs), available in Sunburst finish, Mfg. 1939 to 1957.

14 3/4" body width.

1939-1949		$500	$450	$400	$350	$300	$250	$200
1950-1957		$650	$600	$550	$500	$450	$400	$350

In 1941, 15 1/2" body, tortoise pickguard replaced original part/designs; hand rest removed.
By 1950, 16 3/8" maple body, Tone Spectrum pickup replaced original part/designs.
In 1954, DeArmond pickup, clear barrel knobs replaced original part/designs; Blonde finish was optional.

CENTURY (1958-1970 Mfg.) - 16 3/8" body width, thin hollow body, 25 1/2" scale, dot fingerboard inlay, rosewood bridge/trapeze tailpiece, tortoise pickguard, metal peghead logo plate, P-90 pickup, volume/tone controls, available in Sunburst finish. Mfg. 1958 to 1970.

		$700	$650	$600	$500	$400	$325	$300

CORONET (1939-1949 Mfg.) - non-adjustable single body binding, dot fingerboard inlay, trapeze tailpiece, metal peghead logo plate, volume/tone controls, available in Brown Sunburst finish. Mfg. 1939 to 1949.

14 3/8" body width.

		$500	$450	$400	$375	$325	$300	$250

Epiphone John Lennon Model
courtesy Guitarzan

Emperor Series

The Emperor contemporary re-issue model was introduced in 1982, as the Emperor F and the Emperor (T) models (available in Antique Sunburst). In 1992, Natural finish was introduced; in 1993, the Emperor II (Model ETE2) pre-empted the Emperor. Two years later, jazz guitar great Joe Pass "adopted" the Emperor II as his signature model. The silk-screened signature on the pickguard would begin on models from 1995 production on (models 1992 to 1994 would not have this silk- screened logo on the pickguard).

Epiphone's "Imperial Collection" model Emperor 1930's (Model EIEM) was introduced in 1993. This premium model was built in Japan. The Emperor 1930's was renamed Emperor Re-Issue in 1994, but did not last into 1995 (last retail list was $3,100).

JOE PASS EMPEROR II (Model ETE2, EMPEROR II, EMPEROR) - single round cutaway hollow style, arched bound laminated maple top, 2 f-holes, bound tortoise pickguard with stylized E logo, laminated maple back/sides, 3-piece maple neck, 24 ¾" scale, 20-fret bound rosewood fingerboard with pearl block inlay, adjustable rosewood bridge/stylized trapeze tailpiece, bound peghead with pearl vine/logo inlay, 3-per-side tuners, gold hardware, 2 covered humbucker pickups with exposed screws, 2 volume/tone controls, 3-position switch, available in Natural and Vintage Sunburst finishes. Mfg. 1982 to 1992 (as EMPEROR), 1993 to 1994 (as EMPEROR II), 1995 to date (JOE PASS EMPEROR II).

1982-1992		$500	$400	$350	$300	$275	$250	$225
1993-1994		$600	$500	$400	$350	$325	$285	$250
1995-1997		$800	$700	$625	$525	$450	$350	$275
MSR	$1,149	$800	$700	$625	$525	$450	$350	$275

In 1994, Heritage Cherry Sunburst finish was introduced.
In 1995, silk-screened "Joe Pass" signature added to pickguard.
In 1996, select spruce top replaced laminated maple top; Metallic Gold and Wine Red finishes were introduced.
In 2000, Metallic Gold and Wine Red finishes disc.

Emperor II Left-Handed (Model ETE2L) - Available in Natural finish. Current Mfg.

MSR	$1,199	$850	$725	$650	$550	$475	$375	$300

Epiphone Joe Pass Emperor II
courtesy The Epiphone Co.

GRADING	100% MINT	98% NEAR MINT	95% EXC+	90% EXC	80% VG+	70% VG	60% G

EMPEROR REGENT (Model ETEM) - single round cutaway hollow style, arched bound spruce top, bound f-holes, raised bound black pickguard with stylized E logo, maple back/sides/neck, 20-fret bound rosewood fingerboard with pearl block/abalone triangle inlay, adjustable rosewood bridge/Frequensator tailpiece, bound peghead with pearl vine/logo inlay, 3-per-side tuners, gold hardware, covered humbucker pickup with exposed screws, pickguard mounted volume/tone controls, available in Antique Sunburst, Natural, and Vintage Cherry Sunburst finishes. Mfg. 1994 to date.

MSR $1,399	$1,000	$850	$750	$650	$550	$450	$350

Add $200 for metallic finishes: Black Metallic, Metallic Light Blue, Metallic Burgundy Mist, and Turquoise finishes. Disc. 1998.

Add $300 for metallic flake finishes: Gold Flake and Silver Flake finishes. Disc. 1998.

E

Granada Series

GRANADA - 16 1/4" body width, thin hollow body, dot fingerboard inlay, one f-hole, rosewood bridge/trapeze tailpiece, one Melody Maker pickup, volume/tone controls, available in Sunburst finish. Mfg. 1962 to 1970.

	$500	$450	$400	$375	$350	$325	$300

Granada Cutaway - similar to the Granada, except features a single pointed cutaway. Mfg. 1965 to 1970.

	$600	$550	$500	$400	$375	$350	$325

KENT - single bound laminated arched mahogany body (with flat back), 14/20-fret rosewood fingerboard with dot inlays, single large (non-adjustable) Tone Spectrum pickup, tortoise pickguard, trapeze tailpiece, 3-on-a-strip tuners with plastic buttons, metal peghead logo plate, volume/tone controls (octagon knobs), available in Sunburst finish. Mfg. 1949 to 1954.

15 3/8" body width.

	$500	$450	$400	$375	$350	$325	$300

HARRY VOLPE - bound body, dot fingerboard inlay, trapeze tailpiece, metal peghead logo plate, non-adjustable DeArmond pickup, volume/tone controls, available in Sunburst finish. Mfg. 1955 to 1957.

15 1/4" body width.

	$600	$550	$500	$400	$375	$325	$300

Howard Roberts Series

HOWARD ROBERTS STANDARD - single sharp cutaway hollow style, arched spruce top, bound oval soundhole/body, mahogany back/sides/neck, 20-fret bound rosewood fingerboard with pearl slotted block inlay, adjustable rosewood bridge/trapeze tailpiece, blackface peghead with pearl cloud/logo inlay, 3-per-side tuners, nickel tuners, mini humbucker pickup, volume/tone control, available in Cherry finish. Mfg. 1964 to 1970.

	$1,900	$1,400	$1,080	$900	$720	$650	$595

This instrument was co-designed by Howard Roberts.

In 1965, 3-stripe purfling was introduced, Natural and Sunburst finishes became optional. In 1967, tune-o-matic/rosewood base bridge replaced original part/design. In 1968, Natural and Sunburst finishes became standard, Cherry finish was disc.

HOWARD ROBERTS (Model ETHR) - contemporary re-issue, available in Translucent Black and Wine Red finishes. Disc. 2000.

	$775	$675	$595	$525	$425	$350	$275

Last MSR was $1,099.

NOEL GALLAGHER SUPERNOVA (Model ETSN) - Available in Ebony, Cherry, Metallic Light Blue, and Vintage Sunburst finishes.

MSR $1,299	$900	$775	$675	$595	$500	$425	$325

This model was developed in conjunction with Noel Gallagher (Oasis).

In 1999, the "Union Jack" variation was introduced at no additional cost. In 1999, Ebony, Cherry and Vintage Sunburst finishes were disc.

PROFESSIONAL - 16" body width, thin double rounded cutaway bound body, tune-o-matic bridge, Frequensator tailpiece, single parallelogram fingerboard inlay, mini-humbucker, 2 knobs (treble side), 3 knobs and multiple switches (bass side), multi-prong jack, 1/4" jack, available in Mahogany finish. Mfg. 1961 to 1967.

With Amp	$1,650	$1,400	$1,200	$1,000	$900	$800	$700
Without Amp	$1,000	$850	$750	$700	$600	$500	$450

This guitar model was paired with the Professional model amp, which had no control knobs on the faceplate. All controls were mounted on the front of the guitar, and controlled the amp through the cable attached to the multiprong jack. The amp was rated at 15 watts, and had a 12" speaker. When this combination was introduced in the 1963 Epiphone catalog as the Professional Outfit (Model EA7P), the original retail price was $495.

Riviera Series

RIVIERA - 16" body width, thin double cutaway body, bound fingerboard with single parallelogram inlay, bound body, tune-o-matic bridge/trapeze tailpiece, bound tortoiseshell pickguard, 2 mini-humbucker pickups, volume/tone controls, available in Royal Tan finish. Mfg. 1962 to 1970.

	$1,200	$1,000	$900	$750	$700	$600	$500

RIVIERA (Model ETRI) - contemporary re-issue, available in Cherry, Ebony, Natural, and Vintage Cherry Sunburst finishes. Current Mfg.

MSR $1,099	$775	$675	$595	$525	$425	$350	$275

Add $150 for metallic finishes: Black Metallic, Metallic Light Blue, Metallic Burgundy Mist, and Turquoise finishes. Disc 1998.

Add $250 for metallic flake finishes: Gold Flake and Silver Flake finishes. Disc 1998.

In 2000, Natural and Vintage Cherry Sunburst finishes were disc.

GRADING		100% MINT	98% NEAR MINT	95% EXC+	90% EXC	80% VG+	70% VG	60% G

Riviera with Vibrotone (Model ETRI) - similar to the Riviera, except features a Bigsby-derived Vibrotone tremolo, available in Cherry, Gold Flake, Silver Flake, and Turquoise finishes. Mfg. 1997 to 1998.

		$950	$875	$795	$695	$575	$475	$375

Last MSR was $1,499.

JORMA KAUKONEN RIVIERA DELUXE (Model ETJK) -similar to Model ETRI except has gold hardware, laminated maple body, gold Vibratone tailpiece, Grover machine heads, 2 Epiphone '57 Classic Alnico-V pickups, available in Cherry finish. New 2000.

MSR	$1,159	$825	$600	$550	$500	$450	$400	$350

Riviera 12-string (Model ETR2) - Available in Cherry, Ebony, Natural, and Vintage Cherry Sunburst finishes. Mfg. 1997 to 2000.

		$850	$725	$650	$550	$475	$375	$300

Last MSR was $1,199.

Epiphone Sheraton
courtesy The Epiphone Co.

Sheraton Series

SHERATON - double rounded cutaway, arched bound maple top, f-holes, raised bound tortoise pickguard with stylized E logo, maple back/sides, center block maple neck, 22-fret bound rosewood fingerboard with pearl/abalone block/triangle inlay, tune-o-matic bridge/stop tailpiece, bound peghead with pearl vine/logo inlay, 3-per-side tuners, gold hardware, 2 humbucker covered pickups with exposed screws, 2 volume/tone controls, 3-position switch, available in Cherry and Sunburst finishes. Mfg. 1959 to 1970.

1959-1960		$5,200	$4,850	$4,500	$3,800	$3,100	$2,400	$1,700
1961-1970		$2,800	$2,600	$2,300	$2,000	$1,750	$1,400	$950

Reissued 1980 to 1981. Produced in Japan.

1980-1981		$750	$700	$625	$550	$475	$400	$325

Reintroduced in 1993. Produced in Korea. Mfg. 1993 to 1995.

1993-1995		$520	$390	$325	$260	$235	$215	$195

This model has laminated body and neck wood.
Earlier models have either a Frequensator or gold plated Bigsby vibrato.

SHERATON II (Model ETS2) - contemporary re-issue, available in Ebony, Natural, Pearl White, and Vintage Sunburst finishes. Mfg. 1997 to date.

MSR	$1,049	$735	$625	$550	$475	$400	$325	$275

In 2000, Pearl White finish was disc.

Sheraton II Left-Handed (Model ETS2L) - Available in Vintage Sunburst finish. Mfg. 1997 to date.

MSR	$1,099	$775	$675	$595	$525	$425	$350	$275

JOHN LEE HOOKER SIGNATURE 1964 SHERATON (Model USS1) -faithful reproduction of John Lee Hooker's original 1964 Sheraton, multi-bound original body shape and materials, larger original style headstock, 17 degree angle, top contour bracing, spruce/maple/spruce, original relief cut and spacing, solid center block construction, 1-piece mahogany neck with 14 degree grain orientation, neck joint at 19th fret, rosewood fingerboard with original mother-of-pearl and Abalone block and triangle inlays, 2 gold plated "New York" mini humbucking pickups, 5-layer bound pickguard, gold plated Gibson hardware, Grover machine heads, Switchcraft 3-way toggle, Frequensator tailpiece, Antique Natural Nitro Cellulose Lacquer finish. New 2000.

MSR	$2,995	$2,100	$1,500	$1,200	$1,000	$875	$800	$725

JOHN LEE HOOKER SIGNATURE 1964 SHERATON II (Model USS2) -similar to Model USS1 except has stop tailpiece and is available in Vintage Sunburst finish. New 2000.

MSR	$2,995	$2,100	$1,500	$1,200	$1,000	$875	$800	$725

Sorrento Series

SORRENTO - 16 1/4" body width, thin single pointed cutaway body, 24 3/4" scale, dot fingerboard inlay, tune-o-matic bridge/trapeze tailpiece, tortoiseshell pickguard, metal peghead logo plate, nickel hardware, 2 mini-humbucker pickups, volume/tone controls, pickup selector switch, available in Natural, Sunburst, and Royal Tan finish. Mfg. 1960 to 1970.

		$1,450	$1,000	$800	$750	$700	$600	$500

This model was also available with a single mini-humbucker pickup.
This model was also available in a 3/4" size (22" scale) configuration (Mfg. 1961 to 1962).

SORRENTO (Model ETSO) - contemporary re-issue, available in Antique Sunburst, Cherry, Ebony, Orange, and Vintage Cherry Sunburst. Disc. 2000.

		$700	$595	$525	$450	$395	$325	$250

Last MSR was $999.

Add $150 for metallic finishes: Black Metallic, Metallic Light Blue, Metallic Burgundy Mist, and Turquoise finishes.

Add $250 for metallic flake finishes: Gold Flake and Silver Flake finishes.

Sorrento with Vibrotone (Model ETSO) - similar to Sorrento, except features a Bigsby-derived Vibrotone tremolo, available in Gold Flake, Orange, Silver Flake, and Turquoise finishes. Mfg. 1997 to 1998.

		$950	$875	$795	$695	$575	$475	$375

Last MSR was $1,499.

Epiphone Shenaton-E212T
courtesy Dave Hanson

GRADING	100% MINT	98% NEAR MINT	95% EXC+	90% EXC	80% VG+	70% VG	60% G

Sorrento Left-Handed (Model ETSOL) - similar to Sorrento, except in a left-handed configuration, available in Orange finish. Mfg. 1997 to 1999.

		$775	$675	$595	$525	$450	$350	$275

Last MSR was $1,099.

Zephyr Series

ZEPHYR - maple top, multiple body binding, bound fingerboard with block inlay, bound body, trapeze tailpiece, metal peghead logo plate, 2 knobs on round *Mastervoicer* plate, single oblong pickup, available in Blonde finish. Mfg. 1939 to 1957.

16 3/8" body width.

		$950	$850	$750	$650	$550	$500	$450

By 1948, a 17 3/8" body width, Tone Spectrum pickup replaced original part/designs; Sunburst finish was introduced.

ZEPHYR BLUES DELUXE (Model ETA3) - based on the 1949 Gibson ES-5, Flame Maple top, Flame maple body, maple set neck, rosewood fingerboard with block inlays, bound body and neck, f-holes, 3 Alnico-V P-90 pickups, 3 volume controls and 1 master tone control, gold hardware, available in Natural and Vintage Sunburst finishes. New 1999.

MSR	$1,599	$1,120	$950	$850	$750	$650	$550	$450

Zephyr De Luxe - spruce top, bound rosewood fingerboard with cloud inlay, multiple body binding, bound pickguard, bound peghead with vine inlay, Frequensator tailpiece, gold hardware, oblong pickup with slot head screw poles, volume/tone controls on shared shaft with *Mastervoicer* control plate, available in Blonde finish. Mfg. 1941 to 1954.

17 3/8" body width.

		$1,600	$1,400	$1,200	$1,000	$900	$800	$700

In 1950, this model was available with 2-Tone Spectrum pickups and/or Sunburst finish. In 1954, this model was re-designated the De Luxe Electric.

Zephyr De Luxe Regent - rounded cutaway, laminated spruce top, bound rosewood fingerboard with V-block inlay, multiple body binding, bound pickguard, bound peghead with vine inlay, Frequensator tailpiece, gold hardware, 2 rectangular pickups, 2 knobs, *Mastervoicer* control plates, available in Blonde and Sunburst finishes. Mfg. 1949 to 1958.

17 3/8" body width.

		$2,500	$2,300	$1,900	$1,700	$1,600	$1,400	$1,100

In 1954, this model was re-designated the De Luxe Electric.

Zephyr Emperor Regent - rounded cutaway, laminated spruce top, bound rosewood fingerboard with V-block inlay, multiple body binding, bound pickguard, bound peghead, Frequensator tailpiece, gold hardware, 3 pickups, 2 knobs, 6 push buttons on control plate, available in Blonde and Sunburst finishes. Mfg. 1950 to 1958.

18 1/2" body width.

		$3,200	$2,800	$2,300	$1,700	$1,500	$1,100	$1,000

In 1954, this model was re-designated the Emperor Electric.

Zephyr Regent - rounded cutaway, laminate maple top, 20-fret bound rosewood fingerboard with notched rectangle inlay, single body binding, tortoiseshell pickguard, trapeze tailpiece, nickel hardware, one pickup, volume/tone controls, available in Natural and Sunburst finishes. Mfg. 1950 to 1957.

17 3/8" body width.

		$1,200	$1,000	$900	$800	$750	$700	$625

In 1954, this model was re-designated the Zephyr Electric.

ZEPHYR REGENT (Model ETA2) - florentine body style, laminated maple top, mahogany body, maple set neck, rosewood fingerboard with split parallelogram inlays, bound body and neck, f-holes, 1 Humbucker pickup, gold hardware, white pickguard, available in Ebony (disc. 2000), Natural, and Vintage Sunburst finishes. New 1999.

MSR	$899	$630	$535	$475	$425	$375	$325	$275

ELECTRIC

Models witin this section are listed alphbetically by series. On many models, the Epiphone family model name is listed after the model name/number in parentheses. Also, any older nomenclature may appear within the parentheses.

The **Special II Gig Rig** package (list $529) includes a Special II electric guitar, Studio 10 amplifier, cord, Qwik-Tune quartz tuner, black gig bag, strap, picks, and a 30 minute Guitar Essentials Hal Leonard video tape. The **S-210 Gig Rig** package (list $529) is similar but substitutes an S-210 electric guitar.

For guitarists on the move, Epiphone also offers the **LP PeeWee Rave Rig** package (list $299) that features a Les Paul mini electric guitar, 9-volt Mini-Tweed amplifier, strap, cord, and gig bag.

435i (Korea Mfg.) - offset double cutaway body, bolt-on maple neck, rosewood fingerboard, *Bennder* tremolo system, black hardware, 2 single coil/humbucker pickups, volume/tone controls, 5-way selector switch. Mfg. 1989 to 1992.

		$375	$325	$275	$250	$225	$200	$150

Last MSR was $399.

635i (Korea Mfg.) - similar to the 435i, except features a Floyd Rose tremolo. Mfg. 1989 to 1992.

		$395	$350	$300	$275	$250	$225	$175

Last MSR was $599.

935i (Korea Mfg.) - similar to the 435i, except features single coil/humbucker pickups, Floyd Rose tremolo. Mfg. 1989 to 1992.

		$395	$350	$300	$275	$250	$225	$175

Last MSR was $769.

GRADING	100% MINT	98% NEAR MINT	95% EXC+	90% EXC	80% VG+	70% VG	60% G

America Series

Both the U.S.-built Special and Spirit models have "Epiphone USA" on the headstock.

SPECIAL (U.S. Mfg.) - SG-style body, set-in neck, rosewood fingerboard with dot inlay, chrome hardware, stop tailpiece, 1 (or 2) humbucker pickups. Mfg. 1982 to 1983.

$595 $525 $450 $400 $350 $300 $250

SPIRIT (U.S. Mfg.) - Les Paul-style double cutaway body, set-in neck, bound rosewood fingerboard with dot inlay, stoptail bridge, chrome hardware, 3-per-side tuners, 1 (or 2) humbucker pickups, volume/tone controls. Mfg. 1982 to 1983.

$1,100 $975 $850 $750 $650 $525 $400

This model is similar to the Gibson version Spirit model. Some of the Epiphone models may have bound, figured maple tops.

Coronet Series

CORONET (U.S. Mfg.) - dual cutaway body, glue-in neck, dot fingerboard inlay, bridge/tailpiece combination, metal peghead logo plate, one pickup, volume/tone controls, available in Black and Sunburst finish. Mfg. 1958 to 1969.

$1,200 $1,100 $950 $900 $800 $700 $600

In 1959, P-90 pickups replaced the original part/design.
This model originally was a single pickup Crestwood model.

CORONET (Model EECO) - contemporary re-issue, available in Black Metallic, Metallic Blue, Metallic Green, Metallic Purple, and Red Metallic finishes. Mfg. 1995 to 2000.

$350 $300 $275 $225 $195 $150 $125
Last MSR was $499.

Coronet with Vibrotone (Model EECO) - similar to the Coronet, but equipped with a Bigsby-style Vibrotone tremolo bridge, available in Black Metallic, Metallic Blue, Metallic Green, Metallic Purple, and Red Metallic finishes. Mfg. 1997 to 1999.

$425 $375 $325 $275 $250 $195 $150
Last MSR was $599.

(USA) CORONET (U.S. Mfg.) - offset double cutaway mahogany body, white pickguard, mahogany neck, 24-fret bound rosewood fingerboard with pearl block inlay, tune-o-matic bridge/stop tailpiece, black face reverse peghead with logo/USA inscription, 6-on-a-side tuners, gold hardware, single coil/humbucker exposed pickups, volume/tone control, 5-position switch control, active electronics, available in Black, California Coral, Cherry, Pacific Blue, Sunburst, Sunset Yellow, and White finishes. Mfg. 1991 to 1994.

$675 $550 $450 $360 $325 $300 $275
Last MSR was $900.

Add $100 for double locking Floyd Rose vibrato, black hardware.

Epiphone Zephyr
(1950s Reissue Model)
courtesy The Epiphone Co.

Crestwood Series

CRESTWOOD (U.S. Mfg.) - double cutaway body, set-in neck, 24 3/4" scale, rosewood fingerboard with dot inlay, tune-o-matic bridge, gold hardware, pickguard with stylized 'E', metal logo peghead plate, 2 pickups, volume/tone controls, 3-way switch, available in Sunburst finish. Mfg. 1958 to 1959.

$1,850 $1,600 $1,200 $1,000 $900 $800 $700

In 1959, this model was named the Crestwood Custom (see section below).

CRESTWOOD CUSTOM (U.S. Mfg.) - similar to the Crestwood, except features 2 mini humbuckers, no pickguard logo, no peghead plate, oval fingerboard inlay. Mfg. 1959 to 1969.

$2,000 $1,800 $1,375 $1,150 $1,000 $900 $800

CRESTWOOD DELUXE - offset double cutaway body, set-in neck, bound ebony fingerboard with block inlay, tune-o-matic bridge, 6-on-a-side tuners, bound peghead, pickguard, 3 mini-humbucker pickups, volume/tone controls, pickup selector switch, available in Cherry and White finishes. Mfg. 1963 to 1969.

$2,400 $2,200 $1,800 $1,400 $1,200 $1,000 $800

DEL REY STANDARD (Model EEXC) - Available in Amber, Heritage Cherry Sunburst, Transparent Black, and Wine Red finishes. Mfg. 1995 to 2000.

$525 $450 $400 $350 $300 $250 $195
Last MSR was $749.

DOT (Model ETDT) - Design based on the ES-335, available in Cherry, Ebony, Natural, and Vintage Sunburst finishes. Current Mfg.

MSR $659 $465 $325 $275 $245 $215 $185 $170

ELP 2 (Korea Mfg.) - similar to the Epiphone Les Paul design, but featured a bolt-on neck. Mfg. 1988 to 1989.

$350 $300 $275 $250 $225 $175 $150

Epiphone Coronet Guitar
W/Pacemaker Amp
courtesy Guitarzan

E

GRADING	100% MINT	98% NEAR MINT	95% EXC+	90% EXC	80% VG+	70% VG	60% G

E Series

BASHER -Les Paul style laminated alder/maple body, bolt-on hard maple neck, rosewood fingerboard with dot position markers, 22-frets, 2 open coil humbucking pickups, chrome hardware, 3-per-side tuners, available in Vintage Sunburst, Just Black and Heritage Cherry Sunburst, Blood Stain and Bruise Purple finishes. New 2001.

MSR $299 $210 $175 $150 $125 $95 $75 $50

Add $30 for Blood Stain and Bruise Purple finishes.

BEAST - Explorer style body, solid tonewood, bolt-on hard maple neck, select grade Indian Rosewood fingerboard with dot position markers, 6-on-a-side tuners, 22-frets, string-through-body, 2 covered humbucking pickups, chrome hardware, 1 Volume/1 Tone control, 3-way switch, available in Black Metallic, Red Metallic and Light Blue Metallic. New 2001.

MSR $499 $350 $275 $250 $225 $195 $150 $125

BULLY - double cutaway solid body with G-style design (SG), laminated alder/maple body, bolt-on hard maple neck, 22-fret rosewood fingerboard with dot position markers, 3-per-side tuners, 2 open coil humbucking pickups, chrome plated hardware, 1 Volume/1 Tone control, 3-way switch, available in Just Black, Blood Stain and Bruise Purple finishes. New 2001.

MSR $315 $220 $175 $150 $125 $100 $85 $75

DEMON modified, V-shaped tonewood body, hard rock maple neck, select grade Indian Rosewood fingerboard with dot position markers, 22-frets, 2 covered humbucking pickups, 6-on-a-side tuners, 1 Volume/1 Tone control, 3-way switch, string-through-body construction, chrome plated hardware, available in Black Metallic, Metallic Red and Metallic Light Blue finishes. New 2001.

MSR $499 $350 $275 $250 $225 $195 $150 $125

LP XTREME - Les Paul style solid tonewood body, carved top, select grade Indian Rosewood fingerboard with dot position markers, 22-frets, 3-per-side tuners, 2 exposed coil humbucking pickupd, chrome hardware, available in Black/White Crackle, Blue/Yellow Crackle, Green/Yellow Crackle and Red/Yellow Crackle finishes. New 2001.

MSR $999 $700 $475 $400 $350 $300 $250 $225

SLASHER - double cutaway solid body similar to the Firebird design, solid tonewood body, bolt-on hard maple neck, 22-fret select grade Indian Rosewood fingerboard with dot position markers, 6-on-a-side tuners, string-through-body design, 2 covered humbucking pickups, chrome plated hardware, available in Metallic Red, Light Blue Metallic and Black Metallic finishes. New 2001.

MSR $499 $350 $300 $250 $225 $195 $175 $125

EM Series

Epiphone's EM series is based on the Gibson M-III model.

EM-1 (EM-1 REBEL STANDARD) - offset sweeping double cutaway alder body, bolt-on maple neck, 24-fret rosewood fingerboard with pearl trapezoid inlay, standard vibrato, reverse peghead, 6-on-a-side tuners, gold hardware, humbucker/single coil/humbucker covered pickups, volume/tone control, 5-position/mini switches, available in Black, Red and White finishes. Mfg. 1991 to 1998.

$350 $275 $225 $175 $150 $125 $100

Last MSR was $450.

EM-2 (EM-2 Rebel Custom) - similar to EM-1, except has double locking Floyd Rose vibrato. Mfg. 1991 to 1995.

$450 $325 $275 $225 $200 $175 $150

Last MSR was $550.

EM-3 Rebel Custom - similar to EM-1, except features limba body, Jam-Trem locking tremolo. Mfg. 1994 to 1995.

$475 $350 $300 $250 $225 $195 $175

ES-295 Series

ES-295 WITH VIBROTONE (Model ET29) - single cutaway semi-hollow body, 2 f-holes, 20-fret rosewood fingerboard with parallelogram block inlay, 2 creme-colored P-90-style single coils, Bigsby-styled tremolo system, available in Metallic Gold finish. Mfg. 1998 to 2000.

$1,050 $890 $775 $660 $560 $475 $400

This model is similar to Gibson's ES-295 model.
Last MSR was $1,499.

ET Series

In 1970, prior to the takeover of CMI (Epiphone/Gibson's parent company) by the ECL investment group (later Norlin), the decision was made to close down Kalamazoo production of Epiphones in favor of building them overseas in Japan. Ephiphone reviewed a number of models trademarked **Lyle** (built by Matsumoku of Japan), and decided to offer a "new" line of Japanese-built Epiphones that had more in common with other Japanese copies than previous Epiphone products! Japanese-built Epiphones generally sport a blue label that reads *Epiphone, Inc. Kalamazoo, Michigan* but rarely sport a *Made in Japan* sticker.

ET-270 (Japan Mfg.) - strat-style double cutaway body, bolt-on hardwood neck, rosewood fingerboard with dot inlay, vibrola tremolo, chrome hardware, 2 single coil pickups, volume/tone controls, pickup selector toggle switch, available in Cherry Red finish. Mfg. 1971 to 1975.

$275 $250 $225 $200 $175 $150 $125

ET-275 (Japan Mfg.) - Crestwood Custom-style double cutaway hardwood body, bolt-on hardwood neck, rosewood fingerboard with dot inlay, vibrato bridge, chrome hardware, 2 pickups, volume/tone controls, pickup selector switch, available in Sunburst finish. Mfg. 1971 to 1975.

$300 $275 $250 $225 $200 $175 $150

ET-276 (Japan Mfg.) - Crestwood Custom-style double cutaway hardwood body, bolt-on hardwood neck, rosewood fingerboard with dot inlay, stop tailpiece, chrome hardware, 2 pickups, volume/tone controls, pickup selector switch, available in Mahogany finish. Mfg. 1976 to 1979.

$300 $275 $250 $225 $200 $175 $150

GRADING	100% MINT	98% NEAR MINT	95% EXC+	90% EXC	80% VG+	70% VG	60% G

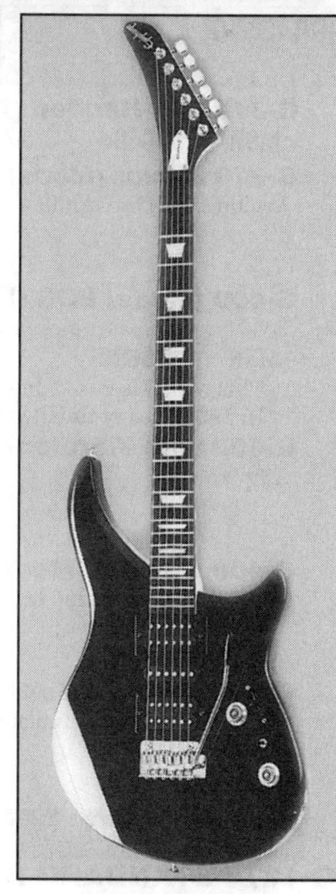

Epiphone EM-1 Rebel Standard courtesy The Epiphone Co.

ET-278 (Japan Mfg.) - Crestwood Custom-style body, bolt-on hardwood neck, bound rosewood fingerboard with dot inlay, chrome hardware, 2 pickups, 2 volume/tone controls, pickup selector toggle switch, available in Ebony finish. Mfg. 1971 to 1975.

$325 $300 $275 $250 $225 $200 $175

ET-290 (Japan Mfg.) - Crestwood Custom-style double cutaway maple body, set-in maple neck, rosewood fingerboard with block inlay, stop tailpiece, gold hardware, 2 pickups, volume/tone controls, pickup selector switch, available in Cherry Sunburst finish. Mfg. 1976 to 1979.

$350 $325 $275 $250 $225 $200 $175

ET-290 N (Japan Mfg.) - similar to the ET-290, except features bound maple fingerboard with black dot inlay, available in Natural finish. Mfg. 1976 to 1979.

$375 $350 $300 $275 $250 $200 $175

Explorer Series

EXPLORER (Model EXP1) - Explorer-style body, chrome hardware, white pickguard, 2 humbuckers, available in Alpine White, Ebony, and Red finishes. Mfg. 1986 to 1989, 1994 to 1998.

$375 $325 $295 $250 $225 $175 $150

Last MSR was $549.

"1958" EXPLORER (Model EXP2) - Explorer-style korina body, set-in mahogany neck, rosewood fingerboard with dot inlay, gold hardware, white pickguard, 2 covered humbuckers, available in Ebony finish. Mfg. 1998 to date.

MSR $729 $500 $375 $325 $275 $225 $200 $175

"1958" Korina Explorer (Model EXP2) - similar to the "1958" Explorer (actually same model, see model code), available in Natural (Korina) finish. Mfg. 1998 to date.

MSR $829 $580 $415 $350 $300 $250 $225 $200

(Epiphone) Flying V Series

"1967" FLYING V (Model EGV1) - Flying V-style mahogany body, available in Alpine White, Ebony, and Red finishes. Mfg. 1989 to 1999.

$440 $380 $340 $295 $250 $200 $160

Last MSR was $629.

In 1998, Vintage White finish replaced the Alpine White finish.

"1958" FLYING V (Model EGV2) - Flying V-style korina body, set-in mahogany neck, rosewood fingerboard with dot inlay, gold hardware, white pickguard, 2 covered humbuckers, available in Ebony finish. Mfg. 1998 to date.

MSR $729 $500 $375 $325 $275 $225 $200 $175

"1958" Korina Flying V (Model EGV2) - similar to the "1958" Flying V (actually same model, see model code), available in Natural (Korina) finish. Mfg. 1998 to date.

MSR $829 $580 $415 $350 $300 $250 $225 $200

Firebird Series

FIREBIRD (Model EGFB) - Available in Ebony, Red, Vintage Sunburst, and White finishes. Mfg. 1995 to 2000.

$475 $425 $375 $325 $275 $225 $175

Last MSR was $649.

'63 FIREBIRD-VII (Model EGF7) -reverse body and headstock, mahogany body and neck, block inlays, 6-on-a-side tuners, 3 Alnico-V Mini-Humbucker pickups, 3 volume, 1 tone, toggle switch, original style Maestro tremelo, white pickguard, gold hardware, available in Antique Ivory, Red, and Black finishes. New 2000.

MSR $819 $575 $425 $350 $300 $275 $250 $225

FIREBIRD 300 (Korea Mfg.) - reverse firebird-style body, laminated mahogany neck-through-body, 25 1/2" scale, 22-fret ebanol fingerboard with dot inlay, Steinberger KB locking tremolo, white pickguard with red firebird graphic, black hardware, single coil/humbucker EMG Select pickups, volume/tone controls, pickup selector switch. Mfg. 1986 to 1988.

$325 $300 $275 $250 $225 $200 $175

Firebird 500 (Korea Mfg.) - similar to the Firebird 300, except has 2 EMG Select humbuckers. Mfg. 1986 to 1988.

$350 $325 $275 $250 $225 $200 $175

G-310 (Model EGG1) - double sharp cutaway alder body, bolt-on mahogany neck, 22-fret rosewood fingerboard with pearl dot inlay, tune-o-matic bridge/stop tailpiece, blackface peghead with logo, 3-per-side tuners, chrome hardware, 2 exposed coil humbucker pickups, 2 volume/2-Tone controls, 3-position switch, available in Black, Red and Vintage White finishes. Mfg. 1989 to date.

MSR $469 $330 $235 $200 $185 $170 $155 $140

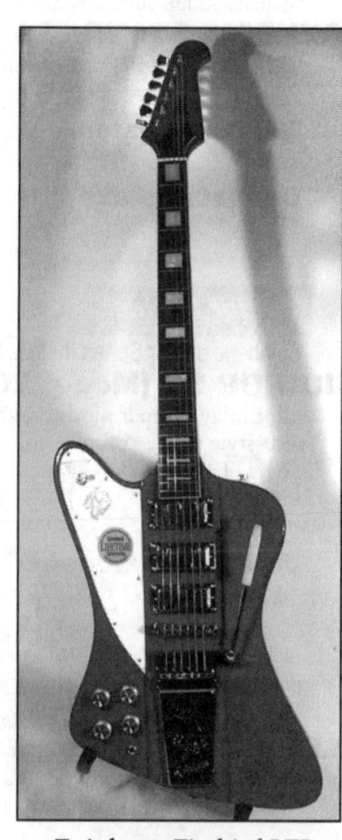

Epiphone Firebird VII courtesy Southpaw Guitars

GRADING		100% MINT	98% NEAR MINT	95% EXC+	90% EXC	80% VG+	70% VG	60% G

G-310 Left-Handed (Model EGG1L) - similar to G-310, except in left-handed configuration, available in Ebony finish. Current Mfg.

MSR	$494	$345	$250	$225	$200	$185	$170	$155

G-310 Junior (Model EGGJ) - similar to G-310, except has a laminated alder/maple SG-style body, available in Ebony, Cherry, and TV Yellow finishes. Disc. 2000.

$160	$140	$120	$100	$80	$70	$50

Last MSR was $229.

G-400 (Model EGG4) - similar to G-310, except has mahogany body, set-in mahogany neck, trapezoid fingerboard inlays, 3-per-side vintage-style tuners, smaller pickguard, 2 covered humbucker pickups, available in Cherry finish. Mfg. 1989 to date.

MSR	$699	$490	$350	$300	$260	$230	$200	$185

This model is based on Gibson's SG model, circa 1962.
In 1998, Ebony finish was introduced.

G-400 with Vibrotone (Model EGG4) - similar to G-400, except has Bigsby-derived tremolo bridge, available in Cherry finish. Mfg. 1997 to 1999.

$475	$425	$375	$325	$275	$225	$175

Last MSR was $699.

G-400 Custom (Model EGG5) - similar to G-400, except has 3 covered humbuckers, white pickguard, gold hardware, fingerboard block inlays, bound neck and headstock, available in Antique Ivory finish. Mfg. 1998 to 2000.

$499	$445	$395	$340	$300	$250	$200

Last MSR was $719.

G-400 Korina (Model EGG4) - similar to G-400, except has korina body, white pickguard, gold hardware, fingerboard block inlays, bound neck and headstock, available in Natural finish. Mfg. 1998 to 2000.

$510	$475	$450	$425	$400	$300	$250

Last MSR was $729.

G-1275 (Doubleneck) Series

G-1275 STANDARD DOUBLENECK (Model EGDS) - SG-style body, 2 bolt-on necks (12-string configuration, 6-per-side tuners; 6-string configuration, 3-per-side tuners), available in Cherry finish. Disc. 1998.

$1,000	$850	$750	$650	$550	$450	$350

Last MSR was $1,399.

G-1275 Custom Doubleneck (Model EGDC) - similar to the G-1275 Standard, except features set-in necks, available in Cherry finish. Disc. 2000.

$1,100	$975	$850	$750	$625	$525	$400

Last MSR was $1,599.

Genesis Series

Genesis series guitars were produced in Taiwan from 1979 to 1981.

GENESIS STANDARD - dual cutaway mahogany body, set-in neck, rosewood fingerboard with dot inlay, 3-per-side tuners, chrome hardware, 2 humbucker pickups, volume/tone control, pickup selector switch, coil tap switch. Mfg. 1979 to 1981.

$325	$300	$275	$250	$225	$200	$175

Genesis Custom - similar to the Genesis Standard, except features bound rosewood fingerboard with crown inlay. Mfg. 1979 to 1981.

$350	$325	$285	$250	$225	$200	$175

Genesis Deluxe - similar to the Genesis Standard, except features bound rosewood fingerboard with block inlay, gold hardware. Mfg. 1979 to 1981.

$375	$350	$295	$250	$225	$200	$175

Junior Series

Epiphone Junior Series models are based on Gibson's Melody Maker instruments.

JUNIOR SC (Model EGJR) - single cutaway laminated alder/maple body, bolt-on mahogany neck, 22-fret rosewood fingerboard with pearl dot inlay, wraparound tune-o-matic bridge, blackface peghead with screened logo, 3-per-side tuners, chrome hardware, black pickguard, 'dog-ear' P-90-style single coil pickup, volume/tone controls, available in Ebony, Cherry, Heritage Cherry Sunburst, TV Yellow, and Vintage Sunburst finishes. Mfg. 1997 to 2000.

$150	$130	$115	$100	$80	$60	$45

Last MSR was $215.

Junior DC (Model EGJC) - similar to Junior SC, except has an offset double cutaway body, available in Ebony, Cherry, and TV Yellow finishes. Mfg. 1997 to 2000.

$160	$140	$120	$100	$80	$60	$50

Last MSR was $229.

(Epiphone) Les Paul Series

LES PAUL 1 (Korea Mfg.) - Les Paul-style basswood body, bolt-on maple neck, 25 1/2" scale, 22-fret rosewood fingerboard with small block inlays, split diamond peghead inlay, black hardware, double locking Steinberger KB tremolo, humbucker pickup, volume control, available in Black, Red and White finishes. Mfg. 1986 to 1989.

$395	$350	$300	$275	$250	$225	$200

Les Paul 2 (Korea Mfg.) - similar to the Les Paul I, except has 2 humbuckers, 2 volume/2-Tone controls, 3-way switch. Mfg. 1986 to 1989.

$395	$350	$300	$275	$250	$225	$200

GRADING		100% MINT	98% NEAR MINT	95% EXC+	90% EXC	80% VG+	70% VG	60% G

Les Paul 3 (Korea Mfg.) - similar to the Les Paul I, except has 2 single coils/Gibson humbucker pickups, volume/tone controls, 3 mini- switches Mfg. 1986 to 1989.

		$395	$350	$300	$275	$250	$225	$200

LES PAUL SIGNATURE (Model ENL 5) - offset double cutaway laminated maple semi-hollow body, laminated maple top, raised creme pickguard, set-in maple neck, 24 ¾" scale, 22-fret bound rosewood fingerboard with trapezoid fingerboard inlay, tune-o-matic bridge/stop tailpiece, unbound peghead, 3-per-side tuners, chrome hardware, 2 low impedance humbuckers, volume/tone controls, 3-way selector toggle switch, varigain selector switch, phase switch, available in Ebony, Metallic Gold, and Vintage Sunburst finishes. Mfg. 1998 to 2000.

		$910	$875	$825	$775	$725	$675	$500

Last MSR was $1,299.

LES PAUL STANDARD (Model ENS-) - Les Paul-style single cutaway mahogany body, figured maple top, raised white pickguard, set-in mahogany neck, 22-fret bound rosewood fingerboard with trapezoid fingerboard inlay, tune-o-matic bridge/stop tailpiece, unbound peghead, 3-per-side tuners, chrome hardware, 2 humbuckers, 2 volume/2-Tone controls, 3-way toggle switch, available in Ebony finish. Mfg. 1989 to date.

MSR	$819	$575	$425	$395	$375	$330	$300	$270

Add $80 for Heritage Cherry Sunburst and Honey Burst finishes.

Les Paul Standard with Vibrotone (Model ENS-) - similar to the Les Paul Standard, except has Bigsby-styled tremolo system, available in Ebony finish. Mfg. 1997 only.

		$700	$625	$550	$475	$425	$350	$275

Last MSR was $949.

Add $100 for Heritage Cherry Sunburst and Honey Burst finishes.

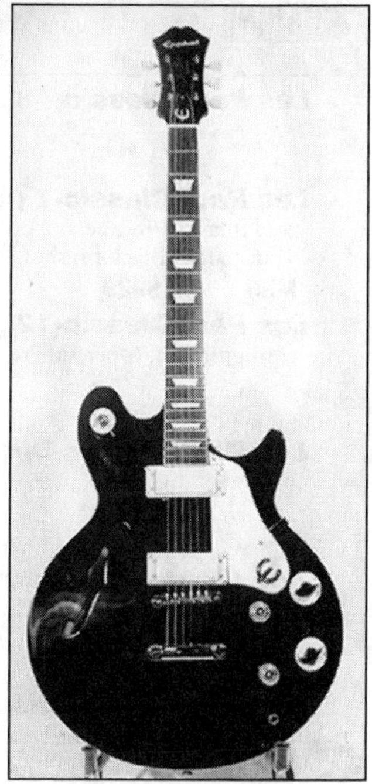
Epiphone Les Paul Signature courtesy Gurney Brown.

Les Paul Standard Left-Handed (Model ENSL) - similar to the Les Paul Standard, except in left-handed configuration, available in Heritage Cherry Sunburst finish only. Mfg. 1996 to date.

MSR	$959	$675	$475	$425	$375	$325	$275	$235

Les Paul Black Beauty with Vibrotone (Model ENS-EB) - similar to the Les Paul Black Beauty, except has Bigsby-styled tremolo system, gold hardware, available in Ebony finish. Mfg. 1997 to 1999.

		$625	$550	$475	$425	$350	$295	$225

Last MSR was $899.

Les Paul Black Beauty (Model ENBB) - similar to the Les Paul Standard, except has gold hardware, 3 humbucker pickups, available in Ebony finish only. Current Mfg.

MSR	$1,029	$725	$525	$450	$400	$365	$335	$295

Les Paul Black Beauty 3 with VibroTone (Model ENBB) - similar to the Les Paul Black Beauty, except has Bigsby-styled tremolo system, gold hardware, 3 humbucker pickups, available in Ebony finish. Mfg. 1997 to 1999.

		$750	$625	$550	$475	$425	$350	$275

Last MSR was $1,049.

Les Paul Standard Goldtop (Model ENS-MG) - similar to the Les Paul Standard, available in Metallic Gold finish only. Mfg. 1995 to 1998.

		$650	$595	$525	$450	$395	$325	$250

Last MSR was $979.

Les Paul '56 Goldtop (Model EN56) - similar to the Les Paul Standard, except features 2 creme-colored P-90-style single coil pickups, creme-colored pickguard, available in Metallic Gold finish only. Mfg. 1998 to date.

MSR	$999	$695	$525	$450	$400	$325	$275	$225

Les Paul Standard Translucent Edition (Model ENST) - Available in Translucent Amber, Translucent Black, Translucent Blue, Translucent Purple, Translucent Red, Transparent Green, and Wine Red finishes. Disc. 2000.

		$660	$560	$485	$435	$360	$300	$225

Last MSR was $959.

Les Paul Standard Translucent Edition with VibroTone (Model ENST) - equipped with Bigsby-derived tremolo bridge, available in Translucent Amber, Translucent Black, Translucent Blue, Translucent Purple, Transluent Red, Transparent Green, and Wine Red finishes. Mfg. 1997 only.

		$700	$650	$575	$500	$425	$350	$275

Last MSR was $1,099.

Les Paul Standard Metal Edition (Model ENSM) - Available in Gold Flake, Blue Flake, Green Flake, Purple Flake, Red Flake, and Silver Flake finishes. Disc. 2000.

		$640	$565	$490	$440	$360	$300	$240

Last MSR was $929.

Les Paul Standard Metal Edition with VibroTone (Model ENSM) - equipped with Bigsby-derived tremolo bridge, available in Gold Flake, Blue Flake, Green Flake, Purple Flake, Red Flake, and Silver Flake finishes. Mfg. 1997 only.

		$800	$750	$675	$575	$500	$400	$325

Last MSR was $1,269.

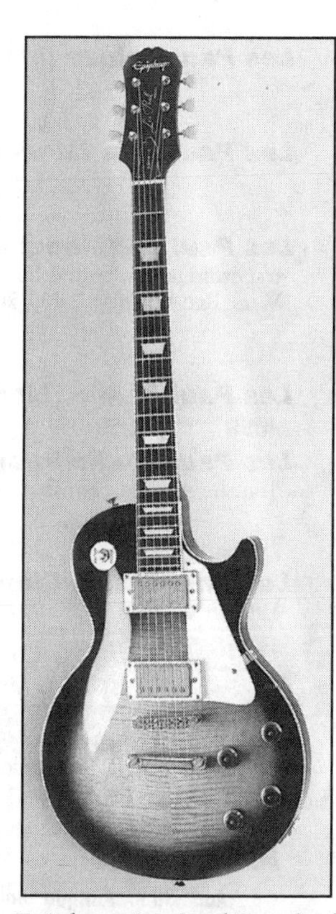
Epiphone Les Paul Standard courtesy The Epiphone Co.

E

GRADING			100% MINT	98% NEAR MINT	95% EXC+	90% EXC	80% VG+	70% VG	60% G

Les Paul Classic - Birdseye Maple top, Available in Amber, Heritage Cherry Sunburst, and Natural finishes. Mfg. 1995 to 1997.

		$575	$525	$475	$425	$350	$275	$225

Last MSR was $899.

Les Paul Classic-7 (Model ENC7) -mahogany body with flamed maple top, mahogany set neck, rosewood fingerboard with pearl trapezoid inlays, 4/3 tuners, 2 open coil humbucking pickups, bound body and neck, white pickguard, chrome hardare, available in Vintage Sunburst and Transparent Black finishes. New 2000.

MSR	$929	$650	$475	$425	$375	$325	$295	$275

Les Paul Classic-12 (12-String) (Model ENL 4) - similar to the Les Paul Standard, except features bound flame maple top, 12-string configuration, 6-per-side tuners, 2 open coil humbuckers, available in Heritage Cherry Sunburst and Vintage Sunburst finishes. Mfg. 1998 to 2000.

		$630	$545	$500	$450	$400	$350	$275

Last MSR was $899.

Les Paul Classic Birdseye (Model ENSB) - Available in Amber, Heritage Cherry Sunburst, and Natural finishes. Mfg. 1996 to 1999.

		$600	$525	$475	$400	$350	$275	$225

Last MSR was $869.

Ace Frehley Les Paul Classic (Model ENAC) - multi-bound, premium Flamed Maple top, rosewood fingerboard with lightning bolt inlays, chrome plated hardware, three Dimarzio USA Super Distortion Humbucker pickups, inlay of Ace's face on the headstock, available in Heritage Cherry Sunburst and Translucent Black finishes. New 1999.

MSR	$1,299	$910	$700	$600	$525	$450	$375	$300

Slash Les Paul Classic (Model ENSH) - Slash Snake graphic on lower bout, flamed maple top, black hardware, no raised pickguard, 2 exposed polepiece humbucker pickups, available in Transparent Red finish. Mfg. 1997 to 2000.

		$699	$599	$525	$450	$375	$325	$250

Last MSR was $999.

Les Paul Custom (Model ENC-) - similar to Les Paul Standard, except has arched bound maple top, raised black pickguard, 22-fret bound rosewood fingerboard with pearl block inlay, bound peghead with pearl split diamond/logo inlay, gold hardware, available in Black and White finishes. Mfg. 1989 to date.

MSR	$999	$695	$525	$450	$400	$325	$275	$225

Les Paul Custom FlameTop (Model ENC-) - similar to the Les Paul Custom, except features highly figured maple top, available in Heritage Cherry Sunburst and Vintage Sunburst finishes. Mfg. 1998 to date.

MSR	$1,099	$775	$575	$500	$450	$400	$365	$335

Les Paul Double Cutaway (Model ELPS) (Also Les Paul Special Double Cutaway) - dual cutaway body, available in Cherry, Ebony, and TV Yellow finishes. Mfg. 1995 to 2000.

		$500	$425	$375	$325	$295	$250	$195

Last MSR was $729.

Les Paul Deluxe (Model ENL3) - Available in Ebony finish. Mfg. 1998 to 2000.

		$575	$525	$475	$425	$375	$300	$200

Last MSR was $819.

Les Paul Elite (Model ENSE) - semi-hollowbody body, single f-hole, gold hardware, available in Ebony finish. Disc. 1999.

		$725	$625	$550	$475	$425	$350	$275

Last MSR was $1,029.

Les Paul ES (Model ENL7) - ES style semi-hollow body, Flame Maple top, mahogany body, maple set neck, rosewood fingerboard with trapezoid inlays, bound body and neck, gold hardware, 2 Humbucker pickups, available in Amber, Heritage Cherry Sunburst, Vintage Sunburst, and Wine Red finishes. 1999-2000.

		$630	$565	$515	$465	$415	$365	$300

Last MSR was $899.

Les Paul Studio (Model ENL1) - Available in Ebony, Heritage Cherry Sunburst, and Vintage Sunburst finishes. Mfg. 1998 to date.

MSR	$699	$490	$375	$335	$300	$275	$250	$225

Les Paul Studio Pearl (Model ENL2) - white Pearloid pickguard/truss rod cover/toggle switch ring, black hardware, available in Translucent Black finishes. Mfg. 1998 to 1999.

		$480	$440	$390	$340	$290	$240	$190

Last MSR was $689.

Les Paul Studio Standard (Model ELSB) - Available in Heritage Cherry Sunburst, Honey Burst, and Metallic Gold finishes. Disc. 1998.

		$500	$450	$400	$350	$300	$250	$195

Last MSR was $769.

LP (Les Paul) Series

The bolt-on neck LP Series models are produced in Korea.

LP-100 (Model ENB-) - Les Paul-style alder/mahogany body, alder/maple top, bolt-on mahogany neck, 2 exposed coil humbucker pickups, available in Ebony, Red, and Pearl White finishes. Mfg. 1994 to date.

MSR	$609	$425	$315	$275	$250	$225	$200	$175

Add $30 for Antique Sunburst, Heritage Cherry Sunburst, and Vintage Sunburst finishes.

Ebony, Red, and Pearl White finishes disc in 2000. In 1998, Antique Sunburst finish was disc.

GRADING		100% MINT	98% NEAR MINT	95% EXC+	90% EXC	80% VG+	70% VG	60% G

LP-100 Left Handed (Model ENBL) - similar to the LP-100, except features left-handed configuration, available in Ebony and Heritage Cherry Sunburst finishes. Current Mfg.

MSR	$633	$445	$325	$295	$260	$230	$200	$175

LP-100 Plus (Model ENBP) - Available in Ebony, Red, and White finishes. Mfg. 1997 to date.

$425	$350	$300	$275	$225	$195	$150

Last MSR was $589.

Add $30 for Heritage Cherry Sunburst and Vintage Sunburst finishes.

LP-300 (Korea Mfg.) - Les Paul-style body, bolt-on neck, bound fingerboard with block inlays. Mfg. 1989 to 1992.

$325	$300	$250	$200	$175	$125	$100

(USA) MAP GUITAR (U.S. Mfg.) - map-shaped mahogany body, set-in neck, chrome hardware, tune-o-matic bridge/stop tailpiece, 2 covered humbucker pickups, 2 volume/2-Tone controls, 3-way selector switch. Mfg. 1983 only.

$1,400	$1,300	$1,200	$1,100	$950	$850	$750

Map guitar models were part of the final production runs at the original Kalamazoo plant prior to its closure in 1984. The Epiphone version of the Map guitar was introduced before the Gibson version, and some Epiphone models "became" Gibson models towards the end of the production run to meet demand.

Nighthawk Series

Epiphone Nighthawk models are based on the popular Gibson Nighthawk Series.

NIGHTHAWK STANDARD (Model ENHS) - Available in Heritage Cherry Sunburst, Translucent Amber, and Vintage Sunburst finishes. Mfg. 1995 to 2000.

$500	$450	$400	$350	$300	$250	$195

Last MSR was $729.

Nighthawk Standard with Tremolo (Model ENHST) - similar to Nighthawk Standard, except features tremolo bridge, available in Heritage Cherry Sunburst, Translucent Amber, and Vintage Sunburst finishes. Disc. 1998.

$550	$500	$450	$400	$325	$275	$200

Last MSR was $849.

Nighthawk Special (Model ENHP) - Available in Ebony and Red finishes. Mfg. 1995 to 1998.

$500	$450	$400	$350	$300	$250	$195

Last MSR was $759.

Nighthawk Special with Tremolo (Model ENHPT) - similar to Nighthawk Special, except features tremolo bridge, available in Ebony and Red finishes. Disc. 1998.

$525	$475	$425	$350	$300	$250	$195

Last MSR was $779.

Olympic Series

OLYMPIC - single cutaway body, set-in neck, rosewood fingerboard with dot inlay, combination bridge/tailpiece, 3-per-side tuners, chrome hardware, one pickup, volume/tone controls, available in Sunburst finish.

(U.S. Mfg.) Mfg. 1960 to 1969.

$650	$600	$550	$500	$475	$425	$375

(Japan Mfg.) Mfg.1977 to 1979.

$500	$450	$400	$350	$300	$265	$225

In 1963, the body style changed to an offset double cutaway design.
In 1964, 6-on-a-side headstock was introduced.

Olympic 3/4 Size (U.S. Mfg.) - similar to Olympic, except features 3/4 size body. Mfg. 1960 to 1964.

$500	$450	$400	$350	$300	$265	$225

Olympic Custom (Japan Mfg.) - similar to Olympic, except features bound neck. Mfg.1977 to 1979.

$950	$900	$850	$800	$700	$650	$575

Olympic Double (U.S. Mfg.) - similar to the Olympic, except features 2 pickups, 3-way selector switch. Mfg. 1960 to 1969.

$700	$650	$600	$550	$500	$425	$375

Olympic Special (U.S. Mfg.) - similar to the Olympic, except features sharper cutaways, one Melody Maker pickup. Mfg. 1962 to 1969.

$600	$550	$500	$450	$400	$350	$300

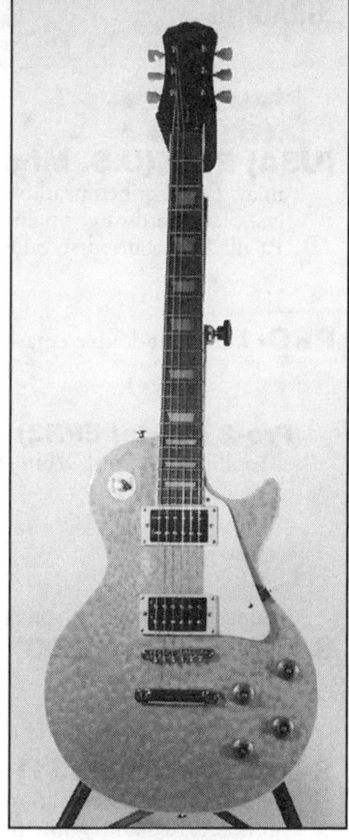

Epiphone Les Paul Birdseye Maple top courtesy Gurney Brown

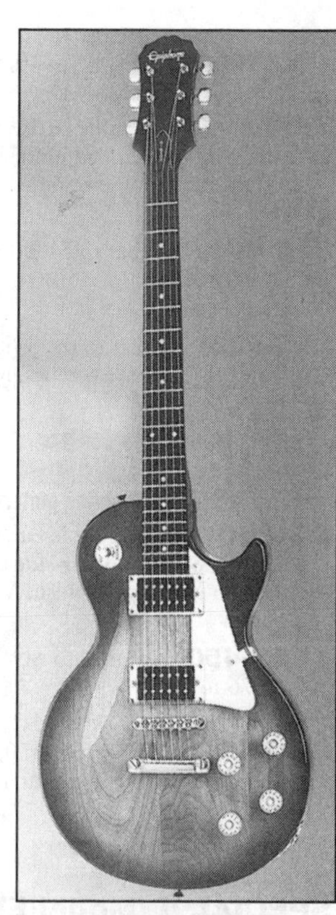

Epiphone LP-100 courtesy The Epiphone Co.

E

GRADING	100% MINT	98% NEAR MINT	95% EXC+	90% EXC	80% VG+	70% VG	60% G

Pro Series

(USA) PRO (U.S. Mfg.) - offset double cutaway poplar body, bolt-on maple neck, 24-fret extended ebony fingerboard with offset pearl dot inlay, *Pro* inscribed pearl block inlay at 24th fret, double locking Floyd Rose vibrato, black face peghead with logo/USA inscription, 6-on-a-side tuners, black hardware, single coil/humbucker exposed pickups, volume/tone control, 3-position switch, available in Black, California Coral, Cherry, Pacific Blue, Sunburst, Sunset Yellow, and White finishes. Mfg. 1989 to 1994.

$395 $350 $300 $250 $225 $195 $150
Last MSR was $600.

PRO-1 - offset double cutaway body, bolt on neck. Mfg. 1995 to 1997.

$495 $425 $400 $350 $295 $250 $195
Last MSR was $749.

Pro-2 (Model EPR2) - similar to Pro-1, except features Steinberger DB bridge, 2 slanted humbucker pickups, available in Black Metallic, Metallic Blue, Pearl White, and Red Metallic finishes. Mfg. 1995 to 1998.

$500 $450 $400 $350 $300 $250 $200
Last MSR was $779.

S Series

S Series instruments are produced in Korea.

S-210 (Model EGSO) - offset double cutaway body, tremolo bridge, available in Ebony, Red, Vintage Sunburst, and Vintage White finishes. Mfg. 1998 to 1999.

$180 $160 $140 $120 $100 $80 $50
Last MSR was $259.

S-310 (Model EGS1) - offset double cutaway maple body, black pickguard, bolt-on maple neck, 22-fret maple fingerboard with black dot inlay, standard vibrato, 6-on-a-side tuners, chrome hardware, 3 single coil exposed pickups, volume/2-Tone controls, 5-way selector switch, available in Black, Red and White finishes. Mfg. 1986 to 1999.

$225 $195 $175 $150 $125 $100 $75
Last MSR was $309.

S-310 Left-Handed (Model EGS1L) - similar to S-310, except features left-handed configuration, available in Black Metallic finish. Disc. 1999.

$225 $200 $175 $150 $125 $100 $85
Last MSR was $334.

S-310 Custom - similar to S-310, except features 2 single coil/humbucker pickups. Mfg. 1995 to 1996.

$250 $200 $175 $150 $125 $100 $90
Last MSR was $349.

S-400 - similar to S-310, except features rosewood fingerboard, *Bender tremolo*, 2 single coil/humbucker pickups. Mfg. 1986 to 1989.

$250 $225 $195 $175 $150 $125 $100

S-600 - offset double cutaway hardwood body, bolt-on maple neck, 25 1/2" scale, 21-fret rosewood fingerboard with white sharktooth inlay, 6-on-a-side tuners, rounded point headstock, black hardware, Steinberger KB tremolo, 2 single coil/humbucker exposed pole piece pickups, volume/2-Tone controls, 5-way selector. Mfg. 1986 to 1989.

$350 $325 $275 $250 $225 $200 $175

S-800 - similar to S-600, except features basswood body, 2 single coil/humbucker covered pickups, volume/tone controls, 3 mini-switches. Mfg. 1986 to 1989.

$350 $325 $275 $250 $225 $200 $175

S-900 - similar to the S-600, except features bound body, maple neck-through-body design, 2 single coil/humbucker covered pickups, volume/tone controls, 3 mini-switches. Mfg. 1986 to 1989.

$375 $350 $275 $250 $225 $200 $175

SC (Scroll) Series

The SC, or Scroll series guitars have a distinct scroll on the upper bass bout, and a carved edge along the top. This series was produced in Japan.

SC-350 - offset double cutaway mahogany body with scrolled bass bout, 3-piece bolt-on mahogany neck, 24-fret ebonized maple fingerboard with white dot inlay, 3-per-side tuners, chrome hardware, wraparound bridge, 2 chrome covered humbuckers, volume/tone controls, 3-way selector, available in Mahogany finish. Mfg. 1976 to 1979.

$325 $275 $250 $225 $200 $175 $150

SC-450 - similar to SC-350, except features maple body, set-in neck, rosewood fingerboard, available in Natural and Mahogany finishes. Mfg. 1976 to 1979.

$325 $275 $250 $225 $200 $175 $150

SC-550 - similar to SC-350, except features maple body, set-in 3-piece maple neck, ebony fingerboard with block inlay, gold hardware, coil tap mini-switch, available in Natural (SC550N) and Ebony (SC550B) finishes. Mfg. 1976 to 1979.

$350 $300 $275 $250 $225 $195 $170

Special II Series

SPECIAL II (Model ENJR) - single cutaway body, bolt-on neck, 2 exposed coil pickups, tune-o-matic bridge/stop tailpiece, volume/tone controls, 3 way selector, available in Ebony, Red, and White finishes. Mfg. 1996 to date.

MSR $299 $210 $160 $135 $120 $105 $90 $75

Add $40 for Heritage Cherry Sunburst, Vintage Sunburst, and Wine Red finishes.

GRADING		100% MINT	98% NEAR MINT	95% EXC+	90% EXC	80% VG+	70% VG	60% G

Special II Left-Handed (Model ENJRL) - similar to the Special II, except in a left-handed configuration, available in Vintage Sunburst finish. Mfg. 1997 to date.

MSR	$364	$255	$185	$160	$145	$130	$120	$110

Special II Plus (Model ENJRP) - similar to the Special II, except features die cast tuners, 2 OBL humbuckers, coil tap capabilities, available in Ebony, Red, and White finishes. Mfg. 1997 to 1999.

$275	$225	$195	$175	$150	$125	$95

Last MSR was $379.

Add $30 for Heritage Cherry Sunburst and Vintage Sunburst finishes.

SPOTLIGHT (KOREA MFG.) - slightly offset double cutaway body, set-in neck, rosewood fingerboard with chevron inlays, 3-per-side headstock, 2 humbucker pickups. Mfg. 1986 to 1989.

$495	$450	$400	$350	$300	$250	$200

T Series

T-310 (Model EGT1) - single cutaway body, fixed bridge, 6-on-a-side tuners, 2 single coil pickups, available in Ebony, French Cream, Red, Vintage Sunburst, and Vintage White finishes. Mfg. 1989 to 2000.

$225	$195	$175	$150	$125	$100	$75

Last MSR was $309.

T-310 Custom - similar to T-310, except featured a chrome covered humbucker in neck position. Mfg. 1995 to 1997.

$225	$195	$170	$150	$125	$100	$80

Last MSR was $339.

V 2 (Korea Mfg.) - Flying V-style body, bolt-on neck, rosewood fingerboard with dot inlay, 6-on-a-side tuners, chrome hardware, standard tremolo, 2 humbucker pickups, volume/tone controls, 3-way switch. Mfg. 1986 to 1989.

$325	$275	$250	$225	$200	$175	$150

Wilshire Series

WILSHIRE - dual cutaway body, set-in neck, rosewood fingerboard with dot inlay, 3-per-side tuners, chrome hardware, tune-o-matic bridge, 2 white P-90 'soapbar' pickups, volume/tone controls, 3-way selector.

(U.S. Mfg.) Mfg. 1959 to 1969.

1959-1969	$950	$875	$800	$675	$550	$425	$300

(Japan Mfg.) Mfg. 1977 to 1979.

1977-1979	$550	$475	$400	$370	$335	$300	$275

In 1961, black P-90 'soapbar' pickups replaced original parts/design.

In 1963, an offset double cutaway body, 2 mini-humbuckers, and 6-on-a-side tuners replaced original parts/design.

Wilshire 12-string (U.S. Mfg.) - similar to the Wilshire, except features a 12-string configuration, 6 per side headstock. Mfg. 1966 to 1968.

$750	$700	$650	$600	$550	$500	$450

X-1000 (KOREA MFG.) - offset double cutaway body, laminated maple neck-through-body, 25 1/2" scale, 24-fret bound ebanol fingerboard with white chevron inlay, 6-on-a-side tuners, bound rounded point headstock, black hardware, Steinberger KB tremolo, 2 single coil/humbucker EMG Select pickups, volume/tone controls, 3 mini-switches. Mfg. 1986 to 1989.

$350	$325	$275	$250	$225	$200	$175

ELECTRIC BASS

On many models, the Epiphone family model name is listed after the model name/number in parentheses. Also, any older nomenclature may appear within the parentheses.

The Accu-Bass Jr. Gig Rig package (list $529) includes an Accu-Bass Jr. electric bass, Studio Bass 10 amplifier, cord, Qwik-Tune quartz tuner, black gig bag, strap, picks, and a 30 minute Guitar Essentials Hal Leonard video tape.

Accu Bass Series

ACCU BASS (Model EBAC) - offset double cutaway maple body, black pickguard with thumb rest, bolt-on maple neck, 20-fret maple fingerboard with black dot inlay, fixed bridge, body matching peghead with logo inscription, 4-on-a-side tuners, chrome hardware, P-style exposed pickup, volume/tone control, available in Black, Red and White finishes. Current Mfg.

MSR	$359	$250	$185	$165	$150	$135	$120	$100

Accu Bass Left-Handed (Model EBACL) - similar to Accu Bass, except features left-handed configuration, available in Ebony finish. Current Mfg.

MSR	$394	$275	$200	$180	$165	$150	$135	$120

Accu Bass Junior (Model EBAJ) - Available in Ebony, Red, Vintage Sunburst, and White finishes. Current Mfg.

MSR	$299	$210	$160	$140	$120	$100	$85	$75

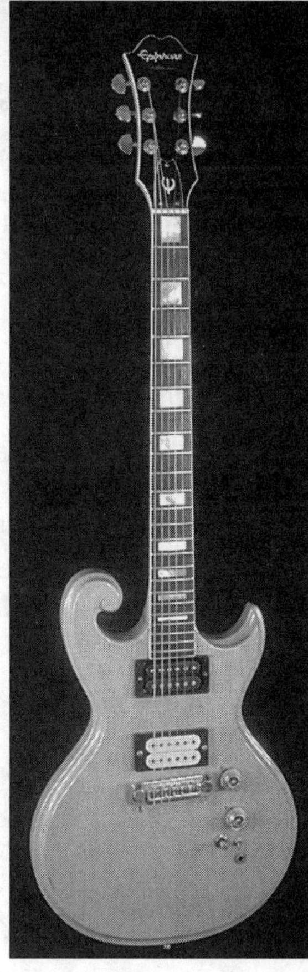

Epiphone Scroll SC-550N
courtesy The Epiphone Co.

Epiphone Special II
courtesy Adele Aust

GRADING		100% MINT	98% NEAR MINT	95% EXC+	90% EXC	80% VG+	70% VG	60% G

EB-0 (Model EBGO, SG-1) - offset double cutaway mahogany body with pointy forward horns, bolt-on mahogany neck, 30" scale, 20-fret rosewood fingerboard with pearl dot inlay, fixed bridge, blackface peghead with screened logo, 2-per-side tuners, chrome hardware, black pickguard, chrome-covered Sidewinder humbucker pickup, volume/tone controls, available in Cherry and Ebony finishes. Mfg. 1998 to date.

MSR	$349	$245	$185	$165	$145	$125	$115	$95

EB-1 (Model EBB1) - viola-shaped mahogany body, bolt-on mahogany neck, painted on 'f-hole', 32" scale, 20-fret rosewood fingerboard with pearl dot inlay, fixed bridge, blackface peghead with screened logo, 2-per-side tuners, chrome hardware, raised black pickguard, chrome-covered Sidewinder humbucker pickup, volume/tone controls, available in Red Brown Mahogany finish. Mfg. 1998 to 2000.

		$420	$375	$325	$275	$225	$200	$150

Last MSR was $599.

This model is equipped with a floor stand (for upright playing.

EB-1 FRETLESS (Model EBB 1F) -same as Model EBB1, but in a fretless configuration. Disc. 2000.

		$425	$350	$300	$260	$220	$185	$155

Last MSR was $599.

EB-3 (Model EBG3) - SG body style, 1 Sidewinder Humbucker pickup and 1 Mini-Humbucker pickup, mahogany body and set neck, rosewood fingerboard with trapezoid inlays, two volume and two tone controls, selector switch, 34" scale, chrome hardware, available in Cherry and Ebony finishes. New 1999.

MSR	$729	$510	$395	$360	$330	$300	$260	$220

EB-3 5-STRING (Model EBG5) -SG body style, 3/2 headstock configuration, set neck, trapezoid inlays, 2 DualRail pickups, 5-way rotary tone selector switch, stop tailpiece, chrome hardware, available in Cherry and Ebony finishes. New 2000.

MSR	$799	$560	$425	$375	$335	$300	$265	$235

EBM Series

EBM-4 (Model EBM4, EBM-4 REBEL STANDARD) - offset sweeping double cutaway basswood body, bolt-on maple neck, 24-fret rosewood fingerboard with pearl offset dot inlay, fixed bridge, blackface reverse peghead, 4-on-a-side tuners, chrome hardware, P/J-style covered pickups, 2 volume/tone controls, available in Cherry, Black, Frost Blue, Pearl White, and Vintage Sunburst finishes. Mfg. 1991 to 1999.

		$395	$325	$295	$250	$225	$175	$150

Last MSR was $559.

EBM-5 (Model EBM5, EBM-5 Rebel Standard) - similar to EBM-4, except has 5-string configuration, 5-per-side tuners, available in Cherry, Black, Frost Blue, Pearl White, and Vintage Sunburst finishes. Mfg. 1991 to 1999.

		$395	$325	$295	$250	$225	$175	$150

Last MSR was $559.

EBM-5 Fretless (Model EBM5F) - similar to EBM-5, except features fretless fingerboard, available in Ebony finish. Disc. 1999.

		$425	$375	$325	$275	$250	$195	$150

Last MSR was $599.

EMBASSY DELUXE - offset double cutaway body, set-in neck, 34" scale, rosewood fingerboard with dot inlay, tune-o-matic bridge chrome hardware, 4-on-a-side tuners, metal hand rest (over strings), 2 Thunderbird-style pickups, volume/tone controls, available in Cherry finish. Mfg. 1962 to 1968.

		$1,500	$1,350	$1,200	$1,100	$1,000	$900	$700

KORINA EXPLORER BASS (Model EBEX) - Korina body, mahogany set neck, rosewood fingerboard with white dot inlays, 34" scale, gold hardware, two Humbucker pickups, available in Natural Korina (disc. 2000) and Ebony finishes. 1999 to date.

MSR	$829	$580	$425	$375	$345	$315	$285	$265

Subtract $100 for Ebony finish.

KORINA FLYING V BASS (EBFV) - Flying V-shaped korina body, mahogany neck, 30.5" scale, 21-fret rosewood fingerboard with pearl dot inlay, fixed bridge, blackface peghead with screened logo, 2-per-side tuners, gold hardware, white pickguard, 2 humbucking pickups, 2 volume/1 tone controls, 3-way selector toggle, available in Ebony and Korina finishes (Korina finish disc. 2000). Mfg. 1998 to date.

MSR	$699	$495	$400	$365	$335	$300	$285	$260

JACK CASADY BASS (Model EBJC) - offset double cutaway semi-hollow laminated maple body, 2 f-holes, set-in mahogany neck, 20-fret rosewood fingerboard with pearl trapezoid inlay, 2-per-side tuners, fixed bridge, creme-colored raised pickguard, chrome hardware, creme-colored low impedance humbucker pickup, volume/tone controls, 3 way impedance boost knob, available in Metallic Gold finish. Mfg. 1997 to date.

MSR	$1,199	$850	$625	$550	$475	$425	$375	$325

LES PAUL SPECIAL BASS (Model EBLP) - Available in Heritage Cherry Sunburst and Vintage Sunburst finishes. Current Mfg.

MSR	$499	$350	$295	$250	$225	$195	$150	$125

LES PAUL STANDARD BASS (Model EBB5) - flame maple top, 2 chrome covered humbuckers, trapezoid fingerboard inlay, available in Ebony, Heritage Cherry Sunburst, and Vintage Sunburst finishes. Mfg. 1998 to date.

MSR	$699	$495	$375	$325	$275	$245	$215	$185

LES PAUL STANDARD 5-STRING BASS (Model EBL5) -mahogany body with flame maple top, maple neck, rosewood fingerboard with trapezoid inlays, 3/2 headstock configuration, 2 DualRail humbucking pickups, 5-way rotary tone switch, stop tailpiece, chrome hardware, available in Transparent Black and Vintage Sunburst finishes. Mfg. 2000 only.

		$500	$450	$400	$365	$335	$300	$275

Last MSR was $699.

GRADING	100% MINT	98% NEAR MINT	95% EXC+	90% EXC	80% VG+	70% VG	60% G

NEWPORT BASS - offset double cutaway body, set-in neck, 30 1/2" scale, rosewood fingerboard with dot inlay, chrome hardware, 2-per-side tuners, combination bridge/tailpiece, chrome hand rest (over strings), rectangular pickup with pole pieces, available in Cherry finish.

(U.S. Mfg.) Mfg. 1961 to 1968.

	$900	$800	$700	$600	$500	$400	$350

Add 20% for custom colors.

(Japan Mfg.) Mfg. 1977 to 1979.

	$275	$250	$225	$200	$175	$150	$125

This model was available with two pickups. In 1963, 4-on-a-side tuners replaced original part/design.

POWER BASS - offset double cutaway maple body, bolt-on maple neck, 20-fret rosewood fingerboard with pearl dot inlay, fixed bridge, body matching peghead with logo inscription, 4-on-a-side tuners, black hardware, P/J-style exposed pickups, 2 volume/1 tone controls, available in Black, Red and White finishes. Disc. 1998.

	$325	$250	$200	$175	$150	$125	$100

Last MSR was $420.

RIPPER (Model EBR2) - slightly offset double cutaway maple body, bolt-on maple neck, 34" scale, 20-fret maple fingerboard with dot inlay, large black pickguard, available in Ebony and Natural finishes. Mfg. 1998 to 2000.

	$350	$275	$225	$200	$175	$150	$125

Last MSR was $499.

This model is based on Gibson's Ripper electric bass.

RIVOLI - thin double cutaway body, 2 f-holes, set-in neck, rosewood fingerboard with dot inlay, chrome hardware, 2-per-side banjo style tuners, oval peghead inlay, one rectangular pickup with pole pieces, volume/tone controls, available in Natural or Sunburst finishes. Mfg. 1959 to 1962, 1963 to 1969, 1970..

	$950	$850	$700	$600	$500	$400	$350

In 1960, right angle tuners replaced original parts/design.
In 1970, two pickups were standard items.

Rivoli Bass (Model EBR1) - contemporary reissue, available in Cherry, Ebony, Natural, and Vintage Cherry Sunburst. Disc. 2000.

	$695	$595	$525	$450	$395	$325	$250

Last MSR was $999.

Rivoli-II Bass (Model EBB6) -thin double cutaway body, set neck, rosewood fingerboard with dot inlays, 2-per-side tuners, 1 Sidewinder humbucking pickup and 1 Mini-Humbucking pickup, 2 volume, 2-Tone, toggle switch, black pickguard, available in Sunburst finish. Disc. 2000.

	$775	$695	$625	$550	$475	$400	$350

Last MSR was $1,099.

ROCK BASS (Model EBRO) - offset double cutaway maple body, bolt-on maple neck, 20-fret rosewood fingerboard with pearl dot inlay, fixed bridge, body matching peghead with logo inscription, 4-on-a-side tuners, black hardware, black pickguard with thumb rest and chrome controls plate, chrome hardware, 2 J-style exposed pickups, 2 volume/1 tone controls, available in Black, Red and White finishes. Disc. 2000.

	$275	$225	$200	$175	$150	$125	$100

Last MSR was $389.

THUNDERBIRD IV BASS (REVERSE, Model EBTB) - reverse Thunderbird body, available in Vintage Sunburst finishes. Current Mfg.

MSR $599	$425	$325	$275	$245	$215	$190	$170

THUNDERBIRD 4 BASS (Model EBT4) - Available in Frost Blue, Sea Foam Green, and Vintage Sunburst finishes. Disc. 1998.

	$495	$450	$395	$350	$295	$250	$195

Last MSR was $719.

Thunderbird 5 Bass (Model EBT5) - similar to Thunderbird 4, except features 5-string configuration, 5-on-a-side tuners, available in Frost Blue, Sea Foam Green, and Vintage Sunburst finishes. Disc. 1998.

	$525	$450	$425	$375	$325	$250	$200

Last MSR was $799.

VIOLA BASS (Model EBV1) - violin-shaped bound laminated maple body, flame maple top, set-in maple neck, 22-fret rosewood fingerboard with dot inlay, 2-per-side tuners, 2 chrome-covered mini-humbuckers, rosewood bridge/chrome tailpiece, chrome hardware, 2 volume/tone controls, pearloid controls plate, available in Vintage Sunburst finish. Current Mfg.

MSR $779	$550	$400	$360	$330	$300	$270	$240

Viola Bass Left-Handed (Model EBVL) - similar to Viola Bass, except features left-handed configuration, available in Vintage Sunburst finish. Disc. 1999.

	$575	$495	$425	$375	$325	$250	$200

Last MSR was $804.

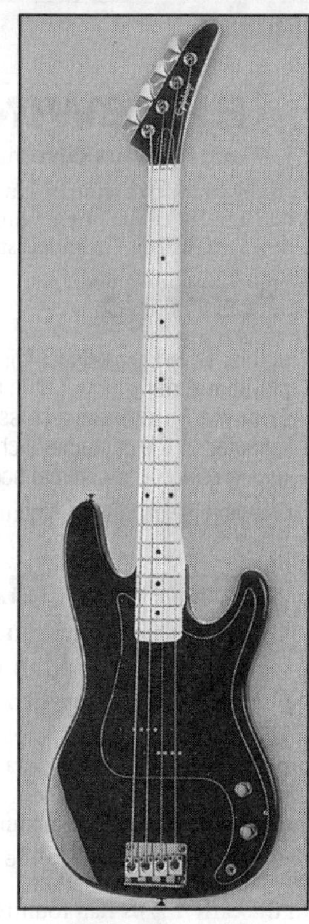

Epiphone Accu Bass
courtesy The Epiphone Co.

1960 Epiphone Rivoli Bass
courtesy The Epiphone Co.

E

GRADING	100% MINT	98% NEAR MINT	95% EXC+	90% EXC	80% VG+	70% VG	60% G

ERLEWINE

Instruments currently built in Austin, Texas since 1973.

Luthier Mark Erlewine began building guitars and basses with his cousin Dan (noted repairman/columnist for *Guitar Player* magazine) in Ypsilanti, Michigan in 1970. Three years later, Mark moved to Austin, Texas and continued building guitars as well as performing repairs and custom work. Erlewine Custom Guitars is still based in Austin, Texas.

ELECTRIC

Luthier Erlewine produces three models. In 1979 Erlewine and Billy Gibbons (ZZ Top) developed the **Chiquita Travel Guitar** (current list price $398), a 27" long playable guitar that will fit in an airplane overhead storage. The Chiquita features a solid hardwood body and one humbucker. Later, the two developed the **Erlewine Automatic**, a cross between the best features of a Strat and a Les Paul. The Automatic is currently offered as a custom built guitar, and the price is reflected in the customer's choice of options (list prices begin at $2,500). In 1982, Erlewine developed the **Lazer** ($1,900), a headless guitar with a reverse tuning bridge and minimal body. The Lazer model is highly favored by Johnny Winter.

Erlewine licensed the Chiquita and Lazer model designs to the Hondo Guitar company in the early 1980s. The licensed models do not have Erlewine's logo on them.

ERNIE BALL/MUSIC MAN

Instruments currently produced in San Luis Obispo, California under the Ernie Ball/Music Man trademark since 1984. Earlier Music Man models were produced in Fullerton, California between 1976 and 1979. Current manufacture and distribution by Ernie Ball/Music Man.

Ernie Ball was born in Cleveland, Ohio in 1930. The American Depression pressured the family to move to Santa Monica, California in 1932. By age nine Ball was practicing guitar, and this interest in music led to a twenty year career as a professional steel guitarist, music teacher, and retailer.

During the 1950s, the steel guitar was a popular instrument to play - but there was some difficulty in obtaining a matched set of strings. Early electric guitar players were also turning to *mixing* sets of strings to get the desired string gauges, but at a waste of the other strings. Ball found great success in marketing prepackaged string sets in custom gauges, and the initial mail order business expanded into a nationwide wholesale operation of strings, picks and other accessories.

In the early 1970s Ball founded the Earthwood company, and produced both electric guitars and acoustic basses for a number of years. After some production disagreements between the original Music Man company and Leo Fender's CLF Research in 1978 (See MUSIC MAN), Fender stopped building instruments exclusively for Music Man, and began designs and production for his final company (G & L). In 1984 Ernie Ball acquired the trademark and design rights to Music Man. Ball set up production in the factory that previously had built the Earthwood instruments. Ernie Ball/Music Man instruments have been in production at that location since 1984.

The first instruments that returned to production were Music Man basses, due to their popularity in the market. By 1987, the first guitar by Ernie Ball/Music Man was released. The Silhouette model was then followed by the Steve Morse model later in that year. Ernie Ball/ Music Man has retained the high level of quality from original Fender/CLF designs, and has introduced some innovative designs to their current line.

ELECTRIC

ALBERT LEE - angular offset double cutaway ash body, aluminum-lined pickguard, bolt-on maple neck, 22-fret maple fingerboard with black dot inlay, strings-through fixed bridge, 4/2-per-side Schaller M6-IND locking tuners, chrome hardware, 3 single coil Seymour Duncan pickups, volume/ tone control, 5-position switch, available in Black, Pearl Blue, Pearl Red, and Translucent Pinkburst finishes. Mfg. 1994 to date.

MSR	$1,400	$1,100	$995	$850	$725	$600	$475	$350

Add $100 for 3-Tone Sunburst finish with shell pickguard.

In 1998, Black, Pearl Red, and Translucent Pinkburst finishes were disc.

The Albert Lee model was designed in conjunction with guitarist Albert Lee.

Albert Lee with Tremolo - similar to the Albert Lee, except has Music Man vintage tremolo. Mfg. 1994 to date.

MSR	$1,500	$1,200	$1,050	$925	$795	$650	$500	$375

AXIS - single cutaway basswood body, bound figured maple top, bolt-on maple neck, 22-fret maple or rosewood fingerboard with black dot inlay, strings through bridge, 4/2-per-side Schaller tuners with pearl buttons, chrome hardware, 2 humbucking DiMarzio pickups, volume control, 3-position switch, available in Translucent Gold, Translucent Purple, Translucent Red, Translucent Sunburst, and Opaque Blacktop finishes. Mfg. 1996 to date.

MSR	$1,600	$1,295	$1,150	$995	$850	$695	$550	$400

In 1998, Translucent Purple, Translucent Red, Translucent Sunburst, and Opaque Blacktop finishes were disc.

This model was formerly known as the Edward Van Halen model. Refer to explanation below.

Axis with Tremolo - similar to Axis, except has Floyd Rose tremolo, available in Translucent Black, Translucent Blue, Translucent Gold, Translucent Natural, Translucent Pink, Translucent Purple, Translucent Red, or Translucent Sunburst finishes. Current Mfg.

MSR	$1,750	$1,400	$1,250	$1,100	$900	$750	$600	$450

In 1998, Translucent Black and Translucent Pink finishes were disc.

AXIS SPORT - similar to Axis, except features ash body, Schaller M6-IND locking tuners, choice of 2 humbuckers, 3 single coils, or 2 single coil/ humbucker configuration, volume and tone controls, 5-way switch, patented "Silent Circuit" noise reduction electronics, available in Black, Ivory, Translucent Blue, Translucent Gold, Translucent Green, Translucent Purple, Translucent Red, and Vintage Sunburst finishes. Mfg. 1997 to date.

MSR	$1,300	$1,100	$900	$775	$675	$550	$450	$325

Add $100 for 3-Tone Vintage Sunburst finish.

In 1998, Opaque Black finish was introduced; Black, Ivory, Translucent Blue, Translucent Gold, Translucent Green, Translucent Purple, and Translucent Red were disc.

GRADING		100% MINT	98% NEAR MINT	95% EXC+	90% EXC	80% VG+	70% VG	60% G

Axis Sport with Tremolo - similar to the Axis Sport, except features Music Man vintage style non-locking tremelo, available in Translucent Blue, Translucent Gold, Translucent Purple, and Translucent Red finishes. Mfg. 1997 to date.

MSR	$1,400	$1,150	$995	$850	$750	$600	$475	$350

AXIS SPORT MM90 - similar to Axis, except features 2 MM90 vintage-style 'soapbar' single coil pickups, available in Platinum and 3-Tone Vintage Sunburst finishes. Mfg. 1998 to date.

MSR	$1,400	$1,150	$995	$850	$750	$600	$475	$350

Axis Sport MM90 with Tremolo - similar to the Axis Sport MM90, except features Music Man vintage style non-locking tremelo, available in Platinum and 3-Tone Vintage Sunburst finishes. Mfg. 1998 to date.

MSR	$1,500	$1,200	$1,050	$925	$775	$650	$500	$375

EDWARD VAN HALEN - single cutaway basswood body, bound figured maple top, bolt-on maple neck, 22-fret maple fingerboard with black dot inlay, strings through bridge, 4/2-per-side Schaller tuners with pearl buttons, chrome hardware, 2 humbucking DiMarzio pickups, volume control (with *Tone* knob!), 3-position switch, available in Translucent Gold, Translucent Purple, and Translucent Red finishes. Mfg. 1991 to 1995.

		$2,200	$1,800	$1,400	$1,100	$N/A	$N/A	$N/A

Last MSR was $1,600.

The Edward Van Halen model was co-designed with Edward Van Halen, and introduced in 1991. Upon dissolution of the endorsement deal, this model was renamed the Axis (see above).

Edward Van Halen with Tremolo - similar to Edward Van Halen, except has Floyd Rose double locking vibrato, available in Black, Metallic Gold, Natural, Sunburst, Translucent Black, Translucent Blue, Translucent Gold, Translucent Pink, Translucent Purple, and Translucent Red finishes. Mfg. 1991 to 1995.

		$2,700	$2,500	$2,100	$1,700	$N/A	$N/A	$N/A

Last MSR was $1,750.

LUKE - offset double cutaway alder body, bolt-on maple neck, 25 1/2" scale, 22-fret rosewood fingerboard with pearl dot inlay, Floyd Rose vibrato, 4/2-per-side Schaller tuners, chrome hardware, 2 single coil/1 humbucker EMG pickups, volume control, 5-position switch, active electronics, available in Pearl Blue and Pearl Red finishes. Mfg. 1994 to date.

1994-1997		$1,100	$950	$875	$795	$675	$525	$375
MSR	$1,600	$1,295	$1,150	$995	$850	$695	$550	$400

In 1998, the Luke model was reconfigured ("Luke II" ?) to feature a Music Man vintage-style tremolo, Schaller M6-IND, locking tuners, custom wound EMG-SLV single coil pickups, volume and tone controls. Luke Blue (Light Pearl Blue) finish was introduced; Pearl Blue and Pearl Red finishes were disc.

The Luke model was designed with artist Steve Lukather (Toto, Los Lobotomys).

SILHOUETTE - offset double cutaway alder, ash or poplar body, aluminum-lined pickguard, bolt-on maple neck, 24-fret maple or rosewood fingerboard with dot inlay, strings-through bridge, 4/2-per-side Schaller tuners, chrome hardware, 2 single coil/1 humbucker DiMarzio pickups, volume/tone control, 5-position switch. Avail able in Black, Natural, Sunburst, Translucent Blueburst, Translucent Teal, Translucent Red, and White finishes. Mfg. 1987 to date.

MSR	$1,125	$900	$795	$695	$575	$475	$375	$275

Add $250 for 3 single coil pickups (this option was disc in 1998).

Add $250 for 2 humbucking pickups (this option was disc in 1998).

In 1996, Natural and Transparent Blueburst finishes were disc.

In 1998, humbucker/single coil/humbucker pickup configuration replaced the 2 single coil/humbucker pickup configuration; Translucent Teal and Translucent Red finishes were disc.

The Silhouette was the first Ernie Ball/Music Man production guitar. Designed by Dudley Gimpel, and developed in part by guitarist Albert Lee, this design was influenced by earlier CLF Research models but a number of modern refinements added.

Silhouette with Tremolo - similar to Silhouette, except has Floyd Rose tremolo. Disc. 1998.

		$975	$850	$725	$625	$525	$400	$300

Last MSR was $1,200.

Add $25 for humbucker/single coil/humbucker pickups.

SILHOUETTE SPECIAL - similar to Silhouette, except has alder body, 22-fret fingerboard, Schaller M6-IND locking tuners, 3 single coil (or 2 single coil/1 humbucker) DiMarzio pickups, patented "Silent Circuit" noise reduction electronics, available in Candy Red, Pearl Blue, Pearl Green, or Pearl Purple finishes. Current Mfg.

MSR	$1,200	$950	$850	$725	$625	$525	$400	$300

Add $100 for 3-Tone Vintage Sunburst finish.

This model is available in a left-handed configuration.

In 1998, Pearl Blue and Pearl Green finishes were disc.

Silhouette Special with Tremolo - similar to Silhouette Special, except has a Music Man vintage-style tremolo. Current Mfg.

MSR	$1,300	$1,100	$900	$795	$675	$550	$450	$325

Early models may feature a Wilkinson VSV tremolo.

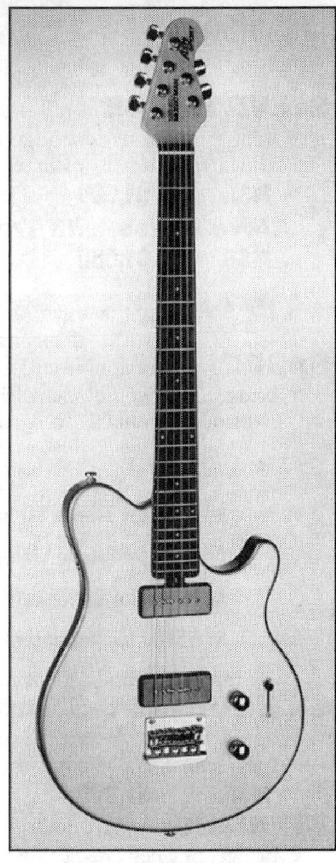

Ernie Ball Axis Sport MM90
courtesy Ernie Ball

E

GRADING		100% MINT	98% NEAR MINT	95% EXC+	90% EXC	80% VG+	70% VG	60% G

STEVE MORSE - offset double cutaway poplar body, black shielded pickguard, bolt-on maple neck, 22-fret rosewood fingerboard with pearl dot inlay, tune-o-matic bridge/stop tailpiece, 4/2-per-side Schaller tuners, chrome hardware, humbucker/slanted single coil/single coil/humbucker DiMarzio pickups, volume/tone control, 3-position selector, and 2 mini switches, available in Translucent Blueburst finish. Mfg. 1988 to date.

MSR	$1,500	$1,200	$1,050	$925	$775	$650	$500	$375

Steve Morse with Tremolo - similar to Steve Morse, except has Floyd Rose tremolo. Current Mfg.

MSR	$1,650	$1,325	$1,150	$1,000	$850	$725	$650	$425

ELECTRIC BASS

SABRE - offset double cutaway alder, ash, or poplar body, 34" scale, bolt-on maple neck, 21-fret maple or rosewood fingerboard with dot inlay, fixed bridge, 3/1 per side Schaller tuners, chrome hardware, 2 Ernie Ball humbucker pickups, volume/treble/mid controls, 5-way selector switch, active electronics, available in Black, Natural, Sunburst, Translucent Blueburst, Translucent Red, and Translucent Teal finishes. Mfg. 1988 to 1991.

$850	$795	$675	$600	$525	$450	$375

Last MSR was $1,095.

Add $60 for 3-band EQ (volume/treble/mid/bass controls).

Add $70 for 3-Tone Vintage Sunburst finish.

Add $100 for Butterscotch finish with shell pickguard.

Add $100 for Translucent White finish with shell pickguard.

This model had an optional fretless pau ferro fingerboard (with or without inlaid fretlines).

SILHOUETTE 6-STRING BASS GUITAR - offset double cutaway poplar body, bolt-on maple neck, 29 5/8" scale, 22-fret maple fingerboard with black dot inlay, strings-through fixed bridge, 4/2-per-side Schaller tuners, chrome hardware, 2 DiMarzio humbucker pickups, volume/tone/series-parallel control, 5-way position switch, available in Black finish. Mfg. 1993 to date.

MSR	$1,800	$1,450	$1,250	$1,100	$950	$775	$625	$450

STERLING - offset double cutaway ash body, pickguard, 34" scale, bolt-on maple neck, 22-fret maple or rosewood fingerboard with dot inlay, fixed bridge, 3/1 per side Schaller tuners, chrome hardware, Ernie Ball humbucker/phantom coil pickups, volume/treble/mid/bass controls, 3-way selector switch, active electronics, available in Black, Pearl Blue, Sunburst, and Translucent Red finishes. Mfg. 1994 to date.

MSR	$1,450	$1,150	$1,000	$895	$750	$625	$495	$375

Add $150 for Natural ash velvet finished body/black pickguard (this option disc in 1998).

This model had an optional fretless pau ferro fingerboard (with or without inlaid fretlines).
The 3-way selector switch has three different pickup selections: both coils, series; single coil; both coils, parallel.

STINGRAY - offset double cutaway ash body, pickguard, bolt-on maple neck, 34" scale, 21-fret maple or rosewood fingerboard with dot inlay, fixed bridge, 3/1 per side Schaller tuners, chrome hardware, humbucker pickup, volume/2-band EQ controls, active electronics, chrome plated brass control cover, available in Black, Sunburst, Translucent Teal, Translucent Red, and White finishes. Current Mfg.

MSR	$1,350	$1,100	$975	$850	$700	$575	$450	$350

Add $50 for 3-band EQ (volume/treble/mid/bass controls).

Add $100 for 3-Tone Vintage Sunburst with black pickguard.

Add $150 for Natural and Natural ash velvet finished body/black pickguard (this option disc in 1998).

In 1998, White finish was disc.
This model has an optional fretless pau ferro fingerboard (with or without inlaid fretlines).
The StingRay model with 3-band EQ is available in a left-handed configuration.

20th Anniversary Sting Ray (1976-1996) - similar to Sting Ray, except has bookmatched figured maple top, black/white/black wood laminate layer, ash body, tortoise shell pickguard, Ernie Ball custom humbucker, volume/treble/mid/bass controls, available in Natural Top/Translucent Red Back finish. Mfg. 1996 only.

$1,600	$1,400	$N/A	$N/A	$N/A	$N/A	$N/A

Last MSR was $1,996.

Only 2,000 models were produced.
This model had an optional fretless pau ferro fingerboard (with or without inlaid fretlines).

Sting Ray 5 - similar to Sting Ray, except has 5-strings, 4/1 per side tuners, volume/3-band EQ controls, 3-position switch. Current Mfg.

MSR	$1,600	$1,200	$800	$770	$600	$540	$495	$450

Add $100 for 3-Tone Vintage Sunburst with black pickguard.

Add $150 for Natural and Natural ash velvet finished body/black pickguard (this option was disc in 1998).

This model is available in a left-handed configuration.
This model has an optional fretless pau ferro fingerboard (with or without inlaid fretlines).
The 3-way selector switch has three different pickup selections: both coils, series; single coil; both coils, parallel.

ERNIE BALL'S EARTHWOOD

Instruments previously produced in San Luis Obispo, California in the early to mid 1970s.

After finding great success with prepackaged string sets and custom gauges, Ernie Ball founded the Earthwood company to produce a four string acoustic bass guitar. George Fullerton built the prototype, as well as helping with other work before moving to Leo Fender's CLF Research company in 1974. Earthwood offered both the acoustic bass guitar and a lacquer finished *solid body* guitar with large sound chambers in 1972, but production was short lived (through February 1973). In April of 1975, bass guitar operations resumed on a limited basis for a number of years.

GRADING	100% MINT	98% NEAR MINT	95% EXC+	90% EXC	80% VG+	70% VG	60% G

Ernie Ball
Steve Morse Model
courtesy Ernie Ball

EROS

Instruments previously produced in Japan between the early 1970s through the early 1980s.

The EROS trademark is the brand name of a UK importer. These guitars were generally entry level copies of American designs.

(Source: Tony Bacon and Paul Day, The Guru's Guitar Guide)

ERRINGTON

Instruments currently produced in North Yorks, England.

Errington offers models in the Herald line such as the Deluxe or the Artizan with a single cutaway routed body, a *cat's eye*-shaped f-hole, bolt-on neck, six per side Gotoh tuners, chrome hardware, volume/tone controls, and a five-way selector switch.

ESTEY

See MAGNATONE.

Instruments previously built in Italy during the late 1960s. Distributed in the U.S. market by Magnatone (Estey Electronics).

Estey thinline electric guitars were offered by Magnatone (Estey Electronics) during the late 1960s. These guitars were imported in from Italy.

(Source: Michael Wright, Vintage Guitar Magazine)

EUGEN

Instruments currently built in Bergen, Norway.

Luthier Henry Eugen began playing guitar in Norway during his teenage years, and built up a guitar collection by age twenty. Customizing existing models led to designing his own guitars, and then learning to build the electric models. In 1979, Eugen began offering his hand crafted solid body electrics. Eugen custom guitars are still produced by him in a one man shop.

ELECTRIC

Eugen currently offers 7 distinct body designs in four different models. The **Basic (#1)** model has a 2-piece laminated body, while the **Paragon (#2)** has an additional maple top, Wood Out Binding or plastic-bound body. The **(#3) Paramount's** maple top is arched instead of flat with the W.O.B., and the **Mr. Eugen (#4)** is the Paramount model with select neck and body wood. The following body designs will indicate model availability.

The **Eugen** model (1-2-3-4) has a slightly offset dual cutaway model with curved forward horns and round lower bout. The set-in neck has a 22-fret fingerboard and 3+3 headstock. Pickups, configuration, and hardware are options discussed with the customer. The **Eugen 10/8** (3-4) is similar to the Eugen, except has 2 large/2 small internal tone chambers.

Eugen's **Little Wing** (1-2) is based on a Gibson Explorer, except the extended upper wing has been caved down to a rounded lower bout - and this model has a 6-on-a-side headstock. The **Classic T** (1-2) is a single cutaway model based on the Tele, while the **Classic S** (1-2-3) is a double cutaway Strat-style guitar (the **Classic S 7/8** has a slightly smaller body).

ELECTRIC BASS

The **Eugen Bass** is available in 4-, 5-, and 6-string configurations, and in the Basic or Paragon model construction.

EUROPA

Instruments previously built in France in the mid 1980s.

This company built high quality Fender-style solid body guitars, and offered both hardware options and choice of a graphite neck.

(Source: Tony Bacon and Paul Day, The Guru's Guitar Guide)

EXCETRO

Instruments previously built in Japan during the mid 1970s.

The EXCETRO company featured a range of medium quality semi-hollowbody guitars based on Rickenbacher-derived designs.

(Source: Tony Bacon and Paul Day, The Guru's Guitar Guide)

EYB GUITARS

Instruments currently built in Leonberg, Germany.

Luthier Gunter Eyb hand crafts custom electric guitar and bass models. Models are constructed using a wide range of clever designs based on classic configurations, and utilize additional piezo pickups and sustainer pickups. For further information concerning specifications and pricing, contact luthier Gunter Eyb directly (see Trademark Index).

E

NOTES

Section F

F GUITARS

Instruments currently built in Hamilton, Ontario (Canada) since 1976.

F Guitars was founded by George Furlanetto (luthier/bassist) and Froc Filipetti (musician) in 1976. Their high quality basses and guitars are the result of their custom building and designing backgrounds. The two designers have over 20 years of collective experience in guitar customizing, and applied that knowledge in designing "the classic vintage sound without the noise, and an even response through the extended range of modern 5- and 6-string basses". F Guitars winds their own pickups, and then matches them to the different wood combinations to achieve specific tonal characteristics.

F Guitars primarily offers 5- and 6-string model basses, but 4-string basses are available by special order (prices start at $2,379). The F Bass preamp was designed by Garry Poplawski of PE-EQ Research, and features one outstanding feature: when the frequencies are varied, the overall level remains constant. Preamps start at a $295 list price.

FM Custom
courtesy Fred Murray

ELECTRIC BASS

Add 10% for left-handed configuration.

Add $100 for gold or black hardware.

Add $150 for Sunburst finish.

Add $200 for Macassar ebony fingerboard.

Add $400 for figured maple top.

Add $400 for "Ceruse" finish (Black and White, Magenta and Black, Turquoise and Black).

Add $500 for neck-through or set-neck construction.

F Bass models are available in Natural Satin, Sunburst, Transparent Electric Blue, Transparent Royal Purple, and Transparent Wine Red finishes. Prices include a high quality Cordura nylon bag with "F" logo.

The **BN-5** 5-string (retail list $3,149) features a solid ash or alder body, 3-piece bolt-on maple neck, 22-fret maple fingerboard, lightweight Hipshot bridge, 2 humcancelling single coil pickups in wooden shells that match the body wood and finish, and a 3-band EQ preamp system with active/passive bypass switch. The **BN-6** 6-string has similar construction except for the 24-fret fingerboard (list $3,649).

The extended range **BNF-5** 5-string has an alder body, 3-piece maple bolt-on neck, 28-fret ebony fingerboard, ebony bridge, black hardware, and 2 humcancelling single coil pickups (list $3,579). The **BNF-6** 6-string has the same construction features (list $4,159).

The 5-string fretted **Studio Model** bass has a 20-fret maple or rosewood finger board, bolt-on maple neck, lightweight Hipshot bridge, and 3-band active EQ (list $3,195).

F Guitars also offers the **Alain Caron** model 6-string Fretless bass. This top-of-the-line model has an acoustically chambered figured maple body, spruce top, bolt-on 3-piece maple neck with oil finish, extended range (28-fret) ebony fingerboard, ebony bridge, black hardware, one magnetic pickup, RMC piezo bridge pickups. The **Alain Caron** model is available in Sunburst finish with matching headstock (retail list $5,599). A 5-string version is available by special order ($4,999). For further information regarding specifications and pricing, please contact F Guitars directly (see Trademark Index).

FM

Instruments currently built in Austin, Texas.

Luthier Fred Murray has been building custom guitars, and repairing or modifying guitars around Austin for a number of years.

FMO

See FACTORY MUSIC OUTLET.

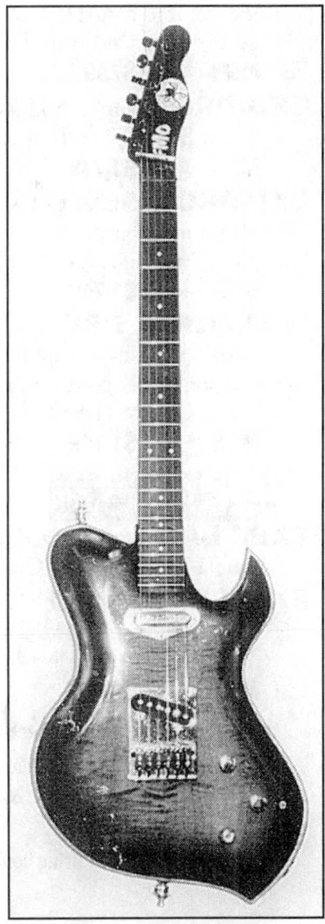

FMO Black Widow
courtesy Carol Lund

FABREGUES BASSES

Basses currently built in Santuce, Puerto Rico.

Pepe Fabregues currently builds basses in 4, 5, or 6-string configurations. They have ash bodies, with maple neck, and ebony, pauferro, or maple fretboards. All hardware and electronics are custom made for Fabregues instruments. Please contact the company directly for current model information and pricing (see Trademark Index).

FACTORY MUSIC OUTLET

Instruments previously built in Kenmore, New York 1981-2000.

Factory Music Outlet was founded in 1981 by Carol Lund. Lund had worked in California with the late Harry Wake. The business began as a hobby, and became a full time business as the need for quality repairs required more of her time. The repair business expanded to include violins, cellos, and all forms of stringed instruments.

As the repair business expanded, Lund realized the need for high quality, one-of-a-kind instruments. Each individual player seemed to have an idea of what their instrument should be. This evolved into a custom building segment of the business. FMO took pride in providing cutting edge innovations for customers. FMO employed the use of graphite and graphite composites for structural integrity as well as tonal quality. They featured graphite reinforced wood necks, bridge plates, cello and violin boards as well as all-graphite necks. FMO used the 2-TEK bridge in many of their custom guitars and basses. The Sabine tuner was also an innovation that FMO used frequently, in both the on board and removable format.

Factory Music Outlet's mission plan was simple: develop and build instruments that are one-of-a-kind. These instruments must be functional and durable as well as aesthetically pleasing.

The model name **Black Widow** is derived from the use of graphite components and American Black Walnut wood. The graphite is black, as is the Walnut when refinished using their *See Through Black* finish. While FMO's original guitars and basses were made exclusively of these materials, they built guitar models using a variety of woods and combinations of wood types.

Factory Music Outlet's other custom built guitar model was the **Tribute to Jerry Guitar** (last retail list $3,000). This model was composed of exotic woods, brass, abalone, and graphite components. It was available as a custom order only, and had many unique features. Price included a deluxe Bullhyde case.

FARMER, SIMON

Instruments currently built in East Sussex, Britian.

In November 1991, a source close to Blue Book Publishing sent in a fax containing a picture and write up of a prototype guitar built by Simon Farmer. The **Guitube**, as the prototype was named, featured a routed Canadian rock maple fingerboard, a Kent Armstrong humbucking pickup, a gas-spring dampened tremolo system, and steel tubing that formed the bouts of the guitar body. The pointed headstock has six-on-a-side tuners. As of this date, the ***Blue Book of Electric Guitars*** has not heard nor seen this prototype or any production designs approaching this model.

In 1997, Farmer was displaying a hand crafted carbon fiber guitar at the January NAMM show. Farmer's current workshop is located in East Sussex, England.

FARNELL GUITARS, INC.

Previously FARNELL CUSTOM GUITARS.

Instruments currently built in Pomona, California. Previous production was based in Rancho Cucamonga, California in the early 1990s.

Designer Al Farnell has been producing guitars that feature synthetic bodies of fiberglass for the past several years. The Farnell guitar features a patent-applied for body that is built of a closed-cell polyfoam material with a mahogany insert called the "Sound Reservoir".

ELECTRIC

EXP-K - double cutaway Endever body style, 2 EMG SAV single coil pickups, EMG 81 or 85 humbucker in the bridge position, GoToh H.A.P. tuners, pearl pickguard, fixed bridge and tailpiece, 6-on-a-side tuners, Graph-Tech graphite nut, 1 vol/1 tone control, 5-way switch, available in Ultra Black, Ultra Green, Ultra Purple, Ultra Blue and Ultra Red finishes. Current Mfg.

MSR $799

EXG-K - similar to EXP, except EMG 89 pickup in the neck position and EMG 85 or 81 pickup in the bridge position, push-pull splitter on the volume control, 1 volume/1 tone, 3-way switch, available in Black Tiger, Purple Tiger, Amber Tiger, Cherry Tiger, Honey Tiger, Burgundy Tiger and Blue Tiger finishes. Current Mfg.

MSR $799

EXG-PRO - similar to EXG, except has Graph-Tech Graphite saddles, After Burner 20 DB Booster and SPC Mid Booster, available in Brown Tiger, Black Tiger, Burgundy Tiger, Purple Tiger, Cherry Tiger and Amber Tiger finishes.

MSR $1,749

EXP-PRO - similar to EXP-K, except has push-pull splitter, quartersawn rock maple neck, slab rosewood fingerboard, gold hardware, EMG 89 humbucker pickup in the bridge position, EMG Afterburner, graphite bridge saddles. Available in Ultra Black, Ultra Green, Ultra Purple, Ultra Blue and Ultra Red finishes. Current Mfg.

MSR $1,749

MILLENIUM PRO the Millennium body, EMG 85 humbucker pickup in the neck position, EMG 89 humbucker pickup in the bridge position, push-pull splitter, GoToh H.A.P. tuners, quartersawn rock maple neck, 1 volume/1 tone, 3-way switch, slab rosewood fingerboard, stop tailpiece, gold hardware, EMG Afterburner, graphite bridge saddles. Available in Black Tiger, Brown Tiger, Burgundy Tiger, Purple Tiger, Cherry Tiger and Amber Tiger finishes. Current Mfg.

MSR $1,749

Bass Guitars

EXPJ BASS - oversized double cutaway Endever body style, EMG P/J pickup combination, 4-on-a-side GoToh H.A.P. mini-tuners, 2 volume/1 tone controls, Graph-Tech graphite nut, available in same colors as EXP. Discontinued.

EXB-4 BASS - double cutaway Endever body style, 2 EMG Soapbar pickups, GoToh mini-tuners, 3-piece quartersawn rock maple neck, rosewood fingerboard, 2 volume/1 tone controls, gold hardware, available in Black Tiger, Brown Tiger, Burgundy Tiger, Purple Tiger, Cherry Tiger and Amber Tiger finishes. Current Mfg.

MSR $1,599

Add $150 for for 5-string configuration (Model EXB-5).

EXB-4K Bass - similar to EXB-4, except has Farnell Ultralight body design, 2 Farnell active soapbar pickups, GoToh Farnell bridge, available in same colors as EXB-4. Current Mfg.

MSR $849

Add $50 for 5-string configuration (Model EXB-5K).

FEDDEN

Instruments currently built in Comack, New York, beginning 1999. Previously built in Port Washington, New York.

Luthier George Fedden is currently producing acrylic *see-through* guitar bodies that feature colored inlays inside the body for a stunning effect. Designs are based on classic American favorites, and feature wood bolt-on necks, gold hardware, and gold-plated Kent Armstrong pickups. Their clarity and clean wiring harnesses will definitely make you take a second look. The overall feel and body weight will make you want to play them! Fedden instruments are available directly from the builder.

FENDER

Instruments currently produced in Corona, California (U.S.), Mexico, Japan, Tianjin (China), and Korea. Distributed by the Fender Musical Instruments Corporation of Scottsdale, Arizona. The Fender trademark established circa 1948 in Fullerton, California.

Clarence Leonidas Fender was born in 1909, and raised in Fullerton, California. As a teenager he developed an interest in electronics, and soon was building and repairing radios for fellow classmates. After high school, Leo Fender held a bookkeeping position while he still did radio repair at home. After holding a series of jobs, Fender opened up a full scale radio repair shop in 1939. In addition to service work, the Fender Radio Service store soon became a general electronics retail outlet. However, the forerunner to the Fender Electric Instruments company was a smaller two-man operation that was originally started as the K & F company in 1945. Leo Fender began modestly building small amplifiers and electric lap steels with his partner, Clayton Orr *Doc* Kaufman. After K & F dissolved, Fender then formed the Fender Electric Instrument company in 1946, located on South Pomona Avenue in Fullerton, California. The company sales, though slow at first, began to expand as his amplifiers and lap steel began meeting acceptance among West Coast musicians. In 1950, Fender successfully developed the first production solid body electric guitar. Originally the Broadcaster, the name was quickly changed to the Telecaster after the Gretsch company objected to the infringement of their *Broadkaster* drum sets.

Soon Fender's inventive genius began designing new models through the early 1950s and early 1960s. The Fender *Precision* Bass guitar was unveiled in 1951. While there is some kind of an existing background for the development of an electric solid body guitar, the notion of a 34" scale instrument with a fretted neck that could replace an upright acoustic doublebass was completely new to the music industry. The Precision bass (so named because players could fret the note 'precisely') coupled with a Fender Bassman amplifier gave the bass player more sonic projection. Fender then followed with another design in 1954, the Stratocaster. The simplicity in design, added to the popular sounds and playability, makes this design the most copied world wide. Other popular models of guitars, basses, and amplifiers soon followed.

Fender "Western Set" Strat courtesy Fender Custom Shop

By 1964, Fender's line of products included electric guitars, basses, steel guitars, effects units, acoustic guitars, electric pianos, and a variety of accessories. Leo's faltering health was a factor in putting the company up for sale, and first offered it to Don Randall (the head of Fender Sales) for a million and a half dollars. Randall opened negotiations with the Baldwin Piano & Organ company, but when those negotiations fell through, offered it to the conglomerate CBS (who was looking to diversify the company holdings). Fender (FEIC) was purchased by CBS on January 5, 1965 (actually in December of 1964) for thirteen million dollars. Leo Fender was kept on as a *special consultant* for five years, and then left when then contract was up in 1970. Due to a ten year *no compete* clause, the next Leo Fender-designed guitars did not show up in the music industry until 1976 (Music Man).

While Fender was just another division of CBS, a number of key figures left the company. Forrest White, the production manager, left in 1967 after a dispute in producing solid state amplifiers. Don Randall left in 1969, disenchanted with corporate life. George Fullerton, one of the people involved with the Stratocaster design, left in 1970. Obviously, the quality in Fender products did not drop the day Leo Fender sold the company. Dale Hyatt, another veteran of the early Fender days, figured that the quality on the products stayed relatively stable until around 1968 (Hyatt left in 1972). But a number of cost-cutting strategies, and attempts to produce more products had a deteriorating effect. This reputation leads right to the classic phrase heard at vintage guitar shows, "Pre-CBS?".

In the early 1980s, the Fender guitar empire began to crumble. Many cost-cutting factors and management problems forced CBS to try various last ditch efforts to salvage the instrument line. In March of 1982, Fender (with CBS' blessing) negotiated with Kanda Shokai and Yamano Music to establish **Fender Japan**. After discussions with Tokai (who built a great Fender Strat replica, among other nice guitars), Kawai, and others, Fender finally chose Fuji Gen Gakki (based in Matsumoto, about 130 miles northwest of Tokyo). In 1983 the **Squier** series was built in Japan, earmarked for European distribution. The Squier trademark came from a string-making company in Michigan (V.C. Squier) that CBS had acquired in 1965.

In 1984 CBS decided to sell Fender. Offers came in from IMC (Hondo, Charvel/Jackson), and the Kaman Music Corporation (Ovation). Finally, CBS sold Fender to an investment group led by William Schultz in March for twelve and a half million dollars. This investment group formally became the Fender Musical Instruments Corporation (FMIC). As the sale did not include production facilities, USA guitar production ceased for most of 1985. It has been estimated that 80% of the guitars sold between late 1984 and mid-1986 were made in Japan. Soon after, a new factory was built in Corona, California, and USA production was restored in 1986 and continues to this day.

In 1990, the Fender (FMIC) company built an assembly facility in Mexico to offset rising costs of oriental production due to the weakening of the American dollar in the international market. Fender also experimented with production based in India from 1989 to 1990. The Fender (FMIC) company currently manufactures instruments in China, Japan, Korea, Mexico, and the U.S.

As reported in the March 1998 edition of **MMR**, Fender CEO Schultz sent out a letter to Fender dealers (dated January 9, 1998) which discussed the company establishing a "limited number" of Fender mail-order catalog dealers. Fender has announced specific guidelines as to what is allowed in mail-order catalog sales. Most importantly, Fender "announced a minimum advertised price (MAP) policy applicable to mail-order catalogs only", stated Schultz, "The MAP for mail-order catalogs is set at a maximum 30 percent off the Fender suggested retail price, and will be enforced unilaterally by Fender". What this does to the Fender retail price overall is basically lower the bar - but the impact on regular guitar stores has not been fully realized. While it's one thing to buy because of a discounted price through a catalog, it's a different situation to walk into a dealer's shop and be able to "test drive" a guitar before it is purchased. Retail music stores have to be aware that there is now an outside source (not under their control) that

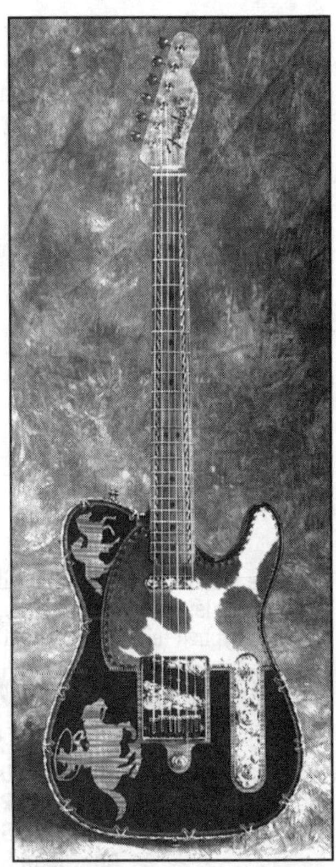

Fender "Western Set" Tele courtesy Fender Custom Shop

F

dictates minimum sales prices - the national catalogs. Of course, retail shops still control the maximum sale price applied to an instrument. Readers familiar to the *Blue Book of Electric Guitars* will note both the Manufacturer's suggest retail price and the appropriate discounted price (100% listing) under currently produced models.

In 1999, Fender changed a significant number of Model Numbers (SKU's). An attempt has been made to update as many of these as possible, but you may encounter a few that have not been changed. We will continue to monitor these changes and stay up-to-date.

(Source for earlier Fender history: Richard R. Smith, Fender: The Sound Heard 'Round the World)

Fender also produced a number of other electric stringed instruments. In early 1956, Fender debuted the solid body Electric Mandolin. This four stringed model originally had a *slab cut* body, but became more contoured like a Stratocaster in 1959. The Electric Mandolin had a four on a side Fender headstock, single coil pickup, volume/tone control, and a 2-screw *shared*-saddle bridge, available in Blond or Sunburst finishes, the Electric Mandolin was in production from 1956 to 1976.

Fender's Electric Violin was first introduced (briefly) in 1958. The first production model had a violin-shaped solid body, single coil pickup, volume/tone controls, and a slotted peghead with four on a side tuners. A revised edition with a scrolled headstock and ebony tuning pegs was produced from 1969 to 1975.

VISUAL IDENTIFICATION FEATURES

When trying to determine the date of an instrument's production, it is useful to know a few things about feature changes that have occurred over the years. The following information may help you to determine the approximate date of manufacture of a Fender instrument by visual observation, without having to handle (or disassemble) the instrument for serial number verification.

Fingerboard Construction

1950 to 1959: All necks were made out of a solid piece of maple with the frets being driven right into the neck. This is the standard design for maple necks.

1959 to 1962: The maple neck was planed flat and a rosewood fingerboard with frets and inlay was glued to the top of the neck. This is known as the *slab top*, or *slab* fingerboard.

1962 to 1983: The maple necks were rounded to the neck's radius and a thinner piece of rosewood was glued to the neck area. This design is called the *veneer* fingerboard.

1983 to date: Fender returned to the *slab top* fingerboard design of the 1959 to 1962 era.

Neckplate Identification

1950 to 1971: The neck was attached to the body by means of a 4-screw neckplate.

1971 to 1981: The neckplate was changed to 3-screws, and a micro neck adjustment device was added.

In 1981: A transition from the 3-screw design back to the 4-screw design began to occur.

By 1983: The 4-screw neckplate was back in standard production, with the micro neck adjuster remaining.

PRODUCTION MODEL CODES

Current Fender instruments are identified by a *part number* that consists of a three digit location/facility code and a four digit model code (the two codes are separated by a hyphen). An example of this would be:

010 - 9200

(The 010-9200 part number is the California-built Stevie Ray Vaughn model.)

As Fender guitars are built in a number of locations worldwide, the three digit code will indicate where production took place (this does not indicate where the parts originated, however; just assembly of components). The first digit differentiates between Fender bridges and Floyd Rose tremolos:

0	**Fender Product, non-Floyd Rose**
1	**Floyd Rose Bridge**
3	**Guild Product**

The second/third digit combination designates the production location:

10	**U.S., Guitar (Corona)**
13	**Mexico, Guitar and Bass (Ensenada)**
19	**U.S., Bass (Corona)**
25	**Japan, Guitar and Bass**
27	**Japan, Guitar and Bass**
33	**Korea, Guitar and Bass**
33	**China, Guitar and Bass**
33	**Indonesia, Guitar and Bass**
50	**Guild Product, Acoustic and Electric (Rhode Island)**
94	**Spain, Acoustic Guitar (Classical)**

The four digits on the other side of the hyphen continue defining the model. The fourth/fifth digit combination is the product designation. The sixth digit defines left-handedness, or key parts inherent to that product. The final seventh digit indicates which type of wood fingerboard. Any digits that follow the second hyphen (eighth/ninth/tenth) are color descriptions (01 = Blond, 02 = Lake Placid Blue, etc.) Happy Hunting!

Production Location by Series Name

Unless otherwise noted, most Series models are produced in the same country of origin. Here is the 1998 unofficial breakdown of Series by country of origin:

American Deluxe Series =	**U.S.A.**
American Plus Series =	**U.S.A.**
American Special Series =	**U.S.A.**
American Standard Series =	**U.S.A.**
American Vintage Series =	**U.S.A.**
Artist Signature Series =	**U.S.A.**

GRADING	100% MINT	98% NEAR MINT	95% EXC+	90% EXC	80% VG+	70% VG	60% G

Fender Coronado II
courtesy San Diego Guitars

California Series = **Corona, California and Ensenada, Mexico**
Collectable Series = **Japan**
Deluxe Series = **Mexico**
Hot Rodded American Series = **U.S.A.**
Limited Edition Artist Series = **Japan**
Standard Series = Mexico

Series names can be cross referenced against production model code to verify country of origin as well.

For further information on Fender acoustic models, please refer to the 7th Edition ***Blue Book of Acoustic Guitars.***

ELECTRIC ARCHTOP

D'AQUISTO ULTRA (Model 010-2070, U.S. Mfg.) - See James D'Aquisto Signature Series (in Electric Guitar section).

ELECTRIC

In late 1997, Fender began marketing the **StratPak** (Model 013-4600-011), an all-in-one package that included a Mexican production Fender Standard Stratocaster, a gig bag, Fender Frontman 15R amplifier (with reverb), tuner, cable, strings, and picks (retail list $650). This all-in-one set helps the guitar student get into an electric guitar package in "one-stop shopping".

In the late 1970s, instrument bodies generally became heavier and less desirable due to their weight. With the higher prices of 1950s and 1960s Stratocasters and Telecasters on today's vintage market (and less access to the average player), however, the 1970s models are beginning to climb in price.

Here's a bit of revisionist history: The 1970s were Fender's "Dark Ages", which lead to players and dealers looking for the models from the '50s and '60s (and the formation of today's vintage guitar market). Now that the source of the sought-after models is drying up or getting "too spendy", those 1970s models aren't looking too bad!

Pricing for Fender Custom Color Finishes (1950s to 1960s) & Refinishing

The most *common* Fender Custom Color finishes from the 1950s/1960s found are Candy Apple Red, Lake Placid Blue and Olympic White. These Custom Colors may not be as highly sought after as other Custom Color finishes, and therefore will not be as highly valued as rarer Custom Colors such as Burgundy Mist.

Add 20%-50% to the price of those vintage Fenders with an original factory Custom Color finish, depending on the rarity of color and original condition. An original custom color Fender's price tag will depend on both the rarity of the finish/model, and the original condition factor.

As a rule, professional refins are worth approximately 50% less than an original model, if the refin is in the original color/finish.

Bullet Series

The Bullet model was introduced in 1983, and was designed by John Page (now with the Fender Custom shop). Originally built in Korea, production was switched back to the U.S. facilities after six months and remained there through 1983. The original design featured a Telecaster-ish body design and slim headstock, a 25 1/2" scale, and two pickups that were "leftovers" from the Mustang production line. The Bullet had a suggested list price of $189, although this amount changed as more models were introduced to the series.

Models in this series have offset double cutaway alder body, white pickguard, bolt-on maple neck, 22-fret maple finger-board with black dot inlay, fixed bridge, telecaster style peghead, 6-on-one-side tuners, chrome hardware, volume/tone control (unless otherwise listed), available in Ivory, Red, Metallic Red, Sunburst, Walnut, and White finishes.

BULLET (First Version) - single cutaway body, 22-fret rosewood fingerboard with pearl dot inlay, 2 single coil covered pickups, 3-position switch. Mfg. 1981 to 1983.

$250 $235 $215 $200 $195 $185 $175

This model was also available with black pickguard.

In 1983, the body was changed to offset double cutaway alder body, known as the 'Second Version' of the Bullet.

Bullet Deluxe - single cutaway mahogany body, 22-fret rosewood fingerboard with pearl dot inlay, strings through bridge, 2 single coil covered pickups, 3-position switch.

$275 $255 $235 $225 $215 $205 $200

This model was also available with black pickguard.

Bullet H-1 - covered humbucker pickup, push button coil split switch. Mfg. 1983 only.

$215 $170 $160 $150 $140 $135 $130

Bullet H-2 - strings through bridge, 2 covered humbucker pickups, 3-position switch, 2 push button coil split switches. Mfg. 1983 only.

$230 $210 $190 $160 $150 $140 $135

Bullet S-2 - laminated plastic pickguard, strings through bridge, 2 single coil covered pickups, 3-position switch. Mfg. 1983 only.

$225 $205 $180 $160 $150 $140 $135

GRADING	100% MINT	98% NEAR MINT	95% EXC+	90% EXC	80% VG+	70% VG	60% G

Bullet S-3 - strings through bridge, 3 single coil covered pickups, 5-position switch. Mfg. 1983 only.

	$250	$225	$200	$175	$165	$160	$150

Coronado Series

CORONADO (U.S. Mfg.) - double rounded cutaway semi hollow bound beech body, arched top, f-holes, raised white pickguard, bolt-on maple neck, 21-fret rosewood fingerboard with pearl dot inlay, adjustable rosewood bridge/trapeze tailpiece, 6-on-one-side tuners, chrome hardware, single coil covered pickup, volume/tone control, available in Cherry, Custom Colors and Sunburst finishes. Mfg. 1966 to 1970.

	$600	$565	$535	$500	$475	$425	$400

This model was also offered with checkered binding, gold pickguard and tune-o-matic bridge/vibrato tailpiece.

Coronado II Wildwood (U.S. Mfg.) - similar to Coronado, except has dye-injected beechwood body, bound f-holes, white pickguard with engraved Wildwood/I-VI, bound fingerboard with block inlay, tune-o-matic bridge/vibrato trapeze tailpiece, pearl tuner buttons, 2 single coil covered pickups, 2 volume/2 tone controls, 3-position switch, available in Natural finish. Mfg. 1967 to 1970.

	$800	$725	$660	$600	$575	$530	$500

The Wildwood finish was the result of a seven year process in Germany where dye was injected into growing beech trees. After the trees were harvested, veneers were cut and laminated to the guitar tops. Pickguard numbers (I-VI) refer to the dye color (primary color of green, blue, and gold) and the applied finish.

Coronado XII Wildwood (U.S. Mfg.) - similar to Coronado, except has 12-string configuration, dye-injected beechwood body, bound f-holes, white pickguard with engraved Wildwood/I-VI, bound fingerboard with block inlay, tune-o-matic bridge/trapeze tailpiece, ebony tailpiece insert with pearl 'F' inlay, 6-per-side tuners with pearl buttons, 2 single coil covered pickups, 2 volume/2 tone controls, 3-position switch, available in Natural finish. Mfg. 1967 to 1970.

	$850	$775	$725	$650	$580	$560	$550

The Wildwood finish was the result of a seven year process in Germany where dye was injected into growing beech trees. After the trees were harvested, veneers were cut and laminated to the guitar tops. Pickguard numbers (I-VI) refer to the dye color (primary color of green, blue, and gold) and the applied finish.

CUSTOM (U.S. Mfg.) - offset double cutaway asymmetrical body with point on bottom bout, tortoise pickguard, bolt-on maple neck, 21-fret bound rosewood fingerboard with pearl block inlay, floating bridge/vibrato with bridge cover, droopy peghead, 3-per-side tuners, chrome hardware, 2 split covered pickups, volume/tone control, 4-position rotary switch, available in Sunburst top/Black back finish. Mfg. 1969 to 1970.

	$1,800	$1,700	$1,600	$1,500	$1,350	$1,175	$1,000

The Custom model was devised by long time Fender employee Virgilio "Babe" Simoni as a method to use up necks and bodies left over from the Electrix XII model. The twelve string peghead was refitted to six strings, and the body was recarved into a different design. The Custom model was originally to be named the "Maverick", which appears on some pegheads. Simoni estimated production to be around 600 to 800 completed pieces.

CYCLONE (Mexico Mfg.) - slightly offset double cutaway poplar body, bolt-on maple neck, 24.75" scale, 22-fret rosewood neck with dot inlay, synchronized tremolo, 6-on-a-side tuners, chrome hardware, brown or white shell pickguard, Tex-Mex single coil/Atomic humbucker pickups, volume/tone controls, 3-position toggle switch, chrome metal controls plate, available in Black, Candy Apple Red, and Arctic White and Brown Sunburst finishes. Mfg. 1998 to date.

MSR $649	$450	$395	$345	$295	$265	$215	$160

(Model 013-5000).

Add $50 for Brown Sunburst finish.

James D'Aquisto Signature Series

James D'Aquisto Signature models were designed by Master Luthier James D'Aquisto, following his initial designs for the Master Series (1984-1985). Current James D'Aquisto Signature Series models are handcrafted in Fender's Custom Shop.

In 1984, Fender contacted D'Aquisto to design three arch top guitar models to be produced in Japan under the **Master Series** designation. The top of the line **Ultra** was an acoustic model with a 17" body width, carved spruce top, carved figured maple back and sides, 25 1/2" scale, and an optional 'floating' pickup attached to the raised pickguard. The **Elite** has a 16" body width, 24 3/4" scale, arched spruce top, one humbucker, and ebony tailpiece/bridge/fingerboard/pickguard. The **Standard** model has a laminated maple top and back, and features 2 humbuckers and rosewood instead of ebony. All Japanese-built **Master Series** models feature a "Designed by D'Aquisto" headstock engraving. It is estimated that only 30 (+/-) Ultra models were built, and 1,000 Elites and Standards. Further research continues on the three **Master Series** models for future editions of the ***Blue Book of Electric Guitars***.

D'AQUISTO DELUXE (U.S. Mfg.) - single round cutaway laminated figured maple body (15 3/4" width), f-holes, maple neck, raised black pickguard, 22-fret bound ebony fingerboard with pearl block inlay, adjustable rosewood bridge/rosewood trapeze tailpiece, black peghead with pearl fan/logo inlay, 3-per-side tuners, chrome hardware, humbucker pickup, volume/tone controls, available in Antique Burst, Black, Natural, and Crimson Red Transparent finishes. Mfg. 1994 to date.

MSR $3,249	$2,275	$2,000	$1,750	$1,550	$1,250	$1,050	$895

(Model 010-2030).

D'Aquisto Standard - single round cutaway laminated maple body, laminated maple top, f-holes, maple neck, raised bound solid rosewood pickguard, 20-fret bound rosewood fingerboard with pearl block inlay, adjustable rosewood bridge/rosewood trapeze tailpiece, bound peghead with pearl fan/logo inlay, 3-per-side tuners with ebony buttons, gold hardware, two humbucker pickups, 2 volume/2 tone controls, available in Black, Natural, and Violin Sunburst finish. Mfg. 1989 to 1994.

	$800	$750	$700	$650	$600	$550	$475

Last MSR was $899.

GRADING	100% MINT	98% NEAR MINT	95% EXC+	90% EXC	80% VG+	70% VG	60% G

D'AQUISTO MASTERBUILT (ULTRA, U.S. Mfg.) - single round cutaway hollow figured maple body (17" width), arched bound spruce top, bound f-holes, set-in maple neck, raised bound ebony pickguard, 22-fret bound ebony fingerboard with pearl block inlay, adjustable ebony bridge/ebony trapeze tailpiece, bound peghead with pearl fan/logo inlay, 3-per-side gold tuners with ebony buttons, available in Antique Burst and Natural finish. Mfg. 1994 to date.

MSR $14,999	$10,499	$7,350	$6,750	$5,750	$5,995	$5,500	$4,995

(Model 010-2070).

Add $1,000 for pickguard mounted custom Kent Armstrong floating pickup (with volume and tone controls) as Model 010-2080 (Mfg. Sug. Retail $15,499).

D'Aquisto Classic Rocker traditional hollow body jazz design, 17" laminated maple hollow body with black and white "Checkerboard" multi-bound top, set three-piece figured maple neck, rosewood fingerboard with special "diamond" inlays, multiple binding, two Custom DeArmond 2000 single coil pickups, Bigsby vibrato tailpiece, chrome hardware, 3-per-side tuners, available in Amber, Black and Crimson Transparent finishes. Current Mfg.

MSR $3,999	$2,800	$2,500	$2,200	$1,900	$1,600	$1,300	$1,000

D'Aquisto Elite (Model 010-4050) - single round cutaway hollow figured maple body, arched bound spruce top, bound f-holes, maple neck, raised bound ebony pickguard, 22-fret bound ebony fingerboard with pearl block inlay, adjustable ebony bridge/ebony trapeze tailpiece, bound peghead with pearl fan/logo inlay, 3-per-side tuners with ebony buttons, gold hardware, humbucker pickup, volume/tone controls, available in Natural finish. Mfg. 1989 to 1994.

	$1,500	$1,300	$1,050	$875	$750	$650	$575

Last MSR was $2,000.

Fender D'Aquisto courtesy Magnolia Music

Duo-Sonic Series

DUO-SONIC (U.S. Mfg.) - offset double cutaway hardwood 3/4 size body, metal pickguard, bolt-on maple neck, 21-fret rosewood fingerboard with pearl dot inlay, fixed bridge with cover, 6-on-one-side tuners with plastic buttons, chrome hardware, 2 single coil pickups, volume/tone control, 3-position switch, available in Desert Sand (most common), Sunburst, or Custom Color (rare) finishes. Mfg. 1956 to 1964.

1956-1960 Long Scale	N/A	$600	$575	$525	$475	$435	$395

This period of Mfg. had a long scale with maple neck.

1956-1960 Short Scale	N/A	$500	$475	$450	$400	$375	$350
1960-1964	N/A	$400	$350	$320	$295	$275	$250

1960-64 Mfg. was produced in Red, Blue, and White colors.

This model was released as a student model. In 1960, tortoise or white plastic pickguard replaced metal pickguard.

Duo-Sonic II (U.S. Mfg.) - similar to Duo-Sonic, except has asymmetrical waist body, restyled plastic/metal pickguard, 22-fret fingerboard, enlarged peghead, 2 pickup selector slide switches, available in Blue, Red and White finishes. Mfg. 1964 to 1969.

	N/A	$500	$480	$460	$440	$420	$410

This instrument had a longer scale length than its predecessor.

DUO-SONIC (Mexico Mfg.) - offset double cutaway poplar body, bolt-on maple neck, 22.7" scale, 21-fret maple neck with black dot inlay, fixed bridge, 6-on-a-side tuners, chrome hardware, white pickguard, 2 single coil pickups, volume/tone controls, 3-position switch, available in Arctic White, Black, and Torino Red finishes. Mfg. 1994 to 1998.

	$200	$175	$150	$135	$115	$95	$75

Last MSR was $289.

(Model 013-0202).

ELECTRIC XII (U.S. Mfg.) - offset double cutaway asymmetrical body, tortoise pickguard, bolt-on maple neck, 21-fret rosewood fingerboard with pearl dot inlay, strings through bridge, droopy peghead, 6-per-side tuners, chrome hardware, 2 split covered pickups, volume/tone controls, 4-position rotary switch, available in Custom Colors and Sunburst finishes. Mfg. 1965 to 1968.

	N/A	$1,700	$1,500	$1,200	$995	$900	$850

In 1965, the fingerboard was bound. In 1966, block fingerboard inlay replaced dot inlay.

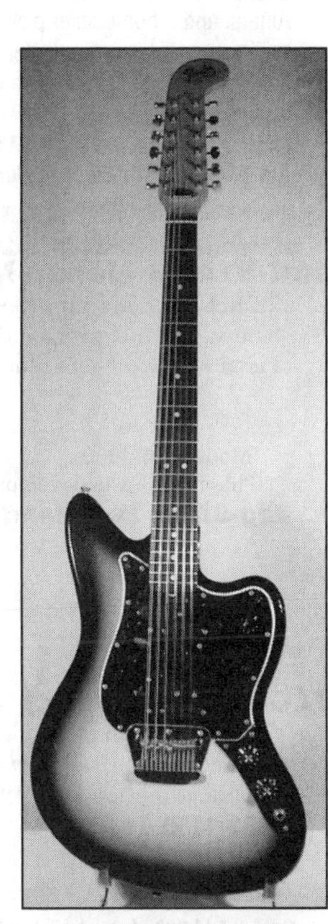
Fender Electric XII courtesy Rod & Hank's Vintage Guitars

F

GRADING	100% MINT	98% NEAR MINT	95% EXC+	90% EXC	80% VG+	70% VG	60% G

Esquire Series

ESQUIRE (U.S. Mfg.) - single cutaway ash body, black pickguard, bolt-on maple neck, 21-fret maple fingerboard with black dot inlay, strings through bridge with cover, 6-on-one-side tuners, chrome hardware, single coil pickup, volume/tone control, 3-position switch, controls mounted on metal plate, available in Butterscotch Blonde finish. Mfg. 1950 to 1969.

1950-1954	N/A	$10,000	$7,500	$5,500	$4,950	$4,250	$3,600
1955-1959	N/A	$7,500	$6,000	$4,500	$3,850	$3,350	$2,800
1960-1964	N/A	$5,000	$4,000	$3,100	$2,800	$2,500	$2,200
1965-1969	N/A	$3,500	$3,000	$2,500	$2,000	$1,850	$1,675

A few early models of this instrument were produced with 2 single coil pickups. First runs on this series were sparse and no instruments were made in the latter part of 1950. In late 1954, white pickguard replaced black pickguard. In 1955, level pole piece pickups were standard. In 1959, rosewood fingerboard with pearl dot inlay replaced the all maple neck. In 1967, maple fingerboard was an option. In 1969, maple fingerboard became standard.

Esquire Custom (U.S. Mfg.) - similar to Esquire, except has bound body, white pickguard, rosewood fingerboard with pearl dot inlay, available in Sunburst finish. Mfg. 1960 to 1970.

1960-1964	N/A	$7,500	$6,500	$5,750	$5,250	$4,750	$4,250
1965-1970	N/A	$5,000	$4,500	$4,000	$3,500	$3,000	$2,650

'54 ESQUIRE REISSUE (Japan Mfg.) - single cutaway ash body, black pickguard, bolt-on maple neck, 21-fret maple fingerboard with black dot inlay, strings through bridge with cover, 6-on-one-side tuners, chrome hardware, single coil pickup, volume/tone control, 3-position switch, controls mounted metal plate, available in Blonde and 2 Tone Sunburst finishes. Disc. 1994.

N/A	$350	$295	$265	$245	$205	$190

Last MSR was $570.

This model was a limited edition instrument available by custom order.

'62 Esquire Custom (Japan Mfg.) - similar to '54 Esquire, except has bound body, white pickguard, rosewood fingerboard with pearl dot inlay, available in Candy Apple Red and 3-Tone Sunburst finishes. Disc. 1994.

N/A	$375	$340	$320	$295	$260	$230

Last MSR was $580.

This model was a limited edition instrument available by custom order.

Esprit and Flame (Master Series) Models

In the early 1980s, Fender offered two models under the Master Series. The Master Series models were produced in Japan. The Esprit and Flame models are dual cutaway, semi-hollow ('tone chambered bodies') alder bodies with spruce or maple tops, set-in maple necks, ebony or rosewood fingerboards, 3-on-a-side tuners, and 2 humbucker pickups.

The Esprit Standard model has the carved maple top and rosewood fingerboard; the Esprit Elite has bridge fine tuners, TBX electronics, and coil-tapping capabilities. The Esprit Ultra has a carved spruce top, ebony fingerboard, and gold hardware.

The Flame models have a smaller body width than the Esprit, with the same model designations and appointments as the Standard/Elite/Ultra designations. Esprit and Flame models have their name designations on the headstock. Updates on the Fender Esprit and Flame models will be featured in future editions of the ***Blue Book of Electric Guitars***.

Jag-Stang Series

JAG-STANG (Japan Mfg.) - offset double cutaway asymmetrical basswood body, bolt-on maple neck, oversized ('60s Strat) headstock, 22-fret rosewood fingerboard with white dot inlay, 24" scale, floating bridge/Fender *Dynamic* vibrato tailpiece, 6-on-a-side tuners, chrome hardware, white pickguard, Vintage Strat single coil/humbucking pickups, volume/tone controls, 2 3-position selector switches, available in Fiesta Red and Sonic Blue. Disc 1999.

$450	$375	$325	$275	$250	$195	$150

Last MSR was $619.

(Model 025-4200).

This model was developed in conjunction with Kurt Cobain (Nirvana).

Jag-Stang Left Hand (Mexico Mfg.) - similar to the Jag-Stang, except in a left-handed configuration. Disc. 1998.

$500	$450	$400	$350	$325	$275	$225

Last MSR was $689.

(Model 013-4220).

Jaguar Series

JAGUAR (U.S. Mfg.) - offset double cutaway asymmetrical alder body, metal/plastic pickguard, bolt-on maple neck, 22-fret rosewood fingerboard with pearl dot inlay, string mute, floating bridge/vibrato, bridge cover plate, 6-on-one-side tuners, chrome hardware, 2 single coil exposed pickups, volume/tone control, volume/tone roller control, preset slide switch, 3 preset slide switches, available in Custom Colors and Sunburst finishes. Mfg. 1962 to 1975.

1962-1965	N/A	$2,200	$1,950	$1,750	$1,550	$1,350	$1,200
1966-1969	N/A	$1,500	$1,250	$1,150	$1,100	$1,050	$975
1970-1975	$1,200	$1,150	$1,100	$1,000	$975	$925	$850

Add 20% for ash body with gold hardware and Blonde finish.

In 1965, the fingerboard was bound. In 1966, block fingerboard inlay replaced dot inlay.

GRADING	100% MINT	98% NEAR MINT	95% EXC+	90% EXC	80% VG+	70% VG	60% G

'62 JAGUAR (U.S. Mfg., No. 010-0900) - alder body with 60's styling, maple neck with rosewood fingerboard, 22 vintage size frets, 24" scale, vintage style tuners, 2 US Jaguar Special Design single-coil pickups, Lead circuit has 2-position tone switch, volume, tone. Rhythm circuit has volume, tone, and circuit selector, brown shell or aged white/black/white pickguard, vintage stlye floating tremolo with tremolo lock button, contoured body with offset waist, available in 3-Color Sunburst, Olympic White, Black, Candy Apple Red, Fiesta Red, and Sherwood Metallic finishes. Case included. Mfg. 1999 to date.

MSR $1,799	$1,350	$995	$895	$795	$695	$550	

Subtract $50 for colors.

In 2001, Inca Silver (-824), Dakota Red (-854) and Ice Blue Metallic (-833) finishes were introduced.

'62 JAGUAR (Jap. Mfg.) - offset double cutaway asymmetrical basswood body, bolt-on maple neck, 24" scale, 21-fret rosewood fingerboard with white dot inlay, string mute, floating bridge/vibrato with 'tremolo lock', bridge cover plate, 6-on-a-side tuners, chrome hardware, metal+plastic pickguard, 2 single coil pickups, volume/tone control, volume/tone roller control, circuit selector slide switch, 3 preset slide switches, available in 3-Tone Sunburst, Candy Apple Red, and Vintage White finishes. Disc. 1998.

$550	$475	$425	$375	$325	$250	$200

Last MSR was $799.

(Model 027-7700).

Jaguar Left Hand (Model 027-7720, Jap. Mfg.) - similar to the Jaguar, except in a left-handed configuration, available in 3-Tone Sunburst finish. Mfg. 1995 to 1998.

$595	$525	$450	$400	$350	$275	$225

Last MSR was $869.

(Model 027-7720).

Fender Jaguar
courtesy Farmhouse Guitars

Jazzmaster Series

JAZZMASTER (U.S. Mfg.) - offset double cutaway asymmetrical alder body, gold metal (or tortoiseshell) pickguard, bolt-on maple neck, 21-fret rosewood fingerboard with pearl dot inlay, floating bridge/vibrato, bridge cover plate, 6-on-one-side tuners, chrome hardware, 2 single coil exposed pickups, volume/tone control, volume/tone roller control, 3-position switch, preset selector slide switch, available in Custom Colors and Sunburst finishes. Mfg. 1958 to 1980.

	100%	98%	95%	90%	80%	70%	60%
1958-1959	N/A	$2,500	$2,150	$1,785	$1,425	$1,285	$1,180
1960-1965	N/A	$2,000	$1,800	$1,600	$1,450	$1,250	$1,200
1966-1969	N/A	$1,500	$1,350	$1,250	$1,100	$1,000	$975
1970-1980	$1,200	$1,100	$1,050	$950	$900	$850	$750

Add 20% for ash body with gold hardware and Blonde finish.

In 1960, tortoise pickguard replaced metal pickguard. In 1965, the fingerboard was bound. In 1966, block fingerboard inlay replaced dot inlay.
In 1976, black pickguard replaced tortoise pickguard.

'62 JAZZMASTER (U.S. Mfg., No. 010-0800) - alder body with 60's styling, maple neck with rosewood fingerboard, 21 vintage size frets, 25.5" scale, vintage style tuners, 2 US Jazzmaster pickups, 3-way switch, Lead circuit has volume and tone, Rhythm circuit has volume, tone and circuit selector, brown shell or aged white/black/white pickguard, vintage style floating tremolo with tremolo lock button, contoured body with offset waist, available in 3-Color Sunburst, Olympic White, Black, Candy Apple Red, Fiesta Red, and Sherwood Metallic finishes. Mfg. 1999 to date.

MSR $1,799	$1,350	$1,150	$1,050	$950	$895	$750	

Subtract $50 for colors.

In 2001, Inca Silver (-824), Dakota Red (-854) and Ice Blue Metallic (-883) finishes were introduced.

'62 JAZZMASTER (Jap. Mfg., No. 027-7800) - offset double cutaway asymmetrical basswood body, bolt-on maple neck, 21-fret rosewood fingerboard with pearl dot inlay, floating bridge/vibrato with 'tremolo lock', bridge cover plate, 6-on-one-side tuners, chrome hardware, tortoiseshell pickguard, 2 single coil pickups, volume/tone control, volume/tone roller control, 3-position switch, preset selector slide switch, available in 3-Tone Sunburst, Candy Apple Red, and Vintage White finishes. Disc. 1999.

$550	$475	$425	$375	$325	$250	$200

Last MSR was $799.

Jazzmaster Left Hand (Jap. Mfg., No. 027-7820) - similar to the '62 Jazzmaster, except in a left-handed configuration, available in 3-Tone Sunburst finish. Mfg. 1995 to 1998.

$595	$525	$450	$400	$350	$275	$225

Last MSR was $869.

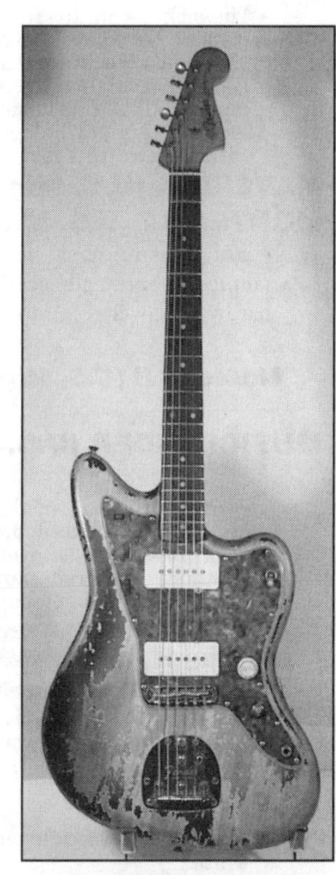

1960 Fender Jazzmaster
courtesy Zeb Cash-Lane

GRADING	100% MINT	98% NEAR MINT	95% EXC+	90% EXC	80% VG+	70% VG	60% G

THE VENTURES LIMITED EDITION JAZZMASTER (Jap. Mfg., No. 027-8200) - offset double cutaway asymmetrical light ash body, bolt-on maple neck, 22-fret rosewood fingerboard with white block inlay, floating bridge/vibrato, bridge cover plate, 6-on-one-side tuners, white shell pickguard, gold hardware, 2 Seymour Duncan JM single coil pickups, volume/tone control, volume/tone roller control, 3-position switch, preset selector slide switch, available in Midnight Black Transparent finish. Mfg. 1996 only.

$1,100 $975 $850 $775 $650 $595 $500

Last MSR was $1,344.

KATANA (Jap. Mfg.) - "wedge" shaped body, maple set neck with rosewood fingerboard, offset triangle position markers, 22 frets, arrowhead shaped headstock, 2 black exposed-coil humbucking pickups, 1 volume/1 tone control, 3-way switch, 2 pivot bridge with vibrato. Mfg. 1985 to 1986

Lead Series

LEAD I (U.S. Mfg.) - offset double cutaway alder body, black pickguard, bolt-on maple neck, 21-fret maple fingerboard with black dot inlay, strings through bridge, 6-on-one-side tuners, chrome hardware, humbucker exposed pickup, 2 two position switches, available in Black and Brown finishes. Mfg. 1979 to 1982.

N/A $350 $300 $275 $250 $225 $200

In 1981, Custom Colors became optional.

Lead II (U.S. Mfg.) - similar to Lead I, except has 2 single coil exposed pickups.

N/A $375 $325 $300 $275 $250 $225

Lead III (U.S. Mfg.) - similar to Lead I, except has 2 humbuckers. Mfg. 1981 to 1982.

N/A $375 $325 $300 $275 $250 $225

LTD (U.S. Mfg.) - single round cutaway hollow figured maple body, arched bound spruce top, f-holes, raised tortoise pickguard, bolt-on maple neck, 20-fret bound ebony fingerboard with pearl "diamond-in-block" inlay, adjustable ebony bridge/metal trapeze tailpiece, ebony tailpiece insert with pearl F inlay, bound peghead with pearl "mirrored F"/logo inlay, 3-per-side tuners with pearl buttons, gold hardware, covered humbucker pickup, volume/tone control, available in Sunburst finish. Mfg. 1968 to 1974.

N/A $3,950 $3,500 $3,000 $2,750 $2,450 $2,150

This model was designed by luthier Roger Rossmeisel, and is very rare.

MARAUDER (U.S. Mfg.) - offset double cutaway asymmetrical alder body, white pickguard, 3 control mounted metal plates, bolt-on maple neck, 21-fret bound rosewood fingerboard with pearl block inlay, strings through bridge with metal cover, 6-on-one-side tuners, chrome hardware, 4 pickups, volume/tone controls on lower treble bout, volume/tone controls, slide switch on upper bass bout, 4 push switches on upper treble bout, available in Custom Colors and Sunburst finishes. Mfg. 1965 to 1966.

Extreme rarity precludes accurate pricing on this model. If and when one surfaces, the asking price could be in the $7,500 - $10,000 range.

The pickups on this instrument were set under the pickguard, making the guitar appear to have no pickups. Due to unknown circumstances, this model never went into full production. There are few of these instruments to be found, and though they were featured in 1965 sales brochures, they would have to be considered prototypes. Most seasoned Fender dealers have never seen a Marauder. In the 1965-1966 catalog, the newly introduced Marauder carried a list price of $479. Compare this to the then- current list price of the Stratocaster's $281! This model had an optional standard vibrato. In 1966, the "second generation" Marauder featured 3 exposed pickups (which replaced original 'hidden' pickups). According to Gene Fields, who was in the Fender R & D section at the time, 8 prototypes were built: 4 with regular frets and 4 with slanted frets. Again, the Marauder was not put into full production.

MAVERICK (U.S. Mfg.) - refer to the Custom Model.

MONTEGO I (U.S. Mfg.) - single round cutaway hollow figured maple body, arched bound spruce top, bound f-holes, raised black pickguard, bolt-on maple neck, 20-fret bound ebony fingerboard with pearl "diamond-in-block" inlay, adjustable ebony bridge/metal trapeze tailpiece, ebony tailpiece insert with pearl F inlay, bound peghead with pearl fan/logo inlay, 3-per-side tuners with pearl buttons, chrome hardware, covered humbucker pickup, volume/tone control, available in Natural and Sunburst finishes. Mfg. 1968 to 1974.

N/A $1,200 $1,100 $950 $900 $850 $800

Montego II (U.S. Mfg.) - similar to Montego I, except has 2 humbucker pickups, 2 volume/2 tone controls, 3-position switch.

N/A $1,400 $1,100 $1,000 $900 $800 $750

MUSICLANDER (U.S. Mfg.) - refer to the Swinger Model.

N/A $1,600 $1,400 $1,300 $1,200 $1,100 $1,000

Fender's Mustang model was initially offered in both the full-scale or 3/4-scale neck. While the Mustangs were in great demand, both necks were produced; but many of the 3/4-scale models were returned from the field due to lack of popularity as compared to the full-scale neck. To salvage leftover parts, Virgilio "Babe" Simoni then redesigned the headstock (which then began to resemble a spear) while another worker redesigned the body. These changes are purely cosmetic; the Musiclander model is basically a Mustang with the 3/4-scale neck and a single pickup. Simoni estimates that all in all perhaps 250 to 300 were built, and even some of these were renamed into the Arrow or Swinger.

Musicmaster/Swinger Series

MUSICMASTER (U.S. Mfg.) - offset double cutaway poplar body, metal pickguard, bolt-on maple neck, 21-fret maple fingerboard with black dot inlay, fixed bridge with cover, 6-on-one-side tuners, chrome hardware, single coil covered pickup, volume/tone control, available in Blonde, Custom Colors and Sunburst finishes. Mfg. 1956 to 1964.

N/A $450 $420 $370 $325 $280 $270

In 1959, rosewood fingerboard with pearl dot inlay replaced maple fingerboard. In 1960, pickguard was changed to plastic: tortoise or white.

GRADING	100% MINT	98% NEAR MINT	95% EXC+	90% EXC	80% VG+	70% VG	60% G

Musicmaster II (U.S. Mfg.) - similar to Musicmaster, except has asymmetrical body, restyled pearloid pickguard, control mounted metal plate, enlarged peghead, available in Blue, Red and White finishes. Mfg. 1964 to 1975.

	N/A	$350	$315	$275	$245	$230	$220

In 1969, 24-fret fingerboard replaced 21-fret fingerboard.

Musicmaster (Mfg. 1975 - 1980) (U.S. Mfg.) - similar to Musicmaster, except has asymmetrical body, black pickguard, 22-fret fingerboard, available in Black and White finishes. Mfg. 1975 to 1980.

	N/A	$275	$240	$215	$195	$185	$175

This model was also available with alder or ash body.

SWINGER (U.S. Mfg.) - offset double cutaway asymmetrical alder body with cutaway on bottom bout, pearloid pickguard, bolt-on maple neck, 21-fret rosewood fingerboard with pearl dot inlay, fixed bridge, pointed peghead, 6-on-one-side tuners, chrome hardware, single coil covered pickup, volume/tone control, available in Black, Blue, Green and Red finishes. Mfg. 1969 only.

	N/A	$1,300	$1,200	$1,100	$1,000	$900	$800

This model was also known as the Arrow and/or the Musicmaster.

ARROW (U.S. Mfg.) - refer to the Swinger model.

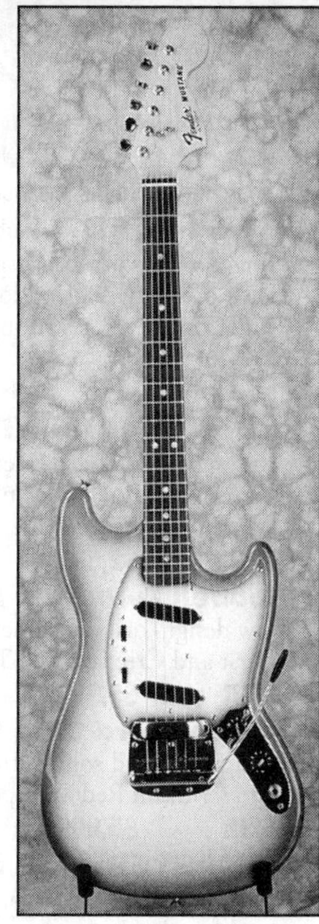

1978 Fender Mustang
courtesy Ryland Fitchett

Mustang/Performer/Prodigy/Bronco Series

MUSTANG (U.S. Mfg.) - offset double cutaway asymmetrical ash body, pearloid or shell pickguard, bolt-on maple neck, 21 or 22-fret rosewood fingerboard with pearl dot inlay, floating bridge/vibrato with bridge cover, 6-on-one-side tuners with plastic buttons, chrome hardware, 2 single coil covered pickups, volume/tone control, 2 selector slide switches, available in Black, Blonde, Blue, Natural, Sunburst, Red, Walnut and White finishes. Mfg. 1964 to 1981.

1964-1969	N/A	$750	$700	$650	$600	$575	$550
1970-1981	N/A	$675	$650	$600	$550	$500	$490

Fender offered the Mustang model in both the full-scale or a student-sized 3/4-scale neck. The Mustang model stayed popular for a number of years with the full-scale neck, but many of the 3/4-scale models were returned from dealers due to lack of acceptance (See MUSICLANDER). As a result, the number of 3/4-scale Mustangs available in the vintage market is a small amount. In 1969, 22-fret fingerboard became standard. In the 1970s, Black, Blonde, Natural, Sunburst and Walnut were the standard finishes. In 1975, tuner buttons became metal; black pickguard replaced original parts/design.

Competition Mustang (U.S. Mfg.) - similar to Mustang, except has Competition finishes (finishes with 3 racing stripes), available in Blue, Burgundy, Orange and Red finishes. Mfg. 1968 to 1973.

	N/A	$800	$725	$650	$630	$610	$600

'69 MUSTANG (Japan Mfg., No. 027-3700) - offset double cutaway slimmed basswood body, bolt-on maple neck, 22-fret rosewood fingerboard with white dot inlay, 24" scale, floating bridge/Fender *Dynamic* vibrato, 6-on-one-side tuners, chrome hardware, tortoiseshell-style pickguard, 2 covered single coil pickups, volume/tone controls, 2 pickup selector on/off slide switches, available in Sonic Blue and Vintage White finishes. Disc. 1999.

	$475	$415	$365	$300	$250	$215	$175

Last MSR was $649.

Mustang Left Hand (Japan Mfg., No. 027-3720) - similar to the Mustang, except in a left-handed configuration. Mfg. 1995 to 1998.

	$450	$425	$375	$325	$275	$225	$175

Last MSR was $719.

PERFORMER (Jap. Mfg.) - offset double cutaway body, maple neck with rosewood fingerboard, arrow-head shaped headstock, string clamp, 24-frets, 6-on-a-side tuners, 1 volume/1 tone control, 3-way switch, 2 angled white pickups, 2 pivot bridge with vibrato. Mfg. 1985 to 1986.

	N/A	$650	$575	$500	$450	$400	$350

PRODIGY (U.S. Mfg.) - offset double cutaway asymmetrical poplar body, black pickguard, bolt-on maple neck, 22-fret rosewood fingerboard with pearl dot inlay, standard vibrato, 6-on-one-side tuners, 2 single coil/1 humbucker exposed pickups, volume/tone controls, 5-position switch, available in Arctic White, Black, Crimson Red Metallic and Lake Placid Blue finishes. Mfg. 1991 to 1995.

	$295	$250	$225	$200	$175	$150	$125

Last MSR was $570.

This model is also available with maple fingerboard with black dot inlay.

BRONCO (U.S. Mfg.) - offset double cutaway poplar body, white pickguard, bolt-on maple neck, 22-fret rosewood fingerboard with pearl dot inlay, standard vibrato, covered single coil pickup, volume/tone control, available in Black, Red and White finishes. Mfg. 1967 to 1980.

	$500	$480	$460	$450	$435	$415	$400

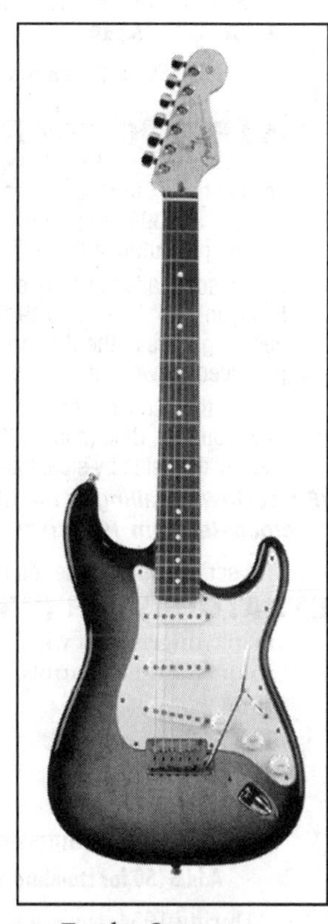

Fender Stratocaster
courtesy Fender

F

GRADING		100% MINT	98% NEAR MINT	95% EXC+	90% EXC	80% VG+	70% VG	60% G

Robben Ford Signature Series

The Robben Ford models were designed with Ford's input and specifications, and are currently built in the Fender Custom Shop.

ROBBEN FORD - double cutaway alder body, hollowed tone chambers, arched bound spruce top, maple neck, 22 jumbo fret bound ebony fingerboard with pearl split block inlay, Robben Ford's signature on the truss rod cover, tune-o-matic bridge/stop tailpiece, bound peghead with pearl stylized fan/logo inlay, 3-per-side tuners with ebony buttons gold hardware, 2 exposed polepiece humbucker pickups, 2 volume/tone controls, 3-position/coil tap switches, available in Antique Burst, Autumn Gold and Black finishes. Mfg. 1989 to 1994.

		N/A	$925	$850	$775	$700	$650	$625

Last MSR was $1,750.

ROBBEN FORD ELITE FM (ELITE, U.S. Mfg., No. 010-3040) - double cutaway mahogany body, arched figured maple top, set-in mahogany neck, 22-fret pau ferro fingerboard with abalone dot inlay, adjustable bridge/tunable tailpiece, blackface peghead with logo inlay, 3-per-side tuners, chrome hardware, 2 Seymour Duncan humbuckers, 2 volume/2 tone controls, 3-position selector, coil tap switch, active electronics, available in Tri-Color Sunburst and Crimson Red Transparent finishes. Mfg. 1994 to date.

MSR	$2,599	$1,825	$1,625	$1,525	$1,425	$1,325	$1,200	$1,000

Robben Ford Ultra FM (U.S. Mfg., No. 010-3060) - similar to Robben Ford Elite, except has internal tone chambers (semi-hollow design), carved flame maple top, multibound ebony fingerboard with pearl block inlay, gold (or nickel) hardware, available in Tri-Color Sunburst and Crimson Red Transparent finishes. Mfg. 1994 to date.

MSR	$5,999	$4,299	$3,795	$3,200	$2,800	$2,400	$2,050	$1,750

Robben Ford Ultra SP (U.S. Mfg., No. 010-3050) - similar to Robben Ford Elite, except has internal tone chambers (semi-hollow design), carved solid spruce top, multibound ebony fingerboard with pearl block inlay, gold hardware, available in Black, Tri-Color Sunburst, and Crimson Red Transparent finishes. Mfg. 1994 to date.

MSR	$5,999	$4,295	$3,795	$3,200	$2,800	$2,400	$2,050	$1,750

STARCASTER (U.S. Mfg.) - offset double cutaway asymmetrical semi-hollow maple body, bound arched top, f-holes, raised black pickguard, bolt-on maple neck, 22-fret maple fingerboard with black dot inlay, fixed bridge, 6-on-one-side tuners, chrome hardware, 2 covered humbucker pickups, master volume plus 2 volume and 2 tone controls, 3-position switch, available in Black, Blonde, Natural, Tobacco Sunburst, Walnut and White finishes. Mfg. 1976 to 1978.

		N/A	$1,475	$1,200	$1,100	$1,000	$950	$900

Designed by Gene Fields, the Starcaster was Fender's answer to Gibson's popular ES-335.

TORNADO (Model 013-0700, Mexico Mfg.) - offset cutaway/sloped shoulder poplar body, bolt-on maple neck, 24.75" scale, 22-fret rosewood neck with dot inlay, strings-through hard tail bridge, 6-on-a-side tuners, chrome hardware, brown shell pickguard, 2 chrome covered Atomic humbucker pickups, 2 volume/2 tone controls, 3-position toggle switch, available in Black, Candy Apple Red, Brown Sunburst, and Arctic White finishes. Mfg. 1998 to date.

MSR	$749	$550	$475	$395	$350	$295	$235	$185

Add $50 for Brown Sunburst finish.

STRATOCASTER SERIES

Leo Fender's Stratocaster was his second guitar design after the Telecaster. The Stratocaster was designed in and around 1953, with actual production beginning in early 1954 (a Fender ad mentioned that "Shipments are expected to begin May 15"). The model went through a series of changes (detailed below) and various permutation through the years.

Here's some additional dates to remember to aid in dating those late 1970s and 1980s Strat variants: Fender's three-way selector switch was updated to the 5-way in 1977. In the mid 1970s the "Thick Skin" high gloss all-polyester finish was introduced. After CBS sold Fender in 1985, there was no production of Fender guitars in the U.S. from February, 1985 to October, 1985. When the Corona plant was started up, only the Vintage Reissue Stratocaster models were produced between late 1985 through 1986.

Finally, the Fender-Lace Sensor was introduced in early 1987. The Lace Sensor was offered in 4 models: the Gold (classic late '50s sound), Silver (more mid-range punch), Blue (a late '50s 'humbucker' sort of sound), and Red (a high output humbucker-ish sound). A "Dually" was created when two Lace Sensors were placed side-by-side, looking like a humbucker but were actually two independent pickups.

(For further detailing of the history of the Stratocaster, see A.R. Duchossoir's book "The Fender Stratocaster". A fact-filled overview of the Stratocaster from 1953 to 1993)

This series has an offset double cutaway body, bolt-on maple neck, 6-on-a-side tuners, 3 single coil pickups (unless otherwise listed).

STRATOCASTER (PRE-CBS, Mfg. 1954 - 1959) - ash body, single ply white pickguard, 4-screw bolt-on maple neck, 21-fret maple fingerboard with black dot inlay, nickel-plated Kluson tuners, strings through bridge, nickel hardware, 3 single coil exposed pickups, 1 volume/2 tone controls, 3-position switch, available in 3-Tone Sunburst nitro-cellulose lacquer finish. Mfg. 1954 to 1959.

1954	N/A	$22,000	$17,000	$16,000	$14,000	$11,000	$8,000
1955-1956	N/A	$15,000	$12,750	$10,500	$8,000	$6,450	$5,400
1957	N/A	$12,500	$9,950	$8,500	$7,000	$5,500	$4,950
1958-1959	N/A	$12,500	$9,950	$8,500	$7,000	$5,500	$4,950
1959/rosewood fingerboard	N/A	$8,000	$7,500	$7,000	$6,500	$6,000	$5,000

Add $150 for standard vibrato with cover.

During 1954, the standard vibrato back cover had round string holes. During 1955, the standard vibrato back cover had oval string holes. From 1954-1958, some models were made with aluminum pickguards - Black and Blonde finishes were special order items. In 1956, gold hardware became an option. In 1956, an alder body replaced the original ash body. Ash wood was used on custom color models, as well as models finished in Blonde. In 1956, Fender offered custom colors in Du-Pont Ducco finish. Black, Dakota Red, Desert Sand, Fiesta Red,

GRADING	100% MINT	98% NEAR MINT	95% EXC+	90% EXC	80% VG+	70% VG	60% G

Lake Placid Blue, Olympic White and Shoreline Gold finishes became an option. In 1957, Fender offered a "deluxe" version with 14 karat gold-plated parts and Blonde (a creamy off-white) finish. This model is unofficially nicknamed the "Mary Kaye" model, due to entertainer Mary Kaye posing with the deluxe model in the 1957 catalog supplement. While Blonde was a standard finish for Telecaster models, it was a custom finish for Stratocasters in the early years. In 1959, 3-layer pickguard replaced original parts/design, rosewood fingerboard became an option.

STRATOCASTER WITH ROSEWOOD FINGERBOARD (PRE-CBS, Mfg. 1959 - 1964) - similar to Stratocaster, except has rosewood fingerboard with pearl dot inlay, 3-ply white pickguard. Mfg. 1959 to 1964.

1960-1962	**N/A**	**$7,500**	**$6,750**	**$6,000**	**$5,500**	**$4,950**	**$4,500**
1963	**N/A**	**$6,500**	**$5,500**	**$4,750**	**$4,200**	**$3,800**	**$3,300**
1964	**N/A**	**$6,000**	**$5,000**	**$4,400**	**$3,900**	**$3,500**	**$3,100**

Add 10% for rosewood 'slab board' fingerboard.

In 1960, some models were issued with tortoise pickguards, but this was not a standard practice. Burgundy Mist, Candy Apple Red, Daphne Blue, Foam Green, Inca Silver, Shell Pink, Sonic Blue and Surf Green finishes became an option. In late 1962, rosewood veneer fingerboard replaced original parts/design.

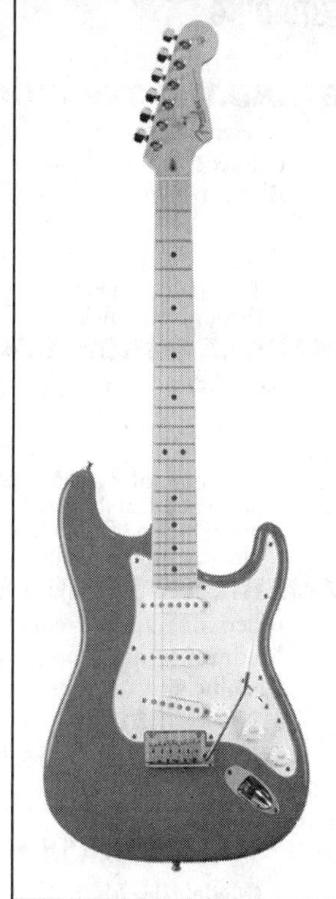

Fender Stratocaster
courtesy Fender

STRATOCASTER W/O TILTED NECK (CBS MFG., Mfg. 1965 - 1971) - similar to Stratocaster, except has smaller body contours, large headstock, rosewood fingerboard with pearl dot inlay. Mfg. 1965 to 1971.

1965 (large headstock)	**N/A**	**$4,500**	**$4,000**	**$3,600**	**$3,300**	**$2,950**	**$2,500**
1966	**N/A**	**$4,500**	**$4,000**	**$3,600**	**$3,300**	**$2,950**	**$2,500**
1967	**N/A**	**$4,000**	**$3,600**	**$3,200**	**$2,950**	**$2,600**	**$2,200**
1968	**N/A**	**$2,350**	**$2,050**	**$1,965**	**$1,525**	**$1,400**	**$1,27**
1969-1971	**N/A**	**$2,500**	**$2,150**	**$1,785**	**$1,400**	**$1,265**	**$1,125**

Currently, the Jimi Hendrix Strat configuration in White (late '60s, early '70s) is very hot, and asking prices are ranging from $5,000 - $7,500.

"CBS Mfg." notation refers to the sale of Fender Electric Instruments Company to the CBS Broadcasting Co. in January, 1965. In 1965, Blue Ice, Charcoal Frost, Firemist Gold, Firemist Silver, Ocean Turquoise and Teal Green finishes became options. In December of 1965, enlarged peghead became standard. In 1967, the maple fingerboard became an option (the one-piece maple neck was optional after 1970). The Stratocaster was also available with a bound fingerboard from roughly 1965 to 1968, but most examples found today are fairly rare.

In 1967, Fender chrome-plated tuning keys ('F' stamped) replaced the original nickel-plated Kluson tuners. In 1968, Polyester finish replaced the original nitro-cellulose finish. In 1970, Blonde, Black, Candy Apple Red, Firemist Gold, Firemist Silver, Lake Placid Blue, Ocean Turquoise, Olympic White and Sonic Blue finishes became options.

STRATOCASTER WITH TILTED NECK AND BULLET HEADSTOCK (CBS MFG., Mfg. 1971 - 1980) - similar to Stratocaster, except has alder or ash body, 3-bolt neck plate with neck adjustment ("Tilt Neck"), large peghead with truss rod adjustment, black logo, maple fingerboard with black dot or rosewood fingerboard with pearl dot inlay, gloss polyester finish. Mfg. 1971 to 1980.

1972-1974	**N/A**	**$1,750**	**$1,500**	**$1,300**	**$1,100**	**$995**	**$850**
1975	**N/A**	**$1,000**	**$800**	**$600**	**$500**	**$425**	**$350**
1976-1977	**N/A**	**$800**	**$700**	**$575**	**$450**	**$375**	**$325**
1978-1980	**N/A**	**$550**	**$475**	**$395**	**$325**	**$275**	**$225**

During Leo Fender's five year consultant contract with CBS/Fender, he developed a neck adjustment system in 1970 that corrected the pitch of the neck in the neck pocket with a micro adjustment in the neckplate (rather than the old-fashioned method of using shims). This device, along with the 3-bolt neck plate, were installed on Stratocasters beginning in mid 1971. In 1972, Natural finish became a standard item. Ash bodies became more predominent in guitar production. In late 1974, flush polepieces replaced staggered polepieces in the pickups. In 1975, pickups were installed that had flat pole pieces along the bobbin top. A 3-ply black pickguard became available. In 1977, the 5-way selector switch replaced the 3-way switch. In 1980, the Fender X-1 lead pickup (hotter output) replaced original parts/design.

STANDARD STRATOCASTER (CBS MFG., "SMITH STRAT", Mfg. 1981 - 1983) - alder body, 21-fret maple fingerboard with black dot or rosewood fingerboard with pearl dot inlay, 4-bolt neckplate, small peghead with black logo, vibrato tailpiece, 3-ply white pickguard, chrome hardware, 3 single coil exposed pickups, volume/2 tone control, 3-position switch, polyurethane finishes. Mfg. 1981 to 1983.

	N/A	**$750**	**$700**	**$650**	**$575**	**$525**	**$475**

Last MSR was $895.

In 1981, Fender hired Dan Smith as Director of Marketing. Smith revised the Standard Stratocaster back to the 4-bolt neckplate, and returned to the smaller (Pre-CBS ?) style headstock.

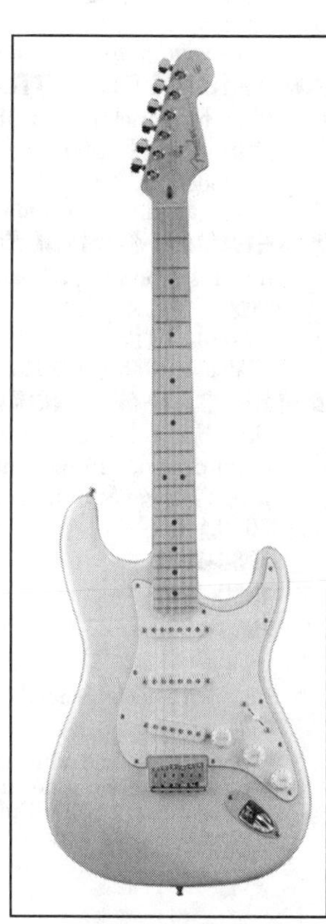

Fender Stratocaster
courtesy Fender

F

GRADING	100% MINT	98% NEAR MINT	95% EXC+	90% EXC	80% VG+	70% VG	60% G

STANDARD STRATOCASTER (CBS MFG., Mfg. 1983 - 1985) - alder body, 21-fret maple fingerboard with black dot or rosewood fingerboard with pearl dot inlay, 4-bolt neckplate, small peghead with silver logo, chrome-plated die-cast tuners, "Freeflyte" vibrato tailpiece, single ply white pickguard, chrome hardware, 3 single coil exposed pickups, volume/tone control, 3-position switch, available in Black, Brown Sunburst, Ivory and Sienna Sunburst polyurethane finishes. Mfg. 1983 to 1985.

	N/A	$600	$550	$500	$475	$425	$375

Last MSR was $699.

This model also featured a vibrato system that was surface mounted and without a vibrato back cavity. The cord receptor was mounted through the pickguard at a right angle.

MARBLE FINISH STANDARD STRATOCASTER ("BOWLING BALL" STRATOCASTER) - similar to the Standard Stratocaster (Mfg. 1983-1984), except featured a novel swirled finish. Mfg. 1984 only.

	$2,500	$2,200	$1,950	$1,600	$1,300	$1,100	$925

Last MSR was $799.

Approximately 225 of these instruments were produced. The unique finish is the result of dipping the (white) primer coated bodies into an oil-based finish that floated on water. After dipping, the guitar received a top coat of polyurethane. Fender produced three dominant colors. The Red finish had black and white swirled in (sometimes resulting in gray areas as well). The Blue finish was mixed with yellow and black, and the Yellow finish was combined with white and silver (sometimes resulting in gold patches).

AMERICAN SERIES STRATOCASTER (U.S. Mfg.) ash or alder body, rosewood fingerboard with dot position markers, hand-rolled fingerboard edges, 3 custom staggered single coil pickups, 5-way switch, two-point synchronized tremelo, staggered tuners, 22 Medium-Jumbo frets, 1 Volume/2 Tone controls, available in 3-Color Sunburst, Hot Rod Red, black, White Blonde, Natural, Aqua Marine Metallic and 2-Color Sunburst finishes. Case included. New 2001.

MSR $1,149	$805	$700	$600	$550	$500	$450	$400

Add $50 for 3-Color Sunburst finish.

Add $150 for 2-Color Sunburst finish.

Add $100 for Left Hand Model with rosewood fingerboard (Model 011-7420) and Left hand Model with maple neck (Model 011-7422).

(Model 011-7400) Also available with maple neck (Model 011-7402). Also available in Hard Tail Model with rosewood fingerboard (Model 011-7430) and Hard Tail Model with maple neck (Model 011-7432).

Hot Rodded American Series Stratocaster

AMERICAN STRAT TEXAS SPECIAL alder or ash body, rosewood fingerboard with dot position markers, deluxe staggered die-cast sealed tuners, 22 Medium-Jumbo frets, 3 Texas Special single coil pickups, 1 Volume/2 Tone controls, Super 5-way switch, two-point synchronized tremelo, available in 3-Color Sunburst, White Blonde, black, Candy Apple Red, Shoreline Gold, and Teal Green Metallic finishes. Case included. New 2001.

MSR $1,299	$910	$800	$700	$600	$550	$500	$400

(Model 011-7300)
Also available with maple neck (Model 011-7302).

AMERICAN FAT STRAT TEXAS SPECIAL similar to American Strat Texas Special except has Seymour Duncan "Pearly Gates Plus" humbucking pickup in the bridge position rosewood fingerboard, case included. New 2001.

MSR $1,299	$910	$800	$700	$600	$550	$500	$400

(Model 011-7900)
Also available with maple neck (Model 011-7902).

AMERICAN DOUBLE FAT STRAT similar to American Fat Strat Texas Special except has two Seymour Duncan humbucking pickups, rosewood fingerboard with dot position markers, case included. New 2001.

MSR $1,399	$980	$850	$750	$650	$550	$500	$450

(Model 011-7200)
Also available in a Hard Tail model (Model 011-7230).

AMERICAN STANDARD STRATOCASTER (FMIC MFG., Mfg. 1986-2000, U.S. Mfg., No. 010-7402) - alder body, 22-fret maple fingerboard with black dot inlay, 4-bolt neck plate, chrome-plated die-cast tuners, standard vibrato with 2 pivot point design, chrome hardware, 3-ply white pickguard, 3 single coil exposed polepiece pickups, 5-position switch, available in Arctic White, Black, Brown Sunburst, Caribbean Mist, Lipstick Red, Midnight Blue, and Midnight Wine polyurethane finishes. Mfg. late 1986, 1987 to 2000.

1986-1989	N/A	$625	$600	$575	$560	$525	$515
1990-1997	N/A	$600	$575	$550	$525	$475	$450
1998-2000	N/A	$700	$625	$525	$450	$395	$325

Last MSR was $999.

Add $150 for Natural Ash finish (1998 to 2000).

This model is also available with rosewood fingerboard with pearl dot inlay (Model 010-7400). In 1997, Candy Apple Red, Inca Silver, Sonic Blue, and Vintage White finishes were introduced; Arctic White, Caribbean Mist, Lipstick Red, Midnight Blue and Midnight Wine finishes were discontinued. In 1998, the DeltaTone system (high output bridge pickup and special "no-load" tone control) electronics was introduced; 3-Color Sunburst, Lake Placid Blue, and Olympic White finishes were introduced; Sonic Blue and Vintage White finishes were discontinued.

GRADING	100% MINT	98% NEAR MINT	95% EXC+	90% EXC	80% VG+	70% VG	60% G

American Standard Stratocaster Hard Tail (U.S. Mfg., No. 010-7432) - similar to the American Standard Stratocaster, except features a fixed bridge/strings through-body (w/ferrules), available in 3-Color Sunburst, Black, Candy Apple Red, Inca Silver, Lake Placid Blue, and Olympic White finishes. Mfg. 1998 to 2000.

$750 $625 $550 $450 $375 $300 $225
Last MSR was $999.

Add $150 for Natural Ash finish (1998 to 2000).

This model is also available with rosewood fingerboard with pearl dot inlay (Model 010-7430).

American Standard Stratocaster Left Hand (U.S. Mfg., No. 010-7422) - similar to the American Standard Stratocaster, except in a left-handed configuration, available in Black, Brown Sunburst, Candy Apple Red, and Vintage White finishes. Disc. 2000.

$685 $625 $560 $485 $415 $340 $265
Last MSR was $1,099.

This model is also available with rosewood fingerboard with pearl dot inlay (Model 010-7420).
In 1998, 3-Color Sunburst and Olympic White finishes were introduced; Brown Sunburst and Vintage White finishes were discontinued.

Deluxe American Standard Stratocaster (U.S. Mfg.) - similar to the American Standard Stratocaster, except features 3 Gold Lace Sensor pickups. Mfg. 1989 to 1990.

$650 $575 $525 $475 $425 $375 $350
Last MSR was $799.

This model was also available with rosewood fingerboard with pearl dot inlay.

American Standard Stratocaster Aluminum Body (U.S. Mfg.) - similar to American Standard Stratocaster, except has a hollow aluminum body, available in Blue Marble, Purple Marble, and Red/Silver/Blue *Flag* graphic anodized finish. Mfg. 1994 only.

Model has not traded sufficiently to quote pricing.
It is estimated that only 400 instruments were produced.

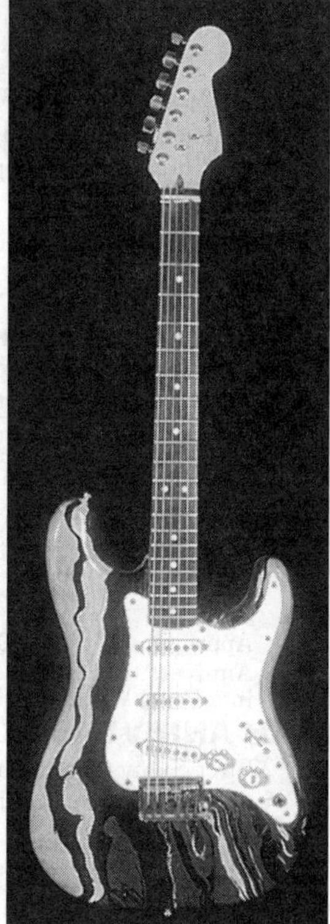

1983 Fender "Bowling Ball" Stratocaster courtesy Dave Rogers

AMERICAN STANDARD STRATOCASTER GR READY (U.S. Mfg., No. 010-7462) - similar to American Standard Stratocaster, except has a Roland GK-2A synth driver mounted behind bridge pickup, 3 synth control knobs, available in Black, Brown Sunburst, Candy Apple Red, and Vintage White finishes. Mfg. 1995 to 1998.

$795 $725 $695 $600 $500 $425 $325
Last MSR was $1,299.

This model was also available with rosewood fingerboard with pearl dot inlay (Model 010-7460).
This model is built pre-wired to drive the Roland GR series guitar synthesizer, as well as perform like a Stratocaster. Roland's GK-2A pickup system can interface with Roland's GR-1, GR-09, and GR-50 synthesizers; as well as the VG-8 guitar system and GI-10 guitar/MIDI interface.

Standard Roland Ready Stratocaster (Mex. Mfg., No. 013-4660) - similar to the American Standard Stratocaster GR Ready, except features poplar body, 21-fret rosewood fingerboard, Standard hardware, available in Artic White, Black, and Brown Sunburst finishes. Mfg. 1998 to date.

MSR $839 $750 $675 $595 $535 $435 $360 $285

Add $50 for Brown Sunburst finish.

This model has a built-in Roland GK-2A pickup and controls, which is pre-wired to drive the Roland GR series guitar synthesizer, as well as perform like a Stratocaster. Roland's GK-2A pickup system can interface with Roland's GR-1, GR-09, and GR-50 synthesizers; as well as the VG-8 guitar system and GI-10 guitar/MIDI interface.

American Deluxe Series

This series represents the ultimate in high performance, classically contoured solid "Tone-Wood" bodies with distinctive neck shapes.

AMERICAN DELUXE STRATOCASTER (U.S. Mfg., No. 010-1000) - premium alder or ash body, one-piece maple neck, rosewwod fingerboard, 25.5" scale, Bi-Flex truss rod, Micro-Tilt neck adjustment, Fender Deluxe locking tuners, 22 medium-jumbo frets, Fender Vintage Noiseless pickups, 5-way switch, Deluxe 2-point synchronized tremolo, Schaller Straplock ready, available in 3-Color Sunburst, Natural, Purple Transparent, White Blonde, Crimson Transparent, Black, and Teal Green Transparent finishes. Current Mfg.

MSR $1,499 $1,125 $950 $895 $850 $795 $750 $650

Add $150 for Natural, White Blonde, and Purple Transparent finishes.

Add $100 for Left Hand Models with rosewood (010-1020) or maple necks (010-1022).

Also available with maple neck (Model 010-1002).

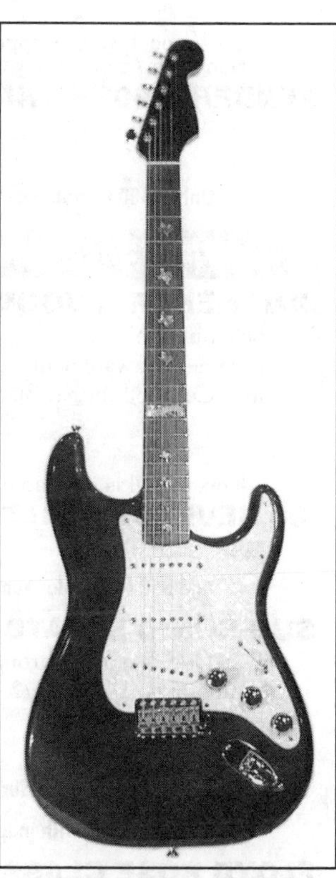

Fender Stratocaster courtesy Jeanne

GRADING	100% MINT	98% NEAR MINT	95% EXC+	90% EXC	80% VG+	70% VG	60% G

American Deluxe Fat Strat (U.S. Mfg., No. 010-1100) - similar to American Deluxe Stratocaster, except has Fender DH-1 Humbucker in the bridge position. The two single coil pickups are wound extra hot for proper balance with the DH-1 Humbucker, LSR roller nut, rosewood fingerboard, available in the same colors as the American Deluxe Stratocaster. Current Mfg.

MSR $1,549	$1,175	$1,025	$925	$875	$825	$775	$675

Add $100 for deluxe locking tremolo, roseood fingerboard (Model 010-1190).

Add $100 for deluxe locking tremolo, maple fingerboard (Model 010-1192).

Also available with maple fingerboard (Model 010-1102).

Anniversary Stratocaster Series

Anniversay Stratocaster models celebrate the introduction of the Stratocaster model in 1954.

25TH ANNIVERSARY STRATOCASTER (U.S. Mfg.) - alder body, black pickguard, black Anniversary logo on bass bout, 21-fret maple fingerboard with black dot inlay, Sperzel tuners, 4-bolt neckplate with "1954 - 1979 25th Anniversary" logo, standard vibrato, chrome hardware, 3 single coil pickups, volume/2 tone controls, 5-position switch, available in Metallic Silver finish. Mfg. 1979 to 1980.

$1,000	$800	$750	$700	$650	$600	$550

Last MSR was $800.

Approximately 10,000 of these instruments were produced. List price included a hardshell case.

Anniversary Stratocaster 6-digit serial numbers begin with a "25". Early models (estimated to be around 500) of this series were finished in a Pearl White finish, which checked and cracked very badly. Most models were returned to the factory to be refinished.

35TH ANNIVERSARY STRATOCASTER (U.S. Mfg.) - quilted maple top/alder body, white pickguard, birdseye maple neck, 22-fret ebony fingerboard with abalone dot inlay, standard vibrato, locking tuners, chrome hardware, 3 single coil Silver Fender Lace Sensors, 5-position selector/mini switches, active electronics, available in 3-Tone Sunburst finish. Mfg. 1989 to 1991.

$1,000	$900	$850	$800	SN/A	SN/A	SN/A

This model was a Custom Shop Limited Edition, based in part on the Strat Plus model. Only 500 instruments were made.

40TH ANNIVERSARY STRATOCASTER (AMERICAN STANDARD EDITION, U.S. Mfg.) - bolt-on maple neck, 3 single coil pickups, volume/tone controls, 5-way switch, stamped neckplate with serial number (# out of 1,954). Mfg. 1994 only.

$1,250	$1,000	$800	$700	$625	$600	$500

Last MSR was $1,800.

It is estimated that Fender produced 1,954 of the American Standard edition 40th Anniversary Stratocasters.

40th Anniversary Stratocaster (Fender Diamond Dealer Edition U.S. Mfg.) - ash body/flamed maple top, bolt-on birdseye maple neck, fancy fingerboard inlay with "1954 - 1994" at 12th fret, gold hardware, gold pickguard, 3 single coil pickups, 5-position switch. Mfg. 1994 only.

$3,500	$3,250	$3,000	$2,800	$2,500	$2,300	$1,850

Last MSR was $6,999.

This model was equipped with a tweed gig bag and flight case. It is estimated that Fender only produced 50 of the Diamond Dealer edition 40th Anniversary Stratocasters.

FENDER'S 50TH ANNIVERSARY MODEL STRATOCASTER (U.S. Mfg.) - Mfg. 1996 only.

$795	$750	$700	$650	$600	$550	$500

Last MSR was $1,299.

Only 2,500 instruments were produced.

American Special Series

JIMI HENDRIX VOODOO STRATOCASTER (U.S. Mfg., No. 010-6602) - (right handed) alder body, (left handed) bolt-on maple neck, 25 1/2" scale, 21-fret maple fingerboard with black dot inlay, vintage-style tremolo, Fender/Schaller vintage 'F' tuners, chrome hardware, white pickguard, 3 Vintage Strat single coil pickups, volume/2 tone controls, VooDoo Strat engraved neckplate, available in 3-Color Sunburst, Black, and Olympic White finishes. Mfg. 1998 to 1999.

$950	$800	$725	$625	$525	$425	$325

Last MSR was $1,349.

This model is available with a rosewood fingerboard (Model 010-6600).

'68 REVERSE STRATOCASTER SPECIAL (U.S. Mfg., No. 011-6602) similar to Jimi Hendrix model. New 2001.

MSR $1,400	$975	$800	$725	$625	$550	$425	$325

Add $50 for 3-color Sunburst.

SUB-SONIC STRATOCASTER HSS (U.S. Mfg., No. 011-04530) alder body, 27" scale, rosewood fingerboard, tuned B-E-A-D-G-B, string through body, hardtail bridge, 1 humbucking pickup and 2 single coil pickups, deluxe die cast sealed tuners, 22 medium-jumbo frets, 1 Volume/2 Tone controls, Special 5-Way switch, available in 3-Color Sunburst, black, Hot Rod Red and Aqua Marine Metallic finishes. New 2001.

MSR $1,399	$979	$875	$775	$675	$575	$475	$395

Add $50 for 3-Color Sunburst finish.

Also available with maple fingerboard (Model 011-4532).

FLOYD ROSE CLASSIC SERIES - please refer to listing under the Floyd Rose Stratocaster Series.

GRADING	100% MINT	98% NEAR MINT	95% EXC+	90% EXC	80% VG+	70% VG	60% G

California Series

The California Strat series was introduced in 1997. The production of this model is a joint effort between Fender's U.S. and Mexican plants.

CALIFORNIA STRAT (U.S. Mfg., No. 010-1402) - alder body, tinted maple neck, 21-fret maple fingerboard with black dot inlay, vintage-style tremolo, chrome hardware, white pickguard, 3 Tex-Mex Trio single coil pickups, volume/2 tone controls, available in Black, Brown Sunburst, Candy Apple Red, Fiesta Red, and Vintage White finishes. Mfg. 1997 to 1999.

$560 $480 $425 $370 $315 $260 $200

Last MSR was $799.

This model is also available with a rosewood fingerboard and white dot inlay (Model 010-1400).

California Fat Strat (U.S. Mfg., No. 010-1502) - similar to the California Strat, except has 2 single coil/humbucker pickups. Mfg. 1997 to 1999.

$600 $525 $450 $395 $335 $275 $215

Last MSR was $849.

This model is also available with a rosewood fingerboard and white dot inlay (Model 010-1500).

Classic Series

The Classic Series is very similar to the California Series.

50's STRATOCASTER (Mex. Mfg., No. 013 -1002) - similar to the California Strat, available in Black, Dakota Red, 2-Color Sunburst, Daphne Blue, and Olympic White. Current Mfg.

MSR $799 $595 $495 $475 $425 $395 $375 $325

In 2001, Surf Green finish was introduced.

Add $50 for 2-Color Sunburst finish.

60's STRATOCASTER (Mex. Mfg., No. 013-1000) - similar to California Strat with rosewood fingerboard, available in Black, Burgundy Mist, 3-Color Sunburst, Shell Pink, and Olympic White. Current Mfg.

MSR $799 $595 $495 $475 $425 $395 $375 $325

In 2001, Lake Placid Blue (-302) finish was introduced.

Add $50 for 3-Color Sunburst finish.

70's STRATOCASTER (Mex. Mfg., No. 013-7000) - "U" shaped neck, large headstock, bullet truss rod, solid ash body, one-piece maple neck, rosewood neck and fingerboard, 25.5" scale, Schaller vintage "F" tuners, 21-frets, 3 vintage strat pickups, 1 volume control, 2 tone controls, 5-way switch, synchronized tremolo, available in 3-Color Sunburst, Olympic White, and Natural finishes. Current Mfg.

MSR $869 $625 $525 $475 $450 $425 $395 $345

This model is also available with a maple neck and fingerboard (Model 013-7002).

Custom Classic Series (U.S. Custom Shop Mfg.)

CLASSIC PLAYER STRAT (No. 015-6600) thin lacquer- finished alder or ash body, lightly figured maple neck, rosewood fingerboard with abalone dot position markers, lightly figured "V" shaped neck, 22 Medium-Jumbo frets, Sperzel Trim-Loc tuners, 3 Custom Shop "Vintage-Noiseless" pickups, gold anodized pickguard, aged white plastic parts, custom vintage two-point synchronized tremelo, available in 3-Color Sunburst, 2-Color Sunburst, black, Bing Cherry Transparent, Cobaly Blue Transparent, Honey Blonde, Midnight Blue, and Midnight Wine finishes. New 2001.

MSR $2,299 $1,600 $1,400 $1,300 $1,200 $1,100 $950 $850

Add $150 for 2-Color Sunburst, Bing Cherry Transparent, Cobalt Blue Transparent and Honey Blonde finishes.

Also available in "V" neck with maple fingerboard (Model 015-6602). Also available with "C" neck with rosewood fingerboard (Model 015-6700) and "C" neck with maple fingerboard (Model 015-6702).

CUSTOM CLASSIC STRATOCASTER (No. 015-6200) custom shop version of the American Series Stratocaster, thin lacquer-finished alder or ash body, lightly figured "V" shaped neck, rosewood fingerboard, 22 Medium-Jumbo frets, Fender Deluxe cast/sealed tuners, 3 Modern Classic single coil pickups including the Hot Classic bridge pickup with custom steel inductance plate, 3-ply parchment pickguard, aged white plastic parts, Custom Classic two-point synchronized tremelo with milled solid stainless steel saddles, solid steel spring block, pop-in tremelo arm, available in 3-Color Sunburst, Daphne Blue, black, Honey Blonde, Cobalt Blue Transparent and Bing Cherry Transparent finishes. New 2001.

MSR $2,069 $1,450 $1,250 $1,150 $995 $895 $795 $650

Also available with "V" neck with maple fingerboard (Model 015-6202). Also available with "C" neck with rosewood fingerboard (Model 015-6300) and "C" neck with maple fingerboard (Model 015-6302).

F

GRADING	100% MINT	98% NEAR MINT	95% EXC+	90% EXC	80% VG+	70% VG	60% G

SUB-SONIC STRATOCASTER (HSS, No. 015-4530) 27" scale tuned B-E-A-D-G-B, rosewood fingerboard, thin lacquer finished alder body, Custom Classic Hardtail bridge, milled solid stainless steel saddles, 1 humbucking pickup and 2 single coil pickups, available in 3-Color Sunburst, Daphne Blue, Black and Candy Apple red finishes. Current Mfg.

MSR $2,299 $1,600 $1,400 $1,200 $1,000 $800 $700 $550

Also available with maple fingerboard (Model 015-4532). Also available with 2 humbucking pickups and rosewood fingerboard, Sub-Sonic Stratocaster HH (Model 015-4630) and with 2 humbucking pickups and maple fingerboard (Model 015-4632).

Deluxe Series

FAT STRAT FLOYD ROSE (Mex. Mfg., 113-3100) - poplar body, 21-fret rosewood fingerboard with dot inlay, large headstock, Floyd Rose locking tremolo, chrome hardware, black pickguard, 2 Tex-Mex single coil/Tex-Mex humbucker pickups, volume/2 tone controls, 5-way selector, available in Black and Arctic White finishes. Mfg. 1998 to date.

MSR $769 $575 $475 $450 $425 $395 $360 $310

Double Fat Strat Floyd Rose (Mex. Mfg., No. 113-3300) - similar to the Fat Strat Floyd Rose, except features 2 Tex-Mex humbucker pickups, available in Black and Arctic White finishes. Mfg. 1998 to date.

MSR $799 $595 $495 $475 $450 $395 $365 $320

DELUXE POWERHOUSE STRAT (Mex. Mfg., No. 013-9502) - poplar body, 21-fret maple fingerboard with black dot inlay, vintage-style tremolo, chrome hardware, white shell pickguard, 3 Powerhouse (ultra quiet) single coil pickups (with hum-cancelling slave coil), master volume/master "no-load" tone/active 12 dB mid-range boost controls, available in Black, Lake Placid Blue, Candy Apple Red, and Arctic White finishes. Mfg. 1998 to date.

MSR $769 $575 $495 $425 $375 $325 $275 $225

This model is also available with a rosewood fingerboard and white dot inlay (Model 013-9500).

DELUXE SUPER STRAT (Mex. Mfg., No. 013-9402) - ash body, tinted maple neck, 21-fret maple fingerboard with black dot inlay, vintage-style tremolo, gold-plated hardware, brown shell pickguard, 3 Super Fat Strat single coil pickups, volume/tone (neck)/tone (middle) controls, push/push switch (bridge pickup activation), available in Black, Brown Sunburst, Crimson Transparent, and Honey Blonde finishes. Mfg. 1998 to date.

MSR $769 $575 $495 $395 $350 $295 $250 $195

This model is also available with a rosewood fingerboard and white dot inlay (Model 013-9400). This model is equipped with "Super Switching", an additional push/push switch for activating the bridge pickup independent of the 5-way selector switch.

Elite Series

The Elite series instruments were Fender's attempt to combine the classic Stratocaster design with active electronics and a revised tremolo system with "drop-in" string loading.

ELITE STRATOCASTER (U.S. Mfg.) - alder body, 21-fret maple fingerboard with black dot inlay, Freeflyte vibrato, chrome hardware, white pickgard, 3 single coil covered Alnico II pickups, volume/2 tone controls, 3 push button pickup selectors, active MDX (midrange) and TBX (high-range) electronics, available in Aztec Gold, Candy Apple Green, Emerald Green, Mocha Brown, Pewter, Ruby Red, Sapphire Blue and Stratoburst finishes. Mfg. 1983 to 1984.

$750 $650 $600 $550 $500 $450 $400
Last MSR was $799.

This instrument was also available with rosewood fingerboard with pearl dot inlay. The output jack was located on the side of the body (instead of the top), and had no rear cover for the drop-in tremolo bridge. There was a backplate for access to the 9-volt battery (required for the active electronics).

Gold Elite Stratocaster (U.S. Mfg.) - similar to Elite Stratocaster, except has pearloid tuner buttons, gold hardware.

$800 $700 $625 $575 $525 $450 $400
Last MSR was $899.

Walnut Elite Stratocaster (U.S. Mfg.) - similar to Elite Stratocaster, except has American black walnut body/neck, ebony fingerboard, pearloid tuner buttons, gold hardware.

$875 $750 $650 $600 $550 $475 $425
Last MSR was $999.

Floyd Rose Stratocaster Series

Floyd Rose, the inventor of the double-locking tremolo, entered into an agreement with Fender (F.M.I.C.) in 1991. The Floyd Rose Classic Stratocaster debuted in 1992.

FLOYD ROSE CLASSIC STRATOCASTER (U.S. Mfg., No. 110-6000) - alder body, 22-fret rosewood fingerboard with pearl dot inlay, Original Floyd Rose tremolo, chrome hardware, 2 American Standard single coil/1 DiMarzio humbucker pickups, volume/2 tone controls, 5-position switch, available in 3-Tone Sunburst, Black, Candy Apple Red, and Vintage White finishes. Mfg. 1992 to 1999.

$950 $825 $725 $625 $525 $440 $350
Last MSR was $1,379.

This model had an optional maple fingerboard with black dot inlay (Model 110-6002).

Floyd Rose Standard Stratocaster (Mex. Mfg., No. 110-6002) - similar to Floyd Rose Classic, except has poplar body, 21-fret fingerboard, Floyd Rose II locking tremolo, 2 single coil/humbucker pickups, available in Arctic White and Black. Mfg. 1994 to 1998.

$375 $325 $275 $250 $200 $175 $125
Last MSR was $529.

This model had an optional maple fingerboard with black dot inlay (Model 113-1102).

GRADING	100% MINT	98% NEAR MINT	95% EXC+	90% EXC	80% VG+	70% VG	60% G

Floyd Rose Standard Stratocaster Foto Flame - similar to Floyd Rose Standard, except has basswood body, 21-fret rosewood fingerboard, Floyd Rose II locking tremolo, available in Antique Foto Flame, Blue Foto Flame, and Crimson Foto Flame finishes. Disc. 1995.

		$375	$325	$295	$250	$225	$195	$150

Last MSR was $639.

FLOYD ROSE CLASSIC STRAT HSS (U.S. Mfg., No. 110-6500) - alder body, 22-fret rosewood fingerboard with pearl dot inlay, Original Floyd Rose double locking tremolo, 3-ply white pickguard, chrome hardware, 2 American Standard single coil/1 Fender DH-1 humbucker pickups, volume/2 tone controls, 5-position switch, available in 3-Tone Sunburst, Black, Candy Apple Red, and Arctic White finishes. Mfg. 1998 to date.

MSR	$1,449	$1,055	$895	$775	$725	$675	$625	$535

This model has an optional maple fingerboard with black dot inlay (Model 110-6502).

Floyd Rose Classic Strat HH (U.S. Mfg., No. 110-6700) - similar to the Floyd Rose Classic Strat HSS, except features 2 Fender DH-1 humbucker pickups, available in 3-Tone Sunburst, Black, Candy Apple Red, and Arctic White finishes. Mfg. 1998 to date.

MSR	$1,499	$1,125	$950	$825	$775	$725	$675	$565

This model has an optional maple fingerboard with black dot inlay (Model 110-6702).

H.M. ('Heavy Metal') Series Strat

Originally produced overseas in 1988, the H.M. Strat series moved to U.S. production from 1989 through 1992. H.M. Series Strats feature a sharply contoured basswood body, 24-fret fingerboard, black headstock finish, and various pickup combinations of DiMarzio humbuckers/American Standard single coils/Fender-Lace Sensor pickups:

H.M. STRAT (JAPAN, U.S. Mfg.) - basswood body, 24-fret maple fingerboard with black dot inlay, double locking Kahler vibrato, black face peghead with 'STRAT' logo, black hardware, various pickup configurations (see above), pickup selector switch, volume/2 tone controls (where applicable), coil tap, available in Black, Blue, Red and White finishes. Mfg. 1988 to 1990.

		$325	$285	$250	$225	$200	$185	$160

This instrument was also available with rosewood fingerboard with pearl dot inlay. U.S.-produced H.M. Strats were available with the following pickup configurations: 1 Silver Fender-Lace Sensor single coil/1 DiMarzio humbucker (Model 10-2200), 2 DiMarzio humbuckers (Model 10-2300), 2 American Standard single coils/1 DiMarzio humbucker pickups (Models 10-2100, 10-2102).

H.M. Strat Ultra (U.S. Mfg., No. 010-2000) - similar to H.M. Strat, except has figured maple top/back, ebony fingerboard with pearl triangle inlay, mother-of-pearl headstock logo, Blue single coil/Gold single coil/2 Red single coil (Dually configuration) Fender-Lace Sensor pickups, volume/2 tone controls, 5-position/mini switches. Mfg. 1990 to 1992.

		$375	$325	$295	$275	$250	$225	$200

Hot Rodded American Models Series

BIG APPLE STRAT (U.S. Mfg., No. 010-7202) - alder body, 22-fret maple fingerboard with black dot inlay, standard vibrato, chrome hardware, brown or white shell pickguard, 2 Seymour Duncan ('59 and Pearly Gates Plus) pickups, 5-position switch, available in Black, Candy Apple Red, Olympic White, Shoreline Gold, and Teal Green Metallic finishes. Mfg. 1997 to 2000.

		$875	$750	$650	$575	$495	$400	$325

Last MSR was $1,249.

Add $80 for 3-Tone Sunburst finish.

Add $150 for BAS-Special w/ash body & rosewood fingerboard & Sienna Sunburst finish (Model 010-7200-822).

This model was also available with a rosewood fingerboard and white dot inlay (Model 010-7200).

Big Apple Strat Hard Tail (U.S. Mfg., No. 010-7232) - similar to the Big Apple Strat, except features a fixed bridge/strings through-body (with ferrules), available in Black, Candy Apple Red, Olympic White, Shoreline Gold, and Teal Green Metallic finishes. Mfg. 1998 to 2000.

		$875	$750	$675	$575	$475	$375	$300

Last MSR was $1,249.

Add $80 for 3-Tone Sunburst finish.

This model is also available with a rosewood fingerboard and white dot inlay (Model 010-7230).

LONE STAR STRAT (U.S. Mfg., No. 010-7902) - alder body, 22-fret maple fingerboard with black dot inlay, standard tremolo, chrome hardware, white (or brown) shell pickguard, 2 Texas Special single coil/1 Seymour Duncan Pearly Gates Plus humbucker pickups, volume/2 tone controls, 5-position switch, available in Black, Candy Apple Red, Olympic White, Shoreline Gold, and Teal Green Metallic finishes. Mfg. 1996 to 2000.

		$840	$725	$650	$550	$475	$395	$300

Last MSR was $1,199.

Add $80 for 3-Tone Sunburst finish.

Add $150 for LSS-Special, ash body with maple neck & Sienna Sunburst finish (Model 010-7902-847).

This model is also available with a rosewood fingerboard and white dot inlay (Model 010-7900).

GRADING	100% MINT	98% NEAR MINT	95% EXC+	90% EXC	80% VG+	70% VG	60% G

ROADHOUSE STRAT (U.S. Mfg., No. 010-7302) - poplar body, (tortoise) shell pickguard, 22-fret maple fingerboard with black dot inlay, tremolo bridge, chrome hardware, 3 Texas Special single coil pickups, 5-position switch, available in Black, Blue, Red, Silver, and White finishes. Mfg. 1997 to 2000.

$825 $725 $625 $525 $450 $375 $285
Last MSR was $1,159.

Add $80 for 3-Tone Sunburst finish.

This model is also available with a rosewood fingerboard and white dot inlay (Model 010-7300).

"HRR" (Hot-Rodded Reissue) Series Stratocaster

"HRR" Stratocaster models feature a double-locking Floyd Rose tremolo and a humbucker in the bridge position. These Japanese-produced models were available from 1990 to 1995.

"HRR" '50s STRATOCASTER (Jap. Mfg., No. 025-1002) - basswood body, 22-fret maple fingerboard with black dot inlay, double locking Floyd Rose vibrato, 2 single coil/1 DiMarzio humbucker pickups, volume/2 tone controls, 5-position/coil split switches, available in Black, Blue Foto Flame, Crimson Foto Flame, Olympic White and 2-Tone Sunburst finishes. Mfg. 1990 to 1995.

$400 $375 $350 $325 $300 $275 $225
Last MSR was $900.

"HRR" '60s Stratocaster (Jap. Mfg., No. 025-1000) - similar to "HRR" '50s Stratocaster, except has rosewood fingerboard with pearl dot inlay, available in Black, Blue Foto Flame, Crimson Foto Flame, Olympic White and 3-Tone Sunburst finishes. Mfg. 1990 to 1994.

$375 $350 $325 $315 $300 $295 $275
Last MSR was $900.

Strat Plus Series

The American-built Strat Plus Series models are the upscale versions of the American Standard Series Stratocasters. Current models all feature Fender-Lace Sensor pickups, LSR roller nuts, and locking tuners.

STRAT PLUS (U.S. Mfg., No. 010-7502) - alder body, 22-fret maple fingerboard with black dot inlay, vibrato bridge, LSR roller nut, Sperzel or Schaller locking tuners, chrome hardware, white shell pickguard, 3 single coil Lace Sensor Gold pickups, volume/2 tone controls, 5-position switch, available in Arctic White, Black, Black Pearl Dust, Blue Pearl Dust, Brown Sunburst, Caribbean Mist, Grafitti Yellow, Lipstick Red, Midnight Blue, and Midnight Wine finishes. Mfg. 1987 to 1999.

$875 $750 $650 $550 $475 $375 $300
Last MSR was $1,199.

Add $50 for 3-Color Sunburst finish.

This model also available with rosewood fingerboard with pearl dot inlay (Model 010-7500). This was the first model to feature Fender Lace sensors. In 1997, Candy Apple Red, Inca Silver, Sonic Blue, and Vintage White finishes were introduced; Arctic White, Black Pearl Dust, Blue Pearl Dust, Caribbean Mist, Lipstick Red, Midnight Blue, and Midnight Wine finishes were discontinued.

Deluxe Strat Plus (U.S. Mfg. No. 110-9502) - similar to Strat Plus, except has ash top/back, alder body, 2 Silver/1 Blue Lace Sensor single coil pickups, available in Antique Burst, Black, Blue Burst, Crimson Burst, Mystic Black, Natural, and Shoreline Gold finishes. Mfg. 1989 to 1999.

$1,050 $895 $795 $675 $575 $475 $375
Last MSR was $1,499.

This model also available with rosewood fingerboard with pearl dot inlay (Model 110-9500). In 1990, this model was released with an alternative set of Lace Sensors: Silver/Blue/Red. Some models may have a Floyd Rose tremolo bridge.

Strat Ultra (U.S. Mfg, No. 110-9800) - similar to Strat Plus, except has figured maple top/back, alder body, ebony fingerboard with abalone dot inlay, Floyd Rose vibrato, 4 Lace Sensor single coil pickups Blue/Silver/2 Red (Dually configuration), mini switch, available in Antique Burst, Black, Blue Burst, and Crimson Burst finishes. Mfg. 1990 to 1999.

$1,250 $1,100 $975 $850 $700 $575 $450
Last MSR was $1,799.

Stratocaster Model Variations

The models below represent variations not categorized in the other subcategories.

1997 COLLECTOR'S EDITION STRATOCASTER (U.S. Mfg., No. 010-1997) - alder body, tinted maple neck, 21-fret rosewood fingerboard with pearl dot inlay/oval-shaped *1997* pearl inlay at 12th fret, vintage-style vibrato, gold hardware, tortoiseshell pickguard, 3 Texas Special single coil pickups, volume/2 tone controls with white knobs, 5-position switch, available in 3-Tone Sunburst nitrocellulose finish. Mfg. 1997 only.

$1,275 $1,100 $900 $800 $700 $600 $450
Last MSR was $1,799.

Production was scheduled for only 1,997 instruments. List price included brown tolex hardshell case.

GRADING	100% MINT	98% NEAR MINT	95% EXC+	90% EXC	80% VG+	70% VG	60% G

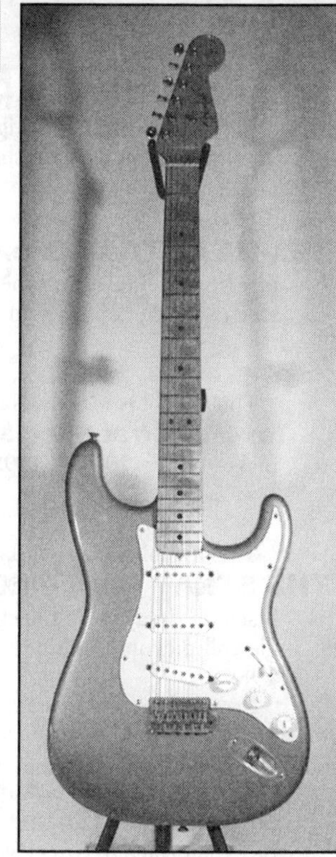
Fender Gold on Gold Strat courtesy Dave Hinson

CONTEMPORARY STRATOCASTER (Jap. Mfg.) - alder body, white pickguard, 22-fret rosewood fingerboard with pearl dot inlay, double locking vibrato, black face peghead, chrome hardware, exposed polepiece humbucker pickup, volume control. Mfg. 1985 to 1987.

	$250	**$230**	**$210**	**$195**	**$185**	**$175**	**$165**

This model was also available with black pickguard, 2 humbucker pickups, volume/tone control, 3-position switch, coil tap configuration; or 2 single coil/1 humbucker pickups, volume/tone control, 5-position switch, coil tap configurations. The Japan Mfg. Contemporary Stratocaster is not to be confused with the U.S. Mfg. Contemporary Strat (available between 1989 to 1991). Research continues on the U.S. Mfg. Contemporary Strat.

GOLD STRATOCASTER (Mfg. 1981-1983, U.S. Mfg.) - alder body, 21-fret maple fingerboard with black dot inlay, 4-bolt neckplate, standard brass vibrato, brass tuners, gold-plated brass hardware, 3-ply white pickguard, 3 single coil exposed pickups, volume/2 tone controls, 5-position switch, available in metallic Gold finish. Mfg. 1981 to 1983.

	$1,100	**$995**	**$850**	**$725**	**$675**	**$650**	**$625**

Last MSR was $975.

This model has been nicknamed the "Gold/Gold" Stratocaster. In 1981, it was offered as a limited edition in the Collector's Series.

"SHORT SCALE" STRAT (Jap. Mfg.) - offset double cutaway ash body, white pickguard, bolt-on maple neck, 22-fret maple fingerboard with black dot inlay, standard vibrato, 6-on-a-side tuners, chrome hardware, 3 single coil pickups, volume/2 tone controls, 5-position switch, available in Arctic White, Black, Frost Red and 3-Tone Sunburst finishes. Disc. 1994.

	$350	**$325**	**$300**	**$275**	**$250**	**$225**	**$200**

Last MSR was $550.

This model had an optional rosewood fingerboard with pearl dot inlay. This model was a limited edition model available through custom order.

STANDARD STRATOCASTER (Mex. Mfg., No. 013-4602) - poplar body, white pickguard, 22-fret maple fingerboard with black dot inlay, vintage-style tremolo, chrome hardware, 6-on-a-side die-cast tuners, 3 single coil pickups, volume/tone contols, 5-position switch, available in Arctic White, Black, Crimson Red Metallic, and Lake Placid Blue finishes. Current Mfg.

MSR **$449**	**$295**	**$260**	**$235**	**$195**	**$170**	**$150**	**$100**

Add $50 for Brown Sunburst finish.

This model also available with optional rosewood fingerboard with pearl dot inlay (Model 013-4600).

Standard Stratocaster Left Hand (Jap. Mfg., No. 027-4620) - similar to the Standard Stratocaster, except in a left-handed configuration with rosewood fingerboard, available in Black finish. Disc. 1998.

	$310	**$275**	**$250**	**$225**	**$175**	**$150**	**$125**

Last MSR was $439.

Also available with maple fingerboard (013-4622).

Standard Stratocaster Left Hand (Mex. Mfg., No. 013-4620) -similar to Standard Stratocaster Japanese Mfg. except Mfg. in Mexico. Current Mfg.

MSR **$499**	**$350**	**$295**	**$275**	**$250**	**$225**	**$195**	**$150**

Also available with maple neck (Model 013-4622) . Current Mfg.

STANDARD FAT STRAT (Mex. Mfg., No. 013-4700) - similar to Standard Stratocaster, except has 2 single coil pickups and 1 humbucking pickup, rosewood fingerboard, available in Black, Brown Sunburst, Midnight Blue, Midnight Wine, and Arctic White finishes. Current Mfg.

MSR **$499**	**$375**	**$295**	**$265**	**$235**	**$210**	**$175**	**$150**

Add $50 for Brown Sunburst finish.

Also available with maple neck and fingerboard (Model 013-4702).

Standard Fat Strat Floyd Rose (Mex. Mfg., No. 113-4700) - similar to Standard Fat Strat, except has Floyd Rose licensed double locking tremolo, rosewood fingerboard. Current Mfg.

MSR **$599**	**$450**	**$375**	**$350**	**$325**	**$295**	**$265**	**$210**

STRATOCASTER SPECIAL (Mex. Mfg., No. 013-5602) - ash veneer body, 21-fret maple fingerboard with black dot inlay, vintage-style tremolo, chrome hardware, 2 single coil/humbucker pickups, volume/2 tone controls, 5-position switch, available in Black, Brown Sunburst, Crimson Transparent, and Vintage Blond transparent finishes. Disc. 1995.

	$325	**$275**	**$250**	**$225**	**$200**	**$175**	**$150**

Last MSR was $559.

This model is also available with a rosewood fingerboard and white dot inlay (Model 013-5600).

GRADING	100% MINT	98% NEAR MINT	95% EXC+	90% EXC	80% VG+	70% VG	60% G

STRATOCASTER XII (Jap. Mfg., No. 027-8900) - alder body, white pickguard, 22-fret rosewood fingerboard with pearl dot inlay, strings through bridge, 6-per-side tuners, chrome hardware, 3 single coil pickups, volume/2 tone controls, 5-position switch, available in Candy Apple Red finish. Mfg. 1988 to 1995.

$675 $550 $485 $420 $355 $290 $225
Last MSR was $919.

TEX-MEX STRAT (Mex. Mfg., No. 013-7602) - poplar body, maple neck, 21-fret maple fingerboard with black dot inlay, vintage-style tremolo, chrome hardware, white pickguard, 3 Tex-Mex Trio single coil pickups, volume/2 tone controls, 5-position switch, available in Black, Brown Sunburst, Candy Apple Red, Sonic Blue, and Vintage White finishes. Mfg. 1996 to 1998.

$400 $350 $325 $275 $225 $195 $150
Last MSR was $599.

This model is also available with a rosewood fingerboard and white dot inlay (Model 013-7600).

Tex-Mex Strat Special (Mex. Mfg., No. 013-7802) - similar to the Tex-Mex Strat, except has 2 single coil/humbucker Tex-Mex pickups. Mfg. 1997 to 1998.

$425 $375 $350 $300 $250 $200 $175
Last MSR was $649.

This model is also available with a rosewood fingerboard and white dot inlay (Model 013-7800).

THE STRAT (CBS MFG., Mfg. 1980 – 1983, U.S. Mfg.) - alder body, white pickguard, 21-fret maple fingerboard with black dot inlay, 4-bolt neck plate, standard brass vibrato, body matching smaller peghead with 'Strat' logo, brass tuners, gold hardware, 3 single coil pickups, volume/tone/rotary controls, 5-position switch, available in Candy Apple Red and Lake Placid Blue finishes. Mfg. 1980 to 1983.

$650 $600 $550 $475 $400 $350 $300
Last MSR was $1,095.

The redesigned wiring of the Strat offers 9 basic and different sounds. The Fender X-1 lead pickup had a 'hotter' output than standard Fender single coil pickups. In 1981, Artic White finish became available.

Walnut Strat (Super Strat, U.S. Mfg.) - similar to The Strat, except has American black walnut body, 1-piece walnut neck, black pickguard/pickup covers, gold hardware, available in Natural finish. Mfg. 1981 to 1983.

$800 $750 $700 $650 $550 $450 $400
Last MSR was $1,195.

A few of these instruments have ebony fingerboards.

TRADITIONAL STRATOCASTER (Mex. Mfg., No. 013-3602) - poplar body, maple neck, 21-fret maple fingerboard with black dot inlay, vintage-style tremolo, chrome hardware, 3-ply white pickguard, 3 single coil pickups, volume/2 tone controls, 5-position switch, available in Arctic White, Black, and Torino Red finishes. Disc. 1998.

$200 $175 $155 $140 $120 $100 $85
Last MSR was $329.

This model is also available with a rosewood fingerboard and white dot inlay (Model 013-3600).

Traditional Stratocaster Left Hand (Mex. Mfg., No. 013-3620) - similar to the Traditional Stratocaster, except in left-handed configuration, rosewood fingerboard only, available in Arctic White or Black finishes. Disc. 1998.

$250 $200 $175 $150 $125 $110 $95
Last MSR was $379.

Traditional Fat Strat (Mex. Mfg., No. 013-3700) - similar to the Traditional Stratocaster, except has a humbucking pickup in the bridge position. Disc. 1998.

$250 $225 $195 $175 $140 $125 $95
Last MSR was $349.

Time Machine Series

Built to exacting specifications of their respective vintages, body contours and radii, neck shape, fingerboard radius, pickups, electronics and hardware. Original materials, tooling and production techniques are employed whenever possible, available in three distinct finish packages: NOS (New-Old Stock), as if the guitar was bought new in its respective year and brought forward to the present day; Closet Classic, asif guitar was bought new in its respective year, played perhaps a dozen times a year and then put carefully away (has a few slight dings, lightly checked finish, oxidized hardware and aged plastic parts; Relic, shows natural wear and tear of years of heavy use-nicks, scratches, worn finish, rusty hardware and aged plastic parts.

'56 STRATOCASTER (NOS, No. 015-0402) - alder or ash body, 10/56 shaped maple neck, single ply white pickguard and original spec pickups, available in White Blonde finish. New 2001.

MSR $2,749 $2,060 $1,750 $1,550 SN/A SN/A SN/A SN/A

Add $220 for Gold hardware (Model 015-0412).

'56 Stratocaster Closet Classic (No. 015-0502) - similar to '56 Stratocaster NOS except in Closet Classic finish, available in 2-Color Sunburst, black, Fiesta Red and Vintage Blonde finishes. New 2001.

MSR $3,059 $2,150 $1,850 $1,650 SN/A SN/A SN/A SN/A

Add $220 for Gold hardware (Model 015-0512).

'56 Stratocaster Relic (No. 015-0602) - similar to '56 Stratocaster NOS except in Relic finish, available in 2-Color Sunburst, black, Vintage Blonde and Fiesta Red finishes. New 2001.

MSR $3,219 $2,250 $1,950 $1,750 SN/A SN/A SN/A SN/A

Add $220 for Gold hardware (Model 015-0612)

GRADING		100% MINT	98% NEAR MINT	95% EXC+	90% EXC	80% VG+	70% VG	60% G

'60 STRATOCASTER (NOS, No. 015-0700) -alder body, "C" shaped neck with rosewood fingerboard, white/black/white pickguard, original specification pickups, available in 3-Color Sunburst, Daphne Blue, Olympic White, and Fiesta Red finishes. New 2001.

MSR	$2,749	$2,060	$1,750	$1,550	$N/A	$N/A	$N/A	$N/A

Add $220 for Gold hardware (Model 015-0710).

'60 Stratocaster Closet Classic - similar to '60 Stratocaster NOS except in Closet Classic finish, available in 3-Color Sunburst, Daphne Blue, Olympis White and Fiesta Red. New 2001.

MSR	$3,059	$2,150	$1,850	$1,650	$N/A	$N/A	$N/A	$N/A

(Model 015-0800)

Add $220 for Gold hardware (Model 015-0810).

'60 Stratocaster Relic - similar to '60 Stratocaster NOS except in Relic finish, available in 3-Color Sunburst, Daphne Blue, Olympis White and Fiesta Red finishes. New 2001.

MSR	$3,219	$2,250	$1,950	$1,750	$N/A	$N/A	$N/A	$N/A

(Model 015-0900).

Add $220 for Gold hardware (Model 015-0910).

'69 STRATOCASTER (NOS, No. 015-1700) - alder body, "U" shaped maple neck, large headstock, round-lam fingerboard rosewood fingerboard, white/black/white pickguard, orifinal specification pickups, available in 3-Color Sunburst, Olympic White and black finishes. New 2001.

MSR	$2,949	$2,065	$1,850	$1,650	$N/A	$N/A	$N/A	$N/A

Also available with maple fingerboard (Model 015-1702)

'69 Stratocaster Closet Classic (No. 015- 1800) - similar to '69 Stratocaster NOS except in Closet Classic finish, rosewood fingerboard. Available in 3-Color Sunburst, Olympic White and Fiesta Red finishes. New 2001.

MSR	$3,259	$2,275	$1,975	$1,775	$N/A	$N/A	$N/A	$N/A

Also available with maple fingerboard (Model 015-1802).

'69 Stratocaster Relic (No. 015-1900) - similar to '69 Stratocaster NOS except in Relic finish, rosewood fingerboard, available in 3-Color Sunburst, Olympic White and Fiesta Red finishes. New 2001.

MSR	$3,419	$2,395	$2,195	$1,995	$N/A	$N/A	$N/A	$N/A

Also available with maple fingerboard (Model 015-1902).

U.S. Vintage Reissue Series

The '57 and '62 Vintage Reissue models were originally produced at the CBS/Fender Fullerton facility (1982-1985). These models were the first Stratocasters of the post-CBS era to be made in the U.S. at the Corona, California production facility.

'57 STRATOCASTER (U.S. Mfg., No. 010-0102/010-0908 - alder body, white pickguard, 21-fret maple fingerboard with black dot inlay, vintage-style vibrato, nickel hardware, 3 American Vintage single coil pickups, volume/2 tone controls, 3-position switch, available in 2-Tone Sunburst, Black, Candy Apple Red, Fiesta Red, Ocean Turquoise, Shoreline Gold, and Vintage White finishes. Mfg. 1982 to 1985 (Fullerton, CA), 1985 to date (Corona, CA).

MSR	$1,699	$1,275	$1,025	$895	$750	$650	$550	$425

Add $200 for the Fullerton-built reissue model (1982-1985).

Add $80 for 2-Color Sunburst finish (1998 to date).

Add $100 for LH configuration, 2-Color Sunburst finish only (Model 010-0122).

In 1997, Shoreline Gold finish was introduced, Ocean Turquoise finish was discontinued. In 1999, White Blonde & Aztec Gold finishes were introduced; Shoreline Gold & Vintage White finishes were discontinued. In 2001, Inca Silver, Dakota Red and Ice Blue Metallic finishes were introduced.

'62 STRATOCASTER (U.S. Mfg., No. 010-0100/010-0909) - alder body, white pickguard, 21-fret rosewood fingerboard with pearl dot inlay, vintage-style vibrato, nickel hardware, 3 American Vintage single coil pickups, volume/2 tone controls, 3-position switch, available in 3-Tone Sunburst, Black, Candy Apple Red, Fiesta Red, Ocean Turquoise, Shoreline Gold, and Vintage White finishes. Mfg. 1982 to 1985 (Fullerton, CA), 1985 to date (Corona, CA).

MSR	$1,699	$1,275	$1,025	$895	$750	$650	$550	$425

Add $200 for the Fullerton-built reissue model (1982-1985).

Add $100 for LH configuration (Model 010-0120).

Add $50 for 3-Color Sunburst finish (1998 to date).

In 1997, Shoreline Gold finish was introduced, Ocean Turquoise finish was discontinued. In 1999, Olympic White & Sherwood Metallic finishes were introduced & Vintage White& Shoreline gold finishes were discontinued. In 2000, Sherwood Metallic finish was discontinued. In 2001, Inca Silver, Dakota Red and Ice Blue Metallic finishes were introduced.

GRADING	100% MINT	98% NEAR MINT	95% EXC+	90% EXC	80% VG+	70% VG	60% G

Fender Japan Limited Edition Series

The following models were limited edition instruments produced by Fender Japan, and available through custom order.

PAISLEY STRAT (Jap. Mfg.) - offset double cutaway ash body, bolt-on maple neck, 21-fret maple fingerboard with black dot inlay, standard vibrato, 6-on-one-side tuners, Paisley pickguard, chrome hardware, 3 single coil pickups, 2 volume/1 tone controls, 5-position switch, available in a Pink Paisley finish. Disc. 1994.

$725 $625 $500 $400 $375 $350 $325
Last MSR was $820.

Blue Flower Strat (Jap. Mfg.) - similar to Paisley Strat, except has Blue Flower pickguard/finish. Disc. 1994.

$750 $625 $500 $450 $425 $400 $375
Last MSR was $720.

F

'72 STRATOCASTER (Jap. Mfg.) - offset double cutaway ash body, bolt-on maple neck, 21-fret maple fingerboard with black dot inlay, '70s oversized headstock, standard vibrato, 6-on-one-side tuners, white pickguard, chrome hardware, 3 single coil pickups, volume/2 tone controls, 5-position switch, available in Natural and Vintage White finishes. Disc. 1995.

$450 $395 $350 $325 $300 $275 $250
Last MSR was $710.

Stratocaster Collectibles Series

Earlier models of the '50s Stratocaster and '60s Stratocaster featured Fender's Foto-Flame finish, which simulated the look of a 'flame' top (i.e., heavily figured maple). Current versions now strive to be a 'vintage replica'. This series has offset double cutaway basswood body, white pickguard, bolt-on maple neck, 21-fret fingerboard, standard vibrato, 6-on-one-side tuners, nickel hardware, 3 single coil pickups, volume/2 tone controls with *aged* knobs, and 5-position switch (unless otherwise listed).

'50s STRATOCASTER (Jap. Mfg., No. 027-1002) - maple fingerboard with black dot inlay, available in 2-Tone Sunburst, Black, Candy Apple Red, Olympic White, Shell Pink, and Sonic Blue finishes. Mfg. 1992 to 1998.

$425 $350 $325 $275 $225 $195 $150
Last MSR was $599.

Earlier models may have a stop tailpiece. Blue and Crimson Foto Flame finishes were discontinued in 1995.

'50s Stratocaster Left Handed (Jap. Mfg., No. 027-1022) - similar to '50s Stratocaster, except in a left-handed configuration, available in 2-Tone Sunburst finish. Disc. 1998.

$475 $400 $350 $300 $275 $225 $175
Last MSR was $669.

'60s STRATOCASTER (Jap. Mfg., No. 027-1000). - rosewood fingerboard with pearl dot inlay, available in 3-Tone Sunburst, Black, Blue Foto Flame, Candy Apple Red, Crimson Foto Flame, Olympic White, Shell Pink, and Sonic Blue finishes. Mfg. 1992 to 1998.

$425 $350 $325 $275 $255 $195 $150
Last MSR was $599.

In 1995, Blue and Crimson Foto Flame finishes were discontinued.

'60s Stratocaster Left Hand (Jap. Mfg., No. 027-1020) - similar to the '60s Stratocaster, except in a left-handed configuration, available in 3-Tone Sunburst finish. Disc. 1998.

$475 $400 $350 $300 $275 $225 $175
Last MSR was $669.

'60s Strat Natural - similar to '60s Stratocaster, except had an alder body, basswood top, available in Natural Foto-Flame finish. Mfg. 1994 to 1995.

$425 $375 $350 $325 $295 $250 $195
Last MSR was $790.

FOTO FLAME STRATOCASTER (Jap. Mfg.) - alder body with basswood top and Foto Flame finish, rosewood fingerboard with pearl dot inlay, white shell pickguard, available in Aged Cherry Sunburst, Autumn Burst, Natural, and Tri-Color Transparent. Disc. 1995.

$400 $350 $325 $300 $275 $250 $195
Last MSR was $799.

'68 STRATOCASTER (Jap. Mfg., No. 027-9202) - ash body, 21-fret maple fingerboard with black dot inlay, oversized (mid '60s) headstock, available in 3-Tone Sunburst, Natural, and Vintage White finishes. Disc. 1999.

$485 $415 $375 $325 $275 $225 $175
Last MSR was $699.

'68 Stratocaster Left Hand (Jap. Mfg., No. 027-9222) - similar to the '68 Stratocaster, except in a left-handed configuration. Disc. 1998.

$450 $400 $350 $325 $295 $250 $195
Last MSR was $749.

The Fender Custom Shop

Prior to the formation of the Custom Shop, the Research & Development section used to construct custom guitars requested by artists. In 1987, Fender brought in Michael Stevens and John Page to start what was envisioned as a boutique lutherie shop - building an estimated 5 or 6 guitars a month. When work orders for the first opening month almost totaled 600, the operation was expanded, and more master builders were added to the Custom Shop. Michael Stevens later left the Custom Shop in the Fall of 1990.

GRADING	100% MINT	98% NEAR MINT	95% EXC+	90% EXC	80% VG+	70% VG	60% G

The Custom Shop quickly began a liaison between artists requesting specific building ideas and Fender's production models. Page eventually became manager of both the Custom Shop and the R & D area, and some model ideas/designs that started on custom pieces eventually worked their way into regular production pieces.

Fender Custom Shop Production Stratocasters

In addition to the custom guitars and Limited Edition runs, the Custom Shop also produces a number of models in smaller production runs. The following models have a Stratocaster offset double cutaway body, bolt-on neck, 6-on-a-side headstock, three single coil pickups, and volume/2 tone controls (unless otherwise specified).

'57 LEFT HAND STRATOCASTER (U.S. Mfg., No. 010-5722) - alder body, white pickguard, 21-fret maple fingerboard with black dot inlay, vintage-style tremolo, chrome hardware, 3 Texas Special single coil pickups, 3-position switch, available in Black and Olympic White finishes. Disc. 1998.

$1,750 $1,525 $1,300 $1,200 $1,050 $850 $625
Last MSR was $2,499.

'62 Left Hand Stratocaster (U.S. Mfg., No. 010-6220) - similar to '57 Left Hand Stratocaster, except has rosewood fingerboard, *aged* pickguard/knobs, available in Black and Olympic White finishes. Disc. 1998.

$1,750 $1,550 $1,350 $1,250 $1,000 $850 $625
Last MSR was $2,499.

'58 STRATOCASTER (U.S. Mfg., No. 010-0802) - ash body, 21-fret maple neck with black dot inlays, vintage-style tremolo, 3 Fat '50s single coil pickups, *aged* pickguard/knobs, available in 3-Tone Sunburst, Black, and Blonde finishes. Disc. 1998.

$1,600 $1,400 $1,300 $1,100 $975 $750 $575
Last MSR was $2,299.

This model was available with gold hardware (Model 010-0812).

CARVED TOP STRATOCASTER (U.S. Mfg., No. 010-9700) - ash body, carved figured maple top, figured maple neck, rosewood fingerboard, deluxe tremolo, chrome hardware, 2 Texas Special single coil/Seymour Duncan JB humbucker pickups, volume/tone controls, 5-way selector, available in Aged Cherry Sunburst, Antique Burst, Crimson Transparent, Natural, and Teal Green Transparent finishes. Disc. 1998.

$2,300 $2,100 $1,800 $1,625 $1,350 $1,100 $825
Last MSR was $3,299.

This model was available with maple neck with black dot inlays (Model 010-9702).

CONTEMPORARY STRATOCASTER (U.S. Mfg., No. 010-9900) - down-sized alder body, 22-fret rosewood fingerboard with pearl dot inlay, Deluxe tremolo, chrome hardware, white pickguard, 2 Texas Special single coil/Seymour Duncan JB humbucker pickups, volume/tone controls, 5-way selector, available in Aged Cherry Sunburst, Natural, Shoreline Gold Metallic, Teal Green Transparent finishes. Mfg. 1989 to 1998.

$1,600 $1,500 $1,300 $1,100 $975 $750 $575
Last MSR was $2,299.

This model was available with optional maple neck with black dot inlays (Model 010-9902), Floyd Rose tremolo, flame maple top (Model 010-9970), and maple neck/flame maple top (Model 010-9972). The U.S.-built Contemporary Stratocaster first debuted circa 1989/1990.

Fender Custom Shop Contemporary Models Series

CARVED TOP STRAT HSS (U.S. Mfg., No. 010-2802) - swamp ash body, carved highly figured book-matched maple top, maple neck, 22-fret maple fingerboard with dot inlay, LSR nut, Fender Deluxe tremolo, locking tuners, chrome hardware, 2 Texas Special single coil/Seymour Duncan JB humbucker pickups, volume/2 tone controls, special switching, available in Antique Burst, Aged Cherry Sunburst, Crimson Transparent, Natural, and Teal Green Transparent finishes. Mfg. 1998.

$2,650 $2,300 $2,000 $1,700 $1,450 $1,275 $1,100
Last MSR was $3,299.

Add $100 for Natural finish.

This model is optional with rosewood neck with pearl dot inlays (Model 010-2800).

Carved Top Strat Dual Humbuckers (U.S. Mfg., No. 010-2902) - similar to the Carved Top Strat HSS, except features 2 Seymour Duncan humbucker pickups, available in Antique Burst, Aged Cherry Sunburst, Crimson Transparent, Natural, and Teal Green Transparent finishes. Mfg. 1998.

$2,650 $2,300 $1,950 $1,650 $1,400 $1,250 $1,075
Last MSR was $3,299.

Add $100 for Natural finish.

This model is optional with rosewood neck with pearl dot inlays (Model 010-2900).

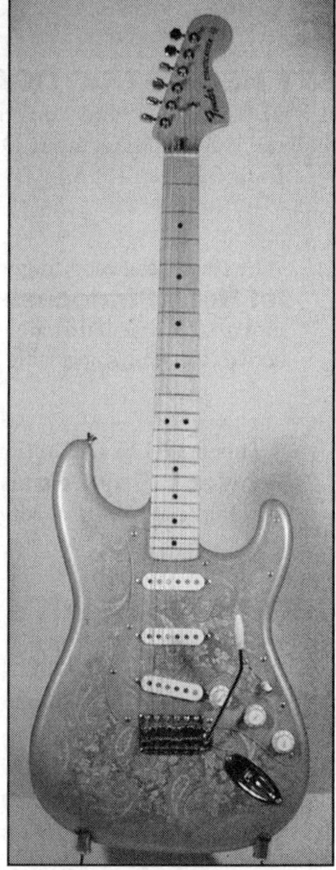

Fender Paisley Strat
courtesy San Diego Guitar

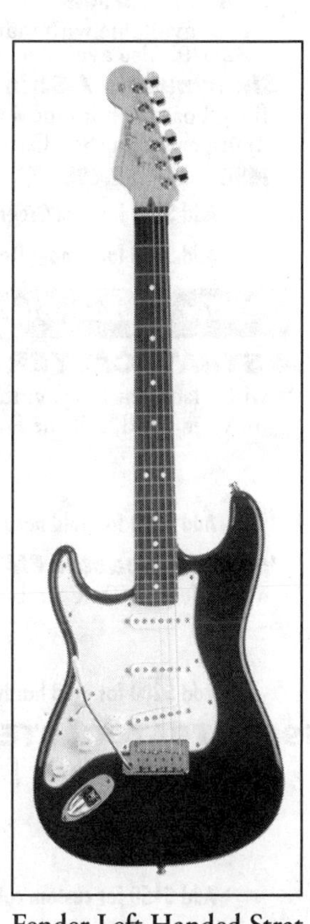

Fender Left Handed Strat
courtesy Fender

GRADING	100% MINT	98% NEAR MINT	95% EXC+	90% EXC	80% VG+	70% VG	60% G

SET NECK STRATOCASTER (U.S. Mfg., No. 010-2700) - ash body, highly figured book-matched maple top, set-in maple neck, 22-fret ebony fingerboard with pearl dot inlay, Fender Deluxe vibrato, LSR roller nut, locking tuners, chrome hardware, 2 Texas Special single coil/Seymour Duncan JB humbucker pickups, volume/2 tone controls, 5-position switch, available in Antique Burst and Natural finishes. Disc. 1998.

$1,950 $1,675 $1,475 $1,250 $995 $795 $600
Last MSR was $2,399.

In 1998, rosewood fingerboard replaced the ebony fingerboard.

Set Neck Stratocaster (U.S. Mfg.) - mahogany body, figured maple top, 22-fret ebony fingerboard with pearl dot inlay, standard vibrato, chrome hardware, 4 single coil Lace Sensor pickups (2 in humbucker configuration), volume/2 tone controls, 5-position/mini switches, active electronics, available in Antique Burst, Natural, Transparent Crimson, and Transparent Ebony finishes. Mfg. 1992 to 1995.

$1,750 $1,550 $1,250 $1,100 $950 $800 $650
Last MSR was $2,150.

This model has an optional gold hardware with Brite White finish.

Set Neck Floyd Rose Strat (U.S. Mfg.) - similar to Set Neck Stratocaster, except has double locking Floyd Rose vibrato, 2 single coil/1 humbucker pickups. Mfg. 1992 to 1995.

$1,500 $1,300 $1,150 $1,000 $875 $725 $595
Last MSR was $2,150.

SHOWMASTER WITH DELUXE TREMOLO (U.S. Mfg., No. 010-4202) - downsized alder body, carved maple top, maple neck, 22-fret maple fingerboard with abalone dot inlay, LSR nut, Fender Deluxe tremolo, Sperzel Trim-Lok tuners, chrome hardware, 2 Custom Shop Fat '50s single coil/Seymour Duncan '59 Trembucker humbucker pickups, volume/2 tone controls, special switching, available in Aged Cherry Sunburst, Bing Cherry Transparent, and Cobalt Blue Transparent finishes. Mfg. 1998 to date.

MSR $2,199 $1,550 $1,350 $1,150 $1,050 $850 $750 $625

This model is optional with rosewood neck with abalone dot inlays (Model 010-4200).

Showmaster with Deluxe Locking Tremolo (U.S. Mfg., No. 010-4292) - similar to the Showmaster with Deluxe Tremolo, except features a Fender Deluxe locking tremolo, available in Aged Cherry Sunburst, Bing Cherry Transparent, and Cobalt Blue Transparent finishes. Mfg. 1998.

$2,400 $2,100 $N/A $N/A $N/A $N/A $N/A
Last MSR was $2,999.

This model is optional with rosewood neck with abalone dot inlays (Model 010-4290).

Showmaster FMT (U.S. Mfg., No. 010-4270) - similar to Showmaster except with figured maple top and Deluxe 2-point synchronized tremelo with pop-in arm, rosewood fingerboard, available in Aged Cherry Sunburst, Antique Burst, Teal Green Transparent, Bing Cherry Transparent and Cobalt Blue Transparent finishes. Current Mfg.

MSR $2,449 $1,725 $1,525 $1,325 $1,125 $925 $825 $695

Also available with maple fingerboard (Model 010-4272). Also available with Set Neck and rosewood fingerboard (Model 010-4390) MSR $2,649. Also available with Set Neck, rosewood fingerboard and stop tailpiece (Model 010-4300) MSR $2,599.

Showmaster 7-String HH (U.S. Mfg., No. 015-4430) - similar to Showmaster except in a 7-string configuration, rosewood finegrboard, 2 humbucking pickups, Hard-tail, available in black, Antique Burst, Teal Green Transparent, Bing Cherry Transparent, Cobalt Blue Transparent finishes. Current Mfg.

MSR $2,499 $1,750 $1,550 $1,350 $1,150 $950 $850 $695

Add $150 for Teal Green Transparent and Bing Cherry Transparent finishes.

Add $100 for Fender Deluxe Locking Tremelo (Model 015-4490).

Fender Custom Shop Custom Classic Series

'54 STRATOCASTER (U.S. Mfg., No. 010-5402) - swamp ash body, lightly figured maple neck, 21-fret maple fingerboard with black dot inlay, vintage-style tremolo, white pickguard, nickel hardware, 3 Custom '50s single coil pickups, 3-position switch, available in Aztec Gold, 2-Tone Sunburst and Vintage Blonde finishes. Disc. 1998.

$1,600 $1,450 $1,300 $1,150 $995 $775 $575
Last MSR was $2,999.

Add $200 for gold hardware (Model 010-5412).

'54 Stratocaster FMT (U.S. Mfg., No. 010-5472) - similar to the '54 Stratocaster, except features a highly figured flame maple top, available in 2-Tone Sunburst, Aged Cherry Sunburst, and Natural finishes. Disc. 1998.

$1,800 $1,600 $1,525 $1,300 $1,075 $850 $625
Last MSR was $2,499.

Add $200 for gold hardware (Model 010-5482).

1960 STRATOCASTER (U.S. Mfg., No. 010-6000) - similar to '54 Stratocaster, except has alder body, rosewood fingerboard with pearl dot inlay, 3 Texas Special single coil pickups with *aged* covers, available in 3-Tone Sunburst, Black, and Olympic White finishes. Disc. 1998.

$1,539 $1,400 $1,250 $1,100 $950 $730 $550
Last MSR was $2,199.

Add $150 for custom color finishes.

Add $200 for gold hardware (Model 010-6010).

Instruments with Olympic White finish have tortoise pickguards and body matching pegheads.

GRADING	100% MINT	98% NEAR MINT	95% EXC+	90% EXC	80% VG+	70% VG	60% G

1960 Stratocaster FMT (U.S. Mfg., No. 010-6070) - similar to the 1960 Stratocaster, except features a highly figured flame maple top, available in 3-Tone Sunburst, Aged Cherry Sunburst, and Natural finishes. Disc. 1998.

	$1,800	$1,500	$1,325	$1,200	$1,075	$850	$625

Last MSR was $2,499.

Add $200 for gold hardware (Model 010-6080).

'69 STRATOCASTER (U.S. Mfg., No. 010-6900) - alder body, maple neck, 21-fret rosewood fingerboard with dot inlay, oversized (late '60s) headstock, chrome hardware, 3 Custom '69 single coil pickups, available in 3-Tone Sunburst, Black, and Olympic White finishes. Disc. 1998.

	$1,850	$1,650	$1,475	$1,275	$1,075	$850	$650

Last MSR was $2,599.

This model was available with maple neck with black dot inlays (Model 010-6902).

AMERICAN CLASSIC STRATOCASTER (U.S. Mfg., No. 010-4702) - alder body, lightly figured maple neck, 22-fret maple fingerboard, chrome American Standard hardware, American Standard tremolo, 3 Texas Special single coil pickups, custom detailing, available in 3-Tone Sunburst, 2-Tone Sunburst, and White Blonde finishes. Disc. 1998.

	$1,195	$1,050	$975	$825	$695	$550	$425

Last MSR was $1,699.

This model was available with a rosewood fingerboard (Model 010-4700). In 1998, the option for gold hardware (Model 010-4712), or rosewood fingerboard/gold hardware (Model 010-4710) was discontinued. Instruments with Olympic White finish have tortoise pickguard. Some early models may have Black Holo- Flake finishes with pearloid pickguards, Olympic White, or custom finishes.

CLASSIC PLAYER STRAT C-NECK (U.S. Mfg., No. 010-0702) - alder or ash body, rounded "C"-shaped maple neck, 22-fret maple fingerboard, chrome hardware, Sperzel Trim-Lok tuners, 2-point vintage-style tremolo, 3 Custom Shop Noiseless single coil pickups, available in Aged Cherry Sunburst, Black, and Teal Green Transparent finishes. New 1998.

MSR $1,999	$1,300	$1,100	$900	$800	$700	$600	$525

Add $150 for custom color finishes.

This model is available with a rosewood fingerboard (Model 010-0700). The Black finish features a gold anodized pickguard; the Aged Cherry Sunburst and Teal Green Transparent finishes each feature a parchment pickguard.

Classic Player Strat V-Neck (U.S. Mfg., No. 010-0602) - similar to the Classic Player Strat C-Neck, except features a soft "V"-shaped maple neck, available in Aged Cherry Sunburst, Black, and Teal Green Transparent finishes. Mfg. 1998 Only.

MSR $1,999	$1,300	$1,100	$900	$800	$700	$600	$525

Add $150 for custom color finishes.

This model is available with a rosewood fingerboard (Model 010-0600). The Black finish features a gold anodized pickguard; the Aged Cherry Sunburst and Teal Green Transparent finishes each feature a parchment pickguard.

N.O.S. (NEW OLD STOCK) STRATOCASTER (U.S. Mfg., No. 010-0502) - alder body, maple neck, 21-fret maple fingerboard, chrome hardware, vintage-style tremolo, 3 Custom '65 (replica) single coil pickups, available in Black, Bleached 3-Color Sunburst, and Olympic White "Thinskin" finishes. Mfg. 1998 only

	$1,825	$1,500	$1,350	$1,150	$950	$850	$750

Last MSR was $2,799.

Add $150 for custom color finishes.

This model was available with a rosewood fingerboard (Model 010-0500).
This model is "a detailed recreation of a mid-1960s Strat", built by using the original tooling and production techniques. There are no N.O.S. parts on this reproduction model.

Fender Custom Shop Limited Edition Stratocasters

The Limited Edition Stratocasters are produced in very limited production runs by Fender's Custom Shop. These models have a finite number produced, are generally labeled # instrument/total amount, and are offered to Fender Diamond level dealers to broker to the public. As such, there is no announced retail price per model - only availability.

The following models have a Stratocaster offset double cutaway body, three single coil pickups, bolt-on neck, and 6-on-a-side headstock (unless otherwise specified).

ALUMINUM BODY STRATOCASTER (U.S. Mfg.) - hollow aluminum body, available in Chrome (with Black Custom Shop pickguard/headstock), Green with Black and Gold swirls, and Jet Black (with chrome pickguard) anodized finishes. Mfg. 1994 only.

	$2,500	$2,200	$1,900	$1,600	$1,400	$1,250	$1,100

'57 Fender Left handed Strat courtesy Thoroughbred Music

Fender Aluminum Body Custom
19th Annual Dallas Show

GRADING	100% MINT	98% NEAR MINT	95% EXC+	90% EXC	80% VG+	70% VG	60% G

BILL CARSON STRATOCASTER (U.S. Mfg.) - similar to the 1957 Reissue, except has neck shaped to Bill Carson's specifications, available in Cimarron red.

$1,700 $1,550 $1,250 $1,000 $900 $800 $700

Only 100 instruments were built. The first 41 were built for Music Trader and have documentation (non-Music Trader models do not have this paperwork). Package includes tweed hardshell case. Guitarist Bill Carson gave advice on the design of the original Stratocaster.

FREDDY TAVARES ALOHA STRATOCASTER (U.S. Mfg., No. 010-4404) - hollow aluminum body, available with Hawaiian scene anodized finish. Mfg. 1993 to 1994.

$2,500 $2,200 $1,850 $1,600 $1,400 $1,200 $1,000

Only 153 instuments were built.

HARLEY DAVIDSON STRATOCASTER (U.S. Mfg., No. 010-4401) - hollow aluminum body, chrome inscribed pickguard, available in Chrome finish only. Mfg. 1993 only.

$22,500 $19,000 $16,000 $13,000 $9,995 $8,500 $7,750

Only 109 instruments were built. The 60 models made available to Diamond Edition dealers carry a Diamond emblem on the headstock. The 40 models available for export, and the 9 that were delivered to the Harley Davidson company do not carry this emblem.

F

JIMI HENDRIX MONTEREY (U.S. Mfg.) - reverse headstock, white pickguard, available in red/green psychadelic-style finish with backstage pass sticker on lower bout. Mfg. 1997 only.

$4,950 $3,850 $3,350 $2,950 $2,650 $2,350 $2,000

Last MSR was $6,999.

Only 210 instruments were built.

Sources have written in to indicate that there was possibly another Hendrix Custom Shop model built circa 1993. This yet-uncomfirmed model was similar to the 1980 Hendrix model, except the '93 version had a maple cap neck and Transition style logo on the headstock. The ***Blue Book of Electric Guitars*** has yet to confirm the existence of the 1993 edition, and is preparing further research into this matter.

HOMER HAYNES LIMITED EDITION (HLE/HLE REISSUE '88, U.S. Mfg.) - gold anodized pickguard, gold hardware, available in Gold finish only. Mfg. 1988 only.

$1,750 $1,500 $1,200 $1,000 $850 $750 $650

Only 500 instruments were built. This model was one of the early Custom Shop limited edition runs, and was based on a 1957 model Stratocaster.

HANK MARVIN SIGNATURE LIMITED EDITION (U.S. Mfg.) - Available in Fiesta Red finish. Mfg. 1995 to 1996.

$1,950 $1,700 $1,300 $1,100 $925 $800 $700

Only 164 instruments were built for European distribution.

PLAYBOY 40TH ANNIVERSARY STRATOCASTER (U.S. Mfg., No. 010-4402) - gold hardware, maple fingerboard with black pearl bunny inlays, available with custom Marilyn Monroe graphic finish. Mfg. 1994 only.

$4,950 $4,200 $3,960 $3,250 $2,850 $2,500 $2,250

Last MSR was $7,999.

Only 175 instruments were built. Package includes red Playboy leather strap, red gig bag, and hardshell case.

STEVENS LJ STRATOCASTER (U.S. Mfg., No. 010-3500) - set-in neck, highly figured top, Brazilian rosewood fingerboard, 2 special design humbuckers, available in Autumn Gold, Antique Burst, Crimson Stain, and Ebony Stain. Mfg. 1987.

N/A $2,750 $2,400 $2,000 $1,650 $1,350 $1,150

Last MSR was $2,799.

The Stevens LJ was the first Custom Shop model released. It is estimated that only 35 to 40 instruments were built. Only 4 additional prototypes of the Stevens LJ II and Stevens LJ III (2 each) were constructed.

Stratocaster "Relic" Series

"Relic" series instruments were cosmetically aged by the Fender Custom Shop. Instruments are stamped on the headstock and into the body (under the pickguard) with the Custom Shop logo to avoid future cases of "mistaken identity" in the Vintage Guitar market. Died-in-the-wool Strat players/collectors don't seem to be satisfied with a 100% "fresh paint" finish, explaining why this series was initially offered. The Relic Series was discontinued in 2000.

'50s "RELIC" STRATOCASTER (U.S. Mfg., No. 010-5802) - light ash body, maple neck, 21-fret maple fingerboard with black dot inlay, vintage-style tremolo, *aged* white pickguard/nickel hardware/knobs/pickup covers/etc., 3 Custom '54 single coil pickups, volume/2 tone controls, available in 2-Color Sunburst and Vintage Blonde finishes. Disc. 2000.

$1,825 $1,550 $1,350 $1,150 $950 $850 $725

Last MSR was $2,599.

Add $200 for aged gold hardware (Model 010-5812).

'60s "Relic" Stratocaster (U.S. Mfg., No. 010-6400) - similar to the '50s Relic Stratocaster, except features an alder body, rosewood 'slab' fingerboard, 3 Custom '60s single coil pickups. Similar distressed aging, available in 3-Color Sunburst and Olympic White finishes. Disc. 2000.

$1,850 $1,600 $1,400 $1,200 $995 $895 $750

Last MSR was $2,599.

Add $200 for aged gold hardware (Model 010-6410).

Add $150 for custom color finish: Burgundy Mist, Daphne Blue, Fiesta Red, and Lake Placid Blue.

GRADING	100% MINT	98% NEAR MINT	95% EXC+	90% EXC	80% VG+	70% VG	60% G

"RELIC" FLOYD ROSE STRATOCASTER (U.S. Mfg., No. 010-6802) - alder body, maple neck, 21-fret maple fingerboard with black dot inlay, Original Floyd Rose tremolo, *aged* white pickguard/chrome hardware/knobs/pickup covers/etc., 2 custom '69 single coil/Seymour Duncan '59 humbucker pickups, volume/2 tone controls, available in Black and Olympic White finishes. Mfg. 1998 only.

		$1,975	$1,695	$1,495	$1,295	$1,095	$995	$850

Last MSR was $2,799.

This model is available with a rosewood fingerboard (Model 110-6800).

Artist Signature Stratocaster Series

Artist Signature Series Stratocasters are designed in collaboration with the artist whose name appears on the headstock. The nature of the Signature Series is to present an instrument that contains the idiosyncrasies similar to the artist's personal guitar.

JEFF BECK (U.S. Mfg., No. 010-9600) - alder body, 22-fret rosewood fingerboard with pearl dot inlay, standard vibrato, LSR roller nut, Jeff Beck's signature on peghead, locking tuners, chrome hardware, 4 single coil Lace Sensor Gold pickups (2 in humbucker configuration), coil tap switch, available in Midnight Purple, Surf Green, and Vintage White finishes. Mfg. 1991 to date.

MSR $1,799 — $1,250 $1,100 $975 $875 $750 $625 $450

RITCHIE BLACKMORE LIMITED EDITION (Jap. Mfg., No. 025-8400) basswood body, oversized headstock, partially scalloped 21-fret rosewood fingerboard with dot inlay, chrome/nickel hardware, white pickguard, 2 Seymour Duncan Quarter Pounder single coils (no middle pickup - cover only), 3-bolt neckplate, black control knobs, available in Olympic White. Mfg. 1997 only.

$800 $750 $700 $650 $600 $500 $450

Last MSR was $1,000.

RITCHIE BLACKMORE (U.S. Mfg., No. 010-2400) ash body, set maple neck, scalloped rosewood fingerboard with dot position markers, 22 jumbo frets, 70's large headstock, deluxe locking tuners, two Gold Fender-Lace Sensor pickups, 1 Volume/2 Tone controls, two-point synchronized tremelo, Dunlop flush-mount straplock system, available in Olmypic White. Current Mfg.

MSR $4,999 — $3,499 $2,995 $2,695 $2,395 $2,095 $1,795 $1,495

Add $400 for Roland GK-2 pickup system. (Roland Ready, Model 010-2460).

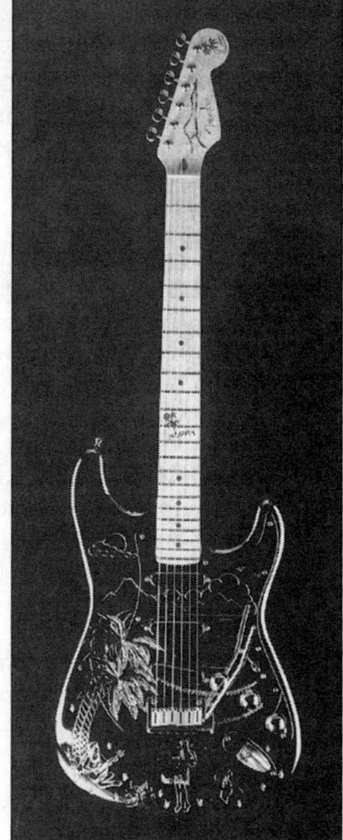

Fender Freddie Tavares 'Aloha' Strat courtesy Fender Custom Shop

ERIC CLAPTON (U.S. Mfg., No. 010-7602) - alder body, 22-fret maple fingerboard with black dot inlay, vintage-style vibrato, Eric Clapton's signature on headstock, chrome hardware, 3 single coil Lace Sensor Gold pickups, active electronics, available in Black, Candy Green, Olympic White, Pewter, and Torino Red finishes. Mfg. 1988 to date.

MSR $1,799 — $1,225 $1,000 $950 $875 $750 $625 $500

ROBERT CRAY (U.S. Mfg., No. 010-9100) - alder body, 21-fret rosewood fingerboard with pearl dot inlay, strings through bridge, Robert Cray's signature on peghead, chrome hardware, 3 single coil exposed pickups, available in Inca Silver, 3-Tone Sunburst and Violet finishes. Mfg. 1990 to date.

MSR $2,749 — $1,950 $1,450 $1,150 $1,050 $950 $800 $700

This model is available by custom order only. In 1998, gold hardware replaced chrome hardware.

DICK DALE (U.S. Mfg., No. 010-6100) - alder body, rosewood fingerboard with pearl dot inlay, standard vibrato, Dick Dale's signature on reverse peghead, chrome hardware, 3 Custom '50s single coil pickups, special switching, available in Chartreuse Sparkle finish. Mfg. 1992 to date.

MSR $2,999 — $2,050 $1,550 $1,250 $1,150 $975 $850 $750

JERRY DONAHUE LIMITED EDITION (Jap. Mfg., No. 025-8900) - basswood body, 21-fret maple fingerboard with dot inlay, LSR nut, midnight blue sparkle pickguard, 3 Seymour Duncan single coil pickups, volume/tone controls, 2 position rotary switch, 5-way selector, available in Transparent Blue Sapphire finish. Mfg. 1997 to 1998.

$800 $695 $625 $525 $450 $375 $295

Last MSR was $1,149.

BUDDY GUY (U.S. Mfg., No. 010-7802) - alder body, 22-fret maple fingerboard with black dot inlay, standard vibrato, Buddy Guy's signature on headstock, chrome hardware, 3 single coil Lace Sensor Gold pickups, active electronics, available in 2-Tone Sunburst (white shell pickguard) and Honey Brown (brown shell pickguard) finishes. Mfg. 1995 to date.

MSR $1,799 — $1,225 $1,000 $950 $875 $750 $625 $500

JIMI HENDRIX TRIBUTE (U.S. Mfg., No. 010-6822) - alder body, 21-fret maple fingerboard with black dot inlay, reverse oversized (late '60s) headstock, vintage-style vibrato, reverse logo/headstock information, chrome hardware, *F* tuning keys, 3 reverse staggered single coil pickups, available in Olympic White finish. Mfg. 1997 to 2000.

$1,125 $950 $800 $750 $700 $650 $600

Last MSR was $1,599.

This model is essentially a left-handed guitar strung right-handed.

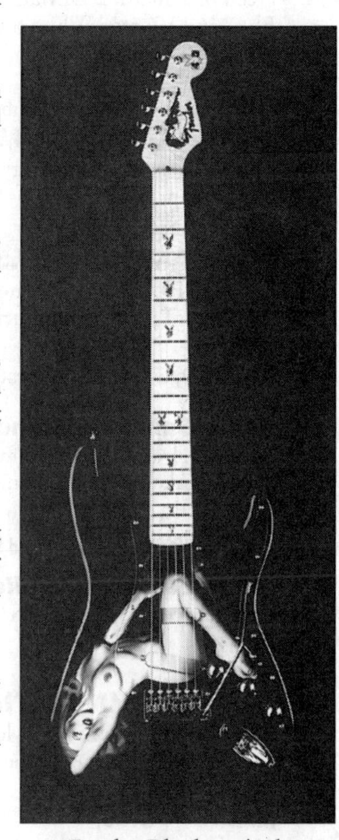

Fender Playboy 40th Anniversary Strat courtesy Fender Custom Shop

GRADING	100% MINT	98% NEAR MINT	95% EXC+	90% EXC	80% VG+	70% VG	60% G

Hendrix Model (1980 Mfg., U.S. Mfg.) - alder body, 21-fret maple fingerboard with black dot inlay, standard vibrato, reverse headstock, 4-bolt neckplate, chrome hardware, white pickguard, 3 single coil pickups, volume/2 tone controls, 5-way selector switch, available in White polyester finish. Mfg. 1980 only.

$995 $900 $825 $775 $725 $675 $625
Last MSR was $1,500.

It is estimated that only 25 instruments were produced. The Hendrix model featured construction similar to the 25th Anniversary model, except had a reverse headstock and an additional body contour on the front.

MATTHIAS JABS (Jap. Mfg., No. 025-7400) - alder body, maple neck, 22-fret rosewood fingerboard with custom Saturn planet inlays, custom shape small headstock, Gotoh vintage locking tuners, vintage tremolo, nickel hardware, single-ply white pickguard, 2 Custom Shop '50s single coil/Seymour Duncan JB humbucker pickups, TBX circuitry, available in Candy Apple Red finish. Mfg. 1998 Only.

$775 $650 $600 $550 $500 $450 $400
Last MSR was $1,099.

F

JOHN JORGENSEN LIMITED EDITION HELLECASTER (Jap. Mfg., No. 025-8800) - maple body, maple neck, large reversed Strat headstock, 22-fret rosewood fingerboard with gold sparkle dot inlays, Schaller locking tuners, two pivot point tremolo, gold hardware, gold sparkle pickguard, 3 split Seymour Duncan single coil pickups, custom wired 5-way selector switch, available in Black Sparkle finish. Mfg. 1997 to 1998.

$850 $750 $650 $600 $550 $500 $450
Last MSR was $1,300.

YNGWIE MALMSTEEN (U.S. Mfg., No. 010-7702) - alder body, 22-fret scalloped maple fingerboard with black dot inlay, American Standard vibrato, brass nut, Yngwie Malmsteen's signature on peghead, chrome hardware, 2 DiMarzio HS-3/1 American Standard Stratocaster single coil pickups, active electronics, available in Candy Apple Red, Sonic Blue, and Vintage White finishes. Mfg. 1988 to 1998.

$1,100 $950 $850 $750 $625 $525 $400
Last MSR was $1,599.

This model is also available with rosewood fingerboard and pearl dot inlays (Model 010-7700).

Yngwie Malmsteen Standard (Jap. Mfg., No. 027-2702) - similar to Yngwie Malmsteen model, except has basswood body, 70's style headstock, no active electronics, available in Black, Sonic Blue, and Vintage White finishes. Mfg. 1991 to 1994.

$650 $575 $480 $435 $385 $340 $290
Last MSR was $960.

YNGWIE MALMSTEEN (U.S. Mfg., No. 010-7102) - alder body, 21-fret scalloped maple fingerboard with black dot inlay, large headstock, vintage vibrato, brass nut, Yngwie Malmsteen's signature on peghead, Schaller 'F' tuners, pre-aged chrome hardware, mint green pickguard, 2 DiMarzio YJM single coil/DiMarzio HS-3 single coil pickups, 3-way selector switch, available in Candy Apple Red, Sonic Blue, and Vintage White finishes. Mfg. 1998 to date.

MSR $1,849 $1,300 $1,100 $1,000 $900 $800 $700 $500

This model is also available with rosewood fingerboard and pearl dot inlays (Model 010-7100).

BONNIE RAITT (U.S. Mfg., No. 010-9300) - alder body, 22-fret rosewood fingerboard with white dot inlay, larger (1960s-style) headstock, vintage-style vibrato, Bonnie Raitt's signature on peghead, chrome hardware, white shell pickguard, 3 Texas Special single coil pickups, available in 3-Tone Sunburst and Desert Sunburst finishes. Mfg. 1996 to date.

MSR $1,799 $1,225 $1,000 $950 $875 $750 $625 $500

RICHIE SAMBORA (U.S. Mfg., No. 010-2602/010-2702) - alder body, 22-fret maple fingerboard with abalone star inlay, Original Floyd Rose vibrato, Richie Sambora's signature on peghead, pearl tuner buttons, chrome hardware, 2 Texas Special single coil/1 DiMarzio PAF Pro humbucker pickups, active electronics, available in Arctic White and Cherry Sunburst finishes. Mfg. 1993 to 1999.

MSR $1,849 $1,375 $1,175 $1,025 $895 $775 $625 $495

In 1999, 3-Color Sunburst, Fiesta Red & Vintage White finishes were introduced; Arctic White & Cherry Sunburst finishes were discontinued.

Richie Sambora Standard (Mex. Mfg., No. 113-2700) - poplar body, 21-fret rosewood fingerboard with pearl dot inlay, Floyd Rose II vibrato, chrome hardware, 2 single coil/1 DiMarzio PAF Pro humbucker pickup, available in Arctic White, Black, Crimson Red Metallic, and Lake Placid Blue finishes. Mfg. 1994 to date.

MSR $799 $575 $475 $425 $375 $325 $250 $195

In 1999, Candy Apple Red finish was introduced and Crimson Red Metallic finish was discontinued.

Richie Sambora Limited Edition Black Paisley (Jap. Mfg., No. 125-2702) - similar to the Richie Sambora Signature model, except features 2 RS Special single coil/custom wound humbucking pickups, available in Black Paisley finish. Mfg. 1996 only.

$795 $700 $625 $550 $495 $425 $350
Last MSR was $1,369.

JIMMY VAUGHN SIGNATURE TEX-MEX (Mex. Mfg., No. 013-9202) - poplar body, 21-fret maple fingerboard with black dot inlay, vintage-style vibrato, Jimmy Vaughn's signature on peghead, nickel hardware, single-ply white pickguard, 3 Tex-Mex single coil pickups, volume/2 tone controls, 5-position switch, special wiring, available in Olympic White and 2-Tone Sunburst finishes. Mfg. 1997 to date.

MSR $769 $545 $450 $395 $350 $295 $250 $185

In 1999, Black, and Candy Apple Red finishes were introduced.

Add $50 for 2-Tone Sunburst finish.

GRADING	100% MINT	98% NEAR MINT	95% EXC+	90% EXC	80% VG+	70% VG	60% G

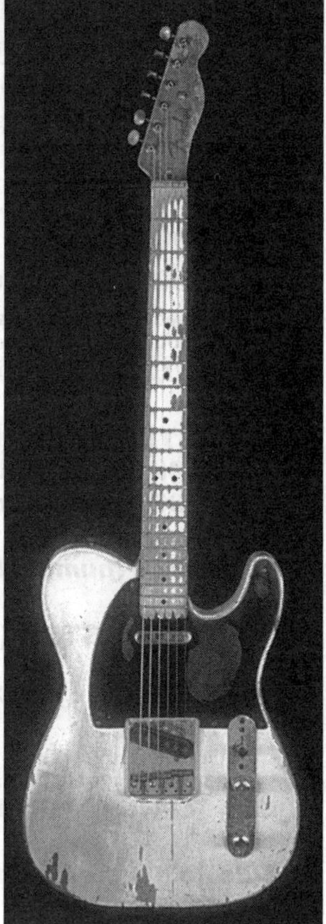

1950 Fender "No-Telecaster"
courtesy Russell Farrow

STEVIE RAY VAUGHN (U.S. Mfg., No. 010-9200) - alder body, 21-fret rosewood fingerboard with clay dot inlay, left-handed vintage-style vibrato, Stevie Ray Vaughn's signature on peghead, gold hardware, black pickguard with SRV logo, 3 Texas Special single coil pickups, volume/2 tone controls, 5-position switch, available in 3-Tone Sunburst finish. Mfg. 1992 to date.

MSR	$1,799	$1,225	$1,000	$950	$875	$750	$625	$500

VENTURE'S LIMITED EDITION (Jap. Mfg., No. 025-8100) - light ash body, 22-fret rosewood fingerboard with white block inlay, vintage-style vibrato, white shell pickguard, gold hardware, 3 Lace Sensor Gold single coil pickups, active electronics, available in Midnight Black Transparent finish. Mfg. 1996 only.

	$1,050	$895	$795	$690	$595	$500	$400

Last MSR was $1,489.

TELECASTER SERIES

All instruments in this series have a single cutaway body, bolt-on maple neck, 6-on-one-side tuners, unless otherwise listed.

BROADCASTER (Mfg. 1950) - ash body, black pickguard, 21-fret maple fingerboard with black dot inlay, fixed bridge with cover, chrome hardware, 2 single coil pickups, 3-position switch, volume/tone control, available in Translucent Butterscotch finish. Mfg. 1950.

	N/A	$20,000	$18,000	$16,000	$15,000	$12,500	$11,000

This model should be determined on a piece-by-piece basis as opposed to the usual market. Prototypes and custom models existed before 1948.

After Fender released the Broadcaster model, the Fred Gretsch company objected to the similarity of the name to their Broadkaster trademark used on Gretsch drums. Fender, the new kids on the block (at that time), complied with the request. In 1951, the Broadcaster name was changed to Telecaster.

"NO"CASTER - similar to Broadcaster, except has Fender name only on the headstock.

	N/A	$15,000	$13,000	$12,000	$10,000	$9,000	$8,000

Add $400-$600 for original case.

Certain very clean/all original models have sold for as high as $14,000. However, this should be determined on a piece-by-piece basis as opposed to the usual market. In the transition period between the Broadcaster and Telecaster model names, Fender continued producing guitars. Leo Fender, never one to throw money away, simply clipped the Broadcaster name off of the labels already in stock. Therefore, the guitars produced between the Broadcaster and Telecaster name changeover have been nicknamed the "No"caster by collectors due to lack of model name after the 'Fender' logo on the headstock.

TELECASTER (FENDER MFG., Mfg. 1951 - 1964) - ash body, black pickguard, 21-fret maple fingerboard with black dot inlay, strings through bridge, chrome hardware, 2 single coil pickups, volume/tone controls, 3-position switch, controls mounted metal plate, available in Blonde finish. Mfg. 1951 to 1964.

1951-1954	N/A	$12,500	$11,000	$9,700	$9,200	$8,750	$8,250
1955-1959	N/A	$7,500	$6,800	$5,700	$5,400	$5,200	$4,900
1960-1964	N/A	$6,500	$6,000	$5,500	$4,500	$4,000	$3,500

In late 1954, white pickguard replaced original parts/design. In 1955, level pole piece pickups became standard.

In 1958, fixed bridge replaced original parts/design. In September 1959, rosewood fingerboard with pearl dot inlay replaced maple fingerboard. In 1960, strings through bridge replaced fixed bridge.

TELECASTER (CBS MFG., Mfg. 1965 - 1983) - similar to original Telecaster, except has F stamp on back of neck plates. Mfg. 1965 to 1983 (referred to as CBS Mfg. because of the sale of Fender Musical Instruments Corp. to the CBS Broadcasting Co. in early 1965).

1965-1969	N/A	$3,500	$3,100	$2,800	$2,500	$2,350	$1,400
1970-1975	N/A	$1,100	$850	$750	$650	$525	$425
1976-1979	N/A	$850	$750	$650	$550	$475	$400
1980-1983	N/A	$575	$475	$400	$350	$295	$250

In 1967, Bigsby vibrato tailpiece was an option. From 1967-1969, maple fingerboard was an option. In 1969, maple fingerboard with black dot inlay replaced original parts/design. In 1975, black pickguard replaced original parts/design. Telecasters with a maple cap fingerboard bring a higher premium.

TELECASTER WITH BIGSBY VIBRATO (CBS MFG., Mfg. 1967 - 1975) - similar to original Telecaster, except has Bigsby vibrato unit. Mfg. 1967 to 1975.

1967-1969	N/A	$2,200	$1,900	$1,600	$1,500	$1,400	$1,250
1970-1975	$1,200	$950	$800	$675	$525	$475	$425

Telecasters with a maple cap fingerboard bring a higher premium.

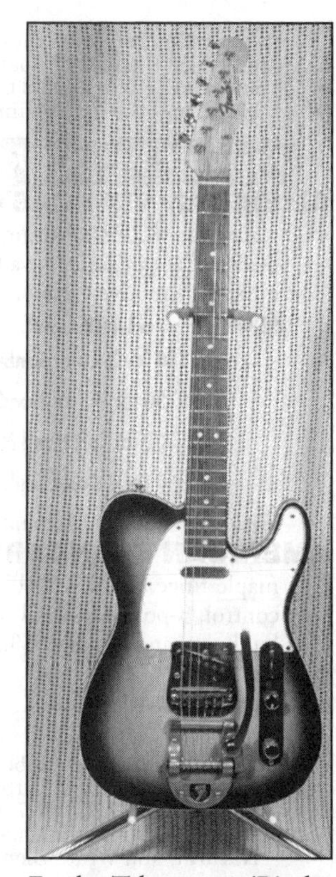

Fender Telecaster w/Bigsby
Blue Book archives

F

GRADING		100% MINT	98% NEAR MINT	95% EXC+	90% EXC	80% VG+	70% VG	60% G

TELECASTER CUSTOM (Mfg. 1959 – 1978) - bound alder body, white pickguard, 21-fret maple fingerboard with pearl dot inlay, strings through bridge, chrome hardware, 2 single coil pickups, volume/tone controls, 3-position switch, controls mounted metal plate, available in Custom Colors finish. Mfg. 1959 to 1972.

1959-1965		**N/A**	**$8,500**	**$7,500**	**$6,500**	**$5,500**	**$5,000**	**$4,500**
1966-1972		**N/A**	**$5,000**	**$4,500**	**$4,000**	**$3,500**	**$3,200**	**$2,875**
1972-1978 (K. Richards)		**N/A**	**$1,200**	**$1,050**	**$900**	**$800**	**$725**	**$650**

Add 10% for rosewood 'slab board' fingerboard.

This model is also available with an ash body. Certain very clean/all original models have sold for as high as $4,000 to $7,000. However, this should be determined on a piece-by-piece basis as opposed to the usual market.

TELECASTER DELUXE (Mfg. 1973 – 1978)

		N/A	**$850**	**$775**	**$725**	**$650**	**$600**	**$550**

TELECASTER THINLINE (Mfg. 1968 - 1978) various finishes, Natural finish was standard, Sunburst and Custom Colors will being 20%-50% premium.

1968-1971 (single coil PUs)

		N/A	**$2,500**	**$2,250**	**$2,000**	**$1,800**	**$1,600**	**$1,500**

1972-1978 (humbuckers)

		N/A	**$1,250**	**$1,100**	**$975**	**$900**	**$825**	**$750**

ELITE TELECASTER (Mfg. 1983 – 1985, U.S. Mfg.) - bound alder body, 21-fret fingerboard with black dot inlay, fixed bridge, chrome hardware, 2 covered humbuckers, 2 volume/2 tone controls, 3-position switch, active electronics, available in Natural and Sunburst finishes. Mfg. 1983 to 1985.

		N/A	**$650**	**$550**	**$500**	**$475**	**$450**	**$400**

This model came with a white pickguard that could be applied with the supplied adhesive backing. This model was also available with rosewood fingerboard with pearl dot inlay.

Elite Telecaster Gold (U.S. Mfg.) - similar to Elite Telecaster, except has pearloid button tuners, gold hardware. Disc.

		N/A	**$700**	**$600**	**$550**	**$500**	**$450**	**$400**

Elite Telecaster Walnut (U.S. Mfg.) - similar to Elite Telecaster, except has walnut body/neck, ebony fingerboard with pearl dot inlay, pearloid button tuners, gold hardware, available in Natural finish. Disc.

		N/A	**$700**	**$550**	**$495**	**$350**	**$300**	**$250**

Marble Finish Telecaster ("Bowling Ball") - similar to the 1983-1984 Telecaster, except featured a novel swirled finish. Mfg. 1984 only.

		N/A	**$3,000**	**$2,500**	**$1,950**	**$1,600**	**$1,300**	**$1,100**

Last MSR was $799.

Approximately 75 of these instruments were produced. The unique finish is the result of dipping the (white) primer coated bodies into an oil-based finish that floated on water. After dipping, the guitar received a top coat of polyurethane. Fender produced three dominant colors. The Red finish had black and white swirled in (sometimes resulting in gray areas as well). The Blue finish was mixed with yellow and black, and the Yellow finish was combined with white and silver (sometimes resulting in gold patches).

American Series Telecasters (U.S. Mfg.)

AMERICAN TELECASTER (U.S. MFG. No. 011-8400) alder or ash body, rosewood fingerboard, Deluxe staggered cast/sealed tuners, 22 Medium-Jumbo frets, American Tele pickups, 1 Volume/1 Tone control, 3-way switch, 6-saddle string through body bridge. Case included, available in 3-Color Sunburst, White Blonde, black, Natural, Hot Rod Red, Aqua marine Metallic and 2-Color Sunburst finishes. New 2001.

MSR	**$1,149**	**$795**	**$650**	**$600**	**$550**	**$500**	**$450**	**$400**

Add $50 for 3-Color Sunburst finish.

Add $150 for White Blonde, Natural, and 2-Color Sunburst finishes.

Add $100 for Left Hand Model (Model 011-8422), available in 3-Color Sunburst, White Blonde, black and Hot Rod Red finishes.

Add $50 for 3-Color Sunburst finish and $150 for White Blonde finish.

Also available with maple fingerboard (Model 011-8402)

AMERICAN STANDARD (U.S. Mfg., Mfg. 1988 – 1999, No. 010-8402) - alder body, bolt-on maple neck, 22-fret maple fingerboard with black dot inlay, fixed bridge, chrome hardware, 2 American Standard Telecaster single coil pickups, volume/tone control, 3-position switch, controls mounted metal plate, available in Black, Caribbean Mist, Lipstick Red, Midnight Blue, Midnight Wine, Sunburst, and Vintage White finishes. Mfg. 1988 to 1999.

1988-1997		**N/A**	**$575**	**$500**	**$450**	**$395**	**$325**	**$275**
1998-1999		**$690**	**$600**	**$525**	**$450**	**$395**	**$325**	**$275**

Last MSR was $999.

This model also available with rosewood fingerboard with pearl dot inlay (Model 010-8400). These were the first Telecasters of the post-CBS era to be made in the U.S. (at the Corona, California production facility). Only the vintage series Telecasters were available between 1986 and 1987. In 1997, Brown Sunburst, Candy Apple Red, Inca Silver, and Sonic Blue finishes were introduced; Caribbean Mist, Lipstick Red, Midnight Blue, Midnight Wine, and Sunburst finishes were discontinued. In 1999, Aqua Marine Metallic, Metallic Purple, Natural, and White Blonde finishes were introduced.

Add $80 for 3-Color Sunburst (1999).

Add $150 for Natural and White Blonde finishes.

GRADING	100% MINT	98% NEAR MINT	95% EXC+	90% EXC	80% VG+	70% VG	60% G

American Standard Left Hand (U.S. Mfg., No. 010-8422) - similar to the American Standard Telecaster, except in a left-handed configuration, available in Black, Brown Sunburst, Candy Apple Red, and Vintage White finishes. Disc. 1999.

$765	$650	$575	$500	$425	$350	$275

Last MSR was $1,099.

In 1999, Metallic Purple and 3-Color Sunburst finishes were introduced and Brown Sunburst and Candy Apple Red finishes were discontinued.

Add $80 for 3-Color Sunburst finish (1999).

American Standard Telecaster Aluminum Body (U.S. Mfg.) - similar to American Standard Telecaster, except has a hollow aluminum body, available in Blue Marble, Purple Marble, and Red/Silver/Blue *Flag* graphic anodized finish. Mfg. 1994 only.

Model has not traded sufficiently to quote pricing.
It is estimated that only 100 instruments were produced.

American Standard B-Bender (U.S. Mfg., No. 010-8442) - similar to the American Standard Telecaster, except has custom designed Parsons/White B-Bender system installed, available in Black, Brown Sunburst, Candy Apple Red, and Vintage White finishes. Mfg. 1995 to 1999.

$790	$675	$595	$525	$450	$375	$285

Last MSR was $1,129.

AMERICAN DELUXE (U.S. Mfg., No. 010-4600) - premium ash or alder body with bound top and contoured back, special shape maple neck, rosewood fingerboard, abalone dot inlays, 25.5" scale, 22 medium-jumbo frets, Deluxe Fender die-cast tuners, 2 Vintage Tele Noiseless pickups, master tone, master volume, 3-ply aged white or Brown shell pickguard, Fender Deluxe Tele bridge, Bi-flex truss rod, Micro-tilt neck adjustment, Schaller Strap-Lock ready, available in 3-Color Sunburst, White Blonde, Natural, Black, Crimson Transparent, Teal Green Transparent, and Purple Transparent finishes. Current Mfg.

MSR	$1,699	$1,275	$1,075	$950	$850	$750	$575	$475

Add $150 for Natural, White Blonde, and Purple Transparent finishes.

Also available with maple fingerboard (Model 010-4602).

American Deluxe Power Tele (U.S. Mfg., No. 010-5700) - similar to American Deluxe Telecaster, except has rosewood fingerboard, Fender/Fishman Power Bridge, 6-Piezo pickup, 3-way mimi toggle for Power Bridge, dual concentric volume and tone controls, available in 3-Color Sunburst, black, White Blonde, Natural, Crimson Transparent and Teal green Transparent finishes. 1999 to date.

MSR	$2,249	$1,575	$1,375	$1,175

Also available with maple fingeboard (Model 010-5702).

U.S. American Fat Tele (U.S. Fat Tele, U.S. Mfg., No. 011-8000/010-8000). - solid alder body, one-piece maple neck, Micro-Tilt neck adjustment, rosewood fingerboard, deluxe Fender die-cast tuners, 22 medium-jumbo frets, 1 American Standard Tele pickup and 1 Fender DH-1 Humbucker pickup, master volume, master tone, 6-saddle string-through-body bridge, white shell pickguard, Schaller Straplock ready, available in 3-Color Sunburst, Candy Apple Red, and Olympic White finishes. Current Mfg.

MSR	$1,299	$975	$850	$750	$625	$525	$450	$350

Add $80 for 3-Color Sunburst finish.

White Blonde finish introduced in 2001.

Also available with maple fingerboard (Model 010-8002, disc. 2000)

AMERICAN NASHVILLE B-BENDER TELE (U.S. Mfg., No. 011-8342) allows for country bends, steel guitar glisses and wild special effects, poplar body, maple fingerboard with black dot position markers, Deluxe cast/sealed tuners, 22 Medium-Jumbo frets, 2 American Tele pickups and 1 Texas Special Strat pickup, 1 Volume/1Tone control, Super 5-way Strat-o-Tele switch, 6-saddle string through body, case included, available in 3-Color Sunburst, Olympic White, black and Candy Apple red finishes. Current Mfg.

MSR	$1,449	$1,015	$895	$795	$750	$695	$650	$595

40th ANNIVERSARY TELECASTER (U.S. Mfg.) - ash body, bound figured maple top, cream pickguard, 22-fret maple fingerboard with black dot inlay, fixed bridge, pearl tuner buttons, gold hardware, 2 single coil pickups, volume/tone control, 3-position switch, available in Antique Two-Tone, Natural and Transparent Red finishes. Mfg. 1988 to 1990.

$1,950	$1,850	$1,750	$1,650	$1,550	$1,450	$1,375

Last MSR was $1,299.

Approximately 300 of these instruments were Mfg.

1998 COLLECTOR'S EDITION TELECASTER (U.S. Mfg., No. 010-1998) - ash body, maple neck, 21-fret rosewood fingerboard with abalone dot inlay and special 12th fret inlay, fixed bridge, gold vintage-style hardware, single-ply white pickguard, 2 vintage-style single coil pickups, volume/tone controls, 3-way selector, controls mounted metal plate, engraved neckplate, available in 2-Color Sunburst finish. Mfg. 1998 Only.

$1,190	$1,000	$900	$800	$700	$600	$500

Last MSR was $1,699.

Production is scheduled for only 1,998 instruments. List price includes brown tolex hardshell case.

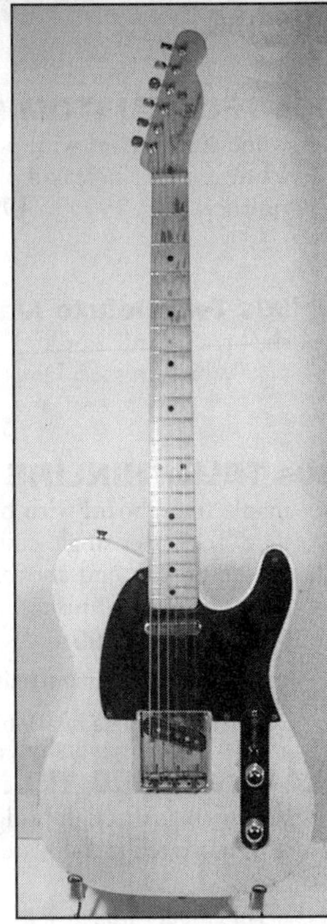

'54 Fender Telecaster
courtesy Austin Vintage

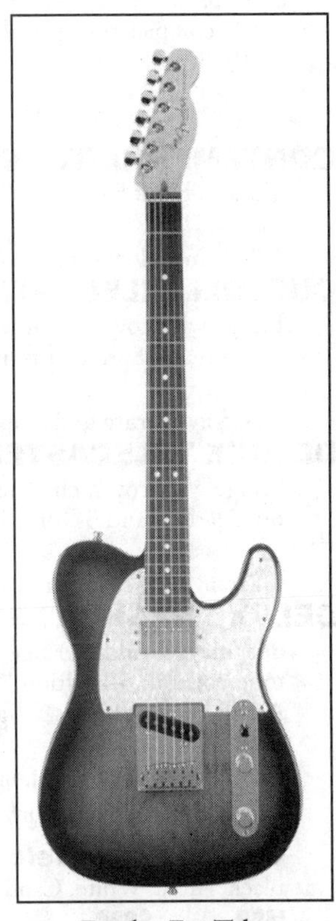

Fender Fat Tele
courtesy Fender

F

GRADING	100% MINT	98% NEAR MINT	95% EXC+	90% EXC	80% VG+	70% VG	60% G

'90s TELE CUSTOM (Jap. Mfg., No. 025-2500) - double bound basswood body, pearloid binding, maple neck, 21-fret rosewood fingerboard with pearl dot inlay, strings through-body bridge, gold hardware, color-matched (to body binding) pearloid pickguard, 2 Vintage Tele single coil pickups, volume/tone controls, 3-way selector, controls mounted metal plate, available in Black and Olympic White finishes. Mfg. 1995 to 1998.

		$450	$400	$375	$325	$295	$250	$195

Last MSR was $749.

'90s Tele Deluxe (Jap. Mfg., No. 025-9000) - similar to the '90s Tele Custom, except has Strat body contours, alder body, white shell pickguard, 2 Strat/1 Tele single coil pickups, 5-way selector, available in 3-Tone Sunburst, Black, Candy Apple Red, Sonic Blue, and Vintage White finishes. Disc. 1998.

		$575	$500	$425	$375	$325	$275	$225

Last MSR was $819.

'90s TELE THINLINE (U.S. Mfg., No. 010-8202) - double bound semi-hollow ash body, f-hole, bolt-on maple neck, 22-fret maple fingerboard with black dot inlay, strings through-body bridge, white or brown shell pickguard, chrome hardware, 2 American Standard Telecaster single coil pickups, volume/tone control, 3-position switch, controls mounted metal plate, DeltaTone system (high output bridge pickup and special "no-load" tone control) electronics, available in 3-Color Sunburst, Black, Crimson Transparent, Natural, and Olympic White finishes. Mfg. 1988 to date.

MSR	$1,899	$1,295	$1,145	$1,025	$875	$725	$595	$465

Add $50 for Natural finish.

This model also available with rosewood fingerboard with pearl dot inlay (Model 010-8200). Models with Natural or Olympic White finishes have brown shell pickguards and matching binding.

BLACK & GOLD TELECASTER (U.S. Mfg.) - hardwood body, black pickguard, 21-fret maple fingerboard with black dot inlay, brass strings through bridge, blackface peghead with logo, gold hardware, 2 single coil pickups, volume/tone control, 3-position switch, controls mounted metal plate, available in Black finish. Mfg. 1981 to 1983.

		$1,250	$1,050	$925	$850	$775	$750	$700

This model was also available with rosewood fingerboard with pearl dot inlay.

CALIFORNIA TELE (U.S. Mfg., No. 010-1602) - alder body, maple neck, 21-fret maple fingerboard with black dot inlay, 6-saddle bridge, chrome hardware, 3-ply white pickguard, Tex-Mex Strat/Tex-Mex Tele single coil pickups, volume/tone control, 3-position switch, controls mounted metal plate, available in Black, Brown Sunburst, Candy Apple Red, Fiesta Red, and Vintage White finishes. Mfg. 1998 Only.

		$569	$475	$425	$375	$325	$250	$200

Last MSR was $799.

This model also available with rosewood fingerboard with pearl dot inlay (Model 010-1600).

California Fat Tele (U.S. Mfg., No. 010-1702) - similar to the California Tele, except features Tex-Mex humbucker/Tex- Mex Tele single coil pickups, special switching, available in Black, Brown Sunburst, Candy Apple Red, Fiesta Red, and Vintage White finishes. Mfg. 1997 to 1998.

		$599	$500	$450	$395	$325	$275	$225

Last MSR was $849.

CONTEMPORARY TELECASTER (Jap. Mfg.) - hardwood body, 22-fret rosewood fingerboard with pearl dot inlay, standard vibrato, black hardware, 2 single coil/1 humbucker pickup, volume/tone controls, 3 mini switches. Mfg. 1985 to 1987.

		N/A	$200	$190	$180	$170	$160	$150

This model was also available with 2 humbucker pickups, 3-position/coil tap switches.

CUSTOM TELECASTER (U.S. Mfg.) - ash body, black pickguard, 21-fret maple fingerboard with black dot inlay, strings through bridge with cover, chrome hardware, humbucker/single coil pickups, 2 volume/2 tone controls, 3-position switch, available in Black, Blonde, Natural and Sunburst finishes. Mfg. 1972 to 1981.

		N/A	$1,200	$1,150	$1,100	$1,000	$925	$850

Bigsby vibrato and maple fingerboard were optional.

DELUXE TELECASTER (U.S. Mfg.) - poplar body, black pickguard, 21-fret maple fingerboard with black dot inlay, strings through bridge with cover, chrome hardware, 2 humbucker pickups, 2 volume/2 tone controls, 3-position switch, available in Blonde, Custom Colors, Natural and 3-Tone Sunburst finishes. Mfg. 1973 to 1981.

		N/A	$1,000	$950	$895	$800	$725	$650

From 1977-1979, Antigua finish was available with matching pickguard.

DELUXE NASHVILLE TELE (Mex. Mfg., No. 013-5302) - alder body, maple neck, 21-fret maple fingerboard with black dot inlay, 6-saddle bridge, chrome hardware, brown shell pickguard, Tex-Mex Tele/Tex-Mex Strat/Tex-Mex Tele single coil pickups, volume/tone control, 5-position "Strat-o-Tone" switch, controls mounted metal plate, available in Black, Brown Sunburst, Candy Apple Red, and Arctic White finishes. Mfg. 1998 to date.

MSR	$649	$450	$375	$350	$300	$275	$225	$165

This model also available with rosewood fingerboard with pearl dot inlay (Model 013-5300).

Add $50 for Brown Sunburst finish (1999).

Deluxe Power Tele (Mex. Mfg., No. 013-5000) - similar to Nashville Tele, except has Fender/Fishman Power Bridge, available in Black, Arctic White, Candy Apple Red, and Brown Sunburst. 1999 to date.

MSR	$959	$675	$625	$575	$525	$475	$425	$375

GRADING	100% MINT	98% NEAR MINT	95% EXC+	90% EXC	80% VG+	70% VG	60% G

Fender Sparkle Telecaster Custom Shop courtesy Brook May's Pro Shop

PINK PAISLEY, BLUE FLORAL TELECASTER (U.S. Mfg.) - ash body, floral/paisley pickguard, 21-fret maple fingerboard with black dot inlay, strings through bridge, chrome hardware, 2 single coil pickups, volume/tone controls, 3-position switch, controls mounted metal plate, available in Blue Floral and Pink Paisley finishes. Mfg. 1968 to 1970.

N/A	$5,000	$4,500	$4,000	$3,600	$3,250	$2,950

PAISLEY TELECASTER (Jap. Mfg.) - single cutaway ash body, paisley pickguard, bolt-on maple neck, 21-fret maple fingerboard with black dot inlay, strings through bridge, 6-on-one-side tuners, chrome hardware, 2 single coil pickups, volume/tone controls, 3-position switch, controls mounted metal plate, available in Paisley finish. Disc. 1994.

N/A	$750	$625	$450	$400	$375	$350

Last MSR was $820.

This model was a limited edition instrument available by custom order.

Blue Flower Telecaster (Jap. Mfg.) - similar to Paisley Tele, except has Blue Floral pickguard/finish. Disc. 1994.

N/A	$750	$625	$450	$400	$375	$350

Last MSR was $720.

This model was a limited edition instrument available by custom order.

PAISLEY TELE (Jap. Mfg., No. 027-4902) - basswood body, bolt-on maple neck, 21-fret maple fingerboard with black dot inlay, strings through bridge, 6-on-a-side tuners, chrome hardware, clear pickguard, 2 single coil pickups, volume/tone controls, 3-position switch, controls mounted metal plate, available in custom Pink Paisley pattern finish. Disc. 1998.

N/A	$650	$575	$425	$375	$350	$325

Last MSR was $759.

ROSEWOOD TELECASTER (U.S. Mfg.) - rosewood body, black pickguard, bolt-on rosewood neck, 21-fret rosewood fingerboard with pearl dot inlay, strings through bridge with cover, chrome hardware, 2 single coil pickups, volume/tone control, 3-position switch, controls mounted metal plate, available in Natural finish. Mfg. 1969 to 1972.

N/A	$5,000	$4,200	$3,800	$3,300	$3,000	$2,750

Certain very clean/all original models have sold for as high as $4,000 to $7,000. However, this should be determined on a piece-by-piece basis as opposed to the usual market. The Rosewood Telecaster was also offered with a hollowed (3 chambers) body between 1971 and 1972.

Rosewood Telecaster (Jap. Mfg.) - single cutaway rosewood body, black pickguard, bolt-on rosewood neck, 21-fret rosewood fingerboard with pearl dot inlay, strings through bridge with cover, chrome hardware, 2 single coil pickups, volume/tone control, 3-position switch, controls mounted metal plate, available in Natural finish. Disc. 1995.

$900	$800	$700	$625	$550	$500	$450

Last MSR was $1,230.

This model was a limited edition instruments available by custom order.

SPARKLE TELECASTER - poplar body, white pickguard, figured maple neck, 21-fret maple fingerboard with black dot inlay, strings through bridge with brass saddles, nickel hardware, 2 single coil pickups, volume/tone control, 3-position switch, available in Champagne Sparkle, Gold Sparkle and Silver Sparkle finishes. Mfg. 1993 to 1995.

N/A	$1,500	$1,290	$1,155	$1,020	$875	$740

Last MSR was $2,150.

This model was available by custom order only.

STANDARD TELECASTER (Mex. Mfg., No. 013-5102/013-5202) - poplar body, bolt-on maple neck, 21-fret maple fingerboard with black dot inlay, fixed bridge, chrome hardware, 3-ply white pickguard, 2 single coil pickups, volume/tone control, 3-position switch, controls mounted metal plate, available in Arctic White, Black, Brown Sunburst, Crimson Red Metallic, and Lake Placid Blue finishes. Current Mfg.

MSR	$449	$335	$285	$245	$210	$165	$140	$110

In 1998, Midnight Blue and Midnight Wine finishes were introduced; Crimson Red Metallic, and Lake Placid Blue finishes were discontinued.

TELE-SONIC (U.S. Mfg., No. 010-1800) - chambered mahogany body, maple neck, 24 3/4" scale, 22-fret rosewood fingerboard with dot inlay, Wilkinson stop tailpiece, die-cast tuners, chrome hardware, black pickguard, 2 DeArmond 2K single coil pickups, 2 volume/2 tone control, 3-position toggle switch, available in Brown Sunburst and Crimson Transparent finishes. Mfg. 1998 to date.

MSR	$1,649	$1,175	$1,050	$950	$850	$750	$675	$625

TELECASTER ACOUSTIC/ELECTRIC (Jap. Mfg., 025-2400) - single round cutaway semi hollow basswood body, bound solid spruce top, f-hole, maple neck, 22-fret rosewood fingerboard with pearl dot inlay, rosewood bridge, 6-on-one-side die-cast tuners, chrome hardware, single coil/piezo bridge pickups, volume/pan/tone controls, available in 3-Tone Sunburst and Black finishes. Mfg. 1995 to 1998.

$375	$325	$275	$250	$225	$200	$175

Last MSR was $699.

GRADING	100% MINT	98% NEAR MINT	95% EXC+	90% EXC	80% VG+	70% VG	60% G

Telecaster Classical Thinline (Jap. Mfg., 025-2800) - similar to the Telecaster Acoustic/Electric, except in a nylon string configuration, 21-fret rosewood fingerboard, piezo bridge pickup (only), volume/tone controls, active electronics, available in 3-Tone Sunburst and Black finishes. Mfg. 1995 to 1998.

	$375	$325	$275	$250	$225	$200	$175

Last MSR was $699.

TELECASTER PLUS (U.S. Mfg., U.S. TELECASTER PLUS, No. 010-8500) - alder body, bound ash veneer top/back, maple neck, 22-fret rosewood fingerboard with pearl dot inlay, fixed bridge, chrome hardware, white pickguard, 3 single coil Lace Sensor pickups, volume/tone control, 3-position switch, controls mounted metal plate, available in Antique Burst, Black, Blue Burst, Crimson Burst, and Teal Green Metallic finishes. Mfg. 1995 to 1998.

	$925	$795	$700	$600	$525	$425	$325

Last MSR was $1,299.

Add $100 for solid ash body with Natural finish.

This model also available with maple fingerboard with black dot inlay (Model 010-8502).

TELECASTER SPECIAL (Mex. Mfg., No. 013-5502) - poplar body, ash top, 22-fret maple fingerboard with black dot inlay, fixed strings through bridge, chrome hardware, humbucker/single coil pickups, volume/tone controls, 3-position switch, available in Natural finish. Mfg. 1994 to 1998.

	$325	$295	$250	$200	$175	$150	$125

Last MSR was $510.

TELECASTER THINLINE (U.S. Mfg.) - ash body with hollowed bass side, f-hole, pearloid pickguard, 21-fret maple fingerboard with black dot inlay, strings through bridge with cover, chrome hardware, 2 single coil pickups, volume/tone control, 3-position switch, available in Custom Colors, Natural and Sunburst finishes. Mfg. 1968 to 1971.

	N/A	$2,500	$2,250	$2,150	$1,950	$1,800	$1,750

Add $300 for Sunburst or Custom Color finishes.

In 1969, rosewood fingerboard with pearl dot inlay became an option.

Telecaster Thinline II (U.S. Mfg.) - similar to Thinline Telecaster, except has 2 humbucker pickups. Mfg. 1972 to 1978.

	N/A	$1,200	$1,100	$1,050	$1,000	$950	$900

Add $100 for Sunburst or Custom Color finishes (except Mocha Brown).

TEX-MEX TELE SPECIAL (Mex. Mfg., 013-7302) - poplar body, bolt-on maple neck, 21-fret maple fingerboard with black dot inlay, vintage-style bridge, chrome hardware, white pickguard, Tex-Mex humbucker/Tex-Mex single coil pickups, volume/tone control, 3-position switch, controls mounted metal plate, available in Black, Brown Sunburst, Candy Apple Red, Sonic Blue, and Vintage White finishes. Mfg. 1997 to 1998.

	$450	$395	$350	$300	$250	$200	$150

Last MSR was $649.

TRADITIONAL TELECASTER (Mex. Mfg., 013-3202) - poplar body, bolt-on maple neck, 21-fret maple fingerboard with black dot inlay, fixed bridge, chrome hardware, 3-ply white pickguard, 2 single coil pickups, volume/tone control, 3-position switch, controls mounted metal plate, available in Arctic White, Black, and Torino Red finishes. Disc. 1998.

	$225	$200	$175	$150	$125	$100	$75

Last MSR was $329.

H.M.T. Series Telecaster Series

H.M.T. (Heavy Metal Telecasters) were available in the late 1980s/early 1990s. Models include the 2 DiMarzio humbucker Model 25-2100, Blue Fender-Lace Sensor single coil Model 25-2200, and piezo bridge/Silver Fender-Lace Sensor Model 25-2300. Future research continues on the H.M.T. Telecaster models.

U.S. Vintage Reissue Series

'52 TELECASTER (U.S. Mfg., No. 010-0202/010-1303) - light ash body, maple neck, 21-fret maple fingerboard with black dot inlay, vintage-style fixed bridge, chrome hardware, black pickguard, 2 American Vintage single coil pickups, volume/tone control, 3-position switch, controls mounted metal plate, available in Black, Butterscotch Blonde, and Copper finishes. Current Mfg.

MSR $1,699	$1,275	$1,075	$850	$750	$650	$525	$425

In 2000, Copper finish was discontinued.

Add $100 for LH configuration (Model 010- 0222).

'52 Tele Special (U.S. Mfg., No. 010-0212-803/010-0212) - premuim ash body, one-piece "U" shape maple neck with truss rod, maple fingerboard, 25.5" scale, 21-frets, gold hardware, gold vintage style tuners, gold original style Tele bridge with gold "ash tray" bridge cover, 1-ply white pickguard, 2 New American Vintage Tele pickups, 3-position switch, master tone, master volume, available in 2-Color Sunburst, Black finish. Case included. Current Mfg.

MSR $1,849	$1,385	$1,175	$975	$875	$775	$675	$525

In 2000, black finish was discontinued.

GRADING	100% MINT	98% NEAR MINT	95% EXC+	90% EXC	80% VG+	70% VG	60% G

Telecaster Collectibles Series

The following models have a Telecaster single cutaway body, two single coil pickups, bolt-on neck, and six on a side headstock (unless otherwise specified).

'50s TELECASTER (Jap. Mfg., No. 027-1202) - basswood body, maple neck, 21-fret maple fingerboard with black dot inlay, vintage-style bridge, chrome hardware, black pickguard, 2 single coil pickups, volume/tone control, 3-position switch, controls mounted metal plate, available in 2-Tone Sunburst, Black, Blonde, Candy Apple Red, Shell Pink, and Sonic Blue finishes. Disc. 1998.

$450 $375 $325 $275 $225 $195 $150
Last MSR was $599.

'50s Telecaster Left Hand (Jap. Mfg., No. 027-1222). - similar to the '50s Telecaster, except in left-handed configuration, available in Blonde finish only. Disc. 1998.

$450 $375 $325 $275 $225 $195 $150
Last MSR was $669.

50'S TELECASTER (Mex. Mfg., No. 013-1202) - solid ash body, one-piece maple neck, Fender vintage style tuners, 25.5" scale, 21 nickel silver frets, single-ply white pickguard, 2 Vintage Tele pickups, master tone, master volume, 3-way switch, 3-saddle string-through-body bridge, available in White Blonde, 2-Color Sunburst, and Black finishes. Current Mfg.

MSR $869 $650 $550 $495 $450 $375 $325 $225

'62 CUSTOM TELECASTER (U.S. Mfg., No. 010-6200) - alder body with maple "C" shape neck, bound top and back, rosewood fingerboard, 25.5" scale, 21 vintage style frets, vintage style tuners, '62 Tele pickups, 3-way switch, master volume, master tone, aged 3-ply pickguard, vintage Tele bridge, available in 3-Color Sunburst, Black, and Candy Apple Red finishes. New 1999.

MSR $1,799 $1,350 $1,150 $950 $850 $750 $650 $500

In 2001, Dakota Red, Inca Silver and Ice Blue Metallic finishes were introduced.

Add $50 for 3-Color Sunburst.

'62 CUSTOM TELECASTER (Jap. Mfg., No. 027-5100) - double bound basswood body, maple neck, 21-fret rosewood fingerboard with white dot inlay, vintage-style bridge, chrome hardware, white pickguard, 2 single coil pickups, volume/tone control, 3-position switch, controls mounted metal plate, available in 3-Tone Sunburst and Candy Apple Red finishes. Disc 1999.

$470 $400 $350 $300 $275 $225 $175
Last MSR was $669.

'62 Custom Telecaster Left Hand (Jap. Mfg., No. 027-5120) - similar to the '62 Custom Telecaster, except in left-handed configuration, available in 3-Tone Sunburst and Candy Apple Red finishes. Disc. 1998.

$525 $450 $395 $350 $295 $250 $175
Last MSR was $739.

'69 TELECASTER THINLINE (Jap. Mfg., No. 027-7702) - semi-hollow mahogany body, f-hole, maple neck, 21-fret rosewood fingerboard with white dot inlay, vintage-style bridge, chrome hardware, white shell pickguard, 2 single coil pickups, volume/tone control, 3-position switch, available in Natural finish. Disc. 1998.

$495 $450 $400 $350 $295 $250 $195
Last MSR was $749.

'69 TELECASTER THINLINE (Mex. Mfg., No. 013-6902) - semi-hollow mahogany or ash body, one-piece maple neck, 25.5" scale Schaller vintage "F" tuners, 21 nickel silver frets, white shell pickguard, 2 Vintage Tele pickups, master tone, master volume, 3-way switch, 3-saddle string-through-body bridge, available in 3-Color Sunburst, Black, and natural finishes. Current Mfg.

MSR $949 $710 $600 $550 $475 $400 $350 $275

'72 Telecaster Thinline (Jap. Mfg., No. 027-3202) - similar to the '69 Telecaster Thinline, exept has 'bullet' truss rod adjustment, semi-hollow ash body, string-through-body fixed bridge, 2 covered humbuckers, available in Natural finish. Disc. 1999.

$560 $475 $425 $375 $325 $250 $200
Last MSR was $799.

'72 Telecaster Thinline (Mex. Mfg., No. 013-7402) - semi-hollow ash body, f-hole, maple neck and fingerboard, 25.5" scale, Bullet truss rod, Fender/Schaller "F" style tuners, 2 Fender Reissue "Wide Range" Humbucker pickups, 3-way switch, master tone, master volume, white Pearloid pickguard, 70's Strat non-tremolo bridge, available in 3-Color Sunburst and Natural finishes. New 1999.

MSR $949 $700 $600 $500 $450 $400 $350 $300

'53 Fender Telecaster (Refinished) courtesy Tom Murphy

F

GRADING	100% MINT	98% NEAR MINT	95% EXC+	90% EXC	80% VG+	70% VG	60% G

'72 TELECASTER CUSTOM (Jap. Mfg., No. 027-7602) - basswood body, maple neck, 21-fret maple fingerboard with black dot inlay, vintage-style bridge, chrome hardware, 3-ply black pickguard, covered humbucker/single coil pickups, 2 volume/2 tone controls, 3-position switch, available in 3-Tone Sunburst and Black finishes. Disc. 1999.

$460 $395 $350 $300 $250 $225 $175

Last MSR was $659.

'72 TELECASTER CUSTOM (Mex. Mfg., No. 013-7502) - poplar or alder body, maple "U" shaped neck, Micro-Tilt neck adjustment, maple fingerboard, 25.5" scale, 21-frets, Bullet truss rod, Fender/Schaller "F" style tuners, 1 Fender "Wide Range" Humbucker pickup and 1 single coil Tele pickup, 3-way switch, 2 volume controls, 2 tone controls, 3-ply pickguard, vintage style 6-saddle Tele bridge, available in 3-Color Sunburst and Black finishes. New 1999.

MSR $849 $650 $550 $475 $425 $375 $325 $225

Add $50 for 3-Color Sunburst finish.

Also available with rosewood fingerboard (Model 013-7500).

F

Fender Custom Shop Contemporary Models Series

In addition to specialty custom guitars and Limited Edition runs, the Custom Shop also produces a number of models in smaller production runs as **Contemporary Models** and **Custom Classics**.

SET NECK TELE JR. (U.S. Mfg., No. 010-3400) - mahogany body with 11 'tone chambers' (semi-hollow design), set-in mahogany neck, 22-fret pau ferro fingerboard with white dot inlay, chrome hardware, tortoiseshell pickguard, 6-on-a-side tuners, American Standard (Strat) bridge, 2 Seymour Duncan P-90 pickups, volume/tone controls, 3-way selector, controls mounted metal plate, available in Antique Burst, Crimson Red Transparent, Natural, and Vintage White finishes. Mfg. 1997 to 2000.

$1,700 $1,450 $1,350 $1,250 $1,150 $1,000 $850

Last MSR was $2,599.

SET NECK TELECASTER (U.S. Mfg.) - mahogany body, bound figured maple top, mahogany neck, 22-fret rosewood fingerboard with pearl dot inlay, strings through bridge, locking tuners, 2 DiMarzio humbucker pickups, volume/tone control, 3-position/coil tap switches, available in Antique Burst, Autumn Gold, Transparent Crimson, Transparent Ebony, and Transparent Sapphire Blue finishes. Mfg. 1990 to 1995.

$1,300 $1,100 $925 $850 $800 $775 $650

Last MSR was $2,150.

This model is also available with double locking Floyd Rose vibrato, roller nut. In 1993, pau ferro fingerboard became standard.

Set Neck Telecaster C/A (U.S. Mfg.) - similar to Set Neck Telecaster, except has tortoise pickguard, pau ferro fingerboard, gold hardware, humbucker/single coil pickups, available in Gold Sparkle, Natural, Silver Sparkle, and Transparent Sunset Orange finishes. Mfg. 1991 to 1995.

$1,300 $1,050 $900 $825 $800 $750 $650

Last MSR was $2,150.

Fender Custom Shop Custom Classic Series

The following Custom Shop prodcution models have a Telecaster single cutaway body, two single coil pickups, bolt-on neck, and six on a side headstock (unless otherwise specified).

'50s TELECASTER (No. 010-5002, U.S. Mfg.) - light ash body, figured maple neck, 21-fret maple fingerboard with black dot inlay, vintage-style bridge, nickel hardware, single ply white pickguard, 2 American Vintage single coil pickups, volume/tone controls, 3-position switch, available in 2-Tone Sunburst, Black, and (White) Blonde finishes. Disc. 1998.

$1,400 $1,250 $1,100 $1,000 $900 $750 $575

Last MSR was $2,299.

Add $200 for gold hardware (Model 010-5012).

'60s Telecaster Custom (No. 010-6300, U.S. Mfg.) - similar to the '50s Telecaster, except has double bound alder body, 21-fret rosewood fingerboard with white dot inlay, 2 Texas Special Tele single coil pickups, available in Custom Colors and 3-Tone Sunburst and Black finishes. Mfg. 1997 to 1998.

$1,900 $1,625 $1,425 $1,250 $1,000 $875 $675

Last MSR was $2,699.

Add $150 for Custom color finishes.

Add $200 for gold hardware (Model 010-6310).

'52 TELE CUSTOM CLASSIC LEFT HAND (U.S. Mfg., No. 010-5222) - alder body, figured maple neck, 21-fret maple fingerboard with black dot inlay, vintage-style bridge, chrome hardware, black pickguard, 2 Texas Special Tele single coil pickups, volume/tone controls, 3-position switch, available in 2-Tone Sunburst and Honey Blonde finishes. Disc. 1998.

$1,750 $1,500 $1,325 $1,150 $975 $800 $625

Last MSR was $2,499.

GRADING	100% MINT	98% NEAR MINT	95% EXC+	90% EXC	80% VG+	70% VG	60% G

AMERICAN CLASSIC TELECASTER (U.S. Mfg., No. 010-4802) - alder body, figured maple neck, 22-fret maple fingerboard with black dot inlay, American Standard Tele bridge, chrome hardware, brown or white shell pickguard, 2 Texas Special Strat/Texas Tele bridge single coil pickups, volume/tone controls, 3-position switch, available in Custom Colors and 2-Tone Sunburst, 3-Tone Sunburst, Blonde, and Olympic White finishes. Disc. 1998.

		$1,275	$1,000	$925	$800	$675	$550	$450

Last MSR was $1,699.

This model is available with rosewood fingerboard (Model 010-4800). In 1998, gold hardware (Model 010-4812), or rosewood fingerboard/gold hardware (Model 010-4810) option was discontinued; Blonde and Olympic White finishes were discontinued; White Blonde finish was introduced. The Sunburst finishes feature a white shell pickguard; the White Blonde finish has a brown shell pickguard.

BAJO SEXTO TELECASTER (U.S. Mfg., No. 010-4002) - swamp ash body, 30.2" scale, 24-fret maple fingerboard with black dot inlay, strings through bridge with brass saddles, nickel hardware, black pickguard, 2 Texas Special single coil pickups, volume/tone control, 3-position switch, series wiring, available in Honey Blonde and 2-Tone Sunburst finishes. Mfg. 1993 to 1998.

		$1,400	$1,200	$1,100	$975	$800	$675	$550

Last MSR was $1,999.

This instrument is a longer scaled (baritone) instrument.

TELECASTER XII (U.S. Mfg., No. 010-4100) - swamp ash body, bolt-on figured maple neck, 22-fret rosewood fingerboard with white dot inlay, chrome hardware, white (or black) pickguard, 6-per-side tuners, vintage-style 12-string bridge, 2 Texas Special single coil pickups, series wiring, volume/tone controls, 3-way selector, controls mounted metal plate, available in 2-Tone Sunburst, 3-Tone Sunburst, Sea Foam Green, and Vintage Blonde finishes. Disc. 1998.

		$1,750	$1,500	$1,325	$1,150	$975	$800	$625

Last MSR was $2,499.

This model is available with a maple fingerboard with black dot inlay (Model 010-4102).

CUSTOM CLASSIC TELECASTER (No. 015-6400) this guitar is the Custom Shop version of the American Series Telecaster. Thin lacquer-finished premium Ash body, lightly figured maple neck, rosewood fingerboard, 22 Medium-Jumbo frets, Fender Deluxe cast/sealed tuners, new "Twisted Tele" neck pickup and new Classic Tele bridge pickup, reverse control plate with 3-way switch towards rear, three-ply parchment pickguard, new Custom Classic bridge with solid steel bridge plate and chrome-plated solid milled brass saddles, available in 3-Color Sunburst, Bing Cherry Transparent, Cobalt Blue Transparent and Honey Blonde finishes. New 2001.

MSR	$2,199	$1,550	$1,350	$1,250	$N/A	$N/A	$N/A	$N/A

Also available with maple fingerboard (Model 015-6402).

SUB-SONIC TELECASTER (No. 015-4732) tuned B-E-A-D-G-B to provide the low growl of a 7-string guitar, 27" scale, maple fingerboard, thin lacquer-finished alder body, available in White Blonde, 2-Color Sunburst, black and Butterscotch Blonde finishes. New 2001.

MSR	$2,379	$1,665	$1,450	$1,250	$N/A	$N/A	$N/A	$N/A

Telecaster Relic Series

Relic series instruments are cosmetically aged by the Fender Custom Shop. Instruments are stamped on the headstock and into the body (under the pickguard) with the Custom Shop logo to avoid future cases of "mistaken identity" in the Vintage Guitar market.

Some debate has begun in regards to grading Relic series instruments. Is proper degradation of the instrument as it occurs at the Fender factory the only damage allowed, or do the dents and chips that occur at a dealer's shop (pre-sale) count? If a Relic series model gets further abused in the hands of a player, does the value go up? How does a dealer determine if the damage was "factory" versus aftermarket in the secondary guitar market? The ***Blue Book of Electric Guitars*** will continue to report on this debate in future editions.

'50s RELIC NO-CASTER (U.S. Mfg., No. 010-5102) - light ash body, maple neck, 21-fret maple fingerboard with black dot inlay, strings through vintage bridge with 3 Gatton saddles, *aged* nickel hardware, 2 Custom '50s single coil pickups, volume/tone control, 3-position switch, controls mounted on metal plate, available in Honey Blonde finish. Disc. 1998.

		$1,950	$1,690	$1,485	$1,250	$1,125	$950	$825

Last MSR was $2,599.

Telecaster Signature Series

Signature Series Telecasters are designed in collaboration with the artist whose name appears on the headstock. The nature of the Signature Series is to present an instrument that contains the idiosyncrasies similar to the artist's guitar.

JAMES BURTON (U.S. Mfg., No. 010-8602) - light ash body, 21-fret maple fingerboard with black dot inlay, strings through bridge, gold hardware, 3 single coil Lace Sensor pickups, volume/tone control, 5-position switch, available in Black with Candy Red Paisley, Black with Gold Paisley, Frost Red, and Pearl White finishes. Mfg. 1990 to date.

MSR	$1,799	$1,250	$1,125	$950	$825	$725	$575	$450

This model features black chrome hardware on the Black with Gold Paisley and Frost Red finishes. In 2000, Frost Red finish was discontinued.

GRADING		100% MINT	98% NEAR MINT	95% EXC+	90% EXC	80% VG+	70% VG	60% G

James Burton Standard (Mex. Mfg., No. 013-8602) - similar to the James Burton, except has poplar body, white pickguard, chrome hardware, 2 Texas Special Tele pickups, available in 2-Tone Sunburst, Black, Candy Apple Red, and Vintage Blonde finishes. Mfg. 1995 to date.

MSR	$769	$550	$475	$450	$350	$300	$250	$175

In 1999, 2-Tone Sunburst, Black, and Vintage Blonde finishes were discontinued.
In 2000, Vintage White finish was introduced.

ALBERT COLLINS (U.S. Mfg., No. 010-8800) - bound ash body, white pickguard, bolt-on maple neck, 21-fret maple fingerboard with black dot inlay, strings through bridge with cover, 6-on-one-side tuners, chrome hardware, humbucker/single coil pickups, volume/tone control, 3-position switch, controls mounted on a metal plate, available in Natural finish. Mfg. 1990 to date.

MSR	$3,599	$2,850	$2,500	$2,250	$1,750	$1,500	$1,200	$900

This guitar is custom order only.

JERRY DONAHUE TELECASTER (U.S. Mfg., No. 010-8902) - ash body, birdseye maple top/back, black pickguard, birdseye maple neck, 21-fret maple fingerboard with black dot inlay, strings through bridge, 6-on-one-side tuners, Jerry Donahue's signature on peghead, gold hardware, 2 Seymour Duncan single coil pickups, volume/tone control, 5-position switch, controls mounted metal plate, available in 3-Tone Sunburst, Crimson Red Transparent, and Sapphire Blue transparent finishes. Mfg. 1992 to date.

MSR	$3,149	$2,500	$2,200	$1,850	$1,650	$1,300	$1,000	$700

J.D. Telecaster (Jap. Mfg., No. 027-9702) - similar to the Jerry Donahue Telecaster, except features bound basswood body, 2 single coil pickups, 5-way switch, special wiring, available in 3-Tone Sunburst, Black, Crimson Red Transparent, and Sapphire Blue Transparent finishes. Mfg. 1992 to 1999.

		$500	$425	$375	$325	$275	$225	$175

Last MSR was $709.

MUDDY WATERS TRIBUTE TELECASTER 2000 (U.S. Mfg.) exact replica of the late '50's Telecaster that was Muddy's signature guitar, every ding, scratch and gouge is present along with amplifier knobs on the controls. Mfg. in 2000 only.

MUDDY WATERS (Mex. Mfg., No. 013-8500) ash body, rosewood fingerboard with dot position markers, vintage machine heads, 21 Medium-Jumbo frets, 2 U.S. Special Vintage Tele pickups, 1 Volume/1 Tone control, 3-way switch, American vintage '52 Tele bridge, available in Candy Apple Red finish only. New 2001.

MSR	$899	$675	$575	$525	$475	$425	$375	$325

NOKIE EDWARDS LIMITED EDITION (Japan Mfg., No. 025-8500) - laminated ash/basswood/rock maple body with flame maple top, (strat-style) back and arm contours, bolt-on 3-ply maple neck, 22-fret ebony fingerboard with pearloid dot inlay and zero fret, tilt back headstock, 6-on-one-side tuners, gold hardware, 2 Seymour Duncan humbucking pickups, volume/push-pull tone (for coil tapping) controls, 3-position switch, available in Natural finish. Mfg. 1996 only.

		$1,750	$1,575	$1,275	$1,125	$1,000	$900	$800

Last MSR was $1,959.

It is estimated that only 35 instruments were produced.

DANNY GATTON (U.S. Mfg., No. 010-8700) - swamp ash body, white pickguard, bolt-on maple neck, 22-fret maple fingerboard with black dot inlay/cubic zirconium side markers, strings through stainless steel bridge, 2 twin blade Joe Barden single coil pickups, volume/tone control, 3-position switch, available in Frost Gold and Honey Blonde finishes. Current Mfg.

MSR	$3,749	$2,650	$2,200	$1,950	$1,650	$1,200	$900	$825

This guitar is custom order only.

MERLE HAGGARD TRIBUTE (U.S. Mfg., No. 010-0402) - laminated figured maple top, ivoroid body binding, set-in maple neck, 22-fret maple fingerboard with dot inlay, abalone "Tuff Dog Tele" headstock inlay, gold hardware, white ivoroid pickguard, 2 Texas Tele pickups, custom 4-way switching, available in 2-Color Sunburst finish. Mfg. 1998 to date.

MSR	$5,749	$4,025	$3,400	$2,900	$2,600	$2,300	$2,000	$1,700

WAYLON JENNINGS TRIBUTE (U.S. Mfg., No. 010-0302) - bound top/back light ash body, 21-fret maple fingerboard with dot inlay/Flying W at 12th fret, Scruggs tuner on low 'E' string, Elite tuning keys with pearloid buttons, chrome hardware, 3-ply white pickguard, 2 Texas Tele pickups, available in Black finish with leather White Rose inlay. Mfg. 1995 to date.

MSR	$4,499	$3,150	$2,600	$2,300	$2,000	$1,850	$1,700	$1,550

JOHN JORGENSON TELECASTER (U.S. Mfg., No. 010-4400) - korina body, maple neck, 22-fret African rosewood fingerboard with pearloid dot inlay, Sperzel TrimLok tuners, vintage-style bridge, chrome hardware, matching sparkle pickguard, 2 custom vintage-looking humbucking pickups, volume/tone controls, 3-position switch, chrome metal controls plate, available in Black, Champagne Sparkle, and Silver Sparkle tops with Natural body finishes. Mfg. 1998 to date.

MSR	$3,999	$2,800	$2,350	$2,000	$1,850	$1,650	$1,550	$1,400

Both the Champagne and Silver Sparkle finishes feature white pearloid binding. The Black finish model has gold sparkle binding and ebony fingerboard with gold sparkle dot inlay. In 2000, Natural finish was discontinued.

BUCK OWENS LIMITED EDITION (Jap. Mfg., No. 025-7500) - basswood body, maple neck, 22-fret rosewood fingerboard with dot inlay, 3-saddle fixed bridge, gold-plated vintage hardware, gold pickguard, 2 Vintage Tele pickups with Alnico magnets, volume/tone controls, 3-way switch, gold-plated metal controls plate, available in Red/Silver/Blue Sparkle finish. New 1998.

MSR	$999	$700	$600	$500	$450	$400	$360	$320

GRADING	100% MINT	98% NEAR MINT	95% EXC+	90% EXC	80% VG+	70% VG	60% G

WILL RAY LIMITED EDITION JAZZ-A-CASTER (Jap. Mfg., No. 025-8700) - basswood body, satin-finished maple neck, small Strat headstock, 22-fret rosewood fingerboard with white pearloid triangle inlay, Schaller tuners, Hipshot B-Bender, chrome hardware, white shell pickguard, 2 Seymour Duncan Jazzmaster pickups, volume/tone controls, 4-position switch, available in Gold Foil finish. Mfg. 1997 to 1998.

$1,000 $850 $725 $650 $600 $550 $500

Last MSR was $1,550.

WILL RAY SIGNATURE MOJO TELE (U.S. Mfg., No. 010-4500) - ash body, maple neck, Strat headstock, 22-fret rosewood fingerboard with pearl VooDoo Skulls inlay, Sperzel TrimLok tuners, custom Tele bridge with 3-string saddles, chrome hardware, white shell pickguard, 2 Custom Shop Jazzmaster pickups, volume/tone select/tone controls, 3-position switch, available in Cadmium Orange, Lime Green, and Ultra Marine Blue finishes with 23kt Gold Foil Leaf applique. Mfg. 1998 to date.

MSR $4,299 $3,000 $2,500 $2,100 $1,850 $1,650 $1,500 $1,350

Add $300 for Hipshot String Bending system (Model 010-4540).

CLARENCE WHITE (U.S. Mfg., No. 010-5602) - ash body, tortoise pickguard, figured maple neck, 21-fret maple fingerboard with black dot inlay, strings through bridge, Parsons-White stringbender, 2 Texas Tele/'54 Strat single coil pickups, volume/tone control, 3-position switch, available in 2-Tone Sunburst finish. Mfg. 1994 to date.

MSR $5,299 $3,700 $2,950 $2,600 $2,300 $1,950 $1,550 $1,350

This instrument has Scruggs banjo tuners on the E strings.

Time Machine Telecaster Series

Time Machine Series Telecasters are built to exacting specifications of their respective vintages, including: body contours and radii, neck shape, fingerboard radius, pickups, electronics and hardware. Original materials, tooling and production techniques are employed whenever possible.

Each model is available in three distinct finish packages: NOS (New Old Stock), as if the guitar was bought new in its respective year and brought forward in time to the present day; Closet Classic, as if the guitar was bought new in its respective year, played perhaps a dozen times a year and then carefully put away - has a few small dings, lightly checked finish, oxidized hardware and aged plastic parts; Relic, shows natural wear and tear of years of heavy use - nicks, dings, scratches, worn finish, rusty hardware, and aged plastic parts.

'51 "NOCASTER" (NOS, No. 015-0102) ash body, "U" shaped maple neck, single ply black pickguard and original specification pickups, available in Vintage Blonde finish. New 2001.

MSR $2,859 $2,000 $1,800 $1,600 $1,400 $1,200 $1,000 $850

'51 "Nocaster" Closet Classic (No. 015-0202) - similar to '51 "Nocaster" (NOS) except in Closet Classic finish, available in Honey Blonde finish. New 2001.

MSR $3,169 $2,225 $1,995 $1,795 $1,575 $1,400 $1,200 $975

'51 "Nocaster" Relic (No. 015-0302) - similar to '51 "Nocaster" (NOS) except in Relic finish, available in Honey Blonde finish. New 2001.

MSR $3,329 $2,330 $2,150 $1,850 $1,625 $1,450 $1,250 $1,025

'63 TELECASTER (NOS, No. 015-1000) - alder body, "C" shaped maple neck with round-lam rosewood fingerboard, white/black/white pickguard and original specification pickups, available in White Blonde finish. New 2001.

MSR $2,859 $2,000 $1,800 $1,600 $1,400 $1,200 $995 $850

'63 Telecaster Closet Classic (No. 015-1100) - similar to '63 Telecaster (NOS) except in Closet Classic finish, available in lake Placid Blue, Candy Apple Red and Vintage Blonde finishes. New 2001.

MSR $3,169 $2,225 $1,995 $1,850 $1,600 $1,400 $1,200 $1,000

Add $150 for Vintage Blonde finish.

'63 Telecaster Relic (No. 015-1200) - similar to '63 Telecaster (NOS) except in Relic finish, available in Lake Placid Blue, Candy Apple red and Vintage Blonde finishes. New 2001.

MSR $3,319 $2,330 $2,150 $1,850 $1,600 $1,400 $1,200 $1,000

Add $150 for Vintage Blonde finish.

ELECTRIC BASS

H.M. Bass/H.M.T. Bass Series

The H.M. and H.M.T. ('Heavy Metal' ?) Bass Series were available in the late 1980s (circa 1987). H.M. models include the 3 Silver Fender-Lace Sensor **Model 19- 4600**, 3 Jazz Bass single coil pickups **Models 19-4500, 19-4400**, and piezo bridge/Silver Fender-Lace Sensor **Model 25-9600**. Future research continues on the H.M. bass models.

GRADING	100% MINT	98% NEAR MINT	95% EXC+	90% EXC	80% VG+	70% VG	60% G

BASS V (U.S. Mfg.) - offset double cutaway elongated ash body, bolt-on maple neck, 15-fret rosewood fingerboard with pearl dot inlay, strings through bridge, coverplate with F logo, 5-on-one-side tuners, chrome hardware, white plastic/metal pickguard, thumb rest, single coil split covered pickup, pickup coverplate, volume/tone control, available in Custom Colors and Sunburst finishes. Mfg. 1965 to 1970.

	100%	98%	95%	90%	80%	70%	60%
	N/A	$2,000	$1,850	$1,700	$1,550	$1,300	$1,100

Add $100 for left-hand version.

In 1966, bound fingerboard with black inlay became standard.

BASS VI (U.S. Mfg.) - offset double cutaway asymmetrical ash body, bolt-on maple neck, 21-fret rosewood fingerboard with pearl dot inlay, floating bridge/vibrato with bridge cover, 6-on-one-side tuners, chrome hardware, tortoise/metal or white pickguard, 3 single coil exposed pickups with metal rings, volume/tone control, 3 on/off pickup selector switches, low cut switch, available in Custom Colors and Sunburst finishes. Mfg. 1961 to 1975.

	100%	98%	95%	90%	80%	70%	60%
1962-1965	N/A	$3,000	$2,575	$2,150	$1,725	$1,550	$1,425
1966-1969	N/A	$2,300	$2,00	$1,750	$1,500	$1,300	$1,200
1970-1975	N/A	$1,500	$1,295	$1,075	$875	$775	$700

In 1963, strings mute and another 2-position switch were added, a maple fingerboard with black dot inlay was made available. In 1965, bound fingerboard with dot inlays became standard. In 1966, bound fingerboard with block inlay became standard. In 1969, Fender locking vibrato was optionally offered. In 1974, a black pickguard became standard.

BASS VI REISSUE (Jap. Mfg., No. 027-7600) - offset double cutaway asymmetrical alder body, bolt-on maple neck, 30.3" scale, 21-fret rosewood fingerboard with pearl dot inlay, floating tremolo with 'trem-lock', 6-on-one-side tuners, chrome hardware, red shell pickguard, 3 single coil pickups, master volume/master tone controls, 3 pickup selector switches, low cut (*strangle*) switch, available in 3-Tone Sunburst finish. Mfg. 1995 to 1998.

100%	98%	95%	90%	80%	70%	60%
$750	$650	$575	$495	$400	$350	$250

Last MSR was $1,000.

Roscoe Beck Signature Series

ROSCOE BECK V BASS (U.S. Mfg., No. 019-6500) - offset double cutaway alder body, bolt-on maple neck with graphite reinforcement, 22-fret pau ferro fingerboard with pearl dot inlay, strings through body bridge, Roscoe Beck's signature on peghead, chrome hardware, mint white (or brown shell) pickguard, 2 Dual Jazz 5 pickups, volume/tone controls pickup selector switch, 2 mini-switches, available in 3-Tone Sunburst, Candy Apple Red, Shoreline Gold, and Teal Green Metallic finishes. Mfg. 1997 to date.

		100%	98%	95%	90%	80%	70%	60%
MSR	$1,799	$1,250	$1,075	$950	$850	$750	$600	$500

Bullet Bass Series

BULLET B30 - offset double cutaway alder body, white pickguard, bolt-on maple neck, 19-fret maple fingerboard with black dot inlay, fixed bridge, tele-style peghead, chrome hardware, 1 split covered pickup, volume/tone control, available in Brown Sunburst, Custom Colors, Ivory, Red and Walnut finishes. Mfg. 1982 to 1983.

100%	98%	95%	90%	80%	70%	60%
N/A	$275	$250	$225	$200	$185	$165

Bullet B34 - similar to Bullet B30, except has a long scale length.

100%	98%	95%	90%	80%	70%	60%
N/A	$325	$300	$275	$250	$225	$210

Bullet B40 - similar to Bullet B30, except has 20-fret fingerboard.

100%	98%	95%	90%	80%	70%	60%
N/A	$300	$275	$250	$225	$200	$175

Coronado Bass Series

CORONADO BASS I (U.S. Mfg.) - double rounded cutaway semi hollow bound maple body, arched top, f-holes, 2 finger rests, bolt-on maple neck, 21-fret rosewood fingerboard with pearl dot inlay, adjustable aluminum bridge/trapeze tailpiece, ebony tailpiece insert with pearl F inlay, 4-on-one-side tuners, chrome hardware, single coil covered pickup, volume/tone control, available in Cherry and Sunburst finishes. Mfg. 1966 to 1970.

100%	98%	95%	90%	80%	70%	60%
N/A	$500	$450	$425	$375	$325	$295

A wide variety of bridge styles was available on this model.

Coronado Bass II (U.S. Mfg.) - similar to Coronado Bass I, except has bound f-holes/fingerboard with block inlay, tune-o-matic bridge, string mutes, 2 single coil covered pickups, 2 volume/2 tone controls, 3-position switch. Mfg. 1967 to 1970.

100%	98%	95%	90%	80%	70%	60%
N/A	$700	$650	$595	$500	$450	$400

Wildwood finishes were optional. The Wildwood finish was the result of a seven year process in Germany where dye was injected into growing beech trees. After the trees were harvested, veneers were cut and laminated to the guitar tops. Pickguard numbers (I-VI) refer to the dye color (primary color of green, blue, and gold) and the applied finish.

Coronado Bass II Antigua (U.S. Mfg.) - similar to Coronado Bass II, except has Antigua (Black to Silver Sunburst) finish. Mfg. 1970 to 1972.

100%	98%	95%	90%	80%	70%	60%
$850	$800	$750	$650	$600	$550	$500

Jazz Series

Instruments in this series have an offset double cutaway (slim waist) body, bolt-on maple neck, 4-on-one-side tuners (unless otherwise specified). Currently, Jazz basses are more popular and desirable than the P Bass.

GRADING		100% MINT	98% NEAR MINT	95% EXC+	90% EXC	80% VG+	70% VG	60% G

JAZZ BASS (FENDER MFG., Mfg. 1960 - 1964) - alder body, tortoise/metal pickguard with finger rest, 20-fret rosewood fingerboard with pearl dot inlay, fixed bridge with string mutes, F logo bridge cover, chrome hardware, 2 J-style pickups, 2 concentric (volume/tone) controls, available in Blonde, Custom Colors and 3-Tone Sunburst finishes. Mfg. 1960 to 1974.

	100%	98%	95%	90%	80%	70%	60%
1960	**N/A**	**$7,000**	**$6,250**	**$5,500**	**$5,200**	**$4,900**	**$4,750**
1961	**N/A**	**$7,000**	**$6,200**	**$5,450**	**$5,100**	**$4,750**	**$4,500**
1962 (Stacked)	**N/A**	**$6,000**	**$5,500**	**$4,900**	**$4,550**	**$4,200**	**$4,000**
1962 (3 Knobs)	**N/A**	**$5,000**	**$4,500**	**$3,750**	**$3,000**	**$2,650**	**$2,425**
1963-1964	**N/A**	**$4,500**	**$4,000**	**$3,500**	**$2,950**	**$2,550**	**$2,325**

Instruments from 1960 and 1961 to mid 1962 have concentric 'stacked' volume and tone knobs. After mid 1962, 2 volume and 1 tone controls replaced the stacked control knobs. In 1962, Blonde and Custom Color finishes were introduced, Blonde finish instruments have ash body. Custom Color finishes have white pickguards. In 1963, string mutes were removed. Certain very clean/all original models in a blonde finish with concentric knobs have sold for as high as $9,000. However, this should be determined on a piece-by-piece basis as opposed to the usual market.

JAZZ BASS (CBS MFG., Mfg. 1965 - 1974) - alder body, tortoise/metal pickguard with finger rest, 20-fret rosewood fingerboard with pearl dot inlay, fixed bridge with string mutes, F logo bridge cover, chrome hardware, 2 J-style pickups, 2 concentric (volume/tone) controls, available in Blonde, Custom Colors and 3-Tone Sunburst finishes. Mfg. 1960 to 1974.

	100%	98%	95%	90%	80%	70%	60%
1965	**N/A**	**$3,500**	**$2,950**	**$2,600**	**$2,250**	**$1,950**	**$1,750**
1966-1969	**N/A**	**$2,500**	**$2,250**	**$2,000**	**$1,665**	**$1,335**	**$1,150**
1970-1974	**$1,250**	**$1,070**	**$895**	**$715**	**$625**	**$575**	**$535**

In 1965, bound fingerboard was added. In 1966, block fingerboard inlay replaced dot inlay. In 1969, black bound maple fingerboard with black block inlay was made optional.

JAZZ BASS (3-BOLT NECK - CBS MFG., Mfg. 1975 - 1980) - similar to Jazz, except has a 3-bolt neck. Mfg. 1975 to 1980.

100%	98%	95%	90%	80%	70%	60%
$1,200	**$1,100**	**$1,000**	**$900**	**$800**	**$750**	**$650**

Jazz Bass Gold (U.S. Mfg.) - similar to Jazz, except has gold hardware, available in Gold finish. Mfg. 1981 to 1984.

100%	98%	95%	90%	80%	70%	60%
$750	**$700**	**$660**	**$540**	**$500**	**$475**	**$450**

JAZZ BASS (ONE PIECE PICKGUARD - CBS MFG., Mfg. 1983 to 1984) - similar to Jazz, except has a one-piece white pickguard (no chrome metal controls plate). Mfg. 1983 to 1984.

100%	98%	95%	90%	80%	70%	60%
$900	**$850**	**$700**	**$600**	**$550**	**$450**	**$350**

AMERICAN JAZZ BASS (AMERICAN STANDARD, U.S. Mfg., No. 019-3400/019-2400). - alder body, bolt-on maple neck with graphite reinforcement, 20-fret rosewood fingerboard with pearl dot inlay, strings through body bridge, chrome hardware, white/metal pickguard, 2 J-style American Vintage Jazz pickups, 2 volume/1 tone controls, available in Arctic White, Black, Brown Sunburst, Caribbean Mist, Lipstick Red, Midnight Blue, and Midnight Wine finishes. Current Mfg.

		100%	98%	95%	90%	80%	70%	60%
MSR	**$1,299**	**$900**	**$750**	**$675**	**$625**	**$550**	**$425**	**$325**

Add $80 for 3-Color Sunburst finish.

Add $150 for Natural Ash finish.

In 1996, Arctic White, Carribbean Mist, Lipstick Red, Midnight Blue, and Midnight Wine colors were discontinued; Candy Apple Red, Vintage White, Crimson burst, and Sonic Blue finishes were introduced. In 1998, Vintage White, Crimson burst, and Sonic Blue finishes were discontinued; 3-Color Sunburst, Inca Silver, Lake Placid Blue, Natural Ash, and Olympic White finishes were introduced.
In 1999, Aqua Marine Metallic, & White Blonde finishes were introduced; Lake Placid Blue finish was discontinued.
In 2000, Inca Silver finish was discontinued.

American Jazz Bass w/Maple Neck (American Standard Jazz, U.S. Mfg., No. 019-3402/019-2402) - similar to the American Standard Jazz, except has maple fingerboard with black dot inlay, available in Black, Brown Sunburst, Candy Apple Red, Inca Silver, Lake Placid Blue, and Olympic White finishes. Mfg. 1997 to date.

		100%	98%	95%	90%	80%	70%	60%
MSR	**$1,129**	**$750**	**$650**	**$575**	**$525**	**$450**	**$375**	**$300**

Add $80 for 3-Color Sunburst finish.

Add $150 for Natural Ash finish.

In 1998, Brown Sunburst finish was discontinued; 3-Color Sunburst and Natural Ash finishes were introduced. In 1999, Aqua Marine Metallic & White Blonde finishes were introduced; Lake Placid Blue finish was discontinued. In 2000, Inca Silver finish was discontinued.

American Jazz Bass Fretless (American Standard, U.S. Mfg., No. 019-3408/019-2408) - similar to American Standard Jazz Bass, except in a fretless configuration, rosewood fingerboard, available in 3-Color Sunburst, Olympic White, Black, and Purple Metallic finishes.

		100%	98%	95%	90%	80%	70%	60%
MSR	**$1,349**	**$1,000**	**$825**	**$750**	**$650**	**$550**	**$450**	**$325**

Add $80 for 3-Color Sunburst finish.

Fender Bass VI
courtesy Oklahoma Guitar Co.

Fender Jazz Bass V
courtesy Marvin C. Mahler

F

GRADING		100% MINT	98% NEAR MINT	95% EXC+	90% EXC	80% VG+	70% VG	60% G

American Jazz Bass V (American Standard, U.S. Mfg., No. 019-3500/019-2500) - similar to the American Standard Jazz, except has 20-fret pao ferro fingerboard, 2 J-style American Vintage Jazz 5 pickups, available in Black, Brown Sunburst, Candy Apple Red, Inca Silver, Lake Placid Blue, and Olympic White finishes. Current Mfg.

MSR	$1,349	$1,000	$825	$750	$650	$550	$400	$300

Add $80 for 3-Color Sunburst finish.

In 1998, Brown Sunburst finish was discontinued; 3-Color Sunburst finish was introduced. In 1999, Aqua Marine Metallic, & White Blonde finishes were introduced; Lake Placid Blue finish was discontinued. In 2000, Hot Rod Red finish was introduced.

AMERICAN DELUXE JAZZ BASS (U.S. Mfg., No. 019-5800) - premium ash or alder body, maple neck with 22 American Standard frets, graphite reinforced neck, rosewood fingerboard with abalone dot inlays, 34" scale, American Deluxe tuners, Fender Noiseless Jazz Bass pickups, pan pot, master volume, 3-band active EQ with treble boost/cut, Mid-boost/cut, and Bass-boost/cut, aged white or brown shell pickguard, deluxe top-load or string- through body bridge. New 1999.

MSR	$1,599	$1,200	$1,025	$950	$850	$750	$600	$500

Add $150 for Natural, White Blonde, and Purple Transparent finishes.

Add $50 for 5-String configuration with pao ferro fingerboard (Model 019-5900)(New 1999).

Add $50 for 5-String configuration with maple fingerboard (Model 019-5902) (New 1999).

Add $50 for Fretless configuration (019-5808) (New 1999).

Add $100 for Left Hand Model (019-5820)

Also available with maple fingerboard (Model 019-5802).

CONTEMPORARY JAZZ BASS (Jap. Mfg., No. 027-9000) - ash body, 20-fret rosewood fingerboard with pearl dot inlay, carbon graphite nut, fixed bridge, chrome hardware, Fender/Gotoh tuners, P/J-style pickups, volume/tone/frequency sweep controls. Mfg. 1987 only.

		$300	$275	$250	$225	$200	$185	$165

This model was also available in a fretless configuration.

DELUXE ACTIVE JAZZ BASS (Mex. Mfg., No. 013-6700) - poplar body, bolt-on maple neck, 20-fret rosewood fingerboard with dot inlay, fixed bridge, chrome hardware, brown shell and metal pickguard, 2 American Deluxe J-Bass pickups, volume/blend/bass/mid/treble controls, active electronics, available in Arctic White, Black, Brown Sunburst, and Candy Apple Red finishes. Mfg. 1998 to date.

MSR	$769	$550	$475	$425	$375	$300	$250	$200

Deluxe Active Jazz Bass V (Mex. Mfg., No. 013-6800) - similar to the Active Jazz Bass, except has 5-string configuration, 5-on-a-side tuners, 20-fret pau ferro fingerboard, 2 American Deluxe J-Bass V pickups, available in Arctic White, Black, Brown Sunburst, and Candy Apple Red finishes. Mfg. 1998 to date.

MSR	$799	$550	$500	$450	$400	$350	$275	$225

JAZZ BASS DELUXE (U.S. Mfg., No. 019-4400) - down-sized alder body, ash veneer top/back, bolt-on tinted maple neck with graphite reinforcement, 22-fret rosewood fingerboard with pearl dot inlay, strings through body bridge, chrome hardware, white (or brown) shell/metal pickguard, 2 J-style Jazz Bass humbucking pickups, 2 volume/3-band EQ controls, active electronics, available in Antique Burst, Black, Blue Burst, Crimson Burst, Shoreline Gold, and Teal Green Metallic finishes. Disc. 1998.

		$875	$750	$675	$575	$495	$400	$325

Last MSR was $1,249.

Jazz Bass Deluxe w/Maple Neck (U.S. Mfg., No. Model 019-4402) - similar to the Jazz Bass Deluxe, except has maple fingerboard with black dot inlay, available in Antique Burst, Black, Blue Burst, Crimson Burst, Shoreline Gold, and Teal Green Metallic finishes. Mfg. 1997 to 1998.

		$875	$750	$675	$575	$495	$400	$325

Last MSR was $1,249.

Jazz Bass Deluxe Fretless (U.S. Mfg., No. 019-4408) - similar to the Jazz Bass Deluxe, except has fretless rosewood fingerboard, available in Antique Burst, Black, Shoreline Gold, and Teal Green Metallic finishes. Disc. 1998.

		$900	$795	$700	$600	$525	$425	$325

Last MSR was $1,299.

Jazz Bass Deluxe V String (U.S. Mfg., No. 019-4500) - similar to the Jazz Bass Deluxe, except has 5-string configuration, 20-fret pau ferro fingerboard, 2 J-style American Vintage Jazz 5 pickups, available in Antique Burst, Black, Blue Burst, Crimson Burst, Shoreline Gold, and Teal Green Metallic finishes. Disc. 1998.

		$900	$795	$700	$600	$525	$425	$325

Last MSR was $1,299.

JAZZ SPECIAL - Precision style basswood body, Jazz Bass style neck, no pickguard, graphite nut, black hardware, P/J pickup configuration. Disc.

		$295	$280	$265	$250	$225	$200	$175

Jazz "Power" Special - similar to Jazz Special, except has triple laminated maple/rosewood/graphite neck, active circuitry. Disc.

		$325	$300	$295	$275	$250	$225	$200

GRADING	100% MINT	98% NEAR MINT	95% EXC+	90% EXC	80% VG+	70% VG	60% G

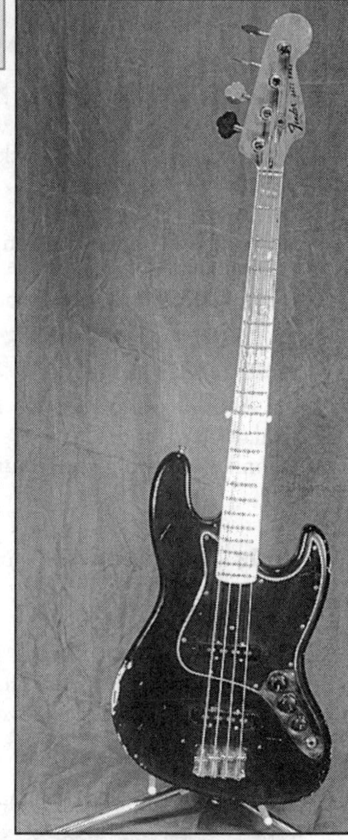
Fender Jazz Bass
Blue Book archives

JAZZ PLUS (U.S. Mfg., No. 019-8402) - alder body, 22-fret rosewood fingerboard with pearl dot inlay, fixed bridge, chrome hardware, 2 J-style Lace Sensor pickups, volume/pan control, concentric treble/bass control, active electronics, available in Arctic White, Black, Black Pearl Burst, Blue Pearl Burst, Brown Sunburst, Caribbean Mist, Lipstick Red, Midnight Blue, Midnight Wine, and Natural finishes. Disc. 1994.

$625 $595 $550 $495 $425 $375 $325
Last MSR was $1,120.

This model was available with a maple fingerboard (Model 19-8400). This model was optional with an ash body and maple fingerboard with black dot inlay (Model 19-8500).

Jazz Plus V (U.S. Mfg.) - similar to Jazz Plus, except has 5-strings, 5-on-one-side tuners. Disc. 1994.

$675 $625 $595 $525 $450 $395 $325
Last MSR was $1,190.

STANDARD JAZZ BASS (Mex. Mfg., No. 013-6500) - poplar body, bolt-on maple neck, 20-fret rosewood fingerboard with white dot inlay, fixed bridge, chrome hardware, 3-ply white/metal pickguard, 2 J-style pickups, 2 volume/1 tone controls, available in Arctic White, Black, Brown Sunburst, Crimson Red Metallic, and Lake Placid Blue finishes. Current Mfg.

MSR $449 $325 $275 $250 $225 $175 $150 $110

In 1998, Midnight Blue and Midnight Wine finishes were introduced; Crimson Red Metallic and Lake Placid Blue finishes were discontinued.

Standard Jazz Bass Left Hand (Mex. Mfg., No. 013-6520) - similar to Standard Jazz Bass, except has left-handed configuration, available in Arctic White, Black, Brown Sunburst, Midnight Blue, and Midnight Wine finishes. Mfg. 1998 to date.

MSR $499 $335 $300 $275 $225 $195 $165 $125

Add $50 for Brown Sunburst finish.

Standard Jazz Bass Fretless (Mex. Mfg., No. 013-6508) - similar to Standard Jazz Bass, except has left-handed configuration, available in Arctic White, Black, Brown Sunburst, Midnight Blue, and Midnight Wine finishes. Mfg. 1998 to date.

MSR $499 $345 $300 $275 $225 $200 $175 $130

Add $50 for Brown Sunburst finish.

Standard Jazz Bass Left Hand (Jap. Mfg., No. 027-6720) - similar to Standard Jazz Bass, except has basswood body, left-handed configuration, available in 3-Color Sunburst and Vintage White finishes. Disc. 1998.

$450 $400 $350 $295 $250 $200 $175
Last MSR was $769.

Standard Jazz Bass Fretless (Jap. Mfg., No. 013-6508) - similar to Standard Jazz Bass, except has basswood body, fretless fingerboard, available in Arctic White and Black finishes. Disc. 1998.

$350 $325 $295 $250 $200 $175 $150
Last MSR was $609.

Standard Jazz Bass V (U.S. Mfg., No. 013-6600) - similar to Standard Jazz Bass, except has 5-string configuration, 5-on-a-side tuners, 20-fret pau ferro fingerboard, available in Arctic White, Black, Brown Sunburst, Midnight Blue, and Midnight Wine finishes. Mfg. 1998 to date.

MSR $549 $375 $325 $295 $250 $225 $175 $145

Add $50 for Brown Sunburst finish.

TRADITIONAL JAZZ BASS (No. 013-3500, Mex. Mfg.) - poplar body, bolt-on maple neck, 20-fret rosewood fingerboard with white dot inlay, fixed bridge, chrome hardware, 3-ply white/metal pickguard, 2 J-style pickups, 2 volume/1 tone controls, available in Arctic White, Black, and Torino Red finishes. Disc. 1998.

$225 $200 $175 $150 $125 $100 $75
Last MSR was $339.

U.S. Vintage Reissue Series

'75 JAZZ BASS (U.S. Mfg., No. 019-0302) ash body, bound maple fingerboard, block position markers, black/white/black pickguard, "bullet" truss rod, 3-bolt "micro-tilt" neck, 2 vintage bi-pole pickups, 20-frets, 2 Volume/1 Tone control, Vintage-4 Saddle bridge, case included, available in 3-Color Sunburst, black and Natural finishes. Current Mfg.

MSR $1,899 $1,325 $1,125 $1,025 $925 $825 $725 $595

Also available with rosewood fingerboard and white/black/white pickguard (Model 019-3000).

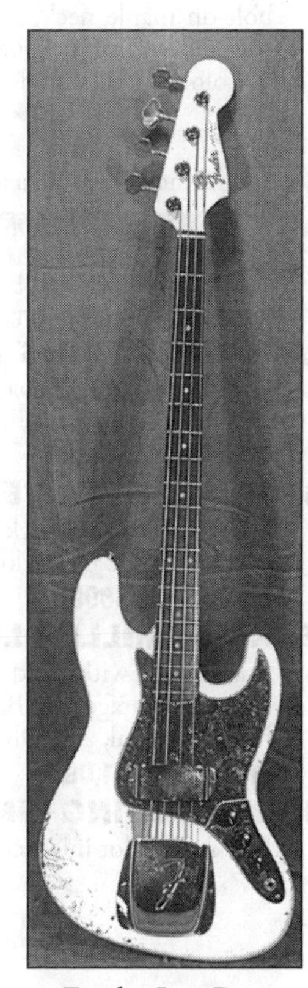
Fender Jazz Bass
Blue Book archives

GRADING		100% MINT	98% NEAR MINT	95% EXC+	90% EXC	80% VG+	70% VG	60% G

'62 JAZZ BASS (U.S. Mfg.) - alder body, bolt-on maple neck, 34" scale, 20-fret rosewood fingerboard with pearl dot inlay, fixed bridge, chrome hardware, white (or black or tortoiseshell)/metal pickguard with finger rest, 2 J-style American Vintage Jazz pickups, 2 volume/tone concentric ('stacked') controls, available in 3-Tone Sunburst, Black, and Vintage White finishes. Current Mfg.

MSR	$1,799	$1,275	$1,075	$950	$800	$675	$550	$425

(Model 019-0209).

In 1996, Vintage White finish was discontinued. In 1999, Lake Placid Blue and Olympic White finishes were introduced. In 2001, Inca Silver, Dakota Red, and Ice Blue Metallic finishes were introduced.

Add $50 for 3-Color Sunburst finish.

Jazz Bass Collectibles Series

'60s JAZZ ('60s Jazz Bass) - basswood body, white/metal pickguard with finger rest, 20-fret rosewood fingerboard with pearl dot inlay, fixed bridge, chrome hardware, 2 J-style pickups, 2 volume/1 tone controls, available in Black, Candy Apple Red, Olympic White, Sonic Blue and 3-Color Sunburst finishes. Disc. 1995.

		$500	$425	$350	$295	$275	$250	$225

Last MSR was $700.

'60s Jazz Natural - similar to Reissue 60's Jazz, except has Foto-Flame finish. Mfg. 1994 to 1995.

		$550	$450	$375	$325	$300	$275	$250

Last MSR was $800.

'75 JAZZ (Jap. Mfg., No. 027-3500) - ash body, bolt-on maple neck, 20-fret rosewood fingerboard with white block inlay, 'bullet' truss rod adjustment, fixed bridge with string mutes, 'F' logo bridge cover, chrome hardware, white/metal pickguard with finger rest, 2 J-style Jazz Bass pickups, 2 volume/1 tone controls, available in 3-Tone Sunburst and Natural finishes. Disc. 1999.

		$569	$475	$425	$375	$325	$250	$200

Last MSR was $799.

This model also available with maple fingerboard (Model 027-3502).

Fender Custom Shop Production Jazz Basses

'62 JAZZ BASS LEFT HAND (U.S. Mfg., No. 019-6120) - left-handed configuration, alder body, bolt-on maple neck, 34" scale, 20-fret rosewood fingerboard with pearl dot inlay, fixed bridge, chrome hardware, tortoiseshell/metal pickguard with finger rest, 2 J-style Vintage Jazz pickups, 2 volume/tone controls, available in Black, and Olympic White finishes. Disc. 1998.

		$2,000	$1,800	$1,650	$1,475	$1,255	$1,050	$850

Last MSR was $2,899.

AMERICAN CLASSIC JAZZ BASS (U.S. Mfg., No. 019-7200) - bound down-sized swamp ash body, graphite reinforced bolt-on maple neck, 34" scale, 22-fret rosewood fingerboard with white shell block inlay, strings through bridge, chrome hardware, tortoiseshell/metal pickguard with finger rest, 2 J-style American Jazz pickups, volume/3-band EQ controls, active elctronics, available in (Tri) 3-Color Sunburst and Natural finishes. Disc. 1998.

		$1,800	$1,650	$1,500	$1,325	$1,125	$950	$750

Last MSR was $2,599.

This model was also available with optional flame maple top (American Classic Jazz Bass FMT).

Limited Edition Jazz Basses

The Limited Edition Jazz Basses are produced in smaller production runs by Fender's Custom Shop. The following models have a Jazz Bass sleek offset double cutaway body, two single coil pickups, bolt-on neck, and four on a side headstock (unless otherwise specified).

JACO PASTORIUS TRIBUTE (U.S. Mfg., No. 019-6108) - select alder body, special shaped maple neck, epoxy coated fretless rosewood fingerboard, replacement P-Bass control knobs, Vintage reversed tuners, 20-fret lines, 2 Volume/1 Tone control, Vintage-4 Saddle bridge, distressed finish, available in 3-Color Sunburst finish.

MSR	$3,899	$2,725	$2,250	$1,950	$1,700	$1,500	$1,300	$1,100

GEDDY LEE LIMITED EDITION (Jap. Mfg., No. 025-7702) - alder body, maple neck, 20-fret black bound maple fingerboard with black block inlay, chrome hardware, BadAss II bridge, 3-ply white pickguard, Fender/Schaller tuners, 2 '62 U.S. Jazz Bass single coil pickups, bakelite knobs, metal controls plate, available in Black finish. Mfg. 1998 to date.

MSR	$899	$675	$575	$475	$450	$425	$400	$350

MARCUS MILLER LIMITED EDITION (Jap. Mfg., No. 025-7802) - ash body, maple neck, 20-fret white bound maple fingerboard with pearloid block inlay, chrome hardware, BadAss II bridge, oversized black pickguard, vintage-style tuners, chrome pickup cover, 2 Vintage Jazz Bass single coil pickups, 2 volume/treble/bass controls, 2-band active EQ with bypass switch, available in 3-Tone Sunburst, Natural, and Olympic White finishes. Mfg. 1998 to date.

MSR	$1,099	$825	$700	$600	$550	$500	$450	$400

NOEL REDDING LIMITED EDITION (Jap. Mfg., No. 025-8600) - alder body, maple neck, 20-fret rosewood fingerboard with dot inlay, chrome/nickel hardware, tortoiseshell pickguard, available in 3-Tone Sunburst finish. Mfg. 1997 only.

		$775	$625	$550	$500	$450	$400	$350

Last MSR was $900.

GRADING	100% MINT	98% NEAR MINT	95% EXC+	90% EXC	80% VG+	70% VG	60% G

THE VENTURES LIMITED (Jap. Mfg., No. 025-8300) - light ash body, white shell/metal pickguard with finger rest, 20-fret rosewood fingerboard with white block inlay, fixed bridge, gold hardware, 2 J-style Fender U.S.A. pickups, volume/tone controls, available in Midnight Black Transparent finish. Mfg. 1996 only.

	$1,100	$925	$800	$700	$625	$550	$500

Last MSR was $1,439.

Time Machine Series

Built to exacting specifications of their respective vintages, including: body contours and radii, neck shape, fingerboard radius, pickups, electronics and hardware. Original materials, tooling, and production techniques are employed whenever possible. 3 finish packages are available-NOS (New Old Stock): as if the guitar was bought new in its respective year and brought forward in time to the present day, Closet Classic: as if the guitar was bought new in its respective year, played perhaps a dozen times each year and then put carefully away, has small dings, lightly checked finish, oxidized hardware, and aged plastic parts. Relic: shows natural wear and tear of years of heavy use - nicks, scratches, worn finish, rusty hardware and aged plastic parts.

'64 JAZZ BASS NOS (NEW OLD STOCK, U.S. CUSTOM SHOP MFG., No. 015-1300) alder body, maple neck with round-lam rosewood fingerboard, brown shell pickguard, original specification pickups, Vintage Reversed tuners, 20-frets, 2 Volume/1 Tone control, Vintage-4 Saddle bridge, available in 3-Color Sunburst and Olympic White finishes. New 2001.

MSR $2,799	$1,960	$1,600	$1,300	$1,100	$900	$750	$650

'64 Jazz Bass Closet Classic (No. 015-1400) - similar to '64 Jazz Bass NOS except with Closet Classic finish, available in 3-Color Sunburst and Olympic White finishes. New 2001.

MSR $3,109	$2,175	$1,700	$1,500	$1,300	$1,100	$950	$850

'64 Jazz Bass Relic (No. 015-1500) - similar to '64 Jazz Bass NOS except with Relic finish, available in 3-Color Sunburst and Olympic White finishes. New 2001.

MSR $3,269	$2,295	$1,800	$1,600	$1,400	$1,200	$1,050	$950

Jazz Relic Series

Relic series instruments were cosmetically aged by the Fender Custom Shop. Instruments are stamped on the headstock and into the body (under the pickguard) with the Custom Shop logo to avoid future cases of "mistaken identity" in the Vintage Guitar market.

'60s "RELIC" JAZZ BASS (U.S. Mfg., No. 019-6300) - alder body, maple neck, 20-fret rosewood fingerboard with dot inlay, *aged* nickel hardware, 2 Vintage Jazz single coil pickups, tortoiseshell pickguard, available in 3-Tone Sunburst and Olympic White finishes. Disc. 1998.

	$1,900	$1,725	$1,550	$1,300	$1,100	$895	$650

Last MSR was $2,599.

JP-90 (No. 14-4100) - offset double cutaway asymmetrical poplar body, black pickguard, bolt-on maple neck, 20-fret rosewood fingerboard with pearl dot inlay, fixed bridge, 4-on-one-side tuners, chrome hardware, P/J-style pickups, volume/tone control, 3-position switch, available in Arctic White, Black and Torino Red finishes. Mfg. 1990 to 1994.

	$300	$275	$250	$225	$200	$185	$165

Last MSR was $530.

MB Series

MB-4 - offset double cutaway asymmetrical basswood body, black pickguard, bolt-on maple neck, 22-fret rosewood fingerboard with pearl dot inlay, fixed bridge, 4-on-one-side tuners, chrome hardware, P/J-style pickups, concentric volume/treble/bass/mix controls, 3-position switch, available in Black, Red and White finishes. Mfg. 1994 to 1995.

	$325	$275	$225	$200	$175	$150	$125

Last MSR was $550.

MB-5 - similar to MB-4, except has 5-string configuration, 5-on-one-side tuners. Mfg. 1994 to 1995.

	$400	$325	$250	$225	$200	$175	$150

Last MSR was $620.

This model has an optional poplar body.

MUSICMASTER (U.S. Mfg.) - offset double cutaway asymmetrical ash body, black pickguard, thumb rest, bolt-on maple neck, 19-fret rosewood fingerboard with pearl dot inlay, fixed bridge, 4-on-one-side tuners, chrome hardware, single coil covered pickup, volume/tone control, available in Black, Blue, Red and White finishes. Mfg. 1970 to 1983.

	$350	$325	$300	$275	$250	$225	$200

GRADING		100% MINT	98% NEAR MINT	95% EXC+	90% EXC	80% VG+	70% VG	60% G

Mustang Bass Series

MUSTANG (U.S. Mfg.) - offset double cutaway poplar body, plastic/metal pickguard, thumb rest, bolt-on maple neck, 19-fret rosewood fingerboard with pearl dot inlay, fixed bridge, 4-on-one-side tuners, chrome hardware, P-style pickup, volume/tone control, available in Antigua, Black, Blonde, Blue, Natural, Red, Sunburst, Walnut, White and Wine finishes. Mfg. 1966 to 1983.

		N/A	$700	$675	$625	$600	$575	$540

Add $45 for left-hand version.

Add $100 for Competition finishes.

In 1969, Competition finishes were introduced. These finishes consist of solid colors (blue, burgundy, orange and red) with racing stripes. The instrument was also referred to as Competition Mustang Bass with these finishes.

PERFORMER - offset dual cutaway asymmetrical hardwood body, white pickguard, bolt-on maple neck, 24-fret rosewood fingerboard with pearl dot inlay, fixed bridge, 4-on-one-side tuners, chrome hardware, 2 single coil covered pickups, 2 volume/1 tone controls, active electronics, available in Sunburst finish. Mfg. 1987 to 1988.

		N/A	$275	$250	$225	$200	$185	$165

Precision Bass Series

All instruments in this series have an offset double cutaway body, bolt-on maple neck, 4-on-one-side tuners, unless otherwise listed.

PRECISION BASS (ORIGINAL DESIGN, Mfg. 1951 - 1954) - ash body, black pickguard, 20-fret maple fingerboard with black dot inlay, strings-through bridge, chrome bridge cover, chrome hardware, single coil exposed pickup with cover, volume/tone controls on metal plate, available in Blonde finish. Mfg. 1951 to 1954.

		N/A	$5,000	$4,250	$3,900	$3,500	$3,250	$3,000

The Precision bass was the first production electric bass with a fretted fingerboard. Early Precision basses have a similar design to Fender's Telecaster guitar (and similar slimmer headstocks). In 1957, the classic Precision design (wider headstock, split pickup, controls/pickup/1/4" socket all mounted on the pickguard) debuted.

PRECISION BASS (FENDER MFG., Mfg. 1954 - 1964) - similar to original design Precision, except has white pickguard and contoured body (similar to the contour of a Fender Stratocaster), available in Blonde, Custom Colors, 2 Tone Sunburst and 3-Tone Sunburst finishes. Mfg. 1954 to 1964.

1954		N/A	$5,000	$4,250	$3,900	$3,500	$3,250	$3,000
1955		N/A	$4,000	$3,400	$2,900	$2,550	$2,300	$2,150
1956		N/A	$4,000	$3,350	$2,850	$2,500	$2,250	$2,100
1957		N/A	$4,000	$3,550	$2,950	$2,650	$2,425	$2,150
1958-1959		N/A	$4,000	$3,500	$2,800	$2,550	$2,400	$2,100
1960-1964		N/A	$3,000	$2,550	$2,300	$2,150	$2,000	$1,750

Black pickguard with Blonde finish was an option. During 1957, a redesigned aluminum pickguard, fixed bridge, strat style peghead and split pickup replaced the original parts/designs. In 1959, rosewood fingerboard with pearl dot inlay replaced maple.

PRECISION BASS (CBS MFG., Mfg. 1965 - 1984) - similar to the 1957 Precision, available in Blonde, Custom Colors, 2 Tone Sunburst and 3-Tone Sunburst finishes. Mfg. 1965 to 1984.

1965		N/A	$2,000	$1,675	$1,325	$1,200	$1,100	$1,000
1966-1969		N/A	$1,500	$1,300	$1,075	$1,000	$950	$875
1970-1974		N/A	$700	$625	$550	$450	$395	$350
1975-1979		N/A	$725	$650	$625	$550	$425	$375
1980-1984		N/A	$575	$450	$425	$395	$350	$325

In 1968, maple fingerboard was an option. In 1970, fretless fingerboard was an option. By 1976, thumb rest on pickguard was standard.

PRECISION BASS (FMIC MFG., Mfg. 1985 - 1995) - similar to the 1957 Precision, available in Blonde, Custom Colors, 2-Tone Sunburst, and 3-Tone Sunburst finishes. Mfg. 1985 to 1995.

		$550	$525	$500	$460	$430	$400	$370

Precision Contemporary - similar to Precision, except has no pickguard and a rosewood fingerboard. Mfg. 1987 only.

		$250	$225	$210	$195	$175	$165	$155

AMERICAN PRECISION BASS (AMERICAN STANDARD, U.S. Mfg., No. 019-3200/019-2200) - alder body, graphite reinforced rosewood neck with vintage decal, 34" scale, 20-fret rosewood fingerboard with pearl dot inlay, strings-through-body bridge, chrome hardware, white pickguard, P-style American Vintage Precision pickup, volume/tone controls, available in Black, Brown Sunburst, Candy Apple Red, Inca Silver, Sonic Blue and Vintage White finishes. Mfg. 1996 to date.

MSR	$1,249	$875	$750	$650	$550	$495	$375	$275

Also available with maple neck (Model 019-3202) (Formerly Model 019-2202). In 1999, 3-Color Sunburst, Aqua Marine Metallic, White Blonde, Natural, Purple Metallic, & Olympic White finishes were introduced. Brown Sunburst, Candy Apple Red, Sonic Blue, and Vintage White finishes were discontinued.

Add $50 for 3-Color Sunburst finish.

Add $150 for Natural (Ash) finish.

GRADING	100% MINT	98% NEAR MINT	95% EXC+	90% EXC	80% VG+	70% VG	60% G

American Standard Precision Left Hand (U.S. Mfg., No. 019-2220) - similar to the American Standard Precision, except in left-handed configuration, available in Black, Brown Sunburst, Candy Apple Red, and Vintage White finishes. Mfg. 1996 to 1999.

$750	$650	$575	$500	$425	$350	$275

Last MSR was $1,079.

American Standard Precision Fretless (U.S. Mfg., No. 019-2208) - similar to the American Standard Precision, except with fretless neck, available in Black, Brown Sunburst, Candy Apple Red, and Vintage White. Mfg. 1996 to 1998.

$725	$625	$575	$495	$425	$350	$250

Last MSR was $1,029.

AMERICAN DELUXE PRECISION BASS (U.S. Mfg., No. 019-5200) - premium ash or alder body, maple neck with 22 American Standard frets, graphite reinforced neck, rosewood fingerboard, 34" scale, American Deluxe tuners, 1 Vintage Spec Split Single-Coil pickup, 1 New Special Design Humbucker pickup, master volume, pan pot, 3-band active EQ with treble boost/cut, mid-boost/cut, bass-boost/cut, aged white or brown shell pickguard, deluxe top-load or string-through-body bridge, available in 3-Color Sunburst, White Blonde, Black, Natural, Crimson Transparent, Teal Green Transparent, and Purple Transparent finishes. Current Mfg.

MSR $1,599	$1,200	$1,050	$950	$850	$750	$650	$525

Add $150 for Natural, White Blonde, and Purple Transparent finishes.

Also available with maple fingerboard (Model 019-5202).

American Deluxe Precision Bass V (U.S. Mfg., No. 019-5300) - similar to American Deluxe Precision Bass, except in a 5-string configuration, rosewood fingerboard. New 1999.

MSR $1,649	$1,225	$1,075	$975	$875	$750	$650	$475

Add $150 for Natural, White Blonde, and Purple Transparent finishes.

Also available with maple fingerboard (Model 019-5302).

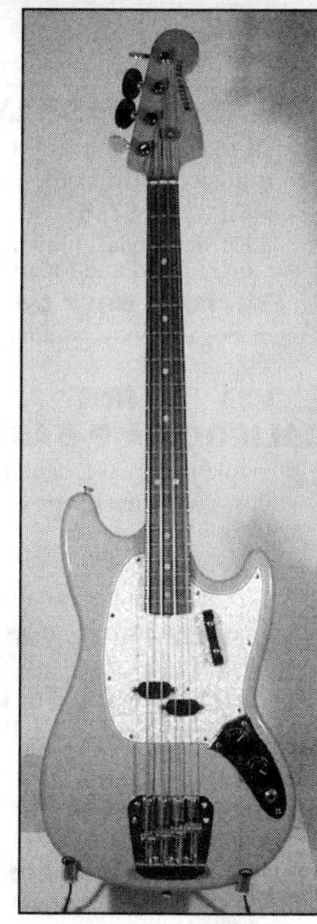

Fender Mustang Bass courtesy Southworth Guitars

HOT ROD P-BASS (U.S. Mfg., No. 019-4800/019-1900) - alder or ash body, maple neck, 20 American Standard frets, rosewood fingerboard, graphite reinforced neck, 34" scale, American Standard tuners, 1 New "Hot-Vintage P-Bass pickup, 1 New "Hot -Vintage" Jazz Bass pickup, 2 volume controls, master tone, Brown shell pickguard, deluxe top-load or string-through bridge, available in 3-Color Sunburst, Olympic White, Black, Natural, and Sunset Orange finishes. New 1999.

MSR $1,399	$975	$850	$750	$650	$550	$475	$425

Add $100 for LH configuration (Model 019-4820) (Formerly Model 019-1920).

Add $80 for 3-Color Sunburst finish.

Add $150 for Natural and Sunset Orange Transparent finishes.

Also available with maple fingerboard (Model 019-4802) (Formerly Model 019-1902).

PRECISION ACOUSTIC/ELECTRIC (Jap. Mfg., No. 027-9608) - hollowed basswood body, bound solid spruce top, f-hole, fretless rosewood fingerboard, strings through acoustic style rosewood bridge, chrome hardware, P-style Silver Fender-Lace Sensor/piezo bridge pickups, volume/tone/pan controls, active electronics, available in Antique Burst and Natural finishes. Disc. 1995.

$700	$600	$500	$450	$375	$325	$300

Last MSR was $1,230.

This model is also available with 20-fret fingerboard.

PRECISION BASS DELUXE (U.S. Mfg., No. 019-4200) - down-sized alder body, ash veneer top/back, graphite reinforced tinted maple neck, 34" scale, 22-fret rosewood fingerboard with pearl dot inlay, fixed bridge, chrome hardware, white (or brown) shell pickguard, P-style American Vintage Precision/humbucker pickups, volume/3-band EQ controls, available in Antique Burst, Black, Blue Burst, Crimson Burst, Shoreline Gold, and Teal Green Metallic finishes. Disc. 1998.

$850	$750	$675	$575	$495	$425	$325

Last MSR was $1,249.

This model is also available with a maple fingerboard with black dot inlay (Model 019-4202).

PRECISION BASS SPECIAL (Mex. Mfg., No. 013-5400) - poplar body, ash veneer top, maple neck, 20-fret rosewood fingerboard with white dot inlay, fixed bridge, chrome hardware, black pickguard, P/J-Style covered pickups, volume/pan/tone controls, available in Black, Brown Sunburst, Crimson Burst, and Vintage Blonde finishes. Disc. 1998.

$350	$325	$300	$275	$225	$175	$150

Last MSR was $569.

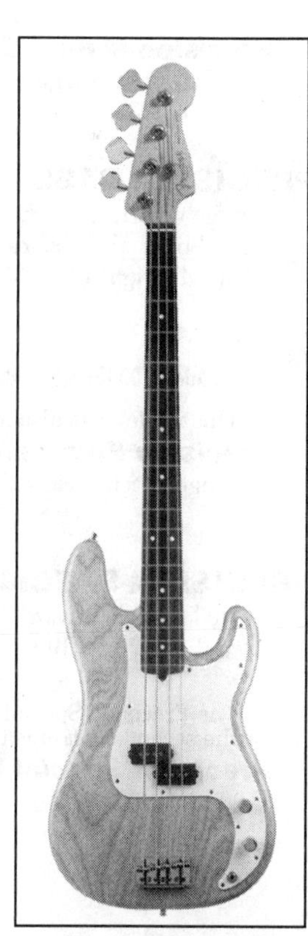

Fender Precision Bass courtesy Fender

GRADING	100% MINT	98% NEAR MINT	95% EXC+	90% EXC	80% VG+	70% VG	60% G

PRECISION BASS LYTE STANDARD (Jap. Mfg., No. 025-9500) - down-sized basswood body, bolt-on maple neck, 22-fret rosewood fingerboard with pearl dot inlay, fixed bridge, chrome hardware, P/J-style covered pickups, volume/treble/bass/pan controls, active electronics, available in Antique Burst, Fiesta Red, Frost White, and Montego Black finishes. Current Mfg.

MSR $756 — $530 $450 $395 $350 $295 $250 $185

Earlier models may have Lace Sensor pickups, and Blue Foto Flame, Crimson Foto Flame, or Frost Red finishes. In 1999, Frost Red was introduced and Fiesta Red was discontinued.

Precision Bass Lyte Deluxe (Jap. Mfg., No. 025-9800) - similar to the Precision Bass Lyte Standard, except has down-sized mahogany body, gold hardware, P-Style/humbucking covered pickups, volume/pan/treble/mid/bass controls, available in Natural finish. Current Mfg.

MSR $899 — $630 $550 $495 $425 $350 $295 $225

CALIFORNIA P-BASS SPECIAL (U.S. Mfg., No. 019-1802) - alder Precision body, bolt-on satin-finished Jazz-style maple neck, 20-fret maple fingerboard with dot inlay, vintage-style bridge, creme pickguard, chrome hardware, Vintage spec P/J-Bass pickups, 2 volume/1 tone controls, available in Black, Brown Sunburst, Candy Apple Red, and Vintage White finishes. Disc. 1998.

$599 $425 $375 $325 $275 $225 $175
Last MSR was $849.

This model is available with a rosewood fingerboard (Model 019-1800).

Precision Elite Series

PRECISION ELITE I - ash body, white pickguard, 20-fret maple fingerboard with black dot inlay, fixed bridge with tuners, die-cast tuners, chrome hardware, P-style covered pickup, volume/tone control, active electronics. Mfg. 1983 to 1985.

N/A $500 $450 $375 $325 $275 $250

Precision Elite II - similar to Precision Elite I, except has 2 P-style pickups, 2 volume/1 tone controls, 3-position mini switch. Disc.

N/A $525 $475 $395 $325 $275 $250

Precision Gold Elite I - similar to Precision Elite I, except has gold hardware. Disc.

N/A $500 $450 $375 $325 $300 $275

Precision Gold Elite II - similar to Precision Elite I, except has gold hardware, 2 P-style pickups, 2 volume/1 tone controls, 3-position mini switch. Disc.

N/A $525 $475 $400 $325 $300 $275

Precision Walnut Elite I - similar to Precision Elite I, except has walnut body/neck, black pickguard, ebony fingerboard with pearl dot inlay, strings through bridge, gold hardware, P-style exposed pickup, volume/treble/bass controls, series/parallel switch, available in Natural finish. Disc.

N/A $500 $450 $375 $325 $295 $275

Precision Walnut Elite II - similar to Precision Elite I, except has walnut body/neck, black pickguard, ebony fingerboard with pearl dot inlay, strings through bridge, gold hardware, 2 P-style exposed pickups, volume/treble/bass controls, series/parallel switch, available in Natural finish. Disc.

N/A $525 $475 $395 $350 $325 $300

PRECISION BASS PLUS (U.S. Mfg., No. 019-7502) - alder body, 22-fret rosewood fingerboard with pearl dot inlay, fixed bridge with tuners, chrome hardware, P/J-style Silver Lace Sensor pickups, volume/tone control, 3-position switch, series/parallel push button, TBX active electronics, available in Arctic White, Black, Black Pearl Burst, Blue Pearl Burst, Brown Sunburst, Caribbean Mist, Lipstick Red, Midnight Blue, Midnight Wine and Natural finishes. Mfg. 1990 to 1994.

N/A $475 $450 $425 $400 $375 $350
Last MSR was $1,000.

Add $100 for ash body with Natural finish.

This model was also available with maple fingerboard with black dot inlay (Model 19-7500).

Precision Plus Deluxe (U.S. Mfg.) - similar to Precision Plus, except has down-sized body style, volume/treble/bass/pan controls, redesigned active electronics. Mfg. 1990 to 1994.

N/A $600 $500 $450 $425 $400 $375
Last MSR was $1,200.

PRECISION SPECIAL (U.S. Mfg.) - alder body, white pickguard, 20-fret maple fingerboard with black dot inlay, fixed bridge, gold-plated brass hardware, P-style exposed pickup, volume/treble/bass controls, on/off mini switch, active electronics, available in Candy Apple Red, Lake Placid Blue, and White finishes with matching headstock finish. Mfg. 1980 to 1983.

N/A $550 $425 $395 $375 $350 $325

The Precision Special functioned in two modes: Active and Passive. In both modes, the volume control remains the same; in Passive mode the second control is the master tone control; in Active mode the second and third controls become the bass/treble controls.

Precision Special Walnut (U.S. Mfg.) - similar to Precision Special, except has walnut body/neck, available in Natural finish. Mfg. 1982 to 1983.

N/A $525 $400 $375 $350 $325 $300

GRADING		100% MINT	98% NEAR MINT	95% EXC+	90% EXC	80% VG+	70% VG	60% G

STANDARD PRECISION BASS (Mex. Mfg., No. 013-6000) - poplar body, bolt-on maple neck, 20-fret rosewood fingerboard with white dot inlay, fixed bridge, chrome hardware, 3-ply white pickguard, P-style pickup, volume/tone control, available in Arctic White, Black, Brown Sunburst, Crimson Red Metallic, and Lake Placid Blue finishes. Mfg. 1987 to date.

MSR	$427	$275	$250	$230	$210	$185	$160	$110

In 1998, Midnight Blue and Midnight Wine finishes were introduced; Crimson Red Metallic, and Lake Placid Blue finishes were discontinued.

Add $50 for Brown Sunburst finish.

Deluxe P-Bass Special (Mex. Mfg., No. 013-5700) - alder P-Bass body, maple Jazz Bass neck with standard truss rod, rosewood fingerboard, 20 medium-jumbo frets, 34" scale, chrome hardware, standard tuners, US Vintage P-Bass bridge, gold anodized pickguard, 1 Vintage Special P-Bass pickup, 1 Vintage Special Jazz Bass pickup 2 volume controls, master tone control, side-mounted jack, US electronic components, available in Black, Candy Apple Red, Brown Sunburst, and Arctic White finishes. Current Mfg.

MSR	$699	$525	$425	$375	$325	$275	$250	$215

Add $50 for Brown Sunburst finish.

Also available with maple fingerboard (Model 013-5702).

TRADITIONAL PRECISION BASS (Mex. Mfg., No. 013-3400) - poplar body, bolt-on maple neck, 20-fret rosewood fingerboard with white dot inlay, fixed bridge, chrome hardware, 3-ply white pickguard, P-style pickup, volume/tone control, available in Arctic White, Black, and Torino Red finishes. Disc. 1998.

		$225	$200	$175	$150	$125	$100	$75

Last MSR was $339.

Fender 1955 Precision Bass courtesy Thoroughbred Music

Time Machine Series

Built to exacting specifications of their respective vintage including body contours and radii, neck shape, fingerboard radius, pickups, electronics and hardware. Original materials, tooling and production techniques are employed whenever possible. Three distinct finish packages are avalable: NOS (New Old Stock) as if the instrument was bought new in its respective year and brought forward in time to the present day; Closet Classic, as if the instrument was bought new in its respective year, played perhaps a dozen times each year and then put carefull away - small dings, lightly checked finish, oxidized hardware and aged plastic parts; Relic, shows natural wear and tear of years of heavy use – nicks, scratches, worn finish, rusty hardware and aged plastic parts.

'59 PRECISION BASS NOS (NEW OLD STOCK, U.S. CUSTOM SHOP MFG., No. 015-2100) - alder or ash body, rosewood fingerboard with dot position markers, Vintage Reversed tuners, 20-frets, Vintage split-coil pickups, 1 Volume/1Tone control, Vintage-4 Saddle bridge, available in 3-Color Sunburst and White Blonde finishes. New 2001.

MSR	$2,749	$1,925	$1,600	$1,375	$1,100	$950	$825	$700

Add $150 for White Blonde finish.

'59 Precision Bass Closet Classic (No. 015-2200) - similar to '59 Precision Bass NOS except with Closet Classic finish, available in 3-Color Sunburst and Vintage Blonde finishes. New 2001.

MSR	$3,059	$2,150	$1,725	$1,475	$1,150	$1,000	$875	$750

Add $150 for Vintage Blonde finish.

'59 Precision Bass Relic (No. 015-2300) - similar to '59 Precision Bass NOS except with Relic finish, available in 3-Color Sunburst and Vintage Blonde finishes. New 2001.

MSR	$3,219	$2,250	$1,825	$1,550	$1,225	$1,075	$925	$800

Add $150 for Vintage Blonde finish.

U.S. Vintage Reissue Series

'57 PRECISION (U.S. Mfg.) - ash body, bolt-on maple neck, 20-fret maple fingerboard with black dot inlay, fixed bridge, gold hardware, gold anodized pickguard with thumb rest, P-style pickup, volume/tone control, available in 2-Tone Sunburst, Blonde, Black, and Vintage White finishes. Mfg. 1982 to date.

MSR	$1,699	$1,200	$1,000	$875	$750	$625	$525	$400

(Model 019-0115).

In 1989, alder body and chrome hardware replaced original parts/designs. In 1994, Blond and Vintage White finishes were discontinued.

In 1999, Candy Apple Red and White Blonde finishes were introduced. In 2001, Inca Silver, Dakota Red and Ice Blue Metallic finishes were introduced.

Add $50 for 2-Color Sunburst.

Add $150 for White Blonde finish.

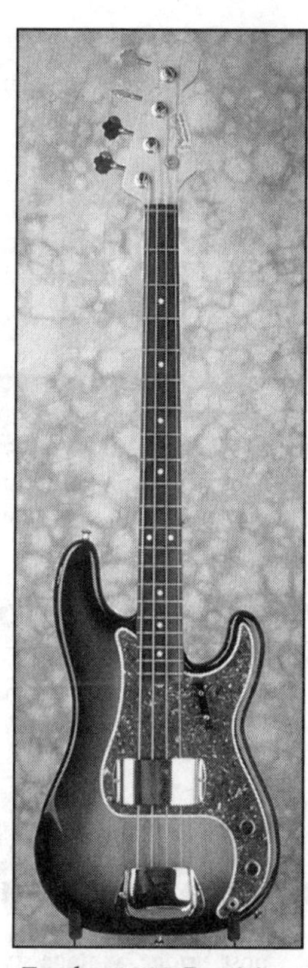

Fender 1982 Precision (Reissue) courtesy Mike Coulson

F

GRADING	100% MINT	98% NEAR MINT	95% EXC+	90% EXC	80% VG+	70% VG	60% G

'62 PRECISION (U.S. Mfg., No. 019-0116) - alder body, bolt-on maple neck, 20-fret rosewood fingerboard with pearl dot inlay, fixed bridge, chrome hardware, tortoise pickguard with thumb rest, P-style pickup, volume/tone control, available in 3-Tone Sunburst, Black, Blonde, and Vintage White finishes. Mfg. 1982 to date.

MSR $1,699	$1,200	$1,000	$875	$750	$625	$525	$400

In 1994, Blonde and Vintage White finishes were discontinued. In 1999, Fiesta Red and Olympic White finishes were introduced. In 2000, Inca Silver, Dakota Red and Ice Blue Metallic finishes were introduced.

Add $50 for 3-Color Sunburst finish.

'62 Precision Left-Hand (U.S. Mfg.) - similar to (U.S. Vintage) '62 Precision, except in a left-handed configuration, available in Black and Olympic white finishes. Disc. 1994.

$1,000	$950	$925	$875	$775	$650	$550

Last MSR was $2,200.

Fender Japan Limited Edition Series

This model was a limited edition that was produced by Fender Japan, and was available by custom order.

'75 PRECISION (Jap. Mfg.) - ash body, bolt-on maple neck, 20-fret maple fingerboard with black dot inlay, strings-through bridge, chrome hardware, black pickguard, P-style pickup, volume/tone controls on metal plate, available in Natural finish. Disc. 1995.

N/A	$500	$395	$300	$275	$225	$175

Last MSR was $720.

This model also available with rosewood fingerboard with pearl dot inlay.

Precision Collectibles Series

'51 P-BASS REISSUE (Jap. Mfg., No. 027-1902) - offset double cutaway ash body, bolt-on maple neck, 20-fret maple fingerboard with black dot inlay, vintage 2-saddle bridge, chrome hardware, black pickguard, single coil exposed pole piece pickup, volume/tone controls on metal plate, available in 2-Tone Sunburst and Blonde finishes. Disc. 1998.

N/A	$495	$450	$395	$350	$295	$250

Last MSR was $739.

Custom Shop '51 Precision (U.S. Mfg.) - similar to the '51 P-Bass Reissue, these models were part of a Custom Shop Limited run.

N/A	$1,500	$1,400	$1,300	$1,200	$1,100	$1,000

'50s PRECISION - basswood body, white pickguard, 20-fret maple fingerboard with black dot inlay, fixed bridge, chrome hardware, P-style exposed pickup, volume/tone control, available in Black, Candy Apple Red, Olympic White, Sonic Blue and 3-Tone Sunburst finishes. Mfg. 1994 to 1995.

N/A	$450	$375	$325	$295	$275	$250

Last MSR was $690.

'60s Precision - similar to Precision Reissue '50s, except has tortoise pickguard, rosewood fingerboard with pearl dot inlay. Mfg. 1994 to 1995.

N/A	$450	$375	$325	$295	$275	$250

Last MSR was $690.

This model also available with white pickguard.

'60s Precision Natural - similar to Precision Reissue '50s, except has tortoise pickguard, rosewood fingerboard with pearl dot inlay, available in Foto-Flame finish. Mfg. 1994 to 1995.

N/A	$500	$400	$350	$325	$300	$275

Last MSR was $800.

Fender Custom Shop Production Precision Basses

'57 PRECISION BASS LEFT HAND (U.S. Mfg., No. 019-5722) - left-handed configuration, alder body, bolt-on maple neck, 20-fret maple fingerboard with black dot inlay, fixed bridge, chrome hardware, gold anodized pickguard with thumb rest, P-style pickup, volume/tone control, available in Black and Olympic white finishes. Disc. 1998.

$1,750	$1,600	$1,450	$1,250	$1,000	$875	$700

Last MSR was $2,499.

VINTAGE PRECISION BASS CUSTOM (U.S. Mfg., VINTAGE PRECISION CUSTOM BASS, No. 019-5602) - swamp ash body, bolt-on figured maple neck, 20-fret maple fingerboard with black dot inlay, fixed bridge, nickel hardware, black pickguard, P/J-style Vintage pickups, volume/tone controls mounted on metal plate, available in 2-Tone Sunburst and Honey Blonde finishes. Mfg. 1993 to 2000.

$1,625	$1,450	$1,275	$1,100	$925	$775	$600

Last MSR was $2,299.

Limited Edition Precision Basses

DONALD "DUCK" DUNN PRECISION BASS LIMITED EDITION (Jap. Mfg., No. 025-7602) - alder body, bolt-on '50s-shaped maple neck, 20-fret maple fingerboard with black dot inlay, Donald "Duck" Dunn signature on headstock, vintage 4-post bridge, vintage-style tuners, chrome-plated nickel hardware, gold anodized pickguard, Vintage P-Bass pickup, volume/tone controls, available in Candy Apple Red finish. Mfg. 1998 Only.

$599	$500	$450	$425	$400	$350	$300

Last MSR was $799.

GRADING	100% MINT	98% NEAR MINT	95% EXC+	90% EXC	80% VG+	70% VG	60% G

Prodigy Series

PRODIGY ACTIVE BASS - offset double cutaway poplar body, bolt-on maple neck, 20-fret rosewood fingerboard with pearl dot inlay, fixed bridge, 4-on-one-side tuners, chrome hardware, P/J-style pickups, concentric volume-pan/treble-bass controls, active electronics, available in Arctic White, Black, Crimson Red Metallic and Lake Placid Blue finishes. Mfg. 1992 to 1995.

N/A $325 $300 $275 $250 $225 $200
Last MSR was $600.

Prophecy Series

PROPHECY I - offset double cutaway asymmetrical basswood body, bolt-on maple neck, 22-fret rosewood fingerboard with pearl dot inlay, fixed bridge, 2-per-side tuners, chrome hardware, P/J-style pickups, volume/treble/bass/mix controls, available in Sunburst finish. Disc. 1995.

N/A $500 $395 $325 $295 $250 $225
Last MSR was $770.

Prophecy II - similar to Prophecy I, except has ash body, gold hardware, active electronics. Disc. 1995.

N/A $550 $475 $395 $300 $275 $250
Last MSR was $870.

Prophecy III - similar to Prophecy I, except has alder/walnut/bubinga body, through body maple neck, gold hardware, active electronics. Disc. 1995.

N/A $675 $600 $525 $475 $450 $425
Last MSR was $1,330.

Telecaster Bass Series

TELECASTER BASS (1st Version, U.S. Mfg.) - offset double cutaway ash body, white pickguard, finger rest, bolt-on maple neck, 20-fret maple fingerboard with black dot inlay, fixed bridge with cover, 4-on-one-side tuners, chrome hardware, single coil exposed pickup with cover, volume/tone control, available in Blonde and Custom Colors finishes. Mfg. 1968 to 1972.

N/A $1,500 $1,350 $1,100 $1,000 $950 $900

In 1970, a fretless fingerboard became optional.

Telecaster Bass (2nd Version, U.S. Mfg.) - similar to Telecaster, except has redesigned pickguard, thumb rest, 2-section bridge, covered humbucker pickup with no separate cover, available in Blonde and Sunburst finishes. Mfg. 1972 to 1979.

N/A $900 $800 $700 $650 $600 $550

Between 1977 to 1979, a 4-section single string groove bridge was available.

Telecaster Bass Paisley, Telecaster Bass Blue Floral (U.S. Mfg.) - similar to Telecaster Bass, except available in Blue Floral and Pink Paisley finishes and had a single coil pickup. Mfg. 1968 to 1970.

N/A $3,000 $2,700 $2,300 $2,000 $1,900 $1,800

Stu Hamm Signature Series

This instrument was designed in collaboration with bassist Stu Hamm, and debuted in 1993.

STU HAMM URGE BASS (U.S. Mfg., No. 019-1400) - down-sized offset double cutaway alder body, bolt-on maple neck, 32" scale, 24-fret pau ferro fingerboard, strings through body gold plated bridge, Stu Hamm's signature on peghead, 4-on-one-side black chrome tuners, white pearloid pickguard, J/P/J-style pickups, volume/pan, treble/bass concentric ('stacked') controls, 3-position mini/rotary switches, active electronics, available in Burgundy Mist, Lake Placid Blue, Montego Black, and Sherwood Green Metallic finishes. Mfg. 1993 to 1999.

$1,125 $825 $750 $675 $600 $550 $500
Last MSR was $1,599.

Stu Hamm Urge Bass II (U.S. Mfg., No. 019-1500) - similar to Stu Hamm Urge Bass, poplar body, 34" scale, rosewood fingerboard, Deluxe Lightweight tuners, 24-frets, 2 Noiseless Jazz pickups and 1 Custom P-Bass pickup, Volume, Blend, 3-band EQ, 3-way mini-toggle, Combo string through body bridge, available in 3-Color Sunburst, black, Bright Amber Metallic and Bright Sapphire Metallic finishes. Current Mfg.

MSR $1,799 $1,260 $1,050 $950 $750 $650 $550 $450

Stu Hamm Urge Standard Bass (Mex. Mfg., No. 013-1400). - similar to Stu Hamm Urge Bass, except has poplar body, rosewood fingerboard, 2 J-style pickups, volume/tone controls, pickup selector mini-switch, active electronics, available in Arctic White, Black, Crimson Red Metallic, and Lake Placid Blue finishes. Mfg. 1994 to 1999.

$420 $375 $325 $295 $250 $225 $175
Last MSR was $599.

GRADING	100% MINT	98% NEAR MINT	95% EXC+	90% EXC	80% VG+	70% VG	60% G

FENIX

Instruments previously built in Korea circa 1989 to 1992, and 1996 to date.

The Fenix trademark was used by instrument manufacturer Young Chang (Korea). Fenix guitars were built at the same time that the factory was producing Squier models for Fender. As a result, models with the Fenix brand name tend to be derived from Fender-based designs. Fenix guitars and basses were popular for a four-year run in England due to their decent quality at a relatively low price. In 1996, U.K. distributors Barnes & Mullins re-introduced the product line.

FENTON-WEILL

Instruments previously built in England from 1959 through the mid 1960s.

Henry Weill's company after collaboration with Jim Burns (BURNS-WEILL trademark) produced a decent range of distinctive solid body designs. While earlier models may seem similar to BURNS-WEILL models, they were soon restyled and other models of "similar character" were added. Fenton-Weill also produced fiber glass bodied guitars under the trademark of FIBRATONE.

As author Tony Bacon has noted, "although UK-made guitars have often offered better value and quality, they apparently lack the mystique of leading USA instruments." Most English-built guitars were destined for English consumption.

(Source: Tony Bacon, The Ultimate Guitar Book)

FERNANDES

Instruments currently produced in Tokyo, Japan since 1969. Distributed in the U.S. by Fernandes Guitars U.S.A. Inc., of Van Nuys, California.

In 1969, Fernandes Company Ltd. (based in Tokyo, Japan) was established to produce quality classical guitars at an affordable price. Over the next twenty years, Fernandes expanded the line and became one of the largest selling guitar manufacturers in the world. Fernandes is the number one selling guitar in Japan, and at times has held as much as 40% of the Japanese market.

In late 1992, Fernandes Company Ltd. began distributing their entire line of guitars to the U.S. market as Fernandes Guitars U.S.A., Inc. Fernandes Company Ltd. uses only the top facilities located in Japan, Taiwan, China, and Korea to produce their guitars. Once the factory is done manufacturing the guitars, they are shipped to the United States where they are inspected and set up again.

In 1998, Fernandes renamed their instruments. For example, the eye-catching **H-80** art-deco-style guitar model became the **Vertigo Deluxe**. In addition to their **RetroRocket** and **Retrospect** series, Fernandes is concentrating on the newer additions to their line like the **P-Project, Native, Dragonfly,** and **Lexington** series. Fernandes also offers five different models of practice amps (15 to 20 watts) for guitars and basses.

(Company history courtesy Bryan Wresinski, Fernandes Guitars U.S.A.)

Fernandes guitars now represent one of the most diverse groups of guitars in the market today. Since its inception, the Fernandes company has consistently raised the bar for the entire industry to follow. No product more typifies this than the Fernandes *Sustainer System*. The Sustainer is a specially designed neck pickup and circuit that allows the guitar to sustain chords or single notes indefinitely, giving the player complete control of sustain and feedback without the excessive volume from an amplifier. The Sustainer operates in three modes: Standard (sustains fundamental pitch or pitches), Harmonic (creates various 3rd and 5th harmonics of the note being sustained), and Mix (a combination of the first two modes).

ELECTRIC

AFR Series

AFR-35 - offset double cutaway alder body, bolt-on maple neck, 25 1/2" scale, 24-fret rosewood fingerboard with dot inlay, standard tremolo, 6-on-a-side tuners, black hardware, black pickguard, 2 single coil/humbucker pickups, volume/tone controls, 5-way switch, available in Black, Metallic Blue, and Metallic Red finishes. Disc. 1998.

$375 $325 $275 $225 $195 $150 $125
Last MSR was $499.

Add $240 for Sustainer Standard pickup system.
Add $280 for Sustainer Custom pickup system.

AFR-45 - offset double cutaway basswood body, bolt-on maple neck, 24-fret rosewood fingerboard with dot inlay, standard tremolo, 6-on-a-side tuners, chrome hardware, 2 single coil/humbucker pickups, volume/tone control, 5-way switch, available in Black, Metallic Red, and Metallic Blue finishes. Disc. 1996.

$300 $250 $225 $200 $175 $150 $100
Last MSR was $459.

AFR-55 - similar to the AFR-45, except features gold hardware, available in Blackburst, Blueburst, and Redburst finishes. Disc. 1996.

$300 $250 $225 $200 $175 $150 $125
Last MSR was $499.

AFR-55GF - similar to the AFR-35, except features a basswood body, gold hardware, no pickguard, available in Black Burst, Blue Burst, and Red Burst finishes. Disc. 1998.

$550 $475 $425 $375 $300 $250 $175
Last MSR was $739.

Add $240 for Sustainer Standard pickup system.
Add $280 for Sustainer Custom pickup system.

GRADING	100% MINT	98% NEAR MINT	95% EXC+	90% EXC	80% VG+	70% VG	60% G

AFR-65 - similar to the AFR-55, except features black hardware, Fernandes double locking tremolo, available in Black, Turquoise Metallic, and Wine Red Metallic finishes. Disc. 1996.

	$375	$325	$295	$250	$225	$175	$150

Last MSR was $599.

AFR-65X - similar to the AFR-55, except features humbucker/single coil/humbucker pickups, 3-way switch, available in Gun Metal Blue, Metallic Black, and Metallic Red finishes. Disc. 1996.

	$395	$325	$295	$250	$225	$195	$150

Last MSR was $599.

AFR-70S - similar to the AFR-45, except features 22-fret fingerboard, black hardware, Fernandes Sustainer/single coil/humbucker pickups, volume/tone/sustainer volume controls, available in Black and Cobalt Blue finishes. Disc. 1996.

	$450	$375	$350	$300	$250	$225	$175

Last MSR was $699.

AFR-75A - similar to the AFR-35, except features a basswood body, gold hardware, no pickguard, available in Black burst, Blue burst, and Red burst finishes. Disc. 1998.

	$595	$550	$495	$425	$350	$275	$225

Last MSR was $869.

Add $240 for Sustainer Standard pickup system.

AFR-80 - offset double cutaway maple (or ash) body, bolt-on maple neck, 24-fret rosewood fingerboard with pearl dot inlay, double locking vibrato, 6-on-a-side tuners, black hardware, 2 stacked coil/humbucker pickups, volume/tone controls, 5-way switch, available in Candy Apple Red, Metallic Blue, Pearl Black, and Pearl White finishes. Mfg. 1991 to 1992.

	$525	$450	$375	$300	$275	$250	$225

Last MSR was $750.

AFR-80S - similar to the AFR-70S, except features ash body, maple fingerboard, chrome hardware, Fernandes Sustainer/2 single coil pickups, available in Natural finish. Disc. 1996.

	$495	$450	$395	$350	$295	$250	$200

Last MSR was $799.

AFR-85 - similar to AFR-80, except has humbucker/stacked coil/humbucker pickups. Disc. 1992.

	$525	$475	$400	$325	$295	$250	$225

Last MSR was $800.

AFR-90S - similar to the AFR-70S, except features gold hardware, double locking tremolo system, available in Black, Summer Green Metallic and Wine Red Metallic finishes. Disc. 1996.

	$550	$495	$450	$395	$325	$275	$225

Last MSR was $899.

AFR-120S - similar to the AFR-75A, except features Monkey Pod body, gold hardware, 22-fret fingerboard, Fernandes Sustainer Custom/single coil/humbucker pickups, volume/tone/sustainer volume controls, 5-way switch, available in Natural finish. Disc. 1998.

	$1,200	$1,100	$950	$875	$725	$595	$450

Last MSR was $1,799.

AFR-150S - similar to the AFR-90S, except features mahogany body, flame maple top, ebony fingerboard, Fernandes Sustainer/single coil/humbucker, available in Natural finish. Disc. 1996.

	$1,250	$1,150	$995	$900	$750	$600	$475

Last MSR was $1,899.

AMG Series

AMG-60 - double cutaway basswood body, set-in maple neck, 24-fret maple fingerboard with black dot inlay, standard vibrato, 3-per-side tuners, gold hardware, 2 humbucker pickups, volume/tone control, 3-position switch, available in Fire Red, Navy Blue, Screaming Yellow, and Snow White finishes. Mfg. 1991 to 1992.

	$500	$450	$375	$295	$250	$225	$200

Last MSR was $730.

AMG-70 - similar to AMG-60, except has ash body, rosewood fingerboard with white dot inlay, black hardware, 2 stacked coil/humbucker pickups, available in Transparent Black, Transparent Green, Transparent Purple, and Transparent Red finishes. Disc. 1993.

	$525	$450	$375	$300	$275	$250	$225

Last MSR was $750.

This model was available with gold hardware (Model AMG-70G).

Decade Series

The Decade Series was introduced in 1997.

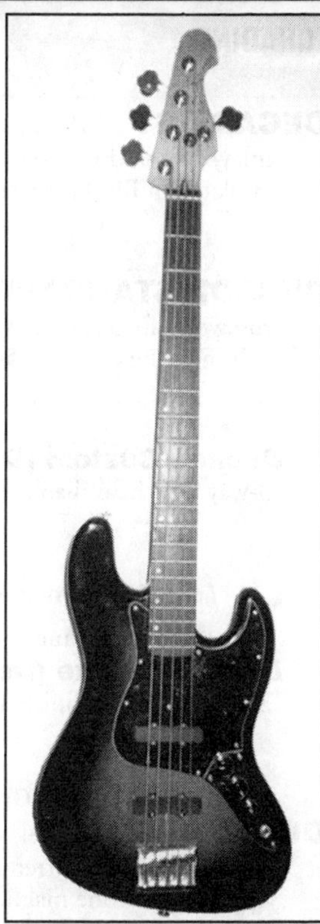

Fenix Bass
courtesy Thomas Bauer

Fernandes AFR-120 S
courtesy
Fernandes Guitars

F

GRADING	100% MINT	98% NEAR MINT	95% EXC+	90% EXC	80% VG+	70% VG	60% G

DECADE-S1 - 7/8 size sleek offset double cutaway basswood body, bolt-on maple neck, 25 1/2" scale, 21-fret rosewood fingerboard with dot inlay, standard tremolo, 6-on-a-side tuners, chrome hardware, white pickguard, 3 single coil pickups, volume/tone controls, 5-way switch, available in Black, Pewter, and Vintage Metallic Blue finishes. Mfg. 1997 to 1998.

$325 $275 $250 $225 $175 $150 $125
Last MSR was $429.

DECADE STANDARD (DECADE-A1) - sleek slightly offset double cutaway alder body, bolt-on maple neck, 25 1/2" scale, 21-fret rosewood fingerboard with dot inlay, vintage tremolo, 6-on-a-side tuners, chrome hardware, white pearloid pickguard, 3 single coil pickups, volume/tone controls, 5-way switch, available in Black, Cream White, and Sea Foam Green finishes. Disc. 1999.

$375 $325 $275 $250 $195 $150 $125
Last MSR was $479.

Decade Custom (Decade-A2) - similar to the Decade Standard, except features a fixed bridge, 2 chrome covered humbucker pickups, 3-way switch, available in Black, Cream White, and Sea Foam Green finishes. Mfg. 1997 to 1999.

$425 $365 $325 $275 $230 $185 $140
Last MSR was $549.

Add $240 for Sustainer Standard pickup system (available 1997 only).

In 1998, Silver and Vintage Metallic Blue finishes were introduced; Cream White and Sea Foam Green finishes were discontinued.

Decade Deluxe (Decade-J1) - similar to the Decade Standard, except Gotoh tuners, 1 volume/2 tone controls, available in Black and 3-Tone Sunburst finishes. Mfg. 1997 to 1999.

$595 $525 $475 $400 $350 $275 $225
Last MSR was $849.

In 1998, Sea Foam Green finish replaced Black finish.

DECADE PRO - sleek slightly offset double cutaway alder body, bolt-on maple neck, 25 1/2" scale, 21-fret rosewood fingerboard with dot inlay, vintage-style tremolo, 6-on-a-side tuners, pearloid pickguard, chrome hardware, Sustainer Transducer/exposed coil humbucker pickups, volume/tone magnetic controls, Sustainer volume control, 3-way pickup selector switch, Sustainer on/off/Sustainer mode selector mini-switches, available in Vintage Metallic Blue finish. Mfg. 1998 to 1999.

$595 $500 $450 $395 $325 $275 $225
Last MSR was $849.

Decade Elite - similar to Decade Pro, except features mahogany body, maple top, 22-fret fingerboard, black Gotoh hardware, black or pearloid pickguard, available in Black Satin, 3-Tone Sunburst and Rust finishes. Mfg. 1998 to 2000.

$950 $825 $725 $625 $550 $450 $350
Last MSR was $1,299.

In 1999, Black Satin and Rust finishes were discontinued.

Deuce Series (Formerly WS Series)

The Deuce Series was introduced in 1997. Early (WS) models were optional with the Sustainer Standard pickup system.

Add $240 for Sustainer Standard pickup system (available 1997 only).

DEUCE STANDARD (WS-500) - dual cutaway alder body, bolt-on maple neck, 24 3/4" scale, 22-fret rosewood fingerboard with dot inlay, stop tailpiece, 3-per-side tuners, chrome hardware, pearloid pickguard, 2 chrome covered humbucker pickups, volume/tone controls, 3-way switch, available in Black and Cream White finishes. Mfg. 1997 to 1999.

$375 $300 $275 $225 $195 $150 $125
Last MSR was $479.

Deuce Deluxe (WS-1000) - similar to the Deuce Standard, except features mahogany body/neck, tunomatic bridge/stop tailpiece, Gotoh tuners, available in Mahogany Brown and Wine Red finishes. Mfg. 1997 to 1999.

$695 $595 $525 $450 $375 $325 $250
Last MSR was $999.

Dragonfly Series (Formerly APG Series)

Early versions of the **APG-50, APG-95GF**, and **APG-145** were optional with the Sustainer Standard pickup system.

Add $240 for Sustainer Standard pickup system.

DRAGONFLY STANDARD (APG-50) - slightly double cutaway alder body, bolt-on maple neck, 25 1/2" scale, 22-fret rosewood fingerboard with dot inlay, stop tailpiece, 3-per-side tuners, chrome hardware, 2 chrome covered humbucker pickups, volume/tone controls, 3-way switch, available in Black, Dark Red, and Gold finishes. Disc. 2000.

$325 $300 $275 $225 $195 $150 $125
Last MSR was $449.

Dragonfly Custom (APG-95GF) - similar to APG-50, except has a basswood body, carved maple Gravure top, 24 3/4" scale, tune-o-matic bridge/stop tailpiece, Gotoh tuners, available in Black Burst, Cherry Sunburst and Tobacco Sunburst finishes. Disc. 1999.

$695 $595 $525 $450 $375 $325 $250
Last MSR was $999.

GRADING	100% MINT	98% NEAR MINT	95% EXC+	90% EXC	80% VG+	70% VG	60% G

Dragonfly Deluxe (APG-145) - similar to APG-50, except has mahogany body, carved maple top, set-in maple neck, 24 3/4" scale, bound body, bound headstock, tune-o-matic bridge/stop tailpiece, Gotoh tuners, coil tap capability, available in Black, Gold, and Lemon Drop finishes. Disc. 1999.

		$1,100	$975	$875	$750	$625	$525	$400

Last MSR was $1,599.

In 1998, Honey Burst finish replace Lemon Drop finish.

DRAGONFLY PRO - slightly double cutaway basswood body, bolt-on maple neck, 25 1/2" scale, 24-fret rosewood fingerboard with dot inlay, vintage-style tremolo, 3-per-side tuners, gold Gotoh hardware, Sustainer Transducer/single coil/humbucker pickups, volume/tone magnetic controls, Sustainer volume control, 5-way pickup selector switch, Sustainer on/off/Sustainer mode selector mini-switches, available in Lava Burst and Ocean Burst finishes. Mfg. 1998 to date.

MSR	$899	$675	$625	$525	$476	$375	$300	$250

In 1999, Ocean Burst finish was discontinued.
In 2000, Metallic Black and Gun Metal Blue finishes were introduced.

Dragonfly Elite - similar to Dragonfly Pro, except features mahogany body, licensed Floyd Rose locking tremolo, available in Gun Metal Blue and Silver finishes. Mfg. 1998 to date.

MSR	$1,449	$1,095	$895	$795	$695	$550	$450	$350

In 1999, Gun Metal Blue and Siver finishes were discontinued.
In 2000, Black Metallic Satin, Dark Green Metallic Satin and Lava Burst finishes were introduced.

Dragonfly X - similar to Dragonfly Pro, except has alder body, 2 high output single coil pickups and 1 high output single coil pickup in the bridge position, black tuners, black hardtail bridge, available in Black Burst, Blue Burst and Red Burst finishes. New 2000.

MSR	$349	$260	$245	$225	$195	$175	$150	$95

In 2001, Metallic Black, Ocean Burst and Lava Burst finishes were introduced. Black Burst and Blue Burst finishes were discontinued.

APG-65S - double cutaway basswood body, bolt-on maple neck, 24-fret rosewood fingerboard with dot inlay, standard tremolo, 3-per-side tuners, black hardware, Fernandes Sustainer/humbucker pickups, volume/tone/sustainer volume controls, 3-way switch, available in Black and Cobalt Blue finishes. Disc. 1996.

		$450	$375	$350	$300	$250	$225	$175

Last MSR was $699.

APG-80 - double cutaway bound mahogany body, maple top, set-in maple neck, 24-fret rosewood fingerboard with pearl dot inlay, double locking vibrato, bound peghead, 3-per-side tuners, gold hardware, stacked coil/humbucker pickups, volume/tone control, 3-position switch, available in Lemon Drop, Transparent Blue, Transparent Purple, and Transparent Red finishes. Mfg. 1991 to 1992.

		$625	$550	$450	$350	$325	$300	$275

Last MSR was $900.

APG-85S - similar to APG-65S, except has mahogany body, gold hardware, double locking tremolo, Fernandes Sustainer/single coil/humbucker pickups, available in Black, Deep Metallic Red, and Wine Red Metallic finishes. Disc. 1996.

		$575	$495	$450	$375	$350	$275	$225

Last MSR was $899.

APG-90FS - similar to APG-80, except has arched maple top, tune-o-matic bridge/stop tailpiece, 2 humbucker pickups, mini switch, active electronics, available in Lemon Drop, Transparent Black, and Transparent Red finishes. Disc. 1993.

		$795	$725	$600	$475	$425	$375	$325

Last MSR was $1,200.

APG-100 - similar to APG-80, except has arched maple top, tune-o-matic bridge/stop tailpiece and 2 humbucker pickups, available in Cherry Sunburst, Lemon Drop, Transparent Black, and Transparent Red finishes. Mfg. 1991 to 1996.

		$750	$650	$595	$525	$450	$375	$300

Last MSR was $1,200.

FSG Series

FSG-60 - offset double cutaway basswood body, bolt-on maple neck, 22-fret rosewood fingerboard with pearl dot inlay, standard vibrato, 6-on-a-side tuners, black hardware, 2 single coil/humbucker pickups, 2 volume/tone control, 3-way switch, 2 mini switches, active electronics, available in Black, Cobalt Blue, and Cream White finishes. Mfg. 1993 to 1994.

		$525	$450	$400	$325	$295	$250	$200

Last MSR was $800.

FSG-80 - similar to FSG-60, except has ash body, available in Tobacco Sunburst, Transparent Black, Transparent Purple, and Transparent Red finishes. Disc. 1994.

		$550	$495	$450	$395	$325	$275	$225

Last MSR was $900.

Fernandes Tele-Style courtesy 24th Annual Dallas Guitar Show

F

GRADING	100% MINT	98% NEAR MINT	95% EXC+	90% EXC	80% VG+	70% VG	60% G

FSG-100 - similar to FSG-60, except has ash body, double locking vibrato, gold hardware, available in Transparent Black, Transparent Purple, Transparent Red, and Tobacco Sunburst finishes. Disc. 1994.

$725 $600 $525 $475 $395 $350 $275
Last MSR was $1,100.

LE Series

LE-1X - classic offset double cutaway alder body, bolt-on maple neck, 25 1/2" scale, 21-fret rosewood fingerboard with dot inlay, standard tremolo, 6-on-a-side tuners, chrome hardware, white pickguard, 3 single coil pickups, volume/2 tone controls, 5-way switch, available in Black, Cream White, Red, 2-Tone Sunburst, and 3-Tone Sunburst finishes. Disc. 1998.

$225 $195 $175 $150 $125 $100 $75
Last MSR was $299.

LE-1 - similar to the LE-1X, except features a basswood body, rosewood or maple fingerboard, available in Black, Cream White, Pewter, Red, Sea Foam Green, Vintage Metallic Blue, and 3-Tone Sunburst finishes. Mfg. 1993 to 1998.

$375 $325 $275 $250 $200 $175 $125
Last MSR was $499.

LE-1G - similar to the LE-1, except features gold hardware, available in Gold finish. Disc. 1998.

$425 $375 $325 $275 $225 $175 $150
Last MSR was $549.

LE-2 - similar to the LE-1, except features 7 1/4" vintage radius on neck, antique finish on neck, available in Black, Cream White, Candy Apple Red, Sonic Blue, Pewter, Sea Foam Green, Vintage Metallic Blue, 2-Tone Sunburst, and 3-Tone Sunburst finishes. Mfg. 1991 to 1998.

$500 $450 $395 $350 $275 $225 $175
Last MSR was $699.

LE-2FS - similar to LE-2, except has active electronics. Disc. 1993.

$495 $425 $350 $275 $250 $225 $200
Last MSR was $710.

LE-2G - similar to LE-2, except has gold hardware, available in Candy Apple Red, Cream White, Gold, Vintage Metallic Blue, and 3-Tone Sunburst finishes. Disc. 1998.

$550 $495 $425 $375 $300 $250 $195
Last MSR was $749.

LE-2L - similar to LE-2, except in left-handed configuration, available in Black, Candy Apple Red, Cream White, Sonic Blue, Vintage Metallic Blue, 2-Tone Sunburst, and 3-Tone Sunburst finishes. Disc. 1998.

$595 $550 $475 $425 $350 $275 $225
Last MSR was $849.

LE-2N - similar to LE-2, except has an ash body, fixed bridge, tortoiseshell pickguard, available in Black, Candy Apple Red, Cream White, Sonic Blue, Vintage Metallic Blue, 2-Tone Sunburst, and 3-Tone Sunburst finishes. Disc. 1998.

$595 $550 $475 $425 $350 $275 $225
Last MSR was $849.

LE-2X - similar to LE-2, except has double locking vibrato, 2 single coil/humbucker pickups, available in Black, Candy Apple Red, Cream, Sonic Blue, and 3-Tone Sunburst finishes. Disc. 1993.

$375 $325 $300 $250 $225 $195 $150
Last MSR was $600.

This model has optional reverse peghead and gold hardware.

LE-3 - offset double cutaway basswood body, white pickguard, bolt-on maple neck, 21-fret maple fingerboard with black dot inlay, standard vibrato, roller nut, 6-on-one-side tuners, chrome hardware, 3 single coil pickups, volume/2 tone controls, 5-position switch, available in Black, Cream White, and Red finishes. Disc. 1993.

$450 $375 $325 $295 $250 $225 $200
Last MSR was $700.

LE-3FS - similar to LE-3, except has active electronics. Disc. 1993.

$625 $550 $495 $425 $350 $325 $275
Last MSR was $1,000.

Lexington Series (BSA Series)

LEXINGTON STANDARD (BSA-100) - slightly offset double cutaway hollow body, arched maple top, maple back/sides, single layer body binding, set-in mahogany neck, 24 3/4" scale, 22-fret ebony fingerboard with dot inlay, bound neck/headstock, tune-o-matic bridge/stop tailpiece, 3-per-side Gotoh tuners, chrome hardware, 2 covered humbucker pickups, 2 volume/2 tone controls, 3-way switch, available in Black and Wine Red finishes. Disc. 1999.

$1,450 $1,225 $1,100 $950 $750 $625 $475
Last MSR was $1,899.

Lexington Deluxe (BSA-135) - similar to the BSA-100, except features gold hardware, gold covered humbuckers, multi-layered body binding, bound neck/headstock/soundholes, triangle trapezoid fingerboard inlays, available in Black finish. Disc. 1999.

$1,650 $1,425 $1,250 $1,100 $900 $725 $550
Last MSR was $2,199.

GRADING	100% MINT	98% NEAR MINT	95% EXC+	90% EXC	80% VG+	70% VG	60% G

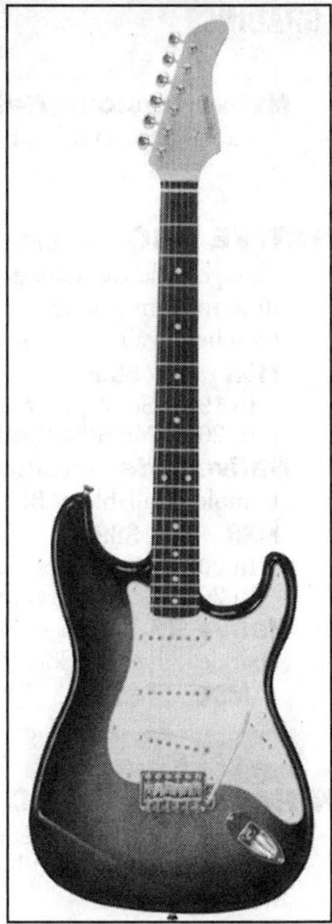
Fernandes LE-2
courtesy
Fernandes Guitars

Monterey Series (LS Series)

Earlier LS Series models were optional with a Sustainer Standard pickup system.

Add $240 for Sustainer Standard pickup system.

LS-50 - single cutaway basswood body, bolt-on maple neck, 25 1/2" scale, 22-fret rosewood fingerboard with dot inlay, stop tailpiece, 3-per-side tuners, chrome hardware, 2 humbucker pickups, volume/tone controls, 3-way switch, available in Black, Dark Red, and Pewter finishes. Disc. 1998.

$295 $275 $250 $225 $195 $150 $125
Last MSR was $429.

MONTEREY STANDARD (LS-75) - single cutaway alder body, bolt-on maple neck, 24 3/4" scale, 22-fret rosewood fingerboard with dot inlay, stop tailpiece, 3-per-side tuners, black pickguard, chrome hardware, 2 chrome covered humbucker pickups, 2 volume/2 tone controls, 3-way switch, available in Black, Tobacco Sunburst, and TV Yellow finishes. Disc. 1999.

$350 $295 $250 $225 $195 $150 $125
Last MSR was $449.

In 1998, Dark Red and Silver finishes were introduced.
Earlier LS-75 models may have a 25 1/2" scale.

Monterey Pro - similar to Monterey Standard, except has Sustainer Driver/Humbucker pickup in the neck position and a high ouput humbucker pickup in the bridge position, volume/tone controls, Suatainer Mode Selector, Sustainer on/off, Sustainer Intensity, available in Metallic Black and Tobacco Sunburst finishes. New specs for 2000.

MSR $849 $635 $550 $499 $450 $399 $350 $299

Monterey X - similar to Monterey Pro, except has 2 high output humbucking pickups, volume/tone controls, 3-way selector switch, available in Black, Dark Green and Tobacco Sunburst finishes. Current Mfg.

MSR $349 $260 $225 $199 $175 $150 $125 $95

In 2000, Dark Green and Tobacco Sunburst finishes were discontinued.
In 2001, Lava Flame and Tobacco Flames finishes were introduced.

Monterey Custom (LS-80) - similar to the LS-75, except features mahogany body, set-in mahogany neck, 2 chrome covered mini humbuckers, pearloid pickguard, Gotoh tuners, available in Wine Red finish. Disc. 1999.

$975 $850 $750 $650 $525 $425 $325
Last MSR was $1,299.

MONTEREY DELUXE (LS-135) - single cutaway mahogany core body, carved quilted maple top and back, set-in mahogany neck, multi-layered body binding, 24 3/4" scale, 22-fret bound ebony fingerboard with triangle trapezoid inlay, bound headstock, stop tailpiece, 3-per-side Gotoh tuners, gold hardware, 2 covered humbucker pickups, 2 volume/2 tone controls, 3-way switch, available in Cherry Sunburst finish. Disc. 1999.

$1,299 $1,100 $975 $850 $725 $600 $475
Last MSR was $1,849.

MONTEREY MAGNACOUSTIC (LSA-50 ELECTRIC/ACOUSTIC) - single cutaway alder body, bolt-on maple neck, 24 3/4" scale, 22-fret rosewood fingerboard with dot inlay, Indian rosewood bridge, 3-per-side tuners, chrome hardware, double-bladed humbucker pickup, Shadow bridge piezo pickup, 2 volume/treble/bass controls, 3-way switch, active preamp, available in Black and Dark Red finishes. Disc. 1999.

$675 $575 $525 $450 $375 $300 $225
Last MSR was $899.

Monterey Elecoustic (LSA-65 Electric/Acoustic) - similar to the LSA-50, except features basswood body, flame maple gravure top, single layer binding, triangle trapezoid inlays, 3-per-side gold Gotoh tuners with tortoise buttons, wood knobs, bridge mounted Shadow piezo pickup, volume/treble/bass controls, Fishman preamp, available in Black, See-Through Blue, See-Through Red, Tobacco Sunburst, and Vintage Natural finishes. Current Mfg.

MSR $1,199 $850 $695 $625 $550 $395 $350 $275

Native Series

The Native model was designed in 1996 at the Fernandes Custom Shop in North Hollywood, California. Early models from 1996-1997 were optional with the Sustainer Standard pickup system.

Add $240 for Sustainer Standard pickup system (1996-1997).

NATIVE STANDARD (NATIVE-A1) - rounded shoulder single cutaway alder body, bolt-on maple neck, 25 1/2" scale, 22-fret rosewood fingerboard with dot inlay, vintage-style tremolo, 3-per-side tuners, pearloid pickguard, chrome hardware, 2 chrome covered humbucker pickups, 2 volume/1 tone controls, 3-way switch, available in Black, Cream White, and Sea Foam Green finishes. Disc. 1999.

$375 $325 $275 $250 $200 $175 $125
Last MSR was $499.

GRADING	100% MINT	98% NEAR MINT	95% EXC+	90% EXC	80% VG+	70% VG	60% G

Native Custom (Native-A2) - similar to Native Standard, except features 2 black Fernandes FP-90 single coil pickups, available in Black, Cream White, and Sea Foam Green finishes. Disc. 1999.

	$450	$395	$350	$295	$250	$200	$150

Last MSR was $599.

NATIVE PRO - rounded shoulder single cutaway alder body, bolt-on maple neck, 25 1/2" scale, 22-fret rosewood fingerboard with dot inlay, vintage-style tremolo, 3-per-side tuners, pearloid pickguard, chrome hardware, Sustainer Transducer/exposed coil humbucker pickups, volume/tone magnetic controls, Sustainer volume control, 3-way pickup selector switch, Sustainer on/off/Sustainer mode selector mini-switches, available in Sea Foam Green finish. Mfg. 1998 to date.

MSR $699	$475	$420	$375	$325	$275	$225	$175

In 1999, Sea Foam green finish was discontinued.
In 2000, Metallic Black and Dark Green Metallic finishes were introduced.

Native Elite - similar to Native Pro, except features basswood body, flame maple gravure top, Gotoh hardware, licensed Floyd Rose locking tremolo, available in Black Burst finish. Mfg. 1998 to date.

MSR $999	$750	$650	$575	$525	$450	$425	$325

In 2000, Lava Burst and Ocean Burst finishes were introduced.
In 2001, Lava Burst and Ocean Burst finishes were discontinued and See Through Red and See Through Blue finishes were introduced.

Native X - similar to Native Pro, except has 2 high output humbucker pickups, black pickguard, available in Metallic Black, Blue Sparkle, Red Sparkle, Silver Sparkle. White pickguard optional. Current Mfg.

MSR $349	$265	$225	$195	$175	$150	$95	$65

Nomad Series

NOMAD STANDARD (ZO-3 TRAVEL GUITAR) - "standing elephant"-shaped hardwood body, bolt-on maple neck, 24" scale, 22-fret rosewood fingerboard with dot inlay, fixed bridge, 6-on-a-side tuners, chrome hardware, humbucker pickup, built-in 3 1/2" speaker, volume control, LED light, on/off switch, available in Black, Cream White, Gold, Red, Silver, and Vintage Metallic Blue finishes. Current Mfg.

MSR $259	$195	$150	$125	$99	$75	$50	$35

The built-in 5 watt amplifier is powered by a 9-volt battery.
Early versions of this model may have Blue, Green, Pewter, Pink, or Yellow finishes.
In 1999, Cream White, Gold, Silver and Vintage Metallic Blue finishes were discontinued.
In 2000, Blue and Sunburst finishes were introduced.
In 2001, Vintage Metallic Blue finish was re-introduced and 3-Tone Sunburst finish was introduced.

Nomad Deluxe - similar to Nomad Standard, except has effects processor controls, available in Metallic Black, Candy Apple Red, Silver, Hot Rod Flame, USA Flag and UK flag.Current Mfg.

MSR $539	$399	$350	$299	$250	$225	$195	$150

Add $20 for hot Rod Flame, USA flag and UK flag.

Nomad Custom - similar to the Nomad Standard, available in UK Flag and USA Flag graphic finishes. Disc. 1999.

	$295	$250	$225	$195	$150	$125	$95

Last MSR was $369.

P-Project Series

P-PROJECT - single cutaway hollowed body, spruce top, mahogany back, bolt-on mahogany neck, 25.5" scale, 22-fret ebony fingerboard, wenge bridge, 6-on-a-side gold Gotoh tuners with tortoise buttons, Fishman bridge piezo pickup, volume control (mounted on bridge), bass/treble tone controls (mounted inside back panel), Fishman preamp, available in Natural finish. Mfg. 1997 (special order), 1998 to 1999.

	$2,100	$1,750	$N/A	$N/A	$N/A	$N/A	$N/A

Last MSR was $2,999.

RetroRocket Series

RETROROCKET ELITE - offset double cutaway basswood body, bolt-on maple neck, 25 1/2" scale, 22-fret rosewood fingerboard with dot inlay, Wilkinson tremolo, 6-on-a-side satin chrome Gotoh tuners, mint green pickguard, Sustainer Transducer/2 double blade stacked humbucker pickups (looks like three single coil pickups from a distance), volume/tone magnetic controls, Sustainer volume control, 5-way pickup selector switch, Sustainer on/off/Sustainer mode selector mini-switches, available in 3-Tone Sunburst and Vintage Metallic Blue finishes. Mfg. 1998 to date.

MSR $1,299	$925	$795	$700	$600	$525	$425	$325

In 2000, 2-Tone Sunburst/maple finish was introduced.
In 2001, 3-Tone Sunburst, Vintage Metallic Blue and 2-Tone Sunburst/maple finishes were discontinued and See Through Red, See Through Blue and Tobacco Sunburst finishes were introduced.

Retrorocket Pro - similar to Retrorocket Elite, except has alder body, 1 Sustainer Driver/Single Coil pickup, 1 high output single coil pickup and 1 high output humbucker pickup in the bridge position, chrome tuners, chrome vintage tremelo, available in Black, Candy Apple red, Vintage Metallic Blue and 3-Tone Sunburst finishes. Current Mfg.

MSR $679	$509	$450	$399	$350	$299	$250	$199

GRADING	100% MINT	98% NEAR MINT	95% EXC+	90% EXC	80% VG+	70% VG	60% G

Retrorocket X - similar to Retrorocket Pro, except has 2 high output single coil pickups and 1 high output humbucking pickup in the bridge position, volume/tone controls, 5-way switch, available in Black, Dark Red, Dark Green, Sonic Blue and 3-Tone Sunburst finishes. Current Mfg.

MSR $299	$225	$195	$175	$150	$125	$95	$65

In 2000, Sonic Blue finish was discontinued.
In 2001, Lava Flame and Blue Flame finishes were introduced.

Retrorocket X One - similar to Retrorocket X, except has 3 single coil high output pickups, available in Black, Cream White, Dark Red and 3-Tone Sunburst finishes. New 2000.

MSR $279	$209	$175	$150	$125	$95	$75	$50

Raven Series

RAVEN ELITE - offset double cutaway maple/mahogany body, bolt-on maple neck, 24 ¾" scale, rosewood fingerboard with dot position markers, 24 large frets, Sustainer Driver/Single Coil pickup in the neck position and high output humbucker in the bridge position, volume/tone controls, Sustainer on/off, Sustainer Intensity and Sustainer Mode Selector switches, black Gotoh tuners, black Wilkinson tremelo bridge, available in Black Burst finish. Current Mfg.

MSR $1,249	$935	$875	$799	$750	$699	$660	$550

Raven Standard - similar to Raven Elite, except has alder body, 2 high output humbucking pickups, volume. 3-way selector switch, available in Metallic Black and Metallic Blue finishes. Mfg. 2000 only.

	$375	$350	$295	$250	$195	$150	$95

Last MSR was $499.

Revolver Series

REVOLVER PRO - offset double cutaway basswood body, bolt-on maple neck, 25 1/2" scale, 22-fret rosewood fingerboard with dot inlay, vintage-style tremolo, 6-on-a-side tuners, black Gotoh hardware, Sustainer Transducer/single coil/humbucker exposed pole piece pickups, volume/tone magnetic controls, Sustainer volume control, 5-way pickup selector switch, Sustainer on/off/Sustainer mode selector mini-switches, available in Black and Cobalt Blue finishes. Mfg. 1998 to date.

MSR $849	$595	$525	$450	$395	$350	$295	$225

In 1999, Black and Cobalt Blue finishes were discontinued.
In 2000, Metallic Black, Dark Green Metallic and Silver finishes were introduced.

Revolver Pro 7 - similar to Revolver Pro, except in a 7-string configuration, available in Metallic Black finish. New 2000.

MSR $949	$710	$650	$595	$550	$495	$450	$395

Revolver X - similar to Revolver Proo, except has 2 high output humbucker pickups, volume/tone controls, 3-way switch, available in Black, Dark Blue and dark Red finishes. New 2000.

MSR $449	$335	$295	$250	$195	$150	$125	$75

Revolver Standard - similar to Revolver Pro, except has basswood body, graphite nut, 2 high output single coil pickups and 1 high output humbucker pickup in the bridge position, volume/tone control, 5-way switch, chrome Gotoh tuners, chrome vintage tremelo, available in Black, Metallic Blue, Metallic Red, and Tobacco Sunburst finishes. Mfg. 2000 only.

	$450	$395	$350	$295	$250	$195	$150

Last MSR was $649.

Add $100 for Left Hand configuration (Model Revolver Standard LH). New 2000.

Revolver Deluxe - similar to Revolver Standard, except has Fernandes/Floyd Rose Licensed Tremelo bridge, available in Gun Metal Blue, Mava Burst, Ocean Burst, and White Pearl finishes. New 2000.

	$635	$595	$550	$495	$450	$395	$350

Last MSR was $849.

Revolver Elite - similar to Revolver Pro, except chrome Gotoh hardware, licensed Floyd Rose locking tremolo, available in Black and Silver finishes. Mfg. 1998 to date.

MSR $1,399	$1,050	$850	$650	$450	$375	$325	$250

In 1999, Black and Silver finishes were discontinued.
In 2000, Metallic Black, Metallic Blue and Metallic Red finishes were introduced.

TE Series

TE-1 - classic single cutaway alder body, white pickguard, bolt-on maple neck, 25 1/2" scale, 21-fret rosewood or maple fingerboard with dot inlay, fixed bridge, 6-on-a-side tuners, chrome hardware, black pickguard, 2 single coil pickups, volume/tone control, 3-way switch, available in Black, Candy Apple Red, Cream White, and Three Tone Sunburst finishes. Mfg. 1993 to 1998.

	$325	$295	$250	$225	$175	$150	$125

Last MSR was $449.

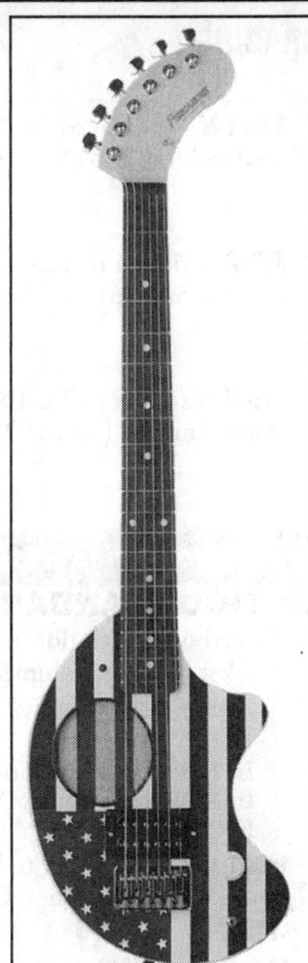

Fernandes Nomad Custom courtesy Fernandes Guitars

F

GRADING	100% MINT	98% NEAR MINT	95% EXC+	90% EXC	80% VG+	70% VG	60% G

TE-1N - similar to the TE-1, except features an ash body, 7 1/4" vintage radius on neck, antique finish on neck, available in Blonde and Vintage Natural finishes. Disc. 1998.

	$550	$500	$450	$395	$325	$250	$200

Last MSR was $799.

TE-2 - similar to TE-1N, except has a bound basswood body, white pickguard, available in Black, Candy Apple Red, Vintage Metallic Blue, and 3-Tone Sunburst finishes. Disc. 1998.

	$500	$475	$425	$375	$300	$250	$195

Last MSR was $749.

TE-3 - similar to TE-1N, except has semi-hollow ash body, pearloid pickguard, available in Black, Candy Apple Red, Natural, and 3-Tone Sunburst finishes. Disc. 1998.

	$675	$625	$550	$475	$395	$325	$250

Last MSR was $949.

F

Vertigo Series (H Series)

VERTIGO STANDARD (H-65) - original ("art deco coffee table") style alder body, bolt-on maple neck, 24 3/4" scale, 22-fret rosewood fingerboard with dot inlay, stop tailpiece, 3-per-side tuners, chrome hardware, upside down 'U' pearloid pickguard, 2 chrome covered humbucker pickups, volume/tone controls, 3-way switch, available in Black, Pale Cobalt, and Vivid Orange finishes. Disc. 2000.

	$395	$300	$275	$225	$195	$165	$125

Last MSR was $499.

In 1998, Dark Red and Vintage Metallic Blue finishes were introduced.
In 1999, pale Cobalt, Vivid Orange, Dark Red and Vintage Metallic Blue Finishes were discontinued.
In 2000, 3-Tone Sunburst and Dark green Metallic finishes were introduced.

Vertigo X - similar to Vertigo Standard, except has 1 high output humbucker pickup in the bridge position, volume control, available in Black and Dark Red finishes. Current Mfg.

MSR $275	$205	$175	$150	$125	$95	$75	$50

Vertigo Elite - similar to Vertigo Deluxe, except has maple bolt-on neck, Sustainer driver/humbucker pickup in the neck position and high output humbucker in the bridge position, Sustainer mode selector, Sustainer Intensity and Sustainer on/off, black pickguard, available in Matte Black finish. Current Mfg.

MSR $1,149	$860	$750	$650	$550	$450	$350	$250

Vertigo Deluxe (H-80) - similar to the H-65, except features mahogany body/neck, bound neck/headstock, forward-pointing pearloid pickguard, Gotoh chrome hardware, 2 mini humbuckers, triangle trapezoid inlays, available in Mahogany Brown and Pewter finishes. Current Mfg.

MSR $799	$599	$499	$450	$395	$350	$295	$195

In 1998, Silver finish replaced Pewter finish.
In 1999, Mahogany Brown and Silver finishes discontinued.
In 2000, Black Sunburst and Red Burst finishes introduced.

H-85 - original (art deco coffee table) style alder body, bolt-on maple neck, 22-fret rosewood fingerboard with dot inlay, double locking vibrato, 3-per-side tuners, black hardware, 2 humbucker pickups, volume/tone controls, 3-way switch, available in Shining Green and Neon Pink finishes. Disc. 1996.

	$675	$550	$495	$425	$375	$325	$250

Last MSR was $999.

VORTEX ELITE - modified "V" shaped alder body, bolt-on maple neck, 24 ¾" scale, rosewood fingerboard with split trapezoid position markers, Sustainer Driver/Humbucker pickup in the neck position and high output humbucker pickup in the bridge position, volume control, Suatainer Mode Selector, Sustainer Intensity and Sustainer on/off controls, black Gotoh tuners, black double locking Fernandes/Floyd Rose Licensed Tremelo bridge, available in Metallic Black finish. Current Mfg.

MSR $1,299	$975	$850	$750	$650	$550	$450	$350

ELECTRIC BASS

AMB Series

AMB-4 - offset double cutaway alder body, bolt-on maple neck, 34" scale, 24-fret rosewood fingerboard with dot inlay, fixed bridge, 2-per-side tuners, chrome hardware, P/J-style passive pickups, 2 volume/tone control, available in Black, Metallic Blue, and Metallic Red finishes. Disc. 1998.

	$350	$300	$275	$225	$195	$150	$125

Last MSR was $469.

AMB-4GF - similar to the AMB-4, except features basswood body, graphic finishes, available in Black Burst, Blue Burst, and Red Burst finishes. Disc. 1998.

	$575	$525	$475	$395	$325	$275	$200

Last MSR was $799.

GRADING	100% MINT	98% NEAR MINT	95% EXC+	90% EXC	80% VG+	70% VG	60% G

AMB-40 - offset double cutaway basswood body, bolt-on maple neck, 24-fret rosewood fingerboard with pearl dot inlay, fixed bridge, 2-per-side tuners, chrome hardware, P/J-style Fernandes pickups, 2 volume/ tone control, available in Black, Blue Sunburst, Fire Red and Snow White finishes. Mfg. 1991 to 1993.

$375 $325 $275 $225 $200 $175 $150
Last MSR was $570.

Add $80 for left-handed configuration (Model AMB-40L).

AMB-45 - similar to AMB-40, except has black hardware, available in Black, Metallic Blue, and Metallic Red finishes. Disc. 1996.

$325 $250 $225 $200 $175 $150 $125
Last MSR was $499.

Add $100 for left-handed configuration (Model AMB-45L).

AMB-55 - similar to AMB-45, available in Black Burst, Blue Burst, and Red Burst finishes. Disc. 1996.

$375 $325 $295 $250 $225 $175 $150
Last MSR was $599.

AMB-60 - similar to AMB-40, except has black hardware. Disc. 1994.

$395 $325 $300 $250 $225 $175 $150
Last MSR was $600.

AMB-70 - similar to AMB-40, except has ash body, active pickups, and gold hardware, available in Transparent Black, Transparent Purple, Transparent White, and Vintage Natural finishes. Disc. 1992.

$495 $450 $400 $325 $295 $250 $200
Last MSR was $800.

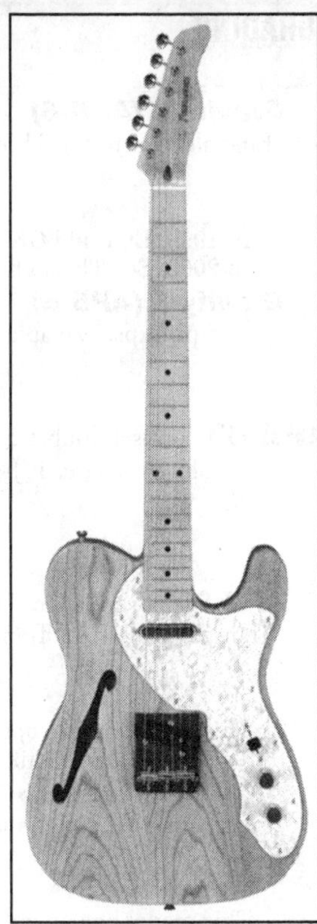

Fernandes TE-3 courtesy Fernandes Guitars

ASB Series

ASB-100 - mahogany body, bolt-on maple neck, 24-fret rosewood fingerboard with dot inlay, fixed bridge, 2-per-side tuners, Fernandes Sustainer/humbucker pickups, volume/tone controls, available in Black finish. Disc. 1996.

$795 $725 $650 $575 $475 $400 $325
Last MSR was $1,299.

This model has an optional fretless fingerboard.

Gravity Series (APB Series)

The Gravity bass model debuted in 1993.

GRAVITY 4 (APB-4) - offset double cutaway ash body, bolt-on 3-piece maple neck, 34" scale, 24-fret rosewood fingerboard with dot inlay, fixed bridge, 2-per-side tuners, gold Gotoh hardware, active P/J-style pickups, volume/blend/treble/bass controls, active pre-amp, available in Black, Emerald Green, See-Through Purple, and Vintage Natural finishes. Disc. 1999.

$895 $750 $675 $575 $495 $400 $325
Last MSR was $1,249.

Gravity 4M (APB-4M) - similar to APB-4, except has maple fingerboard, available in Oil Natural finish. Disc. 2000.

$875 $725 $650 $575 $495 $400 $325
Last MSR was $1,199.

In 2000, Black, Emerald Green, and See-Through Purple finishes introduced.

Gravity 4 Standard - similar to Gravity 4, except has basswood body, 2 volume/1 tone control, available in Black, Metallic Blue, Silver and Tobacco Sunburst finish. Mfg. 2000 only.

$560 $495 $450 $395 $350 $295 $250
Last MSR was $749.

Add $20 for Flame top (Model Gravity 4 Standard GF), available in See through Black Burst, Blue Burst and Red Burst finishes. Mfg. 2000 only.

Add $50 for Quilt top (Model Gravity 4 Standard GQ), available in Ocean Burst, Lava Burst and Purple Burst finishes. Mfg. 2000 only.

Gravity 5 (APB-5) - similar to the APB-4, except has 5-string configuration, 3/2-per-side tuners, 2 active J-style pickups, available in Black, Emerald Green, See-Through Purple, and Vintage Natural finishes. Disc. 1999.

$950 $800 $700 $625 $525 $450 $350
Last MSR was $1,349.

Gravity 5M (APB-5M) - similar to APB-5, except has maple fingerboard, available in Oil Natural finish. Disc. 2000.

$950 $800 $700 $625 $525 $450 $350
Last MSR was $1,349.

In 2000, Black, Emerald Green and See-Through Purple finishes were introduced.

GRADING	100% MINT	98% NEAR MINT	95% EXC+	90% EXC	80% VG+	70% VG	60% G

Gravity 6 (APB-6) - similar to the APB-5, except has 6-string configuration, 3-per-side tuners, 2 J-style passive pickups, available in Black, Emerald Green, See Through Purple, and Vintage Natural finishes. Disc. 2000.

$1,125 $995 $875 $750 $650 $525 $400
Last MSR was $1,599.

In 1999, Emerald Green and Vintage Natural finishes were discontinued.
In 2000, See Through Blue finish was introduced.

Gravity 8 (APB-8) - similar to the APB-4, except has 8-string configuration (4 pairs of strings), 4-per-side tuners, Schaller bridge, active P/J-style pickups, available in Black finish. Disc. 2000.

$1,100 $925 $825 $725 $600 $500 $395
Last MSR was $1,549.

APB-80 - offset double cutaway ash body, bolt-on maple neck, 24-fret rosewood fingerboard with pearl dot inlay, fixed bridge, 2-per-side tuners, gold hardware, P/J-style pickups, 2 volume/tone control, available in Black, Fire Red, Metallic Blue and Snow White finishes. Disc. 1993.

$450 $375 $350 $275 $250 $215 $175
Last MSR was $700.

APB-90 - similar to APB-80, except has active pickups, volume/treble/bass/mix controls, available in Transparent Black, Transparent Blue, Transparent Purple, Transparent Red, Transparent White, Tobacco Sunburst, and Vintage Natural finishes. Disc. 1996.

$625 $525 $475 $415 $350 $300 $250
Last MSR was $959.

This model has an optional fretless fingerboard.
This model also available with maple fingerboard with black dot inlay, 2 J-style pickups (Model APB-90M).

APB-100 - similar to APB-80, except has 5-string configuration, 3/2-per-side tuners, 2 active J-style pickups, available in Transparent Black, Transparent Purple, Transparent White, Tobacco Sunburst, and Vintage Natural finishes. Disc. 1996.

$685 $575 $525 $465 $400 $350 $300
Last MSR was $1,049.

This model has an optional fretless fingerboard.

HB-65 - basswood body, bolt-on maple neck, 24-fret rosewood fingerboard with dot inlay, fixed bridge, 2-per-side tuners, humbucker pickup, volume/tone controls, available in Black and 3-Tone sunburst finishes. Disc. 1996.

$495 $450 $395 $350 $300 $250 $200
Last MSR was $799.

J4-C - offset double cutaway basswood body, bolt-on maple neck, 34" scale, 20-fret rosewood fingerboard with dot inlay, fixed bridge, 4-on-a-side tuners, chrome hardware, white pickguard, 2 J-style passive pickups, 2 volume/tone controls, available in Black, Cream White, Red, and 3-Tone Sunburst. Disc. 1998.

$300 $250 $225 $200 $175 $135 $100
Last MSR was $399.

LEB Series

LEB-J4 - offset double cutaway alder body, bolt-on maple neck, 34" scale, 20-fret rosewood fingerboard with dot inlay, fixed bridge, 4-on-a-side tuners, chrome hardware, white pickguard, 2 J-style passive pickups, 2 volume/tone controls, available in Black, Cream White, Candy Apple Red, Vintage Metallic Blue, and 3-Tone Sunburst. Disc. 1998.

$350 $325 $275 $250 $200 $150 $125
Last MSR was $479.

LEB-J5 - similar to J4-C, except features a 5-string configuration, 4/1 per side tuners, available in Black, Cream White, Candy Apple Red, Vintage Metallic Blue, and 3-Tone Sunburst. Disc. 1998.

$650 $595 $475 $375 $250 $195 $150
Last MSR was $999.

LEB-P4 - offset double cutaway alder body, bolt-on maple neck, 34" scale, 20-fret rosewood fingerboard with dot inlay, fixed bridge, 4-on-a-side tuners, chrome hardware, white pickguard, passive P-style pickups, volume/tone controls, available in Black, Cream White, Candy Apple Red, Vintage Metallic Blue, and 3-Tone Sunburst. Disc. 1998.

$350 $325 $275 $250 $200 $150 $125
Last MSR was $479.

LSB-65 - single cutaway basswood body, bolt-on maple neck, 24-fret rosewood fingerboard with dot inlay, fixed bridge, 2-per-side tuners, humbucker pickup, volume/tone controls, available in Black and 3-Tone sunburst finishes. Disc. 1996.

$425 $375 $350 $300 $250 $225 $175
Last MSR was $699.

NOMAD BASS (PIEZO BASS TRAVEL GUITAR) - "standing elephant"-shaped basswood body, bolt-on maple neck, 25 1/2" scale, 20-fret rosewood fingerboard with dot inlay, rosewood bridge, 4-on-a-side tuners, chrome hardware, Shadow piezo bridge pickup, built-in 4" speaker, volume control, LED light, on/off switch, available in Black, Candy Apple Red, Metallic Blue, and 3-Tone Sunburst. Current Mfg.

MSR $499 $375 $325 $275 $250 $195 $150 $95

The built-in 10 watt amplifier is powered by a 9-volt battery.

GRADING	100% MINT	98% NEAR MINT	95% EXC+	90% EXC	80% VG+	70% VG	60% G

P4-C - offset double cutaway basswood body, bolt-on maple neck, 34" scale, 20-fret rosewood fingerboard with dot inlay, fixed bridge, 4-on-a-side tuners, chrome hardware, white pickguard, passive P-style pickups, volume/tone controls, available in Black, Cream White, Red, and 3-Tone Sunburst. Disc. 1998.

	$300	**$250**	**$225**	**$200**	**$175**	**$135**	**$100**

Last MSR was $399.

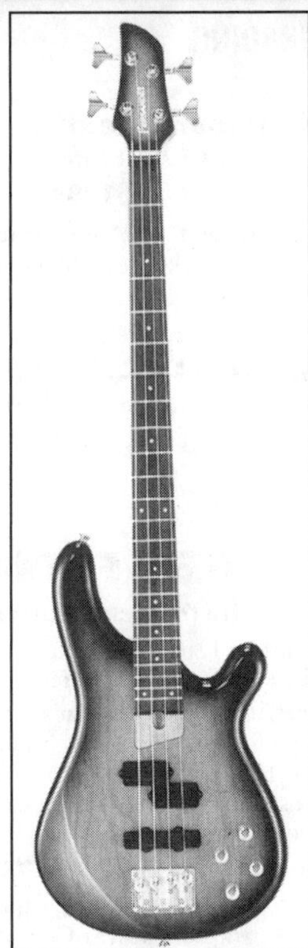

Fernandes APB-90 courtesy Fernandes Guitars

Retrospect Series

RETROSPECT 4 STANDARD - offset double cutaway alder body, bolt-on maple neck, 34" scale, 22-fret rosewood fingerboard with dot inlay, fixed bridge, 4-on-a-side tuners, chrome hardware, white pearloid pickguard, 2 J-style single coil pickups, 2 volume/1 tone controls, series/parallel switch, available in Black, Vintage Metallic Blue, and 3-Tone Sunburst finishes. Disc. 2000.

	$395	**$350**	**$300**	**$275**	**$250**	**$195**	**$150**

Last MSR was $549.

Retrospect 4X - similar to Retrospect 4 Standard, except has passive P-style split-coil pickup mounted mid-body, available in Black, Dark Blue and red finishes. Disc. 2000.

	$299	**$250**	**$199**	**$150**	**$125**	**$95**	**$65**

Last MSR was $399.

Retrospect 5 Standard - similar to Retrospect 4 Standard, except features a 5-string configuration, 4/1 per side tuners, available in Black, Vintage Metallic Blue, and 3-Tone Sunburst finishes. Disc. 2000.

	$565	**$450**	**$395**	**$325**	**$275**	**$225**	**$175**

Last MSR was $749.

In 1999, black finish was discontinued.

RETROSPECT 4 DELUXE - similar to Retrospect 4 Standard, except features a basswood body, flame maple gravure top, 2 passive J-style pickups, Gotoh tuners, mint green pickguard, volume/bass/treble/blend controls, active preamp, available in 3-Tone Sunburst finish with antique finish on neck. Disc. 2000.

	$775	**$675**	**$595**	**$525**	**$425**	**$350**	**$275**

Last MSR was $1,099.

In 1999, 3-Tone Sunburst finish was discontinued.
In 2000, Red Burst and Tobacco Sunburst finishes were introduced.

Retrospect 5 Deluxe - similar to Retrospect 4 Deluxe, except features a 5-string configuration, 4/1 per side tuners, available in 3-Tone Sunburst finish with antique finish on neck. Disc. 2000.

	$895	**$750**	**$675**	**$575**	**$495**	**$400**	**$325**

Last MSR was $1,249.

In 1999, 3-Tone Sunburst finish was discontinued.
In 2000, Red Burst and Tobacco Sunburst finishes were introduced.

TEB-1 - single cutaway basswood body, black pickguard, bolt-on maple neck, 21-fret rosewood or maple fingerboard with dot inlay, fixed bridge, 4-on-one-side tuners, gold hardware, P/J-style pickups, 2 volume/tone controls, available in Black and Cream White finishes. Mfg. 1993 to 1996.

	$500	**$425**	**$375**	**$325**	**$295**	**$250**	**$200**

Last MSR was $779.

Tremor Series

TREMOR 4 - offset double cutaway alder body with rounded cutaway in lower bout, bolt-on maple neck, 34" scale, 24-fret rosewood fingerboard with dot inlay, fixed bridge, 2-per-side tuners, chrome hardware, P/J-style pickups, 2 volume/1 tone controls, series/parallel switch, available in Black, Dark Green Metallic, and Metallic Blue finishes. Mfg. 1998 to 1999.

	$395	**$325**	**$295**	**$250**	**$225**	**$175**	**$150**

Last MSR was $549.

Tremor 4 Standard - similar to Tremor 4, except has black tuners, black traditional bridge, available in Metallic Black, Dark Green Metallic and Metallic Blue finishes. New Specs for 2000.

MSR	**$469**	**$350**	**$325**	**$275**	**$225**	**$195**	**$175**	**$150**

Tremor 4X - similar to Tremor 4 Standard, except has passive P-style pickup mounted mid body, chrome tuners, chrome traditional bridge, available in Black, Dark Blue and red finishes. New 2000.

MSR	**$339**	**$250**	**$225**	**$195**	**$175**	**$150**	**$125**	**$95**

Tremor 4 Deluxe - similar to Tremor 4 Standard, except has bass wood body, 2 Active FGI Technology Soapbar pickups, volume, bass, treble and blend controls, black Gotoh bridge, available in Metallic Black and Dark Red Metallic finishes. Current Mfg.

MSR	**$1,149**	**$899**	**$799**	**$699**	**$650**	**$599**	**$550**	**$450**

Tremor 5 Standard - similar to Tremor 4 Standard except in a 5-string configuration, available in Metallic Black and Dark Green Metallic finishes. New Spec for 2000.

MSR	**$549**	**$410**	**$375**	**$325**	**$275**	**$225**	**$175**	**$125**

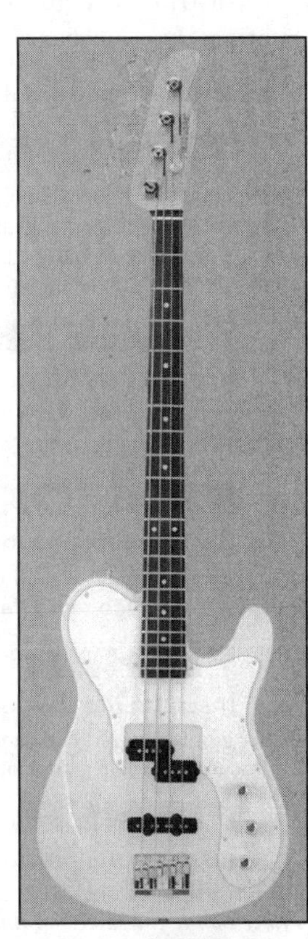

Fernandes TEB-1 courtesy Fernandes Guitars

GRADING		100% MINT	98% NEAR MINT	95% EXC+	90% EXC	80% VG+	70% VG	60% G

Tremor 5 Deluxe - similar to Tremor 4 deluxe, exccept in a 5-string configuration, available in Metallic Black and Dark Metallic Red finishes. Current Mfg.

MSR	$1,199	$899	$750	$650	$550	$450	$350	$295

Tremor 5 - similar to Tremor 4, except features a 5-string configuration, 3/2-per-side tuners, 2 J-style single coil pickups, available in Black and Dark Green Metallic finishes. Mfg. 1998 to 1999.

		$595	$500	$450	$395	$325	$275	$225

Last MSR was $849.

VERTIGO BASS - original ("art deco coffee table") style alder body, bolt-on maple neck, 34" scale, 22-fret rosewood fingerboard with dot inlay, fixed bridge, 2-per-side tuners, chrome hardware, upside down 'U' white pickguard, 2 J-style pickups, 2 volume/1 tone controls, available in Black and Three Tone Sunburst finishes. Mfg. 1998 to 1999.

		$395	$325	$275	$250	$200	$165	$125

Last MSR was $549.

F

FERRINGTON, DANNY

Instruments currently built in Santa Monica, California since 1980.

Luthier Danny Ferrington was born and raised in Louisiana. Ferrington's father, Lloyd, was a cabinet maker who had previously played guitar and bass in a local country western combo. Ferrington's first experiences with woodworking were in his father's shop in Monroe, Louisiana.

Ferrington accepted an apprenticeship in 1975 at the Old Time Pickin' Parlour in Nashville, Tennessee. He spent the next five years working with noted acoustic guitar builder Randy Woods. Ferrington's first acoustic was built in 1977, and he continued to hone his craft.

In 1980, Ferrington moved to Los Angeles, California. Ferrington spent a number of years experimenting with different designs, and tones from instruments, and continued building custom guitars. Many of the features on the custom guitars are developed through discussions with the musician commissioning the piece. It is estimated that by 1992, Ferrington had constructed over one hundred custom instruments.

(Source: Kate Geil, et al, the Ferrington Guitars book)

In the late 1980s, the Kramer guitar company was offering several models designed by Ferrington. After Kramer went under, the Ferrington Guitar Company of Long Branch, New Jersey (phone number was previously listed at 908.870.3800) offered essentially the same models (KFS-1, KFT-1, and KFB-1) with *Ferrington* on the headstock. These models featured a maple neck, rosewood fingerboard, acoustic body, 3-band EQ, and a thinline bridge transducer.

FIBRATONE

See FENTON-WEILL.

These semi-hollow body guitars were built of fiberglass, and produced by the Fenton-Weill company of England in the 1960s.

FICHTER

Instruments currently built in Germany since 1988.

Fichter has been building modern electric upright basses for over twelve years. The Fichter electric upright bass is minimally larger than an electric bass guitar, and can easily fit in the back seat of a mid-sized car.

Fichter estimates that his annual production is now at about fifty instruments a year.

ELECTRIC BASS

Weighing in at around 13 pounds, Fichter's electric bass is constructed of maple and mahogany, and has a 41" contrabass scale. The model features an ebony fingerboard, active preamp and coaxial or magnetic pickup system, and custom Schaller tuners. 4- and 5-string configurations (strung with either high C or low B) are available. A deluxe custom-made bag comes with every bass. Check the Fichter website at http://www.fichterbasses.com for current prices in U.S. dollars (prices are computed in German Marks and vary with the exchange rate).

FINGERBONE

Instruments previously built in England from 1986 to 1989.

The 'Fastback' model was a high quality solid body guitar with an original design and different hardware options.

(Source: Tony Bacon and Paul Day, The Guru's Guitar Guide)

FIREFOX

Instruments previously built in Japan since late 1980s.

These medium quality solid body guitars were based on American designs, and produced in either full size or "mini" versions.

(Source: Tony Bacon and Paul Day, the Guru's Guitar Guide)

FISHER

Instruments previously built in Coalport, Pennsylvania in the early 1990s.

Fisher guitars offered two models of solid body electric guitars that featured American components (hardware and pickups). Further research is pending on this independent guitar building company.

FISHER, ROGER

Instruments previously built in Bellevue, Washington during the late 1980s.

Guitarist Roger Fisher was part of the original line-up in the rock group *Heart*. Fisher left Heart in October, 1979; soon after he founded the *Roger Fisher Band*, and later *Ten Bulls*. In the late 1980s, Fisher became a guitar designer/manufacturer. Known for upgrading and re-working his guitars as early as his Heart playing days, Fisher's Trout guitar featured a variety of non-standard features. The Fisher Trout model's double cutaway custom-shaped body featured an on-board speaker and amp that also doubled as a sustain/feedback device, a 7-band graphic EQ, a headphone output that also doubled as a line-out to mixers or monitor system, a piezo bridge pickup and magnetic pickups, fiber optic position markers, and an asymmetrical neck shaping.

It is estimated that a number of these custom guitars are still in the hands of their original owners, as they rarely show up in the secondary market. The original retail price is still unknown as of this edition.

Fichter Kontrabasse
courtesy Thomas Fichter

FITZPATRICK JAZZ GUITARS

Instruments currently built in Wickford, Rhode Island.

Luthier Charles Fitzpatrick builds acoustic, acoustic-electric, and semi-hollow body electric archtop guitars in 15", 16", 17", and 18" body widths. The **Jazz Box Select** features single cutaway body consisting of fancy quilted or flamed maple with matching rim and neck, solid carved top of North American spruce, fine line black and white body binding, mother-of-pearl block fingerboard inlays, gold tune-o-matic tailpiece, bound tortoiseshell finger rest, and a suspended jazz pickup. List prices range from $3,270 (16"), $3,800 (17"), to $4,500 (18"). The list price includes a hardshell case, and Fitzpatrick offers a range of options and custom inlays.

FIVE STAR

See chapter on House Brands.

While this trademark has been identified as a *House Brand*, the retailer or distributor has not yet been identified. These smaller bodied acoustics have the logo and star position markers painted on, as opposed to the inlay work of a more expensive guitar.

(Source: Willie G. Moseley, Stellas & Stratocasters)

FLEISHMAN

Instruments currently built in Boulder, Colorado.

Luthier Harry Fleishman has been designing and building high quality guitars and basses since 1975. In addition to the electric solid body models that Fleishman is known for, he also builds a small number of acoustic guitars on a yearly basis. Fleishman is also a current columnist for the Guild of American Luthiers newsletter.

Fleishman designed the Flash model for Hondo during the 1980s, a minimalist body reverse-tuned bass with a number of innovative design features.

ELECTRIC BASS

Fleishman currently offers a new upright electric bass model, which is available in 4-, 5-, and 6-string configuration. The 35" (or 42") scale instrument features a neck and body of curly maple, an aged ebony fingerboard, and a combination of electronics to produce a "clear, woody tone". Other models include the **Anti- Gravity Bass**, a hollow body bass with floating tone board; the 4-, 5-, and 6-string **Scroll Bass** with hand carved scroll headstock and ebony fingerboard; and the headless **Jayne** bass, which features an exotic wood body. For more information regarding pricing and model specifications, please contact luthier Fleishman directly (see Trademark Index).

FOCUS

See KRAMER.

Instruments previously built in Japan circa mid to late 1980s.

The Focus series of guitars were built overseas in the ESP factory for Kramer in the mid to late 1980s to supplement the higher end American models. The Kramer company could then offer a wider price range of models to consumers, and still maintain design and quality control over their product.

FODERA

Instruments currently built in Brooklyn, New York since 1983.

Luthiers Vinnie Fodera and Joseph Lauricella founded Fodera Guitars in 1983. Fodera, who had previously worked with Stuart Spector and Ned Steinberger in the late 1970s, focused directly on bass building. Bassists such as Anthony Jackson, Victor Wooten, Lincoln Goines, and Matthew Garrison all swear by their Fodera basses. All Fodera models feature select aged woods and water-based lacquer finishes (a penetrating oil finish is available on request).

New to the Fodera company is the *Diamond Series Bass Strings*, hand wound at the Fodera workshop. Fodera stainless steel and nickel round wound strings are available in 4-, 5-, and 6-string sets in Light to Heavy sizes. "You will Hear and Feel the Difference!"

ELECTRIC BASS

Fodera models are offered in three different construction designs: **Bolt-On** (the neck is bolted on), **Deluxe** (set-in neck), and **Elite** (through-body neck).

Fodera basses are offered with a number of pickup options, as well as custom inlay (call for pricing). All retail prices include a hard case.

Add 15% for left-handed configuration.

Add $250 for fretless fingerboard with inlaid lines.

Add $250 for 5-piece laminated neck.

Add $250 for High Gloss custom color.

Add $300 for maple fingerboard.

Fodera Emperor Bolt-On
5-String
courtesy Fodera Guitars

Add $500 for AAA grade top.

The **Anthony Jackson Contrabass**, designed in conjunction with bassist supreme Anthony Jackson, has a single cutaway alder body, AAA top, 24-fret rosewood fingerboard, 6-string configuration, 3-per-side tuners, Bartolini or Lane Poor pickups (call for retail list price).

Emperor Series

EMPEROR 4-STRING - offset double cutaway alder (or ash or mahogany) body, flamed (or quilted) maple top, 3-piece neck, 34" scale, 21-fret ebony (or rosewood) fingerboard with dot inlay, solid brass nut, 2-per-side tuners, Fodera bridge, Bartolini (or EMG or Lane Poor) pickups, volume/tone controls, Fodera circuitry, available in hand-rubbed clear satin finish. Current Mfg.

Bolt-On

MSR $3,295

Deluxe

MSR $3,465

Elite

MSR $3,905

F

Emperor 5-String - similar to the Emperor 4-String, except has 35" scale, 5-string configuration, 3/2-per-side tuners. Current Mfg.

Bolt-On

MSR $3,995

Deluxe

MSR $4,395

Elite

MSR $4,653

Imperial Series

Imperial Series basses are similar in design to the **Anthony Jackson** contrabass. Imperial models are only available in the **Elite** through-body neck configuration.

IMPERIAL 5-STRING ELITE - single cutaway alder (or ash or mahogany) body, flamed (or quilted) maple top, through-body 3-piece neck, 35" scale, 21-fret ebony (or rosewood) fingerboard with dot inlay, solid brass nut, 2-per-side tuners, Fodera bridge, Bartolini (or EMG or Lane Poor) pickups, volume/tone controls, Fodera circuitry, available in Hand rubbed clear satin finish. Current Mfg.

MSR $5,054

Imperial 6-String Elite - similar to the Imperial 5-String Elite, except has 36" scale, 6-string configuration, 3-per-side tuners. Current Mfg.

MSR $5,494

Monarch Series

Monarch Series basses are similar to the Emperor body design, except have a sleeker profile and slightly further extended horns.

MONARCH 4-STRING - sleek offset double cutaway alder (or ash or mahogany) body, flamed (or quilted) maple top, 3-piece neck, 34" scale, 21-fret ebony (or rosewood) fingerboard with dot inlay, solid brass nut, 2-per-side tuners, Fodera bridge, Bartolini (or EMG or Lane Poor) pickups, volume/tone controls, Fodera circuitry, available in Hand rubbed clear satin finish. Current Mfg.

Deluxe

MSR $3,465

Elite

MSR $3,905

Monarch 5-String - similar to the Monarch 4-String, except has 35" scale, 5-string configuration, 3/2-per-side tuners. Current Mfg.

Deluxe

MSR $4,395

Elite

MSR $4,653

FOSTER

Instruments currently built in Covington, Louisiana.

Luthier Jimmy Foster offers repair and restoration work in addition to his current guitar designs, and has been working in the New Orleans area for over twenty five years. In addition to his standard models (listed below), Foster also offers custom orders available with choice of woods, inlays, and trim. For further information, contact luthier Foster directly (see Trademark Index).

ELECTRIC

AT Archtop Series

Foster's **AT1** features a carved spruce top, carved mahogany back, body binding, 25.5" scale, ebony fingerboard/neck/pickguard, and has an Armstrong humbucking pickup with coil tap capabilities in the neck position. The AT1 is not available in a Natural finish (list $3,450).

The **AT3** features similar construction, except has a carved AA curly maple back, bound ebony fingerboard, ebony headstock overlay, beveled f-holes, and a volume control. The AT3 (list $4,500) is also not available in a Natural finish.

The top-of-the-line **AT5** (list $5,800) has a carved AAA spruce top, carved AAA curly maple back, multi-ply body binding, multi-layer bound ebony headstock overlay/fingerboard/pickguard, bound f-holes, ebony tailpiece, and abalone headstock inlay. A Natural finish is optional for $200; quilted maple back and sides, $350.

Foster AT-S
courtesy Jimmy Foster

Solid Body T Series

The **T Series** models all feature basswood bodies, maple necks, ebony fingerboards, Armstrong humbucking pickup with split coil wiring, 25.5" scale, and volume and tone controls. The **T 1** lists for $1,750. The **T 3** has a bound curly maple top (list $1,950); and the **T 5** has a bound highly figured maple top (list $2,250).

FRAMUS

Instruments currently produced in Markneukirchen, Germany. Distributed by Warwick GmbH & Co. Music Equipment Kg of Markneukirchen, Germany.

Instruments were previously produced in Germany from the late 1940s through the mid 1970s.

In 1996, the trademark was re-introduced in Europe (no U.S. distributors listed to date).

When Frederick Wilfer returned to his home town of Walthersgrun at the end of World War II, he realized that the American-controlled Sudetenland area was soon to fall under control of the Russian forces. With the help of the Americans, Wilfer succeeded in resettling a number of violin makers from Schonbach to Franconia (later in the district of Erlangen). Between 1945 to 1947, Wilfer continued to find homes and employment for the Schonbach violin makers.

In 1946, Wilfer founded the Framus production company, the company name an acronym for Franconian Musical instruments. As the company established itself in 1946, Wilfer drew on the knowledge of his violin builder from Schonbach to produce a range of musical instruments including violins and cellos. The new Framus company expanded out of its first couple of production buildings, eventually building a new factory in Bubenreuth in 1955.

The first Framus electric guitars appeared in the 1950s. Due to the presence of American servicemen stationed there, the influence of rock'n roll surfaced earlier in Germany than other European countries. As a result, German guitar builders had a headstart on answering the demand caused by the proliferation of pop groups during the 1960s. Furthermore, as the German production increased, they began exporting their guitars to other countries (including the U.S.). The Framus company stayed active in producing acoustic and electric guitars, and electric basses until the mid 1970s.

In the 1970s, increased competition and serious price undercutting from firms in the Asian market had a serious effect on established companies. Unfortunately, one aspect was to force a number of firms into bankruptcy - and Framus was one of those companies in 1975. However, Wilfer did have the opportunity to watch his son, Hans-Peter Wilfer, establish his own company in 1982 (see WARWICK). Warwick's success allowed Hans-Peter to re-introduce the Framus trademark to the European musical market in 1996. In honor of his father Frederick, Hans-Peter chose to use the world famous Framus trademark when he began offering guitar models in 1996.

(Source: Hans Peter Wilfer, Warwick GmbH & Co. Music Equipment Kg; and Tony Bacon and Paul Day, The Guru's Guitar Guide)

Current Framus instruments (including the electric guitars, Classic and Folk acoustics, and hand wired tube guitar amps) are produced at the Warwick facility. Currently, Framus instruments are available in England, Germany, Sweden, and Switzerland; worldwide distribution is in the planning stages.

Framus Serialization

In order to properly date the year of issue, most Framus guitars had a separate pair of digits after the main serial number. If the separate pair is present, the two numbers will indicate the year.

ELECTRIC

While the original **Hollywood** series was Gibson-influenced, the later **Strato** series of guitars were strikingly Fender-ish. However, the company did pioneer their own designs such as the **Big 6** double neck model, the **Melodie** 9-string guitar, and the **Billy Lorento** signature model (see BILL LAWRENCE). Research still continues on early Framus models for upcoming editions of the ***Blue Book of Electric Guitars***.

Current high quality solid body Framus models include the single cutaway arched top **Panthera** and double cutaway **Diablo** models. Both models feature the easily recognizable Framus headstock and 3-per-side tuners, good quality woods, pickups, and hardware. For further information regarding the Framus line of instruments, please contact the Framus company directly (see Trademark Index).

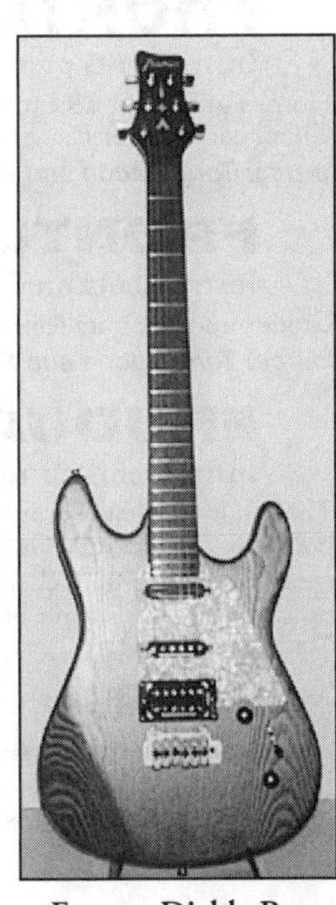

Framus Diable Pro
courtesy
Thomas Bauer

FRANCONIA

Instruments previously built in Japan between 1980 and 1985.

The FRANCONIA trademark was a brand name used by a UK importer. The guitars were generally entry level to mid quality copies of American designs.

(Source: Tony Bacon and Paul Day, The Guru's Guitar Guide)

FREDDY'S FRETS

Instruments currently built in Welland (Ontario), Canada.

Luthier Freddy Gabrsek is currently offfering a number of hand-crafted acoustic and electric guitar models. The Gabrsek Jumbo Steel String is a concert quality acoustic guitar made from the finest materials. (Priced from $2,700).

Electric guitars include the Deluxe Model (List $2,450) featuring mahogany set neck, mahogany body, spectacularly figured maple top with the highest quality hardware. The Standard Model (list $1,950) features a Swamp Ash or alder body with a bolt-on quartered maple neck. For further information regarding specifications and complete pricing, contact Freddy's Frets directly (see Trademark Index).

FRENZ

Instruments currently built in Columbus, Ohio.

Frenz presently builds two hand crafted models, the **Rapier CT 26** and the **Ultimate Custom.** Frenz works directly with the customer specifying the guitar model to insure the proper custom built guitar.

ELECTRIC

The **Rapier CT 26** (list 2,200) is a radical Strat-shaped model with either a mahogany or padauk carved top body, set-in maple neck, 26-fret rosewood fingerboard, and single coil/humbucker pickups. Frenz also offers the custom-built **Ultimate Custom**, which allows the customer choice of scale length, number of frets (up to 40), and any combination of suitable materials. "Your Design or Ours" is Frenz' motto (price quote is based on factors such as design, materials, and hardware).

ELECTRIC BASS

The **Morpheus** bass features a neck-through construction, 34" (or 35" or 36") scale, 2- to 12-string configurations, and choice of woods and electronics. Headless models are offered in 4-, 5-, and 6-string configurations. For further information regarding pricing and specifications, please contact Frenz directly (see Trademark Index).

FRESHER

Instruments previously produced in Japan from the late 1970s to the early 1980s.

Fresher solid body and semi-hollow body guitars were generally medium quality copies of American designs. However, viewing the "Fresher" logo on a strat-style guitar from a distance will make you check your eyesight - and finding a Fresher "Straighter" with built-in effects will make you check your blood pressure!

(Source: Michael Wright, Guitar Stories Volume One)

FRESHMAN

Instruments previously built in Japan in the mid 1960s.

As an inexpensive, entry level guitar, the Freshman trademark is quite apt: a Senior, it isn't. In fact, it's not even close to a Sophomore.

(Source: Tony Bacon and Paul Day, The Guru's Guitar Guide)

FRITZ BROTHERS

Instruments previouslly built in Mobile, Alabama circa 1988.

Luthier Roger Fritz met Marc Fisher in Nashville in 1987. Together with guitarist Roy Buchanan they formed Fritz Brothers guitars, which was relocated to Alabama a year later. During 1988, the Fritz Brothers began building the **Roy Buchanan Bluesmaster** model; Buchanan died later that year (portion of the sales goes to Buchanan's estate).

(Source: Tom Wheeler, American Guitars)

The last given address for Fritz Brothers was c/o Connie Fritz at 10655 Salt Air Road, Theodore, Alabama 36582.

FRONTIER

Instruments previously produced in Japan during the early 1980s.

Frontier guitars are decent to good quality original designs as well as copies of American designs. The puzzling one is the signature model of Norris Fant. Guitar collectors or Fan club members who wish to enlighten us on Mr. Fant are invited to write to the ***Blue Book of Electric Guitars.***

(Source: Tony Bacon and Paul Day, The Guru's Guitar Guide)

FRONTLINE

Instruments previously produced in Korea in the late 1980s.

Guitars under this trademark are medium quality vaguely Fender-ish solid body designs.

(Source: Tony Bacon and Paul Day, The Guru's Guitar Guide)

FRUDUA GUITAR WORKS

Instruments currently built in Imola, Italy.

The Frudua Guitar Works is currently offering a number of Strat-style electric guitars featuring alder bodies and figured maple tops (and lacewood bodies as well). Frudua Guitar Works models also feature high quality pickups and hardware.

Most Frudua bass models all feature a Jazz Bass-style body, graphite-reinforced wood necks, laminated maple/purpleheart necks or hard rock maple necks, and figured maple or spruce tops. For further information regarding specifications and pricing, contact the Frudua Guitar Works directly (see Trademark Index).

FRYE

Instruments currently built in Green Bay, Wisconsin since 1987.

Luthier/repairman Ben Frye has been repairing guitars in the Green Bay area for almost 12 years, and building custom guitars for the past 10 years. Frye estimates that he has built a total of 700 guitars to date (100 built in the last year), and looks forward to a higher production amount this year.

Frye guitars are constructed at The String Instrument Workshop, a shop Ben shares with his father. Lawrence Frye, a repairman and luthier for the past 25 years, was the former teacher at Redwing College's Violin and Guitar Making course between 1974 to 1980. The Workshop, a former bar restored to its turn-of-the-century appearance in Green Bay's downtown area, is the central area to the Fryes' stringed instrument repair.

ELECTRIC

Ben Frye recently attended the Redwing College Guitar course in 1994, but grew up learning and experimenting under his father's supervision. Frye's guitar models feature bolt-on neck construction, Red Rhodes' Velvet Hammer or Lindy Fralin pickups, different electronic packages and hardware, and other customer specified options. Frye turns the necks, and carves and routs out the guitar bodies with templates and power tools instead of using CNC machines.

The **El Pique** (base retail $1,300) is a double cutaway, strat-style solid body with a 25 1/2" scale. A single cutaway model, named the **Over Easy** (list $1,200 and up) is closer to a Tele-influenced model. The Over Easy is also offered with a carved maple top as the **Extra Crispy** model (list $1,800 and up), or as the **Scully** hollowbody (list $1,200). The Scully (named after the first person who ordered one, not the *X-Files* character) is fully hollow, with a solid back/sides and carved out top. Scully models feature a single f-hole, and are constructed of solid spruce, redwood, or cedar. The **Epiphany** (list $1,700) is a wide/thin (2" body depth) electric/acoustic model with a "No Tension Top", and offset soundhole. The **Epiphany** model has a bound top, 3-per-side tuners, and Fishman Matrix pickup.

Frye also offers a double cutaway solid body named the **Top Tone**, that features a 24 3/4" scale and a 3-per-side headstock design starting at $1,200. The Top Tone body shape is reminiscent of a LP Junior or a Rickenbacker. The **Top Tone Ultra** (list $1,900) has a birds-eye maple neck, ebony fingerboard, wood binding, abalone inlay, and exotic wood top.

Any guitar model can be converted to a 30" scale Baritone for an additional $250. Frye also offers his models with hollowed out *tone chambers* which accentuate acoustic properties (dubbed **Fat Free**) for an extra $100.

ELECTRIC BASS

Frye is also offering a bolt-on bass model in 4- or 5-string configurations, as well as a set neck version in 4-, 5-, and 6-string models. The **Big Ben** bass has a smaller, balanced offset waist and extended bass horn. Models range in price from $1,400 to $1,500 (bolt-on), and $1,600 to $2,000 for the set neck models. The options range from wood and pickup types, as well as others.

FURY

Instruments currently built in Saskatoon (Saskatchewan), Canada since 1962.

Luthier Glenn McDougal was born in Wadena (Saskatchewan), Canada on February 13, 1937. He developed his techno-mechanical mind growing up on the family farm. In the mid-to-late 50's McDougal played guitar in a rock and roll band called **Blue Cadillac** which toured throughout Canada and the United States. In 1958, a car accident ended McDougal's career as a player and he turned to guitar design. He married his wife Janet in 1960, and moved to Saskatoon where they live today.

The Fury Guitar Company was founded in 1962. The purpose of the new company was to expand upon the design of specific key components that would improve both sound and performance. The objective was to create a distinctive character that would set the Fury line apart from other makes, yet stay within the boundaries of traditional guitar design. During 1962, McDougal launched the **Fireball**, the first model of his new company. Throughout the history of the company, numerous cutting edge inventions emerged, and continue today, helping to make Fury instruments unique. The decision was made early on to keep the company small, so quality could always be assured. The company is still fully owned and operated by Glenn and Janet McDougall.

Now in its 39th year of operation, Fury is Canada's oldest electric guitar manufacturer, and continues to design and develop instruments with advanced features, making their products desirable to serious players. Fury Guitars introduced solid body 6-string and 12-string guitars, as well as doubleneck models, semi-hollow bodies, and electric bass throughout the 1960s. A new factory was built in the mid 1970s, and the company experienced a major breakthrough in the early 1980s with the development of their ZP pickup.

In 1998, Fury Guitars made their first U.S. show "debut" at the January NAMM industry show. In addition to their new Tornado Bass, McDougall also showcased his limited edition 35th Anniversary Fireball guitar model.

Currently, Fury makes 4 models of 6-strings, a 12-string, baritone and a bass with an optional drop D bridge.

Since 1962 McDougal has built over 6,000 guitars and basses. 8 models are still in production, and now Fury has introduced the Tornado Bass as well. All of these high quality Fury guitars are still produced in Saskatoon, Canada.

Fury pickups are available for players looking to upgrade their sound. Humbucking models include the 50's Rocker, ZP-8, ZP-9, and ZP-20; all models are priced at $130 each. A BBM 3 pickup kit is also available (list $275).

(Source: Sanford Greve, Fury Historian, and Stan Garchinski, Fury Guitars)

ELECTRIC

All Fury list prices include a deluxe hardshell case.

Add $65 for a colored neck.

Add $65 for a colored headstock.

Add $75 for a metallic pickguard.

Add $100 for a Transparent or Natural Blonde finish.

Add $125 for a moderately flamed maple body.

Add $250 for a highly flamed maple body.

Add $325 for 24kt triple plated gold hardware.

20TH CENTURY ARTIST - double cutaway hollowbody 6-string, Honduras mahogany back and sides carved from one solid piece, maple back with tuned reflex chamber, 3-piece rock maple neck with rosewood overlay on angled headstock, 2 stylized f-holes, 22-fret Brazilian rosewood fingerboard with small dot markers on the bass side, 23 3/4" scale length, 3-per-side Grover Roto-matic tuners, two angled black Fury piggyback humbucking pickups, Fury vibrato with pop-out lever, black pinline pickguard, master volume/2 tone controls, 3-position toggle switch, available in a wide variety of lacquer finishes, the most popular being Tobacco Sunburst, Cherry Red, Blonde, and White. Mfg. 1968 to 1989.

BANDIT - single rounded cutaway 6-string, solid basswood or Honduras mahogany body, maple neck, 22-fret Brazilian rosewood fingerboard with small dot markers on bass side, 25.064" scale length, 3-per-side Kluson tuners, 2 black Fury single coil pickups, master volume/master tone controls, 3-position toggle switch, available in a wide variety of lacquer finishes. Mfg. 1967 to 1971.

BANDIT REISSUE (2S, 3S, 2H, HSS) - single rounded cutaway body, 6-string, maple body/neck, 22-fret maple or pau ferro fingerboard with small dot markers on bass side, 25.064" scale length, 6-in-a-line grover mini roto-matic tuners, 3 Fury ZP single coil pickups, master volume/tone controls, 3-position level switch, and rim jack, available in a wide variety of lacquer finishes. New 1999.

MSR $1,230 - $1,395, depending on series

BBM Series

BBM Series models are available in 2 or 3 pickup configurations, and with a standard bridge (S) or tremolo (V).

BBM (2S) - offset rounded double cutaway 6-string, solid soft maple body with rock maple center core, rock maple neck, 22-fret maple or pau ferro fingerboard with small dot markers on bass side, 25.064" scale length, 6-in-line Schaller mini-tuners, Fury ZP9 neck and ZP20 bridge humbucking pickups, master volume/master tone controls, 2 coil tap switches, 3-position toggle switch, Fury high-mass bridge/tailpiece or high-mass vibrato, black plexi pickguard with radius edge (early models without back carve or arm carve), available in a wide variety of lacquer finishes. Mfg. 1985-2000.

Price included hard case.

Last MSR was $1,449.

Add $100 for tremelo.

Add $325 for 24 Kt. gold plated hardware.

Add $75 for matching headstock or neck color.

Add $75 for special effect pickguard.

BBM 12 12-String - same as BBM (2S), except features two Fury piggyback humbucking pickups, Fury high-mass 12-string bridge, 6-per-side Schaller mini-tuners. Mfg. 1995 to date.

Price includes hard case.

MSR $1,650

Add $325 for 24 Kt. gold plated hardware.

Add $75 for matching headstock or neck.

BBM (3S) - same as BBM (2S), except has two ZP5S single coil pickups/ZP20 bridge humbucking pickup, 5-position lever switch, coil tap switch, master volume control. New 1985.

MSR $1,550

Add $100 for tremelo.

Add $325 for 24 Kt. gold plated hardware.

Add $75 for matching headstock or neck color.

Add $75 for special effect pickguard.

CONCORD - double cutaway hollowbody 6-string, Honduras mahogany back and sides carved from one solid piece, maple back with tuned reflex chamber, 3-piece maple neck with rosewood overlay on angled headstock, 2 stylized f-holes, 22-fret African ebony fingerboard with small dot markers on bass side, 23 3/4" or 25" scale length, 3-per-side Grover Roto-matic tuners, two angled black Fury piggyback humbucking pickups, black pinline pickguard, 2 volume/2 tone controls, 3-position toggle switch, Fury trapeze tailpiece, available in a wide variety of lacquer finishes, the most popular being Tobacco Sunburst and Blonde. Mfg. 1974 to 1988.

F12 - double rounded cut-a-way 12-string, solid Honduras mahogany body, rock maple neck, 20-fret maple or Brazilian rosewood fingerboard with small dot markers on bass side, 25.064" scale length, 6-per-side Kluson Deluxe tuners, two Fury piggyback humbucking pickups, master volume/master tone controls, 3-position toggle switch, available in a wide variety of lacquer finishes, the most popular being Tobacco Sunburst and Cherry Red. Mfg. 1966 to 1992.

F22 - double cutaway 6-string, solid Honduras mahogany body, maple neck, 22-fret maple or Brazilian rosewood fingerboard with small dot markers on bass side, 25.064" scale length, 3-per-side Kluson Deluxe tuners, 2 black Fury piggyback humbucking pickups (early models had white pickups), 2 volume/1 tone controls, tone bypass switch, 3-position toggle switch, available in a wide variety of lacquer finishes, the most popular being Cherry Red and California Red. Mfg. 1967 to 1981.

Fireball Series

The original Fireball model was built from 1963 to 1966. In 1990, Fury began offering the Fireball Reissue model, based on the original design.

FIREBALL - offset double cutaway Honduras mahogany body, maple neck, 20-fret rosewood fingerboard with pearl block inlays, 25.064" scale length, 6-in-line Kluson tuners, 2 white Fury single coil pickups, black pinline pickguard, volume control on bass side upper bout, 2 tone controls, tone bypass switch, 3-position toggle switch, available in a wide variety of DuPont Duco lacquer finishes. Mfg. 1962 to 1966.

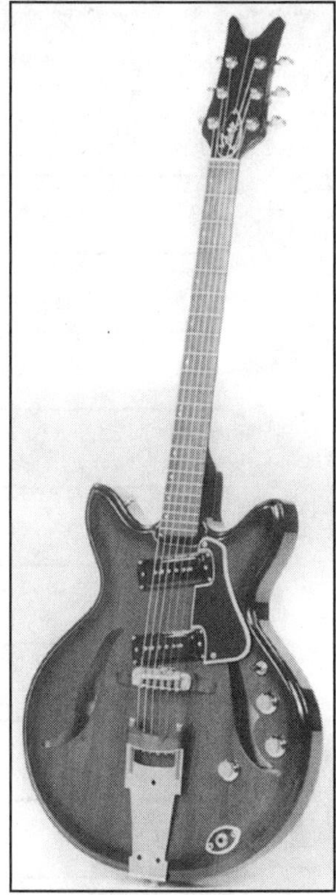

Fury Concord Hollowbody courtesy Fury Guitars

Fireball (S) - offset rounded double cutaway 6-string, solid soft maple body with rock maple center core, rock maple neck, 22-fret maple or pau ferro fingerboard with small dot markers on bass side, 25.064" scale length, 6-in-line Schaller mini-tuners, Fury ZP8 neck and ZP50's Rocker bridge humbucking pickups, master volume control, rim-mount jack, 2 coil tap switches, 3-position toggle switch, no pickguard, Fury high-mass bridge/tailpiece or high-mass vibrato, available in a wide variety of lacquer finishes, the most popular being Tobacco Sunburst, Aztec Gold, and Metallic finishes. Mfg. 1989 to date.

Price includes hard case.

MSR $1,550

Add $100 for tremelo.

Add $325 for 24 Kt. gold plated hardware.

Add $75 for matching headstock or neck color.

Add $75 for special effect pickguard.

Fireball Baritone - offset rounded double cutaway 6-string baritone guitar tuned A to A (a fifth below standard pitch), solid soft maple body with rock maple center core, rock maple neck, 22-fret maple or pau ferro fingerboard with small dot markers on bass side, 29.858" scale length, 4+2 Schaller mini-tuners, Fury ZP8 neck and ZP50's Rocker bridge humbucking pickups, master volume control, 2 coil tap switches, 3-position toggle switch, no pickguard, Fury high-mass bridge/tailpiece, available in a wide variety of lacquer finishes. Mfg. 1991 to date.

MSR $1,550

Price includes hard case.

Add $325 for 24k gold plated hardware.

Add $75 for matching headstock or neck.

ELECTRIC BASS

ANTHEM BASS - double cutaway 4-string bass, soft solid maple body with rock maple center core, 24-fret maple or pau ferro fingerboard, 31.640" scale length, 4-in-line Grover Titan tuners, Fury ZP9B neck and ZP11B bridge humbucking pickups, two volume and one master tone control, 3-position toggle switch, Fury high-mass bridge or Drop-D bridge, available in a wide variety of lacquer finishes. Mfg. 1989 to 1997.

Model has not traded sufficiently to quote pricing.

Last MSR was $1,312.

Add $100 for fretless fingerboard (retail list $1,345).

Add $150 for Drop-D Tuner.

Tornado Bass - same as Anthem Bass, except with deep cutaway on treble side allowing easy access to 24th fret, master volume/master tone controls, 3-position coil tap switch (for single, humbucking, and modified humbucking tones) Fury ZP9B neck pickup, and Fury ZP6B bridge pickup, Hipshot Ultra light tuners and rim-mount jack. Mfg. 1997 to date.

Price includes hard case.

MSR $1,695

Add $100 for Tornado Fretless Bass model with fretless fingerboard.

Add $155 for Drop-D bridge.

Add $325 for 24 Kt. gold plated hardware.

Add $75 for matching headstock or neck.

LS4 BASS - double cutaway with long sharp horns, 4-string fretted or fretless, solid Honduras mahogany body, maple neck, 20-fret maple or Brazilian rosewood fingerboard, ebony or maple fret inlays on fretless model, 31 5/8" scale length, stepped upright-style headstock with 4-in-line Kluson tuners, 1 Fury piggy-back humbucking pickup (later models available with 2 pickups), master volume/master tone controls, available in a wide variety of lacquer finishes, the most popular being Whiskey, White, and Midnight Green. Mfg. 1967 to 1988.

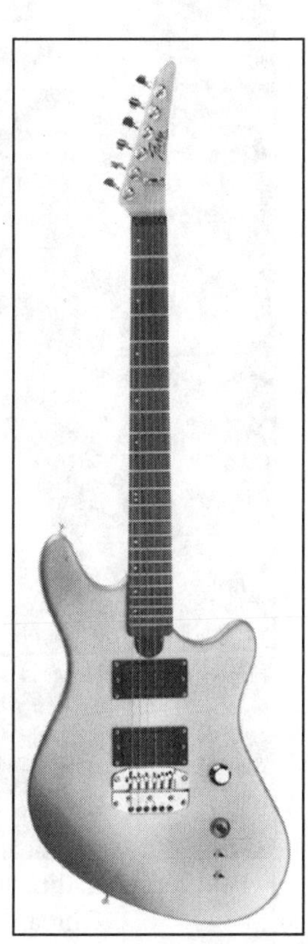

Fury Fireball (Reissue) courtesy Fury Guitars

FUTURAMA

Some guitars may also carry the trademark of GRAZIOSO.

Instruments previosuly built in Czechoslovakia, then Sweden, and finally in Japan between 1958 and 1967.

The FUTURAMA trademark is the brand name of the British importer/distributor Selmer (UK). However, you can also find the GRAZIOSO trademark on some of the real early Czech-built instruments. Production of this line of solid body guitars continued in Eastern Europe until supplanted by some strat-styled models built by HAGSTROM in Sweden. Finally, the Futurama world tour ended on production of small-body model versions built in Japan.

(Source: Tony Bacon, The Ultimate Guitar Book)

NOTES

F

Paul Jernigan, director of marketing for Fender, is shown hamming it up with Daphne Gilman, director of meeting and events, and bass guitar neck.

Section G

GRADING	100% MINT	98% NEAR MINT	95% EXC+	90% EXC	80% VG+	70% VG	60% G

G & L ASAT
1996 Tampa Vintage Show

G

G & L

Instruments currently produced in Fullerton, California since 1980. Distributed by BBE Sound of Huntington Beach, California.

In the late 1970s, the controlling interest at (pre-Ernie Ball) Music Man was making offers to purchase Leo Fender's CLF guitar production facility. Fender and George Fullerton turned down repeated offers, and Music Man began cutting production orders. The controversy settled as CLF Research stopped manufacturing instruments for Music Man in late 1979. In April of 1980 Fender and Fullerton started a new company, G & L (for George & Leo), to continue producing Leo Fender's ongoing design ideas and models. As Fender once again handled R & D in his office/workshop, George Fullerton maintained production management and Dale Hyatt (another ex-Fender company man) was in charge of administrative management and sales.

Between 1980 and 1991, Leo Fender continued to refine his vision of his Fender guitar. Where other people saw individual models, Fender saw an ongoing project that kept refining his ideas about the electric guitar. Clarence L. Fender passed away in March, 1991. As researcher/collector Paul Bechtoldt has noted, "during the eleven years that Fender owned G & L, less than 27,000 guitars were produced. That is less than most companies make in half a year! With monthly production totals less than 800, Leo was making more guitars at his old company in the 1950's than at G & L!"

The G & L company was purchased on December 5, 1991, by John McLaren of BBE Sound, and continues to produce the affordable, quality solid body guitars based on Leo Fender's designs. Leo's wife, Phyllis, remains as Honorary Chairman of G & L, and George Fullerton remains as a permanent consultant. In 1998, G & L opened their Custom Creations Department, a 'custom shop' area for the company.

(Source: Paul Bechtoldt, G&L: Leo's Legacy)

Production Identification Notes

In addition to the G & L bridges, both the Kahler tremolo system (1984-1986) and the Wilkinson roller nut were options on certain models.

In 1998, G & L instruments underwent a major change. All models are now produced with a 4-bolt neckplate, and the serial numbers are applied decals.

Unless otherwise listed, G & L guitars are available with 22-fret maple fingerboard with black dot inlay or rosewood fingerboard with pearl dot inlay. Current models are available in left-handed configurations at no extra charge.

ELECTRIC

The following listed models are available in these **Standard** finishes: Belair Green, Black, Black Silver Swirl, Blue Swirl, Candy Apple Red, Cherryburst, Cobalt Blue, Electric Blue, Emerald Blue, Fullerton Red, Gold Metallic, Gold Metallicburst, Green Swirl, Lake Placid Blue, Pearl White, Red Swirl, Silver Metallic, Sparkle Black, Sparkle Purple, Sparkle Red, Sunburst, Tobacco Sunburst, and White.

G & L also offers a number of **Premier** finishes on certain models. These finishes include: Blonde, Blueburst, Clear Blue, Clear Forest Green, Clear Orange, Clear Red, Honey, Honeyburst, Natural Ash, Natural Satin, and Silver Flake. Premier finishes are also available on the Legacy, ASAT, and ASAT Special (contact dealer for availability).

New colors for 1998 include Pearl White and Honey Blonde finishes.

ASAT Series

In 1998, Bigsby tremolos became optional on ASAT models: **ASAT Special, ASAT Deluxe, ASAT Semi-Hollow,** and **ASAT Deluxe Semi-Hollow.**

ASAT - single cutaway maple body, bolt-on maple neck, 22-fret maple or rosewood fingerboard, 25 1/2" scale, black pickguard, fixed bridge with locking saddles, 6-on-a-side tuners, black hardware, 2 single coil pickups, volume/tone control, 3-position switch. Mfg. 1986 to 1998.

$1,050 $900 $795 $675 $550 $450 $325
Last MSR was $1,300.

In 1992, alder body replaced original parts/design.

ASAT III - similar to ASAT, except has three Magnetic field single coil pickups, chrome hardware, 3-ply white pickguard, and 5-position switch. Mfg. 1995 to 1998.

$1,050 $900 $795 $675 $550 $450 $325
Last MSR was $1,300.

ASAT CLASSIC - similar to ASAT, except has ash body, white pickguard, vintage style fixed bridge, 3-ply white pickguard, chrome hardware. Mfg. 1990 to date.

MSR $1,300 $1,050 $900 $795 $675 $550 $450 $325

This model is currently available in Premier and Standard finishes.

ASAT Bound Classic - similar to ASAT, except has bound ash body, white pickguard. Mfg. 1994 to 1998.

$725 $550 $450 $350 $325 $300 $275
Last MSR was $900.

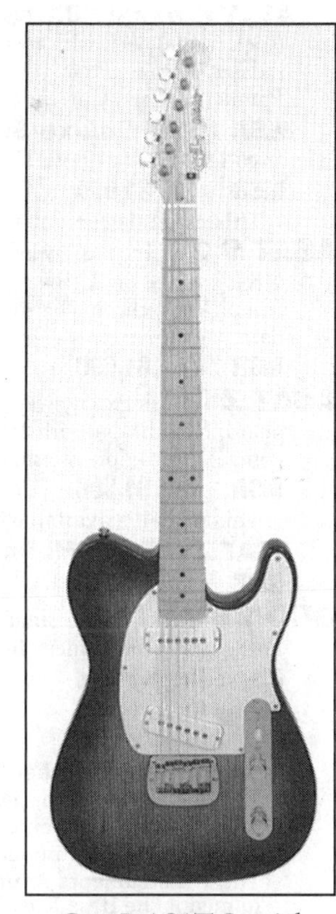
G & L ASAT Special
courtesy G & L

GRADING		100% MINT	98% NEAR MINT	95% EXC+	90% EXC	80% VG+	70% VG	60% G

ASAT Classic Custom - similar to ASAT, except has bookmatched swamp ash top, alder body, top wood binding, 2 Magnetic Field single coil pickups, vintage style fixed bridge, chrome hardware, and pearl pickguard. Mfg. 1995 to 1998.

		$1,125	$1,050	$850	$750	$625	$500	$475

Last MSR was $1,500.

This model is currently available in see-through finishes only, and comes with deluxe Tolex case.

ASAT Special Deluxe similar to ASAT, has maple top on American Tilla back, hard rock maple neck with rosewood or maple fingerboard, dot position markers, 2 large rectangular G&L Magnetic Field high output single coil pickups, Schaller non-locking tuners, G&L patented "Saddle Lock" fixed bridge, 1 voilume/1 tone control, 3-way switch, rear mounted controls, no pickguard, chrome hardware, available in Standard finishes. Molded hard case included. Current Mfg.

ASAT Deluxe - similar to ASAT, except has bound flamed maple top, mahogany body, 2 Seymour Duncan humbuckers, rear loaded controls, no pickguard, chrome hardware, and fixed bridge with saddle lock. Mfg. 1995 to date.

MSR	$1,950	$1,450	$1,100	$875	$725	$650	$595	$525

This model is currently available in see-through finishes only, and comes with deluxe Tolex case.

ASAT Special - similar to ASAT, except has 3-ply white pickguard, and chrome hardware. Mfg. 1994 to date.

MSR	$1,300	$1,050	$900	$775	$660	$550	$435	$325

ASAT Classic "Blues Boy" - similar to ASAT, has alder body on Standard finishes and all solid finishes, Swamp Ash on all Premier finishes, Hard Rock Maple neck with rosewood or maple fingerboard, dot position markers, Schaller non-locking tuners, Traditional "Boxed" steel bridge with six saddles, Seymour Duncan "Seth Lover" 1955 Humbucking neck pickup and G&L Magnetic Field single coil pickup, 1 volume/1 tone control, 3-way switch, Available in Standard and Premier finishes. Current Mfg.

ASAT JUNIOR LIMITED EDITION - single cutaway chambered (semi-hollow) mahogany body, mahogany neck, 22-fret ebony fingerboard, black pickguard, tune-o-matic bridge/stop tailpiece, 6-on-a-side tuners, chrome hardware, 2 black Custom ASAT Special single coil pickups, volume/tone control, 3-way toggle switch. Mfg. 1998 to 1999.

		$1,365	$1,100	$945	$830	$690	$560	$435

Last MSR was $1,950.

Only 250 instruments are scheduled in this Limited Edition.

ASAT SEMI-HOLLOW - single cutaway swamp ash body with 2 'voice chambers' (semi-hollow), f-hole, bolt-on maple neck, 22-fret maple or rosewood fingerboard, 25 1/2" scale, pearl (or black or white or tortoise or vintage) pickguard, fixed bridge with locking saddles, 6-on-a-side tuners, chrome hardware, 2 magnetic field single coil pickups, volume/tone control, 3-position switch, controls mounted on metal plate. Mfg. 1997 to date.

MSR	$1,450	$1,025	$875	$775	$670	$570	$465	$365

This model is currently available in Premier and Standard finishes. All three Semi-Hollow guitar models are available with or without the f-hole.

ASAT Classic Semi-Hollow - similar to the ASAT Semi-Hollow, except features Schaller vintage-style fixed bridge, bird's-eye maple neck. Mfg. 1997 to date.

MSR	$1,450	$1,025	$875	$775	$670	$570	$465	$365

ASAT Classic "Blues Boy" Semi-Hollow similar to ASAT Classic Semi-Hollow, has Swamp Ash body with twin Voice Chambers, Hard Rock Maple neck with roswood or maple fingerboard, dot position markers, Schaller non-locking tuners, Traditional "Boxed" steel bridge with six saddles, 3-way switch, 1 volume/1 tone control, chrome hardware, 3-ply black or white pickguard, with or without f-hole, available in Standard and Premier finishes. Current Mfg.

MSR ASAT Deluxe Semi-Hollow - similar to the ASAT Semi-Hollow, except bound mahogany body, curly maple top, features G & L fixed bridge, 2 Seymour Duncan humbuckers, rear-loaded controls. Mfg. 1997 to date.

MSR	$1,950	$1,350	$1,175	$1,050	$900	$770	$635	$500

This model is currently available in see-through finishes only, and comes with deluxe Tolex case.

ASAT S 3 - single cutaway Swamp Ash or Alder body, Hard Rock Maple neck with rosewood or maple fingerboard, 22-frets, Schaller locking tuners, G&L "Saddle Lock" fixed bridge, volume and tone controls, five-way pickup selector, three large rectangular G&L Magnetic Field high output single coil pickups, chrome hardware, three-ply white pickguard, available in Standard and Premiere finishes. G&L molded hard case included. Mfg. 1998-date.

MSR	$1,500	$1,050	$915	$815	$695	$590	$485	$380

ASAT Z 3 - single cutaway swamp ash or alder body, bolt-on hard rock maple neck, 22-fret maple or rosewood fingerboard, 25 1/2" scale, pearl pickguard, fixed bridge with locking saddles, 6-on-a-side Schaller tuners, chrome hardware, 3 "Z-Coil" magnetic field single coil pickups, volume/tone control, 5-position switch, controls mounted on metal plate. Mfg. 1998 to date.

MSR	$1,500	$1,050	$915	$815	$695	$590	$485	$380

This model is available in Premier or Standard Finishes. Black, White, Tortoise, or Creme pickguards are optional.

ASAT Z 3 Semi-Hollow - similar to the ASAT Z 3, except features with 2 'voice chambers' (semi-hollow), f-hole. Mfg. 1998 to date.

MSR	$1,700	$1,200	$1,045	$930	$790	$665	$545	$425

BROADCASTER - single cutaway alder body, black pickguard, bolt-on maple neck, fixed bridge with locking saddles, body color matching peghead, 6-on-a-side tuners, black hardware, 2 single coil pickups, volume/tone control, 3-position switch, available in Black finish. Mfg. 1985 to 1986.

Maple fingerboard		$1,800	$1,250	$1,100	$900	$725	$650	$595
Ebony fingerboard		$1,400	$1,075	$925	$700	$675	$525	$395

Last MSR was $706.

A Certificate of Authenticity was issued with each instrument.
This model had an optional ebony fingerboard with pearl dot inlay.
42 of these instruments have double locking Kahler vibratos.
Two of these instruments are left handed.
These instruments returned as an embelishment to Leo Fender's original Telecaster design. In 1948, Leo Fender designed a guitar, named it the Broadcaster, and put it into production. After shipping a number of instruments, he was notified that another company had the rights to the name. Fender then changed the Broadcaster to the Telecaster, and the rest is solid body guitar history. In 1985, believing that the Broadcaster name had been abandoned, Fender once again named a production model the Broadcaster. Once again, another company stepped in and informed G & L that the Broadcaster name was taken. Leo's policy was to honor all trademarks, and decided to cease

GRADING	100% MINT	98% NEAR MINT	95% EXC+	90% EXC	80% VG+	70% VG	60% G

using the Broadcaster name within a reasonable amount of time (and after a reasonable number of guitars were sold!). G & L produced this instrument for one year, with all instruments being signed and dated by Leo in the neck pocket of the body. Broadcasters carry their own unique serial number prefix (BC).

G & L decided to manufacture a limited number of instruments. The total number produced was 869. Of these, 308 have maple fingerboards. In late 1986, the Broadcaster was renamed the ASAT.

CAVALIER - offset double cutaway ash body, bolt-on maple neck, 25 1/2" scale, black pickguard, standard vibrato, 6-on-a-side tuners, chrome hardware, 2 slanted humbucker pickups, 1 volume/2 tone control, 5-position switch. Mfg. 1983 to 1986.

$600 $550 $500 $450 $400 $350 $275

It is estimated that 1,400 Cavaliers were produced.

Climax Series

CLIMAX - offset double cutaway ash body, bolt-on maple neck, double locking vibrato, 6-on-a-side tuners, black hardware, 2 single coil/humbucker pickups, volume/tone control, 5-position switch. Mfg. 1993 to 1995.

$800 $575 $525 $400 $350 $325 $275
Last MSR was $1,150.

Climax Plus - similar to Climax, except has humbucker/single coil/humbucker pickups.

$900 $625 $575 $450 $375 $350 $300
Last MSR was $1,250.

Climax XL - similar to Climax, except has 2 humbucker pickups, 3-position switch.

$825 $595 $525 $425 $350 $325 $295
Last MSR was $1,180.

COMANCHE V - offset double cutaway maple body, black pickguard, bolt-on maple neck, 22-fret maple fingerboard with black dot inlay, standard vibrato, 6-on-a-side tuners, chrome hardware, 3 Z-shaped single coil pickups, volume/2 tone controls, 5-position switch, available in Black, Blonde, Cherryburst and Natural finishes. Mfg. 1990 to 1991.

$925 $795 $650 $525 $475 $425 $395
Last MSR was $1,325.

Add $60 for Leo Fender vibrato.

This model also had an optional ebony fingerboard with pearl dot inlays.

Comanche VI - similar to Comanche V, except has 6 mini switches, not the 5-position switch.

$930 $795 $660 $530 $475 $435 $395
Last MSR was $1,325.

Add $60 for Leo Fender vibrato.

The six mini switches offered over 40 different pickup/tone combinations.

COMANCHE (REISSUE) - offset double cutaway swamp ash or alder body, bolt-on hard rock maple neck, 22-fret maple or rosewood fingerboard with dot inlay, Dual Fulcrum vibrato, 3-ply pickguard, 6-on-a-side Schaller locking tuners, chrome hardware, 3 Z-Coil magnetic field single coil pickups, volume/tone controls, 5-position switch, mini-toggle switch. Mfg. 1998 to date.

MSR $1,500

This model is available with Premium and Standard finishes.

COMMEMORATIVE - single cutaway maple body, bolt-on maple neck, 22-fret maple fingerboard with black dot inlays, 25 1/2" scale, white pickguard, *Leo Fender*/1909-1991 with rose inlay on upper bass bout, vintage style bridge, 6-on-a-side tuners, gold hardware, 2 single coil pickups, volume/tone control, 3-position switch. Mfg. 1992 to 1997.

$2,800 $2,400 $2,150 $1,800 $1,525 $1,300 $1,100
Last MSR was $3,200.

F-100 Series

The F-100 series was the first model offered from the G & L company in 1980. The only difference between a model I and a model II is the radius of the fretboard (7 1/2 inches versus 12 inches).

F-100-I - offset double cutaway mahogany body, bolt-on maple neck, 22-fret maple fingerboard (12" radius) with black dot inlay, fixed bridge, 6-on-a-side tuners, chrome hardware, 2 humbucker pickups, volume/tone control, 3-position selector switch, available in Natural and Sunburst finishes. Mfg. 1980 to 1985.

$500 $450 $425 $400 $350 $325 $275

This model was available with a G & L vibrato.

This model may have ash, maple, or mahogany bodies, and maple or ebony fingerboards.

F-100-IE - similar to the F-100-I, except has on-board preamp and additional coil tap/preamp switches.

$550 $500 $450 $400 $375 $350 $300

F-100-II - similar to the F-100-I, except has a 7 1/2-inch radius fretboard.

$500 $450 $425 $400 $350 $315 $255

F-100-IIE - similar to the F-100-II, except has on-board preamp and additional coil tap/preamp switches.

$600 $550 $475 $425 $375 $350 $300

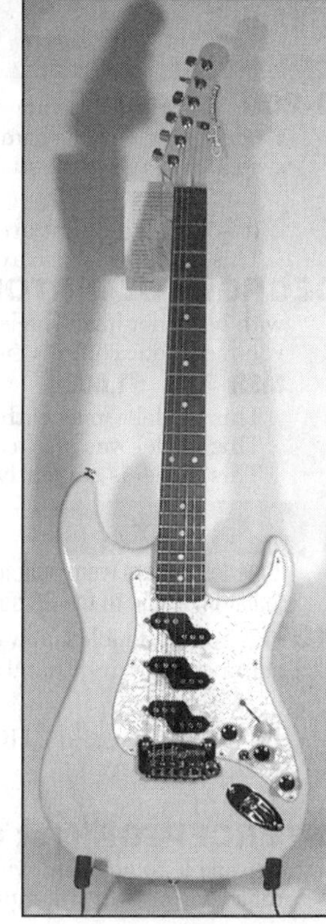

G & L Comanche courtesy Buffalo Bros. Guitars

G & L Commemorative courtesy Eugene Sharpey

G

GRADING	100% MINT	98% NEAR MINT	95% EXC+	90% EXC	80% VG+	70% VG	60% G

G-200 - offset double cutaway mahogany body, bolt-on maple neck, 22-fret maple fingerboard with black dot inlay, 24 3/4" scale, fixed bridge, 6-on-a-side tuners, chrome hardware, 2 humbucker pickups, 2 volume/2 tone controls and jack mounted on black plate on lower bout, 3-position selector switch, available in Natural and Sunburst finishes. Mfg. 1981 to 1982.

$525 $450 $425 $400 $350 $300 $250

It is estimated that around 200 instruments were produced. Between 12 to 20 of the later instruments have rear loaded controls.
This model was also available with an ebony fingerboard with pearl dot inlays.

GEORGE FULLERTON SIGNATURE MODEL - offset double cutaway maple body, bolt-on maple neck, 22-fret maple fingerboard with black dot inlay, single ply white pickguard, standard vibrato, 6-on-a-side tuners, chrome hardware, 3 G & L vintage alnico single coil pickups, 1 volume/2 tone controls, 5-position selector switch. Mfg. 1994 to date.

MSR $1,600 $1,300 $1,125 $1,000 $825 $695 $550 $395

This model comes with an autographed copy of George Fullerton's *Guitar Legends* book.
This model was also available with a rosewood fingerboard with pearl dot inlays.
This model is currently available in Premier and Standard finishes.

HG Series

HG series guitars were built for only one year in 1982. An estimated 1,000 instruments were produced, and more HG-1 models than HG-2. HG series guitars are similar in design to the SC series, except have one or two G & L Magnetic Field humbucking pickups (depending on the model).

G

HG-1 - offset double cutaway maple body, bolt-on maple neck, 22-fret maple fingerboard with black dot inlay, standard vibrato, 6-on-a-side tuners, chrome hardware, 1 humbucker pickup, volume/tone controls and jack mounted on black *quarter moon*-shaped panel. Mfg. 1982 to 1983.

$375 $325 $275 $250 $200 $175 $150

HG-2 - similar to the HG-1, except has two humbucking pickups, and a pickup selector switch mounted on control panel near volume and tone controls.

$400 $350 $325 $295 $250 $225 $195

INTERCEPTOR (1st DESIGN) - radical offset double cutaway ash body, additional shaped armrest on lower bout, bolt-on maple neck, 22-fret maple fingerboard with black dot inlay, 25 1/2" scale, standard vibrato, 6-on-a-side tuners, chrome hardware, 2 humbucker pickups, volume/tone controls and jack mounted on black panel. Mfg. 1983 to 1986.

$1,500 $1,250 $995 $900 $850 $775 $675

The first design Interceptors have more triangular-pointed horns. Also, pickup configuration can and does vary (i.e., 3 single coils).
This model may have ash, maple, or mahogany bodies; and maple or rosewood fingerboards.

Interceptor (2nd Design) - similar to the first Interceptor design, except the horns are slimmer and rounded; controls are rear loaded, and the jack is on the side of the body.

$1,350 $1,050 $900 $825 $725 $650 $595

It is estimated that a total of 67 Interceptors (first and second design) were built.

Interceptor (3rd Design) - offset double cutaway ash body, bolt-on maple neck, 22-fret rosewood fingerboard, standard vibrato, 6-on-a-side tuners, chrome hardware, 2 single coil/humbucking pickups, volume/tone controls, 5-position switch. Mfg. 1987 to 1989.

$1,000 $925 $850 $775 $675 $595 $475

The third Interceptor design is more traditional than the previous two incarnations. The controls are rear loaded, and the top has a carved sloped *ledge* along the bass side.

Invader Series

INVADER (1st Design) - offset double cutaway poplar body, bolt-on maple neck, 25 1/2" scale, 22-fret rosewood fingerboard with pearl dot inlays, double locking vibrato, 6-on-a-side tuners, chrome hardware, 2 single coil/humbucker pickups, 1 volume/2 tone control, 3 pickup selector mini-switches. Mfg. 1984 to 1988.

$525 $475 $425 $395 $350 $300 $250

This model may have ash, maple, or poplar bodies, and maple or rosewood fingerboards.

INVADER (Current Mfg.) - offset double cutaway body, bolt-on maple neck, 25 1/2" scale, 22-fret maple or rosewood fingerboard with dot inlays, double locking Original Floyd Rose vibrato, 6-on-a-side tuners, black or chrome hardware, 2 dual 'blade'/1 TB4 humbucker Seymour Duncan pickups, 1 volume/tone control, 5-way selector, coil tap mini-switch. Mfg. 1997 to date.

MSR $1,900 $1,425 $1,250 $1,100 $950 $775 $625 $475

This model is available in both the Standard and Premier finishes, and comes complete with deluxe Tolex case.

Invader Deluxe - similar to the Invader, except has figured maple top, mahogany body, woodgrain edges around top, bird's-eye maple, rosewood, or ebony fingerboards, available in Blonde, Blueburst, Cherryburst, Clear Blue, Clear Forest Green, Clear Orange, Clear Red, Honey, Honeyburst, Natural Ash, Sunburst, Tobacco Sunburst, and Satin finishes. Mfg. 1997 to 1999.

$1,600 $1,400 $1,225 $1,050 $895 $725 $550

Last MSR was $2,150.

INVADER PLUS - similar to the Invader, except has humbucker/single coil 'blade'/humbucker Seymour Duncan pickups. Mfg. 1997 to date.

MSR $2,000 $1,500 $1,300 $1,150 $995 $825 $650 $500

Invader Plus Deluxe - similar to the Invader Plus, except has figured maple top, mahogany body, woodgrain edges around top, bird's-eye maple, rosewood, or ebony fingerboards, available in Blonde, Blueburst, Cherryburst, Clear Blue, Clear Forest Green, Clear Orange, Clear Red, Honey, Honeyburst, Natural Ash, Sunburst, Tobacco Sunburst, and Satin finishes. Mfg. 1997 to 1999.

$1,700 $1,450 $1,300 $1,100 $925 $750 $575

Last MSR was $2,250.

INVADER XL - similar to the Invader, except has 2 Seymour Duncan humbuckers. Mfg. 1997 to date.

MSR $1,950 $1,475 $1,300 $1,125 $950 $800 $650 $495

GRADING		100% MINT	98% NEAR MINT	95% EXC+	90% EXC	80% VG+	70% VG	60% G

Invader XL Deluxe - similar to the Invader XL, except has figured maple top, mahogany body, woodgrain edges around top, bird's-eye maple, rosewood, or ebony fingerboards, available in Blonde, Blueburst, Cherryburst, Clear Blue, Clear Forest Green, Clear Orange, Clear Red, Honey, Honeyburst, Natural Ash, Sunburst, Tobacco Sunburst, and Satin finishes. Mfg. 1997 to 1999.

		$1,650	$1,425	$1,250	$1,100	$900	$725	$550

Last MSR was $2,200.

LEGACY - offset double cutaway body, white pickguard, bolt-on maple neck, standard vibrato, 6-on-a-side tuners, chrome hardware, 3 vintage Alnico single coil pickups, volume/treble/bass controls, 5-position switch. Mfg. 1992 to date.

MSR	$1,200	$975	$850	$750	$625	$525	$400	$300

Legacy Deluxe similar to Legacy, has maple top on American Tilla back, Hardrock Maple neck with rosewood or maple fingerboard, dot position markers, 2 G&L Vintage style Alnico V single coil pickups and a Seymour Duncan TB4 Humbucking pickup in the bridge position, Schaller non-locking tuners, G&L patented "Dual Fulcrum" tremelo, 5-way selector switch, rear mounted controls, chrome hardware, no pickguard, G&L molded hard case included, available in Standard finishes. Current Mfg.

Legacy HB similar to Legacy, has alder body on all Standard and solid finishes, Swamp Ask body on all Premier finishes, Hard Rock Maple neck with rosewood or maple fingerboard, dot position markers, Schaller non-locking tuners, G&L patented "Dual Fulcrum" tremelo, 2 G&L vintage style Alnico V single coil pickups and a Seymour Duncan TB4 Humbucking pickup in the bridge position. 5-way selector switch, mini-toggle allows the humbucker to be split, volume control, chrome hardware, 3-ply white pickguard, G&L molded case included, available in Standard finishes. Current Mfg.

Legacy 2HB similar to Legacy HB, except a Seymour Duncan 58N humbucking pickup in the neck position and a Seymour Duncan JB humbucking pickup in the bridge position, available in Standard finishes. Current Mfg.

Legacy Special - similar to Legacy, except has graphite nut, locking Sperzel tuners, 2 dual blade/1 humbucking power blade pickups. Mfg. 1993 to date.

MSR	$1,300	$1,050	$900	$795	$675	$550	$450	$325

This model is currently available in Premier and Standard finishes.

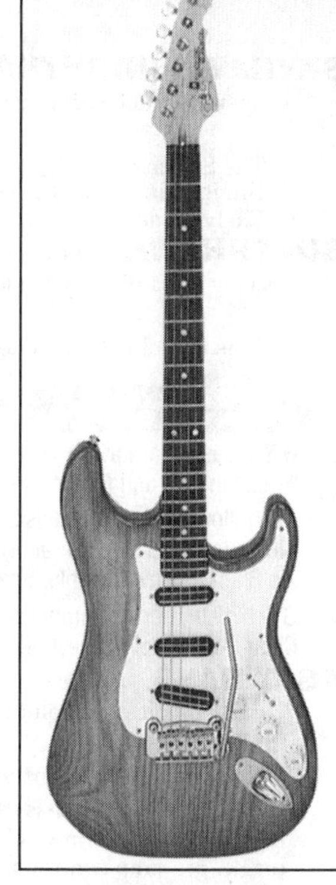

G & L Legacy Special
courtesy G & L

NIGHTHAWK - Refer to the Skyhawk model.

RAMPAGE - offset double cutaway maple body, bolt-on hardrock maple neck, 25 1/2" scale, 22-fret rosewood fingerboard (12" radius) with pearl dot inlays, double locking vibrato, 6-on-a-side tuners, chrome hardware, 1 humbucker pickup, volume control. Mfg. 1984 to 1988.

		$425	$375	$325	$295	$250	$200	$150

This model may have ash, maple, or poplar bodies; and maple or rosewood fingerboards.

S-500 - offset double cutaway body, white pickguard, bolt-on maple neck, 25 1/2" scale, standard vibrato, 6-on-a-side locking Sperzel tuners, chrome hardware, 3-ply white pickguard, 3 vintage Alnico-5 single coil pickups, volume/treble/bass control, 5-position/mini switch. Mfg. 1982 to date.

1982-1985		$625	$550	$500	$450	$400	$375	$275
1986-1996		$775	$650	$550	$500	$450	$400	$325

S-500 Deluxe similar to S-500, except has maple top on American Tilla back. Standard finishes available. Current Mfg.

S-500 (Current) similar to S-500, except has alder or Swamp Ash body depending on finish, hard Rock Maple neck with rosewood or maple fingerboard, Schaller locking tuners, G&L patented "Dual Fulcrum" tremelo, chrome hardware, 3 G&L Magnetic Field single coil pickups, available in Standard finishes. Current Mfg.

MSR	$1,300	$1,050	$900	$795	$675	$550	$450	$325

Early models may have ash, maple, or mahogany bodies, and maple or ebony fingerboards.
This model is currently available in Premier and Standard finishes.

SC Series

The SC series was produced over a period of eighteen months, beginning in 1982. An estimated 1,200 instruments total were produced. SC series guitars have one, two, or three G & L Magnetic Field single coil pickups (depending on the model).

SC-1 - offset double cutaway maple body, bolt-on maple neck, 22-fret maple fingerboard with black dot inlay, standard vibrato, 6-on-a-side tuners, chrome hardware, 1 single coil pickup, volume/tone controls and jack mounted on black *quarter moon*-shaped panel. Mfg. 1982 to 1984.

		$350	$325	$275	$250	$200	$175	$150

Less than 250 SC-1 models were built.

SC-2 - similar to the SC-1, except has two single coil pickups, and a pickup selector switch mounted on control panel near volume and tone controls.

		$400	$375	$325	$295	$250	$225	$195

SC-3 - similar to the SC-1, except has three single coil pickups, and a pickup selector switch mounted on control panel near volume and tone controls.

		$425	$395	$350	$325	$275	$250	$225

G & L S-500
courtesy Phil Willhoite

GRADING	100% MINT	98% NEAR MINT	95% EXC+	90% EXC	80% VG+	70% VG	60% G

SKYHAWK (NIGHTHAWK) - offset double cutaway ash body, white pickguard, 22-fret bolt-on maple neck, 25 1/2" scale, standard vibrato, 6-on-a-side tuners, chrome hardware, 3 single coil pickups, 1 volume/2 tone control, 5-position switch. Mfg. 1983 to 1985.

	$650	$600	$550	$475	$400	$375	$325

The Skyhawk model debuted in 1983 as the Nighthawk. Due to a conflict with a Washington D.C. band of the same name, the name was changed in 1984. It is estimated that 269 Nighthawk-labeled instruments were produced.

Early models may have ash, maple, or mahogany bodies, and maple or ebony fingerboards.

SUPERHAWK - offset double cutaway maple body, bolt-on maple neck, 25 1/2" scale, 22-fret rosewood fingerboard with pearl dot inlays, double locking vibrato, 6-on-a-side tuners, chrome hardware, 2 humbucker pickups, 1 volume/2 tone control, 3-position switch. Mfg. 1984 to 1989.

	$550	$475	$400	$350	$300	$250	$200

This model may have ash, maple, or mahogany bodies, and maple or rosewood fingerboards.

ELECTRIC BASS

G & L basses are available with 21-fret maple fingerboard with black dot inlay or rosewood fingerboard with pearl dot inlay, or ebony fretless (with or without "Ghostlines"), and feature a fixed bridge with locking saddles.

The following listed models are available in these **Standard** finishes: Belair Green, Black, Black Silver Swirl, Blue Swirl, Candy Apple Red, Cherryburst, Cobalt Blue, Electric Blue, Emerald Blue, Fullerton Red, Gold Metallic, Gold Metallicburst, Green Swirl, Lake Placid Blue, Pearl White, Red Swirl, Silver Metallic, Sparkle Black, Sparkle Purple, Sparkle Red, Sunburst, Tobacco Sunburst, and White.

G & L also offers a number of **Premier** finishes on certain models. These finishes include: Blonde, Blueburst, Clear Blue, Clear Forest Green, Clear Orange, Clear Red, Honey, Honeyburst, Natural Satin, and Natural Ash. Premier finishes are also available on the LB-100, SB-1, and SB-2 (contact dealer for availability).

ASAT BASS - single cutaway ash (or maple) body, bolt-on maple neck, 34" scale, 21-fret maple fingerboard, 4-on-a-side tuners, chrome hardware, 2 dual coil pickups, volume/treble/bass controls, pickup/series-parallel/preamp switches, active electronics. Mfg. 1989 to date.

MSR $1,400	$1,150	$1,000	$875	$750	$600	$495	$350

This model is currently available in Premier and Standard finishes.

ASAT Bass Semi-Hollow similar to ASAT Bass, except has Swamp Ash body with twin Voice Chambers, 2 G&L Magnetic Field humbucking pickups, Custom G&L "Ultra-Lite" tuners, G&L patented "Saddle Lock" bridge, G&L Tri-Tone active/passive electronics, series/parallel mini-toggle, pre=amp control mini-toggle, available in Standard finishes.

CLIMAX BASS - offset double cutaway ash body, bolt-on maple neck, 4-on-a-side ultralite tuners, no pickguard/rear loaded controls, chrome hardware, 1 humbucker pickup, volume/treble/bass controls, bypass/preamp switches. Mfg. 1993 to 1995.

	$850	$650	$550	$450	$395	$350	$300

Last MSR was $1,100.

EL TORO - offset double cutaway ash body, bolt-on maple neck, 34" scale, 21-fret maple fingerboard with black dot inlays, fixed bridge, 4-on-a-side tuners, 2 bi-pole smaller humbucker pickups, volume/treble/bass controls, pickup selector switch. Mfg. 1983 to 1985.

	$675	$600	$495	$450	$425	$400	$350

This model may have ash, maple, or mahogany bodies; and ebony, maple, or rosewood fingerboards.

INTERCEPTOR BASS - offset double cutaway maple body, bolt-on maple neck, 34" scale, 21-fret maple fingerboard with black dot inlays, 4-on-a-side tuners, 2 bi-pole smaller humbucker pickups, volume/treble/bass controls, pickup selector switch. Mfg. 1984 to 1989.

	$1,100	$950	$825	$700	$575	$525	$450

The Interceptor Bass shared similar design lines of the third model Interceptor guitar, and the same electronics as the El Toro model bass.

This model may have ash, maple, or mahogany bodies, and ebony, maple, or rosewood fingerboards.

JB-2 BASS – offset double cutaway alder body (Swamp Ash body on Premier finishes), Hard Rock Maple neck with rosewood or maple fingerboard, dot position markers, Custom G&L "Ultra-Lite" tuners, G&L patented "Saddle-Lock" bridge, 2 volume/1 tone control, chrome hardware, no pickguard, available in Standard colors. Current Mfg.

LB-100 (LEGACY BASS) - offset double cutaway alder body, bolt-on maple neck, 21-fret maple or rosewood fingerboard, 4-on-a-side ultralite tuners, white pickguard, chrome hardware, fixed bridge with locking saddles, P-Bass-style split-coil pickup, volume/tone control, passive electronics. Mfg. 1993 to 2001.

	$975	$850	$740	$625	$525	$400	$295

Last MSR was $1,200.

In late 1993, the Legacy Bass was renamed the LB-100.

This model is available in Standard finishes.

L Series

L-1000 - offset double cutaway maple body, bolt-on maple neck, 34" scale, 21-fret maple fingerboard with black dot inlays, 4-on-a-side tuners, humbucker pickup, volume/treble/bass controls, series-parallel switch, available in Natural and Sunburst finishes. Mfg. 1980 to 1994.

	$675	$575	$475	$395	$350	$300	$275

Last MSR was $950.

This model may have ash, maple, or mahogany bodies, and ebony, maple, or rosewood fingerboards.

L-1000 F - similar to the L-1000, except has fretless neck.

	$695	$600	$500	$400	$350	$300	$275

L-1500 - similar to L-1000, except has 5 strings, alder body, no pickguard, rear loaded controls, 3/2-per-side tuners, chrome hardware, G & L magnetic field humbucker, preamp on/off switch, series/parallel switch, volume/treble/bass controls, active/passive electronics. Mfg. 1995 to date.

MSR $1,300	$1,050	$900	$795	$675	$550	$450	$325

This model is currently available in Premier and Standard finishes.

GRADING		100% MINT	98% NEAR MINT	95% EXC+	90% EXC	80% VG+	70% VG	60% G

L-1500 Custom - similar to the L-1500, except has bookmatched ash top, alder body, wood binding, and no contour on top. Mfg. 1996 to 1998.

		$1,100	$850	$700	$650	$525	$475	$375

Last MSR was $1,449.

This model is currently available in see-through finishes only, and comes complete with a deluxe Tolex case.

L-1505 - offset double cutaway American tilia body, swamp ash top, bolt-on maple neck, 21-fret maple or rosewood fingerboard, rear loaded controls, 3/2-per-side tuners, chrome hardware, G & L magnetic field humbucker, preamp on/off switch, series/parallel switch, volume/treble/bass controls, active/passive electronics. Mfg. 1997 to date.

MSR	$1,500	$1,200	$1,050	$925	$795	$650	$500	$375

This model is currently available in Premier and Standard finishes.

L-1505 Custom - similar to the L-1505, except has bookmatched ash top, alder body, bird's-eye maple neck, wood binding. Mfg. 1997 to 1998.

		$1,150	$1,000	$895	$775	$650	$525	$425

Last MSR was $1,649.

This model is currently available in see-through finishes only, and comes complete with a deluxe Tolex case.

In 1998, strings through-body option was introduced; 3/2-per-side headstock was re-designed, eliminating the string retainer.

L-2000 (L-2000 E) - similar to L-1000, except has 2 humbucker pickups, pickup/series-parallel/preamp/treble boost switches, active electronics. Mfg. 1980 to date.

MSR	$1,400	$1,125	$1,000	$875	$750	$600	$495	$350

This model is currently available in Premier and Standard finishes.

The L-2000 E model was introduced in 1981. Further research regarding these two similar yet slighty different models continues for future editions of the ***Blue Book of Electric Guitars***.

L-2000 Custom - similar to the L-2000, except has bookmatched ash top, alder body, wood binding, no top contour. Mfg. 1996 to 1998.

		$1,250	$1,100	$950	$800	$675	$525	$395

Last MSR was $1,549.

This model is currently available in see-through finishes only, and comes with deluxe Tolex case.

L-2000 F - similar to the L-2000, except has fretless neck and passive tone circuitry. Disc. 1998.

		$950	$625	$600	$475	$425	$395	$350

Last MSR was $1,250.

L-2000 FE - similar to the L-2000 E, except has fretless neck. Disc. 1998.

		$950	$625	$600	$475	$425	$395	$350

Last MSR was $1,250.

L-2500 - similar to L-1000, except has 5 strings, no pickguard, rear loaded controls, 3/2-per-side tuners, chrome hardware, 2 magnetic field humbucking pickups, preamp on/off switch, coil tap switch, pickup selector, volume/treble/bass controls, Tri-tone active/passive electronics. Mfg. 1994 to date.

MSR	$1,600	$1,300	$1,125	$1,000	$825	$695	$550	$400

This model is currently available in Premier and Standard finishes.

In 1998, strings through-body option was introduced; 3/2-per-side headstock was re-designed, eliminating the string retainer.

L-2500 Custom - similar to the L-2500, except has bookmatched ash top, alder body, wood binding, and no contour on top. Mfg. 1996 to 1998.

		$1,400	$1,225	$1,100	$925	$750	$600	$450

Last MSR was $1,749.

This model is currently available in see-through finishes only, and comes complete with a deluxe Tolex case.

L-5000 - similar to L-1000, except has 5 strings, alder body, black pickguard, 4/1 per side tuners, volume/tone control, passive electronics. Mfg. 1987 to 1994.

		$875	$825	$775	$650	$450	$375	$275

Last MSR was $950.

This model may have ash, maple, or poplar bodies; and maple, or rosewood fingerboards.

L-5500 - similar to L-1000, except has 5 strings, alder body, no pickguard, rear loaded controls, 4/1 per side tuners, black hardware, 2 EMG 40 DC humbucking pickups, volume/concentric treble-bass/pan control, EMG BTC electronics. Mfg. 1994 to 1997.

		$1,200	$900	$750	$600	$550	$495	$450

Last MSR was $1,550.

This model was available in Premier and Standard finishes.

L-5500 Custom - similar to the L-5500, except has bookmatched ash top, alder body, wood binding, and no contour on top. Mfg. 1996 to 1998.

		$1,500	$1,100	$950	$850	$750	$675	$550

Last MSR was $2,100.

This model was available in see-through finishes only.

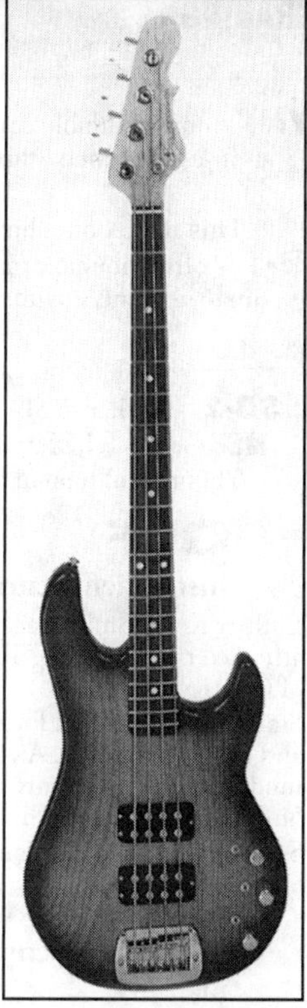

G & L L-2000 Bass
courtesy G & L

G

GRADING	100% MINT	98% NEAR MINT	95% EXC+	90% EXC	80% VG+	70% VG	60% G

LYNX - offset double cutaway maple body, bolt-on hardrock maple neck, 34" scale, 21-fret maple fingerboard with black dot inlays, black pickguard, 4-on-a-side tuners, chrome hardware, 2 single coil pickups, volume/tone control, pickup selector. Mfg. 1984 to 1986.

	$525	$475	$425	$375	$350	$325	$275

This model may have ash, maple, or mahogany bodies, and ebony, maple, or rosewood fingerboards.

SB-1 - offset double cutaway maple body, bolt-on hardrock maple neck, 34" scale, 21-fret maple fingerboard with black dot inlays, black pickguard, 4-on-a-side tuners, chrome hardware, split coil pickup, volume/tone control. Mfg. 1982 to 2001.

	$975	$850	$750	$625	$525	$400	$295

Last MSR was $1,200.

SB-2 - similar to SB-1, except has split coil/single coil pickups, 2 volume controls.

MSR $1,250	$1,000	$875	$775	$650	$525	$425	$300

This model has an optional rosewood fingerboard with pearl dot inlays.

GLF

Instruments currently built in Rogers, Minnesota. Distributed by the GLF Custom Shop of Rogers, Minnesota.

Luthier Kevin Smith began building and *messing around* with guitars since his high school days. Born in Fosston, Minnesota in 1961, Smith later attended the Red Wing Technical College. He spent a number of years as a lighting and guitar tech for the regional band *Encounter*, which was based out of Chicago, Illinois.

Smith opened the GLF Custom Shop in 1984. Although the original focus was on both lighting and guitars, he soon focused directly on guitar repair and custom building. A custom ordered guitar may range between $1,200 and $1,500 (depending on hardware and pickups), but for further details on models and components contact the GLF shop. In addition to his busy schedule, he also provides custom finishes for the Benedict Guitar company. Smith also introduced his **ToneSmith** line of guitars in 1997 (See TONESMITH).

Smith holds the patent on the Combo Rack, a guitar stand that attaches to the player's amplifier and holds the instrument when not in use.

GMP GUITARS

Instruments currently built in San Dimas, California. Distributed by G M Precision Products, Inc. of San Dimas, California.

G M P has been producing high quality guitars since 1990 (first proto-types were built in 1989). G M P has always favored the latest in technology in their designs, including the use of Sperzal locking tuners, Wilkinson vibratos and roller nuts, and other techniques. G M P uses Honduran mahagony, quilted and flamed maple, and select Western alder. Options include Seymour Duncan or Tom Holmes pickups, transparent colors, and special wiring. For further information and specifications, contact G M Precision Products directly (see Trademark Index).

ELECTRIC

All guitar models feature the GMP 'center dipped' 3-per-side headstock, Seymour Duncan pickups, Sperzel locking tuners, Schaller roller bridges or Wilkinson vibratos, Schaller strap locks, hardware choices (color and type), and numerous color finishes. All models are equipped with a hardshell case.

Options include Tom Holmes humbuckers and Van Zandt pickups (call for pricing).

CUSTOM - sleek offset double cutaway mahogany body with pointy forward horns, flame (or quilted) maple top, mahogany neck, 24-fret rosewood or ebony fingerboard with abalone diamond inlay, Wilkinson tremolo or tune-o-matic bridge/strings through-body ferrules, 3-per-side tuners, gold hardware, 2 humbucker pickups, volume/tone controls, 3-way toggle switch, available in (unlimited) Transparent Color finishes. Current Mfg.

MSR $2,150	$1,725	$1,295	$1,095	$995	$895	$795	$695

Classic similar to the Custom, except features an alder or basswood body, maple neck, 24-fret rosewood or maple fingerboard with dot inlay, pickguard, pickguard-mounted electronics, choice of pickup configuration, available in (unlimited) Solid Color finishes. Current Mfg.

MSR $1,550	$1,250	$1,150	$1,050	$950	$850	$750	$595

Inlay Top - similar to the Custom, except features an exotic wood (bird's-eye, flame, or quilted maple)top inlay (on the top of the body), available in (unlimited) Transparent Color finishes. Current Mfg.

MSR $2,350	$1,875	$1,395	$1,195	$1,095	$995	895	$750

ELITE - offset double cutaway mahogany body, flame (or quilted) maple top, mahogany neck, 22-fret rosewood or ebony fingerboard with abalone diamond inlay, Wilkinso tremolo or tune-o-matic bridge/strings through-body ferrules, 3-per-side tuners, gold hardware, 2 humbucker pickups, volume/tone controls, 3-way toggle switch, available in (unlimited) Transparent Color finishes. Current Mfg.

MSR $2,650	$2,125	$1,595	$1,395	$1,295	$1,095	$995	$850

ELITE DOUBLENECK - 6/12 doubleneck version of the Elite, offset double cutaway mahogany body, premium grade quilted or flamed maple tops, mahogany necks, rosewood or ebony 22-fret fingerboards,diamond shaped abalone position markers, string through-body on 12-string side, Wilkinson vibrato tailpiece on 6-string side, 2 exposed zebra coil humbucking pickups, (unlimited) transparent colors. Current Mfg.

MSR $4,300	$3,450	$2,400	$2,100	$1,750	$1,600	$1,500	$1,250

PAWN SHOP - offset single cutaway basswood body, maple neck, 22-fret rosewood fingerboard with abalone dot inlay, tune-o-matic bridge/strings through-body ferrules, 3-per-side tuners, black chrome or chrome hardware, 2 humbucker pickups, 2 volume/2 tone controls, 3-way toggle switch, available in Black, Metallic Blue, Red, and White finishes. Current Mfg.

MSR $1,550	$1,250	$995	$895	$795	$695	$625	$550

This model is available in other optional colors (call for availability and pricing).

Pawn Shop Special - similar to the Pawn Shop, except features a creme bound mahogany body, bound f-hole, mahogany neck, bound ebony fingerboard with abalone dot position markers/abalone diamond inlay at 12th fret, bound headstock, chrome or gold hardware, available in (unlimited) Solid Color finishes. Current Mfg.

MSR $2,450	$1,960	$1,475	$1,275	$1,175	$1,050	$950	$795

Add $100 for flame or quilted maple top.

GRADING	100% MINT	98% NEAR MINT	95% EXC+	90% EXC	80% VG+	70% VG	60% G

GMP "V" "V" shaped mahogany body, mahogany neck, rosewood or ebony 22-fret fingerboard, 3-per-side tuners, abalone diamond shaped position markers, string through-body or stop tailpiece, available in (unlimited) solid colors. Current Mfg.

MSR	$2,450	$1,960	$1,475	$1,275	$1,175	$1,050	$950	$795

Add $100 for quilted or flame maple tops.

ROXIE SS - offset single rounded cutaway mahogany body, creme bound Western maple top, mahogany neck, 22-fret bound rosewood fingerboard with matching metal flake finish color diamond inlay, tune-o-matic bridge/trapeze tailpiece, 3-per-side tuners, bound headstock, chrome hardware, 2 humbucker pickups, volume/tone controls, 3-way toggle switch, available in (unlimited) Metal Flake finishes. Current Mfg.

MSR	$2,550	$2,050	$1,525	$1,325	$1,125	$995	$895	$750

Add $100 for Bigsby tremolo/Schaller roller bridge.

ELECTRIC BASS

Options include Bartolini and EMG pickups (call for pricing).

ROXIE SS BASS - offset dual cutaway body, creme body binding, alder or mahogany body wings, through-body maple neck, 34" scale, 22-fret bound ebony fingerboard with matching metal flake finish color diamond inlay, fixed bridge, 2-per-side tuners, bound headstock, chrome hardware, 2 Seymour Duncan Basslines pickups, volume/tone controls, available in Metal Flake finishes. Current Mfg.

MSR	$2,450	$1,960	$1,475	$1,275	$1,175	$1,050	$950	$795

ELITE offset double cutaway maple and exotic hardwood multi-laminate neck through-body construction, 4, 5, or 6 string, carved quilted or flame maple top, mahogany, alder, or ash sides, ebony or Pau ferro 24-fret fingerboards, EMG or Bartolini pickups available, 34" scale. Oil, wax, or polyurethane finishes available.

MSR	$2,650	$2,125	$1,595	$1,395	$1,295	$1,195	$1,050	$925

Add $100 for 6-string model.

STANDARD - offset double cutaway body, alder or mahogany body wings, flame or quilted maple top, through-body maple neck, 34" scale, 24-fret rosewood or ebony fingerboard, fixed bridge, black hardware, P/J-style Seymour Duncan Basslines pickups, 2 volume/1 tone controls, available in (unlimited) Transparent Colors, Oil & Wax, or Polyurethane finishes. Current Mfg.

4-String, 2-per-side tuners.

MSR	$2,350	$1,880	$1,450	$1,250	$1,150	$995	$895	$750

5-String, 3/2-per-side tuners.

MSR	$2,350	1,880	$1,450	$1,250	$1,150	$995	$895	$750

6-String, 3-per-side tuners.

MSR	$2,450	1,880	$1,450	$1,250	$1,150	$995	$895	$750

GR BASSES

Instruments currently built in San Marcos, California.

GR Basses feature an electric solid body design with an open headstock with sideways mounted tuners (inspired by upright basses) for ideal string tension; other features include a curved heel with five bolts holding the neck stable, and a custom GR bridge with large radius saddles for increased reasonance. As if the open headstock isn't enough of an identification clue, all models have the "GR" logo on the tip of the headstock. For further information regarding pricing and specifications, please contact GR Basses directly (see Trademark Index).

ELECTRIC BASS

GR Basses are also available with alder or poplar body woods. Contact GR Basses for pricing on extra upgrades such as a flamed ash or flamed maple top.

Add $50 for a fretless fingerboard.

Add $50 for pearloid box inlays.

Add $75 for pearloid or tortoise shell pickguard.

Add $150 for dual Bassline Music Man pickups.

Add $200 for Basslines 2-band active EQ (with slap contour).

Add $200 for left-handed configuration.

Add $250 for solid color finish.

Add $300 for High Gloss finish.

GRP (GRT) 4-STRING - offset double cutaway (GRP) or single cutaway body (GRT) solid ash body, bolt-on maple neck, 34" scale, 22-fret rosewood (or ebony or maple) fingerboard with pearl (or abalone or black inlays), 2-per-side open headstock, chrome or black hardware, (Seymour Duncan) Bassline Music Man pickup, volume/tone controls, available in Oil finish. Current Mfg.

MSR $1,249

Add $200 for 5-string configuration

GRD

GUITAR RESEARCH AND DESIGN.

Instruments previously built in South Strafford, Vermont between 1978 to 1982. Distributed initially by United Marketing International of Grapevine, Texas; distribution was later retained by Guitar Reseach and Design.

GRD (Guitar Reseach and Design) was founded in 1978 by luthier/designer Charles Fox. The Guitar Reseach and Design company grew out of the School of Guitar Research and Design Center, which was founded by Fox in South Strafford, Vermont in 1973. The GRD Center was the first guitar building school in North American. The GRD company workforce consisted of graduates from the school.

GRD first advertised in **Guitar Player** magazine in the October 1978 issue, and were distributed by United Marketing International of Grapevine, Texas. This same issue also featured pictures of their Chicago NAMM booth on page 23, while page 24 showed a picture of then-GP columnist and vintage guitar expert George Gruhn holding one of their double cutaway models. The ads in the November and December 1978 issues of **Guitar Player** announced that they were available direct to the musician and to select professional sound shops around the country. A letter to customers during this time period who had requested the company's brochures announced that GRD had broken ties with their distributor.

George Gruhn's January 1979 **Guitar Player** column featured GRD instruments. Gruhn called them "one of the most interesting guitars I saw at the entire (NAMM) show.and are capable of producing almost any type of sound. The instruments are beautifully crafted, and while modernistic in design, they were tasteful, reserved, and elegant. it is a significant instrument that demonstrates the future potential in both electrical and physical design." The last mention of GRD was in the January 1981 issue of **Guitar Player** magazine, in which Jim Nollman stated that Charles Fox was designing him a 3/4-size guitar to use in playing slide guitar in Jim's attempt to communicate with whales. And you thought that slide guitar playing only perked up the ears of dogs in the neighborhood!

GRD closed its doors in 1982, and Fox moved to San Francisco to pursue other interests. Fox became a biofeedback therapist, yoga instructor, and professional gambler as he stayed out of the guitar business. However, the lure of teaching and the world of lutherie beckoned, and Fox started the American School of Luthiery in Healdsburg, California. In 1998, Fox also returned to guitar manufacturing as he founded the CFOX guitar company (see CFOX) which is currently building high quality acoustic guitars.

(Source: Vincent Motel, G R D Historian)

GRD Design Features

Guitar Reseach and Design was an innovative company during the late 1970s. Some of the company's ideas include the thin body acoustic guitar, brass nuts, hexaphonic pickups, and active electronics that featured on-board compression, distortion, and wireless broadcasters. GRD electric guitars utilized fade/mix controls (instead of the usual toggle switches) to blend the pickups' outputs; and featured coil tap (coil split) and phase switches. GRD electric guitars were also available with built-in 6 band graphic equalizers that offered 18 dB of cut or boost, and parametric equalizers with selectable frequency centers and cut or boost controls (these features are usually associated with P.A. mixing boards).

GRD hardware was manufactured in house, and the pickups used on the electric models were specially wound and potted by DiMarzio.

What appears to be binding on the solid body models is actually two laminated layers of maple sandwiching a layer of ebonized maple in the center. GRD instruments all feature the highly noticeable "Omega" headstock cutaway.

ELECTRIC

Standard GRD Series

The 1978 GRD brochure illustrated 3 different solid body styles that had 2 different electronic systems. These two different electronic systems were comprised of the **PF** models, which have wide range parametric variable filters with stacked frequenct "Q" controls which could be set in hi-pass, lo-pass, or band-pass modes. The **EQ** models have 2 modified MXR 6 band graphic equalizers with 18 dB of cut or boost.

All necks and bodies were pattern grade Honduran mahogany, and each body had a thick solid rosewood overlay. Often mistaken for a "really nice piece of ebony", the fingerboards were phenolic resin! GRD electrics feature a unique heel-less neck/body joint, and the head and arm are cut from separate pieces which are spliced rather than being bandsawn from one piece of wood. The 3-per-side headstocks feature gold-plated Schaller tuners.

The nut is 1/4" wide solid brass, and each string has its own separate 1" deep brass bridge block (each block is individually adjustable for height and length). The tailpiece is solid brass, and the rear cover plates are solid brass too. Instead of a toggle switch, there is a fader (mixer) which allows the guitarist to blend the pickups in varying amounts. The magnetic pickups are specially wound and potted DiMarzio units, and there is a transducer pickup mounted in the neck. Pickups have no mounting rings, and are mounted through the back of the instrument. GRD electric models were optionally offered with dual distortion circuits, compressor sustainer units, and hexaphonic pickups.

GRD offered three different solid body models, all of which feature a 645 mm scale and 24-fret fingerboard. The **DC** model has a dual cutaway body reminiscent of the Hamer Artist model (or Gibson Les Paul Double Cutaway). The **SC** model is a single cutaway model similar to a Les Paul; and the unique **M 1** model (featured in Wheeler's American Guitars book) has a rectangular (or wedge) body with large "O" or "Omega" cutaway in its lower bout. Outside of the Bo Diddly- approved **M 1**, all GRD models feature rather traditional body designs.

All 1987 models have active electronics; but instead of on-board batteries, the guitars use a single three conductor cord that runs through a small power supply box between the guitar and the amplifier. Early GRD guitars have a built-in NiCad battery which is always charging when the guitar is played through, or simply plugged into its normal power supply. If the guitar is played without its normal power supply, it is ready with a fully charged battery.

GRD AX Series

The **AX Series** was introduced in early 1979 as a more affordable alternative to the standard series. The **AX Series** was available in all four electric body styles (DC, SC, M 1, and Bass). While the neck/body construction was the same as the **Standard Series**, the hardware was different. Bodies and necks were Honduran Mahogany, and the face woods were Jet Black maple (or Fancy Flamed maple, or rosewood) with fancy interface laminates. There were two different control set- ups available, but the pickups were the same DiMarzio custom design used on all the other guitars. One DiMarzio was a PAF design, while the second model had a hotter output. Active models were powered with a 9-volt battery.

The **Standard AX** had a master volume and 2 tone controls, slide type pickup selector (mixer), 2 Dual Sound switches (one per pickup).

The **Active AX** had a master volume and master tone controls, slide type pickup selector (mixer), 2 Dual Sound switches (one per pickup), EQ/preamp switch, and 6 band graphic equalizer (with 18 dB cut or boost).

GRD Passive Pickup Series

GRD offered passive pickup models starting in 1979 (there was no catalog featuring these particular guitar models). These models were available in either an "Explorer" or "Flying V" body shapes. The customer could choose any pickup configuration, although GRD recommended using different pickups for the neck and bridge positions (for example, a DiMarzio SDHP in the neck position and a DiMarzio X2N in the bridge position). The pickups were mounted with standard mounting rings made of brass, and were also available with the rear mounted specially potted DiMarzio pickups. The pickups also had coil taps for humbucker or single coil operation as well as a phase switch when both pickups were selected.

These guitars still featured brass nuts, Schaller tuners, and featured Schaller wrap-around bridges. Gold-plated hardware was standard, but chrome hardware was available as an option (that's certainly a switch from today's marketplace!). Fine tuners were also optional.

The **Passive** models had the same two piece headstock/neck configuration, and heel-less body joint as the **Active** models. They also had the same mahogany neck/body woods as well as rosewood or maple tops. **Passive** models feature the same 24-fret phenolic fingerboard and scale length as the **Active** models.

ELECTRIC BASS

The electric bass model from 1978 has an 865 mm scale and 24-fret fingerboard. The **B** Bass Guitar was also offered with a fretless fingerboard. All other construction techniques were similar to the electric guitars.

GTX

Instruments currently produced in Korea. Distributed by the Kaman Music Corporation of Bloomfield, Connecticut.

The GTX trademark is the brandname of the Kaman Corporation for this series of Fender-ish and 'superstrat' solid body models. Imported from Korea since the late 1980s, the GTX line offers comfortable feeling and good sounding guitars at reasonable prices.

GALANTI

Instruments previously built in Italy during the early 1960s through the early 1970s.

The Galanti company focused on fairly straightforward original designs on their solid and semi-hollowbody guitars. The company also offered a number of amp designs.

(Source: Tony Bacon, The Ultimate Guitar Book)

GALE, GEOFF

Instruments previously built in England through the 1970s.

Original designs were featured on these solid body guitars, and they carried model designations such as the Magnum, Quasar, Cobra, and Phasar.

(Source: Tony Bacon and Paul Day, The Guru's Guitar Guide)

GEMELLI

Instruments previously produced in Italy during the 1960s.

Guitars bearing this trademark were built by Benito & Umberto Cingolani in Recanti, Italy. Like many other European countries, Italy experienced the 1960s pop music popularity that led to a larger demand for electric guitars. However, many electric guitar builders were also manufacturers of accordions. As a result, many guitars ended up with accordion- style finishes and touches, such as a barrage of buttons for pickup or tone selection. It is up to the individual guitar player to make the choice: play 'em or pose with 'em!

(Source: Tony Bacon, The Ultimate Guitar Book)

GHERSON

Instruments previously produced in Italy from the mid 1970s to early 1980s.

The Gherson company produced a number of good quality copies of American designs in the solid body format.

(Source: Tony Bacon and Paul Day, The Guru's Guitar Guide)

G.H. RENO

Please refer to this listing in the R section.

GIBSON

Current trademark established circa 1896, and manufactured by the Gibson Guitar Corp., with production facilities located in Nashville, TN (beginning 1974), Bozeman, MT (beginning 1989, and Memphis, TN (beginning 2001). Custom shops are located in both Nashville, TN & Bozeman, MT. All Gibson instruments are currently distributed by the Gibson Guitar Corporation located in Nashville, TN.

Gibson instruments were previously produced in Kalamazoo, MI, from 1896 to 1984. The Gibson Mandolin-Guitar Manufacturing Company, Limited (which evolved into the Gibson Guitar Corporation) produced both electric and acoustic instruments in Kalamazoo, MI from 1902 to 1984. Gibson's first electric guitar, the ES-150 (also known as the Charlie Christian model) was manufactured during 1936.

Most acoustic instruments are currently produced in the Bozeman, MT plant - for more information, please refer to the 7th Edition *Blue Book of Acoustic Guitars.*

Luthier Orville H. Gibson was born in Chateaugay, New York. In 1856 he moved west to Kalamazoo, Michigan. City records from 1896-1897 indicate a business address of 114 South Burdick for *O.H. Gibson, Manufacturer, Musical Instruments*. By 1899-1902, the city directories indicate a change to the Second Floor of 104 East Main.

The Gibson Mandolin-Guitar Manufacturing Company, Limited was established at 2:55 p.m. on October 11, 1902. The agreement was formed by John W. Adams (president), Samuel H. Van Horn (treasurer), Sylvo Reams (secretary and also production manager), Lewis Williams (later secretary and General Manager), and Leroy Hornbeck. Orville Gibson was not one of the founding partners, but had a separate contract to be a consultant and trainer. Gibson was also the first to purchase 500 shares of the new company's stock. In 1915, Gibson and the company negotiated a new agreement in which Orville was to be paid a monthly salary for the rest of his life. Orville, who had some troubles with his health back in 1911, was treated in 1916 at the pyschiatric center of St. Lawrence State hospital in Ogdensburg, New York. Orville Gibson died of endocarditis on August 21, 1918.

In 1906 the company moved to 116 East Exchange Place, and the name was changed to Gibson Mandolin Guitar Company. In 1917, production facilities were opened at Parsons Street (the first of a total of five buildings at that location). Chicago Musical Instruments (CMI) acquired controlling interest in Gibson, Inc. in 1944. Maurice H. Berlin (president of CMI) became general secretary and treasurer of Gibson. From this date, the Gibson Sales Department became located in Chicago while the Kalamazoo plant concentrated on production.

In 1935, Gibson began investigating into a prototype electric pickup. Musician Alvino Rey started research with engineers at the Lyon & Healy company (See WASHBURN) in Chicago, and a year later the research was moved in-house to Kalamazoo. In late 1935, Gibson debuted the hexagonal pickup on a lap steel model; this same pickup was applied to an archtop guitar and offered as the ES (Electric Spanish) 150 in 1936. The ES-150 was used by jazz guitarist Charlie Christian, and this model is still known as the "Charlie Christian" model.

After the release of Leo Fender's **Broadcaster** (later **Telecaster**) model, Gibson and guitarist Les Paul collaborated in the release of the solid body Gibson **Les Paul** in 1952. This model was refined with the introduction of the tune-o-matic bridge/stop tailpiece combination, and P.A.F. humbuckers through the 1950s. Under the direction of then Gibson president Ted McCarty, the Gibson company attempted to throw off the tag of being "stodgy" and old fashioned when they introduced the **Flying V** and Explorer models in the late 1950s. In this case, they pre-judged the public's tastes by about 10 years! As guitar players' tastes changed in the late 1950s, Gibson discontinued the single cutaway Les Paul model in favor of the double cutaway SG in 1960. As the popularity of the electric blues (as championed by Eric Clapton and Michael Bloomfield) grew during the 1960s, Gibson reissued the Les Paul in 1968.

Gibson acquired Epiphone in 1957, and production of Gibson-made Epiphones began in 1959, and lasted until 1969. In 1970, production moved to Japan (or, the Epiphone name was then applied to imported instruments).

In December of 1969, E.C.L. Industries, Inc. took control of CMI. Gibson, Inc. stayed under control of CMI until 1974, when it became a subsidiary of NORLIN Industries (Norlin is named after H. Norton Stevens, president of E.C.L. and Maurice H. Berlin, president of CMI). A new factory was opened in Nashville, Tennessee the same year.

In 1980, Norlin decided to sell Gibson. Norlin also relocated some of the sales, marketing, administration, and finance personnel from Chicago to the Nashville plant. Main Gibson production was then handled in Nashville, and Kalamazoo became a specialist factory for custom orders. In 1983, then-Gibson president Marty Locke informed plant manager Jim Deurloo that the Kalamazoo plant would close. Final production was June 1984, and the plant closed three months later. [On a side note: Rather than give up on the 65-year-old facilities, Jim Deurloo, Marv Lamb, and J.P. Moats started the Heritage Guitar Company in April of 1985. The company is located in the original 1917 building.]

In January of 1986, Henry Juszkiewicz (pres), David Berryman (VP of finance and accounting), and Gary Zebrowski (electronics business) bought Gibson for five million dollars. Since the purchase in 1986, the revived **Gibson USA** company has been at work to return to the level of quality the company had reached earlier. Expansion of the acoustic guitar production began at the Bozeman, Montana facilities. Many hard rock bands and guitarists began playing (and posing) with Gibson guitars, again fueling desire among the players.

Gibson's **Historic Collection** models were introduced in 1991, and custom pieces built at Gibson's Custom Shop began sporting their own **Gibson Custom * Art * Historic** logo on the headstock in 1996. This new division is responsible for producing Historic Collection models, commemorative guitars, custom-ordered and special edition guitars, as well as restoration and repair of vintage models.

In the tail end of 1996, both the Dobro production facilities in California and the Montana mandolin guitar facilities were closed down. New production facilities for both named **Original Musical Instruments** (O.M.I.) is expected to be opened in Nashville, Tennessee in late 1998.

In 1998, Gibson opened up a new dealer level for specialty guitars. The Gibson Historic Collection **Award** models are only available through the (estimated) 50 Award Level dealers, and feature specific year/model designated instruments at an upscale price. As noted elsewhere, the antique and vintage firearm market has authentic reproductions of especially prized models. Whether or not Gibson is building "reproductions" with these designated models, the bottom line is that they are damn fine instruments that any Gibson fan would be honored to own (and play).

During 1999, Gibson once again released a large number of new models and finishes, further filling out their electric guitar lineup. In the 7th Edition ***Blue Book of Electric Guitars***, both the Custom Collection and Historic Series Models from the Custom Shop have been grouped in the back of the Gibson section for easier lookup. Since Gibson continues to change their model lineup on a regular basis, it is suggested that a trip to their web site is in order to learn more on what's current, and just as important, what has been discontinued.

Gibson started the new millennium in perhaps its best shape for a long time. With the Montana plant now producing consistently high quality acoustic instruments (perhaps their best ever), and the electric models being led by the extensive offerings from the Gibson Custom, Art, and Historic Division, this legendary American guitar company seems to be in great shape for the next century of guitar manufacturing. Additionally, Gibson recently opened up a new archtop production facility in Memphis, TN during 2001.

(Source: Walter Carter, Gibson Guitars: 100 Years of an American Icon; and Tom Wheeler, American Guitars)

IDENTIFYING FEATURES ON GIBSON MUSICAL INSTRUMENTS

Gibson Headstock Logo

The most consistent and easily found feature that goes across all models of Gibson production is the logo, or lack of one, found on the peghead. The very earliest instruments made are generally found with a star inside a crescent design, or a blank peghead, and labels inside the body. This lasted until approximately 1902.

From 1902 to the late 1920s, The Gibson, inlaid in pearl and placed at a slant, is found on the peghead. In the late 1920s, this style of logo was changed to having *The Gibson* read straight across the peghead as opposed to being slanted. Flat top acoustics production began at approximately this time and these instruments generally do not have *The* on the inlay, it just has *Gibson* in script writing. By 1933, this was the established peghead logo for Gibson. Just before WWII, Gibson began making the lettering on the logo thicker and this became standard on most prewar instruments. Right after WWII, the styling of the logo remained but it became slanted once again.

In 1947, the logo that is still in use today made its debut. This logo has a block styling with the *G* having a tail, the *i* dot is touching the *G*, the *b* and *o* are open and the *n* is connected at the bottom. The logo is still slanted. By 1951, the dot on the *i* was no longer connected to the *G*. In 1967, the logo styling became even more squared (pentographed) with the *b* and *o* becoming closed and the *i* dot being removed.

In 1970, Gibson replaced the black tinted piece of wood that had been used on the peghead face with a black fiber that the logo and other peghead inlay were placed into. With the change in peghead facing came a slightly smaller logo lettering. In 1972, the *i* dot reappeared on the peghead logo. In 1981, the *n* is connected at the top of the *o*. There are a few models through the years that do not follow this timeline, ie: reissues and limited editions, but most of the production instruments can be found with the above feature changes.

Gibson USA
courtesy Gibson USA

Gibson Tuners

The configuration of the Kluson tuners used on Gibson instruments can be used to date an instrument. Before 1959, all Kluson tuners with plastic buttons had a single ring around the stem end of the button. In 1960, this was changed to a double ring configuration.

Gibson Peghead Volute

Another dating feature of Gibsons is the use of a peghead volute found on instruments between 1970 and 1973. Also, in 1965 Gibson switched from 17 degrees to 14 degrees on the tilt of the peghead. Before 1950, peghead thickness varied, getting narrower towards the top of the peghead. After 1950, pegheads all became one uniform thickness, from bottom to top.

Common Gibson Abbreviations

The abbreviations listed below may also be used in sequence (i.e., and ES-150DC is an electric spanish model with cutaway and double pickups).

C - Cutaway
D - Dreadnought or Double Pickup
E - Electric
ES - Electric (Electro) Spanish
GS - Gut String
J - Jumbo
LE - Limited Edition
S - Spanish, Solid Body, Special or Super
SG - Solid Guitar
T - Tremolo or Thinline
V - Venetian or Vibrato

Current Gibson Finishes/Hardware Abbreviations

AB – Ambay Guasu (Smartwood only)
AN – Antique Natural
AW – Alpine White
BA – Banara (Smartwood only)
BC – Black Chrome
BF – Flat Black/Gothic
BG – Bigsby Gold
BG – Bullion Gold
BL – Transulcent Black
BR – Trans Brown
BT – Blue Teal Flip-flop
BU – Translucent Blue
CB – Chicago Blue
CG – Country Gentleman Brown
CH – Cherry
CH – Chrome Hardware
CN – Cinnamon
CR – Crème
CU – Curupay (Smartwood only)
CW – Classic White
DB – Desert Burst (Brown)
EB – Ebony
ED – Emerald Burst (Green)
ES – Ebony Stain
FI – Fireburst
GH – Gold Hardware
HB – Honeyburst
HC – Heritage Cherry
HS – Heritage Cherry Sunburst
LM – Lemonburst
MC – Vibrola Chrome
MD – Midnightburst (Blue)
NA – Natural
NH – Nickel Hardware
NS – Natural Stain

Gibson Doubleneck 6-String
(1 of 40 made)
courtesy Guitar Emporium

GRADING	100% MINT	98% NEAR MINT	95% EXC+	90% EXC	80% VG+	70% VG	60% G

OR – Sunrise Orange
PE – Peroba (Smartwood only)
RB – Lavaburst (red)
RD – Translucent Red (Faded Cherry)
TA – Translucent Amber
TP – Translucent Purple
TR – Translucent Red
VS – Vintage Sunburst
WR – Wine Red

Production Model Codes & Shipment Totals

For ease in identifying current Gibson production guitar models in the Gibson section, the Gibson Family Code (in parenthesis) follows the model's name (in some cases, only the alphabetical prefix is listed, as the individual finishes and/or colors will result in the rest of the code). This also is true when brackets[]are encountered within a family code.

For anyone who is interested in individual Gibson model production totals from 1937-1979 (including guitars, basses, artist models, custom models, mandolins, banjos, ukuleles, steel guitars, effects, and amps), it is recommended to look at *Gibson Shipment Totals 1937-1979* by Larry Meiners. Please use the convenient insert order card in this book to order.

G

ACOUSTIC/ACOUSTIC ELECTRIC

For further information regarding Gibson acoustic and acoustic electric models, please refer to the 7th Edition ***Blue Book of Acoustic Guitars***. Gibson Chet Atkins and the J-160 Series acoustic electric models will be found in the Gibson Acoustic Electric section in the ***Blue Book of Acoustic Guitars***.

ELECTRIC

For organizational consideration, the subcategory names and variations under this Electric category name have been listed in the following sequence: BB. King Series, Barney Kessel Models, Byrdland Model, Centennial Series, Challenger Series, Chet Atkins Models, Corvus Series, Doubleneck Models, ES Series, Electrics: Misc., Explorer Series, Firebird Reverse Series, Firebird Non-Reverse Series, Flying V Series, Howard Roberts Models, Johnny Smith Model, L Series/Le Grande, Les Paul Series, Paul Series, M Series, Melody Maker Series, Moderne Model, Nighthawk Series, RD Series, SG Series, Sonex Series, Spirit Series, and Super 400 CES Models. Musician's models are alphabetized by their first names. The Gibson Custom Shop & Historic Collection Models can be found after these subcategories.

Add 15%-30% for original Natural Blonde finish (depending on rarity & original condition) on all Gibson electrics listed below which were manufactured with this option.

Subtract approx. 50% for refinishing on all models listed below.

Typically subtract 10%-20% for Gibson electric guitars with Kahler or Floyd Rose locking trememlos, as they are not as desirable as those instruments without.

B.B. King Series

For further information on the Little Lucille (introduced 1999), please refer to the Nighthawk Series section later in this text.

B.B. KING STANDARD - double round cutaway semi hollow bound body, arched maple top, raised layered black pickguard, maple back/sides/neck, 22-fret bound rosewood fingerboard with pearl dot inlay, tune-o-matic bridge/tunable stop tailpiece, blackface peghead with pearl Lucille/logo inlay, 3-per-side tuners, chrome hardware, 2 covered humbucker pickups, 2 volume/2 tone controls, 3-position switch, stereo output. Available in Cherry and Ebony finishes. Mfg. 1980 to 1985.

N/A $1,350 $1,175 $925 $750 $650 $575

B.B. King Lucille (ARLC) - similar to B.B. King Standard, except has bound pickguard, bound ebony fingerboard with pearl block inlay, bound peghead, gold hardware, Vari-tone switch. Available in Cherry and Ebony finishes. Mfg. 1980 to date.

MSR $3,152 $2,100 $1,575 $1,400 $1,200 $1,000 $875 $750

From 1980 to 1988, this model was named the B.B. King Custom. Early production models had "Lucille" inlaid into the fretboard.

Barney Kessel Models

BARNEY KESSEL REGULAR - double sharp cutaway semi hollow bound body, arched maple top, bound f-holes, raised layered black pickguard, maple back/sides, mahogany neck, 22-fret bound rosewood fingerboard with pearl block inlay, adjustable rosewood bridge/trapeze tailpiece, wood tailpiece insert with pearl model name inlay, bound blackface peghead with pearl crown/logo inlay, 3-per-side tuners, nickel hardware, 2 covered humbucker pickups, 2 volume/2 tone controls, 3-position switch. Available in Cherry Sunburst finish. Mfg. 1961 to 1974.

N/A $2,500 $2,250 $1,950 $1,600 $1,295 $1,150

Barney Kessel Custom - similar to Barney Kessel Regular, except has bowtie fingerboard inlay, musical note peghead inlay, gold hardware.

N/A $3,400 $2,950 $2,500 $2,200 $1,900 $1,750

Byrdland Model

Please refer to the Custom Shop/Historic Collection section for current Byrdland production information.

BYRDLAND - single round cutaway multi-bound hollow body, solid spruce top, raised bound tortoise pickguard, bound f-holes, maple back/sides/neck, 22-fret multi-bound ebony pointed fingerboard with pearl block inlay, tune-o-matic bridge/rosewood base, trapeze tailpiece, multi-bound blackface peghead with pearl flowerpot/logo inlay, 3-per-side tuners, gold hardware, 2 single coil Alnico pickups, 2 volume/2 tone controls, 3-position switch. Available in Natural and Sunburst finishes. Mfg. 1955 to 1985.

1955-1957	**N/A**	**$7,000**	**$6,500**	**$6,000**	**$5,500**	**$4,600**	**$4,000**
1958-1959	**N/A**	**$6,500**	**$4,900**	**$4,150**	**$3,600**	**$3,250**	**$3,000**
1960-1961	**N/A**	**$5,500**	**$5,000**	**$4,000**	**$3,500**	**$3,000**	**$2,800**
1962-1968	**N/A**	**$3,500**	**$3,200**	**$3,000**	**$2,750**	**$2,500**	**$2,200**
1969-1985	**N/A**	**$3,000**	**$2,600**	**$2,400**	**$2,250**	**$2,000**	**$1,850**

Add 20%-30% for Blonde finish, depending on original condition. Highly flamed maple will also add a premium.

The Byrdland model was designed in conjunction with Billy Byrd and Hank Garland.
In 1958, 2 covered P.A.F. humbucker pickups replaced original part/design.
In 1959, Stereo-Varitone electronics were optionally offered.
In 1960, single sharp cutaway replaced original part/design.
In 1962, Patent Number humbucker pickups replaced the previous P.A.F. humbuckers.
In mid 1968, single round cutaway replaced previous part/design.

'94 Gibson Lucille
courtesy Tracey Cooley

Centennial Series

During 1994, Gibson began offering the electric **Centennial** series models to celebrate Gibson's 100 year anniversary (1894 to 1994). There were 12 models in the program - and were released at the rate of one new model per month. No more than 101 instruments of each model were produced. Gibson's plan was to have 100 dealers that year, with each one committed to a package of 12 guitars. Those dealers received a custom made oak & glass humidfied display cabinet at no charge to display each new model. Since the Custom Shop opened in 1994, the only Custom Shop Centennial model was the L-5 CES. The other 11 models were built by Gibson USA, and include the **Firebird VII** in Vintage Sunburst (Sept.), **Flying V** in Antique Gold (July), **Les Paul Double Cutaway** in Heritage Cherry (Jan.), Les Paul Classic Gold Top (Feb.), ES 350T (March), Explorer in Antique Gold (April), EDS 1275 in Ebony (May), ES 335 in Cherry (June), 1957 Black Beauty with 3 pickups (Nov.), L5 in Ebony (Dec.), and a **Les Paul Standard** in Vintage Sunburst (Oct.). Each instrument in the series retailed for $10,000. The serial numbers run from # 1894 to # 1994.

All Centennial models feature gold-plated hardware, gold control knobs with raised Centennial logo, a diamond dot over the 'i' in the Gibson logo, serial number on tailpiece with numeral '1' in diamonds, medallion on the back of peghead with the image of Orville Gibson, an engraved 100th Anniversary banner inlay on the 12th fret, and a Centennial logo on the pickguard. Centennial models came with a black leather-covered case, a gold signet ring with Centennial logo, and a framed 16 x 20 photograph.

The Centennial Series was discontinued in 1999.

Current values for new in case Centennial Series models can very somewhat, but the Gibson dealers we polled came up with the following price ranges.

LP Special Double Cutaway - $1,500 - $2,000
LP Classic Gold Top - $2,500 - $3,000
ES 350T - $3,000 - $3,500
Explorer - $3,000 - $3,500
EDS 1275 - $2,000 - $2,500
ES 335 - $3,000 - $3,500
Flying V - $2,000 - $2,500
ES 335 - $2,000 - $2,500
Firebird VII - $3,000 - $3,500
LP Standard - $1,750 - $2,250
1957 Black Beauty - $2,000 - $2,500
L5 CES (Custom Shop) - $3,750 - $4,500

Gibson Barney Kessel
courtesy Tam Milano

Challenger Series

CHALLENGER I - single cutaway mahogany body, black pickguard, bolt-on maple neck, 22-fret rosewood fingerboard with pearl dot inlay, tune- o-matic stud tailpiece, 3-per-side tuners, chrome (and silver) hardware, humbucker pickup, volume/tone control. Available in Cherry Red finish. Mfg. 1983 to 1985.

N/A	**$300**	**$250**	**$200**	**$175**	**$150**	**$125**

Challenger II - similar to Challenger I, except has 2 humbucker pickups, 2 volume controls.

N/A	**$325**	**$275**	**$250**	**$215**	**$175**	**$150**

Chet Atkins Models

CHET ATKINS COUNTRY GENTLEMAN (ARCA) - single round cutaway semi hollow bound maple body, bound f-holes, raised bound tortoise pickguard, bound arm rest on bottom bass bout, 3-piece maple neck, 22-fret rosewood fingerboard with offset red block inlay, tune-o-matic bridge/Bigsby vibrato tailpiece, blackface peghead with pearl plant/logo inlay, 3-per-side tuners, gold hardware, 2 covered humbucker pickups, master volume on upper treble bout, 2 volume/1 tone controls, 3-position switch. Available in Country Gentleman Brown (CG), Ebony (EB), Sunrise Orange (OR), and Wine Red (WR) finishes. Mfg. 1987 to date.

MSR	**$4,614**	**$3,100**	**$2,300**	**$2,000**	**$1,650**	**$1,500**	**$1,275**	**$1,075**

In 1994, Ebony finish was discontinued.

GRADING	100% MINT	98% NEAR MINT	95% EXC+	90% EXC	80% VG+	70% VG	60% G

CHET ATKINS TENNESSEAN (ARCT) - single round cutaway semi hollow bound maple body, f-holes, raised pickguard with engraved "Tennessean", arm rest on bottom bass bout, 3-piece maple neck, 22-fret rosewood fingerboard with offset pearl dot inlay, tune-o-matic bridge/stop tailpiece, blackface peghead with signature/pearl logo inlay, 3-per-side tuners with pearl buttons, chrome hardware, 2 covered humbucker pickups, master volume on upper treble bout, 2 volume/1 tone controls, 3-position switch. Available in Ebony (EB) finish. Current Mfg.

MSR $3,460 — $2,350 $1,800 $1,500 $1,275 $1,000 $900 $825

In 1994, Country Gentleman Brown (CG), Sunrise Orange (OR) and Wine Red (WR) finishes became standard, Ebony finish was discontinued.

CHET ATKINS SUPER 4000 - single rounded cutaway hollow body (Super 400 size), bound carved Sitka spruce top, bound f-holes, raised multi-bound tortoiseshell pickguard, carved bookmatched maple back/sides, multiple bound body, 5-piece curly maple neck, 20-fret bound ebony fingerboard, pearl split block fingerboard inlay, adjustable ebony bridge base/gold tune-o-matic bridge, gold trapeze tailpiece with ebony insertsa and abalone fleur-de-lis inlay, multi-bound blackface peghead with pearl 5-piece split diamond/logo inlay, 3-per-side gold Kluson tuners with mother-of-pearl buttons, 'floating' pickup and linear sliding volume control with ebony knob (under raised pickguard), includes authenticity certificate signed by Chet Atkins. Available in Sunburst and Natural finishes. Mfg. 1997 only.

It is estimated that only 25 Super 4000 models were built. Only 20 instruments were available to the public, some dealers may have inventory.

$N/A $17,500 $12,500

Last MSR was $40,000.

Corvus Series

CORVUS I - can opener style hardwood body, black pickguard, bolt-on maple neck, 22-fret rosewood fingerboard with white dot inlay, tune-o-matic stud tailpiece, 6-on-a-side tuners, chrome hardware, covered humbucker pickup, volume/tone control. Available in Silver finish. Mfg. 1983 to 1985.

N/A $400 $325 $275 $225 $195 $150

Corvus II - similar to Corvus I, except has 2 covered humbucker pickups, 3-position switch.

N/A $495 $350 $295 $250 $225 $175

Corvus III - similar to Corvus I, except has 3 exposed single coil pickups, 5-position switch.

N/A $550 $500 $395 $325 $295 $225

Doubleneck Models

DOUBLE TWELVE - double cutaway hollow maple body, carved spruce top, 2-stripe bound body, double neck configuration, 2 bound black pickguards, 3-position neck selector switch, each mahogany neck has 20-fret bound rosewood fingerboard with pearl parallelogram inlay, tune-o-matic bridge/fixed tailpiece, 6-per-side/3-per-side tuners with pearl buttons, chrome hardware, 2 covered humbucker pickups, volume/tone control, 3-position switch. Available in Black, Sunburst and White finishes. Mfg. 1958 to 1962.

$20,000 $18,000 $15,000 $12,500 $10,000 $8,000 $6,500

EDS 1275 - double cutaway mahogany body, double neck configuration, 2 black 3-ply laminated pickguards, 3-position neck/pickup selector switches, 2 volume/2 tone controls, each mahogany neck has 20-fret bound rosewood fingerboard with pearl parallelogram inlay, tune-o-matic bridge/fixed tailpiece, 6-per-side/3-per-side tuners with pearl buttons, chrome hardware, 2 covered humbucker pickups. Available in Jet Black, Sunburst and White finishes. Mfg. 1963 to 1968.

N/A $6,500 $6,000 $5,750 $5,500 $5,250 $4,600

EBSF 1250 - similar to EDS 1275, except has bass configuration instead of twelve string configuration on upper neck, built-in fuzztone. Mfg. 1962 to 1967.

N/A $5,000 $4,750 $4,350 $4,000 $3,850 $3,650

EDS 1275 - similar to EDS 1275, except available in Alpine White, Cherry, Heritage Cherry, Cherry Sunburst, Sunburst, Walnut and White finishes. Mfg. 1977 to date.

1977-1986 — N/A $2,150 $1,850 $1,650 $1,450 $1,325 $1,200
1987-1989 — N/A $1,575 $1,250 $1,100 $925 $825 $725

In 1984, Cherry Sunburst, Walnut and White finishes became standard part/design. In 1987, Cherry finish became an option.
In 1990, Alpine White (with gold hardware) and Heritage Cherry (with chrome hardware) finishes became standard part/design.

1990-1998 — $2,100 $1,600 $1,375 $1,175 $950 $750 $525

Add $200 for Alpine White finish.

EDS 1275 Alpine White (DSED-AW) - gold hardware. Available in Alpine White finish. Current Mfg.

MSR $4,229 — $2,850 $2,100 $1,950 $1,800 $1,600 $1,400 $1,150

EDS 1275 Heritage Cherry (DSED-HC) - chrome hardware. Available in Heritage Cherry Sunburst finish. Current Mfg.

MSR $3,845 — $2,600 $1,925 $1,850 $1,725 $1,500 $1,300 $1,000

ES Series

ES-5 & ES-5 SWITCHMASTER - single round cutaway hollow body, arched figured maple top, bound f-holes, raised layered black pickguard, 3-stripe bound body, figured maple back/sides/neck, 20-fret multi-bound pointed fingerboard with pearl block inlay, adjustable ebony bridge/trapeze tailpiece, bound blackface peghead with pearl crown/logo inlay, 3-per-side tuners with plastic buttons, gold hardware, 3 single coil pickups, tone control on cutaway bout, 3 volume controls. Available in Natural and Sunburst finishes. Mfg. 1949 to 1962.

1949-1956 — N/A $5,500 $4,950 $4,450 $4,100 $3,875 $3,600
1957-1962 — N/A $9,500 $8,600 $7,650 $6,750 $6,350 $6,100

Add $1,200 for Natural finish.

A few early models can be found with unbound f-holes. In 1955, model renamed ES-5 Switchmaster, tune-o-matic bridge, 3 volume/3 tone controls, 4 position switch replaced previous part/design. In 1957, humbucker pickups replaced original part/design.
In 1960, sharp cutaway replaced original part/design.

GRADING	100% MINT	98% NEAR MINT	95% EXC+	90% EXC	80% VG+	70% VG	60% G

ES-100 - arched maple top, f-holes, raised black pickguard, bound body, maple back, mahogany sides/neck, 14/20-fret rosewood fingerboard with pearl dot inlay, adjustable rosewood bridge/trapeze tailpiece, blackface peghead with pearl logo inlay, 3-per-side tuners, nickel hardware, single coil pickup, volume/tone control. Available in Sunburst finish. Mfg. 1938 to 1941.

1938-1939	**N/A**	**$1,000**	**$850**	**$725**	**$575**	**$500**	**$475**
1940-1941	**N/A**	**$650**	**$550**	**$475**	**$375**	**$325**	**$300**

ES-120 T - arched maple top, molded black pickguard, f-hole, maple back, mahogany sides/neck, 14/20-fret rosewood fingerboard with pearl dot inlay, adjustable rosewood bridge/trapeze tailpiece, 3-per-side tuners with plastic buttons, chrome hardware, single coil pickup, volume/tone control. Available in Sunburst finish. Mfg. 1962 to 1971.

N/A $600 $525 $450 $375 $350 $325

Add $100 for 2 pickup versions (ES-120 TD).

ES-125 - arched maple top, f-holes, raised black pickguard, bound body, maple back, mahogany sides/neck, 14/20-fret rosewood fingerboard with pearl dot inlay, adjustable rosewood bridge/trapeze tailpiece, blackface peghead with pearl logo inlay, 3-per-side tuners, nickel hardware, single coil pickup, volume/tone control. Available in Sunburst finish. Mfg. 1946 to 1970.

N/A $800 $725 $650 $575 $525 $500

Some production occurred in 1941, though the majority of production was post-World War II. In 1946, a few models were produced with an all mahogany body.

ES-125 C - similar to ES-125, except has a cutaway body.

N/A $1,000 $825 $675 $575 $500 $450

ES-125 CD - similar to ES-125, except has cutaway body and double pickups.

N/A $1,250 $1,050 $950 $825 $700 $575

ES-125 T - similar to ES-125, except has a thin body. Mfg. 1956 to 1969.

N/A $950 $825 $675 $575 $500 $450

ES-125 TD - similar to ES-125, except has a thin body and double pickups.

N/A $900 $775 $675 $575 $500 $450

ES-125 TDC - similar to ES-125, except has a thin body, cutaway, and double pickups.

N/A $1,250 $1,050 $950 $825 $700 $575

This model has been made popular by George Thoroughgood.

ES-125 T 3/4 - similar to ES-125 T, except has a 3/4 size body. Mfg. 1957 to 1969.

N/A $600 $550 $475 $400 $375 $350

ES-130/ES-135 - arched maple top, layered black pickguard, f-hole, maple back, mahogany sides/neck, 14/20-fret bound rosewood fingerboard with pearl block inlay, adjustable rosewood bridge/trapeze tailpiece, 3-per-side tuners with plastic buttons, nickel hardware, single coil pickup, volume/tone control. Available in Sunburst finish. Mfg. 1954 to 1958.

N/A $900 $875 $800 $750 $725 $695

ES-135 D - similar to ES-135, except had 2 single coil pickups, 2 volume/2 tone controls.

N/A $1,000 $855 $715 $570 $510 $465

ES-135 (ES35) - single sharp cutaway semi-hollow bound maple body, f-holes, raised black pickguard, maple neck, 22-fret rosewood fingerboard with pearl dot inlay, tune-o-matic bridge/trapeze tailpiece, 3-per-side tuners with pearl buttons, chrome hardware, 2 single coil pickups, 2 volume/2 tone controls, 3-position switch. Available in various finishes (including Gothic, 100% satin black finish, black chrome hardware, and 12th fret moon and star inlay), hardshell case became standard in 1998. Current Mfg.

MSR $2,306 $1,600 $1,150 $900 $775 $650 $550 $450

Add $77 for Cherry (ES35-CH) and Vintage Sunburst (ES35-VS) finishes.

Subtract approx. 10% for Gothic finish (matte black, Mfg. 1999 only).

ES-135 w/Humbuckers (ES3H) - similar to ES-135, except has 2 humbucker pickups. Available in Ebony, Vintage Sunburst, Natural, or Wine Red finish. New 1999.

MSR $2,460 $1,700 $1,250 $950 $800 $675 $575 $475

Add $77 for Vintage Sunburst, Natural, or Wine Red finish.

ES-140 3/4 - single sharp cutaway body, arched maple top, raised black pickguard, f-holes, bound body, maple back/sides, mahogany neck, 19-fret rosewood fingerboard with pearl dot inlay, adjustable rosewood bridge/trapeze tailpiece, 3-per-side tuners with plastic buttons, nickel hardware, P-90 single coil pickup, volume/tone control. Available in Natural and Sunburst finishes. Mfg. 1950 to 1957.

N/A $1,000 $925 $845 $750 $625 $490

ES-140 T 3/4 - similar to ES-140 3/4, except had a thin body. Mfg. 1957 to 1968.

N/A $850 $680 $585 $485 $450 $420

Gibson ES-5 (Switchmaster)
courtesy Dave's Music

Gibson ES-125
courtesy C.W. Green

GRADING	100% MINT	98% NEAR MINT	95% EXC+	90% EXC	80% VG+	70% VG	60% G

ES-150 (1936-1942 Mfg.) - spruce top, f-holes, bound black pickguard, bound body, flat maple back, mahogany sides/neck, 14/19-fret bound rosewood fingerboard with pearl dot inlay, adjustable rosewood bridge/trapeze tailpiece, pearl peghead logo inlay, 3-per-side tuners, nickel hardware, single coil pickup, volume/tone control. Available in Sunburst finish. Mfg. 1936 to 1942.

1936-1940 N/A $3,500 $3,300 $3,100 $2,900 $2,750 $2,500

This guitar was informally known as the Charlie Christian model. In 1940, arched back and unbound fingerboard replaced original part/design. In 1941, a different pickup was introduced.

ES-150 (1946-1956 Mfg.) - similar to ES-150 (Pre War model), except has slightly larger body, layered black pickguard, silkscreen peghead logo. Mfg. 1946 to 1956.

N/A $1,700 $1,500 $1,400 $1,300 $1,225 $1,100

In 1950, bound fingerboard with trapezoid inlay replaced original part/design.

ES-150 DC - double cutaway semi hollow style, arched maple top, f-holes, raised layered black pickguard, bound body, maple back/sides, mahogany neck, 22-fret rosewood fingerboard with pearl block inlay, tune-o-matic bridge/trapeze tailpiece, 3-per-side tuners, chrome hardware, 2 covered humbucker pickups, master volume control on upper treble bout, 2 volume/2 tone controls, 3-position switch. Available in Cherry, Natural and Walnut finishes. Mfg. 1969 to 1975.

1969-1970 N/A $1,700 $1,500 $1,450 $1,350 $1,200 $1,100
1971-1975 N/A $1,200 $1,100 $995 $875 $825 $795

ES-165 HERB ELLIS (ARHE) - single sharp cutaway hollow bound maple body, f-holes, raised black pickguard, mahogany neck, 20-fret bound rosewood fingerboard with pearl parallelogram inlay, tune-o-matic metal/rosewood bridge/trapeze tailpiece, peghead with pearl plant/logo inlay, 3-per-side tuners with pearl buttons, gold hardware, 2 covered humbucker pickups, 2 volume/2 tone controls, 3-position switch. Available in Cherry (CH), Ebony (EB), and Vintage Sunburst (VS) finishes. Current Mfg.

MSR $3,229 $2,225 $1,650 $1,400 $1,175 $950 $875 $750

In 1994, Cherry and Ebony finishes were discontinued.

ES-175 - single sharp cutaway body, arched maple top, f-holes, raised layered black pickguard, bound body, maple back/sides, mahogany neck, 20-fret bound rosewood fingerboard with pearl parallelogram inlay, adjustable rosewood bridge/trapeze tailpiece, black face peghead with pearl crown/logo inlay, nickel hardware, single coil pickup, volume/tone control. Available in Natural and Sunburst finishes. Mfg. 1949 to 1971.

1949-1956 (P90 pickup) N/A $2,800 $2,600 $2,350 $2,200 $1,800 $1,600
1957-1962 (PAF pickup) N/A $3,000 $2,375 $2,000 $1,650 $1,300 $1,150
1963-1971 N/A $2,000 $1,750 $1,500 $1,300 $1,150 $1,000

In 1957, P.A.F. humbucker pickup replaced original part/design. In 1962, Pat. No. humbucker pickups replaced previous part/design. This model was also produced in a thinline body, ES-175 T. Further research continues on this configuration for future editions.

ES-175 D (ES75) - similar to ES-175, except has 2 single coil pickups, 2 volume/2 tone controls, 3-position switch. Mfg. 1953 to date.

1953-1956 (P90 pickups) N/A $3,000 $2,400 $2,150 $2,000 $1,775 $1,550
1957-1962 (PAF pickups) N/A $3,500 $3,000 $2,650 $2,325 $1,900 $1,650
1962-1969 (Pat. No. pickups) N/A $2,500 $2,200 $2,000 $1,725 $1,550 $1,350
1970-1997 N/A $2,000 $1,850 $1,375 $1,250 $995 $875
MSR $3,922 $2,650 $2,150 $1,800 $1,575 $1,350 $1,100 $975

Add $76 for Vintage Sunburst finish.

Add $923 for Natural finish.

Current production instruments are produced in either a Wine Red (WR), Vintage Sunburst (VS) or Natural (AN) finish with gold hardware.

In 1957, P.A.F. humbucker pickups replaced original part/design. In 1962, Pat. No. humbucker pickups replaced previous part/design.
In 1974, neck volute was introduced. By 1977, tune-o-matic bridge replaced original part/design. In 1981, neck volute was discontinued.
In 1983, mahogany back/sides replaced original part/design. In 1990, maple back/sides replaced previous part/design.

ES-175 D-AN (ES75-AN) - similar to ES-175 D, except has 2 single coil pickups, 2 volume/2 tone controls, 3-position switch. Available in Antique Natural finish and nickel hardware. Disc. 2000.

$3,625 $2,850 $2,475 $2,100 $1,700 $1,350 $1,100

Last MSR was $5,589.

ES-225 T - single sharp cutaway thin body, arched maple top, f-holes, raised layered black pickguard, bound body, maple back/sides, mahogany neck, 20-fret bound rosewood fingerboard with pearl dot inlay, trapeze wrapover tailpiece, blackface peghead with pearl logo inlay, single coil pickup, volume/tone control. Available in Sunburst finish. Mfg. 1955 to 1959.

N/A $1,300 $1,200 $1,100 $925 $800 $750

ES-225 TD - similar to ES-225T, except has 2 pickups, 2 volume/2 tone controls. Mfg. 1956 to 1959.

N/A $1,875 $1,625 $1,450 $1,250 $1,050 $925

ES-240 - very rare model, only 3 are known to exist.

Extreme rarity factor precludes accurate price evaluation.

ES-250 - jumbo style, spruce top, raised bound black pickguard, 3-stripe bound body, maple back/sides/neck, 14/20-fret bound rosewood fingerboard with pearl open book inlay, adjustable rosewood bridge/trapeze tailpiece, blackface stairstep peghead with pearl logo inlay, 3-per-side tuners, nickel hardware, single coil Charlie Christian pickup, volume/tone control. Available in Natural and Sunburst finishes. Limited Mfg. 1938 to 1940, very rare.

N/A N/A $7,500 $6,200 $5,750 $4,400 $3,650

In 1940, standard style peghead, split half circle fingerboard inlay replaced original part/design.

GRADING	100% MINT	98% NEAR MINT	95% EXC+	90% EXC	80% VG+	70% VG	60% G

ES-295 - single sharp cutaway body, multi-bound maple top, f-holes, raised white pickguard with etched flowers, maple back/sides/neck, 19-fret bound rosewood fingerboard with pearl parallelogram inlay, trapeze wrapover tailpiece, blackface peghead with pearl plant/logo inlay, 3-per-side tuners with pearl buttons, gold hardware, 2 single coil pickups, 2 volume/2 tone controls, 3-position switch. Available in Gold finish. Mfg. 1952 to 1959.

N/A	$5,000	$4,500	$3,900	$3,450	$3,150	$3,000

In 1955, 20-fret fingerboard replaced original part/design. In 1958, humbucker pickups replaced original part/design.

Current production instruments are part of the Historic Collection Series, found at the end of this section.

ES-300 (1940-1942 Mfg.) - spruce top, bound black pickguard, multi-bound body, maple back/sides/neck, 14/20-fret rosewood fingerboard with pearl parallelogram inlay, adjustable rosewood bridge/trapeze tailpiece, bound peghead with pearl crown/logo inlay, 3-per-side tuners, nickel hardware, single coil pickup, volume/tone control. Available in Natural and Sunburst finishes. Mfg. 1940 to 1942.

N/A	N/A	N/A	$2,400	$2,100	$1,500	$1,250

This model was also manufactured with a split diamond peghead inlay.

ES-300 (1946 to 1952 Mfg.) - similar to ES-300 Prewar, except has layered black pickguard, bound fingerboard. Mfg. 1946 to 1952.

N/A	$2,100	$1,650	$1,450	$1,200	$1,000	$925

In 1948, 2 single coil pickups, 2 volume controls replaced original part/design. Tone control moved to upper treble bout.

ES-320 TD - double round cutaway semi-hollow bound body, arched maple top, f-holes, raised black pickguard, maple back/sides/neck, 22-fret rosewood fingerboard with pearl dot inlay, fixed tune-o-matic bridge with logo engraved cover, 3-per-side tuners, nickel hardware, 2 single coil pickups, volume/tone control, 2 slide switches. Available in Cherry, Natural and Walnut finishes. Mfg. 1971 to 1975.

N/A	$750	$625	$500	$425	$350	$295

ES-325 TD - double round cutaway semi-hollow bound body, arched maple top, f-holes, raised layered black pickguard, maple back/sides/neck, 22-fret rosewood fingerboard with pearl dot inlay, tune-o-matic bridge/trapeze tailpiece, 3-per-side tuners with plastic buttons, nickel hardware, 2 mini humbucker pickups, 2 volume/2 tone controls, 3-position switch, control mounted on black plastic plate. Available in Cherry, Walnut, and Wine Red finishes. Mfg. 1972 to 1979.

$850	$750	$650	$550	$475	$375	$325

ES-330 T - double round cutaway semi-hollow bound body, arched maple top, raised bound black pickguard, f-holes, maple back/sides, mahogany neck, 22-fret bound rosewood fingerboard with pearl dot inlay, tune-o-matic bridge/trapeze tailpiece, blackface peghead with pearl logo inlay, 3-per-side tuners with plastic buttons, nickel hardware, single coil pickup, volume/tone control. Available in Cherry, Natural and Sunburst finishes. Mfg. 1959 to 1963.

N/A	$1,700	$1,350	$1,200	$1,100	$1,000	$950

In 1962, block fingerboard inlay, chrome covered pickups replaced original part/design, Cherry finish became an option, Natural finish was discontinued.

ES-330 TD - similar to ES-330 T, except has 2 single coil pickups, 2 volume/2 tone controls, 3-position switch. Mfg. 1959 to 1972.

N/A	$2,000	$1,750	$1,450	$1,150	$1,050	$950

In 1962, pearl block fingerboard inlay replaced original part/design. Between 1967-1969, Sparkling Burgundy finish was an option. In 1968, Walnut finish was an option.

ES-335 S STANDARD (ES-335 SOLID BODY) - double round cutaway maple body, black pickguard, mahogany neck, 22-fret rosewood fingerboard with pearl dot inlay, tune-o-matic bridge/stop tailpiece, 3-per-side tuners, nickel hardware, 2 "exposed" humbucker pickups, 2 volume/2 tone controls, mini switch (for coil tapping), 3-way selector switch. Available in Natural and Sunburst finishes. Mfg. 1980 to 1983.

N/A	$700	$650	$550	$475	$400	$350

This model was clearly based on the popular ES-335 semi-hollow model; the width of the solid body is narrower than the semi-hollow model it is based on.

ES-335 S Custom - similar to the ES-335 S Standard, except features a mahogany body, 2 Gibson "Dirty Finger" humbucking pickups. Mfg. 1981 only.

N/A	$750	$695	$650	$600	$525	$475

ES-335 S Deluxe - similar to the ES-335 S Standard, except features a mahogany body, bound ebony fingerboard, brass nut, TP-6 Fine Tuning tailpiece/tune-o-matic bridge, 2 Gibson "Dirty Finger" humbucking pickups. Mfg. 1980 to 1983.

N/A	$750	$695	$650	$600	$525	$475

Gibson ES-175 D (Current Mfg.) courtesy Gibson USA

Gibson ES-300 (Prewar) courtesy Gary's Classic

G

GRADING		100% MINT	98% NEAR MINT	95% EXC+	90% EXC	80% VG+	70% VG	60% G

ES-335 T (ES-335 TD) - double round cutaway semi-hollow bound body, arched maple top, f-holes, raised layered black pickguard, maple back/sides, mahogany neck, 22-fret rosewood fingerboard with pearl dot inlays, tune-o-matic bridge/stop tailpiece, blackface peghead with pearl crown/logo inlay, 3-per-side tuners, nickel hardware, 2 covered humbucker PAF pickups, 2 volume/2 tone controls, 3-position switch. Available in Cherry, Blonde and Sunburst finishes. Mfg. 1958 to 1960 (as the ES-335 T), 1960 to 1982 (as the ES-335 TD).

1958-1959		**N/A**	**$15,000**	**$13,500**	**$11,500**	**$9,600**	**$7,700**	**$6,800**

In 1958, some models found were unbound. In 1959, Cherry finish was an option. In 1960, the name changed to ES-335 TD, smaller pickguard replaced original part/design.

1960-1961		**N/A**	**$10,000**	**$8,500**	**$7,250**	**$5,750**	**$5,000**	**$4,750**
1962-1964		**N/A**	**$6,500**	**$4,800**	**$4,000**	**$3,300**	**$2,800**	**$2,400**
1965-1968		**N/A**	**$2,500**	**$1,650**	**$1,200**	**$1,000**	**$850**	**$700**
1969-1974		**N/A**	**$1,700**	**$1,500**	**$1,300**	**$1,150**	**$975**	**$850**
1975-1982		**N/A**	**$1,700**	**$1,550**	**$1,400**	**$1,250**	**$1,150**	**$1,000**

In 1962, block fingerboard inlay, Pat. No. pickups replaced original part/design. In 1964, trapeze tailpiece replaced original part/design. In 1967, Walnut finish became an option, some models with slanted block fingerboard inlay. From 1969 to 1970, neck volute was available. In 1977, coil tap switch was added.

In 1982, this original version was discontinued in favor of the ES-335 Dot (a return to the 1960 style with dot fingerboard markers). The ES-335 TD Dot is currently known as the ES-335 TD (ESDT).

ES-335 TD (ESDT) - double round cutaway semi hollow bound maple body, f-holes, raised black pickguard, mahogany neck, 22-fret bound rosewood fingerboard with pearl dot inlay, tune-o-matic bridge/stop tailpiece, blackface peghead with pearl plant/logo inlay, 3-per-side tuners, nickel hardware, 2 covered humbucker pickups, 2 volume/2 tone controls, 3-position switch. Available in Natural, Cherry (CH), Ebony (EB), Trans Brown (BR), Vintage Sunburst (VS), and Gothic (100% satin black finish, black chrome hardware, and 12th fret moon and star inlay) finishes. Mfg. 1982 to date.

1982-1997		**N/A**	**$2,000**	**$1,875**	**$1,750**	**$1,650**	**$1,575**	**$1,500**
MSR	**$3,614**	**$2,450**	**$1,825**	**$1,575**	**$1,350**	**$1,150**	**$950**	**$825**

Subtract approx. 35% for Gothic finish (matte black, Mfg. 1999 only).

In 1994, Ebony finish was discontinued.

ES-335 TD-AN - similar to the ES-335 TD. Available in Antique Natural finish (with nickel hardware). Current Mfg.

MSR	**$4,383**	**$2,975**	**$2,200**	**$1,850**	**$1,600**	**$1,400**	**$1,200**	**$1,000**

ES-335 TD Plain Wood (ESBP/ESDP) - similar to the ES-335 TD, except has plain wood top, and choice of block (ESBP) or dot (ESDP) neck inlays. Available in Trans Blue, Natural, Trans Red, or Ebony (dot neck only) finish. New 1999.

MSR	**$3,075**	**$2,100**	**$1,575**	**$1,375**	**$1,175**	**$975**	**$850**	**$700**

ES-335 TD-12 - similar to the ES-335 TD, except in 12-string configuration, fingerboard block inlay, triangular peghead inlay. Mfg. 1965 to 1971.

		N/A	**$1,500**	**$1,300**	**$1,100**	**$900**	**$825**	**$750**

ES-335 Studio - similar to ES-335 TD, except has no f-holes. Mfg. 1987 to 1994.

		N/A	**$800**	**$700**	**$600**	**$550**	**$475**	**$400**

Last MSR was $900.

ES-340 TD - double round cutaway semi hollow bound body, arched maple top, f-holes, raised layered black pickguard, maple back/sides/neck, 22-fret rosewood fingerboard with pearl dot inlay, tune-o-matic bridge/stop tailpiece, blackface peghead with pearl crown/logo inlay, 3-per-side tuners, nickel hardware, 2 covered humbucker pickups, volume/mixer/2 tone controls, 3-position switch. Available in Natural and Walnut finishes. Mfg. 1969 to 1974.

		N/A	**$1,750**	**$1,500**	**$1,250**	**$1,000**	**$900**	**$825**

ES-345 TD - double rounded cutaway semi-hollow bound body, arched maple top, f-holes, raised layered black pickguard, maple back/sides, mahogany neck, 22-fret bound rosewood fingerboard with pearl parallelogram inlay, tune-o-matic bridge/trapeze tailpiece, blackface peghead with pearl crown/logo inlay, 3-per-side tuners with plastic buttons, gold hardware, 2 covered humbucker pickups, 2 volume/2 tone controls, 3-position/Vari-tone switches, stereo output. Available in Cherry, Natural, Sunburst and Walnut finishes. Mfg. 1959 to 1982.

1959-1964		**N/A**	**$6,500**	**$6,000**	**$4,650**	**$4,150**	**$3,650**	**$3,150**
1965-1969		**N/A**	**$3,500**	**$3,200**	**$2,800**	**$2,400**	**$2,100**	**$1,850**
1970-1982		**N/A**	**$1,800**	**$1,600**	**$1,500**	**$1,300**	**$1,100**	**$995**

In 1959, Cherry finish became an option. In 1969, Walnut finish became an option. In 1982, stop tailpiece replaced original part/design.

ES-347 TD - double rounded cutaway semi-hollow bound body, arched figured maple top, f-holes, raised layered black pickguard, maple back/sides/neck, 22-fret bound ebony fingerboard with pearl block inlay, tune-o-matic bridge/tunable stop tailpiece, bound blackface peghead with pearl crown/logo inlay, 3-per-side tuners, gold hardware, 2 covered humbucker pickups, 2 volume/2 tone controls, 3-position/coil tap switches. Available in Sunburst finish. Mfg. 1978 to 1991.

		N/A	**$1,800**	**$1,550**	**$1,295**	**$1,000**	**$925**	**$800**

ES-350 - single rounded cutaway hollow bound body, arched figured maple top, bound f-holes, raised layered black pickguard, maple back/sides/neck, 22-fret bound rosewood fingerboard with pearl parallelogram inlay, adjustable rosewood bridge/trapeze tailpiece, bound blackface peghead with pearl crown/logo inlay, 3-per-side tuners with plastic buttons, gold hardware, covered single coil pickup, volume/tone controls. Available in Natural and Sunburst finishes. Mfg. 1947 to 1956.

1947-1949 (1 P90 pickup)		**N/A**	**$3,500**	**$3,150**	**$2,800**	**$2,350**	**$2,000**	**$1,750**
1950-1956 (2 pickups)		**N/A**	**$4,000**	**$3,400**	**$3,000**	**$2,600**	**$2,300**	**$2,000**

In 1948, 2 single coil pickups, tone control on cutaway bout, 2 volume controls were introduced. In 1952, 2 volume/2 tone controls 3-position switch replaced previous part/design. In 1956, tune-o-matic bridge replaced original part/design.

GRADING	100% MINT	98% NEAR MINT	95% EXC+	90% EXC	80% VG+	70% VG	60% G

ES-350 T - similar to ES-350, except has thin body, short scale length. Mfg. 1955 to 1963.

	N/A	$4,000	$3,200	$2,800	$2,350	$2,000	$1,750

ES-350 T models with PAF pickups and/or a Blonde finish command a premium.

In 1957, P.A.F. humbucker pickups replaced original part/design. In 1960, sharp cutaway replaced original part/design.

ES-355 TD-SV - double rounded cutaway semi-hollow bound body, arched maple top, bound f-holes, raised layered black pickguard, maple back/sides, mahogany neck, 22-fret bound ebony fingerboard with pearl block inlay, tune-o-matic bridge/Bigsby vibrato tailpiece, bound blackface peghead with pearl split diamond/logo inlay, 3-per-side tuners, gold hardware, 2 covered P.A.F. humbucker pickups, 2 volume/2 tone controls, 3-position/Varitone switches, stereo output. Available in Cherry and Walnut finishes. Mfg. 1958 to 1982.

1958-1962	N/A	$7,500	$6,950	$6,000	$5,250	$4,750	$4,250
1963-1968	N/A	$3,000	$2,800	$2,500	$2,300	$2,100	$1,950
1969-1974	N/A	$2,500	$2,250	$2,150	$1,950	$1,900	$1,750
1975-1982	N/A	$2,000	$1,800	$1,550	$1,350	$1,200	$1,100

This model with mono PAFs and stop tailpiece is the most desirable.

In 1961, side-pull vibrato replaced original part/design. In 1962, Pat. No. humbucker pickups replaced original part/design. In 1963, Vibrola tailpiece with engraved lyre/logo replaced previous part/design.

In 1969, Bigsby vibrato replaced previous part/design, Walnut finish became an option. In 1974, neck volute was introduced. In 1981, neck volute was discontinued.

1964 Gibson ES-335
courtesy Garrie Johnson

ES-369 - double rounded cutaway semi-hollow bound body, arched maple top, f-holes, raised cream pickguard, maple back/sides, mahogany neck, 22-fret bound rosewood fingerboard with pearl trapezoid inlay, tune-o-matic bridge/tunable stop tailpiece, blackface peghead with pearl logo inlay, 3-per-side tuners, chrome hardware, 2 exposed humbucker pickups, 2 volume/2 tone controls, 3-position/coil tap switches. Available in Cherry, Natural, Sunburst and Walnut finishes. Mfg. 1982 only.

	N/A	$1,500	$1,200	$1,100	$950	$775	$725

ES-775 - single sharp cutaway hollow bound maple body, f-holes, raised bound black pickguard, 3-piece figured maple neck, 20-fret bound ebony fingerboard with pearl block inlay, tune-o-matic metal/ebony bridge/trapeze tailpiece, ebony block tailpiece insert, bound peghead with pearl stylized bird/logo inlay, 3-per-side Grover Imperial tuners, gold hardware, 2 covered humbucker pickups, 2 volume/2 tone controls, 3-position switch. Available in Ebony finish. Disc. 1996.

	$2,000	$1,650	$1,450	$1,200	$950	$850	$795

Last MSR was $2,400.

Add $400 for Antique Natural and Vintage Sunburst finishes.

ES ARTIST ACTIVE - double rounded cutaway semi-hollow bound body, arched maple top, raised layered black pickguard, maple back/sides, mahogany neck, 22-fret bound ebony fingerboard with pearl offset dot inlay, tune-o-matic bridge/tunable stop tailpiece, blackface peghead with pearl winged-f/logo inlay, 3-per-side tuners, gold hardware, 2 covered humbucker pickups, 2 volume/1 tone controls, 3-position switch, 3 mini switches, active electronics, stereo output. Available in Cherry, Natural, Sunburst and Walnut finishes. Mfg. 1979 to 1986.

	$1,450	$1,250	$1,100	$875	$725	$595	$450

A few ES Artist models were produced with a unique ES Artist trapeze tailpiece, 3-Tone Sunburst finish, stereo output, and unusual fretboard inlays. This variation is rare, and prices are typically in the $3,250-$4,500 range (or maybe a trade for a Pelham Blue 335 + a few extra buck$!).

Electrics: Misc.

GK-55 - single cutaway mahogany body, bolt-on mahogany neck, 22-fret rosewood fingerboard with pearl dot inlay, tune-o-matic bridge/stop tailpiece, 3-per-side tuners, chrome hardware, 2 exposed humbucker pickups, 2 volume/2 tone controls, 3-position switch. Available in Tobacco Sunburst finish. Mfg. 1979 only.

	$300	$250	$225	$175	$150	$125	$100

KZ II - dual cutaway body, mahogany neck, rosewood fingerboard, 3-per-side tuners, truss rod cover with engraved KZ II logo. Mfg. 1980 only.

According to sources contacted at Gibson, the KZ II was a project at Kalamazoo to use up "leftover parts and pieces". The design was later sold to another company, who produced the model as the Spirit.

Jimmy KcKenzie, a current owner of one of these guitar models, describes the guitar as *having a Les Paul neck affixed to a Melody Maker body.* More research continues into this model.

The relative rarity and scarity of information about this late Kalamazoo era solid body makes pricing difficult.

SR-71 - offset double cutaway, 2 single coil/1 humbucker pickups, Wayne Charvel design. Mfg. 1989 only.

	N/A	$360	$325	$295	$275	$250	$225

While Lockheed made this model famous, Gibson's attempt ended up in a tailspin.

U-2 - offset double cutaway basswood body, maple neck, rosewood fingerboard, Kahler vibrato, 6-on-a-side tuners, black hardware, 2 single coil/humbucker pickups. Mfg. 1987 to 1994.

	$450	$400	$360	$330	$300	$275	$250

Last MSR was $949.

Gibson ES-775
courtesy Gibson USA

GRADING	100% MINT	98% NEAR MINT	95% EXC+	90% EXC	80% VG+	70% VG	60% G

US-1 - offset double cutaway basswood body, bound maple top/back, balsa wood core, ebony fingerboard, 6-on-a-side tuners, 1 humbucker/2 stacked coil humbuckers, with or w/o tremelo, available in Natural top finish. Mfg. 1987 to 1994.

$500 $450 $400 $350 $300 $275 $250
Last MSR was $1,575.

ALL AMERICAN II - dual cutaway (Melody Maker-style) solid mahogany body, mahogany neck, 24 3/4" scale, 22-fret rosewood fingerboard with dot inlay, vibrola (tremolo) bridge, blackface peghead with silkscreened logo, engraved "All American II" on truss rod cover, 3-per-side tuners, chrome hardware, 2 exposed polepiece single coil pickups, volume/tone controls, 3-way toggle switch. Available in Ebony (EB) and Dark Wineburst (DW) finishes. Mfg. 1996 to 1998.

$450 $395 $350 $300 $275 $225 $175
Last MSR was $649.

FUTURA - "can opener"-style hardwood body, black tri-laminated pickguard, through-body maple neck, 22-fret rosewood fingerboard with white dot inlay, tune-o-matic bridge/stop tailpiece, 6-on-a-side tuners, chrome hardware, 2 covered humbucker pickups, 2 volume/1 tone controls, 3-position/rotary coil tap switches. Available in Ebony, Ultraviolet, and White finish. Mfg. 1983 to 1985.

$275 $225 $195 $150 $125 $100 $75

INVADER - single cutaway mahogany body/neck, 22-fret ebony fingerboard with dot inlay, double locking vibrato, 6-on-a-side tuners, black hardware, 2 exposed *Dirty Finger* humbucker pickups, 2 volume/2 tone controls, 3-position switch. Available in Black finish. Mfg. 1983 to 1989.

$350 $300 $250 $200 $175 $125 $100

G

VICTORY MV-2 - offset double cutaway, rosewood fingerboard, 6-on-a-side tuners, 2 humbuckers. Available in Antique Sunburst or Candy Apple Red finishes. Mfg. 1981 to 1984.

$325 $275 $225 $195 $175 $150 $125

Victory MV-10 - similar to Victory MV-2, except has an ebony fingerboard, stacked coil pickup, coil tap switch. Available in Apple Red and Twilight Blue finishes.

$350 $295 $225 $175 $150 $125 $100

Explorer Series

EXPLORER (KORINA) - offset hourglass korina (African limba wood) body, white pickguard, korina neck, 22-fret rosewood fingerboard with pearl dot inlay, tune-o-matic bridge/stop tailpiece, blackface peghead with pearl logo inlay, 6-on-a-side tuners, gold (1958-59) or nickel (1962-63) hardware, 2 P.A.F. (1958-59) or patent number (1962-63) humbucker pickups, 2 volume/1 tone controls, 3-position switch. Available in Natural finish. Mfg. 1958-1959 and 1962-1963 (brown case 1958-59, black case 1962-63).

A few early specimens were produced with a V-shaped peghead and a raised plastic logo. The first prototype was dubbed the Futura.

The Explorer model was introduced shortly after the Flying V and had a 1958 retail price of $247.50. A modernistic concept guitar from Gibson, this model had very limited manufacture (estimated to be under 100 instruments). Original Explorers exhibiting some wear and no problems are currently priced in the $45,000- $55,000 range, and upwards to $100,000. Even though the 1962-1963 period of manufacture was mostly a clean- up of earlier bodies and related parts that were never finished during the first production run, values seem to be the same for both periods. Until someone finds and documents a Moderne, the Explorer (Korina) will continue to be Gibson's most desirable and rarest electric instrument.

Explorer Reissue - similar to Explorer (Korina), except has mahogany body/neck. Available in Black, Natural and White finishes. Mfg. 1975 to 1980.

N/A $1,500 $1,295 $1,100 $950 $850 $750

Explorer II - similar to Explorer (Korina), except has 5-piece laminated walnut/maple body, maple neck, ebony fingerboard with dot inlay, *E 2* engraved truss rod cover, tunable TP-6 stop tailpiece, gold hardware, 2 exposed coil humbucker pickups. Available in Natural finish. Mfg. 1979 to 1984.

N/A $1,100 $1,000 $950 $900 $825 $775

This model was also available with maple neck. Body woods on this model were interchangeable (i.e. walnut or maple used on top). Models with a bound curly maple top may be an Explorer CMT (See model below).

Explorer (I) - similar to Explorer II, except has mahogany body, rosewood fingerboard with dot inlay, decal headstock logo, tune-o-matic bridge/stop tailpiece or black Kahler Flyer tremolo, 2 uncovered humbuckers. Available in Black and White finishes. Mfg. 1981 to 1989.

N/A $900 $850 $795 $750 $700 $675

In 1987, ebony fingerboard replaced rosewood fingerboard; tremolo bridge was discontinued.

This model was also available in a left-handed configuration (Explorer Left Hand), available 1984 to 1987.

EXPLORER KORINA REISSUE (1984 Mfg.) - offset hourglass korina body, black pickguard, korina neck, 22-fret rosewood fingerboard with pearl dot inlay, tune-o-matic bridge/stop tailpiece, blackface peghead with pearl logo inlay, stamped serial number on peghead, 6-on-a-side Schaller tuners, gold hardware, 2 humbucker pickups, 2 volume/1 tone controls, 3-position switch. Available in Antique Natural, Candy Apple Red, Ebony and Ivory finishes. Mfg. 1984 only.

N/A $2,500 $2,200 $1,950 $1,650 $1,500 $1,350

This was Gibson's first Explorer Korina reissue model. In 1984, this Limited Edition was designed as a re-issue of 1958 Explorer.

It is estimated that only 1,000 instruments were produced. Current production instruments (1958 Korina Explorer) are part of the Historic Collection Series, found at the end of this section.

Explorer Heritage (Limited Edition) - similar to Explorer Korina Reissue, except has inked serial number on peghead, pearloid buttons, black control knobs. Available in Antique Natural, Ebony and Ivory finishes. Mfg. 1983 only.

N/A $3,500 $3,000 $2,500 $2,000 $1,800 $1,650

It is estimated that 100 of these instruments were manufactured. Serial numbers on the Explorer Heritage models consist of a single letter followed by 3 digits.

Explorer Heritage (Custom Shop) - similar to Explorer Korina Reissue, except has stamped serial number on peghead, black pickguard, gold hardware. Available in Antique Natural, Ebony and Ivory finishes. Mfg. 1983 only.

N/A $2,000 $1,800 $1,600 $1,400 $1,250 $1,100

It is estimated that 500 of these instruments were manufactured.

GRADING		100% MINT	98% NEAR MINT	95% EXC+	90% EXC	80% VG+	70% VG	60% G

EXPLORER 83 (EXPLORER) - offset hourglass body, mahogany neck, 22-fret rosewood fingerboard with pearl dot inlay, tremolo tailpiece (Kahler and Floyd Rose systems), 6-on-a-side tuners, chrome hardware, 2 exposed coil humbucker pickups, 2 volume/tone controls, 3-position switch. Available in Black and White finishes. Mfg. 1984 to 1989.

		N/A	$750	$675	$595	$525	$450	$425

In 1984, alder body replaced original part/design. When the name was changed from the Explorer 83 to Explorer, this model was offered with optional custom graphics and original artist finishes.

Explorer w/Black Hardware - similar to Explorer 83, except has Kahler tremolo system and black hardware. Mfg. 1985 only.

		N/A	$750	$675	$595	$525	$450	$425

Explorer CMT - similar to Explorer 83, except has bound curly maple top. Mfg. 1984 only.

		N/A	$795	$725	$625	$550	$475	$450

Some models may have *E 2* engraved on the truss rod cover.

EXPLORER III - offset hourglass alder body, white pickguard, korina neck, 22-fret rosewood fingerboard with pearl dot inlay, tune-o-matic bridge/stop tailpiece, peghead logo decal, 6-on-a-side tuners, chrome hardware, 3 'soapbar' P-90 pickups, volume/tone controls, 3-position switch. Available in Natural finish. Mfg. 1984 to 1985.

		N/A	$600	$550	$525	$475	$450	$425

Explorer III w/Black Hardware - similar to Explorer III, except has Kahler tremolo system and black hardware. Mfg. 1985 only.

		N/A	$625	$575	$550	$500	$475	$450

EXPLORER 425 - offset hourglass mahogany body, set-in mahogany neck, white pickguard, 22-fret ebony fingerboard with pearl dot inlay, Kahler vibrato, blackface peghead with pearl logo inlay, 6-on-a-side tuners, black hardware, 2 uncovered single coil/humbucker pickups, volume/tone controls, 3 mini switches. Available in Natural finish. Mfg. 1986 only.

		N/A	$600	$550	$500	$475	$425	$400

XLP Custom - similar to Explorer 425, except has bound top, sharply pointed horns, rounded cutout on lower treble bout, 2 Dirty Fingers exposed coil humbuckers, double locking tremolo system. Mfg. 1985 to 1987.

		N/A	$975	$850	$695	$650	$595	$485

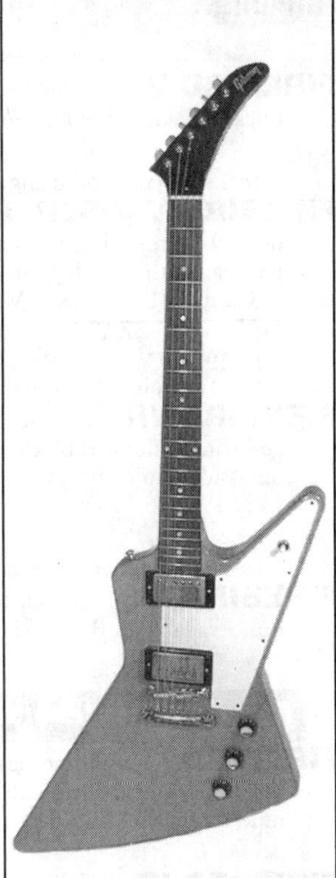
Gibson Explorer
courtesy Dave Hinson

EXPLORER '76 (DSXR, EXPLORER REISSUE) - offset hourglass mahogany body/neck, white pickguard, 22-fret rosewood fingerboard with pearl dot inlay, tune-o-matic bridge/stop tailpiece, blackface peghead with pearl logo inlay, 6-on-a-side tuners, chrome hardware, 2 ceramic (496R and 500T) magnet humbuckers, 2 volume/1 tone controls, 3-position switch. Available in Cherry (CH), Classic White (CW), Ebony (EB), Natural (mfg, 1999-2001), Natural Burst (Mfg. 1999-2001), Vintage Sunburst (VS) or Gothic (satin black finish, black chrome hardware, and 12th fret moon and star inlay) finishes. Mfg. 1990 to date.

MSR	$1,891	$1,200	$950	$850	$725	$625	$525	$425

Add $108 for Classic White finish.

In 1994, Vintage Sunburst finish was discontinued.

GIBSON EXPLORER (DSXR) - mahogany body and neck, 2 ceramic (496R and 500T) magnet humbuckers, rosewood fingerboard, tune-o-matic bridge with stop tailpiece, chrome or gold hardware, various finishes (including Gothic, 100% satin black finish, black chrome hardware, and 12th fret moon and star inlay). New 1998.

MSR	$1,768	$1,175	$925	$825	$725	$625	$525	$425

Add $154 for Gothic finish (limited Mfg.).

EXPLORER 90 DOUBLE - offset hourglass mahogany body/neck, 25 1/2" scale, white pickguard, 22-fret rosewood fingerboard with pearl dot inlay, tune-o-matic bridge/stop tailpiece, blackface peghead with pearl split diamond/logo inlay, 6-on-a-side tuners, gold hardware, 2 humbucker pickups, 2 volume/1 tone controls, 3-position switch. Available in Natural finish. Mfg. 1989 to 1991.

		N/A	$900	$825	$675	$550	$495	$450

Firebird Reverse Series

Firebird guitars were offered in custom colors as well as standard Gibson finishes. The Firebirds were available in these Custom Colors: Amber Red, Cardinal Red, Frost Blue, Golden Mist, Heather, Inverness Green, Kelly Green, Pelham Blue, Polaris Blue, and Silver Mist finishes.

Add 25% - 50% for custom colors (depending on rarity of the custom color).

FIREBIRD I - asymmetrical hourglass style mahogany body, layered white pickguard, through-body mahogany neck, 22-fret Brazilian rosewood fingerboard with pearl dot inlay, wrapover stop tailpiece, partial blackface reverse peghead with pearl logo inlay, 6-on-a-side banjo tuners, nickel hardware, covered humbucker pickup, volume/tone control. Available in Sunburst finish. Mfg. 1963 to 1965.

		N/A	$4,000	$3,500	$3,000	$2,550	$2,200	$2,000

A few of these guitars were produced with vibratos. In 1965, peghead design changed to bass side tuner array. In 1965, some models found with perpendicular to peghead tuners, single coil pickups.

FIREBIRD III - similar to Firebird I, except has bound fingerboard, tune-o-matic bridge/vibrato tailpiece, 2 humbucker pickups, 2 volume/2 tone controls, 3-position switch.

		N/A	$4,000	$3,500	$3,000	$2,500	$2,200	$2,000

In 1965, peghead design changed to bass side tuner array, some models found with perpendicular to peghead tuners, single coil pickups.

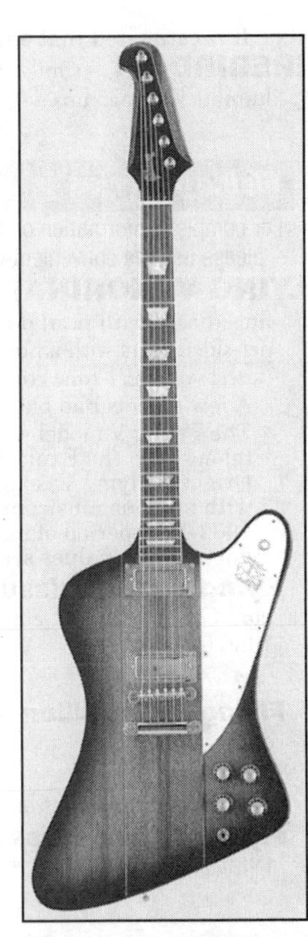
Gibson Firebird (Reissue)
courtesy Gibson USA

GRADING	100% MINT	98% NEAR MINT	95% EXC+	90% EXC	80% VG+	70% VG	60% G

FIREBIRD V - similar to Firebird I, except has bound fingerboard with trapezoid inlay, tune-o-matic bridge/vibrato with engraved cover, 2 humbucker pickups, 2 volume/2 tone controls, 3-position switch.

N/A $5,500 $4,800 $4,100 $3,350 $3,000 $2,800

In 1965, peghead design changed to bass side tuner array.

FIREBIRD V (DSFR, REISSUE) - asymmetrical hourglass style mahogany body, white pickguard with engraved Firebird symbol, through-body 9-piece mahogany/walnut neck, 22-fret rosewood fingerboard with pearl trapezoid inlay, tune-o-matic bridge/stop tailpiece, partial blackface peghead with pearl logo inlay, 6-on-a-side banjo tuners, chrome hardware, 2 covered pickups, 2 volume/2 tone controls, 3-position switch. Available in Cardinal Red, Classic White (CW), Ebony (EB), Heritage Cherry (HC), and Vintage Sunburst finishes. Mfg. 1990 to date.

MSR $2,152 $1,475 $1,075 $950 $825 $750 $675 $575

In 1994, Cardinal Red, Classic White, Ebony and Heritage Cherry finishes were discontinued. Circa 1975, a Firebird V "Reissue" (call it the 1st Reissue?) was briefly offered in a *gold coil* finish - these older reissues are currently selling in the $2,775 range.

FIREBIRD VII - asymmetrical hourglass style mahogany body, layered white pickguard, through-body mahogany neck, 22-fret bound ebony fingerboard with pearl block inlay, tune-o-matic bridge/vibrato tailpiece with engraved cover, partial blackface reverse peghead with pearl logo inlay, 6-on-a-side banjo tuners, gold hardware, 3 covered humbucker pickups, 2 volume/2 tone controls, 3-position switch. Available in Sunburst finish. Mfg. 1963 to 1965.

N/A $8,500 $7,750 $7,200 $6,750 $6,295 $4,750

In 1965, peghead design changed to bass side tuner array.

FIREBIRD '76 - similar to Firebird VII, except has red/white/blue Firebird emblem on pickguard, pearl dot fingerboard inlay, 2 humbucker pickups. Available in Black, Mahogany, Sunburst and White finishes. Mfg. 1976 only.

N/A $1,500 $1,350 $1,200 $1,050 $950 $895

Firebird Non-Reverse Series Solid Bodies

FIREBIRD I - asymmetrical hourglass style mahogany body, layered white pickguard with engraved Firebird logo, mahogany neck, 22-fret Brazilian rosewood fingerboard with pearl dot inlay, compensated bridge/vibrato tailpiece, 6-on-a-side tuners, chrome hardware, 2 single coil pickups, 2 volume/2 tone controls, 3-position switch. Available in Custom Color and Sunburst finishes. Mfg. 1963 to 1969.

N/A $1,300 $1,250 $1,050 $950 $850 $775

FIREBIRD III - similar to Firebird I, except has 3 pickups.

N/A $1,600 $1,450 $1,295 $1,150 $1,050 $975

FIREBIRD V - similar to Firebird I, except has tune-o-matic bridge/vibrato tailpiece with engraved cover, 2 covered original style Firebird humbucking pickups.

N/A $2,000 $1,850 $1,695 $1,475 $1,250 $1,050

FIREBIRD 12 - similar to Firebird I, except has 12 strings, blackface peghead with pearl split diamond inlay, tune-o-matic bridge/fixed tailpiece, 6-on-a-side tuners. Mfg. 1966 to 1967.

N/A $1,100 $950 $795 $625 $575 $525

It is estimated that only 272 instruments were produced.

FIREBIRD VII - similar to Firebird I, except has tune-o-matic bridge/vibrato tailpiece with engraved cover, gold hardware, 3 original style Firebird humbucking pickups.

N/A $2,500 $2,300 $1,950 $1,775 $1,550 $1,375

Flying V Series

For complete information on this unusual Gibson model, it is recommended to read *Flying V - An Illustrated History of the Modernistic Guitar* by Larry Meiners - please use the convenient insert order card in this book to order.

FLYING V (KORINA) - V-shaped korina body, layered white pickguard, rubber strip on treble side of body, korina neck, 22-fret rosewood fingerboard with pearl dot inlay, tune-o-matic bridge, strings through anchoring with V-shaped metal plate, raised plastic lettering on peghead, 3-per-side tuners with amber buttons, gold (1958-59) or nickel (1962-63) hardware, 2 PAF (1958-59) or patent number (1962-63) humbucker pickups, 2 volume/1 tone controls. Available in Natural finish, brown case 1958-59, black case 1962-63. Mfg. 1958 to 1959, 1962 to 1963.

A few models had black pickguards.

The Flying V model was introduced in 1958 and had an original retail price of $247.50 plus $75 for the case. A modernistic concept guitar (along with the Explorer and Moderne) from Gibson, this model had very limited manufacture (estimated to be under 100 instruments). Original Flying Vs exhibiting some wear and no problems are currently priced in the $40,000-$80,000 range, up to $100,000 (even more with a fmous musician premium attached). Recently, an original average condition Flying V case only sold for $10,000! Even though the 1962-1963 period of manufacture was mostly a clean-up of earlier bodies and related parts that were never finished during the first production run, values seem to be the same for both periods.

Flying V (1st Reissue) - similar to Flying V, except has mahogany body/neck, no rubber strip on body, tun-o-matic bridge/stud tailpiece (and Gibson vibrato), embossed logo on truss rod cover, redesigned (shorter and rounder) peghead. Available in Cherry and Sunburst finishes. Mfg. 1966 to 1970.

N/A $9,995 $8,950 $7,950 $7,150 $6,350 $5,750

Flying V Medallion - similar to Flying V (1st Reissue), except has Limited Edition medallion on top, redesigned (shorter) peghead. Mfg. 1971 only.

N/A $5,000 $4,500 $4,150 $3,750 $3,350 $3,000

It is estimated that only 350 instruments were produced.

Flying V (2nd Reissue) - similar to Flying V (1st Reissue). Available in Black, Natural, Tobacco Sunburst and White finishes. Mfg. 1975 to 1980.

N/A $2,000 $1,850 $1,650 $1,500 $1,375 $1,225

GRADING	100% MINT	98% NEAR MINT	95% EXC+	90% EXC	80% VG+	70% VG	60% G

FLYING V II - V-shaped 5-piece laminated walnut/maple body, layered black pickguard, walnut neck, 22-fret ebony fingerboard with pearl dot inlay, tune-o-matic bridge, strings through anchoring with V-shaped metal plate, blackface peghead with pearl logo, "V 2" engraved on truss rod cover, 3-per-side tuners, gold hardware, 2 "V"-shaped humbucker pickups, 2 volume/tone controls, 3-position switch. Available in Natural finish. Mfg. 1979 to 1982.

N/A $1,250 $1,150 $1,000 $925 $875 $825

This model was also available with maple neck. Body woods on this model were interchangeable, i.e. walnut or maple were used for top.
Towards the end of the production run, rectangular humbuckers were substituted for the *V*-shaped original pickups.
Models with a bound curly maple top may be a Flying V CMT (See model below).

FLYING V HERITAGE (LIMITED REISSUE, FLYING V 3RD REISSUE) - V-shaped korina body, layered white pickguard, rubber strip on treble side of body, korina neck, 22-fret rosewood fingerboard with pearl dot inlay, tune-o-matic bridge, strings through anchoring with V-shaped metal plate, raised plastic lettering on peghead, 3-per-side tuners with plastic single ring buttons, gold hardware, 2 humbucker PAF pickups, 2 volume/1 tone gold controls. Available in Antique Natural, Candy Apple Red, Ebony and White finishes. Mfg. 1981 to 1982 (Flying V Heritage), 1983 to 1984 (Flying V 3rd Edition).

N/A $2,750 $2,400 $2,150 $1,900 $1,825 $1,675

Subtract 20% for White finish.

Add 60% for Candy Apple Red finish.

Serial Numbers for the Flying V Heritage consisted of the letter A followed by 3 digits.
In 1983, renamed Flying V (3rd Reissue); black control knobs replaced original part/design.
It is estimated that only 1,000 instruments were produced between 1983 to 1984.
Current production instruments (1958 Korina Flying V) are part of the Historic Collection Series, found at the end of this section.

THE V (1983 Mfg.) - V-shaped mahogany body, bound curly maple top, mahogany neck, 22-fret ebony fingerboard with pearl dot inlay, tune-o-matic bridge/stop tailpiece, 3-per-side tuners, chrome hardware, 2 humbucker pickups, 2 volume/1 tone controls, 3-position switch. Available in Antique Natural, Antique Sunburst and Vintage Cherry Sunburst finishes. Mfg. 1983 only.

N/A $850 $700 $650 $600 $550 $475

FLYING V 83 (FLYING V) - V-shaped alder body, mahogany neck, 22-fret rosewood fingerboard with pearl dot inlay, tremolo tailpiece (Kahler or Floyd Rose), 3-per-side tuners, chrome hardware, peghead logo decal, 2 exposed coil humbucker pickups, 2 volume/1 tone controls, 3-position switch. Available in Ebony and Ivory finishes. Mfg. 1983 (Flying V 83), 1984 to 1989 (Flying V).

N/A $750 $650 $525 $450 $395 $350

In 1984, renamed Flying V, 2 Dirty Fingers humbuckers and tune-o-matic bridge replaced original part/design. Ivory finish discontinued, Alpine White and Red finishes were introduced. In 1984, tremolo and locking nut system were options. In 1984, Custom and Designer finishes were options. This model was also available in a left-handed configuration (Flying V Left Hand), available 1984 to 1989.

Flying V CMT - similar to Flying V, except has bound curly maple top. Available in Antique Sunburst or Vintage Cherry Sunburst finishes. Mfg. 1984 only.

N/A $650 $600 $500 $400 $350 $325

This model had an optional tremolo bridge. Some models may have a *V 2* engraved on the truss rod cover.

Flying V w/Black Hardware - similar to Flying V (circa 1984), except has Kahler locking tremolo, black hardware. Available in Alpine White, Ebony, and Red finishes. Mfg. 1985 only.

N/A $650 $600 $500 $400 $360 $330

FLYING V XPL - V-shaped mahogany body, layered white pickguard, set-in mahogany neck, 22-fret rosewood fingerboard with pearl dot inlay, tune-o-matic bridge/stop tailpiece, 6-on-a-side tuners, black hardware, 2 humbucker pickups, 2 volume/1 tone controls. Available in Night Violet and Plum Wineburst finishes. Mfg. 1984 to 1987.

N/A $650 $600 $525 $450 $400 $350

This model had an optional Kahler tremolo system.

Flying V XPL w/Black Hardware - similar to Flying V XPL, except has locking Kahler tremolo system, black hardware. Available in Alpine White, Ebony, and Red finishes. Mfg. 1985 only.

N/A $650 $600 $525 $450 $400 $350

Flying V 90 Double - similar to Flying V XPL, except has 24-fret ebony fingerboard with pearl split diamond inlay, 25 1/2" scale, strings through anchoring with V-shaped metal plate, blackface peghead with pearl logo inlay, single coil/humbucker pickups, volume/tone control, 3-position switch. Available in Black finish. Mfg. 1989-1992.

$500 $475 $425 $350 $300 $250 $200

FLYING V (1988-1989 Mfg.) - similar to original Flying V, except has a 24-fret ebony fingerboard, Steinberger KB-X vibrato or string through-body design, double coil pickup. Mfg. 1988 to 1989.

N/A $400 $350 $300 $275 $250 $225

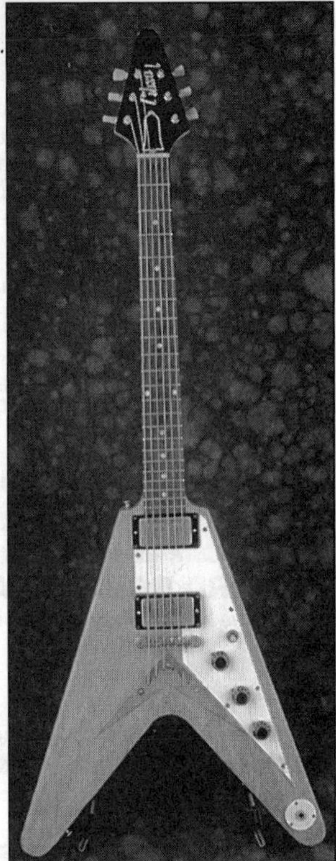

1958 Gibson Flying V
courtesy Southworth Guitars

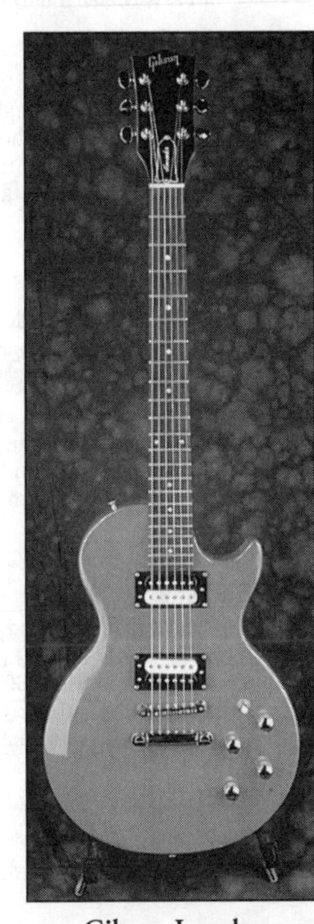

Gibson Invader
courtesy Judy Hill

GRADING			100% MINT	98% NEAR MINT	95% EXC+	90% EXC	80% VG+	70% VG	60% G

FLYING V '67 (DSVR, FLYING V REISSUE) - V-shaped mahogany body, white pickguard, mahogany neck, 22-fret rosewood fingerboard with pearl dot inlay, tune-o-matic bridge/stop tailpiece, arrow style peghead, 3-per-side tuners with pearl buttons, chrome hardware, 2 exposed humbucker pickups, 2 volume/1 tone controls, 3-position switch. Available in Cherry (CH), Classic White (CW), Ebony (EB), Vintage Sunburst (VS), Translucent Purple (Mfg. 1999-2001), Natural Burst (Mfg. 1999-2001) or Gothic (Mfg. 1999-2001, satin black finish, black chrome hardware, and 12th fret moon and star inlay) finish. Mfg. 1990 to date.

MSR	$1,922	$1,350	$995	$875	$775	$675	$595	$450

Add $153 for Classic White finish with gold hardware.

In 1994, Vintage Sunburst finish was discontinued.

FLYING V '98 - mahogany body and neck, 2 ceramic (496R and 500T) magnet humbuckers, rosewood fingerboard, tune-a-matic bridge with stop tailpiece, chrome or gold hardware, finishes include Gothic, (100% satin black finish, black chrome hardware, and 12th fret moon and star inlay), Natural Burst, Translucent Purple, Natural, and Classic White (Disc, 2001). 40th Anniversary Limited Edition. New 1998.

MSR	$1,845	$1,300	$925	$850	$775	$700	$650	$600

Add $153 for Natural finish.

Howard Roberts Models

HOWARD ROBERTS ARTIST - single sharp cutaway body, arched maple top, oval soundhole, raised multi-bound tortoise pickguard, 3-stripe bound body/rosette, maple back/sides/neck, 22-fret bound ebony fingerboard with pearl slot block inlay, adjustable ebony bridge/trapeze tailpiece, wood tailpiece insert with pearl model name inlay, bound peghead with pearl flower/logo inlay, 3-per-side tuners, gold hardware, humbucker pickup, volume/treble/mid controls. Available in Natural, Red Wine and Sunburst finishes. Mfg. 1976 to 1981.

	N/A	$1,800	$1,500	$1,200	$1,075	$950	$875

In 1979, two pickups became an option.

Howard Roberts Custom - similar to Howard Roberts Artist, except has rosewood fingerboard, chrome hardware. Available in Cherry, Sunburst and Wine Red finishes. Mfg. 1974 to 1981.

	N/A	$1,500	$1,200	$975	$795	$650	$595

HOWARD ROBERTS FUSION III (ARFU) - single sharp cutaway semi-hollow bound maple body, f-holes, raised black pickguard, maple neck, 20-fret bound rosewood fingerboard with pearl dot inlay, tune-o-matic bridge/adjustable tailpiece, peghead with pearl plant/logo inlay, 3-per-side tuners, gold hardware, 2 covered humbucker pickups, 2 volume/2 tone controls, 3-position switch. Available in Ebony (EB), Vintage Sunburst, Cherry, and Fireburst finishes. Mfg. 1979 to date.

MSR	$2,614	$1,800	$1,300	$1,100	$995	$850	$725	$625

Add $308 for Cherry (CH) or Vintage Sunburst (VS) finish.

In 1990, 6-finger tailpiece replaced original part/design.

In 1994, Fireburst finish was discontinued.

Johnny Smith Model

JOHNNY SMITH - single rounded cutaway bound hollow body, carved spruce top, bound f-holes, raised bound tortoise pickguard, figured maple back/sides/neck, 20-fret bound ebony fingerboard with pearl split block inlay, adjustable rosewood bridge/trapeze tailpiece, multi-bound peghead with split diamond/logo inlay, 3-per-side tuners, gold hardware, mini humbucker pickup, pickguard mounted volume control. Available in Natural and Sunburst finishes. Mfg. 1961 to 1989.

1961-1968	N/A	$7,500	$6,900	$5,750	$5,225	$4,775	$4,100
1969-1973	N/A	$6,000	$5,500	$5,150	$4,500	$4,250	$3,500
1974-1989	N/A	$4,500	$4,200	$4,100	$3,750	$3,250	$2,850

In 1963, 2 pickup model was introduced. By 1979, 6-finger tailpiece replaced original part/design.

L-Series/Le Grande

L-5 CES - single rounded cutaway bound hollow body, carved spruce top, layered tortoise pickguard, bound f-holes, maple back/sides/neck, 20-fret bound pointed ebony fingerboard with pearl block inlay, ebony bridge with pearl inlay on wings, model name engraved trapeze tailpiece with chrome insert, multibound blackface peghead with pearl flame/logo inlay, 3-per-side tuners, gold hardware, 2 single coil pickups, 2 volume/2 tone controls, 3-position switch. Available in Natural and Sunburst finish. Mfg. 1951 to date.

1951-1959	N/A	$15,000	$12,850	$10,725	$8,575	$7,750	$7,100
1960-1964	N/A	$11,375	$9,750	$8,250	$6,500	$5,850	$5,375
1965-1968	N/A	$7,500	$6,450	$5,350	$4,295	$3,850	$3,550
1969-current (Wine Red)	$4,750	$3,400	$2,950	$2,575	$2,350	$2,150	$1,950

Between 1951-53, P90 pickups were standard, between 1953-57, Alnico pickups were standard. In 1957, humbucker pickups replaced Alnico pickups. In 1960, sharp cutaway replaced original part/design. In 1962, Pat. No. humbucker pickups replaced P.A.F. humbuckers. In 1969, round cutaway replaced previous part/design. In 1974, neck volute was introduced. In 1981, neck volute was discontinued. Current production instruments (L-4 CES and L-5 CES models) are now part of the Historic Collection Series, found at the end of this section.

GRADING	100% MINT	98% NEAR MINT	95% EXC+	90% EXC	80% VG+	70% VG	60% G

L-5 S - single sharp cutaway multi-bound maple body, carved figured maple top, maple neck, 22-fret bound ebony pointed-end fingerboard with abalone block inlay, tune-o-matic bridge/trapeze tailpiece, silver center tailpiece insert with engraved model name, multi bound blackface peghead vase/logo inlay, 3-per-side tuners, gold hardware, 2 covered low impedance or regular humbucker pickups, 2 volume/2 tone controls, 3-position switch. Available in Cherry Sunburst finish. Mfg. 1972 to 1985.

High Impedance pickups	**N/A**	**$2,000**	**$1,800**	**$1,650**	**$1,395**	**$1,100**	**$950**
Low impedance pickups	**N/A**	**$1,500**	**$1,300**	**$1,100**	**$950**	**$850**	**$725**

This model is most desirable with 2 humbuckers and stop tailpiece. In 1974, covered humbucker pickups replaced original low impedance pickups (bridge pickup is diagonal).

In 1975, stop tailpiece replaced the original trapeze tailpiece. In 1976, tunable stop tailpiece replaced the stop tailpiece.

L-5 STUDIO (CSL5[ ]NH) - please refer to the Custom/Historic Collection Series listing.

L-6 S - single sharp cutaway maple body, black pickguard, maple neck, 24-fret maple fingerboard with pearl block inlay, tunable bridge/stop tailpiece, blackface peghead, 3-per-side tuners, chrome hardware, 2 covered humbucker pickups, 2 volume/1 tone controls, rotary switch. Available in Cherry and Natural finishes. Mfg. 1973 to 1980.

N/A	**$500**	**$450**	**$400**	**$350**	**$325**	**$275**

This model was available with ebony fingerboard in Tobacco Sunburst finish. In 1975, pearl dot inlay replaced block inlay, instrument renamed L-6S Custom.

L-6 S Deluxe - similar to L-6 S, except has bolt-on maple neck, pearl dot fingerboard inlay, strings through anchoring, volume/tone control, 3-position switch. Mfg. 1975 to 1980.

N/A	**$375**	**$350**	**$300**	**$250**	**$225**	**$200**

A few of these instruments have set necks. This instrument was also available with rosewood fingerboard.

LE GRAND - single round cutaway body, spruce top, bound f-holes, raised bound tortoise pickguard, figured maple back/sides/neck, 19-fret bound ebony fingerboard with abalone/pearl split block inlay, adjustable ebony bridge with pearl inlay/finger tailpiece, bound blackface peghead with pearl split diamond/logo inlay, 3-per-side tuners, gold hardware, floating single coil pickup. Available in Chablis, Sunrise Orange and Translucent Amber finishes. Mfg. 1994 to 1996.

$4,500	**$4,000**	**$3,750**	**$3,200**	**$2,500**	**$2,300**	**$2,050**

Last MSR was $6,300.

LE GRANDE (HSLGGH) - please refer to listing in the Custom/Historic Collection Series.

Gibson L-5 Custom
courtesy Elliot Rubinson

LES PAUL SERIES

Les Paul Series

The Les Paul model debuted in 1952, and was Gibson's first production solid body electric guitar. Because of the almost endless variations that have been produced over the years, this model has become a field unto itself.

Early models are without binding around the fingerboard and do not have a plastic ring around the selector switch. It has been noted that some of the early models have the Gold finish continuing on the **sides and back** in addition to the top. The original Gold Top finish is prone to a greenish hue around the lower bouts of the instrument where the player's arm(s) rubbed off the clear and/or color coat. Because the color coat was originally mixed with bronze powder, the exposure of the bronze with air will produce a green oxidation (the same type of oxidation that occurs on the metal parts occasionally when the finish is rubbed off). Horizontal weather checking striations are also normal on original Gold Top finishes.

LES PAUL MODEL - single sharp cutaway solid mahogany body, bound carved maple top, raised cream pickguard, one piece mahogany neck, 22-fret bound rosewood fingerboard with pearl trapezoid inlays, trapeze bridge/tailpiece, blackface peghead with holly veneer/pearl logo inlay, silkscreen model name on peghead, 3-per-side Kluson tuners with plastic single ring buttons, nickel hardware, 2 single coil P-90 pickups, 2 volume/2 tone controls, 3-position switch. Available in Gold Top/Natural back finish. Mfg. 1952 to 1958.

1952-1953 Trapeze	**N/A**	**$4,500**	**$4,000**	**$3,500**	**$3,200**	**$2,875**	**$2,450**
1953-1955 Stop Tailpiece	**N/A**	**$7,500**	**$6,500**	**$5,500**	**$4,500**	**$4,000**	**$3,650**
1956	**N/A**	**$10,000**	**$9,000**	**$7,850**	**$7,250**	**$7,000**	**$6,750**
1957-1958	**N/A**	**$20,000**	**$18,750**	**$17,375**	**$16,500**	**$15,250**	**$12,750**

Originally, bridge tailpieces were used with the strings traveling under the bar of the bridge. During 1952 and through most of 1953, the strings were changed to travel over the bridge bar. Special order instruments have Dark Brown back finish. In 1952, these models were not serialized. In 1953, ink stamped serial numbers on back of peghead were introduced, wrapover bridge/tailpiece replaced original part/design.

In 1955, tune-o-matic bridge/stop tailpiece replaced previous part/design. In 1957, humbucker PAF pickups replaced original part/design. Les Paul models in very cleaN/All original condition have sold for as high as $20,000. Instruments should be determined on a piece-by-piece basis as opposed to the usual market.

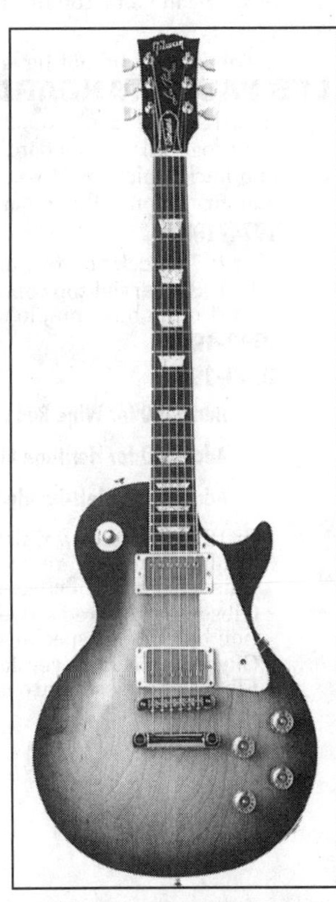

Gibson Les Paul Standard
courtesy Gibson USA

GRADING	100% MINT	98% NEAR MINT	95% EXC+	90% EXC	80% VG+	70% VG	60% G

LES PAUL STANDARD - single sharp cutaway mahogany body, bound carved flame maple top, raised cream pickguard, one piece mahogany neck, 22-fret rosewood fingerboard with pearl trapezoid inlay, tune-o-matic bridge/stop tailpiece, blackface peghead with holly veneer/pearl logo inlay, 3-per-side Kluson tuners with single ring plastic buttons, nickel hardware, 2 covered humbucker PAF pickups, 2 volume/2 tone controls, 3-position switch. Available in Cherry Sunburst finish. Mfg. 1958 to 1960.

These instruments in average (60%-80%) original condition without much flame start in the $40,000 range. 80%-90% original condition with nicely flamed tops are currently in the $60,000 range. Recent flametop sales on strong instruments have been priced between $50,000-$100,000, depending on original condition and amount of flame.

In 1959, large frets replaced original part/design. In 1960, thin neck, double ring tuner buttons replaced original part/design.

It is estimated that Gibson built 1,700 of these beauties between 1958 to 1960; and perhaps only 1,500 have still survived to today. In 1959, they retailed for $279 - the value of a *flame top* Gibson Les Paul Standard today depends on two factors: the degree of *flame* (figuring) in the maple top and the degree of original condition. It's hard to believe that two great bookmatched pieces of figured maple that no one paid much attention to in 1959 will cost you $35,000 extra today.

This particular model has achieved legendary status among guitar collectors, players, and investors throughout the world. This model, more than any other, proves what turbo-charged desirability can do to an instrument's price tag. Needless to say, the ***Blue Book of Electric Guitars*** fully recommends that several professional appraisals be secured before purchasing a collectible guitar of this magnitude.

After Bloomfield and Clapton made the 'Burst popular back in the late 1960s, some musicians were having their gold-tops stripped and refinished to join the craze! Given the magnitude of this particular part of the market, some fakes and re-topped or refinished guitars have surfaced.

LES PAUL (SG BODY STYLE) - double sharp cutaway mahogany body, layered black pickguard, mahogany neck, 22-fret bound rosewood fingerboard with pearl trapezoid inlay, tune-o-matic bridge/side-pull vibrato, blackface peghead with pearl logo inlay, 3-per-side Kluson tuners with double ring plastic tuners, nickel hardware, 2 covered humbucker pickups, 2 volume/2 tone controls, 3-position switch. Available in Cherry finish. Mfg. 1960 to 1963.

	100%	98%	95%	90%	80%	70%	60%
	N/A	**$3,500**	**$3,200**	**$2,750**	**$2,250**	**$1,850**	**$1,355**

In late 1960, the body style was changed to what is now known as the SG body style. The Les Paul logo was still applied on the peghead (see submodel description directly below). In 1961, the Les Paul name was put on truss rod cover, and did not have a model name on the peghead. Pearl crown peghead inlay. In 1962, some models were produced with ebony tailblock and pearl inlay.

In 1963, renamed SG Standard. See SG Series later in text.

LES PAUL STANDARD (1968-1969 Mfg.) - single sharp cutaway solid mahogany body, deeper cutaway binding, bound carved maple top, raised cream pickguard, mahogany neck, 22-fret bound rosewood fingerboard with pearl trapezoid inlay, tune-o-matic bridge/stop tailpiece, blackface peghead with pearl logo inlay, 3-per-side Kluson tuners with double ring plastic buttons, nickel hardware, 2 single coil P-90 pickups, 2 volume/2 tone controls, 3-position switch. Available in Gold Top/Natural Back finish. Mfg. 1968 to 1969.

	100%	98%	95%	90%	80%	70%	60%
1968	**N/A**	**$3,500**	**$3,100**	**$2,750**	**$2,250**	**$2,000**	**$1,900**
1969	**N/A**	**$3,000**	**$2,600**	**$2,200**	**$2,000**	**$1,900**	**$1,800**

This was Gibson's first Gold Top reissue.

LES PAUL STANDARD (1971 Mfg.) - single sharp cutaway solid mahogany body, bound carved maple top, raised cream pickguard, mahogany neck, 22-fret bound rosewood fingerboard with pearl trapezoid inlay, wrapover bridge tailpiece, blackface peghead with pearl logo inlay, 3-per-side Kluson tuners with plastic double ring buttons, nickel hardware, 2 single coil P-90 pickups, 2 volume/2 tone controls, 3-position switch. Available in Gold Top finish. Mfg. 1971 to 1973.

	100%	98%	95%	90%	80%	70%	60%
	N/A	**$2,000**	**$1,650**	**$1,275**	**$1,000**	**$875**	**$800**

This model did not have a neck volute. This model was a reissue of the 1954 Les Paul.

LES PAUL STANDARD (1974-1997 Mfg., LPS-) - single cutaway mahogany body, set-in mahogany (or maple) neck, bound carved 3-piece maple top, 22-fret bound rosewood fingerboard with pearl trapezoid inlay, tune-o-matic bridge/stop tailpiece, blackface peghead with pearl logo inlay, "Standard" engraved on truss rod cover, 3-per-side tuners with pearloid buttons, chrome hardware, cream pickguard, 2 covered humbucker pickups, 2 volume/2 tone controls, 3-position switch. Available in Cherry Sunburst, Dark Sunburst, Ebony (EB), Gold Top, Heritage Sunburst, Honey Burst, Natural, Tobacco Sunburst, TV Yellow, Vintage Sunburst and Wine Red (WR) finishes. Mfg. 1974 to 1997.

	100%	98%	95%	90%	80%	70%	60%
1974-1981	**N/A**	**$1,400**	**$1,175**	**$950**	**$850**	**$800**	**$725**

In 1974, neck volute was introduced, slab cut body replaced original part/design. In 1978, one-piece body replaced original part/design. In 1981, carved top replaced previous part/design, neck volute was discontinued. Gibson's Les Paul Standards made between 1974 to 1981 often have maple necks and three-piece maple tops. These models are viewed as less desireable in the vintage guitar market.

	100%	98%	95%	90%	80%	70%	60%
1982-1989	**N/A**	**$1,200**	**$1,000**	**$925**	**$875**	**$800**	**$700**
1990-1997	**$1,600**	**$1,200**	**$1,100**	**$935**	**$875**	**$770**	**$695**

Add $100 for Wine Red finish (LPS-WR).

Add $300 for Heritage Cherry Sunburst (LPS-HS), Honey Burst (LPS-HB), and Vintage Sunburst (LPS-VS) finishes.

Add $225 for left-handed configuration (production models 1990 to 1997).

In 1990, TV Yellow finish became standard. In 1994, Cherry Sunburst, Dark Sunburst, Gold Top, Heritage Sunburst, Natural, Tobacco Sunburst and TV Yellow finishes were discontinued. In 1998, the Les Paul Standard was redesignated the LPS8, and reduced to only 4 finishes (choice of chrome or gold hardware). See listing below.

Gibson has offered a twelve-string version of the Les Paul in the past. However, these instruments have either been very, very low production batches, or specialty productions, or custom shop orders.

Current Specialty versions of classic Les Paul configurations (Les Paul '56 Gold Top Reissue, Les Paul '59 Flametop Reissue, Les Paul '60 Flametop Reissue) are part of the Historic Collection Series, and can be found at the end of this section.

GRADING	100% MINT	98% NEAR MINT	95% EXC+	90% EXC	80% VG+	70% VG	60% G

LES PAUL STANDARD (1998-Current, LPS/LPS-8) - single cutaway mahogany body, set-in mahogany neck, bound carved maple top, 24.75" scale, 22-fret bound rosewood fingerboard with pearl trapezoid inlay, tune-o-matic bridge/stop tailpiece, blackface peghead with pearl logo inlay, "Standard" engraved on truss rod cover, 3-per-side tuners, chrome hardware, cream pickguard, 2 covered humbucker (490R/498T) pickups, 2 volume/2 tone controls, 3-way toggle switch. Available in Bullion Gold (BG, new 2001), Ebony (EB), Heritage Cherry Sunburst (HS), Honey Burst (HB), Wine Red (WR) Vintage Sunburst (new 1999), Frost and Crimson Sparkle (disc. 2000), Green, Blue, and Diamond Sparkle (Disc. 2001) finishes. New 1998.

MSR $3,075 — $2,150 $1,525 $1,325 $1,125 $925 $800 $650

Add $231 for Vintage Sunburst, Honey Burst, and Heritage Cherry Sunburst.

Add $385 for Bullion Gold finish.

Add $100 for gold hardware (Disc.).

Add $225 for left-handed configuration.

In 1998, the Les Paul Standard was redesignated LPS-8, and was introduced in 3 finishes, and a choice of chrome or gold (disc. 1999) hardware.

Les Paul Standard Raw Power similar to Les Paul Standard, except has Natural Satin finish. New 2001.

MSR $2,845 — $1,950 $1,425 $1,275 $1,075 $900 $800 $650

Les Paul Standard Lite (LPLI) - double cutaway design, carved maple top, mahogany back, 24 3/4 in. scale, includes treble '57 Classic Plus humbucker and rythmn 492R Alnico magnet humbucker pickups, gold hardware, choice of Translucent Amber, Translucent Black, or Translucent Blue finish. Mfg. 1999-2001.

$1,575 $1,250 $1,050 $900 $800 $700 $625

Last MSR was $2,399.

Les Paul Standard Bird's-eye - similar to Les Paul Standard (LPS-), except has bird's-eye maple top. Available in Heritage Sunburst, Honey Burst and Vintage Sunburst finishes. Mfg. 1993 to 1995.

$1,950 $1,350 $1,140 $860 $775 $710 $645

Last MSR was $2,699.

Les Paul Standard Plus (LPS+) - Available in Heritage Cherry Sunburst (HS), Honey Burst (HB), and Vintage Sunburst (VS). Disc. 1997, reintroduced 2001.

MSR $3,614 — $2,450 $1,325 $1,100 $975 $875 $800 $725

LES PAUL ARTISAN - single sharp cutaway mahogany body, multi-bound carved maple top, raised bound black pickguard, mahogany neck, 22-fret bound ebony fingerboard with pearl flowers/heart inlay, tune-o-matic bridge/tunable stop tailpiece, multi-bound peghead with pearl split flowers/heart/logo inlay, 3-per-side tuners, gold hardware, 2 single coil pickups, 2 volume/2 tone controls, 3-position switch. Available in Ebony, Tobacco Sunburst and Walnut finishes. Mfg. 1976 -1982.

N/A $1,850 $1,500 $1,300 $1,075 $895 $785

Originally offered with 3 humbuckers pickups optional, the 3 humbucker configuration became standard in 1979. In 1980, larger tune-o-matic bridge replaced original part/design.

LES PAUL ARTIST - single cutaway mahogany body, multi-bound carved maple top, raised black pickguard, mahogany neck, 22-fret bound ebony fingerboard with pearl block inlay, tune-o-matic bridge/tunable stop tailpiece, multibound blackface peghead with pearl script *LP*/logo, 3-per-side tuners, gold hardware, 2 covered humbucker pickups, volume/treble/bass controls, 3-position selector/3 mini switches, active electronics. Available in Sunburst finish. Mfg. 1979 to 1981.

N/A $1,500 $1,200 $995 $850 $725 $650

In 1980, Ebony and Fireburst finishes became optional.

LES PAUL DELUXE - single sharp cutaway 3-piece mahogany/maple body, deeper cutaway binding, bound carved maple top, raised cream pickguard, mahogany neck, 22-fret bound rosewood fingerboard with pearl trapezoid inlay, tune-o-matic bridge/stop tailpiece, widened blackface peghead with pearl logo inlay, 3-per-side Kluson tuners with plastic double ring buttons, nickel hardware, 2 mini humbucker pickups, 2 volume/2 tone controls, 3-position switch. Available in Blue Sparkle Top, Cherry, Cherry Sunburst, Gold Top, Red Sparkle Top, Tobacco Sunburst, Walnut and Wine Red finishes. Mfg. 1969-1985.

1969-1971 — N/A $2,000 $1,700 $1,500 $1,350 $1,200 $1,000

1972-1985 — N/A $1,250 $1,100 $95 $850 $700 $600

A few of these models were produced with 2 single coil P-90 pickups. In 1971, neck volute was introduced, Cherry, Cherry Sunburst and Walnut finishes became standard. In 1972, the Walnut finish was discontinued, and the Tobacco Sunburst finish became standard. In 1975, Natural and Wine Red finishes became options. In 1977, 2-piece mahogany body replaced original part/design. In 1981, neck volute was discontinued.

Les Paul Pro-Deluxe - similar to Les Paul Deluxe, except has ebony fingerboard, chrome hardware. Available in Black, Cherry Sunburst, Gold Top and Tobacco Sunburst finishes. Mfg. 1978 to 1982.

N/A $1,200 $1,000 $875 $750 $625 $595

LES PAUL DELUXE GOLDTOP - similar to Les Paul Deluxe, except has mini-humbucker pickups, "Hall of Fame" decal on neck bend, and Gold finish. Mfg. circa 1991.

N/A $1,500 $1,200 $995 $850 $725 $650

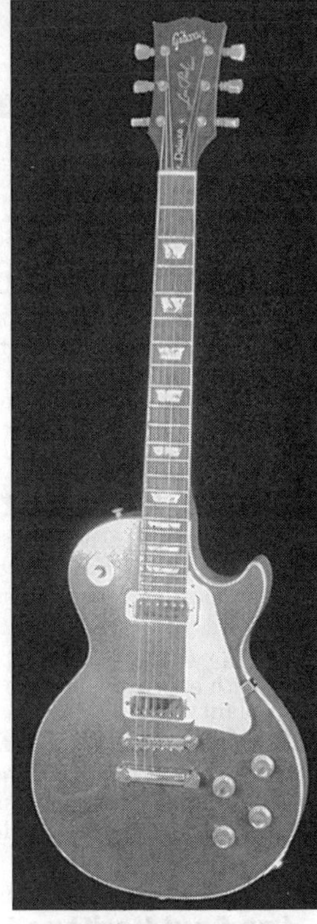

Gibson Les Paul Deluxe courtesy John Miller

1953 Gibson Les Paul Goldtop courtesy Dave Hinson

G

GRADING	100% MINT	98% NEAR MINT	95% EXC+	90% EXC	80% VG+	70% VG	60% G

LES PAUL DELUXE 30th ANNIVERSARY - similar to Les Paul Deluxe, except has mini-humbucker pickups, chrome hardware, standard pearloid trapezoid inlays (w/o anniversary markings), available in nitro-cellulose Ebony, Wine Red, or Bullion Gold (new 2001) finish. New 1999.

MSR $2,922 $2,000 $1,500 $1,300 $1,175 $1,025 $900 $800

Add $531 for Bullion Gold finish.

KALAMAZOO CUSTOM ORDER '59 REISSUE LES PAUL - '59 LP Standard style appointments, highly figured (flame or quilted) maple tops, ebonized holly veneered pegheads, original inked serialization, other '59 Standard features. Mfg. circa 1978-79.

Instruments have not traded extensively to quote accurate pricing.

These instruments are considered desirable because Gibson (unofficially) duplicated an original 1959 Les Paul Standard almost exactly for a few companies (including Leo's in California, The Guitar Trader in New Jersey, and Jimmy Wallace through Arnold and Morgan Music in Texas). These companies custom ordered Les Paul models that were patterned exactly after an original Gibson 1959 Standard Model (and feature individualized truss rod covers). Because of quality and limited manufacture (less than 250 exist), estimated asking prices today are in the $6,500 to $7,500 range.

LES PAUL KALAMAZOO - single sharp cutaway solid mahogany body, bound carved maple top, raised cream pickguard, mahogany neck, 22-fret bound rosewood fingerboard with pearl trapezoid inlay, Nashville tune-o-matic bridge/stop tailpiece, large blackface peghead with pearl logo inlay, "Les Paul K.M." engraved on truss cover, 3-per-side Grover tuners, nickel hardware, 2 cream colored covered humbucker pickups, 2 volume/2 tone controls, 3-position switch. Available in Antique Sunburst, Cherry Sunburst and Natural finishes. Mfg. 1979 only.

N/A $1,500 $1,200 $1,050 $875 $695 $600

This was Gibson's first nationally distributed flame top reissue. The first production run of these instruments exhibited a metal plate with engraved Custom Made logo below the tailpiece. Approximately 1,500 of this model were manufactured in Gibson's Kalamazoo plant.

LES PAUL HERITAGE 80 - single sharp cutaway mahogany body, bound carved flame maple top, raised cream pickguard, 3-piece mahogany neck, 22-fret rosewood fingerboard with pearl trapezoid inlay, tune-o-matic bridge/stop tailpiece, blackface peghead with pearl logo inlay, "Heritage 80" on truss cover, 3-per-side Grover tuners, nickel hardware, 2 covered humbucker pickups, 2 volume/2 tone controls, 3-position switch. Available in Cherry Sunburst and Honey Sunburst finishes. Mfg. 1980-82.

N/A $3,000 $2,570 $2,150 $1,725 $1,550 $1,400

A few of these instruments were produced with Ebony finish and are very rare.

Les Paul Heritage 80 Elite - similar to Les Paul Heritage 80, except has quilted maple top, one piece neck, ebony fingerboard.

N/A $3,000 $2,575 $2,150 $1,750 $1,550 $1,425

LES PAUL LP-XPL - single sharp cutaway solid mahogany body, bound carved maple top, raised cream pickguard, mahogany neck, 22-fret bound ebony fingerboard with pearl dot inlay, tune-o-matic bridge/stop tailpiece, blackface peghead with pearl logo inlay, 6-on-a-side tuners, chrome hardware, 2 single coil pickups, 2 volume/2 tone controls, 3-position switch. Available in Cherry Sunburst finish. Mfg. 1984 to 1987.

N/A $750 $600 $550 $475 $425 $350

This model was also available with double cutaway body. This model was also available with 2 single coil/1 humbucker pickups configuration.

LES PAUL (1985 REISSUE) - similar specifications to the current Gibson Historic Collection Les Paul '59 Flametop Reissue (this was Gibson's first authorized 1959 Les Paul reissue). Mfg. 1985 only.

N/A $3,000 $2,850 $2,600 $2,395 $2,175 $1,850

LES PAUL SMARTWOOD STANDARD (LPSW) - (Alternative wood project Les Paul model) single cutaway mahogany body, carved top, 22-fret fingerboard with pearl dot inlay, tune-o-matic bridge/stop tailpiece, blackface peghead with pearl logo inlay, "SmartWood" engraved on truss rod cover, 3-per-side tuners, gold hardware, 2 covered humbucker pickups, 2 volume/2 tone controls, 3-position switch. Available in Antique Natural (AN) finish. Mfg. 1995-2001.

$2,150 $1,625 $1,450 $1,225 $1,025 $900 $800

Last MSR was $3,299.

SmartWood is a program of the Rainforest Alliances, an international non-profit conservation organization that certifies if certain woods are harvested in a sustainable manner.

LES PAUL SMARTWOOD EXOTIC - single cutaway mahogany body, carved Ambay Guasu, Banara, Cancharana (disc. 2001), Curupay, Peroba, or Taperyva Guasu top, 22-fret Curupay fingerboard with pearloid dot inlay, tune-o-matic bridge/stop tailpiece, blackface peghead with pearl logo inlay, "Exotic Wood" engraved on truss rod cover, 3-per-side tuners with plastic buttons, gold hardware, 2 covered humbucker (490R/498T) pickups, 2 volume/2 tone controls, 3-position switch, includes gig bag. Available in UV-Cured Matte finish. Mfg. 1998 to date.

MSR $1,537 $1,050 $800 $700 $600 $500 $425 $350

LES PAUL SPOTLIGHT SPECIAL - single sharp cutaway mahogany body, bound carved 3-piece maple/mahogany/maple top, raised cream pickguard, mahogany neck, 22-fret rosewood fingerboard with pearl trapezoid inlay, tune-o-matic bridge/stop tailpiece, blackface peghead with pearl logo inlay, 3-per-side tuners with plastic buttons, chrome hardware, 2 covered humbucker pickups, 2 volume/2 tone controls, 3-position switch. Available in Natural finish. Mfg. 1980-85.

N/A $2,250 $1,950 $1,600 $1,295 $1,150 $1,050

Les Paul CMT - similar to Les Paul Spotlight Special, except has maple/walnut/maple body, curly maple top. Mfg. 1986-89.

N/A $2,500 $2,150 $1,795 $1,450 $1,295 $1,200

GRADING	100% MINT	98% NEAR MINT	95% EXC+	90% EXC	80% VG+	70% VG	60% G

THE LES PAUL - single sharp cutaway body, rosewood bound carved 2 piece bookmatched flame maple top/back/sides, mahogany core, raised rosewood pickguard, maple neck, 22-fret bound 3-piece ebony/rosewood/ebony fingerboard with abalone block inlay, tune-o-matic bridge/stop tailpiece, pearl split diamond/logo peghead inlay, 3-per-side Schaller tuners with pearl buttons, serial number engraved pearl plate on peghead back, gold hardware, 2 Super humbucker pickups with rosewood surrounds, 2 volume/2 tone rosewood control knobs, 3-position switch, rosewood control plate on back. Available in Natural and Wine Red finishes. Mfg. 1976 to 1980.

Due to extreme rarity (71 were produced, ser. nos. #61-#68 were made without their rosewood parts), accurate price evaluation is difficult for this model. Since this variation at the time, was perhaps Gibson's most elaborate and ornate (not to mention most expensive) LP, most of these instruments were not played. As a result, remaining specimens are usually in 95%+ condition. Current asking prices for this condition factor are presently in the $9,000 - $15,000 price range, depending on the condition. A few early models had solid figured maple bodies.

In 1978, Schaller tune-o-matic bridge/tunable stop tailpiece replaced original part/design. In 1979, Wine Red finish was discontinued.

Les Paul Anniversary Models

LES PAUL CUSTOM TWENTIETH ANNIVERSARY - single sharp cutaway multi-bound mahogany body with carved top, raised bound black pickguard, mahogany neck, 22-fret bound ebony fingerboard with pearl block inlay, Twentieth Anniversary engraved into block inlay at 15th fret, tune-o-matic bridge/stop tailpiece, multi-bound peghead with pearl split diamond/logo inlay, 3-per-side tuners with plastic buttons, gold hardware, 2 humbucker pickups, 2 volume/2 tone controls, 3-position switch. Available in Black, White, and Cherry Sunburst finishes. Mfg. 1974 only.

N/A $1,800 $1,540 $1,285 $1,025 $925 $845

LES PAUL 25/50 ANNIVERSARY - mahogany body, carved maple top, slashed block fingerboard inlay, 25/50 peghead inlay, 2 humbuckers. Mfg. 1979 only.

N/A $1,750 $1,550 $1,350 $1,200 $1,000 $900

Last MSR was $1,250.

Add $200 for Natural finish.

This guitar commemorated 25 years of the Les Paul model, and 50 years of Les Paul's continuing career.

LES PAUL STANDARD THIRTIETH ANNIVERSARY - single sharp cutaway mahogany body, bound carved maple top, raised cream pickguard, mahogany neck, 22-fret rosewood fingerboard with pearl trapezoid inlay, pearl *Thirtieth Anniversary* inlay at 15th fret, tune-o-matic bridge/stop tailpiece, blackface peghead with pearl logo inlay, 3-per-side tuners with plastic buttons, nickel hardware, 2 covered humbucker pickups, 2 volume/2 tone controls, 3-position switch. Available in Gold Top finish. Mfg. 1982-84.

N/A $1,950 $1,725 $1,500 $1,050 $900 $750

LES PAUL DELUXE THIRTIETH ANNIVERSARY - similar to Les Paul Deluxe, except has mini-humbucker pickups, chrome hardware, standard pearloid trapezoid inlays (w/o anniversary markings), available in Ebony, Wine Red, or Bullion Gold (new 2001) finish. New 1999.

MSR $2,922 $2,000 $1,500 $1,300 $1,175 $1,025 $900 $800

Add $531 for Bullion Gold finish.

LES PAUL CUSTOM THIRTY-FIFTH ANNIVERSARY - similar to original Les Paul Custom Twentieth Anniversary, except has Thirty-Fifth Anniversary etched on peghead inlay, 3 humbucker pickups. Mfg. 1989 only.

N/A $1,600 $1,370 $1,145 $915 $825 $755

LES PAUL STANDARD FORTIETH ANNIVERSARY - similar to Les Paul Standard Thirtieth Anniversary, except has ebony fingerboard, gold hardware, 2 stacked humbucker pickups. Mfg. 1992 only.

N/A $1,500 $1,300 $1,100 $850 $775 $700

Les Paul Custom Shop Signature Series

More more information on the Les Paul Custom Shop Signature Series, please refer to the Custom Shop section later in this text.

Les Paul Classic Series

The various grades of this series can be determined by the hand written initials indicating grade underneath the rythmn pickup (i.e., LPPP refers to Les Paul Premium Plus).

LES PAUL CLASSIC (LPCS) - single sharp cutaway mahogany body, bound carved maple top, bound rosewood fingerboard with pearl trapezoid inlay, tune-o-matic bridge/stop tailpiece, blackface peghead with pearl logo inlay, pearloid button tuners, nickel hardware, cream pickguard with engraved "1960", 2 exposed humbucker pickups, 2 volume/2 tone controls, 3-way toggle selector. Available in Ebony (EB), Honey Burst (HB), Heritage Cherry Sunburst (HS), and Vintage Sunburst (VS) finishes from 1990-98, and Bullion Gold (1998-to date). In 2001, all finishes except Ebony were reintroduced.

MSR $2,537 $1,750 $1,300 $1,100 $975 $850 $775 $700

Add $923 for Bullion Gold finish.

In 1994, Ebony (EB) and Vintage Sunburst (VS) finishes were discontinued. In 1998, Honey Burst (HB) and Heritage Cherry Sunburst (HS) finishes were discontinued.

GRADING	100% MINT	98% NEAR MINT	95% EXC+	90% EXC	80% VG+	70% VG	60% G

Les Paul Classic Plus - similar to Les Paul Classic, except has curly maple top. Available in Honey Burst (disc.), Heritage Cherry Sunburst (disc.), Translucent Amber, Translucent Purple (disc.), Translucent Red and Vintage Sunburst (disc.) finishes. Disc. 1995, retintroduced 1999-2001.

	$1,650	$1,500	$1,300	$1,175	$950	$875	$795

Last MSR was $3,837.

In 1994, Translucent Purple, Translucent Red and Vintage Sunburst finishes were discontinued.

Les Paul Classic Premium Plus (LPPP) - similar to Les Paul Classic, except has higher quality curly maple top. Available in Honey Burst (HB), Heritage Cherry Sunburst (HS), Translucent Amber (TA), Translucent Purple, Translucent Red and Vintage Sunburst finishes. Disc. 1996.

	$2,150	$1,850	$1,650	$1,450	$1,250	$1,050	$900

Last MSR was $5,099.

In 1994, Translucent Purple, Translucent Red and Vintage Sunburst finishes were discontinued.

Les Paul Classic Bird's-eye - similar to Les Paul Classic, except has bird's-eye maple top. Available in Honey Burst, Heritage Cherry Sunburst, Translucent Amber, Translucent Purple, Translucent Red and Vintage Sunburst finishes. Disc. 1994.

	$1,550	$1,300	$1,050	$925	$850	$775	$700

Last MSR was $2,600.

Les Paul Classic Premium Bird's-eye - similar to Les Paul Classic, except has highest quality bird's-eye maple top. Available in Honey Burst, Heritage Cherry Sunburst, Translucent Amber, Translucent Purple, Translucent Red and Vintage Sunburst finishes. Disc. 1994.

	$1,850	$1,650	$1,450	$1,250	$1,050	$900	$800

Last MSR was $4,700.

G

The Les Paul Classic Premium Plus Versus the Les Paul Reissue:

Evolution of the Les Paul Reissue (An Overview)

The origin of the Les Paul Reissue dates back to the mid 1970s when a few vintage-oriented dealers began requesting reproductions of the increasingly precious late 1950s Les Paul Standards. In the early 1980s Gibson added a variation of the model to the product line. At the time, merely applying a figured maple top to the current stock model seemed to suffice. Although it received minor cosmetic and hardware changes through the 1980s, it was not based on accurate 1950s design and detail until 1993. The **Les Paul Reissue** had been distinguishable because of its figured maple top, inked serial number, ABR bridge, etc. until the appearance of the **Les Paul Classic** in the early 1990s.

Designed by J.T. Ribiloff of Gibson R & D, the **Classic** featured a noticeably thinner 1960 neck profile as well as features previously exclusively found on the **Reissue**. To enhance the vintage look, Ribiloff redesigned a smaller headstock with push-in bushing tuners and aged fingerboard inlays. Of course, these features soon made their way to the **Reissue**. It was at this point that the **Reissue** and the **Classic** were structurally very similar.

Originally, the **Classic** was not to have a figured maple top, but the grading standards for the figuring in the tops for the **Reissues** became so high that the tops that did not qualify as Reissue quality were applied to the Classic - thus creating the **Les Paul Classic Plus**. Some of these "Plus" tops would turn out to be more figured than others, and thus became "Premium Plus" tops - and introduced the **Les Paul Classic Premium Plus.**

By 1992, there existed the **Les Paul Classic**, the **Classic Plus**, the **Classic Premium Plus**, and the **Les Paul Reissue** - and one more! The thin profile 1960 "classic" neck was offered on the Reissue, creating the **1960 Reissue**. At this point, there was some confusion between the **1960 Classic** and the **1960 Reissue**.

Gibson actually began addressing the problem as early as 1991, and began blueprinting original instruments in 1992. By the winter NAMM show in 1993, the redesigned **'59 Reissue** (Model LPR9) was introduced.

In the spring of 1993, Gibson changed the model decal on the headstock face of the **Classic** to read **Les Paul Classic**. Reissue Les Paul models in 1993 retained the silkscreened logo (just like the originals). The **Historic Reissue** line can be identified by the "R" plus the model year (R9 = '59 Reissue, R7 = '57 Reissue, R6 = '56 Reissue) stamped into the ledge in the bottom of the control cavity. From 1993 until the spring of 1994 all **Reissues** received a Historic decal on the back of the headstock (some early 1993 models may have the Custom Shop decal instead).

(Reissue Information courtesy Gibson Guitar Corporation)

Les Paul XR Series

LES PAUL XR-I - single cutaway mahogany body, carved maple top, 22-fret rosewood fingerboard with pearl dot inlay, tune-o-matic bridge/stop tailpiece, 3-per-side tuners with pearloid buttons, chrome hardware, 2 exposed humbucker pickups, 2 volume/2 tone controls, 3-position/coil tap switches. Available in Cherry Sunburst, Goldburst and Tobacco Sunburst finishes. Mfg. 1981-83.

	N/A	$650	$575	$500	$495	$400	$350

Les Paul XR-II - similar to Les Paul XR-I, except has bound figured maple top, "Gibson" embossed pickup covers. Available in Honey Sunburst finish.

	N/A	$750	$650	$525	$425	$395	$350

Les Paul Custom Series

LES PAUL CUSTOM - single sharp cutaway multi-bound mahogany body with carved top, raised bound black pickguard, mahogany neck, 22-fret bound ebony fingerboard with pearl block inlay, tune-o-matic bridge/stop tailpiece, multi-bound peghead with pearl split diamond/logo inlay, 3-per-side Deluxe Kluson tuners with plastic single ring buttons, gold hardware, 2 single coil pickups, 2 volume/2 tone controls, 3-position switch. Available in Black finish. Mfg. 1954 to 1960.

1954-1957	N/A	$7,000	$6,250	$5,700	$5,250	$4,400	$4,000
1958-1960	N/A	$12,000	$11,300	$10,200	$9,250	$8,750	$8,000

This guitar was nicknamed the *Black Beauty* and also the *Fretless Wonder.*

In 1957, 3 PAF humbucker pickups replaced 2 pickup configuration. A few models found with 2 humbucker pickups. In 1959, Grover tuners replaced original part/design. Current production instruments (Les Paul Custom Black Beauty '54 Reissue, Les Paul Custom Black Beauty '57 Reissue) are part of the Historic Collection Series, found at the end of this section.

GRADING	100% MINT	98% NEAR MINT	95% EXC+	90% EXC	80% VG+	70% VG	60% G

LES PAUL CUSTOM (SG BODY STYLE) - double sharp cutaway mahogany body, white layered pickguard, mahogany neck, 22-fret bound ebony fingerboard with pearl block inlay, tune-o-matic bridge/side-pull vibrato, multi-bound peghead with pearl split diamond inlay, 3-per-side tuners, gold hardware, 3 covered humbucker pickups, 2 volume/2 tone controls, 3-position switch. Available in Black or White finishes. Mfg. 1961-63.

	100%	98%	95%	90%	80%	70%	60%
	N/A	$4,500	$3,950	$3,500	$3,000	$2,650	$2,300

Models in black finish are very rare. In 1962, some models were produced with pearl inlaid ebony tail-piece insert. In 1963, renamed SG Custom (See SG Series later in text). Current production instruments (SG Les Paul Custom) are part of the Historic Collection Series, found at the end of this section.

LES PAUL CUSTOM 1968 REISSUE - single sharp cutaway mahogany body, multi-bound carved maple top, raised bound black pickguard, one piece mahogany neck, 22 small fret bound ebony fingerboard with pearl block inlay, tune-o-matic bridge/stop tailpiece, multi-bound peghead with pearl split diamond/logo inlay, no neck volute, 3-per-side Grover tuners, gold hardware, 2 humbucker Pat. No. pickups, 2 volume/2 tone controls, 3-position switch. Available in Black finish. Mfg. 1968 only.

	100%	98%	95%	90%	80%	70%	60%
	N/A	$2,800	$2,600	$2,300	$2,200	$2,000	$1,900

This instrument was a reissue of 1957 version of the Les Paul Custom.

LES PAUL CUSTOM 1969 REISSUE (LPC-) - similar to Les Paul Custom 1968 Reissue, except has 3-piece mahogany/maple body, 3-piece neck. Available in Alpine White (AW), Black, Cherry, Cherry Sunburst, Ebony (EB), Heritage Sunburst, Honeyburst, Natural, Tobacco Sunburst, Vintage Sunburst, Walnut, White, and Wine Red (WR) finishes. New 1969.

		100%	98%	95%	90%	80%	70%	60%
1969		N/A	$2,000	$1,750	$1,450	$1,150	$1,000	$925

This period of production can be determined by the heel.

		100%	98%	95%	90%	80%	70%	60%
1970-1989		N/A	$1,400	$1,200	$1,000	$800	$725	$650

This period of production can be determined by neck volute and Made in U.S.A. on back of headstock.

		100%	98%	95%	90%	80%	70%	60%
1990-1998		$1,500	$1,150	$950	$795	$825	$675	$625
MSR	$3,998	$2,700	$1,500	$1,150	$975	$850	$725	$675

Current production models are available in a left-handed configuration at $225 retail upcharge.

In 1971, neck volute was introduced, Cherry and Cherry Sunburst finishes became options. From 1971-1973, 3 humbucker pickup configuration became an option. In 1972, Tobacco Sunburst became an option. In 1975, jumbo frets replaced original part/design, Natural and White finishes became an option. In 1976, Wine Red finish became available. In 1977, one piece mahogany body replaced original part/design, Walnut finish became available. In 1981, neck volute was discontinued. In 1988, Alpine White, Ebony, Heritage Sunburst and Vintage Sunburst finishes became available; gold hardware also became available. In 1990, Honey Burst finish became available. In 1994, Black, Cherry, Cherry Sunburst, Heritage Sunburst, Honeyburst, Tobacco Sunburst, Vintage Sunburst, Walnut and White finishes were discontinued.

Les Paul Custom Plus (LPCC) - similar to Les Paul Custom, except has bound figured maple top and gold hardware. Available in Dark Wineburst, Honey Burst (HB), Heritage Cherry Sunburst (HS), and Vintage Sunburst (VS) finishes. Disc. 1996.

100%	98%	95%	90%	80%	70%	60%
$1,995	$1,750	$1,500	$1,250	$1,050	$925	$800

Last MSR was $4,439.

In 1994, Dark Wineburst finish was discontinued.

Les Paul Custom Premium Plus - similar to Les Paul Custom, except has highest quality bound figured maple top. Available in Dark Wineburst, Honey Burst, Heritage Cherry Sunburst and Vintage Sunburst finishes. Disc. 1994.

100%	98%	95%	90%	80%	70%	60%
$2,095	$1,800	$1,500	$1,200	$1,100	$995	$900

Last MSR was $3,000.

Les Paul Custom Reissue '54 - similar to original Les Paul Custom. Mfg. 1972 to 1977.

100%	98%	95%	90%	80%	70%	60%
N/A	$1,750	$1,550	$1,375	$1,200	$1,050	$925

In 1977, this model was available with a maple fingerboard.

LES PAUL CUSTOM LITE - single sharp cutaway multi-bound mahogany body with carved top, raised bound black pickguard, mahogany neck, 22-fret bound ebony fingerboard with pearl block inlay, tune-o-matic bridge/stop tailpiece, multi-bound peghead with pearl split diamond/logo inlay, 3-per-side tuners with chrome buttons, gold hardware, 2 covered humbucker pickups, volume/tone control, 3-position switch, mini coil tap switch. Available in Black finish. Mfg. 1987-1990.

100%	98%	95%	90%	80%	70%	60%
N/A	$1,250	$1,050	$875	$775	$650	$525

This model was also available with double locking vibrato.

Les Paul Custom Shop Models

Please refer to the listings in the Custom Collection/Historic Series section.

Les Paul DC (Double Cutaway) Series

The Les Paul DC Standard is a Gibson production model; the DC Pro is a Gibson Custom Shop model and will have the Custom Shop logo on the back of the headstock.

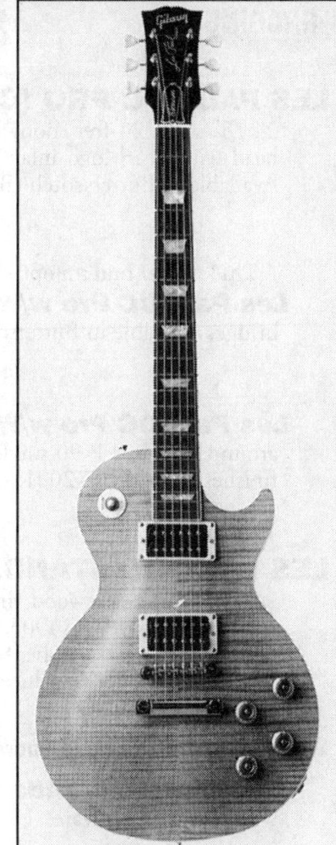

Gibson Les Paul Premium Plus
courtesy Gibson USA

Gibson SG Les Paul Custom
courtesy Gibson USA

GRADING	100% MINT	98% NEAR MINT	95% EXC+	90% EXC	80% VG+	70% VG	60% G

LES PAUL DC PRO (CSDC4TH[ ]NH) - offset double cutaway mahogany back, bound AAA flamed maple top, set-in mahogany neck, 24.75" scale, 24-fret ebony fingerboard with pearl dot inlay, tune-o-matic bridge/stop tailpiece, 3-per-side Schaller mini-tuners, black slimmed peghead with pearl logo inlay, nickel hardware, 2 covered humbuckers ('57 Classic/'97 Classic), master volume/master tone controls, 3-way toggle. Available in Butterscotch (BS), Faded Cherry (FC), Translucent Black (TB), and Translucent Indigo (TI) finishes. Mfg. 1997-2001.

$2,950 $2,500 $2,195 $1,900 $1,650 $1,350 $1,050
Last MSR was $4,195.

This model had an optional 25.5" scale length by special order.

Les Paul DC Pro w/WrapAround Bridge (CSDC4WH[ ]NH) - similar to the Les Paul DC Pro, except features a wraparound bridge. Available in Butterscotch (BS), Faded Cherry (FC), Translucent Black (TB), and Translucent Indigo (TI) finishes. Mfg. 1997-2001.

$2,950 $2,500 $2,195 $1,900 $1,650 $1,350 $1,050
Last MSR was $4,195.

Les Paul DC Pro w/WrapAround Bridge/P-90s (CSDC4WP[ ]NH) - similar to the Les Paul DC Pro, except features a wraparound bridge, 2 P-90 single coil pickups. Available in Butterscotch (BS), Faded Cherry (FC), Translucent Black (TB), and Translucent Indigo (TI) finishes. Mfg. 1997-2001.

$2,775 $2,400 $2,150 $1,900 $1,650 $1,325 $995
Last MSR was $3,950.

LES PAUL DC STANDARD (LPS2) - offset double cutaway mahogany back, AAA flamed maple top, set-in mahogany neck, 24.75" scale, 24-fret bound rosewood fingerboard with pearloid trapezoid inlay, tune-o-matic bridge/stop tailpiece, 3-per-side tuners, black peghead, chrome hardware, 2 covered (490R/498T) humbuckers, volume/tone controls, 3-way toggle. Available in Trans Red (TR), Translucent Amber (TA), Midnight Burst (MD), Amber Serrano (AS, disc.), Blue Diamond (BD, disc.), Black Pepper (BP, disc.), Green Jalapeno (GJ, disc.), and Red Hot Tamale (RT, disc.) lacquer translucent finishes. Mfg. 1998-99, reintroduced 2001.

MSR $2,152 $1,475 $1,075 $950 $875 $800 $700 $600

Add $100 for gold hardware (disc.).

Les Paul DC Standard Sunburst Limited Edition (LPS2) - available in either Tangerineburst with gold hardware or Lemonburst with chrome hardware. Disc. 2000.

$1,625 $1,300 $1,000 $875 $800 $700 $600
Last MSR was $2,409.

Add approx. $100 for Tangerine (LPS2-TN) finish.

Les Paul Studio Series

LES PAUL DOUBLE CUTAWAY STUDIO (LPDS) - offset double cutaway mahogany back, carved maple top, set-in mahogany neck, 24-fret rosewood fingerboard with dot inlay, wrap-around stop tailpiece, 3-per-side tuners, chrome hardware, 2 covered humbuckers, volume/tone controls, 3-way toggle. Available in Ebony (EB), Heritage Cherry Sunburst (HS), Emerald Green, Ruby, and Wine Red (WR) finishes. Mfg. 1997-99.

$875 $795 $700 $625 $550 $450 $350
Last MSR was $1,378.

Add $125 for Heritage Cherry Sunburst finish.

In 1998, Emerald Green (EZ) and Ruby (RZ) finishes were introduced; Wine Red (WR) finish was discontinued.

LES PAUL STUDIO (LPST) - single sharp cutaway mahogany body, carved maple top, raised black pickguard, 22-fret rosewood fingerboard with pearl dot inlay, tune-o-matic bridge/stop tailpiece, 3-per-side tuners, chrome hardware, 2 covered humbucker pickups, 2 volume/2 tone controls, 3-position switch. Available in Alpine White (AW, disc.), Gothic, Ebony (EB), Blue Teal Flip-flop (BT), White (disc. 1994), and Wine Red (WR) finishes. Mfg. 1984 to 1998, reintroduced 2001.

MSR $1,691 $1,200 $850 $775 $700 $650 $600 $550

Add $97 for Blue Teal Flip-flop finish.

Add $231 for Gothic finish.

In 1987, ebony fingerboard replaced rosewood fingerboard. In 1990, trapezoid fingerboard inlay replaced dot inlay.

Les Paul Studio (LPSO) - similar to Les Paul Studio, gold or chrome hardware. Available in Amber (AZ, disc. 1999), Ebony (EB), Emerald (EZ), and Ruby (RZ) finishes. Mfg. 1996-99.

$900 $775 $675 $575 $500 $450 $425
Last MSR was $1,700.

Add $100 for gold hardware.

Add $150 for Amber finish with gold hardware.

Les Paul Studio Custom - similar to Les Paul Studio, except has multi-bound body, bound fingerboard, multi-bound peghead. Available in Cherry Sunburst, Ebony and Sunburst finishes. Mfg. 1984 to 1987.

N/A $675 $595 $495 $395 $350 $325

Les Paul Studio Gem Limited Edition (LPGS) - similar to the Les Paul Studio, except features 2 creme P-90 pickups, cream pickguard, trapezoid fingerboard inlay, and gold hardware. Available in Amethyst (AM), Emerald (EM), Ruby (RU), Sapphire (SP), and Topaz (TO) finishes. Mfg. 1996-98.

$950 $850 $750 $650 $500 $425 $375
Last MSR was $1,639.

GRADING	100% MINT	98% NEAR MINT	95% EXC+	90% EXC	80% VG+	70% VG	60% G

Les Paul Studio Standard - similar to Les Paul Studio, except has bound body. Available in Cherry Sunburst, Sunburst and White finishes. Mfg. 1984 to 1987.

	N/A	$675	$595	$495	$395	$350	$325

Les Paul Studio Lite (LPLT) - similar to Les Paul Studio, except has no pickguard, ebony fingerboard with trapezoid inlay, black chrome hardware, exposed pickups. Available in Translucent Black, Translucent Blue (BU) and Translucent Red finishes. Disc. 1998.

	$995	$900	$800	$695	$575	$450	$400

Last MSR was $1,749.

Add $150 for gold hardware with Heritage Cherry Sunburst (LPLT-HS) and Vintage Sunburst (LPLT-VS) finishes.

In 1994, Translucent Black and Translucent Red finishes were discontinued.

Les Paul Studio Lite/M III - similar to Les Paul Studio, except has no pickguard, exposed humbucker/ single coil/humbucker pickups, volume/tone control, 5-position switch. Disc. 1995.

	$950	$775	$700	$595	$425	$350	$250

Last MSR was $1,350.

LES PAUL STUDIO PLUS - similar to Les Paul Studio, except is available in Desert Burst (DB) and Trans Red (TR) finish, gold hardware. New 2001.

MSR	$2,383	$1,650	$1,200	$1,000	$850	$750	$650	$575

Les Paul Low-Impedance Series

LES PAUL PERSONAL - single cutaway multi-bound mahogany body, carved top, raised bound pickguard, mahogany neck, 22-fret bound ebony fingerboard with pearl block inlay, tune-o-matic bridge/stop tailpiece, multi-bound blackface peghead with pearl diamond/logo inlay, 3-per-side tuners with plastic buttons, gold hardware, 2 low impedance pickups, mic volume control on upper bass bout, volume/decade/treble/bass controls, two 3-position switches, phase slide switch. Available in Walnut finish. Mfg. 1969 to 1971.

	N/A	$1,250	$1,100	$895	$725	$650	$595

This instrument had an optional Bigsby vibrato.

LES PAUL PROFESSIONAL - single cutaway bound mahogany body, raised black pickguard, mahogany neck, 22-fret rosewood fingerboard with pearl trapezoid inlay, tune-o-matic bridge/stop tailpiece, blackface peghead with pearl logo inlay, 3-per-side tuners, nickel hardware, 2 low impedance pickups, volume/decade/treble/ bass controls, two 3-position switches, phase slide switch. Available in Walnut finish. Mfg. 1969 - 1971.

	$900	$795	$650	$525	$475	$425	$375

This instrument had an optional Bigsby vibrato.

LES PAUL RECORDING - single cutaway bound mahogany body, carved top, raised multi-layer pickguard, mahogany neck, 22-fret bound rosewood fingerboard with pearl block inlay, tune-o-matic bridge/stop tailpiece, multi-bound peghead with pearl split diamond/logo inlay, 2 covered low impedance pickups, "Gibson" formed on pickup covers, volume/decade/treble/bass controls, two 3-position switches, impedance/phase slide switches, built-in transformer. Available in Walnut finish. Mfg. 1971 - 1980.

	N/A	$1,000	$900	$795	$700	$650	$575

In 1975, White finish became an option. In 1978, Ebony and Cherry Sunburst finishes became an option.

LES PAUL SIGNATURE - offset double cutaway, arched maple top, raised cream pickguard, f-holes, maple back/sides, mahogany neck, 22-fret bound rosewood fingerboard with pearl trapezoid inlay, tune-o-matic bridge/ stop tailpiece, blackface peghead with pearl logo inlay, 3-per-side tuners with plastic buttons, chrome hardware, 2 low impedance humbucker pickups, plastic pickup covers with stamped logo, volume/tone control, 3-position/ phase/level switches. Available in Gold Top and Sunburst finishes. Mfg. 1973 -78.

	N/A	$2,000	$1,850	$1,675	$1,550	$1,400	$1,300

This model has walnut back/sides with Gold Top finish. After 1976, high and low impedance humbuckers became available.

Les Paul Special Series

LES PAUL SPECIAL - single cutaway mahogany body, multi-layer black pickguard, mahogany neck, 22-fret bound rosewood fingerboard with dot inlay, wrapover stop tailpiece, 3-per-side tuners with plastic buttons, nickel hardware, 2 single coil pickups, 2 volume/2 tone controls, 3-position switch. Available in Limed Mahogany finish. Mfg. 1955-59.

	N/A	$3,500	$2,950	$2,450	$1,975	$1,695	$1,250

In 1959, double round cutaway body replaced original part/design, Cherry finish became available. A few instruments were also made in double cutaway with 2 black soapbar pickups and Cherry Red finish.

LES PAUL SPECIAL (SG BODY STYLE) - double cutaway mahogany body, black pickguard, mahogany neck, 22-fret rosewood fingerboard with pearl dot inlay, tune-o-matic bridge/stop tailpiece, silk-screened model name on peghead, 3-per-side tuners with plastic buttons, nickel hardware, single coil pickup, volume/tone control. Available in Cherry finish. Mfg. 1961-63.

	N/A	$2,000	$1,750	$1,500	$1,300	$1,250	$1,000

Add $1,000 for TV finish.

In 1962, Maestro vibrato became an option. In 1963, renamed SG Special. See SG Series later in text.

Les Paul Special 3/4 - similar to Les Paul Special, except has a 3/4 size body, shorter neck. Available in Cherry Red finish. Mfg. 1959 - 1961.

	N/A	$1,250	$950	$825	$750	$675	$600

Gibson Les Paul Studio
courtesy Gibson USA

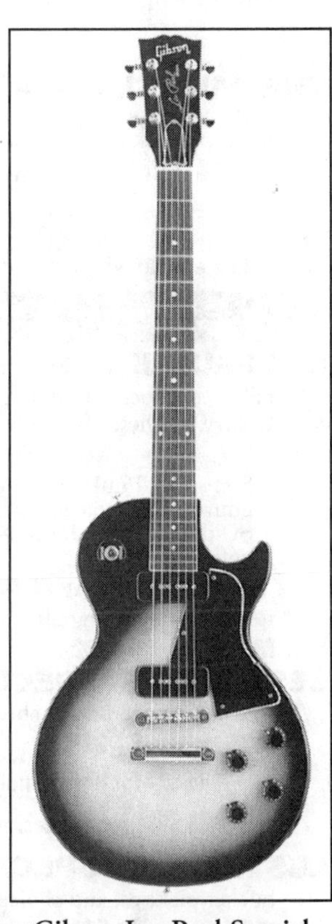

Gibson Les Paul Special
courtesy Gibson USA

G

GRADING	100% MINT	98% NEAR MINT	95% EXC+	90% EXC	80% VG+	70% VG	60% G

LES PAUL SPECIAL similar to Les Paul Special, except has tune-o-matic bridge/stop tailpiece, stacked humbucker pickups, nickel hardware. Available in Ebony, Heritage Cherry (HC), Tobacco Sunburst (TS) and T.V. Yellow (TV) finishes. Mfg. mid 1970s.

N/A $750 $650 $550 $500 $425 $375

LES PAUL SPECIAL (LPJ2) - similar to Les Paul Special, except has tune-o-matic bridge/stop tailpiece, stacked humbucker pickups, nickel hardware. Available in Ebony, Heritage Cherry (HC), Tobacco Sunburst (TS) and T.V. Yellow (TV) finishes. Mfg. 1989 - 1998.

$1,000 $875 $750 $650 $550 $500 $450
Last MSR was $1,239.

Add $400 for T.V. Yellow finish (last LPJ2-TV retail list price was $1,639).

Les Paul Special Double Cutaway (LPJD) - similar to Les Paul Special (LPJ2), except has double cutaway body design instead of single cutaway. Available in Heritage Cherry (HC), and TV Yellow (TV) finishes. Mfg. 1989 - 1998.

$1,150 $975 $875 $795 $650 $500 $375
Last MSR was $1,339.

Add $400 for T.V. Yellow finish (last LPJD-TV retail list price was $1,739).

LES PAUL SPECIAL SL (LPJS) - single cutaway solid mahogany body, set-in mahogany neck, 24.75" scale, 22-fret rosewood fingerboard with pearl dot inlay, tune-o-matic bridge/stop tailpiece, blackface peghead with silkscreened logo, 3-per-side vintage-style tuners, chrome hardware, pearloid pickguard, 2 P-100 stacked humbucker (looks like a black P-90) pickups, 2 volume/2 tone controls, 3-way toggle switch. Available in UV-cured Ebony (EB), Emerald (EX), and Ruby (RX) finishes. Mfg. 1996-99.

$575 $420 $375 $325 $250 $200 $175
Last MSR was $840.

G

The Paul Series

THE PAUL STANDARD - single sharp cutaway walnut body/neck, 22-fret ebony fingerboard with pearl dot inlay, tune-o-matic bridge/stop tailpiece, 3-per-side tuners, chrome hardware, 2 exposed humbucker pickups, 2 volume/2 tone controls, 3-position switch. Available in Natural satin nitrocellulose finish. Mfg. 1978 - 1982.

N/A $425 $375 $300 $250 $225 $200

In 1980, this guitar was renamed Firebrand, with the Firebrand logo burned into the peghead.

The Paul Deluxe - similar to original The Paul Standard, except has mahogany body/neck. Available in Antique Natural, Ebony, Natural and Wine Red finishes. Mfg. 1980 - 1986.

N/A $450 $395 $325 $250 $225 $200

In 1985, Ebony and Wine Red finishes replaced original part/design.

THE PAUL II - single cutaway solid mahogany body, mahogany neck, 24 3/4" scale, 22-fret rosewood fingerboard with dot inlay, tune-o-matic bridge/stop tailpiece, blackface peghead with silkscreened logo, engraved "The Paul II" on truss rod cover, 3-per-side tuners, chrome hardware, 2 exposed pole piece humbucker pickups (490R/498T), 2 volume/2 tone controls, 3-way toggle switch. Available in Ebony (EB) and Wine Red (WR) finishes. Mfg. 1996 to 1998.

$450 $395 $350 $300 $275 $225 $175
Last MSR was $849.

THE PAUL SL (LPTP) - single cutaway solid mahogany body with carved top, mahogany neck, 24.75" scale, 22-fret rosewood fingerboard with pearl dot inlay, tune-o-matic bridge/stop tailpiece, blackface peghead with silkscreened logo, 3-per-side vintage-style tuners, chrome hardware, 2 exposed polepiece humbucker pickups (490R/498T), 2 volume/2 tone controls, 3-way toggle switch. Available in UV-Cured Ebony (EB), Emerald (EX), and Ruby (RX) finishes. Mfg. 1996-99.

$650 $475 $425 $375 $325 $300 $275
Last MSR was $947.

The engraved truss rod cover may (incorrectly) read "The Paul II".

Les Paul Junior Series

LES PAUL JR. - single cutaway mahogany body, black pickguard, mahogany neck, 22-fret rosewood fingerboard with dot inlay, wrapover stop tailpiece, 3-per-side tuners with plastic buttons, nickel hardware, single P-90 coil pickup, volume/tone control. Available in Brown Sunburst and Cherry finishes. Mfg. 1954-1960.

N/A $2,000 $1,675 $1,250 $1,050 $975 $825

Some Les Paul Jr. models were produced with 3/4 scale necks on the full size bodies. In 1958, double round cutaway body, tortoise pickguard replaced original part/design, Cherry finish became available, Sunburst finish was discontinued. In 1961, the body switched to the SG design, with laminated pickguard and Les Paul Jr. peghead logo (available in a Cherry finish). See Les Paul Jr. (SG Body Style) model below.

Les Paul Junior (LPJ-) - similar to Les Paul Jr., except has chrome hardware, available in Vintage Sunburst (VS) or Ebony (EB) finish. Limited Mfg. beginning 2001.

MSR $1,152 $850 $600 $550 $500 $465 $435 $400

LES PAUL JR. SPECIAL (LPJS) - single cutaway mahogany body, mahogany neck, 2 black P-100 stacked humbucker pickups, 22-fret rosewood fingerboard, chrome hardware, choice of Ebony, Cinnamon, or Natural finish, includes gig bag. New 1999.

MSR $1,229 $875 $615 $550 $500 $465 $435 $400

Add $77 for Natural finish.

Add $231 for humbucker pickups (Ebony finish only, new 2000).

LES PAUL JR. SPECIAL PLUS (LPJ+) - similar to Les Paul Junior Special, except has AA figured maple top, 2 covered Alnico humbucker pickups, and choice of Trans Amber (TA) or Trans Red (TR) finish. New 2001.

MSR $1,614 $1,150 $825 $700 $600 $525 $450 $400

GRADING	100% MINT	98% NEAR MINT	95% EXC+	90% EXC	80% VG+	70% VG	60% G

LES PAUL JR. (SG BODY STYLE) - double cutaway mahogany body, black pickguard, mahogany neck, 22-fret rosewood fingerboard with pearl dot inlay, tune-o-matic bridge/stop tailpiece, silkscreened model name on peghead, 3-per-side tuners with plastic buttons, nickel hardware, single coil pickup, volume/tone control. Available in Cherry finish. Mfg. 1961 to 1963.

N/A	$1,550	$1,250	$1,000	$875	$800	$750

In 1962, Maestro vibrato became an option. In 1963, renamed the SG Jr. (See SG Series later in text).

Les Paul Junior 3/4 - similar to Les Paul Junior, except has 3/4 size body, shorter neck. Mfg. 1956 to 1961.

N/A	$1,100	$950	$795	$625	$575	$525

Les Paul Junior II - similar to Les Paul Junior, except has 2 P-100 pickups. Mfg. 1989 only.

N/A	$800	$695	$575	$450	$400	$375

This model is also available in a dual cutaway version.

Les Paul Junior (Reissue) - similar to Les Paul Junior. Available in Cherry, Tobacco Sunburst, TV Yellow or White finishes. Mfg. 1986 to 1996.

$725	$550	$450	$350	$325	$300	$275

Last MSR was $900.

LES PAUL JR. LITE (LPJL) - similar to Les Paul Junior (SG Body Style), except has 2 P-100 pickups, 22-fret rosewood fingerboard, chrome hardware, choice of Ebony, Natural, or Cinnamon finish, includes gig bag. New 1999.

MSR	$996	$725	$500	$450	$415	$385	$360	$340

Add $79 for Natural finish.

LES PAUL TV - similar to the single cutaway Les Paul Jr., except has Limed Mahogany finish. Mfg. 1954 -59.

N/A	$3,500	$3,000	$2,650	$2,200	$2,000	$1,800

A few of these guitars were made with a 3/4 size body. In 1958, double round cutaway body and multi-layer pickguard replaced original part/design. In 1959, the double rounded cutaway horns was renamed the SG TV. (See SG Series later in text).

Gibson Les Paul Jr.
courtesy Kelly Barber

M Series

M III DELUXE - offset double cutaway poplar/maple/walnut body, tortoise pickguard with engraved "M III" logo, maple neck, 24-fret maple fingerboard with wood arrow inlay, double locking Floyd Rose vibrato, reverse blackface peghead with screened logo, 6-on-a-side tuners, black chrome hardware, exposed humbucker/single coil/humbucker pickups, volume/tone control, 5-position/tone selector switches. Available in Antique Natural finish. Disc. 1994.

$500	$450	$400	$350	$300	$250	$200

Last MSR was $1,300.

M III Standard - similar to M III Deluxe, except has solid poplar body. Available in Alpine White, Candy Apple Red and Ebony finishes. Disc. 1994.

$500	$425	$375	$325	$300	$250	$200

Last MSR was $1,080.

Add $55 for Translucent Amber and Translucent Red finishes, no pickguard.

M IV S DELUXE - offset double cutaway black limba body, maple neck, 24-fret ebony fingerboard with pearl arrow inlay, Steinberger vibrato, reverse blackface peghead with screened logo, 6-on-a-side Steinberger locking tuners, black chrome hardware, exposed humbucker/single coil/humbucker pickups, volume/tone control, 5-position/tone selector switches. Available in Natural finish. Mfg. 1994 to 1996.

$900	$795	$700	$650	$600	$550	$495

Last MSR was $2,375.

M IV S Standard - similar to M IV S Deluxe, except has poplar body, pearl dot fingerboard inlay. Available in Ebony finish. Mfg. 1994 to 1996.

$900	$750	$695	$625	$595	$550	$495

Last MSR was $2,100.

MAP - United States-shaped mahogany body, 3-piece maple neck, 22-fret bound rosewood fingerboard with pearl dot inlay, tune-o-matic bridge/stop tailpiece, blackface peghead with pearl logo inlay, chrome hardware, 2 covered humbucker pickups, 2 volume/2 tone controls, 3-position switch. Available in Natural finish. Mfg. 1983 only.

N/A	$1,250	$800	$700	$500	$400	$350

MARAUDER - single cutaway alder body, white pickguard, bolt-on maple neck, 22-fret rosewood fingerboard with pearl dot inlay, tune-o-matic bridge/stop tailpiece, 3-per-side tuners, chrome hardware, humbucker/single coil pickups, volume/tone control, rotary switch. Available in Black and Natural finishes. Mfg. 1975 - 1980.

N/A	$400	$350	$295	$225	$200	$175

Black pickguards were also available on this instrument. In 1978, maple fingerboard replaced original part/design.

Marauder Custom - similar to Marauder, except has bound fingerboard with block inlay, 3-position switch, no rotary switch. Available in Sunburst finish. Mfg. 1976 to 1977.

N/A	$400	$350	$325	$250	$225	$200

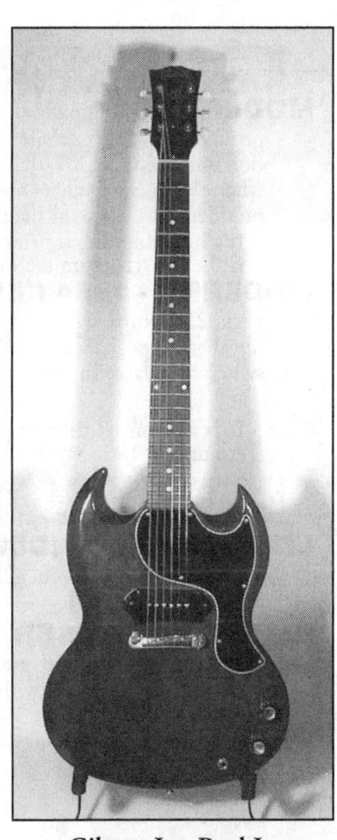
Gibson Les Paul Jr.
(SG Body)
courtesy Rick Wilkiewicz

GRADING	100% MINT	98% NEAR MINT	95% EXC+	90% EXC	80% VG+	70% VG	60% G

Melody Maker Series

All notes on original Melody Maker apply to all instruments in this section, unless otherwise noted.

MELODY MAKER - single or double sharp cutaway mahogany body, black pickguard with model name stamp, mahogany neck, 22-fret rosewood fingerboard with pearl dot inlay, wrapover stop tailpiece, 3-per-side tuners with plastic buttons, nickel hardware, covered single coil pickup, volume/tone control. Available in Sunburst finish. Mfg. 1959 - 1971.

1959-1960	N/A	$750	$625	$550	$400	$325	$275
1961-1965	N/A	$500	$425	$350	$295	$250	$225
1966-1969	N/A	$450	$395	$325	$250	$225	$200
1970-1971	N/A	$400	$350	$295	$225	$200	$175

The single cutaway is the most desirable configuration of this model. In 1960, redesigned narrower pickup replaced original part/design. In 1961, double round cutaway body replaced original part/design. In 1962, Maestro vibrato became an option. In 1963, Cherry finish became available. In 1966, double sharp cutaway body, white pickguard, vibrato tailpiece, Fire Engine Red and Pelham Blue finishes replaced previous part/design. In 1967, Sparkling Burgundy finish became an option. In 1970, only Walnut finish was available.

Melody Maker 3/4 - similar to Melody Maker, except has 3/4 size body. Available in Golden Sunburst finish. Mfg. 1959 - 1970.

1959-1960	N/A	$525	$450	$400	$375	$350	$300
1961-1970	N/A	$400	$350	$295	$225	$200	$175

Melody Maker-D - similar to Melody Maker, except has 2 mini humbucker pickups. Available in Golden Sunburst finish. Mfg. 1960 - 1971.

1960	N/A	$800	$700	$625	$525	$475	$400
1961-1965	N/A	$600	$525	$450	$375	$300	$275
1966-1969	N/A	$450	$375	$300	$250	$225	$200
1970-1971	N/A	$425	$375	$300	$250	$225	$175

Melody Maker III - similar to Melody Maker, except has 3 pickups. Available in Pelham Blue and Sparkling Burgundy finishes. Mfg. 1968 - 1971.

	N/A	$525	$450	$375	$300	$275	$250

Melody Maker-12 - similar to original Melody Maker, except has twelve strings, 6-per-side tuners, 2 mini humbuckers. Mfg. 1967 to 1971.

	N/A	$650	$525	$450	$375	$300	$250

Add $250 for Pelham Blue and Sparkling Burgundy finishes.

In 1970, available in Pelham Blue and Sparkling Burgundy finishes only.

MELODY MAKER REISSUE - single cutaway mahogany body, black pickguard, mahogany neck, 22-fret rosewood fingerboard with pearl dot inlay, tune-o-matic bridge/stop tailpiece, 3-per-side tuners with pearloid buttons, chrome hardware, covered humbucker pickup, volume/tone control. Available in Alpine White, Ebony and Frost Blue finishes. Disc. 2000.

	$600	$450	$375	$300	$275	$250	$225

Last MSR was $750.

Moderne Models

MODERNE - originally designed as one of three Gibson modernistic concept guitars (with the Explorer and Flying V), this instrument was blueprinted in 1958. A debate still rages over whether or not they were actually built, as a 1958 Moderne has not yet been seen. There is some vague mention on a shipping list (that could also apply to the Explorer model). Tom Wheeler, in his book American Guitars, suggests that some were built - and when the music retailers responded in a negative way, Gibson sold some at a cut rate price to employees and destroyed others. Ted McCarty, who was president of Gibson at the time (and part designer of the three models), has guessed that a handful were built as prototypes.

It's hard to hang a price tag on something that hasn't been seen. Until one actually shows up, and can be authenticated by experts (materials, construction techniques, parts) can there be an intelligent conversation about a price.

MODERNE - 1984 REISSUE (MODERNE HERITAGE) - single cutaway sharkfin style korina body, black pickguard, korina neck, 22-fret rosewood fingerboard with pearl dot inlay, tune-o-matic bridge/stop tailpiece, tulip blackface peghead with pearl logo inlay, inked serial number on peghead, 3-per-side tuners with plastic single ring buttons, gold hardware, 2 humbucker pickups, 2 volume/1 tone controls, 3-position switch. Available in Natural finish. Mfg. 1984 only.

	N/A	$2,000	$1,550	$1,250	$1,100	$1,000	$895

It is estimated that only 700 instruments were produced. This is a (re)issue of the 1958 Moderne, with specifications from the blueprint. An actual 1958 original specimen has yet to be verified.

Nighthawk Series

LITTLE LUCILLE (DSLL) - similar to Blueshawk, except has tune-o-matic bridge, and TP-6 tailpiece, 3-way selector switch with 6-position Varitone selector switch, gold hardware, Ebony finish only. New 1999.

MSR $1,845	$1,275	$925	$850	$750	$675	$600	$550

BLUESHAWK (DSBH, DSNB) - single cutaway poplar body, 2 f-holes, bound solid maple top, 25.5" scale, mahogany neck, 22-fret rosewood fingerboard with pearl diamond inlay, fixed bridge with strings through-body ferrules, blackface peghead with pearl double diamond/logo inlay, 3-per-side tuners with plastic buttons, gold hardware, 2 creme-colored P-90-style *Blues 90* pickups with hum-cancelling dummy coil, volume/push-pull tone controls, 3-way selector, 6-position Varitone switch, includes gig bag. Available in Chicago Blue (new 1997), Ebony (EB) and Heritage Cherry (HC) finishes. Current Mfg.

MSR $1,229	$875	$625	$550	$495	$450	$400	$350

Gibson

Shipment Totals 1937-1979

by Larry Meiners is simply a must for all Gibson collectors and players. This new 64-page book finally lets you determine the year of manufacture and production totals on over 1.6 million Gibson instruments (includes guitars, basses, mandolins, steels, banjos, and even amps) built between 1937-1979.

Why guess when you can be sure?

Also Available Online as a Download
www.bluebookinc.com
Good Information Never Sleeps!

Flying "V"

The Illustrated History of this Modernistic Guitar

Gibson's ultimate alternative design, is comprehensively researched by Larry Meiners in this new 72-page book. Includes production figures, serialization, and photos of Jimi Hendrix, Lonnie Mack, Albert King, Michael Shenker, Eric Johnson Foreword by Billy Gibbons. It's all here, and includes 8 pages of color.

Why guess when you can be sure?

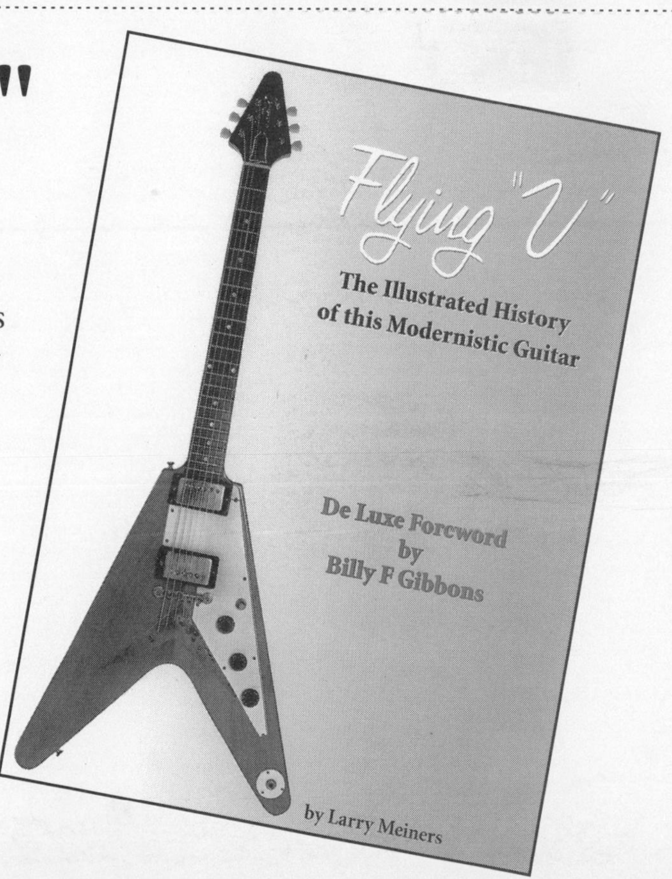

GRADING	100% MINT	98% NEAR MINT	95% EXC+	90% EXC	80% VG+	70% VG	60% G

BluesHawk w/Maestro (DSBH) - similar to BluesHawk (DSBH), except features a gold-plated tune- o-matic bridge/Maestro tremolo. Available in Chicago Blue (CB), Ebony (EB) and Heritage Cherry (HC) finishes. Mfg. 1997-2000.

$1,025 $850 $750 $650 $550 $450 $350
Last MSR was $1,486.

THE HAWK - single cutaway mahogany body, mahogany neck, 25.5" scale, 22-fret rosewood fingerboard with dot inlay, wraparound bridge, blackface peghead with silkscreened logo, engraved "The Hawk" truss rod cover, 3-per-side tuners, chrome hardware, 2 exposed pole piece humbucker (490R) pickups, 1 volume/2 tone controls, 3-way selector. Available in Ebony (EB) and Wine Red (WR) finishes. Disc. 1998.

Rarity and lack of activity in the secondary marketplace precludes accurate pricing on this model.

NIGHTHAWK CUSTOM (DSNC) - single cutaway mahogany body, bound figured maple top, mahogany neck, 22-fret bound ebony fingerboard with pearl crown inlay, strings through bridge, bound blackface peghead with pearl plant/logo inlay, 3-per-side tuners with pearl buttons, gold hardware, 2 humbucker pickups, volume/push-pull tone controls, 5-position switch. Available in Antique Natural (AN), Dark Wineburst, Fireburst (FI), Translucent Red and Vintage Sunburst finishes. Disc. 1999.

$1,025 $850 $750 $650 $550 $450 $350
Last MSR was $2,299.

In 1994, Translucent Amber (TA) finish was introduced, Dark Wineburst, Translucent Red and Vintage Sunburst finishes were discontinued.

Nighthawk Custom 3 Pickup (DSC3) - similar to Nighthawk Custom, except has humbucker/single coil/humbucker pickups. Available in Antique Natural (AN), Fireburst (FI), and Translucent Amber (TA) finishes. Disc. 1999.

$1,025 $850 $750 $650 $550 $450 $350
Last MSR was $2,399.

Nighthawk Custom 3 Pickup/Floyd Rose (DSC3-FG) - similar to Nighthawk Custom 3 Pickup, except has double locking Floyd Rose vibrato and gold hardware. Available in Antique Natural (AN), Fireburst (FI), and Translucent Amber (TA) finishes. Mfg. 1994-99.

$895 $750 $650 $550 $450 $350 $275
Last MSR was $2,499.

NIGHTHAWK LANDMARK (DSLS) - single cutaway mahogany body, bound maple top, mahogany neck, 22-fret rosewood fingerboard with pearl dot inlay, fixed bridge, 3-per-side tuners with pearl buttons, gold hardware, 2 mini humbucker pickups, volume/push-pull tone controls, 5-position switch, Landmark Series decal noting the location of the National Park or Monument specific to each color. Available in Everglades Green (EG), Glacier Blue (GB), Mojave Burst (MB), Navajo Turquoise (NT), and Sequoia Red (SR) finishes. Mfg. 1995-99.

$750 $650 $575 $500 $450 $425 $395
Last MSR was $1,339.

NIGHTHAWK SPECIAL (DSN-) - single cutaway mahogany body, bound maple top, mahogany neck, 22-fret rosewood fingerboard with pearl dot inlay, strings through bridge, blackface peghead with pearl logo inlay, 3-per-side tuners, gold hardware, 2 humbucker pickups, volume/push-pull tone controls, 5-position switch. Available in Ebony (EB), Heritage Cherry (HC), and Vintage Sunburst (VS) finishes. Disc. 1999.

$650 $575 $500 $425 $350 $275 $250
Last MSR was $1,099.

Nighthawk Special 3 Pickup (DSN3) - similar to Nighthawk Special, except has humbucker/single coil/humbucker pickups. Disc. 1999.

$750 $650 $575 $500 $450 $425 $395
Last MSR was $1,199.

NIGHTHAWK STANDARD (DSNS) - single cutaway mahogany body, bound figured maple top, mahogany neck, 22-fret bound rosewood fingerboard with pearl parallelogram inlay, strings through bridge, bound blackface peghead with pearl plant/logo inlay, 3-per-side tuners with pearl buttons, gold hardware, 2 humbucker pickups, volume/push-pull tone controls, 5-position switch. Available in Fireburst (FI), Translucent Amber (TA), Translucent Red, and Vintage Sunburst (VS) finishes. Disc. 1999.

$800 $725 $650 $550 $475 $400 $350
Last MSR was $1,599.

In 1994, Translucent Red finish was discontinued.

Nighthawk Standard 3 Pickup (DSS3) - similar to Nighthawk Standard, except has humbucker/single coil/humbucker pickups. Available in Fireburst (FI), Translucent Amber (TA), and Vintage Sunburst (VS) finishes. Disc. 1999.

$895 $750 $650 $550 $450 $350 $275
Last MSR was $1,739.

Nighthawk Standard 3 Pickup/Floyd Rose (DSS3-FG) - similar to Nighthawk Standard 3 Pickup, except has double locking Floyd Rose vibrato and gold hardware. Available in Fireburst (FI), Translucent Amber (TA), and Vintage Sunburst (VS) finishes. Mfg. 1994-99.

$750 $650 $575 $500 $450 $425 $395
Last MSR was$1,839.

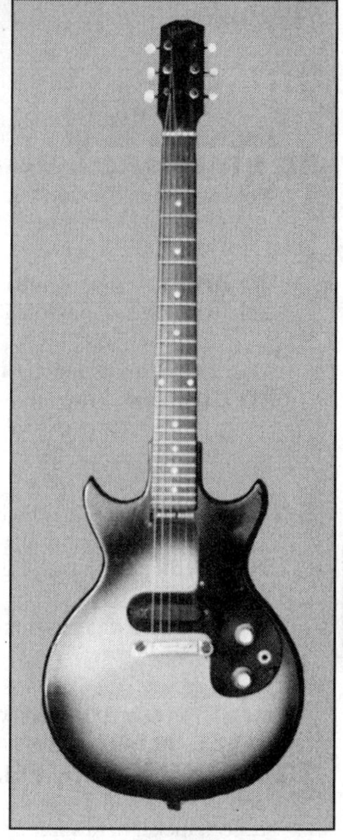

1966 Gibson Melody Maker
courtesy Pressly Lee

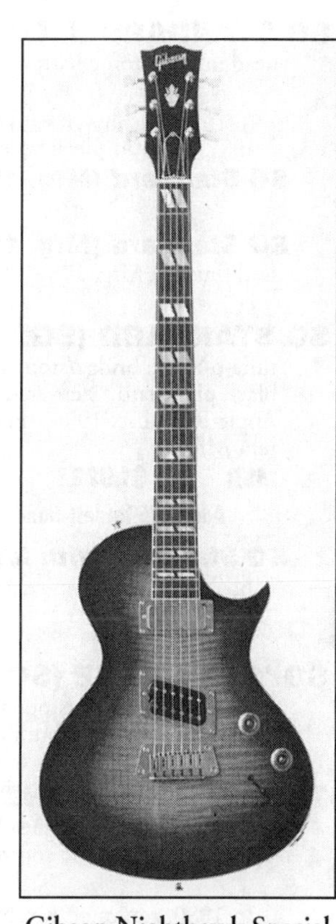

Gibson Nighthawk Special
courtesy Gibson USA

GRADING	100% MINT	98% NEAR MINT	95% EXC+	90% EXC	80% VG+	70% VG	60% G

RD Series

RD STANDARD - single cutaway asymmetrical hourglass style maple body, black pickguard, maple neck, 22-fret rosewood fingerboard with pearl dot inlay, tune-o-matic bridge/stop tailpiece, blackface peghead with logo decal, 3-per-side tuners, nickel hardware, 2 covered humbucker pickups, 2 volume/2 tone controls, 3-position switch. Available in Cherry Sunburst, Ebony, Natural and Tobacco Sunburst finishes. Mfg. 1977-79.

N/A $600 $500 $425 $375 $325 $300

RD Artist - similar to RD Standard, except has an ebony fingerboard with block inlay, multi bound peghead with pearl stylized f-hole/logo inlay, gold hardware, mini switch, active electronics.

N/A $800 $725 $650 $575 $500 $425

In 1978, tunable stop tailpiece replaced original part/design.

RD Custom - similar to RD Standard, except has maple fingerboard, active electronics, mini switch.

N/A $950 $825 $725 $625 $525 $450

S-1 - single cutaway alder body, black tri-lam pickguard, bolt-on maple neck, 22-fret rosewood or maple fingerboard with pearl dot inlay, tune-o-matic bridge/stop tailpiece, 3-per-side tuners, chrome hardware, 3 single coil bar pickups, volume/tone control, 3-position/rotary switches. Available in Natural/Blonde finish. Mfg. 1976 to 1980.

N/A $400 $350 $295 $225 $200 $175

This model was previously endorsed by Ron Wood.

SG Series

In 1961, this new body shape was originally intended to bring a new style to the Les Paul line. But without Les Paul's approval they were renamed the **SG** during 1963. The first two years of instruments in this series have *Les Paul* logos on their pegheads or the area below the fingerboard (see Les Paul section).

SG STANDARD (MFG. 1963-1971) - double sharp cutaway mahogany body, layered black pickguard, one piece mahogany neck, 22-fret bound rosewood fingerboard with pearl trapezoid inlay, tune-o-matic bridge/side-pull vibrato, blackface peghead with pearl logo inlay, 3-per-side tuners, nickel hardware, 2 covered humbucker pickups, 2 volume/2 tone controls, 3-position switch. Available in Cherry finish. Mfg. 1963 - 1971.

1963-1965 N/A $3,500 $3,000 $2,750 $2,500 $2,150 $1,900
1966-1971 N/A $1,800 $1,600 $1,495 $1,150 $1,000 $975

In 1963, some models were produced with ebony tailblock with pearl inlay.

SG Deluxe - double cutaway mahogany body, raised layered black pickguard, mahogany neck, 22-fret bound rosewood fingerboard with pearl block inlay, tune-o-matic bridge/Bigsby-style vibrato tailpiece, blackface peghead with pearl crown/logo inlay, 3-per-side tuners, chrome hardware, 2 covered humbucker pickups, 2 volume/2 tone controls mounted on layered black plate, 3-position switch. Available in Cherry, Natural and Walnut finishes. Mfg. 1971 - 1974.

N/A $750 $695 $525 $450 $400 $325

SG STANDARD (MFG. 1972-1981) - similar to SG Standard, except has pearl block fingerboard inlay, stop tailpiece, pearl crown peghead inlay, chrome hardware. Available in Cherry finish. Mfg. 1972 - 1981.

N/A $750 $650 $575 $500 $450 $425

In 1976, Bigsby vibrato became standard, stop tailpiece was an option, Cherry, Tobacco Sunburst and White finishes became available. In 1977, stop tailpiece became standard, Bigsby vibrato became an option.

SG Standard (Mfg. 1983-87) - same as SG Standard Reissue I. Available in Cherry and Sunburst finishes. Mfg. 1983 - 1987.

N/A $525 $450 $375 $300 $270 $250

SG Standard (Mfg. 1989-1990) - similar to SG Standard Reissue I, except has trapezoid fingerboard inlay. Available in Ebony and Wine Red finishes. Mfg. 1989 - 1990.

N/A $500 $425 $350 $295 $250 $225

SG STANDARD (SGS-) - double cutaway mahogany body, mahogany neck, 22-fret bound rosewood fingerboard with pearl trapezoid inlay, tune-o-matic bridge/stop tailpiece, blackface peghead with pearl crown/logo inlay, 3-per-side tuners with plastic buttons, chrome hardware, layered black pickguard, 2 covered humbucker pickups, 2 volume/2 tone controls, 3-position switch. Available in Candy Apple Blue (disc. 1994), Candy Apple Red (disc. 1994), Ebony (EB), Heritage Cherry (HC), Natural Burst (new 1999, limited edition), and TV Yellow (disc. 1994) finishes. Current Mfg.

MSR $1,922 $1,375 $975 $875 $775 $650 $575 $495

Add $225 for left-handed configuration.

SG Standard With Maestro (SGS-) - similar to SG Standard, except features a Maestro vibrato tailpiece. Available Ebony (EB) finish. Mfg. 1996-2000.

$1,350 $1,050 $950 $850 $725 $600 $475

Last MSR was $2,043.

SG '61 REISSUE (SG61) - double cutaway mahogany body, mahogany neck, 22-fret bound rosewood fingerboard with pearl trapezoid inlay, tune-o-matic bridge/stop tailpiece, blackface peghead with pearl plant/logo inlay, 3-per-side tuner with pearl buttons, nickel hardware, layered black pickguard, 2 covered humbucker pickups, 2 volume/2 tone controls, 3-position switch. Available in Heritage Cherry (HC) finish. New 1986.

MSR $2,383 $1,650 $1,400 $1,200 $995 $850 $700 $600

THE SG (FIREBRAND) - double cutaway walnut body, walnut neck, 22-fret ebony fingerboard with pearl dot inlay, tune-o-matic bridge/stop tailpiece, blackface peghead with pearl crown/logo inlay, 3-per-side tuners, chrome hardware, layered black pickguard, 2 covered humbucker pickups, 2 volume/2 tone controls, 3-position switch. Available in Natural satin nitrocellulose finish. Mfg. 1979 to 1981.

N/A $500 $450 $400 $325 $250 $225

In 1980, renamed Firebrand SG with new name burned into top.

GRADING	100% MINT	98% NEAR MINT	95% EXC+	90% EXC	80% VG+	70% VG	60% G

Gibson SG Standard
courtesy Rick Wilkiewicz

The SG (Deluxe) - similar to The SG (Standard), except has mahogany body/neck. Available in Antique Mahogany, Ebony, Natural and Wine Red finishes. Mfg. 1979 to 1985.

	100%	98%	95%	90%	80%	70%	60%
	N/A	$500	$450	$400	$325	$250	$225

In 1980, renamed Firebrand SG Deluxe with new name burned into top.

SG EXCLUSIVE - similar to the the SG (Standard), except has mahogany body, black finish, cream binding on neck, cream pickguard, cream pickup covers, gold knobs, quail tap switch, TP-6 stop tailpiece, and truss rod cover that reads Exclusive. Mfg. 1979 only.

	100%	98%	95%	90%	80%	70%	60%
	N/A	$800	$695	$625	$550	$500	$450

SG ANGUS YOUNG SIGNATURE - similar to SG Classic, except has two pickups ('57 classic and Angus Young humbuckers), devil decal on headstock, engraved tailpiece with vibrator, includes Angus Young signature on hardshell case, available in Aged Cherry (AC) finish only. New 2000.

	100%	98%	95%	90%	80%	70%	60%
MSR $2,922	$2,000	$1,475	$1,275	$1,075	$950	$875	$800

SG CLASSIC - double sharp cutaway mahogany body, patterned after the late 1960s SG Special, 2 P-90 pickups, 22-fret bound rosewood fingerboard with pearloid dot inlays, tune-o-matic bridge with ABR tailpiece, chrome hardware, includes gig bag, available in Ebony Stain or Heritage Cherry finish. New 1999.

	100%	98%	95%	90%	80%	70%	60%
MSR $1,537	$1,075	$775	$675	$600	$525	$475	$425

SG CUSTOM - double sharp cutaway mahogany body, mahogany neck, 22-fret bound ebony fingerboard with pearl block inlay, tune-o-matic bridge/side-pull vibrato, multi-bound peghead with pearl split diamond inlay, 3-per-side tuners, gold hardware, white layered pickguard, 3 covered humbucker pickups, 2 volume/2 tone controls, 3-position switch. Available in Black, Cherry, Tobacco Sunburst, Walnut, White and Wine Red finishes. Mfg. 1963 to 1980.

	100%	98%	95%	90%	80%	70%	60%
1963-1966	N/A	$3,000	$2,650	$2,300	$2,000	$1,800	$1,700
1967-1970	N/A	$2,000	$1,850	$1,650	$1,450	$1,300	$1,100
1970-1980	N/A	$1,250	$1,000	$875	$725	$575	$500

In 1963, Maestro vibrato replaced original part/design. In 1972, stop tailpiece replaced previous part/design.
In 1976, Bigsby vibrato replaced previous part/design.

SG DELUXE (SGD+) - double cutaway mahogany body, slim tapered mahogany neck, 22-fret rosewood fingerboard with pearl dot inlay, tune-o-matic bridge/Bigsby-style Maestro tremolo, blackface peghead with pearl logo inlay, 3-per-side tuners, chrome hardware, pearloid pickguard, 3 chrome-covered mini-humbucker pickups, volume/tone controls, 6-way rotary "chickenhead" switch. Available in Blue Ice (BI), Ebony (new 1999), and Hellfire Red (HR) finishes. Mfg. 1998-99.

	100%	98%	95%	90%	80%	70%	60%
	$1,400	$1,200	$1,025	$950	$825	$750	$675

Last MSR was $2,141.

SG LES PAUL (SG BODY STYLE) W/DELUXE MAESTRO (SG61) - features traditional SG style with Maestro deluxe vibrola, two '57 Classic humbucker pickups, black pickguard, Hertiage Cherry finish. Mfg. 1999-2000.

	100%	98%	95%	90%	80%	70%	60%
	$1,895	$1,450	$1,275	$1,075	$995	$875	$795

Last MSR was $2,899.

SG JR. - double cutaway mahogany body, mahogany neck, 22-fret rosewood fingerboard with pearl dot inlay, tune-o-matic bridge/stop tailpiece, 3-per-side tuners with plastic buttons, nickel hardware, black pickguard, single coil pickup, volume/tone control. Available in Cherry finish. Mfg. 1963 to 1971.

	100%	98%	95%	90%	80%	70%	60%
1963-1965	N/A	$1,000	$900	$825	$700	$625	$550
1966-1971	N/A	$750	$675	$550	$495	$450	$395

This model had an optional vibrato beginning in 1962. In 1961, The Les Paul Jr. adopted the SG body style, and featured a single P-90 pickup, laminated pickguard, and Les Paul Jr. peghead logo. In 1963, the Les Paul Jr. was renamed the SG Jr. In 1965, vibrato became standard.

SG Jr. (Current Mfg. SGJ-) - double cutaway mahogany body, chrome hardware, current production model with choice of Ebony or Wine Red finish. New 1999.

	100%	98%	95%	90%	80%	70%	60%
MSR $1,075	$775	$525	$450	$400	$350	$295	$250

SG SPECIAL - double cutaway mahogany body, mahogany neck, 22-fret rosewood fingerboard with pearl dot inlay, stop tailpiece, blackface peghead with pearl logo inlay, 3-per-side tuners with plastic buttons, nickel hardware, layered black pickguard, 2 single coil pickups, 2 volume/2 tone control, 3-position switch. Available in Cherry and White finishes. Mfg. 1963 to 1971.

	100%	98%	95%	90%	80%	70%	60%
1963-1965	N/A	$1,800	$1,600	$1,400	$1,250	$1,000	$900
1966-1971	N/A	$1,000	$850	$775	$695	$600	$525

Add $200 for white finish (1963-1965 manufacture).

This model had an optional vibrato. In 1965, vibrato became standard.

SG Special 3/4 - similar to SG Special, except has 3/4 size body, 19-fret fingerboard. Available in Cherry Red finish. Mfg. 1959 to 1961.

	100%	98%	95%	90%	80%	70%	60%
	N/A	$800	$700	$625	$550	$495	$450

SG Professional - similar to SG Special, except has a pearl logo, 2 black soap bar P-90 pickups. Available in Cherry, Natural and Walnut finishes. Mfg. 1971 to 1974.

	100%	98%	95%	90%	80%	70%	60%
	N/A	$475	$400	$350	$275	$250	$225

1972 Gibson SG Deluxe
courtesy David West

GRADING		100% MINT	98% NEAR MINT	95% EXC+	90% EXC	80% VG+	70% VG	60% G

SG Studio - similar to SG Special, except has no pickguard, 2 humbucker pickups, 2 volume/1 tone controls. Available in Natural finish. Mfg. 1978 only.

		N/A	$450	$395	$325	$250	$225	$200

SG SPECIAL (SGSP) - double sharp cutaway mahogany body, maple neck, 22-fret rosewood fingerboard with pearl dot inlay, tune-o-matic bridge/stop tailpiece, blackface peghead with silkscreened logo inlay, 3-per-side tuners, chrome hardware, black pickguard, 2 humbucker pickups, volume/tone controls, 3-position switch. Available in Alpine White (disc. 1998), Ebony (EB), Ferrari Red (FR, disc.), Ebony Stain (Mfg. 1999-2000, limited edition), Plum (Mfg. 1999-2000, limited edition), Creme (Mfg. 1999-2000, limited edition), Wine Red (new 2001), Blue Teal Flip-flop (new 2001), and TV Yellow (disc. 1994) finishes. Current Mfg.

MSR	$1,229	$875	$625	$550	$500	$450	$400	$375

Add $77 for Blue Teal Flip-flop finish.

SG GOTHIC (SGG-) - similar to SG Special, except has Gothic finish, includes gig bag. New 2000.

MSR	$1,383	$975	$675	$600	$525	$475	$415	$385

SG SUPREME (SGSU) - double sharp cutaway mahogany body with AA flame maple top, mahogany slim tapered (1959 style) neck with ebony fingerboard featuring split diamond inlays, bound neck and headstock, 2 P-90A black pickups, tune-o-matic bridge and stop tailpiece, gold hardware, available in Lavaburst (new 2001), Fireburst (FI), Midnight Burst (MD, new 2001), and Emerald Burst (ED, new 2001) finish. New 1999.

MSR	$3,229	$2,200	$1,875	$1,575	$1,375	$1,200	$1,000	$825

Add $79 for 1957 style humbuckers (not available in Fireburst finish).

SG TV - double rounded cutaway mahogany body, mahogany neck, 22-fret rosewood fingerboard with pearl dot inlay, tune-o-matic bridge/stop tailpiece, 3-per-side tuners with plastic buttons, nickel hardware, black pickguard, single coil pickup, volume/tone control. Available in Limed Mahogany and White finishes. Mfg. 1959 to 1968.

	N/A	$2,700	$2,400	$2,100	$1,850	$1,500	$1,250
Limed mahogany	N/A	$2,700	$2,400	$2,100	$1,850	$1,500	$1,250
White	N/A	$1,500	$1,300	$1,100	$950	$825	$700

In 1961, the SG-style body replaced the double rounded cutaway horns. This configuration was available in White finish.
This model is fairly rare, and does not trade too often in the vintage guitar market.

SG-X LIMTED EDITION (SGX-) - double cutaway mahogany body, mahogany neck, 24 3/4" scale, 24-fret rosewood fingerboard with pearl dot inlay, tune-o-matic bridge/stop tailpiece, blackface peghead with logo, 3-per-side tuners, chrome hardware, white pickguard, 500T exposed pole-piece humbucker pickups, volume/tone controls, coil-tap mini-switch. Available in Carribean Blue (SB), Corona Yellow (SY), and Coral (SC) finishes. Mfg. 1998 only.

		$575	$495	$450	$400	$350	$300	$275

Last MSR was $740.

SG-X (SGX-) - similar to the SG-X. Available in Ebony (EB) and Dark Wineburst (DW) finishes. Mfg. 1998 -2000

		$550	$425	$375	$325	$275	$250	$225

Last MSR was $856.

SG-Z (SGZ-) - double cutaway mahogany body, slim tapered mahogany neck, 24-fret bound rosewood fingerboard with pearl split diamond inlay, tune-o-matic bridge/Z-shaped stop tailpiece with strings through-body, blackface peghead with pearl Z/Gibson logo inlay, 3-per-side tuners, black chrome hardware, pearloid pickguard, 500T single coil/490R humbucker exposed polepiece pickups, volume/tone controls, 3-way selector toggle. Available in Platinum (PL) and Verdigris (VG) finishes. Limited Mfg. 1998 only.

Last MSR was $1,365.

SG '90 SINGLE - double sharp cutaway mahogany body, pearloid pickguard, maple neck, 24-fret bound ebony fingerboard with pearl split diamond inlay, strings through anchoring, blackface peghead with pearl crown/logo inlay, 3-per-side tuners, black chrome hardware, humbucker pickup, volume/tone control, 3-position switch. Available in Alpine White, Heritage Cherry and Metallic Turquoise finishes. Mfg. 1989 - 1990.

		N/A	$525	$450	$395	$350	$325	$295

This model had an optional double locking vibrato.

SG '90 Double - similar to SG '90 Single, except has single coil/humbucker pickups. Mfg. 1989 - 1992.

		N/A	$550	$425	$400	$350	$325	$300

SG-100 - double cutaway mahogany body, black pickguard, mahogany neck, 22-fret rosewood fingerboard with dot inlay, tunable stop tailpiece, 3-per-side tuners, nickel hardware, single coil pickup, volume/tone control. Available in Cherry and Walnut finishes. Mfg. 1971 - 1972.

		N/A	$350	$300	$250	$225	$175	$150

SG-200 - similar to SG-100, except has 2 single coil pickups, slide switch.

		N/A	$350	$300	$250	$225	$175	$150

SG-250 - similar to SG-100, except has 2 single coil pickups, 2 slide switches. Available in Cherry Sunburst finish.

		N/A	$350	$300	$250	$225	$175	$150

SG I - double cutaway mahogany body, black pickguard, mahogany neck, 22-fret rosewood fingerboard with dot inlay, tunable stop tailpiece, 3-per-side tuners, nickel hardware, single coil pickup, volume/tone control. Available in Cherry and Walnut finishes. Mfg. 1972-79.

		N/A	$350	$300	$250	$225	$175	$150

SG II - similar to SG I, except has 2 single coil pickups, slide switch.

		N/A	$350	$300	$250	$225	$175	$150

SG III - similar to SG I, except has 2 single coil pickups, 2 slide switches. Available in Cherry Sunburst finish.

		N/A	$350	$300	$250	$225	$175	$150

GRADING	100% MINT	98% NEAR MINT	95% EXC+	90% EXC	80% VG+	70% VG	60% G

Gibson Sonex-180 Custom
courtesy The Music Shoppe

Sonex Series

SONEX-180 CUSTOM - single cutaway composite body, black pickguard, bolt-on maple neck, 22-fret ebony fingerboard with dot inlay, tune-o-matic bridge/stop tailpiece, blackface peghead with decal logo, 3-per-side tuners, chrome hardware, 2 exposed humbucker pickups, 2 volume/2 tone controls, 3-position switch. Available in Ebony and White finishes. Mfg. 1981 to 1982.

N/A	$325	$275	$225	$195	$175	$150

Sonex-180 Deluxe - similar to Sonex-180 Custom, except has 2 ply pickguard, rosewood fingerboard. Available in Ebony finish. Mfg. 1981 to 1984.

N/A	$325	$275	$225	$195	$175	$150

In 1982, a left-handed version of this instrument became available.

Sonex Artist - similar to Sonex-180 Custom, except has rosewood fingerboard, tunable stop tailpiece, 3 mini switches, active electronics. Available in Candy Apple Red and Ivory finishes. Mfg. 1981 to 1984.

N/A	$375	$325	$275	$225	$195	$175

Spirit Series

SPIRIT I - double cutaway mahogany body, bound figured maple top, tortoise shell pickguard, mahogany neck, 2-fret rosewood fingerboard with pearl dot inlay, tunable wrapover bridge, blackface peghead with logo decal, 3-per-side tuners with plastic buttons, chrome hardware, 1 exposed humbucker pickup, volume/tone control. Available in Natural, Red and Sunburst finishes. Mfg. 1982 to 1988.

N/A	$400	$325	$250	$225	$175	$150

In 1983, 6-per-side tuner peghead replaced original part/design, figured maple top was removed.

Spirit II - similar to Spirit I, except has no pickguard, 2 exposed humbuckers pickups, 2 volume/1 tone controls.

N/A	$450	$375	$325	$275	$250	$195

Spirit II XPL - similar to Spirit I, except has bound fingerboard, Kahler vibrato, 6-on-a-side tuners, 2 exposed humbuckers pickups, 2 volume/1 tone controls. Mfg. 1985 to 1987.

N/A	$350	$300	$250	$225	$200	$180

Super 400 CES Model

SUPER 400 CES - single round cutaway grand auditorium style body, arched spruce top, bound f-holes, raised multi-bound mottled plastic pickguard, figured maple back/sides, multiple bound body, 3-piece figured maple/mahogany neck, model name engraved into heel cap, 14/20-fret bound ebony fingerboard with point on bottom, pearl split block fingerboard inlay, adjustable rosewood bridge with pearl triangle wings inlay, gold trapeze tailpiece with engraved model name, multi-bound blackface peghead with pearl split diamond/logo inlay, pearl split diamond inlay on back of peghead, 3-per-side tuners, gold hardware, 2 single coil pickups, 2 volume/2 tone controls, 3-position switch. Available in Ebony, Natural, Sunburst and Wine Red finishes. Mfg. 1951 to 1994.

1951-1954	N/A	$15,000	$13,000	$11,200	$9,300	$7,450	$6,700
1955-1959	N/A	$12,500	$10,750	$8,900	$7,200	$6,500	$5,900
1960-1969	N/A	$13,000	$11,000	$9,600	$8,100	$7,500	$7,000
1970-1974	N/A	$7,500	$6,850	$6,300	$5,750	$5,200	$4,900
1975-1985	N/A	$6,000	$5,300	$4,575	$3,850	$3,500	$3,350
1986-1994	N/A	$5,500	$5,000	$4,500	$4,000	$3,800	$3,650

Last MSR was $5,000.

Between 1951-53, P90 pickups were standard, during 1953-57, Alnico pickups were standard. In 1957, PAF humbucker pickups replaced Alnico pickups. In 1960, sharp cutaway replaced original part/design. In 1962, Pat. No. humbucker pickups replaced previous part/design.

In 1969, round cutaway replaced previous part/design. In 1974, neck volute was introduced.

In 1981, neck volute was discontinued. Super 400 CES models with PAF pickups (1957-1962) have sold for as high as $15,000. Instruments should be determined on a piece-by-piece basis as opposed to the usual market. The Super 400 CES model has been a platform for experimentation - ser. nos. of "one-offs" were custom ordered to special features. Current production instruments are part of the Historic Collection Series, found at the end of this section.

Gibson Super 400
courtesy Dr. Tom Van Hoose

Tal Farlow Model

TAL FARLOW - single round cutaway bound hollow body, arched figured maple top, bound f-holes, scroll style inlay on cutaway, raised black bound pickguard, maple back/sides/neck, 20 bound rosewood fingerboard with pearl reverse crown inlay, tune-o-matic bridge/trapeze tailpiece, rosewood tailpiece insert with pearl engraved block inlay, bound peghead with pearl crown/logo inlay, 3-per-side tuners, chrome hardware, 2 covered humbucker pickups, 2 volume/2 tone controls, 3-position switch. Available in Brown Sunburst finish. Mfg. 1962 to 1971.

N/A	$10,000	$9,200	$8,350	$7,450	$7,000	$6,800

Current production instruments (Tal Farlow Reissue) are part of the Historic Collection Series, found at the end of this section.

GRADING	100% MINT	98% NEAR MINT	95% EXC+	90% EXC	80% VG+	70% VG	60% G

Trini Lopez Models

TRINI LOPEZ STANDARD - double round cutaway semi hollow bound body, arched maple top, bound diamond holes, raised layered black pickguard, maple back/sides, mahogany neck, 22-fret bound rosewood fingerboard with pearl split diamond inlay, tune-o-matic bridge/trapeze tailpiece, ebony tailpiece insert with pearl model name inlay, 6-on-a-side tuners, chrome hardware, 2 covered humbucker pickups, 2 volume/2 tone controls, 3-position switch. Available in Cherry finish. Mfg. 1964 to 1971.

N/A	$1,800	$1,550	$1,400	$1,250	$1,100	$995

Trini Lopez Deluxe - similar to Trini Lopez Standard, except has sharp cutaway, tortoise pickguard, 20-fret ebony fingerboard. Available in Cherry Sunburst finish.

N/A	$2,000	$1,875	$1,725	$1,595	$1,525	$1,475

GIBSON CUSTOM SHOP

The Gibson Guitar Corp. operates 2 Custom Shops - one in Nashville, TN (mostly electric Mfg.), and one in Bozeman, MT only acoustic Mfg. The Custom Shop manufactures instruments for the Gibson Custom, Art, and Historic Division. The Historic Collection specializes in handcrafting exact reproductions of historically significant Gibson instruments, I.e., Les Pauls, SGs, Firebirds, and large body jazz guitars. The Custom Collection focuses on Custom Shop artist signature models and newer variations of some of Gibson's older classics. The Art Guitars are mostly limited edition and one-of-a-kind guitars - most of these involve elaborate painted/inlaid scenes.

Also refer to the 7th Edition ***Blue Book of Acoustic Guitars*** for more information on the acoustic Custom Shop models available from the Bozeman, MT Custom Shop.

Historic & Custom Collection Instruments Mfg. by the Custom Shop

The models listed below are either reproductions of Gibson classics (Historic Collection) or other Custom Shop models manufactured in various configurations, including selected artist signature models. Whenever possible, Gibson factory model nomenclature (in some cases, only prefixes are listed) has been provided at the end of the model name. In some instances, you may see [ ] brackets, which indicates the color/finish abbreviation would appear in that spot.

Historic instruments are manufactured to the exact original specifications and in several cases, use the same tooling when available.

Gibson Custom Shop/Historic Collection instruments are produced in limited quantities. Since most of these instruments see little or no use (the great majority remain NIC), most are in Excellent+ condition, values below will only be listed down to the 95% condition factor.

Custom Shop and Historic Collection instruments listed below can be differentiated by the Custom Shop or Historic Collection model note reference at the end of each model listing.

Current Custom Collection Finishes/Hardware Abbreviations

AN – Antique Natural
BG - Bigsby
BP – Black/White Bullseye
BS – Butterscotch
CB – Caramel Brown
CH - Chrome
CRB – Cranberry
CS – Chablis
CS – Heritage Cherry Sunburst (Elegant Model)
DW – Dark Wineburst
EB – Ebony
EG – Emberglow
FC – Faded Cherry
FM – Firemist
GB – Gingerburst
GH – Gold
GML – Gold Maestro
HB – Honeyburst
HS – Heritage Cherry Sunburst
NA – Natural
NH – Nickel
NM – Nickel Maestro
NML – Nickel Maestro Long
NT – Nickel Trapeze
PK – Peacock
SB – Sienna Burst
TGB – Tangerine Burst
TA – Trans Amber
TBK – Trans Black
TB – Trans Blue
TR – Trans Red
3B – Triburst
TS – Tobacco Burst
VS – Vintage Sunburst
WR – Wine Red

GRADING	100% MINT	98% NEAR MINT	95% EXC+	90% EXC	80% VG+	70% VG	60% G

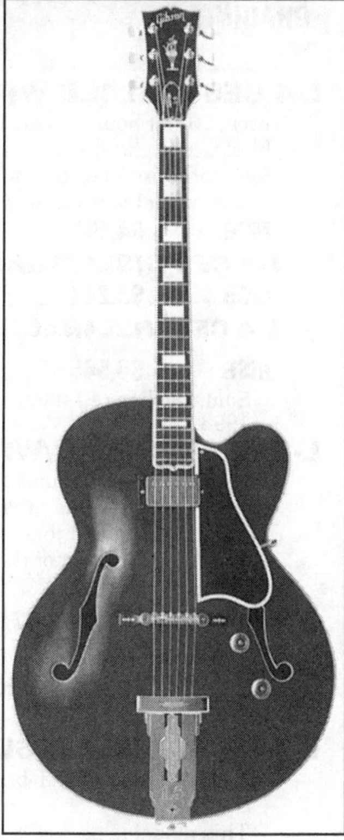
Gibson Byrdland
courtesy Thoroughbred Music

Current Historic Collection Finishes/Hardware Abbreviations

AG – Antique Gold
AN – Antique Natural
BG - Bigsby
BR – Cremona Brown Sunburst
BS – Butterscotch
CH - Chrome
CW – Classic White
EB – Ebony
FC – Faded Cherry
GH – Gold
GML – Gold Maestro
HB – Honeyburst
HD – Heritage Darkburst
NA – Natural
NH – Nickel
NM – Nickel Maestro
NM – Nickel Maestro Long
NT – Nickel Trapeze
OB – Oxblood
TV – TV Yellow
TS – Tobacco Sunburst
VB – Viceroy Brown Sunburst
VS – Vintage Sunburst
WR – Wine Red

Custom Shop/Historic Collection Carved Top Series

BYRDLAND - (HSBYWRGH) - single rounded cutaway multi-ply bound hollow body, solid spruce top, bound f-holes, maple back/sides/neck, 23 1/2" scale, 22-fret multi-ply bound ebony pointed fingerboard with pearl block inlay, ABR-1 bridge with rosewood base/trapeze tailpiece, multi-ply bound blackface peghead with pearl flowerpot/logo inlay, 3-per-side tuners, gold hardware, raised bound tortoise pickguard, 2 covered humbucker ('57 Classic PAF Reissue) pickups, 2 volume/2 tone controls, 3-way selector switch (on treble bout). Available in Wine Red, Natural, or Vintage Sunburst finish. New 1998.

Body Width 17", Body Depth 2 1/4".

This model is part of the Historic Collection.

MSR $8,225 $4,500 $2,950 $2,350

Byrdland (HSBYVSGH) - with Vintage Sunburst finish.

MSR $9,599 $5,250 $3,800 $2,900

Byrdland (HSBYNAGH) - with Natural finish.

MSR $11,232 $6,100 $4,500 $3,450

BYRDLAND FLORENTINE (HSBYFWRGH) - similar to the Byrdland, except features a single Florentine cutaway body. Available in Wine Red, Natural, or Vintage Sunburst finish. New 1998.

Body Width 17", Body Depth 2 1/4".

This model is part of the Historic Collection.

MSR $8,469 $4,650 $3,350 $2,700

Byrdland (HSBYFVSGH) - with Vintage Sunburst finish.

MSR $10,247 $5,600 $4,000 $3,100

Byrdland (HSBYFNAGH) - with Natural finish.

MSR $11,940 $6,600 $4,650 $3,300

WES MONTGOMERY (HSWMWRGH) - single round cutaway hollow body, carved spruce top, bound f-holes, raised bound tortoise pickguard, multibound body, carved flame maple back/sides, 5-piece maple neck, 20-fret multibound ebony fingerboard with pearl block inlay, tune-o-matic bridge on ebony base with pearl leaf inlay, engraved trapeze tailpiece with silver engraved insert, multibound blackface peghead with pearl torch/logo inlay, 3-per-side tuners, gold hardware, humbucker pickup, volume/tone control. Available in Vintage Sunburst, Wine Red, Ebony (disc.), or Natural finish. New 1993.

This model is part of the Historic Collection.

MSR $7,931 $4,350 $3,100 $2,600

Wes Montgomery (HSWMVSGH) - with Vintage Sunburst or Ebony (special order, disc.) finish.

MSR $10,044 $5,500 $4,000 $3,275

Wes Montgomery (HSWMNAGH) - with Natural finish.

MSR $12,565 $6,850 $4,875 $4,000

Gibson Wes Montgomery
courtesy Gibson USA

GRADING	100% MINT	98% NEAR MINT	95% EXC+	90% EXC	80% VG+	70% VG	60% G

L-4 CES (HSL4EB/WRGH) - single sharp cutaway bound body, carved spruce top, layered black pickguard, f-holes, mahogany back/sides/neck, 20-fret bound ebony fingerboard with pearl parallelogram inlay, tune-o-matic bridge on ebony base with pearl inlay on wings, trapeze tailpiece, blackface peghead with pearl crown/logo inlay, 3-per-side tuners with plastic buttons, gold hardware, 2 covered humbucker pickups, 2 volume/2 tone controls, 3-position switch, available in Wine Red, Ebony, Vintage Sunburst, and Natural finish. New 1987.

This model is from the Custom Collection.

MSR $4,195 $2,600 $1,900 $1,550

L-4 CES (HSL4VSGH) - with Vintage Sunburst (VS) finishes.

MSR $5,244 $3,225 $2,325 $1,900

L-4 CES (HSL4NAGH) - with Natural (NA) finishes.

MSR $6,565 $4,000 $3,000 $2,475

Some earlier reissue models were available in Natural (NA) finish. Natural finish was briefly discontinued in 1996, then reintroduced in 1998.

L-5 CES (HSLCEB/WRGH) - single round cutaway bound body, carved spruce top, layered tortoise pickguard, bound f-holes, maple back/sides/neck, 20-fret bound pointed ebony fingerboard with pearl block inlay, ebony bridge with pearl inlay on wings, model name engraved trapeze tailpiece with chrome insert, multi-bound blackface peghead with pearl flame/logo inlay, 3-per-side tuners, gold hardware, 2 covered humbucker pickups, 2 volume/2 tone controls, 3-position switch. Available in Natural, Wine Red, Ebony, and Vintage Sunburst finish. Current Mfg.

This model is part of the Historic Collection.

MSR $8,678 $4,750 $3,400 $2,950

L-5 CES (HSLCVSGH) - with Vintage Sunburst finish.

MSR $11,923 $6,450 $4,650 $3,950

L-5 CES (HSLCNAGH) - with Natural finish.

MSR $14,444 $7,800 $5,750 $4,800

L-5 SIGNATURE (CSL5SGH) - scaled down body variation of the original L-5, spruce top, AAA maple back/rims, two '57 Classic humbucker pickups, ABR-1 bridge, with L-5 style tailpiece, 7-ply top binding, 3-ply back binding, available in Vintage Sunburst or Tangerine Burst. New 2001.

This model is part of the Custom Collection.

MSR $9,685 $6,450 $4,650 $3,950

L-5 STUDIO (CSL5[ ]NH) - single rounded cutaway semi-hollow body, carved spruce top, black body binding, 2 f-holes, 20-fret ebony fingerboard with mother-of-pearl dot inlay, ABR-1 bridge with pearl inlay on wings/metal Bail raised tailpiece, blackface peghead with pearl logo inlay, 3-per-side Schaller tuners, "Ice Cube Marble" pickguard, nickel hardware, 2 covered humbucker ('57 Classic) pickups, 2 volume/2 tone controls, 3-position switch. Available in Autumnburst (AB), Translucent Blue (BU), Translucent Red (TR), or Alpine White (new 1999) finish. Mfg. 1997-2000.

This model was part of the Custom Collection.

$3,150 $2,600 $2,200

Last MSR was $5,226.

Add $546 for Alpine White finish (new 1999).

Early versions of this model were identified as being available in a Classic White finish.

SUPER 400 CES (HSS4EB/WRGH) - single sharp cutaway grand auditorium style body, arched spruce top, bound f-holes, raised multi-bound mottled plastic pickguard, figured maple back/sides, multiple bound body, 3-piece figured maple/mahogany neck, model name engraved into heel cap, 14/20-fret bound ebony fingerboard with point on bottom, pearl split block fingerboard inlay, adjustable rosewood bridge with pearl triangle wings inlay, gold trapeze tailpiece with engraved model name, multi-bound blackface peghead with pearl 5-piece split diamond/logo inlay, pearl 3-piece split diamond inlay on back of peghead, 3-per-side tuners, gold hardware, 2 pickups, 2 volume/2 tone controls, 3-position switch. Available in Natural, Wine Red, Ebony, and Vintage Sunburst finish. Current Mfg.

This model is part of the Historic Collection.

MSR $11,588 $6,250 $4,575 $3,975

Super 400 CES (HSS4VSGH) - with Vintage Sunburst finish.

MSR $14,263 $7,700 $5,650 $4,800

Super 400 CES (HSS4NAGH) - with Natural finishes.

MSR $17,770 $9,600 $7,000 $5,650

Custom Shop/Historic Collection Electric Spanish (ES Model Prefix) Series

ES-5 SWITCHMASTER (HS5SVSGH) - single rounded cutaway body, arched figured maple top, bound f-holes, 3-ply bound body, figured maple back/sides/neck, 20-fret multi-bound pointed fingerboard with pearl block inlay, ABR-1 adjustable bridge/ornate trapeze tailpiece, bound blackface peghead with pearl crown/logo inlay, 3-per-side tuners, gold hardware, raised layered black pickguard, 3 '57 Classic PAF covered pickups, 4-position selector switch on treble cutaway bout, 3 volume/3 tone controls. Available in Vintage Sunburst finish. Disc. 2000.

This model was part of the Historic Collection.

$3,375 $2,800 $2,350

Last MSR was $5,614.

ES-5 Switchmaster (HS5SNAGH) - with Natural finish.

$4,325 $3,600 $3,100

Last MSR was $7,210.

ES-5 Switchmaster P-90 (HS5SP[ ]GH) - similar to the ES-5 Switchmaster, except features P-90 pickups. Available in Vintage Sunburst (VS) and Wine Red (WR) finishes. Disc. 2000.

$3,375 $2,800 $2,350

Last MSR was $5,614.

GRADING	100% MINT	98% NEAR MINT	95% EXC+	90% EXC	80% VG+	70% VG	60% G

ES-5 Switchmaster P-90 (HS5SPNAGH) - with Natural finish.

$4,325 $3,600 $3,100

Last MSR was $7,210.

ES-5 P WITH 3 P-90 PICKUPS (HS5P[ ]GH) - similar to the ES-5 Switchmaster, except has 3 black P-90 pickups, 3 volume controls, 1 master tone control on treble bout, raised tailpiece. Available in Vintage Sunburst (VS) and Wine Red (WR) finishes. Disc. 2000.

This model was part of the Historic Collection.

$3,200 $2,650 $2,150

Last MSR was $5,357.

ES-5 P With 3 P-90 Pickups (HS5PNAGH) - with Natural finish.

$4,175 $3,500 $3,000

Last MSR was $6,953.

ES-5 Alnico (HS5AVSGH) - similar to the ES-5 Switchmaster, except features Alnico pickups. Available in Vintage Sunburst finish. Disc. 2000.

$3,550 $2,900 $2,250

Last MSR was $5,897.

ES-5 Alnico (HS5ANAGH) - with Natural finish.

$4,500 $3,750 $3,150

Last MSR was $7,493.

ES-135 SWINGMASTER - features all maple construction (top, rims, back and neck), slim 22-fret ebony fingerboard, 2 P90 single coil pickups, nickel hardware, including Bigbsy tailpiece with extended arm, multi-ply pickguard, custom pinup decal on upper bout, 4 different finishes. Mfg. 1999-2000.

This model was part of the Custom Collection.

$2,200 $1,825 $1,500

Last MSR was $3,670.

ES-150 CHARLIE CHRISTIAN - styled after the original 1935 ES-150 used by Charlie Christian, features single "bar-style" high output pickup and Golden Sunburst finish, AAA spruce on top, back, and sides, one-piece mahogany neck with rosewood fingerboard and pearl block inlays, nickel hardware, single volume and single tone control. Limited Mfg. 2000.

This model was part of the Custom Collection.

$4,850 $3,250 $2,350

Last MSR was $6,470.

ES-175 SWINGMASTER - features maple top, back, rims, and mahogany neck with 20-fret ebony fingerboard, two '57 Classic humbucker pickups, nickel hardware, including ABR-1 bridge and Bigbsy tailpiece with extended arm, multi-ply pickguard, custom pinup decal on upper bout, 4 different finishes. Mfg. 1999-2000.

This model was part of the Custom Collection.

$2,850 $2,375 $1,975

Last MSR was $4,750.

ES-295 (ES95 prefix) - single sharp cutaway bound maple body, f-holes, raised white pickguard with etched flowers, maple neck, 20-fret bound rosewood fingerboard with pearl parallelogram inlay, tune-o-matic metal/rosewood bridge/trapeze tailpiece, blackface peghead with pearl plant/logo inlay, 3-per-side tuners with pearl buttons, nickel hardware, 2 covered stacked humbucker pickups, 2 volume/2 tone controls, 3-position switch. Available in Antique Gold (AG) finish. Disc. 2000.

This model was part of the Historic Collection.

$3,500 $2,925 $2,400

Last MSR was $5,838.

In 1997, the ES-295 was offered in Bullion Gold finish (ES95AGBN) with a Bigsby tremolo.

ES-295 With Bigsby (ES95A prefix) - similar to the ES-295, except features a Bigsby tremolo bridge. Available in Antique Gold finish. Mfg. 1998-2000.

$3,700 $3,075 $2,500

Last MSR was $6,154.

ES-330 (HS30[ ]NH) - dual rounded cutaway semi-hollow bound body, arched maple top, f-holes, maple back/sides, mahogany neck, 22-fret bound rosewood fingerboard with pearloid dot inlay, ABR-1 bridge/raised trapeze tailpiece, blackface peghead with pearl logo inlay, 3-per-side tuners, nickel hardware, raised bound black pickguard, 2 'dog-eared' P-90 single coil pickups, 2 volume/2 tone controls, 3-way selector switch. Available in Faded Cherry (FC), Viceroy Brown Sunburst (VB), and Vintage Sunburst (VS) finishes. Mfg. 1998-2000.

This model was part of the Historic Collection.

$2,550 $2,125 $1,650

Last MSR was $4,250.

ES-330 (HS30ANNH) - with Antique Natural finish.

$3,050 $2,525 $2,000

Last MSR was $5,075.

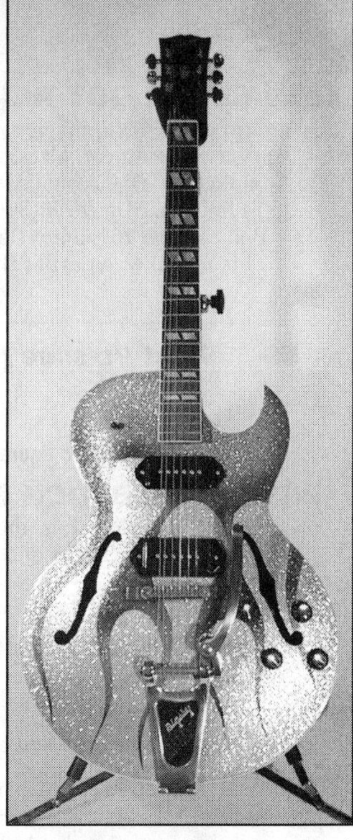

Gibson ES-175 (Custom Shop) courtesy Dave's Guitar Shop

G

GRADING	100% MINT	98% NEAR MINT	95% EXC+	90% EXC	80% VG+	70% VG	60% G

1959 ES-335 DOT REISSUE (HS35P9[ ]NH) - double rounded cutaway semi-hollow bound body, arched maple top, f-holes, arched maple back, maple sides, set-in one-piece mahogany neck, 24 3/4" scale, 22-fret rosewood fingerboard with pearloid dot inlay, tune-o-matic bridge/stop tailpiece, blackface peghead with pearl crown/logo inlay, 3-per-side tuners, nickel hardware, raised layered black pickguard, 2 covered humbucker ('57 Classic PAF Reissue) pickups, 2 volume/2 tone controls, 3-position switch. Available in Faded Cherry (FC) and Vintage Sunburst (VS) finishes. Mfg. 1998-2000.

Body Width 16", Body Depth 1 3/4".

This model was part of the Historic Collection.

$3,400 $2,850 $2,375

Last MSR was $5,665.

ES-335 Dot Reissue (HS35P9ANNH) - with Antique Natural finish.

$3,825 $3,175 $2,550

Last MSR was $6,362.

Add $908 for extra figured wood (Model HS35F9ANNH, Mfg. 1999-2000).

1963 ES-335 BLOCK REISSUE (HS35P0[ ]NH) - similar to the 1959 ES-335 Dot Reissue, except has a 1963-style thin tapered neck, pearloid block fingerboard inlay. Available in Faded Cherry (FC) and Vintage Sunburst (VS) finishes. Mfg. 1998-2000.

This model was part of the Historic Collection.

$3,400 $2,850 $2,375

Last MSR was $5,665.

ES-335 Block Reissue (HS35P0ANNH) - with Antique Natural finish.

$3,825 $3,175 $2,550

Last MSR was $6,362.

Add $908 for extra figured wood (Model HS35FOANNH, Mfg. 1999-2000).

ES-336 (ES36NH) - dual rounded cutaway semi-hollow bound body, carved maple top, 2 f-holes, mahogany back/sides, set-in mahogany neck, 22-fret rosewood fingerboard with pearl dot inlay, tune-o-matic bridge/stop tailpiece, slimmed down blackface peghead with pearl Gibson logo inlay, 3-per-side tuners, nickel hardware, raised layered black pickguard, 2 covered humbucker pickups, 2 volume/2 tone controls, 3-way toggle switch. Available in Emberglow (EG) and Wine Red (WR) finishes. Mfg. 1997-2000.

This model was part of the Custom Collection.

$2,400 $1,950 $1,500

Last MSR was $3,989.

ES-345 (HS45[ ]GH) - double rounded cutaway semi-hollow bound body, arched maple top, f-holes, maple back/sides, mahogany neck, 22-fret bound rosewood fingerboard with pearl parallelogram inlay, ABR-1 bridge/stop tailpiece, blackface peghead with pearl crown/logo inlay, 3-per-side tuners, gold hardware, raised layered black pickguard, 2 covered humbucker ('57 Classic PAF Reissue) pickups, 2 volume/2 tone controls, 3-position selector switch, 6-way Vari-tone rotary switch. Available in Faded Cherry (FC), Viceroy Brown Sunburst (VB), and Vintage Sunburst (VS) finishes. Mfg. 1998-2000.

Body Width 16", Body Depth 1 3/4".

This model was part of the Historic Collection.

$3,300 $2,750 $2,275

Last MSR was $5,501.

ES-345 (HS45ANGH) - with Antique Natural or Vintage Burst (new 1999) finish.

$3,700 $3,100 $2,575

Last MSR was $6,176.

ES-345 WITH BIGSBY (HS45[ ]BG) - similar to the ES-345, except features a Bigsby tremolo bridge. Available in Faded Cherry (FC), Viceroy Brown Sunburst (VB), and Vintage Sunburst (VS) finishes. Mfg. 1998-2000.

This model was part of the Historic Collection.

$3,475 $2,900 $2,400

Last MSR was $5,775.

ES-345 With Bigsby (HS45ANBG) - with Antique Natural or Vintage Burst (new 1999) finish.

$3,875 $3,225 $2,575

Last MSR was $6,450.

ES-345 WITH MAESTRO (HS45[ ]GML) - similar to the ES-345, except features a Maestro tailpiece. Available in Faded Cherry (FC), Viceroy Brown Sunburst (VB), and Vintage Sunburst (VS) finishes. Mfg. 1998-2000.

This model was part of the Historic Collection.

$3,625 $3,025 $2,425

Last MSR was $6,049.

ES-345 With Maestro (HS45ANGML) - with Antique Natural or Vintage Burst (new 1999) finish.

$4,050 $3,375 $2,650

Last MSR was $6,724.

ES-346 (ES346GH) - semi-hollow bound body, carved maple top, mahogany back/sides, set-in mahogany neck, tune-o-matic bridge/stop tailpiece, blackface peghead with pearl Gibson logo inlay, 3-per-side tuners, gold hardware, 2 covered humbucker pickups, volume/tone controls, 3-way toggle switch. Available in Emberglow (EG) or Gingerburst (new 1999) finish. Mfg. 1997-2000.

This model was part of the Custom Collection.

$2,750 $2,300 $1,950

Last MSR was $4,589.

GRADING	100% MINT	98% NEAR MINT	95% EXC+	90% EXC	80% VG+	70% VG	60% G

ES-350 T (HS50[ ]GH) - single rounded cutaway hollow bound body, arched figured curly maple top, multi-ply body binding, 2 bound f-holes, curly maple back/sides/neck, 24 3/4" scale, 22-fret bound rosewood fingerboard with pearl parallelogram inlay, adjustable rosewood bridge/ornate trapeze tailpiece, bound blackface peghead with pearl crown/logo inlay, 3-per-side tuners with plastic buttons, gold hardware, raised layered black pickguard, 2 covered humbucker ('57 Classic PAF) pickups, 2 volume/2 tone controls, 3-way selector toggle. Available in Viceroy Brown Sunburst (VB) and Vintage Sunburst (VS) finishes. Mfg. 1998-2000.

Body Width 17", Body Depth 2 1/4".

This model was part of the Historic Collection.

$3,575 $3,000 $2,475

Last MSR was $5,978.

ES-350 T (HS50ANGH) - with Antique Natural or Vintage Burst (new 1999) finish.

$3,825 $3,250 $2,600

Last MSR was $6,370.

ES-446S - carved spruce top with braces carved into top, one-piece mahogany carved out body, rosewood fingerboard with pearl dot inlays, two '57 Classic humbuckers, nickel hardware, tune-o-matic bridge with bail tailpiece, under 7 1/2 lbs., current finishes includes Emberglow (EG), Faded Cherry (FC), Honeyburst (HB), Natural (NA), and Vintage Sunburst (VS). New 1999.

This model is part of the Custom Collection.

MSR $3,650 $2,775 $1,825 $1,450

TAL FARLOW (HSTFWRNH) - single round cutaway bound hollow body, arched figured maple top, bound f-holes, scroll style inlay on cutaway, raised black bound pickguard, maple back/sides/neck, 20-fret bound rosewood fingerboard with pearl reverse crown inlay, tune-o-matic bridge/trapeze tailpiece, rosewood tailpiece insert with pearl engraved block inlay, bound peghead with pearl crown/logo inlay, 3-per-side tuners, nickel hardware, 2 covered humbucker pickups, 2 volume/2 tone controls, 3-position switch. Available in Wine Red (WR) finish. Current Mfg.

This model is part of the Historic Collection.

MSR $4,429 $2,600 $1,950 $1,475

Tal Farlow (HSTFVSNH) - with Vintage Sunburst finish (with nickel hardware). Current Mfg.

MSR $4,590 $2,700 $2,000 $1,500

Tal Farlow (HSTF prefix) - with Viceroy Brown Sunburst or Natural finish (with nickel hardware). New 1998.

MSR $5,463 $3,200 $2,350 $1,800

PAUL JACKSON, JR. SIGNATURE - similar to ES-346, except made to the artist's specifications, with AAA figured maple top, available in Gingerburst or Wine Red finishes. New 1999.

This model is part of the Custom Collection.

MSR $3,700 $2,800 $2,100 $1,650

LE GRANDE (HSLGGH) - Custom Shop edition of the Le Grand, with gold hardware. Available in Dark Wineburst (DW, new 2000), Vintage Sunburst, Chablis, Natural, or Trans Amber finish. New 1998.

This model is part of the Custom Collection.

MSR $10,694 $6,500 $4,650 $3,300

Add $2,443 for Chablis, Natural, or Trans Amber finish (new 1999).

PAT MARTINO SIGNATURE - carved out mahogany thin body, AAA figured maple top on Custom Model, plain maple top on Standard Model, f-holes, two '57 Classic humbuckers, straight pull peghead, ebony fingerboard w/o inlays, nickel (Standard Model) or gold (Custom Model) hardware, tune-o-matic bridge with stop tailpiece, available in Caramel Brown (CB) or Heritage Cherry Sunburst (HS). New 1999, Standard Model disc. 2000.

This model is part of the Custom Collection.

MSR $3,950 $3,000 $2,200 $1,700

Subtract 10% for Standard Model.

Custom/Historic Collection Designer Series

YAHOO! EXPLORER - limited edition model featuring Yahoo! graphics, purple swirl nitro cellulose finish.

This model is part of the Limited Edition Custom Collection.

Lack of secondary marketplace activity on this model precludes accurate pricing.

1958 KORINA EXPLORER (DSKX prefix) - korina body, white pickguard, korina neck, 22-fret rosewood fingerboard with pearl dot inlay, tune-o-matic bridge/trapeze tailpiece, 6-on-a-side tuners, gold hardware, 2 humbucker pickups, 2 volume/1 tone controls, 3-position switch. Available in Antique Natural finish. Current Mfg.

This model is part of the Historic Collection.

MSR $13,992 $7,600 $5,500 $4,000

1957 Korina Futura (CSM prefix) - similar to the Explorer, except has a split 3-per-side headstock. Available in Antique Natural (with gold hardware) finish. New 1998.

MSR $13,992 $7,600 $5,500 $4,000

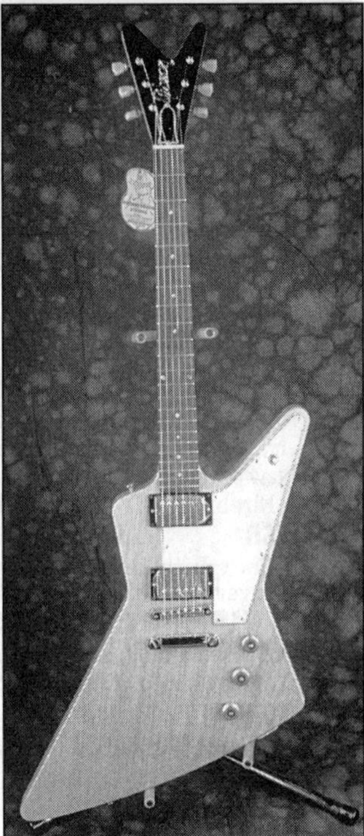

Gibson Historic Reissue Explorer courtesy Ronn David

G

GRADING	100% MINT	98% NEAR MINT	95% EXC+	90% EXC	80% VG+	70% VG	60% G

1958 KORINA FLYING V (DSKV prefix) - V-shaped korina body, white pickguard, korina neck, 22-fret rosewood fingerboard with pearl dot inlay, tune-o-matic bridge/stop tailpiece, 3-per-side tuners with plastic buttons, gold hardware, 2 humbucker pickups, 2 volume/1 tone controls, 3-position switch. Available in Natural finish. Current Mfg.

This model is part of the Historic Collection.

MSR $13,992 $7,600 $5,500 $4,000

1967 FLYING V REISSUE - mahogany V-shaped body, available in Antique Natural, Classic White, Ebony, Faded Cherry, or Tobaccoburst. New 2001.

This model is part of the Historic Collection.

MSR $4,706 $3,000 $2,200 $1,675

1963 FIREBIRD I (HSF1 prefix) - asymmetrical hourglass style mahogany body, through-body 9-ply laminated mahogany neck, 22-fret rosewood fingerboard with pearl dot inlay, wraparound tailpiece, wood/partial blackface reverse peghead with pearl logo inlay, 6 in a line banjo tuners, nickel hardware, multi-ply white pickguard, covered mini-humbucker pickup, volume/tone control. Available in Vintage Sunburst (VS) finish. New 1998.

Firebird I, III, V, and VII are part of the Historic Collection Series, and are an Award level dealer exclusive models.

MSR $3,956 $2,200 $1,650 $1,175

The entire Firebird Series (I, III, V, VII) is available in Custom Colors (Limited Quantities): Cardinal Red, Ebony, Ember Red, Frost Blue, Inverness Green, Kerry Green, Pelham Blue, Polaris White, Golden Mist Poly, Heather Poly, and Silver Mist Poly (polyurethane).

1964 FIREBIRD III (HSF3NM) - similar to the 1963 Firebird I, except features a bound rosewood fingerboard, tune-o-matic bridge/Maestro vibrola tailpiece, 2 covered mini-humbucker pickups, 2 volume/2 tone controls, 3-way selector (mounted on pickguard on treble bout). Available in Vintage Sunburst (VS) finish. New 1998.

MSR $4,848 $2,700 $2,000 $1,475

1965 FIREBIRD V (HSF5NML) - similar to the 1963 Firebird I, except features a bound rosewood fingerboard with pearl trapezoid inlay, ABR- 1 bridge/Maestro deluxe vibrola tailpiece, plastic handle on vibrola arm, 2 covered mini-humbucker pickups, 2 volume/2 tone controls, 3-way selector (mounted on pickguard on treble bout). Available in Vintage Sunburst (VS) finish. New 1998.

MSR $5,726 $3,150 $2,350 $1,850

1965 Firebird VII (HSF7GML) - similar to the 1963 Firebird I, except features a bound ebony fingerboard with pearl block inlay, ABR-1 bridge/Maestro deluxe vibrola tailpiece, plastic handle on vibrola arm, gold hardware, 3 covered mini-humbucker pickups, 2 volume/2 tone controls, 3-way selector (mounted on pickguard on treble bout). Available in Vintage Sunburst (VS) finish. New 1998.

This model is part of the Historic Collection.

MSR $7,490 $4,100 $3,000 $2,350

Custom/Historic Collection SG Series

LES PAUL SG STANDARD REISSUE (SGSR prefix) - reissue of the Les Paul SG Standard, includes historically accurate heel shape, holly peg veneer, tapered peg head, vintage body shape and scarfing, two '57 Classic pickups, pearloid trapezoid inlays on fingerboard, ABR-1 bridge with stop bar or ABR-1 bridge with short Maestro vibrato, available in Faded Cherry, Classic White, or TV Yellow finish. New 2000.

This model is part of the Historic Collection.

MSR $4,159 $2,450 $1,850 $1,425

Add $194 for Maestro vibrato.

Add $324 for aged hardware (SGSRA prefix).

Add $259 for Classic White or TV Yellow finish.

LES PAUL SG SPECIAL REISSUE (SGSPR prefix) - reissue of the Les Paul SG Special, includes historically accurate heel shape, holly peg veneer, tapered peg head, vintage body shape and scarfing, two P-90 pickups, wraparound bridge or vibrato with short Maestro tailpiece, pearl dot inlays, available in Faded Cherry, Classic White, or TV Yellow finish. New 2000.

This model is part of the Historic Collection.

MSR $3,574 $2,100 $1,575 $1,200

Add $325 for Maestro vibrato.

Add $260 for Classic White or TV Yellow finish.

LES PAUL SG CUSTOM REISSUE (SGC-CWGH) - double sharp cutaway mahogany body, white layered pickguard, mahogany neck, 22-fret bound ebony fingerboard with pearl block inlay, model tune-o-matic bridge/stop tailpiece, multi-bound peghead with pearl split diamond inlay, 3-per-side tuners, gold hardware, 3 covered humbucker pickups, 2 volume/2 tone controls, 3-position switch, available in Classic White or Faded Cherry (new 2000) finish. Current Mfg.

This model is part of the Historic Collection.

MSR $4,938 $2,900 $2,100 $1,600

Les Paul SG Custom With Maestro (SGC-CWGML) - similar to the Les Paul SG Custom, except features a Bigsby-style Maestro tremolo bridge. Available in Classic White finish (with gold hardware). Current Mfg.

MSR $5,133 $3,000 $2,200 $1,675

'63 CORVETTE STINGRAY SG LIMITED EDITION double cutaway (SG-style) mahogany body carved to simulate the split rear window of a '63 Stingray Corvette (with simulated chrome windows), set-in mahogany neck, 22-fret bound ebony fingerboard with mother-of-pearl "StingRay" inlay, wraparound bridge, blackface peghead with pearl checkered flag/logo inlay, 3-per-side tuners, chrome hardware, Corvette-style valve cover engraving chrome plated pickup, volume/tone controls, engraved serial number plate. Available in Tuxedo Black, Sebring Silver, and Riverside Red finishes. The 1963 Corvette Guitar was a Gibson Custom Shop model, and was produced in a limited edition of 150 instruments. Mfg. 1996 only.

$2,500 $2,250 $1,975 $1,750 $1,500 $1,350 $1,200

This model comes with a leather case, Certificate of Authenticity, and framed print of the original concept drawing of the Gibson 1963 Corvette Guitar.

GRADING	100% MINT	98% NEAR MINT	95% EXC+	90% EXC	80% VG+	70% VG	60% G

PETE TOWNSHEND SIGNATURE - SG body style, replica of the SG Pete Townshend used during The Who's "Live at Leeds" concert in 1970, features Townshend's signature on back of headstock, includes hand-signed certificate, exclusive flight case and protective cloth guitar cover. Only 250 Mfg. 2000, and sold out.

This model is part of the Custom Collection.

N/A $3,000 $2,250

Last MSR was $4,588.

TONY IOMMI SIGNATURE - SG body style, one-piece solid mahogany body, with original style 1961 neck joint, slim taper mahogany neck, 2 Tony Iommi signature humbucking pickups, ebony fingerboard with sterling silver cross inlays, nickel hardware, ABR-1 bridge with stop tailpiece, right or left-handed, Ebony or Wine Red finish. New 1999.

This model is part of the Custom Collection.

MSR $4,990 $3,800 $2,800 $2,100

Historic Collection Les Paul Series

LES PAUL '52 GOLD TOP REISSUE (LPR2AGNT) - single sharp cutaway solid mahogany body, bound carved maple top, mahogany neck, 22-fret bound rosewood fingerboard with pearl trapezoid inlays, raised trapeze tailpiece, blackface peghead with pearl logo inlay, 3-per-side tuners with plastic buttons, nickel hardware, raised cream pickguard, 2 creme P-90 single coil pickups, 2 volume/2 tone controls, 3-position switch. Available in Antique Gold finish. New 1998.

This model is part of the Historic Collection.

MSR $4,279 $2,500 $1,850 $1,450

LES PAUL '54 GOLD TOP REISSUE (LPR4AGNH) - similar to the Les Paul '52 Gold Top Reissue, except features wraparound bridge, and hardware similar to the original 1954 model. Available in Antique Gold finish. Current Mfg.

MSR $4,517 $2,650 $1,975 $1,475

Les Paul '54 "Oxblood" Reissue (LPR4JBNH) - similar to the Les Paul '54 Gold Top Reissue, except features two '57 Classic PAF Reissue humbucker pickups. Available in Oxblood finish (with nickel hardware). New 1998.

MSR $5,084 $2,950 $2,175 $1,600

LES PAUL CUSTOM BLACK BEAUTY '54 REISSUE (LPB4EBGH) - single sharp cutaway multi-bound mahogany body with carved top, raised bound black pickguard, mahogany neck, 22-fret bound ebony fingerboard with pearl block inlay, tune-o-matic bridge/stop tailpiece, multi-bound peghead with pearl split diamond/logo inlay, 3-per-side tuners with plastic buttons, gold hardware, 2 single coil pickups, 2 volume/2 tone controls, 3-position switch, available in Ebony finish. Current Mfg.

This model is part of the Historic Collection.

MSR $4,671 $2,750 $2,000 $1,525

Add $291 for Gold Bigsby tremolo (Model LPB4EBBG).

LES PAUL '56 GOLD TOP REISSUE (LPR6AGNH) - single sharp cutaway solid mahogany body, bound carved maple top, mahogany neck, 22-fret bound rosewood fingerboard with pearl trapezoid inlays, tune- o-matic bridge/stop bar tailpiece, blackface peghead with pearl logo inlay, 3-per-side tuners with plastic buttons, nickel hardware, raised cream pickguard, 2 single coil pickups, 2 volume/2 tone controls, 3-position switch. Available in Antique Gold Top finish. New 1990.

This model is part of the Historic Collection.

MSR $4,517 $2,650 $1,925 $1,450

Add $3,163 for aged finish by Tom Murphy (LPR6AAGNH).

LES PAUL CUSTOM BLACK BEAUTY '57 REISSUE 2 PICKUP (LPB7EBGH) - single sharp cutaway multi-bound mahogany body with carved top, raised bound black pickguard, mahogany neck, 22-fret bound ebony fingerboard with pearl block inlay, tune-o-matic bridge/stop tailpiece, multi-bound peghead with pearl split diamond/logo inlay, 3-per-side tuners with plastic buttons, gold hardware, 2 humbucker pickups, 2 volume/2 tone controls, 3-position switch, available in Ebony finish. Current Mfg.

This model is part of the Historic Collection.

MSR $4,524 $2,650 $1,925 $1,450

Les Paul Custom Black Beauty '57 Reissue 3 Pickups (LPB3 prefix) - similar to Les Paul Custom Black Beauty '57 Reissue, except has 3 pickups, available with Bigsby tremelo or master tone control. Current Mfg.

MSR $4,671 $2,750 $2,000 $1,550

Add $291 for Gold Bigsby tremolo (Model LPB7EBBG).

Add $825 for master tone (new 1999, Model LPB3MBGH).

LES PAUL '57 CUSTOM REISSUE - reissue of the 1957 Les Paul Custom, gold hardware, available in Faded Cherry (FC) finish only. New 2001.

This model is part of the Historic Collection.

MSR $4,524 $2,650 $1,950 $1,500

Gibson Historic Reissue
Les Paul
courtesy Ronn David

G

GRADING	100% MINT	98% NEAR MINT	95% EXC+	90% EXC	80% VG+	70% VG	60% G

LES PAUL '57 GOLDTOP REISSUE (LPR7AGNH) - single sharp cutaway solid mahogany body, bound carved maple top, raised cream pickguard, mahogany neck, 22-fret bound rosewood fingerboard with pearl trapezoid inlays, tune-o-matic bridge/stop tailpiece, blackface peghead with pearl logo inlay, 3-per-side tuners with plastic buttons, nickel hardware, 2 humbucker pickups, 2 volume/2 tone controls, 3-position switch. Available in Antique Goldtop finish or in darkback configuration (new 2001). Current Mfg.

This model is part of the Historic Collection.

MSR $4,582 $2,700 $2,000 $1,550

Add $3,124 for aged finish by Tom Murphy (LPR7AAGNH, new 2001).

Les Paul '57 Goldtop Reissue with Aging & Amp includes Tom Murphy aging, Reissue case and Gibson amp.

MSR $9,663 $5,500 $4,000 $3,250

LES PAUL '58 PLAINTOP REISSUE (LPR8NH) - similar to the Les Paul '59 Flametop Reissue, except features a much less figured carved maple top. Available in Heritage Cherry Sunburst (HS) and Vintage Red (VR) finishes. Disc. 1999.

Last MSR was $5,450.

Les Paul '58 Figured Top Reissue (LPR8F/LPR8NH) similar to the Les Paul '58 PlainTop Reissue, except features a slightly more figured carved maple top. Available in Butterscotch (BS) and Vintage Red (VR, disc.) finishes (with nickel hardware). Mfg. 1998-99, reintroduced 2001.

MSR $5,700 $4,450 $2,750 $2,150

LES PAUL '59 FLAMETOP REISSUE (LPR9H/LPR9K) - single sharp cutaway solid mahogany body, bound carved curly maple top, raised cream pickguard, mahogany neck, 22-fret bound rosewood fingerboard with pearl trapezoid inlays, tune-o-matic bridge/stop tailpiece, blackface peghead with pearl logo inlay, 3-per-side tuners with plastic buttons, nickel hardware, 2 humbucker pickups, 2 volume/2 tone controls, 3-position switch. Available in Heritage Darkburst (HD, disc. 2000) and Heritage Cherry Sunburst (HS) finishes. Current Mfg.

The Les Paul '59 Series is part of the Historic Collection, and are Award level dealer exclusive models.

MSR $7,500 $5,000 $3,700 $2,950

Les Paul '59 Figured Top Reissue (LPR9F) - similar to the Les Paul '59 Flametop Reissue, except features a less figured carved maple top. Available in Heritage Cherry Sunburst (HS) and Vintage Red (VR) finishes. Mfg. 1999-2000.

$4,950 $4,100 $3,350

Last MSR was $8,162.

Les Paul '59 Plaintop Reissue (LPR9P) - similar to the Les Paul '59 Flametop Reissue, except features a much less figured carved maple top. Available in Heritage Cherry Sunburst (HS) and Vintage Red (VR) finishes. Mfg. 1999-2000.

$3,775 $3,100 $2,500

Last MSR was $6,291.

LES PAUL '60 FLAMETOP REISSUE (LPR0NH) - single sharp cutaway mahogany body, bound carved flame maple top, raised cream pickguard, mahogany neck, 22-fret rosewood fingerboard with pearl trapezoid inlay, tune-o-matic bridge/stop tailpiece, blackface peghead with pearl logo inlay, 3-per-side tuners with plastic buttons, nickel hardware, 2 covered humbucker pickups, 2 volume/2 tone controls, 3-position switch. Available in Heritage Darkburst (HD) and Heritage Cherry Sunburst (HS) finishes. Disc. 2001.

This model was part of the Historic Collection, and was an Award level dealer exclusive model.

$5,000 $3,375 $2,750

Last MSR was $12,620.

1957 LP JUNIOR SINGLE CUTAWAY (LPJRSC prefix) - single cutaway mahogany body, set-in mahogany neck, 22-fret rosewood fingerboard with pearl dot inlay, wraparound tailpiece, 3-per-side tuners with plastic buttons, nickel hardware, black pickguard, black 'dog-eared' P-90 single coil pickup, volume/tone controls. Available in Faded Cherry (FC), Vintage Sunburst (VS) and TV Yellow (TV) finishes. New 1998.

This model is part of the Historic Collection.

MSR $3,080 $1,850 $1,350 $1,050

1958 LP Junior Double Cutaway (LPJRDC prefix) - similar to the 1957 LP Junior Single Cutaway, except features a double cutaway body. Available in Faded Cherry (FC) and TV Yellow (TV) finishes. New 1998.

MSR $3,080 $1,850 $1,350 $1,050

1960 LP SPECIAL SINGLE CUTAWAY (LPSPSCNH) - single cutaway mahogany body, set-in mahogany neck, 22-fret rosewood fingerboard with pearl dot inlay, wraparound tailpiece, 3-per-side tuners with plastic buttons, nickel hardware, black pickguard, 2 black P-90 single coil pickups, 2 volume/2 tone controls, 3-way selector toggle switch. Available in Faded Cherry (FC) and TV Yellow (TV) finishes. New 1998.

This model is part of the Historic Collection.

MSR $3,348 $1,995 $1,450 $1,150

1960 LP Special Double Cutaway (LPSPDCNH) - similar to the 1960 LP Special Single Cutaway, except features an offset double cutaway body. Available in Faded Cherry (FC) and TV Yellow (TV) finishes. New 1998.

MSR $3,348 $1,995 $1,450 $1,150

Custom Collection Les Paul Series

The upscale Les Paul Custom Collection models are produced in limited quantities in the Gibson Custom Shop, and will have the Custom Shop logo on the back of the headstock.

The few Custom Shop models that may show up in the vintage/used market as a rule are usually in 95% or better condition, since they are rarely played.

LES PAUL 1968 CUSTOM FIGURED TOP (CS68LPCF prefix) 1968 Les Paul Custom configuration with carved figured maple top, two '57 Classic humbucker pickups, gold hardware, ABR-1 bridge with stop tailpiece, choice of Antique Natural, Butterscotch, Heritage Cherry Sunburst, or Tri-burst finish. New 2000.

MSR $5,062 $3,100 $2,200 $1,825

GRADING	100% MINT	98% NEAR MINT	95% EXC+	90% EXC	80% VG+	70% VG	60% G

LES PAUL CATALINA (CSCAT[ ]NH) single cutaway mahogany body, internal sound chambers, set-in mahogany neck, white bound carved maple top, 22-fret bound ebony fingerboard with pearl trapezoid inlay, tune-o-matic bridge/stop tailpiece, blackface peghead with pearl Custom Shop/Gibson logo inlays, white pearloid truss rod cover, 3-per-side tuners, nickel hardware, white pearloid pickguard, 2 covered humbucker ('57 Classic) pickups, 2 volume/2 tone controls, 3-way toggle switch. Available in Canary Yellow (CY), Cascade Green (CG), and Riverside Red (RR) finishes. Mfg. 1997-99.

$2,225 $1,850 $1,450

Last MSR was $3,695.

The Riverside Red (RR) finish was a Limited Run finish.

LES PAUL CLASS 5 (CSC5 prefix) features bound figured maple top, 60s profile neck with long tenon, 2 Burstbucker pickups, nickel hardware, single ply crème binding on top/neck, available in Cranberry (CRB), Sienna Burst (SB), Trans Amber (TA), Trans Blue (TB), Trans Black (TBK), or Tangerine Burst (TGB). New 2001.

MSR $4,925 $3,350 $2,400 $1,925

Add $300 for Sienna Burst, Trans Amber, or Tangerine Burst finish.

LES PAUL CLASSIC MAHOGANY - features solid mahogany construction with carved figured mahogany top, and one piece mahogany neck with long tenon, two '57 Classic zebra humbucker pickups, nickel hardware available in Antique Natural (AN), Heritage Sunburst (HS), Trans Red (TR), and Vintage Sunburst (VS). Mfg. 2000 only.

$2,750 $2,250 $1,750

Last MSR was $4,568.

LES PAUL ELEGANT FLAME (CSELNH) OR QUILT (CSELQNH) TOP - single cutaway mahogany body, internal sound chambers, set-in mahogany neck, cream bound carved AAA grade maple top (disc. 2000) or quilt top (new 2001, subject to availability), 22-fret bound ebony fingerboard with abalone trapezoid inlay, tune-o-matic bridge/stop tailpiece, blackface peghead with pearl Custom Shop/Gibson logo inlays, black truss rod cover, 3-per-side tuners, nickel hardware, clear pickguard, 2 covered humbucker ('57 Classic) pickups, 2 volume/2 tone controls, 3-way toggle switch. Available in Heritage Cherry Sunburst (HS, new 2001), Peacock (PK, new 2001), Antique Natural (AN), Butterscotch (BS), Cherry Sunburst (Mfg. 1999-2000), Tobacco Sunburst (Mfg. 1999-2000), and Firemist (FM, disc. 2000) finishes. New 1997.

MSR $5,778 $3,925 $2,900 $2,350

Subtract approx. $500 for flametop configuration.

LES PAUL FLORENTINE (CSF-GH) - single cutaway semi-hollow mahogany body with center block, set-in mahogany neck, bound carved maple top, 2 f-holes (or diamond-shaped f-holes), white body binding (front and back), 22-fret bound ebony fingerboard with pearl block inlay, tune-o-matic bridge/stop tailpiece, bound blackface peghead with pearl split diamond/Gibson logo inlays, engraved "Les Paul Florentine" black truss rod cover, 3-per-side tuners, gold hardware, 2 covered humbucker ('57 Classic) pickups, 2 volume/2 tone controls, 3-way toggle switch. Available in Ebony (EB), Emberglow (EG), Heritage Cherry Sunburst (new 1999) and Wine Red (WR) finishes. Mfg. 1997-2000.

$2,625 $2,150 $1,650

Last MSR was $4,359.

Les Paul Florentine Plus (CSFPGH) - similar to the Les Paul Florentine, except features a figured maple top. Available in Antique Natural (AN), Emberglow (EG), Translucent Black (new 1999), and Heritage Cherry Sunburst (HS) finishes. Mfg. 1997-2000.

$2,995 $2,450 $1,950

Last MSR was $4,926.

LES PAUL ULTIMA (CSUL prefix) - single cutaway mahogany body, set-in mahogany neck, abalone/white bound carved AAA grade maple top, 22-fret bound ebony fingerboard with custom abalone inlay, tune-o-matic bridge/stop tailpiece, blackface peghead with pearl Custom Shop/Gibson logo inlays, choice of butterfly (CSULBHSGH), flame (CSULFHSGH), harp (CSULHHSGH), or tree of life (CSULTHSGH) fretboard inlay, gold truss rod cover, 3-per-side Grover Imperial tuners with metal or pearl buttons, gold hardware, 2 covered humbucker ('57 Classic) pickups, 2 volume/2 tone controls, 3-way toggle switch. Available in Heritage Cherry Sunburst (HS) finish. Mfg. 1997-2001.

$6,100 $4,950 $3,750

Last MSR was $10,170.

Add $260 for gold Ultima trapeze tailpiece (the 8=digit model code is followed by a ET or GT (1999) for "Tailpiece" code).

ACE FREHLEY SIGNATURE LES PAUL (LPAF, LPFR) - single cutaway bound mahogany body, flame maple top, 22-fret bound ebony fingerboard with lightning bolt inlay/Frehley's signature in pearl script at 12th fret, bound black peghead with 'Ace' peghead image, chrome hardware, tune-o-matic bridge/stop tail piece, no pickguard, 3 DiMarzio humbucker pickups, 2 volume/2 tone controls, 3-way toggle. Available in Sunburst finish. Mfg. by the Custom Shop 1997-2001.

$4,000 $3,100 $2,500 $2,100 $1,850 $1,650 $1,425

Last MSR was $6,222.

GRADING	100% MINT	98% NEAR MINT	95% EXC+	90% EXC	80% VG+	70% VG	60% G

JIMMY PAGE SIGNATURE LES PAUL (LPPG) - single cutaway bound mahogany body, AA grade figured maple top, 22-fret bound rosewood fingerboard with trapezoid inlay, bound black peghead, gold hardware, tune-o-matic bridge/stop tail piece, cream pickguard with engraved "Jimmy Page" signature, 2 exposed polepiece humbucker pickups, 2 volume/2 tone controls (all push-pull for custom wiring and coil taps), 3-way selector toggle. Available in Light Honey Burst (LB) finish. Mfg. by the Custom Shop 1995-99.

$4,000 $3,100 $2,500 $2,100 $1,850 $1,650 $1,425

Last MSR was $6,300.

JOE PERRY SIGNATURE LES PAUL (LPJP, LPPR) - single cutaway mahognay body, bookmatched figured maple top, 22-fret rosewood fingerboard with trapezoid inlay, black peghead with white shell truss rod cover, Joe Perry's signature in white on body behind the bridge, black chrome hardware, tune-o-matic bridge/stop tail piece, white shell pickguard, 2 humbucker pickups, 2 volume/2 tone controls (treble tone control is push/pull), active mid-boost circuit, 3-way toggle. Available in hand-stained Translucent Blackburst finish, Mfg. by the Custom Shop 1997-99.

$2,250 $1,600 $1,350 $1,100 $995 $875 $750

Last MSR was $3,296.

ZAKK WYLDE SIGNATURE LES PAUL - features unmistakable B&W bullseye graphics or Natural Rough (disc.) top, 2 EMG black pickups, gold hardware, oiled, raw maple back, Mfg. by the Custom Shop. New 1999.

MSR $4,900 $3,800 $2,725 $2,300 $1,975 $1,675 $1,375 $1,250

Add $800 for Natural Rough top.

GARY MOORE SIGNATURE LES PAUL - features AA carved maple top with Lemonburst finish, exposed Burst-Bucker pickups, Gary Moore signature engraved on truss rod cover. New 2001.

MSR $2,922 $2,000 $1,750 $1,500 $1,200 $1,000 $875 $750

This model is a standard production model, not manufactured by the Custom Shop.

PETER FRAMPTON SIGNATURE LES PAUL - features specially wired 3 pickup configuration with chambered back allowing for lightweight construction, Peter Frampton signature inlaid on 12th fret, Custom style pearloid spilt diamond headstock inlay, available in Ebony finish only. New 2000.

MSR $5,802 $3,575 $2,950 $2,500 $2,150 $1,800 $1,550 $1,275

Custom Collection Les Paul Limited Editions

The Nashville Custom Shop has produced a number of limited editions over the years. These instruments are typically limited to 50 to approx. 300, depending on the configuration and original order. Total production and original MSRs have been provided if known. Secondary marketplace values are difficult to determine, since these instruments are very specialized, and appeal only to a small number of collectors and nitch enthusiasts.

Limited Edition LPs have included a '60 Corvette (total unknown, features distinctive two-tone aqua body and Corvette motifs), a Hard Rock Café, '60 Corvette LP (B&W, Corvette logo inlaid in neck), Dale Earnhardt (333 Mfg. 1999, black body with #3 on front), Dale Earnhardt Intimidator ($4,000 current MSR, 333 Mfg. beginning 2000, anniversary silver with "The Intimidator" inlaid on fretboard), Dale Earnhardt Jr. ($4,000 current MSR, Mfg. beginning 2000, Budweiser logo with #8 on body), X-Men Wolverine (50 Mfg. 2000, features X-Men motifs), Web-Slinger One (150 Mfg., features Spider-Man pattern), Old Hickory (200 Mfg. 1999), Playboy ($7,000 current MSR, 10 Mfg., features black body with white Playboy bunny logo and Playboy inlaid in fretboard), Playboy Rabbit Head (50 Mfg., body is shaped like a black rabbit head), and Playmate of the Year (50 Mfg. beginning 2001, features pink burst glitter finish).

ELECTRIC BASS

EB Series

EB - double sharp cutaway maple body, tortoise pickguard, maple neck, 20-fret maple fingerboard with pearl dot inlay, bar bridge, blackface peghead with logo decal, 2-per-side tuners, chrome hardware, covered humbucker pickup, volume/tone control. Available in Natural finish. Mfg. 1970 only.

N/A $675 $580 $485 $385 $350 $320

EB-O - double round cutaway mahogany body, black pickguard, mahogany neck, 20-fret rosewood fingerboard with pearl dot inlay, bar bridge, blackface peghead with pearl crown/logo inlay, 2-per-side Kluson banjo tuners, nickel hardware, covered humbucker pickup, volume/tone control. Available in Cherry Red finish. Mfg. 1959 to 1979.

1959-1960 N/A $1,500 $1,325 $1,150 $975 $895 $850

1961-1979 N/A $1,000 $825 $775 $595 $525 $450

In 1961, double sharp cutaway body, laminated pickguard, standard tuners replaced original part/design. In 1963, metal handrest was added, metal covered pickup replaced original part/design.

EB-OF - similar to EB-O, except has laminated pickguard, metal handrest, built-in fuzztone electronics with volume/attack controls and on/off switch. Mfg. 1962 to 1965.

N/A $1,200 $1,125 $1,050 $950 $895 $795

EB-OL - similar to EB-O, except has long scale length. Mfg. 1969 to 1979.

N/A $600 $525 $450 $395 $325 $250

EB-1 (GIBSON ELECTRIC BASS) - violin shaped mahogany body, arched top with painted f-hole/purfling, raised black pickguard, mahogany neck, 20-fret rosewood fingerboard with pearl dot inlay, bar bridge, blackface peghead with pearl logo inlay, 2-per-side Kluson banjo tuners, nickel hardware, covered alnico pickup, volume/tone control. Available in Dark Brown finish. Mfg. 1953 to 1958.

N/A $3,500 $3,100 $2,850 $2,500 $2,200 $2,000

This model was originally designated the Gibson Electric Bass. In 1958, after the introduction of the EB-2 model, the Gibson Electric Bass was commonly called the EB-1.

EB-1 (1970-1972 Mfg.) - similar to EB-1, except has standard tuners, one covered humbucker pickup. Mfg. 1970 to 1972.

N/A $1,500 $1,275 $1,050 $850 $775 $700

GRADING	100% MINT	98% NEAR MINT	95% EXC+	90% EXC	80% VG+	70% VG	60% G

EB-2 - double round cutaway semi hollow body, arched maple top, raised laminated pickguard, f-holes, bound body, maple back/sides, mahogany neck, 20-fret rosewood fingerboard with pearl dot inlay, bar bridge, blackface peghead with pearl crown/logo inlay, 2-per-side Kluson banjo tuners, nickel hardware, covered humbucker pickup, volume/tone control. Available in Natural and Sunburst finishes. Mfg. 1958 to 1961.

	N/A	$2,500	$2,000	$1,695	$1,500	$1,250	$1,000

EB-2 models in Natural finish (Model EB-2 N) command a premium.

In 1959, baritone pushbutton control added; Black finish was introduced. In 1960, string mute added, standard tuners, redesigned pickup replaced original part/design; Cherry finish was introduced.

EB-2 (1964-1972 Mfg.) - similar to EB-2, except has standard tuners, metal covered humbucker pickup. Available in Sunburst finish. Mfg. 1964 to 1972.

	N/A	$1,000	$900	$800	$700	$600	$500

In 1965, Cherry finish became an option.

EB-2D - similar to EB-2, except has standard tuners, 2 metal covered humbucker pickups. Available in Cherry and Sunburst finishes. Mfg. 1966 to 1972.

	N/A	$1,250	$1,125	$1,000	$900	$800	$700

In 1969, Burgundy and Walnut finishes were introduced.

EB-3 - double sharp cutaway mahogany body, laminated black pickguard with finger rest, metal hand rest, mahogany neck, 30 1/2" scale, 20-fret rosewood fingerboard with pearl dot inlay, bar bridge, blackface peghead with pearl crown/logo inlay, 2-per-side Kluson tuners, nickel hardware, 2 covered humbucker pickups, 2 volume/tone controls, rotary switch. Available in Cherry finish. Mfg. 1961 to 1979.

1961-1969	N/A	$1,500	$1,200	$995	$875	$750	$650
1970-1979	N/A	$1,000	$875	$750	$650	$525	$495

In 1963, metal pickup covers were added. In 1969, metal bridge cover added, slotted peghead replaced original part/design, handrest, crown peghead inlay were removed. In 1971, Natural finish became available, Walnut finish became an option. In 1972, crown peghead inlay added, solid peghead replaced previous part/design. In 1976, White finish became available.

EB-3L - similar to EB-3, except has a longer 34 1/2" scale length. Mfg. 1969 to 1972.

	N/A	$675	$595	$495	$395	$350	$325

EB-4L - double sharp cutaway mahogany body/neck, black laminated pickguard, 20-fret rosewood fingerboard with pearl dot inlay, bar bridge with metal cover, covered humbucker pickup, volume/tone control, 3-position switch. Available in Cherry and Walnut finishes. Mfg. 1972 to 1979.

	N/A	$550	$450	$385	$275	$235	$200

EB-6 THINLINE - double round cutaway semi-hollow (EB-2 shaped) body, arched maple top, raised laminated pickguard, f-holes, bound body, maple back/sides, mahogany neck, 20-fret rosewood fingerboard with pearl dot inlay, bar bridge, blackface peghead with pearl crown/logo inlay, 3-per-side Kluson tuners with plastic buttons, nickel hardware, covered humbucker pickup, volume/tone control, pushbutton switch. Available in Sunburst finish. Mfg. 1960 to 1961.

	N/A	$2,600	$2,200	$1,900	$1,600	$1,250	$1,050

EB-6 Solid Body - similar to EB-6 Thinline, except has double sharp cutaway solid mahogany (SG shaped) body, all metal tuners. Mfg. 1961 to 1966.

	N/A	$2,500	$2,100	$1,750	$1,500	$1,300	$1,200

In 1962, hand rest and string mute were added, 2 covered humbucker pickups, 2 volume/tone controls, 3-position switch replaced original part/design, pushbutton switch removed.

EB 650 - single sharp cutaway semi hollow bound maple body, arched top, diamond soundholes, maple neck, 21-fret rosewood fingerboard with pearl dot inlay, adjustable rosewood bridge/trapeze tailpiece, blackface peghead with pearl vase/logo inlay, 2-per-side tuners, chrome hardware, 2 covered humbucker pickups, 2 volume/2 tone controls. Available in Translucent Amber, Translucent Black, Translucent Blue, Translucent Purple and Translucent Red finishes. Disc. 1996.

	$1,375	$1,150	$1,000	$850	$750	$695	$625

Last MSR was $2,100.

EB 750 - similar to EB 650, except has deeper body, f-holes, figured maple back/sides, abalone inlay, gold hardware, 2 Bartolini pickups, volume/treble/bass/pan controls, active electronics. Available in Ebony finish. Disc. 1996.

	$1,425	$1,200	$1,050	$895	$795	$725	$650

Last MSR was $2,200.

Add $400 for Antique Natural and Vintage Sunburst finishes.

Electric Bass: Misc.

The instruments included in this subcategory are typically models that are not part of a series, and have not had a lot of production or standardized nomenclature. They will appear in alphabetical order.

EXPLORER BASS - radical offset hourglass alder body, maple neck, 21-fret rosewood fingerboard with pearl dot inlay, fixed bridge, blackface peghead with logo decal, 4-on-a-side tuners, chrome hardware, 2 humbucker pickups, 2 volume/1 tone controls. Available in Ebony and Ivory finishes. Mfg. 1984-87.

	N/A	$550	$475	$395	$325	$295	$250

In 1985 only, a Custom Graphics finish was available.

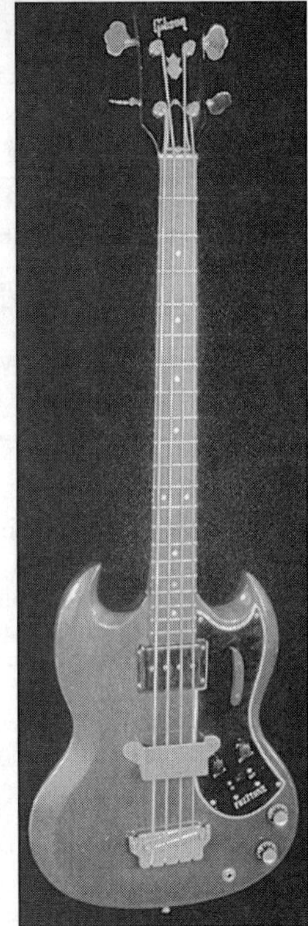

Gibson EB-OF courtesy Thoroughbred Music

G

GRADING	100% MINT	98% NEAR MINT	95% EXC+	90% EXC	80% VG+	70% VG	60% G

FLYING V BASS - V-shaped alder body, maple neck, 21-fret rosewood fingerboard with pearl dot inlay, fixed bridge, blackface arrowhead-shaped headstock with logo decal, 2+2 tuners, chrome hardware, 2 humbucker pickups, volume/tone controls. Available in Ebony, Ivory, and Natural finishes. Mfg. 1978 to 1982.

	N/A	$795	$675	$595	$525	$495	$350

It is estimated that only 300 to 400 of these models were built.

G-3 - similar to Grabber, except has black pickguard, rosewood fingerboard, fixed bridge with cover, blackface peghead with logo decal, 3 single coil pickups, 3-position switch. Available in Natural and Sunburst finishes. Mfg. 1975 to 1982.

	N/A	$275	$225	$195	$150	$125	$100

In 1976, Ebony and Wine Red finishes became available. In 1977, Walnut finish became available.

GIBSON IV BASS - offset double cutaway alder body, maple neck, 22-fret ebony fingerboard with offset pearl dot inlay, fixed bridge, blackface peghead with logo decal, 2-per-side tuners, black hardware, 2 humbucker pickups, 2 volume/1 tone controls. Available in Black, Red and White finishes. Mfg. 1987-89.

	N/A	$700	$600	$500	$400	$350	$325

GIBSON V BASS - similar to Gibson IV, except has 5 strings, 3/2-per-side tuners.

	N/A	$800	$695	$575	$450	$400	$375

GRABBER - offset double cutaway alder body, tortoise or black pickguard, bolt-on maple neck, 20-fret maple fingerboard with pearl dot inlay, tune-o-matic bridge with metal cover, string through-body tailpiece, logo peghead decal, 2-per-side tuners, chrome hardware, 1 movable pickup, volume/tone control. Available in Natural finish. Mfg. 1973 to 1982.

	N/A	$350	$275	$225	$195	$150	$125

In 1975, Ebony and Wine Red finishes became available. In 1976, Black and White finishes became available. In 1977, Walnut finish became available.

L9-S (RIPPER) - offset double cutaway alder body, black pickguard, bolt-on maple neck, 20-fret maple fingerboard with pearl dot inlay, tune-o-matic bridge with metal cover, string through-body tailpiece, blackface peghead with logo decal, 2-per-side tuners, chrome hardware, 2 humbucker pickups, volume/treble/bass controls, rotary switch. Available in Ebony and Natural finishes. Mfg. 1973 to 1982.

	N/A	$475	$350	$275	$225	$195	$175

Add $75 for fretless ebony fingerboard with Sunburst finish.

In 1974, this model was renamed the Ripper. In 1975, fretless ebony fingerboard with Sunburst finish became available. In 1976, Tobacco Sunburst became available.

LELAND SKLAR SIGNATURE BASS (CSLS[ ]SN) offset double cutaway maple body, bolt-on maple neck, 34" scale, 21-fret rosewood fingerboard with pearl dot inlay, fixed bridge, 4-on-a-side tuners, chrome hardware, 2 P-style EMG split-coil pickups, volume/blend/tone controls. Available in Ebony (EB) and TriBurst (TBI) finish. Mfg. 1997-98.

Last MSR was $2,219.

The Leland Sklar Signature Bass was a Gibson Custom Shop model. This model was developed in conjunction with bassist Leland Sklar (Phil Collens, Barefoot Servants).

SG-Z (BAZ-) double sharp cutaway, SG style mahogany body and neck with rosewood fingerboard with split diamond inlays, dual Z-bass pickups, black pearloid pickguard, black chrome hardware, available in Heritage Cherry (HC) and Ebony (EB) finish. New 1998.

MSR $2,152	$1,500	$1,075	$950	$875	$750	$675	$600

Les Paul Bass Series (Mfg. 1969 to 1979)

LES PAUL BASS - single sharp cutaway mahogany body, bound body, control plate, mahogany neck, 24-fret bound rosewood fingerboard with pearl block inlay, fixed bridge with metal cover, bound peghead with pearl split diamond/logo inlay, 2-per-side tuners, chrome hardware, 2 humbucker pickups with metal rings, volume/treble/bass controls, 3-position pickup/tone switches, impedance/phase switches. Available in Walnut finish. Mfg. 1969 to 1976.

	N/A	$650	$555	$465	$370	$335	$305

LES PAUL SIGNATURE BASS - offset double cutaway, arched maple top, raised cream pickguard, f-holes, maple back/sides, mahogany neck, 22-fret rosewood fingerboard with pearl trapezoid inlay, fixed bridge with cover, 2-per-side tuners, chrome hardware, humbucker pickup, plastic pickup cover with stamped logo, volume/tone controls, level switch. Available in Gold Top and Sunburst finishes. Mfg. 1973 to 1979.

	N/A	$1,000	$750	$695	$650	$550	$495

This model had walnut back/sides with Gold Top finish.

LES PAUL TRIUMPH BASS - single sharp cutaway mahogany body, bound body, control plate, mahogany neck, 24-fret bound rosewood fingerboard with pearl block inlay, fixed bridge with metal cover, bound peghead with pearl split diamond/logo inlay, 2-per-side tuners, chrome hardware, 2 humbucker pickups with metal rings, volume/treble/bass controls, 3-position pickup/tone switches, impedance/phase switches. Available in Natural and White finishes. Mfg. 1975 to 1979.

	N/A	$850	$750	$650	$575	$525	$500

Les Paul Bass Series (Recent Mfg.)

LES PAUL SMARTWOOD BASS - single cutaway semi-hollow mahogany body, flat maple top, set-in neck, 34 " scale, 20-fret chechen fingerboard with mother-of-pearl trapezoid inlay, fixed bridge, 2-per-side tuners, gold hardware, 2 Gibson TB+ humbucker pickups, 2 volume/2 tone controls, 3-position pickup selector switch, Bartolini TCT active preamp. Available in Antique Natural, Heritage Cherry Sunburst, Earthburst, Ebony, and Emerald handrubbed finishes (available in polyurethane option).

While advertised in 1998, this model was never produced. SmartWood is a program of the Rainforest Alliances, an international non-profit conservation organization that certifies if certain woods are harvested in a sustainable manner.

LES PAUL SPECIAL BASS single cutaway mahogany body, set-in mahogany neck, 34" scale, 24-fret ebony fingerboard with pearl dot inlay, fixed bridge, 2-per-side tuners, black chrome hardware, 2 TB+ humbucker pickups, volume/blend/bass/treble controls, Bartolini TCT active preamp. Available in Classic White, Ebony, Heritage Cherry Sunburst, and Translucent Amber polyurethane finishes. Mfg. 1997-98.

GRADING	100% MINT	98% NEAR MINT	95% EXC+	90% EXC	80% VG+	70% VG	60% G

Les Paul Special 4-String

	$1,375	$1,175	$975	$875	$775	$700	$650

Last MSR was $2,100.

Les Paul Special 5-String - 3/2-per-side tuners.

	$1,450	$1,225	$1,025	$900	$800	$725	$675

Last MSR was $2,200.

Add $60 for lined fretless fingerboard, $60 for fretless fingerboard (unlined), $100 for chrome hardware, $100 for gold hardware., or $300 for LP Premium Plus flame maple top.

List Prices included a hardshell case.

LES PAUL DELUXE BASS similar to the Les Paul Special, except has pearl trapezoid fingerboard inlays, 2 Bartolini bass humbucker pickups. Available in Clear, Heritage Cherry Sunburst, Honey Burst, Translucent Amber, Translucent Black, Translucent Blue, Translucent Green, Translucent Red, Vintage Sunburst polyurethane or Handrubbed Oil finishes. Mfg. 1997-98.

Les Paul Deluxe 4-String

	$1,525	$1,275	$1,075	$925	$825	$725	$675

Last MSR was $2,300.

Les Paul Special 5-String - 3/2-per-side tuners.

	$1,600	$1,325	$1,125	$950	$850	$750	$700

Last MSR was $2,400.

LES PAUL STANDARD BASS – 4-STRING (BAL3) - similar to the Les Paul Special, except has bound maple top, pearl trapezoid fingerboard inlay, chrome hardware, 2 piece bridge. Available in Clear (disc. 1998), Ebony (disc. 1998), Heritage Cherry Sunburst, Honey Burst, Translucent Amber (disc. 1998), Vintage Sunburst polyurethane or Handrubbed Oil (disc. 1998) finishes. Mfg. 1997 to date.

4-String configuration, 2-per-side tuners.

MSR $2,460	$1,700	$1,225	$1,050	$900	$800	$700	$600

Les Paul Standard Bass – 5-String - 5-String configuration, 3/2-per-side tuners. Disc. 1998.

	$1,750	$1,250	$1,075	$925	$825	$725	$625

Last MSR was $2,630.

Add $100 for chrome hardware.

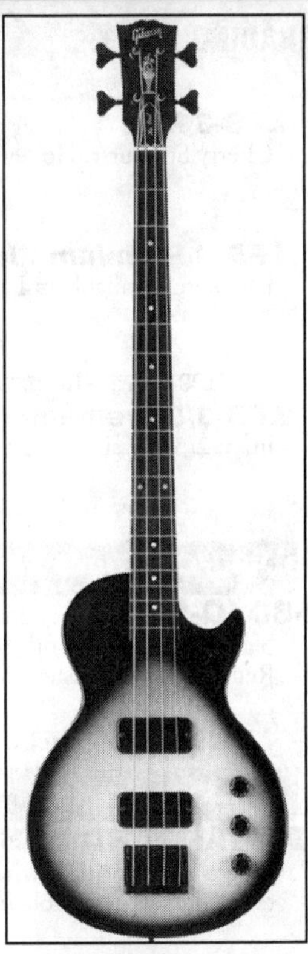

Gibson LPB-1 Bass
courtesy Gibson USA

LPB (Les Paul Bass) Series

LPB-1 - single cutaway mahogany body/neck, 20-fret ebony fingerboard with pearl dot inlay, fixed bridge, black-face peghead with pearl logo inlay, 2-per-side tuners, black hardware, 2 covered humbucker pickups, volume/treble/bass/pan controls, active electronics. Available in Ebony, Classic White, Heritage Cherry and Translucent Amber finishes. Mfg. 1992 to 1996.

	$850	$625	$525	$425	$375	$350	$325

Last MSR was $1,050.

In 1994, Translucent Amber finish was discontinued.

LPB-1/5 - similar to LPB-1, except has 5 strings, 2/3-per-side tuners. Disc. 1996.

	$850	$625	$525	$425	$375	$350	$325

Last MSR was $1,050.

LPB-2 - similar to LPB-1, except has figured maple top, trapezoid fingerboard inlay, Bartolini pickups. Available in Heritage Cherry Sunburst, Translucent Amber, Translucent Black, Translucent Blue and Translucent Red finishes. Disc. 1996.

	$1,100	$895	$800	$650	$575	$525	$475

Last MSR was $1,475.

In 1994, Translucent Amber, Translucent Black, Translucent Blue and Translucent Red finishes were discontinued.

LPB-2/5 - similar to LPB-2, except has 5 strings, 2/3-per-side tuners. Available in Heritage Cherry Sunburst and Translucent Amber finishes. Disc. 1996.

	$1,150	$925	$775	$625	$550	$525	$475

Last MSR was $1,560.

LPB-2 Premium - similar to LPB-1, except has figured maple top, trapezoid fingerboard inlay, Bartolini pickups. Available in Heritage Cherry Sunburst, Honey Burst, Translucent Amber and Vintage Sunburst finishes. Disc. 1996.

	$1,150	$925	$850	$695	$600	$550	$500

Last MSR was $1,560.

In 1994, Honey Burst and Vintage Sunburst finishes were discontinued.

LPB-3 - similar to LPB-1, except has bound maple top, abalone trapezoid fingerboard inlay, chrome hardware. Available in Ebony finish. Disc. 1996.

	$1,250	$995	$825	$650	$595	$550	$495

Last MSR was $1,650.

Add $200 for Heritage Cherry Sunburst, Honey Burst and Vintage Sunburst finishes.

GRADING	100% MINT	98% NEAR MINT	95% EXC+	90% EXC	80% VG+	70% VG	60% G

LPB-3 Plus - similar to LPB-1, except has bound figured maple top, abalone trapezoid fingerboard inlay, chrome hardware. Available in Heritage Cherry Sunburst, Honey Burst, Translucent Amber and Vintage Sunburst finishes. Disc. 1994.

$1,400	$1,195	$1,100	$850	$775	$700	$650

Last MSR was $2,150.

LPB-3 Premium Plus - similar to LPB-1, except has bound highest quality figured maple top, abalone trapezoid fingerboard inlay, chrome hardware. Available in Heritage Cherry Sunburst, Honey Burst, Translucent Amber and Vintage Sunburst finishes. Disc. 1996.

$1,650	$1,450	$1,200	$950	$850	$795	$725

Last MSR was $2,400.

In 1994, Translucent Amber finish was discontinued.

LPB-3/5 Premium Plus - similar to LPB-1, except has 5 strings, bound highest quality figured maple top, abalone trapezoid fingerboard inlay, 2/3-per-side tuners, chrome hardware. Available in Heritage Cherry Sunburst, Honey Burst and Vintage Sunburst finishes. Mfg. 1994 to 1996.

$1,500	$1,350	$1,200	$950	$850	$795	$725

Last MSR was $2,400.

Q-80/Q90 Bass Series

Q-80 (Q-90) - offset double cutaway asymmetrical alder body, bolt-on maple neck, 22-fret rosewood fingerboard with pearl dot inlay, fixed bridge, blackface peghead with screened logo, 4-on-a-side tuners, chrome hardware, 2 humbucker pickups, 2 volume/1 tone controls. Available in Ebony, Red and Black finishes. Mfg. 1987 to 1992.

N/A	$650	$550	$475	$375	$325	$300

In 1988, this model was renamed Q-90. In 1989, fretless fingerboard became available.

RD Bass Series

RD STANDARD BASS - offset hourglass maple body, layered black pickguard, maple neck, 20-fret maple fingerboard with pearl dot inlay, tune-o-matic bridge/strings through anchoring, blackface peghead with pearl logo inlay, 2-per-side tuners, nickel hardware, 2 pickups, 2 volume/2 tone controls. Available in Ebony and Natural finishes. Mfg. 1979 - 1980.

N/A	$500	$450	$375	$325	$275	$225

This model had an ebony fingerboard with Ebony finish only.

RD Artist Bass - similar to RD Standard Bass, except has winged "f" peghead inlay, 3 mini switches, active electronics. Available in Ebony, Fireburst, Natural and Sunburst finishes. Mfg. 1979 - 1982.

N/A	$650	$575	$500	$450	$400	$350

SB Bass Series

SB 300 - double sharp cutaway mahogany body/neck, 20-fret rosewood fingerboard with pearl dot inlay, fixed bridge with metal cover, blackface peghead with screened logo, 2-per-side tuners, chrome hardware, 2 single coil pickups with metal rings, volume/tone control, 3-position switch, control plate. Available in Walnut finish. Mfg. 1971-73.

N/A	$300	$250	$225	$175	$150	$125

SB 400 - similar to SB 300, except has a long scale length. Available in Cherry finish.

N/A	$350	$300	$250	$200	$175	$150

SB 350 - double sharp cutaway mahogany body/neck, thumbrest, 20-fret rosewood fingerboard with pearl dot inlay, bar bridge with metal cover, blackface peghead with pearl logo inlay, 2 covered humbucker pickups, volume/tone control, 2 on/off switches. Available in Cherry, Natural and Walnut finishes. Mfg. 1972 to 1975.

N/A	$325	$275	$225	$195	$175	$150

SB 450 - similar to SB 350, except has a long scale length. Mfg. 1972 to 1976.

N/A	$375	$325	$275	$225	$195	$175

Thunderbird Bass Series

THUNDERBIRD II - asymmetrical hourglass style mahogany body, layered white pickguard with engraved Thunderbird logo, thumb rest, through-body mahogany neck, 20-fret rosewood fingerboard with pearl dot inlay, tune-o-matic bridge/stop tailpiece, 6-on-a-side tuners, chrome hardware, single coil pickups with cover, volume/tone controls. Available in Custom Color and Sunburst finishes. Mfg. 1963 to 1969.

1963-1965	N/A	$3,100	$2,750	$2,300	$1,975	$1,600	$1,295
1966-1969	N/A	$1,800	$1,650	$1,400	$1,300	$1,200	$1,100

In 1965, body/neck were redesigned and replaced original part/design.

THUNDERBIRD IV - similar to Thunderbird II, except has 2 pickups.

1963-1965	N/A	$4,000	$3,600	$3,200	$2,800	$2,300	$2,200
1966-1969	N/A	$1,700	$1,550	$1,400	$1,275	$1,150	$1,000

In 1965, body/neck were redesigned and replaced original part/design.

THUNDERBIRD 1976 BICENTENNIAL - similar to Thunderbird, except has a red/white/blue engraved logo on white pickguard. Available in Black, Natural and Sunburst finishes. Mfg. 1976 only.

N/A	$1,500	$1,295	$1,100	$875	$750	$700

GRADING		100% MINT	98% NEAR MINT	95% EXC+	90% EXC	80% VG+	70% VG	60% G

THUNDERBIRD IV (BAT4) - asymmetrical hourglass style mahogany body, white pickguard with engraved Thunderbird symbol, through-body 9-piece mahogany/walnut neck, 20-fret ebony fingerboard with pearl dot inlay, fixed bridge, partial blackface peghead with pearl logo inlay, 4-on-a-side tuners, black chrome hardware, 2 covered pickups, 2 volume/1 tone controls. Available in Cardinal Red (disc.), Classic White (CW), Ebony (EB), and Vintage Sunburst (VS), Natural (new 1999), Natural Burst (new 1999), and Ebony Stain (new 1999) finishes. Mfg. 1987 to date.

MSR	$2,383	$1,650	$1,200	$1,050	$900	$775	$725	$675

In 1994, Cardinal Red and Vintage Sunburst finishes were discontinued; Tobacco Sunburst (TS) finish was introduced. In 1999, Vintage Sunburst was reintroduced. In 1998, Tobacco Sunburst (TS) finish was discontinued.

THUNDERBIRD NIKKI SIXX SIGNATURE BLACKBIRD - similar to Thunderbird IV, except has flat black finish and black chrome hardware, Thunderbird bridge with Opti-Grab handle, iron cross inlays in ebony fingerboard, on/off toggle switch, dual Thunderbird pickups with "Blackbird" pickguard, includes Nikki Sixx signature hardshell case. New 2000.

MSR	$2,691	$1,850	$1,350	$1,150	$900	$800	$725	$675

Victory Series

VICTORY ARTIST - offset double cutaway asymmetrical alder body, black pickguard, bolt-on maple neck, 24-fret extended rosewood fingerboard with offset pearl dot inlay, fixed bridge, blackface peghead with screened logo, 4-on-a-side tuners, chrome hardware, 2 humbucker pickups, volume/treble/bass controls, electronics/phase switches, active electronics. Available in Antique Fireburst and Candy Apple Red finishes. Mfg. 1981 to 1986.

N/A	$600	$525	$450	$375	$350	$325

Victory Custom - similar to Victory Artist, except has no active electronics. Mfg. 1982 to 1984.

N/A	$525	$450	$375	$300	$275	$250

Victory Standard - similar to Victory Artist, except has 1 humbucker pickup, volume/tone control, phase switch, no active electronics. Available in Candy Apple Red and Silver finishes. Mfg. 1981 to 1987.

N/A	$425	$375	$300	$250	$225	$200

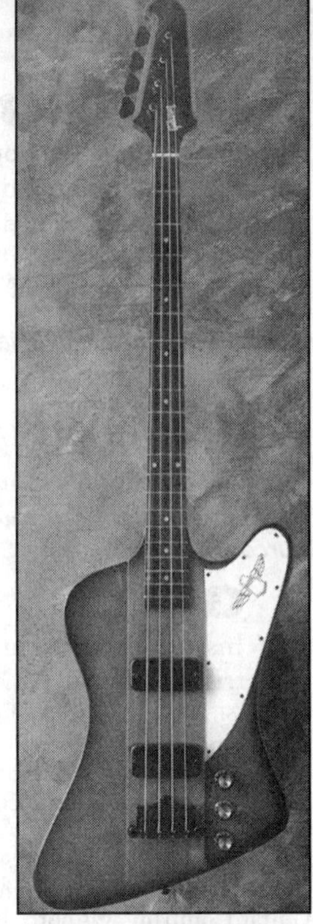

Gibson Thunderbird IV Bass
courtesy Gibson USA

GILCHRIST, STEPHEN

Instruments currently built in Australia. Distributed by the Carmel Music Company of Carmel, California.

Australian luthier Stephen Gilchrist is known for his high qualilty mandolins, mandolas and mandocellos. Gilchrist began building instruments in 1976, and spent 1980 in the U.S. working in Nashville, Tennessee at Gruhn Guitars. After 1980, Gilchrist returned to Australia and continues to produce guitars and mandolins. For further information regarding current model specifications and pricing, contact the Carmel Music Company directly (see Trademark Index).

Gilchrist has built a number of acoustic and electric guitars; most of the electric guitars were built between 1987 to 1988. To make identification of these guitars a bit difficult, some models do not have the Gilchrist name anywhere on the instrument - and none of them have a serial number.

GILES

Instruments previously produced in Bellingham, Massachusetts. Distributed by Giles USA/ AD & G Enterprises of Bellingham, Massachusetts.

Designer/luthier Allen Giles offered a retro-styled/advanced composition guitar model that was reasonably priced. Giles' KL-200 model featured a bolt-on maple neck combined with a resin cast body. The resin cast body was designed to recreate the tonal and sustain qualities of more expensive tone woods. Both the body and the necks were produced in the U.S.A.

If the world's wood supply for guitars is changing and perhaps shrinking, alternative construction technologies may prove necessary in the upcoming years. With major manufacturers like Martin and Gibson embracing the *SmartWood* ideas, and other luthiers experimenting with alternative tone woods (like Modulus Guitars), or alternative body materials (Ibanez' Ergodyne series, or Cort's Luthite models), guitar production may finally get out environmentally friendly!

ELECTRIC

The **KL-200** had an offset double cutaway resin cast body with a cutaway in the lower bout. The bolt-on maple neck had a hand-rubbed oil finish, and featured a 22-fret fingerboard of either maple or rosewood. The chrome (or black) hardware included a vintage-style 6-screw tremolo, and Sperzel locking tuners. The Bill Lawrence pickups were available in either a 3 single coil or 2 single/humbucker configuration; and had volume and tone controls, and a 5-way pickup selector. All electronic elements were mounted to a pearloid pickguard, available in Black, Candy Apple Red, Pearl White, Sea Foam Green, Viper Blue, Gold, Woodland Green, Teal, and Viper Red high gloss finishes. The last retail list price was $850, and Giles offered such custom shop upgrades as painted body color and pickguards, Floyd Rose or Point Technology tremolos, or different pickups.

GRADING	100% MINT	98% NEAR MINT	95% EXC+	90% EXC	80% VG+	70% VG	60% G

GITTLER

Instruments previously handbuilt by Allan Gittler in New York from mid-1970s to mid-1980s. Between 1986 and 1987 the Astron company of Israel produced commercial versions based on the original unique design.

Designer Allan Gittler introduced an electric guitar that expressed its design through function. Gittler produced the first 60 instruments himself and entered into an agreement with an American company that built an additional 100 instruments (which Gittler considers flawed). In 1982, Gittler moved to Israel and took the Hebrew name of Avraham Bar Rashi. Bar Rashi currently offers a new, innovative, wood constructed design that further explores his guitar concepts.

(Information courtesy of Brian Gidyk, Vancouver, Canada)

GLOBE

See also GOODMAN.

See chapter on House Brands.

This trademark has been identified as a *House Brand* of the Goodman Community Discount Center, circa 1958-1960.

(Source: Willie G. Moseley, Stellas & Stratocasters)

GODIN

Instruments currently built in La Patrie and Princeville, Quebec, in Canada; and Berlin, New Hampshire since 1987. Distributed by La Si Do, Inc. of St. Laurent, Canada.

Although the trademark and instruments bearing his name are relatively new, Robert Godin has been a mainstay in the guitar building industry since 1972. Godin got his first guitar at age seven and never looked back. By the time he was 15, he was working at La Tosca Musique in Montreal selling guitars and learning about minor repairs and set up work. Before long, Robert's passion for guitar playing was eclipsed by his fascination with the construction of the instruments themselves. In 1968 Godin set up a custom guitar shop in Montreal called Harmonilab. Harmonilab quickly became known for its excellent work and musicians were coming from as far away as Quebec City to have their guitars adjusted. Harmonilab was the first guitar shop in Quebec to use professional strobe tuners for intonating guitars.

Although Harmonilab's business was flourishing, Robert was full of ideas for the design and construction of acoustic guitars. So in 1972, the **Norman Guitar Company** was born. From the beginning the Norman guitars showed signs of the innovations that Godin would eventually bring to the guitar market. Perhaps the most significant item about the Norman history is that it represented the beginning of guitar building in the village of La Patrie, Quebec. La Patrie has since become an entire town of guitar builders - more on that later.

By 1978, Norman guitars had become quite successful in Canada and France, while at the same time the people in La Patrie were crafting replacement necks and bodies for the electric guitar market. Before long there was a lineup at the door of American guitar companies that wanted Godin's crew to supply all their necks and bodies.

In 1980 Godin introduced the Seagull guitar. With many innovations like a bolt-on neck (for consistent neck pitch), pointed headstock (straight string pull) and a handmade solid top, the Seagull was designed for an ease of play for the entry level to intermediate guitar player. Most striking was the satin lacquer finish. Godin borrowed the finishing idea that was used on fine violins, and applied it to the acoustic guitar. When the final version of the Seagull guitar went into production, Godin went about the business of finding a sales force to help introduce the Seagull into the U.S. market. Several independent U.S. sales agents jumped at the chance to get involved with this new guitar, and armed with samples off they went into the market. A couple of months passed, and not one guitar was sold. Rather than retreat back to Harmonilab, Godin decided that he would have to get out there himself and explain the Seagull guitar concept. So he bought himself an old Ford Econoline van and stuffed it full of about 85 guitars, and started driving through New England visiting guitar shops and introducing the Seagull guitar. Acceptance of this new guitar spread, and by 1985 La Si Do was incorporated and the factory in La Patrie expanded to meet the growing demand. Godin introduced the La Patrie brand of classical acoustic guitars in 1982. The La Patrie trademark was used to honor the town's tradition of luthiery that had developed during the first ten years since the inception of the Norman guitars trademark. In 1985, Godin also introduced the Simon & Patrick line (named after his two sons) for people interested in a more traditional instrument. Simon & Patrick guitars still maintained a number of Seagull innovations.

Since Godin's factory had been producing necks and bodies for various American guitar companies since 1978, he combined that knowledge with his background in acoustic guitar design for an entirely new product. The 'Acousticaster' was debuted in 1987, and represented the first design under the Godin name. The Acousticaster was designed to produce an acoustic sound from an instrument that was as easy to play as the player's favorite electric guitar. This was achieved through the help of a patented mechanical harp system inside the guitar. Over the past few years, the Godin name has become known for very high quality and innovative designs. Robert Godin is showing no signs of slowing down, having recently introduced the innovative models Multiac, LGX, and LGX-SA.

Today, La Si Do Inc. employs close to 500 people in four factories located in La Patrie and Princeville, Quebec (Canada), and Berlin, New Hampshire. Models of the La Si Do guitar family are in demand all over the world, and Godin is still on the road teaching people about guitars. In a final related note, the Ford Econoline van "died" with about 300,000 miles on it about 14 years ago.

(Company History courtesy Robert Godin and Katherine Calder [Artist Relations], La Si Do, Inc., June 5, 1996)

Production Model Codes

Godin is currently using a system similar to the original Gretsch system, in that the company is assigning both a model name and a four digit number that indicates the color finish specific to that guitar model. Thus, the four digit code will indicate which model and color from just one number. References in this text will list the four digit variances for color finish within the model designations.

GRADING	100% MINT	98% NEAR MINT	95% EXC+	90% EXC	80% VG+	70% VG	60% G

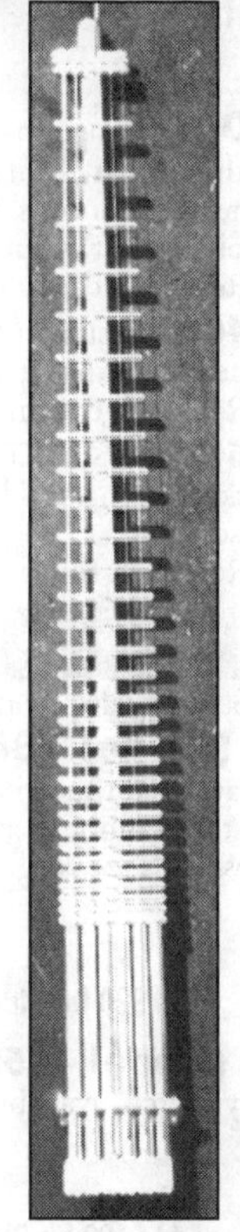
Gittler Guittar
courtesy Brian Gidyk

ELECTRIC

Artisan Series

ARTISAN ST I (model 3990) - offset double cutaway light maple body, carved bird's-eye maple top, bolt-on rock maple neck, 22-fret rosewood or maple fingerboard with offset dot inlay, 21st fret pearl block inlay, Schaller 2000 tremolo, 6-on-a-side locking Schaller tuners, gold hardware, 3 Godin twin blade pickups, volume/tone controls, 5-position switch, available in Antique Violin Brown, Cognacburst, and Transparent Blue finishes. Disc. 1998.

	$875	**$725**	**$625**	**$550**	**$450**	**$375**	**$275**

Last MSR was $1,095.

Early models may have 22-fret ebony fingerboard with offset dot inlay/pearl block inlay at 21st fret, and a Wilkinson vibrato. Models were available in Transparent Black and Transparent Purple finishes.

Artisan ST Signature (Model 11675) - similar to Artisan ST-I, except has carved figured maple top, rock maple neck, maple or rosewood fingerboard, 3 Seymour Duncan Lil '59 pickups. Current Mfg.

Maple fingerboard: Available in Antique Violin Brown (Model 11667), Cognacburst (Model 11681), and Transparent Blue (Model 11675) finishes.

Rosewood fingerboard: Available in Antique Violin Brown (Model 11698), Cognacburst (Model 11711), and Transparent Blue (Model 11704) finishes.

MSR **$1,295**	**$1,050**	**$850**	**$750**	**$650**	**$525**	**$425**	**$325**

Early models may feature a quilted maple top, and ebony fingerboards.
Add $350 for AAA Grade top.

Artisan ST II - similar to Artisan ST I, except has carved arched top, vintage-style vibrato, 6-on-a-side non-locking tuners, 3 Godin twin blade passive pickups, volume/push-pull tone (Michael Braun EQ system) controls, 5-way selector switch, available in Blue and Black finishes. Disc. 1995.

Research continues on the Artisan ST II model and pricing.

Artisan ST II Ultimate - similar to Artisan ST II, except has Wilkinson vibrato, 6-on-a-side staggered locking tuners, available in Blue and Black finishes. Disc. 1995.

Research continues on the Artisan ST II Ultimate model and pricing.

ST IV - similar to Artisan ST I, except has vintage-style Schaller 4000 vibrato, 2 Tetrad (twin) blade/Tetrad Combo humbucker Godin pickups, available in Cognacburst high gloss and Violin Brown satin finishes. Disc. 1997.

	$695	**$550**	**$475**	**$395**	**$350**	**$300**	**$250**

Last MSR was $960.

This model has an optional maple fingerboard with black inlay.

Artisan ST V - similar to Artisan ST I, except has longer bass/shorter treble horns offset cutaway body, Canadian maple top, rosewood fingerboard with offset dot inlay, double locking vibrato, 6-on-a-side non-locking tuners, black hardware, Godin twin blade/Tetrad Combo humbucker pickups, volume/push-pull tone (Michael Braun EQ system) controls, 3-way selector switch, available in Transparent Amber, Transparent Blue and Transparent Green finishes. Disc. 1996.

Research continues on the Artisan ST V model and pricing.

ST VI - similar to Artisan ST V, except has Schaller Floyd Rose II double locking vibrato, non locking tuners, black hardware, Tetrad Combo humbucker/Tetrad blade/Tetrad Combo humbucker Godin pickups, available in Black and Transparent Green finishes. Disc. 1997.

	$700	**$575**	**$500**	**$400**	**$350**	**$300**	**$250**

Last MSR was $990.

The Transparent Green finish was available with a figured maple top.

ARTISAN TC SIGNATURE (Model 4515, ARTISAN TC I) - single cutaway light maple body, carved figured maple top, bolt-on rock maple neck, 22-fret maple or rosewood fingerboard with offset dot inlay, "dish style" fixed bridge, 6-on-a-side tuners, gold hardware, 2 Godin Tetrad twin blade pickups, volume/tone controls, 3-position switch. Disc. 1998.

Maple fingerboard: Available in Antique Violin Brown (Model 4508), Cognacburst (Model 4522), and Transparent Blue (Model 4515) finishes.

Rosewood fingerboard: Available in Antique Violin Brown (Model 4591), Cognacburst (Model 4614), and Transparent Blue (Model 4607) finishes.

	$975	**$750**	**$675**	**$595**	**$495**	**$395**	**$300**

Last MSR was $1,195.

Early TC I models may have ebony fingerboards, bird's-eye maple necks, and the (push-pull) Michael Braun EQ system controls.

Artisan TC II - similar to Artisan TC I, except has carved arched top, 2 Godin twin blade passive pickups, volume/push-pull tone (Michael Braun EQ system) controls, 3-way selector switch, available in White finish. Disc. 1995.

Research continues on the Artisan ST II model and pricing.

G Series

The G Series body shape was derived from the Artisan ST V model.

GRADING	100% MINT	98% NEAR MINT	95% EXC+	90% EXC	80% VG+	70% VG	60% G

G-1000 - (longer bass/shorter treble horns) offset cutaway light maple body, rock maple neck, 24.75" scale, 24-fret maple or rosewood fingerboard with dot inlay, vintage-style tremolo, 6-on-a-side tuners, gold hardware, pickguard, 2 Godin exposed polepiece single coil/humbucker pickups, volume/tone controls, 5-way selector switch, available in Black, Cognacburst, and Transparent Blue high gloss finishes; Transparent Amber and Antique Violin (Burst) satin lacquer finishes. Disc. 1996.

Research continues on the G-1000 model and pricing.

G-4000 - similar to G-1000, except has deluxe Schaller vintage-style tremolo, Schaller locking tuners, available in Black, Cognacburst, Transparent Blue Burst, and Transparent Violet high gloss finishes; Antique Violin (Burst) satin lacquer finish. Disc. 1996.

Research continues on the G-1000 model and pricing.

G-5000 - similar to G-1000, except has 25.5" scale, rosewood fingerboard (only), no pickguard, Tetrad twin blade/Tetrad Combo humbucker pickups, Schaller Floyd Rose II locking tremolo, Schaller locking tuners, MFB mid filter EQ control, available in Black and Red high gloss finishes. Disc. 1996.

Research continues on the G-5000 model and pricing.

LG Series

LG Series models were originally equipped with Godin Tetrad (hum cancelling single coil) pickups. The S designation indicates Seymour Duncan pickups.

LG S (Model 7882) - single cutaway Honduran mahogany body, mahogany neck, 24 3/4" scale, 24-fret Indian rosewood fingerboard with dot inlay, fixed tuneomatic-style bridge, 3-per-side Schaller 'Klouson' Pro Series tuners, matching finish headstock, black hardware, 2 Seymour Duncan custom humbucker pickups, volume/tone controls, 3-position switch, available in Natural (Model 7882) and Transparent Red (Model 7868) semi-gloss finishes. Mfg. 1997 to 1998.

	$600	$525	$450	$395	$325	$250	$175

Last MSR was $725.

Add $20 for Black Pearl (Model 10615) and CognacBurst (Model 7875) high gloss finishes.

LG (Model 4652) - similar to the LG S, except features 2 Godin Tetrad Combo pickups, volume/push-pull tone (MFB mid filter) controls, 5-way switch, available in Natural satin lacquer finish. Disc. 1997.

	$600	$550	$500	$425	$350	$275	$200

Last MSR was $795.

Add $100 for Black (Model 4621), CognacBurst (Model 4645), and Transparent Red (Model 4638) high gloss finishes.

LG (SP90) single cutaway mahogany body, mahogany neck with rosewood fingerboard, 24 ¾" scale, 24-frets, 3-per-side tuners,strings through-body, 1 Volume/1 Tone, 2 Seymour Duncan SP90 single coil pickups, 3-way switch, fixed" tun-o-matic" style bridge, available in natural, Cognac, Dark Gold, Transparent Red and Black Pearl finishes. Current Mfg.

MSR	$725	$550	$415	$350	$295	$265	$235

Add $70 for high gloss finishes.

LGT S (Model 11612) - similar to the LG S, except features a light maple body, Schaller Trem 2000 tremolo, 3-per-side Schaller locking tuners, pickguard, 2 Tetrad blade single coil/Seymour Duncan humbucker pickups, 5-way selector switch, available in Aqua (Model 11612), Black Pearl (Model 11643), Cream (Model 11636), Transparent Blue (Model 11629), and Transparent Red (Model 11650) high gloss finishes. Mfg. 1997 to 1998.

	$650	$575	$500	$425	$350	$275	$200

Last MSR was $795.

LGT (Model 7493) - similar to the LGT S, except features 2 Godin single coil/Tetrad Combo pickups, volume/push-pull tone (MFB mid filter) controls, 5-way switch, available in Aqua (Model 8742), Black (Model 8780), Cream (Model 8759), Transparent Blue (Model 7493), and Transparent Red (Model 7509) high gloss finishes. Disc. 1997.

	$600	$550	$500	$425	$350	$275	$200

Last MSR was $795.

LGX Series

The original **LGX** model featured both magnetic pickups and L.R. Baggs transducer saddles, and offered guitar players both the "electric voice" and the "acoustic voice" in the same instrument. A year later, the **LGX-SA** with Roland-Ready Synth Acess was introduced. The **LGXT** subsitutes a tremolo bridge for a tune-o-matic bridge/strings into-body; and the **LGX3** features 3 single coils instead of the two humbuckers on the LGX-SA.

LGX (Model 7561) - rounded single cutaway mahogany body, carved figured maple top, 25 1/2" scale, mahogany neck, 22-fret rosewood fingerboard with dot inlay, "Godin style" tuneomatic bridge/strings into-body "fingers", 3-per-side tuners, gold hardware, 2 Godin Tetrad (twin blade) pickups, microtransducer bridge pickup, volume/tone/blend controls, 5-way magnetic pickup selector switch, magnetic/mix/transducer mini-switch, volume/treble/mid/bass transducer controls (4 sliders in bass bout), available in Black Pearl (Model 10509), CognacBurst (Model 10486), Mahogany (Model 7578), Transparent Amber (Model 7585), and Transparent Blue (Model 7561) high gloss finishes. Mfg. 1996 to date.

MSR	$1,475	$1,175	$950	$850	$725	$625	$495	$360

Add $50 for 2 Seymour Duncan custom humbucker pickups, available in Black Pearl (Model 10516), CognacBurst (Model 10493), Mahogany (Model 7813), Transparent Amber (Model 7820), and Transparent Blue (Model 7806) high gloss finishes.

Add $350 for AAA Grade top.

LGX Left-Handed (Model 9718) - similar to the LGX-SA, except features a left-handed configuration, available in Mahogany (Model 9718) high gloss finish. Mfg. 1997 to 1998.

	$1,350	$1,200	$1,050	$895	$725	$595	$425

Last MSR was $1,725.

GRADING		100% MINT	98% NEAR MINT	95% EXC+	90% EXC	80% VG+	70% VG	60% G

LGX 3 (Model 11568) - rounded single cutaway maple body, 25 1/2" scale, mahogany neck, 22-fret rosewood fingerboard with dot inlay, "Godin style" tuneomatic bridge/strings into-body "fingers", 3-per-side tuners, gold hardware, 3 Seymour Duncan pickups (Lil '59s/Duckbucker), L.R. Baggs X-Bridge bridge pickup with custom preamp/EQ, volume/blend/tone controls, 5-way magnetic pickup selector switch, magnetic/mix/transducer mini-switch, volume/treble/mid/bass transducer controls (4 sliders in bass bout), available in Black Pearl (Model 10568), Cream (Model 11599), Transparent Blue (Model 11582), and Transparent Red (Model 11575) high gloss finishes. Mfg. 1998 to date.

MSR	$1,250	$935	$695	$650	$595	$550	$495	$425

Add $170 for transparent colors.

LGX-SA WITH SYNTH ACCESS (Model 4904) - rounded single cutaway mahogany body, carved figured maple top, 25 1/2" scale, mahogany neck, 22-fret ebony fingerboard with dot inlay, "Godin style" tuneomatic bridge/strings into-body "fingers", 3-per-side tuners, gold hardware, 2 Godin Tetrad (twin blade) pickups, microtransducer bridge pickup, volume/synth volume/tone controls, 5-way magnetic pickup selector switch, magnetic/mix/transducer mini-switch, Program Up/Down synth control toggle mini-switch, volume/treble/mid/bass transducer controls (4 sliders in bass bout), 13 pin connector for Roland GR series guitar synths, 3 outputs (magnetics, bridge/mix, 13 pin connector), available in Black Pearl (Model 10547), CognacBurst (Model 10523), Mahogany (Model 4911), Transparent Amber (Model 4928), and Transparent Blue (Model 4904) high gloss finishes. Current Mfg.

MSR	$1,875	$1,475	$1,225	$1,075	$895	$750	$625	$475

Add $50 for 2 Seymour Duncan custom humbucker pickups, available in Black Pearl (Model 10554D), CognacBurst (Model 10530), Mahogany (Model 7844), Transparent Amber (Model 7851), and Transparent Blue (Model 7837) high gloss finishes.

Subtract $150 for Black Pearl finish.

LGX-SA With Synth Access Left-Handed (Model 9817) - similar to the LGX-SA, except features a left-handed configuration, available in Mahogany (Model 9817) and Transparent Amber (Model 9824) high gloss finishes. Mfg. 1997 to date.

MSR	$2,125	$1,700	$1,495	$1,300	$1,125	$925	$750	$550

Earlier models may be designated Model 9770.

Add $350 for AAA Grade top.

LGX T (Model 9688) - similar to the LGX-SA, except features maple body (no carved figured maple top), tremolo bridge, L.R. Baggs X-Bridge bridge pickup with custom preamp/EQ, 2 Seymour Duncan custom humbucker pickups, available in Black Pearl (Model 10622), Cream (Model 9701), Transparent Blue (Model 9688), and Transparent Red (Model 9695) high gloss finishes. Mfg. 1997 to date.

MSR	$1,495	$1,200	$1,050	$925	$775	$650	$500	$375

Add $380 for transparent colors.

Add $730 for AAA Grade top and transparent colors.

Godin LGXT
courtesy Godin

Performance Series

RADIATOR single cutaway chambered Silver Leaf Maple body, Rock Maple neck, maple or rosewood fingerboard, dot position markers, 24 ¾" scale, 3-per-side tuners, 24-frets, 2 Godin-designed Low Noise single coil pickups, 2 Volume/1 Tone, full face white or black pearloid pickguard, available in Cream, Black Pearl, Black Chrome, Pace Car Blue, and Black Onyx finishes. Current Mfg.

MSR	$449	$336	$250	$225	$195	$175	$150	$125

Add $20 for Black Chrome finish.

SOLIDAC "2-VOICE" "New Model" - single cutaway Silver Leaf Maple body, mahogany neck with rosewood fingerboard, 22-frets, 25 ½" scale, 3-per-side tuners, tremelo bridge, 2 Volumes/1 Tone, two voice guitar with acoustic sound produced by a transducer equipped bridge and electric sounds by Godin design pickups in a humbucker-single-humbucker configuration, 5-way switch, 2 outputs, available in high gloss Black Pearl, HG Trans Red and HG Trans Purple. Current Mfg.

MSR	$895	$675	$500	$450	$400	$350	$300	$250

GRADING	100% MINT	98% NEAR MINT	95% EXC+	90% EXC	80% VG+	70% VG	60% G

SD Series

SD (Model 8896) - single cutaway light maple body, bolt-on rock maple neck, 24 3/4" scale, 24-fret maple or rosewood fingerboard with dot inlay, vintage-style tremolo bridge, 6-on-a-side tuners, natural headstock finish, chrome hardware, pickguard, 2 Godin single coil/humbucker pickups, volume/tone controls, 5-position switch. Current Mfg.

Maple Fingerboard: Available in Aqua (Model 8872), Banana Cream (Model 10752), Black Pearl (Model 10455), Canary Yellow (Model 10479), Cream (Model 8865), Midnight Blue Pearl (Model 10417), and Powder Blue (Model 11032) high gloss finishes.

Rosewood Fingerboard: Available in Aqua (Model 8803), Banana Cream (Model 10769), Black Pearl (Model 10448), Canary Yellow (Model 10462), Cream (Model 8797), Midnight Blue Pearl (Model 10400), and Powder Blue (Model 11049) high gloss finishes.

MSR	$499	$375	$275	$250	$225	$195	$150	$95

Add $20 for Transparent colors. Maple fingerboard: Extreme Aqua (Model 11117), Extreme Purple (Model 11070), Transparent Blue (Model 8896), Transparent Purple (Model 10431), and Transparent Red (Model 8902) high gloss finishes. Rosewood fingerboard: Extreme Aqua (Model 11124), Extreme Purple (Model 11087), Transparent Blue (Model 8827), Transparent Purple (Model 10424), and Transparent Red (Model 8834) high gloss finishes.

SD With Schaller Floyd Rose (Model 9855) - similar to the SD, except features a Schaller licensed Floyd Rose tremolo, rosewood fingerboard (only), available in Aqua (Model 9831), Black Pearl (Model 10639), and Cream (Model 9879) high gloss finishes. Disc 1999.

		$475	$425	$375	$325	$275	$225	$175

Last MSR was $625.

Add $20 for Transparent Blue (Model 9855) and Transparent Red (Model 9862) high gloss finishes.

ELECTRIC BASS

BG Series

BG IV 4-STRING (Model 8766) - offset double cutaway 3-piece body, rock maple centre/light maple wings, 3-piece maple neck, 34" scale, 22-fret rosewood fingerboard with offset dot inlay, 2-per-side Schaller tuners, Schaller fixed bridge, EMG 40P5/EMG 40 'soapbar' pickups, volume/balance/dual EQ controls, available in Black (Model 8766), Cream (Model 9572), Transparent Blue (Model 7424), and Transparent Red (Model 9565) high-gloss finishes. Current Mfg.

MSR	$1,249	$935	$700	$650	$600	$550	$495	$425

Add $350 for AAA Grade top.

BG V 5-String (Model 8773) - similar to the BG IV, except features a 5-string configuration, 3/2-per-side tuners, available in Black (Model 8773), Cream (Model 9596), Transparent Blue (Model 7455), and Transparent Red (Model 9589) high-gloss finishes. Current Mfg.

MSR	$1,349	$995	$750	$695	$650	$550	$495	$425

Add $350 for AAA Grade top.

SD Bass Series

SD BASS (Model 11735) - offset double cutaway maple body, maple neck, 34" scale, 22-fret rosewood fingerboard with offset dot inlay, 2-per-side tuners, fixed bridge, P/J-style Godin passive pickups, volume/tone controls, available in Black Pearl (Model 11728), Cream (Model 11742), Transparent Blue (Model 11735), and Transparent Purple (Model 11759) high-gloss finishes. Mfg. 1998 to date.

MSR	$595	$450	$350	$295	$250	$195	$150	$95

Add $100 for 5-string model.

SD Pro Bass (Model 11773) - similar to the SD Bass, except features Seymour Duncan Bassline pickups, available in Black Pearl (Model 11766), Cream (Model 11780), Transparent Blue (Model 11773), and Transparent Purple (Model 11797) high-gloss finishes. Mfg. 1998 to 1999.

MSR	$899	$675	$495	$450	$395	$350	$295	$225

GODWIN

Instruments previously built in Italy in the mid 1970s.

In 1967, Bob Murrell produced the first commercially available guitar that made organ sounds, named the **GuitOrgan**. The GuitOrgan featured Japanese-built hollowbody guitars and Baldwin-style circuitry. Following Murrell, the Vox company fused a Phantom model guitar with a Continental model organ around 1970, and named it the **Guitar Organ**. The Godwin company apparently thought that the third time was the charm when they introduced the **Godwin Organ** model guitar in the mid 1970s. Still a bargain if bought by the pound (not by the sound!), the Godwins were only produced for about a year.

The instrument featured a double cutaway wood body, 2 independent single coil pickups, and 13 knobs - plus 19 switches! Even with a large amount of wood removed for the organ circuitry, the fairly deep-bodied guitar is still heavy.

(Source: Tony Bacon, The Ultimate Guitar Book)

GOLDEN WOOD

Instruments currently built in Gualala, California.

The Golden Wood company is currently offering hand crafted guitars. For further information regarding specifications and pricing, please contact the Golden Wood company directly (see Trademark Index).

GRADING	100% MINT	98% NEAR MINT	95% EXC+	90% EXC	80% VG+	70% VG	60% G

GOLDENTONE

Instruments previously produced in Japan during the 1960s.

The Goldentone trademark was used by U.S. importers Elger and its partner Hoshino Gakki Ten as one of the brandnames used in their joint guitar producing venture. Hoshino in Japan was shipping Fuji Gen Gakki-built guitars marketed in the U.S. as Goldentone, Elger, and eventually Ibanez. These solid body guitars featured original body designs in the early to mid 1960s.

(Source: Michael Wright, Guitar Stories Volume One)

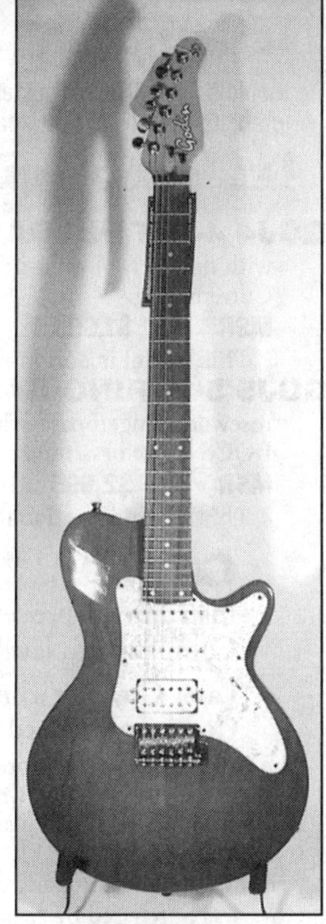

Godin SD
courtesy Brook Mays

GOODFELLOW

See LOWDEN GUITARS.

Instruments currently built in Northern Ireland. Distributed in the U.S. market by Quality First Products of Forest City, North Carolina.

Goodfellow basses were introduced in the 1980s, and caught the eye of Lowden Guitars' Andy Kidd during an exhibit in Manchester. Kidd, originally offering to further *spread the word* and help subcontract some of the building, eventually acquired the company. These high quality basses feature select figured and exotic wood construction, as well as active tone circuitry and humbucking pickups designed by Kent Armstrong, available in 4-, 5-, or 6-string models, the ebony fingerboard spans a two octave neck. For further information, contact Goodfellow directly (see Trademark Index).

GOODMAN

See chapter on House Brands.

This trademark has been identified as a *House Brand* of the Goodman Community Discount Center, circa 1961-1964. Previously, the company used the trademark of GLOBE.

(Source: Willie G. Moseley, Stellas & Stratocasters)

GORDON SMITH

Instruments currently produced in England since 1979.

This company built both original designs and Fender/Gibson-esque designed solid and semi-hollow body guitars. Models feature company's own pickups and hardware, but hardware options changed through the years. Though information is still lacking in model differences, the names retain a certain similarity: The Gypsy, Galaxi, Graduate, Gemini, and GS models.

(Source: Tony Bacon and Paul Day, The Guru's Guitar Guide)

GORDY

Instruments currently built in England since the mid 1980s.

Luthier Gordon Whitham, the *Gordon* of GORDON SMITH fame, is producing a series of high quality instruments. These original design solid body guitars carry such model designations as the Red Shift, 1810, and Xcaster.

(Source: Tony Bacon and Paul Day, The Guru's Guitar Guide)

GOSPEL

Instruments previously built in Bakersfield, California in the late 1960s (a second series was produced in Jonah's Ridge, North Carolina in the early 1980s).

In 1969, luthier Semie Moseley trademarked the Gospel brandname separate from his Mosrite company. Only a handful of late '60s Gospels were produced and featured a design based on Mosrite's Celebrity model guitar. Moseley also produced a Gospel model briefly under his own Mosrite label as well - the rare Gospel (trademark only) does not have the Mosrite name mentioned on the headstock. In the early '80s, Moseley again attempted to offer guitars to the gospel music industry. The Gospel guitars represent Semie Moseley's love of gospel music and his attempt to furnish gospel musicians with quality instruments.

(Information courtesy of Andy Moseley and Hal Hammer, 1996).

Gospel Moseley
courtesy Hal Hammer

G GOULD

Instruments currently built in San Francisco, California. Distributed by G.Gould Music of San Francisco, California.

Bassist/designer Geoff Gould was the founder and president of Modulus Graphite for almost two decades (see MODULUS GRAPHITE). While at Modulus, Gould was responsible for the development of the stringed instrument graphite neck and pioneered the use of the 35" scale length on production bass instruments that featured a low 'B' string.

In addition to his new bass and guitar models, Gould is offering extra long scale (35" scale) 5-string bass string sets in Standard and Taper-Core. For more information regarding the string sets or the G.Gould guitar and bass instruments, please contact Geoff Gould directly (see Trademark Index).

ELECTRIC

Gould's Slant T guitar model is currently available by special order only. This single cutaway model has either specially made OEM Modulus necks, or a maple/graphite composite neck (call for pricing).

ELECTRIC BASS

GGJ4 4-STRING BASS - sleek offset double cutaway ash body, graphite-reinforced hardwood neck, 34" scale, 24-fret rosewood fingerboard with dot inlay, 4-on-a-side tuners, angled back headstock, 2 EMG-JV pickups, volume/tone controls, EMG-BQCS active bass/mid/treble controls. Current Mfg.

MSR $1,995

This model is optional with a flamed maple top.

GGJ5 5-STRING BASS - sleek offset double cutaway alder body, figured maple top, graphite-reinforced hardwood neck, 35" scale, 24-fret rosewood fingerboard with dot inlay, 4/1 per side tuners, angled back headstock, 2 custom EMG 'soapbar' pickups, volume/tone controls, EMG-BQCS active bass/mid/treble controls. Current Mfg.

MSR $2,995

This model is optional in 17.0 mm or 17.5 mm string spacing.

GOYA

Instruments previously produced in Sweden circa 1900s to mid 1960s. Distributed by Hershman Musical Instrument Company of New York.

Later Goya instruments were built in Korea from the early 1970s to 1996, and were distributed by The Martin Guitar Company, located in Nazareth, Pennsylvania.

The Goya trademark was originally used by the Hershman Musical Instrument Company of New York City, New York in the 1950s on models built by Sweden's Levin company (similar models were sold in Europe under the company's Levin trademark). Levin built high quality acoustic flattop, classical, and archtop guitars as well as mandolins. A large number of rebranded *Goya* instruments were imported to the U.S. market.

In the late 1950s, solidbody electric guitars and basses built by Hagstrom (also a Swedish company) were rebranded *Goya* and distributed in the U.S. as well. In 1963 the company changed its name to the Goya Musical Instrument Corporation.

Goya was purchased by Avnet (see **Guild**) in 1966, and continued to import instruments such as the Rangemaster in 1967. By the late 1960s, electric solidbody guitars and basses were then being built in Italy by the EKO company. Avnet then sold the Goya trademark to Kustom Electronics. It has been estimated that the later Goya instruments of the 1970s were built in Japan.

The C. F. Martin company later acquired the Levin company, and bought the rights to the Goya trademark from a company named Dude, Inc. in 1976. Martin imported a number of guitar, mandolin, and banjo string instruments from the 1970s through to 1996. While this trademark is currently discontinued, the rights to the name are still held by the Martin Guitar company.

The Goya company featured a number of innovations that most people are not aware of. Goya was the first classic guitar line to put the trademark name on the headstock, and also created the ball end classic guitar string.

Levin-Era Goya models feature interior paper label with the Goya trademark in a cursive style, and designated "Made by A.B. Herman Carlson Levin - Gothenburg, Sweden". Model and serial number appear on the label, as well as on the neck block.

ELECTRIC

While Goya mainly offered acoustic guitars, the first electrics debuted in the late 1950s. The first series of electrics were built by Hagstrom, and feature a sparkly plastic covering. A later series of electrics such as the Range Masters, were produced from 1967-1969 (by EKO of Italy) and featured pushbutton controls. Other Eko/Goya creations include the Panther, P-26, and P-46. Goya also offered a number of electric guitar amplifiers in the 1950s and 1960s.

GRAFFITI

Instruments previously built in England from the early to late 1980s.

While the instruments were indeed constructed in the UK, the parts themselves were from Italy or Japan. The guitars were medium-to-good quality Fender-styled solid body instruments.

(Source: Tony Bacon and Paul Day, The Guru's Guitar Guide)

GRANT

Instruments previously produced in Japan from the 1970s through the 1980s.

The GRANT trademark was the brandname of a UK importer, and the guitars were medium quality copies of American designs.

(Source: Tony Bacon and Paul Day, The Guru's Guitar Guide)

GRANTSON

Instruments previously produced in Japan during the mid 1970s.

These entry level guitars featured designs based on popular American models.

(Source: Tony Bacon and Paul Day, The Guru's Guitar Guide)

GRAY, KEVIN

Instruments previously built in Dallas, Texas.

Luthier Kevin Gray built custom guitars, as well as performed repairs and restorations on instruments for a number of years.

ELECTRIC

Gray blended state of the art technology with handcrafted exotic wood tops. Standard features included a solid mahogany body and neck, 24-fret rosewood or ebony fingerboard, choice of 24 3/4" or 25 1/2" scale, and mother-of-pearl or abalone inlays. Gray also featured gold-plated hardware, Sperzel locking tuners, Seymour Duncan or Lindy Fralin pickups, and hand-rubbed lacquer finishes.

Gray offered four different variations of his custom guitars. The **Carved Top** (last retail was $2,995) featured an exotic wood top over the mahogany body, and had a set-neck. A **Marquetry Flat Top** (last retail was $2,995) had designs or scenes formed from exotic hardwoods, body binding, and a set-neck. An unsculpted exotic hardwood top and body binding was offered on the **Flat Top** (last retail was $2,795). Gray also built a **Contoured Top/Bolt-on** design (last retail was $2,495) with a carved maple top, maple neck, and either a maple, alder, or basswood body.

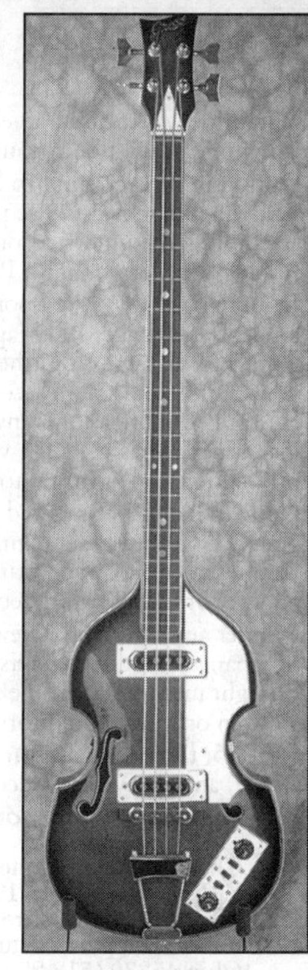

Greco Bass
courtesy Justin Cobb

GRAZIOSO

See FUTURAMA.

GRECO

Instruments previously produced in Japan during the 1960s.

Greco instruments were imported to the U.S. through Goya Guitars/Avnet. Avnet was the same major company that also acquired Guild in 1966.

(Source: Michael Wright, Guitar Stories Volume One)

GREMLIN

Instruments currently built in Asia. Distributed in the U.S. market by Midco International of Effingham, Illinois.

Gremlin guitars are designed for the entry level or student guitarist.

GRENDEL

Instruments currently built in Czechoslovakia. Distributed by Matthews & Ryan Musical Products, Inc., of New York City, New York.

Grendel basses are licensed by Michael Tobias Design (MTD Basses) and are built in the Czech Republic. Grendel basses are also available in the English music market under the Stadium trademark, and are offered through Bass Centre.

Grendel basses are named after the monster character in the literary work *Beowulf*.

ELECTRIC BASS

GR4 4-STRING - offset double cutaway poplar body, bolt-on maple neck, 34" scale, 24-fret (plus 'Zero' fret) wenge fingerboard, 4-on-a-side headstock with wenge overlay, Schaller tuners, 2 single coil Bartolini pickups, volume/tone controls, toggle switch, Bartolini electronics, available in Pilsner Oil or Burgundy Sunburst, Coral Blue, Red, or Red Sunburst See-Through lacquer finishes. Current Mfg.

MSR $1,450

GR4 FL - similar to the GR4, except has a flame maple top. Current Mfg.

MSR $1,510

GR5 5-STRING - similar to the GR4 4-String, except in a 5-string configuration, 4/1 headstock. Current Mfg.

MSR $1,580

GR5 FL - similar to the GR5, except has a flame maple top. Current Mfg.

MSR $1,650

GRENN

Instruments previously built in Japan during the late 1960s.

Grenn guitars were a series of entry level semi-hollow body designs.

(Source: Tony Bacon and Paul Day, The Guru's Guitar Guide)

GRETSCH

Instruments currently produced in the U.S. (three current models) since 1995. Other models produced in Japan from 1989 to date. Distributed by the Fred Gretsch Company of Savannah, Georgia.

Instruments originally produced in New York City, New York from the early 1900s to 1970. Production was moved to Booneville, Arkansas from 1970 to 1979. Gretsch (as owned by D. H. Baldwin Piano Company) ceased production (of guitars) in 1981.

Friedrich Gretsch was born in 1856, and emigrated to America when he was 16. In 1883 he founded a musical instrument shop in Brooklyn which prospered. The Fred Gretsch Company began manufacturing instruments in 1883 (while Friedrich maintained his proper name, he "Americanized" it for the company). Gretsch passed away unexpectedly (at age 39) during a trip to Germany in April 1895, and his son Fred (often referred to as Fred Gretsch, Sr. in company histories) took over the family business (at 15!). Gretsch Sr. expanded the business considerably by 1916. Beginning with percussion, ukeleles, and banjos, Gretsch introduced guitars in the early 1930s, developing a well respected line of archtop orchestra models. In 1926 the company acquired the rights to K. Zildjian Cymbals, and debuted the Gretsch tenor guitar. During the Christmas season of 1929, the production capacity was reported to be 100,000 instruments (stringed instruments and drums); and a new midwestern branch was opened in Chicago, Illinois. In March of 1940 Gretsch acquired the B & D trademark from the Bacon Banjo Corporation. Fred Gretsch, Sr. retired in 1942.

Charles "Duke" Krammer
courtesy Gretsch

William Walter Gretsch assumed the presidency of the company until 1948, and then Fred Gretsch, Jr. took over the position. Gretsch, Jr. was the primary president during the great Gretsch heyday, and was ably assisted by such notables as Jimmy Webster and Charles "Duke" Kramer (Kramer was involved with the Gretsch company from 1935 to his retirement in 1980, and was even involved after his retirement!). During the 1950s, the majority of Gretsch's

GRADING	100% MINT	98% NEAR MINT	95% EXC+	90% EXC	80% VG+	70% VG	60% G

guitar line was focused on electric six string Spanish instruments. With the endorsement of Chet Atkins and George Harrison, Gretsch electrics became very popular with both country and rock-n-roll musicians through the 1960s.

Outbid in their attempt to buy Fender in 1965, the D. H. Baldwin company bought Gretsch in 1967, and Gretsch, Jr. was made a director of Baldwin. Baldwin had previously acquired the manufacturing facilities of England's James Ormstron Burns (Burns Guitars) in September 1965, and Baldwin was assembling the imported Burns parts in Booneville, Arkansas. In a business consolidation, The New York Gretsch operation was moved down to the Arkansas facility in 1970. Production focused on Gretsch, and Burns guitars were basically discontinued.

In January of 1973 the Booneville plant suffered a serious fire. Baldwin made the decision to discontinue guitar building operations. Three months later, long-time manager Bill Hagner formed the Hagner Musical Instruments company and formed an agreement with Baldwin to build and sell Gretsch guitars to Baldwin from the Booneville facility. Baldwin would still retain the rights to the trademark. Another fire broke out in December of the same year, but the operation recovered. Baldwin stepped in and regained control of the operation in December of 1978, the same year that they bought the Kustom Amplifier company in Chanute, Kansas. Gretsch production was briefly moved to the Kansas facility, and by 1982 they moved again to Gallatin, Tennessee. 1981 was probably the last date of guitar production, but Gretsch drum products were continued at Tennessee. In 1983 the production had again returned to Arkansas.

Baldwin had experimented briefly with guitar production at their Mexican organ facilities, producing perhaps 100 *Southern Belle* guitars (basically renamed Country Gentlemans) between 1978 and 1979. When Gretsch production returned to Arkansas in 1983, the Baldwin company asked Charles Kramer to come out of retirement and help bring the business back (which he did). In 1984, Baldwin also sold off their rights to Kustom amps. In 1985 Kramer brokered a deal between Baldwin and Fred Gretsch III that returned the trademark back to the family.

Kramer and Gretsch III developed the specifications for the reissue models that are currently being built by the Terada company in Japan. The majority of Japanese-produced Gretsch models are brokered in the U.S. market; however, there has been some "grey market" Japan-only models that have been brought into the U.S. One such model, the White Penguin Reissue, was briefly offered through Gretsch to the U.S. market - it is estimated that perhaps a dozen or so were sold through dealers.

In 1995, three models were introduced that are currently built in the U.S: **Country Club 1955** (model G6196-1955), **Nashville 1955** (model G6120-1955), and the **White Falcon I - 1955** (model G6136-1955).

(Later company history courtesy Michael Wright, Guitar Stories Volume One)

Charles *Duke* Kramer first joined the Gretsch company at their Chicago office in 1935. When Kramer first retired in 1980, he formed D & F Products. In late 1981, when Baldwin lost a lease on one of their small production plants, Kramer went out and bought any existing guitar parts (about three 42-foot semi-trailers worth!). While some were sold back to the revitalized Gretsch company in 1985, Kramer still makes the parts available through his D & F Products company. D & F Products can be reached at: 6735 Hidden Hills Drive, Cincinnati, Ohio 45230 (513.232.4972).

Initial Production Model Codes

The Gretsch company assigned a name and a four digit number to each guitar model. However, they would also assign a different, yet associated number to the same model in a different color or component assembly. This system helped *expedite the ordering system*, says Charles *Duke* Kramer, *you could look at an invoice and know exactly which model and color from one number.* References in this text, while still incomplete, will list variances in the model designations.

Current Production Model Codes

Current Gretsch models may have a *G* preface to the four digit code, and also letters at the end that designate different bridge configuration (like a Bigsby tremolo), or a cutaway body style. Many of the reissue models also have a hyphen and four digit year following the primary model number designation that indicate a certain vintage-style year.

For further information regarding Gretsch acoustic models, please refer to the 7th Edition ***Blue Book of Acoustic Guitars***.

ELECTRIC

The Gretsch company assigned a name and a four digit number to each guitar model. However, they would also assign a **different, yet associated number to the same model in a different color or component assembly**.

Current Gretsch models may have a *G* preface to the four digit code, and also letters at the end that designate different bridge configuration (like a Bigsby tremolo), or a cutaway body style. Many of the reissue models also have a hyphen and four digit year following the primary model number designation. References in this text (while incomplete) will list the model designation and other related designations (colors) related to the model.

Anniversary Series

ANNIVERSARY (Model 6124) - single round cutaway semi-hollow maple body, arched top, bound body, f-holes, raised white pickguard with logo, mahogany neck, 21-fret ebony fingerboard with pearloid thumbnail inlay, roller bridge/G logo trapeze tailpiece, blackface peghead with logo inlay, peghead mounted nameplate with engraved diamond, 3-per-side tuners, chrome hardware, covered pickup, volume control on cutaway bout, 3-position tone switch, available in Sunburst (Model 6124), Two Tone Green (Model 6125), and Two Tone Tan finishes. Mfg. 1958 to 1972.

	100%	98%	95%	90%	80%	70%	60%
1958-1959	**N/A**	**$1,300**	**$1,000**	**$895**	**$775**	**$695**	**$575**
1960-1964	**N/A**	**$1,100**	**$950**	**$875**	**$750**	**$675**	**$550**
1965-1972	**N/A**	**$1,000**	**$900**	**$800**	**$700**	**$600**	**$550**

Two Tone Green finishes command a higher premium.

In 1960, rosewood fingerboard replaced ebony fingerboard. In 1963, the Two Tone Tan was also designated as Model 6125.

GRADING	100% MINT	98% NEAR MINT	95% EXC+	90% EXC	80% VG+	70% VG	60% G

Double Anniversary (Model 6117) - similar to Anniversary, except has 2 covered pickups, 2 volume controls, 3-position selector switch, available in Sunburst (Model 6117) and Two Tone Green (Model 6118) finishes. Mfg. 1958 to 1975.

1958-1964	N/A	$1,500	$1,285	$1,075	$850	$775	$700
1965-1975	N/A	$750	$650	$525	$425	$395	$350

Two Tone Green finishes command a higher premium.

In 1961, stereo output was optional. The Anniversary Stereo model was offered in Sunburst (Model 6111) and Two Tone Green (Model 6112) until 1963. In 1963, bound fingerboard was added, palm vibrato optional, stereo output was discontinued. In 1963, Two Tone Brown was also designated at Model 6118. In 1972, f-holes were made smaller, adjustable bridge replaced roller bridge, peghead nameplate was removed. In 1974, block fingerboard inlay replaced thumbnail inlay, and the sunburst finish designation became Model 7560.

Anniversary Reissue (Model G6124) - similar to Anniversary, except has rosewood fingerboard, available in Sunburst (Model G6124) and 2 Tone Green (Model G6125) finishes. Disc. 1999.

	$1,200	$900	$750	$600	$550	$495	$450

Last MSR was $1,500.

Double Anniversary Reissue (Model G6117) - similar to Anniversary, except has rosewood fingerboard, 2 pickups, 2 volume controls, 3-position switch, available in Sunburst (Model G6117) and 2 Tone Green (Model G6118) finishes. Disc.

	$1,350	$1,000	$850	$675	$600	$550	$500

Last MSR was $1,700.

Add $100 for 2 Tone Green finish (Model G6118).

Sunburst finish discontinued in 1999. (G6117)

Double Anniversary Reissue Left Hand (Model G6118 LH) - similar to the Double Anniversary Reissue, except in a left-handed configuration. Mfg. 1997 to 1999.

	$1,800	$1,575	$1,375	$1,200	$1,000	$800	$575

Last MSR was $2,250.

ASTRO-JET (Model 6126) - offset double cutaway asymmetrical hardwood body, black pickguard, metal rectangle plate with model name/serial number on bass side cutaway, maple neck, 21-fret bound ebony fingerboard with thumbnail inlay, adjustamatic bridge/Burns vibrato, asymmetrical blackface peghead with silkscreen logo, 4/2-per-side tuners, chrome hardware, 2 exposed pickups, 3 controls, 3 switches, available in Red top/Black back/side finish. Mfg. 1965 to 1968.

	N/A	$900	$850	$725	$575	$525	$475

Gretsch Astro
courtesy Thoroughbred Music

ATKINS AXE (Model 7685) - single sharp cutaway bound hardwood body, white pickguard with logo, maple neck, 22-fret bound ebony fingerboard with white block inlay, tune-o-matic stop bridge, bound black face peghead with logo, 3-per-side tuners, chrome hardware, 2 covered humbucker pickups, 2 volume/2 tone controls, 3-position switch, available in Dark Grey (Model 7685) and Rosewood Stain (Model 7686) finishes. Mfg. 1976 to 1981.

	N/A	$900	$850	$725	$600	$525	$475

Atkins Super Axe (Model 7680) - similar to Atkins Axe, except has black plate with mounted controls, volume/3 effects controls, 2 effects switches, active electronics, available in Red (Model 7680), Dark Grey (Model 7681), and Sunburst (Model 7682).

	N/A	$1,100	$925	$875	$625	$550	$500

AXE REISSUE (Model G7685) - similar to the Atkins Axe. Mfg. 1997 to 1999.

	$1,700	$1,475	$1,300	$1,100	$900	$725	$525

Last MSR was $2,100.

BST (Beast) Series

Baldwin-owned Gretsch introduced the BST series from 1979 to 1981, and the series featured lower line models with a solid body construction and bolt-on necks, as well as higher priced models with neck-through designs.

BST-1000 (SINGLE HUMBUCKER) - single cutaway solid body, bolt-on neck, 24-fret fingerboard, tune-o-matic stop bridge, 3-per-side tuners, chrome hardware, humbucker pickup, volume/tone controls, available in Brown (Model 8210) or Red (Model 8216). Mfg. 1979 to 1981.

	N/A	$425	$350	$300	$250	$200	$150

Last MSR was $299.

BST-1000 (Double Humbucker) - similar to the BST-1000, except has two humbucking pickups, 3-way selector switch, available in Brown (Model 8215) and Red (Model 8211). Mfg. 1979 to 1981.

	N/A	$450	$375	$325	$275	$225	$175

The same model designation (BST-1000) was used on the two pickup version as well as the single pickup model. The four digit model/digit code would be the proper designator.

BST-1500 (Model 8217) - similar to the BST-1000, and featured only one humbucker, available in Brown (Model 8217). Mfg. 1981 only.

	N/A	$375	$325	$275	$225	$175	$125

BST-2000 (Model 8217) - offset double cutaway solid body, bolt-on neck, 22-fret fingerboard, available in Brown (Model 8220) and Red (Model 8221). Mfg. 1979 to 1980.

	N/A	$500	$450	$425	$375	$325	$275

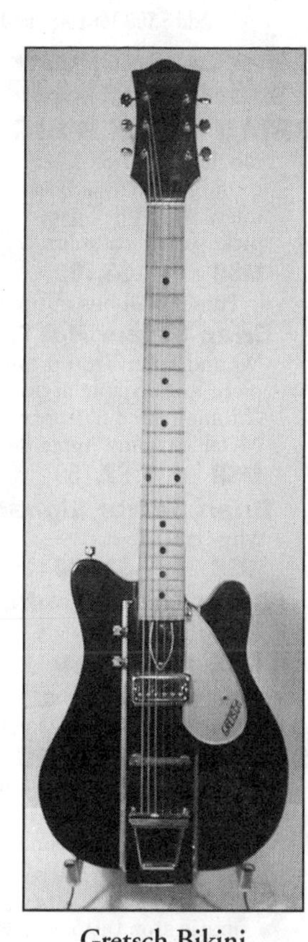

Gretsch Bikini
courtesy Rob Lurvey

G

BST-5000 (Model 8217) - offset double cutaway solid body, laminated neck-through design, 24-fret fingerboard, carved edges around top, available in Red (Model 8250). Mfg. 1979 to 1980.

N/A $500 $450 $425 $375 $325 $275

Last MSR was $695.

BIKINI (Model 6023) - double cutaway slide-and-lock poplar body with detachable poplar center block, raised white pickguard with logo, bolt-on maple neck, 22-fret maple fingerboard with black dot inlay, adjustable ebony bridge/trapeze tailpiece, black face peghead with logo, 3-per-side tuners, chrome hardware, exposed pickup, volume/tone control, available in Black finish. Mfg. 1961 to 1963.

N/A $1,500 $1,200 $1,000 $850 $750 $625

It is estimated that only 35 instruments were produced. The slide-and-lock body is named a "Butterfly" back and is interchangeable with 6-string or bass neck shafts. There is also a "Double Butterfly", able to accommodate both necks (Model 6025). Controls for this instrument are located on top of detachable center block. Double neck Bikini models are priced around $2,000 to $2,500.

Black Falcon Series

BLACK FALCON 1955 SINGLE CUTAWAY (Model G6136 BK) - single round cutaway semi hollow bound maple body, raised gold pickguard with flying falcon, bound f-holes, maple neck, 22-fret bound rosewood fingerboard with pearl block inlay, ebony/metal tune-o-matic bridge/Cadillac tailpiece, bound peghead with pearl gold sparkle logoinlay, 3-per-side tuners, gold hardware, 2 humbucker pickups, master volume/2 volume/1 tone controls, selector switch, available in Black finish. Disc. 1999.

$2,950 $2,600 $2,250 $1,900 $1,600 $1,250 $925

Last MSR was $3,700.

Black Falcon I (Model G7593 BK) - similar to Black Falcon, except has a Bigsby vibrato tailpiece. Disc. 1996.

$2,560 $1,920 $1,600 $1,280 $1,150 $1,055 $960

Last MSR was $3,200.

Black Falcon II (Model G7594 BK) - similar to Black Falcon, except has a double round cutaway body instead of the single cutaway body. Current production.

MSR $3,600 $2,900 $2,500 $2,200 $1,875 $1,550 $1,225 $900

BLACKHAWK (Model 6100) - double round cutaway bound maple body, f-holes, raised silver pickguard with logo, maple neck, 22-fret bound fingerboard with thumbnail inlay, dot inlay above the 12th fret, tuning fork bridge, roller bridge/G logo Bigsby vibrato tailpiece, black face peghead with logo inlay, peghead mounted nameplate, 3-per-side tuners, chrome hardware, 2 covered pickups, volume control on upper bout, 2 volume controls, two 3-position switches, available in Black (Model 6101) and Sunburst (Model 6100) finishes. Mfg. 1967 to 1972.

N/A $1,500 $1,100 $975 $825 $750 $695

The Black finish has a higher premium.

BO DIDDLEY MODEL (Model 6138) faithful reproduction of the famous Bo Diddley rectangular guitar, 17 ¾" X 9 ¼" X 2" rectangular alder body (semi-hollow body), 5-ply maple top, bound top and back, 3-piece rock maple set neck, 1957 style headstock, 3-per-side tuners, ebonized rosewood fingerboard with pearl dot position markers, 22-frets, 25 ½" scale, bone nut, 2 FilterTron pickups with gold covers, 2 Volume/1 Tone control plus master volume, 3-way switch, gold Tune-O-Matic bridge, Gold "G" tailpiece, available in solid red finish. Current Mfg.

MSR $2,500 $1,875 $1,675 $1,475 $1,275 $1,075 $875 $675

Add $300 for Left hand Model (Model G6138LH).

Brian Setzer Series

BRIAN SETZER SIGNATURE (Model G6120-SSL) - single rounded cutaway bound body, arched 5-ply laminated flamed maple top, bound f-holes, 5-ply flame maple back, 7-ply laminated flame maple sides, maple neck, 24.5" scale, 22-fret bound ebony fingerboard with pearl thumbnail inlay, adjustamatic metal bridge with ebony base/Bigsby vibrato tailpiece, bound flame maple veneered peghead with pearl horseshoe/logo inlay, 3-per-side Sperzel locking tuners, gold hardware, raised gold pickguard with artist signature/model name/logo, 2 Gretsch Filtertron humbucker pickups, master volume/2 volume controls, 3-position/tone switches, available in Western Orange Lacquer finish. Mfg. 1994 to date.

MSR $3,700 $2,900 $2,475 $2,200 $1,900 $1,525 $1,225 $875

This model has optional dice volume control knobs (and included).

Brian Setzer Hot Rod (Model 6120SHB, SHT, SHA, & SHP) - similar to Brian Setzer Signature model, except has 2 Specially-Wound Filter-Tron pickups with Alnico Magnets, pickups mounted closer to strings than usual, pickup selector switch, master volume control, 3-piece Rock Maple neck, Ebonized Rosewood fingerboard, silver pickguard with Gretsch logo, oversized f-holes, polished aluminum Bigsby tailpiece, chrome-plated nameplate on headstock, chrome-plated hardware, available in Regal Blue Metallic (G6120SHB), Tangerine Metallic (G6120SHT), Metallic Candy Apple Red (G6120SHA), and Purple Metallic (G6120SHP). New 1999.

MSR $2,750 $2,200 $1,900 $1,700 $1,500

Brian Setzer Signature (Model G6120-SSU) - similar to Brian Setzer Model - SSL, except has Western Orange polyurethane finish. Mfg. 1994 to date.

MSR $3,200 $2,475 $2,075 $1,825 $1,550 $1,300 $1,025 $750

Brian Setzer Limited Edition (Model G6120-SSU GR) - similar to Brian Setzer Model - SSL, except has Green polyurethane finish. Mfg. 1997 to date.

MSR $3,200 $2,475 $2,075 $1,825 $1,575 $1,300 $1,050 $775

Broadkaster Series

BROADKASTER HOLLOW BODY (Model 7607) - double round cutaway semi hollow bound maple body, f-holes, raised black pickguard with logo, maple neck, 22-fret rosewood fingerboard with white dot inlay, adjustable bridge/G logo trapeze tailpiece, blackface peghead with logo, 3-per-side tuners, chrome hardware, 2 covered pickups, master volume/2 volume/2 tone controls, 3-position switch, available in Natural (Model 7607) and Sunburst (Model 7608) finishes. Mfg. 1975 to 1980.

N/A $675 $600 $525 $425 $375 $350

This model was also available with Bigsby vibrato tailpiece in Natural (Model 7603) and Sunburst (Model 7604) finishes. In 1976, tune-o-matic stop tailpiece, 2 covered humbucker DiMarzio pickups replaced original parts/designs. Between 1977 and 1979, a Red finish was offered as Model 7609.

BROADKASTER SOLID BODY (Model 7600) - offset double cutaway maple body, white pickguard, bolt-on maple neck, 22-fret maple fingerboard with black dot inlay, fixed bridge, 3-per-side tuners, chrome hardware, 2 exposed pickups, 2 volume controls, pickup selector/tone switch, available in Natural (Model 7600) and Sunburst (Model 7601) finishes. Mfg. 1975 to 1980.

	N/A	$500	$450	$395	$325	$275	$250

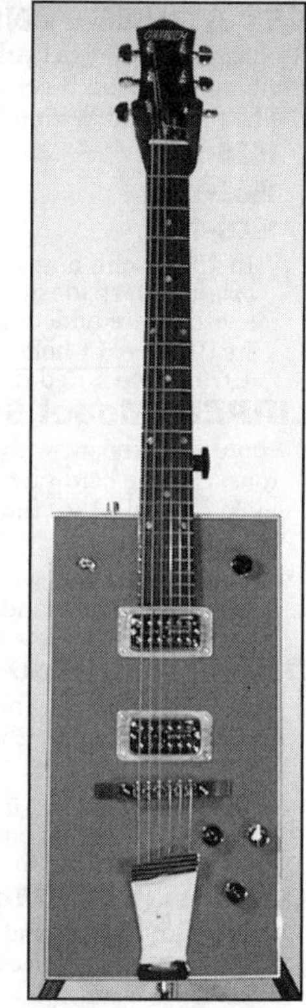

Gretsch Bo Diddley (Model 6138) courtesy Gretsch Guitars

Chet Atkins Models

CHET ATKINS - single cutaway routed mahogany body, bound maple top, raised gold pickguard with signature/logo, G brand on lower bout, tooled leather side trim, maple neck, 22-fret bound rosewood fingerboard with pearl block inlay with engraved western motif, adjustable bridge/Bigsby vibrato tailpiece, bound peghead with maple veneer and pearl steer's head/logo inlay, 3-per-side tuners, gold hardware, 2 exposed DeArmond pickups, control on cutaway bout, 2 volume/tone controls, 3-position switch, available in Red Orange finish. Mfg. 1954 to 1963.

1954-1956	N/A	$4,500	$3,850	$3,250	$2,600	$2,350	$2,125
1957-1960	N/A	$4,500	$3,850	$3,225	$2,575	$2,325	$2,125
1961-1963	N/A	$3,250	$2,800	$2,375	$1,950	$1,725	$1,500

The Bigsby vibrato was available with or without gold-plating. This model was originally issued with a jeweled Western styled strap.

In 1957, an ebony fingerboard with humptop block inlay was introduced, Filter-tron pickups replaced original parts/design, *G* brand and tooled leather side trim were discontinued. In 1958, thumbnail fingerboard inlays replaced block inlays, steer's head peghead inlay replaced horseshoe inlay, tone control replaced by 3-position switch and placed by the pickup selector switch. In 1961, the body was changed to double cutaway style. In 1962, a standby switch was added.

CHET ATKINS COUNTRY GENTLEMAN (Model 6122) - single round cutaway hollow bound maple body, simulated f-holes, gold pickguard with logo, maple neck, 22-fret bound ebony fingerboard with pearl thumbnail inlay, adjustable bridge/Bigsby vibrato tailpiece, bound blackface peghead with logo inlay, peghead mounted nameplate, 3-per-side tuners, gold hardware, 2 covered humbucker pickups, master volume/2 volume controls, two 3-position switches, available in Mahogany and Walnut finishes. Mfg. 1957 to 1981.

1957-1959	N/A	$4,300	$3,700	$3,200	$2,750	$2,250	$1,825
1960-1969	N/A	$2,200	$1,800	$1,450	$1,200	$950	$795
1970-1981	N/A	$1,400	$1,100	$925	$825	$750	$550

A few of the early models had the Chet Atkins signpost signature on the pickguard, but this was not a standard feature. The f-holes on this model were inlaid in early production years, then they were painted on, sometimes being painted as if they were bound. A few models produced during 1960-1961 did have actual f-holes in them, probably special order items. The Bigsby vibrato tailpiece was not gold-plated originally. In 1961, double round cutaway body, bridge mute, standby switch and padded back became available. By 1962, gold-plated vibrato was standard. In 1972, this model became available with open f-holes. Between 1972 to 1980, a Brown finish was offered as Model 7670. In 1975, a tubular arm was added to the Bigsby vibrato. In 1979, vibrato arm was returned to a flat bar.

CHET ATKINS HOLLOW BODY, CHET ATKINS NASHVILLE (Model 6120) - single round cutaway bound maple body, arched top with stylized G brand, bound f-holes, raised gold pickguard with Chet Atkins' sign post signature/logo, maple neck, 22-fret bound rosewood fingerboard with pearl Western motif engraved block inlay, adjustable bridge/Bigsby vibrato tailpiece, bound blackface peghead with steerhead/logo inlay, 3-per-side tuners, gold hardware, 2 exposed DeArmond pickups, volume control on cutaway bout, 2 volume/tone controls, 3-position switch, available in Red, Red Amber and Western Orange finishes. Mfg. 1954 to 1980.

1954-1955	N/A	$7,500	$6,825	$6,300	$5,750	$4,800	$3,900
1956	N/A	$6,950	$5,850	$4,650	$3,850	$3,275	$2,850
1957	N/A	$5,200	$4,785	$4,225	$3,650	$3,100	$2,650
1958-1961	N/A	$4,500	$4,200	$3,725	$2,950	$2,475	$1,850
1962-1967	N/A	$2,500	$2,100	$1,700	$1,450	$1,175	$1,000
1968-1980	N/A	$1,300	$1,100	$975	$850	$725	$650

Some models were available with body matching pegheads. In 1956, engraved fingerboard inlay was discontinued, horseshoe peghead inlay replaced steer's head, vibrato unit was nickel plated. In 1957, humptop fingerboard inlay, Filter-tron pickups replaced original parts/designs, G brand on top discontinued. In 1958, ebony fingerboard with thumbnail inlay and adjustable bar bridge replaced original parts/designs. The tone control changed to a 3-position switch and was placed next to the pickup selector switch. In 1961, body was changed to a double round cutaway semi-hollow style with painted f-holes, pickguard had no signpost around Chet Atkins' signature, string mute, mute/standby switches (a few models were produced with a mute control) and back pad were added. In 1967, this model was renamed the Nashville, with Chet Atkins Nashville on pickguard and peghead mounted nameplate. In 1972, tune-o-matic bridge and elongated peghead were added, string mute and switch, nameplate were removed. Between 1972 to 1979, a Red finish was offered as Model 7660. In 1973, real f-holes were added. In 1975, tubular arm added to vibrato, hardware became chrome plated and the standby switch was removed. In 1979, flat vibrato arm replaced tubular arm.

Gretsch Chet Atkins Country Gentleman courtesy Charlie Wirtz

G

CHET ATKINS TENNESSEAN (Model 6119) - single round cutaway hollow bound maple body, arched top, f-holes, raised black pickguard with Chet Atkins' signpost signature/logo, maple neck, 22-fret ebony fingerboard with pearl thumbnail inlay, adjustable bar bridge/Bigsby vibrato tailpiece, 3-per-side tuners, chrome hardware, exposed pickup, volume control, 3-position switch, available in Cherry, Dark Cherry Stain, Mahogany and Walnut finishes. Mfg. 1958 to 1980.

1958-1961	**N/A**	**$2,500**	**$2,150**	**$1,800**	**$1,425**	**$1,275**	**$1,200**
1962-1968	**N/A**	**$1,250**	**$1,075**	**$895**	**$725**	**$650**	**$595**
1969-1980	**N/A**	**$1,000**	**$850**	**$725**	**$575**	**$500**	**$475**

In 1961, solid maple top with painted f-holes, grey pickguard with logo, bound rosewood fingerboard, tuners with plastic buttons replaced original parts/designs; exposed pickup, 2 volume controls, tone switch were added. In 1962, Chet Atkins signature on pickguard, standby switch were added. In 1963, painted bound f-holes, padded back were added. In 1964, peghead nameplate became available.

In 1970, real f-holes were added. In 1972, adjustamatic bridge replaced bar bridge, peghead nameplate was removed. Between 1972 to 1979, a Dark Red finish was offered as Model 7655.

CLIPPER (Model 6186) - single round cutaway bound maple body, arched top, f-holes, raised pickguard with logo, maple neck, 21-fret ebony fingerboard with white dot inlay, adjustable ebony bridge/trapeze tailpiece, blackface peghead with logo, 3-per-side tuners with plastic buttons, chrome hardware, exposed DeArmond pickup, volume/tone control, available in Natural (Model 6188), Beige/Grey (Model 6187), and Sunburst (Model 6186) finishes. Mfg. 1958 to 1975.

N/A	**$750**	**$675**	**$575**	**$475**	**$375**	**$300**

The original release of this model had a deep, full body. By 1958, the body had a thinner, 335 style thickness to it. In 1963, a palm vibrato was offered as standard, though few models are found with one. In 1968, vibrato was no longer offered. In 1972, 2 pickup models became available. Between 1972 to 1975, a Sunburst/Black finish was offered as Model 7555.

G

COMMITTEE (Model 7628) - double cutaway walnut body, clear pickguard, through-body maple/walnut neck, 22-fret rosewood fingerboard with pearl dot inlay, fixed bridge, bound peghead with burl walnut veneer and pearl logo inlay, 3-per-side tuners, chrome hardware, 2 covered humbucker pickups, 2 volume/2 tone controls, 3-position switch, available in Natural finish. Mfg. 1975 to 1981.

N/A	**$425**	**$375**	**$300**	**$250**	**$225**	**$200**

There are two versions of the Committee model: the dual cutaway body, with a pickguard between the two pickups; and the model with the slightly offset cutaway body (the bass bout is slightly larger than the treble bout). Further research continues on the variations on the Commitee model for future editions of the ***Blue Book of Electric Guitars***.

CONVERTIBLE (Model 6199), SAL SALVADOR MODEL - single round cutaway hollow maple body, spruce top, gold pickguard with logo, bound body/f-holes, maple neck, 21-fret bound rosewood fingerboard with pearl humptop block inlay, adjustable rosewood bridge/G logo trapeze tailpiece, bound blackface peghead with logo inlay, 3-per-side Grover Imperial tuners, gold hardware, exposed DeArmond pickup, volume/tone control, available in Bamboo Yellow and Ivory top with Copper Mist and Sunburst body/neck finishes. Mfg. 1955 to 1968.

1955-1956	**N/A**	**$2,750**	**$2,350**	**$1,975**	**$1,575**	**$1,425**	**$1,295**
1957	**N/A**	**$2,750**	**$2,350**	**$2,000**	**$1,575**	**$1,425**	**$1,300**
1958-1959	**N/A**	**$2,750**	**$2,350**	**$2,000**	**$1,575**	**$1,425**	**$1,300**
1960-1964	**N/A**	**$1,750**	**$1,500**	**$1,250**	**$1,000**	**$900**	**$825**
1965-1968	**N/A**	**$1,750**	**$1,500**	**$1,250**	**$1,000**	**$900**	**$825**

The pickup and controls were pickguard mounted on this instrument. In 1957, ebony fingerboard with thumbnail inlay replaced original fingerboard/inlay. In 1958, this model was renamed the Sal Salvador.

In 1965, block fingerboard inlay replaced thumbnail fingerboard inlay, controls were mounted into the instrument's top.

Corvette Series

CORVETTE (Model 6183) - non-cutaway semi-hollow mahogany body, tortoiseshell pickguard, mahogany neck, 20-fret rosewood fingerboard with pearl dot inlay, 2 f-holes, adjustable rosewood bridge/trapeze tailpiece, black face peghead with logo, 3-per-side tuners with plastic buttons, chrome hardware, single coil pickup, volume/tone control, available in Natural (Model 6183), Sunburst (Model 6182), and Gold (Model 6184) finishes. Mfg. 1954 to 1956.

N/A$	**1,050**	**$950**	**$875**	**$700**	**$650**	**$525**

The semi-hollow Corvette was originally issued as the Electromatic Spanish model. Some models have necks with 21 frets instead of 20.

CORVETTE (Model 6132) - offset double cutaway mahogany body, 2 piece pickguard, mahogany neck, 21-fret rosewood fingerboard with pearl dot inlay, adjustable rosewood bridge/trapeze tailpiece, black face peghead with logo, 3-per-side tuners with plastic buttons, chrome hardware, exposed pickup, volume/tone control, available in Natural (Model 6132) and Platinum Grey (Model 6133) finishes. Mfg. 1961 to 1978.

1961-1962	**N/A**	**$525**	**$450**	**$375**	**$300**	**$270**	**$250**
1963-1964	**N/A**	**$500**	**$425**	**$350**	**$295**	**$250**	**$225**
1965-1969	**N/A**	**$475**	**$400**	**$325**	**$250**	**$225**	**$175**
1970-1978	**N/A**	**$425**	**$375**	**$295**	**$250**	**$195**	**$150**

In 1963, cutaways were sharpened and changed, pickguard styling changed, metal bridge replaced ebony bridge, 1 pickup with vibrato (Model 6134) or 2 pickups (extra tone control and 3-position switch) with vibrato (Model 6135) became optional, Cherry finish was added, and Platinum Grey finish was discontinued. In 1964, peghead shape became rounded with 2/4 tuners per side. In 1966, the Silver Duke with Silver Glitter finish and the Gold Duke with Gold Glitter finish were produced. These guitars were stock 1966 Corvettes (Model 6135) with special finishes that were built specifically for the Sherman Clay Music store chain of the western U.S. Company brochures of the time did not identify the above *Duke* models. These models have been mis-identified as being named after Charles *Duke* Kramer, a long time Gretsch employee - but that was not the case. A small amount of these models exist.

Country Classic Series

COUNTRY CLASSIC SINGLE CUTAWAY (Model G6122 S) - single rounded cutaway semi-hollow bound maple body, bound f-holes, 3-piece maple neck, 22-fret bound ebony fingerboard with pearl thumbnail inlay, ebony/metal tune-o-matic bridge/Bigsby vibrato tailpiece, bound blackface peghead with pearl logo inlay, peghead mounted metal nameplate, 3-per-side tuners, gold hardware, raised gold pickguard with model name/logo, 2 humbucker pickups, master volume/2 volume/1 tone controls, selector switch, available in Walnut Stain finish. Current Mfg.

Body Width 17".

MSR	**$2,700**	**$2,175**	**$1,900**	**$1,675**	**$1,425**	**$1,175**	**$950**	**$675**

Country Classic Double Cutaway (Model G6122) - similar to the Country Classic I, except has double rounded cutaway body.

MSR	**$2,700**	**$2,175**	**$1,900**	**$1,675**	**$1,425**	**$1,175**	**$950**	**$675**

GRADING	100% MINT	98% NEAR MINT	95% EXC+	90% EXC	80% VG+	70% VG	60% G

Gretsch Country Classic Junior courtesy Gretsch

Country Classic 12 String (Model G6122-12) - similar to the Country Classic, except features 12-string configuration, 6-per-side tuners. Mfg. 1997 to date.

MSR $3,100	**$2,500**	**$2,175**	**$1,900**	**$1,600**	**$1,350**	**$1,050**	**$775**

Country Classic 1958 Reissue (Model G6122-1958) - similar to the Country Classic, except features specifications based on the 1958 version. Mfg. 1997 to date.

MSR $2,850	**$2,300**	**$2,000**	**$1,750**	**$1,500**	**$1,250**	**$975**	**$725**

Country Classic 1962 Reissue (Model G6122-1962) - similar to the Country Classic, except features specifications based on the 1962 version.

MSR $2,850	**$2,300**	**$2,000**	**$1,750**	**$1,500**	**$1,250**	**$1,000**	**$725**

Country Classic 1962 Reissue Left-Handed (Model G6122-1962 LH) - similar to the Country Classic 1962 Reissue, except in left-handed configuration. Mfg. late 1994 to 1999.

	$2,625	**$2,325**	**$1,975**	**$1,750**	**$1,425**	**$1,150**	**$825**

Last MSR was $3,300.

COUNTRY CLASSIC JUNIOR (Model G6122 JR) - double rounded cutaway semi-hollow bound body, laminated press-arched maple top and back, 3-ply laminated maple sides (mahogany linings), bound f-holes, set-in 2 piece rock maple neck, 24.6" scale, 22-fret bound ebonized rosewood fingerboard with Neo Classical style pearl (thumbnail) inlay, ebony/metal tune-o-matic bridge/Bigsby vibrato tailpiece, bound peghead with pearl logo inlay, peghead mounted metal nameplate, 3-per-side enclosed tuners, gold hardware, raised gold pickguard with model name/logo, 2 Filtertron pickups, master volume/2 volume/master tone controls, pickup selector switch, available in Walnut and Urethane finishes. Mfg. 1998 to date.

Body Width 14", Body Depth 2 1/4".

MSR $2,200	**$1,750**	**$1,550**	**$1,325**	**$1,125**	**$950**	**$735**	**$525**

Also available in Orange finish (Model G6122 JRO) at no additional cost. Mfg. 2001.

Country Club Series

COUNTRY CLUB (Model 6192) - single round cutaway hollow body, arched laminated maple top, bound body, bound f-holes, raised bound tortoise pickguard, laminated figured maple back/sides, maple neck, 21-fret bound rosewood fingerboard with ivoroid block inlay, Melita bridge/"G" trapeze tailpiece, bound black face peghead with logo, 3-per-side Grover Statite tuners, gold hardware, 2 DeArmond single coil pickups, master volume/2 volume/1 tone controls, 3-position switch, available in Cadillac Green (Model 6196), Natural (Model 6193), and Sunburst (Model 6192) finishes. Mfg. 1954 to 1981.

Body Width 17".

1954	**N/A**	**$3,000**	**$2,750**	**$2,275**	**$1,850**	**$1,375**	**$1,100**
1955-1957	**N/A**	**$2,700**	**$2,450**	**$1,975**	**$1,550**	**$1,050**	**$895**
1958-1959	**N/A**	**$2,500**	**$2,250**	**$1,700**	**$1,375**	**$1,125**	**$950**
1960	**N/A**	**$2,200**	**$1,900**	**$1,400**	**$1,100**	**$975**	**$900**
1961	**N/A**	**$2,100**	**$1,800**	**$1,300**	**$1,050**	**$950**	**$850**
1962-1964	**N/A**	**$2,000**	**$1,700**	**$1,195**	**$1,000**	**$900**	**$825**
1965-1969	**N/A**	**$2,000**	**$1,650**	**$1,150**	**$1,000**	**$900**	**$825**
1970-1974	**N/A**	**$1,800**	**$1,280**	**$1,000**	**$950**	**$895**	**$800**
1975-1979	**N/A**	**$1,400**	**$1,075**	**$950**	**$900**	**$850**	**$775**
1980-1981	**N/A**	**$1,200**	**$1,000**	**$925**	**$875**	**$800**	**$725**

There is a higher premium for the Cadillac Green finish.

In 1955, raised gold pickguard with logo replaced original parts/design. Raised black pickguards may also be found. In 1956, peghead truss rod cover was introduced. In 1958, PAF Filter'Tron humbucker pickups, master/2 volume controls, pickup/tone 3-position switches. In 1959, Grover Imperial tuners replaced original parts/design. By 1960, zero fret was introduced, Pat. Num. Filter'Tron pickups replaced original parts/design. In 1961, thinline body replaced original parts/design. In 1962, padded back, string mute with dial knob, standby switch was introduced. In 1964, Grover "kidney button" tuners replaced original parts/design, padded back, string mute/dial was discontinued. In 1965, deep body replaced original parts/design. In 1968, Cadillac Green finish was discontinued. By 1972, raised grey pickguard with engraved logo, block fingerboard inlay, adjustamatic/rosewood bridge, trapeze tailpiece with logo engraved black plastic insert replaced original parts/design. Between 1972 to 1974, the sunburst designation was changed to Model 7575, and Natural was changed to Model 7576. In 1974, master volume/2 volume/2 tone controls, 3-position switch replaced original parts/designs. In 1975, Antique Stain (Model 7577) finish was introduced, and the Sunburst finish was discontinued. In 1979 only, Walnut finish was available.

Country Club Project-O-Sonic (Model 6101) - similar to Country Club, except has bound ebony fingerboard with pearl thumbnail inlay, Grover Imperial tuners, PAF P.O.S. (Project-O-Sonic) Filter'Tron "stereo" pickups, treble/bass volume controls, 3-position treble/bass/closing switches, available in Cadillac Green (Model 6103), Natural (Model 6102), and Sunburst (Model 6101) finishes. Mfg. 1958 to 1967.

	N/A	**$3,000**	**$2,700**	**$2,300**	**$1,900**	**$1,600**	**$1,250**

In 1959, zero nut, standard Pat. Num. Filter'Tron pickups begin to replace original parts/designs, 3 tone/1 pickup select, 3-position switches replaced original parts/designs.

COUNTRY CLUB (Model G6196CG) single cutaway 17" hollow body design, 2 ¾" depth, 2 Dyna-Sonic pickups, long "G" tailpiece, adjustable bridge, ebony fingerboard with pearl block position markers, 3-per-side tuners, 2 f-holes, detailed binding, gold hardware, available in Cadillac green finish. New 2001.

MSR $3,700	**$2,775**	**$2,475**	**$2,175**	**$1,875**	**$1,575**	**$1,275**	**$950**

Gretsch (USA) Country Club courtesy Fred Gretsch Company

GRADING	100% MINT	98% NEAR MINT	95% EXC+	90% EXC	80% VG+	70% VG	60% G

1955 COUNTRY CLUB CUSTOM REISSUE (Model G6196-1955) - similar to the Country Club, circa 1955. Carved solid spruce top, ebony fingerboard and bridge base, 24K gold plating on hardware, 2 Gretsch Dynasonic pickups, available with hand rubbed lacquer finish, available in Blue Sunburst and Cadillac Green finishes. Mfg. 1995 to 1999.

Body Width 17".

	$6,320	$5,530	$4,820	$4,100	$3,400	$2,690	$1,975

Last MSR was $7,900.

COUNTRY ROC (Model 7620) - single cutaway routed mahogany body, bound arched maple top, raised pickguard with logo, G brand on lower bout, tooled leather side trim, maple neck, 22-fret bound ebony fingerboard with pearl block inlay with engraved western motif, adjustamatic bridge/"G" trapeze tailpiece with western motif belt buckle, bound peghead with figured maple veneer and pearl horseshoe logo/inlay, 3-per-side tuners, gold hardware, 2 exposed pickups, master volume/2 volume/2 tone controls, 3-position switch, available in Red Stain finish. Mfg. 1974 to 1979.

	N/A	$2,250	$1,875	$1,650	$1,525	$1,250	$1,000

DELUXE CHET (Model 7680) - single round cutaway semi-hollow bound maple body, bound f-holes, raised black pickguard with model name/logo, 3-piece maple neck, 22-fret bound ebony fingerboard with pearl thumbnail inlay, tune-o-matic bridge/Bigsby vibrato tailpiece, bound black face peghead with pearl logo inlay, 3-per-side tuners, chrome hardware, 2 exposed pickups, master volume/2 volume/2 tone controls, 3-position switch, available in Dark Red (Model 7680) and Walnut (Model 7681) finishes. Mfg. 1973 to 1975.

1973-1975	N/A	$1,250	$1,050	$900	$750	$625	$550

In 1976, this model was renamed the SUPER AXE, and was discontinued in 1980.

1976-1980	N/A	$1,250	$1,050	$900	$750	$625	$550

DUANE EDDY (Model G6120 DE) - single round cutaway bound body, arched laminated maple top, 7-ply laminated maple back/sides, bound f-holes, raised pickguard with Duane Eddy's signature/logo, rock maple neck, 24.5" scale, 22-fret bound ebony fingerboard with pearl 'hump' block inlay, adjustable Spacer Control bridge/chrome Bigsby vibrato tailpiece, bound blackface peghead, 3-per-side Gotoh tuners, gold hardware, 2 Dynasonic single coil pickups, volume control on cutaway bout, 2 volume/tone controls, 3-position switch, available in Ebony Burst (Model G6120 DE) and Orange (Model G6120 DEO) urethane finishes. Mfg. 1997 to date.

Body Width 16.62", Body Depth 2.8".

MSR $3,700	$3,000	$2,600	$2,250	$1,900	$1,550	$1,225	$925

Duo-Jet Series

These guitars have a single cutaway body, unless otherwise noted. The body construction consists of a top cap over a highly routed body made of pine, maple, mahogany, or spruce. The top was then covered with a plastic material, similar to the covering used by Gretsch on their drums. Duo-Jets also featured a rosewood fingerboard, mahogany neck and 2 DeArmond Dynasonic pickups (again, unless noted otherwise).

DUO-JET (Model 6128) - single cutaway routed mahogany body, bound maple top, raised white pickguard with logo, mahogany neck, 22-fret bound rosewood fingerboard with pearloid block inlay, adjustable bridge/G logo trapeze tailpiece, bound black face peghead with logo, 3-per-side tuners, chrome hardware, 2 exposed DeArmond pickups, master volume/2 volume/1 tone control, 3-position switch, available in Black and Sparkle finishes. Mfg. 1953 to 1971.

1953-1955	N/A	$2,850	$2,450	$2,000	$1,650	$1,475	$1,350
1956	N/A	$2,750	$2,350	$1,950	$1,500	$1,350	$1,250
1957	N/A	$2,500	$2,100	$1,725	$1,350	$1,175	$1,050
1958-1960	N/A	$2,250	$1,950	$1,550	$1,100	$1,075	$975
1961-1962	N/A	$1,900	$1,625	$1,225	$1,025	$975	$850
1963-1966	N/A	$1,650	$1,325	$1,100	$895	$795	$725
1967	N/A	$1,300	$1,075	$995	$900	$825	$750
1968-1971	N/A	$1,050	$895	$825	$775	$625	$575

This model was available as a custom order instrument with Green finish and gold hardware. In 1956, humptop fingerboard inlay replaced block inlay. In 1957, Filter-tron pickups replaced original parts/design. In 1958, thumbnail fingerboard inlay and roller bridge replaced the original parts/designs, 3-position switch replaced tone control and placed by the other switch. In 1961, double cutaway body became available. In 1962, gold pickguard, Burns vibrato, gold hardware and standby switch replaced, or were added, items. From 1963-1966, Sparkle finishes were offered. In 1968, Bigsby vibrato replaced existing vibrato/tailpiece, treble boost switch added.

DUO JET (G6128) - single round cutaway mahogany body, bound arched maple top, raised white pickguard with logo, mahogany neck, 22-fret bound rosewood fingerboard with pearl humpblock inlay, adjustamatic bridge/G logo trapeze tailpiece, bound blackface peghead with pearl horseshoe/logo inlay, 3-per-side tuners, chrome hardware, 2 humbucker pickups, master/2 volume/1 tone controls, selector switch, available in Jet Black top finish. Mfg. 1990 to date.

MSR $1,950	$1,550	$1,375	$1,200	$1,050	$850	$675	$485

Add $150 for optional chrome Bigsby tremolo (Model G6128 T).

Add $50 for Pumpkin finish (Model G6128 PT)

Duo-Jet Doubleneck (G6128T-6/12) - similar to the Duo Jet (G6128), except features two necks (doubleneck configuration). Mfg. 1998 to present.

MSR $4,500	$3,600	$3,100	$2,700	$2,275	$1,900	$1,500	$1,125

DUO JET 1957 REISSUE (Model G6128-1957) - single round cutaway mahogany body, bound arched maple top, raised white pickguard with logo, mahogany neck, 22-fret bound rosewood fingerboard with pearl humpblock inlay, adjustamatic metal bridge with rosewood base/tailpiece, bound blackface peghead with pearl logo inlay, 3-per-side tuners, chrome hardware, 2 humbucker pickups, master volume/2 volume/1 tone controls, 3-position switch, available in Black finish. Mfg. 1994 to date.

MSR $2,500	$1,999	$1,750	$1,525	$1,325	$1,050	$850	$625

Add $100 for optional chrome Bigsby tremolo (Model G6128 T-1957).

This model has an optional G logo trapeze tailpiece.

GRADING		100% MINT	98% NEAR MINT	95% EXC+	90% EXC	80% VG+	70% VG	60% G

Duo Jet 1957 Reissue Left-Handed (Model G6128-1957 LH) - similar to the Duo Jet 1957 Reissue, except in left-handed configuration. Mfg. late 1994 to present.

MSR	$2,950	$2,375	$2,075	$1,825	$1,550	$1,300	$1,000	$750

Duo Jet 1962 Reissue with Bigsby (Model G6128T-1962) - similar to the Duo Jet 1957 Reissue, except features specifications based on the 1962 version. Mfg. 1996 to date.

MSR	$2,200	$1,775	$1,525	$1,325	$1,150	$950	$7275	$550

JET FIREBIRD (Model 6131) - similar to Duo Jet, except has black pickguard with logo, 22-fret bound rosewood fingerboard with pearloid block inlay, adjustable bridge/G logo trapeze tailpiece, bound black face peghead with logo, 3-per-side tuners, chrome hardware, 2 exposed pickups, master/2 volume/1 tone control, 3-position switch, available in Red top/Black back/sides/neck finish. Mfg. 1955 to 1971.

1955-1960	N/A	$2,250	$1,950	$1,600	$1,295	$1,150	$1,100
1961-1964	N/A	$1,550	$1,350	$1,110	$895	$795	$725
1965-1971	N/A	$1,500	$1,295	$1,100	$850	$775	$700

A few models were produced without the logo on the pickguard.

Jet Firebird (Model G6131) - similar to Duo Jet, gold pickguard, gold hardware, available in Cherry Red top finish. Current Mfg.

MSR	$2,050	$1,675	$1,425	$1,275	$1,050	$900	$725	$525

Electromatic (Spanish) Series

ELECTROMATIC SPANISH (Model 6182) - hollow bound maple body, arched spruce top, f-holes, raised tortoise pickguard, maple neck, 14/20-fret rosewood fingerboard with white dot inlay, adjustable rosewood bridge/trapeze tailpiece, blackface peghead with engraved logo, Electromatic vertically engraved onto peghead, 3-per-side tuners with plastic buttons, chrome hardware, exposed DeArmond pickup, volume/tone control, available in Natural (Model 6185N) and Sunburst (Model 6185) finishes. Mfg. 1940 to 1959.

1940-1949	N/A	$850	$700	$650	$600	$525	$475
1950-1959	N/A	$450	$400	$350	$300	$250	$225

The original (1940) version of this model had a larger body style. By 1949, the body style was 16 inches across the bottom bouts. In 1952, the Sunburst finish was redesignated Model 6182, and the Natural finish was redesignated Model 6183. In 1955, this model was renamed Corvette, with a new peghead design. In 1957, a single round cutaway body became available.

Electro II (Model 6187) - similar to Electromatic, except has 2 DeArmond pickups, available in Natural (Model 6188) and Sunburst (Model 6187) finishes. Mfg. 1951 to 1955.

N/A	$1,500	$1,250	$1,100	$895	$750	$625

Electro IIC (Model 6193) - similar to Electromatic, except has single round cutaway, gold hardware, 2 DeArmond pickups, available in Natural (Model 6193) and Sunburst (Model 6192) finishes. Mfg. 1951 to 1953. Body Width 17".

N/A	$900	$850	$740	$675	$550	$425

In 1953, a truss rod was introduced, Melita bridge repaced original parts/design. In 1954, this model was renamed Country Club.

Historic Series

STREAMLINER (G3150) 16" single cutaway hollowbody design, Laminated maple top, back and sides, 24.5" scale, maple neck with rosewood fingerboard, neoclassical position markers, 2 Dynasonic single coil pickups, "G" tailpiece or Bigsby vibrato tailpiece, available in Cherry Red finishes. Current Mfg.

MSR	$1,555	$1,095	$875	$725

Also available in Black finish (Model G3151).

Add $120 for Cherry Red or White finish with Bigsby tailpiece (Models G3155 and G3156 respectively).

Add $370 for Left Hand model in White or Black finish (Models GG3156LH and G 3156BKLH respectively).

SYNCHROMATIC ARCHTOP (G3110) 16 ¼" single cutaway hollow body design, Laminated Spruce top, Laminated Maple back and sides, maple set neck with rosewood fingerboard, neoclassical position markers, 2 Cat's Eye sound holes, synchronized bridge, 2 single coil Dynasonic pickups, available in Tobacco Sunburst finish. Current Mfg.

MSR	$1,620	$1,150	$925	$750

Also available in Thinline models with choice of Orange or Black finishes.

MSR $1,500.

Malcolm Young Signature Series

These models were developed by Gretsch and Malcolm Young (AC/DC), with assistance by Young's guitar technician Alan Rogan. This model is based on Young's early 1960s Jet Firebird that has been modified through the years.

MALCOLM YOUNG SIGNATURE (Model G6131 SMY) - double rounded cutaway bound top, maple top, mahogany back/sides, no f-holes, laminated mahogany neck, 24.5" scale, 22-fret (plus Zero Fret) ebony fingerboard with Neo-Classical (thumbnail) inlays, bound blackface peghead with pearl logo inlay, 3-per-side deluxe enclosed tuners, chrome hardware, BadAss adjustable bridge, Filtertron pickup with Alnico magnets, volume control on cutaway bout, tone control on lower bout, available in Flamed Maple (Model G6131 SMYF), Natural Maple with Satin finish (Model G6131 SMY), and Red (Model G6131 SMYR). Mfg. mid 1996 to date.

MSR	$1,650	$1,300	$1,150	$1.050	$875	$750	$650	$475

Add $100 for Flamed Maple top (Model G6131 SMYF).

Gretsch Duo Jet Double Neck (G6128T-6/12) courtesy Gretsch

GRADING	100% MINT	98% NEAR MINT	95% EXC+	90% EXC	80% VG+	70% VG	60% G

Double Malcolm Young Signature (Model G6131 MY) - similar to the Malcolm Young Signature model, except has two Filtertron pickups, 2 volume/1 tone controls, and pickup selector switch. Available in Flamed Maple (Model G6131 MYF), Natural Maple with matte finish (Model G6131 MY), and Red (Model G6131 MYR). Mfg. mid 1996 to date.

MSR	$1,850	$1,485	$1,285	$1,175	$1,000	$835	$675	$525

Add $100 for Flamed Maple top (Model G6131 MYF)

MONKEES' ROCK-N-ROLL MODEL (Model 6123) - double round cutaway bound maple body, arched top, bound f-holes, raised white pickguard with Monkees/logo, maple neck, 22-fret bound rosewood fingerboard with pearl double thumbnail inlay, adjustable bridge/Bigsby vibrato tailpiece, blackface peghead with pearl logo inlay, peghead mounted nameplate, 3-per-side tuners, chrome hardware, 2 covered pickups, volume control on cutaway bout, 2 volume controls, pickup selector/2 tone switches, available in Red finish. Mfg. 1966 to 1968.

		N/A	$1,295	$1,100	$925	$750	$675	$600

The Monkees' logo appears on the truss rod cover and pickguard.

Nashville Series

NASHVILLE (Model G6120) - single round cutaway semi-hollow bound maple body, raised gold pickguard with logo, bound f-holes, 3-piece maple neck, 22-fret bound ebony fingerboard with pearl block inlay, adjustamatic metal bridge with ebony base/Bigsby vibrato tailpiece, bound blackface peghead with pearl horseshoe/logo inlay, 3-per-side tuners, gold hardware, 2 humbucker pickups, master/2 volume/1 tone controls, selector switch, available in Transparent Orange (Model G6120) or Blue Sunburst (Model G6120 BS) finishes. Mfg. 1991 to date.

MSR	$2,600	$2,075	$1,825	$1,600	$1,350	$1,125	$875	$650

Subtract $50 for Blue Sunburst finish (Model G6120 BS): Retail list price is $2,550.

Keith Scott Nashville (Model 6120KS) - similar to the Nashville, except has brilliant gold top, dark mahogany sides and back, ebony fingerboardwith neoclassical position markers, 16" wide multiple bound body, oversized f-holes, master and individual pickup volume controls, tone control, Gretsch Space Control bridge, Gretsch single coil Dyna-Sonic pickups, 24kt gold-plated hardware, available in Gold Top finish. New 1999.

MSR	$3,700	$3,000	$2,600	$2,300	$2,100	$1,900	$1,600	$1400

Nashville Left-Handed (Model G6120 LH) - similar to the Nashville, except in left-handed configuration. Mfg. late 1994 to present.

MSR	$2,800	$2,250	$1,950	$1,700	$1,450	$1,200	$950	$700

Nashville Double Neck (Model G6120-6/12) - similar to the Nashville, except has a 6-string and 12-string neck configurations. Mfg. 1997 to present.

MSR	$5,000	$4,000	$3,500	$3,100	$2,600	$2,150	$1,700	$1,250

Nashville Western (Model G6120 W) - similar to Nashville, except has stylized G brand on lower bass bout, model name in fence post on pickguard, engraved western motif fingerboard inlay. Current Mfg.

MSR	$2,700	$2,175	$1,900	$1,675	$1,400	$1,175	$925	$675

Nashville Tiger Maple (Model G6120 TM) - similar to Nashville, except has figured maple body/neck. Current Mfg.

MSR	$2,900	$2,335	$2,035	$1,785	$1,550	$1,275	$1,000	$750

Nashville Junior (Model G6120 JR) - similar to Nashville, except features full scale neck/half scale body, available in Brilliant Orange finish. Disc. 1999.

		$1,550	$1,350	$1,175	$1,000	$825	$650	$475

Last MSR was $2,000.

Nashville Junior 2 (G6120-JR2) - similar to Nashville, except features full scale neck/smaller sized body, 2 Filtertron pickups. Mfg. 1998 to date.

MSR	$2,200	$1,750	$1,550	$1,350	$1,100	$900	$800	$650

Nashville 1960 Reissue (Model G6120-1960) - similar to Nashville, except is based on the 1960 model. Current Mfg.

MSR	$2,800	$2,225	$1,975	$1,725	$1,450	$1,200	$950	$700

Nashville 1960 Reissue Left-Handed (Model G6120-1960 LH) - similar to the Nashville 1960 Reissue, except in left-handed configuration. Mfg. late 1994 to present.

MSR	$3,100	$2,475	$2,175	$1,900	$1,600	$1,350	$1,100	$775

1955 NASHVILLE CUSTOM REISSUE (Model G6120-1955) - single round cutaway semi-hollow bound maple body, raised gold pickguard with logo, bound f-holes, 3-piece maple neck, 22-fret bound ebony fingerboard with pearl block inlay, adjustamatic metal bridge with ebony base/Bigsby vibrato tailpiece, bound blackface peghead with pearl horseshoe/logo inlay, 3-per-side tuners, gold hardware, 2 humbucker pickups, master/2 volume/1 tone controls, selector switch, available in Ebony and Transparent Orange finishes. Mfg. 1995 to 1999.

		$6,000	$5,250	$4,575	$3,900	$3,225	$2,550	$1,875

Last MSR was $7,500.

1955 Western Nashville Custom Reissue (Model G6120W-1955) - similar to the 1955 Custom Reissue, except features an authentic 'G' branded top and western motifs. Mfg. 1997 to 1999.

		$6,375	$5,575	$4,850	$4,150	$3,400	$2,725	$2,000

Last MSR was $7,960.

PRINCESS (Model 6106) - offset double cutaway mahogany body, pickguard with "Princess" logo, mahogany neck, 21-fret rosewood fingerboard with pearl dot inlay, adjustable bridge/trapeze tailpiece, Tone Twister vibrato, body matching peghead with logo, 3-per-side tuners with plastic buttons, gold hardware, exposed pickup, volume/tone control, available in Blue, Pink and White finishes. Mfg. 1962 to 1964.

		N/A	$2,200	$1,900	$1,575	$1,250	$1,125	$1,050

Pickguard color on this model was dependent on body color.

GRADING	100% MINT	98% NEAR MINT	95% EXC+	90% EXC	80% VG+	70% VG	60% G

RALLY (Model 6104) - double round cutaway bound maple body, arched top, f-holes, raised pickguard with sportstripes/logo, maple neck, 22-fret bound rosewood fingerboard with pearl thumbnail inlay, dot inlay above 12th fret, adjustable bar bridge/Bigsby vibrato tailpiece, blackface peghead with logo inlay, 3-per-side tuners, chrome hardware, 2 exposed pickups, volume control on cutaway bout, 2 volume/tone controls, pickup selector/treble boost/standby switches, available in Bamboo Yellow top/Copper Mist back/side (Model 6105) and Rally Green (Model 6104) finishes. Mfg. 1967 to 1970.

	100%	98%	95%	90%	80%	70%	60%
	N/A	$1,150	$975	$900	$750	$675	$650

RAMBLER (Model 6115) - single sharp cutaway 3/4 size hollow bound maple body, f-holes, raised black pickguard with logo, maple neck, 20-fret rosewood fingerboard with white dot inlay, adjustable rosewood bridge/G logo trapeze tailpiece, bound blackface peghead with logo inlay, 3-per-side tuners with plastic buttons, chrome hardware, exposed DeArmond pickup, volume/tone control, available in Ivory top/Black body/neck finish. Mfg. 1957 to 1961.

	100%	98%	95%	90%	80%	70%	60%
	N/A	$1,150	$995	$895	$750	$695	$550

In 1960, a round cutaway replaced original style cutaway.

Roc Jet Series

ROC JET (Model 6127) - single cutaway mahogany body, arched bound top, raised silver pickguard with logo, mahogany neck, 22-fret bound ebony fingerboard with pearloid halfmoon inlay and zero fret, adjustable bridge/G logo trapeze tailpiece, bound black face peghead with "Roc Jet" logo, 3-per-side tuners, chrome hardware, model nameplate on peghead, 2 humbucking pickups, 2 volume/2 tone controls, 3-position switch, available in Black (Model 6130) and Orange (Model 6127) finishes. Mfg. 1969 to 1972.

	100%	98%	95%	90%	80%	70%	60%
	N/A	$1,150	$950	$875	$750	$695	$550

ROC JET (Model 7610) - single cutaway mahogany body, arched bound top, raised silver pickguard with logo, mahogany neck, 22-fret bound rosewood fingerboard with pearloid thumbnail inlay, adjustable bridge/G logo trapeze tailpiece, bound black face peghead with logo, nameplate with serial number attached to peghead, 3-per-side tuners, chrome hardware, 2 exposed pickups, master volume on cutaway bout, 2 volume/2 tone controls, 3-position switch, available in Black (Model 7610), Porsche Pumpkin (Model 7611), Red (Model 7612), and Walnut Stain (Model 7613) finishes. Mfg. 1970 to 1980.

	100%	98%	95%	90%	80%	70%	60%
	N/A	$850	$800	$675	$550	$495	$450

In 1972, the pickguard was redesigned, peghead nameplate was removed. In 1978, tune-o-matic stop tailpiece and covered humbucker DiMarzio pickups replaced original parts/designs.

Gretsch (USA) Nashville
courtesy Fred Gretsch Company

Roundup Series

ROUNDUP (Model 6130) - single cutaway routed mahogany body, bound knotty pine top, raised tortoise pickguard with engraved steer's head,"G" brand on lower bout, tooled leather side trim, maple neck, 22-fret bound rosewood fingerboard with pearl block inlay with engraved western motif, adjustable bridge/G logo trapeze tailpiece with western motif belt buckle, bound peghead with pine veneer and pearl steer's head/logo inlay, 3-per-side tuners, gold hardware, 2 exposed DeArmond pickups, control on cutaway bout, 2 volume/tone controls, 3-position switch, available in Orange Stain finish. Mfg. 1954 to 1960.

	100%	98%	95%	90%	80%	70%	60%
	N/A	$4,250	$3,650	$3,100	$2,450	$2,200	$2,000

This model was also available with mahogany and maple tops. This model was originally issued with a jeweled Western styled strap.

ROUNDUP REISSUE (Model G6121) - single round cutaway mahogany body, bound arched maple top, raised gold pickguard with logo, stylized "G" brand on lower bass bout, mahogany neck, 22-fret bound rosewood fingerboard with pearl engraved western motif block inlay, adjustamatic metal bridge with ebony base/Bigsby vibrato tailpiece, bound peghead with pearl horseshoe/logo inlay, 3-per-side tuners, gold hardware, 2 humbucker pickups, master/2 volume/1 tone controls, selector switch, available in Transparent Orange finish. Current Mfg.

	100%	98%	95%	90%	80%	70%	60%
MSR $2,300	$1,825	$1,625	$1,425	$1,225	$1,000	$775	$575

Silver Jet (Sparkle Jet) Series

SILVER JET (Model 6129) - single cutaway routed mahogany body, bound Nitron plastic top, raised white pickguard with logo, mahogany neck, 22-fret bound rosewood fingerboard with pearloid block inlay, adjustable bridge/G logo trapeze tailpiece, bound black face peghead with logo, 3-per-side tuners, chrome hardware, 2 exposed pickups, master/2 volume/1 tone control, 3-position switch, available in Silver Sparkle finish. Mfg. 1955 to 1963.

	100%	98%	95%	90%	80%	70%	60%
1955-1960	N/A	$5,000	$4,300	$3,675	$3,250	$2,700	$2,100
1961-1963	N/A	$3,800	$3,450	$2,850	$2,295	$2,050	$1,895

Any models with Silver Sparkle finish found after 1963 are Duo Jets with Sparkle finish (see Duo Jet models earlier in this section).

SILVER JET (Model G6129) - single round cutaway mahogany body, bound arched maple top, raised white pickguard with logo, mahogany neck, 22-fret bound rosewood fingerboard with pearl humpblock inlay, adjustamatic bridge/G logo trapeze tailpiece, bound blackface peghead with pearl horseshoe/logo inlay, 3-per-side tuners, chrome hardware, 2 humbucker pickups, master/2 volume/1 tone controls, selector switch, available in Silver Sparkle top finish. Current Mfg.

	100%	98%	95%	90%	80%	70%	60%
MSR $2,200	$1,775	$1,525	$1,375	$1,150	$950	$750	$550

Add $150 for optional Bigsby vibrato tailpiece (Model G6129T).

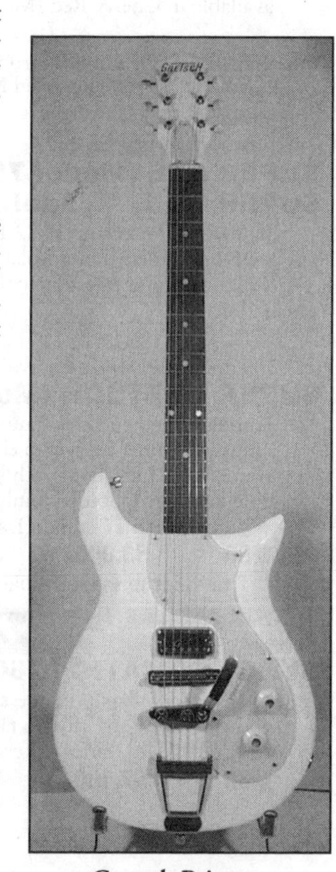

Gretsch Princess
courtesy Wings
Guitar Products

G

GRADING		100% MINT	98% NEAR MINT	95% EXC+	90% EXC	80% VG+	70% VG	60% G

Silver Jet Left-Handed (G6129T-1957LH) - similar to the Silver Jet, except features a left-handed configuration. Mfg. 1998 to present.

MSR	$3,200	$2,575	$2,225	$1,975	$1,650	$1,350	$1,100	$775

SILVER JET 1957 REISSUE (Model G6129-1957) - single round cutaway mahogany body, bound arched maple top, raised white pickguard with logo, mahogany neck, 22-fret bound rosewood fingerboard with pearl humpblock inlay, adjustamatic metal bridge with rosewood base/G logo trapeze tailpiece, bound blackface peghead with pearl logo inlay, 3-per-side tuners, chrome hardware, 2 humbucker pickups, master volume/2 volume/1 tone controls, 3-position switch, available in Silver Sparkle finish. Mfg. 1994 to date.

MSR	$2,600	$1,800	$1,375	$1,175	$925	$825	$750	$675

Silver Jet 1957 Reissue with Bigsby (Model G6129T-1957) - similar to the Silver Jet 1957 Reissue, except has Bigsby tremolo. Mfg. 1994 to date.

MSR	$2,750	$1,825	$1,375	$1,175	$925	$825	$750	$675

Silver Jet 1962 Reissue with Bigsby (Model G6129T-1962) - similar to the Silver Jet 1957 Reissue, except features specifications based on the 1962 version. Mfg. 1996 to date.

MSR	$2,300	$1,835	$1,600	$1,400	$1,200	$1,025	$775	$575

SPARKLE JET (Model G6129TB) - single round cutaway mahogany body, bound arched maple top, raised white pickguard with logo, mahogany neck, 22-fret bound rosewood fingerboard with pearl humpblock inlay, Bigsby tremolo, bound blackface peghead with pearl horseshoe/logo inlay, 3-per-side tuners, chrome hardware, 2 humbucker pickups, master/2 volume/1 tone controls, selector switch, available in Black Sparkle (G6129TB), Champagne Sparkle (G6129TC), Green Sparkle (G6129TG), Gold Sparkle (G6129TAU), Light Blue Pearl Sparkle (G6129TL), and Red Sparkle (G6129TR) top finish. Current Mfg.

MSR	$2,350	$1,875	$1,625	$1,450	$1,250	$1,025	$800	$600

Sparkle Jet 1957 Reissue (Model G6129G-1957) - similar to the Sparkle Jet, except features specifications based on the 1957 Reissue, available in Green Sparkle (G6129G-1957) and Gold Sparkle (G6129AU-1957) top finishes. Current Mfg.

MSR	$2,600	$2,100	$1,825	$1,600	$1,375	$1,150	$900	$675

Streamliner Series

STREAMLINER (Model 6190) - Single cutaway hollow bound body, arched top, f-holes, maple neck, 21-fret bound rosewood fingerboard with pearl 'hump-back' inlay, roller bridge/G logo trapeze tailpiece, blackface peghead with nameplate, 3-per-side tuners with plastic buttons, chrome hardware, plastic pickguard, 1 single coil pickup, volume/tone controls, available in Natural (Model 6191), Yellow/Brown (Model 6189), Gold (Model 6189), and Sunburst (Model 6190) finishes. Mfg. 1954 to 1959.

		N/A	$1,100	$950	$875	$750	$695	$550

In 1958, a humbucker replaced the single coil pickup.

STREAMLINER (Model 6102) - double round cutaway bound maple body, arched top, f-holes, maple neck, 22-fret bound rosewood fingerboard with pearl thumbnail inlay, dot inlay above 12th fret, roller bridge/G logo trapeze tailpiece, blackface peghead with nameplate, 3-per-side tuners with plastic buttons, chrome hardware, 2 covered pickups, master volume/2 volume controls, pickup selector/treble boost/standby switches, available in Cherry Red (Model 6103) and Sunburst (Model 6102) finishes. Mfg. 1969 to 1975.

		N/A	$900	$825	$700	$550	$495	$450

In 1972, dot fingerboard inlay and nameplate were removed, tune-o-matic bridge replaced roller bridge. Between 1972 to 1975, the Red finish was redesignated Model 7566, and the Sunburst finish was redesignated Model 7565.

Super Series

SUPER AXE (Model 7680) - refer to the Deluxe Chet Model.

SUPER CHET (Model 7690) - single round cutaway hollow bound maple body, bound f-holes, raised black pickguard with engraved model name/logo, maple neck, 22-fret bound ebony fingerboard with abalone floral inlay, adjustamatic bridge/trapeze tailpiece with ebony insert with abalone floral inlay, bound blackface peghead with abalone floral/logo inlay, 3-per-side tuners, gold hardware, 2 exposed humbucker pickups, master volume/2 volume/2 tone controls all mounted on the pickguard, available in Red (Model 7690) and Walnut (Model 7691) finishes. Mfg. 1972 to 1980.

		N/A	$1,800	$1,595	$1,275	$1,050	$925	$850

This model was also available with Bigsby vibrato tailpiece.

SUPER GRETSCH (Model G7690) - rounded double cutaway hollow bound body, laminated press-arched maple top and back, 7-ply laminated maple sides, bound f-holes, set-in 2 piece rock maple neck, 25 1/2" scale, 22-fret bound ebony fingerboard with abalone floral inlay, adjustable roller bridge on ebony base/Bigsby tremolo tailpiece, bound peghead with abalone floral/logo inlay, 3-per-side enclosed tuners, gold hardware, raised pickguard with logo, 2 Filtertron pickups, master volume/2 volume/master tone controls (body mounted), pickup selector switch, available in Shaded Golden Sunburst urethane finish. Mfg. 1998 to date.

Body Width 17", Body Depth 2 1/2".

MSR	$3,000	$2,400	$2,100	$1,660	$1,360	$1,200	$1,050	$925

This reissue model is based (in part) on the Super Chet model of the 1970s. Many modern refinements have modified the design.

Synchromatic Series

SYNCHROMATIC (G6040MCSS) - single round cutaway jumbo style, arched maple top, bound 'fang' soundholes, 3-stripe bound body, arched maple back, maple sides/neck, 14/20-fret bound rosewood fingerboard with pearl split humpblock inlay, adjustamatic metal bridge with ebony base/Bigsby vibrato tailpiece, bound blackface peghead with pearl model name/logo inlay, 3-per-side tuners, gold hardware, raised bound tortoise pickguard, humbucker pickup, volume/tone control, pickguard mounted pickup/controls, available in Natural finish. Mfg. 1991 to date.

MSR	$2,500	$2,000	$1,500	$1,250	$1,000	$900	$825	$750

GRADING		100% MINT	98% NEAR MINT	95% EXC+	90% EXC	80% VG+	70% VG	60% G

SYNCHROMATIC JAZZ (G410) (U.S. Mfg.) - single round cutaway multi-bound auditorium style, carved spruce top, f-holes, flame maple back/sides/neck, 20-fret multi-bound ebony fingerboard with pearl split hump block inlay, adjustable ebony stairstep bridge/trapeze tailpiece, multi-bound blackface peghead with pearl logo inlay, 3-per-side Imperial tuners, gold hardware, raised bound flame maple pickguard, humbucker pickup, volume control, pickguard mounted pickup/control, available in Shaded finish. Mfg. 1993 to date.

MSR	$5,700	$4,550	$3,425	$2,850	$N/A	$N/A	$N/A	$N/A

Add $300 for Natural finish. (G410M) 2001.

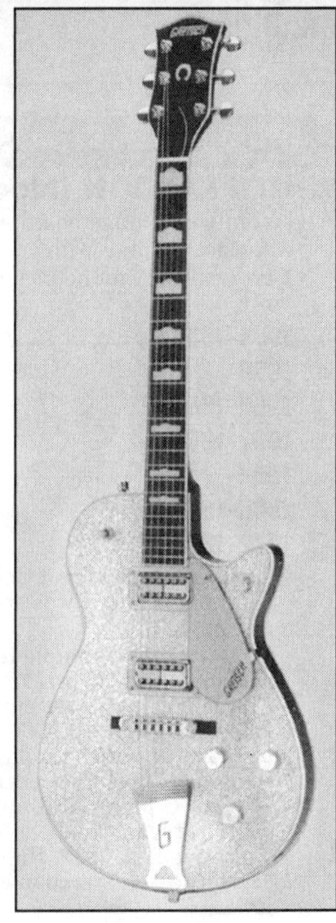
Gretsch Silver Jet
courtesy Fred
Gretsch Enterprises

Tennessee Rose Series

TENNESSEE ROSE (Model G6119) - single round cutaway semi-hollow bound maple body, raised silver pickguard with model name/logo, bound f-holes, maple neck, 22-fret bound rosewood fingerboard with pearl thumbnail inlay, ebony/metal tune-o-matic bridge/Bigsby vibrato tailpiece, black face peghead with pearl logo inlay, 3-per-side tuners, chrome hardware, 2 humbucker pickups, master volume/2 volume/1 tone controls, selector switch, available in Dark Cherry Red Stain finish. Current Mfg.

MSR	$2,300	$1,825	$1,625	$1,425	$1,200	$1,000	$775	$575

Tennessee Rose Left-Handed (G6119 LH) - similar to the Tennessee Rose, except in left-handed configuration. Mfg. late 1994 to date.

MSR	$2,600	$2,075	$1,825	$1,600	$1,350	$1,150	$900	$650

Tennessee Rose 1962 Reissue (G6119-1962) - similar to the Tennessee Rose, except is based on a 1962 configuration. Mfg. 1994 to date.

MSR	$2,400	$1,925	$1,700	$1,475	$1,250	$1,000	$825	$600

TK-300 (Model 7625) - offset double cutaway solid body, white pickguard, bolt-on maple neck, 22-fret rosewood fingerboard with dot inlay, stop bridge, elongated "hockey stick" peghead, 6-on-a-side tuners, chrome hardware, 2 humbucker pickups, volume/tone controls, 3-way pickup selector switch, available in Red (Model 7624) and Natural (Model 7625) finishes. Mfg. 1977 to 1981.

	N/A	$450	$400	$350	$325	$300	$275

VAN EPS (Model 6079) - 7-string configuration, single round cutaway hollow bound maple body, bound f-holes, maple neck, 21-fret bound ebony fingerboard with pearl thumbnail inlay, tuning fork bridge, roller bridge/G logo trapeze tailpiece, bound blackface asymmetrical peghead with pearl logo inlay, peghead mounted nameplate, 4/3-per-side tuners, gold hardware, raised white pickguard with logo, 2 covered humbucker pickups, master volume/2 volume controls, pickup selector/tone/standby switches, available in Sunburst (Model 6079) and Walnut (Model 6080) finishes. Mfg. 1968 to 1979.

1968-1971	N/A	$2,750	$2,275	$1,795	$1,325	$1,100	$925
1971-1979	N/A	$2,350	$1,800	$1,395	$1,125	$995	$875

Walnut finish commands a higher premium.

The above model was a 7-string version. A 6-string version was also offered with 3-per-side tuners in Sunburst (Model 6081) and Brown (Model 6082), though it was discontinued in 1972. In 1972, peghead nameplate, tuning fork bridge and standby switch were removed, ebony bridge and chrome hardware replaced original parts/designs. Between 1972 to 1979, the Brown finish was redesignated Model 7581, and the Sunburst finish was redesignated Model 7580.

VIKING (Model 6187) - double round cutaway hollow bound maple body, f-holes, 21-fret bound ebony fingerboard with pearl thumbnail inlay, offset dot inlay above 12th fret, string mute, roller bridge/Bigsby vibrato tailpiece with telescoping arm, bound blackface peghead with pearl logo inlay, peghead mounted nameplate, 3-per-side tuners, gold hardware, raised pickguard with Viking/logo, 2 covered humbucker rail pickups, master volume/2 volume controls, pickup selector/tone/mute/standby switches, leatherette back pad, available in Cadillac Green (Model 6189), Natural (Model 6188), and Sunburst (Model 6187) finishes. Mfg. 1964 to 1974.

1964-1969	N/A	$1,500	$1,200	$1,00	$925	$850	$775
1970-1974	N/A	$1,200	$1,050	$895	$725	$650	$595

Early models had a Viking ship on the pickguard as well as the logos. In 1966, tuning fork bridge was added. In 1968, flat arm vibrato unit replaced original parts/design. In 1972, string mute, tuning fork and back pad were removed. Between 1972 to 1974, the Natural finish was redesignated Model 7586, and the Sunburst finish was redesignated Model 7585.

GRADING	100% MINT	98% NEAR MINT	95% EXC+	90% EXC	80% VG+	70% VG	60% G

White Falcon Series

WHITE FALCON (Model 6136) - single round cutaway hollow bound maple body, arched spruce top, bound f-holes, maple neck, 21-fret bound ebony fingerboard with pearl "feather engraved" humptop block inlay, adjustable bridge/G logo tubular trapeze tailpiece, bound V styled whiteface peghead with vertical Gold Sparkle wings/logo, 3-per-side Grover Imperial tuners, gold hardware, raised gold pickguard with falcon/logo, 2 exposed DeArmond pickups, master volume on cutaway bout, 2 volume/1 tone control, 3-position switch, available in White finish. Mfg. 1955 to 1981.

	100%	98%	95%	90%	80%	70%	60%
1955-1957	**N/A**	**$18,000**	**$16,000**	**$12,300**	**$10,450**	**$9,700**	**$8,225**
1958	**N/A**	**$15,000**	**$12,000**	**$10,500**	**$9,700**	**$7,850**	**$6,300**
1959-1961	**N/A**	**$12,000**	**$10,575**	**$9,450**	**$8,725**	**$7,450**	**$6,500**
1962-1963	**N/A**	**$6,500**	**$4,925**	**$4,100**	**$3,295**	**$2,950**	**$2,700**
1964	**N/A**	**$5,000**	**$3,425**	**$2,850**	**$2,295**	**$2,100**	**$1,795**
1965-1971	**N/A**	**$3,500**	**$2,800**	**$2,450**	**$2,000**	**$1,650**	**$1,250**
1972-1981	**N/A**	**$3,000**	**$2,275**	**$1,950**	**$1,425**	**$1,100**	**$995**

This instrument had Gold Sparkle binding and jeweled control knobs. The Gold Sparkle binding was not on all bound edges on the earliest models and it was sometimes omitted during this instruments' production run. In 1957, Filter-tron pickups replaced original parts/design.

In 1958, arched maple top, thumbnail fingerboard inlay, horizontal peghead logo, roller bridge and tone switch (placed by pickup selector control) replaced original parts/designs, peghead mounted nameplate was added, though it was not placed on all instruments produced. Stereo output became optional (as Model 6137). In 1959, second version of stereo output offered with 3 tone switches placed by pickup selector switch. In 1960, double mute with 2 controls and back pad were added. In 1962, double round cutaway body and Bigsby vibrato tailpiece became standard, it was offered as an option up to this time. Some models had a *G* logo tubular trapeze tailpiece. Stereo models had master volume control removed and pickup selector switch put in its place. In 1963, mute controls were changed to switches. In 1964, Gretsch G logo vibrato trapeze tailpiece and oval button tuners replaced original parts/designs. In 1965, offset dot fingerboard inlay above 12th fret was added, stereo tone switches were moved to lower bout and controls/switches were reconfigured. In 1966, tuning fork bridge was added. In 1972, Bigsby vibrato unit replaced Gretsch vibrato unit. Between 1972 to 1981, the model was redesignated Model 7594. In 1980, the non-stereo models were discontinued, and the double round cutaway stereo model (Model 7595) was available as a special order item.

White Falcon Reissue - reissue of original White Falcon design, available in White finish. Mfg. 1972 to 1981.

	100%	98%	95%	90%	80%	70%	60%
	N/A	**$4,300**	**$3,700**	**$3,100**	**$2,450**	**$2,200**	**$2,000**

WHITE FALCON 1955 SINGLE CUTAWAY (Model G6136) - single round cutaway semi-hollow bound maple body, bound f-holes, maple neck, 22-fret bound rosewood fingerboard with pearl block inlay, ebony/metal tune-o-matic bridge/Cadillac tailpiece, bound peghead with pearl gold sparkle logo inlay, 3-per-side tuners, gold hardware, raised gold pickguard with flying falcon, 2 humbucker pickups, master volume/2 volume/1 tone controls, selector switch, available in White finish. Mfg. 1991 to date.

	100%	98%	95%	90%	80%	70%	60%
MSR $3,850	**$3,100**	**$2,700**	**$2,350**	**$2,000**	**$1,675**	**$1,325**	**$975**

White Falcon I (Model G7593) - similar to White Falcon 1955 Single Cutaway, except has Bigsby vibrato tailpiece. Mfg. 1991 to date.

	100%	98%	95%	90%	80%	70%	60%
MSR $3,700	**$2,950**	**$2,600**	**$2,250**	**$1,925**	**$1,600**	**$1,250**	**$925**

This reissue model is built in Japan.

White Falcon II (Model G7594) - similar to White Falcon I, except has double round cutaway body and Bigsby tremolo. Mfg. 1991 to date.

	100%	98%	95%	90%	80%	70%	60%
MSR $3,700	**$2,950**	**$2,600**	**$2,250**	**$1,925**	**$1,600**	**$1,250**	**$925**

This reissue model is built in Japan.

Silver Falcon (Model G7594 SL) - similar to White Falcon I, available in Silver finish. Mfg. 1997 to 1999.

	100%	98%	95%	90%	80%	70%	60%
	$2,950	**$2,600**	**$2,250**	**$1,925**	**$1,600**	**$1,250**	**$925**

Last MSR was $3,700.

This reissue model is built in Japan.

WHITE FALCON JR. (Model G7594JR) - similar to White Falcon, except with a smaller, sleeker body, Laminated Maple top and back, gold fleck binding and white/black purfling, 7-ply Laminated Maple sides, f-holes, two-piece Rock Maple set neck, ebony fingerboard, 22-frets, white headstock with gold binding, gold truss rod cover, bone nut, two gold-plated Filtertron pickups, master volume, two pickup volume, master tone, selector switch, gold-plated hardware, available in White urethane finish. New 1999.

	100%	98%	95%	90%	80%	70%	60%
MSR $3,000	**$2,400**	**$2,100**	**$1,900**	**$1,700**	**$1,500**		

1955 WHITE FALCON CUSTOM REISSUE (Model G6136-1955) - similar to White Falcon 1955 Single Cutaway. Carved solid spruce top, ebony fingerboard and bridge base, 24K gold plating on hardware, 2 Gretsch Dynasonic pickups, available with hand rubbed lacquer finish. Mfg. 1995 to 1999.

Body Width 17".

	100%	98%	95%	90%	80%	70%	60%
	$7,125	**$6,250**	**$5,450**	**$4,625**	**$3,825**	**$3,000**	**$2,225**

Last MSR was $8,900.

White Penguin Model

This model debuted at the 1956 Music Industry trade show, and was produced in very small amounts while it was "available" until 1963. The only mention of this model from Gretsch was the appearance on the 1958 and 1959 price lists - it never appeared in any of the Gretsch catalogs.

This guitar is ultra rare; and of the 50 manufactured, only 19 are publicly accounted for. The ***Blue Book of Electric Guitars*** is aware of a small numbers of others not publicly accounted for that are in the hands of private collectors. There are few available (less than a handful) actually on the market as of this edition.

GRADING	100% MINT	98% NEAR MINT	95% EXC+	90% EXC	80% VG+	70% VG	60% G

WHITE PENGUIN (Model 6134) - single cutaway mahogany body, bound arched top, mahogany neck, 22-fret bound ebony fingerboard with pearl *feather engraved* humptop block inlay, adjustable bridge/G logo tubular trapeze tailpiece, bound V styled white face peghead with vertical Gold Sparkle wings/logo, 3-per-side Grover Imperial tuners, gold hardware, raised gold pickguard with penguin/logo, 2 exposed DeArmond pickups, master/2 volume/1 tone control, 3-position switch, available in White finish. Mfg. 1955 to 1963.

	N/A	$80,000	$65,000	$58,500	$47,500	$39,500	$27,500

Originally released with banjo armrest attached to bass lower bout. This instrument had gold sparkle binding and jeweled control knobs. In 1957, Filter-tron pickups replaced original parts/design. In 1958, thumbnail fingerboard inlay, roller bridge replaced the original parts/designs, 3-position switch replaced tone control and was placed by the other switch. In 1959, horizontal logo/metal nameplate was applied to peghead. In 1961, double cutaway body became available.

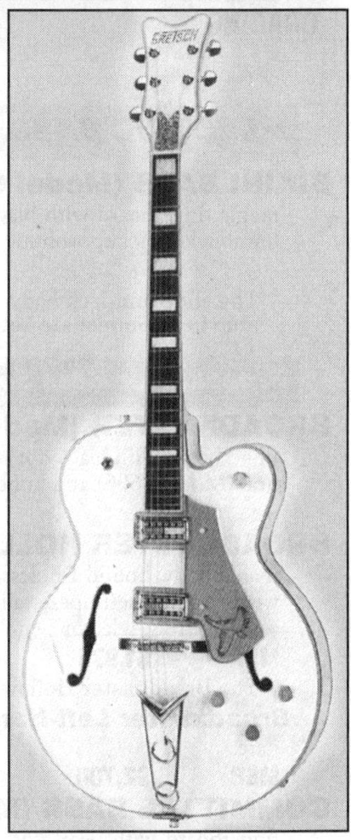

Gretsch White Falcon I (6136) courtesy Fred Gretsch Enterprises

Synchromatic Series

Value line of guitars launched in 2000. Headstocks bear the Synchromatic logo and NOT Gretsch. The Gretsch logo is on the truss rod covers.

BO DIDDLEY (G1810) 17 ¾" X 9 ¾" rectangular body, bolt-on maple neck, rosewood fingerboard with dot position markers, 2 Gretsch humbucker pickups, adjustable bridge, 1 volume and 1 tone control plus master volume and master tone controls, 3-way switch, 3-per-side die-cast tuners, available in Red finish. Mfg. 2000 to date.

MSR	$600	$425	$375	$325	$275	$225	$175	$125

MINI-DIDDLEY (G1850) -compact version of the Bo Diddley model, 8" X 15 ½" body, 20-frets, 1 Gretsch humbucker pickup, bolt-on maple neck with rosewood fingerboard, dot position markers, wraparound tailpiece, 1 volume and 1 tone control, 2-way pickup enhancement switch, die-cast tuners, available in Red finish. Mfg. 2000 to date.

MSR	$450	$315	$275	$250	$225	$195	$150	$110

DOUBLE JET (G1910) double cutaway body, bolt-on maple neck, rosewood fingerboard with dot position markers, 2 Gretsch humbucker pickups, black and white binding, adjustable bridge, pickup selector switch, master volume, 3-per-side die-cast tuners, available in Satin Amber yellow finish. Mfg. 2000 to date.

MSR	$700	$490	$390	$350	$295	$250	$195	$150

Add $50 for Black and Red finishes. New 2001.

Add $100 for Silver Sparkle finish. New 2001.

Add $250 for Silver Sparkle finish and Bigsby tailpiece. New 2001.

JET CLUB (G1413) single cutaway solid body, bolt-on maple neck with rosewood fingerboard, block position markers, 2 gretsch humbucking pickups, chrome Tune-O-Matic bridge, frosted pickguard, 2 volume and 2 tone controls, 3-way switch, 3-per-side die-cast tuners, available in Tobacco Sunburst finish. Mfg. 2000 to date.

MSR	$500	$350	$295	$250	$225	$195	$175	$150

JET PRO (G1514) similar to the other models in the Jet series, except has carved arched top, 2 Gretsch humbucker pickups, set maple neck with rosewood fingerboard, crown position markers, chrome plated Tune-O-Matic bridge, 2 volume and 2 tone controls, 3-way switch, 3-per-side die-cast tuners, available in Cherry Sunburst finish. Mfg. 2000 to date.

MSR	$800	$560	$510	$450	$395	$350	$295	$250

In 2001, Black finish was introduced.

Add $50 for Silver Sparkle finish. New 2001.

Add $150 for Bigsby tailpiece.

JET II (G1315) single cutaway solid body, bolt-on maple neck with rosewood fingerboard, dot position markers, 2 Gretsch humbucker pickups, chrome plated wraparound bridge, frosted pickguard, 1 volume and 1 tone control, 3 -way switch, 3-per-side die-cast tuners, available in Red to Black Sunburst finish. Mfg. 2000 to date.

MSR	$425	$295	$250	$225	$195	$175	$150	$125

JUNIOR JET (G1121) single cutaway solid body, bolt-on maple neck, rosewood fingerboard with dot position markers, chrome plated wraparound bride, 1 Gretsch single coil pickup, frosted pickguard, 1 volume and 1 tone control, 3-per-side die-cast tuners, available in Tobacco Sunburst finish. Mfg. 2000 to date.

MSR	$325	$225	$195	$175	$150	$125	$95	$65

In 2001, Black, Candy Apple Red, Regal Blue, Tangerine and Purple finishes were introduced.

SPARKLE JET (G1615) single cutaway semi-hollow body design, bolt-on maple neck with rosewood fingerboard. Dot position markers, chrome wraparound bridge, 2 volume controls and 1 tone control, master volume, 3-way switch, 3-per-side die-cast tuners, available in Black Sparkle finish. Mfg. 2000 to date.

MSR	$500	$350	$295	$250	$225	$195	$150	$125

Also available in Silver Sparkle, Blue Sparkle, Gold Sparkle, Red Sparkle finishes.

Add $50 for matching sparkle headstock and with 1 f-hole.

Add $150 for Black Sparkle top, back and sides with Bigsby tailpiece. New 2001.

Add $200 for Silver Sparkle top and headstock, with 1 f-hole. New 2001.

1960 Gretsch White Penguin courtesy Art Wiggs

G

GRADING			100% MINT	98% NEAR MINT	95% EXC+	90% EXC	80% VG+	70% VG	60% G

ELECTRIC BASS

BIKINI BASS (Model 6024) - double cutaway slide-and-lock poplar body with detachable poplar center block, bolt-on maple neck, 17-fret maple fingerboard with black dot inlay, adjustable ebony bridge/stop tailpiece, black face peghead with logo, 2-per-side tuners, chrome hardware, humbucker pickup, volume/tone control, available in Black finish. Mfg. 1961 to 1963.

		N/A	$900	$825	$750	$695	$550	$425

The slide-and-lock body is called a Butterfly back and is interchangeable with 6 string or bass shafts. There was also a Double Butterfly, able to accommodate both necks. Controls for this instrument are located on top of detachable center block.

Broadkaster Bass Series

BROADKASTER (Model 7605) - offset double cutaway maple body, white pickguard, bolt-on maple neck, 30 1/2" scale, 20-fret maple fingerboard with black dot inlay, fixed bridge with cover, 2-per-side tuners, chrome hardware, exposed pickup, volume/tone control, available in Natural (Model 7605) and Sunburst (Model 7606) finishes. Mfg. 1975 to 1979.

		N/A	$575	$450	$375	$300	$275	$250

BROADKASTER HOLLOW BODY ELECTRIC BASS (Model G6119-B) - single round cutaway semi hollow bound maple body, bound f-holes, maple neck, 30 1/2" scale, 20-fret bound rosewood fingerboard with pearl thumbnail inlay, adjustamatic metal bridge with ebony base/trapeze tailpiece, blackface peghead with pearl logo inlay, 2-per-side tuners, chrome hardware, 2 humbucker pickups, 2 volume/1 tone controls, selector switch, available in Natural (Model G6119-B) and Transparent Orange (Model 6119-B/O) finishes. Current Mfg.

MSR	$1,975	$1,600	$1,395	$1,225	$1,050	$895	$725	$550

The Broadkaster Hollow Body Electric Bass is also known as the Tennessee Rose/Broadcaster.

Broadkaster Left-Handed (G6119-B LH) - similar to the Broadkaster bass, except in a left-handed configuration. Mfg. late 1994 to date.

MSR	$2,700	$2,175	$1,900	$1,675	$1,425	$1,200	$950	$675

COMMITTEE BASS (Model 7629) - double cutaway walnut body, clear pickguard, through-body maple/walnut neck, 22-fret rosewood fingerboard with pearl dot inlay, fixed bridge, bound peghead with burl walnut veneer and pearl logo inlay, 2-per-side tuners, chrome hardware, exposed pickup, volume/tone control, available in Natural (Model 7629) finish. Mfg. 1977 to 1981.

		N/A	$475	$395	$300	$250	$225	$200

MODEL 6070 (COUNTRY GENTLEMAN BASS) - double round cutaway hollow bound maple body, arched top with painted bound f-holes, finger rests, maple neck, 34" scale, 20-fret rosewood fingerboard with white dot inlay, string mute with switch, roller bridge/G logo trapeze tailpiece, bound blackface peghead with metal nameplate, 2-per-side tuners, gold hardware, covered pickup, volume control, tone/standby switches, round pad on back, available in Amber Red and Sunburst finishes. Mfg. 1962 to 1972.

Body Width 17".

		N/A	$900	$830	$760	$685	$560	$435

After 1972, this model was available only by special order.

Model 6072 - similar to the Model 6070, except has 2 covered pickups, master/2 volume controls, pickup selector/tone/standby switches, available in Sunburst finish. Mfg. 1968 to 1972.

		N/A	$1,200	$1,050	$975	$875	$675	$550

LONG SCALE ELECTRIC BASS REISSUE (MODEL G6072) - double rounded cutaway hollow bound body, laminated maple top and back, 7-ply laminated maple sides, 2 bound f-holes, set-in 3-piece rock maple neck, 34" scale, 20-fret rosewood fingerboard with white dot inlay, adjustable bridge on ebony bass/G logo trapeze tailpiece, 2-per-side tuners, gold hardware, 2 covered pickups, Master volume/2 volume controls, tone/standby/pickup selector switches, round pad on back, available in Shaded Golden Sunburst finishes. Mfg. 1998 to date.

Body Width 17", Body Depth 2".

MSR	$1,975	$1,600	$1,400	$1,300	$1,200	$1,100	$1,000	$850

MODEL 6071 - single round cutaway hollow bound maple body, 29" scale, painted bound f-holes, finger rests, maple neck, 21-fret rosewood fingerboard with white dot inlay, zero fret, string mute with switch, roller bridge/G logo trapeze tailpiece, blackface peghead with logo, 4-on-a-side tuners, gold hardware, covered pickup, volume control, tone/standby switches, available in Red Mahogany finish. Mfg. 1964 to 1972.

Body Width 16".

		N/A	$800	$700	$595	$500	$425	$350

In 1967, chrome hardware replaced gold hardware. After 1972, this model was available only by special order.

Model 6073 - similar to the Model 6071, except has 2 covered pickups, master/2 volume controls, pickup selector/tone/standby switches, available in Mahogany finish. Mfg. 1968 to 1972.

		N/A	$1,000	$895	$725	$650	$525	$425

In 1967, chrome hardware replaced gold hardware.

MODEL 7615 - offset double cutaway asymmetrical mahogany body treble bout cutout, rosewood pickguard with finger rests, mahogany neck, 22-fret bound rosewood fingerboard with white dot inlay, fixed bridge, bound peghead with logo, 2-per-side tuners, chrome hardware, 2 exposed pickups, 2 controls, 3-position switch, available in Mahogany finish. Mfg. 1972 to 1975.

		N/A	$400	$350	$295	$250	$225	$175

TK 300 (Model 7627) - offset double cutaway maple body with divot in bottom, white pickguard, bolt-on maple neck, 20-fret rosewood fingerboard, fixed bridge with cover, chrome hardware, 4-on-a-side tuners, exposed pickup, volume/tone control, available in Autumn Red Stain (Model 7626) and Natural (Model 7627) finishes. Mfg. 1977 to 1981.

		N/A	$375	$325	$275	$250	$225	$175

In 1980, Natural finish was discontinued.

GRADING	100% MINT	98% NEAR MINT	95% EXC+	90% EXC	80% VG+	70% VG	60% G

Synchromatic Bass Series

JUNIOR JET BASS (G1212) single cutaway solid body, bolt-on maple neck, rosewood fingerboard with dot position markers, 2-per-side die-cast tuners, 1 mini-humbucker pickup, adjustable bridge, 1 volume and 1 tone control, available in Black Sunburst finish. Mfg. 2000 to date.

MSR	$379	$265	$225	$175	$150	$125	$95	$65

JUNIOR JET II BASS (G1222) similar to Junior Jet Bass except has 2 humbucking pickups, available in Black Sunburst finish. Mfg. 2000 to date.

MSR	$500	$350	$295	$250	$195	$150	$125	$95

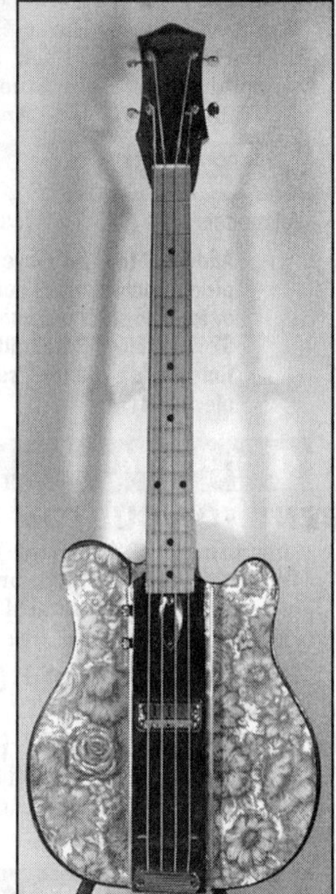

Grosh Bikini Bass
courtesy Jack Wadsworth Jr.

GRIMSHAW

Instruments produced in England from the 1950s through the late 1970s.

While this company is best known for its high quality archtop guitars, they also produced a notable semi-hollowbody design in the mid 1950s called the Short-Scale. In the early 1960s, Emil Grimshaw introduced the Meteor solid body guitar. The company then focused on both original and copies of American designs from the late 1960s on.

(Source: Tony Bacon and Paul Day, The Guru's Guitar Guide)

GRIS GRIS GUITARS

Instruments currently built in New Orleans, Louisiana.

Gris Gris Guitars and Instruments was founded by Ted Graham in 1998. Graham, a rock and rhythm & blues guitar player for the past 33 years, was looking for a guitar with the "perfect look and sound" - so he created one. Using guitar bodies from different sources, Graham commissioned New Orleans Artist Perry Morgan to paint the bodies in one-of-a-kind Voodoo-style designs. Graham also customizes the electronics, to make the guitars "irresistible to the guitar player". All hand-painted instruments are completed in New Orleans. For further information regarding Gris Gris Guitars, contact Ted Graham directly (see Trademark Index).

Perry Morgan is a Magazine Street artist known to Jazzfest fans and others for his ornately painted silks, furniture, and other mediums with a sometime Caribbean tilt. Morgan and Graham attended and studied the 1998 exhibit "The Sacred Arts of Haitian VoDou" at the New Orleans Museum of Art to absorb the themes of the voodoo alters and other art forms from the island. New Orleans still retains its strong Haitian influence, evident today in its food and flavors, architecture, mood, and music.

GROOVE TOOLS

GROOVE TOOLS BY CONKLIN.

Instruments currently built in Korea. Distributed by Westheimer Corporation of Chicago, Illinois.

The Groove Tools line of bass guitars is based on designs from luthier Bill Conklin (see CONKLIN). The instruments are produced in Korea, and re-checked in the U.S. prior to shipping to the dealer thus maintaining a high level of quality.

GT-4 - offset double cutaway Swamp ash body with extended bass bout, figured maple top, bolt-on 5-ply wenge/purpleheart laminated neck with tilt- back headstock, 2-per-side tuners, 34" scale, 24-fret purpleheart fingerboard with dot inlays, fixed bridge, black hardware, 2 Conklin active 'soapbar' pickups, volume/blend/bass/treble controls, available in Clear Hard or Cellophane Magenta finishes. Current Mfg.

MSR $995

GT-5 - similar to the GT-4, except has 5-string configuration, 3/2 headstock. Current Mfg.

MSR $1,095

GT-7 - similar to the GT-4, except has 7-string configuration, 4/3-per-side headstock, 7 piece laminated wenge/purpleheart neck, 2 Bartolini active 'soapbar' pickups. Current Mfg.

MSR $1,695

GT-BD7 Bill Dickens Signature - similar to the GT-4, except has 7-string configuration, 4/3 headstock, 7-piece laminated Maple/Purpleheart neck, through-body design, Swamp ash wings/Curly maple top, gold hardware, 2 Bartolini "Bill Dickens" model pickups, custom Bartolini parametric frequency selector, brilliance/volume/blend/EQ controls, available in Clear Hard or Purple Burst finishes. Current Mfg.

MSR (Club Model) $2,395

Add $100 for fretless model.

This 7-string model was developed in conjunction with bassist Bill Dickens.

Gretsch Long Scale Bass
courtesy Gretsch

GROSH, DON

Instruments currently built in Canyon Country, California since 1992.

Luthier/designer Don Grosh has been repairing and building guitars for the past 15 years. In the 1980s, Grosh worked for a prominent Southern California guitar producer, and has worked with notable guitarists such as Steve Lukather.

For the past five years, Grosh has been offering his fine hand crafted models out of his workshop. Grosh combines state of the art building techniques with quality tone woods and real lacquer finishes for a good looking/good sounding professional instrument.

All models are available with the following standard finishes, unless otherwise listed:

Bursts: Cherry Burst, Honey Burst, Tobacco Burst, Two Color Burst, and Three Color Burst.
Metallic Colors: Black, Blue, Burgundy, Deep Jewel Green, Gold, Purple, Red, and Teal Blue.
Solid Colors: Baby Blue, Black, Vintage Peach, Vintage Red, and Vintage White.
Transparent Colors: Amber, Black, Blonde, Blue, Butterscotch, Cherry, Green, Magenta, Orange, Purple, and Turquoise.

ELECTRIC

All models have a 25 1/2" scale. The following options are available:

Add $160 for bird's-eye maple neck. Add $30 for ebony fingerboard. Add $30 for Jumbo (6100) or Tall Narrow (6105) frets. Add $30 for blend pot (allows pickup combinations not available on standard select switches). Add $30 for locking, standard, or Kluson tuners. Add $50 for white pearl, green pearl, mint, or tortoise shell pickguard. Add $50 for chrome or gold humbucker covers. Add $70 for mahogany or swamp ash body. Add $60 for Wilkinson bridge. Add $240 for Floyd Rose bridge. Add $120 for black hardware. Add $120 for gold hardware. Add $160 for 3 Lindy Fralin single coil pickups. Add $250 for Tie Dye finish. Add $230 for 2 single coil/1 humbucker Lindy Fralin pickups. Add $250 for highly figured (flame or quilt) maple top. Add $600 for RMC MIDI synth electronics.

Bent Top Series

BENT TOP CUSTOM (Model BTC) - offset double cutaway basswood or mahogany body, contoured (bent) figured maple top, bolt-on maple neck, 22-fret maple or rosewood fingerboard with dot position markers, Grosh vintage tremolo or flat mount/string through-body bridge, 6-on-a-side headstock, chrome hardware, white or black pickguard, 3 single coil Seymour Duncan or DiMarzio pickups, volume/tone controls, 5-way selector switch. Current Mfg.

MSR $2,650

Bent Top Custom T (Model BTT) - similar to the Bent Top Custom, except has a single cutaway body design. Current Mfg.

MSR $2,650

FLAT TOP CUSTOM (Model FTC) - single cutaway basswood or mahogany body, figured maple top, bolt-on maple or mahogany neck, 22-fret maple or rosewood fingerboard with dot position markers, stop tail bridge, 6-on-a-side headstock, chrome hardware, 2 humbucking Seymour Duncan or DiMarzio pickups, volume/tone controls, 3-way selector. Current Mfg.

MSR $2,650

Carve Top Series

CUSTOM CARVE TOP (Model CCT) - single cutaway mahogany body, arched (carved) figured maple top, bolt-on maple or mahogany neck, 22-fret maple or rosewood fingerboard with dot position markers, stop tail bridge, 6-on-a-side headstock, chrome hardware, 2 humbucking Seymour Duncan or DiMarzio pickups, volume/tone controls, 3-way selector. Current Mfg.

MSR $2,900

Hollow Carve Top (Model HCT) - similar to the Custom Carve Top, except has hollowed basswood or mahogany body (internal tone chamber).

MSR $2,975

ElectraTone Series

Grosh's new **ElectraTone** series have a retro *Danelectro* feel to them - and that's a good thing! **ElectraTone** models feature a semi-hollow poplar body with a laminated vintage colored top, bolt-on neck, 22-fret rosewood fingerboard, vintage flat-mount bridge. Models are available with a choice of 2 P-90 single coils (**Model GE P-90**), 2 humbuckers (**Model GE H-H**), 2 'lipstick tube' single coils (**Model GE LIPSTICK**), or three single coil pickups (**Model GE SSS**); pickups are mounted to a pickguard. Retail list is $1,195 (the GE SSS 3 retail list is $1,250). A 12-string configuration model (**GE 12**) and a Baritone model (**GE BARATONE**) have been announced for future consideration.

Electric Series

ELECTRIC ACOUSTIC (Model EA) - single cutaway alder body, bolt-on maple or mahogany neck, 22-fret maple or rosewood fingerboard with dot position markers, stop tail bridge, 6-on-a-side headstock, chrome hardware, custom piezo transducer mounted in bridge, volume/tone controls. Current Mfg.

MSR $2,650

Electric Acoustic Trilogy (Model ET) - similar to the Electric Acoustic, except has rosewood bridge and Hipshot Trilogy tuning machine. Current Mfg.

MSR $2,900

Electric Acoustic Hybred (Model ET-H) - similar to the Electric Acoustic, except has magnetic pickups, selector switch. Current Mfg.

MSR $2,900

Electric Classical (Model EC) - similar to the Electric Acoustic, except has rosewood bridge. Current Mfg.

MSR $2,650

Hollow Series

HOLLOW CUSTOM (Model HC) - single cutaway basswood or mahogany hollowed-out body (internal tone chamber), figured maple top, bolt-on maple or mahogany neck, 22-fret maple or rosewood fingerboard with dot position markers, flat mount bridge, 6-on-a-side headstock, chrome hardware, 2 humbucking Seymour Duncan or DiMarzio pickups, volume/tone controls, 3-way selector. Current Mfg.

MSR $2,725

Hollow Silver Sparkle (model HSS) - similar to the Hollow Custom, except has hollowed out alder body, special Silver Sparkle finish on top. Current Mfg.

MSR $2,650

Retro Series

RETRO CLASSIC (Model RC) - offset double cutaway alder body, bolt-on maple neck, 22-fret maple or rosewood fingerboard with dot position markers, Grosh vintage tremolo or flat mount/string through-body bridge, 6-on-a-side headstock, chrome hardware, white or black pickguard, 3 single coil Seymour Duncan or DiMarzio pickups, volume/tone controls, 5-way selector switch. Current Mfg.

MSR $2,250

Retro Classic Pink Sparkle (Model RCPS) - similar to Retro Classic, except has a special Pink Sparkle finish, cream binding on top. Disc.

Last MSR was $2,200.

RETRO CLASSIC VINTAGE T (Model RCVT) - single cutaway alder body, bolt-on maple neck, 22-fret maple or rosewood fingerboard with dot position markers, flat mount/string through-body bridge, 6-on-a-side headstock, chrome hardware, white or black pickguard, 2 single coil Seymour Duncan or DiMarzio pickups, volume/tone controls, 3-way selector switch. Current Mfg.

MSR $2,250

Retro Classic Hollow T (Model RCHT) - similar to the Retro Classic Vintage T, except has hollowed out body (internal acoustic tone chamber). Current Mfg.

MSR $2,450

BARITONE (Model BT) S or T body shape, long scale. Current Mfg.

MSR $2,250

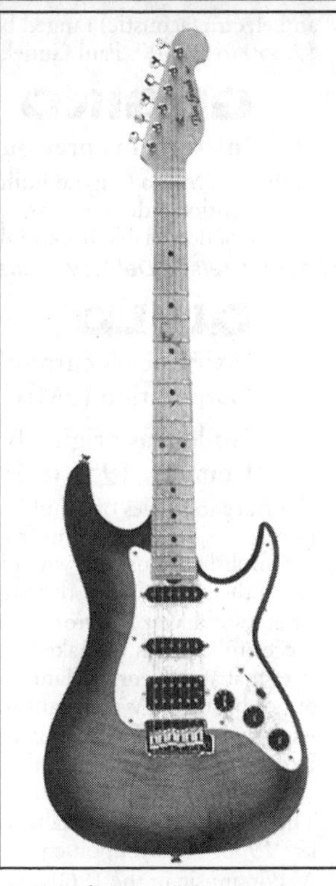

Grosh Bent Top Custom
courtesy Dan Grosh

BASS GUITARS

J4/P4 -retro J or P body style, 4-string, Bad Ass II bridge, Hipshot Ultralight tuners. Current Mfg.

MSR $2,350

J5 - similar to J4, except in a 5-string configuration. 21 or 24-frets, Hipshot 5-string bridge, Hipshot Ultralight tuners. Current Mfg.

MSR $2,600

Add $400 for Quilt or Flame bent "arched" maple top.

GROSSMAN

See chapter on House Brands.

Before World War II, the majority of guitars were sold through mail-order distributors. The Grossman company distributed a number of guitars built for them with their trademark on the headstock.

(Source: Tom Wheeler, American Guitars)

GROVES CUSTOM GUITARS

Instruments currently built in Tucson, Arizona.

Luthier Gordon S. Groves is currently offering hand crafted guitar models. For further information regarding specifications and pricing, please contact luthier Groves directly (see Trademark Index).

GROWLER

See PALMER.

GRUGGETT GUITARS

Instruments currently built since 1961 by Gruggett Guitars located in Bakersfield, California. Distributed by Stark-Marquadt of Bakersfield, California or Jacobson's Service in Denver, Colorado.

Luthier Bill Gruggett originally worked at the Mosrite plant for Semie Moseley beginning in 1962. Gruggett worked his way up to a management position at Mosrite, but when he returned from a vacation in 1966 found that he had been replaced. Gruggett then went to work for another ex-Mosrite employee named Joe Hall, who produced a limited amount of Hallmark "Sweptwing" guitars.

In 1967, Gruggett started his own **Gruggett Guitars**. He built the first forty models of the "Stradette" guitar in his garage, and then moved to a factory in downtown Bakersfield and hired four employees. Between 1967 and 1968, the company started around 300 guitars but only finished 120 of them.

During that same year, Gruggett built thirty-five ES-335-style guitars for Ed Pregor of Hollywood (which carried Pregor's EPCORE label). From 1969 to 1974, Gruggett ran the family's pipe and cable business. Two years later, when Semie Moseley returned to Bakersfield to reopen Mosrite, he called on Gruggett to manage the plant. Unfortunately, Semie's venture ran out of operating capital four months later - and Gruggett was back to building his own models again.

Gruggett Guitars is still in full operation, and luthier Bill Gruggett is building a variety of designs from traditional solid body to hand carved custom guitars.

(Source: Peter Jacobson, Jacobson's Service; and Hal Hammer)

Gruggett Stradette
courtesy Bill Gruggett

GUDELSKY MUSICAL INSTRUMENTS

Instruments previously built in Vista, California from 1985 to 1996.

Luthier Harris Paul Gudelsky (1964-1996) had apprenticed to James D'Aquisto before starting Gudelsky Musical Instruments. Gudelsky's personal goal was to try to build a more modern version of the archtop guitar. Gudelsky offered a small line of instruments exclusively on a customer order basis that included hollow body archtops (acoustic and electric/acoustic) ranged between $4,290 and $5,500; semi hollow bodies ranged from $4,235 to $4,400; and set- neck solid bodies ranged from $2,450 to $3,500. Paul Gudelsky was found fatally shot at his Vista, California home in May, 1996.

GUGINO

Instruments previously built in Buffalo, New York between the 1930s and 1940s.

Luthier Carmino Gugino built instruments that featured high quality conventional building (the frets, finish, carving, etc.) combined with very unconventional design ideas. As detailed by Jay Scott, certain models feature necks that screw on to the body, or have asymmetrical bodies, or an archtop that has a detachable neck/body joint/bridge piece that is removable from the body.

(Source: Teisco Del Rey, Guitar Player magazine)

GUILD

Instruments currently produced in Westerly, Rhode Island since 1969. Distributed by the Fender Musical Instrument Corporation (FMIC) of Scottsdale, Arizona.

Guild was originally located in New York City between 1952 to 1956; production was moved to Hoboken, New Jersey, from late 1956 to 1968. In 1997, Guild (Fender FMIC) opened up a new Custom Shop in Nashville, Tennessee.

Contrary to stories of a guild of old world-style craftsmen gathering to build these exceptional guitars, Guild was founded in 1952 by Alfred Dronge. Dronge, a Jewish emigrant from Europe, grew up in New York City and took jobs working for various music stores on Park Row. Dronge became an accomplished musician who played both banjo and guitar, and loved jazz music. His experience in teaching music and performing in small orchestras led to the formation of the Sagman and Dronge music store.

After World War II, Dronge gave up the music store in favor of importing and distributing Italian accordions. The Sonola Accordion Company was successful enough to make Dronge a small fortune. It is with this reputation and finances that Dronge formed Guild Guitars, Inc. with ex-Ephiphone sales manager George Mann. Incidentally, the *Guild* name came from a third party who was involved with a guitar amplifier company that was going out of business. As the plant was closing down Dronge and Gene Detgen decided to keep the name. The Guild company was registered in 1952.

As the original New York-based Epiphone company was having problems with the local unions, they decided to move production down to Philadelphia. Dronge took advantage of this decision and attracted several of their ex-luthiers to his company. Some of the workers were of Italian ancestry, and felt more comfortable remaining in the *Little Italy* neighborhood rather than moving to Pennsylvania.

The company was originally located in a New York loft from 1952 through 1956. They expanded into a larger workshop in Hoboken, New Jersey, in late 1956. Finally, upon completion of new facilities, Guild moved to its current home in Westerly, Rhode Island, in 1969.

As pop music in the 1960s spurred on a demand for guitars, musical instrument companies expanded to meet the business growth. At the same time, large corporations began to diversify their holdings. Most people are aware of the CBS decision to buy Fender in 1965, or Baldwin Piano's purchase of the Burns trademark and manufacturing equipment in 1967. In 1966 electronic parts producer Avnet Inc. bought Guild Musical Instruments, and Alfred Dronge stayed on as president. Dronge also hired Jim Deurloo (of Gibson and later Heritage fame) as plant manager in December 1969. Deurloo's commitment to quality control resulted in better consistency of Guild products.

Tragedy occurred in 1972 as Alfred Dronge was killed in an aircraft crash. The relationships he built with the members of the company dissipated, and the driving force of twenty years since the inception was gone. However, Leon Tell (Guild's vice president from 1963 to 1973) became the company president in 1973 and maintained that position until 1983.

In mid August of 1986, Avnet sold Guild to a management/investment group from New England and Tennessee. Officers of the newly formed Guild Music Corporation included company President Jerre R. Haskew (previously Chief Executive Officer and President of the Commerce Union Bank of Chattanooga Tennessee), Executive Vice President of Plant and Operations George A. Hammerstrom, and Executive Vice President of Product Development and Artist Relations George Gruhn (Gruhn later left the company in early 1988).

Unfortunately, the remaining members of the investment group defaulted on bank obligations in November of 1988, leading to a court supervised financial restructuring. The Faas Corporation of New Berlin, Wisconsin (now U.S. Musical Corporation) bought Guild in January 1989. Solid body guitar production was discontinued in favor of acoustic and acoustic-electric production (a company strength) although some electric models were reissued in the mid 1990s.

Most recently, the Guild company was purchased by Fender Musical Instrument Corporation in 1995. A recent 1996 catalog shows an arrangement of acoustic and acoustic-electric models, as well as some semi-hollowbody guitars and one solid body electric. Guild has introduced more solid body electrics lately; all current models are based on memorable Guild models from earlier years (such as the Starfire models). In 1997, Guild opened a new Custom Shop in Nashville, Tennessee.

Robert Benedetto signed a formal agreement with the Fender Musical Instrument Corporation (FMIC) on March 5th, 1999 to redesign both the Artist Award and X700 Stuart Models, which will continue to be made at the Guild factory in Westerly, Rhode Island. These newly redesigned models are scheduled for production by 2000. Changes include recarving the tops and backs, changing the bracing, and refining the f-hole and pickguard designs for both models. While the trademark Guild harp-style tailpiece remains, a mother-of-pearl "Benedetto" logo will be inlaid in the 19th fret on both models.

(Reference source for early Guild history: Hans Moust, The Guild Guitar Book; contemporary history courtesy Jay Pilzer; Guild model information courtesy Bill Acton, Guild Guitars, Benedetto information courtesy of Cindy Benedetto.)

IDENTIFYING FEATURES ON GUILD INSTRUMENTS

According to noted authority and Guild enthusiast Jay Pilzer, there are identifying features on Guild instruments that can assist in determining their year of production:

Knobs on Electrics:

1953-58 transparent barrel knobs; 1959-63 transparent yellowish top hat knobs with Guild logo in either chrome or gold; 1964-72 black top hat knobs, Guild logo, tone or vol; circa 1990-present black top hat with Guild logo, no numbers or tone/vol.

Electric Pickguards:

Except for the Johnny Smith/Artist Award (which used the stairstep pickguard), Guild pickguards were rounded, following the shape of the guitar until 1963 when the stairstep became standard on archtop electrics.

Acoustic Pickguards:

Most models have a distinct Guild shape in either tortoise or black with rounded edges that follow the line of guitar, except the F-20, M-20, and new *A* series which have teardrop pickguards.

GRADING	100% MINT	98% NEAR MINT	95% EXC+	90% EXC	80% VG+	70% VG	60% G

Headstock Inlays:

The earliest were simple Guild inverted *V* with triangular insert, with *G* logo below, later the triangular insert disappears, Chesterfield introduced on some models by 1957. In general the more elaborate the headstock, the higher price the instrument.

ELECTRIC ARCHTOPS

CE-100 CAPRI - single sharp cutaway hollow style, arched bound spruce top, raised bound black pickguard, 2 f-holes, maple back/sides/neck, 20-fret bound rosewood fingerboard with pearl block inlay, adjustable rosewood bridge/trapeze tailpiece, blackface peghead with pearl shield/logo inlay, 3-per-side tuners, chrome hardware, single coil pickup, volume/tone control, available in Black, Blonde and Sunburst finishes. Mfg. 1953 to 1984.

N/A $1,500 $1,400 $1,300 $1,250 $1,200 $1,100

This model had an optional Bigsby vibrato. In 1954, harp tailpiece replaced original parts/design. In 1962, humbucker pickup replaced original parts/design.

CE-100 D - similar to CE-100, except has 2 single coil pickups, 2 volume/2 tone controls, 3-position switch. Mfg. 1952 to 1975.

N/A $1,700 $1,600 $1,500 $1,400 $1,300 $1,200

Add $200 for factory-installed DeArmond pickups (a small number were produced with DeArmond pickups at Guild).

In 1962, 2 humbucker pickups replaced original parts/design.

DUANE EDDY 400 - single round cutaway semi-hollow body, arched bound spruce top, f-holes, raised black pickguard with Duane Eddy's signature, maple back/sides, mahogany neck, 20-fret bound rosewood fingerboard with pearl block inlay, adjustable bridge/Bigsby vibrato, bound peghead with pearl Chesterfield/logo inlay, 3-per-side tuners, chrome hardware, 2 covered humbuckers, 2 volume/2 tone controls, 3-position switch, mix control, available in Natural finish. Mfg. 1963 to 1969.

N/A $2,400 $2,300 $2,150 $1,900 $1,700 $1,600

Duane Eddy 500 - similar to Duane Eddy 400, except has figured maple back/sides/neck, ebony fingerboard, gold hardware.

N/A $4,995 $4,800 $4,500 $3,995 $3,600 $3,200

BERT WHEEDON - similar to the Duane Eddy 400, except has a double cutaway and pickguard reads Bert Wheedon. Mfg. 1963 to 1965.

Rarity and lack of activity in the secondary marketplace precludes accurate pricing on this model.
This model was produced for U.K. distribution.

GEORGE BARNES ACOUSTI-LECTRIC - single round cutaway hollow style, arched bound spruce top, bound pickup holes, raised black pickguard with logo, figured maple back/sides/neck, 20-fret bound rosewood fingerboard with pearl block inlay, adjustable rosewood bridge/harp style tailpiece, bound peghead with pearl shield/logo inlay, 3-per-side tuners with pearl buttons, chrome hardware, 2 covered humbucker pickups, 2 volume/2 tone controls, 3-position switch, pickguard mounted controls, available in Natural finish. Mfg. 1964-1967.

Rarity and lack of activity in the secondary marketplace precludes accurate pricing on this model.
Bound slots were placed into the top of this instrument so that the pickups would not touch the top.

GEORGE BARNES Guitar in F - single round cutaway hollow small body, spruce top, bound pickup holes, raised black pickguard with logo, mahogany back/sides/neck, 20-fret bound rosewood fingerboard with pearl block inlay, adjustable rosewood bridge/harp tailpiece, bound blackface peghead with pearl f/logo inlay, 3-per-side tuners, chrome hardware, 2 humbucker pickups, 2 volume/2 tone pickguard mounted controls, 3-position switch. Mfg. 1963 to 1965.

Rarity and lack of activity in the secondary marketplace precludes accurate pricing on this model.
The pickups in this instrument were held in place by a lengthwise support and did not touch the top of the guitar.

M-65 - single round cutaway hollowed mahogany body, bound spruce top, 2 f-holes, raised black laminated pickguard, mahogany neck, 22-fret bound rosewood fingerboard with pearl block inlay, adjustable metal bridge/harp tailpiece, blackface peghead with pearl logo inlay, 3-per-side tuners, nickel hardware, single coil pickup, volume/tone controls, available in Sunburst finish. Mfg. 1962 to 1968.

N/A $1,250 $1,150 $1,050 $950 $850 $800

M-65 3/4 - similar to M-65, except has smaller body/scale length. Mfg. 1962 to 1970.

N/A $1,050 $995 $900 $850 $800 $750

Robert Bendetto Series

BENNY (BENEDETTO BRAND) carved Sitka spruce top, carved mahogany body and neck, ebony fretboard, combination bridge and stopbar, Bendetto pickups, available in Natural or Claret finish.

MSR $5,000

BENNY 7 (BENEDETTO BRAND) similar to Benny model, except has 7 strings.

MSR $6,000

FRATELLO (BENEDETTO BRAND) hand graduated tuned and very select European spruce top, hand carved highly flamed European maple back and sides, ebony fingerrest and fretboard, large block mother-of-pearl inlays, 25 in. scale, Benedetto Model S6 suspended pickup.

MSR $14,000

GRADING	100% MINT	98% NEAR MINT	95% EXC+	90% EXC	80% VG+	70% VG	60% G

MANHATTAN (BENEDETTO BRAND) top-of-the-line Jazz guitar, fine lined binding throughout, hand graduated tuned and very select European spruce top, hand carved highly flamed European maple back and sides, ebony fingerrest and fretboard, 25 in. scale, Benedetto Model S6 suspended pickup, available in Honey Blonde, Antique Burst, or Opulent Brown finish.

MSR $15,000

STUART (BENEDETTO SIGNATURE MODEL)

MSR $9,000

In late 1999, this model was redesigned by Robert Benedetto, with limited production beginning at the Westerly, RI plant. New features include recarved top and back, refined f-hole and pickguard design, changed bracing, and mother-of-pearl "Benedetto" logo inlay on the 19th fret.

M-75 Aristocrat/M-75 Bluesbird/Bluesbird Series

M-75 ARISTOCRAT - single rounded cutaway hollow mahogany body, bound spruce top, raised black laminated pickguard, mahogany neck, 22-fret bound rosewood fingerboard with pearl block inlay, adjustable metal bridge/harp tailpiece, blackface peghead with pearl logo inlay, 3-per-side tuners, gold hardware, 2 single coil pickups, 2 volume/2 tone controls, 3-position switch, available in Natural and Sunburst finishes. Mfg. 1952 to 1963.

N/A $2,150 $2,050 $1,800 $1,700 $1,600 $1,450

The Aristocrat model was often called the Bluesbird.

M-75 Bluesbird Standard - similar to M-75 Aristocrat, except has semi-hollow body construction, pearl Chesterfield/logo inlay, chrome hardware, 2 humbucker pickups. Mfg. 1968 to 1974.

N/A $1,300 $1,250 $1,200 $1,100 $1,025 $975

Last MSR was $425.

M-75 Bluesbird Deluxe (M-75 G Bluesbird) - similar to M-75 Aristocrat, except has pearl Chesterfield/logo inlay, 2 humbucker pickups, gold-plated hardware.

N/A $1,100 $1,050 $995 $895 $825 $775

Last MSR was $495.

The G designation in the production name indicated Gold-plated hardware.

M-75 S BLUESBIRD STANDARD (M-75 CS BLUESBIRD) - single round cutaway bound mahogany solid body, raised black laminated pickguard, mahogany neck, 22-fret bound rosewood fingerboard with pearl block inlay, tune-o-matic bridge/fixed tailpiece, blackface peghead with pearl Chesterfield/logo inlay, 3-per-side tuners, chrome hardware, 2 humbucker pickups, master volume/2 volume/2 tone controls, 3-position switch, available in Sunburst finish. Mfg. 1970 to 1984.

N/A $900 $850 $825 $800 $750 $700

Last MSR was $425.

The S designation in the production name indicated Solid body (instead of semi-hollow); the C designation indicated Chrome hardware.

M-75 S Bluesbird Deluxe (M-75 GS Bluesbird) - similar to M-75 S Bluesbird Standard (CS Bluesbird), except has gold hardware.

N/A $900 $850 $825 $800 $750 $700

Last MSR was $495.

The S designation in the production name indicated Solid body (instead of semi-hollow); the G designation indicated Gold-plated hardware.

BLUESBIRD - similar to the M-75 S Bluesbird (CS Bluesbird), except had 3 single coils (or 2 single coils/humbucker with coil tap switch). Mfg. 1985 to 1988.

N/A $650 $600 $550 $525 $500 $450

BLUESBIRD (Model 350-6400) - single round cutaway bound solid mahogany body, internal sound chambers, carved maple top, raised black pickguard, mahogany neck, 22-fret bound rosewood fingerboard with pearl block inlay, tune-o-matic bridge/stop tailpiece, blackface peghead with pearl Chesterfield/logo inlay, 3-per-side tuners, chrome hardware, 2 Seymour Duncan SH-1 humbucker pickups, 2 volume/2 tone controls, 3-position switch, available in Black (806), Gold Metallic (853), and Transparent Red (838) finishes. Mfg. 1995 to date.

MSR $2,099 $1,575 $1,385 $1,195 $930 $795 $675 $550

Early models may also feature Natural and White finishes.
List Price includes hardshell case.

Bluesbird AAA Top (Model 350-6400) - similar to the Bluesbird, except features a carved AAA grade figured maple top, available in Amber (820), Cherry Sunburst (830), and Tobacco Sunburst (852) finishes. Mfg. 1998 to date.

MSR $2,399 $1,795 $1,495 $1,250 $1,050 $895 $750 $650

List Price includes hardshell case.

Starfire Series

STARFIRE I - single sharp cutaway thin hollow bound maple body, arched top, f-holes, raised black pickguard with star/logo, maple neck, 20-fret bound rosewood fingerboard with pearl dot inlay, adjustable rosewood bridge/harp trapeze tailpiece, bound blackface peghead with pearl Chesterfield/logo inlay, 3-per-side tuners, chrome hardware, single coil pickup, volume/tone controls, available in Cherry Red, Ebony, Emerald Green and Honey Amber finishes. Mfg. 1961 to 1966.

N/A $1,100 $1,025 $925 $875 $825 $775

This model had an optional mahogany body.
In 1962, humbucker pickup replaced original parts/design.

Starfire II - similar to Starfire I, except has 2 single coil pickups, 2 volume/2 tone controls. Mfg. 1961 to 1972.

1961-1972 N/A $1,250 $1,200 $1,150 $1,100 $1,050 $995

Between 1961 to 1962, some models were built with factory-installed DeArmond pickups.
In 1962, 2 humbucker pickups replaced original parts/design.

GRADING		100% MINT	98% NEAR MINT	95% EXC+	90% EXC	80% VG+	70% VG	60% G

Starfire II (Model 350-7200) - single Florentine cutaway thinline hollow body, raised black pickguard, 2 Guild SD-1 humbuckers, adjustable rosewood bridge/harp tailpiece, chrome hardware, 2 volume/2 tone controls, 3-way toggle, available in Antique Burst (837), Black (806), Blonde (801), and Transparent Red (838) finishes. Mfg. 1995 to date.

MSR	$1,999	$1,499	$1,250	$1,100	$850	$750	$625	$500

Left-handed model (Model 350-7220) available at no additional cost.

List Price includes deluxe hardshell case.

Starfire III - similar to Starfire I, except has Guild Bigsby vibrato, 2 single coil pickups, 2 volume/2 tone controls. Mfg. 1961 to 1970.

1961-1970		N/A	$1,350	$1,300	$1,250	$1,175	$1,125	$1,050

Between 1961 to 1962, some models were built with factory-installed DeArmond pickups.

Starfire III (Model 350-7300) - single Florentine cutaway thinline hollow body, raised black pickguard, 2 Guild SD-1 humbuckers, Bigsby bridge/tailpiece, chrome hardware, 2 volume/2 tone controls, 3-way toggle, available in Antique Burst (837), Black (806), Blonde (801), and Transparent Red (838) finishes. Mfg. 1995 to date.

MSR	$2,099	$1,575	$1,325	$1,095	$895	$760	$650	$525

Left-handed model (Model 350-7320) available for an additional $72.

List Price includes deluxe hardshell case.

STARFIRE IV - double round cutaway semi-hollow bound maple body, raised black pickguard, 2 f-holes, 3-piece maple neck, 22-fret bound rosewood fingerboard with pearl dot inlay, tune-o-matic bridge/harp trapeze tailpiece, pearl Chesterfield/logo peghead inlay, 3-per-side tuners, gold hardware, 2 humbucker pickups, 2 volume/2 tone controls, 3-position switch, available in Black, Blonde, Blue, Green, Red and Walnut finishes. Mfg. 1963 to 1994.

1963-1971		N/A	$1,250	$1,200	$1,150	$1,100	$1,050	$995
1972-1980		N/A	$1,250	$1,150	$1,100	$1,050	$995	$950
1981-1990		N/A	$1,100	$1,050	$995	$950	$900	$850
1991-1994		N/A	$1,225	$1,100	$1,025	$925	$850	$750

Last MSR was $1,900.

In 1972, master volume control was introduced. In 1980, ebony fingerboard, stop tailpiece replaced original parts/design, master volume control was discontinued.

Starfire IV (Model 350-7400) - double cutaway thinline hollow body, raised black pickguard, 2 Guild SD-1 humbuckers, bridge/stop tailpiece, chrome hardware, 2 volume/2 tone controls, 3-way toggle, available in Antique Burst (837), Black (806), Blonde (801), and Transparent Red (838) finishes. Mfg. 1995 to date.

MSR	$2,199	$1,650	$1,325	$1,125	$975	$850	$700	$550

Left-handed model (Model 350-7420) available at no additional cost.

List Price includes deluxe hardshell case.

Starfire V - similar to Starfire IV, except has pearl block fingerboard inlay, Guild Bigsby vibrato, master volume control, available in Cherry Red, Ebony, Emerald Green and Honey Amber finishes. Mfg. 1963 to 1972.

		N/A	$1,400	$1,300	$1,250	$1,200	$1,150	$1,100

Add $100 for Amber or Green finish.

Starfire V (New) (Model 350-7600) - similar to Starfire IV, except Curly Maple top and body, rosewood fingerboard with Pearloid block inlays, two SD-1 Humbucker pickups, Guild Bigsby Model 7 Vibrato, chrome hardware, master volume control, available in Blonde (801), Antique Burst (837), and Emerald Green Transparent (848) finishes. New 1999.

MSR	$2,399	$1,795	$1,525	$1,265	$1,075	$915	$775	$650

Left-handed model (Model 350-7620) available for an additional $65.

Starfire VI - similar to Starfire IV, except has bound f-holes, ebony fingerboard with pearl block/abalone wedge inlay, Guild Bigsby vibrato, bound peghead with pearl shield/logo inlay, gold hardware, master volume control, available in Cherry Red, Ebony, Emerald Green and Honey Amber finishes. Mfg. 1963 to 1979.

		N/A	$1,950	$1,800	$1,750	$1,700	$1,625	$1,575

Starfire XII - similar to Starfire IV, except has 12 strings, 6-per-side tuners, available in Cherry Red, Ebony, Emerald Green and Honey Amber finishes. Mfg. 1966 to 1975.

		N/A	$1,300	$1,250	$1,200	$1,125	$1,075	$995

T-100 - single sharp cutaway semi-hollow body, arched bound spruce top, 2 f-holes, mahogany back/sides/neck, 20-fret bound rosewood fingerboard with pearl dot inlay (later production models do not have bound necks), adjustable rosewood bridge/harp tailpiece, blackface peghead with pearl shield/logo inlay (shield does not appear on later models), 3-per-side Grover tuners, chrome hardware, raised black pickguard with 'Guild' in gold lettering, single coil pickup, volume/tone control, serial numbers appear on both back of headstock and on a paper label visible through the upper f-hole. Available in Blonde and Sunburst finishes. Mfg. 1960 to 1972.

		N/A	$975	$925	$875	$800	$775	$725

T-100 D - similar to T-100, except had 2 single coil pickups, 2 volume/2 tone controls, 3-position switch on upper horn.

		N/A	$1,100	$1,025	$975	$925	$875	$750

GRADING		100% MINT	98% NEAR MINT	95% EXC+	90% EXC	80% VG+	70% VG	60% G

G

ST Series

Studio ST 301 - double cutaway archtop laminated maple body (similar to the T-100 with a double cutaway), one single coil or humbucking pickup.

Body Width 16 3/8", Body Depth 1 7/8".

		N/A	$1,100	$1,050	$995	$950	$875	$800

Studio ST 302 - similar to the ST 301, except has 2 pickups.

		N/A	$1,150	$1,100	$1,050	$995	$925	$850

Studio ST 303 - similar to the ST 301, except has 2 pickups and a Bigsby tremolo.

		N/A	$1,250	$1,200	$1,150	$1,100	$1,025	$950

Studio ST 304 - similar to the ST 301, except has 2 pickups and a thicker body.

Body Depth 2 7/8".

		N/A	$1,350	$1,300	$1,250	$1,200	$1,125	$1,050

X-50 GRANADA - hollow style body, arch spruce top, f-holes, raised black pickguard, bound body, mahogany back/sides/neck, 14/20-fret rosewood fingerboard with pearl dot inlay, adjustable rosewood bridge/trapeze tailpiece, blackface peghead with screened logo, 3-per-side tuners, humbucker pickup, volume/tone controls, available in Sunburst finish. Mfg. 1952 to 1970.

		N/A	$950	$900	$850	$800	$725	$700

T-50 - similar to X-50, except had thinline body. Mfg. 1962 to 1982.

		N/A	$700	$650	$600	$550	$495	$450

X-150 SAVOY (Model 350-8400) - single rounded cutaway hollow body, bound laminated flame maple top, 2 f-holes, raised black pickguard, laminated flame maple back/sides, mahogany neck, 20-fret bound rosewood fingerboard with pearl block inlay, adjustable rosewood bridge/engraved harp tailpiece, pearl Chesterfield/logo peghead inlay, 3-per-side tuners, chrome hardware, Guild SD-1 humbucker pickup, volume/tone controls, available in Antique Burst (837) and Blonde (801) finishes. Mfg. 1998 to date.

Body Depth 3 3/8 inches.

MSR	$2,299	$1,725	$1,435	$1,135	$965	$820	$695	$575

Left-handed model (Model 350-8420) available at no additional cost.

List price includes deluxe hardshell case.

1954-1962		N/A	$1,400	$1,200	$995	$850	$700	
1963-1965		N/A	$1,200	$995	$800	$750	$600	

X-150 D Savoy (Model 350-8500) - similar to the X-150 Savoy, except features 2 Guild SD-1 humbucking pickups, available in Antique Burst (837) and Blonde (801) finishes. Mfg. 1998 to date.

Body Depth 3 3/8 inches.

MSR	$2,399	$1,795	$1,490	$1,285	$1,050	$850	$725	$615

Left-handed model (Model 350-8520) available at no additional cost.

List price includes deluxe hardshell case.

X-160 SAVOY - single round cutaway hollow body, bound curly maple archtop, 2 f-holes, bound black pickguard, curly maple back/sides/neck, 20-fret rosewood fingerboard with pearl dot inlay, adjustable rosewood bridge/Bigsby vibrato tailpiece, pearl Chesterfield/logo peghead inlay, 3-per-side tuners, chrome hardware, 2 humbucker pickups, 2 volume/2 tone controls, 3-position switch, available in Black, Blonde and Sunburst finishes. Mfg. 1991 to 1995.

		$1,200	$800	$795	$625	$575	$525	$475

Last MSR was $1,600.

X-170 MANHATTAN (Model 350-8000) - single round cutaway hollow body, bound curly maple archtop, 2 f-holes, black pickguard, curly maple back/sides/neck, 20-fret bound rosewood fingerboard with pearl block inlay, adjustable rosewood bridge/harp tailpiece, pearl Chesterfield/logo peghead inlay, 3-per-side tuners, chrome hardware, 2 Guild SD-1 humbucker pickups, 2 volume/2 tone controls, 3-position switch, available in Antique Burst (837) and Blonde (801) finishes. Mfg. 1988 to date.

Body Width 16 5/8 inches, Body Depth 2 1/2 inches.

MSR	$2,499	$1,875	$1,595	$1,295	$1,050	$850	$750	$625

Left-handed model (Model 350-8020) available at no additional cost.

Earlier models may have a bound black pickguard and gold hardware.
List price includes deluxe hardshell case.

X-170B Manhattan with Bigsby (Model 350-8100) - similar to the X-170 Manhattan, except has Bigsby bridge/tailpiece. Mfg. 1995 to 1998.

Body Width 16 5/8 inches, Body Depth 2 1/2 inches.

		$1,600	$1,450	$1,300	$1,100	$950	$795	$625

Last MSR was $2,099.

X-175 MANHATTAN - single round cutaway hollow body, bound spruce archtop, 2 f holes, black laminated pickguard, maple back/sides, mahogany neck, 20-fret bound rosewood fingerboard with pearl block inlay, adjustable rosewood bridge/harp tailpiece, blackface peghead with pearl logo inlay, 3-per-side tuners, chrome hardware, 2 single coil 'soapbar' pickups, volume/tone controls, 3-position switch, available in Blonde and Sunburst finishes. Mfg. 1954 to 1984.

1954-1962		N/A	$1,800	$1,750	$1,650	$1,550	$1,400	$1,250
1963-1984		N/A	$1,650	$1,600	$1,500	$1,400	$1,150	$1,050

Until 1958, models had 1 volume and 1 tone controls. In 1962, 2 humbucker pickups replaced original parts/design.

GRADING	100% MINT	98% NEAR MINT	95% EXC+	90% EXC	80% VG+	70% VG	60% G

X-60 - similar to the X-150, except has gold finish.

	N/A	$1,500	$1,400	$1,350	$1,250	$1,175	$1,000

X-350 STRATFORD - single round cutaway hollow style, arched spruce top, raised black laminated pickguard, 2 bound f-holes, multibound body, maple back/sides/neck, 20-fret bound rosewood fingerboard with pearl block inlay, adjustable rosewood bridge/harp tailpiece, blackface peghead with pearl shield/logo inlay, 3-per-side tuners, gold hardware, 3 single coil pickups, volume/tone controls, 6 pickup pushbutton switches, available in Natural and Sunburst finishes. Mfg. 1952 to 1973.

	N/A	$2,300	$2,200	$2,100	$2,000	$1,900	$1,800

In 1962, 2 single coil pickups, 3-position switch replaced original parts/designs.

X-400 - similar to the X-175, except had 2 volume/2 tone controls and an early sunburst finish.

	N/A	$1,750	$1,700	$1,600	$1,500	$1,250	$1,150

X-440 - similar to the X-400, except had Blonde finish.

	N/A	$1,650	$1,600	$1,500	$1,400	$1,150	$1,050

X-500 single round cutaway hollow style, bound arched laminated spruce top, 2 bound f-holes, bound tortoise pickguard, maple back/sides/neck, 20-fret bound ebony fingerboard with pearl block/abalone wedge inlay, adjustable ebony bridge, stylized trapeze tailpiece, bound peghead with pearl shield/logo inlay, 3-per-side Imperial tuners, gold hardware, 2 humbucker pickups, 2 volume/2 tone controls, 3-position switch, available in Blonde and Sunburst finishes. Mfg. 1963 to 1995.

1963-1979	N/A	$2,600	$2,275	$2,075	$1,850	$1,650	$1,450
1980-1995	N/A	$2,300	$1,975	$1,775	$1,550	$1,350	$1,150

Last MSR was $3,300.

X-700 STUART (Model 350-8200) - single round cutaway hollow style, bound arched solid spruce top, 2 bound f-holes, bound tortoise pickguard, German maple back/sides, 5-piece maple neck, 20-fret bound ebony fingerboard with pearl block/abalone wedge inlay, adjustable ebony bridge/stylized trapeze tailpiece, bound peghead with pearl shield/logo inlay, 3-per-side Imperial tuners, gold hardware, 2 Guild SD-1 humbucker pickups, 2 volume/2 tone controls, 3-position switch, available in Antique Burst and Blonde finishes. Mfg. 1988 to 1999.

Body Width 16 5/8", Body Depth 3 1/2".

1988-1999 Mfg.	$2,895	$2,460	$2,250	$1,925	$1,625	$1,385	$1,150

Last MSR was $3,856.

X-700 STUART BENEDETTO - please refer to individual listing within the Robert Benedetto Series.

X-770 STUART (Model 395-8201) - this model was advertised by Guild during 1998 with the following specifications: single cutaway hollow style, solid spruce top, 2 f-holes raised pickguard, maple back/sides/neck, 25 1/2" scale, 20-fret bound ebony fingerboard with pearl and abalone inlay, adjustable ebony bridge, engraved harp tailpiece, bound peghead with pearl shield/logo inlay, 3-per-side tuners, gold hardware, Guild SD-1 humbucking pickup, volume/tone controls. Available in Antique Burst (837) and Blonde (801) high gloss finishes.

While advertised, this model has yet to be manufactured.

Body Width 3 1/2".

Guild X-160 Savoy
courtesy Guild Guitars

ELECTRIC

In the late 1980s Guild imported a number of solid body electrics as entry level instruments that had "Burnside by Guild" on the headstock. Further information on these models can be found under the BURNSIDE listing in the ***Blue Book of Electric Guitars***.

Brian May Series

BRIAN MAY - offset double cutaway bound mahogany body, black laminated pickguard, 24-fret ebony fingerboard with pearl dot inlay, tune-o-matic bridge/Brian May vibrato, blackface peghead with pearl logo inlay, 3-per-side tuners, chrome hardware, 3 single coil Seymour Duncan pickups, volume/tone controls, 6 slide switches, available in Black, Transparent Green, Transparent Red and White finishes. Mfg. 1984 to 1988.

	N/A	$2,700	$2,600	$2,500	$2,400	$2,200	$2,050

BRIAN MAY SIGNATURE - offset double cutaway bound mahogany body, black laminated pickguard, 24-fret ebony fingerboard with pearl dot inlay, tune-o-matic bridge/Brian May vibrato, blackface peghead with pearl logo inlay, 3-per-side tuners, chrome hardware, 3 single coil pickups, volume/tone controls, 6 slide switches, available in Transparent Red finish. Mfg. 1994 only.

	$3,500	$3,400	$3,250	$3,150	$3,050	$2,900	$2,750

In 1994, this model was offered in a limited edition of only 1,000 guitars.

BRIAN MAY PRO - offset double cutaway mahogany body, bound mahogany top, black multilaminated pickguard, 24-fret ebony fingerboard with pearl dot inlay, tune-o-matic bridge/Brian May vibrato, mahogany peghead with pearl logo inlay, 3-per-side Schaller tuners, chrome hardware, 3 single coil Seymour Duncan pickups, volume/tone controls, 6 slide switches, available in Black, Transparent Green, Transparent Red and White finishes. Mfg. 1994 to 1995.

	$1,650	$1,475	$1,300	$1,125	$1,050	$995	$950

Last MSR was $1,800.

Brian May Special - similar to Brian May Pro, except has rosewood fingerboard, tune-o-matic bridge/stop tailpiece, available in Natural finish. Mfg. 1994 to 1995.

	$1,350	$1,200	$1,050	$900	$840	$795	$750

Last MSR was $1,500.

Guild X-500 Stuart
courtesy Guild Guitars

GRADING	100% MINT	98% NEAR MINT	95% EXC+	90% EXC	80% VG+	70% VG	60% G

Brian May Standard - offset double cutaway mahogany body, black multilaminated pickguard, 24-fret rosewood fingerboard with pearl dot inlay, tune-o-matic bridge/stop tailpiece, mahogany peghead with pearl logo inlay, 3-per-side Schaller tuners, chrome hardware, 3 single coil pickups, volume/tone controls, 6 slide switches, available in Black, Green, Red and White finishes. Mfg. 1994 to 1995.

	$900	$800	$700	$600	$560	$530	$500

Last MSR was $1,000.

This model has either 1 single coil/1 humbucker pickups or 2 humbucker pickups (both with coil tap). These pickup configurations were optional.

Crossroads Series

CROSSROADS (CR 1) - single cutaway semi-hollow mahogany body, bound figured maple top, figured maple neck, 22-fret bound rosewood fingerboard with pearl dot inlay, rosewood bridge with white black dot pins, blackface peghead with pearl shield/logo inlay, 3-per-side tuners, chrome hardware, humbucker/piezo bridge pickups, 2 volume/1 tone controls, 3-position switch, available in Amber, Black and Natural finishes. Mfg. 1994 to 1995.

	$1,050	$775	$650	$525	$470	$425	$390

Last MSR was $1,300.

CROSSROADS DOUBLE E - double neck configuration, mahogany body with acoustic side routed out, bound spruce top, mahogany neck, bound blackface peghead with pearl Chesterfield/logo inlay, 3-per-side tuners, chrome hardware; acoustic side features: round soundhole, 22-fret rosewood fingerboard with pearl dot inlay, rosewood bridge with white black dot pins, piezo bridge pickups; electric side features: 22-fret bound ebony fingerboard with abalone/pearl wedge/block inlay, tune-o-matic bridge/stop tailpiece, 2 exposed Seymour Duncan humbucker pickups, 2 volume/2 tone controls, two 3-position switches, available in Black and Natural finishes. Mfg. 1993 to 1995.

	$2,250	$1,500	$1,395	$1,195	$1,075	$985	$895

Last MSR was $2,995.

CROSSROADS DOUBLENECK SLASH SIGNATURE MODEL (Model 395-6120) - oversized (shared) single cutaway mahogany body, bound figured maple top, set-in necks, rosewood fingerboards. 12-string configuration (acoustic): round soundhole, spruce braced soundboard, 6-per-side tuners, custom 'pinless' rosewood bridge, Fishman piezo bridge pickup, Fishman preamp. 6-string configuration (electric): 3-per-side tuners, tun-o-matic bridge/stop tailpiece, 2 humbucking pickups, volume/tone controls, 3-way selector switch, available in Black (806) and Crimson Red Transparent (838) high gloss finishes. Mfg. 1997 to date.

MSR	$4,899	$3,675	$3,350	$2,995	$1,820	$1,560	$1,340	$1,095

This model was designed in conjunction with Doug Blair (See BLAIR GUITARS LTD.) and guitarist Slash (Guns 'N Roses).

Crossroads Doubleneck AAA (Model 395-6130) - similar to Crossroads Doubleneck (Model 395-6120), except has AAA Maple solid top. Custom colors upon request, New 1999.

MSR	$4,999	$3,750

Detonator Series

DETONATOR (1ST SERIES) - offset double cutaway poplar body, bolt-on maple neck, 22-fret rosewood fingerboard with dot inlays, black hardware, 6-on-a-side headstock, 2 single coils/1 humbucker EMG active pickups, Floyd Rose locking vibrato. Mfg. 1987 to 1988.

	N/A	$550	$500	$475	$425	$400	$375

In 1988, this model changed designation to the Detonator II.

Detonator - offset double cutaway poplar body, bolt on maple neck, 22-fret rosewood fingerboard with dot inlays, black hardware, 6-on-a-side headstock, 2 single coils/1 humbucker DiMarzio pickups, Guild/Mueller locking vibrato. Mfg. 1988.

	N/A	$495	$450	$425	$375	$350	$325

Liberator Series

LIBERATOR - offset double cutaway poplar body, bolt on maple neck, 22-fret rosewood fingerboard with dot inlays, black hardware, 6-on-a-side headstock, 2 single coils/1 humbucker DiMarzio pickups, Guild/Mueller locking vibrato. Mfg. 1988.

	N/A	$495	$450	$425	$375	$350	$325

Liberator II - offset double cutaway poplar body, bolt on maple neck, 22-fret rosewood fingerboard with dot inlays, black hardware, 6-on-a-side headstock, 2 single coils/1 humbucker EMG active pickups, Floyd Rose locking vibrato. Mfg. 1987 to 1988.

	N/A	$550	$495	$475	$425	$395	$375

Liberator Elite - similar to the Liberator II, except had a flamed maple top, bound ebony fingerboard with rising sun inlays, gold hardware, active Bartolini pickups. Mfg. 1988 only.

	N/A	$650	$595	$575	$525	$495	$475

M-80 Series

M-80 - dual cutaway bound mahogany body, raised black laminated pickguard, mahogany neck, 22-fret bound rosewood fingerboard with pearl block inlay, tune-o-matic bridge/fixed tailpiece, blackface peghead with pearl Chesterfield/logo inlay, 3-per-side tuners, chrome hardware, 2 Guild Xr-7 humbucker pickups, master volume/2 volume/2 tone controls, 3-position switch, available in Black, Natural, Red and White finishes. Mfg. 1975 to 1983.

	N/A	$750	$700	$675	$650	$625	$575

In 1981, this model was offered with a maple top/mahogany back, 24-fret fingerboard, 2 volume/2 tone controls, and a 3-way pickup selector.

M-85 CS - similar to the M-80. Mfg. 1975 to 1980.

	N/A	$680	$750	$725	$700	$525	$475

GRADING	100% MINT	98% NEAR MINT	95% EXC+	90% EXC	80% VG+	70% VG	60% G

Guild Brian May
courtesy Phil Winfield

Nightbird Series

NIGHTBIRD - single cutaway bound chambered mahogany body and carved Sitka spruce or maple top, mahogany neck, 22-fret bound ebony fingerboard with diamond shaped inlays, finetune bridge/stop tailpiece. Mfg. 1985 to 1987.

N/A	$1,600	$1,450	$1,350	$1,250	$1,150	$1,050

Designed in conjunction with vintage guitar expert George Gruhn.

NIGHTBIRD I - similar to the original Nightbird design, except has spruce top, unbound rosewood fingerboard, and unbound headstock, 2 DiMarzio pickups, separate coil tap and phase switches, and chrome hardware. Mfg. 1987 to 1988.

N/A	$950	$825	$775	$725	$675	$650

Nightbird II - similar to the original Nightbird design with carved Sitka spruce top and ebony fingerboard, except has gold hardware. Mfg. 1987 to 1988.

N/A	$900	$775	$725	$675	$625	$600

S Series

While the following models such as the S-250 through the S-284 **Aviator** have no accurate pricing information, there is some increased interest in these Guild solid bodies in the vintage and secondary market.

Most of these 1980s S Series models sell in the range between $350 and $600.

S-25 - offset double cutaway mahogany body, set neck, unbound top, 2 humbuckers, 1 volume and 1 tone control. Mfg. 1981 to 1983.

Rarity and lack of activity in the secondary marketplace precludes accurate pricing on this model.

S-26 - similar to the S-25, except very low production. Mfg. 1983 only.

Rarity and lack of activity in the secondary marketplace precludes accurate pricing on this model.

S-50 JET STAR - offset double cutaway mahogany body with concave bottom bout, black pickguard, built-in stand, mahogany neck, 22-fret rosewood fingerboard with pearl dot inlay, adjustable metal bridge/vibrato tailpiece, 3-per-side tuners, chrome hardware, single coil pickup, volume/tone controls, available in Amber, Black, Cherry Red, Green and Sunburst finishes. Mfg. 1963 to 1967.

N/A	$625	$550	$495	$475	$425	$395

The S-50 Jet Star was the first model of Guild's solid body guitars.

S-56 D - similar to the S-60, except has DiMarzio pickups. Mfg. 1979 to 1982.

Rarity and lack of activity in the secondary marketplace precludes accurate pricing on this model.

S-60 - offset double cutaway mahogany body, black pickguard, mahogany neck, 24-fret rosewood fingerboard with pearl dot inlay, tune-o-matic bridge/fixed tailpiece, 3-per-side tuners, chrome hardware, single pickup, volume/tone controls, available in Black, Red and White finishes. Mfg. 1977 to 1989.

N/A	$425	$400	$350	$325	$275	$250

S-60 D - similar to S-60, except has 2 single coil DiMarzio pickups, 2 volume/2 tone controls, 3-position switch.

N/A	$425	$400	$350	$325	$275	$250

S-70 - similar to S-60, except has 3 single coil pickups, 3-position/2 mini switches.

N/A	$450	$400	$350	$300	$250	$200

S-70 AD - similar to S-70, except has an ash body and DiMarzio pickups. Mfg. 1978 to 1982.

N/A	$450	$400	$350	$300	$250	$200

S-90 - similar to the S-50, except featured a humbucker and a covered bridge/tailpiece assembly. Mfg. 1970 to 1976.

N/A	$525	$450	$400	$375	$325	$300

S-100 POLARA - offset double cutaway mahogany body with concave bottom bout, black laminated pickguard, built-in stand, mahogany neck, 22-fret rosewood fingerboard with pearl dot inlay, adjustable metal bridge/vibrato tailpiece, 3-per-side tuners, chrome hardware, 2 single coil pickups, 2 volume/2 tone controls, 3-position switch, available in Amber, Black, Cherry Red, Green and Sunburst finishes. Mfg. 1963 to 1968.

N/A	$1,225	$1,150	$1,100	$1,050	$995	$950

S-100 POLARA (Model 350-6300) - offset double cutaway mahogany body, set-in mahogany neck, 22-fret bound rosewood fingerboard with pearl block inlay, adjustable metal bridge/stop tailpiece, 3-per-side tuners, chrome hardware, 2 Seymour Duncan humbucking pickups, 2 volume/2 tone controls, 3-way selector switch, available in Black (806), Natural (821), Transparent Red (838), and White (880) finishes. Mfg. 1995 to 2000.

$1,250	$1,050	$900	$775	$675	$550	$475

Last MSR was $1,569.

Subtract $142 for Natural Mahogany finish (S-100 HR).

List Price includes deluxe hardshell case.

S-100 - offset double cutaway mahogany body, black pickguard with logo, mahogany neck, 22-fret bound rosewood fingerboard with pearl block inlay, adjustable metal bridge/vibrato tailpiece, blackface peghead with pearl Chesterfield/logo inlay, 3-per-side tuners, chrome hardware, 2 humbucker pickups, 2 volume/2 tone controls, 3-position switch, available in Amber, Black, Cherry Red, Green and White finishes. Mfg. 1970 to 1974.

N/A	$800	$700	$650	$600	$550	$525

In 1973, phase switch was introduced.

Guild Nightbird II
courtesy Guild Guitars

G

GRADING	100% MINT	98% NEAR MINT	95% EXC+	90% EXC	80% VG+	70% VG	60% G

S-100 C - similar to S-100, except has carved acorn/leaves top, clear pickguard with logo, tune-o-matic bridge/fixed tailpiece, phase switch, stereo output, available in Natural finish. Mfg. 1974 to 1976.

N/A	**$995**	**$900**	**$850**	**$825**	**$775**	**$750**

S-100 Deluxe - similar to S-100, except has Bigsby vibrato tailpiece. Mfg. 1973 to 1975.

N/A	**$825**	**$775**	**$725**	**$700**	**$650**	**$625**

S-100 REISSUE - double cutaway mahogany body, black pickguard, mahogany neck, 22-fret bound rosewood fingerboard with pearl block inlay, tune-o-matic bridge/fixed tailpiece, blackface peghead with pearl Chesterfield/logo inlay, 3-per-side tuners, chrome hardware, 2 humbucker Guild pickups, 2 volume/2 tone controls, 3-position/coil tap switches, available in Black, Green Stain, Natural, Red Stain, Vintage White and White finishes. Mfg. 1994 to 1995.

$800	**$600**	**$500**	**$400**	**$350**	**$325**	**$300**

Last MSR was $1,000.

S-100 G - similar to S-100 Reissue, except has gold hardware. Mfg. 1994 to 1995.

$950	**$725**	**$600**	**$475**	**$425**	**$395**	**$350**

Last MSR was $1,200.

S-200 THUNDERBIRD - offset double cutaway asymmetrical mahogany body with concave bottom bout, black pickguard, built-in stand, mahogany neck, 22-fret bound rosewood fingerboard with pearl block inlay, adjustable metal bridge/vibrato tailpiece, bound blackface peghead with pearl eagle/logo inlay, 3-per-side tuners, chrome hardware, 2 single coil pickups (some with humbuckers), 2 volume/2 tone controls, 3 pickup/1 tone slide switches, available in Amber, Black, Cherry Red, Green and Sunburst finishes. Mfg. 1963 to 1970.

N/A	**$2,100**	**$1,900**	**$1,800**	**$1,700**	**$1,600**	**$1,500**

The Thunderbird model featured a folding stand built into the back of the body. While a unique feature, the stand was less than steady and prone to instability. Be sure to inspect the headstock/neck joint for any indications of previous problems due to the guitar falling over.

S-250 - offset double cutaway mahogany body, set neck, bound top, chrome hardware, 2 humbuckers, 2 volume and 2 tone controls. Mfg. 1981 to 1983.

S-260 - similar to the S-250, except produced in low numbers. Mfg. 1983.

S-270 FLYER (RUNAWAY or SPRINT) - offset double cutaway body, bolt-on neck, 6-on-a-side "Blade" headstock, one EMG pickup, locking tremolo. Mfg. 1983 to 1985.

S-271 Sprint (Flyer) - similar to S-270, except different pickup configuration. Mfg. 1983 to 1985.

S-275 - offset double cutaway body, set neck, bound top, gold hardware, 2 humbuckers, 2 volume/1 tone control, 1 phase (or coil tap) switch. Mfg. 1983 to 1987.

In 1987, pickup configuration changed to 2 single coils/1 humbucker.

S-280 FLYER - offset double cutaway body, bolt-on neck, 22-fret fingerboard, 6-on-a-side headstock, 2 humbuckers, 2 volume/2 tone controls. Mfg. 1983 to 1986.

S-281 Flyer - similar to S-280 Flyer, except has a locking tremolo and 1 volume/1 tone controls. Mfg. 1983 to 1986.

S-282 - similar to S-280 Flyer, except has a set-in neck, 1 volume/1 tone controls. Mfg. 1983 to 1986.

S-284 AVIATOR - symmetrical double cutaway body, set neck, 6-on-a-side "pointed" headstock, locking tremolo, 2 single/humbucker EMG pickups, volume/tone controls. Mfg. 1984 to 1988.

S-285 Aviator - similar to S-284 Aviator, except has bound fingerboard and headstock, fancy fingerboard inlays. Mfg. 1986 to 1987.

S-300 - offset double cutaway mahogany body, distinctly rounded tail end, black pickguard, mahogany neck, 24-fret ebony fingerboard with pearl dot inlay, tune-o-matic bridge/fixed tailpiece, blackface peghead with pearl Chesterfield/logo inlay, 3-per-side tuners, chrome hardware, 2 single coil pickups, 2 volume/2 tone controls, 3-position/phase switches, available in Black, Red and White finishes. Mfg. 1976 to 1989.

N/A	**$600**	**$575**	**$550**	**$525**	**$475**	**$450**

S-300 A - similar to S-300, except has an ash body and maple neck. Mfg. 1977 to 1982.

N/A	**$600**	**$575**	**$550**	**$525**	**$475**	**$450**

S-300 D - similar to S-300, except has 2 DiMarzio humbucker pickups.

N/A	**$600**	**$575**	**$550**	**$525**	**$475**	**$450**

S-400 - similar to the S-300, except has set neck and active electronics. Mfg. 1979 to 1982.

N/A	**$600**	**$575**	**$550**	**$525**	**$475**	**$450**

S-400 A - similar to S-400, except ash body and maple neck. Mfg. 1979 to 1982.

N/A	**$600**	**$575**	**$550**	**$525**	**$475**	**$450**

T Series

T-250 - single cutaway ash body, black pickguard, controls mounted on metal plate, bolt-on maple neck, 22-fret maple fingerboard with black dot inlay, fixed bridge, 6-on-a-side tuners, gold hardware, 2 single coil EMG pickups, volume/tone controls, 3-position switch, available in Black, Blue, Red and White finishes. Mfg. 1986 to circa 1990.

N/A	**$700**	**$675**	**$625**	**$575**	**$525**	**$500**

The T-250 is sometimes referred to as the Roy Buchanan model.

T-200 - similar to the T-250.

N/A	**$775**	**$750**	**$700**	**$650**	**$600**	**$575**

The T-200 is also sometimes called the Roy Buchanan model.

X-79 - offset double cutaway asymmetrical mahogany body with fin like bottom bout, black pickguard, mahogany neck, 24-fret rosewood fingerboard with pearl dot inlay, tune-o-matic bridge/stop tailpiece, blackface peghead with pearl logo inlay, 3-per-side tuners, chrome tuners, 2 single coil pickups, 2 volume/1 tone controls, 3-position switch, available in Black, Green, Red, Sparkle and White finishes. Mfg. 1981 to 1985.

N/A	**$600**	**$550**	**$525**	**$500**	**$475**	**$450**

GRADING	100% MINT	98% NEAR MINT	95% EXC+	90% EXC	80% VG+	70% VG	60% G

X-79-3 - similar to the X-79, except features 3 single coil pickups, volume/tone controls, 3 mini switches. Mfg. 1981 to 1985.

N/A	$600	$550	$525	$500	$475	$450

X Series

X-80 SWAN - possibly related to either the X-79 or X-82. Mfg. 1983 to 1985.

Rarity and lack of activity in the secondary marketplace precludes accurate pricing on this model. Guild records show only 172 models produced.

X-82 NOVA - asymmetrical angular body, 3 point headstock, chrome hardware, stop tailpiece, 2 humbuckers, 2 volume/2 tone controls, phase (or coil tap) switch. Mfg. 1981 to 1984.

N/A	$550	$525	$500	$450	$425	$400

In 1983, a locking tremolo system was added.

X-84 V - bolt neck, Guild or Kahler tremolo. Mfg. 1983 only.

Rarity and lack of activity in the secondary marketplace precludes accurate pricing on this model. In 1983, Guild announced a new line of bolt neck, solid body electrics. To date, research has not indicated further specifications. Future updates will appear in subsequent editions of the ***Blue Book of Electric Guitars***.

X-88 FLYING STAR - "Flying Star" asymmetrical angular body with sharp points, bolt-on neck, locking tremolo, 2 octave fingerboard with star inlays, 1 EMG pickup. Mfg. 1984 to 1985.

N/A	$550	$500	$450	$400	$375	$350

Guitar design was inspired by members of the rock band Motley Crue. Some literature may refer to this model as the Crue Flying Star.

X-88 D Flying Star - similar to X-88 Flying Star, except has DiMarzio pickups. Mfg. 1984 to 1985.

N/A	$550	$500	$450	$400	$375	$350

X-92 CITRON BREAKAWAY - offset solid body (bass side removable for travel), 3 single coil pickups, tremolo, 1 volume/1 tone control, 5-way selector switch. Mfg. 1984 to 1986.

N/A	$625	$585	$545	$515	$485	$465

Designed by luthier Harvey Citron, originally of Veillette-Citron; now currently Citron Enterprises (see CITRON, HARVEY).

The X-92 came with a travel/gig bag.

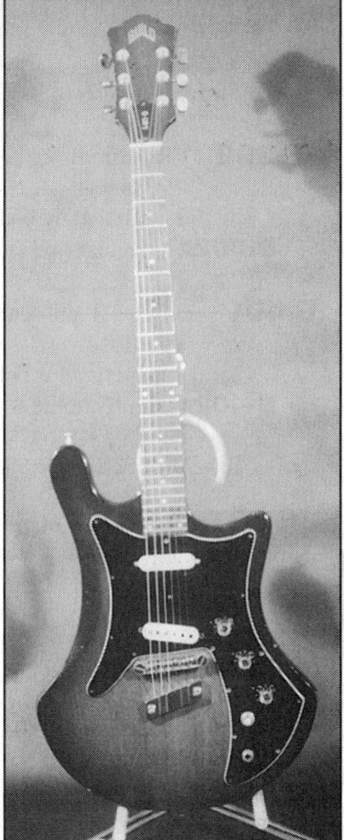

1979 Guild S-60
courtesy Sam J. Maggio

X-97 V - bolt neck, Guild or Kahler tremolo. Mfg. 1983 only.

Rarity and lack of activity in the secondary marketplace precludes accurate pricing on this model. In 1983, Guild announced a new line of bolt neck, solid body electrics.

X-100 BLADERUNNER - asymmetrical angular body that featured triangular sections removed, bolt-on neck, 6-on-a-side pointed headstock, locking tremolo, humbucking pickup, volume/tone controls. Mfg. 1984 to 1985.

$1,175	$1,150	$1,125	$1,100	$1,050	$1,025	$950

Designed by California based design team of David Newell and Andrew Desrosiers (See DAVID ANDREW DESIGN RESEARCH).

X-108 V - bolt neck, Guild or Kahler tremolo. Mfg. 1983 only.

Rarity and lack of activity in the secondary marketplace precludes accurate pricing on this model. In 1983, Guild announced a new line of bolt neck, solid body electrics.

X-2000 NIGHTBIRD - single cutaway routed out mahogany body, bound figured maple top, bound tortoise pickguard, mahogany neck, 22-fret bound ebony fingerboard with pearl block/abalone wedge inlay, tune-o-matic bridge/stop tailpiece, bound peghead with pearl shield/logo inlay, 3-per-side tuners, gold hardware, 2 humbucker pickups, volume/tone control, 3-position/single coil switches, available in Amberburst, Black, Cherry Sunburst and Natural finishes. Disc. 1994.

$1,500	$1,400	$1,300	$1,200	$1,150	$1,100	$1,050

Last MSR was $1,995.

X-3000 Nightingale - similar to X-2000, except has 2 f-holes. Disc. 1994.

$1,700	$1,600	$1,500	$1,400	$1,350	$1,300	$1,250

Last MSR was $1,995.

ELECTRIC BASS

Early Guild basses have a specially designed Guild single coil pickup made by Hagstrom in Sweden that is often mistaken for a humbucker. Some of these basses have an extra switch that activated a passive circuit and eliminated the hum associated with single coil pickups. This feature makes the basses more desirable and collectible.

ASHBORY - small curved teardrop body, neck-through design, 4-on-a-side tuners, chrome hardware, piezo pickup under bridge, volume/tone controls. Mfg. 1986 to 1988.

N/A	$450	$425	$400	$350	$325	$275

It is estimated that only 2,000 instruments were produced. This compact bass had solid silicon tubing for strings, and, oddly enough, can approximate the sound of an upright bass.

B-301 - offset double cutaway mahogany body, black laminated pickguard, mahogany neck, 20-fret rosewood fingerboard with pearl dot inlay, fixed bridge, blackface peghead with pearl Chesterfield/logo inlay, 2-per-side tuners, chrome hardware, single coil pickup, volume/tone controls, available in Black, Natural, White and Red finishes. Mfg. 1977 to 1981.

N/A	$600	$550	$525	$475	$450	$425

In 1980, mahogany body/neck instruments were discontinued.

Guild X-2000 Nightbird
courtesy Guild Guitars

G

GRADING	100% MINT	98% NEAR MINT	95% EXC+	90% EXC	80% VG+	70% VG	60% G

B-301A - similar to B-301, except instrument featured an ash body and maple neck. Mfg. circa 1979 to 1981.

	N/A	$600	$550	$525	$475	$450	$425

B-302 - similar to B-301, except has 2 single coil pickups, 2 volume/2 tone controls, 3-position switch. Mfg. 1977 to 1981.

	N/A	$700	$650	$600	$550	$525	$500

In 1980, mahogany body/neck instruments were discontinued.

B-302A - similar to B-302, except instrument featured an ash body and maple neck. Mfg. circa 1979 to 1981.

	N/A	$650	$600	$575	$525	$500	$475

B-401 - rounded double cutaway body, set neck, 1 pickup. Mfg. 1980 to 1981.

	N/A	$600	$550	$525	$475	$450	$425

Total production for both the B-401 and B-402 was 335 instruments.

B-402 - similar to the B-401, except has 2 pickups. Mfg. 1980 to 1981.

	N/A	$550	$500	$475	$425	$400	$375

Total production for both the B-401 and B-402 was 335 instruments.

JET STAR BASS offset double cutaway companion bass to the S-200 Thunderbird, S-100 Polara, and S-50 Jet Star guitars. It came with a Thunderbird style headstock with 2-per-side tuners until 1966 when it changed to 4 0n 1 side tuners. From 1964-1965 it had a Hagstrom style single co pickup. From 1966 to 1970 it came with Guild Mickey Mouse bass pickups. Mfg. 1964 to 1970

1964-1965	N/A	$1,600	$1,400	$1,200	$1,000	$750	$650
1966-1970	N/A	$1,200	$1,000	$800	$700	$600	$550

JS BASS I - offset double cutaway mahogany body/neck, 21-fret rosewood fingerboard with pearl dot inlay, fixed bridge, blackface peghead with pearl Chesterfield/logo inlay, 2-per-side tuners, chrome hardware, humbucker pickup, volume/tone controls, available in Black, Natural and Sunburst finishes. Mfg. 1970 to 1978.

1964-1970	N/A	$750	$725	$700	$675	$650	$625
1971-1978	N/A	$550	$525	$500	$475	$450	$425

This model had an optional fretless fingerboard. In 1972, tone switch was introduced, redesigned humbucker pickup replaced original parts/design.

JS Bass I LS - similar to JS Bass I, except has long scale length. Mfg. 1976 to 1978.

	N/A	$750	$700	$675	$650	$625	$600

JS BASS II - similar to JS Bass I, except has 2 humbucker pickups, 2 volume/2 tone controls, 3-position switch. Mfg. 1970 to 1978.

	N/A	$750	$725	$700	$675	$650	$625

In 1972, tone switch was introduced, redesigned humbucker pickups replaced original parts/design. In 1974 through 1976, a hand carved acorn/leaves body was offered.

JS Bass II LS - similar to JS Bass I, except has long scale length, 2 humbucker pickups, 2 volume/2 tone controls, 3-position switch. Mfg. 1976 to 1978.

	N/A	$700	$675	$650	$600	$575	$550

M-85 I - similar to the JS Bass I, except has a carved top, single cutaway semi-solid design, rosewood fingerboard with dot inlays, 303/4 inch scale, 1 Hagstrom single coil pickup. Mfg. 1970 to 1980.

	N/A	$1,000	$950	$875	$800	$725	$650

M-85 II - similar to the M-85 I, except has 2 pickups, 2 volume/2 tone controls. Mfg. 1970 to 1980.

	N/A	$1,050	$1,000	$925	$850	$775	$700

Pilot Series

All models in the Pro Pilot series were available fretless at no extra cost.

PRO 4 - offset double cutaway asymmetrical maple body, bolt-on maple neck, 22-fret rosewood fingerboard with pearl dot inlay, fixed bridge, 4-on-a-side tuners, black hardware, 2 J-style active EMG pickups, 2 volume/tone controls, active preamp, available in Amber, Black, Natural and White finishes. Mfg. 1994 to 1995.

	$750	$630	$525	$415	$360	$330	$300

Last MSR was $1,100.

PRO 5 - similar to Pro 4, except has 5 strings, 4/1 per side tuners. Disc. 1995.

	$820	$690	$570	$450	$395	$360	$330

Last MSR was $1,200.

SB-600 PILOT - similar to the Pro 4, except has a poplar body and 2 DiMarzio pickups. Mfg. 1983 to 1988.

	N/A	$500	$450	$400	$375	$350	$325

SB-601 Pilot - similar to SB-600 Pilot, except has 1 pickup. Mfg. 1983 to 1988.

	N/A	$450	$400	$350	$325	$300	$275

SB-602 Pilot - similar to SB-600 Pilot, except has 2 EMG pickups and a bass vibrato. Mfg. 1983 to 1988.

	N/A	$575	$525	$475	$450	$425	$400

SB-603 Pilot - similar to SB-600 Pilot, except has 3 pickups. Mfg. 1983 to 1988.

	N/A	$500	$450	$400	$375	$350	$325

SB-604 Pilot - similar to SB-600 Pilot, except has different headstock design and EMG pickups. Mfg. 1983 to 1988.

	N/A	$550	$500	$450	$425	$400	$375

SB-605 Pilot - similar to SB-600 Pilot, except has 5 strings and EMG pickups. Mfg. 1986 to 1988.

	N/A	$600	$550	$500	$475	$450	$425

GRADING	100% MINT	98% NEAR MINT	95% EXC+	90% EXC	80% VG+	70% VG	60% G

SB-902 ADVANCED PILOT - similar to the SB-600 Pilot, except has a flamed maple body, ebony fingerboard, and Bartolini pickups and preamp. Mfg. 1987 to 1988.

N/A $700 $650 $600 $575 $550 $525

SB-905 Advanced Pilot - similar to SB-902 Advanced Pilot, except has 5 strings. Mfg. 1987 to 1988.

N/A $750 $700 $650 $625 $600 $575

SB Series

Prior to the introduction of the Pilot Bass and subsequent models in 1983, the four models in the SB series sported a vaguely Fenderish body design.

SB-201 - offset double cutaway ash body, set-in maple neck, 2-per-side headstock, 20-fret rosewood fingerboard, Chesterfield logo, split coil pickup, volume/tone controls. Mfg. 1982 to 1983.

N/A $475 $450 $400 $375 $350 $325

Some models have been spotted with a 'soapbar' (large rectangular) pickup.

SB-202 - similar to SB-201, except features 2 pickups, 2 volume/2 tone controls, phase switch. Mfg. 1982 to 1983.

N/A $525 $500 $450 $425 $400 $375

SB-203 - similar to SB-201, except has 1 split coil pickup and 2 single coils, volume/tone controls, 3 mini-switches for pickup selection. Mfg. 1982 to 1983.

N/A $485 $460 $420 $385 $360 $335

SB-502 E - similar to SB-201, except has active electronics. Mfg. 1982 to 1983.

N/A $575 $5500 $500 $475 $450 $425

SB-666 BLADERUNNER BASS - a companion piece to the X-100 Bladerunner guitar, the SB-666 bass shares similar body design features, but only 1 pickup. Mfg. 1984 to 1985.

N/A $1,075 $1,050 $1,025 $1,000 $975 $950

SB-608 FLYING STAR BASS - a companion piece to the X-88 Flying Star guitar, the SB-608 bass shares similar body design features, but only 1 pickup. Mfg. 1984 to 1985.

N/A $625 $600 $575 $550 $510 $475

SB-608 E - similar to the SB-608 Flying Star, except has active EMG pickups. Mfg. 1984 to 1985.

N/A $625 $600 $575 $550 $510 $475

ST 4 - offset double cutaway asymmetrical poplar body, bolt-on maple neck, 22-fret rosewood fingerboard with pearl dot inlay, fixed bridge, 4-on-a-side tuners, black hardware, P/J-style pickups, 2 volume/tone controls, available in Black, Natural and White finishes. Disc. 1994.

$555 $475 $395 $315 $280 $260 $235

This model was also offered with a mahogany body.

Last MSR was $795.

ST 5 - similar to ST 4, except has 5 strings, 4/1 per side tuners. Disc. 1994.

$625 $535 $445 $360 $325 $300 $275

Last MSR was $895.

Starfire Bass Series

STARFIRE BASS I - double round cutaway semi hollow bound maple body, thumb/finger rests, 2 f-holes, 3-piece maple neck, 20-fret rosewood fingerboard with pearl dot inlay, fixed bridge, pearl Chesterfield/logo peghead inlay, 2-per-side tuners, chrome hardware, humbucker pickup, volume/tone controls, available in Cherry Red, Ebony, Emerald Green and Honey Amber finishes. Mfg. 1964 to 1975.

N/A $975 $925 $875 $800 $775 $750

In 1970, Hagstrom-made single coil pickups were featured.
This model also offered a mahogany body.

Starfire Bass II - similar to Starfire Bass I, except has 2 humbucker pickups, master volume control, bass boost switch. Mfg. 1964 to 1977.

N/A $1,000 $950 $875 $850 $825 $800

Starfire Bass II (Model 350-7500) - double cutaway thinline semi-hollow body, laminated mahogany top/back/sides, body binding, 2 f-holes, maple neck, 21-fret rosewood fingerboard with dot inlay, fixed bridge, pearl logo peghead inlay, 2-per-side tuners, chrome hardware, 2 Guild humbucker pickups, 2 volume/2 tone controls, 3-way selector switch, additional switch, available in Antique Burst (837), Black (806), Blonde (801), and Transparent Red (838) finishes. Mfg. 1998 to date.

MSR $2,299 $1,850 $1,550 $1,325 $1,125 $950 $800 $650

Left-handed model (Model 350-7520) available at no additional cost.

List Price includes hardshell case.

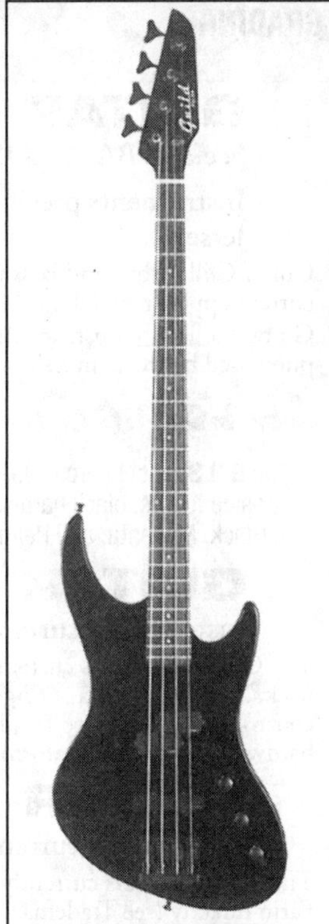

Guild Pilot Bass 602
courtesy Guild Guitars

G

Guild X-702 Bass
courtesy The Music Shoppe

GRADING	100% MINT	98% NEAR MINT	95% EXC+	90% EXC	80% VG+	70% VG	60% G

GUITAR COLLECTION

See also BASS COLLECTION.

Instruments previously manufactured in Japan from 1985 to 1992. Distributed by Meisel Music, Inc. of Springfield, New Jersey.

Guitar Collection (and Bass Collection) instruments are medium grade instruments with good hardware, and a modern, rounded body design. Their current appeal may fall in the range of the novice to intermediate player looking for a solid-feeling instrument.

Guitar Collection instruments were originally distributed by Meisel Music, Inc. for a number of years between 1985 to 1992. Their on-hand stock was purchased by the Sam Ash music store chain of New York in 1994 and sold through the Sam Ash stores.

ELECTRIC

The **G 3 S** model (circa 1992) features a sleek, offset double cutaway alder body, bolt-on maple neck, 24-fret rosewood fingerboard (no inlay), fixed bridge, 3-per-side tuners, black hardware, single coil/humbucker pickups, volume and tone controls, and a 3-way toggle selector switch. The **G 3 S** model was available in Black, Magenta, and Pearl White finishes (original retail list unknown).

GUITAR FACTORY

Instruments currently built in Orlando, Florida.

The Guitar Factory is currently offering an Electric/Acoustic E/A 12 Mono model that features a white limba hollow body, through-body white limba neck, 2 octave red locust fingerboard, red locust bridge, Sperzel tuners, 3 Bartolini single coil pickups/Fishman Matrix acoustic pickup, volume and tone controls. The suggested retail price is $3,600. Various options include pickup configuration, mono or dual outputs, choice of different woods, and hardware. For further information regarding specifications and pricing, contact The Guitar Factory directly (see Trademark Index).

GUITAR FARM

Instruments currently built in Sperryville, Virginia.

The Guitar Farm is currently offering hand crafted guitar models. For further information regarding specifications and pricing, contact The Guitar Farm directly (see Trademark Index).

GUITORGAN

Instruments previously assembled in Waco, Texas between 1969 to 1988 (the guitars were produced in Japan, and the electronics were built and installed in the U.S.). Distributed by Musiconics (MCI) of Waco, Texas.

Inventor Bob Murrell introduced the GuitOrgan prototype at the 1967 Chicago NAMM show, along with partner Bill Mostyn and demonstrator Bob Wiley. Early home-built production began in 1967; a production factory was opened in 1968. Murrell's company started out as Murrell Electronics, which evolved into Musiconics International (MCI). Murrell combined his electronics and musical backgrounds in his vision of a guitar that could also offer Hammond organ-type sounds.

While developing his prototype, Murrell worked with Baldwin for his own organ circuitry (Baldwin was just beginning to import the Burns models to the U.S., and was interested in the various aspects of the guitar market). The finished product featured a fingerboard with segmented frets (six segments, one per string) wired to the internal controls. As a result, when a note or notes are fretted, the organ is triggered - and the note will sustain as long as the note stays fretted. The GuitOrgan allows players the option of either or both sounds of a guitar and the on-board organ. Peavey later approximated this same segmented fret/wired-to-circuitry approach in their own MidiBass (later CyberBass) MIDI controller.

GuitOrgans feature Murrell's own design of organ circuitry, with voices derived from Baldwin products (by permission). Early models were built in various guitars that could house the circuitry. Production models featured the wide hollowbody models from Ventura and Univox, built in Japan. Some models may also be Ibanez or Yamaha.

GuitOrgans have three jacks on the side of the body: Two standard 1/4" phono jacks, and a 3-point electrical jack for the wall plug (power supply). That's right, this guitar plugs into the wall! Using the two jacks, the player can run two amps (or two channels of the same amp). In the late 1980s, Murrell also began wiring the GuitOrgan with MIDI controls; the additional MIDI cost was $480. Murrell would also wire a customer-supplied guitar for $1,200.

(Source: Teisco Del Rey, Guitar Player magazine)

ELECTRIC

The GuitOrgan had a list price of $995 in 1969, and the price rose up to $2,495 retail new by 1984. It is estimated that 3,000 instruments were produced between 1967 to 1984, but the final number is larger due to Murrell offering to build custom orders after 1984.

M-300 - offset double cutaway laminated hollow body, black raised pickguard, 21 (segmented) fret rosewood fingerboard with block inlay, tune-o-matic bridge/raised tailpiece, 3-per-side tuners, chrome hardware, 2 covered humbucker pickups, 2 volume/2 tone controls, 3-position switch, sustain knob/vibrato/8 voice switches, staccato switch, available in Sunburst finish. Mfg. 1969 to circa mid-1970s.

$1,200 $950 $875 $750 $625 $500 $400

The first production run of GuitOrgans were placed in the body of Ventura's Barney Kessel model. Later models were built into Univox's copy of a Gibson 335.

M-340 - similar to the M-300, except features miniturized electronics. Mfg. mid to late 1970s (estimated).

$1,200 $950 $875 $750 $625 $500 $400

B-300 - similar to the M-340, except features Hammond organ-type sounds. Mfg. late 1970s to early 1980s (estimated).

$1,400 $1,050 $950 $850 $750 $675 $600

B-35 - similar to the B-300, except features updated engineering, angled cuts on fret segments. Mfg. mid to late 1980s (estimated).

$1,400 $1,050 $950 $850 $750 $675 $600

GUYA

Instruments previously produced in Japan during the 1960s.

These instruments were generally entry level to good quality guitars based on Rickenbacker designs. Guya was the forerunner to Guyatone labeled guitars, and was built by the same company (see GUYATONE).

(Source: Michael Wright, Guitar Stories Volume One)

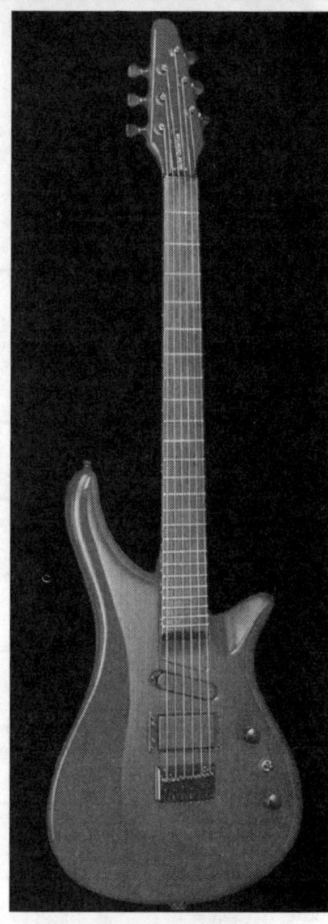

Guitar Collection
G 3 S (MAG)
courtesy Guitar Collection

GUYATONE

Instruments previously built in Japan from late 1950s to the mid 1970s.

The original company was founded by Mitsou Matsuki, an apprentice cabinet maker in the early 1930s. Matsuki, who studied electronics in night classes, was influenced by listening to Hawaiian music. A friend and renowned guitar player, Atsuo Kaneko, requested that Matsuki build a Hawaiian electric guitar. The two entered into business as a company called Matsuki Seisakujo, and produced guitars under the Guya trademark.

In 1948, a little after World War II, Matsuki founded his new company, Matsuki Denki Onkyo Kenkyujo. This company produced electric Hawaiian guitars, amplifiers, and record player cartridges. In 1951, this company began using the Guyatone trademark for its guitars. By the next year the corporate name evolved into Tokyo Sound Company. They produced their first solid body electric in the late 1950s. Original designs dominated the early production, albeit entry level quality. Later quality improved, but at the sacrifice of originality as Guyatone began building medium quality designs based on Fender influences. Some Guyatone guitars also were imported under such brandnames as **Star** or **Antoria**.

(Source: Michael Wright, Guitar Stories Volume One)

While traditional stringed instruments have been part of the Japanese culture, the guitar was first introduced to Japan in 1890. Japan did not even begin to open trade or diplomatic relations with the West until U.S. President Millard Fillmore sent Commodore Matthew C. Perry in 1850. In 1929 Maestro Andres Segovia made his first concert tour in Japan, sparking an interest in the guitar that has been part of the subculture since then. Japanese fascination with the instrumental rock group the Ventures also indicates that not all American design influences would be strictly Fender or Gibson; Mosrite guitars by Semie Moseley also were a large influence, among others.

Classic American guitar designs may have been an influence on the early Japanese models, but the influence was *incorporated* into original designs. The era of copying designs and details began in the early 1970s, but was not the basis for Japanese guitar production. As the entry level models began to get better in quality and meticulous attention to detail, then the American market began to take notice.

Guitorgan B-35
courtesy Grampa's Guitars

NOTES

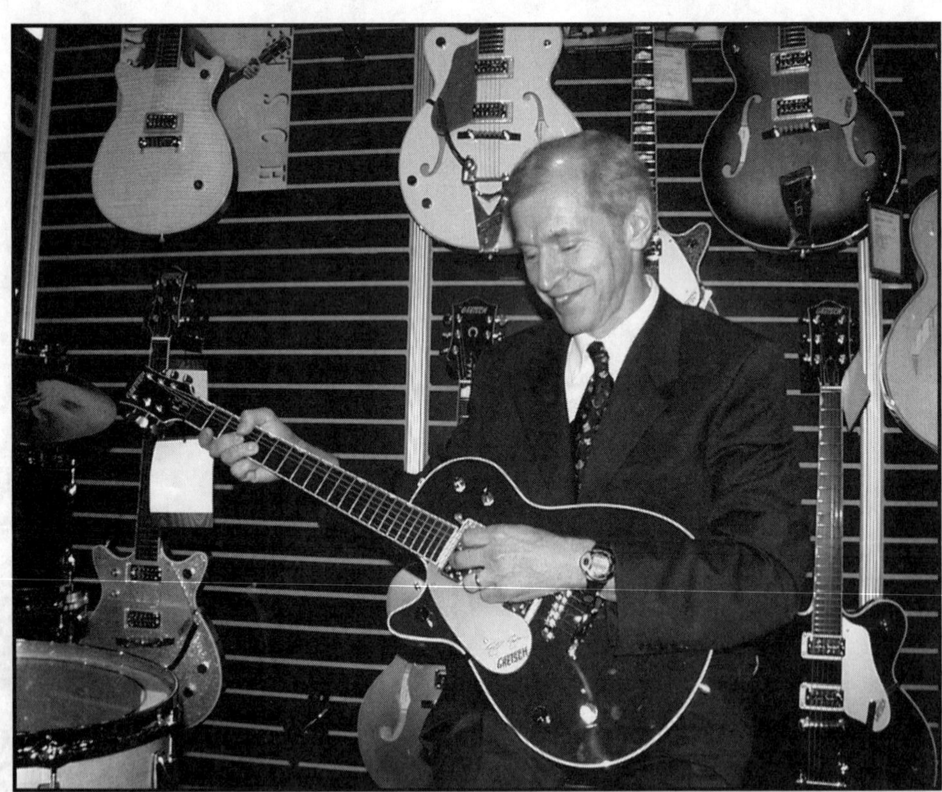

Fred Gretsch, a lefty, always finds time at the shows to enjoy himself with one of his new products. And for good reason, Gretsch guitars have never played better.

Section H

H.M.L. GUITARS

Instruments currently built in Seattle, Washington since 1994.

H.M.L. Guitars was founded in 1994 by Howard Leese (guitarist, and 25 year veteran with the rock group Heart). Leese participates in all aspects of construction as overall quality control inspector. He also allows every customer to help co-design their instruments for a more personal touch. H.M.L. guitars are totally handbuilt in Seattle by luthier Jack Pimentel.

The customer list for H.M.L. guitars includes such notables as Bruce Hastell, Mike Soldano, Val Kolbeck, Billy Gibbons, Jim Fiske, and (of course) Howard Leese himself.

(Company information courtesy Howard Leese, 1996)

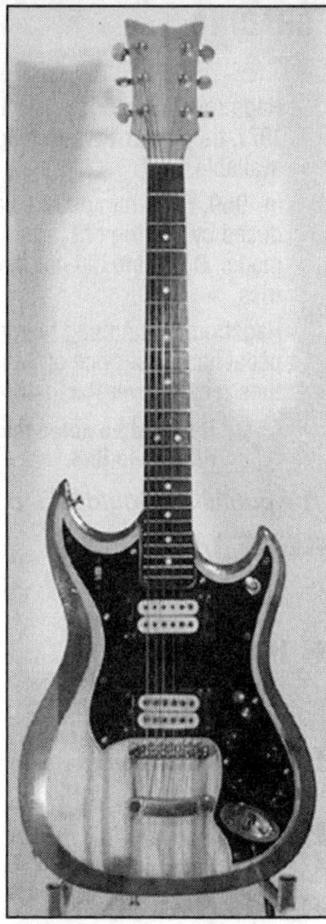

Hagstrom H II N O T
courtesy Richard Blake

ELECTRIC

Designed by Leese, the standard features of the H.M.L. model include a unique set of five hollow chambers placed throughout the body, in areas of acoustical sensitivity to better project "true" sound dissipation. For the fretboards, Leese prefers to use figured cocabola wood on the entire HML line due to its beauty, sound and feel. Other features include a carved tiger flame maple top with matched flame maple neck. Customers can even select their own choice of tops from Howard's personal stock of aged, exotic woods, and can choose specific color finishes, pickups, and electronics. The retail list price starts at $3,000. For further information and pricing, contact H.M.L. Guitars directly (see Trademark Index).

HAGSTROM

Instruments previously produced in Sweden from circa 1957 through the early 1980s.

Early distributors included the Hershman Musical Instrument Company of New York (under GOYA logo) and Selmer, U.K. (under FUTURAMA logo). In the mid 1970s, Ampeg became the U.S. distributor.

Hagstrom first began building guitars and basses in 1957, although many models appeared under the Futurama trademark in England (distributed by Selmer, U.K.) and either Hagstrom or Goya (distributed by Hershman Musical Instrument Company).

Hagstrom produced roughly 130,000 electric guitars and basses from 1958 to 1981 in Alvdalen, Sweden. During the early 80's until 1983, a few instruments were manufactured under the Hagstrom name in Japan. Due to quality concerns and ever increasing competition, the doors were eventually closed in 1983.

Distributors included the Hershman Musical Instrument Company of New York, the Merson Musical Supply Company of Westbury, New York, Selmer, U.K. and eventually Ampeg. The evolution of the Hagstrom line was rapid, and approximately 65 different models of guitars and basses were produced. (Featured here are the more popular and well know models.) Early in its history, guitars were marketed in the U.K. as Futurama and in the US as Goya, Kent (a name that rarely appeared on the guitar and should not be confused with Kent trademark guitars) or Hagstrom. By 1965, all guitars were identified as Hagstrom.

Hagstrom produced both solid body and semi-hollowbody electrics, as well as an archtop model designed by luthier James L D'Aquisto. Also introduced was the first 8 string bass (four pairs of strings) and the "fastest neck in the world" which was accomplished by using an H shape "expander stretcher" truss, a design that has allowed the necks to remain true even to this day.

ELECTRIC

Some Hagstrom models encountered at guitar shops and shows include the 1959 "Les Paul"-styled **ESP 24** hollowbody and 4 pickup **EDP 46 De Luxe**. These have all wood hollowbody interior construction with plastic exterior and were available in sparkle, pearloid or plain with a white pearloid "mother of toilet seat" fingerboard.

Some of the more frequently seen models are the **Kent I** and **H I**, equipped with two single coil pickups and 4 control slide switches. These had a complete Lucite molded top and vinyl back. The **H II** and **H III** models are easy to identify because the name is on the headstock, and the number of pickups corresponds with the model number. (It is important to note that original parts for these guitars, especially the switches, are very difficult to find.) Later came the **H II N** which had two humbucking pickups.

The **Viking I** is equipped with two single coil pickups, one selector switch, individual tone and volume controls for each pickup and six in line tuners. As the Viking line is a semi-hollowbody, these have more of a 335 vibe to them. The **Viking II** is similar to the **V I**, except it has gold hardware and accents. (this is sometimes called the "Elvis guitar" as Elvis briefly played one in his 68 Comeback) The **Viking I N** (or **Scandia**) was equipped with two humbucking pickups, D'Aquisto designed 3 on a side tuners, separate volume and tone controls, pickup selector and a tone selector. It has a plain badge on the headstock. The **Viking** looks identical to the **V I N** except it has a floral headstock badge and a wood center block in the thinline hollowbody.

1963 brought out one of Hagstrom's more unusual desings with the introduction of the **Impala** and **Corvette**. Shaped much like the Fender **Jaguar**, the necks were contoured and filled so they blended and flowed directly into the body. When the guitars began import into the US, the **Corvette** name had to be changed to **Condor**, as Gretsch already had the **Corvette** name registered.

Hagstrom Viking I
courtesy Kwinn Kastrosky

GRADING	100% MINT	98% NEAR MINT	95% EXC+	90% EXC	80% VG+	70% VG	60% G

Hagstrom's **Swede**, a "Les Paul"-derived solidbody electric was introduced in 1970. The suggested list price for the **Swede** (Model 803) in 1975 was $640. In 1977, the **Super Swede** made its debut. 1977 brought about the **Scandi**, a three single coil "strat"-ish style. Most Hagstrom models had a corresponding bass available.

In 1969, Hagstrom debuted an f-hole archtop model designed by James D. A'Quisto. The body, made of nine ply laminate birch, these guitars were actually produced by Bjarton of Bjarnum, Sweden for Hagstrom. In 1976, Hagstrom manufactured and reintroduced the **Jimmy** model and in 1977 added the oval hole model. D'Aquisto did not make these guitars for Hagstrom, however he did purchase bodies from Hagstrom and used them in his own line of hollowbody electrics.

Hagstrom and Ampeg teamed up and introduced the **Patch 2000** guitar and synthesizer system in 1976. This system of a modified **Swede** model plus a footpedal had a list price of $2000 in 1977. Due to the wiring design, it is advisable that you purchase both at the same time if the intention is to use it with a synthesizer, however the instrument plays as any other without the pedal.

It should be noted that the values decrease significantly when the guitars are 80% or less, as replacement parts for Hagstrom guitars and basses are very difficult to find.

The publisher would like to thank Mr. Kwinn Katrosky for his significant contributions to the Hagstrom section.

KENT I/H I (F-11) - double cutaway plastic top vinyl covered back strat-ish style design, 4 control switches, 1 volume control, two single coil, 6 in line tuners.

$650 $600 $450 $375 $200 $150 $75

H II (F-200) - similar to the H I but with all wood body, standand style pickguard and top mount angled jack plate, 4 control switches/1 standby switch.

$600 $550 $400 $300 $175 $150 $100

F12-S - 12-string version of the H II.

$800 $650 $475 $325 $200 $150 $100

H III (F-300) - same as H II except has 3 single coils, 6 control/1 standby switch.

$600 $550 $450 $375 $225 $150 $100

H II N (HG 801) - birch body and neck, 2 humbuckers, 3-way pickups switch, 2 volume/2 tone control, adjustable bridge, Hagstrom "tremar" tremelo.

H II N OT (HG 800) - same as the H II N except without tremelo.

$650 $600 $550 $400 $300 $200 $125

VIKING I - thinline laminate f-hole hollowbody, 3-way toggle, 2 volume/2 tone control, 6 in line tuners, chrome fittings, dot inlays on rosewood fingerboard.

$650 $600 $500 $400 $275 $200 $100

Add $50 if with original Hagstrom Bigsby.

VIKING II - same look as the V I except with gold plated fittings and accessories. Block inlays on ebony fretboard. Mfg. 1967-68.

$800 $750 $600 $450 $300 $200 $100

Add $75 if with original Hagstrom Bigsby.

VIKING I N (HG 802) - 2 humbucking pickups, 2 volume/2 tone controls, 3-position tone/3-position pickup switch, 3 on a side D'AQuisto designed Van Ghent tuners, plain badge on headstock, rosewood bridge base.

VIKING – similar to the Viking I N, but the body contains a solid wood center block, floral design on the headstock instead of the plain badge.

$850 $750 $650 $550 $350 $275 $150

SWEDE - "Les Paul"ish in design, mahogany body and neck, 3-position tone/3-position pickup selector, ebony fretboard w/block inlay, 2 humbucking pickups, 2 volume/2 tone controls, 3 on a side D'Aquisto Van Ghent machine heads, floral design on headstock, bolt on neck.

$1000 $900 $750 $475 $300 $225 $200

Add 20% for Patch 2000.

IMPALA - double cutaway, neck-through design, 2 single coils, 6 inline tuners, 8 control rocker switch bank w/separate volume for rhythm and lead.

$1000 $750 $650 $600 $300 $200 $150

CORVETTE CONDOR - 3 single coil pickups, otherwise identical to the Impala.

$1200 $900 $700 $625 $310 $200 $150

SCANDI - very "Strat"-ish body style, ash body and neck, solid maple fretboard with black dot inlay, 3 covered single coils, 1 volume/3 tone controls, 3 individual pickups selector switches, 6 inline Schaller machines, 2 tail strap buttons.

$1250 $1000 $800 $725 $400 $300 $200

HAGSTROM "JIMMY" D'AQUISTO - single cutaway w/f-holes, laminate birch ached top and back, adjustable ebony saddle and bridge base, 2 humbucking pickups, 2 volume/2 tone contols, 3-position pickup selector, 20-fret birch neck with ebony fretboard, block inlay. 24 3/4" scale.

Body length 20". Width 15 3/4". Depth 2 3/4".

Rarity Factor precludes accurate pricing on this model.

"Jimmy" Oval-hole - same body dimensions as the f-hole but with single oval hole, 1 humbucking pickup mounted in the sound hole, 1 volume/1 tone control mounted on the floating pickguard, nickel plated tailpiece.

$1500 $1250 $1000 $850 $500 $350 $225

GRADING	100% MINT	98% NEAR MINT	95% EXC+	90% EXC	80% VG+	70% VG	60% G

SUPER SWEDE - single cutaway "Les Paul"ish, maple body and neck, zero fret, jumbo silver nickel frets, set neck w/ebony board and block inlay, 2 humbuckers, coil tapping switch, 3-way pickup selector, individual string tailpieces, fully adjustable roller bearing bridge, 2 tail strap buttons.

$2000 $1500 $1250 $1000 $700 $550 $400

ELECTRIC BASS

Many of the Hagstrom six string guitars had a bass model available as well. Similar to the guitar design, these are designated above with a * behind the model. The exception to this is the **Super Swede Bass** and **8 String Bass**. Prices for the bass models are approximately 10% higher than for the six string models.

8 STRING - modeled after the H II, 4 sets of 2 strings, 2 single coil pickups.

$1200 $1000 $900 $750 $400 $300 $200

Hagstrom Jimmy
courtesy Kwinn Kastrosky

HALLMARK

Instruments previously built in Arvin, California during the 1960s.

The Hallmark trademark and design was recently re-introduced in January 1995 on a custom order basis. These custom order Hallmark guitars are built in Bakersfield, California. Distribution by Front Porch Music of Bakersfield, California.

The Hallmark company was founded by Joe Hall, an ex-Mosrite employee, around 1967. The Sweptwing design, in its original dual cutaway glory, is strikingly reminiscent of a Flying V built backwards. According to ads run in Guitar Player magazine back in 1967, the model was available in a six-string, 12 string, bass, semi-hollowbody six-string, and doubleneck configurations. The suggested list price of the semi-hollowbody six-string was $265 in the same ad. According to luthier Bill Gruggett, Hallmark produced perhaps 40 guitars before the company ran out of money.

Models generally featured a 3-tuners-per-side headstock, two humbuckers, a triangular pickguard with the pickup selector mounted in the horn corner, a volume and tone knobs, and a stop tailpiece. The doubleneck version has to be more rare than the standard six string, although vintage Hallmarks don't turn up every day.

If you're still smitten by the original design, the good news is that they're available again! Custom order Hallmarks that feature hardware by the EPM company are now being distributed by Front Porch Music. Interested players are urged to contact the company directly (see Trademark Index).

HAMATAR

Instruments previously built in Spicewood, Texas circa early 1990s - 2000.

Luthier/designer Curt Meyers worked on an innovative design that featured primary and secondary guitar bodies that shared a similar neck. A central fret replaced the conventional nut, and there was a separate scale length for the left hand and the right hand. Dubbed the Model X-15, this guitar can produce two notes on a single string. Last known retail prices on the X-15 ran from $499 up to $4,000.

Meyers also produced a guitar called the **J.H. model** that was designed for players that favor the Jeff Healy fretting technique. The guitar consisted of a central body and a pair of necks that shared the same set of strings. Last known retail prices ranged from $1,400 to $4,000.

HAMBURGUITAR

Instruments currently built in Las Vegas, NV. Previously built in Westland, MI.

Hamburguitar guitar models are custom built by Bernie Hamburger. The instruments are available in 6-, 9-, and 12-string configurations, and feature a large number of configurations and options.

Options include a semi-hollow body choice of pickups, body binding, tremolo (where applicable), and a lacquer finish. For further information regarding pricing and specifications, please contact Bernie Hamburger at Hamburguitar directly (see Trademark Index).

ELECTRIC

Hamburger is currently offering 3 different guitar models, all which feature Seymour Duncan pickups and a handrubed tung oil finish. The **Innovator 9 String** (retail list starting at $2,000) has a bookmatched maple top, figured maple neck, and an ebony fingerboard. The lower 3 strings (E, A, D) are paired with strings tuned one octave above the pitch. Both the New Vintage and the **Model T** feature single cutaway body designs. The Model T (retail starting at $1,700) has a stained bookmatched burl top with binding, mahogany body, maple neck and ebony fingerboard; the **New Vintage** (retail starting at $1,450) has a slab mahogany body, mahogany neck, rosewood fingerboard, and P-90-style pickups.

HAMER

Instruments originally produced in Arlington Heights, Illinois. Current production facilities were moved to New Hartford, Connecticut in 1997. Hamer instruments are distributed by the Kaman Music Corporation of Bloomfield, Connecticut.

Hamer Guitars also has an entry level series of USA-designed guitars and basses that are built in Asia.

Hagstrom Super Swede
courtesy Kwinn Kastrosky

H

Hamer Guitars was co-founded by Paul Hamer and Jol Dantzig in 1976. In the early 1970s, the two were partners in Northern Prairie Music, a Chicago-based store that specialized in stringed instrument repair and used guitars. The repair section had been ordering so many supplies and parts from the Gibson facilities that the two were invited to a tour of the Kalamazoo plant. Later, Northern Prairie was made the first American Gibson authorized warranty repair shop.

Hamer, a regular gigging musician at the time, built a Les Paul-shaped short scale bass with Gibson parts that attracted enough attention for custom orders. By 1973, the shop was taking orders from some professional musicians as well. Hamer and Dantzig were both Gibson enthusiasts. Their early custom guitars were Flying V-based in design, and then later they branched out in Explorer-styled guitars. These early models were basically prototypes for the later production guitars, and featured Gibson hardware, Larry DiMarzio-wound pickups, figured tops, and lacquer finishes.

In the mid 1970s, the prices of used (*beginning to be vintage*) Fenders and Gibsons began to rise. The instruments offered by those same companies was perceived as being of lesser quality (and at higher prices). Hamer and Dantzig saw a market that was ignored by the major companies, so they incorporated Hamer USA. The first shop was set up in Palatine, Illinois. The first Hamer catalog from Fall 1975 shows only an Explorer-shaped guitar dubbed **The Hamer Guitar** (later, it became the **Standard** model) for the retail list price of $799. **Hamer USA** built perhaps 50 Standards between 1975 and 1978, an amount estimated to be 10 to 15 a year. In contrast, Gibson reissued the Explorer from 1976 to 1978 and shipped 3,300 of them! In 1978, Hamer debuted their second model, the Les Paul-ish **Sunburst**. While the Standard had jumped up to a retail price of $1,199, the Sunburst's lower price created new demands. In 1980, the company expanded into larger facilities in Arlington Heights, Illinois.

Paul Hamer left Hamer USA in 1987. A year later, Hamer was acquired by the Kaman Music Corporation. In March of 1997, Hamer production was shifted to new facilities in New Hartford, Connecticut. The Hamer company was given their own workspace, re-installed their same machinery (moved in from Illinois), and they operate their own finishing booth.

The Hamer company was first to offer black chrome hardware and double locking tremolos (right from Floyd Rose's basement!) on production guitars. During the 1980s, customized Hamer guitars sported LED position markers, built-in wireless transmitters, custom colors, custom graphics (like snake or 'dragon' skin).

Serialization

Jol Dantzig estimates that Hamer USA has built 48,000 guitars between 1975 to 1995. Serialization is easy to decipher, as the first digit in the serial number is the year the guitar was built. However, since the cycle repeats itself (0 to 9), knowing when the model was produced becomes the key.

Model Identification

Hamer USA (1975 to 1997): All instruments made in Illinois (1975-1996) and currently Connecticut (1997 to date) display either **Hamer**, or **Hamer USA** logo on the headstock.

1998 to Date: Models after 1997 specifically have the **Hamer USA** logo on the headstock.

Hamer Slammer Series: All instruments in the Slammer series are designed in the U.S., then manufactured overseas and distributed by Hamer. The design specifics on these models are similar to the USA models and have corresponding names, but the materials and components are not of similar quality.

Before 1998: Slammer series instruments up to 1997 have the Hamer Slammer Series logo on the headstock.

1998 to Date: !CUIDADO! In a touching show of Solidarity in 1998, all Slammer series instruments now have a simple **Hamer** logo on the headstock (the serial number is on the back of the headstock). Be especially alert to the **Hamer** versus **Hamer USA** designated headstock logos.

ELECTRIC

Hamer USA Guitars are offered with a variety of options. A Natural finish or Black hardware options are available at no extra charge.

Add $35 for pickguard upgrade (Tortoise shell, Pearloid, and Mint Green).

Add $50 for Seymour Duncan pickup upgrade (per pickup).

Add $75 for EMG pickup upgrade (per pickup).

Add $75 for ebony fingerboard.

Add $100 for color upcharge (color finish not listed by model).

Add $105 for Gold hardware.

Add $135 for crown fingerboard inlays.

Add $425 for left-handed configuration.

Add $500 for Ultimate Grade figured maple body.

Anniversary Series

25th ANNIVERSRY LIMITED EDITION (Model AN25L) - Artist body style and neck made of Honduras Mahogany, Ivoroid bound body, neck, and headstock, sterling silver purfling inside binding, bookmatched flamed maple top with F-hole, ebony fingerboard, crown inlays starting at the first fret, sterling silver truss rod cover with 25th Anniversary engraving, bone nut, pearl inlaid Hamer logo, chrome Grover tuners, Seymour Duncan and Pearly gates pickups, sterling silver back plate with 25th Anniversary engraving, available in Cherry Transparent finish. Silver GC-25 hardshell case included. Mfg. 1999.

MSR $N/A

25th ANNIVERSARY EDITION (Model AN25E) - similar to AN25L except does not have sterling silver purfling,truss rod cover, or back plate. bookmatched "Chevron" mahogany top, covered Seymour Duncan '59 and JB pickups, Grover tuners, tune-o-matic, Stop tailpiece, available in Cherry Transparent finish. Mfg. 1999.

MSR	$1,299	$1,000	$900	$800	$700	$650	$600	$500

GRADING	100% MINT	98% NEAR MINT	95% EXC+	90% EXC	80% VG+	70% VG	60% G

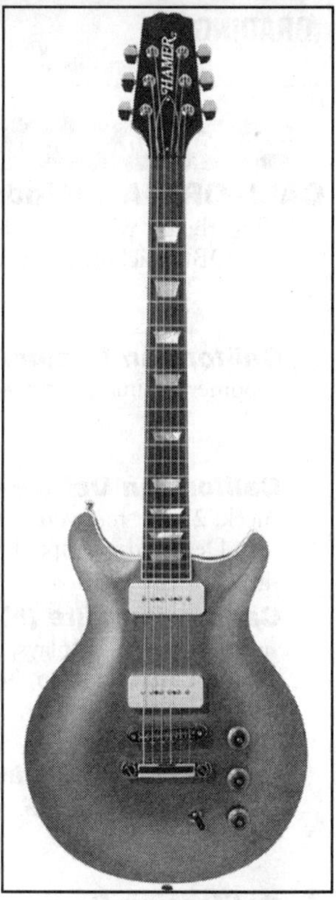
Hamer Archtop GT
courtesy Hamer Guitars

Artist Series

ARTIST CUSTOM (Model GATA) - offset double cutaway mahogany body with sound chamber, arched bound bookmatched flamed maple top, mahogany neck, single f-hole, 22-fret bound rosewood fingerboard with mother-of-pearl crown inlay, tune-o-matic bridge/stop tailpiece, 3-per-side Schaller tuners, chrome hardware, 2 covered Seymour Duncan Seth Lover humbuckers, 1 volume/2 tone controls, 3-position switch, available in '59 Burst (59), Honey (HY), and Natural (NT) lacquer finishes. Natural finish discontinued in 1998. Honey finish discontinued in 1999. In 2001, Honey and Vintage Natural finishes were reintroduced along with the introduction of Red Transparent and Emerald Green finishes. Current Mfg.

MSR $2,899 — $2,175 $1,800 $1600 $1,400 $1,150 $900 $700

Artist Studio (Model GATASO) - similar to the Artist, except has unbound carved bookmatched maple top, unbound fingerboard with pearl dot inlay, Wilkinson Hard Tail wraparound bridge, available in '59 Burst (59), Honey (HY), and Natural (NT) lacquer finishes. Discontinued 1998.

$1,650 $1,425 $1,250 $1,100 $900 $725 $550
Last MSR was $2,199.

ARTIST ULTIMATE (Model ARTULT) - offset double cutaway Honduran mahogany body with sound chamber, arched bookmatched Ultimate Grade figured maple top, mother-of-pearl body binding, set-in 3-piece mahogany neck, one bound f-hole, 24 3/4" scale, 22-fret mother-of-pearl bound ebony fingerboard with mother-of-pearl crown inlays, tune-o-matic bridge/stop tailpiece, 3-per-side Grover Super Rotomatic tuners, gold hardware, 2 covered Seymour Duncan Ultimate humbuckers, volume/2 tone controls, 3-position selector switch, available in Cognac (CN) Lacquer finish. Mfg. 1998 to date.

MSR $4,999 — $3,750 $3,200 $2,900 $2,700 $2,500 $2,200 $2,000

The Duncan Ultimate hand-wound pickups have covers handsigned by Seymour Duncan.

ARTIST (Model GATASO) -offset double cutaway mahogany body, arched flamed maple top, mahogany set neck with rosewood fingerboard, dot inlays, 2 Seymour Duncan Seth Lover pickups, 2 volume/1 tone control, 3-way toggle, Tune-O-Matic bridge, 1 f-hole, tuned sound chamber, Schaller 3 on a side tuners, available in Honey (HY) and 59 Burst (59B) finishes. Current Mfg.

MSR $2,399 — $1,850 $1,600 $1,450 $1,250 $1,150 $1,025 $900

Red Transparent and Emerald Green finishes introduced in 2001.

ARTIST MAHOGANY (Model ARTM) - offset double cutaway finest Honduran mahogany body and neck, book-matched arched top, single f-hole, rosewood fingerboard with mother-of-pearl dot position markers, 2 Seymour Duncan P-90 pickups, 3-per-side Grover tuners, stop tailpiece, Tune-O-Matic bridge, chrome hardware, 2 volume, 1 tone control, available in Silver Sparkle, Cherry Transparent, black, and Jazzburst finishes. New 2001.

MSR $1,499 — $1,125 $1,025 $925 $825 $725 $625 $500

ARTIST MAHOGANY HB (Model ARTHB) - similar to Artist Mahogany except is equipped with two Seymour Duncan humbucking pickups, available in Silver Sparkle, Cherry Transparent, black and Jazzburst finishes. New 2001.

MSR $1,699 — $1,275 $1,175 $1,075 $975 $875 $775 $675

ARTIST KORINA (Model ARTK) - similar to Artist Mahogany except korina body and top, korina neck, 2 Seymour Duncan P-90 pickups, available in Vintage Korina finish. New 2001.

MSR $1,899 — $1,425 $1,325 $1,225 $1,125 $1,025 $925

ARTIST KORINA HB (Model ARTKHB) - similar to Artist Korina except is equipped with two Seymour Duncan humbucker pickups, available in Vintage Korina finish. New 2001.

MSR $1,999 — $1,500 $1,400 $1,300 $1,200 $1,100 $1,000

Blitz Series

BLITZ - radical offset hourglass body, set-in neck, 22-fret rosewood fingerboard with pearl dot inlay, double locking tremolo, 'drooping' peghead with screened logo, 6-on-a-side tuners, black hardware, 2 humbucker pickups, 2 volume/tone controls, 3-position switch, available in Black, Candy Red, Ice Pearl, and Metal Gray finishes. Mfg. 1982 to 1989.

3-per-side headstock

$575 $500 $450 $400 $350 $300 $250

6-on-a-side headstock

$625 $550 $475 $425 $375 $325 $275
Last MSR was $1,125.

The Blitz model was the "updated" version of the Standard.
Early versions of this model have a 3-per-side headstock.

GRADING	100% MINT	98% NEAR MINT	95% EXC+	90% EXC	80% VG+	70% VG	60% G

Californian Series

CALIFORNIAN (Model GCAS) - offset double cutaway mahogany body, bolt-on rock maple neck, 25 1/2" scale, 27-fret rosewood fingerboard with pearl dot inlays, Floyd Rose tremolo, 6-on-a-side Schaller tuners, black hardware, slanted single coil/humbucker Slammer (or OBL) pickups, volume/tone controls, 3-way selector. Mfg. 1988 to 1991.

$975 $825 $725 $650 $550 $475 $375
Last MSR was $1,500.

Californian Custom (Model GCAC) - similar to the Californian, except features a set-in maple neck, ebony fingerboard with pearl boomerang inlay, Trem-single/trembucker Seymour Duncan pickups. Mfg. 1988 to 1993.

$1,100 $900 $825 $750 $650 $575 $500
Last MSR was $2,000.

Californian Deluxe (Model CALDLX) - similar to the Californian, except features a mahogany body, bolt-on ivoroid bound maple neck, 27-fret rosewood fingerboard with boomerang inlays, locking tremelo & nut, 6-on-a-side black tuners 1 humbucker & 1 single coil Duncan Designed pickups, 1 volume control, 3-way toggle, Available in Aztec Gold. Current Mfg.

MSR $789 $600 $500 $450 $400 $350 $300 $250

Californian Elite (Model GCAE) - similar to the Californian, except has mahogany body, maple neck, 27-fret ebony fingerboard with pearl boomerang inlays, Floyd Rose tremolo, Tremstack (stacked single coil)/TrembuckerSeymour Duncan pickups, available in Aztec Gold, Black, Emerald Green, Natural, and Transparent Cherry finishes. Mfg. 1987 to 1996.

$750 $625 $575 $525 $475 $400 $350
Last MSRwas $1,400.

Californian 12-String (Model G12S) - similar to the California Elite, except has 12-string configuration, figured maple top, 6-per-side tuners. Disc. 1992.

$1,100 $925 $825 $750 $650 $525 $425
Last MSR was $1,700.

Californian Doubleneck (Model GDBS) - similar to the Californian Elite, except has doubleneck construction with a variety of configurations (12/6 strings are the most popular), both necks set-in (not bolt-ons). Disc. 1996.

$1,800 $1,650 $1,425 $1,250 $1,000 $875 $675
Last MSR was $2,700.

CALIFORNIAN (Model CAL) - double offset cutaway mahogany body, bolt-on maple neck, slanted 27-fret rosewood fingerboard with dot inlay double locking tremoloe, 6-on-a-side tuners, chrome hardware, single coil/humbucker pickups, 3-position switch, volume control, available in Aztec Gold, Black, and Cherry Transparent finishes. Disc. 1999.

$525 $475 $400 $350 $300 $225 $175
Last MSR was $749.

Centaura Series

CENTAURA (Model GCTS) - offset double cutaway alder body, bolt-on maple neck, 24-fret rosewood fingerboard with pearl offset inlay, Floyd Rose tremolo, reverse headstock, 6-on-a-side Schaller tuners, black hardware, 2 single coil/humbucker Seymour Duncan pickups, volume/tone control, 5-position switch, upper mids boost switch, available in Aztec Gold, Black, Emerald Green, and Transparent Cherry finishes. Mfg. 1988 to 1993.

$800 $750 $675 $595 $500 $425 $350
Last MSR was $1,350.

Centaura Deluxe - similar to Centaura, except has ebony fingerboard, pearl boomerang inlay at 3rd/12th fret, chrome hardware, EMG pickups. Disc. 1993.

$1,100 $995 $875 $750 $650 $550 $450
Last MSR was $1,800.

SLAMMER CENTAURA (Model CTM) - similar to the Centaura, except has maple fingerboard, standard vibrato, reverse headstock, available in Black, Blood Red, Candy Apple Red, 3 Tone Sunburst, and Vintage White finishes. Disc. 1996.

$325 $275 $250 $225 $175 $150 $125
Last MSR was $500.

In 1994, Candy Apple Red and Vintage White finishes were introduced, Blood Red finish was discontinued.

Slammer Centaura C (Model CTR) - similar to the Slammer Centaura, except has locking vibrato, reverse headstock, available in Amber Burst, Black Metalflake, Black Pearl, Candy Red, Cherry Metalflake, Transparent Cherry, Vintage White and 3 Tone Sunburst finishes. Disc. 1994.

$395 $325 $295 $250 $225 $195 $150
Last MSR was $600.

Slammer Centaura Deluxe - similar to the Slammer Centaura, except has curly sycamore body, locking vibrato, regular headstock, available in Transparent Purple and Transparent Walnut finishes. Mfg. 1994 to 1996.

$350 $300 $275 $225 $200 $175 $125
Last MSR was $540.

Slammer Centaura RC - similar to the Slammer Centaura, except has locking vibrato, regular headstock, available in Black and Transparent Cherry finishes. Disc. 1996.

$425 $350 $325 $275 $250 $200 $175
Last MSR was $650.

GRADING	100% MINT	98% NEAR MINT	95% EXC+	90% EXC	80% VG+	70% VG	60% G

Hamer Diablo
courtesy Hamer Guitars

Chaparral Series

CHAPPARRAL (Model GCHS) - offset double cutaway mahogany body, bolt-on maple neck, 25 1/2" scale, 24-fret ebony fingerboard with pearl boomerang inlay, double locking tremolo, 6-on-a-side tuners, black hardware, 2 single coil/humbucker Slammer pickups, volume/tone control, 5-position switch. Mfg. 1988 to 1991.

$825	$675	$625	$550	$495	$425	$375

Last MSR was $1,500.

Chaparral with Sustainiac (Model GCSS) - similar to the Chaparral, except has Sustainiac device in neck pickup position, battery compartment on back. Mfg. 1988 to 1991.

$800	$725	$650	$595	$525	$475	$400

Last MSR was $1,600.

Chaparral Custom (Model GCHC) - similar to the Chaparral, except has set-in maple neck, black hardware, 2 OBL stacked 'blade' single coil/1 Slammer humbucker pickups, volume/tone control, three 3-way mini-switches. Mfg. 1986 to 1988.

$850	$775	$695	$600	$525	$450	$350

Last MSR was $1,750.

The three mini-switches control pickup selection, bridge coil tapping, and single coil phase reversal.

Chaparral Elite (Model GCHE) - similar to the Chaparral, except has alder body, chrome hardware, humbucker/single coil/humbucker pickups, volume/tone control, 5-position/2 mini-switches, active electronics, available in Aztec Gold, Black, Emerald Green, Natural, and Transparent Cherry finishes. Mfg. 1988 to 1990.

$750	$625	$575	$525	$475	$400	$350

Last MSR was $1,400.

Chaparral Elite with Sustainiac (Model GCSE) - similar to the Chaparral Elite, except has Sustainiac device in neck pickup position, battery compartment on back. Mfg. 1989 to 1990.

$1,000	$895	$775	$700	$625	$550	$475

Last MSR was $1,900.

Daytona Series

DAYTONA (Model GDAS) - offset double cutaway alder body, white pickguard, bolt-on maple neck, 25 1/2" scale, 22-fret maple fingerboard with black dot inlay, Wilkinson VS tremolo, 6-on-a-side locking Sperzel tuners, chrome hardware, 3 single coil Seymour Duncan pickups, 1 volume/2 tone controls, 5-position switch, available in 2 Tone Sunburst, Blue Transparent, Emerald Green, Jade Transparent, Kool Blue, Red Transparent, Seafoam Green, Natural, and White Transparent finishes. Mfg. 1994 to 1998.

$800	$695	$600	$525	$450	$375	$295

Last MSR was $1,149.

Add $50 for optional rosewood fingerboard (Model GDAR).

Daytona SV - similar to Daytona, except features 3 active EMG single coil pickups. Mfg. 1994 to 1996.

$750	$650	$600	$550	$500	$450	$400

Last MSR was $1,200.

SLAMMER DAYTONA (Model DAM) - similar to the Daytona, except has maple body, Accutune II tremolo, 3 Slammer single coil pickups, available in Black, Candy Blue, Emerald Green, and Two Tone Burst finishes. Mfg. 1994 to 1998.

$350	$300	$275	$225	$195	$150	$125

Last MSR was $500.

Slammer Daytona (Model DAR) - similar to the Slammer Daytona, except has a rosewood fingerboard, available in Aztec Gold, Black (BK), Candy Blue (CB), Candy Red (CR), and Three Tone Burst (3T) finishes. Mfg. 1994 to date.

MSR	$500	$350	$300	$265	$230	$195	$160	$125

In 1998, Two Tone Sunburst (2T) finish was introduced; Aztec Gold finish was discontinued.

Diablo Series

DIABLO (Model GDBS) - offset double cutaway alder body, bolt-on maple neck, 24-fret rosewood fingerboard with pearl dot inlay, double locking Floyd Rose tremolo, blackface peghead with screened logo, 6-on-a-side tuners, chrome hardware, 2 exposed humbucker DiMarzio pickups, volume/tone controls, 5-position switch, available in Aztec Gold, Black, Cherry Transparent, Emerald Green, Natural, and Red Transparent finishes. Mfg. 1993 to 1996.

$750	$595	$475	$375	$325	$300	$275

Last MSR was $950.

GRADING		100% MINT	98% NEAR MINT	95% EXC+	90% EXC	80% VG+	70% VG	60% G

DIABLO DELUXE (Model DABDLX) - double offset cutaway maple body, ivoroid bound maple bolt-on neck, rosewood fingerboard with boomerang inlays, 2 Duncan Designed humbucker pickups, 2 volume/1 tone control, 3-way toggle, locking nut, Floyd Rose type tremelo bridge, chrome hardware, available in Emerald Green finish. Current Mfg.

MSR	$729	$550	$475	$425	$375	$325	$275	$200

Diablo II (Model GDBS-II) - similar to the Diablo, except has DiMarzio humbucker/single coil/humbucker pickups, available in Aztec Gold, Black, Cherry Transparent, Emerald Green, and Natural finishes. Disc. 1998.

		$800	$725	$650	$595	$500	$400	$325

Last MSR was $1,274.

SLAMMER DIABLO (Model DAB) - offset double cutaway maple body, bolt-on maple neck, 24 3/4" scale, 24-fret rosewood fingerboard with dot inlay, double locking tremolo, 6-on-a-side tuners, chrome hardware, 2 Duncan Designed exposed humbuckers, volume/tone controls, 5-position switch, available in Amberburst, Black (BK), and Emerald Green (EG) finishes. Disc. 1999.

		$485	$425	$375	$300	$250	$200	$150

Last MSR was $689.

In 1995, Amberburst finish was discontinued. Amberburst and Black finishes discontinued in 1998.

Slammer Diablo II (Model DB2) - similar to the Slammer Diablo, except has humbucker/single coil/humbucker pickups, available in Aztec Gold, Black, and Candy Apple Red finishes. Mfg. 1994 to 1996.

		$425	$350	$325	$275	$250	$200	$175

Last MSR was $650.

Slammer Diablo SV (Model DB3) - similar to the Slammer Diablo, except has a standard vibrato, 3 single coil pickups, available in Amberburst, Black, and Candy Apple Red finishes. Mfg. 1994 to 1996.

		$350	$300	$275	$225	$200	$175	$150

Last MSR was $550.

DuoTone Series

DUOTONE (Model GDOS) - double cutaway semi-hollow mahogany body, bound spruce top, 3 round soundholes, mahogany neck, 22-fret bound rosewood fingerboard with pearl dot inlay, strings through rosewood bridge, blackface peghead with screened logo, 3-per-side tuners, chrome hardware, 2 exposed Seymour Duncan humbuckers, piezo bridge pickup, volume/2 tone controls, 3-way magnetic pickup selector, 3-position magnetic/piezo selector switch, on-board 3-band EQ, active electronics, available in '59 Burst, Black, and Natural finishes. Mfg. 1994 to 1998.

		$1,400	$1,300	$1,175	$1,000	$850	$700	$550

Last MSR was $2,199.

The on-board 3-band EQ is accessed through a panel on the rear of the body.

DuoTone P-90 (Model GDOS-90) - similar to the DuoTone, except has 2 single coil P-90-style 'soapbar'pickups, available in '59 Burst, Black, Cherry Transparent, and Natural finishes. Mfg. 1996 only.

		$1,375	$1,200	$1,100	$1,000	$850	$695	$550

Last MSR was $2,099.

DUOTONE CUSTOM (Model DOUC) - double cutaway semi-hollow mahogany body, Ivoroid bound arched spruce top, one f-hole, set-in 3-piece mahogany neck, 24 3/4" scale, 22-fret bound East Indian rosewood fingerboard with pearl crown inlay, strings through rosewood bridge, blackface peghead with screened logo, 3-per-side tuners, chrome hardware, 2 covered Seymour Duncan humbucker ('59/JB) pickups, piezo bridge pickup, volume/2 tone controls, 3-way magnetic pickup selector, 3-position magnetic/piezo selector switch, on-board 3-band EQ, active electronics, available in Jazz Burst (JZ) and Natural (NT) lacquer finishes. Natural finish discontinued 1999. Mfg. 1998 to present.

MSR	$2,799	$2,100	$1,900	$1,800	$1,700	$1,600	$1,450	$1,200

The on-board 3-band EQ is accessed through a panel on the rear of the body.
Red Transparent finish introduced in 2001.

DUOTONE (Model DUO) - modeled after the Duotone Custom, provides electric or acoustic sounds, separately or together, mahogany body with carved spruce top with one f-hole, two Duncan designed humbucker pickups, acoustic bridge mounted Piezo pickup with adjustable 3-band EQ, 3-way mimi toggle switch, available in Jazz Burst finish. Jazz Burst finish discontinued 1999. Cherry Sunburst finished introduced 2000. Mfg. 1999 to present.

MSR	$899	$699	$550	$450	$400	$325	$270	$225

Echotone Series

ECHOTONE (Model ECO) - classically styled , double cutaway design with solid maple bound back and top with bound f-hole, rosewood fingerboard with Mother-of-Pearl dot inlays, 3-per-side tuners, two Duncan designed humbucking pickups with chrome covers, black pickguard, 3-way toggle switch, Keystone tuners, tune-o-matic, Stop tailpiece, available in Cherry Transparent and Two-Tone Sunburst finishes. Mfg. 1999 to present.

MSR	$749	$560	$500	$450	$400	$325	$275	$200

ECHOTONE CUSTOM (Model ECC) - similar to Echotone except has pearl trapezoid fingerboard inlays, gold plated hardware, lyre tailpiece, available in Transparent Cherry finish. Current Mfg.

MSR	$849	$635	$525	$475	$425	$350	$300	$225

H

GRADING	100% MINT	98% NEAR MINT	95% EXC+	90% EXC	80% VG+	70% VG	60% G

Hamer Mirage
courtesy Hamer Guitars

Eclipse Series

ECLIPSE (Model GECS) - offset double cutaway mahogany body, short body horns/rounded lower bout, set-in mahogany neck, 22-fret rosewood fingerboard with pearl dot inlay, Wilkinson Hardtail wrap-around bridge, Lubritrak nut, blackface peghead with screened logo, 3-per-side tuners, chrome hardware, 2 Seymour Duncan mini-humbucker pickups, volume/tone controls, 3-way selector, available in Black, Cherry Transparent (CT), Candy Green (CG), Ferrari Red, and Vintage Orange (VO) finishes. Mfg. 1995 to 1999.

$1,050 $900 $795 $695 $575 $475 $350
Last MSR was $1,399.

In 1998, Black and Ferrari Red finishes were discontinued.

Eclipse 12-String (Model GEC-12) - similar to the Eclipse, except has 12-string configuration, Hamer adjustable bridge, available in Cherry Transparent (CT), Candy Green (CG), and Vintage Orange (VO) finishes. Disc. 1999.

$1,200 $1,050 $925 $795 $675 $525 $400
Last MSR was $1,599.

SLAMMER ECLIPSE (Model ECS) - offset double cutaway mahogany body, short body horns/rounded lower bout, set-in mahogany neck, 22-fret rosewood fingerboard with dot inlay, trapeze bridge/stop tailpiece, 3-per-side tuners, chrome hardware, 2 mini-humbucker pickups, volume/tone controls, 3-way selector, available in Aztec Gold (AG), Black (BK), Cherry Transparent (CT), and Vintage Orange (VO) finishes. Disc. 1999.

$550 $475 $425 $350 $295 $225 $175
Last MSR was $725.

Firebird Series

FB I - asymmetrical hourglass style mahogany body with raised center section, set-in maple neck, 22-fret ebony fingerboard with pearl boomerang inlay, double locking tremolo, reverse peghead, 6-on-a-side tuners, black hardware, Slammmer humbucker pickup, volume/tone control. Mfg. 1986 to 1989.

$750 $675 $625 $575 $525 $475 $400
Last MSR was $1,200.

FB II - similar to the FB I, except has 2 humbuckers, 3-way selector. Mfg. 1987 to 1989.

$795 $725 $650 $600 $550 $525 $450
Last MSR was $1,400.

MAESTRO 7-STRING - offset double cutaway body, set-in neck, reverse headstock, 7 on the other side tuners. Mfg. 1990 to 1991.

$1,300 $1,175 $1,000 $925 $850 $750 $650
Last MSR was $2,600.

The Maestro was a specialty model with a seven-string configuration. The Maestro originally debuted at the 1987 NAMM industry show. More research is being conducted into the specifications.

Mirage Series

MIRAGE (Model GMIR) - offset double cutaway mahogany body, carved figured koa top, mahogany neck, 25 1/2" scale, 22-fret rosewood fingerboard with pearl dot inlay, standard Wilkinson vibrato, 3-per-side Sperzel locking tuners, chrome hardware, 3 Seymour Duncan single coil rail pickups, volume/tone controls, 5-position selector, lead bypass switch, available in Cherry Transparent and Natural finishes. Mfg. 1994 to 1998.

$1,300 $1,150 $1,000 $875 $750 $600 $475
Last MSR was $1,899.

Mirage II (Model GMIR-II) - similar to the Mirage, except has a carved maple top, 2 covered Seymour Duncan humbuckers, 3-way selector, no lead bypass switch, available in '59 Burst, Honey, Kool Blue, Red Transparent, and Tobacco Sunburst finishes. Disc. 1998.

$1,350 $1,200 $1,000 $875 $750 $600 $475
Last MSR was $1,899.

Mirage Maple Top (Model GMIM-II) - similar to the Mirage, except has a carved flame maple top, Wilkinson VS100 tremolo, 3-per-side Schaller locking tuners, 2 covered Seymour Duncan humbucker ('59/JB) pickups, 3-way selector (no lead bypass switch), available in Honey (HY), Kool Blue (KB), and Red Transparent (RT) lacquer finishes. Mfg. 1998 to 1999.

$1,575 $1,350 $1,200 $1,000 $850 $695 $525
Last MSR was $2,099.

GRADING		100% MINT	98% NEAR MINT	95% EXC+	90% EXC	80% VG+	70% VG	60% G

Newport Series

NEWPORT (Model NEW) - double cutaway body style, Ivoroid bound Honduras mahogany neck and body, neck has white dot inlays, hand carved, arched spruse top with two f-holes, two Hamer "Phat Cat" single coil pickups had built in Seymour Duncan's Custom Shop. These are designed so that they can be replaced with humbuckers without altering the pickup cavities. Tune-o-matic bridge and Bigsby vibrato tailpiece. Grover Super Rotomatic tuners. Transparent Orange Sparkle finish. Mfg. 1999 to present.

MSR	$2,199	$1,699	$1,450	$1,350	$1,250	$1,150	$1000	$800

Black Cherry Burst & Jazzburst finishes introduced in 2000.
Vintage Natural finish introduced in 2001.

NEWPORT PRO (Model NEWPRO) - same features as the Newport except has two Seymour Duncan Seth Lover pickups and a tune-o-matic bridge with a stop tailpiece. Mfg. 1999 to present.

MSR	$2,199	$1,699	$1,450	$1,350	$1,250	$1,150	$1000	$800

Black Cherry Burst & Jazzburst finishes introduced in 2000.

NEWPORT PRO CUSTOM (Model NEWPROC) - similar to Newport Pro except has ebony fingerboard, trapezoid position markers, trapeze tailpiece, gold hardware, available in Ruby Red finish. New 2001.

MSR	$2,899	$2,175	$1,975	$1,775	$1,675	$1,575	$1,450	$1,250

NEWPORT 12 STRING (Model NEW12) -similar to Newport Pro except in a 12-string configuration, maple body with Bird's Eye Maple top, maple-set neck, rosewood fingerboard with dot position markers, two Seymour Duncan "Phat Cat" single coil pickups, 1 volume/1 tone control, 3-way toggle, Tune-O-Matic bridge, stop tailpiece, Grover Super Rotomatic tuners, 6-per-side tuners, available in Natural finish. New 2001.

MSR	$2,799	$2,100	$1,900	$1,700	$1,600	$1,500	$1,300	$1,100

Phantom Series

PHANTOM (PHAN) - offset double cutaway Honduran mahogany body, set-in 3-piece mahogany neck, 24 3/4" scale, 22-fret East Indian rosewood fingerboard with pearl dot inlays, tune-o-matic bridge/stop tailpiece, 3-per-side headstock, chrome hardware, black pickguard, Seymour Duncan 'triple coil' (combination single coil and humbucker) pickups, volume/tone controls, 3-way pickup selector, available in 2 Tone Sunburst (2T), Black (BK), and TV Blonde (TV) finishes. Mfg. 1998 Only.

$1,199	$1,000	$900	$800	$700	$600	$450

Last MSR was $1,599.

Phantom Custom (PHANC) - similar to the Phantom, except features a flamed maple top, Seymour Duncan HS-1 single coil/Seymour Duncan 'triple coil' pickups, 5 way rotary switch, available in Amberburst (AM) and Vintage Orange (VO) finishes. Mfg. 1998 to 1999.

$1,425	$1,225	$1,100	$975	$875	$750	$675

Last MSR was $1,899.

PHANTOM A5 - sleek offset double cutaway mahogany body, set-in mahogany neck, 24 3/4" scale, 22-fret rosewood fingerboard with pearl dot inlays, double locking tremolo, 3-per-side headstock, black hardware, black pickguard, single coil/combination single coil and humbucker, volume/tone controls, 3-way pickup selector, 2-way single coil/humbucker mode switch, available in Black, Ice Pearl, Laser Pearl, Midnight Pearl, Red, and White finishes. Mfg. 1982 to 1989.

3-per-side tuners.

$750	$625	$550	$475	$400	$350	$275

6-on-a-side tuners.

$625	$550	$500	$450	$400	$350	$275

Last MSR was $850.

The Phantom A5 was developed in conjunction with guitarist Andy Summers (Police, solo artist).
Earlier versions of the Phantom feature a 3-per-side headstock; later models switched to a 6-on-a-side tuners headstock (estimated circa 1985).

Phantom 12-String - similar to the Phantom A5, except has 12-string configuration, fixed bridge, 6-per-side tuners. Mfg. 1984 to 1989.

$650	$550	$450	$350	$300	$275	$225

Last MSR was $1,100.

Phantom A7 - similar to the Phantom A5, except has both 1/4" phono and 24 pin synth interface, hex bridge pickup, 5-position switch, 3 synth control knobs. Mfg. 1984 to 1989.

$600	$525	$425	$350	$300	$275	$225

Last MSR was $1,700.

The Phantom A7 was equipped to interface with both the Roland G-300 Guitar Synth and the Synclavier system.

Phantom GT - similar to the Phantom A5, except has a single humbucker pickup. Mfg. 1986 to 1989.

$475	$425	$350	$300	$250	$225	$175

Last MSR was $1,450.

This model was developed in conjunction with guitarist Glenn Tipton (Judas Priest).

GRADING	100% MINT	98% NEAR MINT	95% EXC+	90% EXC	80% VG+	70% VG	60% G

Prototype Series

PROTOTYPE - dual cutaway mahogany body, set-in neck, 22-fret rosewood fingerboard with pearl dot inlays, fixed bridge, 3-per-side headstock, chrome hardware, black pickguard, combination single coil and humbucker ('tri-coil'), volume/tone controls, 3-way selector, available in Black, Blue, Red, and White finishes. Mfg. 1981 to 1989.

$600	$525	$450	$350	$300	$250	$195

Last MSR was $850.

This model was available with a locking tremolo system.

Prototype 12-String - similar to the Prototype, except in 12-string configuration, 6-per-side headstock. Mfg. 1982 to 1989.

$700	$625	$550	$450	$400	$350	$295

Last MSR was $1,100.

Prototype II - similar to the Prototype, except has additional single coil pickup (neck position), and additional toggle switch. Mfg. 1984 to 1989.

$600	$525	$450	$350	$300	$250	$195

Last MSR was $850.

Prototype SS - similar to the Prototype, except features rosewood or ebony fingerboard with crown (or dot) inlay, 6-per-side tuners, Floyd Rose or Kahler locking tremolo, 2 single coil/humbucker pickups, 2 selector toggle switches. Mfg. 1985 to 1989.

$650	$575	$495	$400	$350	$300	$250

Last MSR was $1,150.

Scarab Series

SCARAB I - offset single cutaway body with *J-hook* bottom bout, set-in neck, 22-fret rosewood or ebony fingerboard with pearl dot (or pearl crown) inlay, 6-on-a-side tuners, double locking vibrato, chrome hardware, humbucker pickup, volume/tone control, available in various custom Candy, Day-Glo, Pearl, and Phosphorescent finishes. Mfg. 1984 to 1989.

$550	$450	$410	$370	$330	$290	$250

Last MSR was $1,000.

Scarab II - similar to the Scarab I, except has 2 humbucker pickups, 3-way selector. Mfg. 1985 to 1989.

$725	$650	$600	$525	$475	$425	$350

Last MSR was $1,450.

SCEPTER (Model GSRC) - sharply beveled angular mahogany body, set-in rock maple neck, 24 3/4" scale, 24-fret ebony fingerboard with pearl boomerang inlays, Floyd Rose tremolo, 6-on-a-side tuners, black hardware, 2 humbuckers, 3-way selector. Mfg. 1986 to 1988.

$650	$550	$500	$425	$375	$325	$250

Last MSR was $1,650.

Special Series

SPECIAL (Model GSPS) - double cutaway mahogany body, mahogany neck, 22-fret rosewood fingerboard with pearl dot inlay, tune-o-matic bridge/stop tailpiece, blackface peghead with screened logo, 3-per-side tuners, chrome hardware, 2 single coil Seymour Duncan 'soapbar' pickups, 1 volume/2 tone controls, 3-position switch, available in 2 Tone Sunburst, Black, Cherry Transparent (CT), TV Blonde (TV), and Vintage White finishes. Mfg. 1979 to 1998.

$1,050	$900	$795	$675	$575	$450	$350

Last MSR was $1,399.

In 1995, Vintage White finish was discontinued.
In 1998, 2 Tone Sunburst and Black finishes were discontinued.

Special FM (Model GSPS-FM) - similar to Special, except has figured maple top, 2 Seymour Duncan humbucker ('59/JB) pickups, available in '59 Burst (59), Aztec Gold (AG), Blue Transparent, Cherry Transparent, Emerald Green, Natural, Salmon Blush, and Vintage Orange finishes. Mfg. 1994 to 1998.

$1,030	$885	$785	$680	$575	$470	$400

Last MSR was $1,599.

In 1996, Emerald Green, Salmon Blush, Cherry Transparent, and Vintage Orange finishes were discontinued.
In 1998, Blue Transparent and Natural finishes were discontinued.

SLAMMER SPECIAL (Model SPH) - similar to the Special, except has 2 humbucker pickups, available in 3 Tone Sunburst, Black, and Transparent Cherry finishes. Mfg. 1994 to 1995.

$425	$350	$325	$295	$250	$200	$175

Last MSR was $650.

GRADING	100% MINT	98% NEAR MINT	95% EXC+	90% EXC	80% VG+	70% VG	60% G

Standard Series

STANDARD (THE HAMER GUITAR) - explorer-style mahogany body, bound bookmatched curly maple top, mahogany set neck, 24 3/4" scale, 22-fret bound rosewood or ebony fingerboard with pearl dot (or crown) inlay, tune-o-matic bridge/stop tailpiece, chrome hardware, 6-on-a-side hockey stick headstock, 2 humbucking pickups, 2 volume/tone controls, 3-way selector on treble bout, available in Cherry Sunburst, Natural, Opaque Black, Opaque White, and Tobacco Sunburst finishes. Mfg. 1974 to 1989.

	100%	98%	95%	90%	80%	70%	60%
1975-1978	$1,200	$1,000	$925	$850	$725	$650	$550
1979-1989	$1,000	$900	$825	$750	$625	$525	$425

Last MSR was $1,600.

It is estimated that Hamer USA built 50 Standards between 1975 and 1978 (roughly 10 to 15 a year).

STANDARD CUSTOM (Model GSTC) - explorer-style mahogany body, bound bookmatched figured maple top, mahogany set 3-piece mahogany neck, 22-fret bound rosewood fingerboard with pearl crown inlay, tune-o-matic bridge/stop tailpiece, chrome hardware, 6-on-a-side hockey stick headstock, 2 Seymour Duncan exposed pole piece humbucker ('59/JB) pickups, 2 volume/tone controls, 3-way selector on treble bout, available in '59 Burst (59), Black, and Natural finishes. Mfg. 1996 to present.

MSR $2,699	$2,075	$1,825	$1,600	$1,400	$1,100	$850	$675

In 1998, Black and Natural finishes were discontinued.

Standard Dot Inlay (Model GSTS) - similar to the Standard Custom (Model GSTC), except has unbound fingerboard and dot inlays. Mfg. 1996 only.

$1,400	$1,200	$1,100	$950	$750	$625	$475

Last MSR was $1,899.

Standard Korina - similar to the Standard Custom, except features a solid korina (African limba wood) body. Mfg. 1996 only.

Model has not traded sufficiently to quote pricing.
This 1996 Limited Edition was held to 100 pieces.

STANDARD (Model GSTM, STANDARD MAHOGANY) - similar to the Standard Custom, except has solid one-piece mahogany body (no figured maple top), white pickguard, mother-of-pearl fingerboard inlay dots, 2 covered Seymour Duncan humbuckers, available in Black (BK) and Yellow Transparent (YT) finishes. Disc. 1999.

$1,425	$1,250	$1,100	$950	$795	$625	$475

Last MSR was $1,899.

RICK NIELSEN SIGNATURE (Model RNS) - Standard body style with solid maple neck and body, rosewood fingerboard with mother-of-pearl dot inlays, two Duncan designed humbucking pickups, white pickguard with Rick's caricature and facsimile signature, Keystone tuners, three position toggle switch, chrome hardware, available in Aztec Gold (AG) finish. Mfg. 1999 to 2000.

$700	$600	$550	$500	$450	$400	$300

Last MSR was $949.

SLAMMER STANDARD (Model STD) - similar to the Standard (Model GSTM), except has alder body, white dot fingerboard inlay dots, 2 exposed pole piece Duncan Designed humbuckers, available in Aztec Gold (AG) finish. Mfg. 1998 to present.

MSR $799	$600	$500	$450	$400	$350	$300	$250

Black finish introduced in 2001.

STANDARD FLAMETOP (Model STDF) -similar to standard except has ivoroid bound body and neck, flat top, trapezoid position markers, available in Cherry Sunburst finish. New 2001.

MSR $999	$750	$650	$550	$500	$450	$400	$350

JAZZ 5 (Model JZ5) -single cutaway design, finest flamed maple back and sides, arched spruce top, f-holes, bound top, back, and neck, two Duncan designed humbuckers, 3-per-side tuners, maple set neck, rosewood fingerboard with trapezoid position markers, trapeze tailpiece, chrome hardware, black pickguard, available in natural finish. New 2001.

As this edition went to press, prices had yet to be established on this model.

Steve Stevens Series

These models were designed in conjunction with guitarist Steve Stevens (Billy Idol band). A third model, the Steve Stevens Custom (Model GSSC), was issued in 1989 with a retail list price of $1,700.

STEVE STEVENS I - dual cutaway body, set-in neck, 24-fret rosewood or ebony fingerboard with pearl dot (or crown) inlay, 6-on-a-side tuners, double locking tremolo, black hardware, 2 single coil/1 humbucker Slammer pickups, volume/tone controls, 3-way selector, 2-way switch, available in various custom finishes. Mfg. 1984 to 1991.

$600	$500	$425	$350	$300	$250	$225

Last MSR was $1,400.

Steve Stevens II - offset double cutaway mahogany body, set-in rock maple neck, 25 1/2" scale, 22-fret rosewood fingerboard with pearl dot inlays, Floyd Rose tremolo, 6-on-a-side tuners, black hardware, slanted single coil/slanted humbucker pickups, volume/tone control, 3-way selector. Mfg. 1986 to 1991.

$625	$550	$450	$375	$325	$275	$250

Last MSR was $1,500.

This model was also available with an ebony fingerboard with pearl crown inlays.

GRADING	100% MINT	98% NEAR MINT	95% EXC+	90% EXC	80% VG+	70% VG	60% G

Studio Series

Studio Series models, like the Archtop models, feature an arched, figured maple top. In 1998, two Archtop Custom models (the Archtop Custom and the Archtop GT Custom) have been renamed as Studio models.

STUDIO (Model GATS-SO) - slightly offset double cutaway mahogany body, arched flamed maple top, set-in 3-piece mahogany neck, 24 3/4" scale, 22-fret rosewood fingerboard with pearl dot inlay, Wilkinson Hardtail wraparound bridge, 3-per-side tuners, chrome hardware, 2 Seymour Duncan humbucker pickups, volume/2 tone controls, 3-position switch, available in '59 Burst (59), Aztec Gold (AG), Blue Transparent, Cherry Transparent, and Natural finishes. Current Mfg.

MSR	$2,199	$1,699	$1,500	$1,350	$1075	$925	$750	$550

In 1996, tune-o-matic bridge/stop tailpiece replaced the Wilkinson hardtail wraparound.
In 1998, Blue Transparent, Cherry Transparent, and Natural finishes were discontinued.

STUDIO MAHOGANY (Model STUM) - similar to Studio except has book-matched top, Grover tuners, available in black and Cherry Transparent finishes. New 2001.

MSR	$1,699	$1,275	$1,175	$1,075	$975	$875	$775	$675

STUDIO CUSTOM (Model GATC, ARCHTOP CUSTOM) - slightly offset double cutaway mahogany body, arched bound figured maple top, set-in 3-piece mahogany neck, 22-fret bound rosewood fingerboard with mother-of-pearl crown inlay, tune-o-matic bridge/stop tailpiece, 3-per-side tuners, chrome hardware, 2 exposed Seymour Duncan humbuckers, volume/2 tone controls, 3-position switch, available in '59 Burst (59), Aztec Gold, Blue Transparent, Cherry Transparent, and Natural lacquer finishes. Mfg. 1992 to 1997 (as Archtop Custom), 1998 to date (as Studio Custom).

1992-1997		$1,550	$1,325	$1,175	$1,000	$850	$700	$550
MSR	$2,599	$1,975	$1,750	$1,550	$1,350	$1,100	$925	$725

In 1998, Aztec Gold, Blue Transparent, Cherry Transparent, and Natural lacquer finishes were discontinued.

Archtop Standard - similar to Archtop Custom (Model GATC), except has unbound fingerboard with pearl dot inlay, available in '59 Burst, Aztec Gold, Blue Transparent, Cherry Transparent, and Natural lacquer finishes. Disc. 1996.

$950	$795	$650	$525	$475	$425	$395

Last MSR was $1,300.

STUDIO P-90 (Model GAPC, ARCHTOP GT CUSTOM) - similar to Studio Custom, except has 2 creme Seymour Duncan P-90 'soapbar' single coil pickups, available in Gold Top (GT) finishes. Current Mfg.

MSR	$2,149	$1,700	$1,500	$1,300	$1,150	$975	$795	$625

Archtop GT Custom (GAPC) - Similar to the Studio P-90, available in Black and Gold Top finishes. Disc. 1998.

$1,350	$1,150	$1,000	$875	$750	$600	$475

Last MSR was $1,899.

Archtop GT Standard (Model GAPS) - similar to Archtop GT Custom (Model GAPC), except has unbound fingerboard with pearl dot inlay, available in Black and Gold Top finishes. Disc. 1996.

$975	$850	$750	$625	$525	$425	$325

Last MSR was $1,299.

Sunburst Archtop Series

SUNBURST - double cutaway mahogany body, arched bound figured maple top, set-in mahogany neck, 22-fret bound rosewood fingerboard with pearl dot (or crown) inlay, tune-o-matic bridge/stop tailpiece, 3-per-side tuners, chrome hardware, 2 humbucker pickups, 2 volume/1 tone controls, 3-position switch, available in Sunburst finish. Mfg. 1977 to 1989.

$900	$825	$750	$650	$525	$495	$450

Last MSR was $900.

SUNBURST ARCHTOP CUSTOM (Model SBCS) - double cutaway mahogany body, arched bound figured maple top, mahogany neck, 22-fret bound rosewood fingerboard with abalone crown inlay, tune-o-matic bridge/stop tailpiece, 3-per-side tuners, gold hardware, 2 Seymour Duncan humbucker pickups, 2 volume/1 tone controls, 3-position switch, available in '59 Burst, Aztec Gold, Blue Burst, Emerald Green, Natural, Salmon Blush, Transparent Blue, Transparent Cherry, and Vintage Orange finishes. Mfg. 1991 to 1995.

$1,200	$1,000	$925	$825	$700	$575	$450

Last MSR was $1,800.

Sunburst Archtop Standard (Model SBSS) - similar to Sunburst Archtop Custom, except has unbound fingerboard with pearl dot inlay, chrome hardware. Disc. 1995.

$1,100	$950	$850	$750	$625	$525	$400

Last MSR was $1,600.

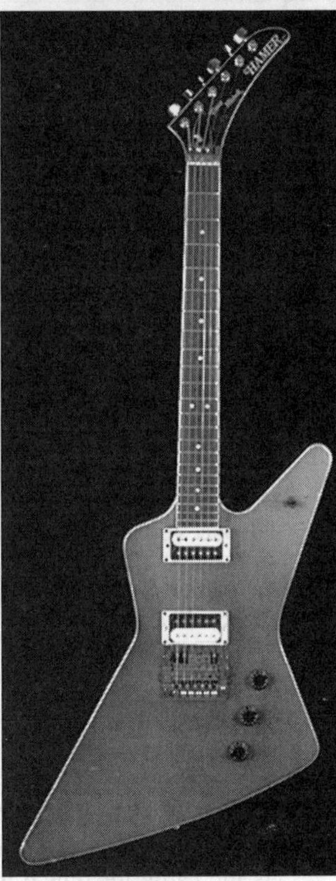

Hamer Standard
courtesy Hyatt W. Finley

H

GRADING		100% MINT	98% NEAR MINT	95% EXC+	90% EXC	80% VG+	70% VG	60% G

Sunburst Archtop Studio - similar to Sunburst Archtop Custom, except has unbound figured maple top, unbound rosewood fingerboard with pearl dot inlay, chrome hardware. Mfg. 1994 to 1995.

		$950	$850	$750	$650	$550	$450	$350

Last MSR was $1,400.

SLAMMER SUNBURST ARCHTOP (Model SAT, SLAMMER ARCHTOP) - slightly offset double cutaway mahogany body, bound carved maple top, mahogany neck, 22-fret rosewood fingerboard with dot inlay, tune-o-matic bridge/stop tailpiece, 3-per-side tuners, chrome hardware, 2 Duncan Designed exposed pole piece humbucker pickups, volume/2 tone controls, 3-position switch, available in Black (BK), Gold Top (GT), and Vintage White finishes. Disc. 1999.

		$485	$400	$350	$275	$225	$200	$150

Last MSR was $699.

In 1995, Vintage White finish was discontinued.

Slammer Archtop Flame Maple (Model SAT-F) - similar to the Slammer (Sunburst) Archtop, except features a carved flame maple top, available in Cherry Sunburst (CS) and Tobacco Sunburst (TS) finishes. Current Mfg.

MSR	$799	$575	$475	$425	$365	$300	$260	$210

Tobacco Sunburst finish discontinued in 2000.
Purpleburst and Blueburst finishes introduced in 2001.

Slammer Sunburst Flat Top (Model SFT) - similar to the Sunburst Archtop, except has a flat top (as opposed to contoured or carved), bound flamed top, available in Aztec Gold (AG), Black (BK), Cherry Sunburst (CS), Cherry Transparent (CT), and Vintage Orange (VO) finishes. Disc. 1999.

		$575	$500	$450	$375	$325	$250	$195

Last MSR was $769.

H

Stellar Series

STELLAR 1 (Model ST1) - double cutaway body design that allows access to all frets, solid maple neck and body, rosewood fingerboard with Mother-of-Pearl dot inlays, two Duncan designed humbucking pickups, silky oak arched top, 3-way toggle switch, chrome deluxe tuners and hardware, tune-o-matic, stop tailpiece, available in Cherry Sunburst and Purpleburst. Mfg. 1999 to 2000.

		$475	$400	$350	$300	$250	$200	$150

Last MSR was $629.

STELLAR 3 (Model ST3) - similar to Stellar 1 except has Duncan designed humbucker and 2 single coil pickups, 5-way switch, mini-toggle coil tap, Wilkinson Tremelo bridge, 1 volume/1 tone control, chrome hardware, available in Cherry Sunburst and black finishes. New 2001.

MSR	$699	$525	$475	$425	$375	$325	$275	$225

T-51 Series

T-51 (Model T51S) - single cutaway alder body, bolt-on hard rock maple neck, 22-fret maple fingerboard with black dot inlay, Wilkinson HT-100 bridge, 6-on-a-side Sperzel tuners, chrome hardware, black bakelite pickguard, 2 Seymour Duncan single coil pickups, volume/tone control, 3-position switch, controls mounted metal plate, available in Black, Butterscotch, Natural, Vintage Orange, and White Transparent finishes. Mfg. 1994 to 1998.

		$800	$695	$600	$550	$450	$375	$295

Last MSR was $1,149.

Add $50 for optional rosewood fingerboard (Model T51R).

T-51 Fishman Power Bridge (Model T51F) - similar to the T-51, except has a bridge-mounted Fishman transducer system. Disc. 1998.

		$950	$850	$750	$650	$550	$450	$350

Last MSR was $1,399.

SLAMMER T-51 (Model T5M) - similar to the T-51, except has swamp ash body, fixed bridge, 2 Slammer single coil pickups, available in 2 Tone Sunburst (2T), Amberburst (AB), and Black (BK) finishes. Mfg. 1994 to 1999.

		$375	$325	$295	$250	$195	$150	$125

Last MSR was $499.

TLE Series

TLE - single cutaway mahogany body, figured maple top, set-in rock maple neck, 24-fret rosewood fingerboard with pearl dot inlay, fixed bridge, black hardware, 6-on-a-side tuners, 3 single coil pickups, volume/tone controls, 5-way selector. Mfg. 1986 to 1989.

		$495	$400	$375	$325	$295	$250	$225

Last MSR was $900.

TLE Custom - single cutaway bound mahogany body, figured maple top, set-in rock maple neck, 24-fret ebony fingerboard with pearl boomerang inlay, Floyd Rose tremolo, black hardware, 6-on-a-side tuners, 2 OBL single coil/Slammer humbucker pickups, volume/tone controls, 5-way selector. Mfg. 1987 to 1989.

		$875	$750	$700	$650	$575	$500	$450

Last MSR was $1,750.

GRADING	100% MINT	98% NEAR MINT	95% EXC+	90% EXC	80% VG+	70% VG	60% G

TRAD '62 (T-62) - double offset cutaway alder body, white pickguard, bolt-on bird's eye maple neck, 22-fret pau ferro fingerboard with pearl dot inlay, standard vibrato, Lubritrak nut, 6-on-a-side locking Sperzel tuners, 3 single coil Alnico pickups, volume control, 5-position switch, 3-band EQ with bypass switch, available in Daphne Blue, Emerald Green, Seafoam Green, 2 Tone Sunburst, 3 Tone Sunburst, Transparent Blue, Transparent White and Vintage White finishes. Mfg. 1992 to 1995.

$950	$800	$725	$625	$550	$450	$350

Last MSR was $1,450.

In 1994, 3 Tone Sunburst was discontinued, Daphne Blue, Emerald Green, 2 Tone Sunburst, Transparent Blue and Transparent White finishes were introduced.

Hamer Slammer Sunburst Flat Top courtesy Hamer Guitars

Vanguard Series

VANGUARD (Model VAN) - trademark double cutaway body style, Honduras Mahogany neck with rosewood fingerboard, semi-hollow body with one f-hole, two Seymour Duncan P-90 pickups with black covers. Unique Silver Sparkle finish covers the entire body, back of neck and headstock. Mfg. 1999 to 2000.

$975	$775	$725	$675	$625	$575	$500

Last MSR was $1,299.

Transparent Cherry finish introduced 2000.

VANGUARD HB (Model VANHB) - similar to Vanguard except has Seymour Duncan '59 pickup in the neck position and Seymour Duncan JB pickup in the bridge position. Mfg. 1999 to 2000.

$1,125	$950	$850	$750	$675	$625	$500

Last MSR was $1,499.

Vector Series

The Vector model was originally available as a custom order only, and then later put into production. Models were built with and without a curly maple top, and with fixed bridge or Kahler tremolo.

VECTOR (MAHOGANY) - flying V-style mahogany body, set-in mahogany neck, 24 3/4" scale, 22-fret rosewood fingerboard with mother-of-pearl inlay, Schaller tuners, string through-body bridge, 2 humbuckers, 2 volume/tone controls, 3-way selector switch, available in Black & White Graphic, Cherry, Sunburst, Opaque Red, Transparent Blue, Transparent Green, and Transparent Yellow finishes. Mfg. 1979 to 1989.

$375	$325	$250	$200	$150	$125	$100

Last MSR was $800.

Vector (Maple Top) - similar to the Vector, except has a curly maple top. Mfg. 1979 to 1989.

$475	$425	$350	$300	$250	$225	$175

Last MSR was $900.

Vector KK (Mahogany) - similar to the Vector, except has a single humbucker pickup. Mfg. 1985 to 1989.

$375	$325	$250	$200	$150	$125	$100

Last MSR was $1,450.

This model was designed in conjunction with guitarist K.K. Downing (Judas Priest).

Vector KK (Maple Top) - similar to the Vector KK, except has a curly maple top, mahogany body. Mfg. 1985 to 1989.

$475	$425	$350	$300	$250	$225	$175

Last MSR was $1,450.

VINTAGE S (Model GVSS) - offset double cutaway figured maple body, bolt-on bird's eye maple neck, 22-fret pau ferro fingerboard with pearl dot inlay, standard ABM vibrato, Lubritrak nut, 6-on-a-side locking Sperzel tuners, 3 Seymour Duncan APS-1 single coil pickups, volume/tone controls, 5-position switch, 3-band EQ with bypass switch, available in '59 Burst, 3 Tone Sunburst, Amberburst, Aztec Gold, Cherry Sunburst, Natural, and Salmon Burst finishes. Disc. 1996.

$1,100	$1,000	$950	$825	$700	$575	$450

Last MSR was $1,800.

In 1994, Aztec Gold, Natural and Salmon Burst finishes were introduced, Cherry Sunburst finish was discontinued.

VIRTUOSO (Model GVTC) - offset double cutaway mahogany body, set-in maple neck, 26 1/4" scale, 36-fret rosewood fingerboard with pearl dot inlay, Floyd Rose tremolo, reverse headstock, 6-on-a-side tuners, humbucker 'rail' single coil pickup, volume controls. Mfg. 1987 to 1991.

$1,200	$1,000	$950	$850	$750	$675	$575

Last MSR was $2,300.

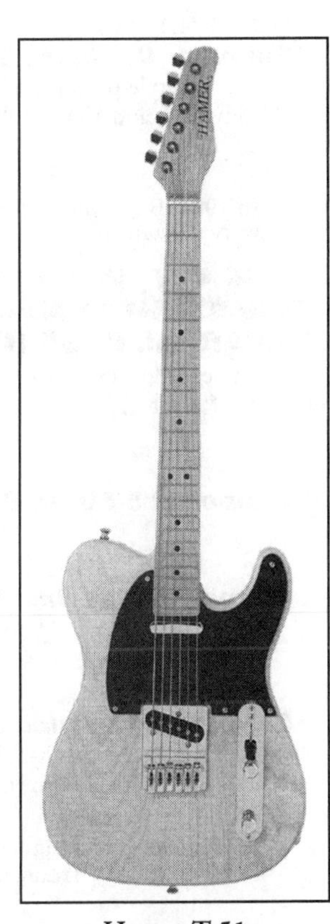

Hamer T-51 courtesy Hamer Guitars

H

GRADING		100% MINT	98% NEAR MINT	95% EXC+	90% EXC	80% VG+	70% VG	60% G

ACOUSTIC ELECTRIC BASS

ACOUSTIC 12-STRING BASS (Model B12A) - single cutaway mahogany body, bound bookmatched figured maple top, maple set neck, 34" scale, round soundhole, 21-fret rosewood fingerboard with pearl dot inlay, fixed bridge, 6-per-side tuners, chrome hardware, 2 EMG pickups (EMG P mounted in soundhole/EMG HB mounted near bridge), 2 volume/tone controls, active electronics. In reality this is a solid body instrument with an acoustic look, available in '59 Burst (59), Black, and White finishes. Mfg. 1991 to 1996, 1998 to date.

MSR $2,799 $2,300 $1,950 $1,650 $1,450 $1,250 $1,000

In 1998, Black and White finishes were discontinued.

ELECTRIC BASS

Hamer USA Basses are offered with a variety of options. A Natural finish or Black hardware options are available at no extra charge.

Add $70 for EMG upgrade (per pickup).

Add $105 for Gold hardware.

BLITZ (Model BBLS) - radical hourglass-shaped mahogany body, set-in maple neck, 34" scale, 21-fret rosewood fingerboard with pearl dot inlay, fixed bridge, 4-on-a-side tuners, chrome hardware, P/J-style pickups, 2 volume/tone control, available in various Hamer custom finishes. Mfg. 1982 to 1991.

$550 $475 $425 $395 $350 $300 $250

Last MSR was $1,050.

Blitz 5 String - similar to the Blitz Bass, except has 5-string configuration. Mfg. 1985 to 1989.

$595 $500 $450 $425 $375 $325 $275

Last MSR was $1,100.

This model was optional with a Kahler tremolo system.

Centaura Bass Series

SLAMMER CENTAURA BASS (Model CB4) - offset double cutaway alder body, bolt-on maple neck, 34" scale, 21-fret maple or rosewood fingerboard with offset dot inlay, fixed bridge, 4-on-a-side tuners, chrome hardware, P/J-style pickups, 2 volume/tone controls, available in 3 Tone Sunburst, Black, Blood Red, Candy Apple Red, and Vintage White finishes. Mfg. 1993 to 1995.

$350 $300 $275 $225 $195 $150 $125

Last MSR was $500.

In 1994, Candy Apple Red and Vintage White finishes were introduced, and Blood Red finish was discontinued.

Slammer Centaura Bass 5 (Model CB5) - similar to the Slammer Centaura Bass, except in a 5-string configuration, reverse headstock, 2 J-style pickups, black hardware, available in 3 Tone Sunburst, Black, Black Metalflake, Black Pearl, Blue Metalflake, Candy Apple Red, Candy Red, and Vintage White finishes. Mfg. 1993 to 1995.

$400 $350 $300 $275 $225 $195 $150

Last MSR was $580.

In 1994, Black and 3 Tone Sunburst finishes were introduced, Black Metalflake, Black Pearl, Blue Metalflake and Candy Red finishes were discontinued.

Chaparral Bass Series

CHAPARRAL BASS (Model BCHS) - offset double cutaway mahogany body, set-in rock maple neck, 20-fret rosewood fingerboard with pearl dot inlay, fixed bridge, 4-on-a-side tuners, chrome hardware, EMG P/J-style pickups, 2 volume/1 tone controls, active electronics. Mfg. 1987 to 1995.

$900 $825 $750 $675 $550 $450 $350

Last MSR was $1,350.

Chaparral 5 String Bass (Model B05S) - similar to Chaparral Bass, except has a 5-string configuration. Mfg. 1987 to 1995.

$1,000 $975 $850 $725 $625 $495 $375

Last MSR was $1,500.

Chaparral Max Bass (Model BCMC) - similar to the Chaparral Bass, except has mahogany or figured maple body, 20-fret ebony fingerboard with pearl boomerang inlays. Mfg. 1987 to 1991.

$1,000 $900 $800 $695 $575 $475 $350

Last MSR was $1,400.

Chaparral 12-String Bass (Model B12L) - similar to Chaparral Bass, except has 12-string configuration, mahogany body, Hamer brass fixed bridge, split-V headstock, 6-per-side Schaller tuners, 2 EMG DC-35 pickups, volume/pan/bass/treble controls, EMG BTS active electronics, stereo output jacks, available in Black (BK) and Cherry Transparent finishes. Current Mfg.

MSR $2,799 $2,300 $2,050 $1,750 $1,500 $1,300 $1,100 $900

This model was designed in conjunction with bassist Tom Petersson (Cheap Trick).

In 1998, Cherry Transparent finish was discontinued.

GRADING	100% MINT	98% NEAR MINT	95% EXC+	90% EXC	80% VG+	70% VG	60% G

CHAPARRAL BASS 9 Bolt Neck, Model B04S) - offset double cutaway alder body, bolt-on maple neck, 21-fret rosewood fingerboard with pearl dot inlay, fixed bridge, 4-on-a-side tuners, chrome hardware, P/J-style EMG pickups, 2 volume/1 tone controls, active electronics, available in Aztec Gold, Black, Candy Red, Natural, 3 Tone Sunburst, Transparent Cherry, Vintage White, and White finishes. Mfg. 1989 to 1995.

		100%	98%	95%	90%	80%	70%	60%
		$900	$850	$750	$650	$575	$450	$350

Last MSR was $1,400.

Chaparral 5-String Bass - similar to Chaparral Bass, except has a 5-string configuration, reverse headstock, additional mix control. Mfg. 1989 to 1995.

		100%	98%	95%	90%	80%	70%	60%
		$1,000	$950	$825	$725	$600	$500	$395

Last MSR was $1,550.

SLAMMER CHAPARRAL BASS (Model CHB) - similar to the Chaparral Bass, except has a maple body, chrome hardware, P/J-style pickups, available in 3 Tone Sunburst, Black, Candy Red, and Vintage White finishes. Disc. 1996.

		100%	98%	95%	90%	80%	70%	60%
		$425	$350	$325	$275	$225	$195	$150

Last MSR was $600.

In 1994, Black, Candy Red and Vintage White finishes were introduced.

Slammer Chaparral Bass 5 (Model CH5) - similar to the Slammer Chaparral Bass, except in a 5-string configuration, reverse headstock, available in 3 Tone Sunburst, Black, and Candy Red finishes. Disc. 1996.

		100%	98%	95%	90%	80%	70%	60%
		$495	$425	$375	$325	$275	$225	$175

Last MSR was $700.

Slammer Chaparral Bass 12 (Model (CH12) - similar to Chaparral 12 Bass except has mahogany body, maple neck with two truss rods, rosewood fingerboard with dot inlays, 2 Duncan Designed humbucker pickups, 1 volume/1 tone, 1 pan with active bass and treble, custom bridge, chrome hardware, available in black and White Pearl finishes. New 2001.

		100%	98%	95%	90%	80%	70%	60%
MSR	$1,299	$975	$875	$775	$675	$575	$475	$375

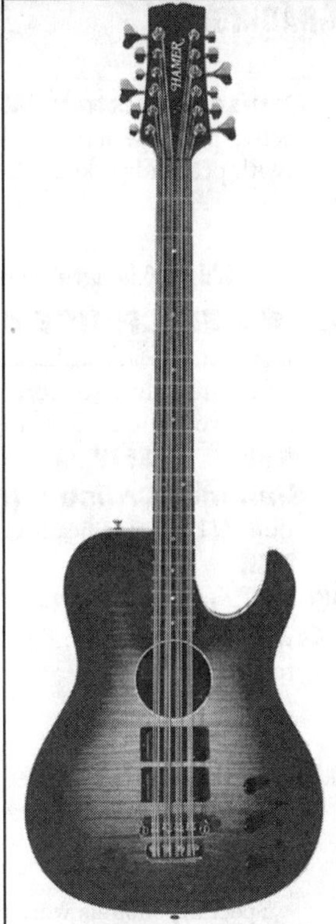

Hamer Acoustic 12-String Bass courtesy Hamer Guitars

Cruisebass Series

CRUISEBASS (Model BCRS) - sleek offset double cutaway alder body, bolt-on maple neck, 34" scale, 22-fret rosewood fingerboard with white dot inlay, 4-on-a-side headstock, Gotoh fixed bridge, chrome hardware, black pickguard, 2 Seymour Duncan J-style pickups, 2 volume/tone controls, available in 2 Tone Sunburst, Black, Black Cherry Burst, Candy Blue, Candy Green, Candy Red, Emerald Green, and White Transparent finishes. Mfg. 1982 to 1989.

		100%	98%	95%	90%	80%	70%	60%
		$850	$750	$650	$575	$475	$375	$295

Last MSR was $1,150.

Cruise Bass (Model BCRT, Cruisebass 2-Tek) - similar to the Cruisebass, except features a 2-Tek bridge, 4-on-a-side Schaller closed housing tuners, available in 2 Tone Sunburst (with tortoise pickguard), Black (with pearloid pickguard), Candy Blue (with pearloid pickguard), and White (with tortoise pickguard) finishes. Disc. 1999.

		100%	98%	95%	90%	80%	70%	60%
		$1,125	$975	$850	$750	$625	$495	$375

Last MSR was $1,499.

Add $100 for an ebony fretless neck with inlaid maple fretlines (Model BCRT-F).

Cruise Custom (Model BCRT-A, Cruisebass Active) - similar to the Cruise Bass (BCRT), except features 2 J-Style EMG active pickups, active EMG electronics, available in 2 Tone Sunburst (with tortoise pickguard), Black (with pearloid pickguard), Candy Blue (with pearloid pickguard), and White (with tortoise pickguard) finishes. Current Mfg.

		100%	98%	95%	90%	80%	70%	60%
		$1,300	$1,150	$1,000	$895	$725	$595	$450

Last MSR was $1,749.

Add $100 for an ebony fretless neck with inlaid maple fretlines (Model BCRT-A-F).

CRUISEBASS 5 - similar to the Cruisebass, except in a 5-string configuration, 5-on-a-side tuners, available in 2 Tone Sunburst, Black, Black Cherry Burst, Candy Blue, Candy Green, Candy Red, Emerald Green, and White Transparent finishes. Mfg. 1982 to 1989.

		100%	98%	95%	90%	80%	70%	60%
		$875	$750	$650	$595	$495	$395	$295

Last MSR was $1,150.

Cruise 5 (Model BC5T, Cruisebass 5 2-Tek) - similar to the Cruisebass, except features a hand carved asymmetrical maple neck, 2-Tek bridge, 5-on-a-side Schaller closed housing tuners, available in 2 Tone Sunburst (with tortoise pickguard), Black (with pearloid pickguard), Candy Blue (with pearloid pickguard), and White (with tortoise pickguard) finishes. Disc. 1999.

		100%	98%	95%	90%	80%	70%	60%
		$1,200	$1,050	$925	$795	$650	$525	$400

Last MSR was $1,599.

Add $100 for an ebony fretless neck with inlaid maple fretlines (Model BC5T-F).

Hamer Slammer Chaparral Bass courtesy Hamer Guitars

GRADING	100% MINT	98% NEAR MINT	95% EXC+	90% EXC	80% VG+	70% VG	60% G

Cruise 5 Custom (Model BC5T-A, Cruisebass 5 Active) - similar to the Cruise 5 (BC5T), except features 2 J-Style EMG active pickups, active EMG electronics, available in 2 Tone Sunburst (with tortoise pickguard), Black (with pearloid pickguard), Candy Blue (with pearloid pickguard), and White (with tortoise pickguard) finishes. Disc. 1999.

$1,500 $1,300 $1,150 $995 $825 $650 $500
Last MSR was $1,999.

Add $100 for an ebony fretless neck with inlaid maple fretlines (Model BC5T-A-F).

SLAMMER CRUISE 4 (Model CRS, SLAMMER CRUISE BASS) - sleek offset double cutaway maple body, bolt-on maple neck, 34" scale, 22-fret rosewood fingerboard with white dot inlay, 4-on-a-side tuners, natural finish headstock, fixed bridge, chrome hardware, white (or tortoiseshell or black) pickguard, 2 J-style pickups, 2 volume/tone controls, available in Black (BK), Candy Blue (CB), and Two Tone Sunburst (2T) finishes. Current Mfg.

MSR $579 $400 $300 $260 $210 $180 $150 $100

Slammer Cruise 5 (Model CRV, Slammer Cruisebass 5) - similar to the Cruisebass 5, except features a five string configuration, 4/1 per side headstock, available in Black (BK), Candy Blue (CB), and Two Tone Sunburst (2T) finishes. Current Mfg.

MSR $679 $465 $390 $340 $285 $235 $175 $125

FB IV - asymmetrical hourglass style mahogany body with raised center section, set-in maple neck, 34" scale, 21-fret rosewood fingerboard with pearl dot inlay, fixed bridge, reverse peghead, 4-on-a-side tuners, black hardware, P/J- style pickups, 2 volume/tone control. Mfg. 1986 to 1989.

$700 $675 $625 $575 $525 $475 $400
Last MSR was $1,200.

H

IMPACT BASS - offset double cutaway mahogany body, set-in hard rock maple neck, 24-fret ebony fingerboard with pearl boomerang inlay, fixed bridge, 2-per-side tuners, gold hardware, 2 EMG pickups, 2 volume/treble/bass controls, active electronics. Mfg. 1991 to 1993.

$1,500 $1,300 $1,100 $1,000 $925 $775 $625
Last MSR was $2,500.

Specialty models were contructed with a neck-through design, pau ferro fingerboard, and used sapelle, purpleheart, and rosewood in their construction.

SCARAB BASS (Model BSCS) - offset single cutaway body with *J-hook* bottom bout, set-in neck, 34" scale, 21-fret rosewood fingerboard with pearl dot inlay, 4-on-a-side tuners, fixed bridge, chrome hardware, P/J-style pickups, 2 volume/tone control, available in various custom Candy, Day-Glo, Pearl, and Phosphorescent finishes. Mfg. 1985 to 1989.

$550 $450 $400 $375 $325 $295 $250
Last MSR was $1,000.

Scarab Bass 5 String - similar to the Scarab Bass, except has 5-string configuration. Mfg. 1985 to 1989.

$600 $500 $450 $425 $375 $350 $300
Last MSR was $1,100.

This model was also offered with a Kahler tremolo bridge.

STANDARD BASS - explorer-style mahogany body, bound bookmatched curly maple top, mahogany set neck, 34" scale, 20-fret bound rosewood or ebony fingerboard with pearl dot inlay, tuneomatic bridge/stop tailpiece, chrome hardware, 4-on-a-side hockey stick headstock, 2 humbucking pickups, 2 volume/tone controls, available in Cherry Sunburst, Natural, Opaque Black, Opaque White, and Tobacco Sunburst finishes. Mfg. 1975 to 1983.

$1,200 $1,000 $925 $850 $750 $675 $550
Last MSR was $1,600.

STANDARD BASS (Model STB) - explored style alder body, flat top, alder set neck with rosewood fingerboard, dot position markers, 2 Duncan Designed humbucker pickups, 2 volume/1 tone control, Gotoh-style tuners, chrome hardware, available in black finish. New 2001.

MSR $899 $675 $575 $525 $475 $425 $375 $325

TWELVE STRING BASS (Short Scale, Model B12S) - double cutaway figured maple body, maple set neck, 30 1/2" scale, 21-fret rosewood fingerboard with pearl dot inlay, fixed bridge, 6-per-side tuners, chrome hardware, 2 EMG pickups, 2 volume/1 tone controls, active electronics, available in '59 Burst, Aztec Gold, Black, Candy Red, Natural, Transparent Cherry, and White finishes. Mfg. 1991 to 1996.

$1,400 $1,200 $1,100 $950 $825 $750 $650
Last MSR was $2,000.

Twelve String Bass (Long Scale) - similar to Twelve String Bass (Short Scale) except has long scale fingerboard.

$1,500 $1,300 $1,200 $1,000 $900 $825 $750
Last MSR was $2,200.

This model was the forerunner to the Chaparral 12-String model.

HAMMERTONE GUITARS

Instruments currently built in Hamilton, Ontario.

Hammertone Guitars builds a 12 string Mando'tar that is tuned an octave higher. For more information regarding this model, please contact the company directly (see Trademark Index).

HAMILTONE

Instruments currently built in Fort Wayne, Indiana.

Luthier James M. Hamilton is currently offering a Limited Edition **SRV** custom guitar similar to the one that the late Stevie Ray Vaughn played on a number of occasions. List price is $5,000. For further information and specifications, please contact luthier Hamilton directly (see Trademark Index).

HANEWINCKEL

Instruments currently built in Artesia, California.

Pete Hanewinckel and Hanewinckel Guitars is currently offering four different models of custom built bass guitars. All four models are all available in 4-, 5-, and 6-string configurations. Basses are constructed with a variety of tonewoods, as well as exotic woods, and feature Bartolini or Lane Poor pickups. Bolt-on models feature 6-bolt neck joints, and neck-through construction is optionally offered.

Retail prices in the Vintage series range between $1,295 up to $1,595; the Classic series prices fall between $1,475 to $1,775; Artist series models are between $1,695 to $1,995; the top-of-the-line Pro series ranges from $1,895 to $2,195. For further information regarding body styles and specifications, please contact Hanewinckel Guitars directly (see Trademark Index).

HANG-DON

Instruments previously built in Vietnam during the 1970s.

These entry level guitars displayed a Fender-ish lean in design, although the composition and materials are basic.

(Source: Tony Bacon, The Ultimate Guitar Book)

HARDBODY COMPOSITE GUITARS

Instruments currently built in Escondido, California. Distributed by Bi-Mar International of Escondido, California.

Designer George M. Clayton is an expert in composite (graphite) materials, and has a background in the aerospace field as well as yacht (Catamaran) building. Clayton was a former vice president and head designer for the Rainsong Guitar Company and currently offers the STS-1 solid body, graphite electric guitar.

The STS-1 ($1,750 new) features a neck-through molded design, ebony fingerboard, abalone inlays, active EMG 89 humbucking pickups, and three custom colors (red, white, or black). Contact Bi-Mar International for distribution and availability.

HARMONIC DESIGN USA

Instruments currently built in Bakersfield, California.

Harmonic Design USA is building two retro-styled guitars for today's players. The **Elektro** (suggested list $1,200) is a semi-hollow body '335' type guitar with a textured multi-flek finish. The **Tweedcaster** (suggested list $1,990) is a Fender-style guitar with aged tweed cloth covering the body and headstock. Retro enough for you? Give Harmonic Design a call!

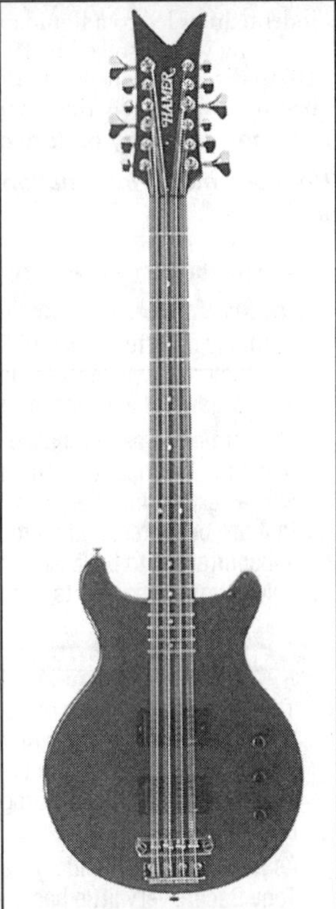

Hamer Short Scale 12-String Bass courtesy Hamer Guitars

HARMONY

Instruments previously produced in the Chicago, Illinois area between the 1890s to 1975.

Harmony, along with Kay, were the two major producers for instrument wholesalers for a number of years (see chapter on House Brands). When the U.S. manufacturing facilities were closed, the Harmony trademark was sold and later applied to Korean-built instruments from the mid 1970s to the late 1980s.

The Harmony Company of Chicago, Illinois was one of the largest American musical instrument manufacturers. Harmony has the historical distinction of being the largest "jobber" house in the nation; producing stringed instruments for a number of different wholesalers. Individual dealers or distributors could get stringed instruments with their own brandname on it (as long as they ordered a minimum of 100 pieces). At one time the amount of instruments being produced by Harmony made up the largest percentage of stringed instruments being manufactured in the U.S. market (archtops, flat-tops, electric Spanish, Hawaiian bodies, ukeleles, banjos, mandolins, violins and more).

Harmony was founded by Wilhelm J.F. Schultz in 1892. Schultz, a German immigrant and former foreman of Lyon & Healy's drum division, started his new company with four employees. By 1884, the number of employees had grown to forty, and Shultz continued to expand into larger and larger factories through 1904. Shultz built Harmony up to a 125 employee workforce (and a quarter of a million dollars in annual sales) by 1915.

In 1916, the Sears, Roebuck Company purchased Harmony, and seven years later the company had annual sales of 250,000 units. Max Adler, a Sears executive, appointed Jay Kraus as vice-president of Harmony in 1925. The following year Jay succeeded founder Wilhelm Schultz as president, and continued expanding production. In 1930, annual sales were reported to be 500,000 units, with 35 to 40 percent being sold to Sears (catalog sales). Harmony had no branch offices, territorial restrictions, or dealer *reps* - wholesalers purchased the musical instruments and aggressively sold to music stores.

Harmony bought several trademarks from the bankrupt Oscar Schmidt Company in 1939, and their Sovereign and Stella lines were Harmony's more popular guitars. In 1940, Krause bought Harmony by acquiring the controlling stock, and continued to expand the company's production to meet the market boom during the 1950s and 1960s. Mr. Kraus remained president until 1968, when he died of a heart attack. Charles Rubovits (who had been with Harmony since 1935) took over as president, and remained in that position for two years. Kraus' trust still maintained control over Harmony, and trust members attempted to form a conglomerate by purchasing Chicago-based distributor Targ & Dinner and a few other companies. Company (or more properly the conglomerate's)

Harmony Archtop courtesy Palm Guitars Holland

H

indebtedness led to a liquidation auction to satisfy creditors - although Harmony continued to turn in impressive annual sales figures right up until the company was dissolved in 1974 (or early 1975). The loss of Harmony in the mid 1970s, combined with the decline of Kay/Valco, Inc. in 1969 (or 1970) definitely left the door wide open for Asian products to gain a larger percentage of the entry or student level guitar market (for example, W.M.I. began using the Kay trademark on Teisco-built guitars as early as 1973; these guitars were sold through department store chains through the 1970s).

(Harmony company history courtesy Tom Wheeler, American Guitars)

(Harmony model information courtesy John Kinnemeyer of JK Lutherie, Ryland Fitchett of Rockohaulix, Ronald Rothman of Rothman's Guitars)

Identifying Re-Branded Harmony Trademarks

Harmony reportedly made 57 "different" brands throughout their productive years. Early models featured the Harmony trademark, or remained unlabeled for the numerous wholesalers. In 1928 Harmony introduced the Roy Smeck Vita series, and two years later the **Grand Concert** and **Hawaiian** models debuted. The **Vagabond** line was introduced in 1931, the **Cremona** series in 1934, and **Patrician** guitars later in 1938.

As Harmony was purchased by Sears, Roebuck in 1916, Harmony built a number of **Silvertone** models. Harmony continued to sell to Sears even after Kraus bought the company. Harmony bought a number of trademarks from the bankrupt Oscar Schmidt Company in 1939 (such as **La Scala, Stella, Sovereign**), as well as expanding their own brandnames with **Valencia, Monterey, Harmony Deluxe, Johnny Marvin, Vogue**, and many (like **Carelli** from the mid 1930s) that are being researched today! Although the Kay company built most of the **Airline** guitars for the Montgomery Ward stores, Harmony would sometimes be subcontracted to build Airlines to meet the seasonal shopping rush. National (Valco) supplied resonator cones for some Harmony resonator models, and probably bought guitar parts from Harmony in return.

Harmony Production, 1961 to 1975

The Harmony company of 4600 South Kolin Avenue in Chicago, Illinois built a great deal of guitars. Harmony catalogs in the early 1960s proudly proclaimed, "We've produced Millions of Instruments but We make them One at a Time." Harmony guitars can be found practically anywhere: the guitar shop, the antique shop, the flea market, the Sunday garage sale right around the corner. Due to the vast numbers of Harmony guitars, and because the majority of them were entry level models, the vintage guitar market's response is a collective shrug of the shoulders as it moves on to the higher dollar American built Fenders and Gibsons, etc.

As a result, the secondary Harmony guitar market is rather hard to pin down. Outside of a few hardy souls like Willie Moseley, Ronald Rothman, Paul Day, and Tony Bacon, very little has been written about Harmony guitar models as a means to identify them. As a result, rather than use the exact **model** designations, most dealers tend to offer a "Harmony Acoustic", or a "'60s Harmony Archtop" through their ads or at guitar shows. It becomes difficult to track the asking prices of various models if the information regarding that model is not available.

The majority of Harmony guitars encountered today are generally part of the millions produced during the 1960s through the company's closing in 1975. As most of them were entry level models, condition (especially physical condition) becomes a bit more critical in pricing. A dead mint Harmony Rocket is worth the money because it's clean - a beat up, player's grade Rocket might not be worth a second look to the interested party. However, the market interest is the deciding factor in pricing - the intrinsic value of (for example) a laminated body Harmony archtop will be the deciding factor in the asking price to the public.

The ***Blue Book of Electric Guitars*** continues to seek out additional input on Harmony models, specifications, dates of production, and any serialization information. This year's section is the starting point for defining Harmony products. Additional information gathered on Harmony will be updated in future editions of the Blue Book of Electric Guitars.

Harmony Pricing Overview

While Harmony did produce a wide range of acoustic archtop and archtop models with pickups, the majority of models were the entry level or student grade instruments. The average Harmony encountered at a guitar show or secondhand store is probably going to be one of the 1960s production models, and for a player's value, most of these will fall in the under $200 range.

Given the interest in other brand name American-produced guitars, there is the faint beginnings of collector desirability on certain Harmony models. Certainly the Pre-war arched (or carved) top acoustics, Rocket series (especially the **H-59 Rocket III model**), or any of the laminated arch tops in mint condition will begin to bring a higher premium. In this case, condition will be everything - the majority of Harmony guitars encountered **have been played** and are not in mint condition.

The Harmony/Silvertone guitar models (offered by Sears) may range in price between $225 to $395, depending on configuration and condition. The Silvertone model with the black finish and single cutaway hollow body with the huge aluminum binding (pickguard and 2 humbuckers) may bring $400 if in clean condition.

Harmony Series Designations

In addition to the Harmony trademark, Harmony models also carry the model (series) designation on the headstock, i.e. **Broadway, Monterey, Patrician, Sovereign**, etc. Some of the Sovereign models may further be designated as "Jet Set variations as well. Keep in mind that there are model distinctions within the series.

For further information regarding Harmony acoustic guitars, please refer to the 7th Edition ***Blue Book of Acoustic Guitars***.

ELECTRIC

Single Cutaway Electric Models

H 62 BLONDE (GRAND AUDITORIUM SIZE) - single cutaway body, laminated curly maple top/laminated spruce back/sides, 2 segmented f-holes, heavy shell edge binding, 14/20-fret rosewood fingerboard with white block inlay, 3-per-side tuners, chrome hardware, adjustable bridge/metal tailpiece, raised black pickguard, 2 Harmony exposed pole piece pickups, 2 volume/2 tone controls, pickup selector switch (mounted on diamond-shaped plate on lower treble bout), available in Natural Blonde finish. Disc. 1966.

Length 41 1/4", Body Width 16 1/4", Body Depth 2 3/4".

The secondary market is still undefined.

Last MSR was $199.50.

H 63 Espanada - similar to H 62 Blonde, except features a 14/20-fret ebonised hard maple fingerboard with pearlette inlay, white body binding, raised white binding, available in Black finish. Disc. 1966.

Length 41 1/4", Body Width 16 1/4", Body Depth 2 3/4".
The secondary market is still undefined.

Last MSR was $199.50.

H 66 VIBRA JET - bound modified single cutaway body, laminated maple top/back/sides, 2 segmented f-holes, 20-fret rosewood fingerboard with white dot inlay, 3-per-side tuners, chrome hardware, adjustable bridge/raised tailpiece, raised bound black pickguard, 2 GoldenTone Indox pickups, 2 volume/2 tone controls ("all in a single row" along lower bout), pickup selector switch (mounted on diamond-shaped plate on lower treble bout), built-in Transistorized Tremolo, Tremolo on/off switch/Tremolo speed/modulation controls mounted on a wedge-shaped controls plate, available in Sunburst Mahogany finish. Mfg. 1961 to 1966.

Length 40 1/2", Body Width 15 3/4", Body Depth 2".
The secondary market is still undefined.

Last MSR was $189.50.

The wedge-shaped ('arrowhead') controls plate in mounted to the top of the guitar, and features an on/off switch, speed and depth control knobs.

Harmony H-66 Vibra Jet
1964 Harmony Catalog

H 68 DEEP BODY CUTAWAY ARTISTS - single cutaway hollow body, bound arched spruce top, 2 bound segmented f-holes, 20-fret rosewood fingerboard with pearlette block inlay, 3-per-side tuners, chrome hardware, adjustable bridge/metal tailpiece, raised black pickguard, 2 DeArmond Golden Tone pickups, 2 volume/2 tone controls, 3-way pickup selector switch (mounted on diamond plate on treble bout), available in Brown Mahogany Shaded Sunburst finish. Mfg. circa 1968 to circa 1971.

Length 41", Body Width 16 1/4", Body Thickness 3 3/8".
The secondary market is still undefined.

Last MSR was $219.50.

H 74 NEO-CUTAWAY (WITH BIGSBY VIBRATO) - modified single cutaway body, laminated maple top/back/sides, 2 segmented f-holes, celluloid edge binding, 20-fret rosewood fingerboard with white dot inlay, 3-per-side tuners, chrome hardware, adjustable bridge/Bigsby tailpiece, raised bound black pick-guard, 2 GoldenTone Indox pickups, 2 volume/2 tone controls, pickup selector switch (mounted on diamond-shaped plate on lower treble bout), available in Sunburst finish. Disc. 1967.

Length 40 1/2", Body Width 15 3/4", Body Depth 2".
The secondary market is still undefined.

Last MSR was $219.50.

Double Cutaway Electric Models

H 60 METEOR (ULTRA THIN DOUBLE CUTAWAY) - dual cutaway hollow bound body, laminated maple top, laminated maple back/sides, 2 bound f-holes, 20-fret ebonized maple fingerboard with white block inlay, 3-per-side tuners, adjustable bridge/metal tailpiece, raised black pick guard, 2 pick-ups, 2 volume/2 tone controls, 3-way pickup selector switch (on treble bout), white truss rod cover, available in Shaded Sunburst finish. Mfg. circa 1968 to 1970.

Length 40 1/2", Body Width 15 3/4", Body Depth 2".
The secondary market is still undefined.

Last MSR was $219.50.

H 60 LH Meteor - similar to the H 60, except features a left-handed configuration, available in Shaded Sunburst finish. Mfg. circa 1968 to circa 1970.

Length 40 1/2", Body Width 15 3/4", Body Depth 2".
The secondary market is still undefined.

Last MSR was $239.50.

H 61 METEOR (ULTRA THIN DOUBLE CUTAWAY) - similar to the H 60 Meteor, except features white dot fingerboard inlay, 2 GoldenTone pickups, black truss rod cover, available in Shaded Sunburst finish. Mfg. 1971 to 1973.

Length 40 1/2", Body Width 15 3/4", Body Depth 2".
The secondary market is still undefined.

Last MSR was $219.50.

H 61 LH Meteor - similar to the H 61, except features a left-handed configuration, available in Shaded Sunburst finish. Mfg. 1971 to 1973.

Length 40 1/2", Body Width 15 3/4", Body Depth 2".
The secondary market is still undefined.

Last MSR was $239.50.

H 64 DOUBLE CUTAWAY ELECTRIC (H 661) - dual cutaway hollow body, bound arched laminated maple top, laminated back/sides, 2 bound segmented f-holes, celluloid binding, 20-fret rosewood fingerboard with white dot inlay, 3-per-side tuners, chrome hardware, adjustable bridge/Bigsby True vibrato tailpiece, raised black pickguard, 2 DeArmond pickups, 2 volume/2 tone controls, 3-way pickup selector switch (mounted on diamond plate on treble bout), available in Shaded Sunburst finish. Mfg. 1967 to 1970.

Length 40 1/2", Body Width 15 3/4", Body Depth 2".
The secondary market is still undefined.

Last MSR was $249.50.

In 1973, the H 64 was redesignated the H6 61.

Harmony H-74 Neo-Cutaway
1964 Harmony Catalog

H

GRADING	100% MINT	98% NEAR MINT	95% EXC+	90% EXC	80% VG+	70% VG	60% G

H 71 - double cutaway body, laminated maple top/back/sides, 24 1/4" scale, 20-fret rosewood fingerboard, 3-per-side Waverly tuners, Bigsby tremolo/adjustable bridge, 2 Harmony pickups, volume/tone controls, pickup selector switch, available in Sunburst finish. Mfg. circa 1971.

Length 40 1/2", Body Width 15 3/4".
The secondary market is still undefined.

Last MSR was $289.50.

This model was available in with a Bigsby tremolo bridge.

H 72 DOUBLE CUTAWAY ARCHED HOLLOW BODY ELECTRIC - dual cutaway hollow bound body, arched laminated maple top, laminated maple back/sides, 2 bound 'S'-shaped f-holes (S-holes?), 24 1/4" scale, 20-fret bound ebonized maple fingerboard with white block inlay, 6-on-a-side Waverly tuners, adjustable bridge/raised art deco metal tailpiece, raised black pickguard, 2 DeArmond Golden Tone pickups, 2 volume/2 tone controls, 3-way pickup selector switch, available in Shaded Burgundy finish. Mfg. 1966 to circa 1971.

Length 40 1/2", Body Width 15 3/4".
The secondary market is still undefined.

Last MSR was $239.50.

H 72 V - similar to the H 72, except features a Bigsby True vibrato bridge, available in Shaded Burgundy finish. Mfg. 1966 to circa 1971.

Length 40 1/2", Body Width 15 3/4".
The secondary market is still undefined.

Last MSR was $289.50.

H 75 - double cutaway body, bound laminated curly maple arched top, laminated maple back/sides, 2 segmented f-holes, 20-fret rosewood fingerboard with white block inlay, 3-per-side tuners, chrome hardware, adjustable bridge/ornamental tailpiece, raised bound black pickguard, 3 DeArmond pickups with exposed pole pieces, 3 volume/3 tone controls, 3 pickup selector switches (mounted on oval plate on lower treble bout), available in Shaded Brown finish. Mfg. 1961 to 1971.

Length 40 1/2", Body Width 15 3/4", Body Depth 2".
The secondary market is still undefined.

Last MSR was $300.

The H 75's finish was also described as "Violin Brown Mahogany Shading with Sunburst Effect".

H 76 - similar to the H 75, except features a Bigsby True vibrato tailpiece, available in Shaded Brown finish. Mfg. 1966 to 1970.

Length 40 1/2", Body Width 15 3/4".
The secondary market is still undefined.

Last MSR was $350.

H 77 - similar to the H 75, available in Shaded Warm Cherry Red finish. Mfg. 1963 to 1970.

Length 40 1/2", Body Width 15 3/4", Body Depth 2".
The secondary market is still undefined.

Last MSR was $300.

H 78 - similar to the H 77, except features a Bigsby True vibrato tailpiece, available in Shaded Warm Cherry Red finish. Mfg. 1966 to 1970.

Length 40 1/2", Body Width 15 3/4".
The secondary market is still undefined.

Last MSR was $350.

H 79 ULTRA THIN DOUBLE CUTAWAY 12-STRING - double cutaway body, bound laminated maple arched top, laminated maple back/sides, 2 segmented f-holes, 24 1/4" scale, 20-fret bound rosewood fingerboard with white block inlay, 6-per-side tuners, slotted headstock, chrome hardware, adjustable bridge/ornamental tailpiece, raised bound black pickguard, 2 DeArmond pickups, 2 volume/2 tone controls, 3-way pickup selector, available in Burgundy Red finish. Mfg. 1966 to 1970.

Length 41", Body Width 15 3/4", Body Depth 2".
The secondary market is still undefined.

Last MSR was $239.50.

Bob Kat, Color Kat Series

In 1963, Harmony debuted the Silhouette Series, which featured three solid body electric models. This Series was renamed the Bob Kat Series in 1969; the models with solid color finishes were renamed the Color Kat Series.

H 15 BOB KAT (H 15 SILHOUETTE) - slightly offset double cutaway maple body, bolt-on hardwood neck, 24 1/4" scale, 20-fret ebonized maple fingerboard with white dot inlay, 6-on-a-side Waverly tuners, adjustable bridge/tailpiece with chrome cover, white pickguard, 2 DeArmond Golden Tone pickups, 2 volume/2 tone controls, 3-way pickup selector toggle, available in Shaded Walnut Wood finish. Mfg. 1963 to circa 1971.

Length 36 3/4", Body Width 12 3/4", Body Thickness 1 1/2".

$125	$100	$90	$80	$65	$50	$35

Last MSR was $87.50.

H 15 V Bob Kat (H 15 Silhouette) - similar to the H 15 Silhouette, except features an adjustable bridge/No. 1750 (Type G/Type W) vibrato tailpiece, available in Shaded Walnut Wood finish. Mfg. 1966 to circa 1971.

Length 36 3/4", Body Width 12 3/4", Body Thickness 1 1/2".

$125	$100	$90	$80	$65	$50	$35

Last MSR was $97.50.

H 14 Bob Kat Single Pickup (H 14 Silhouette) - similar to the H 15 Silhouette, except features one DeArmond Golden Tone pickup, volume/tone controls, rhythm/lead boost slide switch, available in Shaded Walnut Wood finish. Mfg. 1963 to circa 1971.

Length 36 3/4", Body Width 12 3/4", Body Thickness 1 1/2".

$115	$100	$85	$75	$50	$35	$25

Last MSR was $64.50.

GRADING	100% MINT	98% NEAR MINT	95% EXC+	90% EXC	80% VG+	70% VG	60% G

H 14 V Bob Kat (H 14 Silhouette) - similar to the H 14 Silhouette, except features an adjustable bridge/No. 1750 (Type G) vibrato tailpiece, available in Shaded Walnut Wood finish. Mfg. 1966 to circa 1971.

Length 36 3/4", Body Width 12 3/4", Body Thickness 1 1/2".

$115	**$100**	**$85**	**$75**	**$50**	**$35**	**$25**

Last MSR was $74.50.

H 16 COLOR KAT (B, R, W, H 16 SILHOUETTE, H 616) - slightly offset double cutaway maple body, bolt-on hardwood neck, 24 1/4" scale, 20-fret ebonized maple fingerboard with white dot inlay, 6-on-a-side Waverly tuners, adjustable ebonized maple bridge/Type W vibrato tailpiece, white pickguard, 2 DeArmond Golden Tone pickups, 2 volume/2 tone controls, 3-way pickup selector toggle, available in Candy Apple Red (Model H 16 R), Metallic Blue (Model H 16 B), and Gleaming White (Model H 16 W) finishes. Mfg. 1967 to circa 1973.

Length 36 3/4", Body Width 12 3/4", Body Thickness 1 1/2".

$150	**$125**	**$95**	**$80**	**$70**	**$55**	**$35**

Last MSR was $117.50.

The H 16's control knobs are larger than the H 15's 'top hat'-style knobs. The H 16 was redesignated the H 616 in 1973.

H 17 SILHOUETTE - similar to the H 15 Silhouette, except features an adjustable bridge/Type G vibrato with flat metal vibrato arm, available in Shaded Cherry Red finish. Mfg. 1963 to 1966.

Length 36 3/4", Body Width 12 3/4", Body Thickness 1 1/2".

$125	**$100**	**$90**	**$80**	**$65**	**$50**	**$35**

Last MSR was $127.50.

H 19 DE LUXE SILHOUETTE - similar to the H 15 Silhouette, except features larger body dimensions, 20-fret bound rosewood fingerboard with pearlette block inlay, black pickguard, adjustable bridge/Type H (No. 1749B) vibrato, available in Cherry Red finish. Mfg. 1963 to 1968.

Length 39 1/4", Body Width 13 1/4", Body Thickness 1 1/2".

$150	**$125**	**$95**	**$85**	**$70**	**$50**	**$40**

Last MSR was $177.50.

Harmony H-39 Hollywood
1964 Harmony Catalog

Hollywood Electric Series

Hollywood arched (top) models have pickups, laminated hardwood bodies, and "Harmony Hollywood" stencilled on the peghead.

H 37 - arched top hardwood body, 2 f-holes, 20-fret fingerboard with gold block inlay, 3-per-side tuners, chrome hardware, adjustable bridge/raised tailpiece, raised black pickguard, DeArmond pickup, volume/tone controls, available in Metallic Gold finish with Black center panel. Disc. circa 1965.

Length 40", Body Width 15 3/4".
The secondary market is still undefined.

Last MSR was $60.

H 39 - arched top hardwood body, 2 f-holes, 20-fret fingerboard with white block inlay, 3-per-side tuners, chrome hardware, adjustable bridge/raised tailpiece, raised black pickguard, DeArmond pickup, volume/tone controls, available in Shaded Brown Mahogany finish. Disc. circa 1965.

Length 40", Body Width 15 3/4".
The secondary market is still undefined.

Last MSR was $69.50.

H 41 - similar to the H 39, except has 2 DeArmond pickups, raised white pickguard, pointer control (pickup blend). Disc. circa 1968.

The secondary market is still undefined.

Last MSR was $87.50.

Meteor Series

H 70 METEOR - single cutaway body, bound laminated maple top/spruce back/sides, 2 segmented f-holes, 20-fret rosewood fingerboard with white block inlay, 3-per-side tuners, chrome hardware, adjustable bridge/raised tailpiece, raised black pickguard, 2 GoldenTone Indox pickups, 2 volume/2 tone controls, pickup selector switch (mounted on diamond-shaped plate on lower treble bout), available in Sunburst finish. Disc. 1967.

Length 40 1/2", Body Width 15 3/4", Body Depth 2".
The secondary market is still undefined.

Last MSR was $179.50.

H 70 Meteor LH - similar to the H 70 Meteor, except in left-handed configuration, available in Sunburst finish. Disc. 1967.

The secondary market is still undefined.

Last MSR was $199.50.

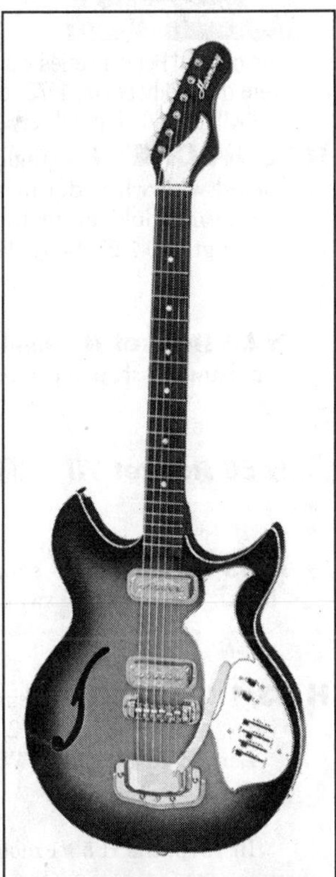

Harmony H683 Rebel
1973 Harmony Catalog

H

GRADING	100% MINT	98% NEAR MINT	95% EXC+	90% EXC	80% VG+	70% VG	60% G

H 71 Meteor (Disc. 1966) - similar to the H 70 Meteor, available in Natural Blonde finish. Disc. 1966.
The secondary market is still undefined.

Last MSR was $199.50.

H 71 Meteor (H6 71) - similar to the H 71 Meteor, except features different Harmony pickups, control knobs, available in Natural Blonde finish. Mfg. circa 1970 to 1972.
The secondary market is still undefined.

Last MSR was $289.50.

Re-designated H6 71 (Mfg. 1973 to 1975).
The secondary market is still undefined.

Last MSR was $329.95.

Rebel Series

Harmony's Rebel Series models featured volume/tone *slider* controls (per pickup) dubbed the "Stick-Shift Controls. "You'll know your settings - Visually," claimed the 1971 catalog. Never mind appealing to the player's aural sense, eh?

H 81 REBEL - offset dual cutaway hollow body, laminated maple top/back/sides, celluloid body binding, hardwood neck, 24 1/4" scale, 20-fret ebonized maple fingerboard with white dot inlay, 6-on-a-side Waverly tuners, adjustable metal bridge/tailpiece with chrome cover, chrome hardware, 2-piece white pickguard, DeArmond pickup, tone change on/off switch, volume/tone slider controls, available in Sunburst finish. Mfg. 1969 to circa 1972.
Length 38", Body Width 14", Body Thickness 1 3/4".

$125 $100 $90 $80 $65 $50 $35
Last MSR was $99.50.

H 82 REBEL (H 682) - offset dual cutaway hollow body, laminated maple top/back/sides, celluloid body binding, hardwood neck, 24 1/4" scale, 20-fret ebonized maple fingerboard with white dot inlay, 6-on-a-side Waverly tuners, adjustable metal bridge/tailpiece with chrome cover, chrome hardware, 2-piece white pickguard, 2 DeArmond pickups, 2 pickup selector on/off switches, 2 volume/2 tone slider controls, available in Sunburst finish. Mfg. 1969 to circa 1972 (as H 82), 1973 to 1975 (as H 682).
Length 38", Body Width 14", Body Thickness 1 3/4".

$175 $150 $100 $85 $75 $50 $35
Last MSR was $119.50.

H 82 G - similar to the H 82, available in Shaded Avocado finish. Mfg. 1969 to circa 1972.
Length 38", Body Width 14", Body Thickness 1 3/4".

$125 $100 $90 $80 $65 $50 $35
Last MSR was $119.50.

Rocket Series

The original Rocket series was discontinued in 1968; however, the "Slash One" series continued on from 1969 to 1972. Two Rocket models (H6 54 and H6 56) were offered between 1973 to 1975. The original Rockets had covered pickups and white control knobs; Slash One models have exposed pole piece pickups and white/gold "Top Hat" style knobs. Body sizes and designs basically remained the same.

H 53 ROCKET I - single cutaway hollow hardwood bodies, celluloid body binding, 2 f-holes, 24 1/4" scale, 20-fret ebonized maple fingerboard with white dot markers, raised white pickguard (marked 'Harmony'), 3-per-side Waverly tuners, adjustable bridge/tailpiece, chrome hardware, Goldentone Indox covered pickup, volume/tone controls, available in Red and Sunburst finishes. Disc. 1968.
Length 40 1/2", Body Width 15 3/4", Body Thickness 2".

$350 $300 $225 $150 $100 $85 $65
Last MSR was $87.50.

H 54 Rocket II - similar to the H 53 Rocket I, except features 2 covered pickups, 2 volume/2 tone controls, pickup selector switch (mounted on diamond-shaped plate on lower treble bout). Disc. 1968.

$395 $325 $250 $175 $125 $95 $75
Last MSR was $119.50.

H 56 Rocket VII - similar to the H 54 Rocket II, except features a vibrato tailpiece. Mfg. 1966 to 1968.

$395 $325 $250 $175 $125 $95 $75
Last MSR was $137.50.

H 59 Rocket III - similar to the H 53 Rocket I, except features 3 covered pickups, 3 volume/3 tone controls ("in a single row" along lower bout), 4 way selector switch (on lower treble bout). Disc. 1968.

$425 $375 $300 $225 $175 $125 $75
Last MSR was $147.50.

H 53/1 ROCKET I - simlar to H 53 Rocket I, except features a GoldenTone exposed pole piece pickup, available in Red and Sunburst finishes. Mfg. 1969 to 1972 (as H 53/1), 1973 to 1975 (as H 654).
Length 40 1/2", Body Width 15 3/4", Body Thickness 2".

$295 $225 $175 $150 $100 $85 $65
Last MSR was $99.50.

In 1973, the H 53/1 model was redesignated the H 654.

GRADING	100% MINT	98% NEAR MINT	95% EXC+	90% EXC	80% VG+	70% VG	60% G

H 54/1 Rocket II (Later H 654) - similar to the H 53/1 Rocket I, except features 2 Goldentone pickups, 2 volume/2 tone controls, 3-way pickup selector switch (mounted on diamond-shaped plate on lower treble bout). Mfg. 1969 to 1972 (as H 54/1), 1973 to 1975 (as H 654).

Length 40 1/2", Body Width 15 3/4", Body Thickness 2".

$325	$250	$195	$150	$100	$85	$65

Last MSR was $134.50.

H 56/1 Rocket VII - similar to the H 54/1 Rocket II, except features a vibrato tailpiece. Mfg. 1969 to 1972 (as H 56/1), 1973 to 1975 (as H 656).

Length 40 1/2", Body Width 15 3/4", Body Thickness 2".

$325	$250	$195	$150	$100	$85	$65

Last MSR was $149.50.

In 1973, the H 56/1 model was redesignated H 656.

H 59/1 Rocket III - similar to the H 53/1 Rocket I, except features 3 Goldentone pickups, 3 volume/3 tone controls, 4 way pickup selector switch (mounted on lower treble bout). Mfg. 1969 to 1970.

Length 40 1/2", Body Width 15 3/4", Body Thickness 2".

$350	$300	$225	$150	$100	$85	$65

Last MSR was $159.50.

Harmony H-59 Rocket III
1964 Harmony Catalog

Silhouette Series

See BOB KAT SERIES.

Roy Smeck Series

Both models were endorsed by guitarist Roy Smeck (the "Wizard of the Strings").

H 57 ROY SMECK (SINGLE PICKUP) - arched auditorium-sized body, celluloid binding, laminated spruce top, 2 segmented f-holes, 20-fret bound rosewood fingerboard with white dot inlay, black peghead marked 'Roy Smeck', 3-per-side tuners, chrome hardware, adjustable bridge/raised tailpiece, raised black pickguard marked 'Harmony', exposed pole piece pickup, volume/tone controls, available in Shaded Brown Mahogany finish. Disc. circa 1965.

Length 40 1/2", Body Width 15 3/4", Body Depth 2".
The secondary market is still undefined.

Last MSR was $105.

H 58 Roy Smeck (Double Pickup) - similar to the H 57 Roy Smeck, except has 2 pickups, 2 volume/2 tone controls, 3-way switch (mounted on diamond-shaped pickguard on lower treble bout), raised white pickguard marked 'Harmony', available in Natural Top/Black back and sides finish. Disc. circa 1965.

The secondary market is still undefined.

Last MSR was $135.

H 73 ROY SMECK ELECTRIC - arched semi-hollow single cutaway body, celluloid binding, laminated maple top, 2 f-holes, 20-fret rosewood fingerboard with white dot inlay, blackface peghead, 'Roy Smeck' logo on upper bass bout, 3-per-side tuners, chrome hardware, adjustable bridge/Type GA vibrato tailpiece, raised white pickguard, 2 DeArmond pickups, 2 volume/2 tone controls, 3-way toggle switch, available in opaque Mandarin Red finish. Mfg. 1963 to circa 1968.

Length 40 1/2", Body Width 15 3/4", Body Depth 2".
The secondary market is still undefined.

Last MSR was $175.

Stratotone Series

Harmony's slab cut solid body Stratotone was available circa mid to late 1950s (discontinued by 1961). While the Stratotone's name was (probably) derived from Fender's Stratocaster model, the slim single cutaway design hearkened back to the Telecaster. Solid body Stratotone models featured Harmony/DeArmond pickups and a 3 on a side headstock.

Solid body Stratotone prices range from $75 up to $175, depending on condition.

Harmony also produced 3 hollow body ('tone chamber') Stratotone models that were discontinued circa 1965. These models featured DeArmond-designed GoldenTone Indox pickups and unique pickup selection/voicing controls.

H 45 STRATOTONE MARS (SINGLE PICKUP) - single cutaway hollow laminated body, white celluloid body binding, hardwood neck, 20-fret ebonised maple fingerboard with white dot inlay, 3-per-side tuners, chrome hardware, adjustable bridge/raised tailpiece, white pickguard, GoldenTone Indox pickup, volume/tone controls, 2 way treble/bass emphasis switch, available in Sunburst finish. Disc. circa 1965.

Length 17 3/4", Body Width 13 1/8", Body Thickness 2".
The secondary market is still undefined.

Last MSR was $72.50.

H 46 Stratotone Mars (Double Pickup) - similar to the H 45 Mars, except has 2 GoldenTone pickups, 3-way switch, 2 stacked control knobs (volume/tone per pickup). Disc. circa 1965.

The secondary market is still undefined.

Last MSR was $98.50.

Harmony H656 Rocket
1973 Harmony Catalog

H 47 STRATOTONE MERCURY - single cutaway hollow body, laminated curly maple top/back, white celluloid body binding, hardwood neck, 20-fret rosewood fingerboard with white pearlette block inlay, 3-per-side tuners, chrome hardware, adjustable bridge/raised tailpiece, white pickguard, GoldenTone Indox pickup, volume/tone controls, 3-way rhythm/treble/bass emphasis switch, available in Sunburst finish. Disc. circa 1965.

Length 17 3/4", Body Width 13 1/8", Body Thickness 2".
The secondary market is still undefined.

Last MSR was $99.50.

The Mercury model's Multi-purpose Switch has three settings: Rhythm (tone preset), Treble (preset with treble emphasis), and Bass (activates the tone control).

H 47 LH Stratotone Mercury - similar to the H 46 Mercury, except in left-handed configuration. Disc. circa 1965.

The secondary market is still undefined.

Last MSR was $117.50.

H 48 Stratotone Mercury - similar to the H 47 Mercury, except has black pickguard, available in Natural Blonde finish. Disc. circa 1965.

The secondary market is still undefined.

Last MSR was $104.50.

H 49 DELUXE STRATOTONE JUPITER - single cutaway hollow body, laminated spruce top/curly maple back, white celluloid body binding, hardwood neck, 20-fret rosewood fingerboard with white block inlay, 3-per-side tuners, chrome hardware, adjustable bridge/raised tailpiece, black pickguard, 2 GoldenTone Indox pickup, 2 volume/2 tone/blender controls, 3-way selector, available in Gold Sunburst finish. Disc. circa 1965.

Length 17 3/4", Body Width 13 1/8", Body Thickness 2".
The secondary market is still undefined.

Last MSR was $147.50.

ELECTRIC BASS

H 22 HI-VALUE - single cutaway semi-hollow body, laminated maple top/back/sides, 2 segmented f-holes, 30" scale, celluloid body binding, 20-fret ebonised maple fingerboard with white dot inlay, 2-per-side Waverly tuners, adjustable rosewood bridge/covered metal endpiece, white "Stealth Fighter Jet"-shaped pickguard, GoldenTone (DeArmond) pickup, volume/tone controls, voicing switch, available in Sunburst Walnut finish. Mfg. 1961 to 1968.

Length 44 1/4", Body Width 15 3/4", Body Thickness 2".

$450 $350 $275 $200 $150 $100 $75

Last MSR was $109.50.

The voicing switch allows the option of the "full bass" or "lighter baritone" registers (possibly a low end filter capacitor control).

H 22/1 Hi-Value - similar to the H 22 Hi-Value, except features dual cutaway semi-hollow body, available in Sunburst finish. Mfg. 1969 to 1972.

Length 44 1/2", Body Width 15 3/4", Body Thickness 2".

$375 $325 $250 $200 $150 $100 $75

Last MSR was $109.50.

H 25 SILHOUETTE DELUXE BASS - offset double cutaway hardwood body, bolt-on hardwood neck, 30" scale, 20-fret rosewood fingerboard with white dot inlay, 4-on-a-side Waverly tuners, adjustable metal bridge/string damper/tailpiece with chrome cover, Golden Tone pickup, volume/tone controls, 2 pushbutton volume/tone preset controls, available in Cherry Red finish. Mfg. 1966 to circa 1972.

Length 44 3/4", Body Width 13", Body Thickness 1 1/2".

$225 $175 $125 $100 $90 $80 $65

Last MSR was $139.50.

H 27 THIN HOLLOW DOUBLE CUTAWAY BASS - dual cutaway hollow body, bound laminated curly maple top, laminated maple back/sides, 2 segmented f-holes, 30" scale, 20-fret bound rosewood fingerboard with white dot inlay, 4-on-a-side Waverly tuners, adjustable metal bridge with nickel-plated cover, 2 GoldenTone pickups, 2 volume/2 tone controls, pickup selector switch, available in Sunburst finish. Mfg. 1966 to circa 1972.

Length 45", Body Width 15 3/4", Body Thickness 2".

$325 $250 $195 $150 $100 $85 $65

Last MSR was $199.50.

HARPERS

Instruments currently built in Apple Valley, California.

Harper's Guitars is a family owned and operated business that designs and builds high quality, solid body electric guitars. According to Jon Harper, Harper's Guitars builds instruments in the traditional manner, by hand - which gives the models a quality, personality, and playability that cannot be obtained in a mass produced instrument. For further information, contact Harper's Guitars directly (see Trademark Index).

A pair of custom built models from Harper's include the Marin ($1,695) that features a figured maple top over a mahogany body, and the Eric Bloom Signature Model ($1,795), which was developed in part with guitarist Eric Bloom (Blue Oyster Cult).

ELECTRIC

Both the **Monterey** and **Sierra** models feature basswood, poplar, or alder bodies, satin tung oil finished maple necks, a 25 1/2" scale, 22-fret maple fingerboards with black dot inlay, Sperzel locking tuners, Schaller non-tremolo bridges, and 2 DiMarzio humbuckers (volume control and 3-way toggle switch). Both models are available in a solid color finish with a suggested retail price of $1,595.

The **Mojave** model is similar to the above models, except features either an ash or mahogany body, 2TEK bridge, hand rubbed oil finish or choice of a translucent finish (retail $1,895). Harper's Guitars offers a wide range of options such as bookmatched tops, different body and neck woods, hardware, and inlays all available at additional costs.

HARPTONE

HARPTONE MANUFACTURING CORPORATION.

Instruments built in Newark, New Jersey 1966 to mid-1970s.

The Harptone company was a commercial successor to the Felsberg Company (circa 1893). During the 1930s, Harptone was more known for musical instrument accessories, although a few guitars were built between 1924 and 1942.

The Harptone Manufacturing Corporation was located at 127 South 15th Street in Newark, New Jersey (07107) during the early to mid 1960s. Harptone's main guitar designer was Stan Koontz (who also designed Standel and his own signature guitars). Harptone's guitar product line consisted of mainly acoustic guitar models, including acoustic archtop models.

When Micro-Frets closed operations in Maryland in either 1974 or 1975, the company assets were purchased by David Sturgill. Sturgill, who served as the company president of Grammer Guitars for three years, let his sons John and Danny gain access to leftover Micro-Frets parts. In addition to those parts, they had also purchased the remains of New Jersey's Harptone guitar company. The two assembled a number of solid body guitars which were then sold under the 'Diamond-S' trademark. Unfortunately, that business venture did not catch on, and dissolved sometime in 1976.

(Company history courtesy Tom Wheeler, American Guitars)

Harper's Marin Model courtesy Harper's Guitars

Harptone instruments were built between 1966 to the mid-1970s. Research continues on the production dates per model, and as such none of the following models below will have an indicated date(s) of manufacture. Instruments can be dated by examining the components (pickups, hardware, tuners) and especially the potentiometers (where applicable). The ***Blue Book of Electric Guitars*** will continue to update further discoveries in future editions.

For further information regarding Harptone acoustic models, please refer to the 7th Edition ***Blue Book of Acoustic Guitars***.

ELECTRIC BASS

400 BASS - semi-acoustic maple body, 30 1/2" scale, 19-fret rosewood fingerboard, adjustable metal bridge, Grover tuners, DeArmond pickup, volume/tone controls.

Body Width 16", Body Thickness 1 3/4" .

The secondary market is still undefined.

Last MSR was $299.95.

HARTKE

Instruments currently built in Syosset, New York.

Hartke makes the XL-4 bass, which features a Vaccaro double T-bar aluminum neck, figured maple neck shell, poplar body, and special electronics. Please contact the company directly for more information, including availability and pricing (see Trademark Index).

HAWK

See FRAMUS and KLIRA.

Instruments previously built in West Germany during the early 1960s.

The Hawk trademark was a brandname used by a UK importer. Instruments imported into England were built by either Framus or Klira in Germany, and are identical to their respective builder's models.

(Source: Tony Bacon and Paul Day, The Guru's Guitar Guide)

R. HAYES INSTRUMENTS

Instruments currently built in Cincinnati, Ohio.

Following three and one-half years of designing, prototyping, and licensing negotiations, Rick Hayes and R. Hayes Instruments of Cincinnati, Ohio, unveiled the first in a series of unique licensed sculpted guitars at the 1998 Summer Session NAMM show in Nashville. Leading the product line is a **Bugs Bunny** model with a worldwide limited edition of only 100 pieces. It is not simply a guitar with characters sculpted into it, it is a character "sculpted" into a guitar - with the integrity of value of the Warner Bros. stamp of approval. This guitar marries artistic form with outstanding musical attributes. Each instrument is part of the complete set of 100, yet the nature of the handwork involved ensures that each is unique in its own right.

As part of the baby boomer generation, Hayes grew up with the Looney Tunes characters - and now he can share them with his teenage sons who find them as captivating as ever. Following a stint with Kenner Products working as a designer on the original Star Wars toy line, Hayes has since managed to keep a hand in music and art related projects at all times. Hayes admits that this has been his most exciting project to date.

Following the **Bugs Bunny** model will be a **Sylvester with Tweety Bird** model, then **Yosemite Sam** and on to several other Warner Bros. character guitars. Negotiations are currently underway with other unrelated licensing entities, as well as other Warner Bros. movie properties. Regardless of the model, only top of the line materials and parts are chosen for their musical and aesthetic qualities. Retail price is $12,000 per instrument, and they will be sold through the R. Hayes website, Warner Bros. Studio stores, and through select retail outlets.

(Company information courtesy Lyn Ebbing, R. Hayes Instruments)

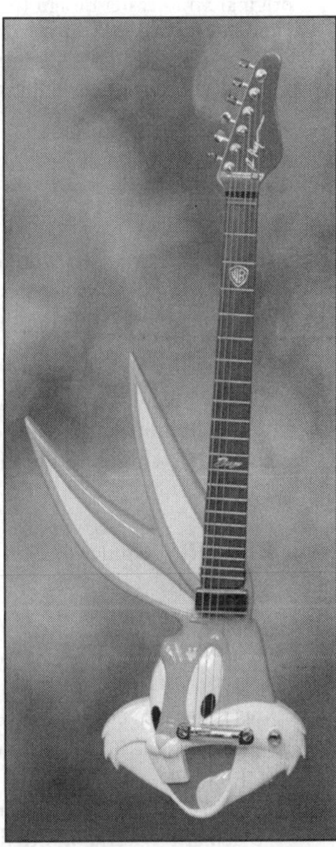

R. Hayes Bugs Bunny Model courtesy R. Hayes Instruments

ELECTRIC

The Bugs Bunny guitar is constructed of top grade AAA maple that is individually carved and painstakingly sanded, then airbrushed, clearcoated, and buffed to a high gloss shine. The Canadian hard rock maple neck is reinforced with a unique two- way double action adjustable truss rod, and topped with a natural ebony fingerboard detailed with intricate mother-

GRADING	100% MINT	98% NEAR MINT	95% EXC+	90% EXC	80% VG+	70% VG	60% G

of-pearl inlay. The neck is then secured with a custom engraved and numbered solid brass neckplate. Added features include a custom wound humbucking pickup, LP JR. bridge, Gotoh locking tuners, and a graphite nut. Retail price is $12,000, and the edition is limited to only 100 pieces.

Each instrument travels in a custom fit Anvil ATA (Air Travel Association) approved flight case with combination lock, and is accompanied by a color Certificate of Authenticity placed in a gold embossed leather portfolio hand signed by Hayes. Additional measures have been taken to provide authenticity protection.

HAYMAN

Instruments previously built in England during the mid 1970s.

In 1969, luthier Jim Burns (ex-Burns, Burns-Weill) was invited into the Dallas-Arbiter organization to develop a new line of guitars under the Hayman trademark. His working collaboration with Bob Pearson (ex-Vox) ultimately developed designs for three guitars and one bass. Woodworking and truss rod work were done by Jack Golder and Norman Holder, who had been with Jim Burns previously.

Instruments were produced from 1970 through 1973. Jim Burns moved on from Dallas-Arbiter in 1971, leaving Pearson to continue developing new ideas. When Dallas-Arbiter folded in the mid 1970s, Pearson joined with Golder and Holder to form the Shergold company. Hayman instruments, while not as flashy as their Burns predecessors, were still solid instruments, and also a link to formation of the later Shergold models.

According to authors Tony Bacon and Paul Day, the last two digits of a Hayman serial number indicate the year of manufacture. This practice began in 1974.

(Source: Paul Day, The Burns Book)

HAYNIE, LES

Instruments currently built in Eureka Springs, Arkansas.

Les Haynie hand crafts custom guitars in his shop in Eureka Springs. For further information concerning models and pricing, please contact luthier Haynie directly (see Trademark Index).

HEART/HEARTWOOD

Instruments previously built in England during the mid to late 1980s. Renamed HEARTWOOD in 1988.

Early models of these high quality original and Fender-style guitars had heart-shaped fretboard and headstock inlays.

(Source: Tony Bacon and Paul Day, The Guru's Guitar Guide)

HEARTFIELD

Instruments previously produced in Japan from 1989 through 1994. Distributed by the Fender Musical Instruments Corporation located in Scottsdale, Arizona.

As part of a reciprocal agreement, the Japanese Fuji Gen Gakki company that produced various Fender models received distribution assistance from FMIC for the Heartfield line. During the mid to late 1980s, various companies such as Jackson/Charvel popularized the "superstrat" concept: different pickup combinations and locking tremolos that updated the original Fender Stratocaster design. As Fender never had much success straying from the original Stratocaster design (like the Katana or Performer models), the Heartfield models filled a niche in promotion of designs "too radical" for the Fender trademark. Heartfield models were designed both at Fender USA and Fender Japan.

Some Heartfield models featured active electronics or other 'non-Fender' associated designs. Later production models may also have **Heartfield by Fender** on the headstock instead of the standard Heartfield logo.

ELECTRIC

Elan Series

ELAN I - double offset cutaway mahogany body, bookmatched figured maple top, mahogany neck, 22-fret ebony fingerboard with pearl dot inlay, fixed bridge, 3-per-side tuners with pearl buttons, gold hardware, 2 humbucker pickups, volume/tone control, 5-position switch, available in Amber, Antique Burst, Crimson Transparent and Sapphire Blue Transparent finishes. Mfg. 1991 to 1993.

$775	$675	$550	$450	$400	$375	$325

Last MSR was $1,120.

From 1991 to 1992, these models featured ivoroid bound figured maple top, bound fingerboard with triangle inlay, and humbucker/single coil/humbucker pickups.

Elan II - similar to Elan I, except has locking Floyd Rose vibrato, locking tuners, chrome hardware.

$795	$725	$595	$475	$425	$395	$325

Last MSR was $1,190.

Elan III - similar to Elan I, except has double locking Floyd Rose vibrato, black hardware, humbucker/single coil/humbucker pickups.

$850	$775	$700	$550	$500	$450	$400

Last MSR was $1,400.

EX Series

This series was produced in 1992 only.

EX I - double offset cutaway basswood body, mahogany neck, 22-fret rosewood fingerboard with pearl dot inlay, double locking Floyd Rose vibrato, 3-per-side tuners, black hardware, 3 single coil pickups, 2 in a humbucker configuration in bridge position, volume/tone/boost control, 5-position switch, series/parallel mini switch, active electronics, available in Black, Chrome Red, Frost Red, Midnight Blue, Montego Black and Mystic White finishes.

$575	$400	$350	$275	$225	$200	$175

GRADING	100% MINT	98% NEAR MINT	95% EXC+	90% EXC	80% VG+	70% VG	60% G

EX II - similar to EX I, except has figured maple top, available in Amber, Antique Burst, Crimson Transparent and Sapphire Blue Transparent finishes.

$600	$425	$350	$300	$250	$225	$195

RR Series

RR 8 - offset double shorthorn cutaway alder body, white pickguard, mahogany neck, 22-fret rosewood fingerboard with pearl dot inlay, fixed bridge, 3-per-side tuners, chrome hardware, humbucker pickup, volume/tone control, 3 mini switches with LED's, active electronics, available in Blue Sparkle, Brite White, Frost Red and Yellow Sparkle finishes. Mfg. 1991 to 1993.

$450	$355	$295	$250	$195	$175	$150

RR 9 - similar to RR 8, except has standard vibrato.

$525	$375	$325	$275	$225	$175	$150

RR 58 - offset double short horn cutaway mahogany body, black pickguard, mahogany neck, 22-fret rosewood fingerboard with abalone dot inlay, fixed bridge, 3-per-side tuners, chrome hardware, 2 humbucker pickups, volume/tone control, 5-position switch, available in Blonde, Crimson Transparent and Emerald Green Transparent finishes. Mfg. 1991 to 1993.

$575	$495	$425	$350	$275	$250	$225

RR 59 - similar to RR 58, except has standard vibrato, locking tuners, 2 humbucker pickups.

$625	$525	$450	$375	$300	$275	$225

Talon Series

TALON - double offset cutaway basswood body, black pickguard, bolt-on maple neck, 22-fret rosewood fingerboard with pearl dot inlay, double locking Floyd Rose vibrato, 6-on-a-side tuners, black hardware, 2 single coil/1 humbucker pickups, volume/tone control, 5-position switch, available in Black, Chrome Red, Frost Red, Midnight Blue, Montego Black and Mystic White finishes. Mfg. 1991 to 1993.

$375	$325	$295	$250	$195	$175	$150

Talon I - similar to Talon, except has humbucker/single coil/humbucker pickups.

$450	$400	$350	$300	$250	$225	$195

Talon II - similar to Talon, except has 24-fret fingerboard, 2 DiMarzio humbucker pickups.

$550	$425	$395	$325	$250	$225	$200

Talon III - similar to Talon, except has humbucker/single coil/humbucker pickups.

$650	$550	$475	$400	$325	$275	$250

Talon III R - similar to Talon III, except has a reverse headstock and no pickguard (rear loaded controls).

$650	$550	$475	$400	$325	$295	$275

TALON IV - double offset cutaway basswood body, black pickguard, bolt-on maple neck, 24-fret rosewood fingerboard with triangle inlay, 12th and 24th frets have additional red triangle inlay, double locking Floyd Rose vibrato, 6-on-a-side tuners, black hardware, humbucker/single coil/humbucker pickups, volume/tone control, 5-position switch, available in Black, Chrome Red, Frost Red, Midnight Blue, Montego Black and Mystic White finishes. Mfg. 1991 to 1993.

$695	$650	$550	$475	$375	$325	$275

Talon V - similar to Talon IV, except has a reverse headstock.

$650	$600	$525	$450	$375	$300	$275

ELECTRIC BASS

DR Series

This series had an offset double cutaway alder body, bolt-on 3-piece maple/graphite neck, rosewood fingerboard with offset pearl dot inlay, fixed bridge, 2 J-style pickups, volume/tone/balance controls, 2 position switch, active electronics. Mfg. 1991 to 1993.

DR 4 - 22-fret fingerboard, 2-per-side tuners, chrome hardware, available in Black Pearl Burst, Blue Pearl Burst, Mystic White and Red Pearl Burst finishes.

$750	$700	$600	$500	$400	$350	$300

DR 5 - 5 strings, 24-fret fingerboard, 2/3-per-side tuners, chrome hardware.

$775	$725	$650	$550	$450	$395	$325

DR 6 - 6 strings, 24-fret fingerboard, 3-per-side tuners, gold hardware, 2 humbucker pickups, available in Black, Chrome Red, Frost Red, Midnight Blue and Mystic White finishes.

$795	$750	$700	$650	$550	$450	$400

H

GRADING	100% MINT	98% NEAR MINT	95% EXC+	90% EXC	80% VG+	70% VG	60% G

DR C Series

This series had an offset double cutaway figured hardwood body, through-body 3-piece maple/graphite neck, 24-fret rosewood fingerboard with offset pearl dot inlay, fixed bridge, gold hardware, 2 J-style pickups, volume/tone/balance controls, 2-position switch, active electronics. This series is custom made, available in Antique Burst, Crimson Stain, Ebony Stain and Natural finishes. Mfg. 1991 to 1993.

DR 4 C - 2-per-side tuners.

$1,200	$1,000	$950	$850	$675	$600	$550

DR 5 C - 5-string configuration, 2/3-per-side tuners.

$1,250	$1,100	$1,000	$900	$725	$650	$595

DR 6 C - 6-string configuration, 3-per-side tuners.

$1,300	$1,150	$1,100	$975	$850	$750	$695

Prophecy Series

PR I - double cutaway basswood body, bolt-on maple neck, 22-fret rosewood fingerboard with pearl dot inlay, fixed bridge, graphite nut, 4-on-a-side tuners, chrome hardware, P-style/J-style pickups, volume/balance control, available in Black, Chrome Red, Frost Red, Midnight Blue and Mystic White finishes. Mfg. 1991 to 1993.

$500	$450	$395	$325	$250	$225	$200

PR II - similar to PR I, except has ash body, gold hardware, volume/treble/bass controls, active electronics, available in Antique Burst, Crimson Transparent, Natural and Sapphire Blue Transparent finishes.

$550	$495	$425	$375	$300	$275	$225

PR III - similar to PR I, except has laminated ash body, through-body laminated maple neck, gold hardware, volume/treble/bass controls, active electronics, available in Antique Burst, Crimson Transparent, Natural and Sapphire Blue Transparent finishes.

$795	$750	$695	$575	$450	$400	$350

HEINS GUITARS

Instruments currently built in Sneek, The Netherlands.

Luthier Wim Heins has been building guitars for the past thirty years - and was motivated to build his first one at an early age because he was too young to actually buy a guitar! After his first experiment, Hein kept building and customizing guitars as a hobby. After one of his guitars Heins built for a friend began to receive some notice, Heins decided to go into business - so what started out as a hobby became a business.

Heins' specialized guitar building and repair shop in The Netherlands offers these hand crafted electric guitar and bass models direct to the player, with no middle man. His current brochure offers an overview of models with the reminder that it can "never be complete or represent the variety in guitars, because all of them are made to the exact specifications of the client".

Personality and originality seem to be big parts of the Heins guitar models, as most of them feature premium figured woods, a sleek offset double cutaway body design, and quality pickups and hardware. Guitar models include the Dick and Zingana, as well as the 7-string Danny model. Basses include the 4-string Noest, 5-string TMF, and 6-string Pookie (which, oddly enough, is this author's nickname for his dog). For further information regarding prices and specifications, please contact Wim Heins at Heins Guitars directly (see Trademark Index).

HEIT DELUXE

Instruments previously produced in Japan circa late 1960s to early 1970s.

The Heit Deluxe trademark is a brand name applied to guitars imported into the U.S. market by an unidentified New York importer. Updated information from noted researcher Michael Wright has confirmed that certain Heit Deluxe models share similarities with Teisco Del Rey guitars, leading to the conclusion that Teisco/Kawai built many of the models for the Heit Deluxe brand name.

(Source: Michael Wright. For further accounts of Japanese guitar production and brand names, see Guitar Stories, Volume One)

HEMBROOK

Instruments currently built in Texas. Distributed by Hembrook Custom Basses and Guitars of Texas.

Ranger Bob, a self-taught luthier, left the U.S. Army in 1992 and returned to the University of Texas. While playing a 5-string bass for a surf-rock band in Austin, Ranger Bob noticed some deficiencies in his instrument - which lead to his discovery that most 5-string basses he encountered were either just retreaded "vintage" designs with an additional string or trendy boutique models that didn't feature very practical designs.

After several years of research and discussion, Ranger Bob began building prototype instruments. During this prototype building, he encountered Texas Mesquite wood (normally considered a pesky shrub in Northern Texas). Mesquite is rare among woods in that it expands and contracts to changes in moisture equally in all directions. Most woods expand 2 or 3 times more across the grain than along the grain - which is why moisture changes can warp necks or bodies. Mesquite is an isometric wood, and thus Ranger Bob argues that it is the ideal neck wood. Through innovation, Ranger Bob and his company search out new components and durable material for their instruments, then integrate the components into the balanced structure.

According to Ranger Bob's web site, Hembrook is not currently taking orders for guitars.

ELECTRIC BASS

Hembrook basses fall in the retail pricing between $1,500 to $2,500, and are offered in 4-, 5-, 6-, and 8-string configurations (as well as a 30" scale baritone model, and two guitar models). Hembrook bass necks feature straight grain Mesquite laminated to figured maple; the bodies are Honduran mahogany with a 1/4" burled Mesquite top. Ranger Bob sourced out parts and electronics from all over the world, and features Seymour Duncan pickups and preamps. Piezo-electric sensors are built in-house. For further information, contact Hembrook Custom Basses and Guitars directly (see Trademark Index).

GRADING	100% MINT	98% NEAR MINT	95% EXC+	90% EXC	80% VG+	70% VG	60% G

HERITAGE

Instruments currently built in Kalamazoo, Michigan since 1984 (serialization begins with "A" serial numbers in 1984). The company was incorporated on April 1st, 1985. The Lasar Music Corporation is the exclusive sales and marketing company for Heritage Guitars, Inc.

Heritage A-555
courtesy Wolfe Guitars

The Gibson guitar company was founded in Kalamazoo in 1902. The young company continued to expand, and built production facilities at 225 Parsons Street (the first of a total of five buildings at that location) in 1917. In 1974, Gibson was acquired by the Norlin corporation, which also opened facilities the same year in Nashville, Tennessee. However, financial troubles led Norlin to consider shutting down either the Kalamazoo or Nashville facilities in the early 1980s. Even though the Kalamazoo plant was Gibson's home since 1917, the decision was made in July of 1983 by Norlin to close the plant. The doors at 225 Parsons Street closed in the fall of 1984.

Heritage Guitar, Inc. opened in 1985 in the original Gibson building. Rather than uproot and move to Tennessee, Jim Deurloo, Marvin Lamb, and J. P. Moats elected to leave the Gibson company, and stay in Kalamazoo to start a new guitar company. Members of the original trio were later joined by Bill Paige and Mike Korpak (other long time Gibson workers). Korpack left the Heritage company in 1985.

Jim Deurloo began working at Gibson in 1958, and through his career was promoted from neck sander to pattern maker up to general foreman of the pattern shop, machine shop, and maintenance. Deurloo was the plant manager at Guild between 1969 to 1974, and had been involved with the opening and tooling up of the newer Nashville facility in 1974. During this time period, Deurloo was also the head of engineering, and was later promoted to assistant plant manager. In 1978 Deurloo was named plant manager at the Kalamazoo facility.

Marv Lamb was hired by Gibson in 1956 to do hand sanding and other jobs in the wood shop (Lamb was one of the workers on the '58 Korina Flying Vs and Explorers). He was promoted through a series of positions to general foreman of finishing and final assembly, and finally to plant superintendent in 1974 (a position he held until Gibson closed the plant in 1984).

J.P. Moats was hired by Gibson in 1957 for sanding and final cleaning. Through promotions, Moats became head of quality control as well as the supervisor of inspectors, and later the wood inspector. While inspecting wood for Gibson, Moats was also in charge of repairs and custom orders.

Bill Paige, a graduate of the business school at Western Michigan University joined Gibson in 1975 as a cost accountant and other capacities in the accounting department. Paige is currently the Heritage controller, and handles all non-guitar manufacturing functions.

All current owners of Heritage continue to design models, and produce various instruments in the production facilities. Heritage continues to develop new models along with their wide range of acoustic, hollow body, semi-hollow, and electric guitar models. Heritage is also one of the few *new* guitar companies with models that are stocked in vintage and collectible guitar stores worldwide.

Heritage offers a wide range of custom features. EMG, HRW, or Seymour Duncan pickups, special colors, special inlays, and choice woods may be ordered (call for custom quote). Unless specified, a hardshell case is optional with the guitar. Cases for the acoustics, jazz guitars, and basses run $170 while the cases for electric guitars are $160; cases for the Super Eagle model are $190.

Var-I-Phase is a Heritage innovation that provides coil tap capabilities as well as the ability to *roll in* the exact amount of in-phase/out-of-phase balance in the player's sound. It is a $300 option on numerous Heritage models.

Add $50 for installed chrome-covered pickups.

Add $100 for an ebony fingerboard.

Add $100 for a pickguard-mounted tone control on jazz models.

Add $150 for gold or black hardware.

Add $300 for left-handed configuration.

Add $500 for Custom-carved left-handed models.

ELECTRIC

ACADEMY CUSTOM - single rounded cutaway style, cream-bound curly maple top, 24 3/4" scale, f-holes, bound maple pickguard, curly maple back/sides, one piece mahogany neck, 22-fret bound rosewood fingerboard with pearl crown inlay, tune-o-matic bridge/stop tailpiece, bound peghead, 3-per-side tuners, gold hardware, 2 humbuckers, 2 volume/tone controls, 3-position switch, available in Almond Sunburst and Antique Sunburst finishes. Mfg. 1992 to date.

Body Width 15", Body Thickness 1 1/2".

MSR	$2,140	$1,250	$1,000	$900	$800	$700	$600	$500

Add $100 for Natural or Translucent Color finishes: Amber Translucent, Black Translucent, Blue Translucent, Cherry Translucent, Emerald Green Translucent, or Vintage Sunburst Translucent.

ALVIN LEE MODEL - 335 style, bound curly maple top/back/sides, f-holes, black pickguard, mahogany neck, 22-fret bound ebony fingerboard with pearl dot inlay, tune-o-matic bridge/stop tailpiece, 3-per-side tuners, chrome hardware, humbucker/single coil/humbucker pickup, 3 volume/2 tone controls, 3-position switch, available in Transparent Cherry finish. Mfg. 1993 to 1996.

$1,500	$1,200	$1,000	$800	$675	$550	$425

Last MSR was $1,885.

Heritage Eagle Archtop
courtesy Buffalo Bros. Guitars

GRADING	100% MINT	98% NEAR MINT	95% EXC+	90% EXC	80% VG+	70% VG	60% G

Eagle Series

EAGLE - single round cutaway hollow style, solid mahogany top/pickguard, 25 1/2" scale, f-holes, cream-bound body, mahogany back/sides/neck, 20-fret rosewood fingerboard with pearl dot inlay, rosewood bridge/trapeze tailpiece, 3-per-side tuners, chrome hardware, pickguard-mounted Heritage jazz pickup, volume control on pickguard, available in Antique Sunburst finish. Mfg. 1986 to date.

Body Width 17", Body Thickness 3".

MSR	$2,730	$2,050	$1,650	$1,525	$1,450	$1,100	$1,000	$850

Add $150 for gold hardware.

Add $200 for Natural or Translucent Color finishes: Cherry Translucent or Vintage Sunburst Translucent.

Eagle Classic - single round cutaway hollow style, solid carved spruce top, 25 1/2" scale, f-holes, bound maple pickguard, bound body, solid curly maple back/sides, 5-piece curly maple neck, 20-fret bound ebony fingerboard, ebony bridge/trapeze tailpiece, bound peghead, 3-per-side tuners, gold hardware, 1 floating (or 2 humbucker) pickups, 2 volume/tone controls, 3-position switch, available in Almond Sunburst and Antique Sunburst finishes. Mfg. 1992 to date.

Body Width 17", Body Thickness 3".

MSR	$3,670	$2,875	$2,050	$1,825	$1,650	$1,400	$1,300	$1,150

Subtract $100 for Black or White finishes.

Add $400 for Natural or Translucent Color finishes: Amber Translucent, Black Translucent, Blue Translucent, Cherry Translucent, Emerald Green Translucent, or Vintage Sunburst Translucent.

H

Eagle TDC - similar to Eagle, except has thinner body style, tune-o-matic bridge, dual top routed pickups, available in Antique Sunburst finish. Current Mfg.

Body Width 17", Body Thickness 2 1/4".

MSR	$2,960	$2,300	$1,650	$1,475	$1,200	$1,100	$1,000	$925

Add $150 for gold hardware.

Add $200 for Natural or Translucent Color finishes: Amber Translucent, Black Translucent, Blue Translucent, Cherry Translucent, Emerald Green Translucent, or Vintage Sunburst Translucent.

AMERICAN EAGLE - single round cutaway hollow style, tap tuned solid spruce carved top, 25 1/2" scale, bound body and f-holes, bound flame maple pickguard with pearl inlay, solid curly or bubbled maple back/sides, 5-piece figured maple neck, 20-fret bound ebony fingerboard with pearl/abalone American heritage inlays, ebony/rosewood bridge with pearl star inlay, Liberty Bell shaped trapeze tailpiece, red/white/blue-bound peghead with pearl eagle, stars, American Flag and Heritage logo inlay, pearl truss rod cover engraved with owner's name, 3-per-side Kluson tuners, gold hardware, pickguard-mounted Heritage jazz pickup with 3 star inlay on cover, volume control on pickguard, available in Natural finish. Mfg. 1986 to date.

MSR	$12,000	$9,500	$8,650	$7,500	$6,500	$5,750	$4,950	$4,250

Price includes hardshell case.

GOLDEN EAGLE - single round cutaway hollow style, solid spruce carved top, 25 1/2" scale, 7-ply bound body, bound f-holes, bound maple pickguard, curly maple back/sides/neck, 20-fret bound ebony fingerboard with pearl cloud inlay, ebony bridge with pearl V inlay, trapeze tailpiece, bound peghead with pearl eagle on tree and logo inlay, eagle inlay on back of headstock (with reg. no.), pearl truss rod cover with owner's name, 3-per-side Kluson tuners, gold hardware, pickguard-mounted Heritage jazz humbucker pickup, pickguard-mounted volume control, available in Antique Sunburst, Sunsetburst, Almond Sunburst, Antique Natural, and Natural finishes. Mfg. 1985 to date.

Body Width 17", Body Thickness 3".

MSR	$4,690	$3,750	$3,050	$2,850	$2,575	$2,200	$1,850	$1,500

Add $300 for Natural or Translucent Color finishes: Amber Translucent, Black Translucent, Blue Translucent, Cherry Translucent, Emerald Green Translucent, or Vintage Sunburst Translucent.

This model is available with a single floating pickup, dual humbucker, or single humbucker pickup configurations.

SUPER EAGLE - single round cutaway hollow style, solid spruce carved top, 25 1/2" scale, bound body and f-holes, bound maple pickguard, curly maple back/sides/neck, 20-fret bound ebony fingerboard with pearl split block inlay, ebony bridge with pearl V inlay, trapeze tailpiece, bound peghead with pearl eagle on tree and logo inlay, pearl truss rod cover with owner's name, 3-per-side Grover Imperial tuners, gold hardware, single floating (or 2 humbucker) pickup(s), volume/tone controls and 3-position switch, available in Antique Sunburst finish. Mfg. 1988 to date.

Body Width 18", Body Thickness 3".

MSR	$5,300	$4,350	$3,400	$3,050	$2,700	$2,195	$1,675	$1,550

Add $400 for Natural or Translucent Color finishes: Amber Translucent, Black Translucent, Blue Translucent, Cherry Translucent, Emerald Green Translucent, or Vintage Sunburst Translucent.

GARY MOORE MODEL - single cutaway mahogany body, bound carved curly maple top, 24 3/4" scale, bound curly maple pickguard, mahogany neck, 22-fret bound rosewood fingerboard with pearl crown inlay, tune-o-matic bridge/stop tailpiece, black peghead with Gary Moore signature imprint, 3-per-side tuners, chrome hardware, 2 EMG humbucker pickups, 2 volume/2 tone controls, 3-position switch, available in Translucent Amber finish. Disc. 1992.

		$1,795	$1,550	$1,350	$1,200	$1,075	$950	$825

Last MSR was $1,415.

This model has a certificate signed by the owners. This model featured a limited production of only 150 instruments: the first group included 75 models in Amber, the second group had 75 models in Almond Sunburst. The series number is stamped on the headstock, beneath ser. no.

GRADING	100% MINT	98% NEAR MINT	95% EXC+	90% EXC	80% VG+	70% VG	60% G

LITTLE-001 - small size asymmetrical double cutaway curly maple body/neck, 22-fret bound rosewood fingerboard with pearl dot inlay, tune-o-matic bridge/stop tailpiece, 3-per-side tuners, chrome hardware, humbucker pickup, volume control, available in Translucent Amber, Translucent Black and Translucent Cherry finishes. Mfg. 1992 to 1994, reintroduced 2000.

MSR $1,075 — $495 $365 $315 $275 $250 $200 $175

List price includes gig bag.

MARK SLAUGHTER ROCK - radical single cutaway mahogany body/neck, 22-fret rosewood fingerboard with pearl dot inlay, tune-o-matic bridge/stop tailpiece, reverse headstock, 6-on-a-side tuners, chrome hardware, 2 single coil/1 humbucker pickups, volume/tone control, 5-position switch, available in Black, Red and White finishes. Mfg. 1992 to 1995.

$750 $595 $550 $425 $395 $350 $325

Last MSR was $1,135.

Add $200 for Kahler Spyder tremolo bridge.

Heritage American Eagle
courtesy
Heritage Guitar Company

Parsons Street Series

PARSONS STREET - offset double cutaway solid mahogany body, curly maple top, 25 1/2" scale, mahogany neck, 22-fret bound rosewood fingerboard with pearl block inlay, tune-o-matic bridge/stop tailpiece, 3-per-side tuners, chrome hardware, 2 single coil/1 humbucker pickups, volume/tone control, 5-position and Var-I-Phase switch, available in Antique Sunburst, Antique Cherry Sunburst and Natural finishes. Mfg. 1989 to 1992.

$875 $800 $695 $600 $500 $450 $395

Last MSR was $1,345.

Parsons Street III - similar to the Parsons Street, except has hardwood body, maple neck, unbound rosewood fingerboard with pearl dot inlay, black chrome hardware, Kahler tremolo bridge, no Var-I-Phase switch, 2 mini switches, available in Black, Red, or White finishes. Disc. 1991.

$625 $525 $475 $375 $325 $275 $250

Last MSR was $1,165.

This model was available with either a Shadow Piezo tremolo pickup or Shadow active humbucking pickup.

Parsons Street V - similar to the Parsons Street, except has bound body, Kahler tremolo bridge, volume/ 2 tone controls, no Var-I-Phase switch, 2 mini switches, available in Antique Sunburst and Antiquê Cherry Burst finishes. Disc. 1991.

$900 $750 $625 $475 $425 $395 $350

Last MSR was $1,300.

This model was available with either a Shadow Piezo tremolo pickup or Shadow active humbucking pickup.

This model was also available in Amber Translucent, Black Translucent, Blue Translucent, Cherry Translucent, Emerald Green Translucent, Almond, Blue, Red, and Vintage Sunburst Translucent finishes.

PROSPECT STANDARD - dual cutaway smaller 335-style, cream-bound curly maple laminate top/ back 24 3/4" scale, f-holes, solid curly maple sides, white pickguard, mahogany neck, 20-fret bound rosewood fingerboard with pearl dot inlay, rollermatic bridge/stop tailpiece, 3-per-side tuners, nickel/chrome hardware, 2 humbucker pickups, 2 volume/tone controls, 3-position switch, available in Almond Sunburst and Antique Sunburst finishes. Mfg. 1991 to date.

Body Width 15", Body Thickness 1 1/2".

MSR $1,785 — $1,375 $1,050 $925 $800 $750 $700 $675

Add $100 for Natural or Translucent Color finishes: Amber Translucent, Black Translucent, Blue Translucent, Cherry Translucent, Emerald Green Translucent, or Vintage Sunburst Translucent.

ROY CLARK MODEL - single round cutaway, bound curly maple top/back/sides, 24 3/4" scale, bound f-holes, bound maple pickguard, mahogany neck, 22-fret bound rosewood fingerboard with mother-of-pearl split block inlay, tune-o-matic roller bridge/stop tailpiece, bound peghead, 3-per-side tuners, gold hardware, 2 humbuckers, 2 volume/tone controls, 3-position switch, available in Almond Sunburst and Antique Sunburst finishes. Mfg. 1992 to date.

Body Width 16", Body Thickness 1 1/2".

MSR $2,550 — $1,975 $1,600 $1,500 $1,375 $1,175 $975 $775

Add $100 for Natural or Translucent Color finishes: Amber Translucent, Black Translucent, Blue Translucent, Cherry Translucent, Emerald Green Translucent, or Vintage Sunburst Translucent.

Heritage Golden Eagle
courtesy
Heritage Guitar Company

GRADING	100% MINT	98% NEAR MINT	95% EXC+	90% EXC	80% VG+	70% VG	60% G

JOHNNY SMITH (THE ROSE) - single round cutaway hollow style, solid spruce carved top, 25" scale, bound body, bound f-holes, bound curly maple pickguard, curly maple back/sides/neck, 20-fret ebony fingerboard with abalone block inlay, ebony bridge, individual finger-style trapeze tailpiece, bound peghead with abalone/pearl rose inlay, 3-per-side tuners, black hardware, pickguard-mounted Heritage jazz humbucker pickup, pickguard-mounted volume control, available in Antique Sunburst finish. Mfg. 1989 to date.

Body Width 17", Body Thickness 3".

MSR $5,710 $4,775 $4,050 $3,625 $3,300 $2,950 $2,550 $2,000

Add $400 for Natural or Translucent Color finishes: Amber Translucent, Black Translucent, Blue Translucent, Cherry Translucent, Emerald Green Translucent, or Vintage Sunburst Translucent.

This model is personally signed by Johnny Smith on the label.

Millennium Series

STANDARD ULTRA - single cutaway semi-hollow body, solid carved multiple white bound ultra curly maple top, single white bound, solid flat mahogany back and solid mahogany sides, f-holes, no pickguard, 1 piece mahogany neck, 24 ¾" scale, white bound ebony fingerboard, mother-of-pearl block position markers, 2 gold plated HRW pickups, 2 Volume/2 Tone controls, 3-way switch. 3-per-side tuners, available in Vintage Sunburst and other finishes. Current Mfg.

MSR $2,600 $1,950 $1,700 $1,500 $1,350 $1,050 $850 $625

LIMITED EDITION 2001 ULTRA - single cutaway semi-hollow body, multiple white bound solid carved ultra curly maple top, single white bound flat ultra curly maple back, solid sides, f-holes, no pickguard, 1-piece mahogany neck, 24 ¾" scale, white bound ebony fingerboard, trapezoid outline markers, the words "Millennium", "2001" and "Kalamazoo" engraved in the last three position markers, 2 gold plated HRW pickups, 2 Volume/2 Tone controls, 3-way switch, individual gold plated tuners, gold plated stop tailpiece, adjustable bridge, 3-per-side tuners, available in Chestnut Sunburst and other finishes. Current Mfg.

MSR $3,200 $2,400 $2,100 $1,800 $1,500 $1,200 $995 $750

BLACK BEAUTY DC - double cutaway semi-hollow body, multiple white bound solid carved maple top, single white bound flat maple back and solid maple sides, f-holes, no pickguard, 1-piece mahogany neck, 24 ¾" scale, white bound ebony fingerboard with mother-of-pearl block position markers, 2 gold plated HRW pickups, 2 Volume/2 Tone controls, 3-way switch, individual gold plated tuners, gold plated stop tailpiece, adjustable bridge, available in Black finish. Current Mfg.

MSR $2,200 $1,650 $1,450 $1,250 $1,050 $850 $650 $500

EAGLE CUSTOM - single cutaway semi-hollow body, solid carved multiple white bound ultra curly maple top, multiple white bound solid carved ultra curly maple back and solid sides, f-holes, no pickguard, 3-piece curly maple neck, 24 ¾" scale, multiple white bound ebony fingerboard, 22-frets, mother-of-pearl split block position markers, 2 gold plated HRW pickups, 2 Volume/2 Tone controls, 3-way switch, individual gold plated Imperial tuners, gold plated Heritage finger tailpiece, adjustable bridge, available in Burnt Amber and other finishes. Current Mfg.

MSR $4,300 $3,350 $2,950 $2,600 $2,300 $2,000 $1,800 $1,600

EAGLE 2000 - single cutaway semi-hollow body, solid carved multiple white bound curly maple top, single white bound solid carved curly maple back and solid sides, no pickguard, 3-piece curly maple neck, 24 ¾" scale white bound ebony fingerboard with 22-frets, abalone block position markers, 2 gold plated Seth Lover pickups, 2 Volume/2 Tone controls, 3-way switch, individual gold plated Grover Imperial tuners, gold plated Heritage bail tailpiece, adjustable bridge, available in Old Style Sunburst and other finishes.

MSR $3,150 $2,365 $2,065 $1,765 $1,450 $1,150 $950 $750

H-155 - single cutaway semi-hollow body, solid carved multiple white bound curly maple top, single white bound flat curly maple back, solid sides, one-piece mahogany neck, single white bound mother-of-pearl headstock inlay, 24 ¾" scale, single white bound ebony fingerboard with mother-of-pearl block position markers, 2 gold plated Seth Lover pickups, 3-way switch, 2 Volume/2 Tone controls, individual gold plated tuners, 3-per-side tuners, gold plated stop tailpiece, adjustable bridge, available in Almond Sunburst and other finishes. Current Mfg.

MSR $2,100 $1,575 $1,350 $1,200 $995 $850 $750 $625 $495

H-158 - single cutaway semi-hollow body with laminated arched top and arched back, single cream bound top and back, no pickguard, 2 f-holes, rosewood cream bound finerboard with 22-frets, mother-of-pearl dot inlays, 2 humbucking pickups, selector switch in horn, 2 volume/2 tone control knobs, chrome plated machine heads, stop bar tailpiece and adj. bridge. New 2001.

MSR $1,785 $1,375 $1,050 $925 $800 $750 $700 $675

SAE CUSTOM - single cutaway mahogany body with carved maple top, 24 3/4" scale, f-holes, bound body, mahogany neck, 22-fret bound rosewood with pearl dot inlay, tune-o-matic bridge/stop tailpiece, 3-per-side tuners, chrome hardware, 2 humbucker pickups, Mike Christian transducer bridge-mounted pickup, 2 volume/1 tone controls, 3 mini toggle switches, available in Antique, Translucent Almond, Translucent Amber, Translucent Blue, Translucent Cherry, and Translucent Emerald Green finishes. Mfg. 1992 to date.

MSR $2,100 $1,675 $1,450 $1,250 $1,075 $875 $675 $500

SAE Cutaway - similar to SAE Custom, except only has a mounted Mike Christian transducer bridge pickup and volume/tone control. Disc. 1994.

$675 $595 $500 $425 $350 $325 $275

Last MSR was $965.

STAT - offset double cutaway bound curly maple/mahogany body, mahogany neck, 22-fret rosewood fingerboard with pearl dot inlay, tune-o-matic bridge/stop tailpiece, 6-on-a-side tuners, chrome hardware, 2 single coil/1 humbucker pickups, volume/tone controls, 3 mini toggle pickup selector/1 mini toggle coil tap switches, available in Antique Sunburst, Antique Cherry Sunburst, and Cherry finishes. Mfg. 1989 to 1991.

$575 $500 $425 $350 $275 $225 $195

Last MSR was $785.

GRADING	100% MINT	98% NEAR MINT	95% EXC+	90% EXC	80% VG+	70% VG	60% G

SWEET 16 - single sharp cutaway hollow style, solid spruce carved top, multiple bound body, bound f-holes, bound curly maple pickguard, curly maple back/sides/neck, 20-fret ebony fingerboard with pearl split block inlay, ebony bridge with pearl 16 inlay, trapeze tailpiece, bound peghead with pearl *Sweet 16* and logo inlay, 3-per-side tuners, gold hardware, pickguard-mounted Heritage jazz humbucker, pickguard-mounted volume control, available in Almond Sunburst and Antique Sunburst finishes. Mfg. 1987 to date.

Body Width 16", Body Thickness 2 3/4".

MSR	$4,180	$3,300	$2,800	$2,400	$1,975	$1,625	$1,275	$925

Add $400 for Natural or Translucent Color finishes: Amber Translucent, Black Translucent, Blue Translucent, Cherry Translucent, Emerald Green Translucent, or Vintage Sunburst Translucent.

This model can be found with either single top routed humbucker or dual top routed humbucker pickup configurations.

V.I.P. (V.I.P.-1) - offset double cutaway curly maple body, bolt-on mahogany neck, 25 1/2" scale, 22-fret rosewood fingerboard with pearl dot inlay, tune-o-matic bridge/stop tailpiece, 6-on-a-side tuners, blackface peghead with "The Heritage" logo, chrome hardware, humbucker pickup, volume/tone controls, coil tap mini toggle switch, phase or standby mini toggle switch, available in Translucent color finishes. Mfg. 1986 to 1990.

$500	$450	$375	$325	$275	$225	$150

Last MSR was $465.

Add $30 for fine tune tailpiece and locking nut.

Add $30 for Kahler Flyer tremolo bridge.

In 1989, Fine Tune tailpiece, and Kahler Flyer tremolo bridge were discontinued.

When both mini-switches are in the Up position, one is a coil tap switch and the other is a standby (signal on/off) switch. When both mini- switches are in the down position, the tone control becomes a Variable Phase control between the two pickup coils (0=out of phase, 10=In phase). A wide variety of tonal capabilities are thus offered to the guitarist.

V.I.P.-2 - similar to the V.I.P., except features 2 humbucker pickups, available in Translucent color finishes. Mfg. 1986 to 1990.

$525	$475	$400	$350	$295	$250	$175

Last MSR was $565.

Add $30 for fine tune tailpiece and locking nut.

Add $30 for Kahler Flyer tremolo bridge.

In 1989, Fine Tune tailpiece, and Kahler Flyer tremolo bridge were discontinued.

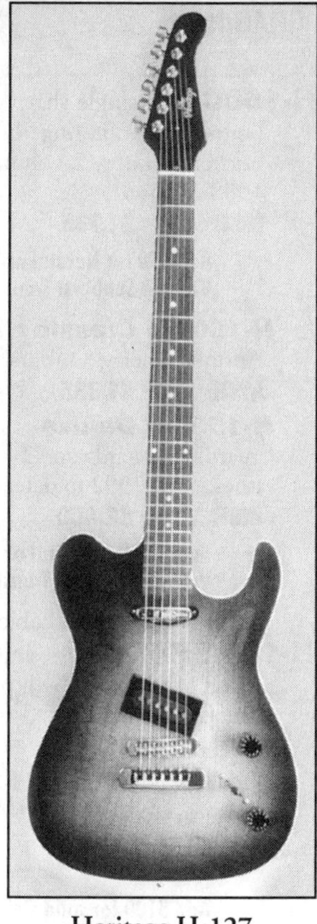

Heritage H-127
courtesy
Heritage Guitar Company

H Series

H-127 CUSTOM - single cutaway mahogany body, bound arch maple top, maple neck, 22-fret maple fingerboard with pearl dot inlay, tune-o-matic bridge/stop tailpiece, 6-on-a-side tuners, chrome hardware, 2 single coil pickups, volume/tone control, 3-position switch, available in Antique Sunburst and Sunsetburst finishes. Mfg. 1992 to 1996.

$750	$625	$600	$550	$450	$395	$325

Last MSR was $1,250.

H-127 Standard - similar to H-127 Custom, except has solid mahogany body. Disc. 1992.

$695	$600	$500	$450	$395	$350	$300

Last MSR was $1,010.

H-140CM - single sharp cutaway mahogany body, bound curly maple top, 24 3/4" scale, white pickguard, mahogany neck, 22-fret rosewood fingerboard with pearl dot inlay, tune-o-matic bridge/stop tailpiece, 3-per-side tuners, chrome hardware, 2 exposed humbucker pickups, 2 volume/2 tone controls, 3-position switch, available in Antique Sunburst and Antique Cherry Sunburst finishes. Mfg. 1985 to date.

MSR	$1,225	$950	$800	$700	$600	$500	$425	$375

Add $50 for Natural or Translucent Color finishes: Amber Translucent, Black Translucent, Blue Translucent, Cherry Translucent, Emerald Green Translucent, or Vintage Sunburst Translucent.

H-140CMV - similar to the H-140CM, except has installed Heritage Var-I-Phase electronics, available in Antique Sunburst, Antique Cherry Sunburst, and Gold Top finishes. Mfg. 1994 to date.

MSR	$1,525	$1,200	$950	$800	$700	$600	$500	$400

H-140 Gold Top - similar to the H-140CM, except has carved plain maple top, available in Gold Top finish. Mfg. 1994 to date.

MSR	$1,225	$950	$800	$700	$600	$500	$425	$375

H-147 - similar to H-140CM, except has plain maple top, bound ebony fingerboard with pearl block inlay, bound peghead and gold hardware. Mfg. 1989 to 1992.

$850	$725	$650	$550	$475	$375	$300

Last MSR was $1,215.

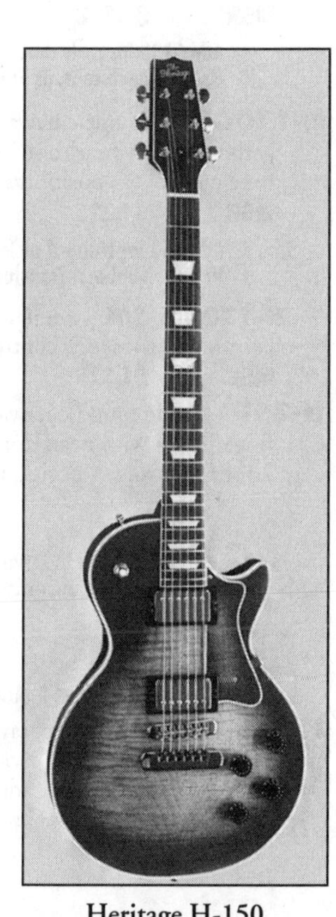

Heritage H-150
courtesy
Heritage Guitar Company

H

GRADING		100% MINT	98% NEAR MINT	95% EXC+	90% EXC	80% VG+	70% VG	60% G

H-150CM - single sharp cutaway mahogany body, bound carved curly maple top, 24 3/4" scale, white pickguard, mahogany neck, 22-fret bound rosewood fingerboard with pearl crown inlay, tune-o-matic bridge/stop tailpiece, 3-per-side tuners, chrome hardware, 2 covered humbucker pickups, 2 volume/2 tone controls, 3-position switch, available in Antique Sunburst and Antique Cherry Sunburst finishes. Mfg. 1988 to date.

MSR	$1,735	$1,325	$1,150	$950	$825	$675	$550	$400

Add $50 for Natural or Translucent Color finishes: Amber Translucent, Black Translucent, Blue Translucent, Cherry Translucent, Emerald Green Translucent, or Vintage Sunburst Translucent.

H-150CM Classic - similar to H-150CM, except has 2 humbucker HRW or Seymour Duncan pickups, available in Antique Sunburst and Antique Cherry Sunburst finishes. Current Mfg.

MSR	$1,835	$1,450	$1,075	$900	$775	$675	$550	$425

H-150CM Deluxe - similar to H-150CM, except has multiple-bound body, bound matching curly maple peghead, bound curly maple pickguard, gold hardware, 2 HRW or Seymour Duncan pickups, available in Almond Sunburst, Antique Sunburst and Antique Cherry Sunburst finishes. Mfg. 1992 to date.

MSR	$2,400	$1,895	$1,595	$1,375	$1,175	$950	$750	$550

Add $50 for Natural or Translucent Color finishes: Amber Translucent, Black Translucent, Blue Translucent, Cherry Translucent, Emerald Green Translucent, or Vintage Sunburst Translucent.

This model is available on a limited basis. Price includes hardshell case.

H-150 SPECIAL - single sharp cutaway poplar body, bound carved plain maple top, 24 3/4" scale, mahogany neck, 22-fret bound rosewood fingerboard with pearl dot inlay, tune-o-matic bridge/stop tailpiece, 3-per-side tuners, chrome hardware, 2 humbucker pickups, 2 volume/2 tone controls, 3-position switch, available in Black and Old Style Sunburst finishes. Mfg. 1994 to date.

MSR	$1,325	$1,000	$875	$750	$650	$550	$425	$325

H-150P - similar to H-150 Special, except has cream-bound solid poplar body, pearl dot fingerboard inlay, available in Blue, Red and White finishes. Mfg. 1992 to 1998.

		$850	$725	$650	$550	$450	$375	$275

Last MSR was $1,050.

Add $100 for solid Gold finish.

H-157 - single sharp cutaway mahogany body, multiple white-bound carved solid maple top, 24 3/4" scale, mahogany neck, 22-fret bound ebony fingerboard with mother-of-pearl block inlay, tune-o-matic bridge/stop tailpiece, bound blackface peghead with pearl diamond/logo inlay, black pickguard, 3-per-side tuners, gold hardware, 2 humbucker pickups, 2 volume/2 tone controls, 3-position switch, available in Black and White finishes. Mfg. 1989 to date.

MSR	$1,940	$1,550	$1,275	$1,100	$895	$725	$575	$425

Add $100 for curly maple top and Natural or Translucent Color finishes: Amber Translucent, Black Translucent, Blue Translucent, Cherry Translucent, Emerald Green Translucent, or Vintage Sunburst Translucent.

H-170CM - double cutaway mahogany body, cream-bound carved solid curly maple top, 24 3/4" scale, mahogany neck, 22-fret rosewood fingerboard with pearl dot inlay, tune-o-matic bridge/stop tailpiece, 3-per-side tuners, chrome hardware, 2 humbucker pickups, 2 volume/2 tone controls, 3-position switch, available in Antique Sunburst and Antique Cherry Sunburst finishes. Mfg. 1996 to date.

MSR	$1,225	$950	$800	$700	$595	$495	$395	$295

Add $50 for Natural or Translucent Color finishes: Amber Translucent, Black Translucent, Blue Translucent, Cherry Translucent, Emerald Green Translucent, or Vintage Sunburst Translucent.

H-170CM SM - similar to the H-170CM, except features 2 Seymour Duncan Stag Mag humbucker pickups, 2 push/pull (coil tap) volume controls, master tone control. Mfg. 1998 to date.

MSR	$1,375	$1,025	$875	$750	$650	$550	$425	$325

H-357 - single round cutaway asymmetrical hourglass style mahogany body, white pickguard, through-body mahogany neck, 22-fret rosewood fingerboard with pearl dot inlay, tune-o-matic bridge/stop tailpiece, 6-on-a-side tuners, chrome hardware, 2 humbucker pickups, 2 volume/2 tone controls, 3-position switch, available in Antique Sunburst, Black, Blue, Red, and White finishes. Mfg. 1989 to 1996.

		$1,000	$775	$650	$500	$450	$425	$375

Last MSR was $1,350.

This model was also available with black pickguard and reverse headstock. Later models have a standard Heritage headstock. It is estimated that only 50 to 75 instruments were produced.

500 Series

Models in the 500 Series feature a semi-hollow body design.

H-516 - single round cutaway semi-hollow body, laminated arched curly maple top and back, solid curly maple sides, f-holes, one-piece mahogany neck, 24 ¾" scale, rosewood fingerboard, mother-of-pearl position markers, 20-frets, individual nickel plated tuners, nickel plated Heritage bail tailpiece, adjustable bridge, 2 chrome plated humbucking pickups, 2 Volume/2 Tone controls, 3-way switch, available in Old Style Sunburst finish. Current Mfg.

MSR	$2,040	$1,530	$1,325	$1,125	$925	$725	$625	$495

GRADING	100% MINT	98% NEAR MINT	95% EXC+	90% EXC	80% VG+	70% VG	60% G

Heritage H-535 EL
courtesy Wolfe Guitars

H-535 - double round cutaway semi-hollow body, cream-bound curly maple laminate top and back, 24 3/4" scale, solid curly maple sides, f-holes, curly maple pickguard, mahogany neck, 22-fret bound rosewood fingerboard with pearl dot inlay, tune-o-matic bridge/stop tailpiece, 3-per-side tuners, chrome hardware, 2 humbucker pickups, 2 volume/tone controls, 3-position switch, available in Antique Sunburst finish. Mfg. 1987 to date.

Body Width 16", Body Thickness 1 1/2".

MSR $1,785 — $1,350 $1,150 $995 $825 $695 $550 $400

Add $100 for Natural or Translucent Color finishes: Amber Translucent, Black Translucent, Blue Translucent, Cherry Translucent, Emerald Green Translucent, or Vintage Sunburst Translucent.

Add $300 for installed Heritage Var-I-Phase and coil tap capabilities.

H-535 Classic - similar to H-535, except has 2 Seymour Duncan humbuckers. Mfg. 1996 to date.

MSR $1,885 — $1,475 $1,225 $1,075 $895 $750 $575 $425

H-535 Custom - similar to H-535, except has pearl diagonal inlay and bound peghead with pearl logo inlay, available in Antique Sunburst and Transparent Black finishes. Mfg. 1991 to 1992.

$1,000 $895 $750 $595 $525 $495 $450

Last MSR was $1,490.

H-555 - similar to H-535, except has bound f-holes, curly maple neck, ebony fingerboard with abalone/pearl diamond/arrow inlay with block after 17th fret, bound peghead with abalone/pearl diamond/arrow and logo inlay, gold hardware, available in Almond Sunburst and Antique Sunburst finishes. Mfg. 1989 to date.

Body Width 16", Body Thickness 1 1/2".

MSR $2,550 — $1,995 $1,675 $1,475 $1,250 $1,000 $800 $595

Add $100 for Natural or Translucent Color finishes: Amber Translucent, Black Translucent, Blue Translucent, Cherry Translucent, Emerald Green Translucent, or Vintage Sunburst Translucent.

Add $300 for installed Heritage Var-I-Phase and coil tap capabilities.

H-574 - single round cutaway hollow style, bound curly maple top/back/sides, f-holes, white pickguard, mahogany neck, 20-fret rosewood fingerboard with pearl dot inlay, tune-o-matic bridge/stop tailpiece, 3-per-side tuners, chrome hardware, 2 humbuckers, 2 volume/tone controls, 3-position switch, available in Antique Sunburst finish. Mfg. 1989 to 1991.

$875 $750 $625 $500 $450 $425 $375

Last MSR was $1,250.

Add $50 for Natural finish.

H-576 - single rounded cutaway semi-hollow style with *floating* center block, cream-bound curly maple laminate top and back, 24 3/4" scale, solid curly maple sides, f-holes, bound curly maple pickguard/peghead, mahogany neck, 20-fret rosewood fingerboard with mother-of-pearl block inlay, bridge/stop tailpiece, 3-per-side tuners, chrome hardware, 2 humbuckers, 2 volume/2 tone controls, 3-position switch, available in Antique Sunburst finish. Mfg. 1990 to date.

Body Width 16", Body Thickness 2 3/4".

MSR $2,190 — $1,725 $1,475 $1,295 $1,100 $895 $700 $525

Add $100 for Natural or Translucent Color finishes: Amber Translucent, Black Translucent, Blue Translucent, Cherry Translucent, Emerald Green Translucent, or Vintage Sunburst Translucent.

Hollow Body Series

H-550 - single round cutaway hollow style, multiple white-bound curly maple laminate braced top, bound curly maple laminate back, 25 1/2" scale, solid curly maple sides, bound f-holes, bound curly maple pickguard, curly maple neck, 20-fret bound ebony fingerboard with pearl split-block inlay, tune-o-matic bridge/trapeze tailpiece, bound peghead with pearl split-block and logo inlay, 3-per-side tuners, chrome hardware, 2 humbucker pickups, 2 volume/tone controls, 3-position switch, available in Antique Sunburst finish. Mfg. 1990 to date.

Body Width 17", Body Thickness 3".

MSR $2,860 — $2,275 $1,900 $1,600 $1,375 $1,095 $850 $625

Add $100 for Natural or Translucent Color finishes: Amber Translucent, Black Translucent, Blue Translucent, Cherry Translucent, Emerald Green Translucent, or Vintage Sunburst Translucent.

Heritage H-575 E
courtesy Wolfe Guitars

H-575 - single sharp cutaway hollow style, cream-bound solid carved curly maple braced top, cream-bound curly maple back, curly maple sides, 24 3/4" scale, f-holes, curly maple pickguard, mahogany neck, 20-fret rosewood fingerboard with pearl dot inlay, rosewood bridge/trapeze tailpiece, 3-per-side tuners, chrome hardware, 2 humbuckers, 2 volume/2 tone controls, 3-position switch, available in Antique Sunburst finish. Mfg. 1987 to date.

Body Width 16", Body Thickness 2 3/4".

MSR $2,250 — $1,750 $1,450 $1,250 $1,050 $850 $675 $500

Add $200 for Natural or Translucent Color finishes: Amber Translucent, Black Translucent, Blue Translucent, Cherry Translucent, Emerald Green Translucent, or Vintage Sunburst Translucent.

GRADING		100% MINT	98% NEAR MINT	95% EXC+	90% EXC	80% VG+	70% VG	60% G

H-575 Classic - similar to the H-575, except has 2 HRW or Seymour Duncan humbuckers. Mfg. 1996 to date.

MSR	$2,350	$1,825	$1,550	$1,295	$1,100	$900	$725	$525

H-575 Custom - similar to the H-575, except has white body binding, bound fingerboard with mother-of-pearl "hash mark" (disc. 1998) or block (standard in 1998) inlays, bound peghead with pearl logo inlay and gold hardware, available in Sunset Burst finish. Mfg. 1989 to date.

MSR	$2,910	$2,295	$1,995	$1,675	$1,400	$1,175	$925	$675

Subtract $100 for Black or White finishes.

Add $200 for Natural or Translucent Color finishes: Amber Translucent, Black Translucent, Blue Translucent, Cherry Translucent, Emerald Green Translucent, or Vintage Sunburst Translucent.

In 1998, block fingerboard inlays replaced the "hash mark" fingerboard inlays, and the headstock inlays were disc.

H-575 Gold Top - similar to the H-575, except has Gold Top. New 2001.

MSR	$2,500	$1,900	$1,600	$1,400	$1,200	$1,000	$800	$595

ELECTRIC BASS

Heritage Electric Bass models are available on a limited basis.

CHUCK JACOBS MODEL - offset double cutaway maple body, 5-piece laminated maple through-body neck, 34" scale, 24-fret bound rosewood fingerboard with pearl dot inlay, 5-string configuration, fixed bridge, bound peghead, 3/2-per-side tuners, black hardware, 2 EMG J-style active pickups, 2 volume/2 tone controls, available in Black, Red, and White finishes. Disc.

$2,100	$1,825	$1,600	$1,350	$1,125	$875	$650

Last MSR was $2,600.

Chuck Jacobs CM - similar to the Chuck Jacobs model, except has curly maple body, available in Translucent Black, Translucent Cherry, and Sunsetburst finishes. Disc.

$2,150	$1,900	$1,650	$1,400	$1,175	$925	$675

Last MSR was $2,700.

HB Series

HB 2 - offset double cutaway hardwood body, bolt-on maple neck, 34" scale, 21-fret rosewood fingerboard with white circle inlays, 4-on-a-side tuners, chrome hardware, fixed bridge, P/J-style pickups, 2 volume/1 tone controls, available in Antique Sun Burst, Antique Cherry Burst, or Black finishes. Disc. 1992.

$650	$575	$525	$475	$425	$375	$325

Last MSR was $755.

HB 1 - similar to the HB 2, except has one split P-style pickup, volume/tone control, series/parallel mini switch. Disc. 1992.

$525	$450	$400	$350	$325	$250	$195

Last MSR was $655.

HB-IV - offset double cutaway maple body, through-body maple neck, 34" scale, 24-fret rosewood fingerboard with pearl dot inlay, fixed bridge, 2-per-side tuners, black hardware, 2 active EMG soapbar pickups, 2 volume/2 tone controls, available in Black, Red and White finishes. Disc.

$1,600	$1,395	$1,225	$1,050	$850	$675	$500

Last MSR was $2,000.

Add $100 for curly maple top and Translucent Color finishes: Black Translucent, Cherry Translucent, Antique Sunburst finishes.

HB-V - similar to HB-IV, except has 5-string configuration, 3/2-per-side tuners, available in Black, Red and White finishes. Disc.

$1,700	$1,495	$1,300	$1,100	$925	$725	$525

Last MSR was $2,125.

Add $100 for curly maple top and Translucent Color finishes: Black Translucent, Cherry Translucent, Antique Sunburst finishes.

HFI, JIRI LEBEDA

Instruments produced in the Czech Republic since 1978.

Luthier Jiri Lebeda Hfi has been offering a wide range of lutherie services in the Czech Republic since the late 1970s. Hfi offers regular lutherie services like set-ups and repair, as well as handcrafting custom instruments and special custom inlay work. Hfi also offers design and technology research of fretted instruments, building prototypes and special series instruments, and building special tools. For further information, contact luthier Jiri Hfi directly (see Trademark Index).

HILL GUITARS

Instruments built in Cleveland, Ohio from 1989 to 1994.

The Hill Guitar Company was founded in Vermilion, Ohio in October of 1989 by luthier Jon Hill, and was open until 1994. Hill's extensive background in custom lutherie and design was an asset when he joined the re-formed Dean Guitars company in 1994. After joining Dean, Hill moved to Florida (the current location of Dean's U.S. Custom Shop). Luthier Hill left the Dean company in late 1997/early 1998.

ELECTRIC

Hill Guitars originally offered eight models of U.S. built guitars that ranged in price from $799 to $2,999; and four models of basses (each available in 4-, 5-, and 6-string configurations) that range from $1,197 to $2,120.

HOFNER

Instruments produced beginning 1887-1949 in Schonbach, and 1950-date in Bubenreuth, and Hagenau, Germany. Current Hofner instruments are distributed in the U.S. by Boosey & Hawkes Musical Instruments, Inc. of Libertyville, Illinois.

The Hofner instrument making company was originally founded by Karl Hofner in 1887. Originally located in Schonbach (in the area now called Czechoslovakia), Hofner produced fine stringed instruments such as violins, cellos, and double basses. Karl's two sons, Josef and Walter, joined the company in 1919 and 1921 (respectively), and expanded Hofner's market to North American and the Far East. Production of guitars began in 1925, in the area that was to become East Germany during the "Cold War" era. Following World War II, the Hofner family moved to West Germany and established a new factory in Bubenreuth in 1948. By 1950, new production facilities in Bubenreuth and Hanenau were staffed by over 300 Hofner employees.

The first Hofner electric archtop debuted in the 1950s. While various guitar models were available in Germany since 1949 (and earlier, if you take in the over 100 years of company history), Hofners were not officially exported to England until Selmer of London took over distributorship in 1958. Furthermore, Selmer's British models were specified for the U.K. only - and differ from those available in the German market.

The concept of a violin-shaped bass was developed by Walter Hofner (Karl's son) in 1956. Walter's idea to electrically amplify a bass was new for the company, but the hollow body model itself was based on family design traditions. The **500/1**. model made its debut at the Frankfurt Music Fair the same year. While most people may recognize that model as the *Beatle Bass* popularized by Paul McCartney, the Hofner company also produced a wide range of solid, semi-hollow, and archtop designs that were good quality instruments.

Until 1997, Hofner products were distributed by EMMC (Entertainment Music Marketing Corporation, which focused on distributing the 500/1 Reissue violin electric bass. In 1998, distribution for Hofner products in the U.S. market was changed to Boosey & Hawkes Musical Instruments, Inc. of Libertyville, Illinois. Boosey & Hawkes wasted no time in introducing three jazz-style semi-hollow guitar models, which includes a **New President** (Model HP-55) model guitar. Boosey & Hawkes is also distributing Thomastik guitar and bass strings along with the Hofner accessories.

(Hofner history source: Gordon Giltrap and Neville Marten, The Hofner Guitar - A History; and Tony Bacon, The Ultimate Guitar Book)

(Current Hofner product information courtesy Rob Olsen, Boosey & Hawkes Musical Instruments, Inc.)

Hofner
courtesy Dennis Swift

Model Dating Information

Hofner began installing adjustable truss-rods in their guitar necks beginning in 1960. Any model prior to that year will not have a truss-rod cover.

Hofner Models (1950s to 1970s)

Between the late 1950s and early 1970s, Hofner produced a number of semi-hollow or hollowbody electric guitars and basses that were in demand in England. English distribution was handled by **Selmer** of London, and specified models that were imported. In some cases, English models are certainly different from the 'domestic' models offered in Germany.

There will always be interest in Hofners; either Paul McCartney's earlier association with the **Beatle Bass** or the thrill of a **Committee** or **Golden Hofner**.

Hofner Models (1960s to 1980s)

From the late 1960s to the early 1980s, the company produced a number of guitar models based on popular American designs. In addition, Hofner also built a number of better quality original models such as **Alpha, Compact**, and **Razorwood** from the late 1970s to the mid 1980s. However, you have to *know 'em before you tag 'em.* The ***Blue Book of Electric Guitars*** recommends discussions with your favorite vintage dealers (it's easier to figure them out when they're in front of you). Other inquiries can be addressed either to Boosey & Hawkes as to models nomenclature and market value.

The models listed below have not been individually priced. In general, acoustic electric archtop models will range from \$750-\$950, semi-acoustic electric archtops from \$750-\$1,250, Hollow body basses from \$850-\$1,500 and solid body basses from \$450-\$650.

Demand is highest in the category of "Violin" basses and weakest in the category of solid body basses. The archtop models are also quite desirable with jazz artists who appreciate quality vintage instruments.

Hofner Models (Non-U.S.)

Hofner (and Boosey & Hawkes) is currently offering a wider range of models outside of the U.S. market. In fact, Hofner has 4 different series of acoustic guitars that are not represented below: the child-sized Jugend-/Schulergitarren (HS Series), classical-style **Konzertgitarren** (HF Series), environment-friendly **Green Line** (HGL Series), and the upscale **Meistergitarrren** (HM Series). Electric models include the **Jazzica Standard** and **Jazzica Special**, **Vice President**, and **New President**, as well as the **Nightingale Standard** and the **Nightingale Special**. Electric bass models are the same.

ELECTRIC GUITARS

Acoustic Electric Archtop Models

Hofner Archtop
courtesy Jimmy Gravity

MODEL 450E - archtop hollowbody, laminated maple top, back & sides, rosewood fingerboard, white celluloid band position markers, bound top, celluloid pickguard, 3-per-side tuners, f-holes, lyre tailpiece, 1 pickup mounted at the fingerboard, no controls, available in sunburst finish & wine red finish on late production models. Mfg. 1954 to 1984.

MODEL 455/S/E1 - archtop hollow body, laminated maple top & back, black & white celluloid bindings on top, back & f-holes, red-white celluloid inlays on the headstock, 3-per-side tuners, white pickguard, lyre tailpiece, celluloid band position markers. 1 adjustable pickup, volume, 3 sliding tone switches, available in cherry red & blonde (Model 455/S/b/E1) finishes. Mfg. early to late 1960's.

MODEL 456/S/b/E2 - archtop hollow body, single cutaway design, flame maple back & sides, bound top, back, fingerboard & f-holes, black pickguard, 3-per-side tuners, red, black, or white headstock, lyre tailpiece, celluloid band position markers, 2 adjustable pickups, 2 volume controls & 3 sliding tone switches or 2 volume & 2 tone controls. Available in blonde finish. Mfg. circa 1961 to 1962.

MODEL 457/S/E1 - archtop hollowbody, single cutaway design, spruce top, flame maple back & sides, bound top, back, fingerboard & f-holes, headstock decorated with gold plated clef & staff, 3-per-side tuners, celluloid band position markers, white pickguard, 1 adjustable pickup, 1 volume control and 3 sliding tone controls, lyre tailpiece, available in brown sunburst finish. Mfg. circa 1961 to 1970.

MODEL 457/S/E2 - same as Model 457/S/E1 except has 2 adjustable pickups & either 2 volume controls & 3 sliding tone switches or 2 volume & 2 tone controls, available in brown sunburst and blonde (Model 457/S/b/E2) finishes. Mfg. circa 1961 to 1970.

MODEL 462/S/E1 - archtop hollow body, selected spruce top, flame maple back & sides, 2-piece tailpiece, elliptical sound holes, bound top, back, fingerboard & f-holes, 3-per-side tuners, headstock has gold plated clef & staff, celluloid band fingerboard inlays (1 wide & 2 narrow), 1 adjustable pickup, 1 volume & 3 sliding tone switches, available in light brown varnish finish. Mfg. circa 1954 to 1970.

MODEL 462/S/E3 - archtop hollow body, same as Model 462/S/E3 except has 3 adjustable pickups & 1 volume & 3 tone controls, pickup selector switch, available in light brown varnish finish. Mfg. circa 1954 to 1970.

MODEL 463/S/E2 - archtop hollow body, single cutaway design, Sapeli Mahogany back & sides, selected spruce top, bound mahogany fingerboard, wooden inlays & celluloid bindings on top & back, wooden inlays around the f-holes, harp tailpiece, 3-per-side tuners, dark pickguard. 2 adjustable pickups, 2 volume & 2 tone controls, available in shaded brown finish. Mfg. circa 1961 to 1970.

MODEL 465/S/E2 - archtop hollow body, single cutaway design, well selected fine spruce top, rosewood back & sides, wood & celluloid bindings on top, back, fingerboard & f-holes, mother-of-pearl headstock inlays (bell-fowers) & fingerboard position markers (1 narrow rectangle flanked by 2 pentagons that resemble arrowheads), ebony fingerboard, 3-per-side tuners, lucite pickguard, 2 pickups, early 1960's models had 2 volume controls & 3 sliding tone controls while late 60's models had 2 volume & 2 tone controls, lyre tailpiece, available in light brown finish. Mfg. circa 1961 to 1970.

MODEL 470/S/E2 - archtop hollow body, single cutaway design, selected spruce top, best quality flame maple back & sides, wooden flower inlays on back, ebony fingerboard & headstock, gold plated hardware, bound top, back, fingerboard & f-holes, 3-per-side tuners, mother-of-pearl headstock inlays (Lillies) and position markers (1 narrow rectangle flanked by 2 pentagons that resemble arrowheads), lucite pickguard, 2 pickups, late 1950's models had 2 volume & 3 sliding tone controls. Mid 60's models had 3 sliding pickup selector switches & 2 volume & 1 tone control. Available in high polish blonde finish. Mfg. circa 1959 to 1994.

MODEL 471/E2 - large archtop hollow body, selected spruce top, flame maple back & sides, florentine cutaway, celluloid binding on top & back, ebony fingerboard with mother-of-pearl inlays, 3-per-side tuners, black pickguard, lyre tailpiece, 2 pickups, 2 volume & 2 tone controls, pickup selector switch, Available in blonde finish. Mfg. circa 1969 to 1977.

MODEL AL2 - archtop hollow body, single cutaway design, spruce top, flame maple back & sides, wooden inlays on back, bound top & back, mother-of-pearl position markers, 1 pickup in the neck position, 1 volume, 1 tone control, 3-per-side tuners, lyre tailpiece, could be ordered with a piezo pickup under the bridge or with stereo output, available in blonde & shaded brown finishes. Mfg. 1978 to 1986.

MODEL AZ - archtop hollow body, single cutaway design, solid spruce top, flame maple back & sides, mother-of-pearl split block position markers, bound top & back, chrome hardware, lyre tailpiece, wooden pickguard, f-holes, 3-per-side tuners, available in black & antique brown finishes. Mfg. 1982 to 1991.

MODEL AZ AWARD - archtop hollow body, same as Model AZ except has V-style tailpiece, ebony fingerboard, gold plated hardware, available in blonde & Bordeaux Red Sunburst finishes. Mfg. 1982 to 1991.

VERYTHIN CLASSIC (Model HVC) - double cutaway semi-hollow bound body, German spruce top, highly flamed African maple back & sides, asymmetrically profiled European maple neck, 22-fret ebony fingerboard with genuine mother-of-pearl inlays, gold plated hardware, solid spruce tone block, individually carved and fitted by hand for a precise match to the top and back, uses no tone bars, specially designed Hofner/Kent Armstrong pickups, contemporary f-hole design, 2 volume & 2 tone controls, toggle switch, lyre tailpiece, gold hardware, available in natural, black, and sunburst finishes. Current Mfg.

MSR $2,495

JAZZICA CUSTOM (Model HJCL/HJ5-I) - single rounded cutaway semi-hollow bound body, solid carved German spruce top, laminated African Anigree back/sides, 2 bound 'cats-eye' f-holes, European hard rock maple neck, 25 3/4" scale, 24-fret bound ebony fingerboard with mother-of-pearl block inlay, 3-per-side Schaller tuners, matching finish peghead, adjustable ebony bridge/raised metal tailpiece, gold hardware, Hofner/Kent Armstrong 'floating' pickup, volume/tone controls, available in Natural finish. Current Mfg.

MSR $3,445

NEW PRESIDENT (Model HNP/HP55-I) - single rounded cutaway semi-hollow bound body, solid carved German spruce top, laminated flamed African Anigree back/sides, 2 f-holes, European hard rock maple neck, 25 3/4" scale, 24-fret bound ebony fingerboard with mother-of-pearl block inlay, 3-per-side Schaller tuners, bound blackface peghead with mother-of-pearl design inlay, adjustable ebony bridge/raised metal tailpiece, gold hardware, raised ebony pickguard, Hofner/Kent Armstrong 'floating' pickup, volume control, available in Natural finish. Current Mfg.

MSR $3,329

VICE PRESIDENT (Model HVP) - single rounded cutaway semi-hollow bound body, solid handcarved German AAA Spruce top, f-holes, highly flamed African maple back & sides, asymmetrically profiled European maple neck, 24-fret ebony fingerboard with genuine mother-of-pearl imlays, nickel plated hardware, mother-of-pearl "lily" inlay on headstock, fully adjustable Hofner/Kent Armstrong floating pickup with individually adjustable pole pieces, non-routed bridge & neck pickups, 3-way pickup selector switch, 2 tone & 2 volume controls, a single bass tonebar braces the top, available in sunburst and black finishes. Current Mfg.

MSR $2,695

NIGHTINGALE (Model HN35-I) - dual rounded cutaway semi-hollow bound body, laminated bird's-eye maple top/back/sides, 2 bound f-holes, solid German spruce sustain block, European hard rock maple neck, 25 3/4" scale, 24-fret bound ebony fingerboard with mother-of-pearl block inlay, 3-per-side Schaller tuners, bound blackface peghead with mother-of-pearl design inlay, tune-o-matic bridge/stop tailpiece with fine tuners, gold hardware, 2 Classic '57 humbucker pickups, 2 volume/2 tone controls, master volume control, 3-way pickup selector, stereo outputs, available in Antique Gold Sunburst finish. Disc.

Last MSR was $3,350.

Hofner Verythin
courtesy J.R. Guitars

Semi Acoustic Electric Archtop Models

MODEL 125 - single cutaway, arched top & back, celluloid bound top & back, 3-per-side tuners, lyre tailpiece, dot position markers, 1 adjustable pickup, 1 volume & 1 tone control, black pickguard, available in shaded brown finish and blonde (Model 125/b/E1). Mfg. 1954 to 1970.

MODEL 126/E2 - same as Model 125 except has 2 pickups, 2 volume & 2 tone controls, available in shaded brown finish. Mfg. 1954 to 1970. Also available in blonde finish (Model 126/b/E2). Mfg. 1956-1967.

MODEL 128/E2 - same basic design as Model 125 except has flame maple back & sides, bound fingerboard, mother-of-pearl headstock inlays and fingerboard position markers, available in gold/red shaded finish with black sides and blonde finish (Model 128/b/E2). Mfg. 1961 to 1970.

MODEL 459 (II) - violin shaped body, 3-per-side tuners, celluloid band position markers, lyre tailpiece, 2 pickups, white pickguard, bound top, available in brown burst finish. Mfg. 1967 to 1970.

MODEL 4572 (II) - arched top, double cutaway design, 2" thick body, 3-per-side tuners, white celluloid binding on top & f-holes, 2 pickups, 2 volume & 2 tone controls with toggle switch or 1 volume & 2 tone controls, f-holes, black pickguard, available in sunburst finish. Mfg. 1969 to 1988.

MODEL 4574 - arched top, double cutaway design, flame maple back & sides, spruce top, 1 ¾" body, bound top, back & f-holes, 3-per-side tuners, celluloid band position markers, mother-of-pearl headstock inlays (bell flowers), 2 pickups, a variety of electronics available, available in wine red shaded finish or brown with black sides. Mfg. 1961 to 1976.

MODEL 4577 - arched top, single florentine cutaway, 3-per-side tuners, 3 dot position markers, f-holes, 2 pickups, 1 volume & 1 tone control & a toggle switch, lyre tailpiece with vibrato bar, black pickguard, available in brown burst finish. Mfg. 1967 to 1992.

T2S - arched top, double cutaway design, flamed maple body with sustain block, bound top, back & f-holes, mother-of-pearl position markers, two 052 pickups, stop tailpiece, 3-per-side tuners, black pickguard, available in walnut brown and Sahara Yellow. Mfg. 1978 to 1980.

ELECTRIC BASS

Hollow Body Models

MODEL 500/1 - violin shaped body, spruce top, maple back & sides, 2 pickups, 2 volume & 2 tone controls on early models, 2 volume & 3 sliding tone controls on production since circa 1959, lyre tailpiece, dot position markers, 2-per-side tuners, Available in shaded brown finish. Mfg. 1956-present.

MODEL 500/2 - single cutaway design similar to Model 125, spruce top, maple back & sides, lyre tailpiece, 2-per-side tuners, dot position markers, 2 pickups, 2 volume controls & 3 sliding tone switches, white pickguard, available in shaded brown finish. Mfg. 1965 to 1970.

MODEL 500/4 - arched top, double cutaway, f-holes, lyre tailpiece, 2-per-side tuners, dot position markers, 2 pickups, 3 rotary controls & a toggle switch, black pickguard, available in brown burst finish. Mfg. 1969 to 1988.

MODEL 500/5 - arched top, single cutaway design, f-holes, 2-per-side tuners, lyre tailpiece, bound top, 2 pickups, 2 volume/2 tone controls, dot position markers, white pickguard, mother-of-pearl headstock inlay (Lillies), available in shaded brown finish. Mfg. 1961 to 1979.

MODEL 500/8 - arched top, double cutaway with florentine style horns, f-holes, celluloid band position markers, 2-per-side tuners, mother-of-pearl headstock inlays (Lillies), 2 pickups, 2 volume/2 tone controls, toggle switch, black pickguard, available in brown burst finish. Mfg. 1969 to 1977.

VINTAGE 63 VIOLIN BASS (Model 500/1-63, BEATLE BASS) - violin-style bound hollow body, arched solid German spruce top, laminated flame maple back/sides, 3-piece laminated maple/beech neck, 22-fret bound rosewood fingerboard with pearl dot inlay, adjustable rosewood bridge/trapeze tailpiece, bound blackface peghead, 2-per-side tuners, nickel hardware, raised pearloid pickguard with engraved logo, 2 "Staple Top" humbucker pickups, 2 volume controls, Rhythm/Solo tone selector switch, Bass On/Treble On pickup selector switches, controls mounted on a pearloid plate, available in Antique Brown Sunburst, transparent red and transparent blue. Current Mfg.

MSR **$2,495**

This model is available in a left-handed configuration with the same specifications.

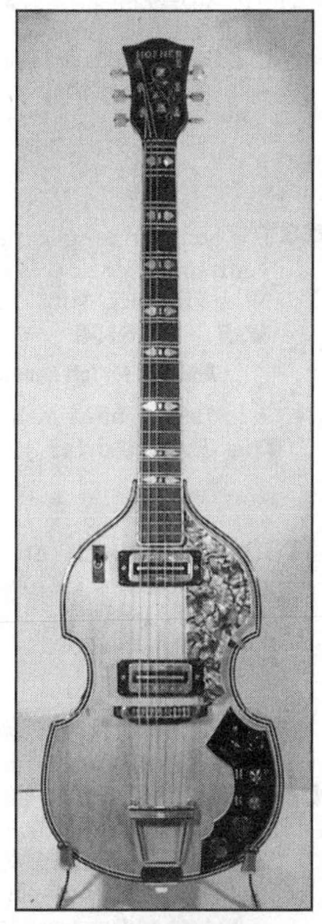

Hofner 459/VTZ
courtesy Debbie Nix

GRADING	100% MINT	98% NEAR MINT	95% EXC+	90% EXC	80% VG+	70% VG	60% G

VINTAGE '62 REISSUE BASS (Model 500/1-62) - violin style bound hollow body, arched solid German spruce top, laminated flame maple back & sides, 2 piece neck, rosewood fingerboard, 22-fret neck, pearl dot position markers, trapeze tailpiece, pearloid pickguard, bound top and back, 2-per-side strip tuners, nickel hardware, 2 "Staple Top" humbucker pickups, 2 volume controls, Rhythm/Solo tone selector switch, Bass On/Treble On pickup selector switches, available in Antique Brown Sunburst finish. Based on Paul McCartney's 1962 Violin Bass. Current Mfg.

MSR $2,695

DELUXE VIOLIN BASS (Model 5000/1) - violin- style bound hollow body, arched German spruce top, tortoise body binding, laminated flame maple back/sides, solid European hard rock maple neck, 22-fret bound ebony fingerboard with pearl double dot inlay, adjustable ebony bridge/raised trapeze tailpiece, bound blackface peghead with mother-of-pearl diamond inlay, 2-per-side tuners, gold hardware, raised black pickguard with engraved logo, 2 "Staple Top" humbucker pickups, 2 volume controls, Rhythm/Solo tone selector switch, Bass On/Treble On pickup selector switches, controls mounted on a black plate, available in Natural finish. Current Mfg.

MSR $2,895

Solid Body Models

MODEL 182 - double cutaway, 1 piece maple neck with rosewood fingerboard, 4-on-a-side tuners, dot position markers, 2 pickups, 2 volume controls & 3 sliding tone controls, black pickguard, available in red, ivory, ice blue, or shaded brown finish. Mfg. 1962 to 1985.

MODEL 183 - shaped similar to Stratocaster, 4-on-a-side tuners, dot position markers, 2 pickups, 2 volume controls and 1 tone switch, white pickgurad. Mfg. 1975 to 1983.

MODEL 185 - offset double cutaway design, 4-on-a-side tuners, celluloid band position markers, 2 pickups, 2 volume/2 tone controls, pickup control switches, black pickguard. Mfg. 1962 to 1983.

MODEL 186 - single cutaway body similar to Telecaster, 4-on-a-side tuners, dot position markers, 2 pickups, 1 volume & 1 tone control, pickup selector switch, covered bridge, available in ivory finish. Mfg. 1971 to 1973.

MODEL 187 (I) - double sutaway design similar to SG, solid mahogany body, 2-per-side tuners, mother-of-pearl block position markers & headstock inlays, 2 pickups, 2 volume & 2 tone controls, toggle switch, white pickguard, covered bridge. Mfg. 1971 to 1972.

MODEL 188 (I) - 6-string bass, offset double cutaway design, 4/2 tuner configuration, celluloid band position markers, 3 pickups, tremelo bridge. Mfg. 1963 only. Also available as Model 188 (II), similar to Model 188 (I) except 6 tuners on one side. Mfg. 1964 to 1970.

HOHNER

Instruments currently produced in Korea, although earlier models from the 1970s were built in Japan. Currently distributed in the U.S. by HSS (a Division of Hohner, Inc.), located in Richmond, Virginia.

The Hohner company was founded in 1857, and is currently the world's largest manufacturer and distributor of harmonicas. Hohner offers a wide range of solidly constructed musical instruments. The company has stayed contemporary with the current market by licensing designs and parts from Ned Steinberger, Claim Guitars (Germany), and Wilkinson hardware.

In addition to their guitar models, Hohner also distributes Sonor drums, Sabian cymbals, and Hohner educational percussion instruments.

ELECTRIC

G3T - Steinberger-style maple body, through-body maple neck, 24-fret rosewood fingerboard with white dot inlay, Steinberger vibrato, black hardware, 2 single coil/humbucker EMG pickups, volume/tone control, 3 mini switches, passive filter in tone control, available in Black and White finishes. Mfg. 1990 to date.

MSR $750 — $575 $495 $425 $375 $325 $250 $195

Add $60 for left handed version (G3TLH).

In 1994, White finish was discontinued.

The Jack Guitar - similar to G3T, except has asymmetrical double cutaway body, available in Black and Metallic Red finishes. Disc. 1994.

$500 $425 $375 $325 $275 $250 $195

Last MSR was $765.

JT60 - offset double cutaway maple body, tortoise pickguard, bolt-on maple neck, 22-fret rosewood fingerboard with pearl dot inlay, standard vibrato, 6-on-a-side tuners, chrome hardware, 3 single coil pickups, 2 volume/tone controls, 5-position switch, advance tone passive electronics, available in Ivory and Sea foam Green finishes. Mfg. 1992 to 1996.

$325 $250 $200 $175 $150 $125 $100

Last MSR was $480.

Caribbean Pearl Series

CARIBBEAN PEARL - single rounded cutaway maple body, bolt-on maple neck, 22-fret rosewood fingerboard with pearloid dot inlay, tune-o-matic bridge/stop tailpiece, 3-per-side die cast tuners, gold hardware, 2 covered humbucker pickups, volume/tone controls, 3-way selector switch, available in Pearl Berry Red (PBR), Pearl Island Blue (PIB), and Pearl Oyster Black (POB) Ivoroid Top (and matching headstock) finishes with matching stained (Blue, Red, Black) backs. Mfg. 1998 to date.

As this edition went to press, prices had yet to be established on this model.

GRADING	100% MINT	98% NEAR MINT	95% EXC+	90% EXC	80% VG+	70% VG	60% G

Hohner Baton Rouge
courtesy Hohner

Classic City Series

THE BATON ROUGE - single cutaway alder body with contoured top, bolt-on maple neck, 22-fret rosewood fingerboard with pearloid dot inlay, wraparound bridge, blackface peghead, 3-per-side die cast tuners, chrome hardware, 2 exposed pole piece humbucker pickups, volume/tone controls, 3-way toggle selector, available in Butterscotch and Cherry Sunburst finishes. Mfg. 1998 to date.

As this edition went to press, prices had yet to be established on this model.

The Springfield - similar to the Baton Rouge, except features 3 single coil pickups, classic-style tremolo bridge, white pickguard, available in Black and Uptown Blue finishes. Mfg. 1998 to date.

As this edition went to press, prices had yet to be established on this model.

THE BIRMINGHAM - slightly offset double cutaway alder body with contoured top, bolt-on maple neck, 22-fret rosewood fingerboard with pearloid dot inlay, wraparound bridge, natural finish peghead, 6-on-a-side die cast tuners, chrome hardware, 2 exposed pole piece humbucker pickups, volume/tone controls, 3-way toggle selector, available in Black and Candy Apple Red finishes. Mfg. 1998 to date.

As this edition went to press, prices had yet to be established on this model.

The Reno - similar to the Birmingham, except features single coil/humbucker pickups, tele-style fixed bridge, black pickguard, available in Vintage Sunburst finish. Mfg. 1998 to date.

As this edition went to press, prices had yet to be established on this model.

HL Series

HL59 - single sharp cutaway solid maple body, bound figured maple top, black pickguard, mahogany neck, 22-fret bound rosewood fingerboard with pearl crown inlay, tune-o-matic bridge/stop tailpiece, bound peghead with pearl pineapple/logo inlay, 3-per-side tuners, chrome or gold hardware, 2 humbucker pickups, 2 volume/tone controls, 3-way switch, available in Black, Cherry Sunburst, Gold Top, Ivory, and Violin finishes. Mfg. 1990 to 1996.

$400 $325 $275 $250 $225 $195 $175
Last MSR was $625.

Add $35 for left-handed version (Model HL59LH).

HLP75 - similar to HL59, except has white pickguard, bolt-on neck, diamond peghead inlay, available in Antique Sunburst and Black finishes. Mfg. 1990 to 1991.

$250 $225 $175 $150 $125 $110 $100
Last MSR was $375.

HL90 - similar to the HL59, except features a bound maple/mahogany body, white pickguard, bound peghead with pearl diamond/logo inlay, 3-per-side tuners, chrome hardware, 2 PAF pickups, available in Gold Top finish. Mfg. 1992 to 1996.

$450 $350 $325 $250 $225 $200 $175
Last MSR was $690.

HL60 - single sharp cutaway maple body, black pickguard, mahogany neck, 22-fret bound rosewood fingerboard with pearl dot inlay, tune-o-matic bridge/stop tailpiece, blackface peghead with pearl coconut/logo inlay, 3-per-side tuners, chrome hardware, 2 single coil pickups, 2 volume/2 tone controls, 3-position switch, available in Cherry Red finish. Mfg. 1994 to 1996.

$375 $325 $275 $225 $200 $175 $150
Last MSR was $575.

HS35 (SE35) - semi-hollow body, maple bound top/back/sides, black pickguard, mahogany neck, 22-fret rosewood fingerboard with pearl dot inlay, tune-o-matic bridge/stop tailpiece, pearl pineapple/logo peghead inlay, chrome hardware, 2 humbucker pickups, 2 volume/tone controls, 3-position switch, available in Natural and Tobacco Sunburst finishes. Mfg. 1990 to date.

MSR $769 $575 $500 $425 $375 $325 $250 $195

Early versions of this model may feature gold hardware, and Black, Sunburst, or White finishes.

HS40 (SE400) - single round cutaway hollow body, maple bound top/back/sides, f-holes, black pickguard, mahogany neck, 22-fret bound rosewood fingerboard with pearl block inlay, tune-o-matic bridge/trapeze tailpiece, bound peghead with pearl pineapple/logo inlay, 2 humbucker pickups, 2 volume/tone controls, 3-position switch, available in Natural and Tobacco Sunburst finishes. Mfg. 1992 to date.

MSR $899 $675 $575 $525 $450 $375 $300 $225

Revelation Series

See REVELATION.

Rockwood (By Hohner) Series

See ROCKWOOD.

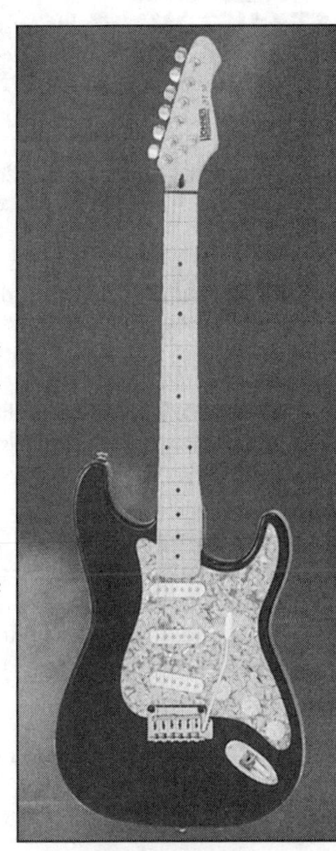

Hohner ST-59
courtesy Hohner

GRADING		100% MINT	98% NEAR MINT	95% EXC+	90% EXC	80% VG+	70% VG	60% G

Standard Series

HS59 (ST59) - double offset cutaway alder body, white pickguard, bolt-on maple neck, 22-fret maple fingerboard with black dot inlay, standard vibrato, 6-on-a-side tuners, chrome hardware, 3 single coil pickups, volume/2 tone controls, 5-way switch, available in Black and Sunburst finishes. Mfg. 1990 to date.

MSR	$479	$375	$300	$250	$225	$175	$150	$125

Add $20 for left-handed configuration with Sunburst finish (Model HS59LH).

Add $20 for pearloid pickguard with Black or Sunburst finish (Model HS59P).

Add $35 for ATN active electronics with Transparent Blue or Transparent Red finishes (Model HS59A).

Add $55 for ATN active electronics and pearloid pickguard with Transparent Blue or Transparent Red finishes (Model HS59AP).

HS65 - rounded single cutaway maple body, flamed maple top, bolt-on maple neck, 22-fret rosewood fingerboard with dot inlay, tremolo, 3-per-side tuners, gold hardware, 2 single coil/humbucker pickups, volume/tone controls, 5-way switch, available in Cherry Sunburst finish. Mfg. 1997 to date.

MSR	$479	$375	$325	$275	$250	$200	$175	$125

HS75 - similar to HS65, except features bird's-eye maple top, set-in neck, chrome hardware, 2 humbuckers, 3-way switch, available in Blonde finish. Mfg. 1997 to date.

MSR	$499	$375	$325	$295	$250	$225	$175	$125

HS85 - similar to HS65, except features pearloid top, 2 single coil pickups, 3-way switch, available in White Pearloid finish. Mfg. 1997 to date.

MSR	$599	$450	$395	$350	$300	$250	$200	$150

HS90 - double offset cutaway maple body, bolt-on maple neck, 24-fret rosewood fingerboard with dot inlay, tremolo, 6-on-a-side tuners, gold hardware, 2 single coil/humbucker pickups, volume/tone controls, 5-way switch, available in Natural Satin finish. Mfg. 1997 to date.

MSR	$549	$425	$350	$325	$275	$225	$175	$125

HT CST - single cutaway alder body, white pickguard, bolt-on maple neck, 22-fret maple fingerboard with black dot inlay, fixed bridge, 6-on-a-side tuners, chrome hardware, 2 single coil pickups, volume/tone controls, 3-way switch, available in Sunburst and Transparent Violet finishes. Current Mfg.

MSR	$525	$395	$350	$300	$275	$225	$175	$125

Add $55 for ATN active electronics and pearloid pickguard with Black finish (Model HT CST AP).

ST Series

ST CUSTOM - double offset cutaway flame maple body, bolt-on maple neck, 22-fret rosewood fingerboard with abalone dot inlay, double locking vibrato, 6-on-a-side tuners, black hardware, 2 single coil/humbucker EMG pickups, volume/tone control, 3 mini switches, available in Cherry Sunburst finish. Mfg. 1990 to 1991.

$675	$625	$525	$425	$375	$350	$325

Last MSR was $1,050.

ST Lynx - similar to ST Custom, except features maple body, 24-fret rosewood fingerboard with white dot inlay, single coil/humbucker EMG pickups, 3-position switch, available in Metallic Blue and Metallic Red finishes. Mfg. 1990 to 1994.

$475	$375	$350	$275	$250	$225	$200

Last MSR was $740.

ST Metal S - similar to the ST Lynx, except features 22-fret rosewood fingerboard with white shark tooth inlay, 2 single coil/1 humbucker EMG pickups, volume/tone control, 3 mini switches, available in Black, Black Crackle, and Pearl White finishes. Mfg. 1990 to 1991.

$425	$375	$325	$250	$225	$200	$175

Last MSR was $630.

ST Victory - similar to the ST Lynx, except features black pickguard, 22-fret rosewood fingerboard with white dot inlay, reverse headstock, humbucker pickup, available in Metallic Dark Purple and Metallic Red finishes. Mfg. 1990 to 1991.

$395	$350	$275	$250	$225	$195	$175

Last MSR was $575.

TE Series

TE CUSTOM - single cutaway bound maple body, white pickguard, bolt-on maple neck, 21-fret rosewood fingerboard with white dot inlay, fixed bridge, 6-on-a-side tuners, chrome hardware, 2 single coil pickups, volume/tone control, 3-position switch, available in 3 Tone Sunburst finish. Mfg. 1992 to 1996.

$375	$250	$225	$175	$150	$125	$100

Last MSR was $500.

TE Custom XII - similar to TE Custom, except has 12-string configuration, black pickguard, 2 humbucker pickups, available in Black finish. Mfg. 1990 to 1993.

$350	$300	$275	$225	$200	$175	$150

Last MSR was $550.

H

GRADING	100% MINT	98% NEAR MINT	95% EXC+	90% EXC	80% VG+	70% VG	60% G

TE Prinz - similar to TE Custom, except features bound flamed maple body, tortoise pickguard, 21-fret maple fingerboard with black dot inlay, available in Natural finish. Mfg. 1990 to 1996.

$350 $275 $250 $200 $175 $150 $125
Last MSR was $565.

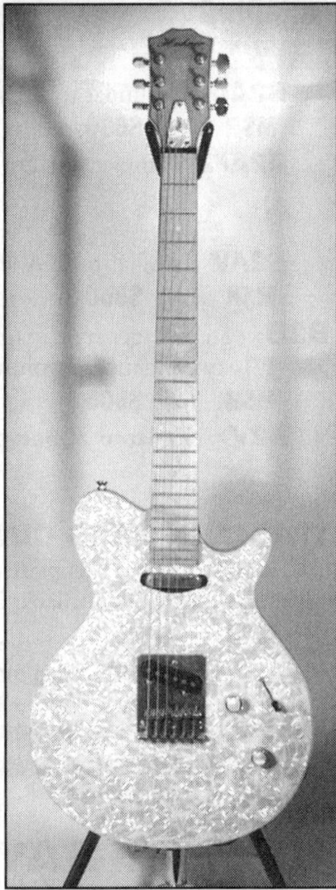

Hohner Pearl
courtesy Mark Rice

ELECTRIC BASS

B BASS - offset double cutaway maple body, through-body maple neck, 24-fret rosewood fingerboard with white dot inlay, Steinberger DB bridge, 2-per-side tuners, black hardware, 2 J-style Designed by EMG pickups, 2 volume/tone controls, active tone electronics with switch and LED, available in Black, Natural Satin, Transparent Black, Transparent Blue, and Transparent Red finishes. Mfg. 1990 to date.

MSR $825 $625 $550 $475 $425 $350 $295 $225

B Bass B - similar to B Bass, except has bolt-on maple neck, available in Lake Placid Blue, Transparent Black, and Transparent Red finishes. Mfg. 1994 to 1996.

$395 $325 $295 $250 $225 $195 $150
Last MSR was $600.

B Bass V - similar to B Bass, except in 5-string configuration, available in Black, Natural Satin, Transparent Black, Transparent Blue, and Walnut Stain finishes. Current Mfg.

MSR $875 $650 $575 $500 $425 $350 $295 $225

B Bass VI - similar to B Bass, except in 6-string configuration, available in Natural finish. Current Mfg.

MSR $1,050 $475 $350 $300 $250 $225 $175 $150

B 500 - sleek offset double cutaway maple body, bolt-on maple neck, 24-fret rosewood fingerboard with white dot inlay, fixed bridge, 2-per-side tuners, chrome hardware, P/J-style pickups, 2 volume/2 tone controls, available in Metallic Red finish. Mfg. 1997 to date.

MSR $549 $425 $350 $325 $275 $225 $175 $125

HPB - offset double cutaway hardwood body, white pickguard, bolt-on maple neck, 20-fret maple fingerboard with black dot inlay, fixed bridge, 4-on-a-side tuners, chrome hardware, P/J-style pickup, volume/tone control, available in Black finish. Current Mfg.

MSR $489 $375 $325 $275 $250 $200 $175 $125

Add $10 for left-handed configuration (HPB LH).

HZB - similar to HPB, except features 2 J-style single coil pickups, tortoiseshell pickguard, 2 volume/tone controls, controls mounted on a metal plate, available in Ivory finish. Current Mfg.

MSR $495 $375 $325 $275 $250 $200 $175 $125

This model is available with a fretless fingerboard (Model HZB FL).

HZAB - similar to HZB, except has 2 J-style Designed by EMG active pickups, available in Vintage Sunburst and Walnut Satin finishes. Current Mfg.

MSR $649 $495 $425 $375 $325 $275 $225 $175

Classic City Series Basses

PHOENIX STANDARD - offset double cutaway agathis body, bolt-on maple neck, 24-fret rosewood fingerboard with offset pearloid dot inlay, fixed bridge, natural finish peghead, 2-per-side die cast tuners, chrome hardware, 2 HPC-4 Deluxe 'soapbar' pickups, 2 volume/tone controls, available in Black and Candy Apple Red finishes. Mfg. 1998 to date.

As this edition went to press, prices had yet to be established on this model.

Phoenix Deluxe - similar to the Phoenix Standard, except features Louisiana swamp ash body, 2 HPC-4 Custom active/passive pickups, gold hardware, abalone fingerboard dot inlay, active electronics LED indicator, available in Desert Walnut Stain finish. Mfg. 1998 to date.

As this edition went to press, prices had yet to be established on this model.

Headless Series

B2 - Steinberger-style maple body, through-body maple neck, 24-fret rosewood fingerboard with white dot inlay, Steinberger bridge, black hardware, 2 humbucker pickups, 2 volume/1 tone controls, available in Black and Red finishes. Mfg. 1990 to 1992.

$350 $300 $275 $225 $200 $175 $125
Last MSR was $550.

B2A - similar to B2, except features mini switch, active electronics, LED lights, available in Black and Red finishes. Mfg. 1990 to 1992.

$450 $375 $300 $250 $225 $200 $150
Last MSR was $625.

Add $35 for left-handed version.

GRADING		100% MINT	98% NEAR MINT	95% EXC+	90% EXC	80% VG+	70% VG	60% G

B2ADB - similar to B2A, except has Steinberger DB bridge, available in Black and Metallic Red finishes. Mfg. 1992 to date.

MSR	$850	$575	$495	$425	$375	$325	$275	$225

B2AFL - similar to B2A, except is fretless with an ebonol fingerboard. Mfg. 1990 to 1992.

		$450	$400	$350	$275	$250	$225	$200

Last MSR was $695.

B2AV - similar to B2A, except features 5-string configuration, available in Walnut Stain finish. Current Mfg.

MSR	$850	$575	$495	$425	$375	$325	$275	$225

B2B - Steinberger style maple body, bolt-on maple neck, 24-fret rosewood fingerboard with white dot inlay, Steinberger bridge, black hardware, P/J-style pickups, 2 volume/tone controls, available in Black finish. Mfg. 1992 to date.

MSR	$565	$425	$375	$325	$275	$250	$195	$150

B2V - similar to B2B, except in a 5-string configuration, available in Black finish. Mfg. 1990 to 1992.

		$450	$400	$350	$275	$250	$225	$200

Last MSR was $675.

THE JACK BASS CUSTOM - offset double cutaway maple body, through-body headless maple neck, 24-fret rosewood fingerboard with white dot inlay, Steinberger bridge, black hardware, 2 J-style pickups, 2 volume/tone controls, active tone electronics with switch and LED, available in Black, Metallic Red, and Natural finishes. Mfg. 1990 to date.

MSR	$875	$650	$575	$450	$375	$300	$275	$225

Add $75 for 5-string configuration (The Jack Bass Custom 5).

H

Rockwood by Hohner Basses

See ROCKWOOD.

HOLIDAY

See chapter on House Brands.

This trademark has been identified as a "House Brand" distributed by Montgomery Wards and Alden's department stores. Author/researcher Willie G. Moseley also reports seeing a catalog reprint showing Holiday instruments made by
Harmony, Kay, and Danelectro. Additional information in regards to instruments with this trademark will be welcome, especially any Danelectro with a 'HOLIDAY' logo on the headstock. Future updates will be included in upcoming editions of the *Blue Book of Electric Guitars*.

(Source: Willie G. Moseley, Stellas & Stratocasters)

HOLLISTER GUITARS

Instruments currently built in Dedham, Massachusetts.

Luthier Kent Hollister is currently offering high quality, custom built guitars such as the **Archtop** ($3,000), **Semi-hollow** ($1,900), **Carved Top Solid Body** ($1,500), and **The Plank** ($1,200). The Plank is an electric solid body with neck-through design. Hollister has also created the **Archtop Bass** ($2,800), which features a central soundhole (as opposed to f-holes). Just the thing to swing with the archtop guitarists! For further information contact luthier Kent Hollister directly (see Trademark Index).

HOLMAN

Instruments previously built in Neodesha, Kansas during the late 1960s. Distributed by Holman-Woodell, Inc. of Neodesha, Kansas.

The Holman-Woodell company built guitars during the late 1960s in Neodesha, Kansas (around 60 miles due south from Topeka). While they were producing guitars for Wurlitzer, they also built their own Holman brand as well as instruments trademarked Alray and 21st Century. The Holman-Woodell company is also famous for building the La Baye "2 x 4" guitars for Wisconsin-based inventor Dan Helland. The Holman-Woodell company also released a number of faux "2 x 4's" built from leftover parts with the "Holman" logo after the La Baye company went under.

(Source: Michael Wright, Guitar Stories Volume One)

HOLMES, TOM

Instruments previously built in Tennessee circa 1970s to 1980s.

Luthier Tom Holmes custom built numerous high quality, solid body guitars for a number of years for artists such as Billy Gibbons (ZZ Top), Bo Diddley, and others. In the mid 1970s, Holmes came up with a design for a "triple coil" (i.e., a pickup that could be split into a single coil and a humbucker instead of just splitting a dual coil), and custom built guitars to bring the idea to the marketplace. The T.H.C. guitars were completely handcrafted (save for the tuners and the bridge) by Holmes, and a majority of the guitars were sold through Larry Henrikson's Ax-in-Hand Guitar Shop in Dekalb, Illinois. Other T.H.C. models include a limited run of Holmes/Gibbons "Cadillac" guitars (based on the Gretsch Cadillac model played by Bo Diddley).

In the mid 1980s, Holmes became involved with the Gibson Guitar company. Holmes designed the tooling for some of the company production, and was a part of Gibson's *'57 Classic* pickup reissue. During his work on the reissue pickup, Holmes worked on a P.A.F. design similar to the original vintage pickups. With the success of his design, Holmes went into business with his own company, hand winding his P.A.F. reproductions and stamping out the proper pickup cover to go with it.

Holmes' pickups have appeared in certain limited production models from the large guitar manufacturing companies, and are very popular in Japan and Germany as aftermarket reissues. For further information on his P.A.F. reproductions, contact Tom Holmes directly (see Trademark Index).

(Collector's tip courtesy David Larson at Audio Restoration, and Larry Henrikson at Ax-in-Hand)

HOLST, STEPHEN

Instruments currently built in Eugene, Oregon since 1984.

Luthier Stephen Holst began building guitars in 1984, and through inspiration and refinement developed the models currently offered. Holst draws on his familiarity of Pacific Northwest tonewoods in developing tonal qualities in his handcrafted instruments. Holst specifically works with the customer commissioning the instrument, tailoring the requests to the specific guitar. In addition, Holst has experimented in other designs such as nylon string, 7- and 12-string, and baritone archtops.

ELECTRIC

Semi-Hollow/Thinline Series

At the request of several jazz performers, Holst designed the **K 250** thinline semi-hollow guitars. The K 250 draws on the inspiration and design of the K 200 archtop, combined with a highly figured black walnut top and peghead overlay. The body width is 15", and the electronics are the Tom Doyle D1 pickup system. List price is $2,200.

Hollister Custom
courtesy Kent Hollister

HONDO

Instruments currently produced in Korea. Distributed by MBT International of Charleston, South Carolina.

Between 1974 to early 1980s some models were produced in Japan.

The Hondo guitar company was originally formed in 1969 when Jerry Freed and Tommy Moore of the International Music Corporation (IMC) of Fort Worth, Texas, combined with the recently formed Samick company. IMC's intent was to introduce modern manufacturing techniques and American quality standards to the Korean guitar manufacturing industry.

The Hondo concept was to offer an organized product line and solid entry level market instruments at a fair market price. The original Korean products were classical and steel-string acoustic guitars. In 1972, the first crudely built Hondo electrics were built. However, two years later the product line took a big leap forward in quality under the new Hondo II logo. Hondo also began limited production of guitars in Japan in 1974.

By 1975, Hondo had distributors in 70 countries worldwide, and had expanded to producing stringed instruments at the time. In 1976, over 22,000 of the Bi-Centennial banjos were sold. The company also made improvements to the finish quality on their products, introduced scalloped bracing on acoustics, and began using a higher quality brand of tuning machines.

Hondo was one of the first overseas guitar builders to feature American-built DiMarzio pickups on the import instruments beginning in 1978. By this year, a number of Hondo II models featured designs based on classic American favorites. In 1979, over 790,000 Hondo instruments were sold worldwide. All guitar production returned to Korea in 1983. At that point, the product line consisted of 485 different models!

In 1985, IMC acquired major interest in the Charvel/Jackson company, and began dedicating more time and interest in the higher end guitar market. The Hondo trademark went into mothballs around 1987. However, Jerry Freed started the *Jerry Freed International* company in 1989, and acquired the rights to the Hondo trademark in 1991 (the "Est. 1969" tagline was added to the Hondo logo at this time). Freed began distribution of a new line of Hondo guitars. In 1993, the revamped company was relocated to Stuart, Florida; additional models added to the line were produced in China and Taiwan.

The Hondo Guitar Company was purchased by the MBT International in 1995. MBT also owns and distributes J.B. Player instruments. The Hondo product line was revamped for improved quality while maintaining student-friendly prices. Hondo celebrated their 25th year of manufacturing electric guitars in 1997.

(Source: Tom Malm, MBT International; and Michael Wright, Guitar Stories Volume One)

Hondo guitars generally carried a new retail price range between $179 and $349 (up to $449). While their more unusual-designed model may command a slightly higher price, the average used price may range between $119 (good condition) up to $199 (clean condition, with case, DiMarzio pickups).

ELECTRIC

Current Hondo electric solid body models include the **H720M** (list $299), a traditional style double cutaway model with bolt-on maple neck, 21-fret rosewood fingerboard, vintage-style tremolo, white pickguard, 3 single coil pickups, volume/2 tone controls, and a 5-way selector switch. The **H715** (list $199) has a plywood body, nato neck, kuku wood fingerboard, black pickguard, humbucker, and volume/tone controls.

All Star Series

The All Star models debuted in the fall of 1983, and featured Fender-based models with a slimmed down Telecaster-ish headstock.

The Paul Dean Series

Paul Dean (Loverboy) endorsed and had a hand in designing two solid body models in 1983. The Hondo version could even be seen as a *dry run* for Dean's later association with the Kramer company. The **Dean II** had a stop tailpiece and two humbuckers, and the **Dean III** featured three single coils and a standard tremolo.

Deluxe Series

The Deluxe Series was first offered in 1982, and featured 11 classical and 22 steel string acoustic models. The electric line featured 9 variations on the Les Paul theme, including the **H-752** double cutaway LP. A 'strat' of sorts carried the des-

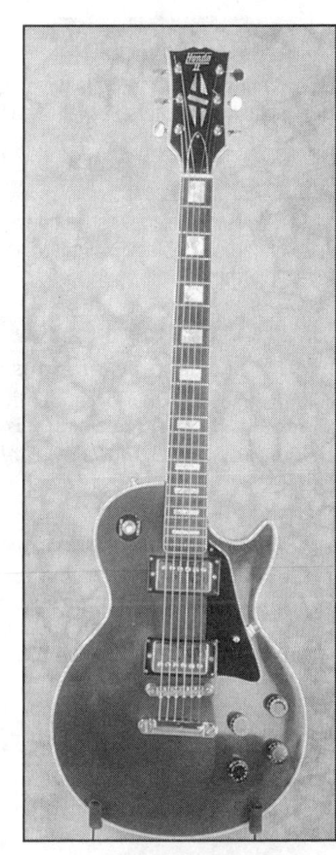

Hondo Deluxe
courtesy David Swadley

GRADING	100% MINT	98% NEAR MINT	95% EXC+	90% EXC	80% VG+	70% VG	60% G

ignation **H-760**, a B.C. Rich inspired model with humbuckers and three mini-switches was the **H-930**, and a 335 repro was designated the **H-935**. Many carried a new list price between $229 and $299.

Erlewine Series

Texas luthier/designer Mark Erlewine licensed a pair of designs to Hondo in 1982 and 1983. His **Chiquita** travel guitar had a scale of 19" and an overall 27 1/2" length; and the headless **Lazer** was a full scale (25 1/2") guitar with an overall length of 31". A third model, named the **Automatic** was offered as well. List prices ranged from $199 to $349.

Fame Series

Unveiled in late 1984, the Fame Series featured Fender-based reproductions with the **Fame** logo in a *spaghetti* looking lettering. However, the spelling and outline would be a give-away from a distance (if their intention was so bold...).

Harry Fleishman Series

In 1985, noted luthier/designer Harry Fleishman licensed the Flash bass, a headless, bodiless, 2 octave neck, Schaller Bridge equipped, magnetic and piezo-driven electric bass that was based on one of his high quality original designs. Fleishman also designed a Tele-ish acoustic/electric similar to the Kramer Ferrington models that were available.

Longhorn Series

H

When is a Danelectro not a Danelectro? The Longhorn series featured a guitar (model **HP 1081**) and bass (model **H 1181**) constructed of solid wood bodies and bolt-on necks. The guitar had a 32-fret neck, single humbucker, fixed bridge, brass nut, volume/tone controls, as well as a coil tap and phase mini switches. The bass model had a 2 octave neck, P-style split pickup, volume/tone controls, and a mini switch. Both were available in Cream Sunburst, Metallic Bronze, and Natural Walnut finishes during the early 1980s.

MasterCaster Series

These mid 1980s models were advertised as having solid ash bodies, Kahler *Flyer* locking tremolos, and Grover tuners.

Professional Series

The Professional Series was introduced in 1982, and had a number of classical and steel string models. More importantly, there was a number of electric Strat-style guitars that were presumably built by Tokai in Japan. Tokai was one of the *reproduction* companies of the mid-to-late 1970s that built pretty good *Strats* - much to Fender's displeasure.

Standard Series

Standard Series guitars were also introduced in the early 1980s, and were Hondo's single or double pickup entry level guitars. The acoustic models were beginner's guitars as well. The Standard line did offer 11 banjo models of different add-ons, and 4 distinct mandolins.

ELECTRIC BASS

New Hondo electric solid body basses feature the **H820M** (list $335), a traditonal style double cutaway model with bolt-on maple neck, 20-fret rosewood fingerboard, black pickguard, P-style pickup, volume and tone controls. The similarly designed H815 (list $249) has a 29 3/4" scale, nato neck, and kuku wood fingerboard.

HOOTENANNY

See chapter on House Brands.

This trademark has been identified as a "sub-brand" from the budget line of CHRIS guitars by the Jackson-Guldan company. However, another source suggests that the trademark was marketed by the Monroe Catalog House.

(Source: Willie G. Moseley, Stellas & Stratocasters)

HOPF

Instruments previously made in Germany from the late 1950s through the mid 1980s.

The Hopf name was established back in 1669, and lasted through the mid 1980s. The company produced a wide range of good quality solid body, semi- hollow, and archtop guitars from the late 1950s on. While some of the designs do bear an American design influence, the liberal use of local woods (such as beech, sycamore, or European pine) and certain departures from conventional styling give them an individual identity.

(Source: Tony Bacon, The Ultimate Guitar Book)

ELECTRIC GUITAR

SATURN 63 - semi-hollow body, 6-on-one-side tuners, two pickups, clear raised pickguard inscribed with 'Hopf', tremolo, one pickup selector switch, one tone switch, and volume knob. Mfg. circa 1950s.

100%	98%	95%	90%	80%	70%	60%
$450	**$375**	**$350**	**$280**	**$220**	**$180**	**$160**

Guitar is equipped with a 3 pin DIN plug instead of a 1/4" jack on control panel. Make sure the original cable is with the guitar when it is purchased!

HOSONO GUITAR WORKS

Instruments previously produced in Glendale, CA.

Hosono Guitar Works produced fine quality instruments for a number of years.

Hopf Saturn 63
courtesy Jimmy Gravity

HOT LICKS

Instruments currently built in Pennsylvania. Distributed by Hot Licks Musical Instruments of Pound Ridge, New York.

The Hot Licks guitar models are the signature series from Arlen Roth (if you have seen any of his videos, then you know the caliber of his playing). These models feature single cutaway bodies and 2 single coil pickups in a decidely 'Tele'-style guitar.

Hot Licks guitars feature lightweight ash bodies, bird's-eye maple necks, and bird's-eye or rosewood fingerboards. Models are available in Classic Sunburst, Safari Green, Roadmaster Red, Vintage Cream, and that well known Del Fuego Black with Flames custom paint finishes. Retail price is $1,695 (the custom Flame job is an additional $300).

HOWARD (JAPAN MFG.)

Instruments previously produced in Japan, circa 1960s.

Instruments under the Japanese-produced Howard trademark thus encountered have been bolt-on neck Fender Strat copies of decent quality. Retail prices in the late 1960s ranged between $79 to $119.

(Source: Roland Lozier, Lozier Piano & Music)

HOYER

Current production instruments are distributed internationally by Mario Pellarin Musikwaren of Cologne, Germany.

Instruments built in West Germany from the late 1950s through the late 1980s.

The Hoyer company produced a wide range of good to high quality solid body, semi-hollow body, and archtop guitars, with some emphasis on the later during the 1960s. During the early 1970s, there was some production of solid bodied guitars with an emphasis on classic American designs.

The Hoyer trademark was re-introduced in the 1990s with the cheerful "A Legend is Back!" motto. Hoyer is currently offering a wide range of acoustic and electric guitars in Europe; a U.S. distributor has not yet been named. Further information on Hoyer instruments is available through the company; contact them directly (see Trademark Index).

(Source: Tony Bacon and Paul Day, The Guru's Guitar Guide)

ELECTRIC

Vintage Electric Series

Hoyer currently is offering a handful of Guild- and Gibson-esque electric guitar models. The semi-hollow single Florentine cutaway Jazz '57 model has a 16" wide body, 2 covered humbuckers, a 3 tuners per side headstock, a 20-fret rosewood fingerboard with white block inlays, and an adjustable rosewood bridge/raised chrome tailpiece. The Jazz '57 is also available with gold hardware, and in Metallic Gold or Tobacco Sunburst finishes. The single rounded cutaway **Cat** model has a 17" body width, and is available in Black, Foam Green, and Wine Red finishes.

On the Gibson front, the single cutaway **Junior 90** model has a solid mahogany body, 2 P-90 'soapbars' or 2 chrome covered humbucker pickups, and Blonde, Wine Red, Black, and Metallic Gold finishes; the **3-35** model is pretty self-explanatory once you remove the dash, and is available in Cherry Red and Tobacco Sunburst finishes.

Hands down '50s cool goes to the Hoyer **Bo** model, a double humbucker, solid alder rectangular, set-in mahogany neck, maraca shakin', Willie and the Hand Jive, Bo Diddley-style guitar!

HUBER, NIK

Instruments currently built in Rodgau, Germany since 1993. Distributed by Nik Huber Guitars of Rodgau, Germany.

Luthier Nik Huber has been building guitars for over 3 years. In addition to his PRS-inspired models, he maintains a repair shop and guitar sales room. Huber's woodworking skills and finishes have attracted notice from many local players as well as notables such as Paul Reed Smith (PRS Guitars).

Huber models are available with numerous custom options, such as gold hardware, Tom Holmes pickups, Mann Made tremolos, L.R. Baggs bridges, custom inlays, quilted maple tops, and others. For further information regarding Nik Huber models, please contact luthier Huber directly (see Trademark Index).

ELECTRIC

Huber offers three distinctive models, all with highly figured wood tops and translucent finishes (a tip of the lutherie cap to PRS). Huber's original design with a slightly offset single cutaway **Dolphin** model has a mahogany body, quilted maple top, mahogany or bird's-eye maple neck, bird's-eye maple or maple-bound rosewood fingerboard, and a dolphin headstock inlay. This model has a 25 1/2" scale length, Wilkinson or Schaller tremolo, and Seymour Duncan (humbucker) pickups. The decidedly single cutaway **Orca** model has a curly maple top, 24 3/4" scale, tune-o-matic bridge/stop tailpiece, 3-per-side Schaller M6 tuners, and Seymour Duncan Antiquity humbuckers.

The offset double cutaway **Steve Lauer** model has a mahogany body, quilted maple top, bird's-eye maple neck/fingerboard, and a bat headstock inlay. This model also has a 25 1/2" scale length, MannMade tremolo, and Joe Barden deluxe pickups.

HUMAN BASE

Instruments currently built in Waldems, Germany. Distributed in the U.S. market by Salwender International of Orange, California.

Human Base produces four models of high quality bolt neck and neck-through bass guitars. Currently, Salwender International is distributing the Base X bolt-on neck model in the U.S. market. Additional specifications and information are available through either Human Base or Salwender International directly (see Trademark Index).

Other Human Base models currently available in Europe (only) include the Jonas model, which has a similar body design as the Base X but upscale hardware and pickups choices. Human Base's Max bass has more of an offset cutaway body, with angular pointed horns and Deep D option. The Deep D is a mechanism that allows access to the lower D at a flip of a switch. Other models include the Class X model, which features higher grade wood and appointments. All models (Base X, Class X, Jonas, and Max) are available in 4-, 5-, and 6- string configurations.

ELECTRIC BASS

Only Human Base's Base X model is currently available in the U.S. market.

Add $200 for high gloss polyester finish.

BASE X - offset double cutaway ash body, bird's-eye maple top, rear-mounted bolt-on neck (neck extends well into the back of the body and bolts in), 22-fret rosewood fingerboard, fixed bridge, 2 Bartolini pickups, volume/tone controls, active electronics, available in various Translucent matte finishes. Current Mfg.

4-string configuration, 2-per-side tuners.

MSR $2,495

5-string configuration, 3/2-per-side tuners.

MSR $2,595

6-string configuration, 3-per-side tuners.

MSR $2,795

HUNTINGTON

Instruments currently distributed by Actodyne General Incorporated.

In 1997, Actodyne General Incorporated debuted a new line of sleek, electric guitar and bass models. Actodyne is the maker of the popular **Lace Helix** guitar pickups. For further information, contact Actodyne General Incorporated directly (see Trademark Index).

HURRICANE

Instruments previously produced in Japan during the late 1980s.

The Hurricane trademark shows up on medium quality *superstrat* and solid body guitars based on popular American designs.

(Source: Tony Bacon and Paul Day, The Guru's Guitar Guide)

HUSKEY

Instruments previously built in Missouri.

Huskey Guitar Works guitar building started in 1979 with one goal - to create a line of instruments that were both innovative and eye catching. Rick and Jackie Huskey found that instruments of the late 1970s did not have the amount of natural sustain that they were looking for.

To increase the amount of sustain, the Huskeys incorporated the same materials used by luthiers for generations in the first of their designs. The **Stormtrooper** design brought about the development of the *SustainArm*, an innovation that increases the sustain of the Huskey guitars by reducing the tension along the neck. The SustainArm is an integral extension of the body, attaching on the low E side of the neck. The SustainArm also enabled them to extend the lower treble side cutaway, and allowed unrestricted access to the fretboard (some fretboards are equipped with as many as 36 frets).

(Company history courtesy Rick and Jackie Huskey)

ELECTRIC

Huskey Guitar Works offered several models of high quality, custom built guitars that featured original designs and neck-through construction. Models include the Axeminister, Keeper, Usurper, Yarnspinner. Last retail prices ranged from $2,599 to $2,699. Guitar models were available in 6-, 9-, and 12-string configurations; left- handed configurations are available at no extra charge.

FREEDOMFIGHTER - wedge-shaped body with sustain arm, through-body neck, 6-on-a-side tuners, Kahler tremolo bridge, EMG 89 humbucker pickup, volume/tone controls.

Last MSR was $2,599.

HARBINGER - dual cutaway maple/mahogany body with sustain arm, 5-piece through-body neck, 6-on-a-side Sperzel locking tuners, Kahler Pro tremolo bridge, 2 EMG (85/89) humbucker pickups, volume/tone controls, 3-way toggle selector.

Last MSR was $2,699.

STORMTROOPER - maple/alder body with sustain arm, 5-piece neck, 29-fret ebony fingerboard, 6-per-side Sperzel locking tuners, Kahler Pro tremolo, leg rest, EMG 89 humbucker, volume/tone controls.

Last MSR was $2,699.

Elder - similar to the Stormtrooper, except features ash and mahogany body.

Last MSR was $2,699.

Peacemaker - similar to the Stormtrooper, except features an alder body.

Last MSR was $2,699.

HUTTL

Instruments previously built in Germany from the 1950s to the 1970s.

The Huttl trademark may not be as well known as other German guitar builders such as Framus, Hopf, or Klira. While their designs may be as original as the others, the quality of workmanship is still fairly rough in comparison. Research continues into the Huttl trademark.

HY-LO

Instruments previously produced in Japan during the mid to late 1960s.

These entry level solid body guitars feature designs based on classic American favorites. One such model (designation unknown) featured an offset double cutaway body and six on a side tuners like a strat, but two single coil pickups and volume and tone controls.

HYUNDAI

Instruments currently built in Korea. Distributed in the U.S. through Hyundai Guitars of West Nyack, New York.

Hyndai offers a range of medium quality guitars designed for beginning students that have designs based on popular American classics.

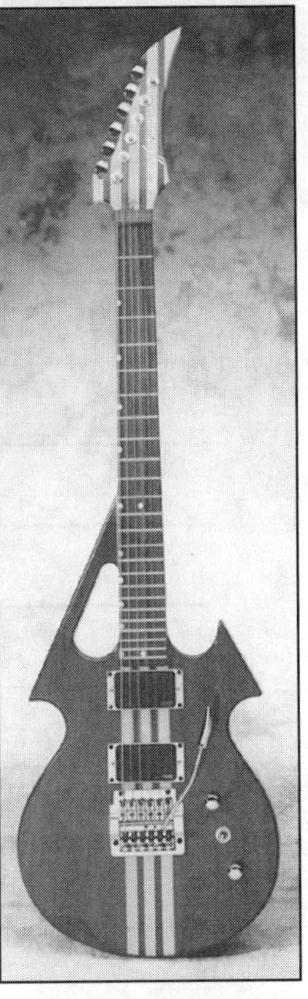

1994 HGW Harbinger
courtesy
Huskey Guitar Works

NOTES

H

Section I

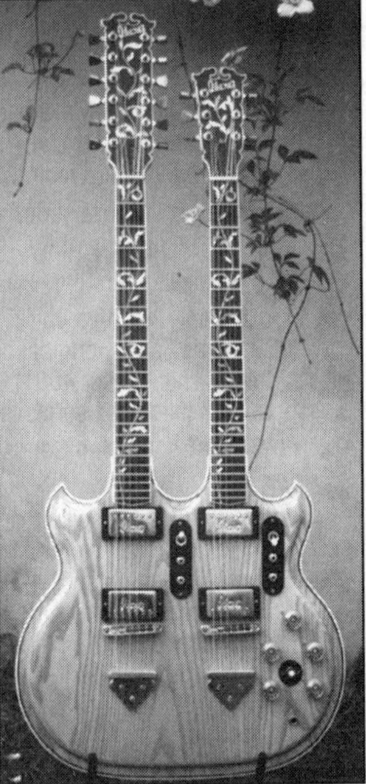

Ibanez Artwood Twin
(Mid-1970's)
courtesy Ibanez USA

IBANEZ

Instruments currently produced in Japan since the early 1960s, and some models produced in Korea since the 1980s. Ibanez guitars are distributed in the U.S. by Ibanez USA (Hoshino) in Bensalem, Pennsylvania. Other distribution offices include Quebec (for Canada), Sydney (for Australia), and Auckland (for New Zealand).

The Ibanez trademark originated from the Fuji plant in Matsumoto, Japan. In 1932, the Hoshino Gakki Ten, Inc. factory began producing instruments under the Ibanez trademark. The factory and offices were burned down during World War II, and were revived in 1950. By the mid 1960s, Hoshino was producing instruments under various trademarks such as Ibanez, Star, King's Stone, Jamboree, and Goldentone.

In the mid-1950s, Harry Rosenbloom opened the Medley Music store outside Philadelphia. As the Folk Music boom began in 1959, Rosenbloom decided to begin producing acoustic guitars and formed the Elger company (named after Rosenbloom's children, Ellen and Gerson). Elger acoustics were produced in Ardmore, Pennsylvania between 1959 and 1965.

In the 1960s, Rosenbloom travelled to Japan and found a number of companies that he contracted to produce the Elger acoustics. Later, he was contacted by Hoshino to form a closer business relationship. The first entry level solid body guitars featuring original designs first surfaced in the mid 1960s, some bearing the Elger trademark, and some bearing the Ibanez logo. One of the major keys to the perceived early Ibanez quality is due to Hoshino shipping the guitars to the Elger factory in Ardmore. The arriving guitars would be re-checked, and set up prior to shipping to the retailer. Many distributors at the time would just simply ship *product* to the retailer, and let surprises occur at the unboxing. By reviewing the guitars in a separate facility, Hoshino/Ibanez could catch any problems before the retailer - so the number of perceived flawed guitars was reduced at the retail/sales end. In England, Ibanez was imported by the Summerfield Brothers, and sometimes had either the CSL trademark or no trademark at all on the headstock. Other U.K. distributors used the **Antoria** brand name, and in Australia they were rebranded with a **Jason** logo.

In the early 1970s, the level of quality rose as well as the level of indebtedness to classic American designs. It has been argued that Ibanez' reproductions of Stratocasters and Les Pauls may be equal to or better than the quality of Norlin era Gibsons or CBS era Fenders. While the ***Blue Book of Electric Guitars*** would rather stay neutral on this debate (we just list them, not rate them), it has been suggested by outside sources that next time *close your eyes and let your hands and ears be the judge*. In any event, the unauthorized reproductions eventually led to Fender's objections to Tokai's imports (the infamous *headstock sawing* rumour), and Norlin/Gibson taking Hoshino/Ibanez/Elger into court for patent infringement.

When Ibanez began having success basically reproducing Gibson guitars and selling them at a lower price on the market, Norlin (Gibson's owner at the time) sent off a cease-and-desist warning. Norlin's lawyers decided that the best way to proceed was to defend the decorative (the headstock) versus the functional (body design), and on June 28th, 1977 the case of Gibson vs. Elger Co. opened in Philadelphia Federal District Court. In early 1978, a resolution was agreed upon: Ibanez would stop reproducing Gibsons if Norlin would stop suing Ibanez. The case was officially closed on February 2, 1978.

The infringement lawsuit ironically might have been the kick in the pants that propelled Ibanez and other Japanese builders to get back into original designs. Ibanez stopped building Gibson exact reproductions, and moved on to other designs. By the early 1980s, certain guitar styles began appealing to other areas of the guitar market (notably the Hard Rock/Heavy Metal genre), and Ibanez's use of famous endorsers probably fueled the appeal. Ibanez's continuing program of original designs and artist involvement continued to work in the mid to late 1980s, and continues to support their position in the market today.

(Source: Michael Wright, Guitar Stories Volume One)

Hardware Dating Identification

It may be easier to date an Ibanez guitar knowing when key hardware developments were introduced.

1977: Ibanez' **Super 80** "Flying Finger" humbuckers with chrome covers.

1980: Ornate (or just large) brass bridges/tailpieces, and brass hardware.

1984: 'Pro Rocker' locking tremolo system.

1985: 'Edge' double locking tremolo system.

1987: Debut of the DiMarzio-made IBZ USA pickups.

1990: 'Lo-Pro' Edge tremolo system.

Model Dating Identification

In addition to the Ibanez company's model history, a serialization chart is provided in the back of the ***Blue Book of Guitars*** to further aid the dating of older Ibanez guitars (not all potentiometer builders use the EIA source code, so overseas-built potentiometer codes on Japanese guitars may not help in the way of clues).

1959-1967: Elger Acoustics are built in Ardmore, Pennsylvania; and are distributed by Medley Music, Grossman Music (Cleveland), Targ and Dinner (Chicago), and the Roger Balmer Company on the west coast. Elger imported from Japan the Tama acoustics, Ibanez acoustics, and some Elger electrics.

1962-1965: Introduction of entry level bolt-neck solid body electrics, and some set-neck archtop electrics by 1965.

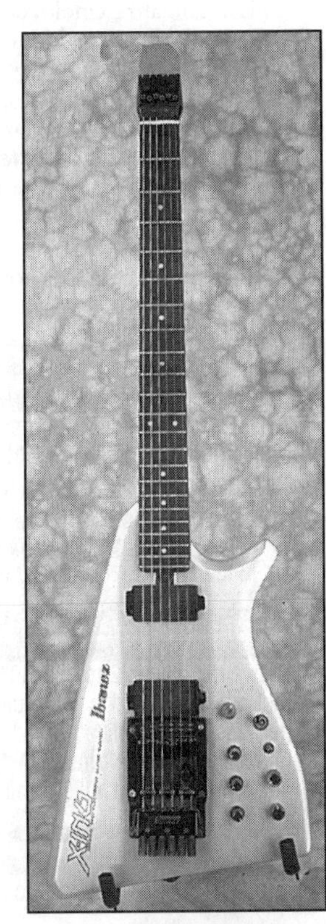

Ibanez IM G2010
courtesy Darryl Alger

GRADING	100% MINT	98% NEAR MINT	95% EXC+	90% EXC	80% VG+	70% VG	60% G

1971-1977: The copy era begins for Ibanez (*Faithful Reproductions*) as solid body electrics based on Gibson, Fender, and Rickenbacker models (both bolt-ons and set-necks) arrive. These are followed by copies of Martin, Guild, Gibson, and Fender acoustics. Ibanez opens an office and warehouse outside of Philadelphia, Pennsylvania to maintain quality control on imported guitars in 1972.

1973: Ibanez's **Artist** series acoustics and electrics are debuted. In 1974, the Artist-style neck joint; later in 1976 an Artist 'Les Paul' arrives. This sets the stage for the LP variant double cutaway Artist model in 1978.

1975: Ibanez began to use a meaningful numbering system as part of their warranty program. In general, the letter stands for the month (January = A, February = B, etc.) and the following two digits are the year.

1977: Ibanez's first original design, the **Iceman**, arrives with a rather *excited* lower bout and *goosebeak* headstock. A bass with the neck-through design (similar to a Rickenbacker 4001) is available, and a full series of neck-through designs are available in the Musician models. The **George Benson GB-10** model and more original design series like the **Performer, Professional, Musician**, and **Concert** also appear.

1979-1980: **Musician** Series basses, Studio Series guitars, and an 8-string bass (MC-980) debut in 1979. The semi-hollowbody AS Series are introduced a year later.

1981-1987: Ibanez switches to the bolt-neck Strat design and other variants in the **Roadster** series, followed by the **Blazer** in 1981, and the **Roadstar II models by 1982. The Pro Line** and **RS** Series solid bodies appears in 1984. The early 1980s are the time for *pointy body designs* such as the **Destroyer II** (Explorer- based model), **X** Series Destroyers, 'headless' Axstar models, and the original extreme pointy-ness of the **XV-500**. Jazz boxes like the **AM** Series semi-hollowbody guitars are introduced in 1982, followed by the **FG** Series a year later. In 1984, the **Lonestar** acoustics are introduced, and Ibanez responds to the MIDI challenge of Roland by unveiling the **IMG-2010** MIDI guitar system.

1987: Ibanez hits the Hard Rock/Heavy Metal route full bore with popular artist endorsements and the **Power, Radius**, and **Saber** (now 'S') series. These models have more in common with the 'superstrat' design than traditional design. The early to mid 1980s is when Ibanez really begins making inroads to the American guitar consumer.

1988: Steve Vai's **JEM** appears on the U.S. market. Ibanez covers the entry level approach with the **EX** Series, built in Korea. The experimental **Maxxas** solid-looking hollow body electric is unleashed.

1990: In 1990, The Steve Vai **JEM 7-string** *Universe* model (it's like six plus one more!) proceeds to pop young guitarists' corks nationwide. The Ibanez **American Master** series, a product of the new American Custom Shop, is introduced.

1991: Reb Beach's **Voyager** model (Ladies and Gentlemen, nothing up my sleeve, and nothing behind the tremolo bridge!) intrigues players who want to bend up several semitones.

1992-1993: The **ATL** acoustic/electric design is unveiled, and **RT** Series guitars debut in 1993.

(This overview, while brief, will hopefully identify years, trends, and series. For further information and deeper clarification, please refer to Michael Wright's Guitar Stories Volume One).

ELECTRIC

JUMP START PACKAGE (IJS40) - offset double cutaway agathis body, bolt-on maple neck, 21-fret maple fingerboard with black dot inlay, standard tremolo, 6-on-a-side tuners, chrome hardware, white pickguard, 2 single coil/humbucker pickups, volume/tone controls, 5-way selector. Available in Black, Jewel Blue, and Candy Apple Red finishes. Current Mfg.

MSR $399 — $320 $275 $250 $230 $215 $185 $140

The Jump Start Package includes the electric guitar, GT10 amplifier with built in Over Drive circuit, gig bag, instructional video, digital auto tuner, strap, cable, picks, chord chart, and a free subscription to Plugged In (the official Ibanez newsletter).

Jump Start Package (IJS70M) - similar to the (IJS40) guitar model, except features humbucker/single coil/humbucker pickups. Available in Black and Metallic Green finishes. Mfg. 1998 to 1999.

$399 $339 $299 $275 $250 $225 $195

Last MSR was $499.

This Jump Start Package includes the electric guitar, GT10 amplifier with built in Over Drive circuit, PL5 PowerLead Distortion foot pedal, gig bag, instructional video, digital auto tuner, strap, cable, picks, chord chart, and a free subscription to Plugged In (the official Ibanez newsletter).

Artist Series (1973 to 1982)

Artist Series models debuted in 1973. By 1977/1978, there were at least three variations being offered: The **Artist (Model 2618)**, which had a dual cutaway body engraved tailpiece, gold hardware, 2 humbuckers with engraved pickup covers, and dot fingerboard inlays. The **Artist EQ (Model 2623)**, a favorite of guitarist Steve Miller during this time period, had an onboard 3-band EQ (three extra knobs).

In 1981, the **Artist Model AR-300** featured a tiger maple (flamed) top and Super 58 humbuckers with coil taps.

Many of the late 1970s Les Paul-styled Artist models are seeing a pricing resurgence of $600 to $800 in the vintage market; actual sales price range from $450 up to $700.

Artist Autograph Series (1975 to 1980)

Between July 1972 to July 1973, luthier Rex Bogue constructed the heavily inlaid doubleneck "Double Rainbow" guitar for jazz guitarist Mahavishnu John McLaughlin (the inlay work alone was over 80 hours!). McLaughlin's doubleneck attracted the attention of Jeff Hasselberger at Ibanez, who received Bogue's permission to duplicate the "look" of the guitar. Ibanez' vaguely SG-shaped doubleneck re-creation debuted in the 1975 Ibanez catalog as the **Model 2670**, under the **Professional** or **Artist Autograph** series. While the **Model 2670** was available from 1975 through 1980, it is estimated that only a dozen were actually produced. The 1975 retail list for the **Model 2670** was $1,500.

Artist Series (Current Mfg.)

The Artist Series was reintroduced by Ibanez in 1997.

GRADING		100% MINT	98% NEAR MINT	95% EXC+	90% EXC	80% VG+	70% VG	60% G

AR200 ARTIST - dual cutaway mahogany body, bound maple top, set-in maple neck, 22-fret rosewood fingerboard with pearl dot inlay, 3-per-side tuners, chrome hardware, Full Tune II bridge/stop tailpiece, 2 humbucker pickups, 2 volume/2 tone controls, 3-way pickup selector. Available in Black and Transparent Red finishes. Mfg. 1997 to 1999.

		$640	$525	$475	$425	$375	$325	$275

Last MSR was $799.

AR700 Artist - similar to the AR200, except features 3-piece maple neck, abalone dot fingerboard inlay, Gibralter II bridge/stop tailpiece, gold hardware, 2 Super 58 humbuckers. Available in Stained Brown Sunburst finish. Mfg. 1997 to 1999.

		$1,050	$850	$750	$650	$595	$525	$450

Last MSR was $1,299.

AR2000 Artist Prestige - similar to the AR200, except features a flamed maple top, 3-piece maple neck, abalone dot fingerboard inlay, Gibralter II bridge/stop tailpiece, gold hardware, 2 Super 58 humbuckers. Available in Vintage Violin finish. Mfg. 1997 to date.

MSR	$1,999	$1,600	$1,250	$1,200	$1,100	$995	$895	$750

Artstar Series

AF80 - single rounded cutaway semi-hollow style, bound maple top, bound f-holes, raised black pickguard, maple back/sides, set-in maple neck, 22-fret bound rosewood fingerboard with pearl dot inlay, adjustable rosewood bridge/trapeze tailpiece, bound blackface peghead with screened flower/logo, 3-per-side tuners, chrome hardware, 2 covered humbucker pickups, 2 volume/2 tone controls, 3-position switch. Available in Vintage Sunburst finish. Mfg. 1994 to 1996.

		$400	$325	$295	$250	$225	$195	$175

Last MSR was $650.

Ibanez AF 200 AV
courtesy Ibanez USA

AF120 - similar to AF80, except features bound spruce top, 20-fret fingerboard with pearl/abalone block inlay, gold hardware, 2 Ibanez Super 58 humbucker pickups. Available in Brown Sunburst finish. Current Mfg.

MSR	$999	$799	$650	$575	$495	$425	$325	$250

AF200 - similar to the AF80, except features bound spruce top, bound f-holes, raised pickguard, 3-piece mahogany/maple set-in neck, 20-fret bound ebony fingerboard with pearl/abalone rectangle inlays, ebony bridge with trapeze tailpiece, gold hardware, 2 Super 58 humbuckers. Available in Antique Violin finish. Mfg. 1991 to 1998.

		$1,500	$1,425	$1,200	$1,000	$900	$725	$550

Last MSR was $2,199.

AF207 7-String - similar to AF200, except features 7-string configuration, 4/3-per-side tuners, one DiMarzio humbucker pickup. Available in Antique Violin finish. Mfg. 1997 todate.

MSR	$2,999	$2,400	$1,950	$1,700	$1,500	$1,300	$N/A	

AF220 - similar to the AF200, except features maple top/back/sides, 20-fret bound rosewood fingerboard with pearl block inlay, adjustable rosewood bridge/GE 103B metal tailpiece. Available in Butterscotch Transparent finish. Mfg. 1998 to 1999.

		$1,525	$1,225	$1,025	$925	$825	$725	$600

Last MSR was $1,899.

AM200 - double cutaway semi-hollow style, burl mahogany top with bound body/f-holes, raised pickguard, burl mahogany back/sides, 3-piece mahogany/maple set-in neck, 20-fret bound rosewood fingerboard with pearl abalone rectangle inlay, tune-o-matic bridge stop tailpiece, bound peghead, 3-per-side nylon head tuners, gold hardware, 2 Super 58 humbuckers, volume/tone control, 3-position selector switch. Available in Antique Violin finish. Mfg. 1991 to 1996.

		$900	$750	$675	$600	$525	$450	$375

Last MSR was $1,500.

AS50 - double cutaway semi-hollow style, maple top/back/sides, f-holes, raised black pickguard, bolt-on maple neck, 22-fret bound rosewood fingerboard with pearl dot inlay, Full Tune II bridge/stop tailpiece, 3-per-side tuners, chrome hardware, 2 humbucker pickups, 2 volume/2 tone controls, 3-position switch. Available in Butterscotch Transparent and Brown Sunburst finishes. Mfg. 1998 to 1999.

		$350	$295	$260	$225	$195	$165	$125

Last MSR was $499.

AS80 - double cutaway semi-hollow style, bound maple top, bound f-holes, raised black pickguard, maple back/sides/neck, set-in neck, 22-fret bound rosewood fingerboard with abalone dot inlay, tune-o-matic bridge/stop tailpiece, bound blackface peghead with screened flower/logo, 3-per-side tuners, chrome hardware, 2 covered Super 58 humbucker pickups, 2 volume/2 tone controls, 3-position switch. Available in Butterscotch Transparent and Vintage Sunburst finishes. Mfg. 1994 to date.

MSR	$799	$650	$525	$450	$395	$325	$275	$200

AS120 - similar to AS80, except features pearl/abalone block fingerboard inlay, gold hardware. Available in Transparent Red finish. Current Mfg.

MSR	$899	$725	$595	$525	$450	$375	$300	$225

AS180 - similar to AS80, except features 3-piece maple/mahogany set-in neck, cream dot fingerboard inlay, Gibralter II tune-o-matic bridge/wrap-around tailpiece. Available in Stained Sunburst finish. Disc. 1999.

		$1,100	$950	$800	$695	$575	$475	$350

Last MSR was $1,399.

Ibanez AS-200 (Artist)
courtesy James Browning

GRADING		100% MINT	98% NEAR MINT	95% EXC+	90% EXC	80% VG+	70% VG	60% G

AS200 - similar to AS80, except features bound flame maple top, flame maple back/sides, 3-piece mahogany/maple neck, pearl/abalone block fingerboard inlay, Gibralter II tune-o-matic bridge/wrap-around tailpiece, gold hardware. Available in Antique Violin finish. Mfg. 1991 to date.

MSR	$2,099	$1,675	$1,350	$1,200	$1,000	$850	$700	$525

Blazer Series

Earlier Blazer models (1980s) featured 2 mini-switches for coil tap and phase functions, and metallic finishes with matching color headstocks. These earlier Blazer models, while note fully profiled for this edition of the ***Blue Book of Electric Guitars***, generally range in price in the secondary market between $125 to $225.

BL850 - offset double cutaway alder body, bolt-on maple neck, 22-fret rosewood fingerboard with pearl dot inlay, 6-on-a-side tuners, chrome hardware, pearloid pickguard, Gotoh 510AT tremolo, humbucker/single coil/humbucker pickups, volume/tone controls, 5-way selector. Available in Black and Vintage Burst finishes. Disc. 1999.

$550 $450 $395 $325 $275 $225 $175
Last MSR was $679.

BL1025 - similar to the BL850, except features Wilkinson VSV tremolo. Available in Cayman Green and Vintage Burst finishes. Disc. 1999.

$799 $650 $575 $495 $425 $325 $250
Last MSR was $999.

Double Axe Series (1974 to 1976)

The Ibanez **Double Axe** model was available from (circa) 1974 to 1976. The **Double Axe** was Ibanez' take on the Gibson EDS-1275; Gibson first produced the EDS-1275 between 1963 to 1968, then discontinued the model. Ibanez began issuing their **Double Axe** in 1974, probably in limited production amounts. Then, in 1977, Gibson again began producing the EDS-1275 (Model DSED currently) and has done so since then. Coincidence? Or to coincide with the Led Zeppelin tours and the frequent use by guitarist Jimmy Page?

The **Double Axe (Model 2402)** was available in a 6-string/12-string doubleneck configuration, a 4-string bass/6-string guitar doubleneck configuration, and an odd dual 6-string doubleneck configuration. All models were available in Cherry or Walnut finishes, with the same list price of $425. All three were also available in a custom Ivory finish for $450.

EX Series

EX Series models were available from 1988 to 1994.

EX160 - offset double cutaway maple body, bolt-on maple neck, 22-fret rosewood fingerboard with pearl dot inlay, standard vibrato, 6-on-a-side tuners, chrome hardware, 2 single coil/1 humbucker pickups, volume/tone control, 5-position switch. Available in Black and Matte Stain finishes. Disc. 1994.

$200 $175 $150 $125 $115 $100 $85
Last MSR was $330.

EX170 - similar to the EX160, except features 22-fret maple fingerboard with black dot inlay, humbucker/single coil/humbucker pickups. Available in Black, Blue Night, and Matte Violin finishes. Disc. 1994.

$215 $175 $160 $140 $125 $105 $90
Last MSR was $350.

EX270 - similar to EX170, except has locking vibrato, black hardware. Available in Black, Blue Night, and Candy Apple finishes. Disc. 1994.

$295 $225 $215 $195 $175 $150 $125
Last MSR was $470.

EX350 - offset double cutaway basswood body, bolt-on maple neck, 22-fret bound rosewood fingerboard with triangle inlay, double locking vibrato, 6-on-a-side tuners, chrome hardware, humbucker/single coil/humbucker Ibanez pickups, volume/tone control, 5-position switch. Available in Black, Burgundy Red, Desert Yellow, and Laser Blue finishes. Disc. 1994.

$350 $300 $275 $250 $215 $180 $150
Last MSR was $570.

EX360 - similar to EX350, except features 2 single coil/humbucker Ibanez pickups. Available in Black, Dark Grey, Jewel Blue, and Purple Pearl finishes. Disc. 1992.

$300 $250 $225 $200 $175 $150 $125
Last MSR was $500.

EX365 - similar to EX350, except features reverse headstock, single coil/humbucker Ibanez pickups. Available in Black, Laser Blue, and Ultra Violet finishes. Disc. 1992.

$295 $250 $225 $195 $175 $150 $125
Last MSR was $480.

EX370 - offset double cutaway basswood body, bolt-on maple neck, 22-fret bound rosewood fingerboard with triangle inlay, double locking vibrato, 6-on-a-side tuners, chrome hardware, humbucker/single coil/humbucker Ibanez pickups, volume/tone control, 5-position switch. Available in Black, Burgundy Red, Jewel Blue, and Ultra Violet finishes. Disc. 1994.

$350 $300 $275 $250 $215 $175 $150
Last MSR was $570.

EX370 FM - similar to EX370, except has flame maple top, gold hardware. Available in Antique Violin, Cherry Sunburst and Wine Burst finishes. Disc. 1994.

$395 $325 $295 $250 $225 $195 $175
Last MSR was $650.

GRADING	100% MINT	98% NEAR MINT	95% EXC+	90% EXC	80% VG+	70% VG	60% G

EX1500 - offset double cutaway maple body, bolt-on maple neck, 22-fret maple fingerboard with black dot inlay, standard vibrato, 6-on-a-side tuners, gold hardware, tortoise pickguard, humbucker/single coil/humbucker pickups, volume/tone control, 5-position switch. Available in Antique Violin and Black finishes. Mfg. 1993 to 1994.

	$250	$225	$200	$175	$150	$125	$110

Last MSR was $430.

EX1700 - similar to EX1500, except has bound body, no pickguard, chrome hardware. Available in Cherry Sunburst and Transparent Turquoise finishes. Mfg. 1993 to 1994.

	$250	$225	$200	$175	$150	$125	$110

Last MSR was $430.

EX3700 - offset double cutaway basswood body, bound flame maple top, bolt-on maple neck, 24-fret maple fingerboard with black dot inlay, double locking vibrato, 6-on-a-side tuners, gold hardware, humbucker/single coil/humbucker Ibanez pickups, volume/tone control, 5-position switch. Available in Transparent Purple, Transparent Red, and Transparent Turquoise finishes. Mfg. 1993 to 1994.

	$395	$325	$295	$250	$225	$195	$175

Last MSR was $650.

Ibanez Doubleneck
courtesy Eric Hoelzeman

FGM (Frank Gambale Signature) Series

The FGM Series was co-designed by guitarist Frank Gambale, and debuted in 1991.

FGM100 - sculpted thin offset double cutaway mahogany body, one piece maple neck, 22-fret bound rosewood fingerboard with body matching color sharktooth inlay, double locking vibrato, 6-on-a-side tuners, black hardware, DiMarzio humbucker/DiMarzio single coil/Ibanez humbucker pickups, volume/tone control, 5-position selector switch. Available in Black, Desert Sun Yellow, Pink Salmon and Sky Blue finishes. Mfg. 1991 to 1994.

	$800	$650	$575	$525	$450	$395	$325

Last MSR was $1,300.

FGM200 - similar to the FGM100, except features unbound 22-fret rosewood fingerboard with clay dot inlay, strings through Gotoh fixed bridge, DiMarzio humbucker/single coil/humbucker pickups. Available in Black and White finishes. Mfg. 1994 to 1996.

	$900	$750	$675	$600	$525	$450	$375

Last MSR was $1,500.

FGM300 - similar to the FGM100, except features 22-fret bound rosewood fingerboard with pearl sharktooth inlay, DiMarzio humbucker/single coil/humbucker pickups. Available in Desert Yellow Sun and Metallic Green finishes. Mfg. 1994 to 1996.

	$1,000	$850	$775	$675	$595	$525	$425

Last MSR was $1,700.

FGM400 - similar to the FGM100, except features a quilted maple top, 22-fret bound rosewood fingerboard with pearl block/Frank Gambale signature inlay at 12th fret, 2 single coil/humbucker Ibanez pickups. Available in Blazer Blue finish. Mfg. 1997 to 1999.

	$1,649	$1,450	$1,275	$1,100	$900	$725	$550

Last MSR was $2,199.

In 1998, Quilted Maple translucent finish was introduced; Blazer Blue finish was discontinued.
When the FGM400 was first introduced, the quilted maple top was a $200 option. This optional model was known as the FGM400 QM, which was available in Quilted Maple finish. A year later, the FGM400 QM model was discontinued; the quilted maple top which was optional before became a production model.

GAX Series

GAX70 ARTIST - dual cutaway agathis body, maple neck, 22-fret rosewood fingerboard with pearl dot inlay, Full Tune II bridge/stop tailpiece, 3-per-side tuners, chrome hardware, 2 exposed pole piece humbucker pickups, 2 volume/2 tone control, 3-position switch. Available in Black, Butterscotch Transparent, Jewel Blue, and Transparent Red finishes. Mfg. 1997 to date.

MSR $279	$195	$175	$155	$135	$115	$95	$75

AX120 - similar to Mpdel GAX70, except has mahogany double cutaway solid body, 22 large frets, 1 ea. IBZ AH 1 and IBZ AH2 humbucking pickups. Available in Black and Gray Nickel finishes. Current Mfg.

MSR $799	$599	$499	$450	$399	$350	$299	$250

AD250 ARTIST - double cutaway select mahogany body, Flamed maple top, 1-piece maple set neck, rosewood fingerboard with pearl dot inlays, 22 large frets, 3-per-side tuners, Full Tune II bridge, 1 ea. IBZ AH-1 and IBZ AH-2 humbucking pickups, chrome hardware. Available in Vintage Burst finish. Current Mfg.

MSR $799	$599	$499	$450	$399	$350	$299	$250

GB (George Benson Signature) Series

The GB Series was co-designed by George Benson. The first model, the **GB10**, was introduced in 1978. Along with the **GB10** was the **GB20**, which featured a 16" body width and a single 'floating' humbucker. The **GB30** was introduced in 1985, and the special **GB12** (celebrating the 12th Anniversary of the GB10) was introduced in 1990.

GRADING	100% MINT	98% NEAR MINT	95% EXC+	90% EXC	80% VG+	70% VG	60% G

GB5 - single round cutaway hollow style, arched spruce top, bound f-holes, raised bound maple pickguard, bound body, maple back/sides, maple/mahogany 3-piece neck, 20-fret bound ebony fingerboard with pearl split block inlay, ebony bridge with pearl curlicue inlay, ebony tailpiece, bound blackface peghead with pearl flower/logo, 3-per-side tuners with pearloid buttons, gold hardware, 2 humbucker Ibanez pickups, 2 volume/2 tone controls, 3-position switch. Available in Brown Sunburst finish. Mfg. 1994 to 1996.

$1,600 $1,450 $1,300 $1,150 $1,000 $875 $725
Last MSR was $2,900.

GB10 - single round cutaway hollow style, arched spruce top, bound f-holes, raised bound black pickguard, bound body, flamed maple back/sides, 3-piece maple/mahogany neck, 22-fret bound ebony fingerboard with pearl/abalone split block inlay/George Benson signature block inlay at 21st fret, ebony bridge with pearl arrow inlays, ebony/metal tailpiece, bound peghead with abalone torch/logo inlay, 3-per-side tuners with pearloid buttons, gold hardware, 2 Ibanez humbucker pickups, 2 volume/2 tone controls, 3-position switch. Available in Brown Sunburst and Natural finishes. Mfg. 1978 to date.

MSR $2,899 $2,325 $1,900 $1,675 $1,425 $1,200 $950 $725

GB10JS - similar to the GB10, except features maple back/sides, bound rosewood fingerboard, rosewood bridge. Available in Brown Sunburst finish. Disc. 1999.

$1,199 $975 $850 $725 $625 $500 $375
Last MSR was $1,499.

GB12 LIMITED EDITION GEORGE BENSON 12th ANNIVERSARY MODEL - single round cutaway hollow style, arched flame maple top/back/sides, abalone and plastic bound body and f-holes, raised matched pickguard, 22-fret ebony fingerboard with special GB-12 inlay/George Benson signature scroll inlay at 21st fret, ebony bridge with flower inlay, gold and ebony tailpiece with vine inlay, bound peghead with abalone logo and George Benson 12th Anniversary Ibanez inlays, 3-per-side nylon head tuners, gold hardware, 2 humbucker Ibanez pickups, 2 volume/tone controls, 3-position switch. Available in Brown Sunburst finish. Mfg. 1990 to 1992.

$1,300 $1,100 $1,000 $850 $750 $625 $500
Last MSR was $2,000.

GB30 - single round cutaway hollow style, arched maple top/back/sides, bound body and f-holes, raised black pickguard, mahogany neck, 22-fret bound ebony fingerboard with offset pearl dot inlay/George Benson signature block inlay at 21st fret, tune-o-matic bridge/stop tailpiece, bound peghead with abalone logo and George Benson standard Ibanez inlay, 3-per-side nylon head tuners, black hardware, 2 humbucker pickups, 2 volume/tone controls, 3-position switch. Available in Black and Transparent Red finishes. Mfg. 1985 to 1992.

$850 $650 $595 $525 $450 $395 $325
Last MSR was $1,300.

GB100 - single round cutaway hollow style, arched flame maple top/back/sides, bound f-holes, abalone bound body, raised maple pickguard, 22-fret bound ebony fingerboard with special pearl GB12 inlay, ebony bridge with flower inlay, metal/ebony tailpiece with pearl vine inlay, bound blackface peghead with abalone torch/logo inlay, 3-per-side tuners with pearloid buttons, gold hardware, 2 humbucker Ibanez pickups, 2 volume/2 tone controls, 3-position switch. Available in Brown Sunburst finish. Mfg. 1993 to 1996.

$1,600 $1,250 $1,100 $995 $875 $750 $625
Last MSR was $2,500.

GB200 - venetian cutaway hollowbody, spruce top, maple back and sides, 3-piece maple/mahogany set neck, bound ebony fingerboard with GB 200 Pearl position markers, 20 medium frets, ebony bridge, 2 IBZ Super 58 humbucking pickups, gold hardware. Available in Brown Sunburst finish. Current Mfg.

MSR $3,399 $2,550 $2,250 $1,850 $1,650 $1,550 $1,450 $1,250

Golden Oldies Series (1974 to 1975)

Proof that Ibanez was willing to take on the established American companies was established in 1974 when Ibanez introduced the **Golden Oldies Series**. The four instruments were modeled after Gibson's stalwart designs, with a little tongue in cheek renaming. The **Rocket Roll** was Ibanez' version of a Flying V, the **Firebrand** was a Firebird copy, the **Deluxe '59er** was a flametop LP with sunburst finish steal (even to the right year in the name!), and the **FM Jr.** was the Ibanez version of the Les Paul TV Junior (FM 'radio' derived from TV - Get it?).

Both the Rocket Roll and the Firebrand had the Ibanez logo on their respective truss rod covers; the Deluxe '59er and FM Jr. had the Ibanez logo across their headstocks. Golden Oldies models featured solid or sunburst finishes, similar to their namesakes.

The **Rocket Roll** model was designated **Model 2387**. Ibanez also had a **Rocket Roll Bass** 4-string model designated **Model 2387-B**, but few have turned up on the secondary market.

Ghostrider Series

The Ghostrider Series was introduced in 1994.

GR320 - double cutaway bound alder body, mahogany neck, 22-fret bound rosewood fingerboard with pearl dot inlay, strings through fixed bridge, 3-per-side tuners, black hardware, 2 Ibanez humbucker pickups, volume/tone control, 3-position switch. Available in Black and Cherry finishes. Mfg. 1994 to 1996.

$425 $350 $325 $275 $250 $215 $175
Last MSR was $700.

GR520 - similar to the GR320, except features bound carved maple top, 22-fret bound rosewood fingerboard with abalone/pearl split block inlay, tune-o-matic bridge/stop tailpiece, bound blackface peghead with screened logo, 3-per-side tuners with pearloid buttons, gold hardware. Available in Orange Sunburst and Vintage Sunburst finishes. Mfg. 1994 to 1996.

$450 $400 $350 $325 $275 $250 $200
Last MSR was $800.

GRX Series

Models RX20, RX20 L, and RX40 were part of the RX Series from 1994 until 1997. In 1998, these models were redesignated with a 'G' prefix and added to the GRX Series.

GRADING		100% MINT	98% NEAR MINT	95% EXC+	90% EXC	80% VG+	70% VG	60% G

Ibanez GB 10 NT courtesy Ibanez USA

GRX20 (RX20) - offset double cutaway agathis body, bolt-on maple neck, 22-fret maple fingerboard with black dot inlay, standard tremolo, 6-on-a-side tuners, chrome hardware, white pickguard, 2 humbucker pickups, volume/tone control, 3-position switch. Available in Black, Blue Night, and Deep Green finishes. Mfg. 1994 to 1999.

		$190	$155	$140	$115	$100	$80	$60

Last MSR was $239.

In 1998, rosewood fingerboard replaced the maple fingerboard; Jewel Blue finish was introduced; Blue Night and Deep Green finishes were discontinued.

GRX20 L (RX20 L) - similar to the RX20, except in left-handed configuration. Available in Black finish. Current Mfg.

MSR	$359	$290	$240	$210	$180	$150	$120	$90

GRX20Z - similar to GRX20 L, except in Right Hand configuration, alder body. Available in black finish. Current Mfg.

MSR	$239	$179	$150	$125	$95	$75	$50	$35

GRX40 (RX40) - similar to the RX20, except features rosewood fingerboard with pearl dot inlay, 2 single coil/humbucker pickups, 5-way selector. Available in Black, Blue Night, and Deep Green finishes. Disc. 1999.

		$215	$175	$155	$135	$115	$90	$70

Last MSR was $269.

In 1998, Candy Apple Red and Jewel Blue finishes were introduced; Blue Night and Deep Green finishes were discontinued.

GRX40Z - similar to GRX40, except has alder body. Available in Black, Metallic Red and Metallic Grape finishes. Current Mfg.

MSR	$269	$199	$175	$150	$125	$95	$75	$50

GRX70 - similar to the RX20, except features rosewood fingerboard with pearl dot inlay, humbucker/single coil/humbucker pickups, 5-way selector. Available in Black and Metallic Green finishes. Mfg. 1998 to 1999.

		$215	$175	$150	$135	$115	$95	$75

Last MSR was $299.

Iceman Series

The original Iceman model (PS10) was introduced in 1978.

IC300 - single horn cutaway asymmetrical bound basswood body with pointed bottom bout, bolt-on maple neck, 22-fret bound rosewood fingerboard with pearl dot inlay, tune-o-matic bridge/stop tailpiece, 3-per-side tuners, chrome hardware, 2 Ibanez humbucker pickups, volume/tone controls, 3-position switch. Available in Black and Blue finishes. Mfg. 1994 to date.

MSR	$649	$525	$425	$375	$325	$275	$225	$175

IC500 - similar to the IC300, except features pearloid bound body, raised pearloid pickguard, abalone dot fingerboard inlay, bound blackface peghead with pearl logo inlay, 3-per-side tuners with pearloid buttons, cosmo black hardware, Available in Black finish. Mfg. 1994 to 1996.

		$800	$650	$595	$525	$450	$400	$325

Last MSR was $1,300.

ICJ100 WZ - single horn cutaway asymmetrical mahogany body with pointed bottom bout, abalone bound maple top/back, set-in maple neck, 22-fret bound rosewood fingerboard with pearl/abalone block inlay, Lo Pro II locking tremolo, 3-per-side tuners, chrome hardware, 2 Ibanez humbucker pickups, volume/tone (push/pull coil tap) controls, 3-position switch. Available in Green Galaxy finishes. Disc. 1999.

		$1,599	$1,299	$1,150	$995	$825	$650	$500

Last MSR was $1,999.

This model was designed in conjunction with J. (White Zombie).

JEM Series

The JEM Series was co-designed by Steve Vai, and introduced in 1987. All models in the series have a *Monkey Grip* hand slot routed in the bodies.

JEM555 - offset double cutaway American basswood body, bolt-on maple neck, 24-fret rosewood fingerboard with pearl dot/vine inlay with Steve Vai signature block inlay at 24th fret, Lo TRS II tremolo, 6-on-a-side tuners, charcoal hardware, humbucker/single coil/humbucker DiMarzio pickups, volume/tone control, 5-position switch. Available in Black and White finishes. Mfg. 1994 to date.

MSR	$1,199	$875	$725	$650	$550	$475	$395	$300

Add $100 for left-handed configuration (Model JEM555L). Available in Black finish only. The left-handed configuration was discontinued in 1998.

JEM7 V - offset double cutaway alder body, pearloid pickguard, bolt-on maple neck, 24-fret ebony fingerboard with pearl/abalone vine inlay, Lo Pro Edge tremolo, 6-on-a-side tuners, gold hardware, humbucker/single coil/humbucker DiMarzio pickups, volume/tone control, 5-position switch. Available in White finish. Mfg. 1994 to date.

MSR	$2,399	$1,700	$1,475	$1,300	$1,100	$950	$750	$595

GRADING		100% MINT	98% NEAR MINT	95% EXC+	90% EXC	80% VG+	70% VG	60% G

JEM7 D - similar to JEM7 V, except has American Basswood body, rosewood fingerboard, screw-head position markers, 2 DiMarzio Breed humbucking pickups and 1 Dimarzio Special single coil in the center position, chrome hardware. Available in Black finish. Current Mfg.

MSR	$1,599	$1,199	$999	$899	$750	$650	$550	$450

JEM7 - similar to the JEM7 V, except features an American basswood body, brushed aluminum pickguard, 24-fret rosewood fingerboard with screw inlay, brushed chrome hardware. Available in Burnt Stain Blue finish. Disc. 1999.

$1,399 $1,199 $1,050 $925 $795 $650 $500
Last MSR was $1,999.

JEM77 GMC (GREEN MULTI-COLOR) - offset double cutaway basswood body, transparent pickguard, bolt-on maple neck, 24-fret rosewood fingerboard with fluorescent vine inlay, double locking vibrato, 6-on-a-side tuners, charcoal hardware, humbucker/single coil/humbucker DiMarzio pickups, volume/tone control, 5-position switch. Available in Green Multi Color finish. Mfg. 1992 to 1994.

$1,250 $1,050 $950 $850 $725 $625 $525
Last MSR was $2,100.

JEM77 BFP (Blue Floral Pattern) - similar to JEM77 GMC, except has maple fingerboard with Blue vine inlay, body matching peghead. Available in Blue Floral Pattern finish. Mfg. 1991 to 1996.

$1,200 $1,000 $900 $800 $700 $600 $500
Last MSR was $2,000.

JEM77 FP (Floral Pattern) - similar to JEM77 GMC, except has green/red vine fingerboard inlay, body matching peghead. Available in Floral Pattern finish. Mfg. 1988 to 1999.

$1,475 $1,275 $1,125 $975 $825 $675 $525

JEM77 PMC (Purple Multi-Color) - similar to JEM77 GMC, except has a maple fingerboard with 3 color pyramid inlay. Available in Purple Multi Color finish. Mfg. 1991 to 1992.

$1,250 $1,050 $950 $850 $725 $625 $525
Last MSR was $2,100.

JEM777 - offset double cutaway basswood body, black pickguard, bolt-on maple neck, 24-fret maple fingerboard with 3 color vanishing pyramid inlay, double locking vibrato, 6-on-a-side tuners, charcoal hardware, humbucker/single coil/humbucker DiMarzio pickups, volume/tone control, 5-position switch. Available in Desert Sun Yellow finish. Mfg. 1992 to 1996.

$1,100 $900 $825 $725 $625 $550 $450
Last MSR was $1,800.

JEM777 V - similar to JEM777, except features alder body. Available in Black finish. Disc. 1994.

$1,000 $850 $750 $675 $595 $525 $425
Last MSR was $1,700.

JPM Series

The JPM Series was co-designed with guitarist John Petrucci (Dream Theatre).

JPM100 - offset double cutaway basswood body, bolt-on 1-piece maple neck, 24-fret bound rosewood fingerboard with offset pearl dot inlay, Lo Pro Edge double locking tremolo, 6-on-a-side tuners, black hardware, 2 DiMarzio humbucker pickups, volume/tone control, 3-position switch.

Available in P4 (Part 4) Black/Green/Blue graphic matte finish Mfg. 1998 to 1999.

$1,100 $950 $825 $725 $600 $495 $375
Last MSR was $1,499.

Available in P3 (Part 3) Black/White graphic finish. Disc. 1997.

$1,100 $1,000 $925 $795 $650 $525 $400
Last MSR was $1,599.

JS (Joe Satriani Signature) Series

The JS Series was co-designed by Joe Satriani, and debuted in 1990.

JS1 - offset double cutaway contoured basswood body, bolt-on maple neck, 22-fret rosewood fingerboard with pearl dot inlay, double locking vibrato, 6-on-a-side tuners, chrome hardware, humbucker/single coil/humbucker DiMarzio pickups, volume/tone control, 5-position switch. Available in Black, Inferno Red and White finishes. Mfg. 1991 to 1994.

$725 $600 $550 $490 $425 $360 $300
Last MSR was $1,200.

JS3 - similar to JS1, except has 2 humbucker DiMarzio pickups, 3-position switch. Available in Custom Graphic finish. Mfg. 1990 only.

$1,400 $1,150 $1,050 $925 $820 $715 $600
Last MSR was $2,300.

JS4 - similar to JS1, except has 2 humbucker DiMarzio pickups, 3-position switch. Available in Electric Rainbow finish. Mfg. 1993 only.

$1,400 $1,150 $1,050 $925 $820 $715 $600
Last MSR was $2,300.

JS5 - similar to JS1, except has 2 humbucker DiMarzio pickups, 3-position switch. Available in Rainforest finish. Mfg. 1992 only.

$1,400 $1,150 $1,050 $925 $820 $715 $600
Last MSR was $2,300.

JS6 - similar to JS1, except has mahogany body, fixed bridge, 2 humbucker DiMarzio pickups, 3-position switch. Available in Oil finish. Mfg. 1993 only.

$1,400 $1,150 $1,050 $925 $820 $715 $600
Last MSR was $2,300.

GRADING		100% MINT	98% NEAR MINT	95% EXC+	90% EXC	80% VG+	70% VG	60% G

JS 10TH ANNIVERSARY CHROME LIMITED EDITION - offset double cutaway contoured luthite body, bolt-on one-piece maple neck, 22-fret rosewood fingerboard with pearl dot inlay, Edge double locking tremolo, 6-on-a-side tuners, chrome hardware, 2 DiMarzio JS10TH humbucker pickups, volume/tone control, 3-position switch. Available in Chrome finish. Mfg. 1998 to 1999.

MSR $2,999 $2,399 $1,925 $N/A $N/A $N/A

JS100 - offset double cutaway contoured basswood body, bolt-on one-piece maple neck, 22-fret rosewood fingerboard with pearl dot inlay/Joe Satriani block inlay at 21st fret, Lo TRS II double locking tremolo, 6-on-a-side tuners, chrome hardware, 2 Ibanez humbucker pickups, volume/tone control, 3-position switch. Available in Black and Transparent Red finishes. Mfg. 1994 to date.

MSR $899 $725 $590 $520 $445 $370 $300 $225

JS600 - similar to JS100, except has strings through fixed bridge. Available in Black and White finishes. Mfg. 1994 to 1996.

$425 $350 $315 $280 $250 $215 $175
Last MSR was $700.

JS700 - similar to JS100, except features mahogany body, one-piece mahogany neck, wraparound bridge, 2 P-90 style single coil pickups. Available in Transparent Red finish. Disc. 1999.

$725 $595 $525 $450 $375 $300 $225
Last MSR was $899.

JS1000 - offset double cutaway contoured mahogany body, bolt-on maple neck, 22-fret rosewood fingerboard with abalone dot inlay/Joe Satriani block inlay at 21st fret, double locking tremolo, 6-on-a-side tuners, charcoal hardware, 2 DiMarzio humbucker (PAF Pro/Fred) pickups, volume/tone control, 3-position switch, hi-pass filter push/pull switch in volume control, coil tap push/pull switch in tone control. Available in Black Pearl and Transparent Blue finishes. Mfg. 1994 to 1996, 1998 to date.

MSR $1,499 $1,050 $899 $795 $695 $585 $475 $375

In 1998, White finish was introduced; Transparent Blue finish was discontinued.

JS6000 - similar to the JS1000, except features strings through fixed bridge. Available in Oil and Transparent Red finishes. Mfg. 1994 to 1996.

$850 $700 $625 $550 $495 $425 $350
Last MSR was $1,400.

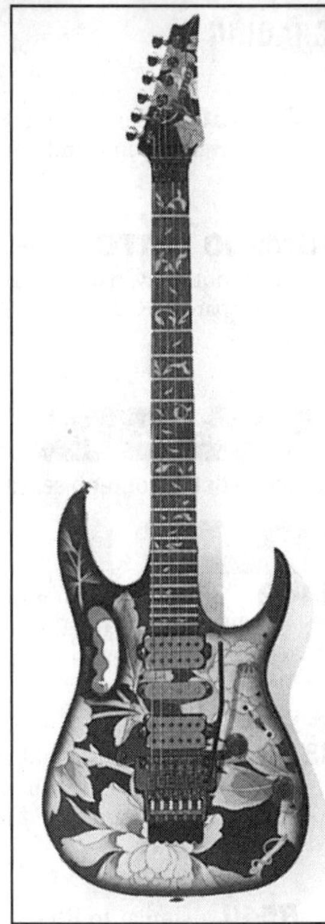

Ibanez JEM 77 FP
courtesy Ibanez USA

Korina Series (1975 to 1977)

Introduced a year after the **Golden Oldies** Series, the **Korina** Series models is another example of Ibanez really sticking it to Gibson. If the series name was the battle cry, then the actual models are the equivalent of the Marines landing. Ibanez introduced three models based on Gibson's futuristic designs of 1958: The **Rocket Roll Sr.** was a copy of the Flying V, the **Futura** was the Moderne copy, and **Destroyer** was their take on the Explorer model. All models had an original retail list price of $395, and featured an Ibanez script logo on the headstock similar (from a distance...hmmm). While one reliable vintage source estimates that the 'Korina' is in fact tinted Japanese ash, interest in these three models has seen a resurgence in the past couple of years.

One note of moderate interest (it'll win you a drink in a bar bet), the **Korina Series** Ibanez Flying V copy was named the **Rocket Roll Sr.** Why Sr.? The first Ibanez **Rocket Roll** model was the solid finish **Golden Oldies Series** model!

The Korina series is again seeing a lot of attention from players and dealers, now in the Vintage Guitar market. The three models all can be found with price tags ranging from $800 to $1,000 at guitar shows; market research has indicated that they actually sell in the area between $550/$600 up to $800.

PM (Pat Metheny Signature) Series

The PM Series was designed in conjunction with Pat Metheny. The PM100 model debuted in 1996.

PM100 PAT METHANY SIGNATURE MODEL - slightly offset semi-hollow body, abalone bound maple top/back/sides, 2 bound f-holes, set-in mahogany neck, 22-fret bound ebony fingerboard with pearl/abalone block inlay/Pat Metheny signature block at 21st fret, raised ebony bridge/metal tailpiece, gold hardware, 3-per-side tuners, black peghead with Ibanez logo/slash diamond inlay, Ibanez Super 58 covered humbucker, volume/tone control. Available in Black and Natural finishes. Mfg. 1996 to date.

MSR $2,899 $2,325 $1,900 $1,675 $1,425 $1,200 $950 $725

PM120 - similar to Model PM100, except has Abalone/Pearl Block position markers, 2 IBZ Silent 58 humbucking pickups. Available in Black and Natural finishes. Current Mfg.

MSR $2,999 $2,250 $1,995 $1,695 $1,495 $1,250 $995 $750

PM20 - similar to the PM100, except features 22-fret bound rosewood fingerboard, rosewood bridge piece, ivoroid body binding. Available in Natural and Transparent Black finishes. Mfg. 1997 to 1999.

$1,125 $925 $800 $695 $575 $475 $350
Last MSR was $1,399.

PGM Series

PGM Series was designed in conjunction with Paul Gilbert (Racer X, Mister Big).

PGM30 - offset double cutaway basswood body, painted f-holes, bolt-on one-piece maple neck, 24-fret rosewood fingerboard with pearl dot inlay, Lo TRS II double locking tremolo, reverse peghead with screened logo, 6-on-the-other-side tuners, chrome hardware, Ibanez humbucker/single coil/humbucker pickups, volume control, 5-position switch. Available in White finish. Disc. 1998. 2000 to date.

MSR $799 $640 $525 $450 $375 $300 $225 $175

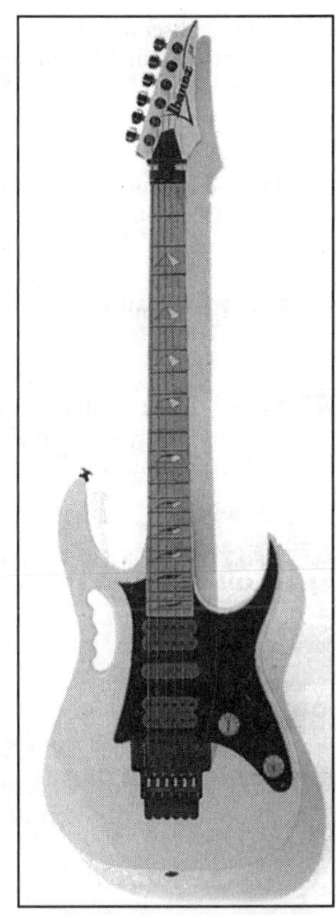

Ibanez JEM 777 DY
courtesy Ibanez USA

GRADING	100% MINT	98% NEAR MINT	95% EXC+	90% EXC	80% VG+	70% VG	60% G

PGM500 - similar to the PGM30, except features strings through fixed bridge, gold hardware, DiMarzio humbucker/single coil/humbucker pickups. Available in Candy Apple finish. Mfg. 1994 to 1996.

$800	$650	$585	$525	$455	$390	$325

Last MSR was $1,300.

PGM900 PMTC - single rounded cutaway mahogany body, 2 painted f-holes, bolt-on one-piece maple neck, 22-fret rosewood fingerboard with pearl dot inlay, fixed bridge, 3-per-side tuners, gold hardware, 2 Ibanez Super 58 humbucker pickups, volume control, 3-position switch. Available in Transparent Red finish. Mfg. 1998 to 1999.

$1,050	$825	$725	$625	$525	$475	$425

Last MSR was $1,299.

Professional Series

See **Artist Autograph** series.

R Series

R442 - offset double cutaway alder body, bolt-on maple neck, 22-fret maple fingerboard with black dot inlay, locking vibrato, 6-on-a-side locking tuners, black hardware, 2 single coil/1 humbucker Ibanez pickups, volume/tone control, 5-position switch. Available in Transparent Blue, Transparent Cherry, and Transparent Sunburst finishes. Mfg. 1992 only.

$425	$350	$325	$275	$250	$200	$175

Last MSR was $700.

R540 LTD - offset double cutaway basswood body, bolt-on maple neck, 22-fret bound rosewood fingerboard with sharktooth inlay, double locking tremolo, 6-on-a-side tuners, black hardware, humbucker/single coil/humbucker Ibanez pickups, volume/tone control, 5-position switch. Available in Black, Candy Apple, and Jewel Blue finishes. Mfg. 1992 to 1996.

$600	$500	$450	$425	$375	$350	$300

Last MSR was $1,000.

R540 - similar to R540 LTD, except has pearl dot inlay, 2 single coil/humbucker Ibanez pickups. Available in Blue Burst finish. Mfg. 1992 only.

$575	$475	$425	$375	$325	$295	$250

Last MSR was $950.

R540 HH - similar to R540, except has 2 Ibanez humbucker pickups. Available in White finish.

$550	$475	$425	$375	$325	$275	$225

Last MSR was $930.

R542 - similar to the R540 LTD, except featured alder body, 22-fret rosewood fingerboard with abalone oval inlay, 3 Ibanez single coil pickups. Available in Blue, Candy Apple and White finishes. Mfg. 1992 only.

$475	$400	$350	$325	$275	$250	$200

Last MSR was $800.

RT150 - offset double cutaway alder body, white pickguard, bolt-on maple neck, 24-fret rosewood fingerboard with pearl dot inlay, standard vibrato, 6-on-a-side tuners, chrome hardware, humbucker/single coil/humbucker pickups, volume/tone control, 5-position switch. Available in Black and Deep Red finishes. Mfg. 1993 only.

$250	$200	$175	$160	$140	$120	$100

Last MSR was $400.

RT450 - similar to RT150, except has tortoise pickguard, locking tuners, Ibanez pickups. Available in Amber, Black and Tobacco Sunburst finishes. Mfg. 1993 only.

$325	$275	$250	$225	$195	$165	$140

Last MSR was $550.

RT452 - similar to RT450, except has 12 strings, fixed bridge, 6-per-side tuners. Available in Amber finish.

$400	$325	$295	$250	$225	$195	$175

Last MSR was $650.

RT650 - offset double cutaway alder body, bound gravure top, pearloid pickguard, bolt-on maple neck, 24-fret bound rosewood fingerboard with pearl dot inlay, standard vibrato, 6-on-a-side locking tuners, chrome hardware, humbucker/single coil/humbucker Ibanez pickups, volume/tone control, 5-position switch. Available in Transparent Blue and Transparent Red finishes. Mfg. 1993 only.

$450	$375	$350	$300	$250	$225	$195

Last MSR was $750.

RV470 - similar to the RT650, except features unbound gravure top, transparent pickguard, 22-fret rosewood fingerboard with pearl dot inlay, gold hardware. Available in Purpleburst and Tobaccoburst finishes. Mfg. 1993 only.

$500	$425	$375	$350	$300	$250	$225

Last MSR was $850.

RG Series

The RG Series debuted in 1985.

RG220 - offset double cutaway basswood body, bolt-on one-piece maple neck, 24-fret rosewood fingerboard with dot inlay, single locking tremolo, 6-on-a-side tuners, chrome hardware, 2 humbucker pickups, volume/tone control, 3-position switch. Available in Black and Metallic Green finishes. Mfg. 1994 to 1999.

$325	$295	$250	$225	$195	$150	$125

Last MSR was $479.

GRADING		100% MINT	98% NEAR MINT	95% EXC+	90% EXC	80% VG+	70% VG	60% G

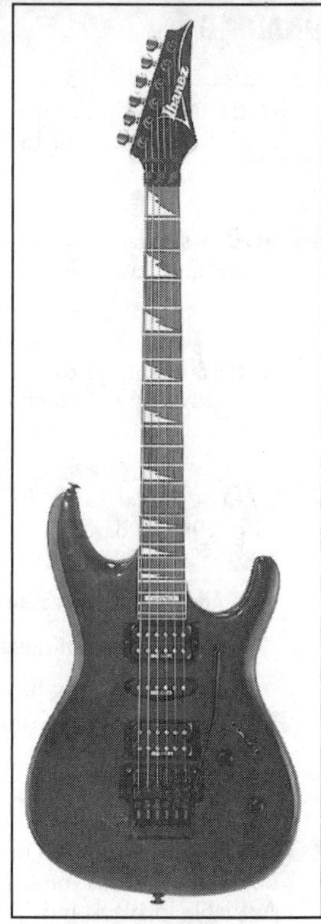
Ibanez 540R LTD
courtesy Ibanez USA

RG170 - similar to the RG220, except features an agathis body, maple fingerboard with black dot inlay, standard tremolo bridge, humbucker/single coil/humbucker pickups, 5-position switch. Available in Black, Jewel Blue, and Metallic Green finishes. Current Mfg.

MSR	$369	$295	$250	$225	$175	$150	$125	$95

In 1998, Metallic Green was discontinued.

RG270 - offset double cutaway basswood body, bolt-on maple neck, 24-fret maple fingerboard with black dot inlay, double locking tremolo, 6-on-a-side tuners, chrome hardware, humbucker/single coil/humbucker pickups, volume/tone control, 5-position switch. Available in Black, Jewel Blue, and Metallic Green finishes. Mfg. 1994 to date.

MSR	$499	$399	$325	$285	$245	$205	$165	$125

Add $50 for 24-fret bound rosewood fingerboard with white sharktooth inlay, black hardware (Model RG270 DX).

Early model may feature Crimson Metallic and Emerald Green finishes.

RG320 - offset double cutaway basswood body, bolt-on maple neck, 24-fret rosewood fingerboard with pearl dot inlay, double Lo TRS II tremolo, 6-on-a-side tuners, chrome hardware, 2 humbucker pickups, volume/tone control, 3-position switch. Available in Grey Pewter matte finishes. Mfg. 1997 to date.

MSR	$599	$425	$375	$325	$295	$250	$195	$150

RG350 DX - similar to the RG320, except features a bound rosewood fingerboard with pearl sharktooth inlay, black hardware, mirror (or white pearloid) pickguard, humbucker/single coil/humbucker pickups. Available in Black and White finishes. Mfg. 1997 to date.

MSR	$679	$475	$425	$375	$325	$275	$225	$175

RG420 - similar to the RG320, except features black hardware, Lo TRS tremolo, 2 humbucker (V7/V8) IBZ pickups. Available in Black and Royal Blue finishes. Mfg. 1997 to 1999.

		$475	$425	$375	$325	$275	$225	$175

Last MSR was $679.

RG450 - offset double cutaway basswood body, transparent pickguard, bolt-on maple neck, 24-fret maple fingerboard with black dot inlay, double locking vibrato, 6-on-a-side tuners, black hardware, humbucker/single coil/humbucker Ibanez pickups, volume/tone control, 5-position switch. Available in Black, Emerald Green and Purple Neon finishes. Mfg. 1994 to 1998.

		$350	$300	$275	$250	$200	$175	$150

Last MSR was $585.

RG450 DX - similar to RG450, except has bound rosewood fingerboard with white sharktooth inlay, black hardware. Available in Black and White finishes. Mfg. 1994 to 1998.

		$595	$495	$425	$375	$300	$250	$195

Last MSR was $749.

RG470 - similar to the RG450, except features 24-fret rosewood fingerboard with pearl dot inlay. Available in Black, Jewel Blue, and Mediterranean Green finishes. Mfg. 1993 to date.

MSR	$699	$550	$450	$400	$350	$295	$225	$175

Add $100 for left-handed configuration (Model RG470 L). Available in Jewel Blue finish only.

Early RG470 models may feature Crimson Metallic and Emerald Green finishes. In 1998, the RG470 L was discontinued in Jewel Blue, and offered in Black finish only.

RG470 FM - similar to RG470, except has bound figured maple top, maple fingerboard with black dot inlay. Available in Transparent Black and Transparent Purple finishes. Mfg. 1994 to 1996.

		$425	$350	$325	$275	$250	$225	$175

Last MSR was $700.

RG470 FX - similar to RG470, except has strings-through fixed bridge. Available in Black and Laser Blue finishes. Mfg. 1994 to 1996.

		$295	$250	$225	$195	$175	$150	$125

Last MSR was $480.

RG520 - offset double cutaway basswood body, bolt-on one-piece maple neck with bubinga reinforcement, 24-fret maple fingerboard with dot inlay, Edge double locking vibrato, 6-on-a-side tuners, chrome hardware, 2 humbucker (V7/V8) IBZ pickups, volume/tone control, 5-position switch. Available in Grey Pewter matte finish. Mfg. 1997 to 1999.

		$550	$475	$425	$375	$300	$250	$200

Last MSR was $799.

RG520 QS - similar to the RG520, except features a mahogany body, quilted sapele top. Available in Transparent Black and Transparent Blue finishes. Mfg. 1997 to date.

MSR	$929	$645	$570	$515	$435	$360	$310	$245

RG550 - offset double cutaway basswood body, black pickguard, bolt-on maple neck, 24-fret maple fingerboard with black dot inlay, double locking vibrato, 6-on-a-side tuners, black hardware, humbucker/single coil/humbucker Ibanez pickups, volume/tone control, 5-position switch. Available in Black finish. Mfg. 1991 to date.

MSR	$819	$650	$525	$475	$400	$350	$275	$200

Early models may feature Electric Blue, Candy Apple, and Desert Sun Yellow finishes.

RG550 DX - similar to RG550, except has body-color-matched mirror pickguard. Available in Laser Blue and Purple Neon finishes. Disc. 1994.

		$500	$425	$375	$350	$300	$250	$225

Last MSR was $850.

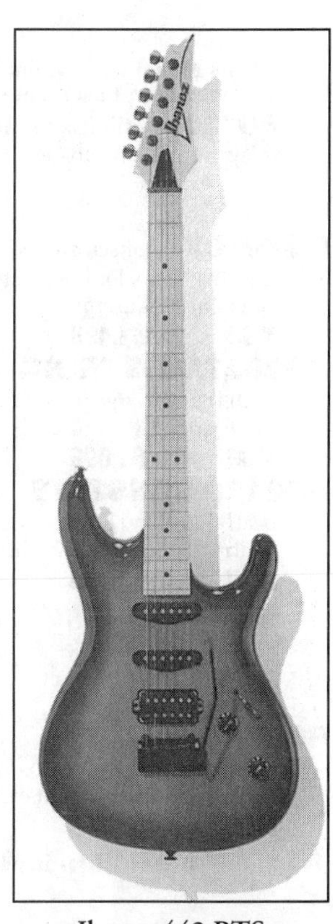
Ibanez 442 RTS
courtesy Ibanez USA

I

GRADING	100% MINT	98% NEAR MINT	95% EXC+	90% EXC	80% VG+	70% VG	60% G

RG550 LTD - similar to RG550, except has body-color-matched mirror pickguard, bound rosewood fingerboard with pearl sharktooth inlay, black hardware. Available in Black and Purple Neon finishes. Mfg. 1994 to 1996.

	$625	$550	$500	$450	$375	$325	$275

Last MSR was $1,000.

RG560 - similar to RG550, except has rosewood fingerboard with pearl dot inlay, 2 single coil/humbucker Ibanez pickups. Available in Black, Candy Apple, and Jewel Blue finishes. Mfg. 1992 only.

	$450	$375	$350	$300	$250	$225	$195

Last MSR was $750.

RG565 - similar to RG550, except has body-color matched fingerboard inlay, reverse headstock, single coil/humbucker Ibanez pickups. Available in Candy Apple, Emerald Green and Laser Blue finishes. Mfg. 1992 only.

	$500	$425	$375	$350	$300	$275	$225

Last MSR was $800.

RG570 - similar to the RG550, except features 24-fret rosewood fingerboard with pearl dot inlay. Available in Black Pearl and Purple Pearl finishes. Mfg. 1992 to date.

MSR $819	$650	$525	$475	$400	$350	$275	$200

Add $80 for Flaked Blue and Flaked Green Metal Flake finishes.

Add $150 for left-handed configuration (Model RG570L). Available in Jewel Blue finish only. The left-handed configuration was discontinued in 1996.

Early models may have Candy Apple, Emerald Green, Jewel Blue, and Purple Neon finishes.

RG570 FM - similar to RG570, except has flame maple top. Available in Amber, Transparent Blue and Transparent Cherry finishes. Mfg. 1992 only.

	$525	$450	$400	$375	$325	$295	$250

Last MSR was $850.

RG750 - offset double cutaway basswood body, bolt-on maple neck, 24-fret bound maple fingerboard with sharktooth inlay, double locking vibrato, bound peghead, 6-on-a-side tuners, black hardware, humbucker/single coil/humbucker Ibanez pickups, volume/tone control, 5-position switch. Available in Black and Candy Apple finishes. Mfg. 1992 only.

	$650	$550	$500	$450	$375	$325	$275

Last MSR was $1,000.

RG760 - similar to RG750, except features rosewood fingerboard, 2 single coil/humbucker Ibanez pickups. Available in Black, Jewel Blue, and Emerald Green finishes.

	$650	$550	$500	$450	$375	$325	$275

Last MSR was $1,000.

RG770 - similar to the RG750, except features 24-fret bound rosewood fingerboard with pearl sharktooth inlay. Available in Black, and Emerald Green finishes. Mfg. 1991 to 1994.

	$650	$550	$500	$450	$375	$325	$275

Last MSR was $1,000.

This Model was available with transparent pickguard, maple fingerboard with body-color-matched sharktooth inlay (Model RG770DX). Available in Laser Blue and Violet Metallic finishes.

RG1200 - similar to the RG750, except features flame maple top, pearloid pickguard, 24-fret bound rosewood fingerboard with abalone oval inlay, humbucker/Ibanez single coil/DiMarzio humbucker pickups. Available in Transparent Red and Transparent Blue finishes. Mfg. 1992 only.

	$850	$675	$600	$550	$475	$425	$350

Last MSR was $1,350.

RG2020X - offset double cutaway mahogany solid body, 3-piece maple neck, rosewood fingerboard, 24 jumbo frets, Wizard neck type, Double Locking Tremelo, L.R. Baggs piezo pickups, Double Edge bridge, 6 on 1 side tuners, 1 ea. V7 and V8 humbucking pickups. Available in Transparent Blue finish. Current Mfg.

MSR $1,499	$1,125	$1,025	$925	$825	$725	$625	$499

RG2027X 7-STRING -offset double cutaway mahogany body, 3-piece maple neck, rosewood fingerboard, abalone offset position marker at the 12th fret, 24 large frets, Wizard 7 neck type, Double Edge 7 bridge, 1 ea IBZ V7-7 & IBZ V8-7 humbucker pickups. Available in Vintage Violin finish. Current Mfg.

MSR $1,699	$1,275	$1,175	$1,075	$975	$875	$750	$625

RG3120 PRESTIGE - offset double cutaway mahogany body, figured maple top, bolt-on 3-piece maple neck, 24-fret rosewood fingerboard with pearl dot inlay, Lo Pro Edge tremolo, 6-on-a-side tuners, chrome hardware, 2 DiMarzio humbucker (PAF PRfo/Tone Zone) pickups, volume/tone control, 3-position switch. Available in Twilight Blue finish. Mfg. 1997 to date.

MSR $1,499	$1,050	$899	$795	$695	$595	$475	$375

RG3220 Prestige - similar to the RG3120, except features a quilted maple top. Available in Twilight Blue and Vintage Red finishes. Mfg. 1998 to 1999.

	$1,150	$975	$850	$750	$625	$500	$395

Last MSR was $1,599.

RG7420 7-STRING - offset double cutaway basswood body, 7-string, one-piece maple neck with Bubinga reinforcement, Wizard-7 All Access neck, rosewood fingerboard, dot position markers, 24 jumbo frets, Lo TRS-7 bridge, 1 ea. IBZ V7-7 & 1 IBZ V8-7 humbucker pickup. Available in Black Pearl and Magenta Crush finishes. Current Mfg.

MSR $799	$599	$550	$499	$450	$399	$350	$299

Deduct $50 for Standard bridge (Model RG7421).

GRADING		100% MINT	98% NEAR MINT	95% EXC+	90% EXC	80% VG+	70% VG	60% G

RG7620 7-STRING - 7-string configuration, offset double cutaway basswood body, bolt-on one-piece maple neck, 24-fret bound maple fingerboard with pearl dot inlay, Lo Pro Edge 7 tremolo, 7-on-a-side tuners, black hardware, 2 DiMarzio Blaze II humbuckers, volume/tone control, 5-position switch. Available in Black and Royal Blue finishes. Current Mfg.

MSR $1,299 $1,050 $850 $745 $640 $535 $430 $325

In 1998, DiMarzio Blaze II humbuckers replaced the DiMarzio RG7 Special humbuckers.

RG7621 7-String - similar to the RG7620, except features a fixed 7-string bridge. Available in Black and White finishes. Mfg. 1997 to 1999.

$699 $599 $525 $450 $395 $325 $250
Last MSR was $999.

RX Series

RX160 - offset double cutaway maple body, bolt-on maple neck, 22-fret rosewood fingerboard with pearl dot inlay, standard vibrato, 6-on-a-side tuners, chrome hardware, humbucker/single coil/humbucker pickups, volume/tone control, 5-position switch. Available in Black, Blue Night and Red finishes. Mfg. 1994 to 1996.

$200 $175 $160 $140 $120 $100 $85
Last MSR was $340.

RX170 - similar to RX160, except has maple fingerboard with black dot inlay. Available in Emerald Green, Transparent Blue, and Transparent Red finishes. Mfg. 1994 to 1996.

$225 $180 $165 $150 $125 $110 $90
Last MSR was $360.

RX270 - similar to RX160, except has bound body, maple fingerboard with black dot inlay. Available in Black, Cherry Sunburst, and Transparent Green finishes. Mfg. 1994 to 1996.

$260 $215 $195 $170 $150 $130 $110
Last MSR was $430.

RX240 - offset double cutaway agathis body, bolt-on maple neck, 22-fret rosewood fingerboard with pearl dot inlay, TZ30 modern tremolo, 6-on-a-side tuners, chrome hardware, white pickguard, 2 single coil/humbucker pickups, volume/tone control, 5-way selector. Available in Candy Apple, Metallic Green, and Sunburst finishes. Disc. 1998.

$325 $250 $225 $195 $165 $135 $100
Last MSR was $399.

RX350 - similar to the RX160, except features pearloid pickguard, 22-fret maple fingerboard with black dot inlay, cosmo black hardware, humbucker/single coil/humbucker Ibanez pickups. Available in Black, Emerald Green, Transparent Red, and Transparent Turquoise finishes. Mfg. 1994 to 1996.

$295 $250 $225 $195 $175 $150 $125
Last MSR was $480.

RX352 - similar to RX350, except has 12 strings, fixed bridge, 6-on-a-side tuners. Available in Black finish. Mfg. 1994.

$350 $295 $250 $225 $200 $175 $150
Last MSR was $580.

RX650 - similar to the RX350, except features bound figured maple top, 22-fret bound rosewood fingerboard with pearl dot inlay. Available in Transparent Green, Transparent Purple, and Transparent Red finishes. Mfg. 1994 to 1996.

$350 $295 $250 $225 $200 $175 $150
Last MSR was $570.

RX750 - similar to the RX350, except features padauk/mahogany/padauk body, 22-fret rosewood fingerboard with pearl dot inlay, gold hardware. Available in Natural finish. Mfg. 1994.

$600 $500 $450 $400 $350 $300 $250
Last MSR was $1,000.

S Series

The S Series was originally introduced as the **Saber** Series in 1987.

SA160 -offset double cutaway mahogany body, 1-piece maple neck, rosewood fingerboard with pearl dot position markers, 22 jumbo frets, TZ30 bridge, 2 PSNDS single coil pickups and 1 PSND-2 humbucking pickup, chrome hardware. Available in Black, Metallic Grape and Vampire Kiss finishes. Current Mfg.

MSR $499 $375 $325 $275 $250 $225 $195 $150

SCA220 -offset double cutaway mahogany body, 1-piece maple neck, rosewood fingerboard with pearl dot position markers, 22 large frets, Short Stop II bridge, 2 IBZ V6 humbucking pickups, chrome hardware. Available in Black Pearl finish. Current Mfg.

MSR $649 $485 $425 $375 $325 $275 $225 $175

S CLASSIC SC420 - thin contoured offset double cutaway mahogany body, one-piece bolt-on maple neck, 22-fret rosewood fingerboard with pearl dot inlay, Short Stop II wraparound bridge, 3-per-side tuners, chrome hardware, 2 Ibanez humbucker pickups, top-mounted volume/tone controls, 3-position switch. Available in Black and Black Cherry finishes. Mfg. 1997 to date.

MSR $999 $810 $660 $585 $495 $400 $325 $250

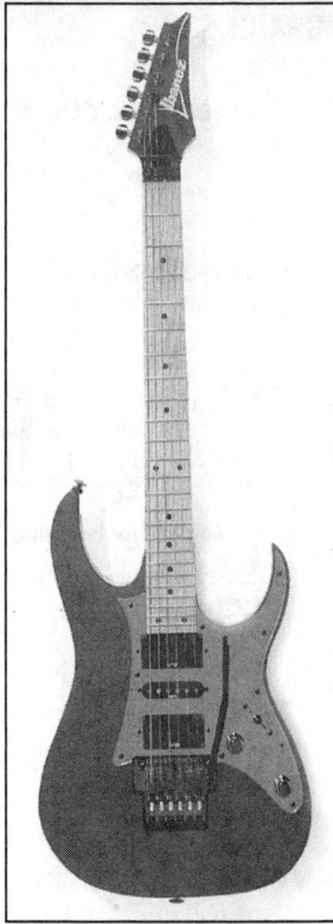

Ibanez RG 550 DX LB
courtesy Ibanez USA

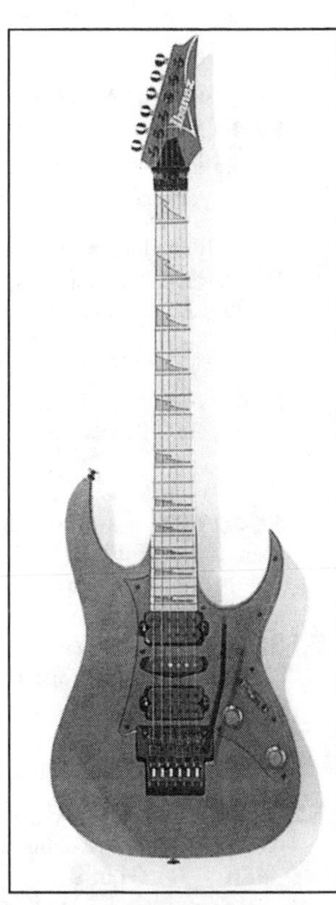

Ibanez RG 770 DX VM
courtesy Ibanez USA

GRADING	100% MINT	98% NEAR MINT	95% EXC+	90% EXC	80% VG+	70% VG	60% G

S Classic SC500 N (Nylon String) - similar to the S Classic SC420, except features a nylon string configuration, spruce top, one-piece mahogany neck, 22-fret bound ebony fingerboard with abalone dot inlay, slotted headstock, gold hardware, piezo bridge pickup, volume/tone controls. Available in Natural finish. Mfg. 1998 to 1999.

	$950	$775	$695	$595	$500	$425	$325

Last MSR was $1,299.

S Classic SC620 - similar to the S Classic SC420, except features bound flame maple top, 22-fret bound ebony fingerboard with abalone/pearl oval inlay, gold hardware. Available in Amber Pearl finish. Mfg. 1997 to 1999.

	$1,125	$925	$800	$695	$575	$475	$350

Last MSR was $1,399.

S470 - sculpted thin offset double cutaway mahogany body, bolt-on maple neck, 22-fret rosewood fingerboard with pearl dot inlay, Lo TRS II double locking tremolo, 6-on-a-side tuners, chrome hardware, humbucker/single coil/humbucker IBZ pickups, volume/tone control, 5-position switch. Available in Black, Jewel Blue, and Mediterranean Green finishes. Mfg. 1991 to date.

MSR $819	$650	$525	$465	$400	$340	$275	$210

Add $80 for left-handed configuration (Model S470 L), available in Black finish only.

Early models may feature Natural Oil, Transparent Blue, and Transparent Red finishes.

S470 FM - similar to S470, except has a flame maple top. Available in British Racing Green finish. Mfg. 1998 to 1999.

	$750	$600	$550	$500	$450	$400	$325

Last MSR was $949.

S470QS similar to Model S470 except, has quilted sapele/mahogany body. Available in Transparent Red finish. Current Mfg.

MSR $949	$715	$625	$550	$450	$350	$295	$250

SF470 - similar to S470, except has tune-o-matic bridge/stop tailpiece. Available in Black and Transparent Red finishes. Mfg. 1991 to 1996.

	$500	$425	$375	$350	$295	$250	$225

Last MSR was $850.

SV420 - similar to S470, except has flamed maple top, 2 Ibanez humbucker pickups, gold hardware, TZ100 modern tremolo. Available in Butterscotch Transparent finish. Disc. 1997.

	$650	$575	$500	$425	$375	$295	$225

Last MSR was $899.

SV470 - similar to S470, except has standard vibrato, locking tuners, gold hardware. Available in Black, Oil and Transparent Red finishes. Mfg. 1993 to 1996.

	$550	$450	$400	$360	$315	$270	$225

Last MSR was $900.

S540 - offset double cutaway mahogany body, bolt-on maple neck, 22-fret maple fingerboard with abalone oval inlay, pearl *Custom Made* inlay at 21st fret, double locking vibrato, 6-on-a-side tuners, cosmo black hardware, humbucker/single coil/humbucker Ibanez pickups, volume/tone control, 5-position switch. Available in Cayman Green, Jade Metallic, and Oil finishes. Mfg. 1987 to 1996.

	$750	$625	$575	$500	$450	$375	$325

Last MSR was $1,200.

In 1994, Cayman Green finish was introduced, Jade Metallic was discontinued.

S540 LTD - similar to S540, except has bound rosewood fingerboard with sharktooth inlay, bound peghead, chrome hardware. Available in Transparent Blue finish. Mfg. 1991 to 1999.

	$1,100	$925	$800	$695	$575	$475	$350

Last MSR was $1,399.

Early models may feature Black, Emerald Green, Jewel Blue, Lipstick Red, and Purple Neon finishes.

S540 BM - similar to S540, except has burl mahogany top, bound rosewood fingerboard, gold hardware. Available in Antique Violin finish. Disc. 1996.

	$850	$650	$595	$525	$450	$395	$325

Last MSR was $1,300.

S540 FM - similar to S540, except has flame maple top, bound rosewood fingerboard with abalone oval inlay, chrome hardware. Available in Transparent Purple and Transparent Turquoise finishes. Disc. 1997.

	$1,100	$950	$825	$725	$600	$495	$375

Last MSR was $1,449.

S540 QM - similar to S540, except has quilted maple top, bound rosewood fingerboard with pearl dot inlay, chrome hardware. Available in Transparent Blue finish. Disc. 1999.

	$995	$850	$750	$650	$550	$450	$350

Last MSR was $1,399.

S1520 offset double cutaway mahogany body, 1-piece maple neck with Bubinga reinforcement, bound rosewood fingerboard, 22 jumbo frets, Wizard All Access neck, "S" Special on 12th fret, Lo Pro Edge bridge, 1 ea. IBZ QM-1 and IBZ QM-2 humbucking pickups. Available in Black Pearl finish. Current Mfg.

MSR $1,199	$899	$799	$699	$650	$599	$550	$499

Add $200 for figured Bubinga top (Model S1520FB).

S2020X offset double cutaway mahogany body, 3-piece maple neck,rosewood fingerboard, 22 jumbo frets, Wizard neck style, Double Edge bridge, 1 ea. MQ-1 and QM-2 humbucking pickups, L.R. Baggs piezo pickup system. Available in Antique Violin finish. Current Mfg.

MSR $1,599	$1,199	$1,099	$999	$899	$799	$699	$550

GRADING	100% MINT	98% NEAR MINT	95% EXC+	90% EXC	80% VG+	70% VG	60% G

S2540 NT S PRESTIGE - sculpted thin offset double cutaway figured sapelle mahogany body, bolt-on 3-piece maple neck, 22-fret bound rosewood fingerboard with pearl 'S' special inlay, Lo Pro Edge double locking tremolo, 6-on-a-side tuners, gold hardware, humbucker/single coil/humbucker IBZ pickups, volume/tone control, 5-position switch. Available in Natural finish. Mfg. 1997 to 1999.

$1,599 $1,399 $1,200 $995 $N/A $N/A $N/A
Last MSR was $1,999.

S7420 7-STRING - offset double cutaway mahogany body, 1-piece maple neck with Bubinga reinforcement, Wizard 7 All Access neck, rosewood fingerboard, 22 jumbo frets, Lo TRS7 bridge, 1 ea. IBZ V7-7 and IBZ V8-7 humbucking pickups. Available in Black Pearl finish. Current Mfg.

MSR $1,299 $975 $875 $775 $675 $550 $450 $350

S5407 7-STRING - sculpted thin offset double cutaway mahogany body, bolt-on maple neck, 7-string configuration, 22-fret rosewood fingerboard with pearl dot inlay, double locking tremolo, 7 on one side tuners, black hardware, 2 single coil/humbucker DiMarzio pickups, volume/tone control, 5-position switch. Available in Black finish. Mfg. 1991 to 1992.

$900 $750 $675 $595 $525 $425 $350
Last MSR was $1,300.

Series II Series (1975 to 1977)

Ibanez had a number of upscale models in the mid 1970s, but it is estimated that only a small number of these models were produced. The **Artwood Nouveau**, perhaps inspired by Ibanez' Rex Bogue-derived **Model 2670**, was a Strat copy with a carved mahogany body and carved headstock. The intriguing **Custom Agent (Model 2405)** featured a bound, ornate Les Paul body and notched headstock. **Custom Agent** models had a retail list price of $448 in 1976. The **Black Eagle Bass** was a Jazz Bass model with maple fingerboard and pearl inlaid pickguard with eagle inlay design.

Talman Series

When this series first debuted in 1994, the bodies were made out of Resoncast, a composite wood material. Later models feature wood construction.

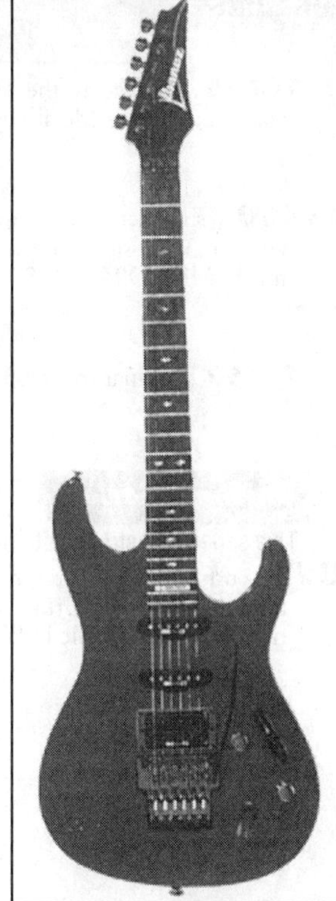

Ibanez 540 S LR
courtesy Ibanez USA

TC420 - offset slight double cutaway basswood body, bolt-on maple neck, 22-fret rosewood fingerboard with pearl dot inlay, Full Action II modern tremolo, 3-per-side tuners, natural wood headstock with screened logo, white pickguard, chrome hardware, 2 chrome cover humbucker pickups, volume/tone control, 3-position switch. Available in Black and Mediterranean Green finishes. Disc. 1999.

$399 $325 $275 $250 $200 $175 $125
Last MSR was $499.

Available in Flaked Silver Metal Flake finish.

$450 $375 $325 $275 $225 $195 $150
Last MSR was $569.

TC420 L - similar to the TC420, except features a left-handed configuration. Available in Mediterranean Green finish. Mfg. 1998 to 1999.

$425 $375 $325 $275 $225 $195 $150
Last MSR was $599.

TC220 - similar to the TC420, except features an agathis body, standard tremolo, 2 exposed pole piece humbucker pickups. Available in Black and Deep Green finishes. Mfg. 1998 to 1999.

$275 $250 $225 $195 $150 $125 $100
Last MSR was $399.

TC5300 - offset double cutaway body, cream pickguard, bolt-on figured maple neck, 22-fret rosewood fingerboard with pearl dot inlay, standard vibrato, 3-per-side tuners, chrome hardware, 3 single coil *lipstick tube* pickups, volume/tone control, 5-position switch. Mfg. 1994 to 1996.

Available in Azure Blue Burst and Royal Orangeburst finishes.

$375 $300 $270 $240 $215 $185 $150
Last MSR was $600.

Available in Black and Pale Blue finishes.

$350 $275 $250 $220 $195 $170 $140
Last MSR was $550.

Available in Gravure Flame Amber finish.

$400 $325 $295 $260 $230 $200 $165
Last MSR was $660.

TC630 - offset slight double cutaway light ash body, bolt-on maple neck, 22-fret rosewood fingerboard with pearl dot inlay, TT50 vintage-style tremolo, 3-per side tuners, natural wood headstock with screened logo, white pearloid pickguard, chrome hardware, 3 single coil *lipstick tube* pickups, volume/tone controls, 5-position switch. Available in Black and Ivory (w/red tortoiseshell pickguard) finishes. Disc. 1998.

$525 $450 $395 $325 $275 $225 $175
Last MSR was $669.

TC740 - similar to the TC630, except features alder body, Gotoh 510AT tremolo, 2 single coil *lipstick tube* chrome cover humbucker pickups. Available in Black and Mint Green finishes. Disc 1999.

$650 $525 $450 $395 $325 $275 $200
Last MSR was $799.

Ibanez Custom Agent
courtesy Glen Perkins

GRADING	100% MINT	98% NEAR MINT	95% EXC+	90% EXC	80% VG+	70% VG	60% G

TC825 - similar to the TC630, except features Bigsby tremolo, 2 chrome cover humbucker pickups, 3-position selector. Available in Flaked Blue and Flaked Silver Metal Flake finishes. Disc. 1999.

	$750	$625	$550	$475	$395	$325	$250

Last MSR was $949.

TV650 - single cutaway bound body, 3-layer white pickguard, bolt-on figured maple neck, 22-fret rosewood fingerboard with pearl dot inlay, standard vibrato, 3-per-side tuners, gold hardware, humbucker/single coil/humbucker pickups, volume/tone control, 5-position switch. Available in White finish. Mfg. 1994 to 1996.

	$425	$350	$325	$275	$250	$200	$175

Last MSR was $700.

TV750 - similar to TV650, except has unbound body. Available in Gravure Quilted Brown Sunburst finish. Mfg. 1994 to 1996.

	$400	$325	$300	$250	$225	$200	$175

Last MSR was $700.

Universe Series

This series of 7-string guitar models was co-designed by Steve Vai, and debuted in 1990.

UV7 - offset double cutaway basswood body, bolt-on maple neck, 24-fret rosewood fingerboard with pearl dot inlay, Lo Pro Edge 7 double locking tremolo, 7-on-a-side tuners, black pickguard, chrome hardware, humbucker/single coil/humbucker DiMarzio pickups, volume/tone control, 5-position switch. Available in Black finish. Mfg. 1990 to 1998.

	$1,400	$1,200	$1,000	$950	$825	$650	$500

Last MSR was $1,999.

UV7 P - similar to UV7, except has white pickguard, pearl abalone pyramid inlay. Available in White finish. Disc. 1994.

	$1,100	$850	$750	$675	$595	$525	$450

Last MSR was $1,700.

UV77 - similar to UV7, except has 3 color pyramid inlay. Available in Multi-colored finish. Disc. 1994.

	$1,300	$1,100	$1,000	$895	$775	$650	$550

Last MSR was $2,200.

UV777 - similar to UV7, except features *disappearing pyramid* fingerboard inlay. Available in Black finish. Current Mfg.

MSR $2,099	$1,675	$1,350	$1,200	$1,000	$850	$695	$525

USA Custom Exotic Wood Series

The Ibanez Custom Shop was moved to North Hollywood, California in 1990. Ibanez **Made in USA** and **American Master** models are produced at this location.

UCEWFM (FLAME MAPLE) & UCEWQM (QUILTED MAPLE) - offset double cutaway mahogany body, highly figured maple top, bolt-on bird's-eye maple neck, 24-fret rosewood fingerboard with pearl dot inlay, double locking tremolo, 6-on-a-side tuners, black hardware, humbucker/Ibanez single coil/DiMarzio humbucker pickups, volume/tone control, 5-position switch. Available in Natural, Transparent Blue, Transparent Ebony, and Transparent Purple finishes. Mfg. 1992 only.

	$1,100	$900	$825	$740	$660	$575	$500

Last MSR was $1,700.

USA Custom Graphic Series

This series was produced in 1992 only.

92 UCGR1 - offset double cutaway basswood body, bolt-on maple neck, 24-fret bound rosewood fingerboard with sharktooth inlay, double locking tremolo, 6-on-a-side tuners, bound peghead, black hardware, DiMarzio single coil/Ibanez humbucker pickups, volume/tone control. Available in "Ice World" finish.

	$950	$825	$750	$675	$595	$525	$425

Last MSR was $1,550.

92 UCGR2 - similar to 92UCGR1, except has reverse headstock, DiMarzio humbucker/Ibanez single coil/DiMarzio humbucker pickups. Available in "No Bones About It" finish.

	$1,000	$850	$775	$695	$625	$525	$450

Last MSR was $1,600.

92 UCGR3 - similar to 92UCGR1, except has reverse headstock, 2 Ibanez humbucker pickups. Available in "Grim Reaper" finish.

	$950	$825	$750	$675	$595	$525	$425

Last MSR was $1,550.

92 UCGR4 - similar to 92UCGR1, except has unbound fingerboard with pearl dot inlay, DiMarzio humbucker/Ibanez single coil/DiMarzio humbucker pickups. Available in "Angel Depart" finish.

	$950	$825	$750	$675	$595	$525	$425

Last MSR was $1,550.

92 UCGR5 - similar to 92UCGR1, except has unbound maple fingerboard with black dot inlay, DiMarzio single coil/humbucker pickups. Available in "Unzipped" finish.

	$925	$800	$725	$650	$550	$475	$400

Last MSR was $1,500.

92 UCGR6 - similar to 92UCGR1, except has unbound rosewood fingerboard with pearl dot inlay, DiMarzio humbucker/Ibanez single coil/DiMarzio humbucker pickups. Available in "Sea Monster" finish.

	$950	$825	$750	$675	$595	$525	$425

Last MSR was $1,550.

GRADING	100% MINT	98% NEAR MINT	95% EXC+	90% EXC	80% VG+	70% VG	60% G

92 UCGR7 - similar to 92UCGR1, except has reverse headstock, DiMarzio humbucker/Ibanez single coil/DiMarzio humbucker pickups. Available in "Alien's Revenge" finish.

$1,000	$850	$775	$695	$625	$525	$450

Last MSR was $1,600.

92 UCGR8 - similar to 92UCGR1, except has unbound maple fingerboard with black dot inlay, 2 DiMarzio humbucker pickups. Available in Cosmic Swirl II finish.

$925	$800	$725	$650	$550	$475	$400

Last MSR was $1,500.

Voyager Series

The Voyager Series was co-designed by Reb Beach, and was introduced in 1991.

RBM1 - offset double cutaway mahogany body with vibrato *wedge* cutaway, metal pickguard, bolt-on maple neck, 22-fret rosewood fingerboard with pearl dot inlay, double locking tremolo, 6-on-a-side tuners, gold hardware, 2 single coil/humbucker pickups, volume control, 5-position switch. Available in Black, Blue, or Candy Apple finishes. Mfg. 1991 to 1994.

$725	$600	$550	$475	$425	$350	$300

Last MSR was $1,200.

RBM2 - similar to RBM1, except has koa top, Bolivian rosewood neck/fingerboard. Available in Natural finish. Disc. 1994.

$1,200	$1,000	$925	$850	$725	$625	$525

Last MSR was $2,100.

RBM10 - offset double cutaway mahogany body with lower wedge cutaway, metal control plate, bolt-on maple neck, 22-fret rosewood fingerboard with pearl dot inlay, double locking tremolo, 6-on-a-side tuners, gold hardware, 2 single coil/humbucker pickups, volume control, 5-position switch. Available in Black and Emerald Green finishes. Mfg. 1994 to 1996.

$475	$400	$350	$325	$275	$250	$200

Last MSR was $800.

RBM400 - similar to RBM10, except has Bolivian rosewood neck/fingerboard, clay dot fingerboard inlay, Ibanez pickups. Available in Oil finish. Mfg. 1994 to 1996.

$900	$750	$675	$600	$525	$450	$375

Last MSR was $1,500.

Ibanez UV 7 BK
courtesy Ibanez USA

ELECTRIC BASS

Ibanez' Jump Start Packages include an electric bass guitar, bass amplifier, gig bag, instructional video, digital auto tuner, strap, cable, picks, and a free subscription to Plugged In (the official Ibanez newsletter).

TR50BK (IJSTR50 JUMP START PACKAGE) - offset double cutaway agathis body, bolt-on maple neck, 22-fret maple fingerboard with black dot inlay, fixed bridge, 4-on-a-side tuners, chrome hardware, black pickguard, P-style pickup, volume/tone controls. Available in Black and Blue Night finishes. Mfg. 1997 only.

$400	$325	$275	$N/A	$N/A	$N/A	$N/A

Last MSR was $499.

JUMP START PACKAGE (IJSB70) - offset double cutaway agathis body, bolt-on maple neck, 22-fret rosewood fingerboard with pearl dot inlay, fixed bridge, 4-on-a-side tuners, chrome hardware, P-style pickup, volume/tone controls. Available in Black and Jewel Blue finishes. Mfg. 1998 to 1999.

$385	$325	$295	$250	$225	$195	$150

Last MSR was $479.

Affirma Series

This series was designed by Swiss luthier, Rolf Spuler. His design incorporates a neck that extends half-way through the body with individual bridges for each string. There is a thumb slot, a pearl/abalone *AFR* insignia, and a pearl block with Ibanez and the serial number inscriptions inlaid into the body, located between the single coil pickup and the bridge system. All models are available in a fretless configuration at no additional charge.

A104 - offset double cutaway asymmetrical saman (or kralo walnut or flame maple) body, maple neck, 24-fret ebony fingerboard with offset pearl inlay at 12th fret, 4 *Mono Rail* bridges, tuning lever on low string bridge, body matching peghead veneer, 2-per-side tuners, black hardware, single coil/4 bridge piezo pickups, volume/concentric treble/bass/mix controls, active electronics. Available in Natural finish. Mfg. 1991 to 1993.

$1,200	$1,000	$900	$800	$700	$600	$500

Last MSR was $1,900.

A105 - similar to A104, except has 5 strings, 5 Mono Rail bridges, 3/2-per-side tuners. Mfg. 1991 to 1993.

$1,400	$1,150	$1,000	$900	$795	$675	$550

Last MSR was $2,000.

ATK Bass Series

ATK Series basses were introduced in 1995.

Ibanez 92 UCGR 1
courtesy Ibanez USA

GRADING		100% MINT	98% NEAR MINT	95% EXC+	90% EXC	80% VG+	70% VG	60% G

ATK300 - offset double cutaway light ash body, bolt-on 3-piece maple neck, 22-fret maple fingerboard with black dot inlay, ATK Custom *surround* fixed bridge, 2-per-side tuners, chrome hardware, triple coil pickup, volume/3-band EQ tone controls, *pickup character* mini switch. Available in Black and Vintage Burst finishes. Disc. 1999.

		$525	$450	$395	$350	$275	$225	$195
						Last MSR was $749.		

ATK305 - similar to the ATK300, except in a 5-string configuration, 2/3-per-side tuners. Disc. 1999.

		$595	$500	$450	$395	$325	$275	$225
						Last MSR was $849.		

BTB Bass Series

BTB500 - offset double cutaway ash body, 4-string, 35" scale, 3-piece maple neck, rosewood fingerboard with Pearl Dot position markers, 24 medium frets, Mono-Rail II bridge, 1 ea. IBZ DFR-N and IBZ DFR-B pickups. Available in Walnut Flat finish. Current Mfg.

MSR	$999	$749	$649	$549	$499	$450	$399	$350

BTB505 - similar to Model BTB500, except in a 5-string configuration. Available in Walnut Flat and Transparent Flat Black finishes. Current Mfg.

MSR	$1,149	$865	$775	$675	$625	$575	$525	$475

CT Bass Series

CTB1 - offset double cutaway maple body, bolt-on 3-piece maple neck, 22-fret rosewood fingerboard with pearl dot inlay, die-cast fixed bridge, 2-per-side tuners, chrome hardware, P/J-style Ibanez pickups, 2 volume/tone controls. Available in Black, Blue Night, Red, and White finishes. Mfg. 1992 only.

		$275	$225	$200	$175	$150	$125	$115
						Last MSR was $450.		

Add $50 for left-handed configuration (Model CTB1L).

CTB3 - similar to CTB1, except has CT Custom fingerboard inlay, black hardware, 2 volume/tone controls. Available in Black, Blue Night, Natural, and Transparent Red finishes. Disc. 1992.

		$350	$300	$275	$250	$225	$175	$150
						Last MSR was $600.		

CTB5 - similar to CTB1 except features CT Custom fingerboard inlay, 5-string configuration, 3/2-per-side tuners, black hardware, 2 J-style EMG pickups, 2 volume/tone controls. Available in Black, Natural, and Transparent Red finishes. Mfg. 1992 only.

		$425	$350	$325	$275	$250	$225	$195
						Last MSR was $700.		

Doug Wimbish Signature Models

DWB-1 - offset double cutaway maple body, 4-string, 5-piece maple/Bubinga neck-thru body, rosewood fingerboard with abalone/pearl position markers, Accu-Cast B20 bridge, 1 ea. IBZ AFR-P and IBZ AFR-J pickups, gold hardware. Available in Transparent Blue finish. Current Mfg.

MSR	$2,999	$2,249	$2,049	$1,849	$1,649	$1,449	$1,249	$1,049

DWB-2 - similar to Model DWB-1, except has bolt-on 3-piece maple neck. Available in Royal Wine Sunburst finish. Current Mfg.

MSR	$1,699	$1,275	$1,075	$875	$750	$695	$650	$595

Gary Willis 5 String Signature Models

GWB1 -offset double cutaway Swamp Ash body, 3-piece maple neck, ebony fretless fingerboard, pearl dot position markers, STD-5 bridge, 1 ea. Bartolini GW and Bartolini NTBT pickups, black hardware. Available in Natural Flat finish. Current Mfg.

MSR	$1,899	$1,425	$1,225	$1,125	$1,025	$925	$825	$725

GWB2 - similar to Model GWB1, except has 24 medium frets. Available in Transparent Black Flat finish. Current Mfg.

MSR	$1,799	$1,349	$1,149	$1,049	$950	$850	$750	$650

Ergodyne Series

Ergodyne Series basses feature **Luthite**, a light weight synthetic body material.

EDB300 - offset double cutaway rounded Luthite body, bolt-on one-piece maple neck, 24-fret rosewood fingerboard with pearl dot inlay, standard fixed bridge, 2-per-side tuners, chrome hardware, 2 Ibanez DX 'soapbar' pickups, 2 volume/tone controls. Available in Black and Jewel Blue finishes. Disc. 1998.

		$450	$350	$325	$275	$225	$175	$150
						Last MSR was $549.		

EDB350 - similar to the EDB300, except features one Ibanez DX pickup, Accu-Cast B20 bridge, black hardware, *Phat* bass boost circuitry. Disc. 1998.

		$500	$425	$375	$325	$275	$225	$175
						Last MSR was $629.		

EDB400 - similar to the EDB300, except features Accu-Cast B20 bridge, black hardware, 2 volume/3-band EQ controls. Available in Black and Jewel Blue finishes. Disc. 1998.

		$525	$450	$395	$325	$275	$225	$175
						Last MSR was $679.		

GRADING	100% MINT	98% NEAR MINT	95% EXC+	90% EXC	80% VG+	70% VG	60% G

EDB405 - similar to the EDB400, except features a 5-string configuration, 3/2-per-side headstock. Disc. 1998.

$575 $525 $450 $395 $325 $250 $200

Last MSR was $799.

EDB500 - offset double cutaway rounded Luthite body with "slap contour area", bolt-on one-piece maple neck, 24-fret rosewood fingerboard with pearl dot inlay, standard fixed bridge, 2-per-side tuners, black hardware, 2 IBZ DXH 'soapbar' pickups, 2 volume/bass/treble controls, PHAT Bass boost active EQ. Available in Gray Pewter matte finish. Mfg. 1998 to date.

MSR $579 $425 $350 $315 $275 $225 $195 $150

EDB600 - similar to the EDB300, except features Accu-Cast B20 bridge, chrome hardware, 2 volume/3-band EQ controls. Available in Gray Pewter and Mystique Purple matte finishes. Mfg. 1998 to date.

MSR $679 $545 $440 $390 $335 $280 $225 $170

EDB605 5-String - similar to the EDB300, except features 5-string configuration, 3/2-per-side tuners, Accu-Cast B25 bridge, 2 volume/3-band EQ controls. Available in Gray Pewter and Mocca matte finishes. Mfg. 1998 to date.

MSR $799 $550 $475 $425 $375 $300 $250 $200

EDB690 - offset double cutaway Luthite body, 5-piece maple and Bubinga neck, rosewood fingerboard with Pearl dot position markers, 24 medium frets, 2-per-side tuners, Accu-Cast B20 bridge, 2 IBZ DXH hign output humbuckers, 3-band active EQ. Available in Burled Art Grain finish. Current Mfg.

MSR $799 $599 $499 $450 $399 $350 $299 $250

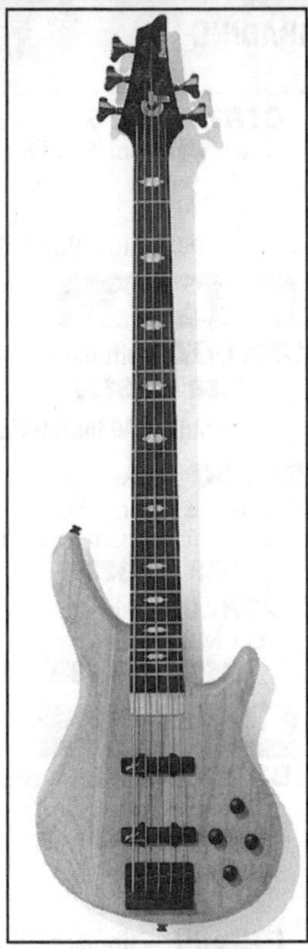

Ibanez CT B5 NT
courtesy Ibanez USA

Ergodyne Contemporary Series

The Ergodyne Contemporary Series models have sleeker bodies than the regular Ergodyne series models, with two contoured areas on the top, extended bass horn, and indented areas under the controls.

EDC700 - sleek offset double cutaway rounded Luthite body with "slap contour areas", bolt-on one-piece maple neck, 24-fret rosewood fingerboard with pearl dot inlay, Accu-Cast B20 bridge, 2-per-side tuners, chrome hardware, 2 IBZ SFR 'soapbar' pickups, 2 volume/bass/treble/Vari-mid controls. Available in Black Pearl and Night Navy finishes. Mfg. 1998 to date.

MSR $849 $600 $525 $475 $400 $350 $295 $225

EDC705 5-String - similar to the EDC700, except features 5-string configuration, 3/2-per-side tuners, Accu-Cast B25 bridge, black hardware, 2 volume/3-band EQ controls. Available in Black Pearl finishes. Mfg. 1998 to date.

MSR $949 $695 $575 $500 $450 $375 $325 $250

EX Bass Series

EXB404 - offset double cutaway maple body, bolt-on 3-piece maple neck, 22-fret rosewood fingerboard with pearl dot inlay, die-cast fixed bridge, 4-on-a-side tuners, chrome hardware, P/J-style pickups, 2 volume/tone controls. Available in Black, Burgundy Red, Crimson Metallic, and Jewel Blue finishes. Disc. 1996.

$275 $225 $200 $180 $160 $135 $115

Last MSR was $450.

Add $50 for left-handed configuration (Model EXB404L). Available in Black finish.

EXB445 - similar to the EXB404, except features 5-string configuration, 4/1 per side tuners, black hardware, 2 J-style EMG pickups. Available in Black, Burgundy Red, and Jewel Blue finishes. Disc. 1996.

$325 $275 $250 $220 $190 $165 $140

Last MSR was $550.

GTR Bass Series

The TR50, TR70, and TR75 models were originally part of the TR Series between 1994 to 1997. In 1998, these models were redesignated the GTR Bass Series models.

GTR50 (TR50) - offset double cutaway agathis body, bolt-on maple neck, 22-fret maple fingerboard with pearl dot inlay, standard fixed bridge, 4-on-a-side tuners, chrome hardware, black pickguard, split P-style pickup, volume/tone controls. Available in Black, Blue Night, and Deep Green finishes. Mfg. 1994 to 1999.

$200 $175 $150 $135 $115 $95 $65

Last MSR was $259.

Add $140 for left-handed configuration (Model GTR50 L). Available in Black finish only.

In 1998, Jewel Blue and Metallic Green finishes were introduced; Blue Night and Deep Green finishes were discontinued.

GTR70 (TR70) - similar to TR50, except features P/J-style pickups. Available in Black, Blue Night, and Deep Green finishes. Disc. 1999.

$240 $195 $175 $150 $125 $100 $75

Last MSR was $299.

In 1998, Jewel Blue finish was introduced; Blue Night and Deep Green finishes were discontinued.

Ibanez EXB 445 BR
courtesy Ibanez USA

GRADING	100% MINT	98% NEAR MINT	95% EXC+	90% EXC	80% VG+	70% VG	60% G

GTR75 (TR75) - similar to TR50, except features 5-string configuration, 4/1 per side headstock, 2 IBZ J-style pickups. Available in Black and Blue Night finishes. Disc. 1999.

$375	$300	$265	$225	$190	$155	$115

Last MSR was $459.

In 1998, Blue Night finish was discontinued.

GSR Series

GSR100Z - similar to Model GSR200, except has 1 PSND-P pickup. Available in Black and Metallic Blue finishes. Current Mfg.

MSR	$259	$195	$175	$150	$125	$95	$75	$50

Add $140 for Left Hand configuration (Model GSR 100L).

GSR200 - offset double cutaway Agatis body, 4 string, 1-piece maple neck, roswood fingerboard with pearl dot position markers, 22 medium frets, 2-per-side tuners, Standard 4-string bridge, 1 ea. PSND-P and PSND-J pickups, chrome hardware. Available in Black, Jewel Blue and Transparent Red finishes. Current Mfg.

MSR	$299	$225	$195	$175	$150	$125	$95	$65

GSR205 - similar to Model GSR200, except in a 5-string configuarion, Standard 5-String bridge, 2 IBZ J5 pickups. Available in Black finish. Current Mfg.

MSR	$459	$345	$295	$250	$225	$195	$150	$99

Iceman Series

ICB300 - single horn cutaway asymmetrical mahogany body with pointed bottom bout, raised cream pickguard, bolt-on maple neck, 22-fret bound rosewood fingerboard with pearl dot inlay, fixed die-cast bridge, 2-per-side tuners, chrome hardware, 2 Ibanez pickups, 2 volume/tone controls, 3-position switch. Available in Black and Blue finishes. Mfg. 1994 to 1996.

$350	$300	$275	$250	$200	$175	$150

Last MSR was $580.

ICB500 - similar to the ICB300, except features pearloid bound mahogany body, raised pearloid pickguard, 22-fret bound rosewood fingerboard with abalone dot inlay, bound blackface peghead with pearl logo inlay, cosmo black hardware. Available in Black finish. Mfg. 1994 to 1996.

$850	$700	$625	$550	$475	$400	$325

Last MSR was $1,300.

S Bass Series

SB1500 - offset double cutaway bubinga (or padauk or wenge) body, bolt-on 5-piece bubinga/wenge neck, 22-fret ebony fingerboard with abalone oval inlays, AccuCast-B bridge, 4-on-a-side tuners, chrome hardware, P/J-style EMG pickups, 2 volume/tone controls, active electronics. Available in Natural finish. Mfg. 1992 only.

$900	$750	$675	$595	$500	$425	$350

Last MSR was $1,500.

SB1200 - similar to the SB1500, except features a mahogany body. Available in Black, Blue, and White finishes. Mfg. 1992 only.

$800	$725	$625	$500	$400	$375	$300

Last MSR was $1,200.

Soundgear Bass Series

Soundgear Series basses were introduced in 1987, and feature the *SD GR* by Ibanez logo on their headstocks.

SR300 - sleek offset double cutaway agathis body, bolt-on 3-piece maple neck, 24-fret rosewood fingerboard with pearl dot inlay, standard fixed bridge, 2-per-side tuners, chrome hardware, P/J-style Ibanez DX pickups, 2 volume/tone controls. Available in Black, Blue Night, and Metallic Green finishes. Disc. 1999.

$325	$250	$225	$200	$175	$125	$100

Last MSR was $399.

Add $100 for left-handed configuration (Model SR300 L). Available in Black finish.

In 1998, Natural finish was introduced; Blue Night and Metallic Green finishes were discontinued; the left-handed option was discontinued.

SR300 DX - similar to the SR300, except features *Phat* bass boost circuitry. Available in Black and Metallic Green finishes. Current Mfg.

MSR	$459	$375	$300	$275	$225	$195	$150	$125

Add $100 for left-handed configuration (Model SR300DXL). Available in Black finish.

In 1998, Jewel Blue finish was introduced, Metallic Green finish was discontinued.

SR305 - similar to the SR300, except features a 5-string configuration, 3/2-per-side tuners, 2 Ibanez DX 'soapbar' pickups. Available in Black and Blue Night finishes. Mfg. 1997 to 1999.

$399	$325	$295	$250	$225	$195	$165

Last MSR was $499.

In 1998, Natural finish was introduced, Blue Night finish was discontinued.

SR305 DX - similar to the SR305, except features *Phat* bass boost circuitry. Available in Black and Metallic Green finishes. Current Mfg.

MSR	$549	$450	$350	$325	$275	$225	$195	$150

In 1998, Jewel Blue finish was introduced, Metallic Green finish was discontinued.

GRADING		100% MINT	98% NEAR MINT	95% EXC+	90% EXC	80% VG+	70% VG	60% G

SR390 - offset double cutaway ash body, bolt-on 3-piece maple neck, 24-fret rosewood fingerboard with pearl dot inlay, standard fixed bridge, 2-per-side tuners, black hardware, 2 IBZ DX 'soapbar' pickups, 2 volume/tone controls, *Phat* bass boost circuitry. Available in Butterscotch and Transparent Red finishes. Mfg. 1998 to 1999.

		$450	$375	$325	$295	$250	$200	$150

Last MSR was $529.

SR400 - offset double cutaway soft maple body, bolt-on 3-piece maple neck, 24-fret rosewood fingerboard with pearl dot inlay, die-cast fixed bridge, 2-per-side tuners, black hardware, P/J-style Ibanez DX pickups, 2 volume/3-band EQ tone controls. Available in Black, Jewel Blue, Mediterranean Green, and Natural finishes. Mfg. 1993 to date.

MSR	$599	$475	$395	$350	$295	$250	$200	$150

Add $50 for left-handed configuration (Model SR400 L) or fretless fingerboard (Model SR400 FL). Both models were only available in a Black finish.

Early models may feature Candy Apple and Crimson Metallic finishes.
In 1997, the left-handed configuration and fretless fingerboard option were both discontinued.
In 1998, Royal Blue finish was introduced, Jewel Blue and Mediterranean Green finishes were discontinued.

SR405 - similar to SR400, except has 5-string configuration, 3/2-per-side tuners, 2 Ibanez DX 'soapbar' pickups. Available in Black, Jewel Blue, and Natural finishes. Mfg. 1994 to date.

MSR	$699	$550	$475	$400	$350	$295	$225	$175

In 1998, Royal Blue finish was introduced, Jewel Blue finish was discontinued.

SR406 - similar to SR400, except has 6-string configuration, 3-per-side tuners, 2 Ibanez DX 'soapbar' pickups. Available in Black finish. Current Mfg.

MSR	$799	$650	$525	$450	$395	$325	$275	$200

In 1998, Natural finish was introduced.

SR480 - offset double cutaway mahogany body, 4-string, 5-piece maple/Wenga neck, rosewood fingerboard with pearl dot position markers, 24 medium frets, Die Cast 4-String bridge, 1 IBZ DXP pickup and 1 IBZ DXJ pickup, EQBIII 3-band active EQ, black hardware. Available in Stained Oil finish. Current Mfg.

MSR	$699	$525	$475	$425	$375	$325	$275	$225

SR485 - similar to Model SR480, except in a 5-string configuration, Die Cast 5-String bridge. Available in Stained Oil finish. Current Mfg.

MSR	$799	$599	$499	$450	$399	$350	$299	$250

SR500 - offset double cutaway maple body, bolt-on 3-piece maple neck, 24-fret rosewood fingerboard with pearl dot inlay, fixed bridge, 2-per-side tuners, black hardware, P/J-style active Ibanez pickups, volume/treble/bass/mix controls, active electronics. Available in Black, Emerald Green, Jewel Blue, Natural, and Transparent Turquoise finishes. Mfg. 1993 to 1996.

		$425	$350	$325	$275	$250	$225	$175

Last MSR was $700.

Add $50 for left-handed configuration (Model SR500 L), available in Black finish.

SR505 - similar to SR500, except has 5-string configuration, 3/2-per-side tuners, 2 J-style EMG pickups. Available in Black, Natural, Transparent Red, and Transparent Turquoise finishes. Mfg. 1993.

		$500	$400	$375	$335	$275	$250	$200

Last MSR was $800.

SR506 - similar to SR500, except has 6-string configuration, 3-per-side tuners, 2 Ibanez ADX active humbucker pickups, Vari-Mid 3-band EQ. Available in Black and Natural finishes. Mfg. 1994 to 1998.

		$750	$625	$575	$495	$425	$325	$250

Last MSR was $999.

SR590 - similar to SR500, except has gold hardware. Available in Natural and Transparent Turquoise finishes. Mfg. 1994 to 1996.

		$450	$375	$350	$300	$250	$225	$195

Last MSR was $750.

SR800 - offset double cutaway basswood body, bolt-on 3-piece maple neck, 24-fret rosewood fingerboard with pearl dot inlay, AccuCast B20 (formerly B IV) bridge, 2-per-side tuners, black hardware, P/J-style Ibanez AFR pickups, volume/blend/Vari-mid 3-band EQ controls. Available in Black, Dark Metallic Green, and Metallic Blue finishes. Current Mfg.

MSR	$799	$640	$525	$460	$395	$330	$265	$200

Add $100 for fretless fingerboard version (Model SR800 F). Mfg. 1992 only.

Add $150 for left handed version (Model SR800 L). Disc. 1994.

Early models may feature Candy Apple, Cayman Green, Jewel Blue, and Royal Blue finishes.
In 1998, Arctic Blue and Cherry Fudge finishes were introduced; Dark Metallic Green and Metallic Blue finishes were discontinued.

SR800 A - similar to SR800, except has ash body. Available in Amber and Transparent Black finishes. Mfg. 1997 to 1999.

		$625	$550	$495	$425	$350	$295	$225

Last MSR was $849.

GRADING		100% MINT	98% NEAR MINT	95% EXC+	90% EXC	80% VG+	70% VG	60% G

SR885 - similar to SR800, except has 5-string configuration, 3/2-per-side tuners, AccuCast B25 bridge, 2 Ibanez ADX active pickups. Available in Black and Metallic Blue finishes. Mfg. 1991 to date.

MSR	$949	$760	$625	$550	$475	$395	$325	$240

Early models may feature Candy Apple, Laser Blue, and Royal Blue finishes.
In 1998, Arctic Blue finish was introduced, Metallic Blue finish was discontinued.

SR886 - similar to SR885, except has 6-string configuration, 3-per-side tuners. Available in Black and Candy Apple finishes. Mfg. 1992 only.

$850 $700 $625 $550 $495 $425 $350
Last MSR was $1,400.

SR890 - offset double cutaway ash body, bolt-on 3-piece maple neck, 24-fret rosewood fingerboard with pearl dot inlay, fixed bridge, 2-per-side tuners, gold hardware, P/J-style Ibanez active pickups, volume/treble/2 mid/bass/mix controls. Available in Transparent Cherry and Transparent Turquoise finishes. Mfg. 1993 only.

$650 $550 $475 $425 $375 $300 $250
Last MSR was $1,000.

SR895 - similar to SR890, except has 5-string configuration, 3/2-per-side tuners. Mfg. 1993 only.

$750 $625 $550 $500 $425 $375 $300
Last MSR was $1,200.

SR900 - similar to the SR890, except features an AccuCast-B bridge, P/J-style Ibanez pickups, 2 volume/tone controls. Available in Emerald Green and Purple Neon finishes. Mfg. 1992 only.

$550 $450 $400 $350 $325 $275 $225
Last MSR was $900.

SR950 - similar to SR900, except has ebony fingerboard with abalone oval inlay, gold hardware. Available in Transparent Cherry and Transparent Turquoise finishes.

$675 $550 $500 $450 $395 $325 $275
Last MSR was $1,000.

SR990 QS - offset double cutaway mahogany body, quilted sapele top, bolt-on 5-piece bubinga/wenge neck, 24-fret wenge fingerboard with abalone oval inlay, AccuCast B20 bridge, 2-per-side tuners, chrome hardware, Ibanez P/J-style AFR pickups, volume/blend/Vari-mid 3-band EQ controls. Available in Stained Oil finish. Mfg. 1998 to 1999.

$695 $575 $525 $450 $375 $325 $250
Last MSR was $949.

SR1010 - offset double cutaway mahogany body, bolt-on 5-piece bubinga/wenge neck, 24-fret wenge fingerboard with abalone oval inlay, AccuCast B20 (previously B IV) bridge, 2-per-side tuners, chrome hardware, Ibanez P/J-style AFR pickups, volume/blend/Vari-mid 3-band EQ controls. Available in Stained Oil finish. Disc. 1999.

$850 $725 $625 $550 $450 $375 $275
Last MSR was $1,099.

In 1998, SFR pickups replaced AFR pickups.

SR1015 - similar to SR1010, except has 5-string configuration, 3/2-per-side tuners, AccuCast B25 bridge, 2 Ibanez ADX humbucker pickups. Available in Stained Oil finish. Disc. 1999.

$1,000 $895 $750 $650 $525 $425 $325
Last MSR was $1,249.

In 1998, SFR pickups replaced ADX pickups.

SR1016 - similar to SR1300, except has 6-string configuration, 3-per-side tuners, die-cast bridge, black hardware, 2 Ibanez ADX humbucker pickups. Available in Stained Oil finish. Disc. 1999.

$1,100 $950 $795 $675 $575 $450 $350
Last MSR was $1,349.

In 1998, DXP pickups replaced ADX pickups.

SR1200 - offset double cutaway mahogany body, figured maple top, through body 5-piece bubinga/wenge neck, 24-fret rosewood fingerboard with abalone oval inlay, die-cast bridge, 2-per-side tuners, black hardware, Ibanez P/J-style AFR pickups, volume/blend/Vari-mid 3-band EQ controls. Available in Butterscotch Transparent and Natural and finishes. Mfg. 1994 to 1998.

$925 $750 $675 $595 $495 $400 $300
Last MSR was $1,199.

SR1205 - similar to SR1200, except has 5-string configuration, 3/2-per-side tuners, 2 Ibanez ADX humbucker pickups. Available in Butterscotch Transparent and Natural finishes. Mfg. 1994 to 1998.

$1,000 $900 $795 $675 $575 $450 $350
Last MSR was $1,349.

SR1300 - offset double cutaway padauk body, bolt-on 5-piece bubinga/wenge neck, 24-fret wenge fingerboard with pearl dot inlay, fixed bridge, 2-per-side tuners, cosmo black hardware, P/J-style Ibanez pickups, volume/treble/2 mid/bass/mix controls. Available in Oil finish. Disc. 1996.

$900 $750 $675 $595 $525 $425 $350
Last MSR was $1,400.

SR1305 - similar to SR1300, except has 5-string configuration, 3/2-per-side tuners, 2 Ibanez active humbucker pickups. Disc. 1996.

$1,000 $800 $725 $650 $550 $475 $400
Last MSR was $1,600.

SR1306 - similar to SR1300, except has 6-string configuration, 3-per-side tuners, 2 Ibanez active humbucker pickups. Disc. 1996.

$1,100 $900 $825 $725 $625 $550 $450
Last MSR was $1,800.

GRADING	100% MINT	98% NEAR MINT	95% EXC+	90% EXC	80% VG+	70% VG	60% G

SR1500 - offset double cutaway bubinga or padauk body, bubinga/wenge 5-piece neck, 22-fret ebony fingerboard with pearl dot inlay, fixed bridge, 2-per-side tuners, black hardware, P/J-style EMG pickups, 2 volume/tone controls. Available in Natural finish. Mfg. 1991 to 1992.

$900	$750	$675	$595	$525	$425	$350

Last MSR was $1,400.

SR2000 - offset double cutaway maple body, through body 5-piece maple/walnut neck, 24-fret wenge fingerboard with abalone oval inlay, fixed bridge, 2-per-side tuners, gold hardware, P/J-style Ibanez pickups, volume/treble/2 mid/bass/mix controls. Available in Oil and Transparent Purple finishes. Mfg. 1993 only.

$1,000	$800	$725	$650	$550	$475	$400

Last MSR was $1,600.

SR2005 - similar to SR2000, except has 5-string configuration, 3/2-per-side tuners, 2 J-style Ibanez pickups. Mfg. 1993 only.

$1,200	$1,000	$895	$795	$695	$575	$475

Last MSR was $1,900.

SR5000 SR PRESTIGE - offset double cutaway mahogany/walnut/mahogany body, bolt-on 5-piece bubinga/wenge neck, 24-fret wenge fingerboard with abalone oval inlay, Monorail bridge pieces with 'D-Tuner', 2-per-side tuners, gold hardware, Ibanez P/J-style AFR pickups, volume/blend/Vari-mid 3-band EQ controls. Available in Mahogany finish. Disc. 1999.

$1,550	$1,250	$1,100	$995	$775	$650	$475

Last MSR was $1,899.

In 1998, 2 IBZ SFR 'soapbar' pickups replaced the P/J-style AFR pickups.

SR5005 SR Prestige - similar to SR5000, except has 5-string configuration, 3/2-per-side tuners, 5 Monorail bridge pieces, 2 Ibanez ADX humbucker pickups. Disc. 1999.

$1,599	$1,299	$1,150	$1,000	$800	$675	$500

Last MSR was $1,999.

In 1998, 2 IBZ SFR 'soapbar' pickups replaced the 2 ADX humbucker pickups.

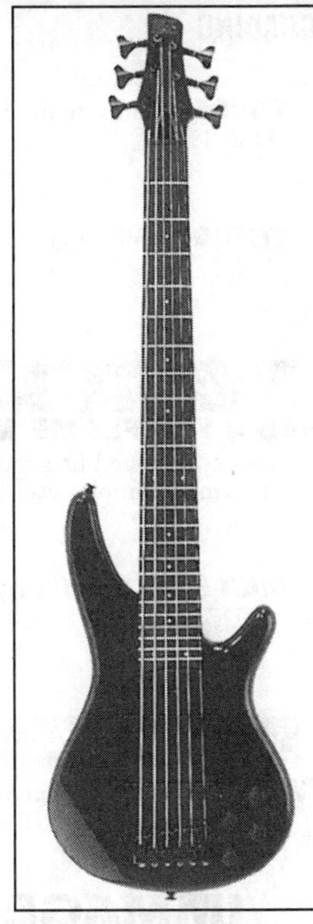

Ibanez SR 886 CA
courtesy Ibanez USA

TR Bass Series

TR Series basses were introduced in 1992, and were originally designated TRB (B for Bass) in the model names.

TRB1 - offset double cutaway alder body, bolt-on maple neck, 22-fret rosewood fingerboard with pearl dot inlay, die cast fixed bridge, 4-on-a-side tuners, black hardware, P/J-style pickups, 2 volume/tone controls. Available in Black, Candy Apple, Jewel Blue, and Transparent Blue finishes. Mfg. 1991 to 1993.

$275	$225	$200	$175	$150	$135	$115

Last MSR was $430.

Add $50 for left-handed version (Model TRB1L), available in Black finish only.

TRB2 - similar to TRB1, except has ash body, gold hardware. Available in Lavender Stain and Walnut Stain finishes. Mfg. 1993 only.

$325	$275	$250	$225	$195	$150	$135

Last MSR was $530.

TRB3 - similar to TRB1, except has basswood body, P/J-style Ibanez pickups, 2 volume/tone controls. Available in Black, Blue and Lipstick Red finishes. Mfg. 1992 only.

$395	$325	$295	$250	$225	$195	$175

Last MSR was $650.

TRB15 - similar to TRB1, except has 5-string configuration, 4/1 per side tuners, 2 J-style pickups. Available in Black and Transparent Red finishes. Mfg. 1993 only.

$325	$275	$250	$225	$195	$150	$125

Last MSR was $530.

TRB100 - offset double cutaway alder body, bolt-on maple neck, 22-fret rosewood fingerboard with pearl dot inlay, fixed bridge, 4-on-a-side tuners, black hardware, P/J-style pickups, volume/tone/mix control. Available in Black, Candy Apple, Jewel Blue, and Transparent Blue finishes. Mfg. 1994 to 1996.

$275	$225	$200	$175	$150	$135	$115

Last MSR was $450.

TRB105 - similar to TRB100, except has 5-string configuration, 4/1 per side tuners, 2 J-style pickups. Available in Black and Transparent Red finishes. Mfg. 1994 to 1996.

$350	$275	$250	$225	$195	$175	$135

Last MSR was $550.

TRB200 - similar to the TRB100, except features an ash body, gold hardware. Available in Lavender Stain and Walnut Stain finishes. Mfg. 1994 to.

$350	$275	$250	$225	$195	$165	$135

Last MSR was $550.

TR500 (TR EXPRESSIONIST) - offset double cutaway alder body, bolt-on maple neck, 22-fret rosewood fingerboard with pearl dot inlay, EB70 Dual Mount bridge, 4-on-a-side tuners, chrome hardware, pickguard, 2 Ibanez PT single coil pickups, volume/tone/3-band EQ controls. Available in Black, Mint Green, and Vintage Burst finishes. Disc. 1998.

$550	$450	$395	$325	$275	$225	$175

Last MSR was $679.

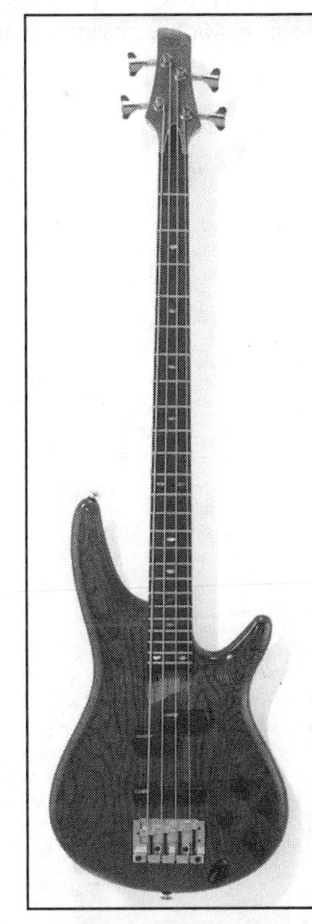

Ibanez SR 950 TT
courtesy Ibanez USA

I

GRADING	100% MINT	98% NEAR MINT	95% EXC+	90% EXC	80% VG+	70% VG	60% G

TR505 - similar to the TR500, except features 5-string configuration, 4/1 per side tuners, tortoiseshell pickguard. Available in Vintage Burst finish. Disc. 1998.

	$650	$525	$450	$395	$325	$275	$200
					Last MSR was $799.		

TR600 - similar to the TR500, except features AccuCast B20 bridge, pearloid pickguard. Available in Cayman Green and Royal Blue finishes. Disc. 1998.

	$650	$525	$450	$395	$325	$275	$200
					Last MSR was $799.		

USA Custom American Master Bass Series

MAB 4 FM (FLAME MAPLE) - offset double cutaway mahogany body, figured maple top, maple/purple heart 3-piece through body neck, 24-fret rosewood fingerboard with pearl dot inlay, Wilkinson fixed bridge, 2-per-side tuners, black hardware, P-style/J-style EMG pickups, 2 volume/tone controls. Available in Natural finish. Disc. 1992.

	$1,500	$1,300	$1,175	$1,050	$925	$775	$650
					Last MSR was $2,600.		

MAB 5 BE (Bird's-eye Maple) - similar to MAB4FM, except has bird's-eye maple top, 5-string configuration, 3/2-per-side tuners. Disc. 1992.

	$1,700	$1,400	$1,275	$1,150	$1,000	$895	$750
					Last MSR was $2,800.		

Verdine White Signature Model

VWB1 - offset double cutaway alder body, 3-piece maple neck, ebony fingerboard with Abalone dot position markers, 24 jumbo frets, Accu-Cast B20 bridge, 1 ea. IBZ AFR-P and IBZ AFR-J pickups, chrome hardware. Available in Cream finish. Current Mfg.

MSR $1,299	$975	$875	$775	$725	$650	$550	$450

I

IMMAGE

Instruments previously built in Taiwan in the mid 1980s.

The Image line consisted of entry level to mid quality designs based on classic American models.

(Source: Tony Bacon and Paul Day, The Guru's Guitar Guide)

IMPERIAL

Instruments previously produced in Italy circa 1963 to 1966 (later models were produced in Japan until circa 1968).

The Imperial trademark is a brand name used by U.S. importer Imperial Accordion Company of Chicago, Illinois. Imperial instruments consisted of solid body electric guitars and basses.

(Source: Michael Wright, Vintage Guitar Magazine)

Section J

GRADING	100% MINT	98% NEAR MINT	95% EXC+	90% EXC	80% VG+	70% VG	60% G

J.B. PLAYER

Instruments currently produced in Asia (specific model Classical guitars are built in Spain). Distributed by MBT International of Charleston, South Carolina.

MBT International, owner of J.B. Player, is the parent company to the Hondo Guitar Company, Musicorp, Engl USA, and MBT Lighting and Sound.

J.B. Player offers a wide range of entry to student level instruments in acoustic or electric solid body guitars and basses. Many higher quality models that are currently offered may appeal to working musicians, and feature such parts as Schaller hardware, Wilkinson bridges, and APC pickups. The current catalog illustrates the four different levels offered: the **JBP Artist**, **Standard**, **Professional**, and **Sledgehammer** series.

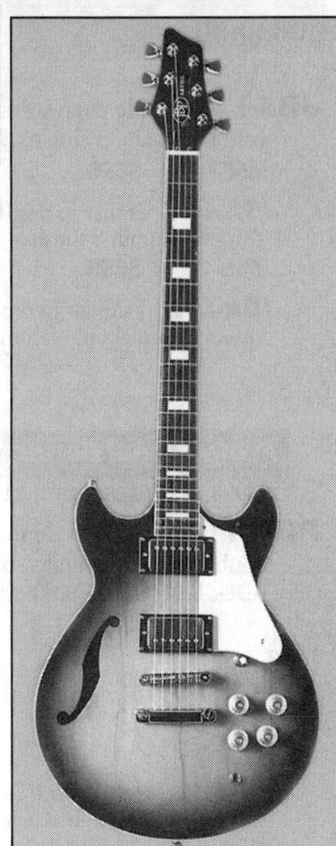

J.B. Player JBA-460
courtesy J.B. Player

ELECTRIC

Artist Series

JB-400-AM - single cutaway semi-hollow body, bound flame maple top, bound 'fang' style soundhole, mahogany back/sides/neck, 22-fret bound ebonized rosewood fingerboard with pearl dot inlay, tune-o-matic bridge/stop tailpiece, bound peghead, 3-per-side tuners, gold hardware, 2 humbucker pickups, volume/tone control, 3-position switch. Available in Natural finish. Disc. 1996.

		100%	98%	95%	90%	80%	70%	60%
		$1,250	$1,050	$935	$825	$700	$590	$475

Last MSR was $1,900.

JB-AL - similar to the JB-400-AM, except features a black bound maple top, basswood back/sides, bolt-on maple neck, 24-fret rosewood fingerboard with pearl dot inlay, single coil/humbucker pickups. Available in White finish. Disc. 1996.

		100%	98%	95%	90%	80%	70%	60%
		$950	$800	$725	$625	$550	$450	$375

Last MSR was $1,475.

JBA-440 - dual cutaway semi-hollow alder body, body binding, one f-hole, alder back/sides, maple neck, 22-fret bound rosewood fingerboard with pearl block inlay, tune-o-matic bridge/stop tailpiece, blackface peghead, 3-per-side tuners, gold hardware, 2 humbucker pickups, volume/tone control, 3-position switch. Available in Black gloss finish. Mfg. 1998 to date.

		100%	98%	95%	90%	80%	70%	60%
MSR	$699	$500	$425	$375	$325	$275	$225	$175

JBA-460 - similar to JBA-440, except features raised white pickguard, 2 volume/2 tone controls. Available in Brown Sunburst finish. Mfg. 1998 to date.

		100%	98%	95%	90%	80%	70%	60%
MSR	$735	$525	$450	$395	$350	$295	$250	$195

JBA-500 - offset double cutaway alder body, carved ash top, maple neck, 22-fret rosewood fingerboard with pearl wedge inlay, standard vibrato, 6-on-a-side tuners, black hardware, humbucker/single coil/humbucker covered APC pickups, volume/tone control, 5-position switch. Available in Amber and Walnut finishes. Mfg. 1994 to 1998.

		100%	98%	95%	90%	80%	70%	60%
		$575	$525	$450	$395	$325	$275	$200

Last MSR was $795.

JBA-600 - offset double cutaway hardwood body, mahogany neck, 24-fret rosewood fingerboard with pearl dot inlay, standard vibrato, 3-per-side tuners, gold hardware, 2 humbucker covered APC pickups, volume/tone control, 3-position switch. Available in Black and Cherryburst finishes. Mfg. 1994 to 1998.

		100%	98%	95%	90%	80%	70%	60%
		$650	$575	$500	$450	$375	$295	$225

Last MSR was $895.

JBA-700 - slightly offset double cutaway alder body, bolt-on maple neck, 22-fret rosewood fingerboard with pearl dot inlay, standard vibrato, 3-per-side tuners, gold hardware, white pearloid pickguard, 3 'lipstick-style' single coil pickups, volume/tone control, 5-position switch. Available in Candy Red and Ivory finishes. Mfg. 1998 to date.

		100%	98%	95%	90%	80%	70%	60%
MSR	$495	$375	$300	$275	$225	$200	$150	$125

JBA-750 - similar to JBS-700, except features Wilkinson tremolo, pearloid pickguard. Available in Candy Red and Dark Metallic Blue finishes. Mfg. 1998 to date.

		100%	98%	95%	90%	80%	70%	60%
MSR	$550	$395	$325	$295	$250	$225	$175	$150

J

GRADING		100% MINT	98% NEAR MINT	95% EXC+	90% EXC	80% VG+	70% VG	60% G

JBA-L3 - single cutaway ash body, bolt-on maple neck, 24-fret rosewood fingerboard with dot inlay, Wilkinson tremolo, 6-on-a-side tuners, gold hardware, 3 single coil pickups, volume/tone control, 5-position switch. Available in Vintage Sunburst finish. Current Mfg.

MSR	$895	$675	$575	$500	$450	$375	$295	$225

JBA-L4 - similar to the JBA-L3, except features tune-o-matic bridge/stop tailpiece, 2 humbuckers, 3-way switch. Available in Vintage Sunburst or Tobacco Sunburst finishes. Current Mfg.

MSR	$695	$525	$450	$395	$350	$275	$225	$175

JBA-LTD - similar to the JBA-L4, except features an alder body, 22-fret rosewood fingerboard, standard vibrato, chrome hardware, 2 covered APC humbucker pickups, volume/tone control, 3-position switch. Available in Natural finish. Mfg. 1994 to 1996.

		$375	$325	$295	$250	$225	$175	$150

Last MSR was $600.

Professional Series

In 1998, the Professional Series PGP-111 models featured advanced "quilted" or "flamed" photo tops, a system that resembles figured maple tops.

PG-111-B3 - offset double cutaway hardwood body, black pickguard, bolt-on maple neck, 22-fret rosewood fingerboard with pearl dot inlay, double locking vibrato, 6-on-a-side tuners, black hardware, 3 single coil pickups, volume/2 tone controls, 5-position switch. Available in Black Pearl, Red Pearl and White Pearl finishes. Mfg. 1994 to 1996.

		$325	$275	$250	$195	$175	$150	$125

Last MSR was $485.

PG-111-HS - similar to PG-111-B3, except has 2 single coil/1 humbucker pickups. Disc. 1996.

		$325	$275	$225	$200	$175	$150	$125

Last MSR was $500.

PG-121 - similar to PG-111-B3, except has no pickguard, volume/tone control, 3 mini switches in place of 5-position switch, coil split in tone control. Available in Black Pearl, Black/White Crackle, Fluorescent Pink, Fluorescent Yellow, Red/White Crackle and White Pearl finishes. Disc. 1996.

		$350	$325	$300	$250	$225	$195	$150

Last MSR was $600.

PGP-111-P - offset double cutaway alder body, bolt-on maple neck, 22-fret rosewood fingerboard with pearl dot inlay, standard vibrato, 6-on-a-side tuners, gold hardware, pearloid pickguard, 3 single coil pickups, volume/2 tone controls, 5-position switch. Available in Amber ("quilted") and Cherry ("flamed") photo top Sunburst finishes. Mfg. 1998 to date.

MSR	$450	$325	$275	$250	$225	$175	$150	$115

PGP-111-DP - similar to PGP-111-P, except has 3 Duncan Designed single coil pickups. Available in Amber ("quilted") and Cherry ("flamed") photo top Sunburst finishes. Mfg. 1998 to date.

MSR	$540	$375	$325	$275	$250	$200	$175	$125

PGP-111-HDP - similar to PGP-111-P, except has 2 Duncan Designed single coil/Duncan Designed humbucker pickups. Available in Amber ("quilted") and Cherry ("flamed") photo top Sunburst finishes. Mfg. 1998 to date.

MSR	$560	$395	$350	$295	$275	$250	$195	$125

PGP-111 - similar to PGP-111-P, except has maple body/neck, neck-through construction, EMG pickups. Available in Black, Black/White Crackle, Fluorescent Yellow, Red, Red/White Crackle, Red/Yellow Crackle, White and White Pearl finishes. Disc. 1994.

		$350	$325	$275	$225	$200	$175	$150

Last MSR was $550.

PGP-112 - single cutaway maple body, ash top and back, bolt-on maple neck, 22-fret maple fingerboard with dot inlay, fixed vibrato, 6-on-a-side tuners, gold hardware, tortoiseshell pickguard, 2 single coil pickups, volume/tone controls, 3-position switch, metal controls plate. Available in Natural and Cherry Sunburst finishes. Mfg. 1998 to date.

MSR	$570	$395	$350	$300	$225	$195	$150	$150

PGP-120 - shark fin style maple body, maple neck, 22-fret rosewood fingerboard with pearl triangle inlay, double locking vibrato, 6-on-a-side tuners, black hardware, 2 single coil/1 humbucker EMG pickups, volume/tone control, 5-position switch. Available in Black, Black Pearl and Black/White Crackle finishes. Disc. 1994.

		$525	$475	$400	$325	$295	$250	$225

Last MSR was $800.

PGP-121 - similar to PG121, except has maple body/neck, neck-through construction, EMG pickups. Available in Black, Black Pearl, Fluorescent Pink, Fluorescent Pink/Blue Crackle, Fluorescent Yellow Crackle, Ultra Violet and White Pearl finishes. Disc. 1994.

		$450	$395	$325	$250	$225	$200	$175

Last MSR was $650.

PGP-150A - offset double cutaway hardwood body, bolt-on maple neck, 24-fret rosewood fingerboard with offset pearl dot inlay, standard vibrato, 6-on-a-side tuners, black hardware, 2 single coil/humbucker pickups, volume/tone controls, 5-position switch. Available in Amber and Cherryburst finishes. Mfg. 1994 to 1996.

		$375	$325	$300	$250	$225	$195	$150

Last MSR was $595.

GRADING	100% MINT	98% NEAR MINT	95% EXC+	90% EXC	80% VG+	70% VG	60% G

J.B. Player JBA-L 3
courtesy J.B. Player

Sledgehammer Series

SHG-111 - offset double cutaway hardwood body, bolt-on maple neck, 22-fret maple fingerboard with black dot inlay, standard vibrato, 6-on-a-side tuners, chrome hardware, white pickguard, 3 single coil pickups, volume/2 tone controls, 5-position switch. Available in Black, Gun Metal Grey, Pink, Phantom Blue, Red, Red/White Crackle, Terminator Red, Ultra Violet, White, 2 Tone Sunburst, and 3 Tone Sunburst finishes. Current Mfg.

MSR $349 — $275 $225 $175 $150 $125 $100 $75

This model also available with rosewood fingerboard with pearl dot inlay.
In 1994, Gun Metal Grey, Pink, Phantom Blue, Red/White Crackle, Terminator Red, Ultra Violet, and White finishes were discontinued.
In 1996, Metallic red, Metallic Blue, and Ivory finishes were introduced; 2 Tone Sunburst finish was discontinued.

SHGL-111 - similar to SHG-111, except features a left-handed configuration. Available in 3-Tone Sunburst, Black, Ivory, Metallic Blue, and Metallic Red finishes. Current Mfg.

MSR $360 — $295 $250 $195 $175 $150 $125 $90

SHG-112 - single cutaway hardwood body, black pickguard, bolt-on maple neck, 22-fret maple fingerboard with black dot inlay, fixed bridge, 6-on-a-side tuners, chrome hardware, 2 single coil pickups, volume/tone controls, 3-position switch. Available in Aged Blonde, Black, Cherry Sunburst, and Natural finishes. Current Mfg.

MSR $349 — $275 $225 $175 $150 $125 $100 $85

In 1996, 3-Tone Sunburst, Ivory, Metallic Blue, and Metallic Red finishes were introduced; Aged Blonde, Cherry Sunburst, and Natural finishes were discontinued.

SHG-112-HSS - similar to SHG-112 (2S), except has 2 single coil/humbucker pickups. Available in Aged Blonde, Black, Cherry Sunburst, and Natural finishes. Disc. 1994.

$275 $225 $200 $175 $150 $125 $100
Last MSR was $430.

SHG-121 - (soloist body style) offset double cutaway hardwood body, ash top, cream binding, bolt-on maple neck, 22-fret rosewood fingerboard with pearl dot inlay, tune-o-matic bridge/stop tailpiece, 6-on-a-side tuners, chrome hardware, 2 humbucker pickups, volume/tone controls, 3-way position switch. Available in Antique Violin, Transparent Black, and Transparent Red finishes. Mfg. 1998 to date.

MSR $349 — $275 $225 $175 $150 $125 $100 $75

SHG-122 - similar to SHG-121, except has 2 single coil/humbucker pickups, volume/2 tone controls, standard tremolo. Available in Antique Violin and Transparent Red finishes. Mfg. 1998 to date.

MSR $369 — $295 $250 $195 $175 $150 $125 $100

SHG-150 - single rounded cutaway nato body, 22-fret rosewood fingerboard with white dot inlay, fixed bridge, 3-per-side die cast tuners, chrome hardware, 2 humbucker pickups, volume/tone controls, 3-position switch. Available in Black Gloss, Transparent Amber, and Wine Red finishes. Mfg. 1998 to date.

MSR $299 — $200 $175 $155 $135 $115 $95 $75

SHG-160 - offset double cutaway nato body, bolt-on maple neck, 22-fret rosewood fingerboard with black dot inlay, standard vibrato, 6-on-a-side tuners, chrome hardware, 2 single coil/humbucker pickups, volume/tone controls, 5-position switch. Available in Metallic Black, Metallic Gold, Cherry Sunburst finishes. Mfg. 1998 to date.

MSR $299 — $200 $175 $155 $135 $115 $95 $75

ELECTRIC BASS

Artist Series Basses

JBA-B1 N - offset double cutaway hardwood body, maple neck, 24-fret rosewood fingerboard with pearl offset dot inlay, fixed bridge, 3/2-per-side tuners, chrome tuners, 2 J-style pickups, 2 volume/2 tone controls. Available in Black and Natural finishes. Mfg. 1994 to 1998.

$625 $550 $475 $425 $350 $275 $225
Last MSR was $850.

JBA-B2 - single cutaway alder body, maple neck, 20-fret rosewood fingerboard with dot inlay, fixed bridge, 2-per-side tuners, gold tuners, 2 J-style pickups, 2 volume/2 tone controls. Available in Black finish. Disc. 1998.

$475 $425 $375 $325 $275 $225 $175
Last MSR was $650.

Add $75 for 5-string configuration (Model JBA-B2V).

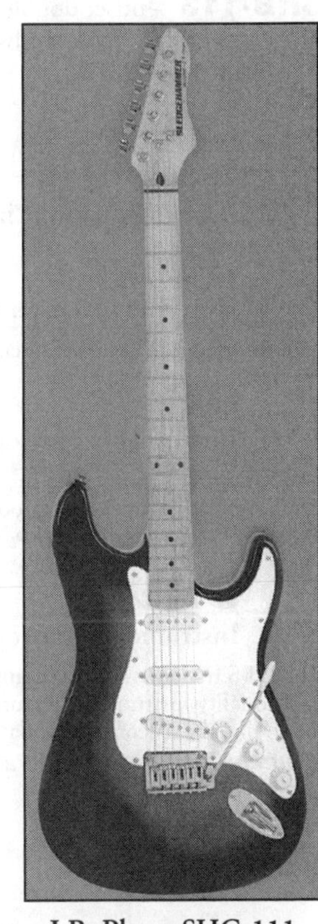

J.B. Player SHG-111
courtesy J.B. Player

GRADING		100% MINT	98% NEAR MINT	95% EXC+	90% EXC	80% VG+	70% VG	60% G

JBA-B3 4-STRING - offset double cutaway solid ash body with extended bass horn, 5-piece maple through-body neck, 24-fret rosewood fingerboard with dot inlay, fixed bridge, 2-per-side tuners, chrome tuners, P/J-style pickups, volume/blend/2 tone controls, active electronics. Available in Natural Gloss (N) and Cherry Matte (CH) finishes. Current Mfg.

MSR	$1,115	$850	$725	$625	$550	$450	$375	$275

JBA-B3 B (Bolt-On) - similar to the JBA-B3, except features bolt-on maple neck, volume/2 tone controls, 3-way switch, active/passive switching. Available in Natural Gloss (N) or Vintage Sunburst (VS) finishes. Current Mfg.

MSR	$660	$495	$425	$375	$325	$275	$225	$175

Add $20 for Transparent Black gloss finish (Model JBA-B3 B T).

JBA-B5 5-STRING - similar to the JBA-B3, except has 5-string configuration, 3/2-per-side tuners. Available in Natural Gloss (N) and Cherry Matte (CH) finishes. Current Mfg.

MSR	$1,195	$900	$795	$675	$575	$495	$395	$300

JBA-B5 B (Bolt-On) - similar to the JBA-B5, except features bolt-on maple neck, volume/2 tone controls, 3-way switch, active/passive switching. Available in Natural Gloss (N) or Vintage Sunburst (VS) finishes. Current Mfg.

MSR	$750	$575	$525	$450	$395	$375	$250	$195

JBA-B6 6-STRING - similar to the JBA-B3, except has 6-string configuration, 3-per-side tuners, 7-piece maple through-body neck, 2 humbucker pickups, 2 volume/2 tone controls. Available in Cherry Matte (CH) finishes. Current Mfg.

MSR	$1,295	$975	$850	$750	$650	$525	$425	$325

Professional Series Basses

PGP-113 - offset double cutaway maple body, black pickguard, bolt-on maple neck, 20-fret rosewood fingerboard with pearl dot inlay, fixed bridge, 4-on-a-side tuners, black hardware, P/J-style EMG pickups, volume/tone control, 3-position switch. Available in Black, Black Pearl, Red, Red Pearl, and White Pearl finishes. Disc. 1994.

$295	$250	$225	$195	$175	$150	$125

Last MSR was $425.

PGP-114 - similar to the PGP-113, except features hardwood body, 24-fret rosewood fingerboard with pearl dot inlay, 2-per-side tuners, chrome hardware, volume/2 tone controls. Available in Black Pearl finish. Mfg. 1994 to 1996.

$325	$275	$250	$225	$195	$175	$150

Last MSR was $495.

Sledgehammer Series Basses

SHB-113 - offset double cutaway hardwood body, black pickguard, bolt-on maple neck, 20-fret rosewood fingerboard with pearl dot inlay, fixed bridge, black hardware, P-style pickup, volume/tone control. Available in Black, Red and White finishes. Current Mfg.

MSR	$379	$295	$250	$225	$195	$150	$125	$95

JD

See JAY DEE.

Instruments built in England.

JDS

Instruments currently built in Asia. Exclusively distributed by Wolf Imports of St. Louis, Missouri.

JDS Limited Edition instruments are medium quality acoustic and solid body electric guitars that feature designs based on popular American classics.

JG

Instruments previously produced in Italy during the late 1960s.

The SA series featured four models of medium quality but original designs. Readers are encouraged to write and share whether or not they also share similarities to other Italian-produced guitars of this era! Results will be published in future editions of the ***Blue Book of Electric Guitars***.

(Source: Tony Bacon and Paul Day, The Guru's Guitar Guide)

JHS

Instruments previously built in Japan during the late 1970s.

The JH S trademark was the initials of the UK importer **John Hornby Skewes**, who founded his import company in 1965 (See ENCORE). The generally good quality instruments featured both original designs and those based on classic American designs. The line focused primarily on solid body guitars, much like the Encore line today.

(Source: Tony Bacon and Paul Day, The Guru's Guitar Guide)

GRADING	100% MINT	98% NEAR MINT	95% EXC+	90% EXC	80% VG+	70% VG	60% G

JP GUITARS

Formerly PIMENTEL GUITARS.

Instruments currently produced in Pullyallup, Washington.

Luthier Jack Pimentel is currently offering the JP and JP II models of stand-up, compact body electric basses. Pimentel's basses share the same dimensions as an original upright bass (same fingerboard radius, neck contour, string spacing, and scale length); however, his models feature a detachable neck for ease in traveling and shipping.

ELECTRIC BASS

All models are constructed of seasoned hardwoods which feature internal tone chambers that enhance the acoustic tonal properties, and feature EMG active EQ circuitry and piezo electric pickups. The **JP I** Upright Bass has a retail list price of $2,200; the **JP II** features a hand carved wood top (list $2,950); and the **JP II Deluxe** has a hand carved flame or quilted maple top and gold hardware (list $3,450). A custom flight case is available for $475, and the upright's stand is $100.

Pimentel also offers his **JP Guitars** ($2,750 for model with fingerboard dot inlay; $3,200 for model with custom fingerboard inlay). For further information regarding bass and guitar model specifications, please contact Jack Pimentel at JP Guitars directly (see Trademark Index).

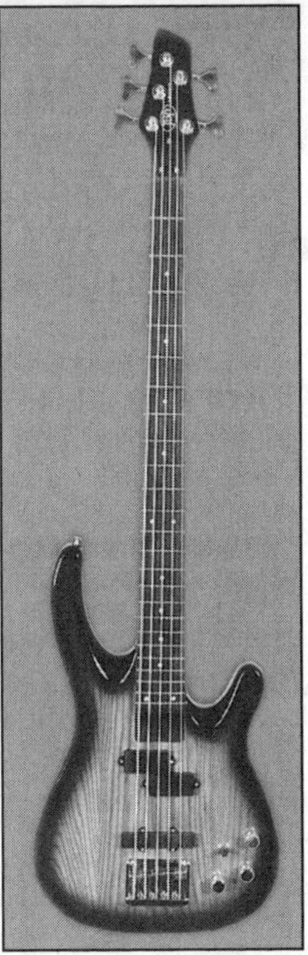

J.B. Player JBA-B5 B
courtesy J.B. Player

JTG OF NASHVILLE

Instruments currently built in Japan. Distributed by JTG of Nashville located in Nashville, Tennessee.

While JTG of Nashville currently imports quality Japanese and Mexican acoustic guitars, they offered a solid body electric during the mid-1980s.

ELECTRIC

The **Infinity** solid body electric guitar was designed by Dave Petschulat, and had a body profile similar to a *sharpened* Explorer. The **Infinity** had a highly angular ash body, curly maple neck, six-on-a-side headstock, one humbucking pickup, a custom tremolo, and was offered with either charcoal gray or white with red accents, and red with a light gray accent. The last suggested retail price (circa mid 1980s) was $595.

JACKSON

Instruments currently built in Ontario, CA & Japan. Jackson USA and Jackson Custom Shop series guitars are built in Ontario, CA. Jackson Professional Series guitars are built in Japan. Distributed in the U.S. market by International Music Corporation (distributor of Ross Electronics and Akai Electronics) of Fort Worth, Texas.

The Charvel/Jackson Guitar company was founded in 1978 after Grover Jackson bought out Wayne Charvel's Guitar Repair shop in Azusa, California. As the bolt-neck custom-built Charvel guitars gained popularity with the up-and-coming West Coast rock musicians, it became a necessity that standardized models were established. By 1983, neck-through designs were introduced with the **Jackson** logo on the headstock. Jackson/Charvel was first licensed (in 1985) and later acquired (in 1986) by the International Music Company (IMC) of Fort Worth, Texas.

In about 1992, upper end Charvels began to be incorporated into the Jackson line (essentially becoming the Jackson Professional Series). American-built models have "Made in U.S.A." logo on the headstock; the Japanese-built Professional series models do not.

ELECTRIC

In 1996, the models in the product line were renamed from their usual name plus designation (ex.: a Rhoads Standard) to a simpler 3 or 4 digit abbreviation (Rhoads Standard = RR2). Older models discontinued prior to 1996 will retain their original designation, while new models and continuing production models will follow the new designation.

AX/S Series

The AX/S Series was introduced in 1999 and offers many outstanding features at very affordable prices.

D10 - Dinky style body constructed of alder with 24-fret maple neck, rosewood fingerboard with dot inlays, JT-480s bridge and two JE10 pickups, chrome hardware. Available in Black, Metallic Blue, and Metallic Red finishes. Disc. 1999.

$300	$250	$225	$200	$175	$150	$100

Last MSR was $425.

D10 PRO - similar to D10 except has shark fin neck inlays, one JA-10N pickup and one JA-10B pickup. JB-480 bridge, chrome hardware, Available in Black, Metallic Red and Metalic Blue finishes. Disc. 1999

$340	$275	$250	$225	$200	$175	$150

Last MSR was $485.

K10 - Kelly body style, alder body, maple neck with rosewood fingerboard, dot inlays, JT-480s bridge, two JE10 pickups, chrome hardware. Available in Black, Metallic Blue and Metallic Red. Disc. 1999.

$350	$285	$260	$240	$210	$185	$160

Last MSR was $495.

GRADING	100% MINT	98% NEAR MINT	95% EXC+	90% EXC	80% VG+	70% VG	60% G

K10 PRO - similar to K10 except has shark fin neck inlays, one JA-10N and one JA-10B pickup, JB-480 bridge, chrome hardware. Available in Black, Metallic Red and Metallic Blue finishes. Disc. 1999.

$390 $325 $275 $250 $225 $200 $175
Last MSR was $555.

R10 - Rhoads body style, alder body, maple neck with rosewood fingerboard, dot inlays, JT-480s bridge and two JE10 pickups, chrome hardware. Available in Black, Metallic Red and Metallic Blue. Disc. 1999.

$350 $285 $260 $240 $210 $185 $160
Last MSR was $495.

R10 PRO - similar to R10 except has shark fin neck inlays, one JA-10 pickup and one JA-10B pickup, JB-480 bridge, chrome hardware. Available in Black, Metallic Red and Metallic Blue. Disc. 1999.

$390 $325 $275 $250 $225 $200 $175
Last MSR was $555.

Concept Series

The Concept series was available briefly from 1993 through late 1994. Continuing popularity led to introduction of the Performer Series in 1995, which combined the best design aspects of the Concept series models with new innovations.

JDR-94 - offset double cutaway poplar body, bolt-on maple neck, 24-fret rosewood fingerboard with pearl offset dot inlay, double locking vibrato, reverse blackface peghead with screened logo, 6-on-a-side tuners, black hardware, humbucker/single coil/humbucker pickups, volume/tone control, 5-position switch. Available in Black, Bright Red and Dark Metallic Blue finishes. Mfg. 1993 to 1994.

$425 $350 $300 $250 $225 $195 $175
Last MSR was $595.

JDX-94 - similar to JDR-94, except has standard fingerboard dot inlay, fixed bridge, standard peghead design, 2 single coil/1 humbucker pickups configuration. Available in Black, Bright Red and Dark Metallic Blue finishes. Mfg. 1993 to 1994.

$375 $325 $275 $225 $200 $175 $150
Last MSR was $550.

J

JRR-94 - shark fin poplar body, black pickguard, bolt-on maple neck, 24-fret rosewood fingerboard with pearl dot inlay, tune-o-matic bridge/strings through-body tailpiece, blackface peghead with screened logo, 6-on-a-side tuners, black hardware, 2 humbucker pickups, 2 volume/1 tone controls, 3-position switch. Available in Black, Bright Red and Dark Metallic Blue finishes. Mfg. 1993 to 1994.

$400 $350 $300 $250 $225 $195 $175
Last MSR was $595.

JSX-94 - offset double cutaway poplar body, bolt-on maple neck, 24-fret rosewood fingerboard with pearl offset dot inlay, double locking vibrato, blackface peghead with screened logo, 6-on-a-side tuners, black hardware, 2 single coil/1 humbucker pickups, volume/tone control, 5-position switch. Available in Black, Bright Red and Dark Metallic Blue finishes. Mfg. 1993 to 1994.

$425 $375 $325 $275 $225 $195 $175
Last MSR was $595.

Performer Series

Continuing popularity of the Concept series led to introduction of the Performer Series in 1995, which combined the best design aspects of the Concept series models with new innovations.

PS-1 - offset double cutaway alder body, bolt-on maple neck, 24-fret rosewood fingerboard with dot inlay, JT490 fulcrum vibrato, blackface peghead with screened logo, 6-on-a-side tuners, black hardware, black pickguard, 2 single coils/1 humbucker pickups, volume/tone control, 5-position switch. Available in Black, Red Violet Metallic, Blue Green Metallic, Black Cherry, and Deep Metallic Blue finishes. Mfg. 1995 to 1999.

$385 $335 $285 $250 $215 $185 $145
Last MSR was $545.

Add $50 for alder body/flamed maple top in Transparent finish (Transparent Blue, Transparent Green, Transparent Purple, and Transparent Red).

PS-2 - similar to PS-1, except has double locking JT500 tremolo and no pickguard. Available in Black, Red Violet Metallic, Blue Green Metallic, Black Cherry, and Deep Metallic Blue finishes. Mfg. 1995 to date.

MSR $595 $415 $350 $315 $265 $240 $210 $165

Add $50 for alder body/flamed maple top in Transparent finish (Transparent Blue, Transparent Green, Transparent Purple, and Transparent Red).

PS-3 - shark fin style alder body, black pickguard, bolt-on maple neck, 24-fret rosewood fingerboard with dot inlay, tune-o-matic bridge/strings through-body tailpiece, blackface peghead with screened logo, 6-on-a-side tuners, black hardware, 2 humbucker pickups, 2 volume/1 tone controls, 3-position switch. Available in Black, Red Violet Metallic, Blue Green Metallic, Black Cherry, and Deep Metallic Blue finishes. Mfg. 1995 to 1999.

$415 $350 $315 $265 $240 $210 $165
Last MSR was $595.

Add $50 for alder body/flamed maple top in Transparent finish (Transparent Blue, Transparent Green, Transparent Purple, and Transparent Red).

GRADING	100% MINT	98% NEAR MINT	95% EXC+	90% EXC	80% VG+	70% VG	60% G

PS-3T - similar to PS-3, except has double locking JT500 tremolo. Available in Black, Red Violet Metallic, Blue Green Metallic, Black Cherry, and Deep Metallic Blue finishes. Mfg. 1995 to date.

MSR	$675	$475	$400	$350	$325	$275	$240	$200

Add $50 for alder body/flamed maple top in Transparent finish (Transparent Blue, Transparent Green, Transparent Purple, and Transparent Red).

PS-4 - offset double cutaway alder body, bolt-on maple neck, 24-fret rosewood fingerboard with offset dot inlay, double locking vibrato, reverse blackface peghead with screened logo, 6 on the other side tuners, black hardware, humbucker/single coil/humbucker pickups, volume/tone control, 5-position switch. Available in Black, Red Violet Metallic, Blue Green Metallic, Black Cherry, and Deep Metallic Blue finishes. Mfg. 1995 to date.

MSR	$645	$450	$400	$350	$325	$275	$225	$175

Add $50 for alder body/flamed maple top in Transparent finish (Transparent Blue, Transparent Green, Transparent Purple, and Transparent Red).

PS-6 - asymmetrical "Kelly"-style alder body, bolt-on maple neck, 24-fret rosewood fingerboard with dot inlay, tune-o-matic bridge/stop tailpiece, blackface peghead with screened logo, 6-on-a-side tuners, chrome hardware, 2 humbucker pickups, 2 volume/1 tone controls, 3-position switch. Available in Black, Red Violet Metallic, Blue Green Metallic, Black Cherry, and Deep Metallic Blue finishes. Mfg. 1997-1998.

$450	$375	$325	$300	$250	$225	$175

Last MSR was $625.

Add $50 for alder body/flamed maple top in Transparent finish (Transparent Blue, Transparent Green, Transparent Purple, and Transparent Red).

PS-6T - similar to the PS-6, except features JT-500 double locking tremolo, black hardware. Mfg. 1997 to date.

MSR	$675	$475	$400	$350	$300	$275	$225	$175

Add $50 for alder body/flamed maple top in Transparent finish (Transparent Blue, Transparent Green, Transparent Purple, and Transparent Red).

PS-7 - offset double cutaway alder body, bolt-on maple neck, 22-fret rosewood fingerboard with dot inlay, Wilkinson VS-50 vibrato, 6-on-a-side tuners, chrome hardware, black pickguard, 2 single coils/humbucker pickups, volume/tone control, 5-position switch. Available in Black, Red Violet Metallic, Blue Green Metallic, Black Cherry, and Deep Metallic Blue finishes. Mfg. 1995 to date.

MSR	$575	$400	$330	$300	$275	$240	$195	$165

Add $50 for alder body/flamed maple top in Transparent finish (Transparent Blue, Transparent Green, Transparent Purple, and Transparent Red).

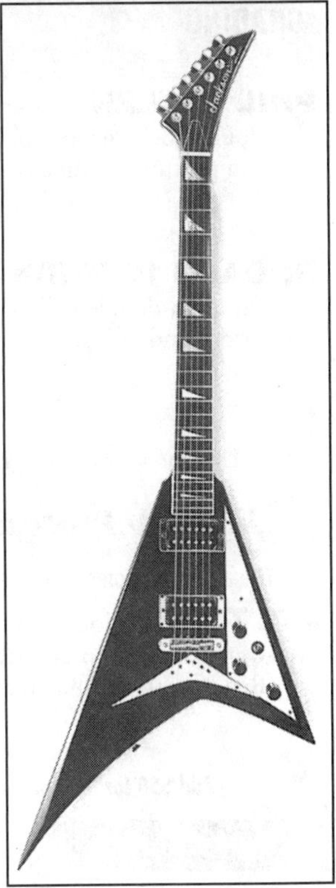

Jackson Original Rhoads
courtesy Jackson

J

Player's Choice Series

The Player's Choice series was released from 1993 to 1995 and incorporated many of the most requested options from the Jackson Custom Shop. Standardization of designs yielded lower retail list prices.

EXOTIC DINKY - offset double cutaway koa body, bound quilted maple top, bolt-on maple neck, 24-fret bound pau ferro fingerboard with offset pearl dot inlay, double locking vibrato, bound peghead with pearl logo inlay, 6-on-a-side tuners, gold hardware, 2 stacked coil/humbucker Seymour Duncan pickups, volume/tone control, 5-position switch. Available in Tobacco Sunburst, Transparent Blue, Transparent Purple and Transparent Red finishes. Mfg. 1993 to 1995.

$1,675	$1,450	$1,200	$950	$850	$795	$725

Last MSR was $2,400.

Flamed Dinky - similar to Exotic Dinky, except has flame maple body, bound ebony fingerboard with pearl sharkfin inlay, black hardware, Jackson pickups. Available in Transparent Black, Transparent Blue and Transparent Purple finishes. Mfg. 1993 to 1995.

$1,550	$1,300	$1,100	$895	$795	$725	$650

Last MSR was $2,200.

KING V - V-style poplar body, through-body maple neck, 22-fret bound ebony fingerboard with pearl sharkfin inlay, fixed locking bridge, bound peghead with pearl logo inlay, 6-on-a-side tuners, black hardware, 2 volume/1 tone controls, 5-position switch with opposite switching. Available in Black finish. Mfg. 1993 to 1995.

$1,500	$1,325	$1,100	$900	$795	$725	$650

Last MSR was $2,200.

ORIGINAL RHOADS - sharkfin style poplar body, gold pickguard, through-body maple neck, 22-fret bound ebony fingerboard with pearl sharkfin inlay, tune-o-matic bridge, strings through tailpiece with V plate, 6-on-a-side tuners, gold hardware, 2 humbucker Seymour Duncan pickups, 2 volume/1 tone controls, 3-position switch. Available in Black finish. Mfg. 1993 to 1995.

$1,600	$1,400	$1,175	$995	$900	$825	$750

Last MSR was $2,200.

GRADING	100% MINT	98% NEAR MINT	95% EXC+	90% EXC	80% VG+	70% VG	60% G

PHIL COLLEN - offset double cutaway maple body, through-body maple neck, 24-fret bound ebony fingerboard with pearl sharkfin inlay double locking vibrato, bound peghead with pearl Jackson logo inlay, 6-on-a-side Gotoh tuners, black hardware, single coil/humbucker Jackson pickups, volume control, 3-position switch. Available in Metallic Black and Pearl White finishes. Mfg. 1993 to 1995.

$1,600 $1,375 $1,150 $925 $850 $750 $675
Last MSR was $2,300.

RHOADS 10 STRING - sharkfin style quilted maple body, through-body maple neck, 22-fret bound ebony fingerboard with pearl sharkfin inlay, double locking vibrato, bound peghead with pearl Jackson inlay, double R truss rod cover, 6-on-a-side tuners, 4 tuners located on bridge end of instrument, gold hardware, volume control, 3-position switch. Available in Transparent Black finish. Mfg. 1993 to 1995.

$1,750 $1,500 $1,250 $1,000 $900 $825 $750
Last MSR was $2,500.

This model was designed in conjunction with guitarist Dan Spitz (Anthrax).

Jackson Professional Series

The Jackson Professional Series is produced in Asia, and features designs based on the Jackson USA models.

AT2 T - offset double cutaway basswood body, bolt-on maple neck, 22-fret rosewood fingerboard with white dot inlay, chrome hardware, wraparound stop tailpiece, 2 chrome covered humbuckers, volume/tone controls, 3-way selector switch. Available in Black, Deep Metallic Red, Cherry Sunburst, and Transparent Purple finishes. Mfg. 1996 to 1998.

$675 $550 $475 $425 $350 $295 $225
Last MSR was $895.

Add $50 for transparent finish and gravure top.

Dinky Series

The Jackson Dinky model is a scaled down 7/8th size 'SuperStrat' model (an updated, modern version of the industry standard 'Strat' - of course, the Dinky body shape is now an industry standard as well), featuring 2 single coils and a humbucker in the bridge condition.

DINKY STANDARD - offset double cutaway basswood body, transparent pickguard, bolt-on maple neck, 24-fret rosewood fingerboard with colored dot inlay, double locking vibrato, 6-on-a-side tuners, black hardware, 2 stacked coil/humbucker Jackson pickups, volume/tone control, 5-position switch. Available in Black, Candy Blue, Dark Metallic Red and Snow White finishes. Mfg. 1991 to 1993.

$625 $525 $450 $350 $325 $300 $275
Last MSR was $895.

DX1 (DINKY XL) - offset double cutaway basswood body, bolt-on maple neck, 24-fret bound rosewood fingerboard with pearl sharkfin inlay, double locking vibrato, 6-on-a-side tuners, black hardware, 2 stacked coil/1 humbucker Jackson pickups, volume/tone control, 5-position switch. Available in Deep Metallic Blue, Metallic Black and Pearl White finishes. Mfg. 1992 to 1998.

$700 $600 $500 $400 $350 $300 $250
Last MSR was $995.

Add $50 for transparent finish.

Dinky XL (Trans) - similar to Dinky XL, except has flame maple top. Available in Cherry Sunburst, Transparent Blue, Transparent Red and Transparent Violet finishes. Mfg. 1993 to 1995.

$650 $595 $550 $425 $395 $350 $300
Last MSR was $1,095.

DX2 (DINKY EX) - offset double cutaway basswood body, black pickguard, bolt-on maple neck, 24-fret rosewood fingerboard with pearl dot inlay, double locking vibrato, 6-on-a-side tuners, black hardware, humbucker/single coil/humbucker Jackson pickups, volume/tone control, 5-position switch. Available in Black, Deep Metallic Blue, Deep Metallic Red and Snow White finishes. Mfg. 1993 to 1998.

$500 $450 $395 $325 $275 $250 $225
Last MSR was $745.

Add $50 for transparent finish.

DR5 (DINKY REVERSE) - offset double cutaway basswood body, bolt-on maple neck, 24-fret maple (or rosewood) fingerboard with offset dot inlay, reverse headstock, double locking vibrato, 6-on-a-side tuners, black hardware, 2 humbucker Jackson pickups, volume/tone control, 3-position switch. Available in Black, Candy Blue, Dark Metallic Violet and Stone finishes. Mfg. 1992 to 1998.

$525 $450 $395 $325 $275 $250 $225
Last MSR was $745.

In 1994, the Stone finish was discontinued.

DR3 (Dinky Reverse - Trans) - similar to Dinky Reverse, except has poplar body, flame maple top. Available in Black, Natural Green Sunburst, Natural Purple Sunburst, Natural Red Sunburst, and Transparent Blue finishes. Mfg. 1994 to date.

MSR $845 $595 $520 $445 $395 $350 $275 $235

Add $50 for transparent finish (Transparent Blue, Transparent Green, Tobacco Sunburst/mahogany body).

In 1998, Transparent Green and Tobacco Sunburst (with mahogany body) finishes were introduced; Natural Green Sunburst, Natural Purple Sunburst, and Natural Red Sunburst finishes were discontinued.

GRADING	100% MINT	98% NEAR MINT	95% EXC+	90% EXC	80% VG+	70% VG	60% G

DR6 - similar to DR3 except string through-body, Tune-O-Matic type bridge. Available in black, Deep Candy Blue and Dark Metallic Red finishes. New for 2000.

MSR $695	$485	$385	$335	$250	$165	$125	$95

Add $50 for Tobacco Sunburst and Burnt Cherry Sunburst finishes.

DR7 7 STRING -similar to DR6 except in a 7-string configuration. Available in black and Deep Candy Blue finishes. Current Mfg.

MSR $895	$626	$500	$425	$350	$275	$200	$125

Add $50 for Transparent Blue and Transparent red finishes.

DK2 (DINKY) - offset double cutaway poplar body, bolt-on maple neck, 22-fret rosewood fingerboard with pearl sharkfin inlay, double locking vibrato, 6-on-a-side tuners, chrome hardware, 2 single coil/humbucker pickups, volume/tone control, 5-position switch. Available in Midnight Blue Sparkle and Deep Metallic Violet finishes. Mfg. 1998 to date.

MSR $895	$625	$550	$500	$425	$375	$275	$225

Add $50 for transparent finish with maple top (Transparent Blue, Transparent Amber, and Transparent Red).

FB Series

FB2 - offset asymmetrical hourglass shaped poplar body, bolt-on maple neck, 24-fret rosewood fingerboard with dot inlays, chrome hardware, JT580 locking tremolo, 2 exposed humbuckers, 1 volume knob, 3-way selector switch. Available in Black, Mint Green, and Vintage White finishes. Mfg. 1996 to 1997.

$525	$475	$450	$425	$375	$325	$275

Last MSR was $795.

FB2 T - similar to the FB2, except has JT390 tune-o-matic/stop tailpiece. Mfg. 1996 to 1997.

$575	$500	$450	$375	$325	$275	$250

Last MSR was $725.

Jackson Dinky XL
courtesy Jackson

J

Fusion Series

FUSION EX - offset double cutaway basswood body, black pickguard, bolt-on maple neck, 24-fret rosewood fingerboard with offset white dot inlay, double locking vibrato, 6-on-a-side tuners, black hardware, 2 single coil/1 humbucker Jackson pickups, volume/tone control, 5-position switch. Available in Black, Deep Metallic Blue, Dark Metallic Red and Snow White finishes. Mfg. 1992 to 1995.

$450	$400	$350	$275	$250	$225	$200

Last MSR was $695.

Fusion HH - offset double cutaway mahogany body, bolt-on maple neck, 24-fret bound rosewood fingerboard with offset pearl dot inlay, double locking vibrato, 6-on-a-side tuners, black hardware, 2 humbucker Jackson pickups, 3-position switch. Available in Black and Transparent Red finishes. Mfg. 1992 to 1995.

$600	$525	$450	$350	$325	$300	$275

Last MSR was $895.

In 1992, basswood body with Black finish was optional.
In 1994, basswood body was discontinued.

FUSION PRO - offset double cutaway basswood body, bolt-on maple neck, 24-fret bound ebony fingerboard with pearl sharkfin inlay, double locking vibrato, bound peghead with pearl Jackson logo inlay, 6-on-a-side tuners, black hardware, 2 stacked coil/humbucker Jackson pickups, volume/tone control, 5-position and bypass switches, active electronics. Available in Bright Red, Candy Blue, Metallic Black and Pearl White finishes. Mfg. 1992 to 1994.

$800	$725	$650	$550	$475	$425	$375

Last MSR was $1,295.

Fusion Pro (Trans) - similar to Fusion Pro, except has flame maple top. Available in Cherry Sunburst, Transparent Amber, Transparent Blue and Transparent Red finishes. Disc. 1994.

$875	$795	$700	$650	$550	$450	$375

Last MSR was $1,395.

FUSION XL - offset double cutaway basswood body, bolt-on maple neck, 24-fret bound ebony fingerboard with pearl sharkfin inlay, double locking vibrato, bound peghead with pearl Jackson logo inlay, 6-on-a-side tuners, black hardware, 2 stacked coil/1 humbucker Jackson pickups, volume/tone control, 5-position switch. Available in Deep Metallic Blue, Dark Metallic Red, Metallic Black and Snow White finishes. Mfg. 1992 to 1994.

$625	$595	$500	$400	$350	$325	$300

Last MSR was $995.

Jackson Fusion HH
courtesy Jackson

GRADING	100% MINT	98% NEAR MINT	95% EXC+	90% EXC	80% VG+	70% VG	60% G

Fusion XL (Trans) - similar to Fusion XL, except has flame maple top. Available in Cherry Sunburst, Transparent Blue, Transparent Red and Transparent Violet finishes. Mfg. 1992 to 1994.

$700 $650 $575 $450 $395 $350 $300
Last MSR was $1,095.

FX1 (FUSION STANDARD) - offset double cutaway basswood body, bolt-on maple neck, 24-fret rosewood fingerboard with pearl offset dot inlay, double locking vibrato, bound peghead with screened Jackson logo inlay, 6-on-a-side tuners, black hardware, 2 stacked coil/1 humbucker Jackson pickups, volume/tone control, 5-position switch. Available in Black, Candy Blue, Dark Metallic Red and Snow White finishes. Mfg. 1992 to 1996.

$700 $550 $495 $375 $295 $250 $225
Last MSR was $895.

INFINITY PRO - double cutaway asymmetrical mahogany body, bound figured maple top, set in mahogany neck, 22-fret bound rosewood fingerboard with pearl diamond/abalone dot inlay, double locking vibrato, bound peghead with pearl Jackson logo inlay, 6-on-a-side tuners, chrome hardware, 2 humbucker Jackson pickups, volume/tone control, 3-position switch. Available in Cherry Sunburst, Star Glo, Transparent Blue, Transparent Red and Transparent Violet finishes. Mfg. 1992 to 1994.

$950 $895 $750 $600 $550 $495 $450
Last MSR was $1,495.

Infinity XL - double cutaway asymmetrical bound basswood body, bolt-on maple neck, 22-fret rosewood fingerboard with abalone dot inlay, double locking vibrato, 6-on-a-side tuners, black hardware, 2 humbucker Jackson pickups, volume/tone control, 3-position switch. Available in Black, Deep Metallic Blue, Dark Metallic Red and Magenta finishes. Mfg. 1992 to 1994.

$695 $595 $500 $400 $350 $325 $300
Last MSR was $995.

JTX STD - single cutaway basswood body, pearloid pickguard, bolt-on maple neck, 24-fret maple fingerboard with black dot inlay, double locking Floyd Rose vibrato, 6-on-a-side tuners, chrome hardware, single coil/humbucker Jackson pickup, volume control, 3-position/mini switches. Available in Black, Deep Metallic Blue, Deep Metallic Red, Magenta, Transparent Pearl Purple and Snow White finishes. Mfg. 1993 to 1995.

$450 $395 $300 $250 $225 $195 $150
Last MSR was $695.

J

In 1994, Transparent Pearl Purple and Snow White finishes were introduced, Deep Metallic Blue and Magenta were discontinued.

JTX (Trans) - similar to JTX, except has ash body. Available in Transparent Black, Transparent Blue, Transparent Pearl Purple and Transparent Red finishes. Mfg. 1993 only.

$450 $395 $325 $250 $225 $200 $175
Last MSR was $645.

JRS-2 - offset double cutaway ash body, bolt-on maple neck, 25 1/2" scale, 22-fret rosewood or maple fingerboard, Wilkinson VS-50 vibrato, reverse natural finish headstock, 6 on the other side tuners, chrome hardware, Kent Armstrong humbucker, volume control. Available in Black, Bright Red, Electric Blue, Transparent Black, and Transparent White finishes. Mfg. 1997 to 1998.

$525 $450 $350 $275 $225 $175 $125
Last MSR was $745.

Add $50 for transparent finish.

Kelly Series

KE4 (KELLY STD) - single sharp cutaway radical hourglass style poplar body, bolt-on maple neck, 24-fret rosewood fingerboard with pearl dot inlay, double locking Floyd Rose vibrato, 6-on-a-side tuners, chrome hardware, 2 humbucker Jackson pickups, volume control, 3-position switch. Available in Black, Deep Metallic Blue, Deep Metallic Red and Deep Metallic Violet finishes. Mfg. 1993 to 1998.

$600 $425 $395 $325 $275 $250 $225
Last MSR was $795.

KE3 (R) (KELLY XL) - similar to Kelly STD, except has pearl sharkfin fingerboard inlay. Available in Black, Dark Metallic Blue and Dark Metallic Violet finishes. Mfg. 1994 to date.

MSR $875 $615 $525 $475 $425 $375 $325 $250

Add $50 for transparent finish (Transparent Blue and Transparent Red).

In 1998, Midnight Blue Sparkle, Transparent Blue, and Transparent Red finishes were introduced; Dark Metallic Blue and Dark Metallic Violet finishes were discontinued.

KV3 - V-style poplar body, bolt-on maple neck, 22-fret rosewood fingerboard with pearl sharkfin inlay, double locking vibrato, 6-on-a-side tuners, chrome hardware, 2 Duncan Design humbucker pickups, volume/tone controls, 3-position switch. Available in Black and Midnight Blue Sparkle finishes. Mfg. 1998 to date.

MSR $875 $615 $525 $475 $425 $375 $325 $250

Add $50 for transparent finishes with maple tops (Cherry Sunburst, Transparent Blue, and Transparent Red).

GRADING	100% MINT	98% NEAR MINT	95% EXC+	90% EXC	80% VG+	70% VG	60% G

PHIL COLLEN MODEL - unbalanced double cutaway poplar body, through-body maple neck, 24-fret bound ebony fingerboard with pearl sharkfin inlay, double locking vibrato, bound peghead with pearl Jackson logo inlay, 6-on-a-side Gotoh tuners, black hardware, single coil/humbucker Jackson pickups, volume control, 3-position switch. Available in Metallic Black, Pearl White and Radiant Red Pearl finishes. Mfg. 1991 only.

	$1,100	$1,000	$850	$675	$600	$550	$500

Last MSR was $1,695.

PC3 PHIL COLLEN - offset double cutaway mahogany body, quilted maple top, bolt-on maple neck, 24-fret quilted maple fingerboard, Wilkinson VS50 tremolo, chrome hardware, 2 single coil/humbucker Duncan Design pickups, volume/tone control, 5-way position switch. Available in Transparent Amber, Transparent Green, and Transparent Red finishes. Mfg. 1998 to date.

MSR $995	$750	$650	$600	$550	$500	$425	$300

Designed in conjunction with Phil Collen (Def Leppard).

Rhoads Series

RR4 (RHOADS EX) - sharkfin style poplar body, bolt-on maple neck, 22-fret rosewood fingerboard with pearl dot inlay, double locking vibrato, 6-on-a-side tuners, black hardware, 2 humbucker Jackson pickups, volume control, 3-position switch. Available in Black, Bright Red, Candy Blue, Snow White and Stone finishes. Mfg. 1992 to 1998.

	$595	$400	$350	$275	$250	$225	$200

Last MSR was $745.

Add $50 for transparent finishes.

RR3 - similar to RR4, except has a maple gravure top and sharkfin inlay. Available in Black and Midnight Blue Sparkle finishes. Mfg. 1995 to date.

MSR $875	$615	$525	$475	$425	$350	$300	$225

Add $50 for transparent finishes (Transparent Blue and Transparent Red).

RWR ROSWELL RHOADS - futuristic rounded sharkfin style poplar body, bolt-on maple neck, 25 1/2" scale, 22-fret rosewood fingerboard with 'crop circle' inlay, tune-o-matic bridge/strings through-body ferrules, 3-per-side tuners, black hardware, Duncan Design humbucker pickups, volume control. Available in Black and Midnight Blue Sparkle finishes.

MSR $975	$685	$575	$525	$450	$400	$325	$275

SC1 SURFCASTER - slightly offset single rounded cutaway semi-hollow mahogany body, bound ash top, bound wedge soundhole, bolt-on maple neck, 25.5" scale, 24-fret bound rosewood (or maple) fingerboard with pearl sharkfin inlay, GTB100 wraparound bridge, bound peghead with screened logo, 3-per-side tuners, squared off headstock, chrome hardware, pearloid pickguard, lipstick-style single coil/chrome covered humbucker pickups, volume/tone control, 3-position switch. Available in Transparent Black, Transparent Green, Transparent Ivory, and Transparent Red finishes. Mfg. 1998 to date.

MSR $1,045	$735	$625	$575	$500	$450	$350	$275

1999-Transparent Green and Transparent Ivory finishes discontinued.

SC3 - similar to SC1 except has two single coil pickups and one humbucking pickup, string through-body. Available in black and Sea Foam Green finishes. Current Mfg.

MSR $995	$750	$600	$550	$500	$450	$400	$325

SC12 12-String -similar to SC3 except in a 12-string configuration, ash body, J370 bridge, 2 Duncan Designed LS101 pickups. Available in black and Sea Foam green finishes. Current Mfg.

MSR $1,245	$925	$750	$675	$575	$500	$425	$350

OC1 - similar to the Surfcaster, except has solid basswood body, 1 Chandler LST lipstick-style single coil/exposed pole piece humbucker. Available in Gun Metal Gray, Metallic Violet, and Vintage White finishes. Mfg. 1996 to 1997.

	$625	$500	$440	$380	$325	$290	$250

Last MSR was $725.

SDK2 - smaller (*Super Dinky*) style, offset double cutaway poplar or ash body, bolt-on maple neck, 24-fret bound rosewood (or maple) fingerboard with pearl sharkfin inlay, double locking vibrato, 6-on-a-side tuners, black hardware, humbucker/single coil/humbucking Jackson pickups, volume/tone control, 5-position switch. Available in Black, Cobalt Blue, Red Pearl Satin, Cobalt Blue Satin, and Graphite finishes. Mfg. 1996 to 1998.

	$475	$375	$325	$295	$250	$225	$175

Last MSR was $625.

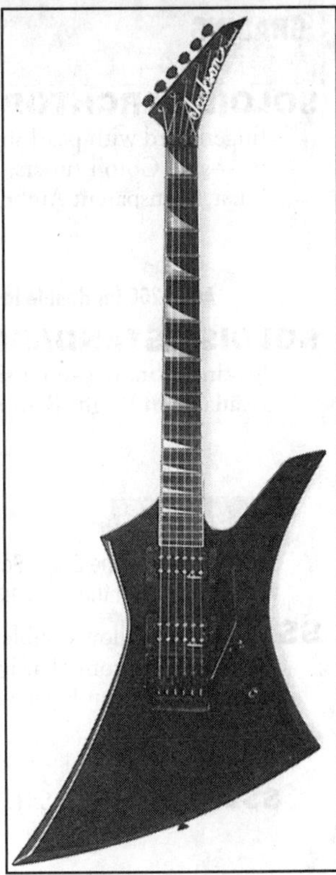

Jackson Kelly XL
courtesy Jackson

J

GRADING	100% MINT	98% NEAR MINT	95% EXC+	90% EXC	80% VG+	70% VG	60% G

SOLOIST ARCHTOP - offset double cutaway mahogany body, arched flame maple top, through-body maple neck, 24-fret bound ebony fingerboard with pearl sharkfin inlay, tune-o-matic bridge with through-body string holders, bound peghead with pearl Jackson logo inlay, 6-on-a-side Gotoh tuners, black hardware, 2 humbucker Jackson pickups, volume/tone control, 3-position switch. Available in Cherry Sunburst, Transparent Amber, Transparent Blue and Transparent Red finishes. Mfg. 1989 to 1991.

$1,000	$895	$750	$600	$550	$495	$450

Last MSR was $1,495.

Add $200 for double locking vibrato.

SOLOIST STANDARD - offset double cutaway poplar body, bolt-on maple neck, 24-fret rosewood fingerboard with dot inlay, double locking vibrato, 6-on-a-side tuners, black hardware, 2 stacked coil/humbucker Jackson pickups, 1 volume/1 tone control, 5-position switch. Available in Bright Red, Deep Metallic Blue, Metallic Blue and Pearl White finishes. Mfg. 1991 to 1995.

$695	$595	$500	$400	$350	$325	$300

Last MSR was $995.

SS Series

Jackson offered the Short Scale series guitars with a scale length of 24 3/4", instead of the usual 25 1/2" scale normally employed. This shorter scale length was an option on the Fusion series for a number of years.

SS1 - offset shallow double cutaway arched basswood or ash body, bolt-on maple neck, 22-fret rosewood fingerboard with dot inlay, 3-per-side headstock, chrome hardware, 2 humbuckers, Wilkinson VS-100 tremolo, volume/tone controls, 3-way switch. Available in Black, Cobalt Blue, Blue Green Pearl, and Red Pearl Satin finishes. Mfg. 1996 to 1997.

$525	$475	$400	$375	$275	$200	$175

Last MSR was $795.

SS2 - similar to the SS1, except has polar body, no arched top, and tune-o-matic stop tailpiece. Mfg. 1996 to 1997.

$450	$375	$325	$275	$175	$150	$125

Last MSR was $695.

TH Series

TH1 (STEALTH EX) - offset double cutaway basswood or ash body, bolt-on maple neck, 22-fret rosewood fingerboard with offset pearl dot inlay, double locking vibrato, 6-on-a-side tuners, black hardware, 2 single coil/humbucker Jackson pickups, volume/tone control, 5-position switch. Available in Black, Metallic Violet, Graphite, Cobalt Blue Satin, and Red Pearl Satin finishes. Mfg. 1991 to 1997.

$595	$400	$350	$275	$250	$225	$200

Last MSR was $795.

Add $100 for left-handed configuration of this model.

TH2 - similar to the TH1, except has Jackson Custom Fulcrum non-locking tremolo and pointy profile *straight pull* 3-per-side headstock. Mfg. 1996 to 1997.

$550	$395	$325	$275	$225	$200	$175

Last MSR was $725.

Stealth Series

STEALTH HX - similar to Stealth EX, except has tune-o-matic bridge, strings through-body tailpiece, 3 humbucker Jackson pickups. Available in Black, Deep Metallic Blue, Deep Metallic Red and Deep Metallic Violet finishes. Mfg. 1991 to 1995.

$425	$375	$300	$250	$225	$195	$175

Last MSR was $595.

STEALTH PRO - offset double cutaway basswood body, bolt-on maple neck, 22-fret ebony fingerboard with offset pearl dot inlay, double locking vibrato, blackface peghead with pearl logo inlay, 6-on-a-side tuners, black hardware, 2 single coil/humbucker Jackson pickups, volume/tone control, 5-position switch. Available in Metallic Blue finish. Mfg. 1991 to 1993.

$795	$725	$600	$495	$425	$375	$325

Last MSR was $1,195.

STEALTH PRO (Trans) - similar to Stealth Pro, except has ash body, body matching peghead without pearl inlay. Available in Transparent Amber finish. Mfg. 1991 to 1993.

$795	$725	$650	$575	$495	$425	$350

Last MSR was $1,295.

This model was available with figured maple top in Transparent Blue and Transparent Violet finishes.

STEALTH XL - similar to Stealth Pro, except has ash body, rosewood fingerboard. Available in Transparent Amber, Transparent Blue, Transparent Red and Transparent Violet finishes. Mfg. 1991 to 1993.

$625	$525	$450	$350	$325	$300	$275

Last MSR was $895.

GRADING	100% MINT	98% NEAR MINT	95% EXC+	90% EXC	80% VG+	70% VG	60% G

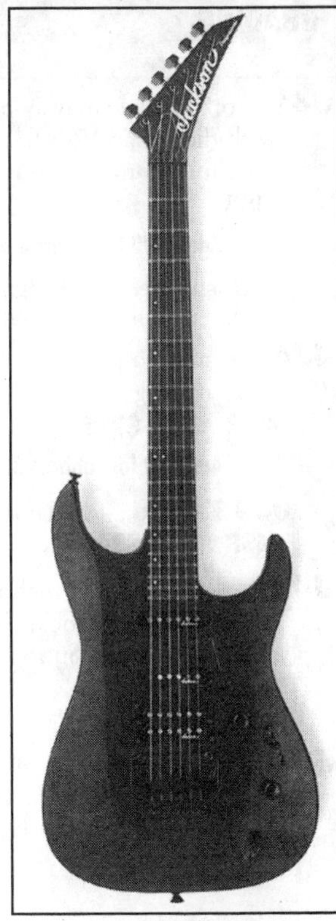
Jackson Stealth EX
courtesy Jackson

WARRIOR PRO - radically offset X-shaped poplar body, through-body maple neck, 24-fret bound ebony fingerboard with pearl sharkfin inlay, double locking vibrato, bound peghead with pearl Jackson logo inlay, 6-on-a-side Gotoh tuners, black hardware, 3 single coil Jackson pickups, volume/tone control, 5-position and mid range sweep switches. Available in Candy Blue, Ferrari Red, Midnight Black, Pearl Yellow and Snow White Pearl finishes. Mfg. 1991 only.

$1,100 $1,000 $895 $775 $650 $550 $475
Last MSR was $1,695.

Jackson Student Series

JS 20 - offset double cutaway alder body, bolt-on maple neck, 22-fret rosewood fingerboard with dot inlay, SG 23 non-locking vibrato, blackface peghead with logo, 6-on-a-side tuners, chrome hardware, 2 single coil/1 humbucker pickups, volume/tone control, 5-position switch. Available in Black, Metallic Blue, and Metallic Red finishes. Mfg. 1996 to date.

MSR $325 $250 $195 $175 $145 $135 $115 $100

JS 30 - similar to JS 20, except features 2 humbuckers. Mfg. 1997 to 1998.

$225 $195 $175 $145 $135 $115 $100
Last MSR was $325.

Jackson U.S.A. Series

Jackson USA models are built in Ontario, California in the same facility as the Jackson Custom Shop.

AT1 - offset double cutaway mahogany (with quilt maple top) or poplar body, bolt-on maple neck, 22-fret ebony fingerboard, chrome hardware, Wilkinson VS-100 tremolo, 2 chrome covered humbuckers, volume/tone controls, 3-way selector switch. Available in Black, Deep Candy Red, Blue Green Pearl, Transparent Blue, Transparent Green, Cherry Sunburst, and Transparent Black finishes. Mfg. 1996 to 1998.

$1,200 $1,000 $950 $850 $750 $675 $550
Last MSR was $1,495.

Add $150 for transparent finish.

AT1 T - similar to the AT1, except features a Wilkinson GB-100 stop tailpiece and chrome humbucker covers. Disc. 1998.

$1,100 $975 $850 $750 $675 $575 $500
Last MSR was $1,445.

Add $150 for transparent finish.

DK1 (DINKY USA) - offset double cutaway poplar body, bound quilted maple top, bolt-on maple neck, 22-fret bound ebony fingerboard with offset pearl dot inlay, Original Floyd Rose vibrato, bound peghead with pearl logo inlay, 6-on-a-side tuners, gold hardware, 2 stacked coil/humbucker Seymour Duncan pickups, volume/tone control, 5-position switch. Available in Black, Deep Candy Red, Blue Green Pearl, Tobacco Sunburst, Transparent Blue, Transparent Purple and Transparent Black finishes. Mfg. 1993-1998.

$1,275 $1,050 $950 $850 $775 $675 $600
Last MSR was $1,695.

Add $100 for transparent finish with maple top (Transparent Black, Blue Burst, Purple Burst, Tobacco Sunburst).

In 1998, bound quilted maple top was only available on transparent finish models.

SDK1 - similar to the DK1, except has smaller (*Super Dinky*) and lighter poplar or ash body, rosewood or maple fingerboard, and humbucker/single coil/humbucking pickups. Available in Black, Cobalt Blue, Orange/Gold Pearl, Gun Metal Grey, Deep Candy Red, and Graphite finishes. Mfg. 1996 to 1997.

$1,000 $875 $750 $675 $595 $500 $475
Last MSR was $1,295.

DR2 - similar to the Dinky Reverse (DR5), except has a poplar (or ash) body, JT580 locking tremolo, 2 Duncan humbuckers, and ebony fingerboard. Available in Black, Ultra Violet Burst, Deep Candy Red, Graphite, and Cobalt Blue Satin finishes. Mfg. 1996-1998.

$1,100 $950 $825 $725 $600 $495 $375
Last MSR was $1,445.

FUSION USA - offset double cutaway basswood body, bolt-on maple neck, 24-fret bound ebony fingerboard with pearl sharkfin inlay, double locking vibrato, bound peghead with pearl Jackson logo inlay, 6-on-a-side tuners, black hardware, 2 stacked coil/1 humbucker Jackson pickups, volume/tone control, 5-position and bypass switches, active electronics. Available in Bright Red, Candy Blue, Metallic Black and Pearl White finishes. Mfg. 1992 to 1994.

$1,650 $1,400 $1,150 $950 $825 $695 $550

GRADING		100% MINT	98% NEAR MINT	95% EXC+	90% EXC	80% VG+	70% VG	60% G

JJ1 - offset dual cutaway poplar or korina body (bass horn slightly extended), bolt-on maple neck, 25 1/2" scale, 22-fret rosewood fingerboard with dice inlay 12th fret markers, 3-per-side headstock, chrome hardware, Wilkinson GTB 100 stop tailpiece, 2 exposed humbuckers, volume/tone control, 3 way selector. Available in Black, Silver Sparkle, and Natural finishes. Mfg. 1996 to date.

MSR	$1,295	$1,000	$895	$775	$675	$575	$495	$400

Add $100 for transparent finish (Transparent Red).

This model was designed in conjunction with Scott Ian (Anthrax).
This model is also available with a Wilkinson VS-100 tremolo as Model JJ1 W (this option was discontinued in 1998).

JJ4 - similar to JJ1 except has string through-body, Tune-O-Matic style bridge, dot position markers. Available in black and Deep Candy Blue. Current Mfg.

MSR	$745	$560	$450	$375	$300	$250	$175	$125

Add $50 for Tobacco Sunburst finish.

JJ4 Tattoo - similar to JJ4 except available in Tattoo finish which is black with intricate white pin-striping job on guitar's top. Current Mfg.

MSR	$845	$635	$510	$425	$350	$275	$200	$150

JJP - single cutaway mahogany body, bolt-on mahogany neck, 24 3/4" scale, 22-fret rosewood fingerboard with dot inlay, 3-per-side tuners, squared off headstock, chrome hardware, DiMarzio humbucker, tune-o-matic bridge/stop tailpiece, volume control. Available in Black, Purple, and Tobacco Sunburst finishes. Mfg. 1997 to 1998.

		$900	$725	$650	$550	$475	$395	$300

Last MSR was $1,195.

JRS-1 - offset double cutaway ash body, bolt-on maple neck, 25 1/2" scale, 22-fret maple fingerboard, Wilkinson VS-100 vibrato, reverse natural finish headstock, 6 on the other side tuners, chrome hardware, Seymour Duncan humbucker, volume control. Available in Black, Electric Blue, Transparent Black, Transparent Red, and Transparent White finishes. Mfg. 1997 to 1998.

		$975	$750	$650	$575	$475	$395	$300

Last MSR was $1,245.

1997 Peter Max Limited Edition JRS-1 - similar to the JRS-1. Available in a hand painted finish by artist Peter Max. Mfg. 1997 only.
Too few of these exist for accurate statistical representation.
In 1997, Jackson offered a very limited series of guitars hand painted by artist Peter Marx. Series I models were to be painted all over, and limited to a total of 12 pieces. Series II models were to be painted on the face of the body only, and limited to 24 pieces. However, a total of only 4 pieces were actually completed out of the entire project. Rare? Yes. Documented? Yes. Price? What the market will bear.

J

KE1 (KELLY PRO) - single sharp cutaway radical hourglass style poplar body, through-body maple neck, 24-fret bound ebony fingerboard with pearl sharkfin inlay, Kahler APM 3310 non-locking fixed bridge, 6-on-a-side tuners, black hardware, Duncan TB4 humbucker pickup, volume control. Available in (Metallic) Black, Transparent Black, and Snow White Pearl finishes. Mfg. 1994 to date.

MSR	$1,695	$1,200	$1,000	$895	$775	$650	$550	$425

Add $100 for transparent finish with maple top (Transparent Black).

Add $150 for Original Floyd Rose tremolo (Model KE1 F) (this option was discontinued in 1998).

This model was designed in conjunction with Marty Freidman (Megadeth).

KE2 - similar to the KE1, except features an Original Floyd Rose tremolo, 2 Seymour Duncan humbucker pickups. Available in Black and Purple Pavo finishes. Mfg. 1998 to date.

MSR	$1,895	$1,325	$1,150	$1,000	$900	$750	$625	$475

KV1 (KING V PRO-MUSTAINE) - V-style poplar body, through-body maple neck, 24-fret bound ebony fingerboard with pearl sharkfin inlay, fixed locking Kahler APM 3310 bridge, bound peghead, 6-on-a-side tuners, black hardware, 2 Seymour Duncan humbucker pickups, 2 volume/1 tone controls, 3-position switch. Available in Black, Cherry Sunburst and Sparkle Silver Metallic finishes. Mfg. 1993 to date.

MSR	$1,795	$1,450	$1,075	$950	$800	$750	$675	$450

Add $100 for Transparent Black finish.
In 1994, Cherry Sunburst finish was introduced.
In 1998, Natural finish with Korina body was introduced; Cherry Sunburst and Sparkle Silver Metallic finishes were discontinued.

KV2 (KING V STD. Mfg. 1993-1997) - V-style poplar body, bolt-on maple neck, 22-fret rosewood fingerboard with pearl dot inlay, double locking Floyd Rose vibrato, 6-on-a-side tuners, black hardware, 2 Jackson humbucker pickups, volume control, 3-position switch. Available in Black, Bright Red, Candy Blue and Snow White finishes. Mfg. 1993 to 1997.

		$595	$425	$375	$300	$275	$250	$200

Last MSR was $795.

KV2 (Mfg. 1998 to Date) - similar to the KV2 (Formerly King V Std.), except features maple through-body neck, 22-fret ebony fingerboard with sharkfin inlay, 2 Seymour Duncan humbucker pickups. Available in Black, Natural, and Purple Pavo finishes. Mfg. 1998 to date.

MSR	$1,895	$1,325	$1,175	$950	$875	$750	$625	$475

GRADING		100% MINT	98% NEAR MINT	95% EXC+	90% EXC	80% VG+	70% VG	60% G

PC1 PHIL COLLEN - offset double cutaway koa body, quilted maple top, bolt-on maple neck, 24-fret quilted maple fingerboard, Original Floyd Rose locking tremolo, gold hardware, Floyd Rose Sustainer pickup/DiMarzio HS-2 single coil/DiMarzio Super 3 humbucker, volume/tone control, 5 way position switch. Available in Au Naturel, Chlorine, Euphoria, Mocha, and Solar Transparent finishes. Mfg. 1996 to date.

MSR	$2,095	$1,750	$1,325	$1,175	$1,000	$850	$700	$550

Designed in conjunction with Phil Collen (Def Leppard).

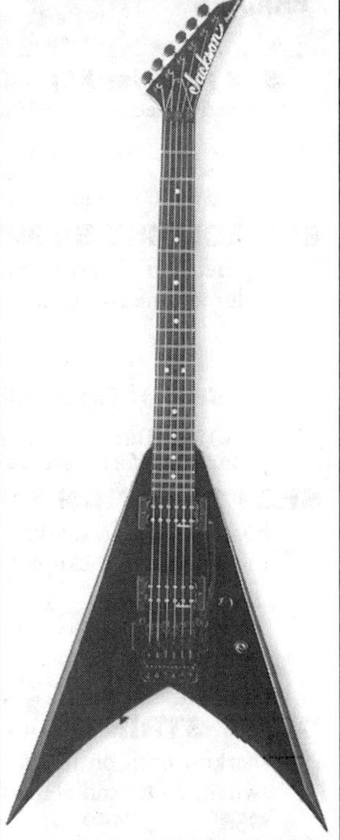

Jackson King V Standard courtesy Jackson

Rhoads Series

RANDY RHOADS LIMITED EDITION - sharkfin style maple body, through-body maple neck, 22-fret bound ebony fingerboard with pearl block inlay, standard vibrato, bound peghead, truss rod cover with overlapping RR stamped into it, 6-on-a-side tuners, gold hardware, 2 humbucker Jackson pickups, 2 volume/tone controls, 3-position switch located on top side of body. Available in White finish with Black pinstriping around body edge. Mfg. 1992 only.

		$1,750	$1,495	$1,250	$1,000	$900	$825	$750

Last MSR was $2,495.

This was a reproduction of the original series that was co-designed by Randy Rhoads and luthier Grover Jackson. Only 200 reproductions were built.

RR1 (RHOADS USA) - similar to Rhoads EX except has black pickguard, bound ebony fingerboard with pearl sharkfin inlay, bound peghead with pearl logo inlay, volume/2 tone controls, 3-way switch. Available in Cobalt Blue, Deep Candy Red, Gun Metal Gray, and Blue Green Metallic finishes. Mfg. 1987 to date.

MSR	$1,895	$1,400	$1,150	$1,000	$900	$775	$725	$475

In 1998, Metallic Black finish was introduced; Gun Metal Gray and Blue Green Metallic finishes were discontinued.

RR1T - similar to RR1 except has a Tunamatic string through-body, SH4B bridge pickup. Available in Blue Green Pearl, black, Black Pearl, Cobalt Blue, Electric Blue Metallic, Ferrari Red, Gun Metal Gray, Metallic Black and Pavo Purple finishes. Current Mfg.

MSR	$1,895	$1,400	$1,150	$1,000	$900	$775	$725	$475

RR2 - similar to RR1, except has maple gravure top, bolt-on neck, 22-fret ebony fingerboard. Available in Black, Deep Metallic Blue, Dark Metallic Red and Snow White finishes. Mfg. 1996 to 1998.

		$1,000	$875	$700	$600	$550	$425	$350

Last MSR was $1,295.

RR3(R) - similar to RR1 except has alder body with flamed maple top, bolt-on rock maple neck with rosewood fingerboard, sharkfin position markers, Duncan Designed 103B and 103N humbucking pickups, JT580LP bridge. Available in black and Deep Candy Blue finishes. Current Mfg.

MSR	$875	$650	$525	$475	$425	$375	$300	$225

Add $50 for Transparent red and Transparent Blue finishes.

RR7 (R) - similar to RR1T except in a 7-string configuration. Available in black and Deep Candy Blue finishes. Current Mfg.

MSR	$895	$675	$550	$475	$425	$400	$325	$250

SDTL1 - single cutaway ash body, bolt-on maple neck, 22-fret maple fingerboard, screened logo, 6-on-a-side tuners, 2 Armstrong single coil pickups/Wilkinson power bridge, 2 volume controls, push/pull pot fader, 3-way selector, stereo output jack, Mfg. 1996 only.

		$1,000	$825	$775	$675	$575	$495	$400

Last MSR was $1,395.

Soloist Series

SOLOIST USA - offset double cutaway poplar body, through-body maple neck, 24-fret bound ebony fingerboard with pearl sharkfin inlay, double locking vibrato, bound peghead with pearl Jackson logo inlay, 6-on-a-side tuners, black hardware, 2 stacked coil/1 humbucker Jackson pickups, volume/tone/mid boost controls, 5-position switch, active electronics. Available in Bright Red, Deep Metallic Blue, Metallic Blue and Pearl White finishes. Mfg. 1991 to 1995.

		$1,300	$1,100	$895	$700	$550	$495	$450

Last MSR was $2,295.

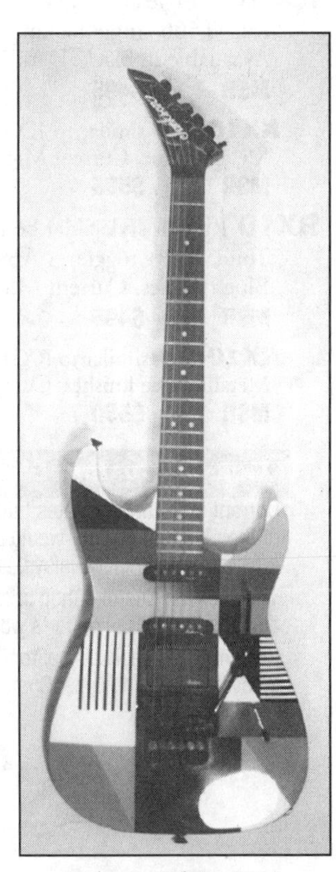

Jackson Soloist USA (Picasso finish) courtesy Jackson

SL1 (SOLOIST USA) - offset double cutaway poplar body, through-body maple neck, 24-fret bound ebony fingerboard with pearl sharkfin inlay, Original Floyd Rose tremelo, bound peghead with pearl Jackson logo inlay, 6-on-a-side tuners, black hardware, 2 Duncan stacked humbuckers/Duncan TB4 humbucker pickups, volume/tone/mid boost controls, 5 way switch, active electronics. Available in Blue Green Pearl, Deep Candy Red, Gun Metal Gray, and Metallic Black finishes. Mfg. 1991 to date.

MSR	$1,795	$1,250	$1,075	$950	$800	$675	$550	$450

This model is available with optional custom graphics.

J

GRADING	100% MINT	98% NEAR MINT	95% EXC+	90% EXC	80% VG+	70% VG	60% G

SL2 (Soloist XL) - similar to SL1, except has ebony fingerboard with no inlays, 2 exposed humbuckers, chrome hardware, screened logo, and no active electronics. Available in Deep Metallic Blue, Dark Metallic Red, Metallic Black and Pearl White finishes. Mfg. 1996 to 1998.

	$1,000	**$875**	**$750**	**$625**	**$575**	**$425**	**$350**

Last MSR was $1,395.

Add $100 for mother-of-pearl sharkfin neck inlay (Model SL2 S).

SLS SOLOIST SUPERLIGHT - offset double cutaway mahogany body, contoured flame maple top, through-body mahogany neck, 24-fret bound rosewood fingerboard, 3-per-side pointed headstock, tune-o-matic bridge/stop tailpiece, chrome hardware, 2 humbuckers, volume/tone controls. Available in Black, Tobacco Sunburst, and Transparent Orange burst finishes. Mfg. 1997-1998.

	$1,250	**$1,000**	**$895**	**$775**	**$650**	**$550**	**$425**

Last MSR was $1,675.

Add $20 for optional flame maple top (this option was discontinued in 1998).

In 1998, Burst Cherry Sunburst and Transparent Black finishes were introduced; Black, Tobacco Sunburst, and Transparent Orange Burst finishes were discontinued.

SHS1 SHANNON SOLOIST - offset double cutaway poplar body, through-body maple neck, 25.5" scale, 24-fret bound ebony fingerboard with pearl sharkfin inlay, 6-on-a-side pointed headstock, Original Floyd Rose tremolo, chrome hardware, 2 single coil/humbucker Seymour Duncan pickups, volume/tone controls, 5 way selector. Available in Black, Blue Ghost Flames, and Slime Green finishes. Mfg. 1998.

	$1,350	**$1,150**	**$1,000**	**$895**	**$750**	**$600**	**$475**

Last MSR was $1,895.

X Series

DX7 7 STRING - offset double cutaway solid body, 7-string configuration, alder body, bolt-on maple neck, rosewood fingerboard with sharkfin position markers, JT790 Tunamatic bridge, string through-body, reverse headstock, 7 on 1 side tuners, 1 Volume/1Tone, 3-way switch, 2 Duncan Designed HB7 humbucking pickups. Available in black, Dark Metallic Blue and Dark Metallic Red finishes. Current Mfg.

MSR $499	**$375**	**$300**	**$250**	**$200**	**$175**	**$150**	**$100**

DX10 - similar to DX7 except in a 6-string cinfiguration, JT500 single locking bridge, Armstrong 213 and Armstrong 214 humbucking pickups, dot position markers. Available in black, Dark Metallic Red and Dark Metallic Blue finishes. Current Mfg.

MSR $425	**$320**	**$255**	**$200**	**$175**	**$150**	**$125**	**$85**

DX10-D - similar to DX10 except has sharkfin position markers. Available in black, Dark Metallic Red and Dark Metallic Blue finishes. Current Mfg.

MSR $485	**$365**	**$290**	**$250**	**$200**	**$175**	**$150**	**$110**

KX10 - single cutaway design with sweeping lower bout, solid alder body, bolt-on maple neck, rosewood fingerboard with dot position markers, JT500 single locking bridge, 1 Volume/1 Tone, 3-way slotted switch, 1 Armstrong 213 and 1 Armstrong 214 humbucking pickups. Avaailable in black, Dark Metallic Red and Dark Metallic Blue finishes. Current Mfg.

MSR $495	**$375**	**$300**	**$250**	**$225**	**$200**	**$175**	**$125**

KX10-D - similar to KX10 except has sharkfin position markers, JT500 double locking bridge. Available in black, Dark Metallic Red and Dark Metallic Blue. Current Mfg.

MSR $555	**$420**	**$335**	**$300**	**$250**	**$225**	**$200**	**$150**

RX10 Rhoads style alder body, bolt-on maple neck, rosewood fingerboard with dot position markers, JT500 single locking bridge, 1 Volume/1 Tone, 3-way toggle, 1 Armstrong 213 and 1 Armstrong 214 humbucking pickups. Available in black, Dark Metallic Red and Dark Metallic Blue finishes. Current Mfg.

MSR $495	**$375**	**$300**	**$250**	**$225**	**$200**	**$175**	**$125**

RX10-D - similar to RX10 except has sharkfin position markers and JT500 double locking bridge. Available in black, Dark Metallic Red and Dark Metallic Blue finishes. Current Mfg.

MSR $550	**$415**	**$$325**	**$275**	**$250**	**$225**	**$200**	**$150**

Jackson Custom Shop Guitars

Current literature indicates that the Jackson Custom Shop has been creating custom guitars longer than any production facility in the U.S. A current example of their custom artistry would be the **Roswell Rhoads**, an advanced sharkfin design machined out of 6061-TS aircraft grade aluminum that features LSR tuners, "crop circle" neck inlays, and a Tom Holmes humbucking pickup.

The Jackson Custom Shop briefly featured custom pyrography finishes, a wood burning technique by artist Dino Muradian that offers a high degree of drawing and shading on the guitar's wood body.

Currently, the Jackson Custom Shop is offering a wide range of body and neck woods, pickup selection, custom wiring, custom or airbrushed finishes, and innovative body designs. Custom guitars take 4 to 12 months for delivery. Contact Jackson Guitars or a local Jackson dealer for a full price quote.

GRADING	100% MINT	98% NEAR MINT	95% EXC+	90% EXC	80% VG+	70% VG	60% G

CUSTOM SHOP GUITAR MODEL (BASE PRICE) - Alder (or basswood or poplar) body, quartersawn maple neck, 25.5" scale, 22 (or 24) fret maple (or rosewood or ebony) fingerboard with sharkfin or dot inlay, Gotoh tuners, chrome or black hardware, choice of pickups and configuration. Available in Solid, Candy Colors, Metallic, or Pearl finishes. Current (specialty) Mfg.

Bolt-On Neck.
MSR $2,300

Bolt-On Neck, figured maple top.
MSR $2,500

Bolt-On Neck, arched figured maple top.
MSR $2,750

Through-body Neck.
MSR $2,750

Through-body Neck, figured maple top.
MSR $2,950

Through-body Neck, arched figured maple top.
MSR $3,100

List prices include an SKB case.

WARRIOR USA - radically offset X-shaped poplar body, through-body maple neck, 24-fret bound ebony fingerboard with pearl sharkfin inlay, double locking vibrato, bound peghead with pearl Jackson logo inlay, 6-on-a-side Gotoh tuners, black hardware, 3 single coil Jackson pickups, volume/tone control, 5-position and midrange sweep switches. Available in Candy Blue, Ferrari Red, Midnight Black, Pearl Yellow and Snow White Pearl finishes. Mfg. circa mid to late 1980s.

$1,995 $1,385 $1,060 $875 $605 $555 $505
Last MSR was $2,950.

This model was available as a custom order only.

ELECTRIC BASS

Concert Series

C 4 P - sleek offset double cutaway poplar body, bolt-on maple neck, 34" scale, 24-fret rosewood fingerboard with pearl dot inlay, chrome hardware, JB340 fixed bridge, 2-per-side tuners, 2 Duncan Design J-style pickups, volume/blend/tone controls. Available in Black, Deep Candy Blue, and Dark Metallic Red finishes. Mfg. 1998 to date.

MSR $645 $450 $400 $350 $325 $275 $225 $175

Add $50 for Transparent Red, Transparent Ivory and Burnt Cherry Sunburst finishes.

C 4 A - similar to the C 4 P, except features 2 Duncan Design SB101 'soapbar' pickups, Armstrong PAB-20 preamp. Available in Black and Deep Candy Blue finishes. Mfg. 1998 to date.

MSR $795 $550 $475 $425 $375 $325 $275 $225

Add $50 for Transparent Red and Tobacco Sunburst (Mahogany body) finishes.

C 4 J - similar to the C 4 P, except features 2 Duncan Design JB104 Alnico J-style pickups. Available in Black, Deep Candy Blue, and Dark Metallic Red finishes. Mfg. 1998.

$500 $425 $350 $300 $250 $200 $175
Last MSR was $725.

Add $50 for Tobacco Sunburst (Mahogany body) finish.

C 5 P 5-STRING - sleek offset double cutaway poplar body, bolt-on maple neck, 34" scale, 24-fret rosewood fingerboard with pearl dot inlay, chrome hardware, JB350 fixed bridge, 3/2-per-side tuners, 2 Duncan Design SB101 pickups, volume/blend/tone controls. Available in Black, Deep Candy Blue, and Dark Metallic Red finishes. Mfg. 1998 to date.

MSR $745 $525 $450 $400 $350 $300 $250 $200

Add $50 for Transparent red, Transparent Ivory and Burnt Cherry Sunburst finishes.

C 5 A - similar to the C 5 P, except features 2 Duncan Design SB101 pickups, Armstrong PAB-20 preamp. Available in Black and Deep Candy Blue finishes. Mfg. 1998 to date.

MSR $845 $595 $495 $450 $400 $350 $275 $225

Add $50 for Transparent Red (Ash body), Transparent Ivory (Ash body) and Tobacco Sunburst (Mahogany body) finishes.

C 20 - sleek offset double cutaway poplar body, bolt-on maple neck, 21-fret rosewood fingerboard with pearl dot inlay, chrome hardware, RBB10 fixed bridge, Jackson P/J-style pickups, volume/blend/tone controls. Available in Black, Metallic Blue, and Metallic Red finishes. Mfg. 1998 to date.

MSR $445 $325 $275 $250 $200 $150 $100 $125

J

GRADING	100% MINT	98% NEAR MINT	95% EXC+	90% EXC	80% VG+	70% VG	60% G

JS Series

JS-40 - offset double cutaway alder body, bolt-on maple neck, 22-fret rosewood fingerboard with white dot inlay, fixed bridge, 4-on-a-side tuners, black hardware, P/J-style pickups, volume/tone/mix control. Available in Black, Metallic Blue, and Metallic Red finishes. Mfg. 1997 to date.

MSR	$395	$295	$240	$215	$185	$155	$130	$100

Performer Series

PS-5 - offset double cutaway alder body, bolt-on maple neck, 22-fret rosewood fingerboard with white dot inlay, fixed bridge, 4-on-a-side tuners, black hardware, Jackson P/J-style pickups, volume/tone/mix control. Available in Black, Deep Metallic Blue, Red Violet Metallic, Blue Green Metallic, and Black Cherry finishes. Mfg. 1997 to 1999.

$415	$340	$310	$265	$245	$220	$175

Last MSR was $595.

Add $50 for alder body/flamed maple top in Transparent finish (Transparent Blue, Transparent Green, Transparent Purple, and Transparent Red).

Professional Series

CONCERT EX - offset double cutaway poplar body, bolt-on maple neck, 22-fret rosewood fingerboard with white dot inlay, fixed bridge, 4-on-a-side tuners, black hardware, Jackson P/J-style pickups, volume/tone/mix control. Available in Black, Bright Red, Candy Blue, Snow White and Stone finishes. Mfg. 1992 to 1995.

$425	$350	$300	$250	$225	$195	$175

Last MSR was $595.

In 1994, Bright Red and Snow White finishes were discontinued.

Concert XL - similar to Concert EX, except has bound fingerboard with pearl sharkfin inlay. Available in Black Cherry, Deep Metallic Blue, Dark Metallic Red, Metallic Black and Pearl White finishes. Mfg. 1992 to 1995.

$575	$525	$450	$375	$325	$300	$275

Last MSR was $895.

In 1994, Pearl White finish was discontinued.

Concert V - similar to Concert EX, except has 5 strings, bound fingerboard with sharkfin inlay, Kahler fixed bridge, volume/treble/bass/mix controls, active electronics. Available in Black Cherry, Dark Metallic Blue and Metallic Black finishes. Mfg. 1992 to 1995.

$595	$525	$475	$400	$375	$325	$300

Last MSR was $995.

EL1 - sleek offset double cutaway basswood body, maple neck, 21-fret rosewood fingerboard, black hardware, fixed bridge, P/J Jackson pickups, volume/blend/tone controls. Available in Black, cobalt Blue, and Red Pearl finishes. Mfg. 1996 to 1998.

$625	$550	$475	$425	$375	$325	$295

Last MSR was $745.

Add $50 for transparent finish.

FUTURA EX (WINGER BASS) - double cutaway asymmetrical offset poplar body, bolt-on maple neck, 22-fret rosewood fingerboard with pearl dot inlay, fixed bridge, 4-on-a-side tuners, black hardware, P/J-style Jackson pickups, volume/tone/mix control. Available in Black, Deep Metallic Blue, Magenta and Snow White finishes. Mfg. 1992 to 1995.

$525	$475	$395	$325	$275	$250	$225

Last MSR was $795.

Add $100 for left-handed version.

The Winger Bass was co-designed in conjunction with Kip Winger.

FUTURA PRO (WINGER BASS) - double cutaway asymmetrical offset maple body, through-body maple neck, 21-fret ebony fingerboard with pearl dot inlay, Kahler fixed bridge, 4-on-a-side tuners, black hardware, 2 EMG pickups, volume/treble/bass/mix control, active electronics. Available in Candy Red, Metallic Black and Pearl White finishes. Mfg. 1992 to 1993.

$1,250	$1,100	$895	$725	$650	$595	$500

Last MSR was $1,795.

Futura Pro (Trans) - similar to Futura Pro, except has lacewood body/neck and has body color matching bound peghead. Available in Carmel Lace, Cinnabar and Natural finishes. Disc. 1993.

$1,300	$1,150	$950	$750	$695	$625	$575

Last MSR was $1,895.

Futura XL - similar to Futura Pro, except has Jackson fixed bridge and P/J-style pickups. Available in Dark Metallic Red, Metallic Black and Pearl White finishes. Disc. 1993.

$900	$795	$675	$525	$475	$425	$375

Last MSR was $1,295.

J

GRADING	100% MINT	98% NEAR MINT	95% EXC+	90% EXC	80% VG+	70% VG	60% G

Futura XL (Trans) - similar to Futura Pro (Trans), except has Jackson fixed bridge and P/J-style pickups. Available in Translucent finishes. Disc. 1993.

		$975	$825	$700	$550	$500	$450	$400

Last MSR was $1,395.

JJ BASS (U.S. Mfg.) - dual cutaway poplar body, bolt-on maple neck, 30" scale, 19-fret rosewood fingerboard with pearl dot inlay, Hipshot fixed bridge, 2-per-side tuners, chrome hardware, Seymour Duncan Basslines humbucking pickup, volume/3 tone controls. Available in Black and Interference Flame finishes. Mfg. 1998 to date.

MSR	$1,695	$1,200	$1,000	$895	$775	$650	$550	$425

Add $200 for Interference Flame finish.

JM6 - offset double cutaway poplar body, bolt-on maple neck, 34" scale, 21-fret rosewood fingerboard with pearl dot inlay, JB340 fixed bridge, 4-on-a-side tuners, natural finish headstock, chrome hardware, Armstrong MM-1 humbucker pickup, volume/tone controls. Available in Black, Retro Green, and Retro Red finishes. Mfg. 1998.

		$425	$375	$325	$295	$250	$195	$150

Last MSR was $595.

JM6 PJ - similar to the JM6, except features Duncan Design P/J-style pickups. Available in Black, Retro Green, and Retro Red finishes. Mfg. 1998.

		$425	$375	$325	$295	$250	$195	$150

Last MSR was $595.

JZB-1 - sleek offset double cutaway alder body, quilted maple top, bolt-on maple neck, 21-fret pau ferro fingerboard, black hardware, fixed bridge, 2 EMG 'soapbar' pickups, volume/blend/tone controls. Available in Amber Sunburst, Transparent Black, and Transparent Purple finishes. Mfg. 1997 to 1998.

		$1,200	$1,000	$900	$795	$675	$550	$425

Last MSR was $1,695.

JZB-2 - similar to the JZB-1, except features an alder (or ash) body, rosewood fingerboard, cream pickguard, 2 Jackson J-style pickups. Available in Black, Electric Blue, Cherry Sunburst, and Tobacco Sunburst finishes. Mfg. 1997 to 1998.

		$975	$800	$725	$625	$525	$425	$325

Last MSR was $1,295.

KB1 KELLY BASS - single sharp cutaway radical hourglass style poplar body, through-body maple neck, 22-fret bound rosewood fingerboard with pearl dot inlay, fixed bridge, 4-on-a-side tuners, black hardware, Jackson P/J pickups, volume/blend/tone controls. Available in Black and Cobalt Blue finishes. Mfg. 1994 to date.

MSR	$745	$525	$450	$400	$350	$300	$250	$200

TBX - single cutaway asymmetrical hourglass poplar body, through-body maple neck, 21-fret bound rosewood fingerboard with pearl sharkfin inlay, fixed bridge, bound blackface peghead with screened logo, 4-on-a-side tuners, black hardware, 2 humbucker EMG pickups, 2 volume/tone controls. Available in Black, Dark Metallic Violet and Scarlet Green Metallic finishes. Mfg. 1994 to 1995.

		$1,100	$925	$850	$675	$600	$550	$495

Last MSR was $1,695.

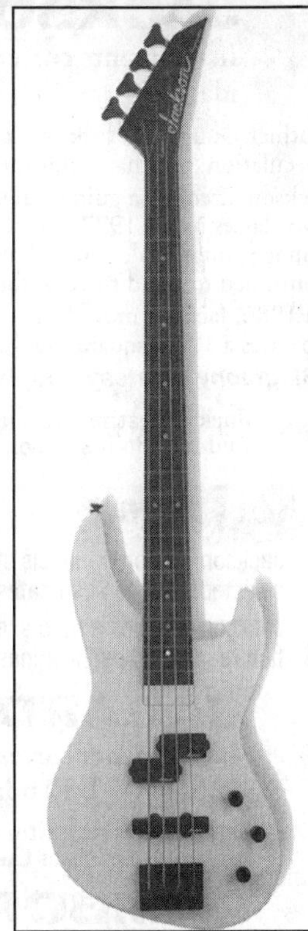

Jackson Futura Ex Bass
courtesy Jackson

Jackson Custom Shop Basses

The Jackson Custom Shop is currently offering a wide range of body and neck woods, pickup selection, custom wiring, custom or airbrushed finishes, and innovative body designs. Custom guitars take 4 to 12 months for delivery. Contact Jackson Guitars or a local Jackson dealer for a full price quote.

CUSTOM SHOP BASS MODEL (BASE PRICE) - Alder (or basswood or poplar) body, quartersawn maple neck, 25.5" scale, 22 (or 24) fret maple (or rosewood or ebony) fingerboard with sharkfin or dot inlay, Gotoh tuners, chrome or black hardware, choice of pickups and configuration. Available in Solid, Candy color, Metallic, or Pearl finishes. Current (specialty) Mfg.

Bolt-On Neck.

MSR $2,200

Bolt-On Neck, figured maple top.

MSR $2,400

Through-body Neck.

MSR $2,500

Through-body Neck, figured maple top.

MSR $2,850

Through-body Neck, arched figured maple top.

MSR $3,050

List prices include an SKB case.

J

JACKSON, DOUGLAS R.

Instruments currently built in Destin, Florida. Distributed through the Douglas R. Jackson Guitar Shop of Destin, Florida.

Luthier Douglas R. Jackson handcrafts his own acoustic and electric guitars, which are built on commission. On occasion, Jackson may build a model on speculation, but that is not the norm. All models are marketed through his guitar shop.

Jackson attended a guitar building school in the Spring of 1977. While enrolled, he was hired by the school to teach and perform repairs. Jackson taught two classes in the 1977 school year, and helped build over 150 instruments (plus his own personal guitars and repairs). Jackson then went to work for a vintage guitar dealer on and off for three years, while he studied just about anything he could get his hands on. During this research phase, Jackson continued to build three or four guitars a year (in addition to his shop repairs).

In 1986, Jackson moved from Arizona to his present location in Destin, Florida (the Pensacola/Fort Walton Beach area). Jackson currently owns and operates a 1,500 square foot building that houses his guitar shop and manufacturing equipment.

(Biography courtesy Douglas R. Jackson)

Jackson estimates that he has built close to 100 instruments consisting of acoustic and electric 6- and 12-string guitars, electric basses and mandolins, resonator guitars, along with a couple of dulcimers (both hammered and Appalachian).

ELECTRIC

Jackson's electric models start at $1,250 for a *set neck* or *neck-through* style, and go up depending on choice of woods, electronics, and the hardware selected. Jackson estimates that the prices of his used electrics range from $600 and up.

Jackson supplies a hard shell case for all of his hand crafted instruments. The majority of instruments are built based on a commission. For further information regarding specifications and pricing, please contact Douglas R. Jackson directly (see Trademark Index).

JAGARD

Instruments currently built in Japan, Taiwan, and China by the Eikosha Musical Instrument Co., Inc. Distributed in the U.S. by V. J. Rendano, located in Boardman, OH.

Jagard electric guitars feature solid ash and solid maple bodies. For more information about current model lineup, availability, and pricing, please contact the distributor directly (see Trademark Index).

JAMBOREE

Instruments previously produced in Japan.

The Jamboree trademark was a brand name used by U.S. importers Elger/Hoshino of Ardmore, Pennsylvania. Jamboree, along with others like Goldentone, King's Stone, and Elger were all used on Japanese guitars imported to the U.S. Elger/Hoshino evolved into Hoshino USA, the distributor of Ibanez guitars.

(Source: Michael Wright, Guitar Stories Volume One)

JAMMER

Instruments currently produced in Asia. Distributed by VMI Industries (Vega Musical Instruments) of Brea, California.

Jammer instruments are designed with the entry level and student guitarist in mind.

JANSEN

Instruments previously produced in Auckland, New Zealand from the 1960s through the 1970s.

Jansen guitars and amplifiers were manufactured by Beverly Bruce and Goldy Ltd., who continued to produce amplifiers and P.A. gear through the late 1980s. During the 1960s and 1970s, Jansen guitars were the most popular brand in New Zealand. One notable U.S. example of Jansen guitars was the *Jazzman* model that was used by the Surfaris.

Jansen guitars were basically Fender-style copies. The Invader model was based on the Stratocaster, while the Beatmaster and Jazzman were based on the Telecaster and Jaguar, respectively. Jansen basses also played "follow the leader", with the Rock Bass and Beat Bass models emulating the Precision and Telecaster basses. Further market surveys will review playability and production quality.

Rarity and lack of activity in the secondary marketplace precludes accurate pricing on this model.

JAROCK

Instruments previously built in Japan during the early 1980s.

These guitars are medium quality Stratocaster-styled solid body guitars.

(Source: Tony Bacon and Paul Day, The Guru's Guitar Guide)

JAROS CUSTOM GUITARS

Instruments currently built in Rochester, Pennsylvania since 1995. Distribution is handled directly at Jaros Custom Guitars, Guitar Land in San Clemente, and Doc's Vintage Guitars in West Los Angeles, California.

Combining years of cabinetmaking and guitar playing, Harry Jaros and his son James decided to build a couple of guitars as a father-and-son project. When the beautifully crafted original models turned out to have great tone and playability, the family hobby quickly became a business venture as they decided to produce more of these handcrafted instruments and make them available for everyone to enjoy!

From coast to coast, Jaros has a pair of guitar players currently endorsing his custom guitars: Jon Butcher, and Bruce Gatewood.

ELECTRIC

Jaros handcrafted guitars feature a 12" neck radius. Both models are available in a semi-hollow ('internal tone chambers') and solid body configurations. Other options include a 24-fret fingerboard; choice of tiger, quilt or bird's-eye maple; translucent lacquer colors; and distinct custom abalone and mother-of-pearl inlay. There are no price up charges for left-handed models.

GRADING	100% MINT	98% NEAR MINT	95% EXC+	90% EXC	80% VG+	70% VG	60% G

CUSTOM 22 CARVE TOP - slightly offset double cutaway mahogany body, bookmatched AAA figured maple carved top, figured maple back, through-body eastern hard rock maple or mahogany neck, 25" scale, 22-fret rosewood (or ebony or paduak) fretboard with original design inlays, chrome or gold hardware, 3-per-side Schaller tuners, two Seymour Duncan humbucking pickups, volume/tone controls (push/pull pots wired for coil tapping), 3-way selector switch. Available in Clear and Sunburst nitrocellulose finishes. Mfg. 1996 to date.

MSR $2,799

List price includes hardshell case.

CUSTOM 22 FLAT TOP - similar to the Custom 22 Carve Top, except has flat bookmatched AAA figured maple top. Mfg. 1995 to date.

MSR $2,799

JAX

Instruments previously produced in Taiwan during the early 1980s.

These solid body guitars consist of entry level designs based on classic American models.

(Source: Tony Bacon and Paul Day, The Guru's Guitar Guide)

JAY DEE

Instruments currently built in Birmingham, England since1977.

The Jay Dee trademark sometimes appears as J D on the headstock of these high quality original design guitars. Luthier John Diggins has been quite successful in building a quality instrument through the years, and has produced some models based on classic American designs as well.

Jay Dee **Supernatural** basses were distributed in the U.S. for a length of time by Aspen & Associates starting in 1985. Aspen & Associates are the non-tube side of Aspen Pittman's Groove Tubes company.

(Source: Tony Bacon and Paul Day, The Guru's Guitar Guide)

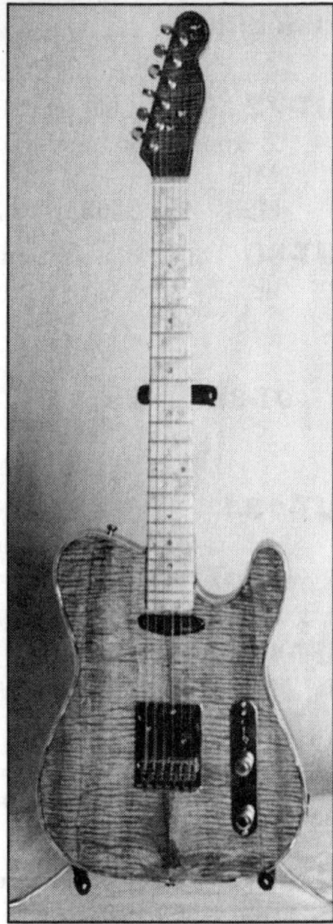

D. Jackson custom Electric courtesy Doug Jackson

JAY G

See chapter on House Brands.

This trademark has been identified as a *sub-brand* from the budget line of CHRIS guitars by the Jackson-Guldan company of Columbus, Ohio.

(Source: Willie G. Moseley, Stellas & Stratocasters)

JAY TURSER

Instruments currently produced in Asia. Distributed by Music Industries Corporation of Floral Park, New York.

Music Industries is currently offering a wide range of Jay Turser solid body electric instruments. These instruments are student and entry level instruments with fairly good quality necks and electronics, and are offered in a good number of finishes.

ELECTRIC

Jay Turser models are offered in the following colors: Antique (ANS), Black (BK), Blue Sparkle (BLSP), Cherry Sunburst (CS), Matt Green (MG), Natural Honey (NH), Purple Sunburst (PS), Red Sunburst (RS), Red Sparkle (RSP), Silver Sparkle (SSP), Transparent Black (TB), Transparent Blue (TBL), Transparent Moss Green (TMG), Transparent Red (TR), Tobacco Sunburst (TS), and Violin Shade (VS) finishes.

JT-10L - 1/2 size LP-style solid body, mahogany neck, rosewood fingerboard, 3-per-side tuners, 2 humbucking pickups, 2 volume/2 tone controls. Available in Black, Purple Sunburst, Transparent Blue, Transparent Red, and Tobacco Sunburst finishes. Current Mfg.

	$135	$110	$95	$85	$65	$50	$35

Last MSR was $179.

JT-30 - 1/2 size Strat-style solid body, maple neck, rosewood fingerboard, 6-on-a-side tuners, 3 single coil pickups, volume/tone controls, 5-way switch. Available in Transparent Black, Transparent Blue, and Transparent Red finishes. Current Mfg.

MSR	$179	$135	$110	$95	$85	$65	$50	$35

JT-50 - double cutaway solid body similar to SG design, maple set neck, rosewood fingerboard, dot position markers, 3-per-side tuners, 2 humbucking pickups, 2 Volume/2 Tone controls, black pickguard, chrome hardware, stop tailpiece. Available in Transparent red finish. Current Mfg.

MSR	$339	$255	$190	$170	$150	$130	$110	$90

JT-50 Custom -Similar to JT-50 except has gold plated tuners and gold hardware. Current Mfg.

MSR	$399	$299	$225	$200	$175	$150	$125	$100

GRADING		100% MINT	98% NEAR MINT	95% EXC+	90% EXC	80% VG+	70% VG	60% G

JT-72 offset double cutaway ash body, flame maple top, 22-fret maple neck, rosewood fingerboard with dot position markers, 3-per-side tuners, 2 exposed coil humbucking pickups, 3-way switch, tremelo tailpiece. Available in transparent Red and Transparent Black finishes. Current Mfg.

MSR	$359	$$275	$210	$180	$150	$130	$110	$90

JT-80 - offset double cutaway 'Rick'-style solid body, maple set neck, rosewood fingerboard, 3-per-side die cast tuners, 3 chrome covered pickups, 2 volume/2 tone controls, mid pickup control. Available in Black and Red Sunburst finishes. Disc. 1999.

$330	$225	$200	$175	$150	$100	$75

Last MSR was $439.

JT-81 - similar to the JT-80, except features double cutaway hollow body. Available in Black and Red Sunburst finishes. Disc. 1999.

$340	$230	$200	$175	$150	$100	$75

Last MSR was $459.

JT-134 - Single cutaway semi-hollow body, contoured top, 22-fret mahogany neck with rosewood fingerboard, dot position markers, 3-per-side tuners, 2 humbucking pickups, Tune-O-Matic bridge, 2 Volume/2 Tone controls, 3-way switch, die-cast tuners, trapeze tailpiece, f-holes, black pickguard. Available in Antique Sunburst finish. Current Mfg.

MSR	$429	$325	$225	$200	$175	$150	$125	$100

JT-134DC - similar to JT-134 except, in a double cutaway version, flame maple top. Available in Antique Sunburst, Cherry Sunburst and Blue finishes. New for 2001.

MSR	$479	$335	$295	$250	$195	$175	$150	$125

JT-134DC Vine - same as Model JT-134DC except, has Abalone and mother-of-pearl vine inlay the full length of the fingerboard. Available in Antique Sunburst and Cherry Sunburst finishes. New for 2001.

MSR	$599	$419	$375	$325	$295	$250	$195	$150

JT-135 - dual cutaway semi-hollow body, arched top, maple set neck, rosewood fingerboard, 3-per-side die cast tuners, tune-o-matic bridge/stop tailpiece, 2 covered humbucker pickups, raised black pickguard, 2 volume/2 tone controls, 3-way toggle switch. Available in Cherry Sunburst, Transparent Red, and Tobacco Sunburst finishes. Current Mfg.

MSR	$409	$310	$210	$185	$165	$140	$90	$65

JT-135D - similar to the JT-135, except features an arched flame maple top. Available in Natural Honey finish. Current Mfg.

MSR	$439	$330	$225	$200	$180	$150	$100	$75

JT-136 - (3" body depth) single cutaway semi-hollow body, arched top, maple set neck, rosewood fingerboard, 3-per-side Kluson tuners, tune-o-matic bridge/stop tailpiece, raised black pickguard, 2 covered humbucker pickups, 2 volume/2 tone controls, 3-way toggle switch. Available in Cherry Sunburst, Transparent Red, and Violin Shade finishes. Current Mfg.

MSR	$449	$335	$235	$205	$185	$155	$100	$75

JT-136 Vine -same as JT-136 except, has vine fingerboard inlay. Available in Cherry Sunburst and Tobacco Sunburst finishes. New for 2001.

MSR	$649	$450	$395	$375	$350	$295	$250	$195

JT-137 semi-acoustic, thin line body with flame maple top, hard maple neck, rosewood fingerboard, 2 covered pickups, 2 Volume/1 Tone control, adjustable bridge, gold die-cast tuners. Available in Black, Tobacco Sunburst and Natural Honey finishes. Current Mfg.

MSR	$529	$375	$325	$275	$225	$175	$125	$75

JT-140 COLONEL - single cutaway hollow body, arched ash top, maple set neck, rosewood fingerboard with pearl block/abalone inlays, 3-per-side tuners, classic jazz-style tremelo, f-holes, 2 humbucking pickups, 2 Volume/2 Tone controls, 3-way switch, gold hardware, black pickguard. Available in white finish. Current Mfg.

MSR	$729	$550	$400	$350	$325	$300	$275	$225

JT-141 MONTERREY - single cutaway hollow body, arched top, maple set neck, rosewood fingerboard with pearl block/abalone inlays, 3-per-side tuners, f-holes, 1 humbucking pickup, 1 Volume/1 Tone control, trapeze tailpiece, gold hardware, black pickguard. Available in Transparent Red, Cherry Sunburst and Tobacco Sunburst finishes. Current Mfg.

MSR	$629	$440	$330	$300	$275	$250	$225	$175

JT-200 (C) - single cutaway solid body, contoured top, mahogany set neck, rosewood fingerboard, 3-per-side covered tuners, tune-o-matic bridge/stop tailpiece, raised black pickguard, 2 covered humbucker pickups, 2 volume/2 tone controls, 3-way toggle switch. Available in Black, Purple Sunburst, and Red Sunburst finishes. Current Mfg.

MSR	$349	$260	$200	$175	$150	$125	$100	$75

JT-200D - similar to the JT-200, except features a flame maple top. Available in Red Sunburst finish. Current Mfg.

MSR	$429	$325	$225	$200	$175	$150	$125	$100

JT-200 PRO - double cutaway lightweight solid body, contoured flame maple top, 22-fret hard maple set neck, rosewood fingerboard with dot position markers, 3-per-side tuners, 2 humbucking pickups, adjustable bridge, 2 Volume/2 Tone controls, 3-way switch, gold die-cast tuners, stop tailpiece, white pickguard. Available in Red Sunburst, Purple Sunburst and black finishes. Current Mfg.

MSR	$429	$300	$225	$200	$175	$150	$125	$100

J

GRADING		100% MINT	98% NEAR MINT	95% EXC+	90% EXC	80% VG+	70% VG	60% G

JT-200 DRAGON - single cutaway solid body with contoured flame maple top, 22-fret mahogany set neck, rosewood fingerboard, 3-per-side tuners, abalone and mother-of-pearl Dragon inlay full length of fingerboard, 2 humbucking pickups, adjustable bridge, 2 Volume/2 Tone controls, 3-way switch, die-cast tuners, gold hardware, black pickguard. Available in Antique Sunburst and Red Sunburst finishes. Disc. 2000.

		$525	$475	$450	$400	$375	$350	$300

Last MSR was $699.

JT-200 Serpent - similar to JT-200 Dragon, solid body with flame maple top, 22-fret mahogany set neck, rosewood fingerboard, 2 humbucking pickups, adjustable bridge, 2 Volume/2 Tone controls, 3-way switch, die-cast tuners, gold hardware, Abalone and mother-of-pearl Serpent inlay full length of fingerboard. Available in Transparent Red, Transparent Black, Purple Sunburst, Red Sunburst and Antique Sunburst finishes. New for 2001.

MSR	$699	$489	$389	$350	$295	$250	$195	$150

JT-250 - offset double cutaway solid ash body, contoured top, maple set neck, rosewood fingerboard, 3-per-side die cast tuners, 2 point tremolo, 2 humbucker pickups, volume/tone controls, 3-way toggle switch. Available in Purple Sunburst, Red Sunburst, Transparent Blue, and Transparent Red finishes. Disc. 1999.

		$365	$275	$250	$225	$200	$175	$125

Last MSR was $489.

JT-250G -similar to Model JT-250 except has gold plated tuners and gold plated hardware. Available in black and Transparent White finishes. Disc. 2000.

		$390	$290	$265	$245	$215	$190	$150

Last MSR was $519.

JT-300 - offset double cutaway solid body, maple set neck, rosewood fingerboard, 6-on-a-side covered tuners, standard tremolo, white pickguard, 3 single coil pickups, volume/2 tone controls, 5-way toggle switch. Available in Black, Natural Honey, Purple Sunburst, Transparent Black, Transparent Blue, Transparent Moss Green, Transparent Red, and Tobacco Sunburst finishes. Current Mfg.

MSR	$249	$185	$150	$125	$100	$75	$65	$50

JT-300QMT similar to JT-300 except, has Quilted Maple Top, pearloid pickguard, gold hardware. Available in Transparent Black, Purple Sunburst, Transparent Blue, Transparent Moss Green, Transparent Red, Natural Honey and Tocbacco Sunburst finishes. New for 2001.

MSR	$299	$210	$175	$150	$125	$95	$75	$50

JT-301 - similar to the JT-300, except features a solid light ash body, white pearloid pickguard. Available in Black finish. Disc. 1999.

		$210	$160	$135	$110	$85	$75	$60

Last MSR was $279.

JT-302 - similar to the JT-300, except features a solid ash body, maple fingerboard, white pearloid pickguard. Available in Natural Honey, Transparent Blue, and Transparent Red finishes. Disc. 2000.

		$250	$190	$165	$150	$125	$100	$75

Last MSR was $329.

JT-700 7-STRING 7-string, offset double cutaway solid body, maple neck, rosewood fingerboard with dot position markers, 7-on-a-side tuners, two exposed coil humbucking pickups, 1 Volume/1 Tone control, 3-way switch, fixed tailpiece. Current Mfg.

MSR	$449	$340	$250	$225	$200	$175	$150	$90

JT-BLUES - sculpted double cutaway solid body, 22-fret bolt-on maple neck, rosewood fingerboard with dot position markers, adjustable nut, 2 humbucking pickups, 1 Volume/1 Tone control, 3-way switch, chrome hardware, die-cast 6-on-a-side tuners, reverse headstock, white pearloid pickguard. Available in Natural, Transparent Red and Transparent Black finishes. Current Mfg.

MSR	$309	$235	$175	$150	$125	$100	$75	$50

JT-BRANSON - same body style as JT-Blues, has two single coil Phantom pickups. Available in Natural, Transparent Red and Transparent Black finishes. Current Mfg.

MSR	$299	$225	$160	$140	$115	$90	$60	$40

JT-CALIFORNIA - same body style as JT-Branson and JT-Blues, has 3 single coil Phantom pickups. Available in Natural, Transparent Red and Transparent Black finishes. Current Mfg.

MSR	$319	$240	$180	$160	$135	$110	$95	$60

JT-HAWK - offset double cutaway solid body, maple neck, rosewood fingerboard, 3-per-side die cast tuners, fixed bridge, white pearloid pickguard, 2 humbucker pickups, volume/tone controls, 3-way toggle switch. Available in Blue Sparkle, Red Sparkle, Silver Sparkle, and Transparent Blue finishes. Disc. 2000.

		$210	$160	$145	$130	$115	$90	$65

Last MSR was $279.

J

GRADING			100% MINT	98% NEAR MINT	95% EXC+	90% EXC	80% VG+	70% VG	60% G

JT-HAWK BB -similar to JT-Hawk except has 3 humbucking pickups, 1 Volume/1Tone, 3-way switch, pearloid pickguard, classic jazz-style tailpiece with tremelo. Disc. 2000.

		$279	$200	$175	$150	$125	$100	$75

Last MSR was $399.

JT-RES - single cutaway acoustic/electric solid poplar body, resonator, hard maple neck, rosewood fingerboard with dot position markers, 1 piezo and 1 covered pickup, 1 volume/2 Tone controls, chrome die cast tuners, 3-per-side tuners. Available in Transparent Red finish. Current Mfg.

MSR	$399	$280	$200	$175	$150	$125	$100	$75

JT-900RES acoustic resonated guitar, 1 lipstick pickup, die-cast tuners, 1 Volume/1 Tone control and mixing control. Available in Cherry Sunburst and Tobacco Sunburst finishes. New for 2001.

MSR	$369	$260	$225	$195	$175	$150	$125	$95

JT-SHARK -solid body instrument with body shaped like a shark, tailfin headstock, 3-per-side tuners, 1 humbucking pickup and 2 single coil pickups, tremelo bridge,

JT-LT -classic single cutaway lightweight solid body design, rosewood fingerboard with dot position markers, 6-on-a-side die-cast tuners, 2 pickups, 3-way switch, white pickguard. Available in Black and Ivory finishes. New for 2001.

MSR	$199	$139	$125	$110	$95	$75	$60	$40

JT-LT Custom - similar to Model JT-LT except, has maple fingerboard, gold hardware, pearloid pickguard. Available in Antique Sunburst finish. New for 2001.

MSR	$249	$175	$150	$125	$95	$75	$50	$35

JT-SOLOSLIM offset double cutaway thinline ash body, 24-fret maple neck with rosewood fingerboard, dot position markers, 2 humbucking and I single coil pickup, floating tremelo, 1 Volume/1 Tone control, 5-way switch, die-cast tuners, 6-on-a-side tuners, chrome hardware. Available in Natural finish. Disc. 2000.

		$325	$240	$210	$180	$155	$125	$95

Last MSR was $429.

JT-HORN -offset double cutaway solid body, 24-fret maple neck, rosewood fingerboard with dot position markers, 1 humbucker and 1 single coil pickup, tremelo, 1 Volume/1 Tone control, 3-way switch, 6-on-a-side die-cast tuners, chrome hardware. Available in Metallic Red and Metallic Blue finishes. Current Mfg.

MSR	$329	$230	$195	$175	$150	$125	$95	$65

JT-SLIMMER -offset double cutaway solid ash body, thin-line design, 22-fret maple neck with rosewood fingerboard, oval position markers, 2 humbuckers and 1 single coil pickup, floating tremelo, 1 Volume/1 Tone control, 5-way switch, die-cast tuners. Available in Transparent Red, Purple Sunburst and Transparent Moss Green finishes. Current Mfg.

MSR	$359	$250	$225	$195	$175	$150	$125	$95

JT-SG - dual cutaway solid body, maple set neck, rosewood fingerboard, 3-per-side die cast tuners, tune-o-matic bridge/stop tailpiece, black pickguard, 2 covered humbucker pickups, 2 volume/2 tone controls, 3-way toggle switch. Available in Transparent Red finish. Disc. 1999.

		$250	$200	$175	$150	$125	$100	$75

Last MSR was $339.

Future Series

JT-SPECTRE -radical offset sweeping solid body design, reverse headstock, 6-on-a-side tuners, 25 ½" scale, rosewood fingerboard with scallop position markers, 1 humbucking pickup and 2 single coil pickups, 1 Volume/1Tone control, 5-way switch, precision vibrato bridge, adjustable nut. Available in Metallic Red, Metallic Black and Metallic Silver finishes. Current Mfg.

MSR	$499	$349	$299	$275	$250	$225	$195	$150

JT-SPIRITE - radical teardrop shaped solid body, reverse headstock, 6-on-a-side tuners, 25 ½" scale, rosewood fingerboard with dot position markers, 1 humbucking pickup and 2 single coil pickups, 1 Volume/1 Tone control, 5-way switch, precision vibrato, adjustable nut. Available in Flourescent Yellow, Flourescent Red and Flourescent Blue finishes. Current Mfg.

MSR	$479	$335	$295	$250	$225	$195	$175	$135

JT-STILETTE - double cutaway sheet aluminum body, reverse headstock, 6-on-a-side tuners, 25 ½" scale, rosewood fingerboard with scallop position markers, 1 humbucking pickup and 2 single coil pickups, 1 Volume/1 Tone control, 5-way switch, precision vibrato, adjustable nut. Available in Aluminum/Black finish. Current Mfg.

MSR	$599	$419	$350	$295	$250	$225	$195	$150

ELECTRIC BASS

JTB-2B - violin-shaped semi-hollow body, maple set neck, rosewood fingerboard, 2-per-side die cast tuners, chrome hardware, white pearloid pickguard, 2 chrome covered humbucker pickup, 2 volume controls, 3 tone slide switches. Available in Violin Shade finish. Current Mfg.

MSR	$409	$305	$230	$200	$175	$150	$125	$100

J

GRADING		100% MINT	98% NEAR MINT	95% EXC+	90% EXC	80% VG+	70% VG	60% G

JTB-40 - 1/2 size P-style solid body, maple neck, rosewood fingerboard, 4-on-a-side tuners, P-style split pickup, volume/tone controls. Available in Transparent Black, Transparent Blue, and Transparent Red finishes. Current Mfg.

MSR	$239	$180	$135	$120	$105	$90	$75	$60

JTB-400 (C) - offset double cutaway solid body, maple neck, rosewood fingerboard, 4-on-a-side tuners, chrome hardware, P-style split pickup, volume/tone controls. Available in Antique, Transparent Moss Green, Natural Honey, Transparent Black, Transparent Red, and Tobacco Sunburst finishes. Current Mfg.

MSR	$299	$225	$170	$150	$130	$110	$90	$70

JTB-400QMT - similar to Model JTB-400 except, has Quilted Maple Top, pearloid pickguard and gold hardware. Available in Tobacco Sunburst, Transparent Black, Transparent Red and Transparent Blue finishes. New for 2001.

MSR	$349	$245	$195	$175	$150	$125	$95	$65

JTB-440 - similar to the JTB-400, except has a exposed pole piece humbucking pickup, round white pickguard, volume/2 tone controls, chrome 1/2-moon controls plate. Available in Purple Sunburst, Transparent Black, Transparent Blue, and Transparent Red finishes. Current Mfg.

MSR	$309	$230	$175	$160	$140	$120	$100	$80

JTB-445 5-String - similar to the JTB-440, except in a 5-string configuration, maple neck, rosewood fingerboard, open back tuners, humbucking pickup, 1 Volume/2 Tone controls. Available in Purple Sunburst, Transparent Blue, Transparent Red and black finishes. Current Mfg.

MSR	$399	$299	$225	$200	$175	$150	$125	$100

JTB-500 4-STRING - offset double cutaway solid body, maple neck, rosewood fingerboard, 2-per-side tuners, black hardware, P/J-style pickup, 2 volume/tone controls. Available in Transparent Black, Transparent Blue, and Transparent Red finishes. Current Mfg.

MSR	$309	$230	$175	$160	$140	$120	$100	$80

JTB-550 5-String - similar to the JTB-500, except has a 5-string configuration, 3/2-per-side tuners. Available in Transparent Black, Transparent Blue, and Transparent Red finishes. Current Mfg.

MSR	$329	$250	$185	$170	$150	$130	$110	$90

JTB-900 - offset double cutaway solid ash body, maple neck, rosewood fingerboard, 2-per-side tuners, matte chrome hardware, P/J-style pickup, 2 volume/tone controls. Available in Natural Honey, Transparent Blue, and Transparent Red finishes. Disc. 2000.

		$300	$225	$200	$175	$150	$125	$100

Last MSR was $399.

JTB-WB - Warwick-style offset double cutaway solid ash body, maple neck, rosewood fingerboard, 2-per-side tuners, matte chrome hardware, 2 J-style pickup, 2 volume/tone controls. Available in Natural Honey and Matt Green finishes. Disc. 1999.

		$260	$200	$175	$150	$125	$110	$90

Last MSR was $349.

Future Series Bass

JT-SCARABE - radical sweeping offset body design similar to the Spectre guitar, reverse headstock, 4 on 1 side tuners, rosewood fingerboard with scallop position markers, 34" scale, 1-twin coil pickup, 1 Volume/1 Tone control. Available in Metallic Black, Metallic Red and Metallic Silver finishes. Current Mfg.

MSR	$529	$375	$325	$275	$250	$225	$195	$150

JAYXZ

Instruments currently built in Lakeland, Florida.

Jeffrey David Patterson was born January 9, 1956 at the tender age of 0 in Lakeland, Florida, where he still manages to survive to this day with the help and understanding of his wife, Mary, and sons, Colin and Kyle (as well as Mom, Dad, brothers, friends, and so on, and so on). Patterson's life was typical of a young boy growing up in central Florida: hanging around orange groves, the Cuban Missile Crisis - and that one fateful Sunday night when the Beatles played on the Ed Sullivan show. Like so many other kids that night, Patterson turned to his parents and said "I wanna guitar for Christmas!" It took a great deal of convincing, but he did get a guitar for Christmas. The first guitar made the most beautiful necklace that any boy could want, but it was not much of a guitar. This began the quest of one little boy that only wanted to get more out of this thing we call guitar.

It was in fact Patterson's second guitar (an unplayable Teisco from W.T. Grant Co.) that inspired him to experiment with the 'action' of a guitar. Matchbook covers, toothpicks, and even small bits of gravel made for good shim stock to improve the playability of the neighbors' cheap "axes-du-joir". At 14, Patterson picked up bass when it was discovered that the Credence Clearwater Revival cover band he was in sucked so bad because there were three rhythm guitars and a drummer. This is what set the stage for the "Component Multineck System" of today.

Patterson began building guitars and other stringed instruments from scratch in 1984 when he became frustrated with the concept of permanent double- neck instruments. 6-string and 12-string necks were an easy choice, but with bass it was a different question altogether. Should the configuration be an 8-string and a 4-string, or fretted and fretless, or what? After thirteen years of hit and miss research, Patterson came up with a new development.

Patterson's Jayxz (pronounced "Jakes") Musical Implements company is currently offering guitars that feature a "Component Multineck System". The CMS concept allows the player to combine various string configuration bodies together to form a doubleneck instrument. Furthermore, Patterson's instruments are also convertible: the tuners and bridge are all mounted on the same easy to remove piece of the instrument called the "Tailstock". After loosening the strings a bit, the tailstock is unbolted and the anchoring hardware is slid off the other end. Patterson estimates that a changeover can be done in less than fifteen minutes.

(Biography courtesy Jeff Patterson, September 1998)

Jayxz CMS models are available in 10 different 'models' (string configurations). Prices per each standard model start at $750. For further information regarding the Jayxz CMS guitars, contact the Jayxz company directly (see Trademark Index).

JEANNIE

Instruments currently built in Pittsburg, California.

The Jeannie Talon VIII 8-string features a jazz-style solid body guitar (different wood choices are available) with a eagle's claw-shaped headstock. This model has an ebony fingerboard, pearl-covered headstock/pickguard/strat-style single coil pickups (with eight pole pieces) and a hand-built custom bridge. The suggested retail price begins at $2,000.

In addition, Jeannie also offers custom pickguards and other guitar parts. Jeannie's pickguards are available with custom engraving, holographic designs, exotic wood pickguards, or custom designs.

JEDSON

Instruments previously produced in Japan from the late 1960s through the late 1970s.

The Jedson trademark appears on entry to student level solid body and semi-hollow body guitars; some models with original design and some models based on classic American designs.

(Source: Tony Bacon and Paul Day, The Guru's Guitar Book)

JEM

Instruments previously built in Carle Place, New York during the mid to late 1980s.

Before Ibanez's Steve Vai Jem model, Jem Custom Guitars was offering custom body designs, paint jobs, and electronic packages. Jem President Joe Despagni's ads used to run "As seen on MTV and on stage with Steve Vai".

Pre-Ibanez Jem guitars are definitely eye-catching, quality built electrics. Prices in the secondary market will reflect quality of workmanship, wood types in construction, and custom work. While the more *custom* body designs may currently be out of fashion with the retro fascination, these are not guitars to sell cheap.

J

JENNINGS

Instruments previously built in Japan, others were assembled in England using Japanese and English parts during the early 1970s.

Jennings produced instruments at different quality levels. On one hand, there's the entry level solid body guitars based on classic American designs; but on the other are some higher quality "tiny-bodied" solid body guitars. Instruments should be examined on an individual basis, and then priced accordingly.

(Source: Tony Bacon and Paul Day, The Guru's Guitar Guide)

JENNINGS, DAVE

Instruments previously built in England during the late 1980s.

Luthier David Jennings produced some very respectable original design solid body guitars. Jennings primarily worked as a custom builder, so the overall number of instruments available might perhaps be rather limited.

(Source: Tony Bacon and Paul Day, The Guru's Guitar Guide)

JENNINGS-THOMPSON

Instruments previously built in Austin, Texas.

Jennings-Thompson was a high quality, limited production company located in Austin. Ross Jennings, a former employee of Wayne Charvel (and also a production manager at B.C. Rich), personally built all his instruments along with another luthier. They limited production to about 30 basses and guitars a year, and worked with the customer to ensure that the commissioned instrument would be exactly tailored to their individual playing style.

Pendulum and Spectrum basses had a retail price beginning at $3,699 (4-string) up to $4,099 (6-string). Their guitars carried a list price of $2,599.

JERRY BIX

Instruments previously built in England during the early 1980s.

While the Musician and Exotic series had some vestiges of Fender-ish styling to them, the Ptera guitars featured original designs. This company also produced some high quality custom models as well.

JERZY DROZD

Instruments currently built in Barcelona, Spain.

Jerzy Drozd offers a handful of **Obsession** Series basses with "unlimited options". Prices range from the $1,725 **Obsession Basic** up to the **Obsession Prodigy Limited Edition** (list $5,525). For additional information regarding model specification and pricing, contact Jerzy Drozd directly (see Trademark Index).

JJ HUCKE GUITARS

Instruments currently built in Shipton on Stour, England.

JJ Hucke Guitars is currently offering three different models of high quality solid body guitars. JJ Hucke models are handcrafted with figured maple tops and translucent finishes. For further information regarding model specification and pricing, contact JJ Hucke directly (see Trademark Index).

ELECTRIC

The sleek double cutaway Antarctica model has a mahogany body, bolt-on maple neck with shaped heel, 24-fret rosewood fingerboard, reverse headstock, 2 humbuckers 5-way 'mega-switch', Schaller Pro licensed Floyd Rose tremolo. A carved maple top is optional on this model.

The Arctic III has similar construction techniques as the Antarctica, except has a rounder lower bout and regular 6-on-a-side tuner headstock. This model is complete with the carved maple top.

The Sahara model has a single rounded cutaway mahogany solid body with a through-body mahogany neck, carved maple top, 24-fret rosewood fingerboard, tune-o-matic bridge/stop tailpiece, 2 Seymour Duncan humbuckers, gold hardware, and 3-per-side Schaller tuners.

JOE'S GUITARS

Instruments previously built in Salt Lake City, Utah.

Joe's Guitars offered a number of handcrafted guitar models and one bass model. All guitar models featured a recessed tune-o-matic bridge, Seymour Duncan pickups, and a hardshell case. Models included the Cobra (last retail was $1,349) and Cobra SX (last retail was $1,699), the hollow body Cobra XT (last retail was $1,995), bolt-on neck model Viper (last retail was $1,349) and the Viper XS (last retail was $1,699).

JOHN BIRCH GUITARS

Instruments currently built in England since 1970.

John Birch Guitars was founded in Birmingham, England in 1970 by luthier John Birch. Birch offered custom repair and guitar building service; the custom guitars were based on popular models (i.e., Fender/Gibson designs) of the day, but featured new construction methods like through-body necks, improved truss rod design, and pickups such as the hyperflux, biflux, and multiflux. In the 1980s he teamed up with Barry Kirby to build the Cobra models, including the highly imaginative Cobra "Rook" for Rook Music (Birch is more renowned for his custom guitar building).

In 1993, John Birch Guitars relocated to Nottingham, England. The company began offering an original series of guitar models as well as MIDI implementation.

(Some historical background courtesy Tony Bacon, The Ultimate Guitar Book)

ELECTRIC

Birch's handcrafted **Classic Guitars** range for 1998 all share the main features of John Birch Guitars. The standard features include through-body neck, sculptured neck-to-body joint, 24-fret fingerboard, full back scratch plate (pickguard), Birch Full Range humbuckers (or single coil), or multimode for MIDI version. Choice of custom color finishes.

Current model designs include the **J1** and **J2** a double cutaway with two humbuckers; the **SG** (traditional SG shape) with 2 humbuckers; the 2 humbucker **LP** (traditional LP shape); and the **ST**, a traditional Strat-style guitar with single coils or humbuckers. Prices for the models with John Birch Pickups and a stop tailpiece begin at $1,297; there is an up charge for the Birch MultiMode pickups and Wilkinson VS-100 tremolo.

ELECTRIC BASS

John Birch basses are offered in 4- and 5-string configurations (6-string available by order). Models feature a 22-fret fingerboard, and are available in the **J1, J2, SG, LP**, and **4001** body styles. Prices for a 4-string with JB Hyperflux (or 2 J-style) pickups starts at $1,375; the 5-string begins at $1,456. There is an up charge for MIDI access and EMG pickups. For further information regarding model specifications and pricing, contact John Birch Guitars directly (see Trademark Index).

JOHNNY REB

Instruments currently produced in Asia. Distributed by Johnny Reb Guitars (L.A. Guitar Works) of Reseda, California.

Those "Rock 'n Rebels" **Johnny Reb** models sport single cutaway 'Tele'-style bodies that combine a wood top to a fiberglass back and sides. The total weight of this traditional design (yet un-traditional production technique) is only 5 pounds - a welcome relief to those "chicken-pickers" playing 4 and 5 hour bar gigs.

The hollow Johhny Reb models are available with ash, figured maple, or mahogany tops with an f-hole, molded fiberglass backs, bolt-on maple necks with rosewood or maple fingerboards, 6-on-a-side chrome tuners, 2 single coil pickups, volume and tone controls, and a 3 way toggle selector. Retail list price is only $399. For further information regarding the Johnny Reb guitars, contact the company directly (see Trademark Index).

JOHNSON

Instruments currently produced in Asia. Distributed by the Music Link of Brisbane, California.

The Music Link's Johnson guitars offer a wide range of acoustic and electric guitars, with prices aimed at the entry level and student guitarists. Please contact Music Link directly for more information (see Trademark Index).

There are also 8 different practice amps in the Johnson line, as well as numerous accessories like cases, Quartz tuners, and tuning machines.

ELECTRIC

Johnson solid body guitars have solid alder bodies and maple necks. The Strat-style **JS-100** retails at $225, and the Tele- style **JT-100** retails at $245.

ELECTRIC BASS

Johnson electric guitars and basses have a pointed headstock, with all tuners on one side. Johnson basses have solid alder bodies and maple necks. The Precision-style **JP-100** retails at $269, and the Jazz-style **JJ-100** also retails at $269.

JOHNSON'S EXTREMELY STRANGE MUSICAL INSTRUMENT COMPANY

Instruments currently built in Burbank, California.

Luthier Bruce Johnson specializes in Scroll Basses, which are distinctive horizontal electric basses with scroll-style headstocks and a warm tone like an upright bass. This bass design was originally manufactured by Ampeg from '66 to '69, and the most common model is known as the AEB-1. Johnson's website has extensive historical and technical information about the Ampeg Scroll Bassses, and he also does restorations and supplies parts for them.

In 1997, Johnson developed and introduced new generations versions of the Scroll Bass design, known as the AEB-2 (fretted) and the AUB-2 (fretless). These basses retain the style and character of the original Ampegs, but have been completely re-engineered to improve the quality, function and tone. These basses are specifically designed to bring out the tone of flatwound strings, and have a rich, cello-like sound. Each of these basses is hand built to order in Johnson's shop in Burbank, CA.

From '97 through '99, Johnson worked in cooperation with St. Louis Music, Inc., and some of those instruments were sold under the Ampeg name. The partnership has been mutually dissolved, and Johnson now sells his instruments directly to musicians worldwide through his website.

In 2000, Johnson introduced the SSB, a unique short scale bass patterened after a rare model that Ampeg manufactured in 1967. In the fall of 2001, Johnson will be introducing a new-generation version of the Ampeg ASB-1 "Devil Bass".

ELECTRIC BASS

J

AEB-2 SCROLL BASS

MSR $2,400

AUB-2 SCROLL BASS (fretless)

MSR $2,200

SSB SHORT SCALE BASS

MSR $1,200

JOKER

See C & R GUITARS.

JOLANA

Instruments previously produced in Czechoslovakia, circa 1960s.

While researching a number of guitar trademarks, associate editor Walter Murray of Frankenstein Fretworks came across two b&w photographs of Jolana instruments in the book **Musical Instruments: An Illustrated History** [Crown Publishers, New York], by Alexander Buchner. The photos illustrate at least four different models of Jolana guitars, ranging from electric models to semi-hollow (or hollow) models. Author Tony Bacon, in **The Ultimate Guitar Book**, calls the two examples he has viewed "Entry level production solid bodies, (but) have original designs with headstocks that seem to echo the Fender *Swinger*". Now that's rocking out behind the Iron Curtain!

(Source: Walter Murray, Frankenstein Fretworks; Alexander Buchner, Musical Instruments: An Illustrated History [Crown Publishers, New York]; and Tony Bacon, The Ultimate Guitar Book)

ELECTRIC

The Jolana solid body electric has an asymmetrical double cutaway body, laminated fingerboard with dot fretmarkers, chrome hardware, adjustable floating bridge/tremolo tailpiece, 3 humbucking pickups, volume and tone controls, four (possibly a fifth) white rocker switches on pickguard.

Jolana hollow or semi-hollow models (**Tornado** model?) feature a Gibson ES-style body, 6-per-side tuners/Strat-style string guides, 21-fret laminated fretboard with dot markers, 2 f-holes, trapeze tailpiece/Bigsby-like tremolo combination, 3 single coil pickups, volume and tone controls, 4 rocker switches on raised pickguard, additional rocker switch/2 finger wheels on upper horn. The "Jolana" logo is located on the lower bout with either a music staff design or in script typeface (without music staff design).

ELECTRIC BASS

The Jolana electric bass model has a maple neck with laminated (darker) wood fingerboard, white or pearloid dot fretmarkers, four on a side tuners with pearloid buttons. No further information ascertained.

GRADING	100% MINT	98% NEAR MINT	95% EXC+	90% EXC	80% VG+	70% VG	60% G

JONES, JERRY

Instruments currently built in Nashville, Tennessee since 1981. Distributed by Jerry Jones Guitars of Nashville, Tennessee.

Luthier Jerry Jones began repair and guitar building at Nashville's Old Time Pickin' Parlour in 1978. By 1980, he had opened his own shop and was building custom guitars as well as designing his own original models. Jones' company has been specializing in reproducing Danelectro models and parts; however, the designs have been updated to improve upon original design flaws and to provide a more stable playing instrument.

Jerry Jones Longhorn Doubleneck courtesy Dave Rogers

ELECTRIC

All instruments in this series are available in: Bahama Green, Black, Copper, Mustard, Red, and Turquoise finishes. The Almond finish is currently discontinued.

Jerry Jones also offers these optional 'Burst finishes: Copperburst, Black/Turquoise, Blood/Cream, and Turquoise/White.

Add $50 for a Neptune bridge (fixed bridge with metal saddles) on below listed models.

Add $75 for Sunburst finish ($150 on the Doubleneck model).

BARITONE - single cutaway poplar body, transparent pickguard, bolt-on poplar neck, 23-fret rosewood fingerboard with pearl dot inlay, fixed bridge with rosewood saddle, 3-per-side tuners, chrome hardware, 2 lipstick pickups, volume/tone controls, 3-position switch. Current Mfg.

MSR	$795	$625	$550	$475	$400	$350	$275	$200

This model is designed to be tuned with a low "B".

DELUXO - single cutaway semi-hollow body, select maple top, carved heel neck joint, 23-fret rosewood fingerboard with pearl dot inlay, fixed metal bridge, 3-per-side tuners, natural finish headstock, chrome hardware, transparent (or matching finish) pickguard with silk-screened Deluxo logo, 2 single coil lipstick pickups, dual concentric volume/tone controls, 3-position selector switch. Mfg. 1998 to date.

6-string guitar.

MSR $895

12-string guitar

MSR $995

Baritone guitar

MSR $895

ELECTRIC SITAR - single cutaway poplar body, transparent pickguard, 13 sympathetic strings with own nut/bridge/lipstick pickup, bolt-on poplar neck, 21-fret rosewood fingerboard with white dot inlay, fixed buzz bridge/through-body tailpiece, 6-on-a-side tuners, chrome hardware, 2 lipstick pickups, 3 volume/tone controls. Available in Black Gator, Original Gator, Turquoise Gator, and White Gator finishes. Current Mfg.

MSR	$1,195	$950	$850	$750	$625	$525	$400	$300

GUITARLIN - deep double cutaway poplar body with hollow sound channels, masonite top/back, transparent pickguard, bolt-on poplar neck, 31-fret rosewood fingerboard with white dot inlay, fixed bridge with rosewood saddle, 3-per-side tuners, chrome hardware, 2 lipstick pickups, volume/tone control, 3-position switch. Current Mfg.

MSR	$795	$625	$550	$475	$400	$350	$275	$200

LONGHORN DOUBLENECK - similar to Guitarlin, except has 2 necks: 6-string guitar configuration and 6-string bass configuration, 3 lipstick tube pickups per guitar neck, 2 lipstick tube pickups per bass neck. Current Mfg.

MSR	$1,665	$1,350	$1,175	$1,000	$885	$750	$595	$450

SHORTHORN - double cutaway poplar body, white pickguard, bolt-on poplar neck, 21-fret rosewood fingerboard with pearl dot inlay, fixed bridge with rosewood saddle, 3-per-side tuners, chrome hardware, 3 lipstick pickups, volume/tone control, 5-position switch. Current Mfg.

MSR	$870	$695	$595	$525	$450	$375	$295	$225

Shorthorn 2 Pickup - similar to Shorthorn, except has 2 lipstick tube single coil pickups. Mfg. 1997 to date.

MSR	$795	$625	$550	$475	$400	$350	$275	$200

SINGLE CUTAWAY - similar to Shorthorn, except has single round cutaway style body. Current Mfg.

MSR	$870	$695	$595	$525	$450	$375	$295	$225

Single Cutaway 2 Pickup - similar to Single Cutaway, except has 2 lipstick tube single coil pickups. Mfg. 1997 to date.

MSR	$795	$625	$550	$475	$400	$350	$275	$200

TWELVE STRING - similar to Single Cutaway, except has 12-string configuration, 6-per-side tuners, fixed bridge with metal saddles, 2 pickups. Current Mfg.

MSR	$895	$725	$625	$550	$475	$395	$300	$225

GRADING		100% MINT	98% NEAR MINT	95% EXC+	90% EXC	80% VG+	70% VG	60% G

ELECTRIC BASS

LONGHORN 4 (SHORT SCALE) - double deep cutaway bound poplar body with hollow sound chambers, transparent pickguard, bolt on poplar neck, 30" scale, 24-fret rosewood fingerboard with white dot inlay, fixed bridge with rosewood saddle, 2-per-side tuners, chrome hardware, 2 lipstick pickups, volume/tone control, 3-position switch. Current Mfg.

MSR	$795	$625	$550	$475	$400	$350	$275	$200

Longhorn 6 - similar to Longhorn 4, except has 6-string configuration, 3-per-side tuners. Current Mfg.

MSR	$795	$625	$550	$475	$400	$350	$275	$200

SINGLE CUTAWAY 4 - similar to Longhorn 4, except has single cutaway style body. Disc. 1992.

		$425	$350	$300	$250	$225	$195	$175

Last MSR was $595.

Single Cutaway 6 - similar to Longhorn 4, except has single cutaway style body, 6-string configuration. Disc. 1992.

		$425	$375	$325	$250	$225	$200	$175

Last MSR was $595.

(Source: Tony Bacon and Paul Day, The Guru's Guitar Guide)

JONES, TED NEWMAN

Instruments currently built in Austin, Texas.

Luthier Ted Newman Jones is offering handcrafted custom instruments in his Austin workshop. For more information regarding Ted Newman Jones, please contact him directly (see Trademark Index).

JOODEE

See DAION.

Instruments previously produced in Japan from the late 1970s through the 1980s.

J

Joodee instruments were produced by luthier Shiro Tsuji and the T & Joodee Guitar company.

Due to the demand in Japan for the Gem B series and others, very few instruments were exported to the U.S. market.

JORDAN GUITARS

Formerly JVE Guitars.

Instruments currently built in Rankin, Illinois.

Luthier Patrick Jordan custom builds guitars, sitars, basses, and *bassitars*, as well as sitars equipped with a tremolo bar. Unlike the Coral/Danelectro design, Jordan places the 12 sympathetic strings to the rear of the instrument. The model for the acoustic sitar came directly from Calcutta.

Jordan features the usual North American hardwoods such as Ash, Alder, Basswood, Cherry, Maple, and Walnut; but others such as Birch, Butternut, Hickory, Poplar, Sycamore, and Sassafras are optional. Jordan's custom template/order sheet gives the player making the commission some control over aspects of the construction, while Jordan maintains control over pickup placement and hardware placement.

For further information, contact Patrick Jordan directly (see Trademark Index).

JUBAL GUITARS

Instruments currently built in Olean, New York.

Jubal's Merlin Deluxe is designed and built by Gregory Swier. This dual cutaway model features a hand-carved mahogany body, mahogany neck-through design, 24-fret ebony fingerboard/ebony headstock overlay, 3-per-side Schaller tuners, Gotoh bridge/stop tailpiece, 'lipstick tube'-style single coil/nickel covered Gibson *Classic '57+* humbucker pickups, volume/tone controls, and a 3-way selector. Available in custom colors, clear lacquer, or oil finishes. The list price of $2,250 includes an ultralite case.

JUDD GUITARS

Instruments currently built in Cranbrook (British Columbia), Canada.

Judd custom instruments are produced in Cranbrook, British Columbia. For information regarding model specifications and pricing, please contact Judd Guitars directly (see Trademark Index).

Section K

K. B. PRO

See KNOWBUDGE.

K I C S (USA)

See R A J GUITAR CRAFTS.

KALAMAZOO

See chapter on House Brands.

In the late 1930s, the Gibson guitar company decided to offer their own entry level guitars. While similar to models built for other distributors (Cromwell, Fascinator, or Capital) in construction, the Kalamazoo line was originally only offered for about five years. Models included flattop and archtop acoustics, lap steels (and amps), and mandolins.

Pre-War Kalamazoo instruments, like other Gibson budget instruments, do not have an adjustable truss rod (a key difference), different construction techniques, and no identifying Gibson logo.

In the mid 1960s, Gibson again released an entry level series of guitars under the Kalamazoo trademark, except all models were electric solid body guitars (except a flattop acoustic) that had a double offset cutaway body, bolt-on necks, 6-on-a-side headstock, and 1 or 2 pickups. The body profile of late 1960s models then switched to even dual cutaways. The second run of Kalamazoo models came to an end in the early 1970s. These Post-War models do feature an adjustable truss rod.

Kalamazoo serial numbers are impressed into the back of the headstock, and feature six digits like the regular Gibson line. However, the Kalamazoo numbers do not match or correspond with the Gibson serialization (in the back of this book). Further information regarding Kalamazoo serialization will appear in future editions of the ***Blue Book of Electric Guitars.***

(Source: Walter Carter, Gibson Guitars: 100 Years of an American Icon)

KALIL

Instruments currently built in McComb, Mississippi.

Luthier Edward E. Kalil builds instruments to custom order. Kalil currently offers acoustic steel and nylon models, as well as solid body electrics. Costs will vary due to complexity of the design and appointments.

Kalil began building guitars after attending a class at Guitar Research and Design (GRD) run by Charles Fox in South Strafford, Vermont. Kalil's class instructor was George Morris. Kalil has been a member of the Guild of American Luthiers (G.A.L.) since 1981, and a member of A.S.I.A. (Association of Stringed Instrument Artisans) since 1988.

Kalil instruments can be easily identified by the 'Kalil' headstock logo. Kalil also offers the Lick En Stik travel guitar, a full scale instrument with a compact body and built in amp (with variable distortion). For further information, contact luthier Edward E. Kalil directly (see Trademark Index).

KAMICO

See chapter on House Brands.

This trademark has been identified as the "House Brand" of the Kay Guitar company. As one of the leading suppliers of "House Brand" guitars, Kay also supplied an entry-level budget line of guitars to various musical instrument distributors.

(Source: Willie G. Moseley, Stellas & Stratocasters)

KAPA

Instruments previously built in Hyattsville, Maryland between 1962 and 1970.

Kapa guitars were designed and built by Kope Veneman and Company, during a successful eight year production. Veneman, a Dutch immigrant, was running a music store during the early 1960s that imported German and Italian guitars. In 1962, Veneman founded his own production facility, and named the company based on initials from his family member's first names: Kope, his son Albert, his daughter Patricia, and his wife Adeline. During the eight year run, the Kapa company produced nearly 120,000 decent quality, fair priced instruments.

ELECTRIC

Kapa guitars were available in four basic body styles, and in three variants thereof (six string, twelve string, and bass guitar). These models include a *mini-Strat* (**Challenger**), a *mini-Jazzmaster* (**Continental**), a teardrop shape (**Minstrel**), and a thinline hollowbody (also a **Challenger**, with different model designations). However, the names are not always consistent with the body styles, and can lead to some confusion. Kapa also produced an unofficial model named the **Cobra**, which is a single pickup model assembled with leftovers from regular production runs.

Kapa guitars were offered with bolt-on necks, 6-on-a-side headstocks (or four, if a bass), and many sported a Jazzmaster-ish tremolo system. Early **Challenger** solid bodies had 2 pickups and a 3-way toggle switch (original retail price $229); *Deluxe* or *Wildcat* models had three (original retail price $275). The **Continental** model debuted around 1966 with a slightly slimmer body and differently cut horns, and sliding on/off pickup switches (original retail price $199). The teardrop-shaped **Minstrel** model (original retail price $269) had three single coil pickups, on/off sliders, master volume, and three tone knobs. Keep in mind, however, that the preceding was a rough approximation - it is possible to find models that have different parts than the standard designs.

(Source: Michael Wright, Guitar Stories Volume One)

KARERA

Instruments currently produced in Korea. Distributed by the V.J. Rendano Music Company, Inc. of Youngstown, Ohio.

Karera offers a wide range of electric guitars and basses that feature classic American designs. These good quality instruments may appeal to entry level up to student guitarist. Suggested new retail prices range from $175 up to $375 on guitar models, $300 to $500 on electric basses.

KASUGA

Instruments previously produced in Japan from the late 1960s through the early 1980s.

Kasuga produced guitars of both original designs and designs based on classic American models. While the quality is medium to good on both solid body or semi-hollowbody guitars, it is generally the "reproduction" models that are found in the music stores. One reader wrote in to report that his Tele-style model plays "pretty good, and has a good feeling neck." Readers with additional photos or information concerning original design Kasuga guitars are invited to write the ***Blue Book of Electric Guitars.***

KAWAI

Instruments previously built in Japan circa 1956 to mid 1970s; imported models since the late 1970s. No current importation. Previously distributed in the U.S. market by Kawai America Corporation of Compton, California.

While Kawai continues to be a dominant company in keyboards (notably their high quality pianos and synthesizers) they have been and continue producing good quality guitars and basses. Although their entire product line is not available in the U.S. market, Kawai does feature a number of startling original designs in addition to a number of models based on classic American design.

The Kawai company began producing their own guitars back in 1956, and had participated in exporting to the American market. In 1967, the Kawai corporation purchased the Teisco company (of *Teisco Del Rey* guitar fame). Kawai continued distributing the Teisco line in the U.S. through 1973, but then concentrated on domestic distribution of Kawai products thereafter.

Kawai returned to the American marketplace in the mid 1980s with a line of quality bass guitar models, and reissued the Teisco Spectrum Five model in the early 1990s.

ELECTRIC BASS

Recent Electric Bass models included the ash body/bolt-on maple neck **Rb 65A** (list $899); the 5-string **RB 865A** (list $1,095); and the koa/maple body, maple/mahogany through-body neck **FIIB 110 KS** (list $1,395).

KAY

See chapter on House Brands.

Instruments previously built between the 1930s and the late 1960s. Kay stringed instruments were manufactured and distributed by the Kay Musical Instrument Company of Chicago, Illinois. Kay, along with Harmony, were the two larger suppliers of "House Brand" instruments for distributors and retailers.

The Kay trademark returned in the 1970s. Currently the instruments are produced in Asia, and are distributed by A.R. Musical Enterprises, Inc. of Fishers, Indiana.

K

The roots of the Kay Musical Instruments company begin back in 1890, when the Groeschel Company of Chicago, Illinois first began building bowl-back (or *potato bug*) mandolins. In 1918 Groeschel was changed to the Stromberg-Voisenet Company, and incorporated in 1921. Vice-president C. G. Stromberg directed production of guitars and banjos under the **Mayflower** trademark (See MAYFLOWER). This Stromberg is not to be confused with luthier Charles Stromberg (and son Elmer) of Boston, Massachusetts. Stromberg-Voisenet introduced the process of laminating wood tops and backs in 1924, and also began arching instruments tops and backs. Henry Kay Kuhrmeyer, who later became company president, offered use of his middle name on the more popular *Kay-Kraft* series of Stromberg-Voisenet's guitars, mandolins and banjos.

The Kay era began when Henry Kay Kuhrmeyer bought the Stromberg-Voisenet company in 1928. Kuhrmeyer renamed the company Kay Musical Instruments in 1931, and began mass-producing stringed instruments in large volume. Kay, like Washburn at the turn of the century, claimed production of almost 100,000 instruments a year by the mid 1930s. Kay instruments were both marketed by the company themselves, or produced for *jobbers* (distributors) and retail houses under various names. Rather than produce a list here, the ***Blue Book of Electric Guitars*** has attempted to identify Kay-produced *House Brands* throughout the alphabetical listing in this text. Many of these instruments were entry level or students instruments then, and should be considered entry level even now. But as Jay Scott (author of **50's Cool: Kay Guitars**) points out, "True, the vast majority of Kay's student-grade and intermediate guitars were awful. But the top of each line - banjo, guitar and mandolin (especially the acoustic and electric jazz guitars and flattop acoustics) - were meritorious pieces of postwar musical art."

Kay introduced upright basses in 1937, and marketed them under both the Kay trademark and K. Meyer (a clever abbreviation of Kuhrmeyer?). After Leo Fender debuted his Precision electric bass at the 1951 NAMM trade show, Kay was the first company to join Fender in the electric bass market as they introduced their K-162 model in 1952. Kay also went on to produce some of the coolest mixtures of classic archtop design and '50s 'modern' acrylic headstocks on the "Gold K" line that debuted in 1957.

The Kay Musical Instrument company was sold to an investment group headed by Sydney Katz in 1955. Katz, a former manager of Harmony's service department, was more aggressive and competitive in the guitar market. Kay's production facilities expanded to try to meet the demand of the guitar market in the late 1950s and early 1960s. A large number of guitars were produced for Sears under their **Silvertone** trademark. At the peak of the guitar boom in 1964, Kay moved into a new million dollar facility located near Chicago's O'Hare Airport.

Unfortunately, by 1965 the guitar market was oversaturated as retail demand fell off. While Kay was still financially sound, Katz sold the company to Seeburg. Seeburg, a large jukebox manufacturer based in Chicago, owned Kay for a period of two years. At this time, the whole guitar industry was feeling the pinch of economics. Seeburg wanted to maintain their niche in the industry by acquiring Valco Guitars, Inc. (See NATIONAL or DOBRO) and producing their own amplifiers to go with the electric Kay guitars. Bob Keyworth, the executive vice-president in charge of Kay, suggested the opposite: Seeburg should sell Kay to Valco.

Robert Engelhardt, who succeeded Louis Dopyera in Valco's ownership in 1962, bought Kay from Seeburg in June 1967. Valco moved into the Kay facilities, but Engelhardt's company was under financed from the beginning. Engelhardt did make some deal with an investment group or financial company, but after two years the bills couldn't be paid. The investment group just showed up one day, and changed the plant locks. By 1969 or 1970, both Valco Guitars Inc., and the Kay trademark were out of business.

The rights to the Kay name were acquired by Sol Weindling and Barry Hornstein, who were importing Teisco Del Rey (Kawai) guitars to the U.S. market with their W.M.I. importing company. W.M.I. begins putting the Kay name on the Teisco products beginning in 1973, and continued on through the 1970s.

GRADING	100% MINT	98% NEAR MINT	95% EXC+	90% EXC	80% VG+	70% VG	60% G

In 1980, Tony Blair of A.R. Enterprises purchased the Kay trademark. The Kay trademark is now on entry level/beginner guitars built in Asia.

(1950s/1960s company history courtesy Jay Scott, 50's Cool: Kay Guitars; contemporary history courtesy Michael Wright, Vintage Guitar Magazine)

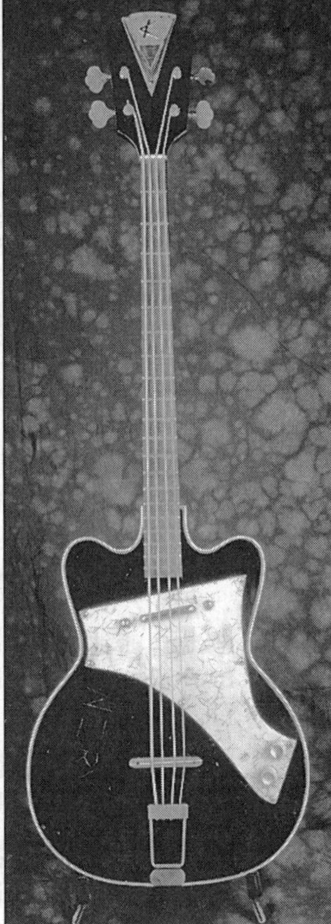

1960 Kay Bass
courtesy Rick King

ELECTRIC

Barney Kessel Models

When guitarist Barney Kessel began endorsing Kay guitars, his signature appeared on the pickguards of the various Barney Kessel guitar models. By 1960, the signature was removed as Kessel had moved on to endorsing Gibson products.

Clean Barney Kessel model guitars range in price from $400 up to $1,000 (although the high end average for sales is around $850).

[BARNEY] KESSEL JAZZ SPECIAL (MODEL 8700 S) - semi-hollow body, 24 3/4" scale, 3-per-side tuners, 2 pickups. Mfg. 1957 to 1960.

The secondary market is still undefined.
This was the premier model of the Gold "K" Line of Barney Kessel guitar models.
This model was also available with a Blonde finish (Model 8700 B).

[Barney] Kessel Jazz Special (Model 8701 S) - similar to the Kessel Jazz Special (Model 8700 S), except features one pickup. Mfg. 1957 to 1960.

The secondary market is still undefined.
This model was also available with a Blonde finish (Model 8701 B).

[BARNEY] KESSEL ARTIST (Model 6700 S) - semi-hollow body, 24 3/4" scale, 3-per-side tuners, 2 pickups. Mfg. 1957 to 1960.

The secondary market is still undefined.
The Artist model was the intermediate sized model of the Gold "K" Line of Barney Kessel guitar models.
This model was also available with a Blonde finish (Model 6700 B).

[Barney] Kessel Artist (Model 6701 S) - similar to the Kessel Artist (Model 6700 S), except features one pickup. Mfg. 1957 to 1960.

The secondary market is still undefined.
This model was also available with a Blonde finish (Model 6701 B).

PRO (Model K172-S, Mfg. 1954 to 1957) - 24 3/4" scale, 3-per-side tuners, one pickup. Mfg. 1954 to 1957.

The secondary market is still undefined.
This model was also available with a Blonde finish (Model K172-B) and Grey Transparent finish called "Harewood" (Model K172-H).

[BARNEY] KESSEL PRO (Model 1700 S, Mfg. 1957 to 1960) - single cutaway LP-style body, 2 pickups. Mfg. 1957 to 1960.

The secondary market is still undefined.
Introduced as a Les Paul-styled guitar in 1954, the Pro became the entry level model in the Gold "K" Line of Barney Kessel guitar models in 1957.
This model was also available with a Blonde finish (Model 1700 B).

[Barney] Kessel Pro (Model 1701 S, Mfg. 1957 - 1960) - similar to the Kessel Pro (Model 1700 S), except features one pickup. Mfg. 1957 to 1960.

The secondary market is still undefined.
This model was also available with a Blonde finish (Model 1701 B).

1958 Kay Barney Kessel
courtesy Rick King

Upbeat Series

Upbeat models also echo some of that '50s coolness, and were available between 1957 through 1960.

UPBEAT (Model K 8980 S) - semi-hollow body, one pickup, 3-per-side tuners on headstock. Mfg. 1957 to 1960.

$400	$325	$285	$250	$215	$195	$175

This model was also available in a Blonde finish (Model K 8980 B), and Jet Black finish as (Model K 8980 J).

Upbeat (Model K 8990 S) - similar to the Upbeat (Model K8980S) except has 2 pickups. Mfg. 1957 to 1961.

$500	$450	$400	$345	$295	$250	$200

This model was also available in a Blonde finish (Model K 8990 B), and Jet Black finish as (Model K 8990 J).

Upbeat (Model K 8995 S) - similar to the Upbeat (Model K8980S) except has 3 pickups. Mfg. 1957 to 1961.

$525	$475	$420	$365	$315	$275	$225

This model was also available in a Blonde finish (Model K 8995 B), and Jet Black finish as (Model K 8995 J).

K

KAY KRAFT

Sometimes hyphenated as KAY-KRAFT.

See KAY.

Instruments previously produced in Chicago, Illinois from the mid 1920s to the mid 1950s.

Henry Kay Kuhrmeyer, who worked his was up from company secretary, treasurer, and later president of Stromberg-Voisenet, lent his middle name to a popular selling line of guitars, mandolins, and banjos. When Kuhrmeyer gained control of Stromberg-Voisenet and changed the name to Kay Musical Instruments, he continued to use the Kay Kraft trademark. Instruments using this trademark could thus be either Stromberg-Voisenet or Kay (depending on the label) but was still produced by the *same* company in the *same* facilities.

KELLER

Instruments currently built in Mandan, North Dakota.

Randall Keller hand crafts custom guitars out of high quality wood and parts as opposed to mass production versions. The **Keller Custom Pro** is offered with a large variety of different woods, hardware choices, and finishes to the customer commissioning the guitar. Prices range around $2,000 new, but contact Keller for a price quote.

KELLETT ALUMINUM GUITARS

Instruments currently manufactured in Santa Clara, California.

Peter Kellett is an established California artist acknowledged for his pioneering work with dye colors on anodized aluminum. Currently, he is making an aluminum instrument patterned after the Stratocaster, with choice of maple or rosewood neck. He also sells the bodies separately, and finishes are multi-colored anodized and/or aluminum nickel. For more information, please contact the company directly (see Trademark Index).

KELLISON, T. R.

Instruments currently built in Billings, Montana since 1978.

Luthier T.R. Kellison has been handcrafting custom instruments since 1978.

KELLY GUITARS

See CARMINE STREET GUITARS.

KEN BEBENSEE GUITARS

Instruments currently built in San Luis Obispo, California.

Luthier Ken Bebensee began building basses and guitars in high school as a musician trying to develop his own style. While studying engineering and industrial technology at Cal Poly State University (San Luis Obispo), Bebensee continued to refine and improve on his designs.

In 1983, Bebensee began offering custom built instruments. Bebensee works out of an old wooden shop in San Luis Obispo, and custom creates a handful of instruments per year. Bebensee's instruments are custom built from the highest grade of sustained yield, exotic woods. For further information (the full color brochure is breathtaking!), please contact luthier Bebensee directly (see Trademark Index).

Bebensee estimates that he has created over 80 instruments since 1983. Bebensee has finished 20 basses and guitars since his color brochure of 1997, most of them custom orders from professional musicians for recording and live performance.

ELECTRIC

Bebensee offers the following as standard features on all his hand crafted instruments: a 24-fret fingerboard, laminated neck-through body design, graphite nut, 100% copper foil shielding in the electronics cavity, Tung Oil/urethane finish, Sperzel locking or Gotoh or Hipshot tuners, Bartolini (or Lane Poor or DiMarzio or Seymour Duncan) pickups, and his own KB bridge. Bebensee also features a list of additional cost options on any of his models.

Bebensee's **Big Fatty Guitar** features neck-through body design combined with a semi-hollow body and 2 f-holes. The **Bear-o-Tone** guitar is a 28" scale baritone with a semi-hollow body, while the similarly shaped **Jazz '96 Guitar** features an ebony tailpiece, 2 active pickups and bridge mounted piezo system. The **Blue Funk Guitar** is a carved solid body model with scrolled horn, Bigsby tremolo, and Blue Metallic polyester finish. A testimony to his craft, the **Gothic Angel** has an elaborately carved body with abalone and mother-of-pearl fingerboard inlays. The **San Luis Archtop** is an acoustic model with a carved spruce top, koa back, cherry sides, and matching set of cats eye f-holes.

The base list prices for an Electric 6-String guitar starts at $2,200 (7-String or Baritone is $2,300). A Flattop Electric/Acoustic guitar starts at $2,440; an Archtop Acoustic model starts at $4,620.

BASS

In addition to his fine guitar models, Bebensee offers a number of high quality electric bass guitars. The **Zeus** combines a sleek, offset double cutaway hollow body with a Bartolini MM magnetic pickup and bridge mounted piezo system, while the **Space Bass** has a carved spruce top and Lane Poor MM pickup. The **Pisces** is a semi-hollow design with Bartolini triple coil pickup, active preamp, 5-position rotary switch, and piezo pickup mounted in the bridge. Other models like the **Deuce, Falcon, Solar**, and **Baroque** are all solid body guitars featuring exotic woods and offset cutaway rounded bodies.

The list prices for a 4-String bass starts at $2,310 (fretted configurations are an additional $100). Bebensee also offers 5-, 6-, and 7-string bass configurations (priced respectively at $2,440, $2,550, and $2,900). An Archtop Acoustic Bass model starts at $3,800.

KENDRICK

Instruments currently built in Pflugerville, Texas since 1994.

In 1989, Gerald Weber started Kendrick Amplifiers in Pflugerville, Texas. Originally dedicated to reproducing the classic Fender tweeds in exact detail, Kendrick has grown to include their own unique designs. Weber was the first designer to build vintage style amp complete with hand-wiring. Weber also joined a network of hand-built amplifier designers that shared an interest in helping musicians gain a knowledge of the workings of their favorite guitar amps.

Weber began writing his monthly column for ***Vintage Guitar Magazine*** over four years ago, which was the first technical article that the magazine had ever printed. Weber is also the author of ***A Desktop Reference of Hip Vintage Guitar Amps and Tube Talk for the Guitarist and Tech,*** both of which gathers together numerous technical tips for tube amplifiers

GRADING	100% MINT	98% NEAR MINT	95% EXC+	90% EXC	80% VG+	70% VG	60% G

Kendrick Continental
courtesy Gerald Weber

ELECTRIC

Beginning in 1994, Weber offered two guitar models in addition to his amplifier line. Kendrick's Continental model was inspired as a tribute to Stevie Ray Vaughan and the Austin blues scene; the Town House model was named after the club in Texas where ZZ Top started their career. Both models are available in other custom colors.

CONTINENTAL - offset angular swamp ash body, maple neck, 22-fret Brazilian rosewood fingerboard with pearl Texas-shaped inlay, 6-on-a-side tuners, chrome hardware, vintage-style tremolo, pickguard, 3 Lindy Fralin single coil *vintage repro* pickups, volume/2 tone controls, 5-way switch. Available in Sunburst nitrocellulose lacquer finish. Mfg. 1994 to date.

MSR $2,200

TOWN HOUSE - single cutaway mahogany body, arched maple top, set-in mahogany neck, 22-fret Brazilian rosewood fingerboard with pearl Texas-shaped inlay, 3-per-side tuners, chrome hardware, tunomatic bridge/stop tailpiece, raised pickguard, 2 Lindy Fralin humbucker pickups, 2 volume/2 tone controls, 3-way selector. Available in Sunburst nitrocellulose lacquer finish. Mfg. 1994, 1996 to date.

MSR $2,500

KENT

Instruments previously produced in Korea and Japan circa 1960s. Distributed in the U.S. by Buegeleisen & Jacobson of New York, New York; Maxwell Meyers in Texas; Southland Musical Merchandise Corporation in North Carolina; and Harris Fandel Corporation in Massachusetts.

The Kent trademark was used on a full line of acoustic and solid body electric guitars, banjos, and mandolins imported into the U.S. market during the 1960s. Some of the earlier Kent guitars were built in Japan by either the Teisco company or Guyatone, but the quality level at this time is down at the entry or student level. The majority of the models were built in Korea.

(Source: Walter Murray, Frankenstein Fretworks; and Michael Wright, Guitar Stories Volume One)

The address for Kent Guitars (as distributed by Buegeleisen & Jacobson) during the 1960s was 5 Union Square, New York (New York 10003).

ELECTRIC

690 - offset double cutaway solid body, 17-fret bolt-on neck with black plastic binding, vertical rectangular position markers, 6-on-a-side tuners, 4 single coil pickups, chrome pickguard, 6 rocker switches for pickup control, 2 roller dials for volume and tone, tremelo tailpiece, adjustable bridge. Available in black/yellow sunburst finish.

830 - maple top/back/sides, 24 3/4" scale, 23-fret rosewood fingerboard, 3-per-side tuners, roller bridge, 2 Kent pickups, volume/tone controls, pickup selector switch. Available in Sunburst finish. Mfg. circa late 1960s to early 1970s.

Length 42 1/2", Body Width 15 5/8", Body Depth 1 5/8".

$175	**$150**	**$115**	**$100**	**$85**	**$65**	**$50**

Last MSR was $99.

831 12-STRING - maple top/back/sides, round soundhole, 24 3/4" scale, 23-fret rosewood fingerboard, roller bridge, 6-per-side tuners, 2 pickups, volume/tone controls, pickup selector switch. Mfg. circa late 1960s to early 1970s.

Length 42 1/2", Body Width 15 5/8", Body Thickness 1 5/8".

$150	**$125**	**$95**	**$85**	**$75**	**$60**	**$50**

Last MSR was $110.

ELECTRIC BASS

832 BASS - semi-acoustic maple body, 30 1/2" scale, 23-fret rosewood fingerboard, 2-per-side tuners, roller bridge, 2 Kent pickups, volume/tone controls, pickup selector switch. Mfg. circa late 1960s to early 1970s.

Length 45 3/4", Body Width 19", Body Depth 1 5/8".

$175	**$150**	**$115**	**$100**	**$85**	**$65**	**$50**

Last MSR was $110.

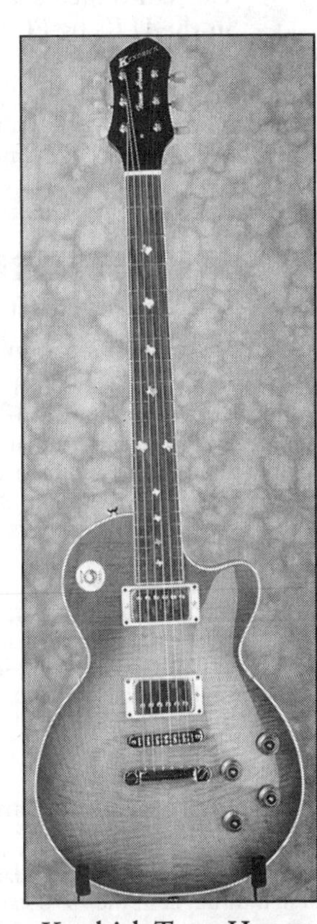

Kendrick Town House
courtesy Gerald Weber

K

KERCORIAN

Instruments previously built in Royal Oak, Michigan 1997-2000.

Jeff Kercorian founded Kercorian Bass Guitars in January of 1997. Kercorian, an electric bassist formany years, handled the bass model designs and electronics; and Jim Sebree, an instrument builder for the past 25 years, constructed the models.

There was no charge for the fretless neck option. Exotic wood tops and backs were also offered.

Add $40 for fretless neck with inlaid lines.

Add $50 for gold hardware.

Add $75 for Hipshot D tuner.

Add $80 for EMG 2-band EQ.

Add $120 for EMG 3-band EQ.

ELECTRIC BASS

SURREALIST - offset double cutaway body with exaggerated bass horn, eastern hard rock maple neck-through design, 34" scale, mahogany body wings, padauk (or purpleheart) top/back, 24-fret ebony fingerboard with mother-of-pearl dot inlay, chrome hardware, 2-per-side headstock, Gotoh tuners, Schaller fixed bridge, active EMG (or passive Bartolini) humbucking pickup, volume/tone controls, Neutrik locking output jack.

Last MSR was $1,299.

This model was also available with bird's-eye maple/walnut top/back, walnut top/maple veneer, lacewood top/back, or walnut top/padauk and maple veneer.

KIMAXE

Instruments currently produced in Korea and China. Distributed by Kenny & Michael's Co., Inc. of Los Angeles, California.

Kimaxe guitars are manufactured by Sang Jin Industrial Company, Ltd., which has a head office in Seoul, Korea and manufacturing facilities in four different places (Inchon, Bupyong, and Kongju, Korea; Tien Jin, China). Sang Jin Industrial Company, Ltd. is better known as a main supplier of guitars to world famous companies such as Fender, Hohner, and other buyers' own brand names for the past ten years. Sang Jin builds almost 10,000 guitars for these accounts each month. In 1994, Sang Jin established its own subsidiary (Kenny and Michael's Company) in Los Angeles in order to distribute their own lines of **Kimaxe** electric guitars and Corina acoustic guitars.

The Kimaxe line mainly offers quality solid body electric guitars and basses with designs based on classic American models at very affordable prices. For further information contact Kenny & Michael's Co., Inc. directly (see Trademark Index).

K

KIMBARA

Instruments previously produced in Japan from the late 1960s to 1990.

Current trademark re-introduced to British marketplace in 1995. Instruments currently produced in China. Distributed in the U.K. by FCN Music.

The Kimbara trademark was a brand name used by a UK importer on these Japanese-produced budget level instruments. Kimbara acoustics were first introduced in England in the late 1960s. During the 1970s, the Kimbara trademark was also applied to a number of solid body guitars based on classic American designs as well. Kimbara instruments are generally mid to good quality budget models, and a mainstay in the British market through 1990. In 1995, FCN Music began importing Chinese-built classical and dreadnought acoustic guitars into England. Retail price-wise, the reborn line is back in its traditional niche.

(Source: Jerry Uwins, Guitar the Magazine [UK])

KIMBERLY

Instruments currently produced in Seoul, Korea. Distributed by the Kimex Trading Co., Ltd. of Seoul, Korea.

Instruments produced in Japan, circa 1960s to early 1970s. Previously distributed by Lafayette Company catalog sales.

Kimberly guitars were originally manufactured by Kawai Guitars (and pianos), located in Hamamatsu, Japan, and imported by Limmco, Inc., owned by Bob Seidman. The company tried to fill the void left by discontinuance of the Kay & Harmony trademarks. Photographic evidence of a Kimberly-branded May Queen (yes, that infamous Teisco model!) arrived at the offices of the *Blue Book of Electric Guitars*. Fellow book enthusiasts are invited to send in photographs and information regarding their Kimberly guitars as well.

(Source: Mr. Bob Seidman, Seidman Sales, Ft. Lauderdale, FL.)

ELECTRIC

Current production of guitars under the Kimberly trademark is the Kimex Trading Co., Ltd. of Seoul, Korea. Kimex produces a number of guitar and bass models that favor classic American designs, and are designed with the entry level guitarist and student in mind.

While some of the currently produced Kimberly models feature solid alder, the majority of bodies are ply-constructed. Retail prices for the **KS-100** strat-styled model begin at $219, while a **KT-200** tele-ish model lists for $329. For further information on models and pricing of current Kimberly instruments, contact the Kimex Trading Co., Ltd. directly (see Trademark Index).

KINAL

Instruments currently produced in Vancouver, British Columbia (Canada), since 1972.

Luthier Mike Kinal has been custom building and designing hand crafted guitars since the late 1960s. Kinal began building 6-string solid body electrics, and produced the **Kinal Standard** in October, 1972. In 1974, Kinal designed the solid body carved top **Kinal Custom**, which became the trademark design throughout the 1970's and 1980's. In 1976, Kinal started to concentrate on bass guitar designs and produced a number of basses. Kinal turned his attention to the creation of the **Voyager Archtop** jazz guitar in 1988.

Mike Kinal now offers a line of guitars and basses with special emphasis on tonality, balance, and comfort. Kinal basses are available with a wide variety of custom finishes including figured and exotic tonewoods tops, headstock laminates, black, gold and two-tone hardware, thumb platforms, neck inlays, and active electronics. Contact Kinal to discuss your custom instrument needs.

(Company history courtesy Mike Kinal, April 1977)

Kinal Voyager Archtop courtesy Kinal

ELECTRIC

The **Voyager Archtop's** body wood is all aged figured maple, and matched for color, tone, and grain pattern. Tops are made from Sitka or Englemann spruce. All tops and backs are hand graduated and tuned. The Voyager archtop is available in single cutaway, or non-cutaway versions, and is available in a 25" or 25 1/2" scale. The fingerboard, bridge, pickguard, and tailpiece are all made from ebony, and the floating-type pickup is a Benedetto or Bartolini. The Voyager archtop is offered in Natural, Violin, or Sunburst finishes with clear coats of nitrocellulose lacquer. In current production, the retail list price is $6,000.

Kinal Solid Body Series

CUSTOM - single cutaway Honduran mahogany body, arched bookmatched figured maple top, set-in Honduran mahogany neck, 22 nickel fret rosewood fingerboard with crown inlays, Schaller tuners and bridge, 2 humbucking pickups, 2 volume/2 tone controls, 3-way selector switch. Available in Sunburst, Translucent Black, and Translucent Red finishes. Current Mfg.

MSR $3,000

STANDARD - offset double cutaway alder, korina, maple, or swamp ash body, set-in neck, 22 nickel fret rosewood fingerboard, chrome hardware, 3 single coil pickups, volume/tone/blend controls, 5-way selector switch. Available in Black, Cherry Red, Cobalt Blue, and Sunburst finishes. Current Mfg.

MSR $1,600

This model is available in a 24 2/3" scale, 25" scale, 25 1/2" scale lengths.

ELECTRIC BASS

MK 4 - offset double cutaway mahogany, alder, or swamp ash body core with bookmatched exotic hardwood top and backs, through-body laminated purpleheart/eastern maple or wenge neck, 34" or 35" scale, ebony fingerboard, 2 pickups, volume/blend/treble/mid/bass controls, active electronics. Available in a highly polished Clear polyester finish. Discontinued.

Last MSR was $2,400.

MK 5 5-String - similar to the MK 4, except in a 5-string configuration. Discontinued.

Last MSR was $2,700.

MK 4-B - offset double cutaway alder, ash, korina or maple body, bolt-on graphite-reinforced hard maple neck, 34" or 35" scale, 24-fret ebony fingerboard, fixed bridge (front or rear loading of strings), 2 single coil Bartolini (or Fralin or Lane Poor) pickups, volume/blend/tone controls. Available in Natural, Sunburst, Translucent Black, Transparent Blue, and Translucent Red finishes. Current Mfg.

MSR $1,550

MK 5-B 5-String - similar to the MK 4-B, except in a 5-string configuration. Current Mfg.

MSR $1,750

MK 6-B 6-String -similar to the MK 4-B, except in a 6-string configuration. Current Mfg.

MSR $1,950

SK 4-B symmetrical double cutaway contour alder, ash, korina or maple body, bolt-on graphite reinforced hard maple neck, 34", 34.5", or 35" scale, 21 or 24-fret ebony, rosewood or maple fingerboard, fixed bridge (front or back loading strings), chrome hardware, 1 single coil/1 humbucking pickup (with coil tap), (Bartolini or Basslines). Available in natural, Burst, or Translucent finishes. Current Mfg.

MSR $1,550

SK 5-B 5-String similar to SK 4-B, except in a 5-string configuration. Current Mfg.

MSR $1,750

SK 6-B 6-String similar to SK 4-B, except in a 6 string configuration. Current Mfg.

MSR $1,950

DK 4-B symmetrical double cutaway, contoured hollow body of alder, ash, maple or mahogany with a spruce top with sound holes. 34", 34.5", and 35" scales, 21 or 24-fret ebony, rosewood or maple fingerboard, chrome hardware, 1 single coil/piezo pickups. Available in natural, Burst, or Translucent finishes. Current Mfg.

MSR $2,250

DK 5-B 5-String similar to DK 4-B, except in a 5-string configuration. Current Mfg.

MSR $2,450

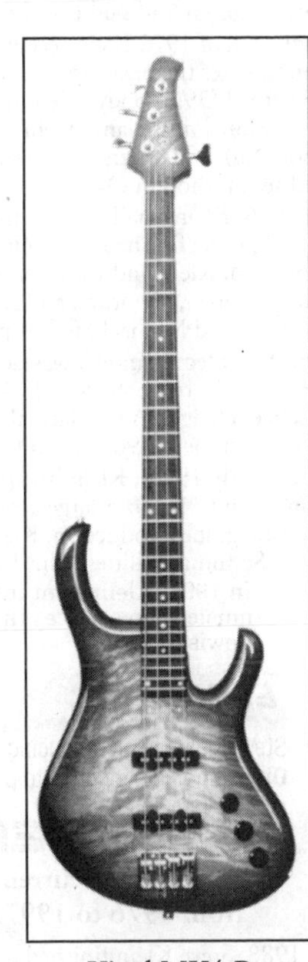

Kinal MK4-B courtesy Kinal

KING, DAVID

Instruments currently built in Portland, Oregon.

Luthier Dave King hand-builds a number of custom basses ranging from minimalist body travel basses to ornately carved and inlaid instruments featuring on board electronic tuners, active electronics, and headphone amplifiers. List prices range from $1,700 to $3,000.

Of the 70 instruments King has built since 1988, only a few have so far come up for resale.

ELECTRIC BASS

David King's philosophy is to build basses that are as comfortable and easy to play as possible. To this end, all specifications such as body dimension, materials, electronics, and finishes are customer specified. King custom machines all of his own headless hardware from solid brass and aluminum. King's designs combine the latest advances in materials and electronics, with non-endangered and certified tonewoods.

The headless **DK** travel bass (retail $1,700) weighs in at 5 pounds. The **Ultralight** headless model (list $1,900) features a khaya, swamp ash, or butternut body, while the **D Bass 4** headless model features exotic wood bodies (list $2,100). The **Kappa** traditional model has a 2-per-side headstock, bolt-on or neck-through design (list $2,200). For further information concerning specifications and pricing, please contact luthier King directly (see Trademark Index).

KING'S STONE

Instruments previously produced in Japan.

The King's Stone trademark was a brand name used by U.S. importers Elger/Hoshino of Ardmore, Pennsylvania. King's Stone, along with others like Goldentone, Jamboree, and Elger were all used on Japanese guitars imported to the U.S. Elger/Hoshino evolved into Hoshino USA, distributor of Ibanez guitars.

(Source: Michael Wright, Guitar Stories Volume One)

KINGSTON

Instruments previously produced in Japan from 1958 to 1967, and distributed in the U.S. by Westheimer Importing Corporation of Chicago, Illinois.

The Kingston brand name was used by U.S. importer Westheimer Importing Corporation of Chicago, Illinois. Jack Westheimer, who was one of the original guitar importers and distributors, is currently president of Cort Musical Instruments of Northbrook, Illinois. The Kingston trademark was used on a product line of acoustic and solid body electric guitars, electric bass guitars, banjos, and mandolins imported into the U.S. market during the 1960s. It has been estimated that 150,000 guitars were sold in the U.S. during the 1960s. Some of the earlier Kingston guitars were built in Japan by either the Teisco company or Guyatone.

(Source: Michael Wright, Guitar Stories Volume One)

KLEIN, STEVE

Instruments currently produced in Sonoma, California since 1976.

Steve Klein first began building electric guitars in Berkeley, California in 1967. A year later, Klein's grandmother introduced him to Dr. Michael Kasha at the University of California in Berkeley. Klein built his first acoustic after that meeting. He briefly attended the California College of Arts and Crafts in 1969, but left to continue building guitars.

In 1970, Klein built his second acoustic guitar. He moved to Colorado in the winter of 1970-1971, but later that summer accepted a job at *The American Dream* guitar shop back in San Diego (this shop was later bought by Bob Taylor and Kurt Listug, and grew into Taylor Guitars).

The third guitar Steve Klein built also had Kasha-inspired designs. Klein travelled to Detroit via Colorado, and met Richard Schneider. Schneider was building Kasha-style classical guitars at the time, and Klein thought that he was going to stay and apprentice with Schneider. Schneider looked at Klein's current guitar and said *Congratulations, You're a guitar builder*, and sent Klein back home.

In the fall of 1972 Klein received his business license. He designed the current acoustic body shape and flying brace, and started work on the Electric Bird guitar. Later the next summer, Klein had finished the first L-457 acoustic; and by 1974 had finished three more acoustics, his first 12 string guitar, and the first small (39.6) body. Klein made a deal with Clayton Johnson (staff member of 'Bill Gramm Presents') to be able to get into concerts to show guitars to professional musicians. Klein got to meet such notables as Stills, Crosby, Young, David Lindly, Doc Watson, Roy Buchanan, John Sebastion (Loving Spoonful), and others. In the summer of 1975, Klein went to Los Angeles with guitars to meet J.D. Souther; he received a commission from Joni Mitchell, and set up shop in Oakland.

In 1976, Klein finally settled into his current shop space in Sonoma. He continued building and designing guitars while doing some repair work. Two years later he finished Joni Mitchell's guitar, and the Electric Bird as well. In 1979, Klein met Steve Kauffman at a G.A.L. convention in Boston. That same year, Klein and Carl Margolis began developing a small electric model that was nicknamed *Lumpy* by David Lindly. Klein also did a side project of antique repair, furniture, and chairs for George Lucas at the Skywalker Ranch. On a more personal note, Klein married Lin Marie DeVincent in the spring of 1985, and Michael Hedges played at their wedding.

The MK Electric model was designed in conjunction with Ronnie Montrose in 1986. By 1988 the small Klein electric design was finished, and was debuted at a trade show in 1989. Klein Electric Division was later started that same year, and Steve Klein began designing an acoustic Harp guitar for Michael Hedges. A year later the acoustic Harp project was dropped in favor of an electrical Harp design instead (Hedges and guitar appeared on the cover of the October 1990 issue of Guitar Player magazine).

In the early 1990s, Klein began designing an acoustic bass guitar *for and with* Bob Taylor of Taylor Guitars. The first prototypes were assembled by Steve Kauffman in 1993. A large acoustic guitar order came in from Japan a year later, and the shipment was sent in 1995. In order to concentrate on the acoustic guitar production, Klein sold his Electric Division to Lorenzo German that same year, and the Electric Division still operates out of the original Klein Sonoma facilities. The Taylor/Klein acoustic bass went into production in 1996, and currently there is a waiting period on acoustic models.

In 1997, Klein went into business with Ed Dufault and opened Klein's Sonoma Music. Located on Broadway in Sonoma, California, the music shop services the local community as well as offering acoustic guitars built by Klein and other high grade builders like Michael Lewis.

ELECTRIC

Steve Klein began producing electric guitars in 1989, and production continued at the Klein facility through 1997. In 1995, Lorenzo German bought the **Electric Division**, and continues to produce high quality electrics. (See KLEIN ELECTRIC GUITARS).

KLEIN ELECTRIC GUITARS

Instruments currently produced in Discovery Bay, California since 1997. Previously produced in Sonoma, California from 1976 to 1997.

In 1988, Steve Klein finished designing a smaller, electric guitar that featured a more ergonomic body style. This model debuted at the 1989 NAMM show, and the Klein Electric Division was later started that same year. In order to concentrate on his acoustic guitar production, Steve Klein sold his Electric Division to Lorenzo German in 1995, and the Electric Division operated out of the original Klein Sonoma facilities through 1997. In 1998, production moved to Discovery Bay, California. Lorenzo German continues to work and promote the high quality electric models.

Current notable guitarists using the Klein electric include David Torn, Bill Frisell, Mick Goodrick, Lou Reed, Henry Kaiser, and Ken Hatfield.

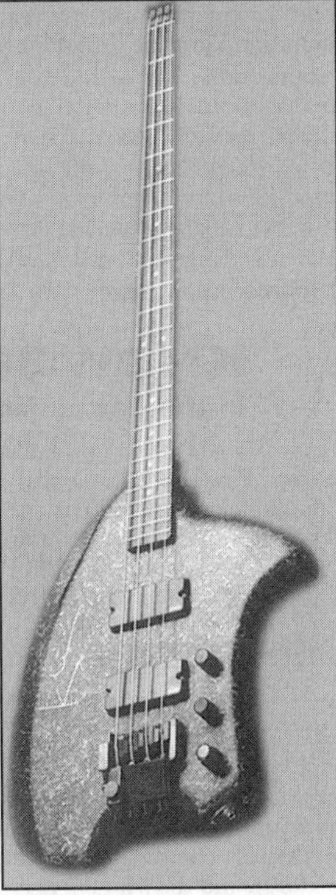

Klein Electric K-Bass
courtesy Lorenzo German

ELECTRIC

The Klein Electric guitar model has an overall length of 31 1/2 inches. Klein electric models are optional with a number of custom features.

Add $133 for a custom finish.

Add $220 for a Novax fingerboard.

Add $352 for a Steinberger Trans-Trem bridge.

BF-96 - offset ergonomic swamp ash body, bolt-on one-piece headless rosewood neck, 25 1/2" scale, 24-fret rosewood fingerboard, Steinberger S-Trem bridge, pickguard, Seymour Duncan Jazz/Alnico II Pro/'59 humbucker pickups, volume/tone controls, 5-way selector switch. Available in Black and Gloss White finishes. Weight 6.5 lbs. Current Mfg.

MSR **$2,574**

Add $169 for a chambered body (internal tone chambers).

Add $297 for Joe Barden pickups.

DT-96 - offset ergonomic alder or basswood body, bolt-on one-piece headless rosewood neck, 25 1/2" scale, 24-fret rosewood fingerboard, Steinberger S-Trem bridge, Seymour Duncan Jazz/'59 humbucker pickups, volume/tone controls, 5-way selector switch. Available in Black and Pearl White finishes. Weight 7.5 lbs. Current Mfg.

MSR **$2,336**

Add $78 for additional Seymour Duncan Alnico Pro II pickup (middle position).

Add $88 for Joe Barden Tele/Two Tone pickups.

ELECTRIC BASS

K BASS 4-STRING - offset ergonomic swamp ash or alder body with extended bass horn, bolt-on Moses Graphite neck, fretless rosewood fingerboard, 2 EMG (35P4/35J) pickups, 2 volume/tone stacked BTC controls. Available in Black and Copper or Metallic Blue zolatone finishes. Current Mfg.

4-String, Steinberger bridge.
MSR **$2,290**

4-String, DB Tuner Steinberger bridge.
MSR **$2,380**

4-String, Steinberger Trans-Trem bridge.
MSR **$2,870**

5-String, Steinberger bridge.
MSR **$2,460**

Add $285 for gloss finish.

Add $786 for maple neck with rosewood or ebony fingerboard.

Add $820 for rosewood neck.

KLIRA

Instruments currently produced in Germany since the late 1950s.

The Klira trademark originated in 1887 by builder Johannes Klier (another text gives "Otto" as his first name). The first company electrics appeared in 1958, and solid body guitars followed in 1960. Throughout the 1960s, Klira produced Fender-ish original designs; but as the 1970s started the emphasis was put on versions of Fender and Gibson designs. Instruments are generally good quality functional guitars, and many have multi-laminate necks (akin to a wood 'butcher block').

(Source: Tony Bacon, The Ultimate Guitar Book)

1970s Knight Electric
courtesy Keith Smart

KNIGHT

Instruments previously made in England during the 1970s and 1980s. Instruments are currently built in Surrey, England.

Luthier Dick Knight (1907-1996) was a well respected British guitar maker, and examples of his work were collected world-wide. Knight (born Stanley Charles Knight) specialized in archtop guitar construction, notably the *Imperial* model. While Knight began building his first guitars in the 1930s, he became more prominent in the 1970s (and 1980s), and featured such clients as Dave Gilmour, Paul McCartney, Pete Townshend, and Mike Rutherford (among others).

During Knight's formative years in the 1930s he worked for Lagonda, the motor vehicle manufacturer. After work, Knight would construct wood items at home, and lost the tips of his fingers in an accident. As this accident prevented him from playing guitar, he turned to making instruments as a hobby.

At the outbreak of World War II Knight met Ben and Lew Davis (the owners of Selmers music shop in London), as well as Joe Van Straten (Selmers' shop manager). In addition to instrument repair, Van Straten suggested the two work on producing a quality English archtop. When finances would not permit the business to carry on, Selmers asked Knight to produce some guitars.

Later, when Knight's wife became ill, he left his work at Selmers and professional guitar making for seventeen years. During this time period, he did produce a number of instruments under the 'KNIGHT' logo. Some of his earliest models do not have a name on the headstock. In addition to his archtop models, Knight produced flattop acoustic, solid body and *335*-style guitars. All Knight's instruments were produced with the same high degree of quality. Recently, Knight's son-in-law Gordon Wells has been continuing to produce guitars and keep the Knight name alive in the guitar-building world.

(Source: Keith Smart, The Zemaitis Guitar Owners Club)

KNOWBUDGE

Instruments currently built in Santa Barbara, California.

KnowBudge Productions builds each guitar over a time period of nine months up to one year. According to a recent letter, their current 1998 6-string electric **Pinaka 411** (retail list $45,936.72) features a sleek Brunzchelle hollow body with ebony fingerboard, 6-on-a-side reverse headstock, fully adjustable non-tremolo bridge, passive electronics (designed for use solely with tube amps), volume control, on/off switch, and a volume bypass switch. The output jack is located towards the rear main fin.

Previously, the 1996 Pinaka T.C. 1-441 had a retail price of $18,369.27. The six-string hollowbody guitar also featured a sculptured Brunzchelle design, 22-fret ebony neck and graphite nut, fixed bridge, and passive electronics (volume control, on/off switch, volume bypass switch).

(Information courtesy KnowBudge Productions, 5-15-97)

KNUTSON LUTHIERY

Instruments currently built in Forrestville, California.

Luthier John Knutson has been building and repairing stringed instruments in and around the San Francisco Bay area since 1978. As a custom builder of acoustic, archtop, and electric instruments, Knutson has produced hundreds of guitars, mandolins, dulcimers, and basses (including custom double- and triple-neck combinations). Knutson is currently producing the Messenger Upright Electric Bass (retail list $2,600), the Songbird Archtop guitar (list $5,000), and the Messenger electric guitar (retail list $1,750). John Knutson holds the exclusive rights to the Songbird, Ecotone, and Messenger trademarks. For further information contact luthier John Knutson directly (see Trademark Index).

KOLL

Instruments currently built in Portland, Oregon.

Luthier Saul Koll combines his background in art (sculpture) and his ten-year experience with instrument repair to design and construct his quality guitars. Most Koll instruments are custom ordered, although he does offer four basic models based on, but not replicas of, vintage style instruments. Koll's guitars are constructed with fine quality tone woods and a glued neck joint design.

K

ELECTRIC

Prices run from $1,499 (**Jr. Glide**) to $1,995 (**Thunder Glide Ali** bass) and $2,399 (**Duo Glide**), up to $3,299 (**Super Glide Almighty**). In addition to the solid and semi-solid instruments mentioned, Koll has specialized in 7-string models since 1992. The current model archtop guitar **Rose City-7** has a list price starting at $3,250. Also, Koll introduced a new solid body model called the **Superior** ($1,699) in 1997.The SPECTROGLIDE lists for $2,499 and the BRIDGETOWN ARCHTOP goes for $4,250.The THUNDERGLIDE ELI CORBET BASS sell for $2,650 and the THUNDERGLIDE ALI ERIC WILSON BASS lists for $3,199. For further information contact luthier Koll directly (see Trademark Index).

KOONTZ

See also STANDEL and HARPTONE.

Instruments previously built in Linden, New Jersey.

Luthier Stan Koontz designed several different models of acoustic and electric guitars and basses for Bob Crooks' Standel company. The instruments were built in Harptone's New Jersey facilities, and have the 'Standel' logo on the peghead. Koontz also built his own custom guitars that featured striking innovations as side-mounted electronics and a hinged internal f-hole cover.

(Source: Tom Wheeler, American Guitars)

KRAMER

Instruments previously produced in Neptune, NJ. Kramer (the original BKL company) was located in Neptune, NJ, since its inception in 1975 to the late 1980s. Production of Kramer (KMI) instruments was at facilities in Eatontown, New Jersey.

Kramer Guitars is currently a division of Gibson Musical Instruments, located in Nashville, Tennessee.

Gary Kramer and Dennis Berardi founded the firm in October of 1975 to produce guitars. Kramer, one of the ex-partners of Travis Bean, brought in his guitar building know-how to Berardi's previous retail experience. In the following April, Peter J. LaPlaca joined the two. LaPlaca had worked his way up through Norlin to vice presidency before joining Kramer and Berardi. The original company is named after their three initials: B, K, L. Kramer (BKL) opened the Neptune factory on July 1, 1976. The first Kramer guitar was co-designed by luthier Phil Petillo, Berardi, and Kramer. Once the prototypes were completed and the factory tooled up, the first production run was completed on November 15, 1976. The first solid body guitars featured an original body design, and a bolt-on aluminum neck with rear wood inlays.

One month after the first production run was finished, Gary Kramer left the BKL company. Guitar production under the Kramer trademark continued. By the early 1980s, the company line consisted of 14 different guitar and bass designs with a price range of $649 to $1,418. Kramer's high profile continued to rise, thanks to an exclusive endorsement deal with Edward Van Halen. In the mid 1980s, the company flourished as they had the sole license to market the Floyd Rose tremolo system.

In 1985, Berardi bought the Spector company; production and distribution of Spector basses then originated from Kramer's facilities in New Jersey. Throughout the late 1980s, Kramer was one of the guitar companies favored by the hard rock/heavy metal bands (along with Charvel/Jackson). However, the company went into bankruptcy in 1989, attempted refinancing several times, and was purchased at auction by a group that incorporated the holdings

GRADING	100% MINT	98% NEAR MINT	95% EXC+	90% EXC	80% VG+	70% VG	60% G

under the company name of Kramer Musical Instruments in 1995. The newly-reformed Kramer (KMI) company had also acquired the rights to the Spector trademark and Spector instruments designs. Kramer (KMI) was located in Eatontown, New Jersey.

Kramer (KMI) re-introduced several new models at industry trade shows in 1995, again sporting an aluminum neck design. However, the company never did directly bring any large amount of products to the musical instrument market.

In 1997, the Gibson corporation acquired the Kramer trademark. By 1998, Gibson was displaying Kramer trademarked models at the Summer NAMM industry show, ads in the print media followed a month later. It has been indicated by some Gibson company officials that the Kramer 'SuperStrat' style models will be produced in Korea (like current Epiphone models).

USA Kramer Baretta
courtesy Brian Goff

Model Identification

Aluminum Neck Models: The first solid body guitars offered in 1975 featured aluminum necks with the open or *prong* V-shape. This is the first identifying clue in comparing a Travis Bean versus a Kramer, as all **Travis Bean** models have a *closed top* (which forms a enclosed 'T'). The first **Kramer** models featured original body designs and two Kramer pickups (they have KRAMER on the pickup covers). In 1978 the **DMZ Custom** series offered DiMarzio pickups.

Wood Neck Models: By 1982, the aluminum neck construction was phased out for a more conventional wood neck/wood body guitars. All high end **Kramer USA** and **Custom** models were produced in America. The **Focus** series of guitars (1985-1989) were built in Japan. **Striker** series and **AeroStar** series (also 1985- 1989) were built in Korea.

1981 Kramer Finishes

When Kramer switched over to the more conventional wood neck/wood body guitars, the Natural finishes that they were using were phased out in favor of new solid finishes (these colors may also be found on the later aluminum neck models as well): Arctic White, Aztec Rust, Electric Yellow, Flame Red, Midnight Black, Pacific Blue, Slate Blue, and Sundance Orange finishes.

ELECTRIC

AeroStar Series

The AeroStar series was produced in Korea during the mid 1980s as an entry level to the more expensive U.S. produced Kramers, and have the EMG Select pickups in them. Used prices run from $175 to $275.

Aluminum Neck Models

Earlier aluminum neck models from 1976 like the **450** feature a laminated "cutting board" style wood body, stop tailpiece, an aluminum plate over the area where the neck bolts to the body, and the 3-per-side "prong" aluminum headstock. The 450 model featured 2 humbuckers, 2 volume and 2 tone controls, and a 3-way pickup selector switch. Other models featured 3 single coil pickups. Research continues on models 250, 350, 450 G, and 650 to designate the differences.

Aluminum neck models are generally priced from $250 to $500 in good condition. While most dealers are happy to sell them, some dealers are holding on to them and cranking up the asking price in the theory that these models may some day be collectible. However, the early models are still "as heavy as a bear" (as we say up north) - and when the neck warms up, the tuning goes out. You be the judge!

K

DMZ Custom Series

DMZ CUSTOM 1000 - offset double cutaway maple body, bolt-on aluminum neck with wood inserts, 21-fret ebanol fingerboard with white dot inlay, *prong* 3-per-side headstock, Schaller tuners, bridge/stop tailpiece, aluminum or stainless steel hardware, 2 DiMarzio Super Distortion humbuckers, volume/tone controls, 3-way selector switch. Available in Natural finish. Mfg. 1978 to 1982.

$550 $475 $410 $345 $280 $215 $150
Last MSR was $629.

DMZ Custom 2000 - similar to the DMZ Custom 1000, except has 2 DiMarzio Dual Sound humbuckers, 2 mini switches (coil taps).

$575 $500 $425 $365 $290 $225 $160
Last MSR was $649.

DMZ Custom 3000 - similar to the DMZ Custom 1000, except has 3 DiMarzio SDS-1 single coil pickups, 5-way selector switch.

$475 $425 $375 $325 $275 $225 $140
Last MSR was $559.

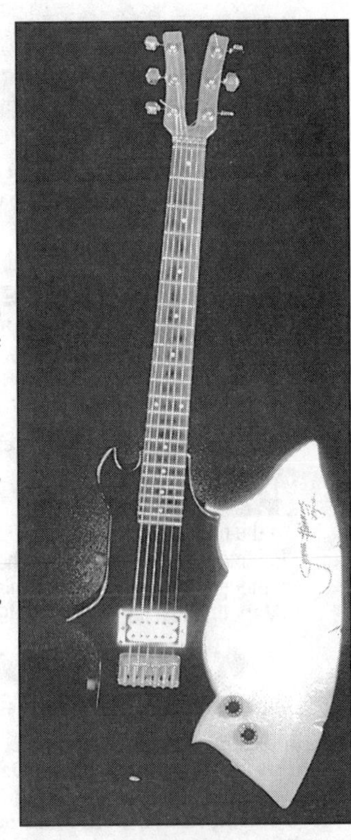
Kramer (Gene Simmons) Axe Guitar
courtesy Thoroughbred Music

Duke Series

Kramer's headless guitars and basses debut between 1981 to 1982. Steinberger's new designs certainly were reviewed throughout the market, apparently. Used prices on the clean ones range from $300 to $350.

Focus Series

Focus series guitars were the Japanese-produced entry level models in 1984. A bit better than the AeroStars, but cheaper price-wise than the U.S. Pacer models.

GRADING	100% MINT	98% NEAR MINT	95% EXC+	90% EXC	80% VG+	70% VG	60% G

Pacer Series

The Pacer series was introduced in 1983, and featured models with specifications similar to the **Custom II**: 6-on-a-side tuners, 'pointy' headstock, maple neck, rosewood fingerboard, 2 single coil/humbucker Seymour Duncan pickups, volume and 2 tone knobs, coil tap switch. Generally pretty good quality guitars now unfairly associated with the 1980s "hair band" heavy metal groups (although some would argue that the "hair bands" were to real metal what dryer lint is to an angora sweater). These guitars now range in price from $350 to $525 (they used to be around $1,200 when they were new).

Signature Series

GORKY PARK - Ballalaika-shaped guitar, bolt-on maple neck. Mfg. 1986 to 1987.

$450	$375	$295	$245	$215	$195	$140

This model was designed in conjunction with the Russian heavy metal band Gorky Park in 1989.

KRAMER-RIPLEY STEREO GUITAR RSG-1 - offset double cutaway body, 6-on-a-side headstock, Floyd Rose locking tremolo, volume/tone controls. Mfg. 1985 to 1987.

$650	$575	$525	$475	$425	$365	$330

Last MSR was $1,349.

Designed by luthier Steve Ripley.
Guitar features a six channel stereo mix, with a panning pot for each string.

PAUL DEAN SIGNATURE - offset double cutaway body, ebony fingerboard, 6-on-a-side pointy headstock, Floyd Rose locking tremolo system, 2 Seymour Duncan Vintage Staggered single coils/Seymour Duncan JB humbucker pickups, volume/tone controls, 3 on/off pickup switches. Mfg. 1986 to 1988.

$550	$495	$455	$415	$385	$335	$295

Last MSR was $1,400.

RICHIE SAMBORA SIGNATURE - offset double cutaway body, maple fingerboard with black star inlays, 6-on-a-side pointy headstock, gold hardware, Floyd Rose locking tremolo system, 2 Seymour Duncan humbucker pickups, volume/tone controls, 5-way selector switch. Mfg. 1988 to 1991.

$475	$425	$350	$295	$245	$215	$185

Last MSR was $1,380.

K

Striker Series

The Striker series, like the AeroStar series, was produced in Korea in the mid 1980s. Similar intent, slightly different features. Used prices run from $175 to $275.

ELECTRIC BASS

DMZ Custom Series

DMZ CUSTOM 4000 - offset double cutaway maple body, bolt-on aluminum neck with wood inserts, 21-fret ebanol fingerboard with white dot inlay, prong 2-per-side headstock, Schaller tuners, bridge/stop tailpiece, aluminum or stainless steel hardware, 2 DiMarzio dual coil humbuckers, volume/tone controls, 3-way selector switch, active EQ. Available in Natural finish. Mfg. 1978 to 1982.

$525	$475	$415	$355	$295	$235	$170

Last MSR was $679.

GENE SIMMONS AXE - "Olde English Executioner Axe"-style maple (or ash) body, bolt-on aluminum neck with rear wood inserts, 22-fret ebanol fingerboard, chrome hardware, 3-per-side "prong" headstock, 2 DiMarzio humbuckers, volume/tone controls, 3-way switch. Available in Black and Silver custom polyester finish. Mfg. 1980 to 1981.

$1,300	$1,150	$975	$800	$700	$625	$525

Last MSR was $799.

Kramer produced a matching guitar model. Both had limited runs of 1000 instruments, numbered and signed by Gene Simmons (KISS).

MIDI

In the mid 1980s Kramer retailed a MIDI interface unit designed by IVL Technologies called the Pitchrider 7000. Ideally, any guitar could be hooked up to the Pitchrider 7000 using a hexaphonic pickup, have guitar information converted to a MIDI signal, and send that signal to any MIDI compatible synthesizer. Although not a guitar *per se*, this tool can add an extra dimension to an existing guitar (providing it tracks the note information properly). In 1988, the Pitchrider (Mark II) had a list price of $649; an additional MFS-40 foot switch was optional for an additional $150.

KRUNDAAL

Instruments previously built in Italy circa early to mid 1960s.

Krundaal instruments designed by Italian motorcycle and guitar appreciator, Wandre' Pelotti (1916-1981). Wandre' instruments may bear a number of different brand names (such as **Davoli, Framez, Avalon,** or **Avanti**), but the Wandre' logo will appear somewhere. Wandre' guitars were personally produced by Pelotti from 1956 or 1957 to 1960; between 1960 to 1963, by Framez in Milan, Italy; from 1963 to 1965 by Davoli. Under the Krundaal logo a stamped *A. Davoli, Made in Italy* designation can be found.

(Source: Tony Bacon, The Ultimate Guitar Book)

GRADING	100% MINT	98% NEAR MINT	95% EXC+	90% EXC	80% VG+	70% VG	60% G

BIKINI - rounded body design, stylized *W* bridge, two single coil *Davoli* pickups. Mfg. circa 1963 to 1965.

$850	**$700**	**$625**	**$550**	**$475**	**$400**	**$325**

This model features an attached portable amplifier.

KUSTOM

Instruments previously built in Chanute, Kansas during the late 1960s.

The Kustom Amplifier company, builders of the famous *tuck-and-roll* covered amps, produced 4 different guitar models in their Kansas factory from 1967 to late 1969. Bud Ross, the founder/designer of Kustom, was a bassist turned second guitarist in the late 1950s who had a knack for electronics and wiring. Ross teamed up with Fred Berry, and Kustom amps debuted at the summer 1965 NAMM show. Eventually the line ranged from small combos to huge P.A.s and bass cabinets (imagine the amp backline at a Creedence Clearwater Revival show, and you'll get an idea about the range of the Kustom product line).

In 1967, Doyle Reeding approached Ross about building guitars. Along with Wesley Valorie, the three began designing electric guitars. Guitar wizard Roy Clark, who later became a Kustom amp endorser, also had input on the Kustom design. These semi-hollowbody guitars featured two-piece carved-out top glued to a two-piece carved-out back (similar to the Microfrets design). Ross estimates that between 2,000 and 3,000 were produced during the two years, all in the Kansas facility.

(Source: Michael Wright, Guitar Stories Volume One)

Kustom K-2000
courtesy John Kinnemeyer

ELECTRIC

All models featured a common body design, and differed in the hardware and pickups that were installed.

K200 A - dual cutaway semi-hollow body, bolt-on maple neck, 22-fret bound rosewood fingerboard with dice dot inlays, cat's eye f-hole, zero fret, chrome-plated nut, 3+3 winged headstock, black pickguard, Bigsby tremolo system, 2 DeArmond humbuckers, 2 volume/2 tone controls, 3-way pickup selector switch. Available in Black, Black Ash, Blue, Natural, Red, Sunburst, White Ash, Wineburst, and Zebra finishes. Mfg. 1967 to late 1969.

$700	**$550**	**$495**	**$450**	**$400**	**$325**	**$265**

The burgundy to green Wineburst finish is also called *Watermelon Burst* by collectors.

K200 B - similar to the K200 A, except has double dot inlay on fingerboard, trapeze tailpiece, and 2 DeArmond single coils. Mfg. 1967 to late 1969.

$625	**$525**	**$475**	**$430**	**$400**	**$325**	**$265**

K200 C - similar to the K200 A, except has smaller unwinged headstock design, white pickguard, and less fancy tuning machines. Mfg. 1967 to late 1969.

$600	**$500**	**$450**	**$400**	**$350**	**$300**	**$245**

ELECTRIC BASS

K200 D - dual cutaway semi-hollow body, bolt-on maple neck, 21-fret rosewood fingerboard with single dot inlays, cat's eye f-hole, zero fret, chrome-plated nut, 2-per-side *winged* headstock, black pickguard, bass bridge/stop tailpiece, 2 DeArmond 4-pole single coil pickups, 2 volume/2 tone controls, 3-way pickup selector switch. Available in Black, Black Ash, Blue, Natural, Red, Sunburst, White Ash, Wineburst, and Zebra finishes. Mfg. 1967 to late 1969.

$700	**$550**	**$495**	**$450**	**$400**	**$325**	**$265**

KYDD

Instruments currently built in Upper Darby, Pennsylvania. Distributed by Modulus Guitars of Novato, California.

Luthier/inventor Bruce Kaminsky, a freelance bassist, designed the Kydd Carry-On bass electric bass to replicate the sounds of an upright acoustic bass in a 6 pound, 35.5 inch overall length instrument. This smaller instrument is set up on a tripod stand, and has a 30" scale (as compared to a 41" plus scale on the old 'doghouse' acoustics). Over the past couple of years, Kaminsky estimates that he has sold at least 100 instruments. Recently, the Modulus Guitars company set up a distribution deal with Kaminsky to further distribute his basses. For further information, please contact luthier Kaminsky directly (see Trademark Index).

ELECTRIC BASS

K BASS - (35.5" overall length) solid hard maple minimalist body/neck, 30" scale, granadillo fingerboard with pearl side position markers, maple adjustable bridge, chrome string clamp and tuning system, Fishman transducers, volume/tone controls. Available in a hand rubbed, ultra-thin finish. Current Mfg.

K 4 4-String.
MSR $1,795

K 5 5-String.
MSR $1,995

K 6 6-String.
MSR $2,195

Add $200 for curly maple body/neck.

List price includes a tripod stand and padded gig bag.

KYLE, DOUG

Instruments currently built in Hampstead (Devon), England.

Doug Kyle is currently offering handcrafted guitars. For additional information regarding models, pricing, and specifications, please contact luthier Kyle directly (see Trademark Index).

Section L

GRADING	100% MINT	98% NEAR MINT	95% EXC+	90% EXC	80% VG+	70% VG	60% G

LTD

Instruments currently built in Korea. Distributed by the ESP Guitar Company, of Hollywood, California.

LTD instruments are designed and distributed by the ESP Guitar Company. All of the designs are based on current ESP models, and offer a cost effective way to own the same ESP style instruments.

ELECTRIC

100 Series

LTD E-100 - single cutaway alder body, bolt-on maple neck, 22-fret rosewood fingerboard with white dot inlay, tune-o-matic bridge/stop tailpiece, 3-per-side headstock, chrome hardware, 2 LTD exposed pole piece humbucker pickups, volume/tone controls, 3-position selector. Available in Black, Candy Apple Red, and Pearl White finishes. Mfg. 1998 to 1999.

		$350	$300	$250	$225	$175	$150	$100

Last MSR was $429.

LTD H-100 - offset double cutaway arched top alder body, bolt-on maple neck, 22-fret rosewood fingerboard with white dot inlay/block inlay on 12th fret, tune-o-matic bridge/stop tailpiece, 'curved point' peghead, 3-per-side tuners, chrome hardware, 2 LTD humbucker pickups, volume/tone controls, 3-way selector toggle. Available in Black, Candy Apple Red, and Pearl White finishes. Mfg. 1998 to date.

MSR $399 — $285 $225 $200 $175 $150 $125 $100

LTD M-100 - offset double cutaway alder body, bolt-on maple neck, 22-fret rosewood fingerboard with white dot inlay (logo block inlay at 12th fret), LTD licensed Floyd Rose tremolo, reverse peghead, 6 on the other side tuners, black hardware, 2 LTD humbucker pickups, volume/tone control, 3-position switch. Available in Black, Candy Apple Red, and Pearl White finishes. Mfg. 1998 to date.

MSR $399 — $275 $225 $190 $175 $150 $100 $75

LTD MH-100 - similar to H-100, except has Floyd Rose Licensed bridge, 24 XJ frets, and two EMG-HZ humbucker pickups. Available in See-Through Black, See-Through Black Cherry, and See-Through Aqua finishes. New 1999.

MSR $499 — $389 $289 $250 $225 $200 $170 $150

200 Series

LTD E-200 (LTD ECLIPSE) - single cutaway alder or mahogany body, bolt-on maple neck, 22-fret bound rosewood fingerboard with white dot inlay (logo block inlay at 12th fret), tune-o-matic bridge/stop tailpiece, 3-per-side headstock, chrome hardware, 2 Duncan Designed exposed pole piece humbucker pickups, volume/tone controls, 3-position selector. Available in Black, Honey Sunburst, See-Through Blue, See-Through Purple, and See-Through Red finishes. Mfg. 1996 to 1999.

$499 $395 $350 $295 $250 $200 $150

Last MSR was $549.

LTD EXP-200 (LTD E.X.P.) - radical offset hourglass alder body, bolt-on maple neck, 22-fret rosewood fingerboard with white dot inlay, tune-o-matic bridge/stop tailpiece, black 'drooping' peghead with screened logo, 6-on-a-side tuners, black hardware, 2 Duncan Designed humbuckers, volume/tone controls, 3-position switch. Available in Black and Olympic White finishes. Mfg. 1996 to 1999.

$599 $500 $425 $375 $300 $250 $175

Last MSR was $719.

LTD F-200 offset double cutaway body with a gothis flavor, basswood body, bolt-on maple neck, rosewood fingerboard with arrowhead position markers, black hardware, Floyd Rose Licensed bridge, 24 XJ frets, 2 humbucking EMG HZ pickups, 3-per-side tuners, locking nut. Available in black, Black Cherry, Midnight Purple and Gunmetal Blue finishes. New 2000.

MSR $699 — $525 $475 $425 $400 $375 $325 $300

GRADING	100% MINT	98% NEAR MINT	95% EXC+	90% EXC	80% VG+	70% VG	60% G

LTD H-200 (LTD HORIZON) - offset double cutaway alder or mahogany arched top body with natural binding, bolt-on maple neck, 24-fret bound rosewood fingerboard with white dot inlay/block inlay on 12th fret, tune-o-matic bridge/stop tailpiece, bound 'curved point' peghead, 3-per-side tuners, chrome hardware, 2 Duncan Designed humbucker pickups, volume/tone controls, 3-way selector toggle. Available in Black, Honey Sunburst, See-Through Blue, See-Through Purple, and See-Through Red finishes. Mfg. 1995 to 2000.

	$409	$3755	$325	$275	$225	$175	$125

Last MSR was $549.

LTD H-201 similar to Model H-200 except has mahogany body with flamed maple top, block position markers and model name inlaid at 12th fret, black hardware, natural top and body binding, Duncan Designed HB-102 pickup set, 1 volume/1 tone control, 5-way Megaswitch. Available in See-Through Green, See-Through Red, See-Through Orange and See-Through Blue. New 2001.

MSR $599	$480	$450	$425	$400	$350	$325	$300

LTD M-2 - offset double cutaway hardwood body, bolt-on neck, 24-fret rosewood fingerboard with white dot inlay (logo block inlay at 12th fret), double locking vibrato, reverse 'pointy' blackface peghead with screened logo, 6-on-the-other-side tuners, black hardware, single coil/humbucker ESP pickups, volume control, 3-position switch. Available in Black finish. Mfg. 1995 to 1998.

	$750	$700	$625	$550	$450	$350	$275

Last MSR was $1,095.

Add $100 for See-Through Blue, See-Through Purple, or See-Through Red finishes.

LTD M-200 - offset double cutaway alder body, bolt-on maple neck, 22-fret rosewood fingerboard with arrowhead inlays (logo block inlay at 12th fret), recessed Floyd Rose Standard tremolo, reverse peghead, 6-on-the-other-side tuners, black hardware, 2 Duncan Designed humbucker pickups, volume/tone control, 3-position switch. Available in Black, Pearl White, See-Through Blue and See-Through Red finishes. Mfg. 1998 to 2000.

	$429	$375	$300	$250	$200	$175	$125

Last MSR was $599.

LTD M-201 similar to Model M-200 except basswood body, white neck binding, EMG HZ H-1 pickup set, 1 volume/1 tone control, 3-way toggle and EMG After Burner. Available in black, Black Gold, Gunmetal Blue and Titanium finishes. New 2001.

MSR $649	$490	$450	$400	$350	$300	$250	$200

LTD M-250 (LTD Mirage) - similar to the LTD M-200, except features 2 rail humbuckers/exposed pole piece humbucker Duncan Designed pickups, 5-way selector switch. Available in Black, Pearl White, See-Through Blue and See-Through Red finishes. Mfg. 1996 to 2000.

	$495	$425	$375	$300	$250	$175	$125

Last MSR was $629.

Early versions of this model may have a Wilkinson tremolo, and (2 single coil/humbucker) ESP pickups.

LTD M-251 similar to Model M201 except has EMG-HZ H-1B, S-1, H-1N pickups, 5-way toggle. Available in black, Black Gold, Gunmetal Blue and Titanium finishes. New 2001.

MSR $679	$510	$450	$400	$350	$300	$250	$200

LTD MH-200 - similar to H-200, except has Floyd Rose Licensed bridge. Available in See-Through Black, See-Through Black Cherry, and See-Through Aqua finishes. Mfg. 1999 to 2000.

	$499	$450	$400	$350	$300	$250	$200

Last MSR was $649.

LTD RS-200 - modified star-shaped mahogany body, maple bolt-on neck with rosewood fingerboard, arrowhead neck inlays, white neck binding, 24 XJ frets, Floyd Rose licensed bridge, twp EMG-HZ humbucker pickups, black hardware. Available in Black, Grey Satin, Midnight Purple, and Gun metal Blue finishes. Mfg. 1999 Only.

	$599	$525	$450	$399	$350	$299	$250

Last MSR was $749.

LTD ULTRA TONE - offset double cutaway hardwood body, 22-fret bound rosewood fingerboard with white dot inlay, tune-o-matic bridge/stop tailpiece, chrome hardware, black/white 'marbleized' pickguard, 3-per-side 'vintage-style' tuners, screened logo/graphic on headstock, 2 covered ESP humbuckers, 2 volume/tone controls, 3-way selector. Available in Black finish. Mfg. 1996 to 1998.

	$625	$575	$500	$450	$375	$300	$225

Last MSR was $895.

LTD Ultra-200 - similar to the LTD Ultra Tone, except features an alder body, white pearloid pickguard, blackface peghead with silk-screened LTD logo, 2 Duncan Designed humbuckers. Available in Black, Pearl White, and Three-Tone Sunburst finishes. Mfg. 1998 to 1999.

	$670	$580	$510	$440	$370	$300	$225

Last MSR was $895.

LTD V-200 - Flying V-shaped alder body, bolt-on maple neck, 22-fret rosewood fingerboard with white dot inlay, tune-o-matic bridge/stop tailpiece, black pointed peghead with screened logo, 3-per-side tuners, chrome hardware, 2 Duncan Designed humbuckers, volume/tone controls, 3-position switch. Available in Black and Olympic White finishes. Mfg. 1998 to 1999.

	$599	$500	$425	$375	$300	$250	$175

Last MSR was $719.

L

GRADING	100% MINT	98% NEAR MINT	95% EXC+	90% EXC	80% VG+	70% VG	60% G

LTD V-250 - similar to V-200, except has mahogany body, arrowhead neck inlays, white neck binding, two EMG-HZ humbucker pickups, Floyd Rose licensed bridge, and black hardware. Available in Black, Grey Satin, Midnight Purple, and Gun metal Blue finishes. Mfg. 1999 to 2000.

	$599	$499	$450	$399	$350	$299	$250

Last MSR was $749.

300 Series

LTD H-300 - similar to H-200, except has mahogany Neck-Through body with Figured Maple top, mahogany neck with rosewood fingerboard, two EMG-HZ humbucker pickups. Available in See-Through Black, See-Through Black Cherry, and See-Through Aqua finishes. Mfg. 1999-2000.

	$600	$500	$450	$400	$350	$325	$300

Last MSR was $749.

LTD H-301 - similar to Model H-300 except has flamed maple top, maple neck, Tune-O-Matic bridge with stop tailpiece, EMG HZ H-1 pickup set. Available in See-Through Green, See-Through Red, See-Through Blue and See-Through Orange finishes. New 2001.

MSR $749	$600	$500	$450	$400	$350	$325	$300

LTD M-300 - similar to M-200, except has mahogany Neck-Through body with Figured Maple top, mahogany neck with rosewood fingerboard, white neck binding, 2 EMG-HZ humbucker pickups. Available in See-Through Black, See-Through Black Cherry, and See-Through Aqua finishes. Mfg. 1999 to 2000.

	$625	$525	$475	$425	$375	$325	$275

Last MSR was $799.

Also available with two EMG-HZ humbucker pickups and one single coil pickup for an additional $30 (LTD M-350). Disc. 2000. Last MSR was $829.

LTD MH-300 - similar to MH-200, except has mahogany Neck-Through body with Figured Maple top, mahogany neck with rosewood fingerboard, and two EMG-HZ pickups. Available in See-Through Black, See-Through Black Cherry, and See-Through Aqua finishes. Mfg. 1999 to 2000.

	$675	$575	$525	$475	$425	$375	$325

Last MSR was $849.

LTD MH-301 similar to Model MH-300 except has quilted maple top, maple neck-through body, EMG-HZ H-1 pickup set. Available in See-Through Purple, See-Through Red, See-Through Green and See-Through Blue finishes. New 2001.

MSR $849	$650	$600	$550	$525	$500	$450	$425

VIPER-300 offset double cutaway design, mahogany body, maple set neck, rosewood fingerboard with dot position markers, Viper 300 inlaid at the 12th fret, black hardware, 3-per-side tuners, Tune-O-Matic bridge, white neck binding, 24 XJ frets, 2 humbucking EMG HZ pickups. Available in black and See-Through Cherry finishes. Mfg. 2000 Only.

	$490	$465	$425	$400	$375	$350	$325

Last MSR was $649.

VIPER-301 similar to Viper 300 except has rosewood fingerboard with flag inlays and model name at the 12th fret, Tune-O-Matic bridge with stop tailpiece, EMG HZ H-1 pickup set, 1 volume/1 tone control, toggle. Available in black and See-Through Black Cherry finishes. New 2001.

MSR $649	$490	$465	$425	$400	$375	$350	$325

EX Series

LTD EX-250 radically shaped mahogany body, maple bolt-on neck, rosewood fingerboard with dot position markers, EX-250 inlaid at the 12th fret, black hardware, Tune-O-Matic bridge, 22 XJ frets, 2 Duncan Designed humbucking pickups, 6-on-a-side tuners, 1 volume/1 tone control, toggle. Available in black, Black Cherry, Midnight Purple and Gunmetal Blue finishes. Mfg. 2000 only.

	$450	$425	$400	$375	$350	$325	$300

Last MSR was $599.

LTD EX-350 similar to Model EX-250 except has mahogany set neck, Floyd Rose Licensed bridge, 2 humbucking EMG HZ pickups. Available in black, Black Cherry, Midnight Purple and Gunmetal Blue. Mfg. 2000 only.

	$600	$550	$500	$450	$400	$375	$350

Last MSR was $799.

L

GRADING		100% MINT	98% NEAR MINT	95% EXC+	90% EXC	80% VG+	70% VG	60% G

MV Series

LTD MV-100 offset double cutaway basswood body, bolt-on maple neck, rosewood fingerboard with offset dot position markers, model name inlaid at 12th fret, black hardware, Tune-O-Matic bridge with string through body, 24 XJ frets, LTD LB-100 and LR-100 pickups, 1 volume/1 tone, 3-way toggle. Available in black, Metallic Gold, Ice Blue and Teal finishes. New 2001.

MSR	$399	$319	$275	$250	$225	$200	$175	$150

LTD MV-200 similar to Model MV-100 except has mahogany body with flamed maple top, natural top and body binding, white binding on neck, Duncan Designed HB-102B and HR-101 pickups. Available in See-Through Red, See-Through Blue, See-Through Purple and See-Through Orange finishes. New 2001.

MSR	$549	$440	$400	$350	$300	$250	$200	$175

LTD MV-300 similar to Model MV-200 except has neck-through body, EMG-HZ H-1B, S-1 pickups. Available in See-Through Red, See-Through Blue, See-Through Purple and See-Through Orange finishes. New 2001.

MSR	$749	$565	$525	$475	$450	$400	$350	$300

Signature Series

LTD GL-500K (George Lynch) offset double cutaway alder body, bolt-on maple neck, rosewood fingerboard with dot position markers, model name at 12th fret, black hardware, Floyd Rose Licensed bridge, 22 XJ frets, Duncan Designed HB-103, SC-101 pickups, 1 volume with push/pull pickup selector, Custom graphics. New 2001.

MSR	$999	$750	$700	$650	$600	$550	$500	$450

LTD GL-500T (George Lynch) similar to Model GL-500K except has different graphic (tiger stripes). New 2001.

MSR	$999	$750	$700	$650	$600	$550	$500	$450

LTD KH-502 (Kirk Hammett) offset double cutaway alder body, maple neck-through body, rosewood fingerboard with dot position markers, skull and crossbones at 12th fet, black hardware, Floyd Rose Licensed bridge, 24 XJ frets, EMG-HZ H-1 pickup set, 2 volume/1 tone control, 3-way slotted switch. Available in Black. New 2001.

MSR	$999	$750	$700	$650	$600	$550	$500	$450

LTD KH-503 (Kirk Hammett) single cutaway alder body, maple neck-through body, rosewood fingerboard with dot position markers and spiders at the 12th fret, black hardware, Floyd Rose Licensed bridge, 24 XJ frets, EMG-HZ H-1 pickup set, 2 volume/1 tone control, 3-way toggle. Available in Black. New 2001.

MSR	$999	$750	$700	$650	$600	$550	$500	$450

LTD MC-500 (Max Cavalera) offset double cutaway alder body, maple neck-through body, rosewood fingerboard with dot position markers and XXX at 12th fret, black hardware, Tune-O-Matic bridge with string-through body, white neck binding, 24 XJ frets, 1 Duncan Designed HB-103B pickup, 1 volume control. Available in Brazil Green finish. New 2001.

MSR	$999	$750	$700	$650	$600	$550	$500	$450

LTD SC-500 (Steven Carpenter) offset double cutaway alder body, maple neck-through body, rosewood fingerboard with model name inlaid at 12th fret, chrome hardware, Tune-O-Matic bridge with string-through body, white neck binding, 24 XJ frets, Duncan Designed HB-102 Set and SC-101 single coil pickup, 1 volume/1 tone control, 3-way slotted switch. Available in black and See-Through green finishes. New 2001.

MSR	$999	$750	$700	$650	$600	$550	$500	$450

LTD TA-500 (Tom Araya) 4-string bass, offset double cutaway alder body, maple neck-through body, rosewood fingerboard with dot inlays and pentagrams at the 12th fret, black hardware, LTD BB-04 bridge, 24 XJ frets, EMG 35-HZ pickup set, volume, pan, B-30 Active EQ. Available in black. New 2001.

MSR	$999	$750	$700	$650	$600	$550	$500	$450

Baritone Models

LTD FB-200 - 27" scale, offset double cutaway basswood body with gothic styling, bolt-on maple neck, rosewood fingerboard with arrowhead position markers, 3-per-side tuners, black hardware, Tune-O-Matic bridge, 24 XJ frets, 2 humbucking EMG HZ pickups, EMG Afterburner Active Gain Boost, 1 volume/1 tone control, toggle. Available in black finish. New 2001.

MSR	$749	$575	$525	$475	$450	$400	$375	$325

LTD VB-300 27" scale, offset double cutaway mahogany body, maple set neck, rosewood fingerboard with dot inlays and model name inlaid at the 12th fret, black hardware, 3-per-side tuners, Tune-O-Matic bridge, white neck binding, 24 XJ frets, 2 humbucking EMG HZ pickups and EMG Afterburner Active gain Boost. Available in black finish. New 2001.

MSR	$749	$575	$525	$475	$450	$400	$375	$325

GRADING	100% MINT	98% NEAR MINT	95% EXC+	90% EXC	80% VG+	70% VG	60% G

7-String Models

LTD M-107 - offset double cutaway basswood body, bolt-on 7-string maple neck, rosewood fingerboard with dot inlays and M-107 at the 12th fret, string through body bridge, 22 XJ frets, 2 humbucking LTD 7 pickups, black hardware, reverse headstock, 7 on 1 side tuners, 1 volume/1tone control, toggle. Available in Black Satin, Blue Satin and Purple Satin finishes. Mfg. 2000 only.

		$375	$350	$325	$300	$275	$250	$225

Last MSR was $499.

LTD M-207 - similar to Model M-107, except has arrowhead position markers, M-207 inlaid at the 12th fret, Floyd Rose Licensed 7 Bridge, 2 humbucking Duncan Design 7 pickups. Available in black, Black Cherry, Midnight Purple and Gunmetal Blue finishes. Mfg. 2000 only.

		$600	$550	$500	$450	$400	$350	$300

Last MSR was $799.

LTD M-307 similar to Model M-207, except has neck-through body, mahogany body, mahogany neck with rosewood fingerboard, white neck binding, M-307 inlaid at the 12th fret, 2 humbucking EMG HZ-707 pickups. Available in black, Black Cherry, Midnight Purple and Gunmetal Blue. Mfg. 2000 to present.

MSR	$849	$650	$600	$550	$500	$450	$400	$375

LTD MH-307 similar to Model M-307, except has mahogany body with figured maple top, block position markers, M-307 inlaid at the 12th fret. Available in See-Through Black, See-Through Black Cherry, See-Through Aqua. Mfg. 2000 to present.

MSR	$899	$675	$625	$575	$525	$475	$425	$375

LTD F-207 offset double cutaway body design with a gothis look, basswood body, bolt-on 7-string maple neck, rosewood fingerboard with arrowhead position markers, black hardware, Floyd Rose Licensed 7 bridge, 24 XJ frets, 2 humbucking EMG HZ-707 pickups, 3 and 4 headstock tuner configuration. Available in black, Black Cherry, Midnight Purple and Gunmetal Blue. Mfg. 2000 only.

		$600	$550	$500	$450	$400	$350	$300

Last MSR was $799.

LTD H-207 offset double cutaway ash body, bolt-on 7-string maple neck, rosewood fingerboard with block inlays, black hardware, Tune-O-Matic 7 bridge, white neck binding, natural body binding, 24 XJ frets, 2 humbucking Duncan Design 7 pickups, 1 volume/1 tone control, toggle, 3 and 4 headstock tuner configuration. Available in See-Through Black, See-Through Black Cherry and See-Through Aqua. Mfg. 2000 only.

		$525	$475	$450	$400	$350	$300	$250

Last MSR was $699.

LTD H-307 similar to Model H-207, except has neck thru body, mahogany body with figured maple top, mahogany neck, 2 humbucking EMG HZ-707 pickups. Available in See-Through Black, See-Through Black Cherry and See-Through Aqua. Mfg. f2000 to date.

MSR	$799	$600	$550	$500	$450	$400	$350	$300

ELECTRIC BASS

LTD H-4 BASS - sleek offset double cutaway hardwood body, maple neck, 24-fret rosewood fingerboard with offset white dot inlay, 2-per-side 'curved point' headstock with screened logo, fixed bridge, black hardware, P/J-style ESP pickups, volume/blend/tone controls. Available in Black, Candy Apple Red, Metallic Purple, and Metallic Blue finishes. Mfg. 1995 to 1998.

		$625	$575	$500	$450	$375	$300	$225

Last MSR was $895.

100 Series Bass

LTD B-100 SPECIAL - slightly offset double cutaway alder body, bolt-on maple neck, 21-fret rosewood fingerboard with white dot inlay, 2-per-side headstock with screened logo, fixed bridge, chrome hardware, LTD exposed pole piece humbucker pickup, volume/tone controls. Available in Black, Candy Apple Red, and Pearl White finishes. Mfg. 1998 to 1999.

		$399	$350	$300	$250	$225	$175	$125

Last MSR was $499.

LTD B-104 BASS - double cutaway basswood body with offset waist, maple bolt-on neck with rosewood fingerboard, dot inlays, 24 XJ frets, 4 String Deluxe Bass bridge, 2 LTD Soapbar pickups with Mid Control, chrome hardware. Available in Black, Grey Satin, Metallic Red, and Electric Blue finishes. New 1999.

MSR	$399	$309	$250	$225	$200	$150	$100	$75

L

GRADING		100% MINT	98% NEAR MINT	95% EXC+	90% EXC	80% VG+	70% VG	60% G

LTD B-105 Bass - similar to B-104 Bass, except in a 5-string configuration. Available in Black, Grey Satin, Metallic Red, and Electric Blue finishes. New 1999.

MSR	$449	$349	$275	$250	$225	$175	$125	$75

200 Series Bass

LTD B-204 BASS - offset double cutaway basswood body, bolt-on maple neck, 24-fret rosewood fingerboard with white dot inlay, 2-per-side headstock with screened logo, fixed bridge, chrome hardware, 2 EMG HZ 'soapbar' pickups, volume/blend/bass/treble controls, EMG active EQ. Available in Red and Natural finishes. Mfg. 1998 to date.

MSR	$649	$559	$480	$420	$350	$290	$220	$170

LTD B-205 Bass - similar to the B-204, except features 5-string configuration, 3/2-per-side tuners. Available in Red and Natural finishes. Mfg. 1998 to date.

MSR	$699	$565	$465	$410	$325	$275	$190	$135

LTD F-204 BASS - offset double cutaway sculpted mahogany body, bolt-on maple neck with rosewood fingerboard, white dot inlays, 24 XJ frets, 4 String Deluxe Bass bridge, two EMG-HZ pickups with 3-band active EQ, black hardware. Available in Black, Grey Satin, Midnight Purple, and Gun metal Blue finishes. New 1999.

MSR	$699	$559	$459	$399	$350	$299	$250	$199

LTD F-205 Bass - similar to F-204 Bass, except in a 5-string configuration. Available in Black, Grey Satin, Midnight Purple, and Gun metal Blue finishes. New 1999.

MSR	$749	$599	$499	$450	$399	$350	$299	$250

300 Series Bass

LTD B-304 BASS - similar to B-204 Bass, except has Neck-Through mahogany body, maple neck with rosewood fingerboard. Available in See-Through Black, See-Through Black Cherry, and 2-Tone Sunburst finishes. New 1999.

MSR	$849	$689	$600	$550	$500	$425	$375	$300

LTD B-305 Bass - similar to B-304 Bass, except in a 5-string configuration. Available in See-Through Black, See-Through Black Cherry, and 2-Tone Sunburst finishes. New 1999.

MSR	$899	$730	$610	$575	$525	$475	$400	$350

LUK

See LAUNHARDT & KOBS.

LA BAYE

Instruments previously built in Neodesha, Kansas in 1967. Designed and distributed by The La Baye Company in Green Bay, Wisconsin. Current information can be obtained through Henri's Music of Green Bay (and Appleton), Wisconsin.

Inventor Dan Helland conceived the notion of a minimal-bodied guitar while working at Henri's Music Shop in Green Bay, Wisconsin during the mid 1960s. After receiving some support from owner Henri Czachor and others, Helland had the Holman-Woodell company of Neodesha, Kansas build the first (and only) run of 45 instruments. La Baye guitars share similar stock hardware pieces and pickups installed on Wurlitzer guitars of the same era, as Holman-Woodell were building a number of different trademarked instruments during the mid to late 1960s.

After receiving the first shipment, Helland attended the 1967 Chicago NAMM show (the same show where Ovation first debuted). Unfortunately, the minimal body concept was so far advanced that the market didn't catch up until Steinberger released his first bass in the 1980s! La Baye instruments were produced in 1967, and a total of 45 were shipped to Helland.

Identification is pretty straight forward, given that the 3+3 headstock will say *La Baye* and sometimes *2 x 4*. The 22-fret neck bolts to the rectangular body, and controls are mounted on top and bottom of the body. There were four models: the six string and twelve string guitars, and the short-scale (single pickup) bass as well as the long-scale (2 pickup) bass. However, keep in mind that there are only 45 official La Baye instruments (others were later offered by Holman and 21st Century, from the same factory that built the initial models).

(Source: Michael Wright, Guitar Stories Volume One)

LACE GUITARS

Also LACE HELIX.

Instruments currently built in Huntington Beach, California. Distributed by AGI (Actodyne General Inc.) of Huntington Beach, California.

AGI's Lace Guitars feature a revolutionary neck design: the ergonomically correct **Lace Helix Twisted Neck**. The Twisted Neck has a 20 degree twist that follows the natural twist of the player's hand as it travels up and down the fingerboard. While the prototypes were introduced during 1997, production finally began in late 1999, after CNC production problems had been solved. Lace also manufactures a Helix 20 degree neck that bolts on to a Fender Stratocaster neck pocket (with clear gloss finish and Jim Dunlop frets). The retail price is $400.

ELECTRIC

Lace guitars feature the patented Lace Helix twisted neck system, with patented dual compound split radius fingerboard. The patented Lace Helix body shape has a unique style and elegance.

GRADING			100% MINT	98% NEAR MINT	95% EXC+	90% EXC	80% VG+	70% VG	60% G

LACE HELIX GLASS - sleek offset double cutaway Avanti lightweight fiberglass body, maple neck, 25 1/2" scale, rosewood fingerboard with offset mother-of-pearl dot inlay, 6-on-a-side Sperzel tuners, fixed bridge, chrome or gold hardware, 2 Lace humbucker pickups, black mini data volume/tone controls, pickup selector switch. Available in Black, Acto-Blue, Red, Yellow, and White finishes.

MSR	$1,995	$1,500	$1,200	$1,000	$825	$700	$600	$550

LACE HELIX WOOD - sleek offset double cutaway mahogany body, maple neck, 25 1/2" scale, rosewood fingerboard with offset mother-of-pearl dot inlay, 6-on-a-side Sperzel tuners, fixed bridge or stop tailpiece, chrome or gold hardware, 3 single coil (or 2 humbucker) Lace pickups, black mini data volume/tone controls, pickup selector switch. Available in Black, Acto-Blue, Red, Yellow, and White finishes.

MSR	$1,995	$1,500	$1,200	$1,000	$825	$700	$600	$550

LG-1 - offset double cutaway alder body, maple neck, 25 1/2" scale, slab rosewood fingerboard with offset mother-of-pearl dot inlay, 6-on-a-side locking Sperzel tuners, ABM bridge, features ActoTone virtual acoustic pickup system, chrome or gold hardware, 3 Lace California convertible pickups, 2 volume/1 tone controls, pickup selector switch.

MSR	$1,300	$925	$800	$700	$600	$500	$400	$350

Add $300 for LG-1 California/Custom (includes carved ash top, and Super Vintage Lace Holy Grail pickups).

California Series

CALIFORNIA CLASSIC offset double cutaway mahogany body, mahogany neck, rosewood fingerboard with dot position markers, 3 Lace PS-900 Ultra Vintage pickups, fulcrum full-contact tremelo or wraparound bridge may be specified, 2-pickup variation may be special ordered. Choice of a variety of traditional nitrocellulose finishes. Current Mfg.

MSR $1,699

CALIFORNIA GOLD RUSH offset double cutaway ash body, bolt-on maple neck with maple fingerboard, 3 Lace Ultra Vintage PS-900 pickups or 3 single coil size Lace Ultra Vintage pickups, full contact tremelo or wraparound bridge. Available in black, red and Three-Tone Vintage Sunburst grain enhanced nitrocellulose translucent finishes. Current Mfg.

MSR $1,799

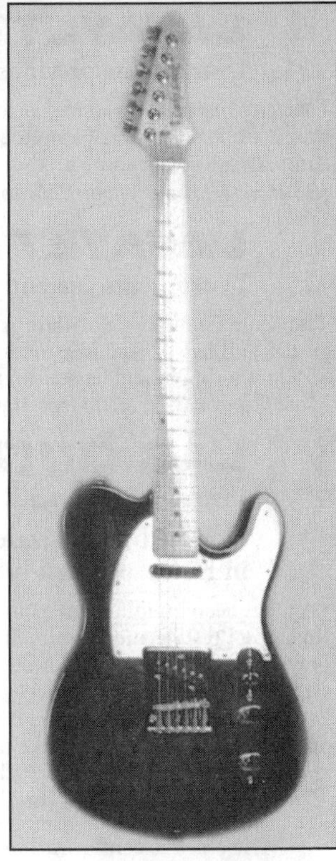

Lady Luck LLT1
courtesy Lady Luck Ind.

LADO

Instruments currently built in Pickering, Ontario. Instruments were previously built in Scarborough, Ontario (Canada) since the early 1970s.

Lado founder and company president Joe Kovacic initially learned the guitar-building craft in Zagreb, Croatia. Kovacic gained luthier experience in Austria and Germany before leaving Europe to move to North America in 1971. Every handcrafted bass and guitar is backed by over thirty years experience, and current suggested retail prices fall between $799 to $999. For further information, please contact Lado directly (see Trademark Index).

LADY LUCK

Instruments currently produced in Korea since 1986. Distributed in the U.S., Europe, and South America by Lady Luck Industries, Inc. of Cary, Illinois.

President Terresa Miller has been offering a wide range of imported, affordable guitars that are designed for beginning students up to working professionals. Lady Luck guitar models are designed in the U.S. (specifications and colors). Lady Luck also offers several models of electric bass guitars along with the line of acoustic and electric guitars.

In addition to the Lady Luck and Nouveau brands, Lady Luck Industries also distributes Adder Plus pickups and EV Star Cables.

ELECTRIC

Lady Luck's **La Femme** model guitars (list $995) feature a female-figure sculpted, styrene body and Bill Lawrence Keystone pickups. Available in White or Black finishes.

Nouveau Series

The **Nouveau** series models like the **LLS-2N** featured an offset double cutaway solid ash body, 2 single coils/humbucker pickups, standard tremolo, and 6-on-a-side tuners. The **LLS-2NFR** model featured a licensed Floyd Rose bridge. Retail list prices begin at $375.

Retrospect Series

LLS- models feature an offset double cutaway body, while the **LLP-** and **LLT-** models feature single cutaway bodies. The **Retrospect** line features designs based on classic American favorites, with prices that begin at $210 (**LLS1**) to $250 (**LLS2**, and up through $280 (**LLT1**). For further information regarding model specifications and pricing, please contact Lady Luck Industries directly (see Trademark Index).

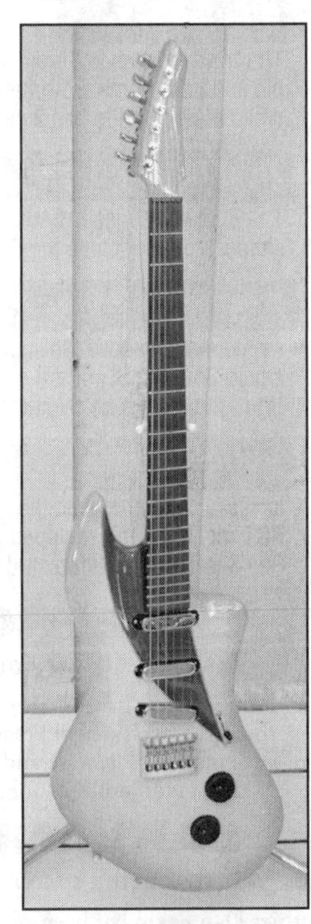

Lace Helix Electric
courtesy S.P. Fjestad

LAFAYETTE (Japan Mfg.)

Instruments previously produced in Japan during the 1960s, and distributed by LaFayette Electronics.

Lafayette instruments were shorter-scaled beginner instruments imported to the U.S. and sold through LaFayette Electronics' catalogs. The LaFayette product line consisted of amplifiers, thinline acoustic/electric archtops, and solid body electric guitars and basses. Many models built by Japan's Guyatone company, although some may also be Teisco models.

(Source: Michael Wright, Vintage Guitar Magazine)

LAFAYETTE (Korea Mfg.)

Instruments currently built in Korea. Distributed by the More Company of Pooler, Georgia.

The More Company, distributors of Synsonic instruments, is also offering a wide range of acoustic and acoustic/electric guitars; and solid body electric guitars and basses. Acoustic models like the **SW 690** have a retail list price of $460; acoustic/electrics start at $500. Solid body electric models range from $350 up to $625, and basses run from $575 to $650. For additional information regarding models, specifications, and pricing, please contact Lafayette (a More Company) directly (see Trademark Index).

LAG GUITARS

Instruments currently built in Bedarieux, France.

Hotline by LAG series is currently produced in Korea (Hotline models are designed in France and built to specifications in Korea). Currently imported and distributed by the Sandell Trading Company, located in Clearwater Beach, Florida.

LAG has been building guitars in France since 1980. LAG began building the high quality **Beast** superstrat designed solid bodies, and later introduced the **Roxanne Prestige** and **Roxanne Classic** double cutaway LP-ish model. One of the more original designs developed by the LAG company was to offer a Floyd Rose locking tremolo on the **Roxanne Prestige**, a move un-duplicated by any of the American companies like Gibson, Hamer, Dean (or others with Gibson-esque guitar designs).

Led by Michael Chavarria, the Bedarieux facility currently has eleven workers. LAG has currently cut back on custom models in favor of offering more options on the four series in the new line. LAG specifically uses flamed maple tops on all of their models, and features electronics by DiMarzio, Fishman, and Seymour Duncan; and Schaller, Sperzel, and Wilkinson hardware.

LAG also produces the "Le Key" portable MIDI keyboard controller, a sleek 37-key model worn on a strap just like a guitar. LAG guitars is also offering a Jumbo style acoustic model with either mahogany or rosewood back and sides. This model is also available in an acoustic/electric configuration.

ELECTRIC

Beast Series

The 'superstrat' **Beast** models feature offset double cutaway basswood bodies, bolt-on maple necks, tremolo bridges, and 6 tuners on a side headstocks. Models include the **Standard**, flamed maple topped **Supreme**, humbucker/single coil/humbucker **Custom**, and the semi-hollow **Thinline**.

Blue Series

The traditional style **Blues** models all feature double cutaway bodies, with distinctive white pearloid pickguards that cover the pickup area forward to the treble and bass horns. Both the **Standard** and **Louisiane** models feature a humbucker/single coil 'SuperTele' configuration (the Louisiane has gold hardware), while the **Nashville** has 2 single coils and a humbucker in the bridge position.

Rockline Series

The Rockline series is LAG's modern 'SuperStrat' models, with a humbucker/single coil/humbucker pickup configuration and sleek double cutaway body shape. Models include the **Standard** and **Avenue**; the **Metalmaster** model has been in production for over ten years.

Roxanne Series

As mentioned above, Roxanne models feature a dual cutaway mahogany body and glued-in neck, and feature two humbuckers and a 3 tuners per side headstock. Both the **Standard** and **Classic** models are straight ahead classic LP-style guitars (the Classic has a flamed maple top and Sunburst finish); the **Prestige** features a tune-o-matic bridge and raised metal tailpiece; and the eye-catching **Floyd** model features a recessed Floyd Rose tremolo.

Hotline Series

In 1994, Lag introduced the new **Hotline** Series. Hotline guitar designs are conceived in France and built to LAG specifications in Korea. Both the **TB1** and the **RK1** models come equipped with the new DUNCAN DESIGNED pickups, and are available in one of three colors: Black See-Through, Green See-Through, or Red See-Through. Interested guitarists are invited to contact the LAG company directly (see Trademark Index).

LAKEFRONT

Instruments previously built in Mossville, Illinois circa early 1980s

Lakefront Musical Instruments offered a number of high quality solid body electric guitars. Instruments featured a neck-through construction, 21-fret fingerboard, 3-per-side gold plated Grover tuner, and laminated body construction that featured oak, zebrawood, rosewood, walnut, curly maple, and bird's-eye maple. Hardware and pickups were specified by the buyer. Suggested list prices are still unknown at this date.

Last given address for Lakefront was Lakefront Musical Instruments, Box 48, Mossville IL 61552.

LAKLAND

Instruments currently built in Chicago, Illinois since 1994.

Luthier Dan Lakin has been playing and buying/selling bass guitars for a number of years. In 1994, he began offering a high quality, custom built electric bass with a design based on Leo Fender's later models.

GRADING	100% MINT	98% NEAR MINT	95% EXC+	90% EXC	80% VG+	70% VG	60% G

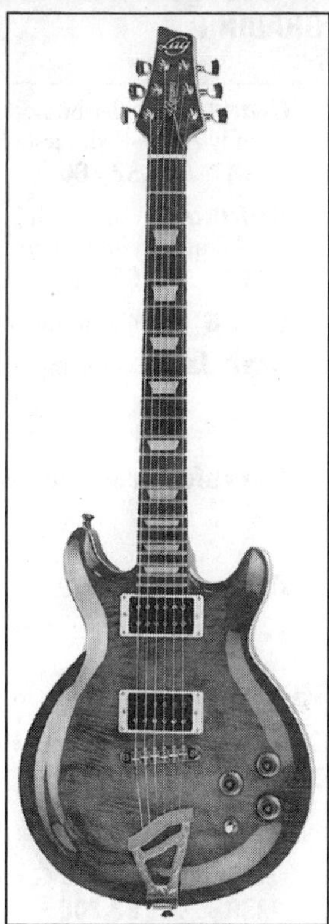
LAG Guitars Roxanne
courtesy LAG Guitars

ELECTRIC BASS

Lakland models are differentiated by the pickup configuration. All models (except the Joe Osborn Signature model) are available in a 4- and 5-string configuration, and in three different appointment levels. 4-String models are optional with a Hipshot Bass Xtender (D-Tuner) for $100.

4-94 - slightly offset double cutaway body, bolt-on quatersawn maple neck with 2 graphite reinforcement bars, 34" scale, 22-fret maple (or rosewood) fingerboard with dot inlay, 4-on-a-side tuners, fixed bridge with round metal plate, chrome hardware, single coil/humbucker Bartolini (or Seymour Duncan Bassline) pickups, volume/pan/bass/mid/treble controls, coil tap switch. Mfg. 1994 to date.

Standard - swamp Ash body with Translucent or Sunburst finish.
MSR $3,000 — $2,250 $1,950 $1,650 $1,450 $1,250 $1,050 $850

Classic - alder body with Metallic finish (with optional white pickguard).
MSR $3,000 — $2,250 $1,950 $1,650 $1,450 $1,250 $1,050 $850

Deluxe - swamp Ash body with quilted or flamed maple top, Translucent or Sunburst finish.
MSR $3,400 — $2,550 $2,250 $1,950 $1,650 $1,350 $1,150 $950

55-94 - similar to the 4-94, except features a 35" scale, 5-string configuration, 3/2-per-side tuners. Mfg. 1994 to date.

Standard - swamp Ash body with Translucent or Sunburst finish.
MSR $3,300 — $2,475 $2,175 $1,875 $1,675 $1,375 $1,075 $875

Classic - alder body with Metallic finish (with optional white pickguard).
MSR $3,300 — $2,475 $2,175 $1,875 $1,675 $1,375 $1,075 $875

Deluxe - swamp Ash body with quilted or flamed maple top, Translucent or Sunburst finish.
MSR $3,800 — $2,850 $2,550 $2,250 $1,950 $1,650 $1,350 $995

4-63 - similar to the 4-94, except features 2 J-style single coil Bartolini (or Basslines or Lindy Fralin) pickups. Current Mfg.

Standard - swamp Ash body with Translucent or Sunburst finish.
MSR $3,000 — $2,250 $1,950 $1,650 $1,450 $1,250 $1,050 $850

Classic - alder body with Metallic finish (with optional white pickguard).
MSR $3,000 — $2,250 $1,950 $1,650 $1,450 $1,250 $1,050 $850

Deluxe - swamp Ash body with quilted or flamed maple top, Translucent or Sunburst finish.
MSR $3,400 — $2,550 $2,250 $1,950 $1,650 $1,350 $1,150 $950

55-63 - similar to the 4-63, except features a 35" scale, 5-string configuration, 3/2-per-side tuners, Bartolini and Bassline pickups. Current Mfg.

Standard - swamp Ash body with Translucent or Sunburst finish.
MSR $3,300 — $2,475 $2,175 $1,875 $1,675 $1,375 $1,075 $875

Classic - alder body with Metallic finish (with optional white pickguard).
MSR $3,300 — $2,475 $2,175 $1,875 $1,675 $1,375 $1,075 $875

Deluxe - swamp Ash body with quilted or flamed maple top, Translucent or Sunburst finish.
MSR $3,800 — $2,850 $2,550 $2,250 $1,950 $1,650 $1,350 $995

4-76 - similar to the 4-94, except features one MM (humbucker) Bartolini (or Basslines) pickup, volume/bass/mid/treble controls. Disc. 2000.

Standard - swamp Ash body with Translucent or Sunburst finish.
$2,150 $1,850 $1,550 $1,250 $1,050 $850 $725
Last MSR was $2,880.

Classic - alder body with Metallic finish (with optional white pickguard).
$2,150 $1,850 $1,550 $1,250 $1,050 $850 $725
Last MSR was $2,880.

Deluxe - swamp Ash body with quilted or flamed maple top, Translucent or Sunburst finish.
$2,850 $2,550 $2,250 $1,950 $1,650 $1,350 $995
Last MSR was $3,300.

4-DUAL J - similar to 4-76 except features two Lindy Fralin "J" style pickups. New 2001.

Standard - swamp Ash body. Available in Translucent White, Translucent Blonde, Amber, Burgundy, Natural, Blue, Three-Tone Sunburst, Tobacco Sunburst, Cherry Sunburst and Teal Sunburst finishes. New 2001
MSR $2,880 — $2,150 $1,850 $1,550 $1,250 $1,050 $850 $725

L

GRADING		100% MINT	98% NEAR MINT	95% EXC+	90% EXC	80% VG+	70% VG	60% G

Classic - alder body. Available in Shoreline Gold, Inca Silver, Teal Green, Sea Foam Green, Lake Placid Blue, Sherwood Green, Burgundy Mist, Candy Apple Red, Fiesta Red, Sonic Blue, Olympic White and black finishes. New 2001.

MSR	$2,880	$2,150	$1,850	$1,550	$1,250	$1,050	$850	$725

Deluxe - swamp Ash body with flame or quilt maple top. Available in Amber, Burgundy, natural, Blue, Three-Tone Sunburst, Tobacco Sunburst, Teal Sunburst and Cherry Sunburst finishes. New 2001.

MSR	$3,300	$2,850	$2,550	$2,250	$1,950	$1,650	$1,350	$995

55-76 - similar to the 4-76, except features a 35" scale, 5-string configuration, 3/2-per-side tuners. Disc. 2000.

Standard - swamp Ash body with Translucent or Sunburst finish.

		$2,400	$2,100	$1,800	$1,500	$1,300	$995	$850

Last MSR was $3,200.

Classic - alder body with Metallic finish (with optional white pickguard).

		$2,400	$2,100	$1,800	$1,500	$1,300	$995	$850

Last MSR was $3,200.

Deluxe - swamp Ash body with quilted or flamed maple top, Translucent or Sunburst finish.

		$2,775	$2,475	$2,175	$1,875	$1,575	$1,275	$975

Last MSR was $3,700.

55-DUAL J - similar to 55-76, except features two Lindy Fralin "J" style pickups. New 2001.

Standard - swamp Ash body. Available in Amber, Burgundy, Natural, Blue, Three Tone Sunburst, Tobacco Sunburst, Cherry Sunburst, Teal Sunburst, Translucent White and Translucent Blonde finishes. New 2001.

MSR	$3,200	$2,400	$2,100	$1,800	$1,500	$1,200	$995	$850

Classic - alder body. Available in Shoreline Gold, Inca Silver, Teal Green, Lake Placid Blue, Sherwood Green, Burgundy Mist, Candy Apple red, Sonic Blue, Seafoam Green, Fiesta Red, Olympic White and black finishes. New 2001.

MSR	$3,200	$2,400	$2,100	$1,800	$1,500	$1,200	$995	$850

Deluxe - swamp Ash body, flame or quilt maple top. Available in Amber, Burgundy, Natural, Blue, Three-Tone Sunburst, Tobacco Sunburst, Cherry Sunburst and Teal Sunburst finishes.

MSR	$3,700	$2,775	$2,475	$2,175	$1,875	$1,575	$1, 375	$1,050

HOLLOWBODY - built in collaboration with Michael Tobias, two Bartolini humbucking pickups, 2-per-side Hipshot Ultra-light tuners, East Indian Rosewood fingerboard with Birdseye Maple position markers, quartersawn Rock Maple neck with graphite reinforcement bars, 1 f-hole. Mfg. 2000 to date.

Standard - carved mahogany back and sides, carved maple top. Available in Shoreline Gold, Inca Silver, Teal Green, Lake Placid Blue, Sherwood Green, Burgundy Mist, Candy Apple Red, Sonic Blue, Seafoam Green, Fiesta Red and Olympic White finishes.

MSR	$3,600	$2,700	$2,400	$2,100	$1,800	$1,500	$1,200	$950

Deluxe - carved mahogany back and sides, carved Maple Top AAA-Flame. Available in Three-Tone Sunburst and Tobacco Sunburst finishes.

MSR	$4,200	$3,150	$2,750	$2,450	$2,150	$1,850	$1,550	$1,250

Deluxe Limited Edition - carved mahogany back and sides, carved Maple top AAAAA-Flame. Available in Three-Tone Sunburst and Tobacco Sunburst finishes.

MSR	$4,800	$3,600	$3,200	$2,800	$2,500	$2,200	$1,900	$1,550

JERRY SCHEFF SIGNATURE -offset double cutaway body, 22-frets, quartersawn Rock maple neck, Birdseye Maple with ebony dots or East Indian Rosewood with Birdseye Maple dots fingerboard, two Kent Armstrong Split-Tube low-output pickups, onboard Bartolini 3-band preamp, white pickguard.

Standard 4 - 34" scale, Swamp Ash body, Hipshot tapered shaft tuners. Available in Amber, Burgundy, Natural, Blue, Three-Tone Sunburst, Tobacco Sunburst, Cherry Sunburst and Teal Sunburst, Translucent White and Translucent Blonde finishes.

MSR	$3,000	$2,250	$1,950	$1,750	$1,450	$1,150	$950	$750

Classic 4 - 34" scale, alder body, Hipshot tapered shaft tuners. Available in Shoreline Gold, Inca Silver, Teal Green, Lake Placid Blue, Seafoam Green, Sherwood Green, Fiesta Red, Burgundy Mist, Candy Apple Red, Sonic Blue, Olympic White and black finishes.

MSR	$3,000	$2,250	$1,950	$1,750	$1,450	$1,150	$950	$750

Deluxe 4 - 34" scale, Swamp Ash body, Hipshot tapered shaft tuners. Available in the same finishes as the Standard Model minus Translucent White and Translucent Blonde. Current Mfg.

MSR	$3,400	$2,550	$2,250	$1,950	$1,650	$1,350	$1,050	$795

Standard 5 - 35" scale, Swamp Ash body, Hipshot Ultralight tuners. Available in the same finishes as its 4-string counterpart.

MSR	$3,300	$2,475	$2,175	$1,875	$1,575	$1,275	$975	$725

Classic 5 - 35" scale, alder body, Hipshot Ultralight tuners. Available in the same finishes as its 4-string counterpart.

MSR	$3,300	$2,475	$2,175	$1,875	$1,575	$1,275	$975	$725

Deluxe 5 - 35" scale, Swamp Ash body, quilt or flame maple top, Hipshot Ultralight tuners. Available in the same finishes as its 4-string counterpart.

MSR	$3,800	$2,850	$2,550	$2, 250	$1,950	$1,650	$1,350	$995

L

BOB GLAUB SIGNATURE - offset diuble cutaway alder or ash body, 34" scale, quartersawn maple neck w/graphite reinforcement, 20-fret East Indian Rosewood fingerboard or maple fingerboard, Lindy Fralin pickups, 1 Volume/1 Tone –passive, Hipshot tapered shaft tuners, Lakland design dual access strings-through body or bridge. Available in 3-Tone Sunburst, black, Olympic White, Candy Apple Red Metallic, Teal Green Metallic, Lake Placid Blue Metallic, Sherwood Green Metallic, Shoreline Gold Metallic, Inca Silver, Burgundy Mist, Translucent White and natural finishes. Current Mfg.

MSR $2,900 $2,175 $1,875 $1,575 $1,275 $1,075 $875 $750

Add $400 for "P & J" configuration with Fralin linear hum-canceling "J" pickup.

JOE OSBORN SIGNATURE - offset double cutaway alder body, bolt-on quatersawn maple neck with 2 graphite reinforcement bars, 34" scale, 20-fret Indian rosewood fingerboard with pearl dot inlay, 4-on-a-side Hipshot tuners, fixed bridge, chrome hardware, tortoiseshell (or vintage white) pick guard, 2 J-style single coil Bartolini (or Lindy Fralin) pickups, 2 stack knob volume/tone controls, metal controls plate. Available in Three Tone Sunburst, Black, Olympic White and Metallic finishes. Current Mfg.

MSR $3,300 $2,475 $2,175 $1,875 $1,575 $1,275 $975 $850

Add $300 for active system with Bartolini pickups and custom made 3-band EQ preamp.

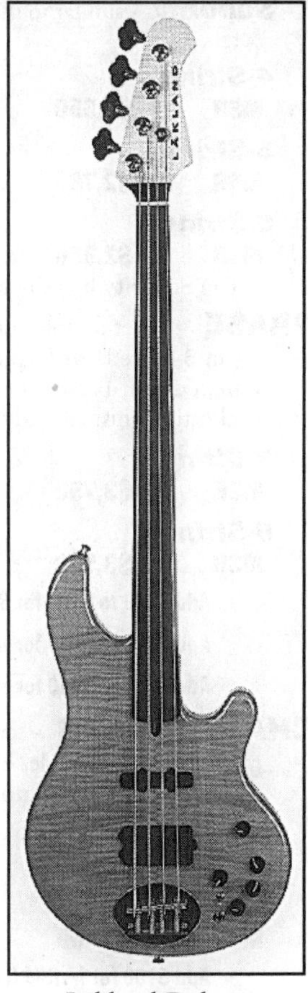

Lakland Deluxe
courtesy Dan Lakin

LAUNAY KING

Instruments previously built in England during the mid 1970s.

These high quality solid body guitars featured original design stylings and "ultra-comprehensive" active circuitry. The entire line consisted of two different series of guitars, the **Swayback** series and the **Prototype** series.

(Source: Tony Bacon and Paul Day, The Guru's Guitar Guide)

LAUNHARDT & KOBS

Instruments currently produced in Wetslar, Germany.

Launhardt & Kobs specialize in high quality acoustic guitar models. Their classical series feature models like the **Prelude, Sarabande, Bourree**, and **Romantika** with slotted headstocks and traditional Spanish-style bodies. The jumbo-style models include the 6-string **Jack D.** and the 12-string **William D.** guitars.

Launhardt & Kobs also produces five Jazz Guitar (archtop) models, all with a 650 mm scale and choice of Attila Zoller or EMG pickups. In addition to the archtop models, Launhardt & Kobs also offers a Strat-style solid body **Model 1** and Tele-ish **Model 2** models under the L U K trademark.

The **Averell D.** akustik (acoustic bass) model has a single rounded cutaway body, and a 865 mm scale length. Both the **Model 3** and **Model 4** solid body electric basses have Jazz bass-stylings.

LAWRENCE, KENNETH

Instruments currently built in Arcata, California since 1986.

Luthier Kenneth Lawrence had a six year background in European style furniture and cabinet building before he began working at Moonstone Guitars. Lawrence worked with owner/luthier Steve Helgeson for five years constructing guitars and basses at Moonstone before starting his own Lawerence Instruments in 1986. Lawerence also draws upon his twenty-eight year bass playing background in his designs. For additional information, contact luthier Kenneth Lawrence directly (see Trademark Index).

ELECTRIC BASS

Lawrence crafts high quality instruments from responsively harvested rainforest hardwoods from southern Mexico and Central America. This forestry project is monitored and endorsed by the Rainforest Alliance. The exotic woods featured in Lawrence's instruments like Grenadillo, Katalox, and Chechen share similar sonic characteristics to traditional hardwood choices. In the past two years, Lawrence increased the scale length on his 5- and 6-string basses to 35" for improving the articulation of the entire instrument (most notably the lower frequencies). Other custom options are available per model (call for pricing and availability).

ASSOCIATE - offset double cutaway 2-piece alder or ash body, bolt-on hard maple neck, 34" (35" on 5- and 6-string models) scale, 24-fret grenadillo or rosewood fingerboard, Gotoh tuners, Gotoh fixed bridge, black hardware, custom Basslines pickups, volume/tone controls, 2-band EQ active electronics. Available in an Oil finished neck/satin finished body. Current Mfg.

4-String

MSR $2,250

5-String

MSR $2,450

6-String

MSR $2,650

Add $35 for gold hardware.

Add $100 for fretless (lined or unlined) fingerboard.

Add $100 for hand rubbed Oil and Wax finish.

Add $180 to $240 for Clear or Transparent color high gloss polyester finish.

Add $200 to $300 for highly figured wood top.

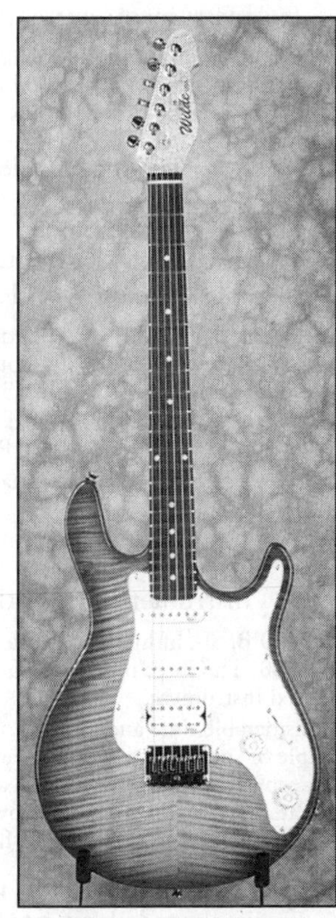

Lawrence Wilde Deluxe
courtesy Bill Lawrence
Guitar Company

L

Sonority - similar to the Associate, except features through-body neck construction. Available in an Oil finished neck/satin finished body. Current Mfg.

4-String
MSR $2,550

5-String
MSR $2,750

6-String
MSR $2,950

The Sonority has the same custom options as the Associate.

BRASE - offset double cutaway 2-piece alder or ash body with upper horn in contact with the neck between the 11th and 15th fret ("braced"), set-in 3-piece hard maple neck with graphite spars, 35" scale, 24-fret grenadillo fingerboard, Gotoh tuners, Gotoh fixed bridge, black hardware, custom Basslines or Lane Poor pickups, volume/tone controls, 3-band EQ active electronics with bypass. Available in an Oil finished neck/satin finished body. Current Mfg.

5-String
MSR $3,750

6-String
MSR $3,950

Add $160 to $200 for Blue, Red, Purple, and Tobacco Burst satin finish.

Add $220 to $260 for Transparent color high gloss polyester finish.

Add $250 to $350 for highly figured wood top.

CHAMBERBASS - sculpted, semi-acoustic offset double cutaway ash or mahogany body, spruce or redwood soundboard (top), set-in hard maple neck, 35" scale, black ebony or katalox fretless fingerboard, Gotoh tuners, Gotoh fixed bridge, black hardware, custom Basslines or Lane Poor pickups/piezo bridge pickup, volume/tone controls. Available in an Oil finished neck/satin finished body. Current Mfg.

5-String
MSR $4,900

6-String
MSR $5,100

Add $100 for fretted fingerboard.

Add $140 for Transparent color high gloss polyester finish.

LEA ELECTRIC GUITARS

Instruments currently built in East Islip, New York.

Solid body and semi-hollow construction guitars are custom made to order. Lea Guitars are hand crafted of exotic and colorful tone woods and feature "through-body" neck construction, bookmatched top, single or double cutaway body designs, choice of body and fingerboard woods, 22 or 24-fret fingerboard, hand rubbed laquer or oil finish, choice of hardware and pickup configurations. The "Century" model is a unique single cutaway design that blends beauty and function. The Century model now features a slightly larger body for improved tone and balance. Base price for the Century model is $1,795. Note: Base price includes a large selection of wood options.

LEDUC

Instruments currently built in France, and distributed by Leduc Instruments of Sun Valley, California. They are also available through World Arts of East Northport, New York.

Luthier/designer Christophe Leduc's high quality electric guitars and basses are built with distinctive tone woods and exacting hand crafting. Leduc's **U-Guitar** features a free-floating soundboard and semi-hollow construction, with pickups and hardware mounted through the soundboard to the body. The U models range in price from $3,295 to $4,195; the semi-acoustic **U (Utopia) Bass** models range in retail price from $2,995 to $3,895.

PAD series basses feature Padauk wood construction in the neck, fingerboard, body, and even the knobs for a unity of resonances. **PAD** basses are offered in 4-, 5-, or 6-string variations. Prices start at $2,150, and on up to $2,895.

Masterpiece models feature a maple and bubinga neck-through-body design. For further information, contact Leduc Instruments directly (see Trademark Index).

LEGEND CUSTOM GUITARS

Instruments currently built in Dartmouth (Nova Scotia), Canada.

Zane O'Brien, luthier and musician behind Legend guitars, has been doing fine woodworking since 1970 and converted over to building electric guitars in 1988. The three man shop turns out high quality electric guitars and basses for the discriminating musician who knows what they want in a finely crafted instrument.

Considerable time and effort is made in selecting only the best grades of woods for the bodies and necks. The book matched tops are ususally figured maple or some exotic wood. The rear mounted pickup design bodies (pickups are installed through the back cavity - a patent is pending) really does a lot to keep the weight down as well as enhances the overall look of the instrument because you only see the top of the pickup when looking at the front of the guitar. This look is similar to how a pickup would look in a pickguard - but without the pickguard. Legend guitar models range in price from $900 to $2,000 (Canadian dollars). For further information regarding pricing and model specifications, please contact Zane O'Brien at Legend Custom Guitars directly (see Trademark Index).

Earlier Legend guitars had Fender style headstocks, but this was changed in 1996. The current "sickle"-style headstock is more unique, simple, and pleasing to the eye.

Hardware and electronics vary depending on customer preferences, price, and availability. Other shape bodies are also available and custom designs are invited. All Legend guitars have a one year limited warranty on material and workmanship. Legend guitars are played and endorsed by such well known artists as George Hebert (Anne Murray Band) and Al McCumber (Lenny Gallant Band), to name a few.

(Company information courtesy Zane O'Brien)

Legend Custom Electric courtesy Legend Custom Guitars

ELECTRIC

The Legend necks are either 25 1/2" or 24 3/4" scale, have a standard 12" radius fingerboard, are either 21 or 22-frets, come with a bi-flex two way adjustable truss rod (no *skunk stripe* on back), six tuners in a line headstock design, and are available in natural maple finish or vintage amber. Necks are available in other exotic fingerboard woods besides rosewood, ebony, maple, etc.

All Legend guitars are produced in a variety of translucent finishes, solid color finishes, metallic finishes, and glitter finishes (all of which are clear coated with a high quality catalyzed urethane lacquer and polished to a glass like deep finish). Many of the guitars have headstocks finished to match the body.

Legend Carved Top Series

The Legend Carved Top/Arch-top is a double cutaway shape like a "strat", but narrower through the waist, has more pronounced horns, deeper, and more rounded. The rear body contour is also deeper and more rounded. The following are examples of current Legend Carved Top models:

The Legend **Purpleheart Carved Top** features a poplar body, purpleheart carved top, rear-routed control and pickup cavities, creme body binding, bolt-on tiger maple neck, 22-fret purpleheart fingerboard with pearl dot inlay, 6-on-a-side Schaller tuners, chrome hardware, strings-through the body fixed bridge, 2 single coil/humbucker pickups, volume/tone controls, 5-way selector switch. This model has a Cherry Burst polyester base/Polyurethane lacquer clear coat (topcoat). The current list price is $875 (Canadian).

The Legend **Bird's-eye Maple** model is similar to the Purpleheart, except features a book matched birds-eye maple top, mahogany body, ebony fingerboard, and 3 active SA EMG single coil pickups. This model has a similar Cherry Burst polyester base/Polyurethane lacquer clear coat (topcoat), and the current list price is $1,375 (Canadian).

The Legend **Tiger Maple** (flamed maple) model is similar to the Purpleheart, except features a book matched tiger maple top over the poplar body, ebony fingerboard, 2 single coil/*Jeff Beck* humbucker Seymour Duncan pickups, and mini-toggle (series/parallel/split humbucker) switch. This model has a Teal Green Burst polyester base/Polyurethan lacquer clear coat (topcoat), and the current list price is $1,375 (Canadian).

Legend "Tele" Series

The "Tele"-style Legend bodies are like the vintage *Fenders*, but with book matched tops, binding, and exotic woods. Here are current Legend "Tele" models for example purposes:

The Legend **Silver Sparkle** Tele features a poplar body, conventional pickup cavities, custom silver sparkle pickguard, black body binding, bolt-on maple neck, 22-fret bound bocote fingerboard with pearl dot inlay, 6-on-a-side Gotoh tuners, black hardware, strings-through the body fixed bridge, 2 single coil pickups, volume/tone controls, 5-way selector switch. This model has a Silver Sparkle polyester base/Polyurethane lacquer clear coat (topcoat). The current list price is $1,250 (Canadian). A similar model with a **Dusty Rose Sparkle/Silver Sparkle Back** finish and Bill Lawrence pickups lists at $1,375 (Canadian)

The Legend **Pau Amarello Tele** model is similar to the Silver Sparkle Tele, except features a book matched Pau Amarello top, white pickguard, white body binding, rosewood fingerboard with gold pearl dot inlay, and chrome hardware. This model has a Natural finish polyester base with an airbrushed brown edging/Polyurethane lacquer clearcoat (topcoat). The current list price is $950 (Canadian).

The Legend **Pearloid-Bound Tele** model is similar to the Silver Sparkle Tele, except features a rosewood fingerboard, pearloid body binding/pearloid pickguard, gold-plated hardware/neck pickup cover, and Schaller tuners. This model has a White polyester base/Polyurethane lacquer clearcoat (topcoat), and the current list price is $975 (Canadian).

LEW CHASE

Instruments previously built in Japan during the late 1970s.

Guitars for the Lew Chase trademark were built by Azumi prior to introduction of their own trademark in the early 1980s. Azumi instruments were generally medium quality solid bodies; expect the same of Lew Chase branded guitars.

(Source: Tony Bacon and Paul Day, The Guru's Guitar Guide)

LIBERTY, GENE

Instruments currently built in Sheridan, Illinois.

Gene Liberty, at the Ultimate Guitar Repair Shop, has been building high-end custom guitars and basses and doing major repair work full-time for over 25 years. Facilities include complete metal and wood-working shops, with custom-built computer controlled machinery for engineering and building prototypes and experimental designs. The shop also designs and builds tools, fixtures and machines specific to guitar construction and repair.

Liberty Archtop with pickups courtesy Gene Liberty

ELECTRIC

Guitars and basses made here are mainly exotic wood, neck-through-body construction, and the buyer can be the designer, with control of all parameters. Some special options can include through-body dovetail neck construction, interchangeable plug-in pickups, custom designed pearl and abalone shell, and gold or silver wire inlay and engraving, non-standard fingerboard radii and fret scale lengths and any type of special wiring. The shop also makes a limited number of acoustic and arch top jazz guitars to order.

The Solid body guitar and bass models have a retail price that starts at $1,800; the Acoustic guitar models start at $2,200; and the Arch top guitar models have a retail price that begins at $3,500.

GRADING	100% MINT	98% NEAR MINT	95% EXC+	90% EXC	80% VG+	70% VG	60% G

LIGHTWAVE SYSTEMS

Formerly AUDIO OPTICS.

Instruments currently manufactured in Japan by Tune Guitar Technology Co., Ltd. The Lightwave pickups (based on optical technology) are built in Santa Barbara, California. Distributed by Lightwave Systems, Inc. of Santa Barbara, California.

The Lightwave pickup system uses a patented new technology of optical scanning in their innovative pickup designs in place of the older magnetic field system. The design team at Lightwave Systems spent ten years creating and perfecting the system, which is composed of optical/piezo sensing elements for each string. The company plans to release their own bass, electroacoustic and electric guitar models, retrofit kits for popular instruments, or as an OEM system for bass and guitar.

According to the company, here's how it works: a string of any composition is illuminated by an infrared light source, so that the string casts a shadow on a pair of high speed photo detectors. When the string is vibrated, the size and shape of the shadow changes in direct proportion to the frequency. This modulates a current passing through the photo sensors - and the current is then amplified. The Lightwave pickup works with any string composition, is totally immune to hum and buzz, and has no self-dampening of string sustains.

ELECTRIC BASS

LIGHTWAVE CUSTOM MANIAC - Exotic hardwood body, 25 fret rosewood fingerboard, bolt-on neck. Pickup system utilizes Lightwave infrared pickups, with piezo sensors; cable and power supply included. Controls include *Ice Tone* (for glassy brilliant highs).

MSR $1,999

Add $1,000 for 5-string configuration.

LINCOLN

Instruments previously produced in Japan between the late 1970s and the early 1980s.

Lincoln instruments featured both original designs and designs based on classic American favorites; most guitars considered good quality.

(Source: Tony Bacon and Paul Day, The Guru's Guitar Guide)

LINDELL

Instruments previously produced in Japan during the mid 1960s.

Research continues into the Lindell trademark, as the producing company in Japan and the American distributor have yet to be identified. Further information will be reported in future editions of the *Blue Book of Electric Guitars*.

LINDERT

Instruments currently built in Chelan, Washington since 1986.

Charles Lindert has been building guitars for the past 15 years in Washington State. The current Loco-Motive Series gets its name in part from the old railway stop near the Chelan Falls facility, near Lake Chelan and the Columbia River.

Now president of his own company, Lindert is ably assisted by Larry Krupla (Production Manager) and Jennifer Sheda (Public Relations). All Lindert instruments are easily recognizable by Lindert's eye-catching *Thumbs Up* patented headstock.

ELECTRIC

Lindert has produced a range of guitar models that run from vintage inspired to advanced, forward-thinking styles. Several of Lindert's models feature the *Missing Link* switch, which allows pickup combinations of neck/bridge, or all three single coils on together (combinations that are not available on traditional 3 single coil pickup systems).

BEACHMASTER - offset double cutaway/offset waist alder body, bolt-on maple neck, 22-fret rosewood fingerboard, 6-on-a-side tuners, fulcrum tremolo bridge, beveled top, chrome hardware, 3 single coil pickups, 1 volume/2 tone controls, 5-way selector/phase/*Missing Link* switch. Available in Black, Blue, Red, Sunburst, and White finishes. Disc. 1995.

$700 $650 $595 $525 $475 $350 $275

Last MSR was $1,099.

Beachmaster II - similar to the Beachmaster, except no phase/*Missing Link* switches. Disc. 1996.

$525 $450 $395 $350 $275 $250 $175

Last MSR was $649.

Levitator Series

The Levitator series offset double cutaway body shape featured louvered soundholes and an integral hand grip on the upper bout. Levitators were optional with a 24-fret fingerboard, a Floyd Rose style tremolo, and Starr pickup selector switches.

LEVITATOR ESCAPE ARTIST - semi hollow offset double cutaway body, bolt-on maple neck, 22-fret rosewood fingerboard, 6-on-a-side tuners, fixed bridge, louvered soundholes and built-in hand grip on the upper bout, chrome hardware, 2 single coil pickups, volume/tone controls, 3-way selector/phase switches. Available in Black, Blue, Red, Sunburst, and White finishes. Disc. 1995.

$700 $650 $575 $525 $475 $350 $275

Last MSR was $1,099.

GRADING	100% MINT	98% NEAR MINT	95% EXC+	90% EXC	80% VG+	70% VG	60% G

Levitator Illusionist - similar to the Levitator Escape Artist, except has 3 single coil pickups, 5-way selector/phase/single-dual switches. Disc. 1995.

$725	$675	$600	$550	$495	$350	$275

Last MSR was $1,099.

Levitator Merlin - similar to the Levitator Escape Artist, except has 2 humbucking pickups, 2 volume/2 tone knobs, 3-way selector/phase/single-dual switches. Disc. 1995.

$725	$675	$600	$550	$495	$350	$275

Last MSR was $1,199.

Levitator Pro-Magician - similar to the Levitator Escape Artist, except has 2 single coil/humbucking pickups, 5-way selector/phase/single-dual switches. Disc. 1995.

$725	$675	$600	$550	$495	$350	$275

Last MSR was $1,299.

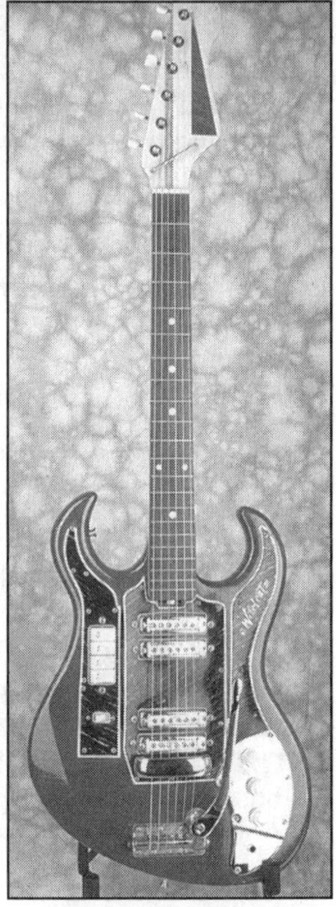

Lindell Wildcat IV
courtesy John Beeson

Locomotive Series

The Locomotive series was originally produced as the Victor series. The series/models were introduced in late 1995, and renamed in 1996. Locomotive models feature a three-piece body construction design similar to '50s Danelectro guitars, and have a 25 1/2" scale.

The Baritone-style **Bass VI** configurations have a 30" scale length, and a 24-fret fingerboard.

LOCOMOTIVE S - offset double cutaway body, bolt-on maple neck, 22-fret rosewood fingerboard, six on one side tuners, chrome hardware, cream colored pickguard, 9 fabric "grille" inserts on top (behind bridge), fixed bridge, 3 single coil pickups, volume/tone controls with chickenhead knobs, 5-way selector switch. Available in textured Beechwood brown finish. Mfg. 1995 to date.

MSR							
$798	$600	$525	$475	$395	$325	$275	$200

Add $184 for extended 30" scale and 24-fret fingerboard (Model LocoMotive S Bass VI).

LocoMotive T - similar to the Locomotive S, except has a single cutaway body, 2 single coil pickups, and 3-way selector. Mfg. 1995 to date.

MSR							
$738	$550	$475	$425	$375	$295	$250	$195

Add $200 for extended 30" scale and 24-fret fingerboard (Model LocoMotive T Bass VI).

Franklin - similar to the Locomotive T, except treble horn has more pronounced point, 2 humbucker pickups, 2 fabric "grille" inserts behind bridge. Mfg. 1996 to date.

MSR							
$858	$650	$550	$495	$425	$350	$295	$225

Add $140 for extended 30" scale and 24-fret fingerboard (Model Franklin Bass VI).

2 Thumbs Up Doubleneck - similar to the Locomotive S, except has double neck configuration, 30" scale upper bass neck/25.5" scale lower guitar neck, 3 single coil pickups (per neck), neck electronics selector, tortoise shell pickguard. Mfg. 1997 to date.

MSR $1,998

CONDUCTOR - similar to the Locomotive T, except treble horn has more pronounced point, 2 humbucker pickups, 'spiderweb'-style 5 large/5 small fabric "grille" inserts behind bridge. Mfg. 1998 to date.

MSR $858

Add $140 for extended 30" scale and 24-fret fingerboard (Model Conductor Bass VI).

DIESEL S - offset double cutaway body, bolt-on maple neck, 22-fret rosewood fingerboard, six on one side tuners, chrome hardware, cream colored pickguard, 6 fabric "grille" inserts on top (behind bridge), fixed bridge, 3 single coil pickups, volume/tone controls with *chickenhead* knobs, 5-way selector switch. Available in textured Beechwood brown finish. Mfg. 1998 to date.

MSR $798

Add $134 for extended 30" scale and 24-fret fingerboard (Model Diesel S Bass VI).

Diesel T - similar to the Diesel S, except has a single cutaway body, 2 single coil pickups, and 3-way selector. Mfg. 1998 to date.

MSR $738

Add $194 for extended 30" scale and 24-fret fingerboard (Model Diesel T Bass VI).

GREENBACK T similar to the Locomotive T, except treble horn has more pronounced point, tonyte dollar green semi-hollowbody model, 3 single coil pickups, 'halfmoon' fabric "grille" inserts behind bridge. Available in Greenback Green/Cream finish. Mfg. 1997 to date.

MSR $990

This model is inspired by the modern art of Diego Rivera.

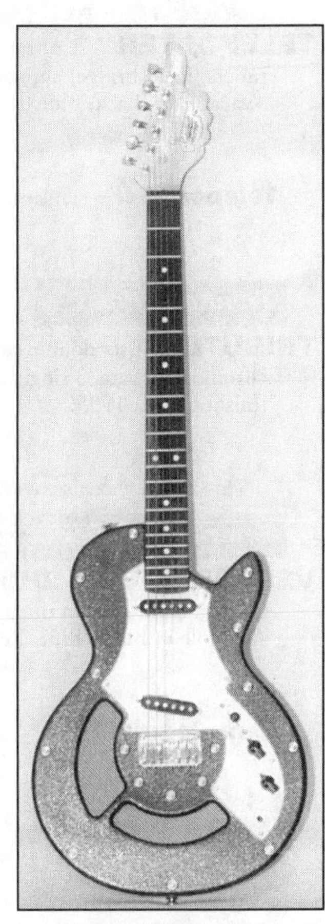

Lindert Victor Model
courtesy Lindert Guitars

L

GRADING	100% MINT	98% NEAR MINT	95% EXC+	90% EXC	80% VG+	70% VG	60% G

SKYLINER - offset double cutaway body, bolt-on maple neck, 25 1/2" scale, 22-fret rosewood fingerboard, six per side tuners, chrome hardware, rocket ship pickguard/*grille* panel, fixed bridge, 2 single coil/humbucker pickups, volume/tone controls with *chickenhead* knobs, 5-way selector switch. Available in textured Beechwood Brown finish. Mfg. 1997 to date.

MSR	$858	$650	$550	$495	$425	$350	$295	$225

Add $140 for extended 30" scale and 24-fret fingerboard (Model Skyliner Bass VI).

Americana Skyliner - similar to Skyliner, except features Red body finish, blue fabric panel inserts, and white pickguard. Mfg. 1997 to 1998.

$600	$525	$475	$400	$325	$275	$225

Last MSR was $859.

TWISTER S - offset double cutaway body, bolt-on maple neck, 22-fret rosewood fingerboard, six on one side tuners, chrome hardware, cream colored pickguard, 6 fabric "grille" inserts on top (behind bridge) in a fan-shaped pattern, fixed bridge, 3 single coil pickups, volume/tone controls with *chickenhead* knobs, 5-way selector switch. Available in textured Beechwood Brown finish. Mfg. 1998 to date.

MSR $798

Add $184 for extended 30" scale and 24-fret fingerboard (Model Twister S Bass VI).

Twister T - similar to the Twister S, except has a single cutaway body, 2 single coil pickups, and 3-way selector. Mfg. 1998 to date.

MSR $738

Add $194 for extended 30" scale and 24-fret fingerboard (Model Twister T Bass VI).

Shooting Star Series

SHOOTING STAR 2HB - assault rifle-style alder body, bolt-on maple neck, 22-fret rosewood fingerboard, 6-on-a-side tuners, fixed bridge, built-in hand grip on the upper bout, chrome hardware, 2 humbucking pickups, 1 volume/2 tone controls, 3-way selector/coil tap switches. Available in Black, Blue, Red, Sunburst, and White finishes. Disc. 1995.

$650	$600	$575	$525	$475	$350	$275

Last MSR was $849.

Shooting Star HSS - similar to the Shooting Star 2HB, except has 2 single coil/humbucking pickups. Disc. 1995.

$675	$625	$595	$550	$495	$350	$275

Last MSR was $899.

Teleporter Series

TELEPORTER - semi-hollow single cutaway body, bolt-on maple neck, 22-fret rosewood fingerboard, 2 f-holes, beveled edges, 6-on-a-side tuners, fixed bridge, chrome hardware, 2 humbucking pickups, 2 volume/2 tone controls, 3-way selector toggle, 2 coil tap mini switches. Available in Black, Blue, Red, Sunburst, and White finishes. Disc. 1995.

$650	$600	$575	$525	$475	$350	$275

Last MSR was $1,099.

Teleporter II - similar to the Teleporter, except has fulcrum tremolo, and no coil tap switches. Disc. 1995.

$525	$450	$395	$350	$275	$250	$175

Last MSR was $599.

Tribute Series

TRIBUTE - offset double cutaway alder body, bolt-on maple neck, 22-fret rosewood fingerboard, 6-on-a-side tuners, fulcrum tremolo bridge, chrome hardware, 3 single coil pickups, 1 volume/2 tone controls, 5-way selector switch. Available in Black, Blue, Red, Sunburst, and White finishes. Disc. 1995.

$650	$600	$550	$475	$395	$350	$275

Last MSR was $949.

This model was also available with a pearloid pickguard as the Tribute Ultra II (retail list was $649).

Ventriloquist Series

VENTRILOQUIST 2HB - flying V-style alder body, bolt-on maple neck, 22-fret rosewood fingerboard, 6-on-a-side tuners, fixed bridge, built-in hand grip on the upper bout, chrome hardware, 2 humbucking pickups, 1 volume/2 tone controls, 3-way selector/coil tap switches. Available in Black, Blue, Red, Sunburst, and White finishes. Disc. 1995.

$650	$600	$575	$525	$475	$350	$275

Last MSR was $1,099.

Ventriloquist HSS - similar to the Ventriloquist 2HB, except has 2 single coil/humbucking pickups. Disc. 1995.

$650	$600	$575	$525	$495	$375	$295

Last MSR was $1,149.

L

BASS

LEVITATOR WAND - semi hollow offset double cutaway body, bolt-on maple neck, 30" scale, 24-fret rosewood fingerboard, 4-on-a-side tuners, fixed bridge, louvered soundholes and built-in hand grip on the upper bout, chrome hardware, 3 single coil pickups, volume/tone controls, 5-way selector/phase/Missing Link switches. Available in Black, Blue, Red, Sunburst, and White finishes. Disc. 1995.

$650 $600 $550 $500 $475 $350 $275

Last MSR was $1,399.

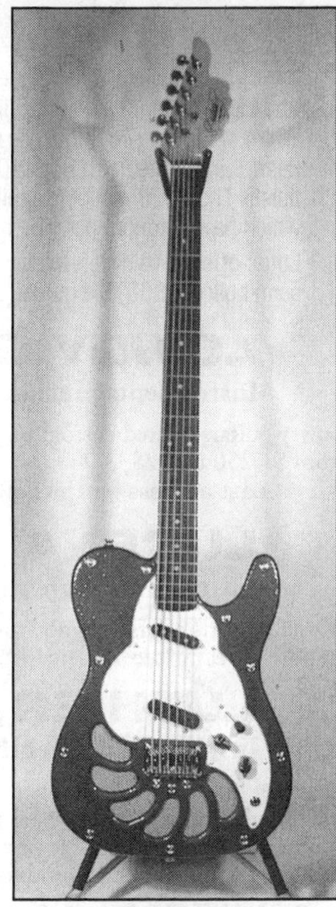

TTTB 6 Bass
(2 0f 2 Made)
courtesy Rick Meyers

LocoMotive Series

LOCOMOTIVE P BASS - offset double cutaway body, bolt-on maple neck, 34" scale, 22-fret rosewood fingerboard, four on one side tuners, chrome hardware, cream colored pickguard, 9 fabric-type grille inserts on top (reversed/before bridge), fixed bridge, split-coil pickup, volume/tone controls with chickenhead knobs. Available in textured Beechwood Brown finish. Current Mfg.

MSR $729 $525 $450 $395 $350 $275 $225 $175

LINN SAHLI

Instruments currently built in Palm Desert, California.

Linn Sahli guitars feature 2 dual coil humbuckers that electronically recreate 14 sound configurations by connecting the individual coils of the pickups in either series or parallel. Thus, the guitar can move from the sound of a 'Strat' to a 'Les Paul' with the change of a pickup selector. Any of these fourteen configurations can be programmed into the six pickup selectors, and an on-board voice will indicate which pickup selection has been chosen during the programming stage.

Linn Sahli guitars also feature 6 individual bridge pieces/string retaining tailpieces, which separate the string "crosstalk" found in one piece bridges.

Current models include the double cutaway Model A (list $3,099) and single cutaway Model T (list $3,099). Both models feature AAA grade flamed maple tops, mahogany bodies, one-piece mahogany necks, and Translucent or Solid Color finishes. Linn Sahli basses are offered in 4- and 5-string configurations. The LSJ model (list $1,999) has a swamp ash or curly maple body, rock maple neck with rosewood fingerboard, and is finished in Translucent colors. The 5-string LSJ-5 Artist (list $2,499) features a through-body neck construction.

LION

See EGMOND.

Instruments previously built in Holland during the late 1960s.

Guitars carrying the Lion trademark were built by the Egmond guitar company during the late 1960s. These low quality to entry level instruments featured both original and designs based on classic American favorites in both solid and semi-hollowbody configurations.

(Source: Tony Bacon and Paul Day, The Guru's Guitar Guide)

LOGABASS

Instruments currently built in Japan, and distributed by Leduc Instruments of Sun Valley, California. Instruments are also available through World Arts of East Northport, New York.

Logabass instruments are high quality basses that feature a 'headless' design and patented bridge/tuning gear. All models have Bartolini electronics, and are available in 4-, 5-, and 6-string configurations (and with fretted or fretless fingerboards. For further information contact Leduc Instruments or World Arts directly (see Trademark Index).

LOPER

Instruments previously built in Hawthorne, Florida 1995-2000. Distributed by Guitar Works of Hawthorne, Florida.

Luthier Joe Loper built high quality custom bass guitars that feature a neck-through design. His original designs contained a number of stylish innovations that indicate fine attention to detail.

LORD

Instruments previously built in Japan.

Guitars with the Lord trademark originated in Japan, and were distributed in the U.S. by the Halifax company.

(Source: Michael Wright, Guitar Stories Volume One)

LOTUS

Instruments currently produced in Korea, China, and India. Distributed by Midco International of Effingham, Illinois.

Lotus guitars are designed for the student or entry level guitarist. Lotus offers a wide range of acoustic and electric guitar models (a little something for everyone!).

In addition to the Electric guitar models, Lotus also offers 4 dreadnought acoustics, 2 banjo models, and 4 mandolins. Lotus Electric Basses are offered in a Precision-style L760, as well as a Jazz-style model L750JSB and two modern design basses (L770 4-string and L780 5-string).

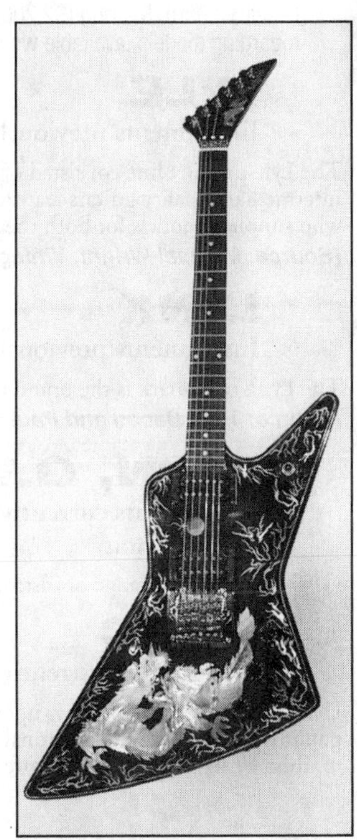

Lotus
courtesy Guitar Recue Society
NAMM 1985 Display Guitar

ELECTRIC

The **L660** Strat-styled guitar (list $235) features a solid ash body, rosewood fingerboard, 3 single coils, and a standard tremolo bridge (available in Black, Red, White, and Tobacco Burst), as well as a left-handed configuration. The upscale **L680** model (list $269) features a pearloid pickguard, and is available in Black Pearl Burst, Blue Pearl Burst, Crimson Burst, Metallic Green, and Silver Red Burst; the **L685** (list $289) has gold hardware and a Transparent Teak woodgrain finish. The **L690** model is similar to the L660, except features 2 single coil and one humbucker pickups. 'SuperStrat' models include the **L1110** and **L1190**, which have 3 tuners per side headstocks, black pickguards, and different pickup configurations.

Lotus offers two different single cutaway body models: the Tele-ish **L590** and the LP-style **L520** models. Lotus also offers a dual cutaway laminated wood semi-hollow **L800TBU** model, as well as 4 "mini" downsized models (list $259 to $289).

LOWRY GUITARS

Instruments previously built in Concord, California from 1975 to early 1990s.

Lowry guitars offered custom built, reverse stringing, *headless* guitar models. The **Modaire** model was offered in several design variations and was priced from $1,250 up to $3,000.

Last address for the Lowry company was given as 2565 Cloverdale Avenue, Unit J, Concord, California 94518 (510.827.4803).

LUCENA

Instruments currently distributed by Music Imports of San Diego, California.

Music Imports offers a number of quality Lucena guitar models. For further information regarding model specifications and pricing, please contact Music Imports directly (see Trademark Index).

LUTHIER, LINC

Instruments currently built in Upland, California since 1991.

Designer Linc Luthier offers handcrafted instruments that feature exotic hardwoods. All bodies are semi-acoustic, and are designed to create an instrument that is lighter in weight as well as possessing greater audio character. Linc also eliminates any plastic, paint, or screws in their quest for functional simplicity - thus, all pickup systems are passive, not active (which requires a battery). Tone is a combination of the overall design coupled with the wood combinations required to produce a certain sound (bright, dark, 'woody', heavy on the mid-range, etc.).

ELECTRIC

Guitar models generally feature a stacked humbucker/dual coil humbucker combination (other custom variations available), with volume and pan controls. Linc features a 24-fret fingerboard, Kahler tremolo or Schaller stop tailpiece, gold hardware, and a clear hand rubbed finish. Retail list prices start at $2,100 for the **Guitar** model, and $2,500 for a **Baritone** configuration.

ELECTRIC BASS

Electric Basses are crafted the same way as the Guitar models, and feature Bartolini pickups and volume/pan controls. **Bass** models are available in 4-string (retail $2,000), 5-string ($2,700), 6-string ($3,100), and 8-string configurations ($3,200); **Double Neck** instruments start at $5,800. For further information regarding models, available woods, and specifications, please contact Linc Luthier directly (see Trademark Index).

LYLE

Instruments previously built in Japan from 1969 to 1980. Distributed by the L.D. Heater company of Portland, Oregon.

The Lyle product line consisted of acoustic and acoustic/electric archtop guitars, as well as solid body electric guitars and basses. These entry level to intermediate quality guitars featured designs based on popular American models. These instruments were manufactured by the Matsumoku company, who supplied models for both the Arai (Aria, Aria Pro II) company and the early 1970s Epiphone models.

(Source: Michael Wright, Vintage Guitar Magazine)

LYNX

Instruments previously produced in Japan during the mid 1970s.

The Lynx trademark is the brand name used by a UK importer, and can be found on very low budget/low quality solid body guitars.

(Source: Tony Bacon and Paul Day, The Guru's Guitar Guide)

LYON, G.W.

Instruments currently built in Korea since the early 1990s. Distributed in the U.S. by Washburn International of Vernon Hills, Illinois.

G.W. Lyon offers a range of instruments designed for the student or beginner guitarist at affordable prices and decent entry level quality.

LYRIC

Instruments currently built in Tulsa, Oklahoma.

Designer John Southern drew upon his personal playing experience in designing the Lyric custom guitar. The primary interest was versatility, so that the guitar would have numerous tonal options available through the pickups and switching system. Southern spent two years developing the prototypes (built in Tulsa by hand), and is now offering six different guitars and one bass model. All guitars come with custom-made hardshell cases.

ELECTRIC

The following listed prices may vary depending on options (call for price quote). Prices include a hardshell tweed case.

The **Jupiter** model (retail list $8,651.10) is the design that Southern started with. The three inch deep AAA-grade Curly maple body is 13" wide across the lower bout, and features a 4/2 (per side tuners) headstock design, 20-fret ebony fingerboard with special *Quasar* position marker inlay, 3 coil-tapped Seymour

Duncan humbuckers, and a bridge mounted piezo pickup. The center humbucker is a custom converted *Woody* acoustic guitar pickup. Controls include two 3-way toggles, two push/pull knobs, and a *Pinky-Knob* master volume control. This ingenious design is complemented by a gold plated Lyric tailpiece and banjo-style custom tuning pegs with abalone buttons.

The **Mars** model is similar in construction, except features a Barcus Berry bridge transducer and a single coil-tapped mini-humbucker. Controls include a blend, push/pull tone, and *Pinky Swell* knobs. The Curly maple body is 1 3/4" deep, and the ebony fingerboard has the Mars Dot inlay pattern. Current list price is $3,221.22.

The **Venus** model (retail list $5,868.16) is an acoustic/electric version of the Jupiter that features a split coil Johnny Smith pickup and an L.R. Baggs bridge transducer and preamp, and a 1 11/16" deep body. It is available in a 3" depth to accommodate an additional graphic EQ, or with an extra magnetic pickup and blend controls.

The Lyric **Lady** (retail list $4,500) is a thicker body version made from hard maple, with a hollower construction and exquisite female figure pearl position markers on ebony. Humbucker pickup placement is conventional neck and bridge, with two coil top option and a blend with a Barcus Berry under saddle thin line pickup. It has no pinky knob and features chrome hardware and Steinberger tuners.

The **Saturn** is a thin 1 3/4" Honduras mahogany body with multiple spiderweb shaped chambers, under an exquisite book matched curly maple cap. The Saturn has a one piece mahogany neck and Quazar fingerboard inlay on finest ebony. The double Johnny Smith custom "Duncan" pickups are coil tapped and floating. The Saturn is priced retail at $2,895. For a moderately priced custom guitar, the Saturn will play rings around its competitors.

The Lyric **Mercury** solid body is offered in a swamp ash, poplar, alder, walnut, or cherry, with a maple or mahogany neck. The pickups are 6 pole piece coil-tapped humbuckers and a stop tail piece. The tuners are conventional Gotoh's, and the specialty colors of clear or copper tone sparkle are offered ($1,795 retail price).

ELECTRIC BASS

The **Zeus** Bass (retail list $3,078.56) features a laminated walnut and maple neck-through design, hollowed curly maple body, 22-fret ebony fingerboard, burled walnut veneer on headstock/rear access panel, EMG active pickups, and an 18 volt on-board preamp.

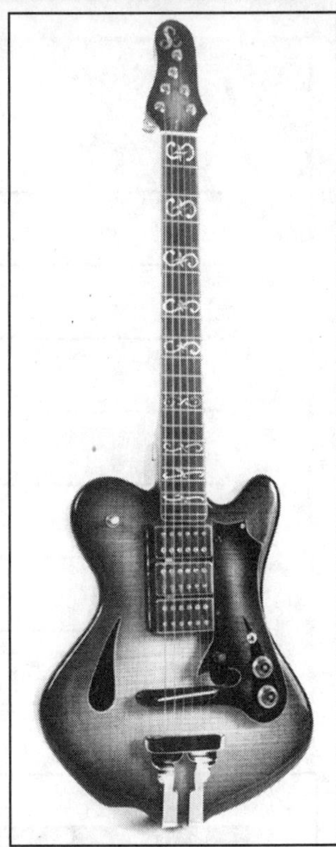

Lyric Guitar
courtesy John Southern

L

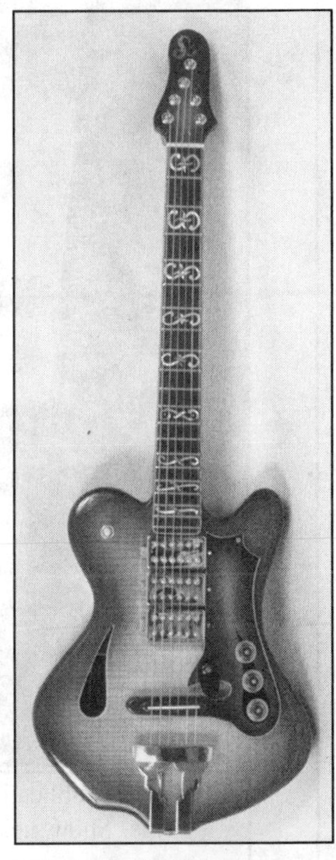

Lyric Guitar
courtesy John Southern

NOTES

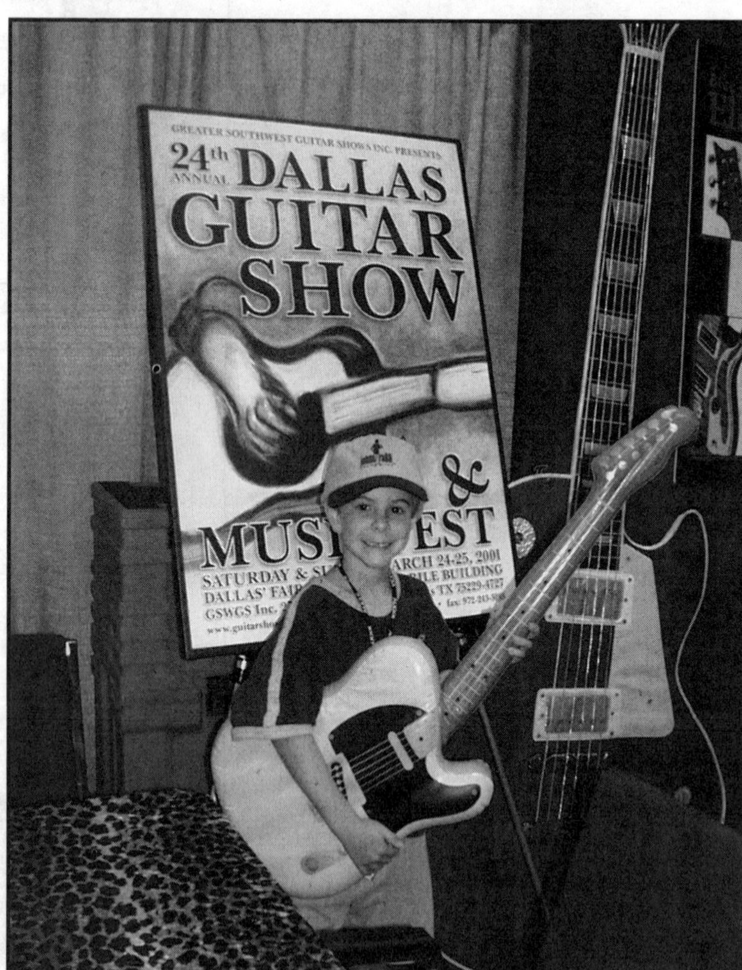

Blue Book Publications, Inc. is a proud sponsor of the Dallas Guitar Show, held each March (www.guitarshow.com)

L

Section M

MD

See METAL DRIVER (Sumer Musical Instruments, Co. Ltd.) & MUSIC DRIVE (Sumer Musical Instruments, Co. Ltd.).

MDX

Instruments currently built in West Point, Massachusetts. Distributed by MDX Sound Lab of West Point, Massachusetts.

Dann Maddox and partners have combined custom guitar and bass building and a computer website to introduce the concept of a "virtual custom shop". After nine years of custom building instruments at the regional level, MDX chose to use the Internet to go international with their handcrafted guitars.

Orders can be received at their address (http://www.mdxguitars.com), and guitars can be designed wholly through the Internet. This allows the customer to interactively design the guitar, and MDX the capabilities to construct it. Maddox can be reached at his E-mail site (dann@mdxguitars.com).

MJ GUITAR ENGINEERING

Instruments currently built in Rohnert Park, California.

MJ Guitars is a small family owned and operated manufacturing company and have been in business for more than 25 years. They specialize in high quality handmade production guitars. For more information, refer to the Trademark Index.

ELECTRIC

Mirage guitars feature a graphite-reinforced *U* shaped open headstock with a logo that reads **M J MIRAGE**, a semi-hollow body, and sleek double cutaway profile. In addition to the listed finishes, Mirage offers Custom Color finishes as well.

MIRAGE STANDARD - sleek offset double cutaway poplar body, carved maple top, set-in maple neck, 24 5/8" scale, 22-fret rosewood fingerboard with cream bar position markers, 3-per-side *open* headstock, Gotoh tuners, chrome hardware, tune-o-matic bridge/stop tailpiece, 2 Seymour Duncan humbuckers, 2 volume/1 tone controls, 3-way selector switch. Current Mfg.

MSR $2,695

Mirage Classic - similar to the Mirage Standard, except features mahogany body, carved maple or mahogany top, maple or mahogany set-in neck, nickel hardware, 2 Seymour Duncan P-90 pickups. Current Mfg.

MSR $2,695

Mirage Custom - similar to the Mirage Standard, except has mahogany body, carved exotic wood top, flame or bird's-eye maple neck, ebony fingerboard, gold hardware. Current Mfg.

MSR $3,695

MIRAGE GT - similar to the Mirage Standard, except features a 25 1/2" scale, internal tone chambers, tele-style bridge, 2 Seymour Duncan Alnico Pro II single coil pickups. Available in Cream, Lake Placid Blue, and Sea Foam Green finishes. Current Mfg.

MSR $2,695

Mirage Rally - similar to the Mirage GT, except has Wilkinson VS100 tremolo, 3 Seymour Duncan single coil pickups, 5-way selector switch. Available in Black, Red, and Silver finishes. Current Mfg.

MSR $2,895

ROADSTER - poplar body, bolt-on maple neck, 25 ½" scale, 2 Seymour Duncan Alnico II Pro pickups, VS100 Tremelo or fixed bridge. Hand made in the U.S.A. Current Mfg.

MSR $1,595

MTD

Instruments currently built in Kingston, New York since 1994.

Luthier Michael Tobias has been handcrafting guitars and basses since 1977. The forerunner of MTD, Tobias Guitars was started in Orlando, Florida in April 1977. Tobias' first shop name was the Guitar Shop, and he sold that business in 1980 and moved to San Francisco to be partners in a short lived manufacturing business called Sierra Guitars. The business made about 50 instruments and then Tobias left San Francisco in May of 1981 to start a repair shop in Costa Mesa, California.

Several months later, Tobias left Costa Mesa and moved to Hollywood. Tobias Guitars continued to repair instruments and build custom basses for the next several years with the help of Bob Lee, and Kevin Almieda (Kevin went on to work for Music Man). The company moved into 1623 Cahuenga Boulevard in Hollywood and after a year quit the repair business. Tobias Guitars added Bob McDonald, lost Kevin to Music Man, and then got Makoto Onishi. The business grew in leaps and bounds. In June of 1988 the company had so many back orders, it did not accept any new orders until the January NAMM show in 1990.

MTD 535 courtesy Michael Tobias Design

After several attempts to move the business to larger, better equipped facilities, Michael Tobias sold Tobias Guitars to Gibson on 1/1/90. Late in 1992, it was decided that in the best corporate interests, Tobias Guitars would move to Nashville. Michael Tobias left the company in December 1992, and was a consultant for Gibson as they set up operations in Nashville.

By contractual agreement, after Tobias' consulting agreement with Gibson was up, he had a 1 year non-competition term. That ended in December 1993. During that time, Tobias moved to The Catskills in upstate New York and set up a small custom shop. Tobias started designing new instruments and building prototypes in preparation for his new venture. The first instruments were named Eclipse. There are 50 of them and most all of them are 35" bolt-ons. There are three neck-throughs. Tobias finally settled on MTD as the company name and trademark. As of this writing (10/1/97) he has delivered 250 MTD instruments delivered, including bolt-on basses, guitars, neck-through basses, and acoustic bass guitars.

Michael Tobias is currently building nearly 100 instruments per year, with the help of Chris Hofschneider (who works two days per week). Chris has at least 15 years experience, having worked for Sam Koontz, Spector Guitars, Kramer, and being on the road with bands like Bon Jovi and other New Jersey-based bands. Michael Tobias is also doing design and development work for other companies, such as Alvarez, Brian Moore Guitars, Modulus Guitars, Lakeland, American Showster (with Chris Hofschneider) and the new Czech-built Grendel basses.

(Source: Michael Tobias, MTD fine hand made guitars and basses)

MTD Bass Specifications

All MTD instruments are delivered with a wenge neck/wenge fingerboard, or maple neck/wenge fingerboard; 21-frets plus a "Zero" fret, 35" scale length. Prices include plush hard shell cases.

The standard finish for body and neck is a tung oil base with a urethane top coat. Wood choices for bodies: swamp ash, poplar, and alder. Other woods, upon request, may require up charges. Exotic tops are subject to availability.

Beginning 2000, all MTD Basses come equipped with the Buzz Feiten Tuning System.

Add $100 for a lined fretless neck.

Add $150 for a hand rubbed oil stain.

Add $200 for satin epoxy coating on lined or unlined fretless fingerboard.

Add $200 for epoxy/oil urethane finished maple fingerboard.

Add $200 for a 24-fret fingerboard.

Add $350 for lacquer finish: sunburst (amber or brown), See-Throughs (transparency) of red, coral blue, or honey gold.

Add $300 for a korina, African satinwood (Avadore), or lacewood body.

Add $350 for a left handed model.

Add $500 for a *10 Top* of burl, flamed, or quilted maple, myrtle, or mahogany.

ELECTRIC BASS

MTD basses feature custom Bartolini active pickups and electronics, volume/pan/treble/mid/bass controls, and internal trim pot to adjust the gain.

435 - 4-string configuration, 2-per-side headstock. Mfg. 1994 to date.

MSR $3,300

535 - 5-string configuration, 2/3-per-side headstock. Mfg. 1994 to date.

MSR $3,500

635 - 6-string configuration, 3-per-side headstock. Mfg. 1994 to date.

MSR $3,700

MTD 735-24

MSR $4,500

KINGSTON - 4- or 5-string Acoustic bass, 24-fret, basswood body, maple necks, rosewood fingerboard, and passive MM style humbucking pickup. New 2001.

MSR $549

Add $50 for 5-string variation.

This model is available through Matthews & Ryan of Brooklyn, NY (716.832.6333).

McCURDY, RIC

Instruments currently built in New York City, New York.

Luthier Ric McCurdy has been producing custom guitars since 1983. Originally based in Santa Barbara, California, he moved to New York City in 1991 where he studied archtop guitar building with Bob Benedetto. Since then, he has been concentrating on building archtops and one-off custom guitars.

Currently using McCurdy guitars are ECM recording artist John Abercrombie and studio ace Joe Beck. All archtops feature the Kent Armstrong adjustable pole piece pickup which can be used with steel or bronze strings.

ELECTRIC

McCurdy's **Perfecta** is a single cutaway model that is 16" across the lower bout, and has bound *Faux Holes*, a single humbucking pickup, maple top/back/sides and neck, 25.5" scale, graphite reinforced neck, ebony fingerboard, and a nitrocellulose lacquer finish (list price $3,000).

The **Monaco** features pickups mounted to the body for added versatility in live performances. The spruce top and flame maple back and sides are augmented by Kent Armstrong or Seymour Duncan humbucker pickups (list $5,000).

McINTURFF, TERRY C.

Instruments currently built in Holly Springs, North Carolina. Distributed by Terry C. McInturff Guitars, Inc. of Holly Springs, North Carolina.

McInturff has been building and servicing guitars since 1977. McInturff's varied luthiery and musical experiences have resulted in the rare opportunities to experiment with guitar designs and to test those designs on stage and in the studio.

McCurdy Perfecta Sunburst courtesy Ric McCurdy

ELECTRIC

All McInturff guitars are standard with full RF shielding and shock protection circuitry. List price includes a deluxe hardshell case. Some options available include upgrading maple tops, adding binding and purfling, optional pickup configurations, neck carves, custom electronics, solo switch and a rainbow of gorgeous nitrocellulose finishes.

TCM POLARIS - offset double cutaway slab Honduran Mahogany body, and Honduran Mahogany graphite reinforced neck, abalone dot inlay, chrome hardware, fixed bridge, TCM Zodiac humbuckers with 5-way switch. Available in 4 transparent colors. Current Mfg.

MSR $1,995

Polaris Pro - similar to the TCM Polaris, except features a ¼" 3A Grade maple top. Available in 22 finishes. Mfg. 1998 to date.

MSR $2,295

TCM MONARCH - offset double cutaway design, solid mahogany body with deep dish carve. Paua™ shell "rope" inlay, chrome hardware, fixed or vibrato bridge, six pickup configurations available at no extra cost. Available in 4 transparent finishes. Current Mfg.

MSR $2,395

TCM EMPRESS - offset double cutaway design with deep dish carved 3A Grade maple top, Paua shell "rope" inlay, chrome hardware, fixed or vibrato bridge, 2 TCM single coil pickups and 1 TCM Zodiac Humbucker in the bridge position. Available in 22 finishes with many options. Current Mfg.

MSR $2,495

TCM ROYAL - offset double cutaway design with deep dish carved mahogany top, features tuned chamber and acoustic port, paua shell "rope" inlay, chrome hardware, fixed bridge, TCM T90 soapbar pickups stock. Available in 4 transparent finishes.

MSR $2,595

TCM GLORY STANDARD - offset double cutaway design with deep dish carved 4A Grade maple top and matching headstock, features semi-hollow chamber, paua shell "slash" inlay, chrome hardware, fixed or vibrato bridge, 2 TCM Zodiac humbucker pickups. Available in 22 finishes with many options. Current Mfg.

MSR $2,995

TCM Glory Custom - offset double cutaway design with deep dish carved 5A Grade maple top and matching headstock, features semi-hollow chamber, Paua shell "slash" inlay, gold hardware, fixed or vibrato bridge, locking tuners, bound neck and headstock, any pickup configuration. Available in 22 finishes. Current Mfg.

MSR $4,200

TCM TAURUS STANDARD - single cutaway design with traditional carved 4A Grade maple top and matching headstock, features "fan-style" tone chambers, 17 degree headstock pitch, paua shell "crest" inlay, chrome hardware, fixed bridge, locking tuners, TCM Zodiac neck and bridge humbuckers, 2 vol/1 tone and blade switch. Available in 22 finishes. Current Mfg.

MSR $3,200

TCM Taurus Standard "T" - similar to Taurus Standard, except features a fully functional vibrato bridge that does not rob the tone, 9 degree pitch headstock, chrome hardware, locking tuners. Available in 22 finishes. Current Mfg.

MSR $3,400

TCM Taurus Custom - similar to Taurus Standard, except has Master Grade maple top and matching headstock, bound body, neck, and headstock, paua shell "slash" inlay, gold hardware. Available in any finish currently offered. Current Mfg.

MSR $6,000

TCM Taurus Tree of Life - similar to taurus Custom, except features reserve stock maple top and matching headstock, exquisite "Tree of Life" inlay features red and green abalone, mother-of-Pearl, and paua shell on an ebony fingerboard framed with paua shell purfling, extends to the peghead for a dramatic but tasteful touch. Current Mfg.

MSR $10,000

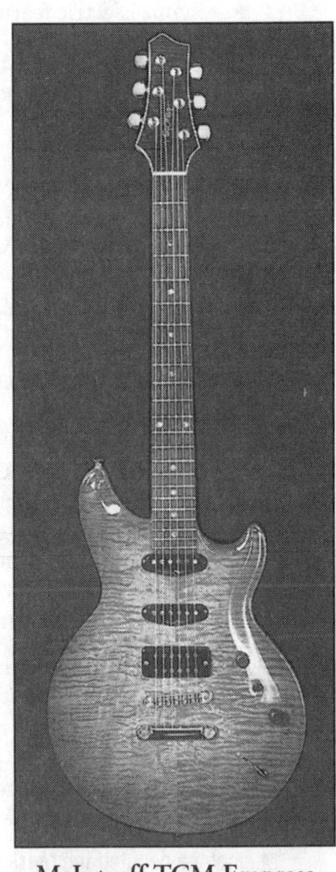

McInturff TCM Empress courtesy Terry McInturrff

M

TCM ZODIAC - body design and liberal design approach similar to the Glory Custom, features best materials and finest grades of woods, 100 piece paua shell, Mother-of-Pearl, and silver zodiac inlay depicts accurate constellations, mountains, planets, and 12th fret sun. Custom birthday inlay available to match the sky on the day you were born. Available in 22 finishes. Current Mfg.

MSR $5,200

TCM Zodiac Custom - same as the TCM Glory, except features solid African Limba wood neck and body. Discontinued.

Last MSR was $5,150.

McLAREN

Instruments currently built in San Diego, California.

Bruce McLaren worked many years as a design engineer in the defense industry and played bass guitar in several amateur bands. When the design of new defense products came to a halt, he started a company (McLaren Products) which manufactures electric bass guitars.

McLaren Products of San Diego, California produces distinctive, highly figured 4- and 5-string basses. Because of a tracer mill type cutting tool developed by Bruce McLaren, a fully carved and beveled body (both front and back) can be produced economically. The body has a unique outline sometimes described as a cross between "an SG and a Strat", and features strips of solid figured hardwoods rather than figured veneer glued on to a lightweight body core (which is done on most figured wood basses being offered today). Due to the extensive carving, the basses weigh in at a light 8 1/2 pounds.

ELECTRIC BASS

The necks are made of hard maple with a carefully designed truss rod arrangement which pulls the fingerboard to the optimum curvature for a very low action. The truss rod is also positioned in the neck so that it will offset the tendency that all basses have for the tuner head to twist (this tendency is caused by the fact that the tension in D strings is about 15 pounds greater than that for E strings). Pickups used are active EMG in a P/J arrangement which makes it possible to individually adjust the volume of each string and gives a wide range of tones. The pickups are fully shielded and produce no hum or buzz either with the hands on or off the strings.

Three body styles are produced, and each are offered with 4- or 5-string configurations - fretted or fretless. The price ranges from $1,530 (**QC4** 4-string) up to $1,850 (**BB5** 5-string).

McSWAIN GUITARS

Instruments currently built in Los Angeles, California.

Luthier Stephen McSwain produces elaborate hand carved guitar bodies that he later builds into full guitars. McSwain's high degree of relief turns the bodies into playable works of art. Contact luthier McSwain for pricing quote and commission date availability directly (see Trademark Index).

MACDONALD, S.B.

Instruments currently built in Huntington (Long Island), New York.

Luthier S.B. MacDonald has been building and restoring stringed instruments for 20 years. His instruments are built by special order and designed around the needs of each customer. MacDonald offers acoustic, electric, and resophonic instruments. He is also a columnist for "20th Century Guitar" and "Acoustic Musician" magazines.

One of MacDonald's custom instruments is the Resonator Electric, a vintage-style semi-hollow body guitar with a resonator cone. The Resonator Electric features a maple neck, 21-fret ebony fingerboard, 6-on-a-side Grover tuners, Tele-style neck pickup/Fishman transducer in resonator cone, volume and tone controls, and cool retro colors. For further information on this model and others, contact luthier S.B. MacDonald directly (see Trademark Index).

MADEIRA

See GUILD.

Instruments previously built in Japan during the early 1970s to late 1980s.

The Madeira line was imported in to augment Guild sales in the U.S. between 1973 and 1974. The first run of solid body electrics consisted of entry level reproductions of classic Fender, Gibson, and even Guild designs (such as the S-100). The electric models were phased out in a year (1973 to 1974), but the acoustics were continued.

The solid body electrics were reintroduced briefly in the early 1980s, and then introduced again in 1990. The line consisted of three guitar models (ME-200, ME-300, ME-500) and one bass model (MBE-100). All shared similar design accoutrements such as bolt-on necks and various pickup configurations.

(Source: Michael Wright, Vintage Guitar Magazine)

MAGNATONE

Instruments previously built in California circa mid 1950s through late 1960s.

Magnatone is more recognized for their series of brown and gold amplifiers produced during the early 1960s than the company's guitars. Magnatone was originally founded as the Dickerson Brothers in Los Angeles, California circa 1937. The company began building phonographs, lap steels, and amplifiers. In 1947 the company was known as Magna Electronics. By the mid 1950s they were offering electric Spanish hollowbody guitars designed by Paul Bigsby. Like Standel (and the early years at Fender), Magnatone wanted a guitar line to offer retailers.

In 1959, Magna Electronics merged with Estey Electronics (which was run by Roy and Ken Chilton). The guitar line was redesigned by Paul Barth in 1961, and four different models were offered. Magnatone also offered **Estey** thinline electric guitars in the late 1960s that were imported in from Italy. Magnatone maintained showrooms on both coasts, with one in West Hempstead, New York, and the other in Torrance, California.

(Source: Tom Wheeler, American Guitars; and Michael Wright, Vintage Guitar Magazine)

ELECTRIC

Mark Series

Magnatone debuted the **Mark** series in 1956, which consisted of single cutaway/one pickup **Mark III Standard**; the single cutaway/two pickup **Mark III Deluxe**; the double cutaway **Mark IV**; and the double cutaway model that was equipped with a Bigsby tremolo called the **Mark V**. Both the Mark IV and the Mark V models were designed by Paul Bigsby.

Starstream Series

In 1962, Paul Barth (of National/Rickenbacker/Bartell fame) designed four models that consisted of a 1- or 2-pickup solid body model, a 3/4 scale beginner's electric guitar, and an electric/acoustic (retail prices ranged from $99 to $299). The guitar line was renamed the **Starstream** series in 1965, and all models were redesigned with a double cutaway body. There were three electric/acoustics models (that ranged from $350 to $420), and three solid body electrics (one a 3/4 size) and a bass guitar (ranging from $170 to $290).

Magnatone Mark III
courtesy Kevin Macy

MAGNUS KREMPEL CUSTOM INSTRUMENTS

Instruments currently built in Weinback, Germany.

Luthier Magnus Krempel is currently offering a number of 4-, 5-, and 6-string electric basses and custom instruments. For additional information regarding specifications and pricing, contact Magnus Krempel directly (see Trademark Index).

MANNE GUITARS

Instruments currently built in Schio, Italy.

Since 1986, Andrea Ballarin and Manne Guitars have been producing hand crafted instruments.

(Model information and pricing courtesy Andrea Ballarin, Manne Guitars)

The following descriptions also contain Export prices (prices in US Dollars) from May 1998; tax, transport and fees are excluded. Prices include a softcase.

ELECTRIC GUITARS

TAOS 'PB - offset double cutaway alder body, bolt-on multi-laminated asymmetrical shaped neck, 640 mm scale, 24-fret phenolic fingerboard, 6-on-a-side tuners, Fishman Powerbridge with piezo pickups, 2 single coils/splittable (coil tap) humbucker, 5-way selector switch. Available in a Satin finish. Current Mfg.

MSR $1,580

The Fishman Powerbridge (with piezo pickups), sends its signal into a specially designed impedance matching transformer, which allows for mixing the signal with the magnetic pick-ups for use into a standard amp input. An additional push-pull tone pot gives you the opportunity to switch to the straight piezo sound, and - if you need to - switch it to a second output jack, to send it to a different channel, amp, or setting.

Taos PB Flame - similar to the Taos '98, except features a mahogany body, flame maple top .Available in a High gloss finish. Current Mfg.

MSR $1,860

SemiAcustica Series

The **SemiAcustica** model is addressed to both folk acoustic and semi-hollow body guitar players. The neck is the same used on the **Taos** models. The offset double cutaway body is constructed with light poplar, and features a spruce top. The body is closed to prevent feedback at loud performances. A special element is placed under the bridge to "dump" top vibrations and simulate the minor sustain, which is a characteristic of acoustic guitars.

This model has a piezo pickup under the bridge and a magnetic pickup near the neck which allows for a mix to get all the different tones (from the full-bodied sound of the humbucker to the crisp and clean sound of the piezo). The bridge has a special design for fast string changing and compensation adjustment. The SemiAcustica model has a retail list price of $1695.00.

ELECTRIC BASS

BASIC XLR - offset double cutaway heavy ash body (45mm thickness), multi-laminated asymmetrical shaped neck, 864 mm scale, 24-fret phenolic fingerboard, 4-on-a-side tuners, 2 epoxy sealed splittable (coil tapped) Manne Soapbar pick-ups (with double shielding), volume/push-pull tone pot, pick-up selector, passive circuitry. Current Mfg.

4-String configuration.

MSR $1,580

5-String configuration

MSR $1,690

An additional balanced XLR output is supplied by an on board specially designed transformer to provide a clean, extended and balanced response output direct to recording desk, P.A. or amp.

AcoustiBass Series

The semi-hollow **AcoustiBass** instrument features an acoustic chamber under the bridge. The strings pass through the body and then over a saddle which has a piezo element. Manne also added a magnetic pick-up in the bridge position that adds an additional mellow tone. The **AcoustiBass** model features the simplified volume, balance, and tone controls, which gives a broad spectrum of sounds (going from a dark, woody double bass sound, to a crisp biting sound). The 4-String version of the AcoustiBass has a retail list price of $1750; the 5-Strings version lists at $1860.

MANSON

A.B. MANSON & COMPANY.

Instruments currently built in Devon, England since the late 1970s. Distributed in the U.S. by S.A. Music of Santa Barbara, California.

Stringed instruments bearing the Manson name come from two separate operations. Acoustic guitars, mandolins, bouzoukis (and even triplenecks!) are built by Andrew Manson at A.B. Manson & Company. Electric guitars and electric basses are built by Hugh Manson at Manson Handmade Instruments. Andrew and Hugh Manson have been aplying their luthier skills for over twenty five years. Both Mansons draw on a wealth of luthier knowledge as they tailor the instrument directly to the player commissioning the work.

Hand sizing (for neck dimensions), custom wiring, or custom choice of wood - it's all done in house. Both facilities are located in Devon, and both Mansons build high quality instruments respective of their particular genre. U.S. retail prices range around $3,275 for various models like the **Dove, Heron,** and **Sandpiper.** For further information regarding model specifications, pricing, and availability, please contact either Andrew or Hugh Manson directly (see Trademark Index).

According to authors Tony Bacon and Paul Day (*The Guru's Guitar Guide*), Manson instruments can be dated by the first two digits of the respective instrument's serial number.

MANTRA

Instruments currently produced in Italy.

The Mantra MG series is constructed of lightweight magnesium alloy, with a bolt-on wood neck. Casting of the innovative body is handled in Italy, while the necks are built in the U.S. by Warmoth Guitars.

MARATHON

See chapter on House Brands.

This trademark had been identified as a *House Brand* previously used by Abercrombie & Fitch during the 1960s by author/researcher Willie G. Moseley. However, a number of newer guitars sporting the same trademark have been recently spotted. These guitars are built in Korea by the Samick company, and serve as an entry level instrument for the novice guitarist.

MARCHIONE

Instruments currently handcrafted in New York (Manhattan), New York.

Stephen Marchione builds recording quality archtop and special commission guitars. Marchione's clientele primarily consists of New York's top studio and stage players, and he has received commissions from the likes of Mark Whitfield, John Abercrombie, Vernon Reed, and Mark Knopfler. Other notables playing Marchione's guitars are George Wadenius (Steely Dan's *Alive in America* CD), Mark Stewart (Bang on a Can's *Music for Airports* CD), and Kenny Brescia and Ira Seigel (sound track for the Broadway smash *Rent*).

Marchione approaches his craft from many different angles. He understands players' sound and comfort needs as a guitar player himself. Marchione also seriously studies the great guitar and violin instruments in order to build archtop guitars that function as pinnacle pieces. When a player brings in a D'Aquisto or D'Angelico to Marchione's Manhattan shop, Marchione scrutinizes the instrument's construction, draws blueprints, and then quizzes the player about the instrument's best qualities. These important elements are then incorporated into his own designs.

The violin tradition has also figured prominently in Marchione's building. A hands-on understanding of cello arching is crucial to Marchione's ability to recreate the arching subtleties that imbue his archtop guitars with full acoustic volume and tambour. Marchione's friendship with violin maker Guy Rabut has impressed upon Marchione the importance of incorporating centuries of stringed instrument knowledge. Their friendship has also given Marchione the opportunity to measure and draw plans from Guarnieri cellows as well as Rabut's renowned instruments.

Personal musicianship, an exacting approach to guitar making, and the experience of hand building almost three hundred acoustic archtops, neck-throughs, and electric guitars are the groundwork for each and every Marchione guitar.

M

(Company information courtesy Stephanie Green)

ELECTRIC

Neck-through-body Electric Models

Marchione's Neck-Through the body construction technique gives the player a wide palette: everything from a fat neck sound to full throttle bridge sound and all the mixes in-between. The comfort and playability of the neck are as integral to Marchione's guitars as great tone, so he cuts the neck to fit the player's hand. The neck is constructed from a three piece Sugar maple laminate, and the 24-fret fingerboard is available with a choice of ebony or rosewood. This three piece neck laminate is ultra stable and delivers clear highs, a responsive midrange, and a deep resonant bass register. The body is constructed of light weight Quilted maple. Aside from the beauty of the quilt figuring, a solid maple body gives the guitar an acoustic quality that is unobtainable with standard electric guitar woods. Spruce wood is used for the body of the Nylon string versions.

The **Neck-through-body** model is available in Steel String and Nylon String configurations. The Steel String version features loft-dried cello-grade highly figured maple body (spruce for Nylon String version), three piece quarter-sawn neck with Brazilian rosewood or ebony fingerboard, and Sperzel tuners. The player commissioning the piece has the choice of bridges, pickups, and configuration. Retail list of the **Neck-Through** model is $6,000.

Bolt-On Neck Electric Models

The **Bolt-On** model is the workhorse of New York's studio and stage players. Marchione builds his Bolt-On neck guitars to deliver incomparable sustain even with a tremolo, clear ringing sound, and easy playing low action. The sustain and sound quality are products of Marchione's full contact press fitting of the neck, machine heads, and bridge posts. When a string is attacked, the tone is transmitted through the instruments instantaneously with nothing lost to sloppy fitting. Marchione levels the fingerboard under string tension to ensure a stable, easy playing, buzz free neck. All electronic components are military grade, and Marchione uses custom audio tapered potentiometers. He also maximizes the signal path by employing a custom wiring configuration.

The **Bolt-On** Neck model features a Swamp ash body, 22-fret one piece maple neck or maple neck with 22-fret Brazilian rosewood fingerboard, Sperzel tuners, and an optional figured maple top. The player commissioning the piece has the choice of bridges, pickups, and configuration. Retail list of the **Neck-Through** model is $3,200.

MARCO POLO

Instruments previously built in Japan circa early 1960s. Distributed by the Marco Polo Company of Santa Ana, California.

The Marco Polo product line offered acoustic flattops, thinline hollowbody acoustic/electric guitars, and solid body electric guitars and basses. These inexpensive Japanese-built instruments were the first to be advertised by its U.S. distributors, Harry Stewart and the Marco Polo company. While the manufacturers are currently unknown, it is estimated that some of the acoustics were built by Suzuki, and some electric models were produced by Guyatone.

(Source: Michael Wright, Vintage Guitar Magazine)

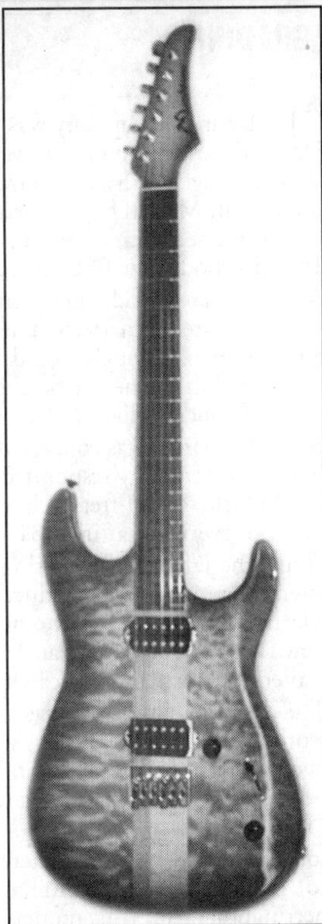

Marchione custom Electric courtesy Marchione Guitars

MARINA

Instruments currently produced in Korea since the late 1980s.

These medium quality solid body guitars sported both original and designs based on classic Fender styles.

(Source: Tony Bacon and Paul Day, The Guru's Guitar Guide)

MARLEAUX

Instruments currently built in Clausthal-Zellerfeld, Germany. Distributed in the U.S. market by the Luthiers Access Group of Chicago, Illinois.

One of Europe's finest custom houses, Marleaux custom basses are now available in the U. S., as distributed by Dan Lenard of Luthiers Access Group. Two basic body styles are offered: The **Consat** and the "headless" **Betra**. Options are the norm - neck-through or bolt-on construction, one piece bodies, or exotic tops and backs (over 40 varieties of tonewoods are available). For additional information regarding model specifications, wood options, and pricing, contact Marleaux directly (see Trademark Index).

MARLIN

Instruments currently produced in Korea. Instruments were previously produced in East Germany.

Since 1989, the trademark "Marlin by Hohner" has been produced in Korea.

The Marlin trademark originally was the brand name of a UK importer. The first **Sidewinder** and **Slammer** series were medium quality strat-styled solid body guitars from East Germany. When production moved to Korea, the models changed to **Blue Fin, Master Class, State of the Art, Loner,** and **Nastie** designations.

In 1989, a variation of the trademark appeared. Headstocks now bore a **Marlin by Hohner** description. Still Korean produced, but whether this is a new entry level series for the Hohner company or a Marlin variant is still being researched. Further updates will appear in the next edition of the ***Blue Book of Electric Guitars.***

(Source: Tony Bacon and Paul Day, The Guru's Guitar Guide)

MARLING

Instruments previously produced in Japan during the mid 1970s.

As the Italian-based EKO guitar company was winding down, they were marketing an EKO guitar copies built in Japan (although they may have been built by EKO). EKO offered a number of Marling acoustic models, as well as electric guitars. These guitar models were poor quality compared to the 1960s Italian EKOs.

(Source: Michael Wright, Guitar Stories Volume One)

MARTIN

Instruments previously produced in Nazareth, Pennsylvania until 1982. C.F. Martin & Company was originally founded in New York in 1833. Acoustic instruments currently built since 1839.

Even though Martin has produced mostly acoustic instruments over the decades, the company information and history have been provided below for the benefit of the reader. Martin made their last pure electric instruments during 1982.

The Martin Guitar company has the unique position of being the only company that has always been helmed by a Martin family member. Christian Frederick Martin, Sr. (1796-1873) came from a woodworking (cabinet making) family background. He learned guitar building as an employee for Johann Stauffer, and worked his way up to Stauffer's foreman in Vienna (Austria). Martin left Stauffer in 1825, and returned to his birthplace in Markneukirchen (Germany). Martin got caught up in an on-going dispute between the violin makers guild and the cabinet makers guild. Martin and his family emigrated to America in the fall of 1833, and by the end of the year set up a full line music store. The Martin store dealt in all types of musical instruments, sheet music, and repairs - as well as Martin's Stauffer-style guitars.

After six years, the Martin family moved to Nazareth, Pennsylvania. C.A. Zoebich & Sons, their New York sales agency, continued to hold "exclusive" rights to sell Martin guitars; so the Martin guitars retained their *New York* labels until a business falling-out occurred in 1898. The Martin family settled outside of town, and continued producing guitars that began to reflect less of a European design in favor of a more straightforward design. Christian Martin favored a deeper lower bout, Brazilian rosewood for the back and sides, cedar for necks, and a squared-off slotted peghead (with 3 tuners per side). Martin's scalloped X-bracing was developed and used beginning in 1850 instead of the traditional "fan" bracing favored by Spanish luthiers (fan bracing is favored on classical guitars today).

In 1852, Martin standardized his body sizes, with "1" the largest and '3" the smallest (size 2 and 2 1/2 were also included). Two years later, a larger "0" and smaller "5" sizes were added as well. Martin also standardized his style (or design) distinctions in the mid 1850s, with the introduction of Style 17 in 1856 and Styles 18 and 27 a year later. **Thus, every Martin guitar has a two-part name: size number and style number.** Martin moved into town in 1857 (a few blocks north of town square), and built his guitar building factory right next door within two years.

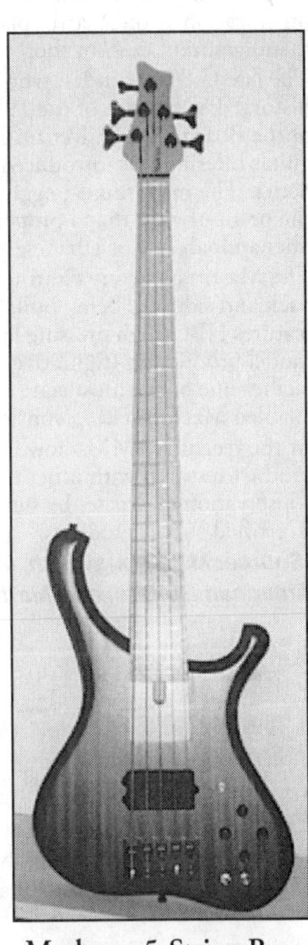

Marleaux 5-String Bass courtesy Thomas Bauer

M

GRADING	100% MINT	98% NEAR MINT	95% EXC+	90% EXC	80% VG+	70% VG	60% G

C.F. Martin & Company was announced in 1867, and in three years a wide range of Styles were available. A larger body size, the 00 debuted in 1877. Under the direction of C.F. Martin, Jr. (1825-1888), the company decided to begin producing mandolins - which caused the business split with their New York sales agency. Martin bowl-back mandolins were offered beginning in 1895, three years before the snowflake inlay **Style 42** became available. Also as important, **Martin began serializing their guitars in 1898**. The company estimated that 8,000 guitars had been built between 1833 to 1898; and so started the serialization with number 8,000. This serialization line is still intact today (!), and functions as a useful tool in dating the vintage models. The 15" wide body **Size 000**, as well as more pearl inlay on Martin guitars were introduced in 1902, which led to the fancier Style 45 two years later.

A major materials change occurred in 1916, as mahogany replaced cedar as the chosen wood for neck building. White celluloid (ivoroid) became the new binding material in 1918. **The Martin company also took a big technological leap in 1922, as they adapted the Model 2 - 17 for steel strings instead of gut strings** (all models would switch to steel string configuration by 1929). To help stabilize the new amount of stress in the necks, an ebony bar was embedded in the neck (the ebony bar was replaced by a steel T-Bar in 1934). Martin briefly built banjos in the early to mid 1920s, and also built a fair share of good quality ukuleles and tiples.

In 1929, Martin was contacted by Perry Bechtel who was looking for a flat top guitar with 14 frets clear of the body (Martin's models all joined at the 12th fret). The company responded by building a 000 model with a slimmed down 14/20-fret neck - announced in the 1930 catalog as the **OM (Orchestra Model)** (the 14/20-fret neck was adopted by almost all models in the production line by 1934). Martin also began stamping the model name into the neck block of every guitar in 1931.

While the Jazz Age was raising a hubaloo, Martin was building arch top guitars. The three C models were introduced in 1931, and the **R-18** two years later. Martin arch top production lasted until 1942. The arch tops of 1931 have since been overshadowed by another model that debuted that year - Martin's 16" wide **Dreadnought** size. Guitar players were asking for more volume, but instead of making a bigger "0000" body, Martin chose to design a new type of acoustic guitar. Martin was already building a similar type of guitar originally as a model for the Oliver Ditson company in 1916; they just waited for the market to catch up to them!

The dreadnought acoustic (so named after large World War I battleships) with X-bracing is probably the most widely copied acoustic guitar design in the world today. A look at today's music market could confirm a large number of companies building a similar design, and the name "dreadnought" has become an industry standard. Back in the 1930s, a singing cowboy of some repute decided to order a dreadnought size guitar in the Style 45. Gene Autry became the first owner of Martin's D-45.

Due to the use of heavy gauge steel strings, the Martin company stopped the practice of "scalloping" (shaving a concave surface) the braces on their guitar tops. 1947 saw the end of herringbone trim on the guitar tops, due to a lack of consistent sources (either German or American). The first two dozen (or so) 1947 D-28 models did have herringbone trim. Some thirty years later, Martin's HD-28 model debuted with the "restored" scalloped bracing and herringbone trim (this model is still in production today).

The folk boom of the late 1950s increased the demand for Martin guitars. The original factory produced around 6,000 guitars a year, but that wasn't enough. Martin began construction on a new facility in 1964, and when the new plant opened a year later, production began to go over 10,000 guitars a year. While expansion of the market is generally a good thing, the limited supply of raw materials is detrimental (to say the least!). In 1969, Brazil put an embargo on rosewood logs exported from their country. To solve this problem, Martin switched over to Indian rosewood in 1969. Brazilian rosewood from legal sources does show up on certain limited edition models from time to time.

The 1970s was a period of fluctuation for the Martin company. Many aggressive foreign companies began importing products into the U.S. market, and were rarely challenged by complacent U.S. manufacturers. To combat the loss of sales in the entry level market, Martin started the **Sigma** line of overseas-produced guitars for dealers. Martin also bought Levin, the Swedish guitar company in 1973. The **Size M**, developed in part by Mark Silber, Matt Umanov, and Dave Bromberg, debuted in 1977. E Series electric guitars were briefly offered beginning in 1979 (up until 1983). A failed attempt at union organization at the Martin plant also occurred in the late 1970s. Martin's Custom Shop was formally opened in 1979, and set the tone for other manufacturers' custom shop concepts.

The late C.F. Martin III, who had steered the company through the Great Depression, said that 1982 was the most devastating year in the company's history. The balance of the 1980s produced some innovations and radical changes at the Martin company. It was 1985 when current CEO and Chairman of the Board Chris F. Martin IV assumed his duties at the youthful age of 28. The Martin Guitar of the Month program, a limited production/custom guitar offering was introduced in 1984 (and continued through 1994, prior to the adoption of the Limited Edition series) as well as the new Jumbo J Series. The most mind-boggling event occurred the next year: The Martin Company adopted the adjustable truss rod in 1985! Martin always maintained the point of view that a properly built guitar wouldn't need one. The Korean-built **Stinger** line of solid body electrics was offered the same year as the **Shenandoah** line of Japanese-produced parts/U.S. assembly.

The Martin company continues producing guitars only in Pennsylvania. The recent **Road** Series models, with their CNC-carved necks and laminated back and sides are being built in the same facilities producing the solid wood bodies and custom shop models. The X Series was introduced in 1998, and features HPL (high pressure laminate) constructed components, decal rosette, screened headstock logo, and patented neck mortise. Martin has brought all model production (figuratively and literally) under one roof. During 1999, Martin proudly opened up its new 85,000 square foot addition, making this facility one of the most state of the art guitar plants on the planet. Production has risen to 225 guitars per day. This new efficient technology also has enabled Martin to keep consistent high quality production within the U.S., while actually lowering consumer costs.

At the recent NAMM show, Martin introduced their new DXM model, a unique instrument with a composite body and top. Martin continues to do product research with other tone woods, and is vitally concerned with dwindling supplies of traditional woods. Martin also adheres to the guidelines and conservation efforts set by such organizations as the Forest Stewardship Council, Rainforest Foundation International, and SmartWood Certified Forestry (Certified Wood products).

(Source: Mike Longworth, Martin Guitars: A History; Walter Carter, The Martin Book: A Complete History of Martin Guitars; and Tom Wheeler, American Guitars, and Martin factory brochures/catalogs.)

M

ELECTRIC

E Series

These models have offset round double cutaway bodies, mahogany necks, round wave cresting style peghead, and 3-per-side tuners.

E-18 - 9-piece maple/rosewood/walnut body, 22-fret rosewood fingerboard with pearl dot inlay, Leo Quan wrapped bridge, brass nut, rosewood peghead veneer with CFM logo decal, Sperzel tuners, chrome hardware, 2 humbucker covered DiMarzio pickups, 2 volume/2 tone controls, 3-position/phase switches. Available in Natural finish. Mfg. 1979 to 1982.

$400	$275	$250	$200	$175	$150	$125

Brass control knobs found on earlier models, replaced by black plastic on later models.

GRADING	100% MINT	98% NEAR MINT	95% EXC+	90% EXC	80% VG+	70% VG	60% G

EM-18 - 9-piece maple/rosewood/walnut body, 22-fret rosewood fingerboard with pearl dot inlay, Leo Quan wrapped bridge, brass nut, rosewood peghead veneer with CFM logo decal, Sperzel tuners, chrome hardware, 2 humbucker exposed DiMarzio pickups, 2 volume/2 tone controls, 3-position/phase/coil tap switches. Available in Natural finish. Mfg. 1979 to 1982.

$450 $325 $275 $225 $195 $175 $150

A few models found with Mighty Mite pickups, brass control knobs found on earlier models, replaced by black plastic on later models.

E-28 - mahogany body, through-body neck, 24-fret ebony fingerboard with pearl dot inlay, Schaller tune-o-matic tailpiece, ebony peghead veneer with CFM logo decal, Schaller tuners, chrome hardware, 2 humbucker exposed Seymour Duncan pickups, 2 volume/treble/bass controls, 3-position/phase/bypass switches, active electronics. Available in Sunburst finish. Mfg. 1981 to 1982.

$650 $475 $395 $325 $250 $225 $200

Martin F-55
courtesy Michael Patton

F Series

These guitars have a 3 on a side traditional squared Martin headstock.

F-50 - single round cutaway semi hollow bound plywood body, f-holes, raised black pickguard, mahogany neck, 20-fret rosewood fingerboard with white dot inlay, adjustable plexiglass bridge/trapeze tailpiece, 3-per-side tuners, chrome hardware, adjustable exposed pickup, volume/tone control. Available in Sunburst finish. Mfg. 1961 to 1965.

$625 $450 $375 $325 $250 $225 $200

Approximately 519 of these instruments were made.

F-55 - similar to F-50, except has 2 pickups, 2 volume/2 tone controls, 3-position switch.

$750 $525 $450 $375 $300 $275 $250

Approximately 665 of these instruments were made.

F-65 - similar to F-50, except has double cutaway, Bigsby style vibrato, 2 pickups, 2 volume/2 tone controls, 3-position switch.

$550 $375 $325 $275 $225 $200 $175

Approximately 566 of these instruments were made.

GT Series

These guitars have a non-traditional large headstock, with 2 sharp upper corners scooping down to the center, and a Lower Bout Width of 16".

GT-70 - single round cutaway semi hollow bound plywood body, arch top, f-holes, raised white pickguard, mahogany neck, 22-fret bound rosewood fingerboard with white dot inlay, adjustable bridge/Bigsby style vibrato, bound peghead with logo decal, 3-per-side tuners, chrome hardware, 2 exposed pickups, 2 volume/2 tone controls, 3-position switch. Available in Black and Burgundy finishes. Mfg. 1965 to 1968.

$750 $525 $450 $375 $300 $275 $250

Approximately 453 of these instruments were made.

GT-75 - similar to GT-70, except has double round cutaways.

$725 $550 $450 $375 $300 $275 $250

Approximately 751 instruments (total) were made.

GT-75-12 - similar to GT-70, except has twelve strings, double round cutaways.

$600 $425 $350 $300 $250 $225 $195

This model had a traditional style headstock.

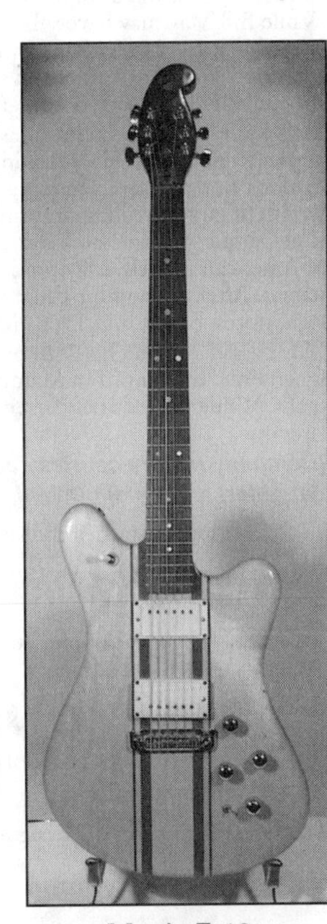

Martin E-18
courtesy Debbie Nix

ELECTRIC BASS

These models have offset round double cutaway body, mahogany neck, round wave cresting style peghead, and 2-per-side tuners.

EB-18 - 9-piece maple/rosewood/walnut body, 22-fret rosewood fingerboard with pearl dot inlay, Leo Quan fixed bridge, brass nut, rosewood peghead veneer with CFM logo decal, Grover tuners, chrome hardware, exposed DiMarzio pickup, volume/tone control, 2-position switch. Available in Natural finish. Mfg. 1979 to 1982.

$425 $295 $250 $200 $175 $150 $125

EB-28 - mahogany body, through-body mahogany neck, 22-fret ebony fingerboard with pearl dot inlay, Schaller tune-o-matic bridge/stop tailpiece, rosewood peghead veneer with CFM logo decal, Schaller tuners, chrome hardware, P/J-style exposed DiMarzio pickups, 2 volume/treble/bass controls, 3-position/phase/bypass switches, active electronics. Available in Sunburst finish. Mfg. 1981 to 1982.

$1,000 $850 $750 $625 $525 $425 $325

Last MSR was $1,254.

This model was also offered with a fretless fingerboard. Approximately 217 of these instruments were made.

M

MARVEL

See also PREMIER.

Instruments previously built in Japan circa 1950s to mid 1960s.

The Peter Sorkin Music Company of New York, New York was an importer/distributor of Premier guitars and amplifiers. Many Premier guitars were built in New York using Italian or other foreign parts, and sometimes the instruments would be rebranded (**Marvel, Royce, Bell-Tone, or Strad-O-Lin**). Marvel guitars have been identified as the budget line distributed by Sorkin. Marvel guitars may be completely imported or have parts that are imported (which would make the guitar partially U.S. built: a helpful tip for all you American xenophobes).

(Source: Michael Wright, Guitar Stories Volume One)

MASTER

Instruments currently built in Los Angeles, California.

Luthier George Gorodnitski has been building fine handcrafted acoustic and semi-hollowbody electric guitars for a number of years. For further information, please contact luthier Gorodnitski directly (see Trademark Index).

MASTER'S BASS

Instruments currently built in Waco, Texas.

For 12 years, the Master's Bass Company has specialized in building handcrafted electric basses. Each Master's bass is a combination of ergonomic design, choice exotic and domestic hardwoods, custom electronics, and the finest bass hardware available.

The **Reality** bass has a 3-piece maple neck and soft maple body wings (retail price $1,995 to $2,250); the **Dream Bass** features a 5-piece neck and bookmatched tops and backs ($3,899 and $4,299); and the top-of-the-line **Fantasy** bass has a 7-piece neck and bookmatched exotic wood tops and backs ($4,599 to $4,999). All basses are offered in 4-, 5-, and 6-string configuration, although 7-string models are an option.

MASTERTONE

See chapter on House Brands.

While the Mastertone designation was applied to high end Gibson banjos in the 1920s, the MASTERTONE trademark was used on a Gibson-produced budget line of electric guitars beginning in 1941. Some acoustic "Hawaiian" guitars from the 1930s by Gibson also carried the Mastertone label. While built to the same standards as other Gibson guitars, they lack the one "true" Gibson touch: an adjustable truss rod. "House Brand" Gibsons were available to musical instrument distributors in the late 1930s and early 1940s.

(Source: Walter Carter, Gibson Guitars: 100 Years of an American Icon)

MATON

Instruments currently produced in Bayswater North, Australia since 1946.

Maton is Australia's longest established guitar manufacturer. The Maton trademark was established in 1946 by British emigre Bill May, a former woodworking teacher. His trademark name was a combination of his last name, and *tone* - just what every luthier seeks.

In the 1940s, it was a commonly held belief among Australian guitarists and musical instrument retailers that American guitars were the best in the world. While Bill May may have subscribed to that general idea, it didn't stop him from questioning why Australians shouldn't build their own guitars. As May related in a 1985 interview, "I wanted to make better guitars, beyond what people thought you had the ability to do. People asked 'How do you think you can do it? You've never been to see how it's done and what do you know about it. And it's Australia. You don't know anything here. If you want good instruments, you have to wait and get them from America'. But I didn't believe that."

May was raised with craftsman skills and a positive attitude, both for his own self esteem and for his country. Bill May originally completed his apprenticeship in cabinet making, and later an honors course in art and graphic design before he spent ten years as a woodwork teacher. When May couldn't find a decent sounding guitar in a reasonable price range, he began building guitars in the garage of his Thornbury home. While there was no wealth of guitar building information back in the 1940s, May learned from the various guitars that passed through his hands. Production tools for the time period were the same sort used by furniture craftsmen, like chisels, planes, or the occasional belt-sander or bench saw. Rather than knock out copies of American models, May produced designs that were distinctive in appearance and sound - and featured Australian woods and distinctly Australian names. After the humble beginnings in his garage, a factory was established outside of Melbourne in 1951. Maton guitars began to be offered through local stores; by the mid 1960s Maton instruments had established a solid reputation throughout Australia.

May passed away on his 75th birthday in 1993, but the company continues to produce quality acoustic guitars. The modern factory located in Bayswater is certainly different from Maton's original site in Canterbury, but the traditional use of hand craftsmanship still co-exists with the new CNC router at the plant. While the focus of current production has been on acoustic guitars, the company also promises that there will be a return of production electrics later on.

(Company history courtesy John Stephenson, The Maton Book (1997); additional model descriptions courtesy Linda Kitchen (Bill May's daughter) and Haidin Demaj, Maton Guitars)

Maton estimates that 80,000 guitars were sold in the past forty years. The current company builds over 400 acoustics per month.

ELECTRIC

A brief listing of their previous quality electric solid body guitars include such models as the **Wedgtail, Flamingo, Fyr Byrd**, and **Ibis**; semi-hollowbodies include the **Slender Line, Starline**, and **Supreme** models.

MAXTONE

Instruments currently produced in Taiwan, and distributed by the Ta Feng Long Enterprises Company, Ltd. of Tai Chung, Taiwan.

Maxtone instruments are designed with the entry level to student quality guitars. For further information, contact Maxtone directly (see Trademark Index).

MAYA

See also EL MAYA.

Instruments previously produced in Japan from the mid 1970s through the mid 1980s.

Maya guitars span the range of entry level to medium quality solid body, semi-hollowbody, and archtops that feature both original designs and other designs based on classic American favorites. The Maya company also produced a secondary trademark called "El Maya" that featured good quality Fender-based designs as well as some originals.

(Source: Tony Bacon and Paul Day, The Guru's Guitar Guide)

MAYFAIR

MAYFAIR

Instruments previously produced in Japan, circa 1960s.

Research continues on the Mayfair trademark.

MEAN GENE GUITARS

Instruments previously built in California between 1989 to 1991.

Gene Baker was a partner in a short lived business arrangement that specialized in guitar building, repair, rehearsal hall rental, and retail sales of guitar-related products. In 1990, Baker also released an instructional video and manual titled *Mean Gene's Insane Lead Guitar Manual.*

(Source: Gene Baker, Baker Guitars U.S.A.)

Baker estimates that about 50 instruments were produced (many with custom colors and graphics), and usually built from ground up on customer's specifications. Baker still services them at his current shop.

MEAZZI

Instruments previously produced in Italy from 1963 to 1969.

The Meazzi company has been a seller, distributor, and even a producer of musical instruments in Italy for over the past 50 years. Between 1963 and 1969, Meazzi offered a wide range of electric guitars and basses. These instruments exude a lot of character (similar to other 1960s production guitars) but offer the vintage guitar collector some real eye-catching models. Best of all, the guitars are pretty good quality for playing, too!

(Source: Marino Meazzi, Meazzi S.P.A. of Paderno, Italy; model text derived from the book celebrating Meazzi's 50th Anniversary, "Meazzi's All Stars" by Marco Cogliati (Paderno, Italy); model dating estimations courtesy Carlos Juan, Collectables & Vintage '95, Stuttgart, Germany)

Most Meazzi models featured an "in-line" tuner headstock and bolt-on neck, similar to Fender style production. Keeping in line with the 1960s designs, many popular Meazzi models had a vague Burns and Fender Jaguar/Jazzmaster design feel. However, pickguard design and appointments are 100% original Meazzi. All hardware is chrome.

Meazzi instruments are more plentiful in Europe than in the U.S. Until the secondary market is defined in the U.S., accurate used market prices are not available.

ELECTRIC

Meazzi offered a number of archtop guitar models between 1964 to 1969. The **Cerri** archtop had a single pickup, and was the top of the line. The two pickup **Zuccheri** was produced in very limited amounts, making it a fairly rare model.

Some of the hollow body guitar models offered between 1964 to 1969 include the **Continental**, which featured 2 pickups and a tremolo bridge; and the 2 pickup model **Sheptre**.

The **Corsair** solid body had an offset double cutaway design, black pickguard, 22-fret fingerboard, 6-on-a-side headstock, metal bridge/mute/tremolo tailpiece, 2 pickups, volume and tone controls. The **Mustang** has a similar body design, but features 3 single coil pickups and a different tremolo bridge configuration. Both models available between 1964 to 1969.

The **Diamond** solid body electric guitar model was briefly produced between 1963 to 1964. The Diamond had one pickup, a sparkle finish top, and a celluloid back overlay.

The **Jupiter** solid body guitar model has an offset double cutaway body (no forward horns), bolt-on neck, 22-fret fingerboard, 6-on-a-side tuners, 2 single coil pickups, half plastic pickguard/half chrome plated pickguard, chrome plate on upper bass bout with a curved slider (fader) volume control, raised metal bridge/tremolo, 2 tone controls, and a curved slider (fader) volume control on lower half of the chrome plated pickguard. This model was also available with 2 DeArmond pickups, or as a hollow body with additional preamp and blend controls. The **Baby Jupiter** guitar model is similar in design, except features a full length white plastic pickguard, one tone control, and a smaller chrome controls plate with a white curved slider (fader) volume control. Both models were produced between 1964 to 1969, and were available in Black, Blue, Green, Red, Red Sunburst, and Yellow Sunburst finishes.

The dual cutaway **Lovely** has a 22-fret fingerboard, 2 single coil pickups, metal bridge/tremolo tailpiece all mounted on an oversized white pickguard/top overlay; the similarly designed **Zephir** features different pickups, and a different metal bridge/mute/tremolo bridge set up. However, the tremolo bridge is mounted on the body.

The **Zodiac** forgoes the sleek body designs of the other models in favor of a single cutaway "artist's palette" shape similar to a *Teisco May Queen.* This solid body model has a 22-fret fingerboard, 2 pickups, metal bridge/mute/tremolo, volume and tone controls. Available between 1964 to 1969.

ELECTRIC BASS

1963 to 1964 Models

The **Diamond** solid body electric bass model, similar to the electric guitar model, was briefly produced between 1963 to 1964. The Diamond Bass had one pickup, a sparkle finish top, and a celluloid back overlay. Another model, the **Double** featured similar construction, but is the rarer of the two.

1964 to 1969 Models

Most Meazzi electric solid body basses featured a rosewood fingerboard with dot position markers and 4-on-a-side tuners. Meazzi basses were available in Black, Green, Red, and Sunburst finishes with matching or natural finished headstock.

The **Jupiter Bass** solid body has an offset double cutaway body (no forward horns), 20-fret fingerboard, 2 pickups, half plastic pickguard/half chrome plated pickguard, chrome plate on upper bass bout with a curved slider (fader) volume control, fixed bridge, chrome bridge cover, 2 tone controls, and a curved slider (fader) volume control on lower half of the chrome plated pickguard. The **Baby Jupiter** is similar in design, except features a full length white plastic pick-guard, one tone control, and a smaller chrome controls plate with a white curved slider (fader) volume control. Both models were produced between 1964 to 1969.

The **Kadett Extra** bass has a dual cutaway solid body, 20-fret fingerboard, large white pickguard, chrome bridge/metal tailpiece, chrome bridge color, 2 gold/chrome colored pickups, volume and tone controls, and a three way selector switch. The Kadett Extra was produced between 1964 to 1969.

The **Meteor** bass was offered in two versions: one pickup (**Meteor Bass I**) or with two pickups as the **Meteor Bass Extra**. Both versions featured an offset double cutaway body (no forward horns), 20-fret fingerboard, oversized white pickguard, fixed bridge, chrome bridge cover, volume and tone controls (the Extra has an additional 3-way toggle switch). Both versions were available between 1964 to 1969.

The offset double cutaway **Tiger** bass has a 21-fret fingerboard and an oversized white pickguard/top overlay - the 2 pickups, volume and tone controls, and metal bridge/tailpiece are all mounted to it. The tailpiece has a chrome cover. While the Tiger was available between 1964 to 1969, it has been noted that very few were actually made.

Other Meazzi bass models issued between 1964 to 1969 include the violin-shaped **Effe** hollow body; and the **Prinz** and **Spezial** hollow body models. All the hollow body basses have two pickups.

MELANCON GUITARS

Instruments currently built in Thibodaux, Louisiana.

Luthier Gerard Melancon's Artist models offer an upscale "version" of Strat- and Tele-style models, with heavily figured (flame and quilt) maple tops over ash (or alder or mahogany) body woods. Melancon also features high grade hardware and pickups in his construction. Melancon offers three different versions of the Artist, like the **Vintage Artist** model (list $2,000), the **Classic Artist** ($2,200), and **Custom Artist** ($2,400). Models differ in their appointments, and Melancon offers a range of custom options to personalize each instrument built.

MELOBAR

Instruments currently built in Sweet, Idaho since the mid 1960s.

Melobar was founded by designer Walt Smith to provide steel guitarists the opportunity to stand up and also be able to play chord voicings without the traditional pedals or knee levers. Smith, a teacher/performer (and cattle rancher), passed away at age 70 in 1990. His son, Ted Smith, continues to operate the family-run business, providing these high quality instruments to steel guitarists.

Walt Smith continued to make improvements on his initial design through the years, and the refinement produced the Powerslide "88 model in the late 1980s. The model can be operated with 10 strings or six, and features a Bill Lawrence pickup. Other model variations featured body designs based on Strat, Explorer, or Flying V shapes; the same designs were offered in a comfortable foam body as well. Some of the original metal acoustic Melobars were built by Dobro, while the first electric solid body models were produced by Semie Mose-ley (of Mosrite fame).

(Source: Teisco Del Rey, Guitar Player magazine)

MELODY

Instruments previously produced in Italy from the late 1970s through to the mid 1980s.

Here's a company with the proper perspective: although their designs were based on classic American favorites were built with medium quality, Melody original design guitars were built much better. The Blue Sage series was introduced in 1982, and included a model called the *Nomad* that featured a built-in amp and speaker.

(Source: Tony Bacon, The Ultimate Guitar Book)

MEMPHIS

Instruments currently produced in Korea (recent circa). Distributed by C. Bruno of Bloomfield, Connecticut.

Memphis electric guitars and basses are entry level to medium quality instruments designed for the student guitarist. Models encountered so far are the bolt-on neck Fender copies (Strats, Teles, P-basses). Headstocks have a silk-screened "Memphis" logo; guitars usually have a thick polyurethane solid finish, so let's not ask how ply the body wood is. One higher end model with a locking tremolo system and two exposed coil humbuckers was recently encountered by contributing writer Walter Murray.

(Source: Walter Murray, Frankenstein Fretworks)

Memphis electric guitars and basses are generally found priced between $79 to $159.

MENKEVICH GUITARS

Instruments currently built in Philadelphia, Pennsylvania.

Luthier Michael Menkevich has been handcrafting quality guitars for a number of years. For more information concerning model specifications and pricing, please contact Michael Menkevich Guitar Workshop directly (see Trademark Index).

MERCHANT

Instruments currently built in New York, New York.

Luthier/designer Steve Merchant has been offering quality, electric, upright basses for a number of years. For further information contact luthier/designer Steve Merchant directly (see Trademark Index).

MERCURY GUITARS

Instruments previously built in Berkeley, California 1994-2000.

Mercury Guitars consisted of three people: Linda Delgado, partner Doug Pelton, and employee Norm Devalier. Mercury Guitars focused on the design of the **Artemis, El Grande**, and **Vintage** guitar models. Mercury Guitars wanted to provide the player with a point of reference from which to begin (hence the reference to the vintage instrument).

The staff at Mercury Guitars hand selected all woods, seeking to use renewable sources while insuring good resonant qualities. Their finish choice also affirmed their commitment to the environment as they utilized a water based product which was specifically engineered for the guitar industry.

ELECTRIC

The Artemis model had a single cutaway alder body, 2 single coil pickups, maple neck with rosewood fingerboard, and one piece bridge (last price $730). The upscale **El Grande** model has an alder body with figured maple top, ebony fingerboard with 26.1" scale length, 2 humbucker pickups, and a tune-o-matic bridge/stop tailpiece. Last list price was $1,550. Mercury also produced a 4-string bass, dubbed the **Casper**, which featured a humbucker pickup.

Mercury El Grande
courtesy Dave Smith

MERLIN

Instruments previously produced in Korea during the late 1970s.

The Merlin trademark was a brand name of a UK importer. The Merlin guitar was an extremely entry level, single pickup solid body guitar. As we like to say up north in the winter time, I prefer to buy my wood by the truckload, not piece by piece.

(Source: Tony Bacon and Paul Day, The Guru's Guitar Guide; Firewood advice courtesy the good ol' boys down at the Manistique General Store 'n Liquor Emporium).

MERMER

Instruments currently built in Sebastian, Florida.

Luthier Richard Mermer, Jr. is producing concert quality, handcrafted instruments designed and built for the individual. Steel string, nylon string, electric-acoustic instruments, and acoustic Hawaiian steel guitars are offered.

All Mermer guitars feature: solid wood construction, choice of select tone woods, decorative wood binding, custom wood and stone inlay, custom scale lengths, fully compensated saddles and precision intonation, adjustable truss rod, choice of hardware and accessories, and optional pickup and microphone installation. For a list of options and additional information, visit Mermer Guitars on the internet; or for color brochure and information write to Mermer Guitars directly (see Trademark Index).

MESSENGER

Instruments previously built in San Francisco, California between 1968 and 1971. Distributed by Musicraft of San Francisco, California.

Messenger guitars and basses featured a single piece metal alloy neck in a design that pre-dated Travis Bean and Kramer instruments. Messenger instruments also feature distinctive f-holes, a thin body, and mono or stereo output. Available in a six or twelve string configuration. Colors included Morning Sunburst, Midnight Sunburst, and Rojo Red. A Brown Sunburst finish has recently been encountered, but has not yet been verified as original.

(Source: Michael Wright, Vintage Guitar Magazine)

MESSENGER UPRIGHT BASS

Instruments currently built in Forestville, California since 1992.

The **Messenger Upright Electric Bass** is a limited edition, hand-crafted, numbered, and signed instrument built by luthier John Knutson. It is designed to make the transition between acoustic and electric playing as natural and rewarding as possible. For more information, please contact the company directly (see Trademark Index).

ELECTRIC BASS

The Messenger Upright Electric Bass is available in 3 configurations: the Original (list price $2,600), the BTS (list price $2,800) and the Custom DLX (list price $3,000). Custom features are also available.

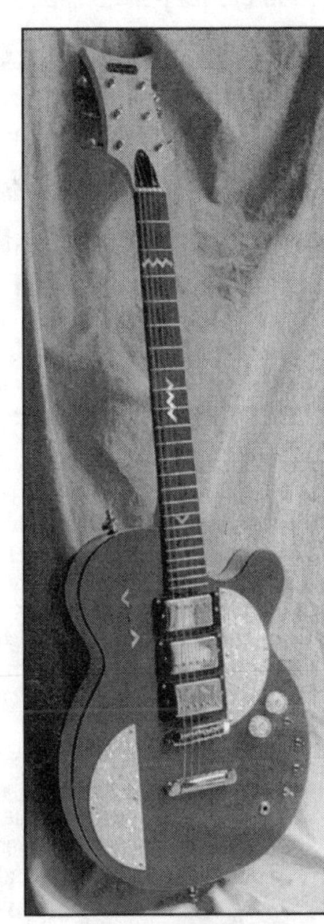

Mercury El Grande
courtesy Linda Delgado and Doug Pelton

METAL DRIVER

Also M D. See MUSIC DRIVE.

Instruments previously built in Korea. Previously distributed by Sumer Musical Instruments Co., Ltd. of Japan.

The Sumer Musical Instruments company briefly offered an aluminum body (with bolt-on wood neck) model which featured the *Abel Axe* aluminum body, also similar to the model offered under the **Rogue** trademark. Other **MD** and **Metal Driver** models during this time period feature wood bodies similar to designs offered by Ibanez and Jackson. All electric guitars and basses were good quality instruments that appealed to the working or semi-professional musician (see MUSIC DRIVE).

M

METROPOLITAN

Instruments currently built in Houston, Texas since 1995. Distributed by Alamo Music Products of Houston, Texas.

Metropolitan Guitars was originally conceived by David Wintz (of Robin Guitars fame), based on the idea that others would find the retro styling of the old National **Glenwood** as appealing as he did. While the original National Glenwood models had a formed plastic body and a bolt-on metal neck, Wintz' current **Tanglewood** model features a "map-shaped" wood body, and a mahogany set-in neck. Wintz debuted the Tanglewood series in March, 1996. Two more series, the Glendale and the Westport, followed a year later. The **Glendale** model has a single cutaway body, more rounded than the Tanglewood, but similar large body dimensions. The **Westport** model has a scaled down, rounded body.

ELECTRIC

All models are available in three configurations. The **Deluxe** configuration features a basswood body, a set-in one piece mahogany neck, rosewood fingerboard with pearl dot inlay, nickel hardware and body molding, custom "Art Deco" tailpiece, truss rod cover, and pickguard. Deluxe configurations have two Rio Grande humbuckers, 2 sets of volume and tone controls, and a 3-way selector switch. All three models in the Deluxe configuration have a retail list price of $1,695 (each).

The **Custom** configuration features a bound rosewood fingerboard with abalone and mother-of-pearl "Butterfly" inlays, as well as polished chrome and nickel hardware. The Custom configuration has a list price on each model at $2,495. A piezo transducer can be mounted in the bridge of a Custom version for an additional $300 (includes volume/tone controls for the piezo). Gold hardware is an additional $400, but well worth the appointment! Metropolitan offers other custom options including See-through finishes on Swamp Ash bodies, metal flake finishes, and Bigsby tailpieces.

MIAMI

Instruments previously produced in Japan during the mid 1970s.

The Miami trademark is the brand name used by a British importer. Instruments tended to be entry level solid body guitars.
(Source: Tony Bacon and Paul Day, The Guru's Guitar Guide)

MICHAEL

Instruments previously built in Japan during the mid 1980s.

The Michael trademark was a brand name used by a UK importer. The "Metro" model was a medium quality strat design solid body.
(Source: Tony Bacon and Paul Day, The Guru's Guitar Guide)

MICHIGAN

Instruments previously produced in East Germany from the late 1950s through the early 1960s.

The Michigan trademark was a brand name utilized by a British importer. Quality ranged from entry level to intermediate on models that were either solid body, semi-hollow, or archtop.
(Source: Tony Bacon and Paul Day, The Guru's Guitar Guide)

MICK, BOB

Instruments currently built in Tucson, Arizona. Distributed directly by Bob Mick Guitars of Tucson, Arizona.

Luthier Bob Mick has a JM-1 ($1,299) short scale bass "built like our top-of-the-line basses, only smaller!" as well as the M-4 ($3,150) neck-through design that features maple and exotic woods in its construction. There are also five and six string versions as well. Furthermore, luthier Mick can custom build any basses from *simple designs to the exotic* in bolt-on or neck-through. Contact Bob Mick directly (see Trademark Index).

M

MICRO-FRETS

Instruments previously built in Frederick, Maryland between 1967 and 1974.

During the expansion of the *pop* music market in the 1960s, many smaller guitar producers entered the electric instrument market to supply the growing public demand for guitars. One such visionary was Ralph J. Jones, who founded the Micro-Frets organization in 1967. Jones, who primarily handled design concepts, electronics, and hardware innovations, received financial backing from his former employer (a successful Maryland real estate magnate). It is estimated that Jones began building his prototypes in 1965, at his Wheaten, Maryland workshop. By 1967 production began at the company factory located at 100 Grove Road in Frederick, Maryland. Ralph J. Jones was the company president and treasurer, and was assisted by F. M. Huggins (vice-president and general manager) and A. R. Hubbard (company secretary) as well as the working staff.

Micro-Frets guitars were shown at the 1968 NAMM show. The company did the greatest amount of production between 1969 and 1971, when 1,700 of the less than 3,000 total guitars were made. Jones passed away sometime in 1973, and was succeeded by Huggins as president.

When Micro-Frets closed operations in Maryland in either 1974 or 1975, the company assets were purchased by David Sturgill. Sturgill, who served as the company president of Grammer Guitars for three years, let his sons John and Danny gain access to leftover Micro-Frets parts. In addition to those parts, they had also purchased the remains of New Jersey's Harptone guitar company. The two assembled a number of solid body guitars which were then sold under the "Diamond-S" trademark. Unfortunately, that business venture did not catch on, and dissipated sometime in 1976.

(Micro-Frets enthusiast Jim Danz, began detailing a listing of Micro-Frets serial numbers. His results appeared in a company history by Michael Wright in Vintage Guitar Magazine)

Micro-Fret Serialization

The entire production of the Micro-Frets company is less than 3,000 guitars and basses produced. As in the case of production guitars, neck plates with stamped serial numbers were pre-purchased in lots, and then bolted to the guitars during the neck attachment. The serial numbers were utilized by Micro-Frets for warranty work, and the four digit numbers do fall roughly in a usable list. **This list should be used for rough approximations only**:

Between the company start-up in 1967 and 1969, serial numbers 1000 to 1300 (around 300 instruments produced). During the transition period, a couple of dozen instruments were produced. From 1969 to 1971, serial numbers 1323 to 3000 (around 1,700 instruments were produced). Finally, in the company's home stretch between 1971 to 1974, serial numbers 3000 to 3670 (roughly 700 instruments were produced).

GRADING	100% MINT	98% NEAR MINT	95% EXC+	90% EXC	80% VG+	70% VG	60% G

Microfrets Signature
courtesy Rick King

Body Construction Styles

Furthermore, a survey of company production indicates **three predominant styles or construction similarities** shared by various production models through the years. Again, this information is a rough approximation based on viewed models, and any errors in it are the fault of this author (so don't blame Jim Danz!):

Style I (1967 to 1969): Most of the Micro-Fret guitars are actually hollow bodied guitars built by joining two separate top and bottom slabs of routed-out solid wood. As a result, earlier models will feature a side *gasket* on the two body halves. The early vibrato design looks similar to a Bigsby. The pickguard will have two levels, and the thumb wheel controls are set into a scalloped edge on the top half. Pickups will be DeArmond, Micro-Frets *Hi-Fis*, or German-made Schallers or possibly Hofners. Tuning pegs will be Grovers (some with pearl grips) or Schallers (on the high end models).

Style II (1969 to 1971): The side gaskets are gone, but side seams should be noticeable. The bi-level pickguard is white, the top half is shorter than the lower, and now conventional knobs are utilized. Guitars now sport only Micro-Fret pickups, but there are a number of different designs. According to Bill Lawrence (Bill Lawrence Guitar Company/Keystone Pickups), Micro-Frets approached him at the 1968 NAMM show and contracted him to design both the pickups and the manufacturing process. Micro-Frets pickups were then produced in-house by the company.

Style III (1971 or 1972 until 1974): No side seams are visible, but by then a number of solid body guitars were being introduced as well. The bi-level pickguard now has a clear plastic short top half. Micro-Fret pickups are again used, although some were built with extra booster coils and three switches for tonal options. There are still some unsubstantiated reports of possible 12-string versions, or even a resonator model!

ELECTRIC

The Orbiter model, with built in wireless transmitter, was only available between 1968 to 1969. This model should be accompanied by a receiver unit.

Orbiter models range from $450 to $900, depending on condition and receiver availability.

CALIBRA I - 22-fret rosewood fingerboard, adjustable metal nut, 6-on-a-side tuners, adjustable bridge, chrome hardware, 2 Micro-Frets pickups, volume/tone controls, pickup selector switch. Mfg. 1969 to circa 1972.

$695 $650 $575 $525 $495 $450 $375
Last MSR was $299.

The Calibra I model was similar to an earlier model, the Golden Comet.

Calibra - similar to the Calibra I, except features a fixed bridge/tailpiece. Mfg. 1971 to circa 1972.

$650 $595 $525 $475 $425 $350 $300
Last MSR was $269.

HUNTINGTON - maple top/back/sides, 22-fret rosewood fingerboard, adjustable metal nut, 6-on-a-side tuners, adjustable bridge, chrome hardware, 2 Micro-Frets pickups, volume/tone controls, pickup selector switch. Mfg. 1967 to circa 1973.

$750 $695 $625 $575 $525 $450 $400
Last MSR was $599.

SIGNATURE - thin dual cutaway hardwood body with pointed horns, maple neck, 22-fret rosewood fingerboard, adjustable metal Micro-nut, 6-on-a-side tuners, Calibrato bridge, chrome hardware, 2 Micro-Frets MF pickups, volume/tone controls, pickup selector switch. Available in Black, Maraschino Cherry, Standard Sunburst, and Walnut finishes. Mfg. 1969 to circa 1972.

$650 $595 $550 $500 $425 $350 $300
Last MSR was $349.

The Signature Model was also offered in a Baritone model (30" scale). Mfg. 1971 to 1974.

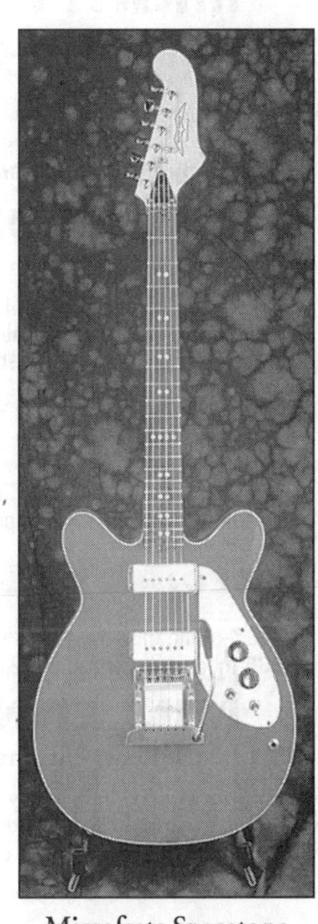

Microfrets Spacetone
courtesy Rick King

SPACETONE - dual rounded cutaway thin body, maple top/back/sides, white celluloid body binding, maple neck, 22-fret rosewood fingerboard, adjustable metal Micro-nut, 6-on-a-side tuners, Calibrato tremolo, chrome hardware, split level white pickguard, 2 Micro-Frets Hi Fi pickups, volume/tone controls, pickup selector switch. Available in Black, Martian Sunburst, and Standard Sunburst finishes. Mfg. 1967 to circa 1973.

$725 $675 $625 $550 $500 $450 $400
Last MSR was $449.

STAGE II - maple top/back/sides, 22-fret rosewood fingerboard, adjustable metal nut, 6-on-a-side tuners, adjustable bridge, chrome hardware, 2 Micro- Frets pickups, volume/tone controls, pickup selector switch. Mfg. 1969 to circa 1971.

$495 $450 $400 $350 $300 $275 $225
Last MSR was $359.

The Stage II Model was also offered in a Baritone model (30" scale). Mfg. 1972 to 1974.

GRADING	100% MINT	98% NEAR MINT	95% EXC+	90% EXC	80% VG+	70% VG	60% G

ELECTRIC BASS

SIGNATURE BASS - (solid) body, 30" (or 34") scale, 20-fret rosewood fingerboard, adjustable metal nut, 4-on-a-side tuners, adjustable bridge, chrome hardware, 2 Micro-Frets pickups, volume/tone controls, pickup selector switch. Mfg. 1969 to circa 1972.

$650	**$575**	**$525**	**$475**	**$425**	**$350**	**$300**

Last MSR was $299.

This model was available with a fretless fingerboard.

STAGE II BASS - slightly offset double cuataway body, maple body, 30" (or 34") scale, maple neck, 20-fret rosewood fingerboard, adjustable metal Micro-nut, 2-per-side tuners, adjustable bridge, chrome hardware, Micro-Frets Hi Fi pickup, volume/tone controls. Available in Black, Maraschino Cherry, Standard Sunburst, and Walnut finishes. Mfg. 1969 to circa 1972.

$500	**$450**	**$375**	**$325**	**$275**	**$250**	**$200**

Last MSR was $299.

This model was available with a fretless fingerboard.

THUNDERMASTER BASS - thin dual rounded cutaway maple body, white celluloid body binding, 30" (or 34") scale, 20-fret rosewood fingerboard, adjustable metal Micro-nut, 2-per-side tuners, adjustable bridge, chrome hardware, 2 Micro-Frets Hi Fi pickups, volume/tone controls, pickup selector switch. Available in Martian Sunburst and Standard Sunburst finishes. Mfg. 1967 to 1973.

$695	**$625**	**$550**	**$500**	**$450**	**$375**	**$325**

Last MSR was $425.

This model was available with a fretless fingerboard.

Rendevous - similar to the Thundermaster, except features one pickup. Mfg. 1967 to 1969.

$625	**$575**	**$525**	**$475**	**$400**	**$350**	**$300**

Last MSR was $295.

MIDI AXE

Instruments currently produced in Everett, Washington. Distributed by the Virtual DSP Corporation of Everett, Washington.

The Virtual DSP Corporation has unveiled a custom electric guitar which incorporates a state of the art pitch-to-MIDI tracking system. The **MIDI Axe features 6 separate RMC piezo electric pickups (built into the tremolo bridge), which combines their signal into a direct output signal.** MIDI Axe is the first MIDI system to allow full software upgradability; software updates are available by download at the company's website. For further information, contact Virtual DSP Corporation directly (see Trademark Index).

MIGHTY MITE

Replacement parts and instruments were previously built in the U.S. during the 1970s and early 1980s. Replacement parts are currently distributed by Westheimer Corporation of Northbrook, Illinois.

The Mighty Mite company was probably better known for its high quality replacement parts it produced rather than the guitars they made available. Mighty Mite parts are still currently offered.

(Source: Tony Bacon and Paul Day, The Guru's Guitar Guide)

MIKE LULL CUSTOM GUITARS

Instruments currently built in Bellevue, Washington.

Luthier Mike Lull has been building guitars for several bands in the Seattle area for years. Lull and two partners opened their own repair shop based on Lull's customizing and repair talents in 1978. Lull has been the sole owner of the Guitar Works since 1983 and still offers repair and restoration services in addition to his custom built instruments.

ELECTRIC

Mike Lull Custom Guitars now offers a number of different guitar models. Prices on the **Classic** models range from $1,695 up to $2,195; the **Modern Soloist** is $2,595, and the **Custom Carved Top** is $2,895. The **Vintage** model definitely brings back the feel of an older Strat. Models feature alder, mahogany, or swamp ash bodies, rock maple necks, maple or rosewood (or ebony) fingerboards, and Seymour Duncan or Van Zandt pickups.

ELECTRIC BASS

The 4-string bass models like the **Modern Jazz** and **Vintage P/J** prices start at $1,695 up to $2,895, and the 5-string **Modern 5** and the 35" scale **Modern 535** models are priced at $2,495 to $2,795. For further information, contact Mike Lull Custom Guitars directly (see Trademark Index).

MILLENNIUM GUITARS

Instruments currently produced in Pasadena, California.

Millennium Guitars have a new Model ML-2000 ($2,880 MSR) that features a body made from polished, clear coated aluminum. The ML-2001 ($2,430 MSR) has traditional construction, and utilizes purple sparkle chip resistant enameled bodies in either gloss or wrinkle finish. For more information, please contact the company directly (see Trademark Index).

GRADING	100% MINT	98% NEAR MINT	95% EXC+	90% EXC	80% VG+	70% VG	60% G

MILLER

Instruments currently built in Rossbach, Germany.

Miller custom instruments are constructed from carbon graphite fibers or hemp, leading to the company's motto "Don't Smoke it, Play it!" Hempline models are semi-hollow in construction, including the neck and headstock. These advanced design aspects place the Miller company on the cutting edge of guitar technology and construction. For additional information concerning models and pricing, contact the Miller company directly (see Trademark Index).

MIRAGE

Instruments previously produced in Taiwan during the late 1980s.

Entry level to intermediate quality guitars based on classic American designs.
(Source: Tony Bacon and Paul Day, The Guru's Guitar Guide)

MIRAGE GUITARS

Instruments previously built in Etters, Pennsylvania circa early 1980s.

Mirage Guitars offered original design electric guitars with see through bodies constructed of acrylic or polyester. The **Mindbender I** had a bolt-on maple neck, 6-on-a-side tuners, and 2 MightyMite humbuckers or 3 single coils. Available in clear, tinted, and opaque. Retail list price began at $795.

The last given address for the company was: Mirage Guitars, R.D. 3, Box 3273, Etters, Pennsylvania (17319).

MODULUS GRAPHITE

See MODULUS GUITARS.

MODULUS GUITARS

Instruments currently built in Novato, California since 1997. Previously built in San Francisco, California 1978-1997.

Modulus Blackknife Classic
courtesy Modulus Guitars

Geoff Gould, an aerospace engineer and bass player, was intrigued by an Alembic-customized bass he saw at a Grateful Dead concert. Assuming that the all wood construction was a heavy proposition, he fashioned some samples of carbon graphite and presented them to Alembic. An experimental model with a graphite neck was displayed in 1977, and a patent issued in 1978. Gould formed the Modulus Graphite company with other ex-aerospace partners to provide necks for Alembic, and also build necks for Music Man's Cutlass bass model as well as their own Modulus Graphite guitars. Modulus Graphite's first products were Fender-style replacement necks, but in the early 1980s five- and six-string bass models were introduced. Since then, the Modulus neck patent has been licensed to several companies, and Modulus has supplied finished necks to Alvarez Yairi, Aria, Cort, Ibanez, Moonstone, Peavey, Status, Steinberger, Tokai, and Zon as well.

ELECTRIC

Blackknife Series

Blackknife series guitars feature bolt-on graphite/epoxy composite necks with phenolic/ebonol fingerboards (unless otherwise listed).

All models are available with the following standard finishes, unless otherwise listed: Amber, Clear Blue, Clear Green, Clear Red, Deep Black, Monza Red, Pure White, Sea Foam Green, Surf Green, and Vintage Pink.

The following options were available on the Blackknife models:

Add $50 for black or gold hardware.

Add $100 for body matching colored neck.

Add $100 for Wilkinson tremolo bridge.

Add $100 for 3-Tone Sunburst or Translucent Cream finish.

Add $100 for Custom Color finishes: Black Cherry, Blue/Greenburst, Blue/Purpleburst, Blue Velvet, Charcoal Metalflake, Cherryburst, Clear Black, Green Velvet, Honeyburst and Purple Metalflake.

Add $150 for Candy Apple Blue, Candy Apple Green, or Candy Apple Red finish.

Add $175 for 2TEK bridge.

Add $200 for double locking tremolo.

CLASSIC (Model BC6) - offset double cutaway alder body, bolt-on graphite neck, 25 1/2" scale, 22-fret phenolic fingerboard with white dot inlay, ABM fixed bridge, 6-on-a-side tuners, chrome hardware, humbucker/single coil/humbucker EMG pickups, volume/tone controls, 5-way selector. Available in Black, Cream, Green, Red, and White finishes. Disc. 1996.

$1,200	$1,000	$900	$800	$700	$600	$500

Last MSR was $1,999.

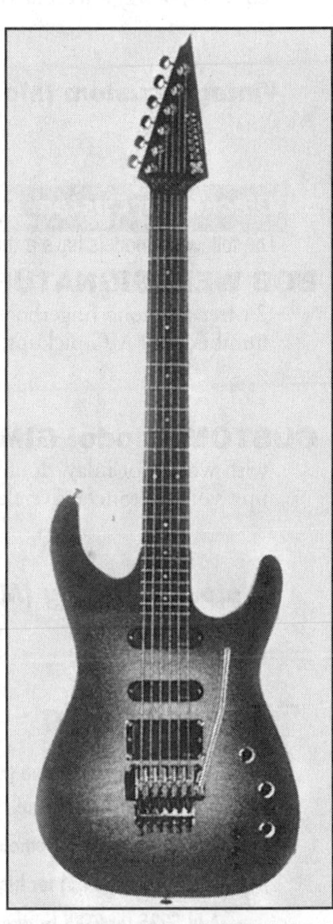

Modulus Blackknife Special 3H
courtesy Modulus Guitars

GRADING	100% MINT	98% NEAR MINT	95% EXC+	90% EXC	80% VG+	70% VG	60% G

Classic (Model GIMCL) - similar to the Classic (Model BC6), except has flamed maple top, gold hardware, Wilkinson VS-100 tremolo, 3 mini-switches. Disc. 1994.

$1,500	**$1,200**	**$1,100**	**$975**	**$850**	**$750**	**$625**

Last MSR was $2,495.

MODEL T (Model MT6/GITNT) - single cutaway alder body, bolt-on graphite neck, 25 1/2" scale, 22-fret phenolic fingerboard with white dot inlay, strings through-body bridge, 6-on-a-side tuners, chrome hardware, 2 Seymour Duncan single coil pickups, volume/tone controls, 3-way selector. Available in Black, Cream, Green, Red, and White finishes. Disc. 1996.

$1,000	**$850**	**$775**	**$695**	**$595**	**$500**	**$425**

Last MSR was $1,699.

Model T Custom (Model GI1NT-C) - similar to Model T, except has figured maple top, black hardware, 1 Seymour Duncan/1 Van Zandt single coil pickups. Disc. 1994.

$1,250	**$1,050**	**$950**	**$850**	**$725**	**$625**	**$525**

Last MSR was $2,095.

SPECIAL (Model BS6) - offset double cutaway alder body, bolt-on graphite neck, 22-fret phenolic fingerboard with white dot inlay, ABM fixed bridge, 6-on-a-side tuners, chrome hardware, 2 HS-2 single coil/1 humbucker DiMarzio pickups, volume/tone controls, 5-way selector. Available in Black, Cream, Green, Red, and White finishes. Mfg. 1994 to 1996.

$1,100	**$950**	**$875**	**$675**	**$600**	**$550**	**$500**

Last MSR was $1,999.

Special 3H (Model GIS3HT) - similar to the Special (Model BS6), except has double locking Floyd Rose tremolo, 2 EMG-SA single coil/1 EMG 85 humbucker pickups, 3 mini-switches. Disc. 1994.

$1,200	**$1,000**	**$900**	**$800**	**$700**	**$600**	**$500**

Last MSR was $1,995.

Special 3H Custom (Model GIS3HT-C) - similar to Special 3H (Model GIS3HT), except has figured maple top, and black hardware. Disc. 1994.

$1,450	**$1,200**	**$1,050**	**$950**	**$850**	**$725**	**$600**

Last MSR was $2,395.

VINTAGE (Model BV6/GIS3VT) - offset double cutaway alder body, bolt-on graphite neck, 25 1/2" scale, 22-fret fingerboard with white dot inlay, vintage-style 2-point tremolo, 3-layer white pickguard, chrome hardware, 3 Van Zandt single coil pickups, volume/2 tone controls, 5-way selector. Available in Black, Cream, Green, Red, and White finishes. Disc. 1996.

$1,050	**$975**	**$850**	**$750**	**$675**	**$575**	**$475**

Last MSR was $1,899.

Vintage Custom (Model GIS3VT-C) - similar to Vintage, except has figured maple top, black hardware. Disc. 1994.

$1,350	**$1,150**	**$1,000**	**$925**	**$800**	**$695**	**$575**

Last MSR was $2,295.

M

Blackknife Custom Series

The following models have a through-body graphite neck. Options are similar to the bolt-on neck Blackknife models.

BOB WEIR SIGNATURE (Model BW6/GIBW) - offset double cutaway alder body, cocabola top, through-body graphite neck, 24-fret phenolic fingerboard with white dot inlay, double locking Floyd Rose tremolo, 6-on-a-side tuners, black hardware, 2 single coil/1 humbucker EMG pickups, volume/tone/active electronics control, 3 mini-switches. Disc. 1996.

$2,100	**$1,750**	**$1,575**	**$1,400**	**$1,225**	**$1,050**	**$875**

Last MSR was $3,499.

CUSTOM (Model GIMCT) - offset double cutaway alder body, figured maple top, through-body neck, 24-fret phenolic fingerboard with white dot inlay, double locking Floyd Rose vibrato, 6-on-a-side tuners, gold hardware, humbucker/single coil/humbucker EMG pickups, volume/tone/active electronics control, 3 mini-switches. Disc. 1994.

$1,800	**$1,500**	**$1,350**	**$1,200**	**$1,050**	**$900**	**$750**

Last MSR was $2,995.

Custom 12-String (Model GIMF-12) - similar to the Custom, except in a 12-string configuration, 6-per-side tuners. Mfg. 1991 to 1992.

$1,600	**$1,350**	**$1,225**	**$1,100**	**$950**	**$800**	**$675**

Last MSR was $2,695.

Genesis Series

Genesis series guitars have a graphite composite central core in the neck surrounded by spruce, cedar, alder, or figured maple; the fingerboard is granadillo.

Add $50 for 2 single coil/1 humbucker DiMarzio pickups (there is no additional charge for substituting 2 DiMarzio humbuckers for the 3 single coils).

Add $100 for ABM tremolo bridge.

Add $200 (and up) for highly figured maple/graphite neck.

Add $225 for 2TEK bridge.

GRADING	100% MINT	98% NEAR MINT	95% EXC+	90% EXC	80% VG+	70% VG	60% G

GENESIS ONE (Model G1/GO6) - offset double cutaway alder body, bolt-on graphite/spruce (or graphite/soma, graphite/alder, or graphite/red cedar) neck, 22-fret granadillo fingerboard with white dot inlay, white (or black) pickguard, ABM fixed bridge, 6-on-a-side Schaller tuners, chrome hardware, 3 DiMarzio dual-blade single coil-sized humbucking pickups, volume/tone controls, 5-way selector. Available in Black, Green, Red, and White finishes. Mfg. 1996 to date.

MSR	$1,699	$1,350	$1,200	$1,050	$895	$725	$575	$425

Add $50 for tortoiseshell, white or black pearl pickguard.

Add $100 for 2-Tone or 3-Tone Sunburst finish.

Add $150 for Candy Apple Blue, Candy Apple Green, or Candy Apple Red finish.

Genesis One with Tremolo (Model G1T) - similar to the Genesis One, except has an ABM tremolo bridge. Mfg. 1997 to date.

MSR	$1,799	$1,450	$1,250	$1,100	$950	$775	$625	$450

GENESIS TWO (Model G2/GT6) - similar to the Genesis One, except has figured maple top, no pickguard (rear-routed body). Available in BlueStone, GreenStone, GrayStone, and RedStone finishes. Mfg. 1996 to date.

MSR	$1,999	$1,600	$1,400	$1,225	$1,050	$850	$675	$500

Add $100 for BlueStoneBurst, GreenStoneBurst, and RedStoneBurst finishes.

Add $200 for highly figured quilt or flamed maple top.

Genesis Two with Tremolo (Model G2T) - similar to the Genesis Two, except has an ABM tremolo bridge. Mfg. 1997 to date.

MSR	$2,099	$1,675	$1,450	$1,275	$1,100	$900	$725	$525

GENESIS THREE (Model G3) - offset double cutaway alder or soma body, set-in graphite/soma (or graphite/red cedar) neck, 25" scale, 22-fret granadillo fingerboard with white dot inlay, black pickguard, fixed bridge, 3-per-side tuners, chrome hardware, 2 custom 'soapbar'-style humbuckers (or 2 full size humbuckers) pickups, 2 volume/1 tone controls, 5-way selector. Available in Black, Blue, Creme, Green, and Red solid finishes; Blue, Green, Honey, and Rose Transparent colors. Mfg. 1998 to date.

MSR	$1,799	$1,375	$1,200	$1,050	$895	$750	$575	$425

Add $100 for Cherryburst and Honeyburst finishes.

Add $200 for quilt or flame maple top.

Modulus Blackknife New Vintage courtesy Modulus Guitars

ELECTRIC BASS

The following options were available on earlier models from Modulus:

Add $100 for Kahler bridge upgrade.

Add $100 for black or gold hardware.

Add $100 for body matching colored neck.

Add $600 for piezo bridge pickup (4-string).

Add $700 for piezo bridge pickup (5-string).

Add $800 for piezo bridge pickup (6-string).

The following options are available on current models:

Add $100 for fretless fingerboard (with or without lines).

Add $100 for BlueStoneBurst, GreenStoneBurst, and RedStoneBurst finishes.

Add $225 for 2TEK bridge.

Add $50 for EMG-DC pickup(s) with active treble/mid/bass controls (BQC).

Add $75 for Bartolini pickups with treble/bass controls (NTBT).

Add $125 for Bartolini pickups with treble/mid/bass controls (NTMB)

There has always been a premium on exotic wood tops throughout the history of Modulus. Here are the current options:

Add $100 for bubinga or purpleheart top (clear finish only).

Add $200 for chakte kok top (clear finish only).

Add $200 (and up) for highly figured quilt or flame maple.

Add $300 for burl or spalted maple (clear finish only).

GRADING		100% MINT	98% NEAR MINT	95% EXC+	90% EXC	80% VG+	70% VG	60% G

Flea Series

FLEA BASS (Model FB4) - offset double cutaway alder body, bolt-on graphite neck, 34" scale, 22-fret phenolic fingerboard with white dot inlay, white (or black) multi-layer pickguard, Gotoh bridge, 4-on-a-side tuners, chrome hardware, Lane Poor MM4 pickup, volume/treble/bass controls, Bartolini NTBT active EQ. Available in Black, Gray, Red, and White Semi-Gloss finishes. Mfg. 1997 to date.

MSR	$1,999	$1,650	$1,500	$1,350	$1,125	$950	$750	$500

Add $50 for Lane Poor MM4 pickup and Bartolini NTMB active EQ (treble/mid/bass controls).

Add $50 for Bartolini MM pickup and Bartolini NTMB active EQ (treble/mid/bass controls).

Add $100 for ABM bridge.

Add $225 for 2TEK bridge.

Add $250 for Blue, Gold, Purple, or Silver Metalflake finish with matching headstock.

This model is also available with Basslines by Seymour Duncan MM pickup and electronics or Bartolini MM pickup/NTBT active EQ at no extra up charge.

Flea Bass 5-String (Model FB5) - similar to the Flea Bass, except has a 5-string configuration. Mfg. 1997 to date.

MSR	$2,199	$1,850	$1,650	$1,425	$1,250	$1,000	$825	$550

J Series

VINTAGE J BASS (Model VJ4/BSJV) - sleek offset double cutaway swamp ash body, bolt-on graphite neck, 34" scale, 21-fret phenolic fingerboard with white dot inlay, Gotoh bridge, 4-on-a-side tuners, tortoiseshell pickguard, chrome hardware, 2 Bartolini J pickups, 2 volume/treble/bass controls. Available in Black, Cream, Green, Red, and White finishes. Mfg. 1994 to date.

MSR	$1,899	$1,425	$1,350	$1,150	$995	$825	$650	$475

In 1996, Green, Red, and White finishes were discontinued. Earlier models may feature 2 EMG-JV pickups and EMG-BTS active electronics.

In 1997, the option of no pickguard/rear-routed controls was offered at no extra premium.

Deluxe J (Model DJ4/BSJV-C) - similar to Vintage J, except has figured maple top, no pickguard (rear-routed body). Available in Amber, Blue, Green, Purple, Red Transparent finishes; Black Cherry, Blue, Blue over Red, Green, Orange Crush, Pink over Blue, Royal Velvet, and Red over Blue Velvet finishes. Mfg. 1994 to 1996.

$1,320	$1,100	$990	$875	$770	$655	$550

Last MSR was $2,199.

M92 Series

M92-4 (Model BSM4) - offset double cutaway alder or poplar body, bolt-on graphite neck, 35" scale, 24-fret phenolic fingerboard with white dot inlay, fixed bridge, 2-per-side tuners, black (or pearloid) pickguard, chrome hardware, EMG-35 DC humbucker pickup, volume/treble/bass controls, active electronics. Mfg. 1994 to 1996.

$1,100	$995	$875	$750	$675	$575	$475

Last MSR was $1,899.

M92-5 (Model BSM5) - similar to M92-4, except has 5 strings, Schaller bridge, 3/2-per-side tuners, EMG-40 DC humbucker pickup. Mfg. 1994 to 1996.

$1,150	$1,000	$950	$850	$725	$625	$525

Last MSR was $2,099.

Genesis MTD Series

The Genesis MTD series was the result of the combined efforts of Modulus Guitars and designer Michael Tobias.

GENESIS MT4 - offset double cutaway alder or light ash body, bolt-on graphite/alder (or graphite/cedar or graphite/spruce) neck, 34" scale, 24-fret granadillo fingerboard with white dot inlay, ABM bridge, 4-on-a-side tuners, black hardware, 2 J-style Bartolini pickups, volume/treble/bass controls. Available in Amber, Blue, Clear Gloss, Clear Satin, Gloss Black, Green, Orange Crush, Purple, and Red finishes. Mfg. 1997 to 1998.

$1,300	$1,150	$1,000	$925	$800	$695	$575

Last MSR was $2,299.

Add $100 for 2-Tone Sunburst, 3-Tone Sunburst, Blue/Green Sunburst, Blue/Purple Sunburst, CherryBurst, or HoneyBurst finish.

Genesis MT5 - similar to the Genesis MT4, except has a 5-string configuration, 35" scale, 22-fret fingerboard, 5-on-a-side tuners. Mfg. 1997 to 1998.

$1,500	$1,250	$1,125	$995	$875	$750	$625

Last MSR was $2,499.

GRADING	100% MINT	98% NEAR MINT	95% EXC+	90% EXC	80% VG+	70% VG	60% G

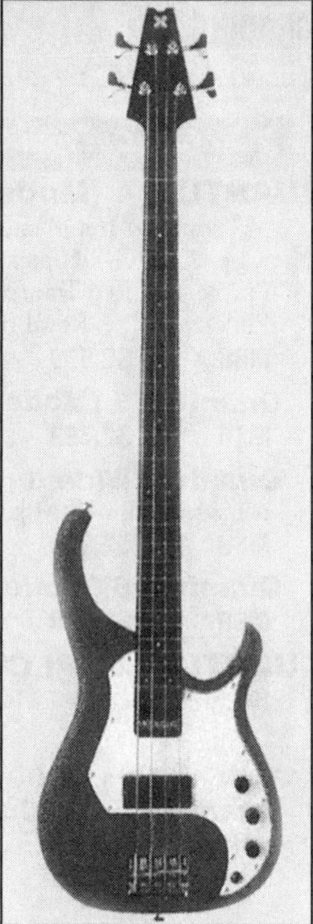

Modulus M92-4
courtesy Modulus Guitars

Oteil Series

OTEIL BASS LIMITED EDITION (Model OB6) - offset double cutaway semi-hollow mahogany body, cedar or spruce top, 'slash'-style f-hole, bolt-on graphite neck, 35" scale, 24-fret phenolic or granadillo fingerboard with white inlay, ABM fixed bridge, 3-per-side tuners, black hardware, 2 Lane Poor 'soapbar' pickups, 2 volume/treble/mid/bass controls. Available in Purpleburst and Deep Transparent Purple finishes. Mfg. 1998 to date.

MSR $3,999

Prime Series

MODULUS PRIME-4 (Model BSP4) - offset double cutaway ash body, bolt-on neck, 24-fret cocabola fingerboard, fixed bridge, 2-per-side tuners, chrome hardware, humbucker pickup, volume/treble/bass controls, active electronics. Available in Natural finish. Mfg. 1994 only.

$1,100	$995	$900	$795	$695	$600	$500

Last MSR was $1,995.

Add $50 for Amber, Blue, Green or Red Clear Color finish.

Add $100 for 2-Tone or Cherry Sunburst finish.

Modulus Prime-5 (Model BSP5) - similar to Modulus Prime-4, except has 5 strings, Schaller bridge, 3/2-per-side tuners. Mfg. 1994 only.

$1,300	$1,100	$995	$875	$750	$675	$550

Last MSR was $2,195.

Modulus Prime-6 (Model BSP6) - similar to Modulus Prime-4, except has 6 strings, APM bridge, 3-per-side tuners. Mfg. 1994 only.

$1,400	$1,250	$1,125	$1,000	$875	$750	$625

Last MSR was $2,495.

SonicHammer Series

The SonicHammer series was originally announced as the **SledgeHammer** series. In 1997, aspects of the SonicHammer design became the foundation for the **Flea Bass**.

SONICHAMMER (SLEDGEHAMMER MODEL SH4) - offset double cutaway alder or swamp ash body, bolt-on graphite neck, 34" scale, 21-fret phenolic fingerboard with white dot inlay, tortoiseshell pickguard, Gotoh bridge, 4-on-a-side tuners, chrome hardware, 3-coil Bartolini pickup, volume/treble/bass controls. Available in Black, Cream, Green, Red, and White finishes. Mfg. 1996 only.

$1,200	$1,100	$995	$895	$775	$650	$550

Last MSR was $2,199.

Deluxe SonicHammer (Deluxe SledgeHammer Model DSH4) - similar to the Sledgehammer, except has a figured maple top, swamp ash body. Available in Amber, Blue, Green, Purple, Red Transparent finishes; Black Cherry, Blue, Blue over Red, Green, Orange Crush, Pink over Blue, Royal Velvet, and Red over Blue Velvet finishes. Mfg. 1996 only.

$1,300	$1,150	$1,000	$950	$850	$725	$600

Last MSR was $2,399.

Quantum Standard Series

QUANTUM 4 SPi STANDARD (Model BSQ4XL) - offset double cutaway alder/poplar body, bolt-on graphite neck, 35" scale, 24-fret fingerboard with white inlay, Modulus/Gotoh fixed bridge, 2-per-side tuners, chrome hardware, 2 active EMG-soapbar pickups, 2 volume/treble/bass controls. Mfg. 1995 to 1996.

$1,300	$1,100	$1,000	$895	$775	$650	$550

Last MSR was $2,199.

The treble/bass controls are concentric in some models.

Quantum 5 SPi Standard (Model BSQ5XL) - similar to Quantum 4 SPi Standard, except has 5 strings, Schaller bridge, 3/2-per-side tuners. Mfg. 1995 to 1996.

$1,400	$1,200	$1,000	$950	$850	$725	$600

Last MSR was $2,399.

Quantum 6 SPi Standard (Model BSQ6XL) - similar to Quantum 4 SPi Standard, except has 6 strings, APM bridge, 3-per-side tuners. Mfg. 1995 to 1996.

$1,500	$1,350	$1,225	$1,000	$950	$800	$675

Last MSR was $2,699.

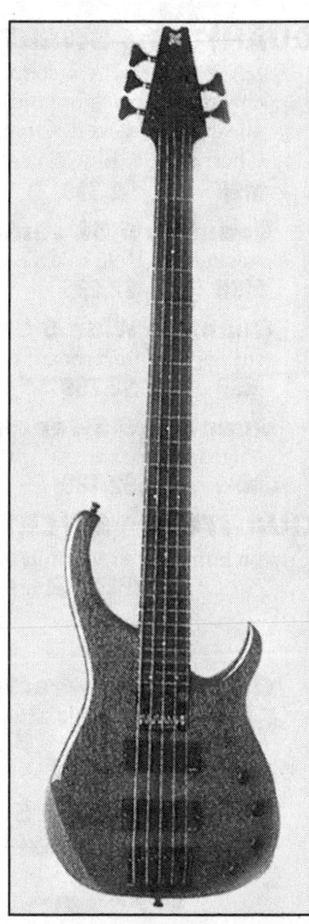

Modulus Quantum 5 SPI Custom
courtesy Modulus Guitars

M

GRADING	100% MINT	98% NEAR MINT	95% EXC+	90% EXC	80% VG+	70% VG	60% G

Quantum Custom Series

QUANTUM 4 (Model Q4) - offset double cutaway alder body, figured maple top, bolt-on graphite neck with relief-adjustment system, 35" scale, 24-fret phenolic or granadillo fingerboard with white inlay, ABM fixed bridge, 2-per-side tuners, chrome (or gold or black) hardware, 2 EMG-DC pickups, volume/balance/treble/bass controls. Available in Amber, Blue, Clear Gloss, Clear Satin, Green, Orange Crush, Purple, and Red Transparent finishes; BlueStone, GrayStone, GreenStone, and RedStone finishes; Black Cherry, Blue, Blue over Red, Green, Pink over Blue, Royal Blue, and Red over Blue Velvet finishes. Mfg. 1996 to date.

MSR	$2,599	$2,000	$1,800	$1,595	$1,350	$1,125	$895	$650

Quantum 5 (Model Q5) - similar to the Quantum 4, except has 5-string configuration, 3/2-per-side headstock. Mfg. 1996 to date.

MSR	$2,799	$2,250	$1,950	$1,700	$1,450	$1,200	$950	$700

Quantum Wide 5 (Model QW5) - similar to the Quantum 4, except has 5-string configuration on a 6-string-sized fingerboard/neck, 3/2-per-side headstock. Mfg. 1996 to date.

MSR	$2,999	$2,400	$2,100	$1,850	$1,550	$1,300	$1,000	$750

Quantum 6 (Model Q6) - similar to the Quantum 4, except has 6-string configuration, 3-per-side headstock. Mfg. 1996 to date.

MSR	$2,999	$2,400	$2,100	$1,850	$1,550	$1,300	$1,000	$750

QUANTUM 4 SPi CUSTOM (Model BSQ4XL-C) - similar to the Quantum 4, except has fixed Modulus/Gotoh bridge, black hardware, 2 active EMG pickups, 2 volume/treble/bass controls. Disc. 1996.

$1,750	$1,375	$1,225	$1,100	$925	$775	$625

Last MSR was $2,499.

Quantum 5 SPi Custom (Model BSQ5XL-C) - similar to Quantum 4 SPi Custom, except has 5 strings, Schaller bridge, 3/2-per-side tuners. Disc. 1996.

$1,600	$1,450	$1,325	$1,150	$995	$850	$675

Last MSR was $2,699.

Quantum 6 SPi Custom (Model BSQ6XL-C) - similar to Quantum 4 SPi Custom, except has 6 strings, APM bridge, 3-per-side tuners. Disc. 1996.

$1,800	$1,650	$1,475	$1,295	$1,100	$925	$750

Last MSR was $2,999.

Quantum SweetSpot Series

QUANTUM 4 SWEETSPOT (Model Q4SS) - offset double cutaway alder body, figured maple top, bolt-on graphite neck with relief-adjustment system, 35" scale, 24-fret composite or granadillo fingerboard with white inlay, ABM fixed bridge, 2-per-side tuners, chrome (or black or gold) hardware, EMG-DC pickup, volume/treble/bass controls, active electronics. Available in Amber, Blue, Clear Gloss, Clear Satin, Green, Orange Crush, Purple, and Red Transparent finishes; BlueStone, GrayStone, GreenStone, and RedStone finishes; Black Cherry, Blue, Blue over Red, Green, Pink over Blue, Royal Blue, and Red over Blue Velvet finishes. Mfg. 1996 to date.

MSR	$2,399	$1,900	$1,650	$1,475	$1,250	$1,000	$825	$600

Quantum 5 SweetSpot (Model Q5SS) - similar to the Quantum 4 SweetSpot, except has 5-string configuration, 3/2-per-side headstock. Mfg. 1996 to date.

MSR	$2,599	$2,100	$1,850	$1,595	$1,350	$1,125	$895	$650

Quantum Wide 5 SweetSpot (Model QW5SS) - similar to the Quantum 4 SweetSpot, except has 5-string configuration on a 6-string- sized fingerboard/neck, 3/2-per-side headstock. Mfg. 1996 to date.

MSR	$2,799	$2,250	$1,950	$1,700	$1,450	$1,200	$950	$700

Quantum 6 SweetSpot (Model Q6SS) - similar to the Quantum 4 SweetSpot, except has 6-string configuration, 3-per-side headstock. Mfg. 1996 to date.

MSR	$2,799	$2,250	$1,950	$1,700	$1,450	$1,200	$950	$700

QUANTUM 4 SWEETSPOT TURBO (Model Q4SST) - similar to the Quantum 4 SweetSpot, except has extra EMG-DC pickup, master volume/balance/treble/bass controls. Available in Amber, Blue, Green, Orange Crush, Purple, Red, and Turquoise Transparent finishes; Black Cherry, Blue, Blue over Red, Green, Pink over Blue, Royal Blue, and Red over Blue Velvet finishes. Mfg. 1996 only.

$1,650	$1,550	$1,375	$1,195	$1,000	$825	$650

Last MSR was $2,599.

Quantum 5 SweetSpot Turbo (Model Q5SST) - similar to the Quantum 4 SweetSpot Turbo, except has 5-string configuration, 3/2-per-side headstock. Mfg. 1996 only.

$1,850	$1,675	$1,495	$1,295	$1,100	$900	$700

Last MSR was $2,799.

Quantum Wide 5 SweetSpot Turbo (Model QW5SST) - similar to the Quantum 4 SweetSpot Turbo, except has 5-string configuration on a 6-string-sized fingerboard/neck, 3/2-per-side headstock. Mfg. 1996 only.

$1,900	$1,750	$1,550	$1,350	$1,125	$900	$750

Last MSR was $2,999.

GRADING	100% MINT	98% NEAR MINT	95% EXC+	90% EXC	80% VG+	70% VG	60% G

Quantum 6 SweetSpot Turbo - similar to the Quantum 4 SweetSpot Turbo, except has 6-string configuration, 3-per-side headstock. Mfg. 1996 only.

$1,950	$1,800	$1,595	$1,375	$1,150	$950	$750

Last MSR was $2,999.

QUANTUM 4 SPi SWEETSPOT CUSTOM (Model BSQ4XL-SS-C) - similar to the Quantum 4 SweetSpot, except has phenolic fingerboard, Modulus/Gotoh fixed bridge, gold or black hardware, volume/treble/bass controls, active electronics. Mfg. 1994 to 1996.

$1,450	$1,150	$1,000	$900	$775	$650	$525

Last MSR was $2,095.

Quantum 5 SPi SweetSpot Custom (Model BSQ5XL-SS-C) - similar to Quantum 4 SPi Sweet Spot Custom, except has 5-string configuration, Schaller bridge, 3/2-per-side tuners. Mfg. 1994 to 1996.

$1,600	$1,275	$1,150	$995	$850	$725	$575

Last MSR was $2,299.

Quantum 6 SPi SweetSpot Custom (Model BSQ6XL-SS-C) - similar to Quantum 4 SPi Sweet Spot Custom, except has 6-string configuration, APM bridge, 3-per-side tuners. Mfg. 1994 to 1996.

$1,650	$1,425	$1,275	$1,150	$975	$800	$650

Last MSR was $2,599.

QUANTUM 4 SPi SWEETSPOT STANDARD (Model BSQ4XL-SS) - similar to the Quantum 4 SPi Sweet Spot Custom, except has alder/poplar body (no figured maple top), chrome hardware. Mfg. 1994 to 1995.

$1,050	$900	$800	$725	$625	$550	$450

Last MSR was $1,799.

Quantum 5 SweetSpot Standard (Model BSQ5XL-SS) - similar to Quantum 4 SPi Sweet Spot Standard, except has 5-string configuration, Schaller bridge, 3/2-per-side tuners. Mfg. 1994 to 1995.

$1,200	$1,000	$900	$800	$700	$600	$500

Last MSR was $1,999.

Quantum 6 SPi SweetSpot Standard (Model BSQ6XL-SS) - similar to Quantum 4 SPi Sweet Spot Standard, except has 6-string configuration, APM bridge, 3-per-side tuners. Mfg. 1994 to 1996.

$1,350	$1,150	$1,050	$925	$800	$695	$575

Last MSR was $2,299.

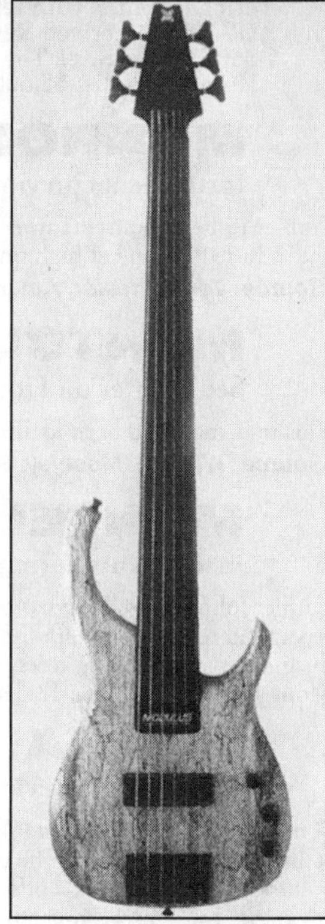

Modulus Quantum 6 SPI Sweetspot Fretless courtesy Modulus Guitars

Quantum Thru-Body Series

Beginning in 1996, neck-through bass and guitar models were available on a custom order basis only.

QUANTUM 4 TBX (Model BIQ4XL) - offset double cutaway alder body, figured maple top, through-body graphite neck, 35" scale, 24-fret phenolic fingerboard with white dot inlay, fixed Modulus/Gotoh bridge, graphite/epoxy nut, 2-per-side Modulus/Gotoh tuners, gold hardware, 2 EMG soapbar humbuckers, 2 volume/treble/bass controls, active EMG-BQCS EQ. Disc. 1996.

$2,750	$2,400	$2,100	$1,800	$1,550	$1,225	$925

Last MSR was $3,699.

Some models may have concentric ("stacked") treble/bass controls.

Quantum 5 TBX (Model BIQ5XL) - similar to 4 TBX, except has 5-string configuration, ABM or Schaller bridge, 3/2-per-side tuners. Disc. 1996.

$3,000	$2,675	$2,350	$2,000	$1,695	$1,350	$1,000

Last MSR was $4,099.

Quantum 6 TBX (Model BIQ6XL) - similar to 4 TBX, except has 6-string configuration, ABM or Kahler bridge, 3-per-side tuners. Mfg. 1992 to 1996.

$3,350	$2,950	$2,575	$2,200	$1,850	$1,495	$1,150

Last MSR was $4,499.

MOLL CUSTOM INSTRUMENTS

Instruments currently built in Springfield, Missouri.

Luthier Bill Moll is currently offering premium custom crafted archtop guitars, carved archtop bass guitars, and solid body electric bass models, as well as repair and restoration services for stringed instruments. Much of Moll's training since 1975 has been in the specific application of acoustical physics, so instruments are built to perform acoustically before electronics are considered. Denise Moll has also been studying lutherie with her husband since 1997, and contributes greatly to the output of the shop. They are one of the few married couples building as a team. Moll still builds custom solid body basses in limited numbers. For more information, including a free color brochure, please contact Bill or Denise Moll directly (see Trademark Index).

Moll Custom Instruments offers 4 archtop models in 16", 17" or 18" lower bout, (a 19" concert grand is optional), and 2 laminated archtop models in 16" or 17" sizes. The Classic (list $3,000, add $300 for 7-string) has a solid carved X-braced spruce top, solid carved maple back/sides/neck, ebony fingerboard, solid brass tailpiece, and Gotoh tuners. The Express (list $5,000, add $500 for 7-string) is a modern

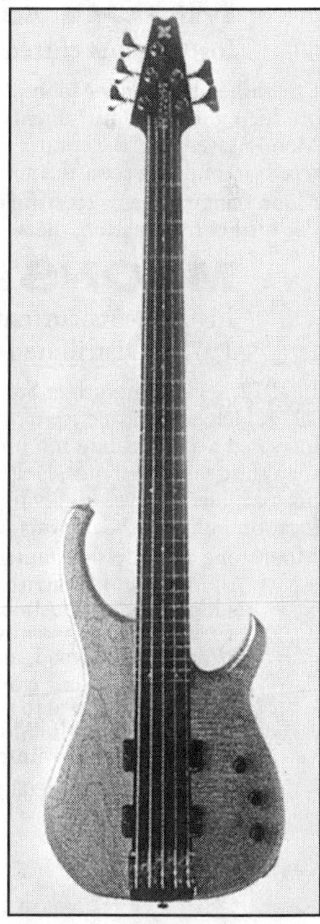

Modulus Quantum 5 TBX courtesy Modulus Guitars

M

design archtop with teardrop-shaped soundholes and no extraneous binding. The Classic Custom (list $5,500, $500 for 7-string). The D'Angelico-derived New Yorker has the fancy inlays and 'stairstep' bridge and pickguard that most jazz players lust after (list $6,500, $500 for 7-string). The John Pizzarelli Model comes in 6-string (list $3,500), and 7-string (list $3,750) variations. The basic Working Class Hero model (list $2,500) is also available in 7-string (list $2,750).

MONROE

Instruments previously built near El Paso, Texas circa late 1980s-1999.

Luthier Robert Monroe Turner was a former apprentice to **Guitar Player** columnist and repairer Dan Erlewine. Turner founded Monroe Guitars in 1988 and debuted his line of high quality, solid body electrics at the 1989 NAMM Show.
(Source: Tom Wheeler, American Guitars)

MONTCLAIR

See chapter on House brands.

This trademark has been identified as a *House Brand* of Montgomery Wards.
(Source: Willie G. Moseley, Stellas & Stratocasters)

MONTELEONE, JOHN

Instruments currently built in Islip, New York.

Luthier John Monteleone has been building guitars and mandolins for almost three decades. A contemporary of James D'Aquisto, Monteleone performed repair and restoration work for a number of years while formulating his own archtop designs. Monteleone's archtop guitars feature such unique ideas as a flush-set truss rod cover, recessed tuning machine retainers, and a convex radiused headstock. For further information, please contact luthier John Monteleone directly (see Trademark Index).

MONZA

Instruments previously built in Holland, circa unknown.

While Monza guitars sports a *Made in Holland* sticker on the back of the headstock, the electronics and tailpiece/bridge on one identified model are clearly Italian (possibly 1960s?). The instrument features 20-fret neck, six on a side headstock and tuners, two pickups, a tremolo/bridge unit, 3 switches, 3 volume/tone knobs, and a offset double cutaway with a scroll on the bass horn reminiscent of the 1960s Premier guitars.
(Source: Teisco Del Rey, Guitar Player, February 1984)

MOON

Instruments currently built in Japan. Distributed in the U.S. market by the Luthiers Access Group of Chicago, Illinois.

The Moon corporation is known primarily for their modern take on the traditional *jazz*-style bass originated by Leo Fender. The last few years has seen Moon develop new modern design basses to compliment these jazz basses. The Climb series, and GLB line offer new choices from Japan's premier bass builder.

MOON GUITARS LTD.

Instruments currently built in Glascow, Scotland.

Established by Jimmy Moon in 1979, the **Moon Guitars** name has become synonymous with custom built instruments of very high quality as they are producing modern instruments with strong traditional roots. Originally, Moon Guitars produced acoustic guitars, mandolins, mandolas, and dulcimers. Moon moved into the electric market during the eighties, producing for an impressive client list of famous names. A shift in the market pre-emptied a return to building acoustics and mandolins (while continuing with custom built electrics, basses, and electric mandolins).
Moon Guitars' latest successful development is the Moon *electro acoustic* mandolin, which comes in various body shapes with a piezo-based pickup system. For further information, please contact Moon Guitars Ltd. directly (see Trademark Index).

MOONSTONE

Instruments currently built in Eureka, California (guitar production has been in different locations in California since 1972). Distributed directly by Moonstone Guitars of Eureka, California.

In 1972, self-taught luthier Steve Helgeson began building acoustic instruments in an old shingle mill located in Moonstone Heights, California. By 1974, Helgeson moved to Arcata, California, and began producing electric Earth Axe guitars. By 1976, Helgeson had moved to a larger shop and increased his model line and production. Helgeson hit boom sales in the early 1980s, but tapered off production after the market shifted in 1985. Rather than shift with the trends, Helgeson preferred to maintain his own designs. In 1988, a major disaster in the form of a deliberately set fire damaged some of his machinery. Steve's highly figured wood supply survived only a minor scorching. Helgeson moved and reopened his workshop in 1990 at the current location in Eureka, California, where he now offers a wide range of acoustic and electric guitars and basses. In addition to the standard models, Moonstone also offers custom guitars designed in accordance with the customer's request. All current prices include a hardshell case.

All Moonstone instruments are constructed from highly figured woods. Where burl wood was not used in the construction, the wood used is highly figured. Almost all necks are reinforced with veneers, or stringers. Bass necks are reinforced with through-body graphite stringers. Moonstone has always utilized exotic woods such as African purpleheart, paduak, wenge, koa, mahogany, Sitka and Engelmann spruce, Myrtlewood, and black burl walnut.

Some older models can also be found with necks entirely made of graphite composite with phenolic fingerboards. Helgeson commissioned Modulus Graphite to produce these necks, and used them on models like the Eclipse Standard, Deluxe Basses, Vulcan Standard and Deluxe guitars, the M-80, D-81 Eagle 6- and 12- string models, as well as the D-81 Standard and the *Moondolin* (mandolin). In 1981, most wood necks were reinforced with a Graphite Aluminum Honeycomb Composite (G.A.H.C.) beam with stainless steel adjustment rod.

For further information regarding current acoustic guitar models, please refer to the 7th Edition ***Blue Book of Acoustic Guitars***.

GRADING	100% MINT	98% NEAR MINT	95% EXC+	90% EXC	80% VG+	70% VG	60% G

Moonstone Eagle
courtesy Steve Helgeson

ELECTRIC

EAGLE - double cutaway hand carved burl maple body, 5-piece maple/padauk neck, 24-fret padauk bound ebony fingerboard with pearl bird inlay, LQBA bridge/tailpiece, walnut burl peghead veneer with pearl half-moon/logo inlay, 3-per-side tuners, gold hardware, 2 humbucker Bartolini pickups, 2 volume/1 tone controls, 3-position switch, push/pull preamp switch in volume control, active electronics. Available in Natural finish. Mfg. 1980 to 1984.

$3,250 $2,650 $2,190 $N/A $N/A $N/A $N/A
Last MSR was $2,780.

A licensed falconer, Helgeson's inspiration for this model came from the training and hunting with his raptors. Only 11 of these guitars were built in this series.

EAGLE LIMITED EDITION - double cutaway hand carved burl maple body, (127 individual hand carved feathers) 5-piece maple/padauk neck, 24-fret bound ebony fingerboard with Moonstone original pearl bird inlay, bridge/tailpiece, walnut burl peghead veneer with pearl halfmoon/logo inlay, 3-per-side tuners, gold hardware, 2 humbucker Bartolini pickups, 2 volume/2 tone controls, 3-position switch, active electronics. Available in Natural finish. Current Mfg.

MSR $7,480

Eclipse Series

ECLIPSE DELUXE - offset double cutaway padauk core body, bookmatch burl top/back, through-body 2-piece maple neck, 24-fret bound ebony fingerboard with pearl diamond/star inlay, LQBA bridge/tailpiece, burl walnut peghead veneer with pearl halfmoon/logo inlay, 3-per-side tuners, gold hardware, 2 humbucker covered Bartolini pickups, 2 volume/2 tone controls, 3-position/phase switches. Available in Natural finish. Mfg. 1979 to 1983.

$1,000 $850 $750 $675 $600 $525 $425
Last MSR was $1,435.

ECLIPSE STANDARD - offset double cutaway mahogany core body, bookmatch burl top/back, through-body 2-piece maple neck, 24-fret rosewood fingerboard with pearl dot inlay, LQBA bridge/tailpiece, burl wood peghead veneer with screened logo, 3-per-side tuners, gold hardware, 2 humbucker covered Bartolini pickups, 2 volume/tone controls, 3-position/phase switches. Available in Natural finish. Mfg. 1979 to 1983.

$875 $725 $660 $585 $535 $475 $400
Last MSR was $1,215.

Eclipse Standard 12 - similar to Standard except has 12 strings, Leo Quan tunable bridge, 6-per-side tuners.

$925 $770 $700 $600 $550 $500 $425
Last MSR was $1,325.

Eclipse Standard Doubleneck - similar to the Standard and the Standard 12 (two necks sharing the same body) with each neck having separate electronics and a 3-position neck selector.

$1,800 $1,425 $1,050 $825 $750 $675 $625
Last MSR was $2,055.

EXPLODER - radical offset hour glass burl wood body, through-body 2-piece maple neck, 24-fret rosewood fingerboard with pearl dot inlay, LQBA bridge/tailpiece, figured wood peghead veneer with screened logo, 3-per-side tuners, gold hardware, 2 humbucker covered Bartolini pickups, 2 volume/1 tone controls, 3-position/phase switches. Available in Natural finish. Mfg. 1980 to 1983.

$975 $780 $785 $585 $550 $520 $490
Last MSR was $965.

This model had DiMarzio pickups as an option.

Moonstone M-80 Custom
courtesy Steve Helgeson

FLAMING V - V-style burl wood body, through-body 2-piece maple neck, 24-fret rosewood fingerboard with pearl dot inlay, LQBA bridge/tailpiece, figured wood peghead veneer with screened logo, 3-per-side tuners, gold hardware, 2 humbucker covered Bartolini pickups, 2 volume/1 tone controls, 3-position/phase switches. Available in Natural finish. Mfg. 1980 to 1984.

$875 $780 $685 $585 $450 $420 $390
Last MSR was $965.

DiMarzio pickups were an option.

M

GRADING	100% MINT	98% NEAR MINT	95% EXC+	90% EXC	80% VG+	70% VG	60% G

M-80 - double cutaway semi hollow body, carved figured maple top/back/sides, f-holes, raised multi layer black pickguard, bound body, 2-piece figured maple neck, 24-fret bound ebony fingerboard with abalone snowflake inlay, LQBA bridge/tailpiece, figured wood peghead veneer with abalone halfmoon/logo inlay, 3-per-side tuners, gold hardware, 2 covered Bartolini humbucker pickups, 2 volume/tone controls, 3-position/phase switches. Available in Natural finish. Mfg. 1980 to 1984.

$1,200 $1,000 $850 $675 $600 $560 $500

Last MSR was $1,690.

Burl walnut pickguard, tunable bridge/tailpiece, PAF pickups, Orange-Honey finish and Tobacco Burst finish were an option.

M-80 REISSUE - double cutaway semi-hollow (with sustain block through-body) or hollow-body (bracing carved in) body, carved figured maple top/back/sides, 25 1/2" scale, f-holes, 2-piece quarterswan hard maple neck, 22-fret bound ebony fingerboard with abalone starflake inlay, tailpiece, ebony peghead veneer with abalone halfmoon/mother-of-pearl logo inlay, 3-per-side Schaller tuners, gold hardware, 2 Seymour Duncan pickups, 2 volume/2 tone controls, 3-position/phase switches. Available in Natural finish.

MSR $3,520

Add $275 for Sunburst finish.

This model is optional with cat's-eye f-holes, pickguard, tune-o-matic bridge/stop tailpiece, pickup selection, and Sunburst or Color toner finishes.

PULSAR - mini radical offset hourglass alder body, black pickguard, maple neck, 24-fret rosewood fingerboard with pearl dot inlay, LQBA bridge/tailpiece, blackface peghead with screened logo, 3-per-side tuners, gold hardware, DiMarzio (or Lawrence) pickup, volume/tone control. Available in Black finish. Mfg. 1980 to 1983.

$850 $675 $600 $525 $475 $400 $350

Last MSR was $810.

PULSAR STANDARD REISSUE similar to Pulsar, available in Natural and Sunburst finish. New 2000.

MSR $2,530

Add $275 for Sunburst finish.

Vulcan Series

VULCAN DELUXE - double cutaway carved burl maple body, 5-piece maple/padauk neck, 24-fret bound ebony fingerboard with pearl diamond/star inlay, LQBA bridge/tailpiece, burl walnut peghead veneer with pearl halfmoon/logo inlay, 3-per-side tuners, gold hardware, 2 humbucker covered Bartolini pickups, master volume/2 volume/2 tone controls, 5 position tone control, 3-position/boost switches, active electronics. Available in Natural finish. Mfg. 1977 to 1984.

$1,175 $1,000 $850 $675 $600 $550 $500

Last MSR was $1,680.

VULCAN STANDARD - double cutaway mahogany body, bound carved bookmatch burl maple top, 2-piece maple neck, 24-fret rosewood fingerboard with pearl dot inlay, LQBA bridge/tailpiece, burl maple peghead veneer with screened logo, 3-per-side tuners, gold hardware, 2 humbucker covered Bartolini pickups, 2 volume/tone controls, 3-position/phase switches. Available in Natural finish. Mfg. 1977 to 1984.

$875 $725 $600 $500 $450 $400 $365

Last MSR was $1,215.

VULCAN STANDARD REISSUE - dual cutaway mahogany body, carved flamed or quilted maple top, set-in mahogany neck, 22-fret bound fingerboard with pearl dot inlay, stop-ABR tailpiece, 3-per-side Grover tuners, gold hardware, 2 Seymour Duncan humbucker pickups, 2 volume/2 tone controls, 3-position switch. Available in Natural finish. Current Mfg.

MSR $2,530

Add $275 for Sunburst finish.

This model is optional with a Madagascar rosewood fretboard, PAF pickups, nickel hardware, and Cherry Mahogany or Honey Sunburst finishes.

Z-80 REISSUE - dual cutaway semi-hollow (parabolic baffles under bridge) body, Englemann spruce "floating" top, 2 7/8" thick rims with *Grill* soundholes in the cutaways, 25 1/2" scale, 2-piece quarterswan figured hard maple neck, 22-fret bound ebony fingerboard with abalone starflake inlay, trapeze tailpiece/ABR1 tune-o-matic bridge, ebony peghead veneer with abalone halfmoon/mother-of-pearl logo inlay, 3-per-side Schaller tuners, gold hardware, 2 Seymour Duncan humbucker pickups, volume/tone controls, 3-position switch. Available in Natural finish.

MSR $4,620+ (base price only)

This reissue is based on the model Helgeson designed in the mid 1980s (only two of the original series were built).

ELECTRIC BASS

Moonstone still offers Exploder & Flaming V models. These are special order custom designed models whose price must be quoted individually upon request.

M-80 BASS - offset double cutaway semi-hollow body, carved flame maple top, mahogany body wings, 35" scale, 2 f-holes, through-body 5-piece maple/purpleheart neck, 22-fret bound ebony fingerboard with abalone large diamond inlay, Alembic tailpiece, 3/2-per-side Schaller tuners, gold hardware, 2 Alembic pickups, 2 volume/2 tone controls, 3-position switch, Alembic electronics. Available in Natural finish.

MSR $3,520 (4-string)

Add $275 for 5-string model.

GRADING	100% MINT	98% NEAR MINT	95% EXC+	90% EXC	80% VG+	70% VG	60% G

ECLIPSE DELUXE - offset double cutaway padauk core body, bookmatch burl top/back, through-body 2-piece maple neck, 24-fret bound ebony fingerboard 24-fret bound ebony fingerboard with pearl diamond/star inlay, fixed bridge, burl walnut peghead veneer with pearl halfmoon/logo inlay, 2-per-side tuners, gold hardware, 2 J-style Bartolini pickups, 2 volume/tone controls, 3-position/phase switches. Available in Natural finish. Mfg. 1980 to 1984.

$1,050 $895 $750 $600 $540 $495 $450
Last MSR was $1,495.

Eclipse Standard - offset double cutaway mahogany core body, bookmatch burl top/back, through-body 3-piece maple/padauk neck with graphite stringers, 24-fret rosewood fingerboard with pearl dot inlay, fixed bridge, burl maple peghead veneer with screened logo, 2-per-side tuners, gold hardware, 2 J-style Bartolini pickups, 2 volume/tone controls, phase switch. Available in Natural finish. Mfg. 1980 to 1984.

$900 $775 $645 $525 $465 $425 $385
Last MSR was $1,295.

EXPLODER - radical offset hour glass burl wood body, through-body 3-piece maple/padauk neck with graphite stringers, 24-fret rosewood fingerboard with pearl dot inlay, fixed bridge, burl maple peghead veneer with screened logo, 2-per-side tuners, gold hardware, 2 J-style Bartolini pickups, 2 volume/1 tone controls, 3-position/phase switches. Available in Natural finish. Mfg. 1980 to 1983.

$875 $750 $625 $500 $450 $400 $375
Last MSR was $1,265.

FLAMING V - V-style burl wood body, through-body 3-piece maple/padauk neck with graphite stringers, 24-fret rosewood fingerboard with pearl dot inlay, fixed bridge, maple burl peghead veneer with screened logo, 2-per-side tuners, gold hardware, 2 J-style Bartolini pickups, 2 volume/1 tone controls, 3-position/phase switches. Available in Natural finish. Mfg. 1981.

$875 $750 $625 $500 $450 $400 $375
Last MSR was $1,265.

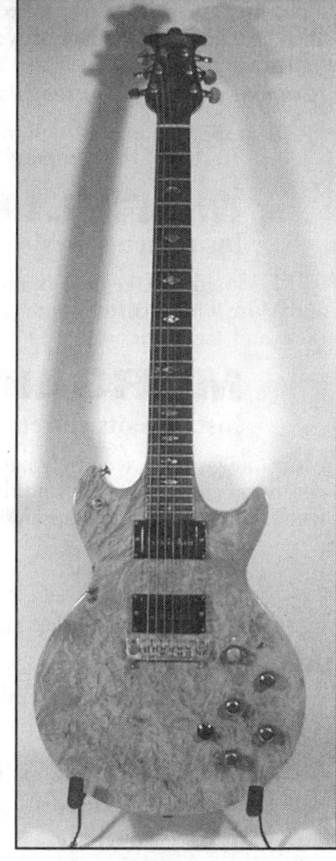

Moonstone Vulcan
courtesy Fly By Nite Music

NEPTUNE - carved figured maple top, swamp ash wings, 5-piece hard rock maple, purple heart stringers, boundy ebony fretboard, graphite reinforced adj. truss rod, ebony head veneer inlaid with mother-of-pearl and abalone crescent, Schaller tuners, Bartollini active pickups and tone circuit, gold ABM bridge. New 2000.

4-String
MSR $3,400
Add $675 for Burst and Thunderbird inlays.

5-String
MSR $3,675
Add $675 for Burst and Thunderbird inlays.

VULCAN - double cutaway burl maple body, 3-piece maple/padauk neck, 24-fret bound ebony fingerboard with pearl diamond/star inlay, fixed bridge, burl walnut peghead veneer with pearl halfmoon/logo inlay, 2-per-side tuners, gold hardware, humbucker covered Bartolini "P" pickup, 2 volume/tone controls, active tone circuit. Available in Natural finish. Mfg. 1982 to 1984.

$750 $625 $525 $475 $425 $350 $300
Last MSR was $1,055.

Vulcan II - similar to Vulcan, except has carved top.

$850 $695 $575 $500 $445 $380 $345
Last MSR was $1,155.

MORALES

Instruments previously produced in Japan by Zen-On circa late 1960s.

The Morales product line offered thinline hollowbody acoustic/electric and hollowbody electric guitars, as well as solid body electric guitars, basses, and mandolins. This brand may not have been imported into the U.S. market.
(Source: Michael Wright, Vintage Guitar Magazine)

MORCH GUITARS

Instruments currently built in Orsted, Denmark since 1970.

In 1970 Johnny Morch started to manufacture electric guitars in cooperation with his father, Arne Morch. The first standard models were made in great numbers in a sort of handmade "batch" production: a carpenter made the body, a painter did the lacquer-work, an engraver cut out the pickguard, and the rest was made by Morch himself (assembling, adjustment, and final delivery to the music shops for retail).
In the middle of 1970 Morch started to cooperate with the guitarist Thomas Puggard-Muller, who designed Morch's "curl"-models which were later published in the Danish Design Index and thus shown all over the world. For years Thomas was involved with the firm, and his close contact with the professional world of music has sold Morch instruments to a great many well-known musicians at home as well as abroad.

Moonstone Vulcan (Reissue)
courtesy Steve Helgeson

M

Since then the firm has expanded in the opposite way of most other companies. Now the entire production takes place exclusively in Morch's workshop, and there is a close contact between the musician and the craftsman. All instruments are literally handmade and adjusted exactly to the needs of the individual musician.

(Company history courtesy Johnny Morch, Morch Guitars)

Importation of Morch instruments to Britain began in 1976. These models may be found in greater abundance in Europe than in the U.S. Currently, the company is offering 2 guitar models, and 4-, 5-, and 6-string bass models. Prices range from $2,600 up to $3,200.

MORELLI, C. M.

Instruments previously built in Port Chester, New York.

C. M. Morelli offered custom models that featured various body and neck materials, hardware, pickup, and finish options. Retail prices started at $1,899, and Morelli built custom body and headstock shapes, 4-, 6-, 8-, 10-, 12-string and double-neck models. C. M. Morelli also offered custom imprinted picks and accessories.

MORGAINE

Instruments currently built in Boppard, Germany. Distributed by CMS (Cotton Music Supply) in Oberursel, Germany.

Morgaine guitars are entirely handmade by experienced Master Luthier Jorg Tandler. Necks are carved the traditional way with a draw knife, body contours carefully shaped, and the arched tops are chiseled similar to the way violin makers carve violin tops. Morgaine guitars feature hand selected woods, Lindy Fralin pickups, Wilkinson VSV tremolos, Schaller or Gotoh tuners, and nitrocellulose lacquer finishes.

ELECTRIC

Morgaine standard finishes include 2-Tone, Cherry, or Tobacco Sunburst finishes. Custom colors include Fiesta Red, Surf Green, and Vintage White.

AUSTIN - Honduran mahogany body/neck, 22-fret Indian rosewood fingerboard with pearl dot inlay, vintage bone nut, tune-o-matic bridge, custom wound Lindy Fralin bridge pickup, volume/tone controls. Mfg. 1997 to date.

MSR **$2,500**

BEAUTY - Honduran mahogany body/neck, American soft maple top, bound Brazilian rosewood fingerboard, 2 custom wound Lindy Fralin humbucker pickups, volume/tone controls. Available in Faded Cherry Sunburst and Tobacco Sunburst finishes. Mfg. 1995 to date.

MSR **$4,195**

STRAT '54 - swamp ash body, hard rock maple neck, 22-fret maple fingerboard, vintage bone nut, Wilkinson VSV tremolo, 3 custom wound Lindy Fralin pickups, volume/tone controls. Available in Sunburst and all custom finishes. Mfg. 1994 to date.

MSR **$3,195**

Strat '57 - similar to Strat '54, except features alder body. Available in Sunburst and all custom finishes. Mfg. 1994 to date.

MSR **$3,195**

Strat '61 - similar to Strat '54, except features alder body, 22-fret Brazilian rosewood fingerboard. Available in Sunburst and all custom finishes. Mfg. 1994 to date.

MSR **$3,195**

MORIDAIRA

See also MORRIS.

Instruments currently produced in Japan.

The Moridaira company is an OEM manufacturer of guitars for other companies, under different trademark names. The company has produced a wide range of entry level to very good quality guitars through the years, depending on the outside company's specifications. Further research continues for upcoming editions of the *Blue Book of Electric Guitars.*

MORRIS

Instruments currently produced in Korea. Distributed by the Moridaira company of Tokyo, Japan.

The Moridaira company offers a wide range of acoustic and solid body electric guitars designed for the beginning student up to the intermediate player under the Morris trademark. Moridaira has also built guitars (OEM) under other trademarks for a number of other guitar companies.

MORTORO, GARY

Instruments currently built in Miami, Florida since 1991.

Luthier Gary Mortoro has been building handcrafted instruments since 1991, under the guidance and direction of Master Luthier and Archtop Builder Robert Benedetto. Gary's dedication to the crafting of his guitars combined with his playing ability has resulted in an instrument not only of fine detail and craftsmanship, but of exquisite sound and beauty. Some of the players who own a Mortoro are George Benson, Tony Mottola, Jimmy Vivino, Rodney Jones, Gene Bertoncini, Joe Cinderella, and Jimmy Buffet.

Mortoro currently offers six different models that are available in carved and laminate versions. For further information, please contact Gary Mortoro directly (see Trademark Index).
The Free Flight retails for $6,500 (carved) and $4,500 (laminate).
The Songbird retails for $8,400 (carved) and $5,000 (laminate).
The Starling retails for $7,800 (carved) and $5,000 (laminate).
The Free Bird retails for $6,500 (carved) and $4,500 (laminate).
The Parrot retails for $7,200 (carved) and $5,000 (laminate).
The Small Starling retails for $7,300 (carved) and $5,000 (laminate).

MOSCATO

Instruments currently built in Uchaux, France.

Jean-Luc Moscato's namesake company offers a number of high quality, unique design electric guitars and basses. Moscato, ably assisted by Paul Lairat, Antoine Drescher, and Jean-Philippe Hubin, produces ornate laminated curved body guitars like the Flame, the **Legend**, and the **Devil In You**; and basses like the **Funk Bass** and the **Legend Bass**. For further information regarding specifications and pricing, please contact Moscato directly (see Trademark Index).

NEAL MOSER GUITARS

Please refer to the N section in this text.

MOSES GRAPHITE MUSICAL INSTRUMENTS

Instruments currently produced in Eugene, Oregon.

Stephen Mosher has been offering high quality replacement graphite necks for several years. Moses, Inc. lists a large number of graphite necks available for 4-, 5-, and 6-string bass, baritone guitars, and 6-string guitars.

ELECTRIC BASS

Moses also produces the **KP Series** graphite upright basses, available in 4-, 5-, and 6-string configurations and a 42-inch scale. Moses Graphite is a full service custom shop, and offers additional luthier supplies. For further information regarding pricing, models, and availability, please contact Moses, Inc. directly (see Trademark Index).

MOSRITE

Instruments previously produced in Bakersfield, California during the 1960s; earlier models built in Los Angeles, California during the mid to late 1950s. Distribution in the 1990s was handled by Unified Sound Association, Inc. Production of Mosrite guitars ceased in 1994.

There were other factory sites around the U.S. during the 1970s and 1980s: other notable locations include Carson City, Nevada; Jonas Ridge, North Carolina; and Booneville, Arkansas (previous home of Baldwin-operated Gretsch production during the 1970s).

Mortoro Parrot
courtesy Mortoro Guitars

Luthier/designer Semie Moseley (1935-1992) was born in Durant, Oklahoma. The family moved to Bakersfield, California when Moseley was 9 years old, and Semie left school in the seventh grade to travel with an evangelistic group playing guitar.

Moseley, 18, was hired by Paul Barth to work at Rickenbacker in 1953. While at Rickenbacker, Moseley worked with Roger Rossmeisl. Rossmeisl's "German carve" technique was later featured on Moseley's guitar models as well. Moseley was later fired from Rickenbacker in 1955 for building his own guitar at their facilities. In the later years, Moseley always credited Barth and Rossmeisl (and the Rickenbacker company) for his beginning knowledge in guitar building.

With the help of Reverend Ray Boatright, who cosigned for guitar building tools at Sears, Moseley began building his original designs. The Mosrite trademark is named after Moseley and Boatright ("-rite"). After leaving Rickenbacker, Moseley built custom instruments for various people around southern California, most notably Joe Maphis (of "Town Hall Party" fame). Moseley freelanced some work with Paul Barth's "Barth" guitars, as well as some neck work for Paul Bigsby.

After traveling for several months with another gospel group, Moseley returned to Bakersfield and again set up shop. Moseley built around 20 guitars for Bob Crooks (STANDEL). When Crooks asked for a Fender-styled guitar model, Moseley flipped a Stratocaster over, traced the rough outline, and built the forerunner to the "Ventures" model!

After Nokie Edwards (Ventures) borrowed a guitar for a recording session, Stan Wagner (Ventures Manager) called Moseley to propose a business collaboration. Mosrite would produce the instruments, and use the Venture's organization as the main distributor. The heyday of the Mosrite company was the years between 1963 and 1969. When the demand set in, the company went from producing 35 guitars a month to 50 and later 300. The Mosrite facility had 105 employees at one point, and offered several different models in addition to the Ventures model (such as the semi-hollowbody Celebrity series, the Combo, and the Joe Maphis series).

In 1963, investors sold the Dobro trademark to Moseley, who built the first 100 or 150 out of parts left over from the Dobro plant in Gardenia. Later Bakersfield Dobros can be identified by the serial number imprinted on the end of the fingerboard. The Mosrite company did not build the amplifiers which bear the Mosrite trademark; another facility built the Mosrite amplifiers and fuzz pedals, and paid for the rights to use the Mosrite name.

The amplifier line proved to be the undoing of Mosrite. While some of the larger amplifiers are fine, one entry level model featured a poor design and a high failure rate. While covering for returns, the Ventures organization used up their line of credit at their bank, and the bank shut down the organization. In doing so, the Mosrite distribution was shut down as well. Moseley tried a deal with Vox (Thomas Organ) but the company was shut down in 1969. Moseley returned to the Gospel music circuit, and transferred the Dobro name to OMI in a series of negotiations.

Between the mid 1970s and the late 1980s, Moseley continued to find backers and sporadically build guitars. In 1972, Guitar Player magazine reported that "Semie Moseley is now working with Reinhold Plastics, Inc. to produce Mosrite of California guitars." Later that year, Moseley set up a tentative deal with Bud Ross at Kustom (Kustom Amplifiers) in Chanute, Kansas. Moseley was going to build a projected 200 guitars a month at his 1424 P Street location, and Ross' Kustom Electronics was going to be the distributor. This deal fell through, leaving Moseley free to strike up another deal in April of 1974 with Pacific Music Supply Company of Los Angeles, California. Pacific Music Supply Company had recently lost their Guild account, and was looking for another guitar line to distribute. One primary model in 1974 was the solid body Model 350 Stereo. The **Brass Rail** model was developed around 1976/1977. While shopping around his new model with "massive sustain", Moseley met a dealer in Hollywood Music in Los Angeles. This dealer had connections in Japan, and requested that Moseley begin recreating the original-style Ventures models. Moseley set out to build 35 to 50 of these reproductions per month for a number of months. Several years after Moseley recovered

Mortoro Small Startling
courtesy Mortoro Guitars

GRADING	100% MINT	98% NEAR MINT	95% EXC+	90% EXC	80% VG+	70% VG	60% G

from an illness in 1983, he began rebuilding his dealer network with a number of models like the **V-88**, **M-88**, and **Ventures 1960's Reissues**. These models were built at his Jonas Ridge location.

Moseley's final guitar production was located in Booneville, Arkansas. The Unified Sound Association was located in a converted Walmart building, and an estimated 90% to 95% of production was earmarked for the Japanese market.

Moseley passed away in 1992. His two biggest loves were Gospel music, and building quality guitars. Throughout his nearly forty year career, he continued to persevere in his guitar building. Unified Sound Association stayed open through 1994 under the direction of Loretta Moseley, and then later closed its doors as well.

(Information courtesy of Andy Moseley and Hal Hammer [1996]; additional information courtesy Willie G. Moseley, Stellas and Stratocasters, and Tom Wheeler, American Guitars; Mosrite catalogs and file information courtesy John Kinnemeyer, JK Lutherie; model dating estimations courtesy Carlos Juan, Collectables & Vintage '95, Stuttgart, Germany)

Mosrite guitars are easily identifiable by the "M" notch in the top of the headstock. Mosrite models produced in the 1960s have a "M" initial in a edged circle, and "Mosrite" (in block letters) "of California" (in smaller script) logo.

Contrary to vintage guitar show information in the current "Age of Fendermania", Mosrite instruments were not available in those (rare) Fender finishes like "Candy Apple Red" and "Lake Placid Blue". Catalog colors were identified as Blue or Red. Mosrite did offer option colored finishes like Metallic Blue and Metallic Red.

Vibrato Identification

Semie's designs offered numerous innovations, most notable being the Vibra-Mute vibrato. This item was designed for the Ventures models and can be used to help identify early Mosrite instruments. The early vibratos (pre-1977) have Vibra-Mute and Mosrite on them, while later vibratos have Mosrite alone on them. More distinction can be made among the earliest instruments with Vibra-Mutes by observing the casting technique used. While the early vibratos were sand-cast, later units were die cast (once funding was available).

Model Designation Description

During the heyday of Mosrite production in Bakersfield, model designations in the catalog would list a **Mark I** to designate a 6-string model, **Mark XII** to indicate the 12-string version, and **Mark X** to designate the bass model within a series. These Mark designations are a forerunner to - but not the same usage as - the later **1967-1969 Mark** "No Logo" series.

Mosrite Production Dates

Mosrite models in this edition of the ***Blue Book of Electric Guitars*** feature estimated dates of production for each model. Just as it is easy to take for granted a sunny day in the Summer until it rains, most dealers and collectors take a Mosrite model as "Just a Mosrite" without really double checking the true nature of which model it really is. Of course, the corollary of this way of thinking is to assume that the Mosrite in question is going to end up in the Far East with the rest of them! Is Johnny Ramone the only current American guitar player to use these guitars? Are there no mega-Mosrite collectors? Ventures fans unite!

The ***Blue Book of Electric Guitars*** is actively seeking additional input on Mosrite models, specifications, date of production, and any serialization information. This year's section is the official "Line Drawn in the Sand" for Mosrite fans - assume that this is Ground Zero, or the foundation to build upon. Any extra information gathered on Mosrite will be updated in future editions of the ***Blue Book of Electric Guitars***. For the time being, assume that **all Production Dates are either CIRCA and/or ESTIMATED.**

For further information regarding Mosrite acoustic and resonator guitar models, please refer to the 7th Edition ***Blue Book of Acoustic Guitars***.

M

ELECTRIC

300 - single cutaway solid body, maple neck, rosewood fingerboard with double dot inlay, 3-per-side tuners, chrome hardware, one exposed pole piece humbucker pickup, volume/tone controls. Available in Natural finish. Mfg. 1973 to 1975.

$600 $550 $475 $425 $350 $275 $200

350 Stereo - similar to the 300, except features white pickguard, 2 exposed pole piece humbucker pickups, 2 volume/2 tone controls, pickup selector toggle switch, on/off switch, 2 side-mounted jacks. Available in Natural Wood finish. Mfg. 1973 to 1975.

$650 $600 $525 $450 $375 $300 $225

All controls are mounted on the pickguard.

BRASS RAIL STANDARD - offset double cutaway hardwood body, maple neck, 22 brass frets mounted into a brass rail running the length of the rosewood fingerboard, 3-per-side tuners, brass hardware, 2 pickups, volume/tone controls, 3-way toggle selector. Available in Natural finish. Mfg. 1976 to 1977.

$1,500 $1,200 $1,000 $850 $700 $600 $500

Brass Rail Deluxe - similar to the Brass Rail, except has active circuitry. Available in Natural finish. Mfg. 1976 to 1977.

$1,700 $1,350 $1,000 $875 $750 $650 $525

It is estimated that only 75 Brass Rail Deluxe models were built.

Celebrity Series

Celebrity Series instruments feature a semi-hollow body, and 2 f-holes. The Celebrity Series featured the CE I, CE II deluxe version and the CE III economical version. Vibrato bridges were offered on each model for an additional $30 (retail list).

GRADING	100% MINT	98% NEAR MINT	95% EXC+	90% EXC	80% VG+	70% VG	60% G

CELEBRITY I (MARK I, CE I, # 202) - arched top and back, 2 3/4" body depth, semi-hollow double cutaway body, spruce top, maple back/sides, double body binding, 2 bound f-holes, maple neck, 24 1/2" scale, zero fret, 22-fret bound rosewood fingerboard, roller bridge/vibrato tailpiece, 3-per-side deluxe chrome tuners, chrome hardware, 2 black single coil pickups with exposed pole pieces, volume/tone controls, white "apostrophe" plastic controls plate on lower bout. Available in Transparent Cherry Red, and Transparent Sunburst finishes. Mfg. 1966 to 1969.

$600 $500 $475 $400 $350 $275 $225
Last MSR was $448.

In 1968, Cherryburst, Deep Black, Metallic Blue, Metallic Red, and Pearl White finishes were introduced.

Celebrity I 12-String (CE I Mark XII, Model 204) - similar to the Celebrity 1, except has 12-string configuration, 6-per-side tuners. Mfg. 1966 to 1969.

$600 $500 $475 $400 $350 $300 $250
Last MSR was $485.

This model had the Moseley vibrato as an option.

CELEBRITY I (1972-1973) - similar to the Celebrity 1 (Model # 202), except features raised black pickguard, volume/tone controls mounted on a rounded "half-moon" plastic controls plate (with 3-way toggle and 1/4" jack. Available in Red and Sunburst finishes. Mfg. 1972 to 1973.

$500 $400 $375 $300 $250 $200 $150
Last MSR was $498.

CELEBRITY (MARK I, CE II, # 211) - bound arched top, 1 13/16" body width, semi-hollow body, spruce top, maple back/sides, maple neck, 2 bound f-holes, 24 1/2" scale, 22-fret bound rosewood fingerboard, roller bridge, vibrato tailpiece, 3-per-side deluxe chrome tuners, raised white pickguard, chrome hardware, 2 adjustable pickups, volume/tone controls, 3-way selector switch, white "apostrophe" plastic controls plate on lower bout. Available in Transparent Cherry Red and Transparent Sunburst finishes. Mfg. 1965 to 1969.

$900 $750 $600 $500 $400 $325 $250
Last MSR was $369.

In 1968, Cherryburst, Deep Black, Metallic Blue, Metallic Red and Pearl White finishes were introduced.

Celebrity 12-String (Mark XII, CE II, # 213) - similar to the Combo, except has 12-string configuration, 6-per-side tuners, adjustable bridge. Mfg. 1965 to 1969.

$850 $700 $550 $475 $375 $300 $225
Last MSR was $419.

This model had the Moseley vibrato as an option.

CELEBRITY (MARK I, CE III, # 220) - similar to the Combo (Mark I) (Model CE II), except features 1 7/8" body depth, maple top, curly maple back/sides, white body purfling, Indian rosewood fretboard, 2 black pickups, adjustable bridge, and 3-per-side enclosed tuners with white buttons. Available in Transparent Cherry Red and Transparent Sunburst finishes. Mfg. 1965 to 1969.

$600 $550 $400 $350 $275 $200 $150
Last MSR was $279.

In 1968, Cherryburst, Deep Black, Metallic Blue, Metallic Red, and Pearl White finishes were introduced.
This model had the Moseley vibrato as an option.

Celebrity (Mark XII, CE III, # 222) - similar to the Combo, except has 12-string configuration, 6-per-side tuners, adjustable bridge. Available in Transparent Cherry Red and Transparent Sunburst finish. Mfg. 1965 to 1969.

$650 $575 $450 $375 $275 $225 $175
Last MSR was $329.

This model had the Moseley vibrato as an option.

Celebrity III (1972-1973) - similar to the Celebrity III (Model # 220), except features adjustable roller bridge/raised tailpiece, raised white pickguard, volume/tone controls mounted on a rounded "half-moon" plastic controls plate (with 3-way toggle and 1/4" jack). Available in Red and Sunburst finishes. Mfg. 1972 to 1973.

$550 $475 $400 $325 $250 $175 $100
Last MSR was $298.

Combo Semi-Acoustic Series

Combo Series models have a semi-acoustic hollow body that is slightly larger than the Mark I solid body.

Mosrite Celebrity
courtesy The Music Shoppe

M

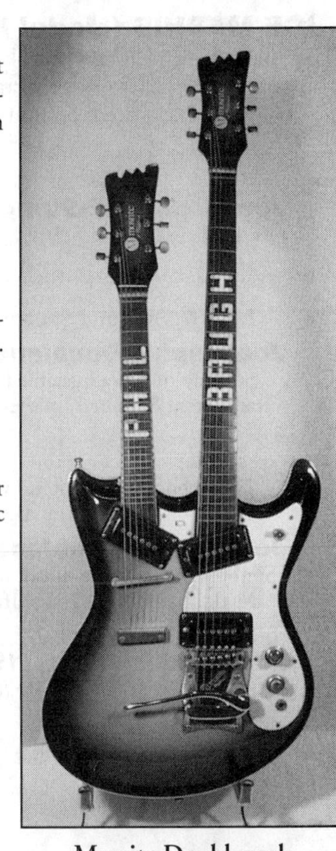

Mosrite Doubleneck
courtesy Eugene

GRADING	100% MINT	98% NEAR MINT	95% EXC+	90% EXC	80% VG+	70% VG	60% G

COMBO I (MARK I, Model 300) - hollow body, 1 1/2" body depth, spruce top, maple back/sides, double body binding, hard rock maple neck, one bound f-hole, zero fret, 24 1/2" scale, 22-fret bound Indian rosewood fingerboard with dot inlay, roller bridge/Mosrite vibrato tailpiece, 3-per-side Kluson deluxe chrome tuners, white pickguard, chrome hardware, 2 adjustable pickups, volume/tone controls, 3-way selector switch. Available in Transparent Cherry Red and Transparent Sunburst finishes. Mfg. 1966 to 1969.

$900 $750 $600 $500 $400 $325 $250
Last MSR was $398.

In 1968, Cherryburst, Deep Black, Metallic Blue, Metallic Red, and Pearl White finishes were introduced.

Combo 1 12-String (Mark XII, Model 302) - similar to the Combo, except has 12-string configuration, 6-per-side tuners, adjustable bridge. Available in Transparent Cherry Red and Transparent Sunburst finish. Mfg. 1965 to 1969.

$850 $700 $550 $475 $375 $300 $225
Last MSR was $448.

This model had the Moseley vibrato as an option.

Gospel Series

In the early 1990s, Moseley offered three models in the **Gospel Victory** series. The **Gospel Victory I** and **Gospel Victory II** had semi-hollow bodies, similar to the original Gospel model. The **Gospel Victory III** model was a solid body version. All three models were briefly built between 1990 to 1992.

GOSPEL (MARK I, Model 600) - bound arched top, arched back, 2 3/4" body width, semi-hollow body, select maple top, maple back/sides, maple neck, 2 bound f-holes, 24 1/2" scale, 22-fret bound rosewood fingerboard, "Mosrite of California/Gospel Guitar" headstock logos, roller bridge/vibrato tailpiece, 3-per-side tuners, raised black pickguard, chrome hardware, 2 black single coil pickups with exposed pole pieces, 2 volume/2 tone controls, 3-way selector switch, black "apostrophe" plastic controls plate on lower bout. Available in Natural finish with tinted Golden Brown headstock. Mfg. 1967 to 1969.

$850 $750 $575 $600 $500 $425 $350
Last MSR was $498.

GOSPEL 12-String (Mark XII, Model 602) - similar to the Gospel, except has 12-string configuration, 6-per-side tuners adjustable bridge. Available in Natural finish. Mfg. 1967 to 1969.

$895 $775 $695 $625 $550 $450 $375
Last MSR was $529.

This model had the Moseley vibrato as an option.

Joe Maphis Models

Joe Maphis Model instruments were designed in conjunction with guitarist Joe Maphis. These semi-hollow models (the walnut back is carved out, and then glued to a spruce top) have controls mounted on the pickguard.

JOE MAPHIS (Model MARK I, # 501) - slightly offset double semi-hollow body, 1 1/2" body depth, bound spruce top, walnut back, hard rock maple neck, 24 1/2" scale, 22-fret celluloid bound rosewood fingerboard, laminated black (or white) shell pickguard, deluxe adjustable roller bridge/vibrato tailpiece, 3-per-side tuners, chrome hardware, 2 adjustable pickups, volume/tone controls. Available in Natural and Transparent Sunburst finishes. Mfg. 1965 to 1969.

$1,200 $1,000 $800 $675 $550 $450 $325
Last MSR was $498.

M

Joe Maphis 12-String (Model Mark XII, # 503) - similar to the Joe Maphis, except has 12-string configuration, 6-per-side tuners. Available in Natural finish. Mfg. 1965 to 1969.

$1,500 $1,300 $1,000 $850 $725 $625 $500
Last MSR was $589.

In 1967, Blue and Sunburst finished were introduced.

Joe Maphis Doubleneck (Model Mark XVIII) - similar to the Joe Maphis, except has 2 necks in a 12-string/6-string configuration, 6-per-side tuners/adjustable bridge (12-string neck), 3-per-side tuners/Moseley vibrato (6-string neck) 1 1/4" body depth. Available in Natural and Transparent Sunburst finishes. Mfg. 1965 to 1969.

$2,000 $1,600 $1,200 $950 $850 $750 $650
Last MSR was $689.

This model was optional with a 4-string Bass neck.
This model was optional with Metallic Blue and Metallic Pearl White finishes (1960s retail list was an additional $30).

Joe Maphis Doubleneck (Model VII) Reissue - similar to the Joe Maphis Doubleneck (Model Mark XVIII). Available in Black, Sunburst, and White finish. Mfg. 1990, 1992 to 1994.

Model has not traded sufficiently to quote pricing.

Last MSR was $3,000.

Joe Maphis JM 65 (1966-1967) - similar to the Joe Maphis, except has 2 necks in a mandolin/6-string configuration, 2-per-side tuners (mandolin neck), 3-per-side tuners (6-string neck). Available in Black and Sunburst finishes. Mfg. 1966 to 1967.

$1,500 $1,200 $1,000 $850 $650 $550 $450

GRADING	100% MINT	98% NEAR MINT	95% EXC+	90% EXC	80% VG+	70% VG	60% G

MOSRITE 1988 GUITAR (M-88) - offset double cutaway basswood body, no German carve body ridge, 3-piece laminated maple neck, zero fret, 22-fret laminated curly maple/rosewood fingerboard, "Mosrite 1988" logo on headstock, vibrato or fixed bridge, 3-per-side tuners, chrome hardware, 2 creme-colored Alnico single coil pickups, volume/tone controls, 3-position switch, side-mounted 1/4" jack. Available in Banana, Diamondized Ebony Black, Diamondized Money Green, Diamondized Ruby Red, and Sunburst finishes. Mfg. circa 1988.

Fixed bridge.

$1,500 $1,250 $1,000 $900 $N/A $N/A $N/A
Last MSR was $1,100.

Vibrato bridge.

$1,800 $1,400 $1,200 $1,000 $N/A $N/A $N/A
Last MSR was $1,260.

The headstock logo on M-88 models reads "Mosrite 1988, Made In U.S.A."

RAMONES MODEL - offset double cutaway basswood or alder body, maple neck, 22-fret rosewood fingerboard with double dot inlay, 3-per-side tuners, natural wood headstock with Mosrite/Ramones logo, tune-o-matic bridge/stop tailpiece, black pickguard, chrome hardware, black covered Mosrite pickup, volume control, top-mounted jack. Available in Gold finish. Mfg. circa 1992.

$2,500 $2,200 $2,000 $N/A $N/A $N/A $N/A

This model was designed in conjunction with long time Mosrite player Johnny Ramone (The Ramones).

Mosrite Joe Maphis 12/6
19th Annual Dallas Show

Ventures Series

In the early 1960s, Semie Moseley entered into an agreement with the Ventures organization to build the Ventures model guitar. Ventures model guitars built between 1959 to 1964 have a **Mosrite of California** logo and "The Ventures Model" on the headstock. After the business agreement with the Ventures faltered, Mosrite produced a **MARK** model (and variants) that were Ventures-style models without the "Ventures" logo or affiliation mentioned.

VENTURES MODEL (1959-1963) - offset double cutaway hardwood body, set-in maple neck, 22-fret bound rosewood fingerboard, (sand casted) Vibramute vibrato bridge, chrome hardware, white pickguard, 2 black single coil pickups, volume/tone controls, 3-position switch. Available in Sunburst finish. Mfg. 1959 to 1963.

Model has not traded sufficiently to quote pricing.
It is estimated that only 40 of these guitars were built.

Ventures Model (1963-1964) - similar to the Ventures Model (1959-1963), except features a bound body, side-mounted jack. Available in Sunburst and White Pearl finishes. Mfg. 1963 to 1964.

$4,500 $4,250 $4,000 $3,500 $3,000 $2,500 $1,800

Ventures Model (1964-1965) - similar to the Ventures Model (1959-1963), except features side-mounted jack, (no body binding). Available in Red, Sunburst, and White Pearl finishes. Mfg. 1964 to 1965.

$3,500 $3,200 $2,750 $2,400 $2,000 $1,600 $1,200

VENTURES (Model MARK I, # 102) - offset double cutaway hardwood body, bolt-on maple neck, 24 1/2" scale, 22-fret bound rosewood fingerboard, deluxe bridge/vibrato tailpiece, "Mosrite of California/The Ventures Model" headstock logo, chrome hardware, white pickguard, 2 black single coil pickups, volume/tone controls, 3-position switch. Available in Metallic Blue, Metallic Red, and Sunburst finishes. Mfg. 1965 to 1967.

With Vibramute bridge

$2,000 $1,500 $1,000 $875 $775 $650 $525
Last MSR was $438.

With Moseley tailpiece

$1,800 $1,250 $950 $850 $750 $625 $500
Last MSR was $398.

Ventures Mark Series models do not have a bound body.

Ventures (Model Mark V, # 101) - similar to the Ventures (Mark I), except features a short scale fingerboard, smaller body, 24 1/2" scale, adjustable bridge. Available in Blue, Red, Sunburst, and White finishes. Mfg. 1963 to 1967.

$1,400 $1,150 $850 $725 $650 $550 $450
Last MSR was $299.95.

Ventures 12-String (Model Mark XII, # 104) - similar to the Ventures (Mark I), except features 12-string configuration, 6-per-side tuners. Available in Metallic Blue, Metallic Red, and Sunburst finishes. Mfg. 1965 to 1967.

With (optional) Vibramute bridge.

$1,000 $900 $800 $675 $575 $475 $375
Last MSR was $489.

With fixed tailpiece.

$1,200 $1,000 $900 $775 $675 $550 $425
Last MSR was $449.

Mosrite Double 12 Hollow
courtesy Abalone Vintage

M

GRADING	100% MINT	98% NEAR MINT	95% EXC+	90% EXC	80% VG+	70% VG	60% G

Ventures Doubleneck (Model Mark XVIII, # 105) - similar to the Ventures (Mark I), except has 2 necks in a 12-string/6-string configuration, 6-per-side tuners (12-string neck), 3-per-side tuners (6-string neck). Available in Metallic Blue, Metallic Red, and Sunburst finishes. Mfg. 1964 to 1967.

$2,000 $1,700 $1,200 $895 $775 $650 $550
Last MSR was $689.

VENTURES II - offset double cutaway hardwood body, bolt-on maple neck, 22-fret rosewood fingerboard, roller bridge/vibrato or Moseley tailpiece, chrome hardware, white pickguard, 2 pickups, volume/tone controls, 3-position switch. Available in Red and Sunburst finishes. Mfg. circa 1974.

$995 $875 $775 $700 $600 $500 $400

Ventures "No Logo" Models: Mark Series (1967-1969)

Between 1967 to 1969, Mosrite continued to produce a Ventures model guitar. However, as the company had no affiliation with the group, the Mark series models have no "The Ventures Model" logo on them.

MARK I - offset double cutaway solid body, bolt-on maple neck, 24 1/2" scale, 22-fret bound Indian rosewood fingerboard, roller bridge/vibrato bridge, chrome hardware, white pickguard, 2 black single coil pickups, volume/tone controls, 3-position switch. Available in Cherryburst, Deep Black, Metallic Blue, Metallic Red, Pearl White, Transparent Cherry Red, and Transparent Sunburst finishes. Mfg. 1967 to 1969.

$900 $800 $750 $650 $575 $500 $425

Mark V - similar to the Mark I, except features a smaller body, 1 1/8" body depth, roller bridge/vibrato tailpiece, 3-per-side tuners with white buttons. Mfg. 1967 to 1969.

$800 $725 $650 $550 $450 $375 $300

Mark XII 12-String - similar to the Mark I, except features 12-string configuration, 6-per-side tuners, adjustable bridge. Mfg. 1967 to 1969.

$850 $775 $700 $600 $500 $425 $350

Mark III (1984-1986) - similar to the Mark I, except features 3 single coil pickups. Available in Sunburst finish. Mfg. 1984 to 1986.

$800 $725 $650 $550 $450 $375 $300

Ventures "No Logo" Models: V Series (1973-1975)

The Mark Series was given humbuckers in place of their usual single coil pickups during production between 1973 to 1975 as the **V-II**. The **V-I Standard**, with two single coil pickups, was offered beginning in 1972.

V-I STANDARD - offset double cutaway solid body, bolt-on maple neck, 22-fret bound rosewood fingerboard with dot inlay, roller bridge/vibrato bridge, 3-per-side tuners, natural finish headstock, white pickguard, chrome hardware, 2 black single coil pickups with exposed pole pieces, 2 volume/1 tone controls, 3-position switch. Available in Red and Sunburst finishes. Mfg. circa 1972 to 1975.

$500 $450 $400 $350 $300 $250 $200
Last MSR was $398.

V-II - offset double cutaway solid body, bolt-on maple neck, 22-fret bound rosewood fingerboard, roller bridge/vibrato bridge, 2-per-side tuners, natural finish headstock, white pickguard, chrome hardware, white pickguard, 2 black humbucker pickups with exposed pole pieces, 2 volume/2 tone controls, 3-position switch, 2 bypass switches. Available in Red and Sunburst finishes. Mfg. 1973 to 1975.

$450 $400 $350 $300 $250 $200 $175
Last MSR was $398.

Ventures Reissue Models (1987, 1988, 1992)

Semie Moseley produced a limited amount of Ventures reissue models in the late 1980s through the early 1990s. It is estimated that a large percentage of these guitars were shipped to, and remain in Japan.

VENTURES EARLY 1960'S REISSUE (BOLT-ON) - offset double cutaway basswood or alder body, bolt-on maple neck, 22-fret rosewood fingerboard, vibrato bridge or tailpiece, 3-per-side tuners, chrome hardware, white pickguard, 2 black Alnico single coil pickups, volume/tone controls, 3-position switch. Available in Black, Sunburst, and White finishes. Mfg. circa 1987 to 1990.

$2,500 $2,200 $2,000 $N/A $N/A $N/A $N/A
Last MSR was $2,200.

VENTURES EARLY 1960'S REISSUE (VENTURES REISSUE '63) - bound offset double cutaway alder body, glued-in maple neck, bound rosewood fingerboard, (original-style sand cast) Vibramute vibrato bridge, 3-per-side tuners, chrome hardware, white pickguard, 2 black Alnico single coil pickups, volume/tone controls, 3-position switch, side-mounted jack. Available in Black, Sunburst, and White finishes. Mfg. circa 1987 to 1990.

$2,800 $2,500 $2,200 $N/A $N/A $N/A $N/A
Last MSR was $2,598.

The announced reserved serial numbers were # 87001 through # 87150. It is unknown at this date how many models were produced.

Ventures 40th Anniversary - similar to the Ventures Reissue '63, except features gold-plated hardware. Available in Black, Sunburst, and White finishes. Mfg. circa 1992.

Lack of secondary marketplace activity precludes accurate pricing on this model.

The 40th Anniversary model celebrated the first Semie Moseley guitar built in 1952 (1952-1992). Research continues on the Ventures 40th Anniversary.

GRADING	100% MINT	98% NEAR MINT	95% EXC+	90% EXC	80% VG+	70% VG	60% G

NOKIE EDWARDS MODEL - bound offset double cutaway alder body, glued-in maple neck, bound rosewood fingerboard, (original-style sand cast) Vibramute vibrato bridge, "Nokie" logo, 3-per-side tuners, chrome hardware, white pickguard, 2 black Alnico single coil pickups, volume/tone controls, 3-position switch, side-mounted jack. Available in Black, Sunburst, and White finishes. Mfg. circa 1989 to 1990.

Lack of secondary marketplace activity precludes accurate pricing on this model.

Last MSR was $2,000.

NOKIE EDWARDS 30TH ANNIVERSAY MODEL - similar to the Nokie Edwards Model, with alder or basswood body, "Nokie Anniversary" logo. Mfg. circa 1992.

Lack of secondary marketplace activity precludes accurate pricing on this model.

VENTURES 1988 (V-88) - offset double cutaway basswood body, 3-piece laminated maple neck, zero fret, 22-fret bound rosewood fingerboard, "Mosrite/The Ventures Model/1988" logo on headstock, vibrato bridge, chrome hardware, white pickguard, 2 black covered Alnico single coil pickups, volume/tone controls, 3-position switch. Available in Banana, Diamondized Ebony Black, Diamondized Money Green, Diamondized Ruby Red, and Sunburst finishes. Mfg. circa 1988.

$2,500 $2,200 $1,800 $1,500 $N/A $N/A $N/A

Last MSR was $1,460.

This model was built close to the same specs as an early 1964 Ventures model.

The next year, the V-89 model debuted, with a list price of $1,998. Research continues on the V-89 model (circa 1989-1990).

Mosrite Celebrity 3 Bass
Short Scale
courtesy Atomic Guitars

ELECTRIC BASS

Celebrity Bass Series

CELEBRITY I BASS (MARK X, Model CE I, # 203) - arched top and back, 2 3/4" body depth, semi-hollow double cutaway body, spruce top, maple back/sides, bound top and back, 2 bound f-holes, maple neck, 30 1/4" scale, 20-fret bound rosewood fingerboard, fixed bridge, chrome bridge cover, 2-per-side tuners, chrome hardware, 2 black pickups with exposed pole pieces, volume/tone controls, 3-way selector switch, white "apostrophe" plastic controls plate on lower bout. Available in Transparent Cherry Red and Transparent Sunburst finishes. Mfg. 1966 to 1969.

$625 $500 $475 $400 $350 $275 $225

Last MSR was $398.

In 1968, Cherryburst, Deep Black, Metallic Blue, Metallic Red, and Pearl White finishes were introduced.

CELEBRITY BASS (MARK X, Model CE II, # 212) - semi-hollow body, spruce top, maple back/sides, double body binding, maple neck, one bound f-hole, bound rosewood fingerboard, 2-per-side tuners, adjustable bridge/metal tailpiece, chrome bridge cover, chrome hardware, 2 adjustable pickups, volume/tone controls, 3-way selector switch. Available in Transparent Cherry Red and Transparent Sunburst finishes. Mfg. 1965 to 1969.

$900 $750 $600 $500 $400 $325 $250

Last MSR was $349.

In 1968, Cherryburst, Deep Black, Metallic Blue, Metallic Red, and Pearl White finishes were introduced.

Celebrity Bass (Mark X, CE III, # 221) - similar to the Combo (Mark I) (Model CE II), except features maple top, curly maple back/sides, white body purfling, Indian rosewood fretboard, 2 black pickups, and 2-per-side enclosed tuners with white buttons. Available in Transparent Cherry Red and Transparent Sunburst finishes. Mfg. 1965 to 1969.

$600 $550 $400 $350 $275 $200 $150

Last MSR was $279.

In 1968, Cherryburst, Deep Black, Metallic Blue, Metallic Red, and Pearl White finishes were introduced.

COMBO 1 BASS (MARK X, 301) - hollow body, spruce top, maple back/sides, double body binding, hard rock maple neck, one bound f-hole, 30 1/4" scale, 20-fret bound rosewood fingerboard, 2-per-side Kluson deluxe chrome tuners, adjustable bridge, chrome bridge cover, chrome hardware, 2 adjustable pickups, volume/tone controls, 3-way selector switch. Available in Transparent Cherry Red and Transparent Sunburst finishes. Mfg. 1966 to 1969.

$900 $750 $600 $500 $400 $325 $250

Last MSR was $369.

GOSPEL BASS (MARK X, 601) - bound arched top, arched back, 2 3/4" body width, semi-hollow body, select maple top, maple back/sides, maple neck, 2 bound f-holes, 30 1/4" scale, 20-fret bound rosewood fingerboard, "Mosrite of California/Gospel Guitar" headstock logos, adjustable bridge, 2-per-side tuners, raised black pickguard, chrome hardware, 2 black pickups with exposed pole pieces, 2 volume/2 tone controls, 3-way selector switch, black "apostrophe" plastic controls plate on lower bout. Available in Natural finish with tinted Golden Brown headstock. Mfg. 1967 to 1969.

$1,000 $900 $850 $750 $675 $600 $500

Last MSR was $469.

M

GRADING	100% MINT	98% NEAR MINT	95% EXC+	90% EXC	80% VG+	70% VG	60% G

JOE MAPHIS BASS (Model MARK X, 502) - semi-hollow body, bound spruce top, 1 1/2" body depth, walnut back, maple neck, 30 1/4" scale, 20-fret rosewood fingerboard, fixed bridge, laminated black (or white) shell pickguard, chrome bridge cover, 2-per-side tuners, chrome hardware, 2 adjustable pickups, volume/tone controls, 3-way selector switch. Available in Natural and Transparent Sunburst finishes. Mfg. 1965 to 1969.

$900 $750 $600 $500 $400 $325 $250
Last MSR was $449.

MOSRITE 1988 BASS (M-88 BASS) - offset double cutaway basswood body, no German carve body ridge, 3-piece laminated maple neck, zero fret, 20-fret laminated curly maple/rosewood fingerboard, "Mosrite 1988" logo on headstock, vibrato or fixed bridge, 2-per-side tuners, chrome hardware, 2 creme colored Alnico pickups, volume/tone controls, 3-position switch, side-mounted 1/4" jack. Available in Banana, Diamondized Ebony Black, Diamondized Money Green, Diamondized Ruby Red, and Sunburst finishes. Mfg. 1988 to 1989.

$1,500 $1,250 $1,000 $900 $N/A $N/A $N/A

The headstock logo on M-88 models reads "Mosrite 1988, Made In U.S.A."

Ventures Bass Series

VENTURES MODEL BASS (1963-1965) - bound offset double cutaway hardwood body, set-in maple neck, 20-fret bound fingerboard, adjustable bridge, chrome hardware, 2-per-side tuners, white pickguard, 2 black pickups, volume/tone controls, 3-position switch, side-mounted jack. Available in Sunburst and White Pearl finishes. Mfg. 1963 to 1965.

$4,500 $4,250 $4,000 $3,500 $3,000 $2,500 $1,800

VENTURES BASS (Model MARK X, # 103) - offset double cutaway hardwood body, bolt-on maple neck, 30 1/4" scale, 20-fret bound rosewood fingerboard with dot inlay, "Mosrite of California/The Ventures" headstock logo, fixed bridge, chrome hardware, white pickguard, 2 black single coil pickups, volume/tone controls, 3-position switch. Available in Metallic Blue, Metallic Red, and Sunburst finishes. Mfg. 1963 to 1966.

$1,500 $1,200 $995 $825 $750 $650 $550
Last MSR was $330.

Ventures Mark Series models do not have a bound body.

MARK X BASS - offset double cutaway solid body, bolt-on maple neck, 30 1/4" scale, 20-fret bound Indian rosewood fingerboard, adjustable bridge, chrome hardware, white pickguard, 2 black pickups, volume/tone controls, 3-position switch. Available in Cherryburst, Deep Black, Metallic Blue, Metallic Red, Pearl White, Transparent Cherry Red, and Transparent Sunburst finishes. Mfg. 1967 to 1969.

$1,200 $1,000 $925 $850 $725 $600 $500

While similar to the 1963-1969 Ventures Bass model, the Mark X Bass does not have a "The Ventures Model" logo on the headstock.

V Bass Series

V-I BASS (V I STANDARD BASS) - offset double cutaway solid body, bolt-on maple neck, 20-fret bound rosewood fingerboard with double dot inlay, adjustable bridge/stop tailpiece, chrome bridge cover, 2-per-side tuners, natural finish headstock, white pickguard, chrome hardware, white pickguard, 2 black pickups with exposed pole pieces, volume/tone controls, 3-position switch. Available in Red and Sunburst finishes. Mfg. circa 1972 to 1975.

$500 $450 $400 $350 $300 $250 $200
Last MSR was $398.

V-II Bass - similar to the V-I Bass, except features 2 black humbucker pickups with exposed pole pieces, 2 pickup bypass switches. Available in Red and Sunburst finish. Mfg. 1973 to 1975.

$550 $475 $425 $375 $325 $250 $200
Last MSR was $398.

Ventures Bass Reissue Models

VENTURES VINTAGE BASS (SET-NECK) - bound offset double cutaway alder body, glued-in maple neck, 20-fret bound rosewood fingerboard, fixed bridge, 2-per-side tuners, chrome hardware, white pickguard, 2 black Alnico single coil pickups, volume/tone controls, 3-position switch, side-mounted jack. Available in Black, Sunburst, and White finishes. Mfg. circa 1990.

$3,000 $2,700 $2,500 $N/A $N/A $N/A $N/A
Last MSR was $2,748.

Ventures Vintage Bass (Bolt-On) - similar to the Ventures Vintage Bass (Set-Neck), except has a bolt-on neck. Mfg. circa 1990.

$2,500 $2,200 $2,000 $N/A $N/A $N/A $N/A
Last MSR was $2,350.

VENTURES 1988 BASS (V-88 BASS) - offset double cutaway basswood body, 3-piece laminated maple neck, 20-fret bound rosewood fingerboard, "Mosrite/The Ventures Model/1988" logo on headstock, 2-per-side tuners, fixed tailpiece, chrome hardware, 2 black pickups, volume/tone controls, 3-position switch. Available in Banana, Diamondized Ebony Black, Diamondized Money Green, Diamondized Ruby Red, and Sunburst finishes. Mfg. circa 1988.

$2,000 $1,700 $1,350 $1,100 $N/A $N/A $N/A
Last MSR was $1,460.

The next year, the V-89 Bass model debuted, with a list price of $2,148. Research continues on the V-89 Bass model (circa 1989-1990).

M

MOURADIAN

Instruments currently built in Cambridge, MA since 1989. Instruments were previously built in Winchester, Massachusetts between 1980, 1982 to 1988.

Mouradian custom basses are high quality instruments generally associated with bassist Chris Squire (Yes) due to his continued use of his CS-74 model. Other noted Mouradian bass players include Pat Badger (Extreme).

Jim Mouradian first built Squire's custom bass in 1980, and formed a production company in 1982. Mouradian Guitars was initially based in Winchester, Massachusetts for the first 6 years, and then moved to Cambridge, Massachusetts in 1989. Jim and his son, Jon, continued to produce custom-built electric basses while offering repair services.

The Mouradian company expanded their production capabilities in 1997/1998 when Jim and John teamed up with Martin Flanders (see FLANDERS ARCHTOP GUITARS) and Pat Badger. Badger, a former employee before his band Extreme hit nationally, has returned to the company that originally hired him.

(Preliminary research courtesy Jeff Meyer; company information courtesy Jon Mouradian)

Mutivox Premier
courtesy Waco Vintage

ELECTRIC BASS

Mouradian **CS-74 "Chris Squire"** basses have an unusual curved body design. The **CS-74** (retail list starting at $3,795) features a neck-through design, graphite-reinforced rock maple neck, 22-fret ebony fingerboard, 3 custom made humcancelling pickups, 3 on/off pickup selector switches, and an active EQ. This model is available with numerous options, including a 5-String configuration (**CS-75**).

Mouradian's newest model is the **Reality Bass**, available in 4-String (retail list $1,895) and 5-String (retail $1,895) configurations. This model has either a swamp ash or alder body, 21-fret rosewood or bird's-eye maple fingerboard, strings through-body bridge, Hipshot Ultralite tuners, EMG 35 P4/35 J pickups, and stacked volume/tone controls. The **Reality Bass** is optional with different electronic packages, exotic woods, custom finishes, or in a fretless configuration. All Mouradian basses are built in the U.S., and are available direct from the company in Massachusetts.

MUDGE BASSES

Instruments currently built in Oakland, California.

Mudge basses are individually handcrafted "one at a time" in the Mudge shop, and feature hand carved bodies and necks. All woods are also hand selected by Mudge. Basses have a mahogany body with exotic or domestic bookmatched top. Necks are handcarved maple with contrasting wood stripes of Walnut or Purpleheart. For further information, contact Mudge Basses directly (see Trademark Index).

ELECTRIC BASS

Mudge bass models are available in the **DN4** 4-string (list $1,800) and 5-string **DN5** (list $2,000) configurations. The off-set double cutaway body is carved from Honduran mahogany and topped with Wenge, Zebrawood, Cocabolo, or Pau Ferro; bird's-eye maple necks feature a Pau Ferro fingerboard and mother-of-pearl side dots. Mudge basses have chrome hardware, Hipshot or Leo Quan BadAss II bridges, 2 EMG J-style pickups, and have hand rubbed oil finishes. The CK Models have the same general specs as the DN's, except the boby material is Ash (list $1,600 4-string) and ($1,800 5-string).

MULTI-STAR

See MUSIMA.

Instruments previously produced in East Germany during the 1970s and 1980s.

The Multi-Star trademark was a brand name used by the Musima company on a series of solid body guitars featuring designs based on popular American classics.

(Source: Tony Bacon and Paul Day, The Guru's Guitar Guide)

MULTIVOX

Instruments previously produced in New York City, New York during the 1950s and 1960s. Later models had imported hardware but were still "built" in New York.

Multivox was the manufacturing subsidiary of the Peter Sorkin Music Company, which built products under the Premier trademark. Sorkin began the Multivox company in the mid 1940s. Multivox eventually established a separate corporate identity, and continued in existence for fourteen or so years after the Sorkin company closed down in the 1970s.

(Source: Michael Wright, Guitar Stories Volume One)

MUNCY

Instruments are currently built in Kingston, Tennessee.

Luthier Gary Muncy designed the solid body "Bout Time" model that features a new innovative neck design. Constructed from CNC machined aluminum, the neck's fretboard is made from bloodwood which is then shaped between the sunken frets similar to scalloping. Fingering notes occurs in the in-between areas so the string makes contact at the raised area.

MURPH

Instruments previously built in San Fernando, California between 1965 and 1966.

Designer/inventor Pat Murphy was responding to his children's musical interests when he began manufacturing Murph guitars in the mid 1960s. Murphy put the family-run shop together with equipment picked up at auctions, and contracted a violin maker named Rick Geiger to help with production. After a falling out with Geiger, Murphy began manufacturing guitars in the midsummer of 1965.

The company originally was to be called York, but a brass instrument manufacturer of the same name caused them to use the Murph trademark. Pat Murphy estimated that perhaps 1,200 to 1,500 guitars were built in the one year production span. Models were built in lots of 50, and a total of nearly 100 guitars were built a week. Bridges and tremolos were from the Gotz company in Germany, and the tuning machines were Klusons. Pickups were hand wound in the guitar production facility. Pat Murphy was also contracted to make a small number of guitars for Sears under the Silvertone label.

(Source: Teisco Del Rey, Guitar Player magazine)

ELECTRIC

Models included the semi-hollow **Gemini**, and the solid body **Squire**. Some of the Squire *seconds* were finished with vinyl upholstery and snap buttons and were designated the **Westerner** model. The Gemini had a retail price of $279, the Squire I (one pickup) at $159.50, and the Squire II (two pickups) listed at $189.50. One model called the **Continental IV** was a single pickup semi-hollowbody design that was priced around $239.

Murphy also produced a full-size kit guitar called the **Tempo**, corresponding bass guitar models for the line, and heart- shaped bodied guitars in six or twelve string configurations.

MUSIC DRIVE

Also M D.

Instruments currently produced in Korea by Sumer Korea. Distributed in the U.S. by Sumer USA, located in Huntington Beach, California.

The Sumer Musical Instruments Co., Ltd. is currently offering a wide range of electric guitar and bass models under the **Music Drive** (or MD) trademark. Most models are good quality designs intended for the intermediate to working professional guitarist. For further information regarding models and prices, please contact Sumer USA (see Trademark Index).

There are a wide range of electric and bass models. Standard Series instruments feature heel-less bolt-on hard maple necks, rosewood fingerboards, chrome hardware, and numerous solid/transparent/metallic finishes.

MUSIC MAN

See ERNIE BALL/MUSIC MAN.

Instruments previously produced in Fullerton, California between 1976 and 1979.

The original Music Man company was put together in March of 1972 by two ex-Fender executives. Tom Walker (a chief salesman) and Forrest White (ex-vice president and general manager of Fender) made their mark early, with a successful line of guitar amplifiers. In 1976, Music Man introduced new solid body guitar models designed and built by Leo Fender. After abiding by a ten year "no compete" clause in the sale of Fender Electrical Instrument Company (1965-1975), Fender's CLF Research factory provided Music Man with numerous guitar and bass models through an exclusive agreement.

Leo Fender and George Fullerton (another ex-Fender employee) began building facilities for CLF Research in December of 1974. Fullerton was made vice president of CLF in March 1976, and the first shipment of instruments from CLF to Music Man was in June of the same year. Some of the notable designs in early Music Man history are the Sabre and Stingray series of guitars and basses.

In 1978, the controlling interest at Music Man expressed a desire to buy the CLF factory and produce instruments directly. Fender and Fullerton turned down repeated offers, and Music Man began cutting production orders. The controversy settled as CLF Research stopped manufacturing instruments for Music Man in late 1979. Fender then began working on new designs for his final company, G & L.

Music Man's trademark and designs were purchased in 1984 by Ernie Ball. The Ernie Ball company, known for its string sets and Earthwood basses, set up production in its San Luis Obispo factory. Ernie Ball/Music Man has retained the high level of quality from original Fender/CLF designs, and has introduced some innovative designs to their current line (See ERNIE BALL/MUSIC MAN).

The three year span of the original Music Man company saw the release of such models as the Sabre I and Sabre II, as well as the Sting Ray I and Sting Ray II guitars. Perhaps even better known are the Sabre Bass, Sting Ray Bass, and Cutlass Bass. The Sting Ray was available with either strings through the body or strings through the bridge. It is estimated that less than 300 Cutlass basses were built.

MUSICIAN SOUND DESIGN

Instruments currently built in Koln (Cologne), Germany.

Musician Sound Design is currently offering a sleek (yet pointy) custom guitar model. For further information, contact Musician Sound Design directly (see Trademark Index).

MUSICVOX

Instruments currently produced in Korea. Distributed by Musicvox of Cherry Hill, New Jersey.

Owner Matt Eichen's new Musicvox Spaceranger guitar features a unique new design that will certainly gather attention any time a player takes it out of the case! Eichen combined the oversized headstock with an equally-oversized treble-side horn for resonance purposes, which gives the Spaceranger design increased sustain.

After two years of expanding into a retail/distributor base, Eichen decided to take the guitars right to the players worldwide with direct sales. As as result, the factory pricing for direct sales has radically reduced the retail list price. Suggested list prices of $750 to $925 are now reduced to $249 to $299, and applies to stock on hand at time of order. Musicvox gig bags are also available ($24.95 to $29.95). Be the first on your block to join the Space Age!

Early versions (1996-1997 Mfg.) of the Spaceranger guitar model featured either an alder or an ultralight ash body. Finishes included solid color urethane colors like *Red Alert, All Systems Green, Black Hole, Ignition Yellow,* and *White Hot.* Nitrocellulose Sunburst and Transparent finishes were also available.

ELECTRIC

The current version **Spaceranger** guitar model features a single cutaway/enlarged lower bout light mahogany body, 24 3/4" scale, bolt-on Canadian maple neck, 21-fret rosewood (or maple) fingerboard with dot (or block) inlays, fixed bridge, 2/4 per side vintage-style keystone tuners on a curved/enlarged head-stock, pickguard, 3-way selector switch, and volume/tone controls. Spacerangers fire up the frequencies via a pair of either black P-90 style single coils, PAF-or mini-style covered humbuckers (chrome or gold covers), or Toaster-style pickups with chrome/black covers. Trapeze and tremolo tailpieces are available by special order.

Finishes include solid colors like Bla*ck (with white body binding)*, *Candy Apple Red*, *Seafoam Green*, *Taxicab Yellow*, and *White (with triple black body binding)*. Transparent finishes include *Bookmatched Flame Maple Top with Cherry Sunburst*, *Fireglow Sunburst*, *Korina*, and *Three Tone Sunburst*. Sparkle Top finishes include *Gold Stardust* and *Silver Stardust*.

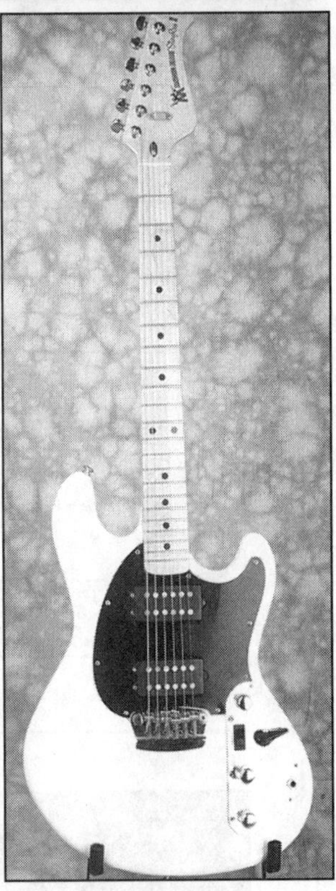

Music Man Stringray II
courtesy John Beeson

ELECTRIC BASS

The **Spaceranger Bass** features a similar construction as the guitar model, except has a 30" scale, 20-fret fingerboard, rosewood bridge/trapeze tailpiece, 1/3-per-side vintage-style keystone tuners, and a pair of either mini-style or large special design covered humbuckers (chrome or gold covers).

Finishes include solid colors like *Black (with white body binding)*, *Candy Apple Red*, and *White (with triple black body binding)*. Transparent finishes include *Bookmatched Flame Maple Top with Cherry Sunburst*, *Korina*, and *Three Tone Sunburst*. Sparkle Top finishes include *Gold Stardust* and *Silver Stardust*.

MUSIMA

Instruments currently produced in Germany since the late 1950s.

The Musima company has been producing a number of solid body and semi-hollowbody guitars with original designs since the late 1950s. It has been reported by other sources that a number of guitars were exported to Britian under the **Otwin & Rellog** trademark. These guitars were available through the early 1960s, then the company issued their own medium quality solid body guitars such as the **707** and **708** during the mid 1960s. The company continues to produce good quality guitars for the international guitar market. Further research is continuing on the Musima company for upcoming editions of the ***Blue Book of Electric Guitars***.

(Source: Tony Bacon, The Ultimate Guitar Book)

M

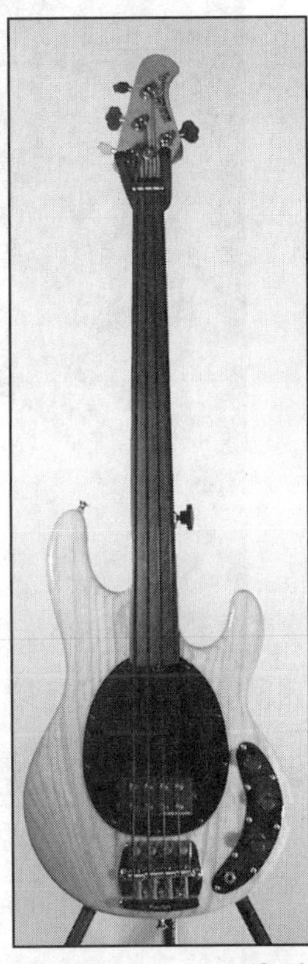

Music Man Stringray (fretless)
courtesy Bass Palace

NOTES

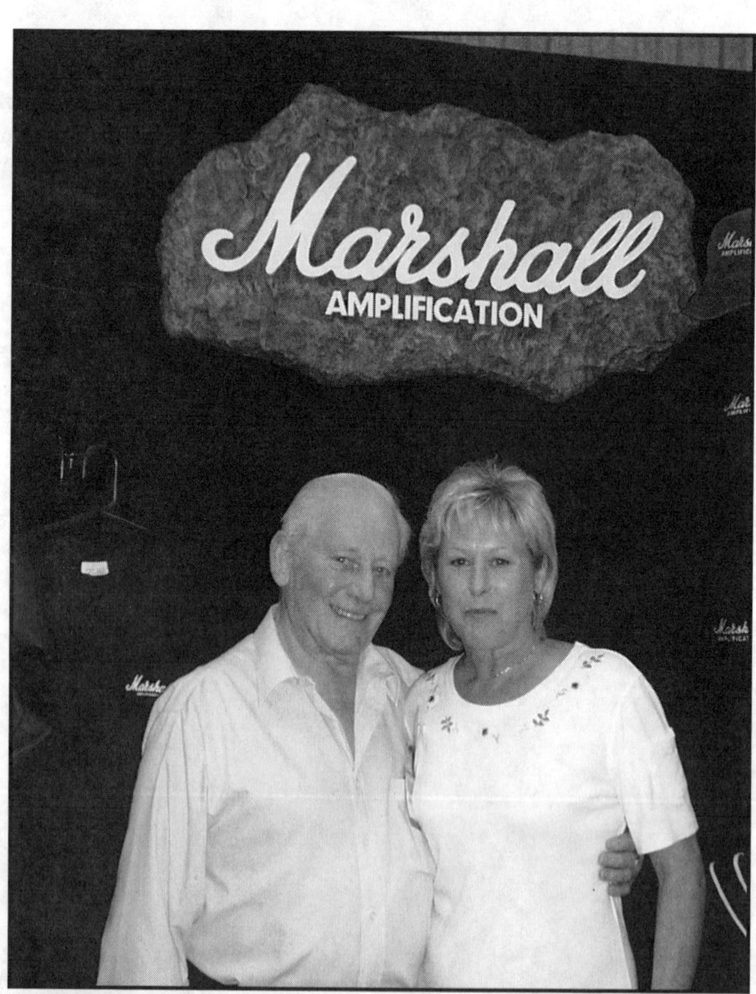

The hardest working couple in the music business, Jim & Phyllis Marshall, finally get a rest from signing Marshall T-shirts. On a good day, he individually personalizes 800 T-shirts and as many posters. Not bad for being 73!

Section N

9STEIN

Instruments currently built in the U.S. Distributed by Michael Reizenstein in Yonkers, New York.

Designer Michael Reizenstein's 9-string combination bass and guitar has an offset, ergonomic body design that features a fully adjustable armrest (which also gives control of the instrument positioning). The guitar features a tune-o-matic bridge/stop tailpiece, humbucker pickup, 5/4 per side headstock, and built-in Boss TU-12 tuner. The 9Stein combination bass and guitar is built by luthier Tommy Doyle. For further information, please contact Michael Reizenstein directly (see Trademark Index).

N.I.C.E.

Instruments currently built in Basel, Switzerland.

N.I.C.E. produces several high quality guitars. For further information regarding model specifications and pricing, please contact N.I.C.E. directly (see Trademark Index).

NS DESIGN

Instruments currently produced in Nobleboro, Maine, and previously produced in Walpole, Maine.

Designer Ned Steinberger founded NS Designs in 1993, as a means to independently develop new and innovative stringed instrument designs. While not really a production center in the factory sense, some of the ideas that are explored here may have an impact on the musical instrument industry again! Currently, the patented 4-string double bass retails for $2,800, $3,200 if with custom EMG magnetic pickups.

NYC MUSIC PRODUCTS

Instruments currently built in Brooklyn, New York. Distributed by Matthews & Ryan Musical Products of Brooklyn, New York.

NYC bass guitars are built by the luthiers at Fodera with a more traditional design, and are designed for the bass player who is looking for the quality of a Fodera bass at a more affordable price.

Before 1998, The Empire bass was offered in 2 variations: the Model 1 (list $2,000), which featured an alder body and a northern rock maple bolt-on neck; and the Model 2 (list $2,000) which had a swamp ash body, northern rock maple bolt-on neck, and a maple fingerboard. The addition of an optional high grade Curly Maple or Quilted Maple top was an extra $500, a Brazilian rosewood fingerboard is an extra $250, and Seymour Duncan Antiquity pickups run an additional $150.

ELECTRIC BASS

Empire Series

The current model **Empire Bass** is offered in a 4-string or 5-string configuration. Both models have either an alder or swamp ash body, bolt-on northern rock maple neck, 21-fret rosewood fingerboard with mother-of-pearl inlay dots (or maple with ebony dots), Seymour Duncan, EMG or Bartolini pickups, black or gold hardware, and a clear Natural satin finish. Models are optionally offered with a Moses Graphite neck (add $270 for a wooden fingerboard). The **Empire** 4-string model (list $2,400) has a scale length of 34"; the **Empire** 5-string model has a 35" scale (list $3,200).

The addition of an optional high grade Curly Maple or Quilted Maple top is an extra $250. Optional urethane lacquer finishes in custom colors are $250, while a high gloss clear finish is $150.

-NYS-

Instruments currently built by Black Creek Musical Instruments, Co., located in Middleburgh, New York.

Blackhawk guitars are handmade in upstate New York by Black Creek Musical Instrument Co. Tone woods include mahogany and finely figured maple. Many finishes and options are available - please contact the company directly for both current information and pricing (see Trademark Index).

NADINE

Instruments previously produced in Japan during the late 1980s.

The Nadine trademark is a brand name used by a British importer. Nadine guitars are good quality Fender-derived and "superstrat" models.

(Source: Tony Bacon and Paul Day, The Guru's Guitar Guide)

N

NADY

Instruments previous manufacturer unknown. Distributed circa mid 1980s by Nady Systems, Inc. of Emeryville, California.

The Nady company is best known for its wireless guitar and microphone systems that were introduced in 1977. In 1985 Nady introduced a guitar model (**Lightning**) and a bass model (**Thunder**) that featured a built-in wireless unit in a production guitar. Nady also offered a 300 watt MOSFET bass amp that was rack mountable, as well as a 100 watt MOSFET rack mountable guitar head.

Nady instrument design featured a maple through-neck design, offset double cutaway alder bodies (or wings), 6-on-a-side (four for the bass) tuning machines, 24-fret ebony fingerboard with mother-of-pearl lightning bolt inlays, black hardware, and a black finish. The Lightning had two humbucking pickups and a locking tremolo system, while the Thunder had a P/J pickup combination. The guitars are equipped with 1/4" jacks so they can still be used conventionally. However, the proper 'complete' package would be the instrument and the 501 VHF receiver. Although Nady instruments came with the 501 VHF receiver, they could be upgraded to the 601 or 701 receivers as well.

Pricing for these instruments depends on condition, playability, working electronics, and receiver (the 501 system was okay for the earlier time period; Nady builds a much better wireless system now). Instrument prices can range between $250 up to $600.

NAPOLITANO, ARTHUR

Instruments currently built in Allentown, New Jersey.

Luthier Arthur Napolitano began building electric guitars in 1967, and offered repair services on instruments in 1978 in Watchung, New Jersey. Napolitano moved to Allentown in 1992, and began building archtop guitars in 1993.

Napolitano currently offers several different archtop models like the **Primavera, Acoustic, Philadelphian, Jazz Box**, and a **Seven-String** model. Prices range from $1,795 to $5,100.

NATIONAL

Instruments previously produced in Los Angeles, California during the mid 1920s to the mid 1930s.

Instruments produced in Chicago, Illinois from mid 1930s to 1969. After National moved production to Chicago in the mid 1930s, they formally changed the company name to VALCO (but still produced 'National' brand guitars).

Instruments produced in Japan circa 1970s. Distributed by Strum'n Drum of Chicago, Illinois. When Valco went out of business in 1969, the National trademark was acquired by Strum'n Drum, who then used the trademark on a series of Japanese built guitars.

The Dopyera family emigrated from the Austro-Hungary area to Southern California in 1908. In the early 1920s, John and Rudy Dopyera began producing banjos in Southern California. They were approached by guitarist George Beauchamp to help solve his "volume" (or lack thereof) problem with other instruments in the vaudeville orchestra. In the course of their conversation, the idea of placing aluminum resonators in a guitar body for amplification purposes was developed. John Dopyera and his four brothers (plus some associates like George Beauchamp) formed National in 1925.

The initial partnership between Dopyera and Beauchamp lasted for about two years, and then John Dopyera left National to form the Dobro company. National's corporate officers in 1929 consisted of Ted E. Kleinmeyer (pres.), George Beauchamp (sec./gen. mngr.), Adolph Rickenbacker (engineer), and Paul Barth (vice pres.). In late 1929, Beauchamp left National, and joined up with Adolph Rickenbacker to form Ro-Pat-In (later Electro String/ Rickenbacker).

At the onset of the American Depression, National was having financial difficulties. Louis Dopyera bought out the National company; and as he owned more than 50% of the stock in Dobro, "merged" the two companies back together (as National Dobro). In 1936, the decision was made to move the company to Chicago, Illinois. Chicago was a veritable hotbed of mass produced musical instruments during the early to pre-World War II 1900s. Manufacturers like Washburn and Regal had facilities, and major wholesalers and retailers like the Tonk Bros. and Lyon & Healy were based there. Victor Smith, Al Frost, and Louis Dopyera moved their operation to Chicago, and in 1943 formally announced the change to VALCO (The initials of their three first names: Victor-Al-Louis Company). Valco worked on war materials during World War II, and returned to instrument production afterwards. Valco produced the National/Supro/Airline fiberglass body guitars in the 1950s and 1960s, as well as wood-bodied models.

In 1969 or 1970, Valco Guitars, Inc. went out of business. The assets of Valco/Kay were auctioned off, and the rights to the National trademark were bought by the Chicago, Illinois-based importers Strum'n Drum. Strum'n Drum, which had been importing Japanese guitars under the **Norma** trademark, were quick to introduce National on a line of Japanese produced guitars that were distributed in the U.S. market. Author/researcher Michael Wright points out that the National "Big Daddy" bolt-neck black LP copy was one of the first models that launched the Japanese "Copy Era" of the 1970s.

(Early company history courtesy Bob Brozman, The History and Artistry of National Resonator Instruments; model descriptions compiled by Dave Hull)

("Copy Era" National information courtesy Michael Wright)

For information regarding the National resonator models, please refer to the 7th Edition ***Blue Book of Acoustic Guitars***.

NEAL MOSER GUITARS

Instruments currently built in Glendora, California. Distributed by GMW Guitar Works of Glendora, California.

Neal Moser Guitars currently features both electric and archtop guitar models, as well as bass models in the **Empire** series. Prices range from $2,250 up to $2,650. For further information on model specifications, please contact Neal Moser Guitars directly (see Trademark Index).

NED CALLAN

See also C M I, SHAFTESBURY, PC, and SIMMS-WATTS.

Instruments previously built in England from the early to late 1970s.

The Ned Callan trademark is a pseudonym for custom luthier Peter Cook. Cook successfully mass-produced enough decent quality solid body guitars to warrant other trademarks: Shaftesbury and Simms-Watts were the brand names of British importers; PC (Cook's initials) and C M I (guessing Cook Musical Instruments - ?) perhaps other marketing devices? Outside of the headstock moniker, the guitars themselves seemed the same.

First Series

The two models in the First Series were produced between 1970 and 1975. Both had 2 single coil pickups, 4 controls, and a selector switch. The **Custom** model featured offset dual cutaways, while the **Salisbury** only had a single cutaway body design.

Second Series

The two models in the Second Series were even more similar: both shared the same rounded body design with two forward horns that earned them the nicknames of "Nobbly Neds"; 2 pickups, and two control switches plus a selector switch. The Hombre had chrome pickups, while the **Cody** had black pickups. Both models were produced from 1973 to 1975.

(Source: Tony Bacon and Paul Day, The Guru's Guitar Guide)

National Bell Air
courtesy Kelly Bar

NEO

Instruments currently produced in Buckingham, Pennsylvania since 1991. Distributed by NEO Products, Inc. of Buckingham, Pennsylvania.

Neo custom guitars and basses feature a body of tough, clear acrylic and a Neon tube (plus power supply) that lights up as the instrument is played. The **Neo** guitars were developed to provide extra visual effects that neon lighting can provide to a musician in the course of a performance. The **Basic** model has a retail price of $1,995, and features a 22-fret ebony fingerboard and 2 EMG humbuckers with active preamp. Additionally, the company has expanded its line to include their new **Spitfire** electric violin (now being distributed through Meisel Music, Inc. of Springfield, New Jersey). For further information, check it out on the Web, or contact Rich Roland at NEO directly (see Trademark Index).

NERVE

Instruments previously built in England during the mid 1980s.

There were three different high quality models produced by Nerve. The original design solid body guitars were "headless", meaning no headstocks at the end of the neck. Model designations were the Energy, Reaction, and the System. Anyone wishing to share knowledge for upcoming editions of the ***Blue Book of Electric Guitars*** is invited to write, and hopefully send photos.

(Source: Tony Bacon and Paul Day, The Guru's Guitar Guide)

NEUSER

Instruments currently built in Bratislava, Slovakia. Distributed by the Neuser Co., Ltd. of Finland.

Neuser handcrafts high quality custom basses that are available in 4-, 5-, and 6-string configurations. Robert Neuser began building bass guitars by himself since 1977. The Neuser Company was originated in 1989. Within a few years the company has brought together a fine team of professional craftsmen. Neuser basses feature a number of body and neck wood combinations as well as finish options (contact the company for a price quote).

The **Crusade** model (list $1,490) features a 2-piece alder body, flame maple top, glued-in 5-piece neck, 22-fret ebony fingerboard, Neuser "soapbar" pickups and EBS active electronics. Basses are finished in high gloss nitrocellulose.

The neck through-body design of the **Courage** has a 2-piece body of ash (or alder or bubinga or mahogany or maple) in different combinations, a 5-piece maple/mahogany neck or bubinga neck, 24-fret ebony fingerboard, and custom Bartolini pickups, EBS or Bartolini active electronics. List price is $2,395.

The **Cloudburst** (list $2,995) has a 9-piece maple/mahogany or bubinga neck through-body construction, 5-piece ash (or alder or bubinga, or mahogany or maple) body in different combinations, 24-fret ebony fingerboard, and Bartolini custom pickups and EBS or Bartolini active electronics. The Cloudburst is available in high gloss nitrocellulose or wax-oil finish.

Neuser's newest design features a combination of a tradition electric bass guitar and a *hammer* system where the player can control the hammers that hits the strings with a piano-like key mechanism. The **Claudia Claw-Hammer** bass (list $4,450) is available in bubinga with a maple plate, Bartolini pickups, active electronics, and a wax-oil finish.

NICKERSON

Instruments currently built in Northampton, Massachusetts since the early 1980s.

Luthier Brad Nickerson, born and raised on Cape Cod, Massachusetts, has been building archtop guitars since 1982. Nickerson attended the Berklee College of Music, and worked in the graphic arts field for a number of years. While continuing his interest in music, Nickerson received valuable advice from New York luthier Carlo Greco, as well as Cape Cod violin builder Donald MacKenzie. Nickerson also gained experience doing repair work for Bay State Vintage Guitars (Boston), and The Fretted Instrument Workshop (Amherst, Massachusetts).

With his partner Lyn Hardy, Nickerson builds archtop, flattop, and electric guitars on a custom order basis. Nickerson is also available for restorations and repair work. For further information regarding specifications and availability, please contact Nickerson Guitars directly (see Trademark Index).

NIEMINEN, KARI

See VERSOUL.

Prior to the introduction of the Versoul trademark, luthier Kari Nieminen of Finland used his name on his hand-built guitars. Nieminen, an industrial designer, teaches at the University of Art and Design in Helsinki.

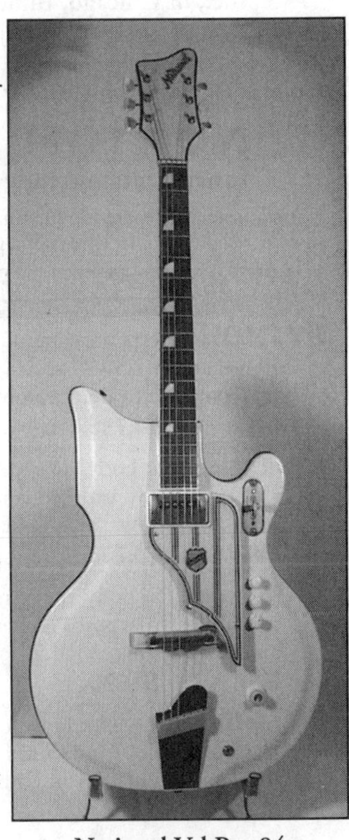

National Val Pro 84
courtesy Dave Jennett

N

NIGHTINGALE

Instruments currently built in England since the late 1980s.

Luthier Bernie Goodfellow features original designs on his high quality solid body guitars.
(Source: Tony Bacon and Paul Day, The Guru's Guitar Guide)

NINETEEN NINETYSEVEN

Previous trademark of instruments (both electric and bass) previously marketed by Akai during 1998.

Previous models included the SB410 Bass, SB511 Bass, SB411 Bass, CG112 Electric, CG112LE Electric, and the SG112 Electric. Limited Mfg. and importation to date.

NINJA

Instruments currently produced in Korea since the late 1980s.

The Ninja trademark is a brandname used by a British importer on these entry level to intermediate quality guitars. The instrument designs are based on classic American favorites.
(Source: Tony Bacon and Paul Day, The Guru's Guitar Guide)

NOBLE

Instruments previously produced in Italy circa 1950s to 1964. Production then shifted to Japan circa 1965 to 1969. Distributed by Don Noble and Company of Chicago, Illinois.

Don E. Noble, accordionist and owner of Don Noble and Company (importers), began business importing Italian accordions. By 1950, Noble was also importing and distributing guitars (manufacturer unknown). In 1962 the company began distributing EKO and Oliviero Pigini guitars, and added Wandre instruments the following year.

In the mid 1960s, the Noble trademark was owned by importer/distributor Strum'N Drum of Chicago. The Noble brand was then used on Japanese-built solid body electrics (made by Tombo) through the late 1960s.

When the Valco/Kay holdings were auctioned off in 1969, Strum'N Drum bought the rights to the National trademark. Strum'N Drum began importing Japanese-built versions of popular American designs under the National logo, and discontinued the Noble trademark during the same time period.
(Source: Michael Wright, Vintage Guitar Magazine)

NOBLES, TONY

Instruments currently built in Austin, Texas.

Shellacious! Luthier Tony Noble builds high quality guitars and also writes a column in *Vintage Guitar Magazine.* For further information, contact Precision Guitarworks directly (see Trademark Index).

NORMA

Instruments previously built in Japan between 1965 to 1970 by the Tombo company. Distributed by Strum'N Drum, Inc., of Chicago, Illinois.

These Japanese built guitars were distributed in the U.S. market by Strum'N Drum, Inc. of Chicago, Illinois. Strum'N Drum also distributed the Japanese-built Noble guitars of the mid to late 1960s, and National solid body guitars in the early 1970s.
(Source: Michael Wright, Guitar Stories Volume One)

NORTON

Instruments currently manufactured in Belgrade, Montana.

Norton instruments are modular in design allowing for switching of pickups and body modules. This is done through a system of metal rails that even allow for changing placement of a pickup.

Modular Electric Guitars

PYTHON - serpentine modular body with snake's head being the upper bout, quartersawn maple neck, rosewood fingerboard with dot position markers, 25 ½ " scale, 6-on-a-side tuners, standard with 2 humbucking pickups, modular system allows for switching of pickups, coil tap, gold hardware, 1 volume/1 tone, 3-way switch. Available in red and black finishes. Current Mfg.

MSR $1,795

AEM - modular body, quartersawn maple neck, rosewood fingerboard with dot position markers, 25 ½" scale, other scales on request, 3-per-side tuners, two exposed coil humbucking pickups, other pickup mudules available, coil tap or phase available, tremelo bridge, 1 volume/1 tone control. Available in black, blue, red, copper, and green finishes. Current Mfg.

MSR $1,795

ADM - modular body, quartersawn maple neck, rosewood fingerboard with dot position markers, 3-per-side tuners, 25 ½" scale, other scales available, two exposed coil humbucking pickups, other pickup modules available, coil tap or phase available, 1 volume/1 tone control, 3-way switch. Available in red, black, and blue finishes. Current Mfg.

MSR $1,695

DR. BILL - modular body, quartersawn maple neck, rosewood fingerboard with dot position markers, 3 per sie tuners, 25 ½" scale, other scales available, 2 humbucking pickups, other pickup modules available, phase and coil tap available, 1 volume/1 tone control, 3-way switch. Available in blue finish. Disc. 2000.

Last MSR was $1,450.

Conventional Electric Guitars

NBG Performer Series

NBG-6 - offset double cutaway body with the look of the modular models, body features a large oval cutout in lower bout, rosewood fingerboard with dot position markers, 6-on-a-side tuners, three humbucking pickups, 1 volume/1 Tone, 3-way switch, stop tailpiece. Available in red and sunburst finishes. Current Mfg.

MSR $899

NFB Performer Series

MARK 1 - offset double cutaway body, maple neck and fingerboard, black dot position markers, 6-on-a-side tuners, 2 exposed coil humbucking pickups, tremelo bridge, 1 volume/1 tone control, 3-way switch. Available in Cherryburst finish. Current Mfg.

MSR $399

MARK II - similar to Mark 1 except has Floyd Rose Licensed tremelo. Available in Sunburst finish. Current Mfg.

MSR $499

MARK III - similar to Mark II except has gold hardware and higher grade top. Available in Redburst finish.

MSR $599

Modular Electric Bass

MERLIN - modular body, quartersawn mapleneck, rosewood fingerboard with dot position markers, 4-on-a-side tuners, two pickups, different pickup modules available, 1 volume/1 tone control, 3-way switch. Available in black finish. Current Mfg.

MSR $1,795

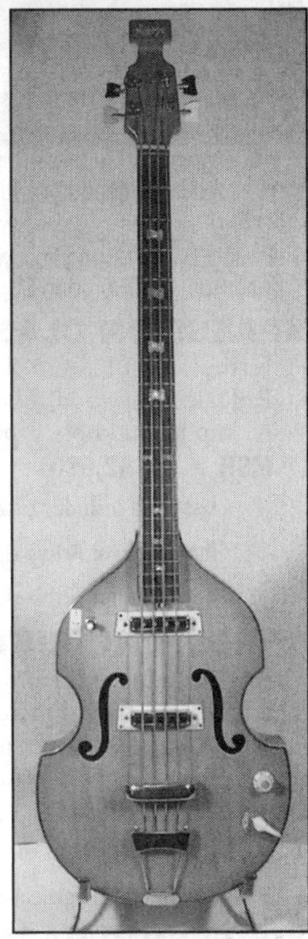

Norma Vidin Bass
courtesy J.R. Guitars

NOUVEAU GUITARS

See LADY LUCK.

NOVA GUITARS

See BUSCARINO.

Instruments currently built in Florida since 1981.

Luthier John Buscarino founded the Nova Guitar Company in 1981, and produced a number of high quality solid body electric guitars under that logo before changing to his current trademark of **Buscarino**.

NOVAX

Instruments currently built in San Leandro, California since 1985.

Novak has built custom guitars since 1970, in locations from New York to California.

Luthier Ralph Novak began playing guitar at age 14 in 1965, and also began experimenting with guitar design, modifying guitars, and making (crude) custom parts.

By age 16, Novak was repairing and customizing guitars for friends, and doing some freelance repair for local music stores. Novak continued part-time repairwork through high school at Stuyvesant in New York, and through college at Brooklyn College, where he studied music as a major. By age 19 Novak was working with Charles LoBue at GuitarLab in Greenwich Village in New York. Later, he quit college to work full-time at GuitarLab, where he worked with some of New York City's finest guitarists and built custom guitars. In his spare time Novak began working on innovative designs with LoBue.

Around 1975, LoBue and GuitarLab moved uptown to Alex's Music on West 48th street. Novak stayed at Alex's for about a year, and then began free lance repair work for several stores on West 48th as well as seeing private clients in his repair shop in a downtown loft.

In 1978, Novak and LoBue moved to the San Francisco Bay area, and worked together until LoBue moved back to New York City. Novak stayed in the Bay area and worked at Subway Guitars in Berkeley, later becoming a partner and helping to build it into the viable repair shop it is today. In 1985 Novak left the partnership to open his own repair shop in Oakland, where he also built several custom instruments a year. In 1989 Novak received a U.S. patent for his "Fanned Fret" system, and began working on prototypes to find the optimum scale length combination for guitar and bass. In 1992 the Novax fretboard was mentioned in **Business Week** magazine's "1992 Idea Winners", and received the Industrial Design Society Award for Excellence in 1993 (the last music-related award was Ned Steinberger's headless bass in 1982).

The first official Novax guitar was completed in 1993, as the result of several years of researching and developing, gathering opinions and suggestions from players of all styles of music. Novak eventually obtained custom hardware for his system, and since then has concentrated on building Expression series and Tribute model guitars and basses. Due to the labor-intensive nature of the work, Novak has "retired" from the daily repair business to focus directly on his guitars.

(Biography courtesy Ralph Novak, 3-18-96)

The patented Novax Fanned Fretboard has been licensed out to such notables as Dingwall Designer Guitars, Klein Custom Guitars, Acacia Instruments, and in late 1995 Moses Graphite announced retrofit epoxy-graphite Novax-style necks for Precision and Jazz basses.

Norma 12-string Model
courtesy John Oldag

ELECTRIC

Expression Series

The Expression Guitars are set-neck models with ergonomic body shapes that are highly carved for comfort and beauty. The new **Expression 8 String** was designed in conjunction with Charlie Hunter, and incorporates 3 bass strings and 5 guitar strings for a wide spectrum of sound. Current retail on this model is $4,500.

Novak's 6- or 7-string hollow body model named the **A-X** which is constructed "under tension" so the finished guitar is bright and responsive. Models range in price from $2,950 up to $3,250.

EXPRESSION CLASSIC - offset double cutaway body features choices of Walnut, Maple, Lacewood, Zebrano, Swamp Ash, or Birch; vertical-grain Eastern Rock Maple neck, patented 22-fret "Fanned Fret" design, choice of fingerboard materials such as Wenge, Purpleheart, Paduak, Rosewood, Ebony, or Bird's Eye Maple; choice of three nut widths, Bartolini pickups, volume knob, rotary switching tone knob, pickup blend knob, 3-per-side headstock design and chrome tuners. Available in Natural finish. Mfg. 1993 to date.

MSR $2,650

List price includes case.

Add $120 for Active circuitry with gain boost and active/passive switching.

Add $175 for Active circuitry with treble and bass boost (16 Db cut/boost).

EXPRESSION CUSTOM - offset double cutaway body features a laminate design of highly figured bookmatched maple over a body core of Paduak, Lacewood, or Purpleheart; vertical-grain Eastern Rock Maple neck, patented 22-fret "Fanned Fret" design, choice of wood-bound fingerboard materials such as Wenge, Purpleheart, Paduak, Rosewood, Ebony, or Bird's Eye Maple; choice of three nut widths, Bartolini pickups, active circuitry (4 different choices), volume knob, rotary switching tone knob, pickup blend knob, gold or black chrome hardware, 3-per-side headstock design. Available in Natural finish. Current Mfg.

MSR $3,150

List price includes case.

Add $200 for vertical-grain Paduak neck.

EXPRESSION BARITONE - offset double cutaway body features choice of Walnut, Birch, or Lacewood; vertical-grain Eastern Rock Maple neck, patented 22-fret "Fanned Fret" design, choice of fingerboard materials such as Wenge, Purpleheart, Paduak, Rosewood, or Ebony; Bartolini "Soapbar" pickups, extra bass-cut circuitry, volume knob, rotary switching tone knob, pickup blend knob, gold or black chrome hardware, 3-per-side headstock design. Available in Natural finish. Current Mfg.

MSR $2,850

List price includes gig bag.

The Baritone model is a specially designed long-scale guitar in "B" tuning.

Tribute Series

The Tribute models are built in tribute to the pioneering work of Leo Fender, and feature bolt-on necks as well as body designs that recall the classic lines of Fender's work.

TRIBUTE GUITAR - Tribute body designs are either single cutaway ("Tele") or double cutaway ("Strat") based solids available in Alder, Ash, or Swamp Ash (body styles are also available in non-traditional laminated exotic woods), Patended "Fanned Fret" fingerboard, Bartolini pickups mounted to the pickguard, Bartolini circuitry, traditional hardware and styling. Current Mfg.

MSR $1,950

Add $500 for laminated body and rear routed electronics (eliminates pickguard).

ELECTRIC BASS

Novak's 5-string electric bass, named the **Mo' B**, is constructed with birch, lacewood, maple, or walnut. Models can be ordered as a Custom, with laminated body and bound fretboard (with wood choices similar to the Expression Custom guitar model).

EXPRESSION BASS 4-STRING - offset double cutaway body features choice of Walnut, Birch, Maple, or Lacewood; vertical-grain Eastern Rock Maple neck, patented "Fanned Fret" design, choice of fingerboard materials such as Wenge, Purpleheart, Paduak, Rosewood, or Ebony; Bartolini "Soapbar" pickups, Bartolini circuitry, volume knob, tone knob, pickup blend knob, 2-per-side headstock design. Available in Natural finish. Current Mfg.

MSR $2,650

Expression Bass 5-String - similar to Expression Bass, except has five strings. Current Mfg.

MSR $2,750

Expression Bass 6-String - similar to Expression Bass, except has six strings. Current Mfg.

MSR $2,850

EXPRESSION CUSTOM BASS - offset double cutaway body features a laminate design of highly figured bookmatched maple over a body core of Paduak, Lacewood, or Purpleheart; vertical-grain Eastern Rock Maple neck, patented "Fanned Fret" design, choice of wood-bound fingerboard materials such as Wenge, Purpleheart, Paduak, Rosewood, Ebony, or Bird's Eye Maple; Bartolini pickups, Bartolini circuitry, volume knob, tone knob, pickup blend knob, gold or black chrome hardware, 2-per-side headstock design. Available in Natural finish. Current Mfg.

MSR $3,150

List price includes case.

Expression Custom Bass 5-String - similar to Expression Custom Bass, except has five strings. Current Mfg.

MSR $3,250

Expression Custom Bass 6-String - similar to Expression Custom Bass, except has six strings. Current Mfg.

MSR $3,350

TRIBUTE BASS - Tribute body designs are a double cutaway ("Precision") or ("Jazz") based solids available in Alder, Ash, or Swamp Ash (body styles are also available in non-traditional laminated exotic woods), Patented "Fanned Fret" fingerboard, Bartolini pickups mounted to the pickguard, Bartolini circuitry, traditional hardware and styling. Current Mfg.

MSR $1,950

Add $500 for laminated body and rear routed electronics (eliminates pickguard).

Add $175 for active tone shaping electronics.

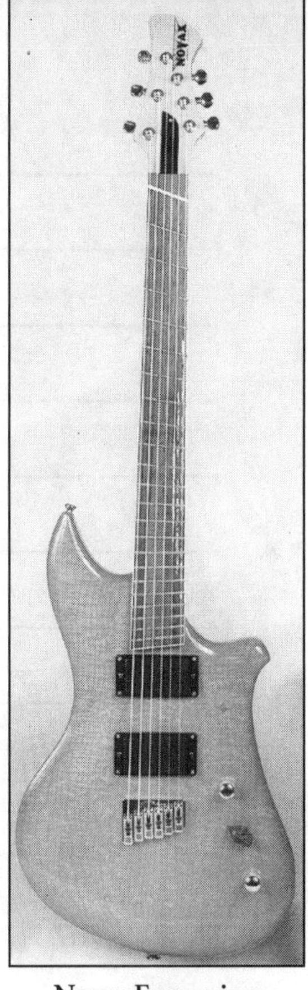

Novax Expression
courtesy Ralph Novak

Novax Charlie Hunter
8-string model
courtesy Novax Guitars

NOTES

Thomas (with Andreas) & Mike (with Triggs) from Mike's Butcher Shop in St. Paul, MN rock during their Saturday breaks in the summertime.

N

Section O

O'HAGAN

Instruments previously built in St. Louis Park (a suburb of Minneapolis), Minnesota from 1979 to 1983. Distributed by the Jemar Corporation of St. Louis Park, Minnesota.

O'Hagan guitars were developed by Jerry O'Hagan. O'Hagan, a former clarinetist and music teacher, began importing the Grande brand acoustic guitars from Japan in 1975. In 1979, the O'Hagan guitar company was formed to build quality, affordable solid body guitars. Two years later, the company incorporated as the Jemar Corporation (this designation can be found on the back of post-1981 models).

In 1983, both a nationwide recession and a resurgence in traditional guitar design (the beginning of"Strat-mania") took a toll on the four year old company. When a bank note became due, the company was unable to pay. The I.R.S. had an outstanding bill due as well, and seized company holdings to auction off. The O'Hagan company, which tried to provide quality guitars at an affordable price, closed its door for good. It is estimated that only 3,000 instruments were produced during the company's four year production, with the majority being the NightWatch models.

Serialization ran one of two ways during the company's production: The first serial number code was *YYMXXX*, with the first two digits indicating the year, the third (and sometimes fourth) digit the month, and the final digits provided the sequential numbering. The second code was probably instituted in the 1980s, as only one digit indicated the year. The second serial code was *MYMXXX*, with the first and third digits indicating the month, the second digit the year, and the last three digits sequential numbering.

(Source: Michael Wright, Guitar Stories Volume One)

VISUAL IDENTIFICATION FEATURES

Headstock Logo

O'Hagan instruments can be identified by the *O'Hagan* decal, or a glued on stylized *O H* logo which also featured a cloverleaf (or sometimes just the cloverleaf). Instruments may also sport a "Jemar Corporation" decal back by the serial number.

Pickup Identification

One dating method to use is based on the instrument's pickup (if the original pickups are still installed). Instruments built between 1979 and 1980 had pickups by Mighty Mite; in 1981 they were switched to DiMarzio; and finally O'Hagan settled on Schaller pickups in 1982 to 1983.

ELECTRIC

The most eye-catching model was the **Shark** (basic retail list $529), which was introduced in 1979. The body design recalls a rounded off Explorer, and features maple and walnut in a neck-through design. The vaguely offset headstock features 3+3 tuning machine alignment, and the guitar has two humbuckers, a 3-way pickup selector switch, two volume knobs and a master tone knob. Other models may feature push/pull coil tap potentiometers (this option cost an extra $90), and a phase switch. O'Hagan also developed the **NightWatch model**, initially a single cutaway LP-style guitar (original retail list $479), and then joined by a dual cutaway model (same retail list price) of the same name.

In 1980, O'Hagan introduced his most popular model, the **Twenty Two** (retail list $529). This model, again built of Maple and Walnut, is based on the popular Flying V design. The **Laser** model, a sort of Strat-based design, featured a six-on-a-side headstock and either three single coils or a humbucker. As O'Hagans were basically hand built custom instruments, various options can be found on existing models, and models were available in a left-handed configuration.

BASS

All guitar models had a bass counterpart (original retail prices ran an additional $10 to $50 extra, depending on the model). Bass models were available as a *Regular*, which had one pickup; or a *Special*, which had two pickups.

OFB GUITARS

See PAT WILKINS.

Instruments previously built in Virginia Beach, Virginia during the early 1990s.

OAHU

Previous trademark of instrument distributed by the Oahu Publishing Company of Cleveland, Ohio.

The Oahu Publishing Company offered Hawaiian and Spanish style acoustic guitars, lap steels, sheet music, and a wide range of accessories during the Hawaiian music craze of pre-War America. Catalogs stress the fact that the company is a major music distributor (thus the question of who built the guitars is still unanswered). Oahu production totals are still unknown.

OAKLAND

Instruments previously produced in Japan from the late 1970s through the early 1980s.

These good quality solid body guitars featured both original designs and designs based on classic American favorites.
(Source: Tony Bacon and Paul Day, The Guru's Guitar Guide)

ODELL

Instrument previous production unknown (possibly produced by the Vega Guitar Company of Boston, Massachusetts). Distributed through the Vega Guitar catalog circa early 1930s to the early 1950s.

Odell acoustic guitars with slotted headstocks were offered through early Vega Guitar catalogs in the early 1930s. In the 1932 catalog, the four Odell models were priced above Harmony guitars, but were not as pricey as the Vega models.
Other Odell *mystery guitars* appear at guitar shows from time to time. David Pavlick is the current owner of an interesting arch top model. The 3 tuners per side headstock features a decal which reads *Odell - Vega Co., - Boston*, and features a 16 1/2" archtop body, one Duo-Tron pickup, 20-fret neck, volume/tone controls mounted on the trapeze tailpiece. Inside one f-hole there is "828H1325" stamped into the back wood. Any readers with further information are invited to write to the *Blue Book of Electric Guitars.*
(Source: David J. Pavlick, Woodbury, Connecticut)

ODYSSEY

Instruments previously built in North Vancouver, British Columbia (Canada), from 1976 to 1981.

Odyssey Guitars, Ltd. was founded in 1976 by partners Attila Balogh (luthier/production manager) and Joe Salley (sales manager). The preliminary guitar model was featured both as a carved top model with body binding and diamond-shaped fingerboard inlays, as well as a non-bound version in Mahogany or Ash body. In 1981 Balogh and Salley parted ways and dissolved the company.
Salley still retains the rights to the Odyssey name, and sells Odyssey Accessories at the Wes-Can company in Surrey, British Columbia. In March 1983, Balogh was commissioned by Paul Dean (Loverboy) to produce a limited run of 50 Paul Dean models. While these models were similar to the custom handcrafted guitar that Paul Dean himself built, they had nothing to do with Odyssey guitars. Balogh then worked with Ray Ayotte to set up the Ayotte Drum Company. Attila Balogh was killed in an accident in November of 1987. Balogh is remembered as being a *true craftsman* in every sense of the word.
(Company history and model information courtesy Mike Kinal, April 1997)

Model Dating Identification

1976-1977: The 3-per-side headstock has a slight dip in the center, bass and treble horns are relatively short.

1978-1979: Redesigned body has lengthened bass and treble horns, center of headstock has a rounded up area.

1980-1981: Introduction of the bolt-neck **Attila** models, headstock has an *AA* logo.

ELECTRIC

The first series of Odyssey guitars featured an ornate carved top/bound body model called the **Carved Guitar**, which had a retail price of $1,195. The non-bound body version was available in a mahogany or ash body. All models featured a 3-per-side headstock, set-neck design, 2 DiMarzio humbuckers, Schaller tuners, brass nut/hardware, and a high gloss hand rubbed finish. The **Mahogany Guitar** model listed for $895, and the **Ash Guitar** was $995. Both non-bound guitar models were offered with a corresponding Bartolini Hi-A pickup equipped 4-string bass model with similar listed prices.

Attila (AA) Series

These models were offered between 1980 and 1981, and featured the Odyssey guitar and bass design with a bolt-on (instead of set-in) neck. Pricing is estimated to be around the Hawk series level.

Carved Top Series 100

In late 1978 the body design was retooled, and the headstock profile was redesigned. The previous Carved Guitar model became the **Carved Top Series 100**.

G100 - carved bookmatched figured maple top, set-in neck, 24 3/4" scale, 3-per-side headstock, herringbone body binding, maple headstock veneer, 24-fret bound ebony fingerboard with mother-of-pearl dot inlays, tune-o-matic bridge/stop tailpiece, brass hardware, Schaller or Grover tuners, 2 DiMarzio Dual Sound humbucking pickups, 2 volume/2 tone controls, 2 coil tap switches, 1 phase switch, 3-way pickup selector switch. Available in Tobacco Shaded (TS) or Wine Shaded (WS) finishes. Mfg. 1978 to 1981.

Last MSR was $1,195.

Carved Ash Series 200

In 1978, the previous Ash Guitar model became the **Carved Top Series 200**.

G200 - double cutaway carved ash body, set-in neck, 24 3/4" scale, 3-per-side headstock, 24-fret bound ebony fingerboard with abalone inlays, tune-o-matic bridge/stop tailpiece, brass hardware, Schaller or Grover tuners, 2 DiMarzio Dual Sound humbucking pickups, 2 volume/2 tone controls, 2 coil tap switches, 1 phase switch, 3-way pickup selector switch. Available in Tobacco Shaded (TS) or Wine Shaded (WS) finishes. Mfg. 1978 to 1981.

Last MSR was $995.

Mahogany Series 300

In 1978, the previous Mahogany Guitar model became the **Mahogany Series 300**.

G300 - double cutaway mahogany body, set-in neck, 24 3/4" scale, 3-per-side headstock, 24-fret bound ebony fingerboard with abalone inlays, tune-o-matic bridge/stop tailpiece, brass hardware, Schaller or Grover tuners, 2 DiMarzio Dual Sound humbucking pickups, 2 volume/2 tone controls, 1 phase switch, 3-way pickup selector switch. Available in Tobacco Shaded (TS) or Wine Shaded (WS) finishes. Mfg. 1978 to 1981.

Last MSR was $895.

ODell-Vega CO. Boston
courtesy David J. Pavlick

Hawk Series 400

Based on Odyssey guitar designs, the Hawk model was designated the economy series with a maple body, natural finish, and different hardware choices.

G400 - double cutaway maple body, set-in neck, 24 3/4" scale, 3-per-side headstock, 24-fret bound ebony fingerboard with dot inlays, tune-o-matic bridge/stop tailpiece, brass hardware, Schaller or Grover tuners, 2 DiMarzio humbuckers, volume/tone controls, 3-way pickup selector switch. Available in Natural finish. Mfg. 1978 to 1981.

Last MSR was $595.

Add $50 for Tobacco Shaded (TS) or Wine Shaded (WS) finishes.

Semi-Acoustic Series 500

This model featured a neck-through body design and a free-floating spruce top.

G500 - double cutaway semi-hollow body, spruce top, neck-through body, 24 3/4" scale, 3-per-side headstock, 24-fret bound ebony fingerboard with mother-of-pearl inlays, hand carved ebony bridge/stop tailpiece, brass hardware, Schaller or Grover tuners, 2 DiMarzio humbucking pickups, 2 volume/ 2 tone controls, 2 coil tap switches, 1 phase switch, 3-way pickup selector switch. Available in Tobacco Shaded (TS) or Wine Shaded (WS) finishes. Mfg. 1978 to 1981.

Last MSR was $1,995.

Add $200 for optional 6-band on board EQ.

Custom Series

Odyssey's **Custom Series 600** offered the customer the choice of any Odyssey guitar style, exotic or noble hardwoods, DiMarzio Dual Sound, PAF, Super II pickups, or Bartolini Hi-A pickups, 2 volume/2 tone controls, 2 coil tap switches, 1 phase switch, 6-band on board graphic EQ, 3-way pickup selector switch. The **G600** guitar or the **B600** bass was available in Tobacco Shaded (TS) or Wine Shaded (WS) finishes, and either model had a list price of $1,495.

Odyssey offered a **Custom V** and **Custom X-plorer** models that featured neck-through body construction, rosewood fingerboards, a bone nut, 2 DiMarzio pickups, Gotoh Gut machine heads, a Leo Quan Badass bridge, volume/tone controls, phase switch, 3-way selector switch. The *V* had a 3+3 "Flying V" headstock, while the *X-plorer* had a six on a side headstock. Both models were offered at $999 with a headshell case.

ELECTRIC BASS

Carved Top Bass Series 100

B100 - carved bookmatched figured maple top, set-in neck, 34" scale, 2-per-side headstock, herringbone body binding, maple headstock veneer, 24-fret bound ebony fingerboard with mother-of-pearl dot inlays, tune-o-matic/stop tailpiece, brass hardware, Schaller or Grover tuners, 2 Bartolini Hi-A pickups, 2 volume/ 2 tone controls, 3-way pickup selector switch. Available in Tobacco Shaded (TS) or Wine Shaded (WS) finishes. Mfg. 1978 to 1981.

Last MSR was $1,195.

Carved Ash Bass Series 200

B200 - double cutaway ash body, set-in neck, 34" scale, 2-per-side headstock, 24-fret bound ebony fingerboard with abalone inlays, tune-o-matic/stop tailpiece, brass hardware, Schaller or Grover tuners, 2 Bartolini Hi-A pickups, 2 volume/2 tone controls, 3-way pickup selector switch. Available in Tobacco Shaded (TS) or Wine Shaded (WS) finishes. Mfg. 1978 to 1981.

Last MSR was $995.

Mahogany Bass Series 300

B300 - double cutaway mahogany body, set-in neck, 34" scale, 2-per-side headstock, 24-fret bound ebony fingerboard with abalone inlays, tune-o-matic/stop tailpiece, brass hardware, Schaller or Grover tuners, 2 Bartolini Hi-A pickups, 2 volume/2 tone controls, 3-way pickup selector switch. Available in Tobacco Shaded (TS) or Wine Shaded (WS) finishes. Mfg. 1978 to 1981.

Last MSR was $895.

Hawk Bass Series 400

B400 - double cutaway maple body, set-in neck, 34" scale, 2-per-side headstock, 24-fret bound ebony fingerboard with dot inlays, Leo Quan Badass bridge, brass hardware, Schaller or Grover tuners, DiMarzio P-bass-style split pickup, volume/tone controls, pickup selector switch. Available in Natural finish. Mfg. 1978 to 1981.

Last MSR was $595.

Add $50 for Tobacco Shaded (TS) or Wine Shaded (WS) finishes.

Semi-Acoustic Bass Series 500

B500 - double cutaway semi-hollow body, spruce top, neck-through body, 34" scale, 2-per-side headstock, 24-fret bound ebony fingerboard with mother-of-pearl inlays, hand carved ebony bridge/stop tailpiece, brass hardware, Schaller or Grover tuners, 2 Bartolini pickups, 2 volume/2 tone controls, 3-way pickup selector switch. Available in Tobacco Shaded (TS) or Wine Shaded (WS) finishes. Mfg. 1978 to 1981.

Last MSR was $1,995.

This model was available with a fretted or unfretted fingerboard.

Add $200 for optional 6-band on board EQ.

OLD KRAFTSMAN

See chapter on House Brands.

This trademark has been identified as a "House Brand" of Speigel, and was sold through the Speigel catalogs. The Old Kraftsman brand was used on a full line of acoustic, thinline acoustic/electric, and solid body guitars from circa 1930s to the 1960s. Old Kraftsman instruments were probably built by various companies in Chicago, including Kay and some models by Gibson.

(Source: Michael Wright, Vintage Guitar Magazine)

ONYX

Instruments previously built in Korea during the 1980s.

The Onyx trademark was the brand name of an Australian importer. These solid body guitars were generally entry level to intermediate quality. However, the late '80s model **1030** bears a passing resemblance to a Mosrite Mark I with modern hardware.

(Source: Tony Bacon, The Ultimate Guitar Book)

OPTEK

See SMARTLIGHT.

OPUS

Instruments currently produced in Japan.

The Opus trademark is a brand name of U.S. importers Ampeg/Selmer.

(Source: Michael Wright, Guitar Stories Volume One)

ORANGE

Instruments previously produced in Korea during the mid 1970s.

While this solid body guitar did feature an original body design and two humbucking pickups, the finish was painted black!

(Source: Tony Bacon and Paul Day, The Guru's Guitar Guide)

ORBIT

See TEISCO DEL REY.

Instruments previously built in Japan during the mid to late 1960s.

The Orbit trademark is the brand name of a UK importer. Orbit guitars were produced by the same folks who built Teisco guitars in Japan; so while there is the relative coolness of the original Teisco design, the entry level quality is the drawback.

(Source: Tony Bacon and Paul Day, The Guru's Guitar Guide)

ORPHEUM

See also LANGE.

Instruments previously manufactured in Chicago, Illinois circa 1930s to 1940s. Distributed by William L. Lange Company of New York, New York, and by C. Bruno & Son.

Instruments later manufactured in Japan circa 1960s. Distributed by Maurice Lipsky Music Company, Inc., of New York, New York.

Orpheum guitars were first introduced by distributor William L. Lange Company of New York in the mid 1930s. The Orpheum brand instruments were also distributed by C. Bruno & Son during this early period. It is estimated that some of the Orpheum models were built in Chicago, Illinois by the Kay company.

Lange's company went out of business in the early 1940s, but New York distributor Maurice Lipsky resumed distribution of Orpheum guitars circa 1944. The Maurice Lipsky Music Company continued distributing Orpheum guitars, through to the 1960s (See also DOMINO).

(Source: Tom Wheeler, American Guitars; Orpheum Manufacturing Company catalog courtesy John Kinnemeyer, JK Lutherie)

Later 1960s products include the Orpheum Conqueror organ (Model 4000), solid state amplifiers for guitars, PA speakers, the model MF 490 Multi-Fuzzzz and model S 470 Sitar Fuzzzz effects pedals. The Orpheum guitar line's three models feature Domino-ish headstocks and Japanese-style electronics. The semi-hollow SL 3 (retail $350) had 3 "Novak designed Jazz pickups" (covered single coils?), 2 channels of 'professional sound', and 3 individual tone controls. "Audiences are captivated by the amazing range of original sound and tone color", claimed the Orpheum flyer (perhaps captivated is too strong of a word, hmm?). Other models include the SL 2 (retail $300) a triple bound fingerboard, and pearl position markers. The Dimension Jazz Bass (model SL 62) has a long scale neck, and 2 Jazz dimension pickups (original retail $300).

Until more research is done in the Orpheum area, prices will continue to fluctuate. Be very cautious in the distinction between the American models and the later overseas models produced in Japan. "What the market will bear" remains the watch word for Orpheums.

OSCAR SCHMIDT

Instruments currently built in Korea, and distributed by Oscar Schmidt International, located in Mundelein, Illinois.

In 1999, Oscar Schmidt released 2 new semi-hollow body electric models, the OE30CH, and the OE30TS. Please contact the distributor directly for more information and current pricing (see Trademark Index).

Old Kraftsman
courtesy John Beeson

OTHON

Instruments currently built in Ovale, California.

Luthier Robert Othon currently offers a range of high quality, solid body guitars that feature a lightweight top of solid rock. Othon's patented process produces a layer of stone so thin that it adds only 6 to 8 ounces to the total weight. Both the Classic (retail list $2,470) and the **Highlander** ($2,630) feature offset double cutaway alder bodies, while the **Viking** ($2,370) has a Honduran mahogany body and a slight flare to the forward horns. The **Traditional** ($2,370) features a single cutaway swamp ash body, 2 single coils, and a fixed bridge. All models feature bolt-on hard rock maple necks and 25 1/2" scale lengths. For further information, contact luthier Robert Othon directly (see Trademark Index).

OTWIN

See MUSIMA.

Instruments previously built in East Germany in the late 1950s to early 1960s.

Instruments with the Otwin brand name were built by the Musima company in Germany during the late 1950s on. Earlier models were available in original designs of both solid body and semi-hollow body configurations through the early 1960s.

(Source: Tony Bacon and Paul Day, The Guru's Guitar Guide)

OVATION

Instruments currently built in New Hartford, Connecticut since 1967. Distribution is handled by the Kaman Music Corporation of Bloomfield, Connecticut.

The Ovation guitar company, and the nature of the Ovation guitar's synthetic back are directly attributed to founder Charles H. Kaman's experiments in helicopter aviation. Kaman, who began playing guitar back in high school, trained in the field of aeronautics and graduated from the Catholic University in Washington, D.C. His first job in 1940 was with a division of United Aircraft, home of aircraft inventor Igor Sikorsky. In 1945, Kaman formed the Kaman Aircraft Corporation to pursue his helicopter-related inventions.

As the company began to grow, the decision was made around 1957 to diversify into manufacturing products in different fields. Kaman initially made overtures to the Martin company, as well as exploring both Harmony and Ludwig drums. Finally, the decision was made to start fresh. Due to research in vibrations and resonances in the materials used to build helicopter blades, guitar development began in 1964 with employees John Ringso and Jim Rickard. In fact, it was Rickard's pre-war Martin D-45 that was used as the"test standard". In 1967, the Ovation company name was chosen, incorporated, and settled into its new facilities in New Hartford, Connecticut. The first model named that year was the Balladeer.

Ovation guitars were debuted at the 1967 NAMM show. Early players and endorsers included Josh White, Charlie Byrd, and Glen Campbell. Piezo pickup equipped models were introduced in 1972, as well as other models. During the early 1970s, Kaman Music (Ovation's parent company) acquired the well-known music distributors Coast, and also part of the Takamine guitar company. By 1975, Ovation decided to release an entry level instrument, and the original Applause/Medallion/Matrix designs were first built in the U.S. before production moved into Korea.

In 1986, Kaman's oldest son became president of Kaman Music. Charles William *Bill* Kaman II had begun working in the Ovation factory at age 14. After graduating college in 1974, Bill was made Director of Development at the Moosup, Connecticut plant. A noted Travis Bean guitar collector (see Kaman's Travis Bean history later in this book), Bill Kaman remained active in the research and development aspect of model design. Kaman helped design the Viper III, and the UK II solid bodies.

Bill Kaman gathered all branches of the company *under one roof* as the Kaman Music Corporation (KMC) in 1986. As the Ovation branch was now concentrating on acoustic and acoustic/electric models, the corporation bought the independent Hamer company in 1988 as the means to re-enter the solid body guitar market. Furthermore, KMC began distributing Trace-Elliot amplifiers the same year, and bought the company in 1992. The Kaman Music Corporation acts as the parent company, and has expanded to cover just about all areas of the music business. As a result, the Ovation branch now concentrates specifically on producing the best acoustic guitars, with the same attention to detail that the company was founded on.

(Source: Walter Carter, The History of the Ovation Guitar)

FOUR DIGIT MODEL CODES

Ovation instruments are identified by a four digit model code. The individual numbers within the code will indicate production information about that model.

The first digit is always 1.

The second digit describes the type of guitar:

1	**Acoustic Roundbacks or Semi-hollow electrics**
2	**Solid Body or Semi-hollow body electrics**
3	**Ultra acoustics**
4	**Solid body**
5	**Acoustic/Electric cutaway Adamas and II/Elite/Ultra electric**
6	**Acoustic/Electric Roundbacks**

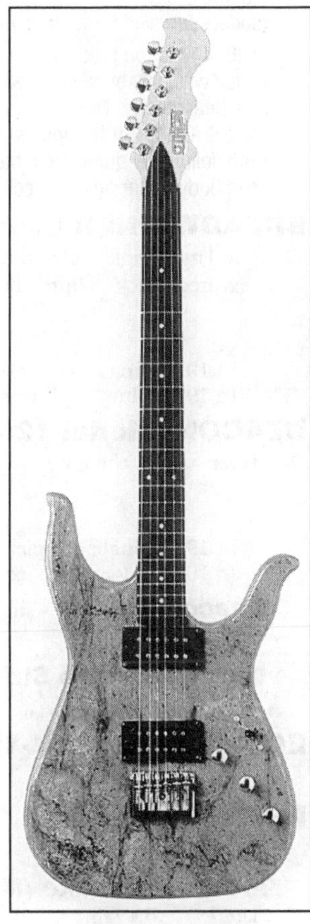

Othon Viking
courtesy Othon Guitars

O

GRADING	100% MINT	98% NEAR MINT	95% EXC+	90% EXC	80% VG+	70% VG	60% G

7 **Deep**
8 **Shallow**

The third digit indicates the depth of the guitar's bowl:

1 **Standard (5 1/2 13/16" deep)**
2 **Artist (5 1/2 1/8" deep)**
3 **Elite/Matrix electric deep bowl**
4 **Matrix shallow bowl**
5 **Custom Balladeer/Legend/Legend 12/Custom Legend 12/Anniversary**
6 **Cutaway electric, deep bowl**
7 **Cutaway electric, shallow bowl**
8 **Adamas (6 1/2 1/16" deep)**

The fourth digit indicates the model (for the first 8 acoustics):

1 **Balladeer**
2 **Deluxe Balladeer**
3 **Classic**
4 **Josh White**
5 **12 String**
6 **Contemporary Folk Classic**
7 **Glen Campbell Artist Balladeer**
8 **Glen Campbell 12 String**

The color code follows the hyphen after the four digit model number. Colors available on Ovation guitars are Sunburst (1), Red (2), Natural (4), Black (5), White (6), LTD Nutmeg/Anniversary Brown/Beige/Tan (7), Blue (8), Brown (9), *Barnwood* [a grey to black sunburst] (B), and Honeyburst (H). Other specialty colors may have a 2- or 3-letter abbreviation.

(Information collected in Mr. Carter's Ovation Appendices was researched and compiled by Paul Bechtoldt)

For further information regarding Ovation acoustic models, please refer to the 7th Edition ***Blue Book of Acoustic Guitars***.

ELECTRIC

Although Ovation's solid body guitars are generally overshadowed by the fine acoustic models, they still are good playable instruments that offer a change of pace from the traditional market favorites. Ovation introduced the **Electric Storm** semi-hollowbody guitars in 1968, and they were available through 1973. The Electric Storm models featured bodies built in Germany, and hardware by Schaller. American-built solid bodies were presented beginning 1972, and various models survived through to 1983. Early models featured an on-board FET preamp, and are probably the first production guitars with "active electronics".

In 1984, Ovation produced the **Hard Body** series, which featured Korean-built necks and bodies, DiMarzio pickups and Schaller hardware. The Hard Body series was only briefly offered for a year, and can be identified by the natural wood strip bearing the Ovation name on the lower section of the four- or six-on-a-side headstocks. The 3+3 headstock looks similar to other Ovation headstocks. Model names range from **GP** (Guitar Paul) which had a retail price of $399, to the **GS** (Guitar Strat) models which ranged in price from $315 to $425. Those names seem pretty self explanatory in regards to the models they resembled. Both solid body guitars and basses were offered. In 1988, Kaman bought the independent **Hamer** company, a move which brought the company back into the solid body guitar field in a competitive way.

BREADWINNER (Model 1251) - "kidney"-shaped mahogany body, mahogany neck, 3-per-side headstock, dot fingerboard inlay, two large single coil pickups, master volume knob, master tone knob, midrange filter switch, three way pickup selector switch. Available in a textured Black, White, Tan, or Blue finish. Mfg. 1972 to 1979.

$375 $335 $275 $245 $225 $175 $140
Last MSR was $349.

In 1975, single coil pickups were replaced by humbuckers.
In 1976, blue finish was discontinued.

O

DEACON (Model 1252) - single cutaway body, diamond shaped position markers, master volume knob, master tone knob, midrange filter switch, three way pickup selector switch. Available in Sunburst finish. Mfg. 1973 to 1980.

$395 $350 $300 $265 $225 $185 $135
Last MSR was $449.

In 1975, single coil pickups were replaced by humbuckers.
In 1976, colors were expanded to Red, Black, and Natural finishes.

Deacon Deluxe - similar to the Deacon, except featured different hardware and pickups. Mfg. 1972 to 1980.

$425 $385 $335 $290 $250 $215 $175

Deacon Twelve String (Model 1253) - similar to the Deacon, except in 12-string configuration. Mfg. 1976 to 1980.

$475 $425 $375 $340 $300 $270 $225

ECLIPSE (Model K-1235) - economy model of the Electric Storm series. Available in Black finish only. Mfg. 1970 to 1973.

$325 $275 $250 $200 $165 $145 $125

PREACHER (Model 1281) - double cutaway mahogany body, 24 1/2" scale, two humbucking pickups. Mfg. 1975 to 1978.

$350 $320 $280 $250 $210 $180 $150

Preacher Deluxe (Model 1282) - similar to the Preacher, except features a series/parallel pickup switch and a midrange control. Mfg. late 1975 to 1978.

$400 $370 $330 $300 $260 $230 $200

GRADING	100% MINT	98% NEAR MINT	95% EXC+	90% EXC	80% VG+	70% VG	60% G

Preacher Deluxe Twelve String (Model 1283) - similar to the Preacher Deluxe, except in a twelve string configuration. Mfg. late 1975 to 1978.

$450 $410 $380 $340 $290 $260 $225

THUNDERHEAD (Model K-1360) - double cutaway semi-hollow body, gold-plated hardware, two DeArmond humbucking pickups, master volume knob, two separate tone control knobs, phase switch on bass bout, pickup balance/blend switch on treble bout. Available in Natural, Nutmeg, or Walnut Green finishes. Mfg. 1968 to 1972.

$250 $225 $200 $175 $150 $135 $125

Thunderhead (Model K-1460) with vibrato was introduced in 1968.

In 1970, the Thunderhead changed designation to K-1213; the Thunderhead with vibrato was designated K- 1212. In 1971, Electric Storm models were offered in Red, Nutmeg, and Black.

In the Spring of 1971, the Thunderhead changed designation to K-1233; the Thunderhead with vibrato was designated K-1234.

Hurricane (Model K-1120) - similar to the Thunderhead, except in a twelve-string variation. Mfg. late 1968 to 1969.

$400 $360 $310 $280 $240 $190 $165

Tornado (Model K-1160) - similar to the Thunderhead model, except features separate volume knobs for each pickup, chrome hardware, and no phase switch. Available in Red or Sunburst finishes. Mfg. late 1968 to 1973.

$275 $245 $225 $200 $165 $145 $125

Tornado (Model K-1260) with vibrato was introduced in 1968.

In 1970, the Tornado changed designation to K-1211; the Tornado with vibrato was designated K-1212.

In the Spring of 1971, the Tornado changed designation to K-1231; the Tornado with vibrato was designated K-1232.

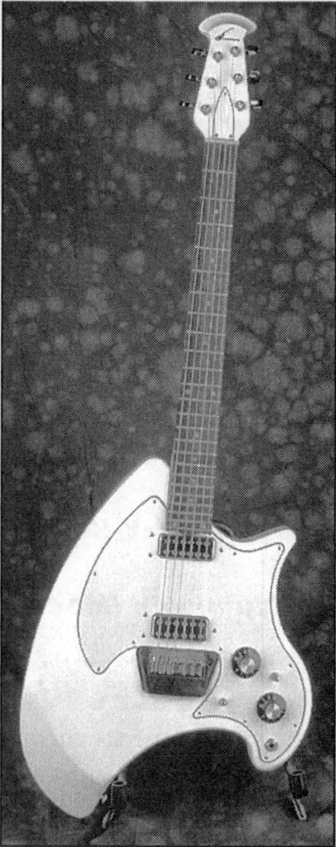

Ovation Breadwinner
courtesy William Kaman II

UK II (Model 1291) - double cutaway Urelite (Urethane) material on an aluminum frame, set-neck design, two humbucking pickups, two volume knobs, two tone knobs, series/parallel pickup switching, three way pickup selector switch on upper bass bout. Mfg. 1980 to 1983.

$375 $335 $295 $250 $215 $185 $160

Last MSR was $550.

The UK II designation was short for Ultra Kaman II.

VIPER (Model 1271) - single cutaway ash body, bolt-on one piece maple neck, maple or ebony fingerboard, two single coil pickups, 25" scale, master volume knob, master tone knob, three way pickup selector switch. Mfg. 1975 to 1983.

$350 $315 $275 $225 $180 $160 $135

Last MSR was $395.

While most bodies were built of ash, some were built using maple or mahogany.

VIPER III (Model 1273) - similar to the Viper, except has three single coil pickups with different individual windings, and three on/off pickup selector switches. Mfg. 1975 to 1983.

$350 $315 $275 $225 $175 $150 $135

ELECTRIC BASS

Magnum Series

MAGNUM I (Model 1261) - double offset cutaway mahogany body, graphite reinforced neck, humbucking pickup (neck position) and double coil pickup (bridge position), stereo output, string mute. Mfg. 1974 to 1978.

$495 $425 $365 $325 $285 $250 $215

Last MSR was $570.

MAGNUM II (Model 1262) - similar to the Magnum I, except featured a 3-band active EQ. Mfg. 1974 to 1978.

$525 $475 $400 $360 $315 $275 $240

Last MSR was $685.

MAGNUM III (Model 1263) - similar to the Magnum I, except features less radical body styling (deeper bass bout cutaway), two split-coil humbuckers. Mfg. 1978 to 1983.

$495 $425 $365 $325 $285 $250 $215

Last MSR was $570.

MAGNUM IV (Model 1264) - similar to the Magnum II, except features less radical body styling (deeper bass bout cutaway), two split-coil humbuckers. Mfg. 1978 to 1983.

$525 $475 $400 $360 $315 $275 $240

Last MSR was $685.

Ovation Viper
courtesy John Beeson

GRADING	100% MINT	98% NEAR MINT	95% EXC+	90% EXC	80% VG+	70% VG	60% G

Typhoon Series

TYPHOON I (Model K-1140) - similar to the Thunderhead guitar model, except in four string bass version. Mfg. late 1968 to 1972.

$275	$235	$200	$185	$160	$140	$115

Typhoon II (Model K-1240) - similar to the Typhoon I model, except initial models have a smaller body and shorter cutaway horns. Mfg. late 1968 to 1969.

$295	$255	$215	$195	$175	$150	$125

Originally catalogued as the Williwaw, which means *Mountain Wind* (in keeping with the Electric Storm *motif*).
In mid 1969, the body design was changed to resemble other Electric Storm models.
In 1970, the Typhoon II changed designation to K-1222.

Typhoon III (Model K-1340) - similar to the Typhoon I, except fretless. Mfg. 1969 to 1970.

$275	$235	$200	$175	$150	$135	$115

Typhoon IV (Model K-1216) - similar to the Typhoon III. Mfg. 1970 to 1972.

$275	$235	$200	$175	$150	$135	$115

Typhoon V (Model K-1217) - Mfg. 1971 to 1972.

$275	$235	$200	$175	$150	$135	$115

OVERWATER BASS

Instruments currently built in the United Kingdom since the late 1970s.

Luthier Chris May has been building high quality guitars and basses since 1978. May has built a number of custom basses with innovative designs, such as the C Bass (1985) which features a lower-than-standard tuning of C-F-Bb-Eb. This 36" scale bass was tuned 2 full steps below conventional 4-string tuning.

In 1995, The Overwater Guitar Company moved to their new headquarters in Carlisle, Cumbria (the last town on A69 before Scotland). The new Overwater Jam Factory, Ltd. features two rehearsal studios, a 24-track recording facility, and a retail outlet for musical equipment sales in addition to May's workshops. May also helped develop the Delta line of bass amplification for Carlsboro.

ELECTRIC

May offers the **Advance** custom guitar and the **"S"** and **"T" Traditional** series models in one of three configurations: The **Standard** has a one-piece neck-through design, and solid wings. The **Deluxe** features a one- or two-piece neck-through design, and an overlaid flat top. The **Pro** configuration is a one- or two-piece neck-through with a carved top. Bolt-on necks are also offered.

Advance necks can be walnut, mahogany, or maple, and the bodies constructed of solid mahogany or walnut (with the option of a flat or carved maple top). Traditional series guitars are generally built with maple necks and either sycamore, light ash, or alder bodies. Fingerboards can be rosewood, ebony, or maple. Customers can specify pickup and electronics, and choice of finish.

ELECTRIC BASS

Chris May is featuring three bass models: the original styles of the **Progress** and **Fusion**, as well as the traditional styled "J" model. Basses are offered in 4-, 5-, 6- , 7-, and 8-string configurations (only 4- and 5-string on the "J" series). Again, there are three different variants in the bass model offering: the **Classic** has a two- or three-piece neck-through design and solid wings. The **Deluxe** features a three-piece neck-through design with laminated wings, and the **Pro** has similar construction with multi-laminated wings. While the "J" series features a bolt-on neck, the body can still be upgraded to a Deluxe or a Pro.

Bass necks can be laminated of maple/walnut or maple/sycamore, and the bodies constructed of sycamore, maple or walnut. The traditional "J" basses are generally built with maple necks and either sycamore, light ash, walnut, or alder bodies. Fingerboards can be rosewood, ebony, or maple. Customers can specify pickup and electronics, and choice of finish.

Section P

PBC

See BUNKER GUITARS.

Instruments previously built in Coopersburg, Pennsylvania from 1989 to 1996.

The PBC Guitar Technology company is the collaboration between John Pearse, Dave Bunker, and Paul Chernay. Pearse and Bunker met at the 1988 NAMM show in California; Pearse promoting his strings and high tech pickups, while Bunker was demonstrating his *Touch* guitar. The two were later joined by Chernay, a longtime friend of Pearse. Luthier Bunker's previous guitar designs, while radical for their time, were designed in a way to solve certain inherent solid body design flaws. PBC Guitar Technology introduced both the *Tension-Free* neck design and the Wishbone hollowbody series.

After the PBC Guitar Technology company went out of business in 1996, Dave Bunker began building guitars under his old **Bunker Guitars** trademark in 1998 (see BUNKER GUITARS). Bunker's new company is planning on offering PBC-style models by late 1998/early 1999.

The Tension-Free design involves a solid 3/8" steel bar that runs inside the length of the neck, and transfers all the string pull directly to the body of the instrument. This leaves the outer wood neck and fretboard free from the loading that would normally lead to neck warpage, and the solid steel core carries all neck vibration to the body. Tension-Free necks have appeared on other manufacturer's models (such as Ibanez' USA Prestige Series models).

ELECTRIC

PBC offered a number of custom options in regards to woods, finishes, electronics, and other player-oriented concerns.

GTS Series

In the early 1990s, PBC offered the GTS electric solid body series. Models featured PBC pickups, 25" scale, 24-fret fingerboards, Tension-Free necks, and six-on-a-side tuners. The **GTS 200** (list $1,095 to $1,595) featured a offset double cutaway body, Floyd Rose tremolo system, 2 PBC Banshee single coils and 1 PBC Spectrutone humbucking pickup.

The **GTS 350** (list $1,195 to $1,695) was a single cutaway model with 2 PBC Spectrutone humbucking pickups, coil taps, Tension-Free neck, and a through-the-body bridge. A semi-hollowbody version, the **GTS 350 SH** (list $1,595 to $1,895) featured similar hardware.

GTX Series

The GTX series of the early 1990s was a marriage of conventional guitar shapes and the Touch series electronics. GTX guitars had a unique angular body design, 25" scale, and 2 *humbuckers* (actually pre-amped Hex pickups similar to the Touch guitar system). The **GTX 200 H** (list $1,895) had the tuning keys on the headstock, while the **GTX Hammer** (list $1,995) featured reverse tuning (tuning keys on the bridge). A fairly advanced system that offered great sustain and keyboard-like note attack - the guitar is actually off until you hammer or pick a note!

Touch Series

The Dave Bunker Signature Series Touch Guitar models offered an instrument that can be played by touching the strings. This innovative instrument combines a 6-string guitar neck, 4-string bass guitar neck, and the PBC Hexaphonic pickups/electronics package. The **GTT 1000** was a high quality, basic model listed at $1,695, and had a solid color finish. The **GTT 2000** (list $2,195) doubled the number of hexaphonic pickups per neck, and thus tripled the tonal options. The top of the line GTT 3000 added a series of adjustable bandpass filters to the 20 hexaphonic pickups, as well as the option of a clear lacquer finish on the natural wood models. The new list price on the **GTT 3000** models ranged from $2,995 to $3,295.

Wishbone Series

Wishbone Hollowbody guitars have an innovative design. Rather than mount the bridge to the solid, carved top like other conventional designs, Bunker's bridge floats on a *wishbone*/multi laminate wood beam that extends from the heel block to the underneath of the bridge. A brass bar couples the block to the bridge, leaving the top of the guitar free to resonate like an acoustic guitar top.

The Wishbone series consists of three hollowbody Archtop models, and an Arlen Roth Signature model. All four models include the Tension-Free neck and Wishbone bridge support beam. Tops are carved from solid bookmatched figured maple, and the bodies are carved from blocks of tone woods.

Add $100 for ebony fingerboard.

Add $100 for AAA grade maple top.

Add $100 for neck binding.

Add $250 for left-handed configuration.

Add $250 for EMG piezo bridge transducer.

P

GRADING	100% MINT	98% NEAR MINT	95% EXC+	90% EXC	80% VG+	70% VG	60% G

AC 200 - 2" deep single cutaway maple (or alder, or walnut) body, carved arched solid figured maple top, 2 f-holes, eastern hard rock maple neck, 25 1/2" scale, 22-fret rosewood (or maple or morado) fingerboard with dot inlay, carved ebony (or rosewood or morado) Wishbone bridge, brass saddles, 3+3 tuners, chrome hardware, Bill Lawrence Keystone pickups, volume/blend/tone controls. Available in Natural, Amberburst, Rubyburst, Vintageburst finishes. Disc. 1996.

$1,000 $925 $750 $675 $600 $550 $495
Last MSR was $1,795.

In 1996, *Jewel Top* finishes were introduced. Finishes include Transparent Amber, Transparent Emerald, and Transparent Ruby tops with natural back and sides.

Arlen Roth Signature AC 200 - similar to the AC 200, except has a 6-on-a-side headstock with screened signature. Available in Rubyburst or satin finish Amberburst. Disc. 1996.

$1,100 $950 $800 $700 $625 $575 $525
Last MSR was $1,795.

AC 300 - similar to the AC-200, except has 3 1/2" body depth. Disc. 1996.

$950 $875 $700 $650 $575 $525 $475
Last MSR was $1,995.

AC 312 - similar to the AC 300, except has 12-string configuration. Disc. 1996.

$1,000 $950 $800 $700 $625 $575 $525
Last MSR was $2,495.

ELECTRIC BASS

GTB Series

Companion basses to the GTS series guitars of the early 1990s can be viewed as forerunners to today's current models. Both the 200 series and the 350 series offered Tension-Free necks and through-the-body bridges, 34" scale, 24-fret fingerboards, and PBC pickups. The **GTB 200** (list $995) featured a offset double cutaway body, four-on-a-side headstock, and chrome hardware. A five string version, the **GTB 205** (list $1,295) featured similar hardware.

Both the four string **GTB 350** and five string **GTB 355** headless models have the same features as the current models. However, the newer designs have a more pronounced inverse body curve by the bridge. Earlier models had prices that ranged from $1,195 to $1,895.

Later GTB models featured Tension-Free necks and through-the-body bridges.

Add $100 for fretted or fretless ebony fingerboards.

Add $100 for AAA grade maple top.

Add $200 for EMG BTC active tone circuit.

Add $350 for left-handed configuration.

Add $900 for patented Hex Mute electronics.

GTB 354 - double cutaway alder body, figured maple top, 5-piece laminated maple and walnut neck, 34" scale, 24-fret rosewood (or maple or morado) fingerboard with dot inlay, PBC through-the-body bridge, 2+2 tuners, gold or chrome hardware, two EMG DC pickups, volume/tone controls, pickup selector switch. Available in Natural, Amberburst, Vintageburst, and Transparent Emerald, Ruby, Sapphire, Amethyst (Purple), or Onyx finishes. Disc. 1996.

$895 $825 $675 $600 $500 $450 $400
Last MSR was $1,495.

This model is available in a headless configuration (tuners on bridge) at no extra charge.

GTB 355 - similar to the GTB 354, except has a 5-string configuration, 3+2 headstock. Disc. 1996.

$900 $825 $700 $600 $500 $450 $400
Last MSR was $1,795.

This model is available in a headless configuration (tuners on bridge) at no extra charge.

GTB 356 - similar to the GTB 354, except has a 6-string configuration, 3-per-side headstock. Disc. 1996.

$975 $900 $750 $650 $550 $500 $450
Last MSR was $2,095.

The GTB 356 is available only in the headless configuration.

Wishbone Series

Both models include the Tension-Free neck and Wishbone bridge support beam. Tops are carved from solid bookmatched figured maple, and the bodies are carved from blocks of tone woods.

Add $100 for *headless* neck.

Add $100 for fretted or fretless ebony fingerboards.

Add $100 for AAA grade maple top.

Add $200 for EMG BTC active tone circuit.

Add $350 for left-handed configuration.

Add $900 for patented Hex Mute electronics.

GRADING	100% MINT	98% NEAR MINT	95% EXC+	90% EXC	80% VG+	70% VG	60% G

AB 400 - 2" deep double cutaway maple (or alder, or walnut) body, carved arched solid figured maple top, 2 f-holes, 5-piece laminated maple and walnut neck, 34" scale, 22-fret rosewood (or maple or morado) fingerboard with dot inlay, carved ebony (or rosewood or morado) Wishbone bridge, brass saddles, 2+2 tuners, chrome hardware, two EMG DC pickups, volume/tone controls, pickup selector switch. Available in Natural, Amberburst, Vintageburst, and Transparent Emerald finishes. Disc. 1996.

$1,200	**$1,000**	**$900**	**$800**	**$700**	**$600**	**$500**

Last MSR was $2,495.

AB 500 - similar to the AB 400, except has a 5-string configuration, 3/2 headstock. Disc. 1996.

$1,250	**$1,100**	**$950**	**$825**	**$725**	**$625**	**$525**

Last MSR was $2,795.

PBC Wishbone AC-300
courtesy Jay Wolfe

PC

See also NED CALLAN.

Instruments previously built in England from the early 1970s through the mid 1980s.

The PC brand is the trademark of custom luthier Peter Cook, who produced the original design Axis solid body guitar for a number of years.

(Source: Tony Bacon and Paul Day, The Guru's Guitar Guide)

PACK LEADER

Instruments previously built in England during the late 1970s.

This high quality solid body guitar was built by luthier Roger Bucknall (Fylde Guitars), and its original design was available in either a Rosewood or Walnut version.

For further information on Roger Bucknall, see FYLDE.

(Source: Tony Bacon and Paul Day, The Guru's Guitar Guide)

PALM BAY

Instruments currently built in England.

Palm Bay is currently offering a number of high quality electric guitars. Models like the Cyclone have an offset double cutaway mahogany body and maple top, maple neck, ebony fingerboard, licensed Floyd Rose bridge, DiMarzio humbuckers, and a Palm Tree inlay at the first fret. Other models include the Cyclone SE-X and Tidal Wave EXP. For further information, please contact Palm Bay Ltd directly (see Trademark Index).

PALMER

Instruments currently produced in Asia from the late 1980s. Distributed by Chesbro Music Company of Idaho Falls, Idaho; and Tropical Music Corporation of Miami, Florida.

Both the Chesbro Music Company and Tropical Music Corporation are distributing Palmer brand acoustic and classical models. These models are geared towards the entry level or student guitarist.

During the late 1980s, Palmer offered instruments that were entry level solid body guitars that feature designs based on traditional American designs. Solid body models were marketed under the trademark (or model designation) of Biscayne, Growler, Baby, and Six. The **Biscayne** trademark is still distributed by Tropical Music Corporation.

Palmer acoustic guitars are usually priced in the used market between $79 up to $299.

PANGBORN

Instruments previously built in England from the late 1970s to the late 1980s.

Luthier Ashley Pangborn has specialized in high quality custom order solid body guitars, as well as standard models such as the Warrior and the Warlord.

(Source: Tony Bacon and Paul Day, The Guru's Guitar Guide)

PARADIS

Instruments currently built in Switzerland.

Luthier Rolf Spuler, designer of the Ibanez AFR Affirma series in the early 1990s, continues to offer advanced design high quality instruments.

PARKER

Instruments currently produced in New York. Distributed by Korg USA of Westbury, New York.

Designer Ken Parker began building unconventional archtop guitars in the 1970s. He then took a job with (now defunct) Stuyvesant Music in New York City, working both in the repair shop as well as building **Guitar Man** instruments. Parker's background in repairing and customizing guitars became the groundwork for the innovative design of the **Fly** guitar.

In 1982, Parker met Larry Fishman (Fishman Transducers) while reviewing a prototype bass. Parker and Fishman joined forces, and attended the 1985 NAMM music industry show to gain financial backing for the new **Fly** model. The new guitar design attracted some interest in the market, but Parker and Fishman were interested in protecting the

P

GRADING	100% MINT	98% NEAR MINT	95% EXC+	90% EXC	80% VG+	70% VG	60% G

design, rather than let unauthorized versions show up in the marketplace. Around 1990, Korg USA (distributor of Marshall amplifiers and Korg keyboards in the U.S. market) took interest in the design and production applications. The Fly guitar debuted at the 1992 NAMM show.

Parker guitars are carved from solid wood, and then have a thin layer of carbon/glass/epoxy composite material applied as a strengthening measure. The fingerboard and peghead veneer on these instruments are made from the same synthetic composite material. While the futuristic design and composite material tends to mystify vintage-minded guitar owners, the Fly is still 95% wood.

ELECTRIC

Fly Series

All instruments in this series have the following specs: offset double cutaway carved poplar one piece body/neck, 24-fret carbon/fiber epoxy fingerboard, blackface peghead with screened logo, 6-on-a-side locking Sperzel tuners, and black hardware. Instruments are finished in a gloss urethane paint.

F - fixed Parker bridge, 2 exposed humbucker pickups, master volume/volume/tone controls, 3-position switch. Mfg. 1994 only.

$1,150 $975 $825 $650 $575 $525 $475
Last MSR was $1,625.

FV - standard Parker vibrato, vibrato tension wheel, 2 exposed humbucker pickups, master volume/volume/tone controls, 3-position switch. Mfg. 1994 only.

$1,300 $1,150 $975 $750 $695 $625 $575
Last MSR was $1,910.

FD - fixed Parker bridge, 2 exposed humbucker/6 piezo bridge pickups, master volume/humbucker volume/tone controls, stacked volume/tone piezo control, two 3-position switches. Mfg. 1994 only.

$1,375 $1,175 $995 $775 $700 $650 $595
Last MSR was $1,960.

FLY DELUXE (FDV) - standard Parker vibrato, vibrato tension wheel, 2 exposed humbucker/6 piezo bridge pickups, master volume/humbucker volume/tone controls, stacked volume/tone piezo control, two 3-position switches. Available in Dusty Black (DB), Majik Blue (MB), Galaxie Gray, Euro Red, Pearl White (PW), Ruby Red (RR), Italian Plum (IP), Emerald Green (EG), and Antique Gold (AG) finishes. Mfg. 1994 to date.

MSR $2,950 $2,250 $1,600 $1,375 $1,195 $995 $795 $600

In 1998, Heather Grey (HG) finish was introduced; Galaxie Gray and Euro Red finishes were disc.
In 2000, Pearl White (PW) finish was disc.

Fly Deluxe Standard (FDVST) - non-piezo model, poplar body and basswood neck, custom wound DiMarzio humbucker pickups, 24 hardened stainless steel frets, Parker vibrato system, locking Sperzel tuners, push/pull tone control coil-tap enables 6 pickup settings. Available in Ruby Red (RR), Dusty Black (DB) & Majik Blue (MB). New 2001.

MSR $2,425 $1,725 $1,400 $1,200 $995 $875 $775 $675

Fly Artist (FAV) - similar to the Fly Deluxe, except features a solid Sitka spruce body, vibrato bridge, piezo bridge mounted pickup, magnetic pickups. Available in Transparent Cherry and Rootbeer Metallic finishes. Mfg. 1996 to date.

MSR $4,167 $2,950 $2,400 $2,000 $1,750 $1,500 $1,200 $895

In 1997, Transparent Butterscotch (BS) finish was introduced; Transparent Cherry and Rootbeer Metallic finishes were disc.

Fly Concert (FCT) - similar to the Fly Deluxe, except features a solid Sitka spruce body, piezo bridge pickups, and no magnetic pickup system. Available in Transparent Cherry and Rootbeer Metallic finishes. Mfg. 1996 to date.

MSR $3,444 $2,000 $1,650 $1,400 $1,225 $1,000 $850 $650

In 1997, Transparent Butterscotch (BS) finish was introduced; Transparent Cherry and Rootbeer Metallic finishes were disc.
In 1998, Ebony (E) - a solid Ebony Pearl finish was introduced.
In 2000, Ebony (E) finish was disc.

Fly Classic (FCV) - similar to the Fly Deluxe, except features a solid mahogany body, and finished top. Available in Transparent Cherry (TC) and Metallic Rootbeer (RB) finishes. Mfg. 1996 to date.

MSR $3,175 $2,300 $1,775 $1,500 $1,250 $1,050 $850 $625

In 1997, Natural Mahogany (NM), Teal (T), Transparent Blue (TB), and Transparent Emerald (TE) finishes were introduced.
In 2000, Transparent Blue, Transparent Emerald, Teal, & Metallic Rootbeer finishes were disc.

Fly Classic Standard (FCVST) - non-piezo model, mahogany body with basswood neck, custom wound DiMarzio humbucker pickups, 24 hardened stainless steel frets, Parker vibrato system, locking Sperzel tuners, push-pull tone control coil-tap enables six pickup settings. Available in transparent cherry & natural mahogany finishes. New 2001.

MSR $2,675 $1,900 $1,500 $1,350 $1,150 $950 $825 $600

Fly Maple Classic (FCVM) - Fly Classic with maple body, Transparent Hazelnut Brown finish. New 1999.

MSR $3,325 $2,400 $1,850 $1,550 $1,250 $1,050 $850 $625

In 2000, Transparent Cherry (TC) finish was introduced.

Fly Maple Custom (FMCV) - select maple body, basswood neck, 2 custom wound DiMarzio humbucking magnetic pickups, Fishmad piezo active preamp/mixer system, parker high performance vibrato. Available in transparent cherry finish. New 2001.

MSR $3,325 $2,425 $1,950 $1,725 $1,550 $1,375 $1,200 $1,050

Fly Supreme (FSV) - similar to the Fly Deluxe, except features a solid maple body, and finished top. Available in Transparent Honey (TH) and Sunburst (SB) finishes. Mfg. 1996 to date.

MSR $5,111 $3,500 $3,200 $2,900 $2,500 $2,200 $1,900 $1,500

In 2000, Sunburst finish was disc.

P

GRADING	100% MINT	98% NEAR MINT	95% EXC+	90% EXC	80% VG+	70% VG	60% G

SPANISH FLY - electric/classical nylon string guitar with solid Sitka spruce body, basswood neck, and ebony bridge with tie block, Butterscotch finish. New 1999.

MSR $4,139	$3,000	$2,700	$2,400	$2,100	$1,800	$1,500	$1,200

MIDIFLY (MIDFV) - features MidiAxe DSP-MIDI guitar system with vibrato, stereo output, Fishman piezo system, and DiMarzio magnetic pickups, Midi in-out, Sunburst, Natural Mahogany or Heather Gray finish. New 1999.

MSR $3,611	$2,500	$2,200	$1,800	$1,500	$1,200	$950	$725

In 2000, Sunbusrt & Natural Mahogany finishes were disc.

FLY DELUXE SINGLE II (FDV2) - solid poplar body with basswood neck, custom wound Dimarzio humbucking & 2 single coil pickups plus 6-element Fishman piezo pickups, Custom Fishman Active Filtering Preamp, 5-way pickup selector, exclusive parker neck with carbon & glass fingerboard, stainless steel frets, presicion aluminum bridge with stainless steel saddles, Sperzel locking tuners, 3 ½-5 lbs. Available in Heather Gray (HG), Dusty Black (DB) & Ruby Red (RR) finishes. New 2000.

MSR $3,050	$2,200	$1,800	$1,575	$1,350	$1,125	$975	$825

FLY HARDTAIL (FHT) - basswood body & basswood neck, custom Sperzel Drop-D tuner, carbon & glass fingerboard, jumbo stainless steel frets, 2 custom wound DiMarzio humbuckers plus Fishman 6-element piezo pickups, Custom Fishman Active Filtering Preamp, non-vibrato bridge with stainless steel saddles. Available in Stealth Gray (SG) finish. New 2000.

MSR $2,972	$2,125	$1,750	$1,500	$1,300	$1,100	$950	$800

FLY HARDTAIL STANDARD (FHTST) - non-piezo model, basswood body and neck, custom wound DiMarzio humbucker pickups, 24 jumbo, hardened stainless steel frets, non-vibrato bridge, locking Sperzel tuners with custom Drop-D, push-pull tone control coil-tap enables 6 pickup settings. Available in Stealth Gray finish. New 2001.

MSR $2,550	$1,825	$1,600	$1,400	$1,200	$1,000	$850	$725

FLY JAZZ (FJZ) - mahogany body and basswood neck, 2 custom wound DiMarzio humbuckers with a specially voiced neck pickup plus Fishman 6-element piezo pickups, Custom Fishman Filtering Preamp, exclusive Parker neck with stainless steel frets, Sperzel locking tuners, carbon & glass fingerboard, precision aluminum bridge with stainless steel saddles. Available in transparent cherry (TC) finish. New 2000.

MSR $3,750	$2,675	$2,300	$1,850	$1,550	$1,250	$975	$750

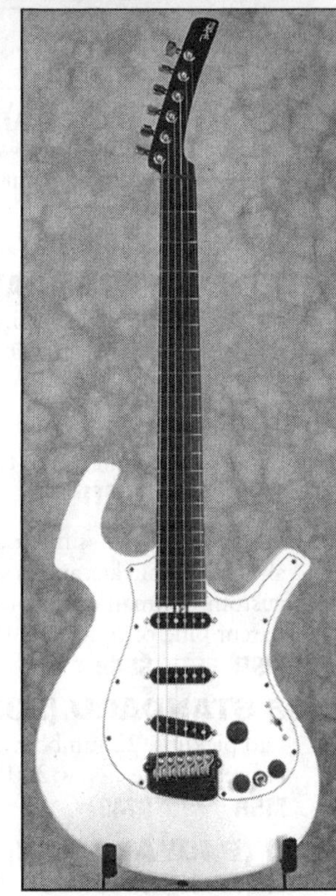

Parker Nitefly courtesy Howie's Guitar Haven

NiteFly Series

The 1997/1998 NiteFly models now have the ability to mix electric and acoustic sound through one amp as well as two in stereo. Parker's **NiteMix** (Model PNM1) magnetic mixer/preamp box is designed specifically for NFV1 and NFV2 Nitefly models to allow the individual outputs to be combined through a single guitar amplifier (list $160).

NIGHTFLY (NFV1) - offset double cutaway solid maple body, bolt-on neck (composed of modulus carbon/glass fiber), 22-fret fingerboard, 6-on-a-side locking Sperzel tuners, pickguard, free-floating vibrato, 3 single coil Dimarzio pickups/Fishman passive piezo-transducer bridge pickup, volume/tone controls, 5-way selector switch (magnetic pickups), piezo volume knob, piezo/magnetic selector switch. Available in Black Pearl, White Pearl, Sunburst, Transparent Red, and Transparent Blue finishes. Mfg. 1996 to 1998.

$975	$775	$675	$595	$495	$395	$300

Last MSR was $1,199.

Nightfly (NFV2) - similar to the NiteFly, except features 2 single coil DiMarzio pickups/DiMarzio humbucker. Mfg. 1996 to 1998.

$1,000	$825	$725	$650	$525	$425	$325

Last MSR was $1,249.

NITEFLY (NFV3) - offset double cutaway solid maple body, bolt-on basswood (reinforced by a back layer of carbon/glass/epoxy composite), 22-fret composite fingerboard, 6-on-a-side locking Sperzel tuners, black pickguard, Parker vibrato, 3 DiMarzio single coil pickups/Fishman piezo transducer bridge pickup, volume/tone controls, 5-way selector switch (magnetic pickups), piezo volume knob, piezo/magnetic selector switch. Available in Black Pearl (B), White Pearl (W), Sunburst (SB), Transparent Red (TR), and Transparent Blue (TB) finishes. Mfg. 1998 to 2000.

$975	$850	$750	$650	$525	$425	$325

Last MSR was $1,299.

Nitefly (NFV4) - similar to the NiteFly, except features 2 single coil DiMarzio pickups/DiMarzio humbucker. Available in Black Pearl (B), White Pearl (W), Sunburst (SB), Transparent Red (TR), and Transparent Blue (TB) finishes. Mfg. 1998 to 2000.

$999	$875	$775	$675	$550	$450	$350

Last MSR was $1,349.

P

GRADING	100% MINT	98% NEAR MINT	95% EXC+	90% EXC	80% VG+	70% VG	60% G

NITEFLY-SA (NFVSA) - Nitefly configuration, carved swamp ash body & mahogany bolt-on neck, carbon & glass fingerboard, stainless steel frets, Nitefly vibrato system with stainless steel saddles, precision aluminum bridge, 2 DiMarzio single coil pickups & 1 DiMarzio humbucker pickup, 6-element Fishman piezo pickup,Sperzel locking tuners. Available in black, sunburst, transparent red & transparent blue. Mfg. 1999 to date.

MSR $1,611 $1,150 $895 $825 $750 $675 $600 $525

NITEFLY-SA STANDARD (NFVSAST) - non-piezo model, swamp ash body, mahogany bolt-on neck, custom wound DiMarzio pickups, 22 hardened stainless steel frets, locking Sperzel tuners, 5-way pickup selector switch. Available in black, sunburst, transparent red & transparent blue. New 2001.

MSR $1,444 $1,025 $800 $725 $675 $600 $650 $495

NITEFLY-M (NFVM) - similar to Nitefly-SA except mahogany body & neck, 2 Dimarzio humbucker pickups. Available in black, sunburst, transparent red & transparent blue. 1999 to date.

MSR $1,611 $1,150 $895 $825 $750 $675 $600 $525

P-38 (P38VA) - similar to Nitefly, select ash body & bolt-on maple neck with rosewood fingerboard, 22 jumbo nickel frets, custom Parker alnico humbucker and 2 single coil pickups,pearloid pickguard, Wilkinson licensed vibrato bridge system featuring Fishman piezo pickups, custom Fishman active preamp with "Smart Switching" output jack for mixing magnetic & piezo signals. Available in black, sunburst, transparent blue & transparent red. New 2000.

MSR $849 $600 $500 $425 $375 $350 $325 $295

P-38 STANDARD (P38VAST) - non-piezo model, ash body, bolt-on maple neck with rosewood fingerboard, custom wound DiMarzio pickups, 22 jumbo nickel-silver frets, Wilkinson licensed vibrato, 5-way pickup selector switch. Available in black, sunbusrt & transparent red finishes. New 2001.

MSR $749 $525 $425 $350 $300 $260 $230 $200

P-40 (P40VA) -ash body, bolt-on maple neck with rosewood fingerboard, 1 humbucking pickup & 2 single coil custom wound Parker alnico magnetic pickups, Wilkinson licensed vibrato with Fishman piezo active preamp/mixer system. Available in transparent red & transparent black finishes. New 2001.

MSR $999

PATRICK EGGLE GUITARS

Instruments currently produced in Coventry, England since 1991.

Luthier Patrick Eggle's background in building guitars began at age fifteen. A number of years later, Eggle formed Patrick Eggle Guitars in 1991. His production guitars were high quality solid body electrics that featured an original style. Eggle later left the guitar company in 1994.

The company continued production of instruments. In January 1997, Patrick Eggle Guitars was purchased by music retailers Musical Exchanges, which has stores in Coventry and Birmingham (England).

Between 1993 to 1994, two models (New York-USA and Los Angeles-USA) were assembled with Patrick Eggle components in Santa Barbara, California. However, full production is again completely centered in England.

ELECTRIC

All models listed below are available in left-handed versions free of charge. There is a $25 charge for Maple Leaf inlays.

BERLIN SERIES

The Berlin model was voted the Making Music *British Guitar of the Year* award in 1995.

DELUXE - offset double cutaway maple body, carved figured maple top, mahogany neck, 24-fret ebony fingerboard with abalone dot inlay, abalone maple leaf inlay on 12th fret, locking Wilkinson vibrato, 3-per-side locking Sperzel tuners, gold hardware, 2 humbucker Eggle pickups, volume/coil tap control, 3-position switch. Available in Antique Gold, Bahamian Blue, Burny Amber, Burgundy Burst, Chardonnay Rouge, Chardonnay Rouge Burst, Cherry, Cherry Burst, Citrus Green, Citrus Green Burst, Deep Sea Blue, Emerald Isle Blue, Pink Glow, Pink Glow Burst, Purple Haze, Shamu Blue, Shamu Blue Burst, Tobacco Burst, Vintage Gold Burst, and Walnut finishes. Disc. 1994.

$980 $840 $700 $560 $505 $460 $420

Last MSR was $1,400.

PLUS - offset double cutaway mahogany body, carved figured maple top, mahogany neck, 24-fret ebony fingerboard with abalone dot inlay, tune-o-matic bridge/stop tailpiece, body matching peghead, 3-per-side locking Sperzel tuners, chrome hardware, 2 humbucker Eggle pickups, volume/tone control, 3-position switch, coil tap in tone control. Available in Antique Gold, Bahamian Blue, Chardonnay Rouge, Cherry, Pink Glow, and Walnut finishes. Disc. 1994.

$560 $480 $400 $320 $290 $265 $240

Add 10% for gold hardware.

Last MSR was $800.

GRADING	100% MINT	98% NEAR MINT	95% EXC+	90% EXC	80% VG+	70% VG	60% G

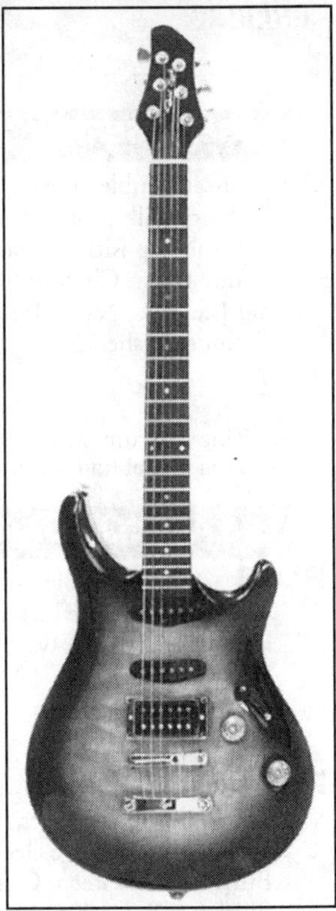
Patrick Eggle Berlin Stage courtesy Patrick Eggle Guitars

PRO - offset double cutaway mahogany body, carved figured maple top, mahogany neck, 22-fret ebony fingerboard with abalone dot inlay, tune-o-matic bridge/stop tailpiece, body matching tailpiece, 3-per-side locking Sperzel tuners, chrome hardware, 2 humbucker Eggle pickups, volume/tone control, 3-position switch. Available in Antique Gold, Bahamian Blue, Burgundy Burst, Chardonnay Rouge, Chardonnay Rouge Burst, Cherry, Cherry Burst, Deep Sea Blue, Emerald Isle Blue, Pink Glow, Pink Glow Burst, Purple Haze, Tobacco Burst, Vintage Gold Burst, and Walnut finishes. Current Mfg.

MSR $2,400 — $2,112 $1,848 $1,775 $1,600 $1,400 $1,150 $975

The Berlin Pro is also offered with a 24-fret fingerboard, gold hardware, or Wilkinson VS 100 tremolo.

STAGE - offset double cutaway mahogany body, carved figured maple top, mahogany neck, 24-fret ebony fingerboard with abalone dot inlay, tune-o-matic bridge/stop tailpiece, body matching tailpiece, 3-per-side locking Sperzel tuners, chrome hardware, 2 humbucker Eggle pickups, volume/tone control, 3-position switch. Available in Antique Gold, Bahamian Blue, Burgundy Burst, Chardonnay Rouge, Chardonnay Rouge Burst, Cherry, Cherry Burst, Deep Sea Blue, Emerald Isle Blue, Pink Glow, Pink Glow Burst, Purple Haze, Tobacco Burst, Vintage Gold Burst, and Walnut finishes. Current Mfg.

MSR $1,400 — $1,232 $1,078 $1,050 $970 $890 $750 $600

STANDARD - offset double cutaway mahogany body, carved figured maple top, mahogany neck, 24-fret ebony fingerboard with abalone dot inlay, tune-o-matic bridge/stop tailpiece, body matching tailpiece, 3-per-side locking Sperzel tuners, chrome hardware, 2 humbucker Eggle pickups, volume/tone control, 3-position switch. Available in Black, Natural and White finishes. Disc. 1994.

$420 $360 $300 $240 $215 $195 $180

Add 10% for gold hardware.

Last MSR was $600.

UK DLX-4HT - offset double cutaway mahogany body, highest quality (AAAA) carved figured maple top, mahogany neck, 22-fret ebony fingerboard with abalone maple leaf inlay, tune-o-matic bridge/stop tailpiece, 3-per-side Sperzel tuners, chrome hardware, 2 humbucker Eggle pickups, volume/tone control, 3-position switch. Available in Natural finish. Disc. 1994.

$1,995 $1,710 $1,425 $1,140 $1,025 $940 $855

Last MSR was $2,850.

UK DLS-4A - similar to UK DLX-4HT, except has Wilkinson vibrato, locking Sperzel tuners. Disc. 1994.

$2,170 $1,860 $1,550 $1,240 $1,115 $1,025 $930

Last MSR was $3,100.

UK PLUS ULTRA - offset double cutaway mahogany body, carved figured maple top, mahogany neck, 22-fret ebony fingerboard with abalone dot inlay, tune-o-matic bridge/stop tailpiece, 3-per-side Sperzel tuners, chrome hardware, 2 humbucker Eggle pickups, volume/tone control, 3-position switch. Available in Antique Gold, Cherry, Cherry Burst and Tobacco Burst finishes. Disc. 1994.

$1,330 $1,140 $950 $760 $685 $625 $570

Last MSR was $1,900.

UK Plus-1A - offset double cutaway mahogany body, carved figured maple top, mahogany neck, 22-fret ebony fingerboard with abalone dot inlay, tune-o-matic bridge/stop tailpiece, 3-per-side Sperzel tuners, chrome hardware, 2 humbucker Eggle pickups, volume/tone control, 3-position switch. Available in Natural finish. Disc. 1994.

$910 $780 $650 $520 $470 $430 $390

Last MSR was $1,300.

UK Plus-2A - similar to Plus-1A, except has higher quality (AA) carved maple top. Disc. 1994.

$1,050 $900 $750 $600 $540 $495 $450

Last MSR was $1,500.

UK Plus-3A - similar to Plus-1A, except has higher quality (AAA) carved maple top, abalone maple leaf fingerboard inlay. Disc. 1994.

$1,360 $1,165 $970 $775 $695 $635 $580

Last MSR was $1,940.

UK PRO ULTRA - offset double cutaway mahogany body, carved figured AAA maple top, mahogany neck, 24-fret ebony fingerboard with abalone dot inlay, locking Wilkinson vibrato, 3-per-side locking Sperzel tuners, chrome hardware, 2 humbucker Eggle pickups, volume/tone control, 3-position switch. Available in Antique Gold, Cherry, Cherry Burst and Tobacco Burst finishes. Disc. 1994.

$1,715 $1,470 $1,225 $980 $875 $805 $735

Last MSR was $2,450.

UK Pro-3A - offset double cutaway mahogany body, carved figured AAA maple top, mahogany neck, 24-fret ebony fingerboard with abalone dot inlay, locking Wilkinson vibrato, 3-per-side locking Sperzel tuners, chrome hardware, 2 humbucker Eggle pickups, volume/tone control, 3-position switch. Available in Natural finish. Disc. 1994.

$1,540 $1,320 $1,100 $880 $790 $725 $660

Last MSR was $2,200.

GRADING	100% MINT	98% NEAR MINT	95% EXC+	90% EXC	80% VG+	70% VG	60% G

LEGEND SERIES

JS - offset double cutaway, maple body, carved figured maple top, figured maple neck, 24-fret ebony fingerboard with pearl maple leaf inlay, locking Wilkinson vibrato, ebony veneer on peghead, 3-per-side locking Sperzel tuners, 2 active humbucker Reflex pickups, volume/tone control, 3-position switch, coil tap in volume control, active electronics. Available in Antique Gold, Bahamian Blue, Burny Amber, Burgundy Burst, Chardonnay Rouge, Chardonnay Rouge Burst, Cherry, Cherry Burst, Citrus Green, Citrus Green Burst, Deep Sea Blue, Emerald Isle Blue, Natural, Pink Glow, Pink Glow Burst, Purple Haze, Shamu Blue, Shamu Blue Burst, Tobacco Burst, Vintage Gold Burst, and Walnut finishes. Disc. 1994.

$1,225 $1,050 $875 $700 $630 $575 $525
Last MSR was $1,750.

This instrument was designed for Big Jim Sullivan.
This model had black hardware as an option.

LOS ANGELES SERIES

PLUS - offset double cutaway maple body, bolt-on maple neck, 24-fret maple fingerboard with black pearl dot inlay, locking Wilkinson vibrato, 3-per-side locking Sperzel tuners, chrome hardware, 3 dual rail pickups, volume/tone control, 5-position rotary switch, mini switch, active electronics. Available in Antique Gold, Cherry, Cherry Burst, Citrus Green, Pink Glow, Purple Haze, Shamu Blue and Shamu Blue Burst finishes. Disc. 1994.

$595 $510 $425 $340 $305 $280 $255
Last MSR was $850.

PRO - offset double cutaway maple body, bolt-on maple neck, 24-fret maple fingerboard with black pearl dot inlay, locking Wilkinson vibrato, ebony peghead veneer, 3-per-side locking Sperzel tuners, gold hardware, 3 stacked coil Reflex pickups, volume/tone control, 5-position rotary switch, active electronics. Available in Antique Gold, Burgundy Burst, Chardonnay Rouge, Chardonnay Rouge Burst, Cherry, Cherry Burst, Citrus Green, Citrus Green Burst, Pink Glow, Pink Glow Burst, Purple Haze, Shamu Blue, Shamu Blue Burst and Vintage Gold Burst finishes. Disc. 1994.

$770 $660 $550 $440 $395 $365 $330
Last MSR was $1,100.

STANDARD - offset double cutaway maple body, bolt-on maple neck, 24-fret maple fingerboard with black pearl dot inlay, locking Wilkinson vibrato, 3-per-side locking Sperzel tuners, chrome hardware, 3 dual rail pickups, volume/tone control, 5-position rotary switch, mini switch, active electronics. Available in Black, Natural, USA Blue, USA Pink, USA Red and USA Yellow finishes. Disc. 1994.

$455 $390 $325 $260 $235 $215 $195
Last MSR was $650.

USA-HT - offset double cutaway alder body, pearloid pickguard, bolt-on maple neck, 22-fret rosewood fingerboard with pearl dot inlay, fixed Wilkinson bridge, 3-per-side Sperzel tuners, 2 single coil/humbucker Seymour Duncan pickups, volume/tone control, 5-position rotary switch, mini switch, active electronics. Available in Calypso Green, Creme, Iris Red, Mauve and Silver Metallic finishes. Disc. 1994.

$770 $660 $550 $440 $395 $365 $330
Last MSR was $1,100.

Creme finish available with tortoise pickguard only.

USA-T - similar to USA-HT, except has locking Sperzel tuners, Wilkinson vibrato. Disc. 1994.

$840 $720 $600 $480 $430 $395 $360
Last MSR was $1,200.

NEW YORK SERIES

DELUXE - offset double cutaway semi hollow mahogany body, carved bound figured maple top, maple/rosewood neck, 22-fret ebony fingerboard with pearl NY inlay at 12th fret, tune-o-matic bridge, string-through body tailpiece, 3-per-side Sperzel tuners, gold hardware, 2 humbucker pickups, volume/tone control, 3-position switch, coil tap in tone control. Available in Antique Gold, Bahamian Blue, Burny Amber, Burgundy Burst, Chardonnay Rouge, Chardonnay Rouge Burst, Cherry, Cherry Burst, Citrus Green, Citrus Green Burst, Deep Sea Blue, Emerald Isle Blue, Pink Glow, Pink Glow Burst, Purple Haze, Shamu Blue, Shamu Blue Burst, Tobacco Burst, Vintage Gold Burst, and Walnut finishes. Disc. 1994.

$420 $360 $300 $240 $215 $195 $180
Last MSR was $600.

PLUS - offset double cutaway mahogany body, pearloid pickguard, bolt-on maple neck, 22-fret rosewood fingerboard with offset pearl dot inlay, tune-o-matic bridge, string-through body tailpiece, 3-per-side Sperzel tuners, chrome hardware, single coil/humbucker pickups, volume/tone control, mini switch, coil tap in tone control. Available in Antique Gold, Burny Amber, Cherry, Citrus Green and Deep Sea Blue. Disc. 1994.

$475 $405 $340 $270 $245 $225 $205
Last MSR was $675.

Add 10% for gold hardware.

P

GRADING	100% MINT	98% NEAR MINT	95% EXC+	90% EXC	80% VG+	70% VG	60% G

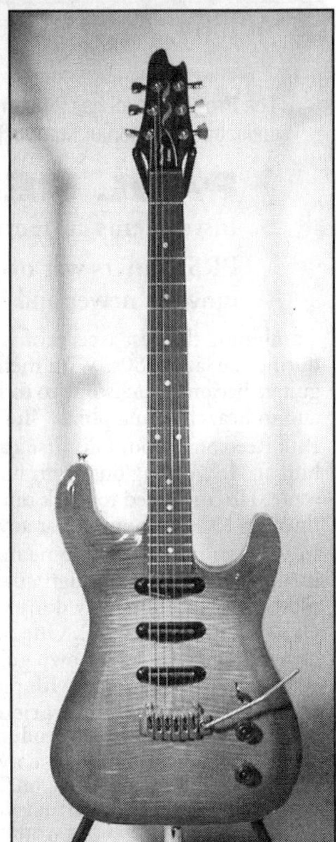
Brian Paul Artist
courtesy Brian Paul

STANDARD - offset double cutaway mahogany body, pearloid pickguard, bolt-on maple neck, 22-fret rosewood fingerboard with offset pearl dot inlay, tune-o-matic bridge, string-through body tailpiece, 3-per-side Sperzel tuners, chrome hardware, single coil/humbucker pickups, volume/tone control, mini switch, coil tap in tone control. Available in Black, Natural, USA Blue, USA Pink, USA Red and USA Yellow finishes. Disc. 1994.

$350	$300	$250	$200	$180	$165	$150

Last MSR was $500.

UK PLUS - offset double cutaway mahogany body, AA figured maple top, bolt-on maple neck, 22-fret rosewood fingerboard with offset pearl dot inlay, tune-o-matic Wilkinson bridge, string-through body tailpiece, 3-per-side Sperzel tuners, chrome hardware, 2 humbucker Seymour Duncan pickups, volume/tone control, 3-position switch. Available in Cherry Burst, Deep Sea Blue and Vintage Gold finishes. Disc. 1994.

$1,050	$900	$750	$600	$540	$495	$450

Last MSR was $1,500.

USA MODEL R - offset double cutaway mahogany body, bolt-on maple neck, 22-fret rosewood fingerboard with offset pearl dot inlay, tune-o-matic Wilkinson bridge/stop tailpiece, 3-per-side Sperzel tuners, chrome hardware, 2 single coil Seymour Duncan pickups, volume/tone control, 3-position switch. Available in Amber, Natural Oil, Red and Red Oil finishes. Disc. 1994.

$700	$600	$500	$400	$360	$330	$300

Last MSR was $1,000.

Add $100 for strings-through body tailpiece.

USA MODEL T - similar to USA Model R, except has single coil/humbucker Seymour Duncan pickups. Disc. 1994.

$700	$600	$500	$400	$360	$330	$300

Last MSR was $1,000.

Add $100 for strings-through body tailpiece.

PATTERSON GUITARS

Instruments currently built in Falcon Heights, Minnesota.

Patterson Guitars is currently offering high quality electric guitars, basses, and archtop models. Options include left-handed configuration, custom inlays, neck scale, and clear or colored lacquer finishes. For further information, please contact Patterson Guitars directly (see Trademark Index).

ELECTRIC

The Patterson **At Series Archtop Jazz Guitars** feature hand-carved German spruce tops, German curly maple back, multi-lined binding throughout, traditionally shaped f-holes, 3 to 5-piece curly maple neck, 22-fret ebony fingerboard, ebony tailpiece, pickguard and bridge, 1 custom-made, dual-coil pickup, gold tuners, and hard shell case. List price is $8,000.

The Patterson **Pt Series Guitars** feature a neck-through, multi-laminated body and graphite reinforced neck with your choice of numerous exotic woods, 24-fret ebony, wenge, or maple fingerboard, custom oil finish, 2 custom-made, humingbucking pickups with Patterson active or passive electronics, light-weight aluminum alloy tuners and precision adjustable bridge. List price is $2,400.

ELECTRIC BASS

The Patterson **Pb Series Basses** feature a bolt-on neck 4-, 5-, and 6-string models, high-gloss base coat/clear urethane finished body, 5-piece graphite reinforced neck, 24-fret ebony, wenge, maple, or phenolic fingerboard front and back peghead veneer, 3-ply laminated pickguard, cast aluminum alloy tuning gears, precision adjustable bridge, fine multi-lined binding, inlaid fret markers, Petterson passive or active high-definition electronics packages, 2 made for Patterson dual coil soapbar pickups. List price is $2,200 to $2,600.

The Patterson **Pt Series Basses** feature a neck-through 4-, 5-, and 6-string models, multi-laminated body and graphite reinforced neck with your choice of numerous exotic woods, 26-fret ebony, wenge, maple or phenolic fingerboard, custom oil finish, 2 custom-made soapbar, dual-coil pickups with Patterson active 4-band EQ or passive electronics, light-weight aluminum alloy tuners and precision adjustable bridge. List price is $2,800 to $3,200.

PAUL, BRIAN

Instruments currently built in Plano, Texas.

Luthier Brian Paul Prokop is currently handcrafting two electric guitar solid body models that feature original designs. Paul originally introduced the **Pro-22**, and this year also unveiled the new **Artist Series** model.

ELECTRIC

Both models feature a carved curly maple top, Honduran mahogany body, mahogany or figured maple neck, 22-fret ebony (or rosewood or maple) fingerboard, abalone and mother-of-pearl fingerboard inlays, Sperzel locking tuners, Seymour Duncan pickups, volume/tone controls, and a Wilkinson bridge (hard tail or floating tremolo system). Guitars are finished in aniline dyes and nitrocellulose lacquer (the current retail price includes a hardshell case).

P

GRADING	100% MINT	98% NEAR MINT	95% EXC+	90% EXC	80% VG+	70% VG	60% G

The **Pro-22** model has 2 humbuckers: Seymour Duncan Pearly Gates and Jeff Beck models. The **Artist Series** model has 3 Seymour Duncan Hot Stack single coils, or the option of humbuckers (like the Pro-22).

PAUL REED SMITH GUITARS (PRS)

Instruments currently produced in Stevensville, Maryland.

PRS Guitars was originally located in Annapolis, Maryland from 1985 to 1996. In 1996, PRS Guitars completed the move to newer and larger facilities in Stevensville, Maryland.

Combining the best aspects of vintage design traditions in modern instruments, luthier Paul Reed Smith devised a guitar that became very influential during the late 1980s. With meticulous attention to detail, design, and production combined with the concept of "graded" figured wood tops, PRS guitars became touchstone to today's high end guitar market. The concept of a "ten top" (denoting the flame in the maple figuring) began at PRS Guitars, and to hear the slang phrase "It's a ten top with birds" is magic at guitar shows nowadays.

Paul Reed Smith built his first guitar for a college music class. Drawing on his high school shop classes and his musical experiences, his first attempt gained him an *A*. Working out of his home attic in the mid 1970s, Smith began designing and revising his guitar models while involved with the guitar repair trade. He continued to work out of a small repair shop for the better part of eight years, and was selling a number of hand crafted guitars between 1976 through 1984 without major advertising. By 1982 he had finished designing and building a guitar that combined his original ideas with traditional ones.

In 1985, Smith received some major financial backing and was able to start limited handmade production of the PRS Custom model. Part of the new finances guaranteed his high quality products would finally see advertising in the major magazines (a corollary to this is the interesting phenomenon that most magazines generally don't review products unless the manufacturer advertises in the magazine - ever see a ***Blue Book of Electric Guitars*** review in *Guitar Player* magazine?). One major difference between PRS and other guitar companies of the 1980s is Smith made, or had exclusively made, all of his own components for his own guitars. Of course, choosing highly figured woods for construction wasn't a bad choice either! Through the years, Smith has continued to experiment with pickup design, body and neck variations, and even amplification and speaker systems.

In addition to the various Limited Edition models, PRS offers the Private Stock models which are available in very limited and very small construction (not production) runs. All models are handcrafted in the factory by custom methods.

PRS Pickups are also available as aftermarket replacement parts. Prices run $100 in black, and $110 for black with gold hardware. Models include the Dragon Treble (ceramic magnet and highest number of windings), Dragon Bass (slightly lower output; Alnico magnet), Artist Treble (warmer vintage style tone), Artist Bass (vintage Alnico style magnets, wound slightly hotter than Dragon Bass), HFS (*Hot, Fat, and Screams* wound hot on ceramic magnets), Vintage Treble (vintage style Alnico magnets, and wound for lower output), Vintage Bass (stock on Custom and CE Bolt-on models), and the Deep Dish II (Alnico magnets, similar in sound to a P-90 single coil).

In 1980, PRS amplifiers were available. The HG-70 Harmonic Generator amplifier head and 4 x 12" cabinet had a retail price of $2,208; the 212 combo version had a list price of $1,795.

Hardware Dating Information

In addition to a fairly straight forward serialization method (see PRS SERIALIZATION), there are a number of ways to supplement guitar dating by inspecting various features on the instrument. In 1991, PRS stopped offering Brazilian rosewood fingerboards, and began offering (very good quality) Indian rosewood. Brazilian rosewood fingerboards are still available through limited edition models or custom built models. PRS began using mother-or-pearl inlay in place of abalone shell inlay. In 1993, PRS introduced the one piece stop tailpiece. In 1995, the large, long neck heel was introduced. The two-piece tremolo bridge replaced the one-piece tremolo bridge.

ELECTRIC

10th ANNIVERSARY MODEL - offset double cutaway mahogany body, carved figured maple top, mahogany neck, 25" scale, abalone bound 22-fret ebony fingerboard with scrimshaw engraved Gold Pearl bird inlays, Gold PRS wrap over bridge/tailpiece, abalone bound peghead with engraved PRS Eagle and mother-of-pearl *10th Anniversary* ribbon inlay, abalone bound truss rod cover, 3-per-side Gold PRS locking tuners, gold hardware, 2 Gold McCarty humbucker pickups, volume and push/pull tone control, 3-position switch. Available in Amber, Dark Cherry Sunburst, Indigo, Purple, and Teal Black finishes. Only 200 Mfg. 1995.

$7,500 $5,800 $4,900 $4,100 $3,200 $2,750 $2,250

Last MSR was $6,600.

Add $200 for a Quilted Maple top.

This model comes complete with hardshell leather case and a Certificate of Authenticity from PRS. This model was also available with semi-hollow body, or a PRS tremolo system.

P

Artist Series

ARTIST - offset double cutaway mahogany body, carved flame maple top, mahogany neck, 24-fret rosewood fingerboard with abalone bird inlay, standard PRS vibrato, abalone signature peghead inlay, 3-per-side locking PRS tuners, chrome hardware, 2 PRS humbucker pickups, volume/tone/5-position control, Certificate of Authenticity. Available in Amber, Dark Cherry Sunburst, Indigo and Teal Black finishes. Mfg. 1990 to 1994.

$2,650 $2,275 $1,895 $1,500 $1,375 $1,250 $1,100

Last MSR was $3,780.

In 1993, curly maple top was introduced, 22-fret maple bound fingerboard replaced original parts/design, semi hollow body, stop tailpiece became an option.

ARTIST II - similar to the Artist, except has carved figured maple top, 25" scale, maple bound 22-fret rosewood fingerboard with abalone bird inlay, PRS wrap over bridge/tailpiece, maple bound peghead with abalone signature inlay, gold hardware, 2 PRS Artist Series humbucker pickups. Available in Amber, Dark Cherry Sunburst, Indigo and Teal Black finishes. Mfg. 1994 to 1996.

$3,400 $3,000 $2,650 $2,200 $1,750 $1,575 $1,450

Last MSR was $4,400.

This model comes complete with a Certificate of Authenticity from PRS. This model was optional with a semi-hollow body, quilted maple top, PRS tremolo system or humbucker/single/humbucker pickup configuration.

GRADING	100% MINT	98% NEAR MINT	95% EXC+	90% EXC	80% VG+	70% VG	60% G

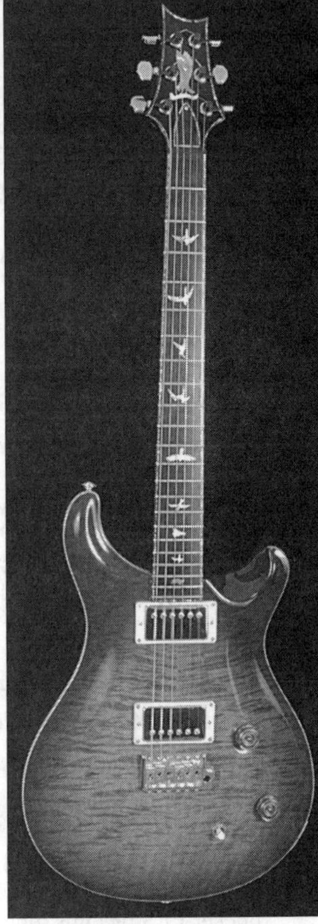
PRS 10th Anniversary courtesy Gary Canady

Artist Ltd. - similar to Artist II, except has 14K gold bird inlays, abalone and mother-of-pearl Eagle headstock inlay, and abalone purfling on the neck, headstock, and truss rod cover. Mfg. 1994 to 1995.

$6,200 $5,400 $4,500 $3,750 $3,000 $2,600 $2,200
Last MSR was $7,000.

A limited quantity of 150 instruments were produced.

ARTIST III - similar to the Artist II, except has paua bound 22-fret rosewood fingerboard with paua shell bird inlay, paua bound peghead with paua signature inlay. Available in Amber, Dark Cherry Sunburst, Indigo and Teal Black finishes. Mfg. 1996 to 1998.

$3,800 $3,350 $2,875 $2,450 $2,150 $1,850 $1,600
Last MSR was $4,800.

Add $240 for quilted maple top.

This model comes complete with hardshell leather case and a Certificate of Authenticity from PRS. This model has the standard PRS tremolo system, or a semi-hollow body optional at no extra charge.

ARTIST IV - similar to the Artist II, except has bound 22-fret rosewood fingerboard with etched solid gold bird inlay, bound peghead with signature inlay, 2 PRS McCarty pickups. Available in Amber, Dark Cherry Sunburst, Indigo and Teal Black finishes. Mfg. 1996 to 1998.

$6,000 $5,300 $4,400 $3,750 $3,000 $2,600 $2,200
Last MSR was $7,600.

Add $240 for quilted maple top.

This model comes complete with hardshell leather case and a Certificate of Authenticity from PRS. This model has the standard PRS tremolo system, or a semi-hollow body optional at no extra charge.

SANTANA MODEL - offset double cutaway mahogany body with Paua shell purfling, carved Artist Grade maple top, mahogany neck, 24 1/2" scale, 24-fret rosewood fingerboard with rippled abalone bird inlays, PRS tremolo system, PRS Eagle inlay on natural wood headstock, abalone OM symbol inlaid on truss rod cover, 3-per-side PRS locking tuners, chrome hardware, 2 Santana Zebra Coil humbucker pickups, volume/tone control, 2 mini switch pickup selectors. Available in Santana Yellow finish (with Natural Mahogany back). Mfg. 1995 to 1998.

$5,750 $5,000 $4,500 $4,000 $3,500 $3,000 $2,500
Last MSR was $6,000.

This model was built by special order only.
In 1998, Brazilian rosewood fingerboard replaced rosewood fingerboard; rosewood headstock overlay replaced natural wood headstock finish; 3-way toggle replaced 2 mini switch pickup selectors. In 1998, The PRS stoptail bridge and gold hardware were optional.
This model is also available in Amber, Black Cherry, Black Sunburst, Cherry Sunburst, Dark Cherry Sunburst, Emerald Green, Grey Black, Orange, Purple, Royal Blue, Scarlet Red, Teal Black, Tobacco Sunburst, Tortoise Shell, Turquoise, Vintage Sunburst, Violin Amber, Violin Amber Sunburst, and Whale Blue finishes. Price includes leather case (this option new in 1998).

SANTANA II MODEL - almost identical to the Santana Model, except has one 3-way selector switch rather than two mini-toggle switches, master volume control, master tone control. Available in Santana Yellow finish. Introduced in 1998.

MSR $8,000 $6,000 $5,000 $4,500 $4,000 $3,500 $3,000 $2,500

This model is offered on a limited Special Order Only basis.
This model is also available in Amber, Black Sunburst, Black Cherry, Dark Cherry Sunburst, Emerald Green, McCarty Sunburst, McCarty Tobacco Sunburst, Teal Black, Tobacco Sunburst, Vintage Sunburst, Violin Amber Sunburst, and Whale Blue finishes. In 2000, Cherry Sunburst, Gray Black, Natural, Orange, Purple, Tortoise Shell, Turquoise, Vintage Yellow, Royal Blue, Scarlet Red finishes introduced.

SANTANA III MODEL - similar to the Santana II model, but less ornate, 1 piece South American mahogany body, two-piece curly maple top, mahogany 24-fret neck, East Indian rosewood fingerboard with abalone bird inlays, two Santana III pickups personally approved by Carlos, 1 volume/1 tone control, 3-way selector, headstock color matches back/neck, PRS tremelo 14-1 low mass locking tuners. Available in Santana Yellow, Amber, Black Cherry, Black Sunburst, Dark Cherry Sunburst, Emerald Green, Gray Black, Natural, Orange, Tri-Color Sunburst, Purple, Teal Black, Tobacco Sunburst, Tortoise Shell, Turquoise, Vintage Sunburst, Vintage Yellow, Whale Blue, Ruby, Royal Blue, Scarlet Red, Tobacco Wrap Around Burst, Violin Amber, Violin Amber Bubrst and Dark Cherry Wrap Around Burst finishes. New 2001.

MSR $3,700 $2,775 $2,575 $2,375 $2,175 $1,975 $1,750 $1,550

Add $550 for 10 top flame.

Add $320 for gold hardware.

SANTANA SE - entry level Santana model, Indonesian Mahogany body, Indonesian Mahogany 22-fret set neck, rosewood fingerboard with SE inlays, gloss black headstock with Santana SE logo, PRS designed tremelo or stop tailpiece, PRS designed non-locking tuners, 2 humbucking pickups, 1 volume/1 tone control, 3-way selector switch. Available in Royal Blue, Grey Black, Teal, and Vintage Cherry finishes. New 2001.

MSR $738 $575 $495 $450 $400 $350 $300 $250

P

GRADING	100% MINT	98% NEAR MINT	95% EXC+	90% EXC	80% VG+	70% VG	60% G

CE (Classic Electric) Bolt-On Series

In 1995, Alder body wood on CE models was changed to Mahogany.

CE 22 (CE 22 BOLT-ON) - offset double cutaway carved alder body, bolt-on maple neck, 22-fret rosewood fingerboard with abalone dot inlay, 25" scale, satin black headstock finish, PRS stoptail or PRS tremolo system, 3-per-side PRS locking tuners, chrome hardware, 2 covered PRS Dragon II humbucker pickups, volume/tone control, 5-position rotary switch. Available in Black Sunburst, Natural, Translucent Green, Translucent Orange, Translucent Purple, Translucent Turquoise, Translucent Blue, Translucent Walnut, and Translucent Vintage Cherry finishes. Mfg. 1994 to 1999.

		100%	98%	95%	90%	80%	70%	60%
		$1,150	$1,000	$900	$825	$695	$575	$425

Last MSR was $1,720.

Add $70 for 3-way toggle selector switch and push/pull tone control (coil tap capabilities).

Add $280 for gold hardware.

This model is available in the following 1998 custom opaque colors: Antique White, Black, Seafoam Green, Ocean Turquoise, Cabernet Metallic, Deep Purple Metallic, Forest Green Metallic, Old Gold Metallic, Orange Mica Pearl Metallic, Platinum Metallic, Royal Blue Metallic, and Strawberry Pearl Metallic finishes. List price includes case.

CE 22 Maple Top (CE 22 Bolt-On Maple Top) - similar to the CE 22 Bolt-on, except has carved figured maple top. Available in Amber, Black Cherry, Black Sunburst, Cherry Sunburst, Dark Blue, Emerald Green, Grey Black, Natural, Orange, Purple, Royal Blue, Scarlet Red, Scarlet Sunburst, Tobacco Sunburst, Tortoise Shell, Vintage Sunburst, and Vintage Yellow finishes. Mfg. 1994 to date.

		100%	98%	95%	90%	80%	70%	60%
MSR	$2,300	$1,750	$1,400	$1,250	$1,050	$900	$725	$575

Add $500 for flame maple 10 top.

Add $700 for quilt maple 10 top.

Add $320 for gold hardware.

In 1998, Turquoise and Whale Blue finishes were introduced; Dark Blue, Natural, and Scarlet Sunburst finishes were disc. This model is also available in the 1998 custom opaque finishes with natural maple edge.

CE 24 (CE BOLT-ON) - offset double cutaway carved alder body, bolt-on maple neck, 24-fret rosewood fingerboard with abalone dot inlay, 25" scale, satin black headstock finish, PRS stoptail or PRS tremolo system, 3-per-side PRS locking tuners, chrome hardware, 2 humbucker PRS pickups (one HFS and one Vintage Bass), volume/tone control, 5-position rotary switch (1st year issue had 3-way switch with large bat). Available in Black, Black Sunburst, Classic Red, Natural, Pearl Black, and Vintage Cherry finishes. Disc. 1999.

		100%	98%	95%	90%	80%	70%	60%
		$1,300	$1,100	$975	$825	$695	$575	$425

Last MSR was $1,720.

Add $70 for 3-way toggle selector switch and push/pull tone control (coil tap capabilities).

Add $320 for gold hardware.

Add $80 for 1996-1997 custom colors (Electric Blue, Electric Red, Pearl White, Black Holoflake, Blue Holoflake, Burgundy Holoflake, Green Holoflake, Gold Holoflake, Red Holoflake, and Silver Holoflake).

In 1998, Translucent Green, Translucent Orange, Translucent Purple, Translucent Turquoise, Translucent Walnut, and (Translucent) Vintage Cherry finishes were introduced; Black, Classic Red, and Pearl Black finishes were disc. This model is available in the following 1998 custom opaque colors: Antique White, Black, Seafoam Green, Ocean Turquoise, Cabernet Metallic, Deep Purple Metallic, Forest Green Metallic, Old Gold Metallic, Orange Mica Pearl Metallic, Platinum Metallic, Royal Blue Metallic, and Strawberry Pearl Metallic finishes.
List price includes case.

CE 24 Maple Top (CE Bolt-On Maple Top) - similar to CE Bolt-On, except has figured maple top. Available in Black Cherry, Black Sunburst, Cherry Sunburst, Dark Blue, Emerald Green, Grey Black, Natural, Orange, Purple, Royal Blue, Scarlet Red, Scarlet Sunburst, Tobacco Sunburst, Tortoise Shell, Vintage Sunburst, and Vintage Yellow finishes. Current Mfg.

		100%	98%	95%	90%	80%	70%	60%
MSR	$2,300	$1,750	$1,400	$1,250	$1,050	$900	$725	$575

Add $260 for mother-of-pearl Bird inlays on neck (this option disc. in 1998).

Add $320 for gold hardware.

Add $500 for flame maple 10 top. (Option disc. 1999).

Add $700 for quilt maple 10 top. (Option disc. 1999).

In 1998, Turquoise and Whale Blue finishes were introduced; Dark Blue, Natural, and Scarlet Sunburst finishes were disc. This model is also available in the 1998 custom opaque finishes with natural maple edge. List price includes case.

Custom Series

CUSTOM 24 (CUSTOM) - offset double cutaway mahogany body, carved maple top, mahogany neck, 24-fret rosewood fingerboard with abalone/pearl moon inlay, 25" scale, PRS tremolo system or PRS stoptail, 3-per-side low mass locking tuners, chrome hardware, 2 humbucker PRS pickups (one HFS and one Vintage Bass), volume/tone control, 5-position rotary switch. Available in Black Cherry, Black Sunburst, Cherry Sunburst, Dark Cherry Sunburst, Emerald Green, Grey Black, Natural, Orange, Purple, Royal Blue, Scarlet Red, Scarlet Sunburst, Tobacco Sunburst, Tortoise Shell, Vintage Sunburst, Vintage Yellow, and Whale Blue finishes with matching headstock. Current Mfg.

		100%	98%	95%	90%	80%	70%	60%
MSR	$2,650	$1,925	$1,550	$1,350	$1,200	$1,000	$750	$650

P

GRADING	100% MINT	98% NEAR MINT	95% EXC+	90% EXC	80% VG+	70% VG	60% G

Add $70 for 3-way toggle selector switch and push/pull tone control (coil tap capabilities).

Add $280 for Abalone bird inlay.

Add $320 for gold hardware.

Add $240 for semi-hollow body (this option disc. in 1998).

Add $550 for flame maple 10 top.

Add $750 for quilt maple 10 top.

Add $1,300 for Artist Package Flame and $1,500 for Artist Package Quilt: Artist Grade flame or quilted maple top, translucent toned back, rosewood headstock veneer, Paua bird inlay in neck, and gold hardware. Available with a leather case.

List price includes case. In 1998, Teal Black, Turqoise, Violin Amber, and Violin Amber Sunburst finishes were introduced; Scarlet Sunburst finish was disc. This model has a Wide-Thin neck optional.

Custom 22 - similar to the Custom, except features a 22-fret fingerboard and 2 covered PRS Dragon II humbucking pickups. Current Mfg.

MSR	$2,650	$1,925	$1,550	$1,350	$1,200	$1,000	$750	$650

Add $70 for 3-way toggle selector switch and push/pull tone control (coil tap capabilities).

Add $320 for gold hardware.

Add $240 for semi-hollow body option.

Add $280 for Abalone bird inlay.

Add $550 for flame maple 10 top.

Add $750 for quilt maple 10 top.

Add $1,300 for Artist Package Flame and $1,500 for Artist Package Quilt: Artist Grade flame or quilted maple top, translucent toned back, rosewood headstock veneer, Paua bird inlay in neck, and gold hardware. Available with a leather case.

List price includes case. This model has a Wide-Thin neck as an option. (Note: The Custom 22 model is essentially the Dragon model without the dragon neck inlay.)

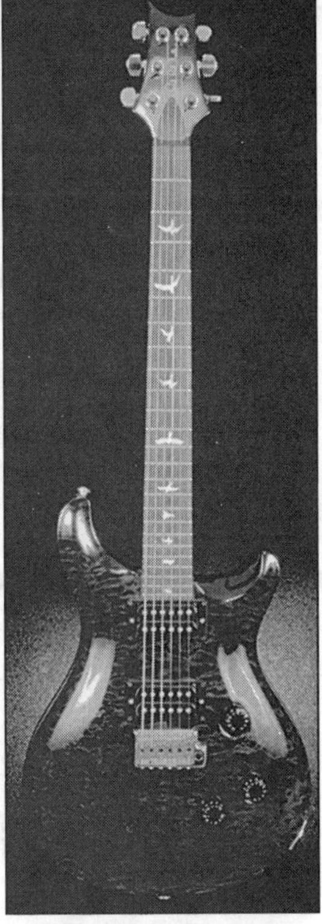

1992 PRS Custom 22
courtesy Gary Canady

CUSTOM 22 SOAPBAR - similar to Custom 22 except has 3 soapbar single coil pickups, 5-way blade pickup selector, 1 volume/1 tone control, rock maple neck, PRS tremelo bridge. 2000 to present.

MSR	$2,800	$2,100	$1,675	$1,450	$1,300	$1,100	$850	$750

Add $200 for Quilt top.

Add $550 for 10 top flame.

Add $750 for 10 top quilt.

Add $200 for rock maple fingerboard with maple tint.

Add $280 for Abalone bird inlays.

Add $320 for gold hardware.

Dragon Series

DRAGON - offset double cutaway mahogany body, arched bound flame maple top, mahogany neck, 22-fret ebony fingerboard with intricate dragon inlay, PRS wrap over bridge/tailpiece, abalone signature inlay on peghead, 3-per-side locking PRS tuners, gold hardware, 2 humbucker PRS pickups, volume/tone control, 5-position rotary control. Available in Amber, Dark Cherry Sunburst, Indigo and Teal Black finishes. Mfg. on a yearly basis, in limited numbers.

The fingerboard dragon inlays on these instruments are made of various seashell, precious metals and stones. Each year the inlay became more elaborate. Dragons have virtually dried up in the used marketplace.

Dragon I (1992 Series) - 100 Mfg. (originally just 50).

$18,000 $15,500 $12,000

Last MSR was $8,000.

Dragon II (1993 Series) - 218-piece fingerboard inlay, 100 Mfg.

$18,000 $15,500 $12,000

Last MSR was $11,000.

Dragon III (1994 Series) - 438-piece fingerboard inlay, 100 Mfg.

$21,000 $18,000 $15,000

Last MSR was $16,000.

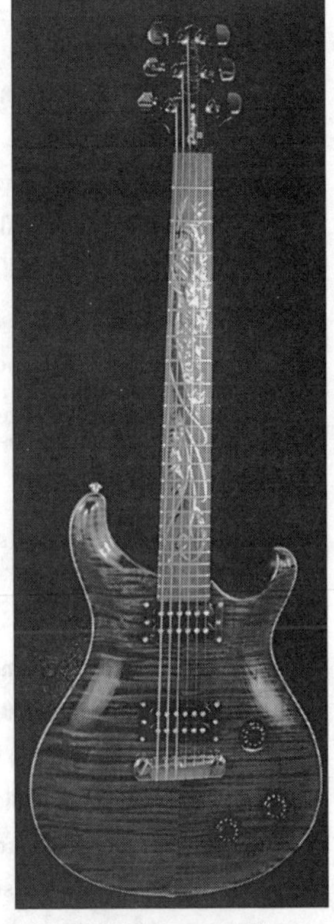

PRS Dragon III
courtesy Gary Canady

P

GRADING	100% MINT	98% NEAR MINT	95% EXC+	90% EXC	80% VG+	70% VG	60% G

EG Bolt-On Series

The EG Bolt-on models had two different body designs (not radically different, just different).

EG BOLT-ON (EG 1) - offset double cutaway alder body, white pickguard, bolt-on maple neck, 22-fret rosewood fingerboard with pearl dot inlay, standard PRS tremolo system, 3-per-side locking PRS tuners, chrome hardware, humbucker/single coil/humbucker pickups, volume control, push-pull tone control, 5-position switch, coil tap in tone control. Available in Black, Black Sunburst, Classic Red, and Seafoam Green finishes. Disc. 1996.

		$800	$650	$575	$475	$395	$350	$300

Last MSR was $1,280.

This model also available with 2 single coil/1 humbucker pickups with coil tap in tone control (EG 2), and 3 single coil pickups with dual tone in tone control (EG 3).

EG Bolt-On LH - similar to EG Bolt-On, except in left-handed configuration. Mfg. 1993 only.

		$750	$700	$625	$500	$450	$400	$350

Last MSR was $1,285.

EG BOLT-ON MAPLE TOP - similar to EG Bolt-On, except has 3-piece maple top. Available in Black Cherry Burst, Black Sunburst, Emerald Green Burst, Grey Black Burst, Purple Burst, Royal Blue Burst, Scarlet Burst, Tri-Color Sunburst and Whale Blue Burst finishes. Disc. 1996.

		$950	$795	$725	$595	$475	$425	$375

Last MSR was $1,580.

In 1994, Black Cherry Burst, Emerald Green Burst, Purple Burst, Royal Blue Burst, Scarlet Burst, Tri-Color Sunburst and Whale Blue Burst finish were introduced.

EG Bolt-On LH Maple Top - similar to EG Bolt-On Maple top, except in left-handed configuration. Available in Black Sunburst and Grey Black Sunburst finishes. Mfg. 1993 only.

		$950	$795	$725	$595	$475	$425	$375

Last MSR was $1,585.

McCarty Series

Introduced in 1994, the McCarty Model instrument was built as a tribute to Ted McCarty, the company president who was responsible for many model and part innovations during his tenure with the Gibson company during the 1950s. In 1998, 3 archtop and 2 hollow body models were introduced to the McCarty Series.

McCARTY (McCARTY MODEL) - offset double cutaway mahogany body, carved figured Michigan maple top, mahogany Wide-Fat neck, 22-fret rosewood fingerboard with pearl and abalone moon inlays, PRS wrap over bridge/tailpiece, blackface peghead with screened logo, 3-per-side vintage-style tuners with plastic buttons, 2 nickel cover McCarty humbucker pickups, volume/push-pull tone (coil tap) control, 3-position switch. Available in McCarty Sunburst and McCarty Tobacco Sunburst finishes. Mfg. 1994 to date.

MSR	$2,840	$2,100	$1,800	$1,500	$1,150	$1,050	$950	$725

Add $200 for PRS tremolo and low mass locking tuners.

Add $280 for abalone bird inlays.

Add $320 for gold hardware.

Add $550 for flame 10 Top.

Add $600 for East Indian rosewood neck (only available with stoptail bridge).

List price includes case. In 1998, headstock matching finishes replaced the blackface peghead; Amber, Black Sunburst, Tortoise Shell, Vintage Yellow, Violin Amber, and Violin Amber Burst finishes were introduced. This model is available in the following 1998 custom opaque colors: Antique White, Black, Seafoam Green, Ocean Turquoise, Cabernet Metallic, Deep Purple Metallic, Forest Green Metallic, Old Gold Metallic, Orange Mica Pearl Metallic, Platinum Metallic, Royal Blue Metallic, and Strawberry Pearl Metallic finishes. This model is also available with additional finishes (10 Top option only): Black Cherry, Dark Cherry Sunburst, Emerald Green, Gray Black, Purple, Turquoise, Teal Black, and Whale Blue.

McCarty Soapbar - similar to McCarty Model, except has mahogany body/carved east coast maple top or carved solid mahogany body, 2 Seymour Duncan 'soapbar' P-90-style single coil pickups, volume/tone controls, 3-way toggle switch. Available in Black Sunburst, Natural, Walnut, and Vintage Cherry finishes (solid mahogany body); Antique White, Black, Seafoam Green, Ocean Turquoise, Cabernet Metallic, Deep Purple Metallic, Forest Green Metallic, Old Gold Metallic, Orange Mica Pearl Metallic, Platinum Metallic, Royal Blue Metallic, and Strawberry Pearl Metallic finishes with natural maple edge (mahogany body/carved maple top). Mfg. 1998 to present.

MSR	$2,840	$2,100	$1,800	$1,500	$1,150	$1,050	$950	$725

Add $200 for PRS tremolo and low mass locking tuners.

Add $550 for flame 10 Top.

Add $280 for abalone bird inlays.

Add $600 for East Indian rosewood neck.

Add $320 for gold hardware.

List price includes case.

P

GRADING	100% MINT	98% NEAR MINT	95% EXC+	90% EXC	80% VG+	70% VG	60% G

McCarty Soapbar Standard -similar to McCarty Soapbar except has carved solid mahogany body (No maple top). Available in Black Sunburst, Natural mahogany, Translucent Blue, translucent Orange, Translucent Purple, Translucent turquoise, translucent Vintage Cherry, Translucent walnut, Crème, Black, Metallic Red, Old Gold Metallic, Platinum Metallic and Metallic green. Current Mfg.

MSR	$2,440	$1,725	$1,500	$1,250	$1,125	$975	$850	$725

Add $280 for Abalone Bird Inlays.
Add $320 for gold hardware.

McCarty Standard - similar to McCarty Model, except has carved solid mahogany body (no maple top). Available in Black, Custom Black, Gold Top, Natural, and Vintage Cherry finishes. Current Mfg.

MSR	$2,440	$1,725	$1,500	$1,250	$1,125	$975	$850	$725

Add $280 for abalone bird inlays.

Add $320 for gold hardware.

List price includes case. In 1998, Black Sunburst, Translucent Green, Translucent Orange, Translucent Purple, Translucent Turquoise, and Translucent Walnut finishes were introduced; Black, Custom Black, and Gold Top finishes were disc. This model is available in the following 1998 custom opaque colors: Antique White, Black, Seafoam Green, Ocean Turquoise, Cabernet Metallic, Deep Purple Metallic, Forest Green Metallic, Old Gold Metallic, Orange Mica Pearl Metallic, Platinum Metallic, Royal Blue Metallic, and Strawberry Pearl Metallic finishes. This model is optional with gold hardware. In 2000, Translucent Green, Deep Purple Metallic, Ocean Turquoise, Forest Green Metallic, Orange Mica Pearl, Royal Blue Metallic, & Strawberry Pearl Metallic finishes were disc. and Translucent Vintage Cherry and Natural Mahogany finishes were introduced.

McCARTY ARCHTOP SPRUCE - offset double cutaway hollow body, carved spruce top, carved mahogany back/sides, *Wide-Fat* mahogany neck, 22-fret rosewood fingerboard with pearl and abalone moon inlays, headstock (matches back/neck), adjustable PRS stoptail bridge, 3-per-side low mass tuners with ebony buttons, 2 McCarty Archtop pickups, volume/tone controls, 3-position toggle switch. Available in Satin Vintage Natural finish. Mfg. 1998 to 2000.

Body Depth (Rim) 2 3/4", Body Depth (Bridge) 4".

$2,600	$2,100	$1,800	$1,600	$1,400	$1,250	$1,000

Last MSR was $3,300.

Add $280 for abalone bird inlays.

Add $320 for gold hardware.

Add $650 for LR Baggs/PRS Piezo bridge system, patent applied for, individual string voicing, real acoustic guitar modeling.

List price includes case.

McCarty Archtop I -similar to McCarty Archtop Spruce except has carved figured maple top, carved mahogany back and sides, 22-fret mahogany neck, rosewood fingerboard, pearl and abalone moon inlays, wide fat neck, rosewood veneer headstock, adjustable PRS stop tailpiece, two McCarty Archtop pickups, 1 volume/1 tone control, 3-way toggle pickup selector. Available in Amber, Black Cherry, Black Sunburst, Dark Cherry Sunburst, Gray Black, McCarty Sunburst, natural, McCarty Tobacco Burst, Teal Black, Tortoise Shell, Turquoise, Vintage Yellow, Whale Blue, Cherry Sunburst, Violin Amber and Violin Amber Burst. Mfg. 2000 Only.

$2,775	$2,575	$2,300	$2,100	$1,900	$1,700	$1,500

Last MSR was $3,700.

Add $200 for quilt top.

Add $550 for 10 top flame.

Add $750 for 10 top quilt.

Add $280 for Abalone bird inlays.

Add $320 for gold hardware.

Add $650 for LR Baggs/PRS piezo bridge system, patent applied for, individual string voicing, real acoustic guitar modeling.

McCarty Archtop II - similar to the McCarty Archtop, except features carved Custom Grade figured maple top and back, rosewood headstock veneer. Available in Amber, Black Cherry, Black Sunburst, Dark Cherry Sunburst, McCarty Tobacco Sunburst, McCarty Sunburst, Natural, Tobacco Sunburst, Vintage Sunburst, Violin Amber, and Violin Amber Burst finishes. Mfg. 1998 to 2000.

$2,600	$2,300	$2,000	$1,800	$1,600	$1,400	$1,200

Last MSR was $3,900.

Add $280 for abalone bird inlays.

Add $1,100 for flame 10 top and back.

Add $1,500 for quilt 10 top and back.

Add $320 for gold hardware.

Add $650 for LR Baggs/PRS piezo bridge system, patent applied for, individual string voicing, real acoustic guitar modeling.

List price includes case.

P

GRADING	100% MINT	98% NEAR MINT	95% EXC+	90% EXC	80% VG+	70% VG	60% G

McCarty Archtop Artist - similar to the McCarty Archtop, except features carved Artist Grade figured maple top and back, 22-fret Brazilia rosewood fingerboard with 14kt gold-outlined abalone bird inlay, rosewood headstock veneer, gold hardware. Available in Amber, Black Cherr Black Sunburst, Dark Cherry Sunburst, Gray Black, McCarty Tobacco Sunburst, McCarty Sunburst, Natural, and Tobacco Sunburst finishes. Mfg 1998 to date.

MSR	$10,000	$7,000	$5,950	$5,500	$5,000	$4,500	$4,000	$3,000

Add $650 for LR Baggs/PRS Piezo bridge system, patent applied for, individual string voicing, real acoustic guitar modeling.

Price includes case.
This model is available by special order only.
"McCarty Archtop Artist" and the instrument's number in this series will be printed on the back of the headstock. This model is optional with flame or quilt top and back (no extra charge). This model is optional in Amber, Black Cherry, Gray Black, McCarty Sunburst, Tiger's Eye, Turquoise, Violin Amber, and Violin Amber Burst double-stained finishes (no extra charge). The double-stained finishes are only available on the McCarty Archtop Artist model and Private Stock models.

McCARTY HOLLOWBODY I - offset double cutaway hollow body, carved spruce top, carved mahogany back/sides, Wide-Fat mahogany neck, 22-fret rosewood fingerboard with pearl and abalone moon inlays, headstock (matches back/neck), PRS stoptail bridge, 3-per-side low mass tuners with ebony buttons, 2 McCarty Archtop pickups, volume/tone controls, 3-position toggle switch. Available in Satin Vintage Natural finish (spruce top); Amber, Black Cherry, Black Sunburst, Dark Cherry Sunburst, McCarty Tobacco Sunburst, McCarty Sunburst Natural, Tobacco Sunburst, Vintage Sunburst, Violin Amber, and Violin Amber Burst high gloss finishes (maple top). Mfg. 1998 to date.

Body Depth (Rim) 1 3/4", Body Depth (Bridge) 3".

MSR	$3,600	$2,650	$2,250	$1,950	$1,750	$1,550	$1,350	$1,150

Add $120 for adjustable PRS stoptail bridge.

Add $280 for abalone bird inlay.

Add $320 for gold hardware.

Add $650 for LR Baggs/PRS Piezo bridge system, patent applied for, individual string voicing, real acoustic guitar modeling.

Add $200 for quilt top.

Add $550 for flame 10 Top.

Add $750 for quilt 10 Top.

List price includes case. This model is optional with gold hardware.

McCarty Hollowbody II - similar to the McCarty Hollowbody, except features carved Custom Grade figured maple top and back, carved mahogany sides. Available in Amber, Black Cherry, Black Sunburst, Dark Cherry Sunburst, McCarty Tobacco Sunburst, McCarty Sunburst, Natural, Tobacco Sunburst, Vintage Sunburst, Violin Amber, and Violin Amber Burst finishes. Mfg. 1998 to date.

MSR	$3,800	$2,800	$2,350	$2,100	$1,900	$1,600	$1,400	$1,200

Add $120 for adjustable PRS stoptail bridge.

Add $280 for abalone bird inlay.

Add $320 for gold hardware.

Add $650 for LR Baggs/PRS Piezo bridge system, patent applied for, individual string voicing, real acoustic guitar modeling.

Add $400 for quilt top and back.

Add $1,100 for flame 10 top and back.

Add $1,500 for quilt 10 top and back.

List price includes case.

McCarty Hollowbody Spruce - similar to McCarty Hollowbody I and II except has carved spruce top. Available in Black Sunburst, Tobacco Sunburst, Tri-Color Sunburst, Vintage Natural, Antique White, Custom Black, Cabernet Metallic and Old Gold Metallic (Gold Top) finishes. New for 2000.

MSR	$3,200	$2,500	$1,900	$2,000	$1,800	$1,600	$1,400	$1,200

Add $280 for Abalone bird inlays.

Add $120 for adjustable PRS stop tailpiece.

Add $320 for gold hardware.

Add $650 for LR Baggs/PRS piezo bridge system, patent applied for, individual string voicing, real acoustic guitar modeling.

ROSEWOOD LTD. - offset double cutaway mahogany body, carved curly maple top, Indian rosewood neck, 22-fret Brazilian rosewood fingerboard with elaborate tree of life (consisting of abalone, Brown Lip mother-of-pearl, coral, gold, and mammoth ivory materials) inlay, PRS wraparound bridge, tree of life and signature peghead inlay, 3-per-side locking PRS tuners with rosewood buttons, gold hardware, 2 PRS McCarty humbuckers, volume/tone controls, 3-position toggle switch. Available in Black Cherry, Grey Black, Purple, Violin Amber, and Violin Amber Sunburst finishes. Mfg. 1996 only.

		$10,500	$9,500	$8,500				

Last MSR was $13,000.

A limited quantity of 100 instruments were produced. This model comes complete with hardshell leather case and a Certificate of Authenticity from PRS.

P

GRADING	100% MINT	98% NEAR MINT	95% EXC+	90% EXC	80% VG+	70% VG	60% G

Single Cut Series

SINGLECUT - single cutaway body design, thick mahogany back, carved maple top, 22-fret mahogany neck, rosewood fingerboard with abalone dot inlays, wide, fat neck, headstock color matches back/neck, PRS stop tailpiece, Vintage tuners, two PRS #7 pickups, 3-way toggle switch on upper bout, 2 volume/2 tone controls. Available in Amber, Black Cherry, Black Sunburst, Cherry Sunburst, Dark Cherry Sunburst, Emerald Green, Gray Black, Natural, Orange, Purple, Teal Black, Tobacco Sunburst, Tortoise Shell, Turquoise, Vintage Sunburst, Vintage yellow, Whale Blue, Royal Blue, Scarlet Red, Violin Amber and Violin Amber Burst finishes. New 2000.

MSR	$3,000	$2,325	$2,050	$1,850	$1,650	$1,550	$1,400	$1,200

Add $200 for quilt top.

Add $550 for 10 top flame.

Add $750 for 10 top quilt.

Add $280 for Abalone bird inlays.

Add $320 for gold hardware.

Add $1,300 for Artist package Flame and $1,500 for Artist package Quilt: Paua bird inlays in neck, rosewood headstock veneer with paua signature, Artist grade top and translucent toned back, gold hardware, leather case.

MARK TREMONTI MODEL - single cutaway design, thick mahogany back with carved maple top, 22-fret mahogany neck, rodewood fingerboard with mother-of-pearl bird inlays, Mark tremonti 12th fret inlay, headstock color matches back/neck, truss rod cover with mother-of-pearl purfling, PRS adjustable stop tailpiece, 14 –1 low mass locking tuners, two Tremonti pickups, 3-way toggle pickup selector, 2 volume/2 tone controls. Available in black finish only. New 2001.

MSR	$3,400	$2,550	$2,350	$2,150	$1,950	$1,750	$1,550	$1,350

Standard Series

STANDARD 22 - offset double cutaway carved mahogany body, set-in mahogany neck, 22-fret rosewood fingerboard with pearl and abalone moon inlay, 25" scale, color-matching headstock, PRS tremolo system or PRS stoptail bridge, 3-per-side locking PRS tuners, chrome hardware, 2 PRS Dragon II humbucker pickups, volume/tone control, 5-position rotary switch. Available in Black, Natural, Pearl Black, and Vintage Cherry finishes. Current Mfg.

MSR	$2,400	$1,750	$1,500	$1,250	$1,000	$900	$800	$600

Add $70 for 3-way toggle selector switch and push/pull tone control (coil tap capabilities).

Add $280 for abalone bird inlays.

Add $320 for gold hardware.

List price includes case.
In 1998, Black Sunburst, Natural, Translucent Green, Translucent Orange, Translucent Purple, Translucent Turquoise, and Translucent Walnut finishes were introduced; Black and Pearl Black finishes were disc. This model is available in the following 1998 custom opaque colors: Antique White, Black, Seafoam Green, Ocean Turquoise, Cabernet Metallic, Deep Purple Metallic, Forest Green Metallic, Old Gold Metallic, Orange Mica Pearl Metallic, Platinum Metallic, Royal Blue Metallic, and Strawberry Pearl Metallic finishes. This model is optional with gold hardware.

Standard 22 Maple Top - similar to the Standard 22, except features mahogany body, carved maple top. Available in Antique White, Black, Seafoam Green, Ocean Turquoise, Cabernet Metallic, Deep Purple Metallic, Forest Green Metallic, Old Gold Metallic, Orange Mica Pearl Metallic, Platinum Metallic, Royal Blue Metallic, and Strawberry Pearl Metallic finishes with natural maple edge (some models may have a natural gloss finish on the back). Mfg. 1998 to 1999.

$1,650	$1,250	$1,150	$950	$850	$750	$600

Last MSR was $2,300.

Add $70 for 3-way toggle selector switch and push/pull tone control (coil tap capabilities).

Add $260 for abalone bird inlays.

Add $280 for gold hardware.

List price includes case.

P

GRADING		100% MINT	98% NEAR MINT	95% EXC+	90% EXC	80% VG+	70% VG	60% G

STANDARD 24 (STANDARD) - offset double cutaway carved mahogany body/neck, 24-fret rosewood fingerboard with pearl and abalone moon inlay, 25" scale, standard PRS tremolo system or PRS stoptail bridge, 3-per-side locking PRS tuners, chrome hardware, 2 humbucker PRS pickups (one HFS and one Vintage Bass), volume/tone control, 5-position rotary switch. Available in Black, Natural, Pearl Black, and Vintage Cherry finishes. Current Mfg.

MSR	$2,400	$1,750	$1,500	$1,250	$1,000	$900	$750	$600

Add $70 for 3-way toggle selector switch and push/pull tone control (coil tap capabilities).

Add $80 for 1996/1997 Custom colors (Custom Black, Electric Blue, Electric Red, Gold Top, Pearl White, Black Holoflake, Blue Holoflake, Burgundy Holoflake, Green Holoflake, Gold Holoflake, Red Holoflake, and Silver Holoflake).

Add $240 for a semi-hollow body (this option disc. in 1998).

Add $280 for abalone Bird inlays on neck.

Add $320 for gold hardware.

List price includes case.

In 1998, Black Sunburst, Natural, Translucent Green, Translucent Orange, Translucent Purple, Translucent Turquoise, and Translucent Walnut finishes were introduced; Black and Pearl Black finishes were disc. This model is available in the following 1998 custom opaque colors: Antique White, Black, Seafoam Green, Ocean Turquoise, Cabernet Metallic, Deep Purple Metallic, Forest Green Metallic, Old Gold Metallic, Orange Mica Pearl Metallic, Platinum Metallic, Royal Blue Metallic, and Strawberry Pearl Metallic finishes.

Standard 24 Maple Top - similar to the Standard 24, except features mahogany body, carved maple top. Available in Antique White, Black, Seafoam Green, Ocean Turquoise, Cabernet Metallic, Deep Purple Metallic, Forest Green Metallic, Old Gold Metallic, Orange Mica Pearl Metallic, Platinum Metallic, Royal Blue Metallic, and Strawberry Pearl Metallic finishes with natural maple edge (some models may have a natural gloss finish on the back). Mfg. 1998 to 1999.

		$1,650	$1,250	$1,150	$950	$850	$750	$600

Last MSR was $2,300.

Add $70 for 3-way toggle selector switch and push/pull tone control (coil tap capabilities).

Add $260 for abalone bird inlays.

Add $280 for gold hardware.

List price includes case.

SWAMP ASH SPECIAL - offset double cutaway carved swamp ash (or black ash) body, bolt-on maple neck, 22-fret maple fingerboard with abalone dot inlay, toned clear headstock finish, PRS stoptail bridge or PRS tremolo, 3-per-side locking PRS tuners, chrome hardware, PRS McCarty humbucker/Seymour Duncan Vintage Rail single coil/PRS McCarty humbucker pickups, volume/push-pull tone (coil tap) controls, 3-position toggle switch. Available in Black, Black Sunburst, and Vintage Cherry finishes. Mfg. 1996 to date.

MSR	$2,400	$1,750	$1,500	$1,250	$1,000	$900	$800	$600

Add $280 for abalone bird inlays.

Add $300 for figured maple neck/figured maple fingerboard.

Add $320 for gold hardware.

In 1998, Natural and Tri-Color Sunburst finishes were introduced; Grey Black finish was disc. (previously 1997 Custom colors). This model is available in the following 1998 custom opaque colors: Antique White, Black, Seafoam Green, Ocean Turquoise, Cabernet Metallic, Deep Purple Metallic, Forest Green Metallic, Old Gold Metallic, Orange Mica Pearl Metallic, Platinum Metallic, Royal Blue Metallic, and Strawberry Pearl Metallic finishes. List price includes case.

ELECTRIC BASS

The PRS Basic electric bass models were available with bolt-on or set-in neck joint configurations. The Bolt-On neck models had alder bodies, or alder bodies with figured maple tops; the Set-In neck models had solid mahogany, or mahogany bodies with maple tops. Desirable options on the PRS bass models include the bird inlays, and a figured maple 10 Top.

ELECTRIC BASS - offset double cutaway alder body, bolt-on rock maple neck, rosewood or rock maple fingerboard, abalone dot inlays, PRS machined brass bridge, 20-1 low mass tuners, 2-per-side tuners, 2 PRS high inductance passive magnetic pickups, 2 volume/1 master tone control. Available in Antique White, black, Cabernet Metallic, Old Gold Metallic, Platinum Metallic & Seafoam Green. New 2000.

MSR	$2,000	$1,500	$1,400	$1,200	$1,000	$900	$800	$700

Add $400 for Swamp Ash Body.

Add $1000 for Figured maple neck with rosewood or figured maple fingerboard.

Add $280 for Abalone bird inlays.

Add $320 for gold hardware.

Add $750 for LR Baggs/PRS piezo bridge system, patent applied for, individual string voicing, 3 band active EQ, selector switch for piezo, magnetic, or both.

Add $200 for Black Sunburst, Translucent Emerald Green, Translucent Vintage Cherry, Tri-Color Sunburst and Translucent Turquoise finishes.

ELECTRIC BASS MAPLE TOP - similar to Electric Bass except, alder back, curly maple inset top. Available in Amber, Black Cherry, Black Sunburst, Dark Cherry Sunburst, Emerald green, Gray Black, Natural, Orange, Purple, Royal Blue, Scarlet Red, Teal Black, Tobacco Sunburst, Tortoise Shell, Turquoise, Vintage Sunburst, Vintage Yellow, Violin Amber, Violin Amber Burst and Whale Blue finishes. New 2000.

MSR	$2,600	$1,950	$1,850	$1,750	$1,500	$1,250	$1,000	$895

GRADING	100% MINT	98% NEAR MINT	95% EXC+	90% EXC	80% VG+	70% VG	60% G

Add $550 for 10 top flame.

Add $1,000 for figured maple neck with rosewood or figured maple fingerboard.

Add $280 for abalone bird inlays.

Add $320 for gold hardware.

Add $750 for LR Baggs/PRS piezo bridge system, patent applied for, individual string voicing, 3-band active EQ, selector switch for piezo, magnetic, or both.

BASIC FOUR - offset double cutaway mahogany body, figured maple top, set-in maple neck, 34" scale, 2-per-side headstock, 3 single coil pickups, volume/tone/pickup selector controls. Available in translucent finishes. Mfg. 1986 to 1987.

$1,800	$1,600	$1,400	$1,200	$1,000	$800	$600

Last MSR was $1,500.

Add $700 for 10 Top w/Birds in 100% condition.

Subtract $200 for alder body/bolt-on neck.

Basic Five - similar to the Basic Four, except has 5-string configuration, 3/2 headstock. Mfg. 1986 to 1987.

$1,300	$1,200	$1,100	$1,000	$800	$600	$400

Last MSR was $1,600.

Subtract $200 for alder body/bolt-on neck.

PRS Basic Five
courtesy Jimmy Gravity

PAWAR GUITARS

Instruments currently built in Willoughby Hills, Ohio.

Pawar Guitars are handcrafted in the U.S., and currently available in 3 models, All models come standard with the Pawar positive tone system (P.T.S.), and feature carved maple tops, lightweight swamp ash backs, maple necks, and rosewood fretboards. Please contact the company directly for more information (see Trademark Index).

TURN OF THE CENTURY PLAYER -offset cutaway solid body, unique scroll upper bout, carved maple top, light weight swamp ash back, maple neck, rosewood fingerboard, 25 ½" scale, jumbo frets, set neck, tunematic bridge, string-through body retainer, Sperzel non-locking tuners, recessed Dunlop strap locks, Pawar Positive Tone System with 20 pre-set classic tones, 2 Seymour Duncan pickups, Gun Metal Gray back. Available in Sterling Silver, Drama Gold, and Midnight Black finishes. Current Mfg.

MSR $2,500

TURN OF THE CENTURY STAGE - similar to Turn Of The Century Player except comes standard with premium hand selected woods and translucent ivory finished back. Available in Copper Tan, Cobalt Blue, and Emeald Green finishes. Current Mfg.

MSR $3,000

TURN OF THE CENTURY PRESTIGE - similar to Turn Of The Century Stage except has highly figured maple top, matching figured maple headstock veneers, premium light weight swamp ash back, ivoroid bound Bird's Eye Maple neck, select rosewood fingerboards. Available in Antiqueburst, natural, Cherryburst, and Tobaccoburst translucent finishes. Current Mfg.

MSR $3,500

Dot Neck Inlay Option $100, all 3 models.
Bigsby B5 Vibrato Tailpiece with Roller Bridge Option $200, all 3 models.
Quilt Maple Top Option $100, Prestige Model Only.
Bird's Eye Maple Top Option $200, Prestige Model Only.

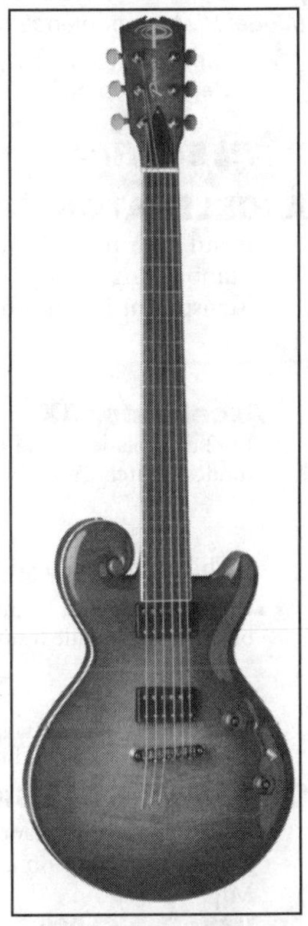

Pawar Prestaige
courtesy Pawar Guitars

PEAR CUSTOM

Instruments currently built in Pleasanton, California.

Luthier Tom Palecki offers custom electric guitar design and construction and custom painting in a wide variety of traditional and high tech colors. Our instruments are exclusively electric and consultations are by appointment only. Prices begin at $2,000 and up for design and construction depending on complexity of design and color. Pear Custom are also the inventors of the TURBOTUNE guitar and bass string winder and TURBOTUNE Drum Key currently licensed to Dean Markley Strings for world wide sales. For further information, please contact Pear Custom Guitars directly (see Trademark Index).

PEARL

Instruments previously produced in Italy starting in the late 1970s (production then moved to Japan). Production ended sometime in the early 1980s.

The Pearl trademark appeared on a number of instruments manufactured (at first) by the Gherson company of Italy. These medium quality guitars featured both original designs on some models, and copies of classic American designs on others. Production of Pearl guitars moved to Japan (circa 1978- 1979) and continued on for another couple of years. Although Italy had a tradition of guitar manufacture throughout the years, the cheaper labor costs that Japan was featuring at the time eventually won out in production considerations.

(Source: Tony Bacon and Paul Day, The Guru's Guitar Guide)

P

GRADING	100% MINT	98% NEAR MINT	95% EXC+	90% EXC	80% VG+	70% VG	60% G

PEAVEY

Instruments currently built in Meridian and Leaksville, Mississippi. Distributed by Peavey Electronics Corporation of Meridian, Mississippi since 1965.

Peavey also has a factory and distribution center in Corby, England to help serve and service the overseas market.

Peavey Electronics is one of the very few major American musical instrument manufacturers still run by the original founding member and owner. Hartley Peavey grew up in Meridian, Mississippi and spent some time working in his father's music store repairing record players. He gained some recognition locally for the guitar amplifiers he built by hand while he was still in school, and decided months prior to college graduation to go into business for himself. In 1965 Peavey Electronics was started out of the basement of Peavey's parents' home. Due to the saturated guitar amp market of the late 1960s, Peavey switched to building P.A. systems and components. By 1968 the product demand was great enough to warrant building a small cement block factory on rented land and hire another staff member.

The demand for Peavey products continued to grow, and by the early 1970s the company's roster had expanded to 150 employees. Emphasis was still placed on P.A. construction, although both guitar and bass amps were doing well. The Peavey company continued to diversify and produce all the components needed to build the finished product. After twelve years of manufacturing, the first series of Peavey guitars was begun in 1977, and introduced at the 1978 NAMM show. An advertising circular used by Peavey in the late '70s compared the price of an American built T-60 (plus case) for $350 versus the Fender Stratocaster's list price of $790 or a Gibson Les Paul for $998.50 (list). In light of those list prices, it's also easy to see where the Japanese guitar makers had plenty of maneuvering room during their "copy" era.

The "T-Series" guitars were introduced in 1978, and the line expanded from three models up to a total of seven in five years. In 1983, the product line changed, and introduced both the mildly wacky Mystic and Razer original designs (the Mantis was added in 1984) and the more conservative Patriot, Horizon, and Milestone guitars. The Fury and Foundation basses were also added at this time. After five years of stop tailpieces, the first Peavey "Octave Plus" vibratos were offered (later superseded by the Power bend model). Pickup designs also shifted from the humbuckers to single or double "blade" pickups.

Models that debuted in 1985 included the vaguely stratish Predator, and the first doubleneck (!), the Hydra. In response to the guitar industry shifting to "superstrat" models, the Impact was introduced in 1986. Guitars also had the option of a Kahler locking tremolo, and two offsprings of the '84 Mantis were released: The Vortex I or Vortex II. The Nitro series of guitars were available in 1987, as well as the Falcon, Unity, and Dyna-Bass. Finally, to answer companies like Kramer or Charvel, the Tracer series and the Vandenberg model(s) debuted in 1988.

As the U.S. guitar market grew more conservative, models like the Generation S-1 and Destiny guitars showed up in guitar shops. Peavey basses continued to evolve into sleeker and more solid instruments like the Palaedium, TL series or B Ninety. 1994 saw the release of the MIDIBASE (later the Cyberbass) that combined magnetic pickups with a MIDI-controller section.

One of Peavey's biggest breakthroughs in recent years was the development of the Peavey EVH amplifier, developed in conjunction with Edward Van Halen. Due to the success and acceptance of the EVH 5150 amplifier, Van Halen withdrew his connection with his signature Ernie Ball model (which is still in production as the Axis model), and designed a "new" **Wolfgang** model with Peavey. This new model had a one year "waiting period" from when it was announced at the NAMM industry trade show to actual production. Many Peavey dealers who did receive early models generally sold them at new retail (no discount) for a number of months due to slow supply.

Rather than stay stuck in a design "holding pattern", Peavey continues to change and revise guitar and bass designs, and they continue the almost twenty year tradition of American built electric guitars and basses.

(Model History, nomenclature, and description courtesy Grant Brown, Peavey Repair section)

Information on virtually any Peavey product, or a product's schematic is available through Peavey Repair. Grant Brown, the head of the Repair section, has been with Peavey Electronics for over eighteen years.

ELECTRIC

AXCELERATOR - offset double cutaway poplar (or swamp ash) body, pearloid pickguard, bolt-on maple neck, 22-fret rosewood fingerboard with pearl dot inlay, Peavey Power Bend III non-locking tremolo, 6-on-a-side locking tuners, chrome hardware, 3 Db2 dual blade humbucking pickups, volume/tone control, 5-position switch. Available in Black, Candy Apple Red, Metallic Gold, Transparent Blue, and Transparent Red finishes. Mfg. 1994 to 1998.

$650 $525 $450 $395 $325 $275 $200
Last MSR was $799.

Axcelerator AX - similar to Axcelerator, except has swamp ash body, Floyd Rose double locking vibrato, non locking tuners, gold hardware 2 Db2 dual blade/1 Db4 quad blade humbucker pickups, 3-way turbo (allows bridge pickup to be tapped as single coil, dual coil, and full humbucking modes) switch. Available in Blonde, Transparent Blue, Transparent Green, and Transparent Red finishes. Mfg. 1995 to 1998.

$650 $525 $450 $395 $325 $275 $200
Last MSR was $799.

This model had maple fingerboard with black dot inlay as an option.

Axcelerator F - similar to Axcelerator, except has swamp ash body, Floyd Rose double locking vibrato, non locking tuners, gold hardware 2 dual blade/1 quad blade humbucker pickups. Available in Blonde, Transparent Blue, Transparent Green, and Transparent Red finishes. Mfg. 1994 only.

$475 $400 $350 $325 $275 $250 $200
Last MSR was $799.

Options such as Swamp Ash body and AX pickup assembly (2 Db2 dual blade and 1 Db4 quad blade humbuckers) were offered on the regular Axcelerator. The Axcelerator F model evolved into the Axcelerator AX model.

CROPPER CLASSIC - single cutaway mahogany body with figured maple top, bolt-on hard rock maple neck, 22-fret rosewood fingerboard, Db2 dual blade humbucker, Db4 quad blade humbucker, gold hardware, master volume and tone controls, 3-way pickup selector switch, two position coil-tap switch. Available in Black, Onion Green, Memphis Sun, and Rhythm Blue finishes. Case included. Current Mfg.

MSR $1,099 $875 $750 $625 $550 $450 $350 $275

This model was designed in conjunction with guitarist Steve Cropper.

GRADING	100% MINT	98% NEAR MINT	95% EXC+	90% EXC	80% VG+	70% VG	60% G

DEFENDER - offset double cutaway poplar body, white laminated pickguard, bolt-on maple neck, 24-fret rosewood fingerboard with pearl dot inlay, double locking Floyd Rose vibrato, 6-on-a-side tuners, chrome hardware, exposed humbucker/single coil/humbucker pickups, volume/tone control, 5-position switch. Available in Black, Candy Apple Red, Cobalt Blue, and White finishes. Mfg. 1994 to 1995.

$350 $295 $250 $225 $200 $175 $150
Last MSR was $590.

Defender F - similar to Defender, except has alder body, black pearloid laminated pickguard, humbucker/single coil rail/humbucker pickups. Available in Metallic Purple, Metallic Silver, Pearl Black, and Pearl White finishes. Mfg. 1994 to 1995.

$475 $400 $350 $325 $275 $250 $200
Last MSR was $799.

DESTINY - offset double cutaway poplar body, through body rock maple neck, 24-fret bound rosewood fingerboard, pearl dot inlays, Kahler double locking vibrato, 6-on-a-side tuners, black hardware, 2 high output single coil/1 Alnico humbucker pickups, volume/tone control, 5-position pickup selector and coil tap switch. Available in Black, Blue, White, and Red finishes. Mfg. 1989 to 1994.

$425 $350 $325 $295 $250 $225 $200
Last MSR was 699.95.

Destiny Custom - offset double cutaway mahogany body, quilted maple top, through body flamed maple neck, 24-fret bound rosewood fingerboard, pearl oval inlay at 12th fret, double locking vibrato, 6-on-a-side tuners, gold hardware, 2 high output single coil/1 Alnico humbucker pickups, volume/tone control, 5-position pickup selector and a coil tap switch. Available in Honey Burst, Transparent Black, Transparent Blue, Transparent Honey Burst, and Transparent Red finishes. Mfg. 1989 to 1994.

$600 $500 $450 $400 $350 $300 $250
Last MSR was $1,000.

Detonator Series

DETONATOR - offset double cutaway poplar body, bolt-on hard rock maple neck, 24-fret rosewood fingerboard with pearl dot inlay, Peavey Floyd Rose double locking tremolo, 6-on-a-side tuners, chrome hardware, ceramic Humbucker/single coil/humbucker configuration, volume/tone control, 5-position switch, white laminated pickguard. Available in Candy Apple Red, Cobalt Blue, Gloss Black, Gloss White finishes. Disc. 1998.

$475 $395 $350 $295 $250 $200 $150
Last MSR was $589.

Detonator AX - similar to the Detonator, except has alder body, Alnico humbucker/Db2 dual blade single coil/Alnico humbucker configuration, Power Bend III tremolo system, locking tuning machines, pearloid pickguard. Available in Metallic Purple, Metallic Silver, Pearl Black, and Pearl White finishes. Disc. 1998.

$625 $500 $450 $375 $325 $250 $195
Last MSR was $779.

Detonator JX - similar to the Detonator, except has poplar body, 2 single coil/humbucker ceramic pickups, Power Bend II tremolo system, non-locking tuning machines, white laminated pickguard. Available in Gloss Black, Gloss Dark Blue, Gloss White, and Gloss Red finishes. Disc. 1998.

$325 $275 $250 $200 $175 $150 $100
Last MSR was $419.

EVH Wolfgang Series

The EVH Wolfgang series was designed in conjunction with Edward Van Halen. Van Halen, who had great success with the Peavey 5150 amplifiers he also helped develop, named the guitar model after his son.

EVH WOLFGANG (Stop Tailpiece/Solid Colors) - offset double cutaway bound basswood body, arched top, bolt-on graphite-reinforced bird's eye maple neck, 22-fret bird's eye maple fingerboard with black dot inlays, 25 1/2" scale, adjustable bridge/stop tailpiece, 3-per-side headstock, chrome tuners, chrome hardware, 2 ceramic humbuckers, volume/tone controls, 3-position pickup selector. Available in Gloss Black and Gloss Ivory finishes. Mfg. 1996 to date.

MSR $1,649 $1,235 $1,050 $890 $750 $635 $510 $385

EVH Wolfgang (Floyd Rose/Solid Colors) - similar to the EVH Wolfgang, except has a Peavey Floyd Rose double locking tremolo system with a "D-Tuner" dropped D tuning knob. Mfg. 1996 to date.

MSR $1,749 $1,310 $1,115 $950 $800 $675 $540 $400

EVH Wolfgang (Stop Tailpiece/Transparent Colors) - similar to the EVH Wolfgang, except features a arched quilted maple top, stop tailpiece/non-tremolo bridge. Available in Transparent Amber, Transparent Purple, Transparent Red, and Sunburst finishes. Mfg. 1996 to date.

MSR $1,879 $1,410 $1,200 $1,025 $875 $750 $600 $450

Peavey EVH Wolfgang
courtesy Peavey

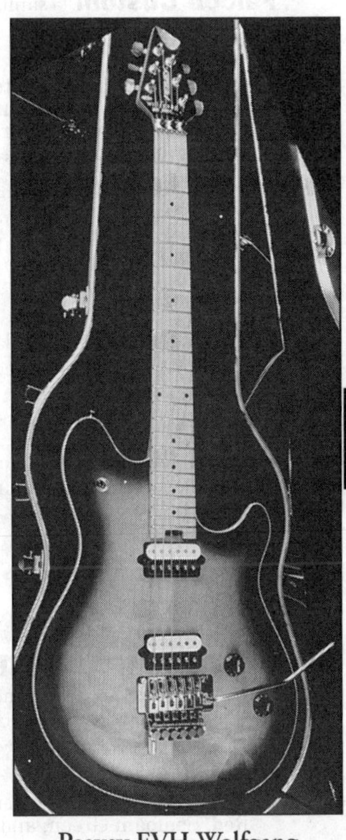

Peavey EVH Wolfgang
courtesy Peavey

P

GRADING		100% MINT	98% NEAR MINT	95% EXC+	90% EXC	80% VG+	70% VG	60% G

EVH Wolfgang (Floyd Rose/Transparent Colors) - similar to the EVH Wolfgang, except has a arched quilted maple top, Peave Floyd Rose double locking tremolo system with a *D-Tuna* dropped D tuning knob. Available in Transparent Amber, Transparent Purple, Transparen Red, and Sunburst finishes. Mfg. 1996 to date.

MSR	$1,979	$1,485	$1,265	$1,075	$915	$775	625	$465

EVH Wolfgang (Stop Tailpiece/Vintage Gold) - similar to the EVH Wolfgang, except has a basswood body, maple top, stop tail-piece/non-tremolo bridge. Available in Gold Top finish. Mfg. 1997 to date.

MSR	$1,879	$1,410	$1,200	$1.025	$875	$750	$600	$450

EVH Wolfgang (Floyd Rose/Vintage Gold) - similar to the EVH Wolfgang, except has a basswood body, maple top, Peavey Floyc Rose double locking tremolo system. Available in Gold Top finish. Mfg. 1997 to date.

MSR	$1,979	$1,485	$1,265	$1,075	$915	$775	$625	$465

EVH WOLFGANG SPECIAL - offset double cutaway basswood body, bolt-on maple neck, 22-fret maple fingerboard with black do inlays, 25 1/2" scale, adjustable bridge/stop tailpiece, 3-per-side headstock, chrome tuners, chrome hardware, 2 humbuckers, volume/tone controls, 3-position pickup selector. Available in Black, Gloss Ivory, Gold, Purple, and Sunburst finishes. Mfg. 1997 to date.

MSR	$1,099	$825	$700	$600	$500	$425	$325	$250

Also available with rosewood fingerboard.

EVH Wolfgang Special Flametop - similar to EVH Wolfgang Special except, has High Grade Flame Maple Top, hand detailed flame body binding, Case included. Available in Gloss Black, Transparent Red, Transparent Purple, Transparent Amber, Transparent Sunburst, and Transparent Dark Cherry Sunburst finishes. Current Mfg.

MSR	$1,499	$1,050	$950	$850	$750	695	$650	$595

Also available with rosewood fingerboard.

EVH Wolfgang Special ST - similar to EVH Wolfgang Special except, has recessed Tune-O-Matic bridge and stop tailpiece, Case included. Available in Gloss Black, Gloss Ivory, Gloss Purple, Vintage Gold, Tobacco Sunburst finishes. Current Mfg.

MSR	$998	$698	$598	$550	$498	$450	$398	$350

Also available with rosewood fingerboard.

Falcon Series

FALCON - double offset cutaway poplar body, bolt-on bi-laminated maple neck, 22-fret maple fingerboard, 25 1/2" scale, 6-on-a-side tuners, three single coil pickups, Kahler locking tremolo system, volume/tone controls, five way pickup selector, white pickguard. Mfg. 1986 to 1988.

$250	$200	$175	$150	$125	$100	$85

Last MSR was $399.50.

Falcon Custom - similar to the Falcon, except featured a rosewood fingerboard and different fingerboard radius. Mfg. 1986 to 1990.

$275	$225	$200	$175	$150	$135	$125

Last MSR was $449.50.

In 1988, the Falcon Custom's body design was restyled into a sleeker profile similar to the Falcon Classic and Falcon Active that were offered that same year. In 1988, Flame Maple neck with Rosewood or Maple fingerboards replaced the standard rock maple neck. In 1989, changes involved a Figured Maple neck with a Rosewood fingerboard, pickups were upgraded to the HRS (Hum Reducing System) models, carved maple top over poplar body, gold hardware, Power Bend II tremolo and locking tuning machines, and a graphite nut.

FALCON ACTIVE - similar to the Falcon, except body was restyled to sleeker design lines, Flame Maple bi-laminated neck with Rosewood or Flame Maple fingerboard, and active Bi-FET pickups replaced the original passive system. Active electronics powered by an on-board 9-volt battery. Mfg. 1988 to 1989.

$325	$275	$250	$225	$195	$175	$150

Last MSR was $549.

Falcon Classic - similar to the Falcon Active, except has Flame Maple bi-laminated neck and Flame Maple fingerboard, 3 passive single coil pickups, Power Bend non-locking tremolo system. Mfg. 1988 to 1989.

$225	$175	$150	$135	$125	$100	$90

Last MSR was $349.50.

Falcon Standard - similar to the Falcon Classic, except has a Figured Maple bi-laminated neck and rosewood fingerboard, 3 HRS (Hum Reducing System) passive single coil pickups, Power Bend II non-locking tremolo and graphite saddles, locking tuning machines. Mfg. 1989 to 1990.

$225	$175	$150	$135	$125	$100	$90

Last MSR was $349.50.

Firenza Series

FIRENZA (IMPACT FIRENZA) - offset double cutaway mahogany body, bolt-on maple neck, 22-fret rosewood fingerboard with pearl dot inlay, 25" scale, recessed tune-o-matic bridge/stop tailpiece, 3-per-side tuners, chrome hardware, 2 "soapbar"single coil pickups, volume/tone control, 3-position selector switch. Available in Ivory, Gloss Black, Sunburst, Transparent Cherry, and Transparent Walnut finishes. Disc. 2000.

$525	$450	$395	$350	$295	$225	$175

Last MSR was $699.

An early Impact Firenza model may have 2 single coil/humbucker pickups, poplar body, or tremolo bridge. Also available in Powder Blue, Red, Seafoam Green, and White finishes.

GRADING	100% MINT	98% NEAR MINT	95% EXC+	90% EXC	80% VG+	70% VG	60% G

Firenza AX (Impact Firenza AX) - similar to the Impact Firenza, except features a swamp ash body, Power Bend III standard tremolo, locking tuners, 2 covered humbucker pickups, 5-way pickup selector. Available in Antique Blonde, Pearl Black, Sunburst, and Transparent Red finishes. Disc. 2000.

$720 $575 $490 $410 $325 $250 $195
Last MSR was $899.

This model was an option with an alder body, and available in Metallic Silver, Pearl Black, or Transparent Grape with pearloid pickguard, or Sunburst with tortoiseshell pickguard finishes.

Firenza JX (Impact Firenza JX) - similar to the Impact Firenza, except features basswood body, fixed bridge, 2 single coil/humbucker pickups, 5-way pickup selector. Available in Gloss Black, Gloss Ivory, and Gloss Red finishes. Mfg. 1997 to 2000.

$480 $390 $345 $295 $250 $200 $150
Last MSR was $599.

G-90 - offset double cutaway poplar body, bolt-on rock maple neck, 24-fret bound rosewood fingerboard with pearl dot inlay, Floyd Rose double locking tremolo, reverse headstock, 6-on-a-side tuners, black hardware, 2 HRS single coil/1 Alnico tapped humbucker pickups, volume/tone control, 5-position pickup selector, coil tap switch. Available in Black, Blue, Eerie Dess Black, Eerie Dess Blue, Eerie Dess Multi, Eerie Dess Red, Pearl White, Raspberry Pearl, and Sunfire Red finishes. Disc. 1994.

$350 $300 $275 $250 $200 $175 $150
Last MSR was $600.

Generation Series

GENERATION S-1 - single cutaway mahogany body, Flame Maple top, bolt-on laminated maple neck, 22-fret rosewood fingerboard with pearl dot inlay, fixed brass bridge, graphlon nut, 6-on-a-side tuners, gold hardware, active single coil/humbucker pickup, volume/tone control, 3-position pickup selector, coil tap switch. Available in Transparent Amber, Transparent Black, Transparent Blue, and Transparent Red finishes. Mfg. 1988 to 1994.

$475 $400 $350 $325 $275 $250 $200
Last MSR was $800.

Generation S-2 - similar to Generation S-1, except has Kahler double locking tremolo system. Mfg. 1990 to 1994.

$475 $400 $350 $325 $275 $250 $200
Last MSR was $800.

Generation S-3 - similar to Generation S-1, except has hollow sound chambers, maple fingerboard with black dot inlay, 3 stacked coil pickups, coil tap in tone control. Available in Transparent Black, Transparent Blue, Transparent Honey Sunburst, and Transparent Red finishes. Mfg. 1991 to 1994.

$300 $250 $225 $200 $175 $150 $125
Last MSR was $500.

Generation Custom - similar to Generation S-1, except has solid Poplar body, Flame Maple neck, Ebony fingerboard, black hardware, Black Chrome Kahler double locking tremolo, Active electronics, Peavey single coil/humbucker pickups, volume/tone controls, 3-way pickup selector, coil tap switch. Mfg. 1989 to 1994.

$475 $400 $350 $325 $275 $250 $200
Last MSR was $799.

Generation Standard - similar to Generation S-1, except has solid Poplar body, Flame Maple bi-laminated neck, 22-fret Flame Maple fingerboard, chrome hardware, 6-on-a-side headstock, 2 single coil pickups, master volume/master tone controls, and 3-way pickup selector. Mfg. 1989 to 1994.

$295 $225 $195 $175 $150 $125 $110
Last MSR was $429.

HORIZON - offset double cutaway hardwood body, bi-laminated hard rock maple neck, 23-fret rosewood neck, 24 3/4" scale, chrome hardware, 6-on-a-side tuners, 2 dual blade humbucking pickups, stop tailpiece, master volume control, two tone controls (one per pickup), 3-way pickup selector. Available in Natural, White, Black, and Sunburst finishes. Mfg. 1983 to 1986.

$225 $195 $175 $150 $125 $100 $85
Last MSR was $379.

The tone control for the humbucking pickups allows the capability of single or dual coil output. Fully opening the pot to *10* achieves single coil mode. Turning counterclockwise to 7 brings the second coil into operation. Tone circuitry is standard in function between 7 and *0*.

Horizon II - similar to the Horizon, except features an extra "single blade"single coil pickup in the middle position (Extra 3-way switch controls the middle pickup only: off/in phase with the other pickups/out-of-phase with the other pickups). Mfg. 1983 to 1986.

$300 $250 $225 $200 $175 $150 $125
Last MSR ranged from $349 to $499.

This model had the option of a Peavey Octave Plus tremolo system.

P

GRADING	100% MINT	98% NEAR MINT	95% EXC+	90% EXC	80% VG+	70% VG	60% G

Horizon II Custom - similar to the Horizon II, except features a black phenolic fingerboard and pearl or metallic finishes. Mfg. 1984 to 1985

$325 $275 $250 $225 $195 $150 $125

Last MSR ranged from $475 to $525.

HYDRA - offset double cutaway hardwood body, bi-laminated hard rock maple necks in a 12/6 configuration, 24-fret maple fingerboards both necks in 24 3/4" scale, 2 dual blade humbuckers per neck, master volume knob, two tone knobs (one per pickup), 3-way pickup selector (6 string), 3-way pickup selector (12-string), 3-way neck selector switch. Mfg. 1984 to 1986.

$650 $550 $495 $450 $395 $325 $275

Last MSR was $1,099.

The tone control for the humbucking pickups allows the capability of single or dual coil output. Fully opening the pot to *10* achieves single coil mode. Turning counterclockwise to *7* brings the second coil into operation. Tone circuitry is standard in function between 7 and *0*.

Jeff Cook Hydra - similar to Hydra, except has Kahler double locking tremolo system on six string neck, as well as Jeff Cook on headstock. Mfg. 1985 to 1986.

$780 $650 $585 $520 $455 $390 $325

Last MSR was $1,299.50.

This model had design input from Jeff Cook (Alabama).

Impact Series

The Impact Series, introduced in 1985, featured "superstrat" styling and a sleek body profile. The later Impact series (Firenza, Milano, and Torino) further explored the Impact body design with other pickup configurations such as dual humbuckers. The Impact Firenza series later evolved into its own Firenza series (See Firenza Series).

IMPACT 1 - offset double cutaway Poplar body, hard rock neck, 22-fret *Polyglide* polymer fingerboard with pearl dot inlay, Kahler locking tremolo system, 6-on-a-side tuners, Black chrome or gold-on-brass hardware, 2 P-6 single coils/1 P-12 humbucker pickups, master volume control, master tone control, three pickup selector mini-switches. Available in Pearl Black and Pearl White finishes. Mfg. 1985 to 1987.

$450 $375 $350 $300 $250 $225 $195

Last MSR was $749.50.

Impact 2 - similar to Impact 1, except has a rosewood fingerboard (instead of synthetic fingerboard). Available in Pearl Black and Pearl White finishes.

$325 $250 $225 $200 $175 $150 $125

Last MSR was $519.

Impact 1 Unity - similar to Impact 1, except has an ebony fingerboard, neck-through design, black chrome hardware, 2 single coil/Alnico humbucker pickups. Available in Pearl Black and Pearl White finishes. Mfg. 1987 to 1989.

$475 $400 $350 $325 $275 $250 $200

Last MSR was $799.

IMPACT MILANO - offset double cutaway maple body, figured maple top, 25" scale, bolt-on rock maple neck, 24-fret rosewood fingerboard with pearl dot inlay, Power Bend III standard vibrato, 6-on-a-side locking tuners, chrome hardware, 2 Alnico exposed humbucker pickups, volume/tone control, 5-position switch. Available in Antique Amber, Metallic Green, Transparent Blue and Transparent Red finishes. Mfg. 1994 to 1995.

$475 $400 $350 $325 $275 $250 $200

Last MSR was $799.

IMPACT TORINO I - offset double cutaway mahogany body, figured maple top, 25" scale, set-in mahogany neck, 24-fret rosewood fingerboard with pearl/abalone 3-D block inlay, tune-o-matic bridge/stop tailpiece, 6-on-a-side tuners, chrome hardware, 2 Alnico exposed humbucker pickups, volume/tone control, 5-position switch. Available in Cherry Sunburst, Honey Sunburst, Metallic Gold, and Transparent Red finishes. Mfg. 1994 to 1995.

$600 $500 $450 $400 $350 $300 $250

Last MSR was $999.

Impact Torino II - similar to Impact Torino I, except had a Power Bend III standard vibrato and locking tuners.

$600 $500 $450 $400 $350 $300 $250

Last MSR was $999.

MANTIS - single cutaway *flying V* ("pointy V"?) hardwood body, bi-laminated hard rock maple neck, 23-fret rosewood neck, 24 3/4" scale, chrome hardware, 6-on-a-side tuners, 1 dual blade humbucking pickup, fixed bridge, master volume control, master tone control. Mfg. 1984 to 1986.

$325 $275 $225 $195 $150 $125 $100

Last MSR was $269.50.

This model had the Octave Plus tremolo system as an option.

Mantis LT - similar to the Mantis, except features a Kahler "Flyer" locking tremolo, black pickguard. Mfg. 1985 to 1986.

$375 $325 $295 $250 $225 $195 $150

P

GRADING	100% MINT	98% NEAR MINT	95% EXC+	90% EXC	80% VG+	70% VG	60% G

MILESTONE - offset double cutaway hardwood body, bi-laminated hard rock maple neck, 24-fret rosewood neck, 24 3/4" scale, chrome hardware, 6-on-a-side tuners, 2 dual blade humbucking pickups, fixed bridge, master volume control, two tone controls (one per pickup), 3-way pickup selector, pickup phase switch (either in or out-of-phase). Mfg. 1983 to 1986.

$275 $225 $200 $175 $150 $125 $100
Last MSR was $449.

This model had the Octave Plus tremolo system as an option. The tone control for the humbucking pickups allows the capability of single or dual coil output. Fully opening the pot to *10* achieves single coil mode. Turning counterclockwise to 7 brings the second coil into operation. Tone circuitry is standard in function between 7 and *0*.

Milestone Custom - similar to the Milestone, except features a phenolic fingerboard. Available in Pearl or Metallic finishes. Mfg. 1985 to 1986.

$295 $250 $225 $200 $175 $150 $125
Last MSR was $499.

Milestone 12 - similar to the Milestone, except features a 12-string configuration. Mfg. 1985 to 1986.

$350 $295 $250 $225 $195 $150 $125
Last MSR was $519.50.

MYSTIC - offset double cutaway-dual *rounded wings* hardwood body, bi-laminated hard rock maple neck, 23-fret rosewood neck, 24 3/4" scale, chrome hardware, 6-on-a-side tuners, 2 dual blade humbucking pickups, fixed bridge, master volume control, two tone controls (one per pickup), 3-way pickup selector. Available in Blood Red, White, Frost Blue, Inca Gold, Silver, Sunfire Red, and Black finishes. Mfg. 1983 to 1986.

$325 $275 $250 $200 $175 $150 $125
Last MSR was $399.

This model had the Octave Plus tremolo system as an option. The tone control for the humbucking pickups allows the capability of single or dual coil output. Fully opening the pot to *10* achieves single coil mode. Turning counterclockwise to 7 brings the second coil into operation. Tone circuitry is standard in function between 7 and *0*.

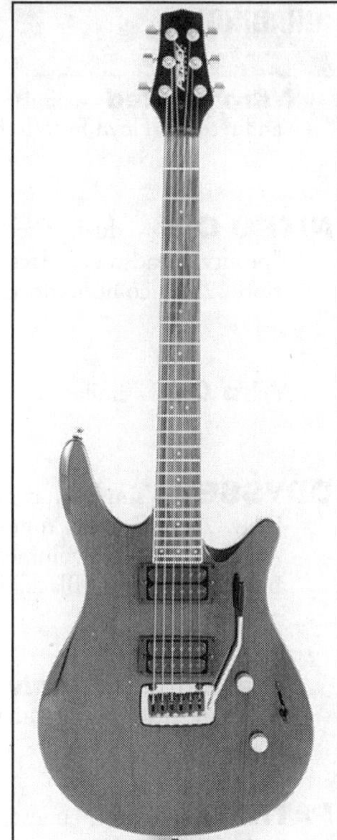

Peavey Impact 2
courtesy Peavey

Nitro Series

The Nitro Series debuted in 1986, and featured a number of models designed towards Hard Rock players.

NITRO I - dual offset cutaway hardwood body, bi-laminated maple neck, 22-fret rosewood fingerboard, 25 1/2" scale, 6-on-a-side "pointy" headstock, black hardware, Peavey Precision tuners, Kahler locking tremolo system, exposed pole piece humbucker, master volume knob. Mfg. 1986 to 1989.

$300 $275 $225 $175 $150 $125 $95
Last MSR was $399.50.

Nitro I Active - similar to the Nitro I, except features active circuitry and an extra tone control knob. System requires a 9-volt battery. Mfg. 1988 to 1990.

$450 $400 $350 $295 $250 $175 $150
Last MSR was $549.

Nitro I Custom - similar to the Nitro I, except features recessed Floyd Rose/Kahler locking tremolo. Mfg. 1987 to 1989.

$350 $300 $275 $200 $150 $125 $100
Last MSR was $499.50.

NITRO II - dual offset cutaway hardwood body, bi-laminated maple neck, 22-fret rosewood fingerboard, 25 1/2" scale, 6-on-a-side "pointy" headstock, black hardware, Peavey Precision tuners, Kahler locking tremolo system, two exposed pole piece humbuckers, master volume knob, master tone knob, 3-way pickup selector switch. Mfg. 1987 to 1989.

$350 $300 $250 $195 $175 $150 $125
Last MSR was $449.50.

NITRO III - dual offset cutaway hardwood body, bi-laminated maple neck, 22-fret rosewood fingerboard, 25 1/2" scale, 6-on-a-side "pointy" headstock, black hardware, Peavey Precision tuners, Kahler locking tremolo system, 2 exposed pole piece single coil pickups, 1 exposed pole piece humbuckers, master volume knob, master tone knob, 3 individual pickup selector mini switches. Mfg. 1987 to 1989.

$375 $325 $275 $225 $195 $175 $125
Last MSR was $499.50.

Nitro III Custom - similar to the Nitro III, except features Alnico pickups and recessed Floyd Rose/Kahler locking tremolo system. Mfg. 1987 to 1989.

$475 $450 $375 $325 $250 $200 $175
Last MSR was $599.50.

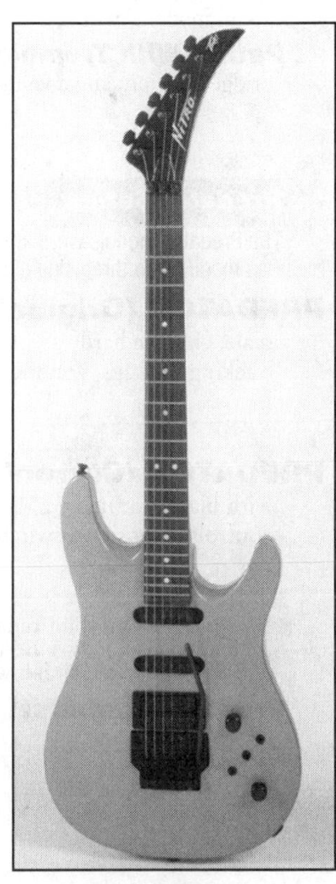

Peavey Nitro
courtesy Peavey

P

GRADING	100% MINT	98% NEAR MINT	95% EXC+	90% EXC	80% VG+	70% VG	60% G

Nitro Limited - similar to the Nitro III, except features 22-fret Ebony fingerboard, gold hardware, neck-through body design, Alnico pickups and recessed Floyd Rose/Kahler locking tremolo system. Mfg. 1987 to 1989.

$650 $525 $475 $425 $350 $300 $250
Last MSR was $1,000.

NITRO C-2 - dual offset cutaway hardwood body, bi-laminated maple neck, 22-fret rosewood fingerboard, 25 1/2" scale, 6-on-a-side "pointy" headstock, black hardware, Peavey Precision tuners, Floyd Rose locking tremolo system, 1 HRS single coil pickup (middle position), 2 Alnico humbuckers, master volume knob, master tone knob, 3 individual pickup selector mini switches. Mfg. 1990 to 1992.

$495 $450 $350 $275 $225 $175 $150
Last MSR was $599.

Nitro C-3 - similar to the Nitro C-2, except features 2 Alnico single coil/Alnico humbucker pickups. Mfg. 1990 to 1992.

$495 $450 $350 $275 $225 $175 $150
Last MSR was $599.

ODYSSEY - single cutaway mahogany body, carved flame maple top, set mahogany neck, 24-fret bound ebony fingerboard with white arrow inlay, 24 3/4" scale, tune-o-matic bridge/stop tailpiece, graphlon nut, bound peghead, 3-per-side tuners, gold hardware, 2 humbucking Alnico pickups, 2 volume/2 tone controls, 3-position and coil split switches, straplocks. Available in '59 Vintage Sunburst, Tobacco Sunburst, Transparent Black, Transparent Blue and Transparent Red finishes. Mfg. 1990 to 1994.

$650 $550 $495 $450 $395 $325 $275
Last MSR was $1,000.

Odyssey 25th Anniversary - similar to Odyssey, except has bound Quilted Maple top, 2 color pearl 3D block fingerboard inlay, black hardware, black pearl tuning machines, straplocks. Available in Transparent Black finish.

$875 $725 $650 $575 $500 $425 $350
Last MSR was $1,300.

PATRIOT - double cutaway hardwood body, bi-laminated hard rock maple neck, 23-fret fingerboard, 23 3/4" scale, chrome hardware, 6-on-a-side headstock, graphlon top nut, black laminated pickguard, 2 single coil blade pickups, volume/tone controls, 3-way pickup selector switch. Mfg. 1983 to 1986.

$225 $195 $175 $150 $125 $100 $75
Last MSR ranged from $229 to $299.

Patriot Plus - similar to the Patriot model, except features dual blade humbucker in the bridge position instead of a single coil, and a 24 3/4" scale. Mfg. 1983 to 1986.

$225 $195 $175 $150 $125 $100 $75
Last MSR was $249.

The tone control for the humbucking pickup allows the capability of single or dual coil output. Fully opening the pot to *10* achieves single coil mode. Turning counterclockwise to *7* brings the second coil into operation. Tone circuitry is standard in function between *7* and *0*.

Patriot With Tremolo - similar to the Patriot model, except features a 24 3/4" scale, a Power Bend standard tremolo, 1 humbucker in the bridge position, and a volume control. Mfg. 1986 to 1990.

$225 $195 $175 $150 $125 $100 $75
Last MSR was $259.50.

Predator Series

The Predator models were introduced in the mid 1980s, and the first model featured a dual humbucker, locking tremolo design. After several years, the design was modified to three single coils pickups instead, and later to the popular single/single/humbucker variant.

PREDATOR (Original Model) - double cutaway hardwood body, bi-laminated hard rock maple neck, 23-fret fingerboard, 24 3/4" scale, chrome hardware, 6-on-a-side headstock, black laminated pickguard, Kahler "Flyer"locking tremolo system, 2 exposed pole piece humbucking pickups, volume control, tone controls, 3-way pickup selector switch. Mfg. 1985 to 1988.

$275 $225 $200 $175 $150 $125 $95
Last MSR was $399.50.

P

PREDATOR (Current Mfg.) - offset double cutaway poplar body, white pickguard, bolt-on maple neck, 22-fret maple fingerboard with black dot inlay, 25 1/2" scale, Power Bend standard vibrato, 6-on-a-side tuners, chrome hardware, 3 single coil pickups, volume/2 tone controls, 5-position switch. Available in Gloss Black, Metallic Red, and Metallic Dark Blue finishes. Mfg. 1990 to 2000.

$240 $200 $175 $150 $125 $100 $75
Last MSR was $299.

In 1996, when the Predator AX was disc., the Predator model was upgraded with the rosewood fingerboard, 2 single coil/1 humbucker pickups, and Power Bend III tremolo system. Early versions of the Predator model were offered in Black, Red, and White finishes. In 1999, Gloss Red finish was added and Metallic Red and Metallic Dark Blue were disc.

Predator Sunburst - similar to the Predator (Current Mfg.). Available in a Sunbust finish. Disc. 1999.

$240 $200 $175 $150 $125 $100 $75
Last MSR was $299.

GRADING	100% MINT	98% NEAR MINT	95% EXC+	90% EXC	80% VG+	70% VG	60% G

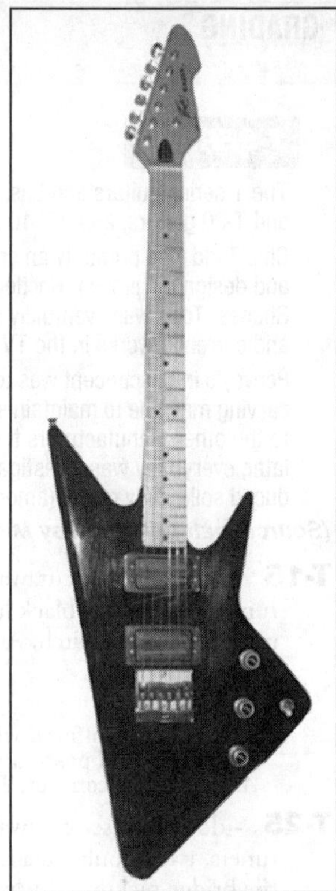

Peavey Razer
courtesy Steve Cherne

Predator AX - similar to Predator, except has rosewood fingerboard with pearl dot inlay, 2 single coil/1 humbucker pickups, volume/tone control, 3-position mini switch. Available in Black, Powder Blue, Red and White finishes. Mfg. 1994 to 1995.

	$225	$195	$175	$150	$125	$100	$85

Last MSR was $349.

Predator DX - similar to Predator AX, except has maple fingerboard. Mfg. 1994 to 1995.

	$225	$195	$175	$150	$125	$100	$85

Last MSR was $349.

Predator HB - similar to Predator Plus except, has 2 high ourput humbucking pickups with black pickup rings, 3-way pickup selector, Master Volume, Master Tone. Available in Gloss Black, Cobalt Blue, Metallic Gold, Metallic garnet Red and Metallic Titanium finishes. Current Mfg.

MSR $299	$209	$150	$130	$110	$90	$70

Predator Plus - similar to Predator, except has solid poplar body, 3-on-a-side headstock with straight string pull and ergonomic tuner placement, master tone and volume control, chrome hardware. Available in Black, Sunburst, Metallic Dark Blue and Metallic Titanium finishes. 1999 to date.

MSR $379	$300	$250	$200	$150	$100	$75	$50

Add $10 for Transparent Red and Transparent Green finishes (Predator Plus Transparent).

Add $10 for maple fingerboard (Predator Plus Maple Fretboard).

Add $30 for Left Hand model (Predator Plus LH).

RAPTOR I - offset double cutaway body, white pickguard, bolt-on maple neck, 21-fret rosewood fingerboard with white dot inlay, 25 1/2" scale, Power Bend standard vibrato, 6-on-a-side tuners, chrome hardware, 3 single coil pickups, volume/2 tone controls, 5-position switch. Available in Gloss Black, Gloss Red, and Gloss White finishes. Disc. 2000.

	$175	$150	$125	$115	$100	$85	$65

Last MSR was $219.

Raptor I Sunburst - similar to the Raptor I. Available in Sunbust finish. Disc. 2000.

	$195	$175	$150	$125	$100	$85	$75

Last MSR was $229.

Raptor Plus - similar to Raptor I, except has multi-lam body, 3-on-a-side headstock with straight string pull and ergonomic tuner placement, master tone control, hum-canceling in positions 2 and 4, master volume control. Available in Sunburst and White finishes. 1999 to date.

MSR $219	$175	$150	$125	$115	$100	$85	$65

Add $10 for Metallic Garnet red finish (Raptor Plus Metallic).

Add $20 for Left Hand model (Raptor Plus LH).

Raptor Plus TK - similar to Raptor Plus except, has covered single coil pickup in the neck position and high output single coil pickup in the bridge position. Available in Glass Black, Cobalt Blue, Metallic Gold, Metallic garnet red and Metallic Titanium finishes. Current Mfg.

MSR $309	$215	$195	$175	$150	$130	$110	$95

RAZER - offset double cutaway-angular hardwood body, bi-laminated hard rock maple neck, 23-fret maple neck with black dot inlays, 24 3/4" scale, chrome hardware, 6-on-a-side tuners, 2 dual blade humbucking pickups, fixed bridge, master volume control, two tone controls (one per pickup), 3-way pickup selector. Available in Blood Red, White, Frost Blue, Silver, Inca Gold, Sunfire Red, and Black finishes. Mfg. 1983 to 1986.

	$325	$275	$225	$175	$150	$125	$100

Last MSR was $399.50.

This model had the Octave Plus tremolo system as an option.
The tone control for the humbucking pickups allows the capability of single or dual coil output. Fully opening the pot to *10* achieves single coil mode. Turning counterclockwise to *7* brings the second coil into operation. Tone circuitry is standard in function between *7* and *0*.

REACTOR - single cutaway poplar body, white pickguard, metal controls mounted plate, bolt-on maple neck, 22-fret maple fingerboard with black dot inlay, 25 1/2" scale, strings-through fixed bridge, 6-on-a-side tuners, chrome hardware, 2 single coil pickups, volume/tone control, 3-position switch. Available in Gloss Black, Gloss Red and Gloss White finishes. Disc. 1999.

	$325	$275	$250	$225	$200	$150	$125

Last MSR was $409.

Reactor AX - similar to Reactor, except has Alder or Swamp Ash body, and 2 Db2-T dual blade humbucking pickups. Available in Gloss Black, Powder Blue, Sea Green (Alder body: pearloid pickguard); Blonde or Sunburst (Swamp Ash: tortoiseshell pickguard). Disc. 1999.

	$450	$375	$325	$275	$225	$175	$150

Last MSR was $559.

P

GRADING	100% MINT	98% NEAR MINT	95% EXC+	90% EXC	80% VG+	70% VG	60% G

T SERIES

The T series guitars and basses were originally designed by Chip Todd in 1977, and debuted at the 1978 NAMM show. The three prototypes shown were T-60 and T-30 guitars, and a T-40 bass.

Chip Todd was primarily an engineer who repaired guitars on the side. Todd was hired out of his Houston guitar repair shop, and initially handled the drafting and design by himself. Hartley Peavey had a great deal of input on the initial designs, and the tone circuit was invented by noted steel guitarist Orville *Red* Rhodes. Todd was eventually assisted by Gerald Pew, Bobby Low, and Charley Gressett. According to researcher Michael Wright, Chip Todd left Peavey in 1981 and currently works in the TV satellite electronics - although he does have a new patent on guitar design that he is considering applying for.

Peavey's initial concept was to use machinery to control efficiency and quality control. Borrowing an idea from gun manufacturing, Peavey bought a controlled carving machine to maintain strict tolerances in design. In a seeming parallel to the Fender debut of *plank guitars* and other derisive comments in 1951 leading to the other manufacturers then building solid body electrics in 1952, the guitar industry first insisted that **you can't build guitars on a computer**! A year later, everybody was investigating numerical controllers (and later the CAD/CAM devices - now CNC machines). If Leo Fender is the father of the mass produced solid body guitar (among other honors), then Hartley Peavey is the father of the modern solid body production technique.

(Source material courtesy Michael Wright, Guitar Stories Volume One)

T-15 - double offset cutaway body, bolt-on bi-laminated rock maple neck, 20-fret fingerboard, 23 1/2" scale, chrome hardware, 6-on-a-side tuners, cream and black laminated pickguard, two oversized "blade" style single coil pickups, master volume knob, master tone knob, 3-way pickup selector switch. Available in Natural finish. Mfg. 1981 to 1983.

$175 $150 $135 $115 $100 $85 $65
Last MSR was $199.50.

The T-15 was offered with the optional Electric Case. The molded plastic case's center area contained a 10 watt amp and 5" speaker, and had a pre- and post-gain controls, and an EQ control. The *Electric Case* can be viewed as Peavey's solid state version of Danelectro's tube *Amp-in-Case* concept. The T-15 Guitar with Electric Case retailed as a package for $259.50.

T-25 - double offset cutaway body, bolt-on bi-laminated rock maple neck, 23-fret fingerboard, 24 3/4" scale, chrome hardware, 6-on-a-side tuners, two "double blade" style humbucking pickups, master volume control, two tone controls (first for the neck pickup and the other for the bridge pickup), 3-way pickup selector switch. Available in Natural, Sunburst, Sunfire Red, and Frost Blue finishes. Mfg. 1982 to 1983.

$225 $195 $175 $150 $135 $115 $95
Last MSR ranged from $299.50 to $374.50.

The tone control for the humbucking pickup allows the capability of single or dual coil output. Fully opening the pot to *10* achieves single coil mode. Turning counterclockwise to 7 brings the second coil into operation. Bridge pickup is full humbucking at the *0* setting.

T-25 Special - similar to the T-25, except features a black phenolic fingerboard and black laminated pickguard. Available in Gloss Black finish. Mfg. 1982 to 1983.

$250 $200 $175 $150 $135 $125 $100
Last MSR was $399.50.

T-26 - double offset cutaway body, bolt-on bi-laminated rock maple neck, 23-fret fingerboard, 24 3/4" scale, chrome hardware, 6-on-a-side tuners, three "blade" style single coil pickups, master volume control, two tone controls (first for the neck pickup and the other for the bridge pickup), five way pickup selector switch. Available in Natural, Sunburst, Sunfire Red, and Frost Blue finishes. Mfg. 1982 to 1983.

$250 $225 $195 $175 $150 $125 $100
Last MSR ranged from $324 to $419.

Both the neck and the bridge single coil pickup have their own tone control. The center pickup does not have a tone control, but functions through either of the two tone controls when employed in the humbucking modes.

T-27 - double offset cutaway body, bolt-on bi-laminated rock maple neck, 23-fret fingerboard, 24 3/4" scale, chrome hardware, 6-on-a-side tuners, two "blade"style single coil pickups and one "double blade" style humbucker, master volume control, two tone controls (first for neck and middle pickups and the other for the bridge pickup), five way pickup selector switch. Available in Natural, Sunburst, Sunfire Red, and Frost Blue finishes. Mfg. 1982 to 1983.

$275 $225 $195 $175 $150 $125 $100
Last MSR ranged from $344 to $419.

The tone control for the humbucking pickup allows the capability of single or dual coil output. Fully opening the pot to *10* achieves single coil mode. Turning counterclockwise to 7 brings the second coil into operation. Bridge pickup is full humbucking at the *0* setting.

T-27 Limited - similar to the T-27, except features upgraded electronics and a rosewood neck. Mfg. 1982 to 1983.

$225 $195 $175 $150 $125 $100 $85
Last MSR was $374.50.

T-30 - double offset cutaway body, bolt-on bi-laminated rock maple neck, 20-fret fingerboard, 23 1/2" scale, 6-on-a-side tuners, three "blade" style single coil pickups, master volume knob, master tone knob, five way pickup selector switch. Available in Natural finish. Mfg. 1981 to 1983.

$175 $150 $125 $115 $100 $85 $75
Last MSR was $259.50.

The T-30 Guitar/Electric Case package retailed at $319.50.

P

GRADING	100% MINT	98% NEAR MINT	95% EXC+	90% EXC	80% VG+	70% VG	60% G

Peavey T-60
courtesy Peavey

T-60 - double offset cutaway body, bolt-on bi-laminated rock maple neck, 23-fret maple fingerboard, 25 1/2" scale, chrome hardware, 6-on-a-side tuners, two "double blade" style humbucking pickups, two volume controls, two tone controls (one per pickup), pickup phase switch, 3-way pickup selector switch. Available in Natural, Black, White, and Sunburst finish. Mfg. 1978 to 1988.

$325 $275 $225 $175 $150 $125 $115

Original MSR was $350 (with case).
Last MSR ranged from $399.50 to $459.50.

Finishes other than Natural command a higher premium.

The T-60 was the first Peavey production guitar, and had a rosewood fingerboard as an option. In 1982, Blood Red and Burgundy finishes were available. The original *Red* Rhodes-designed pickups allows the capability of single or dual coil output. Fully opening the pot to *10* achieves single coil mode. Turning counterclockwise to *7* brings the second coil into operation, and achieving full range humbucking tone. Rotation of the control from *7* to *0* further contours the tone circuit. The Phase switch is a two position switch which reverses the coil relationship in the bridge pickup when the pickup switch is in the middle position: Up is in phase, and Down is out-of-phase.

T-JR (JUNIOR) - similar to the T-60 guitar, except featured an *octave* neck and smaller body dimensions (like a mandolin). Mfg. 1982 to 1983.

$175 $150 $125 $100 $90 $80 $70

Last MSR was $199.95

T-1000 LT - double offset Western Poplar body, rock maple neck, 24-fret rosewood fingerboard, Recessed Floyd Rose licensed Double locking tremolo system, 2 single coil and 1 coil-tapped humbucker pickups, master volume control, master tone control, 5-way pickup selector switch. Mfg. 1992 to 1994.

$425 $350 $325 $275 $250 $200 $175

Last MSR was $699.

The original Tracer model was introduced in 1988. Subsequent models were styled to compete with Charvel/Jackson, Ibanez, and Kramer instruments in the Hard Rock music genre.

TRACER (FIRST VERSION) - offset double cutaway poplar body, bolt-on bi-laminated maple neck, 22-fret maple fingerboard with black dot inlay, 25 1/2" scale, Power Bend standard tremolo, graphlon nut, 6-on-a-side tuners, chrome hardware, 1 humbucker pickup, volume/tone control. Available in Black, Red and White finishes. Mfg. 1988 to 1994.

$225 $195 $175 $150 $125 $115 $100

Last MSR was $299.

Tracer (Second Version): In 1991, after numerous Tracer models had been offered, the original Tracer was *turbo charged* from its basic model design with the addition of 2 single coil pickups, 24-fret maple fingerboard, a new 24 3/4" scale, and a five way pickup selector switch (The Second Version of the Tracer was similar to the Tracer Custom without the Kahler locking tremolo).

Tracer LT - similar to the Tracer (Second Version), except has rosewood fingerboard with white dot inlay, Floyd Rose double locking vibrato, black hardware. Available in Black, Metallic Blue, Metallic Red and White finishes. Mfg. 1991 to 1994.

$300 $250 $225 $195 $175 $150 $125

Last MSR was $424.

TRACER II - similar to the Tracer (First Version), except features single coil/humbucker pickups, 3-way pickup selector switch. Available in Black, Metallic Blue, Metallic Red and White finishes. Mfg. 1989 to 1990.

$300 $250 $225 $195 $175 $150 $125

Last MSR was $359.

Tracer II '89 - similar to the Tracer (Second Version), with the 24 3/4" scale, yet shares all the same hardware and configuration of the previous Tracer II. The only verifiable difference is the scale length. Whip out the measuring stick. Whip it out! Mfg. 1989 to 1991.

$300 $250 $225 $195 $175 $150 $125

Last MSR was $359.

TRACER CUSTOM - similar to the Tracer (Second Version) with the 2 single coil/humbucker pickups, but maintains the original 25 1/2" scale. Other additions include a 5-way pickup selector switch, coil tap, black hardware, Kahler/Floyd Rose double locking tremolo. Mfg. 1989 to 1990.

$425 $400 $350 $275 $225 $175 $125

Last MSR was $529.

P

GRADING	100% MINT	98% NEAR MINT	95% EXC+	90% EXC	80% VG+	70% VG	60% G

Tracer Custom '89 - similar to the Tracer Custom, except has shorter 24 3/4" scale length. Also similar to the revised Tracer (Second Version), except the Custom '89 has a locking Kahler tremolo and the Tracer doesn't. Hmmm. Mfg. 1989 to 1991.

$325	**$295**	**$225**	**$195**	**$175**	**$150**	**$125**

Last MSR was $459.

TRACER DELUXE - similar to the Tracer II, except has a Kahler/Floyd Rose locking tremolo and black hardware; the Deluxe model maintains the original 25 1/2" scale and 22-fret fingerboard. Mfg. 1988 to 1990.

$325	**$275**	**$225**	**$175**	**$150**	**$125**	**$100**

Last MSR was $429.

Tracer Deluxe '89 - similar to the Tracer Deluxe, except has shorter 24 3/4" scale, 24-fret maple fingerboard. Mfg. 1989 to 1991.

$325	**$295**	**$225**	**$195**	**$175**	**$150**	**$125**

Last MSR was $459.

This model has a reverse headstock as an option.

Vandenburg Series

The Vandenburg series of the late 1980s was designed in conjunction with guitarist Adrian Vandenburg.

VANDENBURG SIGNATURE - offset double cutaway poplar body with side slot cuts, bolt-on bi-laminated maple neck, 24-fret ebony fingerboard with pearl dot inlay, 24 3/4" scale, Kahler/Floyd Rose double locking vibrato, reverse headstock, 6-on-the-other-side tuners, black hardware, single coil/Alnico humbucker pickups, volume/tone control, 3-position switch. Available in '62 Blue, Black, Pearl White, Raspberry Pearl, Rock-It Pink, and Sunfire Red finishes. Mfg. 1988 to 1994.

$475	**$425**	**$395**	**$350**	**$275**	**$250**	**$225**

Last MSR was $850.

This model came new with a certificate signed by Adrian Vandenberg.

Vandenburg Custom - offset double cutaway mahogany body with side slot cuts, set maple neck, 24-fret rosewood fingerboard with white stripes and arrows inlay, 24 3/4" scale, Kahler/Floyd Rose double locking vibrato, reverse headstock, 6-on-the-other-side tuners, black hardware, 1 HCS single coil/1 Alnico humbucker pickups, 2 master volume controls, 3-position pickup selector knob. Available in Transparent Honey Sunburst, Transparent Pink and Transparent Violet finishes. Mfg. 1989 to 1994.

$750	**$650**	**$595**	**$525**	**$450**	**$395**	**$325**

Last MSR was $1,299.

The neck pickup volume control has a push-pull coil-tap built in. The coil tap directly affects the bridge humbucker, and converts it from single coil to humbucker mode.

Vandenburg Quilt Top - offset double cutaway mahogany body with side slot cuts, carved Quilted Maple top, set mahogany neck, 24-fret bound rosewood fingerboard with white stripes and arrows inlay, Floyd Rose double locking vibrato, reverse headstock, 6-on-the-other-side tuners, gold hardware, 2 humbucker pickups, volume/tone control, 3-position pickup selector switch, coil tap mini switch. Available in Transparent Honey Sunburst, Transparent Pink and Transparent Violet finishes. Mfg. 1990 to 1994.

$795	**$700**	**$625**	**$550**	**$495**	**$425**	**$350**

Last MSR was $1,399.

Vandenburg Puzzle - similar to the Vandenberg Quilt Top, except features a one piece mahogany body with carved top, and black finish with white puzzle graphics. Mfg. 1989 to 1992.

$850	**$800**	**$725**	**$650**	**$550**	**$475**	**$400**

Last MSR was $1,599.

Vortex Series

VORTEX 1 - single cutaway flared hardwood body, bi-laminated maple neck, 22-fret *Polyglide* polymer fingerboard, 25 1/2" scale, black hardware, 6-on-a-side tuners, Kahler locking tremolo system, two P-12 adjustable pole piece humbucking pickups, master volume knob, master tone knob, 3-way selector switch. Available in Jet Black, Fluorescent Red, Fluorescent Pink, and Pearl White finishes. Mfg. 1985 to 1986.

$425	**$350**	**$325**	**$275**	**$250**	**$200**	**$175**

Last MSR was $699.50.

VORTEX 2 - similar specifications as the Vortex 1, except features a tapered *sharkfin/Flying V* body design. All other pickup and hardware descriptions as previously described. Available in Jet Black, Fluorescent Red, Fluorescent Pink, and Pearl White finishes. Mfg. 1985 to 1986.

$425	**$350**	**$325**	**$275**	**$250**	**$200**	**$175**

Last MSR was $699.50.

ELECTRIC BASS

Axcelerator Series

AXCELERATOR - offset double cutaway poplar body, pearloid pickguard, bolt-on maple neck, 21 rosewood fingerboard with pearl dot inlay, fixed bridge, 4-on-a-side tuners, chrome hardware, 2 VFL active covered humbucker pickups, volume/stacked tone/mix controls. Available in Candy Apple Red, Cobalt Blue, Metallic Gold, Metallic Green and Pearl Black finishes. System requires a 9-volt battery. Mfg. 1994 to 1998.

$475	**$395**	**$350**	**$295**	**$250**	**$200**	**$150**

Last MSR was $600.

P

GRADING	100% MINT	98% NEAR MINT	95% EXC+	90% EXC	80% VG+	70% VG	60% G

Axcelerator Fretless - similar to Axcelerator, except has fretless pau ferro fingerboard. Available in Candy Apple Red, Cobalt Blue, Metallic Gold and Pearl Black finishes. Mfg. 1994 to 1995.

$395	$325	$295	$250	$225	$195	$175

Last MSR was $650.

Axcelerator Plus - similar to Axcelerator, except has swamp ash body and pau ferro fingerboard. Available in Blonde or Sunburst finish with a tortoiseshell pickguard, or Transparent Grape or Transparent Red finish with pearloid pickguard. Disc. 1999.

$650	$525	$450	$395	$325	$275	$200

Last MSR was $799.

Axcelerator 5 - similar to Axcelerator, except has 5 strings, 4/1 per side tuners, 35" scale, Wilkinson WBB5 bridge. Available in Candy Apple Red, Metallic Purple, Metallic Silver and Pearl Black finishes. Disc. 1999.

$615	$500	$440	$380	$315	$260	$195

Last MSR was $769.

The revised design Axcelerator is optional with a fretless neck.

Axcelerator 6 - similar to Axcelerator 5, except has 6 strings, 3-per-side tuners, 35" scale, 21-fret pau ferro fingerboard with white dot inlays, Wilkinson WBB6 bridge, 2 VFL-6 humbucking pickups. Available in Candy Apple Red, Metallic Purple, Metallic Gold and Pearl Black finishes. Mfg. 1997 to 1999.

$875	$725	$625	$550	$450	$375	$275

Last MSR was $1,118.

AXCELERATOR 2-T - offset double cutaway poplar body, pearloid pickguard, bolt-on maple neck, 21 rosewood fingerboard with pearl dot inlay, 2-Tek bridge, 4-on-a-side tuners, chrome hardware, 2 VFL active covered humbucker pickups, volume/stacked tone/mix controls. Available in Candy Apple Red, Cobalt Blue, Metallic Gold, Metallic Green and Pearl Black finishes. System requires a 9-volt battery. Mfg. 1996 to 1999.

$725	$595	$525	$450	$375	$300	$225

Last MSR was $899.

In 1996, the standard Axcelerator model was offered with a 2-Tek bridge. While physically the same specifications as the original, the addition of the 2-Tek technology opens up the sonic qualities by a perceptible amount.

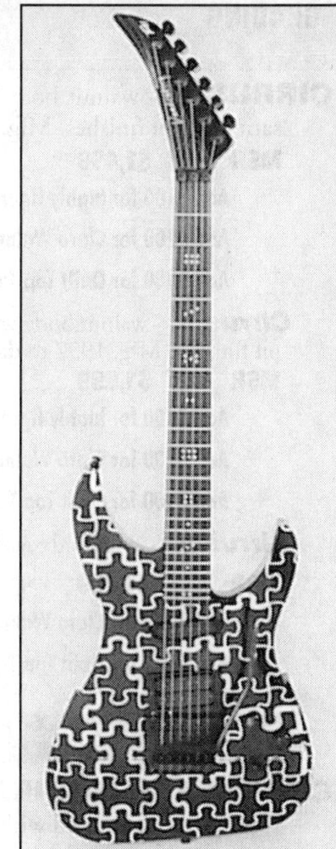

Peavey Vandenburg
courtesy Peavey

B-NINETY - offset double cutaway poplar body with "access scoops", bolt-on bi-laminated maple neck, 21-fret rosewood fingerboard with white dot inlay, 34" scale, fixed bridge, graphlon nut, 4-on-a-side "mini" bass tuners, black hardware, P/J-style pickups, 2 volume/master tone controls. Available in '62 Blue, Black, Charcoal Gray, Pearl White, Raspberry Pearl and Sunfire Red finishes. Mfg. 1990 to 1994.

$300	$250	$225	$200	$175	$150	$125

Last MSR was $499.

This model was optional in a left-handed configuration.

B-Ninety Active - similar to B-Ninety, except has active electronics. Mfg. 1990 to 1994.

$325	$275	$250	$225	$200	$175	$145

Last MSR was $549.

B-QUAD-4 - deep offset double cutaway Flame Maple body, bolt-on Modulus Graphite neck, 24-fret phenolic fingerboard with pearl "B" inlay at 12th fret, fixed bridge, 4-on-a-side tuners, gold hardware, 2 covered active humbucker/4 piezo bridge pickups, master volume, 2 stacked volume/tone controls, piezo volume/tone controls, stereo/mono switch, Dual mono/stereo 1/4" outputs. Available in Transparent Teal and Transparent Violet finishes. Mfg. 1994 to 1998.

$1,700	$1,375	$1,200	$1,050	$875	$700	$525

Last MSR was $2,118.

The B-Quad-4 was designed in conjunction with bassist Brian Bromberg.
This model has black hardware with Natural and White finishes as an option.
Instrument contains on-board 4 x 2 stereo mixing controls for the piezo pickup system. There are four pairs of volume/stereo panning controls on the back plate for adjustment of the stereo field from the dual output jacks.

B-Quad-5 - similar to the B-Quad-4, except has 5-string configuration, 5-on-a-side tuners. Mfg. 1995 to 1998.

$1,950	$1,575	$1,375	$1,195	$995	$795	$600

Last MSR was $2,418.

Cirrus Series

The Cirrus models were introduced in 1997. All models feature a 35" scale, through-body laminated neck (walnut/maple or maple/purpleheart), graphite reinforced neck and peghead, 24-fret pau ferro fingerboard, ABM bridge, 2 VFL humbuckers, volume/balance knobs, treble/mid/bass EQ controls.

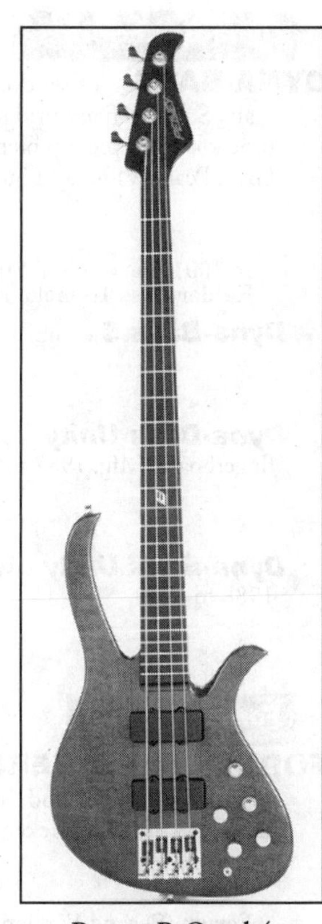

Peavey B-Quad 4
courtesy Peavey

P

GRADING		100% MINT	98% NEAR MINT	95% EXC+	90% EXC	80% VG+	70% VG	60% G

CIRRUS 4 - walnut body with select bookmatched exotic wood tops, 4-string configuration, 2-per-side tuners. Available in hand-rubbed satin and oil finishes. Mfg. 1997 to date.

MSR	$1,499	$1,025	$875	$750	$640	$545	$425	$300

Add $100 for highly figured redwood top (Cirrus 4 Redwood).

Add $200 for Claro Walnut body (Cirrus 4 Claro Walnut).

Add $900 for Quilt Top Tiger Eye option.

Cirrus 5 - walnut body with select bookmatched exotic wood tops, 5-string configuration, 3/2-per-side tuners. Available in hand-rubbed satin and oil finishes. Mfg. 1997 to date.

MSR	$1,699	$1,275	$1,085	$925	$775	$650	$525	$400

Add $100 for highly figured Redwood top (Cirrus 5 Redwood).

Add $200 for Claro Walnut body (Cirrus 5 Claro Walnut).

Add $900 for Quilt Top Tiger Eye option.

Cirrus 6 - alder body with figured redwood wood top, 6-string configuration, 3-per-side tuners. Available in high gloss finish. Mfg. 1997 to date.

MSR	$1,899	$1,425	$1,200	$1,000	$825	$725	$600	$475

Add $200 for Claro Walnut body (Cirrus 6 Claro Walnut).

Add $900 for Quilt Top Tiger Eye option.

Cyberbass Series

CYBERBASS (MIDIBASS) - offset double cutaway poplar body, black pearloid laminated pickguard, bolt-on maple neck, 22-fret rosewood fingerboard with pearl dot inlay, fixed bridge, 4-on-a-side tuners, chrome hardware, 2 covered active humbucker pickups, 2 stacked controls, mini switch. Available in Candy Apple Red, Montana Green and Pearl Black finishes. Mfg. 1994 to 1998.

$1,400	$1,175	$1,000	$895	$750	$595	$450

Last MSR was $1,799.

This model has volume/volume/MIDI volume/master tone controls and can be used to trigger a synthesized sound module, sound bass notes through the conventional magnetic pickups, or combine the two.

Cyberbass 5 - similar to the Cyberbass, except has 5-string configuration, 5-on-a-side tuners. Mfg. 1995 to 1998.

$1,500	$1,200	$1,100	$995	$825	$650	$500

Last MSR was $1,999.

Dyna-Bass Series

DYNA-BASS - offset double cutaway poplar body, bolt-on bi-laminated maple neck, 21-fret rosewood fingerboard with white dot inlay, 34" scale, Schaller fixed bridge, graphlon nut, 4-on-a-side "mini" tuners, gold hardware, 2 active humbucker pickups, volume control, 2 stacked tone controls, pickup blend control, active/passive bypass mini switch. System requires a 9-volt battery. Available in '62 Blue, Black, Charcoal Gray, Pearl White and Sunfire Red finishes. Mfg. 1985 to 1994.

$450	$375	$325	$295	$250	$225	$175

Last MSR was $729.

In 1991, the original Super Ferrite pickups were changed to newer humbucker style. In 1986, the Dyna-Bass was offered with an optional Kahler Bass Tremolo (retail list $929).

Dyna-Bass 5 - similar to Dyna-Bass, except has 5 strings, 4/1 per side tuners, 5 string Schaller bridge, and 34" scale. Mfg. 1987 to 1994.

$475	$400	$350	$325	$275	$250	$200

Last MSR was $799.50.

Dyna-Bass Unity - similar to Dyna-Bass, except has active P/J pickups, neck through construction, black chrome hardware, and 21-fret Ebony fingerboard. Mfg. 1987 to 1990.

$475	$400	$350	$325	$275	$250	$200

Last MSR was $799.

Dyna-Bass Unity Ltd. - similar to Dyna-Bass Unity, except has figured maple top, gold hardware. Available in Honey Sunburst finish. Mfg. 1988 to 1990.

$650	$550	$500	$450	$375	$325	$275

Last MSR was $1,100.

Forum Series

FORUM (FIRST VERSION) - offset double cutaway poplar body, white laminated pickguard, bolt-on bi-laminated Eastern maple neck, 21-fret rosewood fingerboard with pearl dot inlay, 34" scale fixed bridge, graphlon nut, 4-on-a-side tuners, chrome hardware, P-style/J-style ceramic humbucker pickups, 2 volume/tone control. Available in Black, Red and White finishes. Mfg. 1993 to 1998.

$395	$325	$275	$250	$200	$175	$125

Last MSR was $499.

Forum (Second Version): In 1995, the P/J pickup combination was replaced with an active humbucker in the "P-style"position. The three controls switched to volume/treble/bass. This second configuration is the current model.

GRADING	100% MINT	98% NEAR MINT	95% EXC+	90% EXC	80% VG+	70% VG	60% G

Forum 5 - similar to Forum (Second Version), except features 5-String configuration, 35" scale, alder or swamp ash body, Peavey fixed bridge, 2 active VFL-Plus humbuckers, volume/pickup blend/tone controls. Available in Pearl White, Pearl Black (alder bodies); Transparent Grape, Sunburst (swamp ash bodies) finishes. Disc. 1998.

		$625	$525	$450	$395	$325	$275	$200

Last MSR was $789.

Forum AX - similar to Forum (Second Edition), except features alder or swamp ash bodies, ABM fixed bridge, 2 active VFL humbuckers, volume/pickup blend/tone controls. Available in Candy Apple Red, Pearl Black (alder bodies); Blonde, and Sunburst (swamp ash bodies) finishes. Disc. 1998.

		$550	$475	$425	$350	$300	$250	$175

Last MSR was $729.

Forum Plus - similar to Forum (First Version), except has P/J-style active pickups. Available in Candy Apple Red, Cobalt Blue, Metallic Green, and Pearl Black finishes. Mfg. 1993 to 1995.

		$350	$295	$250	$225	$200	$175	$125

Last MSR was $520.

Foundation Series

FOUNDATION - offset double cutaway poplar body, bolt-on maple neck, 21-fret maple fingerboard with black dot inlay, fixed bridge, 34" scale, graphlon nut, 4-on-a-side tuners, chrome hardware, 2 single coil pickups, 2 volume/tone control. Available in Gloss Black, Gloss Red, Sunburst, and Gloss White finishes. Mfg. 1983 to date.

MSR	$599	$475	$360	$295	$250	$225	$175	$150

Add $30 for Foundation model with Rosewood fingerboard.

In 1994, Sunburst finish was disc.

Foundation 5 - similar to Foundation, except has 5 strings, 4/1 per side tuners. Current Mfg.

MSR	$649	$520	$390	$350	$295	$250	$165	$140

Foundation Fretless - similar to Foundation, except has fretless rosewood fingerboard with fret lines. Disc. 1999.

		$350	$275	$250	$225	$175	$150	$125

Last MSR was $429.

Foundation Custom - similar to the Foundation, except features a black phenolic fingerboard and pearly or metallic finishes. Mfg. 1984 to 1985.

		$295	$250	$225	$195	$175	$150	$125

Last MSR ranged from $394.50 to $474.50.

Foundation S - similar to Foundation, except has P/J-style humbucking pickups, hardwood body, 2 volume/tone control. Mfg. 1986 to 1990.

		$350	$300	$275	$225	$175	$150	$100

Last MSR was $419.50.

Foundation S Active - similar to Foundation S, except has active Bi-Fet P/J-style humbucking pickups (system requires a 9-volt battery). Mfg. 1988 to 1990.

		$275	$225	$200	$175	$150	$125	$100

Last MSR was $449.50.

FURY - offset double cutaway poplar body, white pickguard, bolt-on maple neck, 21-fret maple fingerboard with black dot inlay, 34" scale, fixed bridge, graphlon nut, 4-on-a-side tuners, chrome hardware, P-style pickup, volume/tone control. Available in Gloss Black, Gloss Red, Sunburst, and Gloss White finishes. Mfg. 1983 to 1998.

		$325	$250	$195	$175	$150	$125	$100

Last MSR was $399.

The original 1983 Fury model was similar in design to the earlier T-20. In 1994, the Sunburst finish was disc.

FURY II - solid Agathis body with sculpted front and back contours, 34" scale, maple neck, dual expanding truss rod with adjustable wheel, rosewood fingerboard, 21-frets, die-cast bridge with machined steel saddles, mini tuners, 9V powered active pickup and electronics, 8 dB boost/cut for bass, mid, treble, thumb rest, satin chrome plated hardware. Available in Black, Sunburst, Metallic Garnet Red, Metallic Dark Blue and Metallic Titanium finishes. New 1999.

MSR	$399	$300	$250	$225	$200	$175	$150	$100

Add $20 for Left Hand model (Fury II LH).

P

GRADING		100% MINT	98% NEAR MINT	95% EXC+	90% EXC	80% VG+	70% VG	60% G

FURY V QUILT TOP - offset double cutaway solid body, 5-string, 34" scale, 21-frets, Quilted Maple top, solid maple neck with rosewood fingerboard, 2 VFL internally-active pickups, 3-band active EQ, single master volume, mid, bass, and treble controls, satin chrome hardware. Available in Transparent Red, Transparent Blue, Transparent green and Sunburst finishes. Current Mfg.

MSR	$599	$419	$350	$325	$295	$250	$225	$195

Fury VI Quilt Top - similar to Fury V Quilt Top except, in a 6-string configuration. Available in Transparent Red, Transparent Blue, Transparent Green and Sunburst finishes. Current Mfg.

MSR	$699	$489	$425	$375	$350	$325	$295	$250

G Bass Series

G BASS - offset double cutaway solid alder body, bolt-on composite graphite neck, 35" scale, 21-fret pau ferro fingerboard with white dot inlay, fixed bridge, graphlon nut, 4-on-a-side tuners, chrome hardware, VLF Plus humbucker pickup, volume/3 band EQ controls. Available in Holoflack Black, Holoflake Red, and Holoflake Green finishes. Mfg. 1997 to date.

MSR	$918	$700	$595	$525	$450	$395	$325	$250

G 5 Bass - similar to the G Bass, except features 5-string configuration, 5-on-a-side tuners, 2 VFL pickups, ABM bridge, volume/blend/3 band EQ. Available in Holoflack Black, Holoflake Red, Charcoal Grey, Metallic Dark Blue, and Vintage Sunburst finishes. Mfg. 1998 to date.

MSR	$1,399	$1,050	$895	$750	$640	$545	$450	$350

MIDIBASE - offset double cutaway alder body, maple neck, 21-fret rosewood fingerboard with white dot inlay, fixed bridge, graphlon nut, 4-on-a-side tuners, black hardware, 2 humbucker pickups, 2 volume/tone/mix controls, bypass switch. Available in Pearl White finish. Mfg. 1992 to 1993.

		$1,200	$1,000	$895	$775	$675	$550	$450

Last MSR was $1,800.

Basic concept and MIDI controller design by Australian bassist and electrical engineering student Steve Chick. Chick began working on a bass synthesizer in his spare time in 1982, put out his own MB4 retrofit system during the mid 1980s, and began working with the Peavey corporation in 1991. In early 1994, the MidiBass name was changed to Cyberbass (See CYBERBASS).

MILESTONE II - offset double cutaway body, single piece maple neck, 20-fret rosewood fingerboard, 34" scale, fixed bridge, one split-coil pickup, 4-on-a-side tuners, chrome hardware, white laminated pickguard, volume/tone controls. Available in Gloss Black, Gloss Red, Gloss White, and Powder Blue Sunburst finishes. Disc. 1999.

		$215	$175	$155	$135	$115	$95	$75

Last MSR was $269.

Add $10 for Milestone II in Sunburst finish.

MILESTONE III - balanced, comfortable body styling with front and back contours, 34" scale, maple neck, rosewood fingerboard, dual expanding truss rod with adjustable wheel, 2 single coil J-style pickups (hum-cancelling when used together), stamped steel bridge, two volume controls, master tone control, chrome hardware. Available in Black, White, Sunburst, Metallic Garnet Red, and Metallic Dark Blue finishes. New 1999.

MSR	$309	$230	$185	$165	$145	$125	$110	$95

Add $20 for left hand configuration.

Milestone IV - similar to Milestone III, except has 1 split coil P-style pickup. Available in Black, White, Sunburst, Metallic Garnet Red and Metallic Dark Blue finishes. New 1999.

MSR	$299	$225	$180	$160	$140	$120	$100	$85

Add $20 for left hand configuration.

Millennium Series

MILLENNIUM 4BN - offset double cutaway solid alder body, graphite reinforced hard rock maple neck, 35" scale, Birdseye Maple fingerboard, Active VFL pickups, active 3-band EQ, Hipshot bridge. Available in Neon Blue, Gold Sparkle, Charcoal Metallic Violet, Transparent Blonde, Candy Apple Red, Tobacco Sunburst, Peacock Blue Metallic and Pearl Black finishes. Current Mfg.

MSR	$1,299	$900	$800	$700	$650	$600	$550	$500

Millennium 4 Pau Ferro - similar to Millennium 4 BN except, has Pau Ferro fingerboard, same finish options. Current Mfg.

MSR	$1,099	$769	$669	$550	$495	$450	$395	$325

Millennium 4 Maple - similar to Millennium 4 BN except, has maple fingerboard. Same finish options. Current Mfg.

MSR	$1,099	$769	$669	$550	$495	$450	$395	$325

Millennium 4 Plus BN - similar to Millenium 4BN except, has Birdeye Maple neck, Hipshot D-Tuner. Available in Transparent Black Teal, Royal Blue, Tiger Eye, Black Violet, Peacock Blue, Tobacco Sunburst, Vintage Sunburst, Ruby Red, Cashmere Metallic, Harlequin Violet/Gold. Current Mfg.

MSR	$1,599	$1,125	$1,025	$950	$895	$850	$795	$750

Millennium 4 Plus Pau Ferro - similar to Millenium 4 Plus BN except, has Pau Ferro fingerboard, solid alder body with flame maple top. Same finish options. Current Mfg.

MSR	$1,399	$975	$875	$775	$695	$650	$595	$550

P

GRADING		100% MINT	98% NEAR MINT	95% EXC+	90% EXC	80% VG+	70% VG	60% G

Millennium 4 Plus Maple - similar to Millennium 4 Plus BN except, has maple fingerboard, solid alder body with flame maple top. Same finish options. Current Mfg.

MSR	$1,399	$975	$875	$775	$695	$650	$595	$550

Millennium 5 BN - similar to Millennium 4BN except, in a 5-string model. Available in Neon Blue, Gold Sparkle, Charcoal Metallic Violet, Transparent Blonde, Candy Apple Red, Tobacco Sunburst, Peacock Blue Metallic and Pearl Black finishes. Current Mfg.

MSR	$1,599	$1,125	$1,025	$925	$825	$725	$625	$525

Millennium 5 Pau Ferro - similar to Millennium 5 BN except, has Pau Ferro fingerboard. Same finish options. Current Mfg.

MSR	$1,399	$975	$875	$775	$695	$650	$595	$550

Millennium 5 Maple - similar to Millennium 5 BN except, has maple fingerboard. Same finish options. Current Mfg.

MSR	$1,399	$975	$875	$775	$695	$650	$595	$550

Millennium 5 Plus BN - similar to Millennium 5 BN except, has solid alder body with flame maple top. Birdseye Maple fingerboard. Same finish options. Current Mfg.

MSR	$1,899	1,329	$1,229	$1,129	$1,029	$925	$825	$725

Millennium 5 Plus Pau Ferro - similar to Millennium 5 Plus BN except, with Pau Ferro fingerboard. Same finish options. Current Mfg.

MSR	$1,699	$1,195	$1,095	$995	$895	$795	$695	$595

Millennium 5 Plus Maple - similar to Millennium 5 Plus BN except, has maple fingerboard. Same finish options. Current Mfg.

MSR	$1,699	$1,195	$1,095	$995	$895	$795	$695	$595

PALAEDIUM - offset double cutaway three piece alder body, bolt-on maple neck, 21-fret ebony fingerboard with pearl dot inlay, 34" scale, Leo Quan Bad Ass II fixed bridge, graphlon nut, 4-on-a-side tuners, gold hardware, 2 humbucker pickups, volume/tone/mix control. Available in Transparent Amber, Transparent Red and Transparent Violet finishes. Mfg. 1991 to 1994.

		$450	$400	$350	$325	$275	$250	$200

Last MSR was $800.

The Palaedium model was developed in conjunction with bassist Jeff Berlin.

PATRIOT - offset double cutaway maple or southern ash body, bi-laminated maple neck, 21-fret fingerboard, 34" scale, fixed bridge, four on a side tuners, chrome hardware, graphlon nut, one single coil pickup, black laminated pickguard, volume/tone controls. Available in Gloss or Satin finishes. Mfg. 1984 to 1988.

		$200	$175	$150	$125	$115	$100	$85

Last MSR ranged from $225 to $332.

Patriot Custom - similar to the Patriot, except features a rosewood fingerboard and color matched peghead. Mfg. 1986 to 1988.

		$195	$175	$150	$125	$100	$85	$65

Last MSR was $310.

RJ-IV - offset double cutaway maple body, neck-through body bi-laminated maple neck, 21-fret Macassar Ebony fingerboard with pearl arrow inlay, fixed bridge, graphlon nut, 4-on-a-side *mini* tuners, Hipshot Bass Extender Key, black hardware, P/J-style active pickups, volume control, 3 band EQ controls, pickup selector toggle switch. Available in Black Pearl Burst, Blue Pearl Burst, Purple Pearl Burst and Red Pearl Burst finishes. Mfg. 1990 to 1994.

		$600	$525	$475	$425	$375	$325	$275

Last MSR was $1,049.

Model designed in conjunction with bassist Randy Jackson.
This model was optional with a koa body/neck, rosewood fingerboard, and Hipshot D-Tuner.

RSB - offset double cutaway poplar body, bolt-on rock maple neck, 24-fret maple fingerboard with black dot inlay, 34" scale, fixed brass bridge, 4-on-a-side *mini* tuners, gold hardware, graphlon nut, 2 VFL active humbucker pickups, volume/tone/mix controls. Available in Black finish. Mfg. 1993 to 1995.

		$425	$350	$325	$275	$250	$200	$175

Last MSR was $700.

RSB Koa - similar to RSB, except has koa body, pau ferro fingerboard with pearl dot inlay. Available in Oil finish. Mfg. 1993 to 1995.

		$475	$400	$350	$325	$275	$250	$200

Last MSR was $800.

P

GRADING	100% MINT	98% NEAR MINT	95% EXC+	90% EXC	80% VG+	70% VG	60% G

RUDY SARZO SIGNATURE - offset double cutaway ash body, through body maple/purpleheart 5-piece neck, 24-fret ebony fingerboard with pearl oval inlay, fixed Schaller brass bridge, brass nut, 4-on-a-side tuners, gold hardware, 2 ceramic humbucker pickups, volume/tone/3 band EQ controls, bypass switch, active electronics. Available in Transparent Black, Transparent Red, and Transparent Violet finishes. Mfg. 1989 to 1994.

$650 $600 $525 $475 $400 $350 $275
Last MSR was $1,100.

T SERIES

The T series guitars and basses were originally designed by Chip Todd in 1977, and three models debuted in 1978 (T-60 and T-30 guitars, and a T-40 bass).

T-20 - double offset cutaway maple or southern ash body, bi-laminated hard rock maple neck, 21-fret maple fingerboard, 34" scale, chrome hardware, fixed bridge, four on a side headstock, "single blade"single coil pickup, volume knob, tone knob, brown laminated pickguard. Available in Natural, Sunfire Red, and Frost Blue finishes. Mfg. 1982 to 1985.

$250 $195 $175 $150 $135 $115 $95
Last MSR ranged from $299 to $374.

This model was also available with a fretless neck.

T-40 - double offset cutaway body, bolt-on bi-laminated rock maple neck, 23-fret fingerboard, 34" scale, chrome hardware, fixed bridge, four on a side tuners, two "double blade" style humbucking pickups, two volume controls, two tone controls (one per pickup), pickup phase switch, 3-way pickup selector switch, brown laminated pickguard. Available in Natural, White, Black, and Sunburst finishes. Mfg. 1978 to 1988.

$325 $275 $250 $225 $175 $150 $125
Last MSR ranged from $399 to $484 (with case).

The T-40 was the first Peavey production bass. This model was also offered with a fretless neck. In 1982, Blood Red and Burgundy finished were offered. The original *Red* Rhodes-designed pickups allows the capability of single or dual coil output. Fully opening the tone potentiometer to *10* achieves single coil mode. Turning counterclockwise to *7* brings the second coil into operation, and achieving full range humbucking tone. Rotation of the control from *7* to *0* further contours the tone circuit. The Phase switch is a two position switch which reverses the coil relationship in the bridge pickup when the pickup switch is in the middle position (Up is in phase, and Down is out-of-phase).

T-45 - double offset cutaway hardwood body, bi-laminated hard rock maple neck, 21-fret maple fingerboard, 34" scale, chrome hardware, fixed bridge, four on a side tuners, dual blade humbucker, master volume knob, two tone knobs. Available in Black, White, Sunburst, Blood Red, and Burgundy finishes. Mfg. 1982 to 1986.

$275 $225 $200 $175 $150 $125 $100
Last MSR ranged from $434.50 to $459.50.

The humbucking pickup can be used in either single coil or dual coil mode. Fully opening the tone potentiometer to *10* achieves single coil mode. Turning counterclockwise to *7* brings the second coil into operation, and achieving full range humbucking tone. Rotation of the control from *7* to *0* further contours the tone circuit.

TL Series

TL-FIVE - offset double cutaway Eastern Flame Maple body, neck-through body maple/purpleheart 5-piece neck, 24-fret ebony fingerboard with pearl oval inlay, Schaller fixed brass bridge, graphlon nut, 3/2-per-side tuners, gold hardware, 2 Super Ferrite humbucker pickups, volume/blend controls, treble/mid/bass controls, bypass mini-toggle, 3-band active electronics. Available in Honey Sunburst, Transparent Black, Transparent Blue, Transparent Emerald, Transparent Red, and Transparent Violet finishes. Mfg. 1988 to 1998.

$1,300 $1,100 $995 $825 $695 $550 $425
Last MSR was $1,699.

In 1991, the VFL humbuckers were introduced. In 1994, the Transparent Violet finish was disc.

TL-Six - similar to TL-Five, except features 6 strings, pearl arrow fingerboard inlay, 4/2-per-side tuners, Kahler 6-string bridge, gold hardware, 2 P-style pickups. Mfg. 1989 to 1998.

$1,500 $1,250 $1,100 $950 $795 $625 $475
Last MSR was $1,899.

P

Unity Series

UNITY - offset double cutaway poplar body with scoop access styling, neck-through body bi-laminated maple neck, 21-fret rosewood fingerboard with pearl dot inlay, fixed bridge, graphlon nut, 4-on-a-side tuners, black hardware, P/J-style pickups, 2 volume/tone control. Available in '62 Blue, Black, Charcoal Gray, Pearl White, and Sunfire Red finishes. Mfg. 1987 to 1994.

$425 $350 $325 $275 $250 $200 $175
Last MSR was $700.

Unity Koa - similar to Unity, except has koa body, solid koa neck-through design, gold hardware. Available in Natural finish. Mfg. 1988 to 1994.

$450 $375 $350 $300 $250 $225 $195
Last MSR was $750.

GRADING	100% MINT	98% NEAR MINT	95% EXC+	90% EXC	80% VG+	70% VG	60% G

PEDULLA-ORSINI

Instruments previously built in Massachusetts circa 1974 to 1975.

The Pedulla-Orsini trademark was used by Mike Pedulla and Sam Orsini, who collaborated on custom basses, guitars, and banjo construction. Pedulla, a violinist and college music major at the time, teamed up with Orsini, an engineering major. The majority of work that they concentrated on was mostly instrument repair. Pedulla then went on to form M.V. Pedulla Guitars, and became very well known for his high quality bass models.

PEDULLA, M.V.

Instruments currently built in Massachusetts since 1975.

The M.V. Pedulla company was founded back in 1975 by Michael Vincent Pedulla. They originally produced some acoustic guitars, as well as electrics (one model was outfitted with MIDI system compatible with the Roland GR-700 series). Once they discovered the unique design that led to the MVP and Buzz bass models, they began to specialize directly in high quality handcrafted basses.

Stock equipment found on M.V. Pedulla basses include Bartolini pickups and on-board preamps, ABM bridges, and Pedulla/Gotoh tuning machines.

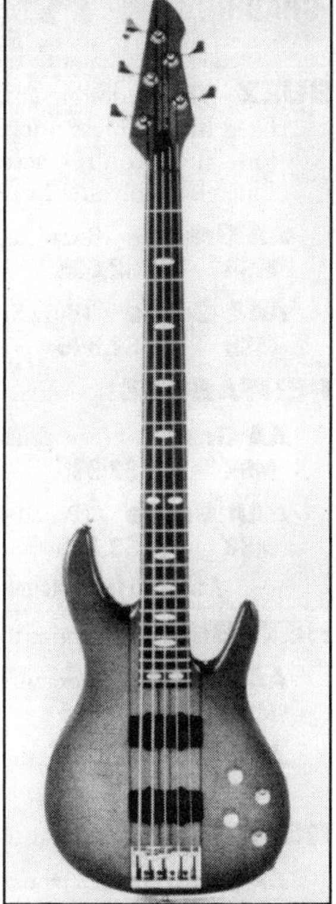

Peavey TL5 Bass
courtesy Peavey

ELECTRIC BASS

All models are available with fretted fingerboards or fretless.

Add $200 for maple fingerboard.

Add $250 for fretless fingerboard with no lines/dot inlay (side dot position markers only).

Add $250 for custom tinted colors: Arctic Night, Charcoal, Emerald Green, Green-Blue Sunburst, Rose, Vintage Cherry, Vintage Cherry Sunburst, or Violet (not available on ET Thunderbass/Thunderbuzz and Rapture series models).

Add $250 for active tone system with treble/bass controls (TBT).

Add $300 for left-handed configuration.

Add $350 for active tone system with treble/mid/bass controls (NTMB).

Add $400 for customer's signature on headstock.

MVP/Buzz Series

This series consists of 2 models, the **MVP** and the **BUZZ**. The **MVP** has a fretted fingerboard, while the **BUZZ** is fretless - all other aspects are identical. Bassists Mark Egan and Tim Landers helped design and perfect the Buzz Bass.

Earlier specifications and nomenclature differ slightly from Pedulla's current model offerings. When the MVP/Buzz **Standard** featured a flame maple body and chrome tuners, the upgrade to black or gold hardware was called the **Deluxe**; a higher grade (AA) flamed maple with black or gold hardware was designated the **Custom**; and the next higher grade (AAA) flame maple with black or gold hardware was labeled a **Signature**. Black or Gold hardware is now standard, and MVP/Buzz basses are offered in the AA or AAA grade flame maple bodies.

Add $800 above the AAA price for AAAAA grade or quilted maple body (the quilted maple body was formerly known as the Limited Edition version).

BUZZ STANDARD - offset double cutaway flame maple body, through body maple laminate neck, fretless ebony fingerboard, fixed bridge, brass nut, 2-per-side tuners, chrome hardware, P/J-style Bartolini pickups, volume/tone/mix control, active electronics. Available in Champagne, Black, Lime Green, Metallic Midnight Blue, Red, and White finishes. Disc. 1994.

$1,400 $1,150 $1,050 $925 $825 $725 $600
Last MSR was $1,775.

This model was optional with 2 J-style or 2 Bartolini humbucker pickups.

Pentabuzz Standard - similar to the Buzz Standard, except features 5-string configuration, 3/2-per-side tuners. Disc. 1994.

$1,650 $1,350 $1,225 $1,100 $950 $825 $700
Last MSR was $2,075.

Hexabuzz Standard - similar to the Buzz Standard, except features 6-string configuration, 3-per-side tuners, 2 J-style Bartolini pickups. Disc. 1994.

$1,800 $1,500 $1,350 $1,200 $1,050 $900 $750
Last MSR was $2,275.

This model had 2 Bartolini humbucker pickups as an option.

Octabuzz Standard - similar to the Buzz Standard, except features 8-string configuration (4 pairs/tuned an octave apart), 4-per-side tuners. Disc. 1994.

$1,675 $1,350 $1,225 $1,100 $975 $850 $700
Last MSR was $2,075.

Pedulla PentaBuzz 5
courtesy M.V.
Pedulla Guitars

P

GRADING		100% MINT	98% NEAR MINT	95% EXC+	90% EXC	80% VG+	70% VG	60% G

BUZZ - offset double cutaway figured Eastern maple body, AA figured, through body quartersawn maple neck, fretless ebony fingerboard, fixed bridge, brass nut, 2-per-side tuners, black or gold hardware, choice of "soapbar" (or P/J-style or J/J-style) Bartolini pickups, volume/tone/blend control, active electronics. Available in Amber, Amber Sunburst, Cherry, Cherry Sunburst, Light Gold, Natural, and Peacock Blue gloss polyester finishes. Current Mfg.

AA Grade - (Buzz Custom) figured maple body.

MSR	$2,695	$2,150	$1,850	$1,600	$1,350	$1,125	$895	$650

AAA Grade - (Buzz Signature) figured maple body.

MSR	$2,995	$2,350	$2,000	$1,775	$1,500	$1,250	$995	$725

PENTABUZZ - similar to the Buzz, except features 5-string configuration, 3/2-per-side tuners. Current Mfg.

AA Grade - (Pentabuzz Custom) figured maple body.

MSR	$2,995	$2,350	$2,000	$1,750	$1,500	$1,250	$995	$725

AAA Grade - (Pentabuzz Signature) figured maple body.

MSR	$3,295	$2,550	$2,100	$1,850	$1,600	$1,300	$1,050	$800

Add $400 for optional wide spacing (19 mm) fingerboard.

HEXABUZZ - similar to the Buzz, except features 6-string configuration, 3-per-side tuners. Current Mfg.

AA Grade - (Hexabuzz Custom) figured maple body.

MSR	$3,195	$2,500	$2,000	$1,750	$1,500	$1,275	$1,000	$795

AAA Grade - (Hexabuzz Signature) figured maple body.

MSR	$3,495	$2,750	$2,225	$1,950	$1,650	$1,400	$1,150	$850

OCTABUZZ - similar to the Buzz, except features 8-string configuration (4 pairs/tuned an octave apart), 4-per-side tuners. Current Mfg.

AA Grade - (Octabuzz Custom) figured maple body.

MSR	$3,295	$2,600	$2,100	$1,850	$1,600	$1,300	$1,050	$800

AAA Grade - (Octabuzz Signature) figured maple body.

MSR	$3,595	$2,800	$2,275	$2,000	$1,725	$1,425	$1,150	$875

MVP4 STANDARD - offset double cutaway flame maple body, through body maple laminate neck, 24-fret ebony fingerboard with pearl dot inlay, fixed bridge, brass nut, 2-per-side tuners, chrome hardware, P/J-style Bartolini pickups, volume/tone/mix control, active electronics. Available in Champagne, Black, Lime Green, Metallic Midnight Blue, Red, and White finishes. Disc. 1994.

		$1,400	$1,150	$1,050	$925	$825	$725	$600

Last MSR was $1,775.

This model was optional with 2 J-style or 2 Bartolini humbucker pickups.

MVP5 Standard - similar to the MVP4 Standard, except features 5-string configuration, 3/2-per-side tuners. Disc. 1994.

		$1,650	$1,350	$1,200	$1,100	$950	$825	$700

Last MSR was $2,075.

MVP6 Standard - similar to the MVP4 Standard, except features 6-string configuration, 3-per-side tuners, 2 J-style Bartolini pickups. Disc. 1994.

		$1,800	$1,500	$1,350	$1,200	$1,050	$900	$750

Last MSR was $2,275.

This model had 2 Bartolini humbucker pickups optional.

MVP8 Standard - similar to the MVP Standard, except features 8-string configuration (4 pairs/tuned an octave apart), 4-per-side tuners. Disc. 1994.

		$1,675	$1,350	$1,225	$1,100	$975	$850	$700

Last MSR was $2,075.

P

MVP4 - offset double cutaway hard Eastern figured maple body, through body quartersawn maple neck, 24-fret ebony fingerboard with pearl dot inlay, fixed bridge, brass nut, 2-per-side tuners, black or gold hardware, choice of "soap bar" (or P/J-style or J/J-style) Bartolini pickups, volume/tone/blend control, active electronics. Available in Amber, Amber Sunburst, Cherry, Cherry Sunburst, Light Gold, Natural, and Peacock Blue gloss polyester finishes. Current Mfg.

AA Grade - (MVP4 Custom) figured maple body.

MSR	$2,695	$2,100	$1,825	$1,600	$1,350	$1,125	$895	$650

AAA Grade - (MVP4 Signature) figured maple body.

MSR	$2,995	$2,350	$2,000	$1,750	$1,500	$1,250	$995	$725

MVP5 - similar to the MVP4, except features 5-string configuration, 3/2-per-side tuners. Current Mfg.

AA Grade - (MVP5 Custom) figured maple body.

MSR	$2,995	$2,350	$2,100	$1,775	$1,500	$1,250	$995	$725

AAA Grade - (MVP5 Signature) figured maple body.

MSR	$3,295	$2,600	$2,100	$1,850	$1,600	$1,300	$1,050	$800

Add $400 for optional wide spacing (19 mm) fingerboard.

GRADING		100% MINT	98% NEAR MINT	95% EXC+	90% EXC	80% VG+	70% VG	60% G

MVP6 - similar to the MVP4, except features 6-string configuration, 3-per-side tuners. Current Mfg.

AA Grade - (MVP6 Custom) figured maple body.

MSR	$3,195	$2,475	$2,000	$1,750	$1,500	$1,250	$1,000	$775

AAA Grade - (MVP6 Signature) figured maple body.

MSR	$3,495	$2,700	$2,200	$1,950	$1,650	$1,400	$1,125	$850

MVP8 - similar to the MVP4, except features 8-string configuration (4 pairs/tuned an octave apart), 4-per-side tuners. Current Mfg.

AA Grade - (MVP8 Custom) figured maple body.

MSR	$3,295	$2,600	$2,100	$1,850	$1,600	$1,300	$1,050	$800

AAA Grade - (MVP8 Signature) figured maple body.

MSR	$3,595	$2,800	$2,275	$2,000	$1,725	$1,425	$1,150	$875

Mark Egan Signature Series

This series is co-designed by bassist Mark Egan.

Add $800 for AAAAA grade or quilted maple body (the quilted maple body was formerly known as the Limited Edition version).

ME 4 - sleek offset double cutaway AAA Grade flame maple body, through body maple neck, 24-fret ebony fingerboard with pearl dot inlay, ebony thumb rest, fixed bridge, brass nut, 2-per-side Gotoh tuners, gold hardware, 2 J-style pickups, volume/tone/mix controls, active electronics. Available in Amber, Amber Sunburst, Cherry, Cherry Sunburst, Light Gold, Natural, and Peacock Blue gloss polyester finishes. Current Mfg.

MSR	$3,395	$2,650	$2,150	$1,900	$N/A	$N/A	$N/A	$N/A

This model is optional with fretless fingerboard as the ME 4-F.

ME 5 - similar to ME 4, except features 5-string configuration, 3/2-per-side tuners. Current Mfg.

MSR	$3,695	$2,875	$2,350	$2,100	$N/A	$N/A	$N/A	$N/A

Add $400 for optional wide spacing (19 mm) fingerboard.

This model is optional with fretless fingerboard as the ME 5-F.

ME 6 - similar to ME 4, except features 6-string configuration, 3-per-side tuners. Current Mfg.

MSR	$3,895	$3,100	$2,500	$2,200	$N/A	$N/A	$N/A	$N/A

This model is optional with fretless fingerboard as the ME 6-F.

ME 4-F+8 Doubleneck - offset double cutaway AAA Grade maple body, doubleneck configuration: fretless 4-string/fretted 8-string. Current Mfg.

MSR	$6,395	$5,100	$4,200	$N/A	$N/A	$N/A	$N/A	$N/A

Rapture Series

Rapture Series pickguard/finish combinations run: Pearl pickguards on solid finishes, Tortoiseshell on Light Gold and Tobacco Sunburst finishes.

RAPTURE RB4 - sleek offset double cutaway soft Eastern curly maple body, bolt-on satin-finished maple neck, 22-fret rosewood fingerboard with pearl dot inlay, fixed bridge, 2-per-side tuners, chrome hardware, pickguard, one Bartolini "soapbar" pickup, volume/treble/bass controls, mid-cut mini switch, TBT electronics. Available in Black, Candy Purple, Candy Red, Candy Teal, Cherry Sunburst, Cool Blue, Light Gold, Planet Green, and Tobacco Sunburst polyester finish. Mfg. 1995 to date.

MSR	$1,495	$1,200	$975	$850	$725	$625	$495	$375

This model is also available with a fretless fingerboard as model RB4-F.

Rapture RB5 - similar to Rapture RB4, except has 5-string configuration, 3/2-per-side tuners. Mfg. 1995 to date.

MSR	$1,695	$1,350	$1,100	$975	$825	$695	$550	$425

This model is also available with a fretless fingerboard as model RB5-F.

RAPTURE RBJ2-4 - similar to the RB4, except features 2 J-style Bartolini pickups, volume/blend/treble/bass controls. Mfg. 1996 to date.

MSR	$1,795	$1,425	$1,200	$1,000	$895	$725	$600	$450

This model is also available with a fretless fingerboard as model RBJ2-4F.

Rapture RBJ2-5 - similar to Rapture RBJ2-4, except has 5-string configuration, 3/2-per-side tuners. Current Mfg.

MSR	$1,995	$1,600	$1,300	$1,150	$1,000	$825	$650	$500

This model is also available with a fretless fingerboard as model RBJ2-5F.

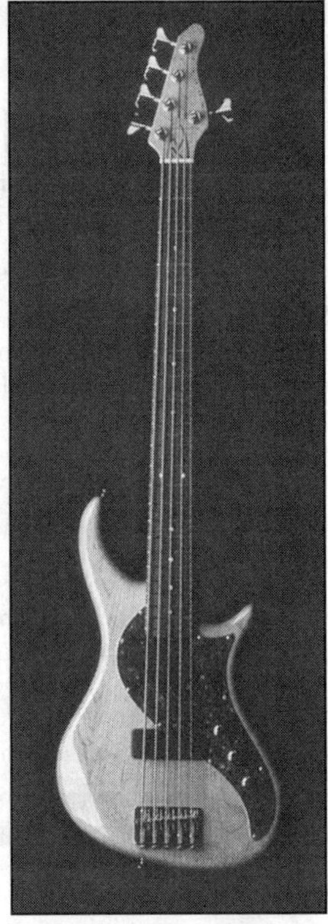

Pedulla Rapture 5
courtesy M.V.
Pedulla Guitars

Pedulla Rapture 5 Sunbrust
courtesy M.V.
Pedulla Guitars

P

GRADING	100% MINT	98% NEAR MINT	95% EXC+	90% EXC	80% VG+	70% VG	60% G

SERIES II Series

Add $200 for "soapbar"or P/J-style active pickups.

Add $200 for A Grade flame maple.

Add $400 for AA Grade flame maple.

S-II 4 - offset double cutaway poplar body, bolt-on maple neck, 22-fret rosewood fingerboard with pearl dot inlay, fixed bridge, brass nut, 2-per-side Gotoh tuners, black hardware, P/J-style Bartolini pickups, volume/tone/mix controls. Available in Black, Champagne, Lime Green, Midnight Blue, Red, Yellow, and White finishes. Disc. 1992.

$900 $775 $650 $575 $N/A $N/A $N/A
Last MSR was $1,295.

This model was optional with a fretless fingerboard as model S-II 4/F.

S-II 5 - similar to S-II 4, except has 5-string configuration, 3/2-per-side tuners. Disc. 1992.

$1,200 $1,050 $875 $750 $N/A $N/A $N/A
Last MSR was $1,695.

This model was optional with a fretless fingerboard as model S-II 5/F.

S-II 6 - similar to S-II 4, except has 6-string configuration, 3-per-side tuners. Disc. 1992.

$1,350 $1,275 $995 $875 $N/A $N/A $N/A
Last MSR was $1,895.

This model was optional with a fretless fingerboard as model S-II 6/F.

ThunderBass/ThunderBuzz Series

This series has 2 variations: the **ThunderBass**, which features a fretted fingerboard, and the **ThunderBuzz**, which is fretless.

THUNDERBASS T4 - sleek offset double cutaway figured maple body, through body maple/bubinga 5-piece neck, 24-fret ebony fingerboard with pearl dot inlay, fixed bridge, 2-per-side MVP/Gotoh tuners, black or gold hardware, 2 Bartolini "soapbar" pickups, volume/tone/pan controls. Available in Amber, Amber Sunburst, Cherry, Cherry Sunburst, Light Gold, Natural, and Peacock Blue gloss polyester finish. Mfg. 1993 to date.

AA Grade - figured maple body.
MSR $2,695 $2,100 $1,750 $1,500 $1,295 $1,100 $850 $650

AAA Grade - figured maple body.
MSR $2,995 $2,300 $1,900 $1,675 $1,425 $1,195 $950 $725

Thunderbass T5 - similar to Thunderbass T4, except has 5-string configuration, 3/2-per-side tuners. Current Mfg.

AA Grade - figured maple body.
MSR $2,995 $2,300 $1,900 $1,650 $1,425 $1,195 $950 $725

AAA Grade - figured maple body.
MSR $3,295 $2,595 $2,150 $1,875 $1,575 $1,325 $1,050 $800

Thunderbass T6 - similar to Thunderbass T4, except has 6-string configuration, 3-per-side tuners. Current Mfg.

AA Grade - figured maple body.
MSR $3,195 $2,500 $2,000 $1,750 $1,500 $1,250 $1,000 $775

AAA Grade - figured maple body.
MSR $3,495 $2,700 $2,200 $1,950 $1,650 $1,400 $1,150 $850

Thunderbass T8 - similar to Thunderbass T4, except has 8-string configuration (4 pairs of strings/tuned an octave apart), 2-per-side tuners, 4 tuners on bottom bout. Mfg. 1994 to date.

AA Grade - figured maple body.
MSR $3,295 $2,550 $2,100 $1,850 $1,575 $1,325 $1,050 $800

AAA Grade - figured maple body.
MSR $3,595 $2,800 $2,300 $2,000 $1,725 $1,450 $1,150 $875

THUNDERBUZZ T4-F - sleek offset double cutaway figured maple body, through body maple/bubinga 5-piece neck, fretless ebony fingerboard, fixed bridge, 2-per-side MVP/Gotoh tuners, black or gold hardware, 2 Bartolini "soapbar"pickups, volume/tone/pan controls. Available in Amber, Amber Sunburst, Cherry, Cherry Sunburst, Light Gold, Natural, and Peacock Blue gloss polyester finish. Mfg. 1993 to date.

AA Grade - figured maple body.
MSR $2,695 $2,100 $1,700 $1,500 $1,300 $1,100 $850 $650

AAA Grade - figured maple body.
MSR $2,995 $2,300 $1,900 $1,650 $1,425 $1,195 $950 $725

Thunderbuzz T5-F - similar to Thunderbuzz T4-F, except has 5-string configuration, 3/2-per-side tuners. Current Mfg.

GRADING		100% MINT	98% NEAR MINT	95% EXC+	90% EXC	80% VG+	70% VG	60% G

AA Grade - figured maple body.

MSR	$2,995	$2,300	$1,900	$1,675	$1,450	$1,195	$950	$725

AAA Grade - figured maple body.

MSR	$3,295	$2,550	$2,100	$1,850	$1,575	$1,350	$1,050	$800

Thunderbuzz T6-F - similar to Thunderbuzz T4-F, except has 6-string configuration, 3-per-side tuners. Current Mfg.

AA Grade - figured maple body.

MSR	$3,195	$2,500	$2,000	$1,750	$1,500	$1,250	$1,000	$775

AAA Grade - figured maple body.

MSR	$3,495	$2,750	$2,225	$1,925	$1,650	$1,400	$1,125	$850

Thunderbuzz T8-F - similar to Thunderbuzz T4-F, except has 8-string configuration (4 pairs of strings/tuned an octave apart), 2-per-side tuners, 4 tuners on bottom bout. Mfg. 1994 to date.

AA Grade - figured maple body.

MSR	$3,295	$2,550	$2,100	$1,850	$1,575	$1,325	$1,050	$800

AAA Grade - figured maple body.

MSR	$3,595	$2,800	$2,300	$2,000	$1,725	$1,450	$1,150	$875

Pedulla ET 5 Zebra
courtesy M.V.
Pedulla Guitars

Exotic Top ThunderBass/ThunderBuzz Series

This series has 2 variations: the **ET ThunderBass**, which features a fretted fingerboard, and the **ET ThunderBuzz**, which is fretless.

Add $300 for AAAAA quilted maple top.

Add $500 for polyester finish (with or without color).

ET4 - sleek offset double cutaway flame maple body, bubinga (or cocobola, AAAAA flame maple, quilted maple, or zebra) top, through body neck, 24-fret ebony fingerboard with pearl dot inlay, fixed bridge, brass nut, 2-per-side Gotoh tuners, chrome hardware, 2 Bartolini humbucker pickups, volume/tone/mix controls, active electronics. Available in Natural oil/urethane finish. Current Mfg.

MSR	$3,095	$2,450	$2,000	$1,750	$1,500	$1,250	$1,000	$750

This model is also available as the Exotic Top Thunderbuzz with a fretless fingerboard (Model ET4-F).

ET5 - similar to ET4, except has 5-string configuration, 3/2-per-side tuners. Current Mfg.

MSR	$3,3295	$2,650	$2,200	$1,950	$1,650	$1,375	$1,100	$825

This model is also available as the Exotic Top Thunderbuzz with a fretless fingerboard (Model ET5-F).

ET6 - similar to ET4, except has 6-string configuration, 3-per-side tuners. Current Mfg.

MSR	$3,595	$2,800	$2,300	$2,000	$1,750	$1,450	$1,150	$875

This model is also available as the Exotic Top Thunderbuzz with a fretless fingerboard (Model ET6-F).

ET 8 - similar to ET4 except has 8-string configuration (4 pairs of strings/tuned an octave apart), 2-per-side tuners on peghead, 4 tuners on bottom bout. Mfg. 1994 to date.

MSR	$3,695	$2,875	$2,350	$2,100	$1,800	$1,475	$1,200	$900

This model is also available as the Exotic Top Thunderbuzz with a fretless fingerboard (Model ET8-F).

Thunderbolt Series

The Thunderbolt Series is the bolt-on neck version of the Thunderbass design.

THUNDERBOLT TB4 - sleek offset double cutaway figured maple body, through body satin-finished neck, 22-fret rosewood fingerboard with pearl dot inlay, fixed bridge, 2-per-side tuners, black or gold hardware, 2 Bartolini "soapbar" pickups, volume/tone/pan controls, mini switch, active electronics. Available in Amber, Amber Sunburst, Cherry, Cherry Sunburst, Light Gold, Natural, and Peacock Blue polyester finish. Mfg. 1994 to date.

AA Grade - figured maple body.

MSR	$2,095	$1,675	$1,350	$1,200	$1,000	$850	$700	$525

AAA Grade - figured maple body.

MSR	$2,395	$1,925	$1,550	$1,350	$1,175	$975	$800	$600

This model is also available with a fretless fingerboard as Model TB4-F.

Thunderbolt TB5 - similar to Thunderbolt TB4, except has 5-string configuration, 3/2-per-side tuners. Current Mfg.

AA Grade - figured maple body.

MSR	$2,195	$1,750	$1,425	$1,250	$1,100	$900	$725	$550

AAA Grade - figured maple body.

MSR	$2,495	$2,000	$1,625	$1,425	$1,225	$1,050	$825	$625

This model is also available with a fretless fingerboard as Model TB5-F.

Pedulla Thunderbolt 5
courtesy M.V.
Pedulla Guitars

P

GRADING			100% MINT	98% NEAR MINT	95% EXC+	90% EXC	80% VG+	70% VG	60% G

Thunderbolt TB6 - similar to Thunderbolt TB4, except has 6-string configuration, 3-per-side tuners. Current Mfg.

AA Grade - figured maple body.

MSR	$2,395	$1,925	$1,550	$1,350	$1,175	$975	$800	$600

AAA Grade - figured maple body.

MSR	$2,695	$2,150	$1,750	$1,550	$1,325	$1,100	$900	$675

This model is also available with a fretless fingerboard as Model TB6-F.

THUNDERBOLT ETB4 - sleek offset double cutaway figured maple body, AAAAA flame maple (or bubinga or cocobola or quilte or zebra) top, bolt-on 5-piece maple/bubinga neck, 24-fret ebony fingerboard with pearl dot inlay, fixed bridge, 2-per-side tuners, black or gold hardware, 2 Bartolini "soapbar" pickups, volume/tone/pan controls, mini switch, active electronics. Available in Oil/urethane finish. Mfg. 1998 to date.

MSR $2,595

This model is also available with a fretless fingerboard as Model ETB4-F.

Thunderbolt ETB5 - similar to Thunderbolt ETB4, except has 5-string configuration, 3/2-per-side tuners. Mfg. 1998 to date.

MSR $2,695

This model is also available with a fretless fingerboard as Model ETB5-F.

Thunderbolt ETB6 - similar to Thunderbolt ETB4, except has 6-string configuration, 3-per-side tuners. Mfg. 1998 to date.

MSR $2,895

This model is also available with a fretless fingerboard as Model ETB6-F.

PENNCO

Instruments previously produced in Japan circa 1970s. Distributed by the Philadelphia Music Company of Philadelphia, Pennsylvania.

This trademark has been identified as a *House Brand* of the Philadelphia Music Company of Philadelphia, Pennsylvania, the U.S. distributor of these Japanese-built instruments. The Pennco (sometimes misspelled *Penco*) brand name was applied to a full range of acoustic and solid body electric guitars, many entry level to intermediate quality versions of popular American designs.

(Source: Michael Wright, Vintage Guitar Magazine)

PENNCREST

See chapter on House Brands.

This trademark has been identified as a *House Brand* of J. C. Penney's.

(Source: Willie G. Moseley, Stellas & Stratocasters)

PENSA CLASSIC

Instruments currently built in New York, New York since 1995. Distributed by Rudy's Music Shop of New York City, New York.

Rudy Pensa continues the tradition of producing high quality custom guitars first started in 1985 with his collaboration with John Suhr under the Pensa-Suhr trademark. Early Pensa-Suhrs were cast in the "superstrat" sort of design, with Floyd Rose tremolos and EMG electronics. When Suhr left in 1990, other builders like Larry Fitzgerald, Mas Hino, and Paul Blomstrom joined the workshop. Today, the Pensa Classic guitar models are beginning to grow more "Gibson-esque" with dual humbuckers and tune-o-matic bridge/stop tailpiece combinations like the Deluxe and Pensa Custom. However, the classic MK model is still being offered.

PENSA-SUHR

Instruments previously produced in New York, New York between the mid 1980s to early 1990s.

Rudy Pensa founded Rudy's Music Shop on West 48th street in New York back in 1978. Rudy's Music Shop features both retail instruments, amps, and effects as well as vintage classics. In 1983 John Suhr added a repair section to the shop, and within two years the pair collaborated on custom guitars and basses. Pensa-Suhr instruments feature exotic woods, pickup and wiring options, and other upgrades that the player could order. Pensa-Suhr instruments were high quality, and built along the lines of classic American designs.

In 1989, John Suhr moved to California and teamed up with Bob Bradshaw to open up a custom pedalboard/custom guitar shop. In 1994, Suhr joined the Fender custom shop as a Master Builder, and has been active in helping modernize the Fender Precision designs as well as his Custom Shop duties. Rudy Pensa maintained Rudy's Music Shop in New York City, and continues producing guitars and basses under the Pensa Classic trademark.

PERFORMANCE

Instruments currently built in Hollywood, California.

The Performance guitar shop has been building custom guitars, doing custom work on guitars, and performing quality repair work for a good number of years.

The **Corsair 22** model features a double cutaway Ash body, 22-fret Maple neck, 2 humbuckers, Schaller Floyd Rose locking tremolo, volume and tone knobs, pickup selector switch and Performance tuners. The guitar comes complete with an oil finish, and has a retail price beginning at $1,850. Performance also offers the **Corsair 24**, a similar model guitar that features a 24-fret fingerboard (two octaves). Retail price begins at $1,950.

P

PERRON

Instruments currently built in Elkhart, Indiana.

Michael Perron is an independent guitar manufacturer that produces five per month, as well as custom guitars and basses. All Perron guitars are high quality instruments that have a solid feel to them. For further information, please contact Michael Perron directly (see Trademark Index).

Pete Back Florid
courtesy Pete Back Guitars

PETE BACK GUITARS

Instruments currently built in Richmond (North Yorkshire), England since 1975.

Luthier Pete Back is noted for his custom handcrafted guitars of the highest quality. His electric, folk and classical guitar construction uses the finest woods available. Pete has his own original designs, but will make whatever the guitarist requires. He also offers repairs (refretting, set-ups, and resprays). Back's prices start at 650 (English pounds), depending on parts and materials.

PETILLO, PHILLIP J.

Instruments currently built in Ocean. NI. Petillo Masterpiece Guitars and Accessories was founded in 1968.

Luthier Phillip J. Petillo has been creating, repairing, and restoring guitars and other instruments for over thirty years. Petillo was one of the original co-designers of the Kramer aluminum neck guitar in 1976, and built the four prototypes for Kramer (BKL). Later, he severed his connections with the company.

Currently, Petillo makes custom handcrafted acoustic carved top and back guitars, flat top acoustics, semi-hollow body guitars, and solid body guitars and basses. Petillo also makes and repairs the bowed instruments. Petillo, a holder of a BS, MS, and PHD in Engineering, also offers his talents in Engineering for product development, research and development, engineering, and prototype building for the musical instruments industry.

Phillip and Lucille Petillo are the founders and officers of a research corporation that develops devices and technology for the medical industry. While seeming unrelated to the music industry, the Phil-Lu Incorporated company illustrates Petillo's problem-solving skills applied in different fields of study.

Petillo estimates that he hand builds between 8 to 20 guitars a year on his current schedule. Prices begin at $1,200 and are priced by nature of design and materials utilized. Custom Marquetry Inlay and other ornamental work is priced by the square inch. Petillo offers 170 different choices of lumbers, veneers, and mother-of-pearl.

Restoration, alteration and repair work are price quoted upon inspection of the instrument. In addition, he markets his patented products such as Petillo Frets, the Acoustic Tonal Sensor, Petillo Strings and Polish, and a fret micro-polishing system.

Some of his clients include: Tal Farlow, Chuck Wayne, Jim Croce, Elvis Presley, James Taylor, Tom Petty, Howie Epstein, Dave Mason, The Blues Brothers, Bruce Springsteen, Gary Talent, Steve Van Zant, Southside Johnny, and many others.

PHANTOM GUITAR WORKS

Instruments previously built in Portland, Oregon from 1995 to 1998.

Phantom Guitar Works produced a number of modern versions of Vox classic designs, keeping true to the spirit of the original model while updating some of the hardware to produce a stabile player's guitar. The ***Blue Book of Electric Guitars*** has been unable to contact the company, leading to some doubt as to whether they are still in business.

Models in the Phantom product line include the **Mandoguitar**, the five sided **Phantom** and **Phantom Bass**, the **Teardrop, Teardrop B.J.**, and the **Teardrop Bass**. The original list prices for these models in standard colors were $995 per instrument, models in the tri-color Sunburst finish were an additional $100.

PHIL

Instruments currently produced in Korea.

The Myung Sung Music Ind. Co., Ltd. is currently offering a wide range of well constructed electric guitar models. There is a large variety of styles, configurations, colors, and affordable price points. Construction utilizes top quality laminates, rosewood, spruce, mahogany, and build quality is top shelf. The **Phil Pro** Series offers models with offset double cutaway bodies, bolt-on necks, and double locking tremolo systems. For more information on the current model lineup, availability, and pricing, please contact The Myung Sung Music Ind. Co., Ltd.

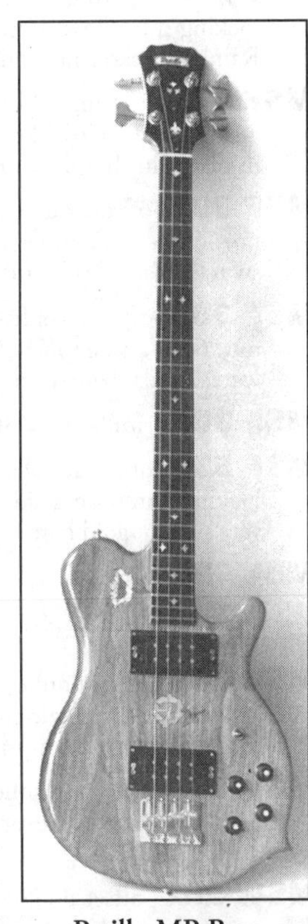

Petillo MP Bass
courtesy Petillo

ELECTRIC

Revival Series

MSG 625 -offset double cutaway solid body with flamed arch top, maple set neck, rosewood fingerboard, 22-frets, pearl block inlays, 3-per-side tuners, 2 humbucking pickups, 2 volume, 1 tone, 3-way switch, gold hardware. Available in Purple Burst finish only. Current Mfg.

MSG 635 offset double cutaway solid body with oak arch top, maple set neck, rosewood fingerboard with dot inlays, 24-frets, 3-per-side tuners, 2 humbucking pickups, 1 volume, 1 tone, 3-way switch, chrome hardware. Available in Cherry Sunburst finish only. Current Mfg.

MSG 640 -offset double cutaway solid body with burled arch top, maple set neck, rosewood fingerboard with dot inlays, 24-frets, 3-per-side tuners, 2 humbucking pickups with exposed coils and 1 single coil pickup, 1 volume, 1 tone, five way switch, vibrato tailpiece, chrome hardware. Available in Transparent Black finish only. Current Mfg.

MSG 650L -offset double cutaway solid body with flame top, maple set neck, rosewood fingerboard with dot inlays, 22-frets, 3-per-side tuners, 1 volume, 1 tone, 3-way switch, pearloid pickguard, 2 humbucking pickups, gold hardware. Available in Blue Burst finish only. Current Mfg.

MSG 655 -offset double cutaway semi-hollowbody design, maple set neck, rosewood fingerboard with dot inlays, 22-frets, 3-per-side tuners, pearloid body binding, single elliptical sound hole, 2 humbucking pickups with exposed zebra coils, gold hardware. Available in Yellow Burst finish only. New 2001.

MSG 678 -offset double cutaway semi-hollowbody design, quilted arch top, maple set neck, rosewood fingerboard with pearloid steer head inlays, 22-frets, 3-per-side tuners, 1 volume, 1 tone, 3-way switch, 2 humbucking pickups with exposed zebra coils, 2 elliptical soundholes, gold hardware, Available in Green Burst finish only. New 2001.

MSG 678A -same as MSG 678 but with Black Pearl hardware and Amber Burst finish. New 2001.

MSG 688 -offset double cutaway solid body with flame top, maple set neck, rosewood fingerboard with pearl block inlays, 22-frets, 3-per-side tuners, string though body, 2 volume, 1 tone, 3-way switch, 2 Seymour Duncan humbucking pickups, pearl body binding, large pearl eagle inlay on guitar top. Available in Transparent Red and Transparent Blue finish. Current Mfg.

PSM 700T -offset double cutaway solid body design, body constructed in laminated bands of maple, walnut and bubinga, arch top, neck through body, neck constructed of maple, walnut and bubinga, rosewood fingerboard with pearl dot inlays, 24-frets, 6-on-a-side tuners, Wilkinson bridge with vibrato bar, 1 volume, 1 tone, five way switch, 2 Bill Lawrence humbucking pickups and 1 single coli alnico pickup, chrome hardware. Available in Natural finish only. New 2001.

Ardent Series

MSF 201 -offset double cutaway solid body, flame top, bolt-on maple neck, rosewood fingerboard with dot inlays, 24-frets, locking nut, 6-on-a-side tuners, Floyd Rose 200 bridge, 1 volume, 1 tone, five way switch, 2 exposed coil humbucking pickups and 1 single coil pickup, gold hardware. Available in Transparent Purple finish only. Current Mfg.

MSF 231 -offset double cutaway solid body, bolt-on maple neck, rosewood fingerboard with offset dot inlays, locking nut, 24-frets, 6-on-a-side tuners, Floyd Rose 200 bridge, 1 volume, 1 tone, five way switch, 2 single coil pickups and 1 exposed coil humbucking pickup, chrome hardware. Available in Dark Metallic Blue finish only. Current Mfg.

MSF 237 -offset double cutaway solid body, bolt-on maple neck, rosewood fingerboard with offset dot inlays, 24-frets, locking nut, 6-on-a-side tuners, Floyd Rose 200 bridge, 1 volume, 1 tone, five way switch, 2 exposed coil humbucking pickups and 1 single coil pickup, black hardware. Available in black finish only. Current Mfg.

MSF 275 -7-string, offset double cutaway solid body, oak top, bolt-on maple neck, rosewood fingerboard with dot inlays, 22-frets, 7-on-a-side tuners, locking nut, Floyd Rose 700 bridge, 1 volume, 1 tone, 3-way switch, 2 exposed coil humbucking pickups and 1 single coil pickup, chrome hardware. Available in Yellow Burst finish only. New 2001.

MSF 276 -7-string, offset double cutaway solid body, bolt-on maple neck with rosewood fingerboard, dot inlays, 24-frets, 7-on-a-side tuners, locking nut, Floyd Rose 700 bridge, 2 exposed coil humbucking pickups, 1 volume, 1 tone, 3-way switch, chrome hardware. Available in Rainbow Pearl finish only. New 2001.

MSF 277 -7-string, offset double cutaway solid body, bolt-on maple neck with rosewood fingerboard, dot inlays, 24-frets, locking nut, 7-on-a-side tuners, Floyd Rose 700 bridge, 2 humbucking pickups with exposed coils, 1 volume, 1 tone, 3-way switch, black hardware. Available in black finish only. Current Mfg.

MSF 301 -offset double cutaway solid body, flamed arch top, bolt-on maple neck with rosewood fingerboard, chevron inlays, 24-frets, locking nut, 6-on-a-side tuners, Floyd Rose 500 bridge, 2 Bill Lawrence humbucking pickups and 1 single coil pickup, 1 volume, 1 tone, five way switch, Black Pearl hardware. Available in Transparent Blue finish only. Current Mfg.

MSF 302 -offset double cutaway solid body with oak arch top, bolt-on maple neck, rosewood fingerboard with dot inlays, 24-frets, locking nut, 6-on-a-side tuners, Floyd Rose bridge, 2 single coil pickups and 1 humbucking pickup, 1 volume, 1 tone, five way switch, chrome hardware. Available in Transparent Amber finish only. Current Mfg.

MSF 303 -similar to MSF 302 except has black hardware and is available in Metallic Green finish only. Current Mfg.

MSF 531 -offset double cutaway solid body, flame double arch top, bolt-on maple neck, rosewood fingerboard with shark fin inlays, 24-frets, locking nut, 6-on-a-side tuners, Floyd Rose 500 bridge, 2 Bill Lawrence humbucking pickups and 1 single coil pickup, 1 volume, 1 tone, five way switch, gold hardware. Available in Transparent Red finish only. Current Mfg.

MSL 988 -Explorer style solid body with flame top, set or bolt-on necks available, rosewood fingerboard with dot inlays, 22-frets, 2 Alnico ZB humbucking pickups with exposed coils, 2 volume, 1 tone, 3-way switch, Black Pearl hardware. Available in Purple Burst finish only. New 2001.

MSS 235 -offset double cutaway solid body, oak top, bolt-on maple neck, rosewood fingerboard with dot inlays, 22-frets, locking nut, 6-on-a-side tuners, 2 single coil pickups and 1 exposed coil humbucking pickup, 1 volume, 1 tone, five way switch, chrome hardware. Available in Transparent Green finish only. Current Mfg.

MSV 983 -V shaped solid body with flame top, available with set or bolt-on maple neck, rosewood fingerboard with dot inlays, 22-frets, 6-on-a-side tuners, 2 exposed coil humbucking pickups, 2 volume, 1 tone, 3-way switch, chrome hardware. Available in Green Burst finish only. Current Mfg.

MSW 202 -offset double cutaway solid body, burl top, bolt-on maple neck, rosewood fingerboard with pearl block inlays, 22-frets, locking nut, 6-on-a-side tuners, Wilkinson bridge, 2 exposed coil humbucking pickups, 1 volume, 1 tone, 3-way switch, gold hardware. Available in Transparent Black finish only. Current Mfg.

MSW 206 -offset double cutaway solid body, flame top, bolt-on maple neck, rosewood fingerboard with offset dot inlays, locking nut, 24-frets, 6-on-a-side tuners, 2 exposed coil humbucking pickups and 1 single coil pickup, 1 volume, 1 tone, five way switch, chrome hardware. Available in Transparent Blue finish only. Current Mfg.

MSW 255 -offset single cutaway body,quilted top, maple through neck, rosewoodfingerboard, 22-frets, 6-on-a-side tuners, Wilkinson bridge, 1 Bill Lawrence humbucking pickup and 2 single coil pickups, 1 volume, 1 tone, five way switch, satin chrome hardware. Available in natural finish only. New 2001.

MSW 577 -offset double cutaway solid body with flame round top, bolt-on 5-piece maple neck, rosewood fingerboard with dot inlays, 22-frets, 6-on-a-side tuners, 2 single coil and 1 humbucking pickup, 1 volume, 1 tone, five way switch, black hardware. Available in Cherry Sunburst finish only. Curent Mfg.

ELECTRIC HOLLOW BODY

FM 800 -double cutaway semi-hollow body, Birdseye Maple top, back and sides, maple set neck, rosewood fingerboard with pearl block inlays, 22-frets 3-per-side tuners, 2 humbucking pickups, lyre tailpiece, 2 volume, 2 tone, 3-way switch, gold hardware. Available in Cherry finish only. Disc. 2000.

FM 805 -double cutaway semi-hollow body, maple top, back, and sides, maple set neck, rosewood fingerboard with pearl block inlays, 22-frets, 3-per-side tuners, 2 humbucking pickups, stop tailpiece, 2 volume, 2 tone, 3-way switch, chrome hardware. Available in black finish only. Disc. 2000.

FM 810 -double cutaway semi-hollow body, flame maple top, maple back and sides, maple set neck, rosewood fingerboard with pearl block inlays, 22-frets, 3-per-side tuners, 2 humbucking pickups, 2 volume, 2 tone, 3-way switch, gold hardware. Available in Transparent Amber finish only. New 2001.

FM 815 -same as FM 805 except has lyre tailpiece and is available in Yellow Burst finish only. Disc. 2000.

FM 820 -double cutaway semi-hollow body, Birds Eye Maple top, back and sides, maple set neck, rosewood fingerboard with pearl block inlays, 22-frets, 3-per-side tuners, 2 humbucking pickups, stop tailpiece, 2 volume, 2 tone, 3-way switch, gold hardware. Available in Cherry Sunburst finish only. Disc. 2000.

FM 827 -double cutaway semi-hollow body, maple top, back and sides, maple set neck, rosewood fingerboard with dot inlays, 22-frets, 3-per-side tuners, 2 humbucking pickups, 2 volume, 2 tone, 3-way switch, chrome hardware. Available in 2 Tone Sunburst finish only. Current Mfg.

FMA 830 -single cutaway semi-hollow body, maple top, maple back and sides, maple set neck, rosewood fingerboard with pearl block inlays, 22-frets, 3-per-side tuners, 2 humbucking pickups, 2 volume, 2 tone, 3-way switch, chrome hardware. Available in 2 Tone Sunburst finish only. Current Mfg.

FMA 850 -single cutaway semi-hollow body, Florentine cutaway, maple top, back, and sides, maple set neck, rosewood fingerboard with pearl block inlays, 3-per-side tuners, 22-frets, vibrato bridge, 2 humbucking pickups, 2 volume, 2 tone, 3-way switch, chrome hardware. Available in Transparent red finish only. Disc. 2000.

FMA 870 -single cutaway semi-hollow body, spruce top, sycamore back and sides, maple set neck, rosewood fingerboard with pearl block inlays, 22-frets, 3-per-side tuners, 2 humbucking pickups, 2 volume, 2 tone, 3-way switch, gold hardware. Available in Transparent Amber finish only. Current Mfg.

FMA 880 -single cutaway semi-hollow body, spruce top, sycamore back and sides, maple set neck, rosewood fingerboard with pearl block inlays, 22-frets, 3-per-side tuners, 1 humbucking pickup, black pickguard, 1 volume, 1 tone, gold hardware. Available in Yellow Burst finish only. Disc. 2000.

ELECTRIC BASS

Command Bass Series

PBM 43T -offset double cutaway solid body, round top, maple set neck, rosewood fingerboard with dot inlays, 24-frets, 2-per-side tuners, 2 pickups, 1 volume, 2 tone, 1 balance, chrome hardware. Available in Rainbow Pearl finish only. New 2001.

PBM 46E -offset double cutaway solid body, mahogany round top, 5-piece set neck, rosewood fingerboard with dot inlays, 24-frets, 2-per-side tuners, 2 pickups, volume, middle, bass, and balance controls, gold hardware. Available in Natural finish only. New 2001.

PBM 47T -offset double cutaway soft maple solid body, maple/walnut/bubinga neck through body, rosewood fingerboard with dot inlays, 24-frets, 2-per-side tuners, 2 Music Man 4 pickups, 1 volume, 2 tone, 1 balance, gold hardware. Available in Natural finish only. Current Mfg.

PBM 48 -offset double cutaway solid body, ash round top, maple bolt-on neck, rosewood fingerboard with dot inlays, 24-frets, 4 on 1 side tuners, 2 pickups, volume, bass,mid, and balance controls, chrome hardware. Available in Natural finish only. New 2001.

P

GRADING	100% MINT	98% NEAR MINT	95% EXC+	90% EXC	80% VG+	70% VG	60% G

PBM 56E -5-string, offset double cutaway solid body, burl round top, maple set neck, rosewood fingerboard with dot inlays, 24-frets, 3/2 tuners, 2 pickups, volume, middle, bass and balance controls, gold hardware. Available in Brown Burst finish only. New 2001.

PBM 58-8 -8-string, offset double cutaway solid body, available with bolt-on or set maple neck, rosewood fingerboard with dot inlays, 24-frets, 4-per-side tuners, 2 GB-4 pickups, controls for volume, treble, mid, bass and balance, chrome hardware. Available in Pearl White finish only. New 2001.

PBM-58-12 -12 string, offset double cutaway solid body, quilted round top, set or bolt-on maple neck, rosewood fingerboard with dot inlays, 24-frets, 6-per-side tuners, 2 GB-4 pickups, volume, mid, bass and balance controls, chrome hardware. Available in Transparent Black finish only. New 2001.

PBM-59T -5-string, offset double cutaway solid body, oak round top, maple/walnut/bubinga neck through body, 24-frets, 3/2 tuners, 2 Music Man 5 pickups, 1 volume, 2 tone, 1 balance, gold hardware. Available in Transparent Amber finish only. Current Mfg.

PHILIP KUBICKI TECHNOLOGY

Instruments currently built in Clifton, New Jersey. Distributed by Philip Kubicki Technology of Clifton, New Jersey.

Luthier Phil Kubicki began building acoustic guitars at age 15. Kubicki was one of the first employees hired by Roger Rossmeisel at Fender, and was part of Rossmeisl's staff during production of the LTD model. After leaving Fender, Kubicki gained a reputation for his custom guitar building. He formed his own company, Philip Kubicki Technology (PKT) to produce acoustic guitars, components (especially high quality necks), and short scale travel electric guitars.

In 1983, Kubicki formalized design plans for the Ex Factor 4 bass. This revolutionary headless-designed bass debuted in 1985. In 1988, Kubicki entered into a trademark and licensing deal with Fender Musical Instruments Corporation which allowed him time for research while Fender built, distributed, and marketed the concept of the Factor bass. By 1992, the deal was dissolved, and Kubicki regained control of his bass designs.

Currently, Kubicki continues to oversee distribution of his namesake basses. In addition, Kubicki is available for guitar repair and refretting of vintage, acoustic, and jazz guitars in Santa Barbara, California.

ELECTRIC

Many people are not aware of the custom guitars that luthier Kubicki has built. There are two models of short scale travel guitars, built in quantities of less than 300: The Arrow (a Flying V) and another based roughly on a Les Paul. Both instruments have high quality pick-ups and hardware, and are generally signed and numbered by Kubicki. Kubicki has also built a number of quality acoustic guitars, again in limited amounts.

ELECTRIC BASS

All instruments are available in Bahama Green, Black, Charcoal Pearl, Midnight Blue Pearl, Red, Tobacco Sunburst, Transparent Blue Burst, Transparent Burgundy, Red, White and Yellow finishes.

Factor Series

EX FACTOR 4 - offset double cutaway wave style maple body with screened logo, laminated maple neck, 32" to 36" scale, 24-fret ebony fingerboard, fixed aluminum bridge with fine tuners (reverse tuning design), 4 string anchors on peghead with low E string clasp (D Tuner), black hardware, 2 Kubicki humbucker pickups, stacked volume/mix control, stacked treble/bass control, 5-position rotary switch, active electronics. Mfg. 1985 to date.

MSR	$2,595	$2,075	$1,675	$1,470	$1,265	$1,050	$855	$650

This model has fretless fingerboard or %-string configuration optional.
The E string clasp allows the player access to the two fret extension (i.e., down to "D"without retuning) on the headstock.

FACTOR 4 - similar to Ex Factor 4, except has no low E string clasp (D Tuner), 34" scale. Current Mfg.

MSR	$2,595	$2,075	$1,675	$1,470	$1,265	$1,050	$855	$650

Key Factor Series

P

KEY FACTOR 4 - offset double cutaway wave style maple body with screened logo, bolt-on laminated maple neck, 24-fret rosewood fingerboard, fixed aluminum bridge, 2-per-side tuners, black hardware, 2 Kubicki humbucker pick ups, stacked volume/mix control, stacked treble/bass control, 5-position rotary switch, active electronics. Mfg. 1994 to date.

MSR	$1,695	$1,350	$1,100	$965	$825	$695	$550	$425

Add $130 for maple fingerboard.
Add $130 for fretless fingerboard.

Key Factor 5 - similar to Key Factor 4, except has 5 strings, 3/2-per-side tuners. Mfg. 1994 to date.

MSR	$1,895	$1,500	$1,225	$1,075	$925	$775	$625	$475

PIGNOSE

Instruments currently produced in Gardena, California. Distributed by Pignose Industries of Gardena, California.

Around 1972, the first 500 handmade Pignose portable amps were constructed by inventors Richard Edlund and Wayne Kimball (model #064 was presented to Keith Richards of the Rolling Stones). Pignose amps have been used by practicing musicians, in studios, and backstage at concerts - anywhere a portable amp could go. As far as using the amp in the studio for rhythm tracks, remember that the case of the regular Pignose can be opened and closed, allowing for different tonal qualities (that's the hot tip for this edition). Pignose Industries currently offers a wide range of Pignose amps.

n 1998, Pignose Industries debuted the **PGG-100**, a mini solid body electric model that features a built-in Pignose mp! The PGG-100 model (list $474) features a 24 1/4" scale, 22-fret rosewood fingerboard, bolt-on maple neck, fixed ridge, 1/4" headphone jack (which also allows the guitar to be plugged into a regular amp), humbucker pickup, built-n amp, and metal pignose volume control (push-pull on/off switch). The 1 watt on board amplifier is powered by a 9-olt battery.

PICKARD

Instruments previously built in England from the late 1970s through the mid 1980s.

These good quality solid body guitars feature original designs, pickups and hardware by custom builder Steve Pickard.
Source: Tony Bacon and Paul Day, The Guru's Guitar Guide)

PLAYER

Instruments previously built in Scarsdale, New York during the mid 1980s.

The Player model MDS-1B attempted to give the musician control over his sound by providing pop-in modules that ield different pickups. The MDS-1B model was routed for two modules (other models were either routed for one or hree). The plastic modules that housed the DiMarzio pickups were inserted from the back of the guitar into mounting ings that had four phospor-bronze self-cleaning contacts. Empty modules were also available if the musician wanted to nstall his own choice of pickups to the guitar.

The offset double cutaway body was one piece Honduran mahogany, and featured a bolt-on neck with either rosewood or ebony or maple fingerboards. The headstock had six on one side Gotoh mini tuners, and the bridge was a Kahler ocking tremolo. The scale length was 25 1/2" and had 22-frets. Controls consisted of a master volume and master tone, individual volume knobs for each pickup, and a 3-way pickup selector switch. The price of $1,100 included a hardshell case, but the pickups were optional!

PLEASANT

Instruments previously produced in Japan circa late 1940s through the mid 1960s.

These Japanese-built solid body guitars were built between 1947 to 1966. The manufacturer is still unknown. There is no evidence of the brand being imported to the American market.
(Source: Michael Wright, Vintage Guitar Magazine)

Premier E-Model
courtesy Abalone Vintage

POOLE CUSTOM GUITARS

Instruments currently built in Kent, England.

Luthier Sid Poole is currently hand crafting custom built electric guitars. Poole bypasses the world of CNC or CAD/CAM and does all the body and neck shaping by hand, as well as spraying the nitrocellulose finishes himself. Poole's guitars feature a choice of pickups, hardware, and electronics. These hand crafted instruments are heavily favored by many of the United Kingdom's guitar players such as Bernie Marsden (Whitesnake) and Geoff Whitehorn (Paul Rodgers Band). For further information regarding specifications and pricing, please contact Sid Poole directly (see Trademark Index).

The majority of Poole's instruments are built on commission basis, and as a custom-built model may feature a wide range of options. It's a fair guess to say that these instruments rarely show up in the secondary market - so eliminate the guesswork and order a new one today!

PREMIER

Instruments currently produced in China. Distributed in the U.S. market by Entertainment Music Marketing Corporation (EMMC) of Deer Park, New York.

Instruments produced in New York during the 1950s and 1960s. Later models manufactured in Japan.

Premier was the brand name of the Louis Sorkin Music Company. Premier-branded solid body guitars were built at the Multivox company of New York, and distribution of those and the later Japanese built Premiers was handled by the Sorkin company of New York City, New York. Other guitars built and distributed (possibly as rebrands) were **ROYCE, STRAD-O-LIN, BELLTONE,** and **MARVEL.**

Current Premier models are built in China, and feature a slimmed (or sleek) strat-style guitar body and P-style bass body. New list prices range from $229 to $289.

Premier solid body guitars featured a double offset cutaway body, and the upper bout had a "carved scroll" design, bolt-on necks, a bound rosewood fingerboard, 3+3 headstocks (initially; later models featured 6-on-a-side), and single coil pickups. Later models of the mid to late 1960s featured wood bodies covered in sparkly plastic.

Towards the end of the U.S. production in the mid 1960s, the **Custom** line of guitars featured numerous body/neck/electronics/hardware parts from overseas manufacturers like Italy and Japan. The guitars were then assembled in the U.S, and available through the early 1970s.

Some models, like the acoustic line, were completely made in Japan during the early 1970s. Some Japanese-built versions of popular American designs were introduced in 1974, but were disc. two years later. By the mid-1970s, both the Sorkin company and Premier guitars had ceased. Multivox continued importing and distributing Hofner instruments as well as Multivox amplifiers through the early 1980s. Hofners are currently distributed by the Entertainment Music Marketing Corporation of New York, as well as the current line of Premier solid body electric guitars and basses.

(Source: Michael Wright, Guitar Stories Volume One)

P

PROFILE

Instruments previously produced in Japan during the mid to late 1980s.

Profile guitars are generally good quality models based on Fender designs.
(Source: Tony Bacon and Paul Day, The Guru's Guitar Guide)

PULSE

Instruments previously built in Korea during the mid to late 1980s.

These entry level to intermediate quality solid body guitars feature designs based on classic American favorites.
(Source: Tony Bacon and Paul Day, The Guru's Guitar Guide)

PURE-TONE

See chapter on House Brands.

This trademark has been identified as a *House Brand* of Selmer (UK).
(Source: Willie G. Moseley, Stellas & Stratocasters)

Talk about a show stopper! Paul Reed Smith, with legendary late Ted McCarty, Nashville Summer NAMM, 2000. For everything else, there's MasterCard.

Section Q

QUEST

Instruments previously built in Japan during the mid 1980s. Distribution in the U.S. market was handled by Primo, Inc. of Marlboro, Massachusetts.

Quest solid body guitars featured some original designs as well as designs based on classic American favorites. Overall, the quality of the instruments were medium to good, a solid playable rock club guitar.

ELECTRIC

Some of the instruments featured in the Quest line while they were briefly imported to the U.S. were an Explorer copy with turned-down point on the treble horn (**ATAK-6X**), and a Bass model similar to a P-Bass with squared off horns and P/J pickup combination (**Manhatten M3-BZ**). Other models will be updated in future editions of the ***Blue Book of Electric Guitars***.

Quest instruments are generally priced between $175 to $350.

QUEST MINI GUITARS

Instruments currently distributed by Music Industries Corporation, located in Floral Park, New York.

These mini instruments come in 2 basic configurations - the AP-5 Traveler guitar, and the AP-7 Baby Shark. Both are 3/4 scale, the AP-5 Traveler features a solid wood body and neck, and both have a built-in amplifier/speaker. For more information, please contact the distributor directly (see Trademark Index).

NOTES

The legendary guitar designer Rick Turner (l) and equally legendary Billy Sheehan (famed bass guitarist), posing with a new Turner 12 string acoustic electric.

Section R

GRADING	100% MINT	98% NEAR MINT	95% EXC+	90% EXC	80% VG+	70% VG	60% G

RWK S.E.T.
courtesy Cathy Shelley

R. HAYES INSTRUMENTS

Please refer to the H section in this text.

R & L

See ROMAN & LIPMAN

Instruments currently built in Danbury, Connecticut since the early 1990s.

RWK

Instruments currently built in Highland Park, Illinois since 1991. Distributed by RWK Guitars of Highland Park, Illinois.

After achieving some success repairing guitars both for himself and friends in the music business, Bob Karger started hand-making guitars in 1991. He wanted to build something that was not only contemporary but would stand the test of time. That is why the company slogan is "Classic Guitars Built Today". The initial design, which to-date is the only design built, is named "SET". This is an acronym for Solid Electric Through-neck.

His goal is to build a guitar which takes advantage of what has been developed so far in the solid electric guitar world and go that extra step. The body is highly contoured, including the noticeable lack of an upper bout, to provide comfort and ease of play. Its through-neck design, along with having the strings anchored through the back of the body, is directly aimed at generating maximum sustain. Because they are handmade, this provides the flexibility of being able to substitute parts and variation in construction aspects, such as neck feel and radius, to easily suit the musician's preference.

(Biography courtesy Bob Karger, RWK Guitars, July 18, 1996)

S.E.T. (Solid Electric Through-neck) - single cutaway ergonomic shaped maple body, solid maple through-neck design, cream top binding, 24-fret bound ebony fingerboard with dot inlay, string through-body bridge, 3-per-side Schaller tuners, gold-plated hardware, 2 humbucker pickups, 2 volume and 2 tone controls, 3-position switch. Translucent Natural finish. Current Mfg.

MSR $799

RAINSONG

Instruments currently produced in Maui, Hawaii since 1994. Distributed by Kuau Technology, Ltd. since 1985. Previous instrument production was a joint effort between facilities in Hawaii and Albuquerque, New Mexico.

Kuau Technology, Ltd. was initially founded in 1982 by Dr. John A. Decker, Jr. to research and provide development on optical instrumentation and marine navigation. Decker, a physicist with degrees in engineering, also enjoys playing classical guitar. Since 1985, the company began concentrating on developing and manufacturing graphite/epoxy Classical and Steel String guitars. Members of the design team included Dr. Decker, as well as noted luthier Lorenzo Pimentel and composite materials expert George M. Clayton. In the company's beginning, the R & D facility was in Maui, Hawaii; and manufacturing was split between Escondido, California and Pimentel and Sons guitar makers of Albuquerque, New Mexico. The California facility handled the work on the composite materials, and the Pimentels in New Mexico supplied the lutherie and finishing work (Pimentel and Sons themselves build quality wooden guitars). The Rainsong All-Graphite acoustic guitar has been commercially available since 1992.

In December 1994, full production facilities were opened in Maui, Hawaii. George Clayton of Bi-Mar Productions assisted in development of the factory and manufacturing processes, then returned to the mainland to continue his own work. The product line has expanded to include classical models, steel string acoustic guitars and basses, acoustic/electric models, and hollowbody electric guitars and basses. Kuau Technologies, Ltd. currently employs ten people on their production staff.

Rainsong guitars and basses feature Rainsong's proprietary graphite/epoxy technology, Schaller tuning machines, optional Fishman transducers, and EMG pickups (on applicable models). Models also available with a single cutaway, in left-handed configurations, a choice of three peghead inlay designs, side-dot fret markers, and wood marquetry rosette. Instruments shipped in a hardshell case.

ELECTRIC

JZ1000 - slim body cutaway jazz guitar design, equipped with EMG dual active humbucking pickups, trapeze tailpiece, all graphite construction. New 1999.

MSR	$2,295	$1,995	$1,750	$1,500	$1,250	$1,100	$995	$775

RAJ GUITAR CRAFTS

Instruments currently built in Asia. Distributed by L.A. Guitar Works of Reseda, California.

All RAJ models are constructed from Southsea hardwoods, and feature meticulously inlaid shells that highlight the body designs. The current models include the **Warbird** ($1,295), which possesses a body design that follows "superstrat" lines. The **Panther** ($1,395) body design is reminiscent of the Fender Jaguar model, albeit more flowing body curves. The **Shark's** ($1,195) original design suggests a cross between a Flying V and Bo Diddley's rectangular guitar of the 1950s (prettier than the description suggests). All models feature a one piece maple neck, or maple with rosewood fingerboard with the S.A.T. (Side Adjustment Truss rod) which allows for neck adjustments while the guitar is still fully strung. For further information, contact L.A. Guitar Works directly (see Trademark Index).

RALEIGH

Instruments currently built in Chicago, Illinois. Distributed by the Aloha Publishing and Musical Instrument Company of Chicago, Illinois.

The Aloha company was founded in 1935 by J. M. Raleigh. True to the nature of a "House Brand" distributor, Raleigh's company distributed both Aloha instruments and amplifiers and Raleigh brand instruments through his Chicago office. Acoustic guitars were supplied by Harmony, and initial amplifiers and guitars for the Aloha trademark were supplied by the Alamo company of San Antonio, Texas. By the mid 1950s, Aloha was producing their own amps, but continued using Alamo products.

(Source: Michael Wright, Vintage Guitar Magazine)

RALSTON

Instruments currently built in Grant Town, West Virginia.

Ralston currently offers three models with regular or figured maple tops, two humbuckers, volume/tone controls, switching for series/parallel or single coil, and rosewood fingerboards. The **R/B** is a double cutaway body style for rock or blues players, while the V is a single cutaway for all styles of music. Ralston's **Original** model is all that (*and a bag of picks*) - a novel eye-catching design with two forward body cutaways as well as two cutaways on the rear bout as well! Contact Ralston for pricing and availability.

RAMIREZ, RAY

Instruments currently built in Humacao, Puerto Rico.

Ray Ramirez is currently producing the Caribbean Series Electric Upright Bass in Wood and also in fiberglass. The instrument is a modern version of the Ampeg Baby Bass. The electronics include a diaphragm pickup for a deep punch and clear sound suitable for Jazz, as well as Latin music.

RAMTRACK

Instruments currently built in Redford, Michigan. Distributed by World Class Engineered Products, Inc. of Redford, Michigan.

The innovative people at Ramtrack have attempted to answer the age-old dilemma of the working musician: how many guitars do you need to bring to a show to convincingly recreate famous guitar sounds? Obviously, a single coil pickup does not sound like a humbucker, and different configurations of pickups exist on a multitude of solid body guitar designs. The Ramtrack guitar design consists of a solid body guitar with cassettes containing different pickup combinations that are removable from the body.

Inventor James Randolph came up with the concept for the Ramtrak when he was faced with compromising his playing style to accommodate the type of guitar loaded with the proper pickups needed to record the tracks for any given song, i.e.: Strats play and sound different than a Les Paul. Though the concept of removable pickups is not a new one, Ramtrack excels in the execution of how the cassettes are installed and removed from the guitar. Ramtrak requires no tools for changing the pickup cassette.

ELECTRIC

Ramtrak guitars (**Model RG1-ST**) feature a pacific maple body, bolt-on hardrock maple neck, 22-fret rosewood fingerboard, standard tremolo, and an aluminum extrusion cassette plate. Pickup cassettes are loaded with the most popular pickups on the market. The guitars are presently manufactured by CNC in Korea, and parts are shipped to Michigan (where final assembly and inspection takes place). For more information on pricing and pickup configurations and products, please contact World Class Engineered Products directly (see Trademark Index).

RANGE RIDER

See chapter on House Brands.

This trademark has been identified as a "House Brand" of the Monroe Catalog House.

(Source: Willie G. Moseley, Stellas & Stratocasters)

RANSOM

Instruments currently built in San Francisco.

Ransom custom builds high quality bass guitars in a 4-, 5-, and 6-string configuration. Basses are constructed of alder bodies with quilted or flame maple tops, 24-fret maple, rosewood, or ebony fingerboards, and feature Bartolini, EMG, or Seymour Duncan pickups. Retail prices range from $1,500 to $2,200. However, for further information, contact Ransom directly (see Trademark Index).

R

RAREBIRD

Instruments currently built in Denver, Colorado since 1978. Distributed by the Rarebird Guitar Laboratory of Denver, Colorado.

Luthier Philip Bruce Clay apprenticed in a small Denver repair shop from 1974 to 1976, where he learned the basics of guitar repair. Later, he attended the Guitar Research and Design Center in Vermont (under the direction of Charles Fox), and graduated in February of 1978.

The **Rarebird** concept has been to build a durable, high quality instrument ever since opening his shop. Custom options are virtually limitless with over 50 species of hardwood on hand, and Clay's 20-plus years of experience can help guide the customer to the tones so desired. Clay's approach is to simply talk the customer through the different options, systematically explaining the combinations. Having built over 1,200 instruments since 1978, Clay is celebrating his 20th Anniversary since Rarebird was established.

Noted **Rarebird** features are multi-laminate necks and graphite reinforcements for stability, heelless bodies - either neck-through or set-in (glued in) for sustain and complete access, and semi-hollow guitar designs to achieve a rich and full balanced tone.

Ramtrak Guitar and Pickup Modules
courtesy Ramtrak Guitars

RAVER

Instruments previously produced in Japan during the mid 1970s.

These very entry level solid body guitars featured 2 pickups - which leads one to ask *why two*? when costs are being cut everywhere else in the overall design.

(Source: Tony Bacon and Paul Day, The Guru's Guitar Guide)

REBETH

Instruments previously built in England during the early 1980s.

Luthier Barry Collier built a number of custom guitars during the early 1980s, and has a strong eye for original designs.

(Source: Tony Bacon, The Ultimate Guitar Book)

REDONDO

See chapter on House Brands.

This trademark has been identified as a *House Brand* of the Tosca Company.

(Source: Willie G. Moseley, Stellas & Stratocasters)

REDWING GUITARS

Instruments currently produced in St. Albans, United Kingdom.

Luthier Patrick Eggle (of Patrick Eggle Guitars fame) left his namesake company in 1994. He continues to focus on high quality solid body electric guitars that feature his original designs.

ELECTRIC

Current models like the **Tornado Signature** and **Ventura Signature** feature alder bodies with figured maple tops, bird's-eye maple necks, Jim Cairnes pickups, Schaller tuners, and Wilkinson bridges. For further information regarding pricing and specifications, please contact luthier Patrick Eggle directly (see Trademark Index).

REEDMAN

Instruments currently built in Korea. Distributed by Reedman America of Whittier, California.

The Reedman Musical Instrument company is currently offering a wide range of good quality acoustic, acoustic/electric, and solid body electric guitars. For further information, please contact Reedman America directly (see Trademark Index).

RELLOG

See MUSIMA.

Instruments previously built in East Germany in the late 1950s to early 1960s.

Instruments with the Rellog brand name were built by the Musima company in Germany during the late 1950s on. Earlier models were available in original designs of both solid body and semi-hollow body configurations through the early 1960s.

(Source: Tony Bacon and Paul Day, The Guru's Guitar Guide)

RENAISSANCE

Instruments previously produced in Malvern, Pennsylvania from 1977 to 1980.

Renaissance guitars was founded by John Marshall, Phil Goldberg, and Dan Lamb in the late 1970s. Marshall, who played guitars in a number of local bands in the 1960s, was friends with local luthier Eric Schulte. Schulte, a former apprentice of Sam Koontz (Harptone and Standel guitars) taught Marshall guitar-building skills. In 1977, Marshall began gathering together information and building jigs, and received some advice from Augustino LoPrinzi on a visit to New Jersey. Goldberg was then a current owner of a northern Delaware music store, and Lamb was a studio guitarist with prior experience from Musitronics (the effects company that built Mu-tron and Dan Armstrong modules). A number of wooden guitar and bass prototypes were built after the decision to use Plexiglass was agreed upon.

In 1979, the then-fledgling company was experiencing financial troubles. Marshall left the company, and a new investor named John Dragonetti became a shareholder. Unfortunately, the company's financial position, combined with the high cost of production, did not provide any stability. Renaissance guitars closed down during the fall of 1980.

In a related sidenote, one of the Renaissance employees was guitarist/designer Dana Sutcliffe. Sutcliffe went on to form his Dana Guitar Design company, and was involved in guitar designs for St. Louis Music's Alvarez line in 1990. One awarding-winning model was the *Dana Scoop* guitar, which won the Music Retailer's *Most Innovative* award in 1992.

(Source: Michael Wright, Guitar Stories Volume One)

Production is estimated to be around 300 to 330 instruments built in the three years. Serialization for Renaissance instruments has one (or two) digits for the month, two following digits for the year, and the remainder of the digits indicating consecutive production (thus, *M(M)YYXXXX*).

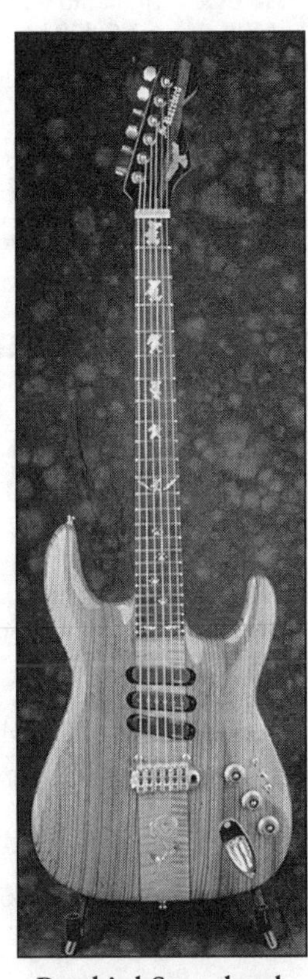

Rarebird Stratohawk
courtesy Bruce Clay

R

ELECTRIC

Renaissance instruments were constructed from either greyish "Bronze", Clear, or "See Through" Black Plexiglass. Necks were built of laminated maple, with ebony fingerboards and brass position markers. The 3-per-side (2-per-side for bass) headstocks had Schaller tuning machines; the instruments featured DiMarzio pickups, a brass nut and bridge, and an active circuit designed by Dan Lamb and Hank Zajac.

The original 1979 product line consisted of the **Model SPG** single cutaway guitar (list $725), the **Model SPB** single cutaway bass with 2 P-Bass DiMarzios (list $750), and the **Model DPB** double cutaway bass with 1 P-Bass DiMarzio (list $625).

A smaller number of pointy horn double cutaway basses and guitars were later developed (**S-100G or B, S-200B, T-100B, and T-200G**).

RENAISSANCE GUITAR COMPANY

Instruments currently built in Santa Cruz, California.

Renaissance Guitars are built by luthier Rick Turner, one of the original three partners that formed Alembic in 1970. In 1978 he left Alembic to form Turner Guitars, and opened a workshop in 1979 in Novato, California. Although artists such as Lindsey Buckingham favored Turner's guitars, the company was closed in 1981. Turner's records show that approximately 130 instruments were built during that time period (1979-1981).

Rick Turner is well-known and respected for his innovative designs that often times utilize a retro style with state of the art construction, materials, and most importantly, his proprietary electronics, which give amazing results. As well as building instruments, Rick Turner has written countless columns on guitar building, repairs, and products profiles in guitar magazines. Turner reopened his guitar shop in 1989, and now offers a range of instruments, under both the Renaissance and Ricker Turner trademarks.

AMPLI-COUSTIC & ELECTRIC

Renaissance Series

The Renaissance series is completed in a semi-hollowbody fashion: the solid Cedar top is glued to a neck extension that runs the length of the rosewood of mahogany body. This design also features the Turner "Reference Piezo" 18-volt system.

Add $450 for New Zealand Paua abalone purfling with contrasting top stripes.

Add $250 for New Zealand Paua abalone purfling on non-slotted pegheads.

RENAISSANCE "AMPLI-COUSTIC" STEEL STRING RS-6 - cedar top with clear poly finish, bolt-on maple neck, walnut or cherry sides/back, Turner designed piezo bridge pickup with 18-volt Highlander pre-amp, low noise, volume and tone controls. Current Mfg.

MSR $1,920

This model is also available in a baritone version with 27 in. scale at no extra charge (Model RS-6B).

RS-6-B - similar to the RS-6, except is baritone. Current Mfg.

MSR $1,920

RS-12 - similar to the RS-6, except is 12-string. Current Mfg.

MSR $2,130

RS-12-B - similar to the RS-12, except is baritone. Current Mfg.

MSR $2,130

RN-6 - similar to RS-6, except is nylon string with bolt-on mahogany neck. Current Mfg.

MSR $1,970

RN-6-H - similar to the RN-6, except has hybrid steel/nylon with slim 14-fret mahogany neck, slot head, and Thomastik/Infeld ropecore strings. Current Mfg.

MSR $2,040

RENAISSANCE STEEL STRING (RSS-1) - cedar top, mahogany laminate back and sides, bound in black, mahogany neck with adjustable truss rod, 24-fret rosewood fingerboard (joins body at 14th fret), 25 21/32" scale, Paua shell dot inlays and side dots, Turner "Reference Piezo" system, 18-volt Highlander Audio buffer electronics, one volume knob. Natural finish. Disc 1998.

Last MSR was $1,675.

RSS-2 - similar to the RSS-1, except features a Rosewood laminate back and sides, ebony fingerboard, Tortoise celluloid binding with half-herringbone purfling around top, multiple veneer overlays on peghead. Disc. 1998.

Last MSR was $2,050.

RENAISSANCE NYLON STRING (RNS-1) - similar to the RSS-1, except rosewood neck width at nut is 2" or 1 7/8", and Paua shell side dots only. Disc. 1998.

Last MSR was $1,650.

RNS-2 - similar to the RNS-1, except features a Rosewood laminate back and sides, ebony fingerboard, Tortoise celluloid binding with half-herringbone purfling around top, multiple veneer overlays on peghead. Disc. 1998.

Last MSR was $2,100.

GRADING	100% MINT	98% NEAR MINT	95% EXC+	90% EXC	80% VG+	70% VG	60% G

Model T series

MODEL T - a new series designed in 1996, with the blues or bottleneck player in mind, the Model T is a modern recreation of the early 1930s George Beauchamp/Paul Barth "double horseshoe" magnetic "Rick" pickup featuring Alnico magnets, affixed to a solid Honduran mahogany or American Swamp Ash (disc.) body that has a colorful front and back laminate of Formica Color-Core. The hard rock maple bolt-on neck features an adjustable truss rod and double graphite reinforcing, and is designed for heavier strings. Though the design screams retro, the hardware is quite modern, including a Wilkinson stop bridge/tailpiece, and Schaller nickel roller bridge. Options include the Wilkinson GTB 100 combination bridge; or Bigsby and Schaller "tune-o-matic" roller bridge combined with either a Turner Bar tailpiece, Bigsby vibrato, or the Hipshot Trilogy (multiple tunings) tailpiece. Standard colors include Rosetta Boomerang, Arctic White, Black, Ferrari Red, and Hawaiian Blue.

MSR $1,500

Add $180 for Bigsby and Schaller roller bridge.

Add $240 with Hipshot Trilogy multi-tuning tailpiece.

Renaissance Ampli-Coustic courtesy Renaissance

ELECTRIC BASS

Electroline Series

Electroline basses feature exotic wood, bolt-on necks, reinforcing graphite bars, and Turner-designed pickups and electronics.

ELECTROLINE 1 - swamp Ash or Honduran mahogany body, bolt-on bird's eye maple neck, fretless Ebony or Pakka wood fingerboard, 34" scale, Wilkinson bridge with Turner Reference Piezo pickups, Schaller or Hipshot Ultra-lite tuning machines, on-board Highlander Audio electronics, multiple veneer overlays on peghead. Available in Vintage Clear, Translucent Maroon, Indigo, or Forest Green. Current Mfg.

MSR $2,190

Add $240 for 5-string configuration (Model EL-15).

ELECTROLINE 2 - similar to the Electroline 1, except features a 21-fret fretted neck, Turner "Diamond T" magnetic pickup system, and blending electronics. Current Mfg.

MSR $2,430

Add $240 for 5-string configuration (Model EL-25).

Add $90 for Gold, Silver Flake, or 3-Tone Sunburst custom color.

Renaissance Bass Ampli-Coustic Series

Add $450 for New Zealand Paua abalone purfling with contrasting top stripes.

Add $250 for New Zealand Paua abalone purfling on non-slotted pegheads.

RENAISSANCE RB-4-FRETTED/FRETLESS BASS - cedar top, maple neck with graphite reinforcement, walnut or cherry sides/back. Current Mfg.

MSR $2,040

RENAISSANCE RB-5 FRETTED/FRETLESS BASS - similar to RB-4, except is 5-string. Current Mfg.

MSR $2,215

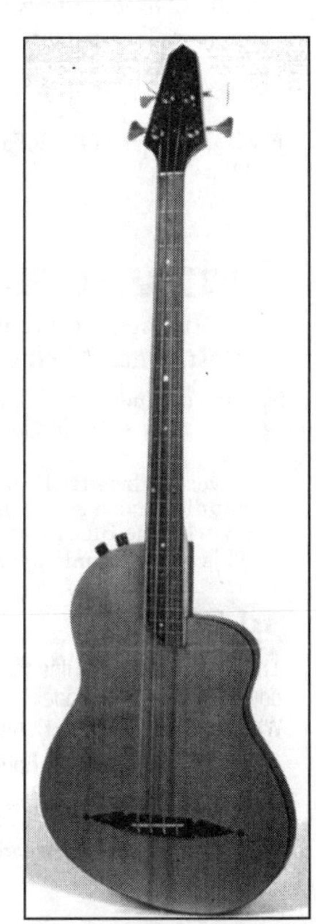

Renaissance Ampli-Coustic Bass courtesy Renaissance

RENO, G.H.

Instruments previously built in Tulsa, Oklahoma.

Gerald H. Reno spent 10 years making a name for himself in the guitar field. In 1984, Jerry, already a working guitarist in Tulsa, Oklahoma, set out to produce his own line of custom built guitars. His idea was a better feeling, playing, and sounding guitar "geared to the experienced player". The modest guitar shop grew into a 4,000 square foot factory, just off the famed Route 66 in Tulsa, Oklahoma.

Standard features on G.H. Reno guitar models consisted of hard rock maple necks, select maple and pau ferro rosewood fingerboards, and hand-wound tuned pickups. Updated features included the 'Glo-Dot' side markers, Sperzel tuners, and 'Single Barrel' or 'Double Barrel' pickups.

ELECTRIC

G.H. Reno guitars were available in Burnt Orange, Light Blue, Light Green, Medium Blue, Metallic Gold, Orange, Transparent Purple, Transparent Blue, and White finishes. Custom colors and other options (like select wood tops, and custom inlays) were also available.

GRADING	100% MINT	98% NEAR MINT	95% EXC+	90% EXC	80% VG+	70% VG	60% G

The Honky Tonk (Last MSR - $1,700) has a single cutaway body style geared for the professional country player, while the Hideaway (Last MSR - $1,700) has an alder body, 3 single coil pickups, and a 4/2 tuners per side headstock. The Rebel is similar to the Hideaway model, except features 2 humbucking pickups (Last MSR - $1,795).

The company also crafted the Twister bass (Last MSR - $1,900). This model has a Northern ash and alder body, bolt-on maple neck, 3/1 tuners per side (or 3/2) headstock, and custom Bartolini pickups. This model was also offered in a doubleneck configuration as the Twister Doubleneck Bass (Last MSR - $3,400).

RESURRECTION GUITARS

Instruments currently built in Jensen Beach, Florida since 1994.

In addition to building custom instruments of every conceivable type, Luthiers Pat O'Donnell and Tim O'Donnell also offer their own line of standard guitars that are true workhorses. The Standard line of guitars starts with The Barebones at $1500, the Standard at $1850, the Stereo Thin Line at $2250 and the Tulip Hollow Body at $3200. Their custom instruments all feature a laminated neck and a plethora of woods to choose from...achieving an amazing sounding instrument and a work of art. Resurrection Guitars has gained a notable reputation for the quality repair work thay have been doing for 15 years.

Resurrection Guitars is authorized by Pete Cripe to build exact replicas of the Jerry Garcia "Lightning Bolt" guitar (which was built for Jerry by Pete's son, the late Steve Cripe). These guitars are available by custom order, and only a very limited number will be obtainable.

REVELATION

Also HSS REVELATION.

Instruments previously built in Czechoslovakia from 1993 to 1996. Distributed by Hohner/HSS, Inc., of Richmond, Virginia.

Revelation series guitars featured designs formulated by the *Hohner Guitar Research Team*, an international group consisting of English, French, German, and U.S. luthiers. Continuing that international flavor, the guitar model itself features European and Indian woods, English pickups, German tuners, American tremolo system/roller nut, and was produced in Czechoslokavia!

ELECTRIC

Both Revelation models feature an on board ATN (Advanced Tonal Network) passive electronic system that is engaged at the push/pull tone switch. In bypass, the signal travels from the pickups to the volume control then directly to the output jack. In active, the signal travels from the pickups to volume to 2 tone controls (then on to the output jack). Tone control 1 is a treble roll-off, while Tone control 2's center detent offers treble cut or pickup resonance.

Revelation Series

RTS - sleek offset double cutaway poplar body, bolt-on maple neck, 25 1/2" scale, 24-fret rosewood fingerboard with offset pearl dot inlay, Wilkinson VS100 tremolo, Wilkinson roller nut, 6-on-a-side Schaller M6 tuners, 3 Entwistle-White single coil pickups, black pickguard, volume/2 tone controls (1 is push/pull), 5-way selector, ATN passive electronic system. Available in Black, Marble Red, Marble White, Red, Sunburst, Transparent Blue, Transparent Honey and Transparent Red polyurethane finishes. Mfg. 1993 to 1996.

$500	$450	$390	$325	$275	$250	$200

Last MSR was $899.

RTX - similar to the RTS, except has middle and bridge pickups in humbucker configuration, 3-way switch, active tone electronics. Mfg. 1993 to 1996.

$525	$475	$425	$325	$275	$250	$200

Last MSR was $899.

REVEREND

Instruments currently built in Eastpointe, Michigan from 1997 to date. Distributed by Reverend Musical Instruments of Eastpointe, Michigan.

Joe Naylor, cofounder of J.F. Naylor Engineering (Naylor Amps) formed Reverend Musical Instruments in March, 1997 to produce American-made, vintage style guitars. Naylor, a graduate of the Roberto-Venn School of Luthiery in 1987, has been designing and custom building guitars for the past ten years.

Reverend briefly offered the Black Cat model, which was similar to the Avenger model. The Black Cat differed in that it had no arm rest, but did have a solid white pickguard, single coil/humbucker pickup combination, volume control (no tone control, and 3-way selector switch. The Black Cat was available in Jet Black finish only (hence the name), and had a retail list price of $598.
This model is only available with a rosewood fingerboard.

ELECTRIC

The **Reverend** guitar line features a wood-based phenolic top and back mated to a six inch wide white mahogany center block (total weight is only 6 1/2 pounds). Reverend models are finished with whitewall sides and *Reflecto-Hyde* tops and backs; this super tough finish is available in '57 Turquoise, Aged White, Fire Engine Red, Hunter Green, Indigo Blue, and Jet Black finishes.

Add $15 for maple fingerboard.

Add $69 for fulcrum tremolo.

Add $70 for Sperzel locking tuners.

R

GRADING	100% MINT	98% NEAR MINT	95% EXC+	90% EXC	80% VG+	70% VG	60% G

AVENGER - slightly offset double cutaway semi-hollow body, *Reflecto-Hyde* phenolic top and back, bolt-on satin finished maple neck, 25 1/2" scale, 22-fret rosewood fingerboard with white dot inlay, fixed bridge, chrome hardware, whitewall sides, white pearloid pickguard, chrome plated arm rest, six on a side sealed die-cast tuners, 3 Kent Armstrong single coil pickups, volume/tone controls, 5-way selector. Available in '57 Turquoise, Aged White (with Tortoiseshell pickguard), Fire Engine Red, Hunter Green, Indigo Blue, and Jet Black. Mfg. 1997 to date.

MSR $899	$719	$650	$595	$550	$495	$450	$375

The Jet Black finish is optional with a Tortoiseshell pickguard.

Avenger GT - similar to the Avenger, except has chrome covered humbucker in the bridge position, coil tap. Mfg. 1997-1999.

Last MSR was $859.

COMMANDO - similar to the Avenger, except has chrome "lipstick tube" single coil/chrome covered humbucker pickups, humbucker coil tap mini switch, 3-way selector switch. Mfg. 1998 to date.

MSR $899	$719	$650	$595	$550	$495	$450	$375

HITMAN - Reverend tele-style bridge pickup, zebra neck humbucker with coil tap, 3-way pickup selector. Available in standard colors. Current Mfg.

MSR $899	$719	$650	$595	$550	$495	$450	$375

ROCCO - similar to the Avenger, except has 2 custom humbuckers with chrome pickup covers, 2 coil tap mini switches, 3-way selector switch. Mfg. 1997 to date.

MSR $899	$719	$650	$595	$550	$495	$450	$375

SLINGSHOT - similar to the Avenger, except has 2 creme colored P-90 pickups, 3-way selector switch. Mfg. 1998 to date.

MSR $899	$719	$650	$595	$550	$495	$450	$375

SPY - similar to the Avenger, except has 3 chrome "lipstick" tube pickups, solid white pickguard. Mfg. 1997 to date.

MSR $899	$719	$650	$595	$550	$495	$450	$375

Resurrection Steve Cripe
courtesy Resurrection

ELECTRIC BASS

RUMBLEFISH BASS - slightly offset double cutaway semi-hollow body, *Reflecto-Hyde* phenolic top and back, bolt-on satin finished maple neck, 34" scale, 21-fret rosewood fingerboard with white dot inlay, fixed bridge, chrome hardware, whitewall sides, white pearloid pickguard, chrome plated arm rest, four on a side sealed die-cast tuners, 2 Kent Armstrong J-style pickups, 2 volume/1 tone controls. Available in '57 Turquoise, Aged White (with Tortoiseshell pickguard), Fire Engine Red, Hunter Green, Indigo Blue, and Jet Black. Mfg. 1998 to date.

MSR $899	$719	$650	$595	$550	$495	$450	$375

The Jet Black finish is optional with a Tortoiseshell pickguard.

RUMBLEFISH XL BASS - similar to Rumblefish except has 1 Volume/1 Tone control, 3-position voicing switch (parallel, single coil, series). Current Mfg.

MSR $929	$735	$625	$550	$495	$450	$395	$350

RUMBLEFISH 5L BASS - 5 string, long scale version of the Rumblefish, with 2 Reverend J-style pickups, 21-fret 35 in. scale aluminum reinforced neck with rosewood fingerboard, lightweight construction. New 1999.

MSR $999	$799	$699	$650	$599	$550	$499	$425

REYNOLDS

Instruments currently built in Austin, Texas.

Luthier Ed Reynolds began repairing instruments in 1974 and then building in 1976. While based in Chicago, Illinois, Reynolds gained a reputation for being a quality repairman. In 1991, Reynolds relocated to Austin, Texas and has continued to build electric guitars and basses. For further information, contact luthier Ed Reynolds directly (see Trademark Index).

RIBBECKE, TOM

Instruments currently built in Healdsburg, California. Previously built in the Santa Rosa and the San Francisco bay area in California.

Luthier Tom Ribbecke has been building and repairing guitars and basses for over twenty three years in the San Francisco bay area. Ribbecke's first lutherie business opened in 1975 in San Francisco's Mission District, and remained open and busy for ten years. In 1985 Ribbecke closed down the storefront in order to focus directly on client commissions.

Resurrection Stereothinline
courtesy Resurrection

R

Ribbecke guitars are entirely hand built by the luthier himself, while working directly with the customer. Beyond his signature and serial number of the piece, Ribbecke also offers a history of the origin of all materials involved in construction.

All prices quoted are the base price new, and does not reflect additions to the commissioned piece. For further information, please contact luthier Tom Ribbecke directly (see Trademark Index).

ELECTRIC

THINLINE STYLE STANDARD (TESTADURA) - Instrument constructed of First Grade Domestic Maple or Rosewood back and sides, solid carved top and back, Ebony pickguard, carbon fiber braced, Master volume and tone controls, dot inlays, and chrome hardware. Available in Natural finish. Current production.

MSR $7,500

Add $400 for Sunburst finish.

Add $450 for wood body binding.

RICH, B.C.

Please refer to the B section of this text.

RICHELIEU

Instruments previously built in Bridgeport, Connecticut from 1982 to 1984.

The Richelieu company was founded by a pair of musicians to produce good quality guitars in their regional area. For a period of about three years, the Richelieu company produced customized neck-through-body **Spectre** guitars. Customers could specify various pickups and finishes. It has been confirmed that the company produced 75 guitars (and a few bass models). A second model, the **Black Rock**, had name badges but the model itself was never produced. Unfortunately, the company ran out of funds before the model design really took off.

Serial numbers are impressed into the back of the headstock.

(Source: David J. Pavlick, Woodbury, Connecticut)

ELECTRIC

Spectre guitars feature a neck-through design, and a Honduran mahogany body shaped roughly like a cross between an SG (dual pointy cutaways) and a Strat (rounded lower bout). Spectres feature a Gibson-esque 3-per-side headstock, chrome hardware, Leo Quan wraparound tailpiece, white pickguard, 2 humbuckers, volume and tone controls, 3-way toggle for pickup selection, and a coil tap mini-switch. Due to production problems with grain-matching the wood, most Spectre models had solid finishes (such as Blue/Gray, White, Purple, and various sparkle finishes) as opposed to a Natural wood finish.

Earlier models have a screened Richelieu logo on a black peghead, block print Spectre badge, one large toggle/one mini- toggle switches, Grover tuning pegs, and DiMarzio pickups.

Later models have a headstock decal that reads "Richelieu USA", an arrowhead-shaped Spectre truss rod cover, one large toggle/two mini-toggle switches, and Schaller tuners. The top cutaway was also opened up for easier playing access.

RICKENBACKER

Instruments currently produced in Santa Ana, California. Distributed by Rickenbacker International Corporation of Santa Ana, California. Rickenbacker instruments have been produced in California since 1931.

In 1925, John Dopyera (and brothers) joined up with George Beauchamp and Adolph Rickenbacker and formed National to build resonator guitars. Beauchamp's attitudes over spending money caused John Dopyera to leave National and start the Dobro company. While at National, Beauchamp, Rickenbacker and Dopyera's nephew, Paul Barth, designed the *Frying Pan* electric lap steel. In 1929 or 1930, Beauchamp was either forced out or fired from National - and so allied himself with Adolph Rickenbacker (National's tool and die man) and Barth to form **Ro-Pat-In**.

In the summer of 1931, Ro-Pat-In started building aluminum versions of the *Frying Pan* prototype. Early models have *Electro* on the headstock. Two years later, *Rickenbacker* (or sometimes *Rickenbacher*) was added to the headstock, and Ro-Pat-In was formally changed to the Electro String Instrument Corporation. Beauchamp left Electro sometime in 1940, and Barth left in 1956 to form his own company.

In December of 1953, F.C. Hall bought out the interests of Rickenbacker and his two partners. The agreement stated that the purchase was complete, and Electro could "continue indefinitely to use the trade name Rickenbacker." Hall, founder of Radio-Tel and the exclusive Fender distributor, had his Fender distributorship bought out by Leo Fender and Don Randall. The Rickenbacker company was formed in 1965 as an organizational change (Electro is still the manufacturer, and Rickenbacker is the sales company). Rickenbacker instruments gained popularity as the Beatles relied on a number of their guitars in the 1960s. One slight area of confusion: the model names and numbers differ from the U.S. market to models imported in to the U.K. market during the short period in the 1960s when Rose Morris represented Rickenbacker in the U.K (at all other times, the model numbers worldwide have been identical to the U.S. market).

In 1984 John Hall (F.C. Hall's son) officially took control by purchasing his father's interests in both the Rickenbacker, Inc. and Electro String companies. Hall formed the Rickenbacker International Corporation (RIC) to combine both interests.

(Source: John C. Hall, Chief Executive Officer, Rickenbacker International Corporation; and Tom Wheeler, American Guitar)

Rickenbacker currently offers the 5002V58 Mandolin, a vintage-style solid body electric mandolin based on a similar model issued in 1958. The current reproduction has a maple and walnut laminated body, 8-string configuration, and single coil pickups. Available in Fireglo or Mapleglo finishes (retail list is $1,489).

Export Model Designations

During the five years in the mid to late 1960s (1964-1969), Rickenbacker exported a handful of models to the Rose, Morris & Company, Ltd. in England for European sales. Many of the export models have a corresponding U.S. model, although the export hollow body models have f-holes rather than the *slash* hole (or none at all). Rickenbacker designated the export models with an *S* after the model number; Rose, Morris gave them a completely different number!

GRADING	100% MINT	98% NEAR MINT	95% EXC+	90% EXC	80% VG+	70% VG	60% G

Rickenbacker Model Rose, Morris Designation

325	**1996**
335	**1997**
336-12	**3262**
345	**1998**
360-12	**1993**
615	**1995**
4000	**1999**
4001	**1999**
4005	**3261**

For further information regarding Rickenbacker acoustic models, please refer to the 7th Edition ***Blue Book of Acoustic Guitars***.

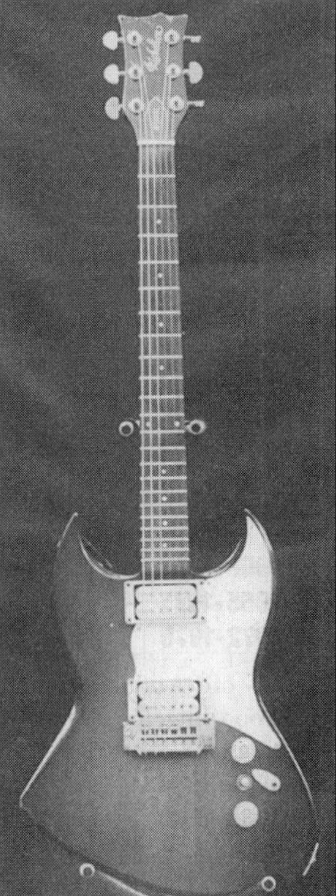

Richelieu Spectre
courtesy Todd Pavlick

ELECTRIC

Rickenbacker pegheads are generally of the same pattern and design. They have 3-per-side tuners and plastic, or metal, logo imprinted plates. Twelve string pegheads, while roughly similar to the six string pegheads, are not the same size and have 6 tuners (3-per-side) running parallel to the peghead face and 6 tuners running perpendicular with routed slots in the peghead face to accommodate string winding.

Most Rickenbacker instrument necks are maple (however, some are maple/shedua laminates). Pickguards and peghead plates are usually color matched, and controls are usually pickguard mounted (any differences will be listed where appropriate). Rickenbacker color finishes include Fireglo, Jetglo, Mapleglo, Midnight Blue, Red, Turquoise, and White. Midnight Blue, Red, and White finishes come standard with black hardware, binding, nameplate, and pickguard. Fireglo, Jetglo, Mapleglo, and Turquoise finishes come standard with chrome hardware, white binding, nameplate, and pickguard. The Vintage Reissue Series models are only available with chrome parts.

In 1964, Rickenbacker's **R** style trapeze tailpieces replaced all other trapeze tailpieces.

ELECTRO SPANISH - folk style, maple top, f-holes, bound body, maple back/sides/neck, 14/19-fret rosewood fingerboard with pearl dot inlay, rosewood bridge/trapeze tailpiece, pearl veneer on classic style peghead with metal logo plate, horseshoe pickup. Available in Stained finish. Mfg. 1932 to 1935.

$1,200 $1,050 $895 $725 $650 $595 $525

In 1934, body binding and volume control were added. This model was superseded by the Ken Roberts model.

KEN ROBERTS ELECTRO-SPANISH - concert style, laminated bound mahogany top, F holes, laminated mahogany back/sides, mahogany neck, 17/22-fret bound rosewood fingerboard with white dot inlay, compensating bridge/Kauffman vibrato tailpiece, pearloid peghead veneer with brass logo plate, 3-per-side tuners, nickel hardware, horseshoe pickup, volume control. Available in Two Tone Brown finish. Mfg. 1935 to 1940.

$750 $700 $650 $600 $500 $425 $375

From 1935-1937, the volume control was octagon shaped.
In 1938, round volume control with ridges replaced original parts/design.

200 Series

220 HAMBURG - double cutaway maple body, through-body maple neck, 24-fret rosewood fingerboard with pearloid dot inlay, fixed bridge, 3-per-side tuners, 2 humbucker pickups, 2 volume/2 tone controls, 3-position switch. Available in Fireglo, Jetglo, Mapleglo, Midnight Blue, Red and White finishes. Mfg. 1987 to 1995.

$675 $450 $325 $300 $275 $250 $225
Last MSR was $900.

260 EL DORADO - similar to 220, except has bound body/fingerboard, gold hardware. Disc. 1995.

$800 $525 $375 $350 $325 $275 $250
Last MSR was $1,050.

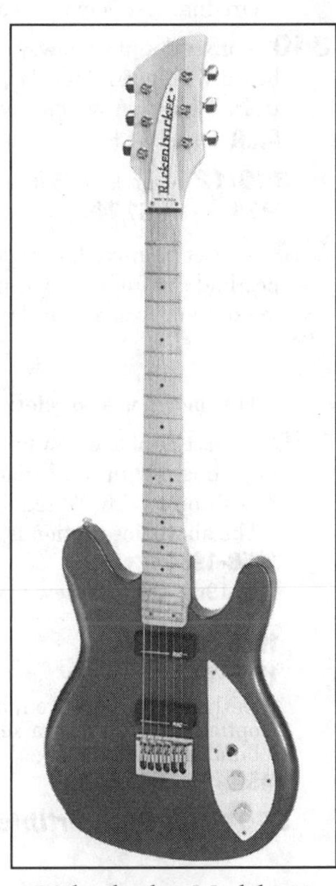

Rickenbacker Model 220
Hamburg
courtesy Rickenbacker

300 Series

This series utilizes a hollow body, white binding, inlaid fingerboard and Rick-o-Sound jacks. These are available in Fireglo or Natural Grain finish (unless otherwise indicated). The 300 Series has also been called the Capri Series.

310 - offset pointed double cutaway semi hollow 3/4 size maple body, 21-fret rosewood fingerboard with white dot inlay, tune-o-matic bridge/trapeze tailpiece, chrome hardware, 2 covered pickups, volume/tone control, 3-position switch. Available in Autumnglo, Fireglo, Mapleglo, Natural or Two-Tone Brown finishes. Mfg. 1958 to 1971. Reintroduced 1981 to 1988.

1958-1964	**$3,000**	**$2,575**	**$2,150**	**$1,725**	**$1,550**	**$1,425**	**$1,295**
1965-1971	**$2,000**	**$1,675**	**$1,950**	**$1,425**	**$1,250**	**$1,125**	**$1,000**

In 1963, a mixer control was added. Instruments were inconsistently produced with and without f-holes.
The 310 model was reintroduced between 1981 to 1988.

1981-1988	**$500**	**$475**	**$425**	**$400**	**$350**	**$300**	**$275**

R

GRADING		100% MINT	98% NEAR MINT	95% EXC+	90% EXC	80% VG+	70% VG	60% G

315 - similar to 310, except has Kauffman vibrato. Mfg. 1958 to 1975.

1958-1964		$3,000	$2,575	$2,150	$1,725	$1,550	$1,425	$1,295
1965-1969		$2,000	$1,675	$1,950	$1,425	$1,250	$1,125	$1,000
1970-1975		$500	$475	$425	$400	$350	$300	$275

320 - offset pointed double cutaway semi hollow 3/4 size maple body, bi-level pickguard, through-body maple neck, 21-fret rosewood fingerboard with pearloid dot inlay, tune-o-matic bridge/R-style trapeze tailpiece, 3-per-side tuners, chrome hardware, 3 chrome bar pickups, 2 volume/2 tone/mix controls, 3-position switch. Available in Fireglo, Jetglo, Mapleglo, Midnight Blue, Red and White finishes. Mfg. 1958 to 1994.

1958-1964		$5,000	$4,375	$4,275	$3,725	$3,050	$2,625	$2,495
1965-1971		$3,500	$3,100	$2,650	$2,225	$2,050	$1,925	$1,725
1972-1994		$800	$675	$575	$450	$400	$375	$325

Last MSR was $1,000.

325 - similar to 320, except has Kauffman vibrato. Available in Fireglo, Mapleglo, Natural or Two-Tone Brown finishes. Mfg. 1958 to 1975.

1958-1964		$6,000	$5,295	$4,575	$3,850	$3,575	$3,350	$3,200
1965-1971		$4,500	$3,795	$3,100	$2,350	$2,075	$1,850	$1,650
1972-1975		$800	$695	$575	$450	$400	$375	$325

330 - offset double cutaway semi hollow maple body, wedge-shaped soundhole, bi-level pickguard, through-body maple neck, 24-fret rosewood fingerboard with pearl dot inlay, tune-o-matic bridge/R-style trapeze tailpiece, 3-per-side tuners, 2 single coil pickups, 2 volume/2 tone/mix controls, 3-position switch. Available in Fireglo, Jetglo, Mapleglo, Midnight Blue, Red and White finishes. Mfg. 1958 to date.

1958-1964		$2,000	$1,650	$1,295	$1,050	$995	$875	$775
1965-1984		$1,000	$925	$875	$800	$725	$675	$550
MSR	$1,419	$1,100	$895	$775	$650	$595	$450	$350

In 1963, a mixer control was added.

330/12 - similar to 330, except has 12-strings, 6-per-side tuners. Mfg. 1965 to date.

1965-1974		$1,300	$1,100	$925	$725	$650	$575	$525
1975-1985		$1,100	$975	$825	$750	$675	$550	$475
1986-1996		$1,000	$895	$800	$675	$600	$525	$425
MSR	$1,529	$1,250	$975	$795	$675	$595	$475	$375

331 - similar to 330, except has Plexiglass top with frequency controlled flashing lights. Mfg. 1970 to 1975.

		$6,000	$5,500	$4,850	$4,250	$3,650	$2,975	$2,450

Originally, this model was released with an external power supply box. This model is nicknamed the Light Show.

340 - offset double cutaway semi hollow maple body, wedge soundhole, bi-level pickguard, through-body maple neck, 24-fret rosewood fingerboard with pearl dot inlay, tune-o-matic bridge/R-style trapeze tailpiece, 3-per-side tuners, 3 single coil pickups, 2 volume/2 tone/mix controls, 3-position switch. Available in Fireglo, Jetglo, Mapleglo, Midnight Blue, Red and White finishes. Mfg. 1994 to date.

MSR	$1,549	$1,195	$995	$850	$750	$625	$500	$400

340/12 - similar to 340, except has 12-strings, 6-per-side tuners. Mfg. 1994 to date.

MSR	$1,749	$1,295	$1,100	$950	$795	$675	$550	$450

350 - offset pointed double cutaway semi hollow maple body, bi-level pickguard, through-body maple neck, 24-fret rosewood fingerboard with pearloid dot inlay, tune-o-matic bridge/R-style trapeze tailpiece, 3 chrome bar pickups, 2 volume/2 tone/mix controls, 3-position switch, stereo output. Available in Fireglo, Jetglo, Mapleglo, Midnight Blue, Red and White finishes. Mfg. 1985 to 1995.

		$950	$725	$575	$450	$400	$350	$325

Last MSR was $1,270.

This model is also referred to as the 350 Liverpool.

360 - offset double cutaway semi hollow maple body, wedge-shaped soundhole, pickguard, through-body maple neck, 21-fret bound rosewood fingerboard with pearl triangle inlay, tune-o-matic bridge/R-style trapeze tailpiece, 2 single coil pickups, 2 volume/2 tone diamond controls, 3-position switch. Wired for stereo. Available in Autumnglo, Black, Fireglo, Natural and Two Tone Brown finishes. Mfg. 1958 to date.

The above description is referred to as the Old Style which ran from 1958-1964:

1958-1964		$3,000	$2,500	$2,000	$1,500	$1,300	$1,150	$1,000

In 1964, the 360 New Style was released and featured an unbound rounded top, bound soundhole and checkered body binding which ran from 1964-1990:

1965-1974		$1,250	$1,100	$895	$650	$525	$475	$395
1975-1990		$850	$725	$575	$525	$495	$450	$400

In the early 1960s, round control knobs and bi-level pickguards began replacing original parts/designs. In 1960, stereo output became optional. In 1963, a mixer control was added. When the model 360 was reissued, the current model has no body binding or slash f-hole binding. Current Mfg.

MSR	$1,549	$1,250	$995	$875	$725	$625	$550	$450

360 6/12 Convertible - 12-string, unique string damping device allows convertible operation from 12 to 6 string.

		$1,850	$1,650	$1,450	$1,200	$995	$850	$725

R

GRADING		100% MINT	98% NEAR MINT	95% EXC+	90% EXC	80% VG+	70% VG	60% G

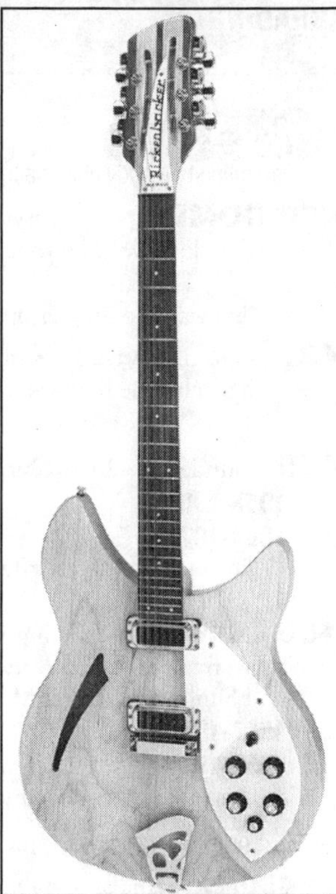
Rickenbacker Model 330/12 courtesy Rickenbacker

360/12 - similar to 360, except has 12-strings, 6-per-side tuners.

		100%	98%	95%	90%	80%	70%	60%
1965-1974		**$1,800**	**$1,525**	**$1,275**	**$1,050**	**$900**	**$825**	**$750**
1975-1990		**$800**	**$675**	**$550**	**$495**	**$450**	**$400**	**$350**

When the model 360/12 was reissued, the current model has no body binding or slash f-hole binding. Current Mfg.

		100%	98%	95%	90%	80%	70%	60%
MSR	**$1,669**	**$1,350**	**$1,150**	**$975**	**$795**	**$675**	**$550**	**$450**

360 WB (365 or 360 VB) - offset double cutaway semi hollow maple body, wedge-shaped soundhole, pickguard, through-body maple neck, 21-fret bound rosewood fingerboard with pearl triangle inlay, tune-o-matic bridge/trapeze tailpiece, 2 single coil pickups, 2 volume/2 tone diamond controls, 3-position switch. Available in Autumnglo, Black, Fireglo, Natural and Two Tone Brown finishes. Mfg. 1958 to 1995.

		100%	98%	95%	90%	80%	70%	60%
1958-1964		**$3,000**	**$2,500**	**$2,000**	**$1,500**	**$1,300**	**$1,150**	**$1,000**
1965-1984		**$1,250**	**$1,235**	**$825**	**$600**	**$525**	**$475**	**$395**
1985-1990		**$700**	**$675**	**$600**	**$525**	**$475**	**$400**	**$375**
		$995	**$675**	**$595**	**$475**	**$425**	**$395**	**$350**

Last MSR was $1,320.

In 1985, this model was reintroduced as 360 VB featuring Old Style body, high gain pickups and R-style tailpiece. In 1991, this model was renamed the 360 WB.

360/12 WB - similar to 360WB, except has 12-strings, 6-per-side tuners. Disc. 1995.

		100%	98%	95%	90%	80%	70%	60%
1958-1963		**$5,200**	**$4,495**	**$3,775**	**$2,950**	**$2,750**	**$2,450**	**$2,250**
1964-1967		**$6,500**	**$5,795**	**$5,000**	**$4,350**	**$3,650**	**$2,900**	**$2,275**
1968		**$5,200**	**$4,495**	**$3,775**	**$2,950**	**$2,775**	**$2,450**	**$2,250**
		$1,150	**$775**	**$675**	**$525**	**$450**	**$400**	**$350**

Last MSR was $1,530.

See Model 365 description history, above.

370 - offset double cutaway semi hollow maple body, wedge-shaped soundhole, pickguard, through-body maple neck, 21-fret bound rosewood fingerboard with pearl triangle inlay, tune-o-matic bridge/R-style trapeze tailpiece, 3 single coil pickups, 2 volume/2 tone diamond controls, 3-position switch. Available in Autumnglo, Black, Fireglo, Natural and Two Tone Brown finishes. Mfg. 1958 to date.

		100%	98%	95%	90%	80%	70%	60%
1958-1964		**$3,000**	**$2,500**	**$2,000**	**$1,500**	**$1,300**	**$1,150**	**$1,000**
1965-1984		**$1,500**	**$1,225**	**$825**	**$600**	**$525**	**$475**	**$395**
1985-1990		**$700**	**$650**	**$600**	**$525**	**$475**	**$400**	**$350**
MSR	**$1,699**	**$1,300**	**$1,100**	**$925**	**$775**	**$650**	**$550**	**$475**

370/12 - similar to 370, except 12-strings, 6-per-side tuners. Current Mfg.

		100%	98%	95%	90%	80%	70%	60%
MSR	**$1,829**	**$1,450**	**$1,150**	**$995**	**$875**	**$695**	**$575**	**$500**

370 WB - similar to 370, except has tune-o-matic bridge/vibrato tailpiece. Mfg. 1994 to 1995.

		100%	98%	95%	90%	80%	70%	60%
		$1,250	**$925**	**$775**	**$625**	**$550**	**$500**	**$450**

Last MSR was $1,555.

370/12 WB - similar to 370, except has 12-strings, tune-o-matic bridge/vibrato tailpiece, 6-per-side tuners. Disc. 1995.

		100%	98%	95%	90%	80%	70%	60%
1958-1968		**$5,200**	**$4,495**	**$3,775**	**$2,950**	**$2,775**	**$2,450**	**$2,225**
		$1,250	**$825**	**$675**	**$525**	**$450**	**$400**	**$350**

Last MSR was $1,655.

380L LAGUNA - offset double cutaway semi-hollow walnut body, slash (wedge-shaped) soundhole, set-in maple neck, 24-fret maple fingerboard with black dot inlay, Rickenbacker fixed bridge, 3-per-side tuners, gold hardware, walnut/maple laminate headstock veneer, 2 humbucker pickups, 2 volume/2 tone controls, 3-position switch. Available in Oil finish. Current Mfg.

		100%	98%	95%	90%	80%	70%	60%
MSR	**$1,699**	**$1,295**	**$1,100**	**$950**	**$795**	**$675**	**$550**	**$425**

380L PZ Laguna - similar to the 380L Laguna, except has bridge-mounted piezo pickups, active electronics. Current Mfg.

		100%	98%	95%	90%	80%	70%	60%
MSR	**$1,999**	**$1,550**	**$1,250**	**$1,100**	**$950**	**$775**	**$650**	**$525**

381 - offset sharp double cutaway semi hollow maple body, carved top, white bi-level pickguard, checkered bound body, bound wedge-shaped soundhole, through-body maple neck, 21-fret bound rosewood fingerboard with pearl triangle inlay, tune-o-matic bridge/trapeze tailpiece, chrome hardware, 2 chrome bar pickups, 2 volume/2 tone/mix controls, 3-position switch. Available in Brownburst and Natural finishes. Mfg. 1958 to 1963.

		100%	98%	95%	90%	80%	70%	60%
1958-1964		**$5,000**	**$4,295**	**$3,575**	**$2,850**	**$2,575**	**$2,350**	**$2,150**
1965-1968		**$4,000**	**$3,450**	**$2,850**	**$2,295**	**$2,050**	**$1,895**	**$1,725**

Reintroduced late 1968 to 1974.

		100%	98%	95%	90%	80%	70%	60%
1969-1974		**$2,500**	**$2,000**	**$1,500**	**$1,300**	**$1,150**	**$1,000**	**$895**

The original run of this series, 1958-early 1960s, had single pickguards, 2 controls. Fingerboard inlay was both dot and triangle. There were also a number of variations that Rickenbacker produced, some with F shaped soundholes and some with vibratos.

R

GRADING	100% MINT	98% NEAR MINT	95% EXC+	90% EXC	80% VG+	70% VG	60% G

400 Series

The tulip style body shape acquired its nickname from the cutaways radiating out at a 45 degree angle, curving outwards to rounded point, then curving back.

400 COMBO - tulip style maple body, gold pickguard, through-body maple neck, 21-fret rosewood fingerboard with white dot inlay, covered pickup, volume/tone control, 2-position switch. Available in Blue Green, Golden and Jet Black finishes. Mfg. 1956 to 1958.

	$1,200	$1,050	$850	$695	$595	$500	$450

This was the first through-body neck construction that Rickenbacker manufactured. In 1957, an extra switch was added.

420 - cresting wave style maple body, white pickguard, through-body maple neck, 21-fret rosewood fingerboard with white dot inlay, fixed bridge, chrome hardware, chrome bar pickup, volume/tone control, 2-position switch. Available in Sunburst finish. Mfg. 1965 to 1984.

	$850	$725	$595	$500	$450	$400	$350

425 - similar to 420, except has vibrato. Mfg. 1958 to 1973.

1958-1963	$875	$725	$575	$500	$475	$425	$375
1964-1973	$450	$325	$275	$200	$175	$150	$125

This model replaced the 400 Combo. In 1965, the vibrato was added, at which time the 420 was introduced as the non-vibrato instrument in this style.

450 COMBO - cresting wave style maple body, white pickguard, through-body maple neck, 21-fret rosewood fingerboard with pearl dot inlay, fixed bridge, chrome hardware, 2 chrome bar pickups, 2 volume/2 tone controls, 3-position switch. Available in Black, Fireglo, Natural and Sunburst finishes. Mfg. 1957 to 1984.

1957-1958	$1,250	$1,000	$850	$700	$600	$525	$450
1959-1984	$700	$595	$525	$475	$425	$375	$295

This model was introduced with a tulip style body, metal pickguard, 2 controls and a rotary switch located on the upper treble bout. It was manufactured this way for one year. In 1958, the cresting wave body style was introduced. In 1966, the 4 controls were introduced. From 1962 to 1977, 3 pickups were optional.

450/12 - similar to 450, except has 12-strings, 6-per-side tuners. Mfg. 1964 to 1985.

	$600	$550	$500	$475	$400	$375	$325

460 - similar to 450, except has bound body, bound fingerboard with pearl triangle inlay, mixer control, mono output jack on pickguard. Available in Black, Fireglo, and Natural finishes. Mfg. 1961 to 1985.

	$750	$675	$625	$575	$525	$495	$450

This model is similar to the model 620 (which has stereo outputs), which may lead to some confusion and/or mis-identification of the proper model designation.

480 - cresting wave style maple body, white pickguard, bolt-on maple neck, 24-fret bound rosewood fingerboard with white dot inlay, covered tune-o-matic bridge/R style trapeze tailpiece, cresting wave style peghead, chrome hardware, 2 single coil exposed pickups, 2 volume/2 tone controls, 3-position switch. Mfg. 1973 to 1984.

	$350	$295	$250	$225	$200	$175	$150

481 - similar to 480, except has bound body, slanted frets, pearl triangle fingerboard inlay, 2 humbucker exposed pickups, phase switch. Mfg. 1973 to 1984.

	$350	$295	$250	$225	$200	$175	$150

483 - similar to the 481, except has three pickups.

	$350	$295	$250	$225	$200	$175	$150

600 Series

600 COMBO - offset double cutaway maple body, carved top, black pickguard, maple neck, 21-fret rosewood fingerboard with white dot inlay, fixed bridge, chrome hardware, single coil horseshoe pickup, volume/tone control, 2-position switch. Available in Blonde finish. Mfg. 1954 to 1959.

	$800	$725	$675	$625	$575	$525	$475

These instruments had both set and bolt-on necks. According to Rickenbacker's own records, there were apparently quite a few variations of this model. These models were on the price lists as having cresting wave style bodies until 1969, though none were ever produced.

610 - cresting wave style maple body, bi-level pickguard, through-body maple neck, 21-fret rosewood fingerboard with pearl dot inlay, tune-o-matic bridge/R-style trapeze tailpiece, 3-per-side tuners, 2 single coil pickups, 2 volume/2 tone/mix controls, 3-position switch. Available in Fireglo, Jetglo, Mapleglo, Midnight Blue, Red and White finishes. Mfg. 1987 to 1998.

	$750	$600	$475	$350	$275	$250	$200

Last MSR was $1,000.

610/12 - similar to 610, except has 12-strings, 6-per-side tuners. Disc. 1998.

	$825	$550	$420	$360	$330	$290	$250

Last MSR was $1,100.

615 (610 VB) - similar to 610, except has roller bridge/vibrato tailpiece, chrome hardware, 2 chrome bar pickups, 2 volume/2 tone controls. Available in Black, Fireglo and Natural finishes. Mfg. 1962 to 1977.

	$725	$595	$525	$495	$450	$400	$375

In 1985, this model was reintroduced as the 610 VB. Mfg. 1985 to 1990.

	$725	$575	$525	$475	$425	$395	$350

R

GRADING		100% MINT	98% NEAR MINT	95% EXC+	90% EXC	80% VG+	70% VG	60% G

620 - similar to 610, except has bound body, bound fingerboard with pearl triangle inlay, 2 single coil exposed pickups. Wired for stereo. Available in Fireglo, Jetglo, Mapleglo, Midnight Blue, Red and White finishes. Mfg. 1977 to date.

MSR	$1,299	$995	$795	$695	$575	$495	$400	$325

620/12 - similar to 620, except has 12-strings, 6-per-side tuners. Mfg. 1981 to date.

MSR	$1,419	$1,100	$875	$750	$650	$550	$450	$350

In 1989, the deluxe trim was replaced by standard trim.

625 (620 VB) - similar to 610, except has bound body, bound fingerboard with pearl triangle inlay, roller bridge/vibrato tailpiece, 2 chrome bar pickups. Available in Fireglo, Jetglo, Mapleglo, Midnight Blue, Red and White finishes. Mfg. 1977 to 1994.

		$475	$450	$425	$375	$325	$300	$250

Last MSR was $1,450.

In 1985, this model was reintroduced as the 620 VB (Mfg. 1985 to 1990).

650 COMBO - offset double sharp cutaway maple body, carved top, pickguard, maple neck, 21-fret rosewood fingerboard with white dot inlay, fixed bridge, single coil horseshoe pickup, volume control. Available in Natural and Turquoise Blue finishes. Mfg. 1957 to 1960.

		$1,100	$995	$825	$750	$595	$525	$450

In late 1957, a chrome bar pickup replaced the horseshoe pickup.

660 - cresting wave style figured ('charactered') maple body, checkered body binding, through-body maple neck, 21-fret bound rosewood fingerboard with pearl triangle inlay, tune-o-matic bridge/trapeze tailpiece, gold bi-level pickguard, gold peghead logoplate, 3-per-side tuners, chrome hardware, 2 vintage-style pickups, 2 volume/2 tone/mix controls, 3-position switch. Available in Fireglo and Jetglo finish. Mfg. 1998 to date.

MSR	$1,879	$1,400	$1,200	$1,100	$1,000	$850	$750	$600

660/12 - similar to the 660, except features 12-string configuration, 6-per-side tuners, 12 saddle bridge. Mfg. 1998 to date.

MSR	$1,999	$1,500	$1,300	$1,200	$1,100	$950	$850	$700

Rickenbacker Model 610
courtesy Rickenbacker

650 Series

All models in this series have a cresting wave style body, pickguard, maple through-body neck, 24-fret maple fingerboard with black dot inlay, fixed bridge, 3-per-side tuners, 2 humbucker pickups, 2 volume/2 tone/mix controls, 3-position switch. Available in Natural finish (unless otherwise listed). Mfg. 1991 to date.

650A ATLANTIS - maple body, 24-frets, chrome hardware and pickplate. Two humbucker pickups. Available in Vintage Turquoise finish only.

MSR	$1,299	$995	$795	$695	$575	$495	$400	$325

650C Colorado - walnut body, 24-frets, two humbucking pickups, chrome hardware and pickplate. Available in Jetglo Black finish only. Mfg. 1994 to date.

MSR	$1,299	$995	$795	$695	$575	$495	$400	$325

650D Dakota - walnut body, 24-frets, two humbucking pickups, walnut peghead laminate, chrome hardware and pickplate. Available in Natural Oil finish.

MSR	$999	$799	$650	$575	$495	$400	$325	$250

650F Frisco (650E Excaliber) - 24-frets, two humbucking pickups, African vermilion body, African vermilion peghead laminate, gold hardware. Available in Clear High Gloss finish.

MSR	$1,419	$1,100	$895	$775	$650	$525	$425	$350

650S Sierra - 24-frets, two humbucking pickups, solid walnut body, walnut peghead laminate, gold hardware. Available in Natural Oil finish.

MSR	$1,099	$895	$750	$625	$550	$450	$375	$275

800 Series

800 (COMBO) - offset double cutaway maple body, carved top, black pickguard, maple neck, 21-fret rosewood fingerboard with white dot inlay, fixed bridge, chrome hardware, double coil horseshoe pickup, 2 volume controls, 2 selector switches. Available in Blonde and Turquoise Blue finishes. Mfg. 1954 to 1959.

		$995	$850	$650	$595	$550	$495	$425

In 1957, the pickguard was enlarged and the controls were mounted on it, a chrome bar pickup replaced one of the "horseshoe" pickups, and Turquoise Blue finish became optional. This model was on the price list through 1969, though it was no longer available.

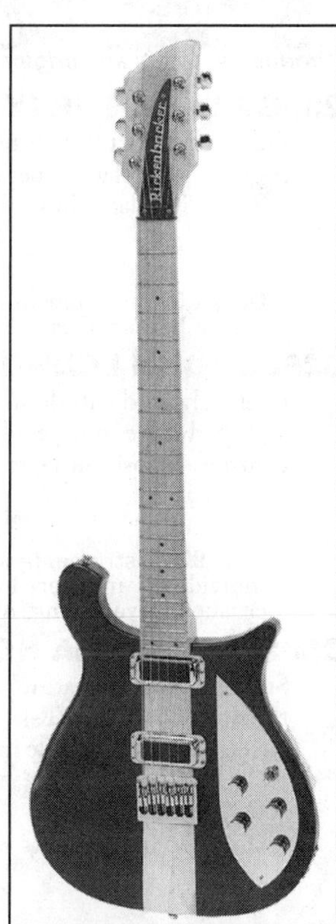

Rickenbacker Model 650 Atlantis
courtesy Rickenbacker

R

GRADING	100% MINT	98% NEAR MINT	95% EXC+	90% EXC	80% VG+	70% VG	60% G

850 COMBO - offset double sharp cutaway maple body, carved top, pickguard, maple neck, 21-fret rosewood fingerboard with white dot inlay, fixed bridge, double coil horseshoe pickup, volume/tone controls, 2 switches. Available in Natural and Turquoise Blue finishes. Mfg. 1957 to 1960.

	$1,295	$1,100	$875	$775	$700	$650	$600

In late 1957, the horseshoe pickup was replaced by a single coil horseshoe and chrome bar pickups. This model was on the price lists through 1967. There were several variations of this model that were made with 3 pickup designs or through-body neck constructions.

900 & 1000 Series

900 - tulip style 3/4 size maple body, white pickguard, through-body maple neck, 21-fret rosewood fingerboard with white dot inlay, fixed bridge, chrome hardware, single coil pickup, volume/tone control, 2-position switch. Available in Black, Brown, Fireglo, Gray and Natural finishes. Mfg. 1957 to 1980.

	$400	$350	$300	$275	$250	$225	$200

In 1958, a chrome bar pickup replaced the original pickup.
In 1961, Fireglo finish became optional. By 1974, cresting wave body style became standard.

950 - similar to 900, except has 2 pickups.

	$450	$400	$350	$325	$300	$275	$250

In 1958, a chrome bar pickup replaced the original pickup. In 1961, Fireglo finish became optional. By 1974, cresting wave body style became standard.

1000 - similar to 900, except has 18 fret fingerboard. Mfg. 1957 to 1971.

	$400	$350	$300	$275	$250	$225	$200

In 1958, a chrome bar pickup replaced the original pickup. In 1961, Fireglo finish became optional.

Export Series

Between 1964 to 1969, Rickenbacker exported a number of models to the Rose, Morris & Company, Ltd. in England for exclusive distribution in the U.K. and European sales. The export models have a corresponding U.S. model, although the export hollow body models have f-holes rather than the slash hole (or none at all).

1997 - offset double cutaway semi-hollow maple body, f-style soundhole, white bi-level pickguard, through-body maple neck, 21-fret rosewood fingerboard with pearl dot inlay, tune-o-matic bridge/trapeze tailpiece, 3-per-side tuners, chrome hardware, 2 pickups, 2 volume/2 tone/mix controls, 3-position switch. Available in Fireglo finish. 1964 to 1969.

1964-1969	$1,500	$1,295	$1,100	$875	$775	$700	$650

In 1966, Autumnglo finish was introduced. The 1997 export model corresponded to the U.S. 335 model.

Limited Edition Series

(Production totals and original list prices courtesy Rickenbacker)

230GF GLENN FREY LIMITED EDITION - (Series 200/2000 style) double cutaway maple body, chrome pickguard with Glenn Frey signature, through-body maple neck, 24-fret maple fingerboard (finished in Gloss Jet Black) with pearl dot inlay, fixed bridge, chrome peghead logo plate, 3-per-side tuners, black hardware, 2 humbucker pickups, chrome volume/tone control, 3-position mini switch. Available in Gloss Jet Black finish. Disc 2000.

	$950	$775	$650	$550	$495	$450	$395

Last MSR was $1,199.

Only 1,000 instruments were scheduled. Each instrument includes a Certificate of Authenticity signed by Glenn Frey. Price included a deluxe hardshell case.

325JL JOHN LENNON LIMITED EDITION - offset double cutaway semi-hollow 3/4 size Eastern rock maple body, white bi-level pickguard with John Lennon signature and graphic, through-body maple neck, 21-fret rosewood fingerboard with pearl dot inlay, tune-o-matic bridge/vintage vibrato, white peghead logoplate, 3-per-side tuners, chrome hardware, 3 vintage-style pickups, 2 volume/2 tone/mix controls, 3-position switch. Available in Jetglo finish. Mfg. 1990 to 1994.

	$1,400	$1,250	$995	$800	$695	$600	$550

Last MSR was $1,700.

Only 974 instruments were produced (953 Model 325JL, 21 Model 325JL LH left-handed configuration). Each instrument includes an individually numbered Certificate of Authenticity. This model was optional with vintage-style hardshell case with silver covering and crushed velvet lining. A total of 2,000 instruments from the John Lennon Series (models 325, 355, 355/12) were produced.

350SH SUSANNA HOFFS LIMITED EDITION - offset sharp double cutaway semi-hollow maple body, bi-level pickguard with Susanna Hoffs signature, checkered body binding, through-body maple neck, 24-fret bound rosewood fingerboard with pearl triangle inlay, tune-o-matic bridge/R-style trapeze tailpiece, 2 'chrome bar'/1 HB-1 humbucker pickups, 2 volume/2 tone/mix controls, 3-position switch, stereo output. Available in Jetglo finish. Mfg. 1988 to 1991.

	$600	$525	$435	$390	$350	$315	$275

Last MSR was $1,279.

Only 250 instruments were produced. Each instrument includes an individually numbered Certificate of Authenticity.

R

GRADING	100% MINT	98% NEAR MINT	95% EXC+	90% EXC	80% VG+	70% VG	60% G

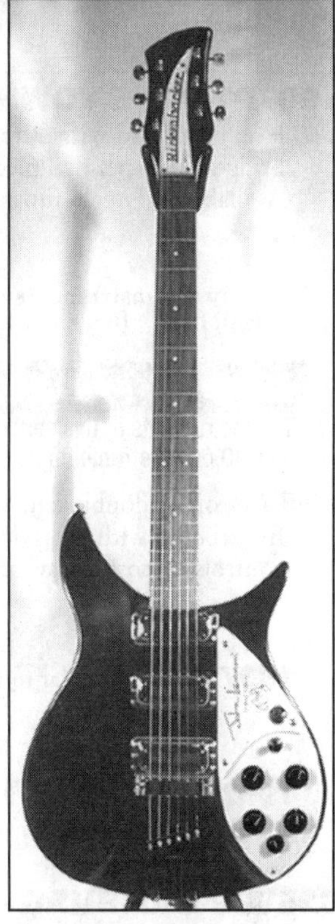

Rickenbacker John Lennon
courtesy John Beeson

355JL JOHN LENNON LIMITED EDITION - offset double cutaway semi-hollow Eastern rock maple body, white bi-level pickguard with John Lennon signature and graphic, through-body maple neck, 21-fret rosewood fingerboard with pearl dot inlay, tune-o-matic bridge/trapeze tailpiece, white peghead logoplate, 3-per-side tuners, chrome hardware, 3 vintage-style pickups, 2 volume/2 tone/mix controls, 3-position switch. Available in Jetglo finish. Mfg. 1990 to 1994.

$1,450 $1,250 $1,000 $875 $775 $700 $650
Last MSR was $1,730.

Only 691 instruments were produced (660 Model 355JL, 8 Model 355JL LH left-handed configuration, 23 Model 355JL VB). Each instrument includes an individually numbered Certificate of Authenticity. This model was optional with vintage-style hardshell case with silver covering and crushed velvet lining.

355/12JL John Lennon Limited Edition - similar to 355JL John Lennon, except has 12-string configuration, 6-per-side tuners. Mfg. 1990 to 1994.

$1,450 $1,250 $1,000 $875 $775 $700 $650
Last MSR was $1,830.

Only 334 instruments were produced (329 Model 355/12JL, 5 Model 355/12JL LH left-handed configuration). Each instrument includes an individually numbered Certificate of Authenticity. This model was optional with vintage-style hardshell case with silver covering and crushed velvet lining.

360CW CARL WILSON LIMITED EDITION - circa 1965 styling, 21-fret, checked binding, vintage pickups, vintage case.

MSR $1,999 $1,500 $1,250 $995

360/12CW CARL WILSON LIMITED EDITION 12-STRINGS - similar to 360CW except in a 12-string configuration.

MSR $2,149 $1,650 $1,350 $1,050

370/12RM ROGER McGUINN LIMITED EDITION - offset double cutaway semi-hollow maple body, bound wedge-shaped soundhole, bi-level pickguard with Roger McGuinn signature, checkered body binding, through-body maple neck, 21-fret bound rosewood fingerboard with pearl triangle inlay, tune-o-matic bridge/R-style trapeze tailpiece, 6-per-side tuners, chrome hardware, 3 vintage-style pickups, 2 volume/2 tone/mix controls, 3-position switch, customized circuitry. Available in Fireglo, Jetglo, and Mapleglo finishes. Mfg. 1988 only.

$1,500 $1,250 $1,075 $895 $775 $650 $525
Last MSR was $1,399.

Add 30% for models in mapleglo finish.

Models with the autographed certificate command a higher premium.

Only 1,000 instruments were produced. Each instrument includes an individually numbered Certificate of Authenticity. The first 250 certificates were signed by Roger McGuinn. This model was optional without the enhanced, customized electronics (retail list price $1,299).

381JK JOHN KAY LIMITED EDITION - double cutaway semi-hollow maple body, carved top/back, checkered body binding, bound wedge style soundhole, silver pickguard with John Kay signature and wolf head logo, through-body maple neck, 21-fret bound rosewood fingerboard with pearl triangle inlay, tune-o-matic bridge/R-style trapeze tailpiece, silver peghead logoplate, 3-per-side tuners, chrome hardware, 2 HB-1 humbucker pickups, 2 volume/2 tone/mix controls, 4-position/phase switches, active electronics, mono or stereo outputs. Available in Jetglo finish. Mfg. 1988 to 1997.

$1,350 $900 $595 $540 $500 $450 $395
Last MSR was $1,699.

Scheduled production amount unknown. Each instrument includes an individually numbered Certificate of Authenticity. Price included a hardshell luggage case.

660/12TP TOM PETTY LIMITED EDITION - cresting wave style figured Eastern rock maple body, checkered body binding, gold bi-level pickguard with Tom Petty signature, checkered body binding, through-body maple neck, 21-fret bound rosewood fingerboard with pearl triangle inlay, tune-o-matic bridge/trapeze tailpiece, gold pickguard, gold peghead logoplate, 6-per-side tuners, chrome hardware, 2 pickups, 2 volume/2 tone/mix controls, 3-position switch. Available in Fireglo and Jetglo finish. Mfg. 1991 to 1997.

$1,475 $1,175 $995 $875 $750 $625 $495
Last MSR was $1,849.

Only 1,000 instruments were produced (807 Model 660/12TP FG, 6 Model 660/12TP LH FG, 186 Model 660/12TP JG, 1 Model 660/12TP LH). Each instrument includes an individually numbered Certificate of Authenticity. Price included a Rickenbacker vintage case.

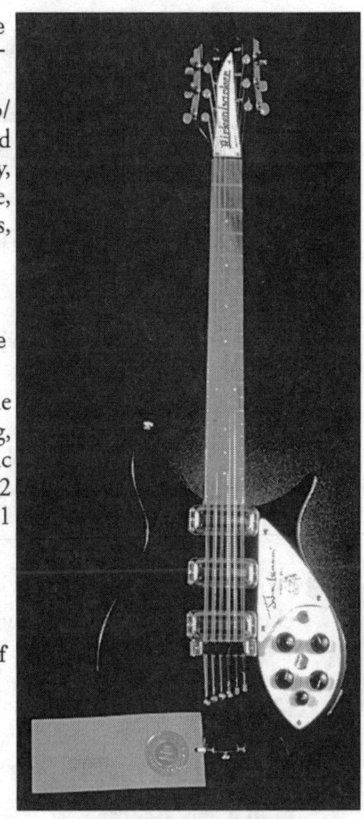

Rickenbacker 325 JL
(John Lennon)
courtesy Joe Chambers

GRADING	100% MINT	98% NEAR MINT	95% EXC+	90% EXC	80% VG+	70% VG	60% G

1997PT PETE TOWNSHEND LIMITED EDITION - offset double cutaway semi-hollow maple body, (violin) f-hole, white bi-level pickguard with Pete Townshend signature, through-body maple neck, 21-fret rosewood fingerboard with pearl dot inlay, tune-o-matic bridge/'R' trapeze tailpiece, 3-per-side tuners, chrome hardware, 3 vintage-style pickups, 2 volume/2 tone/mix controls, 3-position switch. Available in Fireglo finish. Mfg. 1987 only.

$1,500 $1,200 $1,000 $950 $875 $750 $675
Last MSR was $1,225.

Only 250 instruments produced. 1997PT models were individually numbered and came with a Certificate of Authenticity signed by John Hall (CEO, Rickenbacker).

Vintage Reissue Series

The instruments in this series are reproductions from the 1960s, using vintage-style pickups, hardware, and knobs. Rickenbacker typically produces more than 10,000 instruments per year since their debut in 1984. The Vintage Series models are produced in small production lots of 25 to 50 instruments.

1997 - offset double cutaway semi-hollow maple body, (violin) f-hole, white bi-level pickguard, through-body maple neck, 21-fret rosewood fingerboard with pearl dot inlay, tune-o-matic bridge/trapeze tailpiece, 3-per-side tuners, chrome hardware, 2 pickups, 2 volume/2 tone/mix controls, 3-position switch. Available in Fireglo, Jetglo, and Mapleglo finishes. Disc. 2000.

$1,300 $1,100 $895 $775 $650 $525 $475
Last MSR was $1,799.

1997 SPC - similar to 1997, except has 3 pickups. Mfg. 1993 to 2000.

$1,450 $1,100 $975 $850 $695 $550 $500
Last MSR was $1,949.

1997 VB - similar to 1997, except has vibrato tailpiece. Mfg. 1988 to 1995.

$750 $600 $550 $495 $450 $400 $350
Last MSR was $1,500.

325V59 HAMBURG - offset double cutaway semi hollow 3/4 size maple body, gold bi-level pickguard, through-body maple neck, 21-fret rosewood fingerboard with pearl dot inlay, tune-o-matic bridge/Bigsby vibrato tailpiece, 3-per-side tuners, chrome hardware, 3 pickups, 2 volume/2 tone controls, 3-position switch. Available in Jetglo and Mapleglo finishes. Mfg. 1991 to 2000.

$1,750 $1,300 $1,000 $895 $750 $600 $500
Last MSR was $2,069.

This model, a reproduction based on a similar model most popular in 1959, is actually derived from an earlier design.

325V63 MIAMI - similar to 325V59, except has white pickguard, vintage vibrato, 2 volume/2 tone/mix controls. Available in Jetglo finish. Disc. 2000.

$1,700 $1,275 $1,050 $875 $750 $600 $500
Last MSR was $2,069.

This model is derived from the 1959 revision of the Model 325.

350V63 LIVERPOOL - offset sharp double cutaway semi hollow maple body, bi-level pickguard, through-body maple neck, 21-fret rosewood fingerboard with pearloid dot inlay, tune-o-matic bridge/trapeze tailpiece, 3 chrome bar pickups, 2 volume/2 tone/mix controls, 3-position switch, stereo output. Available in Jetglo finish. Mfg. 1994 to present.

MSR $2,129 $1,750 $1,400 $1,150 $1,000 $875 $750 $525

This model is styled after the classic 325 series guitars.

350/12V63 Liverpool 12 - similar to 350V63, except has 12-strings, 6-per-side tuners. Mfg. 1994 to date.

MSR $2,249 $1,800 $1,500 $1,200 $1,000 $895 $775 $550

360V64 - offset double cutaway semi hollow bound maple body, wedge soundhole, white bi-level pickguard, through-body maple neck, 21-fret rosewood fingerboard with pearl triangle inlay, tune-o-matic bridge/trapeze tailpiece, 3-per-side tuners, chrome hardware, 2 pickups, 2 volume/2 tone/mix controls, 3-position switch. Available in Fireglo finish. Disc. 2000.

$1,450 $1,200 $995 $850 $695 $600 $500
Last MSR was $1,949.

This reproduction is based on the 1964 Deluxe 360 model.

360/12V64 - similar to 360V64, except has 12-strings, 6-per-side tuners. Available in Fireglo finish. Mfg. 1985 to 2000.

$1,500 $1,250 $1,050 $900 $750 $650 $550
Last MSR was $2,069.

381V69 - offset double cutaway semi hollow bound maple body, figured maple top/back, bound wedge soundhole, white bi-level pickguard, checkered bound body, through-body maple neck, 21-fret bound rosewood fingerboard with pearl triangle inlay, tune-o-matic bridge/R-style trapeze tailpiece, 3-per-side tuners, chrome hardware, 2 pickups, 2 volume/2 tone/mix controls, 3-position switch. Available in Fireglo, Jetglo and Mapleglo finishes. Mfg. 1987 to date.

MSR $2,859 $2,200 $1,850 $1,450 $1,250 $1,000 $875 $750

This model is derived from a design released in 1957.

381/12V69 - similar to 381V69, except has 12-strings, 6-per-side tuners. Mfg. 1989 to date.

MSR $2,999 $2,300 $1,900 $1,500 $1,300 $1,100 $900 $800

GRADING	100% MINT	98% NEAR MINT	95% EXC+	90% EXC	80% VG+	70% VG	60% G

C SERIES

325C58 HAMBURG - semi hollow body, 21-fret, short scale, 3 pickups, gold pickguard, Kauffman Vibrola. Vintage re-issue case included. Available in Mapleglo and Jetglo finishes. New 2001.

MSR $3,199	$2,400	$2,000	$1,600	$1,400	$1,100	$900	$750

325C64 MIAMI - semi hollow body, 21-fret, short scale, 3 pickups, RIC vibrato, white pickguard. Vintage re-issue case included. Available in Jetglo finish only. New 2001.

MSR $2,999	$2,250	$1,850	$1,450	$1,250	$1,000	$800	$650

360/12V63 - semi-acoustic, 21-frets, full scale, 2 pickups, trapeze tailpiece, double bound. Vintage re-issue case included. Available in Fireglo finish. New 2001.

MSR $3,199	$2,400	$2,000	$1,600	$1,400	$1,100	$900	$750

Double Neck Series

362/12 - offset double cutaway semi hollow checkered bound maple body, bound wedge-shaped soundhole, white pickguard, through-body maple/walnut laminate necks, 24-fret bound rosewood fingerboards with pearl triangle inlay, tune-o-matic bridges/R style tailpieces, 6-per-side/3-per-side tuners, chrome hardware, 2 single coil exposed pickups per neck, 2 volume/2 tone/mix controls, two 3-position switches, stereo output. Available in Natural finish. Mfg. 1975 to 1985.

$2,000	$1,650	$1,175	$995	$875	$795	$700

This was a special order instrument.

4080 - cresting wave style bound maple body, 2-piece black pickguard, maple necks, bound rosewood fingerboards with pearl triangle inlay, fixed bridge for bass neck, tune-o-matic/R style trapeze tailpiece for guitar neck, cresting wave style pegheads, 2-per-side tuners for bass neck, 3-per-side tuners for guitar neck, chrome hardware, 2 single coil exposed pickups per neck, 2 volume/2 tone/1 mix controls, two 3-position switches, stereo output. Available in Natural finish. Mfg. 1975 to 1985.

$1,000	$895	$775	$650	$575	$475	$350

Bass neck may be maple/walnut laminate and had 20-frets. The guitar neck had 24-frets.

4080/12 - similar to 4080, except has 12-strings, 6-per-side tuners on the guitar neck. Mfg. 1978 to 1985.

$1,000	$895	$775	$650	$575	$475	$350

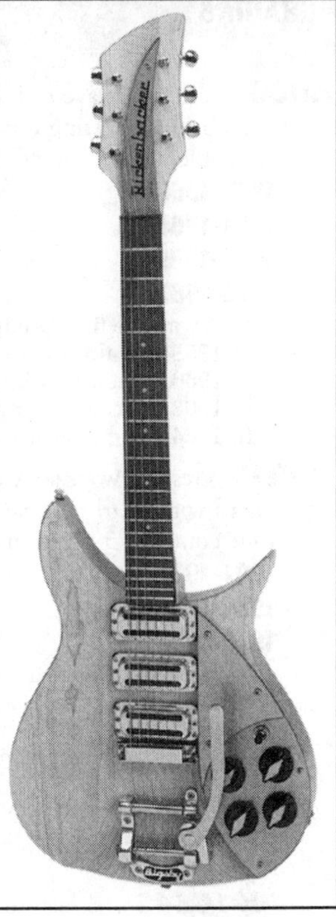

Rickenbacker Model 325V59
courtesy Rickenbacker

ELECTRIC BASS

Research continues into the **3000 Series** (circa 1974 to 1985) for future editions of the ***Blue Book of Electric Guitars***.

2000 Series

2020 HAMBURG - double cutaway maple body, through-body maple neck, 20-fret rosewood fingerboard with pearl dot inlay, fixed bridge, 2-per-side tuners, 2 single coil pickups, 2 volume/2 tone controls, toggle switch, active electronics. Available in Fireglo, Jetglo, Mapleglo, Midnight Blue, Red, and White finishes. Mfg. 1984 to 1995.

$750	$500	$450	$395	$350	$300	$250

Last MSR was $1,000.

2060 EL DORADO - similar to 2020, except has double bound body, bound fingerboard, gold hardware. Disc. 1995.

$850	$575	$525	$475	$400	$350	$300

Last MSR was $1,200.

4000 Series

All models in this series have the following, unless otherwise listed: cresting wave style maple body, pickguard, through-body maple neck, 20-fret rosewood fingerboard, fixed bridge, 2-per-side tuners, single coil/horseshoe pickups, 2 volume/2 tone controls, 3-position switch.

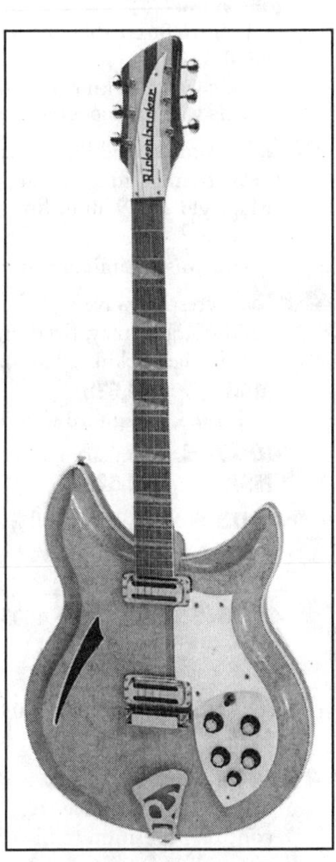

Rickenbacker Model 381V69
courtesy Rickenbacker

R

GRADING	100% MINT	98% NEAR MINT	95% EXC+	90% EXC	80% VG+	70% VG	60% G

4000 - cresting wave style maple body, white pickguard, through-body mahogany neck, 20-fret rosewood fingerboard with white dot inlay, fixed bridge, cresting wave peghead with maple laminate wings, 2-per-side tuners, chrome hardware, horseshoe pickup, volume/tone control. Available in Autumnglo, Brownburst, Black, Fireglo, and Natural finishes. Mfg. 1955 to 1987.

1957-1960	**$5,000**	**$4,450**	**$3,850**	**$3,295**	**$2,850**	**$2,375**	**$1,925**
1961-1965	**$3,000**	**$2,295**	**$2,100**	**$1,650**	**$1,200**	**$1,050**	**$950**
1966-1969	**$2,000**	**$1,425**	**$1,100**	**$995**	**$825**	**$775**	**$625**
1970-1987	**$750**	**$600**	**$500**	**$400**	**$375**	**$325**	**$300**

This was the first production Rickenbacker Bass guitar. In 1955, only a handful of instruments were produced.
In 1958, a walnut neck replaced the mahogany neck.
In 1960, a maple/walnut laminated neck replaced the walnut neck. Fireglo finish became optional.
In 1963, a bridge string mute was added and Autumnglo and Black finishes became optional.
In 1964, the horseshoe pickup was replaced by a single coil pickup with a metal cover.

4001 - cresting wave style checkered bound maple body, white pickguard, through-body maple/walnut neck, 20-fret bound rosewood fingerboard with pearl triangle inlay, fixed bridge, cresting wave peghead, 2-per-side tuners, chrome hardware, bar/horseshoe pickups, 2 volume/2 tone controls, 3-position switch. Available in Fireglo and Natural finishes. Mfg. 1961 to 1986.

1961-1964	**$4,000**	**$3,450**	**$2,850**	**$2,295**	**$2,050**	**$1,895**	**$1,725**
1965-1969	**$3,000**	**$2,575**	**$2,150**	**$1,725**	**$1,550**	**$1,425**	**$1,295**
1970-1986	**$650**	**$550**	**$475**	**$375**	**$300**	**$275**	**$250**

In the early 1960s, a few models had ebony fingerboards.
In 1964, the horseshoe pickup was replaced by a single coil pickup with a metal cover.
In 1965, Natural finish became optional.
Stereo output was originally a special order item on the 4001 until 1971 when it became optional.

4001C64 - similar to 4001 except has horseshoe pickup, Kluson style tuners, neck-through body. Available in Mapleglo and Fireglo finishes. New 2001.

MSR $2,999	**$2,250**	**$2,050**	**$1,850**	**$1,750**	**$1550**	**$1,350**	**$1,050**

4001C64S - similar to 4001C64 except has rehaped body and reversed head. Available in mapleglo finish. New 2001.

MSR $3,199	**$2,400**	**$2,200**	**$2,000**	**$1,850**	**$1,650**	**$1,450**	**$1,150**

4001 FL - similar to 4001, except has a fretless fingerboard.

	$4,000	**$3,450**	**$2,850**	**$2,295**	**$2,050**	**$1,895**	**$1,725**

This model was available only by special order.

4001 S - similar to 4001, except has unbound body, dot fingerboard inlay. Mfg. 1964 to 1967.

1964-1967	**$5,000**	**$4,295**	**$3,575**	**$2,850**	**$2,575**	**$2,350**	**$2,150**

Reintroduced 1980 to 1986.

1980-1986	**$850**	**$750**	**$650**	**$525**	**$475**	**$425**	**$375**

This was also known as the export Model 1999. Original release instruments were manufactured in low quantities and are rare finds.
This was the model made famous by Paul McCartney and Chris Squire.

4002 - similar to 4000, except has checkered bound figured maple body, figured maple/walnut 5-piece neck, bound ebony fingerboard with pearl triangle inlay, 2 humbucker exposed pickups, 2 volume/2 tone controls, 3-position switch, stereo and direct outputs. Available in Mapleglo and Walnut finishes. Mfg. 1981 only.

	$750	**$650**	**$575**	**$495**	**$425**	**$395**	**$350**

This was a Limited Edition instrument.

4003 - cresting wave style bound maple body, 2-piece white pickguard, through-body maple neck, 20-fret bound rosewood fingerboard with pearl triangle inlay, fixed bridge, cresting wave style peghead, 2-per-side tuners, chrome hardware, 2 single coil exposed pickups (metal cover over bridge pickup), 2 volume/2 tone controls, 3-position switch, stereo output. Available in Natural finish. Mfg. 1973 to date.

MSR $1,529	**$1,200**	**$950**	**$795**	**$695**	**$575**	**$475**	**$400**

In 1985, pickguard was replaced with one piece unit.

4003 FL - similar to 4003, except has a fretless fingerboard with pearl dot inlay. Current Mfg.

MSR $1,529	**$1,200**	**$950**	**$795**	**$695**	**$575**	**$475**	**$400**

4003 S - similar to 4003, except has no binding, dot fingerboard inlay, mono output. Available in Red finish. Mfg. 1980 to 1995.

	$850	**$750**	**$650**	**$575**	**$475**	**$395**	**$300**

Last MSR was $1,200.

4003/S5 - similar to 4003, except has 5 string configuration, 3/2-per-side tuners, no binding, dot fingerboard inlay, mono output. Mfg. 1987 to date.

MSR $1,649	**$1,250**	**$995**	**$850**	**$750**	**$625**	**$475**	**$395**

4003/S8 - similar to 4003, except has 8 strings, no binding, dot fingerboard inlay, 4-per-side tuners, mono output. Mfg. 1987 to date.

MSR $1,919	**$1,500**	**$1,275**	**$1,100**	**$895**	**$750**	**$595**	**$475**

4004C CHEYENNE - cresting wave style walnut body, through-body maple neck, 20-fret maple fingerboard with black dot inlay, fixed bridge, cresting wave style peghead with walnut laminates, 2-per-side tuners, gold hardware, 2 humbucker exposed pickups, volume/tone control, 3-position mini switch. Available in Natural finish. Mfg. 1993 to 2000.

	$1,200	**$975**	**$850**	**$750**	**$625**	**$495**	**$395**

Last MSR was $1,569.

R

GRADING	100% MINT	98% NEAR MINT	95% EXC+	90% EXC	80% VG+	70% VG	60% G

4004CII CHEYENNE II - similar to 4004C Cheyenne except has super contoured maple and walnut body, Bubinga fingerboard, gold parts. Available in translucent colors. New 2001.

MSR $1,949	$1,475	$1,250	$1,150	$1,000	$900	$800	$650

4004L Laredo - similar to 4004C, except has hardwood body, chrome hardware. Available in Jetglo finish. Mfg. 1994 to date.

MSR $1,749	$1,350	$1,100	$925	$795	$675	$550	$425

The 4004L Laredo has been available in all standard colors since 1995.

4005 - offset double cutaway semi hollow maple body, rounded top, bound wedge-shaped soundhole, white pickguard, through-body maple/walnut laminate neck, 21-fret bound rosewood fingerboard with pearl triangle inlay, tune-o-matic bridge/R style trapeze tailpiece, cresting wave style peghead, 2-per-side tuners, chrome hardware, 2 single coil exposed pickups, 2 volume/2 tone/mix controls, 3-position switch. Available in Fireglo and Natural finishes. Mfg. 1965 to 1984.

1965-1969	$2,500	$2,150	$1,795	$1,425	$1,295	$1,175	$1,100
1970-1984	$1,250	$1,100	$895	$725	$650	$595	$525

4005 WB - similar to 4005, except has bound body. Mfg. 1966 to 1984.

	$3,000	$2,575	$2,150	$1,725	$1,550	$1,425	$1,295

4005/6 - similar to 4005, except has 6 strings, 3-per-side tuners. Mfg. 1965 to 1978.

	$4,000	$3,500	$2,800	$2,200	$1,800	$1,650	$1,200

4005/8 - similar to 4005, except has 8 strings, 4-per-side tuners. Mfg. 1967 to 1984.

	$3,000	$2,400	$1,895	$1,450	$1,295	$1,175	$1,100

4008 - cresting wave style bound maple body, white pickguard, through-body maple neck, 21-fret bound rosewood fingerboard with pearl triangle inlay, fixed bridge, cresting wave style peghead, 4-per-side tuners, chrome hardware, 2 single coil exposed pickups (metal cover over bridge pickup), 2 volume/2 tone controls, 3-position switch. Available in Fireglo and Natural finishes. Mfg. 1972 to 1984.

	$450	$375	$325	$295	$275	$250	$225

This model was available on special order only.

Rickenbacker Model 4003/S8
courtesy Rickenbacker

Limited Edition Series

2030GF GLENN FREY LIMITED EDITION - double cutaway maple body, chrome pickguard with Glenn Frey signature, through-body maple neck, 20-fret ebony fingerboard with pearl dot inlay, fixed bridge, chrome peghead logoplate, 2-per-side tuners, black hardware, 2 humbucker pickups, chrome volume/tone control, 3-position mini switch. Available in Jetglo finish. Disc. 1995.

	$800	$625	$575	$495	$400	$375	$325

Last MSR was $1,050.

4001CS CHRIS SQUIRE LIMITED EDITION - cresting wave Eastern rock maple body, white pickguard with Chris Squire signature, through-body maple neck, 20-fret vermilion fingerboard with pearl dot inlay, fixed bridge, white peghead logoplate, 2-per-side tuners, chrome hardware, single coil/horseshoe pickups, 2 volume/2 tone controls, 3-position switch. Available in Cream Lacquer finish. Disc. 2000.

	$1,500	$1,350	$1,200	$1,000	$800	$700	$600

Last MSR was $1,899.

Only 1,000 instruments are scheduled.
The fingerboard and peghead on this model are carved from one piece of African vermilion.
Price includes a Rickenbacker vintage case.

4004LK LEMMY KILMISTER LIMITED EDITION - cresting wave style highly carved walnut body, through-body maple neck, 20-fret rosewood fingerboard with pearl dot inlay, fixed bridge, black/white checked body binding, cresting wave style peghead, 2-per-side tuners, gold hardware, 3 humbucker pickups, volume/tone control, 5-position switch. Available in Oil finish. Mfg. 1998 to date.

MSR $2,799	$2,150	$1,950	$1,800	$1,600	$1,400	$1,200	$900

Price includes a standard Rickenbacker case.

Vintage Series

4001V63 - cresting wave style maple body, white pickguard, through-body maple neck, 20-fret rosewood fingerboard with pearl dot inlay, fixed bridge, 2-per-side tuners, chrome hardware, single coil/horseshoe pickups, 2 volume/2 tone controls, 3-position switch. Available in Fireglo and Mapleglo finishes. Mfg. 1984 to 2000.

	$1,575	$1,250	$1,100	$995	$775	$650	$500

Last MSR was $2,069.

This model was derived from the 4001 bass that was popular in 1963.

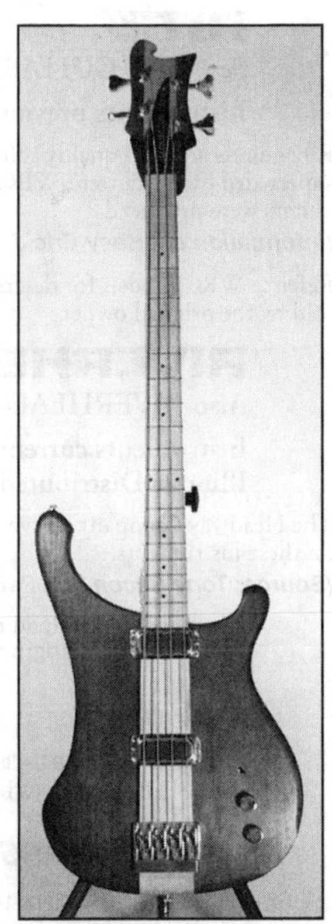

Rickenbacker Cheyenne 4004
courtesy Arlington Guitar Show

R

RICKMANN

Instruments previously built in Japan during the late 1970s.

The Rickmann trademark is a brand name used by a UK importer. Instruments are generally intermediate quality copies of classic American designs.
(Source: Tony Bacon and Paul Day, The Guru's Guitar Guide)

RICO

See B. C. RICH.

RIPLEY, STEVE

Instruments currently built in Tulsa, Oklahoma.

Luthier Steve Ripley had established a reputation as both a guitarist and recording engineer prior to debuting his Stereo Guitar models at the 1983 NAMM show. Ripley's designs were later licensed by Kramer (BKL). In 1986, Ripley moved to Tulsa, Oklahoma and two years later severed his relationship with Kramer. Any other updates will be featured in future editions of the *Blue Book of Guitars*.
(Source: Tom Wheeler, American Guitars)

RITTER

Instruments currently built in Bad Durkheim, Germany since 1991. Distributed worldwide by Ritter Bass Guitars of Bad Durkheim, Germany.

Luthier/designer Jens Ritter originally apprenticed as an traditional woodworker. During his apprenticeship, Ritter was also an accomplished electric bassist who played in German Jazz and Fusion bands.

At the age of eighteen, Ritter began building custom basses for local bass players. After a few years the name Jens Ritter was a synonym for high end custom basses in Europe. In 1999, Ritter invented a new Tremelo System for bass guitars (4-string, 5-string and 6-string). It works with miniature ball bearings. In 2001, he developed a special body sound material called GALPERA. This material has an similar sound characteristic to hard maple and it can be covered with chrome or gold. All instruments are completely hand-made and unique. For further information regarding specifications and pricing, contact Jens Ritter directly (see Trademark Index).

ELECTRIC BASS

Ritter's **Basic-Basses** are a more standardized model from his custom basses. The Basic Bass model has an offset cutaway figured maple (flamed, quilted, bird's-eye, etc.) one (or two) piece hand shaped body, bolt-on graphite neck, 34" scale, fretted phenolic or fretless wood fingerboards, 2 Bartolini soapbar humbuckers, volume/tone controls, 3-band EQ controls with active/passive switch, and a custom built Ritter bridge. Basic Basses are finished in a Balm finish, consisting of an oil and wax application (a high gloss polyester lacquer finish is optional for an additional $200).

The 1998 announced prices run from $3,870 (**4-String fretless**; $4,050 **4-string fretted**) to $4,500 (**5-string fretless**; $4,770 **5-string fretted**) up to $5,200 (**6-string fretless**; $5,490 **6-string fretted**).

In 2001, two basic models are offered, the Classic and the Seal. They have parametric electronics and 2 triblebuckers (3-coil pickups) and are available in Gold and high gloss Piano Lacquer finishes.

RITZ

See WRC GUITARS.

Instruments previously built in Calimesa, California from 1989 to 1990.

Ritz guitars are high quality solid body designs by Wayne R. Charvel (of Charvel/Jackson fame). After a year of production, the Ritz trademark was then superseded by the current **WRC** or **WRC Guitars** (Wayne R. Charvel) trademark. During the year of production under the Ritz name, only a handful of guitars were produced.
(Information courtesy Eric J. Galletta, WRC Guitars)

Refer to WRC models for descriptions and pricing information. Due to the limited supply, these models may not appear in the secondary market unless sold by the original owner.

RIVERHEAD

Also RIVERHEAD GUITARS.

Instruments currently built in Japan since the mid 1980s. Distributed in the U.S. by American Riverhead of Bolingbrook, Illinois. Distributed in Japan by Headway Co., Ltd. of Japan.

The Headway Company's RiverHead guitar models currently feature a number of different designs. Good quality construction and materials are featured on these instruments.
(Source: Tony Bacon and Paul Day, The Guru's Guitar Guide)

An earlier River Head model was the Unicorn, which featured 2 pickups, a smaller original shaped body, and a "headless" neck (no headstock; reverse stringing). Authors Bacon and Day mention a guitar model RUG2090 (Riverhead Unicorn Guitar 2090 perhaps?).

ELECTRIC

The **Diva** series offers a stylistically different take on the conventional strat-style design, while the **Gracia** series of guitars is more "Ernie Ball/Music Man" influenced. Retail list prices begin at $1,099.

ELECTRIC BASS

Gracia basses are based on the offset double cutaway Jazz body design, and are available in 4- and 5-string configuration. Gracia models have alder or quilted maple top/alder bodies, one-piece maple necks, ebony or rosewood or maple fingerboards, Gotoh hardware (black or gold), 2 Alnico J-style pickups, 2 volume/1 tone controls, and translucent colors. Retail list prices begin at $1,049.

GRADING	100% MINT	98% NEAR MINT	95% EXC+	90% EXC	80% VG+	70% VG	60% G

CARLO ROBELLI

Instruments previously produced in Japan circa 1970s. Distributed by Sam Ash of New York, New York.

Carlo Robelli instruments were good quality instruments based on popular American models.
They may look like they were produced in Kalamazoo, but the instruments are definitely Asian in construction. Most instruments are in 80% to 90% condition; and generally priced between $175 to $299.

ROBERTS

Instruments previously built in Brea, California during the early 1990s.

Inventor Curt Roberts and his artist wife, Elizabeth, invented a four-sided guitar neck as a means to supply guitarists with a number of alternative tunings on a single instrument. The **Roto-Caster** was available in 2-, 3-, or 4-neck configurations.

The last given address for Roberts Roto-Neck was 471 West Lambert Rd., Suite 104, Brea, California 92621 (714.256.7276), (FAX) 714.256.7288.

ROBIN GUITARS

Instruments currently built in Houston, Texas since 1982. Distributed by Alamo Music Products of Houston, Texas.

In 1972, David Wintz teamed up with a friend to open a guitar shop in Houston, Texas. After ten years of dealing, repairing, and restoring vintage guitars, Wintz began building quality instruments and offering them for sale. In addition to building guitars, Wintz began offering Rio Grande pickups in 1993. Originated by veteran pickup winder Bart Wittrock, the Rio Grande pickups are offered in a variety of sounds/applications and colors - including sparkle finishes!

As a further supplement to the standard models listed below, Robin's Custom Shop can assemble virtually anything on a special order basis. Custom graphics and a variety of finishes are also available.

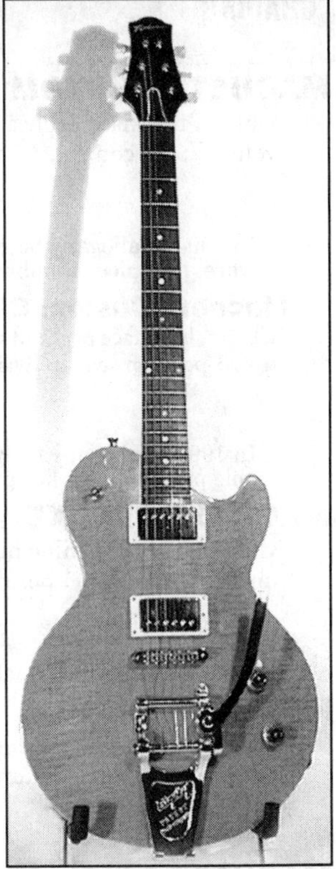

Robin Avalon
courtesy Sam Baker

ELECTRIC

Robin guitars feature Rio Grande pickups as standard equipment.

Avalon Series

AVALON CLASSIC - single cutaway mahogany body, figured maple top, mahogany neck, 22-fret rosewood fingerboard with abalone dot inlay, tune-o-matic bridge/stop tailpiece, blackface peghead with pearl logo inlay, 3-per-side tuners with plastic buttons, nickel hardware, 2 exposed humbucker Seymour Duncan pickups, volume/tone control, 3-position switch. Available in Antique Violinburst, Antique Amber, and Antique Tobaccoburst finishes. Mfg. 1994 to date.

MSR	$2,795	$2,225	$1,825	$1,595	$1,375	$1,150	$925	$700

Add $180 for Bigsby Tailpiece.

Add $400 for abalone dolphin inlay on neck.

AVALON DELUXE - single cutaway ash body, figured maple top, mahogany neck, 22-fret rosewood fingerboard with pearl dot inlay, tune-o-matic bridge/stop tailpiece, blackface peghead with pearl logo inlay, 3-per-side tuners with plastic buttons, nickel hardware, 2 exposed humbucker Seymour Duncan pickups, volume/tone control, 3-position switch. Available in Metallic Gold and Cherry finishes. Mfg. 1994.

MSR	$1,795	$1,450	$1,175	$1,000	$895	$750	$625	$475

Add $180 for Bigsby Tailpiece.

Add $400 for abalone dolphin inlay on neck.

AVALON FLATTOP - single cutaway ash body, tortoise multilam pickguard, mahogany neck, 22-fret rosewood fingerboard with pearl dot inlay, tune-o-matic bridge/stop tailpiece, blackface peghead with screened logo, 3-per-side tuners with plastic buttons, nickel hardware, 2 exposed humbucker Seymour Duncan pickups, volume/tone control, 3-position switch. Available in Old Blonde and Metallic Gold finishes. Mfg. 1994 to date.

MSR	$1,595	$1,275	$1,050	$925	$795	$650	$525	$395

Add $180 for Bigsby Tailpiece.

Add $400 for abalone dolphin inlay on neck.

Machete Series

All models in this series have reverse single cutaway asymmetrical bodies with terraced cuts on front and back. Pegheads are asymmetrically V-shaped.

R

GRADING	100% MINT	98% NEAR MINT	95% EXC+	90% EXC	80% VG+	70% VG	60% G

MACHETE CUSTOM - figured maple body, through-body maple neck, 24-fret ebony fingerboard with pearl dot inlay, double locking vibrato, blackface peghead with screened logo, 4/2-per-side Sperzel tuners, black hardware, 2 Seymour Duncan blade humbucker pickups, volume/tone control, 3-position switch. Available in Antique Amber and Ruby Red finishes. Mfg. 1991 to 1995.

		$1,575	$1,375	$1,150	$950	$850	$795	$725

Last MSR was $2,195.

In 1994, mahogany body, figured maple top, set mahogany neck, rosewood fingerboard, tune-o-matic bridge/stop tailpiece, chrome hardware, pole piece humbucker pickups replaced original parts/designs.

Machete Custom Classic - figured maple body, through-body maple neck, 24-fret ebony fingerboard with pearl dot inlay, double locking vibrato, blackface peghead with screened logo, 4/2-per-side tuners, black hardware, 2 Seymour Duncan blade humbucker pickups, volume/tone control, 3-position switch. Available in Antique Amber and Ruby Red finishes. Mfg. 1991 to 1995.

		$1,725	$1,525	$1,295	$1,100	$975	$895	$800

Last MSR was $2,395.

In 1994, mahogany body, excellent grade figured maple top, set mahogany neck, tune-o-matic bridge/stop tailpiece, chrome hardware, pole piece humbucker pickups replaced original parts/designs.

MACHETE DELUXE - mahogany body, through-body mahogany neck, 24-fret rosewood fingerboard with pearl dot inlay, double locking vibrato, body matching peghead with screened logo, 4/2-per-side tuners, black hardware, 2 Seymour Duncan blade humbucker pickups, volume/tone control, 3-position switch. Available in Cherry finish. Mfg. 1991 to 1995.

		$1,450	$1,250	$1,100	$895	$795	$725	$650

Last MSR was $1,995.

In 1994, poplar body, set maple neck, pole piece humbucker pickups replaced original parts/designs.

MACHETE SPECIAL - ash body, bolt-on maple neck, 24-fret rosewood fingerboard with pearl dot inlay, double locking vibrato, blackface peghead with screened logo, 4/2-per-side tuners, black hardware, 2 humbucker PJ Marx pickups, volume/tone control, 3-position switch. Available in Natural Oil finish. Mfg. 1991 to 1994.

		$695	$595	$500	$400	$350	$325	$300

Last MSR was $995.

MACHETE STANDARD - ash body, bolt-on maple neck, 24-fret rosewood fingerboard with pearl dot inlay, double locking vibrato, body matching peghead with screened logo, 4/2-per-side tuners, black hardware, 2 Seymour Duncan blade humbucker pickups, volume/tone control, 3-position switch. Available in Blue and Cherry finishes. Current Mfg.

MSR	$1,770	$1,425	$1,150	$1,000	$875	$725	$595	$450

Add $400 for abalone dolphin inlays on neck.

Medley Series

All models in this series have V-shaped peghead as an option.

MEDLEY SPECIAL - offset double cutaway ash body, bolt-on maple neck, 24-fret rosewood fingerboard with pearl dot inlay, double locking Floyd Rose vibrato, reverse blade peghead, 6-on-a-side Sperzel tuners, black hardware, single coil/humbucker exposed pickups, volume control, 3-position switch. Available in Oil finish. Mfg. 1991 to 1995.

		$695	$595	$500	$400	$350	$325	$300

Last MSR was $995.

MEDLEY STANDARD - offset double cutaway Swamp Ash or Basswood body, bolt-on maple neck, 24-fret rosewood fingerboard with pearl dot inlay, double locking Floyd Rose vibrato, reverse blade peghead, 6-on-a-side Sperzel tuners, black hardware, single 2 exposed Seymour Duncan humbucker pickups, volume/tone control, 3-position switch. Available in Blue, Cherry, Natural, Pearl Black and Purple finishes. Mfg. 1991 to date.

MSR	$1,770	$1,425	$1,150	$1,000	$875	$725	$595	$450

Add $400 for abalone dolphin inlays on neck.

Medley Standard II-Texas Curly Slabtop - similar to Medley Standard II, except has mahogany body, curly maple top. Available in Natural finish. Disc. 1995.

		$1,270	$1,080	$900	$720	$650	$595	$540

Last MSR was $1,820.

Medley Standard II-Texas Quilted Slabtop - similar to Medley Standard II, except has mahogany body, quilted maple top. Available in Natural finish. Disc. 1995.

		$1,300	$1,110	$925	$750	$675	$600	$550

Last MSR was $1,870.

MEDLEY STANDARD IV - offset double cutaway hardwood body, bolt-on maple neck, 24-fret rosewood fingerboard with pearl dot inlay, double locking Floyd Rose vibrato, reverse blade peghead, 6-on-a-side Sperzel tuners, black hardware, 2 stacked coil rail/1 pole piece Seymour Duncan humbucker exposed pickups, volume/tone control, 5-position switch. Available in Blue, Cherry, Green, Pearl White and Purple finishes. Mfg. 1991 to 1995.

		$1,100	$900	$750	$600	$550	$500	$450

Last MSR was $1,580.

Medley Standard IV-Curly - similar to Medley Standard IV, except has curly maple body. Mfg. 1991 to 1994.

		$1,350	$1,150	$950	$775	$695	$625	$575

Last MSR was $1,920.

GRADING	100% MINT	98% NEAR MINT	95% EXC+	90% EXC	80% VG+	70% VG	60% G

MEDLEY VI EXOTIC TOP - offset double cutaway hardwood body, bound figured maple top, bolt-on maple neck, 24-fret rosewood fingerboard with pearl dot inlay, double locking Floyd Rose vibrato, reverse blade peghead, 6-on-a-side Sperzel tuners, black hardware, single coil rail/exposed pole piece Seymour Duncan humbucker pickups, volume/tone control, 5-position switch. Mfg. 1991 to 1995.

	$1,250	$1,050	$875	$700	$625	$575	$525

Last MSR was $1,790.

MEDLEY STUDIO IV - offset double cutaway ash body, bolt-on maple neck, 24-fret maple fingerboard with black dot inlay, standard Wilkinson vibrato, reverse blade peghead, 6-on-a-side locking Sperzel tuners, chrome hardware, 2 single coil rail/1 exposed pole piece humbucker Seymour Duncan pickups, volume/tone control, 5-position switch. Disc. 1995.

	$1,125	$950	$795	$625	$575	$525	$475

Last MSR was $1,595.

Ranger Series

RANGER - offset double cutaway poplar body, pearloid pickguard, controls mounted on a metal plate, bolt-on maple neck, 22-fret rosewood fingerboard with pearl dot inlay, fixed strings through bridge, reverse peghead, 6-on-a-side tuners, chrome hardware, humbucker/2 single coil pickups, volume/tone control, 5-position switch. Available in Pearl Black, Pearl Red and Pearl White finishes. Mfg. 1991 to date.

MSR $1,595	$1,275	$1,050	$925	$795	$650	$525	$395

Add $100 for ash body.

In 1994, standard peghead replaced original parts/design.

Wrangler - similar to Ranger Standard, except has vintage-style fixed bridge. Available in 3-tone Sunburst, Old Blonde, and Black finishes. Current Mfg.

MSR $1,595	$1,275	$1,050	$925	$795	$650	$525	$395

Add $750 for optional Parson White B-Bender.

RANGER CUSTOM - offset double cutaway bound ash body, white pickguard, metal controls mounted plate, bolt-on figured maple neck, 22-fret rosewood fingerboard with pearl dot inlay, fixed strings through bridge, reverse peghead, 6-on-a-side tuners, chrome hardware, humbucker/2 single coil pickups, volume/tone control, 5-position switch. Available in Cherry, Orange and Three Tone Sunburst finishes. Mfg. 1991 to date.

MSR $1,695	$1,350	$1,100	$975	$825	$695	$550	$425

In 1994, standard peghead replaced original parts/design.

Ranger Custom Exotic Top - similar to Ranger Custom, except has bound figured maple top, pearloid pickguard, standard peghead. Disc. 1995.

	$1,125	$975	$800	$650	$575	$525	$475

Last MSR was $1,620.

RANGER REVIVAL - offset double cutaway hardwood body, pearloid pickguard, bolt-on maple neck, 22-fret rosewood fingerboard with pearl dot inlay, standard vibrato, 6-on-a-side Sperzel tuners, 3 single coil pickups, 1 volume/2 tone controls, 5-position switch. Current Mfg.

MSR $1,595	$1,195	$795	$595	$475	$425	$395	$350

Add $100 for ash body.

RANGER SPECIAL - offset double cutaway ash body, controls mounted on a metal plate, bolt-on maple neck, 22-fret rosewood fingerboard with pearl dot inlay, fixed strings through bridge, reverse peghead, 6-on-a-side tuners, chrome hardware, humbucker/2 single coil pickups, volume/tone control, 5-position switch. Available in Natural Oil finish. Mfg. 1991 to 1995.

	$695	$595	$500	$400	$350	$325	$300

Last MSR was $995.

In 1994, standard peghead replaced original parts/design.

RANGER STUDIO - offset double cutaway ash body, white pickguard, controls mounted on a metal plate, bolt-on maple neck, 22-fret rosewood fingerboard with pearl dot inlay, fixed strings through bridge, reverse peghead, 6-on-a-side locking Sperzel tuners, chrome hardware, 3 single coil pickups, volume/tone control, 5-position switch. Available in Cherry Sunburst, Three Tone Sunburst, Tobacco Sunburst, Two Tone Sunburst, Unburst, Violin Sunburst and the following Transparent finishes: Blue, Bone White, Charcoal Black, Cherry, Green, Honey, Lavender, Natural, Old Blonde, Orange, Purple, Rootbeer, Violet and Yellow. Mfg. 1991 to 1995.

	$1,075	$900	$750	$600	$550	$500	$450

Last MSR was $1,540.

In 1994, standard peghead replaced original parts/design.

1995 Robin Machete
courtesy David Wintz

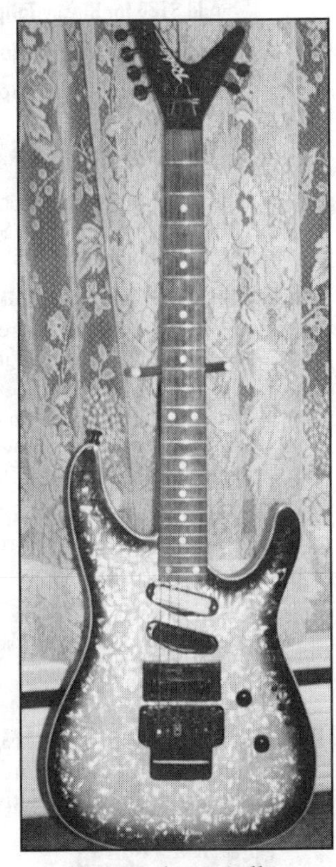

1989 Robin Medley
courtesy Bob Smith

R

GRADING	100% MINT	98% NEAR MINT	95% EXC+	90% EXC	80% VG+	70% VG	60% G

Standard Series

RAIDER STANDARD II - asymmetrical double cutaway reverse hardwood body, bolt-on maple neck, 24-fret rosewood fingerboard with pearl dot inlay, double locking vibrato, reverse headstock, 6-on-a-side tuners, black hardware, 2 humbucker Seymour Duncan pickups, volume/tone control, 3-position switch. Available in Blue, Cherry, Natural, Pearl Black and Purple finishes. Disc. 1992.

		$1,000	$875	$725	$575	$525	$475	$425

Last MSR was $1,450.

Raider Standard IV - similar to Ranger Standard II, except has 2 stacked coil/1 humbucker Seymour Duncan pickups, tone control, 5-position/coil tap switch. Available in Blue, Cherry, Green, Pearl White and Purple finishes. Disc. 1992.

		$1,075	$900	$750	$600	$550	$500	$450

Last MSR was $1,520.

TEDLEY STANDARD VI - single cutaway hardwood body, bolt-on maple neck, 24-fret rosewood fingerboard with pearl dot inlay, double locking vibrato, reverse headstock, 6-on-a-side tuners, black hardware, stacked coil/humbucker Seymour Duncan pickups, volume/tone control, 3-position switch. Available in Cherry, Orange, Pearl Black and Purple finishes. Mfg. 1991 to 1994.

		$1,025	$875	$725	$575	$525	$475	$425

Last MSR was $1,450.

Savoy Series

SAVOY CLASSIC - single cutaway mahogany semi-hollow body, carved curly maple top, mahogany neck, 22-fret rosewood fingerboard with abalone dot inlay, 24.75" scale, tune-o-matic bridge/stop tailpiece, 2 f-holes, blackface peghead with pearl logo inlay, 3-per-side tuners with plastic buttons, nickel hardware, 2 Rio Grande humbuckers, volume/tone control, 3-position switch on upper bass bout. Available in Antique Violinburst, Antique Amber, and Wine Red. Current Mfg.

MSR	$2,995	$2,400	$1,975	$1,725	$1,495	$1,250	$995	$750

Add $180 for Bigsby Tailpiece.

Add $400 for abalone dolphin inlay on neck.

SAVOY DELUXE - single cutaway Swamp Ash (solid) or Poplar (semi-hollow) body, carved arched top, mahogany neck, 22-fret rosewood fingerboard with pearl dot inlay, 2 f-holes, tune-o-matic bridge/stop tailpiece, blackface peghead with pearl logo inlay, 3-per-side tuners with plastic buttons, nickel hardware, 2 Rio Grande humbucker pickups, volume/tone control, 3-position switch on upper bass bout. Available in Metallic Gold, Cherry, Orange, and Old Blonde finishes. Current Mfg.

MSR	$1,995	$1,595	$1,295	$1,125	$975	$825	$650	$500

Add $180 for Bigsby Tailpiece.

Add $400 for abalone dolphin inlay on neck.

Cherry finish can be supplemented with an optional Bigsby and gold-plated hardware.

ELECTRIC BASS

In 1998, Robin Guitars introduced the **Freedom Bass**, a model with classic body styling and Rio Grande 'Powerbucker' passive pickups. The Freedom Bass was offered in a 4-string (list $1,595) and 5-string ($1,695) configurations. The **Freedom Bass Active** was offered with humbucking pickups and active electronics in 4-string (list $1,795) and 5-string (list $1,895) configurations.

JAYBIRD (Ranger Jaybird) - offset double cutaway asymmetrical ash body, pearloid pickguard, controls mounted on a metal plate, bolt-on maple neck, 20-fret rosewood fingerboard with pearl dot inlay, fixed bridge, reverse peghead, 4-on-a-side tuners, chrome hardware, 2 J-style pickups, volume/tone control, 3-position switch. Mfg. 1991 to 1996, 1998 to date.

MSR	$1,595	$1,275	$1,050	$925	$795	$650	$525	$395

This model is similar to the Ranger Bass, but with the Jaybird body style.
In 1994, standard peghead replaced original parts/design.

JAYWALKER (Ranger Jaywalker) - offset double cutaway asymmetrical ash body, figured maple top, bolt-on maple neck, 20-fret ebony fingerboard with pearl dot inlay, fixed bridge, 4-on-a-side tuners, black hardware, 2 J-style Bartolini pickups, volume/treble/bass/mix controls. Mfg. 1991 to 1996.

		$1,395	$1,050	$925	$740	$665	$610	$555

Last MSR was $1,865.

Jaywalker Active - similar to the Jaywalker, except features 'Double J' pickups, active electronics. Available in 3-Tone Sunburst and Tobacco Sunburst finishes.

MSR	$1,995	$1,595	$1,295	$1,125	$975	$825	$650	$500

MACHETE V 5 STRING - reverse single cutaway asymmetrical body with 'terraced' ash body, bolt-on maple neck, 24-fret rosewood fingerboard with pearl dot inlay, fixed Schaller bridge, V-shaped peghead, 3/2-per-side tuners, black hardware, 2 Bartolini pickups, volume/treble/bass/mix controls, active electronics. Available in Transparent Cherry, Transparent Green and Pearl Black finishes. Mfg. 1991 to 1996, 1998 to date.

MSR	$2,195	$1,800	$1,400	$1,175	$995	$875	$675	$550

In 1994, ebony fingerboard replaced original parts/design.

GRADING		100% MINT	98% NEAR MINT	95% EXC+	90% EXC	80% VG+	70% VG	60% G

MEDLEY - offset double cutaway ash body, bolt-on maple neck, 24-fret rosewood fingerboard with pearl dot inlay, fixed bridge, V-shaped peghead, 2-per-side tuners, black hardware, P/J-style pickups, volume/tone control, 3-position switch. Available in Pearl Black, Pearl White, Transparent Blue and Transparent Cherry finishes. Mfg. 1991 to 1996, 1998 to date.

MSR	$1,595	$1,275	$1,050	$925	$795	$650	$525	$395

In 1994, reverse blade peghead replaced original parts/design.

RANGER - offset double cutaway ash body, black pickguard, controls mounted on a metal plate, bolt-on maple neck, 20-fret maple fingerboard with black dot inlay, fixed bridge, reverse peghead, 4-on-a-side Sperzel tuners, chrome hardware, P/J-style pickups, volume/tone control, 3-position switch. Available in Pearl Black, Pearl Red and Transparent Old Blonde finishes. Mfg. 1991 to 1996.

$975	$825	$575	$460	$410	$380	$345

Last MSR was $1,265.

In 1994, standard peghead replaced original parts/design.

Ranger Bass VI - similar to Ranger, except has 24-fret rosewood fingerboard with pearl dot inlay, fixed strings through bridge, 6-on-a-side Sperzel tuners, 3 single coil pickups. Mfg. 1994 to date.

$1,000	$825	$685	$545	$490	$450	$410

Last MSR was $1,365.

Ranger Special - similar to Ranger, except has no pickguard, rosewood fingerboard. Disc. 1994.

$695	$595	$500	$400	$360	$330	$300

Last MSR was $995.

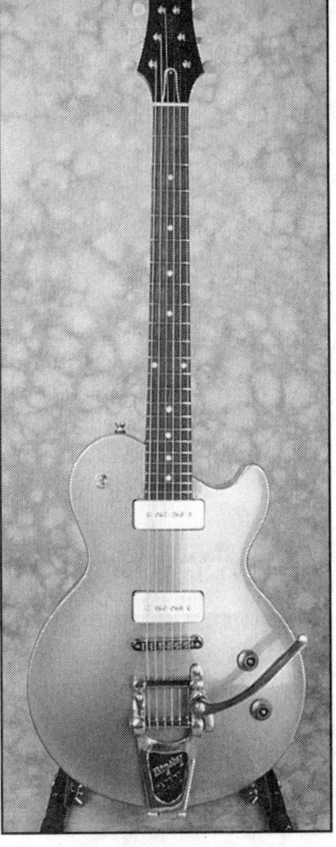

Robin Savoy
courtesy David Wintz

ROBINSON

Instruments currently built in Newburyport, Massachusetts.

Robinson Custom Guitars currently offers two models (SC-1 and SC-2) as well as custom design solid body electrics. Options include choice of woods, figured or exotic tops, hardware, and pickups.

ROCKINGER

Instruments and parts currently produced in Germany since 1978.

Rockinger has been producing numerous high quality replacement parts for a number of years; it seems only natural for them to produce quality original design guitars as well.

(Source: Tony Bacon, The Ultimate Guitar Book)

ROCKOON

Instruments currently produced in Japan by Kawai.

Good quality solid body guitars and basses featuring "superstrat" and original designs. Basses are the sleeker body design prevalent since the mid 1980s (RB series). Superstrats such as the RG, RF, or RGT series feature variations on single/humbucker pickup combinations. Rockoon guitars are equipped with Rockoon/Kawai or Shadow pickups, and Schaller hardware.

ROCKSON

Instruments previously built in Taiwan during the late 1980s.

Rockson solid body guitars featured designs based on the then-popular "superstrat" design, and other Fender-derived designs.

(Source: Tony Bacon and Paul Day, The Guru's Guitar Guide)

ROCKWOOD

See HOHNER.

Instruments currently produced in Korea. Currently distributed in the U.S. by HSS (a Division of Hohner, Inc.), located in Richmond, Virginia.

The Hohner company was founded in 1857, and is currently the world's largest manufacturer and distributor of harmonicas. Hohner offers a wide range of solidly constructed musical instruments. The **Rockwood** (or **Rockwood** Pro) models are good student level Strat-style electrics.

ELECTRIC

Rockwood (by Hohner) Series

LX 100G - double offset cutaway maple body, black pickguard, bolt-on maple neck, 22-fret rosewood fingerboard with pearl dot inlay, standard vibrato, 6-on-a-side tuners, chrome hardware, 3 single coil pickups, 2 volume/tone controls, 5-position switch. Available in Black and Red finishes. Mfg. 1992 to 1996.

$175	$150	$125	$100	$90	$80	$75

Last MSR was $260.

Robin Savoy
courtesy David Wertz

R

GRADING	100% MINT	98% NEAR MINT	95% EXC+	90% EXC	80% VG+	70% VG	60% G

LX 200G - similar to LX100G, except has white pickguard, 2 single coil/humbucker pickups, volume/tone control, coil split switch. Available in Black and White finishes. Mfg. 1992 to 1996.

	$225	$195	$175	$150	$125	$110	$100

Last MSR was $330.

LX 250G - single sharp cutaway bound maple body, white pickguard, mahogany neck, 22-fret bound rosewood fingerboard with pearl crown inlay, tune-o-matic bridge/stop tailpiece, 3-per-side tuners, chrome hardware, 2 humbucker pickups, 2 volume/2 tone controls, 3-position switch. Available in Antique Sunburst and Black finishes. Mfg. 1992 to 1996.

	$250	$195	$175	$150	$125	$115	$100

Last MSR was $375.

RP-150G - double offset cutaway maple body, bolt-on maple neck, 22-fret rosewood fingerboard with dot inlay, vintage-style tremolo bridge, 6-on-a-side tuners, chrome hardware, white pickguard, 3 exposed pole piece single coil pickups, 2 volume/1 tone controls, 5-position switch. Available in Black, Candy Apple Red, Ivory, Metallic Blue, Turquoise, and Two-Tone Sunburst finishes. Current Mfg.

MSR $275	$200	$175	$150	$125	$100	$85	$75

Add $25 for maple fingerboard (Model RP-180G). This model was discontinued in 1997.

ELECTRIC BASS

Rockwood (by Hohner) Bass Series

LX100B - offset double cutaway hardwood body, bolt-on maple neck, 21-fret rosewood fingerboard with white dot inlay, fixed bridge, 4-on-a-side tuners, chrome hardware, P-style pickup, volume/tone control. Available in Black and Red finishes. Mfg. 1992 to 1996.

	$195	$165	$140	$120	$110	$100	$90

Last MSR was $300.

LX200B - similar to LX100B, except has short scale neck. Disc. 1996.

	$175	$150	$135	$110	$100	$90	$80

Last MSR was $270.

LX300B - similar to LX100B, except has white pickguard, P/J-style pickups, 2 volume/tone control. Disc. 1994.

	$240	$210	$185	$150	$135	$120	$110

Last MSR was $370.

RP150B LONG SCALE BASS - offset double cutaway hardwood body, bolt-on maple neck, 21-fret rosewood fingerboard with white dot inlay, fixed bridge, 4 on a side tuners, chrome hardware, P-style pickup, volume/tone controls. Available in Black, Red, and Sunburst finishes. Current Mfg.

MSR $325	$250	$215	$190	$165	$140	$115	$85

RP120B Short Scale Bass - similar to the RP150B, except features 20-fret fingerboard, shorter scale, downsized body. Available in Black finish.

MSR $289	$215	$185	$165	$140	$120	$95	$75

ROGER

Instruments previously built in West Germany from the late 1950s to mid 1960s.

Luthier Wenzel Rossmeisl built very good to high quality archtop guitars as well as a semi-solid body guitar called "Model 54". Rossmeisl derived the trademark name in honor of his son, Roger Rossmeisl.

Roger Rossmeisl (1927-1979) was raised in Germany and learned luthier skills from his father, Wenzel. One particular feature was the "German Carve", a feature used by Wenzel to carve an indented plane around the body outline on the guitar's top. Roger Rossmeisl then travelled to America, where he briefly worked for Gibson in Kalamazoo, Michigan (in a climate not unlike his native Germany). Shortly thereafter he moved to California, and was employed at the Rickenbacker company. During his tenure at Rickenbacker, Rossmeisl was responsible for the design of the Capri and Combo guitars, and custom designs. His apprentice was a young Semie Moseley, who later introduced the "German Carve" on his own Mosrite brand guitars. Rossmeisl left Rickenbacker in 1962 to help Fender develop their own line of acoustic guitars (Fender had been licensing Harmony-made Regals up till then), and later introduced the Montego and LTD archtop electrics.

ROGERS

See chapter on House Brands.

This trademark has been identified as a "House Brand" of Selmer (UK).
(Source: Willie G. Moseley, Stellas & Stratocasters)

ROGUE

Instruments currently produced in Korea. Distributed by Musician's Friend of Medford, Oregon.

Musician's Friend distributes a line of good quality student and entry level instruments through their mail order catalog. Musician's Friend now offers a wide range of good quality guitars at an affordable price. For further information, contact Musician's Friend directly (see Trademark Index).

ROK AXE

Instruments currently produced in Korea. Distributed by Muse of Inchon, Korea.

The Muse company is currently offering a wide range of electric guitar and bass models, as well as a number of acoustic guitar models. Rok Axe models are generally fine entry level to student quality instruments. For further information, contact Rok Axe directly (see Trademark Index).

ROKKOR

Instruments currently produced in Asia. Distributed by the L.A. Guitar Works of Reseda, California.

Rokkor electric guitars are currently offered as part of a guitar & amp package designed for the beginning guitarist. The strat-styled models is available in Candy Red or 3-Tone Sunburst finishes, maple or rosewood fingerboards, and chrome hardware. List price for the guitar/amp package is $338.

ROLAND

Instruments previously built in Japan by Fuji Gen Gakki during the late 1970s through mid 1980s (these instruments feature both a 1/4" phono plug and a 24-pin cable attachment). Distributed in the U.S. by Roland Musical Instruments of Los Angeles, California.

The Roland company was founded in Japan, and has been one of the premier synthesizer builders since its inception in 1974. By 1977, the company began experimenting with guitar synthesis. Traditionally, synthesizers have been linked with keyboards as their key mechanism is easier to adapt to trigger the synthesized voice. Early keys on keyboards were as simple as the lightswitch in your house: press down for "on", release for "off"! As synthesizers continued to evolve (today's model uses microprocessors similar to a home PC computer), the keys provided more information like "velocity"(how hard the key was struck, held, or released - just like a piano).

In 1977, Roland reasoned that the keyboard provided the controlling information to the synthesizer, or was the "controller". In a similar parallel, then, Roland introduced a guitar "controller" and a separate synthesizer. The first system (1977-1980) featured the **GS-500** guitar and the **GR-500** synth, a vaguely Gibsonish single cutaway model with 10 plus switches. The GR-500 featured sounds from the then-current Roland keyboard synths, and the unit was fairly large and full of switches.

Roland's second series (1980-1984) was a direct improvement on their initial design. The **GR-100** (yellow box) and the **GR-300** (blue box) units are much more compact and designed to be placed on the floor - like "synth stompboxes". Roland introduced four guitar models: two models (**202** and **505**) were based on Fender-ish body styles, and the other two (**303** and **808**) were more Gibson-esque in their designs. The first bass-driven synth was also introduced with the **G-33** "controller" and the **GR-33B** synth in a floor package. These specific instruments were built for Roland by Fuji Gen Gakki (builders for Ibanez, Greco, and Fender's Squire series).

The tracking, or reproduction of note(s) struck and when, by these early 1980s systems was better than the GS-500/ GR-500 system. The tracking (response time) has always been the biggest hurdle to overcome in guitar sythesis, with many units being rejected by guitarists because they don't respond quick enough, or with the same dynamics as the original part. Fair enough, but when you consider the amount of information provided by striking one note on a guitar string (pitch, note length, bend, vibrato, etc) you can see the innate difficulty Roland struggled with.

The third series (1984-1986) is the most eye-catching system from Roland. The effects pedal look of the blue and yellow boxes was replaced by the sleek looking **GR-700** and **GR-700B** (bass unit). Standard Fender and Gibson guitar designs were replaced by the **G-707** guitar and **G-77** bass "controllers" which featured an offset design (that made lap placement damn near impossible!), and a "stabilizer bar" that ran from the body to the headstock. The futuristic designs looked exciting, and certainly were high quality, but the unusual appearance led to a quick exit from the market.

One of the key downfalls to the whole Roland system of synthesis was the fact that a guitar player had to buy the full package from Roland. No matter what your favorite guitar was, you could only approach synthesizing sounds through a Roland model guitar. Alternate keyboard controllers had been available to keyboardists for a number of years, and the "controller" just had to be a collection of keys that could trigger a synth. Thanks to the advent of MIDI and formalized MIDI codes beginning in 1982, company A's controller could run Company B and Company C's synthesizers. In 1988 (possibly 1987), Roland made an important breakthrough when they introduced the **GK-1 Synthesizer Driver**. The GK-1 was a small black rectangular decoder unit that was held in place by the strap button on the lower bout of the guitar. Guitar signals were picked up with a hex-designed string pickup that mounted near the bridge of your favorite guitar, as well as a 1/4" phone plug to pick up additional information from the magnetic pickups. The signal ran back to the **GM-70 GR-MIDI Converter** rack unit, and signal information was then split into MIDI and regular guitar signal for additional sound reinforcement. The GK-1 had on board controls for master volume and balance, as well as continuous controller #1 and #2. Just like the previous GR series synths (GR-100, GR-300, GR-700), the GK-1/GM-70 connected with a 24-pin cable. Therefore (and mentioned in the Roland advertising), a "G" Series guitar can also work with the GM-70. While the GS Series forerunner only works with itself, any "G Series guitar can work with any "G" Series synth (just check for the 24-pin connector). At this point, Roland got out of the guitar business, and completely into the guitar synthesis business because they finally supplied a "box" that you could slip on your favorite guitar.

In 1989, modernization stepped in when Roland revamped the **GK-1** with the **GK-2**. Gone was the 24-pin bulky block connector in favor of a slim, rounded 13-pin cable. The GK-2 slimmed into a smaller triangular unit that took up less space on the lower bout of the player's guitar, and the GM-70 evolved into the **GR-50** single space rack unit. Currently, Roland markets an upgraded synth driver (**GK-2A**), which some companies such as Fender and Godin build directly into production models. The rack mounted GR-50 has been redesigned into the **GR-1** floor unit (shades of the GR-100!), and the GR-1's 200 "voices" can be expanded into 400 total with in the unit - as well as driving an external synthesizer. Roland also offers a **GR-09** floor unit, and a single half-rack unit called the **GI-10** (which converts Roland GK-2A information into standard MIDI information). Furthermore, Roland has recently introduced a new unit called the **VG-8** (for virtual guitar) which processes the information sent by a GK-2A driver into different (non-synth) pathways to create a whole new category of "guitar processing".

R

GRADING	100% MINT	98% NEAR MINT	95% EXC+	90% EXC	80% VG+	70% VG	60% G

One of the first things to check for when encountering a Roland synth-guitar is that 24-pin cable. The 24-pin design was proprietary for this system, and does not a similar design available at the local computer store - and they are currently "out of stock" on this crucial item at Roland. So even if you aren't going to use the synthesizer, just having the cable brings the value up!
Original list price of the GR-100 was $595; the GR-300 was $995 (!). There was a splitter box called the US-2 that could be used to patch the two units together.

ELECTRIC/SYNTHESIZER CONTROLLER

Roland's dedication to the guitar synth made them the de facto industry standard. During Roland's second series of guitar synths (1980 to 1984) a number of other guitar builders also produced instruments that could "drive" the Roland **GR-100** and **GR-300** synthesizers (and later the **GR-700**). The following prices listed after each model reflect the 1986 retail price: **Gibson Les Paul** ($1,299) and **Explorer** ($1,049); **Hamer A 7 Phantom** ($1,500); **Modulus Graphite Blacknife Special Synth Controller** ($1,500); **M.V. Pedulla MVP-S** guitar ($1,745) **Steinberger GL2T-GR** ($2,250); **Zion Turbo Synth** ($1,395). If you do find the following instruments, now you know why they have the funny plug and extra knobs on them!

In the mid to late 1980s, Aria built a number of guitar controllers with magnetic pickups, piezo pickups, and a Roland GR- MIDI system all on board. These models may have **Aria Custom Shop** on the headstock. Aria offered the MIDI system in the **PE DLX MID** model, **FL MID** model, and **AVB MID 4** bass model. All have extra synth controlling knobs and both a 1/4" phono and a 13-pin DIN jacks mounted on the sides.

G-202 - offset double cutaway body, 6-on-a-side tuners, 2 humbuckers, pickup selector switch on pickguard's treble bout, 2 volume and 2 tone knobs, three synth dedicated switches. Mfg. 1980 to 1984.

$300 $275 $225 $175 $150 $125 $100

The G-202 guitar controller was designed to be used in conjunction with the GR-100 and GR-300 model synthesizers.

G-303 - slightly offset double cutaway body, 3+3 headstock, 2 humbuckers, pickup selector switch on upper bass bout, 2 volume and 2 tone knobs, chrome hardware, 3 dedicated synth switches, bridge, and stop tailpiece. Mfg. 1980 to 1984.

$300 $275 $225 $175 $150 $125 $100

The G-303 guitar controller was designed to be used in conjunction with the GR-100 and GR-300 model synthesizers.

G-505 - offset double cutaway body, six-on-a-side tuners, 3 single coils, 5-way pickup selector switch on pickguard's treble bout, 2 volume and 2 tone knobs, tremolo bridge, three synth dedicated switches. Mfg. 1980 to 1984.

$350 $325 $275 $225 $175 $150 $125

The G-505 guitar controller was designed to be used in conjunction with the GR-100 and GR-300 model synthesizers.

G-707 - asymmetrical "sharkfin" body with extra "stabilizing" graphite arm that connects to headstock, reverse six on a side headstock, 2 covered humbuckers, selector switch. Mfg. 1983 to 1986.

$300 $275 $225 $175 $150 $125 $100

The G-707 guitar controller was designed to be used in conjunction with the GR-700 model synthesizer. The whole package, when introduced in 1983, had a retail price of $2,995 (Guitar controller, $995; GR-700 floor unit, $1,995).

G-808 - slightly offset double cutaway body, laminated central strip with body "wings", 3+3 headstock, 2 humbuckers, pickup selector switch on upper bass bout, 2 volume and 2 tone knobs, gold hardware, 3 dedicated synth switches, bridge, and stop tailpiece. Mfg. 1980 to 1984.

$300 $275 $225 $175 $150 $125 $100

The G-808 guitar controller was designed to be used in conjunction with the GR-100 and GR-300 model synthesizers.

GS-500 - single cutaway hardwood body, 2 humbuckers, 3+3 headstock, pickup selector switch, 2 volume and 2 tone knobs, extra synth-dedicated knobs and switches. Mfg. 1977 to 1980.

$450 $365 $290 $210 $180 $150 $120

The GS-500 guitar controller was designed to be used in conjunction with the GR-500 model synthesizer.

ELECTRIC BASS/SYNTH CONTROLLER

G-33 - offset double cutaway body, four on a side tuners, 1 magnetic pickup/1 hex MIDI pickup, fixed bridge, 1 volume and 2 tone knobs, assorted synth- dedicated controls. Mfg. 1980 to 1984.

$350 $325 $265 $225 $175 $125 $110

The G-33 guitar controller was designed to be used in conjunction with the GR-33B model synthesizer.

B-88 - Similar to the G-33, except featured a center laminated strip and 2 body "wings", and same pickup/synth configuration. Available in Natural finish. Mfg. 1980 to 1984.

$375 $350 $280 $240 $180 $140 $115

The G-88 guitar controller was designed to be used in conjunction with the GR-33B model synthesizer.

G-77 - asymmetrical "sharkfin" body with extra "stabilizing" graphite arm that connects to headstock, reverse four on a side headstock, 2 pickups, selector switches. Mfg. 1984 to 1985.

$275 $250 $200 $160 $140 $120 $100

The G-77 guitar controller was designed to be used in conjunction with the G-700B model synthesizer.

R

ROMAN, ED

Instruments currently built in Danbury, Connecticut since 1998. Distributed by Ed Roman Guitars of Danbury, Connecticut.

In 1998, luthier/designer Ed Roman opened his own custom guitar company (see ROMAN & LIPMAN). Roman's focus is now on his custom **Edberger** guitar models, which combines Steinberger-style bodies with exotic woods and high quality pickups and hardware. Ed Roman specifically makes a number of trips yearly to gather wood, and personally selects each piece.

Roman is definitely a guitar-oriented individual. His website on the internet is possibly the largest site dedicated to guitars, and features information, articles, opinions, and various services available for custom built guitars. Roman is also a large buyer and seller in the secondary guitar market, and favors good quality, well built guitars.

Ed Roman also maintains another company called Exotic Tonewoods that makes pieces of exotic woods available to custom luthiers and guitar builders.

Due to the variances in wood, hardware, and pickups, the following models show no listed "base" price. However, these high quality instruments are still fairly reasonable for the options available to the player. Certain models have been listed for $1,995 up to $2,995 in past publications. For a proper rate quote, contact Ed Roman Guitars directly (see Trademark Index).

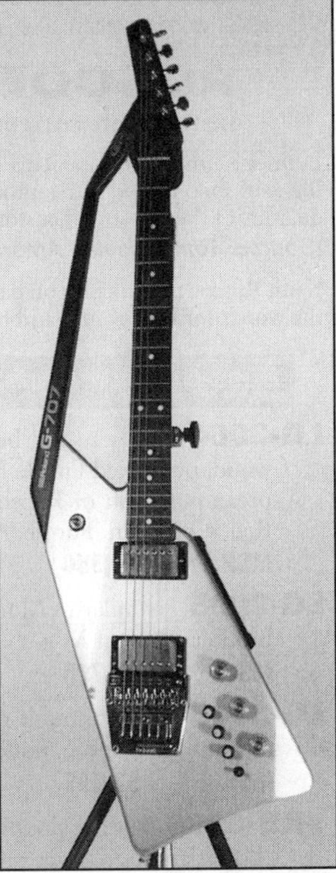

Roland Synth Guitar (G-707)
courtesy Rob's Island Guitars

ELECTRIC

Roman's current custom built model is the **Edberger** which can best be described as a cross between a Steinberger double cutaway model and an Ernie Ball 'Van Halen' model. The **Edberger** has the headless, reverse stringing design of a Steinberger combined with an Original Steinberger TransTrem or S Trem tremolo bridge; but also maintains the offset shallow cutaway feel of the Ernie Ball. **Edberger** models are available with Korina, basswood, alder, mahogany, or swamp ash bodies; Quilted, Burled, Flame, or Spalted maple tops; birds-eye maple or ebony fingerboards; choice of pickups (Tom Holmes, Duncan, EMG, Dimarzio); choice of Original Steinberger TransTrem or S Trem tremolo; solid wood or Strandular Graphite neck; and literally 100 different color finishes. **Edberger** models are available in left-handed and 12-string configurations, or with custom inlays.

Roman also offers other custom built models like the **Fly-berger**, **X-berger**, and Leslie West signature **West-berger** models.

Roman's **Mystery Guitar** model has a solid Honduran mahogany body, neck through design, archtop Quilted or Flamed maple tops, 24-fret bound ebony fingerboard, abalone purfling, and choice of hardware and pickups (Tom Holmes, Duncan, DiMarzio, PRS, or EMG). For further information regarding custom options and pricing, please contact Ed Roman at Ed Roman Guitars directly (see Trademark Index).

ROMAN & LIPMAN

Instruments previously built in Danbury, Connecticut from 1991 to 1997. Distributed by Roman & Lipman Guitars of Danbury, Connecticut.

See ED ROMAN.

Luthier Ed Roman and his partner Barry Lipman founded R & L in the early 1990s to offer custom built instruments to players who were not satisfied with the usual production guitars. R & L, a successful division of the East Coast Music Mall, began offering custom instruments that featured the "most spectacular" wood available. After seven years, Ed Roman left to form his own custom guitar company.

All Roman & Lipman instruments were hand built in the U.S. with American components, with the exception of certain imported exotic woods. Roman & Lipman also offered numerous hardware, pickup, and electronic options. As a result, any Roman & Lipman bass encountered in the secondary market (which is a fairly rare event), must be viewed and priced as a custom built instrument; in other words, priced for what the market will bear.

ELECTRIC

Due to the variances in wood, hardware, and pickups, the following models show no listed "base" price. However, these high quality instruments are still fairly reasonable for the options available to the player. Certain models have been listed for $1,995 up to $2,995 in past publications.

The following model descriptions are the general parameters for the listing as each instrument was basically a custom order. In other words, there is no "standard" base model - guidelines, body designs, and customer satisfaction were the rules of thumb.

The **Penetrator** guitar was first introduced in 1991, and was Roman & Lipman's neck-through solid body guitar. This model boasts a straight string pull with a 3-per-side headstock design; choices of over 15 different body woods, 10 different fingerboard woods, pickups, bridges and electronics. The neck-through design also sports Roman & Lipman's trademarked "No heel neck joint".

The **Sceptre** guitar was introduced in 1992, and was Roman & Lipman's bolt-on neck model. This traditional style guitar boasts high quality tone-wood bodies such as Koa, Quilted Maple and Mahogany combinations, Myrtlewood, Spalted Maple, Burl Maple, and over 10 more choices. Numerous fingerboard materials include Pau Ferro, Brazilian Rosewood, Snakewood, Koa, Macassar Ebony, Flame Maple, Figured Wenge, and others. R & L also offered numerous hardware, pickup, and electronic options.

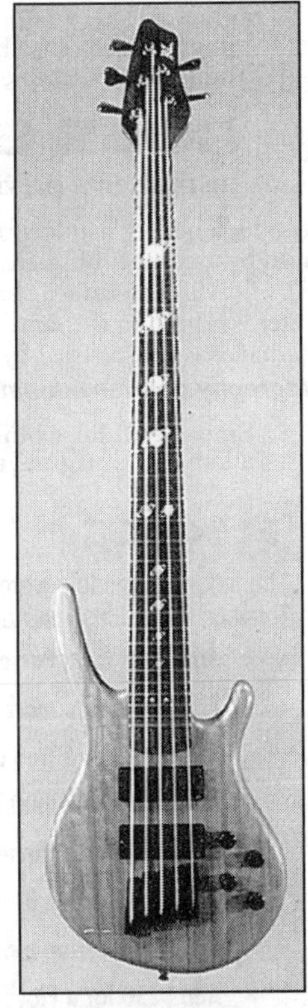
Roman & Lipman
Custom 5 String
courtesy Ed Roman

ELECTRIC BASS

The Intruder bass was offered beginning in 1994 as a four, five, or six string hand constructed instrument. Featuring such tone woods as Quilted Maple, Koa, Korina, Congalo Alves, and Bubinga, these basses have a five piece neck-through-body construction. Different scale lengths, a variety of electronics, pickups combine with R & L's exclusive "Posi-Phase" bridge systems which helps detract the Low B phase cancellation problems on 5 and 6 string models.

The Invader bass was introduced in 1996. A slightly different body design differentiates the Invader from its older brother, the Intruder, but both basses share similar woods, construction, and options.

ROSCOE GUITARS

Instruments currently built in Greensboro, North Carolina since 1971.

Luthier Keith Roscoe opened a shop in Greensboro, North Carolina in 1971 called "The Guitar Shop". From its early origins of four or five guitars a year the workshop turned into a production facility capable of 20 to 30 guitars a month. Roscoe had produced over 900 custom guitars by 1990, and three quarters of them featured custom airbrush or color finishes.

(Source: Tom Wheeler, American Guitars)

Keith Roscoe now focuses on bass guitars. His models feature neck and body woods selected from his collection, and special attention is given to matching the woods for both sound and beauty. For further information, please contact Roscoe Guitars directly (see Trademark Index).

Bass Guitar Models

LG-3000 - offset solid body, choice of Spanish Cedar, mahogany or swamp ash, 4 strings, 24-frets, choice of rosewood, maple, diamond wood, or spalted Purple Heart, 34" scale, small body, figured or flamed maple top, 2 Bartolini pickups plus standard 2-way EQ & Bartolini preamp, Gotoh or Hipshot tuners, black Hipshot bridge. Available in Antique Yellow, Bright Yellow, Emerald Green, Bright Red, Roscoe Red, Cordovan, Purple, Aqua, Cobalt Blue, Faded Blue Jean, Orange, Tobacco Sunburst, Amber and black. Current Mfg.

MSR **$2,350**

LG-3005 - similar to Model LG-300 except in a 5-string configuration, 35" scale, otherwise same features and choice of colors as its 4 string brother. Current Mfg.

MSR **$2,795**

LG-3006 - offset double cutaway LG solid body, similar to LG-3000 and LG-3005 except in a 6-string configuration, same features and colors options as those models, designed in conjunction with Jimmy Haslip. Current Mfg.

MSR **$2,995**

SKB-3006 - offset double cutaway body, standard 6-string design, body slightly larger than LG series basses, 35" scale, 24-frets, same color choices and options as previously listed. Curerent Mfg.

MSR **$2,995**

SKB-3007 - similar to Model SKB-3006 except in a 7-string configuration, can be strung with a low F# or high F, same color options and features as other models. Current Mfg.

MSR **$3,350**

SKB-3008 - similar to Model SKB-3007 except in an 8-string configuration, tuned from low F# to High F (.20 wound), same choice of colors and options as other models. Current Mfg.

MSR **$3,695**

Other options available on all models include ebony, Birdseye Maple, Diamondwood, fretless, and fretless with lines fingerboards, custom inlays, choice of quilted or Birdseye Maple, Cocobola, Burl Maple, Burl Myrtle, Burl Redwood bodies, exhibition grade tops of Quilted Maple, Flame maple, Figured Maple and other exotic woods. Left handed models are available for an additional $135.

ROSE GUITARS

Instruments previously built in Nashville, Tennessee 1981-1998.

These high quality handcrafted guitars feature American made hardware and pickups, as well as highly figured tops. Rose's custom guitars have been played by a number of Nashville's better-known guitar players and session players. Rose, originally an Oregon native, moved to Nashville in the late 1970s. In 1981 he launched both the Rose Guitar Center in Henderson (right outside Nashville) and Jonathan Rose custom guitars. The Rose Guitar Center was been in the same location for the past fifteen years, and featured both new and used instrument sales as well as repair and custom work. Jonathan was ably assisted by his wife Angela, and both could be found either at the shop, or at vintage shows displaying their guitars.

(Biography courtesy Jonathan and Angela Rose, June 1996)

Since 1981, Rose built over 200 custom guitars. Of the 200, 25 were basses. The serialization began in 1981 with #1, and Rose maintained a list of the original specifications, colors, woods, and original owners for each and every one.

ELECTRIC

The following models were all available in Translucent, Emerald Green, Amber, Burgundy, Deep Water Blue, Two-tone Heritage Cherry Burst, and Two-tone Tobacco Burst finishes. Additional custom options include:

Add $595 for a Parsons-White String Bender.

Add $200 for a marbleized finish.

Add $700 for a Tree of Life neck inlay.

Add $375 for a mini Tree of Life inlay.

Add $400 for a Horse and Horse shoe inlay.

Add $100 for top binding.

Add $250 for top binding with Abalone.

Add $250 for a Floyd Rose Tremolo.

Add $200 for a Wilkerson Convertible Bridge.

R

CUSTOM - single cutaway hollow swamp ash body, flamed maple top, two Van Zantz humbucking pickups, one single coil pickup, bird's-eye maple neck with bird's-eye fingerboard, and gold hardware. Disc. Mfg.

Last MSR was $1,695.

ELITE - double cutaway alder or mahogany body, quilted or flamed maple top, two Seymour Duncan pickups, and chrome or gold hardware. Current Mfg.

Last MSR was $2,495.

F-HOLE HOLLOWBODY - hollow swamp ash body, two Van Zantz single coil pickups, bird's-eye maple neck with Brazilian rosewood fingerboard, and chrome hardware. Disc. Mfg.

Last MSR was $1,295.

STANDARD - single cutaway alder body, flame or quilted maple top, contoured back, three Seymour Duncan Alnico pro II single coil pickups, bird's-eye maple neck with ebony fingerboard, and gold hardware. Disc. Mfg.

Last MSR was $1,595.

7/8 STRAT STYLE - offset double cutaway swamp ash body, bird's-eye maple neck, ebony fingerboard, three Seymour Duncan single coil pickups, and chrome hardware. Disc. Mfg.

Last MSR was $1,295.

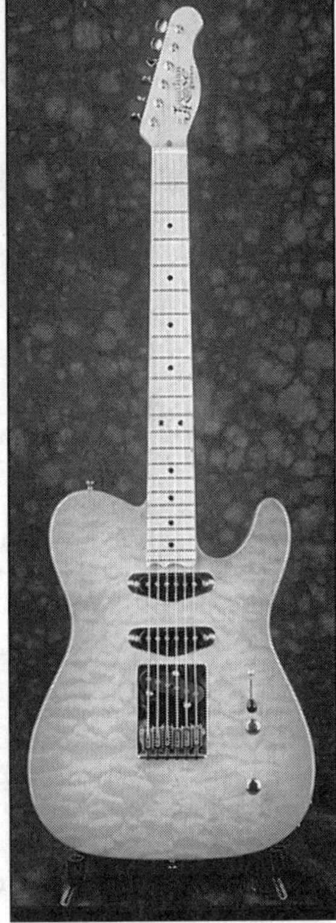

Jonathan Rose Custom
courtesy Rick Kindrel

ROSETTI

See EGMOND and SHERGOLD.

Instruments previously produced in Holland during the early 1960s through the mid 1970s; one solid body model built in England by another company in 1969.

The Rosetti trademark was a brand name used by a UK importer. The Rosetti name turned up on Dutch-built Egmond solid and semi-hollowbody guitars during the 1960s. The same British importer also stocked a Shergold-made solid body model "Triumph" in 1969.

(Source: Tony Bacon and Paul Day, The Guru's Guitar Guide)

ROTOSOUND

Instruments previously built in England in the mid 1970s.

English custom luthier John Birch both designed and built the Rotosound instruments. This high quality solid body did not have any cut-aways in the overall design, and a modular pickup configuration offered the variety of 10 different plug-ins.

(Source: Tony Bacon and Paul Day, The Guru's Guitar Guide)

ROWAN CUSTOM GUITARS

Instruments currently built in Garland, Texas.

Rowan Custom Guitars is a small company in Garland, Texas. Headed by Mike Rowan, this company hand crafts their solid and semi-solid guitars "one at a time" to focus attention to the details and construction techniques.

Rowan offers 4 guitar models: the RSN Set Neck (list $2,300), the RCT-1 (list $1,400), RCT-2 ($1,400), and the RCT-3 ($1,400). For further information regarding specifications and options, contact Rowan Custom Guitars directly (see Trademark Index).

ROY CUSTOM GUITARS

Instruments currently built in Chelmsford (Ontario), Canada.

Roy Custom Guitars offers a completely handcrafted instrument that is available in either left- or right-handed configurations. The **RR Custom Electric Guitar** features a Curly Maple or Cherry wood carved top over a Honduran Mahogany or Alder back. The five piece maple and wenge set-neck has an ebony or rosewood fingerboard, and either gold plated or chromed Gotoh hardware. Retail list price starts at $1,195.

ROYAL

Instruments currently built in England since 1980.

Some of these high quality solid body guitars feature designs based on previous Fender and Gibson favorites. Other original designs include the Medusa and Electra models.

(Source: Tony Bacon and Paul Day, The Guru's Guitar Guide)

ROYALIST

See chapter on House Brands.

This trademark has been identified as a "House Brand" of the RCA Victor Records Store.

(Source: Willie G. Moseley, Stellas & Stratocasters)

RUSTLER

Instruments previously produced in Mason City, Iowa.

Rustler Guitars combined the classic look found in desirable, vintage, single cutaway guitars with the sound, playability, and quality of a custom builder. Instruments were constructed of a curly maple top over alder back and side bodies, and feature gold hardware, 6-on-a-side tuners, and rosewood, maple, or ebony fingerboards.

Rowan Journeyman
courtesy Rowan
Custom Guitars

RYBSKI

Instruments currently built in Wartrace, Tennessee. Distributed by Luthiers Access Group of Chicago, Illinois.

Luthier Slawomir Rybski Waclawik brings close to twenty years of research to the development and custom building of each bass. Waclawik, a bassist himself, combines exotic woods with modern designs.

ELECTRIC BASS

Instruments all feature 34" scale, and a 24-fret (two octave) neck design. Rybski pickups were designed by the luthier and Poland's sound wiz Jan Radwanski. Rybski makes his own pickups and preamp, and the pickups feature a wood cover that match the top of the instrument.

BASIC - cherry (or mahogany or ash) body, padauk neck, 2 Rybski "single coil" pickups, active electronics, master volume/blend/treble/bass controls. Current Mfg.

MSR **$2,750**

Add $200 for 5-string configuration.

Add $350 for 6-string configuration.

PRO - ash (or padauk, or zebrawood, or bubinga) body, padauk (or zebrawood, or purpleheart, or rosewood) top, padauk (or purpleheart or Satinwood) neck, 2 Rybski "double coil" pickups, master volume/blend/treble/bass controls, pickup coil switches, parallel/series switch, active electronics. Current Mfg.

MSR **$3,250**

Add $250 for 5-string configuration.

Add $500 for 6-string configuration.

SPECIAL - zebrawood (or purpleheart, or wenge, or satinwood, or ash) body, zebrawood (or purpleheart, or rosewood, or Bubinga, or wenge) top, purpleheart (or satinwood, or Pau Ferro, or Jatoba) neck, 2 Rybski "double coil" pickups, master volume/blend/treble/mid/bass controls, pickup coil switches, parallel/series switch, active electronics (9 or 18-volt system). Current Mfg.

MSR **$3,650**

Add $250 for 5-string configuration.

Add $500 for 6-string configuration.

Section S

S.D. CURLEE USA

Instruments previously built in Matteson, Illinois from 1975 to 1982.

In the early 1970s, Randy Curlee was the owner of a Chicago based music store. Curlee recognized a need for an inexpensive, hand built quality guitar; and in the late 1970s the instruments he offered ranged in price from $350 (guitar models) to $399 (basses). Curlee thought that the *S.D.* moniker was better than using his first name. Curlee was also the first to plan on overseas *reproductions* occurring, and devised a plan to circumvent that from happening (See S.D. CURLEE INTERNATONAL). After the company closed in 1982, Curlee was involved in Yamaha's guitar production. Curlee also marketed the Zoom sound processors before leaving the music industry.

It is estimated that 15,000 instruments were built during the seven years of production. The majority were basses, and about 3,000 were guitars. Instruments with three digit serial numbers up to around 1000 are the first production models, and serial numbers under 4000 are from the mid to late 1970s. After number 4000, the numbering scheme changed.

(Source: Michael Wright, Guitar Stories Volume One)

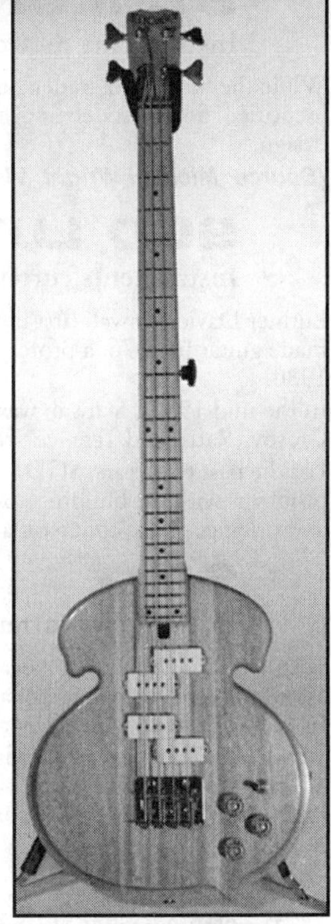

S.D. Curlee Bass
courtesy Guy Bruno

ELECTRIC

Typical of the times when everybody thought that brass parts helped with sustaining properties, S.D. Curlee instruments featured a squared brass nut, brass bridge, brass neck plate and electronics cover. Necks consisted of hard rock maple, and bodies consisted of exotic woods like butcher block Maple, Brazilian or Honduran mahogany, Black walnut, Purpleheart, Koa, and (later models) poplar. Hardware included Schaller tuners, DiMarzio pickups, and BadAss bridges. Headstocks were 3+3 (2+2 on basses), and featured a master volume knob and a tone knob per pickup, as well as a pickup selector toggle. The neck sat halfway into the body in a channel, and had four bolts in a large rear plate (sort of a bolt-on/set-neck hybrid).

Individual models are hard to determine, as there were some variations during production. At least 8 different models were named, although the first three (Standards I, II, and III) are the original models that the following five were variants of. Finally, as the company was closing down in 1982, Curlee built some Destroyer, Flying V, and other original shapes.

S.D. CURLEE INTERNATIONAL

See HONDO.

Instruments previously built in Japan from the late 1970s to the mid 1980s, as well as in Korea during the same time period.

In the mid 1970s, Randy Curlee proposed a deal with Jerry Freed of Hondo Guitars to build licensed designs of his guitars. Curlee planned to beat other unlicensed *copies* to the market, and make money on the reproductions as well. Guitars had similar designs as the S.D. Curlee USA models, except had **S.D. Curlee Design Series** across the peghead, and **Aspen** model designation as well.

Curlee also licensed the design to the Matsumoku company in Japan, who produced similar looking models under the **S.D. Curlee International** logo. The Japanese-produced models were marketed and sold mainly in the Oriental market, while the Hondo versions were distributed in the U.S. as well as the U.K. Some models were distributed by J.C. Penney and Global dealers, and some of the Global dealers even rebranded them under the Global trademark.

(Source: Michael Wright, Guitar Stories Volume One)

ST. BLUES

Instruments previously built in Memphis, Tennessee circa mid to late 1980s. Distributed by S & T Workshop of Memphis, Tennessee.

St. Blues instruments were distributed by the S & T Workshop in Memphis, Tennessee. These high quality electric solid body guitars were favored by such guitarists as Joe Walsh and Jeff Carlisi (.38 Special). Models include the dual cutaway Bluescaster and the single Florentine cutaway Bluesmaster. If you're thinking we're gonna "Tele" ya which Fender-style model they are based on, you're wrong! But consider this: Both models featured maple or rosewood fingerboards, 6-on-a-side tuners, 2 single coil pickups, a fixed bridge, and volume/tone controls plus a three way selector switch mounted on a metal controls plate.you be the judge! Retail list prices were unavailable for comment in this edition.

The last given address for St. Blues/S & T Workshop was 1492 Union, Memphis, Tennessee 38104.

ST. GEORGE

Instruments previously produced in Japan during the mid to late 1960s.

The St. George trademark was a brand name used by U.S. importer Buegeleisen & Jacobson of New York, New York. It has also been reported that instruments bearing the St. George label were imported by the WMI Corporation of Los Angeles, California. These entry level solid body guitars featured some original body designs, but low production quality.

(Source: Michael Wright, Guitar Stories Volume One)

ST. MORITZ

Instruments previously produced in Japan circa 1960s.

While the St. Moritz trademark was a brand name used on Japanese-built guitars, neither the U.S. distributor nor the Japanese manufacturer has been identified. Some models appear to be Teisco/Kawai. Most are the shorter scale beginner's guitar, and are available in a thinline hollowbody or solid body design.

(Source: Michael Wright, Vintage Guitar Magazine)

SGD LUTHERIE

Instruments currently built in Hoboken, New Jersey.

Luthier David Schwab first began repairing and modifying basses and guitars back in 1972. Schwab, who began playing bass in 1969, built his first hand made guitar in 1976, a prototype solid body nylon stringed classical. Another original design was the **MantaRay** 8-string bass, which first debuted in 1980.

In the mid 1980s, Schwab was working at American Showster Guitars, making the '57 **Chevy Tailfin** model for such players as Billy Gibbons, Robin Crosby (Ratt), and Terence Trent D'Arby. The first of these guitars he built appeared in an edition of ***Playboy***, in a section on unique holiday gifts.

For the past two years, SGD Lutherie has been located in a 150 year old building (once the home of Guild Guitars) in Hoboken, New Jersey. After having problems with the building's owners, Schwab has returned to his former location in Orange, New Jersey. For further information regarding current models and pricing, please contact David Schwab directly (see Trademark Index).

SMD

Instruments currently built in New York. Distributed by Toys From the Attic in Shelter Lane, New York.

Luthier Chris Stambaugh began building high quality string instruments for his friends and himself out of necessity: they needed the quality but couldn't afford the retail prices. Stambaugh, born and raised in North Berwick, Maine, started building guitars during his tenure at a furniture building company. In 1995, his band won the Maine Musician's Award for Originality.

Stambaugh is currently attending the Wentworth Institute of Technology and is majoring in Industrial Design. Stambaugh was chosen for the Arioch Scholar program, and is one of three students attending on the program's full scholarship. His stated goal is to craft the highest quality instruments for a fair market price, using environmentally friendly techniques and form and function designs drawn from his educational background.

ELECTRIC

The **SMD Custom** 6-string features a neck-through-body design, and oil finish, Stambaugh's standard peghead and body pattern. Everything else about the guitar is left to the customer's choice: tonewoods, pickups, electronics, hardware, neck inlays, and wiring style is based on the preference of the player commissioning the guitar, and is covered in the base price starting at $1,200. Further options of a gloss finish (add $150) or a tremolo bridge (add $150) are priced extra.

ELECTRIC BASS

Stambaugh's **SMD Custom Bass** is available in 4-, 5-, or 6-string configurations. Similar to the SMD Custom guitar, luthier Stambaugh only specifies an oil finish, peghead and body pattern (the look of the instrument). All other options are left to the customer's choice. While there is no option for a bass tremolo, the gloss finish option is an extra $150. Retail prices start at $1,300 (4-string), $1,450 (5-string), up to $1,600 (6-string model). Luthier Stambaugh is also building custom designed banjos (including a Banjo Bass).

SMT GUITARS

Instruments currently built in Great Falls, Virginia since 1992.

Scientifico Musico Technographique (SMT Guitars) is a full custom guitar manufacturing company that produces 30 instruments a year in limited production. Their instruments are inspired by the work of Paul Bigsby and Nat Daniels (Danelectro) with a touch of Zemaitis thrown in. These instruments are known for their wacky designs, pearl inlay, and excellent playability. Elements of fine art, '40s industrial design, and American hot rod culture are seen in these instruments. SMT has created guitars for Andy Gill (Gang of Four), Chris Isaak, and Billy F. Gibbons (ZZ Top). Due to the customer's involvement in the design process, SMT guitars are not sold in stores and are available directly from the manufacturer.

(Company information courtesy Steven Metz, SMT Guitars)

SSD

See SPECTOR.

Instruments currently built in Korea. Distributed exclusively in North America by Armadillo Enterprises of Clearwater, Florida.

Stuart Spector co-founded Spector Guitars in 1976, and became well known for the sleek, neck-through-body design that proved popular with bass players. In 1985, Kramer (BKL) bought the company while Stuart Spector maintained a consulting position for three years.

In 1989, Spector left Kramer and founded Stuart Spector Designs, Ltd. He introduced the SD bass in 1992, and along with Joe Veillette began handcrafting instruments, using custom made hardware and fine hardwoods. Veillette left SSD in the spring of 1996 to work on his own designs as well as do outside consulting for other firms. Stuart Spector reacquired the rights to his Spector trademark in 1997. Both the U.S. and European produced models became the **Spector** line, while the current Korean produced models retained the **SSD** trademark.

The U.S. built NS and SD series models were previously built in Woodstock, New York from 1992 to 1996; and the Europe series models in Czechoslovakia from 1995 to 1996.

GRADING	100% MINT	98% NEAR MINT	95% EXC+	90% EXC	80% VG+	70% VG	60% G

Sadowsky Vintage Tele Style
courtesy Sadowsky Guitars

ELECTRIC BASS

Korea Series

NS94 (NS-K-4) - offset double cutaway soft maple body, through-body maple neck, rosewood fingerboard with dot inlays, 34" scale, black die cast fixed bridge, blackface peghead with pearl logo inlay, 2-per-side tuners, black hardware, 2 EMG HZ humbucking pickups, two volume/treble/bass EQ controls, active electronics. Available in Gloss Black finish. Disc. 1998.

$750 $675 $595 $500 $425 $325 $250
Last MSR was $950.

NS94S - similar to the NS94. Available in Amber Stain, Black Stain, Blue Stain, Honeyburst, Matte Natural, Natural, Padauk Stain, and Red Stain finishes. Disc. 1998.

$775 $695 $625 $525 $450 $350 $275
Last MSR was $995.

NS95 (NS-K-5) - similar to NS94, except has 5-string configuration, 3/2-per-side tuners. Available in Gloss Black finish. Disc. 1998.

$800 $725 $650 $550 $475 $375 $295
Last MSR was $1,050.

NS95S - similar to NS95. Available in Amber Stain, Black Stain, Blue Stain, Honeyburst, Matte Natural, Natural, Padauk Stain, and Red Stain finishes. Disc. 1998.

$825 $725 $675 $575 $500 $395 $300
Last MSR was $1,095.

SADOWSKY

Instruments currently produced in New York, New York since 1979. Distributed by Sadowsky Guitars Ltd. of Manhattan, New York.

Roger Sadowsky, a noted East Coast repairman and luthier, has been providing quality customizing and repairs in his shop since 1979. Sadowsky originally apprenticed with Master Luthier Augustino LoPrinzi in New Jersey between 1972 to 1974. He then spent five years as the head of the service department for Medley Music Corporation located outside of Philadelphia, Pennsylvania. Upon opening his own shop, Sadowsky initially concentrated on proper instrument set-ups and repair for studio musicians and touring personnel. This background of repair work on top-notch personal instruments became the basis for Sadowsky's later designs.

Sadowsky's instruments are based on time-tested Fender designs, with a primary difference being the attention paid to the choice of woods. The better a guitar sounds acoustically translates into a better sound when used electronically. The nature of custom work versus production line assembly insures that a player will get the features specified, and Sadowsky has also introduced his own custom active preamps and circuitry. Current staff members include Norio Imai and Ken Fallon.

Sadowsky builds an outboard version of his bass preamp for players unable (or unwilling, in the case of a vintage instrument) to have a preamp installed in their instruments. This preamp simply consists of a volume, bass, and treble knobs, but the simplicity of the controls belies the sophisticated nature of the circuitry.

ELECTRIC

THE SADOWSKY GUITAR - offset double cutaway, undersized Strat style alder body, 22-fret maple neck, Morado fingerboard, dot position markers, 6-on-a-side tuners, 3 single coil Sadowsky pickups, vintage style tremelo bridge, by-passable preamp with midrange boost and boost gain. Available in Lake Placid Blue finish. Current Mfg.

MSR $2,500

Add $75 for Swamp Ash body.

Add $200 for bent (arched) maple top.

Add $50 for Black hardware.

Add $75 for Gold Hardware.

Add $200 for Vintage Color Matching Headstock.

VINTAGE TELE - Tele style Swamp Ash body, 22-fret maple neck with maple fingerboard, dot position markers, 6-on-a-side tuners, six-saddle vintage style bridge, 2 Joe Barden pickups, Sadowsky preamp. Available in Transparent White finish. Current Mfg.

MSR $2,600

Add $50 for Black Hardware.

Add $75 for Gold Hardware

Add $200 for Vintage Color Matching Headstock.

S

ELECTRIC NYLON STRING GUITAR - Tele style body, Quilted Maple top on alder, 22-fret maple neck, Morado fingerboard with dot position markers, 6-on-a-side tuners, Piezo crystal transducer with Sadowsky preamp. Available in Cherry Sunburst finish. Current Mfg.

MSR $2,700

Add $500 for MIDI option.

ELECTRIC BASS

THE SADOWSKY BASS - offset double cutaway slightly undersized Jazz Bass style body, 21-fret maple neck, alder body, Sadowsky style pickups, active tone circuit, preamp, 4-string. Available in Candy Apple Red finish. Current Mfg.

MSR $2,425

Add $75 for Swamp Ash body.
Add $275 for bent (arched) maple top.
Add $150 for Vintage Style Basses.
Add $200 for Vintage Color Matching Headstock.
Add $50 for Black Hardware.
Add $75 for Gold Hardware.
Add $100 for Hipshot Bass D-Tuner.
Add $100-250 for Fretless Basses.
Add $100 for Passive Tone/Stacked Preamp.

SAKAI

Instruments previously produced in Japan during the early 1970s.

The Sakai trademark is a brand name of a United Kingdom importer on these entry level to intermediate instruments. The solid and semi-hollowbody guitars have some original designs and designs based on classic American favorites.
(Source: Tony Bacon and Paul Day, The Guru's Guitar Guide)

T. SAKASHTA GUITARS

Instruments currently built in Van Nuys, California. Distribution is directly handled by T. Sakashta Guitars of Van Nuys, California.

Luthier Taku Sakashta builds high quality acoustic Archtop and steel string guitars. All are offered with custom options per model.

ELECTRIC

Jam Master Series

The Jam Master model is a double cutaway archtop semi hollowbody electric guitar, and features differing wood and finish options for the three models. However, the three models do share some similar construction points, such as a Gaboon ebony (or cocobolo) pickguard, Gotoh or Schaller tuning machines, and a Sakashta original design aluminum tailpiece (or Gotoh or Schaller tailpiece). The Jam Master features a Tom Holmes H-450 humbucker in the neck position, and a Tom Holmes H-453 humbucker in the Bridge position. Electronics includes 2 volume knobs, 2 tone knobs with series/parallel switching, and a three way pickup selector toggle switch.

Other options include a maple neck on models two or three, a solid brass tailpiece that replaces stock Gotoh or Schaller, gold hardware, a two tone sunburst, or a three tone sunburst.

The **Jam Master Model One** features a book matched Calelo walnut top, back and matching sides; the bound American black walnut neck has a Gaboon ebony fingerboard and pearl inlays. The Model One is available in high gloss nitrocellulose Natural or Transparent Black finish.

The **Jam Master Model Two** is constructed of book matched bigleaf maple top, back and matching sides; the bound neck is of Honduran mahogany and has a Brazilian rosewood fingerboard with pearl inlays. The Model Two is finished in a high gloss nitrocellulose Blonde, Cherry Red, or Transparent Black finish.

The final **Jam Master, Model Three** sports a book matched Sitka spruce top and bigleaf maple back and matching sides. The bound eastern rock maple neck has a Gaboon ebony fingerboard and pearl inlays, and is offered in a high gloss nitrocellulose Blonde, Cherry Red, or Transparent Black finish.

SAKURA

Instruments previously produced in Japan during the mid 1970s. Production moved to Korea during the 1980s.

The Sakura trademark is a brand name of a UK importer. Entry level to intermediate quality instruments with some original design and others favoring classic American designs.
(Source: Tony Bacon and Paul Day, The Guru's Guitar Guide)

SAMICK

Instruments currently produced in Korea since 1965. Current production of instruments is in Korea and City of Industry, California. Distributed in the U.S. market by Samick Music Corporation of City of Industry, California.

For a number of years, the Samick corporation was the *phantom builder* of instruments for a number of other trademarks. When the Samick trademark was finally introduced to the U.S. guitar market, a number of consumers thought that the company was brand new. However, Samick has been producing both upright and grand pianos, as well as stringed instruments for nearly forty years.

GRADING	100% MINT	98% NEAR MINT	95% EXC+	90% EXC	80% VG+	70% VG	60% G

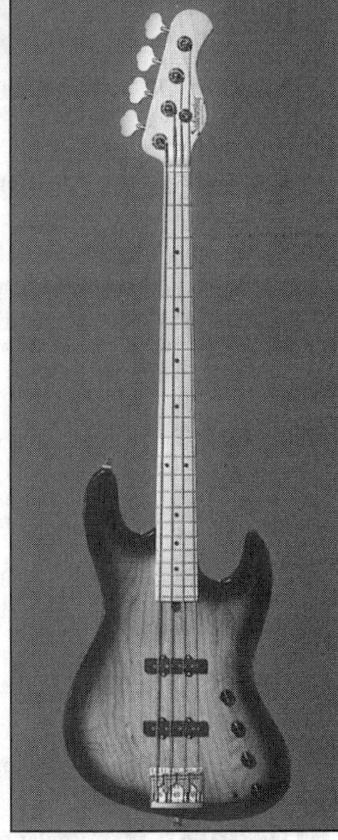
Sadowsky 4-String Bass courtesy Sadowsky Guitars

The **Samick Piano Co.** was established in Korea in 1958. By January of 1960 they had started to produce upright pianos, and within four years became the first Korean piano exporter. One year later in 1965, the company began manufacturing guitars, and by the early 1970s expanded to produce grand pianos and harmonicas as well. In 1973 the company incorporated as the **Samick Musical Instruments Mfg. Co., Ltd.** to reflect the diversity it encompassed. Samick continued to expand into guitar production. They opened a branch office in Los Angeles in 1978, a brand new guitar factory in 1979, and a branch office in West Germany one month before 1981.

Throughout the 1980s Samick continued to grow, prosper, and win awards for quality products and company productivity. The **Samick Products Co.** was established in 1986 as an affiliate producer of other products, and the company was listed on the Korean Stock Exchange in September of 1988. With their size of production facilities (the company claims to be *cranking out over a million guitars a year*, according to a recent brochure), Samick could be referred to as modern day producer of *House Brand* guitars as well as their own brand. In the past couple of years Samick acquired Valley Arts, a guitar company known for its one-of-a-kind instruments and custom guitars. This merger stabilized Valley Arts as the custom shop *wing* of Samick, as well as supplying Samick with quality American designed guitars.

Samick continues to expand their line of guitar models through the use of innovative designs, partnerships with high exposure endorsees (like Blues Saraceno and Ray Benson), and new projects such as the Robert Johnson Commemorative and the D'Leco Charlie Christian Commemorative guitars.

(Samick Company History courtesy Rick Clapper; Model Specifications courtesy Dee Hoyt)

In addition to their acoustic and electric guitars and basses, Samick offers a wide range of other stringed instruments such as autoharps, banjos, mandolins, and violins.

ELECTRIC ARCHTOP

American Classic Charlie Christian Estate Series

All Charlie Christian Estate Series models have a 16" lower body width and 2 1/2" body depth (a portion of Estate Series sales proceeds go directly to respective surviving family members).

CCTS 650 BK - single cutaway hollow body, bound top, solid top/back, set-in neck, 22-fret fingerboard with white split block inlay, 2 f-holes, 3-per-side tuners, tune-o-matic bridge/stop tailpiece, gold hardware, raised matching pickguard, 2 covered humbuckers, 2 volume/2 tone controls (with coil tap), 3-way pickup selector. Available in Black finish. Mfg. 1996-1998.

$900 $775 $690 $600 $520 $435 $350
Last MSR was $1,190.

CCFT 650 GS - similar to the CCTS 650 BK, except has rosewood bridge/gold plated trapeze tailpiece. Available in Golden Sunburst finish. Mfg. 1996-1998.

$900 $775 $690 $600 $520 $435 $350
Last MSR was $1,190.

CCTT 650 WH - similar to the CCTS 650 BK, except has tune-o-matic bridge/trapeze tailpiece. Available in White finish. Mfg. 1996-1998.

$900 $775 $690 $600 $520 $435 $350
Last MSR was $1,190.

ELECTRIC

All American Classics by Valley Arts models are optional with Seymour Duncan pickups as an upgrade.

Add $160 for 2 Seymour Duncan single coil pickups (upgrade).

Add $180 for 3 Seymour Duncan single coil pickups (upgrade).

Add $200 for Seymour Duncan single/single/humbucker pickups (upgrade).

Alternative Series

KJ-540 (AURORA) - offset double cutaway alder body, bolt-on maple neck, 24-fret bound rosewood fingerboard with pearl dot inlay, double locking vibrato, 6-on-a-side tuners, black hardware, single coil/humbucker pickup, volume/tone control, 3-position switch. Available in Aurora finish. Disc. 1994.

$345 $295 $245 $195 $175 $160 $150
Last MSR was $490.

KR-564 GPE (HAWK) - offset double cutaway alder body, bolt-on maple neck, 24-fret bound rosewood fingerboard with pearl triangle inlay, double locking vibrato, 6-on-a-side tuners, black hardware, 2 single coil rail/1 humbucker pickups, volume/2 tone controls, 5-position switch. Available in Hawk Graphic finish. Disc. 1994.

$405 $350 $290 $230 $205 $190 $175
Last MSR was $580.

GRADING	100% MINT	98% NEAR MINT	95% EXC+	90% EXC	80% VG+	70% VG	60% G

KR-654 GPS (Nightbreed) - similar to the Hawk, except features a Nightbreed Graphic finish. Disc. 1994.

		$455	$390	$325	$260	$235	$215	$195

Last MSR was $650.

KR-564 GPSK (Viper) - similar to the Hawk, except features a Viper Graphic finish. Disc. 1994.

		$455	$390	$325	$260	$235	$215	$195

Last MSR was $650.

American Classic Ray Benson Signature Series

Earlier versions of the Ray Benson Signature Series (model DTR-100) featured similar designs like a contoured alder body, but did not include a maple top. Other differing features include 2 single coil pickups and a 3-way selector switch. These models were available in Black (BK) and Tobacco Sunburst (TS) finishes.

STR-100 TS - contoured single cutaway alder body, figured maple top, bolt-on maple neck, 25 1/2" scale, 21-fret maple fingerboard with black dot inlay, fixed bridge, 6-on-a-side die-cast tuners, chrome hardware, violin-shaped white pearloid pickguard, humbucker/Hot Rail single coil Duncan-Designed pickups, volume/tone (push/pull coil tap) control, 5-position switch, controls mounted on metal plate. Available in Tobacco Sunburst finish. Disc. 1999.

		$355	$305	$270	$230	$195	$160	$120

Last MSR was $470.

STR-100 AM - similar to the STR-100 TS, except features flame maple top, humbucker/2 single coil pickups. Available in Amber Flame finish. Current Mfg.

MSR	$750	$575	$475	$425	$375	$325	$275	$195

STR-200 TBK - similar to the STR-100 TS, except features flame maple top, gold hardware, Texas-shaped white pearloid pickguard, humbucker/2 single coil pickups. Available in Transparent Black finish. Current Mfg.

MSR	$825	$625	$525	$475	$425	$375	$325	$250

STR-200KF N - Similar to STR-200 TBK, exceptin Kus finish. This is the NAMM 100th Anniversary Model. 2001 introduction.

MSR	$897	$675	$575	$525	$475	$425	$375	$325

American Classic Blues Saraceno TV Twenty Guitars

Blues Saraceno TV Twenty models may feature a "-cicle" finish, a *Burst*-style finish in non-traditional 'Burst colors.

BS ASH - offset rounded cutaway solid alder body, bolt-on maple neck, 25 1/2" scale, 22-fret maple fingerboard with offset black dot inlay, strings through-body fixed bridge, 3-per-side die-cast tuners, black hardware, 2 single coil/humbucker Duncan-Designed pickups, volume/tone (push/pull coil tap) controls, 5-way selector switch. Available in Black (BK), Raid Red (RA), and White (WH) finishes. Disc. 1999.

		$450	$390	$345	$295	$250	$200	$150

Last MSR was $600.

Add $50 for Black/Red/Grey (BRGR) or Red/Yellow/Black (RYB) Plaid finishes (Model BS ASH PP).

BS AVH - similar to the BS ASH, except features vintage-style tremolo. Available in Black (BK), Raid Red (RA), and White (WH) solid finishes, Berry-cicle (BEC), Cherry-cicle (CHC), Cream-cicle (CRC), Fudge-cicle (FUC), Grape-cicle (GRC), Lemon-cicle (LEC), and Lime-cicle (LIC) "burst" finishes. Disc. 1999.

		$450	$390	$345	$295	$250	$200	$150

Last MSR was $600.

Add $50 for Black (MBKF), Blue (MBLF), Gold (MGF), Green (MGRF), and Silver (MSF) Metal Flake finish (Model BS AVH).

Add $50 for Blue/Burgundy/Black (BLBUBC) or Orange/Green/Gold (OGNGDC) Plaid finishes (Model BS AVH PP).

BS ALG - similar to the BS ASH, except features licensed Floyd Rose locking tremolo, 2 Duncan-Designed humbuckers, volume control, 3-way selector switch. Available in Black (BK), Raid Red (RA), and White (WH) finishes. Disc. 1999.

		$525	$455	$400	$345	$290	$235	$175

Last MSR was $700.

Add $50 for Black/Yellow/Blue (BYBL) or White/Blue/Red (WBLR) Plaid finishes (Model BS ALG PP).

American Classic Jazz Series

HF-650 (BLUENOTE) - single rounded cutaway bound hollow body, arched maple top, raised black pickguard, 2 f-holes, maple back/sides/neck, 22-fret bound rosewood fingerboard with abalone/pearl block inlay, adjustable rosewood bridge/trapeze tailpiece, bound blackface peghead with pearl vines/logo inlay, 3-per-side tuners, gold hardware, 2 covered humbucker pickups, 2 volume/2 tone controls, 3-position switch. Available in Natural (N) and Sunburst (SB) finishes. Current Mfg.

MSR	$1,125	$850	$750	$698	$650	$595	$550	$495

HJ-650 - L-5 style maple body, single rounded cutaway, maple set neck, rosewood fingerboard, 20-frets, 25 ½" scale, block position markers, 3-per-side tuners, 2 f-holes, die-cast tuners, gold hardware, 2 humbucking pickups, 2 volume/2 tone controls, adjustable bridge, trapeze tailpiece. Available in Natural and Tobacco Sunburst finishes. Current Mfg.

MSR	$1,155	$865	$735	$625

S

GRADING	100% MINT	98% NEAR MINT	95% EXC+	90% EXC	80% VG+	70% VG	60% G

Samick HJ-650 N
courtesy Samick

HJ-650/CN - similar to Model HJ-650, except has single Florentine cutaway. Available in Natural finish. Current Mfg.

MSR $1,200 $895 $750 $650

HJ-650 TSB LH - similar to Model HJ-650, except in Left Hand configuration. Available in Tobacco Sunburst finish. Current Mfg.

MSR $1,155 $865 $735 $625

HJ-650 TSB (WABASH) - single round cutaway arched hollow body, maple top, bound holes, raised black pickguard, bound body, 17" lower body bout, maple back/sides/neck, 20-fret bound rosewood fingerboard with pearl block inlay, adjustable rosewood bridge/trapeze tailpiece, bound peghead with pearl flower/logo inlay, 3-per-side tuners, gold hardware, 2 humbucker pickups, 2 volume/2 tone controls, 3-position switch. Available in Natural and Sunburst finishes. Disc. 1999.

$575 $500 $440 $380 $320 $260 $195

Last MSR was $770.

Add $10 for Natural finish (Model HJ-650 N).

HJS-650 TR VS - similar to the HJ-650 TSB, except features abalone bound top/bound raised pickguard, solid spruce top, 17 1/2" lower body bout, bigsby tremolo bridge. Available in Abalone Sunburst finish. Current Mfg.

MSR $1,700 $1,275 $1,100 $965 $830 $695 $560 $425

HJ-660N - similar to HJ-650, except has Tiger top, 3 P-90 pickups and Vintage style tailpiece. Available in Natural finish. New 2001.

MSR $1,275 $950 $815 $695

HJ-850 OR - L-5 style body, arched spruce top, arched maple back and sides, set maple neck, rosewood fingerboard, 20-frets, 25 ½" scale, 2 humbucking pickups, 2 volume/2 tone controls, chrome hardware, Grover tuners, Tune-O-Matic bridge with vibrato. Available in Orange finish. New 2001.

MSR $1,137 $850 $725 $625

SAT-450 (KINGSTON) - double rounded cutaway semi-hollow body, arched flame maple top, bound body, bound f-holes, raised black pickguard, maple back/sides, mahogany neck, 22-fret bound rosewood fingerboard with pearl dot inlay, tune-o-matic bridge/stop tailpiece, bound peghead with pearl leaf/logo inlay, 3-per-side tuners, chrome hardware, 2 humbucker pickups, 2 volume/2 tone controls, 3-position switch. Available in Black, Cherry Sunburst, Golden Sunburst, and Natural finishes. Disc. 1995.

$320 $265 $240 $215 $185 $160 $135

Last MSR was $530.

SAT-650 CSTT (KINGSTON CLASSIC) - double cutaway semi-hollow body, arched tigertail flame maple top, bound f-holes, raised black pickguard, maple back/sides, mahogany neck, 22-fret bound rosewood fingerboard with pearl diamond inlay, tune-o-matic bridge/stop tailpiece, bound peghead with pearl leaf/logo inlay, 3-per-side tuners, gold hardware, 2 humbucker pickups, 2 volume/2 tone controls, 3-position switch. Available in Cherry Sunburst and Natural finishes. Current Mfg.

MSR $1,140 $850 $750 $695 $650 $595 $550 $475

Add $60 for Natural finish (Model SAT-650 TT N).

SAT-650 PBE - similar to SAT-650 CSTT except features Pink Bird's-eye top, back and sides. Current Mfg.

MSR $1,185 $875 $775 $695 $650 $595 $550 $495

SAB-650 BGS - similar to the SAT-650 CSTT, except features bird's-eye maple top/back/sides. Available in Burgundy finish. Disc. 2000.

$595 $515 $450 $390 $325 $265 $200

Last MSR was $790.

American Classic LP Style Series

LP-750 - single cutaway mahogany body, bound mother-of-pearl covered top, set-in mahogany neck, 24 3/4" scale, 24-fret ebony fingerboard with pearl block inlay, bound mother-of-pearl covered headstock, 3-per-side tuners, chrome hardware, tune-o-matic bridge/stop tailpiece, 2 humbucking pickups with chrome covers, 2 volume/2 tone controls, 3-way selector. Current Mfg.

MSR $1,400 $1,050 $900 $790 $680 $570 $460 $350

American Classic Trad-S Style Series

Instruments in this series have an offset double cutaway body, bolt-on maple neck, 21-fret fingerboard, 6-on-a-side tuners, chrome hardware, 3 single coil pickups, 1 volume/2 tone controls, 5-position switch as following features (unless otherwise listed).

GRADING	100% MINT	98% NEAR MINT	95% EXC+	90% EXC	80% VG+	70% VG	60% G

DCL-9500 SDQ AN - carved quilt maple top, abalone body binding, set-in neck, ebony fingerboard, tune-o-matic bridge/stop tailpiece, 2 Duncan humbucker pickups, volume/tone controls, 3-way selector. Disc. 2000.

	$600	$520	$460	$395	$330	$265	$200

Last MSR was $800.

JAD-120 BGS - offset body design, solid maple neck, 25 1/2" scale, 22-fret fingerboard, die-cast tuners, Schaller tremolo, 2 S-90 pickups, volume/tone controls, 3-way selector. Available in Burgundy Sunburst. Mfg. 1997-1998.

	$340	$300	$265	$230	$190	$155	$115

Last MSR was $450.

MFN-130 BLS - solid maple neck, 25 1/2" scale, 22-fret fingerboard, die-cast tuners, Wilkinson tremolo, 3 S-90 pickups, volume/tone controls. Available in Blue Burst finish. Mfg. 1997-1998.

	$375	$325	$285	$245	$205	$165	$125

Last MSR was $500.

RL-660 A TR - plank body, bird's-eye maple neck, 25 1/2" scale, 24-fret ebony fingerboard with white dot inlay, gold hardware, tune-o-matic bridge/stop tailpiece, 2 single coil/humbucker pickups, volume/tone controls. Available in Transparent Red finish. Disc. 1999.

	$375	$325	$285	$245	$205	$165	$125

Last MSR was $500.

SCM-1 G FAM - arched mahogany body, flame maple top, bird's-eye maple neck, 25 1/2" scale, 24-fret ebony fingerboard with white dot inlay, gold hardware, licensed Floyd Rose tremolo, 2 single coil/humbucker Duncan pickups, volume/tone controls. Available in Natural Flame finish. Disc. 1999.

	$450	$390	$345	$295	$250	$200	$150

Last MSR was $600.

SSM-1 - alder body, 22-fret maple fingerboard with black dot inlay, 3 single coil pickups, vintage-style tremolo, white pickguard, 6-on-a-side die-cast tuners. Available in Black, Lake Placid Blue, Metallic Red, Natural Satin, Sea Foam Green, Tobacco Sunburst and White finishes. Mfg. 1994 to date.

MSR $525	$395	$350	$295	$250	$195	$150	$95

In 1999, Florescent Green, Cherry Sunburst, Burgundy Mist finishes were introduced.

SSM-1 LH - similar to the SSM-1, except in a left-handed configuration. Available in Black and Metallic Red finishes. Current Mfg.

MSR $570	$425	$375	$325	$275	$225	$175	$125

SSM-2 - similar to the SSM-1, except features 22-fret rosewood fingerboard with white dot inlay, licensed Floyd Rose tremolo, 2 single coil/humbucker pickups, volume/tone controls. Available in Lake Placid Blue, Metallic Red, and Transparent Black finishes. Mfg. 1994-1998.

	$330	$290	$255	$220	$185	$150	$110

Last MSR was $440.

SSM-3 - similar to the SSM-1, except features 22-fret rosewood fingerboard with white dot inlay, licensed Floyd Rose tremolo, gold hardware, 2 single coil/humbucker pickups, volume/tone controls. Available in Black and Tobacco Sunburst finishes. Mfg. 1994-1998.

	$375	$325	$285	$245	$205	$165	$125

Last MSR was $500.

SMX-3 - bound carved mahogany body, bird's-eye maple neck, 25 1/2" scale, 22-fret bound ebony fingerboard with pearl dot inlay, bound headstock, licensed Floyd Rose tremolo, gold hardware, 2 single coil/humbucker pickups, volume/tone controls. Available in Cherry Sunburst finish. Mfg. 1994 to 1996.

	$390	$325	$295	$260	$225	$195	$165

Last MSR was $650.

SMX-4 - similar to the SMX-3, except features tune-o-matic bridge/stop tailpiece. Available in Transparent Blue and Transparent Red finishes. Mfg. 1994 to 2000.

	$450	$390	$345	$295	$250	$200	$150

Last MSR was $600.

American Classic Trad-T Style Series

Instruments in this series have a single cutaway body design, bolt-on maple neck, 21-fret fingerboard, "Tele"-style fixed bridge, 6-on-a-side tuners, chrome hardware, 2 single coil pickups, volume/tone control, 3-position switch as following features (unless otherwise listed).

TA-630 DLX TR - contoured alder body, flame maple top, rosewood fingerboard with white dot inlay, TM2 tremolo, gold hardware, pearloid pickguard, 3 single coil "lipstick tube" pickups. Available in Transparent Red finish. Disc. 2000.

	$340	$295	$260	$225	$190	$150	$115

Last MSR was $450.

Earlier versions may feature a Purple Burst finish (model TA-630 DLX PS).

TL-650 K N - quilted kusu body, 22-fret rosewood fingerboard with white dot inlay, tune-o-matic bridge/stop tailpiece, die-cast tuners, gold hardware, 2 humbucker pickups. Available in Oyster finish. Mfg. 1994-1998.

	$450	$365	$320	$275	$230	$185	$140

Last MSR was $560.

GRADING	100% MINT	98% NEAR MINT	95% EXC+	90% EXC	80% VG+	70% VG	60% G

SMX-1 - bound carved ash body, 24-fret bound ebony fingerboard with pearl dot inlay, double locking Floyd Rose vibrato, gold hardware, 2 single coil/humbucker pickups, 5-position switch. Available in Cherry Sunburst and Vintage Sunburst finishes. Mfg. 1994 to 1996.

$390	$325	$295	$260	$225	$195	$165

Last MSR was $650.

SMX-2 VS - bound carved ash body, 24-fret maple fingerboard with pearl dot inlay, tune-o-matic bridge/stop tailpiece, die-cast tuners, gold hardware. Available in Vintage Sunburst finish. Mfg. 1994 to 2000.

$425	$370	$325	$280	$235	$190	$145

Last MSR was $570.

This model is available with a 24-fret rosewood fingerboard and Tobacco Sunburst finish (model SMX-2 R TS).

STM-1 - ash body, 22-fret maple fingerboard with black dot inlay, Gotoh locking tuners. Available in Natural finish. Mfg. 1994 to 1996.

$210	$175	$160	$140	$125	$105	$90

Last MSR was $350.

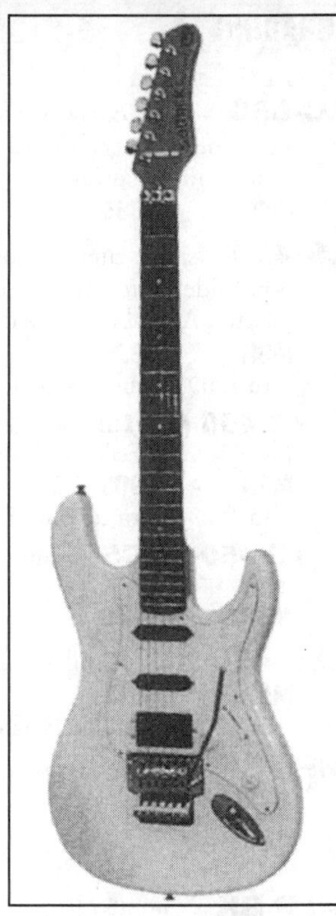

Samick SSM-2 PW
courtesy Samick

Blues Saraceno Radio Ten Artist Series

BS VG - offset rounded cutaway alder body, bolt-on maple neck, 25 1/2" scale, 22-fret maple fingerboard with offset black dot inlay, vintage-style tremolo, 3-per-side die-cast tuners, black hardware, 2 humbucking pickups, volume control, 3-way selector switch. Available in Black (BK), Raid Red (RA), and White (WH) finishes. Disc. 1999.

$265	$230	$205	$175	$150	$120	$90

Last MSR was $350.

Add $50 for Pink (MPF) or Purple (MPUF) Metal Flake finishes (Model BS VG).

Add $50 for White/Blue/Black (WBLB) or White/Red/Black (WRB) Plaid finishes (Model BS VG PP).

BS SH - similar to the BS VG, except features tune-o-matic bridge/stop tailpiece, 2 single coil/humbucker pickups, volume/tone (push/pull coil tap) controls, 5-way selector switch. Available in Black (BK), Raid Red (RA), and White (WH) finishes. Disc. 1999.

$300	$260	$230	$200	$165	$135	$100

Last MSR was $400.

Add $50 for Red (MRF) Metal Flake finish (Model BS SH).

Add $50 for White/Green/Black (WGNB) or White/Orange/Black (WOB) Plaid finishes (Model BS SH PP).

Artist Electric Solid Body Series

DS-100 - offset double cutaway hardwood body, bolt-on maple neck, 25 1/2" scale, 21-fret maple fingerboard with black dot inlay, standard tremolo, 6-on-a-side tuners, chrome hardware, white pickguard, 3 single coil pickups, volume/2 tone controls, 5-position switch. Available in Black, Metallic Red, Sunburst, and White finishes. Mfg. 1994-1998.

$190	$165	$145	$125	$100	$85	$65

Last MSR was $250.

DS-410 - similar to the DS-100, except features 21-fret rosewood fingerboard, 2 single coil/humbucker pickups. Available in Black, Metallic Red, Sunburst, and White finishes. Disc. 1999.

$195	$170	$150	$130	$110	$90	$65

Last MSR was $260.

FV-450 - flying V-style nato body, set-in neck, 24 3/4" scale, 22-fret rosewood fingerboard with white dot inlay, 3-per-side Gotoh tuners, tune-o-matic bridge/stop tailpiece, 2 humbucker pickups, volume/2 tone controls, 3-way selector switch. Available in Black and Metallic Red finishes. Current Mfg.

MSR	$585	$435	$375	$325	$275	$225	$175	$125

KR-660 AC (ICE CUBE) - offset double cutaway acrylic body, bolt-on maple neck, 24-fret bound rosewood fingerboard with pearl *V* inlay, licensed Floyd Rose tremolo, 6-on-a-side die-cast tuners, gold hardware, 2 single coil/humbucker pickups, volume/tone controls, 5-position switch. Available in Clear finish. Disc. 1999.

$525	$455	$400	$345	$290	$230	$175

Last MSR was $700.

KK-660 BB - similar to the KR-660 AC, except features a bamboo body. Available in Natural Bamboo finish. Disc. 1999.

$520	$450	$395	$340	$285	$230	$175

Last MSR was $690.

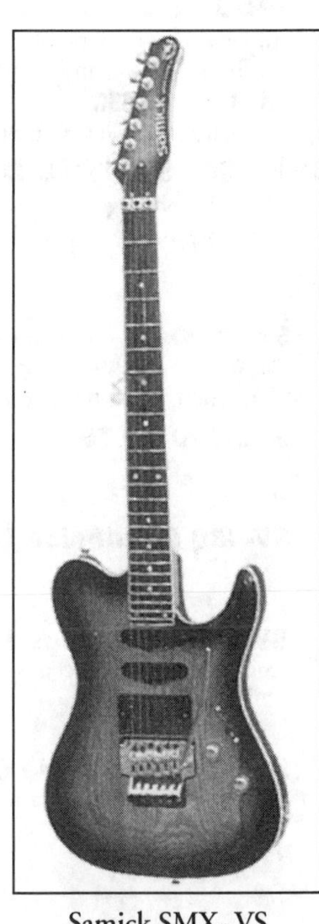

Samick SMX- VS
courtesy Samick

S

GRADING		100% MINT	98% NEAR MINT	95% EXC+	90% EXC	80% VG+	70% VG	60% G

LC-650 - single cutaway body, bound arched top, set-in nato neck, 24 3/4" scale, 22-fret rosewood fingerboard with white block inlay, 3-per-side Gotoh tuners, diamond/logo headstock inlay, gold hardware, tune-o-matic bridge/stop tailpiece, 2 humbucking pickups, 2 volume/2 tone controls, 3-way selector. Available in Black and Cherry Sunburst finishes. Mfg. 1997 to date.

MSR	$855	$650	$550	$495	$450	$395	$350	$275

LS-450 - single cutaway body, bound arched flame top, set-in nato neck, 24 3/4" scale, 22-fret rosewood fingerboard with white block inlay, 3-per-side Gotoh tuners, chrome hardware, tune-o-matic bridge/stop tailpiece, 2 humbucking pickups, 2 volume/2 tone controls, 3-way selector. Available in Cherry Sunburst and Wine Red finishes. Mfg. 1997 to date.

MSR	$825	$595	$495	$450	$395	$350	$295	$250

In 1999, Transparent Burgundy finish was introduced.

LS-450 (Metal Flake) - similar to LS-450, except features bound arched top. Available in Granite Gold, Metallic Green Flake, Metallic Gold, Metallic Gold Flake, and Metallic Red Flake finishes. Mfg. 1997 to date.

MSR	$900	$675	$575	$475	$425	$375	$325	$275

In 1999, Metallic Blue Flake, Bubinga, and Pink Bird's-eye Maple finishes were introduced.

LS-450-12 CS - similar to LS-450, except in a 12-string configuration, 6-per-side tuners. Available in Cherry Sunburst finish. Mfg. 1997 to date.

MSR	$900	$675	$575	$475	$425	$375	$325	$275

LSE-450 HS - similar to LS-450, except features an arched top, bolt-on nato neck. Available in Honey Sunburst finish. Mfg. 1997 to date.

MSR	$570	$425	$375	$325	$275	$225	$175	$125

In 1999, Wine Red finish was introduced.

MFV BK - "mini" flying V-style guitar, 19" scale, stop tailpiece, humbucker pickup, volume/tone control. Available in Black finish. Disc. 2000.

		$200	$175	$155	$135	$115	$190	$70

Last MSR was $270.

MLP BK - "mini" LP-style guitar, 19" scale, stop tailpiece, humbucker pickup, volume/tone control. Available in Black finish. Disc. 2000.

		$200	$175	$155	$135	$115	$190	$70

Last MSR was $270.

MST R - "mini" strat-style guitar, 19" scale, 2 single coil pickups, volume/tone control, 3-way switch. Available in Metallic Red finish. Disc. 2000.

		$200	$175	$155	$135	$115	$190	$70

Last MSR was $270.

SG-450 - dual cutaway SG-style nato body, set-in neck, 24 3/4" scale, 22-fret rosewood fingerboard with white dot inlay, 3-per-side Gotoh tuners, tune-o-matic bridge/stop tailpiece, black pickguard, 2 humbucker pickups, volume/2 tone controls, 3-way selector switch. Available in Black, White, and Wine Red finishes. Mfg. 1997 to date.

MSR	$630	$475	$425	$375	$325	$275	$225	$175

Earlier versions of an SG-style model had white block fingerboard inlay, and were only available in Wine Red finish (model SG 450 WR).

SVE-130 (SOUTHSIDE) - offset double cutaway alder body, bolt-on maple neck, 25 1/2" scale, 21-fret maple fingerboard with black dot inlay, vintage-style tremolo, 6-on-a-side standard tuners, chrome hardware, white pickguard, 3 single coil pickups, volume/2 tone controls, 5-position switch. Available in Black, Metallic Red, Sunburst, and White finishes. Disc. 1999.

		$220	$190	$170	$145	$120	$100	$75

Last MSR was $290.

SVE-130 LH - similar to the SVE-130, except in a left-handed configuration. Available in Black and Metallic Red finishes. Current Mfg.

MSR	$450	$325	$275	$250	$225	$175	$125	$95

In 2000, black finish was Disc.

SVE-130 SD TS - similar to the SVE-130, except features 3 Duncan single coil pickups. Available in Sunburst finish. Disc. 1999.

		$255	$220	$195	$170	$140	$115	$85

Last MSR was $340.

SV-430 (Southside Special) - similar to SVE-130, except has 22-fret rosewood fingerboard with pearl dot inlay. Disc. 1996.

		$165	$135	$120	$110	$95	$80	$70

Last MSR was $270.

SV-460 (Southside Heavy) - similar to SVE-130, except has black pickguard, 22-fret rosewood fingerboard with pearl dot inlay, 2 single coil/1 humbucker pickups. Disc. 1996.

		$170	$140	$125	$115	$100	$85	$70

Last MSR was $280.

SS-430 (Southside Classic) - similar to the SVE-130, except features 22-fret rosewood fingerboard with pearl dot inlay, standard vibrato. Available in Antique Orange, Candy Apple Red, Pacific Blue, SeaMist Green, and Tobacco Sunburst finishes. Disc. 1994.

		$200	$170	$155	$140	$120	$105	$85

Last MSR was $340.

GRADING	100% MINT	98% NEAR MINT	95% EXC+	90% EXC	80% VG+	70% VG	60% G

SS-430 (Southside Legend) - similar to the SVE-130, except features an ash body, 22-fret rosewood fingerboard with pearl dot inlay, standard vibrato. Available in Natural and Transparent Ivory finishes. Disc. 1994.

$200 $170 $155 $140 $120 $105 $85
Last MSR was $340.

TO-120 (UPTOWN) - single cutaway ash body, bolt-on maple neck, 25 1/2" scale, 21-fret maple fingerboard with black dot inlay, fixed bridge, 6-on-a-side tuners, chrome hardware, white pickguard, 2 single coil pickups, volume/tone control, 3-position switch, controls mounted on metal plate. Available in Butterscotch and Transparent Ivory finishes. Disc. 1996.

$175 $145 $130 $115 $105 $90 $75
Last MSR was $290.

TO-120 A N (Uptown Legend) - similar to Uptown, except has alder body, black pickguard, die-cast tuners. Available in Natural finish. Current Mfg.

MSR $540 $395 $350 $295 $250 $195 $150 $95

TO-320 BK (Uptown Classic) - similar to TO-120 A N, except has gold hardware. Available in Black finish. Current Mfg.

MSR $555 $415 $375 $325 $275 $225 $175 $125

Samick TO-120 N
courtesy Samick

Performance Series

KR-664 NM (LEGACY) - offset double cutaway alder body, bolt-on maple neck, 24-fret bound rosewood fingerboard with pearl boomerang inlay, double locking vibrato, 6-on-a-side tuners, gold hardware, 2 single coil rail/1 humbucker pickups, volume/tone control, 5-position/coil tap switches. Available in Natural finish. Disc. 1994.

$340 $280 $255 $225 $200 $170 $140
Last MSR was $560.

KRT-664 (Prophet) - similar to KR-664, except has ash body, through-body neck. Available in Transparent Black and Transparent Red finishes. Disc. 1994.

$360 $300 $270 $240 $210 $180 $150
Last MSR was $600.

KR-665 ARS (Stinger) - similar to the KR-664, except has bound alder body. Available in Antique Red, Sunburst, and Black finishes. Disc. 1994.

$325 $270 $270 $245 $215 $190 $135
Last MSR was $540.

KV-130 (RENEGADE) - offset double cutaway alder body, bolt-on maple neck, 24-fret maple fingerboard with black dot inlay, standard vibrato, 6-on-a-side tuners, chrome hardware, 3 single coil pickups, volume/tone control, 5-position switch. Available in Cobalt Blue and Metallic Red finishes. Disc. 1994.

$230 $190 $170 $155 $135 $115 $95
Last MSR was $380.

KV-450 (Scandal) - similar to Renegade, except has bound rosewood fingerboard, 2 humbucker pickups, 2 volume/1 tone control, 3-position switch. Available in Fluorescent Green and Metallic Black finishes. Disc. 1994.

$180 $150 $135 $120 $105 $90 $75
Last MSR was $300.

SR-660 (SCORPION) - offset double cutaway alder body, bolt-on maple neck, 24-fret bound rosewood fingerboard with pearl boomerang inlay, double locking vibrato, 6-on-a-side tuners, gold hardware, 2 single coil/1 humbucker pickups, volume/tone control, 5-position switch, push/pull coil tap in tone control. Available in Black, Metallic Red, and Pearl White finishes. Disc. 1994.

$315 $260 $235 $210 $185 $160 $130
Last MSR was $520.

YR-660 (Scorpion Plus) - similar to Scorpion, except has sharktooth fingerboard inlay, direct switch. Available in Black, Blue, Metallic Red, and Pearl White finishes. Disc. 1994.

$270 $225 $205 $180 $160 $135 $115
Last MSR was $450.

Standard Electric Solid Body Series

LS-10 - offset double cutaway hardwood body, bolt-on nato neck, 21-fret rosewood fingerboard with white dot inlay, vintage-style tremolo, chrome hardware, 6-on-a-side standard tuners, white pickguard, 3 single coil pickups, volume/tone control, 3-way selector. Available in Black, Metallic Red, Sunburst, and Transparent Cherry finishes. Current Mfg.

MSR $277 $195 $175 $150 $125 $95 $80 $60

In 1999, blue finish was introduced.
Add $18 for Metallic Red, Transparent Cherry and Blue finishes.

S

GRADING	100% MINT	98% NEAR MINT	95% EXC+	90% EXC	80% VG+	70% VG	60% G

LS-11 - offset double cutaway hardwood body, bolt-on maple neck, 25 1/2" scale, 21-fret rosewood fingerboard with white dot inlay, vintage-style tremolo, chrome hardware, 6-on-a-side standard tuners, white pickguard, 3 single coil pickups, volume/2 tone controls, 5-way selector switch. Available in Black, Burgundy Sunburst, Metallic Red, Red Marble, Red Sunburst, Sunburst, and Transparent Cherry finishes. Current Mfg.

MSR $295 — $225 $195 $175 $150 $120 $90 $65

In 1999, Red Sunburst finish was Disc.
Add $12 for Red Marble, Metallic Red and Trans Cherry finishes.

LS-11 D BK LH - similar to the LS-11, except in left-handed configuration, die-cast tuners. Available in Black finish. Current Mfg.

MSR $355 — $265 $225 $175 $150 $125 $95 $75

LS11M - similar to LS-11, except has maple fingerboard. Availvble in Metallic Red, Black and Metallic Dark Blue finishes. New 2001.

MSR $277 — $199 $175 $150 $125 $95 $75 $50

LS-110 - similar to the LS-11, except features 3 Duncan single coil pickups. Available in Black, Red, and Sunburst finishes. Disc. 1999.

$215 $190 $170 $145 $120 $100 $75
Last MSR was $287.

LS-35 BDS (LS-310 DB) - offset double cutaway hardwood body, bolt-on maple neck, 25 1/2" scale, 21-fret rosewood fingerboard with white dot inlay, vintage-style tremolo, black hardware, 6-on-a-side die-cast tuners, pickguard, 2 single coil/humbucker pickups, volume/tone controls, 5-way selector switch. Available in Black, Natural, Orange Sunburst, Transparent Red, and Vintage Sunburst finishes. Mfg. 1997-1998.

$180 $155 $140 $120 $100 $80 $60
Last MSR was $237.

LS-36 D - offset double cutaway hardwood body, oak veneer top, bolt-on maple neck, 25 1/2" scale, 21-fret rosewood fingerboard with white dot inlay, vintage-style tremolo, chrome hardware, 6-on-a-side die-cast tuners, pickguard, 2 single coil/humbucker pickups, volume/tone controls, 5-way selector switch. Available in Brown Sunburst, Orange Sunburst, Transparent Black, Transparent Blue, and Transparent Cherry finishes. Mfg. 1997-1998.

$165 $140 $125 $110 $90 $75 $55
Last MSR was $217.

A similar model, LS-36 SD was announced in 1997, but this model has yet to be manufactured.

LS-40 D - similar to the LS-36 D, except features 2 humbucker pickups, standard tremolo, 3-way selector. Available in Natural, Orange Sunburst, Transparent Blue, and Transparent Cherry finishes. Mfg. 1997-1998.

$165 $140 $125 $110 $90 $75 $55
Last MSR was $217.

LS-45 D - similar to the LS-36 D, except features single body binding, 2 humbucker pickups, standard tremolo. Available in Transparent Blue, Transparent Cherry, and Vintage Sunburst finishes. Mfg. 1997-1998.

$170 $145 $130 $110 $95 $80 $60
Last MSR was $224.

LS-41 DS OS - offset double cutaway hardwood body, bolt-on maple neck, 25 1/2" scale, 21-fret rosewood fingerboard with white dot inlay, vintage-style tremolo, chrome hardware, 6-on-a-side die-cast tuners, pickguard, humbucker/single coil/humbucker pickups, volume/tone controls, 5-way selector switch. Available in Orange Sunburst finish. Mfg. 1997 to 2000.

$170 $150 $135 $115 $100 $80 $60
Last MSR was $226.

LSM-80 T - student 7/8 size offset double cutaway hardwood body, bolt-on nato neck, rosewood fingerboard with white dot inlay, vintage-style tremolo, chrome hardware, 6-on-a-side enclosed gear tuners, white pickguard, single coil/humbucker pickups, volume/tone control, 3-way selector. Available in Black and Red finishes. Mfg. 1997 to date.

MSR $235 — $175 $150 $125 $95 $75 $65 $50

LT-11 BK (P-757 BK) - single cutaway hardwood body, bolt-on maple neck, 25 1/2" scale, 21-fret rosewood fingerboard with white dot inlay, fixed bridge, chrome hardware, 6-on-a-side enclosed gear tuners, white pickguard, 2 single coil pickups, volume/tone control, 3-way selector, controls mounted on a metal plate. Available in Black finish. Current Mfg.

MSR $340 — $255 $225 $195 $150 $125 $95 $75

LT-11 SS - similar to the LT-11 BK. Available in Silver Sunburst finish. Mfg. 1997-1998.

$190 $165 $145 $125 $105 $85 $65
Last MSR was $250.

SL-21 (SL-22) - single cutaway hardwood body (flat, not arched top), nato neck, 24 3/4" scale, 21-fret rosewood fingerboard with white dot inlay, tune-o-matic bridge/stop tailpiece, chrome hardware, 3-per-side standard tuners, 2 humbucker pickups, 2 volume/2 tone control, 3-way selector. Available in Black, Golden Sunburst, Silver Sunburst, and Vintage Sunburst finishes. Current Mfg.

MSR $340 — $250 $195 $175 $150 $125 $95 $70

SL-21 S TC (SL-22 S TC) - similar to the SL-21. Available in Transparent Cherry finish. Current Mfg.

MSR $355 — $265 $225 $195 $150 $125 $95 $75

S

GRADING	100% MINT	98% NEAR MINT	95% EXC+	90% EXC	80% VG+	70% VG	60% G

T Series

RANGER 3 - single cutaway contoured alder body, bolt-on maple neck, 21-fret rosewood fingerboard with pearl dot inlay, strings through fixed bridge, 6-on-a-side tuners, gold hardware, pearloid pickguard, 3 single coil pickups, volume/tone control, 5-position switch. Available in Black and Blue finishes. Mfg. 1994 to 1996.

$300 $250 $225 $200 $175 $150 $125
Last MSR was $500.

ELECTRIC BASS

All American Classics by Valley Arts bass models are optional with Bartolini pickups as an upgrade.

Add $225 for Bartolini P/J pickups for 4-string configuration (upgrade).

Add $235 for Bartolini P/J pickups for 5-string configuration (upgrade).

American Classic Electric Solid Body Bass Series

BTB-460 TS - violin-shaped body, 2 humbucker pickups, 2 volume/2 tone controls. Available in Tobacco Sunburst finish. Mfg. 1997 to 2000.

$595 $515 $455 $390 $325 $265 $200
Last MSR was $790.

CB-630 RSBU N (THUNDER) - sleek offset scooped double cutaway alder body, bubinga top, bolt-on maple neck, 34" scale, 24-fret rosewood fingerboard with pearl dot inlay, fixed bridge, 4-on-a-side die-cast tuners, gold hardware, P/J-style pickups, volume/tone control, 3-position switch. Available in Natural finish. Current Mfg.

MSR $750 $565 $475 $425 $375 $325 $275 $225

Some early models may also feature Black Finishing Net, Granite White Sunburst, and Pearl White finishes.

CB-630 RSQT US - similar to the CB-630 RSBU N, except features a quilted maple top. Available in Light Vapor Green finish. Current Mfg.

MSR $825 $615 $525 $450 $395 $355 $295 $250

FB-430 SQ PS - 7/8 scale sleek offset double cutaway body, quilt top, bolt-on maple neck, 34" scale, 20-fret rosewood fingerboard with pearl dot inlay, fixed bridge, 4-on-a-side die-cast tuners, chrome hardware, P/J-style pickups, 2 volume/tone control. Available in Purple Burst finish. Disc. 2000.

$340 $295 $260 $225 $190 $150 $115
Last MSR was $450.

In 1999, Transparent Red finish was introduced and Purple Burst finish was Disc.

SCBM-1 B TBL - offset double cutaway carved ash body, bolt-on maple neck, 20-fret rosewood fingerboard with pearl dot inlay, fixed bridge, 4-on-a-side tuners, black hardware, P/J-style pickups, 2 volume/1 tone controls, active electronics. Available in Transparent Blue, Transparent Black and Transparent Red finishes. Mfg. 1994 to 2000.

$415 $360 $315 $275 $230 $185 $140
Last MSR was $550.

Add $80 for gold hardware with Transparent Black finish (model SCBM-1 G TB).

In 1996, Transparent Black and Transparent Red finishes were Disc.

SCBM-2 B TBL - similar to SCBM-1 B, except has 5-string configuration, 4/1 per side tuners. Available in Transparent Blue finish. Mfg. 1994 to 2000.

$450 $390 $345 $295 $250 $200 $150
Last MSR was $600.

SCBM-2 G - similar to SCBM-1 B, except has 5-string configuration, 4/1 per side tuners, gold hardware. Available in Transparent Blue and Transparent Red finishes. Mfg. 1994 to 2000.

$450 $390 $345 $295 $250 $200 $150
Last MSR was $600.

Earlier models may also feature Cherry Sunburst and Transparent Black finishes.
In 1999, Transparent Black finish was reintroduced.

SJM-1 - J-style offset double cutaway alder body, bolt-on maple neck, 20-fret rosewood fingerboard with white dot inlay, fixed bridge, pickguard, 4-on-a-side tuners, chrome hardware, 2 J-style pickups, volume/tone controls. Available in Black and 3 Color Sunburst finishes. Disc. 1999.

$300 $260 $230 $200 $165 $135 $100
Last MSR was $400.

Samick Hoo-Doo Man Signature Model
courtesy Hoo-Doo Man

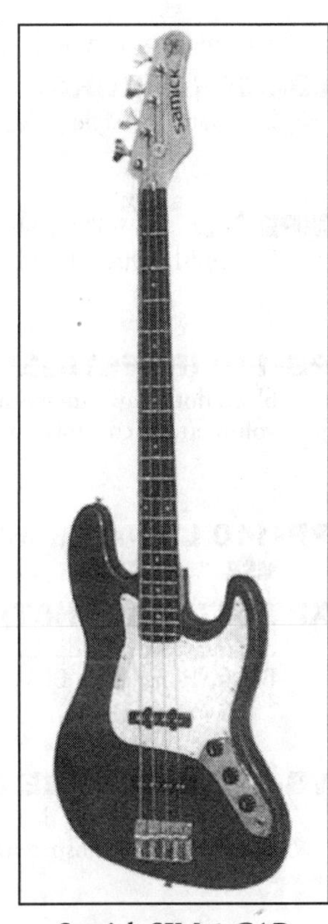

Samick SJM-1 CAR
courtesy Samick

S

GRADING	100% MINT	98% NEAR MINT	95% EXC+	90% EXC	80% VG+	70% VG	60% G

SMBX-1 FCS - offset double cutaway mahogany body, bound carved flame maple top, bolt-on maple neck, 34" scale, 20-fret bound ebony fingerboard with pearl dot inlay, fixed bridge, bound peghead, 4-on-a-side tuners, gold hardware, P/J-style pickups, 2 volume/tone controls, active electronics. Available in Flame Cherry Sunburst finish. Mfg. 1994 to 2000.

$480 $435 $380 $325 $270 $215 $160
Last MSR was $640.

SMBX - similar to SMBX-1 FCS, except has 5-string configuration, 4/1 per side tuners. Available in Flame Cherry Sunburst and Flame Transparent Black finishes. Mfg. 1994 to 2000.

$525 $455 $400 $345 $290 $230 $175
Last MSR was $700.

SPM-1 - contoured offset double cutaway alder body, bolt-on maple neck, 20-fret maple fingerboard with black dot inlay, fixed bridge, pickguard, 4-on-a-side tuners, white pickguard, chrome hardware, P-style split pickup, volume/tone controls. Available in Black and 3 Color Sunburst finishes. Disc. 1999.

$285 $250 $220 $190 $160 $125 $95
Last MSR was $380.

Some early models may also feature Pearl White finish.

YBT-6629 - sleek offset double cutaway ash body, 6-string configuration, through-body maple/walnut neck, 34" scale, 24-fret ebony fingerboard with pearl dot inlay, fixed bridge, 4/2-per-side die-cast tuners, gold hardware, 2 J-style pickups, 2 volume/2 tone controls, 3-way selector, active electronics. Available in Transparent Black and Walnut finishes. Mfg. 1994 to date.

MSR $1,650 $1,250 $1,050 $950 $850 $750 $650 $550

Some early models may also feature a Transparent Red finish. In 1999, Transparent Black finish was Disc.

Artist Electric Solid Body Bass Series

DB-100 - P-style offset double cutaway hardwood body, bolt-on maple neck, 20-fret maple fingerboard with black dot inlay, fixed bridge, pickguard, 4-on-a-side Schaller tuners, white pickguard, chrome hardware, P-style split pickup, volume/tone controls. Available in Black and Metallic Red finishes. Disc. 2000.

$210 $185 $165 $140 $115 $95 $70
Last MSR was $280.

JB-420 (JAVELIN) - offset double cutaway contoured alder body, bolt-on maple neck, 34" scale, 21-fret rosewood fingerboard with white dot inlay, vintage-style fixed bridge, 4-on-a-side tuners, chrome hardware, white pickguard/thumb rest, 2 J-style pickups, 2 volume/tone controls, controls mounted on a metal plate. Available in Black, Pearl White, and Sunburst finishes. Disc. 2000.

$265 $230 $205 $175 $150 $120 $90
Last MSR was $350.

In 1996, Pearl White finish was Disc.

LB-539 (AURORA) - offset double cutaway alder body, maple neck, 24-fret rosewood fingerboard, fixed bridge, 4-on-a-side tuners, black hardware, P/J-style pickup, volume/mid/bass/balance controls. Available in Aurora Multi Palette finish. Disc. 1994.

$325 $270 $245 $220 $190 $165 $130
Last MSR was $520.

MPB MR - "mini" P-style bass, 26" scale, chrome hardware, black pickguard, split P-style pickup, volume/tone controls. Available in Metallic Red finish. Disc. 2000.

$250 $215 $190 $165 $140 $110 $85
Last MSR was $330.

PB-110 (PRESTIGE) - P-style offset double cutaway solid alder body, bolt-on maple neck, 34" scale, 20-fret maple fingerboard with black dot inlay, vintage-style fixed bridge, 4-on-a-side Schaller tuners, chrome hardware, black pickguard/thumb rest, split P-style pickup, volume/tone controls. Available in Black, Metallic Red, and White finishes. Disc. 2000.

$240 $210 $185 $160 $135 $110 $80
Last MSR was $320.

PB-110 LH - similar to the PB-110, except in a left-handed configuration. Available in Black and Metallic Red finishes. Current Mfg.

MSR $495 $375 $325 $275 $225 $175 $125 $95

XBT-637 (PROPHET) - offset double cutaway alder body, through-body 3-piece maple neck, 24-fret rosewood fingerboard with pearl dot inlay, fixed bridge, 4-on-a-side tuners, gold hardware, P/J-style pickups, volume/tone control, 3-position switch. Available in Transparent Black, Transparent Blue, and Transparent Red finishes. Disc. 1994.

$360 $300 $270 $240 $210 $180 $150
Last MSR was $600.

YB-410 (PRESTIGE GT) - sleek contoured offset double cutaway solid alder body, bolt-on maple neck, 34" scale, 24-fret rosewood fingerboard with pearl dot inlay, fixed bridge, 4-on-a-side die-cast tuners, chrome hardware, split P-style pickup, volume/tone controls. Available in Black, Transparent Blue and Tobacco Sunburst finishes. Disc. 2000.

$270 $235 $210 $180 $150 $120 $90
Last MSR was $360.

In 1999, white finish was introduced.

GRADING		100% MINT	98% NEAR MINT	95% EXC+	90% EXC	80% VG+	70% VG	60% G

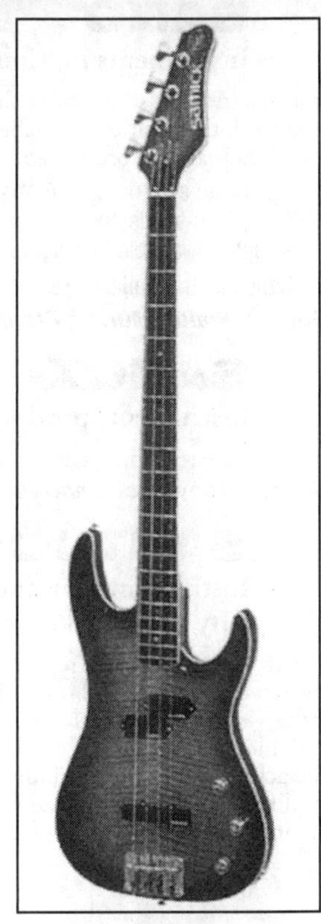

Samick SMBX-1 FCS
courtesy Samick

YB-410 BK LH - similar to the YB-410, except in a left-handed configuration. Available in Black finish. Mfg. 1997 to date.

MSR $540 — $395 $350 $295 $250 $195 $150 $95

YB-430 - similar to the YB-410, except features P/J-style pickups, 3-way selector switch. Available in Tobacco Sunburst and Transparent Blue finishes. Current Mfg.

MSR $570 — $425 $375 $325 $275 $225 $175 $125

In 2000, Tobacco Sunburst finish was Disc.

YB-430 BB - similar to the YB-430, except features bamboo body. Available in Natural finish. Mfg. 1997-1998.

$355 $305 $270 $230 $195 $160 $120

Last MSR was $470.

YB 530 FL - similar to the YB-410, except features P/J-style pickups, fretless rosewood fingerboard, black hardware. Available in Black and Red finishes. Mfg. 1994 to date.

MSR $585 — $435 $375 $325 $275 $225 $175 $125

YB-639 (THUNDERBOLT) - sleek offset double cutaway alder body, bolt-on maple neck, 24-fret rosewood fingerboard with pearl lightning bolt inlay, fixed bridge, 4-per-side tuners, gold hardware, P/J-style active pickups, volume/treble/bass/balance controls. Available in Black, Grayburst, Metallic Red, and Pearl White finishes. Disc. 1994.

$270 $225 $205 $180 $160 $135 $115

Last MSR was $450.

YB5-639 (THUNDER-5) - sleek contoured offset scooped double cutaway solid alder body, 5-string configuration, bolt-on maple neck, 34" scale, 24-fret rosewood fingerboard with pearl dot inlay, fixed bridge, 4/1 on a side die-cast tuners, gold hardware, P/J-style pickups, 2 volume/tone controls, 3-way selector switch, active/passive circuitry. Available in Black, Granite Gold, Metallic Red, and White finishes. Current Mfg.

MSR $780 — $585 $495 $395 $350 $295 $250 $195

YB5-639 BK LH - similar to YB5-639, except in a left-handed configuration. Available in Black finish. Mfg. 1997 to date.

MSR $810 — $595 $495 $395 $350 $295 $250 $195

YB6-629 WA - similar to YB5-639, except features 6-string configuration, 4/2-per-side tuners, 2 J-style pickups, active circuitry. Available in Walnut finish. Mfg. 1997 to date.

MSR $1,350 — $995 $895 $795 $695 $595 $495 $350

A similar model (model YBT6-629) featured maple/walnut through-body neck design, 24-fret ebony fingerboard with pearl dot inlay, and Transparent Black, Transparent Red, and Walnut finishes.

Standard Electric Solid Body Bass Series

LB-11 - P-style offset double cutaway hardwood body, bolt-on maple neck, 34" scale, 20-fret rosewood fingerboard with white dot inlay, vintage-style fixed bridge, 4-on-a-side Schaller tuners, chrome hardware, black pickguard, split P-style pickup, volume/tone controls. Available in Black, Red, and Sunburst finishes. Current Mfg.

MSR $328 — $250 $195 $170 $155 $125 $95 $70

FB-15 S (LB-11 NP) - similar to the LB-11, except features solid maple neck, scooped contoured body, die-cast tuners, no pickguard. Available in Transparent Black, Natural, Transparent Red, and Vintage Sunburst finish. Mfg. 1997 to date.

MSR $355 — $265 $225 $195 $175 $150 $125 $95

LBJ-21 TS - J-style offset double cutaway hardwood body, bolt-on maple neck, 34" scale, 20-fret rosewood fingerboard with white dot inlay, vintage- style fixed bridge, 4-on-a-side die-cast tuners, chrome hardware, pickguard, 2 J-style pickups, volume/tone controls. Available in Tobacco Sunburst finish. Mfg. 1997 to date.

MSR $337 — $250 $225 $195 $175 $150 $125 $95

LBM-10 SB (MPB-11 SB) - short scale P-Style bass, 30" scale, black pickguard, split P-style pickup, volume/tone controls. Available in Sunburst finish. Current Mfg.

MSR $280 — $210 $175 $150 $125 $110 $95 $65

SANDNER

Instruments previously produced between 1948 to 1959.

The Sandner trademark can be found on a series of acoustic archtops. These models may have **Alosa** or **Standard** on the headstock (or tailpiece). Research continues into the Sandner (or Alosa) trademark.

S

SANO

Instruments previously produced in Italy circa late 1960s.

Sano electric models resemble the Fender Jaguar. The Sano 3-way pickup selector toggle switch's positions are labeled as routed inscriptions in the pickguard; the positions are labeled T, ALL, and B. Apparently they stand for "Top", "ALL" (both pickups combined), and "Bottom" - something gets lost in translation from Italian.

The **Sano** electric has an offset double cutaway asymmetrical solid body (wood unknown), bolt-on maple neck, 22-fret rosewood fingerboard with white dot inlay, 6-on-a-side chrome tuners, floating bridge/vibrato tailpiece, w/b/w laminated plastic pickguard, 2 single coil pickups, volume and tone controls, 3-way selector. Available in solid finishes. The neckplate is inscribed "N. 1000", perhaps the model designation.

Sano electric guitars in average condition are worth around $150.

(Source: Walter Murray, Frankenstein Fretworks)

SANOX

Instruments previously produced in Japan from the late 1970s through the mid 1980s.

Intermediate to good quality guitars featuring some original designs and some designs based on American classics.

(Source: Tony Bacon and Paul Day, The Guru's Guitar Guide)

SANTUCCI

Instruments currently produced in Rome, Italy. Distributed in the U.S. market by the Santucci Corporation of New York City, New York.

The 10 string Santucci TrebleBass was developed by Sergio Santucci, a professional musician who has played guitar all over the world. Santucci began to develop the idea of combining the guitar and bass onto a one necked instrument as he was very fond of both. The desire to reproduce the original sound of the 4-string bass together with the guitar was "so strong that I had destroyed five instruments to achieve this project", notes Santucci. The **Treblebass** combines the 6-strings of a guitar with the 4-strings of a bass all on one neck, and is especially designed to expand the two-handed tapping style of play. The active circuitry of the individual guitar/bass pickups are wired to separate outputs (thus processing the two individual outputs to their respective amplification needs), and can be switched on and off independently. The two octave fretboard and custom made Gotoh tremolo/bass tailpiece give any guitarist ample room for exploration across the sonic range. For further information, contact designer Santucci directly (see Trademark Index).

ELECTRIC

TREBLEBASS - offset double cutaway alder body, through-body 5-piece maple neck, 24-fret ebony fingerboard with pearl dot inlay, custom-made Gotoh bridge consisting of: fixed bridge, bass; standard vibrato, guitar; 4/6-per-side tuners, chrome Gotoh hardware, split-bass/single coil/humbucker-guitar EMG pickups, 2 concentric volume/tone controls, 2 mini switches. Available in White, Black, Red, Green, Yellow, and Blue finishes with silk screened logo. Mfg. 1990 to date.

MSR $1,980

SARDONYX

Instruments previously built in New York City, New York circa early 1970s.

Sardonyx custom built guitars and basses were constructed in Greenwich Village in New York City. One source indicates that they were available in Matt Uminov Guitars in the West Village. Further research continues on the Sardonyx trademark.

(Preliminary research courtesy Jeff Meyer)

SARRICOLA

Instruments currently built in Lake Thunderbird, Illinois.

Luthier Bill Sarricola, an ex-Hamer employee, currently offers four different custom built guitar models. Sarricola models feature three different equipment packages on each guitar, as well as other custom options. For further information, contact luthier Bill Sarricola directly (see Trademark Index).

SATELLITE

Instruments previously produced in Japan during the late 1970s. Current production moved to Korea through the early to late 1980s.

The Satellite trademark is the brand name of a United Kingdom importer. These entry level to intermediate quality solid body and semi-hollowbody guitars featured both original and designs based on popular American classics.

(Source: Tony Bacon and Paul Day, The Guru's Guitar Guide)

SAXON

Instruments previously built in Japan during the mid 1970s.

The Saxon trademark is a brand name utilized by a United Kingdom importer. These medium quality solid body guitars featured Gibson-based designs.

(Source: Tony Bacon and Paul Day, The Guru's Guitar Guide)

SCHACK GUITARS

Instruments currently produced in Hammerbach, Germany.

Schack offers handcrafted basses in a 4-, 5-, or 6-string configuration and exotic wood tops. For further information, contact Schack Guitars directly (see Trademark Index).

ELECTRIC

SG 665 BASIC - offset double cutaway asymmetrical figured maple body, maple neck, 24-fret ebony fingerboard, fixed bridge, 3-per-side Sperzel tuners, Schack ETS 2D bridge, chrome hardware, 2 humbucker Seymour Duncan pickups, volume/tone control, 3-position switch. Available in Transparent Stain finish. Current Mfg.

MSR $1,800

Add $230 for tremolo system.

SG 665 CUSTOM - similar to Basic, except has Flamed Maple body and gold hardware. Current Mfg.

MSR $2,030

Add $220 for tremolo system.

SG 665 CLASSIC - similar to Custom, except model features further appointments. Current Mfg.

MSR $2,650

Add $330 for tremolo system.

ELECTRIC BASS

Unique Series

The Unique Series features the basic Unique body design that is offered in both bolt-on and neck-through models. The Unique IV Neck-Through Basic is also available in a Custom, Artwood, and Rootwood configurations (exotic tops). Contact Schack for exotic wood availability, or for a price quote on a bookmatched top/back.

Add $140 for fretless neck with fret inlay stripes.

Add $336 for two piece bookmatched top.

UNIQUE IV BOLT-ON BASIC - offset double cutaway asymmetrical bubinga body, bolt-on maple neck, 24-fret ebony fingerboard, fixed Schack ETS-3D bridge, 2-per-side tuners, black hardware, 2 Basstec JB-4 single coil pickups, 2 volume controls, 3 knob treble/mid/bass EQ control with active electronics. Available in Natural finish. Current Mfg.

MSR $2,800

Unique V Bolt-On Basic - similar to the Unique IV, except has 5-string configuration.

MSR $2,990

Unique VI Bolt-On Basic - similar to the Unique IV, except has 6-string configuration.

MSR $3,475

UNIQUE IV BOLT-ON CUSTOM - similar to the Unique IV Bolt-On Basic, except features exotic wood construction and gold hardware.

MSR $3,460

Unique V Bolt-On Custom - similar to the Unique IV Custom, except has 5-string configuration.

MSR $3,676

Unique VI Bolt-On Custom - similar to the Unique IV Custom, except has 6-string configuration.

MSR $4,130

UNIQUE IV NECK-THROUGH BASIC - offset double cutaway asymmetrical maple body, goncalo alves top, through-body 9 piece maple/bubinga neck, 24-fret ebony fingerboard, fixed bridge, 2-per-side tuners, black hardware, 2 Basstec single coil pickups, 2 volume controls, and a 3 knob treble/mid/bass EQ controls with active electronics. Available in Natural finish. Current Mfg.

MSR $3,590

Unique V Neck-Through Basic - similar to the Unique IV Neck-Through, except has a 36" scale and 5-strings.

MSR $3,930

Unique VI Neck-Through Basic - similar to the Unique IV Neck through, except has a 36" scale and 6-strings.

MSR $4,270

SCHECTER

Instruments currently produced in Los Angeles, California. Production of high quality replacement parts and guitars began in Van Nuys, California in 1976.

The Schecter company, named after David Schecter, began as a repair/modification shop that also did some customizing. Schecter began making high quality replacement parts (such as Solid Brass Hardware, Bridges, Tuners, and the MonsterTone and SuperRock II pickups) and build-your-own instrument kits. This led to the company offering of quality replacement necks and bodies, and eventually to their own line of finished instruments. Schecter is recognized as one of the first companies to market tapped pickup assemblies (coil tapping can offer a wider range of sound from an existing pickup configuration). Other designers associated with Schecter were Dan Armstrong and Tom Anderson.

GRADING	100% MINT	98% NEAR MINT	95% EXC+	90% EXC	80% VG+	70% VG	60% G

In 1994, Michael Ciravolo took over as the new director for Schecter Guitar Research. Ciravolo introduced new guitar designs the same year, and continues to expand the Schecter line with new innovations and designs.
In 1998, Schecter and Maestro Alex Gregory teamed up to offer the 7-String Limited Edition Signature model based on the patented specifications and neck profile of Gregory's original 1989 model. This signature model will be individually numbered, and comes with a signed Certificate of Authenticity (list $2,595).

(Source: Tom Wheeler, American Guitars)

By the mid 1980s, Schecter was offering designs based on early Fender-style guitars in models such as the Mercury, Saturn, Hendrix, and Dream Machine. In the late 1980s Schecter also had the U.S. built Californian series as well as the Japan-made Schecter East models. Currently, the entire Schecter guitar line is built in America.

ELECTRIC

Schecter offers a number of options on their guitar models. Seymour Duncan, EMG, Van Zandt, Lindy Fralin, and Mike Christian piezo pickups are available (call for price quote).

Add $100 for left-handed configuration.

Add 4100 for Sperzel Locking Tuners.

Add $50 for Black or Gold Hardware (Disc. Option).

Add $75 for matching headstock.

Add $175 for Wilkinson VS-100 tremolo (Disc. Option).

Add $250 for Original Floyd Rose tremolo.

Add $300 for Flame Koa or Lacewood top (Disc. Option).

AVENGER - sleek offset double cutaway arched mahogany body, maple neck, 25 1/2" scale, 22-fret rosewood fingerboard with block inlay, 6-on-a-side Sperzel tuners, black headstock with screened logo, tune-o-matic bridge/stop tailpiece, chrome hardware, 2 Seymour Duncan exposed humbuckers, volume/tone controls, 3-way toggle switch. Available in Black, Candy Apple Red, See-Through Red, and Antique Yellow finishes. Mfg. 1997 to date.

MSR $1,895 — $1,600 $1,400 $1,225 $1,050 $850 $675 $500

Add $400 for EMG pickups and reverse headstock (Model Avenger Mach 2).
Add $400 for 7-string configuration (Model Avenger 7).

Contoured Exotic Top Series

C.E.T. - offset double cutaway mahogany or swamp ash body, flame or quilted maple tops, bolt-on bird's-eye maple neck, 22-fret maple or rosewood fingerboard with dot inlay, fixed bridge (or vintage-style tremolo), 6-on-a-side Sperzel locking tuners, chrome hardware, 3 single coil pickups, volume/tone controls with coil tapping capabilities, 5-position switch. Available in Sunburst or Custom See-Through color finishes. Current Mfg.

MSR $2,495 — $1,900 $1,600 $1,395 $1,195 $995 $775 $575

This model is also available with 2 single coil/1 humbucker pickups configuration.
C.E.T. models are also optional with hollow internal "tone" chambers (technically a C.E.T.-H).
In 1996, a version called the C.E.T. Deluxe was offered that specifically featured 3 single coil pickups and a vintage-style tremolo (retail list was also $2,295). This version is inherent in the current listing for the C.E.T. model.
Early versions of this model are available in Black Cherry, Brown Sunburst, Honeyburst, Transparent Aqua, Transparent Purple, Transparent Turquoise, Vintage Cherry Sunburst, and Oil/Wax finishes.

C.E.T.-7 -offset double cutaway 7-string model, semi-hollowbody, rosewood fingerboard with dot position markers, 7 on 1 side tuners, 2 humbucking pickups and 1 single coil pickup in the middle position, 1 Volume/1 Tone control, 5-way switch,choice of finishes. Current Mfg.

MSR $2,695 — $2,150 $1,950 $1,750 $1,550 $1,350 $1,150 $950

C.E.T. PT - similar to the C.E.T., except has single cutaway body, 2 humbucker pickups, 3-way toggle switch. Mfg. 1996 to 1998.

$1,850 $1,600 $1,395 $1,195 $975 $750 $575

Last MSR was $2,295.

Diamond Series

A-1 -offset double cutaway mahogany body, upswept horns, bolt-on maple neck with rosewood fingerboard, diamond position markers, 6-on-a-side tuners, 25 ½" scale, Tune-O-Matic bridge, Grover tuners, black hardware, 24 jumbo frets, 2 Duncan Designed humbucking pickups. Available in Black, Dark Metallic Blue , Metallic Red, Gun Metal Gray and Silver Satin finishes. Disc. 2000.

$485 $450 $395 $350 $295 $250 $175

Last MSR was $649.

A-1 Elite - similar to A-1 model except, has neck through-body. Available in Black, Ultra Voilet and Silver Satin finishes. Current Mfg.

MSR $799 — $599 $550 $495 $450 $395 $350 $295

A-7 - similar to A-1 model except, in a 7-string configuration, Non-Trem 7 bridge. Available in Black, Dark Metallic Blue, Silver Satin, Metallic Red and Gun Metal Gray finishes. Disc. 2000.

$560 $495 $450 $395 $350 $295 $225

Last MSR was $749.

GRADING		100% MINT	98% NEAR MINT	95% EXC+	90% EXC	80% VG+	70% VG	60% G

A-7 Elite - similar to A-1 Elite model except, in a 7-string configuration. Available in Black, Ultra Violet and Silver Satin finishes. Current Mfg.

MSR	$899	$675	$625	$575	$525	$475	$425	$375

AVENGER - similar body design to A-1 and A-7 models except, has basswood body, dot position markers, Crème body biding, 2 Duncan Design pickups, Available in Black Satin, Gray Satin and Walnut Stain finishes. New 2001.

MSR	$569	$425	$375	$325	$275	$225	$175	$150

C-1 - offset double cutaway mahogany body, bolt-on maple neck with rosewood fingerboard, diamond position markers, 3-per-side tuners, 24 jumbo frets, 24 ¾" scale, bound body, Tune-O-Matic bridge, black hardware, 2 Duncan Designed humbucking pickups, string through-body, 1 Volume/1 Tone control, 3-watt switch. Available in Silver Top, Electric Blue, Gray Satin and Black finishes. Current Mfg.

MSR	$599	$450	$395	$350	$295	$250	$195	$165

Add $100 for Left Hand model.

C-1 Plus - similar to C-1 model except, has flame maple top and maple set neck, rosewood fingerboard with Vector position markers, chrome hardware. Available in Charcoal Gray Burst, Vintage Sunburst, Cherry Sunburst and Black Cherry finishes. Current Mfg.

MSR	$749	$560	$495	$450	$395	$350	$295	$225

C-7 -similar to C-1 model except, in a 7-string configuration, ash body, 25 ½" scale, Non-Trem 7 bridge. Available in Black, Gray Satin, See-Through Blue, See-Through Red and Walnut Gloss finishes. Disc. 2000.

		$560	$495	$450	$395	$350	$295	$225

Last MSR was $749.

C-7 Plus - similar to C-1 Plus Model except, in a 7-string configuration, 25 ½" scale, Non-Trem 7 bridge. Available in Charcoal Gray Burst, Vintage Sunburst, Cherry Sunburst and Black Cherry finishes. Current Mfg.

MSR	$799	$599	$550	$499	$450	$399	$350	$299

JERRY HORTON SIGNATURE MODEL - offset double cutaway mahogany body, bolt-on maple neck, rosewood fingerboard with "roach" position marker at the 12th fret, 25 ½" scale, Tune-O-Matic bridge, Grover tuners, black hardware, body and headstock binding, 24 jumbo fets, 2 Seymour Duncan humbucking pickups. Available in Gloss black, Gloss White and Gloss Grey finishes. New 2001.

MSR	$999	$749	$649	$595	$550	$495	$450	$395

M-33 MIKE TEMPESTA SIGNATURE MODEL - slightly offset double cutaway mahogany body with maple top, maple set neck, rosewood fingerboard with "Skulls" position marker at the 12th fret, 24 ¾" scale, Tune-O-Matic bridge, Grover tuners, black hardware, bound body and neck, 22 jumbo frets, 2 Duncan Design humbucking pickups. Available in Black Satin, Gray Satin and Silver Satin finishes. Current Mfg.

MSR	$899	$675	$595	$550	$495	$450	$395	$350

OMEN-6 - offset double cutaway basswood body, bolt-on maple neck, rosewood fingerboard with dot position markers, 3-per-side tuners, 25 ½" scale, Diamond tuners, Chrome hardware, Tune-O-Matic bridge, 24 jumbo frets, 2 Diamond humbucking pickups. Available in Gloss Black, Electric Blue, Black Satin and Walnut Stain finishes. New 2001.

MSR	$469	$349	$275	$250	$225	$195	$175	$150

Omen-7 - similar to Omen-6 model except, in 7-string cinfiguration, black hardware, 2 Duncan Design humbucking pickups. Available in Gloss Black, Walnut Stain, Electric Blue and Black Satin finishes. Current Mfg.

MSR	$599	$449	$399	$349	$299	$249	$199	$175

S-1 - double cutaway mahogany body, bolt-on maple neck with rosewood fingerboard, diamond position markers, 3-per-side tuners, 24 ¾" scale, Grover tuners, chrome hardware, 22 jumbo frets, 2 Duncan Designed humbucking pickups. Available in Black, See-Through Cherry, Violet Burst, Crimson Burst and Army Green Burst finishes. Current Mfg.

MSR	$599	$449	$399	$349	$299	$249	$199	$175

S-1 Plus - similar to S-1 model except, has mahogany body with flame maple top, maple set neck, Cream neck binding. Available in See-Through Black, Black Chery and Trans Green Burst finishes. Current Mfg.

MSR	$749	$560	$495	$450	$395	$350	$295	$250

T-1 - offset double cutaway mahogany body, bolt-on maple neck with rosewood fingerboard, diamond position markers, 22 jumbo frets, 25 ½" scale, Grover Tuners, Tune-O-Matic bridge, 1 Duncan Designed humbucking pickup and 1 Duncan Designed single coil pickup. Available in Black, See-Thru Cherry, Walnut Gloss and Dark Metallic Purple finishes. Disc. 2000.

		$449	$395	$350	$295	$250	$195	$150

Last MSR was $599.

GRADING			100% MINT	98% NEAR MINT	95% EXC+	90% EXC	80% VG+	70% VG	60% G

T-7 - similar to T-I model except, in a 7-string configuration, 24 jumbo frets. Available in Black, See-Through Cherry, Walnut Gloss and Dark Metallic Purple finishes. Disc. 2000.

			$525	$475	$425	$375	$325	$275	$225

Last MSR was $699.

TSH-1 - offset double cutaway semi-hollow mahogany body, flame maple top, bolt-on maple neck with rosewood fingerboard, diamond position markers, 22 jumbo frets, 25 ½" scale, Tune-O-Matic bridge/trapeze, Grover tuners, chrome hardware, 3-per-side tuners, 1 Duncan Designed humbucking pickup and 1 Duncan Designed single coil pickup, white pearloid pickguard. Available in Transparent Honey, See thru Black, Black Cherry and Vintage Trans-Orange finishes. Current Mfg.

MSR	$649		$485	$425	$375	$325	$275	$225	$175

TSH-12 - similar to TSH-1 except, in a 12-string configuration, 6-per-side tuners. Available in Vintage Trans Orange, Black Cherry, See-Through Black and Transparent Honey finishes. Current Mfg.

MSR	$699		$525	$475	$425	$375	$325	$275	$225

TEMPEST - similar to TSH-1 model except, mahogany body, dot position markers, Crème body binding, 2 Duncan Design humbucking pickups. Available in Gloss Black and Gold Top finishes. New 2001.

MSR	$599		$449	$395	$349	$295	$249	$195	$149

V-1 PLUS - offset double cutaway mahogany body with flame maple top, bolt-on maple neck with rosewood fingerboard, diamond position markers, 24 jumbo frets, 25 ½" scale, 6-on-a-side tuners, Floyd Rose bridge with vibrato, 2 Duncan Designed humbucking pickups plus 1 Duncan Designed single coil pickup in the middle position, 1 Volume/1 Tone control, 5-way switch. Available in See-Through Black, Transparent Amber, Trans Purple Burst and Trans Blue Burst finishes. Current Mfg.

MSR	$699		$525	$475	$425	$375	$325	$275	$225

006 - offset double cutaway mahogany body, bolt-on maple neck with rosewood fingerboard, diamond position markers. 3-per-side tuners, 25 ½" scale, Grover tuners, black hardware, non-trem bridge, 22 jumbo frets, 2 Duncan Design pickups, 1 single coil and 1 humbucker. Available in Black Satin, Gray Satin and Walnut Stain finishes. New 2001.

MSR	$599		$449	$395	$349	$295	$249	$195	$149

006 Elite - similar to 006 model except, has mahogany body with flame maple top, maple set neck, diamond position markers at the 12th fret, Tune-O-Matic bridge, bound neck, 24 jumbo frets, 2 Duncan Design pickups, 1 humbucker and 1 single coil. Available in Black Cherry and See-Through Black finishes. New 2001.

MSR	$749		$550	$495	$450	$395	$350	$295	$250

007 - offset double cutaway mahogany body, 7-string, bolt-on maple neck with rosewood fingerboard, diamond position markers, 25 ½" scale, Grover tuners, black hardware, non-tremelo bridge, 24 jumbo frets, 1 Duncan Designed humbucker pickup and 1 Duncan Designed single coil pickup. Available in Black, Walnut Gloss and Black satin finishes. Current Mfg.

MSR	$649		$485	$425	$375	$325	$275	$225	$175

007 Elite - similar to 007 model except, has mahogany body with flame maple top, maple set neck, diamond position markers at the 12th fret. Available in See thru Black and Black Cherry finishes. Current Mfg.

MSR	$799		$595	$525	$475	$425	$375	$325	$275

"H" Series

The "H" Series were offered between 1994 to 1996, and featured 2 hollow internal "tone" chambers, choice of pickup configurations, and transparent finishes. Other options included Wilkinson or Floyd Rose tremolos.

E.T.-H - offset double cutaway mahogany body with 2 internal routed sound chambers, figured maple top, stylized f-hole, bolt-on bird's-eye maple neck, 22-fret maple or rosewood fingerboard with dot inlay, fixed strings through bridge, 6-on-a-side tuners, black hardware, 2 humbucker pickups, volume/tone controls with coil tap capability, 3-position switch. Available in Black Cherry, See-Through Aqua, See-Through Purple, See-Through Turquoise, and Vintage Cherry Sunburst finishes. Mfg. 1994 to 1996.

			$1,535	$1,320	$1,170	$1,000	$860	$700	$550

Last MSR was $2,195.

C.E.T.-H - similar to E.T.-H, except does not have stylized f-hole. Mfg. 1994 to 1996.

			$1,750	$1,500	$1,325	$1,150	$975	$800	$625

Last MSR was $2,495.

This model is also similar to the solid body version C.E.T.

PT C.E.T.-H (PT Hollow) - similar to the C.E.T.-H, except has single cutaway body. Mfg. 1995 to 1996.

			$1,750	$1,500	$1,325	$1,150	$975	$800	$625

Last MSR was $2,495.

Hellcat Series

S

HELLCAT (SPITFIRE) - slightly offset alder body, maple neck, 22-fret rosewood fingerboard with dot inlay, 6-on-a-side locking Sperzel tuners, pearloid pickguard, chrome hardware, Wilkinson VS-100 tremolo, 3 Seymour Duncan covered mini-humbuckers, volume/tone controls, pickup selector switch. Available in Black Sparkle, Blue Sparkle, Burgundy Mist, Candy Apple Red, and White Pearl finishes with matching headstock. Mfg. 1996 to date.

MSR	$1,895		$1,520	$1,325	$1,155	$985	$815	$645	$475

GRADING	100% MINT	98% NEAR MINT	95% EXC+	90% EXC	80% VG+	70% VG	60% G

Subtract $100 for 2 tapped humbuckers or 2 mini humbuckers (Model Hellcat NT).

Hellcat 10 String - similar to Hellcat, except in 10-string configuration, tune-o-matic bridge/string through-body ferrules, 7/3 headstock. Mfg. 1996 to 1999.

	$1,550	**$1,350**	**$1,195**	**$1,000**	**$850**	**$675**	**$495**

Last MSR was $1,895.

Hollywood Series

The Hollywood Series was introduced in 1996. These models are also optional with hollow internal "tone" chambers.

HOLLYWOOD CUSTOM - offset double cutaway mahogany or swamp ash body, highly figured maple tops, bird's-eye maple neck, 22-fret maple or rosewood fingerboard with dot inlay, Wilkinson VS-100 tremolo, 6-on-a-side Sperzel locking tuners, chrome hardware, 2 single coil/1 humbucker pickups, volume/tone controls with coil tapping capabilities, 5-position switch. Available in Vintage Sunburst or Hand Tinted Custom color finishes. Mfg. 1996 to date.

MSR $2,695	**$2,155**	**$1,900**	**$1,655**	**$1,400**	**$1,165**	**$920**	**$675**

Hollywood Classic - similar to the Hollywood Custom, except has arched flame or quilted maple top, 24 3/4" scale, 24-fret fingerboard, 3-per-side tuners, tune-o-matic bridge/strings through-body ferrules, 2 covered humbuckers. Mfg. 1996 to date.

MSR $2,895	**$2,320**	**$2,030**	**$1,770**	**$1,500**	**$1,250**	**$990**	**$725**

This model is also available in a 25 1/2" scale with a 22-fret fingerboard.

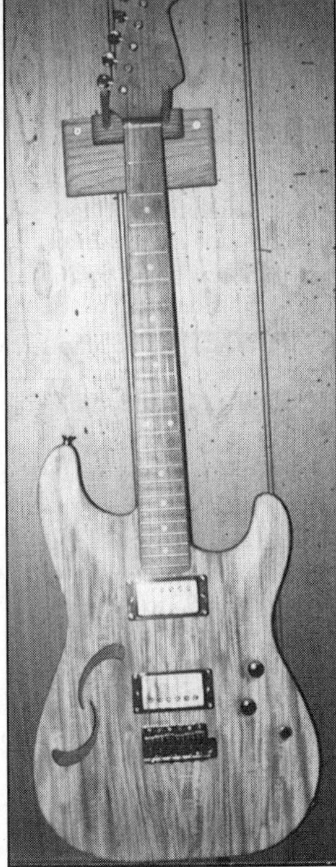

Schecter Custom CET-H
courtesy Bob Smith

Limited Edition Series

CALIFORNIA CUSTOM (CUSTOM) - offset double cutaway figured maple body, bolt-on bird's-eye maple neck, 22-fret rosewood fingerboard with dot inlay, double locking Schaller vibrato, 6-on-a-side tuners, gold hardware, 2 single coil/1 humbucker pickups, volume/tone control, 5-position switch. Available in Black Aqua, Black Cherry, Black Purple, Black Turquoise, Brown Sunburst, Honeyburst, Transparent Turquoise, and Vintage Cherry Sunburst finishes. Disc. 1998.

	$2,100	**$1,800**	**$1,595**	**$1,375**	**$1,100**	**$900**	**$800**

Last MSR was $2,995.

In 1994, Black Aqua and Black Purple finishes were introduced; Black Turquoise, Brown Sunburst and Honeyburst finishes were Disc.

CS-1 - offset double cutaway arched exotic wood body (bird's-eye maple, flamed "Tiger" maple, Hawaiian flamed koa, or flame walnut), set-in neck, 24 3/4" scale, 24-fret rosewood fingerboard with dot inlay, tune-o-matic bridge/string through-body ferrules, 3-per-side Sperzel tuners, gold hardware, 2 Seymour Duncan Seth Lover humbuckers, volume/tone controls, 3-position switch. Available in a hand-rubbed Natural Oil finish. Mfg. 1995 to date.

MSR $3,895	**$2,725**	**$2,300**	**$2,000**	**$1,750**	**$1,450**	**$1,150**	**$995**

Each instrument is hand numbered and comes with a Certificate of Authenticity.

HOLLYWOOD LTD. - offset double cutaway mahogany or swamp ash body, exotic wood tops, bird's-eye maple neck, 22-fret maple or rosewood fingerboard with dot inlay, Wilkinson VS-100 tremolo, 6-on-a-side Sperzel locking tuners, chrome hardware, 2 single coil/1 humbucker pickups, volume/tone controls with coil tapping capabilities, 5-position switch. Available in Custom color finishes. Mfg. 1996 to 1999.

	$2,320	**$2,030**	**$1,770**	**$1,500**	**$1,300**	**$1,045**	**$900**

Last MSR was $2,895.

KORINA CLASSIC - offset double cutaway arched korina body, set-in korina neck, 24 3/4" scale, 22-fret rosewood fingerboard with dot inlay, tune-o-matic bridge/string through-body ferrules, 3-per-side Sperzel tuners, gold hardware, 2 Seymour Duncan Seth Lover humbuckers, 2 volume/1 tone controls, 3-position switch. Available in Antique Yellow finish. Mfg. 1997 only.

MSR $3,895	**$2,750**	**$2,300**

1997 production limited to 12 guitars. Each instrument is hand stamped and comes with a Certificate of Authenticity.

PT CUSTOM - single cutaway mahogany body, carved bound figured maple top, bolt-on birdseye maple neck, 22-fret maple or rosewood fingerboard with dot inlay, tune-o-matic bridge/string through-body ferrules, 6-on-a-side tuners, gold hardware, 2 Seymour Duncan covered humbuckers, volume/tone controls with coil tap capabilities, 3-position switch. Available in Orange Violin, See-Through Black, and Vintage Cherry Sunburst finishes. Mfg. 1992 to 1998.

	$1,750	**$1,500**	**$1,325**	**$1,150**	**$N/A**	**$N/A**	**$N/A**

Last MSR was $2,495.

Schecter Contoured
Exotic Top
courtesy Schecter Guitars

GRADING	100% MINT	98% NEAR MINT	95% EXC+	90% EXC	80% VG+	70% VG	60% G

PT Series

PT (USA) - single cutaway bound alder body, bolt-on maple neck, 22-fret maple or rosewood fingerboard with dot inlay, Tele-style strings-through fixed bridge, 6-on-a-side Sperzel locking tuners, black hardware, 2 humbucker pickups, volume/tone controls with coil tap access, 3-position switch. Available in Gloss Black, Gold, Metallic Blue, Metallic Red, and Snow White finishes. Current Mfg.

MSR	$1,695	$1,425	$1,270	$1,100	$925	$750	$600	$450

This model debuted on The WHO's 1982 farewell tour.

PT CET - similar to PT Model except has contoured exotic top (CET), choice of fingerboard woods, choice of hardware color, choice of pickups, choice of tremelo or hardtail, other options. Available in transparent, sunburst or natural oil finishes. Current Mfg.

MSR	$2,495	$2,000	$1,700	$1,500	$1,300	$1,100	$900	$650

PT S/S (PT/2 S) - similar to PT, except has white pickguard, 2 single coil pickups. Available in 3 Tone Sunburst, Fire Engine Red, Gloss Black, Gold, and Snow White finishes. Mfg. 1994 to 1999.

$1,350	$1,195	$1,050	$895	$725	$575	$425

Last MSR was $1,595.

PT-X - similar to the PT, except has bound mahogany body. Available in Gloss Black, Gold, See-Through Red, Snow White, and Tobacco 'Burst. Mfg. 1995 to 1999.

$1,500	$1,325	$1,150	$1,000	$825	$650	$475

Last MSR was $1,795.

PT-X Deluxe - similar to the PT-X, except has no body binding. Available in Gloss Black, See-Through Blue, See-Through Emerald, See-Through Red, and Tobacco 'Burst finishes. Mfg. 1996 to 1999.

$1,350	$1,195	$1,050	$895	$725	$575	$425

Last MSR was $1,595.

"S"Series

The "S"series was also known as the Standard Series.

"S"STANDARD - offset double cutaway swamp ash body, bolt-on maple neck, 22-fret maple or rosewood fingerboard with dot inlay, fixed bridge (or vintage-style tremolo), 6-on-a-side tuners, chrome hardware, black pickguard, 3 single coil pickups, volume/tone with coil tap control, 5-position switch. Available in Natural Oil finish. Mfg. 1994 to date.

MSR	$1,395	$1,115	$950	$850	$750	$575	$475	$350

This model has 2 single coil/1 humbucker pickups configuration optional.
Early versions of this model have bird's-eye maple necks, and Natural Oil/Wax or Vintage Oil/Wax finishes.

"S"Classic - similar to the "S" Standard, except has arched swamp ash body, 24 3/4" scale, 24-fret maple or rosewood fingerboard, 3-per-side headstock, tune-o-matic bridge/stop tailpiece, 2 exposed humbuckers, 2 volume/1 tone controls, 3-way toggle switch. Mfg. 1996 to date.

MSR	$1,395	$1,200	$1,050	$925	$775	$650	$500	$375

"S"-7 7 String - offsset double cutaway Superstrat body made from Southern Swamp Ash, 25 ½" rock maple neck, maple or rosewood fingerboard, several variations of pickups available, nom-tremelo through-body bridge, Sperzel tuners. Natural and tinted oil finishes available. Current Mfg.

MSR	$1,795	$1,450	$1,225	$995	$800	$700	$600	$450

"S"PT - similar to the "S"Standard, except has single cutaway swamp ash body, black (or white) pickguard/metal controls plate, Tele-style fixed bridge, 2 single coil pickups. Mfg. 1995 to date.

MSR	$1,395	$1,200	$1,050	$925	$775	$650	$500	$375

This model has single coil/humbucker, or humbucker/single coil pickups configuration as an option.

Scorpion Series

The Scorpion Series models feature slightly offset dual cutaway bodies with rounded lower bouts.

SCORPION - double cutaway mahogany body, maple set neck with rosewood fingerboard, diamond position markers at the 12th fret, 25 ½" scale, 24 jumbo frets, 3-per-side tuners, black hardware, 2 Duncan Designed humbucking pickups. Available in Black Satin finish. Current Mfg.

MSR	$699	$525	$475	$425	$395	$350	$325	$275

Scorpion Elite - similar to Scorpion except, has body handbuilt from 1 piece of Honduran Mahogany, highly figured flame maple top, composite center laminate, 24 ¾" medium scale bolt-on quartersawn rock maple neck, Ebony fingerboard, 2 Seymour Duncan Seth Lover humbucking pickups, hard-tail bridge. Available in Transparent finishes. Disc. 2000.

$1,725	$1,525	$1,325	$1,125	$925	$725	$595

Last MSR was $2,295.

SPITFIRE - Refer to the Hellcat model.

S

GRADING	100% MINT	98% NEAR MINT	95% EXC+	90% EXC	80% VG+	70% VG	60% G

Sunset Series

SUNSET CUSTOM - offset double cutaway ash body, rock maple neck, 22-fret maple or rosewood fingerboard with dot inlay, vintage-style tremolo, 6-on-a-side Sperzel locking tuners, chrome hardware, 2 single coil/1 humbucker pickups, volume/tone controls with coil tapping capabilities, 5-position switch. Available in See-Through Black, See-Through Blue, See-Through Green, See-Through Honey Sunburst, See-Through Purple, and See-Through Red finishes with natural binding. Mfg. 1996 to 1999.

		100%	98%	95%	90%	80%	70%	60%
		$1,350	$1,195	$1,050	$895	$725	$575	$425

Last MSR was $1,695.

Add $200 for single coil/humbucker pickup configuration (Model Sunset Custom H/S).

Sunset 7 - body similar to Sunset Classic, hand carved swamp ash body, 25 ½" scale maple neck, rosewood fingerboard, dot position markers, 2 Schecter "tapped" Superock-7 Humbucking pickups, non-trem through body bridge, Sperzel tuners, 5/2 tuner configuration, natural body binding, scouped headstock. Available in soild and transparent finishes. Current Mfg.

		100%	98%	95%	90%	80%	70%	60%
MSR	$1,995	$1,595	$1,350	$1,150	$950	$850	$750	$595

Sunset Classic - similar to the Sunset Custom, except has arched ash body, 24 3/4" scale, 24-fret fingerboard, black headstock with screened logo, 3-per-side tuners, tune-o-matic bridge/strings through-body ferrules, 2 exposed humbuckers. Mfg. 1996 to date.

		100%	98%	95%	90%	80%	70%	60%
MSR	$1,895	$1,525	$1,325	$1,250	$1,050	$875	$675	$500

Schecter PT Series Model courtesy Schecter Guitars

Tempest Series

TEMPEST (USA) - slightly offset mahogany body, maple neck, 25 1/2" scale, 22-fret rosewood fingerboard with dot inlay, 3-per-side Sperzel tuners, black headstock with screened logo, 5-ply black pickguard, tune-o-matic bridge/trapeze tailpiece, chrome hardware, 2 Seymour Duncan P-90 pickups, 2 volume/1 tone controls, 3-way toggle switch. Available in Black, See-Through Red, T.V. Yellow, and Vintage Sunburst finishes. Mfg. 1997 to date.

		100%	98%	95%	90%	80%	70%	60%
MSR	$1,695	$1,450	$1,250	$1,100	$925	$775	$625	$450

Tempest Custom - similar to the Tempest, except has bound maple top, tune-o-matic bridge/stop tailpiece, 2 Seymour Duncan exposed Alnico Pro humbuckers. Available in Black, Burgundy, and Vintage Gold-top finishes. Mfg. 1997 to date.

		100%	98%	95%	90%	80%	70%	60%
MSR	$1,895	$1,600	$1,400	$1,225	$1,050	$875	$675	$500

Traditional Series

Traditional Series models have been the cornerstone of the Schecter company for the past twenty years.

TRADITIONAL - offset double cutaway alder or swamp ash body, bolt-on rock maple neck, 22-fret maple or rosewood fingerboard with dot inlay, vintage-style tremolo, 6-on-a-side Sperzel locking tuners, chrome hardware, white pickguard, 3 single coil pickups, volume/tone controls with coil tapping capabilities, 5-position switch. Available in 2 Tone Sunburst, 3 Tone Sunburst, Burgundy Mist, Candy Red, Gloss Black, Lake Placid Blue, Sea Foam Green, See-Through Aqua, See-Through White, Sonic Blue, Vintage Blonde, and Vintage Red finishes. Current Mfg.

		100%	98%	95%	90%	80%	70%	60%
MSR	$1,795	$1,425	$1,275	$1,100	$950	$775	$600	$450

This model has 2 single coil/1 humbucker pickups configuration as an option.

Early versions of this model have bird's-eye maple necks, and were available in Cherry Sunburst, Metallic Gold, Brownburst, Vintage Black, and Vintage White finishes.

Traditional "PT" - similar to the Traditional, except has single cutaway body, black (or white) pickguard/metal controls plate, Tele-style fixed bridge, 2 single coil pickups. Available in 3 Tone Sunburst, Gloss Black, Natural Gloss, See-Through White, and Vintage Blonde finishes. Mfg. 1996 to date.

		100%	98%	95%	90%	80%	70%	60%
MSR	$1,795	$1,425	$1,275	$1,100	$950	$775	$600	$450

This model has single coil/humbucker, or humbucker/single coil pickups configuration as an option.

ELECTRIC BASS

Schecter also offers options on their bass models. Seymour Duncan and EMG pickups, active EQ circuitry, and custom 4-, 5-, 6-string basses are available (call for price quote).

Add $100% for left-handed configuration.

Add $50 for Black or Gold Hardware.

Add $75 for matching headstock.

Add $100 for Hipshot D-Tuner.

Add $300 for 2-TEK bridge.

Add $300 for Flame Koa or Lacewood top.

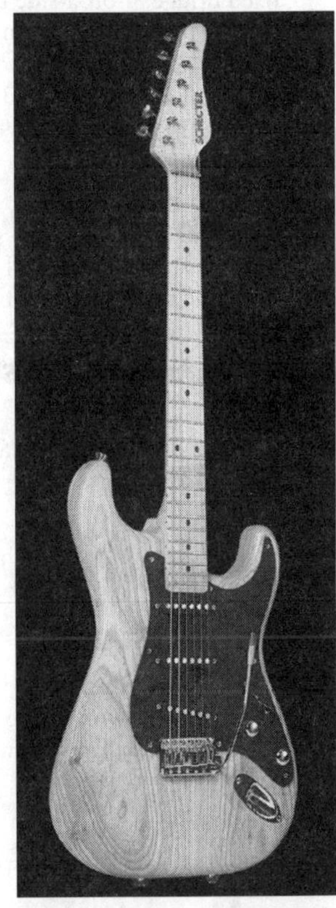

Schecter S Series Model courtesy Schecter Guitars

GRADING	100% MINT	98% NEAR MINT	95% EXC+	90% EXC	80% VG+	70% VG	60% G

BARON 4 (BARON IV) - single cutaway bound mahogany body, bolt-on maple neck, 21-fret maple or rosewood fingerboard with dot inlay, fixed bridge, chrome hardware, 4-on-a-side tuners, Seymour Duncan Basslines humbucker pickup, volume/tone controls, 6 position rotary switch. Available in Antique Yellow, Black, See-Through Red, and Vintage Gold-top finishes. Mfg. 1996 to 2000.

$1,600 $1,400 $1,225 $1,050 $875 $675 $500
Last MSR was $1,895.

Baron 5 (Baron V) - similar to Baron IV, except in 5-string configuration, 5-on-a-side headstock. Mfg. 1996 to 2000.

$1,675 $1,475 $1,275 $1,100 $900 $700 $525
Last MSR was $1,995.

Contoured Exotic Top (C.E.T.) Series

The Contoured Exotic Top model was formerly an option on the Bass/4 model between 1992 to 1994; the C.E.T. model officially debuted in 1995.

C.E.T. 4 - offset double cutaway ash body, flame or quilted maple top, bolt-on bird's-eye maple neck, 21-fret maple or rosewood fingerboard with dot inlay, fixed bridge, 4-on-a-side tuners, chrome hardware, 2 J-style MonsterTone pickups, 2 volume/1 tone controls. Available in Sunburst and Custom See-Through color finishes. Mfg. 1995 to 1998.

$2,000 $1,750 $1,525 $1,300 $1,075 $850 $625
Last MSR was $2,495.

This model is available with P/J-style pickup configuration.

C.E.T. B/4 H - similar to the C.E.T. 4, except has hollow internal "tone" chambers. Available in See-Through Aqua, See-Through Black, See-Through Black Cherry, See-Through Honey, See-Through Honeyburst, See-Through Purple, and See-Through Turquoise finishes. Disc. 1996.

$1,895 $1,625 $1,425 $1,250 $1,050 $875 $675
Last MSR was $2,695.

C.E.T. 5 - similar to C.E.T. 4, except in 5-string configuration, 5-on-a-side headstock. Mfg. 1995 to 1998.

$2,150 $1,895 $1,650 $1,400 $1,150 $925 $675
Last MSR was $2,695.

HELLCAT (SPITFIRE) - slightly offset double cutaway alder body, bolt-on rock maple neck, 21-fret maple or rosewood fingerboard with dot inlay, fixed bridge, 4-on-a-side tuners, chrome hardware, pearloid pickguard, 3 Kent Armstrong "lipstick" pickups, volume/tone controls, 6 position rotary pickup selector. Available in Black Sparkle, Blue Sparkle, Burgundy Mist, Candy Apple Red, and White Pearl finishes with matching headstock. Mfg. 1996 to 2000.

$1,520 $1,330 $1,160 $1,000 $820 $650 $475
Last MSR was $1,895.

MODEL T (USA) - offset double cutaway heavy ash body, bolt-on rock maple neck, 21-fret rosewood or maple fingerboard with dot inlay, fixed bridge, 4-on-a-side tuners, chrome hardware, black pickguard, P/J-style Monstertone pickups, volume/tone controls mounted on metal control plate. Available in 2 Tone Sunburst, Black, Natural Gloss, See- Through White, and Vintage Blonde finishes. Mfg. 1995 to date.

MSR $1,895 $1,575 $1,400 $1,225 $1,050 $875 $675 $500

This model is also available with 2 volume (no tone) controls configuration.
This model was designed in conjunction with Rob DeLeo (Stone Temple Pilots).

"S"Bass Series

"S"STANDARD (-J) - sleek offset double cutaway swamp ash body, bolt-on rock maple neck, 21-fret rosewood or maple fingerboard with dot inlay, fixed bridge, 4-on-a-side tuners, chrome hardware, black pickguard, P/J-style Monstertone pickups, 2 volume/1 tone controls. Available in Natural Oil finish. Mfg. 1995 to date.

MSR $1,395 $1,125 $975 $875 $725 $600 $475 $350

"S" Standard -P ("S" Vintage) - similar to the "S"Standard, except has P-style split pickup, volume/tone controls. Mfg. 1995 to date.

MSR $1,395 $1,125 $975 $875 $725 $600 $475 $350

"S"'51 - similar to the "S"Standard, except has Seymour Duncan vintage single coil pickup, volume/tone controls mounted on chrome control plate. Mfg. 1997 to 1999.

$1,050 $900 $795 $675 $550 $450 $325
Last MSR was $1,295.

"S-Standard-J5 ("S" 5-string) - similar to the "S"Standard, except in 5-string configuration, 5-on-a-side tuners, 2 J-Style pickups. Mfg. 1997 to date.

MSR $1,495 $1,200 $1,050 $925 $775 $650 $500 $375

SUNSET BASS - offset double cutaway ash body, bolt-on bird's eye maple neck, 21-fret maple or rosewood fingerboard with dot inlay, fixed bridge, 4-on-a-side tuners, chrome hardware, P/J-style pickups, 2 volume/1 tone controls. Available in Black, Honeyburst, See-Through Blue, See-Through Green, See-Through Purple, and See- Through Red finishes with natural wood binding. Mfg. 1996 only.

$1,190 $1,000 $885 $770 $655 $540 $425
Last MSR was $1,695.

GRADING	100% MINT	98% NEAR MINT	95% EXC+	90% EXC	80% VG+	70% VG	60% G

TEMPEST - slightly offset double cutaway mahogany body, rock maple neck, 21-fret rosewood fingerboard with pearl dot inlay, fixed bridge, 2-per-side tuners, black headstock with screened logo, chrome hardware, 5-ply black pickguard, covered humbucker/mini-humbucker pickups, 2 volume/tone controls. Available in Antique Yellow, Gloss Black, See-Through Cherry, T.V. Yellow, and Vintage Gold-top finishes. Mfg. 1997 to 1999.

		$1,550	$1,350	$1,150	$1,000	$825	$650	$475

Last MSR was $1,895.

Add $200 for maple top and creme body binding (Model Tempest Custom).

Schecter Bass 5
courtesy Schecter Guitars

Traditional Bass Series

TRADITIONAL J - offset double cutaway alder or swamp ash body, bolt-on rock maple neck, 21-fret rosewood or maple fingerboard with dot inlay, fixed bridge, 4-on-a-side tuners, chrome hardware, black pickguard, 2 J-style Monstertone pickups, 2 volume/1 tone controls mounted on metal control plate. Available in 2 Tone Sunburst, 3 Tone Sunburst, Gloss Black, Natural Gloss, See-Through White, and Vintage White finishes. Mfg. 1994 to date.

MSR	$1,795	$1,425	$1,275	$1,100	$950	$775	$600	$450

Traditional "P" - similar to the Traditional, except has one-piece white pickguard, P-style Monstertone pickup. Available in 2 Tone Sunburst, 3 Tone Sunburst, Gloss Black, Natural Gloss, See-Through White, and Vintage Blonde finishes. Mfg. 1997 to date.

MSR	$1,795	$1,425	$1,275	$1,100	$950	$775	$600	$450

Traditional 5-string - similar to the Traditional, except in 5-string configuration, 5-on-a-side headstock. Mfg. 1995 to 1998.

		$1,475	$1,300	$1,100	$1,000	$800	$650	$475

Last MSR was $1,895.

B/4 (Bass/4) - similar to the Tradition, except has no pickguard/control plate (rear-routed body), P/J-style or 2 J-Style pickups. Available in Gloss Black, Honeyburst, See-Through Blue, See-Through Green, See-Through Purple, and Vintage White finishes. Mfg. 1992 to 1998.

		$1,350	$1,195	$1,000	$875	$725	$575	$425

Last MSR was $1,695.

Early versions of this model have bird's-eye maple necks and ash bodies.
In 1996, Burgundy Mist, See-Through Red, and See-Through White finishes were introduced; Honeyburst, See-Through Green, and See- Through Purple finishes were Disc.

Bass/5 - similar to the Bass/4, except in 5-string configuration, 5-on-a-side headstock. Mfg. 1992 to 1994.

		$1,475	$1,250	$1,100	$975	$825	$675	$525

Last MSR was $2,095.

SCHON

Instruments built in California (later Canada) circa 1987 to 1990.

Schon guitars are so named for their namesake, guitarist Neal Schon (of **Journey** fame). Rather than just sign off on a production guitar, Schon actually put up his own money and design contributions to get the Schon guitar into production.
Schon guitar models were originally built by Charvel/Jackson's west coast production facilities; production later shifted to Larrivee Guitars in Canada during their brief flirtation with electric solid body models (circa 1987-1988).

ELECTRIC

Schon guitar models are generally well crafted instruments; models occasionally turn up at guitar shows and over the Internet.

NS-STD - single cutaway alder body wings, through-body solid maple neck, 25 1/2" scale, 24-fret bound ebony fingerboard with pearl dot inlay, 6-on-a-side Schaller tuners, sloped pointed headstock, chrome hardware, 2 Schon custom humbuckers, tune-o-matic bridge/individual stop *finger* tailpiece, volume/tone controls, five way selector switch. Available in a lacquer finish. Mfg. 1987 to 1990.

		$995	$875	$750	$675	$N/A	$N/A	$N/A

Last MSR was $1,199.

NS-STD W/Tremelo - same as the NS-STD, except has a Kahler tremolo instead of the stylish stop tailpiece.

		$1,050	$900	$775	$700	$N/A	$N/A	$N/A

Last MSR was $1,399.

NS-SC - same as the NS-STD, except has 2 single coils and 1 humbucker, Kahler tremolo.

		$995	$875	$750	$675	$N/A	$N/A	$N/A

Last MSR was $1,499.

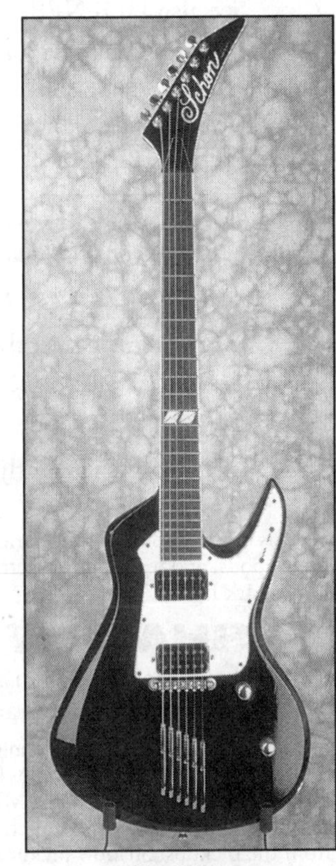

Schon Guitar
courtesy John Beeson

SCHULTE, C. ERIC

Instruments currently built in Frazerview (Malvern), Pennsylvania since the early 1950s.

Luthier Eric Shulte began repairing instruments in the early 1950s, mostly his own and for his close friends. Soon afterward, Schulte began building semi-hollow body guitars of his own design that featured a distinct 6-on-a-side headstock, 2 humbuckers, dual cutaway body with florentine-style horns, and a raised pickguard (a much cooler version of a Gibson Trini Lopez model, if you will). Schulte currently builds a number of different style models now. Schulte is mostly self-taught, although he did learn a good bit in the 1960s while working at the Philadelphia Music Company of Limerick, Pennsylvania. Sam Koontz, the late builder of Koontz guitars also worked there and the two shared *trade secrets*. During the Bluegrass and Folk music heydays Schulte made more than 130 fancy 5-string banjo necks.

Schulte's Music Company of Malvern, Pennsylvania offers both new and used musical instruments, amplifiers, instrument repair and customizing, and his own custom electric guitars and basses. Schulte has been repairing and building guitars for fourty-seven years and is still at it as he enjoys the work, challenges, and the opportunity to meet some wonderful musicians.

Some of Schulte's more notable customers were the late Jim Croce, Paul Stanley (Kiss), Randy Bachmann and Blair Thornton (B.T.O.), Joe Federico, Sergio Franchi, Bill Fisher, Chuck Anderson, *Banjo Joe* Dougherty, Dennis Sandole, and Roger Sprung.

(Biographical information courtesy C. Eric Shulte, July 1997)

SEBRING

Instruments currently built in Korea. Distributed by V.M.I. Industries of Brea, California.

Sebring instruments are designed towards the intermediate level guitar student. For further information, contact V.M.I. Industries directly (se Trademark Index).

SEDONA

Instruments currently built in Asia. Distributed by V M I Industries of Brea, California.

Sedona offers a range of instruments that appeal to the beginning guitarist and entry level player. For further information, contact V.M.I Industries directly (see Trademark Index).

SEIWA

Instruments previously built in Japan during the mid 1980s.

These medium quality solid body guitars featured Fender-based designs, often with two or three single coil pickups.

(Source: Tony Bacon and Paul Day, The Guru's Guitar Guide)

SEKOVA

Instruments previously produced in Japan.

Sekova brand instruments were distributed in the U.S. market by the U.S. Musical Merchandise Corporation of New York, New York.

(Source: Michael Wright, Guitar Stories Volume One)

SELMER LONDON

See also HOFNER.

Instruments previously built in West Germany from the late 1950s to the early 1970s.

Selmer London was the distribution branch of the Selmer company in the United Kingdom. Selmer London distributed the French-built Selmers, as well as imported the Hofner-built semi-hollowbody models. While a number retained the Hofner trademark, some Hofners were rebranded "Selmer". Hofner also produced a number of UK-only export models which were distributed by Selmer London; such as the President and Golden Hofner (top of the hollowbody electric range).

Selmer semi-hollowbody models to watch for include the **Triumph** (single cutaway and a single pickup), **Diplomat** (single cutaway but two pickups), the **Emperor** and the **Astra** (two cutaways and two pickups). In the early 1970s, Selmer also marketed a solid body guitar called the **Studio.**

(Source: Tony Bacon and Paul Day, The Guru's Guitar Guide)

SERIES 10

Instruments currently produced in Korea, and distributed by St. Louis Music of St. Louis, Missouri.

Series 10 instruments are designed for the entry level to intermediate guitar player, and feature designs based on classic American favorites.

SEVER

Instruments currently built in Izola, Slovenia. Distributed by Sever Musical Instruments and Equipment, Ltd. of Izola, Slovenia.

Sever is offering solid body electric guitar models that feature several innovative hardware and design ideas. Sever instruments are hand crafted out of select tone woods, and feature top electronics and hardware. For further information, contact Sever Musical Instruments and Equipment, Ltd. directly (see Trademark Index).

SHADOW

Instruments previously built in West Germany from 1988 through 1994. Disturbed through Shadow Electronics of America, Inc. of Stuart, Florida.

Shadow produced high quality solid body guitars for six years. The company still continues to produce their high quality pickups and transducers, as well as their SH-075 Quick Mount MIDI guitar system. The SH-075 Quick Mount MIDI system combines a hex pickup and the output of a guitar's magnetic pickups to generate a MIDI signal. The SH-075 also has an onboard alphanumeric keypad for sending program changes, assigning MIDI channels, tuning, and other functions. The splitter box at the other end of the MIDI cable decodes the signal into MIDI information and an analog sound from the pickups. Shadow pickups can be ordered as aftermarket replacements, and also can be found in other guitar manufacturers' products.

There is a limited number of high quality guitars still in stock at Shadow Electronics of America in Stuart, Florida. For further information, contact the company directly.

GRADING	100% MINT	98% NEAR MINT	95% EXC+	90% EXC	80% VG+	70% VG	60% G

ELECTRIC

In addition to the numerous high quality guitar models listed below, Shadow also produced a solid body classical guitar. The Shadow **Solid Body Classical** had a retail list price around $1,250.

G Series

All G Series models were available in Blue Stain, Cognac Stain and Red Stain finishes unless otherwise noted.

G 202 - offset double cutaway ash body, bolt-on maple neck, 24-fret rosewood fingerboard with pearl dot inlay, double locking vibrato, 6-on-a-side tuners, chrome hardware, 2 stacked coil/1 active humbucker Shadow pickups, volume/tone control, coil split switch in volume control, on/off switch in tone control, 5-position switch. Available in the three listed finishes, as well as a Black Stain finish. Disc. 1994.

$1,300	**$975**	**$815**	**$650**	**$580**	**$535**	**$485**

Last MSR was $1,625.

This model was also available with black or gold hardware.

G 213 - offset double cutaway Brazilian Cedro body, flame maple top/bolt-on neck, 24-fret rosewood fingerboard with pearl dot inlay, double locking vibrato, 6-on-a-side tuners, gold hardware, 2 stacked coil/1 active humbucker pickups, volume/tone control, coil split switch in volume control, on/off switch in tone control, 5-position switch. Disc. 1994.

$1,300	**$945**	**$890**	**$795**	**$720**	**$660**	**$600**

Last MSR was $1,995.

G 214 - similar to G 213, except has quilted maple top and bird's-eye maple neck.

$1,560	**$1,120**	**$990**	**$880**	**$790**	**$725**	**$660**

Last MSR was $2,200.

G 233 - similar to G 213, except has no magnetic pickups, standard bridge, piezo bridge pickup, volume control, 3-band EQ, active electronics.

$1,100	**$875**	**$780**	**$630**	**$565**	**$515**	**$470**

Last MSR was $1,575.

G 234 - similar to the G 233, except has a quilted maple top and bird's-eye maple neck.

$1,100	**$875**	**$780**	**$630**	**$565**	**$515**	**$470**

Last MSR was $1,575.

G 235 - similar to the G 233, except has a bird's-eye maple top and neck.

$1,100	**$875**	**$780**	**$630**	**$565**	**$515**	**$470**

Last MSR was $1,575.

G 243 - similar to G 233, except has standard bridge, Shadow humbucker with 5-band EQ/piezo bridge pickup with 3-band EQ, 2 volume controls, active electronics. Disc. 1994.

$1,240	**$985**	**$880**	**$705**	**$635**	**$580**	**$530**

Last MSR was $1,770.

G 244 - similar to the G 243, except has a quilted maple top and bird's-eye maple neck.

$1,240	**$985**	**$880**	**$705**	**$635**	**$580**	**$530**

Last MSR was $1,770.

G 245 - similar to the G 233, except has a bird's-eye maple top and neck.

$1,240	**$985**	**$880**	**$705**	**$635**	**$580**	**$530**

Last MSR was $1,770.

Shadow G213G
with SH-015 Midi Pickup
courtesy Steve Cherne

S Series

All S Series models were available in Black, Blue Stain, Blue Thunder, Cognac Stain, Gold, Red Stain, Red Thunder, Tobacco Stain, Violet Stain, White and White Thunder finishes.

All S Series models were available with black, chrome, or gold hardware.

S 100 - offset double cutaway basswood body, bolt-on maple neck, 22-fret rosewood fingerboard with pearl dot inlay, double locking vibrato, 6-on-a-side tuners, 2 single coil/1 humbucker Shadow pickups, volume/tone control, 5-position switch. Disc. 1994.

$750	**$590**	**$500**	**$400**	**$360**	**$330**	**$300**

Last MSR was $995.

S 110 - similar to S 100, except has active humbucker pickup, on/off switch, tone control, active electronics.

$980	**$735**	**$615**	**$490**	**$440**	**$405**	**$370**

Last MSR was $1,225.

S 120 - similar to S 100, except has 2 active humbucker pickups, 2 volume controls and 3-position switch.

$1,050	**$780**	**$660**	**$530**	**$475**	**$435**	**$395**

Last MSR was $1,315.

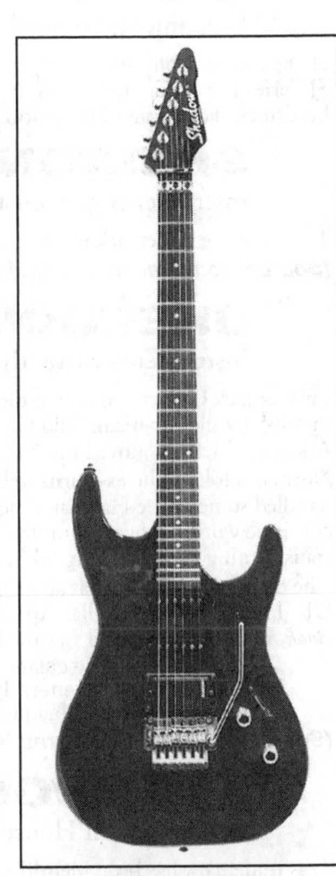

Model S 100
courtesy Shadow Guitars

S

GRADING	100% MINT	98% NEAR MINT	95% EXC+	90% EXC	80% VG+	70% VG	60% G

S 121 - similar to the S 120, except has an alder body.

	$1,240	$985	$880	$705	$635	$580	$530

Last MSR was $1,315.

S 130 (SHP-1) - similar to S 100, except has no magnetic pickups, standard bridge, piezo bridge pickup, volume control, 3-band EQ, active electronics. Mfg. 1990 to 1994.

	$900	$675	$565	$455	$405	$370	$335

Last MSR was $1,125.

S 131 - similar to the S 130, except has an alder body.

	$900	$675	$565	$455	$405	$370	$335

Last MSR was $1,125.

S 140 - similar to S 130, except has standard bridge, Shadow humbucker with 5-band EQ/piezo bridge pickup with 3-band EQ, 2 volume controls, active electronics.

	$1,050	$780	$660	$530	$475	$435	$395

Last MSR was $1,315.

This model is also available with an alder body (S 141).

S 141 - similar to the S 140, except has an alder body.

	$1,050	$780	$660	$530	$475	$435	$395

Last MSR was $1,315.

SHAFTESBURY

See also NED CALLAN.

Instruments previously manufactured in Italy and Japan from the late 1960s to the early 1980s. One English-built model was produced during the overall time period.

The Shaftesbury trademark is the brand name of a UK importer. Shaftesbury instruments were generally medium to good quality versions of American designs. The Shaftesbury line featured both solid and semi-hollowbody guitars and basses. To hazard a guess, I would assume that the Italian production was featured early on in the late 1960s; as costs rose the importer chose to bring in Japanese-built guitars sometime around the mid-to-late 1970s. As luthier Peter Cook was busy during the 1970s mass-producing decent quality guitars under the Ned Callan, Simms-Watts, and CMI brand names the 1970s would be a good "guess-timate" for the introduction of Ned Callan/Shaftesbury model instruments.

(Source: Tony Bacon and Paul Day, The Guru's Guitar Guide)

SHANE

Instruments currently built in Fairfax, Virginia.

Shane has been offering quality custom built guitars for a number of years. Both the **S100 SC** and the **S350 Targa** offer traditional style bodies, while the **SJ Series** features a more modern style. Shane's **SB-1000** bass (retail list $399) has 24-fret fingerboard, 34" scale, P/J-style pickups, and a 2-per-side headstock. For further information, contact Shane Guitars directly (see Trademark Index).

SHELTONE

Instruments previously produced in Japan during the 1960s.

The Sheltone trademark is a brand name used by a UK importer. Sheltone instruments are entry level solid body or semi-hollow body guitars.

(Source: Tony Bacon and Paul Day, The Guru's Guitar Guide)

SHERGOLD

Instruments currently built in England since 1968 (the company is currently concentrating on custom orders).

Luthier Jack Golder was one of the mainstays of the Burns London company during the early 1960s, and stayed with the company when it was purchased in 1965 by the American Baldwin Organ company. Baldwin also acquired Gretsch in 1967. Baldwin was assembling imported Burns parts in Booneville, Arkansas. In 1970 moved the New York Gretsch operation to this facility as it phased out Burns guitar production.

Norman Holder, the ex-Burns mill foreman, rejoined Jack Golder during production of Hayman guitars (and once again affiliated with Jim Burns, who handled some of the Hayman designs). When Dallas-Arbiter, the distributor of Hayman guitars, went under in 1975 both Golder and Holder decided to continue working together on their own line of guitars. Some of the Hayman refinements carried over into the Shergold line (like the Hayman 4040 bass transforming into the Shergold Marathon bass), but the original design concept can be attributed to this team.

The Shergold company has also supplied a number of UK builders with necks and bodies under contract. These companies include BM, Jim Burn's Burns UK, Hayman (under Dallas-Arbiter), Peter Cook's Ned Callan, Pangborn, and Rosetti's "Triumph" model. Author Tony Bacon, in *The Ultimate Guitar Book*, notes that Shergold was the last company to make guitars (and parts) in quantity in the United Kingdom.

Possibly one of the easier trademarks to figure out model designations as the pickguard carries both the "Shergold" and model name on it! Shergold models generally feature a double cutaway solid body, and two humbucking pickups. Models include the Activator, Cavalier, Marathon (bass), Masquerador, Meteor, Modulator, and custom built doublenecks.

(Source: Paul Day, The Burns Book)

SHERWOOD

See chapter on House Brands.

This trademark has been identified as a *House Brand* of Montgomery Wards.

(Source: Willie G. Moseley, Stellas & Stratocasters)

SIEGMUND

Instruments currently built in Austin, Texas.

iegmund Guitars currently produces classic hand crafted archtop, resophonic, and solid body electric guitars, as well s amplifier cabinets and cases. Siegmund features unique and fine quality, original design guitars.

SIERRA (U.S. Mfg.)

SIERRA (EXCALIBER SERIES).

Instruments previously built in San Francisco, California in 1981.

ierra Guitars was a well-conceived but short-lived company that handcrafted the Excaliber line of guitars and basses. ounded in 1981 by Michael Tobias and Ron Armstrong, the San Francisco-based company lasted only one year and roduced 50 instruments.

Model specifications and company history source: Hal Hammer)

ELECTRIC

All Excaliber instruments feature a three piece laminated neck-through design, stainless steel truss rod, chrome plated brass hardware, and select hardwoods. There was a $100 charge for left-handed instruments, and a $100 up charge for a vibrato bridge.

Given the relatively small number of total instruments produced, accurate pricing on the following models is not available. Secondary market prices may have some relationship to the original list prices as offered in 1981.

MODEL 6.1 - Offset double cutaway body, 24 3/4" scale neck, 3-per-side headstock, stop tailpiece, humbucking pickup, volume/tone controls. Available in Natural finish. Mfg. 1981 only.

Last MSR was $1,299.

Model 6.1 A - Similar to the 6.1, except had active electronics and mini toggle switch.

Last MSR was $1,429.

MODEL 6.2 - Offset double cutaway body, 24 3/4" scale neck, 3-per-side headstock, stop tailpiece, 2 humbucking pickups, 2 volume/1 tone controls, selector toggle switch. Available in Natural finish. Mfg. 1981 only.

Last MSR was $1,449.

Model 6.2 A - Similar to the 6.2, except had active electronics and mini toggle switch.

Last MSR was $1,582.

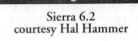

Sierra 6.2
courtesy Hal Hammer

ELECTRIC BASS

There was no charge for the fretless neck option.

MODEL 4.1 - Offset double cutaway body with slightly elongated bass bout, 2-per-side headstock, 2 octave fretted neck, one pickup, volume/tone controls. Available in Natural finish. Mfg. 1981 only.

Last MSR was $1,429.

Model 4.1 A - Similar to the 4.1, except had active electronics and mini toggle switch.

Last MSR was $1,559.

MODEL 4.2 - Offset double cutaway body with slightly elongated bass bout, 2-per-side headstock, 2 octave fretted neck, two pickup, 2 volume/1 tone controls. Available in Natural finish. Mfg. 1981 only.

Last MSR was $1,579.

Model 4.2 A - Similar to the 4.2, except had active electronics and mini toggle switch.

Last MSR was $1,712.

SIERRA (UK Mfg.)

Instruments previously built in England during the early to mid 1960s.

The Jetstar model was a medium quality solid body guitar that featured a design based on Fender; the Jetstar even featured three single coil pickups.

(Source: Tony Bacon and Paul Day, The Guru's Guitar Guide)

SIERRA DESIGNS

Instruments previously built in Portland, Oregon during the early 1980s.

Sierra Designs was founded in 1983 by Gene Fields. Fields, who worked at Fender from 1961 to 1983, eventually joined the Fender R & D section in 1966. Fields was the designer of the Starcaster, Fender's bolt neck answer to the ES-335 in the mid 1970s. The *Blue Book of Electric Guitars* will continue to research Sierra Designs guitars, and updated information will be in future editions.

(Source: Teisco Del Rey, Guitar Player magazine, March 1991)

SIGGI GUITARS

Instruments currently built in Hattenhofen, Germany.

Luthier Siegfried Braun is currently offering a handcrafted electric guitars that feature a direct pull (for strings) headstock, CNS neck system, and flamed or quilted maple tops. For further information regarding model specifications and pricing, contact Siggi Guitars directly (see Trademark Index).

GRADING	100% MINT	98% NEAR MINT	95% EXC+	90% EXC	80% VG+	70% VG	60% G

SIGMA

Instruments previously assembled in Asia, with final finishing/inspection in Nazareth, Pennsylvania. Distributed by the C. F. Martin Guitar Company of Nazareth, Pennsylvania.

In 1970, the Martin Guitar Company expanded its product line by introducing the Sigma line. The instruments begin their assembly in Japan, and then are shipped in to Pennsylvania where the Martin company can oversee the final finishing and setup. Sigma guitars are great introductory models to the classic Martin design.

(Source: Michael Wright, Guitar Stories Volume One)

ELECTRIC

While the focus of the Sigma line has been primarily acoustic guitars (after all, Sigma is a division of the Martin Guitar Company), there were a handful of solid body guitars and basses distributed during the early 1970s. Two models, the SBG2-6 and SBE2-9 resemble Gibson SGs. The **SBE2-9** is similar to the **SBG2-6** except has a Bigsby-style vibrato. The Sigma **SBF2-6** features a telecaster-style body mated to a 3 tuners on a side headstock. The **SBB2-8** electric bass has a vaguely Fender Precision-style body (in the earlier Telecaster bass body style) with a 2 tuners on a side headstock.

SIGNATURE

Instruments currently produced in Canada since the mid 1980s.

The Signature line focuses on high quality "superstrat"solid body designs.

(Source: Tony Bacon and Paul Day, The Guru's Guitar Guide)

SIGNET

Instruments previously produced in Japan circa early 1970s.

The Signet trademark was a brand name used by U.S. importers Ampeg/Selmer.

(Source: Michael Wright, Guitar Stories Volume One)

SILVER CADET

Instruments currently produced in Korea. Distributed in the U.S. market by Ibanez (Hoshino USA) of Bensalem, Pennsylvania.

The Silver Cadet guitar line provides an entry level step into the wonderful world of electric guitars (buy a guitar, plug it into a loud amp, and then tell your parents! They'll either cut your allowance or cut off your electricity). The current quality of these instruments, like other contemporary entry level guitars, is a lot better today than it was twenty or thirty years ago for a beginning student.

ELECTRIC

ZR140 - offset double cutaway hardwood body, black pickguard, bolt-on maple neck, 21-fret rosewood fingerboard with pearl dot inlay, standard vibrato, 6-on-a-side tuners, chrome hardware, 2 single coil/1 humbucker pickups, volume/tone control, 5-position switch. Available in Black, Red and White finishes. Mfg. 1994 to 1996.

$200	$150	$125	$100	$90	$80	$75

Last MSR was $250.

ZR350 - similar to ZR140, except has double locking vibrato, humbucker/single coil/humbucker pickups. Available in Black, Red and White finishes. Mfg. 1994 to 1996.

$325	$250	$225	$175	$150	$125	$100

Last MSR was $430.

ELECTRIC BASS

ZTB100 - offset double cutaway hardwood body, black pickguard, bolt-on maple neck, 22-fret rosewood fingerboard with pearl dot inlay, fixed bridge, 4-on-a-side tuners, chrome hardware, P-style pickup, volume/tone control. Available in Black and Red finishes. Mfg. 1994 to 1996.

$250	$175	$150	$125	$115	$100	$95

Last MSR was $300.

SILVERTONE

See chapter on House Brands.

This trademark has been identified as a "House Brand" owned and used by Sears and Roebuck between 1941 to 1970. There was no company or factory; Sears owned the name and applied it to various products from such manufacturers as HARMONY, VALCO, DANELECTRO, and KAY. Sears and Roebuck acquired Harmony in 1916 to control its respectable ukulele production. Harmony generally sold around 40 percent of its guitar production to Sears. The following is a word of caution: Just because it says **Silvertone**, do not automatically assume it is a Danelectro! In fact, study the guitar to determine possible origin (Harmony, Valco and Kay were originally built in Illinois, Danelectro in New Jersey; so all were U.S. However, mid 1960s models were built in Japan by Teisco, as well!). Best of all, play it! If it looks good, and sounds okay - it was meant to be played. As most Silvertones were sold either through the catalog or in a store, they will generally be entry level quality instruments.

Certain Silvertone models have garnered some notoriety, such as the Danelectro-produced combination of guitar and amp-in-case. Sears also marketed the Teisco company's TRG-1 (or TRE-100) electric guitar with amp built in! This guitar has a six-on-a-side "Silvertone" headstock, and a single cutaway *pregnant Telecaster* body design (the small built-in speaker is in the *tummy*). Harmony produced a number of electric hollowbody guitars (like the Sovereign) for the Silvertone label; Kay also offered a version of their *Thin Twin* model as well as arch top models.

GRADING	100% MINT	98% NEAR MINT	95% EXC+	90% EXC	80% VG+	70% VG	60% G

Silvertone Deluxe (by Harmony) courtesy Daniel Gelabert

ELECTRIC

1300 - single cutaway, U-series body with 13 ¼ inch lower bout width, Masonite semi-solid construction, clear or white pickguard, bolt-on neck, 21-fret rosewood fingerboard with dot inlay, metal trapezoidal bridge with rosewood stick saddle, "Coke-bottle" shaped peghead, 3-per-side tuners with plastic buttons, single coil lipstick tube pickup, volume/tone control with selector switch. Available in Copper (Model 1300) and Black (Model 1302) finishes. Mfd. 1958 to 1959.

N/A $375 $325 $260 $220 $180 $150

1301 - similar to Model 1300 except has 2 single coil lipstick tube pickups, 2 stacked volume/tone controls with 3-position selector switch. Available in Copper (**Model 1301**) and Black (**Model 1303**) finishes. Mfd. 1958 to 1959.

N/A $375 $325 $260 $220 $180 $150

1305 - similar to Model 1300 except has 3 single coil lipstick tube pickups, 3 stacked volume/tone controls. Available in White/Black Sunburst finish. Mfd, 1958 to 1959.

N/A $375 $325 $260 $220 $180 $150

These models are often referred to as U models by collectors because they are almost identical to the U series of guitars that Danelectro manufactured with the Danelectro logo.

1317 - single cutaway with 11 ¾ inch lower bout width, Masonite semi-solid construction, clear pickguard, bolt-on neck, 21-fret rosewood fingerboard with dot inlay, metal trapezoidal bridge with rosewood stick saddle, "Coke-bottle" shaped peghead, 3-per-side tuners with plastic buttons, single coil lipstick tube pickup, volume/tone control with selector switch. Available in Black (**Model 1317**) and Bronze (**Model 1321**) finishes. Mfd. 1957 to 1958.

N/A $375 $325 $260 $220 $180 $150

1319 - similar to Model 1317 except has 2 single coil lipstick tube pickups, 2 stacked volume/tone controls. Available in Black (Model 1319) and Bronze (Model 1323) finishes. Mfd. 1957 to 1958.

N/A $375 $325 $260 $220 $180 $150

These models are similar to the U models except for a shorter lower bout width of 11 ¾ inches and shorter overall length. Collectors call them "peanut body" models.

1357 - single cutaway, solid poplar body covered in vinyl, 11 ¾ inch lower bout width, clear or dark brown pickguard, bolt-on neck, 20-fret rosewood fingerboard with dot inlay, metal trapezoidal bridge with rosewood stick saddle, "Coke-bottle" shaped peghead wider at the bottom, 3-per-side tuners with plastic buttons, single coil lipstick tube pickup, volume/tone control with selector switch. Available in Tan with Ginger sides finish and the following Custom Colors: Flame Red with Black sides, Yellow with black sides, Bronze with Mint Green sides, Coral with White sides (All custom colors Model 1358). Mfd. 1955-1957.

N/A $375 $325 $260 $220 $180 $150

1359 - similar to Model 1357 except has 2 single coil lipstick tube pickups, 2 stacked knob volume/tone controls, 3-position selector switch. Available in Tan with Ginger sides finish and the following Custom Colors: Flame Red with Black sides, Yellow with black sides, Bronze with Mint Green sides, Coral with White sides (All custom colors Model 1360). Mfd. 1955-1957.

N/A $375 $325 $260 $220 $180 $150

1375 - single cutaway, solid poplar body covered in vinyl, 11 ¾ inch lower bout width, white pickguard, bolt-on neck, 20-fret rosewood fingerboard with dot inlay, metal trapezoidal bridge with rosewood stick saddle, "Coke-bottle" shaped peghead covered with white, plastic overlay, lightning bolt under logo and wider at the bottom, 3-per-side tuners with plastic buttons, single coil pickup mounted under pickguard, volume/tone control. Available in Maroon. Mfd 1954 to 1955.

N/A $375 $325 $260 $220 $180 $150

1377 - similar to Model 1375 except has 2 covered pickups, 2 volume/tone controls, 3-position selector switch. Available in Maroon. Mfd. 1954 to 1955.

N/A $375 $325 $260 $220 $180 $150

1417 - single cutaway, U-series body with 13 ¼ inch lower bout width, Masonite semi-solid construction, clear or white pickguard, bolt-on neck, 21-fret rosewood fingerboard with dot inlay, metal trapezoidal bridge with rosewood stick saddle, "dolphin-nose" shaped peghead, 6-on-a-side tuners with plastic buttons, single coil lipstick tube pickup, volume/tone control with selector switch. Available in Bronze (Model 1417) and Black (Model 1419) finishes. Mfd. 1959 to 1960 and 1961-1962.

N/A $375 $325 $260 $220 $180 $150

1415 - identical to Model 1417 except pickguard is cut in a half circle around the lipstick tube pickup instead of flush up against it. Available in Bronze (Model 1415) and Black (Model 1416) finishes. Mfd. 1960 only.

S

GRADING	100% MINT	98% NEAR MINT	95% EXC+	90% EXC	80% VG+	70% VG	60% G

1448 - offset double cutaway asymmetrical body, Masonite semi-solid construction, white pickguard, bolt-on neck, 18-fret rosewood fingerboard with dot inlay, metal trapezoidal bridge with rosewood stick saddle, 6-on-a-side tuners with plastic buttons, single coil lipstick tube pickup, volume/tone control. Available in Black with metallic accents finish. Mfd. 1962 to 1967.

N/A $375 $325 $260 $220 $180 $150

This model is known as an amp-in-case model because the case came fitted with a 3-watt amplifier and a 5-inch speaker.
In 1964, a 6-inch speaker replaced the 5-inch speaker.
In 1964, metal "skatekey" tuners replaced the tuners with plastic buttons.

1449 - similar to Model 1448 except has 21-fret rosewood fingerboard, two single coil lipstick tube pickups, 2 stacked volume/tone controls with 3-position selector switch. Available in Black with metallic accents finish. Mfd. 1963-1964.

N/A $375 $325 $260 $220 $180 $150

This model is known as an amp-in-case model because the case came fitted with a 5-watt amplifier, tremolo and an 8-inch speaker.

1450 - offset double cutaway asymmetrical body, solid wood covered with veneer, tortoise-shell pickguard, bolt-on neck, 21-fret rosewood fingerboard with dot inlay, metal trapezoidal vibrato bridge with rosewood stick saddle, 6-on-a-side metal "skate-key" tuners, 2 single coil lipstick tube pickups with 4 volume/tone controls, 3-position selector switch. Available in Red Sunburst finish. Mfd. 1965-1966

N/A $375 $325 $260 $220 $180 $150

This model was only listed in the 1965 Sears Christmas catalog. However, since 1966 models do exist, it is probable that they were produced and sold in stores to use up available stock.

1451 - offset double cutaway asymmetrical body, solid wood covered with veneer, white pickguard, bolt-on neck, 18-fret rosewood fingerboard with dot inlay, metal trapezoidal bridge with rosewood stick saddle, 6-on-a-side metal "skate-key" tuners, single coil lipstick tube pickup with volume/tone control. Available in Black finish. Mfd. 1967 to 1968.

N/A $375 $325 $260 $220 $180 $150

This model is known as an amp-in-case model because the case came fitted with a 3-watt amplifier and a 6-inch speaker.

1452 - similar to 1451 except 21-fret fingerboard, vibrato bridge, Fender-like peghead shape, 2 single coil lipstick tube pickups with 4 volume/tone controls. Available in Red Sunburst finish. Mfd. 1967 to 1968.

N/A $375 $325 $260 $220 $180 $150

This model is known as an amp-in-case model because the case was fitted with a 5-watt amplifier, tremolo and an 8-inch speaker.

1457 - offset double cutaway asymmetrical body, Masonite semi-solid construction, white pickguard, bolt-on neck, 21-fret rosewood fingerboard with dot inlay, metal trapezoidal bridge with rosewood stick saddle, 6-on-a-side tuners with metal "skate-key" tuners, 2 single coil lipstick tube pickups with stacked volume/tone controls, 3-position selector switch. Available in Red Sunburst with metallic accents finish. Mfd. 1964-1967

N/A $375 $325 $260 $220 $180 $150

This model is known as an amp-in-case model because the case was fitted with a 5-watt amplifier, tremolo and an 8-inch speaker.

1480 - single cutaway, U-series body with 13 ¼ inch lower bout width, Masonite semi-solid construction, clear or white pickguard, bolt-on neck, 18-fret rosewood fingerboard with dot inlay, metal trapezoidal bridge with rosewood stick saddle, dark brown or natural "Coke-bottle" shaped peghead, 3-per-side tuners with plastic buttons, single coil lipstick tube pickup mounted centrally between neck joint and bridge, volume/tone control. Available in Brown with metallic accents finish. Mfd. 1958.

N/A $375 $325 $260 $220 $180 $150

1450 - identical to Model 1480 (Not to be confused with the Model 1450 solidbody above). Mfd 1959.

1456 - identical to Model 1450 except pickguard is cut in a half circle around the lipstick tube pickup instead of flush up against it. Mfd. 1960-1961.

These models were only available through the Sears Christmas catalog. Although they were no longer listed in the Christmas Catalog after 1960, the existence of post-1960 models indicates that they were still being manufactured and sold at Sears stores through at least 1961, probably to use up existing stock.

ELECTRIC BASS

1373 - single cutaway, U-series body with 13 ¼ inch lower bout, Masonite semi-solid construction, clear or white pickguard, bolt-on neck, 24-fret rosewood fingerboard with dot inlay, trapezoidal bridge with rosewood stick saddle, "Coke-bottle" shaped peghead, 3-per-side tuners with plastic buttons, 2 single coil lipstick tube pickups, stacked volume/tone controls with 3-position selector switch. Available in Black finish. Mfd. 1957-1959.

N/A $375 $325 $260 $220 $180 $150

This model was a 6-string bass that was tuned like a guitar, but an octave lower.

1442 - offset double cutaway asymmetrical body, solid wood covered with veneer, white pickguard, bolt-on neck, 30-inch scale, 22-fret rosewood fingerboard with dot inlay, metal trapezoidal bridge with rosewood stick saddle, 4-on-a-side metal tuners, single coil lipstick tube pickup with volume/tone control, selector switch. Available in Brown sunburst finish. Mfd. 1966 to 1968.

N/A $375 $325 $260 $220 $180 $150

1443 - similar to Model 1442 except tortoise-shell pickguard, 34-inch scale, 2 single coil lipstick tube pickups, 4 volume/tone controls with 3-position selector switch. Available in Red Sunburst finish. Mfd. 1966 to 1968.

N/A $375 $325 $260 $220 $180 $150

GRADING	100% MINT	98% NEAR MINT	95% EXC+	90% EXC	80% VG+	70% VG	60% G

1444 - single cutaway, U-series body with 13 ¼ inch lower bout, Masonite semi-solid construction, clear or white pickguard, bolt-on neck, 24-fret rosewood fingerboard with dot inlay, trapezoidal bridge with rosewood stick saddle, "dolphin-nose" shaped peghead, 4-on-a-side tuners with plastic or metal buttons, single coil lipstick tube pickup, volume/tone control. Available in Black finish. Mfd. 1959-1966.

N/A	$375	$325	$260	$220	$180	$150

The publisher would like to thank Scott Sanders for his contributions to the Silvertone section.

(GENE) SIMMON'S PUNISHER BASS

Instruments currently built in California. Distributed by The Punisher (direct sales) of Beverly Hills, California.

As the rock group KISS began their current resurgence in popularity, a series of ads for the Punisher bass appeared in guitar magazines in 1996. The model (available in Natural, Tobacco Sunburst, or Black finish) is available and is identical to the same bass Gene Simmons has used for the past two or three tours. As to date, no information has been revealed as to the builder of the bass, although the headquarters will confirm that it is a company in California. The **Punisher** ($1,500) model features a dual cutaway body with dual cutawy equal-sized horns, EMG P/J pickups, Schaller bridge and hardware, and a hardshell case. No options, no left-handed models, period - just like Gene's!

SIMMS-WATTS

See also NED CALLAN.

Instruments previously produced in England during the mid 1970s.

The Simms-Watts trademark is the brand name used on England's own Ned Callan guitars. In fact, without the difference of the headstock label, the instruments are the same as, and produced by, Ned Callan (Peter Cook).

(Source: Tony Bacon and Paul Day, The Guru's Guitar Book)

SIMPSON

Instruments previously produced in New Zealand during the 1960s.

Luthier Ray Simpson built his first electric guitar in 1941. Production continued throughout the 1960s. A representational model called the **Pan-O-Sonic** combines both strat-designated overtones with original bridge and wiring designs (the three single coil pickups each have their own on/off switch.) If wired differently from a standard 3 or 5-way selector, this switching could offer some pickup combinations not offered traditionally! Anyone with further information on Simpson guitars is invited to write to the *Blue Book of Electric Guitars.*

(Source: Tony Bacon, The Ultimate Guitar Book)

SIMPSON HOT ROD GUITARS

Instruments previously built in Clearwater, Florida.

Sam Simpson offeried some well-built and hand crafted electric guitar models. Most models featured a highly figured maple top and quality pickups and hardware.

SIMPSON-JAMES

Instruments currently built in Westfield, Massachusetts since 1993.

Simpson-James basses are hand built in Westfield, Massachusetts by luthiers Christopher Mowatt and Robert Clarke. The company was established in 1993 with the vision of providing custom electric basses to local professional musicians. The basses produced have been unique in that no two instruments were alike, each being a prototype in design and function. Simpson-James currently offers four different neck-through **SJ-4** 4-string models (list prices range from $1,100 to $1,600), and two **SJ-5** 5-string models (list $2,100). The **Performer Series**, introduced in 1996, is a rebirth of the Great American Workhorse of basses. Offering the same quality in a bolt-neck design, Performer series 4- and 5-strings range from $1,250 to $2,000. According to product director Christopher Mowatt, Simpson-James is currently hand-building between 2 to 5 instruments per month in their efforts to maintain strict quality control.

SMARTLIGHT

Instruments currently produced in Korea. Distributed in the U.S. by Optek Music Systems, Inc. of Raleigh, North Carolina.

Earlier instruments may have the OPTEK or SMARTLIGHT trademark on the headstock. Current models have an "SL" logo on the headstock.

Optek Music Systems was formed by Rusty Shaffer in 1989 as a means to help educate new and existing guitarists through the use of the SmartLIGHT Interactive System(TM) for guitar. The SmartLIGHT guitar has LED lights in the neck that light up guitar fingerings to show guitarists precisely where to place their fingers. The SmartLIGHT connects to a personal computer. Players can learn to play specific songs which have been recorded on MIDI albums by using the company's MIDI driver in conjunction with a general sequencer program. They can also learn chord fingerings of their choice by using software that allows them to choose chords, scales, or notes in any of twelve musical keys and illuminate those fingerings on the guitar.

(Company information courtesy Michelle Gouldsberry)

Three SmartLIGHT electric guitars and one SmartLIGHT bass guitar are offered for all playing levels. The entry level **30-A** electric (factory direct $379.95) has a solid black body with one piezo pickup. The intermediate **30-B** electric ($479.95)

GRADING	100% MINT	98% NEAR MINT	95% EXC+	90% EXC	80% VG+	70% VG	60% G

in Natural or Translucent Blue has one piezo pickup and two single coil pickups. The advanced **30-C** electric ($679.95) in Orange Sunburst has a bird's-eye maple top and back, Seymour Duncan pickups, and gold hardware. The advanced **40-C** electric bass ($699.95) is made of the same materials as the 30-C, and includes the Seymour Duncan Lightnin' Rod bassline active/passive pickup system. The Smartlight guitars are produced in the same Korean factory that makes guitars for companies like Fender, Gibson's Epiphone brand, and Washburn. The U.S. Optek facility checks quality control, assembly, and set-ups prior to shipping.

SMITH, KEN

Instruments currently built in Perkasie, Pennsylvania and Japan. Distributed by Ken Smith Basses, Ltd. of Perkasie, Pennsylvania.

Luthier Ken Smith's original career was as a professional studio musician. Inspired by his need for a better quality bass guitar, he built one! His efforts introduced the concept of a high quality custom bass designed to meet the needs of a professional player.

Smith spent a number of years in the early 1970s researching luthier information and building designs. By 1978 he opened his business, and in 1980 the first Smith basses were introduced.

ELECTRIC BASS

Add $100 for fretless fingerboard models.

Add $200 for left-handed versions.

20TH ANNIVERSARY - offset double cutaway tiger maple body core/black walnut or mahogany laminate, figured (flamed, birds-eye, and charcoal flamed) California redwood top and back, hard rock maple/bubinga laminate neck, 24-fret Macassar ebony fingerboard with mother-of-pearl top and side dot position markers, fixed bridge, figured California redwood peghead with pearl logo inlay, 2-per-side tuners, gold hardware, 2 humbucker pickups, volume/treble/bass/mix controls, series/parallel switches, active electronics. Available in Natural finish. Mfg. 1998 to 1999.

4-string

Last MSR was $6,170.

5-string - 3/2-per-side tuners.

Last MSR was $6,170.

6-string - 3-per-side tuners.

Last MSR was $6,170.

A total of 40 Anniversary basses are scheduled. Serial numbers will designate the order in which the basses were produced, and what string configuration on the backplate.

C.R. CUSTOM IV - double cutaway maple body, figured maple wings, bolt-on 3-piece maple neck, 24-fret pau ferro fingerboard, fixed brass bridge, blackface peghead with pearl logo inlay, 2-per-side tuners, chrome hardware, 2 humbucker pickups, volume/treble/bass/mix controls, active electronics. Available in Natural finish. Mfg. 1993 to date.

MSR	$2,400	$1,925	$1,550	$1,375	$1,200	$935	$760	$675

This model has swamp ash wings as an option.

C.R. Custom V - similar to C.R. Custom IV, except has 5-strings, 3/2-per-side tuners.

MSR	$2,500	$2,000	$1,625	$1,200	$960	$860	$790	$720

C.R. Custom VI - similar to C.R. Custom IV, except has 6-strings, 3-per-side tuners.

MSR	$2,600	$2,075	$1,695	$1,250	$1,000	$900	$825	$750

Burner Series

ARTIST - double cutaway mahogany body with exotic wood top/back, bolt-on maple/walnut 5-piece neck, 24-fret rosewood fingerboard with pearl dot inlay, fixed bridge, 2-per-side tuners, black hardware, 2 humbucker pickups, volume/treble/bass and mix controls, active electronics. Available in Antique Natural finish. Current Mfg.

MSR	$2,399	$1,925	$1,550	$1,000	$800	$720	$660	$600

Artist V - similar to Artist, except has 5-strings, 3/2-per-side tuners.

MSR	$2,499	$2,000	$1,625	$1,050	$840	$755	$690	$630

Artist VI - similar to Artist, except has 6-strings, 3-per-side tuners.

MSR	$2,699	$2,150	$1,750	$1,150	$920	$830	$760	$690

CUSTOM - double cutaway figured maple body, bolt-on maple/walnut 5-piece neck, 24-fret rosewood fingerboard with pearl dot inlay, fixed bridge, 2-per-side tuners, black hardware, 2 J-style pickups, volume/treble/bass and mix controls, active electronics. Available in Transparent Antique Natural, Transparent Candy Red and Transparent Cobalt Blue finishes. Current Mfg.

MSR	$1,999	$1,600	$1,300	$980	$840	$775	$630	$480

Custom V - similar to Custom, except has 5-strings, 3/2-per-side tuners.

MSR	$2,099	$1,675	$1,365	$1,080	$945	$830	$725	$565

Custom VI - similar to Custom, except has 6-strings, 3-per-side tuners.

MSR	$2,299	$1,850	$1,495	$1,150	$980	$850	$760	$670

GRADING		100% MINT	98% NEAR MINT	95% EXC+	90% EXC	80% VG+	70% VG	60% G

DELUXE - double cutaway swamp ash body, bolt-on maple neck, 24-fret pau ferro fingerboard with pearl dot inlay, fixed brass bridge, 2-per-side tuners, black hardware, 2 J-style pickups, 2 volume/1 treble/1 bass controls, active electronics. Available in Antique Natural, Transparent Candy Apple Red, Transparent Cobalt Blue finishes. Current Mfg.

MSR	$1,899	$1,525	$1,235	$1,000	$880	$775	$640	$480

Deluxe V - similar to Deluxe, except has 5-strings, 3/2-per-side tuners.

MSR	$1,999	$1,600	$1,300	$1,050	$920	$800	$680	$530

Deluxe VI - similar to Deluxe, except has 6-strings, 3-per-side tuners.

MSR	$2,199	$1,750	$1,425	$1,140	$1,065	$985	$825	$770

STANDARD - double cutaway alder body, bolt-on maple neck, 24-fret pau ferro fingerboard with pearl dot inlay, fixed brass bridge, 2-per-side tuners, black hardware, 2 J-style pickups, 2 volume/1 treble/1 bass controls, active electronics. Available in Electric Blue, Ivory White, Onyx Black and Scarlet Red finishes. Current Mfg.

MSR	$1,699	$1,350	$1,100	$930	$860	$720	$630	$520

Standard V - similar to Standard, except has 5-strings, 3/2-per-side tuners.

MSR	$1,799	$1,450	$1,150	$975	$880	$750	$665	$550

Standard VI - similar to Standard, except has 6-strings, 3-per-side tuners.

MSR	$1,999	$1,600	$1,300	$1,050	$920	$800	$680	$525

"G" Series

This series has graphite rods adjacent to the truss rod for added strength and durability.

B.M.T. ELITE IV - offset double cutaway mahogany body with walnut/maple veneer, figured maple top/back, through-body 7 piece bubinga/maple/ovankol neck, 24-fret pau ferro fingerboard with pearl dot inlay, fixed brass bridge, blackface peghead with pearl logo inlay, 2-per-side tuners, gold hardware, 2 humbucker pickups, volume/treble/mid/bass/mix controls, active electronics. Available in Natural finish. Mfg. 1993 to date.

MSR	$4,400	$3,525	$2,850	$2,500	$2,175	$1,825	$1,495	$1,150

This model has bubinga, koa, lacewood, pau ferro top/walnut back, ovankol, walnut and zebrawood bodies, ebony fingerboard, black and chrome hardware as an option.

B.M.T. Elite V - similar to B.M.T. Elite IV, except has 5-strings, 3/2-per-side tuners.

MSR	$4,500	$3,600	$2,925	$2,575	$2,225	$1,875	$1,525	$1,175

B.M.T. Elite VI - similar to B.M.T. Elite IV, except has 6-strings, 3-per-side tuners.

MSR	$4,600	$3,675	$2,975	$2,625	$2,265	$1,900	$1,550	$1,200

Smith B.T. Custom "G"
courtesy Ken Smith Basses

B.T. CUSTOM IV - double cutaway mahogany body, figured maple top/back, through-body 5-piece maple/mahogany neck, 24-fret ebony fingerboard with pearl dot inlay, fixed brass bridge, blackface peghead with pearl logo inlay, 2-per-side tuners, black hardware, 2 humbucker Smith pickups, volume/concentric treble-bass/mix controls, active electronics. Available in Charcoal Gray, Electric Blue, Natural and Scarlet Red finishes. Current Mfg.

MSR	$3,900	$3,125	$2,535	$2,225	$1,900	$1,600	$1,285	$975

This model has bubinga, koa, lacewood, pau ferro, ovankol and zebrawood bodies with Natural finish, pau ferro fingerboard, chrome and gold hardware as options.

B.T. Custom V - similar to B.T. Custom IV, except has 5-strings, 3/2-per-side tuners.

MSR	$4,000	$3,250	$2,600	$2,275	$1,950	$1,640	$1,325	$1,000

B.T. Custom VI - similar to B.T. Custom IV, except has 6-strings, 3-per-side tuners.

MSR	$4,100	$3,275	$2,650	$2,335	$2,000	$1,695	$1,375	$1,050

C.R. CUSTOM IV - double cutaway mahogany body, figured maple top/back, through-body 3-piece maple neck, 24-fret pau ferro fingerboard with pearl dot inlay, fixed brass bridge, 2-per-side tuners, chrome hardware, 2 humbucker pickups, volume/treble/bass/mix controls, active electronics. Available in Natural finish. New 1993.

MSR	$2,800	$2,250	$1,825	$1,600	$1,395	$1,175	$965	$750

This group of instruments was formerly the Chuck Rainey Series.
This model has koa, oak and walnut bodies, black and gold hardware as options.

C.R. Custom V - similar to C.R. Custom IV, except has 5-strings, 3/2-per-side tuners. Mfg. 1992 to date.

MSR	$2,900	$2,325	$1,885	$1,650	$1,425	$1,185	$950	$725

C.R. Custom VI - similar to C.R. Custom IV, except has 6-strings, 3-per-side tuners. Mfg. 1992 to date.

MSR	$3,000	$2,400	$1,950	$1,700	$1,475	$1,225	$995	$750

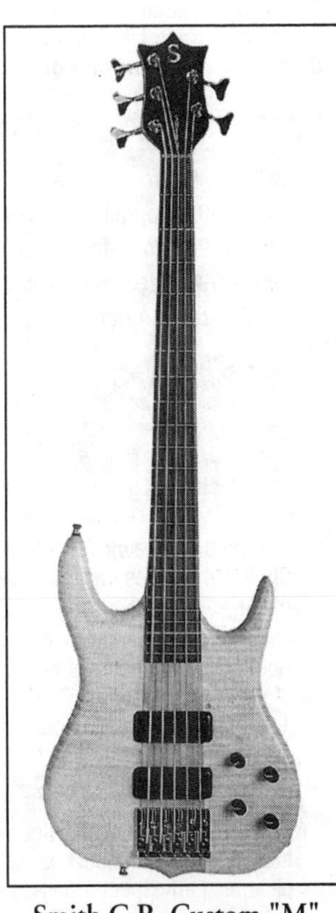

Smith C.R. Custom "M"
courtesy Ken Smith Basses

SOLA-SOUND

Instruments previously produced in Japan during the early 1970s.

The Sola-Sound trademark was a brand name used by a UK importer. These medium quality solid body guitars featured designs based on classic American favorites.

(Source: Tony Bacon and Paul Day, The Guru's Guitar Book)

SONGBIRD GUITARS

Instruments currently made in Asia, and distributed by Songbird Guitars, in Cranberry, Pennsylvania.

Songbird Guitars imports both acoustic and electric instruments. For more information, including model lineup and current prices, please contact the company directly (see Trademark Index).

SONNET

Instruments previously produced in Japan.

Sonnet guitars were distributed in the U.S. by the Daimaru New York Corporation of New York, New York.

(Source: Michael Wright, Guitar Stories Volume One)

SPECTOR

Current trademark owned by Stuart Spector Design, Ltd., located in Saugerties, New York. Instruments are built in Woodstock, New York (USA Handmade Series), THE Czech Republic (Europe Series) Korea (Professional Series) and China (Performance Series).

Instruments originally built in Brooklyn, New York from 1976 through 1985. After Kramer (BKL) bought the company, production moved to Neptune, New Jersey between 1985 to 1989. Some late 1980s Kramer/Spector models were produced in Japan.

Two members of the Brooklyn Woodworkers Co-operative, Stuart Spector and Alan Charney, established Spector Guitars in 1976. The initial SB-1 bass and G-1 guitar both featured neck-through-body design. Another member of the co-op was Ned Steinberger, who was designing and building furniture. Stuart began searching for a new bass design and Ned offered to assist. Ned built a prototype bass that would influence bass guitar design forever. He designed the NS-1 bass. "The idea of attaching the body parts at an angle and then curving the top was intended to give the instrument a more attractive appearance, and the compound curve on the back is for comfort," states Ned. It was this prototype instrument more than any other that set the stage for my work in musical instrument design. The cusved body Spector NS was an instant classic. The NS-1 was updated to the two pickup NS-2, and bolt-on neck versions(NS-1B and NS-2JA) were added to the line in 1982.

Spector sold the company to Kramer Music Products in 1985. Kramer continued to produce the NS-2 bass, and introduced the first imported Spector basses, including the NS-2A, In June, 1987, Stuart debuted the NS-5 5-string bass for Kramer production. All production ceased when Kramer went into bankruptcy in 1989.

Stuart Spector's current company, Stuart Spectpr Designs, Ldt, introduced the new SD bass series in 1991 under the "SSD" name. In December 1992 SSD relaunched the NS bass series.

The Gibson Guitar Corp. purchased the Kramer trademark in 1997, and Stuart Spector Designs purchased the rights to the Spector trademark. All instruments since 1997 sport the original "SS" logo.

(Company information courtesy Stuart Spector)

Model Production by Location Identification

1976-1985: Brooklyn, New York.
1985-1990: Neptune, New Jersey under Kramer.
1991-1996: Woodstock, New York as **S S D**.
1993-1996: Czech Republic as **S S D**.
1997-date: USA Handmade, Czech Republic, Korea and China production with original Spector trademark.

ELECTRIC

Blackhawk Series

The Blackhawk guitar design and development by Chris Hofschneider features a mahogany body with a flame maple top, bolt-on maple neck, rosewood fingerboard, 25.5" scale, black hardware, and Schaller tuners. European production models

like the **Blackhawk CR** with a Wilkinson stop tailpiece lists at $995, while the Blackhawk with Schaller/Floyd Rose tremolo lists at $1,295 (Model BH-FR). Choice of finishes included Black, Blue, and Red Stain finishes, and Cherry Sunburst.

Spector also offers a **Blackhawk Custom USA** (Model BHK-FB) which is built in the U.S. and features Tom Holmes, EMG, or Seymour Duncan P-90 pickups, chrome hardware, and a fixed bridge (list $1,799). The Blackhawk with Original Floyd Rose tremolo (Model BHK-FR) has a list price of $2,029. The optional Gold plated hardware is an additional $80. The U.S.-built Blackhawk guitars are available in Amber Stain, Black & Blue, Black & Teal, Black Cherry, Black Oil, Black Stain, Blueburst, Blue Stain, Cherry Sunburst, Clear Gloss, Forest Green, Golden Stain, Green/Blueburst, Ivory, Magenta Stain, Orange Stain, Red Stain, Teal Stain, Tobacco Sunburst, Teal Stain, and Violet Stain.

ELECTRIC BASS

Ned Steinberger Spector designs from the late 1970s featured models like the **NS-1**, which had a single humbucker pickup, neck-through design, 2-per-side headstock. This model opened the door for others such as the **NS-1 B**, a bolt-on neck model; the **NS-2** (2 humbuckers); and the **NS-2 J** which featured 2 EMG pickups. Early Spector basses still command good money on the vintage market.

NS-2000 Series

NS-2000-4 - offset double cutaway body, through-body neck, 34" scale, 24-fret rosewood fingerboard with pearl dot inlays, fixed bridge, blackface peghead with pearl logo inlay, 2-per-side tuners, chrome hardware, two humbucker pickups, volume/tone controls. Available in Natural finish. Mfg. 1998 to date.

MSR **$995**

Add $100 for 5-string configuration (Model NS2000-5).

This model is produced in Korea.

NS-2000 B - similar to the NS-2000, except features a bolt-on neck. Mfg. 1998 to 1999.

Last MSR was $479.

This model is produced in China.

BOB Series

Stuart Spector designed the BOB models in 1996. These models feature a bolt-on neck design, and are built in the USA.

Add $175 for a high gloss finish (HG).

Add $200 for a figured maple top (FIG-MPL).

BOB 4 - offset double cutaway swamp ash body, 6 bolt, bolt-on maple neck, pau ferro fingerboard, fixed brass bridge, blackface peghead with pearl logo inlay, 2-per-side tuners, gold hardware, EMG DC pickup, volume/treble/bass controls. Available in Matte Natural finish. Mfg. 1996 to 1999.

Last MSR was $1,295.

BOB 4 Deluxe - similar to the BOB 4, except features 2 EMG DC pickups, EMG 3-band EQ. Disc.

Last MSR was $1,565.

BOB 5 - similar to BOB 4, except has 5-string configuration, 3/2-per-side tuners. Mfg. 1996 to 1999.

Last MSR was $1,395.

BOB 5 Deluxe - similar to BOB 4, except has 5-string configuration, 3/2-per-side tuners, 2 EMG DC pickups, EMG 3-band EQ. Disc.

Last MSR was $1,665.

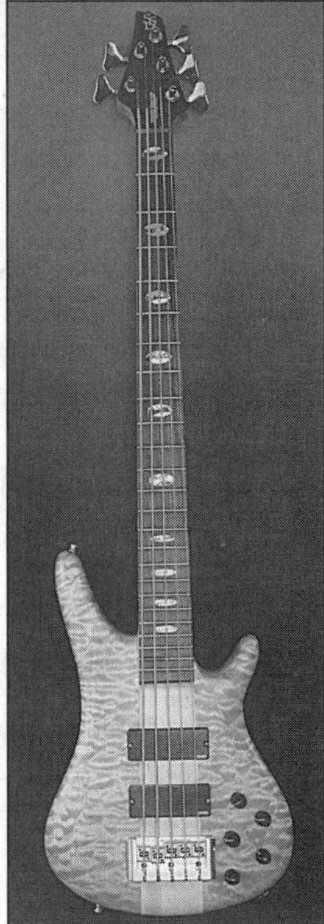

Spector SD Bass courtesy Stuart Spector Design

Europe Series

The NS-CR basses are built in the Czech Republic, and were first offered in 1995.

NS 4 CR - offset double cutaway soft maple body, through-body graphite-reinforced maple neck, rosewood fingerboard with dot inlays, 34" scale, solid fixed brass bridge, blackface peghead with pearl logo inlay, 2-per-side tuners, gold hardware, EMG P/J-style pickups, 2 volume/treble/bass EQ controls, active electronics. Available in Fire Engine Red, Gloss Black, and White finishes. Mfg. 1995 to 1999.

Last MSR was $1,795.

NS 4 CRFM - similar to the NS 4 CR, except features a figured maple body, gold Schaller tuners. Available in Amber, Blackburst, Black Cherry, Black Stain, Clear Gloss, Natural Oil, Plum Stain, and Red Stain finishes. Current Mfg.

MSR **$1,795**

NS 5 CR - similar to NS 4 CR, except has 5-string configuration, 3/2-per-side tuners, EMG 40 DC pickups. Disc. 1999.

Last MSR was $1,995.

NS 5 CRFM - similar to NS 4 CRFM, except has 5-string configuration, 3/2-per-side gold Schaller tuners, EMG 40 DC pickups. Available in Amber, Blackburst, Black Cherry, Black Stain, Clear Gloss, Natural Oil, Plum Stain, and Red Stain finishes. Current Mfg.

MSR **$1,995**

JN Series

In 1995, Spector offered a custom bass series based on a model built for Jason Newsted (Metallica). These neck-through models featured EMG pickups, piezo bridges and electronics, a black oil finish, and fiber optic illuminated side markers. List prices were $4,900 (**JN-4P**), $5,075 (**JN-5P**), and $5,350 (**JN-6P**) respectively.

USA Series

In the USA Series, the NS models were designed by Ned Steinberger (based on his original curved back model from 1976). The SD models were designed by Stuart Spector in 1992. Current U.S. models are optional with bridge-mounted piezo pickup systems.

NS 2 - offset double cutaway figured maple body, through-body 3-piece maple neck, 24-fret pau ferro fingerboard with pearl crown inlays, 34" scale, solid fixed brass bridge, blackface peghead with pearl logo inlay, 2-per-side tuners, gold hardware, P/J-style EMG pickups, volume/mix/stacked 2-band EQ controls, 9-volt active electronics. Available in Natural Oil finish. Current Mfg.

MSR **$3,900**

Add $500 for high gloss finish (Model NS 2 HG). Available in Amber Stain, Black & Blue, Black & Teal, Black Cherry, Black Oil, Black Stain, Blueburst, Blue Stain, Cherry Sunburst, Clear Gloss, Forest Green, Golden Stain, Green/Blueburst, Ivory, Magenta Stain, Orange Stain, Red Stain, Teal Stain, Tobacco Sunburst, Teal Stain, and Violet Stain.

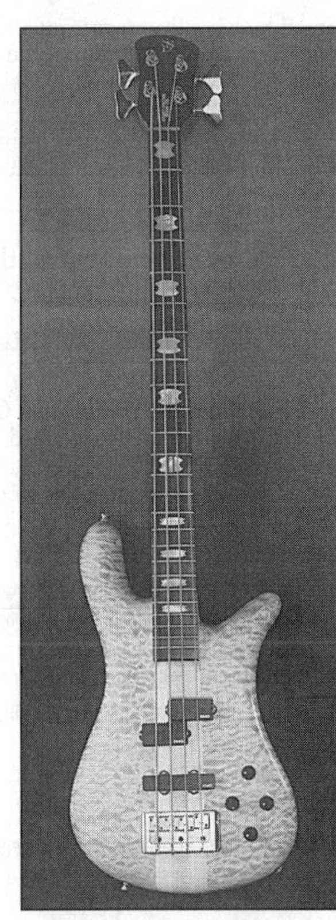

Spector NS Bass courtesy Stuart Spector Design

NS 2 J - similar to the NS 2, except features a bolt-on 3-piece neck, swamp ash body, black hardware, 24-fret pau ferro fingerboard, 2 J-style EMG pickups, EMG active electronics. Available in Natural Oil finish. Current Mfg.

MSR $1,895

Add $175 for high gloss finish (Model NS 2 J HG).

Add $175 for optional curly maple body.

NS 4 - offset double cutaway figured maple body, through-body 3-piece maple neck, 24-fret pau ferro fingerboard with pearl crown inlays, 34 scale, solid fixed brass bridge, blackface peghead with pearl logo inlay, 2-per-side tuners, gold hardware, two EMG 35 DC *soapbar* pickups volume/mix/stacked 2-band EQ controls, 18-volt active electronics. Available in Natural Oil finish. Current Mfg.

MSR $3,900

Add $500 for high gloss finish (Model NS 4 HG).

NS 4-20 Limited Edition 20th Anniversary - similar to the NS 4, except features AAAAA Western quilted maple body, ebony fingerboard with hand cut *swimming trout* inlay of mother-of-pearl/abalone/copper/aluminum. Mfg. 1996 only.

MSR $11,000

This model comes with a Certificate of Authenticity signed by Stuart Spector, and a hardshell case.

NS 5 - similar to NS 4, except has 5-string configuration, 3/2-per-side tuners, EMG 40 DC pickups. Disc. 1999.

Last MSR was $4,000.

Add $500 for high gloss finish (Model NS 5 HG).

NS-6 - similar to NS 4, except has 6-string configuration, 3-per-side tuners, EMG 45 DC pickups. Disc. 1999.

Last MSR was $4,200.

Add $500 for high gloss finish (Model NS 6 HG).

NS 535 5-STRING - offset double cutaway figured maple body, through-body 3-piece maple neck, 24-fret pau ferro fingerboard with pearl crown inlays, 35" scale, solid fixed brass bridge, blackface peghead with pearl logo inlay, 3/2-per-side tuners, gold hardware, two EMG 40 DC *soapbar* pickups, volume/mix/stacked 2-band EQ controls, 18-volt active electronics. Available in Natural Oil finish. Mfg. 1998 to 1999.

SPECIAL

Instruments built in Yugoslavia circa mid 1960s.

These entry level solid body guitars were built by the Muzicka Naklada company, which was based in Yugoslavia. The model 64 sports a vaguely Fender-ish body design and three single coils, as well as 5 knobs and 3 switches.

(Source: Tony Bacon, The Ultimate Guitar Book)

SPIRAL

Instruments currently built in Van Nuys, California. Distributed by Alfa Export Office, Inc. of Van Nuys, California.

Spiral high quality electric guitars are crafted by the same people that build the Xotic custom basses and Trilogic pickups. Spiral's **SEG-Standard** features a two-piece ash or alder double cutaway body, bolt-on neck, 25.5" scale, maple or rosewood fingerboard, 4 Trilogic T/L pickups arranged as a 2 single coil/humbucker configuration, Wilkinson VS-100 G tremolo, master volume/high pass filter/low pass filter controls, coil tap mini-switch, and 5-way pickup selector

(list $1,980). The **SEG-Pro** is similar to the SEG-Standard, except features a flame or quilted maple top over an ash body (list $2,480). Both models are available in Black, Seafoam Green, Red, and White solid finishes; or Black, Blue, Green, Red, White, Yellow, or Special Burst transparent colors.

SQUIER

Instruments currently produced in Mexico, Korea, and China. Distributed by the Fender Musical Instrument company of Scottsdale, Arizona.

Instruments first produced in Japan circa 1982; later production shifted to Korea in 1987 (to the Young Chang Akki factory).

In 1982, the Fender division of CBS established **Fender Japan** in conjunction with Kanda Shokai and Yamano music. Production of the Squier instruments, originally intended for European distribution, began in 1983 at the Fugi Gen Gakki facilities in Matsumoto, Japan. The Squier trademark was based on the V.C. Squire string-making company that produced strings for Fender in the 1950s, and was later acquired by Fender (under CBS) in 1965. What was intended as a *European Commodity* soon became a way for Fender to provide entry level instruments for students and beginning players.

The Squier trademark was introduced in 1983, and Squier II series was introduced circa 1986. In 1996, the Squier line was greatly expanded by Fender, with the introduction of various different series.

Production Model Codes

Fender's current **Squier** instruments are produced in Mexico, Korea and China. Fender products are identified by a *part number* that consists of a three digit location/facility code and a four digit model code (the two codes are separated by a hyphen).

The second/third digit combination designates the production location:

13	**Mexico, Guitar and Bass**
33	**Korea, Guitar and Bass**
33	**China, Guitar and Bass**

The first digit after the hyphen will indicate which country is the place of origin:

0	**China, Guitar and Bass**
1	**Korea, Guitar and Bass**
6	**Korea, Guitar and Bass**

For example, the model designated 033-0600 would be the Chinese-produced Affinity Series Strat.

S

GRADING	100% MINT	98% NEAR MINT	95% EXC+	90% EXC	80% VG+	70% VG	60% G

ELECTRIC

Squier instruments are directly based on Fender designs, and either carry a large **Squier by Fender** or Fender - Squier Series on the headstock.

Affinity Series

DUO-SONIC (Model 033-0702) - hardwood body, maple neck, 22.7" scale, 20-fret fingerboard, fixed bridge, 2 single coil pickups. Available in Black, Arctic White, and Torino Red. Mfg. 1998 to 2000.

		$160	$140	$120	$100	$80	$60	$45

Last MSR was $229.

STRAT (Model 033-0600/Model 031-0600) - offset double cutaway hardwood body, 22-fret rosewood fingerboard with white dot inlay, tremolo, chrome hardware, white pickguard, 3 single coil pickups, volume/2 tone controls, 5-way selector. Available in Arctic White, Black, and Torino Red finishes. Current Mfg.

MSR	$249	$175	$150	$135	$115	$100	$85	$65

In 2001, British Racing Green, Baltic Blue and Galactic Purple finishes were introduced.

FAT STRAT - similar to Affinity Strat, except has a humbucking pickup in the bridge position. Available in Black, Arctic White, British Racing Green, Torino Red and Baltic Blue finishes. New 2001.

MSR $279 $195

TELE (Model 033-0200) - hardwood body, maple neck, 21-fret rosewood fingerboard, 2 single coil pickups. Available in Black, Arctic White, and Torino Red. Mfg. 1998 to 2000.

		$180	$160	$140	$120	$100	$80	$60

Last MSR was $259.

TELE - similar to Affinity Tele (Model 033-0200), except has solid alder body, new die-cast tuners. Available in Black, Baltic Blue, Torino Red and Arctic White finishes. Current Mfg.

MSR $249 $175

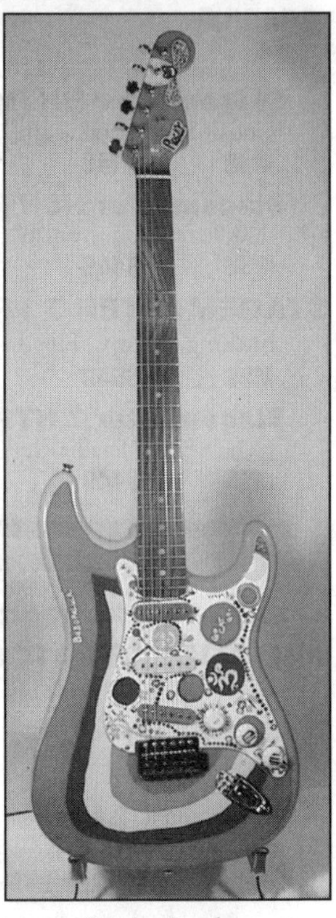

Squier Rocky
courtesy J.R. Guitars

Bullet Series

Squier Bullet guitars and basses were produced in Japan between 1983 to 1988. Bullets have a telecaster-style headstock with a **Squier by Fender - Bullet**/star with a "1" in the center logo. Retail list prices in the early 1980s ranged between $279 up to $419. The average used price today ranges from $125 up to $175.

Stagemaster Series

STAGEMASTER SUB-SONIC DELUXE (Model 032-4805) - offset double cutaway solid basswood body, maple neck through-body with reverse "small" Strat headstock,6-on-a-side tuners, rosewood fingerboard, 27" scale, 24-frets, master volume and tone, 2 exposed coil humbucking pickups. Available in Metallic Black. New 2001.

MSR $699 $489

STAGEMASTER DELUXE HH (Model 132-4800) - offset double cutaway solid basswood body, maple neck through-body with "small" reverse Strat headstock, rosewood fingerboard, 24-frets, 6-on-a-side tuners, Floyd Rose licensed double locking tremelo, master volume and tone, 2 humbucking pickups. Available in Shoreline Gold Metallic, Atlantic Blue Metallic and Wine Red Metallic finishes. Current Mfg.

MSR $599 $419

Stagemaster Deluxe HSH (Model 132-4900) - similar to Stagemaster Deluxe HH, except has 2 humbucking pickups and 1 single coil pickup in the middle position. Available in Pewter Gray Metallic, Black Metallic and Emerald Green Metallic finishes. Current Mfg.

MSR $599 $419

STAGEMASTER HSS (Model 132-3700) - offset double cutaway solid alder body, maple neck with rosewood fingerboard, 24 medium-jumbo frets, 6-on-a-side tuners, 2 single coil pickups and 1 humbucking pickup in the bridge position. Available in Black Metallic, Cobalt Blue Metallic and Purple Metallic finishes. Current Mfg.

MSR $449 $315

Stagemaster HSS NLT (Model 032-2700) - similar to Stagemaster HSS, except has Floyd Rose licensed non-locking twin pivot tremelo. Available in Black Metallic, Cobalt Blue Metallic and Purple Metallic finishes. New 2001.

MSR $349 $245

GRADING	100% MINT	98% NEAR MINT	95% EXC+	90% EXC	80% VG+	70% VG	60% G

Stagemaster HH (Model 132-3800) - similar to Stagemaster HSS, except has 2 humbucking pickups. Available in Black Metallic, Cobalt Blue Metallic and Purple Metallic finishes. Current Mfg.

MSR $449 $315

Stagemaster HSH (Model 132-3900) - similar to Stagemaster HH, except has 2 humbucking pickups and 1 single coil pickup in the middle position. Available in Black Metallic, Cobalt Blue Metallic and Purple Metallic finishes. Current Mfg.

MSR $449 $315

STAGEMASTER 7 FR (Model 132-3807) - similar to Stagemaster HH, except in a 7-string configuration, 2 high-output humbucking pickups, Floyd Rose licensed tremelo. Available in Black Metallic, Cobalt Blue Metallic and Purple Metallic finishes. Current Mfg.

MSR $549 $385

Stagemaster 7 HT (Model 032-3837) - similar to Stagemaster 7 FR, except has a "Hard-Tail" bridge. Available in Black Metallic, Cobalt Blue Metallic and Purple Metallic finishes. Current Mfg.

MSR $449 $315

Stratocaster Series

The following models are based on Fender's Stratocaster design, and all have an offset double cutaway body, bolt-on maple neck, 6-on-a-side tuners, chrome hardware, 3 single coil pickups, volume/2 tone controls, and 5-way selector (unless otherwise listed).

PRO TONE STRATOCASTER (Model 033-2900) - ash body, 21-fret rosewood fingerboard with white dot inlay, gold hardware, white shell pickguard, vintage style tremolo. Available in Crimson Red Transparent and Sapphire Blue Transparent finishes. Disc. 1998.

$375 $325 $275 $250 $200 $175 $125

Last MSR was $529.

This model is also available with a maple fingerboard with black dot inlay (Model 033-2902).

Pro Tone Stratocaster (Model 033-2600) - ash body, 21-fret rosewood fingerboard with white dot inlay, chrome hardware, red shell pickguard. Available in Olympic White with matching headstock. Disc. 1998.

$350 $300 $275 $225 $195 $150 $125

Last MSR was $499.

Pro Tone Stratocaster (Model 033-2700) - ash body, 21-fret rosewood fingerboard with white dot inlay, chrome hardware, white shell pickguard. Available in 3-Tone Sunburst finish. Disc. 1998.

$350 $300 $275 $225 $195 $150 $125

Last MSR was $499.

Pro Tone Stratocaster (Model 033-2802) - ash body, 21-fret maple fingerboard with black dot inlay, chrome hardware, *aged* pickup covers/control knobs, white pickguard. Available in Vintage Blonde finish. Disc. 1998.

$350 $300 $275 $225 $195 $150 $125

Last MSR was $499.

This model is also available in left-handed configuration (Model 033-2822).

Pro Tone Fat Strat (Model 133-3102) - ash body, 22-fret maple fingerboard with black dot inlay, gold hardware, black shell pickguard, licensed Floyd Rose tremolo, 2 single coil/humbucker pickups, volume/tone controls. Available in Black finish. Disc. 1998.

$450 $375 $350 $295 $250 $200 $150

Last MSR was $639.

STANDARD STRATOCASTER (Model 033-1602) - alder body, 21-fret maple fingerboard with black dot inlay, chrome hardware, vintage-style tremolo, 3-ply white pickguard. Available in Arctic White, Black, Brown Sunburst, Midnight Blue, and Midnight Wine finishes. Disc. 1998.

$200 $175 $150 $125 $100 $90 $75

Last MSR was $289.

This model is available with a rosewood fingerboard with white dot inlay (Model 033-1600).
This model is available in a left-handed configuration (Model 033-1620) in Black and Brown Sunburst finishes.

Standard Fat Stratocaster (Model 033-1702) - similar to the Standard Stratocaster, except has 2 single coil/humbucker pickups. Available in Midnight Blue and Midnight Wine finishes. Disc. 1998.

$215 $175 $150 $135 $115 $100 $75

Last MSR was $299.

STANDARD STRATOCASTER (Model 013-2102) - poplar body, 21-fret maple fingerboard with black dot inlay, chrome hardware, vintage-style tremolo, 3-ply white pickguard. Available in Arctic White, Black, Brown Sunburst, Lake Placid Blue, and Crimson Red Metallic finishes. Mfg. 1998 to 2000.

$225 $195 $165 $135 $115 $95 $75

Last MSR was $329.

Add $30 for a left-handed configuration (Model 013-2120) in Black, Arctic White, Brown Sunburst, Crimson Red Metallic, and Lake Placid Blue finishes.

This model is available with a rosewood fingerboard with white dot inlay (Model 013-2100).

GRADING	100% MINT	98% NEAR MINT	95% EXC+	90% EXC	80% VG+	70% VG	60% G

Standard Stratocaster (Model 032-1600) - similar to Standard Stratocaster (Model 013-3102), except hassolid agathis body, maple neck, 22-fret rosewood fingerboard, large headstock, die-cast tuners, twin pivot bridge with satin- anodized saddles, 3 Alnico single coil pickups. Available in 3-Color Sunburst, Sherwood Green Metallic, Candy Apple Red, Black Metallic, Shoreline Gold and Purple Metallic finishes. New 2001.

MSR $349 $245

Also available with maple fingerboard (Model 032-1602).

Add $30 for Left-Hand model (Model 032-1620). Rosewood fingerboard. Available in Black Metallic, Purple Metallic and 3-Color Sunburst finishes.

Add $30 for 3-Color Sunburst finish.

Standard Fat Stratocaster (Model 013-2202) - similar to the Standard Stratocaster, except has 2 single coil/humbucker pickups. Available in Arctic White, Black, Brown Sunburst, Lake Placid Blue, and Crimson Red Metallic finishes. Mfg. 1998 to 2000.

$235 $200 $175 $150 $125 $100 $85
Last MSR was $339.

Add $120 for Floyd Rose II tremolo (Model 113-2202) in Black, Arctic White, Brown Sunburst, Crimson Red Metallic, and Lake Placid Blue finishes. The Standard Fat Strat With Floyd Rose is available with a rosewood fingerboard (Model 113-2200).

STANDARD FAT STRATOCASTER (Model 032-1700) - similar to Standard Fat Stratocaster (Model 013-2202), except has solid agathis body, high-output humbucker in the bridge position, 22-frets, large headstock, black pickguard and knobs, black tremolo tip and pickup covers. Available in 3-Color Sunburst, Shoreline Gold, Black Metallic, Candy Apple Red, Sherwood Green Metallic and Purple Metallic finishes. Upgraded for 2001.

MSR $379 $265

Standard Fat Strat 7 (Model 032-1807) - similar to Standard Fat Stratocaster, except in a seven string configuration. Available in 3-Color Sunburst, Black Metallic, Sherwood Green Metallic, Candy Apple Red, Purple Metallic and Shoreline Gold finishes. Upgraded for 2001.

MSR $449

DOUBLE FAT STRATOCASTER (Model 032-1800) - similar to Standard Fat Stratocaster, except has 2 humbucking pickups. Available in Sherwood Gold, Candy Apple Red, Sherwood Green Metallic, Purple Metallic, 3-Color Sunburst and Black Metallic finishes. Upgraded for 2001.

MSR $379 $265

Standard Double Fat Strat 7HT (Model 032-1837) - similar to Double Fat Stratocaster, except has Hard-Tail bridge. Available in 3-Color Sunburst, Black Metallic and Purple Metallic finishes. Upgraded for 2001.

MSR $449 $315

Telecaster Series

The following models are based on Fender's Telecaster, and all have an single cutaway body, bolt-on maple neck, 6-on-a-side tuners, 2 single coil pickups, tele-style bridge, volume/tone controls, contols mounted on a metal plate, and 3-way selector (unless otherwise listed).

PRO TONE FAT TELE (Model 033-3700) - ash body, 21-fret rosewood fingerboard with white dot inlay, chrome hardware, red shell pickguard, humbucker/single coil pickups. Available in Natural finish. Disc. 1998.

$350 $300 $275 $225 $195 $150 $125
Last MSR was $499.

PRO TONE THINLINE TELE (Model 033-3802) - semi-hollow bound ash body, f-hole, 21-fret maple fingerboard with black dot inlay, gold hardware, white shell pickguard. Available in Crimson Red Transparent finish. Disc. 1998.

$400 $350 $300 $275 $225 $195 $150
Last MSR was $579.

STANDARD TELECASTER (Model 033-1202) - alder body, 21-fret maple fingerboard with black dot inlay, chrome hardware, 3-ply white pickguard, 2 single coil pickups. Available in Black, Blond, Brown Sunburst, and Midnight Wine finishes. Disc. 1998.

$200 $175 $150 $135 $115 $95 $75
Last MSR was $289.

STANDARD TELECASTER (Model 013-2302) - poplar body, 21-fret maple fingerboard with black dot inlay, chrome hardware, 3-ply white pickguard, 2 single coil pickups. Available in Black, arctic White, Brown Sunburst, Lake Placid Blue, and Crimson Red Metallic finishes. Mfg. 1998 to 2000.

$235 $195 $175 $150 $125 $95 $75
Last MSR was $339.

GRADING	100% MINT	98% NEAR MINT	95% EXC+	90% EXC	80% VG+	70% VG	60% G

STANDARD TELECASTER (Model 032-1200) - similar to Standard Telecaster (Model 032-2302), except has solid agathis body, 2 single coil Alnico pickups. Available in 3-Color Sunburst, Sherwood Green Metallic, Vintage Blonde, Black Metallic, Candy Apple Red, and Purple Metallic finishes. Current Mfg.

MSR $349 $245

Add $30 for 3-Color Sunburst and Vintage Blonde finishes.

STANDARD FAT TELECASTER (Model 032-1300) - similar to Standard Telecaster (Model 013-2302), except has 1 humbucking pickup in the neck position and 1 single coil Alnico pickup. Available in 3-Color Sunburst, Shoreline Gold, Sherwood Green Metallic, Vintage Blonde, Black Metallic and Candy Apple Red finishes. Current Mfg.

MSR $379 $265

Add $30 for 3-Color Sunburst and Vintage Blonde finishes.

Double Fat Tele Deluxe - similar to Standard Fat Telecaster, except has solid mahogany carved top body, mahogany set neck, 2 humbucking pickups. Available in Black Metallic, Atlantic Blue Metallic and Frost Red Metallic finishes. Current Mfg.

MSR $549 $385

Vista Series

BULLET (Model 031-0000) - beginner or student level Strat, maple neck, 21-frets, rosewood fingerboard with dot position markers, 3 single coil pickups, 6-on-a-side tuners, 25 ½" scale, hard-tail bridge. Available in Black and Torino Red finishes. Current Mfg.

MSR $199 $139

JAGMASTER (Model 027-1600) - offset double cutaway basswood body, bolt-on maple neck, 24" scale, 22-fret rosewood fingerboard with white dot inlay, 6-on-a-side tuners, vintage-style tremolo, chrome hardware, brown shell pickguard, 2 humbucker pickups, volume/tone controls, 3-way switch. Available in 3-Tone Sunburst, Black, Candy Apple Red, Sonic Blue, and Vintage White finishes. Disc. 2000.

$350 $300 $275 $225 $175 $125 $75

Last MSR was $499.

STANDARD JAGMASTER (Model 032-0700) - similar to Jagmaster, except has solid alder body. Available in Candy Apple Red, Silver Sparkle and Montego Black finishes. Current Mfg.

MSR $399 $279

SUPER-SONIC (Model 027-1500) - rounded double cutaway alder body, bolt-on maple neck, 24" scale, reverse headstock, 22-fret rosewood fingerboard with white dot inlay, 6 on the other side tuners, vintage-style tremolo, chrome hardware, 3-ply white/metal pickguard, 2 humbucker pickups, volume/tone controls, 3-way switch. Available in Black and Olympic White finishes. Disc. 2000.

$350 $300 $275 $225 $175 $125 $75

Last MSR was $499.

Add $100 for Blue Sparkle or Silver Sparkle finishes.

VENUS (Model 027-1700) - double cutaway basswood body with rounded lower bout, bolt-on maple neck, 25 1/2" scale, 22-fret bound rosewood fingerboard with white dot inlay, 6-on-a-side tuners, tune-o-matic bridge/strings through-body ferrules, chrome hardware, white shell pickguard, single coil/humbucker pickups, volume control, 3-way switch. Available in 3-Tone Sunburst, Black, and Surf Green finishes with matching headstock. Disc. 2000.

$350 $300 $275 $225 $175 $125 $75

Last MSR was $499.

Venus XII (Model 027-1800) - similar to Venus, except features 12-string configuration, 6-per-side tuners, 2 Seymour Duncan split single coil pickups, volume/tone controls. Disc. 2000.

$625 $575 $525 $475 $400 $325 $225

Last MSR was $799.

ELECTRIC BASS

Affinity Bass Series

BRONCO BASS (Model 031-0902/Model 033-0902) - hardwood body, maple neck, 30" scale, 19-fret maple fingerboard, single coil pickup. Available in Black, Arctic White, and Torino Red. Mfg. 1998 to date.

MSR $249 $175 $150 $135 $120 $100 $85 $65

In 2000, Arctic White finish Disc.

P-BASS (Model 031-0400/Model 033-0400) - offset double cutaway hardwood body, 21-fret rosewood fingerboard with white dot inlay, fixed bridge, chrome hardware, white pickguard, 1 P-style split pickup, volume/tone controls. Available in Arctic White, Black, and Torino Red finishes. Current Mfg.

MSR $269 $190 $160 $145 $120 $100 $85 $65

In 2001, Baltic Blue finish was introduced.

GRADING	100% MINT	98% NEAR MINT	95% EXC+	90% EXC	80% VG+	70% VG	60% G

P-Bass Special (Model 033-0500) - similar to the P-Bass, except features P/J-style pickups. Available in Black, Arctic White, and Torino Red. Mfg. 1998 to 2000.

	$195	$175	$155	$135	$120	$100	$75

Last MSR was $279.

Standard P-Bass Special (Model 032-1500) - similar to P-Bass Special, except has, solid Agathis body, Jazz Bass neck, 20-frets, standard hardware. Available in 3-Color Sunburst, Sherwood Green Metallic, Candy Apple Red, Black Metallic, Shoreline Gold and Purple Metallic finishes. Current Mfg.

MSR $369 $260

Add $30 for Left-Hand model (Model 032-1520).

Add $60 for 5-string model (Model 032-1505).

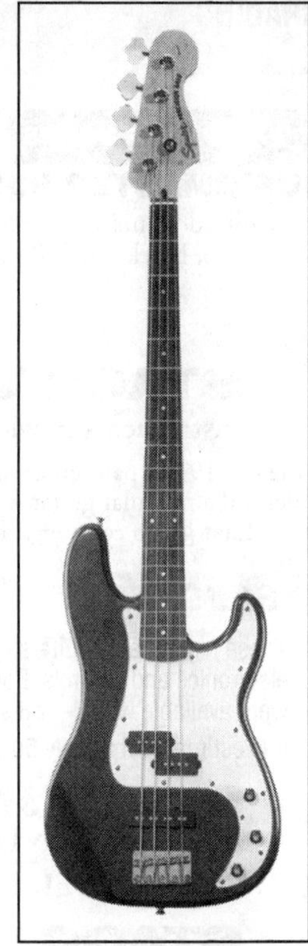

Squier P Bass Special courtesy Fender

Jazz Bass Series

STANDARD JAZZ BASS (Model 033-1500) - sleek offset double cutaway alder body, bolt-on maple neck, 20-fret rosewood fingerboard with white dot inlay, fixed bridge, chrome hardware, white/metal pickguard, 2 single coil pickups, 2 volume/tone controls. Available in Black, Brown Sunburst, and Midnight Wine finishes. Disc. 1998.

	$225	$195	$175	$150	$125	$100	$75

Last MSR was $309.

STANDARD JAZZ BASS (Model 013-2500) - sleek offset double cutaway poplar body, bolt-on maple neck, 20-fret rosewood fingerboard with white dot inlay, fixed bridge, chrome hardware, white/metal pickguard, 2 single coil pickups, 2 volume/tone controls. Available in Black, Brown Sunburst, Arctic White, Crimson Red Metallic, and Lake placid Blue finishes. Disc. 2000.

	$250	$195	$175	$150	$125	$100	$75

Last MSR was $349.

Standard Jazz Bass (New) - similar to Standard Jazz Bass (old), exept has solid agathis body. Available in 3-Color Sunburst, Candy Apple Red, Shoreline Gold, Sherwood Green Metallic, Black Metallic and Purple Metallic finishes. New 2001.

MSR $369 $260

Precision Bass Series

The following models are based on Fender's Precision Bass, and all have an offset double cutaway body, bolt-on maple neck, 34" scale, 4-on-a-side tuners, split single coil pickup, volume/tone controls, unless otherwise listed.

PRO TONE P J BASS (Model 033-5000) - ash body, 20-fret rosewood fingerboard with white dot inlay, chrome hardware, fixed bridge, red shell pickguard, P/J-style Alnico pickups, 2 volume/tone controls. Available in Black finish with matching headstock. Disc. 1998.

	$375	$350	$300	$275	$225	$175	$125

Last MSR was $539.

PRO TONE PRECISION BASS FIVE (Model 033-3802) - ash body, 5-string configuration, 20-fret rosewood fingerboard with white dot inlay, 5-on-a-side tuners, gold hardware, fixed bridge, white shell pickguard, 2 "soapbar" pickups, 2 volume/tone controls. Available in Crimson Red Transparent finish. Disc. 1998.

	$475	$400	$375	$325	$275	$225	$175

Last MSR was $679.

STANDARD PRECISION BASS (Model 033-1400) - alder body, 20-fret rosewood fingerboard with white dot inlay, fixed bridge, chrome hardware, white pickguard, P-style pickup, volume/tone controls. Available in Black, Brown Sunburst, and Midnight Wine finishes. Disc. 1998.

	$200	$175	$150	$135	$125	$100	$75

Last MSR was $299.

This model is available in a left-handed configuration (Model 033-1420) in Brown Sunburst finish.

STANDARD PRECISION BASS (Model 013-2400) - poplar body, 20-fret rosewood fingerboard with white dot inlay, fixed bridge, chrome hardware, whire pickguard, P-style pickup, volume/tone controls. Available in Black, Arctic white, Brown Sunburst, Lake Placid Blue, and Crimson red Metallic finishes. Disc. 2000.

	$250	$195	$175	$150	$125	$100	$75

Last MSR was $339.

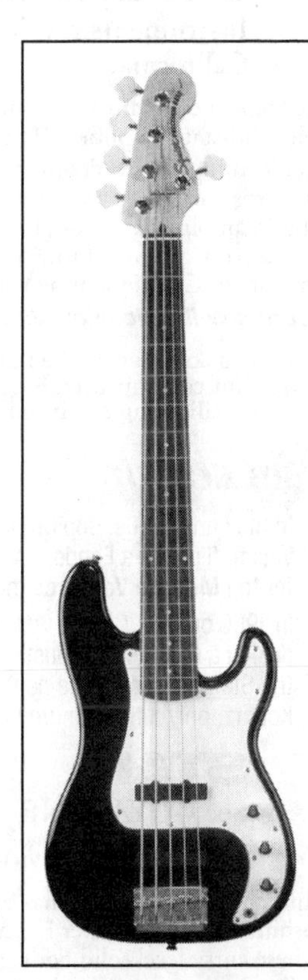

Squier P Bass Special 5 courtesy Fender

S

GRADING	100% MINT	98% NEAR MINT	95% EXC+	90% EXC	80% VG+	70% VG	60% G

Vista Bass Series

MUSICMASTER BASS (Model 033-0300) - sleek double cutaway alder body, 30" scale, 18 fret rosewood fingerboard with white dot inlay, chrome hardware, fixed bridge, white pickguard, Vista-Tone single coil pickup, volume/tone controls. Available in Arctic White, Black, Shell Pink, and Sonic Blue finish with matching headstock. Disc. 2000.

$280	$240	$215	$185	$160	$130	$100

Last MSR was $399.

STACCATO

Instruments previously built in London, England from the early 1980s to around 1986.

In the late 1970s, painter/sculptor/guitarist Pat Townsend designed **Staccato Drums**, asymmetrical shaped drums that flared out from the heads. In 1982, he devised a modular guitar with a fiberglass/polyurethane foam body and magnesium alloy neck section. The necks are interchangeable on the body.

Last given company address for Townsend was: Pat Townsend, 100 Kingsgate Road, London, England (NW6).

ELECTRIC

These high quality guitars featured neck platform of magnesium alloy, which has the pickups and hardware; while the wood or fiberglass solid body has the electronics and controls. Both the bridge (fixed or tremolo) and the nut are magnesium alloy. Neck choices for guitar were 6- or 12-string configuration; basses were available with 4- or 8-string configurations, fretted or fretless. In the early 1980s the Staccato list price was around $1,800 (models were still handmade). It is estimated that only 50 completed instruments were produced.

STADIUM

Also BASS CENTRE STADIUM.

See GRENDEL.

STAGG

Instruments previously built in Japan during the mid 1970s.

The Stagg trademark is a brand name of a UK importer. Stagg instruments were entry level to low quality solid body guitars that featured designs based on popular American classics.

(Source: Tony Bacon and Paul Day, The Guru's Guitar Guide)

STANDEL

Instruments previously produced in Newark, New Jersey during the late 1960s. Distributed by Standel of Temple City, California.

The Standel company was founded by Bob Crooks (an electronics engineer) in the early 1960s, and rose to some prominence in the mid 1960s because of their solid-state amplifiers. The *Standel* name was derived from Crooks' previous radio repair business, Standard Electronics.

After learning electronics from correspondence courses, Crooks began working for Lockheed, and was promoted to engineer in charge of their Electronics Standards Lab. In his spare time, Crooks repaired radios in his garage. He was introduced to Paul Bigsby in the early 1950s, who was looking for someone to build amplifiers. Crooks began experimenting with semi-conductors in 1961, and two years later had developed a high power solid state amp. While the company did well during the 1960s, faulty parts and component failures in 1970 led to erosion of the Standel quality reputation. Crooks later sold the company to CMI in Chicago, and worked for them for two years.

(Source: Willie Moseley, Vintage Guitar magazine)

Crooks later worked at Barcus Berry, and furthered his investigations into tube and transistor amplifiers. Crooks devised a invention that compensated for speaker errors by modifying the signal going into the amplifier. Crooks named the unit the Sonic Maximizer, and it is still being produced by the BBE Sound Corporation of Long Beach, California.

ELECTRIC

In the early 1960s, Bob Crooks asked Semie Moseley (Mosrite) to design a Fender-style solid body guitar for the Standel product line. Moseley's quick response was to flip over a Fender and trace the body outline! Moseley only built about 20 guitars for Crooks, but his *flipped over* original design became the foundation for the **Mosrite Ventures** model.

In 1966 or 1967, Crooks was contacted by the Harptone company of New Jersey with an offer to build guitars for Standel. Harptone hired luthier Stan Koontz to design a number of acoustic and electric guitars and basses for the Standel company. The instruments were built in Harptone's New Jersey facilities, and have the Standel logo on the peghead. Their production began gearing up right as Crooks began having problems with his amplifiers. According to interviews with Koontz, only a few hundred of **Standel** instruments were produced.

STAR

See GUYATONE.

Instruments previously produced in Japan during the early to mid 1960s.

While the Star trademark has been reported as a brand name used by an English importer, the trademark also appeared in the U.S. market distributed by Hoshino Gakki Ten (later Hoshino USA, distributor of Ibanez). No matter how you slice the bread, the loaf comes from the same oven. While the quality of these entry level solid body guitars was okay at best, they at least sported original designs. It is believed that Guyatone (Tokyo Sound Company) built the Star instruments.

GRADING	100% MINT	98% NEAR MINT	95% EXC+	90% EXC	80% VG+	70% VG	60% G

Classic American guitar designs may have been an influence on the early Japanese models, but the *influence* was incorporated into original designs. The era of copying designs and details began in the early 1970s, but was not the basis for Japanese guitar production. As the entry level models began to get better in quality with meticulous attention to detail, then the American market began to take notice.

STARFIELD

Instruments previously produced in Japan and America. Distributed by Starfield America, located in North Hollywood, California.

These higher end guitars were a side project of the Hoshino company, although no brochures directly linked Starfield to Hoshino/Ibanez. Starfield is no longer offered in the U.S. market (Hoshino continued to offer these quality instruments to other markets around the world).

ELECTRIC

Altair Series

AMERICAN CLASSIC - offset double cutaway alder body, white pickguard, bolt on maple neck, 22-fret maple fingerboard with offset black dot inlay, standard Wilkinson vibrato, 3-per-side locking Magnum tuners, chrome hardware, 3 stacked coil Seymour Duncan pickups, volume/tone control, 5-position switch. Available in Pearl White, Pewter, Popsicle, Sail Blue and Tangerine finishes. Disc. 1994.

$700 $600 $500 $400 $360 $330 $300
Last MSR was $1,000.

Ebony fingerboard with offset pearl dot inlay was optional.

American Custom - similar to American Classic, except has mahogany body, flame maple top, no pickguard, gold hardware, 2 humbucker Seymour Duncan pickups. Available in Tobacco Sunburst, Transparent Cherry, Transparent Green and Transparent Grey finishes. Disc. 1994.

$910 $780 $650 $520 $470 $430 $390
Last MSR was $1,300.

American Trad - similar to American Classic, except has mahogany body, black pickguard, fixed bridge, 2 humbucker Seymour Duncan pickups. Available in Transparent Cream, Transparent Green, Transparent Grey, Transparent Mustard and Transparent Red finishes. Disc. 1994.

$700 $600 $500 $400 $360 $330 $300
Last MSR was $1,000.

SJ CLASSIC - offset double cutaway alder body, white pickguard, bolt-on maple neck, 22-fret rosewood fingerboard with offset pearl dot inlay, standard vibrato, 3-per-side tuners, chrome hardware, 3 single coil pickups, volume/tone control, 5-position switch. Available in Black, Blue Mist, Cream, Destroyer Grey, Mint Green and Peach finishes. Disc. 1994.

$280 $240 $200 $160 $145 $130 $120
Last MSR was $400.

SJ Custom - similar to SJ Classic, except has arched swamp ash body, no pickguard, locking Magnum tuners. Available in Transparent Blue, Transparent Cherry, Transparent Cream, Transparent Green and Transparent Grey finishes. Disc. 1994.

$420 $360 $300 $240 $215 $195 $180
Last MSR was $600.

SJ Trad - similar to SJ Classic, except has mahogany body, black pickguard, locking Magnum tuners, 2 single coil/1 humbucker pickups. Available in Transparent Cream, Transparent Green, Transparent Grey, Transparent Mustard and Transparent Red finishes. Disc. 1994.

$420 $360 $300 $240 $215 $195 $180
Last MSR was $600.

Cabriolet Series

AMERICAN SPECIAL - single sharp cutaway asymmetrical mahogany body, carved flame maple top, bolt-on maple neck, 22-fret maple fingerboard with offset black dot inlay, fixed Wilkinson bridge, 3-per-side tuners, chrome hardware, 2 humbucker Seymour Duncan pickups, volume/tone control, 5-position switch. Available in Tobacco Sunburst, Transparent Cherry, Transparent Green and Transparent Grey finishes. Disc. 1994.

$875 $750 $625 $500 $450 $415 $375
Last MSR was $1,250.

Ebony fingerboard with offset pearl dot inlay was optional.

American Standard - similar to American Special, except has alder body, standard Wilkinson vibrato, locking Magnum tuners, 3 stacked coil Seymour Duncan pickups. Available in Pearl White, Pewter, Popsicle, Sail Blue and Tangerine finishes. Disc. 1994.

$665 $570 $475 $380 $345 $315 $285
Last MSR was $950.

GRADING	100% MINT	98% NEAR MINT	95% EXC+	90% EXC	80% VG+	70% VG	60% G

SJ LIMITED - single sharp cutaway asymmetrical semi hollow style, bound bird's-eye maple top, flower petal soundhole, mahogany back, bolt-on maple neck, 22-fret rosewood fingerboard with offset pearl dot inlay, fixed bridge, 3-per-side tuners, chrome hardware, 2 humbucker pickups, volume/tone control, 5-position switch. Available in Tobacco Sunburst, Transparent Cherry, Transparent Green and Transparent Grey finishes. Disc. 1994.

		100%	98%	95%	90%	80%	70%	60%
		$455	$390	$325	$260	$235	$215	$195

Last MSR was $650.

STARFIRE

Instruments currently built in Japan, Taiwan, and China by the Eikosha Musical Instrument Co., Inc. Distributed in the U.S. by V. J. Rendano, located in Boardman, OH.

Starfire electric guitars feature solid ash bodies and maple necks. For more information about current model lineup, availability, and pricing, please contact the distributor directly (see Trademark Index).

STARFORCE

Instruments currently produced in Korea since 1988. Initially exported by Tropical Music of Miami, Florida prior to their purchase of the Dean company.

These medium quality solid body guitars feature designs based on the original Stratocaster, as well as the "superstrat". With the introduction of models such as the 8007 with its more original body design, and several bass guitar models, Starforce seeks to expand its market niche.
(Source: Tony Bacon, The Ultimate Guitar Book)

STARK

Instruments currently produced in Bakersfield, California.

Luthier David Stark offers custom built guitars, as well as guitar refinishing, repairs, and restorations. Stark has been studying under noted luthier Bill Gruggett for three years, and credits his design sense to Gruggett.

STARWAY

Instruments previously manufactured in Japan during the mid 1960s.

The Starway trademark was a brand name used by a UK importer. Starway guitars tend to be entry level solid bodies that sport original designs.
(Source: Tony Bacon and Paul Day, The Guru's Guitar Guide)

STATUS

Also STATUS GRAPHITE.

Formerly STRATA.

Instruments currently built in Essex, England since 1983. Distributed in the U.S. by Trace Elliot USA of Darien, Illinois.

Designer/luthier Rob Green has been building stringed instruments that feature carbon graphite neck-through-body designs since the early 1980s. According to author Tony Bacon, Status was the first British guitar that featured carbon graphite parts. For further information regarding current Status Graphite models, specifications, and pricing, contact Status Graphite directly (see Trademark Index).

Many of these high quality solid body instruments have no headstock (save for 1990s Matrix model) and either two humbuckers or three single coil pickups. The Series II model features wood *wings* on either side of the neck as it passes through the body. The Model 2000 is all graphite in its composition, the Model 4000 is a resin-composite body. Research continues on Status Graphite bass models for future editions of the ***Blue Book of Electric Guitars***.

ELECTRIC BASS

Three new finishes are now available for the Stealth bass model; Amber, Blue, and Red.

Energy Series

ENERGY 4 - offset double cutaway ash body, bolt-on maple neck, 24-fret rosewood fingerboard, fixed bridge, 2-per-side tuners, black hardware, 2 Status pickups, volume/tone/mix controls. Available in Amber, Black, Green, Natural and Red finishes. Current Mfg.

MSR	$1,649	$1,116	$837	$700	$560	$505	$460	$420

This model also available with walnut body and fretless fingerboard.

Energy 5 - similar to Energy 4, except has 5-string configuration, 3/2-per-side tuners.

MSR	$1,899	$1,196	$797	$795	$635	$575	$525	$475

Energy 6 - similar to Energy 4, except has 6-string configuration, 3-per-side tuners.

MSR	$2,099	$1,196	$797	$795	$635	$575	$525	$475

Groove Bass

S

Status introduced the new Groove Bass in 1998. The Groove Bass features an offset double cutaway alder or tulipwood body, and has a *Tri-Max* triple coil pickup (the two outer pickups generate the signal, the middle pickup is the hum-cancelling coil). The Groove Bass is available in 4- (list $1,599) and 5-string (list $1,799) configurations, and in 2-Tone Sunburst, Old English White, and Claret finishes.

GRADING	100% MINT	98% NEAR MINT	95% EXC+	90% EXC	80% VG+	70% VG	60% G

Starforce 6000 (by Palmer) courtesy Bob Dobyne

STAUFER

Instruments currently built in Eschenbach, Germany.

Luthier Andre Waldenmaier is currently offering hand crafted guitars, as well as custom repair services. For additional information regarding the high quality guitars, or the repair services, contact Andre Waldenmaier directly (see Trademark Index).

STEINBERGER

Instruments currently produced in Nashville, Tennessee. Distributed by Gibson Musical Instruments of Nashville, Tennesee (Steinberger is a division of the Gibson Guitar Corporation).

Instruments originally manufactured in New York, then New Jersey. Steinberger was purchased by the Gibson Guitar Corporation in 1987 (after a preliminary 1986 agreement).

Ned Steinberger, like Leo Fender and Nathan Daniels, was an instrument designer who didn't play any instruments. Steinberger revolutionized the bass guitar from the design point-of-view, and popularized the use of carbon graphite in musical instruments.

Ned Steinberger majored in sculpture at the Maryland Institute College of Art. Steinberger moved to New York in the 1970s after graduating, and started working as a cabinet maker and furniture designer. He soon moved into a space at the Brooklyn Woodworkers Co-operative and met a guitar builder named Stuart Spector. In 1976 Steinberger began suggesting ideas that later became the NS-1 bass ("NS" for Steinberger's entails, and "1" for the number of pickups). The NS-2, with two pickups, was introduced later. Steinberger's involvement with the NS design led him to originally consider mounting the tuning machines on the body instead of at the peghead. He produced his first "headless" bass in early 1978, built entirely out of wood. Displeased with the end result due to the conventional "dead spots" on the neck (sympathetic vibrations in the long neck cancel out some fundamentals, also called the "wolf" tone in acoustic guitars), Steinberger took the instrument and covered it in fiberglass. His previous usage of the stiff reinforcing fibers in furniture making and boat building did not prepare him for the improved tone and sustain the covered bass then generated.

In 1978, Steinberger continued to experiment with graphite. Actually, the material is a molded epoxy resin that is strengthened by carbon and glass fibers. This formed material, also popular in boat hulls, is said to have twice the density and ten times the "stiffness"of wood - and to be stronger and lighter than steel! Others who have utilized this material are Geoff Gould of Modulus Graphite, Status (UK), Ovation, and Moses Instruments. Steinberger publicly displayed the instrument at a 1979 U.S. Trade Show, hoping to sell the design to a guitar company. When no offers materialized, he formed the Steinberger Sound Corporation in 1980 with partners P. Robert Young (a plastics engineer) and Hap Kuffner and Stan Jay of Mandolin Brothers.

In 198o, the Steinberger bass was debuted at both the MusicMesse in Frankfurt and the NAMM show in Chicago. One of the hot design trends of the 1980s was the headless, reverse tuning instrument - although many were built of wood. Rather than fight "copycat" lawsuits, Steinberger found it easier to license the body and tuning design to other companies. In 1986 the Gibson Guitar corporation agreed to buy Steinberger Sound, and by 1990 had taken full control of the company. Steinberger continued to serve as a consultant and later developed the Transtrem and DB system detuner bridge.

ELECTRIC

K Series

This series was co-designed by Steve Klein.

GK 4S - radical ergonomic style basswood body, black pickguard, bolt-on Steinberger Blend neck, 24-fret phenolic fingerboard with white dot inlay, Steinberger vibrato, black hardware, 2 single coil/1 humbucker EMG pickups, volume/tone control, 5-position switch. Available in Black and White finishes. Mfg. 1990 to 1994.

$1,260	$1,080	$900	$720	$650	$595	$540

Last MSR was $1,800.

GK 4S-A - similar to GK 4S, except has active electronics. Mfg. 1990 to 1994.

$1,435	$1,230	$1,025	$820	$745	$675	$615

Last MSR was $2,050.

This model had Klein's autograph on the body.

GK 4T - similar to GK 4S, except has TransTrem vibrato. Mfg. 1990 to 1994.

$1,575	$1,345	$1,125	$900	$810	$740	$675

Last MSR was $2,250.

Stark Carve Top courtesy David Stark

S

GRADING		100% MINT	98% NEAR MINT	95% EXC+	90% EXC	80% VG+	70% VG	60% G

L Series

GL 2 (STANDARD) - one piece body/neck construction, rectangular body, 24-fret phenolic fingerboard with white dot inlay, Steinberger vibrato, black hardware, 2 humbucker EMG pickups, volume/tone control, 3-position switch. Available in Black finish. Mfg. 1989 to date.

MSR	$2,150	$1,725	$1,295	$1,075	$860	$775	$710	$645

Add $200 for White finish.

Add $250 for active pickups.

Add $400 for left-handed configuration.

Add $450 for Transtrem bridge.

Add $500 for 12-string version, no vibrato available.

GL 4 (PRO) - one piece body/neck construction, rectangular body, 24-fret phenolic fingerboard with white dot inlay, Transtrem vibrato, black hardware, 2 single coil/1 humbucker EMG pickups, volume/tone control, 5-position switch. Available in Black finish. Mfg. 1989 to date.

MSR	$2,850	$2,250	$1,450	$1,175	$940	$845	$775	$705

GL 7 (ELITE) - one piece body/neck construction, rectangular body, 24-fret phenolic fingerboard with white dot inlay, TransTrem vibrato, black hardware, humbucker/single coil/humbucker EMG pickups, volume/tone control, 5-position/coil split switches, active electronics, gold engraving, signed certificate. Available in Black finish. Mfg. 1989 to date.

MSR	$2,950	$2,350	$1,900	$1,600	$1,280	$1,150	$1,055	$960

M Series

GM 2S - double cutaway maple body, bolt-on Steinberger Blend neck, 24-fret phenolic fingerboard with white dot inlay, Steinberger vibrato, black hardware, 2 humbucker EMG pickups, volume/tone control, 3-position switch. Available in Black, Candy Apple Red, Electric Blue and White finishes. Disc. 1995.

$1,440	$1,080	$900	$720	$650	$595	$540

Last MSR was $1,800.

Add $500 for 12-string version, no vibrato.

GM 2T - similar to GM 2S, except has TransTrem vibrato. Disc. 1995.

$1,800	$1,350	$1,125	$900	$810	$740	$675

Last MSR was $2,250.

GM 4 (STANDARD) - double cutaway maple body, bolt-on Steinberger Blend neck, 24-fret phenolic fingerboard with white dot inlay, Steinberger vibrato, black hardware, 2 single coil/1 humbucker EMG pickups, volume/tone control, 5-position switch. Available in Black, Candy Apple Red, Electric Blue, and White finishes. Mfg. 1988 to date.

MSR	$1,900	$1,525	$1,150	$950	$760	$685	$625	$570

Add $250 for active pickups.

Add $450 for Transtrem bridge.

Add $600 for 12-string configuration.

GM 7S (PRO) - double cutaway maple body, bolt-on Steinberger Blend neck, 24-fret phenolic fingerboard with white dot inlay, Steinberger vibrato, black hardware, humbucker/single coil/humbucker EMG pickups, volume/tone control, 5-position/coil split switches, active electronics. Available in Black, Candy Apple Red, Electric Blue and White finishes. Current Mfg.

MSR	$2,350	$2,075	$1,550	$1,300	$1,040	$935	$860	$780

GM 7T (Pro) - similar to GM 7S, except has TransTrem vibrato, active electronics. Current Mfg.

MSR	$2,800	$2,250	$1,825	$1,425	$1,180	$1,075	$915	$835

R Series

GR 4 - offset double cutaway maple body, bolt-on Steinberger Blend neck, 24-fret phenolic fingerboard with white dot inlay, R Trem vibrato, black hardware, 2 single coil rails/1 humbucker Seymour Duncan pickups, volume/tone control, 5-position switch. Available in Black, Candy Apple Red, Electric Blue and White finishes. Disc. 1995.

$1,000	$835	$695	$555	$495	$455	$415

Last MSR was $1,390.

S Series

S

S STANDARD - offset double cutaway poplar body with bottom bout cutaway, bolt-on Steinberger Blend neck, 24-fret phenolic fingerboard with white dot inlay, standard vibrato, reverse peghead, 6-on-a-side gearless tuners, humbucker/single coil/humbucker exposed pickups, volume/tone control, 5-position/coil split switches. Available in Black and White finishes. Disc. 1995.

$1,500	$1,350	$1,125	$900	$810	$740	$675

Last MSR was $2,250.

GRADING			100% MINT	98% NEAR MINT	95% EXC+	90% EXC	80% VG+	70% VG	60% G

S Pro - similar to S Standard, except has mahogany body, bound maple top, TransTrem vibrato, active electronics. Available in Black, Cherry Sunburst, Fireburst and White finishes. Current Mfg.

		$1,800	$1,560	$1,300	$1,040	$935	$860	$780

Last MSR was $2,600.

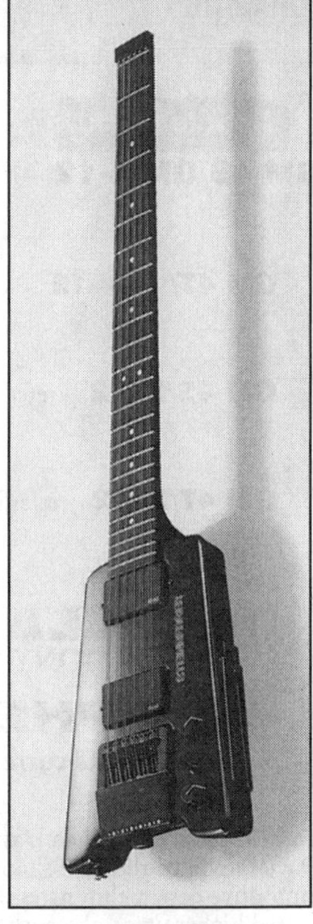

Steinberger GL2-12 courtesy Gibson Guitar Company

GS 7ZA - offset double cutaway hardwood body, bolt-on Steinberger Blend neck, 24-fret phenolic fingerboard with white dot inlay, standard vibrato, reverse headstock, Knife Edge Knut, 6-on-a-side gearless tuners, black hardware, humbucker/single coil/humbucker pickups, volume/tone control, 5-way pickup selector/coil split switches, active electronics. Available in Black, Candy Apple Red, Electric Blue, Purple and White finishes. Disc. 1992.

		$1,715	$1,470	$1,225	$980	$875	$805	$735

Last MSR was $2,450.

GS 7TA - similar to GS 7ZA, except has TransTrem vibrato.

		$1,960	$1,680	$1,400	$1,120	$1,010	$925	$840

Last MSR was $2,800.

ELECTRIC BASS

L Series

XL 2 (STANDARD) - one piece molded body/neck construct, rectangle body, 24-fret phenolic fingerboard with white dot inlay, Steinberger bridge, black hardware, 2 humbucker EMG pickups, 2 volume/1 tone controls. Available in Black finish. Mfg. 1979 to date.

MSR	$2,100	$1,675	$1,250	$1,050	$840	$755	$690	$630

Add $200 for White finish.

Add $200 for fretless fingerboard (lined or unlined).

Add $400 for left-handed configuration.

XL 2D (Pro) - similar to XL 2, except has Steinberger DB bridge. Current Mfg.

MSR	$2,400	$1,925	$1,450	$1,200	$960	$860	$790	$720

XLW 5 - similar to XL 2, except has 5-string configuration. Current Mfg.

MSR	$2,500	$2,000	$1,625	$1,200	$960	$860	$790	$720

M Series

XM 2 - double cutaway maple body, bolt-on Steinberger Blend neck, 24-fret phenolic fingerboard with white dot inlay, Steinberger bridge, black hardware, 2 humbucker EMG pickups, 2 volume/1 tone control. Available in Black, Candy Apple Red, Electric Blue and White finishes. Disc. 1995.

		$1,275	$960	$800	$640	$575	$530	$480

Last MSR was $1,600.

Add $100 for fretless fingerboard.

Add $250 for active electronics.

XM 2D - similar to XM 2, except has Steinberger DB bridge.

		$1,350	$1,025	$850	$680	$610	$560	$510

Last MSR was $1,700.

XM 2-5 - similar to XM 2, except has 5-string configuration.

		$1,450	$1,075	$900	$720	$650	$595	$540

Last MSR was $1,800.

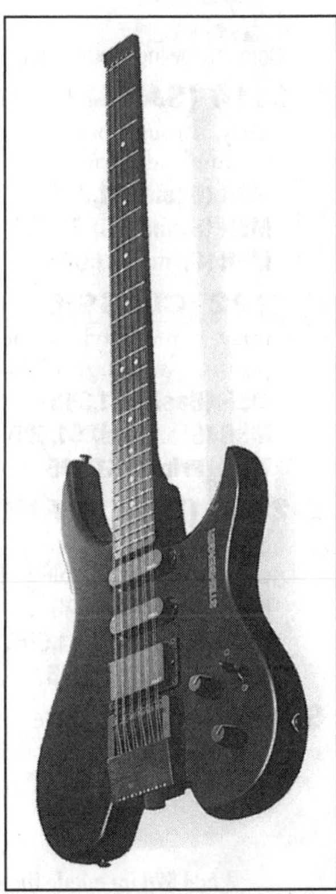

Steinberger GM4-12 courtesy Gibson Guitar Company

Q Series

XQ 2 (STANDARD) - offset double cutaway maple body, bolt-on Steinberger Blend neck, 24-fret phenolic fingerboard with white dot inlay, Steinberger bridge, black hardware, 2 humbucker EMG pickups, 2 volume/1 tone controls. Available in Black, Candy Apple Red, Electric Blue and White finishes. Current Mfg.

MSR	$1,700	$1,350	$1,025	$850	$680	$610	$560	$510

Add $100 for fretless fingerboard.

XQ 2D (Pro) - similar to XQ 2, except has Steinberger DB bridge. Current Mfg.

		$1,450	$1,075	$900	$720	$650	$595	$540

Last MSR was $1,800.

XQ 2-5 - similar to XQ 2, except has 5-string configuration. Current Mfg.

		$1,650	$1,225	$1,025	$820	$745	$675	$615

Last MSR was $2,050.

GRADING	100% MINT	98% NEAR MINT	95% EXC+	90% EXC	80% VG+	70% VG	60% G

Double Neck

GM 4S/GM 4-12 - refer to model GM 4S, in 6 and 12-string versions, in this section for details. Disc. 1995.

$3,275 $2,450 $2,050 $1,640 $1,475 $1,350 $1,230
Last MSR was $4,100.

GM 4T/GM4-12 - refer to model GM 4T, in 6 and 12-string versions, in this section for details. Disc. 1995.

$3,675 $2,750 $2,300 $1,840 $1,655 $1,520 $1,380
Last MSR was $4,600.

GM 4S/XM 2 - refer to models GM 4S and XM 2, in 6-string guitar and 4-string bass models, in this section for details. Disc. 1995.

$3,200 $2,400 $2,000 $1,600 $1,440 $1,320 $1,200
Last MSR was $4,000.

GM 4T/XM 2 - refer to models GM 4T and XM 2, in 6-string guitar and 4-string bass models, in this section for details. Disc. 1995.

$3,600 $2,700 $2,250 $1,800 $1,620 $1,485 $1,350
Last MSR was $4,500.

STELLA

See HARMONY & OSCAR SCHMIDT.

STEPHEN'S

Instruments currently built in Seattle, Washington. Distributed by Stephen's Stringed Instruments, located in Seattle, Washington.

Luthier/designer Stephen Davies created the *Extended Cutaway* (EC) that appears on his own instruments as well as licensed to certain Washburn models. Davies updated the 1950s four bolt rectangular neckplate with a curved "half moon" five bolt that helps lock the neck into the neck pocket. This innovative design eliminates the squared block of wood normally found at the end of a neck pocket, allowing proper thumb/hand placement as notes are fretted higher up on the neck and also avoids the old style side-to-side neck motion.

ELECTRIC

In 1996, the electric guitar models were offered at three different price levels. The **Basic** level offers a straight ahead model with solid hardware and Seymour Duncan pickups. At the next level, the **Standard** offers vintage and custom colors, and hand rubbed finishes in the choice of nitrocellulose lacquers or polyurethane for durability. At the **Prime** level, the instruments are offered with exotic wood necks and bodies. Furthermore, each of the three levels can be upgraded from stock quality parts to an enhanced or custom option depending on the customer's order.

S Series

Some following models may be configured above the Basic level. Contact the company for further information.

S-2114 (SATIN MODEL S) - offset double cutaway alder body, bolt-on maple neck, 22-fret maple or rosewood fingerboard with dot inlay, through-body or stop tailpiece, 6-on-a-side tuners, nickel hardware, either 3 single coil or 2 humbucker Seymour Duncan pickups, 1 volume and 1 tone control, 3 or 5-position switch. Available in oil or satin finish. Mfg. 1995 to date.

MSR (Basic) $1,395
MSR (Standard) $1,695
MSR (Prime) $1,995

S-2122 (CLASSIC DREAM) - offset double cutaway alder body, bolt-on maple neck, 22-fret maple or rosewood fingerboard with dot inlay, vintage-style tremolo, 6-on-a-side tuners, nickel hardware, 3 single coil Seymour Duncan pickups, 1 volume and 1 tone control, 5-position switch. Available in a cream finish. Mfg. 1995 to date.

MSR (Basic) $1,395
MSR (Standard) $1,695
MSR (Prime) $1,995

S-2166 (BLACK AND WHITE) - offset double cutaway alder body, bolt-on maple neck, 22-fret maple fingerboard with dot inlay, Schaller locking tremolo, 6-on-a-side tuners, black hardware, 3 single coil Seymour Duncan pickups, 1 volume and 1 tone control, 5-position switch. Available in black finish. Mfg 1995 to date.

MSR (Basic) $1,395
MSR (Standard) $1,695
MSR (Prime) $1,995

S-22EC - offset double cutaway alder body, bolt-on maple neck, 22-fret ebony fingerboard with pearl dot inlay, double locking vibrato, 6-on-a-side tuners, black hardware, 2 single coil/1 humbucker Seymour Duncan pickups, volume/tone control, 5-position switch. Available in Raw finish. Mfg. 1992 to 1993.

$1,100 $945 $825 $725 $615 $500 $395
Last MSR was $1,575.

Add $20 for maple fingerboard.

Add $170 for figured maple top.

GRADING	100% MINT	98% NEAR MINT	95% EXC+	90% EXC	80% VG+	70% VG	60% G

Subtract $20 for rosewood fingerboard.

Add $70-$100 for Black, Cherry Sunburst, Natural and Tobacco Sunburst finishes.

T Series

Some following models may be configured above the Basic level. Contact the company for further information.

T-3111 (RAW MODEL T) - single cutaway ash or alder body, bolt-on maple neck, 22-fret maple or rosewood fingerboard with dot inlay, vintage-style bridge, 6-on-a-side tuners, nickel hardware, 2 single coil Seymour Duncan pickups, 1 volume and 1 tone control, 3-position switch. Available in tung oil or satin lacquer finish. Mfg. 1995 to date.

MSR (Basic) $1,395
MSR (Standard) $1,695
MSR (Prime) $1,995

T-3315 (BLUES MACHINE) - single cutaway ash body with three internal sound chambers, bolt-on maple neck, 22-fret maple or rosewood fingerboard with dot inlay, vintage-style bridge, 6-on-a-side tuners, nickel hardware, 2 single coil Seymour Duncan pickups, 1 volume and 1 tone control, 3-position switch, optional eight-note f-hole. Mfg. 1995 to date.

MSR (Basic) $1,395
MSR (Standard) $1,695
MSR (Prime) $1,995

T-9111 (HONEY BURST) - Single cutaway flamed maple top over alder body, bolt-on maple neck, 22-fret maple or rosewood fingerboard with dot inlay, vintage-style bridge, 6-on-a-side tuners, gold hardware, 2 single coil Seymour Duncan pickups, 1 volume and 1 tone control, 3-position switch. Mfg. 1995 to date.

MSR (Basic) $1,395
MSR (Standard) $1,695
MSR (Prime) $1,995

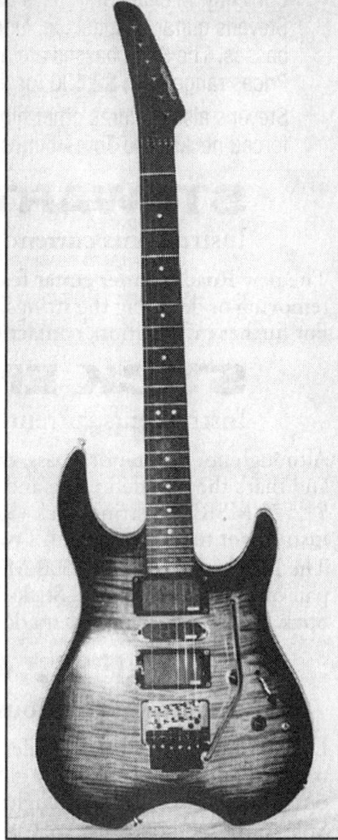

Steinberger S Pro courtesy Gibson Guitar Company

T-22EC - single cutaway ash body, black pickguard, bolt-on maple neck, 22-fret rosewood fingerboard with pearl dot inlay, strings through-body bridge, 6-on-a-side tuners, chrome hardware, 2 single coil Seymour Duncan pickups, volume/tone control, 3-position switch. Available in Black and Natural finishes. Mfg. 1992 to 1993.

	100%	98%	95%	90%	80%	70%	60%
T-22EC	$1,125	$950	$850	$725	$615	$515	$400

Last MSR was $1,595.

Add $20 for maple fingerboard.

Add $30 for ebony fingerboard.

Add $200 for figured maple top.

Add $30 for Butterscotch, Cherry Sunburst and Tobacco Sunburst finishes.

STEVENS ELECTRICAL INSTRUMENTS

Instruments currently built in Alpine, Texas.

For the past thirty years, luthier Michael Stevens has been performing his high quality guitar building and stringed instrument repairs in California and Texas. Stevens, along with John Page, was hired by Fender in 1986 to open their Custom Shop and construct individually-ordered, custom-built instruments.

In 1967, Stevens headed for Berkeley, California to study bronze casting with Peter Voucas, and also to "intercept a woman I was chasing", notes Stevens. Neither of the two happened at the time, but he did run into a great music scene and his life took a turn. While in Berkeley, Stevens met Larry Jameson through a mutual friend - it turned out that they were dating the same woman. Jameson was just starting a guitar repair shop in Oakland near Leo's Music (up above an amp shop called Magic Music Machines). In the long and short of it, Jameson got the girl, but Stevens got a job. Six months later the two moved to the corner of Rose and Grove in Berkeley and opened the Guitar Resurrection. Stevens credits Jameson for teaching him "what a guitar really was" and how to repair guitars by hand. Stevens and Jameson ran the Guitar Resurrection from 1969 to 1974. Stevens recalled a few notable memories during this time period, such as perhaps the first vintage guitar show circa 1970/1971 at Prune Music in Mill Valley, California; and getting vinyl plastic laminated from Hughs Plastic (a chore in itself) being the first to offer routed after market pickguards. After 1974, Stevens left to train Arabian horses for a number of years.

In 1978, Stevens moved to Austin, Texas. One of his early associates was Bill Collings. Stevens continued to make a name for himself performing repairs and building custom guitars for Christopher Cross (a double neck), Paul Glasse (a mandolin model), and Junior Brown's "Guit-Steel" hybrid. Stevens was hired by Fender in 1986 as Senior design engineer for their new Custom shop. While at Fender, Stevens designed the first set-neck Fender model, the LJ (named in honor of Larry Jameson). Perhaps only 35 to 40 of these instruments were constructed. Stevens was the first Master builder at Fender to have his logo on his instruments.

(Biograhy courtesy Michael Stevens)

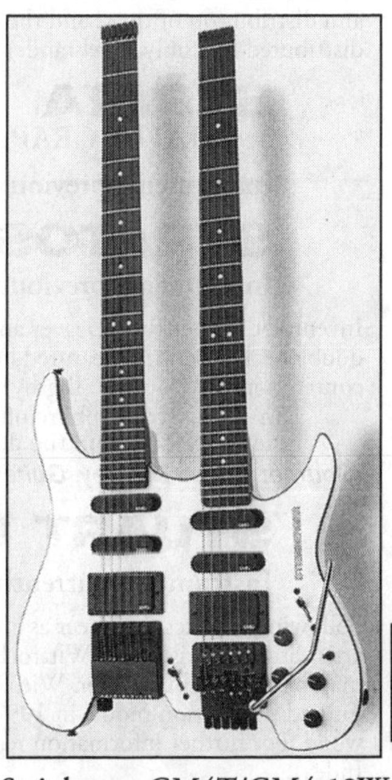

Steinberger GM4T/GM4-12W courtesy Gibson Guitar Company

S

Currently, Michael Stevens is back in Alpine, Texas. After a few years chasing cattle and "recharging his batteries", he is beginning production on a new line of Stevens guitars. Models include the set-neck **LJ** (list price $6,000), the dual cutaway semi-hollowbody **Classic** (list $6,500), and **Slant** series of solid body basses. The Slant basses are available in 4-, 5-, and 6-string configurations, and in bolt-on neck (for the 4- and 5-string) and set-neck (all three) configurations. Prices range from $2,500 for the bolt-on 4-string ($2,900 for set-neck) up to $6,000 for the set neck 6-string with very fancy wood.

Stevens also features other high quality electric guitars. The models in his **Fetish** series feature mahogany or korina bodies, carved maple tops, graphite reinforced necks, and Tom Holmes or Stevens' humbucking pickups. For further information, please contact Michael Stevens directly (see Trademark Index).

STEWART GUITAR COMPANY

Instruments currently built in Swansboro, North Carolina.

The new **Road Runner** guitar features a special tool-free neck connection system which allows the neck to be removed or re-assembled quickly without removing or detuning the strings. This system, dubbed the Clip Joint, allows for a full size guitar to be stored and carried in a briefcase-sized carrying case. For further information, contact the Stewart Guitar company directly (see Trademark Index).

STICK ENTERPRISES, INC.

Instruments currently produced in Woodland Hills, California.

Although not a guitar or a bass, the Stick instrument is a member of the guitar family. Company literature refers to the Stick as a 'Touchboard' instrument, and that's the best definition and description for the various models. Designer/innovator Emmett Chapman designed the 8-string Stick Bass (2001, $1,575 MSR), 10-string Stick ($1,395 MSR, $1,575 for EMG pickup) or 12-string Grand Stick ($1,695 MSR, $1,875 for EMG pickup) as a "Touch" instrument to complement his two-handed guitar style. Stick instruments feature minimalist bodies.

The NS/Stick Model ($1,600 MSR) came about from a collaboration between Emmett Chapman and Ned Steinberger, utilizing a very low action and 2 pair of single coil pickups. Sticks incorporate a unique headstock configuration with a joint reverse-tuning bridge. For further information, please contact Stick Enterprises (see Trademark Index).

STILES, GILBERT L.

Instruments previously built in Independence, West Virginia and Hialeah, Florida between 1960 to 1994.

Luthier/designer Gilbert L. Stiles (1914-1994) had a background of working with wood, be it mill work, logging or house building. In 1960, he set his mind to building a solid body guitar, and continued building instruments for over the next thirty years. In 1963, Stiles moved to Hialeah, Florida. Later on in his career, Stiles also taught for the Augusta Heritage Program at the Davis and Elkins College in Elkins, West Virginia.

Stiles built solid body electrics, arch tops, flattop guitars, mandolins, and other stringed instruments. It has been estimated that Stiles had produced over 1,000 solid body electric guitars and 500 acoustics during his career. His arch top and mandolins are still held in high esteem, as well as his banjos.

Stiles guitars generally have Stiles or G L Stiles on the headstock, or Lee Stiles engraved on a plate at the neck/body joint of a bolt-on designed solid body. Dating a Stiles instrument is difficult, given that only the electric solids were given serial numbers consecutively, and would only indicate which number guitar it was, not when built.

(Source: Michael Wright, Guitar Stories Volume One)

STONEHENGE II

Instruments previously built in Castelfidardo, Italy during the mid 1980s.

Luthier Alfredo Bugari designed his tubular metal-bodied guitar in a semi-solid, semi-hollowbody closed triangular design. A photo of this unique guitar was featured in author/researcher Tony Bacon's 1993 book, ***The Ultimate Guitar Book***.

STRAD-O-LIN

Instruments previously produced in New York during the 1950s and 1960s. Later models manufactured in Japan.

Strad-O-Lin was a brand name of the Peter Sorkin Music Company. A number of solid body guitars were built at the Multivox company of New York, and distribution of those and the later Japanese built models were handled by the Sorkin company of New York City, New York. Other guitars built and distributed (possibly as rebrands) were ROYCE, PREMIER, BELLTONE, and MARVEL.

STRATA

See STATUS GRAPHITE.

Instruments previously made in England during the 1980s.

STRATOSPHERE

Instruments previously built in Springfield, Missouri between 1954 and 1958.

Inventor/designer Russ Deaver and his brother Claude formed the Stratosphere company in 1954, and introduced what is estimated to be the first doubleneck guitar that featured both six- and twelve-string necks. By comparison, Gibson did not release their model until 1958, while other designer contemporaries (Mosrite, Bigsby) had built doublenecks with a smaller octave neck.

In 1955, Stratosphere offered three models: a single neck six string (retail $134.50) called the Standard, the single neck twelve string version ($139.50) and the doubleneck 6/12 ($300). It was estimated that less than 200 instruments were built.

(Source: Teisco Del Rey, Guitar Player magazine)

STUART GUITAR DESIGNS

Instruments currently built in Cincinnati, Ohio.

Following a successful career as a musician in Europe and North America (including composing and performing music for European television and film), artist Stuart Christopher Wittrock returned to Cincinnati, Ohio. Between 1991 to 1997, he performed authorized warranty repairs for virtually every major guitar manufacturer. With 18 months and 2,000 hours design time invested, Wittrock and his team at Stuart Guitar Designs unveiled its first limited production model in 1997. Notable features include a proprietary wood bridge, tone chambers in the neck, "Broken-in" fingerboard, and aged wood. For further information regarding guitar designs and proprietary aging methods, please contact Stuart Guitar Designs directly (see Trademark Index).

(Company information courtesy Stuart C. Wittrock, September 1997)

STUDIO KING

See chapter on House Brands.

While this trademark has been identified as a *House Brand*, the distributor is currently unknown at this time. As information is uncovered, future listings in the ***Blue Book of Electric Guitars*** will be updated.

(Source: Willie G. Moseley, Stellas & Stratocasters)

Stevens LJ
courtesy Jimmy Wallace

STUMP PREACHER GUITARS

Instruments currently produced in Woodinville, Washington.

John Devitry and staff at Stump Preacher Guitars continue to offer an innovative full scale "travel guitar" that is only 27" long! The **Stump Preacher** is currently available in 3 models, the Straight 6 (6 tuners on left or right side of body, $995 MSR), the Stumpy V6 (3 tuners on each side of body, $950 MSR), and the Teardrop V6 (3 tuners on each side of body, $799 MSR). These Stump Preacher models are constructed of high impact polyurethane and feature a neck core which can be adjusted for density, therefore producing different tones. The guitars are equipped with an EMG dual model (disc.) or Lace transducer pickup (various configurations), rosewood fingerboard, Schaller tuners, and a headless neck/reverse tuning system that is highly innovative! Currently, there are 8 different finishes to choose from. All Stump Preacher guitars have a built-in headphone amplifier. For further information, please contact Stump Preacher Guitars directly (see Trademark Index).

SUKOP

Instruments currently built in Angelfire, New Mexico. Distributed by Sukop Electric Guitars of Clifton, New Jersey.

Luthier Stephen Sukop has been building basses for the past 15 years. Sukop is currently offering a number of high quality, custom, handmade bass guitar models. Each Sukop bass is available in a 4-, 5-, or 6-string configuration (fretted or unfretted), and in 34" scale, 35" scale, and 36" scale length. Sukop basses feature a 7-piece laminated neck-through design, Bartolini pickups, Gotoh tuners, and a Kahler bridge. Prices currently range from $2,899 (4-string), $3,149 (5-string) to $3,449 (6-string). For further information, contact luthier Stephen Sukop (see Trademark Index).

SUMBRO

Instruments previously built in Japan during the mid to late 1970s.

The Sumbro trademark is a brand name of UK importer Summerfield Brothers. These entry level to medium quality solid body guitars feature some original designs, as well as designs based on classic American favorites.

(Source: Tony Bacon and Paul Day, The Guru's Guitar Guide)

SUNN

Instruments previously produced in India from 1989 to 1991. Distributed by the Fender Musical Instruments Corporation (FMIC) of Scottsdale, Arizona.

The Sunn trademark, similar to the same used on the line of P.A. and amplifier equipment, was applied to a line of entry level strat replicas built in India. Oddly enough, the strat-styled guitar carries a "Mustang" designation in the headstock.

(Source: Tony Bacon, The Ultimate Guitar Book)

SUNTECH

Instruments previously produced in Japan circa late 1970s to early 1980s.

The only Suntech trademark instruments encountered so far have been bolt-on neck Fender-style Strat copies. These instruments are very nice reproductions of the Strat model. Research continues on the Suntech trademark.

(Source: Roland Lozier, Lozier Piano & Music)

SUPER TWENTY

Instruments previously manufactured in Japan during the mid 1960s.

The Super Twenty trademark is a brand name used by a UK importer. This entry level solid body guitar featured an original design and three single coil pickups.

SUPERIOR

See chapter on House Brands.

While this trademark has been identified as a "House Brand", the distributor is currently unknown. As information is uncovered, future editions of the ***Blue Book of Electric Guitars*** will be updated.

(Source: Willie G. Moseley, Stellas & Stratocasters)

SUPERTONE

See chapter on House Brands.

This trademark has been identified as a *House Brand* of Sears, Roebuck and Company between 1914 to 1941. Instruments produced by various (probably) Chicago-based manufacturers, especially Harmony (then a Sears subsidiary). Sears used the Supertone trademark on a full range of guitars, lap steels, banjos, mandolins, ukuleles, and amplifiers.

In 1940, then-company president Jay Krause bought Harmony from Sears by acquiring the controlling stock, and continued to expand the company's production. By 1941, Sears had retired the Supertone trademark in favor of the new *Silvertone* name. Harmony, though a separate business entity, still sold guitars to Sears for sale under this new brand name.

(Source: Michael Wright, Vintage Guitar Magazine)

SUPRO

See chapter on House Brands.

The Supro trademark was the budget brand of the National Dobro company (See NATIONAL or VALCO), who also supplied Montgomery Wards with Supro models under the **Airline** trademark. National offered budget versions of their designs under the Supro brand name beginning in 1935.

When National moved to Chicago in 1936, the Supro name was on wood-bodied lap steels, amplifiers, and electric Spanish arch top guitars. The first solid body Supro electrics were introduced in 1952, and the fiberglass models began in 1962 (there's almost thirty years of conventionally built guitars in the Supro history).

In 1962, Valco Manufacturing Company name was changed to Valco Guitars, Inc. (the same year that fiberglass models debuted). Kay purchased Valco in 1967, so there are some Kay-built guitars under the Supro brand name. Kay went bankrupt in 1968, and both the Supro and National trademarks were acquired by Chicago's own Strum 'N Drum company. The National name was used on a number of Japanese-built imports, but not the Supro name.

Archer's Music of Fresno, California bought the rights to the Supro name in the early 1980s. They marketed a number of Supro guitars constructed from new old stock (N.O.S.) parts for a limited period of time.

(Source: Michael Wright, Vintage Guitar Magazine)

Some of these Valco-built models were constructed of molded fiberglass bodies and bolt-on wood/metal necks. While Supro pickups may sound somewhat funky to the modern ear, there is no denying the '50s cool appeal. Play 'em or display 'em. Either way, you can't go wrong.

Supros are generally priced between $250 and $650, depending on color and amount of knobs. Decide how you will use them, and pay accordingly.

SURFRITE

Instruments previously built in Bakersfield, California in 1967.

The "Surfrite" prototypes were created by Al Hartel for Mosrite in early 1967, and were built outside the plant. There are five identified prototypes: 2 basses, 2 guitars, and 1 twelve string. The rounded body design also features 2 outside arms that run parallel to the neck and join back behind/part of the headstock. Too labor intensive for production? Well, if they're called prototypes, there's a real good chance that they didn't go into full production.

(Source: Teisco Del Rey, Guitar Player magazine, December 1991)

SURINE

Instruments currently built in Denver, Colorado since 1992.

Scott M. Surine combined his twenty-five years bass playing experience with his graphic arts background in design to offer several models of high quality custom basses. Surine, who holds a Bachelor of Arts degree from Arizona State University, works with luthier Scott Lofquist (a noted Denver guitar builder). Surine basses have been offered since 1992, and a new model was introduced in 1996.

Surine basses are owned and played by musicians such as David Hyde (Delbert McClinton), Me'Shell NdegeOcello (Maverick Recording Artist), Tiran Porter (Doobie Brothers), and Reginald Veal (Branford Marsalis).

Surine basses are available with custom options such as customer-specified string spacing, neck profile contouring, lined or unlined fretless fingerboards, and left-handed versions at no charge. There is a minimal up charge for other variations such as transparent colors, different electronics packages, and some exotic hardwood caps. Hardshell cases and gig bags are available for $150 and $130 respectively.

ELECTRIC BASS

All Surine basses share the same body construction as neck-through design, double cutaway body that reaches to the 24th fret, Bartolini pickups and TCT onboard pre-amp (9-volt), Gotoh tuners, Wilkinson bridge, and double truss rods for 5-, 6-, and 7-string models (a single truss rod is in the 4-string model).

Affinity Series

The Affinity models have symmetrical body horns, and Bartolini BC soapbar pickups.

AFFINITY SERIES I - symmetrical double cutaway Honduras Mahogany body core, choice of exotic woods top and bottom caps and matching headstock, 5-piece flamed maple neck-through construction, 24-fret ebony fingerboard and mother-of-pearl dot inlays, black or gold hardware, brass nut, volume/preamp on-off controls, concentric bass/treble boost/cut controls. Available in Clear Satin Acrylic finish. Current Mfg.

4-String
MSR **$3,095**

5-String
MSR **$3,295**

6-String
MSR **$3,495**

7-String
MSR **$3,695**

AFFINITY SERIES II - symmetrical double cutaway body wings of hard maple, mahogany, southern ash, alder, or walnut with matching headstock; 3-piece hard maple neck-through construction, 24-fret rosewood fingerboard and mother-of-pearl dot inlays, black hardware, brass nut, volume/preamp on-off controls, concentric bass/treble boost/cut controls. Available in Clear Satin Acrylic finish. Current Mfg.

4-String
MSR **$2,495**

5-String
MSR **$2,695**

6-String
MSR **$2,895**

7-String
MSR **$3,095**

AFFINITY SERIES III - symmetrical double cutaway body wings of hard maple, mahogany, or alder, 1-piece hard maple neck-through construction, 24-fret rosewood fingerboard and mother-of-pearl dot inlays, chrome hardware, bone nut, passive Bartolini pickups, volume/bass/treble controls. Available in Hand-Oiled finish. Current Mfg.

4-String
MSR **$1,895**

5-String
MSR **$2,095**

6-String
MSR **$2,295**

Supro Dual Tone
courtesy Michelle Oleck

Esprit Series

Introduced in 1996, the Esprit body design falls somewhere between the Affinity's symmetrical horns and the Protocal's exaggerated top horn. Esprit series basses feature Bartolini Jazz/Jazz pickups.

ESPRIT SERIES I - offset double cutaway Honduras Mahogany body core, choice of exotic woods top and bottom caps and matching headstock, 5-piece flamed maple neck-through construction, 24-fret ebony fingerboard and mother-of-pearl dot inlays, black or gold hardware, brass nut, volume/preamp on-off controls, concentric bass/treble boost/cut controls. Available in Clear Satin Acrylic finish. Current Mfg.

4-String
MSR **$3,095**

5-String
MSR **$3,295**

6-String
MSR **$3,495**

7-String
MSR **$3,695**

ESPRIT SERIES II - offset double cutaway body wings of hard maple, mahogany, southern ash, alder, or walnut with matching headstock; 3-piece hard maple neck-through construction, 24-fret rosewood fingerboard and mother-of-pearl dot inlays, black hardware, brass nut, volume/preamp on-off controls, concentric bass/treble boost/cut controls. Available in Clear Satin Acrylic finish. Current Mfg.

4-String
MSR **$2,495**

5-String
MSR **$2,695**

6-String
MSR **$2,895**

7-String
MSR **$3,095**

ESPRIT SERIES III - offset double cutaway body wings of hard maple, mahogany, or alder; 1-piece hard maple neck-through construction, 24-fret rosewood fingerboard and mother-of-pearl dot inlays, chrome hardware, bone nut, passive Bartolini pickups, volume/bass/treble controls. Available in Hand-Oiled finish. Current Mfg.

4-String
MSR **$1,895**

5-String
MSR **$2,095**

6-String
MSR **$2,295**

Protocol Series

The Protocol model favors an exaggerated top horn, and Bartolini Precision/Jazz pickups.

PROTOCOL SERIES I - offset double cutaway Honduras Mahogany body core, choice of exotic woods top and bottom caps and matching headstock, 5-piece flamed maple neck-through construction, 24-fret ebony fingerboard and mother-of-pearl dot inlays, black or gold hardware, brass nut, volume/preamp on-off controls, concentric bass/treble boost/cut controls. Available in Clear Satin Acrylic finish. Current Mfg.

4-String
MSR **$3,095**

5-String
MSR **$3,295**

6-String
MSR **$3,495**

7-String
MSR **$3,695**

PROTOCOL SERIES II - offset double cutaway body wings of hard maple, mahogany, southern ash, alder, or walnut with matching headstock; 3-piece hard maple neck-through construction, 24-fret rosewood fingerboard and mother-of-pearl dot inlays, black hardware, brass nut, volume/preamp on-off controls, concentric bass/treble boost/cut controls. Available in Clear Satin Acrylic finish. Current Mfg.

4-String
MSR **$2,495**

5-String
MSR **$2,695**

6-String
MSR **$2,895**

7-String
MSR **$3,095**

PROTOCOL SERIES III - offset double cutaway body wings of hard maple, mahogany, or alder; 1-piece hard maple neck-through construction, 24-fret rosewood fingerboard and mother-of-pearl dot inlays, chrome hardware, bone nut, passive Bartolini pickups, volume/bass/treble controls. Available in Hand-Oiled finish. Current Mfg.

4-String
MSR **$1,895**

5-String
MSR **$2,095**

6-String
MSR **$2,295**

SUZUKI

Instruments previously built in Korea. Previously distributed in the U.S. market by Suzuki Guitars of San Diego, California.

Suzuki, noted for their quality pianos, offered a range of acoustic and electric guitars designed for the beginning student to intermediate player. In 1996, the company Disc. the guitar line completely. Suzuki guitars are similar to other trademarked models from Korea at comparable prices.

SYLVAN

Instruments previously built in England during the late 1980s.

The Duke model was a high quality solid body guitar that had a through-body neck as part of its original design.
(Source: Tony Bacon and Paul Day, The Guru's Guitar Guide)

SYNSONICS

Instruments currently built in Korea since 1989. Distributed by The More Company of Pooler, Georgia.

These entry level solid body guitars feature a built in amplifier and three inch speaker that can be defeated by an on/off switch. The overall design is Les Paul-derived with a thinner width body and a bolt-on neck, with the speaker mounted in the body area behind the stop tailpiece. Synsonics also builds a mini solid body guitar dubbed the **Junior Pro.**

S

Section T

21ST CENTURY GUITARS

Instruments previously built in Neodesha, Kansas during the late 1960s. Distributed by Holman-Woodell, Inc. of Neodesha, Kansas.

The Holman-Woodell company built guitars during the late 1960s in Neodesha, Kansas (around 60 miles due south from Topeka). While they were producing guitars for **Wurlitzer**, they also built their own Holman brand as well as instruments trademarked Alray. The Holman-Woodell company is also famous for building the **La Baye** *2 x 4* guitars. The La Baye *2 x 4* guitar model was introduced at the 1967 Chicago NAMM show by inventor Dan Helland. Unfortunately, the radical body-less design proved too far-ahead thinking for the guitar market, and the La Baye trademark officially ended that year. However, the Holman-Woodell company built a number of *2 x 4* guitars out of spare parts, and marketed them first under the Holman trademark. When new owners took over the production facilities, other instruments were released under the **21st Century** trademark. It has been estimated that perhaps up to 100 faux "2 x 4"s were built, but reception of the later instruments was equal to the indifference generated by the first attempt.

(Source: Michael Wright, Guitar Stories Volume One)

TDL GUITAR WORKS

Instruments currently built in Atascadero, California.

Luthier Tony DeLacugo hand-crafts custom guitars and basses that feature an ergonomic body design. Models are available with various pickups, bridges, and hardware options.

ELECTRIC

The **DC Guitar** guitar model features a contoured mahogany body, maple neck, humbucking pickups (with coil taps), and metal-flake finishes (list $3,200). The **Excelsior** guitar model has an ergonomic contoured mahogany body, and a bolt-on maple neck (list $3,500).

ELECTRIC BASS

DeLacugo's Excelsior Bass model features a contoured ergonomic mahogany body, 3-piece bolt-on neck, 24-fret fingerboard, and a Candy Apple metal flake finish (list $3,200).

TV JONES GUITARS

Instruments currently built in Whittier, California.

Luthier Thomas V. Jones has been building quality guitars for a number of years. Jones currently produces Filter'Tron pickups made to the original 50s specs.

ELECTRIC

MODEL 5 BARITONE - single cutaway chambered (semi-hollow) mahogany body, figured maple top, f-hole, set-in maple neck, 29.28" scale, 24-fret ebony fingerboard, 3-per-side tuners, floating ebony bridge/ebony tailpiece, black hardware, EMG 91 pickups, volume/tone controls. Available in Honey finish. Mfg. 1996 to 2000.

Last MSR was $2,100.

Add $150 for fingerboard inlay.

Add $150 for metal bridge/tailpiece.

Add $175 for 2 pickups.

Add $200 for Sunburst finish.

Model 5 Baritone 7-String - similar to the Model 5 Baritone, except features 7-string configuration, 4/3-per-side headstock. Mfg. 1996 to 2000.

Last MSR was $2,400.

MODEL 6 JAZZ - single rounded cutaway semi-hollow laminated body, German spruce top, figured German maple back/sides, basswood body core, 2 f-holes, set-in mahogany neck, 25" scale, ebony fingerboard, 3-per-side tuners, raised ebony fingerboard, floating ebony bridge/ebony tailpiece, black hardware, EMG 91 pickups, volume/tone controls. Available in Honey finish. Mfg. 1996 to date.

Body Width: 16 inches, Body Depth: 2.25 inches.

MSR $6,000

Add $125 for fingerboard inlay.

Add $200 for Sunburst finish.

Add $400 for wood body binding.

GRADING		100% MINT	98% NEAR MINT	95% EXC+	90% EXC	80% VG+	70% VG	60% G

Model 6 Jazz 7-String - similar to the Model 6 Jazz, except features 7-string configuration, 4/3-per-side headstock. Mfg. 1996 to date.

MSR $6,500

SPECTRA SONIC - single cutaway chambered (semi-hollow) body, spruce top, tortoiseshell body binding, set-in alder neck, 24.62" scale, 22-fret padauk fingerboard with white dot inlay, 3-per-side Kluson tuners, tortoiseshell headstock overlay, ABR-1 bridge/Bigsby tremolo, nickel hardware, tortoiseshell pickguard, 2 humbucker pickups, volume/tone controls, 3-way selector switch. Available in Honey finish (Disc.), black and pewter finishes. Mfg. 1996 to date.

MSR $3,500

Add $100 for "tub-tone" 5-way switch.

Add $125 for bound f-hole.

Add $150 for Sparkle finish.

Add $200 for Filter-Tron pickups.

Add $200 for Sunburst finish.

Add $200 for Black lacquer finish.

SPECTRA SONIC "C MELODY" BARITONE - similar to Spectra Sonic, except 29.3" scale and set maple neck, Tone-O-Matic stainless steel saddles, "C melody" pickups. Available in black and pewter finishes. Current Mfg.

MSR $3,700

SPECTRA SONIC BASS - similar to Spectra Sonic, except has 33" scale and set maple neck, 2 TV Jones Filter'Tron pickups with adjustable poles. Available in black and pewter finishes. Current Mfg.

MSR $3,600

TAKEHARU

Instruments previously produced in Japan during the early 1980s.

These good quality solid body and semi-hollowbody guitars featured original designs. Anyone with further information is invited to write to the ***Blue Book of Electric Guitars*** for updates in future editions.

(Source: Tony Bacon and Paul Day, The Guru's Guitar Book)

TALKOVICH, S.

Instruments currently built in Woodstock, Georgia.

Luthier S. Talkovich is currently building guitars in the mold of the classic American designs, but with contemporary parts, hardware, and design features that are the 1990s - not the 1950s. Talkovich features one piece Southern Swamp Ash bodies, Rockwood necks, Lindy Fralin or Rio Grande pickups, Sperzel tuners, and Wilkinson hardware. Rockwood, a process used by Greg Curbow (Curbow String Instruments), is a hardwood composite that is bound by a thermo-setting phenolic resin. This process also eliminates any problems inherent in regular wood necks such as weather fluctuations, humidity, and warping. Talkovich modernized the bolt-on neck process by designing a shifted four bolt pattern, as well as a sculpted neck/heel joint.

Talkovich currently offers two models of his guitars. The **TSS 3** features a one piece Swamp ash body, black Rockwood neck with either a black or Ash Rockwood 21-fret fingerboard, dot inlays, Sperzel tuners, three Lindy Fralin or Rio Grande single coils, Wilkinson bridge, full shielded control cavity, and Graph-tech nut. Finishes include Natural, or a $75 option of a Black top, Tinted finish, or 'Burst finish. Retail lists at $1,775, and includes a deluxe padded gig bag.

The **TSFT 3** is similar to the TSS 3, except that it features a "Fancy Top" of bookmatched American Hard Rock Maple or American Black Walnut. Retail with the deluxe padded gig bag is $1,975.

TANARA

Instruments currently built in Korea and Indonesia. Distributed by the Chesbro Music Company of Idaho Falls, Idaho.

Tanara offers a range of acoustic and electric guitars designed for the entry level to student guitarist.

ELECTRIC

TC80 - single cutaway body, 6-on-a-side covered tuners, tele-style fixed bridge, chrome hardware, pickguard, 2 single coil pickups, volume/tone controls, 3-way selector. Available in Black and Ivory finishes. Current Mfg.

MSR	$309	$230	$200	$175	$155	$130	$105	$80

TG100 - LP-style single cutaway body, carved solid maple top, East Indian rosewood fingerboard, compensating bridge, 3-per-side chrome tuners, 2 humbucking pickups. Available in Black and Cherry Red Sunburst finishes. Current Mfg.

MSR	$389	$295	$250	$220	$190	$160	$130	$100

TS30 - offset double cutaway body, bolt-on mahogany neck, 25 1/2" scale, 21-fret rosewood fingerboard, standard tremolo, 6-on-a-side covered tuners, chrome hardware, pickguard, 3 single coil pickups, volume/2 tone controls. Available in Black and Brown Sunburst finishes. Current Mfg.

MSR	$249	$190	$160	$140	$125	$100	$85	$65

TD33 - similar to the TS30, except features a maple neck. Available in Black and Red finishes. Current Mfg.

MSR	$269	$200	$175	$155	$135	$115	$90	$70

T

TS40 - similar to the TS30, except features 2 single coil/humbucker pickups. Available in Black and Brown Sunburst finishes. Current Mfg.

MSR	$269	$200	$175	$155	$135	$115	$90	$70

GRADING		100% MINT	98% NEAR MINT	95% EXC+	90% EXC	80% VG+	70% VG	60% G

TD44 - similar to the TS40, except features a maple neck. Available in Black and Red finishes. Current Mfg.

MSR	$289	$215	$190	$170	$145	$120	$100	$75

ELECTRIC BASS

TSP25 - offset double cutaway body, bolt-on mahogany neck, 34" scale, 20-fret rosewood fingerboard, fixed bridge, 4-on-a-side die-cast tuners, chrome hardware, pickguard, P-style split pickup, volume/tone controls. Available in Black and Brown Sunburst finishes. Current Mfg.

MSR	$279	$210	$180	$160	$140	$115	$95	$70

TDP30 - similar to the TSP25, except features a maple neck. Available in Black and Red finishes. Current Mfg.

MSR	$299	$225	$195	$170	$150	$125	$100	$75

TSPJ35 - similar to the TSP25, except features P/J-style pickups, 2 volume/1 tone controls. Available in Black and Brown Sunburst finishes. Current Mfg.

MSR	$299	$225	$195	$170	$150	$125	$100	$75

TDPJ40 - similar to the TSPJ35, except features a maple neck. Available in Black and Red finishes. Current Mfg.

MSR	$309	$230	$200	$175	$155	$130	$105	$80

Teisco Del Rey EP-100T courtesy Howie's Guitar Haven

TANGLEWOOD

Instruments currently produced in Korea and Indonesia. Distributed by the European Music Company, Ltd. of Kent, England.

The European Music Company, Ltd. is currently offering a wide range of acoustic and electric guitar models under the **Tanglewood** trademark. These solidly built instruments offer the beginning and intermediate player a quality guitar for the price. For further information regarding model specification and pricing, contact the European Music Company, Ltd. directly (see Trademark Index).

TAUSCH HANDMADE GUITARS

Instruments currently built in Buch, Germany.

Rainer Tausch is currently offering a number of semi-acoustic single cutaway electrics. The **Series 665** model has a maple body (in its basic version), and is available in different body thicknesses, with an additional piezo bridge pickup, and with a tremolo. The 665 is available in a black varnish or oil/wax finish. For further information, contact Rainer Tausch directly (see Trademark Index).

TEIGEN, ROSS

Instruments currently built in Naples, Florida.

Luthier Ross Teigen builds lightweight, distinctly designed custom guitars and basses. Teigen has been building guitars and basses since 1979, and attended the Technical College in Red Wing, Minnesota for stringed instrument construction and repair. Teigen worked in Minneapolis, Naples (Florida), and Miami before establishing Teigen Guitars in 1986 on the edge of the Florida Everglades, where he lives with his wife and three children. For further information on models, prices, and custom options, please contact luthier Teigen directly (see Trademark Index).

TEISCO

See TEISCO DEL REY.

Instruments previously produced in Japan. Distributed in the U.S. by Westheimer Musical Instruments of Evanston, Illinois.

One of the original Teisco importers was George Rose of Los Angeles, California. Some instruments may bear the shortened "Teisco" logo, many others were shipped in unlabeled. Please: no jokes about Teisco "no-casters".

(Source: Michael Wright, Guitar Stories Volume One)

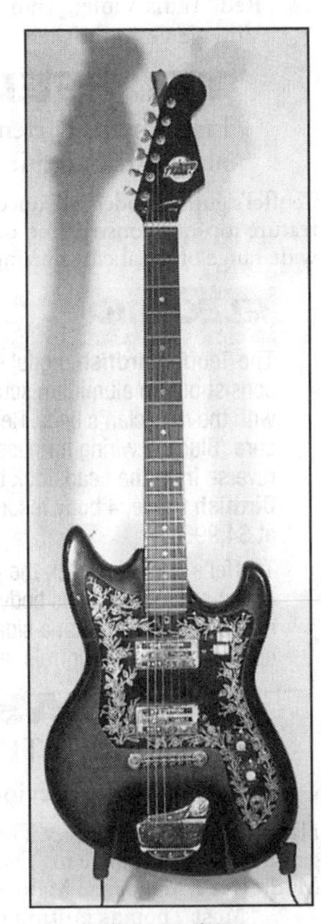

Teisco Del Rey courtesy Nancy Patterson

TEISCO DEL REY

Instruments previously produced in Japan from 1956 to 1973. Distributed in the U.S. by Westheimer Musical Instruments of Evanston, Illinois.

In 1946, Mr. Atswo Kaneko and Mr. Doryu Matsuda founded the Aoi Onpa Kenkyujo company, makers of the guitars bearing the Teisco and other trademarks (the company name roughly translates to the **Hollyhock Soundwave or Electricity Laboratories**). The Teisco name was chosen by Mr. Kaneko, and was used primarily in domestic markets. Early models include lap steel and electric-Spanish guitars. By the 1950s, the company was producing slab-bodied designs with bolt-on necks. In 1956, the company name was changed to the Nippon Onpa Kogyo Co., Ltd. - but the guitars still stayed Teisco!

As the demand for guitars in the U.S. market began to expand, Mr. Jack Westheimer of WMI Corporation of Evanston, Illinois started to import Japanese guitars in the late 1950s, perhaps circa 1958. WMI began importing the Teisco-built Kingston guitars in 1961, and also used the Teisco Del Rey trademark extensively beginning in 1964. Other Teisco-built guitars had different trademarks (a *rebranding* technique), and the different brand names would generally indicate the U.S. importer/distributor. The Japanese company again changed names, this time to the Teisco

Co. Ltd. The Teisco line included all manners of solid body and semi-hollowbody guitars, and their niche in the American guitar market (as entry level or beginner's guitars) assured steady sales.

In 1967, the Kawai Corporation purchased the Teisco company. Not one to ruin a good thing, Kawai continued exporting the Teisco line to the U.S. (although they did change some designs through the years) until 1973. Due to the recent popularity in the Teisco name, Kawai actually produced some limited edition Teisco Spectrum Five models lately in Japan, although they were not made available to the U.S. market.

(Source: Michael Wright, Vintage Guitar Magazine)

One dating method for identifying Teisco guitars (serial numbers are non-existent, and some electronic parts may not conform to the U.S. EIA code) is the change in pickguards that occurred in 1965. Pre-1965 pickguards are plastic construction, while 1965 and post-1965 pickguards are striped metal.

Pricing on Teisco Del Rey models and other Teiscos remains a bit strange. Most models that hang on walls are tagged at $99 (and sometimes lower), but clean cool shaped models sometimes command the $200 to $300 range. However, due to the association of the Spectrum Five model with Eddie Van Halen (he posed with a Spectrum Five on the cover of some German music magazine, if the story is true), some Spectrum Fives are now priced (used) at $1,000!

TELE-STAR

Instruments previously produced in Japan circa late 1960s to 1983.

The Tele-Star trademark was distributed in the U.S. by the Tele-Star Musical Instrument Corporation of New York, New York. Tele-Star offered a full range of acoustic, thinline acoustic/electric hollow body, and solid body electric guitars and basses. Many built by Kawai of Japan, and some models feature sparkle finishes.

(Source: Michael Wright, Vintage Guitar Magazine)

TEMPEST

Instruments previously produced in Japan during the early 1980s.

These entry level to medium quality solid and semi-hollow body guitars featured both original designs and designs based on popular American classics.

(Source: Tony Bacon and Paul Day, The Guru's Guitar Guide)

TERRY ROGERS GUITARS

Instruments currently produced in Tennessee.

Terry Rogers designed the Mallie electric guitar in 1999, and it is currently built by luthier John Suhr. For more information, including availability and pricing, please contact the company directly (see Trademark Index).

ELECTRIC

MALLIE - offset double cutaway solid basswood body, patented body design, best quality bookmatched Flame or Quilted Maple top, ivoroid bound body, straight grain hard maple neck with museum grade Birdseye Maple fingerboard and matching Quilt Maple headstock, 22 medium frets, 3-per-side Sperzel tuners, DiMarzio custom patented design pickups, pickups are split by push-pull tone circuitry, 3-position LP style toggle switch, Floyd Rose design Gotoh locking bridge. Available in Transparent Blue, Trans Green, Trans Purple, Trans Ruby, Trans Red, Trans Violet, Trans Gold, Trans Lemon, Faded Burst, Cherry Burst, '59 Burst, Tobacco, NAMM Flame, Honey Burst, Gloss Black and Vintage Gold finishes. New 2000.

TEUFFEL

Instruments currently built in Germany. Distributed in the U.S. by Salwender International of Trabuco Canyon, California. Distributed in Germany by S K C Graphite of Aschaffenburg, Germany.

Teuffel's guitar models are unconventional new perspectives on the traditional design of the electric guitar. All models are custom built in Germany, and feature top-rate construction details. Teuffel models feature *moveable* Alnico pickups, so the magnetic sources of tone generation can thus be varied for a wide range of tonal customizing.

ELECTRIC

The Teuffel **Birdfish** model has a minimalist metal frame, which reduces the design of an electric guitar to its essential components. The central elements consist of two aluminum sculptures of a *bird* and a *fish*, which provides the *frame* for components to be connected, vibrations transmitted, and interaction with the musician's body. Resonator cylinders (up to two) can be attached across the top of the frame, and consist of both a maple core (Red) and swamp ash core (Blue). A wiring harness provides for interchanging the pickups, and are connected by a central rod for placement by twisting or sliding. Strings are run reverse from the headstock to a Steinberger-style bridge/tailpiece, and the bird's-eye maple neck has 22-frets. The entire **Birdfish** guitar set consists of the **Birdfish** frame, 4 body resonators, five pickups, and a heavily padded and lined nubuk leather bag. The retail list price is quoted at $4,924 (a bass model lists at $4,996).

Teuffel's newest model, the Coco, retains the moveable pickup concept. However, the Coco has an angular body with round pointed horns instead of a minimalist metal body. This body is constructed of a pearwood core, surrounded by a lightweight composite material and a polymer finish. The 22-fret bird's-eye maple neck has a 6-on-a-side headstock and LSR tuners. The Coco (retail list $3,400) has a Wilkinson tremolo bridge/LSR roller nut, 3 splitable Alnico pickups, volume/tone controls, and a five way selector switch.

THOMAS, HARVEY

Also appears as THOMAS CUSTOM GUITARS, or simply THOMAS.

Instruments previously built in Kent, Washington during the early 1960s.

Flamboyant luthier Harvey Thomas built quality semi-hollowbody guitars whose designs bent the "laws of tradition" that conservative semi-hollowbody guitars normally adhere to. Thomas is also well known for his explorations into the solid body design world as well. Models include the **Mandarin**, the **Mod**, **Riot King**, or the **Maltese Surfer.**

Most Thomas guitars feature 6-on-a-side headstocks, a slim neck design, and 21-fret fingerboard that is clear of the body, and glitter or mirror pickguards. The Maltese Surfer looks like a Maltese Cross with a neck attached to one of the four sides. You'll know 'em when you see 'em, but you won't believe what you're looking at!

(Source: Tony Bacon, The Ultimate Guitar Book)

THOMPSON, CARL

Instruments currently built in Brooklyn, New York since 1974.

uthier Carl Thompson moved to New York in 1967, and began working as a repairman in Dan Armstrong's guitar op as a means to round out his income as a musician. In 1971 he formed a new shop with fellow guitarist Joel utkin, and by 1974 was working on his own bass guitar designs. Thompson has built basses for such luminaries as nthony Jackson, Stanley Clarke, and Les Claypool.

uthier Thompson generally produces five or six basses a year. Thompson maintains a small shop in Stahlstown, ennsylvania to rough out body blanks or cut neck blanks, while his final shaping, finishing, and electronics are erformed in his Brooklyn workshop.

Source: Tom Wheeler, American Guitars)

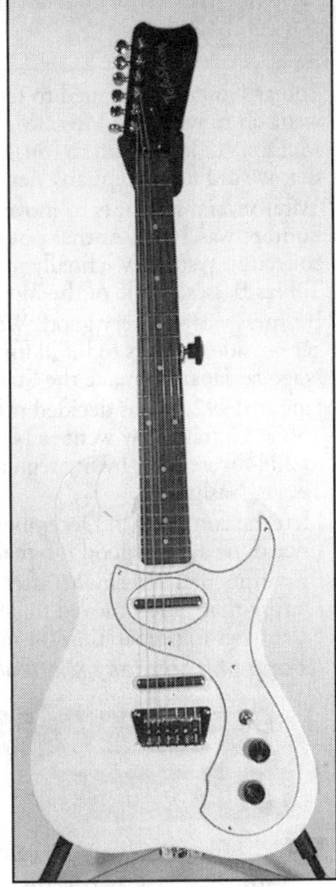

Tele-Star Mona
courtesy Arlington Guitar Show

THORNTON, C. P.

Instruments currently built in Bryant Pond, Maine from mid 1980s.

uthier Charles ("Chuck P.") Thornton began building custom guitars and basses in the mid 1980s that featured neck-hrough designs. While Thornton also worked for Dana Bourgeios in the early 1990s, his current focus is on andcrafted violins. Guitar and bass models are still available on a special order basis.

All Thornton guitar and bass models feature neck-through construction, and have the serial numbers stamped into the fretboard.

Research courtesy Jim Shine, Oxford, Maine)

THUNDER BAY BASSES

Instruments currently built in Asia. Distributed by Sound Trek Distributors of Tampa, Florida.

Thunder Bay instruments are good quality basses designed for the entry or student level up to the medium grade layer. For further information regarding model specifications and pricing, contact Sound Trek Distributors directly see Trademark Index).

TIMTONE

Instruments currently built in Grand Forks (British Columbia), Canada, since 1993.

Timtone guitars are highly regarded hand-crafted instruments designed for each client and built in small batches of our at a time. Luthier Tim Diebert is currently building about twenty instruments a year. He sells direct to the end iser, ensuring a truly personalized, no compromise project. Using either the MK or the MK7 Series, the BT Series and he Rikiyabass body styles as a platform, Tim Diebert offers a large array of base features and options. Base Price ncludes many body shape and top wood choices, pickups and layout, switching choices, scale length, neck shape and ize, fret gauge, tuners, colors and sunbursts, headstock styles, fingerboard wood choices, two styles of forearm rests and lient designated control layout.

The **MK** Series guitar has a base price of $1,950, while the 7-string **MK7** guitar has a base price of $2,400. Options include different bridges, chambered bodies, fingerboard binding, MOP and sterling silver side markers, 2 styles of diamond face markers, fancy custom inlay work, special exotic wood tops, multi-laminated necks and bodies, 24K Gold-plated hardware, including the Steinberger gearless headstock tuners, black hardware, laser engraved cavity cover plate and custom-made cases, special requests and concept instruments.

Electronic options include Varitone controls, dual output piezo bridge saddles, custom Timtone pickups, 3rd or 4th pickup, 3 output MIDI equipped guitar with additional piezo and magnetic outputs or all three signals routing choices and a switchable and adjustable active output.

The **Rikiyabass** model has two main versions, one having the usual headstock and the other being headstockless. Multi-laminated body with fancy maple top over or with laminations showing, 4- or 5-string, fretted or fretless, ebony or Pau Ferro fingerboard, ABM hardware, Seymour Duncan 18V active 2 'soapbar' system with 3-band EQ and balance control and slap contour switch.

The Rikiyabass with headstock and 4-string configuration has a list price of $2,150. The Rikiyabass without a headstock is $2,350 for a 4-string configuration, and $2,550 for a 5-string configuration.

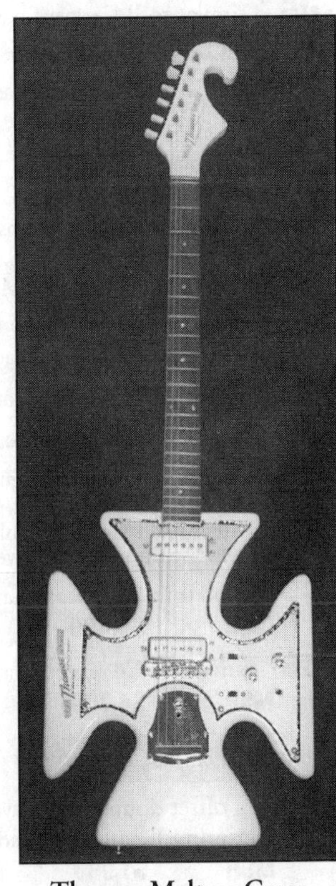

Thomas Maltese Cross
courtesy Brian Goff

TOBIAS

Instruments currently produced in Korea and Nashville, Tennesee. Tobias Guitars are distributed by Gibson Guitar Corporation.

Tobias Basses have been a division of the Gibson Guitar Corporation since January 1990. Production facilities were moved from Hollywood, California to Nashville, Tennessee in 1992.

Prior to purchase by Gibson, Tobias Basses were based in Hollywood, California from 1981 to December 1989.

As related by luthier Michael Tobias, "Tobias Guitars was started in Orlando, Florida in April 1977. The first serial number I used was 0178 - January 1978. After 578, I went back to 179. My first shop name was the Guitar Shop. I sold that business in 1980 and moved to San Francisco to be partners in a short lived manufacturing business called **Sierra Guitars**. We made about 50 instruments. I left San Francisco in May of 1981 and started a repair shop in Costa Mesa, California.

I stayed in Costa Mesa for several months and then moved to Hollywood. The first California serial number was 240, and it was a solid mahogany 6-string guitar. The first South California number was 250. It was a mahogany LP junior style neck through, one of four made.

GRADING	100% MINT	98% NEAR MINT	95% EXC+	90% EXC	80% VG+	70% VG	60% G

Tobias Guitars continued to repair instruments and build custom basses for the next several years with the help of Bob Lee and Kevin Almieda (Kevin went on to work for Music Man). We moved into 1623 Cahuenga Boulevard in Hollywood and after a year quit the repair business. We added Bob McDonald, lost Kevin to Music Man, and then got Makoto Onishi. The business grew by leaps and bounds. In June of 1988, we had so many back orde that we did not accept any new orders until the January NAMM show in 1990.

After several attempts to move the business to larger, better equipped facilities, I sold Tobias Guitars to Gibson on 1/1/90. The first Tobias Gibson seri number was 1094. At that point, Gibson was instrumental in moving us to a bigger shop in Burbank and setting us up with a great spray booth and du collection system. We finally met So. Cal safety codes. Basses built during the 1990-1992 era were built initially by the same crew that had helped establis Tobias Basses as one of the most sought after basses on the planet. We added several people during 1990, and ended up with a great 10 man shop.

Business was still very good. We were not able to make anywhere near enough basses to fill the orders. Instead of trying to jack up production, we tried get outside vendors to build for us. We had 110 **Model T** basses made for us by a very fine builder in New England, and then we got the Terada factory i Nagoya, Japan to make the **Standard** bass for us. This was and is a great bass, but the $/yen ratio killed the project. There were about 400 Standards.

Late in 1992, it was decided that in best corporate interests Tobias Guitars would move to Nashville. After much deliberation, no one from the original Tobias Guitars crew went to Nashville. The final LA Tobias/Gibson serial number is 2044. Despite Gibson's ownership of Tobias, all of the basses made u to 2044 were built by my regular crew. We also built about 60 basses that were not numbered or finished by us. Those would be the first production fror Tobias/Nashville.

I left the company in December of 1992, and was a consultant for Gibson as they set up operations in Nashville. They had some trouble at first, but hav since done a fairly good job making Tobias basses.

By contractual agreement, after my consulting agreement with Gibson was up, I had a one year non competition term. That ended in December of 199 During that time I moved to The Catskills in upstate New York and set up a small custom shop. I started designing new instruments and building prototypes in preparation for my new venture."

(Biography courtesy Michael Tobias, February 22, 1996)

ELECTRIC BASS

Basic Series

B4 - offset double cutaway asymmetrical alder body, through body maple/bubinga neck, 24-fret wenge fingerboard, fixed bridge, 2-per-sid tuners, black hardware, 2 Bartolini pickups, 2 volume/treble/midrange/bass controls, bypass switch, active electronics. Available in Natur finish. Current Mfg.

MSR $3,400 — $2,550 $2,200 $1,925 $1,650 $1,395 $1,125 $850

Add $60 for fretless fingerboard.

Add $200 for polyurethane finish.

Add $250 for left-handed configuration.

This model has bubinga, figured maple, lacewood, walnut, or zebrawood body, maple/purpleheart neck as options.

B5 - similar to B4, except has 5-strings.

MSR $3,600 — $2,700 $2,150 $1,900 $1,650 $1,400 $1,150 $900

B6 - similar to B4, except has 6-strings.

MSR $3,800 — $2,850 $2,275 $2,000 $1,750 $1,475 $1,225 $950

Classic Series

C4 - offset double cutaway asymmetrical laminated body, through body flame maple/purpleheart neck, 24-fret wenge fingerboard, fixed bridge 2-per-side tuners, black hardware, 2 Bartolini pickups, 2 volume/treble/midrange/bass controls, bypass switch, active electronics. Available ir Natural finish. Current Mfg.

MSR $4,100 — $3,075 $2,450 $2,175 $1,900 $1,625 $1,350 $1,075

Add $60 for fretless fingerboard.

Add $200 for polyurethane finish.

Add $250 for left-handed configuration.

This model may have gold or chrome hardware.

Neck may have walnut/purpleheart or walnut/bubinga laminate, maple may replace walnut in some configurations.

This model also available in bird's-eye maple/wenge, bubinga/wenge/alder, flame maple/wenge/walnut, lacewood/wenge/alder, purpleheart/walnut, walnut/wenge/alder, walnut/wenge/walnut, or zebra/wenge/alder laminate body.

C5 - similar to C4, except has 5-strings.

MSR $4,400 — $3,300 $2,650 $2,350 $2,050 $1,725 $1,400 $1,100

C6 - similar to C4, except has 6-strings.

MSR $4,700 — $3,525 $2,825 $2,495 $2,165 $1,825 $1,500 $1,175

Growler Series

GR4 - offset double cutaway body with symmetrical maple/purpleheart neck, 24-fret wenge fingerboard, fixed bridge, 2-per-side tuners, black hardware, 1 Bartolini quad-coil pickup with active 18-volt preamp and 2 contour switches, volume/tone controls. Current Mfg.

MSR $1,900 — $1,450 $1,200 $995 $775 $650 $550 $425

Add $60 for fretless fingerboard.

Add $200 for polyurethane finish.

T

GRADING		100% MINT	98% NEAR MINT	95% EXC+	90% EXC	80% VG+	70% VG	60% G

GR5 - similar to GR4, except features 5-string configuration, 3/2-per-side tuners. Current Mfg.

MSR	$2,100	$1,550	$1,300	$1,050	$875	$725	$600	$475

Killer "B" Series

KB4 - offset double cutaway asymmetrical swamp ash body, bolt-on maple/purpleheart 5-piece neck, 24-fret wenge fingerboard, fixed bridge, 2-per-side tuners, black hardware, 2 Bartolini pickups, 2 volume/treble/midrange/bass controls, bypass switch, active electronics. Available in Oil finish. Current Mfg.

MSR	$2,750	$2,050	$1,650	$1,450	$1,265	$1,075	$885	$695

Add $200 for polyurethane finish.

Add $60 for fretless fingerboard.

Add $250 for left-handed configuration.

This model also available with alder, maple or lacewood body.

KB5 - similar to KB4, except has 5-strings.

MSR	$2,850	$2,150	$1,700	$1,500	$1,300	$1,115	$925	$725

KB6 - similar to KB4, except has 6-strings.

MSR	$2,950	$2,225	$1,775	$1,570	$1,365	$1,160	$955	$750

Pro-Standard Series

PS4 - offset double cutaway asymmetrical figured maple body, through body maple/bubinga 5-piece neck, 24-fret rosewood fingerboard, fixed bridge, 2-per-side tuners, black hardware, 2 Bartolini pickups, volume/mix and 3-band EQ controls, active electronics. Available in Black, Natural, Transparent Candy Amber, Transparent Candy Blue, Transparent Candy Red and White finishes. Mfg. 1994 to 1996.

$1,600	$1,200	$1,000	$800	$720	$660	$600

Last MSR was $2,000.

This model has bubinga or zebra body with Natural finish as options.

PS5 - similar to PS4, except has 5-strings, 3/2-per-side tuners.

$1,675	$1,250	$1,050	$840	$755	$690	$630

Last MSR was $2,100.

PS6 - similar to PS4, except has 6-strings, 3-per-side tuners.

$1,850	$1,375	$1,150	$920	$830	$760	$690

Last MSR was $2,300.

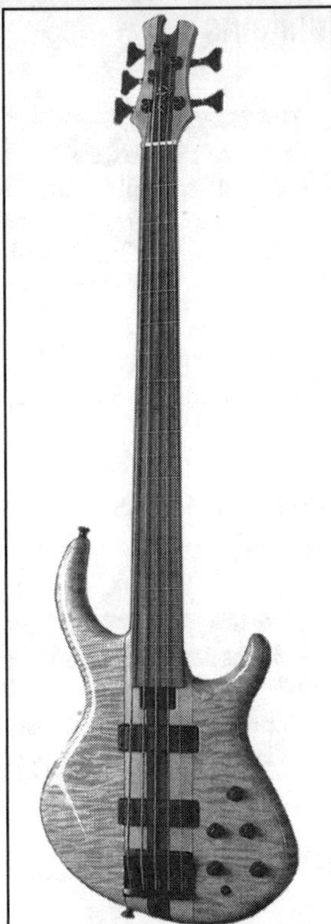
Tobias Basic 4
courtesy Tobias Basses

Renegade Series

Renegade Series instruments were introduced in 1998.

RENEGADE 4 - offset double cutaway alder body, bolt-on maple neck, 24-fret fingerboard, fixed brass bridge, 2-per-side tuners, black hardware, single coil/humbucker Bartolini pickups, 2 volume/push-pull contour tone controls, active electronics. Available in Amber, Black, Blue, Green, and Red finishes. Mfg. 1998 to date.

MSR $1,490

Renegade 5 - similar to Renegade 4, except has 5-string configuration, 3/2-per-side tuners.

MSR $1,590

Signature Series

S4 - offset double cutaway asymmetrical laminated body, through body laminate neck, 24-fret wenge fingerboard, fixed bridge, 2-per-side tuners, black hardware, 2 Bartolini pickups, 2 volume/treble/midrange/bass controls, bypass switch, active electronics. Available in Natural finish. Current Mfg.

MSR	$6,100	$4,750	$3,950	$3,300	$2,925	$2,500	$1,995	$1,425

This model may have gold or chrome hardware.
This model also available in bubinga/wenge/bubinga, lacewood/wenge/lacewood, or zebra/wenge/zebra laminate body.

S5 - similar to S4, except has 5-strings.

MSR	$6,400	$5,300	$4,600	$3,800	$3,250	$2,750	$2,250	$1,600

S6 - similar to S4, except has 6-strings.

MSR	$6,700	$5,700	$5,375	$4,825	$4,295	$3,750	$3,000	$2,575

T

GRADING	100% MINT	98% NEAR MINT	95% EXC+	90% EXC	80% VG+	70% VG	60% G

Standard Series

ST4 - offset double cutaway asymmetrical ash body, through body maple/bubinga 5-piece neck, 24-fret rosewood fingerboard, fixed bridge, 2-per-side tuners, black hardware, 2 Bartolini pickups, volume/mix and 3-band EQ controls, active electronics. Available in Black, Natural, Transparent Candy Amber, Transparent Candy Blue, Transparent Candy Red and White finishes. Disc. 1996.

$1,475 $1,100 $950 $760 $685 $625 $570
Last MSR was $1,850.

This model available in fretless fingerboard at no additional cost.

ST5 - similar to ST4, except has 5-strings.

$1,550 $1,175 $1,000 $800 $720 $660 $600
Last MSR was $1,950.

ST6 - similar to ST4, except has 6-strings.

$1,850 $1,375 $1,150 $920 $830 $760 $690
Last MSR was $2,300.

Toby Deluxe Series

TD4 - offset double cutaway asymmetrical maple body, bolt-on maple neck, 24-fret rosewood fingerboard, fixed bridge, 2-per-side tuners chrome hardware, 2 J-style humbucker pickups, volume/mix/3-band EQ controls, active electronics. Available in Black, Natural, Transparent Candy Amber, Transparent Candy Blue, Transparent Candy Red and White finishes. Mfg. 1994 to 1996.

$725 $550 $450 $360 $325 $300 $275
Last MSR was $900.

TD5 - similar to TD4, except has 5-strings, 3/2-per-side tuners.

$800 $600 $500 $400 $360 $330 $300
Last MSR was $1,000.

Toby Pro Series

TP4 - offset double cutaway asymmetrical maple body, through body maple/wenge 5-piece neck, 24-fret rosewood fingerboard, fixed bridge, 2-per-side tuners, chrome hardware, 2 humbucker pickups, volume/mix/3-band EQ controls, active electronics. Available in Black, Natural, Transparent Candy Amber, Transparent Candy Blue, Transparent Candy Red and White finishes. Mfg. 1994 to 1996.

$950 $725 $600 $480 $430 $395 $360
Last MSR was $1,200.

TP5 - similar to TP4, except has 5-strings, 3/2-per-side tuners.

$1,050 $775 $650 $520 $470 $430 $390
Last MSR was $1,300.

TP6 - similar to TP4, except has 6-strings, 3-per-side tuners.

$1,125 $850 $700 $560 $505 $460 $420
Last MSR was $1,400.

TOKAI

Instruments currently produced in Japan since the early 1960s.

Tokai instruments were very good Fender and Gibson-based replicas produced during the mid to late 1970s. After 1978 the company built instruments based on these classic American designs, then further branched out into some original designs and 'superstrat' models.

TOMKINS

Instruments currently built in Harbord, Australia.

These high quality solid body guitars are custom built by luthier Allan Tomkins, and feature designs based on popular Fender classics. Tomkins' guitars are crafted from exotic Australian hardwoods and softwoods such as Tasmanian King Billy Pine, Black Heart Sassafrass, Queensland Silky Oak, Crab Apple Birch, or Coachwood. Instruments feature Gotoh tuners and bridges, 21-fret necks, Seymour Duncan or Bill Lawrence pickups, and a nitro-cellulose lacquer finish.

TOMMYHAWK

Instruments currently built in New Jersey. Distributed by Tom Barth's Music Box of Dover, New Jersey.

Designer Tom Barth offers a 24" travel-style guitar that is a one-piece carved mahogany body (back, sides, neck, and bracing). The solid spruce top, bridge, and top bracing are then glued on - forming a solid, tone projecting little guitar! In 1997, the soundhole was redesigned into a more elliptical shape. Retail list price on the **Original** is $350. Barth's full size (25 1/2" scale) electric/acoustic has a double cutaway body, 'Tele'-style neck with a 21-fret rosewood or maple fingerboard, and a Seymour Duncan Duckbucker pickup (retail list $595).

TOMMY'S SPECIAL GUITARS

Instruments currently built in Viersen, Germany. Distributed in the U.S. by Salwender International of Orange, California. Distributed in Europe by Tommy's Special Guitars of Viersen, Germany.

Luthier Thomas Metz has been hand crafting high quality solid and semi-solid electric guitars for a number of years. The distinctive feature of the Tommy's Special Guitars model is the systematic respect for the wood and physical sound properties. Each instrument is the technical synthesis of these characteristics. Metz' basic model features an alder, ash or mahogany Strat- or Tele-style body, rock maple neck with rosewood fingerboard, chrome tuners, tunomatic bridge/stop tailpiece (or vintage-style Gotoh tremolo), and EMG pickups. Custom options include a semi-acoustic body with quilted maple top, carved quilted maple top, or bird's-eye maple neck. For more information, contact Thomas Metz directly (see Trademark Index).

Tokai Springy Sound courtesy Austin Vintage

TONEMASTER

See chapter on House Brands.

This trademark has been identified as a "House Brand" ascribed to several distributors such as Harris-Teller of Illinois, Schmidt of Minnesota, and Squire of Michigan. While one recognized source has claimed that instruments under this trademark were built by HARMONY, author/researcher Willie G. Moseley has also seen this brand on a VALCO-made lap steel.

(Source: Willie G. Moseley, Stellas & Stratocasters)

TONESMITH

Instruments currently built in Rogers, Minnesota.

Luthier Kevin Smith opened his GLF Custom shop for guitar repairs and custom building in 1984. In 1996, he began building prototypes for a new guitar design, which in 1997 developed into a full line with different models.

ToneSmith Series

At present, the ToneSmith series consists of 3 different models: The model **316** (the 1997 new offset body shape), model **412** (1996 offset double cutaway body), and the model **510** (a 1996 single cutaway design). All models are available in Guitar, Baritone, and Bass configurations.

After the customer selects the body style and configuration, a decision is made to the level of features. The **Special** (base retail $1,699) has an alder body and top, maple neck with black or ivoroid binding, rosewood fingerboard, pearl dot inlays, solid colors, and nickel or chrome hardware. The **Custom** (base retail $1,999) has a bound mahogany (or alder, or ash) body, flame or bird's-eye maple (or mahogany, alder or ash) top, ivoroid (or pearl or tortoishell) bound maple neck, rosewood fingerboard, pearl diamond wing inlay, semi-transparent or burst finishes, and nickel or chrome hardware. The **Deluxe** (base retail $2,399) is similar to the Custom, except has ebony (or bubinga) fingerboards, sparkle finishes, and optional gold hardware.

All ToneSmith models are optional with an acoustic bridge pickup, Bigsby tremolo, or custom ordered colors. The Ultra Lite Version substitutes a spruce body and spruce or maple top for the regular body and top.

TOP TWENTY

Instruments previously produced in Japan between 1965 to 1976.

The Top Twenty trademark is a brand name used by a UK importer. These entry level quality instruments featured a solid body construction and some original designs.

(Source: Tony Bacon and Paul Day, The Guru's Guitar Guide)

TOTEM

Instruments currently built in Three Rivers, California.

Totem offers several high quality guitars with bolt-neck designs, ash bodies and maple or myrtle tops, and quality hardware.

TOYOTA

Instruments previously produced in Japan circa early 1970s.

Toyota guitars were distributed in the U.S. by the Hershman company of New York, New York. The Toyota trademark was applied to a full range of acoustic, thinline acoustic/electric hollow body, and solid body electric guitars and basses.

(Source: Michael Wright, Guitar Stories Volume One)

TRACE ELLIOT

Instruments currently built in England by STATUS. Distributed in the U.S. market by Trace Elliot USA of Darien, Illinois.

If you're a bass player, you've probably tested or use Trace Elliot amplification. In recent years, Trace has developed amplifiers for both acoustic and electric guitars as well. Now Trace Elliot is offering a line of bass guitars built by the Status company in England.

ELECTRIC BASS

T-Series basses feature bolt-on necks, a new four on one side headstock, and 2 single coil J-style pickups with an additional hum-cancelling *dummy* coil, volume/blend/tone controls, and an active EQ. Retail prices range from $1,899 up to $2,599.

The **T-Bass 1998 Special Edition** features a Candy Apple Red finish with matching headstock, an aged pickguard, and 2 exposed pole Alnico stacked humbucking pickups. Only 100 4-string and 100 5-string models are scheduled.

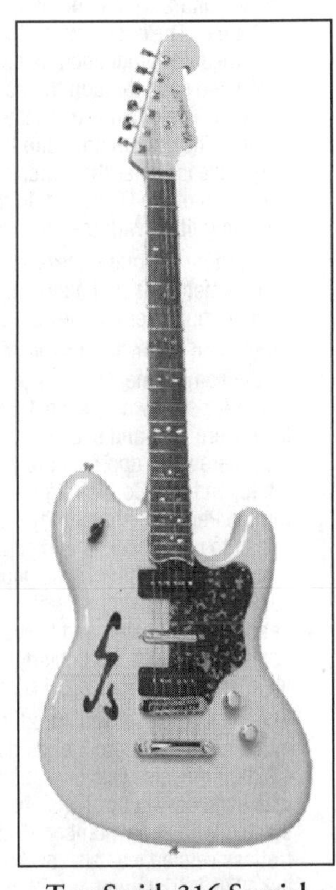

ToneSmith 316 Special courtesy Tone Smith

TRANSPERFORMANCE

Tuning mechanisms currently built in Fort Collins, Colorado.

Transperformance is a Colorado-based company that builds the **L-CAT Automatic Tuning System**. This system is installed in a guitar, and features a computer-controlled bridge and tuning mechanism that can physically change tunings on the instrument. The mechanism comes with 120 factory-programmed alternative tunings, and has memory storage for 240 customer installed others as well. For an example, at the flip of a button you can move from the conventional guitar tuning, to a *dropped D* to an open G - automatically! The system lists for $2,599 (and up).

TRAVELER

Instruments currently built in Redlands, California. Distributed by OMG Music.

Designer J. Corey Oliver offers a full scale travel-style guitar that is only 28 inches in overall length (full size 24 3/4 in. fret board), and two inches thick. Constructed of either maple or mahogany, the Traveler (basic list $399) has a single coil pickup (an optional Fishman transducer is also offered), and a storable lower arm for playing in the sitting position, and a unique Stethophone headset that requires no power source.

TRAVIS BEAN

Instruments previously built in Sun Valley, California from 1974 to 1979.

The following Travis Bean history is reprinted here courtesy of Bill Kaman, who has been a Travis Bean fan from the beginning. Additional information supplied by Richard Oblinger (*Obe*), a Travis Bean employee; and Travis Bean, the man behind it all.

T6061: A Short History on the Travis Bean Guitars

Travis Bean: It's the name of a California motorcycle enthusiast who decided in the early '70s that aluminum would be a step forward in guitar design. He thought that it would be a much more stable material for the necks. Using a neck-through-to-the-bridge design also improved the sound and sustain of the guitars. While Travis played some guitar, he was a drummer and kept a drum kit set up at the factory to back up players when they were there to check out equipment.

The company was founded in 1974 and lasted five years, closing in August of 1979. They produced about 3,650 guitars and basses which are as viable an instrument today in the '90s as they were when they were built. Initial production began in 1974 and continued until December 1977 when the factory was closed for "reorganization". In June 1978 it reopened and continued until August 1979 when the plug was pulled by the investors who had "reorganized" the company. Sashi Pattell, an Indian guy, was the major investor and "drove" the company for the last 12 months. During the first 6 months of 1978, limited "unofficial" production continued with a partial production crew who often took guitars in lieu of wages.

In 1977 the guitars were sold through Rothschild Distribution but that ended with the reorganization. When the company closed in 1979 everything was sold off at auction. Mighty Mite bought about 200 bodies and most of the guitar parts but never really did anything with them. There were about 30 TB500 necks left over and it's not known who bought these. Mighty Mite itself was closed and auctioned off a few years later.

The first guitar Travis ever built was a 'Melody Maker' body shape with Gibson humbucking pickups. The aluminum neck had a welded-on peghead and bolted to the body. The neck attachment plate was inlaid in the body and extended back to under the bridge. After experimenting with this guitar a while the idea of a neck-through-to-the-bridge design began to take shape. A second prototype was built which was much closer to the production design in neck and body configuration. This guitar has a serial number of "1", and used Fender humbucking pickups. After these two guitars, limited production began.

These first "limited production" guitars were TB1000 Artists and were produced in 1974. The serial numbers started with #11 and went to #20.

These guitars were handmade by Travis and Mark McElwee, Travis' partner in the company, and are quite similar in construction to the second pre-production prototype. The bodies were Koa, Teak, Padauk, Zebra wood, and Alder (Guitar #11 and #18 are known to be Padauk). The necks on these were quite different from the later production models produced on a lathe. These were hand carved from a solid block of Reynolds T6061 aluminum and are solid under the fingerboard and solid through the body. The necks have a wide and flat profile which is noticeably thinner than the later production which are much fuller and more rounded. The pickups on these first guitars are humbuckers using Fender bobbins and Alnico magnets; and have 'Travis Bean' engraved on the chrome pickup covers. The guitars are quite thin, about the same thickness as the 1979 final production Artists. Another interesting aspect of these guitars is the peghead. The angle is flatter than later production (about 6 degrees versus a production angle of 12 degrees). There is also about an extra inch between the nut and the beginning of the 'T' cutout. In this extra space there is bolted an aluminum block with 6 holes acting as a string tree to hold the tension over the nut. Later production guitars with the steeper angle didn't need this tie down.

In all, there are quite a few differences between these first 10 prototypes and the production models ranging from the body thickness and top contour, peghead dimensions and angle, neck profile and shape of the body insert piece, to the pickup engraving. These guitars are a bit crude compared to the later production; but after all, they are the first ones made.

Production of the 1000 series continued throughout 1974 with the 1000 Standard being introduced approximately 6 months after the startup. This guitar had all the same dimensions as the 1000 Artist, only differing in that the body was not carved and it had dot fingerboard inlays rather than the large pearl blocks of the Artist. It was a solid 1 3/4" all over. The run of serial numbers on Standards and Artists began with #21 and continued until #1000. At that point the lines were split and each continued with #1001, #1002, etc. While it is unclear if the production records of these first 1000 guitars still exist, it is estimated that there were approximately 1/3 Artists and 2/3 Standards. All the bodies were Koa and most were finished natural; however, the factory did offer black, white, and red. Both straight color and pearl color were offered. There were also several dark blue pearl guitars made (there were two silver guitars made: one for Joe Perry [of Aerosmith] a Standard #1738; and a Wedge Guitar [# 53] for Al Austin). The Koa bodies continued until late 1978 when the painted models began to use magnolia and poplar. The natural finishes continued to use mostly Koa although a natural magnolia is known to exist. All these guitars used black 'speed' knobs which Travis bought directly from Gibson until for some reason Gibson shut them off. After that, clear 'speed' knobs were used. In late 1978 and 1979 black metal knobs were used. Internally, these were referred to as "Sansui" knobs because they looked like they were off a home stereo set! The machine heads were Schaller and Grover and alternated without any pattern throughout the years of production. Towards the end of the company, Gotoh machine heads were used, particularly on the 500 model. The last Artist produced was serial number 1425 and the last Standard produced was serial number 1782. In all, there were about 755 Artists and 1,442 Standards produced.

The TB2000 Bass was introduced in late 1974. The first prototype had serial number "0" and is of similar construction to the first 10 guitars. However, it is much more like a production guitar in that it doesn't have that "handmade" look of the first 10 guitars. This bass is pictured in the first catalogue on the TB2000 models. This bass also had an aluminum nut (the only one made this way). All other production Travis Beans were made with brass nuts. The neck was hand carved by Travis and has a thick squarish feel. It was solid as was the section in the body. The body had a 1/4" edge radius and was Koa. Production started with serial number 11 and the bodies were more rounded and contoured. They were all Koa and made in natural and the same colors as the guitars. A fretless version was also available, as was a short scale model bass. In all about 12 short scale basses were made, two of which were for Bill Wyman in October 1978 (serial number 892 and 893). The last bass made was serial number 1033. In all there were 1,023 basses made.

The 500 model was meant to be a less expensive single coil version of the 1000 model. The first guitars were produced in late 1977, just before the reorganization shutdown. The first 9 guitars were quite different from the balance of production. These had standard 1 3/4" thickness bodies but the aluminum body extension was set in from the top rather than sliding into the middle of the body and being exposed at the back. These guitars had uncoated necks, and the bodies were much more square than later production. Most of these first 500s went to performers like Jerry Garcia and Rory Gallager (who had 3 pickup guitars). Mark McElwee kept one made with a Koa body. In June of 1978 when production resumed with guitar #20 the bodies were more slimmer and had a slanted off center shape. The pickguards also were more stylized, and the majority of the necks were coated with the black Imron paint that was used to give the guitar necks a "warmer" feel. There were several made with three pickups (serial numbers 11, 12, 270). Up until around serial number 290, the pickups had black plastic covers with the pole piece exposed. After #290, the covers were solid black plastic with a molded-in stylized 'Travis Bean' logo. The majority of the 500s had magnolia bodies although there were some made from poplar. Most were painted black, white, or red although there were some naturals made. The last 500 was serial number 362 so there were a total of 351 TB500 guitars produced. There were plans for a 500 model Bass but it was never completed.

The Wedges are perhaps the most unique guitars and basses produced by Travis Bean. They were the "Stage" guitars, and the Travis Bean version of a 'Flying V'. They were introduced in 1976 and built for two years. In total, 45 TB3000 Wedge guitars and 36 TB4000 Wedge basses were produced. All the basses were produced in the 1 3/4" thickness. Most of the guitars were 1 3/4" thick, with the exception of the last few (for example, Wedge guitar #49 is 1 3/4", but the next to the last one produced [# 55] was 1 3/8" thick. Also, # 49 has a one piece fingerboard and # 55 is 2 piece). The majority of the Wedges were produced in pearl colors: white, black, and red. An interesting point is that the bodies were the same overall size for both guitars and bass.

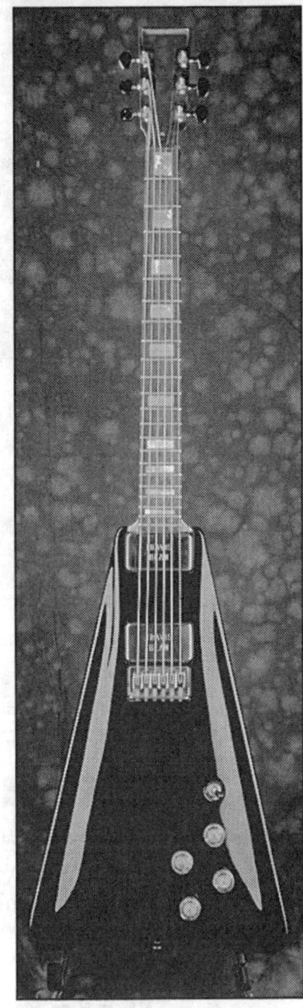

Travis Bean Wedge
courtesy William
Kaman II

There were two doublenecks built. Both were double six strings and used Artist necks. One was a red Wedge and the other a natural Artist. There were also six 5-string guitars made that were Standards and are serial numbered 1732 to 1737. These went to Keith Richards, Travis Bean, Richard Oblinger, Mark McElwee, and Bill Lominic (the head machinist at the company). All these were coated necks and were 1 3/8" thick. Left handed guitars and basses were also available and 'lefty' 1000 Artists and Standards, as well as 2000 basses are known to exist. There were no 'lefty' Wedges or 500s built. There were requests over the years for special custom bodies on guitars, but these requests were turned down. Travis felt that building the custom "one-offs" would dilute the impact of the market place of the standard production. There exist today several instruments with custom bodies (for example: a MAP guitar and a Flying V) but these were retrofitted to existing guitars and not done at the Bean factory.

Throughout the production there were several significant changes that took place. The first change was that the horns of the guitars and basses were widened. This was around mid 1977. This was a suggestion from Rothchild Distributing and it was felt that this would improve playability and sales. An estimate is that this took place on Artists around #1100, Standards #1250, and Basses #440. The second change is that the bodies were made thinner by 3/8". This is estimated to have taken place around #1200 on Artists, #1400 on Standards, and #580 on Basses and was probably phased in around the first part of 1978. The third change was that the fingerboards went to a two piece construction. This took place just about the same time as the thinner bodies. Initially, the fingerboard was rosewood (although some early guitars had ebony; they also experimented with phenolic) and was a standard thickness. The center portion of the neck under the fingerboard was machined away to make it lighter. There was a rib left down the middle to support the fingerboard. On the later version the fingerboard was again rosewood, but half the thickness it had been previously. A thin piece of aluminum was added under the fingerboard to bring the fingerboard assembly back to standard thickness. On these guitars the center rib was not left in the middle of the neck since the aluminum underlay would fully support the wood. Also in 1978, a slight radius was introduced to the fingerboard. Up until this they had all been flat like a classical guitar (except for the prototype bass [#0] which has a 7 degree radius). The fourth change that took place around mid 1977 was the coating of the necks. One of the constant complaints about Travis Beans was that the necks felt "cold" and some found them objectionable (it's a good thing that these complainers didn't play saxophones!). In response to this the company introduced the option of a black Imron coated neck. Imron is a heavy duty automobile enamel. It was felt that this heavy finish would make the necks feel slightly warmer, and since it was a spray-on finish it would be more like a standard guitar neck. This was an option on any guitar or bass (and as mentioned, pretty much a standard on the 500 series).

There was another small change in the machining of the aluminum piece in the body of the guitars. Approximately the first 300 TB1000 guitars made had the aluminum section in the body cavity machined from the side to take out the weight. The middle of the aluminum was cut completely away so there was a back section, visible at the back of the guitar; and a top section, which the pickups sat on. The rear most portion of the extension under the bridge was left solid. This was then glued into the body after it was finished. From around serial number 300, on the body section of the aluminum was machined from the top which created a "U" shaped channel under the guitar top and pickups. The rear end portion under the bridge was again solid. The improvement in this design was that it created a much more rigid structure in the body of the guitar, plus it allowed the body to be screwed to the neck extension by two wood screws through the walls of the "U" channel under the front pickup. Those two screws plus the three that fasten the bridge to the aluminum through the wood body are all that hold it together. This design made it much easier to remove the neck should it need work or work on the body. The pickups sat directly on either side of the "U" channel and were held in place by allen screws mounted from the rear.

The serial number of the guitar is stamped onto the face of the peghead just above the nut. It was also stamped into the aluminum under the neck pickup. On some it was also written on the bottom of the "U" channel. It was written on the body in two places: the interior of the control cavity, and in the space between the pickups on the inside. On the painted bodies the number in the control cavity was often painted over, and therefore not visible. It is interesting to note that bass #477 has body #478 so either bass #478 has #477 body or the #477 body had a problem and they just used the next body on the assembly line. This does prove that necks and bodies are interchangeable.

Where is Travis Bean today? By the time the company was sold at auction, Travis had his fill of production headaches, Music Industry bullshit, and demanding visits from the Taxmen. He took some time off. Being a tinkerer at heart, and someone who is happier using his hands and building things, he eventually began work building sets for the movie studios (which he continues to do today). His personal interest in music has stayed strong, and he has kept playing - focusing mostly on his drumming. Being true to his machinist/designer/tinker side, he has also developed a new style of rack setup for drums that allows for fast set-up and tear-down. So the answer is, Travis is alive and well and still playing in California.

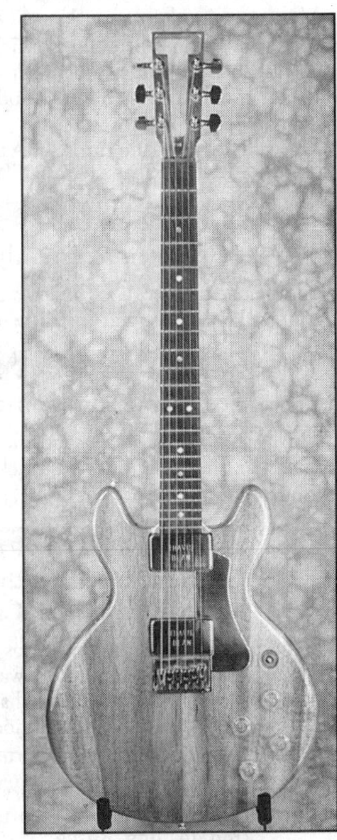

Travis Bean Guitar
courtesy Darryl Alger

(Source: C. William Kaman, II, President (Kaman Music Corporation), May 6, 1994)

Serialization and Model Production

The following chart is a rough accounting of the production by year and serial number:

	1974 to Jan. 1976	Jan. 1976 to Dec. 1977	Jan. 1978 to June 1979	Total
TB500	-	-	11-362	351
TB1000A	11-400	400-1000,1000-1162	1163-1425	755
TB1000S	-	1056	1157-1782	1422
TB2000	11-200	201-763	764-1033	1023
TB3000	-	11-50	51-56	45
TB4000	-	11-47	-	36
	600	1444	1611	3652

ELECTRIC

Travis Bean guitars are offered in the range between $1,000 and $1,250; the rarer Wedge models command a higher price (a total of 45 Wedge guitars and 36 Wedge basses were produced between 1976 and 1978).

TREKER

Instruments currently built in Draper, Utah.

Treker offers a range of quality guitar and bass models that feature the exclusive "Floating Neck" technology. Handcrafted bodies are joined to a neck that has an internal tension bar which offers structural support and allows the fretboard to vibrate free of the traditional static load of the neck/truss rod/ fingerboard design. For further information regarding individual models and specifications, or on the 'Floating Neck' concept, please call Treker directly (see Trademark Index).

TRIGGS, JAMES W.

Instruments currently hand built in Kansas City, KS. Previously manufactured in Nashville, Tennessee.

Luthier Jim Triggs has been building instruments since the mid-1970s. While at Gibson during 1986-1992, Jim wore many hats, including Artist Relations, Custom Shop Manager, Archtop Guitar Supervisor, Custom Mandolin Builder, and Art Guitar Designer. Jim left Gibson in March of 1992, and has been custom building ever since, including for many stars. His more famous clients have included: Alan Jackson, Steve Miller, Elliot Easton, Pat Martino, Mundell Lowe, Vince Gill, and Marty Stuart.

Jim's son Ryan is currently working with him in the shop, and this "team" maybe the only father & son duo currently working on archtops together. The Triggs Boys keep busy with a constant back order of flattops, archtops, and F-5 style mandolins. Much of Jim's time in the shop is spent on design work for other companies. Several models are in Cort Guitars line already, and 4 new Triggs designed "Tradition Guitars" will debut at the Nashville Summer NAMM Show in July, 2001.

The sky's the limit with a Triggs guitar. Electrics start at $3,000. Flattop start at $3,000, archtops around $10,000, and F-5s for around $6,000. Please contact Triggs directly for more information and a personal price quotation (see Trademark Index).

TUBULAR INSTRUMENT CO. INC.

Instruments currently built in Staten Island, NY.

Tubular Instrument Co. builds a unique, light wooden string "Tube Bass". For more information, including current availability and pricing, please contact Pete at Tubular Instrument Co. directly (see Trademark Index).

TRUETONE

See chapter on House Brands.

This trademark has been identified as a "House Brand" of Western Auto. Built by Kay in the 1960s, the six-on-a-side headstock shape shared with this trademark has been dubbed "duck's bill" or "platypus" in reference to the rather bulbous nature of the design.
(Source: Willie G. Moseley, Stellas and Stratocasters)

TRUSSART, JAMES

Instruments currently built in Paris, France. Distributed in the U.S. by Black Market Music of Los Angeles, California and San Francisco, California.

French luthier James Trussart was a custom electric guitar builder who began building in 1980, and rose to some notice during the 1980s in Paris (the "James Trusear Guitar Station" was the name of Trussart's shop). Trussart has created instruments for both Eric Clapton and bassist Nathan East. While it was rumored that Trussart may have retired several years ago, Trussart is still custom crafting the steel bodied instruments that bear his namesake. For further information regarding model designations and pricing, contact James Trussart directly (see Trademark Index).

(Preliminary information courtesy Jeff Meyer)

Trussart created his version of *Str*t* and *T*le* designs that featured exceptional craftsmanship, and were retail priced around $3,000. Trussart's creations feature steel bodies, or engraved metal tops and headstocks over the instrument bodies. Many creations are one-of-a-kind designs. Research still continues on Trussart's custom instruments and the models bearing the James Trusear trademark.

GRADING	100% MINT	98% NEAR MINT	95% EXC+	90% EXC	80% VG+	70% VG	60% G

TUNE GUITAR TECHNOLOGY CO., LTD.

Current trademark of instruments manufactured in Tokyo, Japan since 1983.

Tune Guitar Technology Co., Ltd. offers many different series of high quality basses and guitars. Tune Basses all possess innovative, original designs and quality hardware and electronics. For further information, please contact the company directly (see Trademark Index).

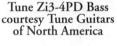

Tune Zi3-4PD Bass courtesy Tune Guitars of North America

ELECTRIC BASS

Bass Maniac Custom Series

TBC-4 S - offset double cutaway walnut/padauk/bubinga body, bolt-on 3-piece maple neck, 25-fret rosewood fingerboard with white dot inlay, fixed Gotoh bridge, 2-per-side Gotoh tuners, black hardware, P/J-style humbucker Tune pickups, volume/treble/bass/mix controls, active electronics. Available in Natural finish. Current Mfg.

MSR	$1,399	$1,050	$850	$750	$650	$550	$450	$350

TBC-5 S - similar to TBC-4 S, except has 5-string configuration, fixed Tune bridge, 3/2-per-side tuners. Current Mfg.

MSR	$1,699	$1,275	$1,025	$900	$775	$650	$525	$425

Kingbass Series

TWB-4 - offset double cutaway walnut/padauk/bubinga body with pointed bottom bout, bolt-on 3-piece maple neck, 24-fret ebony fingerboard with white dot inlay, fixed Gotoh bridge, body matching peghead with raised logo, 2-per-side Gotoh tuners, gold hardware, 2 humbucker Tune pickups, volume/treble/bass/mix/filter controls, active electronics. Available in Natural finish. Current Mfg.

MSR	$2,249	$1,800	$1,350	$1,125	$900	$810	$740	$675

Add $100 for figured maple top.

TWB-5 - similar to TWB-4, except has 5-strings, 3/2-per-side tuners. Current Mfg.

MSR	$2,449	$1,825	$1,470	$1,225	$1,000	$875	$700	$615

TWB-6 - similar to TWB-4, except has 6-strings, 3-per-side tuners. Current Mfg.

MSR	$2,480	$1,860	$1,500	$1,325	$1,150	$975	$800	$620

Zi Neck Through Series

Zi3-4 - offset double cutaway walnut/padauk/bubinga body with pointed bottom bout, through body 3-piece maple neck, 24-fret ebony fingerboard with white dot inlay, fixed Tune bridge, body matching veneered peghead, 2-per-side Gotoh tuners, gold hardware, 2 humbucker Tune pickups, volume/treble/bass/mix/filter controls, active electronics. Available in Natural finish. Current Mfg.

MSR	$2,599	$1,950	$1,600	$1,400	$1,225	$1,025	$850	$650

Zi3-5 - similar to Zi3-4, except has 5-strings, 3/2-per-side tuners. Current Mfg.

MSR	$2,799	$2,100	$1,680	$1,485	$1,290	$1,100	$900	$700

Zi3-6 - similar to Zi3-4, except has 6-strings, 3-per-side tuners. Current Mfg.

MSR	$2,999	$2,250	$1,800	$1,590	$1,380	$1,170	$960	$750

TURNER, RICK

Instruments currently built in Topanga, California. Distributed by Rick Turner Guitars of Topanga, California.

Luthier Rick Turner was one of the original three partners that formed Alembic in 1970. In 1978 he left Alembic to form Turner Guitars, and opened a workshop in 1979 in Novato, California. Although artists such as Lindsey Buckingham favored Turner's guitars, the company was closed in 1981. Turner's records show that approximately 130 instruments were built during that time period (1979-1981).

As well as building instruments, Rick Turner has written countless columns on guitar building, repairs, and products profiles in guitar magazines. Turner reopened his guitar shop in 1989, and now offers a range of instruments.

Please refer to the Renaissance section in this text for more information on these models manufactured by Rick Turner.

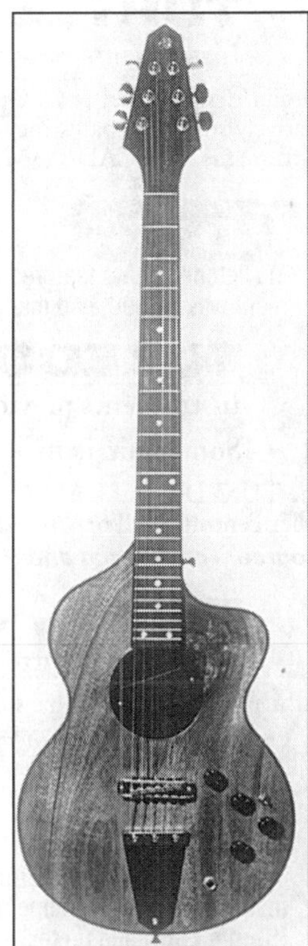

Turner Guitar courtesy Rick Turner

ELECTRIC

Add $400 for AAA flamed or quilted top wood.

Add $200 for Rick Turner Piezo bridge with proprietary blending electronics (BNC electronics only).

Add $250 for matching bird's eye maple peghead, fingerboard, pickup ring, tailpiece, and nickel pickup cover (disc.)

Add $100 for custom colors such as Gold, Silver, Translucent Blue, Translucent Green, or others (disc.).

Add $200 for optional Mike Christian Piezo bridge and Turner blending electronics (disc.).

T

GRADING		100% MINT	98% NEAR MINT	95% EXC+	90% EXC	80% VG+	70% VG	60% G

MODEL ONE - also known as the Lindsey Buckingham guitar, features semi-hollow body and unique rotating single pickup design, trapeze tailpiece, 130 were manufactured before they became a custom shop model. Model One guitars and basses are now available through the custom shop only. Please allow 6-18 months for delivery. This custom shop model carries the Turner brand.

MODEL 1-A - single cutaway arched top mahogany top and back, bound in black, five piece laminated neck with multi layer veneer overlay on peghead, 24-fret black bound rosewood fingerboard (15 frets clear of the body), 24 3/4" scale, nickel plated hardware, single Turner Humbucking pickup, Schaller tuners and roller bridge, Turner "stop" tailpiece, one volume and one tone knob. Available in a deep Red stain on the mahogany body and high gloss urethane finish. Current Mfg.

MSR	$3,450	$3,000	$2,500	$2,250	$1,950	$1,750	$1,600	$1,450

Model 1-B - similar to the Model 1-A, except has an active buffer and line driver preamp.

MSR	$3,695	$3,300	$2,750	$2,375	$2,050	$1,825	$1,700	$1,500

Model 1-C - similar to the Model 1-A, except has a quasi-parametric EQ. This model is the duplicate to the original Model 1 (1979-1981).

MSR	$3,975	$3,550	$2,900	$2,500	$2,150	$1,900	$1,800	$1,550

MODEL 2 - similar to the Model 1-A, except that an added Turner humbucking pickup is added to the bridge position. Disc. 2000.

Last MSR was $2,325.

MODEL 3-A - similar to the Model 1-A, except has an extended 27-fret ebony fingerboard (17 frets clear of the body), 24 3/4" scale. Disc. 2000.

Last MSR was $2,335.

Model 3-B - similar to the Model 3-A, except has an active buffer and line driver preamp. Disc. 2000.

Last MSR was $2,485.

Model 3-C - similar to the Model 3-A, except has a quasi-parametric EQ. Disc. 2000.

Last MSR was $2,585.

Junior Series

The Junior series was offered beginning in 1995. All models have an alder body, one piece maple neck, and no bindings or wood laminates. By saving on labor and some wood costs, the retail price of the Junior series is about $500 less than the Models 1,2, or 3; however, the same hardware and electronic options are offered on the Juniors as is on the regular models.

The **Model 1-A, Jr.** features similar design to the Model 1-A, single pickup, painted alder body, rosewood fingerboard, and passive electronics at a list price of $1,650. The **Model 1-B, Jr.** is the same except has an active buffer and line driver preamp built in ($1,800), and the **Model 1-C, Jr.** features a quasi-parametric EQ ($1,950). All were available in Red, Maroon, Cobalt Blue, or Forest Green. Add $77.25 for a three color sunburst.

This series was discontinued.

TURTLETONE

Instruments previously built in Tempe, Arizona.

Luthier/designer Walter G. Gura produced a number of solid body instruments that feature interesting and innovative designs. Though Turtletone was a relatively small company, they utilized a number of high tech devices like CAD/CAM (Computer Aided Design/Computer Aided Manufacturing) instruments. The CAD/CAM devices also assisted in customer-specified unusual body designs, as the design could be plotted prior to construction.

ELECTRIC

Turtletone guitars featured maple bodies and necks, ebony fingerboards, DiMarzio pickups, and Kahler or Grover hardware. List price for the standard instrument was $1,600, and many special orders/options were available per customer order.

TUXEDO

Instruments previously made in England, West Germany, and Japan during the early to mid 1960s.

Some guitars may also carry the trademark of DALLAS.

The TUXEDO and DALLAS trademarks are the brand names used by a UK importer/distributor. Some of the early solid body guitars were supplied by either Fenton-Weill or Vox in Britain, and other models were imported entry level German and Japanese guitars that featured some original design guitars. ***(Source: Tony Bacon and Paul Day, The Guru's Guitar Guide)***

TYLER, JAMES

Instruments currently built in Van Nuys, California.

Luthier James Tyler and his staff are currently building and offering a fairly wide range of custom solid body guitars and basses.

Models are constructed of quality tonewoods, Wilkinson bridges, Schaller locking tuners, and "Tyler spec'd" Lindy Fralin or Seymour Duncan pickups.

ELECTRIC

Tyler guitars feature an offset, double cutaway body design and bolt-on bird's-eye maple neck. In the **Studio Elite** series, bodies are constructed out of mamywo wood, and some models have a figured maple top "Bent Over Arm Contour". Prices range from $2,495 (**Studio Elite Psychedelic Vomit**) to $2,765 (**Studio Elite**) and up to $3,350 (**Studio Elite Deluxe**).

Tyler's **Mongoose** series is the top of the line Tyler Guitar. Models feature Honduran mahogany bodies, and flame maple tops (except for the **Mongoose Special** and **Mongoose Acoustic Electric**). The maple cap under the **Mongoose Gold Top** is not flamed (nor is the gold finish translucent, if you think about it -

T

so the flame wouldn't be apparent). Prices run from $3,065 on the **Mongoose Gold Top** to $3,550 (**Mongoose Special**). For further information regarding these and other Tyler guitar models, contact Tyler Guitars directly (see Trademark Index).

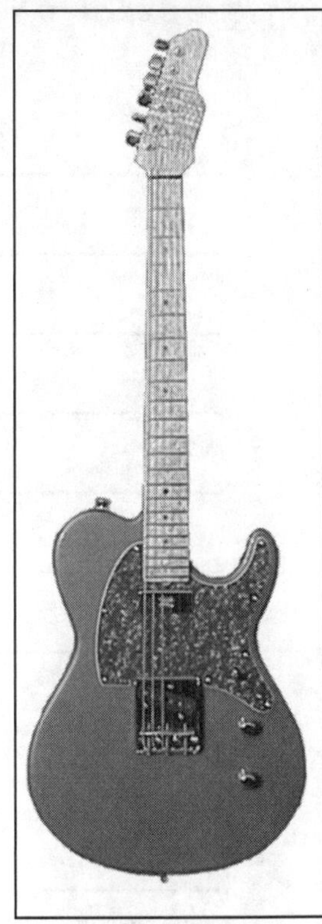

Tyler Mongobastar
courtesy James Tyler Guitars

TYM

Guitars handcrafted in Australia since 1997.

These are in the words of the luthier,Tim, "basically" copies of Mosrites. Production is approximately 25 instruments per year. All models are available in left hand configuration also.

Add $75 for aluminum neck.

Add $35 for rock maple neck.

Add $55 for each Seymour Duncan pickup.

Add $70 for each Seymour Duncan mini-humbucker.

Add $55 for each Kent Armstrong mini-humbucker.

Add $40 for 3-color sunburst finish.

Add $20 for Moseley style Left-Hand tremelo

ELECTRIC

THE JOHNNY MODEL - offset double cutaway body, copy of Johnny Ramone's Mosrite Ventures MKII, solid body with two humbuckers or single coil pickups, Tune-O-Matic bridge, stop tailpiece, Kluson style tuners, 1 volume/1 tone control, 3-way selector switch, black or white 3-ply pickguard. Available in any solid or metallic color. Current Mfg.

MSR $750

The Johnny Deluxe Model - similar to the Johnny Model, except has Moseley type vibrato and cast aluminum top hat knobs, choice of maple or ash neck with a zero fret, a more faithful reproduction of the Mosrite Ventures MK II. Current Mfg.

MSR $830

The Johnny Ramone Model - similar to the Johnny deluxe model, except has 1 Seymour Duncan mini humbucker and 1 DiMarzio "Fat Strat" pickup, Mosrite style bridge and stop tailpiece, Grover style tuners, 1 volume/1 tone control, 3-way selector switch, black or white 3-ply pickguard, available in a selection of body timbers. Available in white, blue or metallic gold finishes. Current Mfg.

MSR $890

THE VERSATONE MODEL - offset double cutaway Mosrite style body, same specs as Johnny Ramone Model, except has angled neck pickup, Tune-O-Matic bridge, Jazzmaster style vibrato. Current Mfg.

MSR $800

The Versatone Deluxe Model - similar to Versatone Model, except has Moseley type vibrato and Mosrite style cast aluminum top hat knobs, zero fret, painted neck binding, 2 P-90 pickups with surrounds, choice of ash or maple body. Current Mfg.

MSR $890

The Versatone Deluxe VIII - copy of Mosrite VIII made in the mid-80's by Semie Moseley, carved top, no pickguard, basswood body, 1 volume control, 3 mini-toggles for pickup on/off, laminated rosewood and maple fingerboard. Current Mfg.

MSR $950

MOSRONG MODEL 500 - Mosrite-ish solid body design, available with 2 single coil pickups or 1 single coil and 1 humbucker in the bridge position, carved top, available with stop tailpiece or Jazzmaster style tremelo. Current Mfg.

MSR $500

T

NOTES

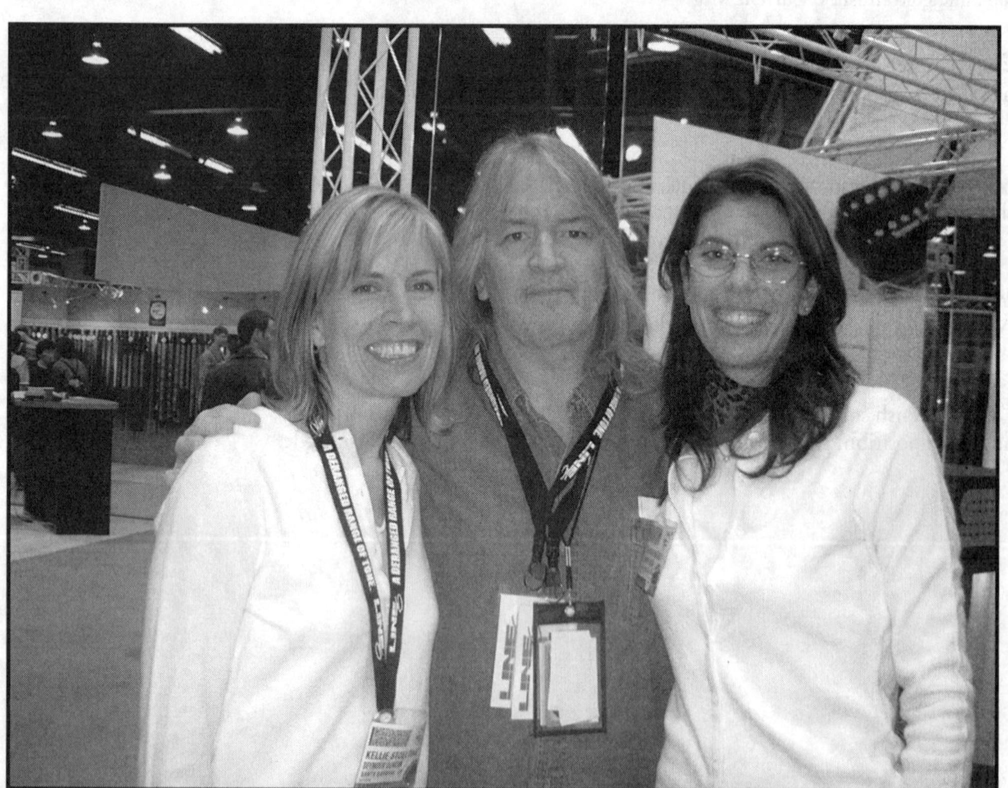

Pickup guru Seymour Duncan, pauses for a pic with several of the lovely Seymour Duncan ladies. If there's anybody cooler than Seymour, We'd like to know about it.

Section U

U.S. MASTERS GUITAR WORKS

Instruments currently built in Middleton, Wisconsin.

The U.S. Masters Guitar Works drew on their retail and repair backgrounds while designing and producing the **Vector** and **Sportster** series of guitars, as well as the EP series 4- and 5-string bass models.

Suggested list prices include a deluxe hardshell case.

ELECTRIC

LeGrand Series

The LeGrand Series is the U.S. Masters re-engineering of the classic 'Strat' design. This model features a locking neck joint to augment the standard bolt-on connection, a low profile heel, and additional pickup blend control. Standard LeGrand finishes include Black, Fine Metallic Candy, Red, Fine Metallic Blue; transparent finishes include Cherry, Purple, and Royal Blue. Deluxe LeGrand finishes are an additional $75, and include Sunburst, Amber, and Emerald Green.

Models include the **LeGrand** (list $1,098), **LeGrand Legend** ($1,345), and the solid curly maple body **LeGrand Custom Legend** ($1,680).

Sportster Series

All three **Sportster** guitar models feature an offset double cutaway select white ash body, bolt-on rock maple necks, maple or Pau ferro fingerboards, and chrome hardware. Standard Sportster opaque finishes include Black, Fine metallic Candy, Red, Fine Metallic Blue; transparent finishes include Cherry, Purple, Royal Blue, and Deep Blue. Deluxe Sportster finishes are an additional $75, and include Sunburst, Amber, Emerald Green, and Clear Gloss.

The **Versatek** model (list $999) has a fixed bridge and 2 HH Versatek pickups; the **Classic** (list $1,074) has a floating tremolo bridge and 2 single coils/humbucker pickup configuration. The **Sportster F Classic** substitutes a Floyd Rose tremolo in place of the floating tremolo bridge, and has a retail list price of $1,345. The **Hammer** model has a similar Floyd Rose tremolo, and features Hammer pickups (list $1,320).

Univox Custom
courtesy The Music Shoppe

Vector Series

Vector model guitars have an offset double cutaway Honduran mahogany bodies and contoured book-matched figured maple tops (*AAA maple tops are available for an extra $300*). Standard Vector opaque finishes include Black, Fine metallic Candy, Red, Fine Metallic Blue; transparent finishes include Amber, Cherry, Emerald Green, Sunburst, Purple, Royal Blue, Deep Blue, and Clear Gloss.

The **Vector Versatek** model (list $1,449) has a fixed bridge and 2 HH Versatek pickups; the **Vector F Classic** (list $1,840) has a Floyd Rose bridge and 2 single coils/humbucker pickup configuration. The **Vector Artist** (list $1,497) has a fixed bridge and 2 single coil/humbucker pickups, while the **Vector Artist Special** substitutes a Point tremolo in place of the fixed bridge, and has a retail list price of $1,680. The **Vector Hammer** model has a similar Floyd Rose tremolo, and features 2 Hammer pickups (list $1,840).

Lacewood Vector Series

These limited edition models are similar to the regular Vector models, but are constructed with solid Australian lacewood. Models include the **Lacewood Versatek** (list $1,160), **Lacewood F Classic** (list $1,490), **Lacewood Artist** (list $1,200), **Lacewood Artist Special** ($1,345), and the **Lacewood Hammer** (list $1,490). Lacewood Vector Transparent gloss finishes are an additional $250, and feature Amber, Cherry, Emerald Green, Royal Blue, and Purple.

ELECTRIC BASS

EP Series

The company also offers a range of bass guitars that feature offset double cutaway contoured bodies, hard maple bodies, Sperzel locking tuners, maple necks. The **EP41 P** has a split P-style pickup (list $1,049), and the **EP41 S** has two 'soapbar' pickups (list $1,245). **EP42** models feature figured wood bodies like curly maple and lacewood; prices range from $1,545 to $1,599.

The EP50 5-String series have a similar construction to the EP40 models, and prices that range from $1,295 (**EP51P**) up to $2,199 (**EP55C**). There is a wide range of bass models and options to choose from. For additional information regarding model specifications and pricing, contact the U.S. Masters directly (see Trademark Index).

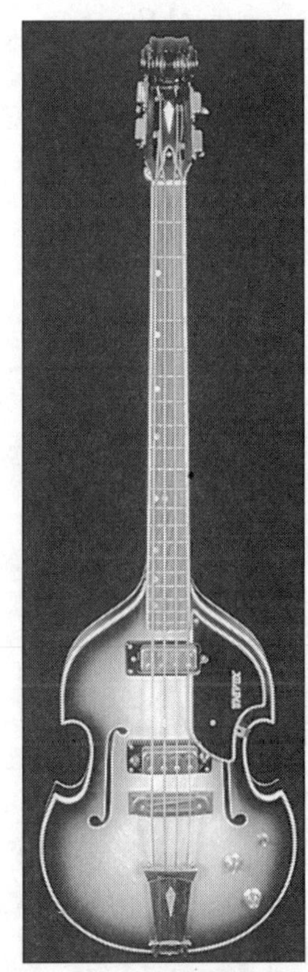

Univox Bass
courtesy Thoroughbred Music

UNICORD

See UNIVOX.

Instruments previously produced in Japan.

The Merson Musical Supply Company of Westbury, New York was the primary importer of Univox guitars. Merson evolved into Unicord, and also became a distributor for Westbury brand guitars.

(Source: Michael Wright, Guitar Stories Volume One)

UNITED

Instruments previously made in Elizabeth, New Jersey during the 1940s.

United guitars was owned by Frank Forcillo, ex-D'Angelico worker and long time friend. D'Angelico put his name on a series of plywood body guitars (Model G-7) that were built at either United or Code (also from New Jersey). The plywood instruments featured solid wood necks fashioned by D'Angelico, but the construction was handled out in the United plant. D'Angelico used to stock these guitars in his showroom/workshop in New York City.

D'Angelicos by United were not numbered or recorded. The body design is perhaps more reminiscent of a Gibson ES-175, and used to carry the designation G 7.

(Source: Paul William Schmidt, Acquired of the Angels)

UNIVOX

Instruments previously built in Japan circa 1969 to 1978. Distributed in the U.S. by the Merson Musical Supply Company of Westbury, New York.

Univox instruments were imported into the U.S. by the Merson Musical Supply Company of Westbury, New York. **Merson Musical Supply** later evolved into the **Unicord** company. The Univox trademark was offered on a full range of acoustic, thinline acoustic/electric hollow body, and solid body electric guitars and basses. The majority of the Univox guitars produced were built by Arai of Japan (See Aria), and are entry level to intermediate quality for players.

(Source: Michael Wright, Guitar Stories Volume One)

Section V

VACCARO

Instruments currently built in Asbury Park, New Jersey. Distributed by the Vaccaro Guitar Company of Asbury Park, New Jersey.

The Vaccaro Guitar Company's debut in 1998 at the music industry NAMM show was one of the most colorful and stylish in years. This new company was formed in April of 1997 to begin producing its vibrant designs and innovative manufacturing techniques. Guitar manufacturing in the United States has been decreasing significantly, and today most of the world's production is done in Korea, Mexico, and Japan. The Vaccaro Guitar company seeks to bring quality guitar building back to America.

The Vaccaro Guitar company was founded by Henry Vaccaro, Sr. (chairman of the board) and Henry Vaccaro, Jr. (president). Henry Vaccaro, Sr. is not new to the guitar industry. Vaccaro, Sr. was one of the original founders of Kramer Music Products, Inc. (KMP), a premier American guitar manufacturing company. Vaccaro, Sr. served as a board member from 1976 to 1982, when he was elected Chairman of KMP's Board of Directors. He successfully guided the company into becoming one of America's largest guitar manufacturers, with sales in 1987 exceeding $15,000,000. Vacarro served as chairman from 1982 to 1988. Vacarro, Sr. was also the founder and president of the Henry V. Vaccarro Corporation, a statewide building construction firm that completed a number of high dollar construction projects. Vaccaro, Sr. dissolved this company when he began testing the prototypes of the new 'V' aluminum neck.

The entire Vaccaro guitar line was conceived by Vaccaro, Jr., stemming from a graphics and fashion background with extensive work in artist management. Vaccaro, Jr. drew from his experience to design a line of stylistic guitars. During the past 5 years, extensive research and testing had been conducted for the development of the Vaccaro 'V' neck that would be featured on all Vaccaro guitars and basses. The stability of the 'V' neck leads to the elimination of frequent adjustments and replacements.

In 1976, Kramer Music Products introduced the patented **Power Forged Aluminum T-Neck** guitar; from 1976 to 1980 total sales were in excess of $6,000,000. In 1981, the aluminum neck was discontinued, as it was too costly to produce compared to the conventional wooden neck. Vacarro, Sr. and luthier Dr. Phillip Petillo re-evaluated the original 1976 aluminum neck while researching the 'V' neck. Part of the problems encountered with the original T-Neck was the heavy weight (21 ounces), high manufacturing costs, and temperature conductibility (the neck would go out of tune under extreme heat or the chill of a cold neck was uncomfortable to guitarists). Vaccaro's new V neck features an aluminum core surrounded by wood (only 2 ounces heavier than a conventional wood neck, which is barely noticeable in a properly balanced body), an Ebanol synthetic fingerboard, and an adjustable truss rod for the desired bow or play in the neck.

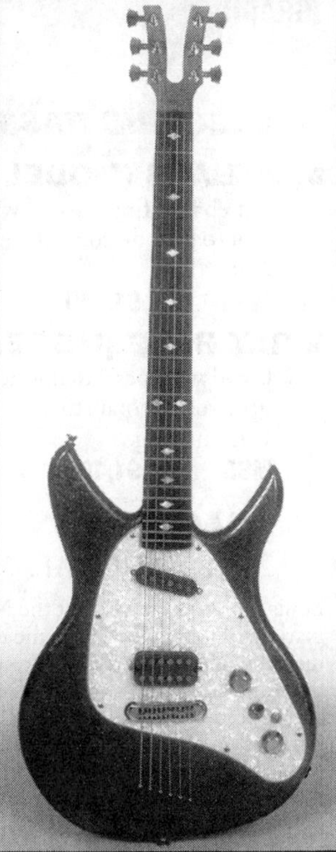

Vaccaro X-Ray
courtesy Henry Vaccaro, Jr.

ELECTRIC

ASTROLITE (MODEL AST) - dual cutaway alder body, bolt-on aluminum/wood 'V' neck, 25 1/2" scale, 22-fret ebanol fingerboard with pearl diamond inlay, Schaller roller saddle bridge/stop tailpiece, 3-per-side tuners, chrome hardware, 2 'soapbar' single coil pickups, volume/tone control, 3-way position toggle switch. Available in Black, Deja Blue, Pepto Pink, Triple Mint, and White finishes. Current Mfg.

MSR $1,349

GENERATOR X (MODEL GX) - offset double cutaway alder body with pointed horns, bolt-on aluminum/wood 'V' neck, 25 1/2" scale, 22-fret ebanol fingerboard with pearl diamond inlay, Schaller roller saddle bridge/Bigsby tremolo, 3-per-side tuners, chrome hardware, 2 single coil/humbucker Rio Grande pickups, volume/tone control, 3-way position toggle switch, 5-way rotary selector. Available in Black, Deja Blue, Fire Burst, Pepto Pink, Orangeade, Retro Burst, and Triple Mint finishes. Current Mfg.

MSR $1,499

GROOVE JET (MODEL GJ) - offset double cutaway alder or mahogany body with pointed horns, bolt-on aluminum/wood 'V' neck, 25 1/2" scale, 22-fret ebanol fingerboard with pearl diamond inlay, Schaller roller saddle bridge/stop tailpiece, 3-per-side tuners, chrome hardware, 2 covered humbucker Seymour Duncan pickups, 2 volume/2 tone control, 3-way position toggle switch. Available in Black, Corduroy, Emerald Stain, Orangeade, Red Glo, Retro Burst, Sapphire Stain, and White finishes. Current Mfg.

MSR $1,349

X-RAY (MODEL XRG) - offset double cutaway alder body, bolt-on aluminum/wood 'V' neck, 25 1/2" scale, 22-fret ebanol fingerboard with pearl diamond inlay, Schaller roller saddle bridge/strings through-body ferrules, 3-per-side tuners, chrome hardware, white pearloid pickguard, single coil/humbucker Rio Grande pickups, volume/tone controls, 3-way position toggle switch, coil tap mini-switch. Available in Black, Blue Sparkle, Green Sparkle, Orange Sparkle, Purple Sparkle, and Red Sparkle finishes. Current Mfg.

MSR $1,399

GRADING	100% MINT	98% NEAR MINT	95% EXC+	90% EXC	80% VG+	70% VG	60% G

ELECTRIC BASS

M-80 BASS (MODEL M-80) - offset double cutaway alder body with pointed horns, bolt-on aluminum/wood 'V' neck, 34" scale, 20-fret ebanol fingerboard with pearl diamond inlay, fixed Schaller bridge, 2-per-side tuners, chrome hardware, P/J-style Basslines pickups, volume/pan/tone controls. Available in Black, Fire Burst, Orangeade, Red Glo, Sapphire Stain, Amber, Emerald Stain, and White finishes. Current Mfg.

MSR $1,549

X-RAY BASS (MODEL XRB) - offset double cutaway alder body, bolt-on aluminum/wood 'V' neck, 34" scale, 20-fret ebanol fingerboard with pearl diamond inlay, fixed Schaller bridge, 2-per-side tuners, chrome hardware, white pearloid pickguard, P/J-style Basslines pickups, volume/pan/tone controls. Available in Black, Blue Sparkle, Green Sparkle, Orange Sparkle, Purple Sparkle, and Red Sparkle finishes. Current Mfg.

MSR $1,499

VALCO

See NATIONAL.

Louis Dopyera bought out the National company, and as he owned more than 50% of the stock in Dobro, "merged" the two companies back together (as National Dobro). In 1936, the decision was made to move the company to Chicago, Illinois. Chicago was a veritable hotbed of mass produced musical instruments during the early to pre-World War II 1900s. Manufacturers like Washburn and Regal had facilities, and major wholesalers and retailers like the Tonk Bros. and Lyon & Healy were based there. Victor Smith, Al Frost, and Louis Dopyera moved their operation to Chicago, and in 1943 formally announced the change to VALCO (the initials of their three first names: V-A-L company). Valco worked on war materials during World War II, and returned to instrument production afterwards. Valco produced the National/Supro/Airline fiberglass body guitars in the 1950s and 1960s, as well as wood-bodied models. In the late 1960s, Valco was absorbed by the Kay company (See KAY). In 1968, Kay/Valco Guitars, Inc. went out of business. Both the National and the Supro trademarks were purchased at the 1969 liquidation auction by Chicago's Strum 'N Drum Music Company.

(Source: Tom Wheeler, American Guitars)

VALLEY ARTS

Instruments currently produced in City of Industry, California since 1993. Previous production was based in North Hollywood, California from 1979 to 1993. Distributed by the Samick Music Corporation of City of Industry, California.

Valley Arts originally began as a North Hollywood teaching studio in 1963. The facilities relocated to Studio City, California and through the years became known as a respected retail store that specialized in professional quality music gear. Production moved back to North Hollywood and into larger facilities in 1989, and luthier/co-owner Michael McGuire directed a staff of 15 employees.

In 1992, the Samick corporation became involved in a joint venture with Valley Arts, and by June of 1993 had acquired full ownership of the company. Samick operates Valley Arts as the custom shop *wing* for the company, as well as utilizing Valley Arts designs for their Samick production guitars built overseas.

All models are available with the following standard finishes, unless otherwise listed: Antique Burst, Antique Natural Burst, AquaMarine Burst, Blue Burst, Blue with Black Burst, Candy Red, Emerald Green, Fire Burst, Green Burst, Green with Black Burst, Green Teen, Kelly Green, Marteen Gold, Midnight Blue, Natural, Orange Teen, Oriental Blue, Purple Teen, Red with Black Burst, Sunset Gold, Transparent Black, Transparent Blue, Transparent Cream, Transparent Green, Transparent Purple, Violet Burst, Watermelon Burst, and White.

ELECTRIC

California Pro Series

CALIFORNIA PRO (Model 7 RS) - 7/8 scale offset double cutaway alder body, bolt-on quartersawn maple neck, 24-fret rosewood fingerboard with abalone inlay, 6-on-a-side tuners, pickguard, gold hardware, stop tail bridge, 2 single coil/humbucker Duncan pickups, volume/tone controls, 5-way selector switch. Available in Antique Burst, Fire Burst, Marteen Gold, Orange Teen, Purple Teen, Transparent Red, and Transparent White transparent finishes; Black, Burgundy, Candy Blue, Candy Red, Hunter Green, and White solid finishes. Current Mfg.

MSR	$1,199	$900	$780	$685	$590	$495	$390	$300

This model is available with a maple fingerboard (Model 7 MS), or with a Wilkinson vintage-style tremolo (Model 7 R; maple fingerboard option is Model 7 M).

California Pro Deluxe (Model Deluxe 7 R) - similar to the California Pro, except has 7/8 scale ash body, Wilkinson vintage-style tremolo, pearloid pickguard. Current Mfg.

MSR	$1,299	$975	$850	$745	$640	$535	$430	$325

This model is available with a maple fingerboard (Model Deluxe 7 M).

California Pro Deluxe (Model Deluxe 8 R) - similar to the California Pro Deluxe (Model Deluxe 7 R), except has full-sized ash body, 22-fret rosewood neck, 3 Duncan single coil pickups. Current Mfg.

MSR	$1,299	$975	$850	$745	$640	$535	$430	$325

This model is available with a maple fingerboard (Model Deluxe 8 M).

California Pro Deluxe T (Model Deluxe 8 R T) - similar to the California Pro Deluxe (Model Deluxe 7 R), except has full-sized ash body, 22-fret rosewood neck, gold tele-style fixed bridge, 2 Duncan single coil pickups. Mfg. 1997 to date.

MSR	$1,299	$975	$850	$745	$640	$535	$430	$325

This model is available with a maple fingerboard (Model Deluxe 8 M T).

GRADING	100% MINT	98% NEAR MINT	95% EXC+	90% EXC	80% VG+	70% VG	60% G

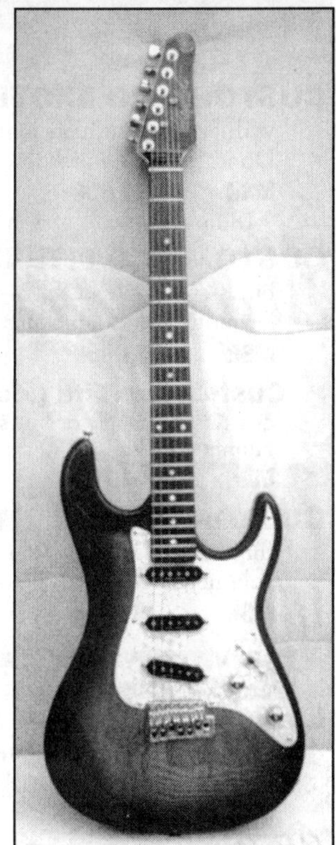

'97 Valley Arts California Pro Deluxe courtesy Bob Dobyne

Custom Pro Series

Both Custom Pro Bent Top and Quilted Maple Top models feature a wide variety of customer-specified options such as pickup configuration, choice of Duncan or EMG pickups, bridge configurations, and finishes.

CUSTOM PRO BENT TOP 'S' (Model C8BS) - offset double cutaway alder body, quilted maple top, bolt-on bird's-eye maple neck, 22-fret ebony fingerboard, 6-on-a-side tuners, gold hardware, volume/tone controls, 5-way selector switch. Current Mfg.

MSR $2,200

Custom Pro Bent Top 'T' (Model C8BT) - similar to the Custom Pro Bent Top 'S', except features a single cutaway body design. Current Mfg.

MSR $2,200

CUSTOM PRO BENT TOP 7/8 'S' (Model C7BS) - similar to the Custom Pro Bent Top 'S', except features a 7/8 scale offset double cutaway body design. Current Mfg.

MSR $2,200

Custom Pro Bent Top 7/8 'T' (Model C7BT) - similar to the Custom Pro Bent Top 'S', except features a 7/8 scale single cutaway body design. Current Mfg.

MSR $2,200

CUSTOM PRO QUILT 'S' (Model C8QS) - offset double cutaway quilted maple body, bolt-on bird's-eye maple neck, 22-fret ebony fingerboard, 6-on-a-side tuners, gold hardware, volume/tone controls, 5-way selector switch. Current Mfg.

MSR $3,100

Custom Pro Quilt 'T' (Model C8QT) - similar to the Custom Pro Quilt 'S', except features a single cutaway body design. Current Mfg.

MSR $3,100

CUSTOM PRO QUILT 7/8 'S' (Model C7QS) - similar to the Custom Pro Quilt 'S', except features a 7/8 scale offset double cutaway body design. Current Mfg.

MSR $3,100

Custom Pro Quilt 7/8 'T' (Model C7QT) - similar to the Custom Pro Quilt 'S', except features a 7/8 scale single cutaway body design. Current Mfg.

MSR $3,100

CUSTOM PRO - offset double cutaway ash body, bolt-on bird's-eye maple neck, 24-fret rosewood fingerboard with pearl dot inlay, double locking vibrato, 6-on-a-side tuners, gold hardware, white or black pickguard, 2 single coil/1 humbucker EMG pickups, volume/tone control, 5-position switch. Available in Burnt Amber, Fireburst, Sunset Gold, Transparent Blue, Transparent Cream, Transparent Green, and Transparent Red finishes. Disc. 1994.

		100%	98%	95%	90%	80%	70%	60%
		$1,200	$1,000	$895	$795	$700	$595	$500

Last MSR was $1,995.

Add $300 for quilted maple body with ebony fingerboard.

STANDARD PRO - offset double cutaway maple body, black pickguard, bolt-on maple neck, 24-fret rosewood fingerboard with pearl dot inlay, double locking vibrato, 6-on-a-side tuners, black or chrome hardware, 2 single coil/1 humbucker EMG pickups, volume/tone control, 5-position switch. Available in Black, Candy Red, Metallic Teal and White finishes. Disc. 1993.

		100%	98%	95%	90%	80%	70%	60%
		$1,200	$1,000	$900	$795	$700	$590	$500

Last MSR was $1,995.

CUSTOM PRO CARVED TOP (Model VACTCP) - offset double cutaway mahogany body, bound flame maple carved top, set-in mahogany/bird's-eye maple neck, 24 3/4" scale, 22-fret bound ebony fingerboard with block inlays, tune-o-matic bridge/stop tailpiece, gold hardware, 2 Seymour Duncan PAF reissue humbuckers, 2 volume/master tone controls, 3-position switch. Mfg. 1997 to date.

		100%	98%	95%	90%	80%	70%	60%
MSR	$3,200	$2,400	$2,080	$1,825	$1,580	$1,315	$1,060	$800

CUSTOM PRO DOUBLE NECK (Model VA12/6BS) - offset double cutaway alder body, quilted top, bolt-on 12-string and 6-string maple necks, 25 1/2" scale, 22-fret ebony fingerboards, chrome hardware; the 12- string neck has a fixed bridge, 3 EMG single coil pickups, volume control, 5-way selector; the 6-string neck has Wilkinson tremolo, 2 single coil/humbucker EMG pickups, volume control, 5-way selector, overall master tone control, 3-way neck selector switch. Mfg. 1997 to date.

		100%	98%	95%	90%	80%	70%	60%
MSR	$4,500	$3,375	$3,000	$2,625	$2,250	$1,875	$1,500	$1,125

GRADING		100% MINT	98% NEAR MINT	95% EXC+	90% EXC	80% VG+	70% VG	60% G

CUSTOM PRO EXOTIC WOOD (Model C7WS41D) - 7/8 scale offset double cutaway walnut body, bolt-on walnut neck with Spanish Luthiers joint, 24-fret ebony fingerboard, Original Floyd Rose tremolo, 6-on-a-side tuners, gold hardware, humbucker/Rail-F Duncan Custom pickups, volume/tone control, 3-position switch. Available in Tung Oil finish. Mfg. 1997 to date.

MSR	$2,200	$1,650	$1,430	$1,255	$1,080	$900	$725	$550

Different species of wood may vary in price.

CUSTOM PRO LITE (Model C7SS25D) - 7/8 scale offset double cutaway swamp ash body, bolt-on (Interlock technology) bird's-eye maple neck, 24-fret ebony fingerboard, Wilkinson vintage tremolo, 6-on-a-side tuners, gold hardware, 2 single coil/humbucker Seymour Duncan pickups, volume/tone control, 5-way switch. Mfg. 1997 to date.

MSR	$1,600	$1,200	$1,040	$915	$785	$660	$530	$400

Custom Pro Lite (Model C7SS41D) - similar to the Custom Pro Lite (Model C7SS25D), except has bolt-on or Interlock neck joint, quartersawn maple or bird's-eye maple neck, rosewood fingerboard, black veneer headstock, Original Floyd Rose tremolo, gold or black hardware, Humbucker/Rail-F Duncan Custom pickups. Mfg. 1997 to date.

MSR	$1,700	$1,275	$1,100	$965	$830	$695	$560	$425

CUSTOM PRO S/L (Model SL8SS22E) - offset double cutaway swamp ash body, bolt-on bird's-eye maple neck, 22-fret ebony fingerboard, Original Floyd Rose vibrato, 6-on-a-side tuners, chrome hardware, black pickguard, 2 single coil/humbucker EMG pickups, volume/tone control, 5-position switch. Available in Fireburst finish (body and neck). Mfg. 1997 to date.

MSR	$1,800	$1,350	$1,170	$1,025	$880	$740	$595	$450

Luthier's Choice Series

LUTHIER'S CHOICE (Model C7-LC) - single cutaway mahogany body, bound carved top, bird's-eye maple neck, 24-fret ebony fingerboard, bound painted headstock, tune-o-matic bridge/stop tailpiece, gold hardware, 2 Duncan P-90 pickups, recessed volume/tone controls, 3-way selector. Available in Antique Burst and Tobacco Sunburst finishes. Current Mfg.

MSR	$2,500	$1,875	$1,625	$1,425	$1,220	$1,015	$825	$625

Luthier's Choice 2 (Model C7-LC2) - similar to the Luthier's Choice, except has herringbone-bound top, 2 single coil/humbucker EMG pickups, 5-way selector. Current Mfg.

MSR	$2,500	$1,875	$1,625	$1,425	$1,220	$1,015	$825	$625

Luthier's Choice Jr. (Model C7-LC/JR) - similar to the Luthier's Choice, except without bound carved top; features mahogany neck, 24-fret rosewood fingerboard, chrome hardware. Mfg. 1997 to date.

MSR	$1,450	$1,100	$945	$830	$715	$600	$480	$365

Master Signature Series

RAY BENSON CUSTOM (Model VARB2) - single cutaway alder body, quilted maple top, maple neck, 25 1/2" scale, 22-fret maple (or rosewood or ebony) fingerboard, 6-on-a-side tuners, fixed bridge, chrome hardware, violin-shaped pearloid pickguard, humbucker/Hot Rail/single coil pickups, volume/tone controls, 5-way selector. Current Mfg.

MSR	$2,200	$1,650	$1,430	$1,255	$1,080	$900	$725	$550

Add $200 for flame maple top.

RAY BENSON CUSTOM TEXAS T (Model VARBTT) - oversized single cutaway alder body, quilted maple top, bird's-eye maple neck, 25 1/2" scale, 22-fret ebony fingerboard, 6-on-a-side tuners, fixed bridge, gold hardware, Texas 'T' or violin-shaped pearloid pickguard, humbucker/Hot Rail/single coil pickups, volume/tone (push/pull) controls, 5-way selector. Current Mfg.

MSR	$2,700	$2,025	$1,755	$1,540	$1,325	$1,100	$890	$675

Add $500 for body and headstock binding.

BLUES SARACENO CUSTOM (Model VABSC) - single rounded cutaway alder body, maple neck, 24 3/4" scale, 24-fret maple or rosewood fingerboard with offset colored position markers, 3-per-side tuners, Floyd Rose tremolo, black hardware, 2 Duncan Trembuckers, volume control, 3-way selector. Current Mfg.

MSR	$1,900	$1,425	$1,235	$1,080	$930	$780	$630	$475

Add $200 for glitter finish.

BLUES SARACENO CUSTOM BENT-TOP (Model VABSCB) - single rounded cutaway alder body, quilted maple top, bird's-eye maple neck, 24 3/4" scale, 24-fret ebony fingerboard with offset abalone position markers, 3-per-side tuners, Floyd Rose tremolo, black hardware, Duncan Trembucker/Duncan 59 humbucker pickups, volume control, 3-way selector. Current Mfg.

MSR	$2,495	$1,870	$1,620	$1,415	$1,225	$1,020	$825	$625

BLUES SARACENO CUSTOM FLAT-TOP (Model VASSH) - single rounded cutaway alder body, quartersawn maple neck, 25 1/2" scale, 22-fret rosewood or maple fingerboard with offset colored position markers, 3-per-side tuners, through-body stringing fixed bridge, black or gold hardware, 2 single coil/1 humbucker pickups, volume control, 5-way selector. Available in all Valley Arts Solid colors plus Berry-cicle, Cherry-cicle, Cream-cicle, Fudge-cicle, Grape-cicle, Lemon-cicle, and Lime-cicle finishes. Current Mfg.

MSR	$1,600	$1,200	$1,040	$915	$785	$660	$530	$400

GRADING			100% MINT	98% NEAR MINT	95% EXC+	90% EXC	80% VG+	70% VG	60% G

STEVE LUKATHER SIGNATURE - offset double cutaway ash body, black pickguard, bolt-on bird's eye maple neck, 24-fret ebony or rosewood fingerboard with pearl dot inlay, double locking vibrato, 6-on-a-side tuners, gold hardware, 2 single coil/1 humbucker EMG pickups, volume/tone control, 5-position switch. Available in Fireburst finish. Disc. 1993.

		$1,245	$1,040	$935	$830	$725	$630	$520

Last MSR was $2,075.

This model was co-designed by Steve Lukather (Toto, Los Lobos) and has his signature on the back of the headstock.

Studio Pro Series

STUDIO PRO (Model SH7SR) - 7/8 scale offset double cutaway hardwood body, bolt-on quartersawn maple neck, 24-fret rosewood fingerboard, 6-on-a-side tuners, black or chrome hardware, vintage-style tremolo, slanted single coil/humbucker Duncan Design pickups, volume/tone controls, 5-way selector switch. Available in Black (BK) or White (WH) finishes. Mfg. 1997 to date.

MSR	$998	$750	$650	$570	$490	$410	$330	$250

Studio Pro (Model HH7TR) - similar to the Studio Pro, except has 7/8 scale single cutaway hardwood body, tune-o-matic bridge, 2 Duncan Design humbuckers. Available in Black (BK) or White (WH) finishes. Current Mfg.

MSR	$998	$750	$650	$570	$490	$410	$330	$250

ELECTRIC BASS

Cal Pro Bass Series

CAL PRO BASS IV (Model BASS IV) - offset double cutaway swamp ash body, bolt-on maple neck, 34" scale, 21-fret rosewood fingerboard, 4-on-a-side Valley Arts tuners, gold hardware, Wilkinson WBB-4 fixed bridge, P/J-style pickups, volume/tone controls. Available in Antique Burst, Fire Burst, Marteen Gold, Orange Teen, Purple Teen, Transparent Red, and Transparent White finishes. Current Mfg.

MSR	$1,399	$1,050	$900	$790	$680	$570	$460	$350

Add $275 for 2TEK bridge.

Cal Pro Bass V (Model BASS V) - similar to the Cal Pro Bass IV, except has 5-string configuration, Wilkinson WBB-5 bridge. Current Mfg.

MSR	$1,499	$1,125	$975	$855	$735	$615	$495	$375

Add $275 for 2TEK bridge.

Custom Pro Bass Series

CUSTOM BASS (Model SKCB) - offset double cutaway mahogany body, bolt-on bird's-eye maple neck, 34" scale, 21-fret ebony fingerboard, fixed bridge, 4-on-a-side tuners, gold hardware, double P-style pickups, volume/tone controls. Current Mfg.

MSR	$1,500	$1,125	$975	$855	$735	$615	$495	$375

CUSTOM BENT BASS (Model BBT) - offset double cutaway alder body, quilted maple top, bolt-on bird's- eye maple neck, 34" scale, 21-fret ebony fingerboard, fixed bridge, 4-on-a-side tuners, gold hardware, P/J-style EMG pickups, volume/tone controls. Current Mfg.

MSR	$2,000	$1,500	$1,300	$1,140	$980	$820	$660	$500

Add $275 for 2TEK bridge.

This model is also available in a 5-string configuration.

CUSTOM QUILT BASS (Model BQB) - offset double cutaway carved herringbone bound quilted maple body, bolt-on bird's-eye maple neck, 34" scale, 21-fret ebony fingerboard with pearl dot inlay, fixed bridge, herringbone bound peghead, 4-on-a-side tuners, gold hardware, P/J-style EMG or Bartolini pickups, volume/tone controls. Current Mfg.

MSR	$3,500	$2,625	$2,275	$2,000	$1,715	$1,435	$1,155	$875

Add $275 for 2TEK bridge.

This model is also available in a 5-string configuration. Earlier versions of this model had black hardware, pickup configurations (2 P-style or 2 J-style), rosewood fingerboards, and active electronics as options.

STUDIO PRO (Model SPB-IV) - offset double cutaway hardwood body, bolt-on quartersawn maple neck, 34" scale, 21-fret rosewood fingerboard, 4-on-a-side tuners, black or chrome hardware, Wilkinson bridge, P-style pickup, volume/tone controls. Available in Black (BK) or White (WH) finishes. Mfg. 1997 to date.

MSR	$998	$750	$650	$570	$490	$410	$330	$250

GRADING	100% MINT	98% NEAR MINT	95% EXC+	90% EXC	80% VG+	70% VG	60% G

VANTAGE

Instruments currently produced in Korea. Original production was based in Japan from 1977 to 1990. Distributed by Music Industries Corporation of Floral Park, New York, since 1987.

This trademark was established in Matsumoku, Japan, around 1977. Instruments have been manufactured in Korea since 1990. Vantage offers a wide range of guitars designed for the beginning student to the intermediate player.

ELECTRIC

100 Series

All models in this series have offset double cutaway laminated body, bolt-on maple neck, 24-fret maple fingerboard with offset black dot inlay, standard vibrato, and 6-on-a-side tuners, unless otherwise listed.

111T - chrome hardware, single coil/humbucker pickup, volume/tone control, 3-position switch. Available in Black, Cherry Sunburst, Red and Tobacco Sunburst finishes. Current Mfg.

MSR	$359	$270	$235	$200	$175	$150	$120	$90

Add $10 for left handed version of this model (Model 111T/LH).

118T - chrome hardware, 2 single coil/1 humbucker pickups, volume/2 tone controls, 5-position switch. Available in Black, Cherry Sunburst and Tobacco Sunburst finishes. Current Mfg.

MSR	$330	$250	$215	$190	$165	$140	$115	$85

118DT - double locking vibrato, black hardware, 2 single coil/1 humbucker pickups, volume/2 tone controls, 5-position switch. Available in Gold Granite, Marble Stone, Metallic Black and Red Granite finishes. Current Mfg.

MSR	$459	$345	$300	$260	$225	$190	$150	$115

200 Series

All models in this series have offset double cutaway alder body, bolt-on maple necks, 24-fret maple fingerboard with offset black dot inlay, standard vibrato, 6-on-a-side tuners, black hardware, volume/2 tone controls, 5-position switch.

213T - 3 single coil pickups. Available in Tobacco Sunburst and Transparent Blue finishes. Current Mfg.

$285	$215	$180	$145	$130	$120	$110

Last MSR was $360.

218T - 2 single coil/1 humbucker pickups. Available in Transparent Black, Transparent Blue and Transparent Red finishes. Current Mfg.

$295	$225	$185	$150	$135	$120	$110

Last MSR was $370.

300 Series

This series is the same as the 200 Series, except has rosewood fingerboards.

311T - single coil/humbucker pickup. Available in Metallic Black Cherry and Metallic Blue finishes. Current Mfg.

$300	$225	$190	$150	$135	$120	$110

Last MSR was $380.

320T - humbucker/single coil/humbucker pickups. Available in Metallic Black, Metallic Black Cherry and Pearl White finishes. Current Mfg.

$315	$235	$195	$155	$140	$125	$115

Last MSR was $390.

400 Series

This series is the same as the 300 Series, except has double locking vibrato.

418DT - 2 single coil/1 humbucker pickups. Available in Black Fishnet, Black Sandstone, Metallic Black and Red Sandstone finishes. Current Mfg.

$385	$285	$240	$190	$170	$155	$145

Last MSR was $480.

600 Series

635V - double cutaway semi hollow style nato body, bound body/F-holes, raised black pickguard, nato neck, 22-fret rosewood fingerboard with offset pearl dot inlay, tunomatic/stop tailpiece, 3-per-side tuners, chrome hardware, 2 humbucker pickups, 2 volume/2 tone controls, 3-position switch. Available in Black, Cherry Sunburst and Walnut finishes. Current Mfg.

MSR	$569	$425	$370	$250	$200	$160	$115	$70

Add $40 for gold hardware with Natural finish.

GRADING	100% MINT	98% NEAR MINT	95% EXC+	90% EXC	80% VG+	70% VG	60% G

700 Series

All models in this series have offset double cutaway alder body, bolt-on maple neck, 24-fret rosewood fingerboard with offset pearl dot inlay, double locking vibrato, 6-on-a-side tuners, black hardware, volume/2 tone controls, 5-position switch, unless otherwise noted.

718DT - 2 single coil/1 humbucker pickups, coil tap. Available in Burgundy, Dark Marble Stone, Transparent Black and Transparent Red finishes. Current Mfg.

$400 $300 $250 $200 $180 $165 $150
Last MSR was $500.

720DT - humbucker/single coil/humbucker pickups, coil tap. Available in Dark Marble Stone, Multi-color and Red Granite finishes. Current Mfg.

$440 $330 $275 $220 $200 $180 $165
Last MSR was $550.

728GDT - figured maple top, bound fingerboard, gold hardware, 2 single coil/1 humbucker pickups, coil tap. Available in Antique Violin finish. Current Mfg.

$500 $375 $315 $250 $225 $205 $190
Last MSR was $630.

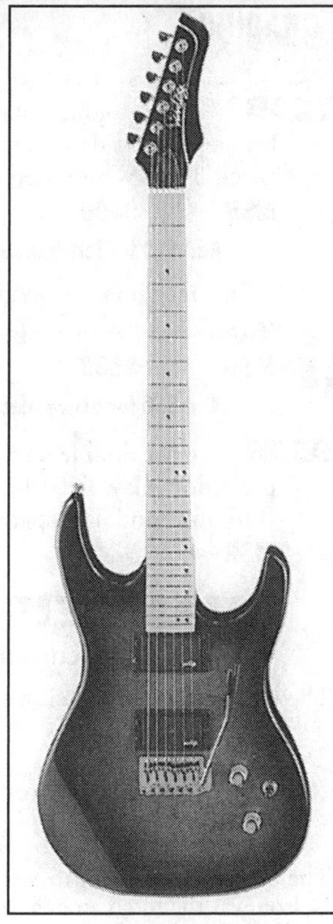

Vantage 115 T
courtesy Vantage

800 Series

All models in this series have offset double cutaway alder body, bound figured maple top, bolt-on maple neck, bound rosewood fingerboard with offset pearl dot inlay, double locking vibrato, body matching bound peghead, 6-on-a-side tuners, volume/2 tone controls, 5-position switch.

818DT - black hardware, 2 single coil/1 humbucker pickups, coil tap. Available in Transparent Black, Transparent Blue and Transparent Red finishes. Current Mfg.

$400 $300 $250 $200 $180 $165 $150
Last MSR was $500.

Add $30 for gold hardware (Model 818GDT).

820GDT - gold hardware, humbucker/single coil/humbucker pickups, coil tap. Available in Transparent Blue and Transparent Burgundy finishes. Current Mfg.

$440 $330 $275 $220 $200 $180 $165
Last MSR was $550.

900 Series

928GDT - offset double cutaway ash body, through body 7-piece maple rosewood neck, 24-fret rosewood fingerboard with offset pearl dot inlay, double locking vibrato, 6-on-a-side tuners, gold hardware, 2 single coil/1 humbucker pickups, volume/2 tone controls, 5-position/coil tap switches. Available in Transparent Burgundy finish. Current Mfg.

$680 $510 $425 $340 $305 $280 $255
Last MSR was $850.

ELECTRIC BASS

225B-1 - offset double cutaway alder body, bolt-on maple neck, 20-fret maple fingerboard with offset black dot inlay, fixed bridge, 2-per-side tuners, chrome hardware, P-style pickup, volume/tone control. Available in Black, Dark Blue Sunburst and Red finishes. Current Mfg.

MSR $399 $295 $220 $165 $130 $120 $110 $100

330B - similar to 225B, except has rosewood fingerboard with offset pearl inlay, black hardware, P-style/J-style pickups, 2 volume/1 tone controls. Available in Transparent Black, Transparent Blue and Transparent Red finishes. Current Mfg.

MSR $459 $350 $300 $265 $225 $190 $155 $115

This model is also available with fretless fingerboard.

525B - similar to 330B, except has higher quality bridge. Available in Black Fishnet and Red Granite finishes. Current Mfg.

$335 $250 $210 $170 $150 $135 $125
Last MSR was $420.

Vantage 635 TG
courtesy Vantage

GRADING	100% MINT	98% NEAR MINT	95% EXC+	90% EXC	80% VG+	70% VG	60% G

725B - offset double cutaway asymmetrical alder body, bolt-on maple neck, 24-fret rosewood fingerboard with offset pearl dot inlay, fixed bridge, 2-per-side tuners, black hardware, P-style/J-style pickups, 2 volume/2 tone controls. Available in Black, Dark Marble Stone, Metallic Black, Pearl White, Red and Transparent Red finishes. Current Mfg.

MSR	$499	$375	$325	$285	$245	$200	$150	$125

Add $20 for left-handed version (Model 725B-LH).

This model is also available with fretless fingerboard.

750B - similar to 725B, except has 5-strings, 3/2-per-side tuners. Available in Blue Marble Stone and Pearl White finishes.

MSR	$539	$400	$350	$300	$265	$225	$175	$135

Add $50 for active electronics.

930B - offset double cutaway asymmetrical ash body, through body 7-piece maple/rosewood neck, 24-fret rosewood fingerboard with offset pearl dot inlay, fixed bridge, 2-per-side tuners, gold hardware, P-style/J-style pickups, 2 volume/2 tone controls. Available in Transparent Burgundy and Transparent Purple finishes. Current Mfg.

MSR	$849	$635	$550	$485	$415	$350	$285	$215

VANTEK

Instruments currently produced in Korea, and distributed by Music Industries Corporation of Floral Park, New York.

These instruments are built with the entry level player or beginning student in mind by Vantage in Korea.

VEGA

Instruments currently built in Korea, and distributed by ANTARES.

Historically, Vega guitars were produced in Boston, Massachusetts.

The predessor company to Vega was founded in 1881 by Swedish immigrant Julius Nelson, C. F. Sunderberg, Mr. Swenson, and several other men. Nelson was the foreman of a 20-odd man workforce (which later rose to 130 employees during the 1920s banjo boom). Nelson, and his brother Carl, gradually bought out the other partners, and incorporated in 1903 as Vega (which means 'star'). In 1904, Vega acquired banjo maker A. C. Fairbanks & Company after Fairbanks suffered a fire, and Fairbank's David L. Day became Vega's general manager.

Vega built banjos under the Bacon trademark, named after popular banjo artist Frederick J. Bacon. Bacon set up his own production facility in Connecticut in 1921, and a year later wooed Day away from Vega to become the vice president in the newly reformed **Bacon & Day** company. While this company marketed several models of guitars, they had no facility for building them. It is speculated that the Bacon & Day guitars were built by the Regal company of Chicago, Illinois.

In the mid 1920s Vega began marketing a guitar called the **Vegaphone**. By the early 1930s, Vega started concentrating more on guitar production, and less on banjo making. Vega debuted its Electrovox electric guitar and amplifier in 1936, and a electric volume control foot pedal in 1937. Vega is reported to have built over 40,000 guitars during the 1930s.

In the 1940s, Vega continued to introduce models such as the Duo-Tron and the Supertron; and by 1949 had become both a guitar producer and a guitar wholesaler as it bought bodies built by Harmony. In 1970 Vega was acquired by the C. F. Martin company for its banjo operations. Martin soon folded Vega's guitar production, and applied the trademark to a line of imported guitars. Ten years later, Martin sold the Vega trademark rights to a Korean guitar production company.

(Source: Tom Wheeler, American Guitars)

VEILLETTE GUITARS

Instruments currently built in Woodstock, New York.

Joe Veillette has worked with both Harvey Citron and Stuart Spector as well as doing custom work under his own brand name. Veillette is co-designer with Michael Tobias of the Alvarez Avante series of acoustic guitars, baritones, and basses. Veillette currently is building his own namesake **Mark III Baritone 12-String, Mark VI Baritone 6-String,** and **Mark IV Bass.** Veillette's baritones are used by Steve Miller, Brad Whitford (Aerosmith), Neal Schon, and John Sebastian. For further information, please contact Veillette Guitars directly (see Trademark Index).

Even though Veillette Guitars appear to be acoustic electric instruments, the company refers to them as electric/acoustic, and because of this, these models are included in the *Blue Book of Electric Guitars.*

One of Veillette's new ideas is a Baritone-scale replacement neck that fits a Strat or Tele model's neck pocket. The Deep Six baritone conversion necks is marketed by WD Products.

ELECTRIC

VEILLETTE MK III BARI-12 - 12-string configuration, semi-solid body design, single cutaway poplar body, figured maple top, bolt-on hard rock maple neck, 26 1/16" scale, 24-fret maple fingerboard, zero fret, rosewood bridge, 6-per-side mini Gotoh tuners, chrome hardware, piezo bridge pickup, volume/3-band active EQ controls. Available in Black stain finish. Mfg. 1997-98.

Last MSR was $1,950.

This model was available as a standard tuned 12-string (list price $1,600) with a 24 1/8" scale, and 22-fret fingerboard, in addition to a 6-string baritone (last MSR was $1,750). Other options included different colors and finishes, fingerboard materials, and a left-handed configuration.

VEILLETTE MK IV 6/12-STRING - 6/12-string configuration, standard tuned, the most recent design evolution. New 1999.

MSR $1,750

Add $150 for 12-string.

VEILLETTE MK IV BARITONE 6/12-STRING - similar to the Mk IV, except features a 6/12-string baritone configuration, 3-per-side tuners. Available in Black stain finish. Mfg. 1998 to date.

MSR $1,750

Add $200 for 12-string (new 1999).

VEILLETTE MK IV 7-STRING - 7-string instrument with 26.1 in. scale length, features System 500 Alvarez piezo preamp combo. New 1999.

MSR $2,050

ELECTRIC BASS

VEILLETTE MK IV BASS - semi-solid body design, single cutaway poplar body, figured maple top, bolt-on hard rock maple neck, 34" scale, 20-fret maple (or rosewood) fingerboard, zero fret, 2-per-side Gotoh tuners, rosewood bridge, chrome hardware, piezo bridge pickup, volume/3-band active EQ controls. Available in Black stain finish. Mfg. 1997 to date.

MSR $1,850

Add $150 for 5-string.

Add $300 for 6-string.

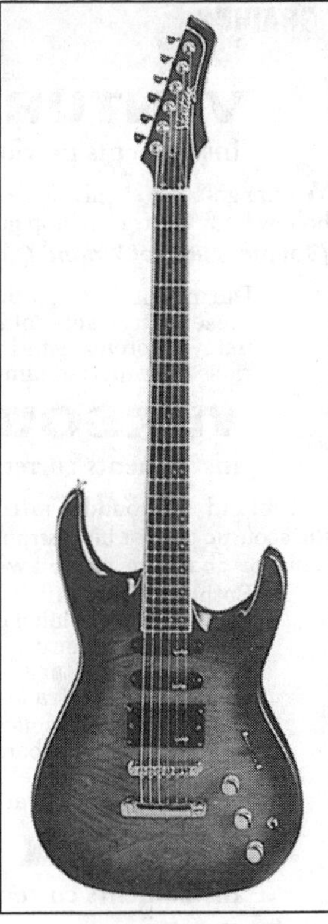

Vantage 728 G
courtesy Vantage

VEILLETTE-CITRON

Instruments previously built in Brooklyn and Kingston, New York from 1976 to 1983.

The Veillette-Citron company was founded in 1975 by namesakes Joe Veillette and Harvey Citron. Rather than copy the current staus quo, both Veillette and Citron built high quality neck-through guitar and bass models that featured brass hardware and their own pickups. The Veillette-Citron company made their official debut at the 1976 NAMM show, and production followed soon after. Working by themselves, and sometimes joined by a workforce of up to five employees, Veillette-Citron instruments were entirely handcrafted.

After the company closed its doors in 1983, Citron went on to write straightforward, fact-filled columns for *Guitar Player* magazine (also *Bass Player* and *Guitar World*) and produced a 90 minute video tape entitled **Basic Guitar Set-Up and Repair** (Homespun Tapes). Citron also licensed the X-92 'Breakaway' to the Guild company in 1985. Citron debuted a new line of guitars and basses in 1994, which featured both bolt-on and neck-through designs and Citron-designed pickups.

Joe Veillette began performing with the musical group the Phantoms during the 1980s, and returned to guitar building in 1991 when he formed a partnership with Stuart Spector. Veillette reintroduced his Shark Baritone guitar, and later left to start his own shop. In addition to custom built guitars, Veillette has also done some consulting work for other instrument manufacturers.

(Source: Baker Rorick, Vintage Guitar Magazine)

VEKTOR ELECTRIC UPRIGHT

Instruments currently built in Viersen, Germany. Distributed in the U.S. market by R2 Musical of Manhattan, New York, L.A. Bass Exchange of Tarzana, California, and Stein on Vine of Hollywood, California.

In 1969, Sven Henrik Gawron began studying the doublebass at the age of 12. Ten years later he attended the Folkwang-Hochschule Conservatory in Essen, Germany, and participated in several modern jazz foundations. Gawron began seriously studying the repair and restoration of acoustic double basses in 1980, which lead to his opening of **Studio fur Kontrabasse** eight years later as a music shop specializing in doublebasses, pickups, and amplification. Gawron collaborated with M. B. Schulz Design in Dusseldorf in 1992 to develop the prototype of the **Vectorbass**, a slim, modern electric upright bass.

ELECTRIC BASS

The **Vektor Electric Upright** is available in 4- or 5-string configurations, with maple body and ebony fingerboard. The retail list price for the 4-string model is $5,500; the 5-string model is $6,500. The new **Vektor Bassett** has a 36" scale and telescope endpin. Retail list price for the 4-string model is $4,400; the 5-string model is $5,400. For additional information, contact Vektor Germany in care of Sven-Henrk Gawron directly (see Trademark Index).

VELENO

Instruments previously built in St. Petersburg, Florida during the early to mid 1970s.

Designer/guitar teacher John Veleno came up with the idea for an aluminum body guitar in 1967, and began producing them in 1970. It is estimated that only 185 instruments were built: 10 are a travel guitar (based on an idea by B.B. King), one is a bass guitar, and two were specially built for Todd Rungren in 1977 that were shaped like an *ankh*.

Veleno guitars were numbered sequentially in the serialization. Production ran from late 1970 through 1975 (maybe 1976).

(Source: Michael Wright, Vintage Guitar Magazine)

Veleno guitars have an equal horn dual cutaway profile body, and are constructed of two halves of routed aluminum blanks that are later combined together. Finished in gold or chrome plating (some have other anodized colors). The neck is an aluminum/magnesium composite, and the 'V'-shaped peghead was designed by Veleno's wife (the red stone on the headstock is a replica of her birthstone, a ruby).

Vantage 928 G
courtesy Vantage

GRADING	100% MINT	98% NEAR MINT	95% EXC+	90% EXC	80% VG+	70% VG	60% G

VENTURA

Instruments previously produced in Japan circa 1970s.

Ventura guitars were distributed in the U.S. market by C. Bruno & Company of New York, New York. Ventura models were both full body and thinline hollow body electric archtop guitars, and generally medium to good quality versions of popular American models.

(Source: Michael Wright, Guitar Stories Volume One; and Sam Maggio)

During the 1970s, a Barney Kessel Custom-style copy (the model is a V-1400, by the way) had a suggested retail price of $199.50. If one of these guitars gets sold at a big guitar show for $200 to $250, does this mean that the guitar *has appreciated in value* or the retail price of today's Korean semi-hollow body guitars has risen over the past twenty five years? Traditionally, there is a ceiling to how high a price can raise on imported laminate wood semi-hollow body guitars - but who can put a price tag on that intangible "funkiness" factor?

VERSOUL, LTD.

Instruments currently built in Helsinki, Finland since 1994.

Versoul Ltd. was founded in 1994 by Kari Nieminen, who has over 20 years background in guitar making and design. Nieminen combines concern for the acoustic tone of his instruments with his innovative designs to produce a masterful instrument. Nieminen's production is on a limited basis (he estimates about one guitar a week) in his humidity controlled workshop.

Both the handcrafted **Zoel** and **Touco** acoustic models reflect his commitment to excellence. Models are available in Silver label (mahogany body), Gold label (Indian rosewood body), and Platinum label (Honduran rosewood body) configurations. The Zoel model has a squared-shoulder design, with spruce top and reverse headstock. Nieminen is also offering an **Acoustic Sitar Guitar**, which provides instant exotic sitar sound with adjustable bridge piece for each string (and 13 sympathetic strings). The fingerboard is scalloped, and the guitar has an extra long scale length for twanging sound.

One of Nieminen's newest model is the electric solid body **Raya**. This model is constructed out of Finnish alder, with a set-in mahogany neck, and 22-fret ebony fingerboard. The Raya features 2 Versoul single coil pickups, and a reverse headstock. Versoul has also recently released a Caspian electric 12-string Sitar, and a Swan Model semi-acoustic guitar. For further information, please contact luthier Nieminen directly (see Trademark Index).

VESTAX

Instruments currently built in Japan. Distributed by the Vestax Corporation of Fairfield, California.

Vestax offers high quality guitars including one model that echos the classic designs of the 1940s and 1950s, as well as a semi-hollow electric model. The D'Angelico-Vestax **Phil Upchurch** model is a single cutaway *New Yorker*-style acoustic with bound body, 2 bound f-holes, bound headstock, 3-per-side gold tuners, 22-fret bound ebony fingerboard with pearl block inlay, raised rosewood pickguard, adjustable rosewood bridge/'stair step' rosewood tailpiece, floating humbucker pickup. Vestax's **Superior Limited Series** semi-hollow **GV-98** looks like a double cutaway 'Strat' or 'PRS' design, but features hollowed out tone chambers under the flamed maple top. The **GV-98** has a Wilkinson VSVG (GG) tremolo bridge, 2 single coil/humbucker pickups, and 22-fret fingerboard. For further information, please contact Vestax directly (see Trademark Index).

VESTER

Instruments previously built in Korea during the early 1990s. Distributed in the U.S. market by Midco International of Effingham, Illinois.

The Vester trademark was established in 1990 by Midco International, and widely distributed these solid body guitars that were designed for the entry level beginner to the intermediate guitarist. Midco discontinued the Vester trademark in 1994 in favor of their popular **LOTUS** line of guitars.

ELECTRIC

JAR 1370 - offset double cutaway carved alder body, bolt-on maple neck, 24-fret rosewood fingerboard with pearl shark tooth inlay, double locking vibrato, 6-on-a-side Gotoh tuners, black hardware, 2 single coil/1 humbucker alnico pickups, volume/tone/preamp controls, 5-position switch. Available in Metallic Ice Blue, Metallic Red and Pearl White finishes. Disc. 1994.

$420	$360	$300	$240	$215	$195	$180

Last MSR was $600.

JAR 1380 - offset double cutaway mahogany body, carved bound figured maple top, bolt-on maple neck, 24-fret rosewood fingerboard with mixed shark tooth/dot inlay, block "Vester" inlay at 24th fret, double locking vibrato, 6-on-a-side tuners, black hardware, 2 active humbucker pickups, volume/tone control, 3-position switch. Available in Cherry Burst, Transparent Black and Transparent Green finishes. Disc. 1994.

$490	$420	$350	$280	$250	$230	$210

Last MSR was $700.

JAR 1400 - offset double cutaway alder body, bolt-on maple neck, 22-fret rosewood fingerboard with mixed pearl shark tooth/dot inlay, double locking vibrato, 6-on-a-side Gotoh tuners, black hardware, 2 single coil/1 humbucker pickups, volume/tone control, 5-position and coil tap switches. Available in Fluorescent Yellow, Metallic Dark Blue, Metallic Red and Pearl White finishes. Disc. 1994.

$420	$360	$300	$240	$215	$195	$180

Last MSR was $600.

JAR 1412 - offset double cutaway alder body, bolt-on maple neck, 24-fret rosewood fingerboard with pearl dot inlay, fixed bridge, 12-string headstock, 6-per-side Gotoh tuners, black hardware, 2 humbucker pickups, volume/tone control, 3-position switch. Available in Metallic Dark Blue, Metallic Red and Pearl White finishes. Disc. 1994.

$420	$360	$300	$240	$215	$195	$180

Last MSR was $600.

GRADING	100% MINT	98% NEAR MINT	95% EXC+	90% EXC	80% VG+	70% VG	60% G

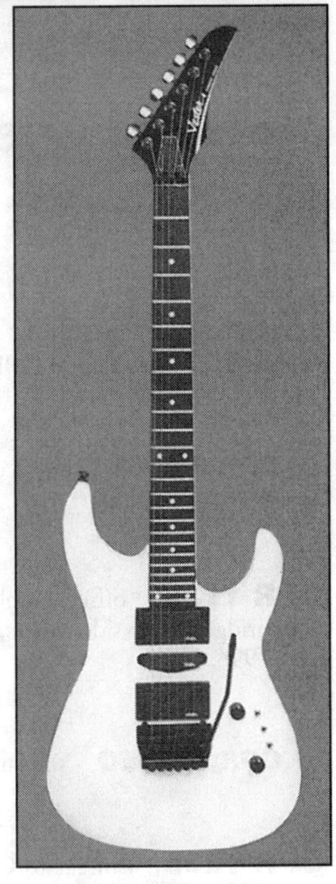

Vester JJR 1050
courtesy Vester

JFA 500 - semi hollow offset double cutaway alder body, bound spruce top, lightning bolt soundhole, maple neck, 22-fret rosewood fingerboard with pearl dot inlay, tunomatic bridge/stop tailpiece, 6-on-a-side tuners, chrome hardware, single coil/humbucker pickups, volume/tone control, 3-position switch, coil split in tone control. Available in Red, Tobacco Sunburst and White finishes. Disc. 1994.

$280 $240 $200 $160 $145 $130 $120
Last MSR was $400.

JJM 1010 - offset double cutaway alder body, black pickguard, bolt-on maple neck, 22-fret maple fingerboard with black dot inlay, standard vibrato, 6-on-a-side tuners, chrome hardware, 2 single coil/1 humbucker pickups, volume/tone control, 5-position switch. Available in Black, Red and White finishes. Disc. 1994.

$210 $180 $150 $120 $110 $100 $90
Last MSR was $300.

JJM 1020 - similar to JJM 1010, except has 24-frets, double locking vibrato, humbucker/single coil/humbucker pickups. Available in Black, Fluorescent Yellow, Red and White finishes. Disc. 1994.

$350 $300 $250 $200 $180 $165 $150
Last MSR was $500.

JJR 550 - offset double cutaway alder body, bolt-on maple neck, 22-fret rosewood fingerboard with pearl dot inlay, double locking vibrato, 6-on-a-side tuners, chrome hardware, single coil/humbucker pickups, volume control, 3-position switch. Available in Blue Green, Metallic Gold and Rubine Red finishes. Disc. 1994.

$235 $200 $170 $135 $125 $115 $105
Last MSR was $340.

Add $30 for Graphic Designs finish.

JJR 1070 - offset double cutaway alder body, bolt-on maple neck, 24-fret rosewood bound fingerboard with pearl inverted V inlay, double locking vibrato, 6-on-a-side tuners, black hardware, humbucker/single coil/humbucker pickups, 3 mini switches. Available in Pearl White finish. Disc. 1994.

$320 $275 $230 $185 $165 $150 $140
Last MSR was $460.

Add $40 for Graphic Designs finish.

JJR 1170 - offset double cutaway alder body, set maple neck, 24-fret rosewood fingerboard with pearl shark tooth inlay, double locking vibrato, 6-on-a-side tuners, black hardware, 2 single coil/1 humbucker alnico pickups, volume/tone and preamp controls, 3 mini switches, active electronics. Available in Black finish. Disc. 1994.

$310 $265 $220 $175 $160 $145 $135
Last MSR was $440.

JJR 1175 - similar to JJR 1170, except has 2 humbucker pickups, no preamp control or mini switches, 5-position switch. Available in Metallic Charcoal Grey and Pearl White finishes. Disc. 1994.

$310 $265 $220 $175 $160 $145 $135
Last MSR was $440.

Subtract $40 for Crackle Blue/Green/Red/Yellow, Crackle Silver/Blue, or Crackle Yellow/Blue finishes.

JJR 1290 - offset double cutaway alder body, bound figured maple top, bolt-on maple neck, 24-fret bound rosewood fingerboard with pearl dot inlay, double locking vibrato, 6-on-a-side Gotoh tuners, black hardware, 2 single coil/1 humbucker pickups, volume/tone control, 5-position switch. Available in Cherry Sunburst, Transparent Blue, Transparent Green and Transparent Red finishes. Disc. 1994.

$330 $280 $235 $190 $170 $155 $140
Last MSR was $470.

Models with the Transparent Red finish have reverse headstocks.

JJR 1462 - doubleneck construction. with one side being similar to JAR 1412 and the other being similar to JJR 1030. Both necks have 22-fret rosewood fingerboards with pearl dot inlay, 3-position neck selector switch included. Available in White finish. Disc. 1994.

$840 $720 $600 $480 $430 $395 $360
Last MSR was $1,200.

OAR 1500 - offset double cutaway asymmetrical mahogany body, carved maple top, set mahogany neck, 24-fret rosewood fingerboard with pearl dot inlay, standard vibrato, 3-per-side Gotoh locking tuners, chrome hardware, 2 humbucker pickups, volume tone control, 3-position and coil split mini switches. Available in Metallic Red, Pearl Blue and Pearl White finishes. Disc. 1994.

$420 $360 $300 $240 $215 $195 $180
Last MSR was $600.

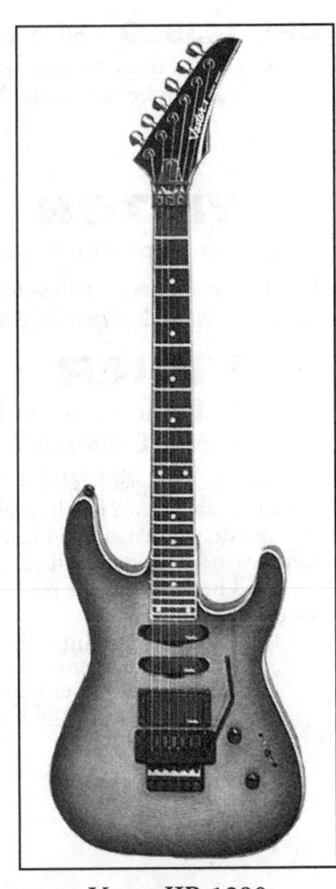

Vester JJR 1290
courtesy Vester

GRADING	100% MINT	98% NEAR MINT	95% EXC+	90% EXC	80% VG+	70% VG	60% G

ELECTRIC BASS

OPR 436 - offset double cutaway asymmetrical maple body, bolt-on maple neck, 24-fret rosewood fingerboard with pearl dot inlay, fixed bridge, 2-per-side tuners, chrome hardware, P-style/J-style pickups, 2 volume/1 tone controls. Available in Black and Metallic Red finishes. Disc. 1994.

$265 $225 $190 $150 $135 $120 $110
Last MSR was $380.

OPR 935 - similar to OPR 436, except has alder body and black hardware. Available in Black, Blue and Metallic Red finishes. Disc. 1994.

$280 $240 $200 $160 $145 $130 $120
Last MSR was $400.

OPR 935EQ - similar to OPR 935, except has volume/treble/bass and mix controls and active electronics. Available in Black and Metallic Red finishes.

$295 $250 $210 $170 $150 $135 $125
Last MSR was $420.

OPR 1135 - offset double cutaway asymmetrical alder body, bolt-on maple neck, 24-fret rosewood fingerboard with pearl dot inlay, fixed bridge, 2-per-side tuners, black hardware, 2 humbucker pickups, 2 volume/1 tone controls. Available in Black and White finishes. Disc. 1994.

$315 $270 $225 $180 $160 $150 $135
Last MSR was $450.

OPR 1135EQ - similar to OPR 1135, except has volume/treble/bass and mix controls and active electronics.

$350 $300 $250 $200 $180 $165 $150
Last MSR was $500.

OPR 1235 - similar to OPR 1135, except has 5-strings, 3/2-per-side tuners, P-style/J-style pickups, 1 volume/2 tone controls, 3-position mini switch. Available in Black and Metallic Red finishes. Disc. 1994.

$350 $300 $250 $200 $180 $165 $150
Last MSR was $500.

OPR 1335EQ - similar to OPR 1235, except has 2 humbucker pickups, volume/treble/bass and mix controls and active electronics. Available in Black and Pearl White finishes. Disc. 1994.

$385 $330 $275 $220 $200 $180 $165
Last MSR was $550.

OPR 1435EQ - offset double cutaway carved alder body, bolt-on 5-piece maple/mahogany neck, 24-fret rosewood fingerboard with pearl dot inlay, fixed bridge, 2-per-side tuners, black hardware, P-style/J-style pickups, volume/treble/bass/mix controls, active electronics. Available in Fluorescent Blue, Metallic Charcoal Grey and Pearl White finishes. Disc. 1994.

$370 $320 $265 $210 $190 $175 $160
Last MSR was $530.

VICTOR

See chapter on House Brands.

This trademark has been identified as a "House Brand" of the RCA Victor Record Stores.
(Source: Willie G. Moseley, Stellas & Stratocasters)

VIGIER

Instruments currently produced in Evry, France since 1980. Distributed in the U.S. by Players International of San Dimas, California.

Luthier Patrice Vigier has been offering high quality solid body instruments since the early 1980s, and features advanced original designs. Vigier guitars and basses are known for the high technology used in their design process. For example, the **Nautilus** model bass that debuted in 1983 had an on board circuitry design that allowed instant access to 19 pre-programmed control settings that were stored by the player. In 1997, Vigier celebrated 10 years that they have been producing their **10/90 Neck**. This neck is composed of 10% carbon graphite, 90% wood; the graphite is used to stabilize and strengthen the wood neck. In just the past few years, a number of the guitar manufacturers in the guitar and bass building industry adopted graphite for the same reason.

In 1980, Vigier introduced the Delta Metal fingerboard. This fingerboard was made from a unique alloy, produced sustain comparable to fretted instruments, was rich in harmonics, featured a uniform hard surface that stayed even (no dips or valleys), and was certainly visually exciting. Vigier has re-issued the *Delta Metal* fingerboard in 1998 as an option on models like the Passion and Arpege. Models like the Excalibur guitar and Excess bass with the *Delta Metal* fingerboard will be called the Surfreter.

GRADING	100% MINT	98% NEAR MINT	95% EXC+	90% EXC	80% VG+	70% VG	60% G

ELECTRIC

ARPEGE III (Model V6ECVC) - offset double cutaway asymmetrical flame maple body, through body maple neck, 22-fret Phenowood fingerboard, double locking vibrato, 3-per-side tuners, black hardware, 2 humbucker pickups, volume/tone/mix controls, 3-position/memory switches, coil split in volume control. Available in Antique Violin, Ash, Aquatic Blue, Burgundy, Emerald Green, French Kiss, Honey, Night Blue, and Red transparent finishes. Current Mfg.

MSR $4,144 $3,300 $2,700 $2,365 $2,000 $1,695 $1,350 $1,025

EXCALIBUR ORIGINAL (Model VE6-CV3) - offset double cutaway ash body, mirrored pickguard, bolt-on maple neck, 24-fret maple fingerboard with black dot inlay, double locking vibrato, 6-on-a-side Gotoh tuners, chrome hardware, 3 single coil Seymour Duncan pickups, volume/tone control, 5-position switch. Available in Black, Honey, Natural Malt, Ocean Blue and Wine Fire finishes. Current Mfg.

MSR $2,016 $1,615 $1,300 $1,140 $980 $825 $660 $500

Add $85 for 2 single coil/humbucker pickup configuration (Model VE6-CV1).

Add $50 for humbucker pickup configuration (Model VE6-CV2).

Excalibur Custom (Model VE6-CVC3) - similar to Excalibur, except has bound flame maple top, body color matching head stock.

MSR $2,422 $1,800 $1,575 $1,385 $1,190 $1,000 $800 $615

Add $50 for 2 single coil/1 humbucker pickup configuration (Model VE6-CVC2).

Add $75 for humbucker/single coil/humbucker pickup configuration (VE6-CVC1)

PASSION III (Model VP6-CVC) - offset double cutaway asymmetrical alder body, half through body carbon fiber weave neck, 24-fret Phenowood fingerboard, double locking vibrato, pearl logo inlay on peghead, 3-per-side tuners with quick winders, chrome hardware, 2 single coil/1 humbucker Seymour Duncan pickups, push/pull volume control with active electronics switch, 6-position rotary tone control with parametric EQ, 3-position switch. Available in Antique Violin, Black, Burnt Metal, Devil Burnt Metal, Ferrari Red, Flip Flop Blue, Fuschia, Lemon, Natural, Night Blue, Pearl White, Peppermint, Silver Black, Sunburst Grey and Transparent Red finishes. Current Mfg.

MSR $3,462 $2,600 $2,250 $1,975 $1,695 $1,425 $1,140 $865

ELECTRIC BASS

ARPEGE III (Model V4ECC) - offset double cutaway asymmetrical flame maple body, through body maple neck, 21-fret Phenowood fingerboard, fixed bridge, 2-per-side tuners, black hardware, 2 single coil pickups, volume/tone/mix/bypass controls, memory switch. Available in Antique Violin, Ash, Aquatic Blue, Burgundy, Devil Burnt, Emerald Green, French Kiss, Honey, Night Blue, and Red transparent finishes. Current Mfg.

MSR $4,052 $3,250 $2,625 $2,300 $1,975 $1,650 $1,325 $1,025

Add $325 for 5-string version of this model (Model V5ECC).

Add $750 for 6-string version of this model (Model V6ECC).

EXCESS (Model VE4EC) - double offset cutaway alder body, bolt-on half-through carbon fiber weave/maple neck, 24-fret maple or rosewood fingerboard, fixed bridge, 4-on-a-side tuners, chrome hardware, black pickguard, 2 single coil pickups, volume/tone/mix controls. Available in Antique Violin, Ash, Black, Clear Black, Clear Red, Natural Matte, and Ocean Blue finishes. Current Mfg.

MSR $2,144 $1,725 $1,400 $1,225 $1,050 $895 $725 $550

During 1998, this model incorporated the Silencer hum canceling system.

PASSION III (Model VP4ECS) - double offset cutaway asymmetrical alder body, half through carbon fiber weave neck, 21-fret Phenowood fingerboard, fixed bridge, 2-per-side tuners, black hardware, 2 single coil pickups, volume/tone/mix controls, parametric EQ/active electronic switches. Available in Antique Violin, Black, Devil Burnt Metal, Ferrari Red, Flip Flop Blue, Fuschia, Lemon, Natural, Night Blue, Pearl White, Peppermint, Silver Black, Sunburst Grey and Transparent Red finishes. Current Mfg.

MSR $3,258 $2,600 $2,125 $1,865 $1,600 $1,340 $1,075 $815

During 1999, this model incorporated the Silencer hum canceling system.

Passion III Custom (Model VP4-ECC) - similar to Passion III, except has flame maple body, chrome hardware. Available in Antique Violin, Aquatic Blue, Ash, Burgundy, Devil Burnt, Emerald Green, French Kiss, Honey, Night Blue and Red finishes.

MSR $3,564 $2,850 $2,325 $2,050 $1,755 $1,470 $1,185 $900

Add $325 for 5-string version of this model (Model VP5-ECC).

Add $625 for 6-string version of this model (Model VP6-ECC).

VINTAGE

Instruments currently produced in Asia. Distributed by John Hornby Skewes & Co., Ltd. of Garforth (Leeds), England.

The **Vintage** trademark is the brand name of UK importer John Hornby Skewes & Co., Ltd.

ELECTRIC & ELECTRIC BASS

Vintage electric guitars and bass come in a variety of styles, models, colors, and options. For more information, including prices, availability, and model specifications, please visit the web site or contact the importer directly (see Trademark Index).

VINTIQUE

Instruments currently manufactured in College Park, Maryland.

Vintique manufactures world class handcrafted guitars - the model is the Vintique Export Series guitar. They also manufacture the Vintique Model 5394 Custom guitar. The price is $POR. For more information regarding this trademark, please contact the company directly (see Trademark Index).

VIRTUOSO

Instruments currently built in England since1986.

Custom builder Jerry Flint produces a number of high quality solid body instruments based on classic Fender designs.

(Source: Tony Bacon and Paul Day, The Guru's Guitar Guide)

VISION

Instruments previously produced in Japan during the late 1980s.

These medium to good quality solid body guitars featured a design based on the classic Stratocaster.

(Source: Tony Bacon and Paul Day, The Guru's Guitar Guide)

VIVI-TONE

Instruments previously built in Kalamazoo, Michigan circa early 1930s.

After pioneering such high quality instruments for Gibson in the 1920s (such as the F-5 Mandolin), Designer/engineer/builder Lloyd Loar founded the Vivi-Tone company to continue exploring designs too radical for Gibson. It is rumored that Loar designed a form of stand-up bass that was amplified while at Gibson, but this prototype was never developed into a production model.

Loar, along with partners Lewis A. Williams and Walter Moon started Vivi-Tone in 1933. Loar continued building his pioneering designs, such as an acoustic guitar with sound holes in the rear, but failed to find commercial success. However, it is because of his early successes at Gibson that researchers approach the Vivi-tone designs with some wonderment instead of discounting the radical ideas altogether.

(Source: Tom Wheeler, American Guitars)

VLINE

Instruments previously built in France circa early 1980s.

Vline headless-style instruments feature an extremely unusual design, and featured all graphite construction. Vline instruments were offered for a limited time prior to problems concerning international copyrights on the tuning systems (See STEINBERGER). Vline instruments were offered in both guitar and bass configurations. It is estimated that only 100 total instruments were produced. Further research continues for future editions of the ***Blue Book of Electric Guitars.***

(Preliminary research courtesy Jeff Meyer)

VOX

Instruments previously built in England from 1961 to 1964; production was then moved to Italy for the U.S. market from the mid 1960s until 1969 or 1970.

After Italian production ceased, some solid body models were built in Japan during the 1980s.

The Vox company, perhaps better known for its amplifier design, also built fashionable and functional guitars and basses during the 1960s. While the early guitar models produced tended to be entry level instruments based on popular Fender designs, later models expressed an originality that fit in well with the 1960s British "Pop" music explosion.

Thomas Walter Jennings was born in London, England on February 28, 1917. During World War II he saw action with the English Royal Engineers, and received a medical discharge in 1941. By 1944 Jennings had a part-time business dealing in secondhand accordions and other musical instruments, and by 1946 had set up shop. Along with fellow musical acquaintance Derek Underdown, Jennings produced the Univox organ in 1951 and formed the Jennings Organ Company not long after. Based on the success of his organs for several years, Jennings teamed up with engineer Dick Denney to build amplifiers under the Vox trademark. In mid 1958, Jennings reincorporated the company as Jennings Musical Instruments (JMI). When rock 'n roll hit Britain, Vox amps were there.

The first Vox guitars were built in 1960 and introduced in 1961. Early models like the **Stroller** or **Clubman** were entry level instruments based on Fender designs. Quality improved a great deal when Vox brought in necks built by EKO in Recanati, Italy. Tom Jennings then assembled a three engineer design team of Bob Pearson (quality and materials control), Mike Bennett (prototypes), and Ken Wilson (styling design) to develop a more original-looking instrument. The resulting 5-sided Phantom in late 1962 featured a Strat-ish three single coil pickup selection and a Bigsby-derived tremolo. Further **Phantom** models were developed in 1963, as well as the **Mark** series ("teardrop" body shapes). When production moved to Italy in 1964, Vox guitars were built by EKO. Vox also offered a 12-string **Mandoguitar**, and a double cutaway 12-string called the **Bouzouki**. A number of hollowbody models such as the **Lynx**, **Bobcat**, and **Cougar** were made by Crucianelli in Italy during the mid 1960s.

In order to generate funds for the company, Jennings sold a substantial amount of shares to the Royston group in 1964, and later that same year the entire shareholding was acquired. JMI was officially renamed Vox Sound Ltd. Thomas Organ was already supplying JMI for organs in the British market, and was looking for a reciprocal agreement to import Vox amps to the U.S. market. However, Joe Benaron (president of Thomas Organ) was really into transistors, and began *supplementing* the British tube models with solid-state amps developed at Thomas laboratories at Sepulveda, California.

The Vox line began the slump that befell other corporate-run music instrument producers during the late 1960s and 1970s. Soon Japanese-built models appeared on the market with Voxton on their headstock, including a Les Paul- derived issued in 1970. Later, the Vox name appeared on a series of original

GRADING	100% MINT	98% NEAR MINT	95% EXC+	90% EXC	80% VG+	70% VG	60% G

design solid body guitars (24 series, 25 series, **White Shadows**) during the early to mid 1980s.These were produced by Aria Pro in Japan. Distribution in the U.S. during this time period was through the Pennino Music Company of Westminster, California; and Allstate Music Supply Corporation of Greensboro, North Carolina.

The Vox trademark was later purchased by the Korg company (Korg USA in the American Market). Korg USA distributes Korg synthesizers, Marshall Amplifiers, Parker guitars, and the new line of Vox amplifiers in the U.S. market. In 1998, Korg/Vox debuted 5 "new" electric guitar models which feature designs based on previous Vox models.

(The Editor wishes to thank Mr. Jim Rhoads of Rhoads Music for his assistance in upgrading this section. For even more information regarding Vox instruments, visit his website at http://members.aol.com/rhoads-musi/store.html and the associated site www.voxshowroom.com.)

Vox's new models include the Mark III model VM3B with Bigsby tremolo (list $1,400), the Mark III model VM3F with fixed tailpiece (list $1,200), the Mark III model VM3CFWD with fixed tailpiece, chrome pickguard, and matching finish headstock (list $1,300), the Mark VI model VM6V with Bigsby tremolo (list $1,400), and the Mark XII model VMXII 12-string guitar (list $1,400).

Model Name Identification

Identification of Vox instruments is fairly easy, as the model names generally appear on the pickguards. However, there are models and configurations that do need to be doublechecked! Collectible Vox guitars seem to be the models built between 1962 and 1969.

ELECTRIC

In general, the Vox solid body guitars that feature Fender-ish designs (like the Clubman or Stroller) in 80% -90% condition are priced between $200 and $300.

ACE - offset double cutaway body, bolt-on neck, 6-on-a-side headstock, 2 single coil pickups, chrome hardware, volume/2 tone controls, 3-way selector switch. Available in White, Red, and Sunburst finishes. Mfg. 1961 to 1966.

$300 $250 $200 $150 $100 $75 $50

Vox Ace
courtesy Keith Smart

Super Ace - similar to the Ace, except has three single coil pickups. Pickup selector switch mounted on lower treble bout. Mfg. 1961 to 1966.

$350 $300 $250 $200 $150 $100 $75

APACHE - asymmetrical rounded body, 6-on-a-side tuners, 3 single coil pickups, chrome hardware, vibrato bridge, volume/2 tone knobs, pickup selector switch. Mfg. 1961 to 1966.

APOLLO - single florentine cutaway hollow body, 6-on-a-side headstock, 1 single coil pickup with black cover, raised white pickguard, 2 f-holes, chrome hardware, trapeze bridge, volume/tone controls. Features an "E tuner" on/off switch, a Treble/Bass boost on/off switch and control, and Distortion on/off switch and control all mounted on a metal plate on lower body bout. Available in Sunburst or Cherry finishes. Mfg. 1967 to 1968.

$600 $500 $450 $400 $350 $300 $250

BOBCAT - dual cutaway hollow body, 3+3 headstock, 3 single coil pickups, raised white pickguard, 2 f-holes, chrome hardware, roller bridge/tremolo system, 2 volume/2 tone controls, pickup selector switch. Mfg. 1965 to 1967.

$600 $500 $450 $400 $350 $300 $250

BOSSMAN - single cutaway hollow body, rounded treble bout, 6-on-a-side headstock, 1 single coil pickup with black cover, raised white pickguard, 2 f- holes, chrome hardware, trapeze bridge, volume/tone controls. Features an "E tuner" on/off switch, a Treble/Bass boost on/off switch and control, and Distortion on/off switch and control all mounted on a metal plate on lower body bout. Available in Sunburst or Cherry finishes. Mfg. 1967 to 1968.

$600 $500 $450 $400 $350 $300 $250

BULLDOG - offset double cutaway body with beveled ridge along top edge, 3+3 headstock, 3 single coils, chrome hardware, vibrato bridge, volume/2 tone controls, pickup selector switch on lower treble bout. Mfg. 1966 only.

$800 $700 $600 $500 $400 $350 $300

The Bulldog model is a relatively rare solid body electric.

A two pickup variation of the Bulldog became the Invader model in 1967. U.K. catalogs also showed a picture of a 2 pickup Bulldog in 1969, which led some people to believe that this configuration was still available in the later time period.

CHEETAH - dual cutaway hollow body, 6-on-a-side headstock, 2 single coil pickups with chrome covers, raised black pickguard, 2 f-holes, chrome hardware, roller bridge/tremolo system, volume/2 tone controls, pickup selector switch, "E tuner" on/off switch mounted on lower treble bout. "On-board" effects mounted on a metal plate features a Treble/Bass boost on/off switch and control, Distortion on/off switch and control, "Repeat Percussion" (a repeating echo-like function) on/off switch and control. Available in Sunburst or Cherry finishes. Mfg. 1967 to 1968.

$600 $500 $450 $400 $350 $300 $250

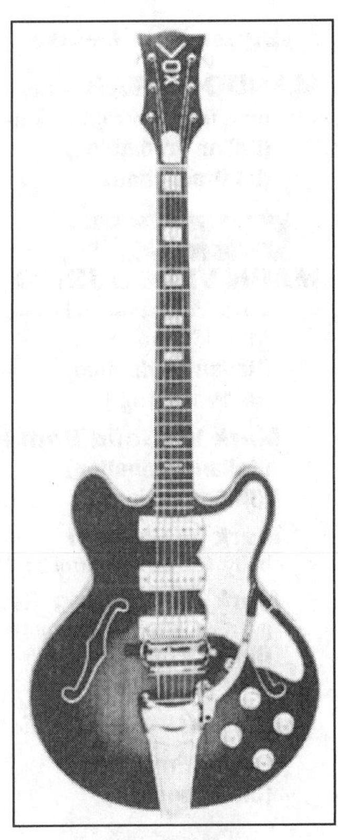

Vox Bobcat
courtesy '60 Vox Catalog

GRADING	100% MINT	98% NEAR MINT	95% EXC+	90% EXC	80% VG+	70% VG	60% G

CLUBMAN - offset double cutaway body, bolt-on neck, 19-fret neck with white dot position markers, 6-on-a-side tuners, chrome hardware, bridge/fixed tailpiece, 2 single coil pickups, 2 volume/1 tone knobs, white pickguard. Available in White or Red finishes. Mfg. 1961 to 1966.

	$300	$250	$200	$150	$100	$75	$50

STROLLER - similar to the Clubman model, except only has one single coil pickup. Available in Red or White finishes. Mfg. 1960 to 1966.

CONSORT (First Series) - similar to the Super Ace, except has smaller rounded off horns, a Bigsby-styled tremolo system, Sycamore neck and rosewood fingerboard. Available in Red or Sunburst finishes. Mfg. 1961 to 1963.

Consort (Second Series) - similar to the Consort (First Series), except has a different Vox vibrato. Mfg. 1963 to 1965.

DELTA - similar to the Phantom model, except has knobs everywhere! Controls mounted on a black pickguard: built-in "E" tuner, distortion booster, treble/bass boost, and "Repeat Percussion". 2 single coil pickups, roller bridge/"Bigsby"-style tremolo. Available in a White finish. Mfg. 1967 to 1968.

	$1,500	$1,350	$1,250	$1,150	$950	$800	$650

GRAND PRIX - single florentine cutaway hollow body, 6-on-a-side headstock, 2 Ferro-Sonic single coil pickups with chrome covers, 21-fret neck with white block inlays, raised black pickguard, 2 f-holes, chrome hardware, roller bridge/tremolo system, hand operated wah-wah control, volume/2 tone controls, pickup selector switch, "E tuner" on/off switch mounted on a small metal plate. "On-board" effects mounted on a metal plate features a Treble/Bass boost on/off switch and control, Distortion on/off switch and control, "Wah Wah" control, and "Repeat Percussion" (a repeating echo-like function) on/off switch and control. Available in Sunburst or Cherry finishes. Mfg. 1967 to 1968.

	$1,500	$1,350	$1,250	$1,150	$950	$800	$650

HARLEM - offset double cutaway body, 6-on-a-side headstock, 2 single coils, chrome hardware, white pickguard, volume/2 tone controls, pickup selector switch located on upper bass bout. Mfg. 1966.

	$500	$400	$350	$300	$250	$200	$150

The fingerboard on the Harlem model is scalloped on the treble side, and straight on the bass side. Retail Price of the Vox Harlem in 1965 was $189!

INVADER - offset Mosrite-styled double cutaway solid body, 6-on-a-side tuners, 22-fret neck with white block inlays, ornate inlaid headstock design, 2 single coil pickups, chrome hardware, Bigsby-styled tremolo, hand operated wah-wah control, 1 volume/2 tone knobs, pickup selector switch, built-in "E" tuner. "On-board" effects mounted on the black pickguard includes a Treble/Bass boost on/off switch and control, Distortion on/off switch and control, "Wah Wah" control, and "Repeat Percussion" (a repeating echo-like function) on/off switch and control. Available in Sunburst finish. Mfg. 1967 to 1968.

	$1,500	$1,300	$1,200	$1,050	$900	$900	$650

LYNX - dual cutaway hollow body, 3+3 headstock, 3 single coil pickups, raised white pickguard, 2 f-holes, chrome hardware, roller bridge/tremolo system, 2 volume/2 tone controls, pickup selector switch. Mfg. 1964 to 1967.

	$600	$500	$400	$300	$250	$200	$100

Super Lynx Deluxe - similar to the Lynx, except has two single coil pickups and black control knobs. Mfg. 1964 to 1967.

MANDOGUITAR - Rounded single cutaway body, 6+6 headstock, octave-sized neck. 2 single coils, chrome hardware, white pickguard, volume/tone controls, pickup selector switch. Mfg. 1964 to 1966

(Italian Production)	$2,500	$2,000	$1,800	$1,600	$1,400	$1,200	$950
(UK Production)	$3,000	$2,700	$2,400	$2,200	$2,000	$1,500	$1,250

Mark Series

MARK VI ACOUSTIC - teardrop shaped semi-hollow body, 6-on-a-side tuners, chrome hardware, roller bridge/tremolo system, f-hole, 3 single coils, raised chrome pickguard, volume/2 tone controls and pickup selector all mounted on metal control plate on lower rear bout. Mfg. 1965 to 1967.

(Italian Production)	$1,000	$800	$700	$600	$500	$400	$300
(UK Production)	$1,500	$1,300	$1,100	$900	$700	$600	$450

Mark VI (Solid Body) - This model was originally called the Phantom MK III. Mfg. 1963 to 1967.

(Italian Production)	$1,000	$800	$700	$600	$500	$400	$300
(UK Production)	$1,500	$1,300	$1,100	$900	$700	$600	$450

Mark VI Special - similar to the Mark VI Acoustic, except has solid body, 6 push buttons mounted on pickguard, controls mounted to the body, and extra control knob near the pickup selector. Mfg. only in the UK. Mfg. 1964 to 1967.

Mark IX (9 String Guitar) - similar to the Mark VI, except has a 3+6 headstock design, 9 strings (3 single bass, 3 pairs treble), white pickguard, volume/2 tone controls, pickup selector switch. Mfg. 1964 to 1967

(Italian Production)	$1,000	$800	$700.	$600	$500	$400	$300
(UK Production)	$1,500	$1,300	$1,100	$900	$700	$600	$450

Mark XII - similar to the Mark IX, except has 6+6 headstock and 12-strings. Mfg. 1964 to 1967

(Italian Production)	$1,000	$800	$700.	$600	$500	$400	$300
(UK Production)	$1,500	$1,300	$1,100	$900	$700	$600	$450

GRADING	100% MINT	98% NEAR MINT	95% EXC+	90% EXC	80% VG+	70% VG	60% G

Phantom (First Series)

The first Phantom series guitars are the first original designs from the Vox company. Some of the other early model solid body guitars introduced prior to 1962 were generally entry level models based on Fender designs.

PHANTOM I - original series solid body electric. Made only in the UK. Mfg. 1962 to 1963.

$2,000	$1,750	$1,500	$1,300	$1,100	$900	$750

Phantom II - similar to the Phantom I, features some variations on the first model. Made only in the UK with Italian necks. Mfg. 1962 to 1963.

$1,500	$1,300	$1,200	$1,100	$1,000	$850	$700

Phantom (Second Series)

PHANTOM VI - 5-sided body, 6-on-a-side "spearpoint" headstock, chrome hardware, roller bridge/tremolo system, 3 single coil pickups, white pickguard, volume/2 tone controls, pickup selector knob. Mfg. 1962 to 1967.

(Italian Production)	$1,000	$800	$700	$600	$500	$400	$300

Phantom XII - similar to the Phantom VI, except has 12-strings. Mfg. 1963 to 1967.

(Italian Production)	$1,000	$800	$700	$600	$500	$400	$300

Phantom XII Stereo - similar to the Phantom XII, except has a stop tailpiece, three split 3+3 single coil pickups, 3 volume/3 tone knobs for bass side pickups mounted on upper forward side of the body, 3 volume/3 tone knobs for treble side pickups mounted on lower rear side of the body, three on/off stereo pickup function selectors, one 5-way pickup selector switch. Mfg. 1966 to 1968.

(Italian Production)	$1,500	$1,300	$1,200	$1,100	$950	$800	$700

Phantom Guitar Organ - similar to the Phantom VI, except has extra tone generating circuitry housed in body, 2 single coil pickups, Organ on/off switch, 3-way pickup selector knob, guitar tone knob, guitar volume knob, organ volume knob, 6 push buttons, octave knob, organ tone knob, flute voice knob, 3 sustain/percussion controls. Mfg. 1966.

(UK Production Only)	$2,000	$1,800	$1,700	$1,600	$1,400	$1,200	$1,000

SHADOW - offset double cutaway body, 6-on-a-side headstock, 3 single coil pickups, chrome hardware, white pickguard, tremolo, squarish tremolo cover has Vox logo on it, volume/2 tone controls, pickup selector knob on lower treble bout. Mfg. 1960 to 1965.

SOUNDCASTER - similar to the Super Ace, except has a mute switch (for introducing "novel banjo effects") built near bridge, and contoured body. Available in Red, White, Blue, and Black finishes. Mfg. 1962 to 1966.

SPITFIRE - offset double cutaway body, 6-on-a-side tuners, chrome hardware, white pickguard, tremolo bridge, 3 single coils, volume/2 tone controls, pickup selector switch located on lower treble bout. Mfg. 1965 to 1967.

$400	$300	$250	$200	$150	$100	$75

Hurricane - similar to the Spitfire, except only has 2 single coil pickups (no mid body pickup). Mfg. 1965 to 1967.

$400	$300	$250	$200	$150	$100	$75

Retail Price of the Vox Hurricane in 1965 was $169.

STARSTREAM - teardrop hollow body, 6-on-a-side headstock, 2 Ferro-Sonic single coil pickups with chrome covers, 21-fret neck with white block inlays, ornate headstock inlays around logo, raised black pickguard, 1 f-hole, chrome hardware, roller bridge/tremolo system, hand operated wah-wah control, volume/2 tone controls, pickup selector switch, "E tuner" on/off switch mounted on a small metal plate. "On-board" effects mounted on a metal plate features a Treble/Bass boost on/off switch and control, Distortion on/off switch and control, "Wah Wah" control, and "Repeat Percussion" (a repeating echo-like function) on/off switch and control. Available in Sunburst and Cherry finishes. Mfg. 1967 to 1968.

$1,500	$1,300	$1,200	$1,000	$800	$700	$550

Starstream XII - similar to the Starstream, except has a 6+6 headstock and 12-string configuration.

TEMPEST XII - offset double cutaway body, 6+6 headstock (12-string), 3 single coil pickups, chrome hardware, tremolo, white pickguard, volume/2 tone controls, pickup selector switch located in lower treble bout. Mfg. 1965 to 1967.

$500	$400	$350	$300	$250	$200	$100

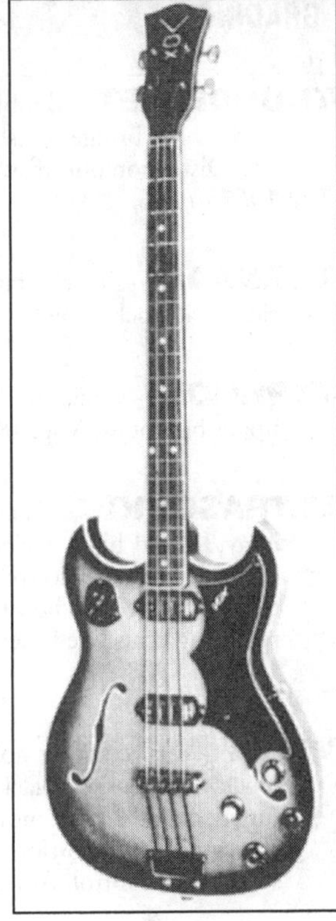

Vox Lynx
courtesy '60 Vox Catalog

Vox Ultrasonic
courtesy Fretware Guitars

GRADING	100% MINT	98% NEAR MINT	95% EXC+	90% EXC	80% VG+	70% VG	60% G

THUNDERJET - double offset cutaway solid body, 22-fret neck with dot inlay, 6-on-a-side tuners, 1 black single coil pickup, chrome hardware, roller bridge/'Bigsby'-styled tremolo system, 1 volume/2 tone knobs, built-in "E" tuner, Treble/Bass boost on/off switch and control and Distortion on/off switch and control. Controls all mounted on a white pickguard. Available in Sunburst, White, or Cherry finishes. Mfg 1967 to 196.

$300 $250 $200 $150 $100 $75 $50

TORNADO - single cutaway semi-hollow body design, 2 f-holes, raised white pickguard, roller bridge/trapeze tailpiece, 3-per-side asymmetrical headstock, 1 pickup (neck position), 1 volume knob and 1 tone knob. Mfg. 1965 to 1967.

$300 $250 $200 $150 100 $75 $50

TYPHOON - similar to the Tornado model, except has a 3+3 headstock, 2 single coil pickups, and the pickup selector switch is located on the upper bass bout. Mfg. 1965 to 1967.

$500 $400 $350 $300 $250 $200 $150

ULTRASONIC - dual cutaway hollow body, 6-on-a-side headstock, 2 single coil pickups with chrome covers, 21-fret neck with white block inlays, raised black pickguard, 2 f-holes, chrome hardware, roller bridge/tremolo system, hand operated wah-wah control, volume/2 tone controls, pickup selector switch, "E tuner" on/off switch mounted on lower treble bout. "On-board" effects mounted on a metal plate features a Treble/Bass boost on/off switch and control, Distortion on/off switch and control, "Wah Wah" control, and "Repeat Percussion" (a repeating echo-like function) on/off switch and control. Available in 6 and 12-string versions. Available in Sunburst or Cherry finishes. Mfg. 1967 to 1968.

$1,500 $1,300 $1,000 $900 $800 $700 $550

VIPER - dual cutaway hollow body, 6-on-a-side headstock, 2 Ferro-Sonic single coil pickups with chrome covers, 21-fret neck with white block inlays, raised black pickguard, 2 f-holes, chrome hardware, trapeze Vox tailpiece, volume/2 tone controls, pickup selector switch, "E tuner" on/off switch mounted on lower treble bout. "On-board" effects mounted on a metal plate features a Treble/Bass boost on/off switch and control, Distortion on/off switch and control, "Wah Wah" control, and "Repeat Percussion" (a repeating echo-like function) on/off switch and control. Available in Sunburst or Cherry finishes. Mfg. 1968.

$600 $500 $400 $300 $250 $200 $150

ELECTRIC BASS

APOLLO IV - single cutaway hollow body, four on a side headstock, 1 single coil pickup, raised white pickguard, 2 f-holes, chrome hardware, roller bridge/trapeze tailpiece, volume/tone controls. "On-board" effects mounted on a metal plate features a "G tuner" on/off switch, Treble/Bass boost on/off switch and control, and Distortion on/off switch and control. Mfg. 1967 to 1968.

$600 $500 $400 $300 $250 $200 $150

ASTRO IV - violin-shaped semi-hollow body, four on a side tuners, 21-fret neck with white dot inlays, 2 single coil pickups, raised black pickguard, trapeze bridge, 1 volume/2 tone knobs, built-in "G" tuner mounted on a small metal plate, pickup selector switch. "On-board" effects mounted on a metal plate features a Treble/Bass boost on/off switch and control, and Distortion on/off switch and control. Mfg. 1967 to 1969.

$600 $500 $400 $300 $250 $200 $150

BASSMASTER - offset double cutaway body, four on a side tuners, 2 single coil pickups, white pickguard, chrome hardware, volume/tone controls. Mfg. 1961 to 1964.

$300 $250 $200 $150 $100 $75 $50

CONSTELLATION IV - teardrop shaped semi-hollow body, four on a side tuners, chrome hardware, fixed bridge, f-hole, 2 chrome covered single coils, raised black pickguard, volume/2 tone controls and pickup selector. "On-board" effects mounted on a metal plate features a "G tuner" on/off switch, Treble/Bass boost on/off switch and control, and Distortion on/off switch and control. Mfg. 1967 to 1968.

$1,500 $1,300 $1,200 $1,100 $1,000 $800 $650

MARK IV - teardrop solid body, four on a side tuners, 2 single coil pickups, fixed bridge, volume/tone controls, pickup selector switch. Mfg. 1965 to 1968.

(Italian Production)	**$1,000**	**$800**	**$700**	**$600**	**$500**	**$400**	**$300**
(UK Production)	**$1,500**	**$1,300**	**$1,200**	**$1,000**	**$900**	**$700**	**$550**

PHANTOM IV - 5-sided body, four on a side tuners, fixed bridge, chrome hardware, white pickguard, 2 single coil pickups, volume/tone controls, pickup selector switch. Mfg. 1965 to 1968.

(Italian Production)	**$1,000**	**$800**	**$700**	**$600**	**$500**	**$400**	**$300**
(UK Production)	**$1,500**	**$1,300**	**$1,200**	**$1,000**	**$900**	**$700**	**$550**

STINGER IV - teardrop shaped semi-hollow body, four on a side tuners, chrome hardware, fixed bridge, f-hole, 2 chrome covered single coils, raised black pickguard, volume/2 tone controls and pickup selector. Mfg. 1968.

$600 $500 $400 $350 $300 $250 $200

GRADING	100% MINT	98% NEAR MINT	95% EXC+	90% EXC	80% VG+	70% VG	60% G

WYMAN BASS - teardrop shaped semi-hollow body, solitary slash f-hole, 2 pickups, 1 volume knob and 1 tone knob, four on a side "spear" headstock. Mfg. 1966 to 1967.

(Italian & UK Production)	**$2,000**	**$1,800**	**$1,600**	**$1,400**	**$1,200**	**$1,000**	**$750**

This model was endorsed by Bill Wyman (Rolling Stones).
A protective snap-on pad was attached to the back of the Wyman bass.

VULCAN

Instruments produced in Korea during the mid 1980s.

Vulcan trademark instruments featured designs based on Fender and Gibson classics. However, these solid body guitars were low to entry level quality, and may appeal to the novice player only.

(Source: Tony Bacon and Paul Day, The Guru's Guitar Guide)

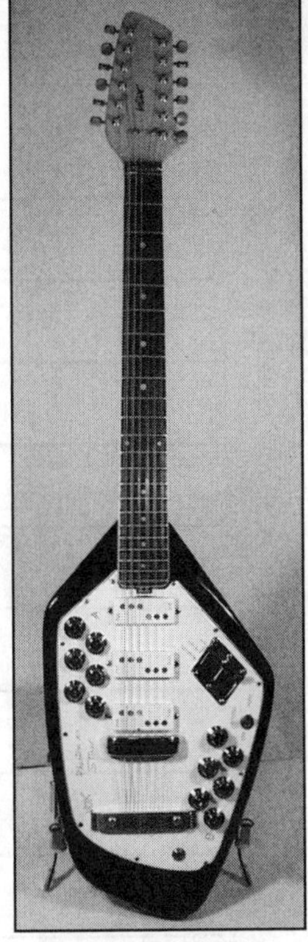

Vox Phantom XII
courtesy Ababue
Vintage

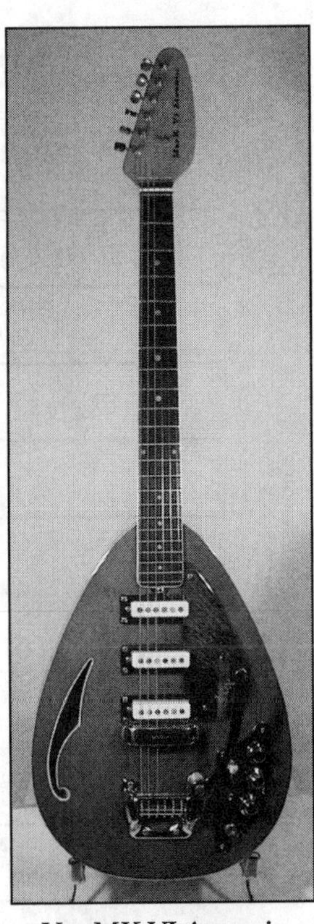

Vox MK VI Acoustic
courtesy Rockohaulix

NOTES

Section W

W

GRADING	100% MINT	98% NEAR MINT	95% EXC+	90% EXC	80% VG+	70% VG	60% G

W. PAUL GUITARS, INC.

Instruments currently built in Waukesha, Wisconsin.

Designer William Paul Jarowsky's objective was to construct a guitar which enhanced the sound quality as well as the playability. Jarowsky developed the patented **Soundport System** electric guitars, which features a contoured semi-hollow body with top soundports hand-sculpted into the hollow chambers between the pickups.

All models feature a through-body neck, and contoured bodies. The **Natural** is the original version of Jarowsky's design, and features a high gloss, satin, or hand-rubbed finish that brings out the grain patterns of the wood. The **Plus** model features a variety of Translucent stains on an all maple or all ash body; the **Ultra** features high gloss solid finishes. Jarowsky's Limited and **Limited** Special models feature selected and exotic woods in their constructions. Currently, the Superior Classic (with elaborate, full length vine inlay) retails for $9,000, including Ameritage case. For additional information regarding wood availability (Timeless Timber wood is sawn from sawmill logs submerged underwater until 1991), and pricing, contact W. Paul Guitars directly (see Trademark Index).

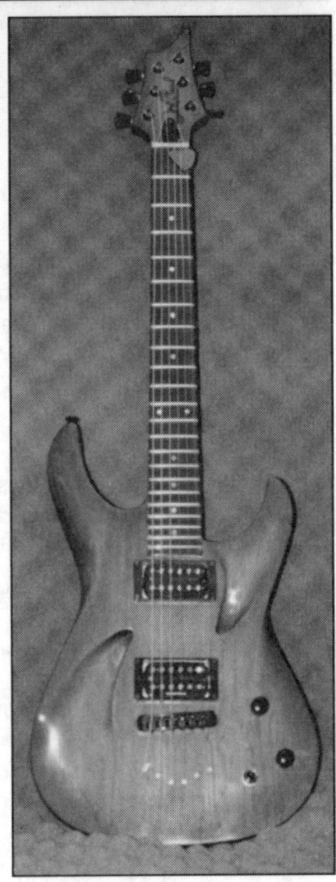

W. Paul Plus (Ash)
courtesy W. Paul Guitars, Inc.

WEM

See WATKINS.

Instruments previously built in England.

W E M (Watkins Electric Music) was the first of two name changes for the Watkins company (1960-1982).

WAL

Instruments currently built by Electric Wood in High Wycombe (Bucks), England since 1978.

In the mid 1970s, Pete Stevens joined London-based repairman Ian Waller to design the Wal Custom bass guitar. In 1978 the two incorporated into the company called Electric Wood, and produced numerous custom basses. Ian Waller later passed away; however, Stevens continues production to date. Wal custom basses are available directly from Electric Wood or through a few selected dealers.

WM GUITARS

Instruments currently built in Santa Fe, New Mexico.

Will Miller and the craftsmen at W M Guitars in Santa Fe are custom building guitar and bass models in the foothills of the Sangre de Cristo mountains. Models are available with set-in or bolt-on necks. Instruments are created with maple, mahogany, wenge, and ebony woods, and feature an oil finish. For further information regarding models and pricing, contact Will Miller at W M Guitars directly (see Trademark Index).

As part of the company's philosophy of ecology, a tree is planted for every instrument the company creates.

WRC GUITARS

Instruments currently built in Calimesa, California since 1990. Distributed by WRC Music International, Inc. of Hemet, California.

After designing guitar models that updated and surpassed their original inspirations, luthier/designer Wayne R. Charvel left his namesake company. Charvel did design one model for Gibson (the US-1) that quite frankly looks like a Charvel Model 6 with "Gibson" on the (Charvel-style) pointy headstock.

In 1989, Wayne Charvel formed a new company that produced guitars under the **Ritz** trademark. Only a handful were built before the logo was changed to **WRC** (Wayne R. Charvel) in 1990. WRC has been producing a number of "one-off" specialty guitars for the past three years. The Neptune Series, which uses seashells as part of the top inlay, was designed in conjunction with current staff member Eric J. Galletta.

WRC Music International also operates the Park Hill Music Studio, a recording studio that has produced a number of recording dates.

ELECTRIC

Classic Series

The Classic series model has the following features optional: standard Wilkinson vibrato, double locking Floyd Rose vibrato, single cutaway body with 2 single coil pickups, volume/tone control, 3-position switch.

WRC CLASSIC - offset double cutaway alder body, bolt-on maple neck, 24-fret rosewood fingerboard with pearl dot inlay, strings through Wilkinson bridge, 3-per-side Grover tuners, chrome hardware, 2 single coil/1 humbucker Kent Armstrong exposed pickups, volume/tone controls, 3 mini switches. Available in Black, Blond, Candy Apple Red, Electric Blue, Seafoam Green, Pearl White, Transparent Blue, Transparent Green, Transparent Tangerine, and White finishes. Mfg. 1994 to date.

MSR	$900	$750	$575	$500	$N/A	$N/A	$N/A	$N/A

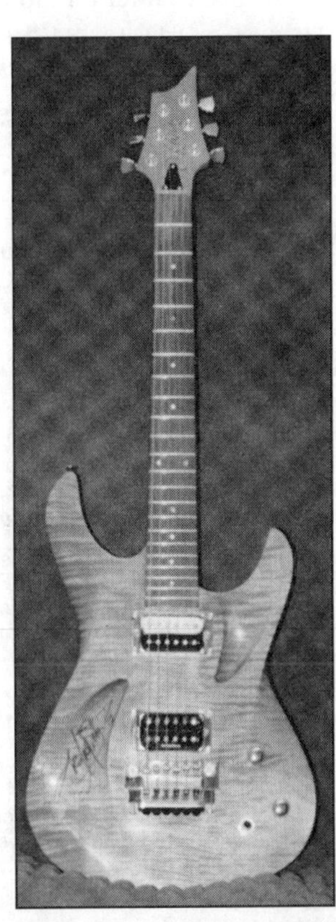

W. Paul Plus (Flame Maple)
courtesy W. Paul Guitars, Inc.

GRADING		100% MINT	98% NEAR MINT	95% EXC+	90% EXC	80% VG+	70% VG	60% G

Exotic Series

The Exotic series model has the following features optional: ebony or maple fingerboards, standard Wilkinson vibrato with locking Gotoh tuners, double locking Floyd Rose vibrato, chrome or gold hardware, single cutaway body with 2 single coil pickups, volume/tone control, 3-position switch.

WRC EXOTIC - offset double cutaway alder body, figured wood top, bolt-on maple neck, 24-fret rosewood fingerboard with pearl dot inlay, strings through Wilkinson bridge, 3-per-side Grover tuners, black hardware, 2 single coil/1 humbucker exposed pickups, volume/tone controls, 3 mini switches. Available in Cherry Burst, Honey Burst, Natural, Tobacco Burst, Transparent Candy Blue, Transparent Candy Green, Transparent Candy Purple, Transparent Candy Red and Transparent Candy Tangerine finishes. Mfg. 1994 to date.

MSR	$1,600	$1,390	$1,250	$1,100	$N/A	$N/A	$N/A	$N/A

Neptune Series

This series, designed by Wayne R.Charvel and Eric J. Galletta, uses Pacific seashells for finish. It is estimated that only 80 Neptune Series models have been built to date. Only the Custom and Deluxe models have the following features optional: standard Wilkinson vibrato with locking Grover tuners or double locking Floyd Rose vibrato, multiple variations of pickup and control configurations.

CUSTOM - offset double cutaway basswood body, bolt-on figured maple neck, 22-fret ebony fingerboard, strings through Wilkinson bridge, 3-per-side Gotoh tuners, gold hardware, 2 Seymour Duncan humbucker pickups, volume/tone controls, 3-position switch. Available in Black Snake, Neptune Avalon, Neptune Gold, Neptune Violet Oyster, Paua, Tiger Cowrie and White Nautilus shell finishes. Current Mfg.

MSR	$3,000	$2,700	$2,400	$2,100	$N/A	$N/A	$N/A	$N/A

This model has the following features optional: 24-fret fingerboard, rosewood or maple fingerboard, abalone or pearl fingerboard inlay, black (or cloud, dolphin, or dot) fingerboard inlay design.

Deluxe - similar to the Custom, except features 24-fret rosewood fingerboard with abalone dot inlay, tune-o-matic bridge/stop tailpiece, black hardware, Seymour Duncan exposed humbucker pickup, volume control. Available in Black Snake, Neptune Avalon, Neptune Violet Oyster and Tiger Cowrie shell finishes. Current Mfg.

MSR	$2,400	$2,100	$1,850	$1,500	$N/A	$N/A	$N/A	$N/A

This model has the following features optional: ebony or maple fingerboard, pearl dot fingerboard inlay, chrome or gold hardware.

Standard - similar to the Custom, except features an alder body, bolt-on maple neck, 24-fret rosewood fingerboard with pearl dot inlay, double locking Floyd Rose vibrato, 3-per-side Grover tuners, chrome hardware. Available in Neptune Avalon shell finish. Current Mfg.

MSR	$2,000	$1,750	$1,500	$1,250	$N/A	$N/A	$N/A	$N/A

This model has standard Wilkinson vibrato with locking Grover tuners as an option.

WABASH

See chapter on House Brands.

This trademark has been identified as a "House Brand" of Wexler.

(Source: Willie G. Moseley, Stellas & Stratocasters)

WANDRE'

See DAVOLI.

See also FRAMEZ.

Instruments previously produced in Italy during the mid 1950s through to the late 1960s. Distributed in the U.S. by Don Noble and Company, and in the U.K. by Jennings Musical Industries, Ltd. (JMI).

Wandre guitars help define where art design and guitar production cross. Designed by Italian motorcycle and guitar appreciator, Wandre' Pelotti (1916-1981) was an artist and sculptor from Milan. Wandre' instruments are oddly shaped thinline hollow body electric or solid body electric guitars with either Framez or Davoli pickups.

Wandre' guitars were personally produced by Pelotti from 1956/1957 to 1960. Between 1960 and 1963, the designs were produced by Framez in Milan, Italy; then by Davoli from 1963 to 1965. Pelotti supervised construction from 1966 to 1969 in his own factory.

Wandre's instruments may bear a number of different brand names, but the Wandre' logo will appear somewhere. Other brand names include Davoli, Framez, JMI, Noble, Avalon, Avanti I, Krundaal, and possibly others.

(Source: Tony Bacon and Paul Day, The Guru's Guitar Guide; and Michael Wright, Vintage Guitar Magazine)

These solid body (and some hollow body) guitars featured aluminum necks (called "Duraluminum") with wood fingerboards, and plastic coverings on the body. Finishes include multi-color or sparkle, as well as linoleum and fiberglass body parts. The **B.B.** model was named in honor of actress Brigitte Bardot. The futuristic body designs of the **Rock Oval, Spazial**, and **Swedenbass** may have some visual appeal, but the level of playing quality isn't as high as the coolness factor may indicate.

WARR

Instruments currently built in Long Beach, California since 1993.

Luthier/designer Mark D.Warr is offering the Touch-style Guitar (Model TSG) instrument that features a conventional body, but can be played in a variety of styles.

Luthier Magnus Krempel is building the Warr Guitar for the European market with permission from Mark Warr. Krempel's Warr models have an additional option of a Wilkinson tremolo system for the four or five high strings (see MAGNUS KREMPEL).

GRADING	100% MINT	98% NEAR MINT	95% EXC+	90% EXC	80% VG+	70% VG	60% G

ELECTRIC

Warr models feature Sperzel locking tuners, Wilkinson bridge, Bartolini stereo pickups, 18-volt active preamp system, and 3- to 5-piece hardwood laminated necks. Prices range from $2,195 (Raptor), $3,390 (Artist with bolt-on neck), to $4,030 (Artist NT with through-body neck design). For additional information, please contact Mark Warr directly (see Trademark Index).

WARRIOR

Instruments currently built in Rossville, Georgia since 1995.

Warrior Annointed Hand Made Instruments is currently offering four high quality custom built bass models that feature bolt-on and neck-through designs, exotic woods, and an innovative "through-body stringing" that corrects the floppy feeling of the low B-string.

ELECTRIC BASS

Warrior's **Standard** model (list $1,950), features bodies with a purpleheart center and mahogany or maple 'wings', a bolt- on neck, figured bookmatched tops, bird's-eye maple or purpleheart fingerboards, Seymour Duncan humbucker pickup, and volume/tone controls.

The **Studio** model has a through-body 3-ply laminated neck with a purpleheart center and choice of mahogany or maple (or wenge or walnut) sides, figured bookmatched tops, wenge, bird's-eye maple or purpleheart fingerboards, and 2 Bartolini or Seymour Duncan pickups (list $2,700).

Both the **Standard Plus** and **Studio Plus** neck-through models are also available in bolt-on neck configurations. These models feature a wide range of figured wood laminated tops and back, and multi-ply necks. The base retail price ranges from $2,900 up to $10,000, depending on the options and wood choices. For further information concerning wood choices and pricing, please contact Warrior Basses directly (see Trademark Index).

WARWICK

Instruments currently produced in Markneukirchen, Germany by Warwick Gmbh & Co., Musicequipment KG since 1982. Distributed exclusively in the U.S. by Dana B. Goods of Santa Barbara, California.

Hans Peter Wilfer, son of Framus' Frederick Wilfer, established the Warwick trademark in 1982 in Erlangen (Bavaria). Wilfer literally grew up in the Framus factories of his father, and learned all aspects of construction and production 'right at the source'. The high quality of Warwick basses quickly gained notice with bass players worldwide.

In 1995, Warwick moved to Markneukirchen (in the Saxon Vogtland) to take advantage of the centuries of instrument-making traditions. Construction of the new plant provided the opportunity to install new state-of-the-art machinery to go with the skilled craftsmen. The Warwick company continues to focus on producing high quality bass guitars; and since 1993, Warwick also offers a full range of bass amplification systems and speaker cabinets.

For information regarding the Warwick **Alien** acoustic bass model, please refer to the 7th *Edition Blue Book of Acoustic Guitars.*

ELECTRIC BASS

An ebony fretless fingerboard is available on all models at no additional charge; the optional ebony fretless fingerboard with inlaid lines costs $210.

The following options are available on all models from Warwick:

Add 15% for left-handed version.

Add $75 for black, chrome, or gold hardware.

Add $125 for dot inlays.

Add $125 for ebony fingerboard on fretted instruments.

Add $125 for a D tuner.

Add $250 for owner's name inlay.

Add $240 for high-polish colors on bolt-on bass models.

Add $400 for high-polish colors on neck-through models.

Add $500 for Bird's eye Maple body upgrade (maple body models only).

Add $650 for LED fret markers.

BUZZARD - offset double cutaway zebrano body, wenge/zebrano neck, 24-fret wenge fingerboard, pearl model name peghead inlay, 4-on-a-side tuners, gold hardware, 2 P-style MEC pickups, volume/treble/mid/bass/mix controls, active electronics. Available in Natural finish. Disc. 1995.

$2,750	**$2,400**	**$2,150**	**$1,850**	**$1,400**	**$1,250**	**$1,100**

Last MSR was $3,900.

This model was designed by John Entwistle (The Who), and is not available with fretless fingerboard.

GRADING	100% MINT	98% NEAR MINT	95% EXC+	90% EXC	80% VG+	70% VG	60% G

W

Corvette Series

Ash bodies and colors are sometimes available on the Corvette Standard models.

CORVETTE PRO LINE - offset double cutaway contoured ash body, 3-piece wenge neck, 24-fret wenge fingerboard, 2-per-side tuners gold hardware, 2 J-style active MEC pickups, 2 volume/1 tone controls. Available in Blue Ocean, Burgundy Red, Honey Violin and Nirvana Black oil finishes. Mfg. 1994 to 1995.

$1,250 $1,000 $850 $675 $600 $550 $500
Last MSR was $1,700.

Corvette Pro Line 5-String - similar to Corvette Pro Line, except has 5 strings, 3/2-per-side tuners. Mfg. 1994 to 1995.

$1,400 $1,250 $1,050 $850 $750 $695 $625
Last MSR was $2,100.

Corvette Pro Line 6-String - similar to Corvette Pro Line, except has 6-strings, 3-per-side tuners. Mfg. 1994 to 1995.

$1,600 $1,350 $1,100 $950 $850 $775 $700
Last MSR was $2,400.

Corvette Limited - similar to Corvette Pro Line, except features a semi-hollowbody design and f-holes. Production was limited to 100 instruments.

There has not been sufficient trading of this model to quote prices.

CORVETTE ALTUS - offset double cutaway contoured ash body, flamed maple top, 3-piece wenge neck, 24-fret wenge fingerboard, 2-per-side tuners, gold hardware, MEC large pole 'soapbar' active pickup, volume/3-band EQ controls, Seymour Duncan Basslines MM electronics. Available in Natural oil finishes. Current Mfg.

MSR $1,499 $1,200 $1,050 $925 $775 $650 $500 $375

Add $125 for Basslines SMB-4A Alnico pickups.

The Altus model features an ash body with flamed maple top separated by a walnut veneer inlay. The fretless fingerboard is ebony.

Corvette Altus 5-String - similar to Corvette Altus, except has 4-piece wenge neck, 5 strings, 3/2-per-side tuners. Current Mfg.

MSR $1,699 $1,350 $1,195 $1,050 $895 $725 $575 $425

Add $125 for Basslines SMB-5A Alnico pickups.

CORVETTE STANDARD - offset double cutaway contoured 2 (or 3) piece bubinga body, bolt-on wenge neck, 24-fret wenge fingerboard, 2-per-side tuners, chrome hardware, 2 J-style passive pickups, 2 volume/1 tone controls. Available in Natural oil finishes. Mfg. 1996 to date.

MSR $999 $725 $550 $475 $395 $350 $275 $250

Corvette Standard (Active) - similar to Corvette Standard, except has 2 active J-style pickups. Mfg. 1996 to date.

MSR $1,299 $1,000 $850 $600 $450 $400 $350 $300

Corvette Standard 5-String - similar to Corvette Standard (Active), except has 5 strings, 3/2-per-side tuners. Mfg. 1996 to date.

MSR $1,499 $1,200 $1,050 $925 $750 $600 $550 $500

Corvette Standard 6-String - similar to Corvette Standard (Active), except has 6-strings, 3-per-side tuners. Mfg. 1996 to date.

MSR $1,699 $1,300 $1,200 $1,000 $895 $825 $750 $700

DOLPHIN PRO I - offset double cutaway asymmetrical boire/rosewood body, half through-body 7-piece wenge/zebrano neck, 24-fret wenge fingerboard with pearl dolphin inlay, 2-per-side tuners, chrome hardware, MEC J-style/humbucker pickups, concentric volume-balance/concentric treble-bass control, MEC active electronics, push/pull electronics switch in volume control, push/pull coil split switch in tone control. Available in Natural oil finish. Current, Mfg.

MSR $3,599 $2,900 $2,500 $2,100 $1,800 $1,425 $N/A $N/A

In 1996, gold hardware replaced chrome.

Dolphin Pro I 5-String - similar to Dolphin Pro I, except has 5 strings, 3/2-per-side tuners. Current, Mfg.

MSR $3,899 $3,100 $2,850 $2,400 $1,900 $1,600 $N/A $N/A

DOLPHIN PRO II - offset double cutaway asymmetrical ash body, bolt-on 3-piece maple neck, 24-fret wenge fingerboard, 2-per-side tuners, chrome hardware, 2 MEC J-style pickups, volume/concentric treble-bass/balance controls, active electronics, push/pull electronics switch in volume control. Available in Black, Black Stain, Blue, Blue Stain, Red Stain and Wine Red finishes. Disc. 1994.

$1,400 $1,200 $1,000 $875 $750 $675 $600
Last MSR was $2,050.

This model had Bartolini or EMG pickups as an option.

Fortress Series

FORTRESS (FORTRESS ONE) - offset double cutaway 3-piece maple body, bolt-on 3-piece wenge neck, 24-fret wenge fingerboard, 2-per-side tuners, chrome hardware, MEC Gold P/J-style active pickups, volume/treble/bass/balance control, active MEC electronics. Available in Black, Blue, Green, Honey, Natural Maple, Red, and Violet satin finishes. Current Mfg.

MSR $1,499 $1,200 $1,050 $875 $650 $600 $550 $500

GRADING		100% MINT	98% NEAR MINT	95% EXC+	90% EXC	80% VG+	70% VG	60% G

Fortress R & B Standard 4-String - similar to Fortress, except has an ash body, and MEC P/J-style passive pickups. Mfg. 1994 to date.

MSR	$1,199	$1,000	$925	$850	$750	$600	$550	$425

Fortress 5 String - similar to Fortress, except has 5 strings, 3/2-per-side tuners, 2 MEC J-style active pickups, active MEC electronics. Mfg. 1994 to date.

MSR	$1,699	$1,350	$1,050	$900	$750	$675	$600	$550

FORTRESS FLASHBACK - offset double cutaway 2 (or 3) piece ash body, bolt-on wenge neck, 24-fret wenge fingerboard, 2-per-side tuners, chrome hardware, celluloid mother-of-pearl pickguard, 2 MEC lipstick tube pickups, passive volume/blend/tone controls. Available in Honey, Natural, and Red finishes. Mfg. 1996 to date.

MSR	$1,499	$1,200	$1,050	$825	$650	$600	$550	$500

Add $200 for 2-Tek bridge upgrade (factory installation).

Fortress Flashback 5 String - similar to Fortress Flashback, except has 5 strings, 3/2-per-side tuners. Mfg. 1996 to date.

MSR	$1,699	$1,350	$1,050	$900	$850	$725	$650	$525

Add $200 for 2-Tek bridge upgrade (factory installation).

FORTRESS MASTERMAN - offset double cutaway 2-piece maple body, bolt-on wenge neck, 24-fret wenge fingerboard, 2-per-side tuners, side dot fret markers, chrome hardware, MEC dual J-style active pickup, volume/blend controls, 2 independent sets of bass/treble controls, 2 preamps. Available in Honey, Natural, and Red finishes. Mfg. 1996 to date.

MSR	$1,699	$1,350	$1,050	$900	$825	$750	$650	$550

Fortress Masterman 5 String - similar to Fortress Masterman, except has 5 strings, 3/2-per-side tuners. Mfg. 1996 to date.

MSR	$1,899	$1,500	$1,350	$1,100	$950	$875	$725	$650

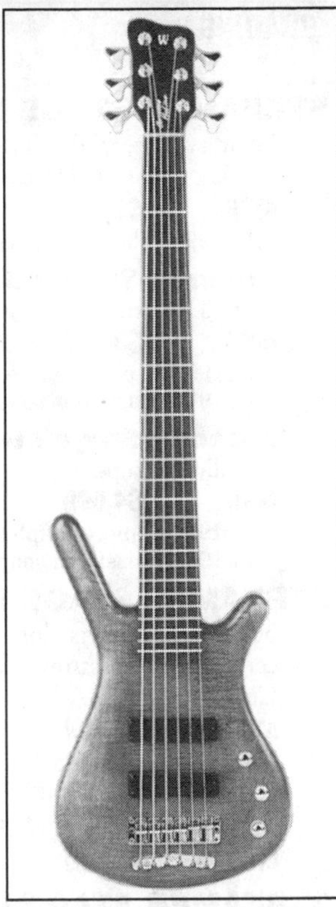

Warwick Corvette Pro
courtesy Warwick

Streamer Series

STREAMER BOLT-ON - offset double cutaway contoured cherry body, bolt-on maple/bubinga neck, 24-fret wenge fingerboard with pearl dot inlay, 2-per-side tuners, chrome hardware, P/J-style active MEC pickups, 2 volume/2 tone controls. Available in Natural finish. Disc. 1996.

		$1,600	$1,250	$1,000	$850	$750	$695	$600

Last MSR was $2,100.

Streamer Bolt-On 5-String - similar to Streamer Bolt-On, except has 5 strings, 3/2-per-side tuners, 2 J-style active MEC pickups. Disc. 1996.

		$1,700	$1,500	$1,300	$1,050	$950	$850	$750

Last MSR was $2,500.

Streamer Bolt-On 6-String - similar to Streamer, except has 6-strings, 7-piece neck, 3-per-side tuners, 2 humbucker active MEC pickups. Mfg. 1994 to 1996.

		$1,800	$1,600	$1,400	$1,150	$1,000	$925	$850

Last MSR was $2,800.

STREAMER LX - offset double cutaway contoured 2-piece flamed maple body, bolt-on wenge neck, 24-fret wenge fingerboard with pearl dot inlay, 2-per-side tuners, chrome hardware, MEC P/J-style active pickups, volume/treble/bass controls, active MEC electronics. Available in High Polish Black, Blue, Green, Honey, Natural Maple, Red, and Violet finishes. Mfg. 1996 to date.

MSR	$1,999	$1,650	$1,425	$1,200	$1,050	$950	$825	$750

Streamer LX 5 String - similar to Streamer LX, except has 5 strings, 3/2-per-side tuners, 2 MEC J-style active pickups. Mfg. 1996 to date.

MSR	$2,199	$1,750	$1,525	$1,300	$1,100	$1,050	$950	$875

Streamer LX 6 String - similar to Streamer LX, except has 6 strings, 3-per-side tuners, 2 Bassline 'soapbar' active pickups. Mfg. 1997 to date.

MSR	$2,399	$1,950	$1,700	$1,500	$1,250	$1,100	$995	$900

STREAMER PRO-M - offset double cutaway contoured 2-piece flamed maple body, bolt-on wenge neck, 24-fret wenge fingerboard, side pearl dot fret markers, 2-per-side Gotoh tuners, brass hardware, MEC dual J-style active pickup, volume/blend controls, separate treble/bass controls, 2 preamp electronics. Available in Black, Blue, Green, Honey, Natural Maple, Red, and Violet satin finishes. Mfg. 1996 to date.

MSR	$1,799	$1,400	$1,150	$1,000	$850	$775	$700	$625

Streamer Pro-M 5 String - similar to Streamer LX, except has 5 strings, 3/2-per-side tuners. Mfg. 1996 to date.

MSR	$1,999	$1,650	$1,425	$1,200	$1,050	$950	$825	$775

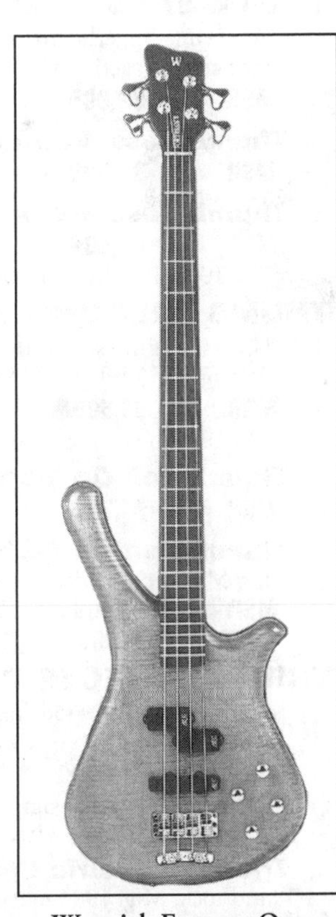

Warwick Fortress One
courtesy Warwick

GRADING	100% MINT	98% NEAR MINT	95% EXC+	90% EXC	80% VG+	70% VG	60% G

STREAMER STAGE I - offset double cutaway contoured maple body, through-body 5-piece maple/bubinga neck, 24-fret wenge finge board with pearl dot inlay, 2-per-side tuners, gold hardware, P/J-style MEC pickups, volume/treble/bass/balance control, active MEC elec tronics, push/pull electronics switch in volume control. Available in Natural finish. Current Mfg.

MSR $2,799 — $2,100 $1,400 $1,325 $1,050 $950 $875 $795

In 1996, Black, Blue, Green, Honey, Natural Maple, Red, and Violet satin finishes were introduced.

Streamer Stage I 5-String - similar to Streamer Stage I, except has 5 strings, 7-piece maple/wenge neck, 3/2-per-side tuners, 2 humbucke Bartolini pickups. Current Mfg.

MSR $3,799 — $2,850 $1,900 $1,850 $1,475 $1,325 $1,200 $1,100

In 1994, 7-piece maple/bubinga neck replaced original parts/design.
In 1996, Basslines soapbar pickups replaced original parts/design.

Streamer Stage I 6-String - similar to Streamer Stage I, except has 6-strings, 7-piece maple/wenge neck, 3-per-side tuners, 2 humbucke Bartolini pickups.

MSR $4,099 — $3,250 $2,550 $2,150 $1,650 $1,350 $1,200 $1,100

In 1994, 7-piece maple/bubinga neck replaced original parts/design.
In 1996, Basslines soapbar pickups replaced original parts/design.

STREAMER STAGE II - offset double cutaway contoured afzelia body, half through 7-piece wenge/afzelia neck, 24-fret ebony finge board with pearl/abalone Tao inlay, abalone W peghead inlay, 2-per-side tuners, gold hardware, 2 MEC J-style active pickups, volume/cor centric treble-bass/mid/balance control, MEC active electronics, push/pull electronics switch in volume control. Available in Natural finish Current Mfg.

MSR $3,399 — $2,750 $2,250 $1,850 $1,650 $1,250 $1,050 $925

This model has Bartolini or EMG pickups as an option.
In 1994, wenge fingerboard replaced original parts/design.

Streamer Stage II 5-String - similar to Streamer Stage II, except has 5 strings, 3/2-per-side tuners. Current Mfg.

MSR $3,699 — $2,925 $2,450 $2,000 $1,850 $1,425 $1,300 $1,100

STREAMER STAGE III - offset double cutaway asymmetrical boire body, half through-body 7-piece wenge/zebrano neck, 24-fret ebon fingerboard with pearl oval inlay, 2-per-side tuners, chrome hardware, 1 single coil/1 humbucker pickups, concentric volume-balance/cor centric treble-bass control, active electronics. Available in Natural finish. Disc. 1990.

$2,500 $2,150 $1,800 $1,450 $1,295 $1,175 $1,100

Last MSR was $3,600.

Thumb Series

THUMB BASS - offset double cutaway asymmetrical contoured 2-piece bubinga body, half through-body 7-piece wenge/bubinga neck, 24 fret wenge fingerboard, 2-per-side tuners, black hardware, 2 MEC Gold J-style pickups, volume/concentric treble-bass/concentric mid-bal ance control, active MEC electronics. Available in Natural oil finish. Current Mfg.

MSR $2,995 — $2,400 $2,100 $1,850 $1,350 $1,150 $950 $875

Thumb Bass 5-String - similar to Thumb Bass, except has 5 strings, 3/2-per-side tuners. Current Mfg.

MSR $3,299 — $2,650 $2,300 $2,000 $1,500 $1,295 $1,100 $950

Thumb Bass 6-String - similar to Thumb Bass, except has 6-strings, 3-per-side tuners, 2 humbucker Bartolini pickups.

MSR $3,599 — $2,895 $2,600 $2,250 $1,800 $1,450 $1,100 $1,000

In 1996, Bassline soapbar pickups replaced the Bartolini humbuckers.

THUMB BOLT ON - offset double cutaway asymmetrical contoured walnut body, bolt-on 3-piece wenge neck, 24-fret wenge fingerboar 2-per-side tuners, chrome hardware, 2 J-style MEC pickups, volume/concentric treble-bass/concentric mid-balance controls, active ME electronics. Available in Natural finish. Mfg. 1994 to date.

MSR $1,599 — $1,250 $1,000 $900 $850 $775 $625 $525

In 1998, black hardware replaced chrome hardware; ovankol body replaced the walnut body.

Thumb Bolt On 5-String - similar to Thumb Bolt On, except has 5 strings, 4-piece wenge neck, 3/2-per-side tuners. Mfg. 1994 to date.

MSR $1,799 — $1,450 $1,150 $1,000 $950 $875 $795 $675

Thumb Bolt On 6-String - similar to Thumb Bolt On, except has 6-strings, 5-piece wenge neck, 3-per-side tuners, 2 humbucker MEC pick ups. Mfg. 1994 to date.

MSR $1,999 — $1,600 $1,400 $1,125 $1,050 $975 $975 $750

In 1996, Bassline Soapbar pickups replaced the MEC humbuckers.

TRIUMPH ELECTRIC UPRIGHT - 3/4 scale (Electric Upright Bass) body, flamed maple body, arched select Bavarian spruce top maple neck, rosewood fingerboard, Rubner satin engraved machine heads, scrolled headstock, Mec quad magnetic pickup/preamp system Mfg. 1996 to date.

MSR $4,999

This model was designed by Hans Peter Wilfer, and was based on a Framus bass designed by his father.
This model comes with a gig bag and stand.

Triumph Electric Upright 5-String - similar to the Triumph Electric Upright, except features 5 string configuration and a 3/2-per-sid headstock. Mfg. 1996 to date.

MSR $5,199

GRADING	100% MINT	98% NEAR MINT	95% EXC+	90% EXC	80% VG+	70% VG	60% G

W

WASHBURN

Instruments currently produced both in Chicago, Illinois and Korea. Distributed by Washburn International, located in Vernon Hills, Illinois.

Historically, Washburn instruments were produced in the Chicago, Illinois area from numerous sources from the late 1800s to 1940s. When the trademark was revived in the 1960s, instruments were produced first in Japan, and then later in Korea.

The Washburn trademark was originated by the Lyon & Healy company of Chicago, Illinois. George Washburn Lyon and Patrick Joseph Healy were chosen by Oliver Ditson, who had formed the Oliver Ditson Company, Inc. in 1835 as a musical publisher. Ditson was a primary force in music merchandising, distribution, and retail sales on the East Coast. In 1864 the Lyon & Healy music store opened for business. The late 1800s found the company ever expanding from retail, to producer, and finally distributor. The Washburn trademark was formally filed for in 1887, and the name applied to quality stringed instruments produced by a manufacturing department of Lyon & Healy.

Lyon & Healy were part of the Chicago musical instrument production conglomerate that produced musical instruments throughout the early and mid 1900s. As in business, if there is demand, a successful business will supply. Due to their early pioneering of mass production, the Washburn facility averaged up to one hundred instruments a day! Lyon & Healy/Washburn were eventually overtaken by the Tonk Bros. company, and the Washburn trademark was eventually discarded.

When the trademark was revived in 1964, the initial production of acoustic guitars came from Japan. Washburn electric guitars were re-introduced to the American market in 1979, and featured U.S. designs on Japanese-built instruments. Production of the entry level models was switched to Korea during the mid to late 1980s. As the company gained a larger foothold in the guitar market, American production was reintroduced in the late 1980s as well. Grover Jackson (ex-Jackson/Charvel) was instrumental in introducing new designs for Washburn for the Chicago series in 1993.

In 1998, Washburn adopted the Buzz Feiten *Tuning System* on the American-produced models. The Buzz Feiten Tuning System is a new 'tempered' tuning system that produces a more "in-tune" guitar.

(Early company history courtesy of John Teagle in his book Washburn: Over One Hundred Years of Fine Stringed Instruments. The actual history is a lot more involved and convoluted than the above outline suggests, and Teagle's book does a fine job of unravelling the narrative)

Washburn HB35
courtesy Washburn

ELECTRIC

Classic Series

HB30 - double cutaway semi hollow style, arched flamed sycamore top, raised black pickguard, bound body/f-holes, flamed sycamore back/sides, maple neck, 20-fret bound rosewood fingerboard with pearl dot inlay, tune-o-matic bridge/stop tailpiece, bound blackface peghead with pearl diamond/W/logo inlay, 3-per-side Grover tuners, chrome hardware, 2 humbucker Washburn pickups, 2 volume/2 tone controls, 3-position switch. Available in Cherry and Tobacco Sunburst & Wine Red finishes. Mfg. 1994 to 1996, 1998 to date.

MSR	$899	$675	$595	$525	$450	$375	$295	$225

Wine red finish discontinued 1999.

HB35 (S) - double cutaway semi hollow style, arched flamed sycamore top, raised black pickguard, bound body/f- holes, flamed sycamore back/sides, maple neck, 20-fret bound rosewood fingerboard with pearl split rectangle inlay, tune-o-matic bridge/stop tailpiece, bound blackface peghead with pearl diamond/W/logo inlay, 3-per-side Grover tuners, gold hardware, 2 humbucker Washburn pickups, 2 volume/2 tone controls, 3-position switch. Available in Natural, Tobacco Sunburst and Wine Red finishes. Current Mfg.

MSR	$1,199	$900	$795	$675	$595	$495	$395	$300

Tobacco Sunburst finish discontinued 1999.

J-6 MONTGOMERY (J-6 S) - single rounded cutaway hollow body, arched spruce top, raised black pickguard, bound body/2 f-holes, maple back/sides, maple neck, 20-fret bound rosewood fingerboard with split rectangle abalone inlay, adjustable tune-o-matic bridge/metal 'W' trapeze tailpiece, bound blackface peghead with abalone diamond/W/logo inlay, 3-per-side Grover tuners, gold hardware, 2 humbucker pickups, 2 volume/2 tone controls, 3-position switch. Available in Natural and Tobacco Sunburst finishes. Current Mfg.

MSR	$1,299	$975	$850	$750	$650	$525	$425	$300

In 1994, flamed sycamore back/sides replaced original parts/design.

J-8 Memphis - similar to the J-6 Montgomery, except features maple top, 2 P-90-style single coil pickups. Available in Black and Natural finishes. Mfg. 1997 to 1999.

$825	$725	$625	$525	$400	$300	$200

Last MSR was $1,099.

Washburn J6 Montgomery
courtesy Washburn

GRADING		100% MINT	98% NEAR MINT	95% EXC+	90% EXC	80% VG+	70% VG	60% G

W

J-9 WASHINGTON - single rounded cutaway hollow body, arched maple top, raised black pickguard, bound body/2 f-holes, maple back/sides, maple neck, 20-fret bound rosewood fingerboard with split rectangle abalone inlay, adjustable tune-o-matic bridge/metal 'W' trapeze tailpiece, bound blackface peghead with abalone diamond/W/logo inlay, 3-per-side Grover tuners, chrome hardware, 2 humbucker pickups, 2 volume/2 tone controls, 3-position switch. Available in Wine Red finish. Mfg. 1997 to date.

MSR	$1,099	$850	$725	$650	$575	$450	$350	$275

Add $50 for gold hardware (Model J-9G Washington). Available in Black and White finishes.

J-9 V G Washington - similar to the J-9 Washington, except features gold hardware, Bigsby tremolo. Available in Black finish. Mfg. 1997 to date.

MSR	$1,199	$925	$775	$675	$575	$450	$350	$250

J-10 - single cutaway hollow style, arched solid spruce top, bound body and f-holes, raised bound tortoise pickguard, flame maple back/sides, multi layer maple neck, 20-fret bound ebony fingerboard with pearl/abalone split rectangle inlay, ebony bridge, trapeze tailpiece, bound peghead with abalone Washburn logo and stylized inlay, 3-per-side pearl button tuners, gold hardware, 2 humbucker pickups, 2 volume/tone controls, 3-position switch. Available in Natural and Tobacco Sunburst finishes. Disc. 1992.

$1,100	$1,000	$900	$725	$650	$595	$550

Last MSR was $1,800.

J-14 REGAL (U.S. Mfg.) - single rounded cutaway hollow body, arched maple top, raised black pickguard, bound body/2 f-holes, maple back/sides, maple neck, 20-fret bound ebony fingerboard with split rectangle abalone inlay, adjustable tune-o-matic bridge/Bigsby tremolo, bound blackface peghead with abalone diamond/W/logo inlay, 3-per-side Grover tuners, chrome hardware, 2 Seymour Duncan humbucker pickups, 2 volume/2 tone controls, 3-position switch & Washburn Reso-Tone Tailpiece. Available in Natural and Transparent Wine Red finishes. Mfg. 1998 to 1999.

$1725	$1525	$1425	$1325	$1200	$1125	$1000

Last MSR was $2,299.

This model features the Buzz Feiten Tuning System.

J-15 Paramount (U.S. Mfg.) - similar to the J-9 Washington, except features adjustable tune-o-matic bridge/metal 'W' trapeze tailpiece, Spruce top & Sycamore back and sides. Lifetime Warranty. Available in Natural and Tobacco Sunburst finishes. Mfg. 1998 to date.

MSR	$2,999	$2250	$1950	$1850	$1750	$1600	$1500	$1300

This model features the Buzz Feiten Tuning System.

WP50 - single cutaway style, carved bound flame maple top, mahogany body/neck, raised white pickguard, 22-fret bound rosewood fingerboard with pearl trapezoid inlay, tune-o-matic bridge/stop tailpiece, 3-per-side pearl button tuners, chrome hardware, 2 humbucker Washburn pickups, 2 volume/tone controls, 3-position switch. Available in Cherry Sunburst and Tobacco Sunburst finishes. Disc. 1992.

$425	$350	$300	$250	$225	$195	$175

Last MSR was $600.

WP80 - similar to WP50, except has carved maple top, black raised pickguard, ebonized fingerboard and gold hardware. Available in Black and White finishes. Disc. 1992.

$475	$400	$350	$275	$225	$200	$175

Last MSR was $680.

WT522 - single cutaway alder body, figured ash top, white pickguard, controls mounted on a metal plate, bolt-on maple neck, 21-fret maple fingerboard with black dot inlay, strings through Wilkinson bridge, 6-on-a-side Grover tuners, chrome hardware, 2 single coil Washburn pickups, volume/tone control. Available in Black, Blonde and Tobacco Sunburst finishes. Mfg. 1994 to 1996.

$375	$300	$250	$200	$175	$150	$125

Last MSR was $500.

Culprit (CP) Series

Culprit Series instruments were the second series of models designed in conjunction with guitarist Dimebag Darrell (Pantera), and were introduced in 1998. The **CP2003** is available in Transparent Bordeaux Red (list $1,099) and Black (list $1,149) finishes.

Dime Series

Dime Series instruments were designed in conjunction with guitarist Dimebag Darrell (Pantera).

DIME3 (U.S. Mfg.) - Flying V with forward treble horn mahogany body, black body binding, set-in mahogany neck, 22-fret rosewood fingerboard with pearl dot inlay, Floyd Rose double locking vibrato, 'V'-shaped peghead, 3-per-side Grover tuners, black hardware, 2 Seymour Duncan humbucker pickups, volume/tone controls, 3-position toggle switch. Available in Dime Slime (Greenish), Dime Bolt (Lightning graphic), and Red Bolt finishes. Current Mfg.

MSR	$2,499	$1,900	$1,500	$1,325	$1,150	$975	$800	$625

This model features the Buzz Feiten Tuning System.

DIME332 - Flying V with forward treble horn alder body, mahogany neck, 22-fret rosewood fingerboard with pearl dot inlay, tune-o-matic bridge/stop tailpiece, 'V'-shaped peghead, 3-per-side Grover tuners, chrome hardware, 2 Washburn humbucker pickups, volume/tone controls, 3-position toggle switch. Available in Black and Red finishes. Mfg. 1998 to date.

MSR	$499	$400	$350	$325	$275	$200	$175	$125

GRADING	100% MINT	98% NEAR MINT	95% EXC+	90% EXC	80% VG+	70% VG	60% G

W

Dime333 - similar to the DIME332, except features a Floyd Rose locking tremolo bridge. Available in BlackJack, DimeSlime Green, and DimeBolt (graphic) finishes. Current Mfg.

MSR $1,129	$850	$675	$595	$525	$450	$375	$295

Falcon Series

FALCON - double cutaway mahogany body, bound carved maple top, through-body mahogany neck, 22-fret bound rosewood fingerboard with brass circle inlay, strings through bridge, bound blackface peghead with screened logo, 3-per-side tuners, chrome hardware, 2 humbucker Washburn pickups, 2 volume/2 tone controls, 3-position switch. Available in Sunburst finish. Mfg. 1980 to 1986.

$250	$175	$150	$125	$100	$90	$75

Falcon Standard - similar to Falcon, except has coil tap switch (in tone controls). Available in Sunburst finish. Mfg. 1980 to 1986.

$300	$200	$175	$150	$125	$100	$85

Falcon Deluxe - similar to Falcon, except has abalone fingerboard inlay, coil tap switch (in tone controls). Available in Sunburst finish. Mfg. 1980 to 1986.

$350	$250	$200	$175	$150	$125	$100

KC Series

KC20 - offset double cutaway hardwood body, arched top and back, scalloped cutaways, bolt-on maple neck, 22-fret rosewood fingerboard with pearl dot inlay, standard vibrato, 6-on-a-side tuners, chrome hardware, 2 single coil/1 humbucker Washburn pickups, volume/tone control, 5-position switch. Available in Black and White finishes. Disc. 1992.

$250	$200	$175	$150	$125	$115	$100

Last MSR was $350.

Add $50 for left-handed configuration (Model KC20 LH).

KC40 - offset double cutaway alder body, arched top and back, bolt-on maple neck, 22-fret rosewood fingerboard with pearl dot inlay, double locking vibrato, 6-on-a-side tuners, chrome hardware, 2 single coil/humbucker Washburn pickups, volume/tone control, 5-position switch. Available in Black and White finishes. Disc. 1992.

$325	$275	$225	$195	$175	$150	$125

Last MSR was $470.

Add $70 for left-handed configuration (Model KC40 LH).

KC42 - similar to KC40, except has reverse peghead. Available in Black, Woodstone Fluorescent Red and Woodstone Fluorescent Yellow finishes. Disc. 1992.

$350	$300	$250	$200	$175	$150	$125

Last MSR was $500.

KC44 - similar to KC40, except has humbucker/single coil/humbucker Washburn pickups. Available in Black Rain and White Rain finishes. Disc. 1992.

$350	$300	$250	$200	$175	$150	$125

Last MSR was $500.

KC70 - similar to KC40, except has black hardware, 3 individual pickup selector and coil tap switches. Available in Black, Metallic Black Cherry, White Rain, Woodstone Brown, Woodstone Red and Woodstone Silver finishes. Disc. 1992.

$450	$395	$325	$250	$225	$200	$175

Last MSR was $650.

Add $100 for left-handed configuration (Model KC70 LH).

KC90 - offset double cutaway alder body, arched top and back, scalloped cutaways, bolt-on maple neck, 24-fret rosewood fingerboard with pearl dot inlay, double locking vibrato, 6-on-a-side tuners, black hardware, 2 Seymour Duncan single coil/1 humbucker pickups, 5-position and coil tap switches. Available in Black, Blond, Metallic Red, Natural Gold, Transparent Red and White. Disc. 1992.

$625	$575	$475	$395	$350	$325	$295

Last MSR was $970.

Laredo Series

All the instruments in this series were hand built in Chicago, and featured Seymour Duncan or Bill Lawrence pickups.

GRADING		100% MINT	98% NEAR MINT	95% EXC+	90% EXC	80% VG+	70% VG	60% G

LT82 - single cutaway alder body, bolt-on maple neck, 22-fret maple fingerboard with black dot inlay, strings through Wilkinson bridge, 6-on-a-side Gotoh tuners, chrome hardware, white pickguard, 2 single coil pickups, volume/tone control, 3-position switch, controls mounted on a metal plate. Available in Black, Natural, Transparent Blue, Transparent Red, Tobacco Sunburst, and Vintage Sunburst finishes. Mfg. 1992 to 1996.

		$600	$475	$400	$325	$295	$250	$225

Last MSR was $800.

This model was optional with an ash body, pearloid pickguard, abalone dot fingerboard inlay, or a rosewood fingerboard with pearl dot inlay.

LT92 - similar to LT82, except features an ash body, pearloid pickguard. Available in Natural and Tobacco Sunburst finishes. Disc. 1996.

		$775	$600	$500	$400	$350	$300	$250

Last MSR was $1,000.

This model has rosewood fingerboard with pearl dot inlay as an option.

Magnum Series

MR250 - single Florentine cutaway semi-hollow mahogany body, 2 small f-holes (near bridge), mahogany neck, 22-fret rosewood fingerboard with pearl dot inlay, tune-o-matic bridge/stop tailpiece, 3-per-side Grover tuners, chrome hardware, 2 exposed coil humbucker pickups, volume/tone controls, 3-position toggle switch. Available in Antique Natural and Transparent Bordeaux Red finishes. Mfg. 1997 to 1999.

		$900	$725	$650	$550	$475	$395	$300

Last MSR was $1,199.

MR400 (U.S. Mfg.) - similar to the MR250, except features 2 P-90-style single coil pickups. Bigsby/Roller Bridge is optional. Available in Honey and Transparent Red finishes. Mfg. 1997 to date.

MSR	$2,199	$1,650	$1,450	$1,200	$1,000	$850	$700	$550

This model features the Buzz Feiten Tuning System.

MR450 (U.S. Mfg.) - similar to the MR250, except features 2 Seymour Duncan humbucker pickups. Available in Honey and Transparent Red finishes. Mfg. 1997 to date.

MSR	$1,999	$1,500	$1,200	$1,050	$925	$795	$650	$500

This model features the Buzz Feiten Tuning System.

Maverick Series

BT2 - slightly offset double cutaway mahogany body, maple neck, 22-fret rosewood fingerboard with pearl dot inlay, tune-o-matic bridge/stop tailpiece, 3-per-side Grover tuners, chrome hardware, 2 exposed coil humbucker pickups, volume/tone controls, 3-position toggle switch. Available in Black, Cherry Sunburst, Caribbean Blue, and Tiffany Blue finishes. Mfg. 1998 to date.

MSR	$299	$225	$175	$150	$125	$110	$95	$75

Add $50 for Metal Flake Blue and Metal Flake Silver finishes.

Caribbean Blue discontinued 1999.

BT2 Q - similar to BT2, except features a quilted maple top. Available in Vintage Sunburst finish. Mfg. 1998 to date.

MSR	$349	$260	$240	$220	$200	$140	$120	$100

BTM Mini - similar to BT2, except features smaller "mini" body. Available in Metallic Dark Blue finish. Mfg. 1998 to date.

MSR	$229	$170	$150	$130	$110	$95	$75	$60

BT3 - similar to BT2, except features tremolo bridge, white pickguard, 3 single coil pickups, volume/2 tone controls, 5-way selector switch. Available in Black, Cherry Sunburst, Ivory, Tiffany Blue, and Red finishes. Mfg. 1997 to 1999.

		$250	$200	$175	$150	$135	$115	$95

Last MSR was $349.

BT4 - similar to BT2, except features tremolo bridge, 2 single coil/humbucker pickups, volume/tone controls, 5-way selector switch. Available in Black, Dark Blue, and Tobacco Sunburst finishes. Mfg. 1997 to date.

MSR	$299	$225	$175	$150	$135	$115	$95	$70

BT4 Q - similar to BT4, except features a quilted maple top. Available in Cherry Sunburst finish. Mfg. 1998 to date.

MSR	$329	$250	$225	$195	$150	$125	$100	$75

BT4 Q LH - similar to BT4, except features a quilted maple top, left-handed configuration. Available in Cherry Sunburst finish. Mfg. 1998 to date.

MSR	$379	$285	$260	$200	$175	$150	$125	$100

BT6 - similar to BT2, except features Floyd Rose tremolo bridge, humbucker/single coil/humbucker pickups, volume/tone controls, 5-way selector switch. Available in Metal Flake Black, Galactic Blue, and Transparent Wine Red finishes. Mfg. 1998 to 1999.

		$450	$375	$325	$295	$250	$195	$150

Last MSR was $599.

BT8 - slightly offset double cutaway mahogany body, bound body, maple neck, 22-fret rosewood fingerboard with pearl dot inlay, tune-o-matic bridge/stop tailpiece, 3-per-side Grover tuners, chrome hardware, 2 exposed coil humbucker pickups, volume/tone controls, 3-position toggle switch. Available in Honey Sunburst, Transparent Red, and Transparent Purple finishes. Mfg. 1997 to 1999.

		$550	$450	$395	$350	$295	$250	$195

Last MSR was $749.

GRADING	100% MINT	98% NEAR MINT	95% EXC+	90% EXC	80% VG+	70% VG	60% G

BT9 - similar to BT8, except features maple fingerboard, black hardware, tremolo bridge, white pickguard, 2 single coil/humbucker pickups, volume/2 tone controls, 5-way selector switch. Available in Transparent Blue and Transparent Red finishes. Mfg. 1997 to 1999.

		$525	$425	$375	$325	$275	$225	$175

Last MSR was $699.

BT10 - similar to BT8, except features Floyd Rose tremolo bridge. Available in Transparent Dark Blue and Transparent Red finishes. Mfg. 1997 to 1999.

		$525	$425	$375	$325	$275	$225	$175

Last MSR was $899.

WM100 (WMSTD, U.S. Mfg.) - slightly offset double cutaway mahogany body, wood body binding, mahogany neck, 22-fret rosewood fingerboard with pearl dot inlay, tune-o-matic bridge/Schaller stop tailpiece, 3-per-side Grover tuners, chrome hardware, 2 Seymour Duncan humbucker pickups, volume/tone controls, 3-position toggle switch. Available in Cobalt Blue, Transparent Bordeaux Red, and Honey finishes. Mfg. 1997 to 1999.

		$1,275	$1,000	$895	$775	$650	$550	$425

Last MSR was $1,699.

This model features the Buzz Feiten Tuning System.

WM200 (WMP, U.S. Mfg.) - similar to WM100, except features swamp ash body, maple neck, white pickguard, 2 single coil/humbucker Seymour Duncan pickups, volume/2 tone controls, 5-way selector switch. Available in Black, Transparent Bordeaux Red, and Vintage Sunburst finishes. Mfg. 1997 to 1999.

		$1,125	$900	$795	$695	$595	$475	$375

Last MSR was $1,499.

This model features the Buzz Feiten Tuning System.

WMS (U.S. Mfg.) - similar to WM200 (MWP), but available in Butterscotch Matte, Natural Matte, & Red Matte finishes. New 1999.

MSR	$999	$750	$600	$500	$400	$350	$300	$250

WM612 (U.S. Mfg.) - similar to WM100, except features one (or 2) Seymour Duncan pickups/piezo bridge pickups, 2 volume/2 tone controls, pickup selector switch(es). Available in Vintage Sunburst finish. Mfg. 1998 to date.

MSR	$3,999	$2,999	$2,699	$2,399

This model features the Buzz Feiten Tuning System.

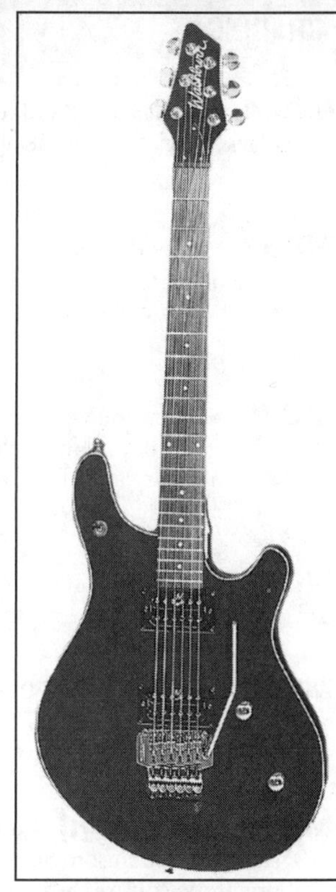

Washburn BT10 TR
courtesy Washburn

Mercury Series

Mercury Series instruments were produced in Asia and U.S. All of the U.S.-built instruments in the Mercury series were produced in Chicago, and featured Seymour Duncan or Bill Lawrence pickups.

MG30 - offset double cutaway hardwood body, bolt-on maple neck, 24-fret rosewood fingerboard with offset pearl dot inlay, double locking vibrato, 6-on-a-side tuners, chrome hardware, 2 single coil/1 humbucker Washburn pickups, volume/tone control, 5-position switch with coil tap. Available in Metallic Red, Pacific Blue Rain and Tobacco Sunburst finishes. Disc. 1994.

		$325	$295	$250	$195	$175	$150	$125

Last MSR was $480.

MG34 - similar to MG30, except has maple fingerboard with black offset dot inlay, humbucker/single coil/humbucker pickups. Available in Black, Metallic Dark Blue and Purple Rain finishes. Disc. 1994.

		$350	$300	$250	$200	$175	$150	$125

Last MSR was $500.

MG40 - offset double cutaway alder body, white pickguard, bolt-on maple neck, 24-fret rosewood fingerboard with offset pearl dot inlay, double locking vibrato, 6-on-a-side tuners, black hardware, volume/tone control, 5-position switch with coil tap. Available in Black, Ice Pearl, Metallic Red and Pearl Blue finishes. Disc. 1994.

		$400	$350	$275	$225	$200	$175	$150

Last MSR was $570.

MG42 - similar to MG40, except has 2 humbucker pickups. Available in Metallic Purple and Midnight Blue Metallic finishes. Disc. 1994.

		$400	$350	$295	$250	$225	$195	$175

Last MSR was $570.

MG43 - similar to MG40, except has maple fingerboard with offset black dot inlay, 3 single coil pickups. Available in Black and Metallic Red finishes. Disc. 1994.

		$350	$325	$275	$225	$200	$175	$150

Last MSR was $550.

GRADING	100% MINT	98% NEAR MINT	95% EXC+	90% EXC	80% VG+	70% VG	60% G

MG44 - similar to MG40, except has maple fingerboard with offset black dot inlay, humbucker/single coil/humbucker pickups. Available in Black, Black Cherry Metallic, Metallic Red and Midnight Blue Metallic finishes. Disc. 1994.

$425	$350	$295	$225	$200	$175	$150

Last MSR was $590.

MG52 - offset double cutaway hardwood body, white pickguard, bolt-on maple neck, 24-fret rosewood fingerboard with offset pearl dot inlay, tune-o- matic bridge/stop tailpiece, 6-on-a-side tuners, chrome hardware, 2 humbucker Washburn pickups, volume/tone control, 5-way switch with coil tap. Available in Metallic Dark Blue and Tobacco Sunburst finishes. Disc. 1994.

$300	$250	$225	$175	$150	$125	$100

Last MSR was $430.

MG70 - offset double cutaway alder body, flamed maple top, transparent pickguard, bolt-on maple neck, 24-fret rosewood fingerboard with offset pearl dot inlay, double locking vibrato, 6-on-a-side tuners, gold hardware, volume/tone control, 5-position switch with coil tap. Available in Transparent Blue and Vintage Sunburst finishes. Disc. 1994.

$495	$425	$350	$275	$250	$225	$200

Last MSR was $700.

MG72 - similar to MG70, except has 2 humbucker pickups. Available in Transparent Purple and Vintage Sunburst finishes. Disc. 1994.

$495	$425	$350	$275	$250	$225	$200

Last MSR was $700.

MG74 - similar to MG70, except has maple fingerboard with offset black dot inlay, humbucker/single coil/humbucker pickups. Available in Transparent Purple and Vintage Sunburst finishes. Disc. 1994.

$500	$425	$350	$295	$250	$225	$200

Last MSR was $720.

MG90 (U.S. Mfg.) - offset double cutaway mahogany body, bolt-on maple neck, 24-fret rosewood fingerboard with offset pearl dot inlay, standard Wilkinson vibrato, 6-on-a-side locking Gotoh tuners, chrome hardware, 2 single coil/humbucker exposed pole piece pickups, volume/tone control, 5-position switch. Available in Natural finish. Mfg. 1994 to 1996.

$675	$550	$450	$350	$325	$300	$275

Last MSR was $900.

MG94 (U.S. Mfg.) - similar to MG90, except features alder body, 24-fret maple fingerboard with offset black dot inlay, double locking vibrato, 6-on-a-side tuners, chrome hardware, humbucker/single coil/humbucker pickups. Available in Green Iridescent, Iridescent, Midnight Blue Metallic and 3 Tone Sunburst finishes. Disc. 1994.

$675	$600	$500	$400	$350	$325	$300

Last MSR was $1,000.

This model has rosewood fingerboard with pearl dot inlay as an option.

MG100 Pro (U.S. Mfg.) - similar to the MG90, except features an ash body. Available in Antique Natural, Transparent Blue, Transparent Red and Vintage Sunburst finishes. Mfg. 1994 to 1996.

$725	$650	$550	$450	$395	$350	$325

Last MSR was $1,199.

MG102 (U.S. Mfg.) - offset double cutaway ash body, bolt-on maple neck, 24-fret rosewood fingerboard with offset pearl dot inlay, standard Wilkinson vibrato, 6-on-a-side locking Gotoh tuners, chrome hardware, 2 humbucker exposed pickups, volume/tone control, 5-position switch. Available in Antique Natural, Transparent Blue and Transparent Red finishes. Mfg. 1994 to 1996.

$725	$600	$550	$450	$395	$350	$325

Last MSR was $1,100.

MG104 (U.S. Mfg.) - offset double cutaway alder body, quilted maple top, bolt-on maple neck, 24-fret maple fingerboard with offset black dot inlay, double locking vibrato, 6-on-a-side tuners, chrome hardware, humbucker/single coil/humbucker pickups, volume/tone control, 5-position switch. Available in Transparent Red and Vintage Sunburst finishes. Disc. 1994.

$725	$600	$550	$450	$395	$350	$325

Last MSR was $1,100.

MG112 (U.S. Mfg.) - offset double cutaway alder body, bound quilted maple top, bolt-on maple neck, 24-fret rosewood fingerboard with offset pearl dot inlay, tune-o-matic bridge/stop tailpiece, 6-on-a-side Gotoh tuners, chrome hardware, 2 humbucker exposed pickups, volume/tone control, 5-position switch. Available in Black, Transparent Blue, Transparent Purple, Transparent Red and Vintage Sunburst finishes. Mfg. 1992 to 1996.

$750	$650	$575	$450	$350	$325	$300

Last MSR was $1,200.

In 1994, ash body, double locking Floyd Rose vibrato replaced original parts/designs, quilted maple top, Transparent Red finish were discontinued.

MG120 (U.S. Mfg.) - offset double cutaway mahogany body, quilted maple top, bolt-on maple neck, 24-fret rosewood fingerboard with offset pearl dot inlay, standard Wilkinson vibrato, 6-on-a-side locking Gotoh tuners, chrome hardware, 2 single coil/humbucker exposed pickups, volume/tone control, 5-position switch. Available in Transparent Blue, Transparent Red and Vintage Sunburst finishes. Mfg. 1994 to 1996.

$750	$675	$625	$550	$475	$425	$395

Last MSR was $1,300.

GRADING	100% MINT	98% NEAR MINT	95% EXC+	90% EXC	80% VG+	70% VG	60% G

MG122 ARTIST (U.S. MFG.) - similar to MG120, except features 2 exposed humbucker pickups. Available in Transparent Purple, Transparent Red and Vintage Sunburst finishes. Mfg. 1994 to 1996.

	$775	$700	$650	$600	$525	$450	$400

Last MSR was $1,499.

MG142 (U.S. Mfg.) - similar to MG120, except features 24-fret ebony fingerboard with offset pearl dot inlay, tune-o-matic bridge/stop tailpiece, graphite nut, 6-on-a-side tuners, 2 humbucker pickups, Available in Transparent Red and Vintage Sunburst finishes. Disc. 1994.

	$800	$725	$650	$600	$525	$450	$400

Last MSR was $1,700.

MG154 (U.S. Mfg.) - similar to MG142, except has double locking vibrato, humbucker/single coil/humbucker pickups. Disc. 1994.

	$825	$750	$700	$650	$550	$475	$425

Last MSR was $1,800.

MG300 - offset double cutaway hardwood body, bolt-on maple neck, 24-fret rosewood fingerboard with offset pearl dot inlay, double locking Floyd Rose vibrato, 6-on-a-side tuners, chrome hardware, 2 single coil/humbucker exposed Washburn pickups, volume/tone control, 5-position switch. Available in Ice Pearl, Metallic Red and Pacific Blue Rain finishes. Mfg. 1994 to 1996.

	$325	$275	$250	$200	$175	$150	$125

Last MSR was $500.

MG340 - offset double cutaway hardwood body, bolt-on maple neck, 24-fret maple fingerboard with offset black dot inlay, double locking Floyd Rose vibrato, 6-on-a-side tuners, chrome hardware, humbucker/single coil/humbucker exposed Washburn pickups, volume/tone control, 5-position switch. Available in Black, Pearl Blue and Purple Rain finishes. Mfg. 1994 to 1996.

	$375	$300	$250	$200	$175	$150	$125

Last MSR was $579.

MG401 - offset double cutaway alder body, figured ash top, bolt-on maple neck, 24-fret rosewood fingerboard with offset pearl dot inlay, standard Schaller vibrato, 6-on-a-side tuners, chrome hardware, 2 single coil/humbucker exposed Washburn pickups, volume/tone with coil tap control, 5-position switch. Available in Antique Natural, Blonde, Natural and Transparent Burgundy finishes. Mfg. 1994 to 1996.

	$450	$350	$300	$250	$225	$195	$175

Last MSR was $699.

MG522 - offset double cutaway alder body, figured ash top, bolt-on maple neck, 24-fret rosewood fingerboard with offset pearl dot inlay, tune-o-matic bridge/stop tailpiece, 6-on-a-side tuners, chrome hardware, 2 humbucker exposed Washburn pickups, volume/tone with coil tap control, 3-position switch. Available in Tobacco Sunburst and Transparent Black finishes. Mfg. 1994 to 1996.

	$350	$300	$275	$225	$195	$175	$150

Last MSR was $530.

MG700 - offset double cutaway alder body, figured sycamore top, bolt-on maple neck, 24-fret rosewood fingerboard with offset pearl dot inlay, double locking Floyd Rose vibrato, 6-on-a-side Grover tuners, gold hardware, 2 single coil/humbucker exposed Washburn pickups, volume/tone control, 5-position switch. Available in Antique Natural and Vintage Sunburst finishes. Mfg. 1994 to 1996.

	$450	$400	$350	$275	$250	$225	$200

Last MSR was $700.

MG701 - similar to MG700, except features a standard Wilkinson vibrato, 6-on-a-side locking Schaller tuners, chrome hardware. Available in Antique Natural, Transparent Blue and Vintage Sunburst finishes. Mfg. 1994 to 1996.

	$475	$400	$375	$295	$250	$225	$200

Last MSR was $730.

MG821 - similar to the MG700, except features a bound figured sycamore top, standard Wilkinson vibrato, 6-on-a-side locking Schaller tuners, chrome hardware, 2 exposed humbucker Washburn pickups, volume/tone with coil tap control, 5-position switch. Available in Tobacco Sunburst and Transparent Burgundy finishes. Mfg. 1994 to 1996.

	$500	$425	$395	$325	$275	$250	$225

Last MSR was $780.

Jennifer Batten Series

JB100 (U.S. Mfg.) - offset double cutaway swamp ash and flamed maple body, maple neck, rosewood fingerboard with dot position markers, 3-per-side tuners, 1 Duncan JB Jr. and 2 Duckbucker pickups, Floyd Rose bridge. locking nut, Buzz Feiten Tuning System, 1 volume/1 tone, slotted switch. Available in Caramel Burst, white and Honey finishes. New 2000.

MSR $1,799	$1,350	$1,150	$1,050	$950	$850	$750	$600

GRADING		100% MINT	98% NEAR MINT	95% EXC+	90% EXC	80% VG+	70% VG	60% G

JB100 MIDI (U.S. Mfg.) - similar to Model JB100 except includes a Roland GK-2 pickup. Available in Caramel Burst, white and honey finishes. New 2000.

MSR	$1,999	$1,499	$1,299	$1,199	$1,099	$1,000	$900	$700

Nuno Bettencourt Series

This series was co-designed with Nuno Bettencourt and features the patented Extended Stephen's Cutaway. All of the U.S.- built instruments in this series were produced in Chicago, and featured Seymour Duncan or Bill Lawrence pickups.

N1 - offset double cutaway alder body, bolt-on maple neck, 22-fret rosewood fingerboard with pearl dot inlay, standard tremolo, reverse headstock, 6-on-a-side Grover tuners, chrome hardware, 2 Washburn humbucker pickups, volume control, 3-position switch. Available in Natural Matte and Padauk Stain finishes. Mfg. 1997 to 1999.

$325 $275 $250 $200 $175 $125 $100
Last MSR was $429.

N2 - similar to the N1, except features a Floyd Rose double locking vibrato, 2 humbucker (Washburn/Bill Lawrence) pickups. Available in Natural Matte and Padauk Stain finishes. Disc. 1999.

$725 $575 $500 $425 $375 $300 $225
Last MSR was $949.

N4E A (U.S. Mfg.) - offset double cutaway alder body, bolt-on maple neck, 22-fret ebony fingerboard with pearl dot inlay, Floyd Rose double locking vibrato, reverse peghead, 6-on-a-side Grover tuners, chrome hardware, 2 Seymour Duncan humbucker pickups, volume control, 3-position switch. Available in Natural Matte finish. Mfg. 1992 to 1998.

$1,125 $975 $850 $725 $625 $495 $375
Last MSR was $1,499.

This model features the Buzz Feiten Tuning System.

N4E P (U.S. Mfg.) - similar to N4EA, except has padauk body. Mfg. 1992 to 1996.

$1,000 $900 $800 $695 $575 $500 $400
Last MSR was $1,599.

N4E SA (U.S. Mfg.) similar to N4EA, except has swamp ash body. Available in Natural Matte, Paduak Stain Natural Matte, and Vintage Sunburst finishes. Mfg. 1994 to date.

MSR	$1,699	$1,275	$1,100	$975	$825	$695	$550	$425

This model features the Buzz Feiten Tuning System.

N4E QM (U.S. Mfg.) - similar to N4EA, except has quilted maple top. Available in Tobacco Sunburst and Wineburst finishes. Mfg. 1997 to 1999.

$1,500 $1,200 $1,050 $900 $775 $625 $500
Last MSR was $1,999.

This model features the Buzz Feiten Tuning System.

Centurian/P Series (Carved Top Electrics)

All P Series models are equipped with the Buzz Feiten Tuning System.

CT2K (P2) - slightly offset single cutaway mahogany body, mahogany neck, 22-fret rosewood fingerboard with pearl dot inlay, tune-o-matic bridge/stop tailpiece, blackface peghead, 3-per-side Grover tuners, chrome hardware, white pickguard, 2 exposed coil humbucker pickups, volume/tone controls, 3-position toggle switch. Available in Black, Tiffany Blue, and Sapphire Blue finishes. Mfg. 1997 to 1999.

$650 $500 $425 $375 $325 $275 $200
Last MSR was $879.

CT290K (P2 90) - similar to P2, except has 2 black P-90-style single coil pickups. Available in Transparent Blue and Transparent Red finishes. Mfg. 1997 to 1999.

$650 $500 $425 $375 $325 $275 $200
Last MSR was $879.

CT2QK (P2 Q) - similar to P2, except has a quilted maple top. Available in Cherry Sunburst finish. Mfg. 1997 to date.

MSR	$939	$700	$550	$450	$400	$350	$300	$250

CTP (Plus/P3, U.S. Mfg.) - slightly offset single cutaway bound sapele body, sapele neck, 22-fret rosewood fingerboard with pearl dot inlay, tune-o-matic bridge/Schaller fine tuner tailpiece, blackface peghead, 3-per-side Grover tuners, chrome hardware, 2 Seymour Duncan humbucker pickups, volume/tone controls, 3-position toggle switch. Available in Antique Natural, Black, and Transparent Bordeaux Red finishes. Mfg. 1997 to 1999.

$1,275 $1,025 $850 $750 $650 $500 $400
Last MSR was $1,699.

CTS (Studio) - similar to CTP. Available in Butterscotch Matte, Natural Matte & Red Matte. New 1999.

MSR	$1,299	$975	$825	$725	$625	$525	$400	$300

GRADING	100% MINT	98% NEAR MINT	95% EXC+	90% EXC	80% VG+	70% VG	60% G

CTSTD (Standard/P4, U.S. Mfg.) - slightly offset single cutaway bound mahogany body, mahogany neck, 22-fret ebony fingerboard with pearl dot inlay, tune-o-matic bridge/Schaller fine tuner tailpiece, blackface peghead, 3-per-side Schaller locking tuners, chrome hardware, 2 Seymour Duncan humbucker pickups, volume/tone controls, 3-position toggle switch. Available in Black, and Cherry Sunburst finishes. Mfg. 1997 to 1999.

$1,425 $1,150 $1,000 $850 $750 $600 $500
Last MSR was $1,899.

CTDLX (P4 DLX, U.S. Mfg.) - similar to P4, except has a bound quilted maple top, bound fingerboard, 2 volume/2 tone controls. Available in Cherry Sunburst, BlueBurst, and Tobacco Sunburst finishes. Mfg. 1997 to 1999.

$1,650 $1,300 $1,150 $975 $800 $625 $550
Last MSR was $2,199.

Paul Stanley (PS) Series

Paul Stanley Series instruments were designed in conjunction with guitarist Paul Stanley (KISS), and were introduced in 1998. The entry level **PS100 B** features an alder body, 2 humbucker pickups and a tune-o-matic bridge (list $599); the **PS500 B** features a mahogany body and neck (list $1,249). The U.S.-built **PS2000 B** has Seymour Duncan pickups, and an ebony fingerboard tempered with the Buzz Feiten Tuning System (list $2,499). All models are available in a Black finish only.

PS2000 ROSE (Paul Stanley Limited Edition of 50) - similar to Model PS2000 except has a recreation of Paul's Rose tattoo on the top just above the tailpiece. Each guitar is hand signed by Paul on the back along with its series number. Comes with certificate of authenticity and a deluxe luggage quality hard case. Limited Mfg. during 2000.

MSR $3,999

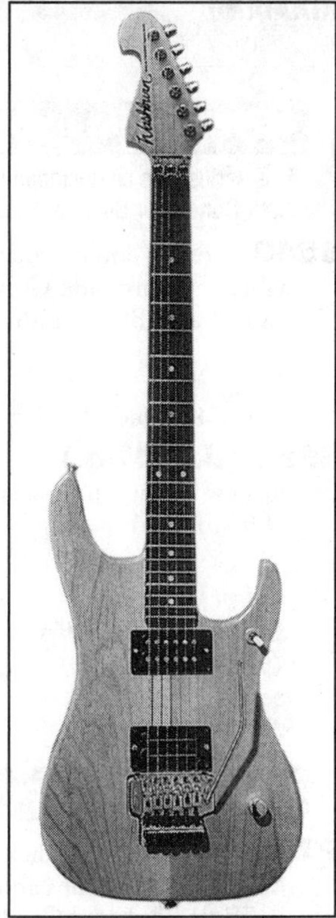

Washburn N2 NM
courtesy Washburn

Shadow Series

Washburn's Shadow Series instruments are double cutaway body models. The **WS4** (list $349) features 3 single coil pickups and a fulcrum tremolo bridge; the **WS6** (list $349) has 2 single coils and a humbucker pickup configuration.

Silverado Series

This series incorporates the Stephen's Extended Cutaway neck joint, and has rosewood or maple fingerboards. All the instruments in this series were hand built in Chicago, and featured Seymour Duncan or Bill Lawrence pickups.

LS93 - offset double cutaway ash body, pearloid pickguard, bolt-on maple neck, 22-fret fingerboard with pearl dot inlay, standard Wilkinson vibrato, 6-on-a-side locking Gotoh tuners, chrome hardware, 3 single coil pickups, volume/2 tone controls, 5-position switch. Available in Black, Natural, Transparent Blue, Transparent Red and Vintage Sunburst finishes. Mfg. 1994 to 1996.

$675 $550 $500 $400 $350 $325 $300
Last MSR was $1,000.

LT93 - similar to the LS93, except features an alder body, 22-fret maple fingerboard with black dot inlay, standard vibrato, 6-on-a-side locking tuners. Available in Black and Tobacco Sunburst finishes. Mfg. 1992 to 1994.

$750 $675 $550 $500 $475 $400 $350
Last MSR was $1,300.

LT103 - similar to LT93, except has flame maple or swamp ash body. Available in Natural and Tobacco Sunburst finishes. Disc. 1994.

$800 $725 $600 $550 $475 $400 $350
Last MSR was $1,600.

Stage Series

Stage Series models were available from Washburn between 1979 to 1986, and represent some of the first electric guitar models from the revamped Washburn company. These models featured U.S. designs, and were produced in Japan.

The **A- 5** had an original retail price of $399; the **A-10** retail list was $599; and the **A-20** had a retail price of $699. Models with a tremolo (vibrato) bridge have a "-V" designation in their model name (for example, A-10-V).

Stage Series models in player's grade condition generally can be found priced between $75 to $175.

Stephen's Extended Cutaway Series

EC26 ATLANTIS - offset double cutaway basswood body, bolt-on maple neck, 26-fret rosewood fingerboard with pearl dot inlay, locking vibrato, 6-on-a-side locking tuners, chrome hardware, single coil/humbucker Seymour Duncan pickup, volume/tone control, 5-position switch. Available in Black, Red and White finishes. Disc. 1991.

$675 $600 $550 $450 $395 $350 $325
Last MSR was $1,100.

This model featured the Stephen's Extended Cutaway neck joint.

GRADING	100% MINT	98% NEAR MINT	95% EXC+	90% EXC	80% VG+	70% VG	60% G

W

Steve Stevens Signature Series

This series was co-designed with Steve Stevens (Billy Idol band). All of the U.S.-built instruments in this series were produced in Chicago, and featured Seymour Duncan or Bill Lawrence pickups.

SS40 - offset double cutaway poplar body, bolt-on maple neck, 22-fret maple fingerboard with abalone inlay, double locking Floyd Rose vibrato, 6-on-a-side Grover tuners, gold hardware, 2 angled humbucker exposed Washburn pickups, volume control, 5-position switch. Available in Black finish. Mfg. 1992 to 1996.

$525	$475	$400	$325	$295	$250	$225

Last MSR was $800.

In 1994, black dot fingerboard inlay replaced the original abalone inlay.

SS80 (U.S. Mfg.) - offset double cutaway poplar body, bolt-on maple neck, 22-fret maple fingerboard with abalone dot inlay, double locking vibrato, 6-on-a-side tuners, gold hardware, 2 humbucker pickups, volume control, 3-position switch. Available in Black finish. Mfg. 1992 to 1996.

$750	$700	$650	$600	$550	$495	$450

Last MSR was $1,500.

SS100 (U.S. Mfg.) - similar to SS80, except has black dot inlay, black hardware. Available in Vintage Frankenstein Graphic finishes. Mfg. 1992 to 1994.

$875	$800	$700	$625	$550	$495	$450

Last MSR was $1,800.

USA Custom Specialties

PT3 (U.S. Mfg.) - heavy offset "V" mahogany body, ½ " maple top, ebony fingerboard with dot position markers, 2 Seymour Duncan humbucking pickups and 1 single coil pickup, Grover 18-1 tuners, 3-per-side tuners, Buzz Feiten Tuning System, black hardware. Available in Triple Black and Candy Apple Red finishes. New 2000.

MSR	$1,499	$1,125	$1,000	$900	$800	$700	$600	$500

PTK (U.S. Mfg.) - similar to Model PT3 except has korina body, ebony set neck, ebony fingerboard, EMG and Duncan pickups, Buzz Feiten Tuning System. Available in Korina Gloss finish. New 2000.

MSR	$1,999	$1,499	$1,300	$1,200	$1,100	$1,000	$900	$750

Wings Series

All of the U.S.-built instruments in this series were produced in Chicago, and featured Seymour Duncan or Bill Lawrence pickups.

SB50 (U.S. Mfg.) - double cutaway mahogany body, black pickguard, mahogany neck, 22-fret rosewood fingerboard with pearl dot inlay, tune-o-matic bridge/stop tailpiece, 3-per-side vintage Keystone tuners, chrome hardware, 2 single coil "soapbar" pickups, volume/2 tone controls, 3-position switch. Available in Ivory, Tobacco Sunburst and Wine Red finishes. Mfg. 1992 to 1994.

$625	$550	$450	$350	$325	$300	$275

Last MSR was $900.

SB100 (U.S. Mfg.) - similar to SB50, except has bound arched figured maple top, no pickguard, bound fingerboard with pearl stylized V inlay, 2 humbucker pickups. Available in Cherry Sunburst and Vintage Sunburst finishes. Mfg. 1992 to 1994.

$1,250	$1,100	$1,000	$900	$800	$725	$650

Last MSR was $2,500.

SB80 - double cutaway mahogany body, arched bound flame maple top, raised white pickguard, mahogany neck, 22-fret bound rosewood fingerboard with pearl wings inlay, tune-o-matic bridge/stop tailpiece, 3-per-side tuners, chrome hardware, 2 humbucker Washburn pickups, 2 volume/2 tone controls, 3-position switch. Available in Natural and Vintage Sunburst finishes. Disc. 1996.

$495	$425	$375	$325	$295	$275	$250

Last MSR was $750.

WR Series

WR150 - offset double cutaway solid body, maple neck, rosewood fingerboard with offset dot position markers, jumbo frets, 6-on-a-side tuners, 2 single coil pickups and 1 humbucking pickup, 1 volume/1 tone, slotted switch, Fulcrum bridge, vibrato tailpiece, chrome hardware. Available in Metallic Blue, Metallic Purple, Metallic Red and Caribbean Blue. New 2000.

MSR	$319	$239	$200	$175	$150	$125	$100	$75

WR150Q - similar to Model WR150 except has quilted top. Available in Tobacco Sunburst finish only. New 2000.

MSR	$369	$275	$225	$200	$175	$150	$125	$100

WG580 - offset double cutaway solid body, maple neck, rosewood fingerboard with dot position markers, jumbo frets, 2 humbucking pickups and 1 single coil pickup, slotted switch, 1 volume/1 tone, 6-on-a-side tuners, black hardware. Available in black, Metallic Blue and Metallic Purple. New 2000.

MSR	$749	$560	$500	$450	$400	$350	$300	$250

GRADING		100% MINT	98% NEAR MINT	95% EXC+	90% EXC	80% VG+	70% VG	60% G

CS780 - offset double cutaway solid body, maple neck, rosewood fingerboard with sharkfin position markers, faceted body, jumbo frets, 6-on-a-side tuners, locking nut, Floyd Rose bridge, 1 volume/1 tone, slotted switch, gold hardware, 2 humbucking pickups and 1 single coil pickup. Available in Metallic Purple and Pearl White. New 2000.

MSR	$849	$635	$575	$525	$475	$425	$375	$300

RS980 - offset double cutaway solid body, maple neck, rosewood fingerboard with sharkfin position markers, jumbo frets, reverse headstock, locking nut, Floyd Rose bridge, 2 humbucking pickups and 1 single coil pickup, black hardware, 1 volume/1 tone, slotted switch. Available in Tobaccp Sunburst and Metallic Gray. New 2000.

MSR	$869	$650	$600	$550	$500	$450	$400	$350

7 String Models

WG587 - offset double cutaway carved mahogany body, maple neck, rosewood fingerboard with dot position markers, Tune-O-Matic bridge, locking nut, vibrato tailpiece, 7 on 1 side tuners, 2 humbucking pickups and 1 single coil pickup, black hardware. Available in Metallic Red and Metallic Gray finishes. New 2000.

MSR	$749	$560	$500	$450	$400	$350	$300	$250

WG587V - similar to WG587 but is equipped with a Floyd Rose bridge. Available in Metallic Red and Metallic Gray. New 2000.

MSR	$899	$675	$600	$550	$500	$450	$400	$300

Sonic 7 (S7) (USA) - offset double cutaway solid mahogany body, maple neck, figured maple fingerboard with black dot position markers, 6 plus 1 headstock tuner configuration, Buzz Feiten Tuning System, hardtail bridge, string-through-body design, 2 humbucking pickups, 2 volume/1 tone, slotted switch, black hardware. Available in Metallic Purple and Heavy Metal finishes. New 2000.

MSR	$1,599	$1,200	$1,000	$900	$850	$800	$700	$550

Deduct $200 for Industrial Black and Industrial Silver finishes.

Sonic 7 (S7V) (USA) - similar to Model S7 except has Floyd Rose bridge. Available in Metallic Purple and Heavy Metal finishes. New 2000.

MSR	$1,699	$1,275	$1,050	$950	$900	$800	$700	$600

Subtract $200 for Industrial Black and Industrial Silver finishes.

ELECTRIC BASS

Axxess Series

XS2 - offset double cutaway hardwood body, maple neck, 24-fret rosewood fingerboard with pearl dot inlay, fixed bridge, 4-on-a-side tuners, chrome hardware, P-style Washburn pickup, push/pull volume/tone control. Available in Black, Red and White finishes. Disc. 1992.

$275	$250	$200	$175	$150	$125	$100

Last MSR was $400.

XS4 - offset double cutaway alder body, maple neck, 24-fret rosewood fingerboard with pearl dot inlay, fixed bridge, 4-on-a-side tuners, chrome hardware, P-style/J-style Washburn pickups, volume/treble/bass controls, active electronics. Available in Black and Red finishes. Disc. 1992.

$325	$295	$250	$195	$175	$150	$125

Last MSR was $480.

XS5 - similar to XS4, except has 5 strings, 4/1 tuners and 2 J-style Washburn pickups. Available in Black, Red and White finishes. Disc. 1992.

$400	$350	$295	$225	$200	$175	$150

Last MSR was $580.

XS6 - similar to XS4, except has 6-strings. Available in Metallic Cherry Black and Pearl White finishes. Disc. 1992.

$425	$350	$300	$250	$225	$195	$175

Last MSR was $600.

XS8 - similar to XS4, except black hardware, 2 single coil Status pickups and active 2-band EQ fader control. Available in Charcoal Rain, Black, and White finishes. Disc. 1992.

$450	$400	$350	$300	$250	$225	$200

Last MSR was $800.

GRADING		100% MINT	98% NEAR MINT	95% EXC+	90% EXC	80% VG+	70% VG	60% G

Bantam Series

XB100 - offset double cutaway asymmetrical mahogany body, bolt-on maple neck, 20-fret rosewood fingerboard with pearl dot inlay, fixed bridge, 2-per-side tuners, chrome hardware, P-style WB100 pickup, volume/tone controls. Available in Black, Metallic Purple, and Black Metal Flake finishes. Mfg. 1997 to date.

MSR $319 — $240 $200 $175 $150 $125 $95 $75

Add $30 for XB100 Flame Tobacco Sunburst finish (New 1999).

XB200 - offset double cutaway asymmetrical hardwood body, bolt-on maple neck, 20-fret rosewood fingerboard with offset pearl dot inlay, fixed bridge, 2-per-side tuners, chrome hardware, P/J-style Washburn WB500 pickups, 2 volume/2 tone controls. Available in Black, Metallic Red, and Pearl Blue finishes. Mfg. 1994 to date.

MSR $499 — $375 $295 $250 $225 $195 $150 $125

Add $50 for left-handed configuration (Model XB200 LH), available in Caribbean Blue finish only.

Add $50 for XB200 Flame Tobacco Sunburst finish (New 1999).

This model is available with a fretless fingerboard (Model XB200 FL). Available in Black finish only.

XB400 - offset double cutaway asymmetrical alder body, figured ash top, bolt-on maple neck, 20-fret rosewood fingerboard with offset pearl dot inlay, fixed bridge, 2-per-side tuners, chrome hardware, 2 Washburn humbucker pickups, 2 volume/2 tone controls, active electronics. Available in Tobacco Sunburst, Transparent Burgundy, and Transparent Blue finishes. Mfg. 1994 to 1999.

$635 $575 $525 $450 $375 $300 $225
Last MSR was $849.

In 1996, Natural Matte and Transparent Red finishes were introduced; Tobacco Sunburst and Transparent Burgundy finishes were discontinued.

XB500 - similar to XB400, except has 5-string configuration, 3/2-per-side tuners. Available in Black and Natural finishes. Mfg. 1994 to 1999.

$675 $550 $495 $425 $350 $295 $225
Last MSR was $899.

In 1996, Transparent Blue and Transparent Red finishes were introduced. Transparent Blue disc. 1998
Early models may feature 2 P-style split coil pickups.

XB600 - similar to XB400, except has 6-string configuration, 3-per-side tuners. Available in Black and Natural finishes. Mfg. 1994 to 1999.

$899 $725 $650 $575 $475 $395 $300
Last MSR was $1,199.

In 1996, Transparent Blue and Transparent Red finishes were introduced. By 1999 offered only in Natural Matte finish.
Early models may feature 2 P-style split coil pickups.

XB800 - offset double cutaway asymmetrical alder body, figured sycamore top, bolt-on maple neck, 24-fret rosewood fingerboard with offset pearl dot inlay, fixed bridge, 2-per-side tuners, gold hardware, 2 humbucker Status pickups, volume/treble/bass/pan controls, active electronics. Available in Antique Natural, Transparent Burgundy, Transparent Blue and Vintage Sunburst finishes. Mfg. 1994 to 1996.

$525 $475 $400 $325 $295 $275 $250
Last MSR was $800.

XB900 (U.S. Mfg.) - offset double cutaway asymmetrical swamp ash body, bolt-on maple neck, 24-fret rosewood fingerboard with offset pearl dot inlay, fixed bridge, 2-per-side tuners, black hardware, Seymour Duncan Bassline 'soapbar' pickup, volume/3-band EQ controls, active electronics. Available in StoneWash Blue and StoneWash Red finishes. Antique Satin added in 1999. Mfg. 1997 to date.

MSR $1,499 — $1,125 $900 $795 $695 $595 $475 $375

This model features the Buzz Feiten Tuning System.

XB900JJ (U.S. Mfg.) - similar to XB900, but has 2 Jazz pickups and is available in Butterscotch Matte and Natural Matte finishes. New 1999.

MSR $1,299 — $975 $850 $750 $650 $525 $425 $325

XB900PJ (U.S. Mfg.) - similar to XB900, but has 1 Jazz and 1 "P" pickup. Available in Butterscotch Matte and natural Matte finishes. New 1999.

MSR $1,299 — $975 $850 $750 $650 $525 $425 $325

XB925 (U.S. Mfg.) - similar to XB900, except has 5-string configuration, 3/2-per-side tuners, Bartolini custom pickups. Available in Antique Stain, Bubinga, Cherry Sunburst, Vintage Sunburst, and African Zebra finishes. Mfg. 1997-1998.

$1,275 $1,000 $895 $775 $650 $550 $425
Last MSR was $1,699.

This model features the Buzz Feiten Tuning System.

XB1000 (U.S. Mfg.) - offset double cutaway asymmetrical ash body, bolt-on maple neck, 24-fret rosewood fingerboard with pearl dot inlay, fixed Wilkinson bridge, blackface peghead with screened logo, 2-per-side Gotoh tuners, chrome hardware, humbucker Bartolini pickup, volume/mid/concentric treble/bass controls. Available in Black, Transparent Blue and Transparent Red finishes. Mfg. 1994 to 1996.

$1,000 $900 $750 $600 $550 $495 $450
Last MSR was $1,500.

GRADING	100% MINT	98% NEAR MINT	95% EXC+	90% EXC	80% VG+	70% VG	60% G

Washburn XB400
courtesy Washburn

Classic Series

B200 - single cutaway alder body, bound carved maple top, 3-piece maple neck, 22-fret bound rosewood fingerboard with pearl dot inlay, fixed bridge, 2-per-side tuners, chrome hardware, 2 Washburn pickups, 2 volume/2 tone controls. Available in Metallic Dark Blue finish. Disc. 1994.

$525 $450 $375 $300 $275 $250 $225
Last MSR was $750.

Mercury Series

MB2 - offset double cutaway hardwood body, bolt-on maple neck, 24-fret rosewood fingerboard with offset pearl dot inlay, fixed bridge, 4-on-a-side tuners, chrome hardware, P-style pickup, volume/tone control. Available in Black, Pacific Blue Rain and White finishes. Disc. 1994.

$325 $275 $225 $195 $175 $150 $125
Last MSR was $470.

MB4 - offset double cutaway alder body, bolt-on maple neck, 24-fret rosewood fingerboard with offset pearl dot inlay, fixed bridge, 4-on-a-side tuners, chrome hardware, P-style/J-style Washburn pickups, volume/treble/bass controls, 3-position switch, active electronics. Available in Black, Black Cherry Metallic, Ice Pearl, Midnight Blue Metallic and Natural finishes. Disc. 1994.

$375 $325 $275 $225 $200 $175 $150
Last MSR was $550.

This model was also available with a maple fingerboard with black dot inlay.

MB5 - similar to MB4, except has 5-string configuration, 4/1 per side tuners, 2 J-style pickups. Available in Black, Ice Pearl and Natural finishes. Disc. 1994.

$475 $400 $325 $275 $250 $225 $200
Last MSR was $670.

MB6 - similar to MB4, except has 6-string configuration, 4/2-per-side tuners, 2 J-style pickups. Available in Natural finish. Disc. 1994.

$525 $450 $375 $300 $275 $250 $225
Last MSR was $750.

MB8 - offset double cutaway alder body, flame maple top, bolt-on maple neck, 24-fret rosewood fingerboard with offset pearl dot inlay, fixed bridge, 4-on-a-side tuners, gold hardware, 2 humbucker active Status pickups, volume/treble/bass/mix controls, active electronics. Available in Tobacco Sunburst, Transparent Blue and Transparent Purple finishes. Disc. 1994.

$550 $475 $400 $325 $295 $275 $250
Last MSR was $800.

This model was also available with a maple fingerboard with black dot inlay.

Shadow Bass Series

Washburn's Shadow Series bass instruments are double cutaway body models. The **WP4** (list $364) features a P-style split pickup and deluxe die cast bridge; the **WJ4** (list $364) has 2 J-style pickups.

Status Series 1000

S60 - offset double cutaway one piece maple body/neck construction, walnut top/back laminates, 24-fret carbonite fingerboard, no headstock, tunable bridge, brass hardware, 2 single coil Status pickups, volume/tone control, active electronics with fader control. Available in Black and White finishes. Disc. 1992.

$700 $600 $500 $400 $350 $325 $300
Last MSR was $1,000.

S70 - similar to S60. Available in Natural, Transparent Blue, and Transparent Red finishes. Disc. 1994.

$800 $725 $600 $500 $425 $375 $350
Last MSR was $1,200.

This model was also available with fretless fingerboard (Model S70 FL).

WATKINS

Instruments previously built in England from circa 1961 to 1982. Trademark was changed to W.E.M. (Watkins Electric Music) in the late 1960s, and then to WILSON in the 1970s.

Watkins (W.E.M.) were known primarily for their amplifiers; however, many players in Great Britain started out on a Watkins Rapier guitar. Borrowing heavily on Leo Fender's Stratocaster design, the guitars were available in 2-, 3-, or 4-pickup models. Guitars were designated by the model number: **Rapier 22** (2 pickups), **Rapier 33** (3 pickups), and **Rapier 44** (4 pickups). Models were available in a Bright Red or Black finish. A bass guitar counterpart was produced, and featured 2 pickups. These instruments started being produced around 1961.

Sid Watkins was responsible for the guitar making, as well as the cabinets for the various W.E.M. amps and W.E.M. CopiCats (an echo effect box distributed in the U.S. by Guild in the mid 1960s). The electronics were fitted to the amps by Sid's brother, Charlie. W.E.M. supplied many festivals in the 1960s with their P.A. systems. Watkins produced one of the first guitar synths. The **Fifth Man** featured a number of effects plus a primitive drum box. The guitar was demonstrated on the British television programme "Tomorrow's World".

At the end of the 1960s, some of the Watkins guitars were branded W.E.M. The last change of name in the 1970s was Wilson (this was the maiden name of Sid's mother). Sid branched out into semi-acoustic guitars which became very popular. These models were favored by Roy Wood of Wizard (The Move). The guitar's popularity grew in Germany, and Sid would load up his V.W. camper to take them over himself.

As a footnote, Watkins made some guitars for VOX, when VOX apparently could not keep up with the demand for their instruments. As another matter of interest, G PLAN (a British furniture company) also produced some guitars for the company.

(Source: Keith Smart, Zemaitis Guitar Owners Club. Smart was an employee at Watkins/W.E.M. during the 1970s. Additional model information courtesy Tony Bacon and Paul Day, The Guru's Guitar Guide)

ELECTRIC

The Watkins trademark appears on entry level to medium quality solid body and semi-hollowbody models that primarily appealed to student players. Models include such designation as the **Rapier, Circuit 4, Mercury, Ranger**, and **Sapphire**. As indicated earlier, production was maintained until 1982 and the trademark name changed (or should we say evolved) twice during this company's history.

WAYNE

Instruments currently built in Paradise, California by Wayne Charvel, and his son Michael Charvel. Mr. Charvel has been building guitars since approximately 1962 and has built custom instruments for a plethora of famous professional guitarists. Over the years, he worked for Fender, Gibson, and B.C. Rich.

ELECTRIC

HYDRA - outrageous body design, Premium grade Alder body, AAA Bird's-eye Maple neck, 22-fret neck, Original Floyd Rose tremolo bridge in chrome or non-tremolo brass bridge, available with the Eddie Van Halen D-tuna which allows the E string to be dropped to D without unclamping, ebony, rosewood, or maple fingerboards, Gotoh tuners, chrome or brass knobs, chrome or brass/gold hardware, one pickup variation available with volume control, two pickup variation has volume control and three-way switch. Available in Jet Black, Bright Red, Candy Red, Corvette Yellow, Orange, Dark Purple, Metallic Lavender, Lime Green, Hand Rubbed Oil, Rock White, and Cherry Sunburst. Custom graphics are also available.

As this edition went to press, retail list prices for this model were not available.

ROCK LEGEND - double cutaway body design, technical specifications are the same as the Hydra Model.

As this edition went to press, retail list prices for this model were not available.

STAR GUITAR - modified star shaped body design, technical specifications are the same as the Hydra Model.

As this edition went to press, retail list prices for this model were not available.

WAYNE SPECIAL - double cutaway body, Flame or Quilted Maple top, Select Alder body, Cream Ivoroid binding and pickup bezels, compound radius fingerboard of ebony, rosewood, or maple. Other specifications are the same as the Hydra Model. Available in Transparent Amber, Transparent Blue, Transparent Purple, Transparent Red, Natural, and Cherry Sunburst finishes.

As this edition went to press, retail list prices for this model were not available.

WEEDON, BERT

Trademark of instruments previously built in West Germany in the mid 1960s.

While the Bert Weedon trademark was a brand name used by a UK importer, Bert Weedon was a famous British guitarist best known for his daily guitar lessons on British radio. Weedon was normally associated with Hofner guitars throughout his career. The **Zero One** model was a semi-hollowbody with a single cutaway and two pickups.

(Source: Tony Bacon and Paul Day, The Guru's Guitar Guide)

WELSON

Instruments previously produced in Italy from the early 1970s to the early 1980s.

The Welson company produced medium quality guitars based on Gibson designs, as well as their own original designs and semi-hollowbody models. Welson also built guitars for the Vox company, and for Wurlitzer (U.S.).

(Source: Tony Bacon and Paul Day, The Guru's Guitar Guide)

WESTBURY

See UNICORD.

Instruments previously produced in Japan between 1978 through 1981.

The Merson Musical Supply Company of Westbury, New York was the primary importer of Univox guitars. Merson evolved into Unicord, and also became a distributor for Westbury brand guitars. Westbury instruments featured a set neck design on both the solid body electric guitars and basses, and generally had two humbuckers on the guitar models (some also had a vari-tone switch). Westbury guitars are generally medium to good quality original designs.

(Source: Michael Wright, Guitar Stories Volume One)

ELECTRIC

CUSTOM - offset dual cutaway body, arched top, set-in neck, 22-fret ebony fingerboard with white block inlay, 3 on a side headstock, bridge/stop tailpiece, chrome hardware, bound black peghead with Westbury logo and *W* design, 2 covered humbucking pickups, 2 volume/2 tone controls, 3-way switch, 5-position pickup tap/phase control. Mfg. 1978 to 1981.

$425 $365 $300 $245 $170 $120 $85

GRADING	100% MINT	98% NEAR MINT	95% EXC+	90% EXC	80% VG+	70% VG	60% G

Custom S - similar to the Custom, except has bound body, rosewood fingerboard, gold hardware, 2 DiMarzio humbuckers. Mfg. 1980 to 1981.

$450	$390	$330	$270	$210	$150	$85

ELECTRIC BASS

TRACK IV BASS - offset dual cutaway body, set-in neck, 20-fret ebony fingerboard with white dot inlay, 2-per-side headstock, fixed bridge, chrome hardware, black peghead with Westbury logo and *W* design, black pickguard, 2 P-style pickups, volume/blend/tone controls. Mfg. 1978 to 1981.

$400	$360	$320	$280	$240	$200	$150

WESTONE

Instruments previously produced in Japan from circa late 1970s to mid 1980s. Subsequent instruments were built in Korea. Distributed in the U.S. by St. Louis Music of St. Louis, Missouri.

Trademark re-introduced to British marketplace in 1996 by FCN Music. Instruments currently produced in Korea.

The Matsumoku company of Japan had been manufacturing guitars for other trademarks (such as Aria, Epiphone, and Vantage) since the 1960s. In 1981, Matsumoku decided to market their own original designs under their own trademark in addition to their current production for others. Westone guitars were originally marketed in the U.K. prior to the U.S. market. Matsumoku guitars are generally well-built, solid playing guitars that featured innovative design ideas.

In 1984, St. Louis Music announced that it would be merging Westone with their Electra brand (which was introduced back in 1971). Through the mid 1980s, models were sold under the Electra/Westone imprint, then Westone only as the Electra brand aspect was discontinued. In 1987 Matsumoku stopped producing instruments, so guitar production switched to Korea.

While the brand is not currently available in the U.S. market, FCN Music recently began importing Korean-built models into England. The current series consists of five models of medium to good quality.

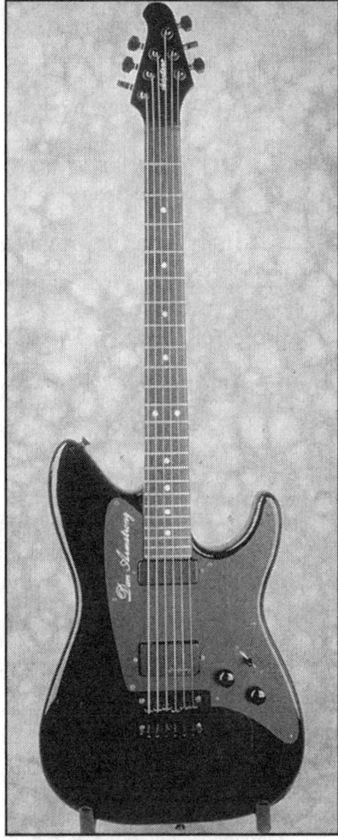

Westone Dan Armstrong courtesy Bob and Matt Brown

ELECTRIC

Most guitars were designed as part of a certain series. The overall body design would then feature different pickup combinations, or the addition of a tremolo; popular series includes the Pantera (1986-1987), Thunder (1981-1987), Spectrum (1984-1987), Phoenix, Dynasty, Futura, Custom Pro, and the Clipper Six (1986-1988). The Clipper Six series was designed by Mark Ray of the United Kingdom.

Many of the guitar series were produced in limited quantities. Matsumoku-produced Electra/Westone guitars should have serialization beginning with a *4* or *84*.

SPECTRUM ST - solid body, 22-fret bolt-on neck, dot position markers, chrome hardware, 6-on-a-side tuners, 1 volume/1 tone control, toggle switch, no pickguard, tremelo, 2 exposed coil humbuckers.

WILDE USA

See BILL LAWRENCE GUITAR COMPANY LLC.

WILKES

Instruments currently built in England since the mid 1970s.

These high quality solid body guitars feature both original and designs based on popular American classics. Models include the Answer, Extrovert, Poet, Skitzo, and the Slut (?!). We know what you're thinking, and you are absolutely correct: Send photos and information for future updates of the Wilkes guitar models to the ***Blue Book of Electric Guitars***!

(Source: Tony Bacon and Paul Day, The Guru's Guitar Book)

WILKINS, PAT

Instruments currently built in Van Nuys, California. Distributed by Wilkins Guitar Finishes of Van Nuys, California.

Instruments previously built in Portsmouth, Virginia.

Luthier Pat Wilkins has been acknowledged as a premier finisher of quality instruments for well over the past ten years. Some of his recent handiwork can be viewed on such models as the U.S. produced Pacifica models for Yamaha, as well as his namesake hand crafted models (other examples occasionally turn up as prototypes displayed at industry trade shows - but no further hints will be dropped).

Prior to moving to California, Wilkins joined former Schecter Research President Bill Ricketts and ex-Zion Guitars luthier Kenny Marshall in custom building limited production guitars and basses in the 1980s. The **OFB Guitars** custom models were built in Portsmouth, Virginia.

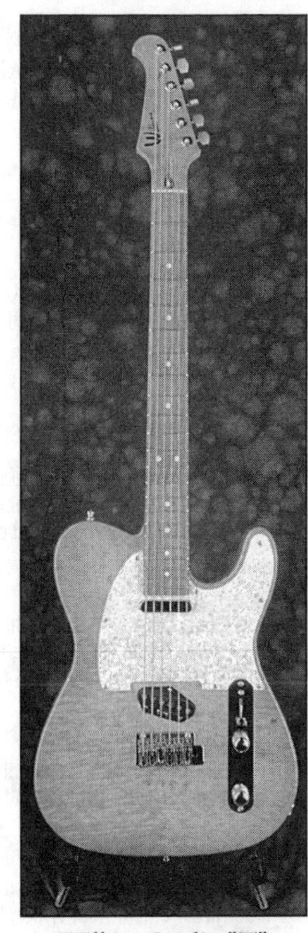

Wilkins Studio "T" courtesy Pat Wilkins

ELECTRIC

Wilkins' former models feature bolt-on neck, tilt-back headstocks, locking machine heads, numerous different pickup combinations, and spectacular finishes. For further information regarding custom finishes, please contact Wilkins Guitar Finishes directly (see Trademark Index).

W

WILSON

See WATKINS.

Instruments previously built in England.

The Wilson logo is the final one used by the Watkins company (1960-1982). Models include the three pickup Sapphire III solid body, and some electric hollowbody designs.

(Source: Tony Bacon, The Ultimate Guitar Book)

WINSTON

Instruments previously produced in Japan circa early 1960s to late 1960s. Distributed in the U.S. by Buegeleisen & Jacobson of New York, New York.

The Winston trademark was a brand name used by U.S. importers Buegeleisen & Jacobson of New York, New York. The Winston brand appeared on a full range of acoustic guitars, thinline acoustic/electric archtops, and solid body electric guitars and basses. Winston instruments are generally the shorter scale beginner's guitar. Although the manufacturers are unknown, some models appear to be built by Guyatone.

(Source: Michael Wright, Vintage Guitar Magazine)

WITTMAN

Instruments currently built in Williamsport, Pennsylvania since the early 1990s.

Wittman basses featured exotic woods and a sleek body profile, and different stringing configurations. The Aurora's sleek profile features an extended bass horn, and slimmed back treble bout cutaway.

ELECTRIC BASS

Models are designed with headstock as well as reverse tuned bridge (headless). The Aurora is available in 4-, 5-, and 6- string configurations. For those seeking a more traditional body shape, Wittman also offers a J/P shape design. Prices range from $1,900 to $2,300 for the different Aurora string configurations, and $1,500 to $1,900 for the traditional design. All models feature walnut, maple, polar, ash, or cherry bodies, a bolt-on neck (neck through is optional), maple, ebony or rosewood fingerboard, EMG DC or Bartolini soapbar pickup, a Spinstrap, and on-board ProTuner. For further information regarding model specifications and pricing, contact Wittman Guitars directly (see Trademark Index).

WOLLERMAN GUITARS

Instruments currently built in Sheffield, Illinois. Wollerman Guitars also builds instruments for SUPERVOLT, STONE AXE, BIGGUN, BRICK, and JUNK trademarks. Wollerman Guitars also markets LEDSLED amplification and V-Max pickups.

Luthier/designer Mark Wollerman has been building handcrafted instruments since 1983. Wollerman, a guitarist himself, built his "new" guitar years ago when his finances were low. The Devastator, Wollerman's first handcrafted guitar, was used constantly as he participated with bands. Outside of a few model revisions, the same guitar is still currently produced. Wollerman founded his company in the early 1980s on the premise of building affordable guitars for musicians.

Wollerman offers over 170 guitar body designs, each which are available in eight different lines and five different sizes. Wollerman also offers electric mandolins and electric violins. Wollerman instruments are currently available both in the U.S., and in 21 countries worldwide. A large 112 page catalog of options and body styles is available for a nominal fee. For further information, please contact Wollerman guitars directly (see Trademark Index).

According to Mark Wollerman, some of the more popular body styles are the **Raider, Swept-Wing, Pro-57, J.P. 63, Blaster, Twister, Torqmaster**, and the **Junkmaster**.

ELECTRIC

All Standard Wollerman guitars feature a 25 1/2" scale, 21-fret rosewood fingerboard, graphite nut, Pro sealed tuning pegs, heavy duty hardtail bridge, chrome hardware, one standard humbucking pickup, and one volume control. Wollerman models have individual unique features that differentiate from model to model. Options can be added or subtracted to come up with custom versions of each model.

Wollerman Series

The **Pearl Deluxe** features the full Power Tone bodies with highly figured tops available in White, Black, Gold, Red, Blue, or Green pearloid. Sides are finished in Black or White Naugahyde, and backs in a Gloss White. The **Super Pearl Deluxe** is an extra cost option of pearloid backs instead of Gloss White. There are many custom paint and solid body options, and the retail price lists at $429 and up.

Biggun Series

The **Biggun** series is a special variation of the **Wollerman, Supervolt, Brick**, and **Rawhide** lines. Models feature a 10% oversized body, 27" scale length, and 1 3/4" neck width (at nut). A true Baritone neck (28 1/2") is also available. Retail prices list at $449 and up.

Supervolt Series

Supervolt models feature bodies similar to the full Power Tone bodies, except have Gloss White textured Fiberglass tops and backs and choice of pickguards/ sidetrim in Black, Red, White, Blue, Yellow, and Green. Other options include color co- ordinated pickup covers, and swirl pickguards. Retail prices begin at $319 and up.

Brick Series

Similar to the Supervolt, except feature tops, backs, and sides that resemble brick walls! Models feature gray "cement lines" and Red, White, Black, or Brown bricks. Retail list begins at $359 and up.

Stone Axe Series

Stone Axe models feature the Full Power Tone bodies and pickguards, but the bodies have a finish like they were carved out of stone. Colors include Turquoise Dust, Red Quartz, Gray Stone, Sandstone, Pueblo Stone, Black Stone, Soap Stone, and Ironstone. Retail prices list at $339 and up.

Rawhide Series

Rawhide series guitars have the Wollerman Full Power Tone bodies with tops and backs constructed of "Leatherwood", and pickguards covered in black or white Naugahyde. Retail list begins at $299 and up.

Junk Series

The Junk guitar and bass series is the "enviromentally conscious" line from Wollerman. These instruments feature a neck- through-body design based on laminating the extra wood left over from other projects. These laminated bodies feature a natural look, durable all wood construction, and decent tone. A number of other guitar companies began building multi-laminated wood body guitars as far back as the 1970s, all with high end prices. However, this series is moderately priced, and begins at $259 and up.

Special Guitar Operations

The Special Guitar Operations is the high end custom shop maintained by Wollerman. **S.G.O. guitars** and **basses** (list $499 and up) feature the best parts, pickups, and woods available - as well as the flexibility for custom designs. Most bass guitar orders are processed through the S.G.O., and **Wollerman basses** (list $299 and up) feature a 34" scale, rosewood fingerboard, chrome hardware, a JB pickup, and one volume control. Most of the guitar designs are available in bass format. Wollerman also produces 4-string **Tenor** guitars (list $239 and up), **Mini** guitars (similar to the full scale models, yet begin at $229 and up), **electric Mandolins** ($199 and up), and **left handed guitars** (most models, and parts are available too - list $219 and up).

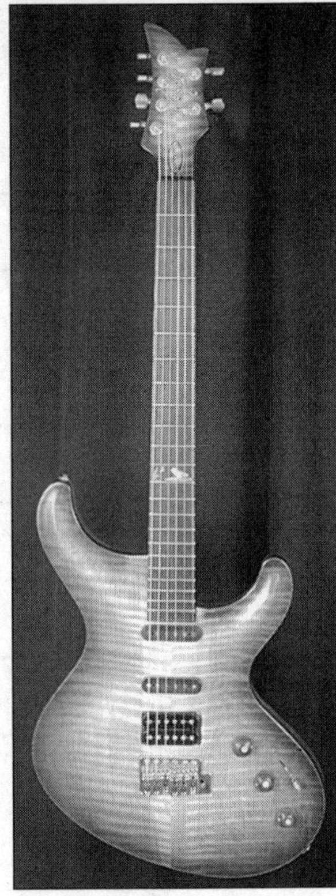

Wood's Custom
courtesy Woody Phiffer

WOODY'S CUSTOM GUITARS

Instruments currently produced in New York City since mid 1970s.

Luthier/designer Woody Phiffer has been building and producing innovative high quality guitars for several years. Phiffer's guitars always feature high quality construction and shaping, and immaculate translucent finishes.

Phiffer's current custom model features a carved top and back, carved pickup covers, exotic woods, mutli-layer body binding, and quality hardware and pickups. The list price begins around $3,900, although prices will change to reflect custom options. For further information, please contact luthier Phiffer directly (see Trademark Index).

WORLD TEISCO

See TEISCO DEL REY.

WRIGHT GUITAR TECHNOLOGY

Instruments currently built in Eugene, Oregon.

Luthier Wright was briefly involved with Stephen Mosher's Moses Graphite necks, and then turned to producing a good quality travel guitar. The **Soloette** model has even traveled on the NASA's space shuttle recently! For more information regarding the Soloette and pricing, contact Wright Guitar Technology directly (see Trademark Index).

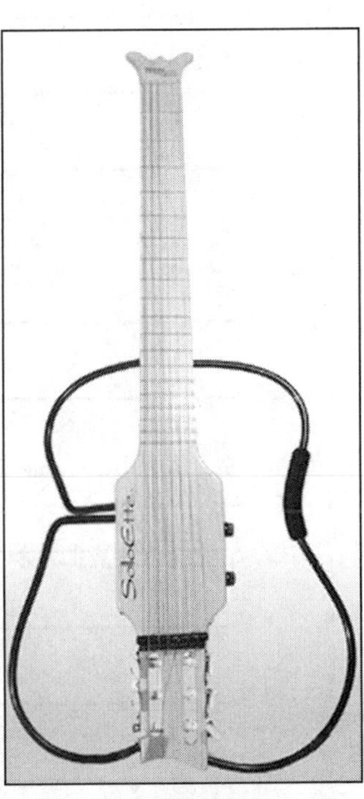

Wright Soloette
courtesy Wright Guitar Tech

WURLITZER

Instruments previously built in America during the 1960s. Wurlitzer then began importing models from Italy during the 1970s.

During the 1960s, Wurlitzer distributed guitars built in the Holman-Woodell facility in Neodesha, Kansas (makers of other trademarks such as Holman, Alray, 21st Century, and La Baye). Instruments were medium quality solid or semi-hollowbody guitars. As U.S. production prices rose, Wurlitzer began importing semi-hollowbody guitars built by the Welson company in Italy in the early 1970s.

W

NOTES

Section X

GRADING	100% MINT	98% NEAR MINT	95% EXC+	90% EXC	80% VG+	70% VG	60% G

XOTIC GUITARS

Instruments currently built in Van Nuys, California. Distributed by Alfa Export Office, Inc. of Van Nuys, California.

Xotic builds high quality basses with exotic woods and premium hardware. Xotic is also building Trilogic pickups and preamps, as well as the Spiral guitar models (See SPIRAL).

ELECTRIC BASS

There is no additional charge for left-handed configurations. Xotic does offer a number of additional custom options per model.

XB-1 - offset double cutaway 2-piece ash or alder body, bolt-on 3-piece maple neck, 34" scale, 24-fret maple fingerboard with black dot inlay, Gotoh bridge, Kent Armstrong pickup, volume/tone controls, Xotic P-1 preamp. Available in Black, Red, White, or Burst finishes. Current Mfg.

4-string - 2 per side Gotoh GB70E tuners.
MSR $1,780

5-String - 3/2 per side tuners.
MSR $1,980

XB-2 STANDARD - offset double cutaway ash or alder body, bolt-on 3-piece maple, 34" scale, 24-fret bird's-eye maple fingerboard with abalone dot inlay, Hipshot Ultralite tuners, Kahler bridge, 2 Kent Armstrong pickups, master volume/blend/master tone controls, 3-band EQ controls, Xotic Super 125 preamp. Available in Transparent color finishes. Current Mfg.

4-string - 2 per side tuners.
MSR $2,480

5-string - 3/2 per side tuners.
MSR $2,680

Add $150 for cocobola, kingwood, or macassar ebony fingerboard.

Add $200 for fretless fingerboard.

Add $300 for custom model with set neck.

XB-2 Custom - similar to the XB-2 Standard, except features exotic wood top and back (bubinga, padauk, quilted maple, or zebrawood), ebony fingerboard with aluminum rings design inlay. Available in Clear Semigloss finish. Current Mfg.

4-string - 2 per side tuners.
MSR $2,950

5-string - 3/2 per side tuners.
MSR $3,100

6-string - 3 per side tuners.
MSR $3,300

XB-2 Premier - similar to the XB-2 Standard, except features maple, ash or alder body, special exotic wood top and back (figured maple, Macassar ebony, Madrone burl, maple burl, spalted maple, or ziricote), set-in maple neck, ebony fingerboard with aluminum rings design inlay. Available in Clear Semigloss finish. Current Mfg.

4-string - 2 per side tuners.
MSR $3,500

5-string - 3/2 per side tuners.
MSR $3,700

6-string - 3 per side tuners.
MSR $3,900

XB-3 STANDARD 5-STRING - offset double cutaway ash or alder body, bolt-on 3-piece maple, 34" scale, 21-fret bird's-eye maple fingerboard with abalone dot inlay, 3/2 per side Hipshot Ultralite tuners, Kahler bridge, 2 original single coil pickups, volume/blend/tone controls. Available in Transparent color finishes. Mfg. 1998 to date.
MSR $2,680

GRADING	100% MINT	98% NEAR MINT	95% EXC+	90% EXC	80% VG+	70% VG	60% G

XB-3 Custom 5-String - similar to the XB-3 Standard 5-String, except features exotic wood top and back (bubinga, padauk, quilted maple or zebrawood), ebony fingerboard with aluminum rings design inlay. Available in Clear Semigloss finish. Current Mfg.
MSR **$3,100**

XB-3 Premier - similar to the XB-3 Standard 5-String, except features maple, ash or alder body, special exotic wood top and back (figured maple, Macassar ebony, Madrone burl, maple burl, spalted maple, or ziricote), set-in maple neck, ebony fingerboard with aluminum rings design inlay. Available in Clear Semigloss finish. Current Mfg.
MSR **$3,700**

X

Section Y

GRADING	100% MINT	98% NEAR MINT	95% EXC+	90% EXC	80% VG+	70% VG	60% G

Yamaha AES 1500 B
courtesy Yamaha

YAMAHA

Instruments currently produced in U.S., Taiwan, and Indonesia. Distributed in the U.S. by the Yamaha Corporation of America, located in Buena Park, California.

Instruments previously produced in Japan. Yamaha company headquarters is located in Hamamatsu, Japan.

Yamaha has a tradition of building musical instruments for over 100 years. The first Yamaha solid body electric guitars were introduced to the American market in 1966. While the first series relied on designs based on classic American favorites, the second series developed more original designs. In the mid 1970s, Yamaha was recognized as the first Oriental brand to emerge as a prominent force equal to the big-name US builders.

Production shifted to Taiwan in the early 1980s as Yamaha built its own facility to maintain quality. In 1990, the Yamaha Corporation of America (located in Buena Park, California) opened the Yamaha Guitar Development (YGD) center in North Hollywood, California. The Yamaha Guitar Development center focuses on design, prototyping, and customizing both current and new models. The YGD also custom builds and maintains many of the Yamaha artist's instruments. The center's address on Weddington Street probably was the namesake of the Weddington series instruments of the early 1990s.

The Yamaha company is active in producing a full range of musical instruments, including band instruments, stringed instruments, amplifiers, and P.A. equipment.

ELECTRIC

AES Series

The two AES Series models debuted in 1998.

AES 500 - single rounded cutaway nato body, bolt-on maple neck, 25 1/2" scale, 22-fret rosewood fingerboard with pearl dot inlay, wraparound bridge, 3-per-side tuners, chrome hardware, pearloid 'stealth fighter'-shaped pickguard, 2 chrome covered humbucker pickups, 2 volume/tone controls, 3-way selector switch. Available in Black, Cream White, Gold, and Silver gloss finishes. Mfg. 1998 to 2000.

$450 $350 $300 $250 $200 $175 $150
Last MSR was $599.

AES 800 - single rounded cutaway alder body, mahogany top, bolt-on maple neck, 25 1/2" scale, 22-fret rosewood fingerboard with pearl dot inlay, tune-o-matic bridge/individual 'fingers' tailpiece, 3-per-side tuners, chrome hardware, tortoiseshell 'jimmy cap'-shaped pickguard, 2 DiMarzio Q-100 hum-cancelling 'soapbar' humbucker pickups, volume/tone/phase controls, 5-way selector switch. Available in Brown Sunburst and Cherry Sunburst finishes. Mfg. 1998 to 2000.

$600 $500 $450 $400 $350 $300 $250
Last MSR was $799.

AES 800 B - similar to AES 800, except has alder body, Bigsby tailpiece, master volume, master tone, coil cut, 3-way selector switch. Available in Blue finish. Disc.

$750 $650 $600 $550 $500 $450 $400
Last MSR was $999.

Image Series

AE 1200 S - single round cutaway hollow body, laminated spruce top, bound body and f-holes, raised bound tortoise pickguard, beech/birch back/sides, mahogany neck, 20-fret bound ebony fingerboard with abalone split block inlay, metal/grenadilla bridge with trapeze tailpiece, bound peghead, 3-per-side tuners, gold hardware, 2 humbucker pickups, 2 volume/tone controls, 3-position switch, coil split in tone controls. Available in Antique Stain and Natural finishes. Disc. 1996.

$1,350 $900 $800 $650 $575 $500 $450
Last MSR was $1,800.

AES 1500 - single round cutaway hollow body, curly maple top, bound body and f-holes, raised black pickguard, maple back/sides, 3-piece maple neck, 22-fret bound rosewood fingerboard with pearl dot inlay, bridge/stop tailpiece, abalone Yamaha symbol and scroll inlay on peghead, 3-per-side tuners, gold hardware, 2 DiMarzio humbucker pickups, 2 volume/tone controls, 3-position switch, coil split in tone controls. Available in Orange Stain and Pearl Snow White finishes. Disc. 1998.

$1,900 $1,525 $1,150 $850 $750 $595 $525
Last MSR was $1,999.

GRADING	100% MINT	98% NEAR MINT	95% EXC+	90% EXC	80% VG+	70% VG	60% G

AES 1500 B - similar to AES 1500, except has Bigsby vibrato. Available in Antique Sunburst, Black, Natural and Orange Stain finishes. Mfg. 1994 to 1998.

$1,395	$1,250	$1,100	$975	$775	$650	$600

Last MSR was $2,399.

AES 1500 (New) - single round cutaway semi-hollow body, arched sycamore top, maple back and sides, set maple/mahogany neck with rosewood fingerboard, 22-frets, 2 DiMarzio Q-100 Humbuckers, gold hardware, 3-way selector switch, 2 volume and 2 tone controls, coil splitting, 3-per-side tuners, tune-o-matic bridge, 24 3/4" scale. Available in Orange, and Pearl Snow White finishes. New features in 1999.

MSR	$2,399	$1,900	$1,535	$1,350	$1,100	$995	$895	$750

AES 1500 B (New) - similar to AES 1500, except has Bigsby B-6 tailpiece. Available in orange and black finishes.

MSR	$2,599	$2,100	$1,650	$1,400	$1,250	$1,100	$995	$895

AEX 500 - single rounded cutaway semi-hollow body, laminated spruce top, bound body, 2 f-holes, laminated back/sides, bolt-on maple neck, 22-fret rosewood fingerboard with pearl dot inlay, adjustable rosewood bridge/metal trapeze tailpiece, blackface peghead with scroll/logo inlay, 3-per-side tuners, gold hardware, covered humbucker/piezo bridge pickups, master volume/pickup blend controls, 3 band EQ controls. Available in Black and Brown Sunburst finishes. Mfg. 1998 to 2000.

$525	$450	$425	$400	$375	$350	$300

Last MSR was $699.

AEX 500 N - nylon string, semi-hollow alder body, laminated spruce top, maple bolt-on neck, rosewood fingerboard, 22-frets, 1-way piezo pickup with 3-band EQ, rosewood bridge, 24 3/4" scale, master volume, gold hardware. Available in Natural gloss and Solid Black finishes. Current Mfg.

MSR	$699	$525	$450	$425	$375	$350	$325	$275

AEX 502 - single cutaway, semi-hollow alder body with maple veneer, f-holes, maple bolt-on neck, rosewood fingerboard, 22-frets, 2 P-90 style pickups with "Dog Ear" covers, Tune-O-Matic bridge with stop tailpiece, 24 3/4" scale, master volume, master tone, 3-way selector switch, gold hardware. Available in Brown Sunburst, Solid Black, and Orange stain finishes. Disc. 2000.

$485	$425	$400	$350	$325	$300	$250

Last MSR was $649.

AEX 520 - similar to AEX 502, except has Mini-Humbucking pickups with covers. Available in Brown Sunburst, Solid Black, and Orange stain finishes. Disc. 2000.

$525	$450	$425	$375	$350	$325	$275

Last MSR was $699.

AEX 1500 - single rounded cutaway hollow body, arched sycamore top, raised black pickguard, bound body and f-holes, figured maple back/sides/neck, 20-fret bound ebony fingerboard with pearl dot inlay, adjustable ebony bridge/trapeze tailpiece, bound blackface peghead with pearl scroll/logo inlay, 3-per-side tuners, gold hardware, humbucker/piezo bridge pickups, humbucker volume/tone controls, piezo volume/tone/3-band EQ controls. Available in Antique Stain, Faded Burst and Natural finishes. Mfg. 1994 to 1998.

$1,250	$1,150	$975	$725	$650	$595	$500

Last MSR was $1,999.

AEX 1500 (New) - jazz archtop body, sycamore top, maple back and sides, ebony fingerboard, 20-frets, Floating Johnny Smith style humbuckers, bridge piezo, gold hardware, humbucker volume, tone, piezo pre-amp system with 3-band EQ, blend, volume, adjustable mid-range, ebony/bone bridge, 24 3'4" scale, co-designed with Martin Taylor. Available in Natural and Antique Sunburst finishes. New features in 1999.

MSR	$1,999	$1,500	$1,300	$1,150	$1,050	$895	$775	$675

Pacifica Series Single Cutaway

Pacifica models are available in single or double cutaway body models.

PAC 102 S - single cutaway alder body, bolt-on maple neck, 22-fret bubinga fingerboard with pearl dot inlay, fixed bridge, 6-on-a-side tuners, chrome hardware, white pickguard, 2 single coil pickups, volume/tone controls, 3-position switch. Available in Black, Brown Satin, and Natural satin finishes. Mfg. 1994 to 2000.

$275	$195	$150	$125	$115	$100	$85

Last MSR was $349.

PAC 120 S - single cutaway alder body, bolt-on maple neck, 22-fret bubinga fingerboard with pearl dot inlay, strings through fixed bridge, 6-on-a-side tuners, chrome hardware, 2 humbucker pickups, volume/tone controls, 3-position switch. Available in Antique Sunburst, Black, and Yellow Natural finishes. Mfg. 1994 to date.

MSR	$339	$250	$195	$175	$150	$125	$100	$90

In 1998, Natural Satin finish was introduced; Antique Sunburst and Yellow Natural finishes were discontinued. In 1999, Brown Satin was introduced.

PAC 302 S - single cutaway bound alder body, bolt-on maple neck, 22-fret rosewood fingerboard with pearl dot inlay, New Vintage fixed bridge, 6-on-a-side tuners, gold hardware, white pearloid pickguard, 2 single coil pickups, volume/tone controls, 3-position switch. Available in Cherry Sunburst, Charcoal Grey, and Translucent Blue finishes. Disc. 1999.

$375	$295	$250	$225	$175	$150	$125

Last MSR was $479.

GRADING			100% MINT	98% NEAR MINT	95% EXC+	90% EXC	80% VG+	70% VG	60% G

PAC 311 MS - Mike Stern body style, alder body with ash veneer, maple neck and fingerboard, 22-frets, 1 Humbucker pickup, 1 "Hot Rail" style pickup, 3-position, selector, master volume, master tone, fixed bridge, black pickguard, chrome hardware. Available in Natural, Vintage Blonde, and Orange Stain finishes. Current Mfg.

MSR $549 $410 $325 $275 $250 $195 $165 $135

PAC 402 S - single cutaway bound alder body with 'high definition' top, bolt-on maple neck, 22-fret rosewood fingerboard with pearl dot inlay, New Vintage fixed bridge, 6-on-a-side tuners, gold hardware, white pearloid pickguard, 2 single coil pickups, volume/tone controls, 3-position switch. Available in High Definition Amber Burst, High Definition Violin Sunburst, and High Definition Translucent Green finishes. Disc.

$425 $350 $300 $250 $200 $175 $150
Last MSR was $579.

812 S - single cutaway alder body, black pickguard, bolt-on maple neck, 24-fret rosewood fingerboard with pearl dot inlay, double locking vibrato, 6-on-a-side tuners, black hardware, 2 stacked coil/1 humbucker pickups, volume/tone control, 5-position switch with coil split. Available in Black, Dark Red Metallic and Lightning Blue finishes. Disc. 1994.

$525 $450 $375 $295 $250 $225 $200
Last MSR was $730.

AES FRANK GAMBALE SIGNATURE MODEL - designed inconjucction with guitarist Frank Gambale, features Fretwaves tuning system, carved top,double cutaway lightweight mahogany body, rear mounted bolt-on neck with ebony fingerboard, 25 ½" scale, 3-per-side tuners, VS-100G bridge, 2 Seymour Duncan Hot Rails and 1 Seymour Duncan JB in the bridge position, master volume, master tone, push-pull coil tap, 5-position switch. Available in black and white finishes. New 2001.

MSR $2,699 $1,889 $1,699 $1,499 $1,299 $1,099 $899 $650

PAC 1511 MS MIKE STERN SIGNATURE MODEL - single cutaway bound 2-piece white ash body, bolt-on maple neck, 22-fret maple fingerboard with dot inlay, New Vintage fixed bridge, 6-on-a-side tuners, chrome hardware, black pickguard, 2 Seymour Duncan single coil pickups, volume/tone controls, 3-position switch. Available in Natural gloss finish. Mfg. 1996 to date.

MSR $1,499 $1,150 $900 $800 $700 $625 $475 $350

RGXTT TY TABOR SIGNATURE MODEL - designed in conjunction with Ty Tabor of King's X, offset double cutaway body constructed of American Basswood wings and a stepped maple center, 2 Seymour Duncan Vintage Rails and 1 Seymour Duncan JB in the bridge position, 4-pole 5-way switch, master volume, master tone, coil capacitor cut push-pull switch, Wilkinson VS100G tremelo bridge, rosewood fingerboard, 22-frets, 3-per-side tuners. Available in Translucent Red Sunburst, Translucent Green Sunburst and Translucent Purple Sunburst finishes. Current Mfg.

MSR $1,599 $1,125 $1,025 $925 $825 $725 $625 $499

RGXTTD6 (Drop 6) Ty Tabor Signature Model - similar to Model RGXTT except, in a 26 ¼" scale, used together with heavier strings to provide deep throated tones. Available in Translucent Green Sunburst and Translucent Purple Sunburst. New 2001.

MSR $1,699 $1,189 $1,075 $975 $875 $775 $675 $550

1221 M S - single cutaway basswood body, black pickguard, bolt-on maple neck, 24-fret maple fingerboard with black slash inlay, double locking vibrato, 6-on-a-side tuners, black hardware, humbucker/stacked coil/humbucker DiMarzio pickups, volume/tone control, 5-position switch with coil split. Available in Black and Yellow Pearl finishes. Disc. 1994.

$725 $625 $525 $425 $375 $350 $325
Last MSR was $1,060.

1230 S - single cutaway basswood body, black pickguard, bolt-on maple neck, 24-fret maple fingerboard with black slash inlay, double locking vibrato, 6-on-a-side tuners, black hardware, 3 DiMarzio humbucker pickups, volume/tone control, 5-position switch with coil split. Available in Black and Dark Blue Metallic finishes. Disc. 1994.

$750 $650 $550 $425 $375 $350 $325
Last MSR was $1,060.

PACIFICA USA 1 - single curved cutaway bound alder body, figured maple top, bolt-on maple neck, 22-fret rosewood fingerboard with pearl dot inlay, Wilkinson VSV vintage tremolo, 6-on-a-side Sperzel Tremlock tuners, gold hardware, white pearloid pickguard, 2 Seymour Duncan single coil/Seymour Duncan custom humbucker pickups, volume/tone controls, 5-position switch, metal controls plate. Available in Natural, Translucent Blue, and Violin Sunburst finishes. Mfg. 1996 to 2000.

$1,550 $1,300 1,150 $N/A $N/A $N/A $N/A
Last MSR was $1,899.

This model is constructed at the U.S. Yamaha Guitar Development center, featuring Warmoth bodies and necks, Seymour Duncan pickups, Wilkinson tremolo bridges, and Sperzel tuners.

Yamaha AEX 1500
courtesy Yamaha

Y

GRADING	100% MINT	98% NEAR MINT	95% EXC+	90% EXC	80% VG+	70% VG	60% G

Pacifica Series Double Cutaway

PAC 112 - offset double cutaway alder body, bolt-on maple neck, 22-fret bubinga fingerboard with pearl dot inlay, standard vibrato, 6-on-a-side tuners, chrome hardware, white pickguard, 2 single coil/humbucker pickups, volume/tone controls, 5-position switch. Available in Antique Sunburst, Black and Yellow Natural finishes. Mfg. 1994 to date.

MSR	$379	$290	$215	$165	$140	$155	$110	$95

Add $70 for left-handed configuration (Model PAC112 L).

Add $20 for maple fingerboard (Model PAC112 M).

In 1999, Natural Satin, Brown Satin & Vintage White finishes were introduced; Antique Sunburst & Natural Yellow finishes were discontinued.

PAC 303-12 12-STRING - offset double cutaway alder body, bolt-on maple neck, 22-fret rosewood fingerboard with pearl dot inlay, fixed bridge, 6-per-side tuners, gold hardware, white pearloid pickguard, 3 single coil pickups, volume/tone controls, 5-position switch. Available in Translucent Blue and Translucent Cherry finishes. Disc. 1999.

		$525	$425	$375	$325	$275	$225	$175

Last MSR was $699.

PAC 303-12 II - double cutaway 12-string, alder body with ash veneer top, maple neck, rosewood fingerboard, 22-frets, 3-single coil pickups, 5-position selector switch, master volume, master tone, bridge with individual intonation adjustment, black pickguard, chrome hardware. Available in Old Violin Sunburst, and Honey Burst. Current Mfg.

MSR	$649	$485	$410	$340	$295	$250	$215	$150

PAC 312 - offset double cutaway alder body, bolt-on maple neck, 22-fret rosewood fingerboard with pearl dot inlay, vintage-style tremolo, 6-on-a-side tuners, gold hardware, white pearloid pickguard, 2 single coil/humbucker pickups, volume/tone controls, 5-position switch. Available in Charcoal Grey, Cherry Sunburst, and Translucent Blue finishes. Disc.

		$375	$300	$275	$225	$195	$150	$125

Last MSR was $499.

PAC 312 II - double cutaway body, alder body with ash veneer top, maple neck with rosewood fingerboard, 22-frets, 2 single coil pickups and 1 Humbucker pickup, 5-position switch, master volume, master tone, vintage tremolo, black pickguard, chrome hardware. Available in Old Violin Sunburst, Translucent Red, and Translucent Dark Green finishes. Current Mfg.

MSR	$539	$400	$325	$295	$250	$225	$175	$145

PAC 412 - offset double cutaway bound alder body with 'high definition' top, bolt-on maple neck, 22-fret rosewood fingerboard with pearl dot inlay, vintage-style tremolo, 6-on-a-side tuners, gold hardware, white pearloid pickguard, 2 single coil pickups, volume/tone controls, 3-position switch. Available in High Definition Amber Burst, High Definition Violin Sunburst, and High Definition Translucent Green finishes. Disc.

		$425	$350	$300	$250	$200	$175	$150

Last MSR was $579.

PAC 604 W - offset double cutaway select alder body, bolt-on maple neck, 22-fret rosewood fingerboard with pearl dot inlay, standard vibrato, 6-on-a-side tuners, chrome hardware, pearloid pickguard, 2 single coil/humbucker pickups, volume/tone control, 5-position switch. Available in Antique Sunburst, Black, Cherry Sunburst and Sea Foam Green finishes. Mfg. 1994 to date.

MSR	$849	$695	$495	$425	$325	$295	$265	$235

In 1998, Translucent Blue finish was introduced; Sea Foam Green finish was discontinued. In 1999, Antique Sunburst finish was discontinued.

PAC 812 W - offset double cutaway select alder body, maple veneer top, bolt-on maple neck, 22-fret rosewood fingerboard with pearl dot inlay, Wilkinson VS100 tremolo, 6-on-a-side tuners, brushed aluminum hardware, white pearloid pickguard, 2 single coil/humbucker Seymour Duncan pickups, volume/tone control, 5-way selector switch. Available in Natural, Translucent Blue, and Violin Sunburst finishes. Mfg. 1998 to date.

MSR	$1,149	$950	$800	$750	$650	$595	$550	$495

821 - offset double cutaway alder body, black pickguard, bolt-on maple neck, 24-fret rosewood fingerboard with pearl dot inlay, double locking vibrato, 6-on-a-side tuners, black hardware, humbucker/stacked coil/humbucker pickups, volume/tone control, 5-position switch with coil split. Available in Black, Dark Red Metallic and Lightning Blue finishes. Disc. 1994.

		$525	$450	$375	$295	$250	$225	$200

Last MSR was $730.

This model was also available with reverse peghead (Model 821R).

904 - offset double cutaway alder body, ash top, white pickguard, bolt-on maple Warmoth neck, 22-fret rosewood fingerboard with pearl dot inlay, 6-on-a-side tuners, nickel hardware, 2 single coil/humbucker pickups, volume/tone controls, 5-position switch. Available in Faded Blue, Faded Burst, Old Violin Sunburst and Translucent Black finishes. Mfg. 1994 to 1996.

		$800	$750	$625	$500	$450	$425	$375

Last MSR was $1,250.

GRADING	100% MINT	98% NEAR MINT	95% EXC+	90% EXC	80% VG+	70% VG	60% G

12 J - offset double cutaway swamp ash body, white pickguard, bolt-on maple neck, 22-fret fingerboard with pearl dot inlay, double locking vibrato, 6-on-a-side tuners, chrome hardware, 2 stacked coil/humbucker DiMarzio pickups, volume/tone control, 5-position switch. Available in Black, Crimson Red, Faded Burst and Translucent Blue finishes. Disc. 1996.

$725 $650 $525 $425 $375 $350 $325
Last MSR was $1,250.

212 - offset double cutaway basswood body, black pickguard, bolt-on maple neck, 24-fret rosewood fingerboard with pearl slash inlay, double locking vibrato, 6-on-a-side tuners, black hardware, 2 stacked coil/humbucker DiMarzio pickups, volume/tone control, 5-position switch with coil split. Available in Black, Dark Blue Metallic and Dark Red Metallic finishes. Disc. 1994.

$750 $625 $525 $425 $375 $350 $325
Last MSR was $1,060.

221 - similar to 1212, except has humbucker/stacked coil/humbucker DiMarzio pickups. Available in Black and Dark Blue Metallic Flake finishes. Disc. 1994.

$750 $650 $525 $425 $375 $350 $325
Last MSR was $1,060.

1221 M - similar to 1221, except has maple fingerboard with black slash inlay. Disc. 1994.

$750 $650 $525 $425 $375 $350 $325
Last MSR was $1,060.

1230 - similar to 1221, except has 3 humbucker DiMarzio pickups. Available in Black, Dark Red Metallic and Lightning Blue finishes. Disc. 1994.

$750 $650 $550 $425 $395 $350 $325
Last MSR was $1,060.

1412 - offset double cutaway mahogany body with 2 tone chambers, arched flame maple top, 7-piece maple/mahogany through body neck, 24-fret bound ebony fingerboard with abalone/pearl block inlay, double locking vibrato, 6-on-a-side tuners, chrome hardware, 2 stacked coil/humbucker DiMarzio pickups, volume/tone control, 5-position switch with coil split. Available in Blonde, Cherry, Faded Burst, Rose Burst, and Transparent Black finishes. Disc. 1994.

$1,300 $1,200 $1,050 $895 $795 $725 $650
Last MSR was $2,200.

PACIFICA USA 2 - offset double cutaway bound basswood body, figured maple top, bolt-on maple neck, 22-fret rosewood fingerboard with pearl dot inlay, Wilkinson VS100 floating tremolo, 6-on-a-side Sperzel Tremlock tuners, gold hardware, white pearloid pickguard, 2 Seymour Duncan single coil/Seymour Duncan custom humbucker pickups, volume/tone controls 5-position switch. Available in Natural, Translucent Blue, and Violin Sunburst finishes. Mfg. 1996 to 2000.

$1,550 $1,300 1,150 $N/A $N/A $N/A $N/A
Last MSR was $1,899.

This model is constructed at the U.S. Yamaha Guitar Development center, featuring Warmoth bodies and necks, Seymour Duncan pickups, Wilkinson tremolo bridges, and Sperzel tuners.

RGZ/RGX Series

RGZ 112 P - offset double cutaway alder body, black pickguard, bolt-on maple neck, 22-fret bubinga fingerboard with pearl dot inlay, standard vibrato, 6-on-a-side tuners, chrome hardware, 2 single coil/humbucker pickups, volume/tone control, 5-position switch. Available in Black, Lightning Blue and Vivid Red finishes. Disc. 1994.

$200 $175 $150 $125 $115 $100 $85
Last MSR was $300.

RGX 120 D - offset double cutaway alder body, bolt-on maple neck, 22-fret bubinga fingerboard with pearl dot inlay, standard vibrato, 6-on-a-side tuners, chrome hardware, 2 humbucker pickups, volume/tone controls, 3-position switch. Available in Black, Vintage Red and White finishes. Mfg. 1994 to 1998.

$250 $200 $175 $150 $125 $115 $100
Last MSR was $349.

RGX 121 D (RGZ 121 P) - similar to RGX 120 D, except has humbucker/single coil/humbucker pickups, 5-position switch. Available in Black, Blue Metallic, Vintage Red and Yellow Natural finishes. Disc. 1998.

$275 $225 $200 $175 $150 $125 $100
Last MSR was $379.

RZX 121 S - similar to RGX 120 D except, has one single coil pickup in the middle position in addition to two humbuckers, rosewood fingerboard, vintage tremelo. Available in Mist Purple, Mist Raspberry, Satin Black and Shelby Blue finishes. Current Mfg.

MSR $499 $349 $299 $249 $199 $149 $99 $65

Yamaha Pacifica 312
courtesy Yamaha

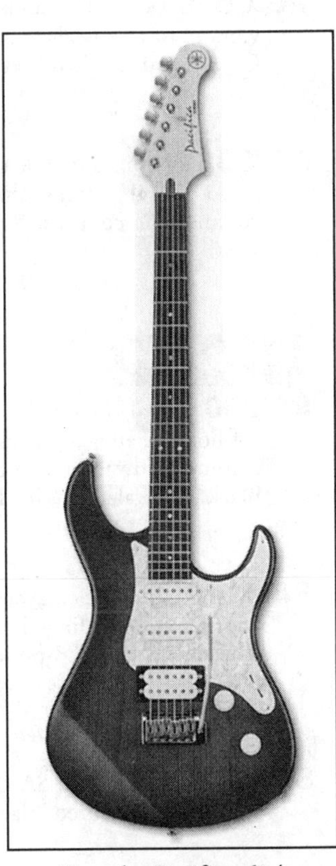

Yamaha Pacifica 604
courtesy Yamaha

GRADING	100% MINT	98% NEAR MINT	95% EXC+	90% EXC	80% VG+	70% VG	60% G

RGZ 321 P - similar to RGZ 120 D, except has double locking vibrato, humbucker/single coil/humbucker pickups, 5-position switc Available in Black, Lightning Blue and 3D Blue. Disc. 1994.

		$325	$275	$225	$195	$175	$150	$125
						Last MSR was $460.		

RGX 420 S - offset double cutaway alder body, bolt-on neck, rosewood fingerboard with dot position markers, 25 ½" scale, 24-frets, 6-o a-side tuners, 2 humbicking pickups, 5-position switch, master volume, master tone, double locking tremelo. Available in Grey Satin, Mi Green and Satin Black finishes. Current Mfg.

MSR	$599	$419	$350	$295	$250	$195	$150	$95

RGX 420 SD6 (Drop 6) - similar to Model RGX 420 S except, has a 26 ¼" scale. The longer scale and heavier strings provide a deep throate tone. New 2001.

MSR	$649	$450	$395	$350	$295	$250	$195	$150

RGX 421 D - offset double cutaway alder body, bolt-on maple neck, 24-fret rosewood fingerboard with pearl dot inlay, double lockir vibrato, 6-on-a-side tuners, chrome hardware, volume/tone controls, 5-position switch. Available in Aqua, Black Pearl, Natural and Re Metallic finishes. Mfg. 1994 to 1998.

		$425	$375	$295	$225	$200	$175	$150
						Last MSR was $599.		

This model was optional with a maple fingerboard (Model RGZ 421 D M).

RGZ 612 P - offset double cutaway alder body, black pickguard, bolt-on maple neck, 24-fret rosewood fingerboard with pearl dot inla double locking vibrato, 6-on-a-side tuners, black hardware, 2 single coil/humbucker pickups, volume/tone control, 5-position switch wi coil split. Available in Black, Dark Red Metallic and Lightning Blue finishes. Disc. 1994.

		$500	$425	$350	$295	$250	$225	$200
						Last MSR was $720.		

RGZ 612 PL - similar to RGZ 612 P, except has a left-handed configuration. Disc. 1994.

		$525	$500	$425	$350	$300	$250	$225
						Last MSR was $830.		

RGX 621 D (RGZ 621 P) - offset double cutaway alder body, bolt-on maple neck, 24-fret rosewood fingerboard with pearl offset do inlay, double locking vibrato, 6-on-a-side tuners, black hardware, humbucker/single coil/humbucker pickups, volume/tone controls, 5-posi tion switch. Available in Antique Sunburst, Black, Blue Metallic and Red Metallic finishes. Disc. 1995

		$500	$400	$350	$295	$250	$225	$200
						Last MSR was $800.		

RGX 820 R - offset double cutaway basswood body, bolt-on maple neck, 22-fret rosewood fingerboard with green dot inlay, double locking vibrato, reverse peghead, 6-on-a-side tuners, black hardware, 2 humbucker pickups, volume control, 3-position switch. Available in Black Green Plaid and Red Metallic finishes. Mfg. 1993 to 1995.

		$725	$625	$525	$450	$375	$350	$300
						Last MSR was $1,050.		

RGX 821 - offset double cutaway alder body, bolt-on maple neck, 24-fret rosewood fingerboard with abalone oval inlay (fingerboard is scalloped from the 20th to the 24th fret), double locking vibrato, 6-on-a-side tuners, gold hardware, humbucker/single coil/humbucker pickups, volume/tone controls, 5-position switch. Available in Antique Sunburst, Blackburst, Faded Blue and Violetburst finishes. Mfg. 1994 to 1996.

		$700	$600	$500	$400	$350	$325	$275
						Last MSR was $1,000.		

SA Series

SA 800 - dual cutaway semi-hollow body, laminated beech/birch top/back, alder center block, laminated mahogany/birch sides, bound body, 2 f-holes, mahogany neck, 22-fret bound rosewood fingerboard with pearl dot inlay, tunomatic bridge/stop tailpiece, 3-per-side tuners, chrome hardware, raised black pickguard, 2 covered humbucker pickups, 2 volume/2 tone controls, 3-position toggle switch. Available in Black, Natural and Wine Red finishes. Mfg. 1983 to 1989.

		$450	$375	$325	$250	$2000	$175	$125
						Last MSR was $699.		

SA 1100 - double cutaway semi hollow body, laminated maple top/back/sides, bound body, raised black pickguard, mahogany neck, 22-fret bound rosewood fingerboard with pearl dot inlay, bridge/stop tailpiece, 3-per-side tuners, chrome hardware, 2 humbucker pickups, 2 volume/tone controls, 3-position switch, coil split in tone controls. Available in Black, Brown Sunburst, Natural and Orange Sunburst finishes. Disc. 1994.

		$735	$630	$525	$420	$380	$345	$315
						Last MSR was $1,050.		

SA 2000 - similar to SA 1100, except has curly maple top, ebony fingerboard with abalone split block inlay, bound peghead with abalone Yamaha logo/stylized inlay, gold hardware. Available in Brown Sunburst and Violin Sunburst finishes. Mfg. 1981 to 1989.

		$675	$595	$540	$460	$385	$315	$250
						Last MSR was $995.		

Add $100 for left-handed configuration (Model SA 2000 L). Mfg. 1982 to 1989.

Early versions feature a laminated beech/birch top and back.

GRADING	100% MINT	98% NEAR MINT	95% EXC+	90% EXC	80% VG+	70% VG	60% G

SA 2100 - similar to SA 1100, except has laminated beech/birch top and back, 2 covered Alnico humbucker pickups, ebony fingerboard with abalone split block inlay, bound peghead with abalone Yamaha logo/stylized inlay, gold hardware. Available in Brown Sunburst and Violin Sunburst finishes. Mfg. 1985 to 1986.

	$750	$650	$575	$525	$450	$350	$275

Last MSR was $1,299.

SA 2200 - similar to SA 1100, except has flame maple top, maple neck, ebony fingerboard with abalone split block inlay, bound peghead with abalone Yamaha logo/stylized inlay, gold hardware. Available in Brown Sunburst and Violin Sunburst finishes. Mfg. 1992 to date.

MSR $2,259	$1,795	$1,275	$1,075	$925	$775	$670	$575

SBG Series

In the 1980s, Yamaha introduced the SG (Solid Body Guitar) models. Guitar fans familiar with those specific initials will recognize that this situation wouldn't last long! The SG Series later became the SBG (Solid Body Guitar) Series.

SBG 500 - dual pointed cutaway agathis body, bound carved maple top, maple neck, 24 3/4" scale, 22-fret bound rosewood fingerboard with pearl dot inlay, tunomatic bridge/stop tailpiece, 3-per-side tuners, chrome hardware, 2 exposed pole piece humbucker pickups, 2 volume/2 tone controls, 3-way toggle switch. Available in Burgundy and Brown Sunburst finishes. Mfg. 1981 to 1983.

	$225	$195	$175	$150	$125	$100	$75

Last MSR was $550.

Add $60 for left-handed configuration (Model SBG 550 L).

SBG 500 B - dual pointed cutaway nato body, bound body, bolt-on nato neck, 24 3/4" scale, 22-fret rosewood fingerboard with pearl dot inlay, tunomatic bridge/stop tailpiece, 3-per-side tuners, chrome hardware, 2 exposed pole piece humbucker pickups, 2 volume/2 tone controls, 3-way toggle switch. Available in Black, Cherry Sunburst, and Gold finishes. Mfg. 1998 to date.

MSR $739	$550	$495	$450	$400	$350	$300	$250

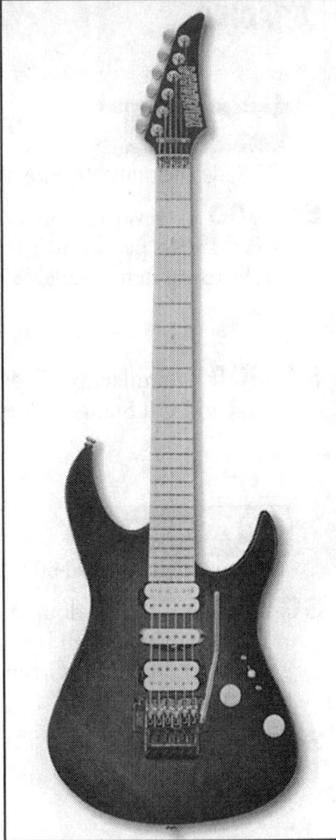

Yamaha RGX 421 DM
courtesy Yamaha

SBG 700 S - dual pointed cutaway mahogany body, bound body, set-in mahogany neck, 24 3/4" scale, 22-fret rosewood fingerboard with pearl dot inlay, tunomatic bridge/stop tailpiece, 3-per-side tuners, gold hardware, 2 exposed pole piece humbucker pickups, 2 volume/2 tone controls (with coil tap capabilities), 3-way toggle switch. Available in Black, Brown Sunburst, Cherry Sunburst, and Translucent Green finishes. Mfg. 1998 to date.

MSR $1,399	$1,050	$925	$875	$795	$725	$675	$625

Brown Sunburst finish discontinued 2000.

SBG 1000 - dual pointed cutaway mahogany body, bound carved maple top, set-in mahogany neck, 24 3/4" scale, 22-fret bound rosewood fingerboard with pearl split triangle inlay, tunomatic bridge/stop tailpiece, 3-per-side tuners, bound headstock, chrome hardware, black pickguard, 2 humbucker pickups, 2 volume/2 tone controls (with coil tap capabilities), 3-way toggle switch. Available in Black and Cherry Sunburst finishes. Mfg. 1982 to 1989.

	$450	$425	$375	$325	$275	$250	$200

Last MSR was $795.

Add $105 for left-handed configuration (Model SBG 1000 L). Mfg. 1983 to 1989.

SBG 2000 - similar to SBG 1000, except features set-in laminated maple/mahogany neck, 22-fret bound ebony fingerboard with pearl split triangle inlay. Available in Black, Brown Sunburst, Cherry Sunburst, and Deep Green finishes. Mfg. 1981 to 1989.

	$525	$475	$425	$375	$325	$275	$225

Last MSR was $1,045.

Add $130 for left-handed configuration (Model SBG 2000 L). Mfg. 1981 to 1989.

SBG 3000 - similar to SBG 1000, except features Mexican abalone body binding, set-in laminated maple/mahogany neck, 22-fret bound ebony fingerboard with mother-of-pearl/Mexican abalone split triangle inlay, gold hardware, engraved stop tailpiece. Available in Metallic Black, Metallic Gold, and Wine Red finishes. Mfg. 1983 to 1989.

	$600	$525	$450	$400	$350	$300	$250

Last MSR was $1,295.

This model was equipped with an optional brass pickguard (to replace the factory installed black plastic pickguard).

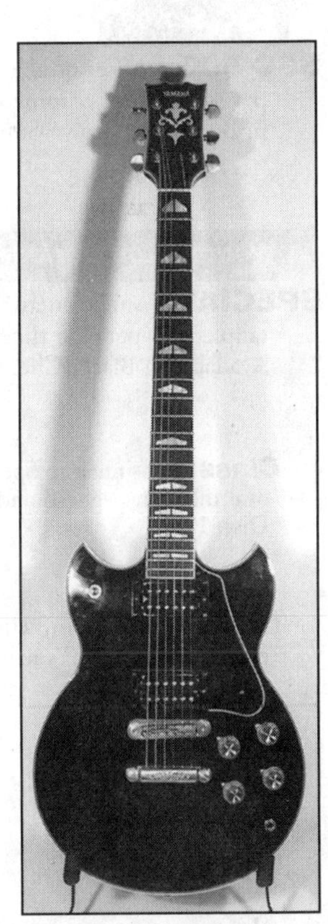

Yamaha SG 2000
courtesy San Diego Guitars

GRADING	100% MINT	98% NEAR MINT	95% EXC+	90% EXC	80% VG+	70% VG	60% G

SC Series

SC Series instruments have a body style reminiscent of a "flipped over" Strat, with the treble bout horn extending further out than the bass horn.

SC 400 - (reversed) offset double cutaway mahogany and ash body, through body mahogany neck, 25 1/2" scale, 22-fret rosewood finge board with pearl dot inlay, fixed bridge, 6-on-a-side tuners, chrome hardware, 3 Alnico 5 single coil pickups, volume/tone controls, 5-wa selector switch. Available in Persimmon Red and Oil Stain finishes. Mfg. 1982 to 1983.

		$225	$195	$175	$150	$125	$100	$75

Last MSR was $475.

SC 600 - similar to SC 400, except features a maple/mahogany/ash/alder laminated body, maple/mahogany neck. Available in Persimmo Red and Oil Stain finishes. Mfg. 1982 to 1983.

		$250	$225	$200	$175	$150	$125	$100

Last MSR was $615.

SGV Series

Reintroduction of a mid-60's design with updated features.

SGV 300 - offset double cutaway alder body, maple neck with rosewood fingerboard, dot position markers, 22-frets, 6-on-a-side tuners Yamaha original ball bearing tremelo system, 3 Yamaha single coil pickups, volume, tone, balance controls, 3-way switch. Available in Black Red Metallic, Pearl Green and CanaryYellow finishes. Current Mfg.

MSR	$549	$385	$325	$275	$225	$195	$125	

SGV 800 - similar to SGV 300 except, has 2 single coil Alnico-5 pickups, 2 Volume/1 Tone control, pearloid pickguard. Available in Blacl Sparkle, Blue Sparkle and Red Sparkle finishes. Current Mfg.

MSR	$699	$489	$425	$375	$325	$275	$225	$175

SHB Series

SHB 400 - offset double cutaway alder body, maple neck, 24 3/4" scale, 22-fret rosewood fingerboard with pearl dot inlay, fixed bridge, 3-per-side tuners, chrome hardware, 2 exposed pole piece humbucker pickups, volume/tone controls, 3-way toggle switch. Available in Chestnut and Natural finishes. Mfg. 1981 to 1983.

		$225	$175	$150	$125	$115	$100	$75

Last MSR was $450.

SSC Series

SSC 500 - offset double cutaway alder body, maple neck, 25 1/2" scale, 21-fret rosewood fingerboard with pearl dot inlay, fixed bridge, 3-per-side tuners, chrome hardware, 3 bar-magnet single coil pickups, volume/tone controls, 3 mini-toggle pickup selector switches. Available in Burgundy, Brown Sunburst, and Natural finishes. Mfg. 1981 to 1983.

		$225	$195	$175	$150	$125	$100	$75

Last MSR was $550.

Weddington Series

SPECIAL - single cutaway mahogany body, set in mahogany neck, 22-fret rosewood fingerboard with pearl dot inlay, adjustable bar bridge/ tailpiece, 3-per-side tuners, chrome hardware, 2 humbucker DiMarzio pickups, 2 volume/tone controls, 5-position switch with coil split. Available in Black, Cherry and Cream White finishes. Disc. 1994.

		$725	$600	$550	$400	$350	$325	$300

Last MSR was $1,000.

Classic - similar to Special, except has arched bound maple top, bound fingerboard with pearl split block inlay, pearl Yamaha symbol and stylized oval inlay on peghead and tunomatic bridge/stop tailpiece. Available in Cherry Sunburst, Metallic Black, Metallic Red top/Natural sides finishes. Disc. 1995.

		$950	$800	$700	$550	$500	$450	$400

Last MSR was $1,600.

Custom - similar to Classic, except has figured maple top, mahogany/maple neck, ebony fingerboard with pearl/abalone inlay, ebony veneer on peghead with pearl Yamaha symbol and stylized scroll inlay. Available in Cherry, Faded Burst and Roseburst finishes. Disc. 1995.

		$1,200	$1,000	$950	$775	$650	$595	$525

Last MSR was $2,200.

GRADING	100% MINT	98% NEAR MINT	95% EXC+	90% EXC	80% VG+	70% VG	60% G

Yamaha SA 2200
courtesy Yamaha

ELECTRIC BASS

Attitude Series

ATTITUDE CUSTOM - offset double cutaway alder body, white pickguard, bolt-on maple neck, 21-fret maple fingerboard with offset black slot inlay, solid brass fixed bridge with 4 built-in piezo electric pickups, 4-on-a-side tuners, chrome hardware, woofer/P-style/piezo DiMarzio pickups, volume/tone control, mini toggle pickup selector switch, stereo outputs. Available in Crimson Red, Dark Blue Metallic and Light Violet Metallic finishes. Disc. 1996.

$1,200 $900 $750 $600 $550 $495 $450
Last MSR was $1,500.

ATTITUDE DELUXE - offset double cutaway alder body, white pickguard, bolt-on maple neck, 21-fret rosewood fingerboard with pearl dot inlay, fixed bridge, 4-on-a-side tuners, chrome hardware, Yamaha "Six Pack" pickup, volume/tone control, 5-position switch. Available in Metallic Black, Metallic Red, Pacific Blue and White finishes. Disc. 1994.

$625 $550 $450 $350 $325 $300 $275
Last MSR was $900.

ATTITUDE LIMITED - offset double cutaway alder body, white pickguard, bolt-on maple neck, 34" scale, 21-fret maple fingerboard with offset black slot inlay, solid brass fixed bridge, 4-on-a-side tuners, "Hipshot" XTender, chrome hardware, Dimarzio bass pickups, 2 volume/tone controls, mini-toggle pickup select switches, stereo outputs. Available in Lightning Red and Thunder Blue finishes. Disc. 1992.

$1,200 $1,000 $900 $750 $650 $595 $550
Last MSR was $1,800.

The Attitude Limited was designed in conjunction with bassist Billy Sheehan (Mr. Big).

ATTITUDE LIMITED II BILLY SHEEHAN SIGNATURE MODEL - similar to Limited, except has pearloid pickguard, scalloped fingerboard from 17th through 21st fret, black hardware. Available in Black and Sea Foam Green finishes. Mfg. 1994 to date.

MSR $1,899 $1,350 $1,100 $950 $775 $650 $575 $450

The Limited II was designed in conjunction with bassist Billy Sheehan (Mr. Big).

ATTITUDE X BILLY SHEEHAN 10TH ANNIVERSARY MODEL - similar to Limited edition II except, features position markers that are Billy's fingerprints, pearloid pickguard. Available in Purple Metallic and Black Metallic. Commemorates the 10th anniversary of the Attitude line. New 2001.

MSR $1,999 $1,399 $1,199 $1,099 $999 $899 $799 $650

ATTITUDE PLUS - offset double cutaway alder body, white pickguard, bolt-on maple neck, 21-fret rosewood fingerboard with pearl dot inlay, fixed bridge, 4-on-a-side tuners, chrome hardware, P-style pickup, volume/tone control. Available in Black, Sea Foam Green, and Red finishes. Current Mfg.

MSR $399 $295 $250 $225 $195 $175 $150 $95

ATTITUDE SPECIAL - offset double cutaway alder body, white pickguard, bolt-on maple neck, 21-fret maple fingerboard with offset black slot inlay, fixed bridge, 4-on-a-side tuners, chrome hardware, DiMarzio Woofer/DiMarzio P-style pickups, 2 volume/1 tone controls. Available in Black, Lightning Red, Sea Foam Green and Thunder Blue finishes. Mfg. 1994 to 1996.

$550 $425 $350 $275 $250 $225 $200
Last MSR was $700.

ATTITUDE STANDARD - offset double cutaway alder body, white pickguard, bolt-on maple neck, 21-fret rosewood fingerboard with pearl dot inlay, fixed bridge, 4-on-a-side tuners, chrome hardware, P/J-style pickups, volume/tone control, 3-position switch. Available in Black Pearl, Crimson Red, Dark Blue Metallic and White finishes. Disc. 1996.

$600 $450 $375 $295 $275 $250 $225
Last MSR was $800.

Standard 5 - similar to Standard, except has 5-string configuration, 4/1 per side tuners. Disc. 1994.

$625 $500 $400 $350 $300 $275 $250
Last MSR was $930.

BB Series

BB200 - offset double cutaway alder body, bolt-on maple neck, 21-fret rosewood fingerboard with pearl dot tuners, fixed bridge, 4-on-a-side tuners, chrome hardware, P-style pickup, volume/tone control. Available in Black, Vivid Red and White finishes. Disc. 1994.

$250 $225 $175 $150 $135 $125 $115
Last MSR was $370.

This model was optional with a fretless fingerboard (Model BB200 F).

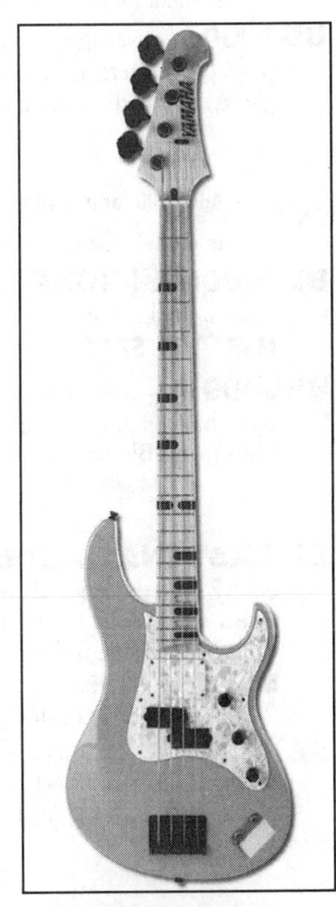

Yamaha ATT LTD II
courtesy Yamaha

GRADING	100% MINT	98% NEAR MINT	95% EXC+	90% EXC	80% VG+	70% VG	60% G

BB300 - similar to BB200, except has redesigned bridge. Disc. 1994.

	$300	$250	$225	$175	$150	$135	$115

Last MSR was $430.

This model was optional in a left-handed version (Model BB300 L).

BB350 - offset double cutaway alder body, bolt-on maple neck, 21-fret rosewood fingerboard with pearl dot inlay, fixed bridge, 4-on-a-sid tuners, chrome hardware, 2 J-style pickups, 2 volume/tone controls. Available in Black, Blue Metallic, Natural and Vintage Red finishes Mfg. 1994 to 1996.

	$400	$300	$250	$225	$175	$150	$125

Last MSR was $500.

Y

BB400 - offset double cutaway alder body, bolt-on maple neck, 33 7/8" scale, 21-fret rosewood fingerboard with pearl dot tuners, fixe bridge, 4-on-a-side tuners, chrome hardware, P-style pickup, volume/tone control. Available in Chestnut and Natural finishes. Mfg. 1981 t 1983.

	$275	$225	$195	$175	$150	$125	$100

Last MSR was $450.

Add $50 for a left-handed configuration (Model BB400 L). Mfg. 1982 to 1983.

BB1000 S - offset double cutaway alder, laminated maple/mahogany through-body neck, 33 7/8" scale, 21-fret rosewood fingerboard with pearl dot tuners, fixed bridge, 4-on-a-side tuners, chrome hardware, P/J-style pickups, volume/tone controls, 3-way selector toggle. Available in Persimmon Red and Brown Stain finishes. Mfg. 1982 to 1989.

	$375	$325	$295	$250	$200	$175	$125

Last MSR was $720.

This model may also have a maple or mahogany body.

BB1200 S - similar to the BB1000 S, except features an ebony fingerboard with pearl oval inlays, P-style pickup, 3-band EQ, on/off mini-switch. Available in Burgundy and Deep Green finishes. Mfg. 1982 to 1989.

	$395	$350	$300	$275	$225	$175	$150

Last MSR was $850.

This model was optional with a fretless fingerboard (Model BB1200 S F).

BB1500 A - offset double cutaway alder body, black lam pickguard, bolt-on maple neck, 21-fret rosewood fingerboard with pearl dot inlay, brass fixed bridge, 4-on-a-side tuners, gold hardware, 2 stacked humbucker pickups, volume/treble/mid/bass/mix controls, active electronics.Available in Black pearl, Natural and Wine Red finishes. Mfg. 1994 to 1996.

	$800	$600	$500	$400	$360	$330	$300

Last MSR was $1,000.

This model was optional with a fretless fingerboard (Model BB1500 A F).

BB2000 - offset double cutaway alder body, laminated maple/mahogany through-body neck, 33 7/8" scale, 21-fret ebony fingerboard with pearl oval tuners, fixed bridge, 4-on-a-side tuners, chrome hardware, P/bar-magnet J-style pickups, volume/tone controls, 3-way selector toggle. Available in Natural and Brown Stain finishes. Mfg. 1982 to 1989.

	$450	$425	$400	$350	$325	$275	$225

Last MSR was $989.

Add $100 for a left-handed configuration (Model BB2000 L). Mfg. 1983 to 1989.

This model was optional with a fretless fingerboard (Model BB2000 F). Mfg. 1983 to 1989.

BB3000MA MICHAEL ANTHONY SIGNATURE MODEL - offset double cutaway neck through body design, 4-on-a-side tuners, nickel hardware, Hipshot D-Tuner, custom chile pepper position markers. Available in Black and Green finishes. New 2001.

MSR $2,999	$2,099	$1,899	$1,699	$1,499	$1,299	$1099	$899

BB5000 A - offset double cutaway alder body, mahogany/maple through body neck, 24-fret ebony fingerboard with pearl oval inlay, 5-string fixed bridge, 4/1 per side tuners, brass hardware, P/J-style pickups, volume/tone/mix controls, active electronics. Available in Cream White, Gun metal Blue and Purple Pearl finishes. Disc. 1994.

	$1,190	$1,020	$850	$680	$610	$560	$510

Last MSR was $1,700.

BB EAST (NATHAN EAST SIGNATURE) - offset double cutaway alder body, figured maple top, bolt-on maple neck, 24-fret ebony fingerboard with pearl block inlay, brass fixed bridge, figured maple veneered peghead with screened artist's signature/logo, 3/2-per-side tuners, gold hardware, 2 humbucker pickups, volume/treble/mid/bass/mix controls, active electronics. Available in Amberburst and Translucent Blue finishes. Mfg. 1994 to date.

MSR $3,199	$2,550	$2,100	$1,800	$1,575	$1,355	$995	$775

This model was co-designed by bassist Nathan East.

BB G 4 - offset double cutaway alder body with 'high definition' top, bolt-on maple neck, 24-fret rosewood fingerboard with pearl dot inlay, vintage-style fixed bridge, 2-per-side tuners, gold hardware, 2 single coil pickups, volume/tone/blend controls. Available in High Definition Amber Burst and High Definition Translucent Blue finishes. Disc.

	$495	$395	$350	$300	$275	$225	$175

Last MSR was $649.

GRADING			100% MINT	98% NEAR MINT	95% EXC+	90% EXC	80% VG+	70% VG	60% G

BB G 4 S - BBN4 upgraded with active electronics, 2 active humbuckers, gold hardware, volume, pan, bass, treble boost/cut, die-cast bridge. Available in Sunburst, Blue, Pearl Snow White, and Black. Current Mfg.

MSR $649 | $450 | $375 | $295 | $275 | $225 | $195 | $165

BB G 5 - similar to the BB G 4, except features a 5-string configuration, 3/2-per-side tuners. Available in High Definition Amber Burst and High Definition Translucent Blue finishes. Disc.

$525 | $450 | $375 | $325 | $295 | $250 | $195

Last MSR was $699.

BB G 5 S - BBN5 upgraded with active electronics, 2 active humbuckers, gold hardware, volume, pan, bass, treble boost/cut, die cast bridge. Available in Sunburst, Blue, Pearl Snow White, and Black. Current Mfg.

MSR $699 | $525 | $425 | $375 | $325 | $295 | $250 | $195

BB N 4 - offset double cutaway alder body, bolt-on maple neck, 24-fret rosewood fingerboard with pearl dot inlay, vintage-style fixed bridge, 2-per-side tuners, chrome hardware, 2 single coil pickups, volume/tone/blend controls. Available in Black, Brown Satin, and Natural Satin finishes. Current Mfg.

MSR $549 | $425 | $325 | $295 | $250 | $225 | $175 | $145

Add $80 for left-handed configuration (Model BB N 4 L).

Fretless fingerboard available at no extra cost (Model BB N 4 F).

BB N 5 - similar to the BB N 4, except features a 5-string configuration, 3/2-per-side tuners. Available in Black, Brown Satin, and Natural Satin finishes. Current Mfg.

MSR $599 | $425 | $350 | $275 | $250 | $200 | $175 | $150

BB N 5 A - similar to the BB N 4, except features figured maple top, 5-string configuration, 3/2-per-side tuners, 2 Alnico active single pickups with dummy coils, master volume, pan, bass cut/boost, treble cut/boost, 3 band EQ controls, active electronics. Available in Amber Burst and Translucent Blue finishes. Disc.

$1,125 | $950 | $850 | $750 | $700 | $600 | $500

Last MSR was $1,499.

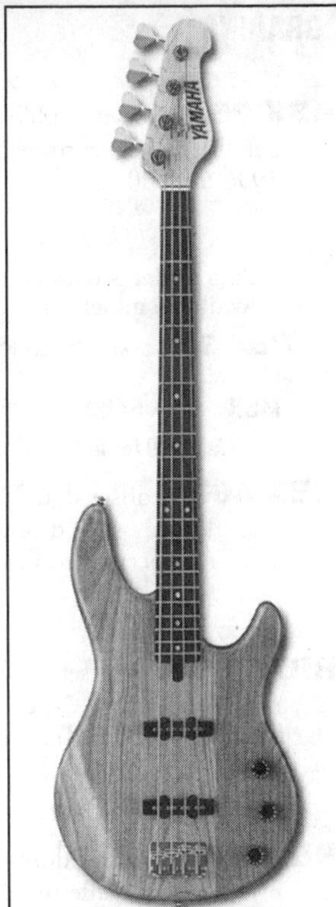

Yamaha BB 350
courtesy Yamaha

BEX Series

BEX 4C - single cutaway hollow alder body, rosewood fingerboard with dot position markers, 21-frets, rosewood bridge, 1 humbucking pickup and 1 piezo pickup on the bridge, Master Volume, Balance, 3 band EQ. Available in Dark Blue Burst, Orange Stain and Brown Sunburst finish. New 2001.

MSR $999 | $699 | $599 | $525 | $475 | $425 | $375 | $325

RBX Series

RBX 6 JM JOHN MYUNG SIGNATURE MODEL - double cutaway alder body with figured maple veneer, maple neck, ebony fingerboard with abalone "infinity" inlays, 24-frets, 2 active double coil pickups, volume, pan, bass, treble boost/cut, solid brass bridge, gold hardware, 35" scale. Available in Turquoise Blue and Ruby Red finishes. Current Mfg.

MSR $1,499 | $1,125 | $995 | $900 | $850 | $795 | $750 | $650

RBX 250 - offset double cutaway alder body, bolt-on maple neck, 22-fret rosewood fingerboard with pearl dot inlay, fixed bridge, 4-on-a-side tuners, chrome hardware, P-style pickup, volume/tone controls. Available in Black, Blue Indo, Crimson Red, Lightning Blue, Natural, and Pearl Snow White finishes. Disc. 1996.

$250 | $195 | $175 | $150 | $125 | $100 | $85

Last MSR was $330.

RBX 350 - similar to RBX 250, except has P/J-style pickups, volume/tone/mix controls. Available in Aqua, Black, Blue Indo, Brown Stain, Crimson Red, Lightning Blue and Pearl Snow White finishes. Disc. 1996.

$325 | $250 | $200 | $175 | $150 | $125 | $100

Last MSR was $400.

RBX 350 L - similar to RBX 350, except has left-handed configuration. Disc. 1996.

$395 | $265 | $235 | $190 | $170 | $155 | $140

Last MSR was $520.

RBX 650 - similar to RBX 350, except has black hardware. Available in Black Pearl, Dark Blue Metallic, Faded Blue, Natural, and Red Metallic finishes. Mfg. 1992 to 1996.

$425 | $350 | $325 | $275 | $250 | $225 | $200

Last MSR was $700.

Yamaha RBX 350 II
courtesy Yamaha

GRADING	100% MINT	98% NEAR MINT	95% EXC+	90% EXC	80% VG+	70% VG	60% G

RBX 260 - offset double cutaway alder body, bolt-on maple neck, 24-fret rosewood fingerboard with pearl dot inlay, low mass fixed bridge, 2-per-side tuners, chrome hardware, P-style pickup, volume/tone controls. Available in Black, Red, Blue Satin, and Natural Satin finishes. Mfg. 1996 to 2000.

	$250	$200	$175	$150	$125	$100	$95

Last MSR was $349.

This model is optional with a fretless fingerboard (Model RBX 260 F) MSR $429.
Available in left-handed configuration (Model RBX 260 L) MSR $449.

RBX 360 - similar to RBX 260, except has P/J-style pickups, volume/tone/pan controls. Available in Black and Brown Satin finishes. Mfg. 1996 to date.

MSR $499	$380	$295	$275	$250	$195	$165	$125

Add $90 for left-handed configuration (Model RBX 360 L). Disc. 1999.

RBX 460 - offset double cutaway alder body with 'high definition' top, bolt-on maple neck, 24-fret rosewood fingerboard with pearl dot inlay, low mass fixed bridge, 2-per-side tuners, gold hardware, P/J-style pickups, volume/tone/blend controls. Available in Translucent Blue and Translucent Red finishes. Disc.

	$450	$350	$300	$275	$225	$195	$150

Last MSR was $579.

RBX 760 A - offset double cutaway alder body, ash veneer top, bolt-on maple neck, 24-fret rosewood fingerboard with pearl dot inlay, low mass fixed bridge, 2-per-side tuners, gold hardware, 2 humbucker pickups, volume/blend/bass/treble controls, active electronics. Available in Translucent Blue, Translucent Green, and Translucent Red finishes. Current Mfg.

MSR $749	$565	$445	$395	$345	$285	$235	$185

Add $100 for 5-string configuration, 3/2-per-side tuners (Model RBX 765 A).

RBX1000 - offset double cutaway sculpted ash body, bolt-on maple neck, 24-fret rosewood fingerboard with pearl dot inlay, fixed brass bridge, 4-on-a-side tuners, chrome hardware, P/J-style pickups, volume/treble/bass/mix controls, active electronics. Available in Blue Stain, Brown Stain, Natural, Translucent Black, and Translucent Violet finishes. Disc. 1996.

	$625	$550	$500	$425	$375	$350	$300

Last MSR was $1,100.

SBV Series

SBV 500 - reintroduction of a mid-60's design, offset radical double cutaway alder body, bolt-on neck, 34" scale, rosewood fingerboard, dot position markers, 20-frets, Vintage bridge, 2 Felight single coil pickups, 2 Volume/1 Tone control. Available in Red Metallic, Shrlby Blue and Canary Yellow. Current Mfg.

MSR $599	$419	$350	$295	$250	$195	$150	$95

TRB Series

TRB 4 - offset double cutaway carved ash body, bolt-on maple neck, 34" scale, 24-fret rosewood fingerboard with pearl dot inlay, brass fixed bridge, 2-per-side brass tuners, gold hardware, 2 stacked humbucker pickups, volume/treble/mid/bass/mix controls, active electronics. Available in Blue Stain, Brown Stain, Cherry Sunburst and Natural finishes. Mfg. 1994 to 1998.

	$1,200	$900	$750	$600	$550	$495	$450

Last MSR was $1,599.

TRB 4 P - similar to TRB 4, except features an offset double cutaway figured maple/rosewood/maple body, maple/mahogany neck through body, 34" scale, 24-fret ebony fingerboard with pearl dot inlay, solid brass bridge, 2-per-side brass tuners, P/J-style/piezo bridge pickups, volume/treble/bass/2 mix controls, piezo pickup switch. Available in Red Blonde, Translucent Blue, and Translucent Red Sunburst finishes. Disc. 1994.

	$1,400	$1,200	$1,000	$800	$720	$660	$600

Last MSR was $2,000.

TRB 4 II - offset double cutaway ash body, maple neck, 35" scale, 24-fret rosewood fingerboard with pearl dot inlay, fixed brass bridge, 2-per-side tuners, gold hardware, 2 humbucker pickups, volume/pan/treble cut and boost/mid/bass controls. Available in Amber Burst, Translucent Blue Burst, and Magenta Burst finishes. Mfg. 1998 to date.

MSR $1,599	$1,195	$1,000	$900	$800	$700	$650	$575

TRB 5 - offset double cutaway carved ash body, bolt-on maple neck, 34" scale, 24-fret rosewood fingerboard with pearl dot inlay, brass fixed bridge, 3/2-per-side brass tuners, gold hardware, 2 stacked humbucker pickups, volume/treble/mid/bass/mix controls, active electronics. Available in Amber Stain, Blue Stain, Charcoal Gray and Cherry Sunburst finishes. Mfg. 1994 to 1998.

	$1,250	$950	$800	$650	$575	$525	$475

Last MSR was $1,699.

TRB5 P - similar to TRB5, except features an offset double cutaway figured maple/rosewood/maple body, maple/mahogany through body neck, 34" scale, 24-fret ebony fingerboard with pearl dot inlay, solid brass bridge, 3/2-per-side brass tuners, P/J-style/piezo bridge pickups, volume/treble/bass/2 mix controls, piezo pickup switch. Available in Red Blonde, Translucent Blue and Translucent Red Sunburst finishes. Disc. 1996.

	$1,500	$1,250	$1,150	$925	$825	$750	$695

Last MSR was $2,500.

GRADING	100% MINT	98% NEAR MINT	95% EXC+	90% EXC	80% VG+	70% VG	60% G

TRB 5 II - offset double cutaway ash body, maple neck, 35" scale, 24-fret rosewood fingerboard with pearl dot inlay, fixed brass bridge, 3/2-per-side tuners, gold hardware, 2 humbucker pickups, volume/pan/treble cut and boost/mid/bass controls. Available in Amber Burst, Translucent Blue Burst, and Magenta Burst finishes. Mfg. 1998 to date.

MSR $1,699 — $1,250 $1,050 $950 $850 $800 $695 $625

TRB 5 F II - similar to the TRB 5 II, except features a fretless fingerboard. Available in Amber Burst, Translucent Blue, Burst, and Magenta finishes. Mfg. 1998 to date.

MSR $1,799 — $1,375 $1,100 $950 $850 $800 $750 $625

In 1999, Magenta finish was discontinued.

TRB 5 P II - similar to Model TRB 5 F II except, available with maple, Bubinga or Ovankol top, neck through body, ebony fingerboard, Yamaha BPZ bridge, 2 double coil Alnico V pickups plus piezo pickup on bridge, 3-band EQ, pickup balance control. Available in Natural finish. Current Mfg.

MSR $3,999 — $2,799 $2,499 $2,199 $1,899 $1,599 $1,299 $999

TRB 5 L II - similar to the TRB 5 II, except features a left-handed configuration. Available in Amber Burst, Translucent Blue Burst, and Magenta finishes. Mfg. 1998 to date.

MSR $1,899 — $1,425 $1,150 $995 $850 $750 $695 $625

In 1999, Magenta finish was discontinued.

TRB 6 - offset double cutaway carved ash body, bolt-on maple neck, 34" scale, 24-fret rosewood fingerboard with pearl dot inlay, brass fixed bridge, 3-per-side brass tuners, gold hardware, 2 stacked humbucker pickups, volume/treble/mid/bass/mix controls, active electronics. Available in Amber Stain and Charcoal Gray finishes. Mfg. 1994 to 1998.

$1,300 $1,000 $900 $725 $650 $595 $550

Last MSR was $1,999.

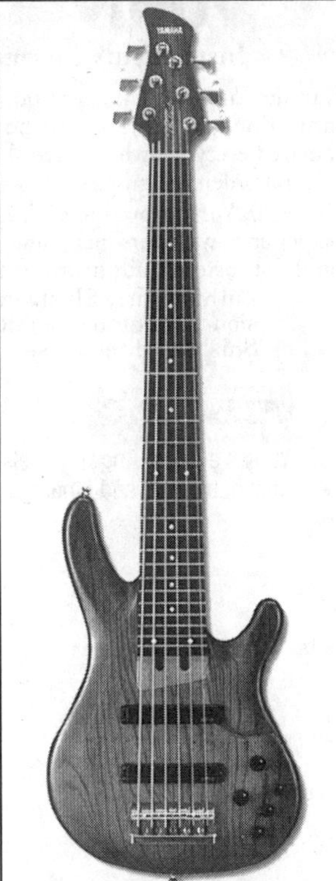

Yamaha TRB 6
courtesy Yamaha

TRB6 P - similar to TRB6, except features an offset double cutaway figured maple/rosewood/maple body, maple/mahogany through body neck, 34" scale, 24-fret ebony fingerboard with pearl dot inlay, solid brass bridge, 3-per-side brass tuners, 2 J-style/piezo bridge pickups, volume/treble/bass/2 mix controls, piezo pickup switch. Available in Red Blonde, Translucent Blue and Translucent Red Sunburst finishes. Disc. 1996.

$1,600 $1,350 $1,200 $1,000 $925 $850 $750

Last MSR was $2,700.

TRB 6 II - offset double cutaway ash body, maple neck, 35" scale, 24-fret rosewood fingerboard with pearl dot inlay, fixed brass bridge, 3-per-side tuners, gold hardware, 2 humbucker pickups, volume/pan/treble cut and boost/mid/bass controls. Available in Amber Burst, Translucent Blue Burst, and Magenta finishes. Mfg. 1998 to date.

MSR $1,999 — $1,495 $1,295 $1,150 $1,050 $925 $875 $675

TRB 6P II - similar to Model TRB 6 II except, has choice of Maple, Bubinga or Ovankol top, neck through body, ebony fingerboard, 2 Double Coil Alnico V pickups plue piezo pickup mounted on the bridge, volume, balance, piezo volume and 3-band EQ. Available in natural finish. Current Mfg.

MSR $4,399 — $3,079 $2,775 $2,475 $2,175 $1,875 $1,575 $1,275

TRB JP (JOHN PATITUCCI SIGNATURE) - offset double cutaway alder body, carved figured maple top, bolt-on maple neck, 34" scale, 24-fret ebony fingerboard with pearl 3/4 oval inlay, brass fixed bridge, figured maple veneered peghead with screened artist's signature/logo, 3-per-side brass tuners, gold hardware, 2 stacked humbucker pickups, volume/treble/mid/bass/mix controls, active electronics. Available in Amber Stain and Charcoal Gray finishes. Mfg. 1994 to date.

MSR $3,399 — $2,700 $2,200 $1,900 $1,675 $1,300 $1,095 $850

This model was co-designed by bassist John Patitucci.

YAMAKI

See DAION.

Instruments previously produced in Japan during the late 1970s through the 1980s.

YAMATO

Instruments previously produced in Japan during the late 1970s to the early 1980s.

Yamato guitars are medium quality instruments that feature both original and designs based on classic American favorites.

(Source: Tony Bacon and Paul Day, The Guru's Guitar Guide)

YUNKER, ERIC

Instruments previously built in San Francisco, California during the early 1980s.

Luthier Eric Yunker (1953-1985) was described as "a man of many skills - poet, printer, inventor, graphic artist, musician, guitar sculptor." Yunker's instruments combined the sculpting aspect of a guitar body with playability, as well. One of the Yunker guitars is on display in the ZZ Top display area at the Rock and Roll Hall of Fame and Museum in Cleveland, Ohio.

(Source: Jas Obrecht, Guitar Player magazine)

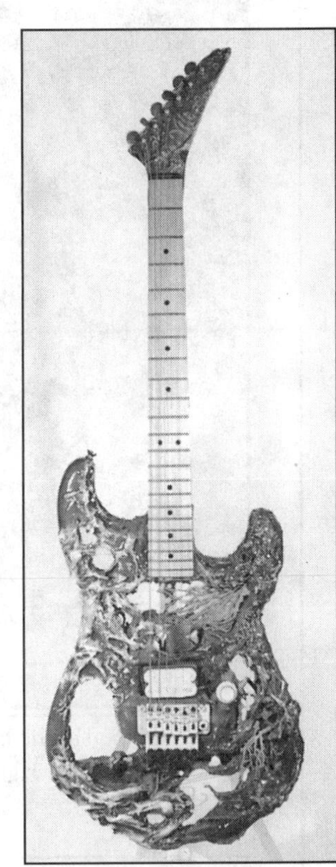

Yile Fish Tank
courtesy Dan Kiblinger

YURIY

Instruments currently built in Wheeling, Illinois since 1990.

Luthier Yuriy Shishkov was born in 1964 in St. Petersburg. As with many other guitar makers, Shishkov began his career from discovering a big personal attraction to music. After spending 10 years playing guitars that he found unsatisfactory, Yuriy attempted to build his own instrument in 1986. The results amazed everyone who played the instrument, including Yuriy himself! From this initial bit of success, Yuriy gained a reputation as a luthier as well as several orders for guitars.

In 1990, Yuriy moved to Chicago, Illinois. A year later, he secured a job at Washburn International, a major guitar company based in Chicago. His experience with personal guitar building lead him to a position of handling the difficult repairs, restorations, intricate inlay work, company prototypes, and the custom-built instruments for the artist endorsees.

Luthier Yuriy Shishkov is currently offering custom designed and construction of instruments from solid body guitars to his current passion of archtop acoustics and hollow body electrics. For additional information regarding pricing and availability, contact luthier Yuriy Shishkov directly (see Trademark Index).

ELECTRIC

Yuriy's electric **Angel** models range in price from $1,950 up to $3,500. Yuriy offers a number of options on his instruments, such as inlays, exotic woods, pickups, hardware, and bindings. He also works with the player commissioning the guitar to insure that the finished result is exactly what the player is specifying.

Even the Nashville cops rock out at the NAMM Show. This officer got caught rockin' right on Broadway with the well-traveled, giant LP!

Section Z

ZAK

Instruments currently built in Gdansk, Poland. Distributed by Mayones Company of Gdansk, Poland.

The Mayones Company (Zenon Dziewulski) is currently offering a number of good quality solid body electric guitar and bass models. Production models feature the 'SuperStrat' styling, while the Custom Shop models are heavily into tone woods and natural finishes. For further information regarding models and pricing, contact the Mayones Company directly (see Trademark Index).

ZEMAITIS

Instruments previously handcrafted in England 1957-2001.

Tony Zemaitis was born Antanus (Anthony) Casimere (Charles) Zemaitis in 1935. While his grandparents were Lithuanian, both Tony and his parents were born in the UK. At age 16 he left college to be an apprentice at cabinet making. As part of a hobby, he refashioned an old damaged guitar found in the family attic. In 1955, the first turning point to luthiery. Zemaitis built his first "half decent" guitar, a classical, nylon string with peghead. In the mid to late 1950s, Zemaitis served for two years in Britian's National Service.

Upon his return to civilian life, Zemaitis continued his guitar building hobby, only now a number of the guitars began turning up onto the folk scene. By 1960 he was selling guitars for the price of the materials, and a number of the originals that Zemaitis calls **Oldies** still exist. Early users include Spencer Davis, Long John Baldry, and Jimi Hendrix. In 1965, Zemaitis' *hobby* had acquired enough interest that he was able to become self employed. By the late 1960s, the orders were coming in from a number of top players such as Ron Wood, Eric Clapton, and George Harrison. The house and shop all moved lock, stock, and barrel to Kent in 1972. A **Student** model was introduced in 1980, but proved to be too popular and time consuming to produce the number of orders, so it was discontinued.

In 1995, Zemaitis celebrated the 40th Anniversary of the first classical guitar he built in 1955. Guitar production was limited to 10 guitars a year. Now over sixty, Zemaitis reports that he is still fit, healthy and going strong, and what started as a pleasant hobby has still remained pleasurable through the years. In 2001, Tony Zemaitis finally decided to retire and enjoy himself. He is still active, contributes to the Zemaitis Club magazine, and loves to read about how well his guitars are doing.

Recently, George Harrison lent 3 of his Zemaitis acoustic models to an exhibition in the U.K. organized by Viscount Linley (Princess Margaret's son).

(Source: Tony Zemaitis, March 1996 and Keith Smart, 2001)

(Information courtesy Keith Smart and Keith Rogers, The Z Gazette: magazine of the Zemaitis Guitar Owners Club based in England)

Zemaitis Superior M/F
courtesy Keith Smart

AUTHENTICITY

In the late 1980s, Zemaitis was surprised to see that his guitars were even more valuable in the secondhand market than originally priced. As his relative output is limited, an alarming trend of forgeries has emerged in England, Japan, and the U.S. Serial numbers identification and dating on guitars will continue to be unreported in this edition, due to the number of forgeries that keep turning up (and we're not going to add tips to the "help-yourself merchants" as Tony likes to call them). To clarify matters simply: Tony Zemaitis has granted NO ONE permission to build reproductions and NO licensing deals have been made to any company.

Points to Consider when Buying a Zemaitis:

Prior to spending a large amount of money on what may very well turn out to be a copy of a Zemaitis, it is always best to ask for advice.

There are German, Japanese, and English copies. At first glance they may look a little like a Zemaitis, but they will not sound like one due to the use of second-rate materials. Because of the mass produced nature of these fakes, the intonation and general finish will be inferior to the genuine article. Even more alarming, what starts out as a cheap copy changes hands once or twice and eventually ends up being advertised as *the real thing* without proper research.

The more difficult *fakes* (?) to spot are the genuine Zemaitis guitars that started life as a cheaper version (Student or Test model), and has been unofficially upgraded. In other words, a plain front guitar suddenly becomes a Pearl Front guitar. While parts and pieces will be genuine, the newer finish and general appearance are nothing like the real thing.

Always ask for a receipt, even if you are not buying from a shop. Always check the spelling of *Zemaitis*. Look at the engraving, and make sure that it is engraved by hand (not photo etching - it is too clean and has not been worked on by hand).

(reprinted courtesy Keith Smart, The Z Gazette)

The ***Blue Book of Electric Guitars*** strongly recommends two or three written estimates of any ZEMAITIS instrument from accredited sources. If possible, ask to see the original paperwork. Here are two more serious tips: Usually the person who commissioned the guitar has their initials on the truss rod cover. Also, review the printed label and logo (there's only one correct spelling for Mr. Zemaitis' name - and contrary to word of mouth, he does not intentionally misspell it on his guitars.

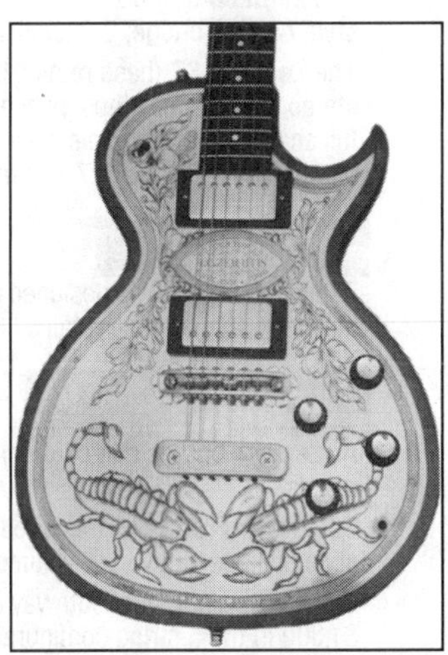

Detail of Danny O'Brien's Engraving
courtesy Keith Smart

MODEL DESCRIPTIONS

Here is a brief overview of model histories and designations. During the late 1950s, a few basic acoustic models were built to learn about sizes, shapes, wood response, and soundholes. From 1960 to 1964, guitar building was still a hobby, so there was no particular standard; also, the paper labels inside are hand labeled.

In 1965, Zemaitis *turned pro* and introduced the **Standard, Superior**, and **Custom** models of acoustic guitars. These terms are relative, not definitive as there is some overlapping from piece to piece. While some soundholes are round, there are a number of acoustic guitars built with the *heart shaped* soundhole.

The electric solidbody guitar was discussed and inspired by Eric Clapton on a visit to Zemaitis' workshop in 1969. The handful of early models had aluminum plates on the faces, and later were followed by solid silver, then finally returned to aluminum as the British tax people proved difficult. Zemaitis' good friend and engraver Danny O'Brien handles the ornate engraving on the M/F (**Metal Front**) models. The first *test* guitar was sold off cheaply at the time, but the second was purchased by Tony McPhee (Groundhogs); the third guitar built was purchased by Ron Wood. The M/F guitar model has since moved worldwide. There is a variation model called the **Disc Front** which has a round faced metal plate around the pickups as opposed to the entire front. An ultimate version called the Pearl Front is just that: a pearl topped solid body guitar - and the written description hardly does justice to the actual piece.

The **Student** model was introduced in 1980. Designed as a basic guitar that could be later upgraded, the model proved so popular that it was quickly discontinued for fear that the production would overtake other work altogether! In the late 1980s, clients began asking for either more decorations or copies of older models. At this point Zemaitis upgraded his system to the **Custom, Deluxe**, and **Custom Deluxe** which are still in use to date. Again, these three models are relative, not definitive as some crossing back and forth does go on.

Z

ZENBU GUITARS

Instruments currently built in California since 1978. Distributed by Zenbu Guitars of Sacramento, California.

Luthier/designer Toshi Hiraoka has been producing custom built guitars for specific clients for the past twenty years. Zenbu Guitars is available by appointment only.

ZEN-ON

Instruments previously produced in Japan circa 1946 to late 1960s.

The Zen-On brand appears on a full range of intermediate quality solid body electric guitars and basses, as well as thinline acoustic/electric hollow body guitars and electric mandolins. By the late 1960s the company began using the Morales trademark (See MORALES). The Japanese manufacturer is unknown, and Zen-On was not heavily imported into the U.S. market.

(Source: Michael Wright, Vintage Guitar Magazine)

ZENTA

Instruments previously produced in Japan in the late 1960s to the late 1970s. During the 1970s, production moved to Korea.

These entry level solid body and semi-hollowbody guitars featured both original design and designs based on classic American favorites.

(Source: Tony Bacon and Paul Day, The Guru's Guitar Guide)

ZENTECH

Instruments currently built in Girdwood, Alaska.

Dave Hill's Zentech Instruments is a small custom shop that specializes in limited production, high quality custom built electric guitars and basses. Zentech combines classic and free-thinking designs, select woods, high tech electronics, and precision bridges and tuners (Schaller, Smith, and Steinberger) in their instruments. In 1996, Zentech began offering archtop acoustics that featured 20-year-old Sitka spruce.

All instruments have a 10 year guarantee, and prices include a hardshell case. Zentech also offers numerous custom options in hardware and exotic woods (call for pricing and availability).

ELECTRIC

The **Zentech SE** (base retail $1,000) has a cedar body and quilted maple top, rosewood fingerboard, inline headstock, chrome or black handware, vintage-style *hardtail* bridge, 2 Chandler Zebra humbuckers, volume/tone controls, and a three way pickup selector.

The **Zentech ST** (base retail $1,200) has an offset double cutaway teak body, maple neck, Schaller tuners, and 2 Chandler Zebra humbuckers. It is wired in stereo, and has coil taps, phase switch, gold hardware, and tune-o-matic bridge/stop tailpiece. Slightly related is the **Tasmanian Micro**, a travel guitar with a full scale (25 1/2") maple neck, smaller teak body, maple fingerboard, chrome hardware, single pickup, and single volume knob. Designed to fit in the overhead bin of a Boeing 727, this model is complete with a padded gigbag for $700.

Artist Series

Zentech's **Shark** was designed in conjunction with Yupik Eskimo artist Jack Abraham. The Shark has the same appointments as the SE model, but a very original body shape (base retail $1,500).

ELECTRIC BASS

All Zentech basses can be ordered in 4-, 5-, 6-, and 7-string configurations, and with any combination of options. The following price quotes reflect the model discussed.

The **Darth Fretless** 5 has a teak body with rather pointy forward horns, a through-body neck, fretless ebony fingerboard, locking tuners, graphite nut, 2 J-style pickups, active EQ, volume/blend/tone controls. This 5-string model has a base retail of $1,350.

A quilted walnut, dual cutaway rounded body signifies the **RB 5** bass. The RB 5 has a similar pickup/EQ/controls package as the Darth, and is priced at $1,300 in the 5-string configuration.

The **Zebra 6** 6-string has an offset cutaway body, through-body rock maple neck, ebony fingerboard, 2 Bartolini pickups, and volume/pan/tone controls. Zebra 6 strings have a base retail of $1,500.

GRADING	100% MINT	98% NEAR MINT	95% EXC+	90% EXC	80% VG+	70% VG	60% G

ZETA

Instruments currently built in Oakland, California since 1982. Distributed by Zeta Music Systems, Inc. of Oakland, California.

Zeta currently offers quality acoustic/electric violins, and a MIDI violin synthesizer in addition to the current Crossover models of electric bass.

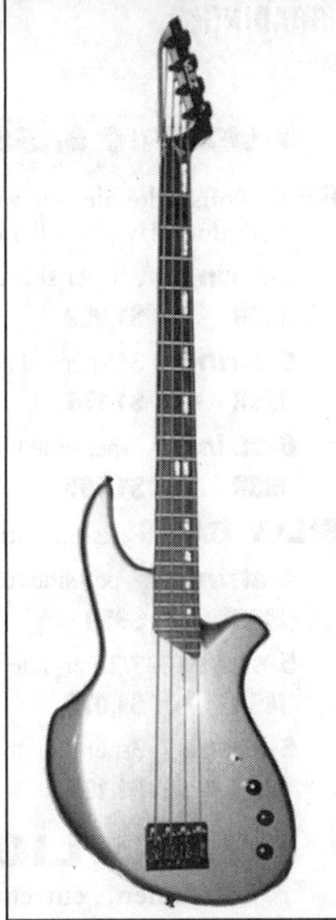

Zeta Prizm
courtesy Steve Cherne

ELECTRIC

MIRROR 6 - rounded asymmetrical double cutaway ash body, bolt-on maple neck with aluminum and graphite headstock reinforcement, 24-fret ebony fingerboard with offset white block inlay, strings through body bridge, reverse headstock, 6 on the other side Gotoh tuners, black hardware, single coil/humbucker EMG pickups, hex MIDI pickup, volume/tone/blend/MIDI controls, 3 on/off switches (pickups or hex/synth). Available in Black, Metallic Grey, Pearl White, Red and Sea Foam Green finishes. Mfg. 1989 to 1994.

$2,000 $1,650 $1,295 $1,095 $875 $750 $625
Last MSR was $2,995.

Add $800 for modified Kahler double locking tremolo.

The Mirror 6 guitar functioned as a MIDI controller, and requires the Mirror 6 rack unit. Programming and parameter editing in the rack unit can be accessed through the guitar controls.

ELECTRIC BASS

Zeta currently offers the **Crossover** bass, which allows bassists the flexibility of two playing positions: either upright (the bass mounted on a specially designed stand) or on a shoulder strap. The 6-string configuration is available as the **Rob Wasserman Signature** model (list price is $3,895). Additionally, Zeta currently manufactures the E-Series Bass ($1,499 MSR), the Performer Bass ($1,999 MSR), Performer Upright ($2,500 MSR), and the Jazz Upright ($5,995).

Add $500 for flame or curly maple top (in Vintage Sunburst).

Add $500 for exotic woods (koa, figured walnut, and zebrawood).

CROSSOVER 4 (Model XB-304) - sleek offset body design, set-in neck, fretless fingerboard, 2-per-side tuners, magnetic pickup, volume/tone controls. Available in hand-oiled Natural, Black, and White finishes. Current Mfg.

MSR $2,895

Crossover 5 (Model XB-305) - similar to the Crossover 4, except in a 5-string configuration. Current Mfg.

MSR $3,395

PRISM - offset double cutaway ash body, bolt-on maple neck, 34" scale, 24-fret rosewood fingerboard with offset white block inlay, Zeta adjustable bridge, graphite laminated reverse headstock with aluminum stabilizing bar, 4 on the other side Gotoh tuners, black hardware, bridge mounted piezo pickups, volume/bass/presence controls, 3-way attentuation switch. Available in Gloss Black, Anthracite Grey, Pearl White, Red and Sea Foam Green finishes. Mfg. 1988 to 1991.

$795 $695 $575 $495 $375 $275 $225
Last MSR was $1,495.

The 3-way attentuation switch was designed to allow switching between a *P-Bass* sound, a *Steinberger*-type sound, or the *acoustic-like* Zeta sound.

ZIM GAR

Instruments previously produced in Japan circa 1960s. Distributed in the U.S. by the Gar Zim Musical Instrument Corporation of Brooklyn, New York.

Zim Gar instruments were distributed by U.S. importer Gar Zim Musical Instrument Corporation of Brooklyn, New York. During the 1960s, Zim Gar offered the shorter scale beginner's solid body electric guitars and basses. The Japanese manufacturer is currently unknown.

Zim Gar budget electric guitars were available through K Mart stores during the 1960s. The 2 pickup model had a list price of $29.95; the 3 pickup model was $39.95.

(Source: Roland Lozier, Lozier Piano & Music; and Michael Wright, Guitar Stories Volume One)

ZIMMERLY, KEVIN

Instruments currently produced in Bay Shore, New York since 1993.

Luthier Kevin Zimmerly has been building high quality custom basses for the last three years. Zimmerly draws on his background of over 22 years in the music industry for design ideas and innovations, and has two current models: The RKZ (an offset double cutaway body) and the "SILLY BASS" (an extreme treble side cutaway design).

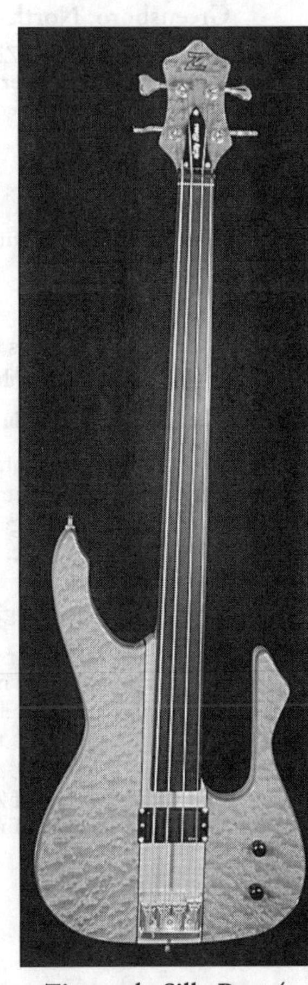

Zimmerly Silly Bass 4
courtesy Kevin Zimmerly

GRADING	100% MINT	98% NEAR MINT	95% EXC+	90% EXC	80% VG+	70% VG	60% G

ELECTRIC BASS

RKZ - offset double cutaway body, ash, (or mahogany, maple, poplar, alder) body wings, through-body 3-piece maple neck, ebony fingerboard with dot inlays, Schaller or Wilkinson bridge, Gotoh tuners, chrome hardware, EMG pickups, volume/tone controls. Current Mfg.

4-string - 3/1 per side tuners.

MSR **$1,059**

5-string - 3/2-per-side tuners.

MSR **$1,175**

6-string - 3-per-side tuners.

MSR **$1,295**

Z

SILLY BASS - similar to the RKZ, except features an offset body with an extreme cutaway on the treble side. Current Mfg.

4-string - 2-per-side tuners.

MSR **$959**

5-string - 3/2-per-side tuners.

MSR **$1,075**

6-string - 3-per-side tuners.

MSR **$1,195**

ZOID LIGHT GUITARS

Instruments currently built in Tampa, Florida. Previous production was located in Melbourne, Florida.

Zoid (Research and Development) **Light Guitars** offers a guitar model that features high density transparent bodies and internal lighting systems. The Light Guitar is available in three body shapes (and thirty-two colors). Current retail prices begin at $1,400 to $1,800.

ZION

Instruments currently built in Greensboro, North Carolina since 1980. Distributed by Zion Guitar Technology of Greensboro, North Carolina.

Luthier Ken Hoover founded Zion Guitar Technology in 1980, after six years of repairs, restorations, and custom building experience. In 1983, Zion was commissioned by **Guitar Player** magazine to build the **Silver Bird** model that was featured on the cover - and commissioned again in 1991 to build the **Burning Desire** model for cover art. Hoover has worked with such artists as Phil Keaggy and Ty Tabor (King's X), as well as custom builders such as Joe Barden and Pat Wilkins.

Zion guitars have been famous for their high quality and amazing custom finishes, and the Zion guitar staff maintains an output of 40 to 50 guitars a month.

From 1980 to 1993, the peghead logo had block lettering and triangular *wings*. In 1994, Zion redesigned their peghead logo to feature a bold signature look, with a large Z.

ELECTRIC

Current price includes a hardshell case (unless otherwise noted).

Add $100 for gold hardware.

Add $100 for glossy, tinted finish on neck.

ACTION SERIES - offset double cutaway basswood body, bolt-on maple neck, 25 1/2" scale, 22-fret rosewood (or ebony or bird's-eye maple) fingerboard, vintage style tremolo, bone nut, pearl pickguard/backplate, 6-on-a-side Sperzel Trim-lok tuners, chrome hardware, 3 Seymour Duncan vintage replica single coil pickups, volume/tone control, 5-way selector switch. Available in Black, Natural, and White finishes. Mfg. 1997 to date.

MSR **$1,150**

Price includes deluxe gig bag.

BURNING DESIRE - offset double cutaway basswood body, bolt-on maple neck, 22-fret ebony fingerboard with pearl dot inlay, standard Kahler vibrato, graphite nut, 6-on-a-side locking Sperzel tuners, chrome hardware, 2 stacked coil/1 humbucker Joe Barden pickups, volume/tone control, 3 pickup selector mini switches, 1 bypass-to-humbucker mini switch. Available in Black with Neon Flames finish. Disc. 1994.

$2,400	$2,100	$1,795	$1,395	$1,175	$995	$895

Last MSR was $2,995.

This model was one of Zion's Limited Edition Series.
The pickup selector mini switch had three positions: series, off, and parallel.

GRADING	100% MINT	98% NEAR MINT	95% EXC+	90% EXC	80% VG+	70% VG	60% G

ICKASSO - similar to Burning Desire, except has black hardware and Zion Versa-Tone pickups. Available in Black, Blue/Purple/Pink and Pink/Orange/Yellow, and White finishes. Disc. 1994.

$2,000 $1,750 $1,450 $1,100 $900 $825 $750
Last MSR was $2,495.

This model was one of Zion's Limited Edition Series.

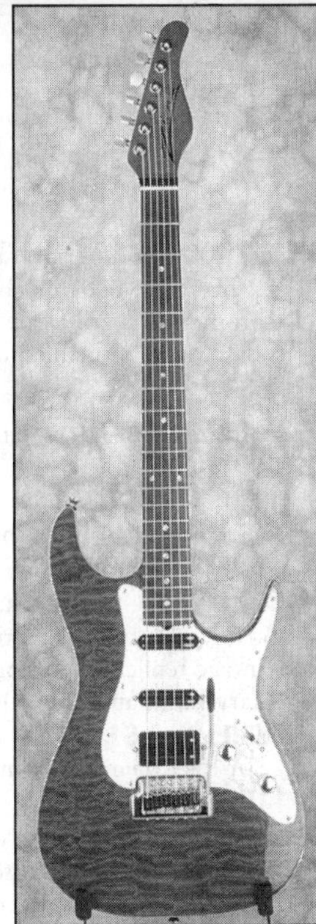
Zion Electric
courtesy Ken Hoover

CLASSIC MAPLE - offset double cutaway basswood body, carved arched bound figured maple top, bolt-on maple neck, 25 1/2" scale, 22-fret ebony (or bird's-eye maple) fingerboard with pearl dot inlay, Kahler *Steeler* locking vibrato, recessed bridge area, 6-on-a-side Sperzel Trim-lok tuners, black hardware, 2 single coil/1 humbucker Seymour Duncan (or Fralin or Barden Deluxe) pickups, volume/tone control, 5-position switch. Available in Amber Top, Black, Transparent Blue Burst, Tobacco Burst and Vintage Burst finishes. Current Mfg.

MSR $2,640 $2,100 $1,850 $1,600 $1,375 $1,125 $895 $650

In 1995, Black, Transparent Blue Burst, and Vintage Burst finishes were discontinued. Honey Burst, Purple Burst, and Transparent Teal finishes were introduced.
Past models were also available with Zion, EMG, Ultrasonic, or PJ Marx pickups.

Frosted Marble - similar to Classic Maple, except has basswood body, Zion Versa-Tone pickups, and custom *Frosted Marble* finish with matching headstock. Available in Deep Blue, Fire Orange, Intense Red, Jade Green, and Purple Frosted Marble finishes. Mfg. 1994 to 1996.

$1,700 $1,550 $1,350 $1,100 $950 $725 $550
Last MSR was $2,195.

Graphic Series - similar to Classic Maple, except has basswood body, choice of 5-way selector or 3 pickup selector mini switches, and a bypass- to-humbucker mini switch, and custom airbrushed design or specialty finish. Available in Frosted Marble, Guilded Frost, Marble Rock, Metal Marble, Splatter Rock and Techno Frost finishes. Disc. 1994.

$1,500 $1,150 $1,000 $895 $750 $600 $475
Last MSR was $1,895.

Available in Burning Desire, Frosted Marble, Metal Marble, and Silverbird graphic finishes. Mfg. 1998 to date.

MSR $2,640 $2,100 $1,850 $1,600 $1,375 $1,125 $895 $650

The current version of the Graphic Series has many custom options, "Features determine the exact price."
The pickup selector mini switch had three positions: series, off, and parallel.

RT Classic - similar to the Classic Maple, except has chrome hardware, bone nut, Mann resophonic tremolo. Available in Amber Top, Honey Burst, Purple Burst, Tobacco Burst, and Transparent Teal finishes. Current Mfg.

MSR $2,640 $2,100 $1,850 $1,600 $1,375 $1,125 $895 $650

RT Classic Professional - similar to the RT Classic, except has swamp ash or mahogany body, Skyway tremolo. Mfg. 1998 to date.

MSR $3,060

METRO - mahogany body, figured maple top, bolt-on maple neck, 25 1/2" scale, 22-fret rosewood (or bird's-eye maple or ebony) fingerboard, Mann resophonic tremolo, bone nut, 6-on-a-side Sperzel Trim-lok tuners, chrome hardware, 2 Barden Deluxe (or Seymour Duncan or Fralin) humbuckers, 2 volume/2 tone push/pull controls, 3-way selector switch. Available in Amber Top, Honey Burst, Purple Burst, Tobacco Burst, and Transparent Teal finishes. Mfg. 1997 to date.

MSR $2,395 $1,900 $1,675 $1,450 $N/A $N/A $N/A $N/A

PRIMERA - single cutaway mahogany body, AAAAA grade figured maple top, set-in mahogany neck, 24 3/4" scale, 22-fret rosewood fingerboard with mother-of-pearl royal crown inlays, tunomatic bridge/stop tailpiece (or Mann resophonic tremolo), 3-on-a-side Sperzel Trim-lok tuners, gold hardware, 2 Joe Barden Two-Tone (or Lindy Fralin) humbuckers, 2 volume/2 tone push/pull controls, 3-way selector switch. Available in Amber Top and Honey Burst finishes. Mfg. 1994 to date.

MSR $3,995 $3,200 $2,800 $2,400 $N/A $N/A $N/A $N/A

Phil Keaggy Signature Model Primera - similar to the Primera, except has 2 custom Seymour Duncan humbuckers, and Phil Keaggy signature imprint on headstock. Mfg. 1997 to date.

MSR $3,995

This is a Limited production model. Model includes a laminated Certificate of Authenticity.
The push/pull controls throw the humbuckers into parallel for a brighter tone.

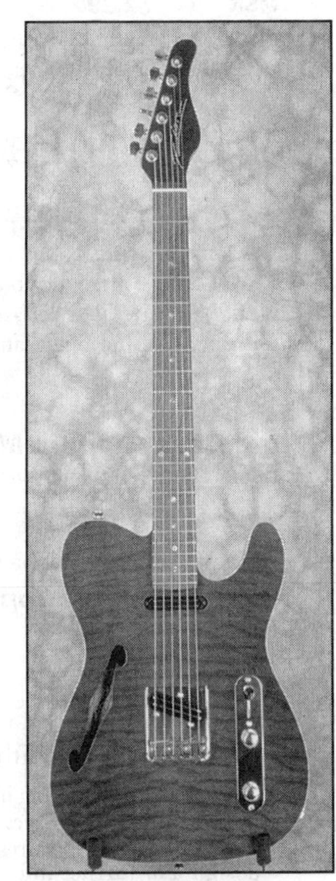
Zion Ninety
courtesy Ken Hoover

T Model Series

T MODEL - offset double cutaway basswood body, pearloid pickguard, bolt-on maple neck, 22-fret ebony (or maple) fingerboard with pearl dot inlay, standard Gotoh vibrato, graphite nut, 6-on-a-side locking Sperzel tuners, 3 stacked coil Zion pickups, volume/tone control, 5-position switch. Available in Black, Cream and Tobacco Burst finishes. Mfg. 1991 to 1996.

$1,275 $1,100 $975 $825 $695 $550 $395
Last MSR was $1,595.

In 1995, Lindy Fralin pickups replaced original parts/designs.

GRADING	100% MINT	98% NEAR MINT	95% EXC+	90% EXC	80% VG+	70% VG	60% G

Maple Top T - similar to T Model, except has figured maple top and Zion vibrato. Available in Blue Burst, Purple Burst, Tobacco Burst and Vintage Burst finishes. Mfg. 1991 to 1995.

	$1,400	$1,195	$1,050	$900	$775	$625	$495

Last MSR was $1,995.

BENT TOP MAPLE T - offset double cutaway basswood body, *Bent* (contoured) figured maple top, bolt-on maple neck, 25 1/2" scale 22-fret rosewood (or ebony or bird's-eye maple) fingerboard, Mann resophonic tremolo, 6-on-a-side Sperzel Trim-lok tuners, bone nut chrome hardware, pearl pickguard and backplate, 3 Lindy Fralin single coil pickups with white 6-hole covers, volume/tone controls, 5-position switch. Available in Blue Burst, Honey Burst, Purple Burst, and Tobacco Burst finishes. Mfg. 1996 to date.

MSR $2,395	$1,900	$1,675	$1,450	$1,250	$1,050	$825	$600

Left Maple Top - similar to the Bent Top Maple T, except in a left-handed configuration. Mfg. 1991 to date.

1991-1995	$1,400	$1,195	$1,050	$900	$775	$625	$495
MSR $2,395	$1,900	$1,675	$1,450	$1,250	$1,050	$825	$600

From 1991 to 1995, the Left Maple Top model was similar to the Maple Top T (except as a left-hander). When the *Bent* or contoured top Maple T was introduced in 1996, the Left Maple Top model followed the new design configuration.

THE FIFTY - single cutaway swamp ash body, bolt-on maple neck, 25 1/2" scale, 22-fret bird's-eye maple (or ebony or rosewood) finger board, tele-style fixed bridge, 6-on-a-side Sperzel Trim-lok tuners, bone nut, chrome hardware, black bakelite pickguard, 2 Seymour Duncan vintage replica single coil pickups, chrome controls plate, volume/tone controls, 3-position switch. Available in Butterscotch, Honey Burst Mary Kaye, and TransOrange finishes. Mfg. 1994 to date.

MSR $1,995	$1,600	$1,400	$1,225	$1,050	$850	$675	$500

In 1997, Zion redesigned their 6-saddle bridge, and replaced it with vintage-styled 3 *shared*-saddle bridge (angled for intonation correction).

THE NINETY - single cutaway swamp ash thin-line body, figured maple top, bolt-on maple neck, 25 1/2" scale, f-hole, 22-fret bird's-eye maple (or ebony or rosewood) fingerboard, tele-style fixed bridge, 6-on-a-side Sperzel Trim-lok tuners, bone nut, gold hardware, 2 Joe Barden Deluxe single coil pickups, gold controls plate, volume/tone controls, 3-position switch. Available in Blue Burst, Honey Burst, Tobacco Burst and TransOrange finishes. Mfg. 1994 to date.

MSR $2,395	$1,900	$1,675	$1,450	$1,250	$1,050	$825	$600

In 1997, Zion redesigned their 6-saddle bridge, and replaced it with vintage-styled 3 *shared*-saddle bridge (angled for intonation correction).

TY TABOR SIGNATURE MODEL - offset double cutaway basswood body, maple top, bolt-on maple neck, 25 1/2" scale, 22-fret rosewood fingerboard with pearl dot inlay, Mann resophonic tremolo, 6-on-a-side Sperzel Trim-lok tuners, gold hardware, black pickguard with *Ty Tabor* signature imprint, 3 Joe Barden Strat Deluxe single coil pickups, special taper tone control, 3 on/off push button pickup selectors with red button caps. Available in Deep Opaque Red with special design position markers on back of neck. Mfg. 1994 to date.

MSR $2,295	$1,850	$1,600	$1,395	$1,195	$995	$775	$575

ULTRA GLIDE - single cutaway basswood body, carved maple top, 24 3/4" scale, 24-fret fingerboard, Kahler "Steeler" tremolo w/auto latch, 2 humbuckers. Mfg. 1991 to 1992.

	$1,300	$1,100	$800	$675	$575	$450	$400

Last MSR was $1,995.

This model was one of Zion's Limited Edition Series.

ELECTRIC BASS

RAD BASS - offset double cutaway basswood body, bolt-on maple neck, 20-fret ebony fingerboard, fixed bridge, 4-per-side Gotoh tuners, black hardware, P-style/J-style EMG pickups, 2 volume/1 tone controls. Available in Amber Top, Classic Black, Purple Burst, Tobacco Burst, Transparent Blue Burst, and Vintage Burst finishes. Disc. 1994.

	$1,400	$1,195	$1,050	$900	$775	$625	$495

Last MSR was $1,995.

Rad Bass Graphic Model - similar to the Rad Bass, except features specialty airbrush design or specialty finish. Available in Frosted Marble Blue, Frosted Marble Purple, Frosted Marble Red, and Techno-Frost finishes. Disc. 1992.

	$1,100	$900	$795	$650	$550	$475	$400

Last MSR was $1,595.

Graphic finishes were available on the Rad Bass starting in 1993.

Rad Bass Maple Top - similar to the Rad Bass, except had a figured maple top over basswood body. Disc. 1992.

	$1,295	$1,100	$995	$825	$750	$650	$575

Last MSR was $1,795.

ZOLLA

Instruments currently built in San Diego, California since 1979.

Zolla Guitars has been building high quality custom guitars, necks, and bodies in Southern California for the past 18 years. Zolla also provides neck and body parts for various companies and individual luthiers.

Zolla's **BZ** series features 3 guitar models with a corresponding bass design. The BZ series overall features an offset, double cutaway body design. For further information regarding finished guitars or basses, or for guitar bodies and neck parts, call Zolla Guitars directly (see Trademark Index).

ZON

Instruments currently built in Redwood City, CA since 1987. Previous production was in Buffalo, New York from 1982 to 1987.

Luthier/musician Joseph M. Zon originally began building instruments in upstate New York back in 1982. Four years later Zon Guitars moved into larger facilities across country in California to meet the greater demand for his high quality basses.

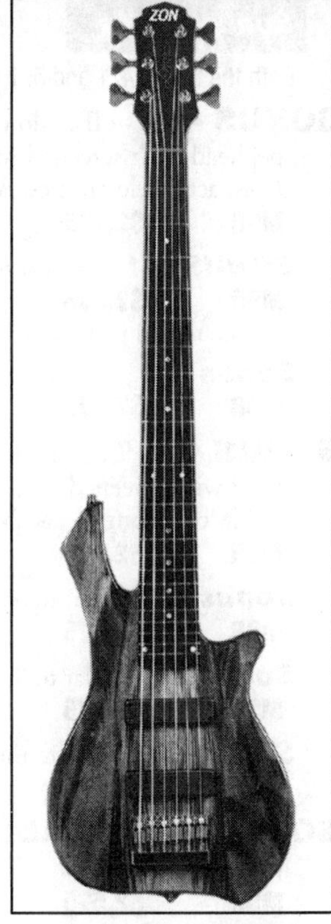

Zon Legacy Elite 6
courtesy Zon Guitars

ELECTRIC BASS

Michael Manring Hyperbass Series

Prior to 1998, the Hyperbass model with detunable keys and bridge was labeled the Version II. Currently, the Version I is featured with detunable or non-detunable keys.

A third version of the Hyperbass, **Version III** featured the detunable Zon/ATB bridge, detunable Zon/Gotoh/Hipshot tuners, and a piezo body pickup (last retail list was $7,995). The Version III was discontinued in 1998; the Zon piezo bridge option is still available for Zon basses.

VERSION I - offset deep cutaway teardrop poplar body, curly maple top, composite neck, fretless phenolic fingerboard, blackface peghead with screened model name/logo, black hardware, humbucker Bartolini pickup, volume/treble/bass controls, ZP2-S active electronics. Available in Natural top/Black back finishes. Current Mfg.

Fixed Schaller bridge, 2-per-side Zon/Gotoh tuners.

MSR **$3,995**

Detunable Zon/ATB bridge, detunable Zon/Gotoh/Hipshot tuners.

MSR **$6,995**

This instrument was co-designed by Michael Manring, and features a 3 octave fingerboard.

Legacy Elite Series

LEGACY ELITE - offset double cutaway poplar-core body, choice of bookmatched figured wood top, composite neck, 34" scale, 24-fret phenolic fingerboard with pearl dot inlay, fixed Zon bridge, blackface peghead with screened model name/logo, 2-per-side Schaller tuners, chrome hardware, 2 Bartolini dual coil pickups, volume/pan/bass/mid/treble boost/cut controls, ZP2-D active electronics. Available in Black, Emerald Green, Heather, Ice Blue, Lazer Blue, Midnight Blue, Mint Green, Mist Green, Natural, Pearl Blue, Porsche Red, Powder Blue, and Yellow finishes. Current Mfg.

MSR **$3,395**

This model is optional with the following tops: bird's-eye maple, California walnut, curly maple, goncalo alves, koa, mangowood, myrtlewood, quilted maple, or zebrawood.

Legacy Elite V - similar to Elite, except has 5 strings, 3/2-per-side tuners. Mfg. 1986 to date.

MSR **$3,895**

Legacy Elite VI - similar to Elite, except has 6 strings, 3-per-side tuners. Mfg. 1988 to date.

MSR **$4,195**

LEGACY ELITE SPECIAL - similar to the Legacy Elite, except features a bookmatched bubinga top, 2 Bartolini multi coil pickups. Available in Natural top/Black back finishes. Current Mfg.

MSR **$3,595**

Legacy Elite V Special - similar to Elite Special, except has 5 strings, 3/2 tuners per side. Current Mfg.

MSR **$4,095**

Legacy Elite VI Special - similar to Elite Special, except has 6 strings, 3 tuners per side. Current Mfg.

MSR **$4,395**

STANDARD - offset double cutaway ash body, bolt-on composite neck, 24-fret phenolic fingerboard, fixed Zon bridge, blackface peghead with screened model name/logo, 2-per-side Zon/Gotoh tuners, chrome hardware, 2 Bartolini humbucker pickups, volume/pan/bass/mid/treble boost/cut controls, ZP2-D active electronics. Available in Natural or Transparent finishes. Current Mfg.

MSR **$2,495**

This model has figured maple body optional.

Standard V - similar to Standard, except has 5 strings, 3/2-per-side tuners.

MSR **$2,795**

Standard VI - similar to Standard, except has 6 strings, 3-per-side tuners.

MSR **$3,095**

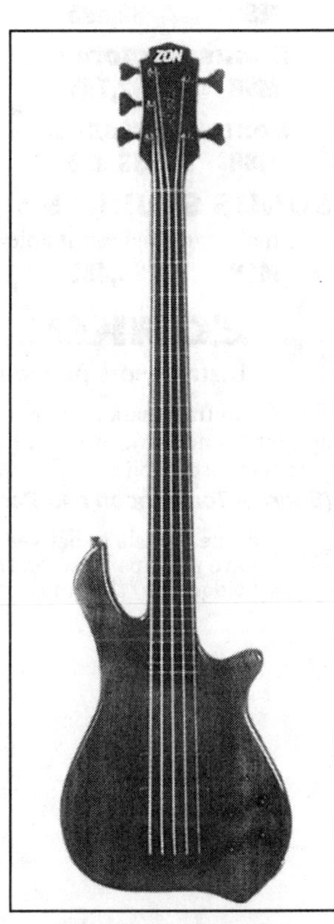

Zon Elite V Special
courtesy Zon Guitars

Sonus Series

Both the Sonus 4/1 and 5/1 feature a single humbucking pickup, while the Sonus and Sonus Special models feature two pickups.

SONUS 4/1 - offset double cutaway alder body, bolt-on composite neck, 34" scale, 24-fret phenolic fingerboard, fixed Zon bridge, blackface peghead with screened model name/logo, 2-per-side Zon/Gotoh tuners, chrome hardware, humbucking pickup, 2 volume/treble/bass controls, active electronics. Available in Dark Metallic Blue, Heather, High Gloss Black, and Metallic Red finishes. Current Mfg.

MSR $2,195

SONUS 5/1 - similar to the Sonus 4/1, except in five string configuration, 3/2-per-side tuners.

MSR $2,395

This model is optional with 22-fret fingerboard and a 35" scale.

Sonus 5/2 - similar to the Sonus 5/1, except has 2 custom wound humbucking pickups. New 1999.

MSR $2,675

SONUS 4 - offset double cutaway ash body, bolt-on composite neck, 34" scale, 24-fret phenolic fingerboard, fixed Zon bridge, blackface peghead with screened model name/logo, 2-per-side Zon/Gotoh tuners, chrome hardware, 2 Bartolini single coil pickups, 2 concentric volume/treble/bass controls, active electronics. Available in Natural or Transparent finishes. Current Mfg.

MSR $2,375

Sonus 5 - similar to Sonus, except has 5 strings, 3/2-per-side tuners. Current Mfg.

MSR $2,675

Sonus 6 - similar to Sonus, except has 6 strings, 3-per-side tuners.

MSR $2,975

Sonus 8 - similar to the Sonus, except has 8 strings, 4 per side tuners, 2 special multi-coil pickups. Available in Natural finish. Current Mfg.

MSR $2,775

SONUS 4 SPECIAL - similar to the Sonus, except features a bookmatched bubinga top, 2 special multi-coil pickups. Available in Natural polyester gloss finish. Current Mfg.

MSR $2,675

Sonus 5 Special - similar to Sonus Special, except has 5 strings, 3/2-per-side tuners. Current Mfg.

MSR $2,975

Sonus 6 Special - similar to Sonus Special, except has 6 strings, 3-per-side tuners. Current Mfg.

MSR $3,375

SONUS CUSTOM - similar to the Sonus, except features a 2-piece swamp ash body, bookmatched figured wood top, 2 special multi-coil pickups. Available in Transparent and custom color finishes. Current Mfg.

MSR $2,595

Sonus Custom 5 - similar to Sonus Custom, except has 5 strings, 3/2-per-side tuners. Current Mfg.

MSR $2,795

Sonus Custom 6 - similar to Sonus Custom, except has 6 strings, 3-per-side tuners. Mfg. 1998 to date.

MSR $3,395

SONUS STUDIO 5 - 5 string model with 2 custom wound dual coil pickups and independent EQ per pickup, 22-fret, 35 in. scale, mahogany/figured maple body. New 1999.

MSR $3,495

ZORKO

Instruments previously built in Chicago, Illinois during the early to mid 1960s.

The Zorko trademark is the brand name of the Dopyera Brothers (See DOBRO and VALCO), and was used to market an electric pickup-equipped upright "mini-bass". In 1962, Everett Hull from Ampeg acquired the rights to the design. Hull improved the design, and Jess Oliver devised a new 'diaphragm-style' pickup. The Ampeg company then marketed the model as the "Baby Bass".

(Source: Tony Bacon and Barry Moorhouse, The Bass Book)

Some models in between 70% to 90% have been seen priced between $650 and $1,200. Pricing depends on condition of the body; also, compare pickups between the Zorko and an Ampeg. There may be retro fit kits from Azola, Clevinger, or some of the pickup companies (piezo bridge kits) that may fit a Zorko *mini-bass*.

SERIALIZATION

POTENTIOMETER CODING: SOURCE DATE CODE

An Important Instrument Dating Breakthrough developed by Hans Moust (author, *The Guild Guitar Book*)

Stamped on every potentiometer (volume and tone *pots*) is a six or seven digit *source code* that tells who made the pot, as well as the week and the year. The *source dating* code is an element of standardization that is administered by the Electronics Industries Association (EIA), formed in 1924. The EIA assigns each manufacturer a three digit code (there are some with one, two or four digits). Moust's research has indicated no source date codes on any guitar pots before the late 1940s, and no single digit year code after 1959 (6 digit source code).

It's fairly easy to crack the source code. The first three digits indicate the company that built the potentiometer. Some times these digits may be separated by a space, a hyphen, or a period. The most common company codes found are:

137	**CTS**	**304**	**Stackpole**
140	**Clarostat**	**134**	**Centralab**
106	**Allen Bradley**	**381**	**Bourns Networks**

If the code is only six digits long, then the fourth digit is the year code (between 1947 and 1959). If the code is seven digits long, then the fourth and fifth digits indicate the year. The final two digits in either of the codes indicate the week of the year the potentiometer was built. Any final two digits with a code number over 52 possibly indicates a part number instead of a week of the year code.

When dating an instrument by the 'pot code', keep two things in mind: The potentiometers must be original to the piece (new solder, or a date code that is off by ten or more years is a good giveaway to spot replacement pots); and that the pot code only indicates when the potentiometer was built! If the pot is an original, it indicates a date that the guitar could not have been built before - so it's always a good idea to have extra reference material around.

Moust's research has indicated that virtually all Fenders from 1966 to 1969 have pots dated from 1966. Moust has speculated that when CBS bought Fender, they found a good deal on pots and bought a three year supply. Guild apparently had the same good fortune in 1979, for when Moust visited the factory they still had a good supply of '79 pots - which explains why every Guild since then has had similar dated pots!

Finally, a word of caution: not all potentiometer manufacturers subscribed to the EIA source code date, and early Japanese components did not use the international coding like the American and European builders. If the code does not fit the above criteria, don't *force it* and skew your dating results.

(Source: George Gruhn and Walter Carter, Guitar Player magazine, October 1990)

ALEMBIC SERIAL NUMBERS

Alembic began developing and installing custom electronics in 1969 as the company was just forming. Alembic continued to customize basses with their active electronics for players like Jack Casady and Phil Lesh, which lead to the creation of Alembic instruments. Every instrument the company has produced has a corresponding instrument file which contains the original work order (specifications), returned warranty, and any other relevant paperwork.

In general, the first two numbers in the serial number are the year the instrument was completed; the letter code designates the model. The final two to five digits indicate the individual instrument and its place in the overall Alembic production. Alembic started with the number 1 in 1972, and has progressed sequentially ever since. An "A" or "B" after the serial number indicates the rare occasion when a serial number has been duplicated.

On new instruments, the serial number is stamped on the truss rod cover and also in the electronics cavity (Epic and Orion models have the number stamped in the back of the peghead and in the electronics cavity). On older instruments, the serial number is stamped directly on the ebony fingerboard below the 24th fret. Earliest Alembic models have serial numbers stamped on top of the headstock.

TOM ANDERSON GUITARWORKS SERIALIZATION

Tom Anderson spent a number of years building necks and guitar bodies before producing completed guitars. Outside of custom built specialties, 1987 was the first year that the volume began to resemble production numbers.

Although every guitar built is tracked in the company files, many are remembered by staff luthiers who had a hand in producing them. Engraved on the neck plate of each guitar is the date it was completed along with *MADE IN CALIFORNIA*.

An example of this would be: 12-21-92P, or 5-27-93A, or 9-15-95N. An A, N, or P lets you know if the instrument was completed in the A.M. (A), P.M. (P) or, if production is moving well, at approximately Noon (N).

B. C. RICH SERIALIZATION

Bernardo Chavez Rico learned his luthier skills from his father, Bernardo Mason Rico. When the B.C. Rich trademark was adopted, Rico built acoustic guitars for the first two years, and then switched to custom built solid body electrics. When production formally commenced in 1972, the first 350 guitars were numbered sequentially.

In 1974, a serial number code was devised. The five digit serial number was encoded YYZZZ, with the first two digits indicating the year and the last three indicating consecutive production. By the late 1970s, demand and production increased enough that the year number began ahead of the date. In 1980, the year digits were two years ahead - and by 1981, they were off by four years!

Currently, the American made B.C. Rich serialization does provide with numbers corresponding to the year, and quantity of guitars built in that year. For example:

953001995	(300th instrument produced)
960021996	(2nd instrument produced)

The serialization on the Import series models is for identification only, and does not depict the year of manufacture. B.C. Rich does maintain records that indicate the year of manufacture (and the manufacturer) if they are needed.

(Source: Bernie Rich, President/Founder of B.C. Rich International; and Michael Wright, Vintage Guitar Magazine)

BENEDETTO SERIAL NUMBERS

To date, Robert Benedetto has completed over 750 musical instruments. 466 are archtop guitars, with the remainder comprising of 51 violins, 5 violas, 1 classical guitar, 2 mandolins, 11 semi-hollow electrics, 209 electric solid body electric guitars and basses, and one cello. The 11 semi-hollow electrics include six unique carved top, semi-hollow electrics made between 1982 and 1986. The other five include three prototypes for, and two finished examples of, his new "benny" semi-hollow electric line introduced in 1998. The 209 electric solid bodies include 157 electric guitars and 52 electric basses. Benedetto began making them in 1986 with John Buscarino. He stopped making them in the Spring of 1987. The 11 semi-hollow electrics and the 1 classical guitar are included in the archtop guitar serial numbering system. The two mandolins have no serial numbers. The violins, violas and cello have their own serial number system (starting with #101) as do the electric solid body guitars and basses (starting with #1001).

Serial Numbers:

All Benedetto archtop guitars (except his first two) are numbered in one series, Electric solidbodies and basses each have their own separate series, as do the violins, violas and cello. Archtop guitars have a 4- or 5- digit serial number with configuration ##(#)yy. 2 (or 3) digits ##(#)=ranking, beginning with #1 in 1968.

Last 2 digits yy=year.

Example: 43599 was made in 1999 and is the 435th archtop made since 1968.

From Robert Benedetto's Archtop Guitar Serial Number Logbook (Note: year listed on the right indicates date shipped, not made).

Serial	Year
0168 (#1)*	1968
0270 (#2)*	1970
0372	1972
0473	1973
0575 through 0676	1976
0777 through 1177	1977
1277 through 2778	1978
2879 through 4279	1979
4380 through 5580	1980
5681 through 7381	1981
7482 through 9582	1982
9682 through 10983	1983
11084 through 11984	1984
12085 through 12885	1985
12986 through 13586	1986
13686 through 13987-A	1987
14087 through 16488	1988
16588 through 19189	1989
19289 through 22490-A	1990
22591 through 25091	1991
25192 through 28092	1992
28193 through 30293	1993
30393 through 32994	1994
33095 through 36595	1995
36696 through 39496	1996
39597 through 40697	1997
40798 through 43498	1998
43599 through 45099	1999

* Actual number in log: Benedetto did not adopt his current serial number system until his third guitar, serial #0372.

Seven guitar serial numbers are follwed by the letter "A". Example: archtop guitar #23891 and #23891-A are two separate instruments even though both are numbered the "238th".

Further information and a full serial number list can be found in Robert Benedetto's book, Making an Archtop Guitar (Center stream Publishing/Hal Leonard, 1994).

CARVIN SERIAL NUMBERS

Originally founded by Lowell C. Kiesel as the pickup-building L. C. Kiesel Company, Carvin has expanded through the years into a full line mail order company that offers guitars, basses, amplifiers, P.A. gear, and replacement parts. The company initially offered kit-built guitars, and by 1964 completed models.

The 2,000 to 4,000 instruments built between 1964 and 1970 did not have serial numbers. The first serial number issued in 1970 was number 5000, and numbers since then have been sequential. Serial numbers were first placed on the end of the fingerboard, and now appear on the neck plate.

Serial	Year
# 5000	1970 (first number issued)
# 11000 - 13000	1980-1983
# 13001 - 15000	1983-1984
# 17000 - 20000	1985-1986
# 22000 - 25000	1988-1989
# 26000 - 33000	1989-1991
# 35000 - on	1992-date

(Source: Michael Wright, Vintage Guitar Magazine)

D'ANGELICO SERIAL NUMBERS

Master Luthier John D'Angelico (1905-1964) opened his own shop at age 27, and every guitar was hand built - many to the specifications or nuances of the customer commissioning the instrument. In the course of his brief lifetime, he created 1,164 numbered guitars, as well as unnumbered mandolins, novelty instruments, and the necks for the plywood semi-hollowbody electrics. The nature of this list is to help identify the numbered guitars as to the date produced.

D'Angelico kept a pair of ledger books and some loose sheets of paper as a log of the guitars created, models, date of completion (or possibly the date of shipping), the person or business to whom the guitar was sold, and the date. The following list is a rough approximation of the ledgers and records.

Serial	Date
First *Loose Sheets*	
1002 through 1073	1932 to 1934
Ledger Book One	
1169 through 1456	1936 to 1939
1457 through 1831	1940 to 1949
1832 through 1849	1950
Ledger Book Two	
1850 through 2098	1950 to 1959
2099 through 2122	1960
2123	1961
Second *Loose Sheets*	
2124 through 2164	Dates not recorded

Again, I must stress that the above system is a guide only. In 1991, author Paul William Schmidt published a book entitled *Acquired of the Angels: The Lives and Works of Master Guitar Makers John D'Angelico and James L. D'Aquisto* (The Scarecrow Press, Inc.; Metuchen, N.J. & London). In appendix 1 the entire ledger information is reprinted save information on persons or business to whom the guitar was sold. This book is fully recommended to anyone seeking information on luthiers John D'Angelico and James L. D'Aquisto.

D'AQUISTO SERIAL NUMBERS

Master Luthier James L. D'Aquisto (1935-1995) met John D'Angelico around 1953. At the early age of 17 D'Aquisto became D'Angelico's apprentice, and by 1959 was handling the decorative procedures and other lutherie jobs.

D'Aquisto, like his mentor before him, kept ledger books as a log of the guitars created, models, date of completion (or possibly the date of shipping), the person or business to whom the guitar was sold, and the date. The following list is a rough approximation of the ledger. As the original pages contain some idiosyncrasies, the following list will by nature be inaccurate as well - and should only be used as a guide for dating individual instruments. The nature of this list is only to help identify the numbered guitars as to the date produced.

Serial	Date
The D'Aquisto Ledger	
1001 through 1035	1965 to 1969
1036 through 1084	1970 to 1974
1085 through 1133	1975 to 1979
1134 through 1175	1980 to 1984
1176 through 1228	1985 to 1990

Beginning in 1988, serial number was 1230. 1257 was D'Aquisto's last serial number on non-futuristic models.

Other guitars that D'Aquisto built had their own serial numbers. For example, solid body and semi-hollow body guitars from 1976 to 1987 had an *E* before the three digit number. D'Aquisto also built some classical models, some flat-top acoustics, and some hollow body electric models (hollowbody guitars run from #1 to #30, 1976 to 1980; and #101 to #118, 1982 to 1988).

In 1991, author Paul William Schmidt published a book entitled *Acquired of the Angels: The Lives and Works of Master Guitar Makers John D'Angelico and James L. D'Aquisto* (The Scarecrow Press, Inc.; Metuchen, N.J. & London). In appendix 2 the entire ledger information is reprinted up to the year 1988 except for information on persons or business to whom the guitar was sold. This book is fully recommended to anyone seeking information on luthiers John D'Angelico and James L. D'Aquisto.

DANELECTRO SERIALIZATION

Danelectro serial numbers are usually located in the neck pocket, although they do also turn up in other hidden areas of the body. Most Danelectros carry a four digit code. The code pattern is *XXYZ*: XX is the week of the year (01-52), Y is still a mystery (Batch code or Designator?), and Z is the last digit of the production years. As the Z number is duplicated every 10 years, model designation and features should also be used in determining the date. Some guitars built during the first nine weeks of each year (01 through 09, XX code) may not have the 0 as the first number.

There are two variations on this code. In late 1967, the **Coral** and **Dane** series were offered, and were numbered with a *ZXX* code. The other original models still maintain their four digit code. However, the **Convertible** model (a Pre-'67 series) was cosmetically changed in 1968 to a Dane-style headstock, and changed to the new three digit code.

(Serialization courtesy of Paul Bechtoldt and Doug Tulloch, Guitars from Neptune. This book is the definitive listing for models, specifications, and company information - plus it carries many examples of the company's advertising as a reference tool)

DEAN SERIALIZATION

Serialization for the *Made in the U.S.A.* instruments is fairly straightforward to decipher. The serial numbers were stamped into the back of the headstock, and the first two digits of the serial number are the year of manufacture. The following five digits represent the instrument number. Examples of this would be:

79 00619	manufactured in 1979
81 39102	manufactured in 1981

The imported Deans do not carry the stamped and year-coded serial numbers, and would have to be dated through configuration, headstock design, and other design factors.

EPIPHONE SERIAL NUMBERS

In 1917, Epaminondas *Epi* Stathopoulos began using the **House of Stathopoulo** brand on the family's lutherie business. By 1923 the business was incorporated, and a year later the new trademark was unveiled on a line of banjos. Stathopoulos combined his nickname *Epi* with the Greek word for sound, *phone*. When the company was recapitalized in 1928, it became the **Epiphone Banjo Company**.

Guitars were introduced in 1930, and were built in New York City, New York through 1953. Company manufacturing was moved to Philadelphia due to union harrassment in New York, and Epiphone continued on through 1957. Serial numbers on original Epiphones can be found on the label.

Epiphone **Electar** electric instruments were numbered consecutively, using a die stamped number on the back of the headstock. The numbering system began at 000 in 1935, terminating at about 9000 in 1944. Between about 1944 and 1950, the two number prefixes 15, 25,26, 60, 75, or 85 were assigned to specific models. These were followed by three digits which were the actual "serial" number. In 1951, electric instruments wer brought under the same numbering system as acoustics, and serial numbers were relocated to a paper label in the instrument's interior. Some transitional instruments bear both impressed numbers and a paper label with differing numbers. The latter are the more accurate for use in dating.

Number	Year
1000 - 3000 [electrics only]	1937-1938
4000 - 5000 [electrics only]	1939-1941
5000 [acoustics]	1932
6000	1933
7000	1934
8000 - 9000	1935
10000	1930-1932, 1936
11000	1937
12000	1938
13000	1939-1940
14000 - 15000	1941-1942
16000 - 18000	1943
19000	1944

In 1944, a change was made in the numbering sequence.

Number	Year
51000 - 52000	1944
52000 - 54000	1945
54000 - 55000	1946
56000	1947
57000	1948
58000	1949
59000	1950
60000 - 63000	1951
64000	1952
64000 - 66000	1953
68000	1954
69000	1955-1957

ELECTRIC INSTRUMENTS (Numbers are approximate):

Number	Year
1935	000 to 249
1936	250 to 749
1937	750 to 1499
1938	1500 to 2499
1939	2500 to 3499
1940	3500 to 4999
1941	5000 to 6499
1942	6500 to 7499
1943	7500 to 8299
1944	8300 to 9000

In May of 1957, Epiphone was purchased by CMI and became a division of Gibson. Parts and materials were shipped to the new home in Kalamazoo, Michigan. Ex-Epiphone workers in New Berlin, New York "celebrated" by hosting a bonfire behind the plant with available lumber (finished and unfinished!).

Gibson built Epiphone guitars in Kalamazoo from 1958 to 1969. Hollow body guitars had the serial number on the label inside, and prefixed with a "A-" plus four digits for the first three years. Electric solid body guitars had the serial number inked on the back of the headstock, and the first number indicates the year: "8" (1958), "9" (1959), and "0" (1960).

In 1960, the numbering scheme changed as all models had the serial number pressed into the back on the headstock. There were numerous examples of duplication of serial numbers, so when dating a Epiphone from this time period consideration of parts/configuration and other details is equally important.

Number	Year
100 - 41199	1961
41200 - 61180	1962
61450 - 64222	1963
64240 - 70501	1964
71180 - 95846	1962* * (Numerical sequence may not coincide to year sequence)
95849 - 99999	1963*
000001 - 099999	1967*
100000 - 106099	1963 or 1967*
106100 - 108999	1963

Number	Year
109000 - 109999	1963 or 1967*
110000 - 111549	1963
111550 - 115799	1963 or 1967*
115800 - 118299	1963
118300 - 120999	1963 or 1967*
121000 - 139999	1963
140000 - 140100	1963 or 1967*
140101 - 144304	1963
144305 - 144380	1963 or 1964
144381 - 145000	1963
147001 - 149891	1963 or 1964
149892 - 152989	1963
152990 - 174222	1964
174223 - 179098	1964 or 1965
179099 - 199999	1964
200000 - 250199	1964
250540 - 290998	1965
300000 - 305999	1965
306000 - 306099	1965 or 1967*
307000 - 307984	1965
309653 - 310999	1965 or 1967*
311000 - 320149	1965
320150 - 320699	1967*
320700 - 325999	1967*
325000 - 326999	1965 or 1966
327000 - 329999	1965
330000 - 330999	1965 or 1967 or 1968*
331000 - 346119	1965
346120 - 347099	1965 or 1966
348000 - 349100	1966
349101 - 368639	1965
368640 - 369890	1966
370000 - 370999	1967
380000 - 380999	1966 to 1968*
381000 - 385309	1966
390000 - 390998	1967
400001 - 400999	1965 to 1968*
401000 - 408699	1966
408800 - 409250	1966 or 1967
420000 - 438922	1966
500000 - 500999	1965 to 1966, or 1968 to 1969*
501009 - 501600	1965
501601 - 501702	1968
501703 - 502706	1965 or 1968*
503010 - 503109	1968
503405 - 520955	1965 or 1968*
520956 - 530056	1968
530061 - 530850	1966 or 1968 or 1969*
530851 - 530993	1968 or 1969
530994 - 539999	1969
540000 - 540795	1966 or 1969*
540796 - 545009	1969
555000 - 556909	1966*
558012 - 567400	1969
570099 - 570755	1966*
580000 - 580999	1969
600000 - 600999	1966 to 1969*
601000 - 606090	1969
700000 - 700799	1966 or 1967*
750000 - 750999	1968 or 1969
800000 - 800999	1966 to 1969*
801000 - 812838	1966 or 1969*
812900 - 819999	1969
820000 - 820087	1966 or 1969*
820088 - 823830	1966*
824000 - 824999	1969
828002 - 847488	1966 or 1969*
847499 - 858999	1966 or 1969*
859001 - 895038	1967*
895039 - 896999	1968*
897000 - 898999	1967 or 1969*
899000 - 972864	1968*

Between 1970-mid 90s, almost all Epiphones were made in either Japan or Korea. Most have a 7 digit serial number, and production records/statistics are not available currently for this time period.

In 1970, production of Epiphone instruments moved to Japan. Japanese Epiphones were manufactured between 1970 to 1983. According to author/researcher Walter Carter, the serial numbers on these are unreliable as a usable tool for dating models. Comparison to catalogs is one of the few means available. Earlier Kalamazoo labels were generally orange with black printing and said "Made in Kalamazoo", while the Japanese instruments featured blue labels which read "Epiphone of Kalamazoo, Michigan" (note that it doesn't say made in Kalamazoo, nor does it say Made in Japan). While not a solid rule of thumb, research of the model should be more thorough than just glancing at the label.

During the early 1980s, the Japanese production costs became pricey due to the changing ratio of the dollar/yen. Production moved to Korea, and again the serial numbers are not an exact science as a dating mechanism. In 1993, a structure was developed where the number (or pair of numbers) following the initial letter indicates the year of production (i.e. "3" indicates 1993, or a "93" would indicate the same).

Some top-of-the-line Epiphones were produced in the U.S. at Gibson's Kalamazoo, Nashville, or Montana facility since the mid 70s. These instruments are the only ones that correspond to the standard post-1977 Gibson serialization. Like Gibson numbers, there are 8 digits in the complete number, and follows the code of YDDDYNNN. The YY (first and fifth) indicate the year built. DDD indicates the day of the year (so DDD can't be above 365), and the NNN indicates the instrument's production ranking for that day (NNN = 021 = 21st guitar built). The Nashville facility begins each day at number 501, and the Montana workshop begins at number 001 (as did Kalamazoo). **However**, in 1994, the Nashville-produced Epiphones were configured as YYNNNNNN: YY = 94 (the year) and NNNNNN is the ranking for the entire year.

Current Epiphones manufactured overseas typically utilize a 7 digit serial number, the first number being the last number of the year of manufacture. Many of these instruments have an alphabetical character designating the manufacturing facility (i.e., S3861789 refer to an instrument mfg. during 1993 by Samick, R5618265 indicates an instrument mfg. during 1995 by Aria.

Information for this chart of Epiphone serial numbers can be found in Walter Carter's book, Epiphone: The Complete History (Hal Leonard, 1995). Not only a fascinating story and chronology of the original Epiphone company and its continuation, but also an overview of product catalogs as well as serial numbers. Walter Carter serves as the Gibson Historian as well as being a noted songwriter and author. He also wrote The Martin Book, and co-authored several with expert George Gruhn including Gruhn's Guide to Vintage Guitars, Acoustic Guitars and Other Fretted Instruments, and Electric Guitars and Basses: A Photographic History (All are available through GPI/Miller-Freeman books).

FENDER SERIALIZATION

Serial numbers, in general, are found on the bridgeplate, the neckplate, the backplate or the peghead. From 1950-1954, serial numbers are found on the bridgeplate or vibrato backplate. From 1954-1976, the serial numbers are found on the neckplate, both top or bottom of the plate. From 1976 to date, the serial number appears with the peghead decal. Vintage Reissues have their serial numbers on the neckplate and have been in use since 1982.

The Fender company also stamped (or handwrote) the production date on the heel of the neck, in the body routs, on the pickups, and near the wiring harness (the body, pickup, and wiring dating was only done sporadically, during certain time periods). However, the neck date (and body date) indicate when the neck (or body) part was completed! Fender produces necks and guitar bodies separately, and bolts the two together during final production. Therefore, the date on the neck will generally be weeks or months before the actual production date.

When trying to determine the manufacturing date of an instrument by serialization, it is best to keep in mind that there are no clear cut boundaries between where the numbers began and when they ended. There were constant overlapping of serial numbers between years and models. The following are approximate numbers and dates.

1950	0001-0750
1951	0200-1900
1952	0400-4900
1953	2020-5030
1954	2780-7340
1955	6600-12800
1956	7800-16000
1957	14900-025200
1958	022700-38200
1959	31400-60600
1960	44200-58600
1961	55500-81700
1962	71600-99800
1963	81600-99200

In 1962, as the serialization count neared 100000, for one reason or another, the transition did not occur. Instead, an L preceded a 5 digit sequence. It ran this way from 1962 to 1965.

1962	L00400-L13200
1963	L00200-L40300
1964	L20600-L76200
1965	L34980-L69900

In 1965, when CBS bought Fender Musical Instruments, Inc., the serialization has come to be known as the F Series, due to an "F" being stamped onto the neckplate. This series of numbers went from 1965 to 1973. The approximate numbers and years are as follows:

1965	100001-147400
1966	112170-600200
1967	162165-602550
1968	211480-627740
1969	238945-290835
1970	278910-305415
1971	272500-380020
1972	301395-412360
1973	359415-418360

In early 1973, Fender stopped the practice of writing/stamping the production date on the heel of the neck (through 1982). The following are rough approximations for the years 1973 to 1976:

Early 1973 to Late 1976:	400000 series
Late 1973 to Late 1976:	500000 series
Mid 1974 to Mid 1976:	600000 series
Mid 1976 to Late 1976:	700000 series

In late 1976, Fender decided to move to a new numbering scheme for their serialization. The numbers appeared on the pegheads and for the remainder of 1976 they had a prefix of 76 or S6 preceding a 5 digit sequence. In 1977, the serialization went to a letter for the decade, followed by a single digit for the year and then 5 to 6 digits. Examples of the letter/digit code follow like this: S for the '70s, E for the '80s, N for the '90s, etc.

1970s	**S** (example) S8 - 1978
1980s	**E** (example) E1 - 1981
1990s	**N** (example) N2 - 1992

While the idea was fine, the actuality was a different matter. Instrument production did not meet the levels for which decals had been produced, so there are several overlapping years. Sometimes several prefixes found within a single year's production. Here is the revised table of letter/digit year codes:

1976	S6 (also 76)
1977	S7 and S8
1978	S7, S8, and S9
1979	S9 and E0
1980-1981	S9, E0, and E1
1982	E1, E2, and E3
1984-1985	E3 and E4
1985-1986	*No U.S. Production
1987	E4
1988	E4 and E8
1989	E8 and E9
1990	E9, N9, and N0
1991	N0 (American Series, plus 6 digits)
1992	N2
1993	N3
1994	N4
1995	N5
1996	N6
1997	N7
1998	N8
1999	N9
2000	Z0
2001	Z1

V Prefixes (introduced circa 1982) designate Vintage Reissue Series. Relic Series instruments are denoted by an R prefix. A D prefix indicates Deluxe. M prefix designates Mexican Mfg. S prefix designates Signature model. For instance, a new Fender Subsonic with serial no. DZ0255356 indicates a deluxe instrument manufactured in 2000.

Serialization on Fender Japan Models

Fender Japan was established in March, 1982, in a negotiation between CBS/Fender, Kanda Shokai, and Yamano Music. Instruments were built by Fuji Gen Gakki, initially for the European market. When the Vintage/Reissues models were offered in the early 1980s, a *V* in the serial number indicated U.S. production, while a *JV* stood for Fender Japan-built models. For the first two years of Japanese production, serial numbers consisted of a 2 letter prefix to indicate the year, followed by five digits. In late 1984, this code was changed to a single letter prefix and six digits. The Japanese Fender production facility is now making instruments for the Asian marketplace only. Note the overlapping year/multi-prefix letter codes:

1982-1984	JV
1983-1984	SQ
1984-1987	E (plus 6 digits)
1985-1986	A, B, and C
1986-1987	F
1987-1988+	G
1988-1989	H
1989-1990	I and J
1990-1991	K
1991-1992	L
1992-1993	M

1993-1994	N
1994-1995	O
1995-1996	P
1996-1997	RESEARCH PENDING
1997-1998	RESEARCH PENDING
1998-1999	RESEARCH PENDING
1999-2000	RESEARCH PENDING

Dating a Fender instrument by serialization alone can get you within an approximate range of years, but should not be used as a definitive means to determine the year of actual production.

(Fender Serialization overview courtesy A.R. Duchossoir; Later year production codes courtesy Michael Wright, Vintage Guitar Magazine)

FRAMUS SERIAL NUMBERS

Framus serial numbers were generally placed on the back of the peghead or on a label inside the body. The main body of the serial number is followed by an additional pair of digits and a letter. This additional pair of numbers indicate the production year.

For example:

51334 63L =	1963
65939 70L =	1970

(Serial number information courtesy Tony Bacon and Barry Moorehouse, The Bass Book, GPI Books, 1995)

G & L SERIAL NUMBERS

According to G & L expert Paul Bechtoldt, all production serial numbers started at #500, as prior numbers were reserved for special instruments or presentations. All G & L models have a date in the neck pocket of the instrument, for reliable dating. Most G & L instruments have both body and neck dating, leading to some confusion as to the actual building date. However, the final authority exists in the G & L log book - manually looking up the serial number of the instrument.

1980-1996: All G & L serial numbers are seven digits long, with the first digit being a letter prefix indicating a guitar ("G") system or bass ("B") system.

1997-Date: In 1997, all guitar models, L-1505 and L-2500 basses, changed to a six-digit sequence beginning with CL (in honor of founder Clarence Leo Fender), followed by four numbers.

The two guitar models to have their own prefix digits and numbering system were the Broadcaster ("BC") and George Fullerton Signature model ("GF").

First Recorded Serial Number For Each Year

YEAR	GUITAR	BASS
1980	G000530	B000518
1981	G003122	B001917
1982	G009886	B008525
1983	G011654	B010382
1984	G013273	B014266
1985	G014690	B016108
1986	G017325	B017691
1987	G020241	B018063
1988	G023725	B019627
1989	G024983	B020106
1990	G026344	B021788
1991	G027163	B023013
1992	G029962	B024288
1993	More research under way	
1994	"	
1995	"	
1996	"	
1997	"	
1998	"	
1999	"	
2000	"	

(Information courtesy Paul Bechtoldt, G & L: Leo's Legacy, Woof Associates, 1994. This book is a must-have for anyone interested in G & L instruments, as the book documents models, variations, and the company history.)

GIBSON SERIALIZATION

Identifying Gibson instruments by serial number is tricky at best and downright impossible in some cases. The best methods of identifying them is by using a combination of the serial number, the factory order number and any features that are particular to a specific time that changes may have occurred in instrument design (i.e. logo design change, headstock volutes, etc). There have been 6 different serial number styles used to date on Gibson instruments.

The first serialization started in 1902 and ran until 1947. The serial numbers started with number 100 and go to 99999. All numbers are approximates. In most cases, only the upper end instruments were assigned identification numbers.

YEAR	LAST #
1903	1150
1904	1850
1905	2550
1906	3350
1907	4250
1908	5450
1909	6950
1910	8750
1911	10850
1912	13350
1913	16100
1914	20150
1915	25150
1916	32000
1917	39500
1918	47900
1919	53800
1920	62200
1921	69300
1922	71400
1923	74900
1924	80300
1925	82700
1926	83600
1927	85400
1928	87300
1929	89750
1930	90200
1931	90450
1932	90700
1933	91400
1934	92300
1935	92800
1936	94100
1937	95200
1938	95750
1939	96050
1940	96600
1941	97400
1942	97700
1943	97850
1944	98250
1945	98650
1946	99300
1947	99999

White oval labels were used on instruments from 1902 to 1954, at which time the oval label was changed to an orange color. On instruments with round soundholes, this label is visible directly below it. On f-hole instruments, it is visible through the upper f-hole. The second type of serial numbers used started with an *A* prefix and ran from 1947 to 1961. The first number is A 100.

YEAR	LAST #
1947	A 1305
1948	A 2665
1949	A 4410
1950	A 6595
1951	A 9420
1952	A 12460
1953	A 17435
1954	A 18665
1955	A 21910
1956	A 24755
1957	A 26820
1958	A 28880
1959	A 32285
1960	A 35645
1961	A 36150

When production of solid body guitars began, an entirely new serial number system was developed. Though not used on the earliest instruments produced (those done in 1952), a few of these instruments have 3 digits stamped on the headstock top. Some time in 1953, instruments were ink stamped on the headstock back with 5 or 6 digit numbers, the first indicating the year, the following numbers are production numbers. The production numbers run in a consecutive order and, aside from a few oddities in the change over years (1961-1962), it is fairly accurate to use them when identifying solid body instruments produced between 1953 and 1961. Examples of this system:

42205 = 1954

614562 = 1956

In 1961 Gibson started a new serial number system that covered all instrument lines. It consisted of numbers that are impressed into the wood. It is also generally known to be the most frustrating and hard to understand system that Gibson has employed. The numbers were used between the years 1961-1969. There are several instances where batches of numbers are switched in order, duplicated, not just once, but up to four times, and seem to be randomly assigned, throughout the decade. In general though, the numbers are approximately as follows:

YEAR	APPROXIMATE SERIAL RANGE
1961	100-42440
1962	42441-61180
1963	61450-64220
1964	64240-70500
1962	71180-96600
1963	96601-99999
1967	000001-008010
1967	010000-042900
1967	044000-044100
1967	050000-054400
1967	055000-063999
1967	064000-066010
1967	067000-070910
1967	090000-099999
1963, 1967	100000-106099
1963	106100-108900
1963, 1967	109000-109999
1963	110000-111549
1963, 1967	111550-115799
1963	115800-118299
1963, 1967	118300-120999
1963	121000-139999

YEAR	APPROXIMATE SERIAL RANGE
1963, 1967	140000-140100
1963	140101-144304
1964	144305-144380
1963	144381-145000
1963	147009-149864
1964	149865-149891
1963	149892-152989
1964	152990-174222
1964, 1965	174223-176643
1964	176644-199999
1964	200000-250335
1965	250336-291000
1965	301755-302100
1965	302754-305983
1965, 1967	306000-306100
1965, 1967	307000-307985
1965, 1967	309848-310999
1965	311000-320149
1967	320150-320699
1965	320700-321100
1965	322000-326600
1965	328000-328500
1965	328700-329179
1965, 1967	329180-330199
1965, 1967, 1968	330200-332240
1965	332241-347090
1965	348000-348092
1966	348093-349100
1965	349121-368638
1966	368640-369890
1967	370000-370999
1966	380000-385309
1967	390000-390998
1965, 1966, 1967, 1968	400001-400999
1966	401000-407985
1966	408000-408690
1966	408800-409250
1966	420000-426090
1966	427000-429180
1966	430005-438530
1966	438800-438925
1965, 1966, 1968, 1969	500000-500999
1965	501010-501600
1968	501601-501702
1965, 1968	501703-502706
1968	503010-503110
1965, 1968	503405-520955
1968	520956-530056
1966, 1968, 1969	530061-530850
1968, 1969	530851-530993
1969	530994-539999
1966, 1969	540000-540795
1969	540796-545009
1966	550000-556910
1969	558012-567400
1966	570099-570755
1969	580000-580999

YEAR	APPROXIMATE SERIAL RANGE
1966, 1967, 1968, 1969	600000-600999
1969	601000-601090
1969	605901-606090
1966, 1967	700000-700799
1968, 1969	750000-750999
1966, 1967, 1968, 1969	800000-800999
1966, 1969	801000-812838
1969	812900-814999
1969	817000-819999
1966, 1969	820000-820087
1966	820088-823830
1969	824000-824999
1966, 1969	828002-847488
1966	847499-858999
1967	859001-880089
1967	893401-895038
1968	895039-896999
1967	897000-898999
1968	899000-899999
1968	900000-902250
1968	903000-920899
1968	940000-941009
1968	942001-943000

YEAR	APPROXIMATE SERIAL RANGE
1968	945000-945450
1968	947415-956000
1968	959000-960909
1968	970000-972864

Gibson's F O N System

In addition to the above serial number information, Gibson also used **Factory Order Numbers (F O N) to track batches of instruments being produced at the time. In the earlier years at Gibson, guitars were normally built in batches of 40 instruments. Gibson's Factory Order Numbers were an internal coding that followed the group of instruments through the factory. Thus, the older Gibson guitars may have a serial number and a F O N. The F O N may indicate the year, batch number, and the ranking (order of production within the batch of 40).**

This system is useful in helping to date and authenticate instruments. There are three separate groupings of numbers that have been identified and are used for their accuracy. The numbers are usually stamped or written on the instrument's back and seen through the lower F hole or round soundhole, or maybe impressed on the back of the headstock.

1908-1923 Approximate #s

YEAR	F O N
1908	259
1909	309
1910	545, 927
1911	1260, 1295
1912	1408, 1593
1913	1811, 1902
1914	1936, 2152
1915	2209, 3207
1916	2667, 3508
1917	3246, 11010
1918	9839, 11159
1919	11146, 11212
1920	11329, 11367
1921	11375, 11527
1922	11565, 11729
1923	11973

F O Ns for the years 1935-1941 usually consisted of the batch number, a letter for the year and the instrument number. Examples are as follows:

722 A 23
465 D 58
863 E 02.

Code Letter and Year

Code	Year
A	1935
B	1936
C	1937
D	1938
E	1939
F	1940
G	1941

Code Letter F O Ns were discontinued after 1941, and any instruments made during or right after World War II do not bear an F O N codes. In 1949, a four digit F O N was used, but not in conjunction with any code letter indicating the year.

From 1952-1961, the F O N scheme followed the pattern of a letter, the batch number and an instrument ranking number (when the guitar was built in the run of 40). The F O N is the only identification number on Gibson's lower grade models (like the ES-125, ES-140, J-160E, etc.) which do not feature a paper label. Higher grade models (such as the Super 400, L-5, J-200, etc.) feature both a serial number <u>and</u> a F O N. When both numbers are present on a higher grade model, remember that the F O N was assigned at the beginning of the production run, while the serial number was recorded later (before shipping). The serial number would properly indicate the actual date of the guitar. F O N examples run thus:

Y 2230 21
V 4867 8
R 6785 15

Code Letter and Year

Code	Year
Z	1952
Y	1953
X	1954
W	1955
V	1956
U	1957
T	1958
S	1959
R	1960
Q	1961

After 1961 the use of FONs was discontinued at Gibson.

When the Nashville Gibson plant was opened in 1974, it was decided that the bulk of the production of products would be run in the South; the Kalamazoo plant would produce the higher end (fancier) models in the North. Of course, many of the older guitar builders and craftsmen were still in Kalamazoo; and if they weren't ready to change how they built guitars, then they may not have been ready to change how they numbered them! Certain guitar models built in the late 1970s can be used to demonstrate the old-style 6 digit serial numbers. **It is estimated that Gibson's Kalamazoo plant continued to use the 6 digit serial numbers through 1978 and 1979.** So double check the serial numbers on those 1970s L-5s, Super 400s, and Super 5 BJBs! It has come to light recently that the Kalamazoo plant did not directly switch over to the "new" 8 digit serialization method in 1977.

From 1970-1975 the method of serializing instruments at Gibson became even more random. All numbers were impressed into the wood and a six digit number assigned, though no particular order was given and some instruments had a letter prefix. The orange labels inside hollow bodied instruments was discontinued in 1970 and were replaced by white and orange rectangle labels on the acoustics, and small black, purple and white rectangle labels were placed on electric models.

In 1970, the words MADE IN USA was impressed into the back of instrument headstocks (though a few instruments from the 1950s also had *MADE IN USA* impressed into their headstocks as well).

Year(s)	Approximate Series Manufacture
1970, 1971, and 1972	100000s, 600000s, 700000s, 900000s
1973	000001s, 100000s, 200000s, 800000s and a few "A" + 6 digit numbers

Year(s)	Approximate Series Manufacture
1974 and 1975	100000s, 200000s, 300000s, 400000s, 500000s, 600000s, 800000s and a few *A-B-C-D-E-F* + 6 digit numbers

During the period from 1975-1977 Gibson used a transfer that had eight digit numbers, the first two indicate the year, 99=1975, 00=1976 and 06=1977, the following six digits are in the 100000 to 200000 range. *MADE IN USA* were also included on the transfer and some models had *LIMITED EDITION* also applied. A few bolt on neck instruments had a date ink stamped on the heel area.

In 1977, Gibson first introduced the serialization method that is in practice today. This updated system utilizes an impressed eight digit numbering scheme that covers both serializing and dating functions. The pattern is as follows:

YDDDYPPP

YY is the production year

DDD is the day of the year

PPP is the plant designation and/or instrument rank.

The numbers 001-499 may also indicate Kalamazoo production, 500-999 may also indicate Nashville production. The Kalamazoo numbers were discontinued in 1984.

On recently manufactured Gibson electrics, 5 or 6 digit numbers are also utilized on custom instruments. Also, there are some exceptions to these rules, including reissues. A '58 LP Reissue may be serial numbered 81XXX - the 8 is the model designator ('58 Reissue), the 1 references the last digit of the year of manufacture (2001, in this case), and the last 3 numbers (XXX) indicate the plant count. An example of a '59 LP Reissue serial number would be 91XXX.

All currently manufactured Gibsons (non-custom shop) are stamped with a hand arbor, and start at 300, and continue until production is finished that day. This hand stamp used to be reset daily at #300 for all the LP style headstocks. The other shapes (Flying V, T-Bird, Explorer, etc.) were started at 700.

When acoustic production began at the plant built in Bozeman, Montana (in 1989), the series' numbers were reorganized. Bozeman instruments began using 001-299 designations and, in 1990, Nashville instruments began using 300-999 designations. It should also be noted that the Nashville plant has not reached the 900s since 1977, so these numbers have been reserved for prototypes. Examples:

70108276 means the instrument was produced on Jan.10, 1978, in Kalamazoo and was the 276th instrument stamped that day.

82765501 means the instrument was produced on Oct. 3, 1985, in Nashville and was the 1st instrument stamped that day.

Current mfg. ES-5 Switchmaster with ser. no. 22280003 indicates an instrument built on the 228th day (Aug. 15th) of 2000, and is instrument #3 of production rank.

00871595 indicates the instrument was built on the March 28th (87th day), 2001, and was the 95th instrument stamped that day in Nashville.

81136 indicates a 1958 Les Paul Resissue manufactured in 2001, and was the 136th instrument stamped that day in Nashville.

There are still some variances that Gibson uses on some instruments produced today, but for the most part the above can be used for identifying instruments.

GRETSCH SERIALIZATION

Before World War II, serial numbers were penciled onto the inside backs of Gretsch's higher end instruments. By 1949, small labels bearing *Fred Gretsch Mfg. Co.*, serial and model number replaced the penciled numbers inside the instruments. This label was replaced by a different style label, an orange and grey one, sometime in 1957. A few variations of this scheme occurred throughout the company's history, the most common being the use of impressed numbers in the headstock of instruments, beginning about 1949. Serial numbers were also stamped into the headstock nameplate of a few models. The numbers remain consecutive throughout and the following chart gives approximations of the years they occurred.

APPROXIMATE SERIALIZATION RANGE	YEARS
001 - 1000	1939-1945
1001 - 2000	1946-1949
2001 - 3000	1950
3001 - 5000	1951
5001 - 6000	1952
6001 - 8000	1953
8001 - 12000	1954
12001 - 16000	1955
16001 - 21000	1956
21001 - 26000	1957
26001 - 30000	1958
30001 - 34000	1959
34001 - 39000	1960
39001 - 45000	1961
45001 - 52000	1962
52001 - 63000	1963
63001 - 78000	1964
78001 - 85000	1965

In the latter part of 1965, Gretsch decided to begin using a date coded system of serialization. It consists of the first digit (sometimes two) that identified the month; the second or third identifying the year, and the remaining digit (or digits) represented the number of the instrument in production for that month. Some examples of this system would be:

997	September, 1969 (7th instrument produced)
11255	November, 1972 (55th instrument produced)

On solid body instruments, impressed headstock numbers were used. In 1967, *Made in USA* was added. Hollow body instruments still made use of a label placed on the inside back of the instrument.

Around circa 1973, the label style changed once again, becoming a black and white rectangle with *Gretsch Guitars* and the date coded serialization on it. A hyphen was also added between the month and the year to help avoid confusion.

Serialization Examples:

12-4387 indicates an instrument built in December, 1974 (387th instrument produced)

3-745 indicates and instrument built in March, 1977 (45th instrument produced)

Contemporary Gretsch serialization beginning in 1989 utilizes 9 digits in a YYMMmmm(m)xxx format. YY indicates the last 2 digits of the year (i.e., 01 = 2001). M or MM indicates the month of the year (1-12). mmm(m) references the model number with either 3 or 4 digits (i.e., a 6136 reads 136). x(xx) refers to a 1-3 digit production count.

A currently manufactured Country Club Model (Model No. 6196) with ser. no. 01319652 indicates it was built in March of 2001, the last 3 numbers of the model number are next - 196. 52 indicates the production count.

A Model No. 6121 Roundup with a ser. no. of 999121447 indicates it was built in Sept. of 1999, 121 represents the last 3 digits of the model number, and 447 is the production count.

GUILD SERIALIZATION

Guild Serialization went through three distinct phases, and can be both a helpful guide as well as confusing when trying to determine the manufacturing date of a guitar. The primary idea to realize is that most Guild models use a separate serial numbering system for each guitar model - there is no "overall system" to plug a number into! While serial numbers are sometimes a helpful tool, other dating devices like potentiomter codes or dating by hardware may be more exact.

1952-1965: Between the inception of the Guild company in 1952 to 1965, the serialization was sequential for all models.

APPROXIMATE LAST NUMBER	YEAR
350	1952
840	1953
1526	1954
2468	1955
3830	1956
5712	1957
8348	1958
12035	1959
14713	1960
18419	1961
22722	1962
28943	1963
38636	1964
46606	1965

1966-1969: While some models retained the serialization from the original series, many models were designated with a 2 letter prefix and an independent numbering series for each individual model between 1966 to 1969.

Continued Original Serialization Series

APPROXIMATE LAST NUMBER	YEAR
46608	1966
46637	1967
46656	1968
46695	1969

The models that were numbered with the new 2 letter prefix started each separate serial number series with 101.

1970-1979: The following chart details the serial numbers as produced through the 1970s. There are no corresponding model names or numbers for this time period.

APPROXIMATE LAST NUMBER	YEAR
50978	1970
61463	1971
75602	1972
95496	1973
112803	1974
130304	1975
149625	1976
169867	1977
190567	1978
211877	1979

1979-1989: In 1979, Guild returned to the separate prefix/serial number system. Serial numbers after the 2 letter prefix in each separate system began with 100001 (thus, you would need a serialization table for each model/by year to date by serialization alone). In 1987, a third system was devised. In some cases, the **Model Designation** became the *prefix* for the serial number. For example:

D300041 D-30, #0041 (41st D-30 instrument produced)

With acoustic models, you can cross-reference the model name to the serial number to judge the rest of the serialization; the resulting serial number must still be checked in the serialization table.

1990-Date: Guild continued with the separate prefix/serialization system. In 1994, only the Model Prefix and last serial numbers for each model were recorded; better records continued in 1995.

Guild Custom Shop: The three Guild Custom Shop models (**45th Anniversary, Deco,** and **Finesse**) all use a completely different serial numbering system. Each instrument has a serial number on the back of the headstock that indicates the "which number out of the complete series". Inside the guitar there is a seven digit code: The first three numbers (starting with #500) indicate the production sequence, while the last four digits indicate the date of production (the 4th and 7th digit **in reverse** indicate the year, the 5th and 6th digits are the month).

Guild has a series of charts available on their website (www.guildguitars.com - Ask Mr. Gearhead) to help date a Guild model during its different manufacturing periods. It is recommended that you refer to this information, as there are many charts needed for the individual model serialization. Through the years (and different owners of the company), some of the historical documentation has been lost or destroyed. However, these tables are some of the most comprehensive available to the public. They are up to date through Dec. of 1997.

(Serialization reference source: Hans Moust, The Guild Guitar Book; and Jay Pilzer, Guild Authority; additional company information courtesy Bill Acton, Guild Guitars)

HAMER SERIALIZATION

Hamer serial numbers are fairly easy to understand, given that the first digit in the instrument's serial number is the last digit of the year the instrument was produced (1986 would be a **6**, for instance). The use of a single digit means that those numbers will cycle every ten years (0 to 9); instrument production dates now have more relevance.

From 1974-1981, Hamer USA employed 2 separate serial numbering systems, one for custom instruments, and one for production models:

Custom Instruments: These instruments are easily recognized by the use of a 4-digit number stamped into the wood on the back of the peghead. The numbers ran from #0000 through #0680. All of the early Hamer USA Standards and 12-string basses, as well as a number of prototype instruments, were included in this serial numbering system.

Production Models: production models are stamped (initially with ink, later in the wood, on the back of the peghead) with either a 5 or 6-digit serial number. The first digit indicates the year that the instrument was built. The next 4 or 5 digits are sequentially stamped in order of production. For example, serial number 7 0001 was built in 1977, and was the first production model guitar built. Similarly, 0 1964 was built in 1980, and was the 1,964th production guitar built. The serial numbering sequence by decade is indicated below:

1970s	7 0001 - 9 1450
1980s	0 1451 - 9 24192
1990s	0 24193 - 9 50155
2000-present	0 50156 - present

(Hamer Serialization courtesy Jol Dantzig & Frank Rindone Hamer USA)

HOFNER DATING INFORMATION

The sequence of Hofner serial numbers do not provide an exact method for dating Hofner guitars. Hofners were available in Germany since 1949 (and earlier, if you take in the over 100 years of company history); but were not officially exported to England until Selmer of London took over distributorship in 1958. Furthermore, Selmer British models were specified for the U.K. only - and differ from those available in the German market.

However, research from author Paul Day indicated a dating scheme based on the pickups installed versus the time period. Keep in mind that there will be transitional models, and combinations do appear. Finally, a quick rule of thumb: Adjustable truss-rods were installed in necks beginning in 1960. Anything prior will not have a truss-rod cover.

DATE	PICKUP STYLE
1953-1959	Six *star-slot* pole piece (built by Fuma)
1957-1960	Black, White, or Brown plastic, with plain tops. Ends can be square or oval.
1960-1961	Rectangular metal case with four black slits in the top. Hofner *diamond* logo.
1961-1963	Rectangular metal case, six slot-screw **or** six rectangular pole pieces. The Hofner *diamond* logo appears on many of these.
1963-1967	Rectangular metal case, six slot-screw **and** six rectangular pole pieces.
1967-1978	Rectangular metal case, a single central bar magnet, plus six small slot-screw pole pieces.

Hofner then introduced a number of guitars based on Classic American favorites in the late 1960s on. These instruments used OEM pickups from Schaller, Shadow, and DiMarzio.

(Information courtesy Paul Day, and was featured in Gordon Giltrap and Neville Marten's The Hofner Guitar - A History (International Music Publications Limited, 1993). The Giltrap and Marten book is an overview of Hofner models produced between the late 1950s and the early 1970s, and a recommended read for those interested in Hofner guitars or British pop and rock from the 1960s)

IBANEZ MODEL NOMENLCATURE & SERIALIZATION

IBANEZ MODEL NUMBERING SYSTEM

Ibanez offers a wide selection of models with a corresponding wide range of features. This means there are a lot of models and, of course, a lot of different model numbers to try and keep track of. Ibanez serial numbers never indicated the model number, and still don't. Most solid body Ibanez guiatrs and basses didn't feature model numbers until recently, and even then, only on Korean made instruments. On some semi-hollow models, some model numbers will appear on the label visible through the f-hole.

Here's how the Ibanez model numbers work (most of the time, of course, there are always exceptions - but for the Ibanez models commonly encountered, this system applies pretty consistently).

SERIES: the first in the model number designate the series: RG550BK, RG Series; SR800BK is a Soundgear, etc. Also, in the Artstar lines, AS indicates (A)rtstar (S)emihollow, AF indicates (A)rtstar (F)ull hollow.

FINISH: the last 2 letters designate the finish: RG550BK, Black finish; RX240CA, Candy Apple. **Exceptions**: finishes such as Amber Pearl and Stained Oil Finish use 3 letters: AMP, SOL, etc. (having offered so many finishes, Ibanez is running out of traditional 2 letter cominations!)

The numbers following the Series letters indicate 2 items:

1. Point of Manufacture

On solid body guitars and basses, the numbers 500 and above indicate Japanese manufacture: RG550BK, SR800BK, BL850VB, the numbers 400 and below indicate Korean manufacture: SR400BK, RX240MG, etc.

This system doesn't apply to hollow bodies, and many signature guitars. J of White Zombie's signature model, the IJ100WZ is made in Japan, as is the JPM100.

2. Pickup Configuration

On solid body guitars only, the last 2 numbers indicate pickup configuration:

20= two humbucking pickups with or w/o pickguard (ex: TC420MD)

30 = three single coils with or w/o pickguard (no current models)

40 = sin/sin/hum with a pickguard (ex: TC740MN)

50 = hum/sin/hum with a pickguard (ex: RG550BK)

60 = sin/sin/hum with no pickguard (no current models)

70 = hum/sin/hum with no pickguard (ex: RG570FBL)

Exceptions: Of course! For example, TC825 (which has 2 humbuckers and a pickguard). BL1025 (hum/sin/hum with a pickguard), etc.

IBANEZ SERIALIZATION

Author/researcher Michael Wright successfully discussed the Ibanez/Hoshino history in his book, *Guitar Stories Volume One* (Vintage Guitar Books, 1995). Early serial numbers and foreign-built potentiometer codes on Japanese guitars aren't much help in the way of clues, but Ibanez did institute a meaningful numbering system as part of their warranty program in 1975.

Before 1987: In general, Ibanez serial numbers between 1975 to 1987 had seven digits, arranged **XYYZZZZ.** The letter prefix "X" stands for the month (January = A, February = B, etc. on to L); the next following two digits "YY" are the year. The last four digits indicate the number of instruments built per month through a particular production date.

An outside source indicated that the month/letter code prefix was discontined in 1988, and the previous dating code was discontinued in 1990. However (or whatever), in 1987 the **XYYZZZZ** still appeared the same, but the new listing shifted to **XYZZZZZ.**

1987 and later: The opening alphabetical prefix "X" now indicates production **location** instead of month: **F** (Fuji, Japan), or **C** (Cort, Korea). The first digit "Y" indicates the year: As in 198Y - and as in 199Y. Bright-eyed serialization students will have already noticed that while the year is obtainable, the decade isn't! Because of this, it is good to have a working knowledge of which models were available approx. which time periods. All following numbers again are the production ranking code (ZZZZZ).

Mid 1997: Ibanez changed the format, and the second two digit after the alphabetical prefix indicate the last 2 digits of the actual year of production (i.e, F0003680 indicates guitar built in Fuji during 2000).

CE Designation: In late 1996, in addition to the serial number on the back of the headstock, Ibanez electric guitars and basses added the "CE" designation. This indicates that the product meets the electronic standards of the European Common Market, similar to our UL approval.

(Source: Michael Wright, Guitar Stories Volume One, Jim Donahue, Ibanez Guitars)

MATSUMOKU SERIAL NUMBERS

(Includes various models from ARIA PRO II, VANTAGE, WASHBURN,WESTONE)

Any Matsumoku-produced instrument will have the first number as the identifier for the year, or possibly a two digit combination. Matsumoku stopped production in Japan in 1987, so an initial digit of "8" cannot be 1988 - the combination of the "8" plus the next digit will give the eighties designation.

The Matsumoku company built guitars for a number of trademarks. Although the Aria Company started their own "ARIA" guitar production in the 1960s, Matsumoku built guitars for them under contract from 1980 to 1987. Matsumoku also built guitars for **Vantage** between 1980 to 1986.

In 1979, the new series of **Washburn** electrics were designed in America, and produced in Japan by Matsumoku. After the success of supplying guitars for other companies' trademarks, Matsumoku marketed their own **Westone** instruments between 1981 to 1987. As Matsumoku stopped production in Japan in 1987, Westone production was moved to Korea.

(Dating information courtesy Tony Bacon and Paul Day, The Guru's Guitar Guide, Bold Strummer Ltd, 1990)

MOONSTONE SERIALIZATION

The most important factor in determining the year of manufacture for Moonstone instruments is that each model had its own set of serial numbers. There is no grouping of models by year of manufacture.

D-81 EAGLE

L001-L004	1981
L005-L011	1982

EAGLE (Electrics)

52950-52952	1980
52953-52954	1981
52955-52959	1982
52960	1983

EARTHAXE
(26 total instruments made)

0001-0013	1975
0014-0026	1976

ECLIPSE Guitar models
(81 total instruments made)

79001-79003	1979
8004-8036	1980
8037-8040	1981
1041-1052	1981
1053-1075	1982
1076-1081	1983

ECLIPSE Bass models
(124 total instruments made)

3801-3821	1980
3822-3828	1981
3029-3062	1981
3063-3109	1982
3110-3118	1983
3119-3123	1984

EXPLODER Guitar models
(65 total instruments made)

7801-7806	1980
7007-7020	1981
7021-7052	1982
7053-7065	1983

EXPLODER Bass models
(35 total instruments made)

6801-6803	1980
6004-6013	1981
6014-6031	1982
6032-6035	1983

FLYING V Guitar models
(52 total instruments made)

5801-5812	1980
5013-5028	1981
5029-5045	1982
5046-5048	1983
5049-5052	1984

FLYING V Bass models
(6 total instruments made)

9001-9006	1981

M-80
(64 total instruments made)

4801-4808	1980
4809-4816	1981
4017-4031	1981
4032-4052	1982
4053-4064	1983

MOONDOLINS

T001-T002	1981
T003-T006	1983
T007	1984

VULCAN Guitar models
(162 total instruments made)

5027	1977
5028-5034	1978
107835-107838	1978
17939-179115	1979
179116-179120	1980
80121-80129	1980
80130-80134	1981
8135-8167	1981
8168-8185	1982
8186-8191	1983
7988-7991	1984

VULCAN Bass models
(19 total instruments made)

V001-V002	1982
V003-V016	1983
V017-V019	1984

MUSIC MAN SERIAL NUMBERS

The serial numbers found on the original Music Man/Leo Fender's CLF produced instruments ("pre-Ernie Ball") are not encoded in a system that indicates the production date, but such information can be found on the end of the neck. As with the earlier Fenders, the neck would have to be removed from the body to view this information.

The Ernie Ball Music Man serialization utilizes a numbering system that indicates the year through the first two digits (for example: 93537 = 1993).

PAUL REED SMITH SERIALIZATION

PRS regular production set neck 5 digit serialization is fairly easy to decipher: The first digit of the instrument's serial number corresponds to the last digit of the year (i.e., 199"X") the guitar was built. The rest of the numbers correspond to that guitar's production number off the line.

Prefix Number	Years of Mfg.
0	1990 or 2000
1	1991 or 2001
2	1992
3	1993
4	1994
5	1985 or 1995
6	1986 or 1996
7	1987 or 1997
8	1988 or 1998
9	1989 or 1999
Example: 7 2385	= 1987, 2,385th guitar built

However, just like the Hamer serialization, this number will cycle every ten years - so knowing when the model was available becomes critical. Keep in mind that the serial numbers from the 1980s will be a relatively low number; serial numbers from the mid-1990s will be much higher.

Example: 7 25385= 1997, 25,385th guitar built

Example: 050427 (McCarty Soapbar) = 2000, 50,427th guitar built

Example: 155765 (Custom Soapbar) = 2001, 55,765th instrument built

Before 1990, serial ranges were approximately 0001-0400 for 1985, 041-1700 for 1986, 1701-3500 for 1987, 3501-5400 for 1988, 5401-7600 for 1989, 7601-10100 for 1990 (start of 5 digit numbers).

PRS CE (Classic Electric) models have one extra number inserted between the first digit (year designator) and befor the number of the guitar. They are numbered in sequence (1988 began with 0001, and 1999 ended at approx. 20,000).

Example: 9 CE19759= 1999, 19,759th guitar built

EG Models manufactured 1990-1995 have their own serial number range, approx. 0001-3300.

PRS bolt-on and set neck basses were manufactured 1989-1991, and also have their own serial number ranges - 0001-0200 for bolt neck, 0001-0800 for set neck. Additionally, swamp ash specials mfg. 1997-1999 have their own range beginning with 00001.

(Source: The PRS Guitar Book by Dave Burrluck, Balafon Books)

PEAVEY SERIAL NUMBERS

While more musicians may be aware of Peavey through the numerous high quality amplifiers and P.A. systems they build, the company has been producing solidbody guitars and basses since 1978. Peavey serial numbers exist more for the company's warranty program than an actual dating system. According to researcher Michael Wright, the earliest serial numbers had six digits; by 1978 the company switched to eight digits. Peavey can supply the shipping date (which is within a few weeks of actual production) for the more inquisitive.

Replacement manuals are generally available for Peavey products. For further information, contact Peavey Electronics through the Index of Current Manufacturers located in the back of this book.

(Information courtesy Michael Wright, Guitar Stories Volume One)

RICKENBACKER SERIAL NUMBERS

Rickenbacker offered a number of guitar models as well as lap steels prior to World War II, such as the **Ken Roberts Spanish** electric f-hole flattop (mid 1930s to 1940) and the **559** model archtop in the early 1940s. The company put production on hold during the war; in 1946, began producing an **Electric Spanish** archtop. Serialization on early Rickenbacker models from 1931 to 1953 is unreliable, but models may be dated by patent information. This method should be used in conjunction with comparisons of parts, and design changes.

In 1953, Rickenbacker/Electro was purchased by Francis C. Hall. The **Combo 600** and **Combo 800** models debuted in 1954. From 1954 on, the serial number appears on the bridge or jackplate of the instrument. The Rickenbacker serial numbers during the 1950s have four to seven digits. The letter within the code indicates the type of instrument (Combo/guitar, bass, mandolin, etc), and the number after the letter indicates the year of production:

Example: X(X)B7XX(A bass from 1957)

1961 to 1986: In 1961, the serialization scheme changes. The new code has <u>two letter</u> prefixes, followed by digits. The first letter prefix indicates the year; the second digit indicates the month of production.

PREFIX	YEAR
A	1961
B	1962
C	1963
D	1964
E	1965
F	1966
G	1967
H	1968
I	1969
J	1970
K	1971
L	1972
M	1973
N	1974
O	1975
P	1976
Q	1977
R	1978
S	1979
T	1980
U	1981
V	1982
W	1983
X	1984
Y	1985
Z	1986
A	January
B	February

PREFIX	YEAR
C	March
D	April
E	May
F	June
G	July
H	August
I	September
J	October
K	November
L	December
M	January
N	February
P	March
Q	April
R	May
S	June
T	July
U	August
V	Septemberr
W	October
X	November
Y	December

In 1987, the serialization was revised, again. The updated serial number code has letter prefix (A to L) that still indicates month; the following digit that indicates the year:

DIGIT	YEAR
0	1987
1	1988
2	1989
3	1990
4	1991
5	1992
6	1993
7	1994
8	1995
9	1996
0	1997
1	1998

The following digits after the month/year digits are production (for example, *L2XXXX* would be an instrument built in December, 1989).

In 1999, the system was changed to a number only system. The 2 digits by themselves are the year, and the first two from the 4-5 set being the week it was made. Example: 0012345 - this instrument would have been made in the 12th week of 2000. Example: a new Ricky Model 620-12 with serial number 0119659 indicates an instrument built in the 19th week of 2001. 659 indicates the internal production number.

(Information courtesy of Tommy Thomasson, Rickenbacker International Corporation.)

WASHBURN SERIALIZATION

The Washburn trademark was introduced by the Lyon & Healy company of Chicago, Illinois in 1864. While this trademark has changed hands a number of times, the historical records have not! Washburn suffered a fire in the 1920s that destoyed all records and paperwork that was on file; in the 1950s, another fire destroyed the accumulated files yet again.

When the trademark was revived yet again in 1964, the first production of Washburn acoustic guitars was in Japan. Washburn electric guitars debuted in 1979, and featured U.S. designs and Japanese production.

Production of Washburn guitars changed to Korea in the mid to late 1980s; a number of U.S.-produced **Chicago Series** models were introduced in the late 1980s as well. Serial numbers from 1988 on use the first two digits of the instrument's serial number to indicate the year the instrument was produced (1988 = 88XXX). This process works for most, but not all, of the instruments since then.

Washburn Limited Editions feature the year in the model name. For example, D-95 LTD is a Limited Edition introduced in 1995. No corresponding serialization information is available at this time.

(Washburn information courtesy Dr. Duck's AxWax)

YAMAHA SERIAL NUMBERS

Yamaha instruments were originally produced in Japan; production switched to Taiwan in the early 1980s. Instruments are currently produced in the U.S., Taiwan, and Indonesia. It is important to recognize that Yamaha uses two different serialization systems.

Yamaha electric guitars and basses have a letter/number (2 letters followed by 5 numbers) code that indicates production date. The first two letters of the serial number indicate the year and month of production (the first letter indicates the year, the second letter indicates the month). Yamaha's coding system substitutes a letter for a number indicating year and month, thus:

CODE LETTER	MONTH or YEAR NUMBER
H	1
I	2
J	3
K	4
L	5
M	6
N	7
O	8
P	9
X	10
Y	11
Z	12

For example, an "H" in the first of two letters would be a "1", indicating the last digit of the year (1981 or 1991). An "H" in the second of two letters would also be a "1", indicating the first month (January). Like Hamer, the digits will cycle around every 10 years.

After the two letter prefixes, 5 digits follow. The first two digits represent the day of the month, and the three digits indicate the production ranking for that day. For example:

NZ19218	December 19, 1987 (or 1997); #218.

The example's code should be properly broken down as N - Z - 27 - 428. The "N" in the first of the two letters would be a "7", indicating the last digit of the year (1987 or 1997). The "Z" in the second of the two letters would be a "12", indicating the 12th month (December). The two digit pair after the letters is the day of the month, the 19th. The final three digits indicate production ranking, therefore this imaginary guitar is the 218th instrument built that day.

Yamaha Acoustics and Acoustic Electrics contain 8 digit serial numbers. In this coding scheme, the first digit represents the last digit of the year (for example, 1987 = 7); the second and third numbers indicate the month (numbers 01 through 12); the fourth and fifth numbers will indicate the day of the month, and the final three digits will indicate the production ranking of the instrument.

This system works for most (but not all) of Yamaha products. If a serial number doesn't fit the coding system, Yamaha offers internal research via their website (www.yamahaguitars.com) - just email your request in.

GUITAR REFERENCES

Maybe the best advice any guitar player/collector will ever get is "For every guitar you purchase, buy 5 guitar books". It's still a good rule of mb. The guitar industry has been very fortunate in that many good reference works have been published within the last several decades. In ms of the major trademarks, it's pretty much over – most of the good books are already out there. All you have to do is buy 'em and read 'em. ne are even out of print, and have already become very collectible (expensive).

If you're a player, collector, or just kind of an all-around average guitar pervert, you gotta do your homework. And there have never been more ys to bone up on your chosen homework assignments. Even though the web does a good job of performing many basic guitar information ser- es, it's still not a book. It's also necessary that you subscribe to a few good magazines within your area (please refer to Periodicals listing).

The following titles represent a good cross sectional cut of those reference that are outstanding in their field(s). Also, don't miss the new list- ;s from Music Sales pictured on page 64. Larry Meiner's new books, *Gibson Shipment Totals 1937-1979* & *Flying "V" – The Illustrated History this Modernistic Guitar* are available directly through us – please use the insert order card located in the G section of this book.

Spending $300 annually to have these valuable books at your fingertips is the cheapest insurance policy you'll every buy. If you're serious about ur guitars, this information could also save you thousands of dollars and a lot of bad attitude. So bone up or bail out! No whining either – it's retty cool homework assignment.

Most of the books listed below can be obtained through:

JK Lutherie
11115 Sand Run
Harrison, OH 45030
Phone: 800.344.8880
www.jklutherie.com
Guitar@jklutherie.com

JK Lutherie also attends many major guitar shows annually, and you may want to stop by the booth to either purchase or inquire about any ew releases. Many video releases are also available, and can be found on his web site.

'he Acoustic Guitar by Nick Freeth & ;harles Alexander, Running Press, 1999, SBN: 0-7624-0419-1

Acoustic Guitars and Other Fretted 'nstruments by George Gruhn & Walter Carter, Miller Freeman Inc., 1993, SBN: 0-87930-240-2

Acquired of the Angels: The lives and works of master guitar makers John D'Angelico and James L. D'Aquisto by Paul William Schmidt, The Scarecrow Press, Inc., 1991, ISBN: 1-57886-002-4

American Guitars by Tom Wheeler, HarperCollins Publishers, 1990, ISBN: 0-06-014996-5

Ampeg: The Story Behind the Sound by Gregg Hopkins & Bill Moore, Hal Leonard Corporation, 1999, ISBN: 0-7935-7951-1

The Bass Book by Tony Bacon & Barry Moorhouse, GPI/Miller Freeman Inc., 1995, ISBN: 0-87930-368-9

The Beauty of the 'Burst by Yasuhiko Iwanade, Rittor Music, 1997

Bizarre Guitars Vol. 2, Rittor Music, 1993

Blue Guitar by Ken Vose, Chronicle Books, 1998, ISBN: 0-8118-1912-4

The Burns Book by Paul Day, The Bold Strummer, Ltd., 1990, ISBN: 0-933224-09-5

'Burst 1958-'60 Sunburst Les Paul by Jay Scott & Vic Da Pra, Seventh String Press, 1994, ISBN: 0-8256-9388-8

Classic Guitars U.S.A. by Willie G. Moseley, Centerstream Publishing, 1992, ISBN: 0-931759-52-8

Collectables & Vintage by Carlos Juan, American Guitar Center, 1995

The Complete Encyclopedia of the Guitar by Terry Burrows, Carlton Books, 1998, ISBN: 0-02-865028-X

The Complete Guitarist by Richard Chapman, DK Publishing, 1993, ISBN: 1-56458-181-0

The Custom Guitar Shop & Wayne Richard Charvel (What's in a Name?) by Frank Wm. Green, Working Musician Publications, 1999

Custom Guitars by David A. Lusterman, String Letter Publishing, 2000, ISBN: 1-890490-29-6

Dangerous Curves: The Art of the Guitar by Darcy Kuronen, MFA Publications, 2000, ISBN: 0-87846-478-6

GUITAR REFERENCES

The Development of the Modern Guitar by John Huber, Kahn & Avril, 1994, ISBN: 0-93224-59-1

The Electric Guitar by Tom Wheeler, et. al., Chronicle Books, 1993, ISBN: 0-8118-0863-7

Electric Guitars by Rob Goudy, Schiffer Publishing, Ltd., 1999, ISBN: 0-7643-0964-1

Electric Guitars and Basses by George Gruhn & Walter Carter, GPI/Miller Freeman Inc., 1994, ISBN: 0-87930-492-8

Epiphone, The Complete History by Walter Carter, Hal Leonard Corporation, 1995, ISBN: 0-7935-4203-0

Epiphone: The House of Stathopoulo by Jim Fisch & L.B. Fred, Amsco Publications (Music Sales Corporation), 1996, ISBN: 0-8256-1453-8

The Fender Bass by Klaus Blasquiz, Hal Leonard Publishing Corp., Milwaukee WI, 1990, ISBN: 0-7935-0757

The Fender Book by Tony Bacon & Paul Day, GPI/Miller Freeman Inc., 1992

The Fender Book by Tony Bacon & Paul Day, Revised Edition, Miller Freeman Books, 1998, ISBN: 0-87930-554-1

Fender Custom Shop Guitar Gallery by Richard R, Smith, Hal Leonard Corporation, 1996, ISBN: 0-7935-5065-3

The Fender Guitar by Ken Achard, The Bold Strummer, Ltd., 1990, ISBN: 0-933224-48-9

Fender: The Inside Story by Forrest White, GPI/Miller Freeman Books, 1994, ISBN: 0-87930-309-3

Fender - The Sound Heard 'Round the World by Richard R. Smith, Garfish Publishing Company, 1995, ISBN: 0-9648612-7-5

The Fender Stratocaster by A.R. Duchossoir, Hal Leonard Publishing Corp., 1989, ISBN: 0-88188-880-X

The Fender Telecaster by A.R. Duchossoir, Hal Leonard Publishing Corp., 1991, ISBN: 0-7935-0860-6

Ferrington Guitars by Kate Giel, et al, HarperCollins, 1992

50 Years of Fender by Tony Bacon, Balafon Books, 2000, ISBN: 0-87930-621-1

'50s Cool: Kay Guitars by Jay Scott, Seventh String Press, 1992, ISBN: 1-880422-01-B

Flying "V" – The Illustrated History of this Modernistic Guitar by Larry Meiners, Flying Vintage Publications, 2001, ISBN: 0-9708273-3-4

G&L: Leo's Legacy by Paul Bechtoldt, Woof Associates, 1994

The Galaxy of Strats by Yasuhiko Iwanade, Rittor Music, 1998, ISBN: 4-8456-0279-2

Gibson Electrics by A.R. Duchossoir, Hal Leonard Publishing Corp., 1981

Gibson Electrics - The Classic Years by A.R. Duchossoir, Hal Leonard Publishing Corp., 1994

The Gibson ES175 by Adrian Ingram, Music Maker Books, 1994, ISBN: 1-870951-11-5

The Gibson Guitar by Ian C. Bishop, The Bold Strummer, Ltd., 1990

The Gibson Guitar From 1950 Vol. 2 b Ian C. Bishop, The Bold Strummer, Lt 1990, ISBN: 0-933224-47-8

Gibson Guitars, 100 Years of an America Icon by Walter Carter, General Publishing, Inc., 1994, ISBN: 1-88164 39-3

The Gibson L-5: Its History and Its Playe by Adrian Ingram, 1997, ISBN: 1-57424-047-1

The Gibson Les Paul Book by Tony Bacc & Paul Day, GPI/Miller Freeman Inc., 1993, ISBN: 0-87930-289-5

Gibson Shipment Totals 1937-1979 by Larry Meiners, Flying Vintage Publications, 2001, ISBN: 0-9708273-4 2

The Gibson Super 400 by Thomas A. Va Hoose, Miller Freeman, Inc., 1991, ISBN: 0-87930-230-5

Gibson's Fabulous Flat-Top Guitars by Erlewine, Vinolpal and Whitford, Mille Freeman Books, 1994, ISBN: 0-87930-321-2

The Gretsch Book by Tony Bacon & Paul Day, GPI/Miller Freeman Inc., 1996, ISBN: 0-87930-408-1

Gruhn's Guide to Vintage Guitars by George Gruhn & Walter Carter, GPI/Miller Freeman Inc., 1991, 1999, ISBN: 0-87930-422-7

The Guild Guitar Book - The Company and the Instruments 1952-1977 by Hans Moust, Guitar Archives Publications, 1995, ISBN: 0-7935-5220-6

The Guitar Book, A Handbook for Electric & Acoustic Guitarists by Tom Wheeler, Harper & Row, 1974 ISBN: 0-06-014559-5

GUITAR REFERENCES

he Guitar Handbook by Ralph Denyer, lfred A. Knopf Inc., 1982, ISBN: 0-79-74275-1

uitar Identification by A.R. Duchossoir, lal Leonard Publishing Corp., 1983, 990, & 1999, ISBN: 0-634-00672-X

uitar Legends by George Fullerton, Centerstream Publishing, 1993, ISBN: 0-6-273352-4

uitar People by Willie G. Moseley, 'intage Guitar Books, 1997, ISBN: 1-84883-06-0

uitar Stories Volume One by Michael Wright, Vintage Guitar Books, 1995, SBN: 1-884883-03-6

Guitars from Neptune - A Definitive ourney Into Danelectro Mania by Paul Bechtoldt & Doug Tulloch, JK Lutherie, 1996

The Guitars of the Fred Gretsch Company by Jay Scott, Centerstream Publishing, 1992, ISBN: 0-931759-62

Guitars from the Renaissance to Rock by Tom & Mary Anne Evans, Facts on File, 1977

Guitars, Guitars, Guitars by Briggs, Brinkman and Crocker, All American Music Publishers, 1988

Guitars of the Stars, Volume 1 Rick Nielsen & Bill Rich, Gots Publishing Ltd., A Division of Rich Specialties, Inc., 1993, ISBN: 0-9635279-0-B

The Guru's Guitar Guide by Tony Bacon & Paul Day, Track Record Publishing, 1990

The History & Artistry of National Resonator Instruments by Bob Brozeman, Centerstream Publishing, 1993, ISBN: 0-931759-65-X

The History and Development of the American Guitar by Ken Achard, The Bold Strummer, Ltd., 1990, ISBN: 0-933224-18-4

The History of the Ovation Guitar by Walter Carter, Hal Leonard Corporation, 1996, ISBN: 0-7935-5948-0

The History of Rickenbacker Guitars by Richard R. Smith, Centerstream Publishing, 1989, ISBN: 0-931759-15-3

The Hofner Guitar - A History by Gordon Giltrap & Neville Marten, International Music Publications Limited, 1993, ISBN: 0-86359-956-7

Hofner Guitars-Made in Germany by Michael Naglav

Hofner Violin 'Beatle' Bass by Joe Dunn, New Cavendish Books, 1996, ISBN: 974-82251-43

How the Fender Bass Changed the World by Jim Roberts, Backbeat Books, 2001, ISBN: 0-87930-630-0

The Larsons' Creations, Guitars and Mandolins by Robert Carl Hartman, Centerstream Publishing, 1995, ISBN: 0-931759-77-3

Making an Archtop Guitar - The Definitive Work on the Design and Construction of an Acoustic Archtop Guitar by Robert Benedetto, Centerstream Publishing/Hal Leonard Corp., 1996

The Martin Book by Walter Carter, GPI/Miller Freeman Inc., 1995, ISBN: 0-87930-354-9

Martin Guitars, a History by Mike Longworth, 4 Maples Press Inc., 1987

Martin Guitars: An Illustrated Celebration of America's Premier Guitarmaker by Jim Washburn, Rodale Press, 1997, ISBN: 0-87596-797-3

My Life & Times with Fender Musical Instruments by Bill Carsonwith Willie G. Moseley, Vintage Guitar Books, 1998, ISBN: 1-884883-10-9

Norman's Rare Guitars by David Swartz with Norman Harris, Swartz, Inc., 1999, ISBN: 0-9669219-0-9

The PRS Guitar Book by Dave Burrluck, Balafon Books, 1999

Pick the Right Guitar – The Guitar Buyer's Handbook by Vern Juran, J-V Publishing, 1997, ISBN: 0-9675609-0-X

The Rickenbacker Book by Tony Bacon & Paul Day, GPI/Miller Freeman Inc., 1994, ISBN: 0-87930-329-8

Stellas & Stratocasters by Willie G. Moseley, Vintage Guitar Books, 1994, ISBN: 1-884883-00-1

The Steve Howe Guitar Collection by Steve Howe, GPI/Miller Freeman, Inc., 1993, ISBN: 0-87930-290-9

The Story of the Fender Stratocaster: Curves, Contours, and Body Horns by Ray Minhinnett, Miller Freeman, 1995, ISBN: 0-87930-349-2

The Ultimate Guitar Book by Tony Bacon, Alfred A. Knopf, Inc., 1991, ISBN: 0-394-58955-6

The Vox Story by David Petersen & Dick Denney, The Bold Strummer, Ltd., 1993, ISBN: 0-933224-70-2

Washburn: Over One Hundred Years of Find Stringed Instruments by John Teagle, Music Sales Corp, 1996, ISBN: 0-8256-1435-X

PERIODICALS LISTINGS

You've bought this book so you're obviously interested in stringed instruments. Being knowledgeable about any subject is a good idea and having the up- the-minute news is the best form of knowledge. We recommend the following publications for instrument information, collecting news, updates and sh announcements, luthier and artist insights and loads of other information that might interest you.

20th Century Guitar
Seventh String Press, Inc., 135 Oser Avenue, Hauppauge, New York 11788
Phone number: 631-273-1674,
Fax: 631-434-9057
www.tcguitar.com
Published monthly. 12 month subscription is $15.00 in the USA.

Acoustic Guitar
String Letter Publishing, Inc., 255 W. End Ave.,
San Rafael, California 94901
Phone number: 415-485-6946,
Fax: 415-485-0831
www.acousticguitar.com
Email: slp@stringletter.com
Published monthly. 12 month subscription is $29.95 in the USA.

Bass Player
2800 Campus Dr.
San Mateo, CA 94403
Phone number: 650.513.4300
Fax: 650.513.4642
www.bassplayer.com
bassplayer@musicplayer.com
Published monthly. 12 month subscription is $29.95

Downbeat
102 N. Haven Road, Elmhurst, Illinois 60126-3379.
630-941-2030 Fax: 630-941-3210
Published monthly.

Gitarre & Bass (Germany)
MM-Musik-Media-Verlag GmbH,
An Der Wachsfabrik 8, Koln, 50996 Germany
Phone number: 011-39-2236-96217
Fax: 011-39-2236-96217-5
Published monthly.

Guitar Digest
P.O. Box 66, The Plains, Ohio 45780
Phone number: 740-797-3351
or 740-592-4614
www.guitardigest.com
www.ottoguitarshow.com
Email: alexmack@frognet.net
Published 6 times a year. A six issue subscription is $10.00 in the USA.

Guitar for the Practicing Musician
Cherry Lane Magazines, LLC,
Six East 32nd St., 11th Flr., New York, NY 10016
Phone number: 212-561-3000
Fax: 212-251-0840
Published monthly. 12 month subscription is $22.95 in the USA, and a two year subscription is $37.95 in the USA.

Guitar One
Cherry Lane Magazines, LLC, Six East 32nd St., 11th Flr., New York, NY 10016
Phone number: 212-561-3000
Fax: 212-251-0840 Published monthly.
Available on the newstands for $4.95 per issue in the USA.

The Guitar Magazine (UK)
IPC Focus House Dingwall Avenue, Croyden CR9 2TA, England.
Phone number: 011.44.208.774.0600
Fax: 011.44.208.774.0934
Published every 4 weeks - 16 per year.

Guitar Player
2800 Campus Dr.
San Mateo, CA 94403
Phone number: 650.513.4300
Fax: 650.513.4642
www.guitarplayer.com
Published monthly. 12 month subscription is $29.95 in the USA.

Guitar World
Harris Publications, Inc.,
1115 Broadway, 8th Flr.
New York, New York 10010
Phone number: 800-866-2886
Email: sounding.board@guitarworld.com
http://www.guitarworld.com
Published monthly. 12 month subscription is $23.94 in the USA.

Guitar World Acoustic
Harris Publications, Inc.,
1115 Broadway, 8th Flr.
New York, New York 10010
Phone number: 212-807-7100,
Fax: 212-627-4678
Email: sounding.board@guitarworld.com
http://www.guitarworld.com
Published monthly. $16.97 for 6 issues, publisher every other month.

Guitarist (UK)
Alexander House, Forehill, Ely,
Cambs CB7 4AF, England
Phone number: 011-44-1353-665577
Fax: 011-44-1353-662489
Email: guitarist@musicians-net.co.uk
Published monthly.

Guitarist (France)
10, Rue De la Paix, Boulogne, France 92100

JazzTimes
8737 Colesville Rd., 5th Floor,
Silver Spring, MD 20910
Phone: 301.588.4114 Fax: 301.588.5531
Wwwjazztimes.com
Published 10 times/year. A one year subscription is $23.95 in the USA.

Just Jazz Guitar
P.O. Box 76053, Atlanta,
Georgia 30358-1053
Phone number: 404-250-9298
Fax: 404-250-9951
www.justjazzguitar.com
Published 4 times a year. A one year subscription is $36 in the USA.

Musico Pro
Music Maker Publications, Inc., 5412 Idylwil Trail, Suite 100, Boulder, Colorado 80301
Phone number: 303-516-9118
Fax: 303-516-9119
www.recordingmag.com
Email: info@recordingmag.com
A music/gear magazine is published in Spanish (available in U.S., Argentine, Chile, Mexico, and Spain).
Published 12 times a year. Subscription is $19.95 in the USA.

Staccato
Manfred Hecker and Carsten Durer, Editors.
Akazienweg 57, Cologne, 50827 Germany
Phone number: 011-39-221-5301560
Fax: 011-39-221-5302286
Email: staccato@vva.com

Vintage Guitar Magazine
Alan J. Greenwood, P.O. Box 7301,
Bismarck, North Dakota 58507
Phone number: 701-255-1197
Fax: 701-255-0250
www.vintageguitar.com
Published monthly. 12 month subscription is $27.95 in the USA.

Vintage Guitar News (Germany)
Verlag Gunter Janssen, Eggensteinerstr. 46,
Stutensee, D-76297 Germany
Phone number: +49-7244-740063,
Fax: +49-7244-740064
Email: 101574.223@compuserve.com
Published six times yearly.

In addition to the regular publications put out by these publishers, most offer Special Edition (i.e., yearly buyers' guides, new product reviews, market overviews, etc.) magazines that are released annually, or bi-annually. Please contact them directly for more information.

Identifying "House Brands" Musical Instruments

The phenomenon of large production companies producing "house brand" instruments dates back to the late 1800s and early 1900s. A "house brand" is defined as a trademark used by distributors, wholesalers, and retailers to represent their respective company instead of the manufacturer. These brands are found (for the most part) on budget instruments, although some models are currently sought after by players and collectors on the basis of playability, tone, or relative degree of "coolness" they project.

In the 1800s, many guitar manufacturers were located in New York and Philadelphia; by the early 1900s large guitar factories were centered in Chicago. The "Big Three" that evolved out of the early 1930s were Harmony, Kay, and Valco. Valco, producer of National and Supro instruments, produced the Airline house brand as well as bodies and resonator parts that were sold to Harmony and Kay. However, the majority of house brand instruments found today probably originated at either Harmony or Kay. On the East Coast, Danelectro was a large builder/supplier to Sears & Roebuck under Sears' Silvertone label (sometimes up to 85 percent of Danelectro's output).

Prior to World War II, Harmony and Kay sold straight to wholesalers like catalogue houses and large distributors. In turn, these wholesalers would send their salesmen and "reps" out on the road to generate sales - no territories, no music store chains - just straight sales. Business was fierce, and companies used their own private labels to denote "their" product. House brands were typically used as a marketing tool for distributors, wholesalers, and/or retailers to try to eliminate consumer shopping for the best price on popular makes and models of the time. How could you shop a trademark that didn't exist anywhere else? Tom Wheeler, in his book, *American Guitars*, quoted former Harmony president Charles A. Rubovits' recollection that the company built 57 private brands for the wholesalers - and sold over five million guitars.

An informative essay about house brands and their place in the vintage guitar spectrum can be found in *Stellas & Stratocasters* (Vintage Guitar Books) by Willie G. Moseley, feature writer/columnist for *Vintage Guitar Magazine*. Moseley's commentary includes a listing of thirty-eight brands and their retailers/distributors, brief anecdotes about the major American manufacturers of budget instruments (Harmony, Kay, etc.) and photos of twenty-five American made house brand instruments.

Since writing that article, Moseley has advised the *Blue Book of Electric Guitars*: "I've come across a couple of other house brands in my travels; one example was a low-end, Stella-type variant with `Superior' sloppily screen-printed on its headstock. It was one of those cheap, beginner's instruments that were and still are at the nadir of American-made guitars, but so far I haven't been able to determine anything about its brand name...not that it matters too much!"

"It's my opinion, and I dare say the opinion of most vintage guitar enthusiasts, that a good rule of thumb concerning the collectibility of house brands would be something along the lines of 'If it was a budget instrument then, it's proportionally a budget instrument now.' Regrettably, as the interest in vintage guitars continues to grow, some individuals and/or businesses tend to assume that simply because an instrument is 'old' and/or 'discontinued' and/or 'American-made', that automatically makes it a 'collector's item' and/or 'valuable'. That's certainly not the case, especially with house brands. It's disheartening to walk into a pawn shop and see a Kay-made Silvertone archtop electric from the Sixties labeled as an 'antique' and priced at $499, when the instrument is worth no more than $100 in the vintage guitar market, and such incidents are apparently on the increase. And that's unfortunate for everybody."

The *Blue Book of Electric Guitars* is continuing to collect data and evaluate the collectibility and pricing on these house brand instruments. Condition is a large factor in the pricing, as a thirty-to-forty year old guitar ordered from a catalog may have been used/abused by younger members of a household (to the detriment of the instrument). House brand guitars may be antiques, they may be somewhat collectible, and they may be "classic pieces of Americana" (as one antique shop's sign declared), but they should still be relatively inexpensive when compared to the rest of the vintage guitar market. We believe Mr. Moseley to be correct in his C-note assessment of this aspect of the vintage market (at 80% to 90% condition); other music markets that service players and students may find pricing at a slightly wider range of $75 to $150 depending on other factors (playability, possessing an adjustable truss rod, appearance/"coolness" factor, a solid wood top versus plywood, veneer sides, additional parts, etc.) This is the bottom line: this book should help identify the brand/original company, give a few hints as to the quality and desirability, and a price range. The rest is up to you! We will continue to survey the market for pricing trends and "hot" models - further information will be included in upcoming editions of the *Blue Book of Electric Guitars.*

Blue Book of Electric Guitars

AMPS/EFFECTS/STRINGS/PICKUPS

Now that you've bought the guitar of your dreams, what are you going to plug it into?
A Quick Reference of Amplifier Manufacturers.

ACOUSTIC
A division of Samick Corp.
18521 Railroad Street
City of Industy CA 91748
626.964.4700
Fax: 626.964.8898
www.acoustic.mu

ACTODYNE GENERAL, INC.
5561 Engineer Drive
Huntington Beach CA 92649
800.575.5223
714.898.2776
Fax: 714.893.1045
www.agilace.com

ADAMAS
Distributed by Kaman Music
860.509.8888

AGUILAR
Aguilar Amplification LLC
599 Broadway, 7th Floor
New York NY 10012
212.757.2823
Fax: 212.431.8201
email: aguilar@interport.net
www.aguilaramp.com

GEORGE ALESSANDRO
Alessandro Corporation
P.O. Box 253
Huntingdon Valley PA 19006
215.355.6424
Fax: 215.355.6424

AMPEG
St. Louis Music (SLM)
1400 Ferguson Avenue
St. Louis MO 63133
800.727.4512
314.727.4512
Fax: 314.727.8929
www.ampeg.com

ART
Applied Research and Technologies
215 Tremont Street
Rochester NY 14608-2366
716.436.2720
Fax: 716.436.3942
artroch@aol.com
www.artroch.com

ASHDOWN
c/o HHB
1410 Centinela Avenue
Los Angeles CA 90025-2501
310.319.9111
Fax: 310.319.1311
sales@hhbusa.com

BAG END LOUDSPEAKERS
P.O. Box 488
Barrington IL 60011
847.897.6766
Fax: 847.382.4551

BEHRINGER
11041 Santa Monica Blvd
Los Angeles CA 90023
310.441.4430
Fax: 310.441.4460
www.behringer.com

BLUE'S PEARL AMP COMPANY
92 Litchfield Ave.
Babylon NY 11702
516.422.8661
Fax: 516.422.7030

BLUESLAND
Tone City Engineering & Mfg.
396 Dewey St.
St. Paul MN 55117
651.645.0030
Fax: 651.647.9603
www.bluesland.com

BOGNER
Bogner Amplification
11411 Vanowen St.
North Hollywood CA 91605
818.765.8929
Fax: 818.765.5299

BOYDEN
Boyden Amplifiers
7883 Hestia Place
Pensacola FL 32506
850.455.1604

TONY BRUNO CUSTOM AMPS
40-33 168th Street
Flushing NY 11358
718.762.7320

BUDDA AMPLIFICATION
37 Joseph Ct.
San Rafael CA 94903
415.492.1935
buddatone@aol.com

CALLAHAM
Callaham Guitars
114 Tudor Drive
Winchester VA 22603
540.955.0294 - shop
540.665.8045 - voicemail
email:
callaham@visuallink.com
www.callahamguitars.com

CARVIN
12340 World Trade Drive
San Diego CA 92128
800.854.2235
619.487.1600
Fax: 619.487.8160
www.carvin.com
www.carvinguitars.com

CARR AMPLIFIERS
433 W. Salisbury Street
Pittsboro, NC 27312
919.545.0747
www.carramps.com
scarr1@mindspring.com

CB LABS, INC.
990 Housatonic Avenue
Bridgeport CT 06606
203.335.1093
Fax: 203.331.9214

CHARLIE STRINGER
Stringer Industries
P.O. Box 4241
Warren NJ 07059
732.469.2828
Fax: 732.469.2828
www.snarlingdogs.com

CLARK AMPLIFIERS
1531 Augusta Road
West Columbia SC 29169

CRATE
St. Louis Music (SLM)
1400 Ferguson Avenue
St. Louis MO 63133
800.727.4512
314.727.4512
Fax: 314.727.8929
www.crateamps.com

CUSTOM AUDIO AMPLIFIERS
19648 Magnolia Boulevard
N. Hollywood CA 91601
818.763.8898
Fax: 818.763.8890

DAEDALUS CABINETS
P.O. Box 124
Newfield NY 14867
Phone/Fax: 607.564.0000
www.daedalusmusic.com
info@daedalusmusic.com

DANELECTRO
P.O. Box 2769
Laguna Hills CA 92654
949.361.2100
Fax: 949.369.8500
www.danelectro.com

DEAN
Dean Musical Instruments
15251 Roosevelt Blvd, Suite 206
Clearwater FL 33760
727.519.9669
Fax: 727.519.9703
www.deanguitars.com
info@deanguitars.com

DIAZ
Diaz Amplifiers
P.O. Box 1315
East Stroudsburg PA 18301
717.476.5338
ampbo@ptd.net

DEAN MARKLEY
Dean Markley Amplifiers
P.O. Box 507
Bloomfield CT 06002-0507
800.647.2244
860.243.7941
Fax: 860.243.7287

DIGITECH
8760 South Sandy Parkway
Sandy UT 84070
801.566.8800
Fax: 801.566.7005
www.digitech.com

DOD
8760 South Sandy Parkway
Sandy UT 84070
801.566.8800
Fax: 801.566.7005
(Int'l Fax) 603.672.4246
www.dod.com

DR. Z AMPS
7523 Grand Division
Cleveland OH 44125
216.429.2922
Fax: 216.581.7577
drz@icgroup.net
www.drzamps.com

EBS
In Sweden:
Framnasbacken 12
Solna S171 42 Sweden
46.873.50010
Fax: 46.873.50015

EDEN
Eden Electronics, Inc.
P.O. Box 338
310 First St.
Montrose MN 55363
612.675.3650
Fax: 612.675.3651

EGNATER
Egnater Amplification
860 Livernois
St. Ferndale MI 48237-1302

EPIPHONE
645 Massman Drive
Nashville TN 37210
615.871.4500
Fax: 615.872.7768
www.epiphone.com

EVANS
Evans Custom Amplifiers
Dept. T2
5900 Barbell Circle
McLeansville NC 27301
800.697.2347

EVI AUDIO
600 Cecil Street
Buchanan MI 49107
800.234.6831
Fax: 616.659.1304

EVIL AMPS
Available through Junglewood Music
708.656.9175

FATBOY
Fatboy Amplifiers
847.509.9404

FENDER
Fender Musical Instruments Corp.
7975 N Hayden Road
Scottsdale AZ 85258
480.596.9690
Fax: 480.596.1384
www.fender.com

FENTON
Fenton Music Group
P.O. Box 669786
Marietta GA 30066
800.336.8662

FERNANDES
12600 Saticoy Street S.
N. Hollywood CA 91605
818.764.8383
Fax: 818.764.0080

HMAN
ANSDUCERS
)-D Fordham Road
lmington MA 01887
3.988.9199
x: 978.988.0770

LDED SPACE
CHNOLOGIES
04 Fairwood Lane
). Box 801008
worth GA 30101
0.427.8288
x: 770.427.5094

JCHS AUDIO
ECHNOLOGY
Collins Ave.
oomfield, NJ 07003
one/Fax: 973.893.0225
ww.fuchsaudiotechnolo-
.com
fo@fuchsaudiotechnolo-
.com

JRMAN SOUND, INC.
97 South McDowell
oulevard
etaluma CA 94954
07.763.1010
ax: 707.763.1310
ww.furmansound.com

ALLIEN-KRUEGER
allien-Krueger, Inc.
240 Paragon Drive
an Jose CA 95131-1306
08.441.7970
ax: 408.441.8085

ENZ BENZ
NCLOSURES
811 E. Pierce Street
cottsdale AZ 85257
80.941.0705
ax: 480.941.2412

GIBSON
818 Elm Hill Pike
Nashville TN 37210
15.871.4500
Fax: 615.889.5509
www.gibson.com

GORILLA
400 W. Alondra Blvd.
Gardena CA 90248
800.9PI.GNOS
213.770.4444
Fax: 310.538.9560

GROOVE TUBES LLC
1543 Truman Street
San Fernando CA 91340
818.361.4500
Fax: 818.365.9884
www.groovetubes.com

HAFLER PROFESSIONAL
546 S. Rockford Drive
Tempe AZ 85281
480.967.3565
Fax: 480.894.1528

HARMONY
MBT-DBA Musicorp
620 Dobbin Road
Charleston SC 29414
843.763.9083
www.mbtinternational.com

HARRY KOLBE
Harry Kolbe, Soundsmith, Inc.
27 West 20th Street
Suite 1005
New York NY 10011
212.627.2740
Fax: 212.627.2741
www.soundsmith.com/

HARTKE
Samson Technologies Corp.
P.O. Box 9031
Syosset, NY 11791-9031
516.364.2244
www.samsontech.com
sales@samsontech.com

HIWATT
Hiwatt Amplification
8163 Lankershim Blvd
North Hollywood CA 91605
www.hiwatt.com
info@hiwatt.com

HOLLAND
Holland Amplifiers
500 Wilson Pike Circle, Suite 204
Brentwood TN 37027
615.377.4913
Fax: 615.373.4986

HONDO
Hondo Amplifiers
P.O. Box 30819
Charleston SC 29417
843.763.9083
Fax: 843.763.9096
www.hondo.com

HUGHES & KETTNER
Hughes & Kettner Inc
P O Box 2297
Des Plains IL 60017-2297
800.HK AMPS 1
847.439.6771
Fax: 847.439.6781
www.hughes-and-kettner.com

IBANEZ
Hoshino USA INC
1726 Winchester Road
Bensalem PA 19020
215.638.8670

JOHNSON
Johnson Amplification
8760 South Sandy Parkway
Sandy UT 84070
801.566.8800
Fax: 801.566.7005
www.johnson-amp.com

KENDRICK
Kendrick Amplifiers
P.O. Box 160
Pflugerville TX 78660
512.990.5486
512.990.0548

KJL
Acoustic Analysis, Inc.
521 Hamilton
Gretna LA 70053
504.363.9143
Fax: 504.363.9165
www.kjlamps.com

KUSTOM
Kustom, Inc
4940 Delhi Pike
Cincinnatti OH 45238
513.451.5000
Fax: 513.347.2298
www.kustom.com
sales@kustom.com

LANEY USA
P O Box 186
Torrington CT 06797
860.626.1277
Fax: 860.626.1278
www.laney.co.uk
laneyus1@aol.com

LEDSLED
Ledsled Amplification
Fax: 815.454.2775

LINE 6
555 St. Charles Drive Suite 100
Thousand Oaks CA 91360
877.865.4636
Fax: 877.381.4681
www.line6.com
info@line6.com

LITTLE LANILEI
Songworks Systems
32158 Camino Capistrano #A274
San Juan Capistrano, CA 92675-3711
949.582.7720
Fax: 949.363.5962
Canada: 604.589.6279
www.songworks.com

LOUIS
Louis Electric Amplifier Company
P.O. Box 188
Bergenfield NJ 07621
201.384.6166

MACKIE DESIGNS, INC.
16220 Wood-Red Road NE
Woodinville WA 98072
800.258.6883
425.487.4333
Fax: 425.487.4337
www.mackie.com

MANN
Mann Pro Sound
2660 E. Ganley
Tuscon AZ 85706
520.295.3920
Fax: 520.295.3924

MARSHALL
Marshall c/o Korg USA
316 South Service Road
Melville NY 11747-3201
800.872.5674
Fax: 800.289.5674
www.marshallamps.com

MATCHLESS
Matchless Amp. Co.
9129 Perkins St.
Pico Rivera CA 90670
562.801.4840
Fax: 562.801.4828

MESA/BOOGIE
1317 Ross Street
Petaluma CA 94954
707.778.6565
Fax: 707.765.1503
www.mesaboogie.com

MUSICLORD, INC.
1761 South Central
Suites 58 & 59
Kent WA 98032
206.878.8038
206.813.9033 - shop

ORANGE
Orange USA
770.457.6890
www.orange-amps.com

PARK
89 Frost St.
Westbury NY 11590
800.645.3188
516.333.9100
Fax: 516.333.9108

PEAVEY
Peavey Electronics
711 A St.
Meridian MS 39301
601.483.5365
Fax: 601.486.1278
www.peavey.com

PIGNOSE
400 W. Alondra Blvd.
Gardena CA 90248
800.9PI.GNOS
213.770.4444
Fax: 310.538.9560

QSC AUDIO PRODUCTS
1675 MacArthur Boulevard
Costa Mesa CA 92626
714.754.6175
Fax: 714.754.6174
www.qscaudio.com

RAEZER'S EDGE
726 Girard Avenue
Swarthmore PA 19081
610.328.5466
Fax: 610.328.3857

RANDALL
Washburn International Inc
444 East Courtland Street
Mundelein IL 60060
800.US SOUND
Fax: 847.949.8444
www.randallamplifiers.com

REDBEAR
Available through Gibson USA
1050 Acorn Drive
Suite A
Nashville TN 37210
800.283.7135
615.871.4500
Fax: 615.872.7768
www.gibson.com

REVEREND
Reverend Musical Instruments
27300 Gloede Unit D
Warren MI 48093
810.775.1025
www.reverendmusical.com

RIVERA
Rivera Research & Development Corporation
13310 Ralston Ave.
Sylmar CA 91342
818.833.7066
Fax: 818.833.9656

RMS
Distributed by Musicorp/MBT
P.O. Box 30819
Charleston SC 29417
803.763.9083
Fax: 803.763.9096

ROCKTRON
Rocktron Corporation
2870 Technology Drive
Rochester Hills MI 48309
800.432.ROCK
248.853.3055
Fax: 248.353.5937
email: rocktron@eagle-quest.com

RODGERS
Rodgers Amplifiers, Inc.
3824 Exchange Ave.
Naples FL 33942
www.rodgersamps.com

ROLAND
Roland Corp. US
5100 S. Eastern Avenue
Los Angeles CA 90040
323.890.3700
www.rolandus.com

SA FLA
Sa Fla Tweed Replicas
Paul Markwalter
954.524.7169

SHERLOCK AUDIO
c/o Rainbow Music & Engineering
1418 Pitt Street
Cornwall Ontario
Canada K6J 3T8
Fax: 613.932.8603

SHRAPNEL
Shrapnel Amplication Company
707.224.0951

SIEGMUND TUBE AMPLIFICATION
818.353.5558
www.siegmundguitars.com

SPEEDSTER AMPLIFIERS
P.O. Box 2012
Gig Harbor, WA 98335
888.472.AMPS
www.speedster-amplifiers.com
info@speedster-amplifers.com

SMICZ AMPLIFICATION
112 Lazy Lane
Southington, CT 06489
860.276.1099
Fax: 860.628.6871
www.smicz-amplification.com
info@ smicz-amplification.com

SOLDANO
Soldano Custom
Amplification
1537 NW Ballard Way
Seattle WA 98107
206.781.4636
Fax: 206.781.5173

SOVTEK
New Sensor Corporation
20 Cooper Square
New York NY 10003
800.633.5477
212.529.0466
Fax: 212.529.0486

SPEEDSTER
Vintage Voicing Technologies
P.O. Box 2012
Gig Harbor WA 98335
www.cyber-tec.com/speedstr

SUNN
c/o Fender Musical Instruments
7975 North Hayden Road
Suite C-100
Scottsdale AZ 85258
602.596.7143
Fax: 602.596.7143
www.fender.com

SWR
SWR Sound Corp.
9130 Glen Oaks Blvd.
Sun Valley CA 91352
818.253.4797
Fax: 818.253.4799

TECH 21
333 West 52nd Street
New York NY 10019
212.315.1116
Fax: 212.315.0825
www.tech21nyc.com
info@tech21nyc.com

THD
THD Electronics, Ltd.
4816 15th Ave. NW
Seattle WA 98107-4717
206.781.5500
FAX 206.781.5508
www.thdelectronics.com

THUNDERFUNK
Thunderfunk Labs
P.O. Box 740
Waukegan IL 60085
847.263.7400
Fax: 847.244.1455

TONE KING
Tone King Amplifier Co.
703 S. Luzerne Ave.
Baltimore MD 21224
410.327.6530
Fax: 410.327.6530

TORRES
Torres Engineering
1630 Palm Avenue
San Mateo CA 94402
650.571.6887
Fax: 650.571.1507
www.torresengineering.com
email: amps007@aol.com

TRACE ELLIOT
Gibson
1818 Elm Hill Pike
Nashville TN 37210
615.871.4500
Fax: 615.889.5509
www.gibson.com

TRAINWRECK
Trainwreck Circuits
59 Preston Road
Colonia NJ 07067-2420
908.381.5126

TRAYNOR
Yorkville Sound Inc
4325 Witmer Industrial Estates
Niagara Falls NY 14305
716.297.2920
Fax: 716.297.3689
sales@yorkville.com

TUBEWORKS
8201 E. Pacific Place
Denver CO 80231
800.326.0269
303.750.3801
Fax: 303.750.2162

VANTAGE
Available through Music Industries
99 Tulip Avenue, Suite 101
Floral Park NY 11001
800.431.6699

VHT
1200 Lawerence Drive #465
Newbury Park CA 91320
805.376.9899
Fax: 805.376.9999

VICTORIA
Victoria Amp Co.
1504 Newman Court
Naperville IL 60564-4132
630.369.3527
Fax: 630.527.2221

VOLTMASTER
Voltmaster Amplifier Company
1101 E. Plano Parkway, Suite H
Plano TX 75074
214.341.8121
www.virtbiz.com/voltmaster

VOX
Available through Korg USA
316 South Service Road
Melville NY 11747-3201
800.872.5674
Fax: 800.289.5674
www.korg.com

WARWICK
Distributed by Dana B. Goods
5427 Hollister Avenue
Santa Barbara CA 93111
805.964.9610
Fax: 805.964.9749

WASHBURN
255 Corporate Woods Parkway
Vernon Hills IL 60061
800.877.6863
708.913.5511
Fax: 708.913.7772

WORKING DOG AMPS
www.alessandro-products.com

YAMAHA
P O Box 6600
Buena Park CA 90620
714.522.9011
Fax: 714.522.9301
www.yamaha.com

YORKVILLE
Yorkville Sound
4625 Witmer Industrial Estate
Niagra Falls NY 14305
716.297.2920
Fax: 800.466.9329
www.yorkville.com

EFFECTS

There are a growing number of companies who are making effects, either in footpedal or rackmount configuration. Effects offer the guitarist or bassist tonal coloration and variety in sounds.
A brief survey of Effects Companies.

ALESIS
3630 Holdrege Avenue
Los Angeles CA 90016
Fax: 310.841.2272
alecorp@alesis1.usa.com

APOGEE SYSTEMS
27 Steere Road
Greenville RI 02828
401.949.4440

ARION
Distributed by Stringer Industries
P.O. Box 4241
Warren NJ 07059
908.469.2828
Fax: 908.469.2882
104466.762@compuserve.com
www.snarlingdogs.com

ART
Applied Research and Technology
215 Tremont Street
Rochester NY 14608
716.436.2720
Fax: 716.436.3942
artrochaol.com
artroch@cis.compuserve.com
www.artroch.com

AUSTONE ELECTRONICS
P.O. Box 300730
Austin, TX 78703
512.402.1381
www.austone-electronics.com
sales@austone-electronics.com

BBE
BBE Sound, Inc.
5381 Production Drive
Huntington Beach CA 92649
714.897.6766
Fax: 714.896.0736

BIXONIC
(The Expandora)
Distributed by Sound Barrier International
P.O. Box 4732
133 Frazier Avenue
Chattanooga TN 37405-0732
423.75.MUSIC
423.756.8742

BLACK CAT
5930 E. Royal Lane #291
Dallas TX 75230
800.929.5889

BLUE'S PEARL AMP COMPANY
92 Litchfield Ave.
Babylon NY 11702
516.422.8661
Fax: 516.422.7030

BOOMERANG
P.O. Box 541595

las TX 75354-1595
.530.4699

SS
tributed by the Roland
rporation
0 Dominion Circle
Angeles CA 90040-
7
.685.5141
: 213.722.9233
and@aol.com
w.rolandus.com

DDA
Joseph Ct.
Rafael CA 94903
5.492.1935
ddatone@aol.com

RL MARTIN
JITAR PEDALS
ropean Musical Imports
c
D Box 68
llsdale NJ 07642
1.594.0817
x: 201.594.0829
fo@europeanmusical.com
w.europeanmusical.com

3 LABS, INC.
0 Housatonic Avenue
idgeport CT 06606
3.335.1093
x: 203.331.9214

HARLIE STRINGER'S
NARLING DOGS
ringer Industries
O. Box 4241
Varren NJ 07059
8.469.2828
x: 908.469.2828
04466.762@
mpuserve.com
ww.snarlingdogs.com

OLORSOUND
30 East Main Street
noka MN 55303
12.427.2411
ax: 612.422.1380

RATE
t. Louis Music (SLM)
400 Ferguson Avenue
t. Louis MO 63133
00.727.4512
14.727.4512
ax: 314.727.8929

CROWTHER AUDIO
The Hotcake)
P.O. Box 96104
Balmoral Auckland 1030
New Zealand

CUSTOM AUDIO AMPLIFIERS
19648 Magnolia Boulevard
N. Hollywood CA 91601
818.763.8898
Fax: 818.763.8890

DANELECTRO
P.O. Box 2769
Laguna Hills CA 92654
949.583.2419

DIGITECH
8760 South Sandy Parkway
Sandy UT 84070
801.566.8919
Fax: 801.566.7005
(Int'l Fax) 603.672.4246
www.digitech.com

DOD
8760 South Sandy Parkway
Sandy UT 84070
801.566.8800
Fax: 801.566.7005
(Int'l Fax) 603.672.4246
www.dod.com

DREDGE-TONE
Dredge-Tone Audio
P.O. Box 8172
Berkeley CA 94707
510.526.8284

DUNLOP
Dunlop Manufacturing Inc
P O Box 846
Benicia CA 94510
707.745.2722
Fax: 707.745.2658
www.jimdulop.com

EBOW
Heet Sound Products
c/o Greg Heet
611 Ducommon Street
Los Angeles CA 90012
213.687.9946
Fax: 213.625.1944
info@ebow.com

ELECTRO-HARMONIX
New Sensor Corporation
20 Cooper Square
Fourth Floor
New York NY 10003
800.633.6477
www.newsensor.com
info@newsensor.com

ELECTRO-VOICE/VEGA
600 Cecil Street
Buchanan MI 49107
800.234.6831
Fax: 616.659.1304

EN ROUTE MUSIC
(The Porch Board Bass)
P.O. Box 8223
Janesville WI 53547
608.752.2229
enroutemsc@aol.com

ENSONIQ
155 Great Valley Parkway
Malvern PA 19355-0735
800.553.5151
Fax: 610.647.8908

EVENTIDE
One Alsan Way
Little Ferry NJ 07643
201.641.1200
Fax: 201.641.1640
www.eventide.com

FISHMAN TRANSDUCERS
340-D Fordham Road
Wilmington MA 01887
508.988.9199
Fax: 508.988.0770

FLIP
c/o Godlyke Inc
P O Box 4677
Wayne NJ 07474-4677
973.835.2100
Fax: 973.835.2100
godlykehq@aol.com
www.guyatone.com

FOLDED SPACE TECHNOLOGIES
1004 Fairwood Lane
P.O. Box 801008
Acworth GA 30101
770.427.8288
Fax: 770.427.5094

FRANTONE
(The Hepcat)
1763 Columbia Avenue
Lancaster PA 17603
Fax: 717.397.2470

FULLTONE CUSTOM EFFECTS
3815 Beethoven St.
Los Angeles CA 90066
310.397.3456
Fax: 310.397.3456
To Send, Press *51
email:
Robintrowr@AOL.com
(Robin Trower)

FURMAN SOUND, INC.
1997 South McDowell Boulevard
Petaluma CA 94954
707.763.1010
Fax: 707.763.1310
www.furmansound.com

GEORGE DENNIS
George Dennis FX Pedals
c/o European Crafts, Inc.
3637 Cahuenga Boulevard
Hollywood CA 90068
213.851.0750
Fax: 216.851.0148

GROOVE TUBES LLC
1543 Truman Street
San Fernando CA 91340
818.361.4500
Fax: 818.365.9884
www.groovetubes.com

GUYATONE
c/o Godlyke Inc
P O Box 4677
Wayne NJ 07474-4677
973.835.2100
Fax: 973.835.2100
www.guyatone.com

HEET
Heet Sound Products
611 Ducommun Street
Los Angeles CA 90012
213.687.9946
Fax: 213.625.1944
www.ebow.com
info@ebow.com

HEIL
(The Talkbox)
Distributed by Jim Dunlop, USA
P.O. Box 846
Benicia CA 94510
707.745.2722
Fax: 707.745.2658
www.jimdunlop,com

HOLLAND
Holland Amplifiers
753 Spence Circle
Virginia Beach VA 23462
804.467.0146
Fax: 804.427.1783

IBANEZ
Hoshino USA
1726 Winchester Road
Bensalem PA 19020
215.638.8670
Fax: 215.245.8583
www.ibanez.com

JGR ELECTRONICS
(The Retro Rocket)
P.O. Box 39
Oak Ridge NJ 07438

JIM DUNLOP, USA
(Hendrix series Effects Pedals)
P.O. Box 846
Benicia CA 94510
707.745.2722
Fax: 707.745.2658
www.jimdunlop,com

KLON
(The Centaur)
P.O. Box 1025
Brookline MA 02146
617.738.8409
Fax: 617.738.8531
klon@delphi.com

LAMARR
7305 Creekview
West Bloomfield MI 48322
810.851.9561
Fax: 810.851.9574

LEXICON
3 Oak Park
Bedford MA 01730-1441
716.280.0300
Fax: 716.280.0490
www.lexicon.com

LINE 6
Line 6 Inc
555 St Charles Drive Suite 100
Thousand Oaks CA 91360
877.865.4636
Fax: 805.381.4681
www.line6.com
info@line6.com

LOVETONE
P.O. Box 102
Henley-on-Thames
Oxfordshire
RG9 1XX England
UK PHONE:
011.44.1491.571411
UK Fax:
011.44.1491.571411
US INFO LINE:
714.509.1718
email:
lovetone@channel.co.uk
http://www.channel.co.uk/lovetone/

MARSHALL
89 Frost St.
Westbury NY 11590
800.645.3188
516.333.9100
Fax: 516.333.9108

MATCHLESS
Matchless Amp. Co.
9129 Perkins St.
Pico Rivera CA 90670
562.801.4840
Fax: 562.801.4828

MESA/BOOGIE
1317 Ross Street
Petaluma CA 94954
707.778.6565
Fax: 707.765.1503
email:
www.mesaboogie.com

MORLEY
185 Detroit Street
Cary IL 60013
847.639.4646
Fax: 847.639.4723

MXR
Distributed by Jim Dunlop, USA
P.O. Box 846
Benicia CA 94510
707.745.2722
Fax: 707.745.2658
www.jimdunlop,com

NOBELS EFFECTS
Distributed by Musicorp/MBT
P.O. Box 30819
Charleston SC 29417
803.763.9083
Fax: 803.763.9096

NUANCE EFFECTS
(410)374-5102
Baltimore, MD
www.nuanceeffects.com

PEAVEY
Peavey Electronics
711 A Street
Meridian MS 39301
601.486.1278
AOL keyword: Peavey
CompuServe: Go Peavey
www.peavey.com

PRESCRIPTION ELECTRONICS
P.O. Box 42233
Portland OR 97242
503.239.9106
Fax: 503.239.9106

PRO CO
135 E. Kalamazoo Avenue
Kalamazoo MI 49007
800.253.7360
Fax: 616.388.9681

RANE
10802 47th Avenue West
Mukilteo WA 98275
206.355.6000
Fax: 206.347.7757

REAL MCCOY CUSTOM 3
(Blues Dog) 713.460.2300
Fax: 713.460.0059

RFX
Rolls Corporation
5143 S. Main Street
Salt Lake City UT 84107-4740
801.263.9053
Fax: 801.263.9068
rollsfx@rolls.com
david@rolls.com
www.xmission.com/~rollsrfx

ROCKMAN
Dept. AP
P.O. Box 846
Benicia CA 94510
707.745.2722
dunlop@a.crl.com

ROCKSON
Distributed by Musicorp/MBT
P.O. Box 30819
Charleston SC 29417
803.763.9083
Fax: 803.763.9096

ROCKTEK
Distributed by Stringer Industries
P.O. Box 4241
Warren NJ 07059
908.469.2828
Fax: 908.469.2828
104466.762@compuserve.com
www.snarlingdogs.com

ROCKTRON
A division of GHS Corporation
2813 Wilbur Avenue
Battle Creek MI 48309
616.968.3351
Fax: 616.968.6913
www.rocktron.com

ROCKER
Distributed by Jim Dunlop, USA
P.O. Box 846
Benicia CA 94510
707.745.2722
Fax: 707.745.2658
www.jimdunlop,com

ROLAND
7200 Dominion Circle
Los Angeles CA 90040-3647
323.685.5141
Fax: 323.722.9233
roland@aol.com
www.rolandus.com

SABINE
13301 Highway 441
Alachua FL 32615-8544
386.418.2000
Fax: 386.418.2001
www.sabine.com

SHERLOCK AUDIO
c/o Rainbow Music & Engineering
1418 Pitt Street
Cornwall Ontario
Canada K6J 3T8
613.932.8603

SNARLING DOGS
Matthews & Ryan
68 34th Street
Brooklyn NY 11232
718.832.6333
Fax: 718.832.5270
www.snarlingdogs.com
sales@snarlingdogs.com

SOBBAT
(The Fuzz Breaker)
A Division of Kinko Music Co., Ltd.
4-2 Bo-jo-cho
Mibu, Nakagyo-ku
Kyoto Japan 604
011.81.75.822.5472
Distributed in the U.S. by
Joe Hertzel
41 Alpine Place
Cheektowaga NY 14225

SOLDANO
Soldano Custom Amplification
1537 NW Ballard Way
Seattle WA 98107
206.781.4636
www.soldano.com

SONY
3 Paragon Drive
Montvale NJ 07645
201.930.1000
201.358.4907

SWEET SOUND ELECTRONICS
P.O. Box 514
Trenton MI 48183-0514
313.676.3106
Fax: 313.676.3106

T C ELECTRONICS
T C Electronics of Denmark
705 Lakefield Road
Westlake Village CA 91361-2611
805.373.1828
Fax: 805.379.2648
tc@tcelectronic.com
www.tcelectronic.com

TECH 21 NYC (SANSAMP)
333 West 52nd Street
New York NY 10019
212.315.1116
Fax: 212.315.0825
www.tech21nyc.com
info@tech21nyc.com

THD ELECTRONICS
THD Electronics, Ltd.
4816 15th Ave. NW
Seattle WA 98107-4717
206.781.5500
FAX: 206.781.5508
www.thdelectronics.com

THEREMIN
The Sound of Sci-Fi
P.O. Box 342502
Milwaukee WI 53234
Fax: 414.327.4141

TONEWORKS
Distributed by Korg USA
316 South Service Road
Melville NY 11747-3201
800.872.5674
Fax: 800.289.5674
www.korg.com

TRACE ELLIOT USA, LTD.
2601 75th Street
Darien IL 60561
630.972.1981
Fax: 630.972.1988

TUBEWORKS
8201 E. Pacific Place
Denver CO 80231
800.326.0269
303.750.3801
Fax: 303.750.2162

VISUAL SOUND
11 Bedford Avenue, Suite R-2
Norwalk CT 06850
800.686.3317
203.866.7101
Fax: 203.852.1123

VOODOO LABS
Digital Music Corporation
5312-J Derry Avenue
Agoura Hills CA 91301
818.991.3881
Fax: 818.991.4185
www.voodoolab.com

VOX
Distributed by Korg USA
316 South Service Road
Melville NY 11747-3201
800.872.5674
Fax: 800.289.5674
www.korg.com

WAY HUGE ELECTRONICS
818.981.1908
www.wayhuge.com/way-huge/

YAMAHA
P.O. Box 6600
Buena Park CA 90602
714.522.9011
Fax: 714.522.9301
www.yamaha.com

ZOOM
Distributed by Samson Technologies Corporation
P.O. Box 9031
Syosset NY 11971
516.364.2244
Fax: 516.364.388

STRINGS

Another aspect of tone generation is Strings. How strings interact with the instrument and the player another crucial portion of the overall "chain" of the sound produced. The following is a brief review of String Companies

ADAMAS
Distributed by Kaman Music (OVATION)
P.O. Box 507
Bloomfield CT 06002-0507
860.509.8888
www.kamanmusic.com

CHARLIE STRINGER SNARLING DOGS STRINGS
Dept. GW
P.O. Box 4241
Warren NJ 07059
908.469.2828
Fax: 908.469.2882

CONCERTISTE
Picato Musician Strings
Unit 24, Treorchy Ind. Est.
Treorchy Mid Glamorgan
United Kingdom CF42 6E
44.144.343.7928
Fax: 44.144.343.3624

J. D'ADDARIO
J. D'Addario & Co.
595 Smith Street
Farmingdale NY 11735
800.323.2746
631.439.3300
Fax: 631.439.3333

ings@daddario.com
ww.daddario.com

AQUISTO
E. Industry Court
). Box 569
eer Park NY 11729
1.586.4426
x: 631.586.4472

EAN MARKLEY
50 Scott Blvd. #45
nta Clara CA 95054
8.988.2456
x: 408.988.0441
ww.deanmarkley.com

R STRINGS
Palisades Avenue
nerson NJ 07630
)1.599.0100
ax: 201.599.0404
ww.drstrings.com
nail: DRStaff@aol.com

LIXIR STRINGS
'. L. Gore & Associates
)1 Airport Rd.
lkton, MD 21921
38.367.5533
nail: mail@goremusic.com
www.goremusic.com

RNIE BALL
O. Box 4117
an Luis Obispo CA
3401
05.544.7726
ax: 805.544.7275
www.ernieball.com

VERLY
verly Music Company
305 West Victory Blvd.
Burbank, CA 91506
88.4EVERLY
www.everlymusic.com

FENDER
Fender Musical Instruments
Corp.
7975 N Hayden Road
Scottsdale AZ 85258
502.596.9690
Fax: 602.596.1385
www.fender.com

GHS
G.H.S. Corporation
P.O. Box 136
2813 Wilber Avenue
Battle Creek MI 49016
800.388.4447
616.968.3351
Fax: 616.968.6913
Strings@GHStrings.com
www.ghsstrings.com

GIBSON
Gibson Strings &
Accessories
A Manufacturing Division
of Gibson Guitar Corp.
1150 Bave Rd.
Elgin IL 60123
800.544.2766
Fax: 847.741.4644
www.gibson.com

JOHN PEARSE STRINGS
Breezy Ridge Instruments
P.O. Box 295
Center Valley PA 18034
610.691.3302
Fax: 610.691.3304
www.johnpearsestrings.com
jpinfo@aol.com

LABELLA
256 Broadway
Newburg NY 12550
845.562.4400
Fax: 845.562.4491
www.labella.com
bellaon@msn.com

MARI
14 W. 71st Street
New York NY 10023-4209
212.799.6781
Fax: 212.721.3932

MARTIN STRINGS
C.F.Martin & Co.
510 Sycamore Street
Nazareth PA 18064
800.633.2060
610.759.5757
info@mguitar.com
www.mguitar.com

MAXIMA
57 Crooks Avenue
Clifton NJ 07011
garpc@ix.netcom.com

PHANTOM STRINGS
80353 Qunicy Mayger Rd.
Clatskanie, OR 97016
503.728.4825
Fax: 503.728.4979
www.phantomguitars.com

SABINE
NitroStasis Strings
13301 Highway 441
Alachua FL 32615-8544
904.418.2000
Fax: 904.418.2001
sabine@sabineinc.com
www.sabineinc.com

S.I.T. STRINGS
815 S. Broadway
Akron OH 44311
330.434.8010
email:
sinfositstrings@aol.com

THOMASTIK-INFELD
P.O. Box 93
Northport NY 11768
800.644.5268
www.thomastik-infeld.com
info@connollyandco.com

YAMAHA STRINGS
6600 Orangethorpe Avenue
Buena Park CA 90620
714.522.9011
Fax: 714.739.2680
The Link between the
Strings and the Amp:
Pickups!
A Review of Pickup
companies

ADDER PLUS
830 Seton Court
Unit 12
Wheeling IL 60090
847.537.0202
Fax: 847.537.0355

KENT ARMSTRONG
Distributed by WD Music
Products, Inc.
4070 Mayflower Road
Fort Myers FL 33916
941.337.7575
941.337.4585
www.kentarmstrong.com
sales@wdmusicproducts.com
Exclusive Distributor for
Kluson tuning machines
Kent Armstrong - Europe
Rainbow Products
Unit 31, Old Surrenden
Manor
Bethersden, Kent
TN26 3DL England
Mike@rainbowproducts.co.uk

AUDIO OPTICS
Audio Optics, Inc.
P.O. Box 691
Santa Barbara CA 93102
800.548.6669
805.563.2202
Fax: 805.569.4060
info@aollightwave.com
www.mallennium.com/aolig
htwave

BARCUS BERRY
Distributed by BBE Sound,
Inc
5381 Production Drive
Huntington Beach CA
92649
800.233.8346
714.897.6766
Fax: 714.896.0736

JOE BARDEN
356 Maple Ave. W.
Vienna VA 22180
703.938.8638
Fax: 703.938.0460
www.joebarden.com
info@joebarden.com

BARTOLINI
Bartolini Pickups and
Electronics
2133 Research Drive #16
Livermore CA 94550
510.443.1037
Fax: 510.449.7692

BENEDETTO
Benedetto Jazz Pickups
13103 Waterford Run Drive
Riverview, FL 33569-5732
813.571.0948
Fax: 813.571.0949
www.benedetto-guitars.com
benedetto@benedetto-guitars.com

CHANDLER
Chandler Guitars
370 Lang Road
Burlingame CA 94010-
2003
415.342.1490
Fax: 415.342.9692

MIKE CHRISTIAN
Mike Christian Guitar
Technology
P.O. Box 1937
West Babylon NY 11704
516.422.4791
Fax: 516.422.5030

DEAN MARKLEY
Dean Markley Strings, Inc.
3350 Scott Blvd. #45
Santa Clara CA 95054
800.800.1008
408.988.2456
Fax: 408.988.0441

DIMARZIO
Dimarzio, Inc.
1388 Richmond Terrace
Staten Island NY 10310
800.221.6468
718.981.9286
Fax: 718.720.5296

T.W. DOYLE
85 Ridgewood Road
Township of Washington
NJ 07675
201.664.3697

SEYMOUR DUNCAN
5427 Hollister Avenue
Santa Barbara CA 93111-
2345
800.SDU.NCAN
800.964.9610
Fax: 805.964.9749

EMG
EMG. Inc.
P.O. Box 4394
Santa Rosa CA 95402
707.525.9941
Fax: 707.575.7046
www.emginc.com

EPM
#6-399 South Edgeware
Road
St. Thomas Ontario
Canada N5P 4B8
519.633.5195
Fax: 519.633.8314
email: info@epm-ltd.com
Web: www.epm-ltd.com

FISHMAN
Fishman Transducers, Inc.
Fishman Audio Division
340-D Fordham Road
Wilmington MA 01887-
2113
508.988.9199
Fax: 508.988.0770

LINDY FRALIN
Lindy Fralin Pickups
2015 W. Laburnum 2nd
Floor
Richmond VA 23227
804.358.2699
Fax: 804.358.3431
www.fralinpickups.com

GUITARSMITH
M.L. Smith
367 North Drive
Norco CA 91760
909.736.0358

GROOVE TUBES LLC
1543 Truman St.
San Fernando, CA 91340
www.groovetubes.com

HIGHLANDER
Highlander Musical Audio
Products
305 Glenwood Avenue
Ventura CA 93003-4426
805.658.1819
Fax: 805.658.6828

TOM HOLMES
P.O. Box 414
Joelton TN 37080
615.876.3453

AMPS/EFFECTS/STRINGS/PICKUPS

LACE MUSIC PRODUCTS
5561 Engineer Drive
Huntington Beach CA 92649
800.575.LACE
714.898.2776
Fax: 714.893.1045
www.lacemusic.com

LANE POOR
Lane Poor Music Co.
347 Pleasant St.
Fall River MA 02721
508.679.1922
Fax: 508.679.1904
www.lanepoor.com
lane@lanepoor.com

WILLIAM LAWRENCE
Also KEYSTONE PICKUPS
William Lawrence Design Corp.
314 Taylor Street
Bethlehem PA 18015
610.866.5211
Fax: 610.866.5495

L. R. BAGGS
L.R. Baggs Co.
483 N Frontage Road
Nipomo CA 93444
805.929.3545
Fax: 805.929.2043
Baggsco@LRBaggs.com

MIMESIS
Mike Vanden
Old School
Strontian
Acharacle
Argyll Scotland PH36 4JA

PAN
Pan Electric
207 Rundlview Dr. N.E.
Calgary AB Canada T1Y 1H7
403.285.8893
www.pan-electric.com
PASC123@telusplanet.net

RIO GRANDE PICKUPS
3526 East T.C. Jester Blvd.
Houston, TX 77018
713.957.0470
Fax: 713.957.3316
www.riograndepickups.com
sales@riograndepickups.com

SENTELL PICKUPS
866.382.2974
www.sentellpickups.com
csentell@excite.com

SHADOW
Shadow Electronics of America
2700 SE Market Place
Stuart FL 34997
407.221.8177
Fax: 407.221.8178

SUNRISE
Sunrise Pickup Systems
8101 Orion Ave. #19
Van Nuys CA 91406
818.785.3428
Fax: 818.785.9972
JimSunrise@earthlink.net
www.Sunrisepickups.com

TV JONES
P.O. Box 163
Whittier, CA 90608
562.693.0068
www.tvjones.com

VAN ZANDT
Distributed and Produced by VAN ZANDT Pickups
205 Robinson Rd.
Combine TX 75159
214.476.8844
Fax: 214.476.8844

ZETA
Zeta Music Systems
2230 Livingston St.
Oakland CA 94606
800.622.6434
510.261.1702
Fax: 510.261.1708

STRINGS/LUTHIER ORGANIZATIONS

Association of Stringed Instrument Artisans (ASIA)
c/o David Vinopal
P.O. Box 341
Paul Smiths, NY 12970
518-891-5379
(*GUITARMAKER* is the quarterly newsletter/publication of ASIA)

Guild of American Luthiers (GAL)
8222 South Park Avenue
Tacoma, WA 98408
206-472-7853
(*AMERICAN LUTHERIE* is the quarterly journal of GAL)

Fretted Instrument Guild of America
c/o Glen Lemmer, Editor
2344 S. Oakley Avenue
Chicago, IL 60608
(*FIGA*, official publication)

TRADEMARK INDEX

·C.E. GUITARS
· Centre Road, #4
·mersworth, NH 03878
·3.692.5971
·x: 603.592.6015
·an@nh.ultranet.com

BASSES
·2 Clark Lane
·altham-Boston, MA
·2154
·1.891.1134
·asses@gis.net
·ww.abasses.com

·BEL AXE
·O. Box 895
·vanston, WY 82931
·07.789.8049
·ax: 307.789.6929

·BILENE
·istributed by Advantage
·orldwide.
·00.MUS.ICAL
·00.687.4225

·BYSS
·35 N. 13th St.
·orest City, IA 50436
·41.582.3718
·ww.abyssguitars.com

·CACIA
·NSTRUMENTS
·.O. Box 162
·outhampton, PA 18966
·15.953.9120
·ax: 215.953.8170
·nfo@acaciainstruments.com
·ww.acaciainstruments.com

·DALBERTO, LAVEZZI
·ia Cav. di Vitt. Veneto 8
·4011 Argenta (FE)
·taly
·532.805845

·LAMO GUITARS
Distributed by Alamo
Music Products
3526 East T.C. Jester Road
Houston, TX 77018
713.957.0470
Fax: 713.957.3316
www.alamoguitars.com
Sales@alamoguitars.com

ALEMBIC, INC.
3005 Wiljan Court,
Building A
Santa Rosa, CA 95407-
5702
707.523.2611
Fax: 707.523.2935
www.alembic.com
info@alembic.com

ALESSI, JOE
Instrumental Music Service
221 High Street
Pottstown, PA 19464
monjakwa@ptd.net

ALLEN, RICHARD C.
2801 New Deal Road
Almonte, CA 91733
818.442.8806

ALLEN, ROB
1423 Harvard, Unit A
Santa Monica, CA 90404
310.453.9135
www.ourworld.com-
puserve.com/homepages/ro
ballenguitars

ALVAREZ
A Division of St. Louis
Music, Inc – see listing.

ALVAREZ, JUAN
CARLOS MORAGA
Rio Blanco 217
Chaiten Chile
jmoraga@entel.cl

AMBUSH CUSTOM
BASSES
Frederick, MD
301.874.2635
www.ambushbass.com
scott@ambushbass.com

AMERICAN
ACOUSTECH
4405 Ridge Road W.
Rochester, NY 14626-
3549
716.352.3225
Fax: 716.352.8614

AMERICAN
SHOWSTER
856 Route 9
Bayville, NJ 08721
732.269.8900
Fax: 732.269.8181
AmShowste@aol.com
www.americanshowster.com

AMIGO
Distributed by Midco
International – see listing.

AMPEG
A Division of St. Louis
Music, Inc. – see listing.
www.ampeg.com

TOM ANDERSON
GUITARWORKS
2697 Lavery Court Unit 27
Newbury Park, CA 91320
805.498.1747
Fax: 805.498.0878
www.andersonguitars.com
aguitar@earthlink.net

ANDRE, RICARDO
FERREIRA
Lisboa Portugal
bizet90@hotmail.com

ANDREAS GUITARS
Distributed by Connolly &
Co.
8 Vernon Valley Road
East Northport, NY 11731
800.644.5268
Fax: 631.757.0021

Dollach 95
9843 Grosskirchheim
Austria
011.43.4825.255
Fax: 011.43.4825.2554
www.andreasguitars.com
Andreas.guitars@utanet.at

ANGELO
T. Angelo Industrial Co.
Ltd.
4862 Soi Phomjit
Rama IV Road
Prakanong Klongtoey
Bangkok 10110
Thailand
662.392.1041
Fax: 662.712.1153
aprasart@loxinfo.co.th

ANTONIO,
SCANDURRA
Via Palazzotto 50
Catania Italy
095.431901

APOLLONIO, NICK
P.O. Box 791
Rockport, ME 04856
207.236.6312

ARBOR
Distributed by Midco
International – see listing.

ARIA
ARIA PRO II
ARIANA
Aria USA/NHF
Distributed by 9244
Commerce Highway
Pennsauken, NJ 08110
800.524.0441
856.663.8900
Fax: 856.663.0436
ariagtrs@aol.com
www.ariausa.com

ARMSTRONG, DAN
Design Consultant
13385 Astoria Street
Sylmar, CA 91342-2436
818.362.6901

ARMSTRONG,
GEORGE DAVID
16783 NW Greenhoot
Yamhill, OR 97148
goldmanarmstrong@
msn.com

ARPEGGIO KORINA
GUITARS
2120 Darby Road
Havertown, PA 19083
610.449.6900
Fax: 610.449.8110
arpkorina1@cs.com
www.arpkorina.com

ARTESE, MARIO
Liutisti & Liutai
Via Cattaneo, 11/g
Cosenza
Italy 87100
maartese@tin.it

ARTISTA
Distributed by
Musicorp/MBT
Hondo Guitar Company
P.O. Box 30819
Charleston, SC 29417
800.845.1922
843.763.9083
Fax: 843.763.9096

ASLIN DANE
David Burns Musical
Instruments Inc.
P.O. Box 136
West Islip, NY 11795
516.376.6020
Fax: 516.376.6017
Catalystin@aol.com

ASPRI CREATIVE
ACOUSTICS
12145 de l'Acadie
Montreal PQ
Canada H3M 2V1
514.333.2853
Fax: 514.333.3153

ASTURIAS
Distributed by J.T.G. of
NASHVILLE
5350 Hillsboro Road
Nashville, TN 37215
615.665.8384
Fax: 615.665.9468

ASTRO GUITARS, INC.
1256 Industrial Blvd.
Port St. Lucie, FL 33452

ATELIER Z
Japan
011.81.3.3377.0157
Fax: 011.81.3.3377.0183
www.atelierz.co.jp
postmaster@atelierz.co.jp

ATLANSIA
Atlansia Instrumental
Technology, Ltd.
5882-2 Sasaga
Matsumoto, Nagano
Japan 399
011.81.263.25.2389
Fax: 011.81.263.25.6644
(Telex)
3342.342.AITECH.J
www.cnet.ne.jp/atlansia
atlansia@po.cnet.ne.jp

ARAM
Phone:
011.82.42.522.4310
Fax: 011.82.42.527.8261
www.aramco.co.kr
aramco@unitel.co.kr

ARCHER GUITARS
Dynamic Music
Distributing, Inc.
P.O. Box 27655
Milwaukee, WI 53227
800.343.3003
Fax: 800.211.5570

AUERSWALD
Gustav-Schwab-StraBe 14
N
D-78467 Konstanz
Germany
011.49.7531.66157
Fax: 011.49.7531.56911

AUSTIN
A Division of St. Louis
Music, Inc. – see listing.

LUE STAR GUITAR OMPANY
98 Bluestar Highway
nnville, MI 49408
6.543.4591
erron@accn.org

LUE STAR MUSIC
). Box 493
7 Main Street
vingston, VA 22949
4.263.6746

LUESOUTH
). Box 3562
orence, AL 35630
5.764.7431
nnie@hiwaay.net

OGART
KC Graphite
detenstr. 29
3785 Obernburg
ermany
6022.649010
ax: 06022.649012
cgraphite@primanet.de
istributed by Salwender
nternational
140 N. Lemon Street #M
range, CA 92867
14.583.1285
ax: 714.583.9331
we@salwender.com
ww.salwender.com

OOGIE BODY
oogie Body Music
roducts
O. Box 2012
ig Harbor, WA 98335
53.851.2267
ww.cyber-tec.com/boogie

ORJES, RALF
)istributed by Dacapo
Musik
Muhlenweg 22
)-26160 Bad
Zwischenahn
Germany
)4403.59691
Fax: 04403.64102
Distributed by Ralf Schulte
2320 Old South Ocean
Blvd.
Palm Beach, FL 33480
Fax: 561.588.8248

BORN TO ROCK
Born to Rock Design Inc.
470 West End, # 8A
New York, NY 10024
800.496.7625
212.496.5342
Fax: 212.496.2780
71271.3051@
compuserve.com
www.webcorp.com/btr

BORYS GUITARS
Roger Borys
420 Pine Street
Burlington, VT 05401

BOSSA
Bossa Company, Ltd.
Maison-Daiwa #301
3-11-4 Minami-Horie
Nishi-ku, Osaka
550 Japan
81.6.539.6741
bossa@netplus.ne.jp
www.iban.com/bossa
Exclusively Distributed by
Soniq Trading, Inc.
11657 Oxnard Street,
Suite 211
North Hollywood, CA
91606
818.761.9260
Fax: 818.761.9282
soniq@ni.net

BOTTELLI, ENRICO
Via Cuzzi 16
20155 Milano
Italy
02.39214715

BOUCHARD, MARIO
295, Avenue Giguere
Suite 005
Vanier Quebec
Canada G1M 1X7
guitar@total.net
www.total.net/~guitar/

BOUVIER
700 Ocean Gate Drive
P.O. Box 743
Ocean Gate, NJ 08740
732.269.8660
Fax: 732.269.2216

BOWN, RALPH S.
The Old Coach House
1, Paver Lane
Walmgate York Y01 2TS
England
01904.621011

BOY LONDON
On You Co., Ltd.
4-33-21 Minamihorie,
Nishi-ku
Osaka Japan 550-0015
011.81.6.6539.6600
Fax: 011.81.6.6539.1310
Onyou@osk3.3web.ne.jp

BOYCE, JAMES C.
North Falmouth, MA
508.563.9494
umboyce@capecod.net

BRADFORD, AARON
Dixieland Guitars
9512 Downing Street
Richmond, VA 23233
bradfor@erols.com

BRANDENBURG STRINGED INSTRUMENTS
7355 Eagle Creek Drive
Centerville, OH 45459
pimmel90@aol.com

BRANDONI MUSIC LTD.
Unit 3.6
Wembley Commercial
Centre
East Lane
Wembley, Middlesex
England HA9 7XJ
011.44.20.8908.2323
roberto@brandonimusic.freeserve.co.uk

BRIAN EASTWOOD GUITARS
408 Newchurch Road
Stacksteads
Bacup OL13 0LD
England
011.44.1706.874549
peterwilliams@ias.u-net.com
www.freespace.virginnet.co.uk/b.eastwood/

BRIAN MOORE CUSTOM GUITARS
South Patterson Business
Park
Route 22
Brewster, NY 10509
914.279.4142
Fax: 914.279.5477
BMCguitars@aol.com
www.BMCGuitars.com

BRIAN PAUL GUITARS
1508 Winding Hollow
Plano, TX 75093
214.761.3626
Fax: 972.250.0073
bripaul@airmail.net

BRIDWELL WORKSHOP
426 W. Wilson Street
Palatine, IL 60067-4920
847.934.0374
Bridwshp@aol.com

BRITO, EDUARDO THIAGO AREAS
Shin QI-08 CONJ-09,
Casa 16
Brasilia, DF 71520-290
botafogo@mre.gov.br

BROWN, JAMES
13174 S. 18th Street
Vicksburg, MI 49097

BRUBAKER GUITARS, INC.
900-A Leidy Road
Westminster, MD 21157
410.857.7600
Fax: 410.857.7622
www.brubakerguitars.com
brubakerguitars@erols.com

BRUNE, RICHARD E.
800 Greenwood Street
Evanston, IL 6021-4312

BRUZE CONTRABASS
6922 Kramer Street
San Diego, CA 92111
619.541.2635

BUNKER GUITARS, LLC
17624 15th Avenue SE
Suite 108A
Mill Creek, WA 98012
425.483.1217
Fax: 425.483.3829
bunker@conceptsnet.com
www.bunker-guitars.com

BURNS
Burns London Ltd.
21 Vernon Close
Ottershaw, Surrey
England KT16 0JD
011.44.1932.875255
Fax: 011.44.1932.873057
www.burns-guitars.co.uk
barry@burns-guitars.co.uk

BUSCARINO GUITARS, INC.
9075-B 130th Avenue
North
Largo, FL 33773
813.586.4992
Fax: 813.581.4535
www.netace.com/buscarino

BUZZART, CRAIG
5235 Diane Way
Santa Rosa, CA 95409-5118
Craig_Buzzart@lamg.com

BYRD GUITAR CO.
Seattle, WA
253.281.2267
www.jamesbyrd.com

CLE GUITARS
RD 4, Box 79A
Moundsville, WV 26041

CADDY, KURT
11852 N. Ridgetop Lane
Brighton, MO 65617
kcaddy@sbuniv.edu

CALKIN, JOHN
P.O. Box 421
Greenville, VA 24440

CALLAHAM GUITARS
114 Tudor Drive
Winchester, VA 22603
540.955.0294
540.665.8045
callaham@visuallink.com
www.visuallink.com
/callaham/

CAMPBELL, FRED W.
F.W. Campbell & Sons
1709 Little Orchard
San Jose, CA 95125
laquerboy@aol.com

CARL THOMPSON GUITARS
171 Court Street
Brooklyn, NY 11201

CARLISLE, STEVE
12510 Sagamore Forest
Lane
Reistertown, MD 23136

CARLSON GUITAR COMPANY
2507 Beechwood Blvd.
St. Joseph, MO 64503
877.232.2324
Custserv@carlsonguitars.com

CARMAN, BOB
Kathy & Bob's Planet
1702 E. Pepper Circle # 3
Mesa, AZ 85203
bobcrmn@worldnet.att.net

CARMINE STREET GUITARS
42 Carmine Street
New York, NY 10014
212.239.3866
619.239.3866

CARMODY GUITARS LTD.
1060 Clearview Avenue
Burlington Ontario
Canada L7T 2J1
ginette.drovin@sympatico.ca

CARODYCE INSTRUMENTS
11 Castle Road
Weybridge
Surrey KT13 9QP
England
www.cybozone.com/fg/deacon.html

CARRETT, JAMES
430 Stenner Street
Toowoomba Queensland
Australia 4350
carrettj@ozemail.com.au

CARRINGTON, CHRISTOPHER
Open Ocean Music
8255 San Cristobal
Dallas, TX 75128
neptune@isource.net
www.isource.net/~neptune

CARRIVEAU
4427 N. 7th Avenue
Phoenix, AZ 85013

CARRUTHERS, JOHN
346 Sunset Avnue
Venice, CA 90291
310.392.3910
Fax: 310.392.0389

CARTWRIGHT, KEN
Cartwright's Music Repair Shop
189 Liberty Street NE
Salem, OR 97301

CARVIN
12340 World Trade Drive
San Diego, CA 92128
800.854.2235
619.487.8700
Fax: 619.487.8160
www.carvinguitars.com

CASELEY GUITAR COMPANY
105 - 272 E. 4th
Vancouver British Columbia
Canada V5T 4S2

CASTRILLON, IGNACIO
Calle 73 #49-60
Medellin Columbia

CASSOTTA, DAVE
SonFather Guitars
5000 Plumbago Place
Rocklin, CA 95677
sfguitar@inreach.com
home.inreach.com/sfguitar/

CATALUNA
Distributed by Reliance International Corporation
3rd Fl., No. 175, Sec. 2,
An-Ho Road
P.O. Box No. 96-140
Taipei
Taiwan R.O.C.
011.886.2.736.8151
Fax: 011.886.2.738.6491
Fax: 886.2.738.2614

CATALYST INSTRUMENTS USA
P.O. Box 136
West Islip, NY 11795
516.376.6020
www.catalyst-instruments.com
Catalystin@aol.com

CATCHINGS GUITARS
330 Jackson Avenue
McComb, MS 39648
tomcat@telapex.com

CECCON, CARLO
Via Alessi, 13
Milan 20123
Italy
39.2.389955409
ceccon@iol.it

CECCONI, CARLO
Via Alpi Apuane 44
Roma 00141
Italy
06.8170176

CHABOT GUITAR CO.
18033 East Gunnison Place
Aurora, CO 80017
guitarmaker@milehigh.net
www.milehigh.net/guitarmaker

CHANDRA, FERNANDEZ SETIAHADI
Perumahan Griya Pabean LI/F55
Sidoarjo Surabaya
East Java
Indonesia

CHAPEC
Chapec Companhia Industrial de Alimentos
Gustavo Antonio De Nadal
Rua Lauro Miller, 304-E, Centro
Chapec SC 89.800-000
55.(049)723.0295

CHAPIN GUITARS
1709-D Little Orchard
San Jose, CA 95125
408.295.6252
shaydz@earthlink.net

CHAPPELL GUITARS
2619 Columbia Avenue
Richmond, CA 94804
510.528.2904
Fax: 510.528.8310
guitarsrus@earthlink.net
www.home.earthlink.net/~guitarsrus

CHATWORTH GUITARS
England
01423.536383

CHORDACOPIA GUITARS
31881 Florida Street
Redlands, CA 92373
peter_roehling@eee.org

CHRIS LARKIN CUSTOM GUITARS
Castlegregory, Co. Kerry
Ireland
Phone/Fax:
011.353.66.713.9330
www.chrislarkinguitars.com
chris@chrislarkinguitars.com

CIGANA
Guitarras Cigana, Lda.
Av. Agostinho Ribeiro
Edificio Sta. Ovaia - BL 4
Felgueiras
Portugal
351.55.925785
Fax: 351.55.925785

CITRON, HARVEY
Harvey Citron Enterprises
282 Chestnut Hill Road #4
Woodstock, NY 12498
914.679.7138
Fax: 914.679.3221
harvey@citron-guitars.com
www.citron-guitars.com

CLARK, EUGENE
P.O. Box 710
El Cerrito, CA 94530

CLARK, NEIL ALEXANDER
Fishguard
West Wales
United Kingdom

CLAXTON GUITARS
2527-C Mission Street
Santa Cruz, CA 95060
408.469.4563
Fax: 408.426.9875

CLEVINGER, AZOLA, & LEE
C.A.L.
See CLEVINGER or AZOLA for product information

CLEVINGER
553 Kenmore Avenue
Oakland, CA 94610
510.444.2542
Fax: 510.444.2542
clevbass@pacbell.net
www.batnet.com/jazmin/clevbass

CLIFTON BASSES & GUITARS
34 Shooters Hill Rd.
Blackheath England SE3 7BD
Phone/Fax:
011.44.20.8858.7795

CLOUTIER GUITARS
Tree Frog Instruments
521 Short Street
Faribault, MN 55021
treefrog@ptel.net
www.means.net/~treefrog/cloutierguitars.html

CLOVER
Zum Wetterschacht 9
45659 Recklinghausen
Germany
011.49.2361.15881
Fax: 011.49.2361.183473
clover@t-online.de
www.clover-guitars.com

COLE, JEFFREY C.
Cole Studios
4862 Country Road 12
Andover, NY 14806
colestu@vivanet.com

COLIN'S GUITAR WORKS
1205-B Antioch Pike
Nashville, TN 37211
cgw@vol.com
www.vol.com/~cgw

COLLIER QUALITY BASSES
Kasteeldreef 119
B-2970 Schilde
Belgium
Phone/Fax:
011.32.3.354.4531
Edcollier@pi.de

COLLOPY GUITARS
301 Balboa Street
San Francisco, CA 9411
415.221.2990
Fax: 415.221.6380
rcollopy@pacbell.net

CONKLIN GUITARS
P.O. Box 1394
Springfield, MO 65801
417.886.3525
Fax: 417.886.2934
conklin@conklinguitars.c
www.conklinguitars.com

CONNER, MIKE
Fretted Instrument Adjustment & Repair
7010 Longshore Avenue
Seneca, SC 29672
j_m_conner@valenite.con

COOG INSTRUMENT
218 Plateau Avenue
Santa Cruz, CA 95060
coog@coog.com
www.coog.com

CORDOBA
Distributed by Guitar Salon International – see listing.

CORREA, HUMBERTO
Flores Condor de Columbia
Carrera 12A #77A-05
Bogota
Columbia

CORT MUSICAL INSTRUMENTS
3451 W. Commercial Avenue
Northbrook, IL 60062
847.498.6491
Fax: 847.498.5370
postmaster@cort.com
www.cort.com

COTE BASSES
Largo, FL

COURA, PETER
Guitar Center
SchumannStr. 15
60325 Frankfurt
Germany
011.49.6975.2744

COWLES, AARON
Aaron's Music Service
13 S. Main
Vicksburg, MI 49097

CRATE
Also CRATE/ELECTRA
Distributed by St. Louis
Music, Inc. – see listing.

CREWS CORPORATION
Crews Maniac Sound
Guitars and Basses
38-5, Kamiuma
Setagayna-ku
Tokyo 154-0011
Japan
011.81.3.34115612
Fax: 011.81.3.34115661

CRIPE, STEVE
P.O. Box 358
Trilby, FL 33593
904.583.4680

CUDNEY GUITARS
P.O. Box 998
Oakley, CA 94561
russ@cudney.net
www.cudney.net

CURBOW
Morgantown, GA

CUSTOM AX GUITARS
Edison, NJ

CUSTOM GUITAR COMPANY
1168 Aster Ave.
Subbyvale, CA 94086

THE CUSTOM JOB
Angwin, CA

CYAMPAGNE, PAUL
8660 Jeanne - Mance
Montreal Quebec
Canada H2P 2S6

D. C. HILDER BUILDER
2 Yorkshire Street N.
Guelph Ontario
Canada N1H 5A5
519.835.2279

D'ANGELICO
Distributed by Vestax
Vestax Corporation
2-37-1 Kamiuma
Setagayaku
Tokyo 154-0011
03.3412.7011
Fax: 03.3412.7013
vestax-corporation@msn.com

D'ANGELICO II
Archtop Enterprises, Inc.
1980 Broadcast Plaza
Merrick, NY 11566
516.868.4877
516.223.3421

D'ARCY GUITARS
Paul Avenell
Belmont Road
Brisbane Queensland
Australia 4153
pavmuse@powerup.com.au

D'LECO GUITARS
2000 NW 15th St.
Oklahoma City, OK
73106
Phone/Fax: 405.524.0448
www.charliechristian.com
jameswdale@netzero.net

DALMEDO, TITO
Preston
England
011.44.1772.718907
011.44.973.163205

DANELECTRO
Evets Corporation
P.O. Box 2769
Laguna Hills, CA 92654-2769
949.498.9854
Fax: 714.369.8500
www.danelectro.com

DARMSTADTER, JAY
1724 Allied Street
Charlottesville, VA 22901

DART, DAVID L.
P.O. Box 322
520 Hwy 128
Navarro, CA 95463
ddart@pacific.net
www.luthier.com

DAVE J. KING GUITARS
4805 N. Borthwick Avenue
Portland, OR 97217
503.282.0327
bgs@teleport.com
www.teleport.com/~bgs

DAVIDSON STRINGED INSTRUMENTS
P.O. Box 150758
Lakewood, CO 80215
303.984.1896
guitars@rmi.net

DAVIES, PETER
23 Heathwood Road
Cardiff
Wales CF4 4JL
United Kingdom
petelorna@aol.com

DAVIS, J. THOMAS
3135 N. High Street
Columbus, OH 43202-1125
614.263.0264
Fax: 614.447.0174
tom@jthomasdavis.com
www.jthomasdavis.com

DAVIS, KYLE
Just Guitars
106 Forest Lane
Madisonville, KY 42431
cbta@vci.net

DAVIS, RICK
Running Dog
RD 2, Box 57
Richmond, VT 05477

DAVIS, WILLIAM
Handbuilt Guitars
57 Main Street
Boxford, MA 01921
508.887.0282
Fax: 508.887.7214

DEAKON ROADS GUITARS
743 Costigan Place
Saskatoon, SK S7J 3R3
306.653.3879
Fax: 306.374.0633
www.furyguitar.com/deakon
deakon@furyguitar.com

DE CAVA FRETTED INSTRUMENTS
P.O. Box 131
Stratford, CT 06497
203.377.0096
888.661.0229
JRDeCava@aol.com

DECK, LOREN PAUL
Wire & Wood Guitars
306 S. Oak Knoll Avenue
Pasadena, CA 91101
wirewood@macconnect.co
www.macconnect.com/~wirewood

DE LORENE ACOUSTICS, INC.
7304 184th Street
Surrey British Columbia
Canada V4N 3G5
604.574.8041
Fax: 604.574.4889

DEAN
Distributed by Armadillo Enterprises
15251 Roosevelt Blvd.
Suite 206
Clearwater, FL 33760
800.793.5273
727.796.8868
Fax: 727.797.9448
gtr&bass@armadilloent.co
www.deanguitars.com

DEAN USA
7091 N.W. 51st Street
Miami, FL 33166
305.594.3909
Fax: 305.594.0786

DE ARMOND
DeArmond By Guild
Distributed by Fender
Musical Instruments
GmbH
Heltorfer StraBe 20
40472 Dusseldorf
Germany
011.49.211.417030
Fax: 011.49.211.4792849
Fax: 011.49.211.4170373

DEIMEL GUITARWORKS
Frank Deimel
Bautzener Str. 14
10829 Berlin
Germany
deimelguitarwoks@berlin.snafu.de

DEVON GUITARS
1372 Lake Park Ct.
Pewaukee, WI 53072
414.228.4513
Fax: 414.228.4398

ERIC DEYOE
Deyoe Guitars
Colfax Guitar Shop
3220 East Colfax Avenue
Denver, CO 80206
303.394.0099
www.colfaxguitarshop.com

DILLON GUITARS
17 Stewart Lane
Bloomsburg, PA 17815
570.784.7552
Fax: 570.784.8328
www.picasso.net/dillon
artranch@aol.com

DINES, ROB
Robz Guitars
473 California Street
Santa Clara, CA 95050
rdines@divi.com

DINGWALL DESIGNER GUITARS
P.O. Box 9194
Saskatoon SK
Canada S7K 7E8
306.242.6201
Fax: 306.242.6404
Dingwallguitars@home.com
www.dingwallguitars.com

DIPINTO HANDMADE GUITARS
631 N. 2nd St.
Philadelphia, PA 19123
215.923.2353
Fax: 215.923.5899
www.dipintoguitars.com

DIXON, MARTIN
England
01487.823182

DOBRO
Distributed by Gibson
Musical Instruments – see listing.

DODGE GUITAR COMPANY
2801 NW 22nd Terrace
Pompano Beach, FL
33069
954.975.3533
Fax: 954.975.3577
650.562.4331
info@dodgeguitars.com
www.dodgeguitars.com

DOLAN, MICHAEL
3222 Airway Dr. #4
Santa Rosa, CA 95403
707.575.0654

DONEFER, GARY
Slugmeister Bass and Guitar
P.O. Box 1718
Mendocino, CA 95460
gdonefer@mcn.org

DRAJAS GUITARS
Hamburg, Germany

DRISKILL GUITARS
2800A Shamrock
Fort Worth, TX 76107
817.336.0600
Joe@driskillguitars.com
www.driskillguitars.com

PHILIPPE DUBREUILLE
25 Denmark Street
1st Floor, Guitar Emporium
London WC 2 H8NJ
England
011.20.7704.81.71
Fax: 011.44.20.7226.5418
www.dubreuille.com
philgood@dubreuille.com

DUESENBERG
KrausenStrasse 35
D-30171 Hannover
Germany
011.49.511.855.226
Fax: 011.49.511.855.249
www.duesenberg.de

DUNWELL GUITARS
Magnolia Star Route
1891 CR 68-J
Nederland CO 80466
303.939.8870
dunwell@jnov.colorado.edu

E. C. POL GUITAR COMPANY
Vancouver British Columbia
Canada
www.personal.smartt.com/~amirault/duncan.html

ESH
ESH Gitarrenkonzeption GmbH
Jakobsspitalchen 3
D-54290 Trier
Germany
011.49.651.41041
Fax: 011.49.651.41042
www.esh-basses.com
esh-basses@t-online.com
Distributed by ESH USA/MTC NYC
495 Lorimer St.
Brooklyn, NY 11211
718.963.2777
Fax: 718.302.4890

ESP GUITAR COMPANY
1536 N. Highland Avenue
Hollywood, CA 90046
800.423.8388
323.969.0877
Fax: 323.969.9335
www.espguitars.com

THE ESP COMPANY, LTD. OF JAPAN
Overseas Department
2-10-11 Takada
Toshima-ku
Tokyo 171 Japan
03.3.982.3684
Fax: 03.3.982.1036

EAGLE
Eagle Country Instruments
Rieslingweg 12C
Murr Germany
011.49.714.424736
Fax: 011.49.714.4209115

CHRIS ECCLESHALL
Unit 2
Webber's Way
Darington, Totnes
Devon
England TQ9 6JY
011.44.1803.862364

ECLECTIC GUITARS BY DESIGN
226 Overhill Drive
Duncan, SC 29334
864.949.0872
eclecticgbd@mindspring.com

ED CLARK GUITARS
520A Hawkins Ave.
Ronkonkoma, NY 11779
631.738.8181
ejcfretwx@aol.com

EDWARDS GUITAR RESEARCH LTD.
8892 N. 56th Street
Temple Terrace, FL 33617

EDWARDS, MICK
48 Dukes Lane
Adelaide
South Australia 5000
micke@adelaide.on.net

EKO MUSICAL INSTRUMENTS
EKO - C.so Persiani, 44
C.P. 58 - 62019 Recanati (MC) ITALY
Tel: +39-0733-226271
Fax: +39-0733-226546
info@eko.it
www.eko.it
www.ekoguitars.com

EL CID
Distributed by L.A. Guitar Works – see listing.

ELDH, KLAS
Friman Vag
Froson Osterund
Sweden 83254
eldh@mail.bip.net
www.home6.swipnet.se/~w-62511/klas/klasbas.htm

ELRICK BASS GUITARS
1906 West Crystal Street #1
Chicago, IL 60622
773.489.5514
Fax: 773.489.5514
www.elrick.com
Distributed by T.J. Wagner & Son
P.O. Box 59
Fairport, NY 14450
716.425.9730
Fax: 716.425.9466

EMERY
Distributed by Resound Vintage Guitars
7438 Hwy. 53
Britt, MN 55710
218.741.9515

EMINENCE
G. Edward Lutherie, Inc.
1620 Central Avenue Northeast
Minneapolis, MN 55413
612.781.5799
gelbass@aol.com
www.gelbass.com

ENCORE
Distributed by John Hornby Skewes & Co., Ltd. – see listing.

ENGLISH GUITARS
14586 Olive Vista Drive
Jamul, CA 91935
Phone/Fax: 619.669.0833
www.englishguitars.com

EPI
Distributed by Gibson Musical Instruments – see listing.

EPIPHONE
Distributed by Gibson Musical Instruments
Epiphone Company
645 Massman Drive
Nashville, TN 37210
800.283.7135
615.871.4500
Fax: 615.872.7768
www.epiphone.com
www.gibson.com

ERIKSSON, MATS
Hansta 3
Vingaker
Sweden S-64391
mats.eriksson@vingaker.mail.telia.com

ERLEWINE GUITARS
4402 Burnet Rd.
Austin, TX 78756-3319
512.302.1225
Fax: 512.371.1655
www.erlewineguitars.com
mark@erlewineguitars.com

ERNIE BALL/MUSIC MAN
151 Suburban Road
P.O. Box 4117
San Luis Obispo, CA 93401
800.543.2255
805.544.7726
Fax: 805.544.7275
ernieball@ernieball.com
www.ernieball.com

ERRINGTON GUITARS
Cravengate
Richmond, North Yorks
England DL10 4RE
01748.824700

EUGEN GUITARS
P.O. Box 1782, Nordnes
5024 Bergen
Norway
011.47.55.23.28.60
Fax: 011.47.55.23.04.35
eugen@abcnett.no
www.eugen.no

EVANS GUITAR PRODUCTS
961 Dunford Avenue
Victoria British Columbia
Canada V9B 2S4

EVD STRING INSTRUMENTS
1869 S. Pearl Street
Denver, CO 80210
evd303@aol.com
www.musicore.com/evd

EYB GUITARS
Schillerstrasse 48
D-71229 Leonberg
Germany
011.49.7152.243.85
Fax: 011.49.7152.243.99
www.eyb-guitars.de

F BASS
Guitar Clinic
16 McKinstry Street
Hamilton, Ontario
Canada L8L 6C1
905.522.1582
Fax: 905.528.5667
www.fbass.com

FM
Austin, TX
312.292.0544

FABREGUES BASSES
Pepe Fabregues
Villa Music World
1853 Ponce de Leon
Santure, PR 00909
787.727.5000
Fax: 787.728.8848
Fabass@coqui.net

FABRICANT, NEIL L.
821 Westfield Avenue
Elizabeth, NJ 07208
drfab@aol.com

MARTIN FAIR
Route 1, Box 174
Santa Fe, NM 87501

FARNELL GUITAR COMPANY
1544 East 1st Street
Pomona, Ca 91766
909.629.9111
Fax: 909.629.6711

FEDDEN
40 Stonywood Road
Commack, NY 11725
516.864.1936

FENDER
Fender Musical Instruments Corporation
7975 North Hayden Road
Scottsdale, AZ 85258-3246
480.596.9690
Fax: 480.596.1384
www.fender.com

FERNANDES GUITARS
12600 Saticoy Street
North Hollywood, CA 91605
800.318.8599
Fax: 818.764.0080
www.fernandesguitars.com

FERRARIS, MARIO ROSAZZA
Via P. Cossa 3
Roma
Italy
06.3230741

FERRINGTON, DANNY
P.O. Box 923
Pacific Palisades, CA 90272
310.454.0692

FICHTER E-KONTRABASSE
Fichter & Jaeger GbR
Hauptstrasse 27a
D-65529 Waldems
Germany
011.49.6126.1570
Fax: 011.49.6126.1819
service@fichterbasses.com
www.fichterbasses.com

LHO, JOSE ANTO-
IO RUOTOLO
ua dos Trilhos, 2096
o Paulo, SP 03168-010
otolo@mandic.com.br

ITZPATRICK JAZZ
UITARS
4 Enfield Avenue
Vickford, RI 02852
01.294.4801

LEISHMAN
NSTRUMENTS
500 Whitney Place
oulder, CO 80303
03.499.1614

LOHR, W.
azzebel
Kerktoren 4
Middelburg Zld
The Netherlands
os1@pi.net

FODERA
68 34th Street
Brooklyn, NY 11232
718.832.3455
Fax: 718.832.3458
www.fodera.com
fodera@interport.net

FONTANILLA, ALAN
P.O. Box 31423
San Francisco, CA 94131
415.642.9375

FOSTER GUITAR
MANUFACTURING
76353 Eugene Wallace
Road
Covington, LA 70435
504.892.9822
guitars@neosoft.com
www.fosterguitars.com

FOTI, MAURIZIO
Via Alessi 13
Milan
Italy 20123
011.39.2.58101241
mf@iol.it

FRAMUS
Postfach 10010
D-08258 Markneukirchen
Germany
011.49.3742.25550
Fax: 011.49.3742.55599
wwpresse@aol.com

FREDDY'S FRETS
2520 Meritt Road
Welland Ontario
Canada L3B 5N5
905.384.0303
Fax: 905.384.0014
freddy@freddyfrets.com
www.freddysfrets.com

FRENZ
P.O. Box 29612
Columbus, OH 43229-0612
614.847.4108

FRISCO GUITAR
WORKS
Frisco, TX

FRUDUA GUITAR
WORKS
Via Zappa Ceroni
18-40026 Imola (BO)
Italy
0542.45002
Fax: 0542.43810
www.ispitalia.it/frudua.htm

FRYE GUITARS
147 N. Broadway
Green Bay, WI 54303
920.433.0710
strgws@netnet.net

FURY
Fury Guitar
Manufacturing, Ltd.
902 Avenue J North
Saskatoon Saskatchewan
Canada S7L 2l2
306.244.4063
Fax: 306.374.0633
info@furyguitar.com
www.furyguitar.com

G & L MUSICAL
PRODUCTS
Distributed by BBE Sound, Inc.
5381 Production Drive
Huntington Beach, CA
92649
714.897.6766
Fax: 714.895.6728
www.glguitars.com

GC GUITARS
5934 El Mio Drive
Los Angeles, CA 90042
gcmqr@earthlink.com

GLF
Distributed by the GLF
Custom Shop
19817 Jackie Lane
Rogers, MN 55374
763.428.8818
glfsmith@aol.com

GMP GUITARS
GM Precision Products
510 E. Arrow Highway
San Dimas, CA 91773
909.592.5144
Fax: 909.599.0798
gmp@gmpguitars.com
www.gmpguitars.com

GMW GUITARWORKS
Empire Guitars
Neal Moser Guitars
220 N. Glendora Avenue
Glendora, CA 91741
818.914.8082
Fax: 818.914.4287

GR BASSES
295 Trade Street
San Marcos, CA 92069
619.761.1131
Fax: 760.761.0137
www.grbasses.com

GTX
Distributed by the Kaman
Music Corporation – see
listing.

GALLACHER GUITARS
255 Kooba Street
Albury NSW
Australia 2640
stuart@dragnet.com.au

GANZ, STEVE
3629 Illinois Lane
Bellingham, WA 98226
sganz_guitars@
geocities.com
www.geocities.com
/vienna/2242/

GARDNER GUITARS
8976 Rosetta Circle
Sacramento, CA 95826
drguitar@midtown.net

GAZELLE GUITARS
Glasco Turnpike
Woodstock, NY 12498
songcraftr@aol.com

GAZER GUITARS
Roanoke, VA

GENTRY, MICK
Flinders Avenue
Molendinar Queensland
Australia 4214
mickgrep@fan.net.au

GGOULD
1315 23rd Avenue
Suite 200 A
San Francisco, CA 94122
800.513.2200
415.759.5199
Fax: 415.759.5399
geoff@ggould.com
www.ggould.com

GHOST INSTRUMENT
COMPANY
P.O. Box 1368
Anaconda, MT 59711
tm51mt@aol.com

GIANCARLO CORTESI
Via Don Carlo 65
Albana S. Alessandro (BG)
Italy 24061
035.580369

GIBSON
Gibson Musical
Instruments
1818 Elm Hill Pike
Nashville, TN 37210-3781
800.846.4376
615.871.4500
Fax: 615.889.5509
jazor@gibson.com
www.gibson.com

GIEBITZ, BILL
Strait Music Company
805 W. 5th Street
Austin, TX 78703
giebitz@dfti.com

GIFFIN GUITARS
Alingsas Sweden

GILET, GERARD
Gilet Guitars &
Guitarwoods
Factory 5/6 Booralee Street
Botany NSW
Australia 2019
www.spirit.com.au/~gra-mac/gilet/giletintro.html

GILLHAM'S GUITAR
WORKS
116 S. Channel Drive
Wrightsville, NC 28480

GIOACHINO,
GIUSSANI
Podere Aile
Anghiari (Ariezzo)
Italy 52031

GIRDIS
8745 Evanston Avenue
North
Seattle, WA 98103
www.cybozone.com/fg
/girdis.html

GITARRENBAU
GleimstraBe 56
10437 Berlin
Germany
030.442.0196

GODIN
Godin Guitars
Distributed by La Si Do,
Inc. – see listing.

THE GOLDEN WOOD
33700 S. Highway One
Gualala, CA 95445
707.884.4213
dbucher@mcn.org

GOLDFINGER CO.
Valervn. 67
Moss
Norway 1537
glennrichardthommassen@
broderdue.com

GOLEBATMAZ,
OZHAN
100 Yil AA-14
Balgat - Ankara
Turkey
c/o: kemal@tel-soft.com

GOMES, ROBERT
914 A Mission Street
Santa Cruz, CA 95060-3504
sequoia@cruzio.com

GOODFELLOW BASSES
Built by the Lowden Guitar
Company
Distributed in the USA by
Quality First Products
137 North Quail Run
Forest City, NC 28043
800.872.5856
Fax: 704.245.8965

GORDON SMITH
GUITARS
Distributed by Machine
Head
2 Bush House
Bush Fair
Harlow, Essex
England CM18 6NS
01279.421744
Fax: 01462.458880

GOUGI FABRICE
L'Atelier de Lutherie
Fabrice Gougi
Rue de la Gare
Penmarsh
France 29760
gougi@wanadoo.fr

GRAINGER, JIM
Custom Fretted
Instruments & Repair
400 Firetower Road
Sparta, TN 38583
customfret@juno.com

GRANATA GUITARS
Oak Ridge, NJ

GREEN, JUSTIN
P.O. Box 513
Choctaw, OK 73020
jgreen@theshop.net

GREGORY, JAMES D.
Jim Gregory Guitar/Repair
17133 West Munyon Road
Cane Hill, AR 72717
jgregory@lincoln.mwsc
.k12.ar.us

GREMLIN
Distributed by Midco
International – see listing.

GRENDEL
Distributed by Matthews
& Ryan Musical Products
68 34th Street
Brooklyn, NY 11232
800.248.4827
718.832.6333
Fax: 718.832.5270
matthewsandryan@
compuserve.com
www.matthewsan
dryan.com

GRETSCH
Fred Gretsch Enterprises,
Ltd.
P.O. Box 2468
Savannah, GA 31402
912.748.7070
Fax: 912.748.6005
www.gretsch.com

GRETZ, JACK
Distributed by Magdon
Music
jackguitrs@aol.com

GRIFFITHS GUITAR WORKS
St. John's, Newfoundland
Canada

GRIS GRIS GUITARS
Morgan-West Stuio Gallery
3326 Magazine Street
New Orleans, LA 70115
504.895.7976
504.288.2364
VoDouDude@aol.com

GROOVE TOOLS
Distributed by the
Westheimer Corporation
3451 W. Commercial
Avenue
Northbrook, IL 60062
847.498.6491
Fax: 847.498.5370
postmaster@cort.com
www.cort.com

GROSH CUSTOM GUITARS
26818 Oak Avenue #F
Canyon Country, CA
91351
661.252.6716
Fax: 661.252.6716
info@groshguitars.com
www.groshguitars.com

GROVES CUSTOM GUITARS
Tuscon, AZ

GRUGGETT, BILL
Bakersfield, CA
805.399.4612
Distributed by Stark-
Marquadt
Productions & Service
Bakersfield, CA
805.831.8613
Distributed by Jacobson's
Service
Fine Guitars
Denver CO
303.935.2007

GUILD
A division of Fender
Musical Instruments
Corporation – see listing.
www.guildguitars.com

GUITAR FACTORY
2816 Edgewater Drive
Orlando, FL 32804
800.541.1070
407.425.1070
Fax: 407.425.7276
felsfam@magicnet.net
members.aol.com/gif89
/index.html

GUITAR FARM
RR 1, Box 60
Sperryville, VA 22740-
9604
540.987.9744
Fax: 640.987.9419

GUITAR SALON INTERNATIONAL
3100 Donald Douglas
Loop North
Santa Monica, CA 90405
310.399.2181
310.396.9283
GSImail@guitarsalon.com
www.guitarsalon.com

GUITARLAB
Kiyoshi Itoh
Funabashi, Chiba
Japan

GUTSCHER, WOLFGANG
33-35 St. John's Square
Unit 51
Pennybank Chambers
London EC1 M4DS
England
wolfgang.gutscher@
easynet.co.uk

GUY, PAUL
Katarina Bangata 65
Stockholm
Sweden 11642
paul@guyguitars.se
www.home3.swipnet.se
/~w-37192/

HML GUITARS
Howard M. Leese Guitars
532 Kennebeck Avenue S.
Kent, WA 98031
253.859.5108
Fax: 253.657.6354

HAGENLOCHER GUITARRAS
Calle Guadarrama 3 Bajo
Granada
Spain E-18009
henner@valnet.es

HALLGREN, PER
Skraddarns Vag 14
Grabo
Sweden
per.hallgren@mbox301.swi
pnet.se

HALLMARK
Exclusively distributed by
Front Porch Music
1711 19th Street
Bakersfield, CA 93301
800.900.2JAM

HAMBURGUITAR
2300 E. Silverado Ranch
Blvd., Apt. 2037
Las Vegas, NV 09123-3974

HAMER GUITARS
Distributed by the Kaman
Music Corporation – see
listing.

HAMILTONE
Hamiltone Guitar
Workshop, Inc.
1910 Spy Run Avenue
Fort Wayne, IN 46805
219.422.2359

HAMMERTONE
Guitar Clinic
16 McKinstry Street
Hamilton, Ontario
Canada L8L 6C1
905.522.1582
Fax: 905.528.5667
www.guitarclinic.com

HANEWINCKEL GUITARS
Mr. Pete Hanewinckel
10002 St. John Cir.
Cypress, CA 90630
714.484.2846
www.hanewinckel
guitars.com
haneguitars@earthlink.net

HANIKA GITARREN
Armin Hanika
Egerstrasse 12A
Baiersdorf Bayern
D-91083 Germany
armin.hanika@t-online.de

HARDBODY COMPOSITE GUITARS
Escondido, California.

HARGREAVES BASS GUITARS
P.O. Box 997
Carlsborg, WA 98324-
0997
jthbass@wolfenet.com
www.wolfenet.com/~
jthbas
www.cybozone.com/fg
/leadingedge.html

HARMONIC DESIGN PICKUPS
325 Jefferson Street
Bakersfield, CA 93305
661.321.0395
Fax: 661.322.2360
pickups@harmonic
design.net
www.harmonicdesign.net

HARPER'S GUITARS
P.O. Box 2877
Apple Valley, CA 92307
760.240.1792
Fax: 760.240.1792
harpergtrs@aol.com
www.harpersguitars.com

HARRIS, RICHARD
7610 Chris Anne Drive
Indianapolis, IN 46237

HARTKE
Samson Technologies Corp
P.O. Box 9031
Syosset, NY 11791-9031
516.364.2244
www.samsontech.com
sales@samsontech.com

R. HAYES INSTRUMENTS
Cincinnati, OH
888.484.4879
www.RHayes
Instruments.com

HAYNIE, LES
Eureka Springs, AR
501.253.8941

HEIDI PULFER
Via Piccinino 3
Rimini
Italy 47037
0541.27997

HEINS GUITARS
Hoogend 26
8601 AE Sneek
The Netherlands
Phone/Fax:
011.31.515.423848
www.heinsguitars.com
info@heinsguitars.com

HEINZ, JOHN
Prototech Engineering
5 Hunter Avenue
Joliet, IL 60436
jwheinz@juno.com

HERITAGE
Heritage Guitar, Inc.
225 Parsons Street
Kalamazoo, MI 49007
616.385.5721
Fax: 616.385.3519
www.heritageguitar.com
Exclusive Sales and
Marketing
Lasar Music Corporation
P.O. Box 2045
Brentwood, TN 37027
615.337.4913
Fax: 615.373.4986

HERNANDEZ, JAVIER
Humlegardsgatan 13
Stockholm
Sweden 12244
x-herdz@swipnet.se

HEWETT GUITARS
12430 Gail St.
New Caney, TX 77357
281.354.7894
guitar@wt.net
www.hewettguitars.com

HFI, JIRI LEBEDA
Jasminova 32
10600 Praha 10
Czech Republic
420.2.7553.472
420.602.255.120

HILL GUITAR COMPANY
702 Hitchcock Street
Plant City, FL 33566
813.754.6499
Fax: 813.759.9112
www.aaei.com/w

HILL, JAMES
The Heron
England
011.44.12.47.469090

HINTON, CHRIS
Hinton Custom Inlays
Ashland, WI 54806
hiton@ncis.net

HOFFMAN, CRAIG
Hoffman Stringed Instruments and Repairs
2660 South Yonkers Road
Raleigh, NC 27604

HOFNER
Karl Hofner GmbH
EgerlandstraBe 38
91083 Baiersdorf-Hagenau
Germany
9131.7758.0
Fax: 9131.7758.58
Distributed by Boosey & Hawkes
1600 Northwind Blvd.
Libertyville, IL 60048
847.816.2500
Fax: 847.816.2514
www.boosey.com
booseyH@aol.com

HOHNER
Exclusively distributed in the U.S. by HSS
(A Division of Hohner, Inc.)
Lakeridge Park
10223 Sycamore Drive
Ashland, VA 23005
800.446.6010
804.550.2700
Fax: 804.550.2670
www.hohnerusa.com

HOLLISTER GUITARS
Dedham, MA

HOLMES, TOM
P.O. Box 414
Joelton, TN 37080
615.876.3453

HOLST, STEPHEN
354 E. 30th Avenue
Eugene, OR 97405
541.687.7845
Fax: 541.687.7845
guitar@rio.com
www.rio.com/~guitars/

HOOD, EDWARD D.
Yondern and Back
1315 1/2 W. 5th Street
Port Angeles, WA 98363
ehood@olypen.com

HONDO
Hondo Guitar Company
Distributed by Musicorp/MBT
P.O. Box 30819
Charleston, SC 29417
800.845.1922
803.763.9083
Fax: 803.763.9096
www.hondo.com

HOT LICKS
P.O. Box 337
Pound Ridge, NY 10576
800.388.3008
914.763.8016
Fax: 914.763.9453
hotlicks@ix.netcom.com
www.hotlicks.com

HOYER
International Distribution by Musikwarengrosshandel
Mario Pellarin
Toyota-Allee 19
D-50858 Koeln (Cologne)
Germany
49.2234.16011
Fax: 49.2234.14042
106131.523@compuserve.com
www.pellarin.de

HUBER, NIK
LudwigstraBe 12
63110 Rodgau
Germany
011.49.6106.649007
Fax: 011.49.6106.648488
nikhuber@aol.com

HUMAN BASE
HauptstraBe 27a
65529 Waldems
Germany
011.49.6126.1570
Fax: 011.49.6126.1819
www.humanbase.de
Distributed by Salwender International
1140 N. Lemon Street #M
Orange, CA 92867
714.583.1285
Fax: 714.583.9331
uwe@salwender.com
www.salwender.com

HUNTER, ROBERT J.
1400 West 3rd Street
Waterloo, IA 50701

HUNTINGTON GUITARS
5561 Engineer Drive
Huntington Beach, CA 92649
800.575.5223
714.898.2776
Fax: 714.893.1045
info@agi-lace.com
www.agi-lace.com

HUSS AND DALTON GUITAR COMPANY
102 Wayne Avenue
(P.O. Box 537)
Stuarts Draft, VA 24477
540.337.3382
Fax: 540.337.3382
hdguitar@cfw.com
www.dezines.com/hdguitar

HWANG-CARLOS GUITARS
Leo Hwang-Carlos
8 Easthampton Road
Northampton, MA 01060
lhwangca@mtholyoke.edu

HYUNDAI
Hyundai Guitars
126 Route 303
West Nyack, NY 10994
914.353.3520
Fax: 914.353.3540

IBANEZ
Hoshino (USA), Inc.
1726 Winchester Road
Bensalem, PA 19020-0886
800.669.4226
215.638.8670
Fax: 215.245.8583
www.ibanez.com
Ibanez Canada
2165-46th Avenue
Lachine Quebec H8T 2P1
Ibanez Australia
88 Bourke Road
Alexandria Sydney NSW 2015
Ibanez New Zealand
5 Amokura Street
Henderson Auckland

J.B. PLAYER
PO Box 30819
Charleston, SC 29417
800.845.1922
843.763.9083
Fax: 843.763.9096
www.jbplayer.com

JDS
Distributed by US Band & Orchestra Supplies, Inc.
1933 Woodson Road
St. Louis, MO 63114
800.844.9653
314.429.3439
Fax: 314.429.3255

JLD RESEARCH AND DEVELOPMENT
2431 S. Lake Letta Drive #2
Avon Park, FL 33825
jldrd@digital.net
www.digital.net/~jlddoc/

JMS CUSTOM GUITARS
1308 Everett Avenue
No. Two
Louisville, KY 40204

JP GUITARS
11917 150th St. Ct. E
Puyallup, WA 98374
253.841.2954
Fax: 253.845.8357

JWL INSTRUMENT
Jokke Lagerqvist
Tallgatan 7
HOK
Sweden 56013
jokke@jwl.pp.se
www.flashback.net/~guitar

JACKSON/CHARVEL GUITAR COMPANY
P.O. Box 961077
Fort Worth, TX 76161-077
www.jacksonguitars.com
Distributed by Akai Musical Instrument Corporation
4710 Mercantile Drive
Fort Worth, TX 76137
800.433.5627
817.831.9203
akaiUSA@ix.netcom.com
www.akai.com/akaipro

JACKSON, DOUGLAS R.
P.O. Box 5149
Destin, FL 32540
Or,
175 Stahlman Avenue
Destin, FL 32541
850.654.1048
Fax: 850.654.1048

JACOBSON, PAUL
www.cybozone.com/fg/jacobson.html

JAEN ARCHTOP GUITARS
Fernando Alonso Jaen
C/Solana de Opanel
14 Bis - 2
Madrid
Spain 28091
falonso@alcatel.es

JAGARD
Distributed by V.J. Rendano – see listing.
Eikosha Musical Instrument Co., Inc.
2, Onaridori 1-chrome
Kitaku, Nagoya, JAPAN
Phone:
011.81.52.911.6456
Fax: 011.81.52.911.6474
Eikosh@aol.com

JAMMER
Distributed by Vega Musical Instruments – see listing.

JARMAN GUITARS
Bexleyheath, Kent
England
jarman@btinternet.com
www.btinternet.com/~sjguitars/

JAROS CUSTOM GUITARS
103 Mary Street
Rochester, PA 15074
412.774.5615

JAY TURSER
Distributed by Music Industries Corporation
99 Tulip Avenue
Suite 101
Floral Park, NY 11001
800.431.6699
516.352.4110
Fax: 516.352.0754

mic@musicindustries.com
www.musicindustries.com

JAYXZ MUSICAL IMPLEMENTS
2028 Nottingham Road
Lakeland, FL 33803
941.686.3229
jayxz@get.net
home1.get.net/jayxz/

JEANNIE
Jeannie Pickguards and Guitar Accessories
292 Atherton Avenue
Pittsburg, CA 94565
510.439.1447

JENKINS, CHRIS
829 Kingston Drive
Mansfield, TX 76063
cjenkins@arlington.net

JERRY JONES GUITARS
(P.O. Box 22507)
913 Church Street
Nashville, TN 37203
615.255.0088
Fax: 615.255.7742

JERZY DROZD
c/Bruselas, 35 Bajos
Barcelona
Spain 08041
+34.93.4504900
Fax: +34.93.4504900

JJ HUCKE GUITARS
J.J. Hucke Limited
Tower Farm
Little Wolford
Shipton-On-Stour, Warwickshire
England CV36 5NR
1608.684887
Fax: 1608.684887
jpinfo@aol.com
www.jjhucke.com

JOHANSEN, LEIF JORGEN
Nordassloyfa 11A
Oslo
Norway 1250
226.22228

JOHANSSON, JENS
Odenskogvagen 84
Ostersund
Sweden
vfhs@algonet.se

JOHN BIRCH GUITARS
MIDI Access Technology
21 A Seymour Road
West Bridgford
Nottingham NG25EE
United Kingdom
0115.9818523
(Mobile) 0468.130420
jc@johnbirchguitars.demon.co.uk
www.johnbirchguitars.demon.co.uk
Distributed in the U.S. by Greg Dorsett
619.229.8709
Fax: 800.579.1611
gd@mysurf.com

JOHN HORNBY SKEWES & CO., LTD.
Salem House
Parkinson Approach
Garforth Leeds
LS25 2HR England
011.44.113.286.5381
Fax: 011.44.113.286.8515
Info@jhs.co.uk
www.jhs.co.uk

JOHN PEARSE GUITARS
Vintage Acoustic Steel Guitars
Distributed by Breezy Ridge Instruments
P.O. Box 295
Center Valley, PA 18034-0295
800.235.33029
610.691.3302
Fax: 610.691.3304
www.jpstrings.com

JOHNNY REB
Distributed by Johhny Reb Guitars/L.A. Guitar Works - see listing.

JOHNSON
Distributed by The Music Link
P.O. Box 162
Brisbane, CA 94005
888.552.5465
650.615.8991
Fax: 650.615.8997
thelink@@musiclinkcorp.com

JOHNSON GUITARS
P.O. Box 222
Talkeetna, AK 99676
907.733.2005
Fax: 907.733.2777
jguitars@alaska.net

JOHNSON'S EXTREMELY STRANGE MUSICAL INSTRUMENT COMPANY
119 West Linden Avenue
Burbank, CA 91502
818.955.8152

JONES GUITARS
Brookfield Road
Brookfield Works
Leeds Yorkshire
England LS6 4EH
cwj27@aol.com

JONES, ARTHUR MILES
Fretworks
4027 4th Street SE
Calgary Alberta
Canada T2G 2W4
fretwork@fretwork.com
www.fretwork.com

JONES, RICK OWEN
Coconut Grove Music
418 Kuulei Road
Kailua, HI 96734

JONES, TED NEWMAN
1310 S. First Street
Austin, TX 78704-3038
512.445.9625
Fax: 512.442.5855

JONGE, SERGIE DE
Oshawa, Ontario
Canada
www.cybozone.com/fg/jonge.html

JUBAL GUITARS
326 S. Union Street
Olean, NY 14760
716.372.7771

JUDD GUITARS
Cranbrook, British Columbia, Canada

JUZEK, BOB
Metropolitan Music Company
P.O. Box 1415
Mountain Road
Stowe, VT 05672-9598

K.D. DAVIS GUITARS
853 Second Street West
Sonoma, CA 95476
inivekdboy@sprynet.com

KGB MUSICAL INSTRUMENTS
61 Derby Road
Birkenhead
Merseyside L42 7HA
England
0151.6473268

KSM GUITARS
349 North Main
Logan, UT 84321

KALIL FINE HANDCRAFTED GUITARS
132 S. Front Street
McComb, MS 39648
601.249.3894
edekalil@aol.com
members.aol.coM/edekalil/kalil.html

KAMAN MUSIC CORPORATION
P.O. Box 507
Bloomfield, CT 06002-0507
800.647.2244
860.509.8888
Fax: 860.509.8891
frindone-KMC@kaman.com
info-kmc@kaman.com
www.kamanmusic.com

KAMBO, VARINDER
15 Scenic Drive
South Salem, NY 10590
vkhalsa@bestweb.net

KARERA
Distributed by V.J. Rendano Music Company, Inc. – see listing.

KAWA, PETER
508.697.8485

KAY
Distributed by A.R. Musical Enterprises, Inc.
9031 Technology Drive
Fishers, IN 46038
800.428.4807
317.577.6999
Fax: 317.577.7288

KELDAY, WILLIAM C.
The Guitar Workshop
Unit 3
Aldessan House
The Clachan Campsie Glen
Glascow G65 7AB
Scotland
billguitmk@aol.com

KELLER CUSTOM GUITARS
P.O. Box 244
Mandan, ND 58554
701.663.1153
Fax: 701.667.2197

KELLER GUITARS
Alphonse J. Keller
Bayreutherstrasse 4-6
Erlangen Bavaria
91054 Germany

KELLETT ALUMINUM GUITARS
415 Mathew St.
Santa Clara, CA 95050
408.988.1910
Fax: 408.988.8606
www.pkselective.com
pkpeter@pkselective.com

KELLISON, T. R.
1739 Grand Avenue
Billings, MT 59102
406.245.4212
www.imt.net/~evolve/guitarshop/index.html

KEN BEBENSEE GUITARS
P.O. Box 12115
San Luis Obispo, CA 93401
805.541.8842
ken@kbguitars.com
www.kbguitars.com

KENDRICK
Kendricks Amplifiers
P.O. Box 160
Pflugerville, TX 78691-0160
512.990.5486
Fax: 512.990.0548
kendrick@inetport.com
www.kendrick-amplifiers.com

KENNETH LAWRENCE INSTRUMENTS
1055 Samoa Blvd.
Arcata, CA 95521
707.822.2543
lawrence@reninet.com

KERSENBROCK GUITARS
111 S. Third
Lindsborg, KS 67456
785.227.2968

KEVIN RYAN GUITARS
14211 Wiltshire Street
Westminster, CA 92683
714.894.0590
Fax: 714.379.0944
ryanguitar@aol.com

IMAXE
istributed by Kenny &
lichael's Company, Inc.
425 S. Hill St.
os Angeles, CA 90007
00.504.9831
13.746.2848
ax: 213.747.1161

IMBARA
)istributed by FCN Music
lorley Road
onbridge
ent TN9 1RA
ngland
1732.366.421

IMBERLY
imex Trading Co., Ltd.
oom 1411, Han Suh
iver Park
1-11, Yeo Eui Do-Dong
eong Deung Po-Ku, Seoul
orea
32.2.786.1014
32.2.783.0408
ax: 82.2.786.5578

INAL, MIKE
3239 E. 52nd Avenue
ancouver British
Columbia
CANADA V5S 1T9
504.433.6544
guitar@istar.ca
www.kinal.com

KINKADE
18 Clevedon Terrace
Kingsdown
Bristol BS6 5TX
England
0117.9243279

KINNAIRD, JOHN
100 Rolling Road
Social Circle, GA 30025
jhkjr@bellsouth.net

KLEIN, STEVE
Klein Acoustic Guitars
2560 Knob Hill Road
Sonoma, CA 95476
707.938.4639
Fax: 707.938.4639
info@kleinguitars.com
www.kleinguitars.com

KLEIN ELECTRIC GUITARS
1207 Marina Circle
Discovery Bay, CA 94514
925.516.9338
Fax: 925.516.7333
klein@genesisnetwork.net

KNATT, THOMAS
Luthiers Workshop
Waltham, MA

KNAUFF, JOHN
Neo CLassic Guitars
6839 Kerrywood Circle
Centreville, VA 20121
jknauff@visa.com

KNIGHT GUITARS
Woodham Lane
New Haw, Weybridge
Surrey, England
01932.353131

KNOWBUDGE PRODUCTIONS
3463 State Street # 305
Santa Barbara, CA 93105
805.963.2908

KNUTSON LUTHIERY
Custom Guitar, Bass, and
Mandolin Works
P.O. Box 945
Forrestville, CA 95436
707.887.2709
john@messengerbass.com
www.messengerbass.com/KnutsonLuthiery

KOCH, MARTIN
Hartbergerstrasse 22
A-8200 Gleisdorf
Austria
koch@kwb.tv-graz.ac.at
www.cis.tv-graz.ac.at
/iwb/martin/welcome.html

KOLEKOLE GUITARS
Norwood, MA

KOLL GUITAR COMPANY
2402 SE Belmont Street
Portland, OR 97214
503.235.9797

KOST, CHRISTOF
Christof Kost Basse
Bachstr. 62-64
52066 Aachen
Germany
011.49.241.531110
Fax: 011.49.241.509150

KOUCKY, BILL
Route #2
Box 424
East Jordan, MI 49072

KRAMER GUITARS
Distributed by Gibson
Musical Instruments – see
listing.

KRAUSE, ERIK
Die Gitarrenwerkstatt
Haslacher Str. 10
79115 Freiburg
Germany
ekrause@ruf.uni-freiburg.de
www.gitarrenwerkstatt.de

KRAWCZAK, KAZIMIERZ M.
63 Marshall Avenue
Warwick, RI 02886
401.739.3215

KREIDER, CRAIG
Lee Harbor, Inc.
1708 Lincoln Avenue
Panama City, FL 33972

KRIMMEL, MAX
Nederland, CO 80466
max@maxkrimmel.com
www.maxkrimmel.com

KROCHMAN, GREG
The Classic Ax
1024 16th Avenue South
Suite 203
Nashville, TN 37212

KRUEGER, JAMES
Broken String Music
133 Imperial Crescent
Bradford Ontario
Canada L3Z 2N3
krugdesn@pathcom.com

KYDD
Kydd Products
P.O. Box 2650
Upper Darby, PA 19082
800.622.KYDD
Distributed by Modulus
Guitars, Inc.
8 Digital Drive
Suite 101
Novato, CA 94949
800.758.2918
415.884.2300
Fax: 415.884.2373
www.modulusguitars.com

KYLE, DOUG
Fursdon, Moreton
Hampstead, Devon
England TQ13 8QT
44.647.70394

L.A. GUITAR WORKS
19320 Vanowen Street
Reseda, CA
818.758.8787
Fax: 818.758.8788

LKS GUITARS & MANDOLINS
8 Mt. Gilead Road
Thirroul NSW
Australia
lksguitars@ozemail.com.au
www.ozemail.com
.au/~lksguit

LTD
Distributed by the ESP
Guitar Company – see listing.

LA ROCQUE GUITARS
Furtwaengler Str. 9A
70195 Stuttgart
Germany
joerg.scherbaum@
metronet.de

LA SI DO, INC.
4240 Sere Street
St. Laurent Quebec
Canada H4T 1A6
514.343.5560
Fax: 514.343.5098
sales@lasido.com
www.lasido.com

LACE HELIX GUITARS
5561 Engineer Drive
Huntington Beach, CA
92649
800.575.5223
714.898.2776
Fax: 714.893.1045
info@agi-lace.com
www.agi-lace.com

LADO MUSICAL INC
205 St. David Street
Lindsay, Ontario
CANADA K9V 5K7
705.328.2005.
Fax: 705.328.0100
www.lado-guitars.com
ladomusic@on.aibn.com

LADY LUCK
Lady Luck Industries, Inc.
P.O. Box 195
Cary, IL 60013
708.639.8907
Fax: 708.639.7010
www.ladyluck.com

LAFAYETTE
A More Company
200 Governor Treutlen
Road
P.O. Box 956
Pooler, GA 31322
912.748.1101
Fax: 912.748.1106
brown@synsonics.com
www.synsonics.com

LAG
Sandell Trading Co.
Clearwater, FL 33767
727.298.0757
Fax: 727.442.3952

LAKLAND BASSES
2044 N. Dominick
Chicago, IL 60614
773.871.9637
Fax: 773.871.6675
lakland@msn.com
www.lakland.com

LANGEJANS GUITARS
P.O. Box 1857
Holland, MI 49422-1857
616.396.1776
Fax: 616.396.3105
langejan@macatawa.org

LARSON, KRISTOPHER
The Loft
315 N. 36th Street
Seattle, WA 98103

LAUGHLIN GUITARS
1551 East 4th Avenue
#163
Vancouver British
Columbia
Canada V5N 1J7
bob_laughlin@douglas.bc.ca
www.douglas.bc.ca
/~laughlin

LAUNHARDT
Gitarrenatelier &
Meisterwerkstatt
Garbenheimer StraBe 34
35578 Wetzlar
Germany
011-49-6441-444440
Fax: 011-49-6441-444441
Launhardt@topmail.de
www.launhardt.de

LAWRENCE FINE GUITARS
Larry Mills
6530 Baywood Lane
North College Hill, OH
45224

LEA ELECTRIC GUITARS
23 Division Street
East Islip, NY 11730
516.581.2804

LEACH, H.G.
P.O. Box 1315
Cedar Ridge, CA 95924
916.477.2938

LEDUC
Leduc Guitars and Basses
1, Place de L'eglise
57100 Thionville
France
+33.382.531616
Fax: +33.382.531717
leduc@wanadoo.fr
www.perso.wanadoo.fr/leduc/
Distributed by Leduc/Logabass Instruments
10121 Stonehurst Avenue
Sun Valley, CA 91352
516.266.1957
Fax: 516.266.2568

LEGEND CUSTOM GUITARS
15 Durham Way
Dartmouth Nova Scotia
Canada B2V 1X1
902.462.6292

LEVESQUE GUITARS
Alan Levesque
6204 Moray Avenue
New Port Richey, FL 34653
levesque@gate.net

LIBERTY, GENE
(P.O. Box 506)
112 S. Bushnell Street
Sheridan, IL 60551
815.496.9092
guitarfix@snd.softfarm.com
mmm.snd.softfarm.com/guitarfix

LIGHTWAVES SYSTEMS
P.O. Box 691
Santa Barbera, CA 93101
800.548.6669
805.563.2202
Fax: 805.569.4060
info@aolightway.com
www.mallennium.com/AOLIGHTWAVE.COM

LILLARD, JAMES D.
Jay Dee's Guitar Repair
1869 Madison Avenue
Memphis, TN 38104-2621
jaydeegtr@aol.com
members.aol.com/jaydeegtr/index.html

LINC LUTHIER
1318 N. Monte Vista Avenue #11
Upland, CA 91786
909.931.0642
Fax: 909.931.1713
LincInc@aol.com
www.members.aol.com/lincinc/lincluthier.html

LINDERT GUITARS, INC.
Box 172
Chelan, WA 98816
888.805.4633
509.682.2360
Fax: 509.682.1209
info@lindertguitars.com
www.lindertguitars.com

LINN SAHLI
73458 Highway 111
Palm Desert, CA 92260
760.346.6901

LINDSEY INSTRUMENTS
Kaono Lindsey
2806 Booth Road
Pauoa Valley, HI 96813
ukuman@lava.net

LIVERMAN, JEFF
1722 Elmsmere
Richmond, VA 23227

LIVESEY, THOMAS B.
T. B. Livesey Guitars
P.O. Box 215
Gin Gin Queensland
Australia 4671
couzens@mpx.com.au
www.mpx.com.au

LOBEN SELS, HANS VAN
Teut 96
Amersfoort 3811 W2
Netherlands
loben@kpd.nl
www.domeinen.net/lobelsels

LOGABASS
Distributed by Leduc/Logabass Instruments
See Listing Under LEDUC
S S S Sound Co., Ltd.
P.O. Box No. 1
Kanie Aichi Japan 497
05675.2.3888

LOPEZ, ABEL GARCIA
Guerrero 383
C.P. 60250
Paracho Michoacan
Mexico
52.(452)50239
Fax: 52.(452)50873

LORENZO, FRIGNANI
Via F. Baracca 38
41031 Camposanto (MO)
Italy
0535.87056

LOTUS
Distributed by Midco International – see listing.

LUCENA
Distributed by Music Imports of San Diego, California.

LUCIANO, LOVADINA
Via Verdi 5
31030 Arcade (TV)
Italy
0422.720212
Fax: 0422.720212

LUCK, CHRISTOPHER
RR #2, Box 1590
South China, ME 04358
celuck@pivot.net

LUIS, ARBAN
Via Darwin 17
52100 Arezzo
Italy
0575.381709

LYON, G.W.
Distributed by Washburn International
255 Corporate Woods Parkway
Vernon Hills, IL 60061-3109
800.US.SOUND
708.913.5511
Fax: 708.913.7772
jhawk103@aol.com
www.washburn.com

LYRIC GUITARS
56 E. 53rd Place
Tulsa, OK 74105
918.747.7380

MB GUITARS
Marion Music
4970 Stack Blvd. # b-3
Melbourne FL 32901
mbeckert@digital.net

MDX
MDX Sound Lab
736 Cromwell Street
West Point, MS 39773
601.494.8777
dann@mdxguitars.com
www.mdxguitars.com

MJ GUITAR ENGINEERING
643 Martin Avenue #2
Rohnert Park, CA 95928
707.588.8075
Fax: 707.588.8160
mjguitar@aol.com
www.mjguitar.com

MTD
Michael Tobias Design
760 Zena Highwoods Road
Kingston, NY 12401
845.246.0670
Fax: 845.246.1670
mike@mtdbass.com
www.mtdbass.com

MCALISTER GUITARS
40 Eucalyptus Dr.
Watsonville, CA 95076
831.761.2519
www.mcalisterguitars.com

McARTHUR, GRAHAM
9 Eileen Street
Modbury South Australia
Australia 5092
grahammc@camtech.net.au

McCOLLUM GUITARS
P.O Box 806
ColFax, CA 95713-0806
530.346.7657
mccollum@netshel.net
www.svlg.org

McCURDY, RIC
19 Hudson Street
New York, NY 10013-3822
212.274.8352
McCurdygtr@aol.com

McDERMOTT GUITARS
Dennis McDermott
Bizarre Guitars
1930 S. Greenwood
Wichita, KS 67211

McDONALD, GRAHAM
P.O. Box 365
Jamison ACT
Australia 2614
www.spirit.com.au/~gramac/instruments.html

McGILL GUITARS
2818 Columbine Place
Nashville, TN 37209
615.385.9071
Fax: 615.352.9876
conecaster@aol.com

McHUGH GUITARS
P.O. Box 2216
Northbrook, IL 60065-2216
847.498.3319

McINTURFF GUITARS
200-C Irving Parkway
Holly Springs, NC 27540
919.552.4586
Fax: 919.552.0542
www.mcinturffguitars.com
info@mcinturffguitars.com

McLAREN
McLaren Products
3519 Mt. Ariane Dr.
San Diego, CA 92111
619.874.8899
Fax: 619.874.8899

McLEOD HANDCRAFTED INSTRUMENTS
37539 97th Street East
Littlerock, CA 93543
dgmcleod@qnet.com

MCPHERSON GUITAR
P.O. Box 367, River Road
Sparta, WI 54655
608.629.2728

McSWAIN GUITARS
1237 Hollywood Way, Apt C
Burbank, CA 91505
818.842.1176
Fax: 818.842.1176
mcswainguitars@worldnet.att.net
www.mcswainguitars.com

MACDONALD, S.B.
22 Fairmont Street
Huntington, NY 11743
516.421.9056
guitardoc@earthlink.net
www.home.earthlink.net/~guitardoc/

M.A.C. SOUND
See PHILLIP MURRAY

MADDEN GUITARS
202 Fifth Avenue North
Franklin, TN 37064
strgwndr@aol.com
www.tndirectory.com/maddenguitars

MAGNUS KREMPEL
Weilburger StraBe 8
35796 Weinback
Germany
011.49.6471.41392

AILLETTE, BENOIT
ustom Hand Made
uitars
9 16th Avenue
oxboro Quebec
anada H8Y 2Y2
nasson@worldnet.att.net
www.home.att.net/~mas-
on/bm.html

AJKOWSKI, GEORGE
3012 Pt. Richmond Drive
NW
Gig Harbor, WA 98332
arek@wolfenet.com

MALLON
Distributed by Menkevich
Guitars
5013 Tulip Street
Philadelphia, PA 19135
215.288.8417

MANNE GUITARS
Andrea Ballarin
Via Paraiso, #28
Schio VI
Italy 36015
+39.445.673872
Fax: +39.445.512452
info@manne.com
www.manne.com

MANSON
A.B. Manson & Co.
Easterbrook, Hittisliegh
Exeter EX6 6LR
England
0647.24139
Fax: 0647.24140
Manson Guitars
Vellake, Sandford
Crediton, Devon EX17
4EH
United Kingdom
44.01363.775603
Distributed in the U.S. by
Eichelbaum Guitars
1735 Mountain Avenue
Santa Barbara, CA 93101
805.563.6028
deguitars@aol.com
www.escribes.com/eichel-
baum

MANZANITA GUITARS
Sellenfried 3
D-37124 Rosdorf
Germany
49.551.782.417
Fax: 49.551.782.417
info@manzanita.de
www.manzanita.de

MARCHIONE GUITARS
20 West 20th Street
Suite 806
New York, NY 10011
212.675.5215
Fax: 212.675.6356
www.marchione.com/

MARINOSSON, EGGERT MAR
Tonastoedin h/f
Skipholt 50 D
Reykjavik
Iceland 105

MARIO, GRIMALDI
Via Lamarmora 2
Trisobbio (AL)
Italy 15070
0143.831947

MARIO, NOVELLI
Via Nogariole 43
Giavera del Montello (TV)
Italy
0422.770216

MARLEAUX BASS GUITARS
Zellweg 20
38678 Clausthal-Zellerfeld
Germany
011.49.5323.8.1747
Fax: 011.49.5323.2379
Distributed through the
Luthiers Access Group
P.O. Box 388798
Chicago, IL 60638-8798
708.974.4022
Fax: 708.974.4022
luacgrp@millnet.net
www.essentialstrings.com/l
uacgrp.htm

MARTELL GUITARS UNLIMITED
2158 East 39th Avenue
Vancouver British
Columbia
Canada V5P 1H7
amirault@smartt.com
www.personal.smartt.com/
~amirault/

MARTIN
The C.F. Martin Guitar
Company
510 Sycamore Street
Nazareth, PA 18064-9233
800.345.3103
610.759.2837
Fax: 610.759.5757
info@mguitar.com
www.mguitar.com

MARTINA, ELLIO
Eefde
The Netherlands

MASTER
Master Handmade Guitars
7336 Santa Monica Blvd.
#663
W. Hollywood, CA 90046
310.228.3185
masterguitars@usa.com
www.masterguitars.hyper-
mart.net

MASTER'S BASS
Master's Bass Company
3001 Fadal Avenue
Waco, TX 76708
817.756.3310

MATLIN GUITARS
Mendocino, CA
www.mcn.org/Men
ComNet
/Business/Retail/matlin/
matlin1.html

MATON GUITARS
9-11 Kelvin Road
North Bayswater, Victoria
Australia 3153
03.97207259
Fax: 03.9720.7273
Haidin@maton.com.au

MAUEL GUITARS
77 Sylvan Vista Drive
Auburn, CA 95603
whmauel@neworld.net

MAUI MUSIC
Maui Music Guitars &
Acoustic Bass
808.667.5711

MAXTONE
Maxtone Musical
Instrument Mfg. Co., Ltd.
(Ta Feng Long Enterprises
Co., Ltd.)
3F, #400 Taichung-Kang
Road, Sec. 1
Tai Chung Taiwan ROC
011.886.4.313.2115
Fax: 011.886.4.313.2493
maxtone@ms7.hinet.net

MAYORCA
Distributed by Tropical
Music Corporation
7091 N.W. 51st Street
Miami, FL 33166-5629
305.594.3909
Fax: 305.594.0786
www.tropicalmusic.com

MEARS, MIKE
Windy Hill GuitarWorks
10160 Hampton Road
FairFax Station, VA 22039
mearsman2@aol.com

MEGAS, TED
Arch Top Guitar Maker
1070 Van Dyke
San Francisco, CA 94124
415.822.3100
Fax: 415.822.1454
tmegas@infinex.com

MELANCON GUITARS
249 W. Main Street
Thibodaux, LA 70301
504.447.4090
Fax: 504.447.4090
melanconguitars@mobile.te
l.com

MELOBAR
Melobar Guitars, Inc.
Distributed by Smith
Family Music Products
9175 Butte Road
Sweet, ID 83670
800.942.6509
208.584.3349
Fax: 208.584.3312
Enhancr@micron.net

MENDEZ, JOSE
Oncativo 2026
Lanus 1824
Buenos Aires
Argentina
cc951048@bed.buenayre.
com.ar

MENKEVICH GUITARS
1401 Church Street
Philadelphia, PA 19124
215.288.8417
menkguitar@icdc.com
www.icdc.com/~menkevich

MERCHANT VERTICAL BASS CO.
208 West 29th St., Ste. 213
New York City, NY 10001
www.merchantbass.com
merchant@pipeline.com

MERKEL, STEVE
Integrity Music
1000 Cody Road
Mobile, AL 36695

MERMER GUITARS
P.O. Box 782132
Sebastian, FL 32958-4014
561.388.0317
mermer@gate.net
www.gate.net/~mermer

MERVI
Guitarras Mervi S.L.
Abellaroi, 3
San Antonio de Benageber
Valencia 46814
Spain
346.1350336
Fax: 346.1350220

MESSENGER
Messenger Upright Electric
Bass & Guitars
P.O. Box 945
Forrestville, CA 95436
707.887.2709
john@messengerbass.com
www.messengerbass.com

METAL DRIVER
Sumer Musical Instruments
Co., Ltd.
#645-55 Airport B/D
3F, Bangwah 2-Dong
Kangseo-Ku
Seoul Korea
2.666.0382
Fax: 2.666.0385

METROPOLITAN
Distributed by Alamo
Music Products
3526 East T.C. Jester Blvd.
Houston, TX 77018
713.957.0470
Fax: 713.957.3316
www.metropolitanguitars.c
om

MICHAUD, SERGE
See SERGE

MICHELE, DELLA GIUSTINA
Via della Seta 35
Italy
0438.912378

MICK, BOB
Bob Mick Guitars
19 East Toole
Tucson, AZ 85701
520.327.5800

MIDCO INTERNATIONAL
P.O. Box 748
908 W. Fayette Avenue
Effingham, IL 62401
800.35.MIDCO
800.356.4326
Fax: 800.700.7006

MIDI AXE

Virtual DSP Corporation
4119 125th Street SE
Everett, WA 98208
425.338.5221
Fax: 425.379.8888
www.midiaxe.com

MIKE LULL CUSTOM GUITARS
Mike Lull's Guitar Works
13240 NE 20th, Suite #2
Bellevue, WA 98005
425.643.8074
Fax: 425.746.5748
guitarwk@mikelull.com
www.mikelull.com

MILBURN GUITARS
28093 Liberty Road
Sweet Home, OR 97386
omilburn@dswebnet.com
www.weber.u.washington.edu/~patm

MILLENIUM GUITARS
P.O. Box 1068
Pasadena, CA 91102
626.574.8350

MILLER
Miller Guitars & Basses
SonnhoglstraBe 7
D-94439 Rossbach
Germany
011.49.8547.7508
Fax: 011.49.8547.7948
info@millerguitars.com
www.millerguitars.com

MITCHNECK, AARON J.
Back Mountain Music Company
433 S. Memorial Highway
Trucksville, PA 18708
ajnemasis@aol.com

MODULUS GUITARS
8 Digital Drive
Suite 101
Novato, CA 94949
800.758.2918
415.884.2300
Fax: 415.884.2373
www.modulusguitars.com

MOJO GUITARS
6630 Sussex Avenue #301
Burnaby British Columbia
Canada V5H 3C6
amirault@smartt.com
www.personal.smartt.com/~amirault

MOLINI CUSTOM GUITARS
441 Briarwood Road
Columbia, SC 29206
molini@mailexcite.com

MOLL CUSTOM INSTRUMENTS
720 E. Cherokee
Springfield, MO 65807-2706
417.883.9946
mollinst@ix.netcom.com
www.mollinst.com

MONCLOA GUITARS
M. Prado Ugarteche 626
La Estancia, La Molina
Lima 12
Peru
511.368.0260
511.479.8456
Fax: 511.479.0266
daniel@net.casopidata.com.pe
www.members.tripod.com/~moncloa

MONIQUE
Distributed by V.J. Rendano Music Company, Inc. – see listing.

MONTELEONE, JOHN
Custom Mandolin and Guitar Maker
(P.O. Box 52
Islip, NY 11751)
41 Degnon Blvd.
Bay Shore, NY 11706
516.277.3620
Fax: 516.277.3639

MOON
Moon Corporation
3F 2-28-7 Akabane Kita-ku
Tokyo Japan T115
81.3.3598.1661
Fax: 81.3.3598.1682
Distributed through the Luthiers Access Group
P.O. Box 388798
Chicago, IL 60638-8798
708.974.4022
Fax: 708.974.4022
luacgrp@millnet.net
www.essentialstrings.com/luacgrp.htm

MOON GUITARS LTD.
974 Pollokshaws Road
Glasgow G41 2HA
Scotland
Phone/Fax:
011.44.141.632.9526

MOONEY, FERGUS
4579 Chatterton Way
Victoria British Columbia
Canada A8X 4Y7
fmooney@direct.ca

MOONSTONE GUITARS
P.O. Box 757
Eureka, CA 95502
707.445.9045
www.moonstoneguitars.com
steve@moonstoneguitars.com

MOORADIAN
Distributed by Matthews & Ryan
800.248.4827

MORCH GUITARS
Voer Faergevej 104
8950 Orsted
Denmark
Phone/Fax:
011.45.86.48.89.23
www.morch-guitars.dk

MORGAINE
Distributed by CMS Cotton Music Supply
Kumeliusstr. 14
61440 Oberursel
Germany
06171.53306
Fax: 06171.53499
Juergen.Kirschner@rhein-main.netsurf.de
www.transfer.de/cms

MORRIS
Moridaira Musical Instrument Company, Ltd.
2-7-4 Iwatioto-Cho
Chiyoda-Ku
Tokyo 101
Japan
81.3.3862.1641
Fax: 81.3.3864.7454
mmi@kiwi.co.jp

MORRONE, MARCELLO
Via Panebianco II Strada 32
Cosenza
Italy 87100
mmorron@tin.it

MORTORO, GARY
P.O. Box 161225
Miami, FL 33116-1225
305.238.7947
Fax: 305.259.8745
mortorogtr@aol.com

MOSCATO
Quartier Roquecourbe
Uchaux
84100 France
04.90.40.6657
Fax: 06.09.33.5686

MOSES, INC.
Moses Graphite Musical Instruments
P.O. Box 10028
Eugene, OR 97440
Phone/Fax: 541.484.6068
Orders@mosesgraphite.com
www.mosesgraphite.com

MOURADIAN GUITARS & BASSES
1904 Mass Avenue
Cambridge, MA 02140
617.547.7500
www.MGuitars.com

MUDGE BASSES
P.O. Box 21279
Oakland, CA 94620
510.581.2825
www.mudgebass.com

MUNCY
Muncy Guitar Company
128 Oak Drive
Kingston, TN 37763
423.717.0165

MUNSON, C. D.
Red Wing Tech Inc.
Hwy. 58 & Pioneer Road
Red Wing, MN 55066

MURRAY, PHILLIP
M.A.C. Sound
No. 17 Idrone Close
Knocklyon
Dublin 16
Ireland
phillip@clubi.ie

MUSIC DRIVE
Sumer Musical Instruments Co. Ltd.
Mori Bldg.
3F 2-6-6 Jingu Atsuta-ku
Nagoya Japan
456
+81.52.682.8905
Fax: +81.52.682.8906
Sumer Korea
#538 Wanggil-Dong
Seo-Ku
Inchon City Korea
+82.32.564.8283
Fax: +82.32.563.8285
Distributed by Sumer USA
9792 Edmonds Way, #126
Edmonds, WA 98020
425.771.4571
Fax: 425.775.8562
amasia@earthlink.net
2017 Seaview Drive
Fullerton, CA 92833
714.278.9082
Fax: 714.879.2763
sumerusa@hotmail.com

MUSICIAN SOUND DESIGN
Lindenstr. 32
50674 Koln (Cologne)
Germany
221.2409614
Fax: 221.2409615

MUSICVOX CORPORATION
600 Kings Hwy N. #PMB-167
Cherry Hill, NJ 08034-1505
609.667.0444
Fax: 609.667.5527
www.musicvox.com
guitar@musicvox.com

MUSIMA
Musikinstrumenten Manufaktur GmbH
PestalozzistraBe 25
D-08258 Markneukirchen
Germany
37.422.5700
Fax: 37.422.2441

MYERS, MATT
609 Pine
Muscatine, IA 52761
319.264.5138

MYHRVOLD, KNUT
Gitar Doktor'n
Haukedalsv. 66
3960 Stathelle
Norway
gitardoktorn@tm.telia.no

MYLES, CHRISTOPHER
P.O. Box 675
Silverton, CO 81433-0675
970.387.0185

YTHIC GUITAR OMPANY
'ind O'Neal
len Burnie, MD 21060
inds@sprynet.com
ome.sprynet.com/sprynet/inds

.I.C.E. GUITARS
andererStrasse 6
H-4057 Basel
witzerland
hone/Fax:
11.41.61.692.2306
liceguitars@active.ch

STEIN
Combination Bass and Guitar
11 Orchard Street
onkers, NY 10703
14.376.4128

NB CUSTOM GUITARS
251 10th Street
Courtenay, British Columbia
Canada V9N 1R8
50.338.6834
nbcustom@island.net
www.island.net/nbcustom/

NS DESIGN
420 Hilltop Road
Nobleboro, ME 045555
207.563.7700
www.nedsteinberger.com

NYC MUSIC PRODUCTS
Matthews & Ryan Musical Products
68 34th Street
Brooklyn, NY 11232
800.248.4827
718.832.6333
Fax: 718.832.5270
matthewsandryan@compuserve.com
www.matthewsandryan.com

NAPOLITANO, ARTHUR
P.O. Box 0294
Allentown, NJ 08501
609.259.8818

NEAL MOSER GUITARS
Distributed by GMW Guitarworks
220 N. Glendora Avenue
Glendora, CA 91740
818.914.8082
Fax: 818.914.4287

NECHVILLE MUSICAL PRODUCTS
10021 Third Avenue S.
Bloomington, MN 55420-4921
612.888.9710
Fax: 612.888.4140

NEO
NEO Products, Inc.
1800 V Mearns Road
Warminster, PA 18974
215.773.9995
Fax: 215.773.9996
neopro@voicenet.com
www.voicenet.com/~neopro

NEUSER BASS GUITARS
Neuser Co., Ltd.
Hulivarinne 9a
02730 Espoo
Finland
011.358.9.599645
Fax: 011.358.9.593322
basses@neuserbasses.com
www.neuserbasses.com

NEWTON, DAVID
Beaumont, TX
d.newton@worldnet.att.net

NICKERSON GUITARS
8 Easthampton Rd.
Northampton MA 01060
413.586.8521

NIGHTINGALE
25 Denmark Street
London WC2H 8NJ
England
0171.379.3572

NIXON CUSTOM GUITARS
47 A McCurtain Street
Cork
Ireland
arthive@indigo.ie

NOBLE GUITARS
The Old Rectory
Alvechurch
Birmingham B48 7SU
United Kingdon
011.44.121.447.8089
Fax: 011.44.121.445.6144

NOBLES, TONY
Distributed by Precision Guitarworks
9705 Burnet Rd. #109
Austin, TX 78758
512.836.4838

NORRIS, SUSAN
Vermont Musical Instrument Builders Cooperative
RD #1, Box 2250
Plainfield VT 05667

NORTH, JAMES
810.227.7072
www.ismi.net/upnorth

NOVAX
Novax Fanned Fret Guitars
940 A Estabrook
San Leandro, CA 94577
Phone/Fax: 510.483.3599
www.novaxguitars.com
novax@netwiz.net

OFB GUITARS
953 REON Drive #B
Virginia Beach, VA 23464-3811
804.523.9278

OLD WOODS GUITARS
Stacy Woods
3354 Bagdad Road
Bagdad, KY 40003
gufb27a@prodigy.com

OPSTAL, GEERT VAN
Berkenlaan 8
Leon op Zand
CH 5175
Netherlands
0130.416362690
luthier@worldonline.nl

OREHEK, TYLER
162 West 54th Street
Suite 10 A
New York, NY 10019
orehek@aol.com

OSCAR SCHMIDT
Oscar Schmidt International
Distributed by Washburn International
255 Corporate Woods Parkway
Vernon Hills, IL 600061-3109
800.877.6863
847.913.5511
Fax: 847.913.7772
washburn@washburn.com
www.washburn.com

OTHON GUITARS
Golden State Art Works
8838 Greenback Lane
Orangevale, CA 95662
916.988.8533
Fax: 916.988.0170

OTTALAGANO, VINCE
Vishnu Music
(P.O. Box 1248)
64 North Main Street
Gloversville, NY 12078
vincent@superior.net

OVATION
Distributed by the Kaman Music Corporation – see listing.

OVERWATER
Atlas Works, Nelson Street
Carlisle, Cumbria
United Kingdom
CA2 5ND
01228.590591
Fax: 01228.590597
www.overwaterbasses.com
info@overwaterbasses.com

OXRIEDER, GREGORY
Handmade Guitars
10617 NE 13th
Bellevue, WA 98004

PBC
PBC Guitar Technology
See BUNKER.
Utah
www.bunker-guitar.com

PALM BAY LTD.
7 Gleneagles Drive
Southwood
Farnborough
Hampshire
GU14 0PH
England
(0) 1252.660530
Fax: (0) 1252.523927
amacbay@aol.com
www.palmbayguitars.com

PALMER
Distributed by Chesbro Music Company
P.O. Box 2009
Idaho Falls, ID 83403
800.CHE.SBRO
800.243.7276
Fax: 208.522.8712
cmc@srv.net
Distributed by Tropical Music Corporation
7091 N.W. 51st Street
Miami, FL 33166-5629
305.594.3909
Fax: 305.594.0786
www.tropicalmusic.com

PALMWOOD GUITARS & STRINGED INSTRUMENTS
92 Thomas Street
Wellington Pt. Queensland
Australia 4159
c/o: j.owens@qca.gu.edu.qu

PAOLO, CORIANI
Via Barchetta 98
Moderna
Italy 41100
075.8041485

PARADIS GUITARWORKS
Waldeggstr. 8
CH 8405 Winterthur
Switzerland
41.52.233.34.43
Fax: 41.52.233.34.43

PARKER GUITARS
Distributed by Korg USA
316 South Service Road
Melville, NY 11747-3201
800.645.3188
516.333.9100
Fax: 516.333.9108
www.korg.com

PARROT PRODUCTIONS
2390 Ocean Pines
Berlin, MD 215811
kraccheo@dmv.com

PASCALI, LUIGI DE
P.O. Box
Avuily - Geneva
Switzerland 1237
41.22.756.25.38

PATRICK EGGLE GUITARS
Queens Chambers
Old Snow Hill
Birmingham B4 6HW
England
0121.2121989
Fax: 0121.2121990

PATTERSON GUITARS
1417 Iowa Avenue West
Falcon Heights, MN 55108
651.647.5701
Fax: 651.647.5701
info@pattersonguitars.com
www.pattersonguitars.com.

PAUL REED SMITH (PRS)
Paul Reed Smith Guitars
380 Log Canoe Circle
Stevensville, MD 21666
410.643.9970
Fax: 410.643.9980
www.prsguitars.com

PAWAR GUITARS
28262 Chardon Rd.
Willoughby Hills, OH
44092
440.953.1999
Fax: 440.953.0183
www.pawarguitars.com
dealerservice@pawar
guitars.com

PAUL'S GUITARS
740 N. 10th Street
Spearfish, SD 57783
ccr7861@mystic.bhsu.edu

PEAR DESIGN
Pear Custom Guitars
1039 Serpentine Ln.
Suite E
Pleasanton, CA 94566
925.462.2857
www.peardesign.com

PEAVEY
Peavey Electronics
Corporation
711 A Street
Meridian, MS 39301
601.483.5365
Fax: 601.486.1278
www.peavey.com

PECK, DARRYL J.
2 Indian Road
Dudley, MA 01571
c-dpeck@ma.ultranet.com

PEDULLA, M.V.
M. V. Pedulla
Guitars, Inc.
P.O. Box 226
Rockland, MA 02370
781.871.0073
Fax: 781.878.4028
christin@pedulla.com
www.pedulla.com

PENSA CLASSIC
Distributed by Rudy's
Music Shop
169 West 48th St.
New York, NY 10036
212.391.1699
Fax: 212.768.3782

PERFORMANCE
3621 Cahuenga Blvd.
Hollywood, CA 90068
213.883.0781
Fax: 213.883.0997

PERRON CUSTOM GUITARS
25471 CR 24
Elkhart, IN 46517
102377.1047@
compuserve.com

PERRY, DARYL
The Guitar Suite
500-100 Arthur Street
Winnipeg Manitoba
Canada R3B 1H3

PETE BACK CUSTOM GUITARS
8 Silver Street
Reeth, Richmond
North Yorkshire
England DL11 6SP
Phone/Fax:
011.44.1748.884887
Guitarman@guitarmaker.
co.uk
www.guitarmaker.co.uk

PETILLO, PHILLIP
Petillo Masterpiece Guitars
1206 Herbert Avenue
Ocean, NJ 07712
908.531.6338

PETTA, MARCO ANTONIO
Av. 1, Hoyada de Milla,
No. 0-259
Merida
Venezuela 5201-A

PHANTOM GUITAR WORKS, INC.
2000 NE 42nd, Suite 231
Portland, OR 97213
503.282.6799
Fax: 503.282.6799

PHIL
Myung Sung Music Ind.
Co., Ltd.
#143 Deung Won Ri
Jori-Myon Paju-City
Kyungki-Do Korea
011.82.348.941.5477
Fax: 011.82.348.941.7938

PHIL HARMONIC GUITARS
4388 County Road 7640
West Plains, MO 65775
sparky@townsqr.com

PHILIP KUBICKI GUITARS
726 Bond Avenue
Santa Barbara, CA 93103
805.963.6703
Fax: 805.963.0380

PHOENIX
Phoenix Guitar Company
6030 E. Le Marche
Scottsdale, AZ 85254
602.553.0005
Fax: 602.553.0646

PICATO
Distributed by Saga
Musical Instruments
429 Littlefield Avenue
South San Francisco, CA
94080
800.BUY.SAGA
415.588.5558
415.871.7590

PIGNOSE INDUSTRIES
400 W. Alondra Blvd.
Gardena, CA 90248
213.770.4444
Fax: 310.538.9560

PLANET GUITARS
1117 Semlin Drive
Vancouver British
Columbia
Canada V5L 4K3
classical@musician.org
www.intergate.bc.ca
/business/magi

POOLE CUSTOM GUITARS
4 Portway Road
Cliffe Woods
Rochester, Kent ME3 8JA
England
011.44.1634.220817
Fax: 011.44.1634.220129
www.poolecustomguitars.co
.uk
sidpoole@poolecustomgui-
tars.co.uk

POSHEK
751 Rembrandt
Laguna Beach, CA 92651
poshek@aol.com

PREMIER
Premier Guitars & Amps
Distributed by the
Entertainment Music
Marketing Corp.
770-12 Grand Blvd.
Deer Park, NY 117219
800.345.6013
516.243.0600
Fax: 516.243.0605

PRICE ENTERPRISES
P.O. Box 1115
Jones, OK 73049
ghprice@telepath.com

PRISLOE, THOMAS
P.O. Box 99
Mesa, CO 81643
prisloe@gj.net
www.gj.net/~prisloe

QUEST
Music Industries
Corporation
99 Tulip Ave.
Floral Park
New York, NY 11001
800.431.6699
516.352.4110
Fax: 516.352.0754
www.musicindustries.com

R & L
See ED ROMAN

RBC
995 W. 3rd Street
North Vancouver British
Columbia
Canada V7P 1E4
amirault@smartt.com
www.personal.smartt.com/~
amirault/rbc.html

RJS GUITARS
Fort Worth, TX 76116
817.738.5780
RJSGuitar@webtv.net

RWK GUITARS
P.O. Box 1068
Highland Park, IL 60035
800.454.7078
www.rwkguitars.com
bob@rwkguitars.com

RAGGHIANTI, FABIO
Via Fornace 10
Caprigna (LU)
Italy 55045
0584.796050

RAIMI, RICHARD
4028 Woodland Park
Avenue N.
Seattle, WA

RAINSONG
Rainsong Graphite Guitars
300 Ohukai Road #C-214
Kihei, HI 96753
rainsongki@aol.com
www.rainsong.com

RAJ GUITAR CRAFTS
Distributed by L.A. Guitar
Works – see listing.

RALSTON
P.O. Box 138
Grant Town, WV 26574
304.278.5645

RAMIREZ, RAY
Ray Ramirez Basses
20 Esmeralda Street
Humacao, Puerto Rico
00791
Phone/Fax: 787.852.1476
Cell: 787.613.0906
rramirez@coqui.net
www.rayramirezbasses.com

RAMTRAK
Distributed by World Cla
Engineered Products
24900 Capital
Redford, MI 48239
313.538.1200
Fax: 313.538.1255
jimgtr@flash.net
www.ramtrak.com

RANSOM
15 LaFayette St.
San Francisco, CA 94103
415.864.3281

RAREBIRD GUITARS
P.O. Box 211094
Denver, CO 80221-9998
303.657.0056
6406 Raleigh Street
Arvada, CO 80003-6435

RASPAGNI, CARLO
Via Vitt. Veneto 7
Vignate (MI)
Italy
02.9566089

RAVEN
c/o Bearingdale Guitars &
Basses
01582.597651
Fax: 01582.599994

RAYA AND RAYA
Paseo del Salon 9
Granada
Spain 18009

READ CUSTOM INSTRUMENTS
Bolton, MA

REBERGEN, JOHAN
Joh. Camphuysstraat 47
Utrecht 3534 ES
Holland

REDWING GUITARS
P.O. Box 125
St. Albans Herts.
AL1 1PX United Kingdom
1727.838.808
Fax: 1727.838.808
101625.516@compuserve.com

EDMAN
stributed by Reedman
nerica
006 Philadelphia Street,
ite 301
hittier, CA 90601
0.698.2645
x: 310.698.1074

ENAISSANCE
UITARS
). Box 7440
nta Cruz, CA 95060-
40
)0.644.5268
x: 510.757.0021
ww.renaissance
itars.com

ESURRECTION
UITARS
334 NE Jensen Beach
lvd. #5
nsen Beach, FL 34957
61.232.0089
ax: 561.287.5343
m@resurrectionguitars.com
ww.resurrectionguitars.com

EVEREND MUSICAL
NSTRUMENTS
3109 Gratiot Ave., Room

astpointe, MI 48201
10.775.1025
ax: 810.775.2991
www.reverendmusical.com
everendmu@aol.com

REYNOLDS MUSICAL
NSTRUMENTS
3905 Sam Carter
Austin, TX 78736
512.288.5298

REYNOLDS, JON
The Custom Job
P.O. Box 872
Angwin, CA 94508
thecustomjob@
angelfire.com
www.angelfire.com/biz/the-
customjob

RHINEHART GUITARS
Billy Rhinehart
14 Second Street
Athens, OH 45701
www.eurekanet.com/~rhine
hart/

RIBBECKE, TOM
P.O. Box 2215
Healdsburg, CA 95448
707.433.3778
Ribguitar@aol.com

RICE, KEN
701 Cypress Wood Cove
Chesapeake, VA 23323
krice@macs.net

RICKENBACKER
Rickenbacker International
Corporation
3895 S. Main Street
Santa Ana, CA 92707-
5710
714.545.5574
Fax: 714.754.0135
info@rickenbacker.com
www.rickenbacker.com

RITTER BASS GUITARS
Holzweg 119
D-67098 Bad Durkheim
Germany
001.49.6322.981364
Fax: 011.49.6322.981365
info@ritter-basses.com
www.ritter-basses.com

RIVERHEAD
Headway Co., Ltd.
6007 Sasaga
Matsumoto, Nagano 399
Japan
0263.26.8798
Fax: 0263.26.8324

RIZSANYI, GEORGE
Hands On Music
50 King Street E.
Bowmanville Ontario
Canada L1N 1C2
fretboy@gsfmicro.com
www.gsfmicro.com

RIZZOLO, GARY
The Guitar Company
113 York Street
Sandy Bay Hobart
Tasmania 7005
rizzolo@netspace.net.au

ROBIN GUITARS
Distributed by Alamo
Music Products
3526 East T.C. Jester Blvd.
Houston, TX 77018
713.957.0470
Fax: 713.957.3316
robintx@io.com
www.io.com/~robintx

ROBINSON CUSTOM
GUITARS
23 Columbus Avenue
Newburyport, MA 01950
508.465.3959
Fax: 508.465.3959

ROBOSSON, THAD
Precision Guitar
4442 N. 7th Avenue
Suite 6
Phoenix, AZ 85013
tmrob@primenet.com

RODRIGUEZ, ALBERTO
PAREDES
Transversal 68D #79A-15
Santafe de Bogot
Bogota
Columbia
albertoparedes@
hotmail.com

RODRIGUEZ GUITARS
929 Meyers Street
Richmond, VA 23230

ROGUE
Distributed in the U.S by
Musician's Friend
931 Chevy Way
Medford, OR 97504
Also:
P.O. Box 4520
Medford, OR 97501
800.776.5176
Fax: 541.776.1370
support@musiciansfriend.
com
www.musiciansfriend.com

ROK AXE
Muse
Namdong Industrial Estate
Inchon
Korea 156
032.811.6481
Fax: 032.811.6488

ROKKOR
Distributed by L.A. Guitar
Works – see listing.

ROLAND
Roland Musical
Instruments
7200 Cominon Circle
Los Angeles, CA 90040-
3696
213.685.5141
Fax: 213.722.0911
rolandpr@aol.com
www.rolandus.com

ROMAN, ED
Ed Roman Guitars
36 Tamarack Avenue
Danbury, CT 06811
203.746.4995
www.edromanguitars.com

ROMANTIC GUITAR &
MANDOLIN CO.
25 Wood Street 2411
Toronto Ontario
Canada M4Y 2P9
romantic@aracnet.net

ROMPRE, JEAN
460 Ste. - Catherine West.
Montreal Quebec
Canada H3B 1A7
ad791876@er.uquam.ca

ROSCOE GUITARS
(P.O. Box 5404)
332 A Tate Street
Greensboro, NC 27435
910.274.8810
Fax: 910.275.4469

ROSE, JONATHAN W.
1208 W. Main Street
Hendersonville, TN 37075
800.597.1720
615.822.6818

ROSE, ROGER
620 B Blandy Drive
Colts Neck, NJ 07722-
5034
rose@myhost.com

ROSENTHAL, GERALD
69 Plympton Street
Waltham, MA 02154

ROWAN CUSTOM
GUITARS
809 Meadowgate Drive
Garland, TX 75040
972.495.2413
www.rowanguitars.com

ROY, RENE
Sudbury, Ontario
Canada
705.521.7328
www.byreneroyguitars.com

ROY CUSTOM
GUITARS
Chelmsford (Ontario),
Canada

RUMER GUITAR
WORKS
P.O. Box 364
Rollinsville, CO 80474
303.642.3665
Fax: 303.234.5488

RYBSKI
Distributed through the
Luthiers Access Group
P.O. Box 388798
Chicago, IL 60638-8798
708.974.4022
Fax: 708.974.4022
luacgrp@millnet.net
www.essentialstrings.com/lu
acgrp.htm

RYDER, STEVE
Steve Ryder Stringed
Instruments
93 Washington Avenue
Portland, ME 04101
strydah@cybertours.com
sjryder.com

ST. LOUIS MUSIC, INC.
1400 Ferguson Avenue
St. Louis, MO 63133
800.727.4512
314.727.4512
Fax: 314.727.8929

SGD LUTHERIE
300 Observer Highway, 4th
Floor
Hoboken NJ 07030
sgd_luth@gate.cybernex.ne
www2.cybernex.net/~sgd_l
uth

SMD
Distributed by Toys From
The Attic
203 Mamaroneck Ave.
White Plains, NY 10601
914.421.0069
Fax: 914.328.3852
Info@tfta.com
www.tfta.com

SMT GUITARS
Scientifico Musico
Technographique
P.O. Box 670
Great Falls, VA 22066-
0670
703.522.7740

SSD
Distributed by Armadillo
Enterprises
15251 Roosevelt Blvd.
Suite 206
Clearwater, FL 33760
800.793.5273
727.796.8868
Fax: 727.797.9448
Stuart Spector Design, Ltd.
1450 Route 212
Saugerties, NY 12477
914.246.1385
Fax: 914.246.0833

SADOWSKY GUITARS LTD.
1600 Broadway #1000 (48-49 St.)
New York, NY 10019
212.586.3960
Fax: 212.765.5231
Roger@sadowsky.com
www.sadowsky.com

SAHLIN, ERIC
4324 E. 37th Avenue
Spokane, WA 99223

T. SAKASHTA GUITARS
Taku Sakashta, Luthier
1905 Sperring Road #21
Sonoma, CA 95476
707.938.8604
Fax: 707.938.5246

SAMICK
Samick Music Corporation
18521 Railroad Street
City of Industry, CA 91748
800.592.9393
626.964.4700
Fax: 626.965.5224
samick_music@earthlink.net

SAMPAOLO, CAMILLO
Viale Isonzo 60
Milano
Italy 20135
sampa@planet.it
members.planet.it/freewww/sampa/home.html

SAMSON, DR. BILL
88 Grove Road
West Ferry
Dundee
Scotland DD5 7AB
wbs@sol.co.uk

SANDEN ACOUSTIC GUITARS
Karl X Gustavs Gata 33
Helsingborg
Sweden 25439

SANTA FE GUITARS
Santa Fe Violin & Guitar Works
1412 Llano St.
Santa Fe, NM 87505
505.988.4240

SANTER GUITARS
2216 Calaveras Avenue
Davis, CA 95616
lewis@davis.com

SANTO, LOVERDE
Via del Ciclamino 42
Catania
Italy 95121
095.451046

SANTUCCI
Santucci Treblebass
69 W. 38th Street
New York, NY 10018
212.302.6805
Fax: 212.581.4617

SAQUI, STEPHEN NEAL
The Blue Guitar
San Diego, CA
saqui@anarchyx.com
www.ax.com/users/saqui/steve

SARRICOLA GUITARS
Available through Sarricola Custom Shop
3 Barbados Court N.
Lake Thunderbird, IL 61560
815.437.2127

SATO, KAZVO
Heiligenstrasse 27
66740 Saarlouis
Saar
Germany

SCHACK GUITARS
Hanauer StraBe 51
Hamersbach
Germany 63546
+49.6185.1744
(FAX:) +49.6185.7959

SCHAEFER GUITARS
1601 Versailles Rd.
Ft. Worth, TX 76116
817.377.3250
www.schaeferguitars.com

SCHATTEN DESIGN
124 Ottawa Street S.
Kitchener Ontario
Canada
ischattn@netcom.ca

SCHECTER GUITAR RESEARCH
1538 N. Highland Avenue
Los Angeles, CA 90028
323.469.8900
Fax: 323.469.8901
www.schecterguitars.com

SCHEL, BRUCE VANDER
West Music Company
1212 5th Street
Coralville, IA 52241
bruce@avalon.net
www.avalon.net/~bruce

SCHMUKLER, IVON
Artisan Fretted Instruments
8 Easthampton Road
Northampton, MA 01060
leeds@crocker.com

SCHRAMM GUITARS
926 West Princeton Avenue
Fresno, CA 93075

SCHULTE, C. ERIC
24 Buttonwood Avenue
Frazerview (Malvern), PA 19355
610.644.9533

SCIPIO, FLIP VAN DOMBURG
Staten Island, NY

SCRAFFORD, ROGER
Seattle, WA

SEBRING
Distributed by Vega Musical Instruments – see listing.

SEDONA
Distributed by Vega Musical Instruments – see listing.

SELMER
The Selmer Co. Inc.
P.O. Box 310
Elkhart, IN 46515
800.348.7426
219.522.1675
www.selmer.com

SELSAM, DOUGLAS SPRIGGS
Selsam Innovations
8211 Michael Drive
Huntington Beach, CA 92647

SERGE GUITARS
63 Rue Boisvert
St. Etienne Quebec
Canada G6J 1G3
smichaud@sympatico.ca
www3.sympatico.ca/smichaud

SERIES 10
A Division of St. Louis Music, Inc. – see listing.

SEVER
Sever Musical Instruments & Equipment
Cankarjev Drevored 34
(P.O. Box 43)
6310 Izola
Slovenia
386.66.645-130
Fax: 386.66.647-400
sever@eunet.si
www.sever.si

SEXAUER GUITARS
724 "H" Street
Petaluma, CA 94952

SHANE
3211 Barbara Lane, Unit 2
FairFax, VA 22031
800.356.1105
Fax: 703.641.4951

SHELTON-FARRETTA GUITARS
5040 SE 115th
Portland, OR 97266
jshelton@teleport.com
www.teleport.com/~jshelton/

SHEPPARD, DAVID
Sheppard Instruments & Repairs
1820 Spring Garden Street
Greensboro, NC 27403

SHIFFLETT, CHARLES R.
H-R Guitars
124 7 Avenue SW
High River Alberta
Canada T1V 1A2
403.652.1526
105025.2644@compuserve.com

SIEGMUND GUITARS
213.876.5239
sigmundgtrs@hotmail.com
www.siegmundguitars.com

SIERRA VISTA GUITAR COMPANY
Tombstone, AZ

SIGGI GUITARS
Schutzenstr. 45
D-73110 Hattenhofen
Germany
011.49.7164.130087
Fax: 011.49.7164.130200
Siggi.guitars@T-online.de

SIGMA
Distributed by the Martin Guitar Company – see listing.

SIGURDSON GUITAR
2158 East 39th Avenue
Vancouver British Columbia
Canada V5P 1H7
amirault@smartt.com
www.personal.smartt.com/amirault/sigurdson.html

SILER, DENNIS
Jack's Music
3190 Highway 95
Hattieville, AR 72063
siler@petit-jean.pjtc.tec.ar.us

SILVER, JOHN
#5 Chester Road
Parkwood
Johannesburg
South Africa

SILVER CADET
Distributed by Ibanez US – see listing.

SIMMONS, GENE
GENE SIMMONS' PUNISHER
P.O. Box 16075
Beverly Hills, CA 90209
609.PUNISHER
609.786.4743

SIMPSON-JAMES GUITARS
17 Spruce Circle
Westfield, MA 01085-2610
413.568.6654
www.connix.com/~sjguitar

SKORSKI, MIKE
Mike's Guitars at Jones Music
161-B Robertsville Road
Oak Ridge, TN 37830
biz2biz@nxs.net

SMART, A. LAWRENCE
501 E. Park
Social Circle, GA 30025
jhkjr@mindspring.com

SMARTLIGHT
Optek Music Systems, Inc.
8109 Ebenezer Church Rd.
Raleigh, NC 27625
800.833.8306
Fax: 919.878.7997
info@optekmusic.com
www.optekmusic.com

SMITH, KEN
Ken Smith Basses, Ltd.
P.O. Box 199

rkasie, PA 18944
0.347.6484
5.453.8887
x: 215.453.8084
pport@kensmith
sses.com
w.kensmithbasses.com

OLID ROCK GUITARS
15 River Street
latka, FL 32177
g@gbso.net

OLOMON, ERICH
307 Kent St.
nchorage, AK 99503
07.563.6548

OMERVELL GUITARS
443 Green Cove Road
rasstown, NC 28902
omervell@grove.net
yattweb.com/freepage/s/so
nervell@grove.net/home.
html

ONGBIRD GUITARS
O. Box 303/Cranberry
Mall
Cranberry, PA 16319
Phone/Fax: 814.678.2028

SPECTOR
Distributed by Armadillo
Enterprises
5251 Roosevelt Blvd.
Suite 206
Clearwater, FL 33760
800.793.5273
727.796.8868
Fax: 727.797.9448
www.armadilloent.com/
music
Stuart Spector Design, Ltd.
1450 Route 212
Saugerties, NY 12477
914.246.1385
Fax: 914.246.0833

SPIRAL
Distributed by Alfa Export
Office, Inc.
7625 Hayvenhurst Avenue
Unit 19
Van Nuys, CA 91406
818.786.1121
Fax: 818.786.6827
xotic@instanet.com
www.xoticguitars.com

SQUIER
Distributed by the Fender
Musical Instruments
Corporation – see listing.

STAGNITTO GUITARS
236 Vernon Avenue
Paterson, NJ 07503
212.822.4533
Fax: 212.822.4503
jstag@prodigy.com

STAMM, LARRY
P.O. Box 561
McBride British Columbia
Canada V0J 2E0
larryst@vis.bc.ca

STANSELL, LES
P.O. Box 6056
Pistol River, OR 97444

STARFIRE
Distributed by V.J.
Rendano Music Company,
Inc. – see listing.
Eikosha Musical
Instrument Co., Inc.
2, Onaridori 1-chrome
Kitaku, Nagoya, JAPAN
Phone:
011.81.52.911.6456
Fax: 011.81.52.911.6474
Eikosh@aol.com

STARFORCE
Distributed by Tropical
Music Corporation
7091 N.W. 51st Street
Miami, FL 33166-5629
305.594.3909
Fax: 305.594.0786
www.tropicalmusic.com

STARK GUITARS
5904 Cedar Glen Lane
Bakersfield, CA 93313
805.831.8613

STARR, JERRY
411 61st Street
Albuquerque, NM 87121

STATUS GRAPHITE
Coleman's Bridge
Colchester Road
Witham Essex England
CM8 3HP
01376.500575
Fax: 01376.500569
Distributed in the U.S. by
Trace Elliot USA
2601 75th Street
Darien, IL 60561
630.972.1981
Fax: 630.972.1988
www.trace-elliot,com

STAUFER GUITARS
Theodor Engel-Str. 46
Escenbach
Germany 73107
07161.45480
Fax: 07161.45480

STAUFFER, JOEL A.
Front Porch Dreams
Guitars
35786 165th Avenue
Goodhue, MN 55027

ST. CYR, BOB
14 Beverly Street
Waterloo Ontario
Canada N2L 2H6
bobstcy@golden.net
www.gsfmicro.com

STEELE GUITARS
641 West D. Street South
Dixon, CA 95620
jwsteele@ucdavis.edu

STEELE GUITARS
K. Doug Steele
112-B Edwardia Drive
Greensboro, NC 27409

STEINBERGER GUITARS
A Division of Gibson
Musical Instruments – see
listing.

STEPHEN'S
Stephen's Stringed
Instruments
1733 Westlake Avenue
North Seattle, WA 98109
206.286.1443
Fax: 206.286.1728
ssinet@aol.com
www.seanet.com/~jsd

STEVENS
Stevens Electrical
Instruments
112 N. Sixth Street
Alpine, TX 79830
915.837.5989
Fax: 915.837.5989

STEVENS, THOM
Hawknest Company
2472 Citation Court
Wexford, PA 15090
hawknest@nauticom.net

STEWART GUITAR CO.
P.O. Box 995
Swansboro, NC 28584
910.362.3575
Fax: 910.326.1938
stewart@onslowonline.net

STICK
Stick Enterprises, Inc.
6011 Woodlake Avenue
Woodland Hills, CA
91367-3238
818.884.2001
Fax: 818.883.0668
stick@earthlink.net
www.stick.com

STICKEL, DANIEL
710 West 15th
Suite 21
North Vancouver
British Columbia
Canada V3M 3K6

STONEHENGE II
Alfredo Bugari
Liutaio
Via Carlo Marx 8
60022 Castelfidardo (AN)
Italy
071.782.07.66

STONEMAN GUITARS
20 Russell Blvd.
Bradford, PA 16701
814.362.8820

STROMBERG, ROGER
Andgraend 28
Lulea
Sweden
roger.stromberg@usa.net

STU ROCK
P.O. Box 4101
Cincinnati, OH 45204-
0101
513.602.9881
www.StuRock.com

STULTZ, BILL
Bill's Guitar Repair
1600 Robin Road
Martinsville, IN 46151
bbstultz@tecwrite.co

STUMP PREACHER GUITARS, INC.
12064 NE 178th St.
Woodinville, WA 98072
800.427.8867
425.402.1935
Fax: 425.486.8262
info@stumppreacher.com
www.stumppreacher.com

SUKOP ELECTRIC GUITARS
57 Crooks Avenue
Clifton, NJ 07011
800.888.1899
201.772.3333
Fax: 201.772.5410

SUMER
Sumer Musical Instruments
Co., Ltd.
#645-55 Airport B/D
3F, Bangwah 2-Dong
Kangseo-Ku
Seoul Korea
2.666.0382
Fax: 2.666.0385
Sumer USA
9792 Edmonds Way, #126
Edmonds, WA 98020
425.771.4571
Fax: 425.775.8562
amasia@earthlink.net

SUPERIOR GUITAR WORKS
4047 Cresson Street, 2nd
Floor
Philadelphia, PA 19127
superiorguitar@pipeline.co
m

SURINE ELECTRIC BASSES
P.O. Box 6440
Denver, CO 80206
Phone/Fax: 303.388.3956
www.surinebasses.com
mail@surinebasses.com

SYDOW, TOM
Tom S. Guitar Works
16105 Castile Drive
Whittier, CA 90603

SYNSONICS
A More Company
P.O. Box 9885
Savannah, GA 31412-
0085
brown@synsonics.com
www.synsonics.com

TDL GUITAR WORKS
6911 Sycamore Road
Atascadero, CA 93422
805.461.3663
Fax: 805.461.3309
tdl@tcsn.net

TPN CUSTOM GUITARS
Wales, MA
413.267.3392

TV JONES GUITARS
P.O. Box 163
Whittier, CA 90608
562.693.0068
Fax: 562.693.1688
www.tvjones.com
tvjones@bigfoot.com

TACCHI, ANDREA
Concert Guitar Maker
Via Monte Oliveto 20
Firenze
Italy 50124
tacchi@dada.it

TALKOVICH, S.
P.O. Box 98
Woodstock, GA 30188
770.926.8876
talkgtr@aol.com

TANARA
Distributed by the Chesbro Music Company
P.O. Box 2009
327 Broadway
Idaho Falls, ID 83403-2009
800.CHE.SBRO
800.243.7276
Fax: 208.522.8712
cmc@srv.net

TANGLEWOOD
Distributed by European Music Company, Ltd.
Unit 6
Concorde Business Centre
Main Road
Biggin Hill
Kent
England TN16 3YN
01959.571600
Fax: 01959.572267

TATE, Z. Q.
Fretted Instrument Engineering
37 Scout Avenue
Auckland
New Zealand
Fax: 64.9.620.8790
croydon-mcrae@xtra.co.nz

TAUBER, CHARLES S.
Hamilton, Ontario
Canada
www.cybozone.com/fg/tauber.html

TAUSCH HANDMADE GUITARS
DorfstraBe 40
Buch-Ritzisried
Germany 89290
011-49-7343-5488
Fax: 011-49-7343-921501
Tauschguitars@nord-schwaben.de
www.tausch-guitars.com

TAYLOR, STEVE
13 Atkins Lane
Newport News, VA 23602

TEIGEN, ROSS
Teigen Guitars
P.O. Box 990421
Naples, FL 33999
941.455.5724

TERRY ROGERS GUITARS
Phone: 931.879.4800/4802
www.terryrogersguitars.com

TEUFFEL ELECTRIC GUITARS
Germany
Fax: 49.7307.21206
Distributed by Salwender International
1140 N. Lemon Street #M
Orange, CA 92867
714.583.1285
Fax: 714.583.9331
uwe@salwender.com
www.salwender.com

TEXARKANA
Distributed by V.J. Rendano Music Company, Inc. – see listing.

THOMAS LLOYD GUITARS
15 Yarra Street
Yarra Glen
Melbourne Victoria
Australia 3775
matty@wire.net.au

THOMAS, OTIS A.
Baddeck, Cape Breton
Nova Scotia
Canada

THRASH, BILL
P.O. Box 1783
Las Cruces, NM 87901
thrash@riolink.com

THUNDER BAY BASSES
Distributed by Sound Trek Distributors U.S.A.
2119 W. Hillsborough Avenue
Tampa, FL 33603
888.466.TREK
www.sound-trek.com

THUNDERHOUSE INSTRUMENTS
2809 Bucklepost Cres.
Mississauga Ontario
Canada L5N 1X6
amatniek@inforamp.net

THURMAN, ROGER
Thurman Guitar & Violin Repair, Inc.
900 Franklin Avenue
Kent, OH 44240
rogluthier@aol.com
members.aol.com/rogluthier/index/html

TICE, ROBERT
HCR #1, Box 465
Sciota, PA 18354
luthier@epix.net

TIMELESS INSTRUMENTS
P.O. Box 51
Tugaske SK
Canada S0H 4B0
888.884.2753
306.759.2042
Fax: 306.759.2729
www3.sk.sympatico.ca/timeless

TIMM, JERRY
4512 47th Street S.E.
Auburn, WA 98092
253.833.8667
Fax: 253.833.1820

TIMTONE CUSTOM GUITARS
P.O. Box 193
19097 Hwy 21 North
Danville, WA 99121
604.442.5651
Fax: 604.442.5651
timtone@wkpowerlink.com
www.netshop.net/~timtone
timtone@gfk.auracom.com
www.stablemusic.com/timtone/

TJELTA, INGVARD
Nadienne GWS
Nordahlgriegsgate 21
Moss
Norway 1524
(47) 69.25.45.84

TOBIAS GUITARS
Distributed by Gibson Musical Instruments – see listing.

TOMAS, OTIS A.
RR 4, Baddeck
Cape Breton Nova Scotia
Canada BO3 1B0

TOMKINS CUSTOM GUITARS & BASSES
17 Eric Street
Harbord
N.S.W. 2096 Australia
61.2.9905.2442
Fax: 61.2.9905.5998

TOMMYHAWK
Tom Barth's Music Box
1910 Rt. 10, Bldg. 1, Ste. 3
Succasunna, NJ 07876
Phone/Fax: 973.927.6711
NJLUCK@aol.com
www.tommyhawk.com

TOMMY'S SPECIAL GUITARS
Gereonsplatz 3
Viersen
Germany 41747
+49.2162.29227
+49.2162.25152
Distributed in the U.S. by Salwender International
1140 N. Lemon Street #M
Orange, CA 92867
714.583.1285
Fax: 714.583.9331
uwe@salwender.com
www.salwender.com

TONESMITH
19817 Jackie Lane
Rogers, MN 55374
763.428.8907
Fax: 763.428.1535
tonesmith@aol.com
www.tonesmith.com

TOPF, RICHARD P.
Topf Tech
2230 East Hamilton Avenue
Orange, CA 92867

TORTORICI GUITARS
2111 Palo Verde Avenue
Long Beach, CA 90815-3323
tortorici@luthiers.com
www.tortorici-guitars.com

TOTEM GUITARS
40861 Ferndale Dr.
Three Rivers, CA 93271
209.561.4009

TRACE ELLIOT
England
01621.851851
Distributed by Trace Elliot (USA) Ltd.
2601 75th Street
Darien, IL 60561
630.972.1981
Fax: 630.972.1988

TRANSPERFORMANCE, LLC
Self-tuning Guitars
217 Racquette Dr., Unit 8
Fort Collins, CO 80524
970.482.9132
Fax: 970.498.8865
www.selftuning.com

TRAUGOTT, JEFF
Jeff Traugott Guitars
2553 B Mission Street
Santa Cruz, CA 95060
408.426.2313
Fax: 408.426.2313

TRAVELER
The Traveler Guitar
325 Alabama, Suite 8
Redlands, CA 92373
909.307.2626
Fax: 909.307.2628
www.travelerguitar.com

TREKER
Treker Manufacturing
12011 S. Hwy. 91
Payson, UT 84651

TRIGGS, JAMES W.
Fine Hand Made Guitars & Mandolins
P.O. Box 6210
Kansas City, KS 66106-0210
Fax: 913.962.2254
www.triggsguitars.com

TRINITY GUITARS
2089 Camp Street
Jamestown, NY
ajrb30a@prodigy.com

TRUSSART, JAMES
3 Villa Poissonniere
Paris
France 75018
33.1.4638.9368
Fax: 33.1.4638.2390
trussart@dunet.com
Distributed in the U.S. by Black Market Music
841 N. La Cienaga Blvd.
Los Angeles, CA 90069
310.659.6795
Fax: 310.659.6796
Black Market Music
1016 Howard Street
San Francisco, CA 94103
415.252.1055
Fax: 415.252.1060

**BULAR
TRUMENT
. INC.**
Pelton Ave.
en Island, NY 10310
ne/Fax: 718.876.7870
w.gettubular.com
e@gettubular.com

GGLE, ROD
Perry Avenue
ssville, IL 60963
7.748.6041

**JNE GUITAR
CHNOLOGY LTD.**
2, 2-9-11 Fukasawa,
agaya
kyo, 158-0081
pan
1.81.3.5758.2565
x: 011.81.3.5758.2566
netech@sepia.ocn.ne.jp

JNG BASSES
3 Ashland Place #1
ew York, NY 11217
8.797.2047
x: 718.797.2162

URNER, RICK
ck Turner Guitars
5 Almar Ave.
nta Cruz, CA 95060
31.460.9144
ax: 831.460.9146
ww.rickturnerguitars.com
turner466@aol.com

YLER, JAMES
166 Sepulveda Blvd.
an Nuys, CA 91411
18.901.0278
ax: 818.901.0294
www.tylerguitars.com

**J.S. MASTERS GUITAR
WORKS**
324 Pinehurst Drive
Jnit B
Middleton, WI 53562
508.836.5505
Fax: 608.836.6530
guitars@usmasters.com
www.usmasters.com

USHER, TREVOR
Sounds in Scale
Trefaes Bella, Sarn
Pwllhei, Gynedd
United Kingdom LL53
8RL

**V.J. RENDANO MUSIC
COMPANY, INC.**
7152 Market Street
Youngstown, OH 44512
800.321.4048
330.758.0881
Fax: 330.758.1096

VACCARO
Vaccaro Guitar Co.
1001 2nd Avenue
Asbury Park, NJ 07712
732.774.8174
Fax: 732.775.2203
Info@vaccaroguitars.com
www.vaccaroguitars.com

VAISTO, JAN
Malvavagen 23
Akersbera
Sweden 18435
jan.vaisto@mailbox.swip-
net.se

VALLEE, ETINNE
25 Jolicouer, Suite 3
Victoriaville Quebec
Canada G6P 2P8

VALLEY ARTS
Distributed by Samick
Music Corporation – see
listing.

**VANTAGE
VANTEK**
Distributed by Music
Industries Corporation
99 Tulip Avenue
Suite 101
Floral Park, NY 11001
800.431.6699
516.352.4110
Fax: 516.352.0754
mic@musicindustries.com
www.musicindustries.com

VEGA, CHARLES
2101 Carterdale Road
Baltimore, MD 21209-
4523
410.664.6506

**VEGA MUSICAL
INSTRUMENTS
(VMI INDUSTRIES)**
P.O. Box 1357
2980-D Enterprise Street
Brea, CA 92822-1357
800.237.4864
714.572.1492
Fax: 714.572.9321

VEILLETTE GUITARS
2628 Route 212
Woodstock, NY 12498
Phone/Fax: 914.679.6154
www.veilletteguitars.com
jv@netstop.net

VEKTOR GERMANY
C/o Sven-Henrik Gawron
Markstr. 5
D-41751 Viersen
Germany
011.49.2162.53309
Fax: 011.49.2162.45692
www.vektor-bass.de
vektor@vektor-bass.de

VERSOUL
Kutomotie 13
Fin-00380 Helsinki
Finland
358.0565.1876
Fax: 358.0565.1876

VESTAX
Vestax Corporation
2-37-1 Kamiuma
Setagayaku
Tokyo 154-0011
03.3412.7011
Fax: 03.3412.7013
vestax-
corporation@msn.com
Vestax Musical Electronics
Corporation
2870 Cordelia Rd., Suite
100
Fairfield, CA 94585
707.427.1920
Fax: 707.427.2023

VIGIER
Vigier Guitars, Basses, and
Strings
27 - 29 Z.A. Des Champs
Elysees
Every
France 91000
33.1.60792364
Fax: 33.1.64979246
www.vigierguitars.com
www.vigier.fr
Distributed in the U.S. by
Players International
111 W. Second Street
San Dimas, CA 91773
909.592.6682
Fax: 909.599.0908

VINCENZO, CIPRIANI
Via Cimabue 5
S. Madrid d. Angeli
Assisi (PG)
Italy 06088
075.8041485

VINTAGE
Distributed by John
Hornby Skewes & Co.,
Ltd. – see listing.

VINTAGE DESIGNS
Route 7, Box 1538-X
Manning, SC 29102-9242
803.473.3707
vin_designs@ftc-i.net
www.geocities.com/nashvill
e/2041

VINTIQUE
P.O. Box 593
College Park, MD 20741-
0593
301.982.9413
jay@vintique.com

VIPUR GUITARS
Pretoria
South Africa

VOLBRECHT GUITARS
130 North Artist Drive
Nashville, IN 47448
ozbond@monroe.lib.in.us

**W. PAUL GUITARS,
INC.**
1018 Madison Street
Waukesha, WI 53188
414.896.7794

WM GUITARS
Rt. 1, Box 174
Santa Fe, NM 87501
Phone/Fax: 505.455.0848

**WRC CUSTOM
GUITARS**
P.O. Box 5247
Hemet, CA 92544
galletta@ivic.net
Wayne R. Charvel
6311 Skyway
Paradise, CA 95969
909.929.8734

WAGNER, MATTHIAS
Ruschstr. 5
Vogtsburg
Germany D-79235
matthias.wagner_lavten@t-
online.de

WAL
Electric Wood
Leigh Court
Leigh Street
High Wycombe, Bucks
England HP11 2RH
01494.442925
Fax: 01494.472468

WARR GUITARS
6933 Keynote St.
Long Beach, CA 90808
310.421.7293
Fax: 310.421.7293

WARRIOR
100 Direct Connection
Drive
Rossville, GA 30741
800.987.7969
706.891.3009
Fax: 706.891.3629
www.warriorinstruments.
com

WARWICK
Warwick GmbH & Co.
Music Equipment KG
Postfach 10010
D-08258 Markneukirchen
Germany
3742.25550
Fax: 3742.55599
Exclusively Distributed in
the U.S. by Dana B. Goods
5427 Hollister Avenue
Santa Barbara, CA 93111-
2345
800.765.8663
805.964.9610
Fax: 805.964.9749
72431.416@compuserve.
com
www.danabgoods.com

WASHBURN
Distributed by Washburn
International
255 Corporate Woods
Parkway
Vernon Hills, IL 60061-
3109
800.US.SOUND
(800.877.6863)
847.913.5511
Fax: 847.913.7772
washburn@washburn.com
www.washburn.com

WATTS GUITARS
2457 NW Grant Avenue
Corvallis, OR 97330

WAYNE GUITARS
6311 Skyway Dr.
Paradise, CA 95969
530.872.5123
www.wayneguitars.com

WEGELIN, RON
1414 W. 14st
Scottsbluff, NV 69361
rwegelin@panesu.esu14.k12.ne.us

WELLS, SYLVAN
618 N. Wild Olive
Daytona Beach, FL 33118
swells@america.com

WENTZELL GUITARS
609 Longstreet Circle
Summerville, SC 29483
wguitars@cchat.com
www.cchat.com/wguitars

WESLEY, STEVE
Taree, NSW
Australia

WESTERMAN, RICH
6780 Warren
St. Anne, IL 60964
musicadtk@keynet.net
www.execpe.com/~danb/mandolin/westerman.html

WESTONE
Distributed by FCN Music
Morley Road
Tonbridge
Kent TN9 1RA
01732.366.421

WHEAT COMPANY
Arroyo Grande, CA

WHITE, J.
England
01252.520911

WHITSETT GUITAR WORKS
2369 Browning Street
Sarasota, FL 34237
ellisjazz@worldnet.att.net

WIESNER, JAMES
Tyrson's Wood
Ojai, CA 93023
tyrswood@pacbell.net
home.pacbell.net/tyrswood/index.html

WILHELMY, RENE
8415 Rue Foucher
Montreal Quebec
Canada H2P 2CZ
rwil@infobahnos.com
www.infobahnos.com/~rwil/

WILKINS, PAT
Wilkins Guitar Finishes
15734 Stagg Street
Van Nuys, CA 91406
818.909.7310
wilkinsguitar@usa.net

WILLIAMS GUITAR MFG. LTD.
Spicer Road RD 3
Kaitaia Northlands
New Zealand 0500
laurie@williams-guitars.co.nz

WILLIAMS GUITARS
209 Rogers Avenue
Mt. Sterling, KY 40353
prwilliams@kih.net

WILLIAMS, SCOTT A.
312 Diamon Road
Jackson, NJ 08527
tabla@mail.superlink.net

WILLIAMS, STAN
9 Belmont Drive
Rome, GA 30165

WILLIAMSON, DAVE
Common Bond, Acoustic Music
Route 1
Troy, MT 59935

WIND MOUNTAIN GUITARS
P.O. Box 477
Carson, WA 98610
williammyres@linkport.com

WINDROSE
Distributed by Vega Musical Instruments – see listing.

WITTMAN BASS GUITARS
Distributed by Spins International, Inc.
691 Woodland Avenue
Williamsport, PA 17701
717.327.1527
717.321.0604
wittbas@csrlink.net

WOLLERMAN GUITARS
P.O. Box 457
Sheffield, IL 61361
815.454.2775
Fax: 815.454.2700

WOODALL, GARY
229 N.W. 19th Street
Richmond, IN 47374
mandolin@infocom.com

WOODY'S GUITARS
55 Railroad Avenue
Building #11
Garnerville, NY 10923
914.942.5123

WORLAND GUITARS
810 N. First Street
Rockford, IL 61107
815.961.8854
worland.james@mcleodusa.net

WRIGHT GUITAR, INC.
3632 Gilham Rd.
Eugene, OR 97408-1631

WYZA GUITARS
Bill Wyza

XOTIC GUITARS
Distributed by Alfa Export Office, Inc.
7625 Hayvenhurst Avenue
Unit 19
Van Nuys, CA 91406
818.786.1121
Fax: 818.786.6827
xotic@instanet.com
www.xoticguitars.com

YAMAHA
Yamaha Corporation of America
6600 Orangethorpe Avenue
Buena Park, CA 90620
800.322.4322
714.522.9011
Fax: 714.522.9587
www.yamahaguitars.com

YANUZIELLO, JOSEPH
Toronto, Canada
Distributed by Elderly Instruments
1100 N. Washington
Lansing, MI 48906
517.372.7890

YELDA, PETER MICHAEL
1127 Peach Street
San Luis Obispo, CA 93401

YONG, C. H. JEFFREY
Guitar Institute Malaysia
55-2, Jalan 5/76 B
Desa Pandan
Kuala Lumpur 55100
tcmych@tm.net.my

YONTZ, GEORGE
George Yontz Guitars
5563 Archer Road
Brethren, MI 49619
yontz@manistee-isd.k12.mi.us

YURIY
P.O. Box 4914
Buffalo Grove, IL 60089
847.670.1169
www.yuriyguitars.com

ZAK
Distributed by Mayones Company
Zueniwuta 11
80 - 354 Gdansk
Poland
+48.58.521476
Fax: +48.58.430783

ZENBU GUITARS
By Appointment Only
2121 Marconi Avenue
Sacramento, CA 95821
916.920.0678
Fax: 916.927.8131

ZENTECH DESIGN GROUP
P.O. Box 751
Zentech Plaza
Girdwood, AK 99587-0751
907.783.2502
zentech@alaska,net
www.alaska.net/~zentechnweb/index.html

ZETA
Zeta Music Systems
2230 Livingston Street
Oakland, CA 94606
800.622.6434
510.261.1702
Fax: 510.261.1708
prices@zetamusic.com
www.zetamusic.com

ZIMMERLY, K.
17 Oswego Drive
Bay Shore, NY 11706
516.968.5523

ZIMNICKI GUITARS
15106 Garfield
Allen Park, MI 48101
www.zimnicki.com
gzim@flash.net

ZOID LIGHT GUITAR
736 S. 50th Street
Tampa, FL 33619

ZION GUITARS, INC.
2606-406 Phoenix Drive
Greensboro, NC 27406
336.852.7603
Fax: 336.852.1889
www.zionguitars.com
khoov@worldnet.att.net

ZOLLA GUITARS
4901 Morena Blvd.
Suite 908
San Diego, CA 92117
619.270.5530
Fax: 619.270.0450
zollaguits@aol.com
www.kewlweb.com/zolla

ZON GUITARS
2688-D Middlefield Road
Redwood City, CA 94063
650.366.3516
Fax: 650.366.9996
jzon@zonguitars.com
www.zonguitars.com

INDEX

A

B

INDEX

C

INDEX

D

INDEX

INDEX

G

INDEX

H

INDEX

INDEX

INDEX

N

O

INDEX

P

Q

R

INDEX

INDEX

INDEX

Pages 867-928

P.S. Guitar Identification 101 (Answers from pg. 576)

1. Tuning machine
2. Head
3. Truss rod adjustment
4. Nut
5. Neck
6. Fingerboard
7. Position marker
8. Fret
9. Neck attachment bolt
10. Neck angle adjustment screw
11. Vibrola springs
12. Detail of back showing vibrola mechanism
13. Pickup selector switch
14. Tone control capacitor
15. Jack socket
16. Potentiometer
17. Control knob
18. String anchor block
19. Bridge unit with adjustable bridge pieces
20. Vibrola arm
21. Pickguard
22. Pickup
23. Solid body
24. Adjustable bridge piece
25. Vibrola arm
26. String
27. Bridge mounting plate
28. Base cover plate
29. Tension adjustment screw
30. Tension spring
31. String anchor block

P.S. Guitar Identification 101

Q: What do internists and advanced guitar perverts have in common?

A: They both know their body parts.

So can you! How many parts/components you can correctly identify in the diagram below? Answers appear on previous page.

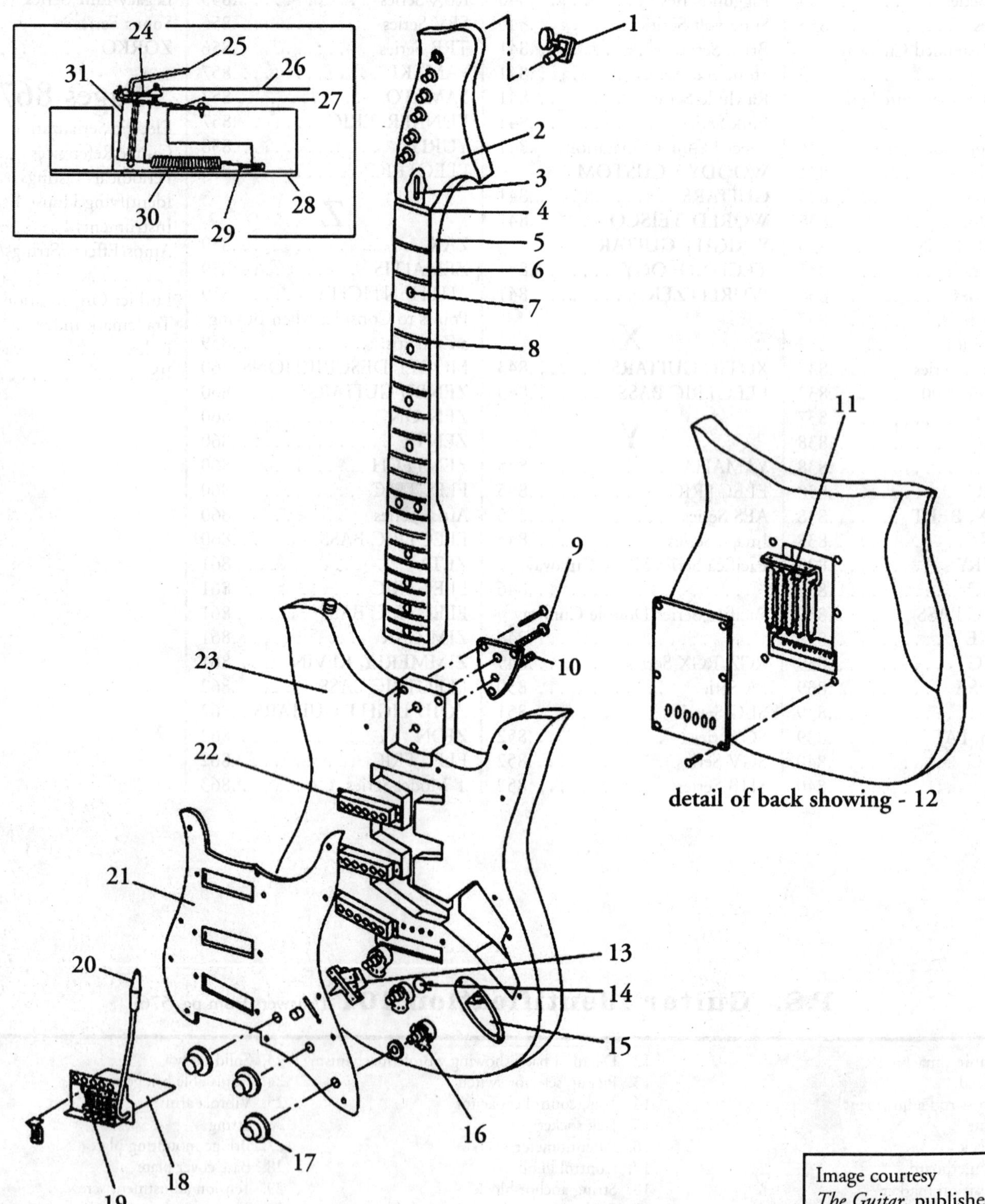

Exposed view of an electric solid body showing construction

Image courtesy *The Guitar*, published by Quarto Marketing, located in New York, NY, 1984 ISBN 0-688-01972-2